SKY SPORTS FOOTBALL YEARBOOK 2003-2004

SKY SPORTS

EDITORS: GLENDA ROLLIN AND JACK ROLLIN

In association with 

headline

Copyright © 2003 HEADLINE BOOK PUBLISHING

First published in 2003
by HEADLINE BOOK PUBLISHING

10 9 8 7 6 5 4 3 2 1

All rights reserved. No part of this publication may be reproduced, stored in a retrieval system, or transmitted, in any form or by any means without the prior written permission of the publisher, nor be otherwise circulated in any form of binding or cover other than that in which it is published and without a similar condition being imposed on the subsequent purchaser.

This publication contains material that is the copyright and database right of the FA Barclaycard Premiership and the Nationwide Football League Limited.

Front cover photographs: (left and background) Ruud Van Nistelrooy (Manchester United); (centre) Frank Lampard (Chelsea); (right) Patrick Vieira (Arsenal) – all *Empics*.

Spine photograph: Zinedine Zidane (Real Madrid) and Edgar Davids (Juventus) *Getty Images*.

Back cover photographs: (top) Dianbobo Balde (Celtic) and Michael Mols (Rangers) *Getty Images*; (bottom) James Beattie (Southampton) and Steven Caldwell (Newcastle United) *Empics*.

Cataloguing in Publication Data is available from the British Library

ISBN 0 7553 1227 9 (hardback)
ISBN 0 7553 1228 7 (trade paperback)

Typeset by Wearset Ltd, Boldon, Tyne and Wear

Printed and bound in Great Britain by
Mackays of Chatham PLC,
Chatham, Kent

HEADLINE BOOK PUBLISHING
A division of Hodder Headline
338 Euston Road
London NW1 3BH

www.headline.co.uk
www.hodderheadline.com

CONTENTS

FOREWORD

I look along my office wall and there they all are, 33 editions of the Football Yearbook that has, largely thanks to Jack Rollin and his daughter Glenda, become the ultimate in football reference. No collector would pay much for my set, all volumes dog-eared from constant use, some actually falling to bits after being travelling companions around the world.

In the early years of my commentating career I used to take all the issues with me, up to around a dozen, just in case I needed to look way back to check a vital piece of information. I stopped that not because the weight became too heavy to bear, though it was getting that way, but because the risk of losing such precious books on my travels became too great. In the early 1980s I left them in my car at Heathrow airport and while I was away the car was stolen. Amazingly the thief took other items, including clothes from a suitcase, but when the vehicle was recovered the set of books was still there. Since that scare it has just been each current edition that has been ever present in my bag.

My connection with the Yearbook goes back to the 4th edition, 1973–74, when I helped read the proofs for Jack who always slaves round the clock from the end of each season to deadline day. Back then he was grateful for any willing assistant. He taught me a lot about attention to detail and factual accuracy for which I will always be grateful. I was a member of his squad in various capacities later in the seventies but for the most part I have simply been an avid devourer of the subject matter, a true fan.

I must thank Rothmans for their support for over thirty years which has given the annual the prestige it now enjoys. Times change, however, and I am delighted that Sky Sports has picked up a dropped baton and is prepared to run with it.

Team Rollin is still in business and every football commentator, indeed every football lover, will be grateful for that.

Martin Tyler, Senior Commentator, Sky Sports

Martin Tyler receives his Commentator of the Decade award from FAPL Chief Executive Richard Scudamore.

INTRODUCTION

In this 34th edition of the Yearbook, firstly we are delighted to welcome our new sponsors, Sky Sports and also to renew the association with both the FA Premier League and Football League. Once again, our new edition features historical and record information for the 92 clubs. Among the innovations are the inclusion of red cards for domestic and international competitions and increased coverage for the Champions League, both past and present. The Who's Who style Players Directory once more provides a season-by-season account of the individual player's appearances and goals. There is also each club's full record in the previous ten seasons and the latest sequences recorded for wins, draws and defeats, plus runs of scoring and non-scoring.

Detailed and varied coverage involves the FA Premier League, Football League, Scottish, Welsh and Irish football, amateur, schools, university, reserve team, extensive non-League information, awards, records and an international directory, Football and the Law, women's football, referees and the work of chaplains.

Transfers fees are given where known. When two clubs have differed as to the amount of a record move, the lower figure has been quoted in both instances. For certain entries, the figure quoted in the list of transfers may be the original one, without extra finance built in for appearances and other reasons, which would appear subsequently as a record fee on the relevant club page. Also, the date when a player is signed often varies from the one given as his registration and the diary occasionally refers to the transfer fee originally discussed, but not ultimately paid.

A frequent question asked is why Football League records have not been changed since the advent of the Premier League. The answer is simple: the Football League still considers its First Division to be a championship which has existed for over 100 years.

The Editors would like to thank Alan Elliott for the Scottish section, Bob Hennessy for the Milestones Diary, Tony Brown for sequences and instances of match results in the Records Section and Ian Nannestad for the Obituaries and additional information on foreign players. Thanks are also due to John English, who provided invaluable and conscientious reading of the proofs. The Editors would like to pay tribute to the following people in the various organisations who have helped to make this edition complete, especially Mike Foster, Zoe Ward and Anthony Walker of the FA Premier League, Debbie Birch and Louise Standing from the Football League, as well as David C. Thomson from the Scottish League.

ACKNOWLEDGEMENTS

The editors would like to express appreciation of the following individuals and organisations for their co-operation: David Barber, Dawn Keleher and Gary Simmonds (Football Association), Heather Elliott, Dr Malcolm Brodie, Wally Goss (AFA), Rev. Nigel Sands, Edward Grayson, Ken Goldman, Grahame Lloyd, Marshall Gillespie, Valery Karpoushkin, Andrew Howe, Mike Kelleher, Ester Kristiansson, Ole Hall and Wendy McCance (Headline Book Publishing).

Special thanks are due to the indefatigable and loquacious Lorraine Jerram, Headline's Senior Editor for her generosity, expertise, constant support, resilience, patience, sincerity, perspicacity and appreciation, not to mention her unfailing humour, stoicism, quick-wittedness and understated authority.

Finally, sincere thanks to John Anderson, Simon Dunnington, Geoff Turner, Brian Tait and the staff at Wearset for their efforts in the production of this book, which was much appreciated throughout the year.

EDITORIAL

If Michelangelo had painted by numbers, you could still have admired his colouring, but it would have been more system than Sistine and while at first sight there is much to be pleased about in present day football, it is a different scenario under the surface.

Active attendance at matches is up again, passive viewing from a variety of television outlets increasing and there is sustained interest at all levels down to the grass roots. There is money continuing to come in. The game has never been more popular on the widest scale.

In statistical terms, crowds in the Premier League reached 13,468,965 over 400,000 higher than in 2001–02 and representing an increase of over three percent. The average attendance of 35,445 was the highest in Europe.

But underneath, as we have said before, the beautiful game attracts ugly people. If they wish to misbehave, it is almost impossible to stop them; the mindless on a carnival of menace. Last season England came a gnat's whisker of being thrown out of Euro 2004 because of the problems surrounding the match with Turkey. This was not an isolated incident. There were others of a completely domestic nature.

Yet the only way to start clawing back the discipline required is to create a better climate by education, then legislation before eradication can be implemented. Alas the will to achieve these aims appears to be as far away as ever. Our society must stop wringing its hands over the situation and start ringing the changes.

In desperation it was found necessary for top players to appeal to so-called fans to behave before the Slovakia match in the light of the heavy fine and threats made by UEFA about our future conduct.

Then there are the outgoings which are outstripping income. Too many balance sheets are wavering in the breeze. The icy draught of the administrator is becoming all too-familiar. In the clamour for success with market forces dictating, unfortunately there is often an early closing day. Painful decisions could be taken to remedy such issues, but again trying to obtain a consensus would seem to be unlikely. Mr Micawber's *laissez-faire* attitude was not the ideal one, but by the dickens it favoured the black against the red.

Not all footballers earn lottery winning size wage packets. It is just that the stars attract the publicity and their incomes analysed. The recent transfer of David Beckham to Real Madrid in a reported £25 million deal certainly included structured payments to the player and of course not all the money went to Manchester United. Some sources have mentioned £17.25 million as being the fee at the basis of the move.

Losing his famous No. 7 shirt and acquiring a new No. 23 brought various thoughts on why he chose it. About the only explanation not forthcoming was that the game's most renowned squad number of all time in the game was arguably the No. 14 worn by Johan Cruyff at Ajax. And mathematicians will have been quick to fathom out that both numbers add up to the famous five . . .

It is generally accepted that there is too much football. But whether to cut down at club or national level is the dilemma. FIFA clearly want fewer domestic matches and more international fixtures, their balancing act coming down harder on clubs. But even national associations fail to help the situation.

While there has been debate over a long period concerning the physical demands on top players it was highlighted in the summer with the tragic death at the age of 28 of the Cameroon international Marc Vivien Foe during a Confederations Cup match, one of those tournaments which are being labelled in some quarters as totally unnecessary.

It is not only the established stars who suffer from a calendar which bulges football all the year round. Last season partly due to success in reaching final tournaments, England teams at various intermediate levels, completed a total of 66 matches. Though large squads are used because of matches in close proximity to each other, the strain was undeniably illustrated by the Under-20s in the Toulon tournament in the middle of June.

Against Argentina, the England team was beaten 8-0. They were not a bunch of beer-bellied lads recruited from the Dog and Duck but included at least half a dozen players who had appeared in first team matches in the Premier League and Football League.

The only explanation must be that they were knackered after a gruelling season. One report, obviously scratching around for a reasonable excuse, referred to the fact that the team was weakened because Wayne Rooney was not playing, though he had not figured in the squad all season.

One solution suggested is to introduce unlimited substitutes. The day of American-style time-outs, endless replacements and players coming back into the reckoning once they have had a rest on the bench may not be in the too far distance. Specialist players could be brought on simply for free-kicks – the ideal job for someone like David Beckham.

Of course the England national team has already practised for this eventuality, using complete teams in each half of a match. The worry is that matches will take much longer, but with the present archaic system of time-keeping, we might find actual playing time being reduced to little more than one half.

If there is a threat to clubs income because of a reduction of league games, the interests of the G-14 clubs should not be ignored. You will have heard about G-8 which used to be G-7, the big boys of the world's finances. However, as you know, too, G-14 which is still known as such except it has increased to 18 members, all football's elite clubs. They want to keep their options open about forming a European League of their own if UEFA start pushing their luck with them. It may yet reach that level especially if the European governing body takes heed – as we will have to do presumably – of FIFA's desire eventually to reduce the number of clubs in European Leagues to sixteen.

UEFA have cut the number of matches in the Champions League for 2003–04, but are to increase those in the UEFA Cup with the introduction of a group stage next season! Presumably the competition will be known as the UEFA League.

Stress levels do not solely exist on the pitch. The two most recent examples of health scares involved Glenn Roeder the West Ham United manager towards the end of last season when he was rushed to hospital and previously Liverpool's Gerard Houllier, neither of them in the category of the most demonstrative on the touchline. And it is no consolation for anyone in any walk of life to be told that death is nature's way of telling you to slow down.

Managers continue to be the scapegoats for a lack of success. Players win things, managers lose them. Some would argue that how could anyone blame a manager for lining up his next job while still employed elsewhere when the likelihood of a long-term association is practically non-existent.

There was media speculation when Chelsea's new owner Roman Abramovich had a meeting with England team manager Sven Goran Eriksson, but there appeared to be no truth in the rumour that the former was heard whistling "Sven will I see you again?"

Manchester United's ninth "League" title – eight Premier and one Champions – in 11 years and Arsenal runners-up, head the first of the levels which exist in the top flight. The next layer includes those striving for a place in the Champions League, followed by the UEFA Cup hopefuls. Then there are those on the fringe of this and finally others happy enough to stay in the Premier League and avoid the trauma of relegation.

Naturally parachute money is helpful, but often clubs find on landing that they need the equivalent of a financial SAS to rescue them. While show business celebrities are keen to reveal their allegiance to football clubs, Uri Geller – famous for bending it like Uri Geller – attached himself to Exeter City, who still fell out of the League.

Apart from a blip two years ago, Manchester United have never been out of the top two in the Premiership, neither have Arsenal in the last six years. But in order to compete in the modern era, it seems that the numbers of those able to find the resources to compete to a sufficiently high standard required of a championship-winning club, are few enough.

It has been whimsically suggested that Manchester United have become so popular worldwide that even if they did not play another serious match, but jet-setted around spreading the gospel according to Old Trafford and performing exhibition matches rather like the Haarlem Globetrotters did for basketball years ago, they would probably continue to make a profit. Jokingly or not, behind the humour is probably the greatest accolade accorded to a football team, which is as much of an institution as anything else.

Of those clubs finishing in the top half last season, only one English manager was in charge. He was Sir Bobby Robson, 70-plus going on 35. A lesson to us all about enjoying the game for all its peripheral faults and guiding his team to third place, while in the process of trying to recover some of his international caps disgracefully stolen during the season.

It was the nearly season for English teams in Europe, United were best of the bunch reaching the quarter-finals of the Champions League. They pushed the talented Real Madrid team to the limit at Old Trafford. Mr Posh did himself a bit of good in Spanish eyes with a couple of goals after appearing as a late substitute.

Strange how Real Madrid then failed against Juventus, who in turn were beaten by AC Milan in the final. It should not be forgotten that Celtic achieved the not entirely expected feat of beating both Blackburn Rovers and Liverpool in a couple of ties inevitably tagged the Championship of Britain, on the journey towards losing the UEFA Cup final against Porto.

Ironically four of the five top finishing teams in the Premiership last season are the only ones to have won European titles in the years since the start of the FA Premier League. In the Champions League, Manchester United did it in 1999, Arsenal the Cup-Winners' Cup in 1994, Chelsea four years later in the same competition and Liverpool in the 2001 UEFA Cup.

We are now well used to foreign players and in the summer one of the biggest favourites was the diminutive, but perfectly-formed Gianfranco Zola of Chelsea and Italy, who has been arguably the greatest of ambassadors from abroad.

'Zo, who is theese Real Madrid?' David Beckham, England's football ambassador at large contemplates leaving No. 7 behind and taking No. 23 in the Spanish capital. (Actionimages)

Last season another foreigner, the Frenchman Thierry Henry made both the players and football writers awards for the outstanding player. We are reliably informed by a welter of facts that he had more shots on and off target than anyone else and came close to finishing as top scorer. Gliding gazelle-like away from defenders, Henry might be accused of having one fault: failing to finish with ferocity, needing to clinch things with the power of a Shire horse; but then any genius will find some critics.

Henry was pipped by one goal by Manchester United's Ruud Van Nistelrooy, in the race for the goal king of the season. A more direct spearhead, the cloned combination of these two would become virtually unplayable.

Because UEFA have a quaint notion about the Champions League and consider the qualifying part of the competition a total irrelevancy, the Dutch striker was deprived of officially equalling the record for being top scorer in the competiton. We have rectified this unfair omission in this edition and he takes his rightful place in the overall list of marksmen.

Were it possible to remedy as easily the many anomalies surrounding the game, now there's a thing.

SKY SPORTS FOOTBALL YEARBOOK HONOURS

Football, as we know, is all about opinions. This year, those members of the Football Writers' Association who selected their team of the season for Sky Sports Football Yearbook could find no room in the team or on the substitutes bench in the final analysis for David Beckham, the Manchester United player transferred to Real Madrid during the summer in a package deal said to have cost £25,000,000. Others who had support but failed to force their way in, included Steven Gerrard and Sami Hyypia (both Liverpool), Ryan Giggs, Rio Ferdinand and Mikael Silvestre (all Manchester United), Gianfranco Zola and John Terry (both Chelsea), plus Wayne Bridge (Southampton).

Once again, Michael Owen was kept out of the twin strikers role and had to be satisfied with a seat on the bench, as he had last year for both the Team of the Season and the Team of the Decade.

For the 2002–03 team of the season, the majority of members once again chose a 4-4-2 formation. Despite Manchester United securing their ninth Premier League title in eleven years, only three of their players, John O'Shea, Paul Scholes and Ruud Van Nistelrooy succeeded in making the first team. Last season's right-back Gary Neville was one of the substitutes, his place going to his Old Trafford colleague O'Shea, the Republic of Ireland international who has become one of the outstanding players over the last year.

Five different clubs were represented in the choice, but Liverpool had only Owen among the list of substitutes. Everton's discovery of the season, Wayne Rooney, did well to be represented as a substitute and the improvement shown by Blackburn Rovers was reflected in them having two players nominated, the United States of America goalkeeper Brad Friedel and Republic of Ireland winger Damien Duff. Manager of the Year was Sir Alex Ferguson, previously Manager of the Decade.

Africa was also represented in Jay-Jay Okocha, the Bolton Wanderers and Nigeria international midfield player.

Of players selected over the last ten years and from last year's honours, only Patrick Vieira of Arsenal has featured again. Arsenal striker Thierry Henry, who was also voted Professional Footballers' Association Footballer of the Year again partnered Van Nistelrooy up front. Arsenal full-back Ashley Cole retained his place, but there was a new pairing in central defence with both Rio Ferdinand transferred to Manchester United and Liverpool's Sami Hyypia losing their places to William Gallas of Chelsea and Sol Campbell of Arsenal. Paul Scholes of Manchester United was another clear winner for a slot in midfield.

Sky Sports Football Yearbook Team of the Season 2002–03

Brad Friedel
(*Blackburn R*)

John O'Shea (*Manchester U*) | Sol Campbell (*Arsenal*) | William Gallas (*Chelsea*) | Ashley Cole (*Arsenal*)

Jay-Jay Okocha (*Bolton W*) | Patrick Vieira (*Arsenal*) | Paul Scholes (*Manchester U*) | Damien Duff (*Blackburn R*)

Ruud Van Nistelrooy (*Manchester U*) | Thierry Henry (*Arsenal*)

Manager:
Sir Alex Ferguson CBE (*Manchester U*)

Substitutes:
Gary Neville *(Manchester U)*
Michael Owen *(Liverpool)*
Wayne Rooney *(Everton)*

THE FOOTBALL RECORDS

CHAMPIONS LEAGUE AND EUROPEAN CUP RECORDS

ALL TIME CHAMPIONS LEAGUE APPEARANCES

(including matches in the Qualifying competitions)

		Games	Goals
BECKHAM, DAVID		**81**	**15**
1994–95	Manchester U	1	1
1996–97	Manchester U	10	2
1997–98	Manchester U	8	0
1998–99	Manchester U	12	2
1999–2000	Manchester U	12	2
2000–01	Manchester U	12	0
2001–02	Manchester U	13	5
2002–03	Manchester U	13	3
MALDINI, PAOLO		**81**	**2**
1992–93	AC Milan	10	1
1993–94	AC Milan	13	1
1994–95	AC Milan	13	0
1996–97	AC Milan	6	0
1999–2000	AC Milan	6	0
2000–01	AC Milan	14	0
2002–03	AC Milan	19	0
NEVILLE, GARY		**80**	**1**
1993–94	Manchester U	1	0
1994–95	Manchester U	2	0
1996–97	Manchester U	10	0
1997–98	Manchester U	8	0
1998–99	Manchester U	12	0
1999–2000	Manchester U	9	0
2000–01	Manchester U	14	0
2001–02	Manchester U	14	0
2002–03	Manchester U	10	1
RAUL, GONZALEZ*		**78**	**43**
1995–96	Real Madrid	8	6
1997–98	Real Madrid	11	2
1998–99	Real Madrid	8	3
1999–2000	Real Madrid	15	10
2000–01	Real Madrid	12	7
2001–02	Real Madrid	12	6
2002–03	Real Madrid	12	9

* *Top scorer in Champions League*

		Games	Goals
de BOER, FRANK		**77**	**9**
1994–95	Ajax	10	2
1995–96	Ajax	9	1
1996–97	Ajax	9	0
1998–99	Ajax	6	0
1999–2000	Barcelona	12	2
2000–01	Barcelona	4	1
2001–02	Barcelona	13	0
2002–03	Barcelona	14	3
ROBERTO CARLOS		**76**	**12**
1997–98	Real Madrid	9	2
1998–99	Real Madrid	8	0
1999–2000	Real Madrid	17	4
2000–01	Real Madrid	14	4
2001–02	Real Madrid	13	1
2002–03	Real Madrid	15	1
GIGGS, RYAN		**74**	**20**
1994–95	Manchester U	3	2
1996–97	Manchester U	7	2
1997–98	Manchester U	5	1
1998–99	Manchester U	9	5
1999–2000	Manchester U	11	1
2000–01	Manchester U	11	2
2001–02	Manchester U	13	2
2002–03	Manchester U	15	5
KAHN, OLIVER		**73**	**0**
1994–95	Bayern Munich	5	0
1997–98	Bayern Munich	8	0
1998–99	Bayern Munich	13	0
1999–2000	Bayern Munich	13	0
2000–01	Bayern Munich	16	0
2001–02	Bayern Munich	12	0
2002–03	Bayern Munich	6	0
SOLSKJAER, OLE GUNNAR		**73**	**18**
1996–97	Manchester U	10	1
1997–98	Manchester U	6	1
1998–99	Manchester U	6	2
1999–2000	Manchester U	11	3
2000–01	Manchester U	11	0
2001–02	Manchester U	15	7
2002–03	Manchester U	14	4
KLUIVERT, PATRICK		**72**	**30**
1994–95	Ajax	10	2
1995–96	Ajax	8	5
1996–97	Ajax	4	2
1999–2000	Barcelona	14	7
2000–01	Barcelona	4	2
2001–02	Barcelona	17	7
2002–03	Barcelona	15	5
SCHOLES, PAUL		**71**	**18**
1994–95	Manchester U	2	0
1996–97	Manchester U	4	0
1997–98	Manchester U	7	2
1998–99	Manchester U	12	4
1999–2000	Manchester U	11	3
2000–01	Manchester U	12	6
2001–02	Manchester U	13	1
2002–03	Manchester U	10	2
STRAND, ROAR		**71**	**13**
1995–96	Rosenborg	8	2
1996–97	Rosenborg	10	1
1997–98	Rosenborg	8	4
1998–99	Rosenborg	8	1
1999–2000	Rosenborg	12	1
2000–01	Rosenborg	10	3
2001–02	Rosenborg	8	1
2002–03	Rosenborg	7	0

TOP TEN ALL TIME EUROPEAN CUP AND CHAMPIONS LEAGUE APPEARANCES

	P	W	D	L	F	A
Real Madrid	263	154	43	66	591	293
Bayern Munich	180	100	44	36	346	175
AC Milan	147	80	34	33	271	128
Manchester United	142	78	35	29	286	147
Juventus	155	77	37	41	260	160
Barcelona	140	78	31	31	269	155
Benfica	149	73	35	41	292	159
Ajax	129	68	31	39	215	116
Dynamo Kiev	144	67	30	47	209	158
Liverpool	99	57	22	20	194	84

ALL-TIME EUROPEAN CUP AND CHAMPIONS LEAGUE TOP SCORERS

Season	Player	Goals
1955–56	Milos Milutinovic (Partizan Belgrade)	8
1956–57	Dennis Viollet (Manchester United)	9
1957–58	Alfredo Di Stefano (Real Madrid)	10
1958–59	Just Fontaine (Reims)	10
1959–60	Ferenc Puskas (Real Madrid)	12
1960–61	Jose Aguas (Benfica)	11
1961–62	Alfredo Di Stefano (Real Madrid)	
	Ferenc Puskas (Real Madrid)	
	Justo Tejada (Real Madrid)	7
1962–63	Jose Altafini (AC Milan)	14
1963–64	Vladimir Kovacevic (Partizan Belgrade)	
	Ferenc Puskas (Real Madrid)	
	Alessandro Mazzola (Internazionale)	7
1964–65	Jose Torres (Benfica)	9
1965–66	Eusebio (Benfica)	
	Florian Albert (Ferencvaros)	7
1966–67	Paul Van Himst (Anderlecht)	
	Jurgen Piepenberg (Vorwaerts)	6
1967–68	Eusebio (Benfica)	6
1968–69	Denis Law (Manchester United)	9
1969–70	Mick Jones (Leeds United)	8
1970–71	Antonis Antoniadis (Panathinaikos)	10
1971–72	Sylvester Takac (Standard Liege)	
	Johan Cruyff (Ajax)	
	Lou Macari (Celtic)	5
1972–73	Gerd Muller (Bayern Munich)	11
1973–74	Gerd Muller (Bayern Munich)	9
1974–75	Gerd Muller (Bayern Munich)	6
1975–76	Josef Heynckes (Moenchengladbach)	
	Carlos Santillana (Real Madrid)	6
1976–77	Gerd Muller (Bayern Munich)	
	Franco Cucinotta (Zurich)	5
1977–78	Allan Simonsen (Moenchengladbach)	5
1978–79	Claudio Sulser (Grasshoppers)	11
1979–80	Soren Lerby (Ajax)	10
1980–81	Karl–Heinz Rummenigge (Bayern Munich)	
	Terry McDermott (Liverpool)	
	Graeme Souness (Liverpool)	6
1981–82	Dieter Hoeness (Bayern Munich)	7
1982–83	Paolo Rossi (Juventus)	6
1983–84	Viktor Sokol (Dynamo Minsk)	6
1984–85	Michel Platini (Juventus)	
	Torbjorn Nilsson (IFK Gothenburg)	7
1985–86	Torbjorn Nilsson (IFK Gothenburg)	7
1986–87	Borislav Cvetkovic (Red Star Belgrade)	7
1987–88	Rabah Madjer (Porto)	
	Jean-Marc Ferreri (Bordeaux)	
	Michel (Real Madrid)	
	Rui Aguas (Benfica)	
	Ally McCoist (Rangers)	
	Gheorghe Hagi (Steaua)	4
1988–89	Marco Van Basten (AC Milan)	10
1989–90	Romario (PSV Eindhoven)	
	Jean-Pierre Papin (Marseille)	6
1990–91	Peter Pacult (Tirol)	
	Jean-Pierre Papin (Marseille)	6
1991–92	Jean-Pierre Papin (Marseille)	7
1992–93	Romario (PSV Eindhoven)	7
1993–94	Ronald Koeman (Barcelona)	
	Wynton Rufer (Werder Bremen)	8
1994–95	George Weah (Paris St Germain)	7
1995–96	Jari Litmanen (Ajax)	9
1996–97	Ally McCoist (Rangers)	6
1997–98	Alessandro Del Piero (Juventus)	10
1998–99	Andrei Shevchenko (Dynamo Kiev)	10
1999–2000	Mario Jardel (Porto)	
	Rivaldo (Barcelona)	
	Raul (Real Madrid)	10
2000–01	Andrei Shevchenko (AC Milan)	
	Mario Jardel (Galatasaray)	9
2001–02	Ruud Van Nistelrooy (Manchester United)	10
2002–03	Ruud Van Nistelrooy (Manchester United)	14

EUROPEAN CUP AND CHAMPIONS LEAGUE RECORDS

CHAMPIONS LEAGUE ATTENDANCES AND GOALS FROM GROUP STAGES ONWARDS

Season	*Attendances*	*Average*	*Goals*	*Games*
1992–93	873,251	34,930	56	25
1993–94	1,202,289	44,529	71	27
1994–95	2,328,515	38,172	140	61
1995–96	1,874,316	30,726	159	61
1996–97	2,093,228	34,315	161	61
1997–98	2,868,271	33,744	239	85
1998–99	3,608,331	42,451	238	85
1999–2000	5,490,709	34,973	442	157
2000–01	5,773,486	36,774	449	157
2001–02	5,417,716	34,508	393	157
2002–03	6,461,112	41,154	431	157

HIGHEST AVERAGE ATTENDANCE IN ONE EUROPEAN CUP SEASON
1959–60 50,545 from a total attendance of 2,780,000.

HIGHEST SCORE IN A EUROPEAN/CHAMPIONS LEAGUE MATCH
Feyenoord (Holland)12, KR Reykjavik (Iceland) 0
(First Round First Leg 1969–70)

HIGHEST AGGREGATE
Benfica (Portugal) 18, Dudelange (Luxembourg) 0
(Preliminary Round 1965–66)

MOST GOALS OVERALL
49 Alfredo Di Stefano (Real Madrid) *(1955–64)*
46 Eusebio (Benfica) *(1959–74)*
43 Raul (Real Madrid) *(1995–2003)*
36 Gerd Muller (Bayern Munich) *(1969–77)*

WINS WITH TWO DIFFERENT CLUBS
Miodrag Belodedici (Steaua) 1986; (Red Star Belgrade) 1991.
Ronald Koeman (PSV Eindhoven) 1988; (Barcelona) 1992.
Dejan Savicevic (Red Star Belgrade) 1991; (AC Milan) 1994.
Marcel Desailly (Marseille) 1993; (AC Milan) 1994.
Frank Rijkaard (AC Milan) 1989, 1990; (Ajax) 1995.
Vladimir Jugovic (Red Star Belgrade) 1991; (Juventus) 1996.
Didier Deschamps (Marseille) 1993; (Juventus) 1996.
Paulo Sousa (Juventus) 1996; (Borussia Dortmund) 1997.
Christian Panucci (AC Milan) 1994; (Real Madrid) 1998.

MOST WINS WITH DIFFERENT CLUBS
Clarence Seedorf (Ajax) 1995; (Real Madrid) 1998; (AC Milan) 2003.

MOST WINNERS MEDALS
6 Francisco Gento (Real Madrid) 1956, 1957, 1958, 1959, 1960, 1966.
5 Alfredo Di Stefano (Real Madrid) 1956, 1957, 1958, 1959, 1960.
5 Jose Maria Zarraga (Real Madrid) 1956, 1957, 1958, 1959, 1960.
4 Jose-Hector Rial (Real Madrid) 1956, 1957, 1958, 1959.
4 Marquitos (Real Madrid) 1956, 1957, 1959, 1960.
4 Phil Neal (Liverpool) 1977, 1978, 1981, 1984.

EUROPEAN CUP AND CHAMPIONS LEAGUE RECORDS– *continued*

MOST GOALS SCORED IN FINALS
7 Alfredo Di Stefano (Real Madrid), 1956 (1), 1957 (1 pen), 1958 (1), 1959 (1), 1960 (3).
7 Ferenc Puskas (Real Madrid), 1960 (4), 1962 (3).

MOST FINAL APPEARANCES PER COUNTRY
Italy 23 (10 wins, 13 defeats).
Spain 19 (10 wins, 9 defeats).
Germany 13 (6 wins, 7 defeats).
England 11 (9 wins, 2 defeats).

MOST CLUB FINAL WINNERS

Real Madrid (Spain)	9	1956, 1957, 1958, 1959, 1960, 1966, 1998, 2000, 2002.
AC Milan (Italy)	6	1963, 1969, 1989, 1990, 1994, 2003.

MOST APPEARANCES IN FINAL
Real Madrid 12; AC Milan 9.

MOST SUCCESSFUL MANAGER
Bob Paisley (Liverpool) 1977, 1978, 1981.

FASTEST GOALS SCORED IN CHAMPIONS LEAGUE

20.07 sec	Gilberto Silva for Arsenal at PSV Eindhoven 25 September 2002.
20.12 sec	Alessandro Del Piero for Juventus at Manchester United 1 October 1997.

MOST SUCCESSIVE CHAMPIONS LEAGUE APPEARANCES
Rosenborg (Norway) 8 1995–96 – 2002–03.

MOST SUCCESSIVE WINS IN THE CHAMPIONS LEAGUE
Barcelona (Spain) 11 2002–03.

LANDMARKS

Wayne Rooney (Everton) became the youngest England international when he made his debut against Australia at the age of 17 years 111 days. James Prinsep had previously held the record since the 19th century, having made his first appearance against Scotland on 5 April 1879 at 17 years 252 days.

Michael Owen celebrated becoming the youngest England international to reach 50 appearances for his country scoring twice against Slovakia and captaining the team at the same time. He is the last England player to score a hat-trick which he achieved against Germany on 1 September 2001.

Two Manchester United players Ryan Giggs and Ole Gunnar Solskjaer reached a century of goals for the club. Giggs, who had at one time been Wales youngest international player at the age of 17 years 321 days also recorded his 500th senior game. Solskjaer once scored four Premier League goals in 13 minutes against Nottingham Forest on 6 February 1999.

Alan Shearer (Newcastle United) continued to achieve personal records. He reached his century of League goals for Newcastle, hit his first hat-trick in Europe for many years and overtook the record of Wyn Davies at the club who had scored ten goals in United's first three seasons of European competition. Shearer also reached his 300th club goal, received the player of the decade award from the PFA and hit the second fastest goal of all-time in the Premier League at 10.4 seconds.

Two of Arsenal's most experienced foreign internationals Dennis Bergkamp (Holland) and Thierry Henry (France) reached 100 goals for the club in the space of a week of each other. Henry took 181 games to reach his target, Bergkamp 296.

Blackpool's youngest ever first team player Philip Doughty was not even registered to play in the Football League when he made his debut in an LDV Vans Trophy match at the age of 16 years 92 days. He followed in a club tradition because on 9 September 1980, Eamon Collins had turned out in an Anglo-Scottish Cup match aged 14 years 323 days.

On 1 February 2003, three own goals in the space of eight minutes by Sunderland players in the home game with Charlton Athletic gave the visitors a fine start. Stephen Wright and Michael Proctor (two) were the culprits.

David Seaman (Arsenal), with intermediate honours added, reached 1000 senior matches By the end of the season his total was 1020 comprising 712 League, 59 League Cup, 81 FA Cup, 73 Europe, 4 Charity Shield, 75 full England caps, 6 B Internationals and 10 Under-21. Though he began with Leeds United, his first League appearances were with Peterbrough United, followed by Birmingham City and Queens Park Rangers.

Manchester United reached their 100th win in Europe. Their first had been in the second leg of their first tie against Anderlecht on 26 September 1956. This 10-0 win remains their highest score in a cup match and helped complete a 12-0 aggregate win.

Dion Dublin (Aston Villa) joined the Premier League's 100 goal club having scored earlier during the period of Premiership matches with initially Manchester United, then Coventry City.

Wayne Rooney also became the youngest player to score in the FA Premier League at 16 years 360 days, but was overtaken by James Milner (Leeds United) at 16 years 357 days. Michael Owen had been the previous youngest at 17 years 144 days.

Arsenal broke the record of consecutive scoring reaching 47 and then extended it to 55. Chesterfield had held the record since 1929–30

Paul Jackson of Stocksbridge Park Steels equalled the FA Cup record by scoring 10 goals in the 17-1 preliminary win over Oldham Town.

Lee Holmes (Derby Co) at 15 years 277 days, became the youngest player to appear in the FA Cup proper. Nine days earlier he had become his club's youngest League debutant.

Gianfranco Zola (Chelsea) in his last season in England reached his 200th League game and 300th senior match for the Stamford Bridge club. He also finished with 59 Premier League goals, more than any other Chelsea player.

Andy Goram completed every domestic cup honour in Scotland by helping Queen of the South to victory in the Bell's Challenge Cup.

Fulham fielded 11 internationals from 11 different countries during the match with Bury in the Worthington Cup, one of 20 cup matches played in four competitions.

Arsenal extended their number of consecutive Premier League victories to 14 on the opening day of the season.

Northern Ireland played their 500th international match against Spain on 11 June 2003.

In Ireland's first ever international against England on 18 February 1882, they fielded the youngest ever player in Samuel Johnston aged 15 years 154 days. The following week he scored the first goal for Ireland against Wales.

OTHER BRITISH FOOTBALL RECORDS

ALL-TIME PREMIER LEAGUE CHAMPIONSHIP SEASONS IN ORDER OF MERIT

	Team	Season	P	W	D	L	F	A	Pts	Pts Av
1	Manchester U	1999–2000	38	28	7	3	97	45	91	2.39
2	Arsenal	2001–02	38	26	9	3	79	36	87	2.26
3	Manchester U	1993–94	42	27	11	4	80	38	92	2.19
4	Manchester U	2002–03	38	25	8	5	74	34	83	2.18
5	Manchester U	1995–96	38	25	7	6	73	35	82	2.15
6	Blackburn R	1994–95	42	27	8	7	80	39	89	2.11
7	Manchester U	2000–01	38	24	8	6	79	31	80	2.09
8	Manchester U	1998–99	38	22	13	3	80	37	79	2.07
9	Arsenal	1997–98	38	23	9	6	68	33	78	2.05
10	Manchester U	1992–93	42	24	12	6	67	31	84	2.00
11	Manchester U	1996–97	38	21	12	5	76	44	75	1.97

TOP TEN WORLD TRANSFERS

	Player	Clubs	Fee (£m)	Year
1	Zinedine Zidane	Juventus to Real Madrid	46.5	2001
2	Luis Figo	Barcelona to Real Madrid	37.4	2000
3	Hernan Crespo	Parma to Lazio	35.7	2000
4	Gianluigi Buffon	Parma to Juventus	34	2001
5	Christian Vieri	Lazio to Internationale	31	1999
6	Rio Ferdinand	Leeds U to Manchester U	30	2002
7	Giazka Mendieta	Valencia to Lazio	29	2001
8	Ronaldo	Internazionale to Real Madrid	28.9	2002
9	Juan Sebastian Veron	Lazio to Manchester United	28.1	2001
10	Rui Costa	Fiorentina to AC Milan	28	2001

Source: National Press.

TOP TEN BRITISH TRANSFERS (incoming only)

	Player	Clubs	Fee (£m)	Year
1	Rio Ferdinand	Leeds U to Manchester U	30	2002
2	Juan Sebastian Veron	Lazio to Manchester U	28.1	2001
3	Ruud Van Nistelrooy	PSV Eindhoven to Manchester U	19	2001
4	Rio Ferdinand	West Ham U to Leeds U	18	2000
5	Alan Shearer	Blackburn R to Newcastle U	15	1996
	Jimmy Floyd Hasselbaink	Atletico Madrid to Chelsea	15	2000
7	Nicolas Anelka	Paris St Germain to Manchester C	13	2002
8	Dwight Yorke	Aston Villa to Manchester U	12	1998
	Tor Andre Flo	Chelsea to Rangers	12	2000
10	Sylvain Wiltord	Bordeaux to Arsenal	11	2000

Source: National Press.

TOP TEN TRANSFER SPENDERS 2002

	Club	Spend (£m)
1	Manchester United	38.6
2	Manchester City	28.74
3	Middlesbrough	21.65
4	Liverpool	19.8
5	Newcastle United	18.5
6	Sunderland	18
7	Birmingham City	10.75
8	Everton	10.6
9	Aston Villa	9.75
10	Tottenham Hotspur	7.9

Source: National Press.

TOP TEN WORLD STARS ANNUAL WAGES

	Player	Club	Wages (£m)
1	David Beckham	Man U/Real Madrid	10.53
2	Zinedine Zidane	Real Madrid	9.83
3	Ronaldo	Real Madrid	8.22
4	Rio Ferdinand	Manchester United	6.75
5	Alessandro Del Piero	Juventus	6.57
6	Hideotoshi Nakata	Parka	6.57
7	Raul	Real Madrid	6.53
8	Christian Vieira	Internazionale	6.52
9	Michael Owen	Liverpool	6.25
10	Roy Keane	Manchester United	6.07

Source: National Press

TOP TEN PREMIER LEAGUE AVERAGE ATTENDANCES 2002–03

1	Manchester U	67,630
2	Newcastle U	51,920
3	Liverpool	43,243
4	Chelsea	39,799
5	Sunderland	39,698
6	Leeds U	39,127
7	Everton	38,468
8	Arsenal	38,040
9	Tottenham H	35,899
10	Aston Villa	35,081

TOP TEN GOALSCORERS IN WORLD CUP FINAL TOURNAMENTS

1	Gerd Muller (West Germany)	1970, 74	14
2	Just Fontaine (France)	1958	13
3	Pele (Brazil)	1958, 70	12
4	Ronaldo (Brazil)	1998, 2002	12
5	Sandor Kocsis (Hungary)	1954	11
6	Jurgen Klinsmann (Germany)	1990, 98	11
7	Helmut Rahn (West Germany)	1954, 58	10
	Teofilo Cubillas (Peru)	1970, 78	10
	Grzegorz Lato (Poland)	1974, 82	10
	Gary Lineker (England)	1986, 90	10
	Gabriel Batistuta (Argentina)	1994, 2002	10

TOP TEN FOOTBALL LEAGUE AVERAGE ATTENDANCES 2002–03

1	Leicester C	29,219
2	Wolverhampton W	25,745
3	Derby Co	25,470
4	Ipswich T	25,455
5	Nottingham F	24,437
6	Norwich C	20,353
7	Sheffield W	20,327
8	Portsmouth	18,934
9	Sheffield U	18,113
10	Crystal Palace	16,867

TOP TEN ALL-TIME ENGLAND GOALSCORERS

1	Bobby Charlton	49
2	Gary Lineker	48
3	Jimmy Greaves	44
4	Tom Finney	30
5	Nat Lofthouse	30
6	Alan Shearer	30
7	Vivian Woodward	29
8	Steve Bloomer	28
9	David Platt	27
10	Bryan Robson	26

TOP TEN AVERAGE ATTENDANCES

1	Manchester United	2002–03	67,630
2	Manchester United	2001–02	67,586
3	Manchester United	2000–01	67,544
4	Manchester United	1999–2000	58,017
5	Manchester United	1967–68	57,552
6	Newcastle United	1947–48	56,283
7	Tottenham Hotspur	1950–51	55,509
8	Manchester United	1998–99	55,188
9	Manchester United	1997–98	55,168
10	Manchester United	1996–97	55,081

TOP TEN AVERAGE WORLD CUP FINAL CROWDS

1	In USA	1994	68,604
2	In Brazil	1950	60,772
3	In Mexico	1970	52,311
4	In England	1966	50,458
5	In Italy	1990	48,368
6	In Mexico	1986	46,956
7	In West Germany	1974	46,684
8	In France	1998	43,366
9	In Argentina	1978	42,374
10	In South Korea/Japan	2002	42,274

TOP TEN ALL-TIME ENGLAND CAPS

1	Peter Shilton	125
2	Bobby Moore	108
3	Bobby Charlton	106
4	Billy Wright	105
5	Bryan Robson	90
6	Kenny Sansom	86
7	Ray Wilkins	84
8	Gary Lineker	80
9	John Barnes	79
10	Stuart Pearce	78

TOP TEN PREMIERSHIP APPEARANCES

1	Gary Speed	376
2	Nigel Winterburn	352
3	David James	345
4	Alan Shearer	344
5	Teddy Sheringham	343
6	Ryan Giggs	342
7	Gareth Southgate	339
8	Tim Sherwood	328
9	David Seaman	325
10	Gary McAllister	325

MOST GOALS FOR IN A SEASON

FA PREMIER LEAGUE		Goals	Games
1999–2000	Manchester U	97	38
FOOTBALL LEAGUE			
Division 1			
1930–31	Aston V	128	42
Division 2			
1926–27	Middlesbrough	122	42
Division 3(S)			
1927–28	Millwall	127	42
Division 3(N)			
1928–29	Bradford C	128	42
Division 3			
1961–62	QPR	111	46
Division 4			
1960–61	Peterborough U	134	46
SCOTTISH PREMIER LEAGUE			
2001–02	Celtic	94	38
SCOTTISH LEAGUE			
Premier Division			
1991–92	Rangers	101	44
1982–83	Dundee U	90	36
1982–83	Celtic	90	36
1986–87	Celtic	90	44
Division 1			
1957–58	Hearts	132	34
Division 2			
1937–38	Raith R	142	34
New Division 1			
1993–94	Dunfermline Ath	93	44
1981–82	Motherwell	92	39
New Division 2			
1987–88	Ayr U	95	39
New Division 3			
1997–98	Alloa	78	36

FEWEST GOALS AGAINST IN A SEASON

FA PREMIER LEAGUE		Goals	Games
1998–99	Arsenal	17	38
FOOTBALL LEAGUE (minimum 42 games)			
Division 1			
1978–79	Liverpool	16	42
Division 2			
1924–25	Manchester U	23	42
2002–03	Wigan Ath	25	46
Division 3(S)			
1921–22	Southampton	21	42
Division 3(N)			
1953–54	Port Vale	21	46
Division 3			
1995–96	Gillingham	20	46
Division 4			
1980–81	Lincoln C	25	46
SCOTTISH PREMIER LEAGUE			
2001–02	Celtic	18	38
SCOTTISH LEAGUE (minimum 30 games)			
Premier Division			
1989–90	Rangers	19	36
1986–87	Rangers	23	44
1987–88	Celtic	23	44
Division 1			
1913–14	Celtic	14	38
Division 3			
1966–67	Morton	20	38
New Division 1			
1996–97	St Johnstone	23	36
1980–81	Hibernian	24	39
1993–94	Falkirk	32	44
New Division 2			
1987–88	St Johnstone	24	39
1990–91	Stirling Alb	24	39
New Division 3			
1995–96	Brechin C	21	36

FEWEST GOALS FOR IN A SEASON

FA PREMIER LEAGUE		Goals	Games
1996–97	Leeds U	28	38
FOOTBALL LEAGUE (minimum 42 games)			
Division 1			
1984–85	Stoke C	24	42
Division 2			
1971–72	Watford	24	42
1994–95	Leyton Orient	30	46
Division 3(S)			
1950–51	Crystal Palace	33	46
Division 3(N)			
1923–24	Crewe Alex	32	42
Division 3			
1969–70	Stockport Co	27	46
Division 4			
1981–82	Crewe Alex	29	46
SCOTTISH PREMIER LEAGUE			
2001–02	St Johnstone	24	38
SCOTTISH LEAGUE (minimum 30 games)			
Premier Division			
1988–89	Hamilton A	19	36
1991–92	Dunfermline Ath	22	44
Division 1			
1993–94	Brechin C	30	44
1966–67	Ayr U	20	34
Division 2			
1923–24	Lochgelly U	20	38
New Division 1			
1980–81	Stirling Alb	18	39
1995–96	Dumbarton	23	36
New Division 2			
1994–95	Brechin C	22	36
New Division 3			
1995–96	Alloa	26	36

MOST GOALS AGAINST IN A SEASON

FA PREMIER LEAGUE		Goals	Games
1993–94	Swindon T	100	42
FOOTBALL LEAGUE			
Division 1			
1930–31	Blackpool	125	42
Division 2			
1898–99	Darwen	141	34
Division 3(S)			
1929–30	Merthyr T	135	42
Division 3(N)			
1927–28	Nelson	136	42
Division 3			
1959–60	Accrington S	123	46
Division 4			
1959–60	Hartlepools U	109	46
SCOTTISH PREMIER LEAGUE			
1999–2000	Aberdeen	83	36
SCOTTISH LEAGUE			
Premier Division			
1984–85	Morton	100	36
1987–88	Morton	100	44
Division 1			
1931–32	Leith Ath	137	38
Division 2			
1931–32	Edinburgh C	146	38
New Division 1			
1988–89	Queen of the S	99	39
1992–93	Cowdenbeath	109	44
New Division 2			
1977–78	Meadowbank T	89	39
New Division 3			
1994–95	Albion R	82	36

GOALS PER GAME (from 1992–93)

Goals per game	Premier Games	Premier Goals	Division 1 Games	Division 1 Goals	Division 2 Games	Division 2 Goals	Division 3 Games	Division 3 Goals
0	387	0	520	0	506	0	487	0
1	830	830	1121	1121	1141	1141	1126	1126
2	1098	2196	1518	3036	1563	3126	1463	2926
3	900	2700	1262	3786	1314	3942	1261	3783
4	615	2460	864	3456	832	3328	765	3060
5	316	1580	465	2325	429	2145	391	1955
6	170	1020	217	1302	169	1014	190	1140
7	72	504	73	511	84	588	81	567
8	31	248	24	192	23	184	27	216
9	7	63	4	36	9	81	8	72
10	0	0	2	20	2	20	2	20
11	0	0	2	22	0	0	1	11
	4426	**11601**	**6072**	**15807**	**6072**	**15569**	**5802**	**14876**

GOALS PER GAME (Football League to 1991–92))

Goals per game	Division 1 Games	Division 1 Goals	Division 2 Games	Division 2 Goals	Division 3 Games	Division 3 Goals	Division 4 Games	Division 4 Goals	Division 3(S) Games	Division 3(S) Goals	Division 3(N) Games	Division 3(N) Goals
0	2465	0	2665	0	1446	0	1438	0	997	0	803	0
1	5606	5606	5836	5836	3225	3225	3106	3106	2073	2073	1914	1914
2	8275	16550	8609	17218	4569	9138	4441	8882	3314	6628	2939	5878
3	7731	23193	7842	23526	3784	11352	4041	12123	2996	8988	2922	8766
4	6230	24920	5897	23588	2837	11348	2784	11136	2445	9780	2410	9640
5	3751	18755	3634	18170	1566	7830	1506	7530	1554	7770	1599	7995
6	2137	12822	2007	12042	769	4614	786	4716	870	5220	930	5580
7	1092	7644	1001	7007	357	2499	336	2352	451	3157	461	3227
8	542	4336	376	3008	135	1080	143	1144	209	1672	221	1768
9	197	1773	164	1476	64	576	35	315	76	684	102	918
10	83	830	68	680	13	130	8	80	33	330	45	450
11	37	407	19	209	2	22	7	77	15	165	15	165
12	12	144	17	204	1	12	0	0	7	84	8	96
13	4	52	4	52	0	0	0	0	2	26	4	52
14	2	28	1	14	0	0	0	0	0	0	0	0
17	0	0	0	0	0	0	0	0	0	0	1	17
	38164	**117060**	**38140**	**113030**	**18768**	**51826**	**18631**	**51461**	**15042**	**46577**	**14374**	**46466**

New Overall Totals (since 1992)		Complete Overall Totals (since 1888–89)	
Games	22372	Games	165491
Goals	57853	Goals	484273

TOP TEN PREMIERSHIP GOALSCORERS

1	Alan Shearer	221	**6**	Dwight Yorke	116
2	Andy Cole	152	**7**	Ian Wright	113
3	Les Ferdinand	136	**8**	Dion Dublin	108
4	Robbie Fowler	136	**9**	Michael Owen	102
5	Teddy Sheringham	129	**10**	Matthew Le Tissier	101

MOST CUP GOALS IN A CAREER

FA CUP (Pre-Second World war)
Henry Cursham 48 (Notts Co)

FA CUP (post-war)
Ian Rush 43 (Chester, Liverpool)

LEAGUE CUP
Geoff Hurst 49 (West Ham U, Stoke C)
Ian Rush 49 (Chester, Liverpool, Newcastle U)

SCORED IN EVERY PREMIERSHIP GAME

Arsenal 2001–02 38 matches

MOST FA CUP FINAL GOALS

Ian Rush (Liverpool) 5: 1986(2), 1989(2), 1992(1)

MOST LEAGUE GOALS IN A SEASON

FA PREMIER LEAGUE		*Goals*	*Games*
1993–94	Andy Cole (Newcastle U)	34	40
1994–95	Alan Shearer (Blackburn R)	34	42
FOOTBALL LEAGUE			
Division 1			
1927–28	Dixie Dean (Everton)	60	39
Division 2			
1926–27	George Camsell (Middlesbrough)	59	37
Division 3(S)			
1936–37	Joe Payne (Luton T)	55	39
Division 3(N)			
1936–37	Ted Harston (Mansfield T)	55	41
Division 3			
1959–60	Derek Reeves (Southampton)	39	46
Division 4			
1960–61	Terry Bly (Peterborough U)	52	46
FA CUP			
1887–88	Jimmy Ross (Preston NE)	20	8
LEAGUE CUP			
1986–87	Clive Allen (Tottenham H)	12	9
SCOTTISH PREMIER LEAGUE			
2000–01	Henrik Larsson (Celtic)	35	37
SCOTTISH LEAGUE			
Division 1			
1931–32	William McFadyen (Motherwell)	52	34
Division 2			
1927–28	Jim Smith (Ayr U)	66	38

MOST LEAGUE GOALS IN A CAREER

FOOTBALL LEAGUE

Arthur Rowley	*Goals*	*Games*	*Season*
WBA	4	24	1946–48
Fulham	27	56	1948–50
Leicester C	251	303	1950–58
Shrewsbury T	152	236	1958–65
	434	619	

SCOTTISH LEAGUE

Jimmy McGrory			
Celtic	1	3	1922–23
Clydebank	13	30	1923–24
Celtic	396	375	1924–38
	410	408	

HAT-TRICKS

Career
34 Dixie Dean (Tranmere R, Everton, Notts Co, England)

Division 1 (one season post-war)
6 Jimmy Greaves (Chelsea), 1960–61

Three for one team one match
West, Spouncer, Hooper, Nottingham F v Leicester Fosse, Division 1, 21 April 1909
Barnes, Ambler, Davies, Wrexham v Hartlepools U, Division 4, 3 March 1962
Adcock, Stewart, White, Manchester C v Huddersfield T, Division 2, 7 Nov 1987
Loasby, Smith, Wells, Northampton T v Walsall, Division 3S, 5 Nov 1927
Bowater, Hoyland, Readman, Mansfield T v Rotherham U, Division 3N, 27 Dec 1932

MOST GOALS IN A GAME

FA PREMIER LEAGUE	
19 Sept 1999	Alan Shearer (Newcastle U) 5 goals v Sheffield W
4 Mar 1995	Andy Cole (Manchester U) 5 goals v Ipswich T
FOOTBALL LEAGUE	
Division 1	
14 Dec 1935	Ted Drake (Arsenal) 7 goals v Aston V
Division 2	
5 Feb 1955	Tommy Briggs (Blackburn R) 7 goals v Bristol R
23 Feb 1957	Neville Coleman (Stoke C) 7 goals v Lincoln C
Division 3(S)	
13 April 1936	Joe Payne (Luton T) 10 goals v Bristol R
Division 3(N)	
26 Dec 1935	Bunny Bell (Tranmere R) 9 goals v Oldham Ath
Division 3	
16 Sept 1969	Steve Earle (Fulham) 5 goals v Halifax T
24 April 1965	Barrie Thomas (Scunthorpe U) 5 goals v Luton T
20 Nov 1965	Keith East (Swindon T) 5 goals v Mansfield T
2 Oct 1971	Alf Wood (Shrewsbury T) 5 goals v Blackburn R
10 Sept 1983	Tony Caldwell (Bolton W) 5 goals v Walsall
4 May 1987	Andy Jones (Port Vale) 5 goals v Newport Co
3 April 1990	Steve Wilkinson (Mansfield T) 5 goals v Birmingham C
5 Sept 1998	Giuliano Grazioli (Peterborough U) 5 goals v Barnet
6 April 2002	Lee Jones (Wrexham) 5 goals v Cambridge U
Division 4	
26 Dec 1962	Bert Lister (Oldham Ath) 6 goals v Southport
FA CUP	
20 Nov 1971	Ted MacDougall (Bournemouth) 9 goals v Margate (*1st Round*)
LEAGUE CUP	
25 Oct 1989	Frankie Bunn (Oldham Ath) 6 goals v Scarborough
SCOTTISH LEAGUE	
Premier Division	
17 Nov 1984	Paul Sturrock (Dundee U) 5 goals v Morton
Division 1	
14 Sept 1928	Jimmy McGrory (Celtic) 8 goals v Dunfermline Ath
Division 2	
1 Oct 1927	Owen McNally (Arthurlie) 8 goals v Armadale
2 Jan 1930	Jim Dyet (King's Park) 8 goals v Forfar Ath
18 April 1936	John Calder (Morton) 8 goals v Raith R
20 Aug 1937	Norman Hayward (Raith R) 8 goals v Brechin C
SCOTTISH CUP	
12 Sept 1885	John Petrie (Arbroath) 13 goals v Bon Accord (*1st Round*)

HIGHEST WINS

Highest win in a First-Class Match
(Scottish Cup 1st Round)

Arbroath	36	Bon Accord	0	12 Sept 1885

Highest win in an International Match

England	13	Ireland	0	18 Feb 1882

Highest win in a FA Cup Match

Preston NE *(1st Round)*	26	Hyde U	0	15 Oct 1887

Highest win in a League Cup Match

West Ham U *(2nd Round, 2nd Leg)*	10	Bury	0	25 Oct 1983
Liverpool *(2nd Round, 1st Leg)*	10	Fulham	0	23 Sept 1986

Highest win in an FA Premier League Match

Manchester U	9	Ipswich T	0	4 March 1995
Nottingham F	1	Manchester U	8	6 Feb 1999

Highest win in a Football League Match
Division 1 – highest home win

WBA	12	Darwen	0	4 April 1892
Nottingham F	12	Leicester Fosse	0	21 April 1909

Division 1 – highest away win

Newcastle U	1	Sunderland	9	5 Dec 1908
Cardiff C	1	Wolverhampton W	9	3 Sept 1955

Division 2 – highest home win

Newcastle U	13	Newport Co	0	5 Oct 1946

Division 2 – highest away win

Burslem PV	0	Sheffield U	10	10 Dec 1892

Division 3 – highest home win

Gillingham	10	Chesterfield	0	5 Sept 1987

Division 3 – highest away win

Barnet	1	Peterborough U	9	5 Sept 1998

Division 3(S) – highest home win

Luton T	12	Bristol R	0	13 April 1936

Division 3(S – highest away win

Northampton T	0	Walsall	8	2 Feb 1947

Division 3(N – highest home win

Stockport Co	13	Halifax T	0	6 Jan 1934

Division 3(N) – highest away win

Accrington S	0	Barnsley	9	3 Feb 1934

Division 4 – highest home win

Oldham Ath	11	Southport	0	26 Dec 1962

Division 4 – highest away win

Crewe Alex	1	Rotherham U	8	8 Sept 1973

Highest wins in a Scottish League Match
Scottish Premier Division – highest home win

Aberdeen	8	Motherwell	0	26 March 1979

Scottish Premier Division – highest away win

Hamilton A	0	Celtic	8	5 Nov 1988

Scottish Division 1 – highest home win

Celtic	11	Dundee	0	26 Oct 1895

Scottish Division 1 – highest away win

Airdrieonians	1	Hibernian	11	24 Oct 1950

Scottish Division 2 – highest home win

Airdrieonians	15	Dundee Wanderers	1	1 Dec 1894

Scottish Division 2 – highest away win

Alloa Ath	0	Dundee	10	8 March 1947

ALL HOME WINS IN A SEASON

Brentford won all 21 games in Division 3(S), 1929–30

RECORD AWAY WINS IN A SEASON

Doncaster R won 18 of 21 games in Division 3(N), 1946–47

CONSECUTIVE AWAY WINS

Arsenal 8 games FA Premier League 2001–02

FEWEST WINS IN A SEASON

		Wins	Games
FA PREMIER LEAGUE			
1993–94	Swindon T	5	42
2002–03	Sunderland	4	38
FOOTBALL LEAGUE			
Division 1			
1889–90	Stoke C	3	22
1912–13	Woolwich Arsenal	3	38
1984–85	Stoke C	3	42
Division 2			
1899–1900	Loughborough T	1	34
1983–84	Cambridge U	4	42
Division 3(S)			
1929–30	Merthyr T	6	42
1925–26	QPR	6	42
Division 3(N)			
1931–32	Rochdale	4	40
Division 3			
1973–74	Rochdale	2	46
Division 4			
1976–77	Southport	3	46
SCOTTISH PREMIER LEAGUE			
1998–99	Dunfermline Ath	4	36
SCOTTISH LEAGUE			
Premier Division			
1975–76	St Johnstone	3	36
1982–83	Kilmarnock	3	36
1987–88	Morton	3	44
Division 1			
1891–92	Vale of Leven	0	22
Division 2			
1905–06	East Stirlingshire	1	22
1974–75	Forfar Ath	1	38
New Division 1			
1988–89	Queen of the S	2	39
1992–93	Cowdenbeath	3	44
New Division 2			
1975–76	Forfar Ath	4	26
1987–88	Stranraer	4	39
New Division 3			
2002–03	East Stirling	2	36

UNDEFEATED AT HOME

Liverpool 85 games (63 League, 9 League Cup, 7 European, 6 FA Cup), Jan 1978–Jan 1981

UNDEFEATED AWAY

Arsenal 19 games FA Premier League 2001–02 (only Preston NE with 11 in 1888–89 had previously remained unbeaten away)

HIGHEST AGGREGATE SCORES

Highest Aggregate Score England
Division 3(N)

Tranmere R	13	Oldham Ath	4	26 Dec 1935

Highest Aggregate Score Scotland
Division 2

Airdrieonians	15	Dundee Wanderers	1	1 Dec 1894

MOST WINS IN A SEASON

		Wins	Games
FA PREMIER LEAGUE			
1999–2000	Manchester U	28	38
FOOTBALL LEAGUE			
Division 1			
1960–61	Tottenham H	31	42
2001–02	Manchester C	31	46
Division 2			
1919–20	Tottenham H	32	42
Division 3(S)			
1927–28	Millwall	30	42
1929–30	Plymouth Arg	30	42
1946–47	Cardiff C	30	42
1950–51	Nottingham F	30	46
1954–55	Bristol C	30	46
Division 3(N)			
1946–47	Doncaster R	33	42
Division 3			
1971–72	Aston V	32	46
Division 4			
1975–76	Lincoln C	32	46
1985–86	Swindon T	32	46
SCOTTISH PREMIER LEAGUE			
2000–01	Celtic	31	38
2002–03	Rangers	31	38
	Celtic	31	38
SCOTTISH LEAGUE			
Premier Division			
1995–96	Rangers	27	36
1984–85	Aberdeen	27	36
1991–92	Rangers	33	44
1992–93	Rangers	33	44
Division 1			
1920–21	Rangers	35	42
Division 2			
1966–67	Morton	33	38
New Division 1			
1998–99	Hibernian	28	36
New Division 2			
1983–84	Forfar Ath	27	39
1987–88	Ayr U	27	39
New Division 3			
1994–95	Forfar Ath	25	36

MOST POINTS IN A SEASON

(three points for a win)

		Points	Games
FA PREMIER LEAGUE			
1993–94	Manchester U	92	42
FOOTBALL LEAGUE			
Division 1			
1998–99	Sunderland	105	46
1984–85	Everton	90	42
1987–88	Liverpool	90	40
Division 2			
1998–99	Fulham	101	46
Division 3			
2001–02	Plymouth Arg	102	46
Division 4			
1985–86	Swindon T	102	46
SCOTTISH PREMIER LEAGUE			
2001–02	Celtic	103	38
SCOTTISH LEAGUE			
Premier League			
1995–96	Rangers	87	36
New Division 1			
1998–99	Hibernian	89	36
New Division 2			
1995–96	Stirling Alb	81	36
New Division 3			
1994–95	Forfar Ath	80	36

MOST POINTS IN A SEASON

(under old system of two points for a win)

		Points	Games
FOOTBALL LEAGUE			
Division 1			
1978–79	Liverpool	68	42
Division 2			
1919–20	Tottenham H	70	42
Division 3			
1971–72	Aston V	70	46
Division 3(S)			
1950–51	Nottingham F	70	46
1954–55	Bristol C	70	46
Division 3(N)			
1946–47	Doncaster R	72	42
Division 4			
1975–76	Lincoln C	74	46
SCOTTISH LEAGUE			
Premier Division			
1984–85	Aberdeen	59	36
1992–93	Rangers	73	44
Division 1			
1920–21	Rangers	76	42
Division 2			
1966–67	Morton	69	38
New Division 1			
1976–77	St Mirren	62	39
1993–94	Falkirk	66	44
New Division 2			
1983–84	Forfar Ath	63	39

FEWEST POINTS IN A SEASON

		Points	Games
FA PREMIER LEAGUE			
1999–2000	Watford	24	38
FOOTBALL LEAGUE (minimum 34 games)			
Division 1			
1984–85	Stoke C	17	42
Division 2			
1904–05	Doncaster R	8	34
1899–1900	Loughborough T	8	34
Division 3			
1997–98	Doncaster R	20	46
Division 3(S)			
1924–25 & 1929–30	Merthyr T	21	42
1925–26	QPR	21	42
Division 3(N)			
1931–32	Rochdale	11	40
Division 4			
1976–77	Workington	19	46
SCOTTISH PREMIER LEAGUE			
2001–02	St Johnstone	21	38
SCOTTISH LEAGUE (minimum 30 games)			
Premier Division			
1975–76	St Johnstone	11	36
1987–88	Morton	16	44
Division 1			
1954–55	Stirling Alb	6	30
Division 2			
1936–37	Edinburgh C	7	34
New Division 1			
1988–89	Queen of the S	10	39
1992–93	Cowdenbeath	13	44
New Division 2			
1987–88	Berwick R	16	39
1987–88	Stranraer	16	39
New Division 3			
2002–03	East Stirling	13	36

FEWEST DEFEATS IN A SEASON

(Minimum 20 games)

FA PREMIER LEAGUE		Defeats	Games
1998–99	Manchester U	3	38
1998–99	Chelsea	3	38
1999–2000	Manchester U	3	38
2001–02	Arsenal	3	38
FOOTBALL LEAGUE			
Division 1			
1888–89	Preston NE	0	22
1990–91	Arsenal	1	38
1987–88	Liverpool	2	40
1968–69	Leeds U	2	42
Division 2			
1893–94	Liverpool	0	28
1897–98	Burnley	2	30
1905–06	Bristol C	2	38
1963–64	Leeds U	3	42
2002–03	Wigan Ath	4	46
Division 3			
1966–67	QPR	5	46
1989–90	Bristol R	5	46
1997–98	Notts Co	5	46
Division 3(S)			
1921–22	Southampton	4	42
1929–30	Plymouth Arg	4	42
Division 3(N)			
1953–54	Port Vale	3	46
1946–47	Doncaster R	3	42
1923–24	Wolverhampton W	3	42
Division 4			
1975–76	Lincoln C	4	46
1981–82	Sheffield U	4	46
1981–82	Bournemouth	4	46
SCOTTISH PREMIER LEAGUE			
2001–02	Celtic	1	38
SCOTTISH LEAGUE			
Premier Division			
1995–96	Rangers	3	36
1987–88	Celtic	3	44
Division 1			
1898–99	Rangers	0	18
1920–21	Rangers	1	42
Division 2			
1956–57	Clyde	1	36
1962–63	Morton	1	36
1967–68	St Mirren	1	36
New Division 1			
1975–76	Partick T	2	26
1976–77	St Mirren	2	39
1992–93	Raith R	4	44
1993–94	Falkirk	4	44
New Division 2			
1975–76	Raith R	1	26
1975–76	Clydebank	3	26
1983–84	Forfar Ath	3	39
1986–87	Raith R	3	39
1998–99	Livingston	3	36
New Division 3			
2000–01	Hamilton A	4	36

MOST LEAGUE MEDALS

Phil Neal (Liverpool) 8: 1976, 1977, 1979, 1980, 1982, 1983, 1984, 1986
Alan Hansen (Liverpool) 8: 1979, 1980, 1982, 1983, 1984, 1986, 1988, 1990
Ryan Giggs (Manchester U) 8: 1993, 1994, 1996, 1997, 1999, 2000, 2001, 2003

LEAGUE CHAMPIONSHIP HAT-TRICKS

Huddersfield T	1923–24 to 1925–26
Arsenal	1932–33 to 1934–35
Liverpool	1981–82 to 1983–84
Manchester U	1998–99 to 2000–01

MOST DEFEATS IN A SEASON

FA PREMIER LEAGUE		Defeats	Games
1994–95	Ipswich T	29	42
FOOTBALL LEAGUE			
Division 1			
1984–85	Stoke C	31	42
2001–02	Stockport Co	32	46
Division 2			
1938–39	Tranmere R	31	42
1992–93	Chester C	33	46
2000–01	Oxford U	33	46
Division 3			
1997–98	Doncaster R	34	46
Division 3(S)			
1924–25	Merthyr T	29	42
1952–53	Walsall	29	46
1953–54	Walsall	29	46
Division 3(N)			
1931–32	Rochdale	33	40
Division 4			
1987–88	Newport Co	33	46
SCOTTISH PREMIER LEAGUE			
2001–02	St Johnstone	27	38
SCOTTISH LEAGUE			
Premier Division			
1984–85	Morton	29	36
Division 1			
1920–21	St Mirren	31	42
Division 2			
1962–63	Brechin C	30	36
1923–24	Lochgelly	30	38
New Division 1			
1988–89	Queen of the S	29	39
1995–96	Dumbarton	31	36
1992–93	Cowdenbeath	34	44
New Division 2			
1987–88	Berwick R	29	39
New Division 3			
1994–95	Albion R	28	36

MOST DRAWN GAMES IN A SEASON

FA PREMIER LEAGUE		Draws	Games
1993–94	Manchester C	18	42
1993–94	Sheffield U	18	42
1994–95	Southampton	18	42
FOOTBALL LEAGUE			
Division 1			
1978–79	Norwich C	23	42
Division 3			
1997–98	Cardiff C	23	46
1997–98	Hartlepool U	23	46
Division 4			
1986–87	Exeter C	23	46
SCOTTISH LEAGUE			
Premier Division			
1993–94	Aberdeen	21	44
New Division 1			
1986–87	East Fife	21	44

LONGEST WINNING SEQUENCE

FA PREMIER LEAGUE	*Team*	*Games*
2001–02 and 2002–03	Arsenal	14
FOOTBALL LEAGUE		
Division 1		
1959–60 (2) and 1960–61 (11)	Tottenham H	13
1891–92	Preston NE	13
1891–92	Sunderland	13
Division 2		
1904–05	Manchester U	14
1905–06	Bristol C	14
1950–51	Preston NE	14
Division 3		
1985–86	Reading	13
FROM SEASON'S START		
Division 1		
1960–61	Tottenham H	11
1992–93	Newcastle U	11
2000–01	Fulham	11
Division 3		
1985–86	Reading	13

LONGEST SEQUENCE OF CONSECUTIVE SCORING (Individual)

FA PREMIER LEAGUE		
Mark Stein (Chelsea)	9 in 7 games	1993–94
Alan Shearer (Newcastle U)	7 in 7 games	1996–97
Thierry Henry (Arsenal)	9 in 7 games	1999–2000
FOOTBALL LEAGUE RECORD		
Tom Phillipson (Wolverhampton W)	23 in 13 games	1926–27

LONGEST UNBEATEN SEQUENCE

FOOTBALL LEAGUE	*Team*	*Games*
Division 1		
Nov 1977–Dec 1978	Nottingham F	42

LONGEST UNBEATEN CUP SEQUENCE

Liverpool 25 rounds League/Milk Cup 1980–84

LONGEST UNBEATEN SEQUENCE IN A SEASON

FOOTBALL LEAGUE	*Team*	*Games*
Division 1		
1920–21	Burnley	30

LONGEST UNBEATEN START TO A SEASON

FOOTBALL LEAGUE	*Team*	*Games*
Division 1		
1973–74	Leeds U	29
1987–88	Liverpool	29

LONGEST SEQUENCE WITHOUT A WIN IN A SEASON

FOOTBALL LEAGUE	*Team*	*Games*
Division 2		
1983–84	Cambridge U	31

LONGEST SEQUENCE WITHOUT A WIN FROM SEASON'S START

FOOTBALL LEAGUE	*Team*	*Games*
Division 1		
1990–91	Sheffield U	16

LONGEST SEQUENCE OF CONSECUTIVE DEFEATS

FOOTBALL LEAGUE	*Team*	*Games*
Division 2		
1898–99	Darwen	18

A CENTURY OF LEAGUE AND CUP GOALS IN CONSECUTIVE SEASONS

George Camsell	*League*	*Cup*	*Season*
Middlesbrough	59	5	1926–27
(101 goals)	33	4	1927–28

(*Camsell's cup goals were all scored in the FA Cup.*)

Steve Bull			
Wolverhampton W	34	18	1987–88
(102 goals)	37	13	1988–89

(*Bull had 12 in the Sherpa Van Trophy, 3 Littlewoods Cup, 3 FA Cup in 1987–88; 11 Sherpa Van Trophy, 2 Littlewoods Cup in 1988–89.*)

PENALTIES

Most in a Season (individual)
Division 1

	Goals	*Season*
Francis Lee (Manchester C)	13	1971–72

Most awarded in one game
Five Crystal Palace (4 – 1 scored, 3 missed) v Brighton & HA (1 scored), Div 2 1988–89

Most saved in a Season
Division 1
Paul Cooper (Ipswich T) 8 (of 10) 1979–80

GOALKEEPING RECORDS

(without conceding a goal)

BRITISH RECORD (all competitive games)
Chris Woods, Rangers, in 1196 minutes from 26 November 1986 to 31 January 1987.

FOOTBALL LEAGUE
Steve Death, Reading, 1103 minutes from 24 March to 18 August 1979.

MOST SUCCESSFUL MANAGERS

Sir Alex Ferguson CBE
Manchester U
15 major trophies in 13 seasons:
8 Premier League, 4 FA Cup, 1 European Cup, 1 Cup-Winners' Cup, 1 League Cup.

Aberdeen
1976–86 – 9 trophies:
3 League, 4 Scottish Cup, 1 League Cup, 1 Cup-Winners' Cup.

Bob Paisley
Liverpool
1974–83 – 13 trophies:
6 League, 3 European Cup, 3 League Cup, 1 UEFA Cup.

MOST LEAGUE APPEARANCES (750+ matches)

1005 Peter Shilton (286 Leicester City, 110 Stoke City, 202 Nottingham Forest, 188 Southampton, 175 Derby County, 34 Plymouth Argyle, 1 Bolton Wanderers, 9 Leyton Orient) 1966–97

931 Tony Ford (355 Grimsby T, 9 Sunderland (loan), 112 Stoke C, 114 WBA, 68 Grimsby T, 5 Bradford C (loan), 76 Scunthorpe U, 103 Mansfield T, 89 Rochdale) 1975–2002

909 Graeme Armstrong (204 Stirling A, 83 Berwick R, 353 Meadowbank T, 268 Stenhousemuir, 1 Alloa) 1975–2001

863 Tommy Hutchison (165 Blackpool, 314 Coventry City, 46 Manchester City, 92 Burnley, 178 Swansea City, 68 Alloa) 1965–91

824 Terry Paine (713 Southampton, 111 Hereford United) 1957–77

782 Robbie James (484 Swansea C, 48 Stoke C, 87 QPR, 23 Leicester C, 89 Bradford C, 51 Cardiff C) 1973–94

777 Alan Oakes (565 Manchester C, 211 Chester C, 1 Port Vale) 1959–84

771 John Burridge (27 Workington, 134 Blackpool, 65 Aston Villa, 6 Southend U (loan), 88 Crystal Palace, 39 QPR, 74 Wolverhampton W, 6 Derby Co (loan), 109 Sheffield U, 62 Southampton, 67 Newcastle U, 65 Hibernian, 3 Scarborough, 4 Lincoln C, 3 Aberdeen, 3 Dumbarton, 3 Falkirk, 4 Manchester C, 3 Darlington, 6 Queen of the South) 1968–96

770 John Trollope (all for Swindon Town) 1960–80†

764 Jimmy Dickinson (all for Portsmouth) 1946–65

761 Roy Sproson (all for Port Vale) 1950–72

760 Mick Tait (64 Oxford U, 106 Carlisle U, 33 Hull C, 240 Portsmouth, 99 Reading, 79 Darlington, 139 Hartlepool U) 1975–97

758 Ray Clemence (48 Scunthorpe United, 470 Liverpool, 240 Tottenham Hotspur) 1966–87

758 Billy Bonds (95 Charlton Ath, 663 West Ham U) 1964–88

757 Pat Jennings (48 Watford, 472 Tottenham Hotspur, 237 Arsenal) 1963–86

757 Frank Worthington (171 Huddersfield T, 210 Leicester C, 84 Bolton W, 75 Birmingham C, 32 Leeds U, 19 Sunderland, 34 Southampton, 31 Brighton & HA, 59 Tranmere R, 23 Preston NE, 19 Stockport Co) 1966–88

† record for one club

CONSECUTIVE

401 Harold Bell (401 Tranmere R; 459 in all games) 1946–55

FA CUP

88 Ian Callaghan (79 Liverpool, 7 Swansea C, 2 Crewe Alex)

MOST SENIOR MATCHES

1390 Peter Shilton (1005 League, 86 FA Cup, 102 League Cup, 125 Internationals, 13 Under-23, 4 Football League XI, 20 European Cup, 7 Texaco Cup, 5 Simod Cup, 4 European Super Cup, 4 UEFA Cup, 3 Screen Sport Super Cup, 3 Zenith Data Systems Cup, 2 Autoglass Trophy, 2 Charity Shield, 2 Full Members Cup, 1 Anglo-Italian Cup, 1 Football League play-offs, 1 World Club Championship)

YOUNGEST PLAYERS

FA Premier League appearance
Gary McSheffery, 16 years, 198 days, Coventry C v Aston Villa, 27.2.99.

FA Premier League scorer
James Milner, 16 years 357 days, Leeds U v Sunderland 26.12.2002

Football League appearance
Albert Geldard, 15 years 158 days, Bradford Park Avenue v Millwall, Division 2, 16.9.29; and Ken Roberts, 15 years 158 days, Wrexham v Bradford Park Avenue, Division 3N, 1.9.51
If leap years are included, Ken Roberts was 157 days

Football League scorer
Ronnie Dix, 15 years 180 days, Bristol Rovers v Norwich City, Division 3S, 3.3.28.

Division 1 appearance
Derek Forster, 15 years 185 days, Sunderland v Leicester City, 22.8.64.

Division 1 scorer
Jason Dozzell, 16 years 57 days as substitute Ipswich Town v Coventry City, 4.2.84

Division 1 hat-tricks
Alan Shearer, 17 years 240 days, Southampton v Arsenal, 9.4.88
Jimmy Greaves, 17 years 10 months, Chelsea v Portsmouth, 25.12.57

FA Cup appearance (any round)
Andy Awford, 15 years 88 days as substitute Worcester City v Boreham Wood, 3rd Qual. rd, 10.10.87

FA Cup proper appearance
Lee Holmes, 15 years 277 days, Derby Co v Brentford 4.1.2003

FA Cup Final appearance
James Prinsep, 17 years 245 days, Clapham Rovers v Old Etonians, 1879

FA Cup Final scorer
Norman Whiteside, 18 years 18 days, Manchester United v Brighton & Hove Albion, 1983

FA Cup Final captain
David Nish, 21 years 212 days, Leicester City v Manchester City, 1969

League Cup Final scorer
Norman Whiteside, 17 years 324 days, Manchester United v Liverpool, 1983

League Cup Final captain
Barry Venison, 20 years 7 months 8 days, Sunderland v Norwich City, 1985

OLDEST PLAYERS

FA Premier League appearance
John Burridge 43 years 5 months, Manchester C v QPR 14.5.1995

Football League appearance
Neil McBain, 52 years 4 months, New Brighton v Hartlepools United, Div 3N, 15.3.47 (McBain was New Brighton's manager and had to play in an emergency)

Division 1 appearance
Stanley Matthews, 50 years 5 days, Stoke City v Fulham, 6.2.65

RECORD ATTENDANCES

FA PREMIER LEAGUE
67,683 Manchester U v Middlesbrough, Old Trafford 23.3.2002

FOOTBALL LEAGUE
83,260 Manchester U v Arsenal, Maine Road 17.1.1948

SCOTTISH LEAGUE
118,567 Rangers v Celtic, Ibrox Stadium 2.1.1939

FA CUP FINAL
126,047* Bolton W v West Ham U, Wembley 28.4.1923

EUROPEAN CUP
135,826 Celtic v Leeds U, semi-final at Hampden Park 15.4.1970

SCOTTISH CUP
146,433 Celtic v Aberdeen, Hampden Park 24.4.37

WORLD CUP
199,854† Brazil v Uruguay, Maracana, Rio 16.7.50

* It has been estimated that as many as 70,000 more broke in without paying.
† 173,830 paid.

SENDINGS-OFF

SEASON
371 (League alone) 1998–99

DAY
15 (all League) 31 Oct 1998
15 (3 League, 12 FA Cup*) 20 Nov 1982
**worst overall FA Cup total*
26 (14 English, 12 Scottish) 16 Oct 1999
(On 17 Oct 1999 a further 1 English made it 27 for the weekend)

WEEKEND
15 (League alone) 22/23 Dec 1990

FA CUP FINAL
Kevin Moran, Manchester U v Everton 1985

QUICKEST
Walter Boyd, Swansea C v Darlington Div 3 as substitute in zero seconds 23 Nov 1999

MOST IN ONE GAME
Five: Chesterfield (2) v Plymouth Arg (3) 22 Feb 1997
Five: Wigan Ath (1) v Bristol R (4) 2 Dec 1997
Five: Exeter C (3) v Cambridge U (2) 23 Nov 2002

MOST IN ONE TEAM
Wigan Ath (1) v Bristol R (4) 2 Dec 1997
Hereford U (4) v Northampton T (0) 11 Nov 1992

PREMIER LEAGUE EVER-PRESENT CLUBS

	P	*W*	*D*	*L*	*F*	*A*	*Pts*
Manchester U	430	269	101	60	863	394	908
Arsenal	430	218	119	93	683	389	773
Liverpool	430	207	110	113	704	449	731
Chelsea	430	179	128	123	637	489	665
Leeds U	430	181	116	133	601	494	659
Aston Villa	430	166	124	140	533	481	622
Tottenham H	430	150	116	164	569	596	566
Everton	430	136	119	175	527	587	527
Southampton	430	132	112	186	509	627	508

FOREIGNERS IN AND OUT

When the FA Premier League was launched in the 1992–93 season, 11 foreigners kicked off on the first day: Anders Limpar (Sweden). John Jensen (Denmark) both Arsenal; Andrei Kanchelskis (Russia), Peter Schmeichel (Denmark) both Manchester U; Jan Stejskal (Czechoslovakia) QPR; Roland Nilsson (Sweden) Sheffield W; Gunnar Halle (Norway) Oldham Ath; Michel Vonk (Holland) Manchester C; Eric Cantona (France), Leeds U; Hans Segers (Holland) Wimbledon; Craig Forrest (Canada) Ipswich T.

During 2002–03 the turnaround was such that as many foreign players were being either transferred, left after the end of their contracts or were loaned to clubs outside England.

These included David Grondin, Arsenal to Dunfermline Ath; Bernard Diomede, Liverpool to Ajaccio (loan); Abel Xavier, Liverpool to Galatasaray (loan); Danny Sjolund, Liverpool to Djurgaarden (loan); Mikael Forssell, Chelsea to Moenchengladbach (loan); Joe-Max Moore, Everton to New England Revolution; Olivier Dacourt, Leeds U to Roma (loan); Laurent Charvet, Manchester C to Sochaux; Sergei Rebrov, Tottenham H to Fenerbahce (loan); Titi Camara, West Ham U to Al Ittihad (loan); Vladimir Labant, West Ham U to Sparta Prague (loan); Andrei Kanchelskis, Southampton to Al Hilal; Diego Gavilan, Newcastle U to Internacional (loan); Marcelino Newcastle U to Polideportivo Ejido.

Football League clubs were also involved in this area with Richard Spong moving from Coventry C to Djurgaarden; Amir Karic, Ipswich T to Maribor; Ian Joy, Kidderminster H to Columbus Crew; Jani Viander, Stoke C to Midtjylland (loan); Richard Offiong, Newcastle U to Motherwell (loan); Thomas Waehler, Wimbledon to Stromsgodset.

RED CARDS RESCINDED 2002–03

The following players had their sendings-off rescinded by the referee after the game during the 2002–03 season:

Collins (Blackpool)	10 August
Cisse (Birmingham C)	18 August
Wright-Phillips (Manchester C)	31 August
Onuora (Sheffield U)	7 September
Campo (Bolton W)	21 September
Davies (Tottenham H)	16 November
Bedeau (Torquay U)	16 November
Pollitt (Rotherham U)	1 February
Marteinsson (Stoke C)	22 February
Tyson (Reading)	22 March

INTERNATIONAL RECORDS

MOST GOALS IN AN INTERNATIONAL

Record/World Cup	Archie Thompson (Australia) 13 goals v American Samoa	11.4.2001
England	Malcolm Macdonald (Newcastle U) 5 goals v Cyprus, at Wembley	16.4.1975
	Willie Hall (Tottenham H) 5 goals v Ireland, at Old Trafford	16.11.1938
	Steve Bloomer (Derby Co) 5 goals v Wales, at Cardiff	16.3.1896
	Howard Vaughton (Aston Villa) 5 goals v Ireland, at Belfast	18.2.1882
Northern Ireland	Joe Bambrick (Linfield) 6 goals v Wales, at Belfast	1.2.1930
Wales	John Price (Wrexham) 4 goals v Ireland, at Wrexham	25.2.1882
	Mel Charles (Cardiff C) 4 goals v Ireland, at Cardiff	11.4.1962
	Ian Edwards (Chester) 4 goals v Malta, at Wrexham	25.10.1978

MOST GOALS IN AN INTERNATIONAL CAREER

		Goals	*Games*
England	Bobby Charlton (Manchester U)	49	106
Scotland	Denis Law (Huddersfield T, Manchester C, Torino, Manchester U)	30	55
	Kenny Dalglish (Celtic, Liverpool)	30	102
Northern Ireland	Colin Clarke (Bournemouth, Southampton, QPR, Portsmouth)	13	38
Wales	Ian Rush (Liverpool, Juventus)	28	73
Republic of Ireland	Niall Quinn (Arsenal, Manchester C, Sunderland)	21	91

HIGHEST SCORES

Record/World Cup Match	Australia	31	American Samoa	0	2001
European Championship	Spain	12	Malta	1	1983
Olympic Games	Denmark	17	France	1	1908
	Germany	16	USSR	0	1912
Other International Match	Libya	21	Oman	0	1966
European Cup	Feyenoord	12	K R Reykjavik	2	1969
European Cup-Winners' Cup	Sporting Lisbon	16	Apoel Nicosia	1	1963
Fairs & UEFA Cups	Ajax	14	Red Boys	0	1984

GOALSCORING RECORDS

World Cup Final	Geoff Hurst (England) 3 goals v West Germany	1966
World Cup Final tournament	Just Fontaine (France) 13 goals	1958
Career	Artur Friedenreich (Brazil) 1329 goals	1910–30
	Pele (Brazil) 1281 goals	*1956–78
	Franz 'Bimbo' Binder (Austria, Germany) 1006 goals	1930–50
World Cup Finals fastest	Hakan Sukur (Turkey) 10.8 secs v South Korea	2002

**Pele subsequently scored two goals in Testimonial matches making his total 1283.*

MOST CAPPED INTERNATIONALS IN THE BRITISH ISLES

England	Peter Shilton	125 appearances	1970–90
Northern Ireland	Pat Jennings	119 appearances	1964–86
Scotland	Kenny Dalglish	102 appearances	1971–86
Wales	Neville Southall	92 appearances	1982–97
Republic of Ireland	Steve Staunton	102 appearances	1988–2002

MILESTONES DIARY 2002–03

July 2002

Wadsworth installed ... Boston suspend Evans ... FL reach for the Sky ... Munich hero dies ... Venables for Leeds ... Hughes quits action ... Hornets choose Lewington ... Ipswich honour Bobby ... £30m fee for Rio ... Albion forfeit bonus ... Ewood for Yorke ... Another Gunner arrives

1 FL are threatening to take legal action against the FA to prevent the introduction here of the transfer window which FIFA want to commence this season. An estimated £200m was staked in Britain on the 64 matches of WC 2002 making it the biggest sports betting event ever. Huddersfield unveil Mick Wadsworth as boss.

2 Man U's Argentine midfielder Veron is to face magistrates in Rome over allegations of illegally acquiring an Italian passport. Leeds' Keane rejects £9m move to Sunderland.

3 Laurent Blanc signs 1-year deal at Man U. Boro agree £13m double swoop for old boy Juninho and Massimo Maccarone.

4 Div 3 newcomers Boston suspend manager Steve Evans pending an FA hearing into financial irregularities at the club. Thirty years after coming to the city to teach at Alsop High School, Gerard Houllier is presented with an honorary degree at the University of Liverpool.

5 Beleagured FL clubs are thrown a lifeline when Sky TV pay £95m to screen games for the next 4 years. Leeds target Martin O'Neill says he will see out the remaining year of his Celtic contract. Des Walker returns to Forest 10 years after leaving.

6 Just 6 days after the WC finale, Fulham kick-off a new season against Haka in the Intertoto Cup. AFC Wimbledon win a £100,000 – plus sponsors' deal – before playing a match.

7 With Steve McClaren stating he is happy at Boro, speculation is rife Leeds will now appoint Terry Venables.

8 Gunners capture £5.5m Frenchman Pascal Cygan from Lille. Former Munich air crash survivor Ray Wood dies peacefully at his London home, aged 71. Leeds, £60m in debt were obliged to announce the appointment on the Stock Exchange of former England coach Venables.

9 FIFA President sacks the organisation's widely respected communications director Keith Cooper. Brum pay £4.5m for Senegal skipper Aliou Cisse.

10 Newly-formed AFC Wimbledon attract 4,657 to their first friendly at Sutton Utd. Mark Hughes officially brings down the curtain on his career to concentrate on managerial duties as Welsh national boss. Led by celebrity chef Delia Smith more than 60 Nationwide League club owners go on the picket line outside ITV's London studios.

11 Watford give the manager's post to staff coach Ray Lewington. Barnet are refused ground sharing plans with Leyton Orient. As from next season the second group phase of the Champions League will cease with the remaining 16 teams engaging in a 2-leg knock-out competition.

12 Ex-Villa and England winger Tony Daley, 34, retires. PFA's Taylor welcomes proposals for a winter break.

13 Celtic treat their London-based fans to a goal feast in 7–3 win at QPR. BBC are to show the Celtic-Rangers clashes throughout Britain as part of their £24m deal to screen SPL action. Bolton's Gudni Bergsson signs a new 12-month deal postponing for the 4th successive year his retirement to Iceland and becoming a lawyer.

14 Fulham sneak into Intertoto Cup 3rd rd drawing 1–1 in Finland.

15 Brighton appoint director of youth football Martin Hinshelwood as manager. Chelsea sack Peter Osgood from PR duties. Arsenal's Wenger is made a member of the *Legion d'Honneur* in Paris.

16 PFA and LMA back moves that officials will be instructed to issue red cards to punish verbal abuse. Bobby Robson unveils a statue of himself outside Ipswich's Portman Rd.

17 Official figures show PFA chief executive Gordon Taylor's annual salary rising to £623,227 at a time when 650 professionals face up to the prospect of unemployment. David Seaman, 39 in September, signs a 1-year extension to his Arsenal contract. The Irish government threatens to overrule a deal between the FAI and Sky to screen live internationals.

18 Man U will host Boca Juniors of Argentina with proceeds going to UNICEF. Carlisle are cleared after an investigation into alleged financial irregularities.

19 Boston receive £100,000 fine and will have 4 pts deducted next season but keep their place in FL Div 3. PFA offer Bradford City a £2m loan in a bid to save the crisis-hit club. Frank Taylor, the only journalist to survive the 1958 Munich air disaster dies, aged 81.

20 Disgraced Roy Keane appears in Man U's Dublin friendly against Shelbourne.

21 Man U finally land Rio Ferdinand paying a British record £30m for the 23 year old defender. At the 11th hour Liverpool call off a £8m deal for Lee Bowyer of Leeds.

22 Graeme Souness commits himself to Blackburn for another 4 years. Leicester give a free transfer to Dennis Wise a year after joining from Chelsea for £1.6m.

23 Gary Lineker cuts the ribbon on the opening of Leicester's new £35m Walkers Stadium. Denis Irwin who won 7 Premiership titles in a 12-year spell at Man U joins Wolves. Arsenal's Wenger reckons Alex Ferguson paid at least £10m over the odds for new signing Ferdinand.

24 Paul Gascoigne touches down in the US to consider a deal with DC United. Burnley put their entire squad on the list.

25 Hammers' goalie Craig Forrest, 34, who battled against and beat testicular cancer has accepted doctors' advice to retire. Albion players are told the £15,000-a-win per man incentive scheme agreed shortly after Premiership promotion was secured, is no longer valid.
26 Blackburn pay £2m for Dwight Yorke – a pale reflection of the £12.6m Man U gave Villa for him 4 years ago. Ossie Ardiles moves back home to coach champions Racing Club, his first job in Argentina since he signed for Spurs 24 years ago. Owner Michael Knighton finally sells Carlisle.
27 Rioting fans from 2 local clubs force Arsenal's friendly at Rapid Vienna to be abandoned after 67 min. Villa and Fulham ease into the semi-final stages of the Intertoto Cup.
28 Villa's George Boateng completes his £5m transfer to Boro. Brazilian WC winner Gilberto Silva seals his £4.5m move to Arsenal signing a 4-year contract.
29 Graham Taylor says he let Peter Schmeichel, 39, leave Villa rather than block the progress of talented 25 year old Peter Enckelman. Boss Parkin sends home 6 Barnsley players from their Scottish tour.
30 Leeds' Alan Smith is dismissed in Bangkok, his 6th red card. Oxford Utd's 18 year old Jamie Brooks, comes off the critical list after contracting the same life-threatening illness which forced Markus Babbel of Liverpool to miss last season. Tim Sherwood is fined £30,000 for publicly slating Tottenham's lack of summer signings.
31 Ten SPL clubs threaten to resign over BBC TV deal.

August 2002

Mighty Mouse returns ... Hefty fine for Arsenal ... Merson heads to coast ... Bradford's money troubles ... More drug tests ... Community Shield for Arsene ... Juninho shock ... FL attracts big crowds ... Premiership spending drops ... New Wombles get support ... Baresi's brief stay ... Lennon death threats ... Flo a Black Cat ... Litmanen leaves ... Keane off again

1 FL lose their £131.9m claim against Carlton and Granada after High Court rule the League failed to extract sufficient written guarantees in the ITV Digital original contract. Tranmere sack Dave Watson.
2 Coach Ray Mathias is in caretaker control at Tranmere. Wolves unveil new signing Paul Ince. Gazza's American venture with DC United falls through. Former Wimbledon manager, Terry Burton, is to become Ray Lewington's No 2 at Watford.
3 Kevin Keegan's managerial return to the Hamburg club where he won successive European Player of the Year awards in the 80's ends in 1–0 defeat.
4 A property tycoon Colchester Utd fan offers to pay Gascoigne £3,000 a week to turn out for the U's.
5 Arsenal's poor disciplinary record gets a £50,000 FA fine, suspended until the end of 2002–03. Paul Merson, 34, links with Pompey. Lincoln come out of administration.
6 FL chairman Keith Harris quits. Geoffrey Richmond steps down admitting he had lost the support of Bradford fans.
7 Fulham's win over Sochaux earns an Intertoto Cup final against Bologna. Villa lose out on a UEFA place as Lille wrap up victory.
8 Richard Scudamore calls for details of players' contracts, wages and bonuses to be made public. Much-travelled Nick Barmby joins Leeds.
9 Debt-ridden Bradford manage 11th hour reprieve after a financial agreement with the PFA enables the club to come out of administration even after 4 pm deadline. FA will increase random drug tests by 20 per cent.
10 Millwall are hit for 6 at home to Rotherham. A protest means just 668 (from 2,476) home supporters watch the Dons lose to the Gills. Boston's 1st point – now they have minus 3.
11 Superior Arsenal capture the Community Shield beating Liverpool. Boro learn that 'home again' Juninho is out for a long period after sustaining cruciate ligament damage in Italian friendly.
12 Burnley ban ITV cameras from Turf Moor. FL attendances totalling 341,669 reach their highest opening day figure since the 1992 formation of the Premiership (238,963).
13 Predictably Man U's Ferguson claims Roy Keane has 'no case to answer' over disturbing autobiography comments about launching a premeditated attack on Alf-Inge Haaland.
14 Man U are humiliated and lose in Budapest to Zalaegerszeg. Trevor Francis may face a police investigation after clipping the ear of his goalie Alex Kolinko.
15 On the verge of a new season start, spending in the Premiership is down more than £100m after a record £259m a year ago.
16 Man City dramatically launch a £5m law suit against Man U and Roy Keane.
17 Solskjaer nets a timely opening day 100th goal in win over WBA. Former England and Man U winger Lee Sharpe scores on his debut for Exeter. Re-formed AFC Wimbledon attract a Combined Counties League record attendance of 2,449 at Sandhurst.
18 Gunners chalk up a record-breaking 14th consecutive top flight win, one better than Spurs, Preston and Sunderland. Ipswich rout Leicester 6–1. David O'Leary refutes Chairman's claims that he had lost the dressing room at Leeds.
19 Dennis Wise will be the first player to undergo a new disciplinary procedure after deciding to appeal against his sacking at Leicester. Grimsby's Steve Livingstone remains in hospital after fracturing his skull against Derby.
20 Franco Baresi's 81-day reign as Fulham director of football, ends by mutual consent.
21 Death threats to Neil Lennon before kick-off forces the new NI skipper out of the Belfast clash with Cyprus. ROI win in Finland. Denmark triumph in Scotland. Former W Ham defender John Charles, 57 loses his battle with lung cancer.

22 FA announce minute's silence for W/E fixtures in memory of the two murdered Cambridgeshire schoolgirls.
23 Leicester are angered with FL decision demanding the reinstatement of sacked Denis Wise. Giggs nets his 100th score for Man U at Chelsea.
24 Gunners extend their unbeaten run to 23 games drawing at W Ham. Hard-up Cambridge Utd appeal for volunteer after-game ground sweepers in return for free entrance. New boys Boston send out plea to fans for match-day stretcher-bearers.
25 Colourful chairman George Reynolds unveils one-time Newcastle favourite Faustino Asprilla in a Darlington shirt – although the move is far from sealed.
26 Four are re-carded in the Wycombe-QPR clash. Unhappy Jari Litmanen clears his locker at Liverpool's training ground intent it seems on an impending exit.
27 Man U gain revenge sweeping aside Zalaegerszeg with the parents of murdered Soham schoolgirl Holly Wells attending to thank Sir Alex for the contribution he and his players made during the search for their daughter wearing a 'Beckham' shirt when she disappeared. FL anticipate UEFA will soon confirm exemption from the transfer window.
28 Ipswich tell their players to bring their passports for the home game with Avenir Beggen to satisfy possible UEFA identity checks. Newcastle reach Champions League big-time but Celtic crash out.
29 FA's Crozier says it will press for a 2-week winter break despite opposition from 20 Premiership chairmen. Sunderland's Stadium of Light is to host England's EC qualifier against Turkey next April. WBA smash their transfer record twice in a day capturing Lee Hughes and Jason Koumas. Ipswich net 8 UEFA cup goals.
30 Spurs finally end search for a striker agreeing £7m deal with Leeds for Robbie Keane. Tore Andre Flo joins from Rangers for £8m taking Sunderland's spending to over £20m in the last 12 months. Bradford City pay players for the first time in nearly 4 months. Jari Litmanen quits Liverpool to join Ajax.
31 At Sunderland it's red card No. 11 for shamed Roy Keane, sent off for elbowing Jason McAteer the player who attacked comments in his book. Anelka nets a Man City hat-trick. Paul Jackson's 10 goals in Sheffield-based non-League side Stocksbridge Park Steels 17–1 preliminary tie thrashing of Oldham Town equals one of the oldest FA Cup scoring records. Chris Marron did it for South Shields (1947) but Ted MacDougall's 9 for Bournemouth (1971) still holds the record for the competition proper.

September 2002

England trim staff ... FA charge Keane ... Scotland's heavy officials ... Loyal Mathias rewarded ... Faroes embarrass Scots ... Rock is Fergy's banker ... Brum chief's lucky escape ... Everton's Chinese interest ... Hutchinson sadness ... Swans entice Flynn ... Bates has a pop ... York's noisy gimmick ... Refs gets glasses help ... FL book Wembley finals ... Gunners scoring record ... Lazio owe Utd ... 'Shearer' demolishes Wembley

1 Caniggia nets 3 in 6–0 Rangers win. Vieira is off in draw at Chelsea. Owls land only their 2nd League win for 23 years in Sheffield derby match with Blades.
2 A hip operation will rule out Man U's Keane for 3 months.
3 FA express concern over £30m in debt Derby's perilous financial plight and revelations that players have not been paid for August. Veteran manager Colin Addison takes charge at Forest Green Rovers. Coach Eriksson dispenses with 3 of England's medical staff including Dr John Crane involved since 1986. WBA scrap their bonus scheme.
4 FA charge Roy Keane over comments in his autobiography ghosted by former Millwall player now broadcaster Eamon Dunphy. Eriksson is 'frustrated' by Ferguson's decision to withdraw England's Beckham and Scholes from Portugal friendly. Villa's Taylor claims the transfer window will lead to increased 'tapping-up.'
5 Four FA officials are forced to get off Scotland's flight because the plane to the Faroe Islands is overweight with excess baggage. Following tug-of-war between club and country FA of Wales pay £8,000 charter flight to Helsinki for Craig Bellamy.
6 Ray Mathias caps 35 years service and 637 games with Tranmere by being handed the managerial job. On eve of Villa Park friendly with Portugal, Eriksson distributes a general questionnaire to his WC squad of 23 which bizarrely also asks if they still want him as boss.
7 Lively Smith scores in England's friendly draw with Portugal. Wales get their campaign off to a flying start winning in Finland. Ferguson saves the Scots from humiliation scraping a late draw in the Faroes. ROI lose qualifier in Russia.
8 Sir Alex Ferguson in Seventh Heaven at Longchamps greeting his Rock of Gibraltar, the colts 7th consecutive Grade One win beating Mill Reef's mark which stood since 1972. Eriksson is blasted for turning a friendly into farce after 18 players were used in the England-Portugal run-out yesterday. The coach has used 46 players in 21 games but has made 86 substitutions in 10 non-competitive fixtures.
9 New Zealand outfit Auckland Kingz snub Paul Gascoigne's hopes of a short-term contract with the club who play in Australia's Premier League.
10 Gunners equal a Man City record having scored in 44 consecutive League matches – an achivement dating back to 1937 when tonight's opposition did it. Brawling between supporters breaks out before Watford-Luton Worthington Cup tie forcing the scrapping of a minute's silence.

11 Bolton pull off an unlikely victory at Man U. FA will be reminding Arsenal's Henry about removing his jersey and revealing specific messages on a T-shirt. Duncan Ferguson's career at Everton is in the balance after being told his troublesome back complaint is inoperable.

12 Cardiff could be £300,000 out of pocket after shirt sponsor Ken Thorne Group go bust. A month into the season and Arsenal's Vieira pleads for a rest. Brum chairman David Gold, a pilot with 30 years' experience, is lucky to escape as his Cessna aircraft crashes at the club's training ground.

13 Ipswich who have a £13m deficit to make up ask all staff to take a pay cut. Soton's James Beattie, 3 times over the limit, receives a two and a half year driving ban.

14 Gills v Brighton ends with 9-a-side. Man U have just 8 pts from their 1st 6 Premiership games their worst start since the elite division kicked off in 1992–93. Wembley is finally given the go-ahead for reconstruction costing £750m and to be opened for the 2006 FA Cup final. Oldham's Clyde Wijnhard scores 4 in 6–1 win. A figure in the region of 1 billion Chinese viewers with a particular interest in Beckham-style pin-up Li Tie take in the Everton-Boro draw.

15 The East Anglian clash ends 1–1. Red-carded defender Tiatto puts his Man City future in doubt says boss Keegan.

16 In the 1st top flight clash between the clubs for 16 years, Villa goalie Enckelman attempts to trap a Brum throw-in only to let the ball run under his foot and, as contact appeared to be made, the goal is given. Steve Coppell joins Swindon as No. 2.

17 Liverpool suffer demolition in Valencia. Gunners triumph over Borussia Dortmund. Rangers suffer in Prague. Aberdeen, in their 100th European tie, draw. Pompey equal 1983 club record with 7th straight win.

18 Newcastle, 2nd best at Dynamo Kiev. Man U gain easy win over Maccabi Haifa. Rangers confirm Advocaat's departure in November for Dutch national post. Coach Stewart Houston leaves Walsall after a month.

19 In Europe Fulham, Chelsea, Leeds, and Celtic triumph. Blackburn draw and Livingston lose. Chelsea legend and master of the long throw Ian Hutchinson, 54, dies from Parkinson's disease. Swansea put Brian Flynn in charge.

20 Millwall rescue Dennis Wise's career. Steve Evans resigns at Boston. Chelsea chairman Ken Bates slams the era of Osgood and Co.

21 Eight successive defeats now for Brighton. Newcastle win the 123rd NE derby against lethargic Sunderland. Gunners equal Chesterfield's record set in 1931 of scoring in 46 consecutive League games.

22 York chairman says it is possible to recreate the noise of 100,000 fans at the push of a button and sanctions taped chants and roars at home matches to urge on the team. Like other strikers Henry and Owen over the weekend, Smith misses a vital penalty as Leeds go under at Blackburn.

23 Israel make formal request to stage their Euro 2004 tie at White Hart Lane. Claudio Ranieri's 100th in charge sees Chelsea draw against Fulham a game with just 4 Englishmen starting. Real Madrid's McManaman says he is unlikely to return to play in England. Scottish refs sign a £1m sponsorship deal with opticians Specsavers.

24 Struggling Newcastle lose 1–0 at home to Feyenoord. Man U win at Bayer Leverkusen. ITV and Sky win the right to screen Champions League action from 2003–06. Watford ask staff to take a wage cut. PFA's Taylor dismisses as 'farcical' FIFA's ruling that dismissals will receive an automatic 1-match ban.

25 Arsenal's Silva nets the fastest ever Champions League goal, 19.4 seconds in 4–0 win at PSV. Liverpool are held at home by Basle. England will play South Africa in Durban on 22 May fulfilling a long-standing pledge to Nelson Mandela. Newcastle's Bellamy gets 3-match UEFA ban.

26 Leeds reveal pre-tax losses of nearly £34m. The Premier League would like to wrestle control of the England team away from the FA. FL commit their 5 annual finals – Nationwide League play-off finals, Worthington Cup and LDV Vans Trophy – to the new 90,000-seater Wembley Stadium for the 20 years after it is completed. Businessman and life-long fan Graham Simpson replaces Elton John as Watford chairman.

27 Dave Beasant, at 43, the oldest in the FL joins Bradford on a pay-as-you-play basis. Refs are to sport adverts on their sleeves next month when the Premier League conclude a £1m sponsorship.

28 Gunners, 4–1 winners at Leeds establish all-time record by scoring in 47 consecutive games, remaining unbeaten in 23 away matches and 29 Premiership fixtures. Owen nets Liverpool hat-trick at Man City. Wise is booked just 180 seconds into his Millwall debut.

29 After being held to a draw at home against the Gills, Trevor Francis says it looked as though his Crystal Palace players preferred to be at home watching the Ryder Cup on TV.

30 Thierry Henry signs a reported 5-year deal with Nike reckoned to be worth £9m. Tony Adams commences a 3-year Sport Sciences degree course at Brunel University. Man U still chasing £12m in unpaid transfer money from Lazio for Jaap Stam. Rangers reveal they are £52m in debt. A 35-ton demolition machine nicknamed 'Shearer' and specially built over 9 months for the task, takes the 1st chunk out of one of Wembley's Twin Towers.

October 2002

Rooney makes history ... Coleman quits ... 'Chopper' slams Bates ... Popular Zola's landmark ... Reid's reign ends ... Wilko is surprise choice ... Davies is tops for Wales ... Burley departs ... England attract peak viewing ... Keane's match ban ... Giggs hits 500 ... Lineker leads Leicester ... Bad boy Smith ... Royle return ... Positive test not named ... Crozier shock exit

1 Man U maul Olympiakos. In marathon 18 shoot-out attempts Oxford spring Worthington Cup surprise beating Charlton 6–5. Cambridge concede 7 to Sunderland. Hammers scrape through in shoot-out at Chesterfield. Wayne Rooney, 16, hits a brace becoming the youngest goal scorer in Everton history since Tommy Lawton over 70 years ago.

2 QPR reject Israel FA's approach to host the upcoming 2004 qualifier against Cyprus. Coventry trounce Rushden & Diamonds 8–0. Palace put 7 past Cheltenham. Bury earn shock win over Bolton. Fulham's Chris Coleman, out 21 months after a car crash, is forced to quit.

3 Chelsea suffer UEFA Cup exit at home to Viking Stavanger. Rangers also go out. Blackburn win on away goals. Leeds, Fulham and Ipswich advance. WC winner Martin Peters resigns his non-executive director role at Spurs. Barnsley go into administration.

4 Arsenal's Wenger and Henry win the Barclaycard manager and player of the month awards. UEFA to act on fresh claims of racist abuse after Ipswich join Arsenal, Liverpool and Fulham who have complained. Legendary Chelsea defender Ron Harris urges Ken Bates to step down following defeat to the Norwegian part-timers.

5 Mansfield score 6. Brum's Aliou Cisse plays despite knowing at least 9 members of his family have perished in a Senegal ferry tragedy with just 65 of 1,034 on board surviving. Exeter sack John Cornforth after home defeat by York.

6 Zola makes his 200th Chelsea league appearance at Anfield. Old Firm serve up a 3–3 television treat screened live for the 1st time to the whole of Britain.

7 In the wake of 6 wins in 2002 and just 9 of the last 31 at home Sunderland sack Peter Reid, seven and a half years in charge and having spent £22m in the last 9 months. Basement boys Brighton appoint Steve Coppell. Dundee Utd sack Alex Smith. Trevor Brooking steps down as chairman of Sport England after 4 years.

8 Yorath given 4 games to save his Sheff Wed job. Fulham's Mohamed Al Fayed persuades Pele to a link with Santos. Plum UEFA Cup draw sets up a Blackburn-Celtic clash. Prime Minister Blair hosts a No. 10 Downing St reception for WC squad.

9 As Euro 2004 qualifiers take centre stage this week FA bosses brace themselves for new book revelations about coach Eriksson's personal life.

10 Howard Wilkinson surprisingly swaps the FA to take charge at Sunderland naming recent Stoke boss Steve Cotterill as his asst. Hull sack manager Jan Molby after just 16 games. Simon Davies of Spurs is the Welsh Footballer of the Year.

11 George Burley, the Premiership Manager of the Year 17 months ago, loses his job after 8 years in charge at Ipswich. Peter Taylor signs 3-year deal as Hull boss.

12 England's black stars are abused during 2–1 win in Slovakia. Vogts secures 1st Scots victory in Iceland. Cambridge crack club record of scoring in 16 successive League games. Stan Ternent's dug-out ban allows a fan to bid £561 at auction and take his place in the hot seat against Walsall.

13 FA claim racist abuse to Heskey and Cole sparked some supporters attacking Slovakians during yesterday's win. Live BBC coverage of England's EC tie in Bratislava sees a peak of 10 million tuning in. Rotherham's Ronnie Moore confirms he was tricked by a telephone hoaxer believing the caller to be the Ipswich chairman.

14 Leicester stave off administration. Walsall buck the trend by announcing a profit for the 11th successive year.

15 FA dish out 5-match ban and record £150,000 fine to Man U's Keane. Barnsley dismiss Steve Parkin after 11 months. Scotland defeat Canada.

16 Amid trail of defensive blunders England are held 2–2 at home against Macedonia. Re-born Wales register vital win over Italy. Home defeats add pressure on Ireland boss McCarthy.

17 Neil McNab comes out on top from 70 applicants to take charge at Exeter. Wise launches £2.3m legal action against his former club Leicester.

18 Villa will foster links with Finnish club TPS Turku.

19 Giggs makes his 500th appearance at Fulham. Wayne Rooney, the youngest player ever at 16 years, 360 days to score in the Premiership nets the Everton winner seconds from time to defeat Arsenal. Shearer bangs in his 300th club goal at Blackburn.

20 Tottenham's £7m striker Keane gets off the mark with a double. Ex-Rangers and Scotland goalie Andy Goram completes a clean sweep of winning every domestic cup honour in Scotland helping Queen of the South to Bells Cup victory over Brechin.

21 Gary Lineker agrees to lead a consortium bidding to save Leicester. Matt Le Tissier signs, on the pitch, for Eastleigh.

22 Gunners lose at home to fluent Auxerre. Owen plunders 3 in Moscow. McManaman scores both Real Madrid goals in 2–2 with AEK Athens. Oldham will call off games if the firefighters' strike goes ahead as Boundary Park is built mainly of wood.

23 Tommy Taylor loses his Darlington job. Wales, conquerors of Italy, rocket 15 places to 61st in the rankings. Palace's Trevor Francis is charged for 'cuffing' his goalie Alex Kolinko. Newcastle shock Juventus. Man U celebrate their 100th win in Europe.

24 Vieira gets a 2-match ban and £25,000 fine. Football-mad Paul Stevenson changes his name to Save Barnsley FC after his home-town club goes into administration.

25 Emile Heskey who left Leicester for Liverpool for £11m pledges £150,000 towards the rescue plan at his old club.

26 Brad Friedel performs heroics in Blackburn win at Highbury. After being criticised for his England dismissal 10 days before, Leeds' Alan Smith is shown his 8th red card at Boro. After 9 months and 23 Premiership outings £7.5m striker Forlan gets Man U equaliser. After waiting 13 years to renew League rivalry, Palace thump Brighton 5–0.

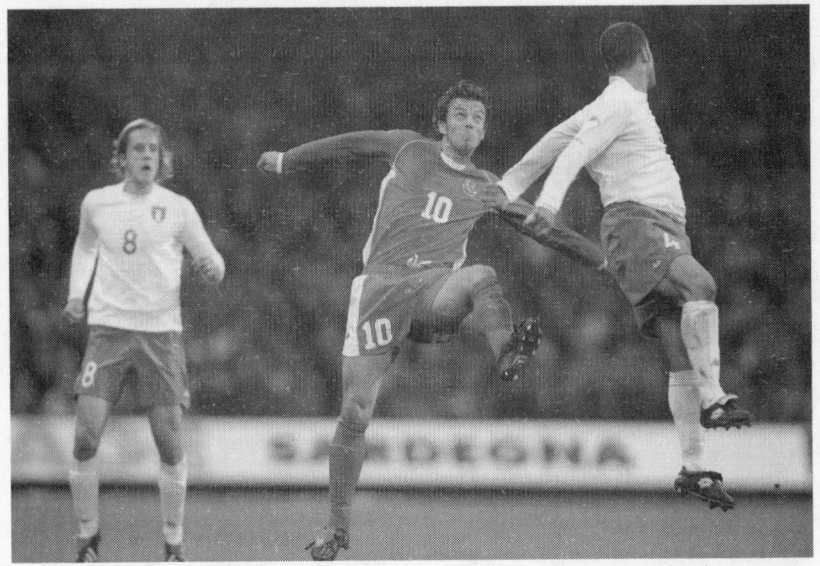

Welsh international football continued its upward spiral last season and Simon Davies (centre) was a successful ingredient. He disputes possession with Italy's Luigi Di Biagio while Massimo Ambrosini looks on in Wales 2-1 win at the Millennium Stadium. (Associated Sports Photography)

27 Veteran goalie Dave Beasant links with Wigan, his 11th club. Beattie fires a hat-trick as Soton come from 2-down to beat Fulham 4–2. Rangers hit Kilmarnock for 6. Marlon King, released just days earlier from prison, appears for the Gills after serving 5 months for handling stolen cars.

28 Leicester's Paul Dickov who has the worst disciplinary record in all 4 divisions is handed a £10,000 club fine. After 17 months absence Joe Royle, 53, agrees a two and a half year contract with Ipswich, 17th in Div 1. Team Bath, the 1st student team in the FA Cup for 122 years beat Horsham to secure a 1st rd tie hosting Mansfield.

29 Ferguson defends fielding a weakened Man U team humiliated 3–0 at Maccabi Haifa. Record low attendance of 849 – which includes 227 visitors and 220 comps – watch Div 1 fixture between Wimbledon and Rotherham. Pompey reach £400,000 settlement figure with former boss Tony Pulis.

30 Gunners experience 4th successive defeat at Borussia Dortmund despite Henry's 22nd goal in 42 Champions League ties. An unnamed player, understood not to be in the Premiership, tests positive for Nandrolone for the 1st time in England. At Anfield, Valencia hand out another lesson to Liverpool.

31 Chief executive Adam Crozier, 38, worn down, insiders say, by criticism and leaks resigns his £613,000 a year FA post he took in January 2000. Fulham, Ipswich, Leeds and Celtic all win in European ties. Terry Yorath hands in his resignation at Sheff Wed.

November 2002

McClaren follows Crozier ... Hindmarch sadness ... McCarthy hounded out ... Macca is Madrid skipper ... Tigana's historic selection ... Owls opt for old boy ... Bosnich tests positive ... Astle's heading caused death ... Magpies fly higher ... Robson's Barca re-union ... Freddie is top Swede ... Ton-Up for Dublin ... Exeter mayhem ... Vauxhall motor over QPR ... Camera catches out Shearer

1 Burley's rejection of the Stoke job opens the door for Tony Pulis, sacked by Pompey in October 2000. Less than 24 hours after Crozier's resignation Steve McClaren quits the England coaching set-up.

2 Posh's Simon Rea becomes the 2nd fastest sending-off from the kick-off in League history after 15 seconds at Cardiff. Eriksson seeks showdown with FA following close friend Crozier's sudden exit. Career appearance No 200 for Tottenham's new signing Robbie Keane. Water-logging ends the Bristol City-Notts County game after 49 minutes.

3 Reassured by senior FA officials at the Fulham-Arsenal game, Eriksson, reportedly approached over the weekend by Italian Federation president Franco Carraro about succeeding Giovanni Trappatoni confirms: 'Everything around me may be changing, but I'm staying the way I am.' Celtic hammer in 7 without reply against Aberdeen. Rooney gains Everton their 1st win at Leeds in 51 years.

4 Man U now fear Keane who has not played since the end of August is out until the New Year not wishing to risk things after a hip operation.

5 FIFA do a U-turn and clear some Wales players to line out with their clubs 4 days ahead of EC qualifier in Azerbaijan. Former Derby player Rob Hindmarch, 41, loses his battle against Motor Neurone disease. In dignified fashion Mick McCarthy, Europe's longest-serving international coach, resigns his ROI job after almost 7 years and, just 4 months after leading his side into the last 16 of the WC. Two empty stands, 161 away supporters and 503 home faithful endure all-time low attendance for stricken Wimbledon at Selhurst Park.

6 Leeds fans vent fury at Ridsdale and Venables after Worthington Cup defeat at Sheff Utd. Burnley turf out Spurs. Sunderland do likewise at Highbury. Oldham put out Hammers. McManaman becomes 1st Englishman to skipper Real Madrid at Oviedo. Tigana creates history fielding 11 internationals from 11 different nations in his Fulham line-up.

7 Sheff Wed install Hartlepool boss Chris Turner as successor to Yorath. John Toshack is given coaching post at Italian Serie B side Catania.

8 Macclesfield midfielder Chris Byrne is seriously ill in hospital after being shot in the leg in an alley in Hulme, Manchester. England is to host the 2005 UEFA Women's Championship. BBC's Grandstand announcers take crash course in Welsh after agreeing to include scores from the League of Wales.

9 City hail the 1st conquest of their illustrious neighbours Utd in 13 years of Manchester clashes. Chelsea's Mark Bosnich, 30, is tested positive for cocaine after failing a routine FA drugs test. Brentford finish with 9 at Crewe. Liverpool's unbeaten Premiership run ends at the Riverside.

10 Hammers still the only side from the top 4 divisions and the Conference yet to win at home, losing again 3–4 to Leeds.

11 Eriksson says he considered walking out had he not been given certain assurances in the wake of recent FA turmoil. Sir Alex can earn as much as £4.5m per year from stud fees following the retirement of his champion racehorse Rock of Gibralter. Coroner rules that former Albion and England striker Jeff Astle, 59, died from brain damage caused by constant heading of a heavy, often wet, leather football. FL want the League Cup back with its traditional name after Worthington's 5-year deal ends this season.

12 Despite coming from 3-down Liverpool fail to progress in Champions League drawing at FC Basle. FAI general secretary Brendan Menton resigns after 'shambles' WC report. Rory Allen tears up his £3,000 weekly Pompey contract retiring at 25 and heading out to join England's Barmy Army of cricket followers in Australia. 'I've never heard anything like it.' says chief executive Peter Storrie.

13 Newcastle make history winning at Feyenoord and qualifying for 2nd phase of the Champions League, after starting with 3 defeats. England line up friendly with Australia on Feb 12 at Upton Park. Goalie Bosnich is in hospital suffering from severe clinical depression.

14 Superior Celtic end Blackburn's UEFA Cup interest. Leeds saunter into next rd against Hapoel Tel Aviv. Neil Ruddock starts legal action against Swindon over alleged unpaid wages.

15 Bobby Robson gets the draw he dreams of with Newcastle meeting Barcelona the club he left in 1997 after winning 3 trophies. Inter and Bayer Leverkusen are also in this tough group.

16 Confirmation that Beckham has a broken rib will mean a possible 4-week lay-off. The 131st fiery north London derby goes to the Gunners. Magpies wrack-up their 800th top flight win at St James' Park and also their 1,400th win at home in all competitions. University side Team Bath, quoted 25,000–1 to lift the FA Cup go out to Mansfield. Vauxhall Motors hold QPR. Oldham held by Burton Albion.

17 Hammers hold Man U snatching a deserved late home equaliser. Bolton lift themselves off the bottom with stunning win at Leeds with chants of 'Time to Go' ringing out from the home support. Sunderland muster not a shot nor gain a corner throughout 90 min holding Liverpool, with 24 attempts on goal, scoreless at Anfield.

18 Burton Albion's heroics win them a £100,000 Sky TV fee for the FA Cup replay with Oldham. Arsenal's Ljungberg is named Swedish Footballer of the Year. France want Man City ban for rebel Anelka who declines late international call-up.

19 Villa's Finnish international goalie Enckelman signs until the end of 2005–6 season. FA are examining the viability of the proposed £80m National Football Centre at Burton-on-Trent. Thierry Henry heads a list of 10 English-based players among the 50 nominations announced for the European Footballer of the Year award. John McCormack is the new manager at Morton.

20 Resilient Wales, 8 games now without defeat, win 2–0 in Azerbaijan. Ex-Old Trafford striker Stuart Pearson retains his MUTV job despite aiming criticism at boss Ferguson. SPL chief executive Roger Mitchell steps down.

21 Mike Newell is the new boss at Hartlepool. Leicester players agree a 30 per cent pay deferral.

22 Houllier takes Eriksson to task for comments on Gerrard's club form. Watford deny claims by Elton John that one player was paid £42,000 a week last season.

23 Looking for a Ist win in over 30 years Newcastle score 3 at Old Trafford but concede 5. Fulham's 2-goal hero Facundo Sava, the Argentine known as 'Zorro' (The Fox) indulges in his trademark celebration of sporting a black and white mask! Stoke crash to 8th successive defeat. Villa's Dublin nets his 100th Premiership goal joining a select band including Shearer and Cole. Arsenal clock up dismissal No 47 at Soton. Five are sent off in a frantic finish at Exeter (3), Cambridge (2).

24 Larsson's double at Livingston sends Celtic back top. Leeds lose at Spurs but will pick up a £25,000 fine for having more than half their side booked.

25 Boro win the right to pursue a compensation claim from Liverpool for Christian Ziege's transfer. Mayor of Barnsley, Peter Doyle, who made his name in the oil and gas industry has agreed in principle to buy the Div 2 club.

26 Basle, conquerors of Celtic and Liverpool stun Man U with a goal after 31 seconds but are floored by Van Nistelrooy's double taking his Champions League tally to 18 from 19 matches. Humiliated QPR make an FA Cup 1st rd exit losing at home on penalties to Vauxhall Motors. House of Lords decide Bruce Grobbleaar must pay £1m – plus legal costs for his ill-fated libel action.

27 Bellamy sees red after 5 minutes as Newcastle are torn apart by Inter. Keegan claims Internet jokers are trying to drive him out of Man City. Huddersfield tell manager Wadsworth to cut costs by not using subs.

28 UEFA charge Shearer for allegedly elbowing Inter's Fabio Cannavaro. Owen sees Liverpool through at Vitesse Arnhem. Spurs tells Ferdinand he can leave.

29 Shearer receives 2-match UEFA ban for violent conduct. Ferguson is given an honorary degree at Edinburgh University.

30 Chelsea refuse to comment on a report they have sacked goalie Mark Bosnich for allegedly testing positive for cocaine. Managerial legends Sir Matt Busby, Bill Shankly and Jock Stein are among the 50 names in the new Scottish Sports Hall of Fame. Pompey maintain their 7-point cushion at the top of Div 1.

December 2002

Shearer's thunderbolt ... Gregory's dealings queried ... Francis' costly cuff ... Boss job for Curle ... Hamilton helps FAI ... A Happy Valley ... Rooney's BBC vote ... Football's gambling culture ... Bowyer's disgrace ... Euro 2008 bid flops ... Boothferry Park bows out ... Wales move up ... Sir Bert dies ... Bellamy fouls up again ... Politician leads FL ... Brum bad boys ... Milner tops Rooney ... Ziege's scare

1 Dudek's blunder puts Man U on course for 2–1 victory at Anfield. Clouds gather over Venables as Leeds lose their 6th in 8 home games. Shearer thumps in an exocet-type volley, reckoned one of the greatest goals seen in front of the famous Gallowgate end, in Magpie win over Everton.

2 Hammers fans call for chairman to quit after last gasp defeat at home to Soton. Arsenal's Cole charged with misconduct for remarks to ref Durkin. Former Albion boss Alan Ashman, 74, dies after suffering a stroke and heart attack. Reading's Alan Pardew is Div 1 Manager of the Month.

3 FA to investigate John Gregory's transfer dealings during his 4-year tenure at Villa. Palace boss Francis gets £1,000 fine for striking his res goalie during a draw in August. Hammers blow as Di Canio now needs a knee operation putting him out for 2 months. Blades have convincing Worthington Cup win to put out Sunderland.

4 Villa ensure no slip-up in League Cup by dismissing PNE 5–0. Liverpool put out Ipswich with the last of 10 penalties. Keith Curle gets the Mansfield job, the club's 4th boss in 3 and a half years.

5 Former NI manager Bryan Hamilton is to assist the FAI in the process of recruiting Mick McCarthy's successor. Man U's Peter Kenyon sparks widespread outrage with his message of gloom predicting only 40 of the 92 League clubs would be able to maintain their professional status.

6 Stats based on results over the last 38 games indicate that Leicester's Micky Adams outshines Houllier, Sir Bobby Robson, Ranieri and McClaren, beaten only by master managers Wenger and Ferguson. Soton's James Beattie is the Barclaycard Player of the Month.

7 Bitter rivals Wenger and Ferguson declare the title race wide open after Man U beat last season's champions who fail to score for the 1st time in 56 matches. On the 10th anniversary of their return to The Valley, Charlton never look like losing to Liverpool. Leeds suffer their 10th Premiership reverse at Fulham. Rangers recover from conceding a goal after 18 seconds, a record for an Old Firm clash, to take full points against Celtic. The Stoke–Coventry match is littered with 13 cautions and culminating in the Potters being reduced to 9 men.

8 Wayne Rooney wins the BBC Young Sports Personality of the Year award, with the Life Achievement going to George Best and recognition to Arsenal's Wenger who clinches the Coach of the Year prize. Jean Tigana offers Fulham access to all his personal bank accounts to clear his name after the club expresses concern about the £11.5m purchase of Steve Marlet to the FA investigators.

9 Promoted Nationwide Conference clubs will be given extra time to improve their ground to the required FL standard. Tottenham's chairman threatens to build their proposed new stadium away from WHL if government do not regenerate the area and improve transport links.

10 On Bobby Robson's emotional return to Barcelona a waterlogged Nou Camp delays for 24 hours Newcastle's Champions League tie. Gunners fluff chances and are held by Valencia. PFA loan £5m to Derby who have the highest wage bill in Div 1.

11 Man U turn on the power against Deportivo La Coruna. Newcastle have no answer to super Barcelona who have lost just 1 in 24 European home ties to English opposition. At Sports Writers Association awards lunch Tony Adams claims gambling is a major problem in football.

12 Television captures Lee Bowyer stamping on a Malaga opponent's head as Leeds, squabbling amongst themselves, go spinning out. One goal away from Ian Rush's all-time record Owen nets his 19th European score in victory over Vitesse Arnhem. Kenny Dalglish claims a 'fix' as the Scotland–Ireland bid to host Euro 2008 trails in a curious 5th of the 7 bidders and way behind winners Austria/Switzerland.

13 Bowyer admits to boss Venables his cowardly head-stamping offence which shames soccer and may spark UEFA into issuing a ban. On eve of North London clash, Hoddle says that he'd prefer to qualify for Europe rather than beat Arsenal. Liverpool and Celtic avoid each other in UEFA Cup 4th rd draw.

14 Bradford avoid a club record 8th successive defeat. Reading concede their 1st League goal in 757 minutes at home to the Blades. Boothferry Park which once housed over 65,000 for an FA Cup 6th rd

tie with Man U hosts its last game in front of 14,162. The Gary Lineker-led consortium gets the go-ahead to clinch a £5m deal to save Leicester. Ryman Premier League leaders Aldershot win before 1,989, the highest non-League attendance in the UK.

15 Celtic fall further behind Rangers held 1–1 at Kilmarnock. Danny Wilson's Bristol City go 16 games unbeaten after win at Cardiff. Outplayed for long periods at Spurs, a Pires penalty salvages a draw for Arsenal. Houllier's team becomes the 1st Liverpool side to lose on Wearside since the 50's.

16 Vale, reportedly £2.4m in debt, go into administration. Ronaldo is named European Footballer of the Year for the 2nd time although only playing 17 top-flight games for Inter and Real Madrid.

17 Forlan's late winner against Chelsea seals Worthington Cup quarter-final place for Man U. In front of a 16,922 record attendance at their JJB Stadium Wigan's League Cup adventure ends. FA receive £9,000 fine for crowd trouble at EC 2004 qualifier against Slovakia. Wales soar from 100th to 52nd in FIFA rankings. Reading's John Mackie makes public apology and volunteers to donate wages to charity for racially abusing Blades' Carl Asaba. John Fashanu buys Welsh Premier club Barry Town.

18 Tributes flow in for Sir Bert Millichip, 88, former chairman of the FA who dies after collapsing at a function in the Midlands. Northumbria police detain Celtic players Bobby Petta, Joos Valgaeren and Johan Mjallby in connection with a nightclub incident. Newcastle's Bellamy is given a second 3-match Champions League suspension of the season. A delay of 80 minutes before Liverpool take a step closer to their 2nd League Cup final in 3 years beating Villa 4–3.

19 Sir Brian Mawhinney, the former NI secretary, is unveiled as the FL's new chairman pledging to maintain a 72-club set-up. Dutch legend Johan Cruyff insists Thierry Henry not Ronaldo deserved the European Players of the Year award. Bergkamp's petulant stamp on a Blackburn player amazingly escapes a ban meriting just a £5,000 fine. Brum are fined £25,000 following crowd misbehaviour. Arthur Rowley, the most prolific scorer in English football with a record 434 in 619 appearances, dies, aged 76.

20 Brum's Bruce defends the fighting spirit of his team who have the Premiership's worse disciplinary record, 42 cautions and 2 reds.

21 Gills grab their 1st win for 10 weeks. Norwich give manager Worthington a new contract just before kick-off against PNE. Midfielder Marcus Browning becomes the 4th player to keep goal for Bournemouth in 3 games in a week. FA secure their 5th and final sponsorship, a £30m deal with Pepsi.

22 Gerrard apologises for his 2-footed horror tackle on Everton's Gary Naysmith. With Keane returning after nearly 4 months Blackburn send Man U to 1st defeat in 12 games.

23 Ziege is off after twice receiving yellow cards for kicking the ball away but Spurs win at Maine Road. Villa still the only team in the Premiership without an away win.

24 Arsenal goalie Rami Shaaban fractures the tibia and fibia bones in his right leg during training and faces months out.

25 Claudio Ranieri has a working Christmas Day studying a video of tomorrow's opponents Soton, 'But my wife was not too happy.' Admits the Chelsea coach.

26 Wayne Rooney, arguably the most watched footballer in Britain, sees red for a lunging tackle on Brum's Vickers. James Milner, aged 16 and 357 days becomes the youngest scorer in the Premiership notching for Leeds in win over Sunderland. A sell-out 22,319 see Hull win at their new Kingston Communication Stadium. Lowly Motherwell hand Rangers their 1st reverse of the season.

27 FA suspend Mark Bosnich from all football activities stating he is not permitted to play again until charges have been heard. Phil Thompson dismisses as 'rubbish' suggestions their title aspirations are finished after Liverpool's 8 League games without a win sequence, representing the club's worst run of results in 50 years.

28 Soton get a lift thanks to Tessem's last-gasp winner which breaks Sunderland's spirit. Relief for Roeder as Defoe snatches an equaliser against Blackburn. Villa's Dublin slots career goal No 200 against Boro as ref Rob Styles takes his booking tally, with another 5, to a seasonal 53 making him the busiest in the Premiership.

29 Jeffers wins late controversial penalty to give Arsenal an equaliser against Liverpool. Tottenham's Ziege reveals it was touch and go whether an amputation was needed after being rushed to hospital late Boxing Day evening after his right leg swelled to an alarming size. Shearer marks his 250th Newcastle appearance with a headed goal.

30 Man City are tipped to prise Robbie Fowler away from Leeds when the transfer window re-opens. Rock-bottom in Div 1 and with debts of over £20m, Sheff Wed will invite worried supporters to a Hillsborough meeting to discuss the crisis with new boss Chris Turner. Harry Redknapp predicts we will never again see a Nationwide club pay a £1m fee.

31 With New Year's morning League positions during the past 5 years 21st, 20th, 22nd, 14th and 14th, Pompey fans are pinching themselves about their top Div 1 spot. Egypt, Libya, Morocco, S Africa and Tunisia were expected to meet tonight's deadline for candidates wanting to stage WC 2010.

January 2003

Semis for new Wembley ... One step for Barca ... Shrews cup shock ... Bosnich drugs test ... Stamford Bridge beach ... Icelander's gambling addiction ... Gazza in China ... Mystery star's card school debts ... Bizarre Scots score ... Poor facilities survey ... League Cup for Durkin ... Attendances on the up ... Irish appoint Kerr ... OT rip-up again ... Riverside's EC tie ... Magpie Woodgate.

1 Arsenal's win over Chelsea produces 4 goals in the final 10 mins. Rain and water logging causes 12 postponements in the top 4 divisions, yet in Manchester supposedly the wettest place in Britain, the Old Trafford pitch needs watering before the match with Sunderland.

2 FA decree that all Cup semi-finals will be played at Wembley to help meet the £757m cost of the new stadium opening in 2006. As demolition of the old Venue of Legends continues, the FA sell one of the 39 steps to Barcelona who lifted the 1992 European Cup there.
3 Cash-strapped Ipswich warn they may be forced to sell players after sacking almost 20 backroom staff.
4 A Carrow Road power cut postpones the Norwich v Brighton FA Cup tie seconds before kick-off. Farnborough Town put out 'Quakers' at Darlington. Argyle held at home by Dagenham & Redbridge. Div 3 strugglers Shrewsbury send Everton tumbling out of the Cup. Bergkamp, signed from Inter Milan for £7.5m in 1995, notches 100th goal for Gunners. School-kid Lee Holmes, Derby's sub midfielder enters the record books as the youngest to appear in the FA Cup proper at Brentford, aged 15 years and 277 days.
5 After 90 mins of pulsating action in the best FA Cup tradition Wolves put out Newcastle.
6 Non-League Farnborough's dream draw with Arsenal, if switched to Highbury, could realise a near £1m windfall. Northampton sack manager Kevan Broadhurst.
7 Chelsea sack Mark Bosnich over his positive drugs test. In League Cup semi-final draw at Old Trafford Blackburn take a deserved away goal back to Ewood Park. Terry Fenwick takes charge at Northampton. Canary fans vote TV cook Delia Smith back on to the Norwich board of directors.
8 Sheffield Utd take a 1st leg League Cup goal advantage to Liverpool. West Ham-bound Lee Bowyer leaves Leeds as he joined them – in disgrace – after UEFA ban him for 6 matches for stamping on an opponent's head. Graeme Souness is charged with misconduct for the 3rd time in less than a year.
9 Soton's Strachan wins the Manager of the Month award. Leeds midfielder Olivier Dacourt joins Roma.
10 Coventry's playing staff including P/manager Gary McAllister take a 12 per cent wage cut. Fulham chairman Mohamed Al Fayed is to turn England's only professional women's side into a semi-pro outfit. Craig Bellamy's new £35,000 a week salary commits him to Newcastle until 2007.
11 Chelsea destroy Charlton on an atrocious, sanded Stamford Bridge pitch described as a 'Copacabana Beach.' Spluttering Liverpool held at home by Villa are now without a win in 11 League games and boasting just 5 points from the past 33. Chelsea's Eider Gudjohnsen confesses blowing £400,000 in a 5-month gambling spree.
12 Henry races to 100 goals in 180 appearance for Arsenal in 4–0 win at Brum. Keane nets a Spurs hat-trick in 4–3 win over Everton. England decline invitation to visit Zimbabwe prior to friendly against S Africa in Durban on May 22. Mark Hughes signs new 4-year contract as Welsh manager.
13 After just 9 wins from 33 games Cheltenham part with manager Graham Allner. Ian Rush who scored a Liverpool record 346 goals from 658 games is to coach the club's forwards on a part-time basis. Ex-striker Tony Cascarino leaks that a 'Big Name' England player involved in a flourishing WC card school in the Far East wrote out a cheque for £30,000 gambling debts.
14 PFA add their support to controlling betting amongst top wage-earning players. FIFA is angry the FA fail to suspend dismissed Chelsea goalie Carlo Cudicini. Gazza jets out to China in an attempt to resurrect his career. Dagenham & Redbridge win cup replay against Plymouth. Bristol City must pay £100,000 after their illegal approach in 1999 for ex-Gillingham boss Tony Pulis.
15 Charlton demand a rematch against Chelsea claiming the completely sanded pitch constituted an artificial surface contrary to the rules of the Premier League (Rule 17, Section 1). Zola is voted Chelsea's best ever player ahead of legends Jimmy Greaves and Peter Osgood.
16 Robbie Fowler's £7m Leeds to Man City deal dramatically collapses at a late stage after a crucial delay by the Maine Road board over the structure of the contract. FA agree to proceed with the £50m training centre academy at Burton. Michael Owen, on a reported £60,000 a week wage, is revealed as the mystery player who lost heavily at cards during England's WC trip to Japan and South Korea.
17 Wayne Rooney, 17, signs first professional Everton contract, a 3½ year deal, shooting his £90-a-week wage to around £14,000 weekly. Sheffield Utd stretch their unbeaten run to 15 matches coming from behind to win the 104th Steel City Derby.
18 Newcastle's Shearer scores in just 10.4 seconds against Man City, second behind the Premiership's 10 second fastest from Tottenham's Ledley King at Bradford City in Dec 2000. Liverpool's worst run of League results in 48 years ends with a 1–0 success at Soton. A bizarre scoreline, witnessed by 452, in Bell's Scottish Div 2 with Brechin hitting 5 at home yet conceding 7 to Cowdenbeath.
19 Arsenal's Bergkamp faces another trial by video after appearing to elbow W Ham's Lee Bowyer in the face. Henry's hat-trick included his 1st headed goal in the Premiership after 9,639 mins. Concerned PFA reveal that as many as 20 of their members are gambling addicts.
20 A 2-year comprehensive survey of football amenities in England reveals a worrying dearth of adequate facilities listing disrepair of pitches, particularly at grass-roots level, a major concern; while the Football Foundation discover 38 per cent of pitches indoor and out, have no changing rooms. Tops for facilities are in Devon, Dorset, Guernsey, Isle of Man, Jersey, Norfolk, Oxfordshire and Suffolk.
21 Owen hits a sublime winner against Sheff Utd to take Liverpool to the Worthington Cup final. Leeds give the all-clear for Brian Kidd to become asst coach to the England team on a part-time basis.
22 Celtic's Martin O'Neill ends speculation about his immediate future, signing a 12-month rolling contract. Bobby Gould is given the manager's job at Cheltenham. Man U sweep past Blackburn to set up a dream League Cup final clash against Liverpool. Ten of the 12 SPL clubs agree to scrap their threat to resign at the end of next season.
23 Villa show a loss of £8.1m for the 6-month period ending 30 Nov 2002. Sunderland describe Man U as 'shabby, despicable, disrespectful, arrogant, and unprofessional' in trying to entice 20 year old David Bellion. Three British players, one figuring in Scotland, have tested positive for marijuana.

24 Paul Durkin will take charge for the Worthington Cup final on 2 Mar. Venables hints the loss of defender Woodgate to Newcastle may trigger his own departure from Elland Road.

25 Gillingham capitalise on Viduka's dismissal by equalising and earning an Elland Road replay. Rochdale and Watford produce the performances of the day both reaching the FA Cup 5th rd. Giving a memorable day out for their 6,000 followers Farnborough, reduced to 10 men after 29 mins, take the cash and souvenirs but there's no romance or glory at Highbury losing 5–1. Over 7 million have watched the Premiership so far; attendances are 2.1 per cent up with last season's 34, 324 average way above Spain (25,700) and Italy (25,200).

26 Zola's brilliance and goals sees Chelsea comfortably through at Shrewsbury. Hammers get a 6–0 Old Trafford mauling.

27 Arsenal and Man U who have met 8 times in the competition with 4 wins apiece are paired in the 5th rd plum tie. Rochdale's P/m Paul Simpson describes as 'fantastic' the trip to Molineux. Reportedly pipping Bryan Robson, Brian Kerr who has steered Ireland's U-16 and U-18 to European titles is named as the successor to Mick McCarthy. Farnborough's boss/chairman Graham Westley quits to become manager at Stevenage.

28 Gudjon Thordarson, sacked 5 days after guiding Stoke to promotion, accepts a £37,500 out-of-court settlement for unfair dismissal. John Toshack resigns from Italian Serie B club Catania. Old Trafford's turf is ripped up after just 11 matches, the 9th time in 4 years the work – estimated to cost £100,000 – has had to be done.

29 At Anfield, Heskey's late headed equaliser pegs back Arsenal. Mike Walsh, former Everton defender, is Southport's new manager. Steve Whitton parts with Colchester after 3 years. Newcastle leapfrog Man U into 2nd place behind Arsenal. Boston Utd's manager Steve Evans is given a 20-month ban from management.

30 England will stage their EC qualifier against Slovakia on 11 June at the Riverside Stadium, the 1st time the national side have been in the town since 1937, at Ayresome Park. Ian McCall is the new manager at Dundee Utd. After his on-off saga move, Robbie Fowler finally links with Man City in £6m package deal from Leeds.

31 On final day of the transfer window Jonathan Woodgate, 23, completes his £9m Leeds to Newcastle move pledging to put his shameful past behind him. Boro snatch Bolton's Michael Ricketts for £3.5m. One-time Luton midfielder Raddy Antic, 54, is the new coach at Barcelona.

February 2003

Boksic bow out ... Cloughie on the mend ... UEFA honour Thierry and Duff ... Lineker helps Leicester ... Colossal Pool sponsorship ... Vialli wants money ... Sherri celebrates ... Goat the hero ... Keane bows out ... England field 2 teams! ... Youngest cap Rooney ... Fergie kick out ... Zola landmark ... Houllier scoffs rumours ... Top earner Becks ... Juninho awakens interest ... Toffees sticking.

1 Sunderland's miserable season descends into farce with 3 og's in 7 mins dropping them bottom of the Premiership. Dave Beasant, at 43, makes his Brighton debut. Under-fire chairman Pete Ridsdale needs a police escort after losing at Everton, their 13th League defeat. Boro's Alen Boksic, 33, announces his retirement, 5 months before his contract is due to expire.

2 Hammers slump to their heaviest home defeat of the season with manager Roeder questioning attitudes of some. Bad weather abandons, after 27 mins, the televised SPL fixture between Dundee and Hibs.

3 Liverpool's Gerrard is given a 3-match suspension for violent conduct. Leeds settle with sacked former manager David O'Leary who had been in dispute over a £2m pay-off. Brian Clough, 67, is discharged from hospital following liver transplant operation. Thierry Henry and Damien Duff are the only Premiership players chosen in the Team of the Year 2002 by almost 1 million votes on UEFA's website.

4 Gary Lineker's 5-man consortium, having raised £4m, is given the go-ahead to take over at Leicester. Mark Bosnich loses his case for unfair dismissal from Chelsea. Some respite for troubled Leeds – they shrug off Gillingham to make the FA Cup 5th rd. Tottenham's Chris Hughton will be Ireland's part-time asst/manager to Brian Kerr.

5 Liverpool celebrate the signing of their Reebok £100m kit deal, the biggest sponsorship in their history, but on the pitch 10-man Palace stun Anfield winning their FA Cup replay 2–0. Soton go through at Millwall.

6 After a series of injuries Scots defender Dominic Matteo quits international football. Blackpool boss Steve McMahon extends his 3-year contract. Chief executive Rick Parry refutes suggestions Gerard Houllier's future is uncertain.

7 Paul Scholes is the Barclaycard Player of the Month for January scoring in all of Man U's games. Luca Vialli, pursuing £1.6m, issues court proceedings over his Watford sacking.

8 Skipper Sheringham reaches the magic figure of 300 goals as Spurs beat Sunderland. Pompey notch 6 against Derby. England's Eriksson's 27-man panel including 17 year old Wayne Rooney will ensure the nation's youngest ever side against Australia.

9 Sub Goater's goal gives City a late equaliser at Old Trafford against Utd in the Manchester derby watched by 67,646. It finishes all square in the Dundee derby clash. Henrik Larsson suffers a double fracture of the jaw against Livingston. Five minutes after cancelling out Henry's 24th min opener. Newcastle's Laurent Robert is sent off in 58th min.

10 Charlton fail to get their Premiership game on the sanded Stamford Bridge surface replayed, but Chelsea are fined £5,000 plus costs. Unable to cope with £15m net loss of income Ipswich, relegated from the Premiership, file for temporary administration.

11 Alex Kolinko is fined 2 weeks wages for refusing to play for Palace at Leicester earlier this month. Oldham, losing £50,000 a week, have ordered manager Iain Dowie to cut members of his backroom staff. England U21's fail to get even a single shot on target losing to a technically superior Italian side in Carrara. Roy Keane performs a U-turn and quits international football.

12 An International reduced to a farce sees England dish out caps sending out 'A' and 'B' teams against Australia at Upton Park but the plan backfires losing 3–1. Everton kid Rooney makes history as the youngest capped, aged 17 years 111 days. Arsenal's Keown is fined £5,000 following his confrontation with Man U's van Nistelrooy.

13 Man City drop plans to sue Roy Keane handing stunned Alfie Haaland 6-month's notice. Following the debacle of the Australia defeat FA announce a series of summit meetings to address the club-versus-country impasse.

14 FL warn forged Worthington Cup final tickets between Liverpool and Man U could be in circulation.

15 A war of words erupts as holders Arsenal book an FA Cup quarter-final spot with a 2–0 win at Old Trafford. Watford pile on more misery for dispirited Sunderland.

16 Chelsea, Wolves and Leeds all progress to the FA Cup quarter-final stage. Postponements make a mockery of the Scottish winter shut-down provoking an urgent enquiry.

17 A tantalising repeat of last year's final between the holders, Arsenal, and the 2000 winners, Chelsea, is the pick of the FA Cup quarter-final draw. Jean Tigana's future remains in doubt as Fulham refuse to give assurances over eventual home and level of ambition. Man U's Ferguson is condemned after frustratingly kicking a dressing-room boot into the face of Beckham after the FA Cup exit by Arsenal.

18 Enthusiastic Newcastle manager Bobby Robson celebrating his 70th birthday maintains today's game is better technically, tactically, financially and physically. Geordies keep alive their Champions League hopes with win at Bayer Leverkusen. TV personality Des Lynam is leading Brighton's fight to move to a new £40m, 25,000 all-seater stadium. Arsenal chuck away 2 more points being held at Highbury by Ajax. A frozen pitch call off at half-time the Brentford–Colchester fixture, the first competitive match to be abandoned at Griffin Park for 35 years.

19 Eclipsed for long periods by Juventus, Man U still gain 2–1 win at Old Trafford. Supporters' group Valiant 2001 win the right to become the new owners of Port Vale. Arsenal's match day announcer is rapped after a jibe at Man U's Ferguson.

20 Hyppia's goal at Auxerre carries Liverpool within sight of UEFA Cup quarter-final. To avoid inflaming any ill-feeling, Newcastle tell recent £8m signing Woodgate to steer clear of Elland Road for Saturday's fixture. Newspaper revelations say England's Eriksson agreed to take over at Man U 6 months before the WC.

21 Boss Roeder is trying to find the Hammers 'mole' who made public an alleged row with defender Gary Breen.

22 After 5-1 thrashing by the Gunners Man City's keeper, Schmeichel says the opposition 'were on a different planet.' Zola, 36, chalks up his 300th outing for Chelsea. Forest put 6 past bottom-placed Stoke.

23 Di Canio throws a touchline tantrum after being subbed in Hammers win at Albion. Gazza nets a hat-trick on his 1st appearance for Chinese club Gansu Tianma.

24 Fulham's draw at Spurs was their 47th game of an eventful packed season. Strugglers Northampton sack Terry Fenwick after 7 weeks. Sheff Utd face their 3rd investigation into crowd trouble this season. Following a disastrous sequence of results, Houllier scoffs at suggestions he is contemplating a return to France with Monaco. A new survey shows Premiership wages rose by a staggering 28 per cent last season with players pocketing an amazing £720m, and Man U's Beckham the highest paid in English history on £90,000 a week.

25 Ken Bates rules out the possibility of Fulham ground-sharing at Chelsea. Man U cruise into the last 8 of the Champions League with a stunning 3–0 victory at Juventus. Colchester who had 72 applications, give the managerial post to Phil Parkinson who has been working with Reading's academy. Juninho's comeback with Boro Reserves, attracts a staggering 20,000 crowd to the Riverside Stadium. Exeter replace boss Neil McNab with Gary Peters.

26 Shearer's 1st hat-trick for 3½ years sinks Bayer Leverkusen. Burnley shock Fulham with 3–0 cup victory leaving them the 1st club from outside the top flight in 11 years to reach the FA Cup final if they win at Watford.

27 Owen's opener in win over Auxerre takes the striker level with Anfield legend Ian Rush on 20 European goals. Celtic's progress against Stuttgart sets up a 'Battle of Britain' UEFA clash with Liverpool.

28 Forged tickets for the Worthington Cup final are trading for £500. Six candidates are set for interviews for the FA chief executive vacancy. Charlton's Alan Curbishley is the Manager of the Month. Everton's dream of building a new stadium at Kings Dock appears doomed. There are no Premiership club applications for the much-maligned Intertoto Cup competition.

March 2003

Robbo caps appeal ... Brum derby mahem ... KK's stance ... Nationwide LC? ... Wilko out ... Shearer's Euro haul ... Black cat McCarthy ... Diouf shame ... Boss' drink lapse ... Bergy in dock ... No SPL break ... El Tel's reign ends ... Inverness Caley shock ... Premiership's highest ... Calm transfer deadline ... Gazza wows Chinese ... Ridsdale quits ... Rams engage Burley.

1 Former Newcastle and Chelsea favourite Gavin Peacock commentates for ESPN, based in Singapore, on today's clash to an audience of 600 million. Juninho scores on his 1st game of his 3rd spell with

Boro. Sir Bobby Robson appeals for the return of 12 England caps stolen during a break-in at his family's Suffolk home 18 months ago.

2 Dudek's heroics assists Liverpool's Worthington Cup final win over Man U. FA confirm La Manga training camp will be used by England ahead of their EC qualifier against Slovakia. Ipswich claim their 1st victory at Carrow Road for 11 years.

3 In the 1st top-flight Brum derby for 16 years Villa finish explosive clash against the Blues with 9 men. Five successive February victories earn Reading's Alan Pardew Nationwide Div 1 Manager of the Month, Ian Holloway (QPR) and Bournemouth's Sean O'Driscoll also earn recognition.

4 West Midlands Police refuse to rule out prosecuting Dion Dublin for head-butting Robbie Savage. Pompey supporters make up 9,000 of the 10,356 at Selhurst Park but endure defeat by The Dons.

5 Boro win the Tees-Tyne derby in front of a sell-out crowd, at 34,814 the highest at the 8-year-old Riverside Stadium. Keegan wins his power struggle at Man City when chairman David Bernstein resigns.

6 Vice-chairman Dein hits back at Ferguson's jibe that Arsenal are arrogant. Sponsors Kingston Communications provide Hull City staff free mobile phones but they don't work around the ground because there is no network coverage. FIFA postpone the 24-team World Youth Championships in UAE. Premier League reveal average attendances reaching 35,151.

7 FIFA confirm their WC finals 2014 will be hosted in S America and likely to be staged jointly by possibly Argentina and Brazil. Swansea City, 91st in the League, included 6 loan players in the 16-man squad against Wrexham when a new ruling states only 5 are permitted. Nationwide express interest in succeeding League Cup sponsor Worthington.

8 Henry is hit by a missile thrown at the Clock end in 2–2 Cup classic clash against Chelsea. Celtic win the Old Firm derby. A leaky roof in the new North Stand delays the kick-off at Ipswich by 15 mins.

9 Blades increase misery on a Leeds team sporting 11 internationals pulling off another shock and powering to the FA Cup semi-finals. Soton and Watford also progress.

10 Howard Wilkinson and assistant Steve Cotterill pay the price for failure at Sunderland having managed to win just 2 of their 20 Premiership matches.

11 Unconvincing Arsenal fail to see off 10-man Roma drawing 1–1 and having won just once in 7 home matches in the competition over 2 seasons. Newcastle's dream is still on, recording a draw at Inter with Shearer's 10th and 11th European scores eclipsing the club record of Wyn Davies. FA announce measures to stop non-League clubs switching Cup ties to Premiership grounds. Blackburn's Stig Inge Bjornebye, 33, capped 78 times for Norway is forced to retire after suffering a fractured eye socket.

12 Former Ireland boss Mick McCarthy who has a rolling contract takes charge at struggling Sunderland, the club's 3rd manager this season. No FA Cup semi-finals will be played in London until the new Wembley is complete in 2006. Gary Neville clocks up a record number of appearances – and scores – in the Champions League against Basle.

13 Diouf brings disgrace on Liverpool by clearly spitting at Celtic fans sparking a police investigation. Watford are hoping to buy back their Vicarage Road ground from the mystery businessman they sold it to for £6m in January.

14 With tomorrow's 12.15 pm clash against Villa their 8th lunch-time kick-off, Man U's Ferguson is unhappy with the situation – and there are 2 more to follow! A Chelsea training ground bust-up involving Carlton Cole knocking out Jesper Gronkjaer is leaked. Sir Bobby Robson tips Alan Curbishley to one day manage England. New boss McCarthy says it will be 'a miracle' if Sunderland stay up – the bookies rate it 10/1. Liverpool to donate the £60,000 club fine – 2 weeks of Diouf's wages – to a charity of Celtic's choice.

15 Sluggish Gunners lose at Blackburn, their 1st defeat in 15 games. Derby, a 7th game without a win, now occupy their lowest League position since Oct 1995.

16 After hinting over the weekend about doing a job for England, Shearer does a U-turn. Rangers beat Celtic to lift the CIS Insurance Cup. On Ranieri's 100th Premiership game Zola, arguably the top oversees import, celebrates with a goal.

17 After missing Saturday's game with Dundee following an alcohol binge, Aberdeen manager Steve Paterson confesses a 'drink problem' vowing to seek professional help. Ferguson taunts Wenger with 'squeeze your bum time' jibes.

18 Gillingham P/manager Andy Hessenthaler chalks up his 500th League appearance. Diouf escapes with 2-game ban for spitting. Former Spurs boss Peter Shreeves resigns at Barnet.

19 Arsenal, with just 1 victory in their last 9 European games, crash out of the Champions League in Valencia. Newcastle's dream also ends against Barcelona.

20 For the 2nd time this season Bergkamp is fined, following an arm-contact incident with Lee Bowyer. Strongbow's refusal to renew £2.5m deal leaves Leeds without a shirt sponsor. SPL January winter break is to be scrapped.

21 Celtic clinch a 2–0 victory at Anfield putting the Scottish champions into their 1st European semi-final since 1974. Announced on the Stock Exchange Venables' 8-month managerial tenure at Leeds is over, with Peter Reid given the caretaker role until the end of the season. Ruud Gullit is to coach Holland's U-20 side. John Gregory is suspended by struggling Derby following 'serious allegations' against him.

22 Man U hit top of the Premiership for the 1st time this season. Chelsea and Newcastle net 5 goals but Wolves go one better mauling The Gills and netting 5 in the opening 30 mins. LMA's John Barnwell reveals that after 17 months Leicester owe sacked manager Peter Taylor £200,000.

23 The biggest upset in Scottish football is provided yet again by Inverness Caledonian Thistle with the Highlanders dumping Celtic out of the Scottish Cup for the 2nd time in 3 years. Saturday's attendance of 67,706 at Old Trafford is the highest in the history of the Premiership.

With Manchester United's Roy Keane, floundering in his wake, Michael Owen powers through for Liverpool in the Worthington Cup Final, the last of the competition under that title and now the Carling Cup. (Actionimages)

24 Hounded Leeds Utd chairman Peter Ridsdale vows to carry on. Lowly Bolton snatch stoppage-time 1-0 penalty winner over Spurs.

25 Arsenal maintain their grip on the FA Cup winning their 6th rd replay thriller at Chelsea. Southend, 14th in Div 3, sack manager Ron Newman. Sorry Wimbledon take just 10 paying fans to Norwich

26 Cash-strapped Huddersfield, struggling in Div 2, sack manager Mick Wadsworth putting Mel Machin in charge. Chelsea investigate an incident in which Arsenal's Henry was struck on the forehead by a cigarette lighter. Amid security fears Wales' EC qualifier against Serbia and Montenegro in Belgrade is cancelled with 20 Aug the new date.

27 Although loans and frees are the order of the day the transfer deadline does show a £900,000 transaction with Ipswich's Hermann Hreidarsson moving to Charlton.

28 Sir Bobby Robson is seething after Hugh Viana dislocates a shoulder and 2-goal Shola Ameobi is sent off. James Beattie collects a striker's Oscar becoming the 1st Premiership player to rack up 20 goals.

29 In EC ties England splutter to win in Liechtenstein. ROI grab win in Georgia but winger Kilbane is hit by an open penknife. Wales sweep aside Azerbaijan. Lee Wilkie makes his Hampden Park debut with a Scotland winner. Sammy McIlroy's side lose yet again in Armenia, completing 702 mins without a goal, a NI record. In Lanzhou, China, a dusty industrial city on the banks of the Yellow River, Gascoigne scores a mesmerising goal, makes another and earns a penalty for Gansu Tianma.

30 Palace's chairman hands Trevor Francis an extraordinary ultimatum to deliver a successful 'blueprint' for the future or face the axe. Eriksson is refusing to bow to opinion and throws in 17 year old Wayne Rooney for the Turkey qualifier. Leeds chairman Peter Ridsdale resigns. Fulham Ladies win penalty shoot-out beating Arsenal in a fiercely-competitive Women's League Cup final.

31 As Prof John McKenzie replaces Ridsdale the Leeds debt has risen to £78.9m. Ron Noades resigns as chairman and director of Brentford. Derby bring in George Burley while manager Gregory is suspended.

April 2003

England crowd disturbances ... 'I'd love it' is top of the pops ... Bizarre Burnley score ... Fergie sorry for rigging slur ... Pool resent criticism ... Gunners and Soton for final ... Premiership Pompey ... Au revior Tigana ... Francis leaves Palace ... Houllier's landmark ... FA job losses ... Top whistler Durkin ... Fergie lets rip ... Newcomers Yeovil ... Henry gets top vote ... Ridsdale benefits ... Ratcliffe resigns.

1 Robbie Keane rejoins the Ireland team in Tirana after the funeral of his father. Jeffers nets his 13th goal in 13 appearances equaling Shearer's U-21 record. Huddersfield players, not paid in full for 5 months forego wages for the rest of the season. Joe Royle is Div 1 Manager of the Month, awards also to Phil Parkinson (Colchester) and Rushden & Diamonds' Brian Talbot.

2 Disgraceful crowd scenes mar England's Rooney-inspired feisty win over Turkey which may lead to playing their next Euro 2004 qualifier behind closed doors. Scotland fail to a penalty in Lithuania.

Teenage wonder boy Wayne Rooney muscles his way past Turkish midfield player Okan during England's impressive 2-0 win in the Euro 2004 qualifier, one of their better performances in recent years. (Associated Sports Photography)

Albania hold listless Ireland. NI, reduced to 9 men, lose to Greece. Kevin Keegan's 'I'd love it, I'd really love it' is to be named the quote of the decade in celebration of the Premiership's 10th anniversary.

3 UEFA probe two pitch invasions at Sunderland during England's victory over Turkey with concern already surfacing amidst taunts of revenge about the October return. The SARS virus sweeping south-east Asia may cancel Everton's China tour in late May.

4 Glenn Roeder is Manager of the Month. Yeovil boss, Gary Johnson, who enjoyed a successful stint as Latvia's national boss between 1999 and 2001 is heading next month to Riga to be a guest of honour at the Eurovision Song Contest. With Galatasaray's Ali Sami Yen stadium, famous for the 'Welcome to Hell' banners due for renovation, England's EC clash is expected to be at Fenerbahce's 50,000 capacity arena.

5 Leeds enjoy their biggest away win in the Premiership having 10 shots on target and scoring 6 at Charlton. Hyypia is red-carded after 4 minutes with the 4–0 Man U win the biggest over Liverpool for 50 years. With 9 goals arriving in the opening half Burnley crash 7–4 at home to Watford. Ferguson sparks a Champions League storm claiming the quarter-finals draw was rigged. SFA's David Taylor brands the country's football anthem 'a bit of a dirge.'

6 An attendance of 50,913 witness Bristol City become the 1st southern club to lift the LDV Vans Trophy in 8 years beating Carlisle. From 184 countries selecting 22 players Man U and Arsenal

dominate the Premier League 10 season domestic and overseas Teams of the Decade, conducted via a website and attracting almost 750,000 votes.

7 Ferguson admits he was wrong to accuse UEFA of rigging Champions League draw. Hamilton's John Walker is hit with a 3 month ban following a positive drug test. Wigan's imminent promotion to Div 1 leads to record losses of £2.7m because of disappointing average crowds of 6,700. Fulham lose at home to Blackburn before the lowest Premiership crowd this season, 14,017.

8 Derby reserve team manager Mark Lillis is planning to extend his stay as assistant to NI manager Sammy McIlroy. Man City's Peter Schmeichel intends going into management. After losing 3-1 to a Real Madrid side turning on the style up front, not in defence, Man U only have a glimmer of hope for the home return.

9 Chris Waddle, 42, signs for Unibond League side Stocksbridge Park Steels.

10 Bergkamp hits back at Ferguson's taunting insisting Arsenal were 'not arrogant, just confident.' The 2003 FIFA World Youth Championships postponed for security is re-scheduled for 27 Nov–19 Dec. Chelsea ban 26 fans for life.

11 A settlement between Wimbledon and Brum is expected within 3 days to bring NI International Michael Hughes out of domestic limbo after a year. Houllier slams the growing list of ex-Liverpool players criticising the club. Soton players can bank £20,000 each if they overcome Watford and reach the FA Cup Final on 17 May.

12 Amidst reports of £38m Real Madrid interest in Beckham. Scholes nets a hat-trick in 6–2 rout of Newcastle. Yeovil finally win promotion to the FL celebrating in style with 4–0 success at Doncaster.

13 Seaman, in his 1,000th senior match helps Arsenal blunt Blades and take their FA Cup Final place where they meet Soton winners over plucky Watford. James Beattie with 22 strikes is nominated with 5 other Premiership players for the PFA Player of the Year award.

14 Graham Barber (Tring) is to referee the 17 May FA Cup Final.

15 With a side assembled for £2.25m, Pompey secure their place back in the top flight for the 1st time since their one brief season in 1988. Wigan gain promotion as a result of Bristol City's 1–1 draw at Crewe. Fulham confirm playing home games at QPR's Loftus Rd for another season. Wales are dealt a Euro 2004 blow with FIFA's decision to suspend Azerbaijan indefinitely threatening to void their results.

16 Campbell is red-carded in Highbury Premiership showdown with Man U. FA Cup finalists Gunners and Soton are locked in a row over a 'lucky' hotel, the 5-star Vale of Glamorgan.

17 Jean Tigana leaves struggling Fulham with former captain Chris Coleman taking temporary charge. Former chairman Ridsdale severs all connections at Leeds resigning from the club and PLC board. Keegan admits embarrassment at Fair Play UEFA Cup place ahead of a team which finishes 10 or 15 pts above Man City.

18 Clubs who go into administration could face a hefty points deduction, relegation or even lose their place in the FL. Trevor Francis leaves Crystal Palace after 18 months in charge. Steve Wignall takes over at Southend Utd. Gazza reports into a rehab clinic in the US suffering from depression.

19 Soton will wear their away strip of yellow and blue for the FA Cup Final – the same colours they wore when upsetting Man U to win in 1976. Ironically, Albion's relegation is confirmed just as they discover the winning habit at Sunderland. Leicester are back in the Premiership. Promotion also for Hartlepool and Rushden & Diamonds. Leeds' Alan Smith sees red yet again, his 3rd this season and 9th in total. Everton lose and finish with 9 men in the Merseyside derby, Houllier's 250th game in sole charge.

20 Holders Rangers reach the Scottish Cup final, then see Celtic's hope of a 3rd successive League title dealt a blow by defeat at Hearts.

21 Glenn Roeder is taken to hospital after collapsing with chest pains at Upton Park following a press conference and win over Boro. Ten years after reaching two Cup finals and entering European competition the following autumn, Sheff Wed slip to Div 2. Grimsby drop out of Div 1 after 5 years. Northampton are relegated to Div 3. Ryan Jarvis, just 16 years and 284 days old, partners 35 year old striker stalwart Iwan Roberts in attack for Norwich.

22 Viduka's double calms the nerves in win over Fulham. Chesterfield's Dave Rushbury resigns after losing 5 games in a row. Three more FA staff are made redundant taking the 3rd wave of job losses to a total of 23. Wolves plan to immortalise 306-goal record-scorer Steve Bull by naming a Molineux stand after him.

23 Beckham is left on the bench until 63rd min, overtakes Gary Neville's record and also contributes 2 goals in an absorbing clash with Man U winning 4–3 but losing 6–5 on agg to Real Madrid, grateful for Ronaldo's hat-trick. Club director Trevor Brooking is considering approaches to temporarily guide managerless Hammers.

24 FL chairman agree to an experiment in Div 3 with playing staff getting no more in wages than 60 per cent of their club's annual turnover. Paul Durkin is named Referee of the Year by a 250-plus panel of football media. Larsson's 40th goal at Boavista, fires Celtic to their 1st European final since 1970.

25 Charlton's ROI goalie Dean Kiely retires from International football to concentrate on his club career. Man U win the FA Youth Cup beating Boro 3–1 on agg. Ferguson lets rip a string of expletives when a radio reporter from Century, which pays Utd £500,000 a season for exclusive rights for all matches, dares to ask about Beckham's future.

26 It's advantage Man U as Arsenal blow a 2-goal lead and allow lively strugglers Bolton to draw level. Tranmere's match with Mansfield is abandoned at half-time after a dare-devil fan climbs onto a pylon then jumps onto a stand roof. Liverpool romp to 6–0 win at Albion with Owen getting the match ball having notched is 100th goal on his 185th appearance. Huddersfield are relegated to the bottom division for the 1st time in 23 years. Having sealed a place in the Conference play-off and sinking £4m

into Doncaster, owner John Ryan, 52, fulfils his lifelong ambition by coming on as late sub against Hereford. Champions and 17 points clear Yeovil attract 8,111 for the visit of Chester. Ryman League side Canvey Island net 10 against Enfield.

27 Pompey clinch the Div 1 title. Arsenal's Henry is the Player of the Year, voted by fellow professionals with Jermaine Jenas (Newcastle) winning the Young Player award. The PFA's Premiership team provokes argument containing 5 from Arsenal and one Scholes, from Man U. Celtic record a vital win at Ibrox.

28 LMA's John Barnwell is campaigning for mangers' contracts to include compulsory cardiovascular tests after 60 per cent of bosses took up the programme and 14 are detected with minor heart problems. A £750,000 bronze depicting Bobby Moore holding aloft the '66 World Cup is unveiled outside Upton Park.

29 Ex-chairman Ridsdale receives a £383,000 golden handshake from Leeds. Shrewsbury's 53-year membership of the FL ends after home defeat by fellow strugglers Carlisle. Banned Bosnich may be allowed to play again after 23 Sept.

30 Manager Kevin Ratcliffe resigns from Shrewsbury. Gunners reveal £9.5m losses. Over 32,000 turn up for Dublin friendly with Duff bagging the winner against Norway. Early blunders cost Scotland, losing at Hampden Park to Austria. Following Eriksson's meeting with 5 top managers, Premiership bosses will be asked to sign an agreement committing their players to the England team.

May 2003

UEFA punish FA ... Dugarry coughs up! ... Grecians drop out ... Man U Champions ... Cloughie acknowledged ... FL crowds rise ... £20m decider ... Derby sacking ... Hammers drop ... Director is national boss ... Colleagues acclaim Moyes ... Taylor exits Villa ... Gunners Cup success ... O'Leary lands job ... Seville turns green ... Beckham wrist fracture ... Gers snatch title ... Wolves wait is over ... FA fear expulsion ... Rangers clean up.

1 UEFA fine the FA £75,000 for the racist abuse towards Turkish supporters and crowd trouble at Sunderland. Man U's Ferguson is also rapped with a paltry £5,000 fine for claiming the Champions League quarter-final draw was fixed. Mark McGhee, Barry Fry and Denis Smith take the respective Nationwide Manager of the Month awards.

2 Former Charlton midfielder Matt Holmes is suing Rangers defender Kevin Muscat for £1m over a challenge 5 years ago which he claims ended his career. Brum's Christophe Dugarry is fined £12,500 but escapes a ban for spitting – because he is a Frenchman!

3 Delight at Newcastle qualifying again for the Champions League. Sunderland's 14th successive defeat confirms they go down as Premierships record-breakers. Di Canio keeps the Hammers dream alive with winner over Chelsea. Exeter lose their League status after 83 years.

4 Boss Ferguson – British footballs' most successful with 27 trophies in 29 years – comes off the golf course to learn that Arsenal's shock 3–2 home defeat to Leeds hands Man U their 8th Premiership title in 11 years, although Wenger churlishly still considers the Gunners the best in the country. Former Rams boss Brian Clough, 35 years a resident, becomes a Freeman of Derby. Pompey players all wear white boots made by Gianluca Festa's sportswear company to mark the Italian's farewell appearance.

5 Sir Bobby Charlton now considers boss Ferguson superior to Sir Matt Busby. Fulham's Ladies team end their professional era completing their second successive League and Cup treble. Doncaster beat Chester to book a place in the Conference play-off final against Dagenham & Redbridge.

6 Europe's top clubs are unanimous in their opposition to plans to increase the WC finals from 32 to 36 teams.

7 In a cup final rehearsal Pires and Pennant net Arsenal hat-tricks against Soton. Leicester give free transfers to 12 players and take-it-or-leave-it offers to six others. Spurs confirm Sheringham can leave. FA decline to name a pro player who refused a drugs test between Jan and Mar. Attendances in the FL rises to 14,871,981, the best figures for the 3 divisions outside the top league since 1964–65; overall, the attendance stats for English football should reach 28.5m, the best since 1972.

8 Eriksson opts not to include players from Cup finalists Arsenal or Soton in the squad to fly to S Africa. Former Bayer Leverkusen coach Klaus Toppmoller is on the short list for Fulham post. Spurs follow Charlton in cancelling a pre-season friendly at Wimbledon's new Milton Keynes base. Liverpool's Houllier claims European success can be helped by having a winter break.

9 Tottenham's Hoddle says he will not quit as pressure on him intensifies. Leeds' Eirik Bakke, guilty of drink-driving, receives 2-year car ban. Lilleshall, once the FA's flagship centre, may be axed in £7m savings. Tomorrow's Chelsea–Liverpool clash with a Champions League spot the prize is being billed as a £20m battle. Derby dismiss manager John Gregory.

10 Doncaster's Golden Goal books a place back in the FL. In the 1st leg play-off Wolves take 2–1 lead over Reading and Forest are held 1–1 by Sheff Utd. Brigg Town win FA Vase final at Upton Park.

11 Bolton's win over Boro condemns Hammers to relegation. Chelsea finish 4th joining Man U, Arsenal and Newcastle in the Champions League; Liverpool, Blackburn and Soton will compete in UEFA Cup. Retiring ref David Elleray urges FIFA to replace yellow cards with sin-bins.

12 After 75 caps spread across 15 years, 39 year old goalie Seaman is omitted from England squad. Roy McFarland takes the managerial post at Chesterfield. Adam Buckley, son of former Lincoln boss Alan, is arrested on suspicion of stealing from the Div 3 club. Stoke director Asgeir Sigurvinsson is appointed Iceland's caretaker coach.

13 Kevin Phillips confirms he will be leaving Sunderland after 6 seasons. Boro's Franck Queudrue receives a 5-match ban for his 3rd red card. BBC's John Motson will overtake Kenneth

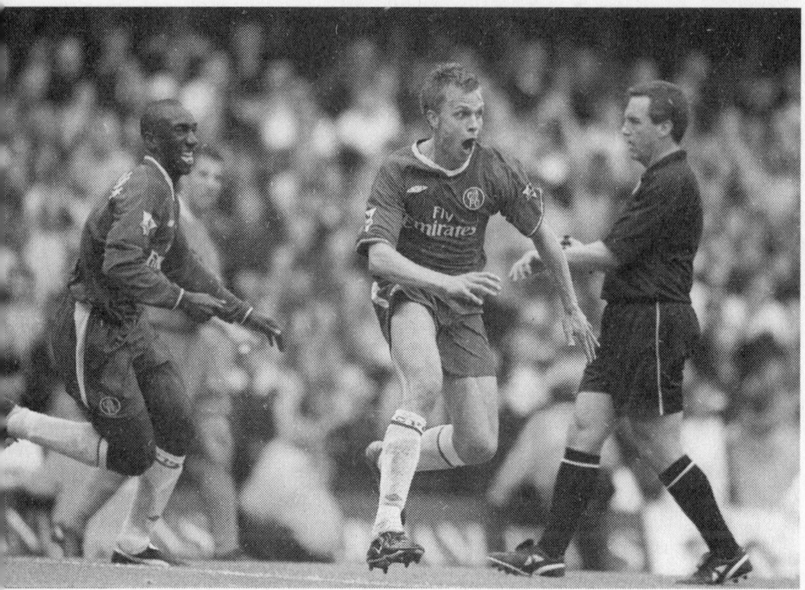

With a place in the Champions League at stake, the Chelsea v Liverpool match at Stamford Bridge took on an even more important aspect at the end of the season. Jesper Gronkjaer shows his delight after making it 2-1 in the Blues favour. (Colorsport)

Wolstenholme's, record when he commentates on his 24th FA Cup final. LMA vote Everton's David Moyes Manager of the Year.

14 Graham Taylor, 58, leaves Villa in frustration after just 15 months into his 2nd spell claiming the club is not run properly. The chairman and co-chairman of Exeter are arrested for alleged fraud at the relegated club.

15 FA confirm 50 year old Mark Palios, a former Tranmere and Crewe midfielder, as chief executive. Ravanelli is one of 10 axed in Derby clear out to save £10m. Fulham make former player Chris Coleman, 32, the youngest manager in the Premiership. Leeds part company with asst Eddie Gray and head coach Brian Kidd.

16 Di Canio, Bowyer and Winterburn are released and 7 others freed as Hammers prepare for life in Div 1. Steve Bruce agrees new 5-year deal with revitalised Brum.

17 In the 122nd FA Cup final, the first beneath a closed roof, Arsenal retain the trophy with Seaman leading the side to a 1–0 defeat of workmanlike Soton; Robert Pires, who missed out last season, nets in the 38th min for their 2nd final triumph in 3 years.

18 Rangers win at Hearts going level with Celtic on both points and goal difference but nudging narrowly ahead having scored one more goal. BBC attracts its best FA Cup final viewing figures for 3 years with 8.3m watching and peaking at 9.6m. FA Trophy travels back with Burscough to the smallest footballing outpost becoming its home since the competition began in 1970.

19 Man City's principal shareholder John Wardle will take the post of chairman succeeding David Bernstein. BBC's TV documentary, *Real Story*, which takes a poll of 700 players shows 46 per cent of professionals are aware of colleagues using recreational drugs.

20 David O'Leary ends his 11-month exile from the Premiership being named Villa's new manager on a 3-year contract. An incredible 50,000–70,000 following, most without tickets, congregate in Seville supporting Celtic who receive a Good Luck fax message from Tony Blair for their UEFA Cup final clash with FC Porto.

21 In their 1st European final for 33 years, Celtic turn Seville into a sea of green but lose 3–2 to an 115th min extra-time goal against FC Porto. Its an FA PR fiasco as 12 players attend but 8 skip meeting with Nelson Mandela in Johannesburg preferring to catch up on some sleep.

22 Beckham fractures right wrist and retires after 50 mins as England beat S Africa in Durban, with Lucas Radebe finally bowing out of the international scene. Heskey's winner is only his 5th scored in 33 appearances. Wales in San Diego, hear from UEFA that home and away successes over Azerbaijan and the 6 goals scored, all stand. Boro axe chief scout Ray Train after 13 years on Teeside.

23 Joe Kinnear and asst Mick Harford have their contracts terminated by Luton's new owners. Palace appoint former player and caretaker boss Steve Kember as manager. Newcastle gamble on signing volatile Lee Bowyer.

24 Cherries skipper Carl Fletcher shows the way with a brace in 5–2 Div 3 play-off final against Lincoln. Speculation breaks that capt Beckham's presence in the game against S Africa was part of a secretly agreed £1m arrangement. Gary Peters, boss of relegated Exeter resigns.

25 The issue on a knife-edge until almost the final kick Rangers dramatically clinch the Championship on goal difference, their 50th league title beating Dunfermline 6–1 and, in spite of Celtic leap-frogging their rivals for 10 mins in 4–0 win at Kilmarnock. Cardiff return to the Div 1 overcoming QPR in extra time to win the play-off final. FA deny appearance fee for Beckham to play in S Africa.

26 Wolves finally end their 19-year wait for top-flight football cruising to a 3–0 play-off victory over Sheff Utd. Celtic's Chris Sutton apologises for accusing Dunfermline of 'lying down' on an emotionally charged final day clash at Rangers. The Sept/Oct Women's WC is re-located from China to the US because of the SARS virus.

27 Scotland are again booed following a lacklustre 1–1 showing against N Zealand. Wales' 10-game 20-month unbeaten run ends with 2–0 defeat in the US. Relegated Shrewsbury appoint Jimmy Quinn manager.

28 No goals in 120 mins as defences rule at Old Trafford before AC Milan eventually convert sufficient spot-kicks beating Juventus and lifting the Champions League trophy. Fearing a UEFA backlash over possible exclusion, Beckham will make a nationwide TV appearance appealing to England fans to behave.

29 Chelsea release Jody Morris and goalie Ed de Goey. Sacked John Gregory is launching legal action against Derby. In a letter to Glasgow Lord Provost Liz Cameron, Seville's mayor praises the 'excellent behaviour' of the estimated 85,000 Celtic fans who flooded the city. Former Welsh centre-forward Trevor Ford dies in Swansea aged 79.

30 Micky Adams signs 3-year Leicester contract. Despite gaining promotion Hartlepool part company with manager Mike Newell. Luton's new owners say supporters can help appoint Joe Kinnear's successor. York sack Terry Dolan.

31 Rangers win the 118th Scottish Cup final beating Dundee and clinching the treble. Glenn Roeder recovering from brain surgery, aims to return the W Ham on 1st July. Owen Hargreaves helps Bayern Munich to German Cup final success.

June 2003

Hundreds out of contract ... Man City back in Europe ... Seaman leaves Arsenal ... Rams boss Burley ... Finnan for Anfield ... Youngest skipper Owen ... Festa heads home ... Beckham for Real ... New fixtures announced ... FA prize money reduced ... Chinese search for Gazza ... Newell gets Luton job ... Real sack coach ... Carling for League Cup ... Man U No. 2 to Real ... Marc-Vivien Foe tragedy ... FIFA reject expansion plans.

1 Rochdale appoint Alan Buckley as manager. PFA's Taylor fears up to 200 players will be forced out this summer with 586 out of contract and available on free transfers. Nationwide League fail in their attempt to get the Premiership to abandon the transfer window system.

2 Liverpool's French coach Jacques Crevoisier leaves for 'family reasons.' Man City will figure in Europe for the 1st time in almost 25 years after England is confirmed winners of UEFA's Fair Play League. Owen and Beckham plead with English supporters to respect the national anthem of opponents. Ossie Ardiles is the new coach at Tokyo Verdy. Farce at Luton as Joe Kinnear and Mick Harford are offered their jobs back.

3 After friendly win over Serbia & Montenegro Eriksson defends using 21 players – and passing the captain's armband from Owen to Heskey, Neville and a bemused Carragher. Arsenal's 75-times capped enthusiastic Seaman, 39, opts for a surprise 1-year contract at Man City. NI lose to under-strength Italy with their scoring drought now stretching 882 minutes.

4 Chris Brass, 27, becomes the youngest boss in FL history after being appointed player/manager at Div 3 York.

5 Derby announce the appointment of their interim manager, George Burley, on a 2-year contract. Steve Coppell agrees a 1-year deal with Brighton. Brazilian coach Marcio Maximo Barcellos rejects a 10-year contract with the Cayman Islands to manage Livingston. FL agree proposals to lower the stadium entry requirements for promoted Conference clubs from 6,000 to 4,000.

6 Premiership allow transfer payments to be spread over the length of a player's contract. Patrik Berger quits Liverpool after 7-years to join Pompey. With a cash shortfall of £3.5m The Dons, desperately searching for investors, opt for administration.

7 Scotland restore some self-belief holding Germany at Hampden Pk. ROI snatch last-gasp vital win over Albania. Turkey reclaim pole position in England's group.

8 With Man U employing super-agent Pini Zahavi, a close friend of boss Ferguson, speculation persists Barcelona are favourites to sign Beckham if AC Milan and Real Madrid keep their cash in their pockets. Luton's new owners suggests merging with Wimbledon.

9 WC winner Gordon Banks describes David James of England as a 'nightmare' goalie. Fulham's Steve Finnan completes a £3.5m move to Liverpool.

10 England U-21's celebrate manager David Platt's 37th birthday beating Slovakia. Chairman Lionel Pickering puts an £8m selling price tag on Derby.

11 Stand-in skipper Owen, winning his 50th cap and becoming at 23 years and 181 days the youngest to captain England in a competitive match, nets twice in 2–1 victory over Slovakia. Villa sack coach John Deehan.

12 Man City's Shaun Goater , an ambassador for grass roots sport in Bermuda, gets an MBE; Arsene Wenger and Gerard Houllier receive honorary OBE's. Real Madrid step up their interest in

Beckham. England could play their Euro grudge tie in Turkey behind closed doors after disturbing crowd trouble in Istanbul.

13 Oldham announce they are on the verge of going out of business. Coach Les Read locks his England U-20 side in the dressing room following an 8–0 Argentina rout in the Toulon Tournament. Pompey's ex-Boro defender Gianluca Festa returns to Cagliari 7 years after leaving.

14 Nigel Pearson is leaving the England set-up to join his former Sheff Wed club. As Man U reveal that they offered Beckham a new contract to prevent him joining Real Madrid, the Spanish giants now claim he signed a pre-contract agreement with them on May 12. Man of the moment, England captain Beckham, is appointed an OBE.

15 Man City are set to become the 1st Premiership club to have two home and away shirt sponsors after losing £3m following the collapse of their current sponsorship deal with First Advice. Adrian Heath is following Peter Reid to Leeds as new chief scout.

16 Charlton complete the £750,000 signing of Ipswich captain Matt Holland. England's final EC 2004 home qualifier against Liechtenstein will be at Old Trafford, Sept 10. Villa's Lee Hendrie is given a 12-month drink-driving ban and fine.

17 A Man U announcement confirms an agreed £25m transfer of 28 year old Beckham to Real Madrid bringing to an end a saga which first came to the boil in April when the two sides were drawn in the Champions League. The player, who will sign a 4-year contract, undertakes a medical on 1st July and be unveiled by the club the next day. Sunderland, despite the worst season in the club's 124-year history, see their fans voted the best in the country in a Premiership survey. Roy Aitken leaves Leeds for Villa as O'Leary's asst.

18 On Aug 20 against Croatia, Portman Road's 30,250-seat ground will become the 13th different stadium to host an England match since the national side has been on the road. David James is joining Miami Dolphins, the American football team, in training. British television viewers will see all Real Madrid matches in the Champions League because ITV and BSkyB will be screening the tournament. Fulham will appeal against FIFA's ruling to pay Valencia £500,000 for pulling out of a deal for striker John Carew.

19 The start of the 2003-04 season will see Bolton travel to Man U for the 3rd successive time; relegated Hammers visit PNE and, after 108 years of existence, Yeovil Town visit Rochdale. Lee Bowyer is to seek an out-of-court settlement with an Asian man who is suing over injuries received when attacked in Leeds in January 2000. Premier League, hopefully maximising their income from the next TV contract, plan an August 2004 bonanza for armchair fans who could view 138 live games, incorporating over the weekend 1 pm or 5.15 pm Saturday starts. PFA pay out £40,000 legal and compensation payment for wrongfully dismissing former chairman Barry Horne.

20 After being cleared of bullying charges and verbal abuse involving 2 youth players, Peter Beardsley is moved from his Newcastle coaching role to a public relations position. Man City's away UEFA tie against Total Networks Solutions may be switched to Wrexham's ground just 50 miles away.

21 Bangor City, with 42 year old manager, Peter Davenport on the bench, lose their opening Inter-Toto Cup tie at Rhyl. Villa make £3m bid for Leeds goalie, Paul Robinson. FA Cup prize money is to be slashed from £12.6m to £10.7m covering the preliminary rounds and 1st and 2nd rounds proper affecting particularly Nationwide League lower division clubs.

22 Real Madrid's 3-1 win over Athletic Bilbao, their 29th La Liga Championship, ensures Champions League action for newcomer Beckham. Chinese B-League team, Gansu Tianma urgently want to hear from missing Gascoigne. FA will be instructing clubs to be more accepting of homosexual players.

23 Mike Newell, dismissed after leading Hartlepool to promotion, is the new boss of Luton after topping a club telephone poll. Holidaying, Teddy Sheringham agrees a 1-year deal, in principle with Pompey. Millwall's Mark McGhee appoints Archie Knox as asst. Real Madrid dramatically sack coach Vicente del Bosque a day after leading them to the championship.

24 Boss Ferguson is resigning himself to losing No. 2 Carlos Queiroz to Real Madrid. Brum, Leicester and Hammers are charged with bad disciplinary records. The League Cup will be known as the Carling Cup after a £10m, 3-year sponsorship which will see every penny go to the cash-strapped Nationwide League.

25 Portuguese striker, Helder Postiga signs for Spurs from FC Porto for £6.25m. Carlos Queiroz is named the new coach at Real Madrid declaring both Beckham and Figo can figure in the same side. Sky Sport will have featured every Premiership club in a live game by the final week of October.

26 Football is in shock as 28 year old former West Ham and Man City midfielder, Marc-Vivien Foe collapses on the pitch and dies after playing for Cameroon against Colombia in the Confederations Cup in Lyon. Former Aberdeen midfielder, Neale Cooper is Hartlepool Utd's new manager.

27 Man City will retire the No. 23 shirt worn by Marc-Vivien Foe last season. Peter Jackson is re-appointed manger of Huddersfield Town.

28 FIFA reject plans to expand the 2006 World Cup from 32 to 36 nations. Bangor's UEFA Cup hopes end losing in Romania in the Inter-Toto Cup.

29 Thierry Henry's 97th min golden goal for France against Cameroon settles a subdued Confederations Cup final in Paris.

30 Sheringham signs 1-year deal at Portsmouth. Former Stoke boss, Gudjon Thordarson is the new manager at Barnsley. Villa ditch £3.25m deal to sign Paul Robinson from Leeds. Mark Hughes says he will not give up his Wales job for a No. 2 position at Man U.

ENGLISH LEAGUE TABLES 2002–03

FA BARCLAYCARD PREMIERSHIP

			Home			*Goals*		*Away*			*Goals*			
		P	W	D	L	F	A	W	D	L	F	A	GD	Pts
1	Manchester U	38	16	2	1	42	12	9	6	4	32	22	40	83
2	Arsenal	38	15	2	2	47	20	8	7	4	38	22	43	78
3	Newcastle U	38	15	2	2	36	17	6	4	9	27	31	15	69
4	Chelsea	38	12	5	2	41	15	7	5	7	27	23	30	67
5	Liverpool	38	9	8	2	30	16	9	2	8	31	25	20	64
6	Blackburn R	38	9	7	3	24	15	7	5	7	28	28	9	60
7	Everton	38	11	5	3	28	19	6	3	10	20	30	–1	59
8	Southampton	38	9	8	2	25	16	4	5	10	18	30	–3	52
9	Manchester C	38	9	2	8	28	26	6	4	9	19	28	–7	51
10	Tottenham H	38	9	4	6	30	29	5	4	10	21	33	–11	50
11	Middlesbrough	38	10	7	2	36	21	3	3	13	12	23	4	49
12	Charlton Ath	38	8	3	8	26	30	6	4	9	19	26	–11	49
13	Birmingham C	38	8	5	6	25	23	5	4	10	16	26	–8	48
14	Fulham	38	11	3	5	26	18	2	6	11	15	32	–9	48
15	Leeds U	38	7	3	9	25	26	7	2	10	33	31	1	47
16	Aston Villa	38	11	2	6	25	14	1	7	11	17	33	–5	45
17	Bolton W	38	7	8	4	27	24	3	6	10	14	27	–10	44
18	West Ham U	38	5	7	7	21	24	5	5	9	21	35	–17	42
19	WBA	38	3	5	11	17	34	3	3	13	12	31	–36	26
20	Sunderland	38	3	2	14	11	31	1	5	13	10	34	–44	19

NATIONWIDE FOOTBALL LEAGUE DIVISION 1

			Home			*Goals*		*Away*			*Goals*			
		P	W	D	L	F	A	W	D	L	F	A	GD	Pts
1	Portsmouth	46	17	3	3	52	22	12	8	3	45	23	52	98
2	Leicester C	46	16	5	2	40	12	10	9	4	33	28	33	92
3	Sheffield U	46	13	7	3	38	23	10	4	9	34	29	20	80
4	Reading	46	13	3	7	33	21	12	1	10	28	25	15	79
5	Wolverhampton W	46	9	10	4	40	19	11	6	6	41	25	37	76
6	Nottingham F	46	14	7	2	57	23	6	7	10	25	27	32	74
7	Ipswich T	46	10	5	8	49	39	9	8	6	31	25	16	70
8	Norwich C	46	14	4	5	36	17	5	8	10	24	32	11	69
9	Millwall	46	11	6	6	34	32	8	3	12	25	37	–10	66
10	Wimbledon	46	12	5	6	39	28	6	6	11	37	45	3	65
11	Gillingham	46	10	6	7	33	31	6	8	9	23	34	–9	62
12	Preston NE	46	11	7	5	44	29	5	6	12	24	41	–2	61
13	Watford	46	11	5	7	33	26	6	4	13	21	44	–16	60
14	Crystal Palace	46	8	10	5	29	17	6	7	10	30	35	7	59
15	Rotherham U	46	8	9	6	27	25	7	5	11	35	37	0	59
16	Burnley	46	10	4	9	35	44	5	6	12	30	45	–24	55
17	Walsall	46	10	3	10	34	34	5	6	12	23	35	–12	54
18	Derby Co	46	9	5	9	33	32	6	2	15	22	42	–19	52
19	Bradford C	46	7	8	8	27	35	7	2	14	24	38	–22	52
20	Coventry C	46	6	6	11	23	31	6	8	9	23	31	–16	50
21	Stoke C	46	9	6	8	25	25	3	8	12	20	44	–24	50
22	Sheffield W	46	7	7	9	29	32	3	9	11	27	41	–17	46
23	Brighton & HA	46	7	6	10	29	31	4	6	13	20	36	–18	45
24	Grimsby T	46	5	6	12	26	39	4	6	13	22	46	–37	39

NATIONWIDE FOOTBALL LEAGUE DIVISION 2

			Home			*Goals*		*Away*			*Goals*			
		P	W	D	L	F	A	W	D	L	F	A	GD	Pts
1	Wigan Ath	46	14	7	2	37	16	15	6	2	31	9	43	100
2	Crewe Alex	46	11	5	7	29	19	14	6	3	47	21	36	86
3	Bristol C	46	15	5	3	43	15	9	6	8	36	33	31	83
4	QPR	46	14	4	5	38	19	10	7	6	31	26	24	83
5	Oldham Ath	46	11	6	6	39	18	11	10	2	29	20	30	82
6	Cardiff C	46	12	6	5	33	20	11	6	6	35	23	25	81
7	Tranmere R	46	14	5	4	38	23	9	6	8	28	34	9	80
8	Plymouth Arg	46	11	6	6	39	24	6	8	9	24	28	11	65
9	Luton T	46	8	8	7	32	28	9	6	8	35	34	5	65
10	Swindon T	46	10	5	8	34	27	6	7	10	25	36	–4	60
11	Peterborough U	46	8	7	8	25	20	6	9	8	26	34	–3	58
12	Colchester U	46	8	7	8	24	24	6	9	8	28	32	–4	58
13	Blackpool	46	10	8	5	35	25	5	5	13	21	39	–8	58
14	Stockport Co	46	8	8	7	39	38	7	2	14	26	32	–5	55
15	Notts Co	46	10	7	6	37	32	3	9	11	25	38	–8	55
16	Brentford	46	8	8	7	28	21	6	4	13	19	35	–9	54
17	Port Vale	46	9	5	9	34	31	5	6	12	20	39	–16	53
18	Wycombe W	46	8	7	8	39	38	5	6	12	20	28	–7	52
19	Barnsley	46	7	8	8	27	31	6	5	12	24	33	–13	52
20	Chesterfield	46	11	4	8	29	28	3	4	16	14	45	–30	50
21	Cheltenham T	46	6	9	8	26	31	4	9	10	27	37	–15	48
22	Huddersfield T	46	7	9	7	27	24	4	3	16	12	37	–22	45
23	Mansfield T	46	9	2	12	38	45	3	6	14	28	52	–31	44
24	Northampton T	46	7	4	12	23	31	3	5	15	17	48	–39	39

NATIONWIDE FOOTBALL LEAGUE DIVISION 3

			Home			*Goals*		*Away*			*Goals*			
		P	W	D	L	F	A	W	D	L	F	A	GD	Pts
1	Rushden & Diamonds	46	16	5	2	48	19	8	10	5	25	28	26	87
2	Hartlepool U	46	16	5	2	49	21	8	8	7	22	30	20	85
3	Wrexham	46	12	7	4	48	26	11	8	4	36	24	34	84
4	Bournemouth	46	14	7	2	38	18	6	7	10	22	30	12	74
5	Scunthorpe U	46	11	8	4	40	20	8	7	8	28	29	19	72
6	Lincoln C	46	10	9	4	29	18	8	7	8	17	19	9	70
7	Bury	46	8	8	7	25	26	10	8	5	32	30	1	70
8	Oxford U	46	9	7	7	26	20	10	5	8	31	27	10	69
9	Torquay U	46	9	11	3	41	31	7	7	9	30	40	0	66
10	York C	46	11	9	3	34	24	6	6	11	18	29	–1	66
11	Kidderminster H	46	8	8	7	30	33	8	7	8	32	30	–1	63
12	Cambridge U	46	10	7	6	38	25	6	6	11	29	45	–3	61
13	Hull C	46	9	10	4	34	19	5	7	11	24	34	5	59
14	Darlington	46	8	10	5	36	27	4	8	11	22	32	–1	54
15	Boston U*	46	11	6	6	34	22	4	7	12	21	34	–1	54
16	Macclesfield T	46	8	6	9	29	28	6	6	11	28	35	–6	54
17	Southend U	46	12	1	10	29	23	5	2	16	18	36	–12	54
18	Leyton Orient	46	9	6	8	28	24	5	5	13	23	37	–10	53
19	Rochdale	46	7	6	10	30	30	5	10	8	33	40	–7	52
20	Bristol R	46	7	7	9	25	27	5	8	10	25	30	–7	51
21	Swansea C	46	9	6	8	28	25	3	7	13	20	40	–17	49
22	Carlisle U	46	5	5	13	26	40	8	5	10	26	38	–26	49
23	Exeter C	46	7	7	9	24	31	4	8	11	26	33	–14	48
24	Shrewsbury T	46	5	6	12	34	39	4	8	11	28	53	–30	41

** Boston U – 4pts deducted at the start of the season.*

FOOTBALL LEAGUE PLAY-OFFS 2002–03

■ *Denotes player sent off.*

DIV 1 SEMI-FINALS FIRST LEG

Saturday, 10 May 2003

Nottingham F (0) 1 *(Johnson 55)*
Sheffield U (0) 1 *(Brown 58 (pen))* 29,064

Nottingham F: Ward; Louis-Jean, Brennan, Williams, Dawson■, Walker, Johnson (Thompson), Scimeca, Huckerby, Harewood, Reid Andy.
Sheffield U: Kenny; Curtis, Kozluk, Brown, Jagielka, Page, Ndlovu, Rankine, Asaba, Windass (Kabba), Tonge.

Wolverhampton W (0) 2 *(Murty 74 (og), Naylor 84)*
Reading (1) 1 *(Forster 25)* 27,678

Wolverhampton W: Murray; Irwin, Naylor, Ince, Butler (Pollet), Lescott, Ndah (Newton), Cameron, Blake, Miller (Sturridge), Kennedy.
Reading: Hahnemann; Murty, Shorey, Brown, Williams, Hughes, Chadwick (Newman), Sidwell, Forster (Tyson■), Harper, Henderson (Cureton).

DIV 2 SEMI-FINALS FIRST LEG

Saturday, 10 May 2003

Cardiff C (0) 1 *(Thorne 74)*
Bristol C (0) 0 19,146

Cardiff C: Alexander; Weston, Barker, Prior, Gabbidon, Whalley, Boland, Kavanagh, Earnshaw (Campbell), Thorne, Legg (Bonner).
Bristol C: Phillips; Carey, Hill, Burnell, Butler, Coles, Murray, Doherty (Tinnion), Peacock, Roberts (Rosenior), Bell.

Oldham Ath (1) 1 *(Eyres 28)*
QPR (0) 1 *(Langley 47)* 12,152

Oldham Ath: Miskelly; Low, Armstrong, Sheridan D (Corazzin), Hall F, Haining, Eyre (Carss), Murray, Wijnhard, Andrews, Eyres.
QPR: Day; Forbes, Williams, Palmer, Shittu, Rose (Pacquette), Bircham, Langley■, Furlong, Gallen, McLeod.

DIV 3 SEMI-FINALS FIRST LEG

Saturday, 10 May 2003

Bury (0) 0
Bournemouth (0) 0 5782

Bury: Garner; Connell, Stuart■, Woodthorpe, Nelson, Redmond, Billy, Forrest, Newby (Nugent), Cramb (Preece), Clegg (Swailes).
Bournemouth: Moss; Young, Cummings, Purches S, Fletcher C, Gulliver, Thomas (O'Connor), Stock (Holmes), Hayter (McDonald), Fletcher S, Elliott.

Lincoln C (2) 5 *(Weaver 15, Mayo 18, Smith 55, Yeo 82, 90)*
Scunthorpe U (1) 3 *(Calvo-Garcia 26, 69, Stanton 70)* 8902

Lincoln C: Marriott; Bailey, Bimson, Weaver, Morgan, Futcher, Butcher, Gain (Willis), Cropper (Yeo), Smith, Mayo.
Scunthorpe U: Evans; Stanton, Dawson, Sparrow (Dalglish), Jackson, Strong, Calvo-Garcia, Kilford, Carruthers (Torpey), Hayes, Beagrie.

DIV 1 SEMI-FINALS SECOND LEG

Wednesday, 14 May 2003

Reading (0) 0
Wolverhampton W (0) 1 *(Rae 81)* 24,060

Reading: Hahnemann; Murty, Shorey, Brown, Williams, Hughes, Little (Chadwick), Sidwell (Watson), Cureton, Harper, Henderson (Rougier).
Wolverhampton W: Murray; Irwin, Naylor, Ince, Butler, Lescott, Newton (Cooper), Cameron, Blake (Sturridge), Miller (Rae), Kennedy.
Wolverhampton W won 3-1 on aggregate.

Thursday, 15 May 2003

Sheffield U (0) 4 *(Brown 60, Kabba 68, Peschisolido 112, Walker 117 (og))*
Nottingham F (1) 3 *(Johnson 30, Reid Andy 58, Page 119 (og))* 30,212

Sheffield U: Kenny; Curtis, Kozluk, Brown, Jagielka, Page, Ndlovu (Peschisolido), Rankine, Asaba (Allison), Windass (Kabba), Tonge.
Nottingham F: Ward; Louis-Jean, Brennan, Williams (Hjelde), Thompson, Walker, Scimeca, Huckerby, Johnson, Harewood (Lester), Reid Andy.
aet; Sheffield U won 5-4 on aggregate.

Gareth Whalley (dark shirt) tries to control the ball for Cardiff City with Queens Park Rangers' Marc Bircham in close attention. City made it to the First Division after a 1-0 win. (Colorsport)

Bournemouth's Stephen Purches emerges from the double intervention of Richard Butcher and Paul Morgan of Lincoln City. Bournemouth won a high-scoring Third Division play-off 5-2. (Actionimages)

DIV 2 SEMI-FINALS SECOND LEG

Tuesday, 13 May 2003

Bristol C (0) 0

Cardiff C (0) 0 16,307

Bristol C: Phillips; Carey, Hill (Beadle), Burnell (Amankwaah), Butler, Coles, Murray, Doherty, Peacock, Roberts (Lita), Tinnion.
Cardiff C: Alexander; Weston (Croft), Barker, Prior, Gabbidon, Whalley, Boland, Kavanagh, Earnshaw (Campbell), Thorne, Legg (Bonner).
Cardiff C won 1-0 on aggregate.

Wednesday, 14 May 2003

QPR (0) 1 *(Furlong 82)*

Oldham Ath (0) 0 17,201

QPR: Day; Kelly, Padula (Williams), Palmer, Shittu, Carlisle, Bircham, Gallen, Furlong, Thomson (Pacquette), McLeod.
Oldham Ath: Pogliacomi; Low, Eyres, Hill, Hall F, Haining, Murray (Carss), Sheridan D (Duxbury), Eyre (Corazzin), Andrews■, Armstrong.
QPR won 2-1 on aggregate.

DIV 3 SEMI-FINALS SECOND LEG

Tuesday, 13 May 2003

Bournemouth (2) 3 *(O'Connor 21, Hayter 38, 60)*

Bury (0) 1 *(Preece 67)* 7945

Bournemouth: Moss; Young, Cummings, Browning, Fletcher C, Gulliver, O'Connor, Purches S, Hayter, Fletcher S, Elliott (Stock).
Bury: Garner; Connell, Woodthorpe, Nelson, Swailes, Redmond (Preece), Billy, Forrest (Nugent), Newby, Cramb, Clegg.
Bournemouth won 3-1 on aggregate.

Wednesday, 14 May 2003

Scunthorpe U (0) 0

Lincoln C (0) 1 *(Yeo 88)* 8295

Scunthorpe U: Evans; Stanton, Dawson (McCombe), Sparrow (Carruthers), Jackson, Strong, Calvo-Garcia, Kilford (Graves), Hayes, Torpey, Dalglish.
Lincoln C: Marriott; Bailey, Bimson, Weaver, Morgan, Futcher, Smith (Bloomer), Butcher, Cropper (Yeo), Mayo, Gain.
Lincoln C won 6-3 on aggregate.

DIV 1 FINAL

Monday, 26 May 2003
(at Millennium Stadium, Cardiff)

Sheffield U (0) 0

Wolverhampton W (3) 3 *(Kennedy 5, Blake 21, Miller 45)* 69,473

Sheffield U: Kenny; Curtis, Kozluk, Brown, Jagielka, Page, Ndlovu (Peschisolido), Rankine (McCall), Asaba (Allison), Kabba, Tonge.
Wolverhampton W: Murray; Irwin, Naylor, Ince, Butler, Lescott, Newton, Cameron, Blake (Proudlock), Miller (Sturridge), Kennedy.

DIV 2 FINAL

Sunday, 25 May 2003
(at Millennium Stadium, Cardiff)

Cardiff C (0) 1 *(Campbell 114)*

QPR (0) 0 66,096

Cardiff C: Alexander; Weston (Croft), Barker, Prior, Gabbidon, Whalley, Boland, Kavanagh, Earnshaw (Campbell), Thorne, Legg (Bonner).
QPR: Day; Kelly, Padula (Williams), Palmer, Shittu, Carlisle, Bircham, Gallen, Furlong, Pacquette (Thomson), McLeod.
aet.

DIV 3 FINAL

Saturday, 24 May 2003
(at Millennium Stadium, Cardiff)

Bournemouth (2) 5 *(Fletcher S 29, Fletcher C 45, 77, Purches S 56, O'Connor 60)*

Lincoln C (1) 2 *(Futcher 35, Bailey 75)* 32,148

Bournemouth: Moss; Young, Cummings, Browning, Fletcher C, Gulliver, O'Connor (Stock), Purches S, Hayter, Fletcher S (Holmes), Elliott (Thomas).
Lincoln C: Marriott; Bailey, Bimson, Weaver (Cornelly), Morgan, Futcher, Butcher, Gain, Cropper (Willis), Smith (Yeo), Mayo.

LEADING GOALSCORERS 2002–03

FA BARCLAYCARD PREMIERSHIP	League	FA Cup	Worthington Cup	Other	Total
Ruud Van Nistelrooy *(Manchester U)*	25	4	1	14	44
Thierry Henry *(Arsenal)*	24	1	0	7	32
James Beattie *(Southampton)*	23	1	0	0	24
Mark Viduka *(Leeds U)*	20	2	0	0	22
Michael Owen *(Liverpool)*	19	0	2	7	28
Alan Shearer *(Newcastle U)*	17	1	0	7	25
Gianfranco Zola *(Chelsea)*	14	2	0	0	16
Paul Scholes *(Manchester U)*	14	1	3	2	20
Robert Pires *(Arsenal)*	14	1	1	0	16
Harry Kewell *(Leeds U)*	14	1	0	1	16
Nicolas Anelka *(Manchester C)*	14	0	0	0	14
Robbie Keane *(Tottenham H)*	14	0	0	0	14
(including 1 League goal for Leeds U)					
Teddy Sheringham *(Tottenham H)*	12	0	1	0	13
Jimmy Floyd Hasselbaink *(Chelsea)*	11	1	2	1	15
Tomasz Radzinski *(Everton)*	11	0	0	0	11
Sylvain Wiltord *(Arsenal)*	10	2	0	1	13
Jason Euell *(Charlton Ath)*	10	1	0	0	11
Dion Dublin *(Aston Villa)*	10	0	4	0	14
Kevin Campbell *(Everton)*	10	0	2	0	12
Eidur Gudjohnsen *(Chelsea)*	10	0	0	0	10
NATIONWIDE DIVISION 1					
Svetoslav Todorov *(Portsmouth)*	26	0	0	0	26
David Johnson *(Nottingham F)*	25	0	2	2	29
David Connolly *(Wimbledon)*	24	0	0	0	24
Marlon Harewood *(Nottingham F)*	20	1	0	0	21
Neil Shipperley *(Wimbledon)*	20	1	3	0	24
Kenny Miller *(Wolverhampton W)*	19	3	1	1	24
Paul Dickov *(Leicester C)*	17	2	1	0	20
Pablo Counago *(Ipswich T)*	17	0	1	3	21
Michael Brown *(Sheffield U)*	16	2	2	2	22
Gareth Taylor *(Burnley)*	16	1	0	0	17
Nicky Forster *(Reading)*	16	0	0	1	17
Richard Cresswell *(Preston NE)*	16	0	0	0	16
Junior *(Walsall)*	15	0	1	0	16
Alan Lee *(Rotherham U)*	15	0	1	0	16
Andy Gray *(Bradford C)*	15	0	0	0	15
Paul McVeigh *(Norwich C)*	14	1	0	0	15
Bobby Zamora *(Brighton & HA)*	14	0	0	0	14
DIVISION 2					
Robert Earnshaw *(Cardiff C)*	31	1	3	0	35
Luke Beckett *(Stockport Co)*	27	1	1	0	29
Sam Parkin *(Swindon T)*	25	0	0	1	26
Mark Stallard *(Notts Co)*	24	0	1	0	25
Rob Hulse *(Crewe Alex)*	22	0	1	4	27
Steve Howard *(Luton T)*	22	0	1	0	23
Simon Haworth *(Tranmere R)*	20	1	1	0	22
Scott Murray *(Bristol C)*	19	3	0	5	27
Iyseden Christie *(Mansfield T)*	18	1	0	0	19
Bruce Dyer *(Barnsley)*	17	1	0	0	18
Martin Smith *(Huddersfield T)*	17	0	0	0	17
John Murphy *(Blackpool)*	16	2	0	1	19
Andy Clarke *(Peterborough U)*	16	1	0	2	19
Andy Liddell *(Wigan Ath)*	16	0	0	0	16
Nathan Ellington *(Wigan Ath)*	15	2	5	0	22
Christian Roberts *(Bristol C)*	13	3	0	1	16
Scott Taylor *(Blackpool)*	13	2	0	1	16
David Eyres *(Oldham Ath)*	13	1	1	1	16
Peter Thorne *(Cardiff C)*	13	1	1	1	16
Tony Thorpe *(Luton T)*	13	1	0	2	16
Kevin Gallen *(QPR)*	13	0	1	0	14
Paul Furlong *(QPR)*	13	0	0	1	14
Wayne Corden *(Mansfield T)*	13	0	0	0	13
DIVISION 3					
Andrew Morrell *(Wrexham)*	34	0	1	0	35
Dave Kitson *(Cambridge U)*	20	1	1	3	25
Martin Carruthers *(Scunthorpe U)*	20	1	0	0	21
Bo Henriksen *(Kidderminster H)*	20	0	0	0	20
Peter Duffield *(Boston U)*	17	0	0	0	17
(including 13 League goals and 2 FA Cup goals for York C)					
Luke Rodgers *(Shrewsbury T)*	16	0	0	4	20
Paul Hall *(Rushden & D)*	16	0	0	0	16
Barry Conlon *(Darlington)*	15	2	0	0	17
Onandi Lowe *(Rushden & D)*	15	1	0	0	16
Lee McEvilly *(Rochdale)*	15	1	0	0	16
Eifion Williams *(Hartlepool U)*	15	0	1	0	16
David Graham *(Torquay U)*	15	0	0	0	15
Duane Darby *(Rushden & D)*	14	0	0	0	14
Martin Gritton *(Torquay U)*	13	3	0	0	16
James Thomas *(Swansea C)*	13	0	1	1	15
Steve Flack *(Exeter C)*	13	0	0	0	13
Mark Tinkler *(Hartlepool U)*	13	0	0	0	13

Other matches consist of European games, LDV Vans Trophy, Community Shield and Football League play-offs. Only goals scored in the respective divisions count in the table. Players listed in order of League goals total.

REVIEW OF THE SEASON

Eight Premiership titles in eleven years and this after their worst start during the lifetime of the league, underlined the fact that you write-off Manchester United at your peril.

With six matches played United had had two of everything: wins, draws and losses. They were ninth and already six points behind the leaders Arsenal.

Once again proving that the championship is a marathon not a sprint, the Old Trafford club judged its final spurt just as manager Sir Alex Ferguson's Rock of Gibraltar would have done and hit the front on 12 April after a lunchtime carnival at Newcastle ending in a 6-2 win.

If there were disappointments they came from other causes, domestic and European, though their hat-trick of reverses were against arguably their most intense rivals. In the Worthington Cup final, soon to become the Carling Cup, United lost 2-0 to Liverpool. The same score saw them crash at home to Arsenal in the FA Cup fifth round and it was in the quarter-final of the Champions League that Real Madrid ended United interest.

For Arsenal to have to settle for runners-up berth must have been a bitter experience following the fluency of their football in the early months of the season. At times during matches they were virtually unplayable.

From the middle of November they had headed affairs and were the favourites. Elsewhere they had lost early interest in the Worthington Cup against lowly Sunderland at Highbury in a 3-2 defeat and in the second stage of the Champions League the Gunners won only one match.

It was left to the FA Cup to provide them with some silverware for their efforts and in a slightly low-key final they beat Southampton 1-0. Arsenal also provided in Thierry Henry both the players' choice and that of the football writers with footballer of the year awards.

In third place Newcastle United enjoyed their highest position for six years and also achieved the feat of losing their initial three games in the first stage of the Champions League, yet still qualified for the second.

The battle for fourth place and its lucrative slot in the Champions League was reserved for the last game of the season at Stamford Bridge. A draw would have been enough for Chelsea, but Liverpool needed victory. Chelsea edged it 2-1.

Chelsea were always within striking distance of the leaders, but faltered after Christmas. For Liverpool even when they were riding high, unbeaten after a dozen games having dropped just three points, there was criticism.

Perhaps because of the high standards set at Anfield, even some of their most fervent supporters were none-too-happy about the style offered to them. Even so, Liverpool won the Worthington Cup and made the graduation from dismissal in the Champions League to reaching the quarter-final of the UEFA Cup, before losing to Celtic. A similar 2-0 defeat had ended their FA Cup hopes against Crystal Palace.

Celebration Ruud Van Nistelrooy style. Manchester United clinched the Premiership title in the 4-1 win over Charlton Athletic on 3 May, aided in no small part by the Dutchman's hat-trick. (Actionimages)

Patrick Vieira turns to avoid the attentions of Newcastle United's Jermaine Jenas and Kieron Dyer during Arsenal's 1-0 win at Highbury early in November. United were ninth at the time, the Gunners in second place. (Actionimages)

Much improved performances came from Blackburn Rovers and Everton. Blackburn in their second season after returning to the FA Premier League might have done even better but for a mid-season hiccup. Everton finished higher than for six years and in Wayne Rooney had the young discovery of the season.

Southampton threatened to force themselves into a European berth, but they had to settle for reaching the FA Cup final. Still Manchester City made it into Europe as winners of UEFA's Fair Play award after a roller-coaster of a season for results.

Tottenham Hotspur finished tenth, their lowest position all season and it was frustrating for them when you consider they were top after four matches.

Failure to produce any meaningful away form restricted Middlesbrough and fortress Riverside was not breached until late in the campaign. Disappointment, too, for Charlton Athletic to slip into the bottom half of the table after five straight wins soon after the turn of the year.

Birmingham City made a successful fight of it to avoid returning to the Football League following more than a decade and a half outside the top flight; after their early adjustment, 13th place was certainly not unlucky for them.

Fulham, heavily involved in a variety of cup matches and with managerial problems, managed to overcome them, while Leeds United, with the black cloud of financial worries constantly hovering over them, had to recruit Peter Reid as manager after Terry Venables left.

Aston Villa, like Middlesbrough, were nervous away from home. Yet their one success was at the Riverside, but enough points in the last nine matches kept them out of trouble.

Back in the Premier for the third time in recent years, Bolton Wanderers were hoping against the hat-trick of relegation and only one reverse in the last nine gave adequate testimony to such avoidance.

West Ham United had to cope with late illness to manager Glenn Roeder and in his absence ex-Upton Park favourite Trevor Brooking tried valiantly to steer them out of danger. But the curse of being bottom at Christmas again proved overwhelming.

Save for three wins on the trot in August and September, West Bromwich Albion were battling against the inevitable and Sunderland's wretched season ended with first Peter Reid and then Howard Wilkinson being shown the door and replaced by Mick McCarthy. They are currently on 15 successive defeats.

Portsmouth, briefly in the old First Division in 1987–88, set their stall out from the onset dropping just two points in their opening nine encounters. With plenty of experience in the team they had breathing space between themselves and Leicester City who bounced back quickly after relegation.

Despite financial problems they maintained a high rating and were never out of the top two after the end of November. This pair were joined via the play-offs by Wolverhampton Wanderers, who all too frequently in the past have flattered without delivering their potential. An improved second half of the season helped.

Sheffield United, who had been Wolves' victims in the play-off final, did well to finish third in the table and reach both domestic semi-finals. In those they were by no means disgraced in losing to Liverpool and Arsenal, respective winners of the League Cup and FA Cup.

A play-off spot was a second half of the season reality for Reading, though Nottingham Forest who almost made it to this stage did not maintain their early season effectiveness.

A valiant attempt to return to the Premier League saw Ipswich Town produce spells of eight and nine games without defeat while fellow East Anglians Norwich City, second in early Autumn, tailed off noticeably.

Millwall finished strongly after a poor start, but Wimbledon with meagre crowds at Selhurst Park because of the split with AFC Wimbledon, saw their push for a play-off place vanish in March.

Gillingham continued to consolidate in their second season in the First Division, but Preston North End had a mid-table look about them at best.

Watford, as high as third in early November did not sustain a challenge afterwards and Crystal Palace's aspirations towards the play-offs evaporated after the turn of the year.

After a bright opening to their programme, Rotherham United ran a little out of steam while Burnley were surprisingly prone to heavy defeats conceding two sevens and two sixes.

Walsall hauled themselves out of trouble in the last six games and Derby County slipping badly at the end were unquestionably relieved at its arrival. Seven consecutive defeats did nothing for Bradford City's morale in mid-season and ten goals in the last 17 matches emphasized where Coventry City's problems lay.

Stoke City rallied dramatically after one run of 16 matches without a win and though they were unbeaten in the last seven matches Sheffield Wednesday were still four points short of salvation.

Brighton & Hove Albion gallantly strove to avoid relegation after winning the Second Division title, but a dozen successive defeats had caused the damage earlier in the season. But it was Grimsby Town who were the first to go, with only three points from their last eight.

One hundred points was the achievement of Wigan Athletic in winning the Second Division title. After two successive defeats at the end of August, they dropped only five points in an unbeaten run to mid-January and remarkably conceded just nine goals away!

Crewe Alexandra did well to make a rapid return to the First Division, heading off other challengers in the last third of the season. They were joined via the play-offs by Cardiff City, who at one stage had appeared capable of automatic promotion, but only two draws and one goal in the last five games ruined any such chance.

Both Bristol City and Queens Park Rangers were just three points behind Crewe, though both failed in the play-offs as did Oldham Athletic just a point further away in a competitive group. Rangers had been as low as tenth in December. Consolation of a kind saw City win the LDV Vans Trophy.

With Everton's Kevin Campbell an interested onlooker, Blackburn Rovers' Craig Short holds off Thomas Gravesen. Both teams gave vastly improved performances during the 2002–03 season. (Actionimages)

Despite staying undefeated during the last 15 matches, Tranmere Rovers had to settle for another try as did Plymouth Argyle, as low as 16th in November.

Sixth was the highest placing Luton Town reached during the term and six straight defeats after a useful opening hit Swindon Town. Peterborough United looked good material for the drop at the half-way mark, but pulled away impressively as did Colchester United after a change of management.

Blackpool did not win one of their last twelve, but four consecutive wins late on helped Stockport County relieve fears of going down. Notts County were another team benefiting from a second half turnaround while Brentford won only two more games from March.

Five wins in a row was Port Vale's best early on and Wycombe Wanderers did not win any of their last eight. Erratic performances had caused Barnsley some worry in the middle of the season and ten matches without a win halted Chesterfield's ambitions, though they did avoid relegation.

Drawn games when wins were desperately required finally doomed Cheltenham Town along with three other Towns: Huddersfield, Mansfield and Northampton.

Huddersfield, bottom in January were unable to scratch around for sufficient points and Mansfield won only one of their last nine, when already relegated. Northampton were goalless in 22 games and had a poor second half of the season.

Replacing them Rushden & Diamonds lasted the pace better than Hartlepool United who had threatened to run away with the Third Division. But the newcomers were unbeaten in the last eleven while Hartlepool won only three of their last thirteen.

Wrexham made it first time as well, undefeated after early March, but Bournemouth had to wait until the play-offs before clinching promotion for themselves.

Scunthorpe United lost interest at this stage after a bright second half showing, as did Lincoln City with a late effort and Bury as high as third early in the New Year. Oxford United missed the cut and they, too, had been third in December.

Too many home drawn matches hit Torquay United, York City were unable to build on a useful start and third place in October flattered Kidderminster Harriers. Boxing Day in third spot was another bad omen for Cambridge United and Hull City at their new ground at least saw support blossom.

Darlington, too, await new premises and will be hoping for more than two wins in a row as experienced in 2002–03. But Boston United, with the handicap of four points deducted, recovered from a mid-season decline.

Macclesfield Town pulled themselves to safety early in March and only eight goals in the last twelve games ended any lingering Southend United hopes toward the play-offs as did their mere three draws.

Leyton Orient won only three of their last sixteen, Rochdale one fewer from the same number yet three wins and a draw ended Bristol Rovers' concerns.

Swansea City won their last two to escape the double drop and two timely away wins near the end saved Carlisle United, beaten finalists in the LDV Vans Trophy.

Exeter City might have won their last three, but it was too little late on and they were joined by Shrewsbury Town, conquerors of Everton in the FA Cup, who did not manage a win in their last 15 outings. Up from the Conference come Yeovil Town those eternal giant-killers and Doncaster Rovers who emerged from the play-offs to resume their Football League status after five years' absence.

Kenny Miller rifles in Wolves' third goal in the emphatic 3-0 win over Sheffield United in the First Division play-off in Cardiff, which sent the midlanders back to the top flight after 20 years. (Colorsport)

INTRODUCTION TO THE CLUB SECTION

The Sky Sports Football Yearbook features a who's who style players directory which incorporates the total appearances and goals for each player as in earlier editions of *Rothmans Football Yearbook*, but additionally, includes more personal information and a season-by-season account of the individual player's record. It is again presented in an A to Z form for easy reference (see pages 428 to 562). There is also each club's full record in the last ten seasons and the latest sequences recorded for wins, draws and defeats, etc. In addition, the individual club's record scoring and non-scoring runs are also included.

The club section again comprises four pages, the first two feature new entries in the *Sky Sports Fact File* and *Did you know?* series. Record transfer fees are usually left to the discretion of the club concerned. The third and fourth pages of this section present a complete record of the League season, including date, venue, opponents, results, half-time score, League position, goalscorers, attendances and complete line-ups including substitutes where used. This comprises every League game in the 2002-03 season. Again, goal times have been added, though not official they give an indication of when goals were scored. These appear as superior figures [10, 20, 30].

An innovation this year is the inclusion of players shown red cards■. This applies throughout the book.

Squad numbers have not been included; those used are the familiar ones, 1–11, while the introduction of a third outfield substitute is recognised as follows:- the first substitute number 12, the second number 13 and the third number 14. However, if there is a subsitute goalkeeper he is represented by number 15, *but only* if he replaces the first choice goalkeeper. Otherwise, he adopts one of the other three substitute numbers, as there have been several instances where a goalkeeper has been used as an outfield player because of injuries during the game. Players replaced are respectively noted with superior figures [1, 2, 3] and [g] for goalkeeper. These third and fourth pages also include consolidated lists of goalscorers for the club in League, Worthington Cup, FA Cup, LDV Vans Trophy and European matches, plus a summary of results in all these major competitions.

The continual increase in the number of matches played on Sundays has resulted in the League positions after every result being taken on that day. Full holiday programmes are also recorded, but the position after mid-week fixtures will not normally have been updated. Attendance figures quoted for the Nationwide Football League are those that appeared in the Press at the time. But those in the FA Barclaycard Premiership are official. The attendance statistics published on pages 590–591 are those officially issued by the FA Premier League but not those concerning the Football League at the end of the season. In the totals at the top of each column on page 4 of the club section, substitute appearances are listed separately by the '+', but have been amalgamated in the totals which feature in the players historical section in the directory mentioned above. Thus, these appearances include those as substitute. In fact, the directory features those names appearing on the FA Premier League and Football League's retained lists, which are published at the end of May. Each player's height and weight where known, plus birth date and place plus source, together with total League goals and appearances for each club represented, can be found as in previous editions. The player's details remain under the club which retain him at the end of the season. An asterisk '*' by a player's name indicates that he was given a free transfer at the end of the 2002–03 season, a dagger '†' against a name means that he is a non-contract player, a double dagger '‡' indicates that the player's registration was cancelled during the season and a section mark '§' shows the player to be a trainee, scholar or associated schoolboy who has made either League or senior appearances. The symbol '#' indicates players 24 and over who are out of contract, but who were offered re-engagement by their clubs. Appearances by players in the play-offs are not included in their career totals. International appearances with foreign players reflect latest information available.

ARSENAL FA Premiership

FOUNDATION

Formed by workers at the Royal Arsenal, Woolwich in 1886, they began as Dial Square (name of one of the workshops), and included two former Nottingham Forest players, Fred Beardsley and Morris Bates. Beardsley wrote to his old club seeking help and they provided the new club with a full set of red jerseys and a ball. The club became known as the 'Woolwich Reds' although their official title soon after formation was Woolwich Arsenal.

Arsenal Stadium, Highbury, London N5 1BU.

Telephone: (020) 7704 4000. ***Fax:*** (020) 7704 4001. ***Box Office:*** (020) 7704 4040. ***Commercial & Marketing:*** (020) 7704 4100. ***Recorded Information:*** (020) 7704 4242.

Ground Capacity: 38,500 all seated.

Record Attendance: 73,295 v Sunderland, Div 1, 9 March 1935.

At Wembley: 73,707 v RC Lens, UEFA Champions League, 25 November 1998.

Record Receipts: £1,026,789 v Manchester U, FA Barclaycard Premiership, 16 May 2003.

Pitch Measurements: 110yd × 73yd.

Chairman: P. D. Hill-Wood. ***Vice-chairman:*** D. Dein. ***Directors:*** R. G. Gibbs, C. E. B. L. Carr, R. C. L. Carr, D. D. Fiszman, K. J. Friar.

Managing Director: K. Edelman.

Manager: Arsène Wenger.

Assistant Manager: Pat Rice.

First Team Coach: Boro Primorac.

Head of Youth Development: Liam Brady.

Physio: Gary Lewin.

Reserve Coach: Eddie Niedzwiecki.

Company Secretary: David Miles.

Commercial Manager: Adrian Ford.

Stadium Manager: John Beattie.

Colours: Red shirts with white sleeves, white shorts, white stockings with red trim.

Change Colours: Yellow shirts with blue trim, blue shorts, yellow stockings with blue trim.

Year Formed: 1886.

Turned Professional: 1891.

Ltd Co: 1893.

Previous Names: 1886, Dial Square; 1886, Royal Arsenal; 1891, Woolwich Arsenal; 1914 Arsenal.

Club Nickname: 'Gunners'.

HONOURS

FA Premier League: Champions 1997–98, 2001–02. Runners-up 1998–99, 1999–2000, 2000–01, 2002–03.

Football League: Division 1 – Champions 1930–31, 1932–33, 1933–34, 1934–35, 1937–38, 1947–48, 1952–53, 1970–71, 1988–89, 1990–91; Runners-up 1925–26, 1931–32, 1972–73; Division 2 – Runners-up 1903–04.

FA Cup: Winners 1930, 1936, 1950, 1971, 1979, 1993, 1998, 2002, 2003; Runners-up 1927, 1932, 1952, 1972, 1978, 1980, 2001.

Double performed: 1970–71, 1997–98, 2001–02.

Football League Cup: Winners 1987, 1993; Runners-up 1968, 1969, 1988.

European Competitions: *Fairs Cup:* 1963–64, 1969–70 (winners), 1970–71. *European Cup:* 1971–72, 1991–92. *UEFA Champions League:* 1998–99, 1999–2000, 2000–01, 2001–02, 2002–03, 2003–04. *UEFA Cup:* 1978–79, 1981–82, 1982–83, 1996–97, 1997–98, 1999–2000 (runners-up). *European Cup-Winners' Cup:* 1979–80 (runners-up), 1993–94 (winners), 1994–95 (runners-up).

SKY SPORTS FACT FILE

On 28 September 2002 Arsenal set an overall League record by scoring in their 47th consecutive match. On 7 December they failed to score for the first time in 56 games overall. To the end of the season, Arsenal had scored in 75 of 77 League matches.

Previous Grounds: 1886, Plumstead Common; 1887, Sportsman Ground; 1888, Manor Ground; 1890, Invicta Ground; 1893, Manor Ground; 1913, Highbury.

First Football League Game: 2 September 1893, Division 2, v Newcastle U (h) D 2–2 – Williams; Powell, Jeffrey; Devine, Buist, Howat; Gemmell, Henderson, Shaw (1), Elliott (1), Booth.

Record League Victory: 12–0 v Loughborough T, Division 2, 12 March 1900 – Orr; McNichol, Jackson; Moir, Dick (2), Anderson (1); Hunt, Cottrell (2), Main (2), Gaudie (3), Tennant (2).

Record Cup Victory: 11–1 v Darwen, FA Cup 3rd rd, 9 January 1932 – Moss; Parker, Hapgood; Jones, Roberts, John; Hulme (2), Jack (3), Lambert (2), James, Bastin (4).

Record Defeat: 0–8 v Loughborough T, Division 2, 12 December 1896.

Most League Points (2 for a win): 66, Division 1, 1930–31.

Most League Points (3 for a win): 87, Premier League 2001–02.

Most League Goals: 127, Division 1, 1930–31.

Highest League Scorer in Season: Ted Drake, 42, 1934–35.

Most League Goals in Total Aggregate: Cliff Bastin, 150, 1930–47.

Most League Goals in One Match: 7, Ted Drake v Aston Villa, Division 1, 14 December 1935.

Most Capped Player: Kenny Sansom, 77 (86), England, 1981–88.

Most League Appearances: David O'Leary, 558, 1975–93.

Youngest League Player: Gerry Ward, 16 years 321 days v Huddersfield T, 22 August 1953 (Jermaine Pennant, 16 years 319 days v Middlesbrough, League Cup, 30 November 1999).

Record Transfer Fee Received: A reported £22,900,000 from Real Madrid for Nicolas Anelka, August 1999.

Record Transfer Fee Paid: A reported £11,000,000 to Bordeaux for Sylvain Wiltord, August 2000.

Football League Record: 1893 Elected to Division 2; 1904–13 Division 1; 1913–19 Division 2; 1919–92 Division 1; 1992– FA Premier League.

MANAGERS

Sam Hollis 1894–97
Tom Mitchell 1897–98
George Elcoat 1898–99
Harry Bradshaw 1899–1904
Phil Kelso 1904–08
George Morrell 1908–15
Leslie Knighton 1919–25
Herbert Chapman 1925–34
George Allison 1934–47
Tom Whittaker 1947–56
Jack Crayston 1956–58
George Swindin 1958–62
Billy Wright 1962–66
Bertie Mee 1966–76
Terry Neill 1976–83
Don Howe 1984–86
George Graham 1986–95
Bruce Rioch 1995–96
Arsène Wenger September 1996–

LATEST SEQUENCES

Longest Sequence of League Wins: 14, 10.2.2002 – 18.8.2002.

Longest Sequence of League Defeats: 7, 12.2.1977 – 12.3.1977.

Longest Sequence of League Draws: 6, 4.3.1961 – 1.4.1961.

Longest Sequence of Unbeaten League Matches: 30, 23.12.2001 – 6.10.2002.

Longest Sequence Without a League Win: 23, 28.9.1912 – 1.3.1913.

Successive Scoring Runs: 55 from 19.5.2001.

Successive Non-scoring Runs: 6 from 25.2.1987.

TEN YEAR LEAGUE RECORD

		P	W	D	L	F	A	Pts	Pos
1993-94	PR Lge	42	18	17	7	53	28	71	4
1994-95	PR Lge	42	13	12	17	52	49	51	12
1995-96	PR Lge	38	17	12	9	49	32	63	5
1996-97	PR Lge	38	19	11	8	62	32	68	3
1997-98	PR Lge	38	23	9	6	68	33	78	1
1998-99	PR Lge	38	22	12	4	59	17	78	2
1999-2000	PR Lge	38	22	7	9	73	43	73	2
2000-01	PR Lge	38	20	10	8	63	38	70	2
2001-02	PR Lge	38	26	9	3	79	36	87	1
2002-03	PR Lge	38	23	9	6	85	42	78	2

DID YOU KNOW?

On 4 January 2003 in a 2-0 FA Cup third round home win over Oxford United, Dennis Bergkamp scored his 100th club goal. The following week Thierry Henry reached his century for Arsenal by scoring in a 4-0 away win at Birmingham City.

ARSENAL 2002–03 LEAGUE RECORD

Match No.	*Date*	*Venue*	*Opponents*	*Result*		*H/T Score*	*Lg. Pos.*	*Goalscorers*	*Attendance*
1	Aug 18	H	Birmingham C	W	2-0	2-0	—	Henry [9], Wiltord [24]	38,018
2	24	A	West Ham U	D	2-2	0-1	4	Henry [65], Wiltord [88]	35,046
3	27	H	WBA	W	5-2	3-0	—	Cole [3], Lauren [21], Wiltord 2 [24, 77], Aliadiere [90]	37,920
4	Sept 1	A	Chelsea	D	1-1	0-1	2	Toure [60]	40,107
5	10	H	Manchester C	W	2-1	2-1	—	Wiltord [26], Henry [42]	37,878
6	14	A	Charlton Ath	W	3-0	1-0	1	Henry [44], Wiltord [67], Edu [88]	26,080
7	21	H	Bolton W	W	2-1	1-0	1	Henry [26], Kanu [90]	37,974
8	28	A	Leeds U	W	4-1	2-0	1	Kanu 2 [9, 86], Toure [20], Henry [47]	40,199
9	Oct 6	H	Sunderland	W	3-1	3-0	1	Kanu 2 [3, 9], Vieira [45]	37,902
10	19	A	Everton	L	1-2	1-1	2	Ljungberg [8]	39,038
11	26	H	Blackburn R	L	1-2	1-1	2	Edu [45]	38,064
12	Nov 3	A	Fulham	W	1-0	1-0	2	Marlet (og) [31]	17,810
13	9	H	Newcastle U	W	1-0	1-0	2	Wiltord [24]	38,121
14	16	H	Tottenham H	W	3-0	1-0	1	Henry [13], Ljungberg [55], Wiltord [71]	38,121
15	23	A	Southampton	L	2-3	1-1	1	Bergkamp [36], Pires [80]	31,797
16	30	H	Aston Villa	W	3-1	1-0	1	Pires [17], Henry 2 (1 pen) [49, 82 (p)]	38,090
17	Dec 7	A	Manchester U	L	0-2	0-1	1		67,650
18	15	A	Tottenham H	D	1-1	1-1	1	Pires (pen) [45]	36,077
19	21	H	Middlesbrough	W	2-0	1-0	1	Campbell [45], Pires [90]	38,003
20	26	A	WBA	W	2-1	0-1	1	Jeffers [48], Henry [85]	26,782
21	29	H	Liverpool	D	1-1	0-0	1	Henry (pen) [79]	38,074
22	Jan 1	H	Chelsea	W	3-2	1-0	1	Desailly (og) [9], Van Bronckhorst [81], Henry [82]	38,096
23	12	A	Birmingham C	W	4-0	2-0	1	Henry 2 [6, 70], Pires [29], Johnson M (og) [67]	29,505
24	19	H	West Ham U	W	3-1	1-1	1	Henry 3 (1 pen) [14 (p), 71, 86]	38,053
25	29	A	Liverpool	D	2-2	1-0	—	Pires [9], Bergkamp [63]	43,668
26	Feb 1	H	Fulham	W	2-1	1-1	1	Pires 2 [17, 90]	38,050
27	9	A	Newcastle U	D	1-1	1-0	1	Henry [35]	52,157
28	22	A	Manchester C	W	5-1	4-0	1	Bergkamp [4], Pires [12], Henry [15], Campbell [19], Vieira [53]	34,960
29	Mar 2	H	Charlton Ath	W	2-0	2-0	1	Jeffers [26], Pires [45]	38,015
30	15	A	Blackburn R	L	0-2	0-1	1		29,840
31	23	H	Everton	W	2-1	1-0	1	Cygan [8], Vieira [64]	38,042
32	Apr 5	A	Aston Villa	D	1-1	0-0	1	Ljungberg [56]	42,602
33	16	H	Manchester U	D	2-2	0-1	—	Henry 2 [51, 62]	38,164
34	19	A	Middlesbrough	W	2-0	0-0	2	Wiltord [48], Henry [82]	34,724
35	26	A	Bolton W	D	2-2	0-0	2	Wiltord [47], Pires [56]	27,253
36	May 4	H	Leeds U	L	2-3	1-1	2	Henry [31], Bergkamp [63]	38,127
37	7	H	Southampton	W	6-1	5-1	—	Pires 3 [9, 23, 47], Pennant 3 [16, 19, 26]	38,052
38	11	A	Sunderland	W	4-0	2-0	2	Henry [7], Ljungberg 3 [39, 78, 88]	40,188

Final League Position: 2

GOALSCORERS

League (85): Henry 24 (3 pens), Pires 14 (1 pen), Wiltord 10, Ljungberg 6, Kanu 5, Bergkamp 4, Pennant 3, Vieira 3, Campbell 2, Edu 2, Jeffers 2, Toure 2, Aliadiere 1, Cole 1, Cygan 1, Lauren 1, Van Bronckhorst 1, own goals 3.
Worthington Cup (2): Jeffers 1, Pires 1.
FA Cup (16): Jeffers 3, Bergkamp 2, Lauren 2, Wiltord 2, Campbell 1, Edu 1, Henry 1, Ljungberg 1, Pires 1, own goals 2.
Community Shield (1): Silva 1.
Champions League (15): Henry 7, Ljungberg 2, Silva 2, Bergkamp 1, Kanu 1, Wiltord 1, Vieira 1.

Seaman D 28	Lauren E 26 + 1	Cole A 30 + 1	Vieira P 24	Campbell S 33	Keown M 22 + 2	Parlour R 14 + 5	Edu 12 + 6	Henry T 37	Bergkamp D 23 + 6	Wiltord S 27 + 7	Toure K 9 + 17	Silva G 32 + 3	Aliadiere J — + 3	Pennant J 1 + 4	Kanu N 9 + 7	Cygan P 16 + 2	Luzhny O 11 + 6	Ljungberg F 19 + 1	Jeffers F 2 + 14	Pires R 21 + 5	Shaaban R 3	Van Bronckhorst G 9 + 11	Taylor S 7 + 1	Garry R 1	Stepanovs I 2	Tavlaridis E — + 1	Hoyte J — + 1	*Match No.*
1	2	3	4	5	6	7	8[2]	9	10[1]	11[3]	13	12	14															1
1	2[1]	3	4	5	6	7[2]	8	9	10[3]	11	12			13	14													2
1	2	3	4[2]	5	6	12	11	10		7[3]	13	8	14		9[1]													3
1	2	3	4■	5	6	7	11[1]			10[2]	12	8	13		9[3]	14												4
1		3	4	5	6		11[1]	9	10	7	12	8					2											5
1		3	4	5	6		12	9	10[2]	11[3]	7[1]	8			13	14	2											6
1	2[1]	3		5	6	4		10	13	7[3]	12	8			9			11[2]	14									7
1	2	3	4	5				10		7[1]	11[2]	8		12	9[3]	6	13		14									8
1	2	3	4	5			12	10[3]		7[1]	13	8			9	6		11[2]	14									9
1	2	3	4	5			12	10		13	7[2]	8			9[3]	6		11[1]	14									10
1	2	3[1]		5			8[3]	10	13	7	12	4			9[2]	6		11		14								11
1	2[3]	3		5			8	9	10[2]	7[1]	12	4			13	6	14	11										12
1		3	4	5			12	9	10[2]	7[1]		8				6	2	11		13								13
		3	4[3]	5				9[1]	10[2]	7		8				6	2	11	12	13	1	14						14
1		3	4	5■			8[1]	9	10[2]	7	12					6	2	11[3]	13	14								15
			4	5	12			9	10[2]	13	7[1]	8				6	2	14		11[3]	1	3						16
		3	4		5			10	12	9[1]	13	8				6	2	7		11[2]	1[G]		15					17
1	2	3		5	6	8		9	10[1]	12	13	4						7[2]		11[3]		14						18
1	2	3		5	6			9		7		8						10		11		4						19
1	2	3	4	5	6			9		7[1]	12	8			13				10[2]	14		11[3]						20
1	2	3	4	5	6			10	12	7[2]		8			9[1]				13	11[3]		14						21
1	12	3	4	5	6			9	10[2]	7[1]	13	8					2			11[3]		14						22
1	2	3		5	6		8[3]	9	10[2]	7	12	4							13	11[1]		14						23
1	2			5	6	12	8[1]	9	10[2]	7[3]		4					13		14	11		3						24
1	2	3	4	5		7		9	10[1]			8				6	12			11								25
1	2[1]	3	4	5	6			9	10	7[2]	12	8[3]							13	11		14						26
1	2	3	4	5	6	12		9	10[2]	7[3]		8[1]							13	11		14						27
	2		4	5	6	14	12	9	10[3]	7[2]		8							13	11[1]		3	1					28
1				5	6	4	8	9		12	2	13						7[1]	10	11[2]		3						29
	2				6[2]	4	8[3]	9	10	12		13				5		7	14	11[1]		3	1					30
	2		4	5		12		9	10[2]		13	8				6		7		11[1]		3	1					31
	2	12	4	5		7[2]		9	10[3]	13	3[1]	8				6		11	14				1					32
	2	3	4[1]	5■	6		12	9	10[2]	13		8			14			7		11[3]			1					33
	2	3[2]		5		8		9[1]	12	10		4				6	13	7		11[3]		14	1					34
1	2[3]	3		5	12	8		10		9		4				6[1]	13	7[2]		11		14						35
1		3			6	8		9	10	7[1]	2[2]	4		12	13		5			11[3]		14						36
						4		10	12		2			7[2]	9		5[3]			11[1]		8	1	3	6	14	13	37
1		3				8[3]		9	10[1]		2	4		13	12		5	7		11[2]		14			6			38

Worthington Cup

Third Round	Sunderland	(h)	2-3

FA Cup

Third Round	Oxford U	(h)	2-0
Fourth Round (at Highbury)	Farnborough T	(a)	5-1
Fifth Round	Manchester U	(a)	2-0
Sixth Round	Chelsea	(h)	2-2
		(a)	3-1
Semi-final (at Old Trafford)	Sheffield U		1-0
Final (at Millennium Stadium)	Southampton		1-0

Champions League

Group A	Borussia Dortmund	(h)	2-0
	PSV Eindhoven	(a)	4-0
	Auxerre	(a)	1-0
		(h)	1-2
	Borussia Dortmund	(a)	1-2
	PSV Eindhoven	(h)	0-0

Champions League

Second Stage Group B	Roma	(a)	3-1
	Valencia	(h)	0-0
	Ajax	(h)	1-1
		(a)	0-0
	Roma	(h)	1-1
	Valencia	(a)	1-2

ASTON VILLA — FA Premiership

FOUNDATION

Cricketing enthusiasts of Villa Cross Wesleyan Chapel, Aston, Birmingham decided to form a football club during the winter of 1874–75. Football clubs were few and far between in the Birmingham area and in their first game against Aston Brook St Mary's Rugby team they played one half rugby and the other soccer. In 1876 they were joined by a Scottish soccer enthusiast George Ramsay who was immediately appointed captain and went on to lead Aston Villa from obscurity to one of the country's top clubs in a period of less than 10 years.

Villa Park, Trinity Road, Birmingham B6 6HE.
Telephone: (0121) 327 2299. ***Fax:*** (0121) 322 2107. ***Commercial Dept:*** (0121) 327 5399. ***Commercial Fax:*** (0121) 328 2099.
Ticket Information: (0121) 327 5353.
Ticketmaster: 0870 998 4552. ***Club Shop:*** (0121) 327 5353.

Website: avfc.co.uk

email addresses: postmaster@astonvilla-fc.co.uk, ticketsales@astonvilla-fc.co.uk

Ground Capacity: 42,602.

Record Attendance: 76,588 v Derby Co, FA Cup 6th rd, 2 March 1946.

Record Receipts: £1,196,712 Portugal v Czech Republic, Euro '96, 23 June 1996.

Pitch Measurements: 115yd × 72yd.

Chairman/Chief Executive: H. D. Ellis.
Deputy Chief Executive and Finance Director: M. J. Ansell. ***Company Secretary:*** Mrs M. Stringer.
Operations Director and Club Secretary: S. M. Stride.

Non Executive Directors: D. M. Owen, A. J. Hales, P. D. Ellis.

Manager: David O'Leary. ***Assistant Manager:*** John Deehan. ***First Team Coach:*** Stuart Gray. ***Coaches:*** Kevin MacDonald, Gordon Cowans, Eric Steele.

Physio: Alan Smith. ***Head of Sports Science:*** Jim Walker.
Reserve Team Manager: Kevin MacDonald. ***Youth Team Manager:*** Tony McAndrew. ***Youth Team Coach:*** Gordon Cowans. ***Youth Development Officer:*** Alan Miller.

Commercial Manager: Abdul Rashid.

Stadium Manager: Tony Diffley.

Football Academy Director: Bryan Jones.

Assistant Academy Director: Steve Burns.

Colours: Claret shirts with blue, white shorts with blue side trim, sky blue stockings with claret turnover.

Change Colours: Yellow shirts with black trim, black shorts with yellow trim to side, black stockings with yellow trim.

Year Formed: 1874. ***Turned Professional:*** 1885.

Ltd Co.: 1896. ***Public Ltd Company:*** 1969.

HONOURS

FA Premier League: Runners-up 1992–93.

Football League: Division 1 – Champions 1893–94, 1895–96, 1896–97, 1898–99, 1899–1900, 1909–10, 1980–81; Runners-up 1888–89, 1902–03, 1907–08, 1910–11, 1912–13, 1913–14, 1930–31, 1932–33, 1989–90; Division 2 – Champions 1937–38, 1959–60; Runners-up 1974–75, 1987–88; Division 3 – Champions 1971–72.

FA Cup: Winners 1887, 1895, 1897, 1905, 1913, 1920, 1957; Runners-up 1892, 1924, 2000.

Double Performed: 1896–97.

Football League Cup: Winners 1961, 1975, 1977, 1994, 1996; Runners-up 1963, 1971.

European Competitions: *European Cup:* 1981–82 (winners), 1982–83. *UEFA Cup:* 1975–76, 1977–78, 1983–84, 1990–91, 1993–94, 1994–95, 1996–97, 1997–98, 1998–99, 2001–02. *World Club Championship:* 1982. *European Super Cup:* 1982–83 (winners). *Intertoto Cup:* 2000, 2001 (winners), 2002.

SKY SPORTS FACT FILE

Dion Dublin registered his 100th FA Premier League goal on 23 November 2002 in the 4-1 win over West Ham United. On 28 December against Middlesbrough he scored his 200th overall in League and Cup games.

Club Nickname: 'The Villans'.

Previous Grounds: 1874 Wilson Road and Aston Park (also used Aston Lower Grounds for some matches); 1876 Wellington Road, Perry Barr; 1897 Villa Park.

First Football League Game: 8 September 1888, Football League, v Wolverhampton W (a) D 1–1 – Warner; Cox, Coulton; Yates, H. Devey, Dawson; A. Brown, Green (1), Allen, Garvey, Hodgetts.

Record League Victory: 12–2 v Accrington S, Division 1, 12 March 1892 – Warner; Evans, Cox; Harry Devey, Jimmy Cowan, Baird; Athersmith (1), Dickson (2), John Devey (4), L. Campbell (4), Hodgetts (1).

Record Cup Victory: 13–0 v Wednesbury Old Ath, FA Cup 1st rd, 30 October 1886 – Warner; Coulton, Simmonds; Yates, Robertson, Burton (2); R. Davis (1), A. Brown (3), Hunter (3), Loach (2), Hodgetts (2).

Record Defeat: 1–8 v Blackburn R, FA Cup 3rd rd, 16 February 1889.

Most League Points (2 for a win): 70, Division 3, 1971–72.

Most League Points (3 for a win): 78, Division 2, 1987–88.

Most League Goals: 128, Division 1, 1930–31.

Highest League Scorer in Season: 'Pongo' Waring, 49, Division 1, 1930–31.

Most League Goals in Total Aggregate: Harry Hampton, 215, 1904–15.

Most League Goals in One Match: 5, Harry Hampton v Sheffield W, Division 1, 5 October 1912; 5, Harold Halse v Derby Co, Division 1, 19 October 1912; 5, Len Capewell v Burnley, Division 1, 29 August 1925; 5, George Brown v Leicester C, Division 1, 2 January 1932; 5, Gerry Hitchens v Charlton Ath, Division 2, 18 November 1959.

MANAGERS

George Ramsay 1884–1926
(Secretary-Manager)
W. J. Smith 1926–34
(Secretary-Manager)
Jimmy McMullan 1934–35
Jimmy Hogan 1936–44
Alex Massie 1945–50
George Martin 1950–53
Eric Houghton 1953–58
Joe Mercer 1958–64
Dick Taylor 1964–67
Tommy Cummings 1967–68
Tommy Docherty 1968–70
Vic Crowe 1970–74
Ron Saunders 1974–82
Tony Barton 1982–84
Graham Turner 1984–86
Billy McNeill 1986–87
Graham Taylor 1987–90
Dr Jozef Venglos 1990–91
Ron Atkinson 1991–94
Brian Little 1994–98
John Gregory 1998–2002
Graham Taylor OBE 2002–03
David O'Leary May 2003–

Most Capped Player: Steve Staunton 64 (102), Republic of Ireland.

Most League Appearances: Charlie Aitken, 561, 1961–76.

Youngest League Player: Jimmy Brown, 15 years 349 days v Bolton W, 17 September 1969.

Record Transfer Fee Received: £12,600,000 from Manchester U for Dwight Yorke, August 1998.

Record Transfer Fee Paid: A reported figure of £9,500,000 to River Plate for Juan Pablo Angel, January 2001.

Football League Record: 1888 Founder Member of the League; 1936–38 Division 2; 1938–59 Division 1; 1959–60 Division 2; 1960–67 Division 1; 1967–70 Division 2; 1970–72 Division 3; 1972–75 Division 2; 1975–87 Division 1; 1987–88 Division 2; 1988–92 Division 1; 1992– FA Premier League.

LATEST SEQUENCES

Longest Sequence of League Wins: 9, 15.10.1910 – 10.12.1910.

Longest Sequence of League Defeats: 11, 23.3.1963 – 4.5.1963.

Longest Sequence of League Draws: 6, 12.9.1981 – 10.10.1981.

Longest Sequence of Unbeaten League Matches: 15, 12.3.1949 – 27.8.1949.

Longest Sequence Without a League Win: 12, 27.12.1986 – 25.3.1987.

Successive Scoring Runs: 35 from 10.11.1895.

Successive Non-scoring Runs: 5 from 29.2.1992.

TEN YEAR LEAGUE RECORD

		P	W	D	L	F	A	Pts	Pos
1993-94	PR Lge	42	15	12	15	46	50	57	10
1994-95	PR Lge	42	11	15	16	51	56	48	18
1995-96	PR Lge	38	18	9	11	52	35	63	4
1996-97	PR Lge	38	17	10	11	47	34	61	5
1997-98	PR Lge	38	17	6	15	49	48	57	7
1998-99	PR Lge	38	15	10	13	51	46	55	6
1999-2000	PR Lge	38	15	13	10	46	35	58	6
2000-01	PR Lge	38	13	15	10	46	43	54	8
2001-02	PR Lge	38	12	14	12	46	47	50	8
2002-03	PR Lge	38	12	9	17	42	47	45	16

DID YOU KNOW ?

On 28 January 2003 Aston Villa, the only team in the FA Premier League without an away win, defeated Middlesbrough 5-2, the sole team unbeaten at home, at the Riverside Stadium after drawing 2-2 at half-time.

ASTON VILLA 2002–03 LEAGUE RECORD

Match No.	*Date*	*Venue*	*Opponents*	*Result*		*H/T Score*	*Lg. Pos.*	*Goalscorers*	*Attendance*
1	Aug 18	H	Liverpool	L	0-1	0-0	—		41,183
2	24	A	Tottenham H	L	0-1	0-1	17		35,384
3	28	H	Manchester C	W	1-0	0-0	—	Vassell 64	33,494
4	Sept 1	A	Bolton W	L	0-1	0-0	16		22,113
5	11	H	Charlton Ath	W	2-0	0-0	—	De la Cruz 70, Moore 83	26,483
6	16	A	Birmingham C	L	0-3	0-1	—		29,505
7	22	H	Everton	W	3-2	1-0	10	Hendrie 2 7, 48, Dublin 85	30,023
8	28	A	Sunderland	L	0-1	0-0	12		40,492
9	Oct 6	H	Leeds U	D	0-0	0-0	14		33,505
10	21	H	Southampton	L	0-1	0-0	—		25,817
11	26	A	Manchester U	D	1-1	1-0	14	Mellberg 35	67,619
12	Nov 3	A	Blackburn R	D	0-0	0-0	15		23,044
13	9	H	Fulham	W	3-1	1-0	14	Angel 20, Allback 66, Leonhardsen 83	29,563
14	16	A	WBA	D	0-0	0-0	14		26,973
15	23	H	West Ham U	W	4-1	1-0	11	Hendrie 29, Leonhardsen 59, Dublin 72, Vassell 80	33,279
16	30	A	Arsenal	L	1-3	0-1	15	Hitzlsperger 64	38,090
17	Dec 7	H	Newcastle U	L	0-1	0-0	15		35,446
18	14	H	WBA	W	2-1	1-1	15	Vassell 16, Hitzlsperger 90	40,391
19	21	A	Chelsea	L	0-2	0-1	15		38,288
20	26	A	Manchester C	L	1-3	1-1	16	Dublin 41	33,991
21	28	H	Middlesbrough	W	1-0	1-0	14	Dublin 11	33,637
22	Jan 1	H	Bolton W	W	2-0	1-0	14	Dublin 8, Vassell 80	31,838
23	11	A	Liverpool	D	1-1	0-1	13	Dublin (pen) 49	43,210
24	18	H	Tottenham H	L	0-1	0-0	14		38,576
25	28	A	Middlesbrough	W	5-2	2-2	—	Vassell 2 24, 81, Gudjonsson 31, Barry 48, Dublin 90	27,542
26	Feb 2	H	Blackburn R	W	3-0	2-0	11	Dublin 2 2, 40, Barry 80	29,171
27	8	A	Fulham	L	1-2	1-2	12	Barry 3	17,902
28	22	A	Charlton Ath	L	0-3	0-0	12		26,229
29	Mar 3	H	Birmingham C	L	0-2	0-0	—		42,602
30	15	H	Manchester U	L	0-1	0-1	14		42,602
31	22	A	Southampton	D	2-2	2-1	14	Hendrie 30, Vassell 36	31,888
32	Apr 5	H	Arsenal	D	1-1	0-0	15	Toure (og) 71	42,602
33	12	A	West Ham U	D	2-2	1-1	14	Vassell (pen) 36, Leonhardsen 53	35,029
34	19	H	Chelsea	W	2-1	1-0	13	Allback 2 11, 78	39,358
35	21	A	Newcastle U	D	1-1	0-1	14	Dublin 69	52,015
36	26	A	Everton	L	1-2	0-0	14	Allback 49	40,167
37	May 3	H	Sunderland	W	1-0	0-0	14	Allback 80	36,963
38	11	A	Leeds U	L	1-3	1-1	16	Gudjonsson 40	40,205

Final League Position: 16

GOALSCORERS

League (42): Dublin 10 (1 pen), Vassell 8 (1 pen), Allback 5, Hendrie 4, Barry 3, Leonhardsen 3, Gudjonsson 2, Hitzlsperger 2, Angel 1, De la Cruz 1, Mellberg 1, Moore 1, own goal 1.
Worthington Cup (14): Dublin 4, Vassell 3 (1 pen), Hitzlsperger 2, Angel 1, Barry 1, De la Cruz 1, Taylor 1, own goal 1.
FA Cup (1): Angel 1.
Intertoto Cup (4): Allback 1, Boulding 1, Staunton 1, Taylor 1.

Enckelman P 33	Delaney M 12	Barry G 35	Mellberg O 38	Alpay O 5	Staunton S 22 + 4	De la Cruz U 12 + 8	Hitzlsperger T 24 + 2	Crouch P 7 + 7	Vassell D 28 + 5	Hendrie L 22 + 5	Samuel J 33 + 5	Hadji M 7 + 4	Allback M 9 + 11	Wright A 9 + 1	Kinsella M 15 + 4	Angel J 8 + 7	Johnsen R 25 + 1	Moore S 7 + 6	Dublin D 23 + 5	Leonhardsen O 13 + 6	Postma S 5 + 1	Taylor I 9 + 4	Edwards R 7 + 1	Cooke S — + 3	Gudjonsson J 9 + 2	Whittingham P 1 + 3	*Match No.*
1	2	3¹	4	5	6	7	8²	9³	10	11	12	13	14														1
1	2	11¹	4		5	7²		9³	10	8	12		13	3	6	14											2
1	2	11	4		5			9	10	7	12		13	3¹	6	8²											3
1	2	11	4		5	12		9²	10¹	7	14		13	3³	6	8											4
1		11	4	5	6	2		12			3		10²		7	9¹	8	13									5
1		11	4	5	6	2			12		3		10²		7	9¹	8		13								6
1		5	4		6	2³		9¹	10²	11	3				7		8	13	12	14							7
1	2¹	11	4		6	12		13	10	8	3				7³		5		9²	14							8
1		11	4		6	2			10	8	3				7	13	5¹		9	12²							9
1▮		11	4	5	6	2¹			10	8²	3	12			7ᴳ			13	9		15						10
1	2	11	4		5		12	13			3				7	14		10³	9²	8¹		6					11
1	2	11	4		5			12			3				8	10²		13	9¹	7		6					12
1	2	11	4		5³		12				3		13		8¹	10²	14		9	7		6					13
1	2	11	4		12		8		13	14	3³		10²				5¹		9	7		6					14
1		3	4		5		8		10²	11¹	2		13		12	14			9³	7		6					15
1			2		5	12	8		10	11¹	3						4		9	7		6					16
1		11¹	4			2	8		10	6	3				12	13	5		9²	7							17
1		11	2		5▮		8		10	6	3						4		9	7							18
1		3	4		5		8		10²	6	2	11	14		12	13			9³	7¹							19
1		6	4		5	2	8¹		10³	13	3	11			7	14			9	12²							20
		11	4			12²	8				3	7¹	13	14	6	10	5³		9		1		2				21
		11	4			7³	8²		12	6	5			3	13	10¹			9		1		2	14			22
1		11	4			12	8		10²	7¹	2			3			5	13	9			6					23
1	2	11	4			12	8	13	14	7¹	3						5	10³	9²			6					24
1	2	11	4		12		8		10	13	3						5	7¹	9						6²		25
1	2¹	11	4		12	13	8		10	14	3						5	7²	9						6³		26
1		11	4			12	8²	13	10	14	3						5	7¹	9				2³		6		27
1		11	4	2		7¹		9	10²		14	12	13	3³	8		5								6		28
1		11	4					12	10	8	2	13		3¹			5	7²	9▮						6▮		29
		11	4				8		10	6	2	7		3			5		9¹		1			12			30
		11	4				8	9¹	10	6²	2	7	12	3			5	13			1						31
1		6	4			2³	8		10	11	3	9²	12				5			13			14		7¹		32
1		6	4		5		8		10	11³	3	7¹	9²							12		13	2		14		33
1		11	4		12		8		10		3		9				5			7			2		6¹		34
1		11³	4		6		8¹		10		3		9				5		12	7		13	2²			14	35
1			4		3		8		12		11		10				5²		9	7¹		13	2³		6	14	36
1			4		3		8³		10	11¹	2		9				5		12	7²		6			13	14	37
		11	4				8		10		2²		9				5¹	7³	12		1	13		14	6	3	38

Worthington Cup

Second Round	Luton T	(h)	3-0
Third Round	Oxford U	(a)	3-0
Fourth Round	Preston NE	(h)	5-0
Fifth Round	Liverpool	(h)	3-4

Intertoto Cup

Third Round	Zurich	(a)	0-2
		(h)	3-0
Semi-final	Lille	(a)	1-1
		(h)	0-2

FA Cup

Third Round	Blackburn R	(h)	1-4

BARNSLEY

Division 2

FOUNDATION

Many clubs owe their inception to the church and Barnsley are among them, for they were formed in 1887 by the Rev. T. T. Preedy, curate of Barnsley St Peter's and went under that name until it was dropped in 1897 a year before being admitted to the Second Division of the Football League.

Oakwell Stadium, Barnsley, South Yorkshire S71 1ET

Telephone: (01226) 211 211. ***Fax:*** (01226) 211 444.
Website: barnsleyfc.co.uk
Email: thereds@barnsleyfc.co.uk
ClubCall: 09068 121 152.

Ground Capacity: 23,186.

Record Attendance: 40,255 v Stoke C, FA Cup 5th rd, 15 February 1936.

Record Receipts: undisclosed.

Pitch Measurements: 110yd × 75yd.

Chairman: J. A. Dennis.

Director: P. O. Doyle.

Manager: Gudjon Thordarson.

First Team Coach: Colin Walker.

Physio: Dave Moore.

General Manager/Secretary: Michael Spinks. ***Sales and Marketing Manager:*** Graham Barlow.

Colours: Red shirts, white shorts, red stockings.

Change Colours: (To be announced.)

Year Formed: 1887. ***Turned Professional:*** 1888. ***Ltd Co.:*** 1899.

Previous Name: 1887, Barnsley St Peter's; 1897, Barnsley.

Club Nickname: 'The Tykes', 'Reds' or 'Colliers'.

First Football League Game: 1 September 1898, Division 2, v Lincoln C (a) L 0–1 – Fawcett; McArtney, Nixon; King, Burleigh, Porteous; Davis, Lees, Murray, McCullough, McGee.

Record League Victory: 9–0 v Loughborough T, Division 2, 28 January 1899 – Greaves; McArtney, Nixon; Porteous, Burleigh, Howard; Davis (4), Hepworth (1), Lees (1), McCullough (1), Jones (2). 9–0 v Accrington S, Division 3 (N), 3 February 1934 – Ellis; Cookson, Shotton; Harper, Henderson, Whitworth; Spence (2), Smith (1), Blight (4), Andrews (1), Ashton (1).

Record Cup Victory: 6–0 v Blackpool, FA Cup 1st rd replay, 20 January 1910 – Mearns; Downs, Ness; Glendinning, Boyle (1), Utley; Bartrop, Gadsby (1), Lillycrop (2), Tufnell (2), Forman. 6–0 v Peterborough U, League Cup 1st rd 2nd leg, 15 September 1981 – Horn; Joyce, Chambers, Glavin (2), Banks, McCarthy, Evans, Parker (2), Aylott (1), McHale, Barrowclough (1).

Record Defeat: 0–9 v Notts Co, Division 2, 19 November 1927.

HONOURS

Football League: Division 1 – Runners-up 1996–97; Division 3 (N) – Champions 1933–34, 1938–39, 1954–55; Runners-up 1953–54; Division 3 – Runners-up 1980–81; Division 4 – Runners-up 1967–68; Promoted 1978–79.

FA Cup: Winners 1912; Runners-up 1910.

Football League Cup: best season: 5th rd, 1982.

SKY SPORTS FACT FILE

Goalkeeper Harry Hough, signed from Thorncliffe Welfare in September 1947, went on to make 364 League and Cup appearances for Barnsley, though initially second choice to Pat Kelly. He missed England B honours with a broken arm.

Most League Points (2 for a win): 67, Division 3 (N), 1938–39.

Most League Points (3 for a win): 82, Division 1, 1999–2000.

Most League Goals: 118, Division 3 (N), 1933–34.

Highest League Scorer in Season: Cecil McCormack, 33, Division 2, 1950–51.

Most League Goals in Total Aggregate: Ernest Hine, 123, 1921–26 and 1934–38.

Most League Goals in One Match: 5, Frank Eaton v South Shields, Division 3N, 9 April 1927; 5, Peter Cunningham v Darlington, Division 3N, 4 February 1933; 5, Beau Asquith v Darlington, Division 3N, 12 November 1938; 5, Cecil McCormack v Luton T, Division 2, 9 September 1950.

Most Capped Player: Gerry Taggart, 35 (50), Northern Ireland.

Most League Appearances: Barry Murphy, 514, 1962–78.

Youngest League Player: Alan Ogley, 16 years 226 days v Bristol R, 18 September 1962.

Record Transfer Fee Received: £4,250,000 from Blackburn R for Ashley Ward, December 1998.

Record Transfer Fee Paid: £1,500,000 to Partizan Belgrade for Georgi Hristov, June 1997.

Football League Record: 1898 Elected to Division 2; 1932–34 Division 3 (N); 1934–38 Division 2; 1938–39 Division 3 (N); 1946–53 Division 2; 1953–55 Division 3 (N); 1955–59 Division 2; 1959–65 Division 3; 1965–68 Division 4; 1968–72 Division 3; 1972–79 Division 4; 1979–81 Division 3; 1981–92 Division 2; 1992–97 Division 1; 1997–98 FA Premier League; 1998–2002 Division 1; 2002– Division 2.

MANAGERS

Arthur Fairclough 1898–1901 *(Secretary-Manager)*
John McCartney 1901–04 *(Secretary-Manager)*
Arthur Fairclough 1904–12
John Hastie 1912–14
Percy Lewis 1914–19
Peter Sant 1919–26
John Commins 1926–29
Arthur Fairclough 1929–30
Brough Fletcher 1930–37
Angus Seed 1937–53
Tim Ward 1953–60
Johnny Steele 1960–71 *(continued as General Manager)*
John McSeveney 1971–72
Johnny Steele *(General Manager)* 1972–73
Jim Iley 1973–78
Allan Clarke 1978–80
Norman Hunter 1980–84
Bobby Collins 1984–85
Allan Clarke 1985–89
Mel Machin 1989–93
Viv Anderson 1993–94
Danny Wilson 1994–98
John Hendrie 1998–99
Dave Bassett 1999–2000
Nigel Spackman 2001
Steve Parkin 2001–02
Glyn Hodges 2002–2003
Gudjon Thordarson July 2003–

LATEST SEQUENCES

Longest Sequence of League Wins: 10, 5.3.1955 – 23.4.1955.

Longest Sequence of League Defeats: 9, 14.3.1953 – 25.4.1953.

Longest Sequence of League Draws: 7, 28.3.1911 – 22.4.1911.

Longest Sequence of Unbeaten League Matches: 21, 1.1.1934 – 5.5.1934.

Longest Sequence Without a League Win: 26, 13.12.1952 – 26.8.1953.

Successive Scoring Runs: 44 from 2.10.1926.

Successive Non-scoring Runs: 6 from 7.10.1899.

TEN YEAR LEAGUE RECORD

		P	W	D	L	F	A	Pts	Pos
1993-94	Div 1	46	16	7	23	55	67	55	18
1994-95	Div 1	46	20	12	14	63	52	72	6
1995-96	Div 1	46	14	18	14	60	66	60	10
1996-97	Div 1	46	22	14	10	76	55	80	2
1997-98	PR Lge	38	10	5	23	37	82	35	19
1998-99	Div 1	46	14	17	15	59	56	59	13
1999-2000	Div 1	46	24	10	12	88	67	82	4
2000-01	Div 1	46	15	9	22	49	62	54	16
2001-02	Div 1	46	11	15	20	59	86	48	23
2002-03	Div 2	46	13	13	20	51	64	52	19

DID YOU KNOW ?

Inside-forward Cecil McCormack had scored 42 League goals in only 50 matches by 1951 when Barnsley had to accept a £20,000 offer for his services from Notts County. The ex-Middlesbrough player had been playing for Chelmsford City previously.

BARNSLEY 2002–03 LEAGUE RECORD

Match No.	Date	Venue	Opponents	Result		H/T Score	Lg. Pos.	Goalscorers	Attendance
1	Aug 10	A	Swindon T	L	1-3	1-1	—	Lumsdon (pen) 30	5702
2	13	H	Cheltenham T	D	1-1	0-0	—	Dyer 51	9641
3	17	H	QPR	W	1-0	0-0	13	Lumsdon 57	9626
4	24	A	Luton T	W	3-2	2-1	10	Perrett (og) 20, Sheron 43, Dyer 58	6230
5	26	H	Notts Co	D	0-0	0-0	9		10,431
6	31	A	Northampton T	L	0-1	0-0	15		5004
7	Sept 7	A	Huddersfield T	L	0-1	0-0	16		11,989
8	14	H	Plymouth Arg	D	1-1	1-1	16	Dyer 10	9134
9	17	H	Blackpool	W	2-1	1-1	—	Sheron 31, Fallon 76	9619
10	21	A	Stockport Co	L	1-4	1-0	14	Fallon 28	5690
11	28	H	Wigan Ath	L	1-3	0-2	17	Betsy 66	9977
12	Oct 5	A	Brentford	W	2-1	1-1	16	Betsy 2 14, 81	5394
13	12	H	Bristol C	L	1-4	0-2	17	Bertos 49	10,495
14	19	A	Tranmere R	L	0-1	0-1	20		6855
15	26	H	Wycombe W	D	1-1	1-1	20	Fallon 33	10,044
16	29	A	Colchester U	D	1-1	1-1	—	Dyer 15	3096
17	Nov 2	A	Chesterfield	L	0-1	0-1	21		4676
18	9	H	Cardiff C	W	3-2	2-2	17	Morgan 2 22, 64, Fallon 30	10,894
19	23	A	Peterborough U	W	3-1	2-0	15	Sheron 2 35, 38, Dyer 90	4449
20	30	H	Oldham Ath	D	2-2	1-1	16	Sheron 28, Dyer 89	11,222
21	Dec 14	A	Crewe Alex	L	0-2	0-1	19		5633
22	21	H	Mansfield T	L	0-1	0-0	19		10,495
23	26	A	Notts Co	L	2-3	1-1	20	Betsy 1, Dyer 62	7413
24	28	H	Port Vale	W	2-1	1-1	16	Fallon 12, Gibbs (pen) 79	9291
25	Jan 1	H	Northampton T	L	1-2	1-1	18	Lumsdon 24	9531
26	11	A	QPR	L	0-1	0-1	20		11,217
27	18	H	Luton T	L	2-3	1-1	22	Betsy 1, Dyer (pen) 76	9079
28	25	A	Port Vale	D	0-0	0-0	20		4033
29	Feb 1	H	Swindon T	D	1-1	1-1	20	Fallon 14	8661
30	8	A	Cardiff C	D	1-1	0-0	22	Dyer (pen) 52	12,759
31	15	H	Chesterfield	W	2-1	2-1	19	Fallon 20, Dyer 33	9373
32	18	A	Cheltenham T	W	3-1	1-1	—	Sheron 18, Dyer 63, Jones Gary 90	3568
33	22	H	Huddersfield T	L	0-1	0-1	15		12,474
34	Mar 1	A	Plymouth Arg	D	1-1	0-1	18	Dyer 66	8228
35	4	A	Blackpool	W	2-1	1-0	—	Sheron 2 41, 62	6827
36	8	H	Stockport Co	W	1-0	1-0	15	Dyer 10	9177
37	15	A	Wycombe W	D	2-2	0-1	16	Sheron 76, Dyer 86	5931
38	18	H	Tranmere R	D	1-1	1-0	—	Dyer 8	8786
39	22	H	Colchester U	D	1-1	1-1	14	Dyer 36	9154
40	29	A	Bristol C	L	0-2	0-1	16		10,232
41	Apr 5	A	Oldham Ath	L	1-2	1-1	16	Mulligan 21	6191
42	12	H	Peterborough U	L	1-2	1-0	19	Dyer (pen) 15	8862
43	19	A	Mansfield T	W	1-0	1-0	18	O'Callaghan 31	4873
44	21	H	Crewe Alex	L	1-2	1-1	19	Ince (og) 33	9396
45	26	H	Brentford	W	1-0	0-0	19	Rankin 90	9065
46	May 3	A	Wigan Ath	L	0-1	0-1	19		12,537

Final League Position: 19

GOALSCORERS

League (51): Dyer 17 (3 pens), Sheron 9, Fallon 7, Betsy 5, Lumsdon 3 (1 pen), Morgan 2, Bertos 1, Gibbs 1 (pen), Jones Gary 1, Mulligan 1, O'Callaghan 1, Rankin 1, own goals 2.
Worthington Cup (1): Rankin 1.
FA Cup (1): Dyer 1.
LDV Vans Trophy (0).

Marriott A 36	Austin N 32 + 2	Gibbs P 23 + 3	Morgan C 36	Flynn M 13 + 1	Jones Gary 31	Lumsdon C 21 + 4	Betsy K 32 + 7	Sheron M 28 + 6	Dyer B 39 + 1	Gorre D 18 + 9	Bertos L 2 + 4	Crooks L 10 + 8	Ward M 22 + 4	Holt A 4 + 3	Curle K 11	Rankin I 1 + 8	Mulligan D 30 + 3	O'Callaghan B 12 + 2	Fallon R 18 + 8	Jones Griff — + 2	Williams R 7 + 1	Hayward S 6	Neil A 30 + 3	Barrowclough C — + 5	Donovan K 20 + 2	Kay A 13 + 3	Ghent M 7	Taylor M 3	Wroe N 1	*Match No.*
1	2	3	4	5	6	7^{1}	8	9	10	11	12																			1
1	2	3	4	5		7	8	9	10	11^{1}		6	12																	2
1	2	3	4			7	8	9^{1}	10	11				6	5	12														3
1	2	6	4			7^{1}	8	9^{2}	10^{3}	11		12		3■	5	13	14													4
1	2	6^{2}	4			7	8	9^{1}	10	11				3	5	12	13													5
1	2	6^{3}	4^{1}	12		7	8	9	10	11^{2}		13		3	5	14														6
1	2^{2}	3			6^{1}	7	8	9^{3}	10		14		13		5	12	11	4												7
1		3		5	8	12	7	9^{1}	10^{2}				4	13	6	11^{3}	2		14											8
1		3		5	7	12	8	9		11^{1}			6	13	4		2		10^{2}											9
1		3^{3}		5	11	12	8	9		7^{1}			4	14	6		2^{2}	13	10											10
1		3		5	6	12	8	9^{2}		11			7■		4		2		10^{1}	13										11
1	2		4		11		8		10^{1}	12			6■		5				9		3	7								12
1	2		4		6^{1}	7	8		10^{2}	11	12				5				9^{3}	13	3		14							13
1		3^{2}	4			7	8		12	11^{1}	5						2	6	9		13		10							14
1		3	4		6^{3}	7	8	12	10	13	11^{2}						2	5	9^{1}				14							15
1		3	4			7	8		10	11			12				2^{1}	5	9				6							16
1	12	3	4			7^{2}	8	14	10	13			6				2	5^{1}	9^{3}				11							17
1	5	3	4			7	8		10			12	6				2^{1}		9				11							18
1		3	4	5	6	7	8	9^{1}	10								2		12				11							19
1		3	4	5	6	7	8	9	10	12							2						11^{1}							20
1		3		5	6	7			10	11		4					2		9				8^{1}	12						21
1		3^{2}	4	5	6	7^{1}	8	9	10	11							2^{3}	14	13				12							22
1		3	4	5	6		8		10									2	9			7^{1}	11		12					23
1	12	3	4	5			8		10	11								2^{1}	9^{2}			7	6	13						24
1	3		4	5		7	8	12	10^{1}	11								2	9^{2}				6^{3}	13		14				25
1	2	3	4		6		9		10^{1}			13						5^{2}	12			8	11	14	7^{3}					26
1	2		4		6		9		10			12						5^{1}	13		3	8	11^{2}	14	7^{3}					27
1	6		4		8				10			5					2		9		3	7^{1}	11		12					28
1	5		4		6^{3}			12	10	13		8	14				2		9^{1}		3		11		7^{2}					29
1	4				11			12	10^{1}			5	8				2		9				3		7	6				30
1	3				8			12	10^{1}			5	6				2		9				11		7	4				31
1	6		4		8			9	10			5	7				3						11		2					32
1	6		4					9^{2}	10	11	13	5^{3}	7			12	3^{1}						8		2	14				33
1	5		4		8		12	9	10				7								3		11		2^{1}	6				34
1	2	12	4		6		13	9	10^{2}				8				3^{1}						11		7	5				35
1	5		4		6		12	9^{1}	10			13	8^{2}				3						11		2	7				36
	5		4		6		12	9	10				8				3						11		7	2^{1}	1			37
	5		4		8		12	9	10			13	7^{2}				3^{1}						11		2	6	1			38
	5		4		8^{2}		7	9	10	12		13					3^{1}						11		2	6	1			39
	5		4		8		7	9	10^{1}	12			3^{2}				13						11		2	6		1		40
	5		4		8	7^{1}	12	9	10			6					3						11^{2}		2	13		1		41
	5		4		8		12	9	10			6	7^{1}				3						11		2			1		42
	2	12				11^{1}	8	9					6				3	5					10		7	4	1			43
	4	12				7^{3}	8	9		13			10^{2}				3	5	14				11		2^{1}	6	1			44
	4		5		8^{1}		10	9^{3}		12			7			13	3		14				11		2^{2}	6	1			45
	4		5				9		10^{1}	11^{2}			7			12			13		3				2	6	1		8	46

Worthington Cup
First Round Macclesfield T (a) 1-4

LDV Vans Trophy
Second Round Bury (a) 0-1

FA Cup
First Round Blackpool (h) 1-4

BIRMINGHAM CITY FA Premiership

FOUNDATION

In 1875, cricketing enthusiasts who were largely members of Trinity Church, Bordesley, determined to continue their sporting relationships throughout the year by forming a football club which they called Small Heath Alliance. For their earliest games played on waste land in Arthur Street, the team included three Edden brothers and two James brothers.

St Andrews, Birmingham B9 4NH.

Telephone: 0121 772 0101. ***Fax:*** (0121) 766 7866.
Website: www.bcfc.com ***ClubCall:*** 09068 121 188.
Club Soccer Shop: 0121 772 0101 (ext. 8).

Ground Capacity: 30,009.

Record Attendance: 66,844 v Everton, FA Cup 5th rd, 11 February 1939.

Record Receipts: £396,113 v Preston NE, (play off semi-final 1st leg), 13 May 2001.

Pitch Measurements: 110yd × 74yd.

Chairman: D. Gold. ***Vice-chairman:*** J. F. Wiseman.
Directors: D. Sullivan, R. Gold, B. Gold, H. Brandman.
Managing Director: K. R. Brady.

Manager: Steve Bruce. ***Coach:*** Mark Bowen.
Reserve Team Coach: Keith Bertschin.
Physio: John Pryce.

General Manager: John Benson.
Safety Officer: Brian Tew. ***Secretary:*** Julia Shelton.

Colours: Blue shirts, white shorts, blue and white stockings.

Change Colours: Yellow shirts, yellow shorts, yellow stockings.

Year Formed: 1875.

Turned Professional: 1885.

Ltd Co.: 1888.

Previous Names: 1875, Small Heath Alliance; 1888, dropped 'Alliance'; 1905, Birmingham; 1945, Birmingham City.

Club Nickname: 'Blues'.

Previous Grounds: 1875, waste ground near Arthur St; 1877, Muntz St, Small Heath; 1906, St Andrews.

First Football League game: 3 September 1892, Division 2, v Burslem Port Vale (h) W 5–1 – Charsley; Bayley, Speller; Ollis, Jenkyns, Devey; Hallam (1), Edwards (1), Short (1), Wheldon (2), Hands.

Record League Victory: 12–0 v Walsall T Swifts, Division 2, 17 December 1892 – Charsley; Bayley, Jones; Ollis, Jenkyns, Devey; Hallam (2), Walton (3), Mobley (3), Wheldon (2), Hands (2). 12–0 v Doncaster R, Division 2, 11 April 1903 – Dorrington; Goldie, Wassell; Beer, Dougherty (1), Howard; Athersmith (1), Leonard (3), McRoberts (1), Wilcox (4), Field (1). Aston, (1 og).

HONOURS

Football League: Promoted from Division 1 (play offs) 2001–02; Division 2 – Champions 1892–93, 1920–21, 1947–48, 1954–55, 1994–95; Runners-up 1893–94, 1900–01, 1902–03, 1971–72, 1984–85; Division 3 Runners-up 1991–92.

FA Cup: Runners-up 1931, 1956.

Football League Cup: Winners 1963; Runners-up 2001.

Leyland Daf Cup: Winners 1991.

Auto Windscreens Shield: Winners 1995.

European Competitions: *European Fairs Cup:* 1955–58, 1958–60 (runners-up), 1960–61 (runners-up), 1961–62.

SKY SPORTS FACT FILE

When Birmingham City won the Second Division championship in 1954–55 from both Luton Town and Rotherham United on 54 points, it was the first time the top three positions in the division had been thus decided by goal average.

Record Cup Victory: 9–2 v Burton W, FA Cup 1st rd, 31 October 1885 – Hedges; Jones, Evetts (1); F. James, Felton, A. James (1); Davenport (2), Stanley (4), Simms, Figures, Morris (1).

Record Defeat: 1–9 v Sheffield W, Division 1, 13 December 1930. 1–9 v Blackburn R, Division 1, 5 January 1895.

Most League Points (2 for a win): 59, Division 2, 1947–48.

Most League Points (3 for a win): 89, Division 2, 1994–95.

Most League Goals: 103, Division 2, 1893–94 (only 28 games).

Highest League Scorer in Season: Joe Bradford, 29, Division 1, 1927–28.

Most League Goals in Total Aggregate: Joe Bradford, 249, 1920–35.

Most League Goals in One Match: 5, Walter Abbott v Darwen, Division 2, 26 November, 1898; 5, John McMillan v Blackpool, Division 2, 2 March 1901; 5, James Windridge v Glossop, Division 2, 23 January 1915.

Most Capped Player: Malcolm Page, 28, Wales.

Most League Appearances: Frank Womack, 491, 1908–28.

Youngest League Player: Trevor Francis, 16 years 7 months v Cardiff C, 5 September 1970.

Record Transfer Fee Received: £3,500,000 from Leicester C for Gary Rowett, July 2000.

Record Transfer Fee Paid: £5,500,000 to Blackburn R for David Dunn, July 2003.

Football League Record: 1892 elected to Division 2; 1894–96 Division 1; 1896–1901 Division 2; 1901–02 Division 1; 1902–03 Division 2; 1903–08 Division 1; 1908–21 Division 2; 1921–39 Division 1; 1946–48 Division 2; 1948–50 Division 1; 1950–55 Division 2; 1955–65 Division 1; 1965–72 Division 2; 1972–79 Division 1; 1979–80 Division 2; 1980–84 Division 1; 1984–85 Division 2; 1985–86 Division 1; 1986–89 Division 2; 1989–92 Division 3; 1992–94 Division 1; 1994–95 Division 2; 1995–2002 Division 1; 2002– FA Premier League.

MANAGERS

Alfred Jones 1892–1908
(Secretary-Manager)
Alec Watson 1908–10
Bob McRoberts 1910–15
Frank Richards 1915–23
Billy Beer 1923–27
Leslie Knighton 1928–33
George Liddell 1933–39
Harry Storer 1945–48
Bob Brocklebank 1949–54
Arthur Turner 1954–58
Pat Beasley 1959–60
Gil Merrick 1960–64
Joe Mallett 1965
Stan Cullis 1965–70
Fred Goodwin 1970–75
Willie Bell 1975–77
Jim Smith 1978–82
Ron Saunders 1982–86
John Bond 1986–87
Garry Pendrey 1987–89
Dave Mackay 1989–91
Lou Macari 1991
Terry Cooper 1991–93
Barry Fry 1993–96
Trevor Francis 1996–2001
Steve Bruce December 2001–

LATEST SEQUENCES

Longest Sequence of League Wins: 13, 17.12.1892 – 16.9.1893.

Longest Sequence of League Defeats: 8, 28.9.1985 – 23.11.1985.

Longest Sequence of League Draws: 8, 18.9.1990 – 23.10.1990.

Longest Sequence of Unbeaten League Matches: 20, 3.9.1994 – 2.1.1995.

Longest Sequence Without a League Win: 17, 28.9.1985 – 18.1.1986.

Successive Scoring Runs: 24 from 24.9.1892.

Successive Non-scoring Runs: 6 from 1.10.1949.

TEN YEAR LEAGUE RECORD

		P	W	D	L	F	A	Pts	Pos
1993-94	Div 1	46	13	12	21	52	69	51	22
1994-95	Div 2	46	25	14	7	84	37	89	1
1995-96	Div 1	46	15	13	18	61	64	58	15
1996-97	Div 1	46	17	15	14	52	48	66	10
1997-98	Div 1	46	19	17	10	60	35	74	7
1998-99	Div 1	46	23	12	11	66	37	81	4
1999-2000	Div 1	46	22	11	13	65	44	77	5
2000-01	Div 1	46	23	9	14	59	48	78	5
2001-02	Div 1	46	21	13	12	70	49	76	5
2002-03	PR Lge	38	13	9	16	41	49	48	13

DID YOU KNOW?

Wombwell-born George Briggs, a utility forward, made over 300 League and Cup appearances for Birmingham and scored more than 100 goals in nine years from 1923 during their lengthy association with the First Division at the time.

BIRMINGHAM CITY 2002–03 LEAGUE RECORD

Match No.	Date	Venue	Opponents	Result	H/T Score	Lg. Pos.	Goalscorers	Attendance
1	Aug 18	A	Arsenal	L 0-2	0-2	—		38,018
2	24	H	Blackburn R	L 0-1	0-1	19		27,527
3	28	A	Everton	D 1-1	0-0	—	John (pen) 50	37,199
4	31	H	Leeds U	W 2-1	1-0	14	Devlin 32, Johnson D 58	27,364
5	Sept 11	A	Liverpool	D 2-2	0-1	—	Morrison 2 61, 90	43,113
6	16	H	Aston Villa	W 3-0	1-0	—	Morrison 31, Enckelman (og) 77, Horsfield 83	29,505
7	21	A	Middlesbrough	L 0-1	0-1	12		29,511
8	28	H	Newcastle U	L 0-2	0-1	14		29,072
9	Oct 5	A	West Ham U	W 2-1	2-1	12	John 2 4, 43	35,010
10	19	A	WBA	D 1-1	0-0	12	Moore (og) 86	26,914
11	26	H	Manchester C	L 0-2	0-1	13		29,316
12	Nov 2	H	Bolton W	W 3-1	0-0	12	Purse 61, Savage 73, Horsfield 83	27,224
13	9	A	Chelsea	L 0-3	0-3	15		35,227
14	17	H	Fulham	D 0-0	0-0	15		26,164
15	23	A	Sunderland	W 1-0	0-0	13	Morrison 89	38,803
16	30	H	Tottenham H	D 1-1	0-0	11	Kenna 68	29,505
17	Dec 7	A	Southampton	L 0-2	0-0	13		31,132
18	15	A	Fulham	W 1-0	1-0	13	Kirovski 7	14,692
19	21	H	Charlton Ath	D 1-1	0-1	13	Devlin (pen) 67	28,837
20	26	H	Everton	D 1-1	1-1	13	Kirovski 45	29,505
21	28	A	Manchester U	L 0-2	0-1	15		67,640
22	Jan 1	A	Leeds U	L 0-2	0-1	15		40,044
23	12	H	Arsenal	L 0-4	0-2	15		29,505
24	18	A	Blackburn R	D 1-1	0-1	16	John 83	23,331
25	Feb 1	A	Bolton W	L 2-4	1-1	16	Savage 44, Morrison 60	24,288
26	4	H	Manchester U	L 0-1	0-0	—		29,475
27	8	H	Chelsea	L 1-3	0-1	16	Savage (pen) 87	29,475
28	23	H	Liverpool	W 2-1	1-0	16	Clemence 34, Morrison 68	29,449
29	Mar 3	A	Aston Villa	W 2-0	0-0	—	Lazaridis 74, Horsfield 77	42,602
30	16	A	Manchester C	L 0-1	0-0	16		34,596
31	22	H	WBA	W 1-0	0-0	15	Horsfield 90	29,449
32	Apr 5	A	Tottenham H	L 1-2	0-1	17	Devlin (pen) 77	36,063
33	12	H	Sunderland	W 2-0	1-0	16	Hughes 43, Dugarry 60	29,132
34	19	A	Charlton Ath	W 2-0	1-0	15	Dugarry 20, Savage (pen) 55	25,699
35	21	H	Southampton	W 3-2	0-1	13	Dugarry 2 75, 82, Hughes 79	29,115
36	26	H	Middlesbrough	W 3-0	2-0	12	Dugarry 18, Clemence 40, Lazaridis 80	28,821
37	May 3	A	Newcastle U	L 0-1	0-1	13		52,146
38	11	H	West Ham U	D 2-2	0-0	13	Horsfield 80, John 88	29,449

Final League Position: 13

GOALSCORERS

League (41): Morrison 6, Dugarry 5, Horsfield 5, John 5 (1 pen), Savage 4 (2 pens), Devlin 3 (2 pens), Clemence 2, Hughes 2, Kirovski 2, Lazaridis 2, Johnson D 1, Kenna 1, Purse 1, own goals 2.
Worthington Cup (3): John 3.
FA Cup (1): John 1.

Vaesen N 27	Kenna J 36 + 1	Grainger M 8 + 1	Cunningham K 31	Purse D 19 + 1	Tebily O 12	Johnson D 28 + 2	Cisse A 21	Horsfield G 15 + 16	John S 20 + 10	Hughes B 10 + 12	Carter D 3 + 9	Lazaridis S 17 + 13	Mooney T — + 1	Savage R 33	Morrison C 24 + 4	Devlin P 20 + 12	Powell D 3 + 8	Kirovski J 5 + 12	Vickers S 5	Woodhouse C — + 3	Sadler M 2	Fagan C — + 1	Johnson M 5 + 1	Hutchinson J 1	Coly F 1	Clemence S 15	Dugarry C 16	Clapham J 16	Bennett I 10	Upson M 14	Swierczewski P — + 1	Marriott A 1	Match No.
1	2	3	4	5	6^{2}	7	8■	9^{1}	10	11	13	12																					1
1		3^{1}	4	5	2	7	8	9^{2}	10	6	11	12	13																				2
1	12	3	4	5	2^{1}	7	11	9^{3}	10	6^{2}	13			8	14																		3
1	2	3	4	5		7	11	12	10^{3}	13		14		8	9^{1}	6^{2}																	4
1	2	3	4	5		11^{2}		12	10^{3}	6^{1}	14	13		8	9	7																	5
1	2	3	4	5		11	6	12	10	13				8^{2}	9^{1}	7^{3}	14																6
1	2^{3}	3^{2}	4	5		11	6	12	10^{1}			13		8	9	7		14															7
1	2		4	5^{2}		11	6	12	10^{1}		3^{3}			8	9	7	13	14															8
1	2		4	5		3	6	12	10^{1}			11^{2}		8	9	7	13																9
1	2				5■			12	10^{3}	13	3	11		8	9	7^{1}	6		4^{2}	14													10
1	2^{2}			5	4		6	12	10	13		11		8	9	7^{1}	3^{3}	14															11
1	2		4	5			6	12	10^{3}	13		11^{1}		8^{2}	9	7	14				3												12
1	3		4	5	2		6	12	10^{3}	14		13		8	9^{1}	7	11^{2}																13
1	3		4	5	2^{2}		6	9	10^{1}	13		11		8^{3}	12	7		14															14
1	3		4	5	2	12	6		10	14		11		8^{2}	9	7^{1}	13^{3}																15
1	3		4	5	2	12	6		10^{2}	13		11^{3}		8	9	7^{1}		14															16
1	3		4	5	2	7^{2}	6^{3}		10	8^{1}	13	11			9			12				14											17
1	3		4	5■	2	11^{1}	6	9^{2}		13				8	10		14	7^{3}		12													18
1	3^{1}		4		2	11^{2}	6	9■				12		8	10	13		7	5														19
1	2		4			11^{1}	6	9^{2}		13		12		8	14	7		10^{3}	5				3										20
1	2		4^{2}				6	12				11^{1}		8	9	7	13	10		14	3^{3}		5										21
1	2	3^{2}				11	6	12						8	9	7	13	10					5^{1}	4									22
1	3	12				7			10						8		13		14	4				5		2^{1}	6^{2}	9^{3}	11					23
	2^{1}					7	6		12			11		8	9	13		14	4^{2}				5^{3}				10	3	1				24
	2		4						12			11		8	9	7^{2}		13								6	10^{1}	3	1	5			25
1	2^{2}		4			7			11^{1}			12		8	9^{3}	13		14								6	10	3		5			26
1	2^{3}		4			7		9^{1}				11		8	12	13										6	10^{2}	3		5	14		27
1	2		4			7		12			13	11		8	9^{3}	14										6^{2}	10^{1}	3		5			28
1	2		4			7		12			13	11^{3}		8^{2}	9^{1}	14										6	10	3		5			29
	2^{3}		4			7^{2}		12	13			11		8	9^{1}	14										6	10	3	1	5			30
	2^{3}		4			11		13	12		14			8	9^{2}	7										6^{1}	10	3	1	5			31
	2^{3}		4			11		9	8^{1}		14	12				7		13								6	10^{2}	3		5		1	32
	2		4					9	12	8^{2}	14	11				7^{1}		13								6	10^{1}	3	1	5			33
	2		4	12		7^{1}		9^{3}	13	11				8		14										6	10^{2}	3	1	5			34
	2^{3}		4			7^{1}		9	12	11		13		8		14										6^{2}	10	3	1	5			35
	2		4			7		9^{3}	12	11^{2}		13		8		14										6	10^{1}	3	1	5			36
	2^{3}			4		7		9	12	11		13		8^{2}									14			6	10^{1}	3	1	5■			37
	2^{3}			4		7		9	12	13		11^{2}		8		14										6	10^{1}	3	1	5			38

Worthington Cup

Second Round	Leyton Orient	(a)	3-2
Third Round	Preston NE	(h)	0-2

FA Cup

Third Round	Fulham	(a)	1-3

BLACKBURN ROVERS FA Premiership

FOUNDATION

It was in 1875 that some Public School old boys called a meeting at which the Blackburn Rovers club was formed and the colours blue and white adopted. The leading light was John Lewis, later to become a founder of the Lancashire FA, a famous referee who was in charge of two FA Cup Finals, and a vice-president of both the FA and the Football League.

Ewood Park, Blackburn BB2 4JF.

Telephone: 08701 113 232. ***Fax:*** (01254) 671 042.
Website: www.rovers.co.uk ***Email:*** enquiries@rovers.co.uk
Ticket Hotline: 08701 123 456. ***ClubCall:*** 09068 121 179.
Mail Order: 08701 123 456. ***Club Shop:*** (01254) 665 606.

Ground Capacity: 31,367.

Record Attendance: 62,522 v Bolton W, FA Cup 6th rd, 2 March 1929.

Record Receipts: £438,868 (gross) v Newcastle U, FA Cup 5th rd, 31 January 2000.

Pitch Measurements: 115yd × 72yd.

Chairman: R. D. Coar BSC.
Vice-chairman: R. L. Matthewman.
Directors: R. D. Coar BSC, R. L. Matthewman, J. O. Williams BSC (Chief Executive), Tom Finn, K. C. Lee, G. R. Root, I. R. Stanners, D. M. Brown.

Manager: Graeme Souness. ***Physio:*** Dave Fevre.
Assistant Manager: Tony Parkes. ***Coach:*** Dean Saunders.

Commercial Manager: Ken Beamish.

Secretary: Tom Finn. ***Stadium Manager:*** J. Newsham.

Colours: Blue and white halved shirts, white shorts with navy blue strip, white stockings with navy blue trim.

Change Colours: Golden amber shirts with black trim, black shorts with golden amber trim, golden amber and black hooped stockings.

Year Formed: 1875.

Turned Professional: 1880.

Ltd Co.: 1897.

Club Nickname: Rovers.

Previous Grounds: 1875, all matches played away; 1876, Oozehead Ground; 1877, Pleasington Cricket Ground; 1878, Alexandra Meadows; 1881, Leamington Road; 1890, Ewood Park.

First Football League Game: 15 September 1888, Football League, v Accrington (h) D 5–5 – Arthur; Beverley, James Southworth; Douglas, Almond, Forrest; Beresford (1), Walton, John Southworth (1), Fecitt (1), Townley (2).

HONOURS

FA Premier League: Champions 1994–95; Runners-up 1993–94.

Football League: Division 1 – Champions 1911–12, 1913–14; 1991–92 (play-offs); Runners-up 2000–01; Division 2 – Champions 1938–39; Runners-up 1957–58; Division 3 – Champions 1974–75; Runners-up 1979–80.

FA Cup: Winners 1884, 1885, 1886, 1890, 1891, 1928; Runners-up 1882, 1960.

Football League Cup: Winners 2002.

Full Members' Cup: Winners 1987.

European Competitions: *European Cup:* 1995–96. *UEFA Cup:* 1994–95, 1998–99, 2002–03.

SKY SPORTS FACT FILE

Blackburn Rovers have been responsible for the following clubs' heaviest defeats: Aston Villa, Birmingham City, Bury, Manchester United, Middlesbrough, Nottingham Forest, Notts County and West Ham United.

Record League Victory: 9–0 v Middlesbrough, Division 2, 6 November 1954 – Elvy; Suart, Eckersley; Clayton, Kelly, Bell; Mooney (3), Crossan (2), Briggs, Quigley (3), Langton (1).

Record Cup Victory: 11–0 v Rossendale, FA Cup 1st rd, 13 October 1884 – Arthur; Hopwood, McIntyre; Forrest, Blenkhorn, Lofthouse; Sowerbutts (2), J. Brown (1), Fecitt (4), Barton (3), Birtwistle (1).

Record Defeat: 0–8 v Arsenal, Division 1, 25 February 1933.

Most League Points (2 for a win): 60, Division 3, 1974–75.

Most League Points (3 for a win): 91, Division 1, 2000–01.

Most League Goals: 114, Division 2, 1954–55.

Highest League Scorer in Season: Ted Harper, 43, Division 1, 1925–26.

Most League Goals in Total Aggregate: Simon Garner, 168, 1978–92.

Most League Goals in One Match: 7, Tommy Briggs v Bristol R, Division 2, 5 February 1953.

Most Capped Player: Henning Berg, 58 (96), Norway.

Most League Appearances: Derek Fazackerley, 596, 1970–86.

Youngest League Player: Harry Dennison, 16 years 155 days v Bristol C, 8 April 1911.

Record Transfer Fee Received: £15,000,000 from Newcastle U for Alan Shearer, July 1996.

Record Transfer Fee Paid: £7,500,000 to Manchester U for Andy Cole, December 2001.

Football League Record: 1888 Founder Member of the League; 1936–39 Division 2; 1946–48 Division 1; 1948–58 Division 2; 1958–66 Division 1; 1966–71 Division 2; 1971–75 Division 3; 1975–79 Division 2; 1979–80 Division 3; 1980–92 Division 2; 1992–99 FA Premier League; 1999–2001 Division 1; 2001– FA Premier League.

MANAGERS

Thomas Mitchell 1884–96
(Secretary-Manager)
J. Walmsley 1896–1903
(Secretary-Manager)
R. B. Middleton 1903–25
Jack Carr 1922–26
(Team Manager under Middleton to 1925)
Bob Crompton 1926–30
(Hon. Team Manager)
Arthur Barritt 1931–36
(had been Secretary from 1927)
Reg Taylor 1936–38
Bob Crompton 1938–41
Eddie Hapgood 1944–47
Will Scott 1947
Jack Bruton 1947–49
Jackie Bestall 1949–53
Johnny Carey 1953–58
Dally Duncan 1958–60
Jack Marshall 1960–67
Eddie Quigley 1967–70
Johnny Carey 1970–71
Ken Furphy 1971–73
Gordon Lee 1974–75
Jim Smith 1975–78
Jim Iley 1978
John Pickering 1978–79
Howard Kendall 1979–81
Bobby Saxton 1981–86
Don Mackay 1987–91
Kenny Dalglish 1991–95
Ray Harford 1995–97
Roy Hodgson 1997–98
Brian Kidd 1998–99
Tony Parkes 1999–2000
Graeme Souness March 2000–

LATEST SEQUENCES

Longest Sequence of League Wins: 8, 1.3.1980 – 7.4.1980.

Longest Sequence of League Defeats: 7, 12.3.1966 – 16.4.1966.

Longest Sequence of League Draws: 5, 11.10.1975 – 1.11.1975.

Longest Sequence of Unbeaten League Matches: 23, 30.9.1987 – 27.3.1988.

Longest Sequence Without a League Win: 16, 11.11.1978 – 24.3.1979.

Successive Scoring Runs: 32 from 24.4.1954.

Successive Non-scoring Runs: 4 from 12.12.1908.

TEN YEAR LEAGUE RECORD

		P	W	D	L	F	A	Pts	Pos
1993-94	PR Lge	42	25	9	8	63	36	84	2
1994-95	PR Lge	42	27	8	7	80	39	89	1
1995-96	PR Lge	38	18	7	13	61	47	61	7
1996-97	PR Lge	38	9	15	14	42	43	42	13
1997-98	PR Lge	38	16	10	12	57	52	58	6
1998-99	PR Lge	38	7	14	17	38	52	35	19
1999-2000	Div 1	46	15	17	14	55	51	62	11
2000-01	Div 1	46	26	13	7	76	39	91	2
2001-02	PR Lge	38	12	10	16	55	51	46	10
2002-03	PR Lge	38	16	12	10	52	43	60	6

DID YOU KNOW ?

On 28 December 2002 Andy Cole became the second FA Premier League player to reach 150 goals in the competition, scoring once in the 2-2 draw with West Ham United. He had previously registered goals with Newcastle United and Manchester United.

BLACKBURN ROVERS 2002–03 LEAGUE RECORD

Match No.	Date	Venue	Opponents	Result		H/T Score	Lg. Pos.	Goalscorers	Attendance
1	Aug 17	H	Sunderland	D	0-0	0-0	—		27,122
2	24	A	Birmingham C	W	1-0	1-0	9	Yorke [13]	27,527
3	28	H	Liverpool	D	2-2	1-1	—	Dunn [16], Grabbi [83]	29,207
4	31	A	Middlesbrough	L	0-1	0-0	10		28,270
5	Sept 11	H	Chelsea	L	2-3	2-1	—	Dunn (pen) [18], Thompson [45]	22,999
6	15	A	Manchester C	D	2-2	1-0	13	Thompson [26], Cole [54]	34,130
7	22	H	Leeds U	W	1-0	1-0	9	Flitcroft [24]	25,415
8	30	A	WBA	W	2-0	0-0	—	Yorke (pen) [72], Duff [76]	25,090
9	Oct 6	H	Tottenham H	L	1-2	0-1	10	Ostenstad [59]	26,203
10	19	H	Newcastle U	W	5-2	2-1	8	Dunn 2 (1 pen) [5 (p), 8], Taylor Martin 2 [55, 74], Griffin (og) [65]	27,307
11	26	A	Arsenal	W	2-1	1-1	7	Edu (og) [6], Yorke [51]	38,064
12	Nov 3	H	Aston Villa	D	0-0	0-0	7		23,044
13	9	A	Southampton	D	1-1	0-1	7	Cole [90]	30,059
14	17	H	Everton	L	0-1	0-1	8		26,494
15	24	A	Charlton Ath	L	1-3	0-0	9	Thompson [60]	26,137
16	30	H	Fulham	W	2-1	1-0	9	Yorke [35], Brevett (og) [77]	21,096
17	Dec 7	A	Bolton W	D	1-1	0-1	10	Short [90]	24,556
18	14	A	Everton	L	1-2	1-2	10	Cole [6]	36,578
19	22	H	Manchester U	W	1-0	1-0	9	Flitcroft [40]	30,475
20	26	A	Liverpool	D	1-1	0-1	10	Cole [77]	43,075
21	28	H	West Ham U	D	2-2	1-1	11	Duff [4], Cole [78]	24,998
22	Jan 1	H	Middlesbrough	W	1-0	0-0	8	Yorke [57]	23,413
23	11	A	Sunderland	D	0-0	0-0	10		36,529
24	18	H	Birmingham C	D	1-1	1-0	9	Duff [19]	23,331
25	29	A	West Ham U	L	1-2	1-0	—	Yorke [38]	34,743
26	Feb 2	A	Aston Villa	L	0-3	0-2	12		29,171
27	8	H	Southampton	W	1-0	1-0	11	Thompson [26]	24,896
28	22	A	Chelsea	W	2-1	0-0	9	Yorke [86], Dunn [90]	40,873
29	Mar 1	H	Manchester C	W	1-0	1-0	8	Dunn [13]	28,647
30	15	H	Arsenal	W	2-0	1-0	7	Duff [22], Tugay [52]	29,840
31	22	A	Newcastle U	L	1-5	0-1	8	Duff [54]	52,106
32	Apr 7	A	Fulham	W	4-0	2-0	—	Dunn (pen) [37], Sukur 2 [42, 54], Duff [53]	14,019
33	12	H	Charlton Ath	W	1-0	1-0	7	Duff [34]	27,506
34	19	A	Manchester U	L	1-3	1-2	7	Berg [24]	67,626
35	21	H	Bolton W	D	0-0	0-0	7		28,862
36	26	A	Leeds U	W	3-2	1-1	7	Dunn (pen) [38], Cole [69], Todd [78]	38,122
37	May 3	H	WBA	D	1-1	1-0	7	Duff [11]	27,470
38	11	A	Tottenham H	W	4-0	2-0	6	Yorke [5], Hignett [45], Duff [48], Cole [60]	36,036

Final League Position: 6

GOALSCORERS

League (52): Duff 9, Dunn 8 (4 pens), Yorke 8 (1 pen), Cole 7, Thompson 4, Flitcroft 2, Sukur 2, Taylor Martin 2, Berg 1, Grabbi 1, Hignett 1, Ostenstad 1, Short 1, Todd 1, Tugay 1, own goals 3.
Worthington Cup (10): Cole 4, Yorke 2, Duff 1, Grabbi 1 (pen), Thompson 1, own goal 1.
FA Cup (9): Yorke 3, Cole 2, Flitcroft 2, Jansen 2.
UEFA Cup (4): Duff 1, Grabbi 1, Ostenstad 1, Thompson 1.

Friedel B 37	Neill L 34	Johansson N 20 + 10	Short C 26 + 1	Taylor Martin 29 + 4	Tugay K 32 + 5	Gillespie K 10 + 15	Dunn D 26 + 2	Cole A 32 + 2	Yorke D 25 + 8	Duff D 26	Hignett C 1 + 2	Flitcroft G 33	Berg H 15 + 1	Grabbi C 1 + 10	Thompson D 23	Mahon A — + 2	Ostenstad E 8 + 9	Danns N 1 + 1	Jansen M — + 7	Curtis J 5	Todd A 7 + 5	Kelly A 1	Douglas J — + 1	McEveley J 9	Gresko V 10	Sukur H 7 + 2	Gallagher P — + 1	*Match No.*
1	2	3	4	5	6	7[1]	8	9	10	11	12																	1
1	2	3	4	5	6[1]		7	9	10	11		8	12															2
1	2	3	4[1]	5	6		7	9	10	11		8		12														3
1	2	3	4	5	12		6	9	10	11		8			7[1]													4
1	2	3[2]	4	5	6[1]	12	11	9	10			8		13	7													5
1	2		4	3	12	7[3]	6	9[2]	10			8	5	13	11[1]	14												6
1	2		4	3	6	7	10[2]					8	5	12	11		9[1]	13										7
1	2	6		3	4	12	10[1]	13	14	11		8[2]	5		7		9[3]											8
1	2	3		4	6	12	10[2]	9[3]		11		8	5[1]	13	7		14											9
1	2	3		4	12	7[1]	6		10[3]			8	5	13	11		9[2]		14									10
1	2	3	12	4	6[2]	13	11[3]		10			8■	5		7		9[1]		14									11
1	2	3	4	5[1]	12	13	6[2]	9	10[3]	11		8			7		14											12
1	2		4	5[2]	6■	7	8	9	10						11		12			3[1]	13							13
1	2	5	4		6		8	9	12	11					7		10			3[1]								14
	2	5	4			12	8	9	13	11				14	7[1]		10[2]			3[3]	6	1						15
1	2	3	4		6		8[1]	9	10	11					7						5		12					16
1	2	12	4	5	13		6[2]	9	10	11		8			7									3[1]				17
1	2■	12	4	5	6	13		9	10	11		8[1]			7									3[2]				18
1	2	3	4	5	6	12	7[1]	9	10	11		8																19
1	2	3[1]	4	5	6			9	10	11		8			7		12											20
1		3	4[3]	5	6	12		9	13	11[1]		8			7		10			2[2]	14							21
1	2	6		5	4	12		9	10[2]			8			11		13	7[1]			14			3[3]				22
1	2[3]	3		5	6	12		9	10	11[2]		8			7[1]	14			13		4							23
1	2	12		5	6			9[2]	10[1]	11		8			7				13		4■			3				24
1	2	12		5	6	7[1]		9	10[2]			8			11		13		14		4			3[3]				25
1		4		5	6	12		9	10			8			7[1]		13		14	2[2]				3	11[3]			26
1	2	12	4	13	6[1]	7[3]		9	10[2]			8	5		11		14								3			27
1	2	11[1]	4		6	12	7	9[3]	13			8	5	10[2]			14								3			28
1	2	12		4	6	7[2]	11	9				8	5				10[3]				13			3[1]		14		29
1		12	4	2	6	7			10[2]	11[1]		8	5												3	9	13	30
1			4	2	6[3]	7[1]	12	13	10[2]	11		8	5	14											3	9		31
1	2[1]		4	12	6[2]	13[3]	7	9		11		8	5	14											3	10		32
1	2		4		6[1]	12	7	9	13	11[3]		8	5	14											3	10[2]		33
1	2		4	12	6		7	9	10	11[2]		8	5[1]												3	13		34
1	2		4	12	6		7	9		11		8	5[1]												3	10		35
1	2	12	4[3]	5	6		7[1]	9	13	11		8									14				3	10[2]		36
1	2	12		5	6		7	9	13	11	14	8[3]									4			3[1]		10[2]		37
1	2	12		5	6		13	9	10	11	7[3]	8[2]							14		4			3[1]				38

Worthington Cup

Third Round	Walsall	(h)	2-2
Fourth Round	Rotherham U	(h)	4-0
Fifth Round	Wigan Ath	(a)	2-0
Semi-final	Manchester U	(a)	1-1
		(h)	1-3

UEFA Cup

First Round	CSKA Sofia	(h)	1-1
		(a)	3-3
Second Round	Celtic	(a)	0-1
		(h)	0-2

FA Cup

Third Round	Aston Villa	(a)	4-1
Fourth Round	Sunderland	(h)	3-3
		(a)	2-2

BLACKPOOL — Division 2

FOUNDATION

Old boys of St John's School who had formed themselves into a football club decided to establish a club bearing the name of their town and Blackpool FC came into being at a meeting at the Stanley Arms Hotel in the summer of 1887. In their first season playing at Raikes Hall Gardens, the club won both the Lancashire Junior Cup and the Fylde Cup.

Bloomfield Road Ground, Seasiders Way, Blackpool FY1 6JJ.

Telephone: 0870 4431953.
Fax: (01253) 405 011. ***Website:*** www.blackpoolfc.co.uk
Email: info@blackpoolfc.co.uk ***ClubCall:*** 09068 121 648

Ground Capacity: 11,000.

Record Attendance: 38,098 v Wolverhampton W, Division 1, 17 September 1955.

Record Receipts: £132,904 v Crystal Palace, FA Cup 3rd rd, January 2003.

Pitch Measurements: 112yd × 74yd.

Chairman: Mr K. Oyston.

Directors: C. Muir OBE, G. Warburton, P. Smith, P. Whitehead.

Manager: Steve McMahon.

Secretary: Peter Collins.

Commercial Director: Geoff Warburton.

Physio: Phil Horner.

Stadium Manager: John Turner.

Colours: Tangerine shirts, white shorts, tangerine stockings.

Change Colours: White shirts, tangerine shorts, white stockings.

Year Formed: 1887.

Turned Professional: 1887.

Ltd Co.: 1896.

Previous Name: 'South Shore' combined with Blackpool in 1899, twelve years after the latter had been formed on the breaking up of the old 'Blackpool St John's' club.

Club Nickname: 'The Seasiders'.

Previous Grounds: 1887, Raikes Hall Gardens; 1897, Athletic Grounds; 1899, Raikes Hall Gardens; 1899, Bloomfield Road.

First Football League game: 5 September 1896, Division 2, v Lincoln C (a) L 1–3 – Douglas; Parr, Bowman; Stuart, Stirzaker, Norris; Clarkin, Donnelly, R. Parkinson, Mount (1), J. Parkinson.

HONOURS

Football League: Division 1 – Runners-up 1955–56; Division 2 – Champions 1929–30; Runners-up 1936–37, 1969–70; Promoted from Division 3 – 2000–01 (play-offs); Division 4 – Runners-up 1984–85.

FA Cup: Winners 1953; Runners-up 1948, 1951.

Football League Cup: Semi-final 1962.

Anglo-Italian Cup: Winners 1971; Runners-up 1972.

LDV Vans Trophy: Winners 2002.

SKY SPORTS FACT FILE

In 1922–23 Harry Bedford scored half of Blackpool's 60 League goals achieved in the Second Division. His total of 32 also put him top scorer in the division. He was twice capped by England during his Bloomfield Road days.

Record League Victory: 7–0 v Reading, Division 2, 10 November 1928 – Mercer; Gibson, Hamilton, Watson, Wilson, Grant, Ritchie, Oxberry (2), Hampson (5), Tufnell, Neal. 7–0 v Preston NE (away), Division 1, 1 May 1948 – Robinson; Shimwell, Crosland; Buchan, Hayward, Kelly; Hobson, Munro (1), McIntosh (5), McCall, Rickett (1). 7–0 v Sunderland, Division 1, 5 October 1957 – Farm; Armfield, Garrett, Kelly (J), Gratrix, Kelly (H), Matthews, Taylor (2), Charnley (2), Durie (2), Perry (1).

Record Cup Victory: 7–1 v Charlton Ath, League Cup 2nd rd, 25 September 1963 – Harvey; Armfield, Martin; Crawford, Gratrix, Cranston; Lea, Ball (1), Charnley (4), Durie (1), Oates (1).

Record Defeat: 1–10 v Small Heath, Division 2, 2 March 1901 and v Huddersfield T, Division 1, 13 December 1930.

Most League Points (2 for a win): 58, Division 2, 1929–30 and Division 2, 1967–68.

Most League Points (3 for a win): 86, Division 4, 1984–85.

Most League Goals: 98, Division 2, 1929–30.

Highest League Scorer in Season: Jimmy Hampson, 45, Division 2, 1929–30.

Most League Goals in Total Aggregate: Jimmy Hampson, 246, 1927–38.

Most League Goals in One Match: 5, Jimmy Hampson v Reading, Division 2, 10 November 1928; 5, Jimmy McIntosh v Preston NE, Division 1, 1 May 1948.

Most Capped Player: Jimmy Armfield, 43, England.

Most League Appearances: Jimmy Armfield, 568, 1952–71.

Youngest League Player: Trevor Sinclair, 16 years 170 days v Wigan Ath, 19 August 1989.

Record Transfer Fee Received: £1,500,000 from Southampton for Brett Ormerod, December 2001.

Record Transfer Fee Paid: £275,000 to Millwall for Chris Malkin, October 1996.

Football League Record: 1896 Elected to Division 2; 1899 Failed re-election; 1900 Re-elected; 1900–30 Division 2; 1930–33 Division 1; 1933–37 Division 2; 1937–67 Division 1; 1967–70 Division 2; 1970–71 Division 1; 1971–78 Division 2; 1978–81 Division 3; 1981–85 Division 4; 1985–90 Division 3; 1990–92 Division 4; 1992–2000 Division 2; 2000–01 Division 3; 2001– Division 2.

MANAGERS

Tom Barcroft 1903–33
(Secretary-Manager)
John Cox 1909–11
Bill Norman 1919–23
Maj. Frank Buckley 1923–27
Sid Beaumont 1927–28
Harry Evans 1928–33
(Hon. Team Manager)
Alex 'Sandy' Macfarlane 1933–35
Joe Smith 1935–58
Ronnie Suart 1958–67
Stan Mortensen 1967–69
Les Shannon 1969–70
Bob Stokoe 1970–72
Harry Potts 1972–76
Allan Brown 1976–78
Bob Stokoe 1978–79
Stan Ternent 1979–80
Alan Ball 1980–81
Allan Brown 1981–82
Sam Ellis 1982–89
Jimmy Mullen 1989–90
Graham Carr 1990
Bill Ayre 1990–94
Sam Allardyce 1994–96
Gary Megson 1996–97
Nigel Worthington 1997–99
Steve McMahon January 2000–

LATEST SEQUENCES

Longest Sequence of League Wins: 9, 21.11.1936 – 1.1.1937.

Longest Sequence of League Defeats: 8, 26.11.1898 – 7.1.1899.

Longest Sequence of League Draws: 5, 4.12.1976 – 1.1.1977.

Longest Sequence of Unbeaten League Matches: 17, 6.4.1968 – 21.9.1968.

Longest Sequence Without a League Win: 19, 19.12.1970 – 24.4.1971.

Successive Scoring Runs: 33 from 23.2.1929.

Successive Non-scoring Runs: 5 from 12.4.1975.

TEN YEAR LEAGUE RECORD

		P	*W*	*D*	*L*	*F*	*A*	*Pts*	*Pos*
1993-94	Div 2	46	16	5	25	63	75	53	20
1994-95	Div 2	46	18	10	18	64	70	64	12
1995-96	Div 2	46	23	13	10	67	40	82	3
1996-97	Div 2	46	18	15	13	60	47	69	7
1997-98	Div 2	46	17	11	18	59	67	62	12
1998-99	Div 2	46	14	14	18	44	54	56	14
1999-2000	Div 2	46	8	17	21	49	77	41	22
2000-01	Div 2	46	22	6	18	74	58	72	7
2001-02	Div 2	46	14	14	18	66	69	56	16
2002-03	Div 2	46	15	13	18	56	64	58	13

DID YOU KNOW ?

Before the Football League changed its rules in 1920 preventing a share of transfer fees, the record received by a player was believed to have been £1,000 paid to Joe Lane signed by Birmingham from Blackpool for only £3,000.

BLACKPOOL 2002–03 LEAGUE RECORD

Match No.	Date	Venue	Opponents	Result		H/T Score	Lg. Pos.	Goalscorers	Atten-dance
1	Aug 10	A	Bristol C	L	0-2	0-0	—		11,891
2	13	H	Luton T	W	5-2	2-1	—	Clarke P 2 [19, 24], Taylor 2 [65, 90], Dalglish [79]	6377
3	17	H	Swindon T	D	0-0	0-0	9		6404
4	23	A	Northampton T	W	1-0	0-0	—	Murphy [90]	5556
5	26	H	Oldham Ath	D	0-0	0-0	6		8201
6	31	A	Huddersfield T	D	0-0	0-0	11		9506
7	Sept 7	H	Tranmere R	W	3-0	0-0	6	Southern [54], Hills (pen) [59], Taylor [83]	6834
8	14	A	Wycombe W	W	2-1	2-1	3	Hills 2 (1 pen) [15 (p), 28]	5815
9	17	A	Barnsley	L	1-2	1-1	—	Murphy [12]	9619
10	21	H	Port Vale	W	3-2	0-1	6	Murphy 2 [63, 64], Clarke P [81]	7756
11	28	A	Chesterfield	L	0-1	0-0	7		4488
12	Oct 5	H	Cheltenham T	W	3-1	1-1	7	Spencer (og) [41], Wellens [64], Walker [83]	6649
13	14	A	QPR	L	1-2	0-1	—	Taylor [63]	11,335
14	19	H	Cardiff C	W	1-0	0-0	7	Hills [52]	7744
15	26	A	Plymouth Arg	W	3-1	2-0	7	Taylor 2 [16, 40], Murphy [87]	8717
16	29	H	Stockport Co	L	1-3	0-0	—	Milligan [90]	7047
17	Nov 2	A	Brentford	L	0-5	0-2	8		5888
18	9	H	Wigan Ath	L	0-2	0-1	8		7676
19	23	A	Crewe Alex	L	0-3	0-1	9		7019
20	30	H	Notts Co	D	1-1	1-0	10	Clarke C [21]	5843
21	Dec 14	A	Mansfield T	L	0-4	0-1	11		4001
22	21	H	Peterborough U	W	3-0	2-0	9	Grayson [17], Bullock [21], Walker [62]	5068
23	26	A	Oldham Ath	D	1-1	1-1	11	Murphy [17]	9415
24	28	H	Colchester U	W	3-1	2-0	9	Walker [34], Grayson [45], Murphy [59]	6040
25	Jan 1	H	Huddersfield T	D	1-1	0-0	12	Hills (pen) [89]	7184
26	18	H	Northampton T	W	2-1	0-1	8	Walker (pen) [77], Murphy [90]	5646
27	22	A	Swindon T	D	1-1	0-1	—	Taylor [61]	4787
28	25	A	Colchester U	W	2-0	0-0	8	Murphy [52], Coid [70]	3305
29	Feb 1	H	Bristol C	D	0-0	0-0	9		7290
30	8	A	Wigan Ath	D	1-1	0-1	9	Taylor [85]	10,546
31	11	A	Luton T	W	3-1	1-0	—	Murphy 3 [10, 52, 74]	6563
32	15	H	Brentford	W	1-0	1-0	7	Murphy [27]	6203
33	22	A	Tranmere R	L	1-2	0-1	7	Evans [59]	9111
34	Mar 1	H	Wycombe W	W	1-0	1-0	7	Murphy [20]	7266
35	4	H	Barnsley	L	1-2	0-1	—	Murphy [56]	6827
36	8	A	Port Vale	L	0-1	0-0	9		4394
37	15	H	Plymouth Arg	D	1-1	1-1	9	Taylor [40]	8772
38	18	A	Cardiff C	L	1-2	1-1	—	Taylor [37]	11,788
39	22	A	Stockport Co	D	2-2	2-1	9	Murphy [32], Grayson [42]	6599
40	29	H	QPR	L	1-3	0-1	10	Taylor [90]	8162
41	Apr 5	A	Notts Co	L	1-3	1-0	10	Robinson [35]	5551
42	12	H	Crewe Alex	L	0-1	0-0	10		7623
43	19	A	Peterborough U	L	0-1	0-1	11		4587
44	21	H	Mansfield T	D	3-3	2-1	11	Blinkhorn 2 [30, 43], Taylor [90]	6173
45	26	A	Cheltenham T	L	0-3	0-2	13		5150
46	May 3	H	Chesterfield	D	1-1	0-1	13	Taylor [64]	7999

Final League Position: 13

GOALSCORERS

League (56): Murphy 16, Taylor 13, Hills 5 (3 pens), Walker 4 (1 pen), Clarke P 3, Grayson 3, Blinkhorn 2, Bullock 1, Clarke C 1, Coid 1, Dalglish 1, Evans 1, Milligan 1, Robinson 1, Southern 1, Wellens 1, own goal 1.
Worthington Cup (0).
FA Cup (8): Murphy 2, Taylor 2, Dalglish 1, Hills 1, own goals 2.
LDV Vans Trophy (3): Milligan 1 (pen), Murphy 1, Taylor 1.

Barnes P 44	Grayson S 44 + 1	Hills J 20 + 7	Collins L 1 + 5	Clarke C 12 + 5	Clarke P 16	Wellens R 36 + 3	Bullock M 34 + 4	Taylor S 30 + 14	Walker R 19 + 13	Southern K 38	Hughes I 13 + 5	Jaszczun T 15 + 6	Dalglish P 20 + 7	O'Kane J 8 + 6	Murphy J 33 + 2	Coid D 31 + 5	Burns J 4 + 3	Milligan J — + 7	Thornton S 1 + 2	McMahon S 3 + 3	Theoklitos M 2	Gulliver P 2 + 1	Blinkhorn M 3 + 4	Richardson L 20	Hendry C 14	Thornley B 7 + 5	Flynn M 21	Evans P 10	Robinson P 5 + 2	Match No.
1	2	3	4■	5	6	7[1]	8■	9[2]	10[3]	11	12	13	14																	1
1	2	11		5	6	7	8	12	9[1]	4		3	10																	2
1	2	11	12		6	7	8	13	9[2]	4[3]	5	3[1]	10	14																3
1			12		6	7	8	13		4	5	3	10[2]	2	9	11[1]														4
1	14		12	13	6	7		9	10	4[2]	5	3	8[3]	2[1]		11														5
1	2		12		6	8[1]		13	9	4	5	3	10[3]	7		11[2]	14													6
1	2	11		12	6	8		9	14	4	5[1]	3[2]	10		13[3]	7														7
1	2	11			6	7	8	12		4		3	10[1]	5	9															8
1	2	11			6	7[1]	8	13	12	4	14	3[3]	10[2]	5	9															9
1	2	3			6	7	8[1]	11		4	5		10		9			12												10
1	2	11			6	7		8	12		5		10[1]	4	9	3														11
1	2	11			6	7		10[1]	12	4	5	3	8		9															12
1	2	11[1]		5		7		10	12	4	6	3	8		9															13
1	2	11[2]		5	6	7		10		4		3	8[1]	12	9	13														14
1	2	11[2]		5	6	7	12	10		4		3	8[1]		9	13														15
1	2			5	6		12	10[2]	13	4		3	8[3]	7[1]	9	11		14												16
1	2	3		5	6	7	8[1]	10[2]	13	4		12	11[3]		9	14														17
1	6	11		5		7	8			4[2]		3[1]	10		9	2			12	13										18
1	2	3■		5		7	8[1]	12		4	13		10[3]	14	9	11			6[2]											19
	2			5		7	8[3]	10[2]	12	4			11[1]		9	3			13		1	6	14							20
	2		12	5■		7	8[2]	10	13	4			11[3]	14	9	3					1	6[1]								21
1	5					7	8[2]	11[1]	10	4			12	13	9	3						14		2	6[3]					22
1	5	12				7	8[1]	11[2]	10	4			13		9	3								2	6					23
1	5	12				7	8[1]	11[2]	10	4	14			13	9	3								2	6[3]					24
1	5	12				7	8[2]	11[3]	10	4			13		9	3[1]								2■	6	14				25
1	5[2]	3[3]				7	12	11[1]	10	4		14	13		9	2											6	8		26
1	5					7[2]	8	12	10[1]	4					9	3								2		13	6	11		27
1	5					7[2]		11	10	4		12	13		9	3[1]								2			6	8		28
1	5					7	12	13	10[2]	4					9	14								2	6	11[3]	3	8[1]		29
1	5					12	8	13	10[2]	4					9	14								2	6	11[3]	3	7[1]		30
1	5			12			8	10		4					9	11								2	6[1]		3	7		31
1	5						8	10		4					9	11								2	6		3	7		32
1	5						8	10[2]	13	4		12			9	11[3]								2[1]	6	14	3	7		33
1	5	11				12■	8[3]		10[2]	4[1]		13			9									2	6	14	3	7		34
1	2	11[1]				12	8	13	10[2]	4					9									3	6	14	5	7[3]		35
1	2			12		11	8	13	10[2]	4					9[1]	3		14							6■	7	5[3]			36
1	2	12					8	10		4			13		9	7[1]								3	6	11[2]	5			37
1	2					7	8	10		4					9	11								3	6		5			38
1	5	12				7	8	10	13	4[1]	14				9[2]	3								2		11[3]	6			39
1	5	3[3]				7	8	11	10[2]							4	14	12					13	2			6		9[1]	40
1	5					7[3]	8	10	12			3[2]				4	13			14				2		11[1]	6		9	41
1	2						8	10			5					7[1]	3	12		13			14	4		11[2]	6		9[3]	42
1	2	3		12			8	11	10[2]		5[1]					7		14					13	4[3]			6		9	43
1	4	12		5		7	8	13								2[1]	3	14		11[3]			10				6		9[2]	44
1	4	12				7	8	13			5			11[2]		2	3[1]			10			9[3]				6		14	45
1	2					7	8	10[2]	12		5				13	3	4[1]			11			9[3]				6		14	46

Worthington Cup
First Round Burnley (a) 0-3

LDV Vans Trophy
First Round Scunthorpe U (a) 3-2
Second Round Crewe Alex (a) 0-2

FA Cup
First Round Barnsley (a) 4-1
Second Round Torquay U (h) 3-1
Third Round Crystal Palace (h) 1-2

BOLTON WANDERERS FA Premiership

FOUNDATION

In 1874 boys of Christ Church Sunday School, Blackburn Street, led by their master Thomas Ogden, established a football club which went under the name of the school and whose president was Vicar of Christ Church. Membership was 6d (two and a half pence). When their president began to lay down too many rules about the use of church premises, the club broke away and formed Bolton Wanderers in 1877, holding their earliest meetings at the Gladstone Hotel.

Reebok Stadium, Burnden Way, Lostock, Bolton BL6 6JW.

Telephone: (01204) 673 673. ***Fax:*** (01204) 673 773. ***Ticket Office:*** (0871) 871 2932. ***ClubCall:*** 09068 121 164.

Ground Capacity: 27,879.

Record Attendance: 69,912 v Manchester C, FA Cup 5th rd, 18 February 1933.

Record Receipts: £335,468 v WBA, Division 1, play-off semi-final, 17 May 2001.

Pitch Measurements: 114yd × 74yd.

President: Nat Lofthouse OBE. ***Chairman:*** P. A. Gartside. ***Directors:*** G. Seymour, G. Warburton, W. B. Warburton, I. Currie, E. Davies OBE, D. McBain.

Team Manager: Sam Allardyce.

Physio: Mark Taylor.

Chief Executive: Allan Duckworth.

Secretary: Simon Marland.

Commercial Director: G. Moores.

Colours: White shirts, white shorts, white stockings.

Change Colours: Yellow shirts with navy sash, navy shorts, yellow stockings.

Year Formed: 1874.

Turned Professional: 1880.

Ltd Co.: 1895.

Previous Name: 1874, Christ Church FC; 1877, Bolton Wanderers.

Club Nickname: 'The Trotters'.

Previous Grounds: Park Recreation Ground and Cockle's Field before moving to Pike's Lane ground 1881; 1895, Burnden Park; 1997, Reebok Stadium.

First Football League Game: 8 September 1888, Football League, v Derby Co (h) L 3–6 – Harrison; Robinson, Mitchell; Roberts, Weir, Bullough, Davenport (2), Milne, Coupar, Barbour, Brogan (1).

Record League Victory: 8–0 v Barnsley, Division 2, 6 October 1934 – Jones; Smith, Finney; Goslin, Atkinson, George Taylor; George T. Taylor (2), Eastham, Milsom (1), Westwood (4), Cook, (1 og).

HONOURS

Football League: Division 1 – Champions 1996–97; Promoted from Division 1 (play-offs) 2000–01. Division 2 – Champions 1908–09, 1977–78; Runners-up 1899–1900, 1904–05, 1910–11, 1934–35, 1992–93; Division 3 – Champions 1972–73.

FA Cup: Winners 1923, 1926, 1929, 1958; Runners-up 1894, 1904, 1953.

Football League Cup: Runners-up 1995.

Freight Rover Trophy: Runners-up 1986.

Sherpa Van Trophy: Winners 1989.

SKY SPORTS FACT FILE

In 2000–01 Bolton Wanderers celebrated promotion back to the FA Premier League with their best record for away wins, notching 14 on travel including another club record of five such consecutive victories.

Record Cup Victory: 13–0 v Sheffield U, FA Cup 2nd rd, 1 February 1890 – Parkinson; Robinson (1), Jones; Bullough, Davenport, Roberts; Rushton, Brogan (3), Cassidy (5), McNee, Weir (4).

Record Defeat: 1–9 v Preston NE, FA Cup 2nd rd, 10 December 1887.

Most League Points (2 for a win): 61, Division 3, 1972–73.

Most League Points (3 for a win): 98, Division 1, 1996–97.

Most League Goals: 100, Division 1, 1996–97.

Highest League Scorer in Season: Joe Smith, 38, Division 1, 1920–21.

Most League Goals in Total Aggregate: Nat Lofthouse, 255, 1946–61.

Most League Goals in One Match: 5, Tony Caldwell v Walsall, Division 3, 10 September 1983.

Most Capped Player: Mark Fish, 34 (60), South Africa.

Most League Appearances: Eddie Hopkinson, 519, 1956–70.

Youngest League Player: Ray Parry, 15 years 267 days v Wolverhampton W, 13 October 1951.

Record Transfer Fee Received: £4,500,000 from Liverpool for Jason McAteer, September 1995.

Record Transfer Fee Paid: £3,500,000 for Dean Holdsworth from Wimbledon, October 1997.

Football League Record: 1888 Founder Member of the League; 1899–1900 Division 2; 1900–03 Division 1; 1903–05 Division 2; 1905–08 Division 1; 1908–09 Division 2; 1909–10 Division 1; 1910–11 Division 2; 1911–33 Division 1; 1933–35 Division 2; 1935–64 Division 1; 1964–71 Division 2; 1971–73 Division 3; 1973–78 Division 2; 1978–80 Division 1; 1980–83 Division 2; 1983–87 Division 3; 1987–88 Division 4; 1988–92 Division 3; 1992–93 Division 2; 1993–95 Division 1; 1995–96 FA Premier League; 1996–97 Division 1; 1997–98 FA Premier League; 1998–2001 Division 1; 2001– FA Premier League.

MANAGERS

Tom Rawthorne 1874–85 *(Secretary)*
J. J. Bentley 1885–86 *(Secretary)*
W. G. Struthers 1886–87 *(Secretary)*
Fitzroy Norris 1887 *(Secretary)*
J. J. Bentley 1887–95 *(Secretary)*
Harry Downs 1895–96 *(Secretary)*
Frank Brettell 1896–98 *(Secretary)*
John Somerville 1898–1910
Will Settle 1910–15
Tom Mather 1915–19
Charles Foweraker 1919–44
Walter Rowley 1944–50
Bill Ridding 1951–68
Nat Lofthouse 1968–70
Jimmy McIlroy 1970
Jimmy Meadows 1971
Nat Lofthouse 1971 *(then Admin. Manager to 1972)*
Jimmy Armfield 1971–74
Ian Greaves 1974–80
Stan Anderson 1980–81
George Mulhall 1981–82
John McGovern 1982–85
Charlie Wright 1985
Phil Neal 1985–92
Bruce Rioch 1992–95
Roy McFarland 1995–96
Colin Todd 1996–99
Sam Allardyce October 1999–

LATEST SEQUENCES

Longest Sequence of League Wins: 11, 5.11.1904 – 2.1.1905.

Longest Sequence of League Defeats: 11, 7.4.1902 – 18.10.1902.

Longest Sequence of League Draws: 6, 25.1.1913 – 8.3.1913.

Longest Sequence of Unbeaten League Matches: 23, 13.10.1990 – 9.3.1991.

Longest Sequence Without a League Win: 26, 7.4.1902 – 10.1.1903.

Successive Scoring Runs: 24 from 22.11.1996.

Successive Non-scoring Runs: 5 from 3.1.1898.

TEN YEAR LEAGUE RECORD

		P	W	D	L	F	A	Pts	Pos
1993-94	Div 1	46	15	14	17	63	64	59	14
1994-95	Div 1	46	21	14	11	67	45	77	3
1995-96	PR Lge	38	8	5	25	39	71	29	20
1996-97	Div 1	46	28	14	4	100	53	98	1
1997-98	PR Lge	38	9	13	16	41	61	40	18
1998-99	Div 1	46	20	16	10	78	59	76	6
1999-2000	Div 1	46	21	13	12	69	50	76	6
2000-01	Div 1	46	24	15	7	76	45	87	3
2001-02	PR Lge	38	9	13	16	44	62	40	16
2002-03	PR Lge	38	10	14	14	41	51	44	17

DID YOU KNOW?

When David Jack scored the goal for Bolton Wanderers which eliminated Manchester City in the 1926 FA Cup final, the ball entered the net at roughly the same point it had done when he scored in the 1923 final.

BOLTON WANDERERS 2002–03 LEAGUE RECORD

Match No.	*Date*	*Venue*	*Opponents*	*Result*		*H/T Score*	*Lg. Pos.*	*Goalscorers*	*Attendance*
1	Aug 17	A	Fulham	L	1-4	1-3	—	Ricketts (pen) [4]	16,338
2	24	H	Charlton Ath	L	1-2	1-1	20	Djorkaeff [2]	21,753
3	Sept 1	H	Aston Villa	W	1-0	0-0	17	Ricketts (pen) [56]	22,113
4	11	A	Manchester U	W	1-0	0-0	—	Nolan [76]	67,623
5	14	H	Liverpool	L	2-3	0-1	14	Gardner [54], Campo [87]	27,328
6	21	A	Arsenal	L	1-2	0-1	17	Farrelly [47]	37,974
7	28	H	Southampton	D	1-1	0-0	17	Djorkaeff [90]	22,692
8	Oct 5	A	Middlesbrough	L	0-2	0-1	18		31,005
9	20	A	Tottenham H	L	1-3	0-0	20	Djorkaeff [63]	35,909
10	28	H	Sunderland	D	1-1	0-1	—	Babb (og) [80]	23,036
11	Nov 2	A	Birmingham C	L	1-3	0-0	20	Okocha [72]	27,224
12	9	H	WBA	D	1-1	0-1	20	Frandsen [89]	23,630
13	17	A	Leeds U	W	4-2	1-1	18	Pedersen 2 [3, 90], Djorkaeff [80], Ricketts (pen) [89]	36,627
14	23	H	Chelsea	D	1-1	0-0	18	Pedersen [63]	25,076
15	30	A	Manchester C	L	0-2	0-1	19		32,661
16	Dec 7	H	Blackburn R	D	1-1	1-0	18	Okocha [8]	24,556
17	16	H	Leeds U	L	0-3	0-2	—		23,201
18	21	A	West Ham U	D	1-1	0-1	19	Ricketts [65]	34,892
19	26	H	Newcastle U	W	4-3	3-1	17	Okocha [5], Gardner [9], Ricketts 2 [45, 63]	27,314
20	28	A	Everton	D	0-0	0-0	17		39,480
21	Jan 1	A	Aston Villa	L	0-2	0-1	17		31,838
22	11	H	Fulham	D	0-0	0-0	17		25,156
23	18	A	Charlton Ath	D	1-1	0-0	17	Djorkaeff [85]	26,029
24	22	A	Newcastle U	L	0-1	0-1	—		52,005
25	28	H	Everton	L	1-2	0-2	—	Bergsson [90]	25,119
26	Feb 1	H	Birmingham C	W	4-2	1-1	17	Cunningham (og) [12], Pedersen [46], Djorkaeff [84], Facey [87]	24,288
27	8	A	WBA	D	1-1	1-0	17	Pedersen [18]	26,627
28	22	H	Manchester U	D	1-1	0-0	17	N'Gotty [61]	27,409
29	Mar 8	A	Liverpool	L	0-2	0-1	17		41,462
30	15	A	Sunderland	W	2-0	0-0	17	Okocha [50], Pedersen [55]	42,124
31	24	H	Tottenham H	W	1-0	0-0	—	Okocha (pen) [90]	23,084
32	Apr 5	H	Manchester C	W	2-0	1-0	16	Pedersen [32], Campo [52]	26,919
33	12	A	Chelsea	L	0-1	0-0	17		39,891
34	19	H	West Ham U	W	1-0	1-0	17	Okocha [38]	27,160
35	21	A	Blackburn R	D	0-0	0-0	16		28,862
36	26	H	Arsenal	D	2-2	0-0	17	Djorkaeff [74], Keown (og) [84]	27,253
37	May 3	A	Southampton	D	0-0	0-0	17		30,951
38	11	H	Middlesbrough	W	2-1	2-0	17	Frandsen [10], Okocha [21]	27,241

Final League Position: 17

GOALSCORERS

League (41): Djorkaeff 7, Okocha 7 (1 pen), Pedersen 7, Ricketts 6 (3 pens), Campo 2, Frandsen 2, Gardner 2, Bergsson 1, Facey 1, Farrelly 1, N'Gotty 1, Nolan 1, own goals 3.
Worthington Cup (0).
FA Cup (1): Ricketts 1.

Jaaskelainen J 38	Mendy B 20 + 1	Charlton S 27 + 4	Frandsen P 34	Bergsson G 31	N'Gotty B 23	Okocha J 26 + 5	Nolan K 15 + 18	Ricketts M 13 + 9	Djorkaeff Y 36	Gardner R 31 + 1	Whitlow M 14 + 3	Pedersen H 31 + 2	Warhurst P 5 + 2	Barness A 21 + 4	Walters J — + 4	Holdsworth D 5 + 4	Campo I 28 + 3	Livesey D — + 2	Farrelly G 6 + 2	Tofting S 2 + 6	Johnson J — + 2	Facey D 1 + 8	Bulent A — + 1	Andre P — + 9	Salva B 1 + 5	Laville F 10	*Match No.*
1	2^{1}	3	4	5	6	7^{2}	8^{3}	9	10	11	12	13	14														1
1		3	8^{2}		6		12	9^{3}	10	11^{1}	5	7	4	2	13	14											2
1		3^{1}	8	5	2		7	9	11	12	6	10	4^{2}	13													3
1		3	4^{2}	5			7	9	10^{1}	11	6	8^{3}	12	2		13	14										4
1		3	4	5			7		10^{1}	11	6^{2}	8		2^{3}	12	9	13	14									5
1		3	8	5		12		13	11^{3}		6	9^{2}		2		10^{1}	4■		7	14							6
1		3	8	5		12		9	11		6	13		2		10^{1}	4		7^{2}								7
1		3^{3}	8^{1}	5		12	7	13	11		6	9		2		10^{2}	4		14								8
1		3		5		12	8	9	10^{1}	11	6			2		13	4^{2}		7								9
1	2^{2}		8		5	12	7^{1}	9	10	3	6			13			4		11								10
1	2	12	8^{1}		5	7	13	9^{3}	10	3■	6^{2}					14	4		11								11
1	6	12	8		5■	7	14	13	10	3^{1}				2		9^{2}	4		11^{3}								12
1	2	3	8		6^{2}	7	11^{1}	12	10			9		5			4			13							13
1		3	8^{2}			7	6^{1}	12	10	11		9	2	5			4			13							14
1		3				7	2^{2}	12	10	11		9^{3}	6	5			4	13		8^{1}	14						15
1		3	8	5		7^{3}	12	13	10	11^{2}		9	6^{1}	2			4			14							16
1		3	8	5	6^{1}	7^{2}			10		12	9		2	13		4		14	11^{3}							17
1		3	4	5	6^{2}	7	8	12	10^{1}	11	13	9		2													18
1		3	4	5		7	12	8	10^{1}	11	2	9^{2}		6								13					19
1		3	6	5		7	8	10^{1}		11		9^{2}		2			4			12		13					20
1		3	4^{1}	5		7	8^{3}	10		11	6	9^{2}		2						12		13	14				21
1		3	6	5		7^{2}	12		10	11		9		2	13		4					8^{1}					22
1	12	3	4	5			7	8	10	11	6	9^{1}		2^{2}								13					23
1	2	3	8^{2}	5	6		7^{3}	12	10	11		9^{1}		4			13					14					24
1	2	3	8	5	6^{2}		12	7	10	11		9^{1}					4					13					25
1	8	3	6	5	2	7			10	11		9^{1}					4					12					26
1	2	3	8	5	6	7^{2}	12		10^{1}	11		9^{3}					4							13	14		27
1	7^{2}	3		5	2	8	12		10^{1}	11		9^{3}		13			4								14	6	28
1	7^{2}	3		5	2	8	12		10	11							4							13	9^{1}	6	29
1	7		8	5	2	11	12		10^{1}	3		9^{2}					4								13	6	30
1	7^{2}		8	5	2	11			10	3^{1}		9		12			4							13		6	31
1	7		8	5	2	11^{1}	12		10^{2}	3		9^{3}					4				13	14				6	32
1	7	12	8^{1}	5		11	13		10	3		9		2^{3}			4^{2}							14		6	33
1	7	3	8	5	2	11^{2}	12		10^{1}			9					4							13		6	34
1	7		8	5	2	11	12		10^{2}	3		9^{1}					4							13		6	35
1	7^{3}		8	5	2	11	12		10	3		9^{2}					4^{1}							14	13	6■	36
1	7^{3}		8	5	2	11^{1}	12		10	3		9^{2}					4							14	13	6	37
1	7^{2}	12	8	5	2	11	13		10^{1}	3	6	9^{3}					4							14			38

Worthington Cup
Second Round Bury (h) 0-1

FA Cup
Third Round Sunderland (h) 1-1
(a) 0-2

BOSTON UNITED Division 3

FOUNDATION

Although it was 1934 before the name Boston United first appeared, football had been played in the town since the late 1800s and indeed, always on the same site as the present York Street stadium. In fact Boston Football Club was established in March 1870 playing their first match against Louth the following month. Before the First World War, there were two clubs, Boston Town, whose headquarters were The Coach and Horses, and Boston Swifts, who used The Indian Queen. In fact, as both public houses were situated on Main Ridge and the pitch was virtually just opposite, it was not surprising that for the first forty years or so, that was what the ground was called. Swifts never reappeared after the First World War and it was left to the club called simply Boston to achieve the first giant-killing in the FA Cup by beating Bradford Park Avenue 1-0 on 12 December 1925. The club was now competing in the Midland League and subsequently reformed under the new title of Boston United.

York Street, Boston, Lincolnshire PE21 6HJ.

Telephone: (01205) 365 525 (match days only).

Fax: (01205) 354 063.

Club Office: (01205) 364 406.

ClubCall: 09068 121 539.

Website: www.bostonunited.co.uk

Ground Capacity: 6,543.

Record Attendance: 10,086 v Corby Town, Friendly, 1955.

President: A. E. Bell.

Chairman: D. Wood.

Directors: R. Jenkin, D. Pickett.

Company Secretary: C. Woodcock.

General Manager/Secretary: John Blackwell.

Merchandising Manager: Becky Thompson.

Manager: Neil Thompson.

Physio: Jim Woods.

Colours: Amber shirts, amber shorts, amber stockings.

Change Colours: White shirts with black and amber trim, white shorts, white stockings.

Year formed: 1934.

SKY SPORTS FACT FILE

England international left-winger Freddy Tunstall rendered yeoman service to Boston United from 1936 and made his last appearance in an emergency at the age of 52 during 1951–52. In addition he was manager, trainer and coach at various times.

Club Nickname: 'The Pilgrims'.

First Football League Game: 10 August 2002, Division 3, v Bournemouth (h), D 2–2 – Bastock; Hocking, Chapman, Morley (Rodwell), Warburton, Ellender, Gould (1), Bennett, Clare, Elding (Cook), Weatherstone S. (1 og).

Record League Victory: 6–0 v Shrewsbury T, Division 3, 21 December 2002 – Bastock; Costello, Chapman, Redfearn (1), Balmer, Hocking (McCarthy), Weatherstone S, Higgins, Douglas (1), Logan (2) (Thompson L), Angel (Gould (1)). (1 og).

Record Transfer Fee Received: £50,000 from Bolton W for David Norris, 2000.

Record Transfer Fee Paid: £14,000 to Wycombe Wanderers for Micky Nuttell.

Football League Record: 2002 Promoted to Division 3.

HONOURS

FA Cup: best season: 3rd rd, 1926, 1956, 1972, 1974.
Football League Cup: never past 1st rd.
Conference: Champions 2001–02.
Dr. Martens: Champions 1999–2000. Runners-up: 1998–99.
Unibond League: Runners-up 1995–96, 1997–98.
Unibond Challenge Cup: Runners-up 1996–97.
FA Trophy: Runners-up 1984–85.
Northern Premier League: Champions 1972–73, 1973–74, 1976–77, 1977–78.
Northern Premier League Cup: Winners 1974, 1976.
Northern Premier League Challenge Shield: Winners 1974, 1975, 1977, 1978.
Lincolnshire Senior Cup: Winners 1935, 1937, 1938, 1946, 1950, 1955, 1956, 1960, 1977, 1979, 1986, 1988, 1989.
Non-League Champions of Champions Cup: Winners 1973, 1977.
East Anglian Cup: Winners 1961.
Central Alliance League: Champions 1961–62.
United Counties League: Champions 1965–66.
West Midlands League: Champions 1966–67, 1967–68.
Eastern Professional Floodlit Cup: Winners 1972.

LATEST SEQUENCES

Longest Sequence of League Wins: 4, 19.4.2003 – 3.5.2003.

Longest Sequence of League Defeats: 6, 29.10.2002 – 14.12.2002.

Longest Sequence of League Draws: 3, 29.3.2003 – 2.4.2003.

Longest Sequence of Unbeaten League Matches: 4, on three occasions.

Longest Sequence Without a League Win: 6, 28.12.2002 – 1.2.2003.

Successive Scoring Runs: 5 from 1.2.2003.

Successive Non-scoring Runs: 5 from 29.10.2002.

MANAGERS

George Kerr/Dave Cusack
Dave Cusack
Peter Morris
Mel Sterland
Greg Fee
Steve Evans 1998–2002
Neil Thompson October 2002–

TEN YEAR LEAGUE RECORD

		P	W	D	L	F	A	Pts	Pos
1993-94	NP pr	42	23	9	10	90	43	78	3
1994-95	NP pr	42	20	11	11	80	43	71	5
1995-96	NP pr	42	23	6	13	86	59	75	2
1996-97	NP pr	44	22	13	9	74	47	79	6
1997-98	NP pr	42	22	12	8	55	40	78	2
1998-99	SL pr	42	17	16	9	69	51	67	2
1999-2000	SL pr	42	27	11	4	102	39	92	1
2000-01	Conf.	42	13	17	12	74	63	56	12
2001-02	Conf.	42	25	9	8	84	42	84	1
2002-03	Div 3	46	15	13	18	55	56	54*	15

**4 pts deducted at start of season.*

DID YOU KNOW?

Boston United's York Street ground was one of the two venues used during the 2002 semi-professional Four Nations Tournament and actually hosted Wales' winning victory over the Republic of Ireland.

BOSTON UNITED 2002–03 LEAGUE RECORD

Match No.	Date	Venue	Opponents	Result		H/T Score	Lg. Pos.	Goalscorers	Attendance
1	Aug 10	H	Bournemouth	D	2-2	0-1	—	Young (og) [52], Gould [54]	4184
2	13	A	Hartlepool U	L	0-2	0-0	—		4841
3	17	A	Wrexham	D	1-1	0-1	24	Rusk [63]	3293
4	24	H	Lincoln C	W	2-0	1-0	24	Weatherstone S [30], Clare [89]	5159
5	26	A	York C	L	0-2	0-1	24		4228
6	31	H	Bury	D	1-1	0-0	24	Weatherstone S [90]	2790
7	Sept 7	A	Kidderminster H	D	0-0	0-0	24		2222
8	14	H	Oxford U	L	1-3	0-3	24	Redfearn [55]	2685
9	18	H	Swansea C	W	1-0	1-0	—	Weatherstone S [36]	2209
10	21	A	Carlisle U	L	2-4	1-4	23	Cook [41], Douglas [69]	3623
11	28	H	Cambridge U	L	1-3	1-2	24	Weatherstone S [43]	3090
12	Oct 5	A	Macclesfield T	L	0-2	0-1	24		1941
13	12	H	Torquay U	W	2-1	0-1	23	Cook [55], Thompson L [63]	2514
14	19	A	Darlington	W	3-2	1-0	21	Thompson L 3 [25, 67, 80]	3033
15	26	H	Rochdale	W	3-1	1-0	21	Weatherstone S [20], Battersby [64], Douglas [90]	2653
16	29	A	Rushden & D	L	0-1	0-1	—		4079
17	Nov 2	H	Exeter C	L	0-3	0-1	22		2474
18	9	A	Scunthorpe U	L	0-2	0-1	23		3730
19	23	A	Hull C	L	0-1	0-0	23		9460
20	30	H	Leyton Orient	L	0-1	0-1	24		2616
21	Dec 14	A	Southend U	L	2-4	0-3	24	Logan [57], Angel [64]	3245
22	21	H	Shrewsbury T	W	6-0	4-0	22	Logan 2 [13, 29], Van Blerk (og) [21], Douglas [41], Redfearn [56], Gould [90]	2155
23	26	H	York C	W	3-0	1-0	20	Douglas 2 [30, 90], Logan [52]	3864
24	28	A	Bristol R	D	1-1	1-0	20	Logan [8]	8311
25	Jan 1	A	Lincoln C	D	1-1	0-1	20	Logan [56]	7846
26	4	H	Hartlepool U	L	0-1	0-0	20		3081
27	18	A	Bury	D	0-0	0-0	22		3024
28	25	H	Bristol R	D	0-0	0-0	23		3209
29	Feb 1	A	Bournemouth	L	1-2	0-0	23	Angel [78]	5180
30	8	H	Scunthorpe U	W	1-0	0-0	20	Logan [90]	3358
31	15	A	Exeter C	W	2-0	1-0	18	Redfearn [44], Douglas [90]	2834
32	22	H	Kidderminster H	W	3-0	2-0	18	Logan 2 [24, 83], Weatherstone S [44]	2485
33	Mar 1	A	Oxford U	L	1-2	0-1	19	Douglas [69]	7157
34	4	A	Swansea C	D	0-0	0-0	—		6642
35	8	H	Carlisle U	D	0-0	0-0	19		3131
36	15	A	Rochdale	L	0-1	0-0	22		2538
37	19	H	Darlington	W	1-0	1-0	—	Greaves [5]	2186
38	22	H	Rushden & D	D	1-1	0-0	18	Jones [67]	3504
39	29	A	Torquay U	D	1-1	0-0	19	Angel (pen) [82]	3039
40	Apr 2	H	Wrexham	D	3-3	1-1	—	Duffield 2 [27, 62], Redfearn (pen) [49]	1919
41	5	A	Leyton Orient	L	2-3	1-2	19	Logan [28], Redfearn [53]	3939
42	12	H	Hull C	L	0-1	0-0	20		3782
43	19	A	Shrewsbury T	W	2-1	1-0	19	Duffield [44], Redfearn [48]	4373
44	21	H	Southend U	W	1-0	0-0	19	Angel (pen) [85]	3247
45	26	H	Macclesfield T	W	2-1	1-0	17	Duffield (pen) [20], Hocking [51]	3825
46	May 3	A	Cambridge U	W	2-1	1-0	15	Angel [37], Rusk [82]	4488

Final League Position: 15

GOALSCORERS

League (55): Logan 10, Douglas 7, Redfearn 6 (1 pen), Weatherstone S 6, Angel 5 (2 pens), Duffield 4 (1 pen), Thompson L 4, Cook 2, Gould 2, Rusk 2, Battersby 1, Clare 1, Greaves 1, Hocking 1, Jones 1, own goals 2.
Worthington Cup (3): Burton 1, Ellender 1, Weatherstone S 1.
FA Cup (2): Battersby 1 (pen), Higgins 1.
LDV Vans Trophy (5): Thompson L 2, Angel 1 (pen), Battersby 1, Weatherstone S 1.

Bastock P 46	Morley B 1+1	Chapman B 37	Hocking M 44+1	Warburton R 16	Ellender P 25+1	Bennett T 29+4	Weatherstone S 43+2	Clare D 7	Elding A 3+5	Gould J 10+10	Rodwell J 2+1	Cook J 6+10	Costello P 13+5	Rusk S 12+6	Burton S 6+2	Angel M 24+7	Thompson N 3	Redfearn N 27+4	Greaves M 24+2	Douglas S 14+15	Clifford M 5+2	Lodge A 1+1	Weatherstone R 2+6	Monington M 1	Thompson L 12+3	Higgins A 13	Battersby T 7+4	McCarthy P 11+1	Logan R 26+1	Balmer S 21	Town D —+8	Duffield P 12+4	George L 1+2	Jones G 2+1	Beevers L —+1	*Match No.*
1	2[1]	3	4	5	6	7	8	9	10[2]	11	12	13																								1
1		3	4	5	6[1]	7	8	9		11	2	10	12																							2
1	12	3[1]	4	5		7	8	9		11[3]	2	13		6	10[2]	14																				3
1			2	5	6	7	8	9						4	10[1]	11	3	12																		4
1			2	5	6	7	8	9		12		13		4	10[3]	11[2]	3[1]	14																		5
1			2	5	6[1]		8	9		11		12		4	10[3]	13		7	3[2]	14																6
1			2	5	10		8			3		12		4[2]		11		7	6	9[1]	13															7
1			2	5	6[1]		8		12			10		13	14		3[3]	11	4	9	7[2]															8
1			12	5	6		8		13	11		7		2	10[2]			4	3[1]	9																9
1			4[3]	5	6		8		12	3		7		2[2]	10[1]			11		9		13	14													10
1				5▮			8		10	12		13	7		14			11	4	9[2]		3[1]	2[3]	6												11
1			4	5		6	10	9	12	3		13	7[3]					8[1]	2		14				11[2]											12
1		3	4			6	10		12	13		9[1]				11[2]			5[3]		2		14		8	7										13
1		3	4			6	10[1]					9				11			5	12	2		13		7[2]	8										14
1		3[3]	4	5		6	10					12				11				13	2		14		7[1]	8	9[2]									15
1		3	4	5		6	10									11				12	2[2]		13		7[1]	8	9									16
1		3	4	5[1]		6	10					13				11[2]			12	14			2		7	8[3]	9									17
1		3	2		6	4	10							12		13			5▮	7					11[1]	8[2]	9									18
1		3	2	5					10[2]			12	4			11				13					7	8	9[1]	6▮								19
1		3	4			12	10						2			11			5						7	8	9[2]	6[1]	13							20
1		3	5				10						2			11		4		12					7	8			9[1]	6						21
1		3	4[3]				7			12			2			11[1]		6		9					13	8		14	10[2]	5						22
1		3	4				7			12			2			11[1]		6		9					13	8[2]	14		10[3]	5						23
1		3	4				7			12			2			11[1]		6		9						8	13	5	10[2]							24
1		3	4			12	7						2			11[2]		6	13	9[3]						8[1]	14	5	10							25
1		3	4			8	7									11		6	2[2]						12		9[1]	5	10		13					26
1		3	4			8	7												2	9[1]					11		12	5	10[2]	6	13					27
1		3	4			8[2]	7[1]			12								13	2	9[3]					11			5	10	6	14					28
1		3	4			12	7			13						11[2]		8	2▮									5	10[3]	6	14	9[1]				29
1		3[2]	4			12	7			13						11		8	2[1]	14								5	10	6[3]		9				30
1		3	4		12	6	7			11								8[1]		13								2	10[2]	5		9[3]	14			31
1		3	4		6	8	7			11[3]										12			13					2	10	5[2]		9[1]	14			32
1		3	4		6[1]	8	7						2					12	5	13									10		14	9[3]	11[2]			33
1		3	2		6	4▮	11						7	12				8		9▮									10[1]	5						34
1		3	2		6	4	7									11		8		9									10[1]	5		12				35
1		3	2[2]		6	4	7							12		11		8											10[1]	5	13	9				36
1		3	2		6		9[2]						12	7[1]		11		8	4										10	5		13				37
1		3	4		6		9							7[1]		11		8	2										10	5				12		38
1		3	2		6	4	11						12			13		8[2]	7[1]										10[3]	5		14		9		39
1		3	4		6	7	11											8	2	12									10[1]	5		13		9[2]		40
1		3	4		6	7	12						13			11		8	2[2]	14									10	5[1]		9[3]				41
1		3	4[1]		6	7	13			14				12		11[3]		8	2										10[2]	5		9				42
1		3	4		6	7	11[2]						13	12				8	2[1]										10	5		9				43
1		3	2		6	7	11[1]							4		12		8		13									10[2]	5	14	9[3]				44
1		3	4		6	8	11						2	7[1]		12				13									10[3]	5	14	9[2]				45
1		3	4		6	8	11						2[2]	7		12			5										10[1]			9			13	46

Worthington Cup

Pr Round	Bristol R	(a)	2-0
First Round	Cardiff C	(h)	1-5

FA Cup

First Round	Northampton T	(a)	2-3

LDV Vans Trophy

First Round	Yeovil T	(h)	4-2
Second Round	Bristol C	(h)	1-2

AFC BOURNEMOUTH Division 2

FOUNDATION

There was a Bournemouth FC as early as 1875, but the present club arose out of the remnants of the Boscombe St John's club (formed 1890). The meeting at which Boscombe FC came into being was held at a house in Gladstone Road in 1899. They began by playing in the Boscombe and District Junior League.

The Fitness First Stadium at Dean Court, Bournemouth, Dorset BH7 7AF.

Telephone: (01202) 726 300. ***Fax:*** (01202) 726 301.
Website: http://www.afcb.co.uk
Email: admin@afcb.co.uk
Ticket Office: (01202) 726 303.

Ground Capacity: 9,600 seats, rising to 12,000 all-seater.

Record Attendance: 28,799 v Manchester U, FA Cup 6th rd, 2 March 1957.

Record Receipts: £96,753 v Bury, Play-off semi-final 2nd leg, 13 May 2003.

Pitch Measurements: 105m × 78m.

Chairman: P. I. Phillips. ***Directors:*** A. H. Kaye (Vice-chairman), A. E. Swaisland, P. E. Hordle, J. C. Saunders, B. J. Bronsdon, D. J. Stone.

Secretary: K. R. J. MacAlister.

Manager: Sean O'Driscoll.

Head Coach: Peter Grant. ***Physio:*** Jim Marshall.

Corporate Manager: Mrs D. Rackley. ***Groundsman:*** D. Edwards.

Colours: Red with black panelled shirts, black shorts, black stockings.

Change Colours: Sky blue and navy shirt, sky blue shorts, sky blue stockings.

Year Formed: 1899.

Turned Professional: 1912.

Ltd Co.: 1914.

Previous Names: 1890, Boscombe St Johns; 1899, Boscombe FC; 1923, Bournemouth & Boscombe Ath FC; 1971, AFC Bournemouth.

Club Nickname: 'Cherries'.

Previous Grounds: 1899, Castlemain Road, Pokesdown; 1910, Dean Court.

First Football League Game: 25 August 1923, Division 3 (S), v Swindon T (a) L 1–3 – Heron; Wingham, Lamb; Butt, C. Smith, Voisey; Miller, Lister (1), Davey, Simpson, Robinson.

Record League Victory: 7–0 v Swindon T, Division 3 (S), 22 September 1956 – Godwin; Cunningham, Keetley; Clayton, Crosland, Rushworth; Siddall (1), Norris (2), Arnott (1), Newsham (2), Cutler (1). 10–0 win v Northampton T at start of 1939–40 expunged from the records on outbreak of war.

HONOURS

Football League: Division 3 – Champions 1986–87; Promoted from Division 3, 2002–03 (play-offs); Division 3 (S) – Runners-up 1947–48; Division 4 – Runners-up 1970–71; Promotion from Division 4 1981–82 (4th).

FA Cup: best season: 6th rd, 1957.

Football League Cup: best season: 4th rd, 1962, 1964.

Associate Members' Cup: Winners 1984.

Auto Windscreens Shield: Runners-up 1998.

SKY SPORTS FACT FILE

In 1946–47 Bournemouth had four ever-present players: Ken Bird, Fred Marsden, Joe Sanaghan and Fred Wilson. Interestingly enough these long-serving favourites all received benefits before the 1949–50 season.

Record Cup Victory: 11–0 v Margate, FA Cup 1st rd, 20 November 1971 – Davies; Machin (1), Kitchener, Benson, Jones, Powell, Cave (1), Boyer, MacDougall (9 incl. 1p), Miller, Scott (De Garis).

Record Defeat: 0–9 v Lincoln C, Division 3, 18 December 1982.

Most League Points (2 for a win): 62, Division 3, 1971–72.

Most League Points (3 for a win): 97, Division 3, 1986–87.

Most League Goals: 88, Division 3 (S), 1956–57.

Highest League Scorer in Season: Ted MacDougall, 42, 1970–71.

Most League Goals in Total Aggregate: Ron Eyre, 202, 1924–33.

Most League Goals in One Match: 4, Jack Russell v Clapton Orient, Division 3S, 7 January 1933; 4, Jack Russell v Bristol C, Division 3S, 28 January 1933; 4, Harry Mardon v Southend U, Division 3S, 1 January 1938; 4, Jack McDonald v Torquay U, Division 3S, 8 November 1947; 4, Ted MacDougall v Colchester U, 18 September 1970; 4, Brian Clark v Rotherham U, 10 October 1972, 4, Luther Blissett v Hull C, 29 November 1988; 4, James Hayter v Bury, Division 2, 21 October 2000.

Most Capped Player: Gerry Peyton, 7 (33), Republic of Ireland.

Most League Appearances: Sean O'Driscoll, 423, 1984–95.

Youngest League Player: Jimmy White, 15 years 321 days v Brentford, 30 April 1958.

Record Transfer Fee Received: £800,000 from Everton for Joe Parkinson, March 1994.

Record Transfer Fee Paid: £210,000 to Gillingham for Gavin Peacock, August 1989.

Football League Record: 1923 Elected to Division 3 (S) and remained a Third Division club for record number of years until 1970; 1970–71 Division 4; 1971–75 Division 3; 1975–82 Division 4; 1982–87 Division 3; 1987–90 Division 2; 1990–92 Division 3; 1992– 2002 Division 2; 2002–03 Division 3; 2003– Division 2.

MANAGERS

Vincent Kitcher 1914–23
(Secretary-Manager)
Harry Kinghorn 1923–25
Leslie Knighton 1925–28
Frank Richards 1928–30
Billy Birrell 1930–35
Bob Crompton 1935–36
Charlie Bell 1936–39
Harry Kinghorn 1939–47
Harry Lowe 1947–50
Jack Bruton 1950–56
Fred Cox 1956–58
Don Welsh 1958–61
Bill McGarry 1961–63
Reg Flewin 1963–65
Fred Cox 1965–70
John Bond 1970–73
Trevor Hartley 1974–75
John Benson 1975–78
Alec Stock 1979–80
David Webb 1980–82
Don Megson 1983
Harry Redknapp 1983–92
Tony Pulis 1992–94
Mel Machin 1994–2000
Sean O'Driscoll August 2000–

LATEST SEQUENCES

Longest Sequence of League Wins: 7, 22.8.1970 – 23.9.1970.

Longest Sequence of League Defeats: 7, 13.8.1994 – 13.9.1994.

Longest Sequence of League Draws: 5, 25.4.2000 – 12.8.2000.

Longest Sequence of Unbeaten League Matches: 18, 6.3.1982 – 28.8.1982.

Longest Sequence Without a League Win: 14, 6.3.1974 – 27.4.1974.

Successive Scoring Runs: 31 from 28.10.2000.

Successive Non-scoring Runs: 6 from 1.2.1975.

TEN YEAR LEAGUE RECORD

		P	W	D	L	F	A	Pts	Pos
1993-94	Div 2	46	14	15	17	51	59	57	17
1994-95	Div 2	46	13	11	22	49	69	50	19
1995-96	Div 2	46	16	10	20	51	70	58	14
1996-97	Div 2	46	15	15	16	43	45	60	16
1997-98	Div 2	46	18	12	16	57	52	66	9
1998-99	Div 2	46	21	13	12	63	41	76	7
1999-2000	Div 2	46	16	9	21	59	62	57	16
2000-01	Div 2	46	20	13	13	79	55	73	7
2001-02	Div 2	46	10	14	22	56	71	44	21
2002-03	Div 3	46	20	14	12	60	48	74	4

DID YOU KNOW ?

On 14 December 2002 Neil Moss kept goal for Bournemouth. Three days later Gareth Stewart broke his leg against Southend United and was replaced by Chris Tardif. On 21 December Tardif had to go off and midfeld player Marcus Browning took over in goal.

AFC BOURNEMOUTH 2002–03 LEAGUE RECORD

Match No.	Date	Venue	Opponents	Result	H/T Score	Lg. Pos.	Goalscorers	Attendance
1	Aug 10	A	Boston U	D 2-2	1-0	—	Maher [9], Stock [54]	4184
2	13	H	Kidderminster H	D 0-0	0-0	—		4771
3	17	H	Cambridge U	D 1-1	0-1	15	Feeney [65]	4315
4	24	A	Swansea C	L 0-2	0-1	22		4325
5	27	H	Oxford U	D 1-1	1-0	—	Holmes [42]	4842
6	31	A	Macclesfield T	W 1-0	1-0	16	Connell [41]	1795
7	Sept 7	A	Exeter C	W 3-1	2-1	9	Connell [36], Elliott (pen) [41], O'Connor [73]	4466
8	14	H	Bury	L 1-2	0-1	14	O'Connor [71]	4851
9	17	H	Rushden & D	W 3-1	1-1	—	Purches S [22], Maher [58], Connell [85]	4527
10	21	A	Darlington	D 2-2	1-1	10	Holmes [27], Connell [82]	2950
11	28	H	Carlisle U	W 3-1	0-0	8	Tindall [62], Connell (pen) [77], Stock [86]	5103
12	Oct 5	A	Lincoln C	W 2-1	1-1	6	Purches S [13], Connell [64]	3273
13	13	H	Hartlepool U	W 2-1	0-1	4	Elliott [61], Widdrington (og) [85]	5998
14	19	A	Leyton Orient	D 0-0	0-0	2		5622
15	26	H	York C	W 1-0	0-0	2	Fletcher S [78]	5755
16	29	A	Torquay U	L 0-4	0-2	—		3543
17	Nov 2	H	Bristol R	W 1-0	1-0	3	Fletcher S [16]	6924
18	9	A	Wrexham	L 2-3	1-1	3	Thomas [30], Hayter [54]	3105
19	23	A	Southend U	W 1-0	0-0	3	O'Connor (pen) [71]	4221
20	30	H	Scunthorpe U	W 2-1	0-1	3	Broadhurst [59], Hayter [66]	6527
21	Dec 14	A	Shrewsbury T	D 0-0	0-0	3		2869
22	21	H	Hull C	D 0-0	0-0	3		6098
23	26	A	Oxford U	L 0-3	0-1	4		8349
24	28	H	Rochdale	D 3-3	2-2	4	Browning [6], Fletcher S [45], O'Connor (pen) [87]	6240
25	Jan 18	H	Macclesfield T	D 2-2	0-2	7	Elliott [68], Hayter [73]	5840
26	Feb 1	H	Boston U	W 2-1	0-0	8	Redfearn (og) [89], Feeney [90]	5180
27	4	A	Kidderminster H	L 0-1	0-0	—		2157
28	8	H	Wrexham	W 2-0	0-0	7	Feeney 2 [52, 55]	5445
29	11	H	Swansea C	W 3-0	1-0	—	Hayter [45], O'Connor 2 (2 pens) [89, 90]	5511
30	15	A	Bristol R	D 0-0	0-0	3		6347
31	22	H	Exeter C	W 2-0	1-0	3	Holmes [36], O'Connor [80]	6674
32	Mar 1	A	Bury	L 1-2	1-1	3	Feeney [12]	2914
33	4	A	Rushden & D	L 1-2	1-1	—	Feeney [43]	4353
34	8	H	Darlington	W 2-0	1-0	3	O'Connor [28], Hayter [67]	5758
35	11	A	Rochdale	D 1-1	1-0	—	Fletcher C [31]	1958
36	15	A	York C	L 0-1	0-0	4		3642
37	18	H	Leyton Orient	W 3-1	2-0	—	Jones (og) [9], Hayter [17], Feeney [60]	5078
38	22	H	Torquay U	D 1-1	0-0	3	Young [90]	7181
39	25	A	Cambridge U	L 1-2	1-1	—	Fletcher S [42]	2885
40	29	A	Hartlepool U	D 0-0	0-0	4		5625
41	Apr 5	A	Scunthorpe U	W 2-0	0-0	3	Hayter [49], Thomas [77]	4488
42	12	H	Southend U	W 1-0	1-0	4	Purches S [9]	6767
43	19	A	Hull C	L 1-3	1-2	4	Fletcher S [5]	15,816
44	21	H	Shrewsbury T	W 2-1	2-1	4	McDonald [22], Elliott [45]	7102
45	26	H	Lincoln C	L 0-1	0-1	4		7578
46	May 3	A	Carlisle U	W 2-0	0-0	4	Hayter 2 [86, 90]	7402

Final League Position: 4

GOALSCORERS

League (60): Hayter 9, O'Connor 8 (4 pens), Feeney 7, Connell 6 (1 pen), Fletcher S 5, Elliott 4 (1 pen), Holmes 3, Purches S 3, Maher 2, Stock 2, Thomas 2, Broadhurst 1, Browning 1, Fletcher C 1, McDonald 1, Tindall 1, Young 1, own goals 3.
Worthington Cup (3): Thomas 2, Connell 1.
FA Cup (8): Fletcher S 2, Broadhurst 1, Browning 1, Elliott 1, Hayter 1, Holmes 1, Thomas 1.
LDV Vans Trophy (7): Hayter 2, Elliott 1, Feeney 1, Fletcher C 1, Fletcher S 1, Purches S 1.
Play-offs (8): Fletcher C 2, Hayter 2, O'Connor 2, Fletcher S 1, Purches S 1.

Tardif C 9	Young N 29 + 3	Purches S 43 + 1	Broadhurst K 20 + 1	Tindall J 24 + 3	Maher S 7 + 1	Stock B 14 + 13	O'Connor G 29 + 12	Hayter J 35 + 10	Feeney W 11 + 10	Elliott W 39 + 5	Browning M 40 + 3	Holmes D 11 + 18	Fletcher C 42	Connell A 10 + 3	Bernard N 3 + 4	Thomas D 30 + 7	Ashdown J 2	Eribenne C — + 6	Moss N 33	Fletcher S 29 + 6	Ridgewell L 2 + 3	Blayney A 2	Buxton L 15 + 2	Cummings W 20	Foyewa A — + 1	McDonald S 3 + 4	Gulliver P 4 + 2	Stewart G — + 1	*Match No.*
1	2	3	4	5	6	7^{1}	8^{2}	9	10	11	12	13																	1
1	2	3		5	6	4^{1}	8	9^{3}	10	11^{2}	12	13	7	14															2
1		3		5	6		8^{2}	9^{1}	11	12	4	10^{3}	7	14	2	13													3
1	2■	6	3	5		12	7^{1}	9	10^{2}	11	4		8	13															4
	2	6	3	5				12		11	4	10	8	9^{1}		7	1												5
	2	6	3	5	12		13	14		11	4	9^{3}	8	10^{1}		7^{2}	1												6
1		3	2	5	6		12	13		11	4	9^{3}	8	10^{2}		7^{1}		14											7
	2^{2}	3		5	6	14	13	12		11■	4^{3}	9	8	10^{1}		7			1										8
	2	3		5	6					11	4	9^{1}	8	10		7		12	1										9
	2	3	12	5	6^{1}	13		14		11^{3}	4	9	8	10		7^{2}			1										10
	2	6	3	5		12	11^{1}	13			4	9^{3}	8	10^{2}		7		14	1										11
	2	3	4			8		9		11^{2}	6		5	10^{3}	12	7^{1}		13	1	14									12
	2	3	4			8	12	9^{2}		11	6^{1}		5	10^{3}		7			1	13	14								13
	2	3	4			8^{3}	12	13		11^{1}	6		5	10^{2}		7			1	14	9								14
	2^{3}	6	3			8	12	9	13	11^{1}	4		5			7^{2}			1	10	14								15
	2^{3}	3	4			14	8	9	12	13	6^{1}		5			7^{2}			1	10	11								16
	2	3	4				8	9^{1}	12	11	6	13	5		14	7^{3}			1	10^{2}									17
	2^{2}	3	4				8	9	12	11^{1}	6	13	5			7^{3}			1	10	14								18
		3	4	12			8	9		11	6		5		2	7^{1}			1	10									19
	2	3	4	12			8	9^{2}		11	6	13	5			7^{1}			1	10									20
	2^{2}	3	4				8	9	12	11	6		5		13	7^{1}			1	10									21
1^{G}	2^{2}	3	4	15			8	9	12	11^{1}	6		5		13	7				10									22
	2^{3}	3		4		12	8	9^{1}	13	11	6■	14	5			7				10^{2}		1							23
	2	3		4			8	9	12	11^{1}	6		5			7				10		1							24
1		3		4		13	8^{1}	9	12	11	6		5		2^{3}	7^{2}				10			14						25
1		3		4		6	8^{1}	9	12	11	13	14	5			7^{3}				10			2^{2}						26
1		3	4^{3}	5		6	8	9^{1}		11		12				7^{2}		13		10				2	14				27
		3^{1}	4	5		7	8^{2}	9	11	12		13							1	10			6	2					28
			4^{1}	5		7	12	9^{2}		11	6	13	8						1	10			3	2					29
				4		7^{2}	12	9	8	11^{1}	6	14	5			13			1	10^{3}			3	2					30
		12		4		7^{2}	13	9^{1}	8	11	6	10^{3}	5						1	14			3	2					31
		3		6		7	8^{1}	9	11	12			5			13			1	10			4^{2}	2					32
		3^{2}		4^{3}			8	9	7^{1}	11	6	13	5			12			1	10			14	2					33
	12	3				13	8^{2}	9^{3}		11^{1}	6	14	5			7			1	10			4	2					34
		3					8	9		11	6	12	5			7^{1}			1	10			4	2					35
		3				12	8	9		11^{3}	6	10	5			7^{1}		13	1	14			4	2^{2}					36
	12	3		4		13	8	9	11^{2}		6	14	5^{1}						1	10^{3}			7	2					37
	12	3^{3}		5^{1}			8	9^{2}	7	11	6	14				13			1	10			4	2					38
	2	3^{2}				11^{1}	8	9		12	6	13	5						1	10			4	7					39
	2	3					8^{1}	9		11^{2}	6		5			12			1	10			4	7		13			40
	2	7					8^{1}	9^{2}		11	6		5			12			1	10^{3}			4	3		13	14		41
	2	6				12		9^{2}		11^{3}	8		5			7^{1}			1	10			4	3		13	14		42
	2	6				12	13	9^{3}		11	8		5			7^{2}			1	10				3^{1}		14	4		43
	2	4				12	8^{1}	13		11	7	14	5						1	10^{3}				3		9^{2}	6		44
	2^{1}	4					13	12		11	8	10^{3}	5			7			1	14				3		9	6^{2}		45
	2	8					12	13		11	4		5			7^{1}			1^{G}	10				3		9^{2}	6	15	46

Worthington Cup

First Round	Brentford	(h)	3-3

LDV Vans Trophy

First Round	Oxford U	(a)	3-2
Second Round	Leyton Orient	(h)	1-0
Quarter-final	Cardiff C	(h)	2-1
Semi-final	Bristol C	(h)	1-3

FA Cup

First Round	Doncaster R	(h)	2-1
Second Round	Southend U	(a)	1-1
		(h)	3-2
Third Round	Crewe Alex	(h)	0-0
		(a)	2-2
Fourth Round	Stoke C	(a)	0-3

BRADFORD CITY — Division 1

FOUNDATION

Bradford was a rugby stronghold around the turn of the century but after Manningham RFC held an archery contest to help them out of financial difficulties in 1903, they were persuaded to give up the handling code and turn to soccer. So they formed Bradford City and continued at Valley Parade. Recognising this as an opportunity of spreading the dribbling code in this part of Yorkshire, the Football League immediately accepted the new club's first application for membership of the Second Division.

Bradford & Bingley Stadium, Valley Parade, Bradford BD8 7DY.

Telephone: (01274) 773 355 (Office). ***Fax:*** (01274) 773 356.
Ticket Office: (01274) 770 022.
Website: www.bradfordcityfc.co.uk
Email: bradfordcityfc@compuserve.com
ClubCall: 09068 888 640.

Ground Capacity: 25,136.

Record Attendance: 39,146 v Burnley, FA Cup 4th rd, 11 March 1911.

Record Receipts: £164,567 v Sheffield Wednesday, FA Cup 5th rd, 16 February 1997.

Pitch Measurements: 110yd × 73yd.

Chairman: Gordon Gibb. ***Directors:*** Julian Rhodes, Prof. David Rhodes, Andrew Richardson.

Managing Director: Shaun Harvey.

HONOURS

Football League: Division 1 – Runners-up 1998–99; Division 2 – Champions 1907–08; Promoted from Division 2 1995–96 (play-offs); Division 3 – Champions 1984–85; Division 3 (N) – Champions 1928–29; Division 4 – Runners-up 1981–82.

FA Cup: Winners 1911.

Football League Cup: best season: 5th rd, 1965, 1989.

European Competitions: *Intertoto Cup:* 2000.

Manager: Nicky Law. ***Assistant Manager:*** Chris Dowhan. ***Physio:*** Steve Redmond.

Secretary: Jon Pollard.

Stadium Manager: Allan Gilliver.

Colours: Claret and amber shirts, claret shorts, claret stockings with amber trim.

Change Colours: Sky blue and navy shirts, navy shorts, sky blue stockings with navy trim.

Year Formed: 1903.

Turned Professional: 1903.

Ltd Co.: 1908.

Club Nickname: 'The Bantams'.

First Football League Game: 1 September 1903, Division 2, v Grimsby T (a) L 0–2 – Seymour; Wilson, Halliday; Robinson, Millar, Farnall; Guy, Beckram, Forrest, McMillan, Graham.

Record League Victory: 11–1 v Rotherham U, Division 3 (N), 25 August 1928 – Sherlaw; Russell, Watson; Burkinshaw (1), Summers, Bauld; Harvey (2), Edmunds (3), White (3), Cairns, Scriven (2).

SKY SPORTS FACT FILE

On 28 January 1939 Bradford City right-back and captain George Murphy had to take over in goal against Accrington Stanley. He saved an 85th minute penalty but conceded the rebound. City still won 3-2.

Record Cup Victory: 11–3 v Walker Celtic, FA Cup 1st rd (replay), 1 December 1937 – Parker; Rookes, McDermott; Murphy, Mackie, Moore; Bagley (1), Whittingham (1), Deakin (4 incl. 1p), Cooke (1), Bartholomew (4).

Record Defeat: 1–9 v Colchester U, Division 4, 30 December 1961.

Most League Points (2 for a win): 63, Division 3 (N), 1928–29.

Most League Points (3 for a win): 94, Division 3, 1984–85.

Most League Goals: 128, Division 3 (N), 1928–29.

Highest League Scorer in Season: David Layne, 34, Division 4, 1961–62.

Most League Goals in Total Aggregate: Bobby Campbell, 121, 1981–84, 1984–86.

Most League Goals in One Match: 7, Albert Whitehurst v Tranmere R, Division 3N, 6 March 1929.

Most Capped Player: Jamie Lawrence, 12, Jamaica.

Most League Appearances: Cec Podd, 502, 1970–84.

Youngest League Player: Robert Cullingford, 16 years 141 days v Mansfield T, 22 April 1970.

Record Transfer Fee Received: £2,000,000 from Newcastle U for Des Hamilton, March 1997 and £2,000,000 from Newcastle U for Andrew O'Brien, March 2001.

Record Transfer Fee Paid: £2,500,000 to Leeds U for David Hopkin, July 2000.

Football League Record: 1903 Elected to Division 2; 1908–22 Division 1; 1922–27 Division 2; 1927–29 Division 3 (N); 1929–37 Division 2; 1937–61 Division 3; 1961–69 Division 4; 1969–72 Division 3; 1972–77 Division 4; 1977–78 Division 3; 1978–82 Division 4; 1982–85 Division 3; 1985–90 Division 2; 1990–92 Division 3; 1992–96 Division 2; 1996–99 Division 1; 1999–2001 FA Premier League; 2001– Division 1.

MANAGERS

Robert Campbell 1903–05
Peter O'Rourke 1905–21
David Menzies 1921–26
Colin Veitch 1926–28
Peter O'Rourke 1928–30
Jack Peart 1930–35
Dick Ray 1935–37
Fred Westgarth 1938–43
Bob Sharp 1943–46
Jack Barker 1946–47
John Milburn 1947–48
David Steele 1948–52
Albert Harris 1952
Ivor Powell 1952–55
Peter Jackson 1955–61
Bob Brocklebank 1961–64
Bill Harris 1965–66
Willie Watson 1966–69
Grenville Hair 1967–68
Jimmy Wheeler 1968–71
Bryan Edwards 1971–75
Bobby Kennedy 1975–78
John Napier 1978
George Mulhall 1978–81
Roy McFarland 1981–82
Trevor Cherry 1982–87
Terry Dolan 1987–89
Terry Yorath 1989–90
John Docherty 1990–91
Frank Stapleton 1991–94
Lennie Lawrence 1994–95
Chris Kamara 1995–98
Paul Jewell 1998–2000
Chris Hutchings 2000
Jim Jefferies 2000–01
Nicky Law January 2002–

LATEST SEQUENCES

Longest Sequence of League Wins: 10, 26.11.1983 – 3.2.1984.

Longest Sequence of League Defeats: 8, 21.1.1933 – 11.3.1933.

Longest Sequence of League Draws: 6, 30.1.1976 – 13.3.1976.

Longest Sequence of Unbeaten League Matches: 21, 11.1.1969 – 2.5.1969.

Longest Sequence Without a League Win: 16, 28.8.1948 – 20.11.1948.

Successive Scoring Runs: 30 from 26.12.1961.

Successive Non-scoring Runs: 7 from 18.4.1925.

TEN YEAR LEAGUE RECORD

		P	*W*	*D*	*L*	*F*	*A*	*Pts*	*Pos*
1993-94	Div 2	46	19	13	14	61	53	70	7
1994-95	Div 2	46	16	12	18	57	64	60	14
1995-96	Div 2	46	22	7	17	71	69	73	6
1996-97	Div 1	46	12	12	22	47	72	48	21
1997-98	Div 1	46	14	15	17	46	59	57	13
1998-99	Div 1	46	26	9	11	82	47	87	2
1999-2000	PR Lge	38	9	9	20	38	68	36	17
2000-01	PR Lge	38	5	11	22	30	70	26	20
2001-02	Div 1	46	15	10	21	69	76	55	15
2002-03	Div 1	46	14	10	22	51	73	52	19

DID YOU KNOW?

Chester-born centre-forward Jack Hallows was a product of Liverpool's Bluecoat FC and was a junior with West Bromwich Albion. But had to go non-league with Grays Thurrock to kick-start his successful career with Bradford City from 1930.

BRADFORD CITY 2002–03 LEAGUE RECORD

Match No.	Date	Venue	Opponents	Result		H/T Score	Lg. Pos.	Goalscorers	Attendance
1	Aug 11	H	Wolverhampton W	D	0-0	0-0	—		13,223
2	13	A	Crystal Palace	D	1-1	0-0	—	Tod [76]	15,205
3	17	A	Stoke C	L	1-2	0-2	18	Gray [90]	12,424
4	24	H	Grimsby T	D	0-0	0-0	19		10,914
5	26	A	Ipswich T	W	2-1	1-1	12	Evans [24], Proctor [83]	25,457
6	31	H	Rotherham U	W	4-2	1-0	9	Ward 2 [24, 86], Uhlenbeek [47], Proctor [56]	12,385
7	Sept 14	A	Walsall	W	1-0	0-0	9	Gray [53]	4678
8	17	A	Leicester C	L	0-4	0-2	—		24,651
9	21	H	Burnley	D	2-2	1-0	10	Gray [17], Proctor [90]	14,561
10	24	H	Coventry C	D	1-1	1-0	—	Evans [25]	11,655
11	28	A	Portsmouth	L	0-3	0-2	13		18,459
12	Oct 5	H	Preston NE	D	1-1	1-1	12	Proctor [20]	13,215
13	12	H	Derby Co	D	0-0	0-0	12		13,385
14	19	A	Sheffield W	L	1-2	1-1	14	Warnock [44]	17,191
15	26	H	Norwich C	W	2-1	1-0	13	Reid 2 [41, 55]	12,888
16	29	A	Reading	L	0-1	0-0	—		12,110
17	Nov 2	A	Brighton & HA	L	2-3	0-2	18	Gray 2 (1 pen) [49, 90 (p)]	6319
18	9	H	Wimbledon	L	3-5	3-2	19	Facey [8], Standing 2 [31, 45]	10,615
19	16	A	Nottingham F	L	0-3	0-3	20		19,653
20	23	H	Sheffield U	L	0-5	0-2	20		13,364
21	30	A	Millwall	L	0-1	0-0	20		8510
22	Dec 7	H	Gillingham	L	1-3	1-0	20	Gray [42]	10,711
23	14	H	Nottingham F	W	1-0	1-0	20	Molenaar [42]	12,245
24	21	A	Watford	L	0-1	0-0	20		12,579
25	26	H	Stoke C	W	4-2	1-2	20	Gray 2 (1 pen) [20 (p), 89], Handyside (og) [67], Jorgensen [70]	14,575
26	28	A	Wolverhampton W	W	2-1	0-0	20	Jorgensen [51], Gray [59]	25,812
27	Jan 18	A	Rotherham U	L	2-3	1-1	20	Jorgensen [2], Gray (pen) [62]	6939
28	25	A	Grimsby T	W	2-1	0-1	19	Gray [57], Jorgensen [90]	5582
29	Feb 1	H	Ipswich T	W	2-0	0-0	19	Jorgensen [62], Forrest [68]	12,080
30	8	A	Wimbledon	D	2-2	1-0	19	Jorgensen [30], Ward [60]	1178
31	15	H	Brighton & HA	L	0-1	0-1	19		11,520
32	22	A	Coventry C	W	2-0	1-0	19	Gray [22], Jorgensen [83]	12,525
33	Mar 1	H	Walsall	L	1-2	0-0	20	Forrest [62]	10,893
34	4	H	Leicester C	D	0-0	0-0	—		11,531
35	8	H	Crystal Palace	W	2-1	0-1	19	Atherton [70], Francis [73]	11,016
36	15	A	Derby Co	W	2-1	1-1	18	Jorgensen [14], Lawrence [90]	23,735
37	18	H	Sheffield W	D	1-1	1-0	—	Gray (pen) [32]	14,452
38	22	H	Reading	L	0-1	0-0	18		11,385
39	25	A	Burnley	W	2-0	1-0	—	Jorgensen [18], Gray [89]	11,095
40	29	A	Norwich C	L	2-3	1-0	15	Forrest [42], Jorgensen (pen) [68]	18,536
41	Apr 5	H	Millwall	L	0-1	0-0	16		10,676
42	19	H	Watford	W	2-1	2-1	17	Jorgensen [13], Gray (pen) [43]	11,145
43	21	A	Gillingham	L	0-1	0-1	17		6281
44	26	A	Preston NE	L	0-1	0-1	18		13,652
45	29	A	Sheffield U	L	0-3	0-0	—		18,297
46	May 4	H	Portsmouth	L	0-5	0-1	19		19,088

Final League Position: 19

GOALSCORERS

League (51): Gray 15 (5 pens), Jorgensen 11 (1 pen), Proctor 4, Forrest 3, Ward 3, Evans 2, Reid 2, Standing 2, Atherton 1, Facey 1, Francis 1, Lawrence 1, Molenaar 1, Tod 1, Uhlenbeek 1, Warnock 1, own goal 1.
Worthington Cup (1): Cadamarteri 1.
FA Cup (1): Danks 1.

Walsh G 3	Uhlenbeek G 42	Emanuel L 25 + 4	Evans P 16 + 3	Wetherall D 16 + 1	Myers A 21 + 3	Gray A 44	Kearney T 4	Ward A 24	Cadamarteri D 14 + 6	Lawrence J 15 + 1	Atherton P 25	Bower M 36 + 1	Tod A 4 + 1	Molenaar R 28 + 1	Davison A 33 + 1	Standing M 14 + 10	Proctor M 10 + 2	Jacobs W 19 + 4	Juanjo 2 + 7	Jorgensen C 28 + 4	Warnock S 12	Banks S 8 + 1	Reid P 7 + 1	Facey D 6	Singh H 3	Francis S 24 + 1	Danks M — + 3	Myhill B 2	Forrest D 10 + 7	Lee A — + 1	Muirhead B 5 + 3	Ten Heuvel L 4 + 1	McHugh F 2	Penford T — + 3	Sanasy K — + 1	*Match No.*
1	2	3	4	5	6	7	8	9	10	11																										1
1	2	3^{1}	4		6	7	8	9	10^{2}	11	5	12	13																							2
1	2	3	4		6	7	8	9	12	11^{2}	5		10^{1}	13																						3
	2		4		3	7	8^{1}	9	10		5			6	1	11	12																			4
	2		4		3	7		9	10^{2}		5^{1}	6			1	11^{3}	8	12	13	14																5
	2		4		3	7		9	10			6		5	1	11^{1}	8			12																6
	2		4			7		9	10		3	6		5	1		8^{1}	12			11															7
	2		12		3	7^{1}		9^{3}	10		6^{2}	4		5	1	13	8		14		11															8
	2		8		6^{1}	7			10■			4■		5	1		9	3		12	11															9
	2		4			7			10			6		5	1^{6}		9	3		8	11	15														10
	2		4^{2}			7			10^{1}			6		5			9	3	12	8	11	1	13													11
	2	7^{1}			6	4		9						5		12	10	3		8	11	1														12
	2	12	8		6	7		9				4		5^{2}			10	3^{1}	13		11	1														13
	2	12	4^{2}		3	7		9				6		5		13	10^{3}	11^{1}	14		8	1														14
	2				3	7		9	10			4		5			12	11^{1}			8	1	6													15
	2	12	13		3^{1}	7		9	10			4		5				11^{3}	14		8	1	6^{2}													16
	2	12	4			3		9^{2}	10^{1}			6		5		13		11	14		8	1	7^{3}													17
	2	3^{1}	4			7			12			6		5	15	10					8	1^{6}		9	11											18
		3	4			7						6		5	1	8			10					9^{1}	11	2	12									19
	2■	3	4^{1}		13	7						6				8		12	10	14				9^{2}	11^{3}	5		1								20
	2	7^{2}			6	10				11	4			5		12		3■						9		8^{1}	13	1								21
		11		12	6	10				8	4			5^{1}	1	13		3		7				9^{3}		2^{2}	14									22
		2			6	10				11	4			5	1	8				7				9		3										23
		3	12			10				7	4	6	9^{1}	5	1	8				11						2										24
	2	7				10				8	4	6^{1}	9	5	1	12		3		11																25
	2	7				10					4	6	9		1	8		3		11						5										26
	2	4				10		9		7	6■			5	1	8^{1}		3		11						12										27
	2					10		9		7	6			5	1	8		3		11						4■										28
	2	7						9				6		5	1	8		3		11						4			10							29
	2	4^{1}				10		9	12		5	6			1	8		3		11									7^{2}	13						30
	2					10		9	7^{1}		5	6			1	8		3		11						4			12							31
	2	3		5		10		9	12	7		6			1					11						4			8^{1}							32
	2	8^{1}		5		10		9	12	7		6			1	13		3^{3}		11						4^{2}			14							33
	2	8		5		10				7	3	6			1					11						4			9							34
	2	7		5	3^{1}	10		9			4	6			1					11						8			12							35
	2	7		5	3^{1}	10		9		13	4	6			1			12		11						8^{2}										36
	2	3^{1}		5		10		9^{2}		7■	4	6			1	12				11						8			13							37
	2			5		10				7	4	3			1	12				11			8^{1}			6			9^{2}		13					38
	2			5		10					4	6			1					11			8			3			9		7					39
	2			5							4	6			1					11			8			3			9		7	10				40
	2	3		5	12	10			13		4	6			1					11			8						9^{2}		7^{1}					41
	2	7		5		10					4	3		6	1					11						8			12			9^{1}				42
	2	7^{2}		5	12	10						3^{1}		4	1					11						6			14		13	9^{3}	8			43
	2^{3}			5	3	10						6		4	1					11						7			12		13	9^{1}	8^{2}	14		44
	2			5	3	10						6		4	1					11						8			9^{2}		7^{1}			12	13	45
	2			5	3	10						6		4^{2}	1					11						8			9^{1}		7	12		13		46

Worthington Cup
First Round Wrexham (a) 1-2

FA Cup
Third Round WBA (a) 1-3

BRENTFORD Division 2

FOUNDATION

Formed as a small amateur concern in 1889 they were very successful in local circles. They won the championship of the West London Alliance in 1893 and a year later the West Middlesex Junior Cup before carrying off the Senior Cup in 1895. After winning both the London Senior Amateur Cup and the Middlesex Senior Cup in 1898 they were admitted to the Second Division of the Southern League.

Griffin Park, Braemar Road, Brentford, Middlesex TW8 0NT.

Telephone: (020) 8847 2511. ***Fax:*** (020) 8568 9940.
Commercial Dept: (020) 8847 2511
Press Office: (020) 8847 2511. ***ClubCall:*** 09068 121 108.

Ground Capacity: 12,500.

Record Attendance: 38,678 v Leicester C, FA Cup 6th rd, 26 February 1949.

Record Receipts: £162,314 v Tottenham H, Worthington Cup 2nd rd, 15 September 1998.

Pitch Measurements: 111yd × 74yd.

Chairman: Eddie Rogers. ***President:*** Denis Smith.
Managing Director: G. Hargraves.
Directors: J. Herting, J. McGlashan, S. Callen, A. Wainwright.

Manager: Wally Downes. ***Coach:*** Garry Thompson.
Director of Youth Football: Geoff Taylor.
Physio: Phil McLoughlin.

HONOURS

Football League: Division 1 best season: 5th, 1935–36; Division 2 – Champions 1934–35; Division 3 – Champions 1991–92, 1998–99; Division 3 (S) – Champions 1932–33, Runners-up 1929–30, 1957–58; Division 4 – Champions 1962–63.

FA Cup: best season: 6th rd, 1938, 1946, 1949, 1989.

Football League Cup: best season: 4th rd, 1983.

Freight Rover Trophy: Runners-up 1985.

LDV Vans Trophy: Runners-up 2001.

Community Officer: Lee Doyle. ***Secretary:*** Lisa Hall. ***Safety Officer:*** Roy King.

Communications Manager: Peter Gilham. ***Corporate Sales Manager:*** Victoria Mountier.

Colours: Red and white vertical striped shirts, black shorts, black stockings.

Change Colours: All old gold and black.

Year Formed: 1889.

Turned Professional: 1899.

Ltd Co.: 1901.

Club Nickname: 'The Bees'.

Previous Grounds: 1889, Clifden Road; 1891, Benns Fields, Little Ealing; 1895, Shotters Field; 1898, Cross Road, S. Ealing; 1900, Boston Park; 1904, Griffin Park.

First Football League Game: 28 August 1920, Division 3, v Exeter C (a) L 0–3 – Young; Hodson, Rosier, Elliott J, Levitt, Amos, Smith, Thompson, Spreadbury, Morley, Henery.

Record League Victory: 9–0 v Wrexham, Division 3, 15 October 1963 – Cakebread; Coote, Jones; Slater, Scott, Higginson; Summers (1), Brooks (2), McAdams (2), Ward (2), Hales (1), (1 og).

SKY SPORTS FACT FILE

George Stewart, early post-war Brentford inside-forward signed from Hamilton Academical, broke one leg on tour in Turkey and the other leg the following year on the same ground. He subsequently played with Queens Park Rangers and Shrewsbury Town.

Record Cup Victory: 7–0 v Windsor & Eton (away), FA Cup 1st rd, 20 November 1982 – Roche; Rowe, Harris (Booker), McNichol (1), Whitehead, Hurlock (2), Kamara, Joseph (1), Mahoney (3), Bowles, Roberts.
N.B. 8–0 v Uxbridge, FA Cup, 3rd Qual rd, 31 October 1903.

Record Defeat: 0–7 v Swansea T, Division 3 (S), 8 November 1924 and v Walsall, Division 3 (S), 19 January 1957.

Most League Points (2 for a win): 62, Division 3 (S), 1932–33 and Division 4, 1962–63.

Most League Points (3 for a win): 85, Division 2, 1994–95 and Division 3, 1998–99.

Most League Goals: 98, Division 4, 1962–63.

Highest League Scorer in Season: Jack Holliday, 38, Division 3 (S), 1932–33.

Most League Goals in Total Aggregate: Jim Towers, 153, 1954–61.

Most League Goals in One Match: 5, Jack Holliday v Luton T, Division 3S, 28 January 1933; Billy Scott v Barnsley, Division 2, 15 December 1934; Peter McKennan v Bury, Division 2, 18 February 1949.

Most Capped Player: John Buttigieg, 22 (98), Malta.

Most League Appearances: Ken Coote, 514, 1949–64.

Youngest League Player: Danis Salman, 15 years 243 days v Watford, 15 November 1975.

Record Transfer Fee Received: £2,500,000 from Wimbledon for Hermann Hreidarsson, October 1999.

Record Transfer Fee Paid: £850,000 to Crystal Palace for Hermann Hreidarsson, September 1998.

Football League Record: 1920 Original Member of Division 3; 1921–33 Division 3 (S); 1933–35 Division 2; 1935–47 Division 1; 1947–54 Division 2; 1954–62 Division 3 (S); 1962–63 Division 4; 1963–66 Division 3; 1966–72 Division 4; 1972–73 Division 3; 1973–78 Division 4; 1978–92 Division 3; 1992–93 Division 1; 1993–98 Division 2; 1998 –99 Division 3; 1999– Division 2.

MANAGERS

Will Lewis 1900–03
(Secretary-Manager)
Dick Molyneux 1902–06
W. G. Brown 1906–08
Fred Halliday 1908–12, 1915–21, 1924–26
(only Secretary to 1922)
Ephraim Rhodes 1912–15
Archie Mitchell 1921–24
Harry Curtis 1926–49
Jackie Gibbons 1949–52
Jimmy Blain 1952–53
Tommy Lawton 1953
Bill Dodgin Snr 1953–57
Malcolm Macdonald 1957–65
Tommy Cavanagh 1965–66
Billy Gray 1966–67
Jimmy Sirrel 1967–69
Frank Blunstone 1969–73
Mike Everitt 1973–75
John Docherty 1975–76
Bill Dodgin Jnr 1976–80
Fred Callaghan 1980–84
Frank McLintock 1984–87
Steve Perryman 1987–90
Phil Holder 1990–93
David Webb 1993–97
Eddie May 1997
Micky Adams 1997–98
Ron Noades 1998–2000
Ray Lewington 2001
Steve Coppell 2001–02
Wally Downes June 2002–

LATEST SEQUENCES

Longest Sequence of League Wins: 9, 30.4.1932 – 24.9.1932.

Longest Sequence of League Defeats: 9, 20.10.1928 – 25.12.1928.

Longest Sequence of League Draws: 5, 16.3.1957 – 6.4.1957.

Longest Sequence of Unbeaten League Matches: 26, 20.2.1999 – 16.10.1999.

Longest Sequence Without a League Win: 16, 19.2.1994 – 7.5.1994.

Successive Scoring Runs: 26 from 4.3.1963.

Successive Non-scoring Runs: 7 from 7.3.2000.

TEN YEAR LEAGUE RECORD

		P	W	D	L	F	A	Pts	Pos
1993-94	Div 2	46	13	19	14	57	55	58	16
1994-95	Div 2	46	25	10	11	81	39	85	2
1995-96	Div 2	46	15	13	18	43	49	58	15
1996-97	Div 2	46	20	14	12	56	43	74	4
1997-98	Div 2	46	11	17	18	50	71	50	21
1998-99	Div 3	46	26	7	13	79	56	85	1
1999-2000	Div 2	46	13	13	20	47	61	52	17
2000-01	Div 2	46	14	17	15	56	70	59	14
2001-02	Div 2	46	24	11	11	77	43	83	3
2002-03	Div 2	46	14	12	20	47	56	54	16

DID YOU KNOW?

Jim Towers and George Francis, the 'Terrible Twins' of Brentford goalscoring fame in the 1950s with respectively 153 and 124 League goals, had played on opposite sides as youngsters with cinema teams: Jim (Gaumont), George (Odeon).

BRENTFORD 2002–03 LEAGUE RECORD

Match No.	*Date*	*Venue*	*Opponents*	*Result*	*H/T Score*	*Lg. Pos.*	*Goalscorers*	*Attendance*
1	Aug 10	A	Huddersfield T	W 2-0	2-0	—	Fullarton[26], Vine[39]	9635
2	13	H	Bristol C	W 1-0	0-0	—	Hunt (pen)[68]	7130
3	17	H	Oldham Ath	D 0-0	0-0	4		5356
4	24	A	Colchester U	W 1-0	1-0	2	Hunt (pen)[45]	3135
5	26	H	Swindon T	W 3-1	2-1	1	Vine 2[7, 14], McCammon[78]	6299
6	31	A	Notts Co	D 2-2	0-1	1	McCammon[56], Williams[78]	5551
7	Sept 7	H	Luton T	D 0-0	0-0	2		7145
8	14	A	Tranmere R	L 1-3	0-1	4	O'Connor[90]	6626
9	17	A	Cardiff C	L 0-2	0-1	—		12,032
10	21	H	Wycombe W	W 1-0	0-0	7	Hunt (pen)[57]	6172
11	28	A	Peterborough U	L 1-5	0-1	9	Vine[86]	5066
12	Oct 5	H	Barnsley	L 1-2	1-1	9	McCammon[26]	5394
13	12	A	Northampton T	W 2-1	2-0	9	Sonko[7], Vine[25]	5739
14	19	H	Port Vale	D 1-1	0-0	9	Hunt (pen)[56]	5177
15	26	A	Stockport Co	W 3-2	1-1	8	McCammon 2[8, 52], Marshall[70]	4601
16	29	H	Plymouth Arg	D 0-0	0-0	—		6431
17	Nov 2	H	Blackpool	W 5-0	2-0	6	Vine[32], Evans 2[37, 90], Sonko 2[60, 86]	5888
18	9	A	Crewe Alex	L 1-2	0-1	7	Sonko[62]	5663
19	23	H	Wigan Ath	L 0-1	0-1	7		5454
20	30	A	Cheltenham T	L 0-1	0-0	9		5013
21	Dec 14	H	Chesterfield	W 2-1	1-1	6	Hunt[6], Vine[48]	5151
22	21	A	QPR	D 1-1	1-1	6	O'Connor[30]	15,559
23	26	A	Swindon T	L 1-2	0-1	9	Vine[76]	6045
24	28	H	Mansfield T	W 1-0	0-0	8	O'Connor[58]	5844
25	Jan 14	A	Oldham Ath	L 1-2	1-1	—	O'Connor[28]	5039
26	18	H	Notts Co	D 1-1	0-1	10	Vine[51]	5112
27	Feb 4	A	Mansfield T	D 0-0	0-0	—		3735
28	8	H	Crewe Alex	L 1-2	1-0	14	Hunt[11]	5424
29	11	A	Bristol C	D 0-0	0-0	—		9084
30	15	A	Blackpool	L 0-1	0-1	13		6203
31	22	A	Luton T	W 1-0	0-0	13	Vine[50]	6940
32	25	H	Huddersfield T	W 1-0	0-0	—	McCammon[56]	4366
33	Mar 1	H	Tranmere R	L 1-2	0-1	12	Sonko[90]	5396
34	4	H	Cardiff C	L 0-2	0-0	—		5727
35	8	A	Wycombe W	L 0-4	0-2	13		5930
36	11	H	Colchester U	D 1-1	1-0	—	McCammon[37]	3990
37	15	H	Stockport Co	L 1-2	1-0	12	Antoine-Curier[39]	4790
38	18	A	Port Vale	L 0-1	0-1	—		3241
39	22	A	Plymouth Arg	L 0-3	0-2	15		6835
40	29	H	Northampton T	W 3-0	0-0	14	Somner[52], Rowlands[77], Hunt[90]	5354
41	Apr 5	H	Cheltenham T	D 2-2	0-2	14	Dobson[63], O'Connor[78]	5011
42	12	A	Wigan Ath	L 0-2	0-0	14		7204
43	19	H	QPR	L 1-2	0-1	17	Peters[81]	9168
44	21	A	Chesterfield	W 2-0	1-0	15	Antoine-Curier 2[36, 55]	3296
45	26	A	Barnsley	L 0-1	0-0	15		9065
46	May 3	H	Peterborough U	D 1-1	0-0	16	Evans[67]	6687

Final League Position: 16

GOALSCORERS

League (47): Vine 10, Hunt 7 (4 pens), McCammon 7, O'Connor 5, Sonko 5, Antoine-Curier 3, Evans 3, Dobson 1, Fullarton 1, Marshall 1, Peters 1, Rowlands 1, Somner 1, Williams 1.
Worthington Cup (4): O'Connor 2 (2 pens), Sonko 1, Vine 1.
FA Cup (7): Hunt 2, Vine 2, McCammon 1, O'Connor 1, Somner 1.
LDV Vans Trophy (4): Hunt 1, McCammon 1, Marshall 1, O'Connor 1.

Smith P 43	Sonko I 37	Dobson M 45 + 1	Somner M 39 + 1	Roget L 14	Hutchinson E 21 + 2	Fullarton J 22 + 5	O'Connor K 44 + 1	McCammon M 31 + 6	Vine R 37 + 5	Hunt S 41 + 1	Smith J 23 + 3	Constantine L 2 + 15	Williams M 4 + 18	Anderson I 9	Hughes S 2 + 1	Evans S 20 + 3	Chorley B 2	Blackman L 1	Marshall S 22 + 2	Peters M 3 + 8	Frampton A 9 + 6	Rowlands M 13 + 5	Tabb J 1 + 4	Julian A 3	Lovett J 1	Traynor R — + 2	Fieldwick L 6 + 1	Antoine-Curier M 11	Match No.
1	4	2	3	5	6	7[1]	8	9[2]	10	11	12	13																	1
1	4	2	3	5	6		8	9	10	11	7																		2
1	4	2	3	5	6		8[1]	9[2]	10	11	7	13	12																3
1	4	2	3	5	6		8	9	10[1]	11	7	12																	4
1	4	2	3	5	6		8	9[1]	10	11	7	12																	5
1	4	2	3	5	6	12	8[2]	9	10	11	7[1]		13																6
1	5	2	4		6	12	8[2]	9	10	11[3]	7[1]		13	3	14														7
1	5	2	4		6[2]	12	8	9	10[3]	11	7[1]	14	13	3															8
1	5	2	4		6[2]	7	8	9[1]	12	11[3]		10	13	3		14													9
1		2		5	6	7	8	9[1]	10	11		12		3			4												10
1		2[1]	12	5	6		8[2]		10	11[3]	7	14	13	3			4	9											11
1	4	2		5	6	7	8	9[1]	10	11[2]		12		3		13													12
1	4	2		5	6	7	8	9[1]	10	11		12		3															13
1	4	2		5[2]	6	7	8[1]	9[3]	10	11			12	3					13	14									14
1		2	4		6	7	8	9	10[1]	3			12			11			5										15
1		2	4		6[1]	7[2]	8	9	10	11			12			3			5		13								16
1	4	2	3			7	8	9[1]	10[2]	11[3]		12	13			6			5		14								17
1	4	2	3[2]			7■	8	9[1]		11		12	10[3]			6			5■		13	14							18
1	4	2	5				8[1]	9	10	11	7[3]		12	3		6[2]						13	14						19
1	4	2	3				8	9[1]	12	11[2]	7					6			5			10	13						20
1	4	3	2			12	9	13	10	11	8[1]					6[2]			5			7							21
1	4	2	3			7	9	12	10	11						6[1]			5			8							22
	4	2	3			7■	9	12	10	11			13			6[1]			5[2]			8		1					23
	4	2	3			7	8[1]	9	10■	11			12			6			5					1					24
1	4	12					8	9		11	7[3]		10[1]			6			5		3	13			2[2]	14			25
1	4	2					8	9[1]	10	11	7		6[2]						5	12	3					13			26
1	4	2	3			7	9		10[1]	11	8	12				6[2]			5			13							27
1	4	2	3			7[1]	8	12	10	9[2]	13					11			5			6■							28
1	4	2	3			7	9	12	10	11	8					6[1]			5										29
1	4	2	3			7	8	12	10	9[2]	11		13		6[1]				5										30
1		2	4		12	7[1]	6	9	10	11	8										3						5		31
1	4	2	3		6		8	9	10	11	7																5		32
1	4	2	3		6[2]		8	9[3]	12		7	10			11[1]				13	14							5		33
1	4	2	3		6		8[1]	9[2]	10		7	13								12	5	11							34
1		2	3		6		8	9[1]	10		7[2]	12							5	13■	4	11							35
1		2	3				8	9[2]	10[1]		12								5	13	4	11					6	7	36
1		2	3		12		8[2]	9	10	13									5		4[1]	11					6	7	37
1	5	2	3		6[2]		8	9	10[1]	11										12	4[3]	13					14	7	38
1	5	2	3				8	9[1]	10	11			12								4	6						7	39
1		2	3	5[2]					10	11	7		12			4					13	8[1]					6	9	40
1	4	2	3	5■		12	13		10	11	7[3]					8[2]					14	6						9[1]	41
1	4	2	3	5		7	10		12[2]	11		13				8						6[1]						9	42
1	4	2	3			7	8			11						12			5	10			6					9[1]	43
1	4	2[2]	3			7	8			11[3]			12			6			5	10[1]	13		14					9	44
	4	2	3			7	8		12	11			13			6			5	10[1]				1				9[2]	45
1	4	2	3				8		10	11			7[2]			6			5	12			13					9[1]	46

Worthington Cup

First Round	Bournemouth	(a)	3-3
Second Round	Middlesbrough	(h)	1-4

LDV Vans Trophy

Second Round	Plymouth Arg	(a)	1-0
Quarter-final	Kidderminster H	(h)	2-1
Semi-final	Cambridge U	(h)	1-2

FA Cup

First Round	Wycombe W	(a)	4-2
Second Round	York C	(a)	2-1
Third Round	Derby Co	(h)	1-0
Fourth Round	Burnley	(h)	0-3

BRIGHTON & HOVE ALBION Division 2

FOUNDATION

A professional club Brighton United was formed in November 1897 at the Imperial Hotel, Queen's Road, but folded in March 1900 after less than two seasons in the Southern League at the County Ground. An amateur team, Brighton & Hove Rangers was then formed by some prominent United supporters and after one season at Withdean, decided to turn semi-professional and play at the County Ground. Rangers were accepted into the Southern League but then also folded June 1901. John Jackson the former United manager organised a meeting at the Seven Stars public house, Ship Street on 24 June 1901 at which a new third club Brighton & Hove United was formed. They took over Rangers' place in the Southern League and pitch at County Ground. The name was changed to Brighton & Hove Albion before a match was played because of objections by Hove FC.

Administration Offices: North West Suite, 8th Floor, Tower Point, 44 North Road, Brighton BN1 1YR.

Ground Address: Withdean Stadium, Tongdean Lane, Brighton BN1 5JD.

Telephone: (01273) 695 400. ***Fax:*** (01273) 648 179.
Website: www.seagulls.co.uk
Ticketline: (01273) 776 992. ***ClubCall:*** 09068 800 609.

Ground Capacity: 6,973 (all seated).

Record Attendance: 36,747 v Fulham, Division 2, 27 December 1958.

Record Receipts: £109,615.65 v Crawley T, FA Cup 3rd rd, 4 January 1992.

Pitch Measurements: 110yd × 70yd.

Directors: Dick Knight (Chairman), Ray Bloom, Derek Chapman, Martin Perry, Bob Pinnock FCA, Kevin Griffiths, Chris Kidger.
Non-executive Director: Sir John Smith QPM.

HONOURS

Football League: Division 1 best season: 13th, 1981–82; Division 2 – Champions 2001–02; Runners-up 1978–79; Division 3 (S) – Champions 1957–58; Runners-up 1953–54, 1955–56; Division 3 – Champions 2000–01; Runners-up 1971–72, 1976–77, 1987–88; Division 4 – Champions 1964–65.

FA Cup: Runners-up 1983.

Football League Cup: best season: 5th rd, 1979.

Manager: Steve Coppell. ***Assistant Manager:*** Bob Booker. ***Director of Football:*** Martin Hinshelwood.
Physio: Malcolm Stuart. ***Youth Team Coach:*** Dean Wilkins.

Chief Executive: Martin Perry. ***Secretary:*** Derek Allan.

Colours: Blue and white striped shirts, white shorts, white stockings.

Change Colours: Yellow shirts, black shorts, black stockings.

Year Formed: 1901.

Turned Professional: 1901. ***Ltd Co.:*** 1904.

Previous Grounds: 1901, County Ground; 1902, Goldstone Ground. ***Club Nickname:*** 'The Seagulls'.

First Football League Game: 28 August 1920, Division 3, v Southend U (a) L 0–2 – Hayes; Woodhouse, Little; Hall, Comber, Bentley; Longstaff, Ritchie, Doran, Rodgerson, March.

SKY SPORTS FACT FILE

Bobby Zamora created an individual scoring record for Brighton & Hove Albion by registering in each of ten consecutive League and Cup matches from October to December 2001. The previous best sequence had been eight.

Record League Victory: 9–1 v Newport Co, Division 3 (S), 18 April 1951 – Ball; Tennant (1p), Mansell (1p); Willard, McCoy, Wilson; Reed, McNichol (4), Garbutt, Bennett (2), Keene (1). 9–1 v Southend U, Division 3, 27 November 1965 – Powney; Magill, Baxter; Leck, Gall, Turner; Gould (1), Collins (1), Livesey (2), Smith (3), Goodchild (2).

Record Cup Victory: 10–1 v Wisbech, FA Cup 1st rd, 13 November 1965 – Powney; Magill, Baxter; Collins (1), Gall, Turner; Gould, Smith (2), Livesey (3), Cassidy (2), Goodchild (1), (1 og).

Record Defeat: 0–9 v Middlesbrough, Division 2, 23 August 1958.

Most League Points (2 for a win): 65, Division 3 (S), 1955–56 and Division 3, 1971–72.

Most League Points (3 for a win): 92, Division 3, 2000–01.

Most League Goals: 112, Division 3 (S), 1955–56.

Highest League Scorer in Season: Peter Ward, 32, Division 3, 1976–77.

Most League Goals in Total Aggregate: Tommy Cook, 114, 1922–29.

Most League Goals in One Match: 5, Jack Doran v Northampton T, Division 3S, 5 November 1921; 5, Adrian Thorne v Watford, Division 3S, 30 April 1958.

Most Capped Player: Steve Penney, 17, Northern Ireland.

Most League Appearances: 'Tug' Wilson, 509, 1922–36.

Youngest League Player: Ian Chapman, 16 years 259 days v Birmingham C, 14 February 1987.

Record Transfer Fee Received: £900,000 from Liverpool for Mark Lawrenson, August 1981.

Record Transfer Fee Paid: £500,000 to Manchester U for Andy Ritchie, October 1980.

Football League Record: 1920 Original Member of Division 3; 1921–58 Division 3 (S); 1958–62 Division 2; 1962–63 Division 3; 1963–65 Division 4; 1965–72 Division 3; 1972–73 Division 2; 1973–77 Division 3; 1977–79 Division 2; 1979–83 Division 1; 1983–87 Division 2; 1987–88 Division 3; 1988–96 Division 2; 1996–2001 Division 3; 2001–02 Division 2; 2002–03 Division 1; 2003– Division 2.

MANAGERS

John Jackson 1901–05
Frank Scott-Walford 1905–08
John Robson 1908–14
Charles Webb 1919–47
Tommy Cook 1947
Don Welsh 1947–51
Billy Lane 1951–61
George Curtis 1961–63
Archie Macaulay 1963–68
Fred Goodwin 1968–70
Pat Saward 1970–73
Brian Clough 1973–74
Peter Taylor 1974–76
Alan Mullery 1976–81
Mike Bailey 1981–82
Jimmy Melia 1982–83
Chris Cattlin 1983–86
Alan Mullery 1986–87
Barry Lloyd 1987–93
Liam Brady 1993–95
Jimmy Case 1995–96
Steve Gritt 1996–98
Brian Horton 1998–99
Jeff Wood 1999
Micky Adams 1999–2001
Peter Taylor 2001–02
Martin Hinshelwood 2002
Steve Coppell October 2002–

LATEST SEQUENCES

Longest Sequence of League Wins: 9, 2.10.1926 – 20.11.1926.

Longest Sequence of League Defeats: 12, 17.8.2002 – 26.10.2002.

Longest Sequence of League Draws: 6, 16.2.1980 – 15.3.1980.

Longest Sequence of Unbeaten League Matches: 16, 8.10.1930 – 28.1.1931.

Longest Sequence Without a League Win: 15, 21.10.1972 – 27.1.1973

Successive Scoring Runs: 31 from 4.2.1956.

Successive Non-scoring Runs: 6 from 8.11.1924.

TEN YEAR LEAGUE RECORD

		P	W	D	L	F	A	Pts	Pos
1993-94	Div 2	46	15	14	17	60	67	59	14
1994-95	Div 2	46	14	17	15	54	53	59	16
1995-96	Div 2	46	10	10	26	46	69	40	23
1996-97	Div 3	46	13	10	23	53	70	47	23
1997-98	Div 3	46	6	17	23	38	66	35	23
1998-99	Div 3	46	16	7	23	49	66	55	17
1999-2000	Div 3	46	17	16	13	64	46	67	11
2000-01	Div 3	46	28	8	10	73	35	92	1
2001-02	Div 2	46	25	15	6	66	42	90	1
2002-03	Div 1	46	11	12	23	49	67	45	23

DID YOU KNOW?

Goalkeeper Harry Baldwin made his first appearance for Brighton & Hove Albion after signing from West Bromwich Albion on the eve of the Second World War in 1939. Apart from wartime games on leave from the Navy he had a long wait for his next 164 League outings.

BRIGHTON & HOVE ALBION 2002–03 LEAGUE RECORD

Match No.	Date	Venue	Opponents	Result		H/T Score	Lg. Pos.	Goalscorers	Attendance
1	Aug 10	A	Burnley	W	3-1	1-0	—	Melton 29, Brooker 65, Zamora 68	14,738
2	13	H	Coventry C	D	0-0	0-0	—		6816
3	17	H	Norwich C	L	0-2	0-0	12		6730
4	24	A	Wimbledon	L	0-1	0-0	16		2522
5	26	H	Walsall	L	0-2	0-2	19		6519
6	31	A	Portsmouth	L	2-4	2-3	22	Cullip 9, Brooker 19	19,031
7	Sept 7	A	Millwall	L	0-1	0-0	22		8822
8	14	H	Gillingham	L	2-4	1-3	23	Brown (og) 27, Hart 80	6733
9	17	H	Stoke C	L	1-2	0-1	—	Carpenter 79	6369
10	21	A	Rotherham U	L	0-1	0-1	23		6696
11	28	H	Grimsby T	L	1-2	0-1	24	Zamora 71	6547
12	Oct 5	A	Watford	L	0-1	0-1	24		15,305
13	19	H	Sheffield U	L	2-4	2-0	24	Hart 23, Barrett 34	6810
14	26	A	Crystal Palace	L	0-5	0-2	24		21,796
15	Nov 2	H	Bradford C	W	3-2	2-0	24	Zamora 2 (2 pens) 10, 55, Rodger 42	6319
16	11	A	Wolverhampton W	D	1-1	1-0	—	Zamora 15	23,016
17	16	H	Derby Co	W	1-0	0-0	24	Mayo 89	6845
18	23	A	Preston NE	D	2-2	0-2	24	Rodger 53, Sidwell 72	13,068
19	27	A	Nottingham F	L	2-3	0-2	—	Sidwell 80, Jones 90	29,137
20	30	H	Reading	L	0-1	0-1	24		6817
21	Dec 7	A	Sheffield W	D	1-1	1-0	24	Hart 20	18,008
22	10	H	Ipswich T	D	1-1	1-0	—	Zamora 45	6377
23	14	A	Derby Co	L	0-1	0-1	23		25,786
24	20	H	Leicester C	L	0-1	0-0	—		6592
25	26	A	Norwich C	W	1-0	1-0	23	Sidwell 38	20,687
26	28	H	Burnley	D	2-2	0-1	23	Sidwell 2 88, 89	6502
27	Jan 11	A	Coventry C	D	0-0	0-0	24		15,951
28	18	H	Portsmouth	D	1-1	0-0	24	Zamora 54	6848
29	Feb 1	A	Walsall	L	0-1	0-1	24		8413
30	4	H	Wimbledon	L	2-3	1-1	—	Brooker 3, Zamora 86	6111
31	8	H	Wolverhampton W	W	4-1	2-0	24	Zamora 31, Blackwell 45, Brooker 47, Hart 67	6754
32	15	A	Bradford C	W	1-0	1-0	22	Zamora 28	11,520
33	22	H	Millwall	W	1-0	0-0	21	Rougier 65	6751
34	Mar 1	A	Gillingham	L	0-3	0-0	21		9178
35	5	A	Stoke C	L	0-1	0-0	—		21,023
36	8	H	Rotherham U	W	2-0	0-0	21	Hurst (og) 56, Zamora 68	6468
37	15	H	Nottingham F	W	1-0	1-0	21	Brooker 16	6830
38	18	A	Sheffield U	L	1-2	1-2	—	Carpenter 14	19,357
39	22	A	Ipswich T	D	2-2	0-1	23	Marshall (og) 66, Rougier 81	26,078
40	25	H	Crystal Palace	D	0-0	0-0	—		6786
41	Apr 4	A	Reading	W	2-1	1-0	—	Brooker 17, Kitson 77	16,133
42	12	H	Preston NE	L	0-2	0-0	22		6669
43	19	A	Leicester C	L	0-2	0-2	22		31,909
44	21	H	Sheffield W	D	1-1	0-1	22	Zamora (pen) 57	6928
45	26	H	Watford	W	4-0	2-0	22	Blackwell 13, Kitson 27, Zamora 72, Oatway 90	6841
46	May 4	A	Grimsby T	D	2-2	1-1	23	Zamora (pen) 45, Cullip 47	6396

Final League Position: 23

GOALSCORERS

League (49): Zamora 14 (4 pens), Brooker 6, Sidwell 5, Hart 4, Blackwell 2, Carpenter 2, Cullip 2, Kitson 2, Rodger 2, Rougier 2, Barrett 1, Jones 1, Mayo 1, Melton 1, Oatway 1, own goals 3.
Worthington Cup (3): Cullip 1, Hammond 1, Wilkinson 1.
FA Cup (1): Pethick 1.

Kuipers M 21	Watson P 45	Mayo K 41	Hinshelwood A 4 + 3	Pethick R 25 + 1	Carpenter R 42 + 2	Melton S 6 + 2	Oatway C 18 + 11	Hart G 27 + 9	Zamora B 35	Brooker P 32 + 5	Rogers P 1 + 3	Wilkinson S 4 + 8	Marney D 6 + 6	Cullip D 44	Harding D — + 1	Kitson P 7 + 3	Petterson A 6 + 1	Jones N 16 + 12	Butters G 6	Barrett G 20 + 10	McPhee C — + 2	Hammond D 1 + 3	Piercy J 1 + 3	Virgo A 3	Blackwell D 18 + 3	Rodger S 27 + 2	Sidwell S 11 + 1	Webb D — + 3	Roberts B 3	Beasant D 16	Ingimarsson I 15	Rougier T 5 + 1	Match No.
1	2	3	4	5	6	7^1	8	9^2	10^3	11	12	13	14																				1
1	2	3		5	6		8	9	10	11	7^1	12		4																			2
1	2	3		5	6		8	9	10^1	11		7^2	12	4	13																		3
1	2	3^2	12	5	6^1	13	8	9^3		11		7	14	4		10																	4
	2		3	5	6	7^1	8			11		12	10	4		9^2	1	13															5
	2			3	6	7^1	8			11		12	10	4			1		5	9■													6
	2			3■	6	7	8			11^1			10^2	4		9	1	12	5		13												7
	2			3	6	7^2	8	12				10^1	13	4		9	1	11^3	5			14											8
	2			3^1	6	7^2	8^3	9				11	10	4			1	12	5		13	14											9
	2	3			6		8	9			12	13	10	4			1	11^2	5				7^1										10
1	2	3			6		8^2	7	10^1	11			12	4						9		13		5									11
1	2	3			6	12		13	10	11^2			7	4						9		8^1		5									12
1	2^1	3	12		6		8	7	10	11^2		13							5	9				4									13
1	2	3			6^3		8^1	7	10	11■	12		13	4						9^2					5	14							14
1■	2	3			6		12	7	10	11^6				4			15			9					5	8^1							15
1	2	3	12	11	6		13	8	10					4						9^2					5^1	7^3	14						16
1	2	3	5^1	11	6			9	10^2					4				12								7	8	13					17
1	2	3		11	6			7	10					4				12							5^1	8	9						18
1	2^2	6		5	12		8^1	9		10				4				3								11	7	13					19
1	2	6		5	8^2			9	10	12				4				3^1								11	7	13					20
1	2	3		5	6			9	10					4				11		12						7^1	8						21
1	2	3		5	6		12		10	7^1				4				11		9^2			13				8						22
1		3	2	5	6^1			12	10	13				4				11^2		9						7	8						23
1	2	3		5	6			12	10	13				4				11^1		9						7	8^2						24
1	2	3		5	6		12	13	10					4				11		9^2						7^1	8						25
1	2	3		5	6		7^1	12	10	13				4				11^2		9							8						26
1	2	3		5	6				10	7				4				11		9							8						27
	2	3		5	6		8^2		10	7				4		12		11		9^1					13				1				28
	2	3		5	6^2		8^3	12	10	7				4				11		9^1					14	13				1			29
	2^2	3		5			6	9■	10	7^1				4				11^3		12			14		13	8				1			30
	2	3		5	8		12	9	10	7^1				4											6	11			1				31
	2	3			8			9	10	7^1				4						12					5	11			1		6		32
	2	3			7				10	11^1				4						9					5	8				1	6	12	33
	2	3^1			7					11^3		14		4				12		9^2			13		5	8				1	6	10	34
	2^2	3			7^1		12		10	11				4						13					5	8				1	6	9	35
	2	3			7				10	11				4											5	8				1	6	9	36
	2^3	3			7		13	12	10	11^2				4				14							5	8				1	6	9^1	37
	2	3			7^1		12	9	10^3	11				4				13		14					5	8^2				1	6		38
	2^2	3			7			9^1		11				4				13		12					5	8				1	6	10	39
	2	3		12	7			9		11				4^1						10					5	8				1	6		40
	2	3			6		12	7^2	10	11				4		14		13		9^3						8^1				1	5		41
	2	3			6			9	10	11^1				4		13		12		7^2						8				1	5		42
	2	3			7		12	9	10^3	11^1				4				13		14					5^2	8				1	6		43
	2^2	3			7			12	10	11^1				4		9				13					5	8				1	6		44
	2	3					12	7^2	10			14		4		9^3		11		13					5	8^1				1	6		45
	2^2	3			12			7	10	13				4		9^3		11^1		14					5	8				1	6		46

Worthington Cup
First Round Exeter C (h) 2-1
Second Round Ipswich T (a) 1-3

FA Cup
Third Round Norwich C (a) 1-3

BRISTOL CITY — Division 2

FOUNDATION

The name Bristol City came into being in 1897 when the Bristol South End club, formed three years earlier, decided to adopt professionalism and apply for admission to the Southern League after competing in the Western League. The historic meeting was held at The Albert Hall, Bedminster. Bristol City employed Sam Hollis from Woolwich Arsenal as manager and gave him £40 to buy players. In 1900 they merged with Bedminster, another leading Bristol club.

Ashton Gate, Bristol BS3 2EJ.

Telephone: (0117) 963 0630 (5 lines).
Fax: (0117) 963 0700. ***Website:*** www.bcfc.co.uk
Commercial: (0117) 963 0600. ***Shop:*** (0117) 963 0637.
ClubCall: 09068 121 176. ***Supporters Club:*** (0117) 966 5554. ***Community Dept:*** (0117) 963 0636.

Ground Capacity: 21,479.

Record Attendance: 43,335 v Preston NE, FA Cup 5th rd, 16 February 1935.

Record Receipts: £251,612 v Everton, FA Cup 4th rd, 23 January 1999.

Pitch Measurements: 115yd × 75yd.

Chairman: S. Lansdown.

Directors: S. Lansdown, K. Dawe, A. Gooch, J. Laycock.

Chief Executive: Colin Sexstone.

Football Secretary: Michelle McDonald.

Manager: Danny Wilson. ***Physio:*** Gill Holt.

Stadium Manager: Dave Lewis.

Commercial Manager: Richard Gould.

Safety Officer: Keith Draisey.

Colours: Red shirts, red shorts, white stockings.

Change Colours: All black.

Year Formed: 1894.

Turned Professional: 1897.

Ltd Co.: 1897. Bristol City Football Club Ltd.

Previous Name: 1894, Bristol South End; 1897, Bristol City.

Club Nickname: 'Robins'.

Previous Grounds: 1894, St John's Lane; 1904, Ashton Gate.

First Football League Game: 7 September 1901, Division 2, v Blackpool (a) W 2–0 – Moles; Tuft, Davies; Jones, McLean, Chambers; Bradbury, Connor, Boucher, O'Brien (2), Flynn.

HONOURS

Football League: Division 1 – Runners-up 1906–07; Division 2 – Champions 1905–06; Runners-up 1975–76, 1997–98; Division 3 (S) – Champions 1922–23, 1926–27, 1954–55; Runners-up 1937–38; Division 3 – Runners-up 1964–65, 1989–90.

FA Cup: Runners-up 1909.

Football League Cup: Semi-final 1971, 1989.

Welsh Cup: Winners 1934.

Anglo-Scottish Cup: Winners 1978.

Freight Rover Trophy: Winners 1986; Runners-up 1987.

Auto Windscreens Shield: Runners-up 2000.

LDV Vans Trophy: Winners 2003.

SKY SPORTS FACT FILE

When Bristol City sold centre-forward Roy Bentley to Newcastle United in 1946, the clubs could not agree the fee of either £8,500 or £8,000. The respective chairmen tossed a coin and United saved themselves £500.

Record League Victory: 9–0 v Aldershot, Division 3 (S), 28 December 1946 – Eddols; Morgan, Fox; Peacock, Roberts, Jones (1); Chilcott, Thomas, Clark (4 incl. 1p), Cyril Williams (1), Hargreaves (3).

Record Cup Victory: 11–0 v Chichester C, FA Cup 1st rd, 5 November 1960 – Cook; Collinson, Thresher; Connor, Alan Williams, Etheridge; Tait (1), Bobby Williams (1), Atyeo (5), Adrian Williams (3), Derrick, (1 og).

Record Defeat: 0–9 v Coventry C, Division 3 (S), 28 April 1934.

Most League Points (2 for a win): 70, Division 3 (S), 1954–55.

Most League Points (3 for a win): 91, Division 3, 1989–90.

Most League Goals: 104, Division 3 (S), 1926–27.

Highest League Scorer in Season: Don Clark, 36, Division 3 (S), 1946–47.

Most League Goals in Total Aggregate: John Atyeo, 314, 1951–66.

Most League Goals in One Match: 6, Tommy 'Tot' Walsh v Gillingham, Division 3S, 15 January 1927.

Most Capped Player: Billy Wedlock, 26, England.

Most League Appearances: John Atyeo, 597, 1951–66.

Youngest League Player: Nyrere Kelly, 16 years 213 days v Hartlepool U, 16 October 1982.

Record Transfer Fee Received: £3,000,000 from Wolverhampton W for Ade Akinbiyi, September 1999.

Record Transfer Fee Paid: £1,200,000 to Gillingham for Ade Akinbiyi, May 1998.

Football League Record: 1901 Elected to Division 2; 1906–11 Division 1; 1911–22 Division 2; 1922–23 Division 3 (S); 1923–24 Division 2; 1924–27 Division 3 (S); 1927–32 Division 2; 1932–55 Division 3 (S); 1955–60 Division 2; 1960–65 Division 3; 1965–76 Division 2; 1976–80 Division 1; 1980–81 Division 2; 1981–82 Division 3; 1982–84 Division 4; 1984–90 Division 3; 1990–92 Division 2; 1992–95 Division 1; 1995–98 Division 2; 1998–99 Division 1; 1999– Division 2.

MANAGERS

Sam Hollis 1897–99
Bob Campbell 1899–1901
Sam Hollis 1901–05
Harry Thickett 1905–10
Sam Hollis 1911–13
George Hedley 1913–17
Jack Hamilton 1917–19
Joe Palmer 1919–21
Alex Raisbeck 1921–29
Joe Bradshaw 1929–32
Bob Hewison 1932–49
(under suspension 1938–39)
Bob Wright 1949–50
Pat Beasley 1950–58
Peter Doherty 1958–60
Fred Ford 1960–67
Alan Dicks 1967–80
Bobby Houghton 1980–82
Roy Hodgson 1982
Terry Cooper 1982–88
(Director from 1983)
Joe Jordan 1988–90
Jimmy Lumsden 1990–92
Denis Smith 1992–93
Russell Osman 1993–94
Joe Jordan 1994–97
John Ward 1997–98
Benny Lennartsson 1998–99
Tony Pulis 1999
Tony Fawthrop 2000
Danny Wilson June 2000–

LATEST SEQUENCES

Longest Sequence of League Wins: 14, 9.9.1905 – 2.12.1905.

Longest Sequence of League Defeats: 7, 3.10.1970 – 7.11.1970.

Longest Sequence of League Draws: 4, 6.11.1999 – 27.11.1999.

Longest Sequence of Unbeaten League Matches: 24, 9.9.1905 – 10.2.1906.

Longest Sequence Without a League Win: 15, 29.4.1933 – 4.11.1933.

Successive Scoring Runs: 25 from 26.12.1905.

Successive Non-scoring Runs: 6 from 10.9.1910.

TEN YEAR LEAGUE RECORD

		P	*W*	*D*	*L*	*F*	*A*	*Pts*	*Pos*
1993-94	Div 1	46	16	16	14	47	50	64	13
1994-95	Div 1	46	11	12	23	42	63	45	23
1995-96	Div 2	46	15	15	16	55	60	60	13
1996-97	Div 2	46	21	10	15	69	51	73	5
1997-98	Div 2	46	25	10	11	69	39	85	2
1998-99	Div 1	46	9	15	22	57	80	42	24
1999-2000	Div 2	46	15	19	12	59	57	64	9
2000-01	Div 2	46	18	14	14	70	56	68	9
2001-02	Div 2	46	21	10	15	68	53	73	7
2002-03	Div 2	46	24	11	11	79	48	83	3

DID YOU KNOW ?

Despite the disappointment in finishing just third in the Second Division in 1920–21, Bristol City could point to their excellent defensive record which saw them concede only 29 goals in their 42 League matches.

BRISTOL CITY 2002–03 LEAGUE RECORD

Match No.	Date	Venue	Opponents	Result		H/T Score	Lg. Pos.	Goalscorers	Attendance
1	Aug 10	H	Blackpool	W	2-0	0-0	—	Peacock [77], Murray [90]	11,891
2	13	A	Brentford	L	0-1	0-0	—		7130
3	17	A	Wigan Ath	L	0-2	0-0	18		6548
4	24	H	Wycombe W	W	3-0	1-0	11	Bell [38], Murray [52], Roberts [72]	9597
5	26	A	Plymouth Arg	L	0-2	0-0	15		11,922
6	31	H	Tranmere R	W	2-0	0-0	10	Tinnion (pen) [70], Murray [74]	9849
7	Sept 6	H	Northampton T	W	3-0	1-0	—	Peacock 2 [7, 76], Clist [87]	11,104
8	14	A	Cheltenham T	W	3-2	2-2	2	Murray [3], Coles [43], Matthews [53]	5895
9	17	A	Oldham Ath	L	0-1	0-0	—		5583
10	21	H	QPR	L	1-3	1-1	9	Murray [11]	12,221
11	28	A	Port Vale	W	3-2	2-0	8	Beadle [18], Murray [40], Lita [90]	4286
12	Oct 5	H	Chesterfield	W	4-0	1-0	6	Roberts [26], Hill [63], Murray 2 [89, 90]	10,107
13	12	A	Barnsley	W	4-1	2-0	5	Butler [19], Roberts 3 [28, 58, 73]	10,495
14	19	H	Swindon T	W	2-0	2-0	3	Murray [12], Tinnion [38]	13,205
15	26	A	Peterborough U	W	3-1	2-1	3	Tinnion [3], Brown A [17], Murray [90]	5332
16	29	H	Huddersfield T	W	1-0	1-0	—	Hill [38]	11,494
17	Nov 9	A	Colchester U	D	2-2	1-0	4	Peacock 2 [42, 58]	3338
18	23	A	Mansfield T	W	5-4	1-1	4	Murray [39], Roberts 2 [50, 90], Tinnion (pen) [87], Lita [89]	4801
19	30	H	Crewe Alex	D	2-2	0-2	4	Murray [48], Peacock [84]	12,585
20	Dec 3	H	Notts Co	W	3-2	1-1	—	Beadle [33], Murray [57], Peacock [83]	10,690
21	14	A	Cardiff C	W	2-0	0-0	2	Tinnion (pen) [49], Roberts [76]	15,239
22	21	H	Luton T	D	1-1	0-0	3	Beadle [90]	14,057
23	26	H	Plymouth Arg	D	0-0	0-0	2		18,085
24	28	A	Stockport Co	W	4-1	3-0	2	Peacock [19], Coles [40], Rosenior [45], Beadle [89]	5100
25	Jan 1	A	Wycombe W	L	1-2	0-0	3	Tinnion (pen) [87]	6785
26	10	H	Wigan Ath	L	0-1	0-0	—		13,151
27	18	A	Tranmere R	D	1-1	1-0	5	Bell [10]	7459
28	25	H	Stockport Co	D	1-1	0-1	5	Roberts [50]	10,831
29	Feb 1	A	Blackpool	D	0-0	0-0	5		7290
30	8	H	Colchester U	L	1-2	0-1	5	Fagan [51]	11,107
31	11	H	Brentford	D	0-0	0-0	—		9084
32	15	A	Notts Co	L	0-2	0-0	5		5754
33	22	A	Northampton T	W	2-1	2-1	5	Robins [12], Tinnion [35]	4688
34	Mar 1	H	Cheltenham T	W	3-1	2-1	5	Robins [2], Brown A [20], Rosenior [90]	11,711
35	4	H	Oldham Ath	W	2-0	0-0	—	Murray [54], Roberts [90]	11,194
36	8	A	QPR	L	0-1	0-1	5		14,681
37	15	H	Peterborough U	W	1-0	1-0	5	Robins [12]	11,231
38	19	A	Swindon T	D	1-1	0-0	—	Robins [48]	8629
39	22	A	Huddersfield T	W	2-1	2-1	5	Hill [17], Peacock [36]	9477
40	29	H	Barnsley	W	2-0	1-0	4	Murray [6], Roberts [63]	10,232
41	Apr 12	H	Mansfield T	W	5-2	2-1	4	Peacock [13], Murray 3 [32, 51, 80], Carey [70]	12,013
42	15	A	Crewe Alex	D	1-1	0-1	—	Roberts [62]	7901
43	19	A	Luton T	D	2-2	0-1	5	Tinnion (pen) [66], Peacock [75]	6381
44	22	H	Cardiff C	W	2-0	0-0	—	Tinnion (pen) [55], Roberts [73]	15,615
45	26	A	Chesterfield	L	0-2	0-0	4		4770
46	May 3	H	Port Vale	W	2-0	2-0	3	Murray [31], Peacock [43]	12,410

Final League Position: 3

GOALSCORERS

League (79): Murray 19, Roberts 13, Peacock 12, Tinnion 9 (6 pens), Beadle 4, Robins 4, Hill 3, Bell 2, Brown A 2, Coles 2, Lita 2, Rosenior 2, Butler 1, Carey 1, Clist 1, Fagan 1, Matthews 1.
Worthington Cup (0).
FA Cup (10): Murray 3, Roberts 3, Lita 2, Tinnion 1 (pen), own goal 1.
LDV Vans Trophy (17): Murray 5, Peacock 3, Bell 2, Burnell 1, Carey 1, Coles 1, Doherty 1, Roberts 1, Robins 1, Rosenior 1.
Play-offs (0).

Phillips S 46	Coles D 38 + 1	Bell M 37 + 1	Burnell J 43 + 1	Millen K 3	Hill M 39 + 3	Murray S 45	Doherty T 38	Peacock L 33 + 4	Roberts C 31 + 13	Brown A 21 + 11	Lita L — + 15	Rosenior L 2 + 19	Fortune C 7 + 3	Woodman C 7 + 3	Matthews L 3 + 4	Hulbert R 2 + 5	Beadle P 11 + 13	Butler T 38	Tinnion B 30 + 10	Clist S — + 3	Carey L 21 + 3	Fagan C 5 + 1	Robins M 6	Amankwaah K — + 1	Match No.
1	2	3	4	5	6	7	8	9	10[1]	11[2]	12	13													1
1	2	3	4[1]	5	6	7	8	9	10[2]	11■	12	13													2
1	2■	3	4	5[3]	6	7	8	9	10[1]	11[2]	13	12	14												3
1	4	3			6	7	8[1]	9[2]	10	11[3]		12	5	2	13	14									4
1	2	3	12		6	7[3]	8[1]	9	10	11			5	4[2]	13		14								5
1		3[1]	2		6	7		9	10[2]				14	4	13	8[3]		5	11	12					6
1			2		6	7	8[1]	9	10[2]					3	13	4	14	5	11[3]	12					7
1	4		7			2	8	9	12	11[1]			6	3	10[2]			5	13						8
1	4		7[2]			2	8■	9[3]	12	13	14		6	3	10[1]			5	11						9
1	4		7		6	2	8	9[2]	12		13	14		3[3]	10[1]			5	11						10
1	4	3	7		6	2[1]	8		10[2]		12					13	9	5	11						11
1	4	3	7		6	2			10	8[2]				12		13	9	5	11[1]						12
1	2	3	4		6	7	8[1]		10	12						13	9[2]	5	11						13
1	4	3[3]	7		6	2	8[1]		10[2]	12	13			14			9	5	11						14
1	2	3	4		6	7	8		9	10[1]	12							5	11						15
1	2	3[2]	4		6	7	8[1]		9	10[3]	12			13		14		5	11						16
1	2	3	4		6	7	8	9	10[2]	12		13						5	11[1]						17
1	2[1]	3	4		6	7			10	8[2]	12	13					9	5	11						18
1	4	3[1]	7		6	2	8[2]	12	10	13	14						9[3]	5	11						19
1	4	3	7		6	2	8	12	10[2]			13					9[1]	5	11						20
1	2	3	4		6	7	8	9	10[1]			12						5	11						21
1	5	3	4[1]		6	7	8	9	10[3]	12		14					13		11[2]		2				22
1	2	3	4		6	7	8[1]	9	10[2]			13					12	5	11						23
1	2	3	4[1]		6	7	8	9		12		10[2]					13	5	11[3]		14				24
1	2	3			6	7	8	9	13[3]	4[1]		10[2]					12	5	11		14				25
1	2[3]	3	4		6	7	8[2]	9		11		12					10[1]	5	13		14				26
1	4	3	8		6	7		9[1]	12				13					5	11		2	10[2]			27
1	4[1]	11	8[3]		6	7			10		12		3[2]					5	13	14	2	9			28
1	4	3	8			7			10[1]				6				9	5	11		2	12			29
1		3	4		6	7	8[2]	12	13				5				10[1]		11		2	9			30
1	5	3	4[1]		6	7	8	12	13								10		11		2	9[2]			31
1	6	3	4[2]			7	8	9	12	11[3]							13	5	14		2	10[1]			32
1	12	3	4[1]		6	7	8	9	13									5	11		2		10[2]		33
1		3	4		6		8	9	7[1]	11		13					12	5			2		10[2]		34
1		3	4		6	7	8[2]	9	12	11								5	13		2		10[1]		35
1		3	4[2]		6	7	8	9	12	11[3]							13	5	14		2		10[1]		36
1		3	4		6	7	8	9[2]	12	11[3]							13	5	14		2		10[1]		37
1	6		4		3	7	8	9	12	11[2]								5	13		2		10[1]		38
1	6		4		3	7	8[3]	9[1]	10[2]	11	12	13						5	14		2				39
1	6[1]	3	4		12	7	8	9	10[2]	11[3]		13						5	14		2				40
1	6	3	4		12	7	8[2]	9	10[3]	13		14						5	11[1]		2				41
1	6	3[1]	4		12	7	8	9	10[3]	13		14						5	11[2]		2				42
1	6		4		3	7	8[1]	9	10[3]	12	13						14	5	11[2]		2				43
1	6		4		3	7	8	9	10[2]	12■		13						5	11[1]		2				44
1	6	12	4		3	7		9[2]	10[1]	8■		13					14	5■	11[3]		2				45
1	6	11	4		3	7[3]		9[2]	10[1]		12						13	5	8		2			14	46

Worthington Cup

First Round	Oxford U	(h)	0-1

FA Cup

First Round	Heybridge S	(a)	7-0
Second Round	Harrogate R	(a)	3-1
Third Round	Leicester C	(a)	0-2

LDV Vans Trophy

First Round	QPR	(a)	0-0
Second Round	Boston U	(a)	2-1
Quarter-final	Wycombe W	(h)	3-0
Semi-final	Bournemouth	(a)	3-1
Southern Final	Cambridge U	(h)	4-2
		(a)	3-0
Final (at Millennium Stadium)	Carlisle U		2-0

BRISTOL ROVERS Division 3

FOUNDATION

Bristol Rovers were formed at a meeting in Stapleton Road, Eastville, in 1883. However, they first went under the name of the Black Arabs (wearing black shirts). Changing their name to Eastville Rovers in their second season, they won the Gloucestershire Senior Cup in 1888–89. Original members of the Bristol & District League in 1892, this eventually became the Western League and Eastville Rovers adopted professionalism in 1897.

Registered Offices: The Memorial Stadium, Filton Avenue, Horfield, Bristol BS7 0BF. (0117) 909 6648.

Ground: The Memorial Stadium.

Training Ground: (0117) 942 1912.

Matchday Ticket Office: (0117) 909 8848.
Fax: (0117) 907 4312.

ClubCall: 09068 121 131. ***Fax:*** (0117) 908 5530.

Community Office: (0117) 907 6555.
Ticket Office: (0117) 924 7474.

Ground Capacity: 11,976.

Record Attendance: 11,433 v Sunderland, Worthington Cup 3rd rd, 31 October 2000 (Memorial Stadium). 9464 v Liverpool, FA Cup 4th rd, 8 February 1992 (Twerton Park). 38,472 v Preston NE, FA Cup 4th rd, 30 January 1960 (Eastville).

HONOURS

Football League: Division 2 best season: 4th, 1994–95; Division 3 (S) – Champions 1952–53; Division 3 – Champions 1989–90; Runners-up 1973–74.

FA Cup: best season: 6th rd, 1951, 1958.

Football League Cup: best season: 5th rd, 1971, 1972.

Record Receipts: £115,000 v Sunderland, Worthington Cup 3rd rd, 31 October 2000.

Pitch Measurements: 101m × 68m.

Vice-presidents: Dr W. T. Cussen, A. I. Seager, R. Redmond, V. Stokes.

Chairman: G. M. H. Dunford. ***Vice-chairman:*** R. Craig. ***Directors:*** D. H. A. Dunford, B. Bradshaw, K. Spencer, C. Williams. ***Associate Director:*** S. Burns.

Director of Football and Team Manager: Ray Graydon. ***Assistant Manager:*** John Still.

Physio: Phil Kite. ***Director of Youth:*** Phil Bater.

Community Scheme Organiser: Peter Aitken.

Club Secretary: Roger Brinsford. ***Office Manager:*** Mrs Angela Mann.

Sales Manager: Graham Bowen.

Colours: Blue and white quartered shirts, white shorts, blue stockings.

Change Colours: Black and yellow shirts, black shorts, black stockings with yellow trim.

Year Formed: 1883. ***Turned Professional:*** 1897. ***Ltd Co.:*** 1896.

Previous Names: 1883, Black Arabs; 1884, Eastville Rovers; 1897, Bristol Eastville Rovers; 1898, Bristol Rovers. ***Club Nickname:*** 'Pirates'.

Previous Grounds: 1883, Purdown; Three Acres, Ashley Hill; Rudgeway, Fishponds; 1897, Eastville; 1986, Twerton Park; 1996, The Memorial Stadium.

First Football League Game: 28 August 1920, Division 3, v Millwall (a) L 0–2 – Stansfield; Bethune, Panes; Boxley, Kenny, Steele; Chance, Bird, Sims, Bell, Palmer.

SKY SPORTS FACT FILE

In 1902–03 'Gentleman Jim' Howie scored 10 goals in 26 League games for Bristol Rovers before signing for Newcastle United where he won League championship and FA Cup medals and was capped by Scotland.

Record League Victory: 7–0 v Brighton & HA, Division 3 (S), 29 November 1952 – Hoyle; Bamford, Fox; Pitt, Warren, Sampson; McIlvenny, Roost (2), Lambden (1), Bradford (1), Petherbridge (2), (1 og). 7–0 v Swansea T, Division 2, 2 October 1954 – Radford; Bamford, Watkins; Pitt, Muir, Anderson; Petherbridge, Bradford (2), Meyer, Roost (1), Hooper (2), (2 og). 7–0 v Shrewsbury T, Division 3, 21 March 1964 – Hall; Hillard, Gwyn Jones; Oldfield, Stone (1), Mabbutt; Jarman (2), Brown (1), Biggs (1p), Hamilton, Bobby Jones (2).
Record Cup Victory: 6–0 v Merthyr Tydfil, FA Cup 1st rd, 14 November 1987 – Martyn; Alexander (Dryden), Tanner, Hibbitt, Twentyman, Jones, Holloway, Meacham (1), White (2), Penrice (3) (Reece), Purnell.
Record Defeat: 0–12 v Luton T, Division 3 (S), 13 April 1936.
Most League Points (2 for a win): 64, Division 3 (S), 1952–53.
Most League Points (3 for a win): 93, Division 3, 1989–90.
Most League Goals: 92, Division 3 (S), 1952–53.
Highest League Scorer in Season: Geoff Bradford, 33, Division 3 (S), 1952–53.
Most League Goals in Total Aggregate: Geoff Bradford, 242, 1949–64.
Most League Goals in One Match: 4, Sidney Leigh v Exeter C, Division 3S, 2 May 1921; 4, Jonah Wilcox v Bournemouth, Division 3S, 12 December 1925; 4, Bill Culley v QPR, Division 3S, 5 March 1927; Frank Curran v Swindon T, Division 3S, 25 March 1939; Vic Lambden v Aldershot, Division 3S, 29 March 1947; George Petherbridge v Torquay U, Division 3S, 1 December 1951; Vic Lambden v Colchester U, Division 3S, 14 May 1952; Geoff Bradford v Rotherham U, Division 2, 14 March 1959; Robin Stubbs v Gillingham, Division 2, 10 October 1970; Alan Warboys v Brighton & HA, Division 3, 1 December 1973; Jamie Cureton v Reading, Division 2, 16 January 1999.
Most Capped Player: Vitalijs Astafjevs, 31 (93), Latvia.
Most League Appearances: Stuart Taylor, 546, 1966–80.
Youngest League Player: Ronnie Dix, 15 years 180 days v Norwich C, 3 March 1928.
Record Transfer Fee Received: £2,000,000 from Fulham for Barry Hayles, November 1998 and £2,000,000 from WBA for Jason Roberts, July 2000.
Record Transfer Fee Paid: £370,000 to QPR for Andy Tillson, November 1992.
Football League Record: 1920 Original Member of Division 3; 1921–53 Division 3 (S); 1953–62 Division 2; 1962–74 Division 3; 1974–81 Division 2; 1981–90 Division 3; 1990–92 Division 2. 1992–93 Division 1; 1993–2001 Division 2; 2001– Division 3.

MANAGERS

Alfred Homer 1899–1920
(continued as Secretary to 1928)
Ben Hall 1920–21
Andy Wilson 1921–26
Joe Palmer 1926–29
Dave McLean 1929–30
Albert Prince-Cox 1930–36
Percy Smith 1936–37
Brough Fletcher 1938–49
Bert Tann 1950–68 *(continued as General Manager to 1972)*
Fred Ford 1968–69
Bill Dodgin Snr 1969–72
Don Megson 1972–77
Bobby Campbell 1978–79
Harold Jarman 1979–80
Terry Cooper 1980–81
Bobby Gould 1981–83
David Williams 1983–85
Bobby Gould 1985–87
Gerry Francis 1987–91
Martin Dobson 1991
Dennis Rofe 1992
Malcolm Allison 1992–93
John Ward 1993–96
Ian Holloway 1996–2001
Garry Thompson 2001
Gerry Francis 2001
Garry Thompson 2001–02
Ray Graydon April 2002–

LATEST SEQUENCES

Longest Sequence of League Wins: 12, 18.10.1952 – 17.1.1953.
Longest Sequence of League Defeats: 8, 26.10.2002 – 21.12.2002.
Longest Sequence of League Draws: 5, 1.11.1975 – 22.11.1975.
Longest Sequence of Unbeaten League Matches: 32, 7.4.1973 – 27.1.1974.
Longest Sequence Without a League Win: 20, 5.4.1980 – 1.11.1980.
Successive Scoring Runs: 26 from 26.3.1927.
Successive Non-scoring Runs: 6 from 14.10.1922.

TEN YEAR LEAGUE RECORD

		P	W	D	L	F	A	Pts	Pos
1993-94	Div 2	46	20	10	16	60	59	70	8
1994-95	Div 2	46	22	16	8	70	40	82	4
1995-96	Div 2	46	20	10	16	57	60	70	10
1996-97	Div 2	46	15	11	20	47	50	56	17
1997-98	Div 2	46	20	10	16	70	64	70	5
1998-99	Div 2	46	13	17	16	65	56	56	13
1999-2000	Div 2	46	23	11	12	69	45	80	7
2000-01	Div 2	46	12	15	19	53	57	51	21
2001-02	Div 3	46	11	12	23	40	60	45	23
2002-03	Div 3	46	12	15	19	50	57	51	20

DID YOU KNOW ?

Joe Nicholls, a goalkeeper who made his name with Tottenham Hotspur from 1926 after Army service, joined Bristol Rovers ten years later and had England trials. While in the Grenadier Guards he had been a heavyweight boxing champion.

BRISTOL ROVERS 2002–03 LEAGUE RECORD

Match No.	Date	Venue	Opponents	Result	H/T Score	Lg. Pos.	Goalscorers	Attendance
1	Aug 10	A	Torquay U	L 1-2	1-1	—	Grazioli [5]	4937
2	13	H	Hull C	D 1-1	1-0	—	Grazioli [30]	7501
3	17	H	Rochdale	L 1-2	1-1	23	Bryant [45]	6478
4	24	A	Carlisle U	D 0-0	0-0	23		6475
5	27	H	Swansea C	W 3-1	1-0	—	Grazioli [33], Tait [52], Astafjevs [84]	6644
6	31	A	Scunthorpe U	D 2-2	0-2	19	Quinn [48], Carlisle (pen) [90]	3178
7	Sept 8	A	Macclesfield T	L 1-2	0-2	21	Carlisle [72]	1814
8	14	H	Exeter C	D 1-1	1-1	19	Tait [39]	6498
9	17	H	Bury	W 2-1	2-0	—	Tait [7], Grazioli [45]	5493
10	21	A	Shrewsbury T	W 5-2	1-0	12	Grazioli 3 [35, 53, 65], Astafjevs [56], Carlisle [80]	3510
11	28	H	Kidderminster H	L 1-2	0-1	15	Tait [74]	9447
12	Oct 5	A	Darlington	L 0-1	0-1	15		2849
13	12	H	Lincoln C	W 2-0	1-0	15	Futcher (og) [17], Grazioli (pen) [52]	6135
14	19	A	York C	D 2-2	2-1	16	U'ddin [40], Astafjevs [44]	3616
15	26	H	Leyton Orient	L 1-2	0-0	16	Coote [54]	6625
16	29	A	Hartlepool U	L 0-2	0-1	—		3889
17	Nov 2	A	Bournemouth	L 0-1	0-1	20		6924
18	9	H	Southend U	L 0-1	0-0	21		5691
19	23	H	Wrexham	L 0-3	0-2	21		6328
20	30	A	Rushden & D	L 1-2	1-1	22	Grazioli (pen) [14]	3960
21	Dec 14	H	Oxford U	L 0-2	0-1	23		5864
22	21	A	Cambridge U	L 1-3	1-1	24	Allen [45]	3701
23	26	A	Swansea C	W 1-0	1-0	21	Tait [30]	5879
24	28	H	Boston U	D 1-1	0-1	21	Carlisle (pen) [87]	8311
25	Jan 4	A	Hull C	L 0-1	0-1	22		14,913
26	14	H	Torquay U	D 1-1	1-1	—	Carlisle (pen) [18]	6196
27	18	H	Scunthorpe U	W 2-1	0-0	20	Astafjevs [85], Carlisle [88]	6617
28	25	A	Boston U	D 0-0	0-0	21		3209
29	Feb 1	H	Carlisle U	L 1-2	1-1	22	Grazioli [33]	7527
30	8	A	Southend U	D 2-2	0-1	24	Barrett [51], Street [56]	4708
31	15	H	Bournemouth	D 0-0	0-0	23		6347
32	22	H	Macclesfield T	D 1-1	0-0	23	Llewellyn [80]	6005
33	Mar 1	A	Exeter C	D 0-0	0-0	23		5759
34	4	A	Bury	W 1-0	0-0	—	Quinn [65]	2425
35	8	H	Shrewsbury T	D 0-0	0-0	20		6839
36	15	A	Leyton Orient	W 2-1	1-1	20	Grazioli [13], Tait [72]	4081
37	18	H	York C	L 0-1	0-1	—		8248
38	22	H	Hartlepool U	W 1-0	1-0	20	Hyde [7]	6557
39	29	A	Lincoln C	L 1-2	1-2	21	Astafjevs [23]	3550
40	Apr 5	H	Rushden & D	L 1-2	1-1	23	Astafjevs [3]	6736
41	8	A	Rochdale	D 1-1	1-1	—	Astafjevs [44]	1658
42	12	A	Wrexham	L 2-3	1-2	22	Llewellyn 2 [44, 82]	5330
43	19	H	Cambridge U	W 3-1	1-0	20	Rammell 2 [29, 65], Astafjevs [82]	7563
44	21	A	Oxford U	W 1-0	0-0	20	Rammell [54]	8732
45	26	H	Darlington	W 2-1	1-0	19	Rammell [23], Carlisle [75]	9835
46	May 3	A	Kidderminster H	D 1-1	0-1	20	Tait [71]	3872

Final League Position: 20

GOALSCORERS

League (50): Grazioli 11 (2 pens), Astafjevs 8, Carlisle 7 (3 pens), Tait 7, Rammell 4, Llewellyn 3, Quinn 2, Allen 1, Barrett 1, Bryant 1, Coote 1, Hyde 1, Street 1, U'ddin 1, own goal 1.
Worthington Cup (0).
FA Cup (6): Allen 1, Barrett 1, Carlisle 1, Gilroy 1, Grazioli 1, Tait 1.
LDV Vans Trophy (0).

Howie S 44	Boxall D 35 + 4	Challis T 16	U'ddin A 17 + 1	Barrett A 45	Quinn R 44	McKeever M 7 + 9	Bryant S 14 + 8	Tait P 33 + 8	Grazioli G 28 + 6	Carlisle W 35 + 6	Astafjevs V 26 + 7	Richards J — + 8	Gilroy D 3 + 8	Hogg L 8 + 9	Gall K — + 9	Warren C — + 2	Austin K 31 + 2	Clarke R 2	Lee D 5	Arndale N 1	Coote A 4 + 1	Plummer C 2	Hyde G 21	Street K 13 + 7	Allen B 5 + 3	Rose R 9	Parker S 13 + 2	Anderson I 14	Llewellyn C 14	Di Piedi M 3 + 2	Hodges L 7 + 1	Rammell A 7	*Match No.*
1	2	3	4	5	6	7	8^{1}	9	10	11^{2}	12	13																					1
1	2	3	4	5	6	7^{1}	8	9	10^{2}	11	12		13																				2
1	2	3	4	5	6	11^{1}	8^{2}	9	10	7		12		13																			3
1	2	3	4	5	6			9^{1}	10	11^{2}	7	12		8	13																		4
1	2	3	4	5	6			9	10^{1}	11	7			8	12																		5
1	2	3	4	5	6	12	13	9	10^{3}	11	7^{1}	14		8^{2}																			6
1	2	3	4	5	6	11^{3}	12	9	10^{2}	7		13		8^{1}		14																	7
1	2	3	4	5	6		8^{1}	9	10^{2}	11	7	13		12																			8
1	2	3	4	5	6		8	9	10	11^{1}	7					12																	9
1	2	3	4	5	6	12	8	9	10^{2}	11^{3}	7^{1}			13	14																		10
1	2^{2}	3^{3}	4	5	6	12	8^{1}	9	10	11	7			13			14																11
1	2^{3}	3	4	5	6		8^{1}	9▮	10^{2}	11	7	13		12			14																12
		3	4	5	6	7^{3}	12	9	10^{2}	11			13	8^{1}	14		2	1															13
	12	3^{1}	4	5	6	7	13		10	11	8^{3}	14					2^{2}	1	9														14
1	2		4	5	6	12	8		10^{2}	7				13					9	3^{1}	11												15
1	2		4	5	6		3	9	12	7^{2}				8	13				10^{1}		11												16
1	2			5	6		4	9	12	7				8			3^{1}		10		11												17
1	2			5	6	11	3	9	12	13				8					7^{2}		10^{1}	4											18
1	2	3		5	6		8	9	10		7						11				12	4^{1}											19
1	2	3^{1}		5	6		12	9	10^{3}		7		13				4						8	11^{2}	14								20
1	2			5					10^{2}	11^{1}	7		13		12		3						8	6	9	4							21
1	2			5	6			9		12	13						4						8▮	11^{2}	10^{1}	3	7						22
1	2			5	6			9		11	12				13		4						8^{1}	7	10^{2}	3							23
1	2			5	6	12		9		11	7		13				4							8^{1}	10^{2}	3							24
1	2^{1}		12	5	6			9	13	11	7				14		4							8	10^{2}	3^{3}							25
1	2			5	6			9^{3}		11	7^{2}		10	13	12		4							8^{1}	14	3							26
1	2			5	6	12		9		11	7		10^{2}				4							8^{1}	13	3							27
1	2			5	6		12	9		11	7^{2}		10^{1}	13			4							8		3							28
1	2		4	5			12	9^{2}	10	11	7^{1}		13				3						6	8									29
1				5	6	12		9	10	7^{1}							4^{2}						8	11		2	13	3					30
1	2			5	6	12		9	10^{2}	7			13				4						8	11^{1}				3					31
1	2			5	6			9^{1}	12	11^{2}	7						4						8					3	10	13			32
1	2				6	12		13	10	7							5						8				4	3	11^{1}	9^{2}			33
1	2			5	6			12	10^{2}	7			13				4						8	11				3		9^{1}			34
1	2^{3}			5	6^{2}			12	10^{1}	7	13						4						8				14	3	11	9			35
1				5	6			9	10^{3}	7^{1}	12			13			4						8	14			3	2	11^{2}				36
1				5^{2}	6^{1}			9	10	7	12						4						8	13			2	3	11				37
1				5	6			9^{1}			7						4						8	12			2	3	10	13	11^{2}		38
1	12			5	6^{2}			14		13	7						4						8				2	3^{1}	10		11^{3}	9	39
1	2			5	6^{1}			12	13	14	7						4						8				3^{3}		10^{2}		11	9	40
1	2			5	6			12	10		7						4						8				3		11			9^{1}	41
1	3			5	6				10^{2}	12	7						4						8^{1}				2		11		13	9	42
1	12			5	6			13			7						4^{1}						8	14			2	3	10		11^{3}	9^{2}	43
1				5	6			12		13	7^{3}						4						8	14			2	3	10		11^{2}	9^{1}	44
1	12			5	6		13			7							4						8^{2}	14			2^{1}	3	10		11^{3}	9	45
1				5	6		8	9		7^{1}							4							12			2	3	10		11		46

Worthington Cup
Pr Round | Boston U | (h) | 0-2

LDV Vans Trophy
First Round | Exeter C | (a) | 0-1

FA Cup
First Round | Runcorn | (h) | 0-0
| | (a) | 3-1
Second Round | Rochdale | (h) | 1-1
| | (a) | 2-3

BURNLEY — Division 1

FOUNDATION

The majority of those responsible for the formation of the Burnley club in 1881 were from the defunct rugby club Burnley Rovers. Indeed, they continued to play rugby for a year before changing to soccer and dropping 'Rovers' from their name. The changes were decided at a meeting held in May 1882 at the Bull Hotel.

Turf Moor, Burnley BB10 4BX.

Telephone: 0870 443 1882. ***Fax:*** 0870 700 014. ***ClubCall:*** 09068 121 153. ***Ticket Office:*** 0870 443 1914. ***Community Programme:*** 0870 443 1882. ***Commercial Department:*** 0870 443 1882.

Ground Capacity: 22,619.

Record Attendance: 54,775 v Huddersfield T, FA Cup 3rd rd, 23 February 1924.

Record Receipts: £183,000 v Preston NE, Division 2, 4 March 2000.

Pitch Measurements: 112yd × 70yd.

Chairman: B. Kilby. ***Vice-chairman:*** R. Ingleby. ***President:*** Dr R. D. Iven MRCS (Eng), LRCP (Lond), MRCGP. ***Directors:*** C. Holt, R. Blakeborough, J. Turkington, M. Hobbs, C. Duckworth.

Manager: Stan Ternent. ***Assistant Manager:*** Sam Ellis.

Chief Executive: A. Watson.

Company Secretary: Cathy Pickup.

Coaches: Ronnie Jepson, Michael Docherty, James Robson, Terry Pashley.

Sales Manager: Anthony Fairclough.

Colours: Claret body with blue sleeves, white shorts, white stockings.

Change Colours: All grey.

Year Formed: 1882.

Turned Professional: 1883. ***Ltd Co.:*** 1897.

Previous Name: 1881, Burnley Rovers; 1882, Burnley.

Club Nickname: 'The Clarets'.

Previous Grounds: 1881, Calder Vale; 1882, Turf Moor.

First Football League Game: 8 September 1888, Football League, v Preston NE (a) L 2–5 – Smith; Lang, Bury, Abrams, Friel, Keenan, Brady, Tait, Poland (1), Gallocher (1), Yates.

Record League Victory: 9–0 v Darwen, Division 1, 9 January 1892 – Hillman; Walker, McFettridge, Lang, Matthews, Keenan, Nicol (3), Bowes, Espie (1), McLardie (3), Hill (2).

HONOURS

Football League: Division 1 – Champions 1920–21, 1959–60; Runners-up 1919–20, 1961–62; Division 2 – Champions 1897–98, 1972–73; Runners-up 1912–13, 1946–47, 1999–2000; Promoted from Division 2, 1993–94 (play-offs); Division 3 – Champions 1981–82; Division 4 – Champions 1991–92. Record 30 consecutive Division 1 games without defeat 1920–21.

FA Cup: Winners 1914; Runners-up 1947, 1962.

Football League Cup: Semi-final 1961, 1969, 1983.

Anglo–Scottish Cup: Winners 1979.

Sherpa Van Trophy: Runners-up 1988.

European Competitions: *European Cup:* 1960–61. *European Fairs Cup:* 1966–67.

SKY SPORTS FACT FILE

On 17 October 1953 Burnley won 5-2 at Arsenal with Bill Holden scoring a hat-trick, while on 17 December 1960 it was another treble for Ray Pointer in a further 5–2 victory at Highbury. In both seasons Burnley finished well above Arsenal.

Record Cup Victory: 9–0 v Crystal Palace, FA Cup 2nd rd (replay), 10 February 1909 – Dawson; Barron, McLean; Cretney (2), Leake, Moffat; Morley, Ogden, Smith (3), Abbott (2), Smethams (1). 9–0 v New Brighton, FA Cup 4th rd, 26 January 1957 – Blacklaw; Angus, Winton; Seith, Adamson, Miller; Newlands (1), McIlroy (3), Lawson (3), Cheesebrough (1), Pilkington (1). 9–0 v Penrith, FA Cup 1st rd, 17 November 1984 – Hansbury; Miller, Hampton, Phelan, Overson (Kennedy), Hird (3 incl. 1p), Grewcock (1), Powell (2), Taylor (3), Biggins, Hutchison.

Record Defeat: 0–10 v Aston Villa, Division 1, 29 August 1925 and v Sheffield U, Division 1, 19 January 1929.

Most League Points (2 for a win): 62, Division 2, 1972–73.

Most League Points (3 for a win): 88, Division 2, 1999–2000.

Most League Goals: 102, Division 1, 1960–61.

Highest League Scorer in Season: George Beel, 35, Division 1, 1927–28.

Most League Goals in Total Aggregate: George Beel, 178, 1923–32.

Most League Goals in One Match: 6, Louis Page v Birmingham C, Division 1, 10 April 1926.

Most Capped Player: Jimmy McIlroy, 51 (55), Northern Ireland.

Most League Appearances: Jerry Dawson, 522, 1907–28.

Youngest League Player: Tommy Lawton, 16 years 174 days v Doncaster R, 28 March 1936.

Record Transfer Fee Received: £750,000 from Luton T for Steve Davis, August 1995.

Record Transfer Fee Paid: £1,000,000 to Stockport C for Ian Moore, October 2000. £1,000,000 to Bradford C for Robbie Blake, January 2002.

Football League Record: 1888 Original Member of the Football League; 1897–98 Division 2; 1898–1900 Division 1; 1900–13 Division 2; 1913–30 Division 1; 1930–47 Division 2; 1947–71 Division 1; 1971–73 Division 2; 1973–76 Division 1; 1976–80 Division 2; 1980–82 Division 3; 1982–83 Division 2; 1983–85 Division 3; 1985–92 Division 4; 1992–94 Division 2; 1994–95 Division 1; 1995–2000 Division 2; 2000– Division 1.

MANAGERS

Arthur F. Sutcliffe 1893–96
(Secretary-Manager)
Harry Bradshaw 1896–99
(Secretary-Manager)
Ernest Magnall 1899–1903
(Secretary-Manager)
Spen Whittaker 1903–10
R. H. Wadge 1910–11
(Secretary-Manager)
John Haworth 1911–25
Albert Pickles 1925–32
Tom Bromilow 1932–35
Alf Boland 1935–39
(Secretary-Manager)
Cliff Britton 1945–48
Frank Hill 1948–54
Alan Brown 1954–57
Billy Dougall 1957–58
Harry Potts 1958–70
(General Manager to 1972)
Jimmy Adamson 1970–76
Joe Brown 1976–77
Harry Potts 1977–79
Brian Miller 1979–83
John Bond 1983–84
John Benson 1984–85
Martin Buchan 1985
Tommy Cavanagh 1985–86
Brian Miller 1986–89
Frank Casper 1989–91
Jimmy Mullen 1991–96
Adrian Heath 1996–97
Chris Waddle 1997–98
Stan Ternent June 1998–

LATEST SEQUENCES

Longest Sequence of League Wins: 10, 16.11.1912 – 18.1.1913.

Longest Sequence of League Defeats: 8, 2.1.1995 – 25.2.1995.

Longest Sequence of League Draws: 6, 21.2.1931 – 28.3.1931.

Longest Sequence of Unbeaten League Matches: 30, 6.9.1920 – 25.3.1921.

Longest Sequence Without a League Win: 24, 16.4.1979 – 17.11.1979.

Successive Scoring Runs: 27 from 13.2.1926.

Successive Non-scoring Runs: 6 from 9.8.1997.

TEN YEAR LEAGUE RECORD

		P	W	D	L	F	A	Pts	Pos
1993-94	Div 2	46	21	10	15	79	58	73	6
1994-95	Div 1	46	11	13	22	49	74	46	22
1995-96	Div 2	46	14	13	19	56	68	55	17
1996-97	Div 2	46	19	11	16	71	55	68	9
1997-98	Div 2	46	13	13	20	55	65	52	20
1998-99	Div 2	46	13	16	17	54	73	55	15
1999-2000	Div 2	46	25	13	8	69	47	88	2
2000-01	Div 2	46	21	9	16	50	54	72	7
2001-02	Div 1	46	21	12	13	70	62	75	7
2002-03	Div 1	46	15	10	21	65	89	55	16

DID YOU KNOW ?

Burnley were involved in a match of twelve goals during the 1897–98 season when they became champions of Division Two. They defeated Loughborough Town 9-3 on 28 March 1898 with Jimmy Ross scoring five of their goals.

BURNLEY 2002–03 LEAGUE RECORD

Match No.	Date	Venue	Opponents	Result		H/T Score	Lg. Pos.	Goalscorers	Attendance
1	Aug 10	H	Brighton & HA	L	1-3	0-1	—	Briscoe [90]	14,738
2	17	A	Wolverhampton W	L	0-3	0-1	24		25,031
3	24	H	Sheffield U	L	0-1	0-1	24		12,868
4	27	A	Reading	L	0-3	0-0	—		12,009
5	31	H	Crystal Palace	D	0-0	0-0	24		12,407
6	Sept 7	A	Derby Co	W	2-1	0-1	23	Blake (pen) [51], Barton (og) [55]	22,343
7	14	H	Stoke C	W	2-1	0-0	20	Gnohere [76], Papadopoulos [81]	14,244
8	17	H	Millwall	D	2-2	1-1	—	West (pen) [18], Moore I [85]	11,878
9	21	A	Bradford C	D	2-2	0-1	20	Blake [57], Taylor [76]	14,561
10	28	H	Wimbledon	W	1-0	0-0	18	Little [51]	12,259
11	Oct 5	A	Sheffield W	W	3-1	1-0	11	Taylor [8], Little [57], Moore I [60]	17,004
12	12	H	Walsall	W	2-1	1-0	9	Blake [42], Davis [69]	12,907
13	19	A	Leicester C	W	1-0	0-0	8	Moore I [55]	26,254
14	22	A	Ipswich T	D	2-2	1-2	—	Gnohere [6], Papadopoulos [90]	22,736
15	26	H	Portsmouth	L	0-3	0-1	10		15,788
16	29	A	Grimsby T	L	5-6	3-4	—	Taylor 2 [22, 49], Moore I [31], Blake 2 (1 pen) [45, 83 (p)]	5620
17	Nov 2	A	Preston NE	L	1-3	0-1	14	Taylor [51]	16,046
18	9	H	Coventry C	W	3-1	2-0	11	Blake (pen) [15], Grant [35], Davenport (og) [86]	13,470
19	16	A	Rotherham U	D	0-0	0-0	11		7575
20	23	H	Norwich C	W	2-0	0-0	9	McGregor [59], Little [85]	16,282
21	30	A	Watford	L	1-2	0-1	9	Taylor [76]	13,977
22	Dec 7	H	Nottingham F	W	1-0	1-0	9	Briscoe [28]	13,869
23	14	H	Rotherham U	L	2-6	0-3	13	Davis 2 [67, 78]	14,121
24	21	A	Gillingham	L	2-4	1-3	15	Taylor [28], Blake (pen) [76]	7905
25	26	H	Wolverhampton W	W	2-1	2-0	13	Taylor [24], West [32]	18,641
26	28	A	Brighton & HA	D	2-2	1-0	12	Little [44], Moore I [71]	6502
27	Jan 11	H	Ipswich T	D	1-1	0-1	14	Blake (pen) [66]	15,501
28	18	A	Crystal Palace	D	1-1	1-0	16	Taylor [44]	16,344
29	Feb 1	H	Reading	L	2-5	0-2	16	Moore I [55], West [90]	14,420
30	8	A	Coventry C	W	1-0	1-0	15	Cox [35]	13,659
31	22	H	Derby Co	W	2-0	2-0	11	Moore I [8], Taylor [23]	15,063
32	Mar 1	A	Stoke C	W	1-0	0-0	11	West [56]	12,874
33	4	A	Millwall	D	1-1	1-0	—	Moore I [18]	6045
34	12	A	Sheffield U	L	2-4	0-2	—	Taylor [64], Blake [90]	17,359
35	15	A	Walsall	L	2-3	0-2	12	Blake (pen) [74], Little [90]	6327
36	18	H	Leicester C	L	1-2	0-0	—	Sinclair (og) [90]	14,554
37	22	H	Grimsby T	D	1-1	0-1	15	Moore A [52]	13,445
38	25	H	Bradford C	L	0-2	0-1	—		11,095
39	Apr 5	H	Watford	L	4-7	4-5	17	Taylor 3 [15, 39, 45], Davis [35]	10,208
40	8	H	Preston NE	W	2-0	1-0	—	Papadopoulos [42], Blake [61]	12,245
41	12	A	Norwich C	L	0-2	0-1	16		20,026
42	15	A	Portsmouth	L	0-1	0-0	—		19,221
43	19	H	Gillingham	W	2-0	1-0	15	Taylor [28], Diallo [50]	14,031
44	21	A	Nottingham F	L	0-2	0-0	16		25,403
45	26	H	Sheffield W	L	2-7	1-3	16	Blake 2 [42, 53]	17,435
46	May 4	A	Wimbledon	L	1-2	1-0	16	Taylor [27]	1972

Final League Position: 16

GOALSCORERS

League (65): Taylor 16, Blake 13 (6 pens), Moore I 8, Little 5, Davis 4, West 4 (1 pen), Papadopoulos 3, Briscoe 2, Gnohere 2, Cox 1, Diallo 1, Grant 1, McGregor 1, Moore A 1, own goals 3.
Worthington Cup (6): Papadopoulos 3, Blake 1, Davis 1, West 1.
FA Cup (13): Moore I 3, Blake 2 (1 pen), Little 2, Moore A 2, Cook 1, Diallo 1, Taylor 1, Weller 1.

Michopoulos N 13	West D 41	Branch G 31 + 1	Grant T 24 + 10	Davis S 25 + 3	Gnohere A 31 + 2	Little G 28 + 5	Blake R 34 + 7	Moore I 35 + 9	Taylor G 38 + 2	Briscoe L 32 + 1	Cox I 23 + 3	Weller P 26 + 8	Papadopoulos D 7 + 27	McGregor M 25 + 5	Cook P 21 + 2	Moore A 14 + 13	Johnrose L 5 + 1	Payton A — + 1	Beresford M 33 + 1	Armstrong G 1 + 5	Maylett B 1 + 5	Diallo D 14	O'Neill M 2 + 5	Chaplow R 2 + 3	Waine A — + 2	Rasmussen M — + 2	*Match No.*
1	2	3^{1}	4	5	6■	7	8^{2}	9^{3}	10	11	12	13	14														1
1	2			5	6	7^{1}		13	9	4	14	10^{3}	12	3	8■	11^{2}											2
1	2	12				7		9	10	3^{1}	5	8^{2}		6	4	11^{3}	13	14									3
1	2		4			7	14	12	9	3	5	13		6	8^{1}	11^{3}	10^{2}										4
1	2		4			7^{2}		12	9	3	5	8	10^{1}	6		13	11										5
	2		4		6	12	10	9		8	3	7		5			11^{1}		1								6
	2		4		6	7	8^{2}	9^{3}	13	11	5		14	3^{1}		12	10		1								7
	2		4		6	7^{1}	12	13	9	3	5		10		14	11^{2}	8^{3}		1								8
	2		4	12	3^{1}	7	13		9	11	5		10^{2}	6^{3}	8	14			1								9
	2^{2}		8	5	6	7	9^{3}	12	10	3	4		14	13		11^{1}			1								10
	2	3		5	6	7	8^{1}	9^{2}	10		4		13	12	11^{3}				1	14							11
	2	3	12	5	6	7	10^{2}	9		13	4	8^{3}			11^{1}				1		14						12
	2	3	12	5	6	7^{2}	8^{1}	9^{3}	10	11	4	13	14						1								13
	2	3		5	6	7^{1}	8	9^{2}	10	11	4	12	13						1								14
	2	3^{3}		5	6	7	8	9^{1}	10	11	4^{2}	12	13						1		14						15
	2	3		5	6^{2}	12	8	9^{1}	10	11		7	14	4^{3}		13			1								16
	2		12	5	6	7	8	9^{3}	10	3^{2}	4^{1}	11	14			13			1								17
	2	3	4	5	6	7^{3}	8^{2}	12	9^{1}	11		10	13						1		14						18
	2	3			6		8^{3}	9	10^{1}	11		7	13	5	4	14			1		12^{2}						19
	2	3^{2}	12		6	7	8	9		11		10	13	5	4^{1}				1								20
	2	3	4	12	6	7	10^{3}	9^{2}	13			8	14	5■		11^{1}			1								21
	2	3		5	6	7^{1}	9^{3}	12	10^{2}	11		8	14		4	13			1								22
	2	3	12	5		7	9		10	11^{1}	4^{3}	8	13		6^{2}	14			1								23
	2■	3	4^{2}		6^{1}	7	8	9^{3}	10■		12	11	13	5		14			1								24
	2		4		6	7^{1}	9^{2}	12	10		5	8	13	3		11			1								25
	2		4		6	7	9^{2}	12	10		5	8	13	3		11^{1}			1								26
1		3	4		6	7	10	9					12	2	8	11^{1}						5					27
	2	3	4^{3}		6		10^{2}	9	7	11			13	14	8^{1}	12			1			5					28
	2		4		6	12	10^{2}	9	7	11^{3}			13	3^{1}	8	14			1			5					29
1	2	3	4				10^{1}	9	7		6		12		8	11^{2}				13		5					30
	2	3	4					9	10	7	6	12		13	8^{2}	11^{1}			1			5					31
	2	3	4					9	10	7	6	12		13	8^{2}	11^{1}			1			5					32
	2	3	4			12	13	9^{1}	10	7	6	14			8^{3}	11^{2}			1			5					33
	2^{2}	3	12	6		7^{3}	13	9	10	11^{1}	4	8			14				1			5					34
		3	4^{1}	13		12	14	9^{3}	10		6^{2}	7		2	8	11			1			5					35
	2		12	4	6^{2}	11	10	9		3^{1}		7	13		8^{3}	14			1			5					36
	2		12	4	6	11	10^{2}	9		3		7	14		8^{1}	13^{3}			1			5					37
	2	3	12	4	13■	11	14	9	10	6^{3}		7			8^{1}				1			5^{2}					38
	2	3^{2}	4^{1}	5	12		8	9	10	11		7	13	6^{3}					1				14				39
1	2	3	12	5			8	9	10	6		7	11^{1}	4													40
1	2	3		5			8	9	10	6^{1}		7	11^{3}	4						12^{2}			14	13			41
1	2	3		5	6^{3}		8	9	10			7	11^{1}	4							12^{2}		13	14			42
1		3		4	6		8^{1}	9	10			7^{2}		2								5	11^{3}	13	12	14	43
1		3		4	6		8	9	10				11^{3}	2						12^{2}		5^{1}	14	7		13	44
1^{6}		3	4	5	6		8	9■	10					2^{2}					15	12	11^{1}		13	7			45
	2	3	4	5^{2}			8	9^{1}	10				12	6					1	7			11		13		46

Worthington Cup

First Round	Blackpool	(h)	3-0
Second Round	Huddersfield T	(a)	1-0
Third Round	Tottenham H	(h)	2-1
Fourth Round	Manchester U	(h)	0-2

FA Cup

Third Round	Grimsby T	(a)	2-2
		(h)	4-0
Fourth Round	Brentford	(a)	3-0
Fifth Round	Fulham	(a)	1-1
		(h)	3-0
Sixth Round	Watford	(a)	0-2

BURY Division 3

FOUNDATION

A meeting at the Waggon & Horses Hotel, attended largely by members of Bury Wesleyans and Bury Unitarians football clubs, decided to form a new Bury club. This was officially formed at a subsequent gathering at the Old White Horse Hotel, Fleet Street, Bury on 24 April 1885.

Gigg Lane, Bury BL9 9HR.

Telephone: (0161) 764 4881. ***Fax:*** (0161) 764 5521.
Commercial Dept: (0161) 705 2144. ***Fax:*** (0161) 763 3103.
Community Programme: (0161) 797 5423.
Info line: 0900 809 0003.

Social Club: (0161) 764 6771.

Ground Capacity: 11,669.

Record Attendance: 35,000 v Bolton W, FA Cup 3rd rd, 9 January 1960.

Record Receipts: £86,000 v Manchester C, Division 1, 12 September 1997.

Pitch Measurements: 112yd × 70yd.

Joint Chairmen: J. Smith, F. Mason.

Manager: Andy Preece. ***Assistant Manager:*** Graham Barrow.
Physios: Lee Nobes, Ian Willcock. ***Youth Development:*** Andy Hill.

Safety Officer: Richard Ambler.

Secretary: Jill Neville.

Commercial Manager: Peter Young.

Colours: White shirts, royal blue shorts, royal blue stockings.

Change Colours: Navy.

Year Formed: 1885.

Turned professional: 1885.

Ltd Co.: 1897.

Club Nickname: 'Shakers'.

Club Sponsors: Bury Metro.

First Football League Game: 1 September 1894, Division 2, v Manchester C (h) W 4–2 – Lowe; Gillespie, Davies; White, Clegg, Ross; Wylie, Barbour (2), Millar (1), Ostler (1), Plant.

Record League Victory: 8–0 v Tranmere R, Division 3, 10 January 1970 – Forrest; Tinney, Saile; Anderson, Turner, McDermott; Hince (1), Arrowsmith (1), Jones (4), Kerr (1), Grundy, (1 og).

Record Cup Victory: 12–1 v Stockton, FA Cup 1st rd (replay), 2 February 1897 – Montgomery; Darroch, Barbour; Hendry (1), Clegg, Ross (1); Wylie (3), Pangbourn, Millar (4), Henderson (2), Plant, (1 og).

HONOURS

Football League: Division 1 best season: 4th, 1925–26; Division 2 – Champions 1894–95, 1996–97; Runners-up 1923–24; Division 3 – Champions 1960–61; Runners-up 1967–68; Promoted from Division 3 (3rd) 1995–96.

FA Cup: Winners 1900, 1903.

Football League Cup: Semi-final 1963.

SKY SPORTS FACT FILE

In 1929–30 John Reid Smith came close to beating Norman Bullock's 31 goals record for the club. One short of the total he broke his nose at Nottingham Forest and his season was prematurely ended as a result.

Record Defeat: 0–10 v Blackburn R, FA Cup pr rd, 1 October 1887. 0–10 v West Ham U, Milk Cup 2nd rd 2nd leg, 25 October 1983.

Most League Points (2 for a win): 68, Division 3, 1960–61.

Most League Points (3 for a win): 84, Division 4, 1984–85 and Division 2, 1996–97.

Most League Goals: 108, Division 3, 1960–61.

Highest League Scorer in Season: Craig Madden, 35, Division 4, 1981–82.

Most League Goals in Total Aggregate: Craig Madden, 129, 1978–86.

Most League Goals in One Match: 5, Eddie Quigley v Millwall, Division 2, 15 February 1947; 5, Ray Pointer v Rotherham U, Division 2, 2 October 1965.

Most Capped Player: Bill Gorman, 11 (13), Republic of Ireland and (4), Northern Ireland.

Most League Appearances: Norman Bullock, 506, 1920–35.

Youngest League Player: Brian Williams, 16 years 133 days v Stockport Co, 18 March 1972.

Record Transfer Fee Received: £1,100,000 from Ipswich T for David Johnson, November 1997.

Record Transfer Fee Paid: £200,000 to Ipswich T for Chris Swailes, November 1997 and to Swindon T for Darren Bullock, February 1999.

Football League Record: 1894 Elected to Division 2; 1895–1912 Division 1; 1912–24 Division 2; 1924–29 Division 1; 1929–57 Division 2; 1957–61 Division 3; 1961–67 Division 2; 1967–68 Division 3; 1968–69 Division 2; 1969–71 Division 3; 1971–74 Division 4; 1974–80 Division 3; 1980–85 Division 4; 1985–96 Division 3; 1996–97 Division 2; 1997–99 Division 1; 1999–2002 Division 2; 2002– Division 3.

MANAGERS

T. Hargreaves 1887
(Secretary-Manager)
H. S. Hamer 1887–1907
(Secretary-Manager)
Archie Montgomery 1907–15
William Cameron 1919–23
James Hunter Thompson 1923–27
Percy Smith 1927–30
Arthur Paine 1930–34
Norman Bullock 1934–38
Jim Porter 1944–45
Norman Bullock 1945–49
John McNeil 1950–53
Dave Russell 1953–61
Bob Stokoe 1961–65
Bert Head 1965–66
Les Shannon 1966–69
Jack Marshall 1969
Les Hart 1970
Tommy McAnearney 1970–72
Alan Brown 1972–73
Bobby Smith 1973–77
Bob Stokoe 1977–78
David Hatton 1978–79
Dave Connor 1979–80
Jim Iley 1980–84
Martin Dobson 1984–89
Sam Ellis 1989–90
Mike Walsh 1990–95
Stan Ternent 1995–98
Neil Warnock 1998–99
Andy Preece May 2000–

LATEST SEQUENCES

Longest Sequence of League Wins: 9, 26.9.1960 – 19.11.1960.

Longest Sequence of League Defeats: 8, 18.8.2001 – 25.9.2001.

Longest Sequence of League Draws: 6, 6.3.1999 – 3.4.1999.

Longest Sequence of Unbeaten League Matches: 18, 4.2.1961 – 29.4.1961.

Longest Sequence Without a League Win: 19, 1.4.1911 – 2.12.1911.

Successive Scoring Runs: 24 from 1.9.1894.

Successive Non-scoring Runs: 6 from 11.1.1969.

TEN YEAR LEAGUE RECORD

		P	*W*	*D*	*L*	*F*	*A*	*Pts*	*Pos*
1993-94	Div 3	42	14	11	17	55	56	53	13
1994-95	Div 3	42	23	11	8	73	36	80	4
1995-96	Div 3	46	22	13	11	66	48	79	3
1996-97	Div 2	46	24	12	10	62	38	84	1
1997-98	Div 1	46	11	19	16	42	58	52	17
1998-99	Div 1	46	10	17	19	35	60	47	22
1999-2000	Div 2	46	13	18	15	61	64	57	15
2000-01	Div 2	46	16	10	20	45	59	58	16
2001-02	Div 2	46	11	11	24	43	75	44	22
2002-03	Div 3	46	18	16	12	57	56	70	7

DID YOU KNOW ?

Centre-half Tom Bradshaw had played for Bury since 1922 before being capped by Scotland against England in the famous Wembley Wizards match of 1928, his only international honour. He later continued with Liverpool.

BURY 2002–03 LEAGUE RECORD

Match No.	*Date*	*Venue*	*Opponents*	*Result*		*H/T Score*	*Lg. Pos.*	*Goalscorers*	*Attendance*
1	Aug 10	A	Oxford U	L	1-2	0-2	—	Clegg [87]	5309
2	13	H	Cambridge U	L	0-1	0-0	—		2650
3	17	H	Swansea C	W	3-2	2-0	16	Clegg [10], Newby [37], Swailes [80]	2348
4	24	A	Hull C	D	1-1	0-1	17	Abbott [64]	8804
5	26	H	Shrewsbury T	W	4-3	1-0	8	Newby 2 [20, 57], Dunfield [46], Abbott [53]	2866
6	31	A	Boston U	D	1-1	0-0	11	Newby [48]	2790
7	Sept 6	H	York C	W	2-1	2-0	—	Newby [21], Abbott [27]	3294
8	14	A	Bournemouth	W	2-1	1-0	6	Forrest (pen) [45], Unsworth [56]	4851
9	17	A	Bristol R	L	1-2	0-2	—	Abbott [90]	5493
10	21	H	Hartlepool U	D	1-1	1-0	9	Abbott [20]	3547
11	28	A	Wrexham	D	2-2	1-2	12	Newby 2 [31, 59]	3941
12	Oct 5	H	Southend U	L	1-3	1-0	14	Nelson [3]	3301
13	12	H	Darlington	D	2-2	0-1	13	Nugent [88], Nelson [90]	2944
14	19	A	Rushden & D	W	1-0	1-0	13	Billy [45]	3925
15	26	H	Macclesfield T	W	2-1	1-0	9	Preece [12], Swailes [84]	3506
16	29	A	Lincoln C	D	1-1	0-1	—	Preece (pen) [77]	2830
17	Nov 2	A	Leyton Orient	W	2-1	1-0	6	Preece [45], Dunfield [85]	4234
18	9	H	Torquay U	L	0-1	0-0	10		3210
19	23	A	Carlisle U	W	2-1	0-0	8	Preece [73], Unsworth [75]	4678
20	30	H	Exeter C	W	1-0	0-0	5	George [82]	2039
21	Dec 14	A	Scunthorpe U	W	1-0	0-0	4	Swailes [73]	3011
22	21	H	Rochdale	D	1-1	0-0	5	Newby [62]	5827
23	26	A	Shrewsbury T	L	1-4	0-1	5	Nugent [87]	4175
24	29	H	Kidderminster H	D	1-1	0-0	6	Newby [77]	3202
25	Jan 1	H	Hull C	W	1-0	0-0	3	Lawson [72]	4290
26	14	A	Swansea C	W	3-2	3-0	—	Billy [2], Nelson [28], Lawson [29]	3555
27	18	H	Boston U	D	0-0	0-0	3		3024
28	25	A	Kidderminster H	L	2-3	0-2	5	Lawson [80], Redmond [89]	2736
29	Feb 4	A	Cambridge U	W	2-1	0-1	—	Nugent [78], Cramb [84]	2875
30	8	A	Torquay U	D	1-1	1-1	3	Billy [44]	3123
31	15	H	Leyton Orient	L	0-1	0-0	4		2707
32	22	A	York C	D	1-1	0-0	4	Clegg [60]	4115
33	Mar 1	H	Bournemouth	W	2-1	1-1	4	Redmond [33], Cramb [84]	2914
34	4	H	Bristol R	L	0-1	0-0	—		2425
35	7	A	Hartlepool U	D	0-0	0-0	—		5734
36	15	A	Macclesfield T	D	0-0	0-0	10		2920
37	18	H	Rushden & D	L	0-1	0-0	—		2291
38	22	H	Lincoln C	W	2-0	2-0	7	Clegg 2 [33, 42]	2776
39	25	H	Oxford U	D	1-1	1-1	—	Abbott [23]	2578
40	29	A	Darlington	L	1-3	1-1	9	Connell [11]	2879
41	Apr 5	A	Exeter C	W	2-1	2-0	9	Billy [23], Newby [30]	3338
42	12	H	Carlisle U	D	1-1	1-0	8	Nugent [33]	3384
43	18	A	Rochdale	W	2-1	1-1	—	Nelson [23], Cramb (pen) [71]	4513
44	21	H	Scunthorpe U	D	0-0	0-0	5		3898
45	26	A	Southend U	W	2-1	1-1	5	Nelson [10], Connell [48]	4707
46	May 3	H	Wrexham	L	0-3	0-1	7		5186

Final League Position: 7

GOALSCORERS

League (57): Newby 10, Abbott 6, Clegg 5, Nelson 5, Billy 4, Nugent 4, Preece 4 (1 pen), Cramb 3 (1 pen), Lawson 3, Swailes 3, Connell 2, Dunfield 2, Redmond 2, Unsworth 2, Forrest 1 (pen), George 1.
Worthington Cup (3): Newby 1, Stuart 1, own goal 1.
FA Cup (0).
LDV Vans Trophy (6): Clegg 1, Dunfield 1, Lawson 1, Newby 1, Nugent 1, Woodthorpe 1.
Play-offs (1): Preece 1.

Garner G 46	Barrass M 16	Stuart J 32 + 5	Unsworth L 34 + 1	Swailes D 38 + 1	Redmond S 26 + 1	Forrest M 22 + 7	Connell L 13 + 1	Newby J 46	Abbott P 17	Clegg G 28 + 3	George L 3 + 5	Hill N 1 + 1	Preece A 11 + 18	Dunfield T 28 + 1	Woodthorpe C 30 + 2	Billy C 33 + 5	Nelson M 38 + 1	Nugent D 11 + 20	Seddon G 2 + 2	Johnrose L 5 + 1	O'Shaughnessy P 6 + 10	Whaley S — + 2	Lawson I 3 + 4	Cramb C 17 + 1	Porter C — + 2	Match No.
1	2^{1}	3	4	5	6	7	8	9	10	11	12															1
1	2	3^{2}	4	5	6^{3}	7	8^{1}	9	10	11	12	13	14													2
1	2	3	4	5	6	7		9	10^{1}	11^{2}			12	8		13										3
1	2^{1}	3	4	5	6	7		9	10	11^{2}				8	12	13										4
1		3	4	5^{2}	6	7^{1}		9	10	11				8	2	12	13									5
1		3	4		6	7		9	10					8	11	2	5									6
1	2	3^{1}	4	12		7		9	10^{2}	11^{3}			13	8	6	14	5									7
1	2		3	5		11		9	10	12				8^{1}	6	7	4									8
1		3^{2}	2	5		11^{1}		9	10				12	8	6	7	4	13								9
1	2	3	4	5		12		9	10^{2}	11^{1}	14		13	8^{3}	6	7										10
1	2		4	5^{2}		7^{1}		9	10	12				8	3	11	6		13							11
1	2^{3}	12	4	5^{1}		7		9	10		13			8	3	11^{2}	6		14							12
1	2^{1}	3	4^{3}	5		12		9	10				13	8		7	6	14	11^{2}							13
1	2	3	11	5				9					12	8^{1}	6	7	4	13	10^{2}							14
1	6	3^{3}	2^{2}	5		12		9^{1}					10	8	11	7	4	13		14						15
1	2^{2}	3	4	5	12			9					10^{1}	8	11	7	6	13								16
1	2	3	4	5		11		9					10^{1}	8^{2}		7	6	12			13					17
1	2^{1}	3^{2}	4	5		8		9					10		11	7	6	12				13				18
1		3	2	5	6			9			11^{1}		10^{2}			7	4	12		8	13					19
1	2	3		5	6^{2}	12		9			11^{1}		10			7	4	13		8						20
1		3	2	5	6			9			11^{1}		10^{3}			7	4	12		8^{2}	13		14			21
1		3	2	5	6			9					10	8		7	4			11						22
1		3■	2	5	6^{2}			9					10	8^{1}	12	7	4	13		11^{3}	14					23
1			2	5	6^{1}			9		11			10^{3}	8^{2}	3	7	4	12			13		14			24
1			2	5	6			9		11^{1}					3	7	4	10			12		8			25
1			3	5	6			9		11			12	8		2	4	7^{1}			13		10^{2}			26
1		12	2	5	6			9		11	13		14	8	3^{1}		4	7^{3}					10^{2}			27
1		3	2	5	6			9		11^{2}				8^{3}	4^{1}	7		13			12		14	10		28
1		3		5	6	12	2	9^{1}		11^{2}				8			4	13			7			10		29
1		3	2	5■	6		12	9		13				8■		14	4	11^{3}			7^{2}			10^{1}		30
1		3	2	5	6			9					12	8		7^{2}	4	13			11			10^{1}		31
1			2		6			9		11					3	7	5	8			4		12	10^{1}		32
1		12	2		6			9		11^{1}				8	3	7	5	13			4^{2}			10		33
1		3	2	5	6^{1}			9		11			12	8		7^{3}	4	13			14			10^{2}		34
1		3	2		6	7		9		11			12		5		4	8						10^{1}		35
1		3^{2}		5		7	2	9		11			12	8^{3}	6		4	13						10^{1}	14	36
1		3		5		7	2	9	8	11					6		4^{1}	10						12		37
1		12		5		11	2^{1}	9^{2}	8	3			13	14	6	7	4							10^{3}		38
1				5		11	2	9	8	3^{1}					6	7	4	12						10		39
1				5		11^{1}	2	9	8^{2}	3			12		6	7	4	13						10		40
1		12		5		11	2	9		3^{1}			13		6	7	4	8^{3}			14			10^{2}		41
1				5		11	2	9		3			12		6	7	4	8						10^{1}		42
1		3	12		6	13	2^{1}	9		11					4	7	5	8^{2}						10		43
1		3			6	12	2	9		11			13		4	7	5	8^{1}						10^{2}		44
1		3			6	8	2	9		11					4	7	5							10		45
1		3	2	5				9^{1}		11		6	10	8	4						7^{2}	12			13	46

Worthington Cup

First Round	Stoke C	(h)	1-0
Second Round	Bolton W	(a)	1-0
Third Round	Fulham	(a)	1-3

FA Cup

First Round	Plymouth Arg	(h)	0-3

LDV Vans Trophy

First Round	Rochdale	(a)	1-0
Second Round	Barnsley	(h)	1-0
Quarter-final	Tranmere R	(h)	2-0
Semi-final	Carlisle U	(a)	2-3

CAMBRIDGE UNITED — Division 3

FOUNDATION

The football revival in Cambridge began soon after World War II when the Abbey United club (formed 1912) decided to turn professional in 1949. In 1951 they changed their name to Cambridge United. They were competing in the United Counties League before graduating to the Eastern Counties League in 1951 and the Southern League in 1958.

Abbey Stadium, Newmarket Road, Cambridge, CB5 8LN.

Telephone: (01223) 566 500. ***Fax:*** (01223) 566 502.
ClubCall: 09068 555 885.
Website: cambridge-united.co.uk

Ground Capacity: 9,247.

Record Attendance: 14,000 v Chelsea, Friendly, 1 May 1970.

Record Receipts: £86,308 v Manchester U, Rumbelows Cup 2nd rd 2nd leg, 9 October 1991.

Pitch Measurements: 110yd × 74yd.

Life President: R. H. Smart.

Chairman: G. G. Harwood. ***Vice-chairman:*** R. F. Hunt.

Directors: J. Howard, R. Hunt, G. Lowe, R. Summerfield, P. S. Barry, R. L. Sargent.

Manager: John Taylor. ***Assistant Manager:*** Dale Brooks.

Physio: Ant Cooke.

Secretary: Andrew Pincher.

Stadium Manager: Ian Darler.

Colours: Amber shirts with black trim, black shorts, black stockings.

Change Colours: All navy with Cambridge blue trim.

Year Formed: 1912.

Turned Professional: 1949.

Ltd Co.: 1948.

Previous Name: 1919, Abbey United; 1951, Cambridge United.

Club Nickname: The 'U's'.

First Football League Game: 15 August 1970, Division 4, v Lincoln C (h) D 1–1 – Roberts; Thompson, Meldrum (1), Slack, Eades, Hardy, Leggett, Cassidy, Lindsey, McKinven, Harris.

HONOURS

Football League: Division 2 best season: 5th, 1991–92; Division 3 – Champions 1990–91; Runners-up 1977–78, 1998–99; Division 4 – Champions 1976–77; Promoted from Division 4 1989–90 (play-offs).

FA Cup: best season: 6th rd, 1990 (shared record for Fourth Division club), 1991.

Football League Cup: best season: 5th rd, 1993.

LDV Vans Trophy: Runners-up 2002.

SKY SPORTS FACT FILE

In the 1957–58 season Cambridge United enjoyed their last term in the Eastern Counties League. Brian Moore scored 49 goals in only 36 matches as the club finished runners-up and entered the Southern League.

Record League Victory: 6–0 v Darlington, Division 4, 18 September 1971 – Roberts; Thompson, Akers, Guild, Eades, Foote, Collins (1p), Horrey, Hollett, Greenhalgh (4), Phillips, (1 og). 6–0 v Hartlepool U, Division 4, 11 February 1989 – Vaughan; Beck, Kimble, Turner, Chapple (1), Daish, Clayton, Holmes, Taylor (3 incl. 1p), Bull (1), Leadbitter (1).

Record Cup Victory: 5–1 v Bristol C, FA Cup 5th rd second replay, 27 February 1990 – Vaughan; Fensome, Kimble, Bailie (O'Shea), Chapple, Daish, Cheetham (Robinson), Leadbitter (1), Dublin (2), Taylor (1), Philpott (1).

Record Defeat: 0–7 v Sunderland, League Cup 2nd rd, 1 October 2002.

Most League Points (2 for a win): 65, Division 4, 1976–77.

Most League Points (3 for a win): 86, Division 3, 1990–91.

Most League Goals: 87, Division 4, 1976–77.

Highest League Scorer in Season: David Crown, 24, Division 4, 1985–86.

Most League Goals in Total Aggregate: John Taylor, 86, 1988–92; 1996–2001.

Most League Goals in One Match: 5, Steve Butler v Exeter C, Division 2, 4 April 1994.

Most Capped Player: Tom Finney, 7 (15), Northern Ireland.

Most League Appearances: Steve Spriggs, 416, 1975–87.

Youngest League Player: Andy Sinton, 16 years 228 days v Wolverhampton W, 2 November 1982.

Record Transfer Fee Received: £1,000,000 from Manchester U for Dion Dublin, August 1992.

Record Transfer Fee Paid: £190,000 to Luton T for Steve Claridge, November 1992.

Football League Record: 1970 Elected to Division 4; 1973–74 Division 3; 1974–77 Division 4; 1977–78 Division 3; 1978–84 Division 2; 1984–85 Division 3; 1985–90 Division 4; 1990–91 Division 3; 1991–92 Division 2; 1992–93 Division 1; 1993–95 Division 2; 1995–99 Division 3; 1999– 2002 Division 2; 2002– Division 3.

MANAGERS

Bill Whittaker 1949–55
Gerald Williams 1955
Bert Johnson 1955–59
Bill Craig 1959–60
Alan Moore 1960–63
Roy Kirk 1964–66
Bill Leivers 1967–74
Ron Atkinson 1974–78
John Docherty 1978–83
John Ryan 1984–85
Ken Shellito 1985
Chris Turner 1985–90
John Beck 1990–92
Ian Atkins 1992–93
Gary Johnson 1993–95
Tommy Taylor 1995–96
Roy McFarland 1996–2001
John Beck 2001
John Taylor January 2002–

LATEST SEQUENCES

Longest Sequence of League Wins: 7, 19.2.1977 – 1.4.1977.

Longest Sequence of League Defeats: 7, 8.4.1985 – 30.4.1985.

Longest Sequence of League Draws: 6, 6.9.1986 – 30.9.1986.

Longest Sequence of Unbeaten League Matches: 14, 9.9.1972 – 10.11.1972.

Longest Sequence Without a League Win: 31, 8.10.1983 – 23.4.1984.

Successive Scoring Runs: 26 from 9.4.2002.

Successive Non-scoring Runs: 5 from 29.9.1973.

TEN YEAR LEAGUE RECORD

		P	W	D	L	F	A	Pts	Pos
1993-94	Div 2	46	19	9	18	79	73	66	10
1994-95	Div 2	46	11	15	20	52	69	48	20
1995-96	Div 3	46	14	12	20	61	71	54	16
1996-97	Div 3	46	18	11	17	53	59	65	10
1997-98	Div 3	46	14	18	14	63	57	60	16
1998-99	Div 3	46	23	12	11	78	48	81	2
1999-2000	Div 2	46	12	12	22	64	65	48	19
2000-01	Div 2	46	14	11	21	61	77	53	19
2001-02	Div 2	46	7	13	26	47	93	34	24
2002-03	Div 3	46	16	13	17	67	70	61	12

DID YOU KNOW ?

As a prelude to the 1976–77 season, Cambridge United tried out their new £6,000 floodlighting system which was three times as powerful as the old one, in a pre-season friendly against the Dutch club Dordrecht on 2 August. United won 4-1.

CAMBRIDGE UNITED 2002–03 LEAGUE RECORD

Match No.	Date	Venue	Opponents	Result		H/T Score	Lg. Pos.	Goalscorers	Attendance
1	Aug 10	H	Darlington	L	1-2	1-1	—	Kitson [6]	4079
2	13	A	Bury	W	1-0	0-0	—	Riza [53]	2650
3	17	A	Bournemouth	D	1-1	1-0	14	Fleming [35]	4315
4	24	H	Leyton Orient	W	2-1	1-0	6	Kitson 2 [6, 55]	4807
5	26	A	Southend U	L	1-2	1-2	11	Riza [28]	4462
6	31	H	Rushden & D	W	4-1	1-0	4	Youngs 2 [21, 77], Riza [63], Kitson [90]	4598
7	Sept 7	H	Hull C	L	1-2	0-0	8	Kitson [90]	4258
8	14	A	Torquay U	L	2-3	0-1	12	Tudor 2 [89, 90]	2557
9	17	A	Rochdale	L	3-4	2-1	—	Bridges [23], Tudor [42], Wanless (pen) [52]	2392
10	21	H	York C	W	3-0	1-0	11	Kitson [13], Tann [82], Bridges [84]	4204
11	28	A	Boston U	W	3-1	2-1	10	Kitson 2 [2, 90], Redfearn (og) [24]	3090
12	Oct 5	H	Wrexham	D	2-2	0-1	12	Youngs [84], Riza [85]	6044
13	12	A	Scunthorpe U	W	2-1	0-1	9	Riza [54], Tudor [82]	3140
14	19	H	Oxford U	D	1-1	1-0	9	Tudor [28]	4621
15	26	A	Kidderminster H	L	1-2	1-2	12	Kitson [8]	2779
16	29	H	Carlisle U	W	2-1	1-1	—	Tudor 2 [25, 63]	3334
17	Nov 2	H	Swansea C	W	1-0	0-0	5	Kitson [53]	3956
18	9	A	Shrewsbury T	L	1-3	0-0	7	Youngs [53]	2928
19	23	A	Exeter C	W	2-1	1-1	6	Tudor [34], Kitson [81]	2722
20	30	H	Macclesfield T	W	3-1	1-1	4	Wanless [29], Kitson [70], Riza (pen) [74]	3834
21	Dec 14	A	Lincoln C	D	2-2	1-1	7	Guttridge [4], Wanless [78]	2845
22	21	H	Bristol R	W	3-1	1-1	4	Parker (og) [17], Youngs [49], Kitson [66]	3701
23	26	H	Southend U	D	1-1	0-1	3	Fleming [63]	6237
24	28	A	Hartlepool U	L	0-3	0-1	5		4805
25	Jan 18	A	Rushden & D	L	1-4	0-1	10	Wanless [87]	5206
26	25	H	Hartlepool U	D	0-0	0-0	12		4543
27	28	A	Leyton Orient	D	1-1	1-0	—	Youngs [35]	3953
28	Feb 4	H	Bury	L	1-2	1-0	—	Youngs [39]	2875
29	8	H	Shrewsbury T	W	5-0	2-0	11	Kitson 2 [4, 59], Riza [45], Youngs 2 [47, 81]	3755
30	15	A	Swansea C	L	0-2	0-0	12		4903
31	22	A	Hull C	D	1-1	1-0	13	Youngs [38]	15,607
32	Mar 1	H	Torquay U	L	0-1	0-1	13		4280
33	4	H	Rochdale	D	2-2	2-1	—	Kitson [4], Tudor [45]	2586
34	8	A	York C	L	1-3	1-0	13	Iriekpen [6]	3394
35	11	A	Darlington	W	2-1	1-0	—	Riza 2 [38, 85]	2076
36	15	H	Kidderminster H	L	0-2	0-0	12		3705
37	18	A	Oxford U	D	1-1	0-0	—	Guttridge [59]	4983
38	22	A	Carlisle U	W	1-0	1-0	12	Kitson [26]	3992
39	25	H	Bournemouth	W	2-1	1-1	—	Kitson [12], Guttridge [83]	2885
40	29	H	Scunthorpe U	D	1-1	1-0	12	Kitson [14]	3951
41	Apr 5	A	Macclesfield T	D	1-1	0-1	12	Riza [67]	2053
42	12	H	Exeter C	W	2-1	0-1	11	Wanless (pen) [69], Turner [90]	5218
43	19	A	Bristol R	L	1-3	0-1	12	Kitson (pen) [90]	7563
44	22	H	Lincoln C	D	0-0	0-0	—		4013
45	26	A	Wrexham	L	0-5	0-3	12		9960
46	May 3	H	Boston U	L	1-2	0-1	12	Riza [72]	4488

Final League Position: 12

GOALSCORERS

League (67): Kitson 20 (1 pen), Riza 11 (1 pen), Youngs 10, Tudor 9, Wanless 5 (2 pens), Guttridge 3, Bridges 2, Fleming 2, Iriekpen 1, Tann 1, Turner 1, own goals 2.
Worthington Cup (3): Duncan 1, Kitson 1, Tudor 1.
FA Cup (8): Tann 2, Youngs 2, Kitson 1, Riza 1, Wanless 1, own goal 1.
LDV Vans Trophy (14): Riza 4, Kitson 3, Fleming 1, Guttridge 1, Tann 1, Tudor 1, Wanless 1, Youngs 1, own goal 1.

Marshall S 45	Goodhind W 34 + 3	Warner P 7 + 1	Duncan A 21 + 2	Angus S 40	Fleming T 42 + 1	Guttridge L 39 + 4	Tudor S 26 + 1	Kitson D 44	Youngs T 31 + 4	Riza O 43 + 3	Scully T 1 + 5	Murray F 25 + 4	Revell A — + 9	Wanless P 27 + 12	Bridges D 6 + 11	Tann A 21 + 4	Nacca F 9 + 8	Chillingworth D 11 + 19	Jordan S 11	Brennan M 1	Newey T 6	Theobald D 1 + 3	Iriekpen E 13	Turner J — + 1	Heathcote J 2	Opara L — + 2	Taylor J — + 1	Match No.
1	2	3	4	5	6	7	8	9	10	11[1]	12																	1
1	2	3		5	6	7[1]	8	9	10[2]	11[3]		4	12	13	14													2
1	2	3	4	5	6	7[2]	8	9[1]	10	11				12	13													3
1	2	3	4	5	6	7[1]	8	9	10	11[2]		13		12														4
1	2	3[2]	4	5	6	7[1]	8	9	10[3]	11	14	13		12														5
1	2	12	4	5	6	7[2]	8	9	10	11		3[1]		13														6
1		2	4	5	6	7[2]	8	9	10	11[1]	12	3			13													7
1	12■	2[2]	4	5	6	7[3]	8	9	10	11		3[1]		13	14													8
1	2		4■	5	12	7[1]	8		10[2]	11		3		6	9	13												9
1	2			5	6		8[2]	9	10	11[3]		3		4[1]	7	12	13	14										10
1	2		13	5	6	12	8[1]	9	10	11[3]		3[2]		4	7			14										11
1	2		4	5	6	12		9	10	11[3]				8	7[1]		14	13	3[2]									12
1	2		4	5	6	7	8	9	10	11									3									13
1	2■		4	5	6	7	8[1]	9	10[2]	11[3]	13			12				14	3									14
1	2			5	6	7[1]	8	9	10[2]	11				12		4	13	14	3[3]									15
1	2		4	5	6	7[1]	8	9		11[3]	10[2]			12			14	13	3									16
1			4	5	3	7	8	9	12	11				6		2		10[1]										17
1			4	5	3	7[1]	8	9	10[2]	11				6	13	2		12										18
1	12		4	5[1]	6	13	8■	9	10■	11[2]				7		2			3									19
1	4			5		7	8	9		11				10[2]	13	2	6[1]	12	3									20
1	5		4		6■	7■	8[3]	9	12	11[1]				13		2	10[2]	14	3									21
1	2		12	5	6	7[2]		9[3]	10	11				8		4[1]	13	14	3									22
1	2		4	5	6	7	8	9	10	11									3									23
1	2		4	5			8	9	10[1]	11				6	13		7[2]	12	3									24
1	2		4	5[2]	3	12	8[3]	9	10	11[1]				7	13	6		14										25
			4		2	7[1]		9	10	11		3	13	6	12	5	8[2]			1								26
1	2			5[1]	3	7		9	10	11[2]		12		8	14	4	6[3]	13										27
1			4	5[1]		7[3]		9	10	11		3	12	6	13	2	8[2]	14										28
1	5				6	2[1]		9[2]	10	11[3]	12	3	13	7	8	4		14										29
1	2				6		12	9	10[3]	11[2]		4	13	7	8[1]	5		14			3							30
1					6	7	8		10	11		2		4		5■	12[2]	9[1]			3	13						31
1	5				6	7	8	9	10[2]	11		3		12		2[1]		13					4					32
1	2			5	6	7	8[1]	9		10		3		12							11		4					33
1	2			5	6	7		9	12	10[2]		3[3]	14	8				13			11[1]		4					34
1	2			5	6	7		9		10		3					8				11		4					35
1	2			5	6	7		9	12	10[2]		3					8[1]	13			11		4					36
1	2[1]			5	6	7		9	11	13		3		8		12		10[2]					4					37
1	2[2]			5	6	7		9[1]	11	12		3		8		13	14	10[3]					4					38
1				5	6[2]	7		9	11	12		3		8		2	13	10[1]					4					39
1				5	6	7		9		11		3		8		2		10					4					40
1	12			5	6	7		9		11		3[1]		8		2		10					4					41
1	3[1]			5	6	7		9		11[2]		12		8		2		10					4	13				42
1	2			5	6	7		9		11		3[1]	12	8				10					4					43
1	2			5	6	7		9		11		3	12	8[1]				10				13	4[2]					44
1	2			5	6[2]	7		9[1]		11[3]			12			4	8	10				13■			3	14		45
1				5	6	7		9		11[2]		3		8		2						4			10[1]	12	13	46

Worthington Cup

First Round	Reading	(h)	3-1
Second Round	Sunderland	(h)	0-7

LDV Vans Trophy

First Round	Rushden & D	(h)	4-0
Second Round	Northampton T	(a)	4-2
Quarter-final	Luton T	(a)	2-1
Semi-final	Brentford	(a)	2-1
Southern Final	Bristol C	(a)	2-4
		(h)	0-3

FA Cup

First Round	Scarborough	(a)	0-0
		(h)	2-1
Second Round	Northampton T	(h)	2-2
		(a)	1-0
Third Round	Millwall	(h)	1-1
		(a)	2-3

CARDIFF CITY — Division 1

FOUNDATION

Credit for the establishment of a first class professional football club in such a rugby stronghold as Cardiff, is due to members of the Riverside club formed in 1899 out of a cricket club of that name. Cardiff became a city in 1905 and in 1908 the South Wales and Monmouthshire FA granted Riverside permission to call themselves Cardiff City. The club turned professional under that name in 1910.

Ninian Park, Cardiff CF11 8SX.

Telephone: (02920) 348 019. ***Fax:*** (02920) 221 001.
Ticket Office: 0845 345 1400.
Website: www.cardiffcityfc.co.uk
Email: reception@cardiffcityfc.co.uk

Ground Capacity: 21,408.

Record Attendance: 62,634, Wales v England, 17 October 1959.

Club Record Attendance: 57,893 v Arsenal, Division 1, 22 April 1953.

Record Receipts: £141,756 v Manchester C, FA Cup 4th rd, 29 January 1994.

Pitch Measurements: 120yd × 72yd.

Owner: Sam Hammam. ***Vice-chairman:*** Steve Borley.
Chief Executive: David Temme.

Directors: Sam Hammam (Owner), Steve Borley (Vice-Chairman), Michael Isaac, Kim Walker, Paul M. Guy, Jonathan Crystal QC. ***Advisor:*** Tony Clemo.

Manager: Lennie Lawrence.
Assistant Manager: Ian Butterworth.
Physio: Clive Goodyear.

Club Secretary: Jason Turner.
Sales Manager: Catherine Scruby.
Press & Media Manager: Neil Hughes.
Business Development Manager: Tony Dilloway.

Colours: Blue shirts, blue shorts, blue stockings.

Change Colours: Yellow shirts, yellow shorts, yellow stockings.

Year Formed: 1899. ***Turned Professional:*** 1910. ***Ltd Co.:*** 1910.

Previous Names: 1899, Riverside; 1902, Riverside Albion; 1908, Cardiff City.

Club Nickname: 'Bluebirds'.

Previous Grounds: Riverside, Sophia Gardens, Old Park and Fir Gardens. Moved to Ninian Park, 1910.

First Football League Game: 28 August 1920, Division 2, v Stockport Co (a) W 5–2 – Kneeshaw; Brittan, Leyton; Keenor (1), Smith, Hardy; Grimshaw (1), Gill (2), Cashmore, West, Evans (1).

Record League Victory: 9–2 v Thames, Division 3 (S), 6 February 1932 – Farquharson; E. L. Morris, Roberts; Galbraith, Harris, Ronan; Emmerson (1), Keating (1), Jones (1), McCambridge (1),

HONOURS

Football League: Division 1 – Runners-up 1923–24; Division 2 – Runners-up 1920–21, 1951–52, 1959–60; Division 2 – 2002–03 (play-offs); Division 3 (S) – Champions 1946–47; Division 3 – Champions 1992–93. Runners-up 1975–76, 1982–83, 2000–01; Division 4 – Runners-up 1987–88.

FA Cup: Winners 1927 (only occasion the Cup has been won by a club outside England); Runners-up 1925.

Football League Cup: Semi-final 1966.

Welsh Cup: Winners 22 times (joint record).

Charity Shield: Winners 1927.

European Competitions: *European Cup-Winners' Cup:* 1964–65, 1965–66, 1967–68 (semi-finalists), 1968–69, 1969–70, 1970–71, 1971–72, 1973–74, 1974–75, 1976–77, 1977–78, 1988–89, 1992–93, 1993–94.

SKY SPORTS FACT FILE

Cardiff City's 74th minute goal in the 1927 final, which took the FA Cup out of England for the first time, was scored by a Scot Hughie Ferguson against Arsenal's Welsh goalkeeper Dan Lewis.

Robbins (5).

Record Cup Victory: 8–0 v Enfield, FA Cup 1st rd, 28 November 1931 – Farquharson; Smith, Roberts; Harris (1), Galbraith, Ronan; Emmerson (2), Keating (3); O'Neill (2), Robbins, McCambridge.

Record Defeat: 2–11 v Sheffield U, Division 1, 1 January 1926.

Most League Points (2 for a win): 66, Division 3 (S), 1946–47.

Most League Points (3 for a win): 86, Division 3, 1982–83.

Most League Goals: 95, Division 3, 2000–01.

Highest League Scorer in Season: Robert Earnshaw, 31, Division 2, 2002–03.

Most League Goals in Total Aggregate: Len Davies, 128, 1920–31.

Most League Goals in One Match: 5, Hugh Ferguson v Burnley, Division 1, 1 September 1928; 5, Walter Robbins v Thames, Division 3S, 6 February 1932; 5, William Henderson v Northampton T, Division 3S, 22 April 1933.

Most Capped Player: Alf Sherwood, 39 (41), Wales.

Most League Appearances: Phil Dwyer, 471, 1972–85.

Youngest League Player: John Toshack, 16 years 236 days v Leyton Orient, 13 November 1965.

Record Transfer Fee Received: £500,000 from Coventry C for Simon Haworth, June 1997.

Record Transfer Fee Paid: £1,700,000 to Stoke C for Peter Thorne, September 2001.

Football League Record: 1920 Elected to Division 2; 1921–29 Division 1; 1929–31 Division 2; 1931–47 Division 3 (S); 1947–52 Division 2; 1952–57 Division 1; 1957–60 Division 2; 1960–62 Division 1; 1962–75 Division 2; 1975–76 Division 3; 1976–82 Division 2; 1982–83 Division 3; 1983–85 Division 2; 1985–86 Division 3; 1986–88 Division 4; 1988–90 Division 3; 1990–92 Division 4; 1992–93 Division 3; 1993–95 Division 2; 1995–99 Division 3; 1999–2000 Division 2; 2000–01 Division 3; 2001–03 Division 2; 2003– Division 1.

MANAGERS

Davy McDougall 1910–11
Fred Stewart 1911–33
Bartley Wilson 1933–34
B. Watts-Jones 1934–37
Bill Jennings 1937–39
Cyril Spiers 1939–46
Billy McCandless 1946–48
Cyril Spiers 1948–54
Trevor Morris 1954–58
Bill Jones 1958–62
George Swindin 1962–64
Jimmy Scoular 1964–73
Frank O'Farrell 1973–74
Jimmy Andrews 1974–78
Richie Morgan 1978–82
Len Ashurst 1982–84
Jimmy Goodfellow 1984
Alan Durban 1984–86
Frank Burrows 1986–89
Len Ashurst 1989–91
Eddie May 1991–94
Terry Yorath 1994–95
Eddie May 1995
Kenny Hibbitt *(Chief Coach)* 1995
Phil Neal 1996
Russell Osman 1996–97
Kenny Hibbitt 1996–98
Frank Burrows 1998–99
Billy Ayre 1999–2000
Bobby Gould 2000
Alan Cork 2000–02
Lennie Lawrence February 2002–

LATEST SEQUENCES

Longest Sequence of League Wins: 9, 26.10.1946 – 28.12.1946.

Longest Sequence of League Defeats: 7, 4.11.1933 – 25.12.1933.

Longest Sequence of League Draws: 6, 29.11.1980 – 17.1.1981.

Longest Sequence of Unbeaten League Matches: 21, 21.9.1946 – 1.3.1947.

Longest Sequence Without a League Win: 15, 21.11.1936 – 6.3.1937.

Successive Scoring Runs: 23 from 24.10.1992.

Successive Non-scoring Runs: 8 from 20.12.1952.

TEN YEAR LEAGUE RECORD

		P	*W*	*D*	*L*	*F*	*A*	*Pts*	*Pos*
1993-94	Div 2	46	13	15	18	66	79	54	19
1994-95	Div 2	46	9	11	26	46	74	38	22
1995-96	Div 3	46	11	12	23	41	64	45	22
1996-97	Div 3	46	20	9	17	56	54	69	7
1997-98	Div 3	46	9	23	14	48	52	50	21
1998-99	Div 3	46	22	14	10	60	39	80	3
1999-2000	Div 2	46	9	17	20	45	67	44	21
2000-01	Div 3	46	23	13	10	95	58	82	2
2001-02	Div 2	46	23	14	9	75	50	83	4
2002-03	Div 2	46	23	12	11	68	43	81	6

DID YOU KNOW ?

Hugh Ferguson, grandson of Hughie Ferguson, Cardiff City's record holder of 32 League and Cup goals in 1926–27, sent a congratulatory message to Robert Earnshaw after the current City striker reached 34 goals in all competitions in 2002–03.

CARDIFF CITY 2002–03 LEAGUE RECORD

Match No.	Date	Venue	Opponents	Result		H/T Score	Lg. Pos.	Goalscorers	Attendance
1	Aug 10	A	Oldham Ath	W	2-1	1-0	—	Campbell [21], Earnshaw [84]	8033
2	13	H	Port Vale	W	3-1	2-1	—	Thorne [4], Fortune-West [9], Legg [69]	13,296
3	17	H	Northampton T	L	1-2	1-1	5	Kavanagh [15]	13,321
4	24	A	Swindon T	W	1-0	1-0	3	Fortune-West [28]	7564
5	26	H	Luton T	D	0-0	0-0	5		13,564
6	31	A	Cheltenham T	D	1-1	1-1	5	Campbell [11]	4395
7	Sept 14	H	Stockport Co	W	2-1	2-1	8	Earnshaw [2], Kavanagh [38]	11,546
8	17	H	Brentford	W	2-0	1-0	—	Legg [28], Earnshaw [73]	12,032
9	21	A	Notts Co	W	1-0	1-0	4	Croft [20]	6118
10	24	A	Plymouth Arg	D	2-2	1-1	—	Earnshaw 2 [2, 67]	11,606
11	28	H	Crewe Alex	W	2-1	0-0	1	Earnshaw 2 [84, 86]	13,208
12	Oct 5	A	Wigan Ath	D	2-2	1-2	2	Earnshaw 2 [20, 86]	8047
13	12	H	Wycombe W	W	1-0	0-0	1	Kavanagh [79]	13,130
14	19	A	Blackpool	L	0-1	0-0	2		7744
15	26	H	Tranmere R	W	4-0	2-0	2	Thorne 2 [29, 82], Earnshaw (pen) [40], Weston [90]	12,096
16	29	A	Mansfield T	W	1-0	0-0	—	Thorne [70]	3441
17	Nov 2	H	Peterborough U	W	3-0	1-0	1	Kavanagh [19], Earnshaw (pen) [54], Weston [58]	12,918
18	9	A	Barnsley	L	2-3	2-2	3	Earnshaw 2 [23, 42]	10,894
19	24	H	Chesterfield	W	1-0	1-0	2	Thorne [12]	13,331
20	29	A	QPR	W	4-0	0-0	—	Earnshaw 3 [59, 65, 87], Campbell [90]	14,345
21	Dec 14	H	Bristol C	L	0-2	0-0	3		15,239
22	20	A	Colchester U	W	2-1	1-0	—	Earnshaw 2 [45, 77]	3096
23	26	A	Luton T	L	0-2	0-0	3		7805
24	29	H	Huddersfield T	W	4-0	2-0	3	Bowen 2 [19, 64], Earnshaw 2 [44, 73]	13,703
25	Jan 1	H	Swindon T	D	1-1	0-0	2	Earnshaw [89]	13,062
26	18	H	Cheltenham T	W	2-1	2-1	4	Thorne [8], Earnshaw [36]	11,605
27	25	A	Huddersfield T	L	0-1	0-0	4		9462
28	31	H	Oldham Ath	D	1-1	1-0	—	Bowen [35]	12,579
29	Feb 4	A	Northampton T	W	1-0	0-0	—	Earnshaw [58]	4553
30	8	H	Barnsley	D	1-1	0-0	3	Gordon [90]	12,759
31	21	H	Plymouth Arg	D	1-1	1-0	—	Earnshaw [42]	14,006
32	25	A	Port Vale	W	2-0	1-0	—	Gordon [35], Thorne [64]	3831
33	Mar 1	A	Stockport Co	D	1-1	0-1	3	Thorne [81]	5385
34	4	A	Brentford	W	2-0	0-0	—	Young [52], Earnshaw [78]	5727
35	8	H	Notts Co	L	0-2	0-0	3		11,389
36	14	A	Tranmere R	D	3-3	1-0	—	Earnshaw 3 [35, 68, 90]	9637
37	18	H	Blackpool	W	2-1	1-1	—	Earnshaw [44], Mahon [51]	11,788
38	21	H	Mansfield T	W	1-0	0-0	—	Earnshaw [62]	13,009
39	Apr 5	H	QPR	L	1-2	0-0	4	Thorne [78]	15,245
40	8	A	Wycombe W	W	4-0	1-0	—	Thorne 2 [5, 81], Mahon [68], Legg [84]	5889
41	13	A	Chesterfield	W	3-0	2-0	3	Kavanagh [24], Thorne 2 [35, 82]	4398
42	16	A	Peterborough U	L	0-2	0-1	—		4984
43	19	H	Colchester U	L	0-3	0-1	3		12,633
44	22	A	Bristol C	L	0-2	0-0	—		15,615
45	26	H	Wigan Ath	D	0-0	0-0	5		14,702
46	May 3	A	Crewe Alex	D	1-1	0-1	6	Earnshaw [64]	9562

Final League Position: 6

GOALSCORERS

League (68): Earnshaw 31 (2 pens), Thorne 13, Kavanagh 5, Bowen 3, Campbell 3, Legg 3, Fortune-West 2, Gordon 2, Mahon 2, Weston 2, Croft 1, Young 1.
Worthington Cup (5): Earnshaw 3, Thorne 1, own goal 1.
FA Cup (9): Campbell 2, Collins 2, Boland 1, Earnshaw 1, Fortune-West 1, Kavanagh 1, Thorne 1.
LDV Vans Trophy (4): Bowen 1, Campbell 1 (pen), Fortune-West 1, Gordon 1.
Play-offs (2): Campbell 1, Thorne 1.

Alexander N 40	Weston R 38	Croft G 39 + 4	Gabbidon D 22 + 2	Barker C 32 + 8	Whalley G 17 + 2	Boland W 40 + 1	Kavanagh G 42 + 2	Fortune-West L 7 + 12	Thorne P 46	Campbell A 10 + 18	Legg A 26 + 9	Collins J — + 2	Earnshaw R 39 + 7	Maxwell L 5 + 11	Prior S 35 + 2	Margetson M 6	Hamilton D 2 + 4	Zhiyi F 6	Bowen J 7 + 4	Young S 11 + 1	Mahon A 13 + 2	Bonner M 7 + 7	Gordon G 3 + 7	Jenkins S 4	Ainsworth G 9	Match No.
1	2	3	4	5	6¹	7	8	9	10²	11³	12	13	14													1
1	2	3	4	5	6²		8	9	10	7¹	11		12	13												2
1	2	3	4	5³	6²		8	9	10	7¹	11		12	13	14											3
1	2²	3	4	12	6		8	9	10¹	7³	11		14	13	5											4
1	2	3	4		6	12	8³	9¹	10	7²	11		13	14	5											5
1	2	3	4		6	7	8	12	10	9²	11¹		13		5											6
1	2	3	4		6²	7	8		10	12	11		9¹	13	5											7
1	2	3	4		6	7	8		10	12	11		9¹		5											8
1	2	3	4	13	6	7	8		10	12	11²		9¹		5											9
1	2	3	4	13	6	7	8		10	12	11²		9¹		5											10
1	2	3	4		6	7³	8	12	10¹	13	11²		9	14	5											11
1	2¹	3	4	12	6	7	8³	9²	10	13			11	14	5											12
	2	3¹	4	12	6²	7	8		10	13	11		9		5	1										13
1	2	3	4		6	7³	8	12	10²	13	11¹		9	14	5											14
1	2	3	4	12		7	8		10	13	11¹		9²	6³	5		14									15
1	2	3	4	6		7	8		10	12			9¹	11²	5		13									16
1	2¹	3	4	12	6²	7	8	14	10³	13			9	11	5											17
1	2	3	4¹	12	6³	7	8	13	10				9	11²	5		14									18
1	2	3		5		7	8		10	12	11		9¹	6²	4		13									19
1	2	3		5		7	8	12	10¹	13	11		9²		4		6									20
1		2		3		7	8		10¹	12	11		9	13³	4		6²	5	14							21
1	2	12		3		6	8	13	10	7¹	11		9²		5			4■								22
1	2			3		4	8	12	10	7¹	11		9		5			6²	13							23
1	2	3		5		7		12	10¹		11		9	13	4³			6²	8	14						24
1	2	3³		5		8	12	13	10	14	11		9		4			6¹	7²							25
1	2			3			6	12	10	8¹	11		9	13	4				7²	5						26
1	2¹	12		3				7²	10	13	11		9		4			6		5	14	8³				27
1	2	3		5		7	8		10		12		9²						11	6	4¹		13'			28
1	2	3		5		7	8		10				9						11	4	6					29
1	2	3¹		5		7³	8		10		12		9						11²	4	6	13	14			30
1	2	3		5		6	8		10		11¹		9		12				7²	4		13				31
1	2	3		5		7	8		10				9¹						12	4		6	11			32
1		3		5		7	8		10		12		9							4	13	6	11²	2¹		33
1		2		3		7	8	12	10			13	9		5²					4	11¹	6				34
1		2¹		3		7	8		10				9		5				13	4	11	6²	12			35
1		2		3		7	8		10				9		5					4	11	6				36
1		3		5		11	8		10		12		9		4						6²	13		2¹	7	37
1		3		5		11	8		10				9		4						6	12		2	7¹	38
		3¹		5		11	8		10		12		9		4	1					6		13	2	7²	39
	2	3	12	5		11	8		10		13		9		4¹	1					6²	14			7³	40
	2	3	12	5		11	8		10				9²		4³	1					6	14	13		7¹	41
	2	3¹	4	5		11	8		10		12		9			1					6		13		7²	42
	2¹	12	4	5	13	11	8		10		3		9			1					6²		14		7³	43
1	2		5	3	12	6¹	8		10	13	11²		9		4										7■	44
1	2	12	5¹	3		6	8		10	13	11		9²		4							14			7³	45
1	2	3		5	6	7¹	12		10	11³	14		13		4							8	9²			46

Worthington Cup

First Round	Boston U	(a)	5-1
Second Round	Tottenham H	(a)	0-1

FA Cup

First Round	Tranmere R	(a)	2-2
		(h)	2-1
Second Round	Margate	(a)	3-0
Third Round	Coventry C	(h)	2-2
		(a)	0-3

LDV Vans Trophy

Second Round	Exeter C	(a)	3-0
Quarter-final	Bournemouth	(a)	1-2

CARLISLE UNITED — Division 3

FOUNDATION

Carlisle United came into being in 1903 through the amalgamation of Shaddongate United and Carlisle Red Rose. The new club was admitted to the Second Division of the Lancashire Combination in 1905–06, winning promotion the following season. Devonshire Park was officially opened on 2 September 1905, when St Helens Town were the visitors. Despite defeat in a disappointing 3-2 start, a respectable mid-table position was achieved.

Brunton Park, Carlisle CA1 1LL.

Telephone: (01228) 526 237. ***Fax:*** (01228) 530 138.
Website: www.carlisleunited.co.uk

Ground Capacity: 13,655.

Record Attendance: 27,500 v Birmingham C, FA Cup 3rd rd, 5 January 1957 and v Middlesbrough, FA Cup 5th rd, 7 February 1970.

Record Receipts: £146,000 v Tottenham H, Coca-Cola Cup 2nd rd, 30 September 1997.

Pitch Measurements: 117yd × 72yd.

Directors: J. Courtenay, A. Jenkins, J. Bourke, Lord Clarke.

Manager: Roddy Collins.

Physio: Neil Dalton.

Secretary: Sarah McKnight.

Colours: Blue shirts, blue shorts, blue stockings.

Change Colours: All white with green and red trim.

Year Formed: 1903.

Ltd Co.: 1921.

Previous Name: 1903, Shaddongate United; 1904, Carlisle United.

Club Nicknames: 'Cumbrians' or 'The Blues'.

Previous Grounds: 1903, Milholme Bank; 1905, Devonshire Park; 1909, Brunton Park.

First Football League Game: 25 August 1928, Division 3 (N), v Accrington S (a) W 3–2 – Prout; Coulthard, Cook; Harrison, Ross, Pigg; Agar (1), Hutchison, McConnell (1), Ward (1), Watson.

Record League Victory: 8–0 v Hartlepool U, Division 3 (N), 1 September 1928 – Prout; Smiles, Cook; Robinson (1) Ross, Pigg; Agar (1), Hutchison (1), McConnell (4), Ward (1), Watson. 8–0 v Scunthorpe U, Division 3 (N), 25 December 1952 – MacLaren; Hill, Scott; Stokoe, Twentyman, Waters; Harrison (1), Whitehouse (5), Ashman (2), Duffett, Bond.

Record Cup Victory: 6–0 v Shepshed Dynamo, FA Cup 1st rd, 16 November 1996 – Caig; Hopper, Archdeacon (pen), Walling, Robinson, Pounewatchy, Peacock (1), Conway (1) (Jansen), Smart (McAlindon (1)), Hayward, Aspinall (Thorpe), (2 og).

HONOURS

Football League: Division 1 best season: 22nd, 1974–75; Promoted from Division 2 (3rd) 1973–74; Division 3 – Champions 1964–65, 1994–95; Runners-up 1981–82; Promoted from Division 3 1996–97; Division 4 – Runners-up 1963–64.

FA Cup: best season: 6th rd 1975.

Football League Cup: Semi-final 1970.

Auto Windscreens Shield: Winners 1997; Runners-up 1995.

LDV Vans Trophy: Runners-up 2003.

SKY SPORTS FACT FILE

In August 1988 teenage defender Dean Holdsworth appeared on the Carlisle United official team photograph. He had been on loan there the previous season. All set to sign he changed his mind and did not play for them.

Record Defeat: 1–11 v Hull C, Division 3 (N), 14 January 1939.

Most League Points (2 for a win): 62, Division 3 (N), 1950–51.

Most League Points (3 for a win): 91, Division 3, 1994–95.

Most League Goals: 113, Division 4, 1963–64.

Highest League Scorer in Season: Jimmy McConnell, 42, Division 3 (N), 1928–29.

Most League Goals in Total Aggregate: Jimmy McConnell, 126, 1928–32.

Most League Goals in One Match: 5, Hugh Mills v Halifax T, Division 3N, 11 September 1937; 5, Jim Whitehouse v Scunthorpe U, Division 3N, 25 December 1952.

Most Capped Player: Eric Welsh, 4, Northern Ireland.

Most League Appearances: Allan Ross, 466, 1963–79.

Youngest League Player: John Slaven, 16 years 162 days v Scunthorpe U, 16 March 2002.

Record Transfer Fee Received: £1,500,000 from Crystal Palace for Matt Jansen, February 1998.

Record Transfer Fee Paid: £121,000 to Notts Co for David Reeves, December 1993.

Football League Record: 1928 Elected to Division 3 (N); 1958–62 Division 4; 1962–63 Division 3; 1963–64 Division 4; 1964–65 Division 3; 1965–74 Division 2; 1974–75 Division 1; 1975–77 Division 2; 1977–82 Division 3; 1982–86 Division 2; 1986–87 Division 3; 1987–92 Division 4; 1992–95 Division 3; 1995–96 Division 2; 1996–97 Division 3; 1997–98 Division 2; 1998– Division 3.

LATEST SEQUENCES

Longest Sequence of League Wins: 6, 27.8.1994 – 17.9.1994.

Longest Sequence of League Defeats: 8, 8.11.1986 – 3.1.1987.

Longest Sequence of League Draws: 6, 11.2.1978 – 11.3.1978.

Longest Sequence of Unbeaten League Matches: 19, 1.10.1994 – 11.2.1995.

Longest Sequence Without a League Win: 14, 19.1.1935 – 19.4.1935.

Successive Scoring Runs: 26 from 23.8.1947.

Successive Non-scoring Runs: 5 from 24.8.1968.

MANAGERS

Harry Kirkbride 1904–05 *(Secretary-Manager)*
McCumiskey 1905–06 *(Secretary-Manager)*
Jack Houston 1906–08 *(Secretary-Manager)*
Bert Stansfield 1908–10
Jack Houston 1910–12
Davie Graham 1912–13
George Bristow 1913–30
Billy Hampson 1930–33
Bill Clarke 1933–35
Robert Kelly 1935–36
Fred Westgarth 1936–38
David Taylor 1938–40
Howard Harkness 1940–45
Bill Clark 1945–46 *(Secretary-Manager)*
Ivor Broadis 1946–49
Bill Shankly 1949–51
Fred Emery 1951–58
Andy Beattie 1958–60
Ivor Powell 1960–63
Alan Ashman 1963–67
Tim Ward 1967–68
Bob Stokoe 1968–70
Ian MacFarlane 1970–72
Alan Ashman 1972–75
Dick Young 1975–76
Bobby Moncur 1976–80
Martin Harvey 1980
Bob Stokoe 1980–85
Bryan 'Pop' Robson 1985
Bob Stokoe 1985–86
Harry Gregg 1986–87
Cliff Middlemass 1987–91
Aidan McCaffery 1991–92
David McCreery 1992–93
Mick Wadsworth *(Director of Coaching)* 1993–96
Mervyn Day 1996–97
David Wilkes and John Halpin (*Directors of Coaching*), and Michael Knighton 1997–99
Martin Wilkinson 1999–2000
Ian Atkins 2000–01
Roddy Collins 2001–02; August 2002–

TEN YEAR LEAGUE RECORD

		P	W	D	L	F	A	Pts	Pos
1993-94	Div 3	42	18	10	14	57	42	64	7
1994-95	Div 3	42	27	10	5	67	31	91	1
1995-96	Div 2	46	12	13	21	57	72	49	21
1996-97	Div 3	46	24	12	10	67	44	84	3
1997-98	Div 2	46	12	8	26	57	73	44	23
1998-99	Div 3	46	11	16	19	43	53	49	23
1999-2000	Div 3	46	9	12	25	42	75	39	23
2000-01	Div 3	46	11	15	20	42	65	48	22
2001-02	Div 3	46	12	16	18	49	56	52	17
2002-03	Div 3	46	13	10	23	52	78	49	22

DID YOU KNOW?

On the opening day of the 2002–03 season Carlisle United's crowd of 10,684 for the visit of Hartlepool United was the best in Division Three, beaten only twice in Division Two and better than three in Division One.

CARLISLE UNITED 2002–03 LEAGUE RECORD

Match No.	Date	Venue	Opponents	Result		H/T Score	Lg. Pos.	Goalscorers	Attendance
1	Aug 10	H	Hartlepool U	L	1-3	0-1	—	Wake 80	10,684
2	13	A	Southend U	W	1-0	0-0	—	McDonagh 85	3881
3	17	A	Lincoln C	W	1-0	0-0	8	Molloy (pen) 66	3034
4	24	H	Bristol R	D	0-0	0-0	8		6475
5	27	A	Darlington	L	0-2	0-0	—		5163
6	31	H	Exeter C	L	0-2	0-2	18		4806
7	Sept 6	H	Rochdale	L	0-2	0-2	—		4501
8	14	A	Hull C	L	0-4	0-1	22		8461
9	17	A	Scunthorpe U	L	1-3	1-1	—	Foran 24	2342
10	21	H	Boston U	W	4-2	4-1	21	Wake 3 14, 34, 45, Foran (pen) 22	3623
11	28	A	Bournemouth	L	1-3	0-0	22	Murphy 90	5103
12	Oct 5	H	Torquay U	L	1-2	1-1	22	Farrell 30	4014
13	12	H	Shrewsbury T	L	1-2	0-1	22	Redmile (og) 56	3484
14	19	A	Macclesfield T	D	2-2	1-1	24	Osman 2, McGill 80	2383
15	26	H	Swansea C	D	2-2	1-1	24	Magennis 3, Farrell (pen) 46	3940
16	29	A	Cambridge U	L	1-2	1-1	—	Sutton 20	3334
17	Nov 2	H	Oxford U	W	1-0	1-0	23	McGill 33	4039
18	9	A	Kidderminster H	W	2-1	1-0	20	Farrell (pen) 15, McDonagh 84	3009
19	23	H	Bury	L	1-2	0-0	20	Murphy 61	4678
20	30	A	York C	L	1-2	0-1	21	Robinson 73	4335
21	Dec 14	H	Wrexham	L	1-2	1-1	22	Foran 5	4480
22	21	A	Rushden & D	D	1-1	1-1	21	Farrell 12	4355
23	26	H	Darlington	D	2-2	2-1	23	Farrell (pen) 9, Hudson 37	6016
24	28	A	Leyton Orient	L	1-2	1-2	23	Shelley 22	4879
25	Jan 1	A	Hartlepool U	L	1-2	1-0	23	Burt 10	5071
26	4	H	Southend U	W	1-0	1-0	21	McCarthy 32	4016
27	18	A	Exeter C	L	0-1	0-0	23		3333
28	25	H	Leyton Orient	W	3-0	0-0	22	Farrell 2 53, 70, Maddison 56	4269
29	Feb 1	A	Bristol R	W	2-1	1-1	19	Farrell 45, Foran 51	7527
30	4	H	Lincoln C	L	1-4	0-2	—	Farrell 90	3567
31	8	H	Kidderminster H	D	2-2	2-1	19	Foran 7, Rundle 41	3882
32	22	A	Rochdale	W	1-0	0-0	20	Green 62	3247
33	Mar 1	H	Hull C	L	1-5	0-3	20	Farrell 90	4678
34	8	A	Boston U	D	0-0	0-0	22		3131
35	11	H	Scunthorpe U	L	1-2	1-1	—	Foran 14	3124
36	15	A	Swansea C	W	2-1	0-0	21	Farrell (pen) 73, McGill 89	5845
37	18	H	Macclesfield T	W	1-0	1-0	—	Birch 8	3773
38	22	H	Cambridge U	L	0-1	0-1	22		3992
39	Apr 1	A	Oxford U	D	0-0	0-0	—		5044
40	12	A	Bury	D	1-1	0-1	21	Foran 80	3384
41	15	H	York C	D	1-1	0-0	—	Kelly 79	4935
42	19	H	Rushden & D	L	1-2	0-0	22	Green 80	5468
43	21	A	Wrexham	L	1-6	0-3	22	Wake 68	6746
44	26	A	Torquay U	W	3-2	3-0	22	Russell 30, Wake 37, Summerbell 45	3761
45	29	A	Shrewsbury T	W	3-2	2-1	—	Wake 3 36, 37, 50	7236
46	May 3	H	Bournemouth	L	0-2	0-0	22		7402

Final League Position: 22

GOALSCORERS

League (52): Farrell 11 (4 pens), Wake 9, Foran 7 (1 pen), McGill 3, Green 2, McDonagh 2, Murphy 2, Birch 1, Burt 1, Hudson 1, Kelly 1, Maddison 1, Magennis 1, McCarthy 1, Molloy 1 (pen), Osman 1, Robinson 1, Rundle 1, Russell 1, Shelley 1, Summerbell 1, Sutton 1, own goal 1.
Worthington Cup (1): McGill 1.
FA Cup (2): Farrell 1, Foran 1.
LDV Vans Trophy (11): McDonagh 3, Farrell 2, Osman 2, Foran 1, McCarthy 1, Robinson 1, Rundle 1.

Keen P 13	Shelley B 32+3	Maddison L 18+3	Whitehead S 9	Andrews L 11+4	McDonagh W 10+14	Baldacchino R 11+11	Birch M 21+3	Foran R 27+4	Molloy T 7	Jack M 3+4	Hevicon R —+1	Galloway M 4+5	Wake B 10+18	Burns J 4+1	Murphy P 38+2	McGill B 22+12	Summerbell M 39	Kelly D 30+2	Nixon M 3+4	Slaven J —+1	Naisbitt D 1	Freeman D 3+1 / Raven P 11	Taylor M 10	Magennis M 6 / Dillon D —+1	Sutton J 7	Farrell C 31+2	Osman L 10+2	Glennon M 32	Byrne D 9+1	Robinson P 1+4	McCarthy J 19+2	Hudson M 14+1	Gulliver P 1	Burt J 4	Rundle A 19+2	Russell C 7+6	Green S 9+1	*Match No.*
1	2	3^{1}	4	5	6	7	8^{2}	9	10	11^{3}	12	13	14																									1
1	2	3^{2}	4	5	12	7	8	9	10			11	13	6^{1}																								2
1	2■	3	4	5	12	7^{1}		9■	10■			11^{3}	13	14	6^{2}	8																						3
1	12	3^{1}	4	5	13		2	9^{3}	10				14	11^{2}	6	8	7																					4
1			4	5^{3}	6		2	9	10			12	13	11^{2}	3	8	7^{1}	14																				5
1			4^{2}	5	6		2			12		11^{1}	9		3	13	7	8	10																			6
1			4	12			2			11^{2}		13	9^{1}	6	3	8	7	5	10																			7
1	3		4				2	9^{1}	10	13		7^{2}	12			8	6	5	11^{3}	14																		8
	3		6	4			2	9	10	12						8^{2}	11	5	13		1	7^{1}																9
1	2^{1}			4	6^{2}		12	9				13	10^{3}		3	8	7	5	14			11																10
1	4				6		2	9^{3}				12	10^{2}		13	8	7^{1}	5	14			11	3															11
1	2			12	13										3	7^{3}	8	5				14	6^{1}	4^{2}	9	10	11											12
1	2				12	7^{1}							13		3	14	8	5					6	4^{3}	9	10^{2}	11											13
	2				12	7^{2}									6	13	8	5					3	4	9	10^{1}	11	1										14
	2				12	13	8^{1}						14		6	7							5	4^{2}	9^{3}	10	11	1	3									15
	2				12	13									6	7	8						5	4^{2}	9^{1}	10	11	1	3									16
	2				12			13							6	7	8■	14					5^{3}	4^{1}	9^{2}	10	11	1	3									17
	2	12			13■	7^{2}		14							6	8	4						5		9^{3}	10	11	1	3^{1}									18
	2	3^{1}				7	12						13		6	8	4	5								10^{2}	11	1		9								19
	2	3^{1}						9							6	8	4						5			10	11	1		12	7							20
	2				7^{2}		12	9■								13	4	5					6			10^{3}	11	1	3^{1}	14		8						21
	2	3			12	13		9							6	11^{3}	4	5								10	14	1			7^{1}	8^{2}						22
	2					7^{1}		9^{2}					12		6	11^{3}	4	5								10	13	1	3		14	8						23
	2	3				12							9		6	11^{1}	4	5^{2}								10		1		13	7	8						24
	2	3^{1}				13									6	11^{3}	4									10		1	12^{2}		7	8	5	9	14			25
	2														6		4	5								10		1	3	12	7	8		9^{1}	11			26
	2				4	12									6	7		5								10^{2}		1	3^{1}			8		9	11	13		27
	2	3			13			7^{3}							6	12	4	5								10		1				8		9^{1}	11^{2}	14		28
	2	3				12		9^{1}							6	13	4	5								10		1			7■	8			11^{2}			29
	2	3^{1}				12		9							6	13	4	5								10		1			7^{2}	8^{3}			11	14		30
	2			12	7			9^{3}							6	13	4	5^{1}								10		1	3			8^{2}			11	14		31
							2	9					13		3	12		5				6				10^{2}		1				8			11^{1}	7	4	32
					12		2^{1}	9							3	7^{2}	4^{3}	5				6				10		1			13	8			11	14		33
							2	12					13		3		4	5				6				10^{2}		1			7	8^{1}			11		9	34
							2^{2}	9					12		3		4	5				6				10^{1}		1			7	13			11		8	35
		12					2	9					14		3^{1}	13	4	5				6				10		1			7^{3}				11^{2}		8	36
	5	3					2	9					13			12	4					6				10^{1}		1			7				11^{3}	14	8^{2}	37
		3					2■	12					13		6		4					5				10		1			7				11^{2}	9	8^{1}	38
							2	9							3		4	5				6				10		1			7				11		8	39
	2				12			9					14		3	13	4	5				6				10^{3}		1			7^{2}				11		8^{1}	40
	2	13			7	12							10^{3}		3		4	5				6^{2}				14		1							11	9	8^{1}	41
		3			8^{3}	12	2						13		6		4■	5								10^{2}		1			7^{1}				11	9	14	42
	2	3		5		12		9^{1}		13			10		6^{2}		4											1			7				11	8		43
	12	3		5		11	2^{1}	9					10^{2}		6		4									13		1			7^{3}				14	8		44
	12	3		13		11	2^{1}	9					10		6		4					5^{2}						1			7					8		45
1	2^{2}			6		11^{3}				4			9		12	8		5	13					14		10					7				3^{1}			46

Worthington Cup

First Round	Rotherham U	(a)	1-3

FA Cup

First Round	Lincoln C	(h)	2-1
Second Round	Scunthorpe U	(a)	0-0

LDV Vans Trophy

First Round	Oldham Ath	(a)	4-3
Second Round	Stockport Co	(h)	1-0
Quarter-final	Wrexham	(h)	2-0
Semi-final	Bury	(h)	3-2
Northern Final	Shrewsbury T	(h)	1-0
		(a)	0-0
Final (at Millennium Stadium)	Bristol C		0-2

CHARLTON ATHLETIC FA Premiership

FOUNDATION

The club was formed on 9 June 1905, by a group of 14- and 15-year-old youths living in streets by the Thames in the area which now borders the Thames Barrier. The club's progress through local leagues was so rapid that after the First World War they joined the Kent League where they spent a season before turning professional and joining the Southern League in 1920. A year later they were elected to the Football League's Division 3 (South).

The Valley, Floyd Road, Charlton, London SE7 8BL.

Telephone: (020) 8333 4000. ***Fax:*** (020) 8333 4001.
Website: www.cafc.co.uk ***Email:*** info@cafc.co.uk
Box Office: (020) 8333 4010. ***ClubCall:*** 09068 121 146.

Ground Capacity: 26,875.

Record Attendance: 75,031 v Aston Villa, FA Cup 5th rd, 12 February 1938 (at The Valley).

Record Receipts: £331,711 v Tottenham H, FA Cup 4th rd, 7 February 2001.

Pitch Measurements: 111yd × 73yd.

Chairman: M. A. Simons.
Deputy Chairman: R. A. Murray.
Group Chief Executive: P. D. Varney.
Directors: R. N. Alwen, G. P. Bone, N. E. Capelin, R. D. Collins, D. J. Hughes, M. C. Stevens, D. C. Sumners, D. G. Ufton, R. C. Whitehand, G. B. C. Franklin, D. White, S. M. Townsend.,

HONOURS

Football League: Division 1 – Champions 1999–2000; Runners-up 1936–37; Promoted from Division 1, 1997–98 (play-offs); Division 2 – Runners-up 1935–36, 1985–86; Division 3 (S) – Champions 1928–29, 1934–35; Promoted from Division 3 (3rd) 1974–75, 1980–81.

FA Cup: Winners 1947; Runners-up 1946.

Football League Cup: best season: 4th rd, 1963, 1966, 1979.

Full Members' Cup: Runners-up 1987.

Manager: Alan Curbishley. ***Assistant Manager:*** Keith Peacock. ***First Team Coach:*** Mervyn Day.
Academy Director: Mick Browne.

Football Secretary: Chris Parkes.

Safety Officer: John Little.

Media and PR: Rick Everitt.

Colours: Red shirts, white shorts, red stockings.

Change Colours: Yellow shirts, yellow shorts, yellow stockings.

Year Formed: 1905.

Turned Professional: 1920. ***Ltd Co.:*** 1919.

Club Nickname: 'Addicks'.

Previous Grounds: 1906, Siemen's Meadow; 1907, Woolwich Common; 1909, Pound Park; 1913, Horn Lane; 1920, The Valley; 1923, Catford (The Mount); 1924, The Valley; 1985, Selhurst Park; 1991, Upton Park; 1992, The Valley.

First Football League Game: 27 August 1921, Division 3 (S), v Exeter C (h) W 1–0 – Hughes; Mitchell, Goodman; Dowling (1), Hampson, Dunn; Castle, Bailey, Halse, Green, Wilson.

SKY SPORTS FACT FILE

On 7 December 2002 Charlton Athletic celebrated the tenth anniversary of their return to The Valley with a 2-0 win over Liverpool. At the time the Merseyside club were fourth and Charlton lying 11th in the table.

Record League Victory: 8–1 v Middlesbrough, Division 1, 12 September 1953 – Bartram; Campbell, Ellis; Fenton, Ufton, Hammond; Hurst (2), O'Linn (2), Leary (1), Firmani (3), Kiernan.

Record Cup Victory: 7–0 v Burton A, FA Cup 3rd rd, 7 January 1956 – Bartram; Campbell, Townsend; Hewie, Ufton, Hammond; Hurst (1), Gauld (1), Leary (3), White, Kiernan (2).

Record Defeat: 1–11 v Aston Villa, Division 2, 14 November 1959.

Most League Points (2 for a win): 61, Division 3 (S), 1934–35.

Most League Points (3 for a win): 91, Division 1, 1999–2000.

Most League Goals: 107, Division 2, 1957–58.

Highest League Scorer in Season: Ralph Allen, 32, Division 3 (S), 1934–35.

Most League Goals in Total Aggregate: Stuart Leary, 153, 1953–62.

Most League Goals in One Match: 5, Wilson Lennox v Exeter C, Division 3S, 2 February 1929; 5, Eddie Firmani v Aston Villa, Division 1, 5 February 1955; 5, John Summers v Huddersfield T, Division 2, 21 December 1957; 5, John Summers v Portsmouth, Division 2, 1 October 1960.

Most Capped Player: Mark Kinsella, 33 (41), Republic of Ireland.

Most League Appearances: Sam Bartram, 583, 1934–56.

Youngest League Player: Paul Konchesky, 16 years 93 days v Oxford U, 16 August 1997.

Record Transfer Fee Received: £4,370,000 from Leeds U for Danny Mills, June 1999.

Record Transfer Fee Paid: £4,750,000 to Wimbledon for Jason Euell, July 2001.

Football League Record: 1921 Elected to Division 3 (S); 1929–33 Division 2; 1933–35 Division 3 (S); 1935–36 Division 2; 1936–57 Division 1; 1957–72 Division 2; 1972–75 Division 3; 1975–80 Division 2; 1980–81 Division 3; 1981–86 Division 2; 1986–90 Division 1; 1990–92 Division 2; 1992–98 Division 1; 1998–99 FA Premier League; 1999–2000 Division 1; 2000– FA Premier League.

MANAGERS

Bill Rayner 1920–25
Alex McFarlane 1925–27
Albert Lindon 1928
Alex McFarlane 1928–32
Jimmy Seed 1933–56
Jimmy Trotter 1956–61
Frank Hill 1961–65
Bob Stokoe 1965–67
Eddie Firmani 1967–70
Theo Foley 1970–74
Andy Nelson 1974–79
Mike Bailey 1979–81
Alan Mullery 1981–82
Ken Craggs 1982
Lennie Lawrence 1982–91
Steve Gritt/Alan Curbishley 1991–95
Alan Curbishley June 1995–

LATEST SEQUENCES

Longest Sequence of League Wins: 12, 26.12.1999 – 7.3.2000.

Longest Sequence of League Defeats: 10, 11.4.1990 – 15.9.1990.

Longest Sequence of League Draws: 6, 13.12.1992 – 16.1.1993.

Longest Sequence of Unbeaten League Matches: 15, 4.10.1980 – 20.12.1980.

Longest Sequence Without a League Win: 16, 26.2.1955 – 22.8.1955.

Successive Scoring Runs: 25 from 26.12.1935.

Successive Non-scoring Runs: 5 from 6.9.1922.

TEN YEAR LEAGUE RECORD

		P	W	D	L	F	A	Pts	Pos
1993-94	Div 1	46	19	8	19	61	58	65	11
1994-95	Div 1	46	16	11	19	58	66	59	15
1995-96	Div 1	46	17	20	9	57	45	71	6
1996-97	Div 1	46	16	11	19	52	66	59	15
1997-98	Div 1	46	26	10	10	80	49	88	4
1998-99	PR Lge	38	8	12	18	41	56	36	18
1999-2000	Div 1	46	27	10	9	79	45	91	1
2000-01	PR Lge	38	14	10	14	50	57	52	9
2001-02	PR Lge	38	10	14	14	38	49	44	14
2002-03	PR Lge	38	14	7	17	45	56	49	12

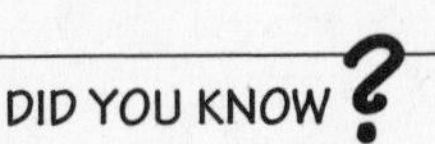

Legendary Charlton Athletic goalkeeper Sam Bartram was an ever-present in five seasons 1936–37, 1938–39, 1947–48, 1949–50 and 1954–55 among his 582 League appearances. He kept a clean sheet in his last game, 2-0 v Arsenal, 15 March 1956.

CHARLTON ATHLETIC 2002–03 LEAGUE RECORD

Match No.	Date	Venue	Opponents	Result		H/T Score	Lg. Pos.	Goalscorers	Attendance
1	Aug 17	H	Chelsea	L	2-3	2-1	—	Konchesky [7], Rufus [33]	25,615
2	24	A	Bolton W	W	2-1	1-1	11	Bart-Williams (pen) [26], Euell [71]	21,753
3	27	H	Tottenham H	L	0-1	0-1	—		26,392
4	31	A	West Ham U	W	2-0	2-0	6	Jensen [4], Fortune [44]	32,424
5	Sept 11	A	Aston Villa	L	0-2	0-0	—		26,483
6	14	H	Arsenal	L	0-3	0-1	15		26,080
7	21	A	Southampton	D	0-0	0-0	16		25,714
8	28	H	Manchester U	L	1-3	1-0	19	Jensen [43]	26,608
9	Oct 6	A	Fulham	L	0-1	0-1	19		14,775
10	20	H	Middlesbrough	W	1-0	1-0	15	Euell [5]	26,242
11	26	A	Newcastle U	L	1-2	1-1	17	Bartlett [30]	51,607
12	Nov 3	H	Sunderland	D	1-1	0-1	16	Rowett [77]	26,255
13	9	A	Everton	L	0-1	0-1	17		37,621
14	16	A	Manchester C	W	1-0	0-0	16	Bartlett [79]	33,455
15	24	H	Blackburn R	W	3-1	0-0	15	Konchesky [59], Rufus [74], Euell [90]	26,137
16	Dec 1	A	Leeds U	W	2-1	0-1	12	Lisbie [80], Parker [90]	35,547
17	7	H	Liverpool	W	2-0	1-0	11	Euell [36], Konchesky [78]	26,679
18	14	H	Manchester C	D	2-2	0-0	11	Euell (pen) [51], Jensen [63]	26,424
19	21	A	Birmingham C	D	1-1	1-0	11	Jensen [37]	28,837
20	26	A	Tottenham H	D	2-2	1-0	12	Euell 2 [14, 49]	36,043
21	28	H	WBA	W	1-0	1-0	12	Lisbie [6]	26,156
22	Jan 11	A	Chelsea	L	1-4	1-3	14	Euell (pen) [42]	37,284
23	18	H	Bolton W	D	1-1	0-0	13	Fish [47]	26,029
24	22	H	West Ham U	W	4-2	2-1	—	Jensen [42], Parker 2 [45, 52], Kishishev [90]	26,327
25	29	A	WBA	W	1-0	0-0	—	Bartlett [60]	25,608
26	Feb 1	A	Sunderland	W	3-1	3-0	8	Wright (og) [24], Proctor (2 og) [29, 32]	36,042
27	8	H	Everton	W	2-1	1-0	8	Kishishev [19], Lisbie [83]	26,607
28	22	H	Aston Villa	W	3-0	0-0	6	Euell [51], Johansson 2 [87, 90]	26,229
29	Mar 2	A	Arsenal	L	0-2	0-2	6		38,015
30	15	H	Newcastle U	L	0-2	0-1	8		26,704
31	22	A	Middlesbrough	D	1-1	1-0	7	Johansson [26]	29,080
32	Apr 5	H	Leeds U	L	1-6	1-3	9	Euell (pen) [45]	26,317
33	12	A	Blackburn R	L	0-1	0-1	10		27,506
34	19	H	Birmingham C	L	0-2	0-1	11		25,699
35	21	A	Liverpool	L	1-2	0-0	12	Bartlett [47]	42,010
36	26	H	Southampton	W	2-1	1-0	9	Parker [32], Lisbie [50]	25,878
37	May 3	A	Manchester U	L	1-4	1-3	12	Jensen [13]	67,721
38	11	H	Fulham	L	0-1	0-1	12		26,089

Final League Position: 12

GOALSCORERS

League (45): Euell 10 (3 pens), Jensen 6, Bartlett 4, Lisbie 4, Parker 4, Johansson 3, Konchesky 3, Kishishev 2, Rufus 2, Bart-Williams 1 (pen), Fish 1, Fortune 1, Rowett 1, own goals 3.
Worthington Cup (0).
FA Cup (3): Johansson 2, Euell 1 (pen).

Kiely D 38	Young L 29 + 3	Powell C 35 + 2	Bart-Williams C 7 + 6	Rufus R 29 + 1	Rowett G 12	Stuart G 3 + 1	Jensen C 32 + 3	Euell J 35 + 1	Johansson J 10 + 21	Konchesky P 17 + 13	Kishishev R 27 + 7	Svensson M 4 + 11	Lisbie K 24 + 8	Brown S — + 3	Fortune J 22 + 4	Robinson J 10 + 3	Bartlett S 25 + 6	Blomqvist J — + 3	Mustoe R 6	Fish M 23	Parker S 28	El Khalej T 2 + 1	Campbell-Ryce J — + 1	Sankofa O — + 1	Roberts B — + 1	Match No.
1	2	3	4^1	5	6	7	8	9^2	10^3	11■	12	13	14													1
1	2	3	4	5	6^3	7^1	8	9	10^2	11		13	12	14												2
1	2	3	4	5			8	9	10^2	11	7^3	13		12	6^1	14										3
1	2	3	4	5			8	9	12		7	10^2			6	11^1	13									4
1	2	3	4^3	5			8	9	12		7^2	10^1		13	6	11	14									5
1	2	3	4^2	5			8	9^1	10^3		13	12	7		6	11		14								6
1	2	3	4	5			8	9	10^2	7			12		6	11^1	13									7
1	2^1	3		5			8	9	12	11	13				6	7	10		4^2							8
1	2^1	3		5			8	9	12	7^2			13			11	10		4	6						9
1	12	3		5	6		8	9			13					2	10		7^1	4	11^2					10
1	3^2			5	6		8	9	12		13					2^3	10	14	7	4	11^1					11
1		3		5	6		8	9	12		13		14			2^1	10^3		7	4	11^2					12
1		3		5			8	9^3	12	13	2^1		10		6		14		7^2	4	11					13
1	2	3		5	6			9	10	12	7		13				8^2			4	11^1					14
1	2	3	12	5				9		13	7		8^1		6^2		10			4	11					15
1	5	3			6		12	9		7	2^1	13	8		14		10^2			4^3	11					16
1	12	3		5	6		13	9		7	2^1	14	8				10^3			4	11^2					17
1	2	3^2		5	6		12	8		13	7^1		9				10			4	11					18
1	2	3	12		6		4		13	11	7^1		9				10^2			5	8					19
1	2	3		5	6		8^3	7		12	14		9		13		10^2			4^1	11					20
1	2	3	12	5	6		8	7	13				9		14		10^2			4^3	11^1					21
1	2	3^1		5			4	8	12	11	7^2		9^3		14		13			6	10					22
1	2^2	3		5			4^1	8	12	13	7	14	9				10^3			6	11					23
1		3		5			7^2	8	12	14	2	13	9^3		4		10^1			6	11					24
1		3		5			7^2	8	12	13	2		9^1		4		10			6	11					25
1		3	14	5			7^2	8	12	13	2		9^1		4		10			6	11^3					26
1		3		5			7^2	8	12	13	2		9		4		10^1			6	11					27
1	2	3	14				4	8	12		7	13	9^1		6		10^2				11^3	5				28
1	2	3^2					4	8	12	13	7	14	9		5		10^1			6	11^3					29
1	2^2	3		12			4	8	10	13	7		14		5		9^3			6^1	11					30
1	13	12		5		7^1	11^2	8	10^3	3	4		9		6		14			2						31
1	4	12		5			7	8	10	3^3	2^1	13	9^2							6	11	14				32
1	2	3		5					12	11	4^2	10	9^3		6	7^1		13			8		14			33
1	2	3					7	8	10	12	4^2	9^3	14		6	13					11	5^1				34
1	2	3		5			4	12	13	11	7		9^2		6	14	10^1				8^3					35
1	5	3					4	8		11	2		9		6		10				7					36
1	5	3	12				4	8^1	13	7	2^3		9^2		6		10				11			14		37
1■	5	3^1				12	4^2	8	13	7	2		9		6		10^G				11				15	38

Worthington Cup
Second Round Oxford U (h) 0-0

FA Cup
Third Round Exeter C (h) 3-1
Fourth Round Fulham (a) 0-3

CHELSEA — FA Premiership

FOUNDATION

Chelsea may never have existed but for the fact that Fulham rejected an offer to rent the Stamford Bridge ground from Mr H. A. Mears who had owned it since 1904. Fortunately he was determined to develop it as a football stadium rather than sell it to the Great Western Railway and got together with Frederick Parker, who persuaded Mears of the financial advantages of developing a major sporting venue. Chelsea FC was formed in 1905, and when admission to the Southern League was denied, they immediately gained admission to the Second Division of the Football League.

Stamford Bridge, London SW6 1HS.

Telephone: (020) 7385 5545. ***Fax:*** (020) 7381 4831.
Blues News 24 Hour Ticket News: 0906 600 7760.
Ticket Credit Card Service: (020) 7386 7799.

Ground Capacity: 42,449.

Record Attendance: 82,905 v Arsenal, Division 1, 12 October 1935.

Record Receipts: £1,824,803 v Manchester U, FA Premier League, 20 April 2002.

Pitch Measurements: 113yd × 74yd.

Chairman: K. W. Bates.

Directors: T. Birch (Chief Executive), Ms Y. S. Todd. M. Woodward (Vice-chairman).

Head Coach: Claudio Ranieri.
Assistant Manager: Gwyn Williams.
First Team Coach: Angelo Antenucci.
Physio: Michael Banks.
Reserve Team Manager: Mick McGiven.

Company Secretary: Alan Shaw.

Club Secretary: David Barnard.

Corporate Sales Manager: Carole Phair.

Safety Officer: Jill Dawson.

Colours: Royal blue shirts and shorts with white trim, white stockings with royal blue trim.

Change Colours: White shirts with royal blue and navy trim, white shorts with royal blue and navy trim, royal blue stockings with white trim.

Year Formed: 1905. ***Turned Professional:*** 1905. ***Ltd Co.:*** 1905. ***Club Nickname:*** 'The Blues'.

First Football League Game: 2 September 1905, Division 2, v Stockport Co (a) L 0–1 – Foulke; Mackie, McEwan; Key, Harris, Miller; Moran, J. T. Robertson, Copeland, Windridge, Kirwan.

HONOURS

Football League: Division 1 – Champions 1954–55; Division 2 – Champions 1983–84, 1988–89; Runners-up 1906–07, 1911–12, 1929–30, 1962–63, 1976–77.

FA Cup: Winners 1970, 1997, 2000; Runners-up 1915, 1967, 1994, 2002.

Football League Cup: Winners 1965, 1998; Runners-up 1972.

Full Members' Cup: Winners 1986.

Zenith Data Systems Cup: Winners 1990.

European Competitions: *Champions League:* 1999–2000. *European Fairs Cup:* 1958–60, 1965–66, 1968–69. *European Cup-Winners' Cup:* 1970–71 (winners), 1971–72, 1994–95, 1997–98 (winners), 1998–99 (semi-finals). *UEFA Cup:* 2000–01, 2001–02, 2002–03. *Super Cup:* 1998–99 (winners).

SKY SPORTS FACT FILE

In the 1998 World Cup finals, Chelsea had ten players appearing for various countries. In 2002 there were five: Marcel Desailly, Celestino Babayaro, Jesper Gronkjaer, Emmanuel Petit and Mario Stanic.

Record League Victory: 9–2 v Glossop N E, Division 2, 1 September 1906 – Byrne; Walton, Miller; Key (1), McRoberts, Henderson; Moran, McDermott (1), Hilsdon (5), Copeland (1), Kirwan (1).

Record Cup Victory: 13–0 v Jeunesse Hautcharage, ECWC, 1st rd 2nd leg, 29 September 1971 – Bonetti; Boyle, Harris (1), Hollins (1p), Webb (1), Hinton, Cooke, Baldwin (3), Osgood (5), Hudson (1), Houseman (1).

Record Defeat: 1–8 v Wolverhampton W, Division 1, 26 September 1953.

Most League Points (2 for a win): 57, Division 2, 1906–07.

Most League Points (3 for a win): 99, Division 2, 1988–89.

Most League Goals: 98, Division 1, 1960–61.

Highest League Scorer in Season: Jimmy Greaves, 41, 1960–61.

Most League Goals in Total Aggregate: Bobby Tambling, 164, 1958–70.

Most League Goals in One Match: 5, George Hilsdon v Glossop, Division 2, 1 September 1906; 5, Jimmy Greaves v Wolverhampton W, Division 1, 30 August 1958; 5, Jimmy Greaves v Preston NE, Division 1, 19 December 1959; 5, Jimmy Greaves v WBA, Division 1, 3 December 1960; 5, Bobby Tambling v Aston Villa, Division 1, 17 September 1966; 5, Gordon Durie v Walsall, Division 2, 4 February 1989.

MANAGERS

John Tait Robertson 1905–07
David Calderhead 1907–33
Leslie Knighton 1933–39
Billy Birrell 1939–52
Ted Drake 1952–61
Tommy Docherty 1962–67
Dave Sexton 1967–74
Ron Suart 1974–75
Eddie McCreadie 1975–77
Ken Shellito 1977–78
Danny Blanchflower 1978–79
Geoff Hurst 1979–81
John Neal 1981–85 *(Director to 1986)*
John Hollins 1985–88
Bobby Campbell 1988–91
Ian Porterfield 1991–93
David Webb 1993
Glenn Hoddle 1993–96
Ruud Gullit 1996–98
Gianluca Vialli 1998–2000
Claudio Ranieri September 2000–

Most Capped Player: Marcel Desailly, 59 (108), France.

Most League Appearances: Ron Harris, 655, 1962–80.

Youngest League Player: Ian Hamilton, 16 years 138 days v Tottenham H, 18 March 1967.

Record Transfer Fee Received: £12,000,000 from Rangers for Tor Andre Flo, November 2000.

Record Transfer Fee Paid: £15,000,000 to Atletico Madrid for Jimmy Floyd Hasselbaink, June 2000.

Football League Record: 1905 Elected to Division 2; 1907–10 Division 1; 1910–12 Division 2; 1912–24 Division 1; 1924–30 Division 2; 1930–62 Division 1; 1962–63 Division 2; 1963–75 Division 1; 1975–77 Division 2; 1977–79 Division 1; 1979–84 Division 2; 1984–88 Division 1; 1988–89 Division 2; 1989–92 Division 1; 1992– FA Premier League.

LATEST SEQUENCES

Longest Sequence of League Wins: 8, 15.3.1989 – 8.4.1989.

Longest Sequence of League Defeats: 7, 1.11.1952 – 20.12.1952.

Longest Sequence of League Draws: 6, 20.8.1969 – 13.9.1969.

Longest Sequence of Unbeaten League Matches: 27, 29.10.1988 – 8.4.1989.

Longest Sequence Without a League Win: 21, 3.11.1987 – 2.4.1988.

Successive Scoring Runs: 27 from 29.10.1988.

Successive Non-scoring Runs: 9 from 14.3.1981.

TEN YEAR LEAGUE RECORD

		P	*W*	*D*	*L*	*F*	*A*	*Pts*	*Pos*
1993-94	PR Lge	42	13	12	17	49	53	51	14
1994-95	PR Lge	42	13	15	14	50	55	54	11
1995-96	PR Lge	38	12	14	12	46	44	50	11
1996-97	PR Lge	38	16	11	11	58	55	59	6
1997-98	PR Lge	38	20	3	15	71	43	63	4
1998-99	PR Lge	38	20	15	3	57	30	75	3
1999-2000	PR Lge	38	18	11	9	53	34	65	5
2000-01	PR Lge	38	17	10	11	68	45	61	6
2001-02	PR Lge	38	17	13	8	66	38	64	6
2002-03	PR Lge	38	19	10	9	68	38	67	4

DID YOU KNOW?

The first match that Chelsea began with 11 internationals was against Coventry City on 15 August 1998. The team comprised three Italians, two Frenchmen, two English caps and one from each of Holland, Nigeria, Spain and Uruguay.

CHELSEA 2002–03 LEAGUE RECORD

Match No.	Date	Venue	Opponents	Result		H/T Score	Lg. Pos.	Goalscorers	Attendance
1	Aug 17	A	Charlton Ath	W	3-2	1-2	—	Zola [43], Cole [84], Lampard [89]	25,615
2	23	H	Manchester U	D	2-2	2-1	—	Gallas [3], Zenden [45]	41,549
3	28	A	Southampton	D	1-1	0-0	—	Lampard [80]	31,208
4	Sept 1	H	Arsenal	D	1-1	1-0	5	Zola [34]	40,107
5	11	A	Blackburn R	W	3-2	1-2	—	Gronkjaer [38], Zola 2 [52, 80]	22,999
6	14	H	Newcastle U	W	3-0	2-0	4	Gudjohnsen 2 [14, 58], Zola [26]	39,756
7	23	A	Fulham	D	0-0	0-0	—		16,503
8	28	H	West Ham U	L	2-3	1-1	5	Hasselbaink (pen) [21], Zola [74]	38,937
9	Oct 6	A	Liverpool	L	0-1	0-0	7		43,856
10	19	A	Manchester C	W	3-0	0-0	6	Zola 2 [69, 84], Hasselbaink [85]	34,953
11	26	H	WBA	W	2-0	1-0	3	Hasselbaink [30], Le Saux [55]	40,893
12	Nov 3	A	Tottenham H	D	0-0	0-0	4		36,047
13	9	H	Birmingham C	W	3-0	3-0	3	Gudjohnsen 2 [3, 31], Zola [42]	35,227
14	16	H	Middlesbrough	W	1-0	0-0	3	Babayaro [47]	39,064
15	23	A	Bolton W	D	1-1	0-0	4	Hasselbaink [90]	25,076
16	30	H	Sunderland	W	3-0	0-0	3	Gallas [58], Desailly [84], Hasselbaink [89]	38,949
17	Dec 7	A	Everton	W	3-1	2-1	2	Stanic [5], Hasselbaink [28], Gronkjaer [90]	39,396
18	14	A	Middlesbrough	D	1-1	1-1	3	Terry [42]	29,160
19	21	H	Aston Villa	W	2-0	1-0	2	Gudjohnsen [42], Lampard [57]	38,288
20	26	H	Southampton	D	0-0	0-0	2		39,442
21	28	A	Leeds U	L	0-2	0-2	2		40,143
22	Jan 1	A	Arsenal	L	2-3	0-1	3	Stanic [85], Petit [86]	38,096
23	11	H	Charlton Ath	W	4-1	3-1	3	Hasselbaink (pen) [3], Gallas [11], Gudjohnsen [34], Le Saux [54]	37,284
24	18	A	Manchester U	L	1-2	1-1	4	Gudjohnsen [30]	67,606
25	28	H	Leeds U	W	3-2	0-1	—	Gudjohnsen [57], Lampard [80], Matteo (og) [83]	39,741
26	Feb 1	H	Tottenham H	D	1-1	1-1	4	Zola [40]	41,436
27	8	A	Birmingham C	W	3-1	1-0	4	Zola [44], Gudjohnsen [49], Hasselbaink (pen) [69]	29,475
28	22	H	Blackburn R	L	1-2	0-0	4	Hasselbaink [90]	40,873
29	Mar 1	A	Newcastle U	L	1-2	1-1	5	Lampard [37]	52,157
30	16	A	WBA	W	2-0	1-0	4	Stanic [38], Zola [56]	26,749
31	22	H	Manchester C	W	5-0	2-0	4	Hasselbaink [37], Terry [43], Stanic [58], Lampard [69], Gallas [79]	41,105
32	Apr 5	A	Sunderland	W	2-1	0-1	4	Zola [52], Cole [85]	40,011
33	12	H	Bolton W	W	1-0	0-0	4	Cole [58]	39,891
34	19	A	Aston Villa	L	1-2	0-1	4	Terry [89]	39,358
35	21	H	Everton	W	4-1	1-0	3	Gudjohnsen [25], Hasselbaink [48], Gronkjaer [62], Zola [90]	40,921
36	26	H	Fulham	D	1-1	1-0	4	Goma (og) [39]	40,792
37	May 3	A	West Ham U	L	0-1	0-0	4		35,042
38	11	H	Liverpool	W	2-1	2-1	4	Desailly [14], Gronkjaer [27]	41,925

Final League Position: 4

GOALSCORERS

League (68): Zola 14, Hasselbaink 11 (3 pens), Gudjohnsen 10, Lampard 6, Gallas 4, Gronkjaer 4, Stanic 4, Cole 3, Terry 3, Desailly 2, Le Saux 2, Babayaro 1, Petit 1, Zenden 1, own goals 2.
Worthington Cup (6): Cole 2, Hasselbaink 2, Petit 1, Stanic 1.
FA Cup (10): Terry 2, Zola 2, Cole 1, Gronkjaer 1, Hasselbaink 1, Lampard 1, Morris 1, Stanic 1.
UEFA Cup (4): De Lucas 1, Hasselbaink 1, Lampard 1, Terry 1.

Cudicini C 36	Ferrer A 3	Babayaro C 16 + 3	Petit E 23 + 1	Gallas W 36 + 2	Desailly M 30 + 1	De Lucas E 17 + 8	Lampard F 37 + 1	Hasselbaink J 27 + 9	Zola G 30 + 8	Zenden B 11 + 10	Gudjohnsen E 20 + 15	Gronkjaer J 20 + 10	Cole C 2 + 11	Melchiot M 31 + 3	Stanic M 13 + 5	Le Saux G 27 + 1	Morris J 19 + 6	Keenan J — + 1	Huth R 2	Oliveira F — + 3	Terry J 16 + 4	De Goey E 2	*Match No.*
1	2	3	4^1	5	6	7	8	9^2	10^3	11	12	13	14										1
1		3	4^1	5	6	7	8	9^2	10^3	11	14	12	13	2									2
1		3		5	6	8	4	9^1	10	11^2	12	7		2	13								3
1	2			5	6	8	4	12	10^1	11^2	9	7		14	13	3^3							4
1		3		5	6	12	8	9	10	13	14	7^3		2	11^2		4^1						5
1				5	6	7	8	12	10^2	11^3	9^1	13		2	3		4	14					6
1				5		7	8	9	10^1	11^2	12	13		2	3		4		6				7
1				5			8	9	12	11^1	10	7		2	3		4		6				8
1			4	5	6		8	9^1	10		12	11		2	7^2	3	13						9
1			4	5	6	7	8	9	10^1					2		3	11			12			10
1			4^1	5	6	11	8	9	10			7^2		2		3	12				13		11
1		3	4	5	6	11^2	8	9^1	10		12			2			7			13			12
1		3	4	5	6^3		8		10		9^2	12	13	2		11^1	7				14		13
1		3	4	5	6		8	12	10		9^1	13		2		11^3	7^2				14		14
1		3^1	4	5	6		8	12	10		9	7^1		2		11^2	13						15
1			12	5	6	7^2	8	9	10		13	11^3		2	14	3	4^1						16
1			4	5	6	7^3	8	9^1	10		12	13		2	11^2	3					14		17
1			4	5		12	8	9^3	10	13	14	7^1		2	11^2	3					6		18
1		12		5			8	9^2	13	11^1	10	14		2	7^3	3	4				6		19
		3	4	12	6	7^3	13	9	10	11^2	14			2^1			8				5	1	20
	2^1			5	6	13	8	12	10		9	7^2			11	3	4					1	21
1		3	4	5	6	7^3	8	9	10^2		12	14		2	13	11^1							22
1		3	4	2	6		8	9	12	13	10	7^2				11^1	14				5^3		23
1		3	4	5	6	12	8	9^2	13	14	10^3	7^1		2		11							24
1		3^2		2	6		8		10^1	12	9	7	13			11	4				5		25
1			4	2	6		8	12	10	11^2	9	7^3	14	13		3^1					5		26
1			4	3	6	12	8^3	13	10^2		9	7^1		2		11	14				5		27
1		12		5			8	9	13	14	10	7^2		2	11^3	3^1	4				6		28
1		3^3		5			8	9	12	13	10	7^1	14	2	11^2		4				6		29
1				5	12	13	8	9	11		10^3	14		4	2^2	3^1	7				6		30
1				5		12	8	9^3	11^1	13	10		14	4	2	3^2	7				6		31
1				3	6	7^2	8	9^3	10^1	12			13	2		11	4			14	5		32
1			4	13	6	12	8	9	11^3	7^1	14		10^2	2		3					5		33
1		12	4	3	6	7	8	13	10^3		14		9	2^2		11^1					5		34
1			4	3	6	7	8	9^1	12		10^2	11^3	13	2		14					5		35
1			4	2^2	6	7^3	8	9	10		12	11^1		13		3	14				5		36
1		3	4	5	6		8	12	10^3	13	9^1		14	2		11	7^2						37
1		3	4	5	6		8	9^2	12		10^1	7^3	13	2	14	11							38

Worthington Cup

Third Round	Gillingham	(h)	2-1
Fourth Round	Everton	(h)	4-1
Fifth Round	Manchester U	(a)	0-1

UEFA Cup

First Round	Viking	(h)	2-1
		(a)	2-4

FA Cup

Third Round	Middlesbrough	(h)	1-0
Fourth Round	Shrewsbury T	(a)	4-0
Fifth Round	Stoke C	(a)	2-0
Sixth Round	Arsenal	(a)	2-2
		(h)	1-3

CHELTENHAM TOWN — Division 3

FOUNDATION

Although a scratch team representing Cheltenham played a match against Gloucester in 1884, the earliest recorded match for Cheltenham Town FC was a friendly against Dean Close School on 12 March 1892. The School won 4–3 and the match was played at Prestbury (half a mile from Whaddon Road). Cheltenham Town played Wednesday afternoon friendlies at a local cricket ground until entering the Mid Gloucester League. In those days the club played in deep red coloured shirts and were nicknamed 'the Rubies'. The club moved to Whaddon Lane for season 1901–02 and changed to red and white colours two years later.

Whaddon Road, Cheltenham, Gloucester GL52 5NA.

Telephone: (01242) 573 558.

Fax: (01242) 224 675.

Website: www.ctfc.com

Ground Capacity: 7,407.

Record Attendance: at Whaddon Road: 8,326 v Reading, FA Cup 1st rd, 17 November 1956; at Cheltenham Athletic Ground: 10,389 v Blackpool, FA Cup 3rd rd, 13 January 1934.

Record Receipts: £78,895 v Burnley, FA Cup 4th rd, 27 January 2002.

Pitch Measurements: 111yd × 72yd.

Chairman: Paul Baker.

Directors: Rod Burge, Colin Farmer, Arthur Hayward, Brian Sandland, John Wood, Barrie Wood, David Reynolds.

Manager: Bobby Gould.

Coach: Bob Bloomer.

Football Co-ordinator: Dave Burnside.

Youth Team Manager: Mike Davis.

Head of Youth: Brian Forsbrook.

Physio: Ian Weston.

Secretary: Paul Godfrey.

Colours: Red and white striped shirts, white shorts, white stockings.

Change Colours: All yellow.

Year Formed: 1892.

Turned Professional: 1932.

HONOURS

Football League: Promoted from Division 3 (play-offs) 2001–02.

FA Cup: best season: 5th rd 2002.

Football League Cup: never past 2nd rd.

Football Conference: Champions 1998–99, runners-up 1997–98.

Trophy: Winners 1997–98.

Southern League: Champions 1984–85; *Southern League Cup:* Winners 1957–58, runners-up 1968–69, 1984–85; *Southern League Merit Cup:* Winners 1984–85; *Southern League Championship Shield:* Winners 1985.

Gloucestershire Senior Cup: Winners 1998–99; *Gloucestershire Northern Senior Professional Cup:* Winners 30 times; *Midland Floodlit Cup:* Winners 1985–86, 1986–87, 1987–88; *Mid Gloucester League:* Champions 1896–97; *Gloucester and District League:* Champions 1902–03, 1905–06; *Cheltenham League:* Champions 1910–11, 1913–14; *North Gloucestershire League:* Champions 1913–14; *Gloucestershire Northern Senior League:* Champions 1928–29, 1932–33; *Gloucestershire Northern Senior Amateur Cup:* Winners 1929–30, 1930–31, 1932–33, 1933–34, 1934–35; *Leamington Hospital Cup:* Winners 1934–35.

SKY SPORTS FACT FILE

In 1933–34 Cheltenham Town, then playing in the Birmingham Combination, reached the FA Cup first round proper to beat Barnet 5-1 and Carlisle United 2-1 before attracting a crowd of 10,000 for the visit of Blackpool.

Ltd Co.: 1937.

Club Nickname: 'The Robins'.

Previous Grounds: Grafton Cricket Ground, Whaddon Lane, Carter's Field (pre 1932).

Record League Victory: 11–0 v Bourneville Ath, Birmingham Combination, 29 April 1933 – Davis; Jones, Williams; Lang (1), Blackburn, Draper; Evans, Hazard (4), Haycox (4), Goodger (1), Hill (1).

Record Cup Victory: 12–0 v Chippenham R, FA Cup 3rd qual. rd, 2 November 1935 – Bowles; Whitehouse, Williams; Lang, Devonport (1), Partridge (2); Perkins, Hackett, Jones (4), Black (4), Griffiths (1).

Record Defeat: 0–7 v Crystal Palace, League Cup 2nd rd, 2 October 2002.
N.B. 1–10 v Merthyr T, Southern League, 8 March 1952.

Most League Points (2 for a win): 60, Southern League Division 1, 1963–64.

Most League Points (3 for a win): 86, Southern League Premier Division, 1994–95.

Most League Goals: 115, Southern League, 1957–58.

Highest League Scorer in Season: Dave Lewis, 33 (53 in all competitions), Southern League Division 1, 1974–75.

Most League Goals in Total Aggregate: Dave Lewis, 205 (290 in all competitions), 1970–83.

Most Capped Player: Michael Duff, 2, Northern Ireland.

Most League Appearances: Roger Thorndale, 523 (702 in all competitions), 1958–76.

Record Transfer Fee Received: £60,000 from Southampton for Christer Warren, 1995.

Record Transfer Fee Paid: £57,000 to West Ham U for Grant McCann, January 2003.

Football League Record: 1999 Promoted to Division 3; 2002 Division 2; 2003– Division 3.

MANAGERS

George Blackburn 1932–34
George Carr 1934–37
Jimmy Brain 1937–48
Cyril Dean 1948–50
George Summerbee 1950–52
William Raeside 1952–53
Arch Anderson 1953–58
Ron Lewin 1958–60
Peter Donnelly 1960–61
Tommy Cavanagh 1961
Arch Anderson 1961–65
Harold Fletcher 1965–66
Bob Etheridge 1966–73
Willie Penman 1973–74
Dennis Allen 1974–79
Terry Paine 1979
Alan Grundy 1979–82
Alan Wood 1982–83
John Murphy 1983–88
Jim Barron 1988–90
John Murphy 1990
Dave Lewis 1990–91
Ally Robertson 1991–92
Lindsay Parsons 1992–95
Chris Robinson 1995–97
Steve Cotterill 1997–2002
Graham Allner 2002–03
Bobby Gould January 2003–

LATEST SEQUENCES

Longest Sequence of League Wins: not more than 3.

Longest Sequence of League Defeats: 5, 13.1.2001 – 13.2.2001.

Longest Sequence of League Draws: 5, 5.4.2003 – 21.4.2003.

Longest Sequence of Unbeaten League Matches: 16, 1.12.2001 – 12.3.2002.

Longest Sequence Without a League Win: 10, 16.4.2002 – 14.9.2002.

Successive Scoring Runs: 15 from 15.2.2003.

Successive Non-scoring Runs: 4 from 12.9.1999.

TEN YEAR LEAGUE RECORD

		P	W	D	L	F	A	Pts	Pos
1993–94	Sth L	42	21	12	9	67	38	75	2
1994–95	Sth L	42	25	11	6	87	39	86	2
1995–96	Sth L	42	21	11	10	76	57	74	3
1996–97	Sth L	42	21	11	10	76	44	74	2
1997–98	Conf	42	23	9	10	63	43	78	2
1998-99	Conf	42	22	14	6	71	36	80	1
1999-2000	Div 3	46	20	10	16	50	42	70	8
2000-01	Div 3	46	18	14	14	59	52	68	9
2001-02	Div 3	46	21	15	10	66	49	78	4
2002-03	Div 2	46	10	18	18	53	68	48	21

DID YOU KNOW ?

In 1957–58 Peter Cleland scored 39 goals for Cheltenham Town and Danny Fowler 31. During the same season the team scored nine goals in three games within the same month and were top scorers in the Southern League.

CHELTENHAM TOWN 2002–03 LEAGUE RECORD

Match No.	*Date*	*Venue*	*Opponents*	*Result*		*H/T Score*	*Lg. Pos.*	*Goalscorers*	*Attendance*
1	Aug 10	H	Wigan Ath	L	0-2	0-2	—		5138
2	13	A	Barnsley	D	1-1	0-0	—	Naylor [86]	9641
3	17	A	Tranmere R	L	0-1	0-0	22		6807
4	24	H	Plymouth Arg	L	1-2	1-0	22	Spencer [33]	4713
5	27	A	Crewe Alex	L	0-1	0-1	—		5488
6	31	H	Cardiff C	D	1-1	1-1	24	Howarth [32]	4395
7	Sept 7	A	Colchester U	D	1-1	1-0	23	Naylor [45]	2845
8	14	H	Bristol C	L	2-3	2-2	24	Alsop 2 [2, 23]	5895
9	17	H	Swindon T	W	2-0	1-0	—	McAuley [30], Milton [65]	5761
10	21	A	Mansfield T	W	2-0	0-0	18	Victory [71], McAuley [84]	4116
11	28	H	Notts Co	L	1-4	0-2	22	Alsop [65]	4565
12	Oct 5	A	Blackpool	L	1-3	1-1	24	Spencer [30]	6649
13	12	A	Luton T	L	1-2	1-0	24	Milton [12]	6447
14	19	H	QPR	D	1-1	0-1	24	Devaney [64]	6382
15	26	A	Northampton T	W	2-1	1-1	23	Alsop [31], Forsyth [62]	5354
16	29	H	Port Vale	L	0-1	0-1	—		3852
17	Nov 2	H	Huddersfield T	W	1-0	0-0	22	Brayson [71]	4322
18	9	A	Stockport Co	D	1-1	1-1	23	Alsop [31]	4531
19	23	A	Oldham Ath	D	0-0	0-0	21		6575
20	30	H	Brentford	W	1-0	0-0	20	Alsop [90]	5013
21	Dec 14	A	Peterborough U	L	1-4	0-3	23	Forsyth [46]	4522
22	21	H	Wycombe W	D	0-0	0-0	21		4303
23	26	H	Crewe Alex	L	0-4	0-3	23		5548
24	28	A	Chesterfield	D	2-2	0-0	23	Spencer 2 [55, 70]	4092
25	Jan 1	A	Plymouth Arg	L	1-3	1-2	23	Worrell (og) [13]	10,927
26	18	A	Cardiff C	L	1-2	1-2	23	Finnigan [19]	11,605
27	25	H	Chesterfield	D	0-0	0-0	24		4423
28	Feb 1	A	Wigan Ath	D	0-0	0-0	24		6171
29	4	H	Tranmere R	W	3-1	1-0	—	Brown [8], Naylor [64], Devaney [72]	3936
30	8	H	Stockport Co	L	0-2	0-0	24		4692
31	15	A	Huddersfield T	D	3-3	2-0	24	McCann 2 [37, 71], Alsop [40]	9309
32	18	H	Barnsley	L	1-3	1-1	—	Naylor [2]	3568
33	22	H	Colchester U	D	1-1	1-1	24	Alsop [2]	3607
34	Mar 1	A	Bristol C	L	1-3	1-2	24	McCann [45]	11,711
35	8	H	Mansfield T	W	3-1	2-0	24	Devaney [2], Brown [38], Spencer [90]	3881
36	12	A	Swindon T	W	3-0	2-0	—	Devaney [32], Brough [40], Spencer [90]	5583
37	15	H	Northampton T	D	1-1	0-0	22	Yates [60]	4917
38	18	A	QPR	L	1-4	1-2	—	Devaney [5]	11,370
39	22	A	Port Vale	W	2-1	1-0	21	McCann [43], Alsop [81]	4800
40	Apr 5	A	Brentford	D	2-2	2-0	21	McCann (pen) [23], Devaney [29]	5011
41	8	H	Luton T	D	2-2	1-2	—	McCann (pen) [27], Alsop [81]	3762
42	12	H	Oldham Ath	D	1-1	1-1	21	Yates [2]	4439
43	19	A	Wycombe W	D	1-1	0-1	21	Naylor [89]	6070
44	21	H	Peterborough U	D	1-1	0-0	21	Duff M [86]	4809
45	26	H	Blackpool	W	3-0	2-0	21	Victory [37], Duff M [48], Naylor [65]	5150
46	May 3	A	Notts Co	L	0-1	0-1	21		9710

Final League Position: 21

GOALSCORERS

League (53): Alsop 10, Devaney 6, McCann 6 (2 pens), Naylor 6, Spencer 6, Brown 2, Duff M 2, Forsyth 2, McAuley 2, Milton 2, Victory 2, Yates 2, Brayson 1, Brough 1, Finnigan 1, Howarth 1, own goal 1.
Worthington Cup (3): Naylor 2, McAuley 1.
FA Cup (4): Alsop 1, Brayson 1, Devaney 1, Yates 1.
LDV Vans Trophy (5): Brayson 2 (1 pen), Alsop 1, Forsyth 1, McCann 1.

Book S 36	Howarth N 26 + 1	Victory J 45	Finnigan J 34 + 3	Walker R 15	Duff M 44	Milton R 15 + 6	Brayson P 14 + 6	Alsop J 32 + 5	Naylor T 19 + 11	Yates M 34 + 3	Williams L 6 + 7	Devaney M 35 + 5	Spencer D 10 + 20	McAuley H 15 + 4	Griffin A 8 + 3	McCann G 27	Brough J 21 + 8	Jones S 5	Forsyth R 12	Simpkins M 2	Duff S 15 + 3	Brown M 11 + 4	Strong G 3 + 1	Bird D 12 + 2	Higgs S 10	*Match No.*
1	2	3	4	5	6	7^{1}	8^{2}	9^{3}	10	11	12	13	14													1
1	2	3	4	5	6	7^{1}		9	12	11	10	8														2
1	2	3	4^{3}	5	6	12	13	9	10	11	7^{1}	8^{2}		14												3
1	2	3	4^{3}	5	6	12	8		10	11	7^{1}	13	9^{2}	14												4
1	2	3	12	5	6	7^{1}	8		9	11	4^{2}	13		10												5
1	2	3	12	5	6	7^{1}	8^{2}	9	10	11	13			4												6
1	2	3		5	6	7	8^{1}	9	10^{2}	11	12	13		4												7
1	2	3	4	5	6	7^{2}	13	9	10^{3}	11	12		14	8^{1}												8
1	2^{1}	3	4	5	6	7		9^{2}	10	11	12		13	8												9
1		3	4	5	6	7		9	10	11				8	2											10
1		3	4	5	6	7^{2}	12	9	10	11	13		14	8^{1}	2^{3}											11
1		3	7	2	6		12		10^{1}	11	13	14	9^{3}			8	4	5^{2}								12
1	2	3^{2}	4	5	6	7	12	9	10^{1}		11^{3}		14				13		8							13
1	2	3	7	5	6		10^{1}	9	12			8				11			4							14
1	5	3	7		6		10	9				8^{1}			2	11	12		4							15
1	2	3	7^{2}	5^{3}	6		10	9	12	13		8^{1}				11	14		4							16
1	2	3	7		6		10^{1}	9				8	12			11	5		4							17
1	2	3	4		6		10	9		7		8				11	5									18
1	2	3	7		6		10^{1}	9				8	12			11	5		4							19
1	2	3	7		6		10^{1}	9		12		8				11■	5		4							20
1	2	3	7		6		10^{3}	9		11^{1}		8	14	12	13		5^{2}		4							21
1	2	3	7		6			9				8	10	11			5		4							22
1	2■	3	7		6■			9				8	10^{1}	11^{2}			12		4	5	13					23
1	2	3			6			9		11		8	10	7					4	5						24
1	2	3			6		12	9		11		8	10^{1}	7^{2}			5		4		13					25
1		3	7			10^{2}		9	12	11^{3}	4^{1}	8	13	14	2		5				6					26
1		3	4		6	7	10^{1}	9	12			8		11	2		5									27
1		3	4		6	7^{1}		9		12		8	10^{3}		2	11	5^{2}				13	14				28
1		3			6			9	10	7		8			2	11					5^{1}	4	12			29
1		3			6	12		9	10	7		8	13		2	11^{1}						4^{2}	5			30
1		3			6			9	10	7^{1}		8		4		11						12	5	2		31
1					6			9	10^{1}			8	12	7		11	5	2				4	3			32
1		3			6			9	10^{1}	7		8^{2}	12	4^{3}		11		2			5	13		14		33
1		3	4		6^{2}			9	12	7		8^{3}	10^{1}			11	13	2			5			14		34
		3	4		6				12	7		8	13			11	9^{2}				5	10^{1}		2	1	35
		3			6	4				7		8	12			11	9				5	10^{1}		2	1	36
	12	3	13		6	4^{2}				7		8	14			11	9				5	10^{3}		2^{1}	1	37
	2	3	4		6^{1}			12		7		8	10			11	9				5				1	38
1	6	3	4					12	13	7		8			14	11	9^{1}				5	10^{2}		2^{3}		39
1		3	4		6			12■		7		8	13			11	9^{1}				5	10^{2}		2		40
		3	4		6			12	13	7		8				11	9				5	10^{2}		2^{1}	1	41
		3	4		6			9^{1}		7		8	12		13	11	10^{3}	5^{2}				14		2	1	42
		3	4		6	12			13	7		8^{2}	14			11	9^{3}				5	10^{1}		2	1	43
		3	4		6	12			13	7		8^{2}	9^{3}			11^{1}	14				5	10		2	1	44
	6	3	4		9	12			10^{2}	7		8	13			11^{1}	14				5^{3}			2	1	45
	6^{1}	3	4		9^{2}			12	10	7		8	14			11	13				5			2^{3}	1	46

Worthington Cup

First Round	Norwich C	(a)	3-0
Second Round	Crystal Palace	(a)	0-7

LDV Vans Trophy

First Round	Colchester U	(h)	4-1
Second Round	Wycombe W	(h)	1-2

FA Cup

First Round	Yeovil T	(a)	2-0
Second Round	Oldham Ath	(a)	2-1
Third Round	Sheffield U	(a)	0-4

CHESTERFIELD Division 2

FOUNDATION

Chesterfield are fourth only to Stoke, Notts County and Nottingham Forest in age for they can trace their existence as far back as 1866, although it is fair to say that they were somewhat casual in the first few years of their history playing only a few friendlies a year. However, their rules of 1871 are still in existence showing an annual membership of 2s (10p), but it was not until 1891 that they won a trophy (the Barnes Cup) and followed this a year later by winning the Sheffield Cup, Barnes Cup and the Derbyshire Junior Cup.

Recreation Ground, Chesterfield S40 4SX.

Telephone: (01246) 209 765. ***Fax:*** (01246) 556 799.
Commercial Dept: (01246) 231 535.
ClubCall: 09068 555 818.

Ground Capacity: 8,502.

Record Attendance: 30,968 v Newcastle U, Division 2, 7 April 1939.

Record Receipts: £75,000 v West Ham U, Worthington Cup, 2nd rd, 1 October 2002.

Pitch Measurements: 113yd × 71yd.

President: His Grace the Duke of Devonshire MC, DL, JP.

Chief Executive: Alan Walters.

Manager: Roy McFarland. ***Assistant Manager:*** Lee Richardson.
Physio: Jamie Hewitt.

Secretary: Alan Walters. ***Commercial Manager:*** Jim Brown. ***Stadium Manager:*** W. W. Kenworthy.

Colours: Blue shirts, blue shorts, white stockings.

Change Colours: All white.

Year Formed: 1866.

Turned Professional: 1891.

Ltd Co: 1871.

Previous Name: Chesterfield Town.

Club Nicknames: 'Blues' or 'Spireites'.

First Football League Game: 2 September 1899, Division 2, v Sheffield W (a) L 1–5 – Hancock; Pilgrim, Fletcher; Ballantyne, Bell, Downie; Morley, Thacker, Gooing, Munday (1), Geary.

Record League Victory: 10–0 v Glossop NE, Division 2, 17 January 1903 – Clutterbuck; Thorpe, Lerper; Haig, Banner, Thacker; Tomlinson (2), Newton (1), Milward (3), Munday (2), Steel (2).

Record Cup Victory: 5–0 v Wath Ath (a), FA Cup 1st rd, 28 November 1925 – Birch; Saxby, Dennis; Wass, Abbott, Thompson; Fisher (1), Roseboom (1), Cookson (2), Whitfield (1), Hopkinson.

HONOURS

Football League: Division 2 best season: 4th, 1946–47; Division 3 (N) – Champions 1930–31, 1935–36; Runners-up 1933–34; Promoted to Division 2 (3rd) – 2000–01; Division 4 – Champions 1969–70, 1984–85.

FA Cup: Semi-final 1997.

Football League Cup: best season: 4th rd, 1965.

Anglo-Scottish Cup: Winners 1981.

SKY SPORTS FACT FILE

Runners-up in the Third Division (North) in 1933–34, Chesterfield had the best defence in the entire League conceding only 43 goals. In 1935–36 as winners they did it again, letting in just 39.

Record Defeat: 0–10 v Gillingham, Division 3, 5 September 1987.

Most League Points (2 for a win): 64, Division 4, 1969–70.

Most League Points (3 for a win): 91, Division 4, 1984–85.

Most League Goals: 102, Division 3 (N), 1930–31.

Highest League Scorer in Season: Jimmy Cookson, 44, Division 3 (N), 1925–26.

Most League Goals in Total Aggregate: Ernie Moss, 161, 1969–76, 1979–81 and 1984–86.

Most League Goals in One Match: 4, Jimmy Cookson v Accrington S, Division 3N, 16 January 1926; 4, Jimmy Cookson v Ashington, Division 3N, 1 May 1926; 4, Jimmy Cookson v Wigan Borough, Division 3N, 4 September 1926; 4, Tommy Lyon v Southampton, Division 2, 3 December 1938.

Most Capped Player: Walter McMillen, 4 (7), Northern Ireland; Mark Williams, 4 (17), Northern Ireland.

Most League Appearances: Dave Blakey, 613, 1948–67.

Youngest League Player: Dennis Thompson, 16 years 160 days v Notts Co, 26 December 1950.

Record Transfer Fee Received: £750,000 from Southampton for Kevin Davies, May 1997.

Record Transfer Fee Paid: £250,000 to Watford for Jason Lee, August 1998.

Football League Record: 1899 Elected to Division 2; 1909 failed re-election; 1921–31 Division 3 (N); 1931–33 Division 2; 1933–36 Division 3 (N); 1936–51 Division 2; 1951–58 Division 3 (N); 1958–61 Division 3; 1961–70 Division 4; 1970–83 Division 3; 1983–85 Division 4; 1985–89 Division 3; 1989–92 Division 4; 1992–95 Division 3; 1995–2000 Division 2; 2000–01 Division 3; 2001– Division 2.

MANAGERS

E. Russell Timmeus 1891–95 *(Secretary-Manager)*
Gilbert Gillies 1895–1901
E. F. Hind 1901–02
Jack Hoskin 1902–06
W. Furness 1906–07
George Swift 1907–10
G. H. Jones 1911–13
R. L. Weston 1913–17
T. Callaghan 1919
J. J. Caffrey 1920–22
Harry Hadley 1922
Harry Parkes 1922–27
Alec Campbell 1927
Ted Davison 1927–32
Bill Harvey 1932–38
Norman Bullock 1938–45
Bob Brocklebank 1945–48
Bobby Marshall 1948–52
Ted Davison 1952–58
Duggie Livingstone 1958–62
Tony McShane 1962–67
Jimmy McGuigan 1967–73
Joe Shaw 1973–76
Arthur Cox 1976–80
Frank Barlow 1980–83
John Duncan 1983–87
Kevin Randall 1987–88
Paul Hart 1988–91
Chris McMenemy 1991–93
John Duncan 1993–2000
Nicky Law 2000–02
Dave Rushbury 2002–03
Roy McFarland May 2003–

LATEST SEQUENCES

Longest Sequence of League Wins: 10, 6.9.1933 – 4.11.1933.

Longest Sequence of League Defeats: 9, 22.10.1960 – 27.12.1960.

Longest Sequence of League Draws: 5, 19.9.1990 – 6.10.1990.

Longest Sequence of Unbeaten League Matches: 21, 26.12.1994 – 29.4.1995.

Longest Sequence Without a League Win: 18, 11.9.1999 – 3.1.2000.

Successive Scoring Runs: 46 from 25.12.1929.

Successive Non-scoring Runs: 7 from 23.9.1977.

TEN YEAR LEAGUE RECORD

		P	W	D	L	F	A	Pts	Pos
1993-94	Div 3	42	16	14	12	55	48	62	8
1994-95	Div 3	42	23	12	7	62	37	81	3
1995-96	Div 2	46	20	12	14	56	51	72	7
1996-97	Div 2	46	18	14	14	42	39	68	10
1997-98	Div 2	46	16	17	13	46	44	65	10
1998-99	Div 2	46	17	13	16	46	44	64	9
1999-2000	Div 2	46	7	15	24	34	63	36	24
2000-01	Div 3	46	25	14	7	79	42	80*	3
2001-02	Div 2	46	13	13	20	53	65	52	18
2002-03	Div 2	46	14	8	24	43	73	50	20

**9 pts deducted.*

DID YOU KNOW ?

From Christmas Day 1929 to Boxing Day 1930 Chesterfield scored in 46 consecutive League matches in Division Three (South). When Arsenal topped this record in 2002–03 manager David Rushbury faxed congratulations to Highbury.

CHESTERFIELD 2002–03 LEAGUE RECORD

Match No.	*Date*	*Venue*	*Opponents*	*Result*		*H/T Score*	*Lg. Pos.*	*Goalscorers*	*Attendance*
1	Aug 10	A	QPR	L	1-3	0-0	—	Ebdon (pen) [55]	12,603
2	13	H	Swindon T	L	2-4	0-3	—	Hurst 2 (1 pen) [56 (p), 75]	3189
3	17	H	Port Vale	W	2-1	0-0	20	Edwards [46], Brandon [86]	3598
4	24	A	Mansfield T	W	2-0	1-0	12	Payne [39], Davies [54]	7258
5	27	H	Northampton T	W	4-0	3-0	—	Hurst 2 [22, 90], Hudson [28], Brandon [42]	3585
6	31	A	Luton T	L	0-3	0-1	12		6060
7	Sept 7	A	Crewe Alex	D	0-0	0-0	12		5837
8	14	H	Wigan Ath	D	0-0	0-0	13		4124
9	17	H	Stockport Co	W	1-0	1-0	—	Brandon [44]	4088
10	21	A	Plymouth Arg	W	1-0	0-0	8	Ebdon [69]	8547
11	28	H	Blackpool	W	1-0	0-0	5	Reeves [49]	4488
12	Oct 5	A	Bristol C	L	0-4	0-1	8		10,107
13	12	H	Tranmere R	W	1-0	0-0	7	Howson [85]	4111
14	18	A	Colchester U	L	0-2	0-0	—		3211
15	26	H	Notts Co	D	0-0	0-0	9		4539
16	29	A	Wycombe W	L	0-2	0-0	—		4897
17	Nov 2	H	Barnsley	W	1-0	1-0	9	Burt [10]	4676
18	9	A	Peterborough U	L	0-1	0-0	9		4359
19	24	A	Cardiff C	L	0-1	0-1	10		13,331
20	30	H	Huddersfield T	W	1-0	1-0	8	Dawson [33]	4194
21	Dec 14	A	Brentford	L	1-2	1-1	9	Brandon [13]	5151
22	21	H	Oldham Ath	L	0-1	0-1	11		4052
23	26	A	Northampton T	W	1-0	0-0	10	Bradley [88]	5282
24	28	H	Cheltenham T	D	2-2	0-0	11	Bradley [72], Howson [74]	4092
25	Jan 1	H	Luton T	W	2-1	0-1	9	Hurst [55], Reeves [59]	4638
26	4	A	Swindon T	L	0-3	0-1	9		4544
27	18	H	Mansfield T	L	1-2	1-1	11	Ebdon (pen) [39]	6813
28	25	A	Cheltenham T	D	0-0	0-0	12		4423
29	Feb 2	H	QPR	L	2-4	1-2	13	Hurst [11], Brandon [90]	4395
30	8	H	Peterborough U	D	0-0	0-0	13		3515
31	11	A	Port Vale	L	2-5	2-4	—	Edwards [34], Ebdon [45]	3039
32	15	A	Barnsley	L	1-2	1-2	14	Brandon [18]	9373
33	22	H	Crewe Alex	L	0-2	0-1	14		3956
34	Mar 1	A	Wigan Ath	L	1-3	0-2	14	Reeves (pen) [66]	6384
35	4	A	Stockport Co	L	1-2	1-1	—	Reeves [6]	4428
36	8	H	Plymouth Arg	W	3-2	2-1	16	Payne [10], Reeves 2 [17, 49]	3668
37	15	A	Notts Co	D	1-1	1-0	17	Folan [11]	6801
38	18	H	Colchester U	L	0-4	0-1	—		3226
39	22	H	Wycombe W	W	4-0	1-0	16	Close [28], Reeves [53], Brandon [67], Hudson [86]	3081
40	29	A	Tranmere R	L	1-2	0-1	17	Reeves [78]	8238
41	Apr 5	A	Huddersfield T	L	0-4	0-2	18		9098
42	13	H	Cardiff C	L	0-3	0-2	20		4398
43	19	A	Oldham Ath	L	0-4	0-2	20		6885
44	21	H	Brentford	L	0-2	0-1	20		3296
45	26	H	Bristol C	W	2-0	0-0	20	Hurst [86], Hudson [90]	4770
46	May 3	A	Blackpool	D	1-1	1-0	20	Douglas [39]	7999

Final League Position: 20

GOALSCORERS

League (43): Reeves 8 (1 pen), Brandon 7, Hurst 7 (1 pen), Ebdon 4 (2 pens), Hudson 3, Bradley 2, Edwards 2, Howson 2, Payne 2, Burt 1, Close 1, Davies 1, Dawson 1, Douglas 1, Folan 1.
Worthington Cup (2): Allott 1, Brandon 1.
FA Cup (1): Davies 1.
LDV Vans Trophy (3): Brandon 2, Allott 1.

Muggleton C 26	Booty M 35 + 3	Edwards R 25 + 4	Dawson K 26	Blatherwick S 30 + 1	Howson S 32 + 1	Brandon C 35 + 1	Ebdon M 21 + 3	Allott M 24 + 9	Hurst G 27 + 5	Payne S 34	Innes M 5 + 5	Howard J 1 + 8	Hudson M 23 + 1	Burt J 11 + 5	Davies G 27 + 7	Reeves D 36 + 4	Rushbury A 23 + 7	O'Hare A 18 + 4	Rowland K — + 3	Richmond A 6 + 1	Bradley S 1 + 8	Wilkinson S — + 1	Williams B 14	Warne S 2 + 1	Folan C 9 + 4	Close B 8	Douglas J 7	*Match No.*
1	2	3	4	5^1	6	7	8	9^2	10	11	12	13																1
1	2	3	4		6	7^1		9	10	5	11^2	12	8	13														2
1	2	3	4		6	7			10	5		12	8		11^1	9												3
1	2	3^2	4		6	7		12	10	5	13		8		11	9^1												4
1	2		4		6	7^1			10	5	11		8	12	3	9												5
1	2		4		6	7^1		12	10	5	11^3	13	8		3^2	9	14											6
1	2		4		6	7				5		10^1	8	12	3	9	11											7
1	2^1		4		6	7	12		13	5			8	10^2	3	9	11											8
1			4		6	7^1	11	9		5			8	12	2	10	3											9
1	2		4	12	6		7	9		5^1				8	3	10	11											10
1	2	13	4	5	6		7^1	9					12	8^2	3	10	11											11
1	7	12	4	5	6	13	11	9					8^2		2^1	10	3											12
1	7	3	4	5	6	10							8	12	2^1	9	11											13
1	2	3		5	6	7	8	12					4	10^1		9	11^2	13										14
1	12		4		6	7	2^1			5		13	8	10	11^2	9	14	3^3										15
1	2		4^1		6	7				5			8	10	11^2	9	12	3	13									16
1	2^3		4		6	7		12		5		13	8	10^2	3	9^1	11		14									17
1	7		4		6	11		12		5		13	8^3	10^2	2	9^1	3		14									18
1	2	3	4	5	6	7		9	10	11					8													19
1	2	3	4	5	6	7	8	9	10	11																		20
1^6	2	3■	4^1	5■	6	7	8	9		11				10	12					15								21
	2^2	3		5	6	7	8	9^1	10	4^3					11	12				1	13	14						22
	12	3		5	6	7	8		10	4				11^1	2	9^2				1	13							23
	3			5	6	7	8		10	4				11^1	2	9				1	12							24
	4	11		5	6	7	8		10						2	9^1		3			12		1					25
		11			6	7^1	8	12	10	5					2	9^2	4^3	3			13		1	14				26
	2^1	11		5	6	7	8		10	4						9^2	12	3			13■		1					27
	2	3		5^2		7	8		10	6^1					4	12	11	13			9		1					28
	4	3			6	7	8	12	10						2	9	11^1	5					1					29
	2	3		5	6	7	8^1	12	10						13	9	11^2	4					1					30
	2	3		5	6	7	8	12	10						13	9^1	11^2	4					1					31
	2	3		5■		7	8	9	10^2							14	12	4			13^3		1	6^1	11			32
	2	3	4^1	5		7	8^2	9	10^3						12		13	6			14		1		11			33
	4	3	6		12			8		5	13	14			2^1	9	11^2						1	7^3	10			34
	7	3		5	6			8	12	4					2	9	11						1		10^1			35
		3		5	6^2	7		8	12	4						9	11	13					1		10^1	2		36
	12	3^1		5		7		8		4						9	11	6					1		10	2		37
			4^3	5		7		8	12	6	13				14	9	11	2^1					1		10^2	3		38
		3^2		5		7		11	12	4			8			9	13	6		1					10^1	2		39
				5				11	10	4			8		7^1	9	3	6		1					12		2	40
	4			5				11	10	6	12		8		13	9^2	3^1			1					7		2	41
1	3			5				11	10	4			8		2^1	9		6							12		7	42
1				5				11	10	4			8		12	9^2	7^1	6							13	3	2	43
1			4	5		7	12	11^1	10^3	6^2			8			9		13							14	3	2	44
1	2	12	4	5			13	9^3	10		11^1		8			14		3								6^2	7	45
1	2	12	4	5					10		11^1		8			9		3								6	7	46

Worthington Cup

First Round	Grimsby T	(a)	1-0
Second Round	West Ham U	(h)	1-1

FA Cup

First Round	Morecambe	(h)	1-2

LDV Vans Trophy

First Round	Halifax T	(h)	2-0
Second Round	Port Vale	(a)	1-1

COLCHESTER UNITED Division 2

FOUNDATION

Colchester United was formed in 1937 when a number of enthusiasts of the much older Colchester Town club decided to establish a professional concern as a limited liability company. The new club continued at Layer Road which had been the amateur club's home since 1909.

Layer Road Ground, Colchester, Essex CO2 7JJ.

Telephone: (01206) 715 301. ***Fax:*** (01206) 715 303.
Club Shop: (01206) 715 309.
Soccer Centre: (01206) 572 378. ***Lottery:*** (01206) 715 320.

Ground Capacity: 7,341.

Record Attendance: 19,072 v Reading, FA Cup 1st rd, 27 November 1948.

Record Receipts: £35,431 v Burnley, Div 2, 26 February 2000.

Pitch Measurements: 110yd × 71yd.

Patron: The Mayor of Colchester.

Chairman: Peter Heard.

Directors: John Worsp, Peter Powell.

Chief Executive: Marie Partner.

Manager: Phil Parkinson.

Assistant Manager/Coach: Geraint Williams.

Director of Youth: Micky Cook.

Physio: Graham Jones.

Consultant Physio: Ray Cole.

Secretary: Miss Sonya Constantine.

Corporate and Promotions Consultant: John Schultz.

Commercial and Marketing Manager: Jerry Carter.

Stadium Manager: David Blacknall.

Colours: Blue and white striped shirts, navy shorts, white stockings.

Change Colours: White shirts, navy shorts, navy stockings.

Year Formed: 1937.

Turned Professional: 1937.

Ltd Co.: 1937.

Club Nickname: 'The U's'.

First Football League Game: 19 August 1950, Division 3 (S), v Gillingham (a) D 0–0 – Wright; Kettle, Allen; Bearryman, Stewart, Elder; Jones, Curry, Turner, McKim, Church.

HONOURS

Football League: Promoted from Division 3 – 1997–98 (play-offs); Division 4 – Runners-up 1961–62.

FA Cup: best season: 6th rd, 1971.

Football League Cup: best season: 5th rd, 1975.

Auto Windscreens Shield: Runners-up 1997.

GM Vauxhall Conference: Winners 1991–92.

FA Trophy: Winners 1992.

SKY SPORTS FACT FILE

On 14 February 2003 Mick Stockwell, Colchester United's acting player-coach, celebrated his 38th birthday during the 1-0 win over Mansfield Town. But he had to watch from the bench from half-time after a recurrence of a back injury.

Record League Victory: 9–1 v Bradford C, Division 4, 30 December 1961 – Ames; Millar, Fowler; Harris, Abrey, Ron Hunt; Foster, Bobby Hunt (4), King (4), Hill (1), Wright.

Record Cup Victory: 7–1 v Yeovil T (away), FA Cup 2nd rd (replay), 11 December 1958 – Ames; Fisher, Fowler; Parker, Milligan, Hammond; Williams (1), McLeod (2), Langman (4), Evans, Wright. 7–1 v Yeading, FA Cup 1st rd (replay), 22 November 1994 – Cheesewright; Betts, English, Cawley, Caesar, Locke (Dennis), Fry, Brown (2), Whitton (2) (Thompson), Kinsella (1), Abrahams (2).

Record Defeat: 0–8 v Leyton Orient, Division 4, 15 October 1989.

Most League Points (2 for a win): 60, Division 4, 1973–74.

Most League Points (3 for a win): 81, Division 4, 1982–83.

Most League Goals: 104, Division 4, 1961–62.

Highest League Scorer in Season: Bobby Hunt, 38, Division 4, 1961–62.

Most League Goals in Total Aggregate: Martyn King, 130, 1956–64.

Most League Goals in One Match: 4, Bobby Hunt v Bradford C, Division 4, 30 December 1961; 4, Martyn King v Bradford C, Division 4, 30 December 1961; 4, Bobby Hunt v Doncaster R, Division 4, 30 April 1962.

Most Capped Player: None.

Most League Appearances: Micky Cook, 613, 1969–84.

Youngest League Player: Lindsay Smith, 16 years 218 days v Grimsby T, 24 April 1971.

Record Transfer Fee Received: £2,250,000 from Newcastle U for Lomano Lua-Lua, September 2000.

Record Transfer Fee Paid: £50,000 to Norwich C for Adrian Coote, December 2001.

Football League Record: 1950 Elected to Division 3 (S); 1958–61 Division 3; 1961–62 Division 4; 1962–65 Division 3; 1965–66 Division 4; 1966–68 Division 3; 1968–74 Division 4; 1974–76 Division 3, 1976–77 Division 4; 1977–81 Division 3; 1981–90 Division 4; 1990–92 GM Vauxhall Conference; 1992–98 Division 3; 1998– Division 2.

MANAGERS

Ted Fenton 1946–48
Jimmy Allen 1948–53
Jack Butler 1953–55
Benny Fenton 1955–63
Neil Franklin 1963–68
Dick Graham 1968–72
Jim Smith 1972–75
Bobby Roberts 1975–82
Allan Hunter 1982–83
Cyril Lea 1983–86
Mike Walker 1986–87
Roger Brown 1987–88
Jock Wallace 1989
Mick Mills 1990
Ian Atkins 1990–91
Roy McDonough 1991–94
George Burley 1994
Steve Wignall 1995–99
Mick Wadsworth 1999
Steve Whitton 1999–2003
Phil Parkinson February 2003–

LATEST SEQUENCES

Longest Sequence of League Wins: 7, 29.11.1968 – 1.2.1969.

Longest Sequence of League Defeats: 8, 9.10.1954 – 4.12.1954.

Longest Sequence of League Draws: 6, 21.3.1977 – 11.4.1977.

Longest Sequence of Unbeaten League Matches: 20, 22.12.1956 – 19.4.1957.

Longest Sequence Without a League Win: 20, 2.3.1968 – 31.8.1968.

Successive Scoring Runs: 24 from 15.9.1962.

Successive Non-scoring Runs: 5 from 7.4.1981.

TEN YEAR LEAGUE RECORD

		P	W	D	L	F	A	Pts	Pos
1993-94	Div 3	42	13	10	19	56	71	49	17
1994-95	Div 3	42	16	10	16	56	64	58	10
1995-96	Div 3	46	18	18	10	61	51	72	7
1996-97	Div 3	46	17	17	12	62	51	68	8
1997-98	Div 3	46	21	11	14	72	60	74	4
1998-99	Div 2	46	12	16	18	52	70	52	18
1999-2000	Div 2	46	14	10	22	59	82	52	18
2000-01	Div 2	46	15	12	19	55	59	57	17
2001-02	Div 2	46	15	12	19	65	76	57	15
2002-03	Div 2	46	14	16	16	52	56	58	12

DID YOU KNOW?

The 1956–57 season was a record-breaking one for Colchester United and included remaining unbeaten at home. They conceded only 56 goals overall and finished just a point behind the top two teams.

COLCHESTER UNITED 2002–03 LEAGUE RECORD

Match No.	Date	Venue	Opponents	Result		H/T Score	Lg. Pos.	Goalscorers	Attendance
1	Aug 10	H	Stockport Co	W	1-0	0-0	—	Pinault[58]	3300
2	13	A	Tranmere R	D	1-1	0-1	—	Keith[53]	7499
3	17	A	Crewe Alex	L	0-2	0-1	15		5138
4	24	H	Brentford	L	0-1	0-1	19		3135
5	26	A	Peterborough U	W	1-0	0-0	12	Keith[80]	4203
6	31	H	Wigan Ath	W	1-0	1-0	8	Morgan[41]	2721
7	Sept 7	H	Cheltenham T	D	1-1	0-1	11	Keith (pen)[59]	2845
8	14	A	Port Vale	L	0-1	0-0	14		3328
9	17	A	Northampton T	L	1-4	1-3	—	Sampson (og)[38]	3663
10	21	H	Oldham Ath	L	0-1	0-0	16		3021
11	28	A	QPR	L	0-2	0-1	20		12,906
12	Oct 5	H	Wycombe W	L	0-1	0-1	20		3252
13	12	A	Swindon T	D	2-2	1-0	21	McGleish[3], Pinault[49]	4152
14	18	H	Chesterfield	W	2-0	0-0	—	Izzet 2[58, 73]	3211
15	26	A	Huddersfield T	D	1-1	1-0	19	Rapley[11]	8912
16	29	H	Barnsley	D	1-1	1-1	—	Stockley[10]	3096
17	Nov 1	A	Mansfield T	L	2-4	2-3	—	Keith (pen)[25], Rapley[31]	3414
18	9	H	Bristol C	D	2-2	0-1	21	Pinault[55], Bowry[66]	3338
19	23	A	Notts Co	W	3-2	2-2	19	Morgan 2[7, 35], McGleish[83]	4626
20	30	H	Plymouth Arg	D	0-0	0-0	19		3714
21	Dec 14	A	Luton T	W	2-1	1-1	15	Duguid[45], Morgan[58]	5890
22	20	H	Cardiff C	L	1-2	0-1	—	Stockwell[52]	3096
23	26	H	Peterborough U	D	1-1	1-0	17	Izzet[45]	3760
24	28	A	Blackpool	L	1-3	0-2	18	Izzet[71]	6040
25	Jan 4	H	Tranmere R	D	2-2	1-1	17	McGleish[12], Keith (pen)[69]	2846
26	11	H	Crewe Alex	L	1-2	1-0	19	Stockwell[41]	2949
27	18	A	Wigan Ath	L	1-2	0-1	21	Keith (pen)[90]	5792
28	25	H	Blackpool	L	0-2	0-0	22		3305
29	Feb 1	A	Stockport Co	D	1-1	0-1	21	Keith[88]	4011
30	8	A	Bristol C	W	2-1	1-0	20	McGleish[12], Pinault[82]	11,107
31	14	H	Mansfield T	W	1-0	0-0	—	McGleish[88]	3247
32	22	A	Cheltenham T	D	1-1	1-1	18	Williams[44]	3607
33	Mar 1	H	Port Vale	W	4-1	2-0	17	Williams 3[7, 36, 72], Keith[53]	3581
34	4	H	Northampton T	W	2-0	1-0	—	Williams[28], McGleish[76]	3408
35	8	A	Oldham Ath	L	0-2	0-2	17		5223
36	11	A	Brentford	D	1-1	0-1	—	Keith (pen)[84]	3990
37	15	H	Huddersfield T	W	2-0	0-0	15	Izzet[74], McGleish[81]	3835
38	18	A	Chesterfield	W	4-0	1-0	—	Izzet[43], Williams[48], Payne (og)[68], Morgan[81]	3226
39	22	A	Barnsley	D	1-1	1-1	13	McGleish[38]	9154
40	29	H	Swindon T	W	1-0	0-0	11	Izzet[57]	3787
41	Apr 5	A	Plymouth Arg	D	0-0	0-0	11		7122
42	12	H	Notts Co	D	1-1	1-1	11	Duguid[7]	3435
43	19	A	Cardiff C	W	3-0	1-0	10	Duguid[4], Izzet[61], Morgan[73]	12,633
44	21	H	Luton T	L	0-5	0-4	10		3967
45	26	A	Wycombe W	D	0-0	0-0	10		6283
46	May 3	H	QPR	L	0-1	0-0	12		5047

Final League Position: 12

GOALSCORERS

League (52): Keith 9 (5 pens), Izzet 8, McGleish 8, Morgan 6, Williams 6, Pinault 4, Duguid 3, Rapley 2, Stockwell 2, Bowry 1, Stockley 1, own goals 2.
Worthington Cup (0).
FA Cup (0).
LDV Vans Trophy (1): McGleish 1.

McKinney R 20 + 1	Warren M 20	Keith J 36	Pinault T 32 + 10	Johnson G 8	White A 41	Duguid K 26 + 1	Bowry B 33 + 2	Rapley K 14 + 7	McGleish S 38 + 5	Stockwell M 30 + 10	Morgan D 22 + 15	Coote A 7 + 9	Izzet K 43 + 2	Brown S 26 + 1	Steele D 6 + 2	Opara L — + 5	Odunsi L 3 + 3	Stockley S 31 + 2	Baldwin P 13 + 6	Richards J — + 2	Keeble C — + 3	Fitzgerald S 26	Atangana S 1 + 5	Chilvers L 6	Williams G 6 + 2	Jackson J 8	May B 4 + 2	Edwards M 3 + 2	Canham M 2 + 1	Halford G 1	*Match No.*
1	2	3	4	5	6	7	8	9^{1}	10^{2}	11^{3}	12	13	14																		1
1^{G}	2	3	4	5	6	7^{1}	8	9^{2}	10	11	13		12	15																	2
1	2	3	4	5	6		8^{1}	12	10^{2}	11	9	13	7																		3
1	2^{2}	3	4	5	6		8	12		11^{1}	9	10^{3}	7		13	14															4
1	2■	3	4^{3}	5	6		8	12	13	11	9^{1}	10^{2}	7				14														5
1	2	3	4	5	6		8		12	11	9^{2}	10^{1}	7			13															6
1	2	3	4	5	6		8	12	10^{1}	11^{3}	9^{2}		7			13		14													7
1	4	3		5^{2}	6		8	12	10	11	14		7				9^{1}	2	13^{3}												8
1	5	3			6		8		10	11	9		7			12	4^{1}	2													9
	3■		4		6		8	12	10^{2}	11^{1}	9	13	7	1	5			2													10
	3		4		6		8	9^{3}	10^{2}	11^{1}	13	12	7	1	5	14		2													11
		3	4^{1}		6		8	9	10	11	12		7	1	5			2													12
		3	4		6		8	9^{2}	10^{1}	11	12	13	7	1	5			2													13
		3	4		6		8	9	10	11			7	1	5			2													14
	5	3	4		6		8	9^{1}	10^{3}	11	12		7	1			13	2^{2}		14											15
		3	4^{2}		6		8	9^{1}	10	11			7	1	5■		12	2	13												16
		3	4		6■		8	9^{2}	10^{3}	11	13		7	1	12		2^{1}		5	14											17
		3	4		6		8	9	10	11^{1}	12		7	1				2	5												18
	5	3	12		6		8	9	13	11^{1}	10^{2}		7	1				2	4												19
	4	3	7		6		8	9	12	11^{2}	10			1				2^{1}	5		13										20
	4^{3}		12		6	2	8	9^{1}		11^{2}	10	13	7	1				3	14			5									21
	4		12		6	2	8	9■		11^{1}	10^{3}	13	7	1				3^{2}				5	14								22
		3	12		6	2	8	13	10	11^{1}			7	1					4			5	9^{2}								23
		3	12		6	2	8		10^{3}	13	9^{2}	14	7	1				11^{1}	4			5									24
	6	3	12			2	8^{1}		9	11^{2}		10	7	1					4		13	5									25
	6	3	12			2	8^{1}		9	11^{3}	13	10	7	1					4^{2}		14	5									26
	4	3			6	2	8		9	11^{1}	12	10^{2}	7	1								5	13								27
	4^{2}	3				2■	8		12	11^{1}		10^{3}	7	1					13			5	14	6	9						28
		3	8		6	2			10^{2}	11^{1}	9^{3}	13	7	1				12				5	14	4							29
		3	8		6		12		10	11^{1}	9^{2}		7	1				2				5		4	13						30
		3	8		6	12			10	11^{1}	9^{2}		7	1				2				5		4	13						31
		3	8		6	11			10	12	13		7	1				2^{1}				5		4	9^{2}						32
		3	8		6	11	12		10	13			7	1				2				5		4^{2}	9^{1}						33
		3	8		6	11			10				7	1				2	4			5			9						34
15		3	8		6■	11			10^{2}		12		7	1^{G}				2	4			5	13		9^{1}						35
1		11	12		6	7	8^{1}		10	13	9^{2}		4					2				5				3					36
1		11	4		6	7			10	12	9^{1}		8					2				5				3					37
1		11	4		6	7			10^{1}	12	13		8					2				5			9^{2}	3					38
1		11	4			9	8^{1}		10	12			7					2	6			5				3					39
1		11^{1}	4			7			10	12			8					2	6			5				3	9				40
1			12		6	7			10^{3}	13	14		8					2				5				11^{2}	9	3	4^{1}		41
1			4		6	7			10		11		8					2				5				3	9^{1}	12			42
1			4		6	11	8		10^{1}		9		7^{2}					2				5				3^{3}	12	14	13		43
1			12		6	7			10		11		8						13			5					9	3	4^{1}	2^{2}	44
1			4		6	11	8		10		9		7					2	12			5						3^{1}			45
1			4		6	11	8^{1}		10^{2}	12	9		7					2	3			5					13				46

Worthington Cup
First Round Coventry C (a) 0-3

LDV Vans Trophy
First Round Cheltenham T (a) 1-4

FA Cup
First Round Chester C (h) 0-1

COVENTRY CITY Division 1

FOUNDATION

Workers at Singers' cycle factory formed a club in 1883. The first success of Singers' FC was to win the Birmingham Junior Cup in 1891 and this led in 1894 to their election to the Birmingham and District League. Four years later they changed their name to Coventry City and joined the Southern League in 1908 at which time they were playing in blue and white quarters.

Highfield Road Stadium, King Richard Street, Coventry CV2 4FW.

Telephone: (024) 7623 4000. ***Fax:*** (024) 7623 4099. ***Ticket Office:*** (024) 7623 4020. ***Ticket Office Fax:*** (024) 7623 4023. ***Sales & Marketing:*** (024) 7623 4010. ***ClubCall:*** 09068 121 166. ***Website:*** http://www.ccfc.co.uk ***Email:*** info@ccfc.co.uk

Ground Capacity: 23,633.

Record Attendance: 51,455 v Wolverhampton W, Division 2, 29 April 1967.

Record Receipts: £405,369 v Charlton Ath, FA Cup 5th rd, 29 January 2000.

Pitch Measurements: 110yd × 75yd.

President: G. Robinson MP.

Chairman: M. C. McGinnity.
Deputy Chairman: J. F. W. Reason.
Directors: A. M. Jepson, J. F. W. Reason, D. A. Higgs, Miss B. Price, G. P. Hover.
Chief Executive: Graham Hover.

Manager: Gary McAllister. ***Assistant Manager:*** Eric Black. ***Physio:*** Stuart Collie.

Stadium Manager: Don Blair.

Club Statistician: Jim Brown.

Colours: Sky blue shirts with navy and white pinstripe, navy sleeves, navy shorts, sky blue stockings with navy and white turnover.

Change Colours: To be announced.

Year Formed: 1883.

Turned Professional: 1893.

Ltd Co.: 1907.

Previous Names: 1883, Singers FC; 1898, Coventry City FC.

Club Nickname: 'Sky Blues'.

Previous Grounds: 1883, Binley Road; 1887, Stoke Road; 1899, Highfield Road.

First Football League Game: 30 August 1919, Division 2, v Tottenham H (h) L 0–5 – Lindon; Roberts, Chaplin, Allan, Hawley, Clarke, Sheldon, Mercer, Sambrooke, Lowes, Gibson.

Record League Victory: 9–0 v Bristol C, Division 3 (S), 28 April 1934 – Pearson; Brown, Bisby; Perry, Davidson, Frith; White (2), Lauderdale, Bourton (5), Jones (2), Lake.

HONOURS

Football League: Division 1 best season: 6th, 1969–70; Division 2 – Champions 1966–67; Division 3 – Champions 1963–64; Division 3 (S) – Champions 1935–36; Runners-up 1933–34; Division 4 – Runners-up 1958–59.

FA Cup: Winners 1987.

Football League Cup: Semi-final 1981, 1990.

European Competitions: *European Fairs Cup:* 1970–71.

SKY SPORTS FACT FILE

The visit of championship challengers Luton Town to Coventry City on 27 April 1936 (1-1) attracted more spectators than the London derby between Arsenal and Chelsea. Highfield Road had 42,809, Highbury 40,402.

Record Cup Victory: 8–0 v Rushden & D, League Cup 2nd rd, 2 October 2002 – Debec; Caldwell, Quinn, Betts (1p), Konjic (Shaw), Davenport, Pipe, Safri (Stanford), Mills (2) (Bothroyd (2)), McSheffery (3), Partridge.

Record Defeat: 2–10 v Norwich C, Division 3 (S), 15 March 1930.

Most League Points (2 for a win): 60, Division 4, 1958–59 and Division 3, 1963–64.

Most League Points (3 for a win): 66, Division 1, 2001–02.

Most League Goals: 108, Division 3 (S), 1931–32.

Highest League Scorer in Season: Clarrie Bourton, 49, Division 3 (S), 1931–32.

Most League Goals in Total Aggregate: Clarrie Bourton, 171, 1931–37.

Most League Goals in One Match: 5, Clarrie Bourton v Bournemouth, Division 3S, 17 October 1931; 5, Arthur Bacon v Gillingham, Division 3S, 30 December 1933.

Most Capped Player: Magnus Hedman 44 (49), Sweden.

Most League Appearances: Steve Ogrizovic, 507, 1984–2000.

Youngest League Player: Ben Mackey, 16 years 167 days v Ipswich T, 12 April 2003.

Record Transfer Fee Received: £12,500,000 from Internazionale for Robbie Keane, July 2000.

Record Transfer Fee Paid: £6,000,000 to Wolverhampton W for Robbie Keane, August 1999.

Football League Record: 1919 Elected to Division 2; 1925–26 Division 3 (N); 1926–36 Division 3 (S); 1936–52 Division 2; 1952–58 Division 3 (S); 1958–59 Division 4; 1959–64 Division 3; 1964–67 Division 2; 1967–92 Division 1; 1992–2001 FA Premier League; 2001– Division 1.

MANAGERS

H. R. Buckle 1909–10
Robert Wallace 1910–13
(Secretary-Manager)
Frank Scott-Walford 1913–15
William Clayton 1917–19
H. Pollitt 1919–20
Albert Evans 1920–24
Jimmy Kerr 1924–28
James McIntyre 1928–31
Harry Storer 1931–45
Dick Bayliss 1945–47
Billy Frith 1947–48
Harry Storer 1948–53
Jack Fairbrother 1953–54
Charlie Elliott 1954–55
Jesse Carver 1955–56
Harry Warren 1956–57
Billy Frith 1957–61
Jimmy Hill 1961–67
Noel Cantwell 1967–72
Bob Dennison 1972
Joe Mercer 1972–75
Gordon Milne 1972–81
Dave Sexton 1981–83
Bobby Gould 1983–84
Don Mackay 1985–86
George Curtis 1986–87
(became Managing Director)
John Sillett 1987–90
Terry Butcher 1990–92
Don Howe 1992
Bobby Gould 1992–93
Phil Neal 1993–95
Ron Atkinson 1995–96
(became Director of Football)
Gordon Strachan 1996–2001
Roland Nilsson 2001–02
Gary McAllister April 2002–

LATEST SEQUENCES

Longest Sequence of League Wins: 6, 25.4.1964 – 5.9.1964.

Longest Sequence of League Defeats: 9, 30.8.1919 – 11.10.1919.

Longest Sequence of League Draws: 6, 28.9.1996 – 16.11.1996.

Longest Sequence of Unbeaten League Matches: 25, 26.11.1966 – 13.5.1967.

Longest Sequence Without a League Win: 19, 30.8.1919 – 20.12.1919.

Successive Scoring Runs: 25 from 10.9.1966.

Successive Non-scoring Runs: 11 from 11.10.1919.

TEN YEAR LEAGUE RECORD

		P	W	D	L	F	A	Pts	Pos
1993-94	PR Lge	42	14	14	14	43	45	56	11
1994-95	PR Lge	42	12	14	16	44	62	50	16
1995-96	PR Lge	38	8	14	16	42	60	38	16
1996-97	PR Lge	38	9	14	15	38	54	41	17
1997-98	PR Lge	38	12	16	10	46	44	52	11
1998-99	PR Lge	38	11	9	18	39	51	42	15
1999-2000	PR Lge	38	12	8	18	47	54	44	14
2000-01	PR Lge	38	8	10	20	36	63	34	19
2001-02	Div 1	46	20	6	20	59	53	66	11
2002-03	Div 1	46	12	14	20	46	62	50	20

DID YOU KNOW?

Vicente Engonga made his debut for Coventry City at the age of 37 years 179 days on 15 February 2003 at Rotherham United, the third player over 37 to turn out for them in the season after Gary McAllister and Steve Walsh.

COVENTRY CITY 2002–03 LEAGUE RECORD

Match No.	Date	Venue	Opponents	Result		H/T Score	Lg. Pos.	Goalscorers	Attendance
1	Aug 10	H	Sheffield U	W	2-1	2-1	—	Bothroyd [16], McSheffrey [40]	18,839
2	13	A	Brighton & HA	D	0-0	0-0	—		6816
3	17	A	Reading	W	2-1	0-1	5	Davenport [74], Bothroyd [81]	14,712
4	24	H	Crystal Palace	W	1-0	1-0	4	Hughes (pen) [5]	15,526
5	26	A	Watford	L	2-5	0-3	6	McSheffrey [86], Eustace [90]	11,136
6	31	H	Nottingham F	L	0-1	0-1	8		13,732
7	Sept 14	H	Grimsby T	W	3-2	0-0	5	Mills [49], McAllister (pen) [69], Bothroyd [87]	12,403
8	18	H	Sheffield W	D	1-1	0-0	—	Normann [76]	14,178
9	21	A	Wimbledon	W	1-0	1-0	6	McAllister (pen) [8]	2077
10	24	A	Bradford C	D	1-1	0-1	—	Bothroyd [83]	11,655
11	28	H	Millwall	L	2-3	2-1	7	McSheffrey [31], Mills [45]	13,562
12	Oct 5	A	Gillingham	W	2-0	0-0	6	Bothroyd [46], Pipe [53]	7722
13	19	A	Portsmouth	D	1-1	0-0	7	Davenport [60]	18,837
14	23	H	Norwich C	D	1-1	1-0	—	Partridge [22]	16,409
15	26	H	Walsall	D	0-0	0-0	7		14,544
16	29	A	Leicester C	L	1-2	0-0	—	Partridge [53]	27,139
17	Nov 2	H	Rotherham U	W	2-1	1-1	7	McAllister 2 [38, 82]	13,179
18	9	A	Burnley	L	1-3	0-2	8	McAllister (pen) [66]	13,470
19	16	H	Wolverhampton W	L	0-2	0-1	10		18,998
20	23	A	Ipswich T	L	1-2	0-1	12	Eustace [74]	23,633
21	30	H	Preston NE	L	1-2	0-1	15	Davenport [80]	13,313
22	Dec 7	A	Stoke C	W	2-1	2-1	14	Bothroyd 2 [16, 21]	12,760
23	14	A	Wolverhampton W	W	2-0	1-0	12	McAllister [8], Partridge [65]	25,577
24	21	H	Derby Co	W	3-0	2-0	10	McAllister [30], Hignett [35], Bothroyd [54]	13,185
25	26	H	Reading	W	2-0	1-0	6	Hignett [39], Partridge [52]	19,526
26	28	A	Sheffield U	D	0-0	0-0	8		20,465
27	Jan 1	A	Crystal Palace	D	1-1	0-0	8	McSheffrey [69]	17,362
28	11	H	Brighton & HA	D	0-0	0-0	6		15,951
29	18	A	Nottingham F	D	1-1	0-1	6	Sara [87]	24,487
30	Feb 1	H	Watford	L	0-1	0-0	9		17,393
31	8	H	Burnley	L	0-1	0-1	11		13,659
32	15	A	Rotherham U	L	0-1	0-1	11		6524
33	22	H	Bradford C	L	0-2	0-1	13		12,525
34	Mar 1	A	Grimsby T	W	2-0	1-0	13	Ford (og) [17], Eustace (pen) [63]	5736
35	5	A	Sheffield W	L	1-5	0-1	—	Joachim [54]	19,536
36	8	H	Wimbledon	D	2-2	1-1	13	Eustace [21], Joachim [74]	11,796
37	15	A	Norwich C	L	0-2	0-1	15		20,099
38	19	H	Portsmouth	L	0-4	0-3	—		13,922
39	22	H	Leicester C	L	1-2	0-0	16	Jansen [71]	16,610
40	Apr 5	A	Preston NE	D	2-2	0-1	18	Pead 2 [52, 62]	13,026
41	12	H	Ipswich T	L	2-4	2-0	19	Jansen [23], Gordon [44]	13,968
42	15	A	Walsall	D	0-0	0-0	—		7337
43	19	A	Derby Co	L	0-1	0-0	19		23,921
44	21	H	Stoke C	L	0-1	0-0	20		12,675
45	26	H	Gillingham	D	0-0	0-0	20		14,795
46	May 4	A	Millwall	L	0-2	0-0	20		9220

Final League Position: 20

GOALSCORERS

League (46): Bothroyd 8, McAllister 7 (3 pens), Eustace 4 (1 pen), McSheffrey 4, Partridge 4, Davenport 3, Hignett 2, Jansen 2, Joachim 2, Mills 2, Pead 2, Gordon 1, Hughes 1 (pen), Normann 1, Pipe 1, Sara 1, own goal 1.
Worthington Cup (11): McSheffrey 4, Mills 3, Bothroyd 2, Betts 1 (pen), McAllister 1.
FA Cup (5): Bothroyd 1, Fowler 1, Holdsworth 1, Mills 1, McAllister 1 (pen).

Hyldgaard M 27	Shaw R 27 + 2	Gordon D 30	Eustace J 23 + 9	Konjic M 42	Davenport C 26 + 6	Delorge L 2	McAllister G 41	Bothroyd J 24 + 9	Joachim J 10 + 1	Chippo Y 20 + 3	McSheffrey G 14 + 15	Mills L 11 + 7 / Mackey B — + 3	Quinn B 13 + 5	Thompson D 4 / Bates T — + 1	Hughes L 3 + 1	Safri Y 24 + 3 / Cooney S — + 1	Walsh S 1 + 1	Pead C 17 + 7	Caldwell G 36	Pipe D 11 + 10	Normann R 2 + 1	Debec F 11 / Noon M — + 2	Partridge R 23 + 4	Kerr B 2 + 1 / Osbourne I 2	Hignett C 7 + 1	McMaster J 2 / Stanford E — + 1	Montgomery G 8	Holdsworth D 13 + 4	Strachan G — + 1	Betts R 1	Sara J 1 + 2	Fowler L 1	Whing A 13 + 1	Engonga V 5 + 3	Yulu C 1 + 2	Jansen M 8 + 1	Jephcott A — + 1	*Match No.*
1	2	3	4	5	6	7¹	8	9²	10	11³	12	13	14																									1
1	2	3	4	5	6■		8	9¹	10²		14		12	7³	13	11																						2
1	2	3	4	5	6		8²	12	10¹	13				7	9	11																						3
1	2	3	4	5	6			12	10²	11¹			13	7	9³	8■	14																					4
1	2	3	4		6		8	10¹			12		13	7	9	11³	5²	14																				5
1	5	3	4				8	9¹		7	10³	12	2			11²		13	6	14																		6
1	4	3	7¹	5			8	9		2		10				11			6	12																		7
1		3²	14	5	6	7¹	8	9³		2		10				11			4	12	13																	8
		3		5	6		8	9¹		7	10²	12				11			4	13	2	1																9
		3		5	6		8	9		7²	10	12				11			4	13	2¹	1																10
		3		5	6		8	9¹		2²	10	7	12			11			4			1	13															11
	12			5	6		4	13³		14	10²	9	3			8			2	7¹		1	11															12
				5	6		10	12		4	13	9¹	3			8			2	7²		1	11															13
			12	5	6		8¹	13		4	10³	9²	3			7			2	14		1	11															14
1		3	12	5	6			9¹		4²	10³	13				8			2	7			11	14														15
1		3	4	5	6		10	12				9¹				8			2	13			11²	7														16
1		3	4²	5	6		10		12			9				8			2				11	7¹	13													17
		3	12	5	6		4			13	14	9²				8¹			2³	7		1	11		10■													18
		3	12	5	6		4¹			7	13	9³				8²			2	14		1	11		10													19
		3	12	5	6		4	13		7	10					8¹			2	14		1	11³			9²												20
		3	4¹	5	6		8	13		7	10³					12			2				14			9²	1	11										21
1	6			5			4	9					3			8		12	2				11		7¹			10										22
1	6			5			4	9²			12		3			8		13	2				11		7			10¹										23
1	6		12	5			4¹	9³				13	3					8	2				11		7			10²	14									24
1	6		12	5			4	9²					3			13		8¹	2				11		7			10										25
1	6	3■	12	5			4	9			13					8		14	2				11²		7³			10¹										26
1	6	3		5			8	7¹			12	9						4	2				11					10										27
1	6		4¹	5			8				13	12	3					7					11					10		2	9²							28
1	6	3		5	12		8	9²			13							7¹	4■				11³					10			14	2						29
1	6	3¹		5	12		4	9²		7■	10		2³					8					11					13			14							30
1	6			5	12		4	13			9		3¹					8	11	7³			14					10²					2					31
1	6		4	5			8	9					3²						2	7			12					10¹						11	13			32
1	6			5	12		4		9				3¹					7²	2				11					13						8		10		33
			4	5	6				9	7								8¹	2			1	11										3	12		10		34
			4	5	6				9	7	12							8¹	2			1	11					13					3			10²		35
1	6		4	5¹	12		8³		9	7²	10■							13	2				11					14					3					36
1	5		4		6		8		9	7						12		13	3				11¹					10					2²					37
1	5		4		6		8		9	7²	12					11¹		2	3									10					13					38
1	6	3	4	5			8	9²								11		7¹		10													2			12	13	39
	6	3	4	5			8	9			12							11		7¹							1						2	13		10²		40
	6	3	4	5	12		8	9²				13		14				11³		7¹							1						2			10		41
	6	3	7	5			8	9			12							11	4								1						2			10¹		42
	6	3	7	5			8	9			10²							11	4								1						2¹	12	13			43
		3	7	5	6						9	13						11	4	12							1						2	8²	10¹			44
		3		5²	6		8³					12				13			4	9		14		11			1						2	7		10¹		45
	12	3³		5	6		8												4	9		13		11¹		14	1						2	7²		10		46

Worthington Cup

First Round	Colchester U	(h)	3-0
Second Round	Rushden & D	(h)	8-0
Third Round	Crystal Palace	(a)	0-3

FA Cup

Third Round	Cardiff C	(a)	2-2
		(h)	3-0
Fourth Round	Rochdale	(a)	0-2

CREWE ALEXANDRA Division 1

FOUNDATION

The first match played at Crewe was on 1 December 1877 against Basford, the leading North Staffordshire team of that time. During the club's history they have also played in a number of other leagues including the Football Alliance, Football Combination, Lancashire League, Manchester League, Central League and Lancashire Combination. Two former players, Aaron Scragg in 1899 and Jackie Pearson in 1911, had the distinction of refereeing FA Cup finals. Pearson was also capped for England against Ireland in 1892.

Football Ground, Gresty Road, Crewe CW2 6EB.

Telephone: (01270) 213 014. ***ClubCall:*** 09068 121 647.

Website: www.crewealex.net

Email: info@crewealex.net

Ground Capacity: 10,046.

Record Attendance: 20,000 v Tottenham H, FA Cup 4th rd, 30 January 1960.

Record Receipts: £102,877 v Everton, FA Cup 5th rd replay, 26 February 2002.

Pitch Measurements: 112yd × 74yd.

President: N. Rowlinson.

Chairman: J. Bowler.

Vice-chairman: N. Hassall.

Directors: D. Rowlinson, R. Clayton, J. McMillan, D. Gradi.

Manager: Dario Gradi MBE.

Business Operations Manager: Alison Bowler.

Finance Operations Manager: Andrew Blakemore.

Stadium Operations Manager: Cliff Simpson.

Colours: Red shirts, white shorts, red stockings.

Change Colours: Silver shirts, navy shorts, silver stockings.

Year Formed: 1877.

Turned Professional: 1893.

Ltd Co.: 1892.

Club Nickname: 'Railwaymen'.

First Football League Game: 3 September 1892, Division 2, v Burton Swifts (a) L 1–7 – Hickton; Moore, Cope; Linnell, Johnson, Osborne; Bennett, Pearson (1), Bailey, Barnett, Roberts.

Record League Victory: 8–0 v Rotherham U, Division 3 (N), 1 October 1932 – Foster; Pringle, Dawson; Ward, Keenor (1), Turner (1); Gillespie, Swindells (1), McConnell (2), Deacon (2), Weale (1).

HONOURS

Football League: Divison 2 – Runners-up 2002–03; Promoted from Division 2 1996–97 (play-offs).

FA Cup: Semi-final 1888.

Football League Cup: best season: 3rd rd, 1975, 1976, 1979, 1993, 1999, 2000, 2002.

Welsh Cup: Winners 1936, 1937.

SKY SPORTS FACT FILE

In 1938–39 Crewe Alexandra had four players achieving hat-tricks: Tom Foster (one), Lee Stevens (two plus four goals), Matthew Johnson (two) and Arthur Rice (one four). The club finished eighth.

Record Cup Victory: 8–0 v Hartlepool U, Auto Windscreens Shield 1st rd, 17 October 1995 – Gayle; Collins (1), Booty, Westwood (Unsworth), Macauley (1), Whalley (1), Garvey (1), Murphy (1), Savage (1) (Rivers (1p)), Lennon, Edwards, (1 og). 8–0 v Doncaster R, LDV Vans Trophy 3rd rd, 10 November 2002 – Bankole; Wright, Walker, Foster, Tierney; Lunt (1), Brammer, Sorvel, Vaughan (1) (Bell); Ashton (3) (Miles), Jack (2) (Jones (1)).

Record Defeat: 2–13 v Tottenham H, FA Cup 4th rd replay, 3 February 1960.

Most League Points (2 for a win): 59, Division 4, 1962–63.

Most League Points (3 for a win): 86, Division 2, 2002–03.

Most League Goals: 95, Division 3 (N), 1931–32.

Highest League Scorer in Season: Terry Harkin, 35, Division 4, 1964–65.

Most League Goals in Total Aggregate: Bert Swindells, 126, 1928–37.

Most League Goals in One Match: 5, Tony Naylor v Colchester U, Division 3, 24 April 1993.

Most Capped Player: Clayton Ince (29), Trinidad & Tobago.

Most League Appearances: Tommy Lowry, 436, 1966–78.

Youngest League Player: Steve Walters, 16 years 119 days v Peterborough U, 6 May 1988.

Record Transfer Fee Received: £3,000,000 Derby Co for Seth Johnson, May 1999.

Record Transfer Fee Paid: £650,000 to Torquay U for Rodney Jack, June 1998.

Football League Record: 1892 Original Member of Division 2; 1896 Failed re-election; 1921 Re-entered Division 3 (N); 1958–63 Division 4; 1963–64 Division 3; 1964–68 Division 4; 1968–69 Division 3; 1969–89 Division 4; 1989–91 Division 3; 1991–92 Division 4; 1992–94 Division 3; 1994–97 Division 2; 1997–2002 Division 1; 2002–03 Division 2; 2003– Division 1.

MANAGERS

W. C. McNeill 1892–94 *(Secretary-Manager)*
J. G. Hall 1895–96 *(Secretary-Manager)*
R. Roberts *(1st team Secretary-Manager)* 1897
J. B. Blomerley 1898–1911 *(Secretary-Manager, continued as Hon. Secretary to 1925)*
Tom Bailey *(Secretary only)* 1925–38
George Lillycrop *(Trainer)* 1938–44
Frank Hill 1944–48
Arthur Turner 1948–51
Harry Catterick 1951–53
Ralph Ward 1953–55
Maurice Lindley 1956–57
Willie Cook 1957–58
Harry Ware 1958–60
Jimmy McGuigan 1960–64
Ernie Tagg 1964–71 *(continued as Secretary to 1972)*
Dennis Viollet 1971
Jimmy Melia 1972–74
Ernie Tagg 1974
Harry Gregg 1975–78
Warwick Rimmer 1978–79
Tony Waddington 1979–81
Arfon Griffiths 1981–82
Peter Morris 1982–83
Dario Gradi June 1983–

LATEST SEQUENCES

Longest Sequence of League Wins: 7, 30.4.1994 – 3.9.1994.

Longest Sequence of League Defeats: 10, 16.4.1979 – 22.8.1979.

Longest Sequence of League Draws: 5, 31.8.1987 – 18.9.1987.

Longest Sequence of Unbeaten League Matches: 17, 25.3.1995 – 16.9.1995.

Longest Sequence Without a League Win: 30, 22.9.1956 – 6.4.1957.

Successive Scoring Runs: 26 from 7.4.1934.

Successive Non-scoring Runs: 9 from 6.11.1974.

TEN YEAR LEAGUE RECORD

		P	*W*	*D*	*L*	*F*	*A*	*Pts*	*Pos*
1993-94	Div 3	42	21	10	11	80	61	73	3
1994-95	Div 2	46	25	8	13	80	68	83	3
1995-96	Div 2	46	22	7	17	77	60	73	5
1996-97	Div 2	46	22	7	17	56	47	73	6
1997-98	Div 1	46	18	5	23	58	65	59	11
1998-99	Div 1	46	12	12	22	54	78	48	18
1999-2000	Div 1	46	14	9	23	46	67	51	19
2000-01	Div 1	46	15	10	21	47	62	55	14
2001-02	Div 1	46	12	13	21	47	76	49	22
2002-03	Div 2	46	25	11	10	76	40	86	2

DID YOU KNOW?

On 22 September 1957 Crewe Alexandra beat Wrexham 1-0 with a goal from Arthur Rowley (!) away and then completed their first League double for five years by winning the return match 2-0 on 2 October, courtesy of Mike Moran and Stan Smith.

CREWE ALEXANDRA 2002–03 LEAGUE RECORD

Match No.	Date	Venue	Opponents	Result		H/T Score	Lg. Pos.	Goalscorers	Attendance
1	Aug 10	A	Northampton T	D	1-1	1-0	—	Sorvel [30]	5694
2	13	H	Notts Co	L	0-3	0-2	—		6141
3	17	H	Colchester U	W	2-0	1-0	14	Hulse [9], Bell [81]	5138
4	24	A	Huddersfield T	D	1-1	1-1	16	Hulse [17]	8467
5	27	H	Cheltenham T	W	1-0	1-0	—	Jack [44]	5488
6	31	A	Mansfield T	W	5-0	3-0	4	Walker [30], Jack [36], Hulse [38], Foster [48], Lunt [65]	4183
7	Sept 7	H	Chesterfield	D	0-0	0-0	5		5837
8	14	A	Peterborough U	D	0-0	0-0	8		4345
9	17	A	Wycombe W	W	2-1	2-1	—	Hulse 2 [26, 31]	4909
10	21	H	Tranmere R	W	2-0	0-0	5	Curtis (og) [57], Hulse [73]	6875
11	28	A	Cardiff C	L	1-2	0-0	6	Hulse [48]	13,208
12	Oct 5	H	QPR	W	2-0	1-0	5	Jones 2 [29, 69]	7683
13	12	A	Stockport Co	W	4-1	2-0	4	Lunt [6], Hulse 2 [31, 85], Jones [53]	6468
14	19	H	Plymouth Arg	L	0-1	0-1	6		6733
15	26	A	Port Vale	W	2-1	1-0	5	Hulse 2 [32, 81]	6374
16	29	H	Luton T	L	0-1	0-0	—		6030
17	Nov 2	A	Wigan Ath	L	0-2	0-2	7		7086
18	9	H	Brentford	W	2-1	1-0	5	Hulse 2 [21, 82]	5663
19	23	H	Blackpool	W	3-0	1-0	5	Hulse [8], Sodje [59], Tierney [63]	7019
20	30	A	Bristol C	D	2-2	2-0	5	Foster [32], Hulse [35]	12,585
21	Dec 14	H	Barnsley	W	2-0	1-0	5	Foster [17], Jack [82]	5633
22	21	A	Swindon T	W	3-1	2-0	5	Ashton [18], Foster [40], Jack [59]	4957
23	26	A	Cheltenham T	W	4-0	3-0	4	Ashton [6], Vaughan [38], Jack [40], Brammer (pen) [67]	5548
24	29	H	Oldham Ath	L	1-2	0-1	5	Hulse [56]	9006
25	Jan 1	H	Mansfield T	W	2-0	0-0	5	Walton [60], Miles [90]	6931
26	11	A	Colchester U	W	2-1	0-1	3	Jones 2 [56, 62]	2949
27	18	H	Huddersfield T	W	1-0	0-0	3	Jones [89]	5819
28	25	A	Oldham Ath	W	3-1	0-0	2	Hulse 2 [60, 86], Ashton [88]	7597
29	Feb 1	H	Northampton T	D	3-3	2-1	2	Jones 2 [39, 70], Vaughan [41]	6164
30	4	A	Notts Co	D	2-2	2-0	—	Jones [2], Hulse [13]	3875
31	8	A	Brentford	W	2-1	0-1	3	Lunt 2 (1 pen) [52, 64 (p)]	5424
32	22	A	Chesterfield	W	2-0	1-0	2	Wright [33], Jack [85]	3956
33	25	H	Wigan Ath	L	0-1	0-1	—		8917
34	Mar 1	H	Peterborough U	L	0-1	0-0	2		5704
35	4	H	Wycombe W	W	4-2	2-1	—	Ashton 2 [8, 62], Lunt (pen) [24], Hulse [59]	5398
36	8	A	Tranmere R	L	1-2	0-1	2	Hulse [47]	8670
37	15	H	Port Vale	D	1-1	0-0	2	Sorvel [54]	8146
38	18	A	Plymouth Arg	W	3-1	2-0	—	Jack [4], Ashton 2 [13, 68]	7777
39	22	A	Luton T	W	4-0	2-0	2	Ashton 2 [7, 21], Vaughan [50], Jack [78]	6607
40	29	H	Stockport Co	W	1-0	0-0	2	Jack [77]	7336
41	Apr 12	A	Blackpool	W	1-0	0-0	2	Lunt [69]	7623
42	15	H	Bristol C	D	1-1	1-0	—	Lunt (pen) [15]	7901
43	19	H	Swindon T	L	0-1	0-0	2		6384
44	21	A	Barnsley	W	2-1	1-1	2	Sorvel [34], Hulse [62]	9396
45	26	A	QPR	D	0-0	0-0	2		16,921
46	May 3	H	Cardiff C	D	1-1	1-0	2	Walker [45]	9562

Final League Position: 2

GOALSCORERS

League (76): Hulse 22, Ashton 9, Jack 9, Jones 9, Lunt 7 (3 pens), Foster 4, Sorvel 3, Vaughan 3, Walker 2, Bell 1, Brammer 1 (pen), Miles 1, Sodje 1, Tierney 1, Walton 1, Wright 1, own goal 1.
Worthington Cup (4): Jack 3, Hulse 1.
FA Cup (6): Ashton 2, Brammer 1 (pen), Jones 1, Rix 1, Sodje 1.
LDV Vans Trophy (16): Ashton 5, Hulse 4, Jack 4, Jones 1, Lunt 1, Vaughan 1.

Ince C 43	Wright D 31	Sodje E 23 + 7	Brammer D 41	Foster S 35	Vaughan D 28 + 4	Rix B 17 + 6	Lunt K 46	Hulse R 35 + 3	Ashton D 24 + 15	Sorvel N 39 + 4	Bell L 3 + 14	Little C 3 + 3	Jones S 18 + 13	Burton S 1	Miles J — + 5	Walker R 31 + 4	Jack R 35 + 3	Walton D 27 + 1	White A — + 2	Tierney P 14 + 3	Bankole A 2 + 1	Edwards P — + 2	Milosevic D 1	Tomlinson S — + 1	McCready C 6 + 2	Robinson J — + 1	Oakes S 3 + 4	*Match No.*
1	2	3	4	5	6	7^{1}	8	9	10	11^{2}	12	13																1
1	2	3	4^{2}	5	6^{1}	7	8	9	10	11	12		13															2
1	2	3	4	5	6		8	9^{3}	10	11^{1}	12		13	7^{2}	14													3
1	2	3	4	5	12	7^{1}	8	9	10^{2}	11						6	13											4
1	2		4	5	3	7^{1}	8	9^{2}	10^{3}		12		13		14	6	11											5
1	2		4	5	3		8^{1}	9^{3}		11	12	7	13		14	6	10^{2}											6
1	2	3	4^{2}	5			8		10	11		7^{1}	12		13	6	9											7
1	2		4	5	3		8	9		11		7^{1}	12			6	10											8
1	2	3	4	5		7^{1}	8	9	12	11						6	10											9
1	2	3	4	5		7^{1}	8	9^{2}	12	11	13					6	10											10
1	2	3	4	5			8	9	10	11			12			6	7^{1}											11
1	2	3	4	5		7^{3}	8	9	12		14	13	10^{2}			6	11^{1}											12
1	2	3	4	5		7^{1}	8	9	13	12			11^{2}			6	10											13
1	2	3	4	5		7	8	9	12				11				10^{1}	6										14
1	2	3	4	5		12	8	9	13	11^{1}			10^{2}			6	7											15
1	2	3	4	5		12	8	9	13	11^{1}			10^{2}			6	7											16
1	2	3^{1}	4	5		7^{2}	8	9	12	11						6■	10^{3}	13	14									17
1	2		4	5		7^{1}	8	9	13	11^{2}			12				10	6		3								18
1		2^{2}	4^{1}	5	7		8	9^{3}	10	12						13	11	6	14	3								19
1	2		4	5	11		8	9	10^{1}	12							7	6		3								20
1	2		4	5	12	7^{1}	8		10	11							9	6		3								21
1	2		4	5	7	12	8		10	11							9^{1}	6		3								22
1		2	4	5	7		8^{3}		10	11	14		13			12	9	6^{1}		3^{2}								23
1	2		4	5■	12		8	9	10^{1}	11^{2}			13				7	6		3								24
1	2	12	4	5	11	7	8			13			10^{3}		14		9^{2}	6		3^{1}								25
1	2	12	4	5	13	7^{2}	8	9^{1}		11	14		10^{3}					6		3								26
	2^{2}	3	4	5	7		8	9		11			10^{1}			12		6			1	13						27
	2		4	5		7^{1}	8	9	12	11			10			13		6^{2}		3			1^{G}	15				28
	2		4		7		8	9	12	11^{1}			10			6	13			3^{2}	1				5			29
1	2	12	4		3		8	9		11			10			6	7^{1}								5			30
1	2	12			3	7^{2}	4	9	13^{3}	11	14		10^{1}			6	8	5										31
1	2				3		4	9^{1}	10	11^{2}	12		8			6	7^{3}	5		13					14			32
1		2■			3		4	9	13	11	7^{1}		10^{3}			6	8	5		14					12^{2}			33
1		12			3		4	9^{2}	13	11	7		10^{3}			6	8	5							2^{1}	14		34
1	2^{1}	12			3		4	9	10^{2}	11	7		13^{3}			6	8	5		14								35
1^{G}		2	4^{1}		3		7	9	10	11	12					6	8	5			15							36
1			4		7		8		10	11						6	9	5		3					2			37
1		12	4				8		10^{3}	11	13					6	9	5		3^{1}		14			2		7^{2}	38
1			4		7		8		10^{2}	11		12				6	9^{1}	5		3					2		13	39
1		2	4	3			8	12	10	11						6	9	5									7^{1}	40
1		2^{1}	4	3	7		8	12	10^{2}	11						6	9	5									13	41
1		3	4	2	7^{3}		8^{1}	12	10^{2}	11			13			6	9	5									14	42
1			4	2	3	12	8	9	10^{1}	11			7			6		5										43
1			4	2	3	12	8	9^{2}	10^{1}	11			7			6		5									13	44
1			4	2	3	12	8	9		11			13			6	10^{1}	5									7^{2}	45
1		2	4^{2}	5	3	7^{3}	8	9^{1}	12	11	14		10			6	13											46

Worthington Cup

First Round	Port Vale	(a)	2-0
Second Round	Manchester C	(a)	2-3

FA Cup

First Round	Port Vale	(a)	1-0
Second Round	Mansfield T	(h)	3-0
Third Round	Bournemouth	(a)	0-0
		(h)	2-2

LDV Vans Trophy

First Round	Mansfield T	(a)	4-0
Second Round	Blackpool	(h)	2-0
Quarter-final	Doncaster R	(h)	8-0
Semi-final	Shrewsbury T	(a)	2-4

CRYSTAL PALACE Division 1

FOUNDATION

There was a Crystal Palace club as early as 1861 but the present organisation was born in 1905 after the formation of a club by the company that controlled the Crystal Palace (building), had been rejected by the FA who did not like the idea of the Cup Final hosts running their own club. A separate company had to be formed and they had their home on the old Cup Final ground until 1915.

Selhurst Park, London SE25 6PU.

Telephone: (020) 8768 6000. ***Fax:*** (020) 8771 5311.
Club Shop: (020) 8768 6100.
Dial-A-Seat Ticketline: (020) 8771 8841.
Communications: (020) 8768 6020.
Fax: (020) 8768 6114. ***ClubCall:*** 09068 400 333.
Website: www.cpfc.co.uk
Email: info@cpfc.co.uk

Ground Capacity: 26,400.

Record Attendance: 51,482 v Burnley, Division 2, 11 May 1979.

Record Receipts: £327,124 v Manchester U, FA Premier League, 21 April 1993 (League); £336,583 v Chelsea, Coca-Cola Cup 5th rd, 6 January 1993.

Pitch Measurements: 110yd × 74yd.

Chairman: Simon Jordan.

Manager: Steve Kember.

Physio: George Cooper.

Stadium Manager: Kevin Corner.

Communications Manager: Terry Byfield.

Colours: Red and blue vertical striped shirts, red shorts, red stockings with blue tops.

Change Colours: All white with red and blue sash on shirt.

Year Formed: 1905. ***Turned Professional:*** 1905. ***Ltd Co.:*** 1905.

Club Nickname: 'The Eagles'.

Previous Grounds: 1905, Crystal Palace; 1915, Herne Hill; 1918, The Nest; 1924, Selhurst Park.

First Football League Game: 28 August 1920, Division 3, v Merthyr T (a) L 1–2 – Alderson; Little, Rhodes; McCracken, Jones, Feebury; Bateman, Conner, Smith, Milligan (1), Whibley.

Record League Victory: 9–0 v Barrow, Division 4, 10 October 1959 – Rouse; Long, Noakes; Truett, Evans, McNichol; Gavin (1), Summersby (4 incl. 1p), Sexton, Byrne (2), Colfar (2).

Record Cup Victory: 8–0 v Southend U, Rumbelows League Cup 2nd rd (1st leg), 25 September 1989 – Martyn; Humphrey (Thompson (1)), Shaw, Pardew, Young, Thorn, McGoldrick, Thomas, Bright (3), Wright (3), Barber (Hodges (1)).

HONOURS

Football League: Division 1 – Champions 1993–94; Promoted from Division 1, 1996–97 (play-offs); Division 2 – Champions 1978–79; Runners-up 1968–69; Division 3 – Runners-up 1963–64; Division 3 (S) – Champions 1920–21; Runners-up 1928–29, 1930–31, 1938–39; Division 4 – Runners-up 1960–61.

FA Cup: Runners-up 1990.

Football League Cup: Semi-final 1993, 1995, 2001.

Zenith Data Systems Cup: Winners 1991.

European Competition: *Intertoto Cup:* 1998.

SKY SPORTS FACT FILE

In 1926 Crystal Palace were honoured by having goalkeeper Billy Callender chosen for the Football League representative team. He had joined them in 1923 and was to make over 200 League appearances, before dying in tragic circumstances.

Record Defeat: 0–9 v Burnley, FA Cup 2nd rd replay, 10 February 1909. 0–9 v Liverpool, Division 1, 12 September 1990.

Most League Points (2 for a win): 64, Division 4, 1960–61.

Most League Points (3 for a win): 90, Division 1, 1993–94.

Most League Goals: 110, Division 4, 1960–61.

Highest League Scorer in Season: Peter Simpson, 46, Division 3 (S), 1930–31.

Most League Goals in Total Aggregate: Peter Simpson, 153, 1930–36.

Most League Goals in One Match: 6, Peter Simpson v Exeter C, Division 3S, 4 October 1930.

Most Capped Player: Aleksandrs Kolinko 23 (38), Latvia.

Most League Appearances: Jim Cannon, 571, 1973–88.

Youngest League Player: Phil Hoadley, 16 years 112 days v Bolton W, 27 April 1968.

Record Transfer Fee Received: £4,500,000 from Tottenham H for Chris Armstrong, June 1995.

Record Transfer Fee Paid: £2,750,000 to RC Strasbourg for Valerien Ismael, January 1998.

Football League Record: 1920 Original Members of Division 3; 1921–25 Division 2; 1925–58 Division 3 (S); 1958–61 Division 4; 1961–64 Division 3; 1964–69 Division 2; 1969–73 Division 1; 1973–74 Division 2; 1974–77 Division 3; 1977–79 Division 2; 1979–81 Division 1; 1981–89 Division 2; 1989–92 Division 1; 1992–93 FA Premier League; 1993–94 Division 1; 1994–95 FA Premier League; 1995–97 Division 1; 1997–98 FA Premier League; 1998– Division 1.

LATEST SEQUENCES

Longest Sequence of League Wins: 8, 9.2.1921 – 26.3.1921.

Longest Sequence of League Defeats: 8, 10.1.1998 – 14.3.1998.

Longest Sequence of League Draws: 5, 21.9.2002 – 19.10.2002.

Longest Sequence of Unbeaten League Matches: 18, 22.2.1969 – 13.8.1969.

Longest Sequence Without a League Win: 20, 3.3.1962 – 8.9.1962.

Successive Scoring Runs: 24 from 27.4.1929.

Successive Non-scoring Runs: 9 from 19.11.1994.

MANAGERS

John T. Robson 1905–07
Edmund Goodman 1907–25 *(had been Secretary since 1905 and afterwards continued in this position to 1933)*
Alec Maley 1925–27
Fred Mavin 1927–30
Jack Tresadern 1930–35
Tom Bromilow 1935–36
R. S. Moyes 1936
Tom Bromilow 1936–39
George Irwin 1939–47
Jack Butler 1947–49
Ronnie Rooke 1949–50
Charlie Slade and Fred Dawes *(Joint Managers)* 1950–51
Laurie Scott 1951–54
Cyril Spiers 1954–58
George Smith 1958–60
Arthur Rowe 1960–62
Dick Graham 1962–66
Bert Head 1966–72 *(continued as General Manager to 1973)*
Malcolm Allison 1973–76
Terry Venables 1976–80
Ernie Walley 1980
Malcolm Allison 1980–81
Dario Gradi 1981
Steve Kember 1981–82
Alan Mullery 1982–84
Steve Coppell 1984–93
Alan Smith 1993–95
Steve Coppell *(Technical Director)* 1995–96
Dave Bassett 1996–97
Steve Coppell 1997–98
Attilio Lombardo 1998
Terry Venables *(Head Coach)* 1998–99
Steve Coppell 1999–2000
Alan Smith 2000–01
Steve Bruce 2001
Trevor Francis 2001–03
Steve Kember June 2003–

TEN YEAR LEAGUE RECORD

		P	W	D	L	F	A	Pts	Pos
1993-94	Div 1	46	27	9	10	73	46	90	1
1994-95	PR Lge	42	11	12	19	34	49	45	19
1995-96	Div 1	46	20	15	11	67	48	75	3
1996-97	Div 1	46	19	14	13	78	48	71	6
1997-98	PR Lge	38	8	9	21	37	71	33	20
1998-99	Div 1	46	14	16	16	58	71	58	14
1999-2000	Div 1	46	13	15	18	57	67	54	15
2000-01	Div 1	46	12	13	21	57	70	49	21
2001-02	Div 1	46	20	6	20	70	62	66	10
2002-03	Div 1	46	14	17	15	59	52	59	14

DID YOU KNOW?

Crystal Palace goalkeeper John Jackson made 393 League and Cup appearances for the club between 1964–65 and 1973–74 including five successive seasons in which he did not miss a single match.

CRYSTAL PALACE 2002–03 LEAGUE RECORD

Match No.	*Date*	*Venue*	*Opponents*	*Result*	*H/T Score*	*Lg. Pos.*	*Goalscorers*	*Attendance*
1	Aug 10	A	Preston NE	W 2-1	0-0	—	Powell [69], Kabba [86]	14,663
2	13	H	Bradford C	D 1-1	0-0	—	Popovic [80]	15,205
3	17	H	Portsmouth	L 2-3	2-0	11	Freedman [40], Popovic [43]	18,315
4	24	A	Coventry C	L 0-1	0-1	14		15,526
5	27	H	Leicester C	D 0-0	0-0	—		15,440
6	31	A	Burnley	D 0-0	0-0	18		12,407
7	Sept 14	H	Wolverhampton W	W 4-2	2-1	15	Routledge [1], Freedman 2 (1 pen) [36, 62 (p)], Thomson [71]	16,961
8	17	H	Derby Co	L 0-1	0-0	—		14,948
9	21	A	Watford	D 3-3	3-2	16	Mullins 2 [24, 45], Granville [41]	12,153
10	25	A	Sheffield W	D 0-0	0-0	—		16,112
11	29	H	Gillingham	D 2-2	0-1	16	Granville [47], Routledge [70]	15,699
12	Oct 5	A	Stoke C	D 1-1	0-0	17	Adebola [77]	14,214
13	19	A	Wimbledon	D 2-2	1-0	17	Gray [15], Johnson [71]	6538
14	26	H	Brighton & HA	W 5-0	2-0	15	Johnson 3 (1 pen) [4, 35, 55 (p)], Freedman (pen) [51], Gray [57]	21,796
15	29	A	Walsall	W 4-3	1-2	—	Johnson 3 [29, 64, 90], Freedman [58]	6368
16	Nov 3	A	Ipswich T	W 2-1	1-1	12	Johnson [19], Butterfield [78]	24,941
17	9	H	Nottingham F	D 0-0	0-0	12		18,971
18	16	A	Norwich C	L 0-2	0-1	13		20,907
19	23	H	Grimsby T	W 2-0	1-0	11	Derry [39], Adebola [61]	20,093
20	26	H	Reading	L 0-1	0-1	—		15,712
21	30	A	Sheffield U	L 1-2	0-1	14	Riihilahti [69]	16,686
22	Dec 7	H	Millwall	W 1-0	0-0	12	Granville [73]	19,301
23	14	H	Norwich C	W 2-0	2-0	10	Adebola [6], Black [27]	16,791
24	22	A	Rotherham U	W 3-1	2-0	9	Black 2 [12, 51], Gray [45]	6829
25	26	A	Portsmouth	D 1-1	1-1	11	Gray [30]	19,217
26	28	H	Preston NE	W 2-0	1-0	7	Black 2 [38, 55]	18,484
27	Jan 1	H	Coventry C	D 1-1	0-0	7	Akinbiyi [72]	17,362
28	18	H	Burnley	D 1-1	0-1	9	Popovic (pen) [62]	16,344
29	Feb 1	A	Leicester C	L 0-1	0-0	11		27,005
30	8	A	Nottingham F	L 1-2	0-1	13	Johnson (pen) [74]	26,012
31	22	H	Sheffield W	D 0-0	0-0	12		16,707
32	Mar 1	A	Wolverhampton W	L 0-4	0-1	14		26,010
33	5	A	Derby Co	W 1-0	0-0	—	Black [61]	22,682
34	8	A	Bradford C	L 1-2	1-0	16	Whelan [24]	11,016
35	11	H	Ipswich T	D 1-1	1-0	—	Johnson [20]	15,990
36	15	A	Reading	L 1-2	0-0	13	Johnson [76]	18,063
37	18	H	Wimbledon	L 0-1	0-1	—		13,713
38	22	H	Walsall	W 2-0	1-0	13	Freedman (pen) [33], Routledge [89]	19,102
39	25	A	Brighton & HA	D 0-0	0-0	—		6786
40	Apr 5	H	Sheffield U	D 2-2	2-1	13	Adebola [15], Whelan [28]	15,377
41	8	H	Watford	L 0-1	0-1	—		14,051
42	12	A	Grimsby T	W 4-1	3-0	11	Routledge [18], Whelan [34], Gray [35], Freedman [89]	4707
43	19	H	Rotherham U	D 0-0	0-0	11		15,508
44	21	A	Millwall	L 2-3	1-2	15	Freedman [22], Roberts (og) [49]	10,670
45	26	H	Stoke C	W 1-0	0-0	12	Adebola [82]	16,064
46	May 4	A	Gillingham	L 1-2	1-2	14	Freedman (pen) [30]	9315

Final League Position: 14

GOALSCORERS

League (59): Johnson 11 (2 pens), Freedman 9 (4 pens), Black 6, Adebola 5, Gray 5, Routledge 4, Granville 3, Popovic 3 (1 pen), Whelan 3, Mullins 2, Akinbiyi 1, Butterfield 1, Derry 1, Kabba 1, Powell 1, Riihilahti 1, Thomson 1, own goal 1.
Worthington Cup (15): Johnson 3, Adebola 2, Black 2, Freedman 2, Gray 1, Mullins 1, Popovic 1, Powell 1, own goals 2.
FA Cup (5): Black 2, Gray 2, own goal 1.

Clarke M 6	Fleming C 9 + 2	Granville D 30 + 5	Mullins H 43	Popovic T 36	Powell D 39	Butterfield D 46	Derry S 36 + 3	Freedman D 22 + 7	Johnson A 27 + 1	Riihilahti A 15 + 10	Thomson S 18 + 9	Black T 20 + 16	Kabba S — + 4	Austin D — + 3	Adebola D 32 + 7	Routledge W 13 + 13	Kolinko A 26 + 2	Rubins A — + 2	Frampton A — + 1	Gray J 29 + 6	Michopoulos N 5	Antwi W — + 4	Symons K 21 + 4	Williams G — + 5	Borrowdale G 8 + 5	Togwell S — + 1	Akinbiyi A 2 + 8	Berthelin C 9	Whelan N 7 + 1	Smith J 2	Hunt D 2	Watson B 3 + 2	Match No.
1	2	3	4	5	6	7	8	9^1	10^2	11^3	12	13	14																				1
1	2^3	3	4	5	6	7	8	9	10^2	12		11^1	13	14																			2
1	12	3	4	5	6^3	7	8^1	9		11	2^2		13	14	10																		3
1	2^3	3	4	5	6	7	8^1	9	12	11^2	14	13			10																		4
1	2	3	4	5	6	7^2	8^1	9	10	12	11^3				13	14																	5
1^6	2	3	4	5	6	7^1		9^2	10	11	12				8	13	15																6
	2	3	4	5	6	7		9^1	10^2		8	12			13	11^3	1	14															7
	2	3	4^1	5	6	7		9	10^3		8	12			13	11^2	1		14														8
	2^3	3	4	5	6	7		9^1	10^2		8			12	13	11■	1			14													9
		3	4	5	6	2		12	9^1	13	8^2				10	11	1			7													10
		3	4	5	6	2	12	9		8		13			10^1	7				11^2	1												11
	2	3	4	5	6	7^2	8^1	9	11^3	12		13			10					14	1												12
		3	4	5		2	8	12	9	6					10	11^1				7	1												13
		3^3	4	5	6	2	8	9	10^2			13			12	7^1	1	14		11													14
		3	4	5	6^1	2	8	9^3	11	12		13			10^2		1			7		14											15
		3^1	4	5	6	2	8	9	11	7^3		13			10^2		1			12			14										16
		3	4	5	6	2	8		9	12	7^2		14		10^3					11^1	1		13										17
		3			6	2	8^1		9	12	4	7^3			10					11	1	13	5^2	14									18
			4		6	2	8		9^2	12	3	11^1			10		1			7^3			5	13	14								19
		3	4		6	2	8		9		11^2	12			10	13	1			7^1			5										20
		3	11	5	6	2	8^2		9	12		13			10	7^1	1						4										21
		3	7	5	6	2	13			11		9			10	12^2	1			8^1			4										22
		3	7	5^1	6	2	12		9	11		8^3			10^2		1			13			4	14									23
			7		6	2^1	8			11		10			9		1			3			4		5	12							24
			7	5	6	2	8			11		10^1			9		1			3			4				12						25
		3	7	5	6^3	2	8			14		10^2			9^1	12	1			11			4				13						26
		3	6	5		2	8			11		10			9^2	12	1			7^1			4				13						27
		12	6	5		2	8		10	11^2		7			9^3	13				3^1			4				14	1					28
	12	3^2	7	5	6	2^3	8		11^1			10			9					13			4				14	1					29
			7	5^3	6	2	8	9^2	11		12	13			10					3			4^1				14	1					30
		5	4		6	2			9	11	7^1	8			13	12^2				3^3					14		10	1					31
			7	5	6	2	8		10^3	11^2		12			9^1	13				3			4				14	1					32
		12	4	5	6^3	2	8				7	10^1			9^2					11			14		3		13	1					33
		12	6	5		2	8	14			7^3	13								3^1			4^2		11		10	1	9				34
		3	4	5	6	2	8	12	10		13	7^2								11^3					14			1	9^1				35
			4	5^2	6	2	8	12	10		7^1					11	15						13		3			1^6	9				36
		12	5		6^1	2	8	9	10^2			7				13	1			11			4		14					3^3			37
		6				2	8	9^2			12	11^3			10	13	1			3		14	4		7					5^1			38
		6■			5	2	8				11	7^1			9^3		1			3^2		12	4	14	13				10				39
			6	5		2	8	12			14	13			9^2		1			11			4		3				10^3		7^1		40
			6	5		2	8^2	9			12				10	13	1			11			4						14		3^3	7^1	41
			4	5^2	6	2		12			8				9	7	1			11					3				10^1			13	42
		12	5		6	2	8	9				13			10^3	14	1			11			4^1		3^2							7	43
		6	5		4	2	8	9			11^1	10				7	1			3^2				12								13	44
			4	5	6^1	2	8	9			12	11			13	7	1												10^2			3	45
			4	5	6	2	8	9			7	11			10	3^1	1			12													46

Worthington Cup

First Round	Plymouth Arg	(h)	2-1
Second Round	Cheltenham T	(h)	7-0
Third Round	Coventry C	(h)	3-0
Fourth Round	Oldham Ath	(h)	2-0
Fifth Round	Sheffield U	(a)	1-3

FA Cup

Third Round	Blackpool	(a)	2-1
Fourth Round	Liverpool	(h)	0-0
		(a)	2-0
Fifth Round	Leeds U	(h)	1-2

DARLINGTON Division 3

FOUNDATION

A football club was formed in Darlington as early as 1861 but the present club began in 1883 and reached the final of the Durham Senior Cup in their first season, losing to Sunderland in a replay after complaining that they had suffered from intimidation in the first. On 5 April 1884, Sunderland had defeated Darlington 4-3. Darlington's objection was upheld by the referee and the replay took place on 3 May. The new referee for the match was Major Marindin, appointed by the Football Association to ensure fair play. Sunderland won 2-0. The following season Darlington won this trophy and for many years were one of the leading amateur clubs in their area.

Reynolds Arena, Hurworth Moor, Neasham Road, Darlington DL2 1GR.

Telephone: (01325) 387 000. ***Fax:*** (01325) 355 969.

Ground Capacity: 25,294.

Record Attendance: 21,023 v Bolton W, League Cup 3rd rd, 14 November 1960.

Record Receipts: £32,300 v Rochdale, Division 4, 11 May 1991.

Pitch Measurements: 105m × 68m.

President: A. Noble.

Chairman: George Reynolds.

Vice-chairman: Gordon Hodgson.

Directors: B. Lowery, S. Reynolds, L. Raine, R. Tennick, I. Robinson.

Manager: Mick Tait. ***Player-Coach:*** Craig Liddle.

Youth Team Coach: Martin Gray. ***Physio:*** Steve Collins.

PR Director: Luke Raine. ***Football Secretary:*** Lisa Charlton.

Finance/Ticketing: Carol Barnett. ***Safety Officer:*** Paul Murphy.

Youth Development Officer: Dave Cowling.

Colours: White and black with red piping.

Change Colours: Red, black and white.

Year Formed: 1883. ***Turned Professional:*** 1908. ***Ltd Co.:*** 1891.

Previous Grounds: Feethams Ground; 2003, Reynolds Arena, Hurworth Moor.

Club Nickname: 'The Quakers'.

First Football League Game: 27 August 1921, Division 3 (N), v Halifax T (h) W 2–0 – Ward; Greaves, Barbour; Dickson (1), Sutcliffe, Malcolm; Dolphin, Hooper (1), Edmunds, Wolstenholme, Winship.

Record League Victory: 9–2 v Lincoln C, Division 3 (N), 7 January 1928 – Archibald; Brooks, Mellen; Kelly, Waugh, McKinnell; Cochrane (1), Gregg (1), Ruddy (3), Lees (3), McGiffen (1).

HONOURS

Football League: Division 2 best season: 15th, 1925–26; Division 3 (N) – Champions 1924–25; Runners-up 1921–22; Division 4 – Champions 1990–91; Runners-up 1965–66.

FA Cup: best season: 5th rd, 1958.

Football League Cup: best season: 5th rd, 1968.

GM Vauxhall Conference: Champions 1989–90.

SKY SPORTS FACT FILE

Before the start of their 18 January 2003 match with Kidderminster Harriers, Darlington introduced their 1966 promotion team to the crowd. They stayed to see a switch of two-goal centre-back Matt Clarke up front, securing a 2-1 win.

Record Cup Victory: 7–2 v Evenwood T, FA Cup 1st rd, 17 November 1956 – Ward; Devlin, Henderson; Bell (1p), Greener, Furphy; Forster (1), Morton (3), Tulip (2), Davis, Moran.

Record Defeat: 0–10 v Doncaster R, Division 4, 25 January 1964.

Most League Points (2 for a win): 59, Division 4, 1965–66.

Most League Points (3 for a win): 85, Division 4, 1984–85.

Most League Goals: 108, Division 3 (N), 1929–30.

Highest League Scorer in Season: David Brown, 39, Division 3 (N), 1924–25.

Most League Goals in Total Aggregate: Alan Walsh, 90, 1978–84.

Most League Goals in One Match: 5, Tom Ruddy v South Shields, Division 2, 23 April 1927; 5, Maurice Wellock v Rotherham U, Division 3N, 15 February 1930.

Most Capped Player: Jason Devos, 3, Canada.

Most League Appearances: Ron Greener, 442, 1955–68.

Youngest League Player: Dale Anderson, 16 years 254 days v Chesterfield, 4 May 1987.

Record Transfer Fee Received: £400,000 from Dundee U for Jason Devos, October 1998.

Record Transfer Fee Paid: £95,000 to Motherwell for Nick Cusack, January 1992.

Football League Record: 1921 Original Member Division 3 (N); 1925–27 Division 2; 1927–58 Division 3 (N); 1958–66 Division 4; 1966–67 Division 3; 1967–85 Division 4; 1985–87 Division 3; 1987–89 Division 4; 1989–90 GM Vauxhall Conference; 1990–91 Division 4; 1991– Division 3.

LATEST SEQUENCES

Longest Sequence of League Wins: 6, 6.2.2000 – 7.3.2000.

Longest Sequence of League Defeats: 8, 31.8.1985 – 19.10.1985.

Longest Sequence of League Draws: 5, 31.12.1988 – 28.1.1989.

Longest Sequence of Unbeaten League Matches: 17, 27.4.1968 – 19.10.1968.

Longest Sequence Without a League Win: 19, 27.4.1988 – 8.11.1988.

Successive Scoring Runs: 22 from 3.12.1932.

Successive Non-scoring Runs: 7 from 5.9.1975.

MANAGERS

Tom McIntosh 1902–11
W. L. Lane 1911–12
(Secretary-Manager)
Dick Jackson 1912–19
Jack English 1919–28
Jack Fairless 1928–33
George Collins 1933–36
George Brown 1936–38
Jackie Carr 1938–42
Jack Surtees 1942
Jack English 1945–46
Bill Forrest 1946–50
George Irwin 1950–52
Bob Gurney 1952–57
Dick Duckworth 1957–60
Eddie Carr 1960–64
Lol Morgan 1964–66
Jimmy Greenhalgh 1966–68
Ray Yeoman 1968–70
Len Richley 1970–71
Frank Brennan 1971
Ken Hale 1971–72
Allan Jones 1972
Ralph Brand 1972–73
Dick Conner 1973–74
Billy Horner 1974–76
Peter Madden 1976–78
Len Walker 1978–79
Billy Elliott 1979–83
Cyril Knowles 1983–87
Dave Booth 1987–89
Brian Little 1989–91
Frank Gray 1991–92
Ray Hankin 1992
Billy McEwan 1992–93
Alan Murray 1993–95
Paul Futcher 1995
David Hodgson/Jim Platt
(Director of Coaching) 1995
Jim Platt 1995–96
David Hodgson 1996–2000
Gary Bennett 2000–01
Tommy Taylor 2001–02
Mick Tait June 2003–
(previously caretaker)

TEN YEAR LEAGUE RECORD

		P	W	D	L	F	A	Pts	Pos
1993-94	Div 3	42	10	11	21	42	64	41	21
1994-95	Div 3	42	11	8	23	43	57	41	20
1995-96	Div 3	46	20	18	8	60	42	78	5
1996-97	Div 3	46	14	10	22	64	78	52	18
1997-98	Div 3	46	14	12	20	56	72	54	19
1998-99	Div 3	46	18	11	17	69	58	65	11
1999-2000	Div 3	46	21	16	9	66	36	79	4
2000-01	Div 3	46	12	13	21	44	56	49	20
2001-02	Div 3	46	15	11	20	60	71	56	15
2002-03	Div 3	46	12	18	16	58	59	54	14

DID YOU KNOW ?

Goalkeeper John Hope played in all four divisions of the Football League in seven matches: Darlington's last game of 1966–67 (Div 3), first four 1967–68 (Div 4), one with Newcastle United (Div 1) 1969 and one Sheffield United (Div 2) 1970–71.

DARLINGTON 2002–03 LEAGUE RECORD

Match No.	Date	Venue	Opponents	Result		H/T Score	Lg. Pos.	Goalscorers	Attendance
1	Aug 10	A	Cambridge U	W	2-1	1-1	—	Clark [44], Nicholls [77]	4079
2	13	H	Swansea C	D	2-2	0-0	—	Clark [65], Liddle [71]	3913
3	17	H	Oxford U	L	0-1	0-1	13		3533
4	24	A	Rochdale	D	1-1	1-1	12	Nicholls [13]	2834
5	27	H	Carlisle U	W	2-0	0-0	—	Naylor 2 [56, 81]	5163
6	31	A	Kidderminster H	D	1-1	0-0	9	Conlon [61]	2488
7	Sept 14	A	Hartlepool U	L	1-4	1-2	16	Clark [27]	6360
8	17	A	York C	L	0-1	0-0	—		4128
9	21	H	Bournemouth	D	2-2	1-1	19	Fenton [35], Conlon [74]	2950
10	24	H	Wrexham	L	0-1	0-1	—		2573
11	28	A	Leyton Orient	L	1-2	1-0	20	Conlon [45]	3975
12	Oct 5	H	Bristol R	W	1-0	1-0	17	Conlon [19]	2849
13	12	A	Bury	D	2-2	1-0	19	Valentine [34], Clark (pen) [73]	2944
14	19	H	Boston U	L	2-3	0-1	20	Clark [85], Conlon [87]	3033
15	26	A	Exeter C	W	4-0	2-0	17	Liddle [35], Clarke [42], Conlon [68], Nicholls [90]	2757
16	29	H	Scunthorpe U	D	1-1	1-1	—	Clark (pen) [28]	3059
17	Nov 2	H	Lincoln C	D	0-0	0-0	19		3277
18	9	A	Rushden & D	L	0-2	0-0	19		3911
19	23	A	Shrewsbury T	D	2-2	0-2	18	Conlon [63], Keltie [82]	2755
20	30	H	Southend U	W	2-1	1-0	17	Conlon [37], Nicholls [87]	2830
21	Dec 14	A	Hull C	W	1-0	1-0	16	Betts [45]	14,162
22	21	H	Macclesfield T	D	0-0	0-0	17		3079
23	26	A	Carlisle U	D	2-2	1-2	17	Offiong 2 (1 pen) [19, 63 (p)]	6016
24	28	H	Torquay U	D	1-1	1-0	16	Nicholls [34]	3506
25	Jan 14	A	Oxford U	D	1-1	0-0	—	Hodgson [87]	4968
26	18	H	Kidderminster H	W	2-1	0-0	16	Clarke 2 [61, 83]	2630
27	25	A	Torquay U	L	1-3	1-3	16	Conlon [18]	2628
28	Feb 4	A	Swansea C	L	0-1	0-1	—		5553
29	8	H	Rushden & D	D	2-2	0-0	16	Hodgson [51], Clark [69]	2742
30	11	H	Rochdale	L	0-1	0-1	—		2479
31	15	A	Lincoln C	D	1-1	1-1	17	Conlon [22]	3193
32	23	A	Wrexham	D	0-0	0-0	17		4079
33	Mar 1	H	Hartlepool U	D	2-2	1-0	17	Conlon [36], Liddle [60]	5832
34	4	H	York C	W	2-1	1-0	—	Mellanby [30], Conlon [87]	3434
35	8	A	Bournemouth	L	0-2	0-1	17		5758
36	11	H	Cambridge U	L	1-2	0-1	—	Mellanby [82]	2076
37	15	H	Exeter C	D	2-2	0-1	17	Mellanby 2 [47, 52]	2476
38	19	A	Boston U	L	0-1	0-1	—		2186
39	22	A	Scunthorpe U	W	1-0	0-0	16	Keltie [81]	3904
40	29	H	Bury	W	3-1	1-1	15	Corbett [20], Naylor [87], Liddle (pen) [90]	2879
41	Apr 5	A	Southend U	L	0-2	0-2	15		3053
42	12	H	Shrewsbury T	W	5-1	3-0	15	Nicholls [20], Conlon 2 [33, 88], Maddison [37], Pearson [74]	2660
43	19	A	Macclesfield T	L	0-1	0-1	16		1967
44	21	H	Hull C	W	2-0	0-0	15	Newey [56], Conlon [90]	3487
45	26	A	Bristol R	L	1-2	0-1	15	Keltie [67]	9835
46	May 3	H	Leyton Orient	D	2-2	1-2	14	Corbett [44], Wainwright [76]	5723

Final League Position: 14

GOALSCORERS

League (58): Conlon 15, Clark 7 (2 pens), Nicholls 6, Liddle 4 (1 pen), Mellanby 4, Clarke 3, Keltie 3, Naylor 3, Corbett 2, Hodgson 2, Offiong 2 (1 pen), Betts 1, Fenton 1, Maddison 1, Newey 1, Pearson 1, Valentine 1, Wainwright 1.
Worthington Cup (0).
FA Cup (8): Conlon 2, Offiong 2, Clark 1, Hodgson 1, Liddle 1, Nicholls 1.
LDV Vans Trophy (0).

Collett A 38	Betts S 40	Valentine R 43	Liddle C 42	Clarke M 35 + 3	Maddison N 25 + 3	Wainwright N 21 + 12	Nicholls A 40 + 1	Conlon B 41	Rundle A 3 + 2	Clark I 23 + 10	Porter C 2 + 1	Keltie C 27 + 3	Naylor G 1 + 12	Cullen J 2 + 1	Hadland P 4 + 2	Ford M 10 + 1	Alexander J — + 1	Hodgson R 22 + 5	McGurk D 3 + 1	Fenton G 4 + 2	Sheeran M — + 4	Reed A — + 1	Whitehead S 23	Mellanby D 6 + 7	Campbell P 3 + 2	Ingham M 3	Pearson G 19 + 2	Offiong R 7	Lonergan A 2	Russell S 1	Corbett J 9 + 1	Newey T 7	*Match No.*
1^{6}	2	3	4	5	6	7	8	9	10^{1}	11^{2}	15	12	13																				1
	2	3	4	5	6	7	8	9	10	11	1																						2
1	2	3	4	5	6	7^{1}	8^{2}	9		11			12	10	13																		3
1	2	3	4	5	6	7	8	9		10		12			11^{1}																		4
1	2	3	4	5	6^{1}		8	9		10			12		11	7																	5
1	2	3	4	5	6	12		9		11^{1}			10^{2}	7^{3}	13	8	14																6
1	2	3	4	5	6	7^{3}		9		10^{1}			12	13	11^{2}	8		14															7
1	2	3	4^{2}	5	6			9		10			12		11^{1}	7		8^{3}	13	14													8
1	2	3		5	6		8	9		11			12			7			4	10^{1}													9
1	2	3		5	6	12	8^{1}	9		11^{2}						7		13	4	10^{3}	14												10
1	2	3		5^{3}		7^{2}	8	9		11			12			6		10^{1}	4	13		14											11
1	2	3	4		6	7^{1}	12	9		11^{2}						8		13		10^{3}	14		5										12
1	2	3	4	5	7			9	12	11^{1}			13			8				10^{2}			6^{3}	14									13
1	2	3	4^{1}	12	6	7^{2}		9	11	10						8							5	13									14
1	2	3	4	12		13	8	9		10^{3}		6	14					11					5^{1}		7^{2}								15
1	2	3	4	5		12	8	9		10^{2}		6	13					11							7^{1}								16
1	2	3	4	5		7	8	9	12	10^{2}		6	13					11^{1}															17
1	2	3	4	5		10^{1}	8	9		12		7				13		11^{2}					6										18
	2	3	4			7	8	9		10		6						11								1	5						19
	2	3		5		7	8	9				6						11^{1}					4			1	12	10					20
	2	3	4■	5		12	8	9				7						11					6			1		10^{1}					21
	2	3	4	5^{1}		13	8	9■		12		7						11					6					10^{2}	1				22
			4	5		7	8	9				6						11					3				2	10	1				23
	2	3	4	12		7^{1}	8	9		13		6						11^{3}					5				14	10^{2}		1			24
1	2	3	4	5	9^{1}	7	8											11						12			6	10					25
1	2	3	4	5	13		9			12		7						11					6				8^{2}	10^{1}					26
1	2	3	4	10	12^{2}	7^{1}	8	9		13		6						11					5■										27
1	2	3	4			7	8	9		10^{1}		6						11			12		5										28
1	2	3	4			7	8	9		10		6						11									5						29
1	2	3	4			7^{1}	8	9		10		6						11			12		5										30
1	2	3	4		7		8	9		10		6^{1}											5		12		11						31
1	2	3	4	9	10	7	8											11^{1}					5^{2}	13	12		6■						32
1	2	3■	4	5	11		8	9				7						12						10^{1}			6						33
1	2	3	4	5	11		8^{2}	9		12		7						13						10^{1}			6						34
1	2	3	4	5	11	12	8^{1}	9		13		7						10^{2}									6						35
1	2	3	4	5		12	8	9■		10		6						11^{2}						13	7^{1}								36
1	2		4	5		7	8	9		12		6						11^{1}						10^{2}			3				13		37
1	2	3^{1}	4	5		12	8	9				7												10			6				11		38
1	2	3	4	5	11		8	9				7															6				10		39
1	2		4		11		8					7	12										5	10^{1}			6				9	3	40
1	2^{1}	3	4		8	12	7			13													5	10^{2}			6				9	11	41
1		3	4	5	8		7	9															6				2				10	11	42
1		2	4	5	11		8^{2}	9				12											6	13			7^{1}				10	3	43
		2	4	5			8	9			1	7											6				11				10	3	44
1		2^{2}	4	5	11	12	8^{1}	9				7											6	13							10	3	45
1		2^{1}	4	5	14	12	8	9		13		7^{3}											6				11				10	3^{2}	46

Worthington Cup

First Round	Huddersfield T	(a)	0-2

LDV Vans Trophy

First Round	Stockport Co	(a)	0-1

FA Cup

First Round	Wrexham	(a)	2-0
Second Round	Stevenage B	(h)	4-1
Third Round	Farnborough T	(h)	2-3

DERBY COUNTY Division 1

FOUNDATION

Derby County was formed by members of the Derbyshire County Cricket Club in 1884, when football was booming in the area and the cricketers thought that a football club would help boost finances for the summer game. To begin with, they sported the cricket club's colours of amber, chocolate and pale blue, and went into the game at the top immediately entering the FA Cup.

Pride Park Stadium, Derby DE24 8XL.

Telephone: (01332) 202 202. ***Fax:*** (01332) 667 519. ***ClubCall:*** 09068 121 187.

Ground Capacity: 33,597.

Record Attendance: 41,826 v Tottenham H, Division 1, 20 September 1969.

Record Receipts: £425,804 v Huddersfield T, FA Cup 5th rd replay, 24 February 1999.

Pitch Measurements: 110yd × 72yd.

Chairman: L. V. Pickering.

Director: F. Vinton.

Manager: George Burley.

First Team Coach: Billy McEwan.

Medical Manager: Peter Melville.

Secretary: Keith Pearson ACIS.

General Sales Manager: Andy Dawson.

Colours: White shirts with black piping, black shorts, white stockings.

Change Colours: Navy blue shirts, navy blue shorts with white trim, navy blue stockings.

Year Formed: 1884.

Turned Professional: 1884.

Ltd Co.: 1896.

Club Nickname: 'The Rams'.

Previous Grounds: 1884, Racecourse Ground; 1895, Baseball Ground; 1997, Pride Park.

First Football League Game: 8 September 1888, Football League, v Bolton W (a) W 6–3 – Marshall; Latham, Ferguson, Williamson; Monks, W. Roulstone; Bakewell (2), Cooper (2), Higgins, H. Plackett, L. Plackett (2).

HONOURS

Football League: Division 1 – Champions 1971–72, 1974–75; Runners-up 1895–96, 1929–30, 1935–36, 1995–96; Division 2 – Champions 1911–12, 1914–15, 1968–69, 1986–87; Runners-up 1925–26; Division 3 (N) Champions 1956–57; Runners-up 1955–56.

FA Cup: Winners 1946; Runners-up 1898, 1899, 1903.

Football League Cup: Semi-final 1968.

Texaco Cup: Winners 1972.

European Competitions: *European Cup:* 1972–73, 1975–76. *UEFA Cup:* 1974–75, 1976–77. *Anglo-Italian Cup:* Runners-up 1993.

SKY SPORTS FACT FILE

The unavailability of Jimmy Hagan to play for Derby County on Christmas Day 1941 gave an unexpected chance for 16-year-old Bemrose schoolboy Tommy Powell (father of Steve), who became a post-war regular at inside or outside-right.

Record League Victory: 9–0 v Wolverhampton W, Division 1, 10 January 1891 – Bunyan; Archie Goodall, Roberts; Walker, Chalmers, Roulstone (1); Bakewell, McLachlan, Johnny Goodall (1), Holmes (2), McMillan (5). 9–0 v Sheffield W, Division 1, 21 January 1899 – Fryer; Methven, Staley; Cox, Archie Goodall, May; Oakden (1), Bloomer (6), Boag, McDonald (1), Allen, (1 og).

Record Cup Victory: 12–0 v Finn Harps, UEFA Cup 1st rd 1st leg, 15 September 1976 – Moseley; Thomas, Nish, Rioch (1), McFarland, Todd (King), Macken, Gemmill, Hector (5), George (3), James (3).

Record Defeat: 2–11 v Everton, FA Cup 1st rd, 1889–90.

Most League Points (2 for a win): 63, Division 2, 1968–69 and Division 3 (N), 1955–56 and 1956–57.

Most League Points (3 for a win): 84, Division 3, 1985–86 and Division 3, 1986–87.

Most League Goals: 111, Division 3 (N), 1956–57.

Highest League Scorer in Season: Jack Bowers, 37, Division 1, 1930–31; Ray Straw, 37 Division 3 (N), 1956–57.

Most League Goals in Total Aggregate: Steve Bloomer, 292, 1892–1906 and 1910–14.

Most League Goals in One Match: 6, Steve Bloomer v Sheffield W, Division 1, 2 January 1899.

Most Capped Player: Deon Burton, 40, Jamaica.

Most League Appearances: Kevin Hector, 486, 1966–78 and 1980–82.

Youngest League Player: Lee Holmes, 15 years 268 days v Grimsby T, 26 December 2002.

Record Transfer Fee Received: £7 million rising to £9 million for Seth Johnson from Leeds U, October 2001.

Record Transfer Fee Paid: £3,000,000 rising to £4,000,000 for Lee Morris from Sheffield U, October 1999.

Football League Record: 1888 Founder Member of the Football League; 1907–12 Division 2; 1912–14 Division 1; 1914–15 Division 2; 1915–21 Division 1; 1921–26 Division 2; 1926–53 Division 1; 1953–55 Division 2; 1955–57 Division 3 (N); 1957–69 Division 2; 1969–80 Division 1; 1980–84 Division 2; 1984–86 Division 3; 1986–87 Division 2; 1987–91 Division 1; 1991–92 Division 2; 1992–96 Division 1; 1996–2002 FA Premier League; 2002– Division 1.

MANAGERS

W. D. Clark 1896–1900
Harry Newbould 1900–06
Jimmy Methven 1906–22
Cecil Potter 1922–25
George Jobey 1925–41
Ted Magner 1944–46
Stuart McMillan 1946–53
Jack Barker 1953–55
Harry Storer 1955–62
Tim Ward 1962–67
Brian Clough 1967–73
Dave Mackay 1973–76
Colin Murphy 1977
Tommy Docherty 1977–79
Colin Addison 1979–82
Johnny Newman 1982
Peter Taylor 1982–84
Roy McFarland 1984
Arthur Cox 1984–93
Roy McFarland 1993–95
Jim Smith 1995–2001
Colin Todd 2001–02
John Gregory 2002–03
George Burley June 2003–

LATEST SEQUENCES

Longest Sequence of League Wins: 9, 15.3.1969 – 19.4.1969.

Longest Sequence of League Defeats: 8, 12.12.1987 – 10.2.1988.

Longest Sequence of League Draws: 6, 26.3.1927 – 18.4.1927.

Longest Sequence of Unbeaten League Matches: 22, 8.3.1969 – 20.9.1969.

Longest Sequence Without a League Win: 20, 15.12.1990 – 23.4.1991.

Successive Scoring Runs: 29 from 3.12.1960.

Successive Non-scoring Runs: 8 from 30.10.1920.

TEN YEAR LEAGUE RECORD

		P	W	D	L	F	A	Pts	Pos
1993-94	Div 1	46	20	11	15	73	68	71	6
1994-95	Div 1	46	18	12	16	66	51	66	9
1995-96	Div 1	46	21	16	9	71	51	79	2
1996-97	PR Lge	38	11	13	14	45	58	46	12
1997-98	PR Lge	38	16	7	15	52	49	55	9
1998-99	PR Lge	38	13	13	12	40	45	52	8
1999-2000	PR Lge	38	9	11	18	44	57	38	16
2000-01	PR Lge	38	10	12	16	37	59	42	17
2001-02	PR Lge	38	8	6	24	33	63	30	19
2002-03	Div 1	46	15	7	24	55	74	52	18

DID YOU KNOW ?

Lee Holmes at 15 years 268 days became the youngest player to turn out for the Derby County first team on Boxing Day 2002, beating Steve Powell's record when he was introduced at 16 years 33 days v Arsenal on 23 October 1971.

DERBY COUNTY 2002–03 LEAGUE RECORD

Match No.	Date	Venue	Opponents	Result		H/T Score	Lg. Pos.	Goalscorers	Attendance
1	Aug 10	H	Reading	W	3-0	0-0	—	Lee [61], Ravanelli [63], Christie [72]	33,016
2	13	A	Gillingham	L	0-1	0-1	—		8775
3	17	A	Grimsby T	W	2-1	1-1	7	Bolder 2 [43, 75]	5810
4	24	H	Wolverhampton W	L	1-4	1-1	9	Christie [45]	29,954
5	26	A	Rotherham U	L	1-2	0-0	13	Strupar [47]	8408
6	31	H	Stoke C	W	2-0	0-0	10	Christie 2 [82, 84]	21,723
7	Sept 7	H	Burnley	L	1-2	1-0	13	Bolder [8]	22,343
8	14	A	Leicester C	L	1-3	1-1	16	Riggott [23]	31,049
9	17	A	Crystal Palace	W	1-0	0-0	—	Kinkladze [83]	14,948
10	21	H	Preston NE	L	0-2	0-1	13		29,257
11	28	A	Ipswich T	W	1-0	1-0	9	Carbonari [45]	24,439
12	Oct 5	H	Walsall	D	2-2	1-0	10	Christie 2 [19, 53]	25,247
13	12	A	Bradford C	D	0-0	0-0	11		13,385
14	20	H	Nottingham F	D	0-0	0-0	11		30,547
15	26	A	Millwall	L	0-3	0-1	14		8116
16	30	H	Sheffield U	W	2-1	1-1	—	McLeod [36], Burton [86]	23,525
17	Nov 2	A	Sheffield W	W	3-1	2-0	10	Morris 2 [7, 29], McLeod [48]	19,747
18	9	H	Portsmouth	L	1-2	1-1	13	Higginbotham (pen) [16]	26,587
19	16	A	Brighton & HA	L	0-1	0-0	14		6845
20	25	H	Wimbledon	W	3-2	1-1	—	Elliott [17], Burton [48], Morris [80]	25,597
21	30	A	Norwich C	L	0-1	0-0	16		20,522
22	Dec 7	H	Watford	W	3-0	1-0	13	Morris [4], Riggott [62], Burton [71]	21,653
23	14	H	Brighton & HA	W	1-0	1-0	11	Higginbotham (pen) [30]	25,786
24	21	A	Coventry C	L	0-3	0-2	13		13,185
25	26	H	Grimsby T	L	1-3	1-1	15	Morris [32]	27,141
26	28	A	Reading	L	1-2	1-1	17	Burley (pen) [8]	16,299
27	Jan 1	A	Wolverhampton W	D	1-1	1-0	15	Christie [15]	26,442
28	11	H	Gillingham	D	1-1	0-0	16	Zavagno (pen) [64]	22,769
29	18	A	Stoke C	W	3-1	0-0	15	Christie [50], Zavagno [74], Morris [89]	17,308
30	Feb 1	H	Rotherham U	W	3-0	2-0	14	Kinkladze [16], Bolder [45], McLeod [49]	26,257
31	8	A	Portsmouth	L	2-6	0-3	14	Morris [58], Kinkladze (pen) [67]	19,503
32	15	H	Sheffield W	D	2-2	0-1	15	Bolder 2 [53, 70]	26,311
33	22	A	Burnley	L	0-2	0-2	16		15,063
34	Mar 1	H	Leicester C	D	1-1	0-1	15	Burley [90]	24,307
35	5	H	Crystal Palace	L	0-1	0-0	—		22,682
36	8	A	Preston NE	L	2-4	0-3	18	Ravanelli 2 [75, 90]	14,003
37	15	H	Bradford C	L	1-2	1-1	20	Morris [28]	23,735
38	19	A	Nottingham F	L	0-3	0-2	—		29,725
39	22	A	Sheffield U	L	0-2	0-1	20		18,401
40	Apr 5	H	Norwich C	W	2-1	1-1	19	Burley [24], Kenton (og) [57]	23,643
41	12	A	Wimbledon	W	2-0	1-0	17	Valakari [29], Boertien [57]	1934
42	16	H	Millwall	L	1-2	1-1	—	Kinkladze [8]	21,014
43	19	H	Coventry C	W	1-0	0-0	18	Ravanelli [62]	23,921
44	21	A	Watford	L	0-2	0-1	18		11,909
45	26	A	Walsall	L	2-3	0-1	19	Valakari [59], Ravanelli [83]	8416
46	May 4	H	Ipswich T	L	1-4	1-3	18	Lee [22]	28,785

Final League Position: 18

GOALSCORERS

League (55): Christie 8, Morris 8, Bolder 6, Ravanelli 5, Kinkladze 4 (1 pen), Burley 3 (1 pen), Burton 3, McLeod 3, Higginbotham 2 (2 pens), Lee 2, Riggott 2, Valakari 2, Zavagno 2 (1 pen), Boertien 1, Carbonari 1, Elliott 1, Strupar 1, own goal 1.
Worthington Cup (4): Christie 1, Evatt 1, Higginbotham 1 (pen), Morris 1.
FA Cup (0).

Poom M 13	Barton W 39	Boertien P 42	Riggott C 21 + 1	Higginbotham D 22 + 1	Bolder A 38 + 7	Murray A 17 + 7	Lee R 34 + 1	Christie M 24	Ravanelli F 16 + 3	Morris L 26 + 4	Jackson R 16 + 5	Evatt I 18 + 12	Twigg G 1 + 7	Tudgay M — + 8	Strupar B 4 + 1	Grenet F 2 + 1	Oakes A 7	Kinkladze G 22 + 6	Grant L 26 + 3	O'Neil B 3	Hunt L 7 + 3	Carbonari H 2	McLeod I 20 + 9	Burton D 4 + 3	Elliott S 21 + 2	Burley C 20	Mills P 12 + 4	Holmes L — + 2	Zavagno L 6 + 3	Chadwick N 4 + 2	Mooney T 7 + 1	Robinson M — + 1	Ritchie P 7	Valakari S 5 + 1	Camp L — + 1	*Match No.*
1	2	3^{1}	4	5	6	7	8	9^{2}	10	11^{3}	12	13	14																							1
1	2	3		5	6	7^{3}	8	9	10^{2}	11	4^{1}	12		14	13																					2
1	2	3^{2}		5	6	7^{1}	8	9	10	11		4	12			13																				3
	2			5	6	7^{2}	8	9		12		4	11^{1}	13	10	3	1																			4
	2	11		5	6	12	8^{1}	9		7		4	13		10	3^{2}	1																			5
1	2	11	4	5	6	7^{1}	8	9^{2}			3	13			10			12																		6
	2	11	4	5	6	7^{1}	8	9		12	3				10		1^{G}		15																	7
1	2	3	4	5	6		8^{1}	9		11		12	13					10^{2}		7																8
1	2	3	4	5	6	7		9		11		12						10^{1}		8^{2}	13															9
1	2▮	3	4	5	6^{2}	12	8	9		11								10		7^{1}	13															10
1	2	3	4	5	11	7	8	9^{1}				12										6	10													11
1		3	4	5	11	7^{2}	8	9				12	14					13			2	6^{1}	10^{3}													12
1		3	4	5	11	7▮	8▮	9^{1}		12		6									2		10													13
		3	4	5	11	7^{1}	8	9				6						12	1		2		10													14
1▮	2		4^{2}	5	11	7				9	3^{1}	6	12					8	15		13		10^{G}													15
1	4	3		5	11		7			9^{1}		6						8			2		10^{2}	12	13											16
1	4	3		5	11		7			9^{1}		6	13					8			2		10^{3}	12^{2}	14											17
	4	3	12	5	11		7		13	9		6^{2}						8	1		2^{1}		10^{3}	14												18
	2^{1}	3	4		11		7	9▮			12	6						8	1					10	5											19
	2	3	4	12	13		7	9^{3}		14		6^{1}							1				10	8	5	11^{2}										20
	2	3^{2}	4	5	12		7			9		13							1				10	8^{1}	6	11										21
	2^{1}	3	4	5	12		7^{2}	9		10^{3}		13							1				14	8	6	11										22
	2	3	4^{1}	5^{3}		13	7^{2}	9		8		12							1				10		6	11	14									23
	2	3^{1}	4		11			9		8		5							1				10		6	7	12									24
	2	3^{3}	4		10^{2}		7	9		8		5^{1}						12	1				13		6	11		14								25
	2		4		6^{1}	7		9		8		12		13					1				10^{2}		5	11	3									26
	2		4		11	7		9		8^{1}		5							1				10		6		3	12								27
	2	11	4^{1}		7			9^{2}		10	12	5		13				8	1						6				3							28
		11		5	6	12		9^{2}		10^{3}	2	4		13				8^{1}	1				14			7			3							29
	2^{3}	11			6		7		12	9^{2}	14	5		13				8	1				10^{1}		4				3							30
	2	11			6		7			9		5						8	1				10		4				3							31
	5▮	11			6		7		12	9^{2}	2			13				8	1				10^{1}		4		14		3^{3}							32
	5	11			6	12	7^{1}		10	9	2							8	1						4				3							33
		3			6		7		10	9	2							8^{1}	1						4	11	5			12						34
		3^{1}			6	8^{3}	7		10		2			13					1				12		4	11	5		14	9^{2}						35
	2	3			6		7		10									8	1				12		4	11	5			9^{1}						36
	2	3			6^{2}		7		10	8								13	1				12		4	11	5^{3}		14	9^{1}						37
	2	3^{1}			6		7		10^{2}										1				8		4	11	5		12	13	9					38
	4^{1}	3			11	8	7				13							12	1		2		10^{3}		6		5^{2}			9		14				39
	2	3			12				10^{1}		5						1	8					13		4	11					9^{2}		6	7		40
	4	3			8^{2}	13			9^{1}		2						1	10					12			11					5		6	7		41
	4^{1}	3			8				9		2						1^{G}	10	15							11	12				5		6	7		42
	4	3			12		7^{2}		9		2							10	1							11	8				5^{1}		6	13		43
	4^{3}	3			8^{2}	13	12		9		2							10	1							11	5				14		6	7^{1}		44
		3			12	8			9		2								1^{G}				10			11	4				5^{1}		6	7	15	45
	4^{1}	3			13		7		10^{3}		2	12^{2}					1	8					14			11	5				9		6			46

Worthington Cup

First Round	Mansfield T	(a)	3-1
Second Round	Oldham Ath	(h)	1-2

FA Cup

Third Round	Brentford	(a)	0-1

DONCASTER ROVERS Division 3

FOUNDATION

In 1879, Mr Albert Jenkins assembled a team to play a match against the Yorkshire Institution for the Deaf. The players remained together as Doncaster Rovers, joining the Midland Alliance in 1889 and the Midland Counties League in 1891.

Belle Vue, Doncaster, DN54 5HT.

Telephone: (01302) 539 441.

Fax: (01302) 539 679.

Website: www.doncasterroversfc.co.uk

Email: info@doncasterroversfc.co.uk

Ground Capacity: 7,219 (1,252 seated).

Record Attendance: 3,7149 v Hull C, Division 3 (N), 2 October 1948.

Record Receipts: £22,000 v QPR, F.A. Cup 3rd rd, 5 January 1985.

Pitch Measurements: 110yd x 76yd.

Chairman: John Ryan.

Directors: M. Collett, S. Highfield JP, K. Chappell MBE, P. Hepworth, A. Liney, J. Ryan, R. Thomas, P. Wetzel, T. Milton.

Financial Controller: D. Morris.

Company Football Secretary: Joan Odale.

Manager: Dave Penney.

Assistant Manager: Mickey Walker.

Physio: Barry Windle.

Stadium Manager: A. Paget.

Colours: Red and white broad hooped shirts, red shorts, red stockings.

Change Colours: All blue.

Year Formed: 1879.

Turned Professional: 1885.

Ltd Co.: 1905 & 1920.

Club Nickname: 'Rovers'.

HONOURS

Football League: Division 2 best season: 7th, 1901–02; Division 3 (N) Champions – 1934–35, 1946–47, 1949–50; Runners-up: 1937–38, 1938–39; Division 4 Champions 1965–66, 1968–69; Runners-up: 1983–84. Promoted 1980–81 (3rd).

F.A. Cup: best season 5th rd, 1952, 1954, 1955, 1956.

Football League Cup: best season: 5th rd, 1976.

Sheffield County Cup: Winners 1891, 1912, 1936, 1938, 1956, 1968, 1976, 1986.

Midland Counties League: Champions 1897, 1899.

Conference Trophy: Winners 1999, 2000.

Sheffield & Hallamshire Senior Cup: Winners 2001, 2002.

SKY SPORTS FACT FILE

On 17 February 1953, Doncaster Rovers Midland League fixture against Lincoln City reserves was played under floodlights for the first time at the Belle Vue ground. The match ended in a 2-2 draw before a crowd of 2,170.

Previous Grounds: Intake Ground 1880–1916; Benetthorpe Ground 1920–1922; Low Pasture, Belle Vue 1922.

Record League Victory: 10–0 v Darlington, Division 4, 25 January 1964: Potter; Raine, Meadows, Windross (1), White, Ripley (2), Robinson, Book (2), Hale (4), Jeffrey, Broadbent (1).

Record Cup Victory: 7–0 v Blyth Spartans, FA Cup 1st rd, 27 November 1937: Imrie; Shaw, Rodgers, McFarlane, Bycroft, Cyril Smith, Burton (1), Killourhy (4), Morgan (2), Malam, Dutton.

Record Defeat: 0–12 v Small Heath, Division 2, 11 April 1903.

Most League Points (2 for a win): 72, Division 3 (N), 1946–47.

Most League Points (3 for a win): 85, Division 4, 1983–84.

Most League Goals: 123, Division 3 (N), 1946–47.

Highest League Scorer in Season: Clarrie Jordan, 42, Division 3 (N), 1946–47.

Most League Goals in Total Aggregate: Tom Keetley, 180, 1923–29.

Most Capped Player: Len Graham, 14, Northern Ireland.

Most League Appearances: Fred Emery, 417, 1925–36.

Record Transfer Fee Received: £250,000 from QPR for Rufus Brevett, February 1991.

Record Transfer Fee Paid: £100,000 to Rushden & D for Justin Jackson, September 2001.

Football League Record: 1901 Elected to Division 2; 1903 Failed re-election; 1904 Re-elected; 1905 Failed re-election; 1923 Re-elected to Divison 3 (N); 1935–37 Division 2; 1937–47 Division 3 (N); 1947–48 Division 2; 1948–50 Division 3 (N); 1950–58 Division 2; 1958–59 Division 3; 1959–66 Division 4; 1966–67 Division 3; 1967–69 Division 4; 1969–71 Division 3; 1971–81 Division 4; 1981–83 Division 3; 1983–84 Division 4; 1984–88 Division 3; 1988–92 Division 4; 1992–98 Division 3; 1998–2003 Conference; 2003– Division 3.

MANAGERS

Arthur Porter 1920–21
Harry Tufnell 1921–22
Arthur Porter 1922–23
Dick Ray 1923–27
David Menzies 1928–36
Fred Emery 1936–40
Bill Marsden 1944–46
Jackie Bestall 1946–49
Peter Doherty 1949–58
Jack Hodgson & Sid Bycroft (*Joint Managers*) 1958
Jack Crayston 1958–59 (*continued as Secretary-Manager to 1961*)
Jackie Bestall (TM) 1959–60
Norman Curtis 1960–61
Danny Malloy 1961–62
Oscar Hold 1962–64
Bill Leivers 1964–66
Keith Kettleborough 1966–67
George Raynor 1967–68
Lawrie McMenemy 1968–71
Morris Setters 1971–74
Stan Anderson 1975–78
Billy Bremner 1978–85
Dave Cusack 1985–87
Dave Mackay 1987–89
Billy Bremner 1989–91
Steve Beaglehole 1991–93
Ian Atkins 1994
Sammy Chung 1994–96
Kerry Dixon (*Player–Manager*) 1996–97
Dave Cowling 1997
Mark Weaver 1997–98
Ian Snodin 1998–99
Steve Wignall 1999–2001
Dave Penney March 2002–

LATEST SEQUENCES

Successive Scoring Runs: 27 from 10.11.1934.

Successive Non-scoring Runs: 7 from 27.9.1947.

TEN YEAR LEAGUE RECORD

		P	*W*	*D*	*L*	*F*	*A*	*Pts*	*Pos*
1993-94	Div 3	42	14	10	18	44	57	52	15
1994-95	Div 3	42	17	10	15	58	43	61	9
1995-96	Div 3	46	16	11	19	49	60	59	13
1996-97	Div 3	46	14	10	22	52	65	52	19
1997-98	Div 3	46	4	8	34	30	113	20	24
1998-99	Conf.	42	12	12	18	51	55	48	16
1999-2000	Conf.	42	15	9	18	46	48	54	12
2000-01	Conf.	42	15	13	14	47	43	58	9
2001-02	Conf.	42	18	13	11	68	46	67	4
2002-03	Conf.	42	22	12	8	73	47	78	3

DID YOU KNOW ?

In 1950–51 season, Doncaster Rovers attracted an average attendance of 22,838 while finishing 11th in the table, the club's highest crowd figure throughout their Football League history.

EVERTON

FA Premiership

FOUNDATION

St Domingo Church Sunday School formed a football club in 1878 which played at Stanley Park. Enthusiasm was so great that in November 1879 they decided to expand membership and changed the name to Everton playing in black shirts with a scarlet sash and nicknamed the 'Black Watch'. After wearing several other colours, royal blue was adopted in 1901.

Goodison Park, Liverpool L4 4EL.

Telephone: (0151) 330 2200. ***Fax:*** (0151) 286 9112.
Website: www.evertonfc.com
Email: everton@evertonfc.com

Ground Capacity: 40,170.

Record Attendance: 78,299 v Liverpool, Division 1, 18 September 1948.

Record Receipts: £730,000 v Manchester U, FA Premier League, 16 September 2000.

Pitch Measurements: 110yd × 70yd.

Chairman: Sir Philip Carter CBE.

Deputy-chairman: Bill Kenwright CBE.

Directors: Keith Tamlin, Arthur Abercromby, Paul Gregg, Jon Woods.

Manager: David Moyes.

Assistant Manager: Alan Irvine.

Chief Executive: Michael J. Dunford.

Club Secretary: David Harrison.

Stadium Manager: Alan Bowen.

Head of Marketing: Andy Hosie.

Head of Corporate Affairs & PR: Ian Ross.

Head of Physiotherapy: Mick Rathbone, Bsc (Hons), MCSP.

Colours: Royal blue shirts, white shorts with blue trim, blue stockings with white trim.

Change Colours: Amber shirts, royal blue shorts, amber stockings.

Year Formed: 1878.

Turned Professional: 1885.

Ltd Co.: 1892.

Previous Name: 1878, St Domingo FC; 1879, Everton.

Club Nickname: 'The Toffees'.

Previous Grounds: 1878, Stanley Park; 1882, Priory Road; 1884, Anfield Road; 1892, Goodison Park.

First Football League Game: 8 September 1888, Football League, v Accrington (h) W 2–1 – Smalley; Dick, Ross; Holt, Jones, Dobson; Fleming (2), Waugh, Lewis, E. Chadwick, Farmer.

HONOURS

Football League: Division 1 – Champions 1890–91, 1914–15, 1927–28, 1931–32, 1938–39, 1962–63, 1969–70, 1984–85, 1986–87; Runners-up 1889–90, 1894–95, 1901–02, 1904–05, 1908–09, 1911–12, 1985–86; Division 2 – Champions 1930–31; Runners-up 1953–54.

FA Cup: Winners 1906, 1933, 1966, 1984, 1995; Runners-up 1893, 1897, 1907, 1968, 1985, 1986, 1989.

Football League Cup: Runners-up 1977, 1984.

League Super Cup: Runners-up 1986.

Simod Cup: Runners-up 1989.

Zenith Data Systems Cup: Runners-up 1991.

European Competitions: *European Cup:* 1963–64, 1970–71. *European Cup-Winners' Cup:* 1966–67, 1984–85 (winners), 1995–96. *European Fairs Cup:* 1962–63, 1964–65, 1965–66. *UEFA Cup:* 1975–76, 1978–79, 1979–80.

SKY SPORTS FACT FILE

On 1 October 2002 at Wrexham in the League Cup, Wayne Rooney at 16 years 342 days became the youngest goalscorer in Everton history, beating Tommy Lawton's record on his debut at 17 years 130 days on 13 March 1937.

Record League Victory: 9–1 v Manchester C, Division 1, 3 September 1906 – Scott; Balmer, Crelley; Booth, Taylor (1), Abbott (1); Sharp, Bolton (1), Young (4), Settle (2), George Wilson. 9–1 v Plymouth Arg, Division 2, 27 December 1930 – Coggins; Williams, Cresswell; McPherson, Griffiths, Thomson; Critchley, Dunn, Dean (4), Johnson (1), Stein (4).

Record Cup Victory: 11–2 v Derby Co, FA Cup 1st rd, 18 January 1890 – Smalley; Hannah, Doyle (1); Kirkwood, Holt (1), Parry; Latta, Brady (3), Geary (3), Chadwick, Millward (3).

Record Defeat: 4–10 v Tottenham H, Division 1, 11 October 1958.

Most League Points (2 for a win): 66, Division 1, 1969–70.

Most League Points (3 for a win): 90, Division 1, 1984–85.

Most League Goals: 121, Division 2, 1930–31.

Highest League Scorer in Season: William Ralph 'Dixie' Dean, 60, Division 1, 1927–28 (All-time League record).

Most League Goals in Total Aggregate: William Ralph 'Dixie' Dean, 349, 1925–37.

Most League Goals in One Match: 6, Jack Southworth v WBA, Division 1, 30 December 1893.

Most Capped Player: Neville Southall, 92, Wales.

Most League Appearances: Neville Southall, 578, 1981–98.

Youngest League Player: Joe Royle, 16 years 282 days v Blackpool, 15 January 1966.

Record Transfer Fee Received: £10,000,000 from Arsenal for Francis Jeffers, June 2001.

Record Transfer Fee Paid: £5,750,000 to Middlesbrough for Nick Barmby, October 1996.

Football League Record: 1888 Founder Member of the Football League; 1930–31 Division 2; 1931–51 Division 1; 1951–54 Division 2; 1954–92 Division 1; 1992– FA Premier League.

MANAGERS

W. E. Barclay 1888–89
(Secretary-Manager)
Dick Molyneux 1889–1901
(Secretary-Manager)
William C. Cuff 1901–18
(Secretary-Manager)
W. J. Sawyer 1918–19
(Secretary-Manager)
Thomas H. McIntosh 1919–35
(Secretary-Manager)
Theo Kelly 1936–48
Cliff Britton 1948–56
Ian Buchan 1956–58
Johnny Carey 1958–61
Harry Catterick 1961–73
Billy Bingham 1973–77
Gordon Lee 1977–81
Howard Kendall 1981–87
Colin Harvey 1987–90
Howard Kendall 1990–93
Mike Walker 1994
Joe Royle 1994–97
Howard Kendall 1997–98
Walter Smith 1998–2002
David Moyes March 2002–

LATEST SEQUENCES

Longest Sequence of League Wins: 12, 24.3.1894 – 13.10.1894.

Longest Sequence of League Defeats: 6, 26.12.1996 – 29.1.1997.

Longest Sequence of League Draws: 5, 4.5.1977 – 16.5.1977.

Longest Sequence of Unbeaten League Matches: 20, 29.4.1978 – 16.12.1978.

Longest Sequence Without a League Win: 14, 6.3.1937 – 4.9.1937.

Successive Scoring Runs: 40 from 15.3.1930.

Successive Non-scoring Runs: 6 from 3.3.1951.

TEN YEAR LEAGUE RECORD

		P	W	D	L	F	A	Pts	Pos
1993-94	PR Lge	42	12	8	22	42	63	44	17
1994-95	PR Lge	42	11	17	14	44	51	50	15
1995-96	PR Lge	38	17	10	11	64	44	61	6
1996-97	PR Lge	38	10	12	16	44	57	42	15
1997-98	PR Lge	38	9	13	16	41	56	40	17
1998-99	PR Lge	38	11	10	17	42	47	43	14
1999-2000	PR Lge	38	12	14	12	59	49	50	13
2000-01	PR Lge	38	11	9	18	45	59	42	16
2001-02	PR Lge	38	11	10	17	45	57	43	15
2002-03	PR Lge	38	17	8	13	48	49	59	7

DID YOU KNOW ?

Though former schoolboy international wing-half Alec Farrall made his Everton debut at only 17 years 51 days on 22 April 1953 against Lincoln City, his next four League games came in successive seasons until 1956–57.

EVERTON 2002–03 LEAGUE RECORD

Match No.	Date	Venue	Opponents	Result	H/T Score	Lg. Pos.	Goalscorers	Attendance
1	Aug 17	H	Tottenham H	D 2-2	1-0	—	Pembridge [37], Radzinski [81]	40,020
2	24	A	Sunderland	W 1-0	0-0	6	Campbell [28]	37,698
3	28	H	Birmingham C	D 1-1	0-0	—	Unsworth [90]	37,199
4	31	A	Manchester C	L 1-3	1-2	12	Unsworth (pen) [29]	34,835
5	Sept 11	A	Southampton	L 0-1	0-0	—		29,190
6	14	H	Middlesbrough	W 2-1	1-1	10	Campbell 2 [32, 77]	32,440
7	22	A	Aston Villa	L 2-3	0-1	13	Radzinski [51], Campbell [66]	30,023
8	28	H	Fulham	W 2-0	2-0	9	Campbell [44], Gravesen [45]	34,380
9	Oct 7	A	Manchester U	L 0-3	0-0	—		67,629
10	19	H	Arsenal	W 2-1	1-1	9	Radzinski [22], Rooney [90]	39,038
11	27	A	West Ham U	W 1-0	0-0	8	Carsley [70]	34,117
12	Nov 3	A	Leeds U	W 1-0	0-0	6	Rooney [80]	40,168
13	9	H	Charlton Ath	W 1-0	1-0	4	Radzinski [31]	37,621
14	17	A	Blackburn R	W 1-0	1-0	4	Campbell [19]	26,494
15	23	H	WBA	W 1-0	1-0	3	Radzinski [35]	40,113
16	Dec 1	A	Newcastle U	L 1-2	1-0	5	Campbell [17]	51,607
17	7	H	Chelsea	L 1-3	1-2	5	Naysmith [43]	39,396
18	14	H	Blackburn R	W 2-1	2-1	4	Carsley [12], Rooney [25]	36,578
19	22	A	Liverpool	D 0-0	0-0	4		44,025
20	26	A	Birmingham C	D 1-1	1-1	4	Radzinski [44]	29,505
21	28	H	Bolton W	D 0-0	0-0	5		39,480
22	Jan 1	H	Manchester C	D 2-2	1-1	5	Watson [6], Radzinski [90]	40,163
23	12	A	Tottenham H	L 3-4	1-1	6	McBride [10], Watson [58], Radzinski [74]	36,066
24	18	H	Sunderland	W 2-1	0-1	5	McBride 2 [51, 57]	37,049
25	28	A	Bolton W	W 2-1	2-0	—	Watson 2 [33, 39]	25,119
26	Feb 1	H	Leeds U	W 2-0	0-0	5	Unsworth (pen) [55], Radzinski [67]	40,153
27	8	A	Charlton Ath	L 1-2	0-1	5	McBride [69]	26,607
28	22	H	Southampton	W 2-1	0-1	5	Radzinski 2 [83, 90]	36,569
29	Mar 1	A	Middlesbrough	D 1-1	1-0	4	Watson [23]	32,467
30	15	H	West Ham U	D 0-0	0-0	5		40,158
31	23	A	Arsenal	L 1-2	0-1	6	Rooney [56]	38,042
32	Apr 6	H	Newcastle U	W 2-1	1-1	5	Rooney [18], Unsworth (pen) [65]	40,031
33	12	A	WBA	W 2-1	2-1	5	Hoult (og) [23], Campbell [45]	26,713
34	19	H	Liverpool	L 1-2	0-1	6	Unsworth (pen) [58]	40,162
35	21	A	Chelsea	L 1-4	0-1	6	Carsley [77]	40,921
36	26	H	Aston Villa	W 2-1	0-0	6	Campbell [59], Rooney [90]	40,167
37	May 3	A	Fulham	L 0-2	0-2	6		18,385
38	11	H	Manchester U	L 1-2	1-1	7	Campbell [8]	40,168

Final League Position: 7

GOALSCORERS

League (48): Radzinski 11, Campbell 10, Rooney 6, Unsworth 5 (4 pens), Watson 5, McBride 4, Carsley 3, Gravesen 1, Naysmith 1, Pembridge 1, own goal 1.
Worthington Cup (7): Campbell 2, Rooney 2, Naysmith 1, Unsworth 1 (pen), Watson 1.
FA Cup (1): Alexandersson 1.

Wright R 33	Hibbert T 23 + 1	Naysmith G 24 + 4	Stubbs A 34 + 1	Weir D 27 + 4	Li Tie 28 + 1	Gravesen T 30 + 3	Rooney W 14 + 19	Campbell K 31 + 5	Radzinski T 27 + 3	Pembridge M 19 + 2	Rodrigo — + 4	Alexandersson N 4 + 3	Unsworth D 32 + 1	Linderoth T 2 + 3	Simonsen S 2	Gerrard P 2	Li Weifeng 1	Carsley L 21 + 3	Yobo J 22 + 2	Pistone A 10 + 5	Watson S 14 + 4	Gemmill S 10 + 6	Baardsen E 1	Osman L — + 2	McBride B 7 + 1	Ferguson D — + 7	Chadwick N — + 1	*Match No.*
1	2	3	4	5	6¹	7	8²	9	10³	11	12	13	14															1
1	2	3	4	5	6²	8	12	9	10	11		7¹		13														2
	2	3¹	4▮	5	6	7	8	9	10		12		11		1													3
	2	3	4	5	6³	8	12	9	10		13	7¹	11²	14	1													4
	2			5	6	8	12	9	10	11	13	7¹	3²			1	4											5
	2		4	5	6	8	12	9	10²	11		7¹	3			1		13										6
1	2		4	5	6	7	8¹	9	10	11		12	3															7
1	2			5	8	7		9	10	11			3					4	6									8
1	2			5▮	7	8	12	9	10¹	11			3					4	6									9
1	2		12	5	4³	8	13	9	10²	11			3	14				7¹	6									10
1	2		4		8²		12	9	10¹	11			3	6				7	5	13								11
1	2	12	4		8¹		13	9	10²	11			3	6				7	5									12
1	2	12	4²	13	6¹	8	14	9	10³	11			3					7	5									13
1	2	3²	4	12	6³	8	13	9	10¹				11					7	5		14							14
1	2	3²	4		6	8	12	9	10¹				11					7	5	13								15
1	2		4	12	6	8	13	9	10²	11			3					7¹	5▮									16
1	2	11	4		6²	8	12	9	10¹				3▮					7	5			13						17
1	2³	11	4	12	6¹	8	10²	9	13				3					7	5	14								18
1	2²	11	4	5		8	12	9	10¹	6								7		3	13							19
1		11	4	5		8	12▮	9	10¹	6²								7	2	3	13							20
1		11²	4	5	6	8	10	9¹	12	13		14						7³	2	3								21
1		3	4	5	6	8³	10	9¹	12	11								13	2²		7	14						22
		11	4		6²				10				3					12	5¹	2	7	8	1	13	9			23
1		11	4	5	6¹	12		13	10				3							2	7	8			9²			24
1		11¹	4²	5	6				10	12			3						13	2	7	8			9			25
1		11	4	5	6			12	10				3							2	7	8			9¹			26
1		11	4³	5	6	7	12	13	10				3¹						14	2		8²			9			27
1		11³	4	5	6¹	12	14	13	10				3							2	7	8			9²			28
1		11	4	5		6¹	12	9²	10				3							2	7	8			13			29
1	2	11³	4	5	12	6	13	14	10				3								7	8¹			9²			30
1			4	5	6¹	8	10	9		11			3						2		7²	12				13		31
1		12	4	5		8	10	9		11¹			3					6	2		7							32
1		12	4	5		8²	10	9		11¹			3					6	2		7³	13				14		33
1		11▮	4	5▮		8¹	10	9					3					6	2		7²	12				13		34
1	12	11	4	5	6³	13	10	9					3¹					7	2²			8				14		35
1	2	11	4	5		8	10¹	9					3³					6			7²	12		13		14		36
1	2²		4			6	10	9		11¹			3					7	5	12	13	8³				14		37
1	2	11¹	4			8³	10	9²					3					6	5	12	7					13	14	38

Worthington Cup

Second Round	Wrexham	(a)	3-0
Third Round	Newcastle U	(a)	3-3
Fourth Round	Chelsea	(a)	1-4

FA Cup

Third Round	Shrewsbury T	(a)	1-2

EXETER CITY

Conference

FOUNDATION

Exeter City was formed in 1904 by the amalgamation of St Sidwell's United and Exeter United. The club first played in the East Devon League and then the Plymouth & District League. After an exhibition match between West Bromwich Albion and Woolwich Arsenal was held to test interest as Exeter was then a rugby stronghold, Exeter City decided at a meeting at the Red Lion Hotel to turn professional in 1908.

St James Park, Exeter EX4 6PX.

Telephone: (01392) 411 243.

Fax: (01392) 413 959.

ClubCall: 09068 121 634.

Website: www.exetercityfc.co.uk

Training Ground: (01395) 232784.

Ground Capacity: 9,036.

Record Attendance: 20,984 v Sunderland, FA Cup 6th rd (replay), 4 March 1931.

Record Receipts: £59,862.98 v Aston Villa, FA Cup 3rd rd, 8 January 1994.

Pitch Measurements: 114yd × 73yd.

Chairman: J. Russell.

Director: M. Lewis.

Associate Directors: M. Shelbourne, P. Dobson, J. Tagg, S. Perryman, D. Newbery.

Manager: Eamonn Dolan.

Physio: Damien Davey.

Company Secretary: P. Carter.

Secretary: Sally Cooke.

Colours: Red and white shirts, white shorts, white stockings.

Change Colours: Purple and white.

Year Formed: 1904.

Turned Professional: 1908.

Ltd Co.: 1908.

Club Nickname: 'The Grecians'.

First Football League Game: 28 August 1920, Division 3, v Brentford (h) W 3–0 – Pym; Coleburne, Feebury (1p); Crawshaw, Carrick, Mitton; Appleton, Makin, Wright (1), Vowles (1), Dockray.

HONOURS

Football League: Division 3 best season: 8th, 1979–80; Division 3 (S) – Runners-up 1932–33; Division 4 – Champions 1989–90; Runners-up 1976–77.

FA Cup: best season: 6th rd replay, 1931, 6th rd 1981.

Football League Cup: never beyond 4th rd.

Division 3 (S) Cup: Winners 1934.

SKY SPORTS FACT FILE

Full-back Wilf Lowton who signed for Exeter City in 1925 after local schoolboy honours, was transferred to Wolverhampton Wanderers, became captain and led them to promotion before returning to Exeter to end his career.

Record League Victory: 8–1 v Coventry C, Division 3 (S), 4 December 1926 – Bailey; Pollard, Charlton; Pullen, Pool, Garrett; Purcell (2), McDevitt, Blackmore (2), Dent (2), Compton (2). 8–1 v Aldershot, Division 3 (S), 4 May 1935 – Chesters; Gray, Miller; Risdon, Webb, Angus; Jack Scott (1), Wrightson (1), Poulter (3), McArthur (1), Dryden (1), (1 og).

Record Cup Victory: 14–0 v Weymouth, FA Cup 1st qual rd, 3 October 1908 – Fletcher; Craig, Bulcock; Ambler, Chadwick, Wake; Parnell (1), Watson (1), McGuigan (4), Bell (6), Copestake (2).

Record Defeat: 0–9 v Notts Co, Division 3 (S), 16 October 1948. 0–9 v Northampton T, Division 3 (S), 12 April 1958.

Most League Points (2 for a win): 62, Division 4, 1976–77.

Most League Points (3 for a win): 89, Division 4, 1989–90.

Most League Goals: 88, Division 3 (S), 1932–33.

Highest League Scorer in Season: Fred Whitlow, 33, Division 3 (S), 1932–33.

Most League Goals in Total Aggregate: Tony Kellow, 129, 1976–78, 1980–83, 1985–88.

Most League Goals in One Match: 4, Harold 'Jazzo' Kirk v Portsmouth, Division 3S, 3 March 1923; 4, Fred Dent v Bristol R, Division 3S, 5 November 1927; 4, Fred Whitlow v Watford, Division 3S, 29 October 1932.

Most Capped Player: Dermot Curtis, 1 (17), Eire.

Most League Appearances: Arnold Mitchell, 495, 1952–66.

Youngest League Player: Cliff Bastin, 16 years 31 days v Coventry C, 14 April 1928.

Record Transfer Fee Received: £500,000 from Manchester C for Martin Phillips, November 1995.

Record Transfer Fee Paid: £65,000 to Blackpool for Tony Kellow, March 1980.

Football League Record: 1920 Elected Division 3; 1921–58 Division 3 (S); 1958–64 Division 4; 1964–66 Division 3; 1966–77 Division 4; 1977–84 Division 3; 1984–90 Division 4; 1990–92 Division 3; 1992–94 Division 2; 1994–2003 Division 3; 2003– Conference.

MANAGERS

Arthur Chadwick 1910–22
Fred Mavin 1923–27
Dave Wilson 1928–29
Billy McDevitt 1929–35
Jack English 1935–39
George Roughton 1945–52
Norman Kirkman 1952–53
Norman Dodgin 1953–57
Bill Thompson 1957–58
Frank Broome 1958–60
Glen Wilson 1960–62
Cyril Spiers 1962–63
Jack Edwards 1963–65
Ellis Stuttard 1965–66
Jock Basford 1966–67
Frank Broome 1967–69
Johnny Newman 1969–76
Bobby Saxton 1977–79
Brian Godfrey 1979–83
Gerry Francis 1983–84
Jim Iley 1984–85
Colin Appleton 1985–87
Terry Cooper 1988–91
Alan Ball 1991–94
Terry Cooper 1994–95
Peter Fox 1995–2000
Noel Blake 2000–01
John Cornforth 2001–02
Neil McNab 2002–03
Gary Peters 2003
Eamonn Dolan June 2003–

LATEST SEQUENCES

Longest Sequence of League Wins: 7, 23.4.1977 – 20.8.1977.

Longest Sequence of League Defeats: 7, 14.1.1984 – 25.2.1984.

Longest Sequence of League Draws: 6, 13.9.1986 – 4.10.1986.

Longest Sequence of Unbeaten League Matches: 13, 23.8.1986 – 25.10.1986.

Longest Sequence Without a League Win: 18, 21.2.1995 – 19.8.1995.

Successive Scoring Runs: 22 from 15.9.1958.

Successive Non-scoring Runs: 6 from 24.11.1923.

TEN YEAR LEAGUE RECORD

		P	*W*	*D*	*L*	*F*	*A*	*Pts*	*Pos*
1993-94	Div 2	46	11	12	23	52	83	45	22
1994-95	Div 3	42	8	10	24	36	70	34	22
1995-96	Div 3	46	13	18	15	46	53	57	14
1996-97	Div 3	46	12	12	22	48	73	48	22
1997-98	Div 3	46	15	15	16	68	63	60	15
1998-99	Div 3	46	17	12	17	47	50	63	12
1999-2000	Div 3	46	11	11	24	46	72	44	21
2000-01	Div 3	46	12	14	20	40	58	50	19
2001-02	Div 3	46	14	13	19	48	73	55	16
2002-03	Div 3	46	11	15	20	50	64	48	23

DID YOU KNOW?

In 1932–33 Exeter City scored a club record at the time of 88 goals in 42 matches and also had their best defensive season in conceding just 48 goals in finishing runners-up to Brentford in Division Three (South).

EXETER CITY 2002–03 LEAGUE RECORD

Match No.	Date	Venue	Opponents	Result	H/T Score	Lg. Pos.	Goalscorers	Attendance
1	Aug 10	A	Shrewsbury T	L 0-1	0-1	—		3781
2	13	H	Scunthorpe U	D 1-1	0-0	—	Thomas ^{90}	3722
3	17	H	Hull C	W 3-1	2-1	11	Sharpe ^{21}, Flack ^{45}, Whittle (og) ^{46}	4257
4	24	A	Kidderminster H	L 3-4	2-2	15	Flack ^{3}, Thomas ^{15}, Roscoe ^{78}	2195
5	26	H	Torquay U	L 1-2	1-2	19	Coppinger ^{41}	6065
6	31	A	Carlisle U	W 2-0	2-0	13	Goodman ^{42}, Gaia ^{45}	4806
7	Sept 7	H	Bournemouth	L 1-3	1-2	17	Roscoe ^{7}	4466
8	14	A	Bristol R	D 1-1	1-1	18	Flack ^{27}	6498
9	17	A	Wrexham	L 0-4	0-2	—		2968
10	21	H	Leyton Orient	W 1-0	0-0	18	Walker J (pen) ^{70}	2784
11	28	A	Southend U	L 0-1	0-1	19		3364
12	Oct 5	H	York C	L 0-1	0-1	21		3178
13	12	H	Rushden & D	D 1-1	1-1	21	Flack ^{6}	2884
14	19	A	Lincoln C	L 0-1	0-0	22		2979
15	26	H	Darlington	L 0-4	0-2	23		2757
16	29	A	Rochdale	D 3-3	1-1	—	Flack 2 $^{1, 75}$, Thomas ^{79}	1944
17	Nov 2	A	Boston U	W 3-0	1-0	21	Hocking (og) ^{35}, Moor 2 $^{54, 81}$	2474
18	9	H	Hartlepool U	L 1-2	0-0	22	Moor ^{49}	2778
19	23	H	Cambridge U	L 1-2	1-1	22	Flack ^{11}	2722
20	30	A	Bury	L 0-1	0-0	23		2039
21	Dec 14	H	Swansea C	W 1-0	0-0	20	Roscoe ^{73}	2625
22	21	A	Oxford U	D 2-2	0-0	20	Flack ^{58}, Walker J (pen) ^{89}	7057
23	28	H	Macclesfield T	D 1-1	0-1	22	Coppinger ^{63}	3017
24	Jan 11	A	Hull C	D 2-2	0-0	22	Partridge ^{68}, Flack ^{90}	13,667
25	18	H	Carlisle U	W 1-0	0-0	21	Partridge ^{60}	3333
26	21	A	Scunthorpe U	D 1-1	0-1	—	Devine ^{75}	2461
27	25	A	Macclesfield T	D 1-1	0-0	20	Devine ^{90}	2035
28	Feb 1	H	Shrewsbury T	D 1-1	1-0	21	Devine ^{19}	3587
29	8	A	Hartlepool U	L 1-2	0-0	22	Walker J (pen) ^{83}	5058
30	11	A	Torquay U	L 0-1	0-1	—		5761
31	15	H	Boston U	L 0-2	0-1	24		2834
32	18	H	Kidderminster H	L 2-5	1-3	—	Devine ^{3}, Coppinger ^{47}	1957
33	22	A	Bournemouth	L 0-2	0-1	24		6674
34	Mar 1	H	Bristol R	D 0-0	0-0	24		5759
35	4	H	Wrexham	W 1-0	0-0	—	Flack ^{73}	2537
36	8	A	Leyton Orient	D 1-1	0-1	24	Devine ^{90}	3667
37	15	A	Darlington	D 2-2	1-0	23	Pettefer ^{19}, Devine ^{70}	2476
38	18	H	Lincoln C	W 2-0	2-0	—	Coppinger ^{22}, Sheldon ^{37}	4009
39	22	H	Rochdale	D 1-1	1-1	23	Walker J (pen) ^{15}	4003
40	29	A	Rushden & D	L 0-1	0-0	24		4921
41	Apr 5	H	Bury	L 1-2	0-2	24	Flack ^{52}	3338
42	12	A	Cambridge U	L 1-2	1-0	24	Iriekpen (og) ^{1}	5218
43	19	H	Oxford U	D 2-2	2-1	24	Devine ^{10}, Walker J ^{24}	4900
44	21	A	Swansea C	W 1-0	0-0	23	Devine ^{69}	9115
45	26	A	York C	W 2-0	1-0	23	Flack ^{5}, Coppinger ^{55}	4840
46	May 3	H	Southend U	W 1-0	0-0	23	Flack ^{90}	9036

Final League Position: 23

GOALSCORERS

League (50): Flack 13, Devine 8, Coppinger 5, Walker J 5 (4 pens), Moor 3, Roscoe 3, Thomas 3, Partridge 2, Gaia 1, Goodman 1, Pettefer 1, Sharpe 1, Sheldon 1, own goals 3.
Worthington Cup (1): McConnell 1 (pen).
FA Cup (6): Gaia 1, Lock 1, McConnell 1, Moor 1, Sheldon 1, Walker 1 (pen).
LDV Vans Trophy (1): Sheldon 1.

Miller K 46	McConnell B 13 + 8	Power G 27 + 3	Gaia S 33	Curran C 10 + 3	Walker J 35 + 4	Cronin G 28 + 11	Taylor C 1 + 2	Coppinger J 35 + 8	Goodman D 11 + 2	Roscoe A 23 + 10	Thomas M 22 + 4	Flack S 39 + 1	Sheldon G 7 + 12	Sharpe L 4	Whitworth N 7 + 1	Watson A 3	Ampadu K 18 + 5	Harries P — + 1	Breslan G — + 10	Hiley S 37	Simpkins M 4 + 1	Moor R 2 + 15	Lock M 1 + 2	Buxton L 4	Pettefer C 30 + 1	Pilkington G 7	Barnard L 3	Alcide C 1	Fraser S — + 1	Virgo A 8 + 1	Partridge S 2 + 2	Devine S 21 + 2	Whitbread A 7	Todd C 12	Kilheeney C — + 4	Baker P 5 + 1	*Match No.*
1	2	3	4▮	5	6[1]	7	8[2]	9	10	11[3]	12	13	14																								1
1	2	3	4	5	6[1]	8		7	10[2]		12	9	13	11																							2
1	2	3	4	5	6	8		7	10[1]	13	12	9[3]	14	11[2]																							3
1	2	3		5	6	8[1]		7		13	10	9	12	11[2]	4																						4
1	2	3	4		6[3]		12	7		13	10	9	8[1]	11[2]		5	14																				5
1	2	3	4			6	12	7[2]	10[3]	11	8	9[1]	13			5	14																				6
1	2	3	4▮		12	6		7	10	11[3]	8[1]	9[2]	13			5	14																				7
1	2	3	4	5	6	8		9		11	7[1]	10[2]					12	13																			8
1	2[3]	3	4	5▮	6	8		9	12	11[2]	7[1]	10			13				14																		9
1	12	3			6	13		7[3]	10	11[1]		9			4		8[2]		14	2	5																10
1		3			6[2]	12		7	10	11[1]		9[3]			4		8		13	2	5	14															11
1	12	3			6	13		7	10	11[3]		9[2]	14		4		8			2[1]	5																12
1			4		6[3]	8		7	10[2]	11[1]		9			5		12			2	3	13	14														13
1		3[2]	4		6	7		10		11[3]		9	12		5▮		8[1]			2	14	13															14
1			4		6			10		12	8	9	7[1]							2		13	3[2]	5	11												15
1			4[1]	12	6[2]	8		14		13	7	9			3[3]					2		10		5	11												16
1						8		2		3	7	9								4		12		5	11	6	10[1]										17
1	12	13				4		9		3[2]	7									2		8		5	11	6		10[1]									18
1▮			4		6	8▮		7[1]		3[3]		9	12▮							2		13			11	5	10[2]		14								19
1			4		6[3]	8		12		3[1]		9[2]								2		13	14		11	5	10			7							20
1	4[1]		6					10[2]		3	7	9					8		13	2		12			11	5											21
1	12[2]		4[3]		6			10		3[1]	7	9					8			2		13			11	5				14							22
1	2[1]				6	8[3]		10[2]			7	9	13						14	3		12			11	5				4							23
1		12▮	4		6[1]	8		10[3]			7	9	2[2]							3					11					5	13	14					24
1		3	4		12	6		13			7[1]	9								2					11					5	10	8[2]					25
1		3	4[1]		12	6		13			7	9								2					11					5	10[2]	8					26
1	12				6[1]	8				3[3]	7[2]	9▮								2		13			11					5	14	10	4				27
1			4		6[1]	8		12			7	9								2					11					5		10	3				28
1		3	4		12	8		9			7[1]									2		13			11					5[2]		10	6				29
1	12	3[1]	4		6	8		7[2]	9											2		13			11							10	5				30
1	12	3[1]	4		6	8			9	13	7[2]									2					11							10	5				31
1			4		6	8▮		13		3[1]	12	9	7[2]							2					11							10	5				32
1	7	3[2]	4		6	8		12	13			9[1]								2					11							10	5				33
1	7[2]	3	4	5	6	8		13		12		9								2					11[1]							10					34
1		3	4					8		7[2]		9	13				6[3]		14	2		12			11							10[1]		5			35
1		3[2]	4	12				8[3]		11	7[1]	9					6		14	2		13										10		5			36
1		3	4			12				7[2]	8[1]	9	14				6		13	2					11							10[3]		5			37
1		3	4[1]	12	6	13		7[3]					9				8[2]		14	2					11							10		5			38
1		3		4	6	12		7		13			9[3]				8[1]			2					11[2]							10		5	14		39
1		3		4	6	12		7[3]		13		9					8[1]			2					11[2]							10		5	14		40
1		3[2]		4[3]	6	8[1]		7		12		9					11			2					13							10		5		14	41
1					6[1]	12		10		3		9	7[2]				8[3]		14	2					11							13		5		4	42
1	12				6			7		3[1]		9					8			2					11							10		5		4	43
1		12	4[1]		6	13		7				9					8			2					11							10[2]		3		5	44
1			4		6	12		7[2]				9					8			2					11							10[1]		3	13	5	45
1			4[2]		6	12		7				9					8[1]			2					11							10		3	13	5	46

Worthington Cup

First Round	Brighton & HA	(a)	1-2

FA Cup

First Round	Forest Green R	(a)	0-0
		(h)	2-1
Second Round	Rushden & D	(h)	3-1
Third Round	Charlton Ath	(a)	1-3

LDV Vans Trophy

First Round	Bristol R	(h)	1-0
Second Round	Cardiff C	(h)	0-3

FULHAM — FA Premiership

FOUNDATION

Churchgoers were responsible for the foundation of Fulham, which first saw the light of day as Fulham St Andrew's Church Sunday School FC in 1879. They won the West London Amateur Cup in 1887 and the championship of the West London League in its initial season of 1892–93. The name Fulham had been adopted in 1888.

South Africa Road, London W12 7PA. (QPR)

Telephone: (020) 7893 8383. ***Fax:*** (020) 7384 4715.
Website: http://www.fulhamfc.co.uk
ClubCall: 09068 440 044.

Ground Capacity: 19,148.

Record Attendance: 49,335 v Millwall, Division 2, 8 October 1938.

Record Receipts: £139,235 v Watford, Division 2, 2 May 1998.

Pitch Measurements: 110yd × 75yd.

Chairman: M. Al Fayed.

Directors: W. F. Muddyman (Vice-chairman), Stuart Benson, Andy Muddyman, Tim Delaney, Lee Hoos, Andy Ambler, Juliet Slot, Mark Collins, Moody Fayed, Bruce Langham.

Chief Executive: Bruce Langham.

Manager: Chris Coleman.

Chief Scout: John Marshall. ***Academy Director:*** Steve Kean.

Community Department Manager: Gary Mulcahey (020) 7384 4759.
Stadium Manager: Francis Broughton. ***Club Secretary & Deputy Managing Director:*** Lee Hoos.
Sales and Marketing Director: Juliet Slot. ***Head of Communications:*** Sarah Brookes.

Colours: White shirts, black trim, black shorts, white stockings red and black trim.

Change Colours: Red and black striped shirts, red shorts and stockings.

Year Formed: 1879.

Turned Professional: 1898.

Ltd Co.: 1903.

Reformed: 1987.

Previous Name: 1879, Fulham St Andrew's; 1888, Fulham.

Club Nickname: 'Cottagers'.

Previous Grounds: 1879, Star Road, Fulham; c.1883, Eel Brook Common, 1884, Lillie Road; 1885, Putney Lower Common; 1886, Ranelagh House, Fulham; 1888, Barn Elms, Castelnau; 1889, Purser's Cross (Roskell's Field), Parsons Green Lane; 1891, Eel Brook Common; 1891, Half Moon, Putney; 1895, Captain James Field, West Brompton; 1896, Craven Cottage.

First Football League Game: 3 September 1907, Division 2, v Hull C (h) L 0–1 – Skene; Ross, Lindsay; Collins, Morrison, Goldie; Dalrymple, Freeman, Bevan, Hubbard, Threlfall.

Record League Victory: 10–1 v Ipswich T, Division 1, 26 December 1963 – Macedo; Cohen, Langley; Mullery (1), Keetch, Robson (1); Key, Cook (1), Leggat (4), Haynes, Howfield (3).

HONOURS

Football League: Division 1 – Champions 2000–01; Division 2 – Champions 1948–49, 1998–99; Runners-up 1958–59; Division 3 (S) – Champions 1931–32; Division 3 – Runners-up 1970–71, 1996–97.

FA Cup: Runners-up 1975.

Football League Cup: best season: 5th rd, 1968, 1971, 2000.

European Competitions: *UEFA Cup:* 2002–03. *Intertoto Cup:* 2002 (winners)

SKY SPORTS FACT FILE

Fulham played 20 cup matches in 2002–03 beginning with the Intertoto Cup in the summer, which they won, continued in the UEFA Cup, then the League Cup and ended on 26 February in an FA Cup replay at Burnley.

Record Cup Victory: 7–0 v Swansea C, FA Cup 1st rd, 11 November 1995 – Lange; Jupp (1), Herrera, Barkus (Brooker (1)), Moore, Angus, Thomas (1), Morgan, Brazil (Hamill), Conroy (3) (Bolt), Cusack (1).

Record Defeat: 0–10 v Liverpool, League Cup 2nd rd 1st leg, 23 September 1986.

Most League Points (2 for a win): 60, Division 2, 1958–59 and Division 3, 1970–71.

Most League Points (3 for a win): 101, Division 2, 1998–99.

Most League Goals: 111, Division 3 (S), 1931–32.

Highest League Scorer in Season: Frank Newton, 43, Division 3 (S), 1931–32.

Most League Goals in Total Aggregate: Gordon Davies, 159, 1978–84, 1986–91.

Most League Goals in One Match: 5, Fred Harrison v Stockport Co, Division 2, 5 September 1908; 5, Bedford Jezzard v Hull C, Division 2, 8 October 1955; 5, Jimmy Hill v Doncaster R, Division 2, 15 March 1958; 5, Steve Earle v Halifax T, Division 3, 16 September 1969.

Most Capped Player: Johnny Haynes, 56, England.

Most League Appearances: Johnny Haynes, 594, 1952–70.

Youngest League Player: Tony Mahoney, 17 years 38 days v Cardiff C, 6 November 1976.

Record Transfer Fee Received: £800,000 from Bristol C for Tony Thorpe, February 1998.

Record Transfer Fee Paid: £11,500,000 to Lyon for Steve Marlet, August 2001.

Football League Record: 1907 Elected to Division 2; 1928–32 Division 3 (S); 1932–49 Division 2; 1949–52 Division 1; 1952–59 Division 2; 1959–68 Division 1; 1968–69 Division 2; 1969–71 Division 3; 1971–80 Division 2; 1980–82 Division 3; 1982–86 Division 2; 1986–92 Division 3; 1992–94 Division 2; 1994–97 Division 3; 1997–99 Division 2; 1999–2001 Division 1; 2001– FA Premier League.

MANAGERS

Harry Bradshaw 1904–09
Phil Kelso 1909–24
Andy Ducat 1924–26
Joe Bradshaw 1926–29
Ned Liddell 1929–31
Jim MacIntyre 1931–34
Jimmy Hogan 1934–35
Jack Peart 1935–48
Frank Osborne 1948–64
(was Secretary-Manager or General Manager for most of this period)
Bill Dodgin Snr 1949–53
Duggie Livingstone 1956–58
Bedford Jezzard 1958–64
(General Manager for last two months)
Vic Buckingham 1965–68
Bobby Robson 1968
Bill Dodgin Jnr 1969–72
Alec Stock 1972–76
Bobby Campbell 1976–80
Malcolm Macdonald 1980–84
Ray Harford 1984–96
Ray Lewington 1986–90
Alan Dicks 1990–91
Don Mackay 1991–94
Ian Branfoot 1994–96
(continued as General Manager)
Micky Adams 1996–97
Ray Wilkins 1997–98
Kevin Keegan 1998–99
(Chief Operating Officer)
Paul Bracewell 1999–2000
Jean Tigana 2000–03
Chris Coleman April 2003–

LATEST SEQUENCES

Longest Sequence of League Wins: 12, 7.5.2000 – 18.10.2000.

Longest Sequence of League Defeats: 11, 2.12.1961 – 24.2.1962.

Longest Sequence of League Draws: 6, 14.10.1995 – 18.11.1995.

Longest Sequence of Unbeaten League Matches: 15, 26.1.1999 – 13.4.1999.

Longest Sequence Without a League Win: 15, 25.2.1950 – 23.8.1950.

Successive Scoring Runs: 26 from 28.3.1931.

Successive Non-scoring Runs: 6 from 21.8.1971.

TEN YEAR LEAGUE RECORD

		P	W	D	L	F	A	Pts	Pos
1993-94	Div 2	46	14	10	22	50	63	52	21
1994-95	Div 3	42	16	14	12	60	54	62	8
1995-96	Div 3	46	12	17	17	57	63	53	17
1996-97	Div 3	46	25	12	9	72	38	87	2
1997-98	Div 2	46	20	10	16	60	43	70	6
1998-99	Div 2	46	31	8	7	79	32	101	1
1999-2000	Div 1	46	17	16	13	49	41	67	9
2000-01	Div 1	46	30	11	5	90	32	101	1
2001-02	PR Lge	38	10	14	14	36	44	44	13
2002-03	PR Lge	38	13	9	16	41	50	48	14

DID YOU KNOW 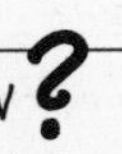

On 6 November 2002 in the League Cup against Bury, Fulham included 11 full internationals from different countries: Cameroon, Denmark, Eire, France, Jamaica, Japan, Latvia, Morocco, Northern Ireland, Scotland and Wales.

FULHAM 2002–03 LEAGUE RECORD

Match No.	Date	Venue	Opponents	Result	H/T Score	Lg. Pos.	Goalscorers	Atten-dance
1	Aug 17	H	Bolton W	W 4-1	3-1	—	Saha (pen) [11], Legwinski 2 [33, 79], Marlet (pen) [38]	16,338
2	24	A	Middlesbrough	D 2-2	0-1	3	Davis [89], Sava [90]	28,588
3	31	A	WBA	L 0-1	0-0	13		25,440
4	Sept 11	H	Tottenham H	W 3-2	0-2	—	Inamoto [68], Malbranque (pen) [84], Legwinski [90]	16,785
5	14	A	Sunderland	W 3-0	1-0	6	Inamoto [34], Hayles [54], Marlet [78]	35,432
6	23	H	Chelsea	D 0-0	0-0	—		16,503
7	28	A	Everton	L 0-2	0-2	8		34,380
8	Oct 6	H	Charlton Ath	W 1-0	1-0	5	Sava [36]	14,775
9	19	H	Manchester U	D 1-1	1-0	7	Marlet [35]	18,103
10	23	H	West Ham U	L 0-1	0-0	—		15,858
11	27	A	Southampton	L 2-4	2-2	11	Clark [15], Malbranque [25]	26,188
12	Nov 3	H	Arsenal	L 0-1	0-1	11		17,810
13	9	A	Aston Villa	L 1-3	0-1	13	Boa Morte [51]	29,563
14	17	A	Birmingham C	D 0-0	0-0	13		26,164
15	23	H	Liverpool	W 3-2	2-0	12	Sava 2 [5, 68], Davis [38]	18,144
16	30	A	Blackburn R	L 1-2	0-1	14	Marlet [60]	21,096
17	Dec 7	H	Leeds U	W 1-0	1-0	12	Djetou [10]	17,499
18	15	H	Birmingham C	L 0-1	0-1	14		14,692
19	21	A	Newcastle U	L 0-2	0-1	14		51,576
20	26	A	West Ham U	D 1-1	0-0	15	Sava [49]	35,025
21	28	H	Manchester C	L 0-1	0-0	16		17,937
22	Jan 11	A	Bolton W	D 0-0	0-0	16		25,156
23	19	H	Middlesbrough	W 1-0	1-0	15	Davis [39]	14,253
24	29	A	Manchester C	L 1-4	1-1	—	Malbranque [2]	33,260
25	Feb 1	A	Arsenal	L 1-2	1-1	15	Malbranque [29]	38,050
26	8	H	Aston Villa	W 2-1	2-1	15	Malbranque (pen) [14], Harley [36]	17,902
27	19	H	WBA	W 3-0	0-0	—	Saha [72], Wome [74], Malbranque (pen) [76]	15,799
28	24	A	Tottenham H	D 1-1	1-1	—	King (og) [15]	34,701
29	Mar 1	H	Sunderland	W 1-0	0-0	12	Saha [85]	16,286
30	15	H	Southampton	D 2-2	1-0	13	Saha [44], Svensson M (og) [52]	18,031
31	22	A	Manchester U	L 0-3	0-1	13		67,706
32	Apr 7	H	Blackburn R	L 0-4	0-2	—		14,019
33	12	A	Liverpool	L 0-2	0-1	15		42,121
34	19	H	Newcastle U	W 2-1	0-1	14	Legwinski [69], Clark [86]	17,900
35	22	A	Leeds U	L 0-2	0-1	—		37,220
36	26	A	Chelsea	D 1-1	0-1	15	Boa Morte [66]	40,792
37	May 3	H	Everton	W 2-0	2-0	15	Stubbs (og) [34], Wright (og) [43]	18,385
38	11	A	Charlton Ath	W 1-0	1-0	14	Saha (pen) [33]	26,089

Final League Position: 14

GOALSCORERS

League (41): Malbranque 6 (3 pens), Saha 5 (2 pens), Sava 5, Legwinski 4, Marlet 4 (1 pen), Davis 3, Boa Morte 2, Clark 2, Inamoto 2, Djetou 1, Harley 1, Hayles 1, Wome 1, own goals 4.
Worthington Cup (4): Stolcers 2, Boa Morte 1, Clark 1.
FA Cup (7): Malbranque 4 (2 pens), Goldbaek 1, Saha 1, Sava 1.
Intertoto Cup (11): Inamoto 4, Legwinski 2, Marlet 2, Davis 1, Hayles 1, Saha 1.
UEFA Cup (9): Malbranque 3 (1 pen), Marlet 3, Boa Morte 2, Hayles 1.

Van der Sar E 19	Finnan S 32	Brevett R 20	Melville A 24 + 2	Goma A 29	Davis S 28	Legwinski S 33 + 2	Malbranque S 35 + 2	Saha L 13 + 4	Marlet S 28	Boa Morte L 25 + 4	Inamoto J 9 + 10	Sava F 13 + 7	Knight Z 12 + 5	Wome P 13 + 1	Collins J — + 5	Hayles B 4 + 10	Ouaddou A 9 + 4	Djetou M 22 + 3	Stolcers A — + 5	Clark L 9 + 2	Goldbaek B 8 + 2	Willock C — + 2	Taylor M 18 + 1	Hammond E 3 + 7	Harley J 11	Herrera M 1 + 1	*Match No.*
1	2	3	4	5	6	7	8^{1}	9^{2}	10	11	12	13															1
1	2	3	4	5	6	7	8^{1}	9	10^{2}	11	12	13															2
1	2	3	4^{1}	5	6	7	12	13	10	11	8^{3}	9^{2}	14														3
1	2			5	6	7	12	9^{3}		11^{1}	8	10	4	3^{2}	13	14											4
1		3		5	6	7	11		9		8^{2}	12	4		13	10^{1}	2										5
1				5	6	7	11		9	12	8^{1}		4	3		10	2										6
1	2		12	5^{1}	6	7	11		9	13	8^{2}	14	4	3		10^{3}											7
1		3	4		6^{3}	7	8		9	11^{1}	12	10^{2}	5	14		13	2										8
1	7	3		5	6	8	11		9			10^{1}	4			12	2										9
1	2		4			7	6		9	11^{2}	8^{1}		5■	3		10		12	13								10
1	2	3		5		7	11		9	10			4^{2}			12	13	6^{1}		8							11
1	2	3	4	5		7	11^{1}		9	10	13					12	6	8^{2}									12
1	7	3	4	5		8	11		9	10^{2}	12	13					2^{3}	6^{1}	14								13
1	2	3■	4	5		8^{2}	11		9■	10^{3}	12		14					13		6	7^{1}						14
1	2	3		5■	6		11		9		12	10^{1}	4					8		13	7^{2}						15
1	2	3	4	5	6	7	11		9	10	12									8^{1}							16
1	2	3	4		6	8	9			10				11				5			7						17
1	2	3	4^{1}	5	6	7	9			10	13^{3}			11^{2}				8		12		14					18
1^{6}		3	4	5	6	8	10^{1}		9					11■				2			7	12	15				19
	2	3	4	5	6	8^{1}	7^{2}		9			10^{3}		11				12			13		1	14			20
	2	3		5	6	12	11^{2}		9			10	4					8^{1}			7		1	13			21
	2	3		5	6	8	11	9		12		10^{1}						4			7		1				22
	2	3		5	6	8	11		9	12		10^{1}						4			7		1				23
	2	3		5	6	8	11		9	10								4			7		1				24
	2		12	5	6	7^{1}	8	13	9	11		10^{2}						4					1		3		25
	2		4	5	6		7	9^{1}	10^{2}	11^{3}		12	13					8			14		1		3		26
	2		4	5^{1}			11^{2}	9	7		8	10		3			12	6	13				1				27
	2				6	8	7	12	9^{1}	11		10^{6}	13	3			5	4^{2}					1■			15	28
	2		4			6	7^{3}	9			8^{1}	10^{2}		11			12	5	14				1	13	3		29
			4	5		8	7	9	10		12^{2}			11^{1}			2	6	13						3	1	30
			4			8	7	9	10	11			5				2	6					1		3		31
	2			5		12	7	9	10^{2}	11			4					8		6^{1}			1	13	3		32
	2		4		6	8	7	9	10^{1}	11^{3}		12		3^{2}			13	5					1	14			33
	2		4		6	8	7^{1}	9^{3}		11^{2}					13	12		5		10			1	14	3		34
	2		4		6	7				11	8^{1}		13			12		5^{2}		10			1	9	3		35
	2		4	5	6	7	8^{2}			11^{1}					13	12				10			1	9	3		36
	2		4	5	6	7	8^{2}	12		11						13				10			1	9^{1}	3		37
	2		4	5	6^{1}	7	8	9^{3}		11^{2}					13	12				10			1	14	3		38

Worthington Cup

Third Round	Bury	(h)	3-1
Fourth Round	Wigan Ath	(a)	1-2

Intertoto Cup

Second Round	Haka	(h)	0-0
		(a)	1-1
Third Round	Egaleo	(h)	1-0
		(a)	1-1
Semi-final	Sochaux	(h)	1-0
		(a)	2-0
Final	Bologna	(a)	2-2
		(h)	3-1

FA Cup

Third Round	Birmingham C	(h)	3-1
Fourth Round	Charlton Ath	(h)	3-0
Fifth Round	Burnley	(h)	1-1
		(a)	0-3

UEFA Cup

First Round	Hajduk Split	(a)	1-0
		(h)	2-2
Second Round	Dynamo Zagreb	(a)	3-0
		(h)	2-1
Third Round	Hertha Berlin	(a)	1-2
		(h)	0-0

GILLINGHAM

Division 1

FOUNDATION

The success of the pioneering Royal Engineers of Chatham excited the interest of the residents of the Medway Towns and led to the formation of many clubs including Excelsior. After winning the Kent Junior Cup and the Chatham District League in 1893, Excelsior decided to go for bigger things and it was at a meeting in the Napier Arms, Brompton, in 1893 that New Brompton FC came into being, buying and developing the ground which is now Priestfield Stadium. Changed name to Gillingham in 1913, when they also changed their strip from black and white stripes to predominantly blue.

Priestfield Stadium, Gillingham, ME7 4DD.

Telephone: (01634) 300 000.
Fax: (01634) 850 986. ***ClubCall:*** 09068 332 211.

Ground Capacity: 11,000.

Record Attendance: 23,002 v QPR, FA Cup 3rd rd, 10 January 1948.

Record Receipts: £80,184 v Sheffield W, FA Cup 3rd rd, 7 January 1995.

Pitch Measurements: 114yd × 75yd.

Chairman/Chief Executive: P. D. P. Scally.

Directors: P. A. Spokes, N. Carter (Finance), M. J. Quarlington (Non-executive).
Associate Director: Yvonne Paulley.

Player Manager: Andy Hessenthaler.

Coach: Wayne Jones.

Physio: George Johnson.

Secretary: Mrs G. E. Poynter.

Colours: Blue/black.

Change Colours: White/yellow.

Year Formed: 1893.

Turned Professional: 1894.

Ltd Co.: 1893.

Previous Name: 1893, New Brompton; 1913, Gillingham.

Club Nickname: 'The Gills'.

First Football League Game: 28 August 1920, Division 3, v Southampton (h) D 1–1 – Branfield; Robertson, Sissons; Battiste, Baxter, Wigmore; Holt, Hall, Gilbey (1), Roe, Gore.

Record League Victory: 10–0 v Chesterfield, Division 3, 5 September 1987 – Kite; Haylock, Pearce, Shipley (2) (Lillis), West, Greenall (1), Pritchard (2), Shearer (2), Lovell, Elsey (2), David Smith (1).

Record Cup Victory: 10–1 v Gorleston, FA Cup 1st rd, 16 November 1957 – Brodie; Parry, Hannaway; Riggs, Boswell, Laing; Payne, Fletcher (2), Saunders (5), Morgan (1), Clark (2).

HONOURS

Football League: Promoted from Division 2 1999–2000 (play-offs); Division 3 – Runners-up 1995-96; Division 4 – Champions 1963–64; Runners-up 1973–74.

FA Cup: best season: 6th rd, 2000.

Football League Cup: best season: 4th rd, 1964, 1997.

SKY SPORTS FACT FILE

Hughie Russell scored nine goals for Gillingham in a 12-1 win over Gloucester City on 9 November 1946. He also missed a penalty. That season he registered 33 goals for the Southern League side.

Record Defeat: 2–9 v Nottingham F, Division 3 (S), 18 November 1950.

Most League Points (2 for a win): 62, Division 4, 1973–74.

Most League Points (3 for a win): 85, Division 2, 1999–2000.

Most League Goals: 90, Division 4, 1973–74.

Highest League Scorer in Season: Ernie Morgan, 31, Division 3 (S), 1954–55; Brian Yeo, 31, Division 4, 1973–74.

Most League Goals in Total Aggregate: Brian Yeo, 135, 1963–75.

Most League Goals in One Match: 6, Fred Cheesmur v Merthyr T, Division 3S, 26 April 1930.

Most Capped Player: Tony Cascarino, 3 (88), Republic of Ireland.

Most League Appearances: John Simpson, 571, 1957–72.

Youngest League Player: Billy Hughes, 15 years 275 days v Southend U, 13 April 1976.

Record Transfer Fee Received: £1,500,000 from Manchester C for Robert Taylor, November 1999.

Record Transfer Fee Paid: £600,000 to Reading for Carl Asaba, August 1998.

Football League Record: 1920 Original Member of Division 3; 1921 Division 3 (S); 1938 Failed re-election; Southern League 1938–44; Kent League 1944–46; Southern League 1946–50; 1950 Re-elected to Division 3 (S); 1958–64 Division 4; 1964–71 Division 3; 1971–74 Division 4; 1974–89 Division 3; 1989–92 Division 4; 1992–96; Division 3; 1996–2000 Division 2; 2000– Division 1.

MANAGERS

W. Ironside Groombridge 1896–1906 *(Secretary-Manager)* *(previously Financial Secretary)*
Steve Smith 1906–08
W. I. Groombridge 1908–19 *(Secretary-Manager)*
George Collins 1919–20
John McMillan 1920–23
Harry Curtis 1923–26
Albert Hoskins 1926–29
Dick Hendrie 1929–31
Fred Mavin 1932–37
Alan Ure 1937–38
Bill Harvey 1938–39
Archie Clark 1939–58
Harry Barratt 1958–62
Freddie Cox 1962–65
Basil Hayward 1966–71
Andy Nelson 1971–74
Len Ashurst 1974–75
Gerry Summers 1975–81
Keith Peacock 1981–87
Paul Taylor 1988
Keith Burkinshaw 1988–89
Damien Richardson 1989–93
Mike Flanagan 1993–95
Neil Smillie 1995
Tony Pulis 1995–99
Peter Taylor 1999–2000
Andy Hessenthaler June 2000–

LATEST SEQUENCES

Longest Sequence of League Wins: 7, 18.12.1954 – 29.1.1955.

Longest Sequence of League Defeats: 10, 20.9.1988 – 5.11.1988.

Longest Sequence of League Draws: 5, 28.8.1993 – 18.9.1993.

Longest Sequence of Unbeaten League Matches: 20, 13.10.1973 – 10.2.1974.

Longest Sequence Without a League Win: 15, 1.4.1972 – 2.9.1972.

Successive Scoring Runs: 20 from 31.10.1959.

Successive Non-scoring Runs: 6 from 11.2.1961.

TEN YEAR LEAGUE RECORD

		P	*W*	*D*	*L*	*F*	*A*	*Pts*	*Pos*
1993-94	Div 3	42	12	15	15	44	51	51	16
1994-95	Div 3	42	10	11	21	46	64	41	19
1995-96	Div 3	46	22	17	7	49	20	83	2
1996-97	Div 2	46	19	10	17	60	59	67	11
1997-98	Div 2	46	19	13	14	52	47	70	8
1998-99	Div 2	46	22	14	10	75	44	80	4
1999-2000	Div 2	46	25	10	11	79	48	85	3
2000-01	Div 1	46	13	16	17	61	66	55	13
2001-02	Div 1	46	18	10	18	64	67	64	12
2002-03	Div 1	46	16	14	16	56	65	62	11

DID YOU KNOW?

Inside-forward Harry Anstiss played in schoolboy international trials but was found to be nine days too old to be capped. His subsequent long career embraced nine clubs and more than 100 League goals. His last club was Gillingham in 1934–35.

GILLINGHAM 2002–03 LEAGUE RECORD

Match No.	Date	Venue	Opponents	Result		H/T Score	Lg. Pos.	Goalscorers	Attendance
1	Aug 10	A	Wimbledon	W	1-0	0-0	—	Ipoua [49]	2476
2	13	H	Derby Co	W	1-0	1-0	—	Shaw [16]	8775
3	17	H	Millwall	W	1-0	0-0	1	Ipoua [61]	7543
4	24	A	Norwich C	L	0-1	0-1	5		20,588
5	26	H	Preston NE	D	1-1	0-0	5	Saunders [62]	7785
6	31	A	Leicester C	L	0-2	0-2	7		30,067
7	Sept 7	H	Portsmouth	L	1-3	0-2	10	James [68]	8797
8	14	A	Brighton & HA	W	4-2	3-1	6	Shaw 2 [11, 36], Perpetuini [12], James [90]	6733
9	18	A	Nottingham F	L	1-4	1-3	—	Hessenthaler [6]	16,073
10	21	H	Sheffield U	D	1-1	1-0	9	Shaw [16]	7497
11	29	A	Crystal Palace	D	2-2	1-0	10	Perpetuini [23], Mullins (og) [70]	15,699
12	Oct 5	H	Coventry C	L	0-2	0-0	13		7722
13	12	A	Rotherham U	D	1-1	1-1	13	Wallace [17]	6094
14	19	H	Watford	W	3-0	2-0	11	Sidibe [2], Ipoua [33], James [90]	8728
15	26	A	Ipswich T	W	1-0	1-0	9	Sidibe [34]	24,176
16	29	H	Wolverhampton W	L	0-4	0-2	—		10,036
17	Nov 2	A	Grimsby T	D	1-1	0-0	13	Saunders [89]	5715
18	9	H	Reading	L	0-1	0-0	14		8511
19	16	H	Sheffield W	D	1-1	1-0	15	Johnson T [24]	8028
20	23	A	Walsall	L	0-1	0-1	16		6630
21	30	H	Stoke C	D	1-1	0-0	17	Shaw [52]	8150
22	Dec 7	A	Bradford C	W	3-1	0-1	17	King 2 (1 pen) [59 (p), 74], Wallace [90]	10,711
23	14	A	Sheffield W	W	2-0	1-0	16	Wallace [5], Smith [74]	17,715
24	21	H	Burnley	W	4-2	3-1	12	Wallace [17], Shaw [41], Smith [45], King [64]	7905
25	26	A	Millwall	D	2-2	1-1	12	Saunders [8], King (pen) [60]	10,947
26	Jan 11	A	Derby Co	D	1-1	0-0	15	Ipoua [57]	22,769
27	18	H	Leicester C	W	3-2	2-0	14	Ipoua [32], Elliott (og) [45], Sidibe [86]	8609
28	Feb 1	A	Preston NE	L	0-3	0-2	15		12,121
29	10	A	Reading	L	1-2	1-1	—	Wallace [10]	11,030
30	15	H	Grimsby T	W	3-0	3-0	14	Wallace 2 [6, 14], Hope [45]	7158
31	22	A	Portsmouth	L	0-1	0-0	15		19,521
32	25	H	Norwich C	W	1-0	0-0	—	Wallace [75]	7935
33	Mar 1	H	Brighton & HA	W	3-0	0-0	9	Shaw [47], Johnson T (pen) [60], Southall [76]	9178
34	4	H	Nottingham F	L	1-4	0-2	—	Wallace [79]	7277
35	11	H	Wimbledon	D	3-3	0-1	—	Shaw 2 [59, 80], Wallace [75]	7884
36	15	H	Rotherham U	D	1-1	1-1	10	Wallace [22]	7284
37	18	A	Watford	W	1-0	0-0	—	Shaw [65]	10,492
38	22	A	Wolverhampton W	L	0-6	0-5	10		25,171
39	25	A	Sheffield U	D	2-2	0-1	—	Osborn [53], Shaw [69]	15,799
40	29	H	Ipswich T	L	1-3	1-1	9	Smith [28]	8508
41	Apr 5	A	Stoke C	D	0-0	0-0	9		12,746
42	12	H	Walsall	L	0-1	0-0	13		6972
43	19	A	Burnley	L	0-2	0-1	14		14,031
44	21	H	Bradford C	W	1-0	1-0	13	Shaw [29]	6281
45	26	A	Coventry C	D	0-0	0-0	13		14,795
46	May 4	H	Crystal Palace	W	2-1	2-1	11	Nosworthy 2 [3, 5]	9315

Final League Position: 11

GOALSCORERS

League (56): Shaw 12, Wallace 11, Ipoua 5, King 4 (2 pens), James 3, Saunders 3, Sidibe 3, Smith 3, Johnson T 2 (1 pen), Nosworthy 2, Perpetuini 2, Hessenthaler 1, Hope 1, Osborn 1, Southall 1, own goals 2.
Worthington Cup (4): Hessenthaler 1, Ipoua 1, Johnson T 1, King 1.
FA Cup (6): Ipoua 2, King 2 (1 pen), Hope 1, Sidibe 1.

Brown J 39	Nosworthy N 37 + 2	Edge R 34	Hope C 46	Ashby B 38	Osborn S 15 + 3	Smith P 45	Hessenthaler A 32 + 1	Sidibe M 24 + 6	Ipoua G 22 + 11	Shaw P 44	Johnson T 12 + 14	Saunders M 28 + 6	James K 5 + 10	Perpetuini D 13 + 16	Patterson M 1 + 1	Wallace R 17 + 5	Bartram V 7 + 1	Pennock A 2 + 1	Johnson L 8 + 10	Awuah J 1 + 3	Rose R — + 2	King M 9 + 1	Spiller D 5 + 5	Southall N 22 + 2	Edusei A — + 2	*Match No.*
1	2	3	4	5	6	7	8	9[1]	10[2]	11	12	13														1
1	2	3	4	5	6	7	8[2]	9	10[1]	11	12	13														2
1	2	3	4	5	6[3]	7	8[2]	9[1]	10	11	12	13	14													3
1	2	3[3]	4	5	6[2]	7	8	9	10[1]	11	12	13	14													4
1	2	3	4	5		7	8[2]	9[1]	10	11	12	6		13												5
1	2	3[1]	4	5		7	8		10[2]	11	9	6			12	13										6
		3[1]	4	5		7	8		10	11	9[2]	6	13	12	2		1									7
1		3	4	5		7	8		10[2]	11		6■	9■	2[1]				13	12							8
1		3	4	5		7	8		10[1]	11		6	9	2						12						9
1		3	4	5		7			10[2]	9		6	8	11[1]				2	12	13						10
1[G]	2		4	5		7			10	8	12			11		9[1]	15	6	3							11
1	2		4	5[3]		7	6		10	8	12		13	11		9[2]			3[1]		14					12
1	2		4	5		7	8[1]		10	11		6	12	3		9										13
1	2		4	5		7	8	9[1]	10[2]	11	12	6	13	3[3]					14							14
1	2		4	5		7	8	9[1]		11	10[3]	6[2]	12	3					13			14				15
1	2■		4	5		7[2]	8	9	10[1]	11[3]	12	6	13	3									14			16
1	2		4	5		7	8	9	10[2]	11[1]	12	6	13	3												17
1	2		4	5		7	8[1]	9	12		13	6	11	3								10[2]				18
1		3	4	5		7	8■	12		11	9[1]	6		2								10[2]	13			19
1	12	3	4	5		7	8[2]	13	14	11	9[3]	6		2[1]								10				20
1	2	3	4			7		9[2]		11	8[1]	6	12			13			5			10				21
1	2	3	4			7	8[3]	9[1]	12	11		6				13			5			10[2]		14		22
1	2		4	5		7	8[3]		12	11[2]		6		13		9[1]			3			10		14		23
1	3		4	5		7	8[2]		12	11		6		13		9[1]						10		2		24
1	3		4	5		7	8		12	11[2]		6		13		9[1]						10		2		25
1	3		4	5		7	8	12	9[1]	11		6										10		2		26
1		3	4	5		7	8	9[2]	10[1]	11		6[3]				12			13				14	2		27
1	12	3[2]	4	5		7	8[1]	9	10	11[3]		6		13		14								2		28
1	2	3	4			7	8[2]	9[1]	12				6	13		10			5					11		29
1	2	3	4	5		6	8[3]	12	10	11[2]				13		9[1]							14	7		30
1	2	3	4	5		7	8	12	10[1]	11						9								6		31
1	2	3	4	5[1]		7	8	9		11		12		13		10[2]								6		32
1	2	3	4	5	12	7[3]		9[2]		11[1]	13	6		14		10								8		33
1	2	3	4	5[3]	12	7				11	10[1]	6[2]		13		9			14					8		34
1		3	4	5[2]	10[1]	7	8		12	11		6				9			13					2		35
1	5	3	4		12	7	8		10[2]	11	13	6[1]				9								2		36
1	5	3	4		6	7	8	12	13	11	10[1]					9[2]								2		37
	5	3	4		8	7		9	12	11	10[1]	6					1							2		38
	5	3	4		8[1]	7		9		11[2]	10	12		13			1		6					2		39
	2	3	4		6	7			12	11	10	8[2]		13		9[1]	1		5							40
	2	3	4	5[2]	6[3]	8		9		11	12					10[1]	1		13				14	7		41
	2	3	4	5	6			9		11[2]	10[1]						1		12				8	7	13	42
	10	3	4	5	6	7		9[1]		11[2]				14			1			12			8	2[3]	13	43
1	10	3	4	5	6	7		9		11													8	2		44
1	10	3	4	5	6	7				11				12					13	9[1]			8[2]	2		45
1	10	3	4	5	6[1]	7[3]	12	9		11[2]				13							14		8	2		46

Worthington Cup

First Round	Torquay U	(a)	1-0
Second Round	Stockport Co	(a)	2-1
Third Round	Chelsea	(a)	1-2

FA Cup

Third Round	Sheffield W	(h)	4-1
Fourth Round	Leeds U	(h)	1-1
		(a)	1-2

GRIMSBY TOWN — Division 2

FOUNDATION

Grimsby Pelham FC, as they were first known, came into being at a meeting held at the Wellington Arms in September 1878. Pelham is the family name of big landowners in the area, the Earls of Yarborough. The receipts for their first game amounted to 6s. 9d. (approx. 39p). After a year, the club name was changed to Grimsby Town.

Blundell Park, Cleethorpes, North East Lincolnshire DN35 7PY.

Telephone: (01472) 605 050. ***Fax:*** (01472) 693 665. ***ClubCall:*** 09068 555 855.

Ground Capacity: 10,033.

Record Attendance: 31,657 v Wolverhampton W, FA Cup 5th rd, 20 February 1937.

Record Receipts: £119,799 v Aston Villa, FA Cup 4th rd, 29 January 1994.

Pitch Measurements: 111yd × 75yd.

Life President: T. J. Lindley.

Chairman: P. W. Furneaux.

Directors: J. Fenty, M. Rouse, J. Elsom, M. C. Chapman.

Manager: Paul Groves.

Assistant Manager: Graham Rodger.

Chief Executive/Company Secretary: Ian Fleming.

Physio: Paul Mitchell.

Commercial Manager: Tony Richardson.

Press Officer: Tim Harvey.

Colours: Black and white striped shirts, black shorts, black stockings with red turnover.

Change Colours: Sky blue shirts with navy trim, sky blue shorts with navy trim, sky blue stockings with navy trim.

Year Formed. 1878.

Turned Professional: 1890. ***Ltd Co.:*** 1890.

Previous Name: 1878, Grimsby Pelham; 1879, Grimsby Town.

Club Nickname: 'The Mariners'.

Previous Grounds: 1880, Clee Park; 1889, Abbey Park; 1899, Blundell Park.

First Football League Game: 3 September 1892, Division 2, v Northwich Victoria (h) W 2–1 – Whitehouse; Lundie, T. Frith; C. Frith, Walker, Murrell; Higgins, Henderson, Brayshaw, Riddoch (2), Ackroyd.

Record League Victory: 9–2 v Darwen, Division 2, 15 April 1899 – Bagshaw; Lockie, Nidd; Griffiths, Bell (1), Nelmes; Jenkinson (3), Richards (1), Cockshutt (3), Robinson, Chadburn (1).

HONOURS

Football League: Division 1 best season: 5th, 1934–35; Division 2 – Champions 1900–01, 1933–34; Runners-up 1928–29; Promoted from Division 2 1997–98 (play-offs); Division 3 (N) – Champions 1925–26, 1955–56; Runners-up 1951–52; Division 3 – Champions 1979–80; Runners-up 1961–62; Division 4 – Champions 1971–72; Runners-up 1978–79; 1989–90.

FA Cup: Semi-finals, 1936, 1939.

Football League Cup: best season: 5th rd, 1980, 1985.

League Group Cup: Winners 1982.

Auto Windscreen Shield: Winners 1998.

SKY SPORTS FACT FILE

Inside-forward Charlie Craven had been a prolific scoring schoolboy in the Boston area but was working in an office when Grimsby Town persuaded him to sign professional forms in 1930. In four years he became a reserve for England v Holland.

Record Cup Victory: 8–0 v Darlington, FA Cup 2nd rd, 21 November 1885 – G. Atkinson; J. H. Taylor, H. Taylor; Hall, Kimpson, Hopewell; H. Atkinson (1), Garnham, Seal (3), Sharman, Monument (4).

Record Defeat: 1–9 v Arsenal, Division 1, 28 January 1931.

Most League Points (2 for a win): 68, Division 3 (N), 1955–56.

Most League Points (3 for a win): 83, Division 3, 1990–91.

Most League Goals: 103, Division 2, 1933–34.

Highest League Scorer in Season: Pat Glover, 42, Division 2, 1933–34.

Most League Goals in Total Aggregate: Pat Glover, 180, 1930–39.

Most League Goals in One Match: 6, Tommy McCairns v Leicester Fosse, Division 2, 11 April 1896.

Most Capped Player: Pat Glover, 7, Wales.

Most League Appearances: John McDermott, 532, 1987– .

Youngest League Player: Tony Ford, 16 years 143 days v Walsall, 4 October 1975.

Record Transfer Fee Received: £1,500,000 from Everton for John Oster, July 1997.

Record Transfer Fee Paid: £500,000 to Preston NE for Lee Ashcroft, August 1998.

Football League Record: 1892 Original Member Division 2; 1901–03 Division 1; 1903 Division 2; 1910 Failed re-election; 1911 re-elected Division 2; 1920–21 Division 3; 1921–26 Division 3 (N); 1926–29 Division 2; 1929–32 Division 1; 1932–34 Division 2; 1934–48 Division 1; 1948–51 Division 2; 1951–56 Division 3 (N); 1956–59 Division 2; 1959–62 Division 3; 1962–64 Division 2; 1964–68 Division 3; 1968–72 Division 4; 1972–77 Division 3; 1977–79 Division 4; 1979–80 Division 3; 1980–87 Division 2; 1987–88 Division 3; 1988–90 Division 4; 1990–91 Division 3; 1991–92 Division 2; 1992–97 Division 1; 1997–98 Division 2; 1998–2003 Division 1; 2003– Division 2.

MANAGERS

H. N. Hickson 1902–20
(Secretary-Manager)
Haydn Price 1920
George Fraser 1921–24
Wilf Gillow 1924–32
Frank Womack 1932–36
Charles Spencer 1937–51
Bill Shankly 1951–53
Billy Walsh 1954–55
Allenby Chilton 1955–59
Tim Ward 1960–62
Tom Johnston 1962–64
Jimmy McGuigan 1964–67
Don McEvoy 1967–68
Bill Harvey 1968–69
Bobby Kennedy 1969–71
Lawrie McMenemy 1971–73
Ron Ashman 1973–75
Tom Casey 1975–76
Johnny Newman 1976–79
George Kerr 1979–82
David Booth 1982–85
Mike Lyons 1985–87
Bobby Roberts 1987–88
Alan Buckley 1988–94
Brian Laws 1994–96
Kenny Swain 1997
Alan Buckley 1997–2000
Lennie Lawrence 2000–01
Paul Groves December 2001–

LATEST SEQUENCES

Longest Sequence of League Wins: 11, 19.1.1952 – 29.3.1952.

Longest Sequence of League Defeats: 9, 30.11.1907 – 18.1.1908.

Longest Sequence of League Draws: 5, 6.2.1965 – 6.3.1965.

Longest Sequence of Unbeaten League Matches: 19, 16.2.1980 – 30.8.1980.

Longest Sequence Without a League Win: 18, 10.10.1981 – 16.3.1982.

Successive Scoring Runs: 33 from 6.10.1928.

Successive Non-scoring Runs: 6 from 11.3.2000.

TEN YEAR LEAGUE RECORD

		P	W	D	L	F	A	Pts	Pos
1993-94	Div 1	46	13	20	13	52	47	59	16
1994-95	Div 1	46	17	14	15	62	56	65	10
1995-96	Div 1	46	14	14	18	55	69	56	17
1996-97	Div 1	46	11	13	22	60	81	46	22
1997-98	Div 2	46	19	15	12	55	37	72	3
1998-99	Div 1	46	17	10	19	40	52	61	11
1999-2000	Div 1	46	13	12	21	41	67	51	20
2000-01	Div 1	46	14	10	22	43	62	52	18
2001-02	Div 1	46	12	14	20	50	72	50	19
2002-03	Div 1	46	9	12	25	48	85	39	24

DID YOU KNOW?

Grimsby Town are the only Football League club to have won matches 6-5 at home and away in the competition. They won by that score at West Bromwich Albion on 30 April 1932 and again on 29 October 2002 against Burnley.

GRIMSBY TOWN 2002–03 LEAGUE RECORD

Match No.	*Date*	*Venue*	*Opponents*	*Result*	*H/T Score*	*Lg. Pos.*	*Goalscorers*	*Attendance*
1	Aug 10	A	Norwich C	L 0-4	0-2	—		19,869
2	13	H	Wimbledon	D 0-0	0-0	—		4625
3	17	H	Derby Co	L 1-2	1-1	21	Barnard [37]	5810
4	24	A	Bradford C	D 0-0	0-0	21		10,914
5	26	H	Portsmouth	L 0-1	0-0	21		5770
6	31	A	Millwall	L 0-2	0-1	23		6677
7	Sept 14	A	Coventry C	L 2-3	0-0	24	Kabba [47], Pouton [70]	12,403
8	17	A	Sheffield U	L 1-2	1-0	—	Robinson [8]	14,208
9	21	H	Nottingham F	L 0-3	0-1	24		7072
10	28	A	Brighton & HA	W 2-1	1-0	23	Barnard [2], Pouton [80]	6547
11	Oct 5	H	Reading	L 0-3	0-2	23		5582
12	8	H	Ipswich T	W 3-0	2-0	—	Kabba 2 [8, 61], Pouton (pen) [18]	4688
13	12	A	Watford	L 0-2	0-1	23		13,821
14	19	H	Rotherham U	D 0-0	0-0	23		6418
15	26	A	Wolverhampton W	L 1-4	1-1	23	Kabba [2]	23,875
16	29	H	Burnley	W 6-5	4-3	—	Kabba 2 [3, 31], Livingstone [28], Campbell [36], Pouton (pen) [56], Ford [72]	5620
17	Nov 2	H	Gillingham	D 1-1	0-0	22	Oster [77]	5715
18	9	A	Stoke C	W 2-1	2-0	21	Livingstone [14], Campbell [22]	11,488
19	16	H	Preston NE	D 3-3	1-1	21	Campbell [3], Ford [59], Mansaram [80]	5774
20	23	A	Crystal Palace	L 0-2	0-1	21		20,093
21	30	H	Leicester C	L 1-2	0-1	21	Oster [54]	7310
22	Dec 7	A	Walsall	L 1-3	1-1	21	Livingstone [38]	5888
23	14	A	Preston NE	L 0-3	0-2	21		12,420
24	21	H	Sheffield W	W 2-0	0-0	21	Santos [49], Mansaram [52]	8224
25	26	A	Derby Co	W 3-1	1-1	21	Oster 2 [3, 64], Soames [89]	27,141
26	28	H	Norwich C	D 1-1	0-0	21	Oster [77]	8306
27	Jan 11	A	Wimbledon	D 3-3	1-0	21	Boulding [35], Andersen (og) [52], Campbell [72]	1336
28	18	H	Millwall	L 0-2	0-1	21		4993
29	25	H	Bradford C	L 1-2	1-0	21	Boulding [15]	5582
30	Feb 1	A	Portsmouth	L 0-3	0-1	22		19,428
31	8	H	Stoke C	W 2-0	2-0	21	Boulding [4], Thompson [40]	5657
32	15	A	Gillingham	L 0-3	0-3	21		7158
33	22	A	Ipswich T	D 2-2	2-1	22	Groves [8], Boulding [24]	24,118
34	Mar 1	H	Coventry C	L 0-2	0-1	22		5736
35	4	H	Sheffield U	L 1-4	1-3	—	Campbell [34]	6897
36	10	A	Nottingham F	D 2-2	1-1	—	Groves [44], Pouton [48]	25,507
37	15	H	Watford	W 1-0	0-0	23	Groves [64]	4847
38	18	A	Rotherham U	W 1-0	0-0	—	Oster [90]	6239
39	22	A	Burnley	D 1-1	1-0	22	Campbell [43]	13,445
40	Apr 5	A	Leicester C	L 0-2	0-0	23		31,014
41	8	H	Wolverhampton W	L 0-1	0-1	—		4983
42	12	H	Crystal Palace	L 1-4	0-3	24	Chettle [48]	4707
43	19	A	Sheffield W	D 0-0	0-0	24		26,082
44	21	H	Walsall	L 0-1	0-0	24		4618
45	26	A	Reading	L 1-2	0-2	24	Keane [90]	20,273
46	May 4	H	Brighton & HA	D 2-2	1-1	24	Keane (pen) [23], Hughes [60]	6396

Final League Position: 24

GOALSCORERS

League (48): Campbell 6, Kabba 6, Oster 6, Pouton 5 (2 pens), Boulding 4, Groves 3, Livingstone 3, Barnard 2, Ford 2, Keane 2 (1 pen), Mansaram 2, Chettle 1, Hughes 1, Robinson 1, Santos 1, Soames 1, Thompson 1, own goal 1.
Worthington Cup (0).
FA Cup (2): Cooke 1 (pen), Mansaram 1.

Coyne D 46	McDermott J 35	Gallimore T 38	Groves P 32 + 4	Chettle S 18 + 2	Coldicott S 26 + 5	Cooke T 15 + 10	Pouton A 25	Livingstone S 21 + 9	Robinson P 5 + 7	Campbell S 45	Ford S 35 + 4	Rowan J 2 + 7	Barnard D 21 + 8	Jevons P — + 3	Taylor R 1	Kabba S 13	Mansaram D 21 + 13	Raven P 6 + 1	Santos G 24 + 2	Ward I 9 + 2	Gavin J 8 + 2	Oster J 17	Parker W 1 + 4	Soames D — + 10	Bolder C 7 + 5	Boulding M 10 + 2	Thompson C 3 + 3	Hughes R 12	Keane M 7	Young G 1	Hockless G 1	Sagare J 1	*Match No.*
1	2	3	4	5^1	6	7	8	9	10^2	11^3	12	13	14																				1
1	2	3	4	5	6	7^2	8	9		11		10^1	13	12																			2
1	2	3	4	5^3	6^1	8		9^2	12	7	14	10	11	13																			3
1	2	3	4	5	6	8			12	7		13	11		9^2	10^1																	4
1	2	3	4	5	6^1	8			12	7	9	13	11^2			10																	5
1	2	3	4	5^1	6	12	8^3		13	7	9		11^2	14		10																	6
1	2	3^1	4	5	6		8		9^3	7	12	13	11^2			10	14																7
1	2		4	5	6	12	8		9	7^3	3	13	11^1			10^2	14																8
1	2	3▮	4	5^1	6^2		8		9	7	12		11			10	13																9
1	2	3	4^2		6		8		9^1	7	5	12	11				10	13															10
1	2				6	7^2	8		12	11	4		3			10	9^1	5	13														11
1					12	7	6	13	14	11	4		3			10^3	9^2	5	8	2^1													12
1					12	7^2	6	14	13	11	4		3			10	9^3	5^1	8	2													13
1		3			12	13	6	9^1		7	4		11			10^3	14	5▮	8▮	2^2													14
1		3			12		6	9		7	4		11^2			10	13	5	8	2^1													15
1		3			6	12	8	9		7	4		11			10		5^1		2													16
1	2	3			6		8	9^1		7	4					10	12				5	11											17
1		3	8		6			9		7	4		12				10^1			2	5	11											18
1		3^2	12		6^1		8	9		7	4▮		13				10				5	11	2										19
1	2^2	3	12		6^1		8	9^3		7	4						10				5	11	13	14									20
1	2	3	4^1		6		8	9		7			11								5	10		12									21
1	2^1	3			6		8	9		7	4		11^2						12		5	10		13									22
1		3	4^1		6	12	8▮	9			2						10^2		11	13	5	7											23
1					6		8	9		7	5		3				10		4	2^1	12	11											24
1			8	6		7^1				11	3						10^2		4	2^3	5	9	12	13	14								25
1	2		8^1		6	12		9		7	5		3^2				10^3		4		13	11		14									26
1	2	3	8	5	6^1	7		9		11	4		12				13									10^2							27
1	2	3	4	5		8^1		9		7	6		11				12							13		10^2							28
1			4	5		7^1		9▮		11	6		3				12			2				13	8	10^2							29
1	2	3	4	5				9		7	6						10		8^1	12				13	11^2								30
1	2	3	4			7	8^3			11	5	12							6					13	14	9^1	10^2						31
1	2	3^2	4	12	8	7^1				11	5		13						6					14		9^3	10						32
1	2	3	4^1		8					7	5								6			10			12	9		11					33
1	2	3	12		6^1		8^3	13		7	5						14		4			10				9^2		11					34
1	2	3	12				4▮	9^2		7^1	5						8		6			10					13	11					35
1	2	3	4				8^2	12		7	5		13				9^1		6			10						11					36
1	2	3	4				8^1			7	5		12				9		6			10						11					37
1	2	3	4		12			13		7	5		11^1				9^2		6			10						8					38
1	2	3	4		8^2			12		7	5						9^1		6			10			13			11					39
1	2	3	4^3			12		13		7	5						9^2		6						10^1	14		8	11				40
1	2	3	4					12		7	5						9		6						10^2	13		8	11^1				41
1	2	3^3	4	5		12		13		7^1	6						8						14		10	9			11^2				42
1	2	3	4	5						7							12		6						10^1	9		8	11				43
1	2	3	4	5		12		10		7^1							13		6							9^3	14	8^2	11				44
1	2	3		12		8				7							13		6						4		14		11	5^1	9^3	10^2	45
1	2^3	3	4	5^2		12				7							10		6				14		13		9	8	11^1				46

Worthington Cup
First Round Chesterfield (h) 0-1

FA Cup
Third Round Burnley (h) 2-2
(a) 0-4

HARTLEPOOL UNITED — Division 2

FOUNDATION

The inspiration for the launching of Hartlepool United was the West Hartlepool club which won the FA Amateur Cup in 1904–05. They had been in existence since 1881 and their Cup success led in 1908 to the formation of the new professional concern which first joined the North-Eastern League. In those days they were Hartlepools United and won the Durham Senior Cup in their first two seasons.

Victoria Park, Clarence Road, Hartlepool TS24 8BZ.

Telephone: (01429) 272 584. ***Fax:*** (01429) 863 007.
Commercial Dept: (01429) 272 584.
Website: www.hartlepoolunited.co.uk
Email: info@hartlepoolunited.co.uk
Football in the Community: (01429) 862 595.

Ground Capacity: 7,629.

Record Attendance: 17,426 v Manchester U, FA Cup 3rd rd, 5 January 1957.

Record Receipts: £59,800 (inc. VAT) v Cheltenham T, Play-off semi-final, 27 April 2002.

Pitch Measurements: 100 × 66 metres.

Chairman: K. Hodcroft.

Directors: H. Hornsey, I. Prescott.

Manager: Neale Cooper.

Youth Coach: Martin Scott.

Physios: John Murray, Ian Gallagher.

Commercial Manager: John Breward.

Secretary: Maureen Smith.

Football in the Community Officers: Keith Nobbs, Peter Smith.

Safety Officer: Maurice Russell.

Colours: Royal blue and white striped shirts.

Change Colours: All red.

Year Formed: 1908.

Turned Professional: 1908.

Ltd Co.: 1908.

Previous Names: 1908, Hartlepools United; 1968, Hartlepool; 1977, Hartlepool United.

Club Nickname: 'The Pool'.

First Football League Game: 27 August 1921, Division 3 (N), v Wrexham (a) W 2–0 – Gill; Thomas, Crilly; Dougherty, Hopkins, Short; Kessler, Mulholland (1), Lister (1), Robertson, Donald.

Record League Victory: 10–1 v Barrow, Division 4, 4 April 1959 – Oakley; Cameron, Waugh; Johnson, Moore, Anderson; Scott (1), Langland (1), Smith (3), Clark (2), Luke (2), (1 og).

HONOURS

Football League: Division 3 – Runners-up 2002–03; Division 3 (N) – Runners-up 1956–57.

FA Cup: best season: 4th rd, 1955, 1978, 1989, 1993.

Football League Cup, best season: 4th rd, 1975.

SKY SPORTS FACT FILE

Hartlepool United doubled up in 2002–03, the seniors winning promotion to the Second Division of the Football League and the youth team taking the Youth Alliance north-east conference title.

Record Cup Victory: 6–0 v North Shields, FA Cup 1st rd, 30 November 1946 – Heywood; Brown, Gregory; Spelman, Lambert, Jones; Price, Scott (2), Sloan (4), Moses, McMahon.

Record Defeat: 1–10 v Wrexham, Division 4, 3 March 1962.

Most League Points (2 for a win): 60, Division 4, 1967–68.

Most League Points (3 for a win): 85, Division 3, 2002–03.

Most League Goals: 90, Division 3 (N), 1956–57.

Highest League Scorer in Season: William Robinson, 28, Division 3 (N), 1927–28; Joe Allon, 28, Division 4, 1990–91.

Most League Goals in Total Aggregate: Ken Johnson, 98, 1949–64.

Most League Goals in One Match: 5, Harry Simmons v Wigan Borough, Division 3N, 1 January 1931; 5, Bobby Folland v Oldham Ath, Division 3N, 15 April 1961.

Most Capped Player: Ambrose Fogarty, 1 (11), Republic of Ireland.

Most League Appearances: Wattie Moore, 447, 1948–64.

Youngest League Player: Steven Istead, 16 years 187 days v Bristol R, 29 October 2002.

Record Transfer Fee Received: £750,000 from Ipswich T for Tommy Miller, July 2001.

Record Transfer Fee Paid: £75,000 to Notts Co for Gary Jones, March 1999; £75,000 to Mansfield T for Darrell Clarke, July 2001.

Football League Record: 1921 Original Member of Division 3 (N); 1958–68 Division 4; 1968–69 Division 3; 1969–91 Division 4; 1991–92 Division 3; 1992–94 Division 2; 1994–2003 Division 3; 2003– Division 2.

LATEST SEQUENCES

Longest Sequence of League Wins: 7, 30.3.2002 – 13.8.2002.

Longest Sequence of League Defeats: 8, 27.1.1993 – 27.2.1993.

Longest Sequence of League Draws: 5, 24.2.2001 – 17.3.2001.

Longest Sequence of Unbeaten League Matches: 21, 2.12.2000 – 31.3.2001.

Longest Sequence Without a League Win: 18, 9.1.1993 – 3.4.1993.

Successive Scoring Runs: 17 from 28.2.1964.

Successive Non-scoring Runs: 11 from 9.1.1993.

MANAGERS

Alfred Priest 1908–12
Percy Humphreys 1912–13
Jack Manners 1913–20
Cecil Potter 1920–22
David Gordon 1922–24
Jack Manners 1924–27
Bill Norman 1927–31
Jack Carr 1932–35
(had been Player-Coach since 1931)
Jimmy Hamilton 1935–43
Fred Westgarth 1943–57
Ray Middleton 1957–59
Bill Robinson 1959–62
Allenby Chilton 1962–63
Bob Gurney 1963–64
Alvan Williams 1964–65
Geoff Twentyman 1965
Brian Clough 1965–67
Angus McLean 1967–70
John Simpson 1970–71
Len Ashurst 1971–74
Ken Hale 1974–76
Billy Horner 1976–83
Johnny Duncan 1983
Mike Docherty 1983
Billy Horner 1984–86
John Bird 1986–88
Bobby Moncur 1988–89
Cyril Knowles 1989–91
Alan Murray 1991–93
Viv Busby 1993
John MacPhail 1993–94
David McCreery 1994–95
Keith Houchen 1995–96
Mick Tait 1996–99
Chris Turner 1999–2002
Mike Newell 2002–03
Neale Cooper June 2003–

TEN YEAR LEAGUE RECORD

		P	*W*	*D*	*L*	*F*	*A*	*Pts*	*Pos*
1993-94	Div 2	46	9	9	28	41	87	36	23
1994-95	Div 3	42	11	10	21	43	69	43	18
1995-96	Div 3	46	12	13	21	47	67	49	20
1996-97	Div 3	46	14	9	23	53	66	51	20
1997-98	Div 3	46	12	23	11	61	53	59	17
1998-99	Div 3	46	13	12	21	52	65	51	22
1999-2000	Div 3	46	21	9	16	60	49	72	7
2000-01	Div 3	46	21	14	11	71	54	77	4
2001-02	Div 3	46	20	11	15	74	48	71	7
2002-03	Div 3	46	24	13	9	71	51	85	2

DID YOU KNOW ?

Jimmy Sloan, signed from Newcastle United the previous month, scored four goals for Hartlepools United in a 6-0 FA Cup first round match against North Shields on 30 November 1946 in front of a crowd of 8,459.

HARTLEPOOL UNITED 2002–03 LEAGUE RECORD

Match No.	Date	Venue	Opponents	Result	H/T Score	Lg. Pos.	Goalscorers	Attendance
1	Aug 10	A	Carlisle U	W 3-1	1-0	—	Tinkler 2 [44, 71], Humphreys [47]	10,684
2	13	H	Boston U	W 2-0	0-0	—	Watson 2 (1 pen) [55, 77 (p)]	4841
3	17	H	Macclesfield T	L 0-2	0-0	4		4684
4	24	A	Torquay U	D 1-1	0-0	3	Humphreys [47]	2403
5	26	H	Hull C	W 2-0	1-0	2	Williams E [32], Watson [63]	4236
6	31	A	Oxford U	W 1-0	1-0	1	Watson [38]	4768
7	Sept 7	A	Swansea C	D 2-2	2-2	2	Tinkler [14], Watson [44]	3370
8	14	H	Darlington	W 4-1	2-1	1	Williams E 2 [3, 35], Humphreys [59], Tinkler [83]	6360
9	17	H	Lincoln C	W 2-1	0-1	—	Boyd [62], Williams E [66]	4248
10	21	A	Bury	D 1-1	0-1	1	Boyd [82]	3547
11	28	H	Rushden & D	L 1-2	1-0	1	Boyd [31]	5502
12	Oct 5	A	Shrewsbury T	W 1-0	0-0	1	Williams E [55]	3142
13	13	A	Bournemouth	L 1-2	1-0	1	Williams E [17]	5998
14	19	H	Wrexham	W 4-3	3-1	1	Tinkler 3 [14, 41, 52], Richardson [19]	4506
15	25	A	Southend U	W 1-0	1-0	—	Williams E [1]	5168
16	29	H	Bristol R	W 2-0	1-0	—	Arnison [41], Williams E [64]	3889
17	Nov 1	H	York C	D 0-0	0-0	—		5789
18	9	A	Exeter C	W 2-1	0-0	1	Tinkler [63], Richardson [66]	2778
19	23	A	Leyton Orient	W 2-1	1-0	1	Williams E 2 [26, 72]	4009
20	30	H	Kidderminster H	W 2-1	2-0	1	Humphreys [3], Tinkler [15]	4296
21	Dec 14	A	Rochdale	L 0-4	0-2	1		3059
22	21	H	Scunthorpe U	D 2-2	1-1	1	McCombe (og) [45], Henderson [89]	4089
23	26	A	Hull C	L 0-2	0-1	2		22,319
24	28	H	Cambridge U	W 3-0	1-0	1	Williams E [45], Tinkler [83], Clarke (pen) [87]	4805
25	Jan 1	H	Carlisle U	W 2-1	0-1	1	Lee [50], Williams E [80]	5071
26	4	A	Boston U	W 1-0	0-0	1	Clarke [70]	3081
27	18	H	Oxford U	W 3-1	2-1	1	Humphreys [24], Richardson 2 [43, 90]	5049
28	21	A	Macclesfield T	W 1-0	1-0	—	Williams E [16]	1576
29	25	A	Cambridge U	D 0-0	0-0	1		4543
30	Feb 1	H	Torquay U	W 3-2	0-1	1	Clarke 2 [56, 69], Richardson [79]	4975
31	8	H	Exeter C	W 2-1	0-0	1	Humphreys [79], Boyd [80]	5058
32	15	A	York C	D 0-0	0-0	1		5953
33	22	H	Swansea C	W 4-0	2-0	1	Humphreys 3 [11, 40, 69], Widdrington [72]	4486
34	Mar 1	A	Darlington	D 2-2	0-1	1	Boyd (pen) [48], Clarke [53]	5832
35	4	A	Lincoln C	L 0-3	0-1	—		3409
36	7	H	Bury	D 0-0	0-0	—		5734
37	15	H	Southend U	W 2-1	1-0	1	Humphreys 2 [36, 49]	4868
38	18	A	Wrexham	L 0-2	0-1	—		4658
39	22	A	Bristol R	L 0-1	0-1	1		6557
40	29	H	Bournemouth	D 0-0	0-0	1		5625
41	Apr 5	A	Kidderminster H	D 2-2	0-2	1	Clarke [63], Williams E [90]	2900
42	12	H	Leyton Orient	W 4-1	1-0	1	Tinkler 2 (1 pen) [10, 66 (p)], Lee [61], Clarke [90]	4795
43	19	A	Scunthorpe U	L 0-4	0-1	2		5280
44	21	H	Rochdale	D 2-2	1-2	2	Widdrington 2 [42, 52]	5408
45	26	H	Shrewsbury T	W 3-0	2-0	2	Williams E [36], Tinkler [45], Henderson [79]	5384
46	May 3	A	Rushden & D	D 1-1	0-1	2	Westwood [90]	6291

Final League Position: 2

GOALSCORERS

League (71): Williams E 15, Tinkler 13 (1 pen), Humphreys 11, Clarke 7 (1 pen), Boyd 5 (1 pen), Richardson 5, Watson 5 (1 pen), Widdrington 3, Henderson 2, Lee 2, Arnison 1, Westwood 1, own goal 1.
Worthington Cup (1): Williams E 1.
FA Cup (2): Barron 1, Richardson 1.
LDV Vans Trophy (0).

Williams A 46	Barron M 42	Robinson M 38	Lee G 45	Westwood C 46	Sweeney A 2 + 2	Clarke D 45	Tinkler M 45	Williams E 44 + 1	Watson G 12 + 5	Humphreys R 46	Arnison P 9 + 10	Henderson K 5 + 25	Easter J — + 8	Smith P 15 + 9	Widdrington T 26 + 6	Boyd A 11 + 11	Simms G — + 1	Richardson M 20 + 4	Istead S — + 6	Barry-Murphy B 7	Bass J 2 + 2	*Match No.*
1	2	3	4	5	6^1	7	8	9^2	10^3	11	12	13	14									1
1	6	3	4	5	12	7	8	9^2	10^3	11	2^1	13	14									2
1	6	3^1	4	5		7	8	9^2	10	11	2^3	12	13	14								3
1	6	3^1	4	5		7	8	9	10	11	2			12								4
1	2^1	3	4	5		7	8	9^3	10	11	12			6^2	13	14						5
1	2	3	4	5		7^2	8	9	10^1	11	13	12		6^3	14							6
1	2	3	4	5		6	8	9^1	10^2	11	7	12				13						7
1	2	3	4	5		7^2	8	9^1	10^3	11	13	12			6	14						8
1	2	3	4	5		7^1	8	9		11					6	10	12					9
1	6		4	5	12	7	8	9		11	2^1				3	10						10
1	2	3^1	4	5		7	8	9		11		13		12	6	10^2						11
1	2	3^1	4	5		7	8	9		11				12	6	10^2		13				12
1	2■	3	4	5		7	8	9^1		11		12		13	6^2	10^3		14				13
1	2	3	4	5		7	6	9^1		8		12		11^2	13	14		10^3				14
1	2	3	4	5		7^2	6	9^3		8	13		14	11^1	12			10				15
1		3	4	5		7^2	6	9^1		8	2		12	11				10	13			16
1		3	4	5		7^1	6	9		8	2			11				10	12			17
1	6		4	5		2	8	9		7				11^2		12		10^1	13	3		18
1	2		4	5		7	6	9^1		8				11		12		10		3		19
1	2		4	5		7^2	6	9		8				11^1	12			10		3	13	20
1			4	5			8	9		11	2				7	12		10^1	13	3	6^2	21
1	2		4	5		7^2	6	9		8		12		11				10^1	13	3		22
1	2		4	5		7^2	6	9		8		10^3		11^1	12			14	13	3		23
1	2		4	5		7	6	9^1		11		12			8	13		10^2		3		24
1	2^2	3	4	5		7	6	9		11			12		8			10^1			13	25
1	2	3	4	5		7	6	9^1		11		12			8			10				26
1	4	3		5		7	6	9		11					8			10			2	27
1	2	3	4	5		7	6	9		11					8			10				28
1	2	3	4	5		7	6	9^1		11					8	12		10				29
1	2	3	4	5	6	7		9^2		11		12			8	13		10^1				30
1	2	3	4	5		7	6			11		12			8	9		10^1				31
1	2	3	4	5		7	6	9		11		12			8	10^1						32
1	2	3	4	5		7	6	9^3		11	12	13			8^1	10^2		14				33
1	2	3	4	5		7	6^2	9		11	13	12			8	10^1						34
1	2	3	4	5		7	6	9		11		12			8	10^1						35
1	2	3	4	5		7	6	9^1	12	11		13			8	10^2						36
1	2	3	4	5		7	6	9^1		11^2	12	14		13	8			10^3				37
1	2	3	4	5		7	6	9^1	12	11		13		14	8^3			10^2				38
1	2	3	4	5		7	6	9		11		12		13	8^2			10^1				39
1	2^2	3	4	5		7	6	9^1	10	8	13	12		11								40
1		3	4	5		7	6	12	9^1	8	2	10		11								41
1	2	3	4	5		7	6	9^2	12	11		10^1	13		8							42
1	2	3^1	4	5		7	6	9	12	11		10			8							43
1	2	3	4	5		7	6	9^1	12	11		10		13	8^2							44
1	2	3	4	5		7	6^1	9^2	10^3	8	12	13		11		14						45
1	2	3	4	5		7^2	6	9	10^1	8		12	13	11								46

Worthington Cup
First Round Tranmere R (h) 1-2

LDV Vans Trophy
First Round Tranmere R (a) 0-5

FA Cup
First Round Southend U (a) 1-1
(h) 1-2

HUDDERSFIELD TOWN Division 3

FOUNDATION

A meeting, attended largely by members of the Huddersfield & District FA, was held at the Imperial Hotel in 1906 to discuss the feasibility of establishing a football club in this rugby stronghold. However, it was not until a man with both the enthusiasm and the money to back the scheme came on the scene, that real progress was made. This benefactor was Mr Hilton Crowther and it was at a meeting at the Albert Hotel in 1908, that the club formally came into existence with a capital of £2,000 and joined the North-Eastern League.

The Alfred McAlpine Stadium, Leeds Road, Huddersfield HD1 6PX.

Telephone: (01484) 484 100. ***Fax:*** (01484) 484 101.

Ticket Office: (01484) 484 123.

Club Shop: (01484) 484 144.

ClubCall: 09068 121 635.

Ground Capacity: 24,500.

Record Attendance: 67,037 v Arsenal, FA Cup 6th rd, 27 February 1932 (at Leeds Road);
23,678 v Liverpool, FA Cup 3rd rd, 12 December 1999 (at Alfred McAlpine Stadium).

Record Receipts: £243,081 v Liverpool, FA Cup 3rd rd, 12 December 1999.

Pitch Measurements: 115yd × 76yd.

Manager: Peter Jackson.

Assistant Manager: Terry Yorath.

Secretary: Ann Hough.

Physio: Alex Moreno.

Stadium Manager: Phil Armitage.

Colours: Blue and white striped shirts, white shorts, white stockings with blue trim.

Change Colours: Black shirts and shorts with royal blue trim, black stockings with royal blue turnover.

Year Formed: 1908.

Turned Professional: 1908. ***Ltd Co.:*** 1908.

Club Nickname: 'The Terriers'.

Previous Ground: 1908, Leeds Road; 1994, The Alfred McAlpine Stadium.

First Football League Game: 3 September 1910, Division 2, v Bradford PA (a) W 1–0 – Mutch; Taylor, Morris; Beaton, Hall, Bartlett; Blackburn, Wood, Hamilton (1), McCubbin, Jee.

Record League Victory: 10–1 v Blackpool, Division 1, 13 December 1930 – Turner; Goodall, Spencer; Redfern, Wilson, Campbell; Bob Kelly (1), McLean (4), Robson (3), Davies (1), Smailes (1).

HONOURS

Football League: Division 1 – Champions 1923–24, 1924–25, 1925–26; Runners-up 1926–27, 1927–28, 1933–34; Division 2 – Champions 1969–70; Runners-up 1919–20, 1952–53; Promoted from Division 2 1994–95 (play-offs); Division 4 – Champions 1979–80.

FA Cup: Winners 1922; Runners-up 1920, 1928, 1930, 1938.

Football League Cup: Semi-final 1968.

Autoglass Trophy: Runners-up 1994.

SKY SPORTS FACT FILE

On 1 April 1989, Huddersfield Town won 6-0 at Bury. It was their highest winning margin since another away success whey they defeated Sheffield United 7-1 at Bramall Lane on 12 November 1927.

Record Cup Victory: 7–0 v Lincoln U, FA Cup 1st rd, 16 November 1991 – Clarke; Trevitt, Charlton, Donovan (2), Mitchell, Doherty, O'Regan (1), Stapleton (1) (Wright), Roberts (2), Onuora (1), Barnett (Ireland).
N.B. 11-0 v Heckmondwike (a), FA Cup pr rd, 18 September 1909 – Doggart; Roberts, Ewing; Hooton, Stevenson, Randall; Kenworthy (2), McCreadie (1), Foster (4), Stacey (4), Jee.

Record Defeat: 1–10 v Manchester C, Division 2, 7 November 1987.

Most League Points (2 for a win): 66, Division 4, 1979–80.

Most League Points (3 for a win): 82, Division 3, 1982–83.

Most League Goals: 101, Division 4, 1979–80.

Highest League Scorer in Season: Sam Taylor, 35, Division 2, 1919–20; George Brown, 35, Division 1, 1925–26.

Most League Goals in Total Aggregate: George Brown, 142, 1921–29; Jimmy Glazzard, 142, 1946–56.

Most League Goals in One Match: 5, Dave Mangnall v Derby Co, Division 1, 21 November 1931; 5, Alf Lythgoe v Blackburn R, Division 1, 13 April 1935.

Most Capped Player: Jimmy Nicholson, 31 (41), Northern Ireland.

Most League Appearances: Billy Smith, 520, 1914–34.

Youngest League Player: Denis Law, 16 years 303 days v Notts Co, 24 December 1956.

Record Transfer Fee Received: £2,700,000 from Sheffield W for Andy Booth, July 1996.

Record Transfer Fee Paid: £1,200,000 to Bristol R for Marcus Stewart, July 1996.

Football League Record: 1910 Elected to Division 2; 1920–52 Division 1; 1952–53 Division 2; 1953–56 Division 1; 1956–70 Division 2; 1970–72 Division 1; 1972–73 Division 2; 1973–75 Division 3; 1975–80 Division 4; 1980–83 Division 3; 1983–88 Division 2; 1988–92 Division 3; 1992–95 Division 2; 1995–2001 Division 1; 2001–03 Division 2; 2003– Division 3.

MANAGERS

Fred Walker 1908–10
Richard Pudan 1910–12
Arthur Fairclough 1912–19
Ambrose Langley 1919–21
Herbert Chapman 1921–25
Cecil Potter 1925–26
Jack Chaplin 1926–29
Clem Stephenson 1929–42
David Steele 1943–47
George Stephenson 1947–52
Andy Beattie 1952–56
Bill Shankly 1956–59
Eddie Boot 1960–64
Tom Johnston 1964–68
Ian Greaves 1968–74
Bobby Collins 1974
Tom Johnston 1975–78
(had been General Manager since 1975)
Mike Buxton 1978–86
Steve Smith 1986–87
Malcolm Macdonald 1987–88
Eoin Hand 1988–92
Ian Ross 1992–93
Neil Warnock 1993–95
Brian Horton 1995–97
Peter Jackson 1997–99
Steve Bruce 1999–2000
Lou Macari 2000–02
Mick Wadsworth 2002–03
Peter Jackson June 2003–

LATEST SEQUENCES

Longest Sequence of League Wins: 11, 5.4.1920 – 4.9.1920.

Longest Sequence of League Defeats: 7, 8.10.1955 – 19.11.1955.

Longest Sequence of League Draws: 6, 3.3.1987 – 3.4.1987.

Longest Sequence of Unbeaten League Matches: 27, 24.1.1925 – 17.10.1925.

Longest Sequence Without a League Win: 22, 4.12.1971 – 29.4.1972.

Successive Scoring Runs: 21 from 5.12.1931.

Successive Non-scoring Runs: 7 from 22.1.1972.

TEN YEAR LEAGUE RECORD

		P	*W*	*D*	*L*	*F*	*A*	*Pts*	*Pos*
1993-94	Div 2	46	17	14	15	58	61	65	11
1994-95	Div 2	46	22	15	9	79	49	81	5
1995-96	Div 1	46	17	12	17	61	58	63	8
1996-97	Div 1	46	13	15	18	48	61	54	20
1997-98	Div 1	46	14	11	21	50	72	53	16
1998-99	Div 1	46	15	16	15	62	71	61	10
1999-2000	Div 1	46	21	11	14	62	49	74	8
2000-01	Div 1	46	11	15	20	48	57	48	22
2001-02	Div 2	46	21	15	10	65	47	78	6
2002-03	Div 2	46	11	12	23	39	61	45	22

DID YOU KNOW ?

In 1909–10 Huddersfield Town signed one-time Sunderland centre-forward Jack Foster from West Ham United. He played centre-half for a few matches and still managed 27 goals including 11 in the FA Cup.

HUDDERSFIELD TOWN 2002–03 LEAGUE RECORD

Match No.	Date	Venue	Opponents	Result		H/T Score	Lg. Pos.	Goalscorers	Attendance
1	Aug 10	H	Brentford	L	0-2	0-2	—		9635
2	13	A	Plymouth Arg	L	1-2	0-0	—	Thorrington [89]	8953
3	17	A	Peterborough U	W	1-0	1-0	19	Mattis [10]	5205
4	24	H	Crewe Alex	D	1-1	1-1	18	Booth [26]	8467
5	26	A	Tranmere R	L	1-2	1-0	19	McDonald [44]	7534
6	31	H	Blackpool	D	0-0	0-0	20		9506
7	Sept 7	H	Barnsley	W	1-0	0-0	17	Smith [59]	11,989
8	14	A	Northampton T	D	0-0	0-0	17		4679
9	17	A	QPR	L	0-3	0-2	—		11,010
10	21	H	Luton T	L	0-1	0-0	21		9249
11	28	A	Oldham Ath	L	0-4	0-2	23		7643
12	Oct 5	H	Port Vale	D	2-2	2-2	22	Smith [12], Baldry [17]	9091
13	12	H	Notts Co	W	3-0	2-0	19	Stead 2 [15, 73], Moses [25]	9984
14	19	A	Mansfield T	W	2-0	0-0	17	Smith 2 [53, 61]	4998
15	26	H	Colchester U	D	1-1	0-1	16	Stead [90]	8912
16	29	A	Bristol C	L	0-1	0-1	—		11,494
17	Nov 2	A	Cheltenham T	L	0-1	0-0	19		4322
18	9	H	Wycombe W	D	0-0	0-0	20		8695
19	23	H	Swindon T	L	2-3	1-2	22	Smith [36], Stead [90]	8334
20	30	A	Chesterfield	L	0-1	0-1	23		4194
21	Dec 14	H	Stockport Co	W	2-1	1-0	22	Smith 2 [27, 83]	7978
22	21	A	Wigan Ath	L	0-1	0-1	23		6013
23	26	H	Tranmere R	L	1-2	0-0	24	Smith [78]	11,002
24	29	A	Cardiff C	L	0-4	0-2	24		13,703
25	Jan 1	A	Blackpool	D	1-1	0-0	24	Booth [75]	7184
26	11	H	Peterborough U	L	0-1	0-0	24		9022
27	18	A	Crewe Alex	L	0-1	0-0	24		5819
28	25	H	Cardiff C	W	1-0	0-0	23	Booth [80]	9462
29	Feb 4	H	Plymouth Arg	W	1-0	0-0	—	Smith (pen) [82]	7294
30	8	A	Wycombe W	D	0-0	0-0	23		5886
31	15	H	Cheltenham T	D	3-3	0-2	23	Irons [54], Smith 2 [56, 59]	9309
32	22	A	Barnsley	W	1-0	1-0	21	Booth [26]	12,474
33	25	A	Brentford	L	0-1	0-0	—		4366
34	Mar 1	H	Northampton T	W	2-0	2-0	19	Baldry [44], Smith [45]	9651
35	4	H	QPR	L	0-3	0-2	—		8695
36	8	A	Luton T	L	0-3	0-0	21		6122
37	15	A	Colchester U	L	0-2	0-0	23		3835
38	18	H	Mansfield T	D	1-1	0-0	—	Smith [51]	8756
39	22	H	Bristol C	L	1-2	1-2	24	Smith (pen) [20]	9477
40	29	A	Notts Co	L	2-3	2-1	24	Booth [19], Schofield [37]	5872
41	Apr 5	H	Chesterfield	W	4-0	2-0	22	Smith 2 [17, 53], Stead 2 [23, 66]	9098
42	12	A	Swindon T	W	1-0	0-0	22	Smith [87]	4760
43	19	H	Wigan Ath	D	0-0	0-0	22		13,769
44	21	A	Stockport Co	L	1-2	1-0	22	Booth [3]	7159
45	26	A	Port Vale	L	1-5	1-2	22	Gavin [45]	5925
46	May 3	H	Oldham Ath	D	1-1	1-0	22	Schofield [26]	11,271

Final League Position: 22

GOALSCORERS

League (39): Smith 17 (2 pens), Booth 6, Stead 6, Baldry 2, Schofield 2, Gavin 1, Irons 1, Mattis 1, McDonald 1, Moses 1, Thorrington 1.
Worthington Cup (2): Baldry 1, own goal 1.
FA Cup (0).
LDV Vans Trophy (1): Mattis 1.

Bevan S 30	Sharp K 38 + 1	Jenkins S 26	Irons K 29 + 6	Moses A 40	Youds E 25	Thorrington J 16 + 15	Holland C 33 + 1	Booth A 32 + 1	Smith M 35 + 3	McDonald S 7 + 6	Mattis D 27 + 6	Stead J 28 + 14	Heary T 14 + 6	Worthington J 10 + 12	Scott P 2 + 11	Baldry S 14 + 8	Schofield D 25 + 5	Gallacher K 5 + 2	Brown N 36 + 2	Dyson J 2 + 1	Macari P — + 5	Clarke N 2 + 1	Ashcroft L 4	Senior P 16 + 2	Labarthe G — + 3	Gavin J 10	Mirfin D — + 1	McCombe J — + 1	*Match No.*
1	2	3	4[1]	5	6	7	8	9	10[2]	11	12	13																	1
1	2	3[1]	4	5	6	7	8	9		11[2]	10[3]	13	12	14															2
1	2	3[2]	4	5	6	7	8	9		11[1]	10[3]	12	13		14														3
1	2	3	4[2]	5	6	7	8	9[1]		11[3]	10	12			13	14													4
1	2	3	4[1]	5	6	7[2]	8			11	10	9[3]			12	13	14												5
1	2	3	4	5	6	7	8[3]			11	10[2]	12			13		14	9[1]											6
1	2	3	4	5	6	7[3]	8		14	12		10[1]		13			11	9[2]											7
1	2	3	4		6	12	8		13	14		10[3]				7[1]	11	9[2]	5										8
1	2	3	4		6[1]	7[3]	8	12		13	10			14			11	9[2]	5										9
1	2	3	4			7[2]	8	10				12					11	9[1]	5	6	13								10
1	2	3	4[1]				7	8	13	10[3]	12	9[2]					11	14	5	6									11
1	2	3				12	4		10		8	9[2]	6[3]		14	7	11[1]	13	5										12
1	2	3	12	5		11	6		10[1]	13	8	9[3]				7[2]			4		14								13
1	2	3		5		11[2]	6		10	12	8	9[1]				7	13		4										14
1	2	3		5		11	6		10[1]	12	8	9				7[3]	13		4[2]	14									15
1	2	3[1]	12	5		7[2]	6[3]		10		8	9				13	11		4		14								16
1	3		12	5			6		10		8	9			7[2]	2[1]	11		4[3]		13	14							17
1	2	3	12	5		7			10		8[1]	9		11[2]	4		13					6							18
1	2	3		5	6	12	4[1]		10		8	9		13		7[2]	11[3]		14										19
1	2[1]	3	7	5	6	13			10		8	12		11[2]		14	9[3]		4										20
1	2	3	8[3]	5	6			9	7[2]			12		13	14		11		4				10[1]						21
1	2	3	7[1]	5	6			9[2]	10			8[3]		12	13		11		4		14								22
1	2	3	8[1]	5	6			9	10		12	13					11		4				7[2]						23
1	2	3	4[2]	5	6	12		9	10[1]		13			14			11■		8				7[3]						24
1	2	3		5		7		9	10		6	12					11		4				8[1]						25
1		3	4[3]	5	6	7[2]	12	9	10		8[1]	11		14		13			2										26
1■	2	3	4[2]	5	6		8	9[1]	10		11					7			12					13					27
1	3		4	5	6	12[2]	8	9[3]	11		7	10[1]	13			14			2										28
	3		4[1]	2	6	12	8	9	11[3]		7	10[2]	14			13			5					1					29
1	3		4[1]	2	6		8[2]	9	11		7	10[3]	13	12		14			5										30
1[6]	3		4	2	6	12		9	10				8	11[3]		7			5					15					31
	3		4		6			9	10[1]		8	12	2			11			5			7		1					32
	3		4[1]	2	6	12		9[3]	10[2]		8	13	11			7			5					1	14				33
	3		4[3]	2	6	12		9	8[2]			10[1]	11	13		7			5					1	14				34
	2[3]		4[2]	5		12		9	8		7	10[1]	3	13		11			6					1	14				35
	2		4■	5			8[2]	9	10[1]		7	12	3[3]	14	13	11			6					1					36
	3■			2			6	9			8	10[1]		7	12		11		4					1		5			37
	3		4[3]	2		12	8	9	10		7[1]	13	14				11[2]		6					1		5			38
	3			2		12	8	9	7			10	6				11[1]		4					1		5			39
			12	2	6	13	3	9	10[1]			8[2]		7			11		4					1		5			40
			12	6			8	9[2]	11[1]			10	3	7	13		2		4					1		5			41
				4[1]			8	9	11		12	10	2	7[2]	13		3		6					1		5			42
				4			8	9	11			10	3	7			2		6					1		5			43
				6		12	8	9	11			10	2	7			3[1]		4					1		5			44
	12			6			8	9	11			10	2■	7[1]			3		4					1		5			45
			7[1]	4			8	9	11		12	10[2]	6				3		2[3]					1		5	14	13	46

Worthington Cup

First Round	Darlington	(h)	2-0
Second Round	Burnley	(h)	0-1

LDV Vans Trophy

First Round	Wrexham	(a)	1-2

FA Cup

First Round	Swindon T	(a)	0-1

HULL CITY

Division 3

FOUNDATION

The enthusiasts who formed Hull City in 1904 were brave men indeed. More than that they were audacious for they immediately put the club on the map in this Rugby League fortress by obtaining a three-year agreement with the Hull Rugby League club to rent their ground! They had obtained quite a number of conversions to the dribbling code, before the Rugby League forbade the use of any of their club grounds by Association Football clubs. By that time, Hull City were well away having entered the FA Cup in their initial season and the Football League, Second Division after only a year.

Kingston Communications Stadium, The Circle, Walton Street, Hull HU3 6HV.

Telephone: 0870 837 0003. ***Fax:*** (01482) 304 882. ***Club Shop:*** 0870 837 0005.

Ground Capacity: 25,404.

Record Attendance: 55,019 v Manchester U, FA Cup 6th rd, 26 February 1949.

Record Receipts: £79,604 v Liverpool, FA Cup 5th rd, 18 February 1989.

Pitch Measurements: 105m × 68m.

Chairman/Chief Executive: Adam Pearson.

Manager: Peter Taylor.

Assistant Manager: Colin Murphy.

First Team Coach: Steve Butler.

Physio: Keith Warner.

Sales Director: John Holmes.

Football in the Community Office: John Davies (01482) 568 088.

Marketing Manager: Rob Smith. ***Ticket Office Manager:*** Carol Taylor.

Club Secretary: Phil Hough.

Hon. Medical Officers: Mr F. R. Howell MA, FRCS, Dr T. Jackson.

Colours: Black, amber and white shirts, black shorts, black stockings.

Change Colours: All white.

Year Formed: 1904. ***Turned Professional:*** 1905.

Ltd Co.: 1905.

Club Nickname: 'The Tigers'.

Previous Grounds: 1904, Boulevard Ground (Hull RFC); 1905, Anlaby Road (Hull CC); 1944, Boulevard Ground; 1946, Boothferry Park; 2002, Kingston Communications Stadium.

First Football League Game: 2 September 1905, Division 2, v Barnsley (h) W 4–1 – Spendiff; Langley, Jones; Martin, Robinson, Gordon (2); Rushton, Spence (1), Wilson (1), Howe, Raisbeck.

Record League Victory: 11–1 v Carlisle U, Division 3 (N), 14 January 1939 – Ellis; Woodhead, Dowen; Robinson (1), Blyth, Hardy; Hubbard (2), Richardson (2), Dickinson (2), Davies (2), Cunliffe (2).

HONOURS

Football League: Division 2 best season: 3rd, 1909–10; Division 3 (N) – Champions 1932–33, 1948–49; Division 3 – Champions 1965–66; Runners-up 1958–59; Division 4 – Runners-up 1982–83.

FA Cup: Semi-final 1930.

Football League Cup: best season: 4th, 1974, 1976, 1978.

Associate Members' Cup: Runners-up 1984.

SKY SPORTS FACT FILE

In the close season of 1939, Hull City laid plans to move from Anlaby Road to Boothferry Park, the site of an old golf course. Because of the Second World War it did not happen until 1946. Then in 2002 they moved again.

Record Cup Victory: 8–2 v Stalybridge Celtic (a), FA Cup 1st rd, 26 November 1932 – Maddison; Goldsmith, Woodhead; Gardner, Hill (1), Denby; Forward (1), Duncan, McNaughton (1), Wainscoat (4), Sargeant (1).

Record Defeat: 0–8 v Wolverhampton W, Division 2, 4 November 1911.

Most League Points (2 for a win): 69, Division 3, 1965–66.

Most League Points (3 for a win): 90, Division 4, 1982–83.

Most League Goals: 109, Division 3, 1965–66.

Highest League Scorer in Season: Bill McNaughton, 39, Division 3 (N), 1932–33.

Most League Goals in Total Aggregate: Chris Chilton, 195, 1960–71.

Most League Goals in One Match: 5, Ken McDonald v Bristol C, Division 2, 17 November 1928; 5, Simon 'Slim' Raleigh v Halifax T, Division 3N, 26 December 1930.

Most Capped Player: Theo Whitmore, Jamaica.

Most League Appearances: Andy Davidson, 520, 1952–67.

Youngest League Player: Matthew Edeson, 16 years 63 days v Fulham, 10 October 1992.

Record Transfer Fee Received: £750,000 from Middlesbrough for Andy Payton, November 1991.

Record Transfer Fee Paid: £210,000 to Leicester C for Lawrie Dudfield, July 2001.

Football League Record: 1905 Elected to Division 2; 1930–33 Division 3 (N); 1933–36 Division 2; 1936–49 Division 3 (N); 1949–56 Division 2; 1956–58 Division 3 (N); 1958–59 Division 3; 1959–60 Division 2; 1960–66 Division 3; 1966–78 Division 2; 1978–81 Division 3; 1981–83 Division 4; 1983–85 Division 3; 1985–91 Division 2; 1991–92 Division 3; 1992–96 Division 2; 1996– Division 3.

MANAGERS

James Ramster 1904–05
(Secretary-Manager)
Ambrose Langley 1905–13
Harry Chapman 1913–14
Fred Stringer 1914–16
David Menzies 1916–21
Percy Lewis 1921–23
Bill McCracken 1923–31
Haydn Green 1931–34
John Hill 1934–36
David Menzies 1936
Ernest Blackburn 1936–46
Major Frank Buckley 1946–48
Raich Carter 1948–51
Bob Jackson 1952–55
Bob Brocklebank 1955–61
Cliff Britton 1961–70
(continued as General Manager to 1971)
Terry Neill 1970–74
John Kaye 1974–77
Bobby Collins 1977–78
Ken Houghton 1978–79
Mike Smith 1979–82
Bobby Brown 1982
Colin Appleton 1982–84
Brian Horton 1984–88
Eddie Gray 1988–89
Colin Appleton 1989
Stan Ternent 1989–91
Terry Dolan 1991–97
Mark Hateley 1997–98
Warren Joyce 1998–2000
Brian Little 2000–02
Jan Molby 2002
Peter Taylor October 2002–

LATEST SEQUENCES

Longest Sequence of League Wins: 10, 23.2.1966 – 20.4.1966.

Longest Sequence of League Defeats: 8, 7.4.1934 – 8.9.1934.

Longest Sequence of League Draws: 5, 30.3.1929 – 15.4.1929.

Longest Sequence of Unbeaten League Matches: 19, 13.3.2001 – 22.9.2001.

Longest Sequence Without a League Win: 27, 27.3.1989 – 4.11.1989.

Successive Scoring Runs: 26 from 10.4.1990.

Successive Non-scoring Runs: 6 from 13.11.1920.

TEN YEAR LEAGUE RECORD

		P	*W*	*D*	*L*	*F*	*A*	*Pts*	*Pos*
1993-94	Div 2	46	18	14	14	62	54	68	9
1994-95	Div 2	46	21	11	14	70	57	74	8
1995-96	Div 2	46	5	16	25	36	78	31	24
1996-97	Div 3	46	13	18	15	44	50	57	17
1997-98	Div 3	46	11	8	27	56	83	41	22
1998-99	Div 3	46	14	11	21	44	62	53	21
1999-2000	Div 3	46	15	14	17	43	43	59	14
2000-01	Div 3	46	19	17	10	47	39	74	6
2001-02	Div 3	46	16	13	17	57	51	61	11
2002-03	Div 3	46	14	17	15	58	53	59	13

DID YOU KNOW ?

In 1948–49 Hull City enjoyed their highest average crowd at the time of 36,763 in winning the Third Division (North) title. But the following season in the Second Division attendances increased to average 37,319.

HULL CITY 2002–03 LEAGUE RECORD

Match No.	Date	Venue	Opponents	Result		H/T Score	Lg. Pos.	Goalscorers	Attendance
1	Aug 10	H	Southend U	D	2-2	1-0	—	Green [8], Elliott [68]	10,449
2	13	A	Bristol R	D	1-1	0-1	—	Johnson [85]	7501
3	17	A	Exeter C	L	1-3	1-2	19	Green [10]	4257
4	24	H	Bury	D	1-1	1-0	21	Johnson [36]	8804
5	26	A	Hartlepool U	L	0-2	0-1	22		4236
6	31	H	Leyton Orient	D	1-1	1-1	22	Keates [38]	7684
7	Sept 7	A	Cambridge U	W	2-1	0-0	18	Whittle [71], Smith [74]	4258
8	14	H	Carlisle U	W	4-0	1-0	13	Alexander 3 [20, 49, 73], Dudfield [78]	8461
9	17	H	Macclesfield T	L	1-3	1-0	—	Green [16]	8703
10	21	A	Oxford U	D	0-0	0-0	16		5445
11	28	H	Swansea C	D	1-1	1-0	16	Jevons [27]	8070
12	Oct 5	A	Kidderminster H	L	0-1	0-0	18		3787
13	12	H	Rochdale	W	3-0	2-0	17	Jevons [28], Branch 2 [45, 84]	9057
14	19	A	Torquay U	W	4-1	1-0	15	Ashbee [45], Jevons [47], Anderson [68], Green [85]	3607
15	26	H	Rushden & D	D	1-1	1-1	15	Green [1]	10,659
16	29	A	Shrewsbury T	D	1-1	0-0	—	Elliott [59]	3086
17	Nov 2	H	Scunthorpe U	W	2-0	0-0	11	Branch [85], Alexander [90]	11,885
18	9	A	Lincoln C	D	1-1	1-1	14	Alexander [22]	6271
19	23	H	Boston U	W	1-0	0-0	11	Delaney [49]	9460
20	30	A	Wrexham	D	0-0	0-0	12		4412
21	Dec 14	H	Darlington	L	0-1	0-1	12		14,162
22	21	A	Bournemouth	D	0-0	0-0	12		6098
23	26	H	Hartlepool U	W	2-0	1-0	11	Keates [21], Green [75]	22,319
24	28	A	York C	D	1-1	0-1	13	Keates [51]	7856
25	Jan 1	A	Bury	L	0-1	0-0	13		4290
26	4	H	Bristol R	W	1-0	1-0	10	Alexander [25]	14,913
27	11	H	Exeter C	D	2-2	0-0	9	Elliott 2 [61, 67]	13,667
28	18	A	Leyton Orient	L	0-2	0-2	11		5125
29	25	H	York C	D	0-0	0-0	13		18,437
30	Feb 1	A	Southend U	L	0-3	0-3	14		4534
31	8	H	Lincoln C	L	0-1	0-0	14		13,728
32	15	A	Scunthorpe U	L	1-3	0-0	15	Forrester [65]	6284
33	22	H	Cambridge U	D	1-1	0-1	14	Forrester (pen) [51]	15,607
34	Mar 1	A	Carlisle U	W	5-1	3-0	14	Walters 2 [20, 67], Elliott 2 [39, 48], Forrester [45]	4678
35	4	A	Macclesfield T	W	1-0	1-0	—	Elliott [45]	2229
36	8	H	Oxford U	D	0-0	0-0	12		17,404
37	15	A	Rushden & D	L	2-4	0-1	13	Otsemobor [59], Walters [63]	4713
38	18	H	Torquay U	D	1-1	0-0	—	Elliott [54]	13,310
39	22	H	Shrewsbury T	W	2-0	0-0	13	Otsemobor [81], Keates (pen) [90]	13,253
40	Apr 5	H	Wrexham	L	1-2	0-0	14	Otsemobor [55]	15,002
41	12	A	Boston U	W	1-0	0-0	13	Elliott [73]	3782
42	19	H	Bournemouth	W	3-1	2-1	13	Walters [31], Elliott 2 [35, 46]	15,816
43	21	A	Darlington	L	0-2	0-0	13		3487
44	26	H	Kidderminster H	W	4-1	2-0	13	Burgess 3 (1 pen) [6 (p), 38, 88], Walters [80]	14,544
45	29	A	Rochdale	L	1-2	0-2	—	Burgess [65]	2225
46	May 3	A	Swansea C	L	2-4	2-2	13	Elliott [9], Reeves [25]	9585

Final League Position: 13

GOALSCORERS

League (58): Elliott 12, Alexander 6, Green 6, Walters 5, Burgess 4 (1 pen), Keates 4 (1 pen), Branch 3, Forrester 3 (1 pen), Jevons 3, Otsemobor 3, Johnson 2, Anderson 1, Ashbee 1, Delaney 1, Dudfield 1, Reeves 1, Smith 1, Whittle 1.
Worthington Cup (2): Alexander 1, Ashbee 1.
FA Cup (0).
LDV Vans Trophy (1): Donaldson 1.

Glennon M 9	Edwards M 3 + 3	Smith S 17 + 5	Ashbee I 31	Anderson J 42 + 1	Strong G 3	Greaves M 3 / Burgess B 7	Williams R 14 + 9	Dudfield L 7 + 14 / Russell S — + 1	Elliott S 30 + 6	Green S 27 + 1	Philpott L — + 1	Bradshaw G 2 + 3	Whittle J 34 + 5	Price M 1 + 2	Johnson S 4 + 8	Regan C 33 + 5	Alexander G 21 + 4	Petty B 2	Morrison O 1 + 1	Keates D 36	Jevons P 13 + 11	Peat N — + 1	Musselwhite P 20	Branch M 6 + 1	Burton S 2 + 9	Delaney D 30	Melton S 19 + 6	Joseph M 22 + 1	Webb D 4 + 8	Holt A 5 + 1	Forrester J 11	Fettis A 17	Donaldson C — + 2	Appleby R 6	Walters J 11	Reeves M 5 + 3	Otsemobor J 8 + 1	Match No.
1	2	3	4▮	5	6	7	8[1]	9	10	11	12																											1
1	2	3[1]	4	5	6▮	7[2]		9[3]	10	11		8	12	13	14																							2
1		3	4	5	6[3]		12	8[1]	10[2]	11▮			14	7	13	2	9																					3
1		3		5		7		12		8		13	6	14	10[1]	2	9	4[2]	11[3]																			4
1			4	5			12	8		11		13	6		10[2]	2	9[1]	3		7																		5
1		3	4	5			7	12				11[1]	6		10[2]	2	9		13	8																		6
1	12	3	4	5			7						6		11[2]	2	9			8	10[1]	13																7
1	12	3	4	5			7	13		11			6		14	2[1]	9[3]			8	10[2]																	8
1		3	4	5			8[2]	12		11			6		13	2	9			7	10[1]																	9
		3	4	5			11[2]	12		7			6		13	2	9[1]			8	10		1															10
	12	3[1]	4	5			11[3]	13		7			6		14	2	9[2]			8	10		1															11
	3[1]	12	4	5				13	10[2]	7			6		14	2				11	8[3]		1	9														12
			4	5			12		8[1]	7			6		13	2	14			11	10[3]		1	9[2]	3													13
			4	5			12		8[1]	7			6			2	13			11	10[2]		1	9[3]	14	3												14
			4	5			12		8[1]	7		13	6			2	9			11[3]	10[2]		1		14	3												15
			4	5			8		10[1]	7			6			2	9			11[2]	12		1		13	3												16
			4	5			8[2]		12	7			6			2	9			11	10[1]		1	13		3												17
				5			8		12	7[2]			6			2	9			11	13		1	10[1]	3	4												18
			4	5					12	7			6			2	9[2]			11	13		1	10[1]		3	8											19
			4	5						7			6			2	9[1]			11	12		1	10[2]		3	8	13										20
		3	4	5[3]					13	7			12			2	9[1]			11[2]	10		1				8	6	14									21
			4	5					9	7						2	12			11	10[1]		1			3	8	6										22
			4	5				12	10[2]	7[1]			13			2	9[3]			11	14		1			3	8	6										23
			4	5				12		13			6[2]			2	9[1]			11[3]	10		1			3	8	7		14								24
			4	5				12	9[2]	10			6[1]			2	13						1			3	8	7		11								25
		12	4	5				10[1]	11[3]	7						2	9[2]				13		1			3	8	6	14									26
			4	5			13	12	10[1]	7						2	9[2]						1			6	8		11	3								27
			4	5[2]			12	13	11	7						14	9[1]						1			6	8[3]	2	10	3								28
			4	5[1]			11[3]		10	7			12			2							1			8	13	6	14	3[2]	9							29
				12			11		10[3]	7[1]			6			2									13	4	8	5	14	3[2]	9	1						30
			4	5			11[1]	7	12				6							8						3[2]		2	10		9	1	13					31
		3[3]	4				11[1]	13	12				6			2				8						7	14	5	10		9[2]	1						32
				5			12	8[2]	10				6			14				11	13					3	7	2[3]			9	1		4[1]				33
		3		5				12	8				6			13				11							7	2	14		9[1]	1		4[2]	10[3]			34
		3	4	5					8				6			12				11								2			9	1		7[1]	10			35
		12	4[1]	5					8				6							11						3	13	2[2]			9	1		7[3]	10	14		36
		12		5					8				6▮							11						3	13				9	1		4[1]	10	7[2]	2	37
				5					8				6							11	13					3	12				9[2]	1		4[1]	10	7	2	38
				5					8							12				11	13				14	3	4	6			9[2]	1			10[1]	7[3]	2	39
				5		9	12		8[2]											11	13				14	3	4[3]	6				1			10	7[1]	2	40
		3		5		9			8				6			2				11						7		4				1	12		10[1]			41
		3[3]		5		9			8				6			7				11[2]						4	12	2				1			10[1]	13	14	42
		12		5		9			10				6			7				11[2]	13					4	8	2				1					3[1]	43
						9		14	8[2]				6			7				11					12	3	4	5[1]	13			1			10[3]		2	44
				5		9[3]			8				6			7[2]				11					12	3	4[1]		14			1			10	13	2	45
		3				9[2]			10				6							11					12	8	4	5	13			1				7	2[1]	46

Worthington Cup
First Round Leicester C (h) 2-4

LDV Vans Trophy
First Round Port Vale (a) 1-3

FA Cup
First Round Macclesfield T (h) 0-3

IPSWICH TOWN — Division 1

FOUNDATION

Considering that Ipswich Town only reached the Football League in 1938, many people outside of East Anglia may be surprised to learn that this club was formed at a meeting held in the Town Hall as far back as 1878 when Mr T. C. Cobbold, MP, was voted president. Originally it was the Ipswich Association FC to distinguish it from the older Ipswich Football Club which played rugby. These two amalgamated in 1888 and the handling game was dropped in 1893.

Portman Road, Ipswich, Suffolk IP1 2DA.

Telephone: (01473) 400 500 (4 lines).
Fax: (01473) 400 040. ***Ticket Office:*** (01473) 400 555.
Website: www.itfc.co.uk ***Email:*** enquiries@itfc.co.uk
Hospitality and Events: (01473) 400 510/400 580.

Ground Capacity: 30,311.

Record Attendance: 38,010 v Leeds U, FA Cup 6th rd, 8 March 1975.

Record Receipts: £105,950 v AZ 67 Alkmaar, UEFA Cup Final 1st leg, 6 May 1981.

Pitch Measurements: 101m × 65m.

Chairman: David Sheepshanks.

Chief Executive: Derek Bowden.

Vice-presidents: Kenneth H. Brightwell, Harold R. Smith.

Directors: P. Hope-Cobbold, R. Moore, John Kerr MBE, R. J. Finbow, Lord Ryder OBE.

Manager: Joe Royle. ***Assistant Manager:*** Willie Donachie.

First Team Coach: Tony Mowbray.
Reserve Team Coach: Steve McCall.

Chief Scout: Colin Suggett. ***Academy Director:*** Bryan Klug. ***Physio:*** Dave Williams.

Secretary: David C. Rose.

Publications Manager: Mike Noye.

Director of Commercial Affairs: Paul Clouting. ***Director of Finance:*** Mike Cooper.

Colours: Blue shirts, white shorts, blue stockings.

Change Colours: Wine red shirts with navy sleeves and white trim, navy shorts, white stockings.

Year Formed: 1878.

Turned Professional: 1936.

Ltd Co.: 1936.

Club Nicknames: 'Blues' or 'Town' or 'Tractor Boys'.

HONOURS

Football League: Division 1 – Champions 1961–62; Runners-up 1980–81, 1981–82; Promoted from Division 1 1999–2000 (play-offs); Division 2 – Champions 1960–61, 1967–68, 1991–92; Division 3 (S) – Champions 1953–54, 1956–57.

FA Cup: Winners 1978.

Football League Cup: Semi-final 1982, 1985.

Texaco Cup: Winners 1973.

European Competitions: *European Cup:* 1962–63. *European Cup-Winners' Cup:* 1978–79. *UEFA Cup:* 1973–74, 1974–75, 1975–76, 1977–78, 1979–80, 1980–81 (winners), 1981–82, 1982–83, 2001–02, 2002–03.

SKY SPORTS FACT FILE

Mancunian full-back Billy Dale served both city clubs initially for Manchester United and made FA Cup final appearances with City before joining Ipswich Town during their first season in the Football League 1938–39.

MANAGERS

Mick O'Brien 1936–37
Scott Duncan 1937–55
(continued as Secretary)
Alf Ramsey 1955–63
Jackie Milburn 1963–64
Bill McGarry 1964–68
Bobby Robson 1969–82
Bobby Ferguson 1982–87
Johnny Duncan 1987–90
John Lyall 1990–94
George Burley 1994–2002
Joe Royle October 2002–

First Football League Game: 27 August 1938, Division 3 (S), v Southend U (h) W 4–2 – Burns; Dale, Parry; Perrett, Fillingham, McLuckie; Williams, Davies (1), Jones (2), Alsop (1), Little.

Record League Victory: 7–0 v Portsmouth, Division 2, 7 November 1964 – Thorburn; Smith, McNeil; Baxter, Bolton, Thompson; Broadfoot (1), Hegan (2), Baker (1), Leadbetter, Brogan (3). 7–0 v Southampton, Division 1, 2 February 1974 – Sivell; Burley, Mills (1), Morris, Hunter, Beattie (1), Hamilton (2), Viljoen, Johnson, Whymark (2), Lambert (1) (Woods). 7–0 v WBA, Division 1, 6 November 1976 – Sivell; Burley, Mills, Talbot, Hunter, Beattie (1), Osborne, Wark (1), Mariner (1) (Bertschin), Whymark (4), Woods.

Record Cup Victory: 10–0 v Floriana, European Cup prel. rd, 25 September 1962 – Bailey; Malcolm, Compton; Baxter, Laurel, Elsworthy (1); Stephenson, Moran (2), Crawford (5), Phillips (2), Blackwood.

Record Defeat: 1–10 v Fulham, Division 1, 26 December 1963.

Most League Points (2 for a win): 64, Division 3 (S), 1953–54 and 1955–56.

Most League Points (3 for a win): 87, Division 1, 1999–2000.

Most League Goals: 106, Division 3 (S), 1955–56.

Highest League Scorer in Season: Ted Phillips, 41, Division 3 (S), 1956–57.

Most League Goals in Total Aggregate: Ray Crawford, 203, 1958–63 and 1966–69.

Most League Goals in One Match: 5, Alan Brazil v Southampton, Division 1, 16 February 1981.

Most Capped Player: Allan Hunter, 47 (53), Northern Ireland.

Most League Appearances: Mick Mills, 591, 1966–82.

Youngest League Player: Jason Dozzell, 16 years 56 days v Coventry C, 4 February 1984.

Record Transfer Fee Received: £6,000,000 from Newcastle U for Kieron Dyer, July 1999; £6,000,000 from Arsenal for Richard Wright, July 2001.

Record Transfer Fee Paid: £4,750,000 to Sampdoria for Matteo Sereni.

Football League Record: 1938 Elected to Division 3 (S); 1954–55 Division 2; 1955–57 Division 3 (S); 1957–61 Division 2; 1961–64 Division 1; 1964–68 Division 2; 1968–86 Division 1; 1986–92 Division 2; 1992–95 FA Premier League; 1995–2000 Division 1; 2000–02 FA Premier League; 2002– Division 1.

LATEST SEQUENCES

Longest Sequence of League Wins: 8, 23.9.1953 – 31.10.1953.

Longest Sequence of League Defeats: 10, 4.9.1954 – 16.10.1954.

Longest Sequence of League Draws: 7, 10.11.1990 – 21.12.1990.

Longest Sequence of Unbeaten League Matches: 23, 8.12.1979 – 26.4.1980.

Longest Sequence Without a League Win: 21, 28.8.1963 – 14.12.1963.

Successive Scoring Runs: 28 from 1.5.1953.

Successive Non-scoring Runs: 7 from 28.2.1995.

TEN YEAR LEAGUE RECORD

		P	W	D	L	F	A	Pts	Pos
1993-94	PR Lge	42	9	16	17	35	58	43	19
1994-95	PR Lge	42	7	6	29	36	93	27	22
1995-96	Div 1	46	19	12	15	79	69	69	7
1996-97	Div 1	46	20	14	12	68	50	74	4
1997-98	Div 1	46	23	14	9	77	43	83	5
1998-99	Div 1	46	26	8	12	69	32	86	3
1999-2000	Div 1	46	25	12	9	71	42	87	3
2000-01	PR Lge	38	20	6	12	57	42	66	5
2001-02	PR Lge	38	9	9	20	41	64	36	18
2002-03	Div 1	46	19	13	14	80	64	70	7

DID YOU KNOW ?

Ipswich Town's first venture into the FA Cup was on 4 October 1890 and a first qualifying round tie with Reading, who were seasoned campaigners in the competition. But goals by George Sherrington and Stan Turner gave Ipswich a 2-0 win.

IPSWICH TOWN 2002–03 LEAGUE RECORD

Match No.	Date	Venue	Opponents	Result		H/T Score	Lg. Pos.	Goalscorers	Attendance
1	Aug 10	A	Walsall	W	2-0	1-0	—	Ambrose [37], Bent M [62]	5253
2	18	H	Leicester C	W	6-1	1-1	6	Holland 2 [45, 57], Ambrose [69], George [75], Counago 2 [85, 90]	27,374
3	24	A	Millwall	D	1-1	0-1	8	Bent D [55]	8097
4	26	H	Bradford C	L	1-2	1-1	8	Bent D [14]	25,457
5	Sept 1	A	Preston NE	D	0-0	0-0	12		15,357
6	15	H	Norwich C	D	1-1	0-0	14	Counago [90]	29,112
7	22	A	Stoke C	L	1-2	0-1	19	Holland [68]	14,587
8	28	H	Derby Co	L	0-1	0-1	21		24,439
9	Oct 6	A	Wimbledon	W	1-0	0-0	19	Ambrose [90]	3238
10	8	A	Grimsby T	L	0-3	0-2	—		4688
11	12	H	Sheffield W	W	2-1	2-0	14	Counago 2 [30, 35]	23,410
12	19	A	Reading	L	1-3	0-2	15	Ambrose [61]	19,524
13	22	H	Burnley	D	2-2	2-1	—	McGreal [2], Ambrose [16]	22,736
14	26	H	Gillingham	L	0-1	0-1	17		24,176
15	Nov 3	H	Crystal Palace	L	1-2	1-1	20	Ambrose [39]	24,941
16	9	A	Sheffield U	D	0-0	0-0	20		15,884
17	17	A	Watford	W	2-0	0-0	18	Armstrong [51], Clapham [57]	16,184
18	23	H	Coventry C	W	2-1	1-0	17	Bent D [10], Counago [83]	23,633
19	30	A	Nottingham F	L	1-2	0-1	18	Williams (og) [89]	24,898
20	Dec 7	H	Rotherham U	L	1-2	1-2	19	Wilnis [11]	22,770
21	10	A	Brighton & HA	D	1-1	0-1	—	Magilton [78]	6377
22	14	H	Watford	W	4-2	2-0	19	Miller T [23], Naylor [40], Counago [67], Bent M [87]	22,985
23	21	A	Portsmouth	D	1-1	0-1	18	Gaardsoe [54]	19,130
24	26	A	Leicester C	W	2-1	0-0	16	Gaardsoe [84], Ambrose [88]	31,426
25	28	H	Walsall	W	3-2	1-0	14	Counago 2 [45, 85], Gaardsoe [60]	26,550
26	Jan 1	H	Millwall	W	4-1	0-0	12	Miller T 2 (1 pen) [57, 87 (p)], Wright [75], Bent M [79]	26,040
27	11	A	Burnley	D	1-1	1-0	12	Counago [22]	15,501
28	18	H	Preston NE	W	3-0	1-0	11	Bent M [30], Bent D 2 [74, 86]	24,666
29	Feb 1	A	Bradford C	L	0-2	0-0	12		12,080
30	8	H	Sheffield U	W	3-2	0-1	9	Bent D 2 [57, 88], Ambrose [88]	26,151
31	19	H	Wolverhampton W	L	2-4	2-1	—	Bent M [2], Holland [45]	27,700
32	22	H	Grimsby T	D	2-2	1-2	9	Bent D 2 [12, 89]	24,118
33	Mar 2	A	Norwich C	W	2-0	0-0	8	Wilnis [72], Bent D [90]	21,243
34	5	A	Wolverhampton W	D	1-1	0-0	—	Naylor [84]	26,901
35	8	H	Stoke C	D	0-0	0-0	7		24,547
36	11	A	Crystal Palace	D	1-1	0-1	—	Bent M [67]	15,990
37	15	A	Sheffield W	W	1-0	1-0	7	Holland [17]	24,726
38	18	H	Reading	W	3-1	2-1	—	Gaardsoe [1], Holland [31], Magilton [70]	24,108
39	22	H	Brighton & HA	D	2-2	1-0	7	Bent M [20], Reuser [85]	26,078
40	29	A	Gillingham	W	3-1	1-1	7	Counago 2 [32, 73], Bent M [78]	8508
41	Apr 5	H	Nottingham F	L	3-4	2-3	7	Miller T 2 (1 pen) [14, 26 (p)], Bent M [60]	29,503
42	12	A	Coventry C	W	4-2	0-2	7	Bent M 2 [51, 68], Counago 2 [55, 65]	13,968
43	18	H	Portsmouth	W	3-0	3-0	—	Reuser [11], Miller T [27], Counago [30]	29,396
44	21	A	Rotherham U	L	1-2	1-0	7	Counago [31]	7519
45	26	H	Wimbledon	L	1-5	0-1	7	Bent D [79]	25,564
46	May 4	A	Derby Co	W	4-1	3-1	7	Counago [32], Bent D [37], Magilton [41], Holland [90]	28,785

Final League Position: 7

GOALSCORERS

League (80): Counago 17, Bent D 12, Bent M 11, Ambrose 8, Holland 7, Miller T 6 (2 pens), Gaardsoe 4, Magilton 3, Naylor 2, Reuser 2, Wilnis 2, Armstrong 1, Clapham 1, George 1, McGreal 1, Wright 1, own goal 1.
Worthington Cup (7): Bent D 2, Ambrose 1, Clapham 1, Counago 1, Gaardsoe 1, Miller T 1.
FA Cup (7): Bent D 3, Ambrose 1, Clapham 1, Gaardsoe 1, Miller 1 (pen).
UEFA Cup (12): Counago 3, Miller T 2, Ambrose 1, Armstrong 1, Bent D 1, Bent M 1 (pen), Brown 1, McGreal 1, Stewart 1.

Marshall A 40	Wilnis F 33 + 2	Clapham J 26	Magilton J 39 + 1	Gaardsoe T 37	Hreidarsson H 28	Holland M 45	Bent D 24 + 11	Counago P 28 + 11	Bent M 25 + 7	Ambrose D 20 + 9	Wright J 25 + 14	Miller T 24 + 6	Armstrong A 9 + 10	Venus M 8	Stewart M 3	George F 3 + 7	Brown W 7 + 2	McGreal J 16	Makin C 33	Westlake I — + 4	Gerrard P 5	Naylor R 11 + 6	Richards M 10 + 3	Reuser M 6 + 10	Pullen J 1	Bowditch D — + 5	Collins A — + 1	Murray A — + 1	*Match No.*
1	2^{1}	3	4	5	6	7	8	9^{2}	10^{3}	11	12	13	14																1
1		11	4^{2}	5	3	7	10	12		8	2	13		6^{3}	9^{1}	14													2
1		3		5	6	7	10	12	8^{2}	11	2	4			9^{1}	13													3
1	12	3	4	5	6	7	10		13	8	2^{2}				9	11^{1}													4
1		11	4	5	3	7	10^{1}	12	9	8	2						6												5
1		3	11^{1}		6	7	10	12	9^{2}	8	2		13	4				5											6
1	2	3	12		6	7	13	9		8		11^{1}	10^{2}	4^{3}			14	5											7
1	2^{1}	11	6		3^{2}	7	10	9^{3}		8	12		14			13	4	5											8
1		3				8		9^{1}	10	13	7	6	12			11^{2}	4	5	2										9
1		3				8		9^{1}	10	13	7	6^{2}	12			11	4	5	2										10
1		3		5		8		9^{1}	10^{2}	11	7	14	12	6^{3}		13	4		2										11
1		3	8^{2}		6	7		9■	10^{3}	11	13		14	4^{1}		12		5	2										12
1		3			6	8	12	9		11	7^{2}	13	10^{1}	4^{3}			14	5	2										13
1		11^{1}			3	6	12	9		8	7^{2}	14	10				4	5	2^{3}	13									14
1		11	4	5	3	7	9			8	12		10^{1}			13	6		2^{2}										15
1	12	3	7	5	6	8	9						10^{2}	11		13		4	2^{1}										16
	2	11	8	6	3	7	9	12					10^{1}					5	4		1								17
	2	11	7	6	3	8	9	12					10^{1}					5	4		1								18
	2^{2}	11	7	6	3^{3}	8	9^{1}	12		14	13		10					5	4		1								19
	2^{1}	11	7	6	3	8	10	9		13			12	4^{2}				5			1								20
	2	3	7	4	6	8	9^{1}	12		13	11		10^{3}					5^{2}			1	14							21
1	2	3	7	5	6	8	12	9^{1}	13		11	4										10^{2}							22
1	2	11	7^{3}	5	3	6	12	9^{1}	13		14	8							4■			10^{2}							23
1	2^{1}	11	7^{2}	5	3	6		9	10^{3}	12	13	8							4			14							24
1	2	3	7	5	4	6		9	12		13	8^{2}							11			10^{1}							25
1	2^{3}	11	7	5^{1}	3	6		9	13	14	12	8							4			10^{2}							26
1	2		4	5	3	6	12	9^{1}	10	11^{2}	7	8											13						27
1	2		7^{2}	5	3	6	12	9^{1}	10	13	11	8							4										28
1	2^{1}		7^{3}	5	3■	6	12	9^{2}	10	13	11	8							4					14					29
1	2		7^{1}	5	3	6	10	9■	12	11	13	8							4^{2}										30
1	2		7	5		6	9	12	10	11^{1}		8						4	3^{2}					13					31
	2		7^{1}	5		6	9		10	11^{3}	12	8						4^{2}	3			13		14	1				32
1	3		7^{1}	5		6	9			10^{2}	11	4							2			12	8			13			33
1	3^{1}		7^{3}	5		6	9			10^{2}	11	4							2			12	8	13		14			34
1	3		7	5	8^{1}	6	9		10		11	4^{3}							2			13	12^{2}	14					35
1	3		4	5		6	9^{2}	12	10	11^{3}	7								2^{1}			8	14	13					36
1	2		7	5		6	9^{1}	12	10^{3}		11									13		4	3	8^{2}		14			37
1	2		7	5		6	12	9^{1}	10		11								3			4		8					38
1	2		7^{2}	5		6	12	9^{1}	10		11	13							3			4		8					39
1	2		7	5^{3}			10^{1}	9^{2}	12		11	6							3	13		4	8	14					40
1	2^{1}		7			6		9	10		11	8	12						5			4	3^{2}	13					41
1	2		7^{1}	5		8		9^{3}	10		12	11							6			4^{2}	3	13		14			42
1	2		7^{1}	5		6		9	10^{2}		12	8	13						4	14			3	11^{3}					43
1	2^{2}		7	5		6		9	10		12	8^{1}							4				3	11		13			44
1	2^{1}		7	5		6	12	9	10		8								4				3	11					45
1	2		7	5		6	8^{2}	9	10^{1}			11^{3}							4				3	12			13	14	46

Worthington Cup

Second Round	Brighton & HA	(h)	3-1
Third Round	Middlesbrough	(h)	3-1
Fourth Round	Liverpool	(a)	1-1

FA Cup

Third Round	Morecambe	(h)	4-0
Fourth Round	Sheffield U	(a)	3-4

UEFA Cup

First Qualifying Round	Avenir Beggen	(a)	1-0
		(h)	8-1
First Round	Sartid	(h)	1-1
		(a)	1-0
Second Round	Slovan Liberec	(h)	1-0
		(a)	0-1

KIDDERMINSTER HARRIERS Division 3

FOUNDATION

Kidderminster Harriers were originally formed as a rugby team and played their first game as a soccer club on 18 September 1886 away to Wilden. Harriers won 2-1 with goals from Arthur Millward and William Colsey. Millward was vice-captain and later Kidderminster's first representative on the executive of the Birmingham County FA in 1897. Colsey was to die in tragic circumstances following an accidental injury sustained in a match only two months later.

Aggborough Stadium, Hoo Road, Kidderminster DY10 1NB.

Telephone: (01562) 823 931.

Fax: (01562) 827 329.

Website: www.harriers.co.uk

Email: info@harriers.co.uk

Ground Capacity: 6,500.

Record Attendance: 9,155 v Hereford U, 27 November 1948.

Chairman: Colin Youngjohns.

Vice-chairman: Barry Norgrove.

Director: Richard Painter.

General Manager: Jim Conway.

Manager: Ian Britton.

Youth Team Manager: John Deakin.

Medical Officer: Dr. V. P. Schreiber.

Physio: Jim Conway.

Football Secretary: Roger Barlow.

Stadium Manager: Roger Barlow.

Media Manager: Steve Thomas.

Year Formed: 1886.

HONOURS

FA Cup: best season: 5th rd 1994

Football League Cup: never past 2nd rd.

Conference: – Champions 1993–94, 1999–2000; Runners-up 1996–97.

FA Trophy: 1986–87 (winners); 1990–91, 1994–95 (runners-up).

Spalding Challenge Cup: Winners 1996–97.

Welsh FA Cup: Runners-up 1985–86, 1988–89.

Southern League Cup: Winners 1979–80.

Worcester Senior Cup: (22)

Birmingham Senior Cup: (7)

Staffordshire Senior Cup: (4)

West Midland League: Champions (6); Runners-up (3)

Southern Premier: Runners-up (1)

West Midland League Cup: Winners (7)

Keys Cup: Winners (7)

Border Counties Floodlit League: Champions: (3)

Camkin Floodlit Cup: Winners (3)

Bass County Vase: Winners (1)

Conference Fair Play Trophy: (5)

SKY SPORTS FACT FILE

The last non-league club to reach the fifth round of the FA Cup was Kidderminster Harriers in 1993–94. Their victims were Chesham United, Kettering Town, Woking, Birmingham City and Preston North End before losing 1-0 to West Ham United.

Club Nickname: 'Harriers'.

First Football League Game: 12 August 2000, Division 3, v Torquay U (h) W 2–0 – Clarke; Clarkson, Stamps, Webb, Hinton, Smith, Bennett, Horne (1), Foster, Hadley (1), Ducros (Bird).

Record League Victory: 4–0 v Swansea C (a), Division 3, 29 October 2002 – Brock; Coleman, Shilton (1), Stamps, Hinton (Bennett), Ayres, Melligan (1), Flynn, Broughton (1) (Foster), Henriksen (1), Williams (Parrish).

Record Cup Victory: 4–0 v Halesowen T, FA Cup 1st rd replay, 16 November 1987.
N.B. 25–0 v Hereford, Birmingham Senior Cup, 1889–90.

Record Defeat: 0–13 v Darwen, FA Cup 1st rd replay, 24 January 1891.

MANAGERS

Leslie Smith
Amos Moss
John Spilsbury
Dudley Kernick
Archie Styles
Stan Lloyd
Harold Cox
Stan Jones
Ron Whitehouse
Alan Grundy
John Chambers
Graham Allner 1983–99
Jan Molby 1999–2002
Ian Britton May 2002–

Most League Points (3 for a win): 66, Division 3, 2001–02.

Most League Goals: 62, Division 3, 2002–03.

Record Transfer Fee Received: £380,000 from WBA for Lee Hughes, 1997.

Record Transfer Fee Paid: £100,000 to Nuneaton Borough for Andy Ducros, July 2000.

Colours: Red shirts with white flash, white shorts, red stockings with white trim.

Change Colours: Black shirts, black shorts, black stockings.

Football League Record: 2000 Promoted to Division 3.

LATEST SEQUENCES

Longest Sequence of League Wins: 4, 3.11.2001 – 24.11.2001.

Longest Sequence Without a League Win: 8, 25.2.2001 – 24.3.2001

Longest Sequence of League Draws: 4, 26.8.2002 – 14.9.2002.

Longest Sequence of Unbeaten League Matches: 9, 24.8.2002 – 5.10.2002.

Successive Scoring Runs: 10 from 3.11.2001.

Successive Non-scoring Runs: 4 from 10.3.2001.

TEN YEAR LEAGUE RECORD

		P	W	D	L	F	A	Pts	Pos
1993-94	Conf.	42	22	9	11	63	35	75	1
1994-95	Conf.	42	16	9	17	63	61	57	11
1995-96	Conf.	42	18	10	14	78	66	64	7
1996-97	Conf.	42	26	7	9	84	42	85	2
1997-98	Conf.	42	11	14	17	56	63	47	17
1998-99	Conf.	42	14	9	19	56	52	51	15
1999-2000	Conf.	42	26	7	9	75	40	85	1
2000-01	Div 3	46	13	14	19	47	61	53	16
2001-02	Div 3	46	19	9	18	56	47	66	10
2002-03	Div 3	46	16	15	15	62	63	63	11

DID YOU KNOW ?

Kidderminster Harriers' most famous son was centre-forward Gerry Hitchens, signed as a 17-year-old in September 1953 and sold for a then club record fee of £1,500 in January 1955. He subsequently won full England caps in a lengthy career.

KIDDERMINSTER HARRIERS 2002–03 LEAGUE RECORD

Match No.	*Date*	*Venue*	*Opponents*	*Result*		*H/T Score*	*Lg. Pos.*	*Goalscorers*	*Attendance*
1	Aug 10	H	Lincoln C	D	1-1	0-1	—	Henriksen [59]	2687
2	13	A	Bournemouth	D	0-0	0-0	—		4771
3	17	A	Rushden & D	L	1-3	0-1	20	Williams [77]	3329
4	24	H	Exeter C	W	4-3	2-2	13	Henriksen 2 [29, 53], Ayres 2 [35, 68]	2195
5	26	A	Leyton Orient	D	0-0	0-0	15		4147
6	31	H	Darlington	D	1-1	0-0	15	Foster (pen) [53]	2488
7	Sept 7	H	Boston U	D	0-0	0-0	14		2222
8	14	A	Scunthorpe U	D	1-1	1-0	17	Shilton [45]	2676
9	17	A	Southend U	W	2-0	1-0	—	Flynn [45], Melligan [49]	2959
10	21	H	Rochdale	D	0-0	0-0	13		2685
11	28	A	Bristol R	W	2-1	1-0	11	Melligan [27], Henriksen [75]	9447
12	Oct 5	H	Hull C	W	1-0	0-0	8	Henriksen [60]	3787
13	12	H	Macclesfield T	L	0-2	0-1	11		2521
14	19	A	Shrewsbury T	W	3-2	2-2	7	Henriksen [5], Williams [45], Artell (og) [55]	3507
15	26	H	Cambridge U	W	2-1	2-1	3	Melligan 2 [4, 27]	2779
16	29	A	Swansea C	W	4-0	1-0	—	Shilton [28], Henriksen [52], Broughton [57], Melligan [62]	3421
17	Nov 9	H	Carlisle U	L	1-2	0-1	6	Flynn [66]	3009
18	19	A	Torquay U	D	2-2	0-2	—	Henriksen [61], Bishop [72]	2629
19	30	A	Hartlepool U	L	1-2	0-2	10	Parrish [47]	4296
20	Dec 14	H	York C	L	1-2	1-1	11	Bishop [40]	2304
21	21	A	Wrexham	W	2-0	1-0	10	Parrish [44], Melligan [89]	3734
22	26	H	Leyton Orient	W	3-2	1-1	10	Bennett [39], Shilton [78], Henriksen [84]	3821
23	29	A	Bury	D	1-1	0-0	10	Henriksen (pen) [49]	3202
24	Jan 11	H	Rushden & D	L	0-2	0-1	12		3417
25	18	A	Darlington	L	1-2	0-0	13	Henriksen [50]	2630
26	25	H	Bury	W	3-2	2-0	11	Parrish [21], Bishop 2 [45, 62]	2736
27	28	H	Oxford U	L	1-3	0-2	—	Parrish [52]	2991
28	Feb 4	H	Bournemouth	W	1-0	0-0	—	Henriksen [83]	2157
29	8	A	Carlisle U	D	2-2	1-2	12	Henriksen [30], Scott [83]	3882
30	15	H	Torquay U	W	2-0	1-0	11	Melligan [20], Henriksen [69]	3039
31	18	A	Exeter C	W	5-2	3-1	—	Henriksen 3 (1 pen) [25, 45 (p), 56], Whitbread (og) [39], Broughton [57]	1957
32	22	A	Boston U	L	0-3	0-2	9		2485
33	Mar 1	H	Scunthorpe U	L	1-3	0-2	11	Henriksen [49]	2834
34	4	H	Southend U	W	1-0	0-0	—	Melligan [76]	2006
35	15	A	Cambridge U	W	2-0	0-0	9	Melligan [66], Morgan [73]	3705
36	18	H	Shrewsbury T	D	2-2	0-2	—	Broughton 2 [62, 68]	3284
37	22	H	Swansea C	D	2-2	2-2	9	Shilton [8], Smith [32]	3172
38	25	A	Lincoln C	L	0-1	0-1	—		4092
39	29	A	Macclesfield T	L	0-2	0-0	11		2069
40	Apr 5	H	Hartlepool U	D	2-2	2-0	11	Henriksen [22], Bishop [27]	2900
41	12	A	Oxford U	L	1-2	1-1	12	Henriksen [45]	6820
42	15	A	Rochdale	W	1-0	0-0	—	Shilton [83]	1810
43	19	H	Wrexham	L	0-2	0-1	11		3689
44	21	A	York C	D	0-0	0-0	11		4069
45	26	A	Hull C	L	1-4	0-2	11	Parrish [60]	14,544
46	May 3	H	Bristol R	D	1-1	1-0	11	Melligan [15]	3872

Final League Position: 11

GOALSCORERS

League (62): Henriksen 20 (2 pens), Melligan 10, Bishop 5, Parrish 5, Shilton 5, Broughton 4, Ayres 2, Flynn 2, Williams 2, Bennett 1, Foster 1 (pen), Morgan 1, Scott 1, Smith 1, own goals 2.
Worthington Cup (0).
FA Cup (3): Broughton 2, own goal 1.
LDV Vans Trophy (7): Broughton 2, Melligan 2, Bennett 1, Sall 1, Shilton 1.

Brock S 35	Smith A 28 + 2	Stamps S 19 + 4	Williams D 43 + 2	Hinton C 44	Sall A 4	Bennett D 28 + 4	Flynn S 45	Broughton D 28 + 9	Henriksen B 36 + 1	Parrish S 21 + 8	Shilton S 39 + 2	Doyle D 1 + 4	Joy I 2 + 4	Ayres L 22 + 7	Foster I 7 + 22	Lewis M — + 2	Ducros A 2	Clyde M 4	Melligan J 28 + 1	Coleman K 13 + 2	Bishop A 22 + 7	Digby F 11	Scott D 19	Morgan W 5	McAuley H — + 4	Heath N — + 1	Khela I — + 1	Match No.
1	2	3	4	5	6	7	8	9	10	11																		1
1	2	3	4	5	6	7^{1}		9	10	8	11^{2}	12	13															2
1	2	3	4	5	6^{1}	7^{2}	8	9■	10	11				12	13													3
1	2	3	4		6	7^{1}	8	9	10^{2}	11		12		5	13													4
1	4	2	6				8	9		11	12	7^{1}	3	5	10^{2}	13												5
1	2	3	4	5			8		10	11				6	9^{1}	12	7											6
1	2	3	4	5			8	9	10	11				6	12		7^{1}											7
1		3	4	5			8	9	10^{1}		11			6	12			2	7									8
1			4	5			8	9	10^{1}		11		12	6	7			3	2									9
1		3	4	5^{1}		12	8	9	10		11			6	13			2	7^{2}									10
1		6	8	5		2	11	9	10^{1}		3			4	12				7									11
1	12	3	4	5^{1}		13	8	9	10		11			2				6	7^{2}									12
1	12	6	11^{1}	5			8		10		3	13		2	9				7	4^{2}								13
1	2	6^{1}	4	5			8	9	10		11			3					7	12								14
1			7^{1}	5		2	8	9	10^{2}	12	3			6	13				11	4								15
1		4	11^{1}	5^{2}		13	8	9^{3}	10	12	3			6	14				7	2								16
1		2■	7^{1}	5			8■	9		12	3			4	10				11	6								17
1	2		7	5		8	11	9^{1}	10^{2}		3		13	4	12					6^{3}	14							18
1			4	5		2	8	9	10^{1}	11	12		3	6							7							19
1				5		2	8	9■		11	3			6					7	4	10							20
1			12	5		2^{1}	8	13	9^{2}	11	3			6					7	4	10							21
1			12	5		2^{2}	8		9^{3}	11^{1}	3	14		6	13				7	4	10							22
1			11	5		2^{1}	8		9		3		12	6					7	4	10							23
1			11	5		2^{1}	8		9		3			6	12				7	4	10							24
1	2		4	5		12	8		9	11	3^{2}			13	14				7^{1}	6	10^{3}							25
1	6		7	5		2	8		9^{1}	11	3^{2}			13	12					4	10							26
1	6^{2}		7	5		2^{3}	8	12	9^{1}	11	3			13	14					4	10							27
	6		7	5		2	8	12	9	11	3^{2}			13							10^{1}	1	4					28
	6		7	5		2^{3}	8	12	9	11	3^{2}				13				14		10^{1}	1	4					29
	6		11	5		2	8	9^{1}	10^{2}		3				12				7		13	1	4					30
	6		11	5		2	8	9	10^{3}	12	3^{2}			13					7^{1}		14	1	4					31
	6		11	5		2	8	9^{3}	10	12	3^{1}			13					7^{2}		14	1	4					32
	6		11^{1}	5			8		9	12	3								7		10	1	4	2				33
	6^{2}		11	5			8	9	10^{1}	12	3^{3}								7	13	14	1	4	2				34
	2		11	5			8	12		13	3				9				7^{2}		10^{1}	1	4	6				35
	6		11	5			8	9			3								7		10	1	4	2				36
	6	12	11	5			8	9^{2}	13		3				14				7		10^{3}	1	4	2^{1}				37
	2	12	7	5			8	13		11	3			6^{1}	9^{2}						10	1	4					38
1	6		7	5		2	8	9		11^{3}	3^{2}				12						10^{1}		4		13	14		39
1	6	12	11	5		2	8	13	9^{2}		3								7		10^{1}		4					40
1	6		11	5		2	8	12	9		3								7		10^{1}		4					41
1	6^{1}	12	11	5		2	8	9	10^{2}		3								7		13		4					42
1	6^{1}	2	9	5		7	8			11	3				12						10^{2}		4		13			43
1		6	7	5		2^{2}	8	9		11^{3}	3				12						10^{1}		4		13		14	44
1		6	7	5		2	8	9	10	11^{2}	3^{1}				12						13		4^{3}		14			45
1		6	11	5		2	8	12	9^{2}		3				13				7		10^{1}		4					46

Worthington Cup

First Round	Nottingham F	(a)	0-4

FA Cup

First Round	Rushden & D	(h)	2-2
		(a)	1-2

LDV Vans Trophy

First Round	Dagenham & R	(a)	3-1
Second Round	Swindon T	(h)	3-2
Quarter-Final	Brentford	(a)	1-2

LEEDS UNITED — FA Premiership

FOUNDATION

Immediately the Leeds City club (founded in 1904) was wound up by the FA in October 1919, following allegations of illegal payments to players, a meeting was called by a Leeds solicitor, Mr Alf Masser, at which Leeds United was formed. They joined the Midland League playing their first game in that competition in November 1919. It was in this same month that the new club had discussions with the directors of a virtually bankrupt Huddersfield Town who wanted to move to Leeds in an amalgamation. But Huddersfield survived even that crisis.

Elland Road, Leeds LS11 0ES.

Telephone: (0113) 367 6000. ***Fax:*** (0113) 367 6050.

Website: www.leedsunited.com

Ticket Information: 0845 121 1992.

Ticket Email: tickets@leedsunited.com

Ground Capacity: 40,296.

Record Attendance: 57,892 v Sunderland, FA Cup 5th rd (replay), 15 March 1967.

Record Receipts: £781,445 v Liverpool, FA Cup 4th rd, 27 January 2001.

Pitch Measurements: 105m × 68m.

President: The Right Hon. The Earl of Harewood KBE, LLD.

Chairman: J. McKenzie.

Directors: S. Harrison, A. Hudson, I. Silvester, D. Walker.

Manager: Peter Reid.

Assistant Manager: Kevin Blackwell.

Club Secretary: Ian Silvester.

Physio: Dave Hancock.

Business Development Manager: Phil Brining.

Stadium Manager: Harry Stokey.

Colours: All white with royal blue trim.

Change Colours: All blue with yellow trim.

Year Formed: 1919, as Leeds United after disbandment (by FA order) of Leeds City (formed in 1904).

Turned Professional: 1920.

Ltd Co.: 1920.

Club Nickname: 'The Whites'.

HONOURS

Football League: Division 1 – Champions 1968–69, 1973–74, 1991–92; Runners-up 1964–65, 1965–66, 1969–70, 1970–71, 1971–72; Division 2 – Champions 1923–24, 1963–64, 1989–90; Runners-up 1927–28, 1931–32, 1955–56.

FA Cup: Winners 1972; Runners-up 1965, 1970, 1973.

Football League Cup: Winners 1968; Runners-up 1996.

European Competitions: *European Cup:* 1969–70, 1974–75 (runners-up). *Champions League:* 1992–93, 2000–01 (semi-finalists). *European Cup-Winners' Cup:* 1972–73 (runners-up). *European Fairs Cup:* 1965–66, 1966–67 (runners-up), 1967–68 (winners), 1968–69, 1970–71 (winners). *UEFA Cup:* 1971–72, 1973–74, 1979–80, 1995–96, 1998–99, 1999–2000 (semi-finalists), 2001–02, 2002–03.

SKY SPORTS FACT FILE

On Boxing Day 2002 James Milner aged 16 years 257 days became the youngest scorer in FA Premier League history in the 2-1 win at Sunderland, eclipsing Everton's Wayne Rooney who had registered earlier in the season at 16 years 360 days.

First Football League Game: 28 August 1920, Division 2, v Port Vale (a) L 0–2 – Down; Duffield, Tillotson; Musgrove, Baker, Walton; Mason, Goldthorpe, Thompson, Lyon, Best.

Record League Victory: 8–0 v Leicester C, Division 1, 7 April 1934 – Moore; George Milburn, Jack Milburn; Edwards, Hart, Copping; Mahon (2), Firth (2), Duggan (2), Furness (2), Cochrane.

Record Cup Victory: 10–0 v Lyn (Oslo), European Cup 1st rd 1st leg, 17 September 1969 – Sprake; Reaney, Cooper, Bremner (2), Charlton, Hunter, Madeley, Clarke (2), Jones (3), Giles (2) (Bates), O'Grady (1).

Record Defeat: 1–8 v Stoke C, Division 1, 27 August 1934.

Most League Points (2 for a win): 67, Division 1, 1968–69.

Most League Points (3 for a win): 85, Division 2, 1989–90.

Most League Goals: 98, Division 2, 1927–28.

Highest League Scorer in Season: John Charles, 42, Division 2, 1953–54.

Most League Goals in Total Aggregate: Peter Lorimer, 168, 1965–79 and 1983–86.

Most League Goals in One Match: 5, Gordon Hodgson v Leicester C, Division 1, 1 October 1938.

Most Capped Player: Lucas Radebe, 58 (70), South Africa.

Most League Appearances: Jack Charlton, 629, 1953–73.

Youngest League Player: Peter Lorimer, 15 years 289 days v Southampton, 29 September 1962.

Record Transfer Fee Received: £30,000,000 from Manchester U for Rio Ferdinand, July 2002.

Record Transfer Fee Paid: £18,000,000 to West Ham United for Rio Ferdinand, November 2000.

Football League Record: 1920 Elected to Division 2; 1924–27 Division 1; 1927–28 Division 2; 1928–31 Division 1; 1931–32 Division 2; 1932–47 Division 1; 1947–56 Division 2; 1956–60 Division 1; 1960–64 Division 2; 1964–82 Division 1; 1982–90 Division 2; 1990–92 Division 1; 1992– FA Premier League.

MANAGERS

Dick Ray 1919–20
Arthur Fairclough 1920–27
Dick Ray 1927–35
Bill Hampson 1935–47
Willis Edwards 1947–48
Major Frank Buckley 1948–53
Raich Carter 1953–58
Bill Lambton 1958–59
Jack Taylor 1959–61
Don Revie OBE 1961–74
Brian Clough 1974
Jimmy Armfield 1974–78
Jock Stein CBE 1978
Jimmy Adamson 1978–80
Allan Clarke 1980–82
Eddie Gray MBE 1982–85
Billy Bremner 1985–88
Howard Wilkinson 1988–96
George Graham 1996–98
David O'Leary 1998–2002
Terry Venables 2002–03
Peter Reid March 2003–

LATEST SEQUENCES

Longest Sequence of League Wins: 9, 26.9.1931 – 21.11.1931.

Longest Sequence of League Defeats: 6, 6.4.1996 – 2.5.1996.

Longest Sequence of League Draws: 5, 19.4.1997 – 9.8.1997.

Longest Sequence of Unbeaten League Matches: 34, 26.10.1968 – 26.8.1969.

Longest Sequence Without a League Win: 17, 1.2.1947 – 26.5.1947.

Successive Scoring Runs: 30 from 27.8.1927.

Successive Non-scoring Runs: 6 from 30.1.1982.

TEN YEAR LEAGUE RECORD

		P	*W*	*D*	*L*	*F*	*A*	*Pts*	*Pos*
1993-94	PR Lge	42	18	16	8	65	39	70	5
1994-95	PR Lge	42	20	13	9	59	38	73	5
1995-96	PR Lge	38	12	7	19	40	57	43	13
1996-97	PR Lge	38	11	13	14	28	38	46	11
1997-98	PR Lge	38	17	8	13	57	46	59	5
1998-99	PR Lge	38	18	13	7	62	34	67	4
1999-2000	PR Lge	38	21	6	11	58	43	69	3
2000-01	PR Lge	38	20	8	10	64	43	68	4
2001-02	PR Lge	38	18	12	8	53	37	66	5
2002-03	PR Lge	38	14	5	19	58	57	47	15

DID YOU KNOW ?

Alan Smith scored all four goals for Leeds United in their 4-1 UEFA Cup second round second leg tie against Hapoel Tel Aviv. It was the best individual scoring performance by a Leeds player in any European match.

LEEDS UNITED 2002–03 LEAGUE RECORD

Match No.	Date	Venue	Opponents	Result		H/T Score	Lg. Pos.	Goalscorers	Attendance
1	Aug 17	H	Manchester C	W	3-0	2-0	—	Barmby [15], Viduka [45], Keane [80]	40,195
2	24	A	WBA	W	3-1	1-0	1	Kewell [39], Bowyer [52], Viduka [70]	26,598
3	28	H	Sunderland	L	0-1	0-0	—		39,929
4	31	A	Birmingham C	L	1-2	0-1	4	Bowyer [50]	27,364
5	Sept 11	A	Newcastle U	W	2-0	1-0	—	Viduka [5], Smith [87]	51,730
6	14	H	Manchester U	W	1-0	0-0	3	Kewell [67]	39,622
7	22	A	Blackburn R	L	0-1	0-1	5		25,415
8	28	H	Arsenal	L	1-4	0-2	7	Kewell [84]	40,199
9	Oct 6	A	Aston Villa	D	0-0	0-0	9		33,505
10	19	H	Liverpool	L	0-1	0-0	10		40,197
11	26	A	Middlesbrough	D	2-2	1-1	12	Viduka (pen) [11], Bowyer [56]	34,723
12	Nov 3	H	Everton	L	0-1	0-0	13		40,168
13	10	A	West Ham U	W	4-3	4-1	10	Barmby [11], Kewell 2 [28, 41], Viduka [45]	33,297
14	17	H	Bolton W	L	2-4	1-1	10	Smith [4], Kewell [84]	36,627
15	24	A	Tottenham H	L	0-2	0-2	14		35,720
16	Dec 1	H	Charlton Ath	L	1-2	1-0	16	Kewell [42]	35,547
17	7	A	Fulham	L	0-1	0-1	16		17,499
18	16	A	Bolton W	W	3-0	2-0	—	Mills [12], Fowler [16], Wilcox [75]	23,201
19	21	H	Southampton	D	1-1	0-0	16	Kewell [73]	36,687
20	26	A	Sunderland	W	2-1	0-1	14	Milner [51], Fowler (pen) [80]	44,029
21	28	H	Chelsea	W	2-0	2-0	13	Gallas (og) [30], Milner [45]	40,143
22	Jan 1	H	Birmingham C	W	2-0	1-0	11	Bakke [6], Viduka [67]	40,044
23	11	A	Manchester C	L	1-2	0-1	12	Kewell [90]	34,884
24	18	H	WBA	D	0-0	0-0	11		39,708
25	28	A	Chelsea	L	2-3	1-0	—	Kewell [18], Lucic [66]	39,741
26	Feb 1	A	Everton	L	0-2	0-0	13		40,153
27	8	H	West Ham U	W	1-0	1-0	13	Johnson Seth [20]	40,126
28	22	H	Newcastle U	L	0-3	0-1	14		40,025
29	Mar 5	A	Manchester U	L	1-2	0-1	—	Viduka [64]	67,626
30	15	H	Middlesbrough	L	2-3	1-2	15	Viduka 2 [24, 76]	39,073
31	23	A	Liverpool	L	1-3	1-2	16	Viduka [44]	43,021
32	Apr 5	A	Charlton Ath	W	6-1	3-1	14	Kewell 2 [12, 76], Harte (pen) [34], Viduka 3 (1 pen) [42, 53, 56 (p)]	26,317
33	12	H	Tottenham H	D	2-2	1-2	13	Viduka 2 (1 pen) [31, 76 (p)]	39,580
34	19	A	Southampton	L	2-3	0-2	16	Kewell [80], Barmby [90]	32,032
35	22	H	Fulham	W	2-0	1-0	—	Viduka 2 [4, 49]	37,220
36	26	H	Blackburn R	L	2-3	1-1	16	Viduka [21], Smith [90]	38,122
37	May 4	A	Arsenal	W	3-2	1-1	16	Kewell [5], Harte [48], Viduka [88]	38,127
38	11	H	Aston Villa	W	3-1	1-1	15	Harte [8], Barmby [81], Viduka [90]	40,205

Final League Position: 15

GOALSCORERS

League (58): Viduka 20 (3 pens), Kewell 14, Barmby 4, Bowyer 3, Harte 3 (1 pen), Smith 3, Fowler 2 (1 pen), Milner 2, Bakke 1, Johnson Seth 1, Keane 1, Lucic 1, Mills 1, Wilcox 1, own goal 1.
Worthington Cup (1): own goal 1.
FA Cup (7): Bakke 2, Viduka 2 (1 pen), Kelly 1, Kewell 1, Smith 1.
UEFA Cup (8): Smith 5, Bakke 1, Barmby 1, Kewell 1.

Robinson P 38	Mills D 32 + 1	Harte I 24 + 3	Bakke E 31 + 3	Radebe L 16 + 3	Matteo D 20	Bowyer L 15	Smith A 33	Viduka M 29 + 4	Kewell H 31	Barmby N 16 + 3	Keane R — + 3	Johnson Seth 3 + 6	Woodgate J 18	Dacourt O 4 + 3	McPhail S 7 + 6	Kelly G 24 + 1	McMaster J — + 4	Duberry M 11 + 3	Lucic T 16 + 1	Bridges M 1 + 4	Wilcox J 23 + 2	Milner J 1 + 17	Burns J 2	Fowler R 2 + 6	Okon P 15	Bravo R 5	Kilgallon M — + 2	Johnson Simon 1 + 3	Match No.
1	2	3	4	5	6	7	8	9[1]	10	11[2]	12	13																	1
1	2	3	4	12	6	7	8	9	10[2]	11	13		5[1]																2
1	2	3	4[2]	5	6	7	8	9	10	11[1]	12			13															3
1	2	3	4[1]		6	7	8	9	10	11			5	12															4
1	2	3	12		6	7	8	9[1]	10	11			5	4															5
1	2	3	12	13	6[2]	7	8	9[3]	10	11[1]			5	4	14														6
1	2	3[2]	4	5		10	8	9[3]		11			6	7[1]	12	13	14												7
1	3		4	5[2]	6	11	8	9	10					7[1]	12	2		13											8
1	2	3	4		6	7	9	12	10	11			5		8[1]														9
1	2	3	4			7	9[1]	12	10	11			5	13	8[2]				6										10
1	2		12	5		7	8■	9[2]	10	11			6		4[1]				3	13									11
1	2	12	4	5		7	8[2]	9[3]	10	11			6				13		3[1]	14									12
1		3	4	5		8		9[2]	10[1]	7					12	2			6	13	11[3]	14							13
1							8	9	10	7			5		4[2]	2		12	3[1]		11	13	6						14
1			4			7	9	12[2]	10				5		8	2			3		11	13	6[1]						15
1		3	4			7[2]	9		10				5		8[1]	2		6		12	11			13					16
1	12	3[1]	4				9[3]						5		8[2]	2		6		10	11	13		14	7				17
1	2	3	4						10			12	5			7			6		11			9[1]	8				18
1	2	3					8	12	10				5			7			6		11			9[1]	4				19
1	5	3[1]	4				8[3]	9[2]	10							2		12	6		11	14		13	7				20
1	5		4[1]				8	9[2]	10[3]			12	6			2			3		11	14		13	7				21
1	5	3	4[1]				8	9	10				6			2					11	12			7				22
1	5		4[2]		3		8[3]	9[1]	10			12	6			2					11	14		13	7				23
1			4[1]	5	6		8	9	10			12				2			3		11[3]	14		13	7[2]				24
1	5		4		6		8	9[2]	10			12				2			3		11	13			7[1]				25
1	5	12	4[3]	13	6[2]		8	9	10							2			3[1]		11	14			7				26
1	2		10[1]		6[2]							4				7	12	5			11	9			8	3	13		27
1	2			5[3]			9		10	12		4				7		6	14		11[2]	13			8[1]	3			28
1	2	3		5			7	9		10[2]		8			12				6			13			4	11[1]			29
1	2		4	5			8	9		10[1]									6		11	12			7	3			30
1	2	12	4	5			10	9		7[2]							14		6		11	13			8[3]	3[1]			31
1	2	3	4[2]	5	11		8[3]	9	10[1]							7		6			12	13						14	32
1	2[2]	3[1]	4	5	11		8	9	10							7		6			12	13							33
1	5[1]	3	4		7		8■	9	10	12						2		6			11								34
1	2	3	4		6		8	9	10							7		5			11								35
1	2	3	4[1]		6		8	9	10							7		5			11							12	36
1	2	3	8	5	6			9	10[1]							7		4			11							12	37
1	2[1]	3	8[2]	5	6[3]			9		12					13	7		4			11						14	10	38

Worthington Cup

Third Round	Sheffield U	(a)	1-2

UEFA Cup

First Round	Metalurg Zapor	(h)	1-0
		(a)	1-1
Second Round	Hapoel Tel Aviv	(h)	1-0
		(n)	4-1
Third Round	Malaga	(a)	0-0
		(h)	1-2

FA Cup

Third Round	Scunthorpe U	(a)	2-0
Fourth Round	Gillingham	(a)	1-1
		(h)	2-1
Fifth Round	Crystal Palace	(a)	2-1
Sixth Round	Sheffield U	(a)	0-1

LEICESTER CITY FA Premiership

FOUNDATION

In 1884 a number of young footballers who were mostly old boys of Wyggeston School, held a meeting at a house on the Roman Fosse Way and formed Leicester Fosse FC. They collected 9d (less than 4p) towards the cost of a ball, plus the same amount for membership. Their first professional, Harry Webb from Stafford Rangers, was signed in 1888 for 2s 6d (12p) per week, plus travelling expenses.

The Walkers Stadium, Filbert Way, Leicester LE2 7FL.

Telephone: 0870 040 6000. ***Ticket Office:*** 0870 040 6000. ***ClubCall:*** 09068 121 185.
24hr Ticket Information: 09068 121 028.
Website: www.lcfc.com

Ground Capacity: 32,500.

Record Attendance: 47,298 v Tottenham H, FA Cup 5th rd, 18 February 1928.

Record Receipts: £377,467 v Aston Villa, League Cup semi-final, 2nd leg, 2 February 2000.

Pitch Measurements: 110yd × 76yd.

President: T. W. Shipman.

Chief Executive: Tim Davies.
Directors: M. George, P. Hockenhull, J. Holmes (non-executive chairman) T. Lander, P. Mace, T. Wheeler, M. Glenn, J. Johnson.

Manager: Micky Adams. ***Assistant Manager:*** Alan Cork.
Reserve Team Coach: Peter Shirtliff.
Director of Football: Dave Bassett.
Physios: David Rennie and Mick Yeoman.

HONOURS

Football League: Division 1 – Runners-up 1928–29; Promoted from Division 1 1993–94 (play-offs) and 1995–96 (play-offs); Division 2 – Champions 1924–25, 1936–37, 1953–54, 1956–57, 1970–71, 1979–80; Runners-up 1907–08.

FA Cup: Runners-up 1949, 1961, 1963, 1969.

Football League Cup: Winners 1964, 1997, 2000; Runners-up 1965, 1999.

European Competitions: *European Cup-Winners' Cup:* 1961–62. *UEFA Cup:* 1997–98, 2000–01.

Head of Media and Communications: Bob Walker. ***Director of Football Administration and Club Secretary:*** Andrew Neville. ***Stadium Manager:*** David Butcher.

Colours: Royal blue shirts, white shorts, blue stockings.

Change Colours: White shirts, royal blue shorts, white stockings.

Year Formed: 1884.

Turned Professional: 1888. ***Ltd Co:*** 1897.

Previous Name: 1884, Leicester Fosse; 1919, Leicester City.

Club Nickname: 'Foxes'.

Previous Grounds: 1884, Victoria Park; 1887, Belgrave Road; 1888, Victoria Park; 1891, Filbert Street.

First Football League Game: 1 September 1894, Division 2, v Grimsby T (a) L 3–4 – Thraves; Smith, Bailey; Seymour, Brown, Henrys; Hill, Hughes, McArthur (1), Skea (2), Priestman.

Record League Victory: 10–0 v Portsmouth, Division 1, 20 October 1928 – McLaren; Black, Brown; Findlay, Carr, Watson; Adcock, Hine (3), Chandler (6), Lochhead, Barry (1).

SKY SPORTS FACT FILE

On 23 October 1957 the floodlights were switched on at Filbert Street for the friendly visit of German champions Borussia Dortmund. A crowd of 18,398 saw Willie Gardiner's goal divide the teams at 1-0.

Record Cup Victory: 8–1 v Coventry C (a), League Cup 5th rd, 1 December 1964 – Banks; Sjoberg, Norman (2); Roberts, King, McDerment; Hodgson (2), Cross, Goodfellow, Gibson (1), Stringfellow (2), (1 og).

Record Defeat: 0–12 (as Leicester Fosse) v Nottingham F, Division 1, 21 April 1909.

Most League Points (2 for a win): 61, Division 2, 1956–57.

Most League Points (3 for a win): 77, Division 2, 1991–92.

Most League Goals: 109, Division 2, 1956–57.

Highest League Scorer in Season: Arthur Rowley, 44, Division 2, 1956–57.

Most League Goals in Total Aggregate: Arthur Chandler, 259, 1923–35.

Most League Goals in One Match: 6, John Duncan v Port Vale, Division 2, 25 December 1924; 6, Arthur Chandler v Portsmouth, Division 1, 20 October 1928.

Most Capped Player: John O'Neill, 39, Northern Ireland.

Most League Appearances: Adam Black, 528, 1920–35.

Youngest League Player: Dave Buchanan, 16 years 192 days v Oldham Ath, 1 January 1979.

Record Transfer Fee Received: £11,000,000 from Liverpool for Emile Heskey, March 2000.

Record Transfer Fee Paid: £5,000,000 to Wolverhampton W for Ade Akinbiyi, July 2000.

Football League Record: 1894 Elected to Division 2; 1908–09 Division 1; 1909–25 Division 2; 1925–35 Division 1; 1935–37 Division 2; 1937–39 Division 1; 1946–54 Division 2; 1954–55 Division 1; 1955–57 Division 2; 1957–69 Division 1; 1969–71 Division 2; 1971–78 Division 1; 1978–80 Division 2; 1980–81 Division 1; 1981–83 Division 2; 1983–87 Division 1; 1987–92 Division 2; 1992–94 Division 1; 1994–95 FA Premier League; 1995–96 Division 1; 1996–2002 FA Premier League; 2002–03 Division 1; 2003– FA Premier League.

MANAGERS

Frank Gardner 1884–92
Ernest Marson 1892–94
J. Lee 1894–95
Henry Jackson 1895–97
William Clark 1897–98
George Johnson 1898–1912
Jack Bartlett 1912–14
Louis Ford 1914–15
Harry Linney 1915–19
Peter Hodge 1919–26
Willie Orr 1926–32
Peter Hodge 1932–34
Arthur Lochhead 1934–36
Frank Womack 1936–39
Tom Bromilow 1939–45
Tom Mather 1945–46
John Duncan 1946–49
Norman Bullock 1949–55
David Halliday 1955–58
Matt Gillies 1958–68
Frank O'Farrell 1968–71
Jimmy Bloomfield 1971–77
Frank McLintock 1977–78
Jock Wallace 1978–82
Gordon Milne 1982–86
Bryan Hamilton 1986–87
David Pleat 1987–91
Gordon Lee 1991
Brian Little 1991–94
Mark McGhee 1994–95
Martin O'Neill 1995–2000
Peter Taylor 2000–01
Dave Bassett 2001–02
Micky Adams April 2002–

LATEST SEQUENCES

Longest Sequence of League Wins: 7, 28.2.1993 – 27.3.1993.

Longest Sequence of League Defeats: 8, 17.3.2001 – 28.4.2001.

Longest Sequence of League Draws: 6, 21.8.1976 – 18.9.1976.

Longest Sequence of Unbeaten League Matches: 19, 6.2.1971 – 18.8.1971.

Longest Sequence Without a League Win: 18, 12.4.1975 – 1.11.1975.

Successive Scoring Runs: 31 from 12.11.1932.

Successive Non-scoring Runs: 7 from 21.11.1987.

TEN YEAR LEAGUE RECORD

		P	*W*	*D*	*L*	*F*	*A*	*Pts*	*Pos*
1993-94	Div 1	46	19	16	11	72	59	73	4
1994-95	PR Lge	42	6	11	25	45	80	29	21
1995-96	Div 1	46	19	14	13	66	60	71	5
1996-97	PR Lge	38	12	11	15	46	54	47	9
1997-98	PR Lge	38	13	14	11	51	41	53	10
1998-99	PR Lge	38	12	13	13	40	46	49	10
1999-2000	PR Lge	38	16	7	15	55	55	55	8
2000-01	PR Lge	38	14	6	18	39	51	48	13
2001-02	PR Lge	38	5	13	20	30	64	28	20
2002-03	Div 1	46	26	14	6	73	40	92	2

DID YOU KNOW ?

Scottish-born left-back Sandy Wood was forced to play for Leicester City as an amateur in 1932 and he was the first naturalised American to appear in English football. He had been capped for the USA v Uruguay.

LEICESTER CITY 2002–03 LEAGUE RECORD

Match No.	Date	Venue	Opponents	Result	H/T Score	Lg. Pos.	Goalscorers	Attendance
1	Aug 10	H	Watford	W 2-0	0-0	—	Deane 2 [47, 55]	31,022
2	14	A	Stoke C	W 1-0	1-0	—	Scowcroft [8]	14,028
3	18	A	Ipswich T	L 1-6	1-1	8	Stevenson [45]	27,374
4	24	H	Reading	W 2-1	2-1	6	Deane [3], Dickov (pen) [5]	22,978
5	27	A	Crystal Palace	D 0-0	0-0	—		15,440
6	31	H	Gillingham	W 2-0	2-0	3	Lewis [11], Dickov [42]	30,067
7	Sept 7	A	Wimbledon	W 3-2	2-2	2	Benjamin [44], Izzet (pen) [45], Stewart [81]	2165
8	14	H	Derby Co	W 3-1	1-1	2	Izzet [28], Deane [79], Dickov [86]	31,049
9	17	H	Bradford C	W 4-0	2-0	—	Deane [27], Elliott [28], Dickov (pen) [67], Scowcroft [90]	24,651
10	21	A	Sheffield W	D 0-0	0-0	2		22,219
11	28	H	Wolverhampton W	W 1-0	1-0	2	Dickov (pen) [6]	32,082
12	Oct 5	A	Norwich C	D 0-0	0-0	2		20,952
13	19	H	Burnley	L 0-1	0-0	3		26,254
14	26	A	Nottingham F	D 2-2	2-0	3	Deane [23], Dickov [41]	29,497
15	29	H	Coventry C	W 2-1	0-0	—	Taggart [76], Deane [89]	27,139
16	Nov 2	A	Portsmouth	W 2-0	2-0	2	Scowcroft [13], Elliott [39]	19,107
17	9	H	Walsall	W 2-0	0-0	2	Heath [57], Scowcroft [67]	25,243
18	16	A	Millwall	D 2-2	2-1	2	Heath [1], Stewart [3]	10,772
19	23	H	Rotherham U	W 2-1	0-0	2	Dickov [50], Stewart [64]	31,714
20	26	A	Preston NE	L 0-2	0-0	—		13,048
21	30	A	Grimsby T	W 2-1	1-0	2	Scowcroft [2], Izzet [74]	7310
22	Dec 7	H	Sheffield U	D 0-0	0-0	2		26,718
23	14	H	Millwall	W 4-1	2-1	2	Scowcroft 2 [10, 52], Elliott [25], Dickov [78]	31,904
24	20	A	Brighton & HA	W 1-0	0-0	—	Deane [72]	6592
25	26	H	Ipswich T	L 1-2	0-0	2	Dickov (pen) [55]	31,426
26	28	A	Watford	W 2-1	1-1	2	Elliott [34], Deane [66]	16,017
27	Jan 11	H	Stoke C	D 0-0	0-0	2		25,038
28	18	A	Gillingham	L 2-3	0-2	2	Sinclair [50], Wright [61]	8609
29	28	A	Reading	W 3-1	3-0	—	Dickov 2 (1 pen) [17, 26 (p)], Heath [34]	17,156
30	Feb 1	H	Crystal Palace	W 1-0	0-0	2	Dickov [77]	27,005
31	8	A	Walsall	W 4-1	2-0	2	Dickov [41], Scowcroft 2 [45, 83], Elliott [72]	8741
32	17	H	Portsmouth	D 1-1	1-0	—	Benjamin [9]	31,775
33	22	H	Wimbledon	W 4-0	2-0	2	Dickov 3 (2 pens) [34 (p), 41 (p), 90], Benjamin [48]	31,438
34	Mar 1	A	Derby Co	D 1-1	1-0	2	Deane [26]	24,307
35	4	A	Bradford C	D 0-0	0-0	—		11,531
36	8	H	Sheffield W	D 1-1	0-1	2	McLaren (og) [50]	27,463
37	15	H	Preston NE	W 2-1	1-1	2	Deane 2 [43, 56]	30,713
38	18	A	Burnley	W 2-1	0-0	—	Dickov [79], Benjamin [83]	14,554
39	22	A	Coventry C	W 2-1	0-0	2	McKinlay [48], Scowcroft [68]	16,610
40	Apr 5	H	Grimsby T	W 2-0	0-0	2	Benjamin [61], Davidson [71]	31,014
41	8	H	Nottingham F	W 1-0	1-0	—	Wright [37]	32,065
42	12	A	Rotherham U	D 1-1	0-0	1	Benjamin [75]	9888
43	19	H	Brighton & HA	W 2-0	2-0	1	Izzet [10], Stewart [45]	31,909
44	21	A	Sheffield U	L 1-2	1-1	2	Deane [4]	21,277
45	27	H	Norwich C	D 1-1	1-0	2	Benjamin [20]	31,369
46	May 4	A	Wolverhampton W	D 1-1	0-0	2	Benjamin (pen) [86]	28,190

Final League Position: 2

GOALSCORERS

League (73): Dickov 17 (7 pens), Deane 13, Scowcroft 10, Benjamin 8 (1 pen), Elliott 5, Izzet 4 (1 pen), Stewart 4, Heath 3, Wright 2, Davidson 1, Lewis 1, McKinlay 1, Sinclair 1, Stevenson 1, Taggart 1, own goal 1.
Worthington Cup (6): Rogers 2, Benjamin 1, Dickov 1, Izzet 1, Scowcroft 1.
FA Cup (3): Dickov 2 (1 pen), Elliott 1.

Walker I 46	Sinclair F 31 + 2	Rogers A 41	Elliott M 43 + 1	Taggart G 33 + 4	Marshall L 1	Summerbee N 7 + 22	Izzet M 38	Dickov P 42	Deane B 31 + 1	Scowcroft J 43	McKinlay B 29 + 8	Stewart J 28 + 9	Benjamin T 18 + 17	Stevenson J — + 6	Ashton J — + 2	Oakes S 1 + 4	Impey A 27 + 5	Lewis J 5 + 4	Wright T 2 + 11	Heath M 9 + 2	Davidson C 28 + 2	Reeves M — + 3	Jones M 3 + 3	O'Grady C — + 1	Flowers T — + 1	Petrescu T — + 1	*Match No.*
1	2	3	4^{1}	5	6	7	8	9^{2}	10^{3}	11	12	13	14														1
1	2	3	4	5		7^{1}	8	9^{2}	10	11	6	12		13													2
1	2	3	4	5^{2}		6^{1}	8^{3}	9	10	7		11		12	13	14											3
1		3	4	5				9	10^{2}	7	6	11^{1}				12	2	8	13								4
1		3	4	5▮				9^{2}		7	6	11^{1}	10			12	2	8		13							5
1		3	4	5			6^{1}	9	10^{2}	7	12	11^{3}	13				2	8			14						6
1	2	11^{2}	4	5^{3}			6		10	9	12	13	14				7	8^{1}			3						7
1	5	11^{3}	4			12	6	9	10	7^{1}	13	14					2	8^{2}			3						8
1	5	11^{3}	4			12	8	9	10^{1}	7	6^{2}						2	13			3	14					9
1	5	11^{2}	4	12		7^{3}	8	9		10	6	13	14				2^{1}				3						10
1	2	11^{1}	4	5		12	8▮	9^{2}	10^{3}	7	6		13								3	14					11
1	2	11	4	5		12	8	9^{1}	10^{2}	7	6		13								3						12
1	2	11^{1}	4	5^{3}		12		9^{2}	10	7	6		13			8	14				3						13
1	2	3^{2}	4	5		12		9	10	11^{1}	6	14				13	7^{3}				8						14
1	2	11	4	5		12▮	8	9^{1}	10		6			13			7^{2}				3						15
1	2	11	4	5			8^{2}	9^{1}	10	7	6	13	12								3						16
1	4	11^{1}				12	8	9	10^{2}	7	6^{3}		13				2	14		5	3						17
1	5	3					8	9^{1}	10▮	11^{3}		7	12				2	13		4	6^{2}	14					18
1	4	3	12	5			8^{2}	9^{3}	10	7	13	11					2^{1}		14		6						19
1	2	3^{1}	4	5			8	9	10^{3}	7	12	6^{2}	13	14							11						20
1	2▮	3^{1}	4	5			8	9		7	6	12	10^{2}				13				11						21
1	2	3	4	5		12	8	9		7	6	13	10^{1}								11^{2}						22
1		3	4			7	8^{2}	9^{1}		10	6^{3}	11		12			2	13		5			14				23
1		3	4			12	8	9^{1}	10^{2}	7	6	11	13				2			5							24
1		3	4			12	8	9	10^{1}	7	6^{2}	11	13				2			5							25
1		3	4			12	8	9^{2}	10	7^{1}	6^{3}	11	13				2			5	14						26
1	5	3	4	12▮		7^{2}		9	10		6	11^{1}	13				2						8				27
1	2	3	4	5			8	9	10^{1}		6						7		12		11						28
1	2	3	4				8	9		7		11	10^{1}						12	5	6						29
1	2	3	4	12			8	9^{1}		7		11	10^{2}						13	5^{3}	6		14				30
1	2		4^{3}	5		12	7	9^{2}		11	6	3	10	13						14			8^{1}				31
1	2	3	4	5		12	8	9^{2}		7	6		10^{1}						13		11						32
1	2	3	4	5^{2}		12	8	9		7	6^{3}	11	10^{1}				13						14				33
1	2	3	4	5		12	6	9	10^{1}	7		11	8														34
1		3	4	5		12	6	9	10	7		11	8^{1}				2										35
1		3^{2}	4	5		12	8	9^{1}	10	7	6	11	13				2										36
1			4	5			8	9	10	7	6	11					2				3						37
1	12		4	5		13	8	9	10^{2}	7	6^{3}	11	14				2^{1}				3						38
1			4	5		12	8	9^{1}		7	6	11	10				2				3						39
1	12	3	4	5		7^{1}	8			9		11	10^{2}				2^{3}		13		6			14			40
1	2	3	4	5			8			7		11	10						9		6						41
1	2^{1}	3	4	5^{2}			8	9		7	12	11^{3}	10				13		14		6						42
1	2	3^{2}	4	5			8	9^{3}	12	7		11	10^{1}				13		14		6						43
1		3	4	12				9^{3}	10^{2}	7	13	11	8^{1}				2		14	5	6▮						44
1		3	4	5		12^{2}		9	10	7	6	11^{1}	8^{3}		14		2		13								45
1^{6}	2^{1}		4	5		12			10^{2}	7	6		8				3		9				11		15	13	46

Worthington Cup

First Round	Hull C	(a)	4-2
Second Round	Sheffield W	(a)	2-1
Third Round	Manchester U	(a)	0-2

FA Cup

Third Round	Bristol C	(h)	2-0
Fourth Round	Wolverhampton W	(a)	1-4

LEYTON ORIENT Division 3

FOUNDATION

There is some doubt about the foundation of Leyton Orient, and, indeed, some confusion with clubs like Leyton and Clapton over their early history. As regards the foundation, the most favoured version is that Leyton Orient was formed originally by members of Homerton Theological College who established Glyn Cricket Club in 1881 and then carried on through the following winter playing football. Eventually many employees of the Orient Shipping Line became involved and so the name Orient was chosen in 1888.

Leyton Stadium, Brisbane Road, Leyton, London E10 5NE.

Telephone: (020) 8926 1111. ***Fax:*** (020) 8926 1110. ***ClubCall:*** 09068 121 150. ***Website:*** leytonorient.com ***Email:*** info@leytonorient.net

Ground Capacity: 11,127.

Record Attendance: 34,345 v West Ham U, FA Cup 4th rd, 25 January 1964.

Record Receipts: £87,867.92 v West Ham U, FA Cup 3rd rd, 10 January 1987.

Pitch Measurements: 110yd × 80yd.

Chairman: Barry Hearn.

Chief Executive: Steve Dawson.

Directors: David Dodd, Steve Davis, Nick Levene.

Manager: Paul Brush. ***First Team Coach:*** Martin Ling. ***Physio:*** Tony Flynn.

Secretary: Kirstine Nicholson.

Colours: Red shirts with black panels under arm, red shorts with black panels down sides, red stockings.

Change Colours: Black and red.

Year Formed: 1881. ***Turned Professional:*** 1903. ***Ltd Co.:*** 1906.

Previous Names: 1881, Glyn Cricket and Football Club; 1886, Eagle Football Club; 1888, Orient Football Club; 1898, Clapton Orient; 1946, Leyton Orient; 1966, Orient; 1987, Leyton Orient.

Club Nickname: 'The O's'.

Previous Grounds: 1884, Glyn Road; 1896, Whittles Athletic Ground; 1900, Millfields Road; 1930, Lea Bridge Road; 1937, Brisbane Road.

First Football League Game: 2 September 1905, Division 2, v Leicester Fosse (a) L 1–2 – Butler; Holmes, Codling; Lamberton, Boden, Boyle; Kingaby (1), Wootten, Leigh, Evenson, Bourne.

Record League Victory: 8–0 v Crystal Palace, Division 3 (S), 12 November 1955 – Welton; Lee, Earl; Blizzard, Aldous, McKnight; White (1), Facey (3), Burgess (2), Heckman, Hartburn (2). 8–0 v Rochdale, Division 4, 20 October 1987 – Wells; Howard, Dickenson (1), Smalley (1), Day, Hull, Hales (2), Castle (Sussex), Shinners (2), Godfrey (Harvey), Comfort (2). 8–0 v Colchester U, Division 4, 15 October 1988 – Wells; Howard, Dickenson, Hales (1p), Day (1), Sitton (1), Baker (1), Ward, Hull (3), Juryeff, Comfort (1). 8–0 v Doncaster R, Division 3, 28 December 1997 – Hyde; Channing, Naylor, Smith (1p), Hicks, Clark, Ling, Joseph R, Griffiths (3) (Harris), Richards (2) (Baker (1)), Inglethorpe (1) (Simpson).

HONOURS

Football League: Division 1 best season: 22nd, 1962–63; Division 2 – Runners-up 1961–62; Division 3 – Champions 1969–70; Division 3 (S) – Champions 1955–56; Runners-up 1954–55; Promoted from Division 4 1988–89 (play-offs).

FA Cup: Semi-final 1978.

Football League Cup: best season: 5th rd, 1963.

SKY SPORTS FACT FILE

On 1 January 1955 Leyton Orient beat Bristol City 4-1 and, for the first time in the club's history, from 15 January to 26 February the League team and Combination side topped their respective competitions.

Record Cup Victory: 9–2 v Chester, League Cup 3rd rd, 15 October 1962 – Robertson; Charlton, Taylor; Gibbs, Bishop, Lea; Deeley (1), Waites (3), Dunmore (2), Graham (3), Wedge.

Record Defeat: 0–8 v Aston Villa, FA Cup 4th rd, 30 January 1929.

Most League Points (2 for a win): 66, Division 3 (S), 1955–56.

Most League Points (3 for a win): 75, Division 4, 1988–89.

Most League Goals: 106, Division 3 (S), 1955–56.

Highest League Scorer in Season: Tom Johnston, 35, Division 2, 1957–58.

Most League Goals in Total Aggregate: Tom Johnston, 121, 1956–58, 1959–61.

Most League Goals in One Match: 4, Wally Leigh v Bradford C, Division 2, 13 April 1906; 4, Albert Pape v Oldham Ath, Division 2, 1 September 1924; 4, Peter Kitchen v Millwall, Division 3, 21 April 1984.

Most Capped Players: Tunji Banjo, 7 (7), Nigeria; John Chiedozie, 7 (9), Nigeria; Tony Grealish, 7 (45), Eire.

Most League Appearances: Peter Allen, 432, 1965–78.

Youngest League Player: Paul Went, 15 years 327 days v Preston NE, 4 September 1965.

Record Transfer Fee Received: £600,000 from Notts Co, for John Chiedozie, August 1981.

Record Transfer Fee Paid: £175,000 to Wigan Ath for Paul Beesley, October 1989.

Football League Record: 1905 Elected to Division 2; 1929–56 Division 3 (S); 1956–62 Division 2; 1962–63 Division 1; 1963–66 Division 2; 1966–70 Division 3; 1970–82 Division 2; 1982–85 Division 3; 1985–89 Division 4; 1989–92 Division 3; 1992–95 Division 2; 1995– Division 3.

MANAGERS

Sam Omerod 1905–06
Ike Ivenson 1906
Billy Holmes 1907–22
Peter Proudfoot 1922–29
Arthur Grimsdell 1929–30
Peter Proudfoot 1930–31
Jimmy Seed 1931–33
David Pratt 1933–34
Peter Proudfoot 1935–39
Tom Halsey 1939
Bill Wright 1939–45
Willie Hall 1945
Bill Wright 1945–46
Charlie Hewitt 1946–48
Neil McBain 1948–49
Alec Stock 1949–59
Les Gore 1959–61
Johnny Carey 1961–63
Benny Fenton 1963–64
Dave Sexton 1965
Dick Graham 1966–68
Jimmy Bloomfield 1968–71
George Petchey 1971–77
Jimmy Bloomfield 1977–81
Paul Went 1981
Ken Knighton 1981
Frank Clark 1982–91 *(Managing Director)*
Peter Eustace 1991–94
Chris Turner/John Sitton 1994–95
Pat Holland 1995–96
Tommy Taylor 1996–2001
Paul Brush October 2001–

LATEST SEQUENCES

Longest Sequence of League Wins: 10, 21.1.1956 – 30.3.1956.

Longest Sequence of League Defeats: 9, 1.4.1995 – 6.5.1995.

Longest Sequence of League Draws: 6, 30.11.1974 – 28.12.1974.

Longest Sequence of Unbeaten League Matches: 13, 30.10.1954 – 19.2.1955.

Longest Sequence Without a League Win: 23, 6.10.1962 – 13.4.1963.

Successive Scoring Runs: 24 from 3.5.2003.

Successive Non-scoring Runs: 8 from 19.11.1994.

TEN YEAR LEAGUE RECORD

		P	*W*	*D*	*L*	*F*	*A*	*Pts*	*Pos*
1993-94	Div 2	46	14	14	18	57	71	56	18
1994-95	Div 2	46	6	8	32	30	75	26	24
1995-96	Div 3	46	12	11	23	44	63	47	21
1996-97	Div 3	46	15	12	19	50	58	57	16
1997-98	Div 3	46	19	12	15	62	47	66	11
1998-99	Div 3	46	19	15	12	68	59	72	6
1999-2000	Div 3	46	13	13	20	47	52	52	19
2000-01	Div 3	46	20	15	11	59	51	75	5
2001-02	Div 3	46	13	13	20	55	71	52	18
2002-03	Div 3	46	14	11	21	51	61	53	18

DID YOU KNOW ?

Tommy Mills, a Welsh schoolboy international inside-forward, moved to London and was playing for the Trocadero in the London Hotels League when Clapton Orient signed him in 1929. He was subsequently fully capped by Wales.

LEYTON ORIENT 2002–03 LEAGUE RECORD

Match No.	*Date*	*Venue*	*Opponents*	*Result*		*H/T Score*	*Lg. Pos.*	*Goalscorers*	*Attendance*
1	Aug 10	A	Rochdale	L	0-1	0-0	—		3252
2	13	H	Macclesfield T	W	3-2	3-0	—	Smith[18], Thorpe[30], Lockwood (pen)[44]	3880
3	17	H	Scunthorpe U	W	2-0	1-0	3	Martin[38], Lockwood (pen)[82]	4028
4	24	A	Cambridge U	L	1-2	0-1	9	Campbell-Ryce[50]	4807
5	26	H	Kidderminster H	D	0-0	0-0	7		4147
6	31	A	Hull C	D	1-1	1-1	10	Toner[19]	7684
7	Sept 7	A	Shrewsbury T	L	1-2	1-0	13	Lockwood[5]	2756
8	14	H	Lincoln C	D	1-1	0-0	15	Thorpe[89]	4579
9	17	H	Oxford U	L	1-2	0-1	—	Thorpe[90]	3758
10	21	A	Exeter C	L	0-1	0-0	22		2784
11	28	H	Darlington	W	2-1	0-1	17	Hutchings[60], Nugent[73]	3975
12	Oct 5	A	Rushden & D	L	0-2	0-0	19		4381
13	12	A	Wrexham	D	0-0	0-0	20		3495
14	19	H	Bournemouth	D	0-0	0-0	19		5622
15	26	A	Bristol R	W	2-1	0-0	19	Campbell-Ryce[57], Nugent[67]	6625
16	29	H	Southend U	W	2-1	2-0	—	Iriekpen[2], Whelan (og)[45]	5343
17	Nov 2	H	Bury	L	1-2	0-1	17	Thorpe[83]	4234
18	9	A	York C	L	2-3	1-1	18	Nugent[9], Martin[58]	3304
19	23	H	Hartlepool U	L	1-2	0-1	19	Canham[69]	4009
20	30	A	Boston U	W	1-0	1-0	18	Tate[5]	2616
21	Dec 14	H	Torquay U	W	2-0	2-0	17	Canham[3], Tate[17]	4443
22	21	A	Swansea C	W	1-0	0-0	14	Tate[54]	4120
23	26	A	Kidderminster H	L	2-3	1-1	15	Ibehre 2[19, 60]	3821
24	28	H	Carlisle U	W	2-1	2-1	14	Ibehre[25], Smith[34]	4879
25	Jan 11	A	Scunthorpe U	L	1-2	1-1	14	Smith[39]	3242
26	18	H	Hull C	W	2-0	2-0	14	Thorpe[24], Ibehre[27]	5125
27	25	A	Carlisle U	L	0-3	0-0	15		4269
28	28	H	Cambridge U	D	1-1	0-1	—	Ibehre[76]	3953
29	Feb 8	H	York C	L	0-1	0-0	15		4260
30	15	A	Bury	W	1-0	0-0	14	Martin[88]	2707
31	22	H	Shrewsbury T	L	0-2	0-0	15		3939
32	25	H	Rochdale	L	0-1	0-1	—		2633
33	Mar 1	A	Lincoln C	D	1-1	0-0	15	Brazier[65]	3130
34	4	A	Oxford U	W	2-0	1-0	—	Tate[17], Harris[54]	5013
35	8	H	Exeter C	D	1-1	1-0	15	Thorpe[45]	3667
36	11	A	Macclesfield T	L	1-3	1-1	—	Thorpe[22]	1676
37	15	H	Bristol R	L	1-2	1-1	16	Lockwood (pen)[42]	4081
38	18	A	Bournemouth	L	1-3	0-2	—	Thorpe[90]	5078
39	22	A	Southend U	L	0-1	0-1	17		4148
40	Apr 5	H	Boston U	W	3-2	2-1	16	Purser 3[2, 33, 79]	3939
41	12	A	Hartlepool U	L	1-4	0-1	17	Heald[63]	4795
42	19	H	Swansea C	W	3-1	1-1	17	Tate 2[10, 65], Turner[52]	4480
43	21	A	Torquay U	D	2-2	1-1	17	Alexander[41], Fletcher[73]	3379
44	26	H	Rushden & D	D	0-0	0-0	16		5180
45	29	H	Wrexham	L	0-1	0-1	—		3766
46	May 3	A	Darlington	D	2-2	2-1	18	Lockwood[26], Alexander[37]	5723

Final League Position: 18

GOALSCORERS

League (51): Thorpe 8, Tate 6, Ibehre 5, Lockwood 5 (3 pens), Martin 3, Nugent 3, Purser 3, Smith 3, Alexander 2, Campbell-Ryce 2, Canham 2, Brazier 1, Fletcher 1, Harris 1, Heald 1, Hutchings 1, Iriekpen 1, Toner 1, Turner 1, own goal 1.
Worthington Cup (5): Campbell-Ryce 1, Fletcher 1, Ibehre 1, Nugent 1, Thorpe 1.
FA Cup (1): Martin 1.
LDV Vans Trophy (3): Barnard 1, Iriekpen 1, Lockwood 1.

Evans R 7	Joseph M 37	Lockwood M 42 + 1	Smith D 27	Harris A 43 + 2	Campbell-Ryce J 16 + 1	Hutchings C 21 + 7	Martin J 21 + 11	Fletcher G 7 + 5	Thorpe L 27 + 11	Brazier M 33	McLean A — + 8	Canham S 9 + 7	Nugent K 10 + 9	Toner C 22 + 3	Barnard D 22 + 7	McGhee D 3	Watts S 2 + 4	Morris G 22 + 1	Jones B 22 + 2	Ibehre J 11 + 14	Miller J 19	Forbes B — + 3	Hatcher D 1 + 5	Iriekpen E 5	Stephens K 2 + 1	Barrett S 11	Tate C 19 + 4	Alexander G 12 + 5	Downer S 8	Harrison L 6	Zakuani G — + 1	Turner M 7	Heald G 5	Purser W 7	*Match No.*
1	2	3	4	5	6^{1}	7	8^{2}	9^{3}	10	11	12	13	14																						1
1	2	3^{1}	4	5	6^{2}	7	8	9^{3}	10	11			14	12	13																				2
1	2	3	4	5	6^{1}	7	8	9^{2}	10	11	13			12																					3
1	2	3	4	5	6	7	8^{1}	9^{2}	10	11			13	12																					4
1		3	4	5	6	7	12		10	11^{1}	13		9^{2}	8		2																			5
1	2^{2}	3	4	6	12	7			10	11				8	13	5	9^{1}																		6
1	2	3	4	6	8	7	12		10■	11^{1}	13					5	9^{2}																		7
	2		4	6	5	7	8^{1}	9^{2}	10	11			12					1	3	13															8
	2^{1}		4	8	6	7	12	9^{3}	10	11			13					1	3^{2}	14	5														9
	2■		4	11	6^{2}	7	8^{3}					10^{1}	9		12			1	3	13	5	14													10
		3	4	2	6	7			10	11			9	8^{1}	12			1			5														11
		3	4	8	6	7			12	11			9		2^{1}			1		10	5														12
		3	4	6	7	8			10^{2}	11			9^{1}		2			1		12	5		13												13
		3	4	6	7	8	12		10^{2}	11^{1}			9^{3}		2		14	1		13	5														14
		3	4	7	11^{3}		8					12	9^{2}	10^{1}	2		13	1			5		14	6											15
		3	4	7	10^{3}		8					12	9^{2}	11^{1}	2		13	1			5		14	6											16
		3		4	10^{2}		8		12			7	9^{1}	11^{3}	2		13	1			5		14	6											17
		3	4■	7			8		10^{1}			12	9	11^{2}	2			1			5		13		6										18
	2	3		4			8	9				12		11^{1}							5	13	7^{2}	6		1	10								19
	4	3		7						11	12	8	13		2				14	10^{1}	5^{3}			6		1	9^{2}								20
	6	3	4	7					12	11		8	13		2					10^{2}	5					1	9^{1}								21
	5	2	4	6			12		13	11		8■			7				3	10^{1}						1	9^{2}								22
	5^{1}	3	4	7			13		12	11^{2}		8			2				6	10						1	9■								23
	5	3	4	7			8		12			11	13		2				6	10^{2}						1	9^{1}								24
	5	3	4	7		12	8		10	11^{1}	13		14		2^{2}				6^{3}	9						1									25
	5	3	4	7		12	8^{1}		10	11	13				2				6	9^{2}						1									26
	5	3	4	7		12	8^{2}		10^{3}	11	13	14			2^{1}				6	9						1									27
	5^{1}	3	4	7		12	8^{3}		10^{2}	11					2				6	9						1	13	14							28
	2	3	4	6		8^{1}	12		13	11^{3}					7					10^{2}	5					1	14	9							29
	5	3	4	7		12	8		10^{2}			11^{1}			2			1	6	13							14	9^{3}							30
	2^{1}	3		5		12	8		10^{3}			11^{2}			7			1	6	13							14	9	4						31
	5	3		7			8		12			13		11	2^{3}			1	6	14							10	9^{1}	4^{2}						32
	2	3		4		7			10	11				8				1	6								9		5						33
	2	3		5		7			10^{2}	11				8^{1}	12			1	6	13							9		4						34
	2	3		5		7			10^{3}	11				8^{1}	12			1	6	13							9^{2}	14	4						35
	2	12		5		7			10	11				8	3^{2}			1	6	13							9^{3}	14	4^{1}						36
	2	3		5		7	12		10	11^{1}				8					6	13							9^{3}	14	4^{2}	1					37
	5	3		7		12	8		10					11	2^{1}				6						4^{3}		9^{2}	13		1	14				38
	2	3		5		7	12		10	11^{2}				8^{1}					6	13					14			9	4^{3}	1					39
	2	3		6				13		11				8^{1}	12												10^{2}	9		1		4	5	7	40
	2	3		6			12		13	11				8^{1}					14								10	9^{2}		1		4^{3}	5	7	41
	2	3					12		13	11				8^{1}				15			4						10^{2}	9		1^{6}		6	5	7	42
	2	3		12			8^{1}	13	10^{3}	11								1		14	4^{2}							9				6	5	7	43
	2	3		12				13		11^{2}				8				1			4^{1}						10	9				6	5	7	44
	2	3		11				13	12					8^{2}				1	5		4■	14					10^{1}	9^{3}				6		7	45
	2	3		11				12						8				1	5^{1}		4						10	9				6		7	46

Worthington Cup
First Round | QPR | (h) | 3-2
Second Round | Birmingham C | (h) | 2-3

FA Cup
First Round | Margate | (h) | 1-1
 | | (a) | 0-1

LDV Vans Trophy
First Round | Peterborough U | (h) | 3-2
Second Round | Bournemouth | (a) | 0-1

LINCOLN CITY — Division 3

FOUNDATION

The original Lincoln Football Club was established in the early 1860's and was one of the first provisional clubs to affiliate to the Football Association. In their early years, they regularly played matches against the famous Sheffield Club and later became known as Lincoln Lindum. The present organisation was formed at a public meeting held in the Monson Arms Hotel in June 1884 and won the Lincolnshire Cup in only their third season. They were founder members of the Midland League in 1889 and that competition's first champions.

Sincil Bank, Lincoln LN5 8LD.

Telephone: (01522) 880 011. ***Fax:*** (01522) 880 020.
Website: www.redimps.com ***ClubCall:*** 09066 555 900.

Ground Capacity: 10,147.

Record Attendance: 23,196 v Derby Co, League Cup 4th rd, 15 November 1967.

Record Receipts: £44,184.46 v Everton, Coca-Cola Cup 2nd rd 1st leg, 21 September 1993.

Pitch Measurements: 110yd × 71yd.

President: J. Jennison. ***Patron:*** Graham Taylor OBE.

Chairman: R. Bradley. ***Vice-chairman:*** J. Hicks.

Directors: K. Roe, S. Wright, K. Cooke, S. Tindall.
Hon. Consultant Surgeon: Mr Brian Smith.
Hon. Club Doctor: Chris Batty.
Company Secretary: P. Bloomfield.

Manager: Keith Alexander.

Physio: Keith Oakes.

Commercial Manager: W. Bavin.

Secretary: F. J. Martin. ***Stadium Manager:*** Nigel Dennis.

Colours: Red and white striped shirts, black shorts, red stockings.

Change Colours: Dark blue shirts, white shorts, dark blue stockings.

Year Formed: 1884. ***Turned Professional:*** 1892.

Ltd Co.: 1895.

Club Nickname: 'The Red Imps'.

Previous Grounds: 1883, John O'Gaunt's; 1894, Sincil Bank.

First Football League Game: 3 September 1892, Division 2, v Sheffield U (a) L 2–4 – W. Gresham; Coulton, Neill; Shaw, Mettam, Moore; Smallman, Irving (1), Cameron (1), Kelly, J. Gresham.

Record League Victory: 11–1 v Crewe Alex, Division 3 (N), 29 September 1951 – Jones; Green (1p), Varney; Wright, Emery, Grummett (1); Troops (1), Garvey, Graver (6), Whittle (1), Johnson (1).

Record Cup Victory: 8–1 v Bromley, FA Cup 2nd rd, 10 December 1938 – McPhail; Hartshorne, Corbett; Bean, Leach, Whyte (1); Hancock, Wilson (1), Ponting (3), Deacon (1), Clare (2).

HONOURS

Football League: Division 2 best season: 5th, 1901–02; Promotion from Division 3, 1997–98; Division 3 (N) – Champions 1931–32, 1947–48, 1951–52; Runners-up 1927–28, 1930–31, 1936–37; Division 4 – Champions 1975–76; Runners-up 1980–81.

FA Cup: best season: 1st rd of Second Series (5th rd equivalent), 1887, 2nd rd (5th rd equivalent), 1890, 1902.

Football League Cup: best season: 4th rd, 1968.

GM Vauxhall Conference: Champions 1987–88.

SKY SPORTS FACT FILE

Andy Graver, legendary post-war striker in three spells with Lincoln City, first shot to prominence playing in the north-east for Southmoor Juniors, scoring eight goals in one match for the club.

Record Defeat: 3–11 v Manchester C, Division 2, 23 March 1895.

Most League Points (2 for a win): 74, Division 4, 1975–76.

Most League Points (3 for a win): 77, Division 3, 1981–82.

Most League Goals: 121, Division 3 (N), 1951–52.

Highest League Scorer in Season: Allan Hall, 41, Division 3 (N), 1931–32.

Most League Goals in Total Aggregate: Andy Graver, 143, 1950–55 and 1958–61.

Most League Goals in One Match: 6, Frank Keetley v Halifax T, Division 3N, 16 January 1932; 6, Andy Graver v Crewe Alex, Division 3N, 29 September 1951.

Most Capped Player: David Pugh, 3 (7), Wales; George Moulson, 3, Republic of Ireland.

Most League Appearances: Grant Brown, 407, 1989–2002.

Youngest League Player: Shane Nicholson, 16 years 172 days v Burnley, 22 November 1986.

Record Transfer Fee Received: £500,000 from Port Vale for Gareth Ainsworth, September 1997.

Record Transfer Fee Paid: £75,000 to Carlisle U for Dean Walling, September 1997; £75,000 to Bury for Tony Battersby, August 1998.

Football League Record: 1892 Founder member of Division 2. Remained in Division 2 until 1920 when they failed re-election but also missed seasons 1908–09 and 1911–12 when not re-elected. 1921–32 Division 3 (N); 1932–34 Division 2; 1934–48 Division 3 (N); 1948–49 Division 2; 1949–52 Division 3 (N); 1952–61 Division 2; 1961–62 Division 3; 1962–76 Division 4; 1976–79 Division 3; 1979–81 Division 4; 1981–86 Division 3; 1986–87 Division 4; 1987–88 GM Vauxhall Conference; 1988–92 Division 4; 1992–98 Division 3; 1998–99 Division 2; 1999– Division 3.

MANAGERS

David Calderhead 1900–07
John Henry Strawson 1907–14
(had been Secretary)
George Fraser 1919–21
David Calderhead Jnr. 1921–24
Horace Henshall 1924–27
Harry Parkes 1927–36
Joe McClelland 1936–46
Bill Anderson 1946–65
(General Manager to 1966)
Roy Chapman 1965–66
Ron Gray 1966–70
Bert Loxley 1970–71
David Herd 1971–72
Graham Taylor 1972–77
George Kerr 1977–78
Willie Bell 1977–78
Colin Murphy 1978–85
John Pickering 1985
George Kerr 1985–87
Peter Daniel 1987
Colin Murphy 1987–90
Allan Clarke 1990
Steve Thompson 1990–93
Keith Alexander 1993–94
Sam Ellis 1994–95
Steve Wicks *(Head Coach)* 1995
John Beck 1995–98
Shane Westley 1998
John Reames 1998–99
Phil Stant 2000–01
Alan Buckley 2001–02
Keith Alexander May 2002–

LATEST SEQUENCES

Longest Sequence of League Wins: 10, 1.9.1930 – 18.10.1930.

Longest Sequence of League Defeats: 12, 21.9.1896 – 9.1.1897.

Longest Sequence of League Draws: 5, 21.2.1981 – 7.3.1981.

Longest Sequence of Unbeaten League Matches: 18, 11.3.1980 – 13.9.1980.

Longest Sequence Without a League Win: 19, 22.8.1978 – 23.12.1978.

Successive Scoring Runs: 37 from 1.3.1930.

Successive Non-scoring Runs: 5 from 15.11.1913.

TEN YEAR LEAGUE RECORD

		P	*W*	*D*	*L*	*F*	*A*	*Pts*	*Pos*
1993-94	Div 3	42	12	11	19	52	63	47	18
1994-95	Div 3	42	15	11	16	54	55	56	12
1995-96	Div 3	46	13	14	19	57	73	53	18
1996-97	Div 3	46	18	12	16	70	69	66	9
1997-98	Div 3	46	20	15	11	60	51	72	3
1998-99	Div 2	46	13	7	26	42	74	46	23
1999-2000	Div 3	46	15	14	17	67	69	59	15
2000-01	Div 3	46	12	15	19	58	66	51	18
2001-02	Div 3	46	10	16	20	44	62	46	22
2002-03	Div 3	46	18	16	12	46	37	70	6

DID YOU KNOW?

Lincoln City lost their Second Division status in 1908 to Tottenham Hotspur, but only after two tied ballots and the Management Committee voting 5-3 against them. However, the Imps bounced back in the Midland League and were re-elected the following year to the Football League.

LINCOLN CITY 2002–03 LEAGUE RECORD

Match No.	Date	Venue	Opponents	Result		H/T Score	Lg. Pos.	Goalscorers	Attendance
1	Aug 10	A	Kidderminster H	D	1-1	1-0	—	Logan 11	2687
2	13	H	Rochdale	W	2-0	0-0	—	Yeo 58, Cropper 81	2894
3	17	H	Carlisle U	L	0-1	0-0	12		3034
4	24	A	Boston U	L	0-2	0-1	19		5159
5	26	H	Macclesfield T	W	3-0	1-0	6	Yeo 2 41, 83, Willis 51	2444
6	31	A	Shrewsbury T	W	2-1	0-1	5	Mike 68, Sedgemore (pen) 80	3168
7	Sept 7	H	Scunthorpe U	W	1-0	1-0	4	Futcher 43	4204
8	14	A	Leyton Orient	D	1-1	0-0	4	Futcher 75	4579
9	17	A	Hartlepool U	L	1-2	1-0	—	Mike 2	4248
10	21	H	Southend U	W	2-1	0-0	4	Gain 62, Yeo 71	3151
11	28	A	Torquay U	D	0-0	0-0	6		3428
12	Oct 5	H	Bournemouth	L	1-2	1-1	10	Cropper 17	3273
13	12	A	Bristol R	L	0-2	0-1	12		6135
14	19	H	Exeter C	W	1-0	0-0	11	Willis 75	2979
15	26	A	Wrexham	W	2-0	0-0	5	Cropper 48, Smith P 77	3312
16	29	H	Bury	D	1-1	1-0	—	Sedgemore (pen) 24	2830
17	Nov 2	A	Darlington	D	0-0	0-0	8		3277
18	9	H	Hull C	D	1-1	1-1	9	Futcher 7	6271
19	23	H	Rushden & D	L	1-2	0-1	12	Gain 83	3198
20	30	A	Oxford U	L	0-1	0-0	13		4923
21	Dec 14	H	Cambridge U	D	2-2	1-1	13	Butcher 34, Weaver 67	2845
22	20	A	York C	D	1-1	1-0	—	Watts 8	3411
23	26	A	Macclesfield T	W	1-0	0-0	13	Gain 83	2187
24	28	H	Swansea C	W	1-0	0-0	12	O'Leary (og) 90	4553
25	Jan 1	H	Boston U	D	1-1	1-0	12	Weaver 10	7846
26	18	H	Shrewsbury T	D	1-1	1-0	12	Butcher 33	2885
27	21	A	Rochdale	W	1-0	0-0	—	Futcher 83	2122
28	25	A	Swansea C	L	0-2	0-1	8		5099
29	Feb 4	A	Carlisle U	W	4-1	2-0	—	Ward 6, Willis 34, Gain 67, Smith P 71	3567
30	8	A	Hull C	W	1-0	0-0	6	Bimson (pen) 65	13,728
31	15	H	Darlington	D	1-1	1-1	9	Ward 31	3193
32	22	A	Scunthorpe U	D	0-0	0-0	11		5141
33	Mar 1	H	Leyton Orient	D	1-1	0-0	10	Futcher 88	3130
34	4	H	Hartlepool U	W	3-0	1-0	—	Pearce 44, Gain 83, Bloomer 88	3409
35	8	A	Southend U	W	1-0	1-0	4	Futcher 10	3912
36	15	H	Wrexham	D	1-1	0-0	6	Weaver 51	3916
37	18	A	Exeter C	L	0-2	0-2	—		4009
38	22	A	Bury	L	0-2	0-2	10		2776
39	25	H	Kidderminster H	W	1-0	1-0	—	Bradley 15	4092
40	29	H	Bristol R	W	2-1	2-1	5	Webb 21, Futcher 29	3550
41	Apr 5	H	Oxford U	L	0-1	0-1	8		3990
42	12	A	Rushden & D	L	0-1	0-1	10		4962
43	19	H	York C	W	1-0	1-0	8	Futcher 41	4653
44	22	A	Cambridge U	D	0-0	0-0	—		4013
45	26	A	Bournemouth	W	1-0	1-0	7	Butcher 28	7578
46	May 3	H	Torquay U	D	1-1	0-1	6	Yeo 86	7906

Final League Position: 6

GOALSCORERS

League (46): Futcher 8, Gain 5, Yeo 5, Butcher 3, Cropper 3, Weaver 3, Willis 3, Mike 2, Sedgemore 2 (2 pens), Smith P 2, Ward 2, Bimson 1 (pen), Bloomer 1, Bradley 1, Logan 1, Pearce 1, Watts 1, Webb 1, own goal 1.
Worthington Cup (1): Mike 1.
FA Cup (1): Futcher 1.
LDV Vans Trophy (5): Yeo 2, Buckley 1, Futcher 1, own goal 1.
Play-offs (8): Yeo 3, Bailey 1, Futcher 1, Mayo 1, Smith 1, Weaver 1.

Marriott A 46	Bailey M 45	Bimson S 41 + 1	Weaver S 44	Morgan P 45	Logan R 10	Smith P 21 + 16	Willis S 23 + 7	Cropper D 24 + 5	Yeo S 22 + 15	Gain P 43	Sedgemore B 23 + 5	Mayo P 5 + 10	Buckley A — + 3	Futcher B 41 + 2	Battersby T 1	Mike A 5 + 12	Black K — + 1	Camm M 3 + 10	Thompson T — + 1	Ward C 5 + 1	Butcher R 23 + 3	Watts S 5	Pearce A 9 + 7	Cornelly C 9 + 7	Dykes D 2 + 1	Cornwall L 1 + 2	Bloomer M 3 + 10	Bradley S 3	Webb D 4 + 1	*Match No.*
1	2	3	4	5	6	7	8	9■	10^{1}	11	12																			1
1	2	3	4	5	6^{2}	7	8	9	10^{1}	11	13	12																		2
1	2^{1}	3^{2}	4■	5	6^{3}	7	8	9	10	11		12	13	14																3
1	2^{2}	3	4	5	6^{3}	7	8		10■	11		12		13	9^{1}	14														4
1	2	3	4	5			8^{2}	9^{1}	10	11	7			6		12	13													5
1	2	3		5	6^{1}	12	8^{3}	9^{2}	10	11	7			4		13		14												6
1	2	3		5	6	10^{1}	8^{3}	9^{2}		11	7	12		4		13		14												7
1	2	3	4	5	6		8	9^{1}		11		12		7		10														8
1	2^{2}	3	4	5	6^{1}		8^{3}	12	10	11		13		7		9		14												9
1	2	3	4	5	6^{1}	7^{3}	12	13	10	11				8		9^{2}		14												10
1	2	3^{1}	4	5	6^{2}	7		9	10	11		12		8				13												11
1	2	3	4^{1}	5		7		9	10^{3}	11	12		13	6		14		8^{2}												12
1	2	3	4^{2}	5		7^{1}		9	10	11	8			6		13		12												13
1	2^{3}	3^{1}	4	5		12	8	13	10	11	7			6		9^{2}		14												14
1	2		4	5		12	8	9^{2}	10^{1}	3	7			6		13		11												15
1	2^{2}		4	5		12	8^{3}	9	10^{1}	11	7			6		13		3	14											16
1	2	3	4	5		7^{1}		9		11	8			6		10^{2}		12		13										17
1	2	3	4	5■		12	8^{3}	9^{2}	10^{1}	11	7			6		13		14												18
1	2^{3}	3	4			7^{2}	12	9	10	11	8^{1}		13	6		14					5									19
1	2	3	4	5		12	13	9^{3}	10^{1}	11	8^{2}			6		14					7									20
1	2^{2}	3	4	5		7	12■		10^{3}		8^{1}			6							11	9	13	14						21
1	2	3	4	5			12	9^{2}	13	11	8^{1}			6							7	10^{3}			14					22
1	2^{2}	3	4	5				12	13	11	8			6							7	9^{1}		14	10^{3}					23
1	2^{1}	3	4	5		13			12	11	6							14			7	8		9^{3}	10^{2}					24
1	2	3	4	5		7			12	11				6		13					8	9^{2}		10^{1}						25
1	2	3	4	5				9	10^{2}	11	8^{1}			6							7			12		13				26
1	2	3^{2}	4	5		12		9	10	11				6							7					8^{1}	13			27
1	2	3	4^{3}	5		7		9	10^{2}	11	12			6							8^{1}			13		14				28
1	2	3	4	5		7^{1}	10^{2}		13	11	12			6						9^{3}	8						14			29
1	2	3	4	5			8^{2}		12	11				6						9^{3}	7		13	10^{1}			14			30
1	2^{1}	3	4	5		7	10		12	11				6						9^{2}	8			13						31
1	2	3	4	5		7	8^{1}			11	10			6						9^{2}			12				13			32
1	2	3	4^{1}	5		7^{2}	9			11	8			6						10^{3}			13	12			14			33
1	2	3	4	5		12	7^{2}			11	8			6							13		10^{1}				14	9^{3}		34
1		3	4	5			7^{1}			11	8	12		6							13		10				2	9^{2}		35
1	2	3	4	5		12	7		13	11^{1}	8^{3}			6							14		10^{2}						9	36
1	2	3	4	5		12	7^{2}		13		8^{3}			6							11		10^{1}	14					9	37
1	2	3	4^{2}	5		12	7^{3}		13		8^{1}	14		6							11		10						9	38
1	2		4	5		12			13	11		3		6							7		10^{1}	8^{2}				9^{3}	14	39
1	2	12	4	5		13				11		3		6							7		10^{2}	8^{1}					9	40
1	2		4^{3}	5		12	14		13	11		3		6							7		10^{1}	9			8^{2}			41
1	2	3	4	5				12	10^{2}	11		14		6							7		13	9^{3}			8^{1}			42
1	2	3	4	5		12		9^{2}		11				6							7		10^{1}	8■			13			43
1	2	3	4	5^{3}		10	12	9^{1}	13	11				6							7			8^{2}			14			44
1	2	3	4	5		10^{2}		9^{3}	12	7		11^{1}		6							8		13				14			45
1	2	3	4^{1}	5		10^{2}		9	12	8		11		6							7		13^{3}				14			46

Worthington Cup
First Round | Stockport Co | (h) | 1-3

LDV Vans Trophy
First Round | York C | (h) | 4-3
Second Round | Shrewsbury T | (h) | 1-2

FA Cup
First Round | Carlisle U | (a) | 1-2

LIVERPOOL

FA Premiership

FOUNDATION

But for a dispute between Everton FC and their landlord at Anfield in 1892, there may never have been a Liverpool club. This dispute persuaded the majority of Evertonians to quit Anfield for Goodison Park, leaving the landlord, Mr John Houlding, to form a new club. He originally tried to retain the name 'Everton' but when this failed, he founded Liverpool Association FC on 15 March 1892.

Anfield Road, Liverpool L4 0TH.

Telephone: (0151) 263 2361. ***Fax:*** (0151) 260 8813. ***Website:*** www.liverpoolfc.tv ***ClubCall:*** 09068 121 184. ***Ticket and Match Information:*** 0870 444 4949 (24-hour service) or 0870 220 2345 (office hours). ***Credit Card Bookings:*** 0870 220 2151. ***International Supporters Club:*** (0151) 261 1444. ***Museum and Stadium Tours:*** (0151) 260 6677. ***LFC Direct Mail Order:*** (0990) 532 532.

Ground Capacity: 45,362.

Record Attendance: 61,905 v Wolverhampton W, FA Cup 4th rd, 2 February 1952.

Record Receipts: £604,048 v Celtic, UEFA Cup, 30 September 1997.

Pitch Measurements: 111yd × 74yd.

Chairman: D. R. Moores.

Chief Executive: Rick Parry BSC, FCA.

Director of Finance: Les Wheatley BSC, FCA.

Directors: N. White FSCA, T. D. Smith, J. Burns, K. E. B. Clayton FCA.

Vice-presidents: H. E. Roberts, J. T. Cross.

Manager: Gerard Houllier.

Assistant Manager: Phil Thompson.

First Team Coach: Cristian Damiano.

Physio: Dave Galley.

Secretary: Bryce Morrison.

Press Officer: Ian Cotton.

Stadium Manager: Ged Poynton.

Academy Director: Steve Heighway.

Colours: All red.

Change Colours: (To be announced.)

Year Formed: 1892. ***Turned Professional:*** 1892. ***Ltd Co.:*** 1892.

Club Nicknames: 'Reds' or 'Pool'.

HONOURS

Football League: Division 1 – Champions 1900–01, 1905–06, 1921–22, 1922–23, 1946–47, 1963–64, 1965–66, 1972–73, 1975–76, 1976–77, 1978–79, 1979–80, 1981–82, 1982–83, 1983–84, 1985–86, 1987–88, 1989–90 (Liverpool have a record number of 18 League Championship wins); Runners-up 1898–99, 1909–10, 1968–69, 1973–74, 1974–75, 1977–78, 1984–85, 1986–87, 1988–89, 1990–91, 2001–02; Division 2 – Champions 1893–94, 1895–96, 1904–05, 1961–62.

FA Cup: Winners 1965, 1974, 1986, 1989, 1992, 2001; Runners-up 1914, 1950, 1971, 1977, 1988, 1996;

Football League Cup: Winners 1981, 1982, 1983, 1984, 1995, 2001, 2003; Runners-up 1978, 1987.

League Super Cup: Winners 1986.

European Competitions: *European Cup:* 1964–65, 1966–67, 1973–74, 1976–77 (winners), 1977–78 (winners), 1978–79, 1979–80, 1980–81 (winners), 1981–82, 1982–83, 1983–84 (winners), 1984–85 (runners-up). *Champions League:* 2001–02, 2002–03. *European Cup-Winners' Cup:* 1965–66 (runners-up), 1971–72, 1974–75, 1992–93, 1996–97 (s-f.). *European Fairs Cup:* 1967–68, 1968–69, 1969–70, 1970–71. *UEFA Cup:* 1972–73 (winners), 1975–76 (winners), 1991–92, 1995–96, 1997–98, 1998–99, 2000–01 (winners), 2002–03. *Super Cup:* 1977 (winners), 1978, 1984, 2001 (winners). *World Club Championship:* 1981 (runners-up), 1984 (runners-up).

SKY SPORTS FACT FILE

On 11 June 2003 Liverpool's Michael Owen celebrated his 50th international appearance for England with two goals against Slovakia and became the youngest in the country's history to reach his half century.

First Football League Game: 2 September 1893, Division 2, v Middlesbrough Ironopolis (a) W 2–0 – McOwen; Hannah, McLean; Henderson, McQue (1), McBride; Gordon, McVean (1), M. McQueen, Stott, H. McQueen.

Record League Victory: 10–1 v Rotherham T, Division 2, 18 February 1896 – Storer; Goldie, Wilkie; McCartney, McQue, Holmes; McVean (3), Ross (2), Allan (4), Becton (1), Bradshaw.

Record Cup Victory: 11–0 v Stromsgodset Drammen, ECWC 1st rd 1st leg, 17 September 1974 – Clemence; Smith (1), Lindsay (1p), Thompson (2), Cormack (1), Hughes (1), Boersma (2), Hall, Heighway (1), Kennedy (1), Callaghan (1).

Record Defeat: 1–9 v Birmingham C, Division 2, 11 December 1954.

Most League Points (2 for a win): 68, Division 1, 1978–79.

Most League Points (3 for a win): 90, Division 1, 1987–88.

Most League Goals: 106, Division 2, 1895–96.

Highest League Scorer in Season: Roger Hunt, 41, Division 2, 1961–62.

Most League Goals in Total Aggregate: Roger Hunt, 245, 1959–69.

Most League Goals in One Match: 5, Andy McGuigan v Stoke C, Division 1, 4 January 1902; 5, John Evans v Bristol R, Division 2, 15 September 1954; 5, Ian Rush v Luton T, Division 1, 29 October 1983.

Most Capped Player: Ian Rush, 67 (73), Wales.

Most League Appearances: Ian Callaghan, 640, 1960–78.

Youngest League Player: Max Thompson, 17 years 128 days v Tottenham H, 8 May 1974.

Record Transfer Fee Received: £12,500,000 from Leeds U for Robbie Fowler, November 2001.

Record Transfer Fee Paid: £11,000,000 to Leicester C for Emile Heskey, March 2000.

Football League Record: 1893 Elected to Division 2; 1894–95 Division 1; 1895–96 Division 2; 1896–1904 Division 1; 1904–05 Division 2; 1905–54 Division 1; 1954–62 Division 2; 1962–92 Division 1; 1992– FA Premier League.

MANAGERS

W. E. Barclay 1892–96
Tom Watson 1896–1915
David Ashworth 1920–23
Matt McQueen 1923–28
George Patterson 1928–36
(continued as Secretary)
George Kay 1936–51
Don Welsh 1951–56
Phil Taylor 1956–59
Bill Shankly 1959–74
Bob Paisley 1974–83
Joe Fagan 1983–85
Kenny Dalglish 1985–91
Graeme Souness 1991–94
Roy Evans January 1994–98
(then Joint Manager)
Gerard Houllier July 1998–

LATEST SEQUENCES

Longest Sequence of League Wins: 12, 21.4.1990 – 6.10.1990.

Longest Sequence of League Defeats: 9, 29.4.1899 – 14.10.1899.

Longest Sequence of League Draws: 6, 19.2.1975 – 19.3.1975.

Longest Sequence of Unbeaten League Matches: 31, 4.5.1987 – 16.3.1988.

Longest Sequence Without a League Win: 14, 12.12.1953 – 20.3.1954.

Successive Scoring Runs: 29 from 27.4.1957.

Successive Non-scoring Runs: 5 from 22.12.1906.

TEN YEAR LEAGUE RECORD

		P	*W*	*D*	*L*	*F*	*A*	*Pts*	*Pos*
1993-94	PR Lge	42	17	9	16	59	55	60	8
1994-95	PR Lge	42	21	11	10	65	37	74	4
1995-96	PR Lge	38	20	11	7	70	34	71	3
1996-97	PR Lge	38	19	11	8	62	37	68	4
1997-98	PR Lge	38	18	11	9	68	42	65	3
1998-99	PR Lge	38	15	9	14	68	49	54	7
1999-2000	PR Lge	38	19	10	9	51	30	67	4
2000-01	PR Lge	38	20	9	9	71	39	69	3
2001-02	PR Lge	38	24	8	6	67	30	80	2
2002-03	PR Lge	38	18	10	10	61	41	64	5

DID YOU KNOW ?

Michael Owen equalled Ian Rush's record of scoring 20 goals in European matches for Liverpool in the 67th minute on 27 February 2003 against Auxerre. Rush had scored in all three major European tournaments.

LIVERPOOL 2002–03 LEAGUE RECORD

Match No.	*Date*	*Venue*	*Opponents*	*Result*	*H/T Score*	*Lg. Pos.*	*Goalscorers*	*Attendance*
1	Aug 18	A	Aston Villa	W 1-0	0-0	—	Riise [47]	41,183
2	24	H	Southampton	W 3-0	1-0	2	Diouf 2 [3, 51], Murphy (pen) [90]	43,058
3	28	A	Blackburn R	D 2-2	1-1	—	Murphy [31], Riise [77]	29,207
4	Sept 2	H	Newcastle U	D 2-2	0-0	—	Hamann [53], Owen (pen) [73]	43,241
5	11	H	Birmingham C	D 2-2	1-0	—	Murphy [25], Gerrard [49]	43,113
6	14	A	Bolton W	W 3-2	1-0	5	Baros 2 [45, 72], Heskey [88]	27,328
7	21	H	WBA	W 2-0	0-0	2	Baros [56], Riise [90]	43,830
8	28	A	Manchester C	W 3-0	1-0	2	Owen 3 [4, 64, 89]	35,131
9	Oct 6	H	Chelsea	W 1-0	0-0	2	Owen [90]	43,856
10	19	A	Leeds U	W 1-0	0-0	1	Diao [66]	40,197
11	26	H	Tottenham H	W 2-1	0-0	1	Murphy [72], Owen (pen) [86]	44,084
12	Nov 2	H	West Ham U	W 2-0	1-0	1	Owen 2 [28, 55]	44,048
13	9	A	Middlesbrough	L 0-1	0-0	1		34,723
14	17	H	Sunderland	D 0-0	0-0	2		43,074
15	23	A	Fulham	L 2-3	0-2	2	Hamann [62], Baros [86]	18,144
16	Dec 1	H	Manchester U	L 1-2	0-0	2	Hyypia [82]	44,250
17	7	A	Charlton Ath	L 0-2	0-1	4		26,679
18	15	A	Sunderland	L 1-2	0-1	5	Baros [68]	37,118
19	22	H	Everton	D 0-0	0-0	5		44,025
20	26	H	Blackburn R	D 1-1	1-0	5	Riise [17]	43,075
21	29	A	Arsenal	D 1-1	0-0	6	Murphy (pen) [70]	38,074
22	Jan 1	A	Newcastle U	L 0-1	0-1	7		52,147
23	11	H	Aston Villa	D 1-1	1-0	7	Owen [38]	43,210
24	18	A	Southampton	W 1-0	1-0	6	Heskey [14]	32,104
25	29	H	Arsenal	D 2-2	0-1	—	Riise [52], Heskey [90]	43,668
26	Feb 2	A	West Ham U	W 3-0	2-0	6	Baros [7], Gerrard [9], Heskey [67]	35,033
27	8	H	Middlesbrough	D 1-1	0-1	6	Riise [74]	42,247
28	23	A	Birmingham C	L 1-2	0-1	7	Owen [77]	29,449
29	Mar 8	H	Bolton W	W 2-0	1-0	6	Diouf [44], Owen [67]	41,462
30	16	A	Tottenham H	W 3-2	0-0	6	Owen [51], Heskey [72], Gerrard [82]	36,077
31	23	H	Leeds U	W 3-1	2-1	5	Owen [12], Murphy [20], Gerrard [73]	43,021
32	Apr 5	A	Manchester U	L 0-4	0-1	6		67,639
33	12	H	Fulham	W 2-0	1-0	6	Heskey [36], Owen [59]	42,121
34	19	A	Everton	W 2-1	1-0	5	Owen [31], Murphy [64]	40,162
35	21	H	Charlton Ath	W 2-1	0-0	5	Hyypia [86], Gerrard [90]	42,010
36	26	A	WBA	W 6-0	1-0	5	Owen 4 [15, 49, 61, 67], Baros 2 [47, 84]	26,852
37	May 3	H	Manchester C	L 1-2	0-0	5	Baros [59]	44,220
38	11	A	Chelsea	L 1-2	1-2	5	Hyypia [11]	41,925

Final League Position: 5

GOALSCORERS

League (61): Owen 19 (2 pens), Baros 9, Murphy 7 (2 pens), Heskey 6, Riise 6, Gerrard 5, Diouf 3, Hyypia 3, Hamann 2, Diao 1.
Worthington Cup (13): Diouf 3 (1 pen), Baros 2, Gerrard 2, Murphy 2, Owen 2, Berger 1, Mellor 1.
FA Cup (1): Murphy 1 (pen).
Community Shield (0).
Champions League (12): Owen 4, Heskey 2, Baros 1, Cheyrou 1, Diao 1, Hyypia 1, Murphy 1, Smicer 1.
UEFA Cup (6): Owen 3, Heskey 1, Hyypia 1, Murphy 1.

Dudek J 30	Xavier A 4	Traore D 30 + 2	Hamann D 29 + 1	Henchoz S 19	Hyypia S 36	Murphy D 36	Gerrard S 32 + 2	Diouf E 21 + 8	Owen M 32 + 3	Riise J 31 + 6	Carragher J 34 + 1	Heskey E 22 + 10	Cheyrou B 8 + 11	Smicer V 10 + 11	Diao S 13 + 13	Berger P — + 2	Baros M 17 + 10	Babbel M 2	Kirkland C 8	Biscan I 3 + 3	Mellor N 1 + 2	Vignal G — + 1	*Match No.*
1	2	3	4	5	6	7	8	9^{1}	10^{2}	11	12	13											1
1	2	3	4	5	6	7	8^{2}	9^{3}	10^{1}	12		11	13	14									2
1	2	3	4	5	6	7	8	9^{2}	10^{1}	11^{3}		12		13	14								3
1	2	3	4	5	6	7	8^{2}	12	10			11	13	9^{1}									4
1		3	4	5^{1}	6	7	8	9^{3}	10	11^{2}	2	12			13	14							5
1		3	4		6	7	8			12	2	11	10^{1}		5		9						6
1			4	5	6	7	8		10	3	2	12	11^{2}		13		9^{1}						7
1		5	4		6	7	8^{2}	12	10	3	2	11			13		9^{1}						8
1		12	4	5^{1}	6	7^{2}	8		10	3	2	9	11^{3}		13		14						9
1		5	4		6	7		10	12	3	2		11		8		9^{1}						10
1		5	4		6	11	7^{1}	9^{2}	10	3	2			12	8		13						11
1		5	4		6	7	12		10	3	2	11		9^{1}	8								12
1		5	4		6	11^{2}	7^{1}		10	3	2	9		12	8		13						13
1		5	4		6	7		12	10	13	3^{2}	11		9^{1}	8			2					14
1		5	4		6	7	12		10	11	3	9^{2}		13	8^{1}		14	2^{3}					15
1		3^{2}	4	5	6	11	7	14	10	13	2	12		8^{3}			9^{1}						16
		3^{2}	4	5	6	7	8	9	10	12	2	11^{1}					13		1				17
		6	4^{1}	5		7	8	13	10	12	2			11^{3}	14		9		1	3^{2}			18
		3^{1}		5	6	7	8		10	11	2	12		13	4^{2}		9		1				19
		3^{1}		5	6	7	4	12	10	11	2	9^{2}		8^{3}			13		1	14			20
		12		5	6	7	8	13	10^{2}	3	2		11^{1}		4		9^{3}		1	14			21
				5	6		8	10^{3}		3	2		11^{1}	12	4■		9^{2}		1	7	13	14	22
				5	6	7	8	11^{3}	10	3	2	12	13	14	4^{2}				1		9^{1}		23
		3		5	6	7	4	8	10	11	2	9							1				24
1				5	6	7^{1}	4	8^{2}	10	3	2	9	11^{3}	14	12		13						25
1			12	5	6	7^{1}	4	8	13	3	2	9	14	11^{3}			10^{2}						26
1			4	5	6	7		8	10	3	2	9^{1}		11^{2}	13		12						27
1		5	4		6	7			12	3	2^{1}	9	11^{2}		8		10				13		28
1		5	4		6	7	8^{1}	9	10	3	2		13	11^{2}	12								29
1		5	4^{1}		6	11	8	7	10	3	2	9			12								30
1		5	4^{1}		6	11	8	7	10	3	2	9^{2}			12		13						31
1		5	4		6■	7^{1}	8	11^{2}		3	2	9	12	13			10^{3}			14			32
1		5	4		6		8		10	3	2	7	12	11^{1}			9						33
1		5	4			11	8	12	10	3	2	7			13		9^{1}			6^{2}			34
1		5	4		6	11^{3}	8	7^{1}	10	3	2	9^{2}	12	14			13						35
1		5	4		6	11^{2}	8	7^{1}	10	3^{3}	2	12	13		14		9						36
1		5	4^{2}		6	11	8	7^{1}	10	3	2	12	13				9						37
1		5			6	11	8■	7^{3}	10	3^{2}	2	12	13		4^{1}	14	9						38

Worthington Cup

Third Round	Southampton	(h)	3-1
Fourth Round	Ipswich T	(h)	1-1
Fifth Round	Aston Villa	(a)	4-3
Semi-final	Sheffield U	(a)	1-2
		(h)	2-0
Final (at Millennium Stadium)	Manchester U		2-0

Champions League

Group B	Valencia	(a)	0-2
	Basle	(h)	1-1
	Spartak Moscow	(h)	5-0
		(a)	3-1
	Valencia	(h)	0-1
	Basle	(a)	3-3

FA Cup

Third Round	Manchester C	(a)	1-0
Fourth Round	Crystal Palace	(a)	0-0
		(h)	0-2

UEFA Cup

Third Round	Vitesse	(a)	1-0
		(h)	1-0
Fourth Round	Auxerre	(a)	1-0
		(h)	2-0
Quarter-final	Celtic	(a)	1-1
		(h)	0-2

LUTON TOWN Division 2

FOUNDATION

Formed by an amalgamation of two leading local clubs, Wanderers and Excelsior a works team, at a meeting in Luton Town Hall in April 1885. The Wanderers had three months earlier changed their name to Luton Town Wanderers and did not take too kindly to the formation of another Town club but were talked around at this meeting. Wanderers had already appeared in the FA Cup and the new club entered in its inaugural season.

Kenilworth Road Stadium, 1 Maple Road, Luton, Beds LU4 8AW.

Telephone: (01582) 411 622. ***Ticket Office:*** (01582) 416 976. ***Credit Hotline:*** (01582) 307 48 (24 hrs). ***ClubCall:*** 09068 121 123.

Ground Capacity: 9,975.

Record Attendance: 30,069 v Blackpool, FA Cup 6th rd replay, 4 March 1959.

Record Receipts: £115,541.20 v West Ham U, FA Cup 6th rd, 23 March 1994.

Pitch Measurements: 110yd × 72yd.

Chairman: M. Watson-Challis.

Directors: E. Hood, R. Stringer, Y. Fletcher, R. H. G. Kelly, C. Newbery.

Manager: Mike Newell.

Secretary: Cherry Newbery.

Commercial Manager: Peter Davis.

Safety Officer: Geoff Lovell.

Colours: White shirts with orange and black trim, black shorts with orange and white trim, black stockings with two white hoops.

Change Colours: Orange shirts with white and royal trim, royal shorts with orange and white trim, royal stockings with two white hoops.

Year Formed: 1885.

Turned Professional: 1890.

Ltd Co.: 1897.

Club Nickname: 'The Hatters'.

Previous Grounds: 1885, Excelsior, Dallow Lane; 1897, Dunstable Road; 1905, Kenilworth Road.

First Football League Game: 4 September 1897, Division 2, v Leicester Fosse (a) D 1–1 – Williams; McCartney, McEwen; Davies, Stewart, Docherty; Gallacher, Coupar, Birch, McInnes, Ekins (1).

Record League Victory: 12–0 v Bristol R, Division 3 (S), 13 April 1936 – Dolman; Mackey, Smith; Finlayson, Nelson, Godfrey; Rich, Martin (1), Payne (10), Roberts (1), Stephenson.

HONOURS

Football League: Division 1 best season: 7th, 1986–87; Division 2 – Champions 1981–82; Runners-up 1954–55, 1973–74; Division 3 – Runners-up 1969–70, 2001–02; Division 4 – Champions 1967–68; Division 3 (S) – Champions 1936–37; Runners-up 1935–36.

FA Cup: Runners-up 1959.

Football League Cup: Winners 1988; Runners-up 1989.

Simod Cup: Runners-up 1988.

SKY SPORTS FACT FILE

In addition to the famous 'ten-goal Joe Payne match', Luton Town were also involved in a match of twelve goals on 2 September 1933 when they defeated Torquay United 10-2 with Andy Rennie scoring four goals.

Record Cup Victory: 9–0 v Clapton, FA Cup 1st rd (replay after abandoned game), 30 November 1927 – Abbott; Kingham, Graham; Black, Rennie, Fraser; Pointon, Yardley (4), Reid (2), Woods (1), Dennis (2).

Record Defeat: 0–9 v Small Heath, Division 2, 12 November 1898.

Most League Points (2 for a win): 66, Division 4, 1967–68.

Most League Points (3 for a win): 97, Division 3, 2001–02.

Most League Goals: 103, Division 3 (S), 1936–37.

Highest League Scorer in Season: Joe Payne, 55, Division 3 (S), 1936–37.

Most League Goals in Total Aggregate: Gordon Turner, 243, 1949–64.

Most League Goals in One Match: 10, Joe Payne v Bristol R, Division 3S, 13 April 1936.

Most Capped Player: Mal Donaghy, 58 (91), Northern Ireland.

Most League Appearances: Bob Morton, 495, 1948–64.

Youngest League Player: Mike O'Hara, 16 years 32 days v Stoke C, 1 October 1960.

Record Transfer Fee Received: £2,500,000 from Arsenal for John Hartson, January 1995.

Record Transfer Fee Paid: £850,000 to Odense for Lars Elstrup, August 1989.

Football League Record: 1897 Elected to Division 2; 1900 Failed re-election; 1920 Division 3; 1921–37 Division 3 (S); 1937–55 Division 2; 1955–60 Division 1; 1960–63 Division 2; 1963–65 Division 3; 1965–68 Division 4; 1968–70 Division 3; 1970–74 Division 2; 1974–75 Division 1; 1975–82 Division 2; 1982–96 Division 1; 1996–2001 Division 2; 2001–02 Division 3; 2002– Division 2.

MANAGERS

Charlie Green 1901–28
(Secretary-Manager)
George Thomson 1925
John McCartney 1927–29
George Kay 1929–31
Harold Wightman 1931–35
Ted Liddell 1936–38
Neil McBain 1938–39
George Martin 1939–47
Dally Duncan 1947–58
Syd Owen 1959–60
Sam Bartram 1960–62
Bill Harvey 1962–64
George Martin 1965–66
Allan Brown 1966–68
Alec Stock 1968–72
Harry Haslam 1972–78
David Pleat 1978–86
John Moore 1986–87
Ray Harford 1987–89
Jim Ryan 1900–91
David Pleat 1991–95
Terry Westley 1995
Lennie Lawrence 1995–2000
Ricky Hill 2000
Lil Fuccillo 2000
Joe Kinnear 2001–03
Mike Newell June 2003–

LATEST SEQUENCES

Longest Sequence of League Wins: 12, 19.2.2002 – 6.4.2002.

Longest Sequence of League Defeats: 8, 11.11.1899 – 6.1.1900.

Longest Sequence of League Draws: 5, 28.8.1971 – 18.9.1971.

Longest Sequence of Unbeaten League Matches: 19, 8.4.1969 – 7.10.1969.

Longest Sequence Without a League Win: 16, 9.9.1964 – 6.11.1964.

Successive Scoring Runs: 25 from 24.10.1931.

Successive Non-scoring Runs: 5 from 10.4.1973.

TEN YEAR LEAGUE RECORD

		P	W	D	L	F	A	Pts	Pos
1993-94	Div 1	46	14	11	21	56	60	53	20
1994-95	Div 1	46	15	13	18	61	64	58	16
1995-96	Div 1	46	11	12	23	40	64	45	24
1996-97	Div 2	46	21	15	10	71	45	78	3
1997-98	Div 2	46	14	15	17	60	64	57	17
1998-99	Div 2	46	16	10	20	51	60	58	12
1999-2000	Div 2	46	17	10	19	61	65	61	13
2000-01	Div 2	46	9	13	24	52	80	40	22
2001-02	Div 3	46	30	7	9	96	48	97	2
2002-03	Div 2	46	17	14	15	67	62	65	9

DID YOU KNOW?

Though naturally overshadowed by Joe Payne, Jack Ball had two more than useful scoring spells with Luton Town: in 1934–35, 30 goals in 31 League games; in 1935–36, 8 in 19 and after a spell with Excelsior Roubaix, 8 in 15 in 1936–37.

LUTON TOWN 2002–03 LEAGUE RECORD

Match No.	Date	Venue	Opponents	Result		H/T Score	Lg. Pos.	Goalscorers	Attendance
1	Aug 10	H	Peterborough U	L	2-3	0-2	—	Crowe [48], Brkovic [82]	7860
2	13	A	Blackpool	L	2-5	1-2	—	Howard [6], Thorpe [71]	6377
3	17	A	Plymouth Arg	L	1-2	0-0	23	Howard [67]	10,973
4	24	H	Barnsley	L	2-3	1-2	23	Nicholls (pen) [43], Spring [61]	6230
5	26	A	Cardiff C	D	0-0	0-0	24		13,564
6	31	H	Chesterfield	W	3-0	1-0	21	Perrett [36], Howard [69], Crowe [84]	6060
7	Sept 7	A	Brentford	D	0-0	0-0	21		7145
8	14	H	Notts Co	D	2-2	0-2	21	Perrett [78], Howard [86]	6456
9	17	H	Mansfield T	L	2-3	0-2	—	Howard [85], Nicholls [87]	6004
10	21	A	Huddersfield T	W	1-0	0-0	19	Howard [90]	9249
11	28	H	Swindon T	W	3-0	1-0	15	Howard [14], Fotiadis [47], Robinson (pen) [87]	6393
12	Oct 5	A	Stockport Co	W	3-2	1-2	14	Spring [14], Fotiadis 2 [71, 74]	5932
13	12	H	Cheltenham T	W	2-1	0-1	10	Coyne [54], Fotiadis [70]	6447
14	19	A	Oldham Ath	W	2-1	1-1	10	Fotiadis [33], Thorpe [58]	6916
15	26	H	Wigan Ath	D	1-1	1-0	10	Skelton [24]	7364
16	29	A	Crewe Alex	W	1-0	0-0	—	Howard [85]	6030
17	Nov 2	A	Northampton T	L	0-3	0-2	10		5750
18	9	H	Port Vale	D	0-0	0-0	10		6112
19	23	H	QPR	D	0-0	0-0	8		9477
20	30	A	Tranmere R	W	3-1	0-1	7	Spring [70], Brkovic [79], Howard [89]	8273
21	Dec 14	H	Colchester U	L	1-2	1-1	8	Fotiadis [35]	5890
22	21	A	Bristol C	D	1-1	0-0	8	Howard [53]	14,057
23	26	H	Cardiff C	W	2-0	0-0	6	Thorpe [80], Howard [90]	7805
24	28	A	Wycombe W	W	2-1	2-0	6	Howard 2 [21, 34]	7740
25	Jan 1	A	Chesterfield	L	1-2	1-0	6	Brkovic [8]	4638
26	18	A	Barnsley	W	3-2	1-1	7	Spring [45], Thorpe 2 [50, 64]	9079
27	25	H	Wycombe W	W	1-0	0-0	7	Spring [57]	7351
28	Feb 1	A	Peterborough U	D	1-1	1-1	8	Howard [12]	6760
29	8	A	Port Vale	W	2-1	0-0	7	Thorpe [49], Nicholls (pen) [76]	4714
30	11	H	Blackpool	L	1-3	0-1	—	Thorpe [48]	6563
31	15	H	Northampton T	W	3-2	1-1	8	Hughes 2 [26, 84], Nicholls [58]	7048
32	22	H	Brentford	L	0-1	0-0	9		6940
33	25	H	Plymouth Arg	W	1-0	0-0	—	Thorpe [50]	7589
34	Mar 1	A	Notts Co	L	1-2	0-0	9	Thorpe [88]	6778
35	4	A	Mansfield T	L	2-3	1-2	—	Thorpe 2 [13, 82]	4829
36	8	H	Huddersfield T	W	3-0	0-0	8	Thorpe [50], Holmes [71], Howard [89]	6122
37	15	A	Wigan Ath	D	1-1	0-0	8	Howard [57]	7087
38	18	H	Oldham Ath	D	0-0	0-0	—		6142
39	22	H	Crewe Alex	L	0-4	0-2	8		6607
40	Apr 5	H	Tranmere R	D	0-0	0-0	8		6326
41	8	A	Cheltenham T	D	2-2	2-1	—	Hughes [12], Forbes [38]	3762
42	12	A	QPR	L	0-2	0-1	8		15,786
43	19	H	Bristol C	D	2-2	1-0	9	Howard 2 [2, 82]	6381
44	21	A	Colchester U	W	5-0	4-0	8	Howard 3 [14, 45, 90], Griffiths [21], Nicholls (pen) [43]	3967
45	26	H	Stockport Co	D	1-1	0-0	8	Howard [61]	6010
46	May 3	A	Swindon T	L	1-2	1-2	9	Thorpe [31]	6455

Final League Position: 9

GOALSCORERS

League (67): Howard 22, Thorpe 13, Fotiadis 6, Nicholls 5 (3 pens), Spring 5, Brkovic 3, Hughes 3, Crowe 2, Perrett 2, Coyne 1, Forbes 1, Griffiths 1, Holmes 1, Robinson 1 (pen), Skelton 1.
Worthington Cup (2): Howard 1, Spring 1.
FA Cup (4): Brkovic 2, Spring 1, Thorpe 1.
LDV Vans Trophy (7): Brkovic 3, Thorpe 2, Deeney 1, Holmes 1.

Emberson C 18 + 2	Neilson A 21 + 5	Kimble A 8 + 4	Spring M 41	Perrett R 19 + 1	Coyne C 38 + 2	Nicholls K 35 + 1	Robinson S 23 + 6	Howard S 41	Thorpe T 28 + 2	Winters R 1	Fotiadis A 8 + 9	Crowe D 17 + 10	Brkovic A 29 + 7	Bayliss D 7 + 6	Holmes P 8 + 9	Boyce E 33 + 1	Davis S 34	Roberts B 5	Hughes P 30 + 5	Hillier I 12 + 10	Berthelin C 9	Skelton A 5 + 3	Ovendale M 5 + 1	Mansell L — + 1	Willmott C 12 + 1	Hirschfeld L 5	Jupp D 2 + 3	Forbes A 3 + 2	Igoe S 2	Beckwith R 4	Foley K — + 2	Griffiths C 3	Judge M — + 1	Match No.
1	2	3	4[1]	5	6	7	8[2]	9	10	11[3]	12	13	14																					1
1	2[1]	3	4[2]		6	7		9	10		13	12	8	5	11[3]	14																		2
1	12		4[2]	5	6■	7[1]	8	9	10[3]			13	11	14		2	3																	3
			4	5	6	7[1]	8	9	10		12	13	11[2]			2	3	1																4
			4	5	6	7	12	9				10	8			2	3	1	11[1]															5
	12		4	5		7	13	9				10	8	6		2[1]	3	1	11[2]															6
	12		4	5		7	13	9				10	8[2]	6		2	3	1	11[1]															7
15	2[2]		4	5	13	7		9			12	10	8	6			3	1[G]	11[1]															8
1			4	5	12	7	13	9			14	10	8[3]	6[2]		2	3		11[1]															9
1			4	5	6	7	8[3]	9			12	10[1]			14	2	3[2]		11	13														10
1			4	5	6	7[2]	8	9			10[1]	12			13	2	3		11															11
	2		4		6		8	9			10[1]	12				5	3		11	7	1													12
	5[1]		4		6		7	9			10[2]	12	13		14	2	3		11[3]		1	8												13
			4	5	6		7		12		10	9[1]	13		11[3]	2	3			14	1	8[2]												14
			4	5	6		8	9			10				11	2	3				1	7												15
			4		6		7	9	12		10[1]		8			5	3			11	1	2												16
	12		4		6	13	7[3]	9	10				8[2]		14	5	3			11	1	2[1]												17
	4			5	6	7	8	9	10						11[1]	2	3		12		1													18
	2		4		6	7■	8	9■	10[1]		12[2]		11			5	3			13	1													19
	2	12	4		6	7	8	9	10[3]		14		11[2]			5	3[1]		13		1													20
	2	3	4[1]		6	7	8				10	9	11			5			12				1											21
1	5[2]	12			6		4	9	10[1]			7	8			2	3■		11	13														22
1		3			6		4	9	10			7	8			2			11	5														23
1		12			6		4	9	10[2]		13	7[3]	8[1]			2	3		11	5				14										24
1					6		4	9	10		7[1]		8	12		2	3		11	5														25
1■	2	3	4		6	7	8[G]	9	10[2]			13		12					11	5[1]			15											26
1	5	3	4		6	7	8[1]	9	10				12			2			11															27
	2	3	4		6[2]		7[1]	9	10			12	8			5			11				1		13									28
	3		4		6	7		9	10			12	8			2			11[1]				1		5									29
	3		4		6	7		9	10			8	11[1]			2				12			1		5									30
1	3		4		6	7			10			9	8			2[1]			11	12					5									31
1	2		4[2]		6	7	12		10			9[1]	8				3		11	13					5									32
			4[1]		6	7		9	10			8	12				3		11	2					5	1								33
			4		6	7		9	10			8[1]	12				3		11[2]	2					5	1	13							34
			4	12	6	7			10			9[1]	8		13		3		11[2]						5	1	2							35
1			4	5	6	7	12	9	10				8[1]		13		3		11[2]	14							2[3]							36
			4	5	6	7	8	9	10				11	2						3[1]						1	12							37
15			4	5	6	7		9	10				8		12		3		11[1]	2						1[G]								38
1			4	5	6	7		9	10				11[2]	14	13		3[3]		12	2								8[1]						39
1			4	5	6	7		9	10[3]				8[1]			2[2]	3		12	13								14■	11					40
1			4	5[1]	6	7		9							14		3		11	12[2]					2		13	10[3]	8					41
	12		4		6	7		9							8	2	3		11[1]				1		5			10						42
	5	12	4			7		9							8[2]	2	3		11[1]						6					1	13	10		43
	5		4[2]			7		9						12	8	2[1]	3		11			13			6					1		10[3]	14	44
	5		4			7		9					13	12	8	2	3		11[2]			14			6[1]					1		10[3]		45
	5	3	4[1]			7		9	10				8[2]	6		2[3]			11			12						13		1	14			46

Worthington Cup

First Round	Watford	(a)	2-1
Second Round	Aston Villa	(a)	0-3

FA Cup

First Round	Guiseley	(h)	4-0
Second Round	Wigan Ath	(a)	0-3

LDV Vans Trophy

First Round	Woking	(a)	2-0
Second Round	Stevenage B	(a)	4-3
Quarter-final	Cambridge U	(h)	1-2

MACCLESFIELD TOWN — Division 3

FOUNDATION

From the mid-19th Century until 1874, Macclesfield Town FC played under rugby rules. In 1891 they moved to the Moss Rose and finished champions of the Manchester & District League in 1906 and 1908. By 1911, they had carried off the Cheshire Senior Cup five times. Macclesfield were founder members of the Cheshire County League in 1919.

The Moss Rose Ground, London Road, Macclesfield, Cheshire SK11 7SP.

Telephone: (01625) 264 686. ***Fax:*** (01625) 264 692.

Website: www.mtfc.co.uk

Email: office@mtfc.co.uk

Commercial Office: (01625) 264 693.

Social Club: (01625) 424 324.

Press Box: (01625) 264 690/1.

Ground Capacity: 6,235 (seated 2,537, standing 3,698).

Record Attendance: 9,008 v Winsford U, Cheshire Senior Cup 2nd rd, 4 February 1948.

Pitch Measurements: 100m × 66m.

Chairman: Rob Bickerton

Chief Executive: Colin Garlick.

Directors: A. Cash, G. Findlow, P. Moors, M. Rance, J. Turner, D. Astbury, A. Alkadhi, B. Alkadhi.

Director of Football: Gil Prescott.

Manager: David Moss.

Reserve Team Manager: John Askey.

Youth Team Coaches: Steve Carroll, Colin Brookes

Company Secretary: Barrie Darcey.

Administration Manager: Dianne Hehir.

Commercial Manager: Matthew Lenton.

Club Doctors: Dr Mike Whiteside, Mike Hughes.

Physio: Paul Lake. ***Assistant Physio:*** Eric Campbell.

Colours: Royal blue shirts, white shorts, blue stockings.

Change Colours: All tangerine.

HONOURS

Football League: Division 3 – Runners-up 1997–98.

FA Cup: best season: 3rd rd, 1968, 1988, 2002, 2003.

Football League Cup: never past 2nd rd.

Vauxhall Conference: Champions 1994–95, 1996–97.

FA Trophy: Winners 1969–70, 1995–96; Runners-up 1988–89.

Bob Lord Trophy: Winners 1993–94; Runners-up 1995–96, 1996–97.

Vauxhall Conference Championship Shield: Winners 1996, 1997, 1998.

Northern Premier League: Winners 1968–69, 1969–70, 1986–87; Runners-up 1984–85.

Northern Premier League Challenge Cup: Winners 1986–87; Runners-up 1969–70, 1970–71, 1982–83.

Northern Premier League Presidents Cup: Winners 1986–87; Runners-up 1984–85.

Cheshire Senior Cup: Winners 20 times; Runners-up 11.

SKY SPORTS FACT FILE

In 1985–86 a serious facial injury to goalkeeper Alan Zelem forced Macclesfield Town to switch midfield maestro Nigel Shaw, player of the year and second top scorer, into goal for the last ten matches.

Year formed: 1874.

Club Nickname: 'The Silkmen'.

Previous Ground: 1874, Rostron Field; 1891, Moss Rose.

First Football League Game: 9 August 1997, Division 3, v Torquay U (h) W 2–1 – Price; Tinson, Rose, Payne (Edey), Howarth, Sodje (1), Askey, Wood, Landon (1) (Power), Mason, Sorvel.

Record League Victory: 5–2 v Mansfield T, Division 3, 2 November 1999 – Martin; Ingram, Rioch, Collins, Tinson, Sedgemore (1), Askey (1), Priest (1), Barker (2), Davies (Wood), Durkan.

Record Win: 15–0 v Chester St Marys, Cheshire Senior Cup, 2nd rd, 16 February 1886.

Record Defeat: 1–13 v Tranmere R reserves, 3 May 1929.

Most League Points (3 for a win): 82, Division 3, 1997–98.

Most League Goals: 66, Division 3, 1999–2000.

Highest League Scorer in Season: Richard Barker, 16, Division 3, 1999–2000.

Most League Goals in Total Aggregate: John Askey, 31, 1997–2003.

Most Capped Player: George Abbey, Nigeria.

Most League Appearances: Darren Tinson, 263, 1997–2003.

Youngest League Player: Peter Griffiths, 18 years 44 days v Reading, 26 September 1998.

Record Transfer Fee Received: £300,000 from Stockport Co for Rickie Lambert, June 2002.

Record Transfer Fee Paid: £35,000 to Vauxhall Motors for Matt Haddrell, March 2003.

Football League Record: Promoted to Division 3 1997; 1998–99 Division 2; 1999– Division 3.

MANAGERS

Since 1967
Keith Goalen 1967–68
Frank Beaumont 1968–72
Billy Haydock 1972–74
Eddie Brown 1974
John Collins 1974
Willie Stevenson 1974
John Collins 1975–76
Tony Coleman 1976
John Barnes 1976
Brian Taylor 1976
Dave Connor 1976–78
Derek Partridge 1978
Phil Staley 1978–80
Jimmy Williams 1980–81
Brian Booth 1981–85
Neil Griffiths 1985–86
Roy Campbell 1986
Peter Wragg 1986–93
Sammy McIlroy 1993–2000
Peter Davenport 2000
Gil Prescott 2001
David Moss November 2001–

LATEST SEQUENCES

Longest Sequence of League Wins: 5, 16.10.1999 – 6.11.1999.

Longest Sequence of League Defeats: 6, 26.12.1998 –6.2.1999.

Longest Sequence of League Draws: 3, 27.9.1997 – 11.10.1997.

Longest Sequence of Unbeaten League Matches: 8, 16.10.1999 – 27.11.1999.

Longest Sequence Without a League Win: 10, 21.11.1998 – 6.2.1999.

Successive Scoring Runs: 9 from 12.9.2000.

Successive Non-scoring Runs: 5 from 18.12.1998.

TEN YEAR LEAGUE RECORD

		P	W	D	L	F	A	Pts	Pos
1993-94	Conf.	42	16	11	15	48	49	59	7
1994-95	Conf.	42	24	8	10	70	40	80	1
1995-96	Conf.	42	22	9	11	66	49	75	4
1996-97	Conf.	42	27	9	6	80	30	90	1
1997-98	Div 3	46	23	13	10	63	44	82	2
1998-99	Div 2	46	11	10	25	43	63	43	24
1999-2000	Div 3	46	18	11	17	66	61	65	13
2000-01	Div 3	46	14	14	18	51	62	56	14
2001-02	Div 3	46	15	13	18	41	52	58	13
2002-03	Div 3	46	14	12	20	57	63	54	16

DID YOU KNOW ?

Inside-forward Lennie Butt resurrected his Football League career with a rewarding spell at Macclesfield Town in 1931–32 at the age of 21 while on Stockport County's transfer list. Huddersfield Town signed him in 1935.

MACCLESFIELD TOWN 2002–03 LEAGUE RECORD

Match No.	Date	Venue	Opponents	Result		H/T Score	Lg. Pos.	Goalscorers	Attendance
1	Aug 10	H	York C	D	1-1	1-0	—	Tipton [18]	2586
2	13	A	Leyton Orient	L	2-3	0-3	—	Glover [49], Lightbourne [77]	3880
3	17	A	Hartlepool U	W	2-0	0-0	10	Adams [85], Whitaker [86]	4684
4	24	H	Wrexham	L	0-1	0-0	16		2592
5	26	A	Lincoln C	L	0-3	0-1	20		2444
6	31	H	Bournemouth	L	0-1	0-1	23		1795
7	Sept 8	H	Bristol R	W	2-1	2-0	19	Tipton (pen) [10], Byrne [17]	1814
8	14	A	Southend U	L	0-1	0-1	20		3249
9	17	A	Hull C	W	3-1	0-1	—	Welch [47], Lightbourne [50], Askey [90]	8703
10	21	H	Scunthorpe U	L	2-3	0-2	20	Whitaker (pen) [82], Lightbourne [87]	1929
11	28	A	Rochdale	L	1-3	1-1	21	Welsh [34]	3090
12	Oct 5	H	Boston U	W	2-0	1-0	16	Whitaker [6], Welsh [73]	1941
13	12	A	Kidderminster H	W	2-0	1-0	16	Welch [31], Eaton [71]	2521
14	19	H	Carlisle U	D	2-2	1-1	17	Eaton [30], Priest [59]	2383
15	26	A	Bury	L	1-2	0-1	18	Lightbourne [52]	3506
16	29	H	Oxford U	W	2-1	0-0	—	Lightbourne [66], Whitaker [88]	1583
17	Nov 2	H	Shrewsbury T	L	1-2	0-1	16	Whitaker [80]	2218
18	9	A	Swansea C	L	0-1	0-0	17		3526
19	23	H	Torquay U	D	3-3	1-3	17	Eaton [31], Macauley [75], Lightbourne [87]	1835
20	30	A	Cambridge U	L	1-3	1-1	19	Tipton [44]	3834
21	Dec 14	H	Rushden & D	L	0-1	0-0	19		1839
22	21	A	Darlington	D	0-0	0-0	19		3079
23	26	H	Lincoln C	L	0-1	0-0	19		2187
24	28	A	Exeter C	D	1-1	1-0	19	Lightbourne [27]	3017
25	Jan 1	A	Wrexham	W	3-1	1-1	19	Pejic (og) [10], Tipton [46], Eaton [88]	3445
26	18	A	Bournemouth	D	2-2	2-0	19	Whitaker [27], Priest [43]	5840
27	21	H	Hartlepool U	L	0-1	0-1	—		1576
28	25	H	Exeter C	D	1-1	0-0	19	Whitaker [56]	2035
29	Feb 2	A	York C	L	1-2	0-1	20	Welch [60]	4009
30	8	H	Swansea C	L	1-3	1-1	21	O'Leary (og) [45]	2515
31	22	A	Bristol R	D	1-1	0-0	22	Lightbourne [77]	6005
32	Mar 1	H	Southend U	W	2-1	0-0	21	Eaton [69], Lightbourne [80]	1917
33	4	H	Hull C	L	0-1	0-1	—		2229
34	8	A	Scunthorpe U	D	1-1	0-0	23	Tipton [71]	3398
35	11	H	Leyton Orient	W	3-1	1-1	—	Whitaker [18], Tipton 2 [54, 67]	1676
36	15	H	Bury	D	0-0	0-0	19		2920
37	18	A	Carlisle U	L	0-1	0-1	—		3773
38	22	A	Oxford U	W	1-0	1-0	19	Tipton [39]	5691
39	29	H	Kidderminster H	W	2-0	0-0	18	Miles [52], Whitaker [54]	2069
40	Apr 5	H	Cambridge U	D	1-1	1-0	18	Lightbourne [41]	2053
41	12	A	Torquay U	D	2-2	2-1	18	Miles [10], Lightbourne [26]	2970
42	15	A	Shrewsbury T	W	3-2	2-2	—	Abbey [6], Miles 2 [40, 90]	4100
43	19	H	Darlington	W	1-0	1-0	15	Whitaker [13]	1967
44	21	A	Rushden & D	L	0-3	0-1	16		4494
45	26	A	Boston U	L	1-2	0-1	18	Little [61]	3825
46	May 3	H	Rochdale	W	3-2	0-1	16	Hockenhull (og) [48], Askey [88], Tipton [90]	2873

Final League Position: 16

GOALSCORERS

League (57): Lightbourne 11, Whitaker 10 (1 pen), Tipton 9 (1 pen), Eaton 5, Miles 4, Welch 3, Askey 2, Priest 2, Welsh 2, Abbey 1, Adams 1, Byrne 1, Glover 1, Little 1, Macauley 1, own goals 3.
Worthington Cup (5): Whitaker 3, Lightbourne 1, Tipton 1.
FA Cup (5): Lightbourne 2, Tipton 2, Whitaker 1.
LDV Vans Trophy (1): Tipton 1.

Wilson S 44	Hitchen S 32 + 1	Adams D 45	Welch M 38 + 1	Tinson D 45	O'Neill P 11 + 1	Munroe K 20 + 5	Priest C 34 + 3	Tipton M 28 + 8	Glover L 5	Whitaker D 41	Askey J 1 + 8	Lightbourne K 39 + 5	Came S 1	Aldridge P — + 1	Hardy L 8 + 8	Ridler D 16 + 1	Robinson N 2 + 8	Byrne C 2 + 1	Welsh A 4 + 2	Abbey G 16 + 6	Eaton D 8 + 12	Macauley S 20	Little C 4 + 2	Brackenridge S — + 2	Carr M 4	Dunning D 17	Ross N 6 + 2	Nash M 1 + 4	Smith D 3	Haddrell M 2 + 2	Miles J 7 + 1	Martin L 2	*Match No.*
1	2	3	4	5	6	7	8	9^{1}	10^{2}	11	12	13																					1
1	2	3	4		6	7^{2}	8	9^{1}	10	11		12	5	13																			2
1	2	3	4	5	6	7	8^{1}		10	11	12	9																					3
1	2	3	4	5	6	7	8^{3}	9^{2}	10^{1}	11	13	12			14																		4
1	2	3	4^{2}	5	6^{3}	7^{1}			10	11		12			14	9	8	13															5
1	2	3	4^{3}	5		7	12	9		11^{1}		13			8	6	10^{2}		14														6
1	2	3	4	5			8	9^{1}		11		10			13	6	12	7^{2}															7
1	2	3	4	5			8	9^{1}		11		10				6	12	7^{2}	13														8
1	2	3	4	5		12	8	9^{2}		11	14	10^{3}				6	13		7^{1}														9
1	2	3	4	5			8	9^{1}		11	12	10			13	6^{2}			7														10
1	2	3	4	5			8	9^{1}		11	12	10				6^{2}	13		7														11
1	2^{1}	3	7	5	4			9		11		10				6			8	12													12
1	2	3	7	5	4			9^{3}		11^{1}		10			8^{2}	6	12			13	14												13
1	2	3		5	4	12	8	9^{3}		11	10^{1}				14	6	13				7^{2}												14
1	2	3	7	5	4	12	8	9^{3}		11^{1}	13	10^{2}				6					14												15
1	2	3	7	5	4		8	9		11		10				6																	16
1	2	3	7	5	4^{2}		8^{1}	9		11		10			12	6					13												17
1	2	3	7	5		4	8^{1}	9		11		10				6					12												18
1	2	3	7^{2}	5		8^{1}	12	9		11		10				6					13	4											19
1	2	3	4	5		7		9		11■		10								12	8^{1}	6											20
1	2	3	4	5		7^{3}	8					10			12^{2}					14	9	6	11^{1}	13									21
1	2	3	4	5			8	9				10								6	7				11■								22
1	2	3	4	5			8	9				10			12					6	7				11^{1}								23
1	2	3	4	5		7	12			10		9			8						6^{2}			13	11^{1}								24
1	2	3	4	5	12	13	8	9^{3}		11		10			6^{1}						14				7^{2}								25
1	2	3		5			8	9		11^{1}		10			7^{2}					12		6				4	13						26
1	2	3		5			8^{1}	9^{2}		11		10			7						12	6				4		13					27
1	2	3	4	5				12		11		10			7^{2}							6				8	9^{1}	13					28
1	2	3	4	5				12				10			11^{3}						13	6				8	9^{1}	14	7^{2}				29
1		3	2	5			8					10^{1}					12			13	14	6				4^{3}	9	7	11^{2}				30
1	2		4	5			8			11		10				6				3	12					7	9^{1}						31
1	2	3	4	5			8	12		11		10									9^{1}	6				7							32
1	2	3	4	5				12		11		10									9	6				8			7^{1}				33
1		3	4^{3}	5		12	8^{1}	13		11		10								2		6				7	9^{2}	14					34
1		3	4	5			8	9^{1}		11		10								2	12	6				7							35
1	12	3^{1}	4	5			8	9		11		10								2		6				7							36
1		3	4	5			8	9		11						12	13			2	14	6^{1}				7^{3}	10^{2}						37
1		3	4	5		6	8	9		11		10								2						7							38
1		3		5		4	8^{1}	9^{2}		11		10								2		6				7				12	13		39
1		3		5		4	8			11		10								2^{1}		6				7				12	9		40
1		3		5		4		12		11		10^{2}								2			7			8	13			6	9^{1}		41
1		3	12	5		4				11		10								2			7^{1}			8				6	9		42
		3	4	5		7	8			11		10								2		6									9	1	43
		3	4^{1}	5		7	8			11		10								2		6	12								9	1	44
1		3	4	5		7	8	12		11^{2}		10^{1}								2		6	13								9		45
1		3		5		4^{1}	8	12		11	13	10^{2}								2		6	7								9		46

Worthington Cup

First Round	Barnsley	(h)	4-1
Second Round	Preston NE	(h)	1-2

LDV Vans Trophy

Second Round	Tranmere R	(h)	1-2

FA Cup

First Round	Hull C	(a)	3-0
Second Round	Vauxhall Motors	(h)	2-0
Third Round	Watford	(h)	0-2

MANCHESTER CITY FA Premiership

FOUNDATION

Manchester City was formed as a Limited Company in 1894 after their predecessors Ardwick had been forced into bankruptcy. However, many historians like to trace the club's lineage as far back as 1880 when St Mark's Church, West Gorton added a football section to their cricket club. They amalgamated with Gorton Athletic in 1884 as Gorton FC. Because of a change of ground they became Ardwick in 1887.

City of Manchester Stadium, Rowsley Street, Eastlands, Manchester M11 3FF.

Telephone: (0161) 231 3200. ***Fax:*** (0161) 438 7999.
Website: www.mcfc.co.uk ***Email:*** mcfc@mcfc.co.uk

Ground Capacity: 48,000.

Record Attendance: 84,569 v Stoke C, FA Cup 6th rd, 3 March 1934 (British record for any game outside London or Glasgow).

Record Receipts: £512,235 Manchester U v Oldham Ath, FA Cup semi-final replay, 13 April 1994.

Acting Chairman: J. Wardle.
Directors: J. Wardle, D. Tueart, A. Lewis, A. Thomas, B. Bodek, A. Mackintosh.
General Secretary: J. B. Halford.

Manager: Kevin Keegan. ***Assistant Manager:*** Arthur Cox.
Reserve Team Coach: Asa Hartford. ***Physio:*** Rob Harris.
Youth Team Coach: Alex Gibson.
Youth Academy Director: Jim Cassell.

Colours: Sky blue shirts, white shorts, sky blue stockings.

Change Colours: Black and red vertical striped shirts, black shorts, black stockings.

Year Formed: 1887 as Ardwick FC; 1894 as Manchester City.

Turned Professional: 1887 as Ardwick FC.

Ltd Co.: 1894.

Previous Names: 1887, Ardwick FC (formed through the amalgamation of West Gorton and Gorton Athletic, the latter having been formed in 1880); 1894, Manchester City.

Club Nicknames: 'Blues' or 'The Citizens'.

Previous Grounds: 1880, Clowes Street; 1881, Kirkmanshulme Cricket Ground; 1882, Queens Road; 1884, Pink Bank Lane; 1887, Hyde Road (1894–1923 as City); 1923, Maine Road; 2003, City of Manchester Stadium.

First Football League Game: 3 September 1892, Division 2, v Bootle (h) W 7–0 – Douglas; McVickers, Robson; Middleton, Russell, Hopkins; Davies (3), Morris (2), Angus (1), Weir (1), Milarvie.

Record League Victory: 10–1 v Huddersfield T, Division 2, 7 November 1987 – Nixon; Gidman, Hinchcliffe, Clements, Lake, Redmond, White (3), Stewart (3), Adcock (3), McNab (1), Simpson.

HONOURS

Football League: Division 1 – Champions 1936–37, 1967–68, 2001–02; Runners-up 1903–04, 1920–21, 1976–77, 1999–2000; Division 2 – Champions 1898–99, 1902–03, 1909–10, 1927–28, 1946–47, 1965–66; Runners-up 1895–96, 1950–51, 1987–88; Promoted from Division 2 (play-offs) 1998–99.

FA Cup: Winners 1904, 1934, 1956, 1969; Runners-up 1926, 1933, 1955, 1981.

Football League Cup: Winners 1970, 1976; Runners-up 1974.

European Competitions: *European Cup:* 1968–69. *European Cup-Winners' Cup:* 1969–70 (winners), 1970–71. *UEFA Cup:* 1972–73, 1976–77, 1977–78, 1978–79.

SKY SPORTS FACT FILE

Beginning with a 2-2 draw at Stoke City on 3 October 1936, Manchester City completed 44 consecutive scoring League games, up to beating Blackpool 2-1 on 9 October 1937. During this period they were First Division champions.

Record Cup Victory: 10–1 v Swindon T, FA Cup 4th rd, 29 January 1930 – Barber; Felton, McCloy; Barrass, Cowan, Heinemann; Toseland, Marshall (5), Tait (3), Johnson (1), Brook (1).

Record Defeat: 1–9 v Everton, Division 1, 3 September 1906.

Most League Points (2 for a win): 62, Division 2, 1946–47.

Most League Points (3 for a win): 99, Division 1, 2001–02.

Most League Goals: 108, Division 2, 1926–27, 108, Division 1, 2001–02.

Highest League Scorer in Season: Tommy Johnson, 38, Division 1, 1928–29.

Most League Goals in Total Aggregate: Tommy Johnson, 158, 1919–30.

Most League Goals in One Match: 5, Fred Williams v Darwen, Division 2, 18 February 1899; 5, Tom Browell v Burnley, Division 2, 24 October 1925; 5, Tom Johnson v Everton, Division 1, 15 September 1928; 5, George Smith v Newport Co, Division 2, 14 June 1947.

Most Capped Player: Colin Bell, 48, England.

Most League Appearances: Alan Oakes, 565, 1959–76.

Youngest League Player: Glyn Pardoe, 15 years 314 days v Birmingham C, 11 April 1961.

Record Transfer Fee Received: £4,925,000 from Ajax for Georgi Kinkladze, May 1998.

Record Transfer Fee Paid: £3,000,000 to Portsmouth for Lee Bradbury, July 1997.

Football League Record: 1892 Ardwick elected founder member of Division 2; 1894 Newly-formed Manchester C elected to Division 2; Division 1 1899–1902, 1903–09, 1910–26, 1928–38, 1947–50, 1951–63, 1966–83, 1985–87, 1989–92; Division 2 1902–03, 1909–10, 1926–28, 1938–47, 1950–51, 1963–66, 1983–85, 1987–89; 1992–96 FA Premier League; 1996–98 Division 1; 1998–99 Division 2; 1999–2000 Division 1; 2000–01 FA Premier League; 2001–02 Division 1; 2002– FA Premier League.

MANAGERS

Joshua Parlby 1893–95
(Secretary-Manager)
Sam Omerod 1895–1902
Tom Maley 1902–06
Harry Newbould 1906–12
Ernest Magnall 1912–24
David Ashworth 1924–25
Peter Hodge 1926–32
Wilf Wild 1932–46
(continued as Secretary to 1950)
Sam Cowan 1946–47
John 'Jock' Thomson 1947–50
Leslie McDowall 1950–63
George Poyser 1963–65
Joe Mercer 1965–71
(continued as General Manager to 1972)
Malcolm Allison 1972–73
Johnny Hart 1973
Ron Saunders 1973–74
Tony Book 1974–79
Malcolm Allison 1979–80
John Bond 1980–83
John Benson 1983
Billy McNeill 1983–86
Jimmy Frizzell 1986–87
(continued as General Manager)
Mel Machin 1987–89
Howard Kendall 1990
Peter Reid 1990–93
Brian Horton 1993–95
Alan Ball 1995–96
Steve Coppell 1996
Frank Clark 1996–98
Joe Royle 1998–2001
Kevin Keegan May 2001–

LATEST SEQUENCES

Longest Sequence of League Wins: 9, 8.4.1912 – 28.9.1912.

Longest Sequence of League Defeats: 8, 23.8.1995 – 14.10.1995.

Longest Sequence of League Draws: 6, 5.4.1913 – 6.9.1913.

Longest Sequence of Unbeaten League Matches: 22, 16.11.1946 – 19.4.1947.

Longest Sequence Without a League Win: 17, 26.12.1979 – 7.4.1980.

Successive Scoring Runs: 44 from 3.10.1936.

Successive Non-scoring Runs: 6 from 30.1.1971.

TEN YEAR LEAGUE RECORD

		P	*W*	*D*	*L*	*F*	*A*	*Pts*	*Pos*
1993-94	PR Lge	42	9	18	15	38	49	45	16
1994-95	PR Lge	42	12	13	17	53	64	49	17
1995-96	PR Lge	38	9	11	18	33	58	38	18
1996-97	Div 1	46	17	10	19	59	60	61	14
1997-98	Div 1	46	12	12	22	56	57	48	22
1998-99	Div 2	46	22	16	8	69	33	82	3
1999-2000	Div 1	46	26	11	9	78	40	89	2
2000-01	PR Lge	38	8	10	20	41	65	34	18
2001-02	Div 1	46	31	6	9	108	52	99	1
2002-03	PR Lge	38	15	6	17	47	54	51	9

DID YOU KNOW ?

On 8 February 1964 Manchester City were losing 1-0 to Bury (courtesy of soon-to-be City man Colin Bell). Goalkeeper Harry Dowd injured his shoulder, went to centre-forward and equalised seven minutes from time.

MANCHESTER CITY 2002–03 LEAGUE RECORD

Match No.	*Date*	*Venue*	*Opponents*	*Result*		*H/T Score*	*Lg. Pos.*	*Goalscorers*	*Attendance*
1	Aug 17	A	Leeds U	L	0-3	0-2	—		40,195
2	24	H	Newcastle U	W	1-0	1-0	12	Huckerby [36]	34,776
3	28	A	Aston Villa	L	0-1	0-0	—		33,494
4	31	H	Everton	W	3-1	2-1	7	Anelka 2 [14, 16], Radzinski (og) [85]	34,835
5	Sept 10	A	Arsenal	L	1-2	1-2	—	Anelka [29]	37,878
6	15	H	Blackburn R	D	2-2	0-1	11	Anelka [80], Goater [90]	34,130
7	21	A	West Ham U	D	0-0	0-0	14		35,050
8	28	H	Liverpool	L	0-3	0-1	15		35,131
9	Oct 5	A	Southampton	L	0-2	0-2	16		31,009
10	19	H	Chelsea	L	0-3	0-0	18		34,953
11	26	A	Birmingham C	W	2-0	1-0	16	Jihai [24], Anelka [87]	29,316
12	Nov 2	A	WBA	W	2-1	0-0	14	Anelka [51], Goater [71]	26,907
13	9	H	Manchester U	W	3-1	2-1	12	Anelka [5], Goater 2 [26, 50]	34,649
14	16	H	Charlton Ath	L	0-1	0-0	12		33,455
15	23	A	Middlesbrough	L	1-3	0-0	16	Anelka [68]	31,502
16	30	H	Bolton W	W	2-0	1-0	13	Howey [25], Berkovic [56]	32,661
17	Dec 9	A	Sunderland	W	3-0	1-0	—	Foe [44], Jihai [62], Goater [87]	36,511
18	14	A	Charlton Ath	D	2-2	0-0	12	Foe 2 [73, 87]	26,424
19	23	H	Tottenham H	L	2-3	1-1	—	Howey [29], Benarbia [90]	34,563
20	26	H	Aston Villa	W	3-1	1-1	11	Foe 2 [15, 80], Benarbia [78]	33,991
21	28	A	Fulham	W	1-0	0-0	9	Anelka [84]	17,937
22	Jan 1	A	Everton	D	2-2	1-1	10	Anelka [33], Foe [82]	40,163
23	11	H	Leeds U	W	2-1	1-0	9	Goater [29], Jensen [50]	34,884
24	18	A	Newcastle U	L	0-2	0-1	10		52,152
25	29	H	Fulham	W	4-1	1-1	—	Anelka [21], Benarbia [47], Foe [61], Wright-Phillips [70]	33,260
26	Feb 1	H	WBA	L	1-2	1-1	10	Gilchrist (og) [22]	34,765
27	9	A	Manchester U	D	1-1	0-1	10	Goater [86]	67,646
28	22	H	Arsenal	L	1-5	0-4	11	Anelka [87]	34,960
29	Mar 1	A	Blackburn R	L	0-1	0-1	11		28,647
30	16	H	Birmingham C	W	1-0	0-0	12	Fowler [72]	34,596
31	22	A	Chelsea	L	0-5	0-2	12		41,105
32	Apr 5	A	Bolton W	L	0-2	0-1	12		26,919
33	12	H	Middlesbrough	D	0-0	0-0	12		34,596
34	18	A	Tottenham H	W	2-0	2-0	—	Sommeil [3], Barton [21]	36,075
35	21	H	Sunderland	W	3-0	2-0	10	Foe 2 [36, 80], Fowler [38]	34,596
36	27	H	West Ham U	L	0-1	0-0	11		34,815
37	May 3	A	Liverpool	W	2-1	0-0	8	Anelka 2 (1 pen) [74 (p), 90]	44,220
38	11	H	Southampton	L	0-1	0-1	9		34,957

Final League Position: 9

GOALSCORERS

League (47): Anelka 14 (1 pen), Foe 9, Goater 7, Benarbia 3, Fowler 2, Howey 2, Jihai 2, Barton 1, Berkovic 1, Huckerby 1, Jensen 1, Sommeil 1, Wright-Phillips 1, own goals 2.
Worthington Cup (3): Berkovic 1, Huckerby 1, own goal 1.
FA Cup (0).

Nash C 9	Wright-Phillips S 23 + 8	Jensen N 32 + 1	Jihai S 25 + 3	Howey S 24	Distin S 34	Benarbia A 21 + 12	Berkovic E 27	Anelka N 38	Foe M 35	Horlock K 22 + 8	Huckerby D 6 + 10	Dunne R 24 + 1	Shuker C 1 + 2	Schmeichel P 29	Tiatto D 10 + 3	Goater S 14 + 12	Bischoff M 1	Mettomo L 3 + 1	Wiekens G 5 + 1	Macken J — + 5	Belmadi D 2 + 6	Sommeil D 14	Fowler R 12 + 1	Barton J 7	Jordan S — + 1	*Match No.*
1	2	3	4^{1}	5^{2}	6	7	8^{3}	9	10	11	12	13	14													1
	2	3	4	5	6	7	8^{1}	9	11	12	10			1												2
	2	3	4	5	6	7	8^{1}	9	11		10^{2}			1	12	13										3
	2■	3	4	5	6	7^{3}	8^{1}	9	11	12	10^{2}			1	13	14										4
	2	3	4	5^{1}	6	7■	8	9	11	12	10^{2}			1		13										5
	2	3	4		6	7	8	9	11				10^{2}	1	12■	13	5^{1}									6
	2	3	4	5	6	7^{1}	8	9	11	10	12			1												7
	2	3	4	5^{2}	6		8	9	11	7	10^{1}		13	1		12										8
	2^{1}	3	4	5^{2}	6	7	8	9	10	11	12			1				13								9
	2	3	4	5	6	7	8	9	11		12			1		10^{1}										10
1		3^{1}	2	5	6		8	9	7	12	13	4			11	10^{2}										11
1		3	2	5	6		8	9	7	12		4			11^{1}	10										12
	12	3	2				8^{1}	9	7	13		4		1	11^{2}	10		6	5							13
	2	3	4			12	8^{1}	9	7^{2}	13	14	5		1	11	10^{3}		6								14
	2■	3	4			12	8	9		7	13	5		1	11	10^{2}		6^{1}								15
			2	5	6	12	8	9	7	11		4		1	3	10^{1}										16
			2	5	6		8	9	7	11		4		1	3	10										17
			2	5^{1}	6	12	8	9	7	11		4		1	3	10										18
			2^{1}	5	6	12	8	9	7	11	13	4		1	3	10^{2}										19
	2^{2}	12		5	6	13	8	9	7	11	14	4		1	3^{1}	10^{3}										20
	12	3	13	5	6	7^{3}	8^{2}	9	4	11	10^{1}	2		1					14							21
	10	3	2	5	6	7		9^{1}	8	11	12	4		1												22
	12	3	2	5	6	13	8^{2}	9	7	11		4		1		10^{1}										23
1		3	2^{1}	5	6	7		9	8	11		4				10^{2}				12	13					24
1	12	3		5	6	7^{1}		9^{2}	8	11		2				13					10	4				25
1	12	3^{2}		5	6	7^{3}		9	8	11		2^{1}				13					14	4	10			26
1	12	3	2	5	6	13	8^{2}	9	7	11^{1}						14						4	10^{3}			27
1	12	3	2	5		13	8	9	11			4^{1}									7^{2}	6	10			28
1	12	3	2^{1}		6	13	8^{2}	9	7	11						14			5^{3}			4	10			29
	2	3■	12		6	7		9	8	11				1					5			4	10^{1}			30
	2^{1}	3	12■		6	7		9	8	11^{3}				1		13			5		14	4	10^{2}			31
	2				3	12	8	9		11^{3}		4		1					5^{1}	13		6	10^{2}	7	14	32
	7	3			5	12	8^{1}	9^{2}	11			2		1		13				14		4	10^{3}	6		33
	11	3			5	7		9	8			2		1						12		4	10^{1}	6		34
	11	3			5	7		9	8			2^{1}		1							12	4	10	6		35
	11	3^{1}			5	7^{2}		9	8			2		1		12				14	13	4	10^{3}	6		36
	11	3			5	7		9		8		2		1								4	10	6		37
	7	3			5	8		9	11	12		2^{1}		1		10^{3}					13	4	14	6^{2}		38

Worthington Cup

Second Round	Crewe Alex	(h)	3-2
Third Round	Wigan Ath	(a)	0-1

FA Cup

Third Round	Liverpool	(h)	0-1

MANCHESTER UNITED FA Premiership

FOUNDATION

Manchester United was formed as comparatively recently as 1902 after their predecessors, Newton Heath, went bankrupt. However, it is usual to give the date of the club's foundation as 1878 when the dining room committee of the carriage and waggon works of the Lancashire and Yorkshire Railway Company formed Newton Heath L and YR Cricket and Football Club. They won the Manchester Cup in 1886 and as Newton Heath FC were admitted to the Second Division in 1892.

Sir Matt Busby Way, Old Trafford, Manchester M16 0RA.

Telephone: (0161) 868 8000. ***Fax:*** (0161) 868 8804.
Website: www.manutd.com ***Email:*** enquiries@manutd.co.uk
Textphone for Deaf/Impaired Hearing: (0161) 868 8668.
Ticket and Match Information: (0870) 757 1968.
Membership and Supporters Club Enquiries: (0870) 442 1994.

Ground Capacity: 68,210.

Record Attendance: 76,962 Wolverhampton W v Grimsby T, FA Cup semi-final, 25 March 1939.
Club Record Attendance: 70,504 v Aston Villa, Division 1, 27 December 1920.

Record Receipts: £1,124,195.24 (net of VAT), £1,320,929.99 (including VAT) v Olympiakos, European Champions League Group G, 23 October 2001.

Pitch Measurements: 116yd × 76yd.

Chief Executive: Peter Kenyon.

Managing Director: David Gill.

Group Finance Director: Nick Humby.

Directors: J. M. Edelson, Sir Bobby Charlton CBE, E. M. Watkins LL.M., R. L. Olive.

Manager: Sir Alex Ferguson CBE.

Secretary: Kenneth Merrett. ***Stadium Manager:*** Alan Bird.

Colours: Red shirts, white shorts, black stockings.

Change Colours: Black shirts, black shorts, black stockings.

Year Formed: 1878 as Newton Heath LYR; 1902, Manchester United.

Turned Professional: 1885. ***Ltd Co.:*** 1907.

Previous Name: 1880, Newton Heath; 1902, Manchester United.

Club Nickname: 'Red Devils'.

Previous Grounds: 1880, North Road, Monsall Road; 1893, Bank Street; 1910, Old Trafford (played at Maine Road 1941–49).

HONOURS

FA Premier League – Champions 1992–93, 1993–94, 1995–96, 1996–97, 1998–99, 1999–2000, 2000–01, 2002–03; Runners-up 1994–95, 1997–98.

Football League: Division 1 – Champions 1907–08, 1910–11, 1951–52, 1955–56, 1956–57, 1964–65, 1966–67; Runners-up 1946–47, 1947–48, 1948–49, 1950–51, 1958–59, 1963–64, 1967–68, 1979–80, 1987–88, 1991–92. Division 2 – Champions 1935–36, 1974–75; Runners-up 1896–97, 1905–06, 1924–25, 1937–38.

FA Cup: Winners 1909, 1948, 1963, 1977, 1983, 1985, 1990, 1994, 1996, 1999; Runners-up 1957, 1958, 1976, 1979, 1995.

Football League Cup: Winners 1992; Runners-up 1983, 1991, 1994, 2003.

European Competitions: *European Cup:* 1956–57 (s-f), 1957–58 (s-f), 1965–66 (s-f), 1967–68 (winners), 1968–69 (s-f). *Champions League:* 1993–94, 1994–95, 1996–97 (s-f), 1997–98, 1998–99 (winners), 1999–2000, 2000–01, 2001–02 (s-f), 2002–03. *European Cup-Winners' Cup:* 1963–64, 1977–78, 1983–84, 1990–91 (winners). 1991–92. *Inter Cities Fairs Cup:* 1964–65. *UEFA Cup:* 1976–77, 1980–81, 1982–83, 1984–85, 1992–93, 1995–96. *Super Cup:* 1991 (winners), 1999 (runners-up). *Inter-Continental Cup:* 1999 (winners), 1968 (runners-up).

SKY SPORTS FACT FILE

On 17 August 2002 Ole Gunnar Solksjaer scored his 100th goal for Manchester United. A week later Ryan Giggs reached his century and on 19 October made his 500th appearance in all matches for the club.

MANAGERS

J. Ernest Mangnall 1903–12
John Bentley 1912–14
John Robson 1914–21
(Secretary-Manager from 1916)
John Chapman 1921–26
Clarence Hilditch 1926–27
Herbert Bamlett 1927–31
Walter Crickmer 1931–32
Scott Duncan 1932–37
Walter Crickmer 1937–45
(Secretary-Manager)
Matt Busby 1945–69
(continued as General Manager then Director)
Wilf McGuinness 1969–70
Sir Matt Busby 1970–71
Frank O'Farrell 1971–72
Tommy Docherty 1972–77
Dave Sexton 1977–81
Ron Atkinson 1981–86
Sir Alex Ferguson November 1986–

First Football League Game: 3 September 1892, Division 1, v Blackburn R (a) L 3–4 – Warner; Clements, Brown; Perrins, Stewart, Erentz; Farman (1), Coupar (1), Donaldson (1), Carson, Mathieson.

Record League Victory (as Newton Heath): 10–1 v Wolverhampton W, Division 1, 15 October 1892 – Warner; Mitchell, Clements; Perrins, Stewart (3), Erentz; Farman (1), Hood (1), Donaldson (3), Carson (1), Hendry (1).

Record League Victory (as Manchester U): 9–0 v Ipswich T, FA Premier League, 4 March 1995 – Schmeichel; Keane (1) (Sharpe), Irwin, Bruce (Butt), Kanchelskis, Pallister, Cole (5), Ince (1), McClair, Hughes (2), Giggs.

Record Cup Victory: 10–0 v RSC Anderlecht, European Cup prel. rd 2nd leg, 26 September 1956 – Wood; Foulkes, Byrne; Colman, Jones, Edwards; Berry (1), Whelan (2), Taylor (3), Viollet (4), Pegg.

Record Defeat: 0–7 v Blackburn R, Division 1, 10 April 1926. 0–7 v Aston Villa, Division 1, 27 December 1930. 0–7 v Wolverhampton W, Division 2, 26 December 1931.

Most League Points (2 for a win): 64, Division 1, 1956–57.

Most League Points (3 for a win): 92, FA Premier League, 1993–94.

Most League Goals: 103, Division 1, 1956–57 and 1958–59.

Highest League Scorer in Season: Dennis Viollet, 32, 1959–60.

Most League Goals in Total Aggregate: Bobby Charlton, 199, 1956–73.

Most Capped Player: Bobby Charlton, 106, England.

Most League Appearances: Bobby Charlton, 606, 1956–73.

Youngest League Player: Jeff Whitefoot, 16 years 105 days v Portsmouth, 15 April 1950.

Record Transfer Fee Received: £25,000,000 from Real Madrid for David Beckham, July 2003.

Record Transfer Fee Paid: £30,000,000 to Leeds U for Rio Ferdinand, July 2002.

Football League Record: 1892 Newton Heath elected to Division 1; 1894–1906 Division 2; 1906–22 Division 1; 1922–25 Division 2; 1925–31 Division 1; 1931–36 Division 2; 1936–37 Division 1; 1937–38 Division 2; 1938–74 Division 1; 1974–75 Division 2; 1975–92 Division 1; 1992– FA Premier League.

LATEST SEQUENCES

Longest Sequence of League Wins: 14, 15.10.1904 – 3.1.1905.

Longest Sequence of League Defeats: 14, 26.4.1930 – 25.10.1930.

Longest Sequence of League Draws: 6, 30.10.1988 – 27.11.1988.

Longest Sequence of Unbeaten League Matches: 29, 26.12.1998 – 25.9.1999.

Longest Sequence Without a League Win: 16, 19.4.1930 – 25.10.1930.

Successive Scoring Runs: 27 from 11.10.1958.

Successive Non-scoring Runs: 5 from 22.2.1902.

TEN YEAR LEAGUE RECORD

		P	W	D	L	F	A	Pts	Pos
1993-94	PR Lge	42	27	11	4	80	38	92	1
1994-95	PR Lge	42	26	10	6	77	28	88	2
1995-96	PR Lge	38	25	7	6	73	35	82	1
1996-97	PR Lge	38	21	12	5	76	44	75	1
1997-98	PR Lge	38	23	8	7	73	26	77	2
1998-99	PR Lge	38	22	13	3	80	37	79	1
1999-2000	PR Lge	38	28	7	3	97	45	91	1
2000-01	PR Lge	38	24	8	6	79	31	80	1
2001-02	PR Lge	38	24	5	9	87	45	77	3
2002-03	PR Lge	38	25	8	5	74	34	83	1

DID YOU KNOW?

During 2002–03 Manchester United celebrated their 100th win in Europe by beating Olympiakos 3-2 and recorded their best result in the FA Cup for 32 years when defeating West Ham United 6-0 in the fourth round on 26 January.

MANCHESTER UNITED 2002–03 LEAGUE RECORD

Match No.	*Date*	*Venue*	*Opponents*	*Result*		*H/T Score*	*Lg. Pos.*	*Goalscorers*	*Attendance*
1	Aug 17	H	WBA	W	1-0	0-0	—	Solskjaer [78]	67,645
2	23	A	Chelsea	D	2-2	1-2	—	Beckham [26], Giggs [66]	41,549
3	31	A	Sunderland	D	1-1	1-0	8	Giggs [7]	47,586
4	Sept 3	H	Middlesbrough	W	1-0	1-0	—	Van Nistelrooy (pen) [28]	67,508
5	11	H	Bolton W	L	0-1	0-0	—		67,623
6	14	A	Leeds U	L	0-1	0-0	9		39,622
7	21	H	Tottenham H	W	1-0	0-0	7	Van Nistelrooy (pen) [63]	67,611
8	28	A	Charlton Ath	W	3-1	0-1	4	Scholes [54], Giggs [83], Van Nistelrooy [90]	26,608
9	Oct 7	H	Everton	W	3-0	0-0	—	Scholes 2 [86,89], Van Nistelrooy (pen) [90]	67,629
10	19	A	Fulham	D	1-1	0-1	4	Solskjaer [62]	18,103
11	26	H	Aston Villa	D	1-1	0-1	4	Forlan [77]	67,619
12	Nov 2	H	Southampton	W	2-1	1-1	3	Neville P [15], Forlan [85]	67,691
13	9	A	Manchester C	L	1-3	1-2	5	Solskjaer [8]	34,649
14	17	A	West Ham U	D	1-1	1-0	5	Van Nistelrooy [38]	35,049
15	23	H	Newcastle U	W	5-3	3-1	5	Scholes [25], Van Nistelrooy 3 [38, 45, 53], Solskjaer [55]	67,625
16	Dec 1	A	Liverpool	W	2-1	0-0	4	Forlan 2 [64, 67]	44,250
17	7	H	Arsenal	W	2-0	1-0	3	Veron [22], Scholes [77]	67,650
18	14	H	West Ham U	W	3-0	2-0	2	Solskjaer [15], Veron [17], Schemmel (og) [61]	67,555
19	22	A	Blackburn R	L	0-1	0-1	3		30,475
20	26	A	Middlesbrough	L	1-3	0-1	3	Giggs [60]	34,673
21	28	H	Birmingham C	W	2-0	1-0	3	Forlan [37], Beckham [73]	67,640
22	Jan 1	H	Sunderland	W	2-1	0-1	2	Beckham [81], Scholes [90]	67,609
23	11	A	WBA	W	3-1	2-1	2	Van Nistelrooy [8], Scholes [23], Solskjaer [55]	26,936
24	18	H	Chelsea	W	2-1	1-1	2	Scholes [39], Forlan [90]	67,606
25	Feb 1	A	Southampton	W	2-0	2-0	2	Van Nistelrooy [15], Giggs [22]	32,086
26	4	A	Birmingham C	W	1-0	0-0	—	Van Nistelrooy [56]	29,475
27	9	H	Manchester C	D	1-1	1-0	2	Van Nistelrooy [18]	67,646
28	22	A	Bolton W	D	1-1	0-0	2	Solskjaer [90]	27,409
29	Mar 5	H	Leeds U	W	2-1	1-0	—	Radebe (og) [20], Silvestre [79]	67,626
30	15	A	Aston Villa	W	1-0	1-0	2	Beckham [12]	42,602
31	22	H	Fulham	W	3-0	1-0	2	Van Nistelrooy 3 (1 pen) [45 (p), 68, 90]	67,706
32	Apr 5	H	Liverpool	W	4-0	1-0	2	Van Nistelrooy 2 (2 pens) [5, 65], Giggs [78], Solskjaer [90]	67,639
33	12	A	Newcastle U	W	6-2	4-1	1	Solskjaer [32], Scholes 3 [34, 38, 52], Giggs [44], Van Nistelrooy (pen) [58]	52,164
34	16	A	Arsenal	D	2-2	1-0	—	Van Nistelrooy [24], Giggs [63]	38,164
35	19	H	Blackburn R	W	3-1	2-1	1	Van Nistelrooy [20], Scholes 2 [42, 61]	67,626
36	27	A	Tottenham H	W	2-0	0-0	1	Scholes [69], Van Nistelrooy [90]	36,073
37	May 3	H	Charlton Ath	W	4-1	3-1	1	Beckham [11], Van Nistelrooy 3 [32, 37, 53]	67,721
38	11	A	Everton	W	2-1	1-1	1	Beckham [43], Van Nistelrooy (pen) [79]	40,168

Final League Position: 1

GOALSCORERS

League (74): Van Nistelrooy 25 (8 pens), Scholes 14, Solskjaer 9, Giggs 8, Beckham 6, Forlan 6, Veron 2, Neville P 1, Silvestre 1, own goals 2.
Worthington Cup (9): Scholes 3, Forlan 2, Beckham 1 (pen), Richardson 1, Solskjaer 1, Van Nistelrooy 1 (pen).
FA Cup (10): Van Nistelrooy 4 (2 pens), Giggs 2, Beckham 1, Neville P 1, Scholes 1, Solskjaer 1.
Champions League (37): Van Nistelrooy 14 (1 pen), Giggs 5, Solskjaer 4, Veron 4, Beckham 3, Scholes 2, Blanc 1, Brown 1, Forlan 1 (pen), Neville G 1, own goal 1.

Carroll R 8 + 2	Neville P 19 + 6	Silvestre M 34	O'Shea J 26 + 6	Keane R 19 + 2	Blanc L 15 + 4	Beckham D 27 + 4	Veron J 21 + 4	Van Nistelrooy R 33 + 1	Butt N 14 + 4	Giggs R 32 + 4	Scholes P 31 + 2	Forlan D 7 + 18	Solskjaer O 29 + 8	Ferdinand R 27 + 1	Barthez F 30	Chadwick L — + 1	Neville G 19 + 7	Pugh D — + 1	Fortune Q 5 + 4	Brown W 22	Roche L — + 1	Richardson K — + 2	May D — + 1	Stewart M — + 1	Ricardo — + 1	*Match No.*
1	2^{1}	3^{2}	4	5	6	7	8^{3}	9	10	11	12	13	14													1
1	2	3	4	5	6	7	12	9^{3}	8	11^{1}	10^{2}	14	13													2
1	2^{1}	3^{2}	13	5■	6	7	8	9		11		12	10	4												3
	2	3	12		6	7^{1}	8	9^{2}	5	11	10^{3}	14	13	4	1											4
	2	3			6	7	8^{1}	9	5	11		12	10	4	1											5
	8	3	2		6	7		9^{1}	5^{2}	11		12	10	4	1	13										6
	2	3	6			7	8^{2}	9	5	11^{3}		12	10^{1}	4	1		13	14								7
	3		2		6	7		12	5^{2}	11	10	8^{1}	9	4	1		13									8
	12	3	4		6	7	8^{2}	9^{1}	5^{3}	11	10	14	13		1		2									9
	5^{2}	3^{1}	4		6	7	8			11	10	12	9		1		2		13							10
	5^{1}	3			6	7	8				10	11	9	4	1		2		12							11
	5^{1}	3^{2}	14		6	7	8	9^{3}		11	10	12	13	4	1		2									12
	5	3	12		6		7^{2}	9		11	8	13	10	4	1		2^{1}									13
		3	2		6		8	9		11	7		10		1				5	4						14
		3	2		6^{2}		12	9^{3}		11	8	10^{1}	7		1				5	4	13	14				15
	12	3	2					9^{2}		11	8	10^{3}	7		1		6		5^{1}	4			13	14		16
	5	6	3				8	9		11	7		10		1		2			4						17
	5	6	3^{2}		13	12	8	9		11	10^{3}	14	7^{1}		1		2			4						18
	5^{2}	6	3	12	13	14		9		11^{3}	8	10^{1}	7		1		2			4						19
			3^{2}	5	6	12	8	9		11	10		7	13	1		2^{1}			4						20
	12	3	2	5^{2}		7	8			13	11^{3}	10	9^{1}	6	1					4		14				21
15		3	2^{1}	5		7	8^{2}			12	11	10	9	6	1^{G}		13			4						22
	8	3	12	5^{1}		7		9			11	13	10^{2}	6	1		2			4						23
	8^{2}	3^{1}		5		7	12	9^{3}		13	10	14	11	6	1		2			4						24
15		3	4	5		7^{1}	8	9^{2}		11	12	13	10	6	1^{G}		2									25
1		3		5		7	8	9^{1}		11	10		12	6			2			4						26
1		3		5		7	8^{2}	9	13	10^{1}	11		12	6			2			4						27
	12		3	5		7	8^{2}	9	13	11^{3}		14	10	6	1		2			4^{1}						28
	12	3	2	5		7	4^{1}	9^{3}	8	13	10			6	1		14		11^{2}							29
		6	3			7		9	5	11	8		10	4	1		2									30
			3			7		9	5	11	8		10	6	1		2			4						31
	8^{1}	3^{2}	13	5		12		9	14	11	10^{3}		7	6	1		2			4						32
		6	3^{3}	5	12			9	8	11^{2}	10	13	7	4	1		14			2^{1}						33
		6	3^{1}	5				9	8	11	10		7	4	1		12			2						34
	3	6		12		7		9	8^{1}	11^{2}	10		13	4	1^{G}				5	2					15	35
1		6	3	5		7		9		10	8		11^{2}	4			12		13	2^{1}						36
1		6	3	5		7	12	9	13	10^{2}	8^{1}	14	11^{3}	4						2						37
1	12	6	3^{2}	5	13	7		9		11	8		10^{3}	4					14	2^{1}						38

Worthington Cup

Third Round	Leicester C	(h)	2-0
Fourth Round	Burnley	(a)	2-0
Fifth Round	Chelsea	(h)	1-0
Semi-final	Blackburn R	(h)	1-1
		(a)	3-1
Final (at Millennium Stadium)	Liverpool		0-2

Champions League

Third Qualifying Round	Zalaegerszeg	(a)	0-1
		(h)	5-0
Group F	Maccabi Haifa	(h)	5-2
	Leverkusen	(a)	2-1
	Olympiakos	(h)	4-0
		(a)	3-2
	Maccabi Haifa	(n)	0-3
	Leverkusen	(h)	2-0

FA Cup

Third Round	Portsmouth	(h)	4-1
Fourth Round	West Ham U	(h)	6-0
Fifth Round	Arsenal	(h)	0-2

Champions League

Second Stage Group D	Basle	(a)	3-1
	La Coruna	(h)	2-0
	Juventus	(h)	2-1
		(a)	3-0
	Basle	(h)	1-1
	La Coruna	(a)	0-2
Quarter-final	Real Madrid	(a)	1-3
		(h)	4-3

MANSFIELD TOWN Division 3

FOUNDATION

The club was formed as Mansfield Wesleyans in 1897, and changed their name to Mansfield Wesley in 1906 and Mansfield Town in 1910. This was after the Mansfield Wesleyan Chapel trustees had requested that the club change its name as 'it has no longer had any connection with either the chapel or school'. The new club participated in the Notts and Derby District League, but in the following season 1911–12 joined the Central Alliance.

Field Mill Ground, Quarry Lane, Mansfield NG18 5DA.

Telephone: 0870 756 3160. ***Fax:*** (01623) 482 495.
Marketing: 0870 756 3160. ***ClubCall:*** 09068 121 311.
Football in the Community: (07977) 428 147.

Ground Capacity: 9,990.

Record Attendance: 24,467 v Nottingham F, FA Cup 3rd rd, 10 January 1953.

Record Receipts: £46,915 v Sheffield W, FA Cup 3rd rd, 5 January 1991.

Pitch Measurements: 114yd × 70yd.

Chairman/Chief Executive: Keith Haslam.

Associate Directors: K. Woodcock, S. Whetton, M. Murphy.

Manager: Keith Curle.

Physio: Jan Pearce.

Community Scheme Organiser: Mark Hemingray.

Secretary: Christine Reynolds.

Commercial Manager: Bob Gorrill.

Colours: Amber shirts with royal blue trim, royal blue shorts with amber trim, amber stockings with blue trim.

Change Colours: All navy.

Year Formed: 1897.

Turned Professional: 1906.

Ltd Co.: 1922.

Previous Name: 1897, Mansfield Wesleyans; 1906, Mansfield Wesley; 1910, Mansfield Town.

Previous Grounds: 1897–99, Westfield Lane; 1899–1901, Ratcliffe Gate; 1901–12, Newgate Lane; 1912–16, Ratcliffe Gate.

Club Nickname: 'The Stags'.

First Football League Game: 29 August 1931, Division 3 (S), v Swindon T (h) W 3–2 – Wilson; Clifford, England; Wake, Davis, Blackburn; Gilhespy, Readman (1), Johnson, Broom (2), Baxter.

Record League Victory: 9–2 v Rotherham U, Division 3 (N), 27 December 1932 – Wilson; Anthony, England; Davies, S. Robinson, Slack; Prior, Broom, Readman (3), Hoyland (3), Bowater (3).

HONOURS

Football League: Division 2 best season: 21st, 1977–78; Division 3 – Champions 1976–77; Promoted to Division 2 (3rd) 2001–02; Division 4 – Champions 1974–75; Division 3 (N) – Runners-up 1950–51.

FA Cup: best season: 6th rd, 1969.

Football League Cup: best season: 5th rd, 1976.

Freight Rover Trophy: Winners 1987.

SKY SPORTS FACT FILE

Unluckily for Bertie Mee, later to become long-serving Arsenal manager, he had his Football League career cut short with injury at Mansfield Town at the age of 18 in February 1939 after 13 League games.

Record Cup Victory: 8–0 v Scarborough (a), FA Cup 1st rd, 22 November 1952 – Bramley; Chessell, Bradley; Field, Plummer, Lewis; Scott, Fox (3), Marron (2), Sid Watson (1), Adam (2).

Record Defeat: 1–8 v Walsall, Division 3 (N), 19 January 1933.

Most League Points (2 for a win): 68, Division 4, 1974–75.

Most League Points (3 for a win): 81, Division 4, 1985–86.

Most League Goals: 108, Division 4, 1962–63.

Highest League Scorer in Season: Ted Harston, 55, Division 3 (N), 1936–37.

Most League Goals in Total Aggregate: Harry Johnson, 104, 1931–36.

Most League Goals in One Match: 7, Ted Harston v Hartlepools U, Division 3N, 23 January 1937.

Most Capped Player: John McClelland, 6 (53), Northern Ireland.

Most League Appearances: Rod Arnold, 440, 1970–83.

Youngest League Player: Cyril Poole, 15 years 351 days v New Brighton, 27 February 1937.

Record Transfer Fee Received: £655,000 from Tottenham H for Colin Calderwood, July 1993.

Record Transfer Fee Paid: £150,000 to Carlisle U for Lee Peacock, October 1997.

Football League Record: 1931 Elected to Division 3 (S); 1932–37 Division 3 (N); 1937–47 Division 3 (S); 1947–58 Division 3 (N); 1958–60 Division 3; 1960–63 Division 4; 1963–72 Division 3; 1972–75 Division 4; 1975–77 Division 3; 1977–78 Division 2; 1978–80 Division 3; 1980–86 Division 4; 1986–91 Division 3; 1991–92 Division 4; 1992–93 Division 2; 1993–2002 Division 3; 2002–03 Division 2; 2003– Division 3.

MANAGERS

John Baynes 1922–25
Ted Davison 1926–28
Jack Hickling 1928–33
Henry Martin 1933–35
Charlie Bell 1935
Harold Wightman 1936
Harold Parkes 1936–38
Jack Poole 1938–44
Lloyd Barke 1944–45
Roy Goodall 1945–49
Freddie Steele 1949–51
George Jobey 1952–53
Stan Mercer 1953–55
Charlie Mitten 1956–58
Sam Weaver 1958–60
Raich Carter 1960–63
Tommy Cummings 1963–67
Tommy Eggleston 1967–70
Jock Basford 1970–71
Danny Williams 1971–74
Dave Smith 1974–76
Peter Morris 1976–78
Billy Bingham 1978–79
Mick Jones 1979–81
Stuart Boam 1981–83
Ian Greaves 1983–89
George Foster 1989–93
Andy King 1993–96
Steve Parkin 1996–99
Bill Dearden 1999–2002
Stuart Watkiss 2002
Keith Curle December 2002–

LATEST SEQUENCES

Longest Sequence of League Wins: 7, 13.9.1991 – 26.10.1991.

Longest Sequence of League Defeats: 7, 18.1.1947 – 15.3.1947.

Longest Sequence of League Draws: 5, 18.10.1986 – 22.11.1986.

Longest Sequence of Unbeaten League Matches: 20, 14.2.1976 – 21.8.1976.

Longest Sequence Without a League Win: 14, 25.3.2000 – 2.9.2000.

Successive Scoring Runs: 27 from 1.10.1962.

Successive Non-scoring Runs: 8 from 25.3.2000.

TEN YEAR LEAGUE RECORD

		P	*W*	*D*	*L*	*F*	*A*	*Pts*	*Pos*
1993-94	Div 3	42	15	10	17	53	62	55	12
1994-95	Div 3	42	18	11	13	84	59	65	6
1995-96	Div 3	46	11	20	15	54	64	53	19
1996-97	Div 3	46	16	16	14	47	45	64	11
1997-98	Div 3	46	16	17	13	64	55	65	12
1998-99	Div 3	46	19	10	17	60	58	67	8
1999-2000	Div 3	46	16	8	22	50	65	56	17
2000-01	Div 3	46	15	13	18	64	72	68	13
2001-02	Div 3	46	24	7	15	72	60	79	3
2002-03	Div 2	46	12	8	26	66	97	44	23

DID YOU KNOW?

In 1950–51 as well as reaching the fifth round of the FA Cup, Mansfield Town were unbeaten at home in the Third Division (North) and overall conceded just 48 goals in their 46 League matches.

MANSFIELD TOWN 2002–03 LEAGUE RECORD

Match No.	Date	Venue	Opponents	Result		H/T Score	Lg. Pos.	Goalscorers	Attendance
1	Aug 10	H	Plymouth Arg	W	4-3	1-1	—	White A 2 [32, 67], Disley [51], Larkin [55]	5309
2	13	A	Wigan Ath	L	2-3	1-2	—	Larkin 2 [45, 54]	5837
3	17	A	Wycombe W	D	3-3	1-2	11	Corden 2 [6, 86], Christie [74]	5057
4	24	H	Chesterfield	L	0-2	0-1	17		7258
5	26	A	Stockport Co	L	0-2	0-1	20		5190
6	31	H	Crewe Alex	L	0-5	0-3	22		4183
7	Sept 7	H	QPR	L	0-4	0-1	22		4581
8	14	A	Oldham Ath	L	1-6	1-3	23	Corden [19]	5490
9	17	A	Luton T	W	3-2	2-0	—	Lawrence [9], Sellars [23], Christie [50]	6004
10	21	H	Cheltenham T	L	0-2	0-0	24		4116
11	28	A	Northampton T	L	0-2	0-1	24		5594
12	Oct 5	H	Tranmere R	W	6-1	0-1	23	MacKenzie [46], Sellars [52], Lawrence [61], Christie 2 [69, 78], Larkin [75]	3668
13	12	A	Peterborough U	D	0-0	0-0	23		5067
14	19	H	Huddersfield T	L	0-2	0-0	23		4998
15	26	A	Swindon T	L	1-2	1-1	24	Lawrence [2]	4136
16	29	H	Cardiff C	L	0-1	0-0	—		3441
17	Nov 1	H	Colchester U	W	4-2	3-2	—	Christie 4 [19, 25, 29, 64]	3414
18	9	A	Notts Co	D	2-2	1-0	24	Lawrence [43], Christie [90]	10,302
19	23	H	Bristol C	L	4-5	1-1	24	Corden 2 (1 pen) [38, 68 (p)], Christie 2 [62, 76]	4801
20	30	A	Port Vale	L	2-4	1-2	24	Corden [1], Christie [67]	3880
21	Dec 14	H	Blackpool	W	4-0	1-0	24	Christie [9], Lawrence [56], Larkin 2 [74, 76]	4001
22	21	A	Barnsley	W	1-0	0-0	24	White A [50]	10,495
23	26	H	Stockport Co	W	4-2	1-2	21	Christie [6], Corden 2 (1 pen) [48 (p), 79], Disley [54]	6434
24	28	A	Brentford	L	0-1	0-0	21		5844
25	Jan 1	A	Crewe Alex	L	0-2	0-0	21		6931
26	11	H	Wycombe W	D	0-0	0-0	22		4811
27	18	A	Chesterfield	W	2-1	1-1	18	Disley [43], Lawrence [90]	6813
28	28	H	Wigan Ath	L	1-2	0-2	—	Christie [50]	5524
29	Feb 1	A	Plymouth Arg	L	1-3	1-1	22	Lawrence [11]	8030
30	4	H	Brentford	D	0-0	0-0	—		3735
31	8	H	Notts Co	W	3-2	0-0	17	White A [52], Mitchell [65], Corden [71]	8134
32	14	A	Colchester U	L	0-1	0-0	—		3247
33	22	A	QPR	D	2-2	1-1	22	Christie 2 [25, 50]	11,942
34	Mar 1	H	Oldham Ath	L	0-1	0-0	22		5712
35	4	H	Luton T	W	3-2	2-1	—	Day [9], Christie [29], Corden [79]	4829
36	8	A	Cheltenham T	L	1-3	0-2	22	Lawrence [83]	3881
37	15	H	Swindon T	W	2-1	2-1	21	Mendes [15], Corden (pen) [39]	4471
38	18	A	Huddersfield T	D	1-1	0-0	—	Corden (pen) [79]	8756
39	21	A	Cardiff C	L	0-1	0-0	—		13,009
40	29	H	Peterborough U	L	1-5	1-3	22	Corden (pen) [17]	5653
41	Apr 5	H	Port Vale	L	0-1	0-1	23		4538
42	12	A	Bristol C	L	2-5	1-2	23	Disley [37], Butler (og) [61]	12,013
43	19	H	Barnsley	L	0-1	0-1	23		4873
44	21	A	Blackpool	D	3-3	1-2	23	Clarke [13], Larkin [46], White A [86]	6173
45	29	A	Tranmere R	L	1-3	0-1	—	Lawrence (pen) [54]	10,418
46	May 3	H	Northampton T	W	2-1	0-1	23	White A [62], Lawrence (pen) [77]	3928

Final League Position: 23

GOALSCORERS

League (66): Christie 18, Corden 13 (5 pens), Lawrence 10 (2 pens), Larkin 7, White A 6, Disley 4, Sellars 2, Clarke 1, Day 1, MacKenzie 1, Mendes 1, Mitchell 1, own goal 1.
Worthington Cup (1): Moore 1.
FA Cup (4): Lawrence 2, Christie 1, own goal 1.
LDV Vans Trophy (0).

Pilkington K 32	Jervis D 4+1	Disley C 39+3	Reddington S 5+2	Moore N 18 Buxton J 3	Williamson L 28+12	Corden W 37+7	MacKenzie N 16+8	White A 19+9	Larkin C 13+9	Sellars S 12+2 Hankey D —+1	Bacon D —+6	Christie I 29+8	Lawrence L 40+3	Lever M 15	Holyoak D —+2	Clarke J 17+4	Hassell B 19+1	Clark P 2+1	Delaney D 7	Glover L —+2	White J —+1	Van Heusden A 5	Hurst M 1	Vaughan T 4	Little C 5	Gadsby M 13+7	Day R 23	Curle K 11+3	Eaton A 20	Curtis T 23	Beardsley C 1+4	Doane B 11	Mitchell C 3+12	Mendes J 18	Welch K 9	Jones A —+1	John-Baptiste A 4	*Match No.*
1	2	3	4	5	6	7	8	9^1	10^2	11^3	12	13	14																									1
1	2	3	4	5	6	12	8^1	9^2	10	11■		13	7																									2
1	2	3	4	5	6	7	8^1	9^2	10^3	12	14	13	11																									3
1	2^1	3	12	5	6	7	13	9^3	10	11^2		14	8	4																								4
1		3	2	5	6	7	8	9^1	10			12	11	4																								5
1		3	2	5	6	7^1	8	9	10^2			13	11	4^3	14	12																						6
1		8		5	6	7		9^2				10	11			12	2^1	3	4	13																		7
1		10		5	6^2	7^1	8			12		9	11			2		3	4	13																		8
1		10	12	5	6		8	13		11^2		9	7	4^1		3			2																			9
1^6		10		5	6	12	8	13	9^2	11			7	4		2^1			3		15																	10
		6		5		12	8		10	11^1		9	7	4		2			3			1																11
		6^2		5		12	8		10	11^1		9	7	4^3	14	2		13	3			1																12
		6		5			8		10	11		9	7	4		2			3			1																13
		6^3		5	12	13	8^1	14	10	11^2		9	7	4		2						1	3															14
		7		5	6	12	8^1			11			9	4		2						1		3	10													15
1		8		5	6	7	12			11^1		9	2	4										3	10													16
1		8		5	6	7	12			11^1	13	9^2	2	4		14								3^3	10													17
1		8			7	11	12					9	3	4		2								6^1	10	5												18
1	12	8		5	6■	7			10^1		13	9^2	11	4		2										3												19
1		8			7	11			12			9	3	4		2	13								10^1	5	6^2											20
1		8				11	6	10^1	12			9	7				2										5	4	3									21
1		8			12	11		10^2	13			9	7				2										4	5	3	6^1								22
1		8^1			12	11		10^2	13			9	7				2									14	4	5	3	6^3								23
1		8			12	11^1		10^3			13	9	7				2										4	5	3	6^2	14							24
1		8^2			10	11	13				12	9■	7^3													2^1	4	5	3	6	14							25
1		8^2			13	11		10	12			9	7^1			14										2	4	5^3	3	6								26
1		8				11		10					7			2										5	4			6	9^1	3	12					27
1		8			12	11		10^3				9^2	7				2									5	4			6^1	13	3	14					28
1		8^1			12	11		10^2					7				2									5	4			6	13	3	14	9^3				29
1					8	11		10^1					7													5	4		3	6		2	12	9				30
1		12			8	11		10^3					7^1													5^2	4	13	3	6		2	14	9				31
		12			8	11		10^2				13	7^1													5^3	4	14	3	6		2		9	1			32
		8			7	11^2						9					2									6	4	5	3				12	10^1	1	13■		33
		8^1			12	11^2						9	7													13	4■	5■	3	6		2	14	10^3	1			34
					7	11^1		13				9	12				2^3									14	4	5	3	6			8^2	10	1			35
					8^2	11	13	12				9	7			2										5	4		3	6				10^1	1			36
		8			12	11^3						9^2	7				2									14	4		5	6		3	13	10^1	1			37
		8			12	11^3			13			9	7^2				2									14	4		5	6		3^1		10	1			38
		8			12	11^3			13			9	7				2										4		5	6		3^1	14	10^2	1			39
		8				11		12				9	13				2^3										4	14	5	6		3	10^2	7^1	1			40
1		8			7	11	13	12				9^3					2										4	5	3^1	6^2			14	10				41
1		8			7	11	10^2	13				12					2									14	4	5	3^3	6^1				9				42
1		8			12	11^3			13			9	7			3^1	2												5	6			14	10^2			4	43
1		12		5	8^1	11		14	13				7			3	2													6			10^3	9^2			4	44
1		8		5	11^1	12	14	10					7			3	2									13				6				9^3			4^2	45
1				5	6	11^2	8	10		13			7			3	2																12	9^1			4	46

Worthington Cup

First Round	Derby Co	(h)	1-3

LDV Vans Trophy

First Round	Crewe Alex	(h)	0-4

FA Cup

First Round	Team Bath	(a)	4-2
Second Round	Crewe Alex	(a)	0-3

MIDDLESBROUGH FA Premiership

FOUNDATION

A previous belief that Middlesbrough Football Club was founded at a tripe supper at the Corporation Hotel has proved to be erroneous. In fact, members of Middlesbrough Cricket Club were responsible for forming it at a meeting in the gymnasium of the Albert Park Hotel in 1875.

Riverside Stadium, Middlesbrough, TS3 6RS.
Telephone: (01642) 877 700. ***Fax:*** (01642) 877 840.
Website: www.mfc.co.uk ***ClubCall:*** 09068 121 181.
Ticket Office: (01642) 877 745.
Ticket Information Line: (01642) 877 809.
Club Tours: (01642) 877 730.
Stadium Store: (01642) 877 720.
Town Centre Store: (01642) 877 849.
Mail Order: (01642) 866 642.
Lottery Office: (01642) 877 790.

Ground Capacity: 35,120.

Record Attendance: Ayresome Park: 53,536 v Newcastle U, Division 1, 27 December 1949. Riverside Stadium: 34,814 v Newcastle U, FA Premier League, 5 March 2003.

Record Receipts: £486,229 v Newcastle U, FA Premier League, 6 December 1998.

Pitch measurements: 105m × 68m.

Chairman: Steve Gibson. ***Chief Executive:*** Keith Lamb.
Secretary: Karen Nelson.

Manager: Steve McClaren.
Assistant Manager: Bill Beswick. ***First Team Coach:*** Steve Harrison.
Reserve Team Coach: Steve Round. ***Youth Academy Director:*** David Parnaby.
Chief Scout: Ray Train.

Commercial Manager: Graham Fordy. ***Media & Communications Manager:*** Dave Allan.
Stadium Manager: Terry Tasker. ***Head of Finance & Administration:*** Alan Bage.

Colours: Red and white.

Change Colours: All navy blue with maroon trim.

Year Formed: 1876; re-formed 1986.

Turned Professional: 1889; became amateur 1892, and professional again, 1899.

Ltd Co: 1892. ***Club Nickname:*** 'Boro'.

Previous Grounds: 1877, Old Archery Ground, Albert Park; 1879, Breckon Hill; 1882, Linthorpe Road Ground; 1903, Ayresome Park; 1995, Cellnet Riverside Stadium.

First Football League Game: 2 September 1899, Division 2, v Lincoln C (a) L 0–3 – Smith; Shaw, Ramsey; Allport, McNally, McCracken; Wanless, Longstaffe, Gettins, Page, Pugh.

Record League Victory: 9–0 v Brighton & HA, Division 2, 23 August 1958 – Taylor; Bilcliff, Robinson; Harris (2p), Phillips, Walley; Day, McLean, Clough (5), Peacock (2), Holliday.

HONOURS

Football League: Division 1 – Champions 1994–95; Runners-up 1997–98; Division 2 – Champions 1926–27, 1928–29, 1973–74; Runners-up 1901–02, 1991–92; Division 3 – Runners-up 1966–67, 1986–87.

FA Cup: Runners-up 1997.

Football League Cup: Runners-up 1997, 1998.

Amateur Cup: Winners 1895, 1898.

Anglo-Scottish Cup: Winners 1976.

Zenith Data Systems Cup: Runners-up 1990.

SKY SPORTS FACT FILE

On 25 April 1953 Middlesbrough needed at least one point to be sure of avoiding relegation. They beat Manchester United 5-0, then won their last game 4-1 at Portsmouth to finish as high as 13th.

Record Cup Victory: 7–0 v Hereford U, Coca-Cola Cup 2nd rd, 1st leg, 18 September 1996 – Miller; Fleming (1), Branco (1), Whyte, Vickers, Whelan, Emerson (1), Mustoe, Stamp, Juninho, Ravanelli (4).

Record Defeat: 0–9 v Blackburn R, Division 2, 6 November 1954.

Most League Points (2 for a win): 65, Division 2, 1973–74.

Most League Points (3 for a win): 94, Division 3, 1986–87.

Most League Goals: 122, Division 2, 1926–27.

Highest League Scorer in Season: George Camsell, 59, Division 2, 1926–27 (Second Division record).

Most League Goals in Total Aggregate: George Camsell, 325, 1925–39.

Most League Goals in One Match: 5, Andy Wilson v Nottingham F, Division 1, 6 October 1923; 5, George Camsell v Manchester C, Division 2, 25 December 1926; 5, George Camsell v Aston Villa, Division 1, 9 September 1935; 5, Brian Clough v Brighton & HA, Division 2, 22 August 1958.

Most Capped Player: Wilf Mannion, 26, England.

Most League Appearances: Tim Williamson, 563, 1902–23.

Youngest League Player: Stephen Bell, 16 years 323 days v Southampton, 30 January 1982; Sam Lawrie, 16 years 323 days v Arsenal, 3 November 1951.

Record Transfer Fee Received: £12,000,000 from Atletico Madrid for Juninho, July 1997.

Record Transfer Fee Paid: £8,100,500 to Empoli for Massimo Maccarone, July 2002.

Football League Record: 1899 Elected to Division 2; 1902–24 Division 1; 1924–27 Division 2; 1927–28 Division 1; 1928–29 Division 2; 1929–54 Division 1; 1954–66 Division 2; 1966–67 Division 3; 1967–74 Division 2; 1974–82 Division 1; 1982–86 Division 2; 1986–87 Division 3; 1987–88 Division 2; 1988–89 Division 1; 1989–92 Division 2; 1992–93 FA Premier League; 1993–95 Division 1; 1995–97 FA Premier League; 1997–98 Division 1; 1998– FA Premier League.

MANAGERS

John Robson 1899–1905
Alex Mackie 1905–06
Andy Aitken 1906–09
J. Gunter 1908–10
(Secretary-Manager)
Andy Walker 1910–11
Tom McIntosh 1911–19
Jimmy Howie 1920–23
Herbert Bamlett 1923–26
Peter McWilliam 1927–34
Wilf Gillow 1934–44
David Jack 1944–52
Walter Rowley 1952–54
Bob Dennison 1954–63
Raich Carter 1963–66
Stan Anderson 1966–73
Jack Charlton 1973–77
John Neal 1977–81
Bobby Murdoch 1981–82
Malcolm Allison 1982–84
Willie Maddren 1984–86
Bruce Rioch 1986–90
Colin Todd 1990–91
Lennie Lawrence 1991–94
Bryan Robson 1994–2001
Steve McClaren July 2001–

LATEST SEQUENCES

Longest Sequence of League Wins: 9, 16.2.1974 – 6.4.1974.

Longest Sequence of League Defeats: 8, 26.12.1995 – 17.2.1996.

Longest Sequence of League Draws: 8, 3.4.1971 – 1.5.1971.

Longest Sequence of Unbeaten League Matches: 24, 8.9.1973 – 19.1.1974.

Longest Sequence Without a League Win: 19, 3.10.1981 – 6.3.1982.

Successive Scoring Runs: 26 from 21.9.1946.

Successive Non-scoring Runs: 4 from 24.11.1923.

TEN YEAR LEAGUE RECORD

		P	W	D	L	F	A	Pts	Pos
1993-94	Div 1	46	18	13	15	66	54	67	9
1994-95	Div 1	46	23	13	10	67	40	82	1
1995-96	PR Lge	38	11	10	17	35	50	43	12
1996-97	PR Lge	38	10	12	16	51	60	39	19
1997-98	Div 1	46	27	10	9	77	41	91	2
1998-99	PR Lge	38	12	15	11	48	54	51	9
1999-2000	PR Lge	38	14	10	14	46	52	52	12
2000-01	PR Lge	38	9	15	14	44	44	42	14
2001-02	PR Lge	38	12	9	17	35	47	45	12
2002-03	PR Lge	38	13	10	15	48	44	49	11

DID YOU KNOW ?

Juninho made a scoring return to first team action after injury, coming on as a half-time substitute and equalising for Middlesbrough against Everton on 1 March 2003. His previous game for Boro was on 14 May 2000 when he scored at Everton.

MIDDLESBROUGH 2002–03 LEAGUE RECORD

Match No.	*Date*	*Venue*	*Opponents*	*Result*		*H/T Score*	*Lg. Pos.*	*Goalscorers*	*Atten-dance*
1	Aug 17	A	Southampton	D	0-0	0-0	—		28,341
2	24	H	Fulham	D	2-2	1-0	13	Maccarone 2 [32, 51]	28,588
3	31	H	Blackburn R	W	1-0	0-0	9	Job [90]	28,270
4	Sept 3	A	Manchester U	L	0-1	0-1	—		67,508
5	10	H	Sunderland	W	3-0	2-0	—	Nemeth 2 [17, 66], Maccarone [37]	32,167
6	14	A	Everton	L	1-2	1-1	8	Nemeth [10]	32,440
7	21	H	Birmingham C	W	1-0	1-0	6	Queudrue [29]	29,511
8	28	A	Tottenham H	W	3-0	1-0	3	Maccarone [33], Geremi [55], Job [58]	36,082
9	Oct 5	H	Bolton W	W	2-0	1-0	3	Ehiogu [23], Geremi [68]	31,005
10	20	A	Charlton Ath	L	0-1	0-1	5		26,242
11	26	H	Leeds U	D	2-2	1-1	6	Job [25], Southgate [83]	34,723
12	Nov 4	A	Newcastle U	L	0-2	0-1	—		51,558
13	9	H	Liverpool	W	1-0	0-0	6	Southgate [82]	34,723
14	16	A	Chelsea	L	0-1	0-0	7		39,064
15	23	H	Manchester C	W	3-1	0-0	6	Ehiogu [53], Boksic [62], Geremi [84]	31,502
16	30	A	WBA	L	0-1	0-0	7		26,833
17	Dec 7	H	West Ham U	D	2-2	0-0	9	Nemeth [58], Ehiogu [88]	28,283
18	14	H	Chelsea	D	1-1	1-1	9	Geremi [32]	29,160
19	21	A	Arsenal	L	0-2	0-1	10		38,003
20	26	H	Manchester U	W	3-1	1-0	8	Boksic [44], Nemeth [48], Job [85]	34,673
21	28	A	Aston Villa	L	0-1	0-1	10		33,637
22	Jan 1	A	Blackburn R	L	0-1	0-0	12		23,413
23	11	H	Southampton	D	2-2	0-1	11	Whelan [73], Maccarone (pen) [82]	27,443
24	19	A	Fulham	L	0-1	0-1	12		14,253
25	28	H	Aston Villa	L	2-5	2-2	—	Maccarone [33], Greening [35]	27,542
26	Feb 8	A	Liverpool	D	1-1	1-0	14	Geremi [38]	42,247
27	22	A	Sunderland	W	3-1	2-0	13	Riggott 2 [21, 28], Christie [59]	42,134
28	Mar 1	H	Everton	D	1-1	0-1	13	Juninho [74]	32,467
29	5	H	Newcastle U	W	1-0	0-0	—	Geremi [62]	34,814
30	15	A	Leeds U	W	3-2	2-1	11	Maccarone (pen) [36], Juninho [45], Geremi [64]	39,073
31	22	H	Charlton Ath	D	1-1	0-1	11	Christie [57]	29,080
32	Apr 5	H	WBA	W	3-0	1-0	10	Christie [36], Greening [76], Nemeth [87]	30,187
33	12	A	Manchester C	D	0-0	0-0	9		34,596
34	19	H	Arsenal	L	0-2	0-0	10		34,724
35	21	A	West Ham U	L	0-1	0-0	11		35,019
36	26	A	Birmingham C	L	0-3	0-2	13		28,821
37	May 3	H	Tottenham H	W	5-1	3-0	10	Christie [23], Juninho [26], Nemeth [28], Maccarone 2 [51, 75]	30,230
38	11	A	Bolton W	L	1-2	0-2	11	Ricketts [61]	27,241

Final League Position: 11

GOALSCORERS

League (48): Maccarone 9 (2 pens), Geremi 7, Nemeth 7, Christie 4, Job 4, Ehiogu 3, Juninho 3, Boksic 2, Greening 2, Riggott 2, Southgate 2, Queudrue 1, Ricketts 1, Whelan 1.
Worthington Cup (5): Downing 1, Marinelli 1, Queudrue 1, Whelan 1, Wilson 1.
FA Cup (0).

Schwarzer M 38	Stockdale R 12 + 2	Murphy D 4 + 4	Southgate G 36	Ehiogu U 31 + 1	Boateng G 28	Geremi 33	Marinelli C 3 + 4	Whelan N 2 + 13	Maccarone M 26 + 8	Greening J 38	Cooper C 14 + 6	Nemeth S 15 + 13	Boksic A 13 + 5	Wilson M 4 + 2	Job J 22 + 6	Queudrue F 29 + 2	Vidmar T 9 + 3	Wilkshire L 7 + 7	Parnaby S 21	Windass D — + 2	Davies A 1	Riggott C 4 + 1	Ricketts M 5 + 4	Christie M 11 + 1	Eustace J — + 1	Juninho 9 + 1	Doriva 3 + 2	Downing S — + 2	*Match No.*
1	2	3^{1}	4	5	6	7	8	9^{2}	10^{3}	11	12	13	14																1
1	2		4	5	6	7	8^{2}	12	10^{1}	11	3		9^{3}	13	14														2
1	2		4	5	6	7	8^{2}		10^{1}	11	13		9		12	3													3
1	2		4	5	8	7	12	13	10^{2}	11	6				9	3^{1}													4
1	2		4	5		7		12	10	11	6	9^{1}		13	8^{2}	3													5
1	2		4^{1}	5		7	13	12	10^{2}	11	6	9	14		8^{3}	3													6
1	2			5		7			10	11	6	9^{1}	12		8^{2}	3	4	13											7
1	2		4	5	6^{1}	7			10	11			9		8	3		12											8
1	2^{2}		4	5	6	7		12	10^{1}	11	13	14	9^{3}		8	3													9
1	2^{2}		4	5	6	7	12	14	10^{1}	11	13	9^{3}			8	3													10
1			4	5	6	7			10	11		12	9^{1}		8	3■			2										11
1			4	5	6	7	12		10	11		9^{1}			8	3■			2										12
1			4	5	6	7			10^{1}	11		9^{2}	12		8		3	13	2										13
1			4	5	6	7		12	10^{1}	11		9^{3}	14		8	13	3		2^{2}										14
1			4	5	6	7		12	10	11			9^{1}		8		3		2										15
1			4	5	6	7		12	10^{1}	11	13	14	9^{3}		8		3		2^{2}										16
1			4	5	8	7		12	10^{3}	11		13	9^{1}			3	6^{2}	14	2										17
1			4	5	6	7		12	10^{1}	11		8	9			3			2										18
1			4	5	6^{1}	7				11		10^{2}	9^{3}		12	3	13	8■	2	14									19
1			4	5		7			12	11		10^{1}	9^{2}	6	8	3		13	2										20
1			4	5		7		12	14	11		9^{1}		6■	8	3	13	10^{2}	2^{3}										21
1			4	5^{2}		7			10^{1}	11		12	9	6	8^{3}	3	13		2	14									22
1		14	4			7		12	13	11		10^{3}	9^{2}		8^{1}	3	5	6	2										23
1			4			7		9^{1}	10	11		12		6	13	3	5	8^{2}	2										24
1		12			6	7			10	11		9			8^{1}	3	5		2		4								25
1	2	3	4		8	7				11	6				10^{1}							5	9	12^{2}	13				26
1		13	4		8	7				11	6	12				3^{2}			2			5	10	9^{1}					27
1			4	12	8	7			13	11	6^{3}					3			2			5^{1}	10	9^{2}		14			28
1		12	4	5	6	7			10^{1}	11						3			2				9			8			29
1		3	4	5	6	7			10^{3}	11	12	13							2^{1}				14	9^{2}		8			30
1		3^{1}	4	5	6	7			10^{3}	11	2	13				12							14	9^{2}		8			31
1	12		4	5		7			13	11	2	14			10^{3}	3								9^{2}		8^{1}	6		32
1			4	5		7^{2}				11	2	12			10^{1}	3		13						9		8	6		33
1			4	5	8				12	11	2	7			13	3		14						9^{2}		10^{1}	6^{3}		34
1	12		4	5	7				10	11	2				13	3^{1}		6					14	9^{3}		8^{2}			35
1			4	5	7				12	11	6^{3}	13			8^{1}	3			2				10^{2}	9			14		36
1	2		4	5^{2}	6				12	11		10				3		7^{3}				13		9^{1}		8		14	37
1			4		6				10^{1}	11^{3}						3■		7	2			5	12	9^{2}		8	13	14	38

Worthington Cup

Second Round	Brentford	(a)	4-1
Third Round	Ipswich T	(a)	1-3

FA Cup

Third Round	Chelsea	(a)	0-1

MILLWALL — Division 1

FOUNDATION

Formed in 1885 as Millwall Rovers by employees of Morton & Co, a jam and marmalade factory in West Ferry Road. The founders were predominantly Scotsmen. Their first headquarters was The Islanders pub in Tooke Street, Millwall. Their first trophy was the East End Cup in 1887.

Millwall Football & Athletic Company (1985) plc, The Den, Zampa Road, Bermondsey SE16 3LN.

Telephone: (020) 7232 1222. ***Fax:*** (020) 7231 3663. ***Ticket Office:*** (020) 7231 9999. ***ClubCall:*** 09068 400 300. ***Club Shop:*** (020) 7231 9845.

Ground Capacity: 20,146 (all-seater).

Record Attendance: 20,093 v Arsenal, FA Cup 3rd rd, 10 January 1994.

Record Receipts: undisclosed.

Pitch Measurements: 100m × 68m.

Chairman: Theo Paphitis. ***Life President:*** Reg Burr. ***Directors:*** Peter Mead, Doug Woodward, David Sullivan. ***Secretary:*** Yvonne Haines.

Manager: Mark McGhee. ***Assistant Manager:*** Steve Gritt. ***Physio:*** Gerry Docherty.

Youth Development Officer & Senior Scout: Bob Pearson. ***Assistant Youth Development Officer:*** Dave Mehmet. ***Hon. Medical Officer:*** Dr. Des Thompson.

Stadium Manager: Colin Sayer. ***Sales and Promotions Manager:*** Mark Cole.

Colours: Blue shirts, white shorts.

Change Colours: Green and white striped shirts, green shorts, green stockings.

Year Formed: 1885. ***Turned Professional:*** 1893. ***Ltd Co.:*** 1894.

Previous Names: 1885, Millwall Rovers; 1889, Millwall Athletic; 1985, Millwall Football & Athletic Company.

Club Nickname: 'The Lions'.

Previous Grounds: 1885, Glengall Road, Millwall; 1886, Back of 'Lord Nelson'; 1890, East Ferry Road; 1901, North Greenwich; 1910, The Den, Cold Blow Lane; 1993, The Den, Bermondsey.

First Football League Game: 28 August 1920, Division 3, v Bristol R (h) W 2–0 – Lansdale; Fort, Hodge; Voisey (1), Riddell, McAlpine; Waterall, Travers, Broad (1), Sutherland, Dempsey.

Record League Victory: 9–1 v Torquay U, Division 3 (S), 29 August 1927 – Lansdale, Tilling, Hill, Amos, Bryant (3), Graham, Chance, Hawkins (3), Landells (1), Phillips (2), Black. 9–1 v Coventry C, Division 3 (S), 19 November 1927 – Lansdale, Fort, Hill, Amos, Collins (1), Graham, Chance, Landells (4), Cock (2), Phillips (2), Black.

HONOURS

Football League: Division 1 best season: 3rd, 1993–94; Division 2 – Champions 1987–88, 2000–01; Division 3 (S) – Champions 1927–28, 1937–38; Runners-up 1952–53; Division 3 – Runners-up 1965–66, 1984–85; Division 4 – Champions 1961–62; Runners-up 1964–65.

FA Cup: Semi-final 1900, 1903, 1937 (first Division 3 side to reach semi-final).

Football League Cup: best season: 5th rd, 1974, 1977, 1995.

Football League Trophy: Winners 1983.

Auto Windscreens Shield: Runners-up 1999.

SKY SPORTS FACT FILE

In the 1926–27 FA Cup after beating First Division opposition in Huddersfield Town 3-1 and Derby County 2-0 (away), Millwall of Division Three (South) defeated Second Division Middlesbrough 3-2 at The Den, the visitors missing two penalties.

Record Cup Victory: 7–0 v Gateshead, FA Cup 2nd rd, 12 December 1936 – Yuill; Ted Smith, Inns; Brolly, Hancock, Forsyth; Thomas (1), Mangnall (1), Ken Burditt (2), McCartney (2), Thorogood (1).

Record Defeat: 1–9 v Aston Villa, FA Cup 4th rd, 28 January 1946.

Most League Points (2 for a win): 65, Division 3 (S), 1927–28 and Division 3, 1965–66.

Most League Points (3 for a win): 93, Division 2, 2000–01.

Most League Goals: 127, Division 3 (S), 1927–28.

Highest League Scorer in Season: Richard Parker, 37, Division 3 (S), 1926–27.

Most League Goals in Total Aggregate: Teddy Sheringham, 93, 1984–91.

Most League Goals in One Match: 5, Richard Parker v Norwich C, Division 3S, 28 August 1926.

Most Capped Player: Eamonn Dunphy, 22 (23), Republic of Ireland.

Most League Appearances: Barry Kitchener, 523, 1967–82.

Youngest League Player: Moses Ashikodi, 15 years 240 days v Brighton & HA, 22 February 2003.

Record Transfer Fee Received: £2,300,000 from Liverpool for Mark Kennedy, March 1995.

Record Transfer Fee Paid: £800,000 to Derby Co for Paul Goddard, December 1989.

Football League Record: 1920 Original Members of Division 3; 1921 Division 3 (S); 1928–34 Division 2; 1934–38 Division 3 (S); 1938–48 Division 2; 1948–58 Division 3 (S); 1958–62 Division 4; 1962–64 Division 3; 1964–65 Division 4; 1965–66 Division 3; 1966–75 Division 2; 1975–76 Division 3; 1976–79 Division 2; 1979–85 Division 3; 1985–88 Division 2; 1988–90 Division 1; 1990–92 Division 2; 1992–96 Division 1; 1996–2001 Division 2; 2001– Division 1.

MANAGERS

F. B. Kidd 1894–99
(Hon. Treasurer/Manager)
E. R. Stopher 1899–1900
(Hon. Treasurer/Manager)
George Saunders 1900–11
(Hon. Treasurer/Manager)
Herbert Lipsham 1911–19
Robert Hunter 1919–33
Bill McCracken 1933–36
Charlie Hewitt 1936–40
Bill Voisey 1940–44
Jack Cock 1944–48
Charlie Hewitt 1948–56
Ron Gray 1956–57
Jimmy Seed 1958–59
Reg Smith 1959–61
Ron Gray 1961–63
Billy Gray 1963–66
Benny Fenton 1966–74
Gordon Jago 1974–77
George Petchey 1978–80
Peter Anderson 1980–82
George Graham 1982–86
John Docherty 1986–90
Bob Pearson 1990
Bruce Rioch 1990–92
Mick McCarthy 1992–96
Jimmy Nicholl 1996–97
John Docherty 1997
Billy Bonds 1997–98
Keith Stevens May 1998–2000
(then Joint Manager)
(*plus* Alan McLeary 1999–2000)
Mark McGhee September 2000–

LATEST SEQUENCES

Longest Sequence of League Wins: 10, 10.3.1928 – 25.4.1928.

Longest Sequence of League Defeats: 11, 10.4.1929 – 16.9.1929.

Longest Sequence of League Draws: 5, 22.12.1973 – 12.1.1974.

Longest Sequence of Unbeaten League Matches: 19, 22.8.1959 – 31.10.1959.

Longest Sequence Without a League Win: 20, 26.12.1989 – 5.5.1990.

Successive Scoring Runs: 22 from 8.12.1923.

Successive Non-scoring Runs: 6 from 20.12.1947.

TEN YEAR LEAGUE RECORD

		P	*W*	*D*	*L*	*F*	*A*	*Pts*	*Pos*
1993-94	Div 1	46	19	17	10	58	49	74	3
1994-95	Div 1	46	16	14	16	60	60	62	12
1995-96	Div 1	46	13	13	20	43	63	52	22
1996-97	Div 2	46	16	13	17	50	55	61	14
1997-98	Div 2	46	14	13	19	43	54	55	18
1998-99	Div 2	46	17	11	18	52	59	62	10
1999-2000	Div 2	46	23	13	10	76	50	82	5
2000-01	Div 2	46	28	9	9	89	38	93	1
2001-02	Div 1	46	22	11	13	69	48	77	4
2002-03	Div 1	46	19	9	18	59	69	66	9

DID YOU KNOW ?

In 1898–99 Millwall's reserve team produced one of the most incredible list of results for a first-class club. They won all 30 League matches for a goals total of 212 scored and only 13 conceded.

MILLWALL 2002–03 LEAGUE RECORD

Match No.	Date	Venue	Opponents	Result		H/T Score	Lg. Pos.	Goalscorers	Attendance
1	Aug 10	H	Rotherham U	L	0-6	0-2	—		7177
2	13	A	Watford	D	0-0	0-0	—		11,187
3	17	A	Gillingham	L	0-1	0-0	23		7543
4	24	H	Ipswich T	D	1-1	1-0	22	May [4]	8097
5	27	A	Sheffield U	L	1-3	0-0	—	Ifill [89]	13,024
6	31	H	Grimsby T	W	2-0	1-0	21	Claridge 2 [7, 60]	6677
7	Sept 7	H	Brighton & HA	W	1-0	0-0	15	Ward [73]	8822
8	14	A	Portsmouth	L	0-1	0-0	18		17,201
9	17	A	Burnley	D	2-2	1-1	—	Livermore [31], Davies [64]	11,878
10	21	H	Walsall	L	0-3	0-2	21		7525
11	28	A	Coventry C	W	3-2	1-2	19	Davies [38], Kinet [50], Harris [85]	13,562
12	Oct 5	H	Nottingham F	L	1-2	1-0	20	Davies [44]	10,521
13	12	H	Wimbledon	D	1-1	0-0	20	Nethercott [82]	8248
14	19	A	Norwich C	L	1-3	0-1	20	Claridge [50]	20,448
15	26	H	Derby Co	W	3-0	1-0	19	Wise [43], Harris 2 (1 pen) [81 (p), 90]	8116
16	30	A	Sheffield W	W	1-0	1-0	—	Claridge [19]	16,791
17	Nov 2	A	Reading	L	0-2	0-1	19		13,081
18	9	H	Preston NE	W	2-1	2-0	16	Ifill [10], Wise [16]	7554
19	16	H	Leicester C	D	2-2	1-2	16	Reid [28], Wise [81]	10,772
20	23	A	Stoke C	W	1-0	1-0	13	Reid [2]	13,776
21	30	H	Bradford C	W	1-0	0-0	10	Harris [82]	8510
22	Dec 7	A	Crystal Palace	L	0-1	0-0	15		19,301
23	14	A	Leicester C	L	1-4	1-2	17	Claridge [1]	31,904
24	21	H	Wolverhampton W	D	1-1	1-1	17	Roberts [43]	9091
25	26	H	Gillingham	D	2-2	1-1	18	Ryan [41], Harris [58]	10,947
26	28	A	Rotherham U	W	3-1	1-0	15	Harris [40], Reid [48], Claridge [58]	6448
27	Jan 1	A	Ipswich T	L	1-4	0-0	16	Reid [64]	26,040
28	11	H	Watford	W	4-0	2-0	13	Claridge [10], Ryan [41], Ifill [78], Sweeney [89]	9030
29	18	A	Grimsby T	W	2-0	1-0	13	Claridge 2 (1 pen) [43, 84 (p)]	4993
30	Feb 1	H	Sheffield U	W	1-0	0-0	10	Ifill [63]	9102
31	8	A	Preston NE	L	1-2	0-2	12	Kinet [88]	13,117
32	15	H	Reading	L	0-2	0-1	12		7038
33	22	A	Brighton & HA	L	0-1	0-0	14		6751
34	Mar 1	H	Portsmouth	L	0-5	0-4	15		9697
35	4	H	Burnley	D	1-1	0-1	—	Sadlier [84]	6045
36	8	A	Walsall	W	2-1	0-0	14	Harris [59], Ifill [62]	6647
37	15	A	Wimbledon	L	0-2	0-1	17		2952
38	18	H	Norwich C	L	0-2	0-2	—		6854
39	22	H	Sheffield W	W	3-0	2-0	14	Reid 2 [42, 45], Ifill [54]	7338
40	Apr 5	A	Bradford C	W	1-0	0-0	12	Harris [90]	10,676
41	12	H	Stoke C	W	3-1	1-0	10	Harris [19], Roberts [49], Livermore [55]	8725
42	16	A	Derby Co	W	2-1	1-1	—	Harris [6], McCammon [63]	21,014
43	19	A	Wolverhampton W	L	0-3	0-1	9		27,015
44	21	H	Crystal Palace	W	3-2	2-1	9	Harris (pen) [39], McCammon [43], Cahill [74]	10,670
45	26	A	Nottingham F	D	3-3	1-2	9	Nethercott [25], Cahill [67], Harris [87]	29,463
46	May 4	H	Coventry C	W	2-0	0-0	9	Craig [51], Cahill [54]	9220

Final League Position: 9

GOALSCORERS

League (59): Harris 12 (2 pens), Claridge 9 (1 pen), Ifill 6, Reid 6, Cahill 3, Davies 3, Wise 3, Kinet 2, Livermore 2, McCammon 2, Nethercott 2, Roberts 2, Ryan 2, Craig 1, May 1, Sadlier 1, Sweeney 1, Ward 1.
Worthington Cup (0).
FA Cup (6): Claridge 3 (1 pen), Ifill 1, Reid 1, Robinson 1.

Warner T 46	Lawrence M 31 + 2	Bull R 9 + 3	Cahill T 9 + 2	Nethercott S 34 + 2	Ward D 36 + 3	Ifill P 45	Livermore D 41	Harris N 34 + 6	Claridge S 31 + 13	Ryan R 36 + 5	Sadlier R 2 + 3	Tuttle D 1	May B 4 + 6	Roberts A 31 + 2	Sweeney P 1 + 4	Kinet C 10 + 10	Davies K 6 + 3	Braniff K 5 + 5	Wise D 28 + 1	Johnson G 7 + 1	Phillips M 7	Robinson P 12 + 2	Reid S 19 + 1	Dolan J 2	Hearn C 6 + 3	Baltacha S 1 + 1	Dunne A 3 + 1	Ashikodi M — + 5	McCammon M 7	Craig T 2	Elliott M — + 1	*Match No.*
1	2	3[1]	4	5	6	7	8	9	10	11	12																					1
1	2	3	4	5	6	7	8■	9	10[1]			11	12																			2
1	2	3[2]	4	5	6	7	8	9	12	13			10[1]	11[3]	14																	3
1	2		4	5	6	7	8	9	12	3			10[1]	11																		4
1	2	12	4	5	6	7		9	13	3			10[2]	8		11[1]																5
1	2		4	5	6	7	8	9[1]	10	3			12	11																		6
1	2	12	4[1]	5	6	7	8[3]	9[2]	10	3			13	11		14																7
1	2[2]	3		5	6	7	8	12	9					4		11[1]	10	13														8
1	2	3		5	6	7	8	12	9[1]					4		11	10															9
1	2	3		5	6	7	8	12	9					4		11[1]	10															10
1	2	3[2]		5	6	7	4	9	12	13				14		11[3]	10[1]		8													11
1	2■			5	6	7	4	9	12	3						11[1]	10		8													12
1	2			5	6	7		9[1]	12	3				4		11	10		8													13
1				5	6	7	4	9[2]	10	3				11[1]			13	12	8	2												14
1				5		7	4	9	10	3				11					8	2	6											15
1	2			5	12	7	4	9[2]	10[1]	3				11			13		8		6											16
1				5	12	7	4	9	10[3]	3				11[2]		13	14		8	2	6[1]											17
1				5	6[1]	7	4	9	10	3				11					8	2		12										18
1	2			5		7	4	9[2]	10	6[3]			13	11[1]		12			8	3			14									19
1				5		7	4	9	10	3									8	2			11	6								20
1	12			5		7	4	13	10	3[2]						14		9[3]	8	2			11	6[1]								21
1	2[2]			5		7	4	12	10	3			9[1]						8	13	6		11									22
1	2[2]			5		7		9	10	3				4					8		6[1]	12	11		13							23
1	2[1]			5		7			10	3				4	12			9	8		6		11									24
1	2			5	12	7		13	10	3				4				9[2]	8		6[1]		11									25
1	2			5	6	7	8	9	10[1]	3				4				12					11									26
1	2			5	6	7	4	9	10[1]	13				3		12			8[2]				11									27
1	2				6	7[2]	4		10	3					12			9	8			5	11[1]		13							28
1	2	12			6	7	4		10	3[1]								9[2]	8			5	11			13						29
1	2				6	7	4		10	3					9[1]	12			8			5			11							30
1					6	7	4		10[3]	3[2]			12			13			8			5	11		9[1]	2	14					31
1		10[1]			6		4		9	3					13	11[2]		12				5	7		8		2					32
1					6	7	4	9[2]	10	3						12						5	11[1]		8		2	13				33
1					6	7	4	9	10[1]	2	12					11			8			5	3									34
1					6	7[1]	4	9	10[3]	3	14			13		12			8[2]			5	11				2					35
1					6	7	8	9	12	2	10[1]			4								5	3		11							36
1	2				6	7	8	9[2]	12	3	10[1]			11		13			14			5			4[3]							37
1		2[1]		13	6[2]	7	8	9	10				12	4		11[3]						5	3		14							38
1				12	6	7	11	9	10[2]	2				4					8			5[1]	3					13				39
1	12			5	6	11	7	9		2				4					8				3[2]					13	10[1]			40
1	2			5	6	7[2]	11	9	12	3				4				13	8										10[1]			41
1	2			5	6	7	11	9[2]	12	3				4					8									13	10[1]			42
1	2		12	5	6	7	11	9		3[1]				4					8										10			43
1	2[1]		12	5	6	7	11	9[2]	13	3				4					8										10			44
1	2		4[3]	5	6	7	8	9	12	13				11															10[1]	3[2]	14	45
1	2		4	5	6	7	11	9[1]	12	13				8														14	10[3]	3[2]		46

Worthington Cup

First Round	Rushden & D	(a)	0-0

FA Cup

Third Round	Cambridge U	(a)	1-1
		(h)	3-2
Fourth Round	Southampton	(a)	1-1
		(h)	1-2

NEWCASTLE UNITED FA Premiership

FOUNDATION

It stemmed from a newly formed club called Stanley in 1881. In October 1882 they changed their name to Newcastle East End to avoid confusion with two other local clubs, Stanley Nops and Stanley Albion. Shortly afterwards another club Rosewood merged with them. Newcastle West End had been formed in August 1882 and they played on a pitch which was part of the Town Moor. Moved to Brandling Park 1885 and St James' Park 1886 (home of Newcastle Rangers). West End went out of existence after a bad run and the remaining committee men invited East End to move to St James' Park. They accepted and, at a meeting in Bath Lane Hall in 1892, changed their name to Newcastle United.

St James' Park, Newcastle-upon-Tyne NE1 4ST.
Telephone: (0191) 201 8400. ***Fax:*** (0191) 201 8600.
ClubCall: 09068 121 190. ***Box Office:*** (0191) 261 1571.
Mail Order: 0870 442 1892. ***Club Shop:*** (0191) 201 8426.
Football in the Community: (0191) 222 0134.
Travel Club: (0191) 201 8550.
Magpies Club: (0191) 201 8472.
Corporate Hospitality: (0191) 201 8704.
Conference and Banqueting: (0191) 201 8525.
Club United: (0191) 201 8581. ***Press Office:*** (0191) 201 8420.
Commercial Department: (0191) 201 8421.
Lottery Office: (0191) 201 8502.
Photographic Dept: (0191) 201 8579.

Ground Capacity: 52,193.

Record Attendance: 68,386 v Chelsea, Division 1, 3 September 1930.

Record Receipts: £1,521,801 v Manchester U, FA Premier League, 12 April 2003.

Pitch Measurements: 105m × 68m.

President: Sir John Hall.

Chairman: W. F. Shepherd. ***Deputy Chairman:*** D. S. Hall.

Directors: R. Cushing, K. Slater (Finance Director).

Manager: Sir Bobby Robson CBE.

Director of Football: Gordon Milne. ***Chief Scout:*** Charlie Woods.

Coaches: John Carver, Tommy Craig, Simon Smith. ***Academy Director:*** Kenny Wharton.

Senior Physio: Derek Wright. ***Physio:*** Paul Ferris. ***Fitness Coach:*** Paul Winsper.

Chief Operating Officer: Russell Cushing. ***Director of Commercial Affairs:*** Trevor Garwood.

Safety Officer: Dave Pattison. ***Team Administrator:*** Tony Toward. ***Assistant Secretary:*** Lee Charnley.

Colours: Black and white striped shirts, black shorts, black stockings.

Change Colours: Black shirts with white piping, black shorts with white piping, black stockings with white tops.

Year Formed: 1881. ***Turned Professional:*** 1889. ***Ltd Co.:*** 1890.

Previous Names: 1881, Stanley; 1882, Newcastle East End; 1892, Newcastle United.

HONOURS

FA Premier League: Runners-up 1995–96, 1996–97; *Football League:* Division 1 – Champions 1904–05, 1906–07, 1908–09, 1926–27, 1992–93; Division 2 – Champions 1964–65; Runners-up 1897–98, 1947–48.

FA Cup: Winners 1910, 1924, 1932, 1951, 1952, 1955; Runners-up 1905, 1906, 1908, 1911, 1974, 1998, 1999.

Football League Cup: Runners-up 1976.

Texaco Cup: Winners 1974, 1975.

European Competitions: *Champions League:* 1997–98, 2002–03. *European Fairs Cup:* 1968–69 (winners), 1969–70, 1970–71. *UEFA Cup:* 1977–78, 1994–95, 1996–97, 1999–2000. *European Cup Winners' Cup:* 1998–99. *Anglo-Italian Cup:* Winners 1972–73. *Intertoto Cup:* 2001 (runners-up).

SKY SPORTS FACT FILE

On 16 November 2002 Newcastle United's 2-1 win over Southampton was their 800th in the top flight at St James' Park and their 1400th at home in all competitions. The first home League win had been 6-0 v Royal Arsenal on 30 September 1893.

Club Nickname: 'The Magpies'.

Previous Grounds: 1881, South Byker; 1886, Chillingham Road, Heaton, 1892, St James' Park.

First Football League Game: 2 September 1893, Division 2, v Royal Arsenal (a) D 2–2 – Ramsay; Jeffery, Miller; Crielly, Graham, McKane; Bowman, Crate (1), Thompson, Sorley (1), Wallace. Graham and not Crate scored according to some reports.

Record League Victory: 13–0 v Newport Co, Division 2, 5 October 1946 – Garbutt; Cowell, Graham; Harvey, Brennan, Wright; Milburn (2), Bentley (1), Wayman (4), Shackleton (6), Pearson.

Record Cup Victory: 9–0 v Southport (at Hillsborough), FA Cup 4th rd, 1 February 1932 – McInroy; Nelson, Fairhurst; McKenzie, Davidson, Weaver (1); Boyd (1), Jimmy Richardson (3), Cape (2), McMenemy (1), Lang (1).

Record Defeat: 0–9 v Burton Wanderers, Division 2, 15 April 1895.

Most League Points (2 for a win): 57, Division 2, 1964–65.

Most League Points (3 for a win): 96, Division 1, 1992–93.

Most League Goals: 98, Division 1, 1951–52.

Highest League Scorer in Season: Hughie Gallacher, 36, Division 1, 1926–27.

Most League Goals in Total Aggregate: Jackie Milburn, 177, 1946–57.

Most League Goals in One Match: 6, Len Shackleton v Newport Co, Division 2, 5 October 1946.

Most Capped Player: Shay Given, 43 (52), Republic of Ireland.

Most League Appearances: Jim Lawrence, 432, 1904–22.

Youngest League Player: Steve Watson, 16 years 223 days v Wolverhampton W, 10 November 1990.

MANAGERS

Frank Watt 1895–32
(Secretary-Manager)
Andy Cunningham 1930–35
Tom Mather 1935–39
Stan Seymour 1939–47
(Hon. Manager)
George Martin 1947–50
Stan Seymour 1950–54
(Hon. Manager)
Duggie Livingstone 1954–56
Stan Seymour 1956–58
(Hon. Manager)
Charlie Mitten 1958–61
Norman Smith 1961–62
Joe Harvey 1962–75
Gordon Lee 1975–77
Richard Dinnis 1977
Bill McGarry 1977–80
Arthur Cox 1980–84
Jack Charlton 1984
Willie McFaul 1985–88
Jim Smith 1988–91
Ossie Ardiles 1991–92
Kevin Keegan 1992–97
Kenny Dalglish 1997–98
Ruud Gullit 1998–99
Sir Bobby Robson
September 1999–

Record Transfer Fee Received: £8,000,000 from Liverpool for Dieter Hamann, July 1999.

Record Transfer Fee Paid: £15,000,000 to Blackburn R for Alan Shearer, July 1996.

Football League Record: 1893 Elected to Division 2; 1898–1934 Division 1; 1934–48 Division 2; 1948–61 Division 1; 1961–65 Division 2; 1965–78 Division 1; 1978–84 Division 2; 1984–89 Division 1; 1989–92 Division 2; 1992–93 Division 1; 1993– FA Premier League.

LATEST SEQUENCES

Longest Sequence of League Wins: 13, 25.4.1992 – 18.10.1992.

Longest Sequence of League Defeats: 10, 23.8.1977 – 15.10.1977.

Longest Sequence of League Draws: 4, 20.1.1990 – 24.2.1990.

Longest Sequence of Unbeaten League Matches: 14, 22.4.1950 – 30.9.1950.

Longest Sequence Without a League Win: 21, 14.1.1978 – 23.8.1978.

Successive Scoring Runs: 25 from 15.4.1939.

Successive Non-scoring Runs: 6 from 31.12.1938.

TEN YEAR LEAGUE RECORD

		P	*W*	*D*	*L*	*F*	*A*	*Pts*	*Pos*
1993-94	PR Lge	42	23	8	11	82	41	77	3
1994-95	PR Lge	42	20	12	10	67	47	72	6
1995-96	PR Lge	38	24	6	8	66	37	78	2
1996-97	PR Lge	38	19	11	8	73	40	68	2
1997-98	PR Lge	38	11	11	16	35	44	44	13
1998-99	PR Lge	38	11	13	14	48	54	46	13
1999-2000	PR Lge	38	14	10	14	63	54	52	11
2000-01	PR Lge	38	14	9	15	44	50	51	11
2001-02	PR Lge	38	21	8	9	74	52	71	4
2002-03	PR Lge	38	21	6	11	63	48	69	3

DID YOU KNOW ?

In 2002–03 Alan Shearer scored his 300th career club goal, became the first player to score a century of Premier League goals for two clubs, equalled its fastest goal and scored his first European match hat-trick for Newcastle United.

NEWCASTLE UNITED 2002–03 LEAGUE RECORD

Match No.	Date	Venue	Opponents	Result		H/T Score	Lg. Pos.	Goalscorers	Attendance
1	Aug 19	H	West Ham U	W	4-0	0-0	—	Lua-Lua 2 61, 72, Shearer 76, Solano 86	51,072
2	24	A	Manchester C	L	0-1	0-1	10		34,776
3	Sept 2	A	Liverpool	D	2-2	0-0	—	Speed 80, Shearer 88	43,241
4	11	H	Leeds U	L	0-2	0-1	—		51,730
5	14	A	Chelsea	L	0-3	0-2	19		39,756
6	21	H	Sunderland	W	2-0	2-0	15	Bellamy 2, Shearer 39	52,181
7	28	A	Birmingham C	W	2-0	1-0	10	Solano 34, Ameobi 90	29,072
8	Oct 5	H	WBA	W	2-1	1-1	8	Shearer 2 45, 69	52,142
9	19	A	Blackburn R	L	2-5	1-2	11	Shearer 2 (1 pen) 36 (p), 48	27,307
10	26	H	Charlton Ath	W	2-1	1-1	9	Griffin 37, Robert 59	51,607
11	Nov 4	H	Middlesbrough	W	2-0	1-0	—	Ameobi 20, Caldwell 87	51,558
12	9	A	Arsenal	L	0-1	0-1	9		38,121
13	16	H	Southampton	W	2-1	1-1	6	Ameobi 41, Hughes 54	51,812
14	23	A	Manchester U	L	3-5	1-3	8	Bernard 35, Shearer 52, Bellamy 75	67,625
15	Dec 1	H	Everton	W	2-1	0-1	6	Shearer 86, Li Tie (og) 89	51,607
16	7	A	Aston Villa	W	1-0	0-0	6	Shearer 82	35,446
17	14	A	Southampton	D	1-1	0-0	6	Bellamy 50	32,061
18	21	H	Fulham	W	2-0	1-0	6	Solano 8, Bellamy 70	51,576
19	26	A	Bolton W	L	3-4	1-3	6	Shearer 2 8, 79, Ameobi 71	27,314
20	29	H	Tottenham H	W	2-1	1-0	4	Speed 17, Shearer 58	52,145
21	Jan 1	H	Liverpool	W	1-0	1-0	4	Robert 13	52,147
22	11	A	West Ham U	D	2-2	1-2	4	Bellamy 9, Jenas 81	35,048
23	18	H	Manchester C	W	2-0	1-0	3	Shearer 1, Bellamy 64	52,152
24	22	H	Bolton W	W	1-0	1-0	1	Jenas 18	52,005
25	29	A	Tottenham H	W	1-0	0-0	—	Jenas 90	36,084
26	Feb 9	H	Arsenal	D	1-1	0-1	3	Robert 53	52,157
27	22	A	Leeds U	W	3-0	1-0	3	Dyer 2 17, 48, Shearer 54	40,025
28	Mar 1	H	Chelsea	W	2-1	1-1	3	Hasselbaink (og) 31, Bernard 53	52,157
29	5	A	Middlesbrough	L	0-1	0-0	—		34,814
30	15	A	Charlton Ath	W	2-0	1-0	3	Shearer (pen) 31, Solano 49	26,704
31	22	H	Blackburn R	W	5-1	1-0	3	Solano 24, Robert 61, Jenas 85, Gresko (og) 89, Bellamy 90	52,106
32	Apr 6	A	Everton	L	1-2	1-1	3	Robert 40	40,031
33	12	H	Manchester U	L	2-6	1-4	3	Jenas 21, Ameobi 89	52,164
34	19	A	Fulham	L	1-2	1-0	3	Shearer 39	17,900
35	21	H	Aston Villa	D	1-1	1-0	4	Solano 37	52,015
36	26	A	Sunderland	W	1-0	1-0	3	Solano (pen) 43	45,067
37	May 3	H	Birmingham C	W	1-0	1-0	3	Viana 42	52,146
38	11	A	WBA	D	2-2	1-0	3	Jenas 44, Viana 80	26,773

Final League Position: 3

GOALSCORERS

League (63): Shearer 17 (2 pens), Bellamy 7, Solano 7 (1 pen), Jenas 6, Ameobi 5, Robert 5, Bernard 2, Dyer 2, Lua-Lua 2, Speed 2, Viana 2, Caldwell 1, Griffin 1, Hughes 1, own goals 3.
Worthington Cup (3): Dyer 2, own goal 1.
FA Cup (2): Jenas 1, Shearer 1 (pen).
Champions League (21): Shearer 7 (2 pens), Ameobi 3, Bellamy 2, Dyer 2, Lua-Lua 2, Viana 2, Solano 1, Speed 1, own goal 1.

Given S 38	Hughes A 35	Bernard O 24 + 6	Dabizas N 13 + 3	Bramble T 13 + 3	Solano N 29 + 2	Dyer K 33 + 2	Jenas J 23 + 9	Shearer A 35	Lua-Lua L 5 + 6	Viana H 11 + 12	McClen J — + 1	Ameobi F 8 + 20	Elliott R — + 2	Speed G 23 + 1	Griffin A 22 + 5	Bellamy C 27 + 2	Robert L 25 + 2	O'Brien Andy 26	Caldwell S 12 + 2	Acuna C 2 + 2	Kerr B 4 + 4	Cort C — + 1	Woodgate J 10	Ambrose D — + 1	Chopra M — + 1	Match No.
1	2	3	4	5	6^{1}	7	8	9	10^{2}	11^{3}	12	13	14													1
1	2	3^{2}	4	5	6	7	8	9	10^{1}	14		12		11^{3}	13											2
1	2	3	4	5	6^{1}	7	12	9	10^{2}	11^{3}				8		13	14									3
1	2	3		5	6	7		9		12		10^{2}		8^{1}	14	13	11	4^{3}								4
1	2	3	4		6^{2}	7	13	9		12		14		8		10^{3}	11^{1}	5								5
1	3		4		6^{3}	7	14	9		12		13		8	2	10^{2}	11^{1}	5								6
1	3		4		6^{2}	7	13	9	10^{1}	14		12		8	2		11^{3}	5								7
1	3	12	4		6^{2}	7	13	9	14					8	2	10^{3}	11^{1}	5								8
1	3^{3}	14	4■	12	6		7	9		13				8	2^{1}	10	11^{2}	5								9
1	3	12		4	6^{2}		7	9		13		10		8	2		11^{1}	5								10
1	5	3			6^{2}	13	7	9		12		10		8	2		11^{1}		4							11
1	3	12	4		6^{2}	10	7	9		11^{1}		13		8	2			5								12
1	3	12	13			7	6	9		11^{1}		10		8	2			5^{2}	4							13
1	3	11^{1}	4		12	7	6	9						8	2	10		5								14
1		3			6	7		9		12		13		8^{1}	2	10	11	5	4^{2}							15
1	5	3			6	7	8	9							2	10	11	4								16
1	3					7	6	9						8	2	10	11	5	4							17
1	3				6^{2}	7^{1}	12	9				13		8^{3}	2	10	11	5	4	14						18
1	3				6^{1}	7	12	9	13			10^{2}		8	2		11	5	4							19
1	2	3	12		6^{3}	7^{1}	13	9	14					8^{2}		10	11	5	4							20
1	6	3					8	9				12	13		2	10	11	5		4^{2}	7^{1}					21
1	6	3				7	8		12			9^{2}			2	10	11		5	4^{1}		13				22
1	2	3	4		6^{1}	7	8	9								10	11		5		12					23
1	2	3	4		6^{1}	7	8	9								10	11		5		12					24
1		3	4	5	12	7	8	9								10	11	2			6^{1}					25
1	2	3		5	6^{1}	7	8	9^{2}				13		12		10	11■	4								26
1	3		12	5		7^{3}		9				13		8	2^{1}	10	11	4		14	6^{2}					27
1	2	3		12	6^{3}	7^{2}		9		11^{1}		13		8	14	10		5					4			28
1	2	3		5		7	6	9		12		13		8^{1}		10	11^{2}						4			29
1	2	3		5	6^{2}	12	7	9		11^{3}		13		8^{1}	14	10							4			30
1	3			5	6^{2}	7	13	9^{3}		12		14		8	2	10	11^{1}						4			31
1		3		5		7	8	9				12			13	10	11	2^{2}			6^{1}		4			32
1	2	3		5	6^{1}	7	8	9	14	13^{3}		12				10	11^{2}						4			33
1	8	3			6^{2}	7		9		11^{1}		12			2■	10		5	13				4			34
1	3	11^{2}		12	6	7		9^{3}	13	8		14			2	10		5					4^{1}			35
1	3	12			6	7	8	9^{2}		11^{1}		13			2	10		5^{3}	14				4			36
1	2	3			6^{2}	7	8			11^{1}		9				10	12		5		13		4			37
1	3				6^{2}	7^{1}	8		10^{3}	11		9			2			5	4		12			13	14	38

Worthington Cup

Third Round	Everton	(h)	3-3

Champions League

Third Qualifying Round	Zeljeznicar	(a)	1-0
		(h)	4-0
Group E	Dynamo Kiev	(a)	0-2
	Feyenoord	(h)	0-1
	Juventus	(a)	0-2
		(h)	1-0
	Dynamo Kiev	(h)	2-1
	Feynoord	(a)	3-2

FA Cup

Third Round	Wolverhampton W	(a)	2-3

Champions League

Second Stage Group A	Internazionale	(h)	1-4
	Barcelona	(a)	1-3
	Leverkusen	(a)	3-1
		(h)	3-1
	Internazionale	(a)	2-2
	Barcelona	(h)	0-2

NORTHAMPTON TOWN — Division 3

FOUNDATION

Formed in 1897 by school teachers connected with the Northampton and District Elementary Schools' Association, they survived a financial crisis at the end of their first year when they were £675 in the red and became members of the Midland League – a fast move indeed for a new club. They achieved Southern League membership in 1901.

Sixfields Stadium, Upton Way, Northampton NN5 5QA.

Telephone: (01604) 757 773. ***Fax:*** (01604) 751 613.
Website: www.ntfc.co.uk
Email: via website.
Ticket Office: (01604) 588 338.

Ground Capacity: 7,653 (all seated).

Record Attendance: (at County Ground): 24,523 v Fulham, Division 1, 23 April 1966; (at Sixfields Stadium): 7,557 v Manchester C, Division 2, 26 September 1998.

Record Receipts (at Sixfields): £102,979 v Tottenham H, Worthington Cup 3rd rd, 27 October 1998.

Pitch Measurements: 116yd × 72yd.

Chairman: D. Cardoza.
Directors: T. Cardoza, T. Clarke MP, B. Stonhill, B. Hancock, B. Egan.

Company Secretary: Norman Howells.

Manager: Martin Wilkinson.
Assistant: Manager: Richard Hill.
Coach: Mark Kearney.
Physio: Denis Casey.

Sales Manager: Paul Martin.

Stadium Manager: Tom Holland.

Colours: Claret shirts with thin white piping, white shorts, claret stockings.

Change Colours: All white.

Year Formed: 1897.

Turned Professional: 1901.

Ltd Co.: 1901.

Previous Ground: 1897, County Ground; 1994, Sixfields Stadium.

Club Nickname: 'The Cobblers'.

First Football League Game: 28 August 1920, Division 3, v Grimsby T (a) L 0–2 – Thorpe; Sproston, Hewison; Jobey, Tomkins, Pease; Whitworth, Lockett, Thomas, Freeman, MacKechnie.

Record League Victory: 10–0 v Walsall, Division 3 (S), 5 November 1927 – Hammond; Watson, Jeffs; Allen, Brett, Odell; Daley, Smith (3), Loasby (3), Hoten (1), Wells (3).

HONOURS

Football League: Division 1 best season: 21st, 1965–66; Division 2 – Runners-up 1964–65; Division 3 – Champions 1962–63; Promoted from Division 3 1996–97 (play-offs); Division 3 (S) – Runners-up 1927–28, 1949–50; Division 4 – Champions 1986–87; Runners-up 1975–76.

FA Cup: best season: 5th rd, 1934, 1950, 1970.

Football League Cup: best season: 5th rd, 1965, 1967.

SKY SPORTS FACT FILE

Centre-half Frankie Howard was the first player transferred by Northampton Town. In the 1898–99 season he was sold to Derby County for £50, made one appearance and returned to Northampton via Wellingborough.

Record Cup Victory: 10–0 v Sutton T, FA Cup prel rd, 7 December 1907 – Cooch; Drennan, Lloyd Davies, Tirrell (1), McCartney, Hickleton, Badenock (3), Platt (3), Lowe (1), Chapman (2), McDiarmid.

Record Defeat: 0–11 v Southampton, Southern League, 28 December 1901.

Most League Points (2 for a win): 68, Division 4, 1975–76.

Most League Points (3 for a win): 99, Division 4, 1986–87.

Most League Goals: 109, Division 3, 1962–63 and Division 3 (S), 1952–53.

Highest League Scorer in Season: Cliff Holton, 36, Division 3, 1961–62.

Most League Goals in Total Aggregate: Jack English, 135, 1947–60.

Most League Goals in One Match: 5, Ralph Hoten v Crystal Palace, Division 3S, 27 October 1928.

Most Capped Player: E. Lloyd Davies, 12 (16), Wales.

Most League Appearances: Tommy Fowler, 521, 1946–61.

Youngest League Player: Adrian Mann, 16 years 297 days v Bury, 5 May 1984.

Record Transfer Fee Received: £265,000 from Watford for Richard Hill, July 1987.

Record Transfer Fee Paid: £150,000 to FC Utrecht for Jamie Forrester, July 2000.

Football League Record: 1920 Original Member of Division 3; 1921 Division 3 (S); 1958–61 Division 4; 1961–63 Division 3; 1963–65 Division 2; 1965–66 Division 1; 1966–67 Division 2; 1967–69 Division 3; 1969–76 Division 4; 1976–77 Division 3; 1977–87 Division 4; 1987–90 Division 3; 1990–92 Division 4; 1992–97 Division 3; 1997–99 Division 2; 1999–2000 Division 3; 2000–03 Division 2; 2003– Division 3.

MANAGERS

Arthur Jones 1897–1907
(Secretary-Manager)
Herbert Chapman 1907–12
Walter Bull 1912–13
Fred Lessons 1913–19
Bob Hewison 1920–25
Jack Tresadern 1925–30
Jack English 1931–35
Syd Puddefoot 1935–37
Warney Cresswell 1937–39
Tom Smith 1939–49
Bob Dennison 1949–54
Dave Smith 1954–59
David Bowen 1959–67
Tony Marchi 1967–68
Ron Flowers 1968–69
Dave Bowen 1969–72
(continued as General Manager and Secretary to 1985 when joined the board)
Billy Baxter 1972–73
Bill Dodgin Jnr 1973–76
Pat Crerand 1976–77
Bill Dodgin Jnr 1977
John Petts 1977–78
Mike Keen 1978–79
Clive Walker 1979–80
Bill Dodgin Jnr 1980–82
Clive Walker 1982–84
Tony Barton 1984–85
Graham Carr 1985–90
Theo Foley 1990–92
Phil Chard 1992–93
John Barnwell 1993–95
Ian Atkins 1995–99
Kevin Wilson 1999–2001
Kevan Broadhurst 2001–03
Terry Fenwick 2003
Martin Wilkinson April 2003–

LATEST SEQUENCES

Longest Sequence of League Wins: 8, 27.8.1960 – 19.9.1960.

Longest Sequence of League Defeats: 8, 26.10.1935 – 21.12.1935.

Longest Sequence of League Draws: 6, 18.9.1983 – 15.10.1983.

Longest Sequence of Unbeaten League Matches: 21, 27.9.1986 – 6.2.1987.

Longest Sequence Without a League Win: 18, 26.3.1969 – 20.9.1969.

Successive Scoring Runs: 27 from 23.8.1986.

Successive Non-scoring Runs: 7 from 7.4.1939.

TEN YEAR LEAGUE RECORD

		P	*W*	*D*	*L*	*F*	*A*	*Pts*	*Pos*
1993-94	Div 3	42	9	11	22	44	66	38	22
1994-95	Div 3	42	10	14	18	45	67	44	17
1995-96	Div 3	46	18	13	15	51	44	67	11
1996-97	Div 3	46	20	12	14	67	44	72	4
1997-98	Div 2	46	18	17	11	52	37	71	4
1998-99	Div 2	46	10	18	18	43	57	48	22
1999-2000	Div 3	46	25	7	14	63	45	82	3
2000-01	Div 2	46	15	12	19	46	59	57	18
2001-02	Div 2	46	14	7	25	54	79	49	20
2002-03	Div 2	46	10	9	27	40	79	39	24

DID YOU KNOW ?

In 1975–76 Northampton Town were unbeaten at home in Division Four with club records established from 68 points, 29 overall wins and only seven defeats. As runners-up they were promoted.

NORTHAMPTON TOWN 2002–03 LEAGUE RECORD

Match No.	Date	Venue	Opponents	Result	H/T Score	Lg. Pos.	Goalscorers	Attendance
1	Aug 10	H	Crewe Alex	D 1-1	0-1	—	Gabbiadini [87]	5694
2	13	A	Wycombe W	D 1-1	0-0	—	Forrester [69]	5993
3	17	A	Cardiff C	W 2-1	1-1	8	Gabbiadini 2 [10, 50]	13,321
4	23	H	Blackpool	L 0-1	0-0	—		5556
5	27	A	Chesterfield	L 0-4	0-3	—		3585
6	31	H	Barnsley	W 1-0	0-0	16	McGregor [74]	5004
7	Sept 6	A	Bristol C	L 0-3	0-1	—		11,104
8	14	H	Huddersfield T	D 0-0	0-0	18		4679
9	17	H	Colchester U	W 4-1	3-1	—	Gabbiadini 3 [15, 45, 60], One [23]	3663
10	21	A	Swindon T	L 0-2	0-1	15		4719
11	28	H	Mansfield T	W 2-0	1-0	12	Gabbiadini (pen) [3], Trollope [80]	5594
12	Oct 5	A	Plymouth Arg	D 0-0	0-0	11		8530
13	12	H	Brentford	L 1-2	0-2	14	Asamoah [90]	5739
14	19	A	Notts Co	L 1-2	0-0	16	Asamoah [79]	6009
15	26	H	Cheltenham T	L 1-2	1-1	18	Forrester [24]	5354
16	29	A	Oldham Ath	L 0-4	0-1	—		5512
17	Nov 2	H	Luton T	W 3-0	2-0	16	Forrester 2 [9, 19], Gabbiadini [50]	5750
18	9	A	QPR	W 1-0	0-0	14	Trollope [61]	11,947
19	23	H	Port Vale	W 3-0	1-0	12	Gabbiadini 2 [38, 56], Forrester [89]	4357
20	30	A	Wigan Ath	L 0-1	0-1	14		6032
21	Dec 14	H	Tranmere R	L 0-4	0-1	16		4268
22	20	A	Stockport Co	L 0-4	0-1	—		4516
23	26	H	Chesterfield	L 0-1	0-0	19		5282
24	28	A	Peterborough U	D 0-0	0-0	20		7767
25	Jan 1	A	Barnsley	W 2-1	1-1	14	Lumsdon (og) [45], Stamp [70]	9531
26	4	H	Wycombe W	L 0-5	0-2	15		4679
27	18	A	Blackpool	L 1-2	1-0	16	Stamp [33]	5646
28	25	H	Peterborough U	L 0-1	0-0	19		5906
29	Feb 1	A	Crewe Alex	D 3-3	1-2	19	Gabbiadini (pen) [45], Hope [63], Asamoah [81]	6164
30	4	H	Cardiff C	L 0-1	0-0	—		4553
31	8	H	QPR	D 1-1	1-0	21	Rahim [16]	5859
32	15	A	Luton T	L 2-3	1-1	22	Burgess [23], Johnson (pen) [71]	7048
33	22	H	Bristol C	L 1-2	1-2	23	McGregor [45]	4688
34	Mar 1	A	Huddersfield T	L 0-2	0-2	23		9651
35	4	A	Colchester U	L 0-2	0-1	—		3408
36	8	H	Swindon T	W 1-0	0-0	23	Harsley [61]	5566
37	15	A	Cheltenham T	D 1-1	0-0	24	Harsley [75]	4917
38	18	H	Notts Co	W 2-0	1-0	—	Asamoah [24], Sampson [82]	5254
39	22	H	Oldham Ath	L 0-2	0-0	23		5646
40	29	A	Brentford	L 0-3	0-0	23		5354
41	Apr 4	H	Wigan Ath	L 0-2	0-2	—		5822
42	12	A	Port Vale	L 2-3	0-1	24	Gabbiadini [62], Dudfield [88]	4209
43	18	H	Stockport Co	L 0-3	0-3	—		5873
44	21	A	Tranmere R	L 0-4	0-0	24		7348
45	26	H	Plymouth Arg	D 2-2	0-1	24	Stamp [66], Morison [72]	5063
46	May 3	A	Mansfield T	L 1-2	1-0	24	Stamp [1]	3928

Final League Position: 24

GOALSCORERS

League (40): Gabbiadini 12 (2 pens), Forrester 5, Asamoah 4, Stamp 4, Harsley 2, McGregor 2, Trollope 2, Burgess 1, Dudfield 1, Hope 1, Johnson 1 (pen), Morison 1, One 1, Rahim 1, Sampson 1, own goal 1.
Worthington Cup (0).
FA Cup (5): Asamoah 1, Gabbiadini 1, Hargreaves 1, Harsley 1, Stamp 1.
LDV Vans Trophy (6): Forrester 2 (1 pen), Asamoah 1, Gabbiadini 1, Hargreaves 1, Rickers 1.

Harper L 31	Gill J 41	Spedding D 9 + 2	Harsley P 41 + 4	Hope R 17 + 6	Marsh C 15	McGregor P 17 + 6	Trollope P 41	Forrester J 18 + 7	Stamp D 12 + 10	Hargreaves C 36 + 3	Carruthers C 26 + 7	Asamoah D 20 + 22	Gabbiadini M 33 + 8	Burgess D 24 + 1	Morison S 4 + 9	Sampson I 31 + 2	Rickers P 8 + 3	One A 6	Abbey N 4 + 1	Frain J 13 + 1	Lincoln G 5 + 7	Thompson G 11	Reid P 19	Turner A — + 3	Rahim B 6	Johnson R 5 + 1	Dudfield L 8 + 2	Youngs T 5	Chambers L — + 1	*Match No.*
1	2	3	4^{1}	5	6	7^{2}	8	9	10^{3}	11	12	13	14																	1
1	2	3	4	5	6		8	9		11			12	7	10^{1}															2
1	2	3	7		6^{1}		8	9^{2}		11	12	13	10^{3}	5	14	4														3
1	2	3	4		6^{1}	12	7	9^{2}		11		13	10	5		8														4
1	2	3	7^{1}			12	8	9^{3}		11	6	13	10^{2}	5	14	4														5
1	2	3	6			12	7	9^{2}		11	13	8^{3}	10^{1}	5	14	4■														6
1	2	3	7			8		12		11	6	9^{1}	10^{2}	5■		4	13													7
1	2		4			7^{2}	8	12		11	6	13	10	5			3	9^{1}												8
1	2		6			7	8	12		11	3	13	10^{1}	5^{3}		4	14	9^{2}												9
1■	2	3	4			7^{2}	8	12		11	5	13	10^{6}			6		9^{1}	15											10
1	2		6	12			8	13		11	3	14	10^{2}	5		4	7^{1}	9^{3}												11
	2		6				8			11	3	12	10	5		4	7	9^{1}	1											12
1	2		6^{3}	14			8	12		11	3	13	10	5		4	7^{2}	9^{1}												13
1	2			12			8	9		11	3	7	10	5^{1}	13	4	6^{2}													14
1			12	5			8	9^{3}		11	6	13	10	2	14	4	7^{1}			3^{2}										15
1			6	5			8	9		11		12	10^{2}	2		4	7^{1}			3	13									16
1	2		6	12			8	9		11	13	7^{3}	10^{1}	5		4	14			3^{2}										17
1	2		6	12			8	9^{2}		11	3	13	10^{1}	5		4	7^{3}				14									18
1	2		6				8	9	12	11	3	7^{1}	10	5		4														19
1	2	12	6				8	9	13	11^{1}	3	7^{2}	10■	5		4														20
	2	3^{1}	6			7^{2}	8	9^{3}	10	11	12	13		5		4					14	1								21
	2		4	5	6	7^{2}	8	9		11	3	10^{1}			12						13	1								22
	2		6	4	3	12	8	9^{1}	10^{3}	11	13	7		5^{2}	14							1								23
	2		6	4	5	11	8	9^{1}	12		3	13	10								7^{2}	1								24
	2		6	5	3		8		9	11		12	10^{1}			4						1	7							25
	2^{2}		6	5^{1}	3		8^{3}	12	9	11	14	13	10			4						1	7							26
			6	5	2	11		9^{3}	8^{1}		3	7	10^{2}			12			1	13			4	14						27
	2		6	5		11^{1}			9■		3	8	10	12					1				4	13	7^{2}					28
	2		6	5		11	8				3	9	10^{1}								12	1	4		7					29
	2		6^{1}	5		11^{3}	8		12		3	9	10^{2}								13	1	4	14	7					30
	2		12	5		11^{1}	8				3	9	10									1	4		7	6				31
	2		12			11^{1}	8		10		3	9		5								1	4		7	6				32
	2		12			11	8^{3}		13	14	3	9	10	5					1				4		7^{2}	6^{1}				33
1	2		6			9^{2}	8^{3}		12	11	7^{1}		10	5						3	13		4			14				34
1	2		6^{2}			9	8		12	11		13	10^{1}	5^{3}		14				3			4			7				35
1	2		6			12	8		10^{2}	11		9^{1}	13			5				3			4			7				36
1	2		6				8		10^{1}	11^{2}		9	12			5				3	7		4				13			37
1	2	12	6				8^{3}		13	14		7	10^{1}			5				3	11		4				9^{2}			38
1	2		8		6^{1}	12				11	3	7	10^{2}		13	5							4				9			39
1	2		8		6^{1}					11		12			7	5				3			4				9	10		40
1	2		6^{1}				8			12		13	14		11^{3}	5				3	7		4				9^{2}	10		41
1	2		6				8		12	11			10^{1}			5				3	7^{2}		4				13	9		42
1	2		6	12			8		13	11		14	10^{3}			5				3			4^{1}				9	7^{2}		43
1	2^{2}		7	4	6		8			11		13	12			5				3							9	10^{1}		44
1			6	4	2		8		10	11	3	7^{2}	12		13	5											9^{1}			45
			6	4	2		8		10^{1}	11	3		12		7	5						1					9^{2}		13	46

Worthington Cup

First Round	Wigan Ath	(h)	0-1

LDV Vans Trophy

First Round	Hereford U	(a)	4-3
Second Round	Cambridge U	(h)	2-4

FA Cup

First Round	Boston U	(h)	3-2
Second Round	Cambridge U	(a)	2-2
		(h)	0-1

NORWICH CITY — Division 1

FOUNDATION

Formed in 1902, largely through the initiative of two local schoolmasters who called a meeting at the Criterion Cafe, they were shocked by an FA Commission which in 1904 declared the club professional and ejected them from the FA Amateur Cup. However, this only served to strengthen their determination. New officials were appointed and a professional club established at a meeting in the Agricultural Hall in March 1905.

Carrow Road, Norwich NR1 1JE.

Telephone: (01603) 760 760. ***Fax:*** (01603) 613 886.
Box Office: 0870 444 1902. ***ClubCall:*** 09068 121 144.

Ground Capacity: 21,468.

Record Attendance: 43,984 v Leicester C, FA Cup 6th rd, 30 March 1963.

Record Receipts: £339,005 v Chelsea, FA Cup 3rd rd, 5 January 2002.

Pitch Measurements: 114yd × 74yd.

President: G. C. Watling. ***Chairman:*** R. J. Munby.
Vice-chairman: B. J. Skipper.
Chief Executive: N. A. Doncaster.
Company Secretary: S. O'Hara.
Directors: M. M. Foulger, M. Wynn Jones, D. Smith.

First Team Manager: Nigel Worthington.
Assistant Manager: Doug Livermore. ***First Team Coach:*** Steve Foley.
Director of Academy: Sammy Morgan.
Coach: Keith Webb. ***Physio:*** Neil Reynolds, MCSP, SRP.

Club Secretary: Kevan Platt.

Colours: Yellow shirts, green shorts, yellow stockings.

Change Colours: All green.

Year Formed: 1902.

Turned Professional: 1905.

Ltd Co.: 1905.

Club Nickname: 'The Canaries'.

Previous Grounds: 1902, Newmarket Road; 1908, The Nest, Rosary Road; 1935, Carrow Road.

First Football League Game: 28 August 1920, Division 3, v Plymouth Arg (a) D 1–1 – Skermer; Gray, Gadsden; Wilkinson, Addy, Martin; Laxton, Kidger, Parker, Whitham (1), Dobson.

Record League Victory: 10–2 v Coventry C, Division 3 (S), 15 March 1930 – Jarvie; Hannah, Graham; Brown, O'Brien, Lochhead (1); Porter (1), Anderson, Hunt (5), Scott (2), Slicer (1).

HONOURS

FA Premier League: best season: 3rd 1992–93.

Football League: Division 2 – Champions 1971–72, 1985–86; Division 3 (S) – Champions 1933–34; Division 3 – Runners-up 1959–60.

FA Cup: Semi-finals 1959, 1989, 1992.

Football League Cup: Winners 1962, 1985; Runners-up 1973, 1975.

European Competitions: *UEFA Cup:* 1993–94.

SKY SPORTS FACT FILE

At the start of the 2002–03 season Norwich City were undefeated in their first six League matches during which time they fielded the same starting line-up and replaced the same three players by the same three substitutes.

Record Cup Victory: 8–0 v Sutton U, FA Cup 4th rd, 28 January 1989 – Gunn; Culverhouse, Bowen, Butterworth, Linighan, Townsend (Crook), Gordon, Fleck (3), Allen (4), Phelan, Putney (1).

Record Defeat: 2–10 v Swindon T, Southern League, 5 September 1908.

Most League Points (2 for a win): 64, Division 3 (S), 1950–51.

Most League Points (3 for a win): 84, Division 2, 1985–86.

Most League Goals: 99, Division 3 (S), 1952–53.

Highest League Scorer in Season: Ralph Hunt, 31, Division 3 (S), 1955–56.

Most League Goals in Total Aggregate: Johnny Gavin, 122, 1945–54, 1955–58.

Most League Goals in One Match: 5, Tommy Hunt v Coventry C, Division 3S, 15 March 1930; 5, Roy Hollis v Walsall, Division 3S, 29 December 1951.

Most Capped Player: Mark Bowen, 35 (41), Wales.

Most League Appearances: Ron Ashman, 592, 1947–64.

Youngest League Player: Ryan Jarvis, 16 years 282 days v Walsall, 19 April 2003.

Record Transfer Fee Received: £5,000,000 from Blackburn R for Chris Sutton, July 1994.

Record Transfer Fee Paid: £1,000,000 to Leeds U for Jon Newsome, June 1994.

Football League Record: 1920 Original Member of Division 3; 1921 Division 3 (S): 1934–39 Division 2; 1946–58 Division 3 (S); 1958–60 Division 3; 1960–72 Division 2; 1972–74 Division 1; 1974–75 Division 2; 1975–81 Division 1; 1981–82 Division 2; 1982–85 Division 1; 1985–86 Division 2; 1986–92 Division 1; 1992–95 FA Premier League; 1995– Division 1.

MANAGERS

John Bowman 1905–07
James McEwen 1907–08
Arthur Turner 1909–10
Bert Stansfield 1910–15
Major Frank Buckley 1919–20
Charles O'Hagan 1920–21
Albert Gosnell 1921–26
Bert Stansfield 1926
Cecil Potter 1926–29
James Kerr 1929–33
Tom Parker 1933–37
Bob Young 1937–39
Jimmy Jewell 1939
Bob Young 1939–45
Cyril Spiers 1946–47
Duggie Lochhead 1947–50
Norman Low 1950–55
Tom Parker 1955–57
Archie Macaulay 1957–61
Willie Reid 1961–62
George Swindin 1962
Ron Ashman 1962–66
Lol Morgan 1966–69
Ron Saunders 1969–73
John Bond 1973–80
Ken Brown 1980–87
Dave Stringer 1987–92
Mike Walker 1992–94
John Deehan 1994–95
Martin O'Neill 1995
Gary Megson 1995–96
Mike Walker 1996–98
Bruce Rioch 1998–2000
Bryan Hamilton 2000
Nigel Worthington January 2001–

LATEST SEQUENCES

Longest Sequence of League Wins: 10, 23.11.1985 – 25.1.1986.

Longest Sequence of League Defeats: 7, 1.4.1995 – 6.5.1995.

Longest Sequence of League Draws: 7, 15.1.1994 – 26.2.1994.

Longest Sequence of Unbeaten League Matches: 20, 31.8.1950 – 30.12.1950.

Longest Sequence Without a League Win: 25, 22.9.1956 – 23.2.1957.

Successive Scoring Runs: 25 from 31.8.1963.

Successive Non-scoring Runs: 5 from 21.2.1925.

TEN YEAR LEAGUE RECORD

		P	W	D	L	F	A	Pts	Pos
1993-94	PR Lge	42	12	17	13	65	61	53	12
1994-95	PR Lge	42	10	13	19	37	54	43	20
1995-96	Div 1	46	14	15	17	59	55	57	16
1996-97	Div 1	46	17	12	17	63	68	63	13
1997-98	Div 1	46	14	13	19	52	69	55	15
1998-99	Div 1	46	15	17	14	62	61	62	9
1999-2000	Div 1	46	14	15	17	45	50	57	12
2000-01	Div 1	46	14	12	20	46	58	54	15
2001-02	Div 1	46	22	9	15	60	51	75	6
2002-03	Div 1	46	19	12	15	60	49	69	8

DID YOU KNOW ?

On 13 September 1952, Norwich City enjoyed their best away win by beating Shrewsbury Town 8-1 at Gay Meadow. Tom Johnston scored four of the goals and the victory was achieved despite Don Pickwick breaking his leg before half-time.

NORWICH CITY 2002–03 LEAGUE RECORD

Match No.	Date	Venue	Opponents	Result		H/T Score	Lg. Pos.	Goalscorers	Attendance
1	Aug 10	H	Grimsby T	W	4-0	2-0	—	Mulryne 2 [30, 60], McVeigh 2 [42, 70]	19,869
2	13	A	Rotherham U	D	1-1	0-0	—	Nielsen [87]	7687
3	17	A	Brighton & HA	W	2-0	0-0	2	McVeigh [59], Easton [67]	6730
4	24	H	Gillingham	W	1-0	1-0	2	McVeigh [39]	20,588
5	26	A	Stoke C	D	1-1	0-0	3	Drury [47]	13,931
6	31	H	Watford	W	4-0	1-0	2	McVeigh [29], Roberts [49], Mulryne [66], Nielsen [88]	20,563
7	Sept 7	H	Sheffield U	L	2-3	0-3	3	McVeigh [85], MacKay [90]	20,075
8	15	A	Ipswich T	D	1-1	0-0	3	MacKay [79]	29,112
9	18	A	Reading	W	2-0	2-0	—	McVeigh [3], Mulryne [5]	14,335
10	21	H	Portsmouth	W	1-0	0-0	3	Roberts [81]	21,335
11	28	A	Preston NE	W	2-1	1-0	3	Nielsen [35], McVeigh [54]	13,550
12	Oct 5	H	Leicester C	D	0-0	0-0	3		20,952
13	19	H	Millwall	W	3-1	1-0	2	Nielsen 2 [43, 59], Kenton [73]	20,448
14	23	A	Coventry C	D	1-1	0-1	—	McVeigh [90]	16,409
15	26	A	Bradford C	L	1-2	0-1	2	Abbey [70]	12,888
16	29	H	Nottingham F	D	0-0	0-0	—		20,986
17	Nov 2	A	Wimbledon	L	2-4	0-3	4	Henderson [71], Nielsen [79]	3908
18	9	H	Sheffield W	W	3-0	2-0	3	Roberts 2 (1 pen) [31 (p), 82], McVeigh [44]	20,667
19	16	H	Crystal Palace	W	2-0	1-0	3	McVeigh [9], Roberts [87]	20,907
20	23	A	Burnley	L	0-2	0-0	3		16,282
21	30	H	Derby Co	W	1-0	0-0	4	MacKay [82]	20,522
22	Dec 7	A	Wolverhampton W	L	0-1	0-1	3		25,753
23	14	A	Crystal Palace	L	0-2	0-2	4		16,791
24	21	H	Walsall	W	2-1	0-0	4	MacKay [55], Mulryne [60]	19,872
25	26	H	Brighton & HA	L	0-1	0-1	5		20,687
26	28	A	Grimsby T	D	1-1	0-0	4	Abbey [51]	8306
27	Jan 11	H	Rotherham U	D	1-1	0-1	4	McVeigh [59]	19,452
28	19	A	Watford	L	1-2	0-1	5	Cox (og) [53]	13,338
29	Feb 1	H	Stoke C	D	2-2	2-0	7	Roberts [2], MacKay [23]	20,186
30	8	A	Sheffield W	D	2-2	2-0	5	Healy [18], Roberts [43]	19,114
31	22	A	Sheffield U	W	1-0	0-0	7	McVeigh [69]	19,020
32	25	A	Gillingham	L	0-1	0-0	—		7935
33	Mar 2	H	Ipswich T	L	0-2	0-0	7		21,243
34	5	H	Reading	L	0-1	0-0	—		18,970
35	12	A	Portsmouth	L	2-3	0-0	—	Easton [58], Rivers [62]	19,221
36	15	H	Coventry C	W	2-0	1-0	8	Nedergaard [33], Drury [90]	20,099
37	18	A	Millwall	W	2-0	2-0	—	MacKay [8], Abbey [38]	6854
38	22	A	Nottingham F	L	0-4	0-2	8		27,296
39	25	H	Wimbledon	W	1-0	1-0	—	Healy [40]	21,059
40	29	H	Bradford C	W	3-2	0-1	8	Rivers 2 (1 pen) [49 (p), 86], Abbey [54]	18,536
41	Apr 5	A	Derby Co	L	1-2	1-1	8	McVeigh [10]	23,643
42	12	H	Burnley	W	2-0	1-0	8	Nedergaard [3], Abbey [67]	20,026
43	19	A	Walsall	D	0-0	0-0	8		7018
44	21	H	Wolverhampton W	L	0-3	0-0	8		20,843
45	27	A	Leicester C	D	1-1	0-1	8	Rivers [74]	31,369
46	May 4	H	Preston NE	W	2-0	0-0	8	Mears (og) [46], Mulryne [63]	20,232

Final League Position: 8

GOALSCORERS

League (60): McVeigh 14, Roberts 7 (1 pen), MacKay 6, Mulryne 6, Nielsen 6, Abbey 5, Rivers 4 (1 pen), Drury 2, Easton 2, Healy 2, Nedergaard 2, Henderson 1, Kenton 1, own goals 2.
Worthington Cup (0).
FA Cup (4): Mulryne 2, Abbey 1, McVeigh 1.

Green R 46	Nedergaard S 34 + 1	Drury A 45	Kenton D 36 + 1	Fleming C 28 + 2	Holt G 45	Rivers M 28 + 2	Mulryne P 31 + 2	Roberts I 33 + 10	McVeigh P 38 + 6	Easton C 23 + 3	Notman A 2 + 6	Nielsen D 11 + 22	Heckingbottom P 7 + 8	MacKay M 35 + 2	Russell D 16 + 5	Emblen N 5 + 7	Southall N 4 + 5	Abbey Z 12 + 18	Llewellyn C 2 + 3	Henderson I 4 + 16	Briggs K 1 + 1	Healy D 10 + 3	Sinclair D 1 + 1	Bromby L 5	Shackell J 2	Jarvis R 2 + 1	Match No.
1	2	3	4	5	6	7[1]	8	9[2]	10	11[3]	12	13	14														1
1	2	3	4	5	6	7[1]	8	9	10[3]	11[2]	12	14	13														2
1	2	3	4	5	6	7[1]	8	9	10[2]	11[3]	12	13	14														3
1	2	3	4	5	6	7[2]	8	9	10[3]	11[1]	12	13	14														4
1	2	3	4	5	6	7[1]	8	9	10[2]	11[3]	12	13	14														5
1	2	3	4	5	6	7[1]	8	9	10[2]	11[3]	12	13	14														6
1	2	3	4	5[1]	6		8	9	10[3]	11[2]	7	13		12	14												7
1	2[2]	3	4		6		8	9	10[1]		7[3]	12	11	5	14	13											8
1	2	3	4		6		8	9	10	12			11[1]	5	7[2]	13											9
1	2	3	4		6		8	9	10[2]	12		13	11	5		7[1]											10
1	2	3	4	12	6		8		10[1]			9[3]	11	5		7[2]	13	14									11
1	2	3	4		6		8	9	11			10[2]		5		7[1]	12		13								12
1	2	3	4		6		8	9	10[1]	11		12		5			7										13
1	2[2]	3	4		6		8	9	12			10	11[1]	5		13	7[3]			14							14
1	2	3[1]	4		6		8[2]	9	11[3]			10	12	5		13	7	14									15
1	2	3	4[1]	12	6	13	8[2]	9	11			10		5		7[3]	14										16
1	2	3		4	6			9[3]	10[2]	11[1]		12	8	5			7	14		13							17
1	2	3	4	5	6	7[3]	8[2]	9	11			10[1]					14	12		13							18
1	2	3	4	5[1]	6	7[2]	8	9	11			10[3]		12			13	14									19
1	2	3	4	5	6	7[2]		9	11			10[3]			13	8[1]		14		12							20
1	7[1]	3	2	4	6	11[3]	8	9[2]	10			12		5				13		14							21
1	7[2]	3	2	4	6		8	9[3]	10			12	11[1]	5				14		13							22
1		3	2	4	6	7	8	9[2]	10[1]	11[3]		12		5				14		13							23
1		3	2	4	6	7	8[1]	9[1]	10[2]	11				5				12		13							24
1		3	2[2]	4	6	7	8	9[3]	10	11[1]		12		5				14		13							25
1		3		4	6		8		12			10	13	5	2			9[2]	11	7[1]							26
1		3		4	6	7	8	12	13			14		5	2			9[1]	11[2]	10[3]							27
1		3	2	4	6	7[3]	8	9[1]				10		5	11[2]			12	14	13							28
1		3[1]	2	4	6	7[3]		9	11					5	8			13	12		14	10[2]					29
1	12	3	2	4[1]	6		8	9[2]	11[3]			13		5	7			14				10					30
1	7	3	2	4	6			9	10	11				5						12		8[1]					31
1	7	3	2	4				9[3]	10	11		12		5				14		13		8[1]	6[2]				32
1		3	2	4[1]	6	7[2]	12	9	10	11[3]								14		13		8		5			33
1	2	3	4		6	7	8	12	10[2]	11[3]		13		5	14			9[1]									34
1	2[1]	3			6	7		12	10[2]	11		13		5	8[3]	14		9						4			35
1	2	3			6	7[2]			12	11				5	8			9				10[1]	13	4			36
1	2	3			6	7[2]		12	10	11				5	8			9[1]				13		4			37
1	2	3	12		6	7		13	14	11[3]				5	8			9[2]				10		4[1]			38
1	2	3	4		6	7		12	11			13		5	8			9[1]				10[2]					39
1	2	3	4		6	7[3]		12		11[2]		10[1]		5	8	14		9		13							40
1	2[2]		4		6	7[3]		12	10	11				5	8	13		9[1]				14			3		41
1	2	3	4		6	7[1]		12	11[2]	13				5	8			9		14		10[3]					42
1	2	3		4	6		12	13	10	11[1]				5	7			9[2]				8[3]				14	43
1		3	2	4	6	7	8	9[2]	11[1]					5				13		12		14				10[3]	44
1		3		4	6	12	8	9	13					5	7					11[2]					2	10[1]	45
1		3		4	6	7[3]	8	9[2]	11[1]			12		5	14			13		10	2						46

Worthington Cup
First Round Cheltenham T (h) 0-3

FA Cup
Third Round Brighton & HA (h) 3-1
Fourth Round Dagenham & R (h) 1-0
Fifth Round Southampton (a) 0-2

NOTTINGHAM FOREST Division 1

FOUNDATION

One of the oldest football clubs in the world, Nottingham Forest was formed at a meeting in the Clinton Arms in 1865. Known originally as the Forest Football Club, the game which first drew the founders together was 'shinney', a form of hockey. When they determined to change to football in 1865, one of their first moves was to buy a set of red caps to wear on the field.

City Ground, Nottingham NG2 5FJ.
Telephone: (0115) 982 4444. ***Fax:*** (0115) 982 4455.
Information Desk: (0115) 982 4449.
Commercial Office: (0115) 982 4450. ***Fax:*** (0115) 982 4410. ***Ticket Office:*** (0115) 982 4445. ***Souvenir Shop:*** (0115) 982 4447. ***Junior Reds:*** (0115) 982 4400.
ClubCall: 09068 121 174.
Website: www.nottinghamforest.co.uk

Ground Capacity: 30,602.

Record Attendance: 49,946 v Manchester U, Division 1, 28 October 1967.

Record Receipts: £499,099 v Bayern Munich, UEFA Cup quarter-final 2nd leg, 19 March 1996.

Pitch Measurements: 112yd × 74yd.

Chairman: N. E. Doughty.
Chief Executive: M. A. Arthur.
Finance Director: J. D. Pelling.
Board of Directors: N. E. Doughty, M. A. Arthur, J. D. Pelling, N. G. Candeland.

Manager: Paul Hart. ***First Team Coaches:*** Ian Bowyer, Liam O'Kane. ***Reserve Team Coach:*** Ian McParland.
Goalkeeping Coach: Andy Beesley.
Physios: Gary Fleming, Steve Devine.

Secretary: Paul White. ***Press Officer:*** Fraser Nicholson.

Colours: Red shirts, white shorts, red stockings.

Change Colours: All white.

Year Formed: 1865. ***Turned Professional:*** 1889.

Ltd Co.: 1982. ***Club Nickname:*** 'Reds'.

HONOURS

Football League: Division 1 – Champions 1977–78, 1997–98; Runners-up 1966–67, 1978–79; Division 2 – Champions 1906–07, 1921–22; Runners-up 1956–57; Division 3 (S) – Champions 1950–51.

FA Cup: Winners 1898, 1959; Runners-up 1991.

Football League Cup: Winners 1978, 1979, 1989, 1990; Runners-up 1980, 1992.

Anglo-Scottish Cup: Winners 1977;

Simod Cup: Winners 1989.

Zenith Data Systems Cup: Winners: 1992.

European Competitions: *European Fairs Cup:* 1961–62, 1967–68. *European Cup:* 1978–79 (winners), 1979–80 (winners), 1980–81. *Super Cup:* 1979–80 (winners), 1980–81 (runners-up). *World Club Championship:* 1980. *UEFA Cup:* 1983–84, 1984–85, 1995–96.

Previous Grounds: 1865, Forest Racecourse; 1879, The Meadows; 1880, Trent Bridge Cricket Ground; 1882, Parkside, Lenton; 1885, Gregory, Lenton; 1890, Town Ground; 1898, City Ground.

First Football League Game: 3 September 1892, Division 1, v Everton (a) D 2–2 – Brown; Earp, Scott; Hamilton, A. Smith, McCracken; McCallum, W. Smith, Higgins (2), Pike, McInnes.

Record League Victory: 12–0 v Leicester Fosse, Division 1, 12 April 1909 – Iremonger; Dudley, Maltby; Hughes (1), Needham, Armstrong; Hooper (3), Marrison, West (3), Morris (2), Spouncer (3 incl. 1p).

Record Cup Victory: 14–0 v Clapton (away), FA Cup 1st rd, 17 January 1891 – Brown; Earp, Scott; A. Smith, Russell, Jeacock; McCallum (2), 'Tich' Smith (1), Higgins (5), Lindley (4), Shaw (2).

SKY SPORTS FACT FILE

Despite dominating much of Midlands regional soccer in the First World War winning three trophies and the Victory Shield against Everton, Nottingham Forest were disappointed at failing to get elected to an expanded First Division.

Record Defeat: 1–9 v Blackburn R, Division 2, 10 April 1937.

Most League Points (2 for a win): 70, Division 3 (S), 1950–51.

Most League Points (3 for a win): 94, Division 1, 1997–98.

Most League Goals: 110, Division 3 (S), 1950–51.

Highest League Scorer in Season: Wally Ardron, 36, Division 3 (S), 1950–51.

Most League Goals in Total Aggregate: Grenville Morris, 199, 1898–1913.

Most League Goals in One Match: 4, Enoch West v Sunderland, Division 1, 9 November 1907; 4, Tommy Gibson v Burnley, Division 2, 25 January 1913; 4, Tom Peacock v Port Vale, Division 2, 23 December 1933; 4, Tom Peacock v Barnsley, Division 2, 9 November 1935; 4, Tom Peacock v Port Vale, Division 2, 23 November 1935; 4, Tom Peacock v Doncaster R, Division 2, 26 December 1935; 4, Tommy Capel v Gillingham, Division 3S, 18 November 1950; 4, Wally Ardron v Hull C, Division 2, 26 December 1952; 4, Tommy Wilson v Barnsley, Division 2, 9 February 1957; 4, Peter Withe v Ipswich T, Division 1, 4 October 1977.

Most Capped Player: Stuart Pearce, 76 (78), England.

Most League Appearances: Bob McKinlay, 614, 1951–70.

Youngest League Player: Craig Westcarr, 16 years 257 days v Burnley, 13 October 2001.

Record Transfer Fee Received: £8,500,000 from Liverpool for Stan Collymore, June 1995.

Record Transfer Fee Paid: £3,500,000 to Celtic for Pierre van Hooijdonk, March 1997.

Football League Record: 1892 Elected to Division 1; 1906–07 Division 2; 1907–11 Division 1; 1911–22 Division 2; 1922–25 Division 1; 1925–49 Division 2; 1949–51 Division 3 (S); 1951–57 Division 2; 1957–72 Division 1; 1972–77 Division 2; 1977–92 Division 1; 1992–93 FA Premier League; 1993–94 Division 1; 1994–97 FA Premier League; 1997–98 Division 1; 1998–99 FA Premier League; 1999– Division 1.

MANAGERS

Harry Radford 1889–97 *(Secretary-Manager)*
Harry Haslam 1897–1909 *(Secretary-Manager)*
Fred Earp 1909–12
Bob Masters 1912–25
John Baynes 1925–29
Stan Hardy 1930–31
Noel Watson 1931–36
Harold Wightman 1936–39
Billy Walker 1939–60
Andy Beattie 1960–63
Johnny Carey 1963–68
Matt Gillies 1969–72
Dave Mackay 1972
Allan Brown 1973–75
Brian Clough 1975–93
Frank Clark 1993–96
Stuart Pearce 1996–97
Dave Bassett 1997–98 *(previously General Manager from February)*
Ron Atkinson 1998–99
David Platt 1999–2001
Paul Hart July 2001–

LATEST SEQUENCES

Longest Sequence of League Wins: 7, 9.5.1979 – 1.9.1979.

Longest Sequence of League Defeats: 14, 21.3.1913 – 27.9.1913.

Longest Sequence of League Draws: 7, 29.4.1978 – 2.9.1978.

Longest Sequence of Unbeaten League Matches: 42, 26.11.1977 – 25.11.1978.

Longest Sequence Without a League Win: 19, 8.9.1998 – 16.1.1999.

Successive Scoring Runs: 22 from 28.3.1931.

Successive Non-scoring Runs: 6 from 2.9.1970.

TEN YEAR LEAGUE RECORD

		P	*W*	*D*	*L*	*F*	*A*	*Pts*	*Pos*
1993-94	Div 1	46	23	14	9	74	49	83	2
1994-95	PR Lge	42	22	11	9	72	43	77	3
1995-96	PR Lge	38	15	13	10	50	54	58	9
1996-97	PR Lge	38	6	16	16	31	59	34	20
1997-98	Div 1	46	28	10	8	82	42	94	1
1998-99	PR Lge	38	7	9	22	35	69	30	20
1999-2000	Div 1	46	14	14	18	53	55	56	14
2000-01	Div 1	46	20	8	18	55	53	68	11
2001-02	Div 1	46	12	18	16	50	51	54	16
2002-03	Div 1	46	20	14	12	82	50	74	6

DID YOU KNOW ?

When Nottingham Forest met the Old Etonians in the FA Cup semi-final at Kennington Oval on 22 March 1879, they became the first provincial club to appear in the Metropolis in a cup tie. Forest had to put off a friendly with Southwell on the day!

NOTTINGHAM FOREST 2002–03 LEAGUE RECORD

Match No.	*Date*	*Venue*	*Opponents*	*Result*	*H/T Score*	*Lg. Pos.*	*Goalscorers*	*Atten-dance*
1	Aug 10	A	Portsmouth	L 0-2	0-2	—		18,910
2	14	H	Preston NE	D 2-2	0-1	—	Johnson D ^{69}, Jess ^{83}	18,065
3	17	H	Sheffield W	W 4-0	1-0	—	Johnson D ^{3}, Lester ^{47}, Scimeca 2 $^{69, 73}$	21,129
4	24	A	Walsall	L 1-2	0-1	12	Prutton ^{83}	5096
5	28	H	Wimbledon	W 2-0	2-0	—	Johnson D 2 $^{16, 45}$	16,431
6	31	A	Coventry C	W 1-0	1-0	6	Scimeca ^{16}	13,732
7	Sept 14	H	Watford	L 0-1	0-1	11		17,865
8	18	H	Gillingham	W 4-1	3-1	—	Harewood 3 (1 pen) $^{4, 17 (p), 65}$, Johnson D ^{39}	16,073
9	21	A	Grimsby T	W 3-0	1-0	7	Johnson D 3 (1 pen) $^{17, 86 (p), 90}$	7072
10	25	A	Stoke C	D 2-2	2-1	—	Dawson ^{35}, Johnson D ^{45}	14,554
11	28	H	Rotherham U	W 3-2	3-1	4	Johnson D 2 $^{3, 39}$, Bopp ^{18}	25,089
12	Oct 5	A	Millwall	W 2-1	0-1	4	Johnson D 2 $^{65, 85}$	10,521
13	20	A	Derby Co	D 0-0	0-0	4		30,547
14	26	H	Leicester C	D 2-2	0-2	6	Johnson D (pen) ^{76}, Lester ^{90}	29,497
15	29	A	Norwich C	D 0-0	0-0	—		20,986
16	Nov 2	H	Sheffield U	W 3-0	0-0	5	Lester 2 $^{54, 61}$, Harewood ^{63}	22,579
17	9	A	Crystal Palace	D 0-0	0-0	5		18,971
18	16	H	Bradford C	W 3-0	3-0	4	Lester ^{18}, Johnson D ^{25}, Louis-Jean ^{36}	19,653
19	23	A	Wolverhampton W	L 1-2	1-0	4	Harewood ^{45}	27,953
20	27	H	Brighton & HA	W 3-2	2-0	—	Harewood ^{8}, Johnson D ^{45}, Lester ^{76}	29,137
21	30	H	Ipswich T	W 2-1	1-0	3	Johnson D 2 $^{5, 63}$	24,898
22	Dec 7	A	Burnley	L 0-1	0-1	3		13,869
23	14	A	Bradford C	L 0-1	0-1	3		12,245
24	21	H	Reading	W 2-0	1-0	3	Johnson D ^{4}, Harewood ^{67}	25,831
25	26	A	Sheffield W	L 0-2	0-1	4		26,362
26	28	H	Portsmouth	L 1-2	0-0	5	Dawson ^{90}	28,165
27	Jan 1	H	Walsall	D 1-1	1-0	4	Thompson J ^{15}	28,441
28	18	H	Coventry C	D 1-1	1-0	4	Williams ^{33}	24,487
29	25	A	Preston NE	D 1-1	1-1	4	Johnson D ^{16}	13,508
30	Feb 1	A	Wimbledon	W 3-2	2-0	4	Harewood 2 $^{29, 32}$, Johnson D ^{90}	3382
31	8	H	Crystal Palace	W 2-1	1-0	4	Dawson ^{4}; Harewood ^{58}	26,012
32	22	H	Stoke C	W 6-0	4-0	4	Harewood 4 (1 pen) $^{13, 24, 28, 45 (p)}$, Johnson D ^{53}, Jess ^{85}	24,085
33	Mar 1	A	Watford	D 1-1	0-1	5	Huckerby ^{66}	17,944
34	4	A	Gillingham	W 4-1	2-0	—	Huckerby 2 $^{7, 17}$, Harewood ^{46}, Thompson J ^{55}	7277
35	10	H	Grimsby T	D 2-2	1-1	—	Reid Andy ^{23}, Williams ^{90}	25,507
36	15	A	Brighton & HA	L 0-1	0-1	5		6830
37	19	H	Derby Co	W 3-0	2-0	—	Harewood 2 (1 pen) $^{13, 49 (p)}$, Huckerby ^{15}	29,725
38	22	H	Norwich C	W 4-0	2-0	5	Huckerby ^{11}, Harewood ^{22}, Williams ^{56}, Brennan ^{82}	27,296
39	Apr 5	A	Ipswich T	W 4-3	3-2	4	Thompson J ^{27}, Harewood 2 $^{29, 75}$, Naylor (og) ^{32}	29,503
40	8	A	Leicester C	L 0-1	0-1	—		32,065
41	11	H	Wolverhampton W	D 2-2	1-2	—	Johnson D ^{40}, Dawson ^{74}	27,209
42	15	A	Sheffield U	L 0-1	0-0	—		23,317
43	18	A	Reading	L 0-1	0-0	—		21,612
44	21	H	Burnley	W 2-0	0-0	6	Dawson ^{75}, Johnson D ^{90}	25,403
45	26	H	Millwall	D 3-3	2-1	6	Jess ^{19}, Bopp ^{22}, Johnson D ^{72}	29,463
46	May 4	A	Rotherham U	D 2-2	0-0	6	Lester ^{63}, Westcarr ^{66}	9942

Final League Position: 6

GOALSCORERS

League (82): Johnson D 25 (2 pens), Harewood 20 (3 pens), Lester 7, Dawson 5, Huckerby 5, Jess 3, Scimeca 3, Thompson J 3, Williams 3, Bopp 2, Brennan 1, Louis-Jean 1, Prutton 1, Reid Andy 1, Westcarr 1, own goal 1.
Worthington Cup (5): Johnson 2, Lester 2 (1 pen), Scimeca 1.
FA Cup (2): Harewood 1, Reid Andy 1.
Play-offs (4): Johnson 2, Reid Andy 1, own goal 1.

Ward D 45	Louis-Jean M 41	Brennan J 45	Williams G 39 + 1	Hjelde J 19 + 7	Walker D 29 + 2	Prutton D 24	Scimeca R 40	Johnson D 40 + 2	Thompson J 18 + 2	Hall M 1	Lester J 20 + 13	Harewood M 42 + 2	Jess E 17 + 15	Reid Andy 22 + 8	Dawson M 38	Bopp E 10 + 3	Doig C 4 + 6	Westcarr C 2 + 9	Oyen D — + 4	Huckerby D 9	Roche B 1	Cash B — + 1	*Match No.*
1	2	3^{1}	4	5	6	7	8	9	10^{2}	11	12	13											1
1	2	3	4	5	6	7	8^{2}	9			10^{1}	11	12	13									2
1	2	3	4	5	6	7	8	9^{1}			10	11	12										3
1	2	3	4	5■	6	7	8	9			10^{2}	11^{1}	12	13									4
1	2	3	4	5	6	7	8	9			10^{1}	11	12										5
1	2	3	4	5	6	7	8	9			12	10^{2}	11^{1}	13									6
1	2	3			6	7■	4^{1}	9			10■	12	11	13	5	8^{2}							7
1	2	3^{3}	4	12	6^{1}	7		9^{2}			13	10	11		5	8	14						8
1	2	3	4	12	6^{1}	7		9				10	11		5	8							9
1	2	3	4	12	6	7		9^{2}			13	10^{1}	11^{3}	14	5	8							10
1	2	3	4	12	6		7	9^{1}				10	11		5	8							11
1	2	3	4		6		7	9				10	11		5	8							12
1	2	3	12		6	7	4	9			13	10	11^{2}		5	8^{1}							13
1	2	3	4		6	7	8	9			12	10	11^{1}		5								14
1	2	3	4		6	7	8	9			11	10			5								15
1	2^{2}	3	4		6	7	8	9^{1}			11	10	12		5		13						16
1	2	3	4		6	7	8	9^{1}			11	10	12		5								17
1	2	3^{2}	4		6	7	8	9^{1}			11	10^{3}	12	14	5		13						18
1	2	3	4		6	7	8	9^{1}			11	10	12		5								19
1	2	3	4^{2}		6	7	8	9^{3}			11	10^{1}	12	13	5			14					20
1	2	3	4		6	7■	8	9			11	10			5								21
1	2	3	4		6		8	9			7^{1}	10	11	12	5								22
1	2	3	4	12	6		8	9			7^{2}	10	13	11^{3}	5^{1}			14					23
1	2	3	4	6			8	9			7■	10	12	11^{1}	5								24
1	2	3	4	6		7	8	9			11^{1}	10	12		5								25
1	2^{1}	3	4		6^{2}	7		9	12		10		11^{3}	8	5		13	14					26
1	2	3	4			7		9^{2}	11		12	10		8^{1}	5		6	13					27
1		3	4	12	6^{3}	7	8		2			10	13	11^{1}	5		14	9^{2}					28
1		3	4			7	8	9^{1}	2			10		11	5		6	12					29
1	2	3	4				8	9	7			10		11	5		6						30
1	2	3	4	6			8	9	7			10		11^{1}	5		12						31
1	2	3	4	6			8	9^{2}	7^{3}			10^{1}	12	11	5			13	14				32
1		3	4	6			8		2			10	7^{1}	11	5				12	9			33
1		3	4	6			8		2			10	7^{1}	11^{3}	5	12		13	14	9^{2}			34
1	2	3	4	6^{1}			8	12	7			10		11	5					9			35
1	2	3	4	12			6	8^{2}	7^{1}		13	10		11	5					9			36
1	2	3	4	6			8	7^{1}				10	12	11^{2}	5				13	9			37
1	2	3	4	6			8	7				10		11	5					9			38
1	2	3	4	6			7^{1}	8^{2}	12		13	10		11	5					9			39
1	2	3	4	6^{1}	12			8^{2}	7		13	10		11	5					9			40
1	2	3			6		8	9	4		7	10		11	5								41
1	2	3		5	6		8	9^{2}	4		7^{1}	10		11		12		13					42
1	2	3					8	12	4		13	10	11^{1}	7	5	6				9^{2}			43
1	2^{1}	3	4^{3}		12		8	9	6		13	10	7^{2}	11	5	14							44
1		3			6		8	9^{2}	2		12	10	7^{1}	11	5	4		13					45
	2			5	6		8		7^{1}		10		11			4	3	9			1	12	46

Worthington Cup

First Round	Kidderminster H	(h)	4-0
Second Round	Walsall	(h)	1-2

FA Cup

Third Round	West Ham U	(a)	2-3

NOTTS COUNTY — Division 2

FOUNDATION

According to the official history of Notts County 'the true date of Notts' foundation has to be the meeting at the George Hotel on 7 December 1864'. However, in the same opening chapter is the following: *The Nottingham Guardian* on 28 November 1862 carried the following report: 'The opening of the Nottingham Football Club commenced on Tuesday last at Cremorne Gardens. A side was chosen by W. Arkwright and Chas Deakin. A very spirited game resulted in the latter scoring two goals and two rouges against one and one'.

Meadow Lane, Nottingham NG2 3HJ.

Telephone: (0115) 952 9000. ***Fax:*** (0115) 955 3994.
Ticket Office: (0115) 955 7210. ***ClubCall:*** 09068 888 684.
Football in the Community: (0115) 955 7215.
Supporters Club: (0115) 955 7255.

Ground Capacity: 20,300.

Record Attendance: 47,310 v York C, FA Cup 6th rd, 12 March 1955.

Record Receipts: £124,539.10 v Manchester C, FA Cup 6th rd, 16 February 1991.

Pitch Measurements: 113yd × 72yd.

Chairman: Albert Scardino.
Directors: B. Barrowcliffe, P. Joyce, D. Rhodes, J. Scardino, D. Ward.

Manager: Billy Dearden. ***Assistant Manager:*** Gary Brazil.
Youth Coach: John Gaunt. ***Secretary:*** Tony Cuthbert.
Physio: Roger Cleary.

Commercial Manager: Shuna Thompson.
Conference & Banqueting Manager: Matthew Foote.
Stadium Manager: Bob Davy.

Colours: Black with white striped shirts, black shorts, black stockings.

Change Colours: All amber.

Year Formed: 1862* (*see Foundation*).

Turned Professional: 1885. ***Ltd Co.:*** 1888. ***Club Nickname:*** 'Magpies'.

Previous Grounds: 1862, The Park; 1864, The Meadows; 1877, Beeston Cricket Ground; 1880, Castle Ground; 1883, Trent Bridge; 1910, Meadow Lane.

First Football League Game: 15 September 1888, Football League, v Everton (a) L 1–2 – Holland; Guttridge, McLean; Brown, Warburton, Shelton; Hodder, Harker, Jardine, Moore (1), Wardle.

Record League Victory: 11–1 v Newport Co, Division 3 (S), 15 January 1949 – Smith; Southwell, Purvis; Gannon, Baxter, Adamson; Houghton (1), Sewell (4), Lawton (4), Pimbley, Johnston (2).

Record Cup Victory: 15–0 v Rotherham T (at Trent Bridge), FA Cup 1st rd, 24 October 1885 – Sherwin; Snook, H. T. Moore; Dobson (1), Emmett (1), Chapman; Gunn (1), Albert Moore (2), Jackson (3), Daft (2), Cursham (4), (1 og).

HONOURS

Football League: Division 1 best season: 3rd, 1890–91, 1900–01; Division 2 – Champions 1896–97, 1913–14, 1922–23; Runners-up 1894–95, 1980–81; Promoted from Division 2 1990–91 (play-offs); Division 3 (S) – Champions 1930–31, 1949–50; Runners-up 1936–37; Division 3 – Champions 1997–98; Runners-up 1972–73; Promoted from Division 3 1989–90 (play-offs); Division 4 – Champions 1970–71; Runners-up 1959–60.

FA Cup: Winners 1894; Runners-up 1891.

Football League Cup: best season: 5th rd, 1964, 1973, 1976.

Anglo-Italian Cup: Winners 1995; Runners-up 1994.

SKY SPORTS FACT FILE

In 1896–97 Notts County scored in each of their 30 Division Two matches in winning the championship. Their first two home games were actually played at Forest's Town Ground because Trent Bridge was required for cricket.

Record Defeat: 1–9 v Blackburn R, Division 1, 16 November 1889. 1–9 v Aston Villa, Division 1, 29 September 1888. 1–9 v Portsmouth, Division 2, 9 April 1927.

Most League Points (2 for a win): 69, Division 4, 1970–71.

Most League Points (3 for a win): 99, Division 3, 1997–98.

Most League Goals: 107, Division 4, 1959–60.

Highest League Scorer in Season: Tom Keetley, 39, Division 3 (S), 1930–31.

Most League Goals in Total Aggregate: Les Bradd, 124, 1967–78.

Most League Goals in One Match: 5, Robert Jardine v Burnley, Division 1, 27 October 1888; 5, Daniel Bruce v Port Vale, Division 2, 26 February 1895; 5, Bertie Mills v Barnsley, Division 2, 19 November 1927.

Most Capped Player: Kevin Wilson, 15 (42), Northern Ireland.

Most League Appearances: Albert Iremonger, 564, 1904–26.

Youngest League Player: Tony Bircumshaw, 16 years 54 days v Brentford, 3 April 1961.

Record Transfer Fee Received: £2,500,000 from Derby Co for Craig Short, September 1992.

Record Transfer Fee Paid: £685,000 to Sheffield U for Tony Agana, November 1991.

Football League Record: 1888 Founder Member of the Football League; 1893–97 Division 2; 1897–1913 Division 1; 1913–14 Division 2; 1914–20 Division 1; 1920–23 Division 2; 1923–26 Division 1; 1926–30 Division 2; 1930–31 Division 3 (S); 1931–35 Division 2; 1935–50 Division 3 (S); 1950–58 Division 2; 1958–59 Division 3; 1959–60 Division 4; 1960–64 Division 3; 1964–71 Division 4; 1971–73 Division 3; 1973–81 Division 2; 1981–84 Division 1; 1984–85 Division 2; 1985–90 Division 3; 1990–91 Division 2; 1991–95 Division 1; 1995–97 Division 2; 1997–98 Division 3; 1998– Division 2.

LATEST SEQUENCES

Longest Sequence of League Wins: 10, 3.12.1997 – 31.1.1998.

Longest Sequence of League Defeats: 7, 3.9.1983 – 16.10.1983.

Longest Sequence of League Draws: 5, 2.12.1978 – 26.12.1978.

Longest Sequence of Unbeaten League Matches: 19, 26.4.1930 – 6.12.1930.

Longest Sequence Without a League Win: 20, 3.12.1996 – 31.3.1997.

Successive Scoring Runs: 35 from 26.4.1930.

Successive Non-scoring Runs: 5 from 30.11.1912.

MANAGERS

Edwin Browne 1883–93 *(Secretary-Manager)*
Tom Featherstone 1893 *(Secretary-Manager)*
Tom Harris 1893–1913 *(Secretary-Manager)*
Albert Fisher 1913–27
Horace Henshall 1927–34
Charlie Jones 1934–35
David Pratt 1935
Percy Smith 1935–36
Jimmy McMullan 1936–37
Harry Parkes 1938–39
Tony Towers 1939–42
Frank Womack 1942–43
Major Frank Buckley 1944–46
Arthur Stollery 1946–49
Eric Houghton 1949–53
George Poyser 1953–57
Tommy Lawton 1957–58
Frank Hill 1958–61
Tim Coleman 1961–63
Eddie Lowe 1963–65
Tim Coleman 1965–66
Jack Burkitt 1966–67
Andy Beattie *(General Manager)* 1967
Billy Gray 1967–68
Jimmy Sirrel 1969–75
Ron Fenton 1975–77
Jimmy Sirrel 1978–82 *(continued as General Manager to 1984)*
Howard Wilkinson 1982–83
Larry Lloyd 1983–84
Richie Barker 1984–85
Jimmy Sirrel 1985–87
John Barnwell 1987–88
Neil Warnock 1989–93
Mick Walker 1993–94
Russell Slade 1994–95
Howard Kendall 1995
Colin Murphy June 1995 *(continued as General Manager to 1996)*
Steve Thompson 1996
Sam Allardyce 1997–99
Gary Brazil 1999–2000
Jocky Scott 2000–01
Gary Brazil 2001
Billy Dearden January 2002–

TEN YEAR LEAGUE RECORD

		P	W	D	L	F	A	Pts	Pos
1993-94	Div 1	46	20	8	18	65	69	68	7
1994-95	Div 1	46	9	13	24	45	66	40	24
1995-96	Div 2	46	21	15	10	63	39	78	4
1996-97	Div 2	46	7	14	25	33	59	35	24
1997-98	Div 3	46	29	12	5	82	43	99	1
1998-99	Div 2	46	14	12	20	52	61	54	16
1999-2000	Div 2	46	18	11	17	61	55	65	8
2000-01	Div 2	46	19	12	15	62	66	69	8
2001-02	Div 2	46	13	11	22	59	71	50	19
2002-03	Div 2	46	13	16	17	62	70	55	15

DID YOU KNOW ?

The first four-figure transfer fee received by Notts County was £1,500 and came from the sale of Jimmy Cantrell to Tottenham Hotspur in October 1912. This former Aston Villa forward led Spurs' attack in the 1921 FA Cup final.

NOTTS COUNTY 2002–03 LEAGUE RECORD

Match No.	Date	Venue	Opponents	Result		H/T Score	Lg. Pos.	Goalscorers	Attendance
1	Aug 10	H	Wycombe W	D	1-1	0-0	—	Cas [59]	6012
2	13	A	Crewe Alex	W	3-0	2-0	—	Allsopp 2 [40, 53], Stallard [41]	6141
3	17	A	Stockport Co	D	0-0	0-0	7		5047
4	24	H	Wigan Ath	L	0-2	0-0	13		6302
5	26	A	Barnsley	D	0-0	0-0	13		10,431
6	31	H	Brentford	D	2-2	1-0	17	Stallard [10], Heffernan [47]	5551
7	Sept 7	H	Oldham Ath	L	1-3	1-2	20	Heffernan [28]	5435
8	14	A	Luton T	D	2-2	2-0	19	Bolland [26], Allsopp [45]	6456
9	17	A	Port Vale	L	2-3	1-1	—	Bolland [26], Allsopp [49]	3505
10	21	H	Cardiff C	L	0-1	0-1	22		6118
11	28	A	Cheltenham T	W	4-1	2-0	19	Stallard 2 [2, 87], Allsopp 2 [3, 56]	4565
12	Oct 5	H	Peterborough U	D	2-2	0-1	19	Stallard [63], Cas [75]	6548
13	12	A	Huddersfield T	L	0-3	0-2	20		9984
14	19	H	Northampton T	W	2-1	0-0	18	Stallard [50], Heffernan [83]	6009
15	26	A	Chesterfield	D	0-0	0-0	17		4539
16	29	H	Swindon T	D	1-1	0-1	—	Bolland [76]	4797
17	Nov 9	H	Mansfield T	D	2-2	0-1	19	Liburd [63], Caskey [85]	10,302
18	23	H	Colchester U	L	2-3	2-2	20	Allsopp [16], Brough [18]	4626
19	30	A	Blackpool	D	1-1	0-1	21	Baraclough [71]	5843
20	Dec 3	A	Bristol C	L	2-3	1-1	—	Stallard 2 [19, 80]	10,690
21	14	H	QPR	W	3-0	2-0	20	Liburd [7], Fenton [14], Allsopp [83]	5343
22	21	A	Tranmere R	D	2-2	1-2	20	Stallard 2 (1 pen) [27 (p), 90]	8275
23	26	H	Barnsley	W	3-2	1-1	16	Stallard (pen) [14], Richardson [78], Baraclough [89]	7413
24	28	A	Plymouth Arg	L	0-1	0-0	17		11,901
25	Jan 1	A	Wigan Ath	L	1-3	0-1	19	Stallard [90]	6009
26	18	A	Brentford	D	1-1	1-0	19	Fenton [45]	5112
27	21	H	Stockport Co	W	3-2	0-2	—	Stallard [55], Heffernan [67], Caskey [75]	4392
28	25	H	Plymouth Arg	L	0-2	0-1	16		6329
29	Feb 1	A	Wycombe W	L	1-3	0-2	17	Stallard [70]	5690
30	4	H	Crewe Alex	D	2-2	0-2	—	Caskey (pen) [61], Allsopp [87]	3875
31	8	A	Mansfield T	L	2-3	0-0	18	Stallard 2 [79, 87]	8134
32	15	H	Bristol C	W	2-0	0-0	15	Stallard (pen) [51], Heffernan [67]	5754
33	22	A	Oldham Ath	D	1-1	0-1	16	Heffernan [85]	5657
34	Mar 1	H	Luton T	W	2-1	0-0	15	Heffernan 2 [79, 84]	6778
35	4	H	Port Vale	W	1-0	0-0	—	Stallard [59]	6302
36	8	A	Cardiff C	W	2-0	0-0	14	Stallard 2 (1 pen) [62 (p), 80]	11,389
37	15	H	Chesterfield	D	1-1	0-1	14	Stallard [79]	6801
38	18	A	Northampton T	L	0-2	0-1	—		5254
39	22	A	Swindon T	L	0-5	0-1	17		4246
40	29	H	Huddersfield T	W	3-2	1-2	15	Heffernan [31], Stallard 2 (2 pens) [71, 90]	5872
41	Apr 5	H	Blackpool	W	3-1	0-1	13	Heffernan [51], Ireland [72], Fenton [82]	5551
42	12	A	Colchester U	D	1-1	1-1	12	Stallard [45]	3435
43	19	H	Tranmere R	L	0-1	0-0	14		5715
44	21	A	QPR	L	0-2	0-1	16		13,585
45	26	A	Peterborough U	L	0-1	0-0	18		5381
46	May 3	H	Cheltenham T	W	1-0	1-0	15	Allsopp [40]	9710

Final League Position: 15

GOALSCORERS

League (62): Stallard 24 (6 pens), Allsopp 10, Heffernan 10, Bolland 3, Caskey 3 (1 pen), Fenton 3, Baraclough 2, Cas 2, Liburd 2, Brough 1, Ireland 1, Richardson 1.
Worthington Cup (2): Heffernan 1, Stallard 1.
FA Cup (2): Allsopp 2.
LDV Vans Trophy (2): Bolland 1, Richardson 1.

Garden S 18	Stone D 11 + 4	Nicholson K 34 + 3	Caskey D 33 + 6	Fenton N 40	Ireland C 35 + 2	Cas M 10 + 8	Bolland P 27 + 2	Stallard M 43 + 2	Allsopp D 28 + 5	Baraclough I 33 + 1	Holmes R 2 + 2	Brough M 26 + 5	Liburd R 26 + 6	Ramsden S 21 + 11	Hefferman P 25 + 11	Richardson I 30 + 4	Hackworth T 4 + 5	Whitley J 12	Ashton J 4	Jupp D 6 + 2	Mildenhall S 21	Riley P 2 + 1	Francis W 2 + 8	Harrad S — + 5	Deeney S 7	McCarthy P 6	Match No.
1	2	3	4	5	6	7	8	9	10	11																	1
1	2^{1}	3	4	5	6	7	8^{3}	9	10	11^{2}	12	14	13														2
1	2	3	4	5	6	7	8	9	10	11																	3
1	2^{2}	3	4^{3}	5	6	7	8	9	10	11^{1}			12	13	14												4
1	2	3	4	5	6^{2}	7^{1}	8	9	10	11			12			13											5
1	2	3	4	5	6^{1}		8^{2}	9	10	11				13	7	12											6
1	2^{2}	3^{3}	4	5	6	7^{1}		9	10	11			12	14	8	13											7
1		3	4	5	6		8	12	10	11^{2}		13	7	2	9^{1}												8
1		3^{1}	4	5	6		8	9	10			11^{2}	7	2	12	13											9
1		3^{3}	4	5		7^{1}	8	9^{2}	10			13	11	2	12	6	14										10
1	2	3	4	5	12	13	8^{2}	9^{3}	10			7^{1}	11		14	6											11
1	2	3	4	5	12	13	8^{2}	9	10			7	11^{3}		14	6^{1}											12
1	2	3	4^{1}	5		7^{2}	12	9	10			8	11^{3}	14	13	6											13
1		3		5		12	8	9	10			4		2	7^{1}	6		11									14
1		3	12	5			8	9	10			4		2	11^{1}	6■		7									15
1	12	3	13	5		14	8	9	10^{3}			4^{2}		2^{1}	11	6		7									16
1	5	3^{1}	12			7	8^{3}	9	13			4	14	2	10^{2}			11	6								17
1			4	5		12		13	10	11		7		2^{1}	9			8	6	3^{2}							18
				5				9	10	11		7^{1}			8	6			4	2	1	3	12				19
			12	5				9	10	11				8	13	6		7	4^{1}	2^{2}	1	3^{3}	14				20
			7	5	6			9	10	11			3			4		8		2	1						21
		12	8	5^{1}	6	7^{2}		9		11			2			4	10	3			1			13			22
			4		6	12		9		11		5^{1}	7■	2		3	10^{2}	8			1			13			23
	12	3^{3}	4		6	13				11		10	7^{1}	2		5	9^{2}	8			1			14			24
		12	4		6	14		9	10	11		8^{1}	3^{2}	2		5		7		13^{3}	1						25
		3		5	6			9	10	11		4		2	12			8		7^{1}	1						26
		3	8	5	6			9	10	11		4^{1}		12	13	2				7^{2}	1						27
		3^{1}	8	5	6			9	10	11			12	2	7	4					1						28
		12	8	5	6			9		11	2^{2}		3	7	10^{3}	4^{1}				13	1			14			29
		3	4	5	6		12	9	13	11	8^{1}		7	2^{2}	10^{3}						1			14			30
			4	5	6		8^{1}	9	10^{2}	11		12	7	2	13	3					1						31
			4	5	6		8^{1}	9		3		7	11^{2}	12	10	2					1		13				32
			4	5	6		8^{1}	9^{2}		3		7^{3}	11	13	10	2	12				1		14				33
		3	4		6		8	9		11			7^{2}	12	10	5					1	13	2^{1}				34
	12	3	4^{2}		6		2	9		11^{1}		8	7	13	10	5					1						35
		3		5	6		7	9				8	11	2	10	4					1						36
		3	12	5	6		7^{2}	9				8	11^{1}	2	10	4					1		13				37
			4	5	6		8^{1}	9		12		7	11	2^{2}	10	3	13				1						38
	12	3	4	5^{1}	6		2^{3}	9			14	7	11^{2}		10		13				1		8				39
		3^{2}		5	6		8	9		11		12	7^{1}		10	4							13		1	2	40
		3		5	6		8^{3}	9^{1}	12^{2}	11			7		10	4	13						14		1	2	41
		3		5	6		8^{1}	9	12	11			7		10	4									1	2	42
		3	12	5	6			9	10	11		4^{2}	7	13			8^{1}								1	2	43
		3	8	5	6			9	10	11		7^{1}			12	4									1	2	44
		3	8■	5^{2}	6			9	12	11		7^{1}		13	10	4									1	2	45
		3	4	5	6			9^{1}	10	11		7		2	8								12		1		46

Worthington Cup
First Round Oldham Ath (a) 2-3

LDV Vans Trophy
First Round Wigan Ath (h) 2-3

FA Cup
First Round Southport (a) 2-4

OLDHAM ATHLETIC — Division 2

FOUNDATION

It was in 1895 that John Garland, the landlord of the Featherstall and Junction Hotel, decided to form a football club. As Pine Villa they played in the Oldham Junior League. In 1899 the local professional club, Oldham County, went out of existence and one of the liquidators persuaded Pine Villa to take over their ground at Sheepfoot Lane and change their name to Oldham Athletic.

Boundary Park, Oldham OL1 2PA.

Telephone: 0870 753 2000, ***07000 Latics:*** 0161 624 4972. ***Fax:*** (0161) 627 5915. ***Website:*** www.oldhamathletic.co.uk ***ClubCall:*** 09068 121 142. ***Commercial Office:*** (0161) 627 1802. ***Fax:*** (0161) 652 6501.

Ground Capacity: (all seated) 13,559.

Record Attendance: 46,471 v Sheffield W, FA Cup 4th rd, 25 January 1930.

Record Receipts: £138,680 v Manchester U, FA Premier League, 29 December 1993.

Pitch Measurements: 110yd × 74yd.

Directors: Paul Thompson, Jean Howard.

Associate Directors: C. E. Moore *(Joint President)* G. T. Butterworth *(Joint President)*.

Manager: Iain Dowie.

Coaches: Lee Duxbury, John Sheridan.

Marketing and Public Relations Manager: Sean Jarvis.

Stadium Manager: George Furniss.

Safety Officer: Peter Davis.

Club Accountant: Neil Joy.

Chief Scout: Gil Prescott.

Colours: All blue with white trim.

Change Colours: All yellow with blue trim.

Year Formed: 1895.

Turned Professional: 1899.

Ltd Co.: 1906.

Previous Name: 1895, Pine Villa; 1899, Oldham Athletic.

Club Nickname: 'The Latics'.

Previous Grounds: 1895, Sheepfoot Lane; 1900, Hudson Field; 1906, Sheepfoot Lane; 1907, Boundary Park.

First Football League Game: 9 September 1907, Division 2, v Stoke (a) W 3–1 – Hewitson; Hodson, Hamilton; Fay, Walders, Wilson; Ward, W. Dodds (1), Newton (1), Hancock, Swarbrick (1).

HONOURS

Football League: Division 1 – Runners-up 1914–15; Division 2 – Champions 1990–91; Runners-up 1909–10; Division 3 (N) – Champions 1952–53; Division 3 – Champions 1973–74; Division 4 – Runners-up 1962–63.

FA Cup: Semi-final 1913, 1990, 1994.

Football League Cup: Runners-up 1990.

SKY SPORTS FACT FILE

Oldham Athletic spectacularly ended Cambridge United's home record of not conceding a goal in 1,159 minutes of play with four goals in eight minutes during their 4-1 victory on 14 May 1983, the last day of the season.

Record League Victory: 11–0 v Southport, Division 4, 26 December 1962 – Bollands; Branagan, Marshall; McCall, Williams, Scott; Ledger (1), Johnstone, Lister (6), Colquhoun (1), Whitaker (3).

Record Cup Victory: 10–1 v Lytham, FA Cup 1st rd, 28 November 1925 – Gray; Wynne, Grundy; Adlam, Heaton, Naylor (1), Douglas, Pynegar (2), Ormston (2), Barnes (3), Watson (2).

Record Defeat: 4–13 v Tranmere R, Division 3 (N), 26 December 1935.

Most League Points (2 for a win): 62, Division 3, 1973–74.

Most League Points (3 for a win): 88, Division 2, 1990–91.

Most League Goals: 95, Division 4, 1962–63.

Highest League Scorer in Season: Tom Davis, 33, Division 3 (N), 1936–37.

Most League Goals in Total Aggregate: Roger Palmer, 141, 1980–94.

Most League Goals in One Match: 7, Eric Gemmell v Chester, Division 3N, 19 January 1952.

Most Capped Player: Gunnar Halle, 24 (64), Norway.

Most League Appearances: Ian Wood, 525, 1966–80.

Youngest League Player: Wayne Harrison, 15 years 11 months v Notts Co, 27 October 1984.

Record Transfer Fee Received: £1,700,000 from Aston Villa for Earl Barrett, February 1992.

Record Transfer Fee Paid: £750,000 to Aston Villa for Ian Olney, June 1992.

Football League Record: 1907 Elected to Division 2; 1910–23 Division 1; 1923–35 Division 2; 1935–53 Division 3 (N); 1953–54 Division 2; 1954–58 Division 3 (N); 1958–63 Division 4; 1963–69 Division 3; 1969–71 Division 4; 1971–74 Division 3; 1974–91 Division 2; 1991–92 Division 1; 1992–94 FA Premier League; 1994–97 Division 1; 1997– Division 2.

MANAGERS

David Ashworth 1906–14
Herbert Bamlett 1914–21
Charlie Roberts 1921–22
David Ashworth 1923–24
Bob Mellor 1924–27
Andy Wilson 1927–32
Jimmy McMullan 1933–34
Bob Mellor 1934–45
(continued as Secretary to 1953)
Frank Womack 1945–47
Billy Wootton 1947–50
George Hardwick 1950–56
Ted Goodier 1956–58
Norman Dodgin 1958–60
Jack Rowley 1960–63
Les McDowall 1963–65
Gordon Hurst 1965–66
Jimmy McIlroy 1966–68
Jack Rowley 1968–69
Jimmy Frizzell 1970–82
Joe Royle 1982–94
Graeme Sharp 1994–97
Neil Warnock 1997–98
Andy Ritchie 1998–2001
Mick Wadsworth 2001–02
Iain Dowie May 2002–

LATEST SEQUENCES

Longest Sequence of League Wins: 10, 12.1.1974 – 12.3.1974.

Longest Sequence of League Defeats: 8, 15.12.1934 – 2.2.1935.

Longest Sequence of League Draws: 5, 26.12.1982 – 15.1.1983.

Longest Sequence of Unbeaten League Matches: 20, 1.5.1990 – 10.11.1990.

Longest Sequence Without a League Win: 17, 4.9.1920 – 18.12.1920.

Successive Scoring Runs: 25 from 15.1.1927.

Successive Non-scoring Runs: 6 from 4.2.1922.

TEN YEAR LEAGUE RECORD

		P	W	D	L	F	A	Pts	Pos
1993-94	PR Lge	42	9	13	20	42	68	40	21
1994-95	Div 1	46	16	13	17	60	60	61	14
1995-96	Div 1	46	14	14	18	54	50	56	18
1996-97	Div 1	46	10	13	23	51	66	43	23
1997-98	Div 2	46	15	16	15	62	54	61	13
1998-99	Div 2	46	14	9	23	48	66	51	20
1999-2000	Div 2	46	16	12	18	50	55	60	14
2000-01	Div 2	46	15	13	18	53	65	58	15
2001-02	Div 2	46	18	16	12	77	65	70	9
2002-03	Div 2	46	22	16	8	68	38	82	5

DID YOU KNOW ?

Stewart Littlewood squeezed some two seasons for Oldham Athletic from January 1929 to March 1931, but arguably saved them from relegation in the first and pushed them to third in the next full season, scoring 45 goals in 78 League matches.

OLDHAM ATHLETIC 2002–03 LEAGUE RECORD

Match No.	*Date*	*Venue*	*Opponents*	*Result*	*H/T Score*	*Lg. Pos.*	*Goalscorers*	*Attendance*
1	Aug 10	H	Cardiff C	L 1-2	0-1	—	Duxbury [90]	8033
2	13	A	Peterborough U	W 1-0	0-0	—	Killen [62]	5204
3	17	A	Brentford	D 0-0	0-0	12		5356
4	24	H	Tranmere R	W 2-0	0-0	9	Hill [69], Wijnhard [77]	5933
5	26	A	Blackpool	D 0-0	0-0	7		8201
6	31	H	Wycombe W	L 0-2	0-1	14		5963
7	Sept 7	A	Notts Co	W 3-1	2-1	10	Eyres [34], Sheridan D [36], Killen [65]	5435
8	14	H	Mansfield T	W 6-1	3-1	5	Wijnhard 4 (1 pen) [10, 26 (p), 36, 70], Corazzin [80], Andrews W (pen) [84]	5490
9	17	H	Bristol C	W 1-0	0-0	—	Wijnhard [70]	5583
10	21	A	Colchester U	W 1-0	0-0	3	Andrews W [64]	3021
11	28	H	Huddersfield T	W 4-0	2-0	3	Wijnhard 2 [1, 57], Eyres [18], Lourenco [80]	7643
12	Oct 5	A	Swindon T	W 1-0	1-0	1	Duxbury [6]	4326
13	12	A	Port Vale	D 1-1	0-0	3	Holden [49]	5563
14	19	H	Luton T	L 1-2	1-1	4	Holden [4]	6916
15	26	A	QPR	W 2-1	2-1	4	Low [29], Duxbury [38]	15,491
16	29	H	Northampton T	W 4-0	1-0	—	Andrews W [28], Corazzin [61], Eyres (pen) [71], Eyre [84]	5512
17	Nov 2	H	Stockport Co	W 2-0	1-0	2	Hall F [40], Vernon [90]	8251
18	9	A	Plymouth Arg	D 2-2	0-2	2	Eyres (pen) [74], Andrews W [76]	8216
19	23	H	Cheltenham T	D 0-0	0-0	3		6575
20	30	A	Barnsley	D 2-2	1-1	3	Baudet [27], Killen [81]	11,222
21	Dec 14	H	Wigan Ath	L 0-2	0-1	4		8269
22	21	A	Chesterfield	W 1-0	1-0	4	Hall F [22]	4052
23	26	H	Blackpool	D 1-1	1-1	5	Haining [45]	9415
24	29	A	Crewe Alex	W 2-1	1-0	4	Corazzin [26], Eyres (pen) [61]	9006
25	Jan 1	A	Tranmere R	W 2-1	1-0	4	Eyres (pen) [37], Baudet [76]	9795
26	4	H	Peterborough U	D 0-0	0-0	3		5922
27	14	H	Brentford	W 2-1	1-1	—	Hall F [22], Duxbury [46]	5039
28	18	A	Wycombe W	D 2-2	1-0	2	Andrews W [26], Carss [84]	6226
29	25	H	Crewe Alex	L 1-3	0-0	3	Armstrong [64]	7597
30	31	A	Cardiff C	D 1-1	0-1	—	Eyres [87]	12,579
31	Feb 8	H	Plymouth Arg	L 0-1	0-1	4		6657
32	15	A	Stockport Co	W 2-1	1-0	4	Murray [9], Eyres [89]	8168
33	22	H	Notts Co	D 1-1	1-0	4	Andrews W [44]	5657
34	Mar 1	A	Mansfield T	W 1-0	0-0	4	Hall F (pen) [88]	5712
35	4	A	Bristol C	L 0-2	0-0	—		11,194
36	8	H	Colchester U	W 2-0	2-0	4	Eyre [13], Eyres [19]	5223
37	15	H	QPR	D 0-0	0-0	4		7242
38	18	A	Luton T	D 0-0	0-0	—		6142
39	22	A	Northampton T	W 2-0	0-0	4	Andrews W 2 [67, 89]	5646
40	29	H	Port Vale	D 1-1	1-1	5	Eyres [28]	7209
41	Apr 5	H	Barnsley	W 2-1	1-1	3	Andrews W [4], Low [56]	6191
42	12	A	Cheltenham T	D 1-1	1-1	5	Eyres [31]	4439
43	19	H	Chesterfield	W 4-0	2-0	4	Andrews W [20], Wijnhard 2 [26, 75], Eyres [79]	6885
44	21	A	Wigan Ath	L 1-3	1-1	5	Andrews W [1]	12,783
45	26	H	Swindon T	W 4-0	2-0	3	Low [27], Eyres [31], Haining [79], Corazzin [83]	6873
46	May 3	A	Huddersfield T	D 1-1	0-1	5	Carss [68]	11,271

Final League Position: 5

GOALSCORERS

League (68): Eyres 13 (4 pens), Andrews W 11 (1 pen), Wijnhard 10 (1 pen), Corazzin 4, Duxbury 4, Hall F 4 (1 pen), Killen 3, Low 3, Baudet 2, Carss 2, Eyre 2, Haining 2, Holden 2, Armstrong 1, Hill 1, Lourenco 1, Murray 1, Sheridan D 1, Vernon 1.
Worthington Cup (6): Wijnhard 2 (1 pen), Carss 1, Corazzin 1, Eyres 1, Killen 1.
FA Cup (5): Eyres 1, Haining 1, Hall F 1, Low 1, Wijnhard 1.
LDV Vans Trophy (3): Vernon 2, Andrews 1.
Play-offs (1): Eyres 1.

Pogliacomi L 37	Clegg M 7 + 1	Carss T 16 + 10	Beharall D 30 + 2	Hall F 40	Baudet J 21 + 3	Sheridan J 3 + 2	Appleby M 11 + 1	Eyre J 27 + 4	Killen C 11 + 16	Eyres D 40	Lourenco 1 + 6	Duxbury L 16 + 18	Corazzin C 21 + 18	Hill C 17	Low J 19 + 2	Wijnhard C 24 + 1	Andrews W 28 + 9	Sheridan D 29 + 4	Holden D 2 + 4	Armstrong C 33	Haining W 25 + 1	Murray P 29 + 1	Vernon S 2 + 6	Burgess B 6 + 1	Miskelly D 9 + 2	Boshell D 2	Hall D — + 2	Match No.
1	2	3^{1}	4	5	6	7^{2}	8	9	10^{3}	11	12	13	14															1
1	2	12	4	5		7^{2}	8	9	10^{3}	3	14	13	11^{1}	6														2
1	2	12	4	5■		7^{1}	8	9^{3}	10^{2}	3		13	11	6	14													3
1	2	12	4	5			8	13	10^{3}	3		11^{1}	14	6	7	9^{2}												4
1	2^{1}		4	5	13	12	8■		10^{3}	3		11	14	6	7^{2}	9												5
1	2^{1}		4		5	12	8		10^{2}	3	11		13	6	7^{3}	9	14											6
1		12	4	5			8	11	10	3			13	6	7	9^{2}		2^{1}										7
1		12	4	5			8^{1}	11		3		13	10	6	2^{2}	9^{3}	14	7										8
1			4	5			8	11		3		12	10^{2}	6	2^{1}	9	13	7										9
1		7	4	5	12			11		3^{3}			10^{1}	6■	2^{2}	9	13	8	14									10
1		8		5	4^{3}			11		3	12	13	10	6		9	2^{1}	7^{2}	14									11
1		8	4^{2}	5	6■			11^{1}	12	3		2	10			9		7	13									12
1		11		5	6				12	3	13	7^{2}	10^{1}			9		8	2	4								13
1		8		5				11	9	3	12	2^{3}	10^{2}				13	7	4^{1}	6	14							14
1				5				11	12	3		4	10	6	2		9^{1}	7		8								15
1				5^{2}				11	12	3		4^{3}	10	6	2		9^{1}	7	13	8		14						16
1				5				11	12	3			10	6	2		9^{2}	8^{1}		4		7	13					17
1			4	5				11^{2}	12	3			10	6	2		9	13		8		7^{1}						18
1			4		5			11^{1}		3	13	12	10^{3}	6		14	9	8		2		7^{2}						19
1	3		4	5	7			11^{1}	13			12	14	6		9^{3}	10^{2}	8		2								20
1			4^{3}	5	6			11^{1}	9^{2}	3		12	10				13	8■		7		2	14					21
1			4	5	7^{2}				12	11		13	14				9^{1}	8		3	6	2	10^{3}					22
1	12		2^{1}	5	4					11		13	14				9	8^{2}		3	6	7	10^{3}					23
1			2	5	4^{2}			8	12	11		13	10^{1}				9			3	6	7						24
1			2	5	4			8		11			10^{1}				9	12		3	6	7						25
1			2^{3}	5	4			8^{2}	12	11		13	10^{1}				9	14		3	6	7						26
1■		12	2	5	4^{1}				10^{G}			11						8		3	6	7		9	15			27
1		12	4	5	7■			8				11					9^{1}			3	6	2	13	10^{2}				28
1		12	4	5■	7^{2}			8^{3}		3		13	14				10			11	6	2		9^{1}				29
		12	4^{2}	5					13	3		7^{1}					10	8		11	6	2		9	1			30
		11	4					12	13	3		7^{2}					10	8		5	6	2		9^{1}	1			31
		11	4				12	13	10^{2}	3			14				9^{3}	8^{1}		5	6	2			1	7		32
1		8	12	5			2^{2}		13	3			14				10			11	6	7		9^{3}		4^{1}		33
1		11	4	5					12	3■		7	13			9^{2}	10^{1}			8	6	2						34
1		11	4^{2}	5	7^{3}				12	3		14	13			9	10^{1}			8	6	2						35
1		2^{2}		5			8^{1}	11		3		12	10			9	13			4	6	7						36
1		3	4^{1}					11				7	10^{2}		12	9	13	8		5	6	2						37
1		3	4					11				7				9	10	8		5	6	2						38
1		3		5				11^{1}					12		2^{3}	9^{2}	10	8		4	6	7		13			14	39
1^{G}				5^{2}					12	3		11^{1}			2	9	10	8		4	6	7	13		15			40
				5						3		7^{2}	12		11	9	10^{1}	8		4	6	2			1		13	41
				5	7^{1}					3			12		2	9	10	8		4	6	11			1			42
			12	5	7^{2}					3		13			2	9	10^{3}	8		4	6^{1}	11	14		1			43
				5	11^{3}			14		3		12	13		2^{1}	9	10	8^{2}		4	6	7			1			44
		12		5	13			11^{1}		3			14		7	9^{3}	10	8^{2}		4	6	2			1			45
		11		5	8					3^{3}			10^{1}	4	2	9	12	13			6^{2}	7	14		1			46

Worthington Cup

First Round	Notts Co	(h)	3-2
Second Round	Derby Co	(a)	2-1
Third Round	West Ham U	(a)	1-0
Fourth Round	Crystal Palace	(a)	0-2

LDV Vans Trophy

First Round	Carlisle U	(h)	3-4

FA Cup

First Round	Burton Alb	(h)	2-2
		(a)	2-2
Second Round	Cheltenham T	(h)	1-2

OXFORD UNITED — Division 3

FOUNDATION

There had been an Oxford United club around the time of World War I but only in the Oxfordshire Thursday League and there is no connection with the modern club which began as Headington in 1893, adding 'United' a year later. Playing first on Quarry Fields and subsequently Wootten's Fields, they owe much to a Dr Hitchings for their early development.

The Kassam Stadium, Grenoble Road, Oxford OX4 4XP.

Telephone: (01865) 337 500. ***Fax:*** 01865 337 555.
Ticketline: 01865 337 533.
Website: www.oufc.co.uk
Email: admin@oufc.co.uk

Ground Capacity: 12,450.

Record Attendance: 22,730 v Preston NE, FA Cup 6th rd, 29 February 1964.

Record Receipts: £136,423 v Chelsea, FA Cup 4th rd, 25 January 1999.

Pitch Measurements: 115yd × 74yd.

Chairman: Firoz Kassam.

Directors: F. Higgins, A. Tawakley. ***Associate Directors:*** B. Cross, Lord Faulkner, B. Smith.

Manager: Ian Atkins.

Physio: Neal Reynolds.

Secretary: Mick Brown.

Stadium Manager: Tony Ashley.

Colours: Yellow shirts with navy trim, navy shorts, navy stockings.

Change Colours: Navy shirts with white trim, white shorts, white stockings.

Year Formed: 1893.

Turned Professional: 1949.

Ltd Co.: 1949.

Club Nickname: 'The U's'.

Previous Names: 1893, Headington; 1894, Headington United; 1960, Oxford United.

Previous Grounds: 1893, Headington Quarry; 1894, Wootten's Field; 1898, Sandy Lane Ground; 1902, Britannia Field; 1909, Sandy Lane; 1910, Quarry Recreation Ground; 1914, Sandy Lane; 1922, The Paddock Manor Road; 1925, Manor Ground; 2001, The Kassam Stadium.

First Football League Game: 18 August 1962, Division 4, v Barrow (a) L 2–3 – Medlock; Beavon, Quartermain; R. Atkinson, Kyle, Jones; Knight, G. Atkinson (1), Houghton (1), Cornwell, Colfar.

Record League Victory: 7–0 v Barrow, Division 4, 19 December 1964 – Fearnley; Beavon, Quartermain; R. Atkinson (1), Kyle, Jones; Morris, Booth (3), Willey (1), G. Atkinson (1), Harrington (1).

HONOURS

Football League: Division 1 best season: 12th, 1997–98; Division 2 – Champions 1984–85; Runners-up 1995–96; Division 3 – Champions 1967–68, 1983–84; Division 4 – Promoted 1964–65 (4th).

FA Cup: best season: 6th rd, 1964 (shared record for 4th Division club).

Football League Cup: Winners 1986.

SKY SPORTS FACT FILE

In 1953–54 the then Headington United's left-back was Ted Croker, later FA Secretary, who made 53 first team appearances that season including nine in the FA Cup before taking up a coaching appointment with the club.

Record Cup Victory: 9–1 v Dorchester T, FA Cup 1st rd, 11 November 1995 – Whitehead; Wood (2), Ford M (1), Smith, Elliott, Gilchrist, Rush (1), Massey (Murphy), Moody (3), Ford R (1), Angel (Beauchamp (1)).

Record Defeat: 0–7 v Sunderland, Division 1, 19 September 1998.

Most League Points (2 for a win): 61, Division 4, 1964–65.

Most League Points (3 for a win): 95, Division 3, 1983–84.

Most League Goals: 91, Division 3, 1983–84.

Highest League Scorer in Season: John Aldridge, 30, Division 2, 1984–85.

Most League Goals in Total Aggregate: Graham Atkinson, 77, 1962–73.

Most League Goals in One Match: 4, Tony Jones v Newport Co, Division 4, 22 September 1962; 4, Arthur Longbottom v Darlington, Division 4, 26 October 1963; 4, Richard Hill v Walsall, Division 2, 26 December 1988; 4, John Durnin v Luton T, 14 November 1992.

Most Capped Player: Jim Magilton, 18 (52\), Northern Ireland.

Most League Appearances: John Shuker, 478, 1962–77.

Youngest League Player: Jason Seacole, 16 years 149 days v Mansfield T, 7 September 1976.

Record Transfer Fee Received: £1,600,000 from Leicester C for Matt Elliott, January 1997.

Record Transfer Fee Paid: £475,000 to Aberdeen for Dean Windass, August 1998.

Football League Record: 1962 Elected to Division 4; 1965–68 Division 3; 1968–76 Division 2; 1976–84 Division 3; 1984–85 Division 2; 1985–88 Division 1; 1988–92 Division 2; 1992–94 Division 1; 1994–96 Division 2; 1996–99 Division 1; 1999–2001 Division 2; 2001– Division 3.

MANAGERS

Harry Thompson 1949–58
(Player-Manager) 1949-51
Arthur Turner 1959–69
(continued as General Manager to 1972)
Ron Saunders 1969
Gerry Summers 1969–75
Mick Brown 1975–79
Bill Asprey 1979–80
Ian Greaves 1980–82
Jim Smith 1982–85
Maurice Evans 1985–88
Mark Lawrenson 1988
Brian Horton 1988–93
Denis Smith 1993–97
Malcolm Crosby 1997
Malcolm Shotton 1998–99
Denis Smith 2000
David Kemp 2000–01
Mark Wright 2001
Ian Atkins November 2001–

LATEST SEQUENCES

Longest Sequence of League Wins: 6, 6.4.1985 – 24.4.1985.

Longest Sequence of League Defeats: 7, 4.5.1991 – 7.9.1991.

Longest Sequence of League Draws: 5, 7.10.1978 – 28.10.1978.

Longest Sequence of Unbeaten League Matches: 20, 17.3.1984 – 29.9.1984.

Longest Sequence Without a League Win: 27, 14.11.1987 – 27.8.1988.

Successive Scoring Runs: 17 from 10.9.1983.

Successive Non-scoring Runs: 6 from 26.3.1988.

TEN YEAR LEAGUE RECORD

		P	*W*	*D*	*L*	*F*	*A*	*Pts*	*Pos*
1993-94	Div 1	46	13	10	23	54	75	49	23
1994-95	Div 2	46	21	12	13	66	52	75	7
1995-96	Div 2	46	24	11	11	76	39	83	2
1996-97	Div 1	46	16	9	21	64	68	57	17
1997-98	Div 1	46	16	10	20	60	64	58	12
1998-99	Div 1	46	10	14	22	48	71	44	23
1999-2000	Div 2	46	12	9	25	43	73	45	20
2000-01	Div 2	46	7	6	33	53	100	27	24
2001-02	Div 3	46	11	14	21	53	62	47	21
2002-03	Div 3	46	19	12	15	57	47	69	8

DID YOU KNOW ?

On Bank Holiday Monday 5 May 1986 Oxford United entertained Arsenal needing a win to have any hope of avoiding relegation. But goals from Ray Houghton (2 mins), John Alridge (71 penalty) and Billy Hamilton (81) provided the necessary salvation.

OXFORD UNITED 2002–03 LEAGUE RECORD

Match No.	Date	Venue	Opponents	Result		H/T Score	Lg. Pos.	Goalscorers	Attendance
1	Aug 10	H	Bury	W	2-1	2-0	—	Crosby (pen) [30], Omoyinmi [34]	5309
2	13	A	Wrexham	L	0-1	0-0	—		3591
3	17	A	Darlington	W	1-0	1-0	6	Basham [45]	3533
4	24	H	Southend U	L	0-1	0-1	10		5162
5	27	A	Bournemouth	D	1-1	0-1	—	Basham [47]	4842
6	31	H	Hartlepool U	L	0-1	0-1	17		4768
7	Sept 7	H	Torquay U	D	2-2	0-0	15	Omoyinmi [81], Powell [88]	5260
8	14	A	Boston U	W	3-1	3-0	10	Powell [16], Scott 2 [24, 36]	2685
9	17	A	Leyton Orient	W	2-1	1-0	—	Scott [8], Crosby (pen) [57]	3758
10	21	H	Hull C	D	0-0	0-0	8		5445
11	28	A	York C	W	1-0	0-0	7	Gordon [61]	3962
12	Oct 5	H	Scunthorpe U	L	0-1	0-0	11		5658
13	12	H	Swansea C	W	1-0	0-0	8	Louis [73]	5440
14	19	A	Cambridge U	D	1-1	0-1	6	Scott [81]	4621
15	26	H	Shrewsbury T	D	2-2	2-2	8	Scott [7], Louis [16]	5559
16	29	A	Macclesfield T	L	1-2	0-0	—	Louis [90]	1583
17	Nov 2	A	Carlisle U	L	0-1	0-1	12		4039
18	9	H	Rochdale	W	2-0	1-0	11	Hunt [17], Basham [70]	4547
19	30	H	Lincoln C	W	1-0	0-0	11	Crosby (pen) [90]	4923
20	Dec 14	A	Bristol R	W	2-0	1-0	9	Robinson [12], Louis [49]	5864
21	21	H	Exeter C	D	2-2	0-0	9	Steele [78], Bound [83]	7057
22	26	H	Bournemouth	W	3-0	1-0	6	Whitehead [30], Hunter [74], Oldfield [76]	8349
23	28	A	Rushden & D	W	2-0	2-0	3	Savage [13], Oldfield [30]	4891
24	Jan 14	H	Darlington	D	1-1	0-0	—	Basham [49]	4968
25	18	A	Hartlepool U	L	1-3	1-2	6	Barron (og) [36]	5049
26	21	A	Southend U	L	1-2	0-1	—	Basham [89]	3203
27	25	H	Rushden & D	W	3-0	0-0	6	Crosby (pen) [51], Savage 2 [84, 87]	6508
28	28	A	Kidderminster H	W	3-1	2-0	—	Basham [21], Hinton (og) [29], Scott [61]	2991
29	Feb 4	H	Wrexham	L	0-2	0-0	—		5532
30	8	A	Rochdale	L	1-2	0-1	5	Savage [71]	2764
31	22	A	Torquay U	W	3-2	0-0	7	Scott [56], Steele 2 [81, 90]	3372
32	Mar 1	H	Boston U	W	2-1	1-0	6	Crosby [16], Ford [54]	7157
33	4	H	Leyton Orient	L	0-2	0-1	—		5013
34	8	A	Hull C	D	0-0	0-0	8		17,404
35	15	A	Shrewsbury T	W	2-1	1-1	5	Waterman [21], Louis [46]	3520
36	18	H	Cambridge U	D	1-1	0-0	—	Louis [65]	4983
37	22	H	Macclesfield T	L	0-1	0-1	8		5691
38	25	A	Bury	D	1-1	1-1	—	McNiven [35]	2578
39	28	A	Swansea C	L	2-3	1-1	—	Scott 2 [25, 82]	5982
40	Apr 1	H	Carlisle U	D	0-0	0-0	—		5044
41	5	A	Lincoln C	W	1-0	1-0	7	Scott [4]	3990
42	12	H	Kidderminster H	W	2-1	1-1	5	McCarthy [38], Omoyinmi [88]	6820
43	19	A	Exeter C	D	2-2	1-2	5	Crosby (pen) [9], Scott [68]	4900
44	21	H	Bristol R	L	0-1	0-0	7		8732
45	26	A	Scunthorpe U	L	0-2	0-1	8		5629
46	May 3	H	York C	W	2-0	1-0	8	Basham 2 [3, 63]	6905

Final League Position: 8

GOALSCORERS

League (57): Scott 11, Basham 8, Crosby 6 (5 pens), Louis 6, Savage 4, Omoyinmi 3, Steele 3, Oldfield 2, Powell 2, Bound 1, Ford 1, Gordon 1, Hunt 1, Hunter 1, McCarthy 1, McNiven 1, Robinson 1, Waterman 1, Whitehead 1, own goals 2.
Worthington Cup (1): Hunt 1.
FA Cup (2): Louis 1, Oldfield 1.
LDV Vans Trophy (2): Crosby 1 (pen), Waterman 1.

Woodman A 45	McNiven S 44	Robinson M 42	Crosby A 46	Bound M 41	Waterman D 27 + 2	Whitehead D 9 + 9	Hunt J 39	Omoyinmi M 4 + 13	Oldfield D 19 + 9	Savage D 43	Basham S 25 + 6	Scott A 29 + 9	Ford B 31 + 6	Hackett C 1 + 11	Ricketts S — + 2	Viveash A 11	Powell P 4 + 10	Louis J 12 + 22	Gordon G 3 + 3	Hunter R 12 + 5	Sall A — + 1	Steele L 3 + 7	Edwards C 5 + 1	Judge A 1	Foley D 4 + 2	McCarthy P 6	Match No.
1	2	3	4	5	6	7	8	9[1]	10[2]	11[3]	12	13	14														1
1	2	3	4	5	6[2]	7	8	9[1]	10[3]	11	13	12	14														2
1	2	3	4	5	6	12	8		10	11[1]	9[2]	7[3]		13	14												3
1	2	3	4	5	6[3]		8	12	10	11[2]	9[1]	7	14	13													4
1	2	3	4	5	6■	7[1]	8		10	11	9[2]	13	12														5
1	2	3	4	5			8	12	10[2]	11	9[1]	7	6	13													6
1	2	3	4			7[2]	8	12	10	11[1]		9[3]	6			5	13	14									7
1	2		4	5			8	12[2]	10	11		9[1]	7			6	3	13									8
1	2		4	5			8		10	11		9	7			6	3										9
1	2		4	5			8	12	10[1]	11[2]		9	7			6	3	13									10
1	2	3	4	5			8	9[1]	10[2]	11			7			6	12		13								11
1	2	3[2]	4	5[3]			8	12	13	11[1]		9	7			6	14		10								12
1	2	3	4	5		7[3]	8	9[2]	12	11			6	13				14	10[1]								13
1	2	3	4	5[2]			8		10[1]	11		9		12		6	13	7									14
1	2	3	4	5[1]		13	8		12	11		9[3]		7■		6		10[2]	14								15
1	2	3	4	5[1]			8		10[3]	11		9[2]		12		6		7	13	14							16
1	2	3	4		6		8			11[1]	13	9		14		5	12	7[3]	10[2]								17
1	2	3	4	5	12	7[2]	8		10	11[1]	9[3]					6	13	14									18
1	2	3	4	5	6[2]	12	8		10[3]	11	9		7[1]				13	14									19
1	2[2]	3	4	5	6	11[1]					9	12	7		13			10[3]		8	14						20
1	2	3	4	5	6[1]		8			11[3]	9[2]	12	7	13				10				14					21
1	2	3	4	5	6	12[2]	8[1]		14		9	13	11					10[3]		7							22
1	2	3	4	5	6	12			10	11[3]	9[2]	13	7[1]					14		8							23
1		3	4	5	6	2			12	11	9[2]		7					10[1]		8		13					24
1	2	3	4	5		12			13	11	9	14	7					10[2]		8[1]			6[3]				25
1	2	3	4	5[3]	6		8[1]		12	11[2]	9	10	7					13					14				26
1	2	3	4	5			8			11	9	10[1]						12		7			6				27
1	2	3	4	5	12		8		13	11[1]	9	10[2]								7			6				28
1	2		4	5[2]			8			11[1]	9[3]	10	12				3	13		7		14	6				29
1	2[1]	3	4	5[3]			8			11	9[2]	10	12					13		7		14	6				30
1	2	3	4	5	6[1]		8			11	9[2]	10[3]	7					12		13		14					31
1	2	3	4	5	6		8			11	9[2]	10	7[1]							12		13					32
1		3	4	5	6		8[1]			11	9[2]	10[3]	7	12				13		2		14					33
1	2	3	4	5	6		8			11	9[2]	13	7					12				10[1]					34
1[3]	2	3	4	5	6	12	8		10[2]	11			7■					13		14		9[1]					35
	2[2]	3	4	5	6		8			11	12		7				13	10				9[1]		1			36
1	2	3[1]	4[2]	5	6		8	12		11[3]	9		7	13			14	10									37
1	2	3	4	5	6		8			11	9[1]	10[2]	7					12							13		38
1	2	3	4	5[3]			8	12		11[2]	9[1]	10	7					13							14	6	39
1	2	3	4				8[1]	12		11		9					13	10[2]		6					7	5	40
1	2	3	4	5	6					11		10	7[2]					12		13					9[1]	8	41
1	2[3]	3	4	5	8	12		13		11[1]		10	7	14											9[2]	6	42
1	2	3	4	5	6	12		13		11[2]		10	7[1]					14		8					9[3]		43
1	2	3	4	5[2]	6		8	12	9[3]	11[1]	13	10	7					14									44
1	2	3	4		6[2]		8■	12	9[3]	11[1]	13	10	7					14								5	45
1	2	3	4		6	7	8		12		9[1]	10[2]	11					13								5	46

Worthington Cup

First Round	Bristol C	(a)	1-0
Second Round	Charlton Ath	(a)	0-0
Third Round	Aston Villa	(h)	0-3

LDV Vans Trophy

First Round	Bournemouth	(h)	2-3

FA Cup

First Round	Dover Ath	(a)	1-0
Second Round	Swindon T	(h)	1-0
Third Round	Arsenal	(a)	0-2

PETERBOROUGH UNITED Division 2

FOUNDATION

The old Peterborough & Fletton club, founded in 1923, was suspended by the FA during season 1932–33 and disbanded. Local enthusiasts determined to carry on and in 1934 a new professional club, Peterborough United, was formed and entered the Midland League the following year. Peterborough's first success came in 1939–40, but from 1955–56 to 1959–60 they won five successive titles. During the 1958–59 season they were undefeated in the Midland League. They reached the third round of the FA Cup, won the Northamptonshire Senior Cup, the Maunsell Cup and were runners-up in the East Anglian Cup.

London Road Ground, Peterborough PE2 8AL.

Telephone: 08700 550 442. ***Fax:*** (01733) 344 140.

ClubCall: 09068 121 654.

Website: www.theposh.com

Email: info@pufc-theposhisp.com

Ground Capacity: 15,314.

Record Attendance: 30,096 v Swansea T, FA Cup 5th rd, 20 February 1965.

Record Receipts: £51,315 v Brighton & HA, FA Cup 5th rd, 15 February 1986.

Pitch Measurements: 112yd × 71yd.

Chairman: Alfred Hand.

Vice-chairman: Ian Forsythe.

Directors: A. Hand, P. Sagar.

Company Secretary: Karen Haylock.

Club Secretary: Julie Etherington.

First Team Manager: Barry Fry.

Head Coach: Phil Chapple.

Physio: Paul Showler.

Colours: Blue shirts, blue shorts, blue stockings.

Change Colours: White shirts, white shorts, white stockings.

Year Formed: 1934.

Turned Professional: 1934.

Ltd Co.: 1934.

Club Nickname: 'The Posh'.

First Football League Game: 20 August 1960, Division 4, v Wrexham (h) W 3–0 – Walls; Stafford, Walker; Rayner, Rigby, Norris; Hails, Emery (1), Bly (1), Smith, McNamee (1).

HONOURS

Football League: Division 1 best season: 10th, 1992–93; Division 2 1991–92 (play-offs). Promoted from Division 3 1999–2000 (play-offs); Division 4 – Champions 1960–61, 1973–74.

FA Cup: best season: 6th rd, 1965.

Football League Cup: Semi-final 1966.

SKY SPORTS FACT FILE

The first five-figure attendance at Peterborough United was 10,380 for a benefit match for three Posh players Bernie Bryan, Cyril Parrot and Cliff Woods. It was in April 1951 against Hull City who included Raich Carter in their team.

Record League Victory: 9–1 v Barnet (a) Division 3, 5 September 1998 – Griemink; Hooper (1), Drury (Farell), Gill, Bodley, Edwards, Davies, Payne, Grazioli (5), Quinn (2) (Rowe), Houghton (Etherington) (1).

Record Cup Victory: 7–0 v Harlow T, FA Cup 1st rd, 16 November 1991 – Barber; Luke, Johnson, Halsall (1), Robinson D, Welsh, Sterling (1) (Butterworth), Cooper G (2 incl. 1p), Riley (1) (Culpin (1)), Charlery (1), Kimble.

Record Defeat: 1–8 v Northampton T, FA Cup 2nd rd (2nd replay), 18 December 1946.

Most League Points (2 for a win): 66, Division 4, 1960–61.

Most League Points (3 for a win): 82, Division 4, 1981–82.

Most League Goals: 134, Division 4, 1960–61.

Highest League Scorer in Season: Terry Bly, 52, Division 4, 1960–61.

Most League Goals in Total Aggregate: Jim Hall, 122, 1967–75.

Most League Goals in One Match: 5, Guiliano Grazioli v Barnet, Division 3, 5 September 1998.

Most Capped Player: Tony Millington, 8 (21), Wales.

Most League Appearances: Tommy Robson, 482, 1968–81.

Youngest League Player: Matthew Etherington, 15 years 262 days v Brentford, 3 May 1997.

Record Transfer Fee Received: £700,000 from Tottenham H for Simon Davies, December 1999.

Record Transfer Fee Paid: £350,000 to Walsall for Martin O'Connor, July 1996.

Football League Record: 1960 Elected to Division 4; 1961–68 Division 3, when they were demoted for financial irregularities; 1968–74 Division 4; 1974–79 Division 3; 1979–91 Division 4; 1991–92 Division 3; 1992–94 Division 1; 1994–97 Division 2; 1997–2000 Division 3; 2000– Division 2.

MANAGERS

Jock Porter 1934–36
Fred Taylor 1936–37
Vic Poulter 1937–38
Sam Madden 1938–48
Jack Blood 1948–50
Bob Gurney 1950–52
Jack Fairbrother 1952–54
George Swindin 1954–58
Jimmy Hagan 1958–62
Jack Fairbrother 1962–64
Gordon Clark 1964–67
Norman Rigby 1967–69
Jim Iley 1969–72
Noel Cantwell 1972–77
John Barnwell 1977–78
Billy Hails 1978–79
Peter Morris 1979–82
Martin Wilkinson 1982–83
John Wile 1983–86
Noel Cantwell 1986–88 *(continued as General Manager)*
Mick Jones 1988–89
Mark Lawrenson 1989–90
Chris Turner 1991–92
Lil Fuccillo 1992–93
John Still 1994–95
Mick Halsall 1995–96
Barry Fry May 1996–

LATEST SEQUENCES

Longest Sequence of League Wins: 9, 1.2.1992 – 14.3.1992.

Longest Sequence of League Defeats: 5, 8.10.1996 – 26.10.1996.

Longest Sequence of League Draws: 8, 18.12.1971 – 12.2.1972.

Longest Sequence of Unbeaten League Matches: 17, 17.12.1960 – 8.4.1961.

Longest Sequence Without a League Win: 17, 23.9.1978 – 30.12.1978.

Successive Scoring Runs: 33 from 20.9.1960.

Successive Non-scoring Runs: 6 from 13.8.2002.

TEN YEAR LEAGUE RECORD

		P	*W*	*D*	*L*	*F*	*A*	*Pts*	*Pos*
1993-94	Div 1	46	8	13	25	48	76	37	24
1994-95	Div 2	46	14	18	14	54	69	60	15
1995-96	Div 2	46	13	13	20	59	66	52	19
1996-97	Div 2	46	11	14	21	55	73	47	21
1997-98	Div 3	46	18	13	15	63	51	67	10
1998-99	Div 3	46	18	12	16	72	56	66	9
1999-2000	Div 3	46	22	12	12	63	54	78	5
2000-01	Div 2	46	15	14	17	61	66	59	12
2001-02	Div 2	46	15	10	21	64	59	55	17
2002-03	Div 2	46	14	16	16	51	54	58	11

DID YOU KNOW ?

In 1959–60 Jim Rayner scored in 14 consecutive League and Cup matches for Peterborough United in the Midland League in a total of 21 during this sequence. His overall achievement for the season was 42.

PETERBOROUGH UNITED 2002–03 LEAGUE RECORD

Match No.	Date	Venue	Opponents	Result		H/T Score	Lg. Pos.	Goalscorers	Atten-dance
1	Aug 10	A	Luton T	W	3-2	2-0	—	Green [2], Newton [30], Clarke A [68]	7860
2	13	H	Oldham Ath	L	0-1	0-0	—		5204
3	17	H	Huddersfield T	L	0-1	0-1	17		5205
4	24	A	QPR	L	0-2	0-0	21		11,510
5	26	H	Colchester U	L	0-1	0-0	21		4203
6	31	A	Port Vale	L	0-1	0-0	23		3862
7	Sept 14	H	Crewe Alex	D	0-0	0-0	22		4345
8	17	H	Plymouth Arg	W	2-0	0-0	—	Clarke A [58], Green [84]	4298
9	21	A	Wigan Ath	D	2-2	0-1	23	Newton [63], Clarke A [76]	5797
10	28	H	Brentford	W	5-1	1-0	18	Rea [1], Bullard (pen) [48], Allen [68], Farrell [77], Clarke A [90]	5066
11	Oct 5	A	Notts Co	D	2-2	1-0	18	Allen [45], Rea [53]	6548
12	8	A	Stockport Co	L	1-2	0-1	—	Clarke A [79]	4726
13	12	H	Mansfield T	D	0-0	0-0	18		5067
14	19	A	Wycombe W	L	2-3	1-2	21	Allen [40], Bullard [90]	5539
15	26	H	Bristol C	L	1-3	1-2	22	Clarke A [43]	5332
16	29	A	Tranmere R	D	1-1	0-0	—	Farrell [88]	5980
17	Nov 2	A	Cardiff C	L	0-3	0-1	23		12,918
18	9	H	Chesterfield	W	1-0	0-0	22	Clarke A [82]	4359
19	23	H	Barnsley	L	1-3	0-2	23	Lee [71]	4449
20	30	A	Swindon T	D	1-1	0-0	22	Bullard [73]	4709
21	Dec 14	H	Cheltenham T	W	4-1	3-0	21	Lee 2 [19, 37], Clarke A 2 [28, 90]	4522
22	21	A	Blackpool	L	0-3	0-2	22		5068
23	26	A	Colchester U	D	1-1	0-1	22	Clarke A [82]	3760
24	28	H	Northampton T	D	0-0	0-0	22		7767
25	Jan 1	H	QPR	L	0-2	0-1	22		6210
26	4	A	Oldham Ath	D	0-0	0-0	21		5922
27	11	A	Huddersfield T	W	1-0	0-0	17	Edwards [83]	9022
28	18	H	Port Vale	L	1-2	0-0	20	Clarke A [82]	4770
29	25	A	Northampton T	W	1-0	0-0	17	Clarke A [55]	5906
30	Feb 1	H	Luton T	D	1-1	1-1	15	Fenn [39]	6760
31	8	A	Chesterfield	D	0-0	0-0	16		3515
32	22	H	Stockport Co	W	2-0	0-0	17	Arber [53], Fotiadis [83]	4386
33	Mar 1	A	Crewe Alex	W	1-0	0-0	16	McKenzie [90]	5704
34	4	A	Plymouth Arg	L	1-6	0-4	—	McKenzie [70]	6931
35	8	H	Wigan Ath	D	1-1	0-0	18	McKenzie [70]	4970
36	15	A	Bristol C	L	0-1	0-1	19		11,231
37	18	H	Wycombe W	L	1-2	1-1	—	Clarke A [43]	3627
38	22	H	Tranmere R	D	0-0	0-0	20		4158
39	29	A	Mansfield T	W	5-1	3-1	18	Rea [8], McKenzie [37], Hendon [44], Clarke A [82], Fotiadis [90]	5653
40	Apr 5	H	Swindon T	D	1-1	1-0	20	Shields [35]	4310
41	12	A	Barnsley	W	2-1	0-1	18	Arber (pen) [60], Crooks (og) [77]	8862
42	16	H	Cardiff C	W	2-0	1-0	—	Gill [38], McKenzie [70]	4984
43	19	H	Blackpool	W	1-0	1-0	13	Farrell [12]	4587
44	21	A	Cheltenham T	D	1-1	0-0	14	Clarke A [64]	4809
45	26	H	Notts Co	W	1-0	0-0	11	Scott [73]	5381
46	May 3	A	Brentford	D	1-1	0-0	11	Clarke A [57]	6687

Final League Position: 11

GOALSCORERS

League (51): Clarke A 16, McKenzie 5, Allen 3, Bullard 3 (1 pen), Farrell 3, Lee 3, Rea 3, Arber 2 (1 pen), Fotiadis 2, Green 2, Newton 2, Edwards 1, Fenn 1, Gill 1, Hendon 1, Scott 1, Shields 1, own goal 1.
Worthington Cup (0).
FA Cup (2): Clarke A 1, Fenn 1.
LDV Vans Trophy (2): Clarke A 2.

Tyler M 29	Gill M 41	Pearce D 2	Forsyth R 6 + 2	Joseph M 16 + 1	Rea S 35 + 2	Bullard J 26	Danielsson H 15 + 3	Clarke A 41 + 4	Green F 8 + 11	Newton A 31 + 5	Lee J 12 + 13	MacDonald G 5 + 3	Shields T 29 + 4	Farrell D 21 + 16	Clarke L — + 1	Edwards A 23	Willis R 1 + 3	Fenn N 8 + 6	Burton S 28 + 3	Jelleyman G 30 + 2	Allen B 10 + 1	Hyde G 8 + 1	Semple R 1 + 2	Connor D 4	McGovern B 1	Arber M 24 + 1	Harrison L 12	McKenzie L 6 + 5	Scott R 13 + 3	Hendon I 7	Fotiadis A 6 + 5	Strachan G 1 + 1	St Ledger-Hall S — + 1	Boucaud A 5 + 1	Scully T — + 3	Murphy B 1	*Match No.*
1	2^1	3^2	4	5	6	7^3	8	9	10	11	12	13	14																								1
1	2		4	5	6		8^1	9^3	10	11	13	3	12	7^2	14																						2
1	2^2		4	5			8	9^1	10	11		3	7	13		6	12																				3
1			4^1	2	5	7	8^2	9^3	10	11		3	12	13		6	14																				4
1	2		4	5^1	12	7	8	13	10^3	11		3				6	9^2	14																			5
1		3	4	2	5^2	7		12	10^1	11		14	9			6^3	13		8																		6
1	2			4		7	8	12	13	11	9^1					5		14	6	3^3	10^2																7
1	3			2		7	8^1	12	10	4	9	13		11^2		5			6																		8
1	2			4		7		9	10^1	3	8^2			11		5			6		12	13															9
1	3		12	2	5	7		9	13	8^2				11		6		14			10^3	4^1															10
1	3			2	5	7		9^1	12	8				11		6		13			10^2	4															11
1	2■		13	4		7		9	12	8		3		11^3		5				14	10^1	6^2															12
1	2			4	5	7		9^3	12	8			13	11				14	3		10^1	6^2															13
1	2			12	5	7		9	13	14			8	11		6^3			3^1		10	4^2															14
1	3			2	5		12	9			13		8^1	11		6					10	4	7^2														15
1	3^1			2	5	7		9			12		8^3	13					6	11^2	10	4	14														16
1	2			4	5■	7		9^3		12	13		8	14					6	3	10^2	11^1															17
1	2				5	7	8	9			12		11	13		6			4	3^2	10^1																18
	2				5	7	12^1	9^1		8	10			11		6		4		13				1	3^2												19
	2				5	7				8	9		4	11		6		10		3				1													20
	2				6	7		9		8	10		4	11		5				3				1													21
	2				5^3	7		9	12	8^2	10		4	11^1		6			13	3				1		14											22
	2				5^3	8		9		12	10		11	13		6			7^1	3^2						4	1	14									23
	2					8		9	12	7	10		6^2	11^1		5			13	3						4	1										24
	2					8		9		7	10		6^1	11		5			12	3						4	1										25
	2					8		9					11			5		10	6	3						4	1		7								26
	2					8		9		12			7	13		5		10	6	3^2						4	1		11^1								27
	2^1				12	8	14	9	13^3	3			7	11		5■		10^2	6							4	1										28
	2				5	7		9					8					10	6	3						4	1		12	11^1							29
	2^2				5		8	9					11	12				10	6	3^1			13			4	1		7								30
	2^1				5		8	9		12			11^3	13				10	6	3^2						4	1		7		14						31
	2				5		8	9^3		7	12		11^2					13	6	3						4	1	14			10^1						32
	2				5		8	9^1		7	12		11						6	3						4	1	13			10^2						33
	2				5		8	9^1		7^2	12			13					6^3	3						4	1	14	11		10						34
1	2				5		8	9		7			11^3	13					6	3						4		12^2	14		10^1						35
1	2				5		8^3	9		7	12			13					6	3^2						4			11		10^1	14					36
1	2				5^2			9		7	10^1									3						4			11	6	12	8	13				37
1	2				5			9		7^2	12■		8	11						3						4		10^1		6	13						38
1	2				5			9^1					8^3	12					6	3						4		10^2	11	7	13			14			39
1	2				5			9					8	12					6	3^1						4		10	11^2	7					13		40
1	2				5			9					8	12					6	3^1						4		10	11^2	7					13		41
1	2				5			9^2					8	12					6^1	3						4		10		7^3	13			11	14		42
1					5			9^1	13	7	12		8	11						3						4		10^2	2					6			43
1					5			9		7	10			11					6	3						4			2					8			44
1	2^2				5			9	12	7				11					6	3						4			13		10^1			8			45
					5			9		7	12		8	11					6	3						4			2					10^1		1	46

Worthington Cup
First Round — Portsmouth — (a) — 0-2

LDV Vans Trophy
First Round — Leyton Orient — (a) — 2-3

FA Cup
First Round — Rochdale — (a) — 2-3

PLYMOUTH ARGYLE Division 2

FOUNDATION

The club was formed in September 1886 as the Argyle Football Club by former public and private school pupils who wanted to continue playing the game. The meeting was held in a room above the Borough Arms (a Coffee House), Bedford Street, Plymouth. It was common then to choose a local street/terrace as a club name and Argyle or Argyll was a fashionable name throughout the land due to Queen Victoria's great interest in Scotland.

Home Park, Plymouth, Devon PL2 3DQ.

Telephone: (01752) 562 561. ***Fax:*** (01752) 606 167.
Pilgrim Shop: (01752) 558 292.

Ground Capacity: 20,134.

Record Attendance: 43,596 v Aston Villa, Division 2, 10 October 1936.

Record Receipts: £128,000 v Burnley, Division 2 play-off, 18 May 1994.

Pitch Measurements: 110yd × 72yd.

Chairman: Paul Stapleton. ***Vice-chairman:*** Peter Jones.

Directors: Phil Gill, Nick Warren, Rt Hon Michael Foot, Robert Dennerly.
Associate Directors: Ken Jones, John McNulty, David Tall.

Chief Executive: John McNulty. ***Secretary:*** Carole Rowntree.

Manager: Paul Sturrock.
Assistant Manager: Kevin Summerfield. ***Physio:*** Paul Maxwell.

Colours: Green shirts, white shorts, green stockings.

Change Colours: Tangerine shirts, green shorts, tangerine stockings.

Year Formed: 1886.

Turned Professional: 1903. ***Ltd Co.:*** 1903.

Previous Name: 1886, Argyle Athletic Club; 1903, Plymouth Argyle.

Club Nickname: 'The Pilgrims'.

First Football League game: 28 August 1920, Division 3, v Norwich C (h) D 1–1 – Craig; Russell, Atterbury; Logan, Dickinson, Forbes; Kirkpatrick, Jack, Bowler, Heeps (1), Dixon.

Record League Victory: 8–1 v Millwall, Division 2, 16 January 1932 – Harper; Roberts, Titmuss; Mackay, Pullan, Reed; Grozier, Bowden (2), Vidler (3), Leslie (1), Black (1), (1 og). 8–1 v Hartlepool U (a), Division 2, 7 May 1994 – Nicholls; Patterson (Naylor), Hill, Burrows, Comyn, McCall (1), Barlow, Castle (1), Landon (3), Marshall (1), Dalton (2).

HONOURS

Football League: Division 2 best season: 4th, 1931–32, 1952–53; Division 3 (S) – Champions 1929–30, 1951–52; Runners-up 1921–22, 1922–23, 1923–24, 1924–25, 1925–26, 1926–27 (record of six consecutive years): Division 3 – Champions 1958–59, 2001–02; Runners-up 1974–75, 1985–86, Promoted 1995–96 (play-offs).

FA Cup: Semi-final 1984.

Football League Cup: Semi-final 1965, 1974.

SKY SPORTS FACT FILE

In 1922–23 Plymouth Argyle's runners-up position in Division Three (South) was due in part to their home record where they dropped only three points in drawn matches and conceded just six goals at Home Park.

Record Cup Victory: 6–0 v Corby T, FA Cup 3rd rd, 22 January 1966 – Leiper; Book, Baird; Williams, Nelson, Newman; Jones (1), Jackson (1), Bickle (3), Piper (1), Jennings.

Record Defeat: 0–9 v Stoke C, Division 2, 17 December 1960.

Most League Points (2 for a win): 68, Division 3 (S), 1929–30.

Most League Points (3 for a win): 102, Division 3, 2001–02.

Most League Goals: 107, Division 3 (S), 1925–26 and 1951–52.

Highest League Scorer in Season: Jack Cock, 32, Division 3 (S), 1926–27.

Most League Goals in Total Aggregate: Sammy Black, 180, 1924–38.

Most League Goals in One Match: 5, Wilf Carter v Charlton Ath, Division 2, 27 December 1960.

Most Capped Player: Moses Russell, 20 (23), Wales.

Most League Appearances: Kevin Hodges, 530, 1978–92.

Youngest League Player: Lee Phillips, 16 years 43 days v Gillingham, 29 October 1996.

Record Transfer Fee Received: £750,000 from Southampton for Mickey Evans, March 1997.

Record Transfer Fee Paid: £250,000 to Hartlepool U for Paul Dalton, June 1992.

Football League Record: 1920 Original Member of Division 3; 1921–30 Division 3 (S); 1930–50 Division 2; 1950–52 Division 3 (S); 1952–56 Division 2; 1956–58 Division 3 (S); 1958–59 Division 3; 1959–68 Division 2; 1968–75 Division 3; 1975–77 Division 2; 1977–86 Division 3; 1986–95 Division 2; 1995–96 Division 3; 1996–98 Division 2; 1998–2002 Division 3; 2002– Division 2.

MANAGERS

Frank Brettell 1903–05
Bob Jack 1905–06
Bill Fullerton 1906–07
Bob Jack 1910–38
Jack Tresadern 1938–47
Jimmy Rae 1948–55
Jack Rowley 1955–60
Neil Dougall 1961
Ellis Stuttard 1961–63
Andy Beattie 1963–64
Malcolm Allison 1964–65
Derek Ufton 1965–68
Billy Bingham 1968–70
Ellis Stuttard 1970–72
Tony Waiters 1972–77
Mike Kelly 1977–78
Malcolm Allison 1978–79
Bobby Saxton 1979–81
Bobby Moncur 1981–83
Johnny Hore 1983–84
Dave Smith 1984–88
Ken Brown 1988–90
David Kemp 1990–92
Peter Shilton 1992–95
Steve McCall 1995
Neil Warnock 1995–97
Mick Jones 1997–98
Kevin Hodges 1998–2000
Paul Sturrock October 2000–

LATEST SEQUENCES

Longest Sequence of League Wins: 9, 8.3.1986 – 12.4.1986.

Longest Sequence of League Defeats: 9, 12.10.1963 – 7.12.1963.

Longest Sequence of League Draws: 5, 26.2.2000 – 14.3.2000.

Longest Sequence of Unbeaten League Matches: 22, 20.4.1929 – 21.12.1929.

Longest Sequence Without a League Win: 13, 27.4.1963 – 2.10.1963.

Successive Scoring Runs: 39 from 15.4.1939.

Successive Non-scoring Runs: 5 from 20.9.1947.

TEN YEAR LEAGUE RECORD

		P	W	D	L	F	A	Pts	Pos
1993-94	Div 2	46	25	10	11	88	56	85	3
1994-95	Div 2	46	12	10	24	45	83	46	21
1995-96	Div 3	46	22	12	12	68	49	79	4
1996-97	Div 2	46	12	18	16	47	58	54	19
1997-98	Div 2	46	12	13	21	55	70	49	22
1998-99	Div 3	46	17	10	19	58	54	61	13
1999-2000	Div 3	46	16	18	12	55	51	66	12
2000-01	Div 3	46	15	13	18	54	61	58	12
2001-02	Div 3	46	31	9	6	71	28	102	1
2002-03	Div 2	46	17	14	15	63	52	65	8

DID YOU KNOW?

On 19 February 1983 Plymouth Argyle goalkeeper Geoff Crudgington suffered second degree burns saving his home from fire. After treatment he played a heroic role in the 3-1 win over Bradford City.

PLYMOUTH ARGYLE 2002–03 LEAGUE RECORD

Match No.	Date	Venue	Opponents	Result		H/T Score	Lg. Pos.	Goalscorers	Attendance
1	Aug 10	A	Mansfield T	L	3-4	1-1	—	Evans [24], Friio [86], Lowndes [90]	5309
2	13	H	Huddersfield T	W	2-1	0-0	—	Friio [58], Wotton [90]	8953
3	17	H	Luton T	W	2-1	0-0	6	McGlinchey [57], Wotton [82]	10,973
4	24	A	Cheltenham T	W	2-1	0-1	4	Coughlan [61], Wotton [74]	4713
5	26	H	Bristol C	W	2-0	0-0	3	Wotton (pen) [65], Coughlan [81]	11,922
6	31	A	QPR	D	2-2	1-0	2	Friio [33], Hodges [59]	14,001
7	Sept 14	A	Barnsley	D	1-1	1-1	7	Sturrock [38]	9134
8	17	A	Peterborough U	L	0-2	0-0	—		4298
9	21	H	Chesterfield	L	0-1	0-0	12		8547
10	24	H	Cardiff C	D	2-2	1-1	—	Wotton [8], Coughlan [90]	11,606
11	28	A	Wycombe W	L	1-2	0-1	11	Friio [60]	6708
12	Oct 5	H	Northampton T	D	0-0	0-0	10		8530
13	12	H	Wigan Ath	L	1-3	1-1	13	Stonebridge [18]	8746
14	19	A	Crewe Alex	W	1-0	1-0	11	Norris [45]	6733
15	26	H	Blackpool	L	1-3	0-2	12	Keith [60]	8717
16	29	A	Brentford	D	0-0	0-0	—		6431
17	Nov 2	A	Tranmere R	L	1-2	1-0	15	Adams [6]	7083
18	9	H	Oldham Ath	D	2-2	2-0	16	Stonebridge [4], Friio [7]	8216
19	23	H	Stockport Co	W	4-1	3-1	13	Goodwin (2 og) [6, 60], Keith [13], Adams [42]	7746
20	30	A	Colchester U	D	0-0	0-0	13		3714
21	Dec 14	H	Swindon T	D	1-1	0-0	12	Hodges (pen) [90]	8111
22	21	A	Port Vale	W	2-1	2-1	12	Evans [2], Keith [40]	4892
23	26	A	Bristol C	D	0-0	0-0	12		18,085
24	28	H	Notts Co	W	1-0	0-0	12	Aljofree [61]	11,901
25	Jan 1	H	Cheltenham T	W	3-1	2-1	10	Phillips [22], Stonebridge [35], Norris [53]	10,927
26	18	H	QPR	L	0-1	0-0	12		10,249
27	25	A	Notts Co	W	2-0	1-0	10	Norris 2 [38, 50]	6329
28	Feb 1	H	Mansfield T	W	3-1	1-1	10	Lawrence (og) [2], Phillips [68], Evans [84]	8030
29	4	A	Huddersfield T	L	0-1	0-0	—		7294
30	8	A	Oldham Ath	W	1-0	1-0	8	Evans [39]	6657
31	15	H	Tranmere R	L	0-1	0-0	10		8590
32	21	A	Cardiff C	D	1-1	0-1	—	Wotton [86]	14,006
33	25	A	Luton T	L	0-1	0-0	—		7589
34	Mar 1	H	Barnsley	D	1-1	1-0	10	Coughlan [14]	8228
35	4	H	Peterborough U	W	6-1	4-0	—	Keith [9], Burton (og) [25], Gill (og) [42], Wotton [45], Friio [62], Bent [72]	6931
36	8	A	Chesterfield	L	2-3	1-2	10	Keith 2 [15, 74]	3668
37	15	A	Blackpool	D	1-1	1-1	10	Keith [29]	8772
38	18	H	Crewe Alex	L	1-3	0-2	—	Stonebridge [47]	7777
39	22	H	Brentford	W	3-0	2-0	10	Keith 2 [12, 47], Smith [28]	6835
40	29	A	Wigan Ath	W	1-0	1-0	9	Keith [35]	7203
41	Apr 5	H	Colchester U	D	0-0	0-0	9		7122
42	12	A	Stockport Co	L	1-2	0-1	9	Keith [72]	5484
43	19	H	Port Vale	W	3-0	0-0	8	Coughlan [56], Norris [67], Wotton [77]	7775
44	23	A	Swindon T	L	0-2	0-1	—		5057
45	26	A	Northampton T	D	2-2	1-0	9	Norris [19], Stonebridge [55]	5063
46	May 3	H	Wycombe W	W	1-0	0-0	8	Lowndes [75]	10,129

Final League Position: 8

GOALSCORERS

League (63): Keith 11, Wotton 8 (1 pen), Friio 6, Norris 6, Coughlan 5, Stonebridge 5, Evans 4, Adams 2, Hodges 2 (1 pen), Lowndes 2, Phillips 2, Aljofree 1, Bent 1, McGlinchey 1, Smith 1, Sturrock 1, own goals 5.
Worthington Cup (1): Sturrock 1.
FA Cup (8): Wotton 3 (1 pen), Stonebridge 2, Evans 1, Friio 1, own goal 1.
LDV Vans Trophy (2): Evans 1, Keith 1.

Larrieu R 43	Worrell D 43	McGlinchey B 11 + 8	Friio D 33 + 3	Wotton P 41 + 2	Coughlan G 42	Bent J 23 + 2	Hodges L 38 + 1	Stonebridge I 30 + 7	Evans M 35 + 7	Adams S 36 + 1	Broad J 1 + 4	Phillips M 14 + 10	Lowndes N 6 + 10	Malcolm S 3	Sturrock B 5 + 15	Keith M 20 + 17	Beresford D 6 + 10	Aljofree H 19	Lopes O 4 + 5	Norris D 29 + 4	McCormick L 2 + 1	Milosevic D 1	Barras T 4	Bernard P 7 + 3	Smith G 4 + 1	Connolly P 2	McAnespie K 2 + 2	Yetton S — + 1	Taylor C 1	Capaldi T 1	*Match No.*
1	2	3	4	5	6[1]	7[2]	8	9[3]	10	11	12	13	14																		1
1	2	3■	4	5		12	8		10[2]	11		7[1]	9	6	13																2
1	2	3	4	5		8	12		10[2]	11		7[1]	9[3]	6	13	14															3
1	2	3[2]	4	5	6	8	10		9[3]	11		12			13	14	7[1]														4
1	2		4[2]	5	6	11[1]	8		10	3	13	7	9[3]		12		14														5
1	2		4	5	6		8		10[2]	11	14	12			9[1]	13	7[3]	3													6
1	2		4	5	6		8	12	10[1]	11	13	7[3]			9[2]			3	14												7
1	2		4	5	6		8[1]	12		11		13	9		10[2]		7[3]	3	14												8
1	2		4	5	6		8[2]	9	10[1]	11[3]		7			12		13	3	14												9
1	2		4	5	6		8	9[1]	10	11[2]		7[3]	13		12			3	14												10
1	2		4	5	6		8	9[2]	10[1]	11		7[3]			12	13	14	3													11
1	2			5	6		8	9[1]	10[2]	11		7			12	13	14	3	4[3]												12
1	2	3	4	5	6		8[3]	9	10[2]	11		7[1]			12	13			14												13
1	2		4	5	6		8[1]	9	12	11					10			3		7											14
1	2		4	5[2]	6		8	9	12	11		13			10[1]	14		3[3]		7											15
	2	3	4	5	6		8		9	11						10				7	1										16
	2	3	4	5	6		8	12	9[2]	11					13	10[1]				7	1										17
	2	12	4	5	6		3	9	10	11						13			8[2]	7[1]	15	1[6]									18
1	2		4	5	6		3	9[1]	10[2]	11			12			8	13			7											19
1	2			5	6		3	9	10	11						8				7			4								20
1	2			5[3]	6		3	9[2]	10	11			12		13	8[1]	14			7			4								21
1	2			5	6		3	9	10[1]	11					12	8				7			4								22
1	2	12		5	6	8	3	13	9[2]	11					14	10[3]				7			4[1]								23
1		12		5	6		3[1]	9	10	11		13						2	8[2]	7				4							24
1	2		12	5	6	4		9[2]	10[3]	11		7[1]			13	14		3		8											25
1	2	12	4	5	6		3[1]	9	10[3]	11		7[2]			13	14				8											26
1	2		4	5	6	8	3	9	10[1]	11						12				7											27
1	2	12	4		6	8		9[3]	10	3		13				14	11[2]	5		7[1]											28
1	2	12	4	5	6	8[2]		9[3]	10	11		13				14		3[1]		7											29
1	2	12	4	5	6	8		13	9[3]	11						10[1]		3		7[2]				14							30
1	2	12	4	5	6	8[2]		9[3]	10	11		13				14		3[1]		7											31
1	2	3[2]	4	5	6	8	11	9[3]	10[1]	12			14			13				7											32
1	2[2]	3[1]	4	5	6	8	11	9	10				13			12				7											33
1	2	3	12	5	6	8		9[3]	10			13	14			11[2]				7				4[1]							34
1	2		4[2]	5	6	8	3	12	9[1]	11		7	14			10[3]				13											35
1	2		4[2]	5	6	8[3]	3	12	9[1]	11		7	14			10				13											36
1	2			5	6	12	8	9[2]	13	3						10				7				4	11[1]						37
1	2[1]			5	6	8	3	9	12	11		7[3]				10				13				4[2]	14						38
1				12	6[1]	8	3	9	13	4						10[2]	14	5		7					11[3]	2					39
1	2		4		6	8[1]	3	9								10		5		7				12	11						40
1	2		4[2]	5		8	3	9[1]	12							10		6	7	13					11[3]		14				41
1	2				6	8■	3[1]		9					5		10	12			7				11			4				42
1	2		12	5	6	8[1]	3		10[2]				9			13	11			7				4							43
1	2[1]		4	12	6		3[2]						9			10	11[3]	5		7				8			13	14			44
1			4[2]	5			3	9			8					10	12			7				13		2	11[1]		6		45
1	2	3	4	5	6	8		9[1]	12				13			10[2]	14			7										11[3]	46

Worthington Cup

First Round	Crystal Palace	(a)	1-2

FA Cup

First Round	Bury	(a)	3-0
Second Round	Stockport Co	(a)	3-0
Third Round	Dagenham & R	(h)	2-2
		(a)	0-2

LDV Vans Trophy

First Round	Chester C	(a)	2-1
Second Round	Brentford	(h)	0-1

PORTSMOUTH — FA Premiership

FOUNDATION

At a meeting held in his High Street, Portsmouth offices in 1898, solicitor Alderman J. E. Pink and five other business and professional men agreed to buy some ground close to Goldsmith Avenue for £4,950 which they developed into Fratton Park in record breaking time. A team of professionals was signed up by manager Frank Brettell and entry to the Southern League obtained for the new club's September 1899 kick-off.

Fratton Park, Frogmore Road, Portsmouth PO4 8RA.
Telephone: (023) 9273 1204. ***Fax:*** (023) 9273 4129.
Ticket Office: (023) 9261 8777.
Box Office Fax: (023) 9275 0825.
Community Office: (023) 9277 8526.
Pompey Shop: (023) 9273 8358.
Football in the Community: (023) 9277 8557.
Corporate Sales: (023) 9277 8564/(023) 9277 8556.
Website: www.pompeyfc.co.uk
Email: info@pompeyfc.co.uk

ClubCall: 09068 121 182.

Ground Capacity: 19,179.

Record Attendance: 51,385 v Derby Co, FA Cup 6th rd, 26 February 1949.

HONOURS

Football League: Division 1 – Champions 1948–49, 1949–50, 2002–03; Division 2 – Runners-up 1926–27, 1986–87; Division 3 (S) – Champions 1923–24; Division 3 – Champions 1961–62, 1982–83.

FA Cup: Winners 1939; Runners-up 1929, 1934.

Football League Cup: best season: 5th rd, 1961, 1986.

Record Receipts: £233,000 v Chelsea, FA Cup 6th rd, 9 March 1997.

Pitch Measurements: 110yd × 72yd.

Chairman: Milan Mandaric.

Directors: F. Dinenage, T. Brady.

Chief Executive: Peter Storrie.

Manager: Harry Redknapp. ***Assistant Manager:*** Jim Smith.

Goalkeeper Coach: Alan Knight.

Secretary: Paul Weld.

Youth Team Manager: Mark O'Connor.

Physio: Gary Sadler.

Colours: Blue shirts, white shorts, red stockings.

Change Colours: Gold and navy shirts, gold and navy shorts, navy stockings.

Year Formed: 1898.

Turned Professional: 1898. ***Ltd Co.:*** 1898.

Club Nickname: 'Pompey'.

First Football League Game: 28 August 1920, Division 3, v Swansea T (h) W 3–0 – Robson; Probert, Potts; Abbott, Harwood, Turner; Thompson, Stringfellow (1), Reid (1), James (1), Beedie.

SKY SPORTS FACT FILE

In successive seasons in Division Three (South) 1921–22 and 1922–23, Portsmouth were the best starters in the Football League, unbeaten in respectively ten and eight matches in those seasons and again with nine in 2002–03.

Record League Victory: 9–1 v Notts Co, Division 2, 9 April 1927 – McPhail; Clifford, Ted Smith; Reg Davies (1), Foxall, Moffat; Forward (1), Mackie (2), Haines (3), Watson, Cook (2).

Record Cup Victory: 7–0 v Stockport Co, FA Cup 3rd rd, 8 January 1949 – Butler; Rookes, Ferrier; Scoular, Flewin, Dickinson; Harris (3), Barlow, Clarke (2), Phillips (2), Froggatt.

Record Defeat: 0–10 v Leicester C, Division 1, 20 October 1928.

Most League Points (2 for a win): 65, Division 3, 1961–62.

Most League Points (3 for a win): 98, Division 1, 2002–03.

Most League Goals: 97, Division 1, 2002–03.

Highest League Scorer in Season: Guy Whittingham, 42, Division 1, 1992–93.

Most League Goals in Total Aggregate: Peter Harris, 194, 1946–60.

Most League Goals in One Match: 5, Alf Strange v Gillingham, Division 3, 27 January 1923; 5, Peter Harris v Aston Villa, Division 1, 3 September 1958.

Most Capped Player: Jimmy Dickinson, 48, England.

Most League Appearances: Jimmy Dickinson, 764, 1946–65.

Youngest League Player: Clive Green, 16 years 259 days v Wrexham, 21 August 1976.

Record Transfer Fee Received: £4,500,000 from Aston Villa for Peter Crouch, March 2002.

Record Transfer Fee Paid: £1,400,000 to Yokohama Marinos for Yoshikatsu Kawaguchi, October 2001.

MANAGERS

Frank Brettell 1898–1901
Bob Blyth 1901–04
Richard Bonney 1905–08
Bob Brown 1911–20
John McCartney 1920–27
Jack Tinn 1927–47
Bob Jackson 1947–52
Eddie Lever 1952–58
Freddie Cox 1958–61
George Smith 1961–70
Ron Tindall 1970–73
(General Manager to 1974)
John Mortimore 1973–74
Ian St John 1974–77
Jimmy Dickinson 1977–79
Frank Burrows 1979–82
Bobby Campbell 1982–84
Alan Ball 1984–89
John Gregory 1989–90
Frank Burrows 1990–91
Jim Smith 1991–95
Terry Fenwick 1995–98
Alan Ball 1998–99
Tony Pulis 2000
Steve Claridge 2000–01
Graham Rix 2001–02
Harry Redknapp March 2002–

Football League Record: 1920 Original Member of Division 3; 1921 Division 3 (S); 1924–27 Division 2; 1927–59 Division 1; 1959–61 Division 2; 1961–62 Division 3; 1962–76 Division 2; 1976–78 Division 3; 1978–80 Division 4; 1980–83 Division 3; 1983–87 Division 2; 1987–88 Division 1; 1988–92 Division 2; 1992–2003 Division 1; 2003– FA Premier League.

LATEST SEQUENCES

Longest Sequence of League Wins: 7, 17.8.2002 – 17.9.2002.

Longest Sequence of League Defeats: 9, 21.10.1975 – 6.12.1975.

Longest Sequence of League Draws: 5, 16.12.2000 – 13.1.2001.

Longest Sequence of Unbeaten League Matches: 15, 18.4.1924 – 18.10.1924.

Longest Sequence Without a League Win: 25, 29.11.1958 – 22.8.1959.

Successive Scoring Runs: 23 from 30.8.1930.

Successive Non-scoring Runs: 6 from 14.1.1939.

TEN YEAR LEAGUE RECORD

		P	W	D	L	F	A	Pts	Pos
1993-94	Div 1	46	15	13	18	52	58	58	17
1994-95	Div 1	46	15	13	18	53	63	58	18
1995-96	Div 1	46	13	13	20	61	69	52	21
1996-97	Div 1	46	20	8	18	59	53	68	7
1997-98	Div 1	46	13	10	23	51	63	49	20
1998-99	Div 1	46	11	14	21	57	73	47	19
1999-2000	Div 1	46	13	12	21	55	66	51	18
2000-01	Div 1	46	10	19	17	47	59	49	20
2001-02	Div 1	46	13	14	19	60	72	53	17
2002-03	Div 1	46	29	11	6	97	45	98	1

DID YOU KNOW ?

Inside-right Jack Smith had had 12 years in the Football League before he won his first full England cap. He cost South Shields £5 in 1919 and went to Portsmouth in 1928, making exactly 261 League appearances for each club.

PORTSMOUTH 2002–03 LEAGUE RECORD

Match No.	Date	Venue	Opponents	Result		H/T Score	Lg. Pos.	Goalscorers	Attendance
1	Aug 10	H	Nottingham F	W	2-0	2-0	—	Burton ^{8}, Pericard ^{45}	18,910
2	13	A	Sheffield U	D	1-1	1-1	—	Burton ^{25}	16,093
3	17	A	Crystal Palace	W	3-2	0-2	—	Foxe ^{68}, Crowe 2 $^{69, 72}$	18,315
4	24	H	Watford	W	3-0	2-0	3	Merson (pen) ^{42}, Todorov ^{45}, Burton ^{47}	17,901
5	26	A	Grimsby T	W	1-0	0-0	1	Burchill ^{85}	5770
6	31	H	Brighton & HA	W	4-2	3-2	1	Taylor ^{3}, Merson (pen) ^{26}, Todorov ^{45}, Crowe ^{52}	19,031
7	Sept 7	A	Gillingham	W	3-1	2-0	1	Merson ^{29}, Burchill ^{45}, O'Neil ^{79}	8797
8	14	H	Millwall	W	1-0	0-0	1	Todorov ^{50}	17,201
9	17	H	Wimbledon	W	4-1	3-1	—	Pericard ^{3}, Todorov ^{31}, Davis (og) ^{39}, Taylor ^{72}	18,837
10	21	A	Norwich C	L	0-1	0-0	1		21,335
11	28	H	Bradford C	W	3-0	2-0	1	Quashie 2 $^{17, 58}$, Pericard ^{21}	18,459
12	Oct 5	A	Rotherham U	W	3-2	3-1	1	Pericard ^{15}, Todorov ^{23}, Merson (pen) ^{45}	8604
13	19	H	Coventry C	D	1-1	0-0	1	Pericard ^{51}	18,837
14	26	A	Burnley	W	3-0	1-0	1	Quashie ^{21}, Todorov ^{58}, Harper ^{86}	15,788
15	29	H	Preston NE	W	3-2	3-1	—	Stone ^{23}, Merson (pen) ^{26}, Taylor ^{34}	18,637
16	Nov 2	H	Leicester C	L	0-2	0-2	1		19,107
17	6	A	Wolverhampton W	D	1-1	0-0	—	Merson ^{56}	27,022
18	9	A	Derby Co	W	2-1	1-1	1	Todorov ^{27}, Burchill ^{51}	26,587
19	16	H	Stoke C	W	3-0	0-0	1	Burchill ^{49}, Pericard ^{87}, Todorov ^{90}	18,701
20	23	A	Sheffield W	W	3-1	1-1	1	Todorov 2 $^{11, 50}$, O'Neil ^{64}	16,602
21	30	H	Walsall	W	3-2	1-1	1	Quashie ^{45}, Todorov ^{58}, Taylor ^{76}	17,701
22	Dec 7	A	Reading	D	0-0	0-0	1		23,462
23	14	A	Stoke C	D	1-1	0-1	1	Crowe ^{74}	13,330
24	21	H	Ipswich T	D	1-1	1-0	1	Todorov ^{19}	19,130
25	26	H	Crystal Palace	D	1-1	1-1	1	Merson ^{27}	19,217
26	28	A	Nottingham F	W	2-1	0-0	1	Taylor ^{56}, Pericard ^{87}	28,165
27	Jan 1	A	Watford	D	2-2	0-0	1	Burton ^{54}, Harper ^{58}	15,048
28	13	H	Sheffield U	L	1-2	0-1	—	O'Neil ^{78}	18,872
29	18	A	Brighton & HA	D	1-1	0-0	1	Todorov ^{64}	6848
30	Feb 1	H	Grimsby T	W	3-0	1-0	1	Yakubu ^{4}, Ford (og) ^{75}, Quashie ^{90}	19,428
31	8	H	Derby Co	W	6-2	3-0	1	Merson ^{3}, Yakubu 2 $^{17, 80}$, Taylor ^{22}, Todorov 2 $^{73, 85}$	19,503
32	17	A	Leicester C	D	1-1	0-1	—	Taylor ^{65}	31,775
33	22	H	Gillingham	W	1-0	0-0	1	De Zeeuw ^{58}	19,521
34	Mar 1	A	Millwall	W	5-0	4-0	1	Yakubu 2 $^{15, 25}$, Sherwood ^{31}, Todorov ^{45}, Merson (pen) ^{72}	9697
35	4	A	Wimbledon	L	1-2	1-0	—	Merson ^{26}	10,356
36	12	H	Norwich C	W	3-2	0-0	—	Yakubu ^{57}, Todorov 2 $^{59, 72}$	19,221
37	15	H	Wolverhampton W	W	1-0	1-0	1	Stone ^{4}	19,558
38	19	A	Coventry C	W	4-0	3-0	—	Caldwell (og) ^{14}, Stone ^{17}, Harper ^{23}, Merson ^{68}	13,922
39	22	A	Preston NE	D	1-1	1-0	1	Yakubu ^{4}	16,665
40	Apr 5	A	Walsall	W	2-1	2-1	1	Harper ^{15}, Todorov ^{33}	7899
41	12	H	Sheffield W	L	1-2	1-0	2	Bradbury ^{20}	19,524
42	15	H	Burnley	W	1-0	0-0	—	Todorov ^{73}	19,221
43	18	A	Ipswich T	L	0-3	0-3	—		29,396
44	21	H	Reading	W	3-0	2-0	1	Pericard 2 $^{19, 45}$, Todorov ^{71}	19,535
45	27	H	Rotherham U	W	3-2	3-2	1	Merson (pen) ^{11}, Todorov 2 $^{22, 45}$	19,420
46	May 4	A	Bradford C	W	5-0	1-0	1	Festa ^{20}, Todorov 3 (1 pen) $^{48, 49, 58 (p)}$, Stone ^{68}	19,088

Final League Position: 1

GOALSCORERS

League (97): Todorov 26 (1 pen), Merson 12 (6 pens), Pericard 9, Taylor 7, Yakubu 7, Quashie 5, Burchill 4, Burton 4, Crowe 4, Harper 4, Stone 4, O'Neil 3, Bradbury 1, De Zeeuw 1, Festa 1, Foxe 1, Sherwood 1, own goals 3.
Worthington Cup (3): Pericard 1, Primus 1, Quashie 1.
FA Cup (1): Stone 1.

Hislop S 46	Howe E 1	Taylor M 35	Robinson C 11 + 4	Foxe H 30 + 2	De Zeeuw A 35 + 3	O'Neil G 11 + 20	Merson P 44 + 1	Pericard V 18 + 14	Burton D 11 + 4	Quashie N 42	Primus L 39 + 1	Hughes R 4 + 2	Todorov S 43 + 2	Burchill M 4 + 14	Crowe J 7 + 9	Festa G 27	Harper K 21 + 16	Tiler C — + 2	Ritchie P 8 + 4	Diabate L 16 + 9	Stone S 18	Buxton L — + 1	Tavlaridis E 3 + 1	Yakubu A 12 + 2	Sherwood T 17	Heikkinen M — + 2	Bradbury L 3	Kawaguchi Y — + 1	*Match No.*
1	2^{1}	3	4	5	6	7	8	9	10	11	12																		1
1		3	4^{2}	5	6	7	8	9^{1}	10^{3}	11	2	13	12	14															2
1		3	4^{2}	5	6	7^{3}	8	9^{1}	10	11	2	13	12		14														3
1		3	12	5	6	13	8^{2}		10^{3}	7		11^{1}	9	14	2	4													4
1		3	12	5	6		8		10^{2}	11		7	9^{1}	13	2^{3}	4	14												5
1		3	12	5	6		8		10^{2}	7		11	9^{1}	13	2^{3}	4	14												6
1		3			6	12	8			7	5	11	9	10^{1}	2^{2}	4	13												7
1		3	7^{2}		6	13	8	10^{1}		11	5		9^{3}	12		4	2	14											8
1		3	7		6	12	8	9		11^{1}	5		10^{2}	13		4	2^{3}	14											9
1		3	7^{2}		6	10^{3}	8	12		11	5		9^{1}	13		4	2		14										10
1		3	7^{1}		6	12	8	9		11	5		10^{2}	13		4^{3}	2		14										11
1		3			6		8	9		11	2		10^{1}			4	12		5	7									12
1		3			6	2^{2}	8	9		11	5		10^{1}	12		4			13	7									13
1		3	12		6		8	9		11	5		10^{2}				13		4	7^{1}	2								14
1		3			6	12	8	9^{2}		11			10^{1}			5	13		4	7	2								15
1		3			6	12	8	9		11	5		10^{2}	13		4^{3}			14	7^{1}	2								16
1		3	4^{2}			12	8	9		11	5		10^{3}	14			13		6	7^{1}	2								17
1		3		12	6		8	13		11	5		10^{3}	9^{2}			14		4^{1}	7	2								18
1		3		4	6	12	8	13		11	5		10^{1}	9^{2}	14		2^{3}			7									19
1		3	11	4	6	12	8^{1}	9			5^{3}		10^{2}	13	14		2			7									20
1		3		5		12	8^{2}	9^{1}		11			10^{3}	13	4		2		6	7		14							21
1		3	7	5	6		8			11	2		10	9^{1}			12		4										22
1			2^{1}	4	6		8		9	11	5		10		13		12		3^{2}	7									23
1		3		4	6	12	8^{1}		9^{2}	11	5		10	13			14			7	2^{3}								24
1		3		4	6	12	8	13	9^{2}	11	5		10		2^{3}		14			7^{1}									25
1		3		4	6	8		12	9^{1}	11	5		10		13		2^{2}			7									26
1		3		4	6^{3}	8	12	13	9^{2}	11	5		10^{1}		14		2			7									27
1		3		4		7	8	9	12	11	5		10^{1}			6^{3}	13				2^{2}		14						28
1		3		4			8	9^{3}		11	5		10		12		13			7	2^{2}		6^{1}	14					29
1		3		4^{2}			8	12		11	5		10		14		2^{3}			13			6	9^{1}	7				30
1		3		4			8			11^{1}	5		10				2			12			6^{2}	9	7	13			31
1		3		4	6		8	12		11	5		10^{2}				2			13				9^{1}	7				32
1		3			6	13	8^{2}	12		11	5		10			4	2							9^{1}	7				33
1		3			6		8^{2}	12		11	5		10^{1}		14	4	2^{3}			13				9	7				34
1		3			6	12	8	13		11	5		10^{2}		2^{1}	4								9	7				35
1		3		12	6	13	8^{1}			11^{3}	5		10			4	2^{2}			14				9	7				36
1				4	6	11	8		12		5^{2}		10^{1}			3	13			14	2			9^{3}	7				37
1				5	6^{3}	11	8	12					10^{1}			4	2			13	3^{2}			9	7	14			38
1				4		11	8		12		5		10^{1}			6	3				2			9	7				39
1				4		12	8^{1}		13	11	5		10			6	3				2			9^{2}	7				40
1				4	12		8			11	5		10			6	3^{1}				2				7		9		41
1				4	6		8	12		11	5		10			3					2				7		9^{1}		42
1				4	6^{3}	14	8^{2}	12		11	5		10			3	13				2				7		9^{1}		43
1				4	12	13	8^{3}	9		11^{2}	5		10			6	3^{1}			14	2				7				44
1				4	12		8	9^{2}		11	5		10			6	3^{1}				2			13	7				45
1^{G}				4^{1}	6	12	8			11	5		10			3^{2}				13	2			9	7			15	46

Worthington Cup

First Round	Peterborough U	(h)	2-0
Second Round	Wimbledon	(h)	1-3

FA Cup

Third Round	Manchester U	(a)	1-4

PORT VALE — Division 2

FOUNDATION

Formed in 1876 as Port Vale, adopting the prefix 'Burslem' in 1884 upon moving to that part of the city. It was dropped in 1909.

Vale Park, Hamil Road, Burslem, Stoke-on-Trent ST6 1AW.

Telephone: (01782) 655 800. ***Fax:*** (01782) 834 981. ***ClubCall:*** 09068 121 636. ***Club Shop:*** (01782) 833 545. ***Community:*** (01782) 575 594. ***Marketing Dept:*** (01782) 835 524. ***Marketing Fax:*** (01782) 836 875.

Ground Capacity: 17,677.

Record Attendance: 49,768 v Aston Villa, FA Cup 5th rd, 20 February 1960.

Record Receipts: £170,349 v Everton, FA Cup 4th rd, 14 February 1996.

Pitch Measurements: 114yd × 75yd.

Manager: Brian Horton. ***Physio:*** Matthew Radcliffe.

Medical Officer: Dr D. Phillips.

Secretary: F. W. Lodey.

Safety Officer: W. Stevenson.

Groundsman: S. Speed.

Community Scheme Officer: Jim Cooper (01782 575594).

Colours: White shirts, black shorts, black and white stockings.

Change Colours: All sky blue.

Year Formed: 1876.

Turned Professional: 1885.

Ltd Co.: 1911.

Previous Name: 1876, Port Vale; 1884, Burslem Port Vale; 1909, Port Vale.

Club Nickname: 'Valiants'.

Previous Grounds: 1876, Limekin Lane, Longport; 1881, Westport; 1884, Moorland Road, Burslem; 1886, Athletic Ground, Cobridge; 1913, Recreation Ground, Hanley; 1950, Vale Park.

First Football League Game: 3 September 1892, Division 2, v Small Heath (a) L 1–5 – Frail; Clutton, Elson; Farrington, McCrindle, Delves; Walker, Scarratt, Bliss (1), Jones. (Only 10 men).

Record League Victory: 9–1 v Chesterfield, Division 2, 24 September 1932 – Leckie; Shenton, Poyser; Sherlock, Round, Jones; McGrath, Mills, Littlewood (6), Kirkham (2), Morton (1).

Record Cup Victory: 7–1 v Irthlingborough, FA Cup 1st rd, 12 January 1907 – Matthews; Dunn, Hamilton; Eardley, Baddeley, Holyhead; Carter, Dodds (2), Beats, Mountford (2), Coxon (3).

HONOURS

Football League: Division 2 – Runners-up 1993–94; Division 3 (N) – Champions 1929–30, 1953–54; Runners-up 1952–53; Division 4 – Champions 1958–59; Promoted 1969–70 (4th).

FA Cup: Semi-final 1954, when in Division 3.

Football League Cup: best season: 3rd rd 1992, 1997.

Autoglass Trophy: Winners 1993.

Anglo-Italian Cup: Runners-up 1996.

LDV Vans Trophy: Winners 2001.

SKY SPORTS FACT FILE

In 1958–59 Port Vale, sporting new black and amber stripes, had five players with double figure goals: Stan Steele 22, Jack Wilkinson 21, Graham Barnett 20, Harry Poole 16 and Dickie Cunliffe 15.

Record Defeat: 0–10 v Sheffield U, Division 2, 10 December 1892. 0–10 v Notts Co, Division 2, 26 February 1895.

Most League Points (2 for a win): 69, Division 3 (N), 1953–54.

Most League Points (3 for a win): 89, Division 2, 1992–93.

Most League Goals: 110, Division 4, 1958–59.

Highest League Scorer in Season: Wilf Kirkham 38, Division 2, 1926–27.

Most League Goals in Total Aggregate: Wilf Kirkham, 154, 1923–29, 1931–33.

Most League Goals in One Match: 6, Stewart Littlewood v Chesterfield, Division 2, 24 September 1922.

Most Capped Player: Tony Rougier, Trinidad & Tobago.

Most League Appearances: Roy Sproson, 761, 1950–72.

Youngest League Player: Malcolm McKenzie, 15 years 347 days v Newport Co, 12 April 1966.

Record Transfer Fee Received: £2,000,000 from Wimbledon for Gareth Ainsworth, October 1998.

Record Transfer Fee Paid: £500,000 to Lincoln C for Gareth Ainsworth, September 1997.

Football League Record: 1892 Original Member of Division 2. Failed re-election in 1896; Re-elected 1898; Resigned 1907; Returned in Oct, 1919, when they took over the fixtures of Leeds City; 1929–30 Division 3 (N); 1930–36 Division 2; 1936–38 Division 3 (N); 1938–52 Division 3 (S); 1952–54 Division 3 (N); 1954–57 Division 2; 1957–58 Division 3 (S); 1958–59 Division 4; 1959–65 Division 3; 1965–70 Division 4; 1970–78 Division 3; 1978–83 Division 4; 1983–84 Division 3; 1984–86 Division 4; 1986–89 Division 3; 1989–94 Division 2; 1994–2000 Division 1; 2000– Division 2.

MANAGERS

Sam Gleaves 1896–1905
(Secretary-Manager)
Tom Clare 1905–11
A. S. Walker 1911–12
H. Myatt 1912–14
Tom Holford 1919–24
(continued as Trainer)
Joe Schofield 1924–30
Tom Morgan 1930–32
Tom Holford 1932–35
Warney Cresswell 1936–37
Tom Morgan 1937–38
Billy Frith 1945–46
Gordon Hodgson 1946–51
Ivor Powell 1951
Freddie Steele 1951–57
Norman Low 1957–62
Freddie Steele 1962–65
Jackie Mudie 1965–67
Sir Stanley Matthews
(General Manager) 1965–68
Gordon Lee 1968–74
Roy Sproson 1974–77
Colin Harper 1977
Bobby Smith 1977–78
Dennis Butler 1978–79
Alan Bloor 1979
John McGrath 1980–83
John Rudge 1984–99
Brian Horton February 1999–

LATEST SEQUENCES

Longest Sequence of League Wins: 8, 8.4.1893 – 30.9.1893.

Longest Sequence of League Defeats: 9, 9.3.1957 – 20.4.1957.

Longest Sequence of League Draws: 6, 26.4.1981 – 12.9.1981.

Longest Sequence of Unbeaten League Matches: 19, 5.5.1969 – 8.11.1969.

Longest Sequence Without a League Win: 17, 7.12.1991 – 21.3.1992.

Successive Scoring Runs: 22 from 12.9.1992.

Successive Non-scoring Runs: 4 from 10.2.1896.

TEN YEAR LEAGUE RECORD

		P	W	D	L	F	A	Pts	Pos
1993-94	Div 2	46	26	10	9	79	46	88	2
1994-95	Div 1	46	15	13	18	58	64	58	17
1995-96	Div 1	46	15	15	16	59	66	60	12
1996-97	Div 1	46	17	16	13	58	55	67	8
1997-98	Div 1	46	13	10	23	56	66	49	19
1998-99	Div 1	46	13	8	25	45	75	47	21
1999-2000	Div 1	46	7	15	24	48	69	36	23
2000-01	Div 2	46	16	14	16	55	49	62	11
2001-02	Div 2	46	16	10	20	51	62	58	14
2002-03	Div 2	46	14	11	21	54	70	53	17

DID YOU KNOW ?

On 21 September 1914, Port Vale recorded their highest score in a competitive match by beating Burton Rangers 14-1 in a Birmingham Cup game; ex-Tottenham Hotspur forward Chris Young scoring seven goals.

PORT VALE 2002–03 LEAGUE RECORD

Match No.	Date	Venue	Opponents	Result		H/T Score	Lg. Pos.	Goalscorers	Attendance
1	Aug 10	H	Tranmere R	L	1-4	1-2	—	Brooker [26]	5629
2	13	A	Cardiff C	L	1-3	1-2	—	Bridge-Wilkinson (pen) [40]	13,296
3	17	A	Chesterfield	L	1-2	0-0	24	Angell (pen) [90]	3598
4	24	H	Stockport Co	L	0-1	0-1	24		4070
5	26	A	Wigan Ath	W	1-0	1-0	22	Armstrong [45]	6532
6	31	H	Peterborough U	W	1-0	0-0	19	Angell [85]	3862
7	Sept 7	A	Swindon T	W	2-1	1-1	15	Bridge-Wilkinson 2 [9, 68]	5029
8	14	H	Colchester U	W	1-0	0-0	11	Collins [47]	3328
9	17	H	Notts Co	W	3-2	1-1	—	Angell 2 [6, 81], Paynter [58]	3505
10	21	A	Blackpool	L	2-3	1-0	10	Collins [23], Bridge-Wilkinson [71]	7756
11	28	H	Bristol C	L	2-3	0-2	13	Paynter [61], Cummins [89]	4286
12	Oct 5	A	Huddersfield T	D	2-2	2-2	12	Collins [5], Paynter [29]	9091
13	12	H	Oldham Ath	D	1-1	0-0	12	McPhee [66]	5563
14	19	A	Brentford	D	1-1	0-0	14	Paynter [68]	5177
15	26	H	Crewe Alex	L	1-2	0-1	14	Angell [56]	6374
16	29	A	Cheltenham T	W	1-0	1-0	—	Bridge-Wilkinson (pen) [33]	3852
17	Nov 2	H	QPR	D	0-0	0-0	13		4394
18	9	A	Luton T	D	0-0	0-0	13		6112
19	23	A	Northampton T	L	0-3	0-1	16		4357
20	30	H	Mansfield T	W	4-2	2-1	12	Cummins 2 [30, 33], Armstrong [50], Paynter [66]	3880
21	Dec 14	A	Wycombe W	L	1-3	0-1	14	Armstrong [49]	5229
22	21	H	Plymouth Arg	L	1-2	1-2	15	Brooker [26]	4892
23	26	H	Wigan Ath	L	0-1	0-0	18		6395
24	28	A	Barnsley	L	1-2	1-1	19	Bridge-Wilkinson [43]	9291
25	Jan 1	A	Stockport Co	D	1-1	0-1	17	Brooker [71]	4390
26	18	A	Peterborough U	W	2-1	0-0	15	Brooker [73], Bridge-Wilkinson [90]	4770
27	25	H	Barnsley	D	0-0	0-0	15		4033
28	Feb 1	A	Tranmere R	L	0-1	0-1	16		7461
29	8	H	Luton T	L	1-2	0-0	19	Boyd [87]	4714
30	11	H	Chesterfield	W	5-2	4-2	—	McPhee [2], Boyd 2 [10, 66], Armstrong [14], Brooker [18]	3039
31	15	A	QPR	L	0-4	0-0	17		13,703
32	22	H	Swindon T	D	1-1	0-0	19	Armstrong [46]	4085
33	25	H	Cardiff C	L	0-2	0-1	—		3831
34	Mar 1	A	Colchester U	L	1-4	0-2	20	Bridge-Wilkinson [55]	3581
35	4	A	Notts Co	L	0-1	0-0	—		6302
36	8	H	Blackpool	W	1-0	0-0	19	Bridge-Wilkinson (pen) [49]	4394
37	15	A	Crewe Alex	D	1-1	0-0	20	Brisco [73]	8146
38	18	H	Brentford	W	1-0	1-0	—	Collins [36]	3241
39	22	H	Cheltenham T	L	1-2	0-1	19	McPhee [74]	4800
40	29	A	Oldham Ath	D	1-1	1-1	19	Cummins [36]	7209
41	Apr 5	A	Mansfield T	W	1-0	1-0	17	Durnin [45]	4538
42	12	H	Northampton T	W	3-2	1-0	16	Walsh [11], Clarke [89], Littlejohn [90]	4209
43	19	A	Plymouth Arg	L	0-3	0-0	19		7775
44	21	H	Wycombe W	D	1-1	1-0	18	Littlejohn [5]	3590
45	26	H	Huddersfield T	W	5-1	2-1	16	Armstrong 2 [18, 59], Littlejohn [31], Collins [82], Charnock [87]	5925
46	May 3	A	Bristol C	L	0-2	0-2	17		12,410

Final League Position: 17

GOALSCORERS

League (54): Bridge-Wilkinson 9 (3 pens), Armstrong 7, Angell 5 (1 pen), Brooker 5, Collins 5, Paynter 5, Cummins 4, Boyd 3, Littlejohn 3, McPhee 3, Brisco 1, Charnock 1, Clarke 1, Durnin 1, Walsh 1.
Worthington Cup (0).
FA Cup (0).
LDV Vans Trophy (5): Angell 2, Armstrong 1, Boyd 1, Carragher 1.

Goodlad M 36 + 1	Cummins M 29 + 1	Charnock P 14 + 4	Collins S 44	Walsh M 17	Brightwell I 34 + 1	Boyd M 19 + 1	Durnin J 25 + 3	McPhee S 35 + 5	Brooker S 21 + 5	Bridge-Wilkinson M 29 + 2	Angell B 13 + 2	McCarthy J 5 + 3	Brisco N 23 + 1	Ingram R 3 + 1	Armstrong I 20 + 9	Rowland S 22 + 3	Carragher M 34 + 1	Burns L 14 + 2	McClare S 9 + 8	Paynter B 16 + 15	Ashcroft L 3	Eldershaw S — + 2	Byrne P 6 + 2	Birchall C — + 2	Clarke P 13	Littlejohn A 12 + 1	Delany D 10	Brown R — + 1	Reid L — + 1	Match No.
1	2	3^{1}	4	5	6	7^{2}	8	9	10	11	13	12																		1
1	2	3	4■	5	6		8	12	10	11^{2}	9^{1}	13	7																	2
1	2		4	5	6^{1}		8	9		11^{2}	10	12	7	3	13															3
1	12	13	4	5			8^{1}	9		14	10	7	3^{3}	2^{2}	11	6														4
1	2		3	5^{1}				9		11		7	8		10	6	4	12												5
1	2	12		5				9		11	13	7	8	6	10^{2}	3^{1}	4													6
1	2		6	5	3			9		11	10	7	8^{1}	12■			4													7
1	2		5		3			9		11	10	7^{1}	8			6	4		12											8
1	2		5		6			9^{1}		11	10		8			3	4		7	12										9
1	2		5		6^{1}		13			11	10		8		12	3	4		7^{2}	9										10
1	2	12	5		6					11	10		8^{1}		7	3	4			9										11
1	2	3	4		6		8				10				7^{1}	11	5		12	9										12
1	2	3	4		6		8	12			10					11^{1}	5			9	7									13
1	2	3	4		6		8^{1}	11			10					12	5			9	7									14
1	2^{3}		4		6	14				11^{2}	10		8		12	3	5		13	9	7^{1}									15
1	2		4		6		8			7	10					11	3	5		9										16
1	2		4		6^{1}		8^{2}	10		11					12	3	7	5	13	9										17
1	2		4		6		8	9	12	11						3	7	5		10^{1}										18
1	2	3	4		6	7	8	9	12						11			5^{1}		10										19
1	2	3	4		6^{1}	7	8	9							11			5	12	10										20
1	2	3	4			7	8		10^{2}						11	6^{1}		5	12	9		13								21
1	2	3	4			7	8^{2}	12	10						11^{1}	6		5	13	9										22
1	2^{2}	3^{3}	4		6	7		9	10	12						11		5	13	8^{1}		14								23
1		3^{2}	4		6^{3}	7		9	10^{1}	11						2		5	8	12			13	14						24
1			4		6		8^{1}	9	10	11						2■		5	7	12			3							25
1			4		6	7		9	10	11					12		2	5	8^{1}				3							26
1			4		6^{1}	7		9	10	11					12		2	5	8				3							27
1			5		6	7^{1}	12	9	10	11					8	13	2^{2}		4^{3}	14			3							28
1			5		6	7		9	10	11					4	2^{1}	12			8			3							29
1			4		6^{2}	7	8	9	10						3^{1}	14	2	5^{3}	11	12			13							30
1			4			7	8^{1}	9^{2}	10				12		11	6	2		5^{3}	13			3	14						31
1			4		6	7	8	12	10				11		3		2								5	9^{1}				32
			4			7		9	10	11			8^{1}		3	6	2			12					5		1			33
			4			7		9	10	11			8^{1}		6	3	2			12					5		1			34
			4	5	6	7		12	10^{1}	11			8^{2}				2			9					3	13	1			35
15			4	5	8	7		9	10	11							2								6	3	1^{G}			36
				5^{2}	6	7^{1}	12	9	10	11			4				2	13							3	8	1			37
			4	5	6			9	10^{1}	11			7				2			12					3	8	1			38
			4	5	6			9	10^{1}	11			7		13		2^{2}			12					3	8	1			39
	2		4		3		8	9		11			7				5	6								10	1			40
1	2		4	5			8	9^{1}	12	11^{2}			7		13		6								3	10				41
	2		4	5^{1}			8	9					7		11		6			12					3	10	1			42
	2	11	4	5^{2}			8^{1}	9					7		12		6			13					3	10	1			43
1	2	12	4		6		8^{1}	9	13				7■		11^{3}		5			14					3	10^{2}				44
1	2	3	4	5	13		8	9^{1}	12						11^{3}		6			14					7	10^{2}				45
1	2	11^{1}	4	5	3^{2}		8^{3}	9							7		6			12						10		13	14	46

Worthington Cup
First Round | Crewe Alex | (h) | 0-2

FA Cup
First Round | Crewe Alex | (h) | 0-1

LDV Vans Trophy
First Round | Hull C | (h) | 3-1
Second Round | Chesterfield | (h) | 1-1
Quarter-final | Shrewsbury T | (a) | 1-2

PRESTON NORTH END

Division 1

FOUNDATION

North End Cricket and Rugby Club which was formed in 1863, indulged in most sports before taking up soccer in about 1879. In 1881 they decided to stick to football to the exclusion of other sports and even a 16–0 drubbing by Blackburn Rovers in an invitation game at Deepdale, a few weeks after taking this decision, did not deter them for they immediately became affiliated to the Lancashire FA.

Deepdale, Preston PR1 6RU.

Telephone: 0870 442 1964. ***Fax:*** (01772) 693 366.
Website: www.pne.com ***Email:*** enquiries@pne.com
Ticket Enquiries: 0870 442 1966.
Ticket Office Credit Card Bookings: 0870 442 1966.
Corporate Hospitality: 0870 442 1964.
Media/Press: 0870 442 1964.
Community: 0870 442 1964.
Ground Capacity: 22,226.

Record Attendance: 42,684 v Arsenal, Division 1, 23 April 1938.

Record Receipts: £108,920 v Stockport Co, FA Cup 3rd rd, 6 January 2001.

Pitch Measurements: 110yd × 77yd.

President: Sir Tom Finney OBE, JP.

Chairman: Derek Shaw.

Director: Simon Beard. ***Non-Executive:*** D. Taylor, S. Jackson.

Manager: Craig Brown.
Assistant Manager: Kelham O'Hanlon.

Coach: Billy Davies. ***Physio:*** Andrew Balderston.

Secretary: G. E. Harrison.

Colours: White shirts, navy shorts, white stockings.

Change Colours: Navy shirts, white shorts, navy stockings.

Year Formed: 1881. ***Turned Professional:*** 1885. ***Ltd Co.:*** 1893.

Club Nicknames: 'The Lilywhites' or 'North End'.

First Football League Game: 8 September 1888, Football League, v Burnley (h) W 5–2 – Trainer; Howarth, Holmes; Robertson, W. Graham, J. Graham; Gordon (1), Ross (2), Goodall, Dewhurst (2), Drummond.

Record League Victory: 10–0 v Stoke, Division 1, 14 September 1889 – Trainer; Howarth, Holmes; Kelso, Russell (1), Graham; Gordon, Jimmy Ross (2), Nick Ross (3), Thomson (2), Drummond (2).

Record Cup Victory: 26–0 v Hyde, FA Cup 1st rd, 15 October 1887 – Addision; Howarth, Nick Ross; Russell (1), Thomson (5), Graham (1); Gordon (5), Jimmy Ross (8), John Goodall (1), Dewhurst (3), Drummond (2).

Record Defeat: 0–7 v Blackpool, Division 1, 1 May 1948.

Most League Points (2 for a win): 61, Division 3, 1970–71.

HONOURS

Football League: Division 1 – Champions 1888–89 (first champions) 1889–90; Runners-up 1890–91, 1891–92, 1892–93, 1905–06, 1952–53, 1957–58; Division 2 – Champions 1903–04, 1912–13, 1950–51, 1999–2000; Runners-up 1914–15, 1933–34; Division 3 – Champions 1970–71, 1995–96; Division 4 – Runners-up 1986–87.

FA Cup: Winners 1889, 1938; Runners-up 1888, 1922, 1937, 1954, 1964.

Football League Cup: best season: 4th rd, 2003.

Double Performed: 1888–89.

Football League Cup: best season: 4th rd, 1963, 1966, 1972, 1981.

SKY SPORTS FACT FILE

Scottish-born wing-half Bobby Crawford had a remarkably consistent record with Preston North End for more than ten years from 1921–22. His 392 League games included missing just one game in six seasons and playing 186 in succession.

Most League Points (3 for a win): 95, Division 2, 1999–2000.

Most League Goals: 100, Division 2, 1927–28 and Division 1, 1957–58.

Highest League Scorer in Season: Ted Harper, 37, Division 2, 1932–33.

Most League Goals in Total Aggregate: Tom Finney, 187, 1946–60.

Most League Goals in One Match: 4, Jimmy Ross v Stoke, Division 1, 6 October 1888; 4, Nick Ross v Derby Co, Division 1, 11 January 1890; 4, George Drummond v Notts Co, Division 1, 12 December 1891; 4, Frank Becton v Notts Co, Division 1, 31 March 1893; 4, George Harrison v Grimsby T, Division 2, 3 November 1928; 4, Alex Reid v Port Vale, Division 2, 23 February 1929; 4, James McClelland v Reading, Division 2, 6 September 1930; 4, Dick Rowley v Notts Co, Division 2, 16 April 1932; 4, Ted Harper v Burnley, Division 2, 29 August 1932; 4, Ted Harper v Lincoln C, Division 2, 11 March 1933; 4, Charlie Wayman v QPR, Division 2, 25 December 1950; 4, Alex Bruce v Colchester U, Division 3, 28 February 1978.

Most Capped Player: Tom Finney, 76, England.

Most League Appearances: Alan Kelly, 447, 1961–75.

Youngest League Player: Steve Doyle, 16 years 166 days v Tranmere R, 15 November 1974.

Record Transfer Fee Received: £1,250,000 from WBA for Kevin Kilbane, June 1997.

Record Transfer Fee Paid: £1,500,000 to Manchester U for David Healy, December 2000.

Football League Record: 1888 Founder Member of League; 1901–04 Division 2; 1904–12 Division 1; 1912–13 Division 2; 1913–14 Division 1; 1914–15 Division 2; 1919–25 Division 1; 1925–34 Division 2; 1934–49 Division 1; 1949–51 Division 2; 1951–61 Division 1; 1961–70 Division 2; 1970–71 Division 3; 1971–74 Division 2; 1974–78 Division 3; 1978–81 Division 2; 1981–85 Division 3; 1985–87 Division 4; 1987–92 Division 3; 1992–93 Division 2; 1993–96 Division 3; 1996–2000 Division 2; 2000– Division 1.

MANAGERS

Charlie Parker 1906–15
Vincent Hayes 1919–23
Jim Lawrence 1923–25
Frank Richards 1925–27
Alex Gibson 1927–31
Lincoln Hayes 1931–32
Run by committee 1932–36
Tommy Muirhead 1936–37
Run by committee 1937–49
Will Scott 1949–53
Scot Symon 1953–54
Frank Hill 1954–56
Cliff Britton 1956–61
Jimmy Milne 1961–68
Bobby Seith 1968–70
Alan Ball Sr 1970–73
Bobby Charlton 1973–75
Harry Catterick 1975–77
Nobby Stiles 1977–81
Tommy Docherty 1981
Gordon Lee 1981–83
Alan Kelly 1983–85
Tommy Booth 1985–86
Brian Kidd 1986
John McGrath 1986–90
Les Chapman 1990–92
Sam Allardyce 1992 (*Caretaker*)
John Beck 1992–94
Gary Peters 1994–98
David Moyes 1998–2002
Kelham O'Hanlon 2002 (*Caretaker*)
Craig Brown April 2002–

LATEST SEQUENCES

Longest Sequence of League Wins: 14, 25.12.1950 – 27.3.1951.

Longest Sequence of League Defeats: 8, 22.9.1984 – 27.10.1984.

Longest Sequence of League Draws: 6, 24.2.1979 – 20.3.1979.

Longest Sequence of Unbeaten League Matches: 23, 8.9.1888 – 14.9.1889.

Longest Sequence Without a League Win: 15, 14.4.1923 – 20.10.1923.

Successive Scoring Runs: 30 from 15.11.1952.

Successive Non-scoring Runs: 6 from 8.4.1897.

TEN YEAR LEAGUE RECORD

		P	W	D	L	F	A	Pts	Pos
1993-94	Div 3	42	18	13	11	79	60	67	5
1994-95	Div 3	42	19	10	13	58	41	67	5
1995-96	Div 3	46	23	17	6	78	38	86	1
1996-97	Div 2	46	18	7	21	49	55	61	15
1997-98	Div 2	46	15	14	17	56	56	59	15
1998-99	Div 2	46	22	13	11	78	50	79	5
1999-2000	Div 2	46	28	11	7	74	37	95	1
2000-01	Div 1	46	23	9	14	64	52	78	4
2001-02	Div 1	46	20	12	14	71	59	72	8
2002-03	Div 1	46	16	13	17	68	70	61	12

DID YOU KNOW ?

In 1970–71 Preston North End won the Division Three title with 21 clean sheets in conceding only 39 goals. They overhauled Fulham the leaders for 24 weeks of the season, beating them 1-0 at Craven Cottage when a draw would have won it for Fulham.

PRESTON NORTH END 2002–03 LEAGUE RECORD

Match No.	Date	Venue	Opponents	Result		H/T Score	Lg. Pos.	Goalscorers	Attendance
1	Aug 10	H	Crystal Palace	L	1-2	0-0	—	Fuller [68]	14,663
2	14	A	Nottingham F	D	2-2	1-0	—	Fuller [31], Etuhu [48]	18,065
3	17	A	Rotherham U	D	0-0	0-0	16		6885
4	24	H	Stoke C	W	4-3	2-1	10	Healy 2 [12, 24], Fuller [60], Cresswell [90]	15,422
5	26	A	Gillingham	D	1-1	0-0	11	Cresswell [90]	7785
6	Sept 1	H	Ipswich T	D	0-0	0-0	14		15,357
7	14	H	Sheffield W	D	2-2	1-1	17	Fuller [13], Cresswell [84]	13,632
8	17	H	Watford	D	1-1	0-1	—	Cresswell [73]	12,408
9	21	A	Derby Co	W	2-0	1-0	12	Etuhu [41], Healy [77]	29,257
10	24	A	Wolverhampton W	L	0-4	0-2	—		23,695
11	28	H	Norwich C	L	1-2	0-1	17	Cresswell [52]	13,550
12	Oct 5	A	Bradford C	D	1-1	1-1	18	Alexander (pen) [39]	13,215
13	19	A	Walsall	D	3-3	1-3	18	Healy [38], Lucketti [75], Alexander [88]	6832
14	26	H	Reading	W	1-0	1-0	16	Cresswell [22]	13,021
15	29	A	Portsmouth	L	2-3	1-3	—	Cresswell [12], Alexander (pen) [47]	18,637
16	Nov 2	H	Burnley	W	3-1	1-0	15	Fuller 2 [3, 66], McKenna [62]	16,046
17	9	A	Millwall	L	1-2	0-2	17	Fuller [89]	7554
18	16	A	Grimsby T	D	3-3	1-1	17	Cresswell [27], Alexander (pen) [84], Etuhu [88]	5774
19	23	H	Brighton & HA	D	2-2	2-0	18	Lucketti [16], Cresswell [36]	13,068
20	26	H	Leicester C	W	2-0	0-0	—	Fuller 2 [48, 90]	13,048
21	30	A	Coventry C	W	2-1	1-0	12	Cresswell [7], Lewis [88]	13,313
22	Dec 7	H	Wimbledon	L	3-5	2-1	16	Abbott [11], McKenna [41], Alexander (pen) [56]	12,415
23	14	H	Grimsby T	W	3-0	2-0	14	Alexander (pen) [12], Cresswell [26], Healy [59]	12,420
24	21	A	Sheffield U	L	0-1	0-0	16		16,342
25	26	H	Rotherham U	L	0-2	0-0	17		15,452
26	28	A	Crystal Palace	L	0-2	0-1	18		18,484
27	Jan 1	A	Stoke C	L	1-2	0-2	18	Abbott [90]	14,862
28	18	A	Ipswich T	L	0-3	0-1	18		24,666
29	25	H	Nottingham F	D	1-1	1-1	18	Lynch [30]	13,508
30	Feb 1	H	Gillingham	W	3-0	2-0	18	Lewis [29], Alexander (pen) [38], Ashby (og) [55]	12,121
31	8	H	Millwall	W	2-1	2-0	18	Lewis [15], Cartwright [25]	13,117
32	22	H	Wolverhampton W	L	0-2	0-0	18		16,070
33	Mar 1	A	Sheffield W	W	1-0	0-0	18	Cresswell [79]	18,912
34	4	A	Watford	W	1-0	1-0	—	Alexander (pen) [19]	11,101
35	8	H	Derby Co	W	4-2	3-0	12	Alexander [14], Etuhu [26], Koumantarakis [39], Cresswell [51]	14,003
36	15	A	Leicester C	L	1-2	1-1	14	Lewis [20]	30,713
37	18	H	Walsall	W	5-0	2-0	—	Alexander (pen) [14], Etuhu [28], Cresswell [63], Koumantarakis 2 [73, 85]	11,170
38	22	H	Portsmouth	D	1-1	0-1	12	McKenna [89]	16,665
39	Apr 5	H	Coventry C	D	2-2	1-0	14	Cresswell [27], Abbott [90]	13,026
40	8	A	Burnley	L	0-2	0-1	—		12,245
41	12	A	Brighton & HA	W	2-0	0-0	12	Jackson [71], Cresswell [86]	6669
42	15	A	Reading	L	1-5	0-2	—	Mears [83]	14,012
43	19	H	Sheffield U	W	2-0	0-0	10	Etuhu [61], Lewis [87]	14,793
44	21	A	Wimbledon	L	0-2	0-0	12		1053
45	26	H	Bradford C	W	1-0	1-0	11	Abbott [13]	13,652
46	May 4	A	Norwich C	L	0-2	0-0	12		20,232

Final League Position: 12

GOALSCORERS

League (68): Cresswell 16, Alexander 10 (8 pens), Fuller 9, Etuhu 6, Healy 5, Lewis 5, Abbott 4, Koumantarakis 3, McKenna 3, Lucketti 2, Cartwright 1, Jackson 1, Lynch 1, Mears 1, own goal 1.
Worthington Cup (6): Fuller 2, Alexander 1 (pen), Jackson 1, Lewis 1, Skora 1.
FA Cup (1): Anderson 1.

Moilanen T 14 + 1	Alexander G 45	Edwards R 26	Murdock C 24	Lucketti C 43	Jackson M 21 + 1	Skora E 30 + 6	Rankine M 11 + 8	Cresswell R 42	Fuller R 18	McKenna P 39 + 2	Anderson I — + 8	Healy D 12 + 12	Etuhu D 33 + 6	Keane M 1 + 4	Cartwright L 13 + 9	Broomes M 21 + 7	Lewis E 34 + 4	Mears T 11 + 11	Lucas D 19 + 2	Abbott P 6 + 10	Barry-Murphy B 2	Gould J 13 + 1	Eaton A — + 1	O'Neil B 12 + 3	Lynch S 6 + 11	Koumantarakis G 10	Bailey J — + 1	Match No.
1	2	3^{1}	4	5	6	7■	8	9	10^{2}	11^{3}	12	13	14															1
1	2	3	4	5	6	7	8	9	10				11^{1}	12														2
1	2	3	4	5	6	7	8	9^{1}	10			12	11															3
1	2	3	4	5			8	9	10	11		7^{2}	6^{1}	12	13													4
1	2	3		5^{2}	6	7		9	10	11		8	12	13		4^{1}												5
1	2	3	4	5		7	8	9	10	6		11^{1}	12															6
1	2	3^{3}	4	5		6	8^{2}	9	10	7		12	13			14	11^{1}											7
1	2		4	5		6		9	10	7		12	8	11^{1}		3												8
1	2	3^{3}	4^{1}	5		7	12	9	10^{2}	11		13	8			6	14											9
1	2		4	5	6^{3}	7^{1}	13	9	10	11		12	8^{2}			3	14											10
1	2		4	5		7^{1}	13	9	10	11		12	8^{2}			6	3											11
1	2		4	5		7		9^{2}	10■	11	12	13	8^{1}			6	3											12
1	2		4^{2}	5		6	7	9		11	12	10	8^{1}			3		13										13
	2	3	4	5		6	8	9^{2}		7		10^{3}				12	11^{1}	13	1	14								14
	2	3^{1}	4	5	12	10	8^{2}	9		7			13			6	11^{3}		1	14								15
	2	3	4	5		6^{1}	12	9	10^{2}	7		13	8			14	11^{3}		1									16
	2	3	4			6^{1}		9	10	7		12	8			5	11		1									17
1	2	3			6	4^{1}		9	10	7		12	8			5	11											18
	2	3	4	5		6^{1}	12	9	10	7			8				11		1									19
	2	3	4	5		6		9	10^{2}	7			8		13	12	11^{1}		1									20
	2	3	4	5		6^{1}	12	9	10^{2}	7		13	8		14		11^{3}		1									21
	2	3		5		6	12			7		10	8^{1}			4	11		1	9								22
	2	3	4	5		6^{2}	12	9		7^{1}		10^{3}	8				11	13	1	14								23
	2		4	5			8■	9			12	10	6			3^{1}	11	7	1									24
	2	3^{3}		5		6^{1}		9		7	12	10	8			4	11^{2}	14	1	13								25
	2		4	5		6^{2}		9		7	12	10^{1}	8^{3}			3	13	11	1	14								26
15	2			5			8	9^{1}		7		10	6^{2}			4	11	13	1^{G}	12	3							27
			4			2					12	10			8	5	11^{1}	7^{2}		9^{3}	3	1	13	6	14			28
	2		4	5						7	12				8		11^{1}	3		13		1		6	9	10^{2}		29
	2			5	6	12		9		7					8	3^{2}	11	13				1		4^{1}	14	10^{3}		30
	2	3		5	6			9					8		7		11^{1}	12				1		4	13	10^{2}		31
	2	3		5	6	12		9		7					8^{1}		11					1		4	13	10^{2}		32
	2	3^{1}		5	6			9		8					7^{2}	12	11^{3}	13				1		4	14	10		33
	2			5	6	12		9		8^{1}					7^{2}	3	11	13				1		4		10		34
	2			5	6			9		8^{1}			4	12	7	3	11		15			1^{G}			13	10^{2}		35
	2			5	6	12		9		8			4^{1}		7	3^{2}	11		15			1^{G}			13	10		36
	2	3		5	6^{1}			9		8^{2}			4		7	12	11^{3}	13	1						14	10		37
	2	3		5				9		8			4		7^{1}	6^{3}	11	12	1					14	13	10^{2}		38
	2	3^{1}		5	6			9		8			4		7^{2}		11		1	12				13	10			39
	2			5	6	12		9		7			8^{2}		13		11^{1}	4	1	14				3	10^{3}			40
	2			5	6	7^{2}		9		8			13		12		11^{1}	3	1	10				4				41
	2			5	6■	4		9		8^{G}			11^{2}		7		12	3	1■			15		13	10^{1}			42
	2			5	6	7^{1}		9^{3}		12			8		13		11^{2}	3		10		1		4	14			43
	2			5	6	7^{1}				12			8		13		11	3		9^{3}		1		4^{2}	10		14	44
	2			5	6	12		9		7^{1}			8		13		11^{2}	3		10^{3}		1		4	14			45
	2	4^{3}		5		6^{2}		9		7			8		12	14	11^{1}	3		13		1			10			46

Worthington Cup

First Round	Scunthorpe U	(h)	2-1
Second Round	Macclesfield T	(a)	2-1
Third Round	Birmingham C	(a)	2-0
Fourth Round	Aston Villa	(a)	0-5

FA Cup

Third Round	Rochdale	(h)	1-2

QUEENS PARK RANGERS Division 2

FOUNDATION

There is an element of doubt about the date of the foundation of this club, but it is believed that in either 1885 or 1886 it was formed through the amalgamation of Christchurch Rangers and St Jude's Institute FC. The leading light was George Wodehouse, whose family maintained a connection with the club until comparatively recent times. Most of the players came from the Queen's Park district so this name was adopted after a year as St Jude's Institute.

South Africa Road, London W12 7PA.

Telephone: (020) 8743 0262. ***Fax:*** (020) 8749 0994.
Club Shop: (020) 8749 2509. ***Box Office:*** (020) 8740 2575.
Supporters Club: (020) 8740 2534.
Commercial: (020) 8740 2588. ***ClubCall:*** 09068 121 162.

Ground Capacity: 19,148.

Record Attendance: 35,353 v Leeds U, Division 1, 27 April 1974.

Record Receipts: £218,475 v Manchester U, FA Premier League, 5 February 1994.

Pitch Measurements: 112yd × 72yd.

Directors: Nick Blackburn, David Davies, Ross Jones, Lyndon Fuller, Kevin McGrath.

Manager: Ian Holloway. ***Secretary:*** Sheila Marson.
Physio: Prav Mathema.

Commercial and Marketing Director: Samantha Taylor.

Year Formed: 1885* (*see Foundation*). ***Turned Professional:*** 1898. ***Ltd Co.:*** 1899.

Previous Name: 1885, St Jude's; 1887, Queens Park Rangers. ***Club Nicknames:*** 'Rangers' or 'Rs'.

Colours: Blue and white hooped shirts, white shorts and stockings.

Change Colours: Red and black half shirts, black shorts, black stockings.

Previous Grounds: 1885* (*see Foundation*), Welford's Fields; 1888–99; London Scottish Ground, Brondesbury, Home Farm, Kensal Rise Green, Gun Club Wormwood Scrubs, Kilburn Cricket Ground; 1899, Kensal Rise Athletic Ground; 1901, Latimer Road, Notting Hill; 1904, Agricultural Society, Park Royal; 1907, Park Royal Ground; 1917, Loftus Road; 1931, White City; 1933, Loftus Road; 1962, White City; 1963, Loftus Road.

First Football League Game: 28 August 1920, Division 3, v Watford (h) L 1–2 – Price; Blackman, Wingrove; McGovern, Grant, O'Brien; Faulkner, Birch (1), Smith, Gregory, Middlemiss.

Record League Victory: 9–2 v Tranmere R, Division 3, 3 December 1960 – Drinkwater; Woods, Ingham; Keen, Rutter, Angell; Lazarus (2), Bedford (2), Evans (2), Andrews (1), Clark (2).

Record Cup Victory: 8–1 v Bristol R (away), FA Cup 1st rd, 27 November 1937 – Gilfillan; Smith, Jefferson; Lowe, James, March; Cape, Mallett, Cheetham (3), Fitzgerald (3) Bott (2). 8–1 v Crewe Alex, Milk Cup 1st rd, 3 October 1983 – Hucker; Neill, Dawes, Waddock (1), McDonald (1), Fenwick, Micklewhite (1), Stewart (1), Allen (1), Stainrod (3), Gregory.

HONOURS

Football League: Division 1 – Runners-up 1975–76; Division 2 – Champions 1982–83; Runners-up 1967–68, 1972–73; Division 3 (S) – Champions 1947–48; Runners-up 1946–47; Division 3 – Champions 1966–67.

FA Cup: Runners-up 1982.

Football League Cup: Winners 1967; Runners-up 1986. (In 1966–67 won Division 3 and Football League Cup).

European Competitions: *UEFA Cup:* 1976–77, 1984–85.

SKY SPORTS FACT FILE

Queens Park Rangers Third Division championship season of 1966–67 was achieved without an entry into the transfer market during the close season. A largely settled team had ten players each making more than 40 appearances in the League.

Record Defeat: 1–8 v Mansfield T, Division 3, 15 March 1965. 1–8 v Manchester U, Division 1, 19 March 1969.

Most League Points (2 for a win): 67, Division 3, 1966–67.

Most League Points (3 for a win): 85, Division 2, 1982–83.

Most League Goals: 111, Division 3, 1961–62.

Highest League Scorer in Season: George Goddard, 37, Division 3 (S), 1929–30.

Most League Goals in Total Aggregate: George Goddard, 172, 1926–34.

Most League Goals in One Match: 4, George Goddard v Merthyr T, Division 3S, 9 March 1929; 4, George Goddard v Swindon T, Division 3S, 12 April 1930; 4, George Goddard v Exeter C, Division 3S, 20 December 1930; 4, George Goddard v Watford, Division 3S, 19 September 1931; 4, Tom Cheetham v Aldershot, Division 3S, 14 September 1935; 4, Tom Cheetham v Aldershot, Division 3S, 12 November 1938.

Most Capped Player: Alan McDonald, 52, Northern Ireland.

Most League Appearances: Tony Ingham, 519, 1950–63.

Youngest League Player: Frank Sibley, 16 years 97 days v Bristol C, 10 March 1964.

Record Transfer Fee Received: £6,000,000 from Newcastle U for Les Ferdinand, June 1995.

Record Transfer Fee Paid: £2,750,000 to Stoke C for Mike Sheron, July 1997.

Football League Record: 1920 Original Members of Division 3; 1921–48 Division 3 (S); 1948–52 Division 2; 1952–58 Division 3 (S); 1958–67 Division 3; 1967–68 Division 2; 1968–69 Division 1; 1969–73 Division 2; 1973–79 Division 1; 1979–83 Division 2; 1983–92 Division 1; 1992–96 FA Premier League; 1996–2001 Division 1; 2001– Division 2.

MANAGERS

James Cowan 1906–13
Jimmy Howie 1913–20
Ted Liddell 1920–24
Will Wood 1924–25 *(had been Secretary since 1903)*
Bob Hewison 1925–30
John Bowman 1930–31
Archie Mitchell 1931–33
Mick O'Brien 1933–35
Billy Birrell 1935–39
Ted Vizard 1939–44
Dave Mangnall 1944–52
Jack Taylor 1952–59
Alec Stock 1959–65 *(General Manager to 1968)*
Bill Dodgin Jnr 1968
Tommy Docherty 1968
Les Allen 1968–71
Gordon Jago 1971–74
Dave Sexton 1974–77
Frank Sibley 1977–78
Steve Burtenshaw 1978–79
Tommy Docherty 1979–80
Terry Venables 1980–84
Gordon Jago 1984
Alan Mullery 1984
Frank Sibley 1984–85
Jim Smith 1985–88
Trevor Francis 1988–90
Don Howe 1990–91
Gerry Francis 1991–94
Ray Wilkins 1994–96
Stewart Houston 1996–97
Ray Harford 1997–98
Gerry Francis 1998–2001
Ian Holloway February 2001–

LATEST SEQUENCES

Longest Sequence of League Wins: 8, 7.11.1931 – 28.12.1931.

Longest Sequence of League Defeats: 9, 25.2.1969 – 5.4.1969.

Longest Sequence of League Draws: 6, 29.1.2000 – 5.3.2000.

Longest Sequence of Unbeaten League Matches: 20, 11.3.1972 – 23.9.1972.

Longest Sequence Without a League Win: 20, 7.12.1968 – 7.4.1969.

Successive Scoring Runs: 33 from 9.12.1961.

Successive Non-scoring Runs: 6 from 18.3.1939.

TEN YEAR LEAGUE RECORD

		P	W	D	L	F	A	Pts	Pos
1993-94	PR Lge	42	16	12	14	62	61	60	9
1994-95	PR Lge	42	17	9	16	61	59	60	8
1995-96	PR Lge	38	9	6	23	38	57	33	19
1996-97	Div 1	46	18	12	16	64	60	66	9
1997-98	Div 1	46	10	19	17	51	63	49	21
1998-99	Div 1	46	12	11	23	52	61	47	20
1999-2000	Div 1	46	16	18	12	62	53	66	10
2000-01	Div 1	46	7	19	20	45	75	40	23
2001-02	Div 2	46	19	14	13	60	49	71	8
2002-03	Div 2	46	24	11	11	69	45	83	4

DID YOU KNOW?

In the summer of 1901, Queens Park Rangers signed John Bowman a right-half from Stoke City and he was subsequently appointed player-secretary, staying four seasons and making 110 League and Cup appearances in the Southern League.

QUEENS PARK RANGERS 2002–03 LEAGUE RECORD

Match No.	Date	Venue	Opponents	Result		H/T Score	Lg. Pos.	Goalscorers	Attendance
1	Aug 10	H	Chesterfield	W	3-1	0-0	—	Furlong [72], Langley [88], Gallen [90]	12,603
2	13	A	Stockport Co	D	1-1	0-0	—	Connolly (pen) [71]	5811
3	17	A	Barnsley	L	0-1	0-0	10		9626
4	24	H	Peterborough U	W	2-0	0-0	6	Gallen 2 [59, 70]	11,510
5	26	A	Wycombe W	L	1-4	1-1	11	Furlong [44]	8383
6	31	H	Plymouth Arg	D	2-2	0-1	13	Thomas [69], Pacquette [90]	14,001
7	Sept 7	A	Mansfield T	W	4-0	1-0	7	Furlong [6], Shittu [48], Gallen [85], Thomson [89]	4581
8	14	H	Swindon T	W	2-0	0-0	6	Gallen [50], Langley [56]	11,619
9	17	H	Huddersfield T	W	3-0	2-0	—	Shittu [4], Williams [32], Carlisle [73]	11,010
10	21	A	Bristol C	W	3-1	1-1	1	Connolly 2 [23, 48], Gallen [53]	12,221
11	28	H	Colchester U	W	2-0	1-0	2	Connolly [39], Gallen [72]	12,906
12	Oct 5	A	Crewe Alex	L	0-2	0-1	4		7683
13	14	H	Blackpool	W	2-1	1-0	—	Langley [18], Clarke C (og) [66]	11,335
14	19	A	Cheltenham T	D	1-1	1-0	5	Thomas [11]	6382
15	26	H	Oldham Ath	L	1-2	1-2	6	Rose [2]	15,491
16	29	A	Wigan Ath	D	1-1	1-1	—	Thomson [45]	6241
17	Nov 2	A	Port Vale	D	0-0	0-0	5		4394
18	9	H	Northampton T	L	0-1	0-0	6		11,947
19	23	A	Luton T	D	0-0	0-0	6		9477
20	29	H	Cardiff C	L	0-4	0-0	—		14,345
21	Dec 14	A	Notts Co	L	0-3	0-2	7		5343
22	21	H	Brentford	D	1-1	1-1	7	Bircham [18]	15,559
23	26	H	Wycombe W	W	2-1	2-0	7	Rose [12], Gallen [30]	14,874
24	28	A	Tranmere R	L	0-3	0-0	10		8434
25	Jan 1	A	Peterborough U	W	2-0	1-0	7	Carlisle [44], Langley [79]	6210
26	4	H	Stockport Co	W	1-0	0-0	6	Gallen (pen) [89]	10,387
27	11	H	Barnsley	W	1-0	1-0	6	Pacquette [11]	11,217
28	18	A	Plymouth Arg	W	1-0	0-0	6	Pacquette [51]	10,249
29	25	H	Tranmere R	L	1-2	0-0	6	Palmer [60]	12,249
30	Feb 2	A	Chesterfield	W	4-2	2-1	6	Pacquette [13], Shittu [22], Furlong [83], Thomson [89]	4395
31	8	A	Northampton T	D	1-1	0-1	6	Furlong [60]	5859
32	15	H	Port Vale	W	4-0	0-0	6	Shittu [52], Furlong [61], Padula [79], Gallen [89]	13,703
33	22	H	Mansfield T	D	2-2	1-1	6	Furlong [20], Gallen [90]	11,942
34	Mar 1	A	Swindon T	L	1-3	1-1	6	Shittu [15]	7716
35	4	A	Huddersfield T	W	3-0	2-0	—	Furlong 2 [5, 90], Shittu [38]	8695
36	8	H	Bristol C	W	1-0	1-0	6	Gallen (pen) [19]	14,681
37	15	A	Oldham Ath	D	0-0	0-0	6		7242
38	18	H	Cheltenham T	W	4-1	2-1	—	Gallen [40], Duff M (og) [45], Cook [55], Furlong [63]	11,370
39	22	H	Wigan Ath	L	0-1	0-0	6		14,703
40	29	A	Blackpool	W	3-1	1-0	6	Langley 3 [35, 65, 85]	8162
41	Apr 5	A	Cardiff C	W	2-1	0-0	6	Furlong [64], Langley [89]	15,245
42	12	H	Luton T	W	2-0	1-0	6	McLeod 2 [39, 83]	15,786
43	19	A	Brentford	W	2-1	1-0	6	Shittu [8], Bircham [90]	9168
44	21	H	Notts Co	W	2-0	1-0	4	Furlong [16], Langley [90]	13,585
45	26	H	Crewe Alex	D	0-0	0-0	6		16,921
46	May 3	A	Colchester U	W	1-0	0-0	3	Furlong [52]	5047

Final League Position: 3

GOALSCORERS

League (69): Furlong 13, Gallen 13 (2 pens), Langley 9, Shittu 7, Connolly 4 (1 pen), Pacquette 4, Thomson 3, Bircham 2, Carlisle 2, McLeod 2, Rose 2, Thomas 2, Cook 1, Padula 1, Palmer 1, Williams 1, own goals 2.
Worthington Cup (2): Gallen 1, Thomson 1 (pen).
FA Cup (1): Thomson 1.
LDV Vans Trophy (0).
Play-offs (2): Furlong 1, Langley 1.

Culkin N 17	Forbes T 38	Murphy D 4 + 7	Palmer S 46	Shittu D 43	Rose M 25 + 3	Bircham M 34 + 2	Daly W 3 + 3	Thomson A 7 + 14	Gallen K 41 + 1	Connolly K 12 + 4	Williams T 22 + 4	Langley R 38 + 1	Furlong P 27 + 6	Dodou E 3 + 7	Padula G 17 + 4	Royce S 16	Pacquette R 4 + 7	Bean M 4 + 3	Thomas J 5 + 1	Carlisle C 34 + 2	Oli D 8 + 10	Digby F 1 + 2	Griffiths L 3 + 3	Willock C 3	Burgess O 2 + 3	Angell B 8 + 5	Cook L 13	Walshe B 1	Plummer C — + 2	Day C 12	McLeod K 8	Kelly S 7	*Match No.*
1	2	3^{1}	4	5	6	7	8^{2}	9^{3}	10	11	12	13	14																				1
1	2		4	5	6	7			10	11^{1}	3	8	9	12																			2
1	2		4	5	6	7			10	11	3^{1}	8	9^{2}	12	13																		3
	2		4	5	6	7			10		3	8	9^{1}	11		1	12																4
	2		4	5	6	7■			10	11^{2}	3	8^{1}	9	12		1		13■															5
	2		4	5	6	7		12	10	13	3		9^{1}	11^{3}		1	14		8^{2}														6
	2		4	5		7		12	10^{1}	13	3	8	9			1		6^{3}	11^{2}	14													7
	2		4	5	7			12	9	11	3	8				1				6	10^{1}												8
	2	13	4	5	7^{2}				9	11	3	8				1	12			6	10^{1}												9
	2	14	4	5	7	12		13	9	11^{2}	3	8^{3}				1				6	10^{1}												10
	2		4	5	7				9	11	3	8	12			1				6	10^{1}												11
	2^{1}		4	5	7	13		12	10	11^{3}	3	8	9							6^{2}	14	1											12
	2		4	5	7^{1}			12	10	13	3	8	9^{3}			1			11^{2}	6	14												13
	2		4	5	7			12	9^{1}	11^{2}	3	8				1			10	6■	13												14
	2		4	5^{1}	7			9		10	3^{2}	8			13	1^{G}			11	6	12	15											15
	2		4	5	7			9		11^{1}	3	8				1			12	6	10												16
	2		4	5	7			9^{1}			3	8		12	11^{G}	1■				6	10^{2}	15	13										17
	2^{1}		4^{2}	5	7	8		9		14	3			11^{3}		1				6	12			10	13								18
	2		4	5		7		9^{1}	13^{3}		3		12			1				6	14			8	11	10^{2}							19
	2		4	5		7			9		3	8	12			1				6	13			11^{2}		10^{1}							20
1	2	3	4		6^{2}	7	12	13	9			8	14							5	11^{1}					10^{3}							21
1	2	3	4		6	7		12	10			8	9							5							11^{1}						22
1	2		4	5	3	7^{2}	13	12	10			8	9^{3}							6						14	11^{1}						23
1	2	12	4	5^{3}	3		7^{2}		10			8	9■	14						6	13						11^{1}						24
1	2	12	4	5	3	7			9			8								6^{1}						10	11						25
1	2	12	4	5	3	7^{3}			9			8					13			6					14	10^{2}	11^{1}						26
1	2		4		6^{1}		12		9			8^{3}			3		10			5	7^{2}				14	13	11						27
1	2	12	4	5		7			9						3^{1}		8^{2}			6	13					10	11■						28
1	2	3	4	5		8		12	7								9^{1}			6			13			10	11^{2}						29
1	2		4	5		7		12	8				13		3		9	14							6^{3}	10^{2}		11^{1}					30
1	2		4	5		6	8^{2}	7^{3}	10				9	12	3			13					11^{1}						14				31
1	2		4	5		6			10			8	9	12	3			7^{1}					11										32
1	2	12	4	5^{2}		6			10			8	9		3^{1}			7^{3}		13	14		11										33
1			4	5		6			10		12	8	9^{3}		3^{2}		13	7		2						14	11^{1}						34
	2		4	5		7			10		12	8	9		3					6							11^{1}			1			35
	2		4	5		7			10		3	8	9							6			12				11^{1}			1			36
	2		4	5		7			10		3^{2}	8	9		12					6						13	11^{1}			1			37
	2		4	5		7		12	10^{1}		3^{2}	8	9^{3}		13					6						14	11			1			38
	2		4	5		7		12	10			8^{1}	9		3					6										1	11		39
			4	5	12	7			10			8	9^{1}		3					6										1	11	2	40
			4	5	12	7			10			8	9		3					6										1	11^{1}	2	41
			4	5		7			10			8	9		3					6										1	11	2	42
			4	5		7			10			8	9		3					6										1	11	2	43
			4	5		7			10			8	9		3					6										1	11	2	44
			4	5	13	7			10		12	8^{2}	9^{3}		3		14			6■										1	11^{1}	2■	45
			4	5	6	7			10			8^{1}	9		3		12												13	1	11	2^{2}	46

Worthington Cup				
First Round	Leyton Orient	(a)	2-3	
LDV Vans Trophy				
First Round	Bristol C	(h)	0-0	

FA Cup			
First Round	Vauxhall M	(a)	0-0
		(h)	1-1

READING Division 1

FOUNDATION

Reading was formed as far back as 1871 at a public meeting held at the Bridge Street Rooms. They first entered the FA Cup as early as 1877 when they amalgamated with the Reading Hornets. The club was further strengthened in 1889 when Earley FC joined them. They were the first winners of the Berks and Bucks Cup in 1878–79.

Madejski Stadium, Junction 11, M4, Reading, Berks RG2 0FL.

Telephone: (0118) 968 1100. ***Fax:*** (0118) 968 1101.

ClubCall: 09068 121 000. ***Website:*** www.readingfc.co.uk
Email: comments@readingfc.co.uk
Ticket Office: (0118) 968 1000.
Ticket Office Fax: (0118) 968 1001.

Ground Capacity: 24,200.

Record Attendance: 33,042 v Brentford, FA Cup 5th rd, 19 February 1927.

Record Receipts: £171,203 v Manchester C, Division 2, 27 March 1999.

Pitch Measurements: 102m × 68m.

President: F. Orton.

Chairman: John Madejski OBE, DL.

Director: I. Wood-Smith.

Manager: Alan Pardew.

Chief Executive: Nigel Howe.

Physio: Jon Fearn.

Commercial Manager: Kevin Girdler.

Secretary: Ms Sue Hewett.

Colours: Hooped royal blue and white shirts, blue shorts, white stockings.

Change Colours: Black shirts, shorts and stockings all with light blue trim.

Year Formed: 1871.

Turned Professional: 1895.

Ltd Co.: 1895.

Club Nickname: 'The Royals'.

Previous Grounds: 1871, Reading Recreation; Reading Cricket Ground; 1882, Coley Park; 1889, Caversham Cricket Ground; 1896, Elm Park; 1998, Madejski Stadium.

First Football League Game: 28 August 1920, Division 3, v Newport Co (a) W 1–0 – Crawford; Smith, Horler; Christie, Mavin, Getgood; Spence, Weston, Yarnell, Bailey (1), Andrews.

HONOURS

Football League: Division 1 – Runners-up 1994–95; Division 2 – Champions 1993–94; Runners-up 2001–02; Division 3 – Champions 1985–86; Division 3 (S) – Champions 1925–26; Runners-up 1931–32, 1934–35, 1948–49, 1951–52; Division 4 – Champions 1978–79.

FA Cup: Semi-final 1927.

Football League Cup: best season: 5th rd, 1996.

Simod Cup: Winners 1988.

SKY SPORTS FACT FILE

Five new signings by Reading in 1939 were to make just those abortive pre-war games for the club: goalkeeper George Gale, full-backs Joe Wilson and Alf Fenwick, left-half Len Edwards and inside-right Ernie Whittam.

Record League Victory: 10–2 v Crystal Palace, Division 3 (S), 4 September 1946 – Groves; Glidden, Gulliver; McKenna, Ratcliffe, Young; Chitty, Maurice Edelston (3), McPhee (4), Barney (1), Deverell (2).

Record Cup Victory: 6–0 v Leyton, FA Cup 2nd rd, 12 December 1925 – Duckworth; Eggo, McConnell; Wilson, Messer, Evans; Smith (2), Braithwaite (1), Davey (1), Tinsley, Robson (2).

Record Defeat: 0–18 v Preston NE, FA Cup 1st rd, 1893–94.

Most League Points (2 for a win): 65, Division 4, 1978–79.

Most League Points (3 for a win): 94, Division 3, 1985–86.

Most League Goals: 112, Division 3 (S), 1951–52.

Highest League Scorer in Season: Ronnie Blackman, 39, Division 3 (S), 1951–52.

Most League Goals in Total Aggregate: Ronnie Blackman, 158, 1947–54.

Most League Goals in One Match: 6, Arthur Bacon v Stoke C, Division 2, 3 April 1931.

Most Capped Player: Jimmy Quinn, 17 (46), Northern Ireland.

Most League Appearances: Martin Hicks, 500, 1978–91.

Youngest League Player: Peter Castle, 16 years 49 days v Watford, 30 April 2003.

Record Transfer Fee Received: £1,575,000 from Newcastle U for Shaka Hislop, August 1995.

Record Transfer Fee Paid: £800,000 to Brentford for Carl Asaba, August 1997.

Football League Record: 1920 Original Member of Division 3; 1921–26 Division 3 (S); 1926–31 Division 2; 1931–58 Division 3 (S); 1958–71 Division 3; 1971–76 Division 4; 1976–77 Division 3; 1977–79 Division 4; 1979–83 Division 3; 1983–84 Division 4; 1984–86 Division 3; 1986–88 Division 2; 1988–92 Division 3; 1992–94 Division 2; 1994–98 Division 1; 1998–2002 Division 2; 2002– Division 1.

MANAGERS

Thomas Sefton 1897–1901
(Secretary-Manager)
James Sharp 1901–02
Harry Matthews 1902–20
Harry Marshall 1920–22
Arthur Chadwick 1923–25
H. S. Bray 1925–26
(Secretary only since 1922 and 1926–35)
Andrew Wylie 1926–31
Joe Smith 1931–35
Billy Butler 1935–39
John Cochrane 1939
Joe Edelston 1939–47
Ted Drake 1947–52
Jack Smith 1952–55
Harry Johnston 1955–63
Roy Bentley 1963–69
Jack Mansell 1969–71
Charlie Hurley 1972–77
Maurice Evans 1977–84
Ian Branfoot 1984–89
Ian Porterfield 1989–91
Mark McGhee 1991–94
Jimmy Quinn/Mick Gooding 1994–97
Terry Bullivant 1997–98
Tommy Burns 1998–99
Alan Pardew October 1999–

LATEST SEQUENCES

Longest Sequence of League Wins: 13, 17.8.1985 – 19.10.1985.

Longest Sequence of League Defeats: 7, 10.4.1998 – 15.8.1998.

Longest Sequence of League Draws: 6, 23.3.2002 – 20.4.02.

Longest Sequence of Unbeaten League Matches: 19, 21.4.1973 – 27.10.1973.

Longest Sequence Without a League Win: 14, 30.4.1927 – 29.10.1927.

Successive Scoring Runs: 32 from 1.10.1932.

Successive Non-scoring Runs: 6 from 13.4.1925.

TEN YEAR LEAGUE RECORD

		P	W	D	L	F	A	Pts	Pos
1993-94	Div 2	46	26	11	9	81	44	89	1
1994-95	Div 1	46	23	10	13	58	44	79	2
1995-96	Div 1	46	13	17	16	54	63	56	19
1996-97	Div 1	46	15	12	19	58	67	57	18
1997-98	Div 1	46	11	9	26	39	78	42	24
1998-99	Div 2	46	16	13	17	54	63	61	11
1999-2000	Div 2	46	16	14	16	57	63	62	10
2000-01	Div 2	46	25	11	10	86	52	86	3
2001-02	Div 2	46	23	15	8	70	43	84	2
2002-03	Div 1	46	25	4	17	61	46	79	4

DID YOU KNOW?

In 1983–84 Reading were unbeaten in League matches at Elm Park during their promotion season and equalled their achievements in consecutive seasons 1933–34 and 1934–35 when finishing respectively third and second in Division Three (South).

READING 2002–03 LEAGUE RECORD

Match No.	Date	Venue	Opponents	Result		H/T Score	Lg. Pos.	Goalscorers	Attendance
1	Aug 10	A	Derby Co	L	0-3	0-0	—		33,016
2	13	H	Sheffield W	W	2-1	0-1	—	Cureton 2 [47, 78]	13,638
3	17	H	Coventry C	L	1-2	1-0	15	Cureton (pen) [13]	14,712
4	24	A	Leicester C	L	1-2	1-2	20	Cureton (pen) [22]	22,978
5	27	H	Burnley	W	3-0	0-0	—	Cureton 2 [55, 90], Butler [87]	12,009
6	31	A	Walsall	W	2-0	0-0	11	Hughes 2 [79, 90]	5327
7	Sept 7	A	Rotherham U	D	0-0	0-0	8		6154
8	14	H	Wimbledon	L	0-1	0-0	12		14,832
9	18	H	Norwich C	L	0-2	0-2	—		14,335
10	21	A	Wolverhampton W	W	1-0	0-0	11	Hughes [58]	25,560
11	28	H	Stoke C	D	1-1	1-1	12	Rougier [11]	13,646
12	Oct 5	A	Grimsby T	W	3-0	2-0	9	Hughes [13], Forster [32], Pouton (og) [90]	5582
13	19	H	Ipswich T	W	3-1	2-0	10	Forster 3 [28, 40, 69]	19,524
14	26	A	Preston NE	L	0-1	0-1	12		13,021
15	29	H	Bradford C	W	1-0	0-0	—	Shorey [71]	12,110
16	Nov 2	H	Millwall	W	2-0	1-0	8	Forster [6], Hughes [90]	13,081
17	9	A	Gillingham	W	1-0	0-0	6	Rougier [82]	8511
18	23	H	Watford	W	1-0	0-0	7	Watson [61]	17,465
19	26	A	Crystal Palace	W	1-0	1-0	—	Forster [39]	15,712
20	30	A	Brighton & HA	W	1-0	1-0	5	Salako [22]	6817
21	Dec 7	H	Portsmouth	D	0-0	0-0	5		23,462
22	14	H	Sheffield U	L	0-2	0-0	6		18,534
23	21	A	Nottingham F	L	0-2	0-1	6		25,831
24	26	A	Coventry C	L	0-2	0-1	7		19,526
25	28	H	Derby Co	W	2-1	1-1	6	Tyson [5], Cureton [90]	16,299
26	Jan 11	A	Sheffield W	L	2-3	2-0	7	Forster [9], Butler [19]	17,715
27	18	H	Walsall	D	0-0	0-0	7		11,786
28	28	H	Leicester C	L	1-3	0-3	—	Hughes [54]	17,156
29	Feb 1	A	Burnley	W	5-2	2-0	5	Sidwell 2 [37, 79], Salako 2 [45, 52], Henderson [90]	14,420
30	10	H	Gillingham	W	2-1	1-1	—	Chadwick [13], Salako [88]	11,030
31	15	A	Millwall	W	2-0	1-0	4	Forster [45], Henderson [83]	7038
32	18	A	Sheffield U	W	3-1	1-1	—	Forster 2 [35, 81], Williams [74]	16,884
33	22	H	Rotherham U	W	3-0	3-0	3	Harper [15], Hughes [32], Forster [40]	14,816
34	Mar 1	A	Wimbledon	L	0-2	0-1	3		3869
35	5	A	Norwich C	W	1-0	0-0	—	Kenton (og) [74]	18,970
36	12	H	Wolverhampton W	L	0-1	0-1	—		19,731
37	15	H	Crystal Palace	W	2-1	0-0	3	Brown [66], Harper [90]	18,063
38	18	A	Ipswich T	L	1-3	1-2	—	Forster [16]	24,108
39	22	A	Bradford C	W	1-0	0-0	4	Forster [66]	11,385
40	Apr 4	H	Brighton & HA	L	1-2	0-1	—	Cureton [84]	16,133
41	15	H	Preston NE	W	5-1	2-0	—	Forster 3 [30, 42, 58], Shorey (pen) [57], Henderson [90]	14,012
42	18	H	Nottingham F	W	1-0	0-0	—	Hughes [74]	21,612
43	21	A	Portsmouth	L	0-3	0-2	5		19,535
44	26	H	Grimsby T	W	2-1	2-0	4	Little [2], Hughes [22]	20,273
45	30	A	Watford	W	3-0	1-0	—	Rougier [27], Henderson [70], Cureton [90]	11,814
46	May 4	A	Stoke C	L	0-1	0-0	4		20,477

Final League Position: 4

GOALSCORERS

League (61): Forster 16, Cureton 9 (2 pens), Hughes 9, Henderson 4, Salako 4, Rougier 3, Butler 2, Harper 2, Shorey 2 (1 pen), Sidwell 2, Brown 1, Chadwick 1, Little 1, Tyson 1, Watson 1, Williams 1, own goals 2.
Worthington Cup (1): Upson 1.
FA Cup (1): own goal 1.
Play-offs (1): Forster 1.

Whitehead P 4	Murty G 43 + 1	Shorey N 43	Mackie J 20 + 5	Williams A 38	Watson K 24 + 8	Igoe S 8 + 7	Hughes A 41 + 2	Butler M 12 + 9	Harper J 34 + 2	Salako J 33 + 10	Parkinson P — + 6	Cureton J 13 + 14	Henderson D 1 + 21	Forster N 35 + 5	Rougier T 13 + 7	Smith A — + 1	Hahnemann M 41	Newman R 21 + 7	Upson M 13 + 1	Tyson N 9 + 14	Ashdown J 1	Brown S 21	Sidwell S 13	Chadwick L 15	Viveash A 4 + 1	Little G 6	Campbell D — + 1	Castle P — + 1	*Match No.*
1	2	3	4	5	6^{1}	7^{2}	8	9^{3}	10	11	12	13	14																1
1	2	3	4	5	6^{3}	12	7	9^{2}	8^{1}	11	14	10	13																2
1	2	3	4	5	6^{1}	7	8	9		11^{3}	12	10^{2}		13	14														3
1	2	3^{2}	4	5	6		8	9^{1}		11		10		7	12	13													4
	2	3	4	5	6^{2}	12	8	9		11	13	10		7^{1}			1												5
	2	3	4	5	6	12	8	9		11	13	10^{2}		7^{1}			1												6
		3^{3}	4	5	6		8^{1}	9^{2}		11	12	10		7	13		1	2	14										7
	12	3	4	5	6	7^{2}	8^{1}	9^{3}		11		10		13	14		1	2											8
	2		4■	5	6^{3}	7	8			11^{2}		10^{1}		12	9		1	14	3	13									9
	2		4	5	6		8			11		10^{1}	13	12	9^{2}		1	7	3										10
	2		4	5	6^{2}		8			11		10		12	9^{1}		1	7	3	13									11
	2	3		5	6^{1}		8		12	11			13	10	9^{2}			7	4		1								12
	2	3		5	6	12		13	8^{3}	11		14		10^{2}	9^{1}		1	7	4										13
	2	3	12	5	6^{3}		8		13	11^{1}		14		10	9^{2}		1	7	4										14
	2	3		5	6^{1}		8	12	10	11^{3}		13		9^{2}			1	7	4	14									15
	2	3		5	6		8	12	11	13				9			1	7^{1}	4	10^{2}									16
	2	3	12	5	6^{2}		8	13	10	11^{3}				9	14		1	7	4^{1}										17
	2	3		5	6	12	8^{2}	9	7	11^{1}		10^{3}			14		1		4	13									18
	2	3		5	6^{2}		8^{1}	12	7	11				10	9		1	13	4										19
	2	3		5	6^{2}		8	12	7	11				10	9^{1}		1	13	4										20
	2	3		5	12		8^{3}	13	10	11		14		9	7^{2}		1	6^{1}	4										21
	2	3	4	5	6		8	12	10	11^{2}		13		9	7^{1}		1												22
	2	3	4	5	6	12	8		10	11^{2}		13		9^{3}	7^{1}		1			14									23
	2	3		5	6^{2}		8		10	11^{3}		9	13		12		1	7^{1}		14		4							24
	2	3		5	12	7		9^{3}	8^{1}	13		10	14				1	6		11^{2}		4							25
	2	3^{3}	4			7	12	9	8	13			14	10			1	6^{1}		11^{2}		5							26
	2	3	4			7	8	9^{3}	11	12		13		10^{2}			1	6^{1}		14		5							27
	2	3		5		7^{2}	8	12	6^{1}			13		9	11		1	14				4^{3}	10						28
	2	3	12	5			8^{2}		6^{1}	11			13	9			1	7				4	10						29
	2	3		5			12		8^{2}	11			13	9			1	6		14		4	10^{1}	7^{3}					30
	2	3		5			8		6	11			12	9^{2}			1			13		4	10	7^{1}					31
	2	3		5			8		6	11^{2}			12	9^{1}			1			13		4	10	7					32
	2	3		5	12		8^{2}		6	11^{1}			13	9^{3}			1			14		4	10	7					33
	2	3	12	5			8		6	11			13	9			1			14		4^{1}	10^{3}	7^{2}					34
	2	3	4	5^{3}			8		6	12			13	9^{2}			1			11^{1}			10	7	14				35
	2	3	4		12		8		6^{1}	13			14	9			1			11^{3}		5	10^{2}	7					36
	2	3	4		12		8		6	13				9			1			11^{2}		5	10^{1}	7					37
	2	3			12		8		6	13				9			1	14		11^{2}		4	10^{3}	7^{1}	5■				38
	2	3				12	8		10	7^{1}			13	9^{2}			1	6		11■		4			5				39
	2	3		5	12		8^{2}		10			13		9			1	6^{1}		14		4		7^{3}		11			40
	2	3		5			8		6	11		12	13	9^{2}			1			14		4		7^{1}		10^{3}			41
	2	3	4^{1}	5			8		10	13			14	9			1	12				6		7^{2}		11^{3}			42
	2	3	12	5			8^{2}		10	13			14	9			1	6				4^{1}		7^{3}		11			43
	2	3		5^{3}			8		6	11		12	13	9^{2}			1	14				4		7		10^{1}			44
		3			6^{2}		8					12	7		9^{1}		1	4		11^{3}		2	10		5		13	14	45
	2	3	4		12				6^{1}	11^{3}		13	14	9			1						10	7^{2}	5	8			46

Worthington Cup			
First Round	Cambridge U	(a)	1-3

FA Cup			
Third Round	Walsall	(a)	0-0
		(h)	1-1

ROCHDALE Division 3

FOUNDATION

Considering the love of rugby in their area, it is not surprising that Rochdale had difficulty in establishing an Association Football club. The earlier Rochdale Town club formed in 1900 went out of existence in 1907 when the present club was immediately established and joined the Manchester League, before graduating to the Lancashire Combination in 1908.

Spotland, Sandy Lane, Rochdale OL11 5DS.

Telephone: (01706) 644 648. ***Fax:*** (01706) 648 466.
Website: www.rochdaleafc.co.uk
Email: office@rochdalefc.co.uk

Commercial: (01706) 647 521.

Ground Capacity: 10,208.

Record Attendance: 24,231 v Notts Co, FA Cup 2nd rd, 10 December 1949.

Record Receipts: £46,000 v Burnley, Division 4, 5 May 1992.

Pitch Measurements: 114yd × 76yd.

President: Mrs L. Stoney.

Chairman: D. F. Kilpatrick.

Directors: G. R. Brierley, C. Dunphy, J. Marsh, G. Morris, R. Bott, I. H. Stott.

Manager: Alan Buckley.

Secretary: Hilary Molyneux Dearden.

Lottery and Merchandising Manager: P. Woodhouse.

Advertising and Sponsorship Manager: L. Duckworth.

Physio: Andy Thorpe.

Colours: Blue shirts with white trim, blue shorts, blue stockings with white hoop on turnover.

Change Colours: All black with fluorescent trim.

Year Formed: 1907.

Turned Professional: 1907.

Ltd Co.: 1910.

Club Nickname: 'The Dale'.

First Football League Game: 27 August 1921, Division 3 (N), v Accrington Stanley (h) W 6–3 – Crabtree; Nuttall, Sheehan; Hill, Farrer, Yarwood; Hoad, Sandiford, Dennison (2), Owens (3), Carney (1).

Record League Victory: 8–1 v Chesterfield, Division 3 (N), 18 December 1926 – Hill; Brown, Ward; Hillhouse, Parkes, Braidwood; Hughes, Bertram, Whitehurst (5), Schofield (2), Martin (1).

HONOURS

Football League: Division 3 best season: 9th, 1969–70; Division 3 (N) – Runners-up 1923–24, 1926–27.

FA Cup: best season: 5th rd, 1990, 2003.

Football League Cup: Runners-up 1962 (record for 4th Division club).

SKY SPORTS FACT FILE

John Hall scored a hat-trick on his debut for Rochdale in an FA Cup tie against Skelmersdale on 17 November 1923. Rochdale won 4-0 and for the player these three goals were one more goal than he managed throughout his League career.

Record Cup Victory: 8–2 v Crook T, FA Cup 1st rd, 26 November 1927 – Moody; Hopkins, Ward; Braidwood, Parkes, Barker; Tompkinson, Clennell (3) Whitehurst (4), Hall, Martin (1).

Record Defeat: 1–9 v Tranmere R, Division 3 (N), 25 December 1931.

Most League Points (2 for a win): 62, Division 3 (N), 1923–24.

Most League Points (3 for a win): 78, Division 3, 2001–02.

Most League Goals: 105, Division 3 (N), 1926–27.

Highest League Scorer in Season: Albert Whitehurst, 44, Division 3 (N), 1926–27.

Most League Goals in Total Aggregate: Reg Jenkins, 119, 1964–73.

Most League Goals in One Match: 6, Tommy Tippett v Hartlepools U, Division 3N, 21 April 1930.

Most Capped Players: Patrick McCourt, 1, Northern Ireland and Lee McEvilly, 1, Northern Ireland.

Most League Appearances: Graham Smith, 317, 1966–74.

Youngest League Player: Zac Hughes, 16 years 105 days v Exeter C, 19 September 1987.

Record Transfer Fee Received: £400,000 from West Ham U for Stephen Bywater, August 1998.

Record Transfer Fee Paid: £150,000 to Stoke C for Paul Connor, March 2001.

Football League Record: 1921 Elected to Division 3 (N); 1958–59 Division 3; 1959–69 Division 4; 1969–74 Division 3; 1974–92 Division 4; 1992– Division 3.

MANAGERS

Billy Bradshaw 1920
Run by committee 1920–22
Tom Wilson 1922–23
Jack Peart 1923–30
Will Cameron 1930–31
Herbert Hopkinson 1932–34
Billy Smith 1934–35
Ernest Nixon 1935–37
Sam Jennings 1937–38
Ted Goodier 1938–52
Jack Warner 1952–53
Harry Catterick 1953–58
Jack Marshall 1958–60
Tony Collins 1960–68
Bob Stokoe 1967–68
Len Richley 1968–70
Dick Conner 1970–73
Walter Joyce 1973–76
Brian Green 1976–77
Mike Ferguson 1977–78
Doug Collins 1979
Bob Stokoe 1979–80
Peter Madden 1980–83
Jimmy Greenhoff 1983–84
Vic Halom 1984–86
Eddie Gray 1986–88
Danny Bergara 1988–89
Terry Dolan 1989–91
Dave Sutton 1991–94
Mick Docherty 1995–96
Graham Barrow 1996–99
Steve Parkin 1999–2001
John Hollins 2001–02
Paul Simpson 2002–03
Alan Buckley May 2003–

LATEST SEQUENCES

Longest Sequence of League Wins: 8, 29.9.1969 – 3.11.1969.

Longest Sequence of League Defeats: 17, 14.11.1931 – 12.3.1932.

Longest Sequence of League Draws: 6, 17.8.1968 – 14.9.1968.

Longest Sequence of Unbeaten League Matches: 20, 15.9.1923 – 19.1.1924.

Longest Sequence Without a League Win: 28, 14.11.1931 – 29.8.1932.

Successive Scoring Runs: 29 from 8.1.1927.

Successive Non-scoring Runs: 9 from 14.3.1980.

TEN YEAR LEAGUE RECORD

		P	*W*	*D*	*L*	*F*	*A*	*Pts*	*Pos*
1993-94	Div 3	42	16	12	14	63	51	60	9
1994-95	Div 3	42	12	14	16	44	67	50	15
1995-96	Div 3	46	14	13	19	57	61	55	15
1996-97	Div 3	46	14	16	16	58	58	58	14
1997-98	Div 3	46	17	7	22	56	55	58	18
1998-99	Div 3	46	13	15	18	42	55	54	19
1999-2000	Div 3	46	18	14	14	57	54	68	10
2000-01	Div 3	46	18	17	11	59	48	71	8
2001-02	Div 3	46	21	15	10	65	52	78	5
2002-03	Div 3	46	12	16	18	63	70	52	19

DID YOU KNOW ?

In a busy 1961–62 season for Rochdale the club completed 61 League and Cup fixtures. Only one player was an ever present – Ron Cairns who also finished as top scorer with 21 goals in all competitions.

ROCHDALE 2002–03 LEAGUE RECORD

Match No.	Date	Venue	Opponents	Result	H/T Score	Lg. Pos.	Goalscorers	Atten-dance
1	Aug 10	H	Leyton Orient	W 1-0	0-0	—	Connor [90]	3252
2	13	A	Lincoln C	L 0-2	0-0	—		2894
3	17	A	Bristol R	W 2-1	1-1	7	Platt [36], Simpson [78]	6478
4	24	H	Darlington	D 1-1	1-1	7	McEvilly [7]	2834
5	26	A	Wrexham	W 5-2	4-2	4	McEvilly [17], Simpson 3 (2 pens) [22, 42 (p), 59 (p)], Griffiths [24]	4340
6	31	H	Southend U	L 1-2	0-1	6	Griffiths [84]	2852
7	Sept 6	A	Carlisle U	W 2-0	2-0	—	Platt [11], Simpson [21]	4501
8	14	H	Shrewsbury T	D 1-1	0-1	3	Simpson (pen) [79]	2914
9	17	H	Cambridge U	W 4-3	1-2	—	Bridges (og) [6], Simpson [60], Townson [89], Oliver [90]	2392
10	21	A	Kidderminster H	D 0-0	0-0	3		2685
11	28	H	Macclesfield T	W 3-1	1-1	2	Connor 2 [21, 65], Platt [81]	3090
12	Oct 5	A	Swansea C	D 1-1	0-1	4	Connor [71]	3732
13	12	A	Hull C	L 0-3	0-2	5		9057
14	19	H	Scunthorpe U	L 1-2	0-0	5	Simpson [86]	3442
15	26	A	Boston U	L 1-3	0-1	10	Flitcroft [81]	2653
16	29	H	Exeter C	D 3-3	1-1	—	Beech [41], Simpson [59], Griffiths [86]	1944
17	Nov 2	H	Rushden & D	L 0-1	0-0	13		2628
18	9	A	Oxford U	L 0-2	0-1	16		4547
19	23	H	York C	L 0-1	0-0	16		3056
20	30	A	Torquay U	D 2-2	0-0	15	Connor [74], Griffiths [78]	2754
21	Dec 14	H	Hartlepool U	W 4-0	2-0	15	Platt [24], McEvilly 2 [43, 62], Connor [56]	3059
22	21	A	Bury	D 1-1	0-0	15	McEvilly [66]	5827
23	26	H	Wrexham	D 2-2	2-1	14	Connor 2 [2, 18]	3727
24	28	A	Bournemouth	D 3-3	2-2	15	Flitcroft [16], McEvilly (pen) [45], Platt [73]	6240
25	Jan 18	A	Southend U	L 0-1	0-0	17		3645
26	21	H	Lincoln C	L 0-1	0-0	—		2122
27	Feb 8	H	Oxford U	W 2-1	1-0	17	Oliver [44], Melaugh [89]	2764
28	11	A	Darlington	W 1-0	1-0	—	Platt [21]	2479
29	22	H	Carlisle U	L 0-1	0-0	16		3247
30	25	A	Leyton Orient	W 1-0	1-0	—	McEvilly (pen) [45]	2633
31	Mar 1	A	Shrewsbury T	L 1-3	0-2	16	McEvilly [84]	3423
32	4	A	Cambridge U	D 2-2	1-2	—	McEvilly [2], McCourt [51]	2586
33	11	H	Bournemouth	D 1-1	0-1	—	Griffiths [49]	1958
34	15	H	Boston U	W 1-0	0-0	15	McEvilly (pen) [75]	2538
35	18	A	Scunthorpe U	L 1-3	1-2	—	McCourt [13]	3616
36	22	A	Exeter C	D 1-1	1-1	15	Connor (pen) [30]	4003
37	24	A	Rushden & D	D 3-3	1-0	—	Simpson [27], Grand [63], Connor [87]	3444
38	Apr 5	H	Torquay U	L 0-2	0-1	17		2216
39	8	H	Bristol R	D 1-1	1-1	—	Connor [21]	1658
40	12	A	York C	D 2-2	1-1	16	Connor [3], McEvilly (pen) [70]	3966
41	15	H	Kidderminster H	L 0-1	0-0	—		1810
42	18	H	Bury	L 1-2	1-1	—	Stuart (og) [34]	4513
43	21	A	Hartlepool U	D 2-2	2-1	18	Grand [23], McEvilly [45]	5408
44	26	H	Swansea C	L 1-2	1-1	20	Griffiths [43]	2777
45	29	H	Hull C	W 2-1	2-0	—	McEvilly [6], Hockenhull [18]	2225
46	May 3	A	Macclesfield T	L 2-3	1-0	19	McEvilly 2 (1 pen) [36 (p), 70]	2873

Final League Position: 19

GOALSCORERS

League (63): McEvilly 15 (5 pens), Connor 12 (1 pen), Simpson 10 (3 pens), Griffiths 6, Platt 6, Flitcroft 2, Grand 2, McCourt 2, Oliver 2, Beech 1, Hockenhull 1, Melaugh 1, Townson 1, own goals 2.
Worthington Cup (0).
FA Cup (12): Connor 3, Platt 3, Beech 1, Griffiths 1, McCourt 1, McEvilly 1, Melaugh 1, Simpson 1.
LDV Vans Trophy (0).

Edwards N 26	Evans W 40	Beech C 16+2	Hodges L 3+4	Macauley S 6	Griffiths G 41+1	Doughty M 39+2	Flitcroft D 40+1	Platt C 40+2	Townson K 5+19	Simpson P 30+5	McCourt P 12+14	Connor P 30+9	Oliver M 17+3	McEvilly L 27+10	Duffy L 19+3	Warner S 6+1	Bishop I 5+3	Jobson R 15+1	Gilks M 19+1	Cansdell-Sheriff S 3	Melaugh G 17+2	Patterson R 2+6	Grand S 22+1	Hill S 9+1	Andrews L 8	Hockenhull D 6+1	Taylor M 2	Bennett N 1	*Match No.*
1	2	3	4^{1}	5	6	7	8	9^{2}	10	11	12	13																	1
1	2	3	4^{1}	5	6	7	8	9	10	11		12																	2
1	2	3^{2}		5	6	7	4	9		11		12	8	10^{1}	13														3
1	2			5	6	3	7	9		11		12	8	10^{1}	4														4
1	2			5	6	3	7	9	12	11^{1}		13	8^{3}	10^{2}	4	14													5
1	2^{3}			5	6	3	7^{2}	9	12	11		13	8	10^{1}	4		14												6
1	2				6	3	7	9		11		10	8		12		4^{1}	5											7
1	2				6	3	7	9	12	11	13	10^{1}	8		4^{2}			5											8
1	2				6	3	7	9^{1}	12	11	4	10^{2}	8	13				5											9
1	2				6	3	7	9		11	4	10^{1}	8	12				5											10
1	2		12		6	3	7^{3}	9	13	11	4^{1}	10^{2}	8				14	5											11
1	2				6	3	7	9■		11		10	8				4	5											12
1	2		12		6	3^{1}	7	9	13	11^{2}		10	8				4	5											13
	2^{3}		11^{1}		6	3	7		13	12	14	10^{2}	8	9			4	5	1										14
1					6	3	7		10^{1}	11	13	9	8^{2}	12	2		4	5											15
1	5	4^{2}			6	3	7	9		11	12	10^{1}		8	2		13												16
1	5	4			6	3	7	9	12	11		10^{1}		8	2														17
1	2	4			6	3		9		11		10		7^{1}						5	8	12							18
1	2	4			6^{1}	3	12	9	13	11^{2}		10		14	7^{3}					5	8								19
1	4	8^{3}			6■	3	7	9	12		14	10^{1}		13	2^{2}					5	11								20
1	4					3	7	9^{2}	12		13	10		8^{1}	2			5			11		6^{3}	14					21
1	4					3	7	9	10^{1}		12			11	2			5			8		6						22
1	4				12	3	7	9		13	14	10^{3}		11^{2}	2^{1}			5			8		6						23
1	4				5	3	7	9				10	12	11		2					8^{1}		6						24
1	4					3	7	9^{2}	12	13		10	8	11		2^{1}		5					6						25
1	4		12		5	3^{2}	7	9	14	13		10^{1}	8	11^{3}		2							6						26
1^{G}	4		12		5			9		11^{1}		10^{2}	7	13		2			15		8		6	3					27
	4	3			5^{1}	12		9	10	11			8^{2}		13	2			1				6	7					28
	4				5		7	9^{1}	12	11^{3}	13			10		2^{2}			1		8	14	6	3					29
	2				5		7			11^{1}	10			9					1		8	12	6	3	4				30
	2				5		7	9^{2}			11		12	10					1		8	13	6	3^{1}	4				31
	4				5	3^{1}	7	9			11		12	10	6				1		8				2				32
	4^{2}				5	3	7	9^{1}			11	12		10	2				1		8		13		6				33
	4^{2}				5	3	7	9		13	11	12		10	2				1		8^{1}				6				34
					5	3	7	12	13	11	8^{2}	10		9^{1}	2				1				6		4				35
		8			5^{2}	3	7	9		11^{1}	12	10			2			13	1				6		4				36
		8				3	7^{1}	9^{2}		11^{3}	12	10		13	2			5	1		14		6		4				37
		2			5^{1}	3			12	11	13	10		9					1		8^{2}		6			7	4		38
					5	3	7	12		11	13	10		9^{1}	2				1		8^{2}		6				4		39
	2				5	3	8	9		11	4	10		15					1^{G}				6			7			40
	2	12			5	3^{2}	8^{1}	9	13	11	4	10^{3}		14									6			7		1	41
	2	12			5	3	8	9		11	4^{1}	10		13					1				6			7^{2}			42
	2	4			5	3^{1}	8	9	12					10					1			7	6	11					43
	2	4			5	3^{1}	8	9	12			13		10					1			7^{3}	6	11^{2}		14			44
	2	4^{1}			5		8	9^{2}				10		11					1		12	13	6	3		7			45
	2	4^{2}			5	12		9				10		11				6	1		8	13		3^{1}		7			46

Worthington Cup

First Round	Sheffield W	(a)	0-1

LDV Vans Trophy

First Round	Bury	(h)	0-1

FA Cup

First Round	Peterborough U	(h)	3-2
Second Round	Bristol R	(a)	1-1
		(h)	3-2
Third Round	Preston NE	(a)	2-1
Fourth Round	Coventry C	(h)	2-0
Fifth Round	Wolverhampton W	(a)	1-3

ROTHERHAM UNITED — Division 1

FOUNDATION

Rotherham were formed in 1870 before becoming Town in the late 1880s. Thornhill United were founded in 1877 and changed their name to Rotherham County in 1905. The Town amalgamated with Rotherham County to form Rotherham United in 1925.

Millmoor Ground, Rotherham S60 1HR.
Telephone: (01709) 512 434. ***Fax:*** (01709) 512 762.
Ticket Office: (01709) 309 440.
Commercial Dept: (01709) 512 760.
Fax: (01709) 512 763. ***Website:*** www.themillers.co.uk
ClubCall: 09068 121 637.

Football in the Community: (01709) 512 761.

Ground Capacity: 11,499.

Record Attendance: 25,170 v Sheffield U, Division 2, 13 December 1952.

Record Receipts: £106,182 v Southampton, FA Cup 3rd rd, 16 January 2002.

Pitch Measurements. 115yd × 70yd.

Chairman: K. F. Booth. ***Directors:*** C. A. Luckock, T. Smallwood OBE.

Chief Executive: Phil Henson.

Manager: Ronnie Moore.
Assistant Manager: John Breckin.

Youth Development Coach: John Bilton.
Physios: Denis Circuit, Ian Bailey.

HONOURS

Football League: Division 2 – runners-up 2000–01; Division 3 – Champions 1980–81; Runners-up 1999–2000; Division 3 (N) – Champions 1950–51; Runners-up 1946–47, 1947–48, 1948–49; Division 4 – Champions 1988–89; Runners-up 1991–92.

FA Cup: best season: 5th rd, 1953, 1968.

Football League Cup: Runners-up 1961.

Auto Windscreens Shield: Winners 1996.

Stadium Manager: Peter Chapman. ***Safety Officer:*** David Sumner.

Commercial Manager: D. Nicholls. ***Media Officer:*** Gerry Somerton.

Year Formed: 1870. ***Turned Professional:*** 1905. ***Ltd Co.:*** 1920. ***Club Nickname:*** 'The Merry Millers'.

Colours: Red and white.

Change Colours: Black and blue striped shirts, black shorts, black stockings.

Previous Names: 1877, Thornhill United; 1905, Rotherham County; 1925, amalgamated with Rotherham Town under Rotherham United.

Previous Ground: 1870, Red House Ground; 1907, Millmoor.

First Football League Game: 2 September 1893, Division 2, Rotherham T v Lincoln C (a) D 1–1 – McKay; Thickett, Watson; Barr, Brown, Broadhead; Longden, Cutts, Leatherbarrow, McCormick, Pickering, (1 og). 30 August 1919, Division 2, Rotherham Co v Nottingham F (h) W 2–0 – Branston; Alton, Baines; Bailey, Coe, Stanton; Lee (1), Cawley (1), Glennon, Lees, Lamb.

Record League Victory: 8–0 v Oldham Ath, Division 3 (N), 26 May 1947 – Warnes; Selkirk, Ibbotson; Edwards, Horace Williams, Danny Williams; Wilson (2), Shaw (1), Ardron (3), Guest (1), Hainsworth (1).

Record Cup Victory: 6–0 v Spennymoor U, FA Cup 2nd rd, 17 December 1977 – McAlister; Forrest, Breckin, Womble, Stancliffe, Green, Finney, Phillips (3), Gwyther (2) (Smith), Goodfellow, Crawford (1). 6–0 v Wolverhampton W, FA Cup 1st rd, 16 November 1985 – O'Hanlon; Forrest, Dungworth, Gooding (1), Smith (1), Pickering, Birch (2), Emerson, Tynan (1), Simmons (1), Pugh. 6–0 v Kings Lynn, FA Cup 2nd rd, 6 December 1997 – Mimms; Clark, Hurst (Goodwin), Garner (1) (Hudson) (1), Warner (Bass), Richardson (1), Berry (1), Thompson, Druce (1), Glover (1), Roscoe.

SKY SPORTS FACT FILE

On the opening day of the 1938–39 season, Rotherham United beat Rochdale 7-1 at Millmoor. At the start of the 2002-03 term they equalled the margin of victory winning 6-0 at Millwall in the First Division.

Record Defeat: 1–11 v Bradford C, Division 3 (N), 25 August 1928.

Most League Points (2 for a win): 71, Division 3 (N), 1950–51.

Most League Points (3 for a win): 91, Division 2, 2000–01.

Most League Goals: 114, Division 3 (N), 1946–47.

Highest League Scorer in Season: Wally Ardron, 38, Division 3 (N), 1946–47.

Most League Goals in Total Aggregate: Gladstone Guest, 130, 1946–56.

Most League Goals in One Match: 4, Roland Bastow v York C, Division 3N, 9 November 1935; 4, Roland Bastow v Rochdale, Division 3N, 7 March 1936; 4, Wally Ardron v Crewe Alex, Division 3N, 5 October 1946; 4, Wally Ardron v Carlisle U, Division 3N, 13 September 1947; 4, Wally Ardron v Hartlepools U, Division 3N, 13 October 1948; 4, Ian Wilson v Liverpool, Division 2, 2 May 1955; 4, Carl Gilbert v Swansea C, Division 3, 28 September 1971; 4, Carl Airey v Chester, Division 3, 31 August 1987; 4, Shaun Goater v Hartlepool U, Division 3, 9 April 1994; 4, Lee Glover v Hull C, Division 3, 28 December 1997; 4, Darren Byfield v Millwall, Division 1, 10 August 2002.

Most Capped Player: Shaun Goater 14 (19), Bermuda.

Most League Appearances: Danny Williams, 459, 1946–62.

Youngest League Player: Kevin Eley, 16 years 72 days v Scunthorpe U, 15 May 1984.

MANAGERS

Billy Heald 1925–29 *(Secretary only for long spell)*
Stanley Davies 1929–30
Billy Heald 1930–33
Reg Freeman 1934–52
Andy Smailes 1952–58
Tom Johnston 1958–62
Danny Williams 1962–65
Jack Mansell 1965–67
Tommy Docherty 1967–68
Jimmy McAnearney 1968–73
Jimmy McGuigan 1973–79
Ian Porterfield 1979–81
Emlyn Hughes 1981–83
George Kerr 1983–85
Norman Hunter 1985–87
Dave Cusack 1987–88
Billy McEwan 1988–91
Phil Henson 1991–94
Archie Gemmill/John McGovern 1994–96
Danny Bergara 1996–97
Ronnie Moore May 1997–

Record Transfer Fee Received: £325,000 from Sheffield W for Matt Clarke, July 1996.

Record Transfer Fee Paid: £150,000 to Millwall for Tony Towner, August 1980; £150,000 to Port Vale for Lee Glover, August 1996; £150,000 to Burnley for Alan Lee, September 2000.

Football League Record: 1893 Rotherham Town elected to Division 2; 1896 Failed re-election; 1919 Rotherham County elected to Division 2; 1923–51 Division 3 (N); 1951–68 Division 2; 1968–73 Division 3; 1973–75 Division 4; 1975–81 Division 3; 1981–83 Division 2; 1983–88 Division 3; 1988–89 Division 4; 1989–91 Division 3; 1991–92 Division 4; 1992–97 Division 2; 1997–2000 Division 3; 2000–01 Division 2; 2001– Division 1.

LATEST SEQUENCES

Longest Sequence of League Wins: 9, 2.2.1982 – 6.3.1982.

Longest Sequence of League Defeats: 8, 7.4.1956 – 18.8.1956.

Longest Sequence of League Draws: 6, 13.10.1969 – 22.11.1969.

Longest Sequence of Unbeaten League Matches: 18, 13.10.1969 – 7.2.1970.

Longest Sequence Without a League Win: 14, 8.10.1977 – 2.1.1978.

Successive Scoring Runs: 30 from 3.4.1954.

Successive Non-scoring Runs: 5 from 4.4.1986.

TEN YEAR LEAGUE RECORD

		P	W	D	L	F	A	Pts	Pos
1993-94	Div 2	46	15	13	18	63	60	58	15
1994-95	Div 2	46	14	14	18	57	61	56	17
1995-96	Div 2	46	14	14	18	54	62	56	16
1996-97	Div 2	46	7	14	25	39	70	35	23
1997-98	Div 3	46	16	19	11	67	61	67	9
1998-99	Div 3	46	20	13	13	79	61	73	5
1999-2000	Div 3	46	24	12	10	72	36	84	2
2000-01	Div 2	46	27	10	9	79	55	91	2
2001-02	Div 1	46	10	19	17	52	66	49	21
2002-03	Div 1	46	15	14	17	62	62	59	15

DID YOU KNOW?

Centre-back John Green, one of the youngest captains in Rotherham United's history, scored the goal which put the team ahead against Arsenal in the 3-1 League Cup win on 30 August 1978 and hit two goals in three minutes v Blackburn Rovers on 8 May 1982.

ROTHERHAM UNITED 2002–03 LEAGUE RECORD

Match No.	*Date*	*Venue*	*Opponents*	*Result*		*H/T Score*	*Lg. Pos.*	*Goalscorers*	*Attendance*
1	Aug 10	A	Millwall	W	6-0	2-0	—	Byfield 4 [23, 52, 80, 81], McIntosh [43], Sedgwick [71]	7177
2	13	H	Norwich C	D	1-1	0-0	—	Lee [68]	7687
3	17	H	Preston NE	D	0-0	0-0	9		6885
4	24	A	Sheffield W	W	2-1	1-1	7	Lee (pen) [29], Garner [90]	22,873
5	26	H	Derby Co	W	2-1	0-0	2	Lee 2 [64, 82]	8408
6	31	A	Bradford C	L	2-4	0-1	5	Barker R [71], Robins [82]	12,385
7	Sept 7	H	Reading	D	0-0	0-0	4		6154
8	14	A	Sheffield U	L	0-1	0-0	8		19,948
9	17	A	Walsall	W	4-3	3-2	—	Byfield 2 [14, 23], Lee 2 (1 pen) [30, 78 (p)]	4648
10	21	H	Brighton & HA	W	1-0	1-0	4	Lee [20]	6696
11	28	A	Nottingham F	L	2-3	1-3	5	Barker R [44], Byfield [59]	25,089
12	Oct 5	H	Portsmouth	L	2-3	1-3	8	Byfield [34], Lee (pen) [73]	8604
13	12	H	Gillingham	D	1-1	1-1	8	Ashby (og) [13]	6094
14	19	A	Grimsby T	D	0-0	0-0	9		6418
15	26	H	Stoke C	W	4-0	2-0	8	Barker R 2 [15, 53], Lee [39], Swailes [87]	7078
16	29	A	Wimbledon	L	1-2	0-1	—	Lee [89]	849
17	Nov 2	A	Coventry C	L	1-2	1-1	11	Daws [37]	13,179
18	9	H	Watford	W	2-1	1-0	9	McIntosh [41], Barker R [67]	6790
19	16	H	Burnley	D	0-0	0-0	9		7575
20	23	A	Leicester C	L	1-2	0-0	10	McIntosh [66]	31,714
21	30	H	Wolverhampton W	D	0-0	0-0	11		6736
22	Dec 7	A	Ipswich T	W	2-1	2-1	10	Talbot [25], Barker R [45]	22,770
23	14	A	Burnley	W	6-2	3-0	8	Lee 2 [12, 59], Mullin 2 [27, 30], Byfield 2 [84, 89]	14,121
24	22	H	Crystal Palace	L	1-3	0-2	11	Byfield [69]	6829
25	26	A	Preston NE	W	2-0	0-0	10	Robins [56], Barker R [85]	15,452
26	28	H	Millwall	L	1-3	0-1	11	Hurst [81]	6448
27	Jan 1	H	Sheffield W	L	0-2	0-0	11		11,480
28	11	A	Norwich C	D	1-1	1-0	11	Garner [33]	19,452
29	18	H	Bradford C	W	3-2	1-1	12	McIntosh [21], Garner [50], Byfield (pen) [60]	6939
30	Feb 1	A	Derby Co	L	0-3	0-2	13		26,257
31	8	A	Watford	W	2-1	0-0	10	McIntosh [69], Swailes [75]	15,025
32	15	H	Coventry C	W	1-0	1-0	6	Byfield [33]	6524
33	22	A	Reading	L	0-3	0-3	8		14,816
34	28	H	Sheffield U	L	1-2	0-1	—	Lee (pen) [81]	10,797
35	Mar 4	H	Walsall	D	0-0	0-0	—		5792
36	8	A	Brighton & HA	L	0-2	0-0	9		6468
37	15	A	Gillingham	D	1-1	1-1	11	Warne [12]	7284
38	18	H	Grimsby T	L	0-1	0-0	—		6239
39	22	H	Wimbledon	W	2-1	1-0	11	Robins [19], Branston [48]	5896
40	Apr 5	A	Wolverhampton W	D	0-0	0-0	10		25,934
41	9	A	Stoke C	L	0-2	0-2	—		19,553
42	12	H	Leicester C	D	1-1	0-0	14	Lee [54]	9888
43	19	A	Crystal Palace	D	0-0	0-0	13		15,508
44	21	H	Ipswich T	W	2-1	0-1	11	Mullin [85], Robins [87]	7519
45	27	A	Portsmouth	L	2-3	2-3	14	Branston [16], Swailes [29]	19,420
46	May 4	H	Nottingham F	D	2-2	0-0	15	Lee [55], Robins [69]	9942

Final League Position: 15

GOALSCORERS

League (62): Lee 15 (4 pens), Byfield 13 (1 pen), Barker R 7, McIntosh 5, Robins 5, Garner 3, Mullin 3, Swailes 3, Branston 2, Daws 1, Hurst 1, Sedgwick 1, Talbot 1, Warne 1, own goal 1.
Worthington Cup (10): Monkhouse 3, Barker R 2, Robins 2 (1 pen), Lee 1, Swailes 1, Warne 1.
FA Cup (0).

Pollitt M 41	Scott R 23	Hurst P 44	Sedgwick C 42 + 1	Swailes C 43	McIntosh M 42	Mullin J 31 + 3	Warne P 21 + 19	Lee A 38 + 3	Byfield D 24 + 13	Talbot S 8 + 7	Barker R 23 + 14	Robins M 6 + 10	Garner D 20 + 6	Monkhouse A 11 + 9	Daws N 30 + 3	Beech C 1 + 1	Bryan M 12 + 4	Branston G 13 + 2	Woodhouse C 11	Gray I 5 + 1	Barker S 11	Farrelly G 6	Match No.
1	2	3	4	5	6	7	8	9^{1}	10^{2}	11^{3}	12	13	14										1
1	2	3	4	5	6	7	8	9	10	11													2
1	2	3	4	5	6	7^{3}	8	9^{1}	10^{2}	11	12	13	14										3
1	2	3	4^{3}	5	6	7	8	9^{1}	10	11^{2}	12		13	14									4
1	2	3	4	5	6	7	8	9	10^{1}		12		11										5
1	2	3	4	5	6	7^{3}	8	9^{1}	10^{2}		12	13	11		14								6
1	2	3	4	5	6	7	8	9	10^{1}			12			11								7
1	2	3	4^{1}	5	6	7	8	9	13		12				11^{2}	10							8
1	2	3	4	5	6	7^{2}	8	9^{1}	10		12		11		13								9
1	2	3	4	5	6		8	9^{1}	10^{2}		12		11	13	7								10
1	2	3	4	5	6		8^{2}		10^{1}		9	12	11	13	7								11
1	2	3	4^{1}	5■	6	12	8	13	10^{2}		9		11	14	7^{3}								12
1	2^{1}	3	4	5	6	12	8	9^{2}	10^{3}		13		11	14	7								13
1		3	4		6	12	8^{3}	9	10^{2}			13	11^{1}	14	7		2	5					14
1	2	3	4^{1}	5	6		12	9	13		10^{3}		11^{2}	8	7		14						15
1	2	3		5	6	7^{2}	8^{1}	9	12	13	10			4	11								16
1	2	3	4	5			12	9	13		10^{2}		11	8^{1}	7			6					17
1	2	3	4^{1}	5	6			9		12	10		11	8	7								18
1	2^{3}	3	4	5	6		12	9^{2}	13		10		11	8^{1}	7		14						19
1	2	3^{1}	4	5	6		12		10^{2}		9	13	11		7			8					20
1	2	3	4	5			12	9			10		11	8^{1}	7			6					21
1	2	3	4^{2}	5	6	7	12	9		11^{1}	10				8	13							22
1	2	3	4^{1}	5	6	7	12	9	13		10^{2}			8^{3}	11		14						23
1	2^{3}	3		5	6	7	8^{1}	9	12	13	10			11	4^{2}		14						24
1		2	4^{1}	5	6	7	12				9	10	13	8^{2}	11		3						25
1		3	4	5	6	7	12	9	10^{1}	11		13		8^{2}			2^{3}	14					26
1		3	4^{2}	5	6	7^{1}	8^{3}	9			10	13	12		11		2	14					27
1		3	4^{1}	5	6	7	12		10^{2}		9	13	11		8		2						28
1		3	4^{1}	5	6^{2}	7	12		10	13	9		11		8		2						29
1■		3	4^{2}	5	6		12	13	10^{1}		9^{G}		11		7		2		8	15			30
1		3	4	5	6	7	12	9	10^{1}				11^{2}	13			2		8				31
1		3	4	5	6	7		9	10				11				2		8				32
1		3	4	5	6	7		9	10^{1}		12		11^{2}	13			2		8				33
1		3	4	5	6	7	12	9	10^{2}		13			11^{1}			2		8				34
1		3	4^{1}	5	6	7	11	9	10		12						2		8				35
1		3	4^{2}	5	6	7	11	9^{1}	10		12		13						8		2		36
1		3			6	7	8	9^{1}			10				12			5■	4		2	11	37
1		3	12		6	7	8^{1}	9^{2}	13		10							5	4		2	11	38
1		3	4^{1}	5		7	12	13		14	9^{2}	10			8			6			2	11^{3}	39
1		3	4^{1}	5		7	12	9	13	14	10^{2}				2				8^{3}		6	11	40
1			4^{1}	5	3	7■	12	9^{3}	13		14	10^{2}			8			6			2	11	41
			4	5	3			9				10			7			6	8	1	2	11	42
		11	4^{1}	5	3	7		9	13	12	10^{2}				8			6		1	2		43
		11	4^{1}	5	3	7		9	12			10			8			6		1	2		44
		11	4^{2}	5	3		12	9		7^{1}	10			13	8			6		1	2		45
		11	4^{1}	5	3		12	9^{2}	13	7		10			8			6		1	2		46

Worthington Cup

First Round	Carlisle U	(h)	3-1
Second Round	Wolverhampton W	(h)	4-4
Third Round	Wimbledon	(a)	3-1
Fourth Round	Blackburn R	(a)	0-4

FA Cup

Third Round	Wimbledon	(h)	0-3

RUSHDEN & DIAMONDS Division 2

FOUNDATION

Rushden & Diamonds were formed in 1992 from an amalgamation of Rushden Town and Irthlingborough Diamonds. At the end of 1990–91, Rushden Town had been relegated to the Southern League Midland Division as their ground was unfit for Premier Division football. Irthlingborough Diamonds were competing in the United Counties League at the time. The idea for this merger came from Max Griggs (owner of Dr Martens), a local multi-millionaire businessman. He invested several million pounds and they were able to achieve Football League status in nine years.

Nene Park, Diamond Way, Irthlingborough, Northants NN9 5QF.

Telephone: (01933) 652 000.

Fax: (01933) 650 418.

Website: www.thediamondsfc.com

Radio Diamonds: (01933) 653 535.

Ground Capacity: 6,441.

Record Attendance: 6,431 v Leeds U, FA Cup 3rd rd, 2 January 1999.

Record Receipts: £46,592 v Rochdale, Division 3 Play-off semi-final first leg, 27 April 2002.

Pitch Measurements: 111yd x 75yd.

Directors: W. M. Griggs CBE, MA (Chairman), M. G. Darnell (Managing), S. W. Griggs, H. M. Johnstone, A. C. Jones, R. W. Langley, C. M. Smith.

Manager: Brian Talbot.

First Team Coach: Steve Spooner.

Youth Team Coach: Neville Hamilton.

Physio: Simon Parsell.

Secretary: David Joyce.

Colours: White shirts with blue trim and red piping, blue shorts, white stockings.

Change Colours: Yellow shirts with black sleeves, black shorts, yellow stockings.

Year formed: 1992.

HONOURS

Football League: Division 3 – Champions 2002–03

FA Cup: best season 3rd rd 1999.

Football League Cup: never past 2nd rd.

Conference: Champions 2000–01.

Conference Championship Shield: Winners 2001.

Southern League Midland Division: Champions 1993–94.

Premier Division: Champions 1995–96.

FA Trophy: Semi-finalists 1994.

Northants FA Hillier Senior Cup: Winners 1993–94, 1998–99.

Maunsell Premier Cup: Winners 1994–95, 1998–99; Finalists 2001–02.

SKY SPORTS FACT FILE

The Rushden Town portion of the club's history found itself drawn against neighbours Kettering Town in preliminary stages of the FA Cup in six of eight seasons from 1946–47 apart from the 1949–50 and 1951–52 seasons.

MANAGERS

Roger Ashby 1992–97
Brian Talbot 1997–

Turned Professional: 1992.

Ltd Co.: 1992.

Club Nickname: 'The Diamonds'.

First Football League Match: 11 August 2001, Division 3, v York C (a) W 1–0 – Turley; Mustafa, Underwood, Talbot (Setchell), Peters, Rodwell, Butterworth, Brady, Patmore (1) (Darby), Jackson, Mills (Carey).

Record League Victory: 7–0 v Redditch U, Southern League, Midland Division, 7 May 1994 – Fox; Wooding (1), Johnson, Flower (1), Beech, Page, Coe, Mann (2), Nuttell (1), Watkins (1), Keast (1).

Record Cup Victory: 8–0 v Desborough T, Northants FA Hillier Senior Cup, 1st rd, 27 September 1994 – Fox; Wooding, Johnson, Flower, Keast, Page, Collins, Butterworth, Nuttell (2), Watkins (2), Mann (2). Subs:– Capone (2), Mason.

Record Defeat: 0–8 v Coventry C, League Cup 2nd rd, 2 October 2002.

Most League Points (3 for a win): 98, Southern League Midland Division, 1993–94.

Most League Goals: 109, Southern League Midland Division, 1993–94.

Highest League Scorer in Season: Darren Collins, 30 (40 in all competitions), Southern League Premier Division, 1995–96.

Most League Goals in Total Aggregate: Darren Collins, 112 (153 in all competitions), 1994–2000.

Most Capped Player: Paul Hall, 5 (41), Jamaica.

Most League Appearances: Garry Butterworth, 286 (371 in all competitions), 1994–2002.

Record Transfer Fee Received: £25,000 from Kettering T for Darren Collins, November 2000.

Record Transfer Fee Paid: Undisclosed to Kansas City Wizards for Onandi Lowe, February 2002.

Football League Record: 2001 Promoted to Division 3; 2003– Division 2.

LATEST SEQUENCES

Longest Sequence of League Wins: 6, 29.10.2002 – 14.12.2002.

Longest Sequence of League Defeats: 4, 27.8.2001 – 15.9.2001.

Longest Sequence of League Draws: not more than 2.

Longest Sequence of Unbeaten League Matches: 12, 18.9.2001 – 20.11.2001.

Longest Sequence Without a League Win: 7, 16.8.2001 – 18.9.2001

Successive Scoring Runs: 16 from 26.1.2002.

Successive Non-scoring Runs: 2 from 26.12.2002.

TEN YEAR LEAGUE RECORD

		P	W	D	L	F	A	Pts	Pos
1993-94	SL mid	42	29	11	2	109	37	98	1
1994-95	SL pr	42	19	11	12	99	65	68	5
1995-96	SL pr	42	29	7	6	99	41	94	1
1996-97	Conf.	42	14	11	17	61	63	53	12
1997-98	Conf.	42	23	5	14	79	57	74	4
1998-99	Conf.	42	20	12	10	71	42	72	4
1999-2000	Conf.	42	21	13	8	71	42	76	2
2000-01	Conf.	42	25	11	6	78	36	86	1
2001-02	Div 3	46	20	13	13	69	53	73	6
2002-03	Div 3	46	24	15	7	73	47	87	1

DID YOU KNOW?

Rushden & Diamonds manager Brian Talbot's first connection with the club was when he was a guest player on the official opening of Irthlingborough Diamonds floodlights at Nene Park.

RUSHDEN & DIAMONDS 2002–03 LEAGUE RECORD

Match No.	Date	Venue	Opponents	Result		H/T Score	Lg. Pos.	Goalscorers	Attendance
1	Aug 10	A	Swansea C	D	2-2	1-1	—	Lowe [13], Underwood [90]	6327
2	13	H	Torquay U	W	3-0	1-0	—	Darby [6], Wardley [57], Hall [75]	3602
3	17	H	Kidderminster H	W	3-1	1-0	1	Flynn (og) [17], Gray (pen) [65], Darby [81]	3329
4	24	A	Shrewsbury T	D	1-1	0-0	1	Darby [72]	3548
5	26	H	Scunthorpe U	W	2-0	1-0	1	Lowe [10], Burgess [50]	3849
6	31	A	Cambridge U	L	1-4	0-1	3	Wardley [83]	4598
7	Sept 7	H	Southend U	W	3-0	2-0	1	Gray 2 (1 pen) [10 (p), 34], Hall [83]	4176
8	14	A	York C	D	0-0	0-0	2		4102
9	17	A	Bournemouth	L	1-3	1-1	—	Dempster [31]	4527
10	21	H	Wrexham	D	2-2	1-1	6	Hall 2 [43, 80]	4090
11	28	A	Hartlepool U	W	2-1	0-1	5	Peters [48], Hall [84]	5502
12	Oct 5	H	Leyton Orient	W	2-0	0-0	3	Darby 2 [79, 87]	4381
13	12	A	Exeter C	D	1-1	1-1	3	Darby [28]	2884
14	19	H	Bury	L	0-1	0-1	4		3925
15	26	A	Hull C	D	1-1	1-1	4	Gray [38]	10,659
16	29	H	Boston U	W	1-0	1-0	—	Lowe [10]	4079
17	Nov 2	A	Rochdale	W	1-0	0-0	2	Darby [64]	2628
18	9	H	Darlington	W	2-0	0-0	2	Lowe [79], Clarke (og) [87]	3911
19	23	A	Lincoln C	W	2-1	1-0	2	Bell [27], Wardley [56]	3198
20	30	H	Bristol R	W	2-1	1-1	2	Lowe [22], Hall [72]	3960
21	Dec 14	A	Macclesfield T	W	1-0	0-0	2	Lowe [81]	1839
22	21	H	Carlisle U	D	1-1	1-1	2	Lowe [16]	4355
23	26	A	Scunthorpe U	D	0-0	0-0	1		4096
24	28	H	Oxford U	L	0-2	0-2	2		4891
25	Jan 1	H	Shrewsbury T	W	5-1	3-0	2	Darby 2 [9, 39], Gray [41], Lowe [61], Hall [70]	4144
26	4	A	Torquay U	D	1-1	0-1	2	Darby [57]	2651
27	11	A	Kidderminster H	W	2-0	1-0	2	Hall 2 [15, 69]	3417
28	18	H	Cambridge U	W	4-1	1-0	2	Gray [39], Bell [59], Hall 2 [85, 90]	5206
29	25	A	Oxford U	L	0-3	0-0	2		6508
30	Feb 1	H	Swansea C	D	1-1	0-1	2	Hall [71]	4046
31	8	A	Darlington	D	2-2	0-0	2	Gray (pen) [56], Hall [84]	2742
32	22	A	Southend U	L	1-2	1-2	2	Hunter [38]	6453
33	Mar 1	H	York C	W	2-1	1-0	2	Wardley [45], Brass (og) [75]	4463
34	4	H	Bournemouth	W	2-1	1-1	—	Darby [20], Lowe (pen) [84]	4353
35	8	A	Wrexham	L	0-3	0-1	2		3441
36	15	H	Hull C	W	4-2	1-0	2	Delaney (og) [2], Hall [68], Lowe [87], Wardley [90]	4713
37	18	A	Bury	W	1-0	0-0	—	Darby [70]	2291
38	22	A	Boston U	D	1-1	0-0	2	Darby [79]	3504
39	24	H	Rochdale	D	3-3	0-1	—	Hall [49], Lowe 2 [65, 73]	3444
40	29	H	Exeter C	W	1-0	0-0	2	Darby [58]	4921
41	Apr 5	A	Bristol R	W	2-1	1-1	2	Lowe 2 [37, 68]	6736
42	12	H	Lincoln C	W	1-0	1-0	2	Lowe [18]	4962
43	19	A	Carlisle U	W	2-1	0-0	1	Wardley [55], Edwards [63]	5468
44	21	H	Macclesfield T	W	3-0	1-0	1	Holdsworth 2 [43, 70], Bell [66]	4494
45	26	A	Leyton Orient	D	0-0	0-0	1		5180
46	May 3	H	Hartlepool U	D	1-1	1-0	1	Hall [29]	6291

Final League Position: 1

GOALSCORERS

League (73): Hall 16, Lowe 15 (1 pen), Darby 14, Gray 7 (3 pens), Wardley 6, Bell 3, Holdsworth 2, Burgess 1, Dempster 1, Edwards 1, Hunter 1, Peters 1, Underwood 1, own goals 4.
Worthington Cup (0).
FA Cup (5): Duffy 3, Lowe 1, Wardley 1.
LDV Vans Trophy (0).

Turley B 43 + 1	Underwood P 40	Bignot M 33	Tillson A 5	Hunter B 40	Gray S 34 + 4	Hall P 44 + 1	Wardley S 36 + 3	Darby D 35 + 2	Lowe O 38 + 1	Talbot D 5 + 8	Dempster J 11 + 5	Partridge S 2 + 5	Mills G 23 + 7	Sambrook A 6 + 9	Burgess A 19 + 8	Mustafa T 10 + 1	Peters M 25 + 2	Bell D 26 + 4	Setchell G 7 + 4	Solkhon B 1	Duffy R 3 + 9	Sollitt A 3	Battersby T 2 + 3	Edwards A 11 + 1	Holdsworth D 4 + 3	*Match No.*
1	2	3	4^1	5■	6	7	8	9^2	10	11^3	12	13	14													1
1	2	3^3		5	6	7	8	9^1	10	11^2	4	12	13	14												2
1	2			5	6	7	8^1	9^3	10	11^2	4	14	12	3	13											3
1	2		5		6	7		9^2	10	11^1	4		8	3■	12	13										4
1	2			5■	6	7		9^1	10		4		8		11	3	12									5
1	2		4	5	6^1	7	12	9^2	10	14		13	8		11^3	3										6
1	2			5	6	7	8	9	10				11^1			3	4	12								7
1	2				6	7	8	9	10		4		11			3	5									8
1	2				6	7	8^2	9^1	10		4	12	11		13	3	5									9
1	2			5^2		7	8		10	12	13	9^1	11			3	4^3	6	14							10
1	9			5	6	7	8			12			11			2	4		3	10^1						11
1				5	6	7	8	9	10				11			2	4		3							12
1	2^2			5	6	7	8	9^1		12			11			3	4		10		13					13
1	2		5		6	7	8^1	9	10	11^2			12			3	4		13							14
		2	5		6	7	12	9	10				11				4	8^1	3			1				15
1		2		5		7	8	9	10	12			11				4	6^1	3							16
1		2		5		7	8	9^1	10				11				4	6	3		12					17
1	2	3		5	6		8	9	10				11				4	7								18
1	2	3		5	6	12	8	9^1		13			11				4	7			10^2					19
1	2	3		5	6^3	7	8	12	10		13		11				4^2	14			9^1					20
	2	3		5		7	8	9	10				11				4	6				1				21
15	2	3		5		7	8		10				11		12		4	6^1			9	1^6				22
1	2	3		5	12	7	8	9	10				11^1				4	6								23
1	2	3		5	6^1	7	8	9	10						12		4	11								24
1	2	3		5	6	7	8	9^1	10^3					14	13		4	11^2			12■					25
1	2	3		5	6	7	8	9	10					12	11^1		4									26
1	2	3		5	6	7	8	9^1	10^2					13			4	11			12					27
1	2^3	3		5^2	6	9			10^1	12	13			7	11		4	8	14							28
1	2	3		5	6	9			10^1					8	11		4	7^2	13		12					29
1	2	3		5	6	7	12		10			9^2	8		11^1		4	13								30
1	2	3		5	6	9	8				12		11		13		4^1	7^2					10			31
1	2	3		5	6	9	8	12			4^2		11^3		14		13	7^1					10			32
1	2	3		5		7	8	9^1	10		4				11			6					12			33
1	2	3		5		7	8	9^1	10		4				11			6					12			34
1				5	6^2	9	8		10		4^1		12	2	11			7	3^3				13	14		35
1	2	3		5	12	7	8	9	10						11			6^1						4		36
1	2^1	3		5		7	8	9^2	10				11	12				6			13			4		37
1		2		5	12	7^1	8	9	10					3	11			6						4		38
1	2	3		5	12	7	8	9	10						11			6^1						4		39
1	2	3		5	6	7^1	8	9^2	10^3				12		11						13			4	14	40
1	2	3		5	6	7^2	8		10					13	11						12			4	9^1	41
1	2^1	3		5	6	7	8	9^2	10					12	11									4	13	42
1	2	3^3		5	6	7	8^1	9					13	14	11^2			12						4	10	43
1	2	3^2			6^1	7		9^3		12	5			13	11			8			14			4	10	44
1	2	3		5	6	7		9	12						11			8						4	10^1	45
1	2	3		5	6	7		9	10^1						11			8						4	12	46

Worthington Cup

First Round	Millwall	(h)	0-0
Second Round	Coventry C	(a)	0-8

LDV Vans Trophy

First Round	Cambridge U	(a)	0-4

FA Cup

First Round	Kidderminster H	(a)	2-2
		(h)	2-1
Second Round	Exeter C	(a)	1-3

SCUNTHORPE UNITED Division 3

FOUNDATION

The year of foundation for Scunthorpe United has often been quoted as 1910, but the club can trace its history back to 1899 when Brumby Hall FC, who played on the Old Showground, consolidated their position by amalgamating with some other clubs and changing their name to Scunthorpe United. The year 1910 was when that club amalgamated with North Lindsey United as Scunthorpe and Lindsey United. The link is Mr W. T. Lockwood whose chairmanship covers both years.

Glanford Park, Scunthorpe, North Lincolnshire DN15 8TD.

Telephone: (01724) 848 077. ***Fax:*** (01724) 857 986. ***ClubCall:*** 09068 121 652.

Ground Capacity: 9,183.

Record Attendance: Old Showground: 23,935 v Portsmouth, FA Cup 4th rd, 30 January 1954. Glanford Park: 8,775 v Rotherham U, Division 4, 1 May 1989.

Record Receipts: £47,252 v Burnley, Division 2, 6 May 2000.

Pitch Measurements: 110yd × 71yd.

Vice-presidents: I. T. Botham, G. Johnson, A. Harvey, R. Ashman, K. Waters, J. Brownsword, B. Heywood, Dr J. Zacarias.

Chairman: K. Wagstaff. ***Vice-chairman:*** R. Garton.

Directors: J. B. Borrill, B. Collen, J. A. C. Godfrey CBE, J. S. Wharton, C. Holland.

Team Manager: Brian Laws.

Chief Executive/Secretary: A. D. Rowing.

Commercial Manager: A. D. Rowing.

Colours: White shirts with claret and blue trim, white shorts with claret and blue trim, white stockings with claret and blue top.

Change Colours: Lime green shirts with navy trim, navy shorts with lime trim, navy stockings with lime top.

Year Formed: 1899. ***Turned Professional:*** 1912.

Ltd Co.: 1912.

Club Nickname: 'The Iron'.

Previous Names: Amalgamated first with Brumby Hall then North Lindsey United to become Scunthorpe & Lindsey United, 1910; dropped '& Lindsey' in 1958.

Previous Ground: 1899, Old Showground; 1988, Glanford Park.

First Football League Game: 19 August 1950, Division 3 (N), v Shrewsbury T (h) D 0–0 – Thompson; Barker, Brownsword; Allen, Taylor, McCormick; Mosby, Payne, Gorin, Rees, Boyes.

HONOURS

Football League: Division 2 best season: 4th, 1961–62; Division 3 (N) – Champions 1957–58. Promoted from Division 3 1998–99 (play-offs).

FA Cup: best season: 5th rd, 1958, 1970.

Football League Cup: never past 3rd rd.

SKY SPORTS FACT FILE

Scunthorpe United's most emphatic League result was achieved at the start of their championship-winning season of 1957–58. They beat Darlington 5-0 with goals from Jackie Marriott (2), Ronnie Waldock (2) and Doug Fletcher.

Record League Victory: 8–1 v Luton T, Division 3, 24 April 1965 – Sidebottom; Horstead, Hemstead; Smith, Neale, Lindsey; Bramley (1), Scott, Thomas (5), Mahy (1), Wilson (1). 8–1 v Torquay U (a), Division 3, 28 October 1995 – Samways; Housham, Wilson, Ford (1), Knill (1), Hope (Nicholson), Thornber, Bullimore (Walsh), McFarlane (4) (Young), Eyre (2), Paterson.

Record Cup Victory: 9–0 v Boston U, FA Cup 1st rd, 21 November 1953 – Malan; Hubbard, Brownsword; Sharpe, White, Bushby; Mosby (1), Haigh (3), Whitfield (2), Gregory (1), Mervyn Jones (2).

Record Defeat: 0–8 v Carlisle U, Division 3 (N), 25 December 1952.

Most League Points (2 for a win): 66, Division 3 (N), 1956–57, 1957–58.

Most League Points (3 for a win): 83, Division 4, 1982–83.

Most League Goals: 88, Division 3 (N), 1957–58.

Highest League Scorer in Season: Barrie Thomas, 31, Division 2, 1961–62.

Most League Goals in Total Aggregate: Steve Cammack, 110, 1979–81, 1981–86.

Most League Goals in One Match: 5, Barrie Thomas v Luton T, Division 3, 24 April 1965.

Most Capped Player: None.

Most League Appearances: Jack Brownsword, 595, 1950–65.

Youngest League Player: Mike Farrell, 16 years 240 days v Workington, 8 November 1975.

Record Transfer Fee Received: £350,000 from Aston Villa for Neil Cox, February 1991.

Record Transfer Fee Paid: £200,000 to Bristol C for Steve Torpey, February 2000.

Football League Record: 1950 Elected to Division 3 (N); 1958–64 Division 2; 1964–68 Division 3; 1968–72 Division 4; 1972–73 Division 3; 1973–83 Division 4; 1983–84 Division 3; 1984–92 Division 4; 1992–99 Division 3; 1999–2000 Division 2; 2000– Division 3.

MANAGERS

Harry Allcock 1915–53
(Secretary-Manager)
Tom Crilly 1936–37
Bernard Harper 1946–48
Leslie Jones 1950–51
Bill Corkhill 1952–56
Ron Suart 1956–58
Tony McShane 1959
Bill Lambton 1959
Frank Soo 1959–60
Dick Duckworth 1960–64
Fred Goodwin 1964–66
Ron Ashman 1967–73
Ron Bradley 1973–74
Dick Rooks 1974–76
Ron Ashman 1976–81
John Duncan 1981–83
Allan Clarke 1983–84
Frank Barlow 1984–87
Mick Buxton 1987–91
Bill Green 1991–93
Richard Money 1993–94
David Moore 1994–96
Mick Buxton 1996–97
Brian Laws February 1997–

LATEST SEQUENCES

Longest Sequence of League Wins: 6, 18.10.1969 – 25.11.1969.

Longest Sequence of League Defeats: 8, 29.11.1997 – 20.1.1998.

Longest Sequence of League Draws: 6, 2.1.1984 – 25.2.1984.

Longest Sequence of Unbeaten League Matches: 15, 13.11.1971 – 26.2.1972.

Longest Sequence Without a League Win: 14, 22.3.1975 – 6.9.1975.

Successive Scoring Runs: 23 from 18.8.1951.

Successive Non-scoring Runs: 7 from 19.4.1975.

TEN YEAR LEAGUE RECORD

		P	W	D	L	F	A	Pts	Pos
1993-94	Div 3	42	15	14	13	64	56	59	11
1994-95	Div 3	42	18	8	16	68	63	62	7
1995-96	Div 3	46	15	15	16	67	61	60	12
1996-97	Div 3	46	18	9	19	59	62	63	13
1997-98	Div 3	46	19	12	15	56	52	69	8
1998-99	Div 3	46	22	8	16	69	58	74	4
1999-2000	Div 2	46	9	12	25	40	74	39	23
2000-01	Div 3	46	18	11	17	62	52	65	10
2001-02	Div 3	46	19	14	13	74	56	71	8
2002-03	Div 3	46	19	15	12	68	49	72	5

DID YOU KNOW ?

When Scunthorpe United changed their claret and blue strip in 1960, a gypsy curse foretold many lean years without success. In 1982 they reverted to their former colours and were rewarded with promotion.

SCUNTHORPE UNITED 2002–03 LEAGUE RECORD

Match No.	Date	Venue	Opponents	Result		H/T Score	Lg. Pos.	Goalscorers	Attendance
1	Aug 10	H	Wrexham	D	1-1	1-0	—	Calvo-Garcia [14]	3879
2	13	A	Exeter C	D	1-1	0-0	—	Carruthers [81]	3722
3	17	A	Leyton Orient	L	0-2	0-1	21		4028
4	24	H	York C	W	2-1	2-1	14	Smith (og) [1], Carruthers [40]	3540
5	26	A	Rushden & D	L	0-2	0-1	18		3849
6	31	H	Bristol R	D	2-2	2-0	20	Dawson [16], Carruthers [25]	3178
7	Sept 7	A	Lincoln C	L	0-1	0-1	23		4204
8	14	H	Kidderminster H	D	1-1	0-1	21	Brough [70]	2676
9	17	H	Carlisle U	W	3-1	1-1	—	Torpey 2 [13, 75], Carruthers [72]	2342
10	21	A	Macclesfield T	W	3-2	2-0	14	Carruthers [30], Torpey 2 [45, 60]	1929
11	28	H	Shrewsbury T	D	1-1	0-1	14	Sparrow [53]	2988
12	Oct 5	A	Oxford U	W	1-0	0-0	13	Beagrie (pen) [58]	5658
13	12	H	Cambridge U	L	1-2	1-0	14	Sparrow [30]	3140
14	19	A	Rochdale	W	2-1	0-0	14	Carruthers 2 [50, 72]	3442
15	26	H	Torquay U	W	5-1	2-1	7	Carruthers [39], Torpey 3 [45, 82, 90], McCombe [73]	2911
16	29	A	Darlington	D	1-1	1-1	—	Carruthers [5]	3059
17	Nov 2	A	Hull C	L	0-2	0-0	10		11,885
18	9	H	Boston U	W	2-0	1-0	8	Beagrie (pen) [16], Torpey [66]	3730
19	23	H	Swansea C	W	2-0	2-0	7	Carruthers (pen) [23], Sparrow [45]	2886
20	30	A	Bournemouth	L	1-2	1-0	9	Sparrow [25]	6527
21	Dec 14	H	Bury	L	0-1	0-0	10		3011
22	21	A	Hartlepool U	D	2-2	1-1	11	Brough [25], Carruthers [49]	4089
23	26	H	Rushden & D	D	0-0	0-0	12		4096
24	29	A	Southend U	W	2-1	0-1	11	Carruthers [75], Torpey [81]	4248
25	Jan 1	A	York C	W	3-1	2-1	7	Torpey (pen) [14], Carruthers [37], Graves [50]	4554
26	11	H	Leyton Orient	W	2-1	1-1	3	Sparrow [27], Kilford [67]	3242
27	18	A	Bristol R	L	1-2	0-0	5	Carruthers [64]	6617
28	21	H	Exeter C	D	1-1	1-0	—	Carruthers [28]	2461
29	25	H	Southend U	W	4-1	3-1	3	Carruthers [11], Kilford [36], Calvo-Garcia [43], Hayes [70]	3096
30	Feb 1	A	Wrexham	L	1-2	0-1	4	Sparrow [83]	3129
31	8	A	Boston U	L	0-1	0-0	9		3358
32	15	H	Hull C	W	3-1	0-0	8	Hayes [50], Sparrow 2 [76, 82]	6284
33	22	H	Lincoln C	D	0-0	0-0	8		5141
34	Mar 1	A	Kidderminster H	W	3-1	2-0	5	Beagrie 2 (1 pen) [32, 73 (p)], Carruthers [33]	2834
35	8	H	Macclesfield T	D	1-1	0-0	7	Hayes [53]	3398
36	11	A	Carlisle U	W	2-1	1-1	—	Beagrie [18], Dawson [67]	3124
37	15	A	Torquay U	D	1-1	1-0	3	Sparrow [8]	2486
38	18	H	Rochdale	W	3-1	2-1	—	Hayes 2 [10, 66], Kilford [31]	3616
39	22	H	Darlington	L	0-1	0-0	4		3904
40	29	A	Cambridge U	D	1-1	0-1	6	Hayes [67]	3951
41	Apr 5	H	Bournemouth	L	0-2	0-0	10		4488
42	12	A	Swansea C	D	1-1	0-1	9	Carruthers [75]	6014
43	19	H	Hartlepool U	W	4-0	1-0	7	Hayes [32], Carruthers 2 [72, 82], Calvo-Garcia [86]	5280
44	21	A	Bury	D	0-0	0-0	6		3898
45	26	H	Oxford U	W	2-0	1-0	6	Hayes [30], Dalglish [90]	5629
46	May 3	A	Shrewsbury T	W	2-1	0-1	5	Dalglish 2 [50, 81]	4127

Final League Position: 5

GOALSCORERS

League (68): Carruthers 20 (1 pen), Torpey 10 (1 pen), Sparrow 9, Hayes 8, Beagrie 5 (3 pens), Calvo-Garcia 3, Dalglish 3, Kilford 3, Brough 2, Dawson 2, Graves 1, McCombe 1, own goal 1.
Worthington Cup (1): Torpey 1.
FA Cup (4): Torpey 3 (1 pen), Carruthers 1.
LDV Vans Trophy (2): Dawson 1, Torpey 1.
Play-offs (3): Calvo-Garcia 2, Stanton 1.

Evans T 46	Stanton N 42	Dawson A 43	Sparrow M 42	Jackson M 32 + 1	Cotterill J 7 + 2	Calvo-Garcia A 28 + 7	Graves W 35 + 6	Carruthers M 42 + 3	Wheatcroft P 2 + 2	Beagrie P 29 + 5	Brough S 10 + 13	McCombe J 23 + 8	Torpey S 26 + 2	Barwick T 1 + 4	Ryan L — + 2	Wright S 2	Ridley L 9 + 2	Parton A — + 8	Balmer S 6	Featherstone L 10 + 10	Kilford I 27 + 1	Byrne C 13	Hayes P 15 + 3	O'Connor A — + 3	Taylor R 4 + 4	Dalglish P 5 + 3	Strong G 7	*Match No.*
1	2	3	4	5	6	7	8	9	10^{1}	11^{2}	12	13																1
1	2	3	4	5	6	7	8	9	10^{1}	11	12																	2
1	2	3	4	5	6	7^{3}	8^{2}	9^{1}	12	11	13		10	14														3
1	2	3	4^{1}	5	6	7	8	9		11^{2}	12		10	13														4
1	2	3	4^{1}	5	6^{3}	7	8^{2}	9	12	11	13	14	10															5
1	2■	3	4	5	6	7^{3}	8	9^{1}		11^{2}	13	12	10	14														6
1	2	3	4	5	6^{1}	7	8	9^{2}		11^{3}	13	12	10		14													7
1		3^{1}		5		7	8	9		11^{2}	4	6	10			2	12	13										8
1		3	4	5		7	8	9^{1}			11	6	10		12	2												9
1	2	3	4	5		7^{1}	8^{2}	9			11	6	10	12				13										10
1	2	3	4	5		7	8	9		12	11^{1}	6	10															11
1	2	3	4	5		7	8	9		11		6	10															12
1	2	3	4			7	8	9^{1}		11		6	10						5	12								13
1	2	3	4■			7	8	9^{1}		11^{2}	12	6	10						5	13								14
1	2	3	4			7	8^{1}	9^{2}		11	12	6	10						5	13								15
1	2	3	4			7	8	9		11^{1}		6	10						5■	12								16
1	2	3				7	8	9		11^{1}	12	6	10	4^{2}					5	13								17
1	2	3				7	8^{1}	9		11		6	10						5	4	12							18
1	2	3	4				8	9				6	10							11	7	5						19
1	2	3	4			12		9^{2}			11^{1}	6	10					13		7	8	5						20
1	2		4				11^{2}	9			7^{1}	6	10				3				8	5	12	13				21
1	2	3	4	12			8	9^{3}			11^{2}	6^{1}	10							13	7	5		14				22
1	2	3	4	5		11	12	9^{1}			7^{2}		10					13		8		6						23
1	2	3	4	5			8	9^{2}			12		10					13		11	7^{1}	6						24
1	2	3^{3}	4	5		12	8	9^{2}			14	13	10							11■	7^{1}	6						25
1	2	3	4	5		12	8	9					10					13		11^{2}	7^{1}	6						26
1	2	11	4^{1}	5		12	8■	9^{2}					10				3				7	6		13				27
1	2	3	4	5			8	9		12		13	10							11^{1}	7	6^{2}						28
1	2	3		5		11	8^{2}	9		12	4	6								10^{1}	7		13					29
1		3■	4	5		11		9		12	7^{1}	6								10^{2}	8	2	13					30
1	2	3	4	5		7		9		11		12									8	6■	10^{1}					31
1	2		4	5		7	12	9^{2}		11^{3}	14	13					3				8^{1}	6	10					32
1	2	3	4	5		7	12	9		11		6									8^{1}		10					33
1	2	3	4	5	13		7^{1}	9		11							6	12			8		10^{2}					34
1	2	3	4	5		12	8^{1}	9^{2}		11							6				7		10		13			35
1	2	3	4	5		12	8	9^{3}		11							6^{1}			13	7		10^{2}		14			36
1	2	3	4	5		12	8	9^{2}		11							6			13	7^{1}		10^{3}		14			37
1	2	3	4	5			8	12		11^{2}		6								13	7		10		9^{1}			38
1	5	3	4		12		8^{3}	9		11		6					2^{1}				7		10^{2}		13	14		39
1	2	3	4				12			11		6									7^{1}		10		9	8	5	40
1	2	3	4				12	13		11■		6									8		10		9^{2}	7^{1}	5	41
1	2	3	4				8	12		11		6									7^{2}		10		9^{1}	13	5	42
1	2^{1}	3^{2}	4	5		7	12	9									13				8		10			11	6	43
1			4	5		7	2	9^{2}		12							3	13			8		10			11^{1}	6	44
1	2	3	4	5		7		9^{1}		11^{2}			12								8		10			13	6	45
1	2	3	4^{1}	5		7		9		11^{2}			12							13	8					10	6	46

Worthington Cup

First Round	Preston NE	(a)	1-2

LDV Vans Trophy

First Round	Blackpool	(h)	2-3

FA Cup

First Round	Northwich Vic	(a)	3-0
Second Round	Carlisle U	(h)	0-0
		(a)	1-0
Third Round	Leeds U	(h)	0-2

SHEFFIELD UNITED Division 1

FOUNDATION

In March 1889, Yorkshire County Cricket Club formed Sheffield United six days after an FA Cup semi-final between Preston North End and West Bromwich Albion had finally convinced Charles Stokes, a member of the cricket club, that the formation of a professional football club would prove successful at Bramall Lane. The United's first secretary, Mr J. B. Wostinholm was also secretary of the cricket club.

Bramall Lane Ground, Sheffield S2 4SU.

Telephone: 0870 7871960. ***Fax:*** 0870 7873345.
Website: www.sufc.co.uk ***Email:*** info@sufc.co.uk
ISDN: (0114) 221 3148. ***Box Office:*** 0870 7873345.
Promotions: 0870 4428803. ***Superstore:*** 0870 4428705.
Commercial: 0870 4428812. ***Catering:*** 0870 4573627.
Academy: 0870 4447091. ***Hall of Fame:*** 0870 4428805.
Publicity: 0870 4428255.
Football in the Community: 0870 4428807.

Ground Capacity: 30,945.

Record Attendance: 68,287 v Leeds U, FA Cup 5th rd, 15 February 1936.

Record Receipts: £397,478 v Nottingham F, Play-off 2nd leg, 15 May 2003.

Pitch Measurements: 112yd × 72yd.

Chairman: D. Dooley (football club), K. McCabe (plc).

Directors: K. McCabe, A. Laver, M. Dudley, A. Bamford, S. Slinn, C. Steer, S. Bean.

Football Executive: Terry Robinson.

Manager: Neil Warnock.

Assistant Manager: David Kelly.

Physios: Dennis Pettitt, Nigel Cox.

Estates Manager: Steve Hicks.

General Manager, Commercial: Andy Daykin.

Secretary: D. Fletcher.

Community Programme Organiser: Tony Currie, Tel: 0870 4428807.

Colours: Red and white striped shirts with white trim, white shorts, white stockings.

Change Colours: All navy with red trim.

Year Formed: 1889.

Turned Professional: 1889.

Ltd Co.: 1899.

Club Nickname: 'The Blades'.

First Football League Game: 3 September 1892, Division 2, v Lincoln C (h) W 4–2 – Lilley; Witham, Cain; Howell, Hendry, Needham (1); Wallace, Dobson, Hammond (3), Davies, Drummond.

HONOURS

Football League: Division 1 – Champions 1897–98; Runners-up 1896–97, 1899–1900; Division 2 – Champions 1952–53; Runners-up 1892–93, 1938–39, 1960–61, 1970–71, 1989–90; Division 4 – Champions 1981–82.

FA Cup: Winners 1899, 1902, 1915, 1925; Runners-up 1901, 1936.

Football League Cup: semi-final 2003.

SKY SPORTS FACT FILE

No other Football League team has been able to equal Sheffield United in being the longest remaining unbeaten team from the start of the season four years in a row from 1896–97 to 1899–1900 inclusive.

Record League Victory: 10–0 v Burslem Port Vale (a), Division 2, 10 December 1892 – Howlett; Witham, Lilley; Howell, Hendry, Needham; Drummond (1), Wallace (1), Hammond (4), Davies (2), Watson (2).

Record Cup Victory: 6–1 v Lincoln C, League Cup, 22 August 2000 – Tracey; Uhlenbeek, Weber, Woodhouse (Ford), Murphy, Sandford, Devlin (pen), Ribeiro (Santos), Bent (3), Kelly (1) (Thompson), Jagielka, og (1). 6–1 v Loughborough, FA Cup 4th qualifying rd, 6 December 1890; 6–1 v Scarborough (a), FA Cup 1st qualifying rd, 5 October 1889.

Record Defeat: 0–13 v Bolton W, FA Cup 2nd rd, 1 February 1890.

Most League Points (2 for a win): 60, Division 2, 1952–53.

Most League Points (3 for a win): 96, Division 4, 1981–82.

Most League Goals: 102, Division 1, 1925–26.

Highest League Scorer in Season: Jimmy Dunne, 41, Division 1, 1930–31.

Most League Goals in Total Aggregate: Harry Johnson, 205, 1919–30.

Most League Goals in One Match: 5, Harry Hammond v Bootle, Division 2, 26 November 1892; 5, Harry Johnson v West Ham U, Division 1, 26 December 1927.

Most Capped Player: Billy Gillespie, 25, Northern Ireland.

Most League Appearances: Joe Shaw, 629, 1948–66.

Youngest League Player: Steve Hawes, 17 years 47 days v WBA, 2 September 1995.

Record Transfer Fee Received: £2,700,000 from Leeds U for Brian Deane, July 1993.

Record Transfer Fee Paid: £1,200,000 to West Ham U for Don Hutchison, January 1996.

Football League Record: 1892 Elected to Division 2; 1893–1934 Division 1; 1934–39 Division 2; 1946–49 Division 1; 1949–53 Division 2; 1953–56 Division 1; 1956–61 Division 2; 1961–68 Division 1; 1968–71 Division 2; 1971–76 Division 1; 1976–79 Division 2; 1979–81 Division 3; 1981–82 Division 4; 1982–84 Division 3; 1984–88 Division 2; 1988–89 Division 3; 1989–90 Division 2; 1990–92 Division 1; 1992–94 FA Premier League; 1994– Division 1.

MANAGERS

J. B. Wostinholm 1889–99 *(Secretary-Manager)*
John Nicholson 1899–1932
Ted Davison 1932–52
Reg Freeman 1952–55
Joe Mercer 1955–58
Johnny Harris 1959–68 *(continued as General Manager to 1970)*
Arthur Rowley 1968–69
Johnny Harris *(General Manager resumed Team Manager duties)* 1969–73
Ken Furphy 1973–75
Jimmy Sirrel 1975–77
Harry Haslam 1978–81
Martin Peters 1981
Ian Porterfield 1981–86
Billy McEwan 1986–88
Dave Bassett 1988–95
Howard Kendall 1995–97
Nigel Spackman 1997–98
Steve Bruce 1998–99
Adrian Heath 1999
Neil Warnock December 1999–

LATEST SEQUENCES

Longest Sequence of League Wins: 8, 14.9.1960 – 22.10.1960.

Longest Sequence of League Defeats: 7, 19.8.1975 – 20.9.1975.

Longest Sequence of League Draws: 6, 6.5.2001 – 8.9.2001.

Longest Sequence of Unbeaten League Matches: 22, 2.9.1899 – 13.1.1900.

Longest Sequence Without a League Win: 19, 27.9.1975 – 7.2.1976.

Successive Scoring Runs: 34 from 30.3.1956.

Successive Non-scoring Runs: 6 from 4.12.1993.

TEN YEAR LEAGUE RECORD

		P	W	D	L	F	A	Pts	Pos
1993-94	PR Lge	42	8	18	16	42	60	42	20
1994-95	Div 1	46	17	17	12	74	55	68	8
1995-96	Div 1	46	16	14	16	57	54	62	9
1996-97	Div 1	46	20	13	13	75	52	73	5
1997-98	Div 1	46	19	17	10	69	54	74	6
1998-99	Div 1	46	18	13	15	71	66	67	8
1999-2000	Div 1	46	13	15	18	59	71	54	16
2000-01	Div 1	46	19	11	16	52	49	68	10
2001-02	Div 1	46	15	15	16	53	54	60	13
2002-03	Div 1	46	23	11	12	72	52	80	3

DID YOU KNOW ?

In 1981–82 Sheffield United's championship season in Division Four included one match of four goals scored in a spell of six minutes in the first half on 3 April 1982 at home to Torquay United during a 4-1 win.

SHEFFIELD UNITED 2002–03 LEAGUE RECORD

Match No.	*Date*	*Venue*	*Opponents*	*Result*		*H/T Score*	*Lg. Pos.*	*Goalscorers*	*Atten-dance*
1	Aug 10	A	Coventry C	L	1-2	1-2	—	Asaba ^{13}	18,839
2	13	H	Portsmouth	D	1-1	1-1	—	Ndlovu ^{12}	16,093
3	17	H	Walsall	D	1-1	1-1	17	McGovern ^{40}	14,011
4	24	A	Burnley	W	1-0	1-0	11	Onuora ^{35}	12,868
5	27	H	Millwall	W	3-1	0-0	—	Asaba ^{77}, Tonge ^{82}, Ndlovu ^{90}	13,024
6	Sept 1	A	Sheffield W	L	0-2	0-0	13		27,075
7	7	A	Norwich C	W	3-2	3-0	6	Brown M ^{1}, Tonge ^{6}, Asaba (pen) ^{31}	20,075
8	14	H	Rotherham U	W	1-0	0-0	4	Ndlovu ^{74}	19,948
9	17	H	Grimsby T	W	2-1	0-1	—	Allison ^{82}, Tonge ^{89}	14,208
10	21	A	Gillingham	D	1-1	0-1	5	Allison ^{60}	7497
11	28	H	Watford	L	1-2	1-2	6	Allison ^{10}	16,301
12	Oct 5	A	Wolverhampton W	W	3-1	1-1	5	Tonge 2 $^{45, 50}$, Allison ^{48}	24,625
13	19	A	Brighton & HA	W	4-2	0-2	5	Brown M ^{70}, Asaba 3 (2 pens) $^{77, 86 (p), 88 (p)}$	6810
14	23	H	Stoke C	W	2-1	0-0	—	Handyside (og) ^{62}, Brown M (pen) ^{70}	15,163
15	26	H	Wimbledon	D	1-1	0-1	4	Asaba ^{90}	17,372
16	30	A	Derby Co	L	1-2	1-1	—	Murphy ^{23}	23,525
17	Nov 2	A	Nottingham F	L	0-3	0-0	6		22,579
18	9	H	Ipswich T	D	0-0	0-0	7		15,884
19	23	A	Bradford C	W	5-0	2-0	6	Kabba ^{14}, Windass ^{40}, Murphy ^{59}, Brown M (pen) ^{80}, Asaba ^{88}	13,364
20	30	H	Crystal Palace	W	2-1	1-0	6	Windass ^{45}, Allison ^{89}	16,686
21	Dec 7	A	Leicester C	D	0-0	0-0	7		26,718
22	14	A	Reading	W	2-0	0-0	5	Harley ^{59}, Windass ^{76}	18,534
23	21	H	Preston NE	W	1-0	0-0	5	Alexander (og) ^{58}	16,342
24	26	A	Walsall	W	1-0	0-0	3	Brown M ^{72}	10,459
25	28	H	Coventry C	D	0-0	0-0	3		20,465
26	Jan 13	A	Portsmouth	W	2-1	1-0	—	Ndlovu ^{24}, Brown M ^{87}	18,872
27	17	H	Sheffield W	W	3-1	0-0	—	Kabba ^{62}, Brown M ^{65}, Allison ^{78}	29,179
28	Feb 1	A	Millwall	L	0-1	0-0	3		9102
29	8	A	Ipswich T	L	2-3	1-0	3	Ndlovu ^{45}, Windass ^{50}	26,151
30	18	H	Reading	L	1-3	1-1	—	Brown M ^{3}	16,884
31	22	H	Norwich C	L	0-1	0-0	5		19,020
32	28	A	Rotherham U	W	2-1	1-0	—	Brown M (pen) ^{17}, Kabba ^{62}	10,797
33	Mar 4	A	Grimsby T	W	4-1	3-1	—	Windass ^{12}, Kabba ^{25}, Kozluk ^{32}, Brown M ^{86}	6897
34	12	H	Burnley	W	4-2	2-0	—	Brown M 2 $^{17, 36}$, Ndlovu 2 $^{66, 72}$	17,359
35	15	A	Stoke C	D	0-0	0-0	4		14,449
36	18	H	Brighton & HA	W	2-1	2-1	—	Windass ^{5}, Brown M ^{34}	19,357
37	22	H	Derby Co	W	2-0	1-0	3	Tonge ^{18}, Kabba ^{55}	18,401
38	25	H	Gillingham	D	2-2	1-0	—	Kabba ^{44}, Peschisolido ^{81}	15,799
39	Apr 5	A	Crystal Palace	D	2-2	1-2	3	Popovic (og) ^{21}, Kabba ^{87}	15,377
40	7	A	Wimbledon	L	0-1	0-1	—		1325
41	15	H	Nottingham F	W	1-0	0-0	—	Asaba ^{62}	23,317
42	19	A	Preston NE	L	0-2	0-0	3		14,793
43	21	H	Leicester C	W	2-1	1-1	3	Asaba 2 $^{15, 90}$	21,277
44	26	H	Wolverhampton W	D	3-3	1-2	3	Peschisolido 2 $^{2, 90}$, Brown M (pen) ^{56}	22,211
45	29	H	Bradford C	W	3-0	0-0	—	Brown M 2 (1 pen) $^{60, 79 (p)}$, Ndlovu ^{64}	18,297
46	May 4	A	Watford	L	0-2	0-0	3		14,320

Final League Position: 3

GOALSCORERS

League (72): Brown M 16 (5 pens), Asaba 11 (3 pens), Ndlovu 8, Kabba 7, Allison 6, Tonge 6, Windass 6, Peschisolido 3, Murphy 2, Harley 1, Kozluk 1, McGovern 1, Onuora 1, own goals 3.
Worthington Cup (14): Brown 2, Peschisolido 2, Tonge 2, Allison 1, Asaba 1, Boulding 1, Jagielka 1, McGovern 1, Montgomery 1, Murphy 1, Ndlovu 1.
FA Cup (11): Kabba 3, Brown 2, Jagielka 1, McGovern 1, Mooney 1, Murphy 1, Ndlovu 1, Peschisolido 1.
Play-offs (5): Brown 2 (1 pen), Kabba 1, Peschisolido 1, own goal 1.

Kenny P 45	Yates S 11+1	Ullathorne R 12	Tonge M 40+4	Murphy S 42+1	Page R 33+1	Jagielka P 41+1	Brown M 39+1	Asaba C 16+12	Onuora I 7	Ndlovu P 30+9	Kozluk R 29+3	Peschisolido P 4+19	Allison W 15+19	Doane B 2+3	McCall S 32+2	McGovern J 11+4	Javary J 2+4	Ten Heuvel L —+5	Montgomery N 15+8	Smith G 1+2	Cryan C —+2	Boulding M 3+3	Harley J 8+1	Windass D 20	Kabba S 19+6	Quinn W 6	Mooney T 2+1	Edghill R —+1	Cas M 3+3	Morrison O 3+5	Curtis J 9+3	Rankine M 5+1	Kelly G 1	Match No.
1	2	3	4^1	5	6^2	7	8	9	10^3	11	13	12	14																					1
1	6	3^2	4^3	5		7	8	9	10	11^1	2			13	14	12																		2
1	6		4	5		8	11^1	9		12	3		10^2	2		7^3	14	13																3
1	6	3^1	11^3	5		8		9	10^2		2		13	12	4	7			14															4
1	6	3	11	5		8		9^2	10^1	12	2				4	7				13														5
1	6^3	3	11	5		8^1	12	9	10	13	2			14	4	7^2																		6
1		3	11	5		6	8^1	12	9■		2				4	7^3	13		10^2		14													7
1		3	11	5		6	8	9	10^2	12	2	13^3			4	7^1			14															8
1		3	11	5		6	8	9^1		12	2	10^3	13		4	7^2		14																9
1		3	11	5		6	8			9	2	12	10		4				7^1															10
1		3	11	5	12	6■	8			9	2^2		10		4^3	7^1			13			14												11
1		3	11^2	5	6	2	7			8			10		4				12	13		9^1												12
1	2	3^2	11	5	6		7	12		8	13		10		4^3	14						9^1												13
1	3		11^2	5	6	4	8	9^1		12	2		10		13	7^3						14												14
1	3		11	5	6	4	8	12		9^3	2					7^2		13		10^1		14												15
1	3		11	5	6	7	8	9		13^3	2				4^1	12		14				10^2												16
1	12		11	5	6^1	2	8	9				13	10		4^3	7^2			3				14											17
1			11	5	6	2	8	12		7		9^1	10^2		4			13					3											18
1			11^3	5	6	2	8	12		7			13		4	14							3	9^2	10^1									19
1			11	5	6	2	8	12		7^1		13	14		4								3	9^3	10^2									20
1			11	5	6	2	8	12		7^3			13		4				14				3	9^2	10^1									21
1			11	5	6	2		12		7			13		4				8				3	9^2	10^1									22
1			11	5	6	2	8	12		7^3		13	10				14		4^1				3		9^2									23
1			14	5	6	2	8	9^2		7^1	12		10		4				11				3■		13^3									24
1			11	5	6	2	8			7		12	10		4								3		9^1									25
1			9	5	6	2	8			7			10		4				11							3								26
1			11	5	6	2	8			7		12	13		4^3				14					9^2	10^1	3								27
1			11	5		6	8			7	2^1	12	13		4									9^2	14	3	10^3							28
1			11	5	6	2	8			7			12		4									9^1	10^2	3^3	13	14						29
1			11	5	6	2	8					12	13		4		7^3							9^2	10^1	3			14					30
1	5^2		11^1		6		8			7■	2		10		4^3				12		13					3■	9			14				31
1				5	6	2	8			7	3	12	13		4				11					9^2	10^1									32
1				5	6	2	8			7^2	3^3	12			4				11					9	10^1					13	14			33
1			11	5	6	2	8			12	3		13		4^1				7^3					9^2	10						14			34
1			11	5	6	2	8			7^3	3	12	13											9^2	10^1					14	4			35
1			11	5	6	2	8			7^2	3	12			4^3									9	10^1					13	14			36
1			7	5	6	4	8				3	12	13				14							9^2	10^3					11^1	2			37
1			11	5	6	4	8			7^1	3	12	13											9^2	10				14		2^3			38
1			11	5	6	2^2		12		7	3		10^1		4				8^3						9				13			14		39
1			12	5	6			13		14		10		3^1			4^3		7					9^2					2	11		8		40
1			11	12	6	5	4	9^2		7^3	3								14					10^1	13						2	8		41
1			11	6		5	4	12			3	13	10^1						7						9^2				8^3	14	2			42
1			11	5		6	4	9		7	3^1		12											10^2	13						2	8		43
1			12	5^2	6	13	7				3	10	14						4^3						9					11^1	2	8		44
1			11		6	5	8	9		7^3	3	13	12		4^1									10^2	14						2			45
			12		6			10		7	3	13			4^1				11					9^2	14				5		2	8^3	1	46

Worthington Cup

First Round	York C	(h)	1-0
Second Round	Wycombe W	(h)	4-1
Third Round	Leeds U	(h)	2-1
Fourth Round	Sunderland	(h)	2-0
Fifth Round	Crystal Palace	(h)	3-1
Semi-final	Liverpool	(h)	2-1
		(a)	0-2

FA Cup

Third Round	Cheltenham T	(h)	4-0
Fourth Round	Ipswich T	(h)	4-3
Fifth Round	Walsall	(h)	2-0
Sixth Round	Leeds U	(h)	1-0
Semi-final (at Old Trafford)	Arsenal		0-1

SHEFFIELD WEDNESDAY Division 2

FOUNDATION

Sheffield being one of the principal centres of early Association Football, this club was formed as long ago as 1867 by the Sheffield Wednesday Cricket Club (formed 1825) and their colours from the start were blue and white. The inaugural meeting was held at the Adelphi Hotel and the original committee included Charles Stokes who was subsequently a founder member of Sheffield United.

Hillsborough, Sheffield S6 1SW.

Telephone: (0114) 221 2121. ***Fax:*** (0114) 221 2122.
ClubCall: 09068 121 186. ***Website:*** www.swfc.co.uk
Email: enquiries@swfc.co.uk
Ticket Office: (0114) 221 2400.

Ground Capacity: 39,859.

Record Attendance: 72,841 v Manchester C, FA Cup 5th rd, 17 February 1934.

Record Receipts: £533,918 Sunderland v Norwich C, FA Cup semi-final, 5 April 1992.

Pitch Measurements: 115yd × 74yd.

President: K. T. Addy.

Chairman: G. K. Hulley. ***Vice-chairman:*** K. T. Addy.

Directors: G. K. Hulley, R. M. Grierson FCA, K. T. Addy, D. E. D. Allen, M. G. Wright.

Manager: Chris Turner.
Assistant Manager: Colin West. ***Physio:*** John Dickens.

Chief Executive: Alan D. Sykes. ***Commercial Director:*** Kaven Walker.
Operations Manager: Alan Roberts.

Colours: Blue and white striped shirts, black shorts, blue stockings.

Change Colours: Ecru shirts, navy shorts, navy stockings.

Year Formed: 1867 (fifth oldest League club).

Turned Professional: 1887.

Ltd Co.: 1899.

Former Names: The Wednesday until 1929.

Club Nickname: 'The Owls'.

Previous Grounds: 1867, Highfield; 1869, Myrtle Road; 1877, Sheaf House; 1887, Olive Grove; 1899, Owlerton (since 1912 known as Hillsborough). Some games were played at Endcliffe in the 1880s. Until 1895 Bramall Lane was used for some games.

First Football League Game: 3 September 1892, Division 1, v Notts Co (a) W 1–0 – Allan; Tom Brandon (1), Mumford; Hall, Betts, Harry Brandon; Spiksley, Brady, Davis, R. N. Brown, Dunlop.

Record League Victory: 9–1 v Birmingham, Division 1, 13 December 1930 – Brown; Walker, Blenkinsop; Strange, Leach, Wilson; Hooper (3), Seed (2), Ball (2), Burgess (1), Rimmer (1).

HONOURS

Football League: Division 1 – Champions 1902–03, 1903–04, 1928–29, 1929–30; Runners-up 1960–61; Division 2 – Champions 1899–1900, 1925–26, 1951–52, 1955–56, 1958–59; Runners-up 1949–50, 1983–84.

FA Cup: Winners 1896, 1907, 1935; Runners-up 1890, 1966, 1993.

Football League Cup: Winners 1991; Runners-up 1993.

European Competitions: *European Fairs Cup:* 1961–62, 1963–64. *UEFA Cup:* 1992–93. *Intertoto Cup:* 1995.

SKY SPORTS FACT FILE

Derek Dooley scored five goals in the 6-0 win by Sheffield Wednesday over Notts County on 3 November 1951. All his goals came in the second half after 50, 62, 68, 78 and 82 minutes of the Second Division match.

Record Cup Victory: 12–0 v Halliwell, FA Cup 1st rd, 17 January 1891 – Smith; Thompson, Brayshaw; Harry Brandon (1), Betts, Cawley (2); Winterbottom, Mumford (2), Bob Brandon (1), Woolhouse (5), Ingram (1).

Record Defeat: 0–10 v Aston Villa, Division 1, 5 October 1912.

Most League Points (2 for a win): 62, Division 2, 1958–59.

Most League Points (3 for a win): 88, Division 2, 1983–84.

Most League Goals: 106, Division 2, 1958–59.

Highest League Scorer in Season: Derek Dooley, 46, Division 2, 1951–52.

Most League Goals in Total Aggregate: Andy Wilson, 199, 1900–20.

Most League Goals in One Match: 6, Doug Hunt v Norwich C, Division 2, 19 November 1938.

Most Capped Player: Nigel Worthington, 50 (66), Northern Ireland.

Most League Appearances: Andrew Wilson, 501, 1900–20.

Youngest League Player: Peter Fox, 15 years 269 days v Orient, 31 March 1973.

Record Transfer Fee Received: £2,750,000 from Blackburn R for Paul Warhurst, September 1993.

Record Transfer Fee Paid: £4,500,000 to Celtic for Paolo Di Canio, August 1997.

Football League Record: 1892 Elected to Division 1; 1899–1900 Division 2; 1900–20 Division 1; 1920–26 Division 2; 1926–37 Division 1; 1937–50 Division 2; 1950–51 Division 1; 1951–52 Division 2; 1952–55 Division 1; 1955–56 Division 2; 1956–58 Division 1; 1958–59 Division 2; 1959–70 Division 1; 1970–75 Division 2; 1975–80 Division 3; 1980–84 Division 2; 1984–90 Division 1; 1990–91 Division 2; 1991–92 Division 1; 1992–2000 FA Premier League; 2000–03 Division 1; 2003– Division 2.

MANAGERS

Arthur Dickinson 1891–1920
(Secretary-Manager)
Robert Brown 1920–33
Billy Walker 1933–37
Jimmy McMullan 1937–42
Eric Taylor 1942–58
(continued as General Manager to 1974)
Harry Catterick 1958–61
Vic Buckingham 1961–64
Alan Brown 1964–68
Jack Marshall 1968–69
Danny Williams 1969–71
Derek Dooley 1971–73
Steve Burtenshaw 1974–75
Len Ashurst 1975–77
Jackie Charlton 1977–83
Howard Wilkinson 1983–88
Peter Eustace 1988–89
Ron Atkinson 1989–91
Trevor Francis 1991–95
David Pleat 1995–97
Ron Atkinson 1997–98
Danny Wilson 1998–2000
Peter Shreeves (Acting) 2000
Paul Jewell 2000–01
Peter Shreeves 2001
Terry Yorath 2001–02
Chris Turner November 2002–

LATEST SEQUENCES

Longest Sequence of League Wins: 9, 23.4.1904 – 15.10.1904.

Longest Sequence of League Defeats: 8, 9.9.2000 – 17.10.2000.

Longest Sequence of League Draws: 5, 24.10.1992 – 28.11.1992.

Longest Sequence of Unbeaten League Matches: 19, 10.12.1960 – 8.4.1961.

Longest Sequence Without a League Win: 20, 11.1.1975 – 30.8.1975.

Successive Scoring Runs: 40 from 14.11.1959.

Successive Non-scoring Runs: 8 from 8.3.1975.

TEN YEAR LEAGUE RECORD

		P	W	D	L	F	A	Pts	Pos
1993-94	PR Lge	42	16	16	10	76	54	64	7
1994-95	PR Lge	42	13	12	17	49	57	51	13
1995-96	PR Lge	38	10	10	18	48	61	40	15
1996-97	PR Lge	38	14	15	9	50	51	57	7
1997-98	PR Lge	38	12	8	18	52	67	44	16
1998-99	PR Lge	38	13	7	18	41	42	46	12
1999-2000	PR Lge	38	8	7	23	38	70	31	19
2000-01	Div 1	46	15	8	23	52	71	53	17
2001-02	Div 1	46	12	14	20	49	71	50	20
2002-03	Div 1	46	10	16	20	56	73	46	22

DID YOU KNOW

In 1935 Ellis Rimmer, the Sheffield Wednesday left-winger, became the second player to score in every round of the FA Cup when he had eight of the club's goals on their way to winning the trophy at Wembley.

SHEFFIELD WEDNESDAY 2002–03 LEAGUE RECORD

Match No.	Date	Venue	Opponents	Result		H/T Score	Lg. Pos.	Goalscorers	Attendance
1	Aug 10	H	Stoke C	D	0-0	0-0	—		26,746
2	13	A	Reading	L	1-2	1-0	—	Sibon [18]	13,638
3	17	A	Nottingham F	L	0-4	0-1	22		21,129
4	24	H	Rotherham U	L	1-2	1-1	23	Armstrong [8]	22,873
5	27	A	Wolverhampton W	D	2-2	1-0	—	Kuqi 2 [9, 63]	27,096
6	Sept 1	H	Sheffield U	W	2-0	0-0	20	Owusu [73], Kuqi [82]	27,075
7	14	A	Preston NE	D	2-2	1-1	21	Kuqi [35], McLaren [76]	13,632
8	18	A	Coventry C	D	1-1	0-0	—	Knight [58]	14,178
9	21	H	Leicester C	D	0-0	0-0	22		22,219
10	25	H	Crystal Palace	D	0-0	0-0	—		16,112
11	28	A	Walsall	L	0-1	0-1	22		6792
12	Oct 5	H	Burnley	L	1-3	0-1	22	Donnelly [67]	17,004
13	12	A	Ipswich T	L	1-2	0-2	22	Donnelly [58]	23,410
14	19	H	Bradford C	W	2-1	1-1	21	Sibon 2 (1 pen) [34, 87 (p)]	17,191
15	26	A	Watford	L	0-1	0-1	22		15,058
16	30	H	Millwall	L	0-1	0-1	—		16,791
17	Nov 2	H	Derby Co	L	1-3	0-2	23	Hamshaw [61]	19,747
18	9	A	Norwich C	L	0-3	0-2	23		20,667
19	16	A	Gillingham	D	1-1	0-1	23	Knight [90]	8028
20	23	H	Portsmouth	L	1-3	1-1	23	Knight [27]	16,602
21	30	A	Wimbledon	L	0-3	0-1	23		2131
22	Dec 7	H	Brighton & HA	D	1-1	0-1	23	Kuqi [90]	18,008
23	14	H	Gillingham	L	0-2	0-1	24		17,715
24	21	A	Grimsby T	L	0-2	0-0	24		8224
25	26	H	Nottingham F	W	2-0	1-0	24	Sibon [45], Johnston [55]	26,362
26	28	A	Stoke C	L	2-3	1-1	24	Sibon [23], Proudlock [72]	16,042
27	Jan 1	A	Rotherham U	W	2-0	0-0	23	Kuqi [68], Proudlock [90]	11,480
28	11	H	Reading	W	3-2	0-2	23	Quinn [52], Sibon [69], Johnston [71]	17,715
29	17	A	Sheffield U	L	1-3	0-0	—	Quinn [47]	29,179
30	Feb 1	H	Wolverhampton W	L	0-4	0-2	23		21,381
31	8	H	Norwich C	D	2-2	0-2	23	Robinson [66], Quinn [76]	19,114
32	15	A	Derby Co	D	2-2	1-0	24	Barton (og) [16], Crane [83]	26,311
33	22	A	Crystal Palace	D	0-0	0-0	23		16,707
34	Mar 1	H	Preston NE	L	0-1	0-0	24		18,912
35	5	H	Coventry C	W	5-1	1-0	—	Reddy [8], Kuqi 2 [52, 69], McLaren [60], Bradbury [63]	19,536
36	8	A	Leicester C	D	1-1	1-0	23	McLaren [25]	27,463
37	15	H	Ipswich T	L	0-1	0-1	24		24,726
38	18	A	Bradford C	D	1-1	0-1	—	Crane [82]	14,452
39	22	A	Millwall	L	0-3	0-2	24		7338
40	29	H	Watford	D	2-2	0-1	24	Bradbury (pen) [66], Maddix [90]	17,086
41	Apr 5	H	Wimbledon	W	4-2	1-0	24	Reddy [40], Owusu 2 [48, 72], Bradbury [76]	17,649
42	12	A	Portsmouth	W	2-1	0-1	23	Westwood [76], Reddy [90]	19,524
43	19	H	Grimsby T	D	0-0	0-0	23		26,082
44	21	A	Brighton & HA	D	1-1	1-0	23	Holt [16]	6928
45	26	A	Burnley	W	7-2	3-1	23	McLaren [3], Westwood [5], Wood R [32], Evans R [47], Haslam [66], Gnohere (og) [73], Quinn [80]	17,435
46	May 4	H	Walsall	W	2-1	0-0	22	Owusu [66], Quinn [76]	20,864

Final League Position: 22

GOALSCORERS

League (56): Kuqi 8, Sibon 6 (1 pen), Quinn 5, McLaren 4, Owusu 4, Bradbury 3 (1 pen), Knight 3, Reddy 3, Crane 2, Donnelly 2, Johnston 2, Proudlock 2, Westwood 2, Armstrong 1, Evans R 1, Hamshaw 1, Haslam 1, Holt 1, Maddix 1, Robinson 1, Wood R 1, own goals 2.
Worthington Cup (2): Sibon 2.
FA Cup (1): Sibon 1.

Pressman K 38	Geary D 24 + 2	Beswetherick J 5 + 1	Soltvedt T 21	Bromby L 26 + 1	Burrows D 13	Armstrong C 17	Donnelly S 10 + 5	Sibon G 23 + 2	Kuqi S 34 + 6	Quinn A 33 + 4	Crane T 13 + 6	Haslam S 18 + 8	McLaren P 31 + 5	Knight L 14 + 10	Westwood A 22 + 1	Hendon I 9	Owusu L 12 + 20	Hamshaw M 4 + 11	Maddix D 22 + 1	Green R 4	Monk G 15	Johnston A 12	Proudlock A 3 + 2	Stringer C 1 + 2	Bradbury L 10 + 1	Morrison O — + 1	Di Piedi M 1 + 1	Robinson C 4	Powell D 8	Barry-Murphy B 17	Reddy M 13 + 2	Evans P 7	Smith D 14	Holt G 3 + 4	Evans R 3 + 1	Wood R 2 + 1	Shaw J — + 1	*Match No.*
1	2	3	4	5	6	7	8	9	10	11																												1
1	2	3	4^{1}	5	6	7	8^{2}	9	10	11■	12	13																										2
1	2	3^{1}	4	5	6	7	8^{2}	9■	10	11			12	13																								3
1	2	3^{1}		5	6	4		9	10	11			12	8	7																							4
1	2		7	5	6	3		9	10				11	8	4																							5
1			4^{1}	3	6	7	8^{3}		10	12			11	9	5	2^{2}	13	14																				6
1			4^{1}	5	3	7		9	10	12			8	11^{2}		2	13		6																			7
1	12			5	3	7		9^{2}	10	11			4	8^{3}		2^{1}	14	13	6																			8
1	3			2	6	7		9^{1}	10	11			4	8^{2}			13	12	5																			9
1	12			5	3	7^{3}		9^{2}	10	11			4^{1}	8		2	14	13	6																			10
1	2			5	3^{3}	7^{1}	12		10	11			4	13	14		9	8^{2}	6																			11
1	2			5		3	12	8	10	11			4	7			9^{1}		6																			12
1	3		4^{1}	5			10	9		11		8	12	7^{3}		2^{2}	13	14	6																			13
1	3		4	5			10	8	9	11^{2}		2	12	7^{1}			13		6■																			14
1	3^{1}		4	5			7	9	10	11^{2}		2	8^{3}	14			13	12	6																			15
1	3		4^{1}	5			7	8	10	11^{2}			12	9^{3}		2	14	13	6																			16
1	3		4	5		11	7^{1}	9^{2}	10			6	8			2	13	12																				17
1	3		4	5		11		8^{1}	10■			6	7	12		2	9																					18
1	3	12	4	5		7		8	10^{2}		11	6		13		2^{1}	9																					19
1	2	3^{2}		5		7	12	8		11	6	4		10			9^{1}	13																				20
1	3		7	5■				12	10^{1}	11	6	4		8^{2}			9	13		2																		21
1	2		4		3	7		12	13		6	8^{3}	11	10^{2}			9^{1}	14		5																		22
1			4		3^{1}			9^{2}	10		6	12	8					7		2	5	11	13															23
1	3		4					9	10^{2}		6	2	8	12				7^{1}			5	11	13															24
1^{G}	3		4					9^{2}		12	6	2	8					7^{1}			5	11	10	15	13													25
	3		4					9^{1}			6	2	8								5	11	10	1	7	12												26
1	3		4	12					9	13	6		8^{2}		5						2	11	10		7^{1}													27
1	3		4					9^{3}	10	8	6^{2}			12	2				13	7^{1}	5	11					14											28
1	3								10	7				12	2				6		5	11					9^{1}	4	8									29
1									10	8		12			5^{1}		13		6		3	11						4	7	2	9^{2}							30
1									10^{1}	8					2		12		6		5	11						4	7	3	9							31
									13	8	12				2		10^{2}		6		5	11						4	7	3	9^{1}	1						32
									13	7	12		8		2		10^{2}		6		5	11								3	9^{1}	1	4					33
									10^{2}	7	12		8^{3}		2		13				5	11			9^{1}				6	3	14	1	4					34
									10	11^{2}		12	8	13	2^{1}		14				5				9^{3}				4	3	7	1	6					35
									10^{1}	11	12		8		2						5				9				4	3	7	1	6					36
									10^{2}	11	13	12	8		2^{3}		14				5				9				4^{1}	3	7	1	6					37
							12			11	10	6^{1}	8		2				5						9					3	7	1	4					38
1							6^{2}		12	11	10^{3}	13	8		2		14		5						9^{1}					3	7		4					39
1							12				10^{2}	6^{1}	8		2		13^{3}		5						9					3	7		4	14	11			40
1									12	11^{2}		13	8		2		10^{3}		5						9^{1}					3	7		4	14	6			41
1				6					10^{2}	11		7	8		2		9^{1}		5											3	12		4	13				42
1				2					10^{1}	11		12	8	13			9^{3}		5											3	7		4	14	6^{2}			43
1				2					12	11		7	8		5^{3}		13		6											3	9^{2}		4	10^{1}		14		44
1^{6}				6					10	11		2	8		5		12							15						3			4^{2}	7^{1}	13	9		45
1				5					10^{1}	11		7	8		2		12													3			4	9^{2}		6	13	46

Worthington Cup

First Round	Rochdale	(h)	1-0
Second Round	Leicester C	(h)	1-2

FA Cup

Third Round	Gillingham	(a)	1-4

SHREWSBURY TOWN — Conference

FOUNDATION

Shrewsbury School having provided a number of the early England and Wales international players it is not surprising that there was a Town club as early as 1876 which won the Birmingham Senior Cup in 1879. However, the present Shrewsbury Town club was formed in 1886 and won the Welsh FA Cup as early as 1891.

Gay Meadow, Shrewsbury SY2 6AB.

Telephone: (01743) 360 111. ***Fax:*** (01743) 236 384.
Commercial Dept: (01743) 356 316.
ClubCall: 09068 121 194.
Community Officer: Brian Williams (01743) 356 623.

Ground Capacity: 8,000.

Record Attendance: 18,917 v Walsall, Division 3, 26 April 1961.

Record Receipts: £80,610 v Arsenal, FA Cup 5th rd, 27 February 1991.

Pitch Measurements: 114yd × 74yd.

Life Vice-presidents: Dr J. Millard Bryson, G. W. Nelson, W.H. Richards.

Chairman: R. Wycherley.

Directors: A. Hopkins, M. J. Starkey, K. R. Woodhouse, T. J. Allen, K. J. Sayfritz. ***Associate Directors:*** M. R. Ashton, H. J. Wilson, A. T. Jones.

Manager: Jimmy Quinn.

Physio: Simon Shakeshaft. ***Coach:*** Dave Fogg.

Commercial Manager: M. Thomas. ***Secretary:*** Mrs J. Shone. ***Operations Manager:*** M. R. Ashton.

Chaplain: Rev. Tim Welch.

Colours: Amber and blue shirts, blue shorts, blue stockings with amber trim.

Change Colours: All white.

Year Formed: 1886.

Turned Professional: 1896.

Ltd Co.: 1936.

Club Nickname: 'Town', 'Blues' or 'Salop'. The name 'Salop' is a colloquialism for the county of Shropshire. Since Shrewsbury is the only club in Shropshire, cries of 'Come on Salop' are frequently used!

Previous Ground: Old Shrewsbury Racecourse.

First Football League Game: 19 August 1950, Division 3 (N), v Scunthorpe U (a) D 0–0 – Egglestone; Fisher, Lewis; Wheatley, Depear, Robinson; Griffin, Hope, Jackson, Brown, Barker.

HONOURS

Football League: Division 2 best season: 8th, 1983–84, 1984–85; Division 3 – Champions 1978–79, 1993–94; Division 4 – Runners-up 1974–75.

FA Cup: best season: 6th rd, 1979, 1982.

Football League Cup: Semi-final 1961.

Welsh Cup: Winners 1891, 1938, 1977, 1979, 1984, 1985; Runners-up 1931, 1948, 1980.

Auto Windscreens Shield: Runners-up 1996

SKY SPORTS FACT FILE

On 4 January 2003 Shrewsbury Town beat Everton 2-1 in an FA Cup third round tie at Gay Meadow. Kevin Ratcliffe the Shrewsbury manager was a former Everton centre-back, his opposite number David Moyes a former Town centre-back.

Record League Victory: 7–0 v Swindon T, Division 3 (S), 6 May 1955 – McBride; Bannister, Skeech; Wallace, Maloney, Candlin; Price, O'Donnell (1), Weigh (4), Russell, McCue (2).

Record Cup Victory: 11–2 v Marine, FA Cup 1st rd, 11 November 1995 – Edwards, Seabury (Dempsey (1)), Withe (1), Evans (1), Whiston (2), Scott (1), Woods, Stevens (1), Spink (3) (Anthrobus), Walton, Berkley, (1 og).

Record Defeat: 1–8 v Norwich C, Division 3 (S), 13 September 1952. 1–8 v Coventry C, Division 3, 22 October 1963.

Most League Points (2 for a win): 62, Division 4, 1974–75.

Most League Points (3 for a win): 79, Division 3, 1993–94.

Most League Goals: 101, Division 4, 1958–59.

Highest League Scorer in Season: Arthur Rowley, 38, Division 4, 1958–59.

Most League Goals in Total Aggregate: Arthur Rowley, 152, 1958–65 (thus completing his League record of 434 goals).

Most League Goals in One Match: 5, Alf Wood v Blackburn R, Division 3, 2 October 1971.

Most Capped Player: Jimmy McLaughlin, 5 (12), Northern Ireland; Bernard McNally, 5, Northern Ireland.

Most League Appearances: Mickey Brown, 418, 1986–91; 1992–94; 1996–2001.

Youngest League Player: Graham French, 16 years 177 days v Reading, 30 September 1961.

Record Transfer Fee Received: £500,000 from Crewe Alex for Dave Walton, October 1997.

Record Transfer Fee Paid: £100,000 to Aldershot for John Dungworth, November 1979 and £100,000 to Southampton for Mark Blake, August 1990.

Football League Record: 1950 Elected to Division 3 (N); 1951–58 Division 3 (S); 1958–59 Division 4; 1959–74 Division 3; 1974–75 Division 4; 1975–79 Division 3; 1979–89 Division 2; 1989–94 Division 3; 1994–97 Division 2; 1997–2003 Division 3; 2003– Conference.

MANAGERS

W. Adams 1905–12
(Secretary-Manager)
A. Weston 1912–34
(Secretary-Manager)
Jack Roscamp 1934–35
Sam Ramsey 1935–36
Ted Bousted 1936–40
Leslie Knighton 1945–49
Harry Chapman 1949–50
Sammy Crooks 1950–54
Walter Rowley 1955–57
Harry Potts 1957–58
Johnny Spuhler 1958
Arthur Rowley 1958–68
Harry Gregg 1968–72
Maurice Evans 1972–73
Alan Durban 1974–78
Richie Barker 1978
Graham Turner 1978–84
Chic Bates 1984–87
Ian McNeill 1987–90
Asa Hartford 1990–91
John Bond 1991–93
Fred Davies 1994–97
(previously Caretaker-Manager 1993–94)
Jake King 1997–99
Kevin Ratcliffe 1999–2003
Jimmy Quinn May 2003–

LATEST SEQUENCES

Longest Sequence of League Wins: 7, 28.10.1995 – 16.12.1995.

Longest Sequence of League Defeats: 8, 9.4.2003 – 3.5.2003.

Longest Sequence of League Draws: 6, 30.10.1963 – 14.12.1963.

Longest Sequence of Unbeaten League Matches: 16, 30.10.1993 – 26.2.1994.

Longest Sequence Without a League Win: 17, 25.1.1992 – 11.4.1992.

Successive Scoring Runs: 28 from 7.9.1960.

Successive Non-scoring Runs: 6 from 1.1.1991.

TEN YEAR LEAGUE RECORD

		P	W	D	L	F	A	Pts	Pos
1993-94	Div 3	42	22	13	7	63	39	79	1
1994-95	Div 2	46	13	14	19	54	62	53	18
1995-96	Div 2	46	13	14	19	58	70	53	18
1996-97	Div 2	46	11	13	22	49	74	46	22
1997-98	Div 3	46	16	13	17	61	62	61	13
1998-99	Div 3	46	14	14	18	52	63	56	15
1999-2000	Div 3	46	9	13	24	40	67	40	22
2000-01	Div 3	46	15	10	21	49	65	55	15
2001-02	Div 3	46	20	10	16	64	53	70	9
2002-03	Div 3	46	9	14	23	62	92	41	24

DID YOU KNOW ?

The first full international for Shrewsbury Town was left-winger Charlie Bowdler for Wales. He was capped once before joining Wolverhampton Wanderers then Blackburn Rovers and again on returning to Shrewsbury.

SHREWSBURY TOWN 2002–03 LEAGUE RECORD

Match No.	Date	Venue	Opponents	Result		H/T Score	Lg. Pos.	Goalscorers	Attendance
1	Aug 10	H	Exeter C	W	1-0	1-0	—	Rodgers [44]	3781
2	13	A	York C	L	1-2	1-0	—	Moss [13]	3463
3	17	A	Southend U	W	3-2	1-1	5	Rodgers 2 [40, 57], Atkins [77]	3150
4	24	H	Rushden & D	D	1-1	0-0	5	Rodgers [70]	3548
5	26	A	Bury	L	3-4	0-1	9	Jemson 3 [65, 72, 73]	2866
6	31	H	Lincoln C	L	1-2	1-0	14	Rodgers [3]	3168
7	Sept 7	H	Leyton Orient	W	2-1	0-1	10	Rodgers [46], Jemson [76]	2756
8	14	A	Rochdale	D	1-1	1-0	11	Van Blerk [39]	2914
9	17	A	Torquay U	L	1-2	0-1	—	Jemson [53]	2528
10	21	H	Bristol R	L	2-5	0-1	17	Murray [47], Rodgers [72]	3510
11	28	A	Scunthorpe U	D	1-1	1-0	18	Rodgers [19]	2988
12	Oct 5	H	Hartlepool U	L	0-1	0-0	20		3142
13	12	A	Carlisle U	W	2-1	1-0	18	Murray [1], Artell [78]	3484
14	19	H	Kidderminster H	L	2-3	2-2	18	Lowe 2 [18, 44]	3507
15	26	A	Oxford U	D	2-2	2-2	20	Woan [21], Drysdale [27]	5559
16	29	H	Hull C	D	1-1	0-0	—	Stevens [89]	3086
17	Nov 2	A	Macclesfield T	W	2-1	1-0	18	Lowe [33], Woan [63]	2218
18	9	H	Cambridge U	W	3-1	0-0	15	Jemson 2 [67, 88], Woan [77]	2928
19	23	H	Darlington	D	2-2	2-0	15	Rodgers [2], Stevens [25]	2755
20	30	A	Swansea C	L	0-2	0-1	16		3638
21	Dec 14	H	Bournemouth	D	0-0	0-0	18		2869
22	21	A	Boston U	L	0-6	0-4	18		2155
23	26	H	Bury	W	4-1	1-0	18	Wilding [12], Lowe 3 [69, 83, 90]	4175
24	Jan 1	A	Rushden & D	L	1-5	0-3	18	Rodgers [46]	4144
25	14	H	Southend U	L	0-1	0-1	—		2699
26	18	A	Lincoln C	D	1-1	0-1	18	Jagielka [73]	2885
27	Feb 1	A	Exeter C	D	1-1	0-1	18	Jemson (pen) [55]	3587
28	8	A	Cambridge U	L	0-5	0-2	18		3755
29	11	H	York C	D	2-2	1-0	—	Rodgers 2 [31, 74]	2599
30	22	A	Leyton Orient	W	2-0	0-0	19	Moss [65], Redmile [70]	3939
31	Mar 1	H	Rochdale	W	3-1	2-0	18	Jagielka 2 [5, 40], Lowe [67]	3423
32	8	A	Bristol R	D	0-0	0-0	18		6839
33	11	A	Wrexham	D	3-3	2-1	—	Woan [3], Tolley J [33], Jemson [67]	7024
34	15	H	Oxford U	L	1-2	1-1	18	Tolley J [45]	3520
35	18	A	Kidderminster H	D	2-2	2-0	—	Wilding [7], Rodgers [15]	3284
36	22	A	Hull C	L	0-2	0-0	21		13,253
37	25	H	Torquay U	L	2-3	0-1	—	Wilding [76], Rodgers (pen) [83]	2694
38	Apr 5	H	Swansea C	D	0-0	0-0	21		4645
39	9	H	Wrexham	L	1-2	0-1	—	Tolley J [59]	5451
40	12	A	Darlington	L	1-5	0-3	23	Lowe [53]	2660
41	15	H	Macclesfield T	L	2-3	2-2	—	Aiston [15], Jemson [42]	4100
42	19	H	Boston U	L	1-2	0-1	23	Lowe [72]	4373
43	21	A	Bournemouth	L	1-2	1-2	24	Aiston [6]	7102
44	26	A	Hartlepool U	L	0-3	0-2	24		5384
45	29	H	Carlisle U	L	2-3	1-2	—	Jemson (pen) [31], Rodgers [84]	7236
46	May 3	H	Scunthorpe U	L	1-2	1-0	24	Rodgers [43]	4127

Final League Position: 24

GOALSCORERS

League (62): Rodgers 16 (1 pen), Jemson 11 (2 pens), Lowe 9, Woan 4, Jagielka 3, Tolley J 3, Wilding 3, Aiston 2, Moss 2, Murray 2, Stevens 2, Artell 1, Atkins 1, Drysdale 1, Redmile 1, Van Blerk 1.
Worthington Cup (0).
FA Cup (9): Jemson 5, Wilding 2, Tolley J 1, Van Blerk 1.
LDV Vans Trophy (11): Rodgers 4, Lowe 4, Atkins 1 (pen), Jemson 1, Moss 1.

Dunbavin I 33	Thompson A 16	Van Blerk J 17 + 6	Redmile M 39	Heathcote M 6	Tolley J 38 + 1	Woan I 33 + 3	Atkins M 29 + 1	Rodgers L 36	Jemson N 38 + 2	Aiston S 11 + 10	Drysdale L 11 + 8	Stevens I 4 + 14	Moss D 35 + 5	Lowe R 27 + 12	Murray K 17 + 11	Wilding P 28 + 5	Artell D 27 + 1	Tolley G — + 1	Mortimer A — + 1	Murphy C — + 3	Jagielka S 12 + 11	Smith A 13	Cartwright M 13	Talbot S 5	Holt A 9	Watts S 3 + 4	Partridge S 2 + 2	Hulbert R 4 + 3	Edwards D — + 1	Stephens R — + 1	*Match No.*
1	2	3^1	4	5	6	7	8	9^3	10	11^2	12	13	14																		1
1	2	3^3	4	5	6	11	8		12		14	9^1	7^2	10	13																2
1	2	3^1	4	5	6^2	11	8	9^3	10		12		7	14	13																3
1	2	3^2	4	5	6	7	8	9	10^1		13	12	14	11^3																	4
1	3		4	5^2	6	7^1	8	9	10		2		12	11	13																5
1	2	3	4	5	6	7^3	8	9^1	10			13	12^2	11	14																6
1	3	11	4				8	9	10		2			7	6	5															7
1	3	11	4		6		8		10			9^1	2	12	7	5															8
1	3	11^1	4		6	12	8		10		13	9^2	2	14	7	5^3															9
1	3^2	12	4		6	7	5	9	10				2	11^1	8	13															10
1	3		4		6^1	11	8	9^2	10^3			14	2	13	7	12	5														11
1	3^1		4		6	7	8	9^2	10				2	13	11^3	12	5	14													12
1		3^2	4		6	11	8		10^1			12	2	9	7		5		13												13
1		3^1	4			7^2	8	9	10		12		2	11	6		5			13											14
1		3^1	4			7	8	9	10^3		12	13	2	11	14	6^2	5														15
1			4		12	7	8	9	10^2		3	13	2	11		6^1	5														16
1			4		6	7	8	9^2	10		3		2	11^1		12	5			13											17
1			4		6	7	8	9	10		3		2	11			5														18
1		11^1	4		6		8	9			3	10	2	7^2	12		5				13										19
1		11^3	4		6		8	9	10^1		3	12	2		13	7^2	5				14										20
1		11	4		6		8	9					2	10			5				7	3									21
1		11^3	4		6	12	8	9		13			2	10		14	5^2				7^1	3									22
1					6	7^1	8	9		12			2	10		4	5				11	3									23
1						7^2	8	9	10^1	12			2	11	13	4	5				6	3									24
1					6^2	7	8^1	9	10	12			2	11^3	13	4	5				14	3									25
1			4				8	9^1	10^2		3	13	2	12	7	6	5				11										26
1		12			6	11			10	8^2	2			9^1	7	4	5			13		3									27
1			4		6	7	8^1	9	10		2			11^2	12		5				13	3									28
			4		6^1	7		9	10				2	11	12	5						3	1	8							29
		12	4		7	11		9	10^2			13	2^3			6	5				14	3^1	1	8							30
1			4			7	12	9^2	10^3	13		14	2	11		5					6	3		8^1							31
		12	4		7^3	11		9^2	10	13			2			6	5				14	3^1	1	8							32
		12	4		7	11		9^2	10				2	13		6	5				14	3^1	1	8^3							33
			4		6	11		9■	10^2	8^1		12	2^3	13		5	14				7	3	1								34
		3^1	4		7^3	11	8	9^2	10	12			2	13		6	5				14		1								35
		3^1	4			11^2	8	9	10	13	12		2		7		5				6		1								36
					6	11		9	10^2	12	3	13	2	7^1		4	5				8		1								37
		12	4		7					11^1		13	2	14		6	5				8		1		3	9^2	10^3				38
			4		7					11			2	12		6	5				8		1		3	9	10^1				39
			4		7	11			12	13			2	10^1		6	5^2						1		3	9^3	14	8			40
1			4		7	11			10	8			2^1	9^3	5	6					13				3		14	12^2			41
1	2		4		8^1	11^2			10	7				9	5	6					12				3			13			42
1	2		4		7			9	10^2	8					5	6					12				3	13		11^1			43
1	2^3		4		7	12■		9	10^2	8					5	6					11^1				3	13		14			44
	2^2				4	7^3		9	10^1	11			13	12■	5	6							1		3	14		8			45
					6^3			9	10^2	11			2	7^1	5	4							1		3	13		8	14	12	46

Worthington Cup

First Round	Walsall	(a)	0-1

FA Cup

First Round	Stafford R	(h)	4-0
Second Round	Barrow	(h)	3-1
Third Round	Everton	(h)	2-1
Fourth Round	Chelsea	(h)	0-4

LDV Vans Trophy

First Round	Morecambe	(h)	3-0
Second Round	Lincoln C	(a)	2-1
Quarter-final	Port Vale	(h)	2-1
Semi-final	Crewe Alex	(h)	4-2
Northern Final	Carlisle U	(a)	0-1
		(h)	0-0

SOUTHAMPTON FA Premiership

FOUNDATION

Formed largely by players from the Deanery FC, which had been established by school teachers in 1880. Most of the founders were connected with the young men's association of St Mary's Church. At the inaugural meeting held in November 1885 the club was named Southampton St Mary's and the church's curate was elected president.

The Friends Provident St Mary's Stadium, Britannia Road, Southampton SO14 5FP.

Telephone: (0870) 2200 000. ***Fax:*** (023) 8072 7727.
Website: www.saintsfc.co.uk ***Email:*** sfc@saintsfc.co.uk
ClubCall: 09068 121 178.
Recorded Ticket Information: 0870 220 0150.

Ground Capacity: 32,689.

Record Attendance: 32,104 v Liverpool, FA Premier League, 18 January 2003.

Record Receipts: £819,209 v Wolverhampton W, FA Cup 6th rd, 9 March 2003.

Pitch Measurements: 112yd × 74yd.

President: E. T. Bates. ***Chairman:*** R. J. G. Lowe.
Vice-chairman: B. H. D. Hunt.
Directors: I. L. Gordon, K. St. J. Wiseman, M. R. Richards FCA, A. Cowen, R. M. Withers.

Manager: Gordon Strachan.

Assistant Manager: Gary Pendrey.

Academy Director: Huw Jennings.

Physios: Jim Joyce, Phil Wilson.

Secretary: Liz Coley.

Colours: Red and white striped shirts, black shorts, white stockings with black and red trim.

Change Colours: White with red shoulder markings, red shorts with white trim, red stockings.

Year Formed: 1885.

Turned Professional: 1894.

Ltd Co.: 1897.

Previous Name: 1885, Southampton St Mary's; 1897, Southampton.

Club Nickname: 'The Saints'.

Previous Grounds: 1885, Antelope Ground; 1897, County Cricket Ground; 1898, The Dell; 2001, St Mary's.

First Football League Game: 28 August 1920, Division 3, v Gillingham (a) D 1–1 – Allen; Parker, Titmuss; Shelley, Campbell, Turner; Barratt, Dominy (1), Rawlings, Moore, Foxall.

HONOURS

Football League: Division 1 – Runners-up 1983–84; Division 2 – Runners-up 1965–66, 1977–78; Division 3 (S) – Champions 1921–22; Runners-up 1920–21; Division 3 – Champions 1959–60.

FA Cup: Winners 1976; Runners-up 1900, 1902, 2003.

Football League Cup: Runners-up 1979.

Zenith Data Systems Cup: Runners-up 1992.

European Competitions: *European Fairs Cup:* 1969–70. *UEFA Cup:* 1971–72, 1981–82, 1982–83, 1984–85. *European Cup-Winners' Cup:* 1976–77.

SKY SPORTS FACT FILE

Locally born centre-half Alec Campbell had two spells with Southampton. During his first he was an amateur international cap in 1909 while still at school and in the second from 1922 played in the full international trial.

Record League Victory: 9–3 v Wolverhampton W, Division 2, 18 September 1965 – Godfrey; Jones, Williams; Walker, Knapp, Huxford; Paine (2), O'Brien (1), Melia, Chivers (4), Sydenham (2).

Record Cup Victory: 7–1 v Ipswich T, FA Cup 3rd rd, 7 January 1961 – Reynolds; Davies, Traynor; Conner, Page, Huxford; Paine (1), O'Brien (3 incl. 1p), Reeves, Mulgrew (2), Penk (1).

Record Defeat: 0–8 v Tottenham H, Division 2, 28 March 1936. 0–8 v Everton, Division 1, 20 November 1971.

Most League Points (2 for a win): 61, Division 3 (S), 1921–22 and Division 3, 1959–60.

Most League Points (3 for a win): 77, Division 1, 1983–84.

Most League Goals: 112, Division 3 (S), 1957–58.

Highest League Scorer in Season: Derek Reeves, 39, Division 3, 1959–60.

Most League Goals in Total Aggregate: Mike Channon, 185, 1966–77, 1979–82.

Most League Goals in One Match: 5, Charlie Wayman v Leicester C, Division 2, 23 October 1948.

Most Capped Player: Peter Shilton, 49 (125), England.

Most League Appearances: Terry Paine, 713, 1956–74.

Youngest League Player: Danny Wallace, 16 years 313 days v Manchester U, 29 November 1980.

Record Transfer Fee Received: £8,000,000 from Tottenham H for Dean Richards, October 2001.

Record Transfer Fee Paid: £4,000,000 to Derby Co for Rory Delap, July 2001.

Football League Record: 1920 Original Member of Division 3; 1921–22 Division 3 (S); 1922–53 Division 2; 1953–58 Division 3 (S); 1958–60 Division 3; 1960–66 Division 2; 1966–74 Division 1; 1974–78 Division 2; 1978–92 Division 1; 1992– FA Premier League.

MANAGERS

Cecil Knight 1894–95
(Secretary-Manager)
Charles Robson 1895–97
E. Arnfield 1897–1911
(Secretary-Manager)
(continued as Secretary)
George Swift 1911–12
Ernest Arnfield 1912–19
Jimmy McIntyre 1919–24
Arthur Chadwick 1925–31
George Kay 1931–36
George Gross 1936–37
Tom Parker 1937–43
J. R. Sarjantson stepped down from the board to act as Secretary-Manager 1943–47 with the next two listed being team Managers during this period
Arthur Dominy 1943–46
Bill Dodgin Snr 1946–49
Sid Cann 1949–51
George Roughton 1952–55
Ted Bates 1955–73
Lawrie McMenemy 1973–85
Chris Nicholl 1985–91
Ian Branfoot 1991–94
Alan Ball 1994–95
Dave Merrington 1995–96
Graeme Souness 1996–97
Dave Jones 1997–2000
Glenn Hoddle 2000–01
Stuart Gray 2001
Gordon Strachan October 2001–

LATEST SEQUENCES

Longest Sequence of League Wins: 6, 3.3.1992 – 4.4.1992.

Longest Sequence of League Defeats: 5, 16.8.1998 – 12.9.1998.

Longest Sequence of League Draws: 7, 28.12.1994 – 11.2.1995.

Longest Sequence of Unbeaten League Matches: 19, 5.9.1921 – 31.12.1921.

Longest Sequence Without a League Win: 20, 30.8.1969 – 27.12.1969.

Successive Scoring Runs: 24 from 5.9.1966.

Successive Non-scoring Runs: 5 from 1.9.1937.

TEN YEAR LEAGUE RECORD

		P	*W*	*D*	*L*	*F*	*A*	*Pts*	*Pos*
1993-94	PR Lge	42	12	7	23	49	66	43	18
1994-95	PR Lge	42	12	18	12	61	63	54	10
1995-96	PR Lge	38	9	11	18	34	52	38	17
1996-97	PR Lge	38	10	11	17	50	56	41	16
1997-98	PR Lge	38	14	6	18	50	55	48	12
1998-99	PR Lge	38	11	8	19	37	64	41	17
1999-2000	PR Lge	38	12	8	18	45	62	44	15
2000-01	PR Lge	38	14	10	14	40	48	52	10
2001-02	PR Lge	38	12	9	17	46	54	45	11
2002-03	PR Lge	38	13	13	12	43	46	52	8

Wayne Bridge, the Southampton and England left wing-back, created an FA Premier League record by playing 112 matches without being substituted. The run ended with injury against Liverpool on 18 January 2003.

SOUTHAMPTON 2002–03 LEAGUE RECORD

Match No.	Date	Venue	Opponents	Result	H/T Score	Lg. Pos.	Goalscorers	Attendance
1	Aug 17	H	Middlesbrough	D 0-0	0-0	—		28,341
2	24	A	Liverpool	L 0-3	0-1	15		43,058
3	28	H	Chelsea	D 1-1	0-0	—	Fernandes 51	31,208
4	31	A	Tottenham H	L 1-2	1-1	19	Taricco (og) 30	35,573
5	Sept 11	H	Everton	W 1-0	0-0	—	Pahars (pen) 73	29,190
6	14	A	WBA	L 0-1	0-0	17		26,377
7	21	H	Charlton Ath	D 0-0	0-0	18		25,714
8	28	A	Bolton W	D 1-1	0-0	18	Bridge 82	22,692
9	Oct 5	H	Manchester C	W 2-0	2-0	13	Ormerod 2 2, 43	31,009
10	21	A	Aston Villa	W 1-0	0-0	—	Beattie (pen) 48	25,817
11	27	H	Fulham	W 4-2	2-2	10	Beattie 3 (1 pen) 27 (p), 42, 53, Ormerod 72	26,188
12	Nov 2	A	Manchester U	L 1-2	1-1	10	Fernandes 18	67,691
13	9	H	Blackburn R	D 1-1	1-0	11	Beattie (pen) 38	30,059
14	16	A	Newcastle U	L 1-2	1-1	11	Beattie 2	51,812
15	23	H	Arsenal	W 3-2	1-1	10	Beattie 2 (1 pen) 45, 59 (p), Toure (og) 67	31,797
16	Dec 2	A	West Ham U	W 1-0	0-0	—	Beattie 90	28,844
17	7	H	Birmingham C	W 2-0	0-0	8	Beattie 2 (1 pen) 60 (p), 82	31,132
18	14	H	Newcastle U	D 1-1	0-0	8	Marsden 52	32,061
19	21	A	Leeds U	D 1-1	0-0	7	Fernandes 89	36,687
20	26	A	Chelsea	D 0-0	0-0	9		39,442
21	28	H	Sunderland	W 2-1	0-0	7	Beattie 73, Tessem 90	31,423
22	Jan 1	H	Tottenham H	W 1-0	0-0	6	Beattie 82	31,890
23	11	A	Middlesbrough	D 2-2	1-0	5	Beattie 2 40, 60	27,443
24	18	H	Liverpool	L 0-1	0-1	8		32,104
25	28	A	Sunderland	W 1-0	0-0	—	Beattie 50	34,102
26	Feb 1	H	Manchester U	L 0-2	0-2	7		32,086
27	8	A	Blackburn R	L 0-1	0-1	9		24,896
28	22	A	Everton	L 1-2	1-0	10	Beattie 33	36,569
29	Mar 1	H	WBA	W 1-0	1-0	10	Beattie 8	31,915
30	15	A	Fulham	D 2-2	0-1	9	Beattie 81, Svensson M 90	18,031
31	22	H	Aston Villa	D 2-2	1-2	9	Beattie 40, Davies 90	31,888
32	Apr 5	H	West Ham U	D 1-1	1-0	11	Beattie 44	31,941
33	19	H	Leeds U	W 3-2	2-0	8	Ormerod 31, Beattie 45, Svensson A 53	32,032
34	21	A	Birmingham C	L 2-3	1-0	9	Svensson A 26, Ormerod 77	29,115
35	26	A	Charlton Ath	L 1-2	0-1	10	Beattie 90	25,878
36	May 3	H	Bolton W	D 0-0	0-0	11		30,951
37	7	A	Arsenal	L 1-6	1-5	—	Tessem 35	38,052
38	11	A	Manchester C	W 1-0	1-0	8	Svensson M 34	34,957

Final League Position: 8

GOALSCORERS

League (43): Beattie 23 (5 pens), Ormerod 5, Fernandes 3, Svensson A 2, Svensson M 2, Tessem 2, Bridge 1, Davies 1, Marsden 1, Pahars 1 (pen), own goals 2.
Worthington Cup (7): Ormerod 3, Delgado 1, Fernandez 1, Marsden 1, Svensson M 1.
FA Cup (13): Oakley 2, Svensson A 2, Tessem 2, Beattie 1, Davies 1, Marsden 1, Ormerod 1, Svensson M 1, own goals 2.

Jones P 13 + 1	Dodd J 13 + 2	Bridge W 34	Marsden C 30	Lundekvam C 33	Williams P 10 + 1	Fernandes F 35 + 2	Delap R 22 + 2	Beattie J 35 + 3	Pahars M 5 + 4	Svensson A 26 + 7	Telfer P 26 + 7	Tessem J 9 + 18	Svensson M 33 + 1	Ormerod B 22 + 9	Kanchelskis A — + 1	Oakley M 28 + 3	El Khalej T — + 1	Niemi A 25	Delgado A 2 + 4	Davies K 1 + 8	Benali F 2	Higginbotham D 3 + 6	Prutton D 9 + 3	Baird C 1 + 2	Monk G 1	*Match No.*
1	2	3	4	5	6	7^{1}	8	9	10^{2}	11	12	13														1
1		3	4	5^{2}	6	7	8	9	10^{1}	11	2	12	13													2
1		3	4		6	7	8	9	10^{1}	11	2	12^{2}	5	13												3
1		3	4		6	7	8	9		11	2		5■	10												4
1	2^{1}	3	4	5	6	7	8	9	13	11^{2}	12			10^{3}	14											5
1	2^{2}	3	4^{3}	5	6■		8	9	10	12	7			13		11^{1}	14									6
		3	4	5	6	7^{2}	8	13	10	12	2	9				11^{1}		1								7
		3	4	5		7	8	12		11	2	9^{1}	6	13		10^{2}		1								8
	2	3	4	5		7	8	9^{3}	12■	11^{2}		14	6	10^{1}		13		1								9
	2	3	4	5^{1}	12	7^{2}	8	9		11	13	14	6	10^{3}				1								10
	2	3	4	5		7		9		11			6	10^{1}		8		1	12							11
	2	3	4^{2}	5		7	12	9		11			6	10^{1}		8		1	13							12
	2	3	4	5		7		9	12	11			6	10^{1}		8		1								13
	2^{2}	3	4	5		7		9	12	11^{1}	13		6	10^{3}		8		1	14							14
	2	3	4	5		7^{1}	8	9			12		6	13		11		1	10^{2}							15
	2	3	4	5		7^{2}	8	9		12	13		6	14		11^{3}		1	10^{1}							16
1	2	3		5		7^{1}	8	9		11	12	13	6	10^{2}		4										17
1		3	4	5		7	8	9		11	2	12	6	10^{1}												18
		3	4^{1}	5		7	8	9		12	2	13	6	10^{2}		11		1								19
		3	4	5		7	8	9		12	2	10^{2}	6			11^{1}		1		13						20
		3	4	5		7	8	9		11^{1}	2	13	6	10^{2}		12		1								21
		3	4	5		7^{2}	8	9			2	12	6	10^{1}		11		1		13						22
		3	4	5		7	8	9			2	10^{1}	6	12		11		1								23
		3^{3}	4^{1}	5		7	8	9		12	2	10^{2}	6	13		11		1	14							24
	12		4		5	7^{1}	8^{2}	9^{3}		10	2	13	6			11		1		14	3					25
15			4	5		7		9		11	2	10^{1}	6			8		1^{6}		12	3					26
			4	5		7^{2}		9		11^{1}	2	10	6	12		8		1				3	13			27
	12			5		7^{1}		9		8^{3}	2	13	6	10^{2}		4		1		14		3	11			28
		3	4	5		7^{2}		9		11^{3}	2	12	6	10^{1}		8		1				13	14			29
	2^{3}	3		5		7^{1}		9			4	12	6	10		8		1		13		14	11^{2}			30
		3		5		7^{1}		9			2	8^{2}	6	10		4		1		12		13	11^{3}	14		31
		3	4	5		7^{1}		9		12	2		6	10^{2}		8		1		13			11			32
1		3		5		7	12	9		8^{1}	2		6	10		4							11			33
1		3		5		7^{3}	8^{2}	9		10	2^{1}	12	6	13		4						14	11			34
1		3	4	5		12		9		11^{1}		13	6	10		8							7		2^{2}	35
		3	4^{2}		5^{3}	7		9		11^{1}	2	12	6	10		8		1				14	13			36
1		11			5	7^{3}		12		4^{2}	2	9	6			13				10^{1}		3	8	14		37
1		3		5		12		9		11^{2}	2	13	6	10^{1}		4						14	8^{3}	7		38

Worthington Cup

Second Round	Tranmere R	(h)	6-1
Third Round	Liverpool	(a)	1-3

FA Cup

Third Round	Tottenham H	(h)	4-0
Fourth Round	Millwall	(h)	1-1
		(a)	2-1
Fifth Round	Norwich C	(h)	2-0
Sixth Round	Wolverhampton W	(h)	2-0
Semi-final (at Villa Park)	Watford		2-1
Final (at Millennium Stadium)	Arsenal		0-1

SOUTHEND UNITED Division 3

FOUNDATION

The leading club in Southend around the turn of the century was Southend Athletic, but they were an amateur concern. Southend United was a more ambitious professional club when they were founded in 1906, employing Bob Jack as secretary-manager and immediately joining the Second Division of the Southern League.

Roots Hall Football Ground, Victoria Avenue, Southend-on-Sea SS2 6NQ.

Telephone: 0870 174 2000. ***Fax:*** (01702) 304 124. ***Commercial:*** 0870 174 2002. ***Ticket Office:*** 0870 174 2001.

Ground Capacity: 12,343.

Record Attendance: 31,090 v Liverpool, FA Cup 3rd rd, 10 January 1979.

Record Receipts: £83,999 v West Ham U, Division 1, 7 April 1993.

Pitch Measurements: 110yd × 74yd.

Deputy-chairman: G. King.
Directors: D. M. Markscheffel, R. J. Osborne, P. Robinson, D. A. J. Wilshire, F. Van Wezel, A. Vine, R. Martin.

Secretary: Miss Helen Giles.

Manager: Steve Wignall.

First Team Coach: Stewart Robson: ***Physio:*** John Stannard.

Commercial Manager: Brian Wheeler. ***Safety Officer:*** David Jobson.

Club Nickname: 'The Blues' or 'The Shrimpers'.

Colours: Navy blue.

Change Colours: All white.

Year Formed: 1906. ***Turned Professional:*** 1906.

Ltd Co.: 1919.

Previous Grounds: 1906, Roots Hall, Prittlewell; 1920, Kursaal; 1934, Southend Stadium; 1955, Roots Hall Football Ground.

First Football League Game: 28 August 1920, Division 3, v Brighton & HA (a) W 2–0 – Capper; Reid, Newton; Wileman, Henderson, Martin; Nicholls, Nuttall, Fairclough (2), Myers, Dorsett.

Record League Victory: 9–2 v Newport Co, Division 3 (S), 5 September 1936 – McKenzie; Nelson, Everest (1); Deacon, Turner, Carr; Bolan, Lane (1), Goddard (4), Dickinson (2), Oswald (1).

Record Cup Victory: 10–1 v Golders Green, FA Cup 1st rd, 24 November 1934 – Moore; Morfitt, Kelly; Mackay, Joe Wilson, Carr (1); Lane (1), Johnson (5), Cheesmuir (2), Deacon (1), Oswald. 10–1 v Brentwood, FA Cup 2nd rd, 7 December 1968 – Roberts; Bentley, Birks; McMillan (1) Beesley, Kurila; Clayton, Chisnall, Moore (4), Best (5), Hamilton. 10–1 v Aldershot, Leyland Daf Cup Prel rd, 6 November 1990 – Sansome; Austin, Powell, Cornwell, Prior (1), Tilson (3), Cawley, Butler, Ansah (1), Benjamin (1), Angell (4).

HONOURS

Football League: Division 1 best season: 13th, 1994–95. Division 3 – Runners-up 1990–91; Division 4 – Champions 1980–81; Runners-up 1971–72, 1977–78.

FA Cup: best season: old 3rd rd, 1921; 5th rd, 1926, 1952, 1976, 1993.

Football League Cup: never past 3rd rd.

SKY SPORTS FACT FILE

Southend United ended Corinthians' participation in the FA Cup. The famous amateur club's last two matches resulted in a 2-0 defeat on 27 November 1937 and 3-0 on 26 November 1938 when Alf Smirk scored all three United goals.

Record Defeat: 1–9 v Brighton & HA, Division 3, 27 November 1965.

Most League Points (2 for a win): 67, Division 4, 1980–81.

Most League Points (3 for a win): 85, Division 3, 1990–91.

Most League Goals: 92, Division 3 (S), 1950–51.

Highest League Scorer in Season: Jim Shankly, 31, 1928–29; Sammy McCrory, 1957–58, both in Division 3 (S).

Most League Goals in Total Aggregate: Roy Hollis, 122, 1953–60.

Most League Goals in One Match: 5, Jim Shankly v Merthyr T, Division 3S, 1 March 1930.

Most Capped Player: George Mackenzie, 9, Eire.

Most League Appearances: Sandy Anderson, 452, 1950–63.

Youngest League Player: Phil O'Connor, 16 years 76 days v Lincoln C, 26 December 1969.

Record Transfer Fee Received: £3,570,000 from Nottingham F for Stan Collymore, June 1993.

Record Transfer Fee Paid: £750,000 to Crystal Palace for Stan Collymore, November 1992.

Football League Record: 1920 Original Member of Division 3; 1921–58 Division 3 (S); 1958–66 Division 3; 1966–72 Division 4; 1972–76 Division 3; 1976–78 Division 4; 1978–80 Division 3; 1980–81 Division 4; 1981–84 Division 3; 1984–87 Division 4; 1987–89 Division 3; 1989–90 Division 4; 1990–91 Division 3; 1991–92 Division 2; 1992–97 Division 1; 1997–98 Division 2; 1998– Division 3.

MANAGERS

Bob Jack 1906–10
George Molyneux 1910–11
O. M. Howard 1911–12
Joe Bradshaw 1912–19
Ned Liddell 1919–20
Tom Mather 1920–21
Ted Birnie 1921–34
David Jack 1934–40
Harry Warren 1946–56
Eddie Perry 1956–60
Frank Broome 1960
Ted Fenton 1961–65
Alvan Williams 1965–67
Ernie Shepherd 1967–69
Geoff Hudson 1969–70
Arthur Rowley 1970–76
Dave Smith 1976–83
Peter Morris 1983–84
Bobby Moore 1984–86
Dave Webb 1986–87
Dick Bate 1987
Paul Clark 1987–88
Dave Webb *(General Manager)* 1988–92
Colin Murphy 1992–93
Barry Fry 1993
Peter Taylor 1993–95
Steve Thompson 1995
Ronnie Whelan 1995–97
Alvin Martin 1997–99
Alan Little 1999–2000
David Webb 2000–01
Rob Newman 2001–03
Steve Wignall May 2003–

LATEST SEQUENCES

Longest Sequence of League Wins: 7, 27.4.1990 – 18.9.1990.

Longest Sequence of League Defeats: 6, 29.8.1987 – 19.9.1987.

Longest Sequence of League Draws: 6, 30.1.1982 – 19.2.1982.

Longest Sequence of Unbeaten League Matches: 16, 20.2.1932 – 29.8.1932.

Longest Sequence Without a League Win: 17, 31.12.1983 – 14.4.1984.

Successive Scoring Runs: 24 from 23.3.1929.

Successive Non-scoring Runs: 6 from 28.10.1933.

TEN YEAR LEAGUE RECORD

		P	*W*	*D*	*L*	*F*	*A*	*Pts*	*Pos*
1993-94	Div 1	46	17	8	21	63	67	59	15
1994-95	Div 1	46	18	8	20	54	73	62	13
1995-96	Div 1	46	15	14	17	52	61	59	14
1996-97	Div 1	46	8	15	23	42	86	39	24
1997-98	Div 2	46	11	10	25	47	79	43	24
1998-99	Div 3	46	14	12	20	52	58	54	18
1999-2000	Div 3	46	15	11	20	53	61	56	16
2000-01	Div 3	46	15	18	13	55	53	63	11
2001-02	Div 3	46	15	13	18	51	54	58	12
2002-03	Div 3	46	17	3	26	47	59	54	17

On 14 December 2002 Southend United centre-back Leon Cort scored a hat-trick against Boston United in a 4-2 win. They were all headed goals and he became the first Blues defender to register a treble in the club's history.

SOUTHEND UNITED 2002–03 LEAGUE RECORD

Match No.	Date	Venue	Opponents	Result		H/T Score	Lg. Pos.	Goalscorers	Attendance
1	Aug 10	A	Hull C	D	2-2	0-1	—	Jenkins [62], Bramble [90]	10,449
2	13	H	Carlisle U	L	0-1	0-0	—		3881
3	17	H	Shrewsbury T	L	2-3	1-1	22	Jenkins [9], Bramble (pen) [81]	3150
4	24	A	Oxford U	W	1-0	1-0	18	Rawle [20]	5162
5	26	H	Cambridge U	W	2-1	2-1	10	Broad [7], Smith J [30]	4462
6	31	A	Rochdale	W	2-1	1-0	7	Rawle [36], Bramble [83]	2852
7	Sept 7	A	Rushden & D	L	0-3	0-2	11		4176
8	14	H	Macclesfield T	W	1-0	1-0	8	Cort [26]	3249
9	17	H	Kidderminster H	L	0-2	0-1	—		2959
10	21	A	Lincoln C	L	1-2	0-0	15	Jenkins [76]	3151
11	28	H	Exeter C	W	1-0	1-0	13	Jones [43]	3364
12	Oct 5	A	Bury	W	3-1	0-1	9	Jones [67], Jenkins [79], Bramble [84]	3301
13	12	H	York C	W	1-0	0-0	6	Belgrave [90]	4411
14	19	A	Swansea C	L	0-1	0-0	8		3623
15	25	H	Hartlepool U	L	0-1	0-1	—		5168
16	29	A	Leyton Orient	L	1-2	0-2	—	Belgrave [73]	5343
17	Nov 2	H	Wrexham	L	0-1	0-1	15		3727
18	9	A	Bristol R	W	1-0	0-0	13	Bramble [78]	5691
19	23	H	Bournemouth	L	0-1	0-0	14		4221
20	30	A	Darlington	L	1-2	0-1	14	Bramble [90]	2830
21	Dec 14	H	Boston U	W	4-2	3-0	14	Cort 3 [7, 23, 88], Rawle [39]	3245
22	21	A	Torquay U	L	1-3	0-1	16	Bramble [60]	2244
23	26	A	Cambridge U	D	1-1	1-0	16	Rawle [10]	6237
24	29	H	Scunthorpe U	L	1-2	1-0	17	Cort [39]	4248
25	Jan 4	A	Carlisle U	L	0-1	0-1	17		4016
26	14	A	Shrewsbury T	W	1-0	1-0	—	Smith J [20]	2699
27	18	H	Rochdale	W	1-0	0-0	15	Bramble [89]	3645
28	21	H	Oxford U	W	2-1	1-0	—	Rawle [45], Bramble [70]	3203
29	25	A	Scunthorpe U	L	1-4	1-3	14	Smith J [17]	3096
30	Feb 1	H	Hull C	W	3-0	3-0	10	Smith J 2 (1 pen) [22, 45 (p)], Rawle [41]	4534
31	8	H	Bristol R	D	2-2	1-0	13	Belgrave [36], Maher [76]	4708
32	15	A	Wrexham	L	0-3	0-1	13		3109
33	22	H	Rushden & D	W	2-1	2-1	12	Rawle [4], Searle [6]	6453
34	Mar 1	A	Macclesfield T	L	1-2	0-0	12	Jenkins [88]	1917
35	4	A	Kidderminster H	L	0-1	0-0	—		2006
36	8	H	Lincoln C	L	0-1	0-1	14		3912
37	15	A	Hartlepool U	L	1-2	0-1	14	Sutch [74]	4868
38	18	H	Swansea C	L	0-2	0-0	—		2832
39	22	H	Leyton Orient	W	1-0	1-0	14	Salter [5]	4148
40	29	A	York C	L	0-2	0-2	14		4312
41	Apr 5	H	Darlington	W	2-0	2-0	13	Maher [40], Jenkins [42]	3053
42	12	A	Bournemouth	L	0-1	0-1	14		6767
43	19	H	Torquay U	W	3-0	2-0	14	Rawle 2 [2, 40], Jenkins [88]	3594
44	21	A	Boston U	L	0-1	0-0	14		3247
45	26	H	Bury	L	1-2	1-1	14	Cort [13]	4707
46	May 3	A	Exeter C	L	0-1	0-0	17		9036

Final League Position: 17

GOALSCORERS

League (47): Bramble 9 (1 pen), Rawle 9, Jenkins 7, Cort 6, Smith J 5 (1 pen), Belgrave 3, Jones 2, Maher 2, Broad 1, Salter 1, Searle 1, Sutch 1.
Worthington Cup (1): Rawle 1.
FA Cup (6): Bramble 2, Rawle 2, Cort 1, own goal 1.
LDV Vans Trophy (1): Jones 1.

Flahavan D 41	Broad S 17	Searle D 39 + 5	Maher K 42	Cort L 46	Whelan P 13 + 1	Clark S 20 + 13	Selley I 11	Rawle M 33 + 1	Jones G 18 + 3	Jenkins N 29 + 5	Thurgood S 7 + 20	Bramble T 31 + 3	Beard M 29 + 7	Maye D — + 2	Smith J 30 + 1	Belgrave B 6 + 15	Scully T 8	Salter M 5 + 8	McSweeney D 15 + 2	Tilson S 2 + 1	Marney D 13 + 4	Gay D 5	Sutch D 16	Kelly S 10	Foley D 5	Darby B 6 + 4	Strachan G 6 + 1	Henry R 3	Jordan T — + 1	Kightly M — + 1	Match No.
1	2^1	3	4	5	6	7^2	8	9	10	11	12	13																			1
1	2	3	4	5	6	7^1	8	9	10	11^2	13	12																			2
1	2^3	3	4	5	6^2	7	8^1		10	11	12	9	14	13																	3
1		3	4^2	5	6	12		9^1	10	11	13	7	2		8																4
1	6	3	4	5		7^2		9^1		11	12	10	2		8	13															5
1	6	3	4	5				9	10^1	11	12	7	2		8																6
1	6^3	3	4	5	12	13		9	10	11^2		7	2^1		8	14															7
1	6	3	4	5				9	10	11		7	2		8																8
1	6	3	4	5		7^1		9	10	11^2			2	13	8	12															9
1	6	12	4	5			8^1	9	10^2	3	13	7	2		11																10
1	11		4	5	6	12	8^3	9^2	13	3	14	10	2^1		7																11
1	2	12	4	5	6		8		10^3	11^1	13	9	3		7^2	14															12
1	4	12	7	5	6^1	13	8^2		10^3	3		9	2		11	14															13
1	2	3	7	5	6	12	8^2			11	13		4^1		10	9															14
1	4^2	12	7	5	6	13	8^1	14	10	3		9^3	2		11																15
1	4	12	7	5	6^1	13	8^2	9^3	10	3			2		11	14■															16
1	6	3	4	5		12			10^1	11^2			2		8	9	7	13													17
1	6	3		5			8			11	12	9	2		4	10	7^1														18
1		3	4	5		7			10^1			9	2		8		11	12	6												19
1		3	4	5					12	11^1		9	2		8	10	7		6												20
1		3	4	5		12		11^3	10		8	9^2	2				7^1	13	6	14											21
1		3	4	5				9	10		8	11	2^1		12		7^3	13	6^2		14										22
1		3	4	5	6			9				10	2		8	12			7		11^1										23
1		3	4	5	6^3			9	12			10	7		8^2	13	11^1		2		14										24
		3		5	6^2			9	10			12	2		8		7^1		13	11	14	1	4^3								25
		3		5		11		9				10	2		8	12			6		7^1	1	4								26
		3	4	5		11^1		9^2		12		10	2^3		8	13			14		7	1	6								27
		3	4	5		11^1		9^3		12	13	10			8	14			2		7^2	1	6								28
		3	4	5		11		9^1				10	2		8	12					7	1	6								29
1		3	4	5		11^1		9^2			12	10■			8	13					7		2	6							30
1		3	4	5		11		9							8	10		12			7^1		2	6							31
1		3	4	5		11		9^2					12		8^1	13					7		2	6	10						32
1		3	4	5		11^1		9			13		12		8^2						7		2	6	10						33
1			4	5		11		9		12	13				8^2			14		3^1	7		2	6	10^3						34
1		3	4	5		11^1		9^3		12	13	7			8^2						14		2	6	10						35
1		3	4	5		11^1				12	8	9									7		2	6	10						36
1		3		5						11	8	9	2					10			7^1		4	6		12					37
1		3	4	5		12				11^1	8	9						10			7^2		2	6		13					38
1		3	4	5		7^1				11	8	9^2	12					10					2	6		13					39
1		3	4	5		12		9		11	8^1	7				10^2			6				2^3			13	14				40
1		3	4	5		7^1		9		11	12		13						6							10^2	8	2			41
1		3	4	5		7^3		9		11			12					13	6							10^2	8	2^1	14		42
1		3	4	5				9		11	12		13					10	6							7	8^1	2^2			43
1		3	4	5		12		9		11			2			13		10^2	6							7^1	8				44
1		3	4	5		12		9		11	13	10	2^2					14	6							7^1	8^3				45
1		3	4	5				9^2		11	12	10	2						6							7^1	8			13	46

Worthington Cup

First Round	Wimbledon	(h)	1-4

LDV Vans Trophy

First Round	Swindon T	(a)	1-6

FA Cup

First Round	Hartlepool U	(h)	1-1
		(a)	2-1
Second Round	Bournemouth	(h)	1-1
		(a)	2-3

STOCKPORT COUNTY Division 2

FOUNDATION

Formed at a meeting held at Wellington Road South by members of Wycliffe Congregational Chapel in 1883, they called themselves Heaton Norris Rovers until changing to Stockport County in 1890, a year before joining the Football Combination.

Edgeley Park, Hardcastle Road, Stockport, Cheshire SK3 9DD.

Telephone: (0161) 286 8888. ***Fax:*** (0161) 286 8900.
Club Shop: (0161) 286 8899. ***ClubCall:*** 09068 121 638.
Website: www.stockportcounty.com

Ground Capacity: 10,817.

Record Attendance: 27,833 v Liverpool, FA Cup 5th rd, 11 February 1950.

Record Receipts: £181,449 v Middlesbrough, Coca-Cola Cup Semi-final 1st leg, 26 February 1997.

Pitch Measurements: 111yd × 72yd.

Hon. Vice-presidents: Freddie Pye, Andrew Barlow, Graham White.

Chairman: Brendan Elwood.

Directors: Mike Baker, Michael Rains.

Secretary: Gary Glendenning BA (HONS), FCCA.

Manager: Carlton Palmer. ***Assistant Manager:*** Kevin Richardson. ***Physio:*** Rodger Wylde.

Assistant Secretary: Andrea Dawson. ***Commercial Manager:*** John Rutter.
Marketing Manager: Steve Bellis. ***Programme Editor:*** Des Hinks.

Year Formed: 1883.

Turned Professional: 1891. ***Ltd Co.:*** 1908.

Previous Names: 1883, Heaton Norris Rovers; 1888, Heaton Norris; 1890, Stockport County.

Club Nicknames: 'County' or 'Hatters'.

Colours: Royal blue shirts with white trim, royal blue shorts with white trim, white stockings with blue trim.

Change Colours: White shirts with black trim, black shorts with white trim, white stockings with black trim.

Previous Grounds: 1883 Heaton Norris Recreation Ground; 1884 Heaton Norris Wanderers Cricket Ground; 1885 Chorlton's Farm, Chorlton's Lane; 1886 Heaton Norris Cricket Ground; 1887 Wilkes' Field, Belmont Street; 1889 Nursery Inn, Green Lane; 1902 Edgeley Park.

First Football League Game: 1 September 1900, Division 2, v Leicester Fosse (a) D 2–2 – Moores; Earp, Wainwright; Pickford, Limond, Harvey; Stansfield, Smith (1), Patterson, Foster, Betteley (1).

Record League Victory: 13–0 v Halifax T, Division 3 (N), 6 January 1934 – McGann; Vincent (1p), Jenkinson; Robinson, Stevens, Len Jones; Foulkes (1), Hill (3), Lythgoe (2), Stevenson (2), Downes (4).

HONOURS

Football League: Division 1 best season: 8th, 1997–98; Division 2 – Runners-up 1996–97; Division 3 (N) – Champions 1921–22, 1936–37; Runners-up 1928–29, 1929-30, 1996–97; Division 4 – Champions 1966–67; Runners-up 1990–91.

FA Cup: best season: 5th rd, 1935, 1950, 2001.

Football League Cup: Semi-final 1997.

Autoglass Trophy: Runners-up 1992, 1993.

SKY SPORTS FACT FILE

On 8 February 2003 away to Cheltenham Town and despite losing player-manager Carlton Palmer in the 38th minute for two bookable offences, Stockport County scored twice in the second half for a 2-0 win.

Record Cup Victory: 5–0 v Lincoln C, FA Cup 1st rd, 11 November 1995 – Edwards; Connelly, Todd, Bennett, Flynn, Gannon (Dinning), Beaumont, Oliver, Ware, Eckhardt (3), Armstrong (1) (Mike), Chalk, (1 og).

Record Defeat: 1–8 v Chesterfield, Division 2, 19 April 1902.

Most League Points (2 for a win): 64, Division 4, 1966–67.

Most League Points (3 for a win): 85, Division 2, 1993–94.

Most League Goals: 115, Division 3 (N), 1933–34.

Highest League Scorer in Season: Alf Lythgoe, 46, Division 3 (N), 1933–34.

Most League Goals in Total Aggregate: Jack Connor, 132, 1951–56.

Most League Goals in One Match: 5, Joe Smith v Southport, Division 3N, 7 January 1928; 5, Joe Smith v Lincoln C, Division 3N, 15 September 1928; 5, Frank Newton v Nelson, Division 3N, 21 September 1929; 5, Alf Lythgoe v Southport, Division 3N, 25 August 1934; 5, Billy McNaughton v Mansfield T, Division 3N, 14 December 1935; 5, Jack Connor v Workington, Division 3N, 8 November 1952; 5, Jack Connor v Carlisle U, Division 3N, 7 April 1956.

Most Capped Player: Jarkko Wiss, 9 (36), Finland.

Most League Appearances: Andy Thorpe, 489, 1978–86, 1988–92.

Youngest League Player: Jimmy Collier, 16 years 227 days v Bristol R, 8 April 1969.

Record Transfer Fee Received: £1,600,000 from Middlesbrough for Alun Armstrong, February 1998.

Record Transfer Fee Paid: £800,000 to Nottingham F for Ian Moore, July 1998.

Football League Record: 1900 Elected to Division 2; 1904 Failed re-election; 1905–21 Division 2; 1921–22 Division 3 (N); 1922–26 Division 2; 1926–37 Division 3 (N); 1937–38 Division 2; 1938–58 Division 3 (N); 1958–59 Division 3; 1959–67 Division 4; 1967–70 Division 3; 1970–91 Division 4; 1991–92 Division 3; 1992–97 Division 2; 1997–2002 Division 1; 2002– Division 2.

MANAGERS

Fred Stewart 1894–1911
Harry Lewis 1911–14
David Ashworth 1914–19
Albert Williams 1919–24
Fred Scotchbrook 1924–26
Lincoln Hyde 1926–31
Andrew Wilson 1932–33
Fred Westgarth 1934–36
Bob Kelly 1936–38
George Hunt 1938–39
Bob Marshall 1939–49
Andy Beattie 1949–52
Dick Duckworth 1952–56
Billy Moir 1956–60
Reg Flewin 1960–63
Trevor Porteous 1963–65
Bert Trautmann *(General Manager)* 1965–66
Eddie Quigley *(Team Manager)* 1965–66
Jimmy Meadows 1966–69
Wally Galbraith 1969–70
Matt Woods 1970–71
Brian Doyle 1972–74
Jimmy Meadows 1974–75
Roy Chapman 1975–76
Eddie Quigley 1976–77
Alan Thompson 1977–78
Mike Summerbee 1978–79
Jimmy McGuigan 1979–82
Eric Webster 1982–85
Colin Murphy 1985
Les Chapman 1985–86
Jimmy Melia 1986
Colin Murphy 1986–87
Asa Hartford 1987–89
Danny Bergara 1989–95
Dave Jones 1995–97
Gary Megson 1997–99
Andy Kilner 1999–2001
Carlton Palmer November 2001–

LATEST SEQUENCES

Longest Sequence of League Wins: 8, 26.12.1927 – 28.1.1928.

Longest Sequence of League Defeats: 10, 24.11.2001 – 13.01.2002

Longest Sequence of League Draws: 7, 17.3.1989 – 14.4.1989.

Longest Sequence of Unbeaten League Matches: 18, 28.1.1933 – 28.8.1933.

Longest Sequence Without a League Win: 19, 28.12.1999 – 22.4.2000.

Successive Scoring Runs: 24 from 8.9.1928.

Successive Non-scoring Runs: 7 from 10.3.1923.

TEN YEAR LEAGUE RECORD

		P	W	D	L	F	A	Pts	Pos
1993-94	Div 2	46	24	13	9	74	44	85	4
1994-95	Div 2	46	19	8	19	63	60	65	11
1995-96	Div 2	46	19	13	14	61	47	70	9
1996-97	Div 2	46	23	13	10	59	41	82	2
1997-98	Div 1	46	19	8	19	71	69	65	8
1998-99	Div 1	46	12	17	17	49	60	53	16
1999-2000	Div 1	46	13	15	18	55	67	54	17
2000-01	Div 1	46	11	18	17	58	65	51	19
2001-02	Div 1	46	6	8	32	42	102	26	24
2002-03	Div 2	46	15	10	21	65	70	55	14

DID YOU KNOW?

In 1929–30 Stockport County achieved a home and away double against Port Vale the Division Three (North) champions, recording 2-1 away and 4-2 home victories. They were the only double defeats suffered by Vale.

STOCKPORT COUNTY 2002–03 LEAGUE RECORD

Match No.	Date	Venue	Opponents	Result		H/T Score	Lg. Pos.	Goalscorers	Attendance
1	Aug 10	A	Colchester U	L	0-1	0-0	—		3300
2	13	H	QPR	D	1-1	0-0	—	Beckett [62]	5811
3	17	H	Notts Co	D	0-0	0-0	21		5047
4	24	A	Port Vale	W	1-0	1-0	15	Beckett [17]	4070
5	26	H	Mansfield T	W	2-0	1-0	8	Reddington (og) [39], Beckett [55]	5190
6	31	A	Swindon T	W	1-0	0-0	6	Beckett [56]	5456
7	Sept 14	A	Cardiff C	L	1-2	1-2	12	Beckett [16]	11,546
8	17	A	Chesterfield	L	0-1	0-1	—		4088
9	21	H	Barnsley	W	4-1	0-1	11	Goodwin 2 [63, 72], Beckett 2 [66, 75]	5690
10	28	A	Tranmere R	L	0-1	0-1	14		7513
11	Oct 5	H	Luton T	L	2-3	2-1	17	Beckett [19], Daly [45]	5932
12	8	H	Peterborough U	W	2-1	1-0	—	Beckett 2 [14, 60]	4726
13	12	H	Crewe Alex	L	1-4	0-2	11	Daly [65]	6468
14	19	A	Wigan Ath	L	1-2	1-0	15	Beckett [4]	7276
15	26	H	Brentford	L	2-3	1-1	15	Beckett [45], Palmer [90]	4601
16	29	A	Blackpool	W	3-1	0-0	—	Ellison [46], Gibb [74], Beckett [89]	7047
17	Nov 2	A	Oldham Ath	L	0-2	0-1	14		8251
18	9	H	Cheltenham T	D	1-1	1-1	15	Burgess [40]	4531
19	23	A	Plymouth Arg	L	1-4	1-3	18	Wotton (og) [11]	7746
20	30	H	Wycombe W	W	2-1	2-0	15	Beckett [10], Ross [39]	4731
21	Dec 14	A	Huddersfield T	L	1-2	0-1	17	Briggs [74]	7978
22	20	H	Northampton T	W	4-0	1-0	—	Beckett 3 [23, 46, 60], Burgess [77]	4516
23	26	A	Mansfield T	L	2-4	2-1	13	Day (og) [3], Burgess (pen) [17]	6434
24	28	H	Bristol C	L	1-4	0-3	14	Beckett [57]	5100
25	Jan 1	H	Port Vale	D	1-1	1-0	15	Burgess (pen) [31]	4390
26	4	A	QPR	L	0-1	0-0	16		10,387
27	18	H	Swindon T	L	2-5	0-2	17	Lescott [83], Lambert [89]	4318
28	21	A	Notts Co	L	2-3	2-0	—	Beckett 2 [15, 30]	4392
29	25	A	Bristol C	D	1-1	1-0	18	Beckett [22]	10,831
30	Feb 1	H	Colchester U	D	1-1	1-0	18	Beckett [36]	4011
31	8	A	Cheltenham T	W	2-0	0-0	15	Daly [76], Wild [90]	4692
32	15	H	Oldham Ath	L	1-2	0-1	18	Daly [46]	8168
33	22	A	Peterborough U	L	0-2	0-0	20		4386
34	Mar 1	H	Cardiff C	D	1-1	1-0	21	Clark [26]	5385
35	4	H	Chesterfield	W	2-1	1-1	—	Beckett [40], Daly [84]	4428
36	8	A	Barnsley	L	0-1	0-1	20		9177
37	15	A	Brentford	W	2-1	0-1	18	Beckett 2 [51, 54]	4790
38	18	H	Wigan Ath	D	1-1	0-0	—	Welsh [70]	6719
39	22	H	Blackpool	D	2-2	1-2	18	Lambert [45], Beckett [77]	6599
40	29	A	Crewe Alex	L	0-1	0-0	20		7336
41	Apr 5	A	Wycombe W	W	4-1	0-0	19	Beckett [78], Greer [85], Wilbraham 2 [88, 90]	5632
42	12	H	Plymouth Arg	W	2-1	1-0	17	Wilbraham [40], Daly (pen) [86]	5484
43	18	A	Northampton T	W	3-0	3-0	—	Wilbraham 2 [7, 24], Goodwin [14]	5873
44	21	H	Huddersfield T	W	2-1	0-1	13	Daly [79], Wilbraham [81]	7159
45	26	A	Luton T	D	1-1	0-0	14	Challinor [83]	6010
46	May 3	H	Tranmere R	L	2-3	2-0	14	Wilbraham [7], Welsh [21]	7236

Final League Position: 14

GOALSCORERS

League (65): Beckett 27, Daly 7 (1 pen), Wilbraham 7, Burgess 4 (2 pens), Goodwin 3, Lambert 2, Welsh 2, Briggs 1, Challinor 1, Clark 1, Ellison 1, Gibb 1, Greer 1, Lescott 1, Palmer 1, Ross 1, Wild 1, own goals 3.
Worthington Cup (4): Beckett 1, Clare 1, Daly 1, Palmer 1.
FA Cup (4): Burgess 2 (1 pen), Beckett 1, Fradin 1.
LDV Vans Trophy (1): Briggs 1.

Jones L 24	Lescott A 36 + 5	Clare R 31 + 5	Challinor D 46	Palmer C 22	Clark P 21	McLachlan F 18 + 4	Lambert R 22 + 7	Daly J 25 + 10	Beckett L 41 + 1	Pemberton M 15 + 5	Gibb A 43 + 2	Briggs K 13 + 6	Burgess B 17 + 2	Goodwin J 22 + 11	Ellison K 17 + 6	Hardiker J 19 + 4	Ross N 1 + 3	Tonkin A 23 + 1	Welsh A 7 + 6	Spencer J 1	Fradin K 8 + 1	Blayney A 2	Jones B 1	Thomas A 1 + 1	Tidman O 18	Wilbraham A 8 + 7	Wild P — + 3	Williams C — + 1	Greer G 4 + 1	*Match No.*
1	2^{1}	3	4	5	6	7■	8^{2}	9^{3}	10	11	12	13	14																	1
1	12^{2}	3	4	8	6	7^{1}		14	10^{3}	11	5	2	9	13																2
1		3^{2}	4	5	6^{1}	7	12		10	11^{3}	8	2	9	13	14															3
1	12	6	4	5	11		8^{1}	13	10		2	3	9^{2}			7														4
1	12	3	4	5	6		8^{1}		10		2	7	9	13		11^{2}														5
1	2	3	4^{1}	5			12	13	10^{2}		7	11	9^{3}	8		6	14													6
1	2	6	4	5				12	10	11	7	3^{2}	9^{1}	13	14	8^{3}														7
1	2	12	4	5				9	10	11	3			6	8^{1}	7														8
1	2^{1}	3	4	5				9	10	11	7	12		6	13	8^{2}														9
1	12	6^{1}	4	5				9	10	11^{2}	7	2		8	13			3												10
1	11		4	5				9	10		2	7		6	12	8^{1}		3												11
1	2		4	5				9^{2}	10	12	7	11^{1}		6	8		13	3												12
1	2	13	4	5				12	10		7	14		6	8^{1}	11^{2}		3	9^{3}											13
1	8	6	4	5		7	11	9^{1}	10		2^{2}		12	13	14			3^{3}												14
	2		4	5			11	12	10		7		9^{1}		8			3		1	6									15
	2	12	4	5^{1}		8			10		7		9		11			3			6	1								16
1	2^{2}	5	4			11			10		7	12	9	13	8^{1}			3			6									17
		5	4					12	10^{1}		2	7	9	8		11		3			6	1								18
1	12		4■			7^{2}		8^{3}	10		2	13	9^{1}	6		5	14	3			11									19
1	2		4	5		8^{1}			10		7	11		12			9	3			6									20
1	7	6^{2}	4	5			8		10	11^{1}	2	12	9			13		3												21
1	2	5	4				8^{2}	12	10^{1}	11^{3}	7	6	9	13		14		3												22
1	2	5	4^{2}				8^{1}		10	11	7	6	9			13		3			12									23
		5	4				8^{1}	12	10	11^{2}	7		9	13		2		3			6		1							24
1	8		4	5					10	12	7		9	6	11^{1}	2		3												25
1	8		4	5					10		7		9	6	11	2		3												26
1	8		4	5^{2}			12	9	10	3^{1}	7			6	11	2								13						27
1	2	5	4			8^{2}	12	9^{1}	10		7			13	11			3			6									28
	2■	5	4			6	8^{1}	9^{2}	10	12	7			13	11^{3}			3							1	14				29
	2	5	4			6	8	9^{2}	10	12	7				11^{1}			3							1	13				30
		2	4	5■	3	6	8	9^{1}	10	11^{2}	7														1	12	13			31
	2	5	4		3	6^{1}	8	9	10	11^{2}	7														1	12	13			32
		2	4		3	12	8^{3}	9^{2}	10	11	7				6^{1}									5	1	13	14			33
	6	5	4		3		8		10		7			2	11^{1}				12						1	9				34
	2	5	4		3		8	12	10		7			6	11^{2}				13						1	9^{1}				35
	6	5	4		3		8	9	10		7			2^{1}	11^{2}			13	12						1					36
	6	5	4		3		8	9	10		7			2	11^{1}				12						1					37
	6	5	4		3	12	8	9	10		7					2^{1}			11						1					38
	6	5	4		3	12	8	9^{3}	10	13	7					2^{1}			11^{2}						1	14				39
	6	5	4		3	12	8		10		7					2^{1}			11						1	9^{2}		13		40
	6	5	4		3		8^{1}	9^{2}	10		7			2		12			11^{3}						1	13			14	41
	6		4		3	8		9						2		5		11							1	10			7	42
	6		4		3	8		9^{1}	12^{2}		14			2		7^{3}		11	13						1	10			5	43
	6	12	4		3^{1}	8^{2}	13	9			7			2				11^{3}	14						1	10			5	44
	6	12	4		3	8^{1}	13	9			7			2					11^{2}						1	10			5	45
	6^{1}	5	4		3	8	12	9			7			2					11						1	10				46

Worthington Cup

First Round	Lincoln C	(a)	3-1
Second Round	Gillingham	(h)	1-2

LDV Vans Trophy

First Round	Darlington	(h)	1-0
Second Round	Carlisle U	(a)	0-1

FA Cup

First Round	St Albans C	(h)	4-1
Second Round	Plymouth Arg	(h)	0-3

STOKE CITY — Division 1

FOUNDATION

The date of the formation of this club has long been in doubt. The year 1863 was claimed, but more recent research by Wade Martin has uncovered nothing earlier than 1868, when a couple of Old Carthusians, who were apprentices at the local works of the old North Staffordshire Railway Company, met with some others from that works, to form Stoke Ramblers. It should also be noted that the old Stoke club went bankrupt in 1908 when a new club was formed.

Britannia Stadium, Stoke-on-Trent ST4 4EG.

Telephone: (01782) 592 222. ***Fax:*** (01782) 592 221.
Commercial Dept: (01782) 592 211.
Football in the Community: (01782) 592 255.
ClubCall: 09068 121 040. ***Website:*** www.stokecityfc.com

Ground Capacity: 28,218.

Record Attendance: 51,380 v Arsenal, Division 1, 29 March 1937.

Record Receipts: £379,000 v Everton, FA Cup 3rd rd, 5 January 2002.

Pitch Measurements: 116yd × 70yd.

Club President: Gordon Banks OBE.

Chairman: Gunnar Thor Gislason.

Vice-chairman: Stefan Geir Thorisson.

Directors: Asgeir Sigurvinsson, Peter Coates, Keith Humphreys.

Chief Executive: Jonathan Fuller.

Manager: Tony Pulis. ***Physio:*** Rick Carter.

Stadium Manager/Safety Officer: J. Alcock.

Colours: Red and white striped shirts, white shorts, red and white hooped stockings.

Change Colours: Blue shirts and shorts with red and white stripe on left hand side, white stockings with blue turnover.

Year Formed: 1863 *(*see Foundation*). ***Turned Professional:*** 1885. ***Ltd Co.:*** 1908.

Previous Names: 1868, Stoke Ramblers; 1870, Stoke; 1925, Stoke City.

Club Nickname: 'The Potters'.

Previous Grounds: 1875, Sweeting's Field; 1878, Victoria Ground (previously known as the Athletic Club Ground); 1997, Britannia Stadium.

First Football League Game: 8 September 1888, Football League, v WBA (h) L 0–2 – Rowley; Clare, Underwood; Ramsey, Shutt, Smith; Sayer, McSkimming, Staton, Edge, Tunnicliffe.

Record League Victory: 10–3 v WBA, Division 1, 4 February 1937 – Doug Westland; Brigham, Harbot; Tutin, Turner (1p), Kirton; Matthews, Antonio (2), Freddie Steele (5), Jimmy Westland, Johnson (2).

HONOURS

Football League: Division 1 best season: 4th, 1935–36, 1946–47; Division 2 – Champions 1932–33, 1962–63, 1992–93; Runners-up 1921–22; Promoted 1978–79 (3rd), Promoted from Division 2 (play-offs) 2001–02; Division 3 (N) – Champions 1926–27.

FA Cup: Semi-finals 1899, 1971, 1972.

Football League Cup: Winners 1972.

Autoglass Trophy: Winners: 1992.

Auto Windscreens Shield: Winners: 2000.

European Competitions: *UEFA Cup:* 1972–73, 1974–75.

SKY SPORTS FACT FILE

On 16 February 1952 Stoke City goalkeeper Dennis Herod broke two fingers in the match at Aston Villa. Substitutes were not permitted and he was put out on the wing and scored the winning goal in the 3-2 win.

Record Cup Victory: 7–1 v Burnley, FA Cup 2nd rd (replay), 20 February 1896 – Clawley; Clare, Eccles; Turner, Grewe, Robertson; Willie Maxwell, Dickson, A. Maxwell (3), Hyslop (4), Schofield.

Record Defeat: 0–10 v Preston NE, Division 1, 14 September 1889.

Most League Points (2 for a win): 63, Division 3 (N), 1926–27.

Most League Points (3 for a win): 93, Division 2, 1992–93.

Most League Goals: 92, Division 3 (N), 1926–27.

Highest League Scorer in Season: Freddie Steele, 33, Division 1, 1936–37.

Most League Goals in Total Aggregate: Freddie Steele, 142, 1934–49.

Most League Goals in One Match: 7, Neville Coleman v Lincoln C, Division 2, 23 February 1957.

Most Capped Player: Gordon Banks, 36 (73), England.

Most League Appearances: Eric Skeels, 506, 1958–76.

Youngest League Player: Peter Bullock, 16 years 163 days v Swansea C, 19 April 1958.

Record Transfer Fee Received: £2,750,000 from QPR for Mike Sheron, July 1997.

Record Transfer Fee Paid: £600,000 to Orgryte for Brynjar Gunnarsson, December 1999.

Football League Record: 1888 Founder Member of Football League; 1890 Not re-elected; 1891 Re-elected; relegated in 1907, and after one year in Division 2, resigned for financial reasons; 1919 re-elected to Division 2; 1922–23 Division 1; 1923–26 Division 2; 1926–27 Division 3 (N); 1927–33 Division 2; 1933–53 Division 1; 1953–63 Division 2; 1963–77 Division 1; 1977–79 Division 2; 1979–85 Division 1; 1985–90 Division 2; 1990–92 Division 3; 1992–93 Division 2; 1993–98 Division 1; 1998–2002 Division 2; 2002– Division 1.

MANAGERS

Tom Slaney 1874–83
(Secretary-Manager)
Walter Cox 1883–84
(Secretary-Manager)
Harry Lockett 1884–90
Joseph Bradshaw 1890–92
Arthur Reeves 1892–95
William Rowley 1895–97
H. D. Austerberry 1897–1908
A. J. Barker 1908–14
Peter Hodge 1914–15
Joe Schofield 1915–19
Arthur Shallcross 1919–23
John 'Jock' Rutherford 1923
Tom Mather 1923–35
Bob McGrory 1935–52
Frank Taylor 1952–60
Tony Waddington 1960–77
George Eastham 1977–78
Alan A'Court 1978
Alan Durban 1978–81
Richie Barker 1981–83
Bill Asprey 1984–85
Mick Mills 1985–89
Alan Ball 1989–91
Lou Macari 1991–93
Joe Jordan 1993–94
Lou Macari 1994–97
Chic Bates 1997–98
Chris Kamara 1998
Brian Little 1998–99
Gary Megson 1999
Gudjon Thordarson 1999–2002
Steve Cotterill 2002
Tony Pulis November 2002–

LATEST SEQUENCES

Longest Sequence of League Wins: 8, 30.3.1895 – 21.9.1895.

Longest Sequence of League Defeats: 11, 6.4.1985 – 17.8.1985.

Longest Sequence of League Draws: 5, 21.3.1987 – 11.4.1987.

Longest Sequence of Unbeaten League Matches: 25, 5.9.1992 – 20.2.1993.

Longest Sequence Without a League Win: 17, 22.4.1989 – 14.10.1989.

Successive Scoring Runs: 21 from 24.12.1921.

Successive Non-scoring Runs: 8 from 29.12.1984.

TEN YEAR LEAGUE RECORD

		P	*W*	*D*	*L*	*F*	*A*	*Pts*	*Pos*
1993-94	Div 1	46	18	13	15	57	59	67	10
1994-95	Div 1	46	16	15	15	50	53	63	11
1995-96	Div 1	46	20	13	13	60	49	73	4
1996-97	Div 1	46	18	10	18	51	57	64	12
1997-98	Div 1	46	11	13	22	44	74	46	23
1998-99	Div 2	46	21	6	19	59	63	69	8
1999-2000	Div 2	46	23	13	10	68	42	82	6
2000-01	Div 2	46	21	14	11	74	49	77	5
2001-02	Div 2	46	23	11	12	67	40	80	5
2002-03	Div 1	46	12	14	20	45	69	50	21

DID YOU KNOW?

Apart from two pre-war seasons with Blackburn Rovers, Tommy Sale scored 282 goals in 483 matches for Stoke City (including wartime football) from Christmas Day 1930 until his last match on 8 April 1946. He continued with Northwich and Hednesford.

STOKE CITY 2002–03 LEAGUE RECORD

Match No.	Date	Venue	Opponents	Result	H/T Score	Lg. Pos.	Goalscorers	Attendance
1	Aug 10	A	Sheffield W	D 0-0	0-0	—		26,746
2	14	H	Leicester C	L 0-1	0-1	—		14,028
3	17	H	Bradford C	W 2-1	2-0	13	Cooke [4], Marteinsson [34]	12,424
4	24	A	Preston NE	L 3-4	1-2	13	Clarke 2 (2 pens) [7, 65], Cooke [89]	15,422
5	26	H	Norwich C	D 1-1	0-0	15	Commons [74]	13,931
6	31	A	Derby Co	L 0-2	0-0	19		21,723
7	Sept 14	A	Burnley	L 1-2	0-0	22	Gudjonsson [74]	14,244
8	17	A	Brighton & HA	W 2-1	1-0	—	Mooney (pen) [17], Cooke [76]	6369
9	22	H	Ipswich T	W 2-1	1-0	15	Shtanyuk [17], Cooke [80]	14,587
10	25	H	Nottingham F	D 2-2	1-2	—	Shtanyuk [13], Goodfellow [72]	14,554
11	28	A	Reading	D 1-1	1-1	14	Van Deurzen [39]	13,646
12	Oct 5	H	Crystal Palace	D 1-1	0-0	15	Iwelumo [85]	14,214
13	19	H	Wolverhampton W	L 0-2	0-0	19		16,885
14	23	A	Sheffield U	L 1-2	0-0	—	Greenacre [84]	15,163
15	26	A	Rotherham U	L 0-4	0-2	20		7078
16	30	H	Watford	L 1-2	0-2	—	Mooney [72]	11,215
17	Nov 2	A	Walsall	L 2-4	0-0	21	Cooke [77], Greenacre [81]	6391
18	9	H	Grimsby T	L 1-2	0-2	22	Mooney (pen) [50]	11,488
19	16	A	Portsmouth	L 0-3	0-0	22		18,701
20	23	H	Millwall	L 0-1	0-1	22		13,776
21	30	A	Gillingham	D 1-1	0-0	22	Clarke [56]	8150
22	Dec 7	H	Coventry C	L 1-2	1-2	22	Hoekstra [35]	12,760
23	14	H	Portsmouth	D 1-1	1-0	22	Gunnarsson [34]	13,330
24	21	A	Wimbledon	D 1-1	0-0	22	Iwelumo [88]	1697
25	26	A	Bradford C	L 2-4	2-1	22	Marteinsson [9], Henry [23]	14,575
26	28	H	Sheffield W	W 3-2	1-1	22	Iwelumo 2 [16, 66], Gunnarsson [90]	16,042
27	Jan 1	H	Preston NE	W 2-1	2-0	22	Gunnarsson [43], Hoekstra [45]	14,862
28	11	A	Leicester C	D 0-0	0-0	22		25,038
29	18	H	Derby Co	L 1-3	0-0	22	Greenacre [63]	17,308
30	Feb 1	A	Norwich C	D 2-2	0-2	21	Gunnarsson [63], Mills [88]	20,186
31	8	A	Grimsby T	L 0-2	0-2	22		5657
32	22	A	Nottingham F	L 0-6	0-4	24		24,085
33	26	H	Walsall	W 1-0	1-0	—	Mills [19]	10,409
34	Mar 1	H	Burnley	L 0-1	0-0	23		12,874
35	5	H	Brighton & HA	W 1-0	0-0	—	Greenacre [83]	21,023
36	8	A	Ipswich T	D 0-0	0-0	22		24,547
37	15	H	Sheffield U	D 0-0	0-0	22		14,449
38	18	A	Wolverhampton W	D 0-0	0-0	—		25,235
39	22	A	Watford	W 2-1	1-0	21	Hoekstra 2 (1 pen) [34 (p), 49]	12,570
40	Apr 5	H	Gillingham	D 0-0	0-0	22		12,746
41	9	H	Rotherham U	W 2-0	2-0	—	Warhurst [21], Cooke [40]	19,553
42	12	A	Millwall	L 1-3	0-1	21	Shtanyuk [73]	8725
43	19	H	Wimbledon	W 2-1	2-0	21	Gunnarsson [29], Akinbiyi [45]	12,587
44	21	A	Coventry C	W 1-0	0-0	21	Iwelumo (pen) [57]	12,675
45	26	A	Crystal Palace	L 0-1	0-0	21		16,064
46	May 4	H	Reading	W 1-0	0-0	21	Akinbiyi [55]	20,477

Final League Position: 21

GOALSCORERS

League (45): Cooke 6, Gunnarsson 5, Iwelumo 5 (1 pen), Greenacre 4, Hoekstra 4 (1 pen), Clarke 3 (2 pens), Mooney 3 (2 pens), Shtanyuk 3, Akinbiyi 2, Marteinsson 2, Mills 2, Commons 1, Goodfellow 1, Gudjonsson 1, Henry 1, Van Deurzen 1, Warhurst 1.
Worthington Cup (0).
FA Cup (6): Iwelumo 3 (1 pen), Greenacre 2, Hoekstra 1.

Cutler N 20	Gunnarsson B 40	Clarke C 27 + 4	Henry K 15 + 3	Handyside P 44	Shtanyuk S 44	Gudjonsson B 25 + 11	O'Connor J 43	Goodfellow M 6 + 14	Iwelumo C 15 + 17	Commons K 6 + 2	Wilson B 1 + 2	Van Deurzen J 7 + 5	Cooke A 24 + 7	Neal L 7 + 9	Marteinsson P 7 + 5	Thomas W 41	Hoekstra P 26 + 4	Mooney T 11 + 1	Greenacre C 18 + 12	Crossley M 12	Banks S 14	Hall M 23 + 1	Richardson F 6 + 1	Mills L 7 + 4	Williams M 5 + 1	Warhurst P 4 + 1	Akinbiyi A 4	Wilson M 4	Match No.
1	2	3	4	5	6	7¹	8	9	10	11²	12	13																	1
1	2	3	4³	5	6	7²	8	10¹	12	11	13		9	14															2
1	2	3	4		6	12	8	13	10²	11	5¹		9		7														3
1	4³	3	7¹	5	6	12	8	10		11²		13	9	14		2													4
1	4	3	7¹	5	6	12	8	10²	13	11			9			2													5
1	4	3	7	5	6	12	8	10		11¹			9			2													6
1	4³	3		5	6	7	8	12		13		11²	9¹			2	14	10■											7
1	4	3	12	5	6	7¹	8		13			11²	9			2		10											8
1	4	3	13	5	6	7	8			12²		11¹	9			2		10											9
1		3	4	5	6	7	8	12	13			11¹	9²			2	14	10³											10
1		3	4	5	6	7	8	12	13			11³	9²	14		2	10¹												11
1		3	4	5	6	7	8	12	13			11¹	9²			2	10												12
1	4	3		5	6	7¹	8	12				11²	9	13		2	10³		14										13
1	4	3		5	6	7¹	8	12					9²			2	11	10	13										14
1	4	3		5	6	7	8	12				13	9²			2	11¹	10³	14										15
1	5	3	4		6	12	8	7¹	13				9²	11³		2		10	14										16
1	4	3		5	6	7¹	8		9²				12	11		2		10	13										17
1	4	3		5	6	7²	8		12				13			2	11	10	9¹										18
1	4	3	2	5		7¹	8		12			13			10³	6	11²	9	14										19
1	4	3		5	6	7	8		9²				12			2¹	11	10	13										20
	4	3¹	12	5	6	7	8		9						11	2			10	1									21
	4■			5	6	7	8	12	9²				13			2■	11¹		10		1	3							22
	4		8¹	5	6	7		12					9	11³	14	2		13	10²		1	3							23
			2	5	6	7	8		12			13	9¹	11³	4		10²		14		1	3							24
			4	5	6	12	8		9					7²	11¹	2	13		10		1	3							25
	4			5	6	7¹	8		9						12	2	11		10		1	3							26
	4			5	6	7	8		9					12		2	11¹		10		1	3							27
	4			5■	6		8	12	9						13	2	11²		10¹		1	3	7						28
	4			5	6	7¹	8	12	9²							2			10		1	3	11	13					29
	4			5	6		8		9²						12	2	11		10¹		1	3	7	13					30
	4			5	6■	12	8		9²							2	11		13		1	3	7¹	10					31
			4	5		12	8							13	6■	2	11²		10¹		1	3	7	9					32
	4			5	6	7	8		12					13		2	11		10²		1	3		9¹					33
	4			5	6	7	8		12				13			2	11		10²		1	3		9¹					34
	4			5	6	7	8		12					13		2³	11²		10		1	3	14	9¹					35
	4	3		5	6		8		12				13	14	11³				10¹	1		2	7	9²					36
	4			5	6	12	8		10¹				9			2	11		13	1		3						7²	37
	7	11		5	6		8						9¹			2			12	1		3			4			10	38
	7	3		5	6		8	12	13				9²		14	2	11¹			1					4			10³	39
	7	3		5	6	12			9²							2	11			1		13		14		4	10³	8¹	40
	7	12		5	6								9	8¹		2	11		10	1		3				4			41
	7	12		5	6		8						9			2	13			1		3		14	4²	11¹	10³		42
	7	12		5	6	13	8						9			2	11³			1		3			14	4¹	10²		43
	7	11		5	6		8		12							2	10²		13	1		3		9¹	4				44
	7	11		5	6		8	12	13				9³			2			10²	1		3			4¹	14			45
	4	12		5	6		8						13	7¹		2	11		10	1		3					9²		46

Worthington Cup
First Round Bury (a) 0-1

FA Cup
Third Round Wigan Ath (h) 3-0
Fourth Round Bournemouth (h) 3-0
Fifth Round Chelsea (h) 0-2

SUNDERLAND — Division 1

FOUNDATION

A Scottish schoolmaster named James Allan, working at Hendon Board School, took the initiative in the foundation of Sunderland in 1879 when they were formed as The Sunderland and District Teachers' Association FC at a meeting in the Adults School, Norfolk Street. Due to financial difficulties, they quickly allowed members from outside the teaching profession and so became Sunderland AFC in October 1880.

Sunderland Stadium of Light, Sunderland, Tyne and Wear SR5 1SU.

Telephone: (0191) 551 5000. ***Fax:*** (0191) 551 5123.
Website: www.safc.com ***ClubCall:*** 09068 121 140.
Ticket Office: (0191) 551 5151.
Club Shop: (0191) 551 5050.
Tour Hotline: (0191) 551 5055.

Ground Capacity: 48,353

Record Attendance: Stadium of Light: 48,353 v Liverpool, FA Premier League, 13 April 2002. FA Premier League figure (46,062). Roker Park: 75,118 v Derby Co, FA Cup 6th rd replay, 8 March 1933.

Record Receipts: £862,840 v Manchester U, FA Premier League, 13 October 2001.

Pitch Measurements: 105m × 68m.

Chairman: R. S. Murray. ***Vice-chairman:*** John Fickling.

Directors: Jim Slater, Lesley Callaghan, Mark Blackbourne, Peter Walker.
Associate Directors: G. S. Wood, J. G. Wood.

Manager: Mick McCarthy.

First Team Coach: Ian Evans.

Reserve Team Manager: Jocky Scott.

Physio: Mark Leather.

Academy Director: Kees Zwamborn.

Community Programme Officer: Bob Oates.

Secretary: Jane Purdon.

Marketing Director: Jim Slater.

Safety Officer: John Davidson.

Colours: Red and white striped shirts, black shorts, black stockings.

Change Colours: Navy blue shirts with red trim, navy shorts, navy blue stockings with red trim.

Year Formed: 1879.

Turned Professional: 1886. ***Ltd Co.:*** 1906.

Previous Name: 1879, Sunderland and District Teacher's AFC; 1880, Sunderland.

Previous Grounds: 1879, Blue House Field, Hendon; 1882, Groves Field, Ashbrooke; 1883, Horatio Street; 1884, Abbs Field, Fulwell; 1886, Newcastle Road; 1898, Roker Park; 1997, Stadium of Light.

HONOURS

Football League: Division 1 – Champions 1891–92, 1892–93, 1894–95, 1901–02, 1912–13, 1935–36, 1995–96, 1998–99; Runners-up 1893–94, 1897–98, 1900–01, 1922–23, 1934–35; Division 2 – Champions 1975–76; Runners-up 1963–64, 1979–80; 1989–90 (play-offs). Division 3 – Champions 1987–88.

FA Cup: Winners 1937, 1973; Runners-up 1913, 1992.

Football League Cup: Runners-up 1985.

European Competitions: *European Cup-Winners' Cup:* 1973–74.

SKY SPORTS FACT FILE

Hugh Wilson, signed by Sunderland from Newmilns in May 1890 and already a Scottish international wing-half, was the player thought to be largely responsible for perfecting the two-handed throw-in.

First Football League Game: 13 September 1890, Football League, v Burnley (h) L 2–3 – Kirtley; Porteous, Oliver; Wilson, Auld, Gibson; Spence (1), Miller, Campbell (1), Scott, D. Hannah.

Record League Victory: 9–1 v Newcastle U (a), Division 1, 5 December 1908 – Roose; Forster, Melton; Daykin, Thomson, Low; Mordue (1), Hogg (3), Brown, Holley (3), Bridgett (2).

Record Cup Victory: 11–1 v Fairfield, FA Cup 1st rd, 2 February 1895 – Doig; McNeill, Johnston; Dunlop, McCreadie (1), Wilson; Gillespie (1), Millar (5), Campbell, Hannah (3), Scott (1).

Record Defeat: 0–8 v Sheff Wed, Division 1, 26 December 1911. 0–8 v West Ham U, Division 1, 19 October 1968. 0–8 v Watford, Division 1, 25 September 1982.

Most League Points (2 for a win): 61, Division 2, 1963–64.

Most League Points (3 for a win): 105, Division 1, 1998–99 (Football League Record).

Most League Goals: 109, Division 1, 1935–36.

Highest League Scorer in Season: Dave Halliday, 43, Division 1, 1928–29.

Most League Goals in Total Aggregate: Charlie Buchan, 209, 1911–25.

Most League Goals in One Match: 5, Charlie Buchan v Liverpool, Division 1, 7 December 1919; 5, Bobby Gurney v Bolton W, Division 1, 7 December 1935; 5, Dominic Sharkey v Norwich C, Division 2, 20 February 1962.

Most Capped Player: Charlie Hurley, 38 (40), Republic of Ireland.

Most League Appearances: Jim Montgomery, 537, 1962–77.

Youngest League Player: Derek Forster, 15 years 184 days v Leicester C, 22 August 1964.

Record Transfer Fee Received: £5,600,000 from Leeds U for Michael Bridges, July 1999.

Record Transfer Fee Paid: £8,000,000 to Rangers for Tore Andre Flo, August 2002.

Football League Record: 1890 Elected to Division 1; 1958–64 Division 2; 1964–70 Division 1; 1970–76 Division 2; 1976–77 Division 1; 1977–80 Division 2; 1980–85 Division 1; 1985–87 Division 2; 1987–88 Division 3; 1988–90 Division 2; 1990–91 Division 1; 1991–92 Division 2; 1992–96 Division 1; 1996–97 FA Premier League; 1997– 99 Division 1; 1999–2003 FA Premier League; 2003– Division 1.

MANAGERS

Tom Watson 1888–96
Bob Campbell 1896–99
Alex Mackie 1899–1905
Bob Kyle 1905–28
Johnny Cochrane 1928–39
Bill Murray 1939–57
Alan Brown 1957–64
George Hardwick 1964–65
Ian McColl 1965–68
Alan Brown 1968–72
Bob Stokoe 1972–76
Jimmy Adamson 1976–78
Ken Knighton 1979–81
Alan Durban 1981–84
Len Ashurst 1984–85
Lawrie McMenemy 1985–87
Denis Smith 1987–91
Malcolm Crosby 1992–93
Terry Butcher 1993
Mick Buxton 1993–95
Peter Reid 1995–2002
Howard Wilkinson 2002–03
Mick McCarthy March 2003–

LATEST SEQUENCES

Longest Sequence of League Wins: 13, 14.11.1891 – 2.4.1892.

Longest Sequence of League Defeats: 15, 18.1.2003 – 11.5.2003 (ongoing).

Longest Sequence of League Draws: 6, 26.3.1949 – 19.4.1949.

Longest Sequence of Unbeaten League Matches: 19, 3.5.1998 – 14.11.1998.

Longest Sequence Without a League Win: 20, 21.12.2002 – 11.5.2003 (ongoing).

Successive Scoring Runs: 29 from 8.11.1997

Successive Non-scoring Runs: 10 from 27.11.1976.

TEN YEAR LEAGUE RECORD

		P	*W*	*D*	*L*	*F*	*A*	*Pts*	*Pos*
1993-94	Div 1	46	19	8	19	54	57	65	12
1994-95	Div 1	46	12	18	16	41	45	54	20
1995-96	Div 1	46	22	17	7	59	33	83	1
1996-97	PR Lge	38	10	10	18	35	53	40	18
1997-98	Div 1	46	26	12	8	86	50	90	3
1998-99	Div 1	46	31	12	3	91	28	105	1
1999-2000	PR Lge	38	16	10	12	57	56	58	7
2000-01	PR Lge	38	15	12	11	46	41	57	7
2001-02	PR Lge	38	10	10	18	29	51	40	17
2002-03	PR Lge	38	4	7	27	21	65	19	20

DID YOU KNOW ?

On 5 February 2003 Kevin Phillips' 10th minute goal for Sunderland against Blackburn Rovers in the FA Cup fourth round was his 10th in the competition, the highest total for one player for the club since 1945–46.

SUNDERLAND 2002–03 LEAGUE RECORD

Match No.	Date	Venue	Opponents	Result	H/T Score	Lg. Pos.	Goalscorers	Attendance
1	Aug 17	A	Blackburn R	D 0-0	0-0	—		27,122
2	24	H	Everton	L 0-1	0-0	14		37,698
3	28	A	Leeds U	W 1-0	0-0	—	McAteer [46]	39,929
4	31	H	Manchester U	D 1-1	0-1	11	Flo [70]	47,586
5	Sept 10	A	Middlesbrough	L 0-3	0-2	—		32,167
6	14	H	Fulham	L 0-3	0-1	18		35,432
7	21	A	Newcastle U	L 0-2	0-2	19		52,181
8	28	H	Aston Villa	W 1-0	0-0	16	Bellion [70]	40,492
9	Oct 6	A	Arsenal	L 1-3	0-3	17	Craddock [82]	37,902
10	19	H	West Ham U	L 0-1	0-1	19		44,352
11	28	A	Bolton W	D 1-1	1-0	—	Gray [45]	23,036
12	Nov 3	A	Charlton Ath	D 1-1	1-0	18	Flo [15]	26,255
13	10	H	Tottenham H	W 2-0	0-0	16	Phillips [60], Flo [62]	40,024
14	17	A	Liverpool	D 0-0	0-0	17		43,074
15	23	H	Birmingham C	L 0-1	0-0	17		38,803
16	30	A	Chelsea	L 0-3	0-0	18		38,949
17	Dec 9	H	Manchester C	L 0-3	0-1	—		36,511
18	15	H	Liverpool	W 2-1	1-0	17	McCann [36], Proctor [85]	37,118
19	21	A	WBA	D 2-2	0-2	17	Phillips 2 [56, 64]	26,448
20	26	H	Leeds U	L 1-2	1-0	18	Proctor [34]	44,029
21	28	A	Southampton	L 1-2	0-0	18	Flo [77]	31,423
22	Jan 1	A	Manchester U	L 1-2	1-0	18	Veron (og) [5]	67,609
23	11	H	Blackburn R	D 0-0	0-0	18		36,529
24	18	A	Everton	L 1-2	1-0	18	Kilbane [34]	37,049
25	28	H	Southampton	L 0-1	0-0	—		34,102
26	Feb 1	H	Charlton Ath	L 1-3	0-3	20	Phillips (pen) [81]	36,042
27	8	A	Tottenham H	L 1-4	1-2	20	Phillips [26]	36,075
28	22	H	Middlesbrough	L 1-3	0-2	20	Phillips [56]	42,134
29	Mar 1	A	Fulham	L 0-1	0-0	20		16,286
30	15	H	Bolton W	L 0-2	0-0	20		42,124
31	22	A	West Ham U	L 0-2	0-1	20		35,033
32	Apr 5	H	Chelsea	L 1-2	1-0	20	Thornton [12]	40,011
33	12	A	Birmingham C	L 0-2	0-1	20		29,132
34	19	H	WBA	L 1-2	0-2	20	Stewart [70]	36,025
35	21	A	Manchester C	L 0-3	0-2	20		34,596
36	26	H	Newcastle U	L 0-1	0-1	20		45,067
37	May 3	A	Aston Villa	L 0-1	0-0	20		36,963
38	11	H	Arsenal	L 0-4	0-2	20		40,188

Final League Position: 20

GOALSCORERS

League (21): Phillips 6 (1 pen), Flo 4, Proctor 2, Bellion 1, Craddock 1, Gray 1, Kilbane 1, McAteer 1, McCann 1, Stewart 1, Thornton 1, own goal 1.
Worthington Cup (10): Stewart 4, Flo 2, Arca 1, Kyle 1, McCann 1, Reyna 1.
FA Cup (8): Phillips 3, Proctor 2, Arca 1, McCann 1, Stewart 1.

Sorensen T 21	Wright S 25 + 1	Gray M 32	McCann G 29 + 1	Babb P 26	Bjorklund J 19 + 1	McAteer J 9	Reyna C 11	Phillips K 32	Butler T 7	Kilbane K 30	Quinn N — + 8	Kyle K 9 + 8	Piper M 8 + 5	Thirlwell P 12 + 7	Arca J 7 + 6	Flo T 23 + 6	Stewart M 9 + 10	Bellion D 5 + 6	Williams D 12 + 4	Craddock J 25	Myhre T 1 + 1	Macho J 12 + 1	McCartney G 16 + 8	Proctor M 11 + 10	Oster J 1 + 2	Thornton S 11	Clark B — + 1	El Karkouri T 8	Emerson 1	Poom M 4	Dickman J — + 1	Ryan R — + 2	Black C 2	Match No.
1	2	3	4	5	6	7	8	9	10	11[1]	12																							1
1	2	3	4	5	6	7[2]	8	9	11		13	10[1]	12																					2
1	2	3		5	6	7	8	9[1]	11			12	10[2]	4	13																			3
1	2	3		5	6	7	4	9	11		12		8[2]	13		10[1]																		4
1	2	3		5	6	7	4		11[1]				8			10	9	12																5
1	2	3	12	5	6	7[1]	4		11[2]		13		8			10	9																	6
1	2	3	4	5	6[2]	7[1]	8			11	12		10			9[3]	14		13															7
1	2[2]		4	5			8			3	12		7		11	10[1]	14	9[3]	13	6														8
1[G]			4	5			8			3	12		13	10[2]	11	9[1]		7	2	6	15													9
	2	3	4	5			8[2]	10		11	12		7[3]	13			9[1]	14		6		1												10
	2	11	4	5			8[2]	10[1]		7				13		12		9		6	1[G]	15	3											11
	2	3	8	5	6			10[2]		7			13	11[1]		9			12	4		1												12
	2	11	4	5				10[2]		7		13		12		9				6		1	3	8[1]										13
		11	4	5	2			10[1]		7		13		12		9[2]	14			6		1	3	8[3]										14
	2	11	4	5				10		7						9		12		6		1	3	8[1]										15
	2	3	4	5	11[1]			10		7[2]				8		9		12		6		1	13											16
	2	11[2]		5	6			10[1]		8		14		4		9[3]	13	12				1	3	7										17
	2	11[2]	4	5	6			10		8				7		9[1]	12					1	3	13										18
	2	11	4	5				10		8				7		9		12		6		1	3[1]											19
	2	3	4	5				10		11		12		8[2]		9[1]	14			6		1	13	7[3]										20
	2	11[2]	4	5	12			10[3]		8		9[1]		7		13				6		1	3	14										21
	2		4[1]	5				10		11				8		7[2]	9[3]		12	6		1	3	13	14									22
1			4	5				10						8	12	9	13		2	6			3	7[2]	11[1]									23
1			4	5				10		11				8[1]	12	9[2]			2	6			3	13		7								24
1		2	4	5[1]				10		11[3]		13		12	8		9[2]			6			3	7			14							25
1	2	3	4	5				10		11[2]					8	9	12			6			13	7[1]										26
1	2		8[2]					10					12	13	11	14				6			3	9[3]		7		5	4[1]					27
1	2	3[1]	4			8		10		11[3]			13		12	9		7[2]		6				14				5						28
1	2	3[1]	4			8		10		11			7[2]			9				6			12	13				5						29
1	2[1]	11			6			10				13			12	9[3]	14		4				3	7[2]		8		5						30
1		11			6			10	4[1]	7		13				9[2]	12		2				3[3]	14		8		5						31
1		3	4		6			10		11[1]		9					8		2				12			7		5						32
	12	3	4		6[2]			10		11		9					8[■]		2				13			7		5[1]		1				33
		3	4[1]					10		11		9[3]			12		8		2	6			13	14		7		5[2]		1				34
		3						10		11		9[2]			4[3]	12	8[1]		2	6			5	13		7				1	14			35
1		3			6					11		9			4[1]	12		7	2	5				10[2]		8						13		36
		3	4		6			10		11		9[1]				12			2	5				13		8				1			7[2]	37
1		3	4		6			10		11		9							2[1]	5			12		13	8[3]						14	7[2]	38

Worthington Cup

Second Round	Cambridge U	(a)	7-0
Third Round	Arsenal	(a)	3-2
Fourth Round	Sheffield U	(a)	0-2

FA Cup

Third Round	Bolton W	(a)	1-1
		(h)	2-0
Fourth Round	Blackburn R	(a)	3-3
		(h)	2-2
Fifth Round	Watford	(h)	0-1

SWANSEA CITY

Division 3

FOUNDATION

The earliest Association Football in Wales was played in the Northern part of the country and no international took place in the South until 1894, when a local paper still thought it necessary to publish an outline of the rules and an illustration of the pitch markings. There had been an earlier Swansea club, but this has no connection with Swansea Town (now City) formed at a public meeting in June 1912.

Vetch Field, Swansea SA1 3SU.
Telephone: (01792) 633 400. ***Fax:*** (01792) 646 120.
Website: www.swanseacity.net
Email: admin@swanseacityafc.fsnet.co.uk
Club Shop: (01792) 633 425.
Commercial Department: (01792) 633 413.
Youth Development: (01792) 633 420/1.

Ground Capacity: 11,807.

Record Attendance: 32,796 v Arsenal, FA Cup 4th rd, 17 February 1968.

Record Receipts: £36,477.42 v Liverpool, Division 1, 18 September 1982.

Pitch Measurements: 112yd × 74yd.

President: Professor David Farmer.

Directors: Huw Jenkins, David Morgan, Leigh Dineen, Brian Katzen

Non-Executive Directors: Donald Keefe, Steve Penny.

Director of Football: Brian Flynn.

First Team Coach: Kevin Reeves.

Assistant Coach: Alan Curtis.

Physio: Richard Evans.

Youth Development Officer: Wayne Powell.

Football Development Officer: Lyndon Jones.

Club Secretary: Jackie Rockey.

Commercial Manager: Dianne Griffiths. ***Safety Officer:*** John Morgan.

Programme Editor: Colin Jones (01792) 633 419.

Colours: All white with black trim.

Change Colours: All black with white trim.

Year Formed: 1912. ***Turned Professional:*** 1912. ***Ltd Co.:*** 1912.

Previous Name: Swansea Town until February 1970. ***Club Nicknames:*** 'The Swans', 'The Jacks'.

First Football League Game: 28 August 1920, Division 3, v Portsmouth (a) L 0–3 – Crumley; Robson, Evans; Smith, Holdsworth, Williams; Hole, I. Jones, Edmundson, Rigsby, Spottiswood.

Record League Victory: 8–0 v Hartlepool U, Division 4, 1 April 1978 – Barber; Evans, Bartley, Lally (1) (Morris), May, Bruton, Kevin Moore, Robbie James (3 incl. 1p), Curtis (3), Toshack (1), Chappell.

HONOURS

Football League: Division 1 best season: 6th, 1981–82; Division 2 – Promoted 1980–81 (3rd); Division 3 (S) – Champions 1924–25, 1948–49; Division 3 – Champions 1999–2000; Promoted 1978–79 (3rd); Division 4 – Promoted 1969–70 (3rd), 1977–78 (3rd), 1987–88 (play-offs).

FA Cup: Semi-finals 1926, 1964.

Football League Cup: best season: 4th rd, 1965, 1977.

Welsh Cup: Winners 10 times; Runners-up 8 times.

Autoglass Trophy: Winners 1994.

European Competitions: *European Cup-Winners' Cup:* 1961–62, 1966–67, 1981–82, 1982–83, 1983–84, 1989–90, 1991–92.

SKY SPORTS FACT FILE

Despite a goal-starved start to 1920–21 in which they managed only ten goals in ten games including a 5-2 win, the then Swansea Town finished a creditable fifth in the inaugural season of the Third Division.

Record Cup Victory: 12–0 v Sliema W (Malta), ECWC 1st rd 1st leg, 15 September 1982 – Davies; Marustik, Hadziabdic (1), Irwin (1), Kennedy, Rajkovic (1), Loveridge (2) (Leighton James), Robbie James, Charles (2), Stevenson (1), Latchford (1) (Walsh (3)).

Record Defeat: 0–8 v Liverpool, FA Cup 3rd rd, 9 January 1990. 0–8 v Monaco, ECWC, 1st rd 2nd leg, 1 October 1991.

Most League Points (2 for a win): 62, Division 3 (S), 1948–49.

Most League Points (3 for a win): 85, Division 3, 1999–2000.

Most League Goals: 90, Division 2, 1956–57.

Highest League Scorer in Season: Cyril Pearce, 35, Division 2, 1931–32.

Most League Goals in Total Aggregate: Ivor Allchurch, 166, 1949–58, 1965–68.

Most League Goals in One Match: 5, Jack Fowler v Charlton Ath, Division 3S, 27 December 1924.

Most Capped Player: Ivor Allchurch, 42 (68), Wales.

Most League Appearances: Wilfred Milne, 585, 1919–37.

Youngest League Player: Nigel Dalling, 15 years 289 days v Southport, 6 December 1974.

Record Transfer Fee Received: £400,000 from Bristol C for Steve Torpey, August 1997.

Record Transfer Fee Paid: £340,000 to Liverpool for Colin Irwin, August 1981.

Football League Record: 1920 Original Member of Division 3; 1921–25 Division 3 (S); 1925–47 Division 2; 1947–49 Division 3 (S); 1949–65 Division 2; 1965–67 Division 3; 1967–70 Division 4; 1970–73 Division 3; 1973–78 Division 4; 1978–79 Division 3; 1979–81 Division 2; 1981–83 Division 1; 1983–84 Division 2; 1984–86 Division 3; 1986–88 Division 4; 1988–92 Division 3; 1992–96 Division 2; 1996–2000 Division 3; 2000–01 Division 2; 2001– Division 3.

MANAGERS

Walter Whittaker 1912–14
William Bartlett 1914–15
Joe Bradshaw 1919–26
Jimmy Thomson 1927–31
Neil Harris 1934–39
Haydn Green 1939–47
Bill McCandless 1947–55
Ron Burgess 1955–58
Trevor Morris 1958–65
Glyn Davies 1965–66
Billy Lucas 1967–69
Roy Bentley 1969–72
Harry Gregg 1972–75
Harry Griffiths 1975–77
John Toshack 1978–83
(resigned October re-appointed in December) 1983–84
Colin Appleton 1984
John Bond 1984–85
Tommy Hutchison 1985–86
Terry Yorath 1986–89
Ian Evans 1989–90
Terry Yorath 1990–91
Frank Burrows 1991–95
Bobby Smith 1995
Kevin Cullis 1996
Jan Molby 1996–97
Micky Adams 1997
Alan Cork 1997–98
John Hollins 1998–2001
Colin Addison 2001–02
Nick Cusack 2002
Brian Flynn September 2002–

LATEST SEQUENCES

Longest Sequence of League Wins: 9, 27.11.1999 – 22.01.2000.

Longest Sequence of League Defeats: 9, 26.1.1991 – 19.3.1991.

Longest Sequence of League Draws: 5, 5.1.1993 – 5.2.1993.

Longest Sequence of Unbeaten League Matches: 19, 19.10.1970 – 9.3.1971.

Longest Sequence Without a League Win: 15, 25.3.1989 – 2.9.1989.

Successive Scoring Runs: 27 from 28.8.1947.

Successive Non-scoring Runs: 6 from 6.2.1996.

TEN YEAR LEAGUE RECORD

		P	W	D	L	F	A	Pts	Pos
1993-94	Div 2	46	16	12	18	56	58	60	13
1994-95	Div 2	46	19	14	13	57	45	71	10
1995-96	Div 2	46	11	14	21	43	79	47	22
1996-97	Div 3	46	21	8	17	62	58	71	5
1997-98	Div 3	46	13	11	22	49	62	50	20
1998-99	Div 3	46	19	14	13	56	48	71	7
1999-2000	Div 3	46	24	13	9	51	30	85	1
2000-01	Div 2	46	8	13	25	47	73	37	23
2001-02	Div 3	46	13	12	21	53	77	51	20
2002-03	Div 3	46	12	13	21	48	65	49	21

DID YOU KNOW?

In their 1924–25 Division 3 (South) championship-winning season Swansea Town were unbeaten at home, dropping just four points. In 1948–49 when they were again top they did even better and were only held to a draw on one occasion at the Vetch.

SWANSEA CITY 2002–03 LEAGUE RECORD

Match No.	Date	Venue	Opponents	Result		H/T Score	Lg. Pos.	Goalscorers	Attendance
1	Aug 10	H	Rushden & D	D	2-2	1-1	—	Thomas [15], Reid [64]	6327
2	13	A	Darlington	D	2-2	0-0	—	Smith D [61], Watkin [89]	3913
3	17	A	Bury	L	2-3	0-2	18	Thomas [64], Swailes (og) [78]	2348
4	24	H	Bournemouth	W	2-0	1-0	11	Wood [1], Mumford [83]	4325
5	27	A	Bristol R	L	1-3	0-1	—	Moss [80]	6644
6	31	H	York C	L	1-2	0-1	21	Moss [77]	4086
7	Sept 7	H	Hartlepool U	D	2-2	2-2	22	Cusack [28], Wood (pen) [43]	3370
8	14	A	Wrexham	L	0-4	0-3	23		3515
9	18	A	Boston U	L	0-1	0-1	—		2209
10	21	H	Torquay U	L	0-1	0-1	24		3872
11	28	A	Hull C	D	1-1	0-1	23	Thomas [52]	8070
12	Oct 5	H	Rochdale	D	1-1	1-0	23	Thomas [32]	3732
13	12	A	Oxford U	L	0-1	0-0	24		5440
14	19	H	Southend U	W	1-0	0-0	23	Thomas (pen) [52]	3623
15	26	A	Carlisle U	D	2-2	1-1	22	Thomas 2 [8, 65]	3940
16	29	H	Kidderminster H	L	0-4	0-1	—		3421
17	Nov 2	A	Cambridge U	L	0-1	0-0	24		3956
18	9	H	Macclesfield T	W	1-0	0-0	24	Murphy [84]	3526
19	23	A	Scunthorpe U	L	0-2	0-2	24		2886
20	30	H	Shrewsbury T	W	2-0	1-0	20	Murphy [42], Richards [70]	3638
21	Dec 14	A	Exeter C	L	0-1	0-0	21		2625
22	21	H	Leyton Orient	L	0-1	0-0	23		4120
23	26	H	Bristol R	L	0-1	0-1	24		5879
24	28	A	Lincoln C	L	0-1	0-0	24		4553
25	Jan 14	H	Bury	L	2-3	0-3	—	Smith J 2 [68, 78]	3555
26	18	A	York C	L	1-3	1-2	24	Parkin (og) [14]	4611
27	25	H	Lincoln C	W	2-0	1-0	24	Nugent [44], Williams [67]	5099
28	Feb 1	A	Rushden & D	D	1-1	1-0	24	Nugent [16]	4046
29	4	H	Darlington	W	1-0	1-0	—	Nugent [37]	5553
30	8	A	Macclesfield T	W	3-1	1-1	23	Watkin [41], Smith J [52], Martinez [67]	2515
31	11	A	Bournemouth	L	0-3	0-1	—		5511
32	15	H	Cambridge U	W	2-0	0-0	19	Richards 2 [58, 82]	4903
33	22	A	Hartlepool U	L	0-4	0-2	21		4486
34	Mar 1	H	Wrexham	D	0-0	0-0	22		6463
35	4	H	Boston U	D	0-0	0-0	—		6642
36	8	A	Torquay U	D	0-0	0-0	21		3287
37	15	H	Carlisle U	L	1-2	0-0	24	Thomas [90]	5845
38	18	A	Southend U	W	2-0	0-0	—	Thomas (pen) [60], Nugent [64]	2832
39	22	A	Kidderminster H	D	2-2	2-2	24	Johnrose [22], Martinez [35]	3172
40	28	H	Oxford U	W	3-2	1-1	—	Richards 2 (1 pen) [35, 62 (p)], Johnrose [55]	5982
41	Apr 5	A	Shrewsbury T	D	0-0	0-0	20		4645
42	12	H	Scunthorpe U	D	1-1	1-0	19	Richards [14]	6014
43	19	A	Leyton Orient	L	1-3	1-1	21	Thomas [8]	4480
44	21	H	Exeter C	L	0-1	0-0	21		9115
45	26	A	Rochdale	W	2-1	1-1	21	Nugent [18], Richards [68]	2777
46	May 3	H	Hull C	W	4-2	2-2	21	Thomas 3 (1 pen) [8, 45 (p), 57], Johnrose [48]	9585

Final League Position: 21

GOALSCORERS

League (48): Thomas 13 (3 pens), Richards 7 (1 pen), Nugent 5, Johnrose 3, Smith J 3, Martinez 2, Moss 2, Murphy 2, Watkin 2, Wood 2 (1 pen), Cusack 1, Mumford 1, Reid 1, Smith D 1, Williams 1, own goals 2.
Worthington Cup (2): Thomas 1, Wood 1.
FA Cup (1): Murphy 1.
LDV Vans Trophy (1): Thomas 1.

Freestone R 33	Jenkins L 26 + 6	Smith D 3 + 1	Smith J 27	O'Leary K 29 + 4	Evans T 25 + 2	Phillips G 19 + 8	Murphy M 9 + 3	Thomas J 34 + 5	Wood J 13 + 4	Reid P 18 + 2	Williams J 11 + 16	Sharp N 4 + 3	Watkin S 15 + 11	Mumford A 17 + 7	Theobald D 9 + 1	Howard M 36 + 2	Moss D 3 + 6	Keaveny J 4 + 5	Cusack N 4 + 1	Lacey D 7 + 3	De-Vulgt L 3 + 1	Cash B 5	Jackson M — + 1	Jones S 5 + 1	Tate A 27	Richards M 14 + 3	Stiens C — + 3	Britton L 25	Durkan K 4 + 2	Nugent K 15	Johnrose L 15	Martinez R 19	Hylton L 7 + 1	Cutler N 13	Maylett B 6	Coates J 2 + 1	Match No.
1	2	3	4	5■	6	7	8	9[1]	10[2]	11	12	13																									1
1	2	3	4[1]	5	6	7[3]	8	9	10[2]	11	13	12	14																								2
1	2	3[3]	4	5[1]	6	7[2]	8	9		11	13	12	10■	14																							3
1	2				6	7		9[1]	10[2]	11	12	4		8[3]	5	3	14	13																			4
1	2				6	7[1]				11	9[2]	4	10[3]	8	5	3	13	12	14																		5
1	2[1]				6		8[2]			11	13	4		12	5	3	9	10	7																		6
1				5	7	12	13		10	11	14	6[1]			4	3	8	9[3]	2[2]																		7
1	2			5	6	7		9	10[1]	11[2]					13	3	8[3]	12	4	14																	8
1	12			2	6	13	8[3]	9	10■	11[1]					5	3	14		4	7[2]																	9
1	2	12		4	6	7		9	13		8[2]		10		5	3				11[1]																	10
1	2			5	6	7		9		12	8[1]		10		4	3	13			11[2]																	11
1	2		4	5	6	7[2]		9					10	8		3	12	13		11[1]																	12
1			4	5	6[2]			9		11			10	7		3	12	8[1]		2	13																13
1	2		4	5				9		11[3]	12			7		3		8[1]		14	6[2]	10	13														14
1	3			5		7	12	9[3]	13	11			10[2]	8	6					14		4		2[1]													15
1	2		4	5		12		9	10	11	13			8[1]		3					6	7[2]															16
1	2		4	5		7	12	9	11[3]		13			8[2]		3		14			6	10[1]															17
1	2[1]		4	5		7	8	9	13	11				12		3						10[2]		6													18
1	12		4	5[3]		7	8[1]	9	10				13	14		3								2	6	11[2]											19
1			4		6	7	8	9						11		2				3					5	10											20
1				5	2	11	8[1]	9	10[3]	13			12	6[2]		3									4		14	7									21
1					6	7[1]		9	8[3]	11	13		10[2]	12	2	3									5		14	4									22
1	12			4[2]	5			9	10	11[3]				7[1]		3								13	6	8	14	2									23
1	2[3]			5	12	13		9[2]	10■				14			3				4[1]				7	6	8		11									24
1			2		12	7		9		8	14		13			3								6[1]	5	10[2]		4	11[3]								25
1	12		6		2	7[1]		9[3]		11[2]	10			13		3									5	14		4		8							26
1			2		6			9			10			8		3									5			4		7	11						27
1			2	13	6			9[1]			10[3]		12			3[2]									5			4	14	8	11	7					28
1			2		6			9[2]	13		14		12			3									5			4	11[3]	8[1]	10	7					29
1			2	5	6	12		9					10			3												4[1]	11		8	7					30
1			2		6	12		9[3]			13		10			3									5	14		4			11[1]	7	8[2]				31
1			2	12	6[1]			13			9		10[2]	8		3									5	11		4				7					32
1[6]			2	15	6	12		13			9[2]			8[1]		3									5	10■		4		11		7					33
			2	6				12			9			8											5	10[1]		4		11		7	3	1			34
	13[3]		2	6[2]				12			9[1]		14	8											5	11		4		10		7	3	1			35
	12		2[1]	6				9[2]					10	8		13									5			4		11		7	3	1			36
	2■			6				13			12		10[2]												5			4		9[1]	8	7	3	1	11		37
	2			6				10[1]					12												5			4		9■	8	7	3	1	11		38
	2			6				10								12									5			4		9	8	7	3[1]	1	11		39
	2		6			12										3									5	10		4[1]		9	8	7		1	11		40
	2		4			6[2]					12		10[1]	13		3									5	9					8	7		1	11		41
	2		6										10[1]			3									5	9		4	12		8	7		1	11		42
	2		6[1]	12				10			14		13			3									5	9[2]		4	11[3]		8	7		1			43
	2			6							10[2]		12			3[1]									5	9		4		11	8	7		1		13	44
	2			6				9[1]								3									5	12		4		10	8	7	13	1		11[2]	45
	2			6				9								3									5			4		10	8	7		1		11	46

Worthington Cup
First Round — Wolverhampton W — (h) — 2-3

LDV Vans Trophy
First Round — Stevenage B — (a) — 1-2

FA Cup
First Round — York C — (a) — 1-2

SWINDON TOWN Division 2

FOUNDATION

It is generally accepted that Swindon Town came into being in 1881, although there is no firm evidence that the club's founder, Rev. William Pitt, captain of the Spartans (an offshoot of a cricket club) changed his club's name to Swindon Town before 1883, when the Spartans amalgamated with St Mark's Young Men's Friendly Society.

County Ground, Swindon, Wiltshire SN1 2ED.

Telephone: 0870 443 1969. ***Fax:*** (01793) 333 703.

Marketing: (01793) 333 718. ***Fax:*** (01793) 333 703.

Superstore: 0870 443 1554. ***Fax:*** (01793) 333 780.

Ticket Office: 0870 443 1894.

Community Office: (01793) 421 303.

ClubCall: 09068 121 640.

Ground Capacity: 15,728.

Record Attendance: 32,000 v Arsenal, FA Cup 3rd rd, 15 January 1972.

Record Receipts: £149,371 v Bolton W, Coca-Cola Cup semi-final, 1st leg, 12 February 1995.

Pitch Measurements: 110yd × 70yd.

Chief Executive: Mark Devlin.

Chairman: Willie Carson.

Directors: R. Holt, Sandy Gray, James Wills, Mark Devlin, Willie Carson.

Manager: Andy King.

Assistant Manager: Malcolm Crosby.

Player-Coach: Alan Reeves.

Physio: Dick Mackey.

Company Secretary: Sandy Gray.

Colours: Red shirts, white shorts, red stockings.

Change Colours: Black and gold striped shirts, black shorts and black stockings.

Year Formed: 1881* (*see Foundation*).

Turned Professional: 1894. ***Ltd Co.:*** 1894.

Club Nickname: 'Robins'.

Previous Ground: 1881, The Croft; 1896, County Ground.

First Football League Game: 28 August 1920, Division 3, v Luton T (h) W 9–1 – Nash; Kay, Macconachie; Langford, Hawley, Wareing; Jefferson (1), Fleming (4), Rogers, Batty (2), Davies (1), (1 og).

HONOURS

FA Premier League: best season: 22nd 1993–94; Division 1 – 1992–93 (play-offs).

Football League: Division 2 – Champions 1995–96; Division 3 – Runners-up 1962–63, 1968–69; Division 4 – Champions 1985–86 (with record 102 points).

FA Cup: Semi-finals 1910, 1912.

Football League Cup: Winners 1969.

Anglo-Italian Cup: Winners 1970.

SKY SPORTS FACT FILE

Winger Bertie Denyer was the first London boy to win schoolboy international honours in 1907 against Wales. After serving in the Sportsmen's Battalion in the First World War he spent nine years with Swindon Town.

Record League Victory: 9–1 v Luton T, Division 3 (S), 28 August 1920 – Nash; Kay, Macconachie; Langford, Hawley, Wareing; Jefferson (1), Fleming (4), Rogers, Batty (2), Davies (1), (1 og).

Record Cup Victory: 10–1 v Farnham U Breweries (away), FA Cup 1st rd (replay), 28 November 1925 – Nash; Dickenson, Weston, Archer, Bew, Adey; Denyer (2), Wall (1), Richardson (4), Johnson (3), Davies.

Record Defeat: 1–10 v Manchester C, FA Cup 4th rd (replay), 25 January 1930.

Most League Points (2 for a win): 64, Division 3, 1968–69.

Most League Points (3 for a win): 102, Division 4, 1985–86.

Most League Goals: 100, Division 3 (S), 1926–27.

Highest League Scorer in Season: Harry Morris, 47, Division 3 (S), 1926–27.

Most League Goals in Total Aggregate: Harry Morris, 216, 1926–33.

Most League Goals in One Match: 5, Harry Morris v QPR, Division 3S, 18 December 1926; 5, Harry Morris v Norwich C, Division 3S, 26 April 1930; 5, Keith East v Mansfield T, Division 3, 20 November 1965.

Most Capped Player: Rod Thomas, 30 (50), Wales.

Most League Appearances: John Trollope, 770, 1960–80.

Youngest League Player: Paul Rideout, 16 years 107 days v Hull C, 29 November 1980.

MANAGERS

Sam Allen 1902–33
Ted Vizard 1933–39
Neil Harris 1939–41
Louis Page 1945–53
Maurice Lindley 1953–55
Bert Head 1956–65
Danny Williams 1965–69
Fred Ford 1969–71
Dave Mackay 1971–72
Les Allen 1972–74
Danny Williams 1974–78
Bobby Smith 1978–80
John Trollope 1980–83
Ken Beamish 1983–84
Lou Macari 1984–89
Ossie Ardiles 1989–91
Glenn Hoddle 1991–93
John Gorman 1993–94
Steve McMahon 1994–99
Jimmy Quinn 1999–2000
Colin Todd 2000
Andy King 2000–01
Roy Evans 2001
Andy King January 2002–

Record Transfer Fee Received: £1,500,000 from Manchester C for Kevin Horlock, January 1997.

Record Transfer Fee Paid: £800,000 to West Ham U for Joey Beauchamp, August 1994.

Football League Record: 1920 Original Member of Division 3; 1921–58 Division 3 (S); 1958–63 Division 3; 1963–65 Division 2; 1965–69 Division 3; 1969–74 Division 2; 1974–82 Division 3; 1982–86 Division 4; 1986–87 Division 3; 1987–92 Division 2; 1992–93 Division 1; 1993–94 FA Premier League; 1994–95 Division 1; 1995–96 Division 2; 1996–2000 Division 1; 2000– Division 2.

LATEST SEQUENCES

Longest Sequence of League Wins: 8, 12.1.1986 – 15.3.1986.

Longest Sequence of League Defeats: 6, 2.5.1993 – 25.8.1993.

Longest Sequence of League Draws: 6, 22.11.1991 – 28.12.1991.

Longest Sequence of Unbeaten League Matches: 22, 12.1.1986 – 23.8.86.

Longest Sequence Without a League Win: 19, 30.10.1999 – 4.3.2000.

Successive Scoring Runs: 31 from 17.4.1926.

Successive Non-scoring Runs: 5 from 16.11.1963.

TEN YEAR LEAGUE RECORD

		P	W	D	L	F	A	Pts	Pos
1993-94	PR Lge	42	5	15	22	47	100	30	22
1994-95	Div 1	46	12	12	22	54	73	48	21
1995-96	Div 2	46	25	17	4	71	34	92	1
1996-97	Div 1	46	15	9	22	52	71	54	19
1997-98	Div 1	46	14	10	22	42	73	52	18
1998-99	Div 1	46	13	11	22	59	81	50	17
1999-2000	Div 1	46	8	12	26	38	77	36	24
2000-01	Div 2	46	13	13	20	47	65	52	20
2001-02	Div 2	46	15	14	17	46	56	59	13
2002-03	Div 2	46	16	12	18	59	63	60	10

DID YOU KNOW ?

Maurice Owen made a dramatic impact with Swindon Town in 1946–47. The wartime ex-Chindit scored on his Colts debut, hit four in one reserve game against Cardiff City, one against Leyton Orient and a hat-trick on his League debut v Watford on 11 January.

SWINDON TOWN 2002–03 LEAGUE RECORD

Match No.	*Date*	*Venue*	*Opponents*	*Result*		*H/T Score*	*Lg. Pos.*	*Goalscorers*	*Attendance*
1	Aug 10	H	Barnsley	W	3-1	1-1	—	Parkin 3 (1 pen) [33, 51, 88 (p)]	5702
2	13	A	Chesterfield	W	4-2	3-0	—	Invincibile 2 [11, 39], Sabin [42], Parkin [57]	3189
3	17	A	Blackpool	D	0-0	0-0	2		6404
4	24	H	Cardiff C	L	0-1	0-1	5		7564
5	26	A	Brentford	L	1-3	1-2	10	Davis J [17]	6299
6	31	H	Stockport Co	L	0-1	0-0	18		5456
7	Sept 7	H	Port Vale	L	1-2	1-1	19	Gurney [7]	5029
8	14	A	QPR	L	0-2	0-0	20		11,619
9	17	A	Cheltenham T	L	0-2	0-1	—		5761
10	21	H	Northampton T	W	2-0	1-0	17	Jackson [31], Parkin (pen) [79]	4719
11	28	A	Luton T	L	0-3	0-1	21		6393
12	Oct 5	H	Oldham Ath	L	0-1	0-1	21		4326
13	12	H	Colchester U	D	2-2	0-1	22	Gurney [66], Sabin [68]	4152
14	19	A	Bristol C	L	0-2	0-2	22		13,205
15	26	H	Mansfield T	W	2-1	1-1	21	Parkin [21], Sabin [46]	4136
16	29	A	Notts Co	D	1-1	1-0	—	Parkin [32]	4797
17	Nov 2	A	Wycombe W	W	3-2	1-1	17	Davis J [12], Parkin 2 [79, 90]	6021
18	9	H	Tranmere R	D	1-1	1-0	18	Parkin [2]	5077
19	23	A	Huddersfield T	W	3-2	2-1	17	Duke [1], Gurney (pen) [24], Parkin [89]	8334
20	30	H	Peterborough U	D	1-1	0-0	18	Parkin (pen) [79]	4709
21	Dec 14	A	Plymouth Arg	D	1-1	0-0	18	Gurney [77]	8111
22	21	H	Crewe Alex	L	1-3	0-2	18	Parkin (pen) [75]	4957
23	26	H	Brentford	W	2-1	1-0	15	Gurney [2], Parkin [66]	6045
24	28	A	Wigan Ath	L	0-2	0-1	15		6114
25	Jan 1	A	Cardiff C	D	1-1	0-0	16	Parkin [70]	13,062
26	4	H	Chesterfield	W	3-0	1-0	14	Parkin [33], Invincibile [52], Reeves [87]	4544
27	18	A	Stockport Co	W	5-2	2-0	14	Parkin [7], Robinson S [12], Reeves [74], Hewlett [85], Sabin [90]	4318
28	22	H	Blackpool	D	1-1	1-0	—	Miglioranzi [20]	4787
29	25	H	Wigan Ath	W	2-1	2-0	11	Invincibile [24], Gurney [35]	5238
30	Feb 1	A	Barnsley	D	1-1	1-1	11	Invincibile [34]	8661
31	8	A	Tranmere R	W	1-0	0-0	11	Gurney [50]	7181
32	15	H	Wycombe W	L	0-3	0-1	12		6239
33	22	A	Port Vale	D	1-1	0-0	11	Parkin [54]	4085
34	Mar 1	H	QPR	W	3-1	1-1	11	Robinson S [18], Parkin [64], Heywood [68]	7716
35	8	A	Northampton T	L	0-1	0-0	11		5566
36	12	H	Cheltenham T	L	0-3	0-2	—		5583
37	15	A	Mansfield T	L	1-2	1-2	13	Reeves [45]	4471
38	19	H	Bristol C	D	1-1	0-0	—	Parkin [66]	8629
39	22	H	Notts Co	W	5-0	1-0	11	Parkin 3 [43, 61, 89], Gurney [59], Duke [69]	4246
40	29	A	Colchester U	L	0-1	0-0	12		3787
41	Apr 5	A	Peterborough U	D	1-1	0-1	12	Invincibile [71]	4310
42	12	H	Huddersfield T	L	0-1	0-0	13		4760
43	19	A	Crewe Alex	W	1-0	0-0	12	Miglioranzi [75]	6384
44	23	H	Plymouth Arg	W	2-0	1-0	—	Invincibile [38], Parkin [68]	5057
45	26	A	Oldham Ath	L	0-4	0-2	12		6873
46	May 3	H	Luton T	W	2-1	2-1	10	Miglioranzi [41], Parkin [43]	6455

Final League Position: 10

GOALSCORERS

League (59): Parkin 25 (4 pens), Gurney 8 (1 pen), Invincibile 7, Sabin 4, Miglioranzi 3, Reeves 3, Davis J 2, Duke 2, Robinson S 2, Hewlett 1, Heywood 1, Jackson 1.
Worthington Cup (1): Willis 1.
FA Cup (1): Gurney 1.
LDV Vans Trophy (8): Invincibile 2, Davis J 1, Heywood 1, Jackson 1, Miglioranzi 1, Parkin 1, Young 1.

Griemink B 44	Edds G 8 + 6	Duke D 44	Miglioranzi S 39 + 2	Heywood M 46	Willis A 9 + 6	Robinson S 42 + 2	Parkin S 41 + 2	Sabin E 27 + 12	Invincibile D 37 + 5	Hewlett M 39 + 1	Davis J 10 + 3	Young A — + 11	Edwards N — + 3	Gurney A 41	Reeves A 35 + 1	Jackson J 12 + 1	Bampton D — + 3	Sutton J — + 1	Nightingale L 2 + 1	Marney D 8 + 1	Ifil J 5 + 4	Beswetherick J 3	Lewis J 9	Dykes D 1 + 1	Herring I 2 + 2	Taylor C — + 4	Farr C 2	Garrard L — + 1	Match No.
1	2	3	4	5	6	7	8	9	10^{1}	11	12																		1
1	2	3	4	5	6	7	8	9	10	11^{1}	12																		2
1	2	3	4	5	6	7	8	9^{1}	10^{2}		11	12	13																3
1	2	3	8	5	6	7^{1}	12	9	10^{2}		11	13		4															4
1	2	3	8	5	6	7^{1}	10	9	12		11			4															5
1	2	3	8	6	12	7^{1}	10	9			11			4	5														6
1	2^{2}	3	7	6	12	8	10	9			11	13		4	5^{1}														7
1	12	3^{1}	7	6		2	10	9		11^{2}		13		4	5	8													8
1	2	3		5		6	10■	9	7	11				4		8													9
1		3	12	5	6	7^{1}	10	9	8	11				2		4													10
1	12	3		5	6	7^{1}	10	9	8^{2}	11		13		2		4													11
1	12	2	7^{1}	4	6			9	10	11				8	5	3													12
1		3		4		7		9	10	11	8			2	5	6													13
1		3	4^{2}	6		8		9	10^{1}	11	7	12		2	5	13													14
1		3	4^{2}	6		13	10	9	12	11	7^{1}			2	5	8													15
1		3	12	6		7	8	9	10^{2}	11	13			2	5	4^{1}													16
1		3		6		7	8	9^{1}	12	11	2			4	5	10													17
1		3		6		7	9		10^{1}	11	8	12		2	5	4													18
1	12	3^{1}	8	4		7	13	9^{2}	10	11				2	5	6													19
1		3	7	6		12	8	9	10	11^{1}				2	5	4													20
1		3	7	4		6^{1}	8	9	10	11				2	5		12												21
1		3	4	6		7	8	9^{1}	10	11				2	5			12											22
1		3	4	6		7	8	12	10	11				2	5				9^{1}										23
1			4	6	12	7^{1}	8	13	10	11				3	5				9^{2}	2									24
1		3	4	6	12	7^{1}	9	13	10^{2}	11				2	5					8									25
1		3	4^{2}	6	12	7^{1}	9	13	10	11				2	5					8									26
1		3	7	6		8	9^{2}	12	10^{1}	11				4	5				13	2									27
1	12	3	7	6		8	9	13	10^{2}	11				4	5					2^{1}									28
1		3	7	6	12	8	9		10	11				4	5					2^{1}									29
1		3	7	4	6^{1}	8	9		10	11				2	5						12								30
1		3^{2}	7	6		8	9	12	10^{1}	11				4	5					2	13								31
1		3	7	6		8	9	12	10	11^{1}				4	5					2^{2}	13								32
1		3	7	6		8	9	12	10^{1}	11				4	5					13	2^{2}								33
1		2	7	6		8	10	9		11				4	5						12	3^{1}							34
1		2	7	6		8	10	9	12	11				4	5							3^{1}							35
1		2	7	6		8	9	12	10	11^{1}				4	5							3■							36
1		3	7^{1}	6		8	9	12	10	11				4	5						2								37
1		3	7	6		8	9		10					4	5						2		11						38
1		3	7	6		8^{3}	9	12	10^{1}	13		14		4	5						2		11^{2}						39
1		3	4	5			8	9^{3}	10^{2}	11		13		6	12						2^{1}		7	14					40
1		3^{1}	7	6		2	10	9■	12	11			13	4	5								8^{2}						41
1	12		4^{2}	6		7	8	9^{3}	10	11		13	14	2									5	3^{1}					42
1		3^{1}	7	6		8	9		10	11					5								4		2	12			43
		3	7^{3}	6		8	9		10^{1}	11		12			5		13						4		2^{2}	14	1		44
		3	7^{2}	6		8^{1}	9		10	11				2^{3}	5								4		12	13	1	14	45
1		3	4^{3}	5		7	8	9^{2}	10^{1}	11				2			12						6		13	14			46

Worthington Cup

First Round	Wycombe W	(h)	1-2

LDV Vans Trophy

First Round	Southend U	(h)	6-1
Second Round	Kidderminster H	(a)	2-3

FA Cup

First Round	Huddersfield T	(h)	1-0
Second Round	Oxford U	(a)	0-1

TORQUAY UNITED Division 3

FOUNDATION

The idea of establishing a Torquay club was agreed by old boys of Torquay College and Torbay College, while sitting in Princess Gardens listening to the band. A proper meeting was subsequently held at Tor Abbey Hotel at which officers were elected. This was on 1 May 1899 and the club's first competition was the Eastern League (later known as the East Devon League). As an amateur club it played at Teignmouth Road, Torquay Recreation Ground and Cricket Field Road before settling down for four years at Torquay Cricket Ground where the rugby club now plays. They became Torquay United in 1921 after merging with Babbacombe FC.

Plainmoor Ground, Torquay, Devon TQ1 3PS.

Telephone: (01803) 328 666. ***Fax:*** (01803) 323 976.
Website: www.torquayunited.com

Ground Capacity: 6,283.

Record Attendance: 21,908 v Huddersfield T, FA Cup 4th rd, 29 January 1955.

Record Receipts: £57,517 v Exeter C, Division 3, 11 February 2003.

Pitch Measurements: 110yd × 74yd.

Chairman/Managing Director: M. Bateson.

Financial Director: Mrs H. Kindeleit-Badcock.

Directors: Mrs S. Bateson, M. Benney, I. Hayman, B. Palk.

First Team Coach: Leroy Rosenior.

Physio: Norman Medhurst.

Company Secretary: Mrs H. Kindeleit-Badcock.

Colours: Yellow shirts with royal blue side inserts and collar, royal blue shorts with yellow side inserts, yellow stockings.

Change Colours: Black and white striped shirts with yellow trim, black shorts with yellow stripes to sides, black stockings with yellow and white stripes top and bottom.

Year Formed: 1899.

Turned Professional: 1921. ***Ltd Co.:*** 1921.

Previous Name: 1910, Torquay Town; 1921, Torquay United.

Club Nickname: 'The Gulls'.

Previous Grounds: 1899, Teignmouth Road; 1900, Torquay Recreation Ground; 1904, Cricket Field Road; 1906, Torquay Cricket Ground; 1910, Plainmoor Ground.

First Football League Game: 27 August 1927, Division 3 (S), v Exeter C (h) D 1–1 – Millsom; Cook, Smith; Wellock, Wragg, Connor, Mackey, Turner (1), Jones, McGovern, Thomson.

HONOURS

Football League: Division 3 best season: 4th, 1967–68; Division 3 (S) – Runners-up 1956–57; Division 4 – Promoted 1959–60 (3rd), 1965–66 (3rd), 1990–91 (play-offs).

FA Cup: best season: 4th rd, 1949, 1955, 1971, 1983, 1990.

Football League Cup: never past 3rd rd.

Sherpa Van Trophy: Runners-up 1989.

SKY SPORTS FACT FILE

In the 1923–24 season Billy Kellock scored ten goals for Torquay United in their FA Cup run which took them from the extra preliminary stage to the fourth qualifying round. His total included a four and a three.

Record League Victory: 9–0 v Swindon T, Division 3 (S), 8 March 1952 – George Webber; Topping, Ralph Calland; Brown, Eric Webber, Towers; Shaw (1), Marchant (1), Northcott (2), Collins (3), Edds (2).

Record Cup Victory: 7–1 v Northampton T, FA Cup 1st rd, 14 November 1959 – Gill; Penford, Downs; Bettany, George Northcott, Rawson; Baxter, Cox, Tommy Northcott (1), Bond (3), Pym (3).

Record Defeat: 2–10 v Fulham, Division 3 (S), 7 September 1931. 2–10 v Luton T, Division 3 (S), 2 September 1933.

Most League Points (2 for a win): 60, Division 4, 1959–60.

Most League Points (3 for a win): 77, Division 4, 1987–88.

Most League Goals: 89, Division 3 (S), 1956–57.

Highest League Scorer in Season: Sammy Collins, 40, Division 3 (S), 1955–56.

Most League Goals in Total Aggregate: Sammy Collins, 204, 1948–58.

Most League Goals in One Match: 5, Robin Stubbs v Newport Co, Division 4, 19 October 1963.

Most Capped Player: Rodney Jack, St Vincent.

Most League Appearances: Dennis Lewis, 443, 1947–59.

Youngest League Player: David Byng, 16 years 36 days v Walsall, 14 August 1993.

Record Transfer Fee Received: £500,000 from Crewe Alex for Rodney Jack, July 1998.

Record Transfer Fee Paid: £70,000 to Barry T for Eifion Williams, March 1999.

Football League Record: 1927 Elected to Division 3 (S); 1958–60 Division 4; 1960–62 Division 3; 1962–66 Division 4; 1966–72 Division 3; 1972–91 Division 4; 1991– Division 3.

MANAGERS

Percy Mackrill 1927–29
A. H. Hoskins 1929 *(Secretary-Manager)*
Frank Womack 1929–32
Frank Brown 1932–38
Alf Steward 1938–40
Billy Butler 1945–46
Jack Butler 1946–47
John McNeil 1947–50
Bob John 1950
Alex Massie 1950–51
Eric Webber 1951–65
Frank O'Farrell 1965–68
Alan Brown 1969–71
Jack Edwards 1971–73
Malcolm Musgrove 1973–76
Mike Green 1977–81
Frank O'Farrell 1981–82 *(continued as General Manager to 1983)*
Bruce Rioch 1982–84
Dave Webb 1984–85
John Sims 1985
Stuart Morgan 1985–87
Cyril Knowles 1987–89
Dave Smith 1989–91
John Impey 1991–92
Ivan Golac 1992
Paul Compton 1992–93
Don O'Riordan 1993–95
Eddie May 1995–96
Kevin Hodges *(Head Coach)* 1996–98
Wes Saunders 1998–2001
Roy McFarland 2001–02
Leroy Rosenior June 2002–

LATEST SEQUENCES

Longest Sequence of League Wins: 8, 24.1.1998 – 3.3.1998.

Longest Sequence of League Defeats: 8, 30.9.1995 – 18.11.1995.

Longest Sequence of League Draws: 8, 25.10.1969 – 13.12.1969.

Longest Sequence of Unbeaten League Matches: 15, 5.5.1990 – 3.11.1990.

Longest Sequence Without a League Win: 17, 5.3.1938 – 10.9.1938.

Successive Scoring Runs: 19 from 3.10.1953.

Successive Non-scoring Runs: 7 from 8.1.1972.

TEN YEAR LEAGUE RECORD

		P	*W*	*D*	*L*	*F*	*A*	*Pts*	*Pos*
1993-94	Div 3	42	17	16	9	64	56	67	6
1994-95	Div 3	42	14	13	15	54	57	55	13
1995-96	Div 3	46	5	14	27	30	84	29	24
1996-97	Div 3	46	13	11	22	46	62	50	21
1997-98	Div 3	46	21	11	14	68	59	74	5
1998-99	Div 3	46	12	17	17	47	58	53	20
1999-2000	Div 3	46	19	12	15	62	52	69	9
2000-01	Div 3	46	12	13	21	52	77	49	21
2001-02	Div 3	46	12	15	19	46	63	51	19
2002-03	Div 3	46	16	18	12	71	71	66	9

DID YOU KNOW ?

Torquay United owed their Football League election in 1927 in part to the decline of the South Wales mining industry in the depression. The ballot had United and Aberdare with 27 votes. United won the re-run by seven.

TORQUAY UNITED 2002–03 LEAGUE RECORD

Match No.	*Date*	*Venue*	*Opponents*	*Result*	*H/T Score*	*Lg. Pos.*	*Goalscorers*	*Attendance*
1	Aug 10	H	Bristol R	W 2-1	1-1	—	Gritton [45], Russell (pen) [74]	4937
2	13	A	Rushden & D	L 0-3	0-1	—		3602
3	17	A	York C	L 3-4	0-1	17	Hankin [56], Richardson [64], Hockley [65]	3203
4	24	H	Hartlepool U	D 1-1	0-0	20	Richardson [51]	2403
5	26	A	Exeter C	W 2-1	2-1	13	Graham [26], Bedeau [45]	6065
6	31	H	Wrexham	W 2-1	2-1	8	Hill [22], Graham [29]	2283
7	Sept 7	A	Oxford U	D 2-2	0-0	7	Graham [48], Bedeau [79]	5260
8	14	H	Cambridge U	W 3-2	1-0	7	Graham 2 [41, 69], Hill [62]	2557
9	17	H	Shrewsbury T	W 2-1	1-0	—	Fowler [19], Graham [77]	2528
10	21	A	Swansea C	W 1-0	1-0	2	Graham [31]	3872
11	28	H	Lincoln C	D 0-0	0-0	3		3428
12	Oct 5	A	Carlisle U	W 2-1	1-1	2	Graham [2], Gritton [90]	4014
13	12	A	Boston U	L 1-2	1-0	2	Hockley [6]	2514
14	19	H	Hull C	L 1-4	0-1	3	Hill [65]	3607
15	26	A	Scunthorpe U	L 1-5	1-2	6	Graham [30]	2911
16	29	H	Bournemouth	W 4-0	2-0	—	Gritton [30], Graham 2 [34, 77], Russell [47]	3543
17	Nov 9	A	Bury	W 1-0	0-0	4	Graham [57]	3210
18	19	H	Kidderminster H	D 2-2	2-0	—	Russell [23], Gritton [32]	2629
19	23	A	Macclesfield T	D 3-3	3-1	4	Graham [2], Fowler [7], Woozley [10]	1835
20	30	H	Rochdale	D 2-2	0-0	6	Gritton [52], Hazell [90]	2754
21	Dec 14	A	Leyton Orient	L 0-2	0-2	8		4443
22	21	H	Southend U	W 3-1	1-0	7	Osei-Kuffour [21], Dunning [65], Bedeau [78]	2244
23	28	A	Darlington	D 1-1	0-1	7	Fowler [74]	3506
24	Jan 4	H	Rushden & D	D 1-1	1-0	8	Fowler (pen) [39]	2651
25	11	H	York C	W 3-1	3-1	4	Gritton 2 [6, 21], Bedeau [24]	2663
26	14	A	Bristol R	D 1-1	1-1	—	Russell [6]	6196
27	18	A	Wrexham	L 1-2	1-1	4	Bedeau [18]	3006
28	25	H	Darlington	W 3-1	3-1	4	Gritton [22], Russell (pen) [31], Woozley [38]	2628
29	Feb 1	A	Hartlepool U	L 2-3	1-0	5	Graham [8], Gritton [58]	4975
30	8	H	Bury	D 1-1	1-1	8	Russell (pen) [13]	3123
31	11	H	Exeter C	W 1-0	1-0	—	Gritton [28]	5761
32	15	A	Kidderminster H	L 0-2	0-1	5		3039
33	22	H	Oxford U	L 2-3	0-0	10	Russell (pen) [70], Wills [75]	3372
34	Mar 1	A	Cambridge U	W 1-0	1-0	7	Osei-Kuffour [4]	4280
35	8	H	Swansea C	D 0-0	0-0	9		3287
36	15	H	Scunthorpe U	D 1-1	0-1	11	Clist [83]	2486
37	18	A	Hull C	D 1-1	0-0	—	Hill [90]	13,310
38	22	A	Bournemouth	D 1-1	0-0	11	Bedeau [68]	7181
39	25	A	Shrewsbury T	W 3-2	1-0	—	Gritton [20], Russell [57], Woozley [90]	2694
40	29	H	Boston U	D 1-1	0-0	7	Russell [68]	3039
41	Apr 5	A	Rochdale	W 2-0	1-0	5	Griffiths (og) [18], Clist [52]	2216
42	12	H	Macclesfield T	D 2-2	1-2	6	Osei-Kuffour [4], Gritton [61]	2970
43	19	A	Southend U	L 0-3	0-2	10		3594
44	21	H	Leyton Orient	D 2-2	1-1	10	Osei-Kuffour [26], Graham [65]	3379
45	26	H	Carlisle U	L 2-3	0-3	10	Murphy (og) [69], Osei-Kuffour [77]	3761
46	May 3	A	Lincoln C	D 1-1	1-0	9	Gritton [31]	7906

Final League Position: 9

GOALSCORERS

League (71): Graham 15, Gritton 13, Russell 9 (4 pens), Bedeau 6, Osei-Kuffour 5, Fowler 4 (1 pen), Hill 4, Woozley 3, Clist 2, Hockley 2, Richardson 2, Dunning 1, Hankin 1, Hazell 1, Wills 1, own goals 2.
Worthington Cup (0).
FA Cup (6): Gritton 3, Fowler 1, Osei-Kuffour 1, Russell 1 (pen).
LDV Vans Trophy (0).

Dearden K 26 + 1	Hazell R 46	Hockley M 25 + 15	Hankin S 17 + 2	Woozley D 45 + 1	Russell A 39	Fowler J 40	Gritton M 39 + 4	Bedeau A 38 + 2	Prince N 3 + 4	Hill K 37 + 2	Richardson M 3 + 6	Benefield J — + 8	Ashington R — + 2	Attwell J 2 + 2	Forinton H 1	Canoville L 36	Graham D 26 + 8	Douglin T 1 + 4	Holmes P 7	Stevens D — + 3	Brown M 2 + 2	Bond K — + 1	Osei-Kuffour J 18 + 12	Van Heusden A 15	Dunning D 4 + 3	Welch K 3	Wills K 5 + 15	Woods S 5 + 4	Amankwaah K 6	Clist S 11	Taylor C 5	Camara B — + 2	Killoughery G 1 + 2	*Match No.*
1	2	3	4	5	6	7	8	9	10^{1}	11	12																							1
1	2	3^{1}	4	5	6	7	8^{2}	9	10^{3}	11	12	13	14																					2
	2	3	4	5	6	7		9^{2}	10^{1}	11	12		13	1	8																			3
1	2	12	4	5	6	7■	13	9		11	10^{2}					3	8^{1}																	4
1	2	12	4	5	6^{1}	8	13	9		11	10					3	7^{2}																	5
1	2	12	4^{3}	5	6^{1}	8	13	9		11	10^{2}					3	7	14																6
1	2	3	4	5			8^{1}	9		11	12					7	10		6															7
1	4	12		5	6	7	8	9	13	11^{2}						3^{1}	10^{3}		2	14														8
1	2	3^{1}	4	5	6	7	8	9	12								10		11															9
1	2	3	4^{2}	5	6	7	8^{1}	9			12						10	13	11															10
1	2		4	5	6	7	8^{1}	9■		11	12					3	10																	11
1	2	12	4	5	6	7^{1}	8	9		11						3	10^{2}				13													12
1	2	3		5	6	7	8		12	11^{1}						4			10^{2}		9	13												13
1	2	12		5	6	7^{1}	8		13	11						3	9		4^{2}		10^{3}		14											14
	4	6		5		8	10	7^{2}		11^{1}				1		2	9		3		12		13											15
1^{6}	4	3		5	6	8	10	7^{1}		11				15		2	9	12																16
	4	2		5	6	8	10	7^{1}		11						3	9							1	12									17
	4	2		5	6	8	10	7		11				15		3^{1}	9							1^{6}	12									18
	2	4		5	6	8	10					12					9	3					7^{1}		11	1								19
	4	2^{1}	6	5	3		10	7				13					9	12					11^{2}		8^{3}	1	14							20
	2	3	4	12	6	7^{3}	8	9^{2}									10						13		11^{1}	1	14	5						21
15	2	3	4	5		7	8^{1}	9		11						6							10^{2}	1^{6}	12			13						22
1	2	3^{1}	4^{2}	5		8		9		11						6							10		7		12	13						23
1	2	4	12	5		8^{2}		9		11		13				3^{3}				14			10				7^{1}	6						24
1	2	12	4	5	7	8^{1}	10^{2}	9^{3}				13				3							14				11	6						25
1	2	12		5	6	7^{2}	10	9		11						3							13				8^{1}	4						26
1	2	3	4	5		8^{1}	10	9^{3}		11		12				7^{2}				14			13					6						27
1	4	12		5	6^{1}	7	8^{3}	9		11						3	13						10^{2}				14		2					28
1	4		12	5	6	8	10	7		11^{2}						3^{1}	9^{3}						13				14		2					29
1	4			5	6	8	10	7		11^{1}						3	9						12				13		2^{2}					30
1	4	12		5	6	8	10	7^{1}		11						3	9^{2}						13						2					31
1	4	12		5	6	8	10	7^{2}		11^{3}						3	9^{1}						13				14		2					32
1	4			5	6	8	10	7^{1}								3	9^{2}						12				13		2	11				33
1	4	12		5	6		9^{2}	13		11						3	14						7^{1}				10^{3}			8	2			34
	4	2		5	6		10	7^{1}		11^{3}		13					12						9	1			14			8^{2}	3			35
	2	12		5		6	10			11^{1}						3	9^{2}						8	1						7	4	13		36
	2	7^{3}		5	6	8	10^{2}			13						3	12						9^{1}	1				14		11	4			37
	2			5	6	8	10^{2}	12		13						3	9^{1}						7^{3}	1				14		11	4			38
	2			5	6	4	10^{2}	7		11						3	12						9^{1}	1			13			8				39
	2	3		5	6	4	10	7^{2}		11							12						9^{1}	1			13			8^{3}			14	40
	2	4		5	6		10^{1}	7		11						3							9	1			12			8				41
	2	4^{1}		5	6		10	7		11						3	12						9	1			13			8^{2}				42
	2	12		5^{1}	6	4	10	7^{3}		11						3	9^{2}						8	1			13						14	43
	2	4		5	6	8	10^{1}			11		13				3	12						9	1									7^{2}	44
	2	12		5	6	4^{1}	13	7		11						3	9^{3}						10	1			14			8^{2}				45
	2	4		5	6^{1}	8	10	7		11						3							12	1			9^{2}					13		46

Worthington Cup
First Round | Gillingham | (h) | 0-1

LDV Vans Trophy
First Round | Wycombe W | (h) | 0-4

FA Cup
First Round | Boreham Wood | (h) | 5-0
Second Round | Blackpool | (a) | 1-3

TOTTENHAM HOTSPUR FA Premiership

FOUNDATION

The Hotspur Football Club was formed from an older cricket club in 1882. Most of the founders were old boys of St John's Presbyterian School and Tottenham Grammar School. The Casey brothers were well to the fore as the family provided the club's first goalposts (painted blue and white) and their first ball. They soon adopted the local YMCA as their meeting place, but after a couple of moves settled at the Red House, which is still their headquarters, although now known simply as 748 High Road.

Bill Nicholson Way, 748 High Road, Tottenham, London N17 0AP.

Telephone: (020) 8365 5000. ***Fax:*** (020) 8365 5175.
Spurs Ticket Line: 0870 420 5000.
Spurs Line: 09068 100 500. ***Members Office:*** (020) 8365 5150.
Commercial Dept: (020) 8365 5010.

Ground Capacity: 36,236.

Record Attendance: 75,038 v Sunderland, FA Cup 6th rd. 5 March 1938.

Record Receipts: undisclosed.

Pitch Measurements: 110yd × 73yd.

Chairman: Daniel Levy.

Football Director: D. J. Pleat.
Finance Director: P. L. Viner.
Property Director: P. Z. Kemsley.

Non-Executive Director: D. Buchler (Vice-chairman).

President: W. E. Nicholson OBE.

Honorary Vice-presidents: N. Solomon, D. A. Alexiou, A. G. Berry.

Manager: Glenn Hoddle. ***Assistant Manager:*** John Gorman.
First Team Coach: Chris Hughton.
Reserve Team Manager: Colin Calderwood.
Chief Physio: Alasdair Beattie.

Club Secretary: John Alexander.
Director of Corporate Hospitality: Mike Rollo.

Press Officer: John Fennelly.

Colours: White shirts, navy blue shorts, white stockings.

Change Colours: Sky blue shirts, sky blue shorts, sky blue stockings.

Year Formed: 1882. ***Turned Professional:*** 1895. ***Ltd Co.:*** 1898.

Previous Name: 1882–84, Hotspur Football Club. ***Club Nickname:*** 'Spurs'.

Previous Grounds: 1882, Tottenham Marshes; 1888, Northumberland Park; 1899, White Hart Lane.

First Football League Game: 1 September 1908, Division 2, v Wolverhampton W (h) W 3–0 – Hewitson; Coquet, Burton; Morris (1), D. Steel, Darnell; Walton, Woodward (2), Macfarlane, R. Steel, Middlemiss.

HONOURS

Football League: Division 1 – Champions 1950–51, 1960–61; Runners-up 1921–22, 1951–52, 1956–57, 1962–63; Division 2 – Champions 1919–20, 1949–50; Runners-up 1908–09, 1932–33; Promoted 1977–78 (3rd).

FA Cup: Winners 1901 (as non-League club), 1921, 1961, 1962, 1967, 1981, 1982, 1991; Runners-up 1987.

Football League Cup: Winners 1971, 1973, 1999; Runners-up 1982, 2002.

European Competitions: *European Cup:* 1961–62. *European Cup-Winners' Cup:* 1962–63 (winners), 1963–64, 1967–68, 1981–82, 1982–83, 1991–92. *UEFA Cup:* 1971–72 (winners), 1972–73, 1973–74 (runners-up), 1983–84 (winners), 1984–85, 1999–2000. *Intertoto Cup:* 1995.

SKY SPORTS FACT FILE

Teddy Sheringham's 84th minute goal for Tottenham Hotspur against Sunderland on 8 February 2003 was his 300th career League and Cup goal and the 100th for Spurs in the Premier League under manager Glenn Hoddle.

Record League Victory: 9–0 v Bristol R, Division 2, 22 October 1977 – Daines; Naylor, Holmes, Hoddle (1), McAllister, Perryman, Pratt, McNab, Moores (3), Lee (4), Taylor (1).

Record Cup Victory: 13–2 v Crewe Alex, FA Cup 4th rd (replay), 3 February 1960 – Brown; Hills, Henry; Blanchflower, Norman, Mackay; White, Harmer (1), Smith (4), Allen (5), Jones (3 incl. 1p).

Record Defeat: 0–8 v Cologne, UEFA Intertoto Cup, 22 July 1995.

Most League Points (2 for a win): 70, Division 2, 1919–20.

Most League Points (3 for a win): 77, Division 1, 1984–85.

Most League Goals: 115, Division 1, 1960–61.

Highest League Scorer in Season: Jimmy Greaves, 37, Division 1, 1962–63.

Most League Goals in Total Aggregate: Jimmy Greaves, 220, 1961–70.

Most League Goals in One Match: 5, Ted Harper v Reading, Division 2, 30 August 1930; 5, Alf Stokes v Birmingham C, Division 1, 18 September 1957; 5, Bobby Smith v Aston Villa, Division 1, 29 March 1958.

Most Capped Player: Pat Jennings, 74 (119), Northern Ireland.

Most League Appearances: Steve Perryman, 655, 1969–86.

Youngest League Player: Ally Dick, 16 years 301 days v Manchester C, 20 February 1982.

Record Transfer Fee Received: £5,500,000 from Lazio for Paul Gascoigne, May 1992.

Record Transfer Fee Paid: £11,000,000 to Dynamo Kiev for Sergei Rebrov, May 2000.

Football League Record: 1908 Elected to Division 2; 1909–15 Division 1; 1919–20 Division 2; 1920–28 Division 1; 1928–33 Division 2; 1933–35 Division 1; 1935–50 Division 2; 1950–77 Division 1; 1977–78 Division 2; 1978–92 Division 1; 1992– FA Premier League.

MANAGERS

Frank Brettell 1898–99
John Cameron 1899–1906
Fred Kirkham 1907–08
Peter McWilliam 1912–27
Billy Minter 1927–29
Percy Smith 1930–35
Jack Tresadern 1935–38
Peter McWilliam 1938–42
Arthur Turner 1942–46
Joe Hulme 1946–49
Arthur Rowe 1949–55
Jimmy Anderson 1955–58
Bill Nicholson 1958–74
Terry Neill 1974–76
Keith Burkinshaw 1976–84
Peter Shreeves 1984–86
David Pleat 1986–87
Terry Venables 1987–91
Peter Shreeves 1991–92
Ossie Ardiles 1993–94
Gerry Francis 1994–97
Christian Gross *(Head Coach)* 1997–98
George Graham 1998–2001
Glenn Hoddle April 2001–

LATEST SEQUENCES

Longest Sequence of League Wins: 13, 23.4.1960 – 1.10.1960.

Longest Sequence of League Defeats: 7, 1.1.1994 – 27.2.1994.

Longest Sequence of League Draws: 6, 9.1.1999 – 27.2.1999.

Longest Sequence of Unbeaten League Matches: 22, 31.8.1949 – 31.12.1949.

Longest Sequence Without a League Win: 16, 29.12.1934 – 13.4.1935.

Successive Scoring Runs: 32 from 24.2.1962

Successive Non-scoring Runs: 6 from 28.12.1985

TEN YEAR LEAGUE RECORD

		P	*W*	*D*	*L*	*F*	*A*	*Pts*	*Pos*
1993-94	PR Lge	42	11	12	19	54	59	45	15
1994-95	PR Lge	42	16	14	12	66	58	62	7
1995-96	PR Lge	38	16	13	9	50	38	61	8
1996-97	PR Lge	38	13	7	18	44	51	46	10
1997-98	PR Lge	38	11	11	16	44	56	44	14
1998-99	PR Lge	38	11	14	13	47	50	47	11
1999-2000	PR Lge	38	15	8	15	57	49	53	10
2000-01	PR Lge	38	13	10	15	47	54	49	12
2001-02	PR Lge	38	14	8	16	49	53	50	9
2002-03	PR Lge	38	14	8	16	51	62	50	10

DID YOU KNOW ?

Cousins Clive and Paul Allen played for Tottenham Hotspur in the 1987 FA Cup final. Paul's uncle Les Allen had been in the Spurs final team of 1961 and in 1982 Clive had played for Queens Park Rangers against Spurs in that final.

TOTTENHAM HOTSPUR 2002–03 LEAGUE RECORD

Match No.	*Date*	*Venue*	*Opponents*	*Result*	*H/T Score*	*Lg. Pos.*	*Goalscorers*	*Attendance*
1	Aug 17	A	Everton	D 2-2	0-1	—	Etherington[63], Ferdinand[74]	40,020
2	24	H	Aston Villa	W 1-0	1-0	8	Redknapp[26]	35,384
3	27	A	Charlton Ath	W 1-0	1-0	—	Davies[8]	26,392
4	31	H	Southampton	W 2-1	1-1	1	Ferdinand[10], Sheringham (pen)[90]	35,573
5	Sept 11	A	Fulham	L 2-3	2-0	—	Richards[36], Sheringham[44]	16,785
6	15	H	West Ham U	W 3-2	0-0	2	Davies[62], Sheringham (pen)[71], Gardner[89]	35,996
7	21	A	Manchester U	L 0-1	0-0	3		67,611
8	28	H	Middlesbrough	L 0-3	0-1	6		36,082
9	Oct 6	A	Blackburn R	W 2-1	1-0	4	Keane[6], Redknapp[89]	26,203
10	20	H	Bolton W	W 3-1	0-0	3	Keane 2[58, 74], Davies[90]	35,909
11	26	A	Liverpool	L 1-2	0-0	5	Richards[82]	44,084
12	Nov 3	H	Chelsea	D 0-0	0-0	5		36,047
13	10	A	Sunderland	L 0-2	0-0	8		40,024
14	16	A	Arsenal	L 0-3	0-1	9		38,121
15	24	H	Leeds U	W 2-0	2-0	7	Sheringham[12], Keane[41]	35,720
16	30	A	Birmingham C	D 1-1	0-0	8	Sheringham[55]	29,505
17	Dec 8	H	WBA	W 3-1	2-0	7	Ziege[3], Keane[30], Poyet[80]	35,994
18	15	H	Arsenal	D 1-1	1-1	7	Ziege[11]	36,077
19	23	A	Manchester C	W 3-2	1-1	—	Perry[38], Davies[48], Poyet[84]	34,563
20	26	H	Charlton Ath	D 2-2	0-1	7	Keane[68], Iversen[87]	36,043
21	29	A	Newcastle U	L 1-2	0-1	8	Dabizas (og)[73]	52,145
22	Jan 1	A	Southampton	L 0-1	0-0	9		31,890
23	12	H	Everton	W 4-3	1-1	8	Poyet[14], Keane 3[50, 68, 83]	36,066
24	18	A	Aston Villa	W 1-0	0-0	7	Sheringham[70]	38,576
25	29	H	Newcastle U	L 0-1	0-0	—		36,084
26	Feb 1	A	Chelsea	D 1-1	1-1	9	Sheringham[18]	41,436
27	8	H	Sunderland	W 4-1	2-1	7	Poyet[14], Doherty[45], Davies[67], Sheringham[84]	36,075
28	24	H	Fulham	D 1-1	1-1	—	Sheringham (pen)[40]	34,701
29	Mar 1	A	West Ham U	L 0-2	0-1	9		35,049
30	16	H	Liverpool	L 2-3	0-0	10	Taricco[49], Sheringham[87]	36,077
31	24	A	Bolton W	L 0-1	0-0	—		23,084
32	Apr 5	H	Birmingham C	W 2-1	1-0	8	Keane[7], Poyet[88]	36,063
33	12	A	Leeds U	D 2-2	2-1	8	Sheringham[37], Keane[39]	39,580
34	18	H	Manchester C	L 0-2	0-2	—		36,075
35	21	A	WBA	W 3-2	1-1	8	Keane 2[45, 85], Sheringham[63]	26,569
36	27	H	Manchester U	L 0-2	0-0	8		36,073
37	May 3	A	Middlesbrough	L 1-5	0-3	9	Redknapp[60]	30,230
38	11	H	Blackburn R	L 0-4	0-2	10		36,036

Final League Position: 10

GOALSCORERS

League (51): Keane 13, Sheringham 12 (3 pens), Davies 5, Poyet 5, Redknapp 3, Ferdinand 2, Richards 2, Ziege 2, Doherty 1, Etherington 1, Gardner 1, Iversen 1, Perry 1, Taricco 1, own goal 1.
Worthington Cup (2): Poyet 1, Sheringham 1.
FA Cup (0).

Keller K 38	Carr S 30	Taricco M 21	Gardner A 11 + 1	Richards D 26	Bunjevcevic G 31 + 4	Davies S 33 + 3	Redknapp J 14 + 3	Iversen S 8 + 11	Sheringham T 34 + 2	Etherington M 15 + 8	Thatcher B 8 + 4	Acimovic M 4 + 13	Ferdinand L 4 + 7	Ziege C 10 + 2	Doherty G 7 + 8	Blondel J — + 1	Perry C 15 + 3	Keane R 29	Freund S 13 + 4	Poyet G 22 + 6	Anderton D 18 + 2	King L 25	Slabber J — + 1	Toda K 2 + 2	*Match No.*
1	2^{1}	3	4	5	6	7	8	9^{2}	10^{3}	11	12	13	14												1
1		2	4	5	12	7	8		10	11^{1}	13	6	9^{3}	3^{2}	14										2
1		2	4	5	6	7	8		10	11			12	3	9^{1}										3
1		2^{1}		5	12	7	8	13	10	11	3	4^{3}	9^{2}		6	14									4
1			4	5	6	7		12	10	11^{1}	3	8^{2}	9	13	14		2^{3}								5
1		2^{2}	4		6	7	8	12	10	11^{1}	13			3	14		5^{3}	9							6
1				5	6	2	8	7^{1}	10^{2}	11	3	13	12		4			9							7
1				5	6	2	8	7^{2}	12	11	4	13	10^{1}	3^{3}	14			9							8
1		2^{2}		5	6	7	8	12	10		3	11^{1}					13	9	4						9
1	2			5	3	7	8		10	11^{1}							6	9	4	12					10
1	2			5	3	7	8^{1}		10^{3}	12		13	14				6	9	4	11^{2}					11
1	2			5	3	7	8		10^{2}			12	13				6	9	4	11^{1}					12
1	2			5	12	11		13	10		3^{2}	14					6	9	4^{3}	8^{1}	7				13
1	2			5	3	7■	8^{1}	12	10^{3}	11^{2}								9	4	13	14	6			14
1	2			5	6	14	12	13	10					3^{3}				9	8	11^{2}	7^{1}	4			15
1	2			5	6		12	13	10			14		3				9^{2}	8	11^{3}	7^{1}	4			16
1	2			5		11	8	12	10^{2}					3			6	9		13	7	4^{1}			17
1	2			5	6	12			10					3				9	8	11	7^{1}	4			18
1	2			5		7		10^{1}						3■			6	9	8	12	11	4			19
1	2				6	12		13	10^{3}				14	3■			5	9	8^{2}	11	7^{1}	4			20
1	2	3			6	7		10^{3}	12			13	14				5	9^{2}	8	11^{1}		4			21
1	2	3^{3}		5	11^{1}			8^{2}	10			13					6	9	7	12	14	4			22
1	2				6	7		10^{1}				12			5		3	9		8	11	4			23
1	2	3		5	6	7			10									9	12	8^{1}	11	4			24
1	2		4	5	6	7			10						12			9^{1}		8	11	3			25
1	2	3	4^{2}		6	7		9^{1}	10	12					13					8	11	5			26
1	2	3		5	6^{1}	7			10	13					14			9^{3}	12	8^{2}	11	4			27
1	2	3		5	6	7			10	13		12^{2}			9					8^{1}	11■	4			28
1	2	3		5	6^{1}	7			10	8^{2}	12	13			9^{3}				14		11	4			29
1	2	3^{1}			6	7			10	11	5				9^{2}				12	8		4	13		30
1	2	3			6	7			10	12	5^{2}				13			9		8	11^{1}	4			31
1	2	3^{1}			6	7			10	12							5	9		8	11	4			32
1	2	3	4		6	7			10	12								9		8^{1}	11	5			33
1	2	3^{2}	4		6^{3}	7			10			12					13	9		8^{1}	11	5		14	34
1	2		3	5^{2}	6	7			10	11							13	9		12		4		8^{1}	35
1	2	3	12	5^{1}	13	7		14	10	11^{3}								9		8		4		6^{2}	36
1	2	3	6		8	7	12		10^{2}	13							5■	9		11^{1}		4			37
1	2	3^{1}				7	6^{2}		10	11				12			5	9		8■		4		13	38

Worthington Cup

Second Round	Cardiff C	(h)	1-0
Third Round	Burnley	(a)	1-2

FA Cup

Third Round	Southampton	(a)	0-4

TRANMERE ROVERS Division 2

FOUNDATION

Formed in 1884 as Belmont they adopted their present title the following year and eventually joined their first league, the West Lancashire League in 1889–90, the same year as their first success in the Wirral Challenge Cup. The club almost folded in 1899–1900 when all the players left en bloc to join a rival club, but they survived the crisis and went from strength to strength winning the 'Combination' title in 1907–08 and the Lancashire Combination in 1913–14. They joined the Football League in 1921 from the Central League.

Prenton Park, Prenton Road West, Prenton, Wirral CH42 9PY.

Telephone: (0151) 609 3333. ***Fax:*** (0151) 608 4385. ***Shop:*** (0151) 609 3311. ***Ticket Office:*** (0151) 609 3322. ***ClubCall:*** 09068 121 646.

Ground Capacity: 16,587 (all seated).

Record Attendance: 24,424 v Stoke C, FA Cup 4th rd, 5 February 1972.

Record Receipts: £268,946 v Liverpool, FA Cup 6th rd, 11 March 2001.

Pitch Measurements: 110yd × 70yd.

Chairperson: Lorraine Rogers.

Directors: Lorraine Rogers, Mick Horton, Richard Hughes.

Secretary: Mick Horton.

Manager: Ray Mathias.

Youth Development Officer: Warwick Rimmer.

Coach and Chief Scout: Dave Philpotts.

Reserve Team Coach: John McMahon.

Physio: Les Parry.

Colours: White shirts and shorts with blue trim.

Change Colours: All yellow.

Year Formed: 1884.

Turned Professional: 1912.

Ltd Co.: 1920.

Previous Name: 1884, Belmont AFC; 1885, Tranmere Rovers.

Club Nickname: 'The Rovers'.

Previous Grounds: 1884, Steeles Field; 1887, Ravenshaws Field/Old Prenton Park; 1912, Prenton Park.

HONOURS

Football League Division 1 best season: 4th, 1992–93; Promoted from Division 3 1990–91 (play-offs); Division 3 (N) – Champions 1937–38; Promotion to 3rd Division: 1966–67, 1975–76; Division 4 – Runners-up 1988–89.

FA Cup: best season: 6th rd, 2000, 2001.

Football League Cup: Runners-up, 2000.

Welsh Cup: Winners 1935; Runners-up 1934.

Leyland Daf Cup: Winners 1990; Runners-up 1991.

SKY SPORTS FACT FILE

Cyril Done scored 14 FA Cup goals for Tranmere Rovers including a hat-trick against Accrington Stanley in three seasons from 1952–53 to 1954–55. He averaged two goals every three matches during his time at Prenton Park.

First Football League Game: 27 August 1921, Division 3 (N), v Crewe Alex (h) W 4–1 – Bradshaw; Grainger, Stuart (1); Campbell, Milnes (1), Heslop; Moreton, Groves (1), Hyam, Ford (1), Hughes.

Record League Victory: 13–4 v Oldham Ath, Division 3 (N), 26 December 1935 – Gray; Platt, Fairhurst; McLaren, Newton, Spencer; Eden, MacDonald (1), Bell (9), Woodward (2), Urmson (1).

Record Cup Victory: 13–0 v Oswestry U, FA Cup 2nd prel rd, 10 October 1914 – Ashcroft; Stevenson, Bullough, Hancock, Taylor, Holden (1), Moreton (1), Cunningham (2), Smith (5), Leck (3), Gould (1).

Record Defeat: 1–9 v Tottenham H, FA Cup 3rd rd (replay), 14 January 1953.

Most League Points (2 for a win): 60, Division 4, 1964–65.

Most League Points (3 for a win): 80, Division 4, 1988–89; Division 3, 1989–90; Division 2, 2002–03.

Most League Goals: 111, Division 3 (N), 1930–31.

Highest League Scorer in Season: Bunny Bell, 35, Division 3 (N), 1933–34.

Most League Goals in Total Aggregate: Ian Muir, 142, 1985–95.

Most League Goals in One Match: 9, Bunny Bell v Oldham Ath, Division 3N, 26 December 1935.

Most Capped Player: John Aldridge, 30 (69), Republic of Ireland.

Most League Appearances: Harold Bell, 595, 1946–64 (incl. League record 401 consecutive appearances).

Youngest League Player: Iain Hume, 16 years 167 days v Swindon T, 15 April 2000.

Record Transfer Fee Received: £3,300,000 from Everton for Steve Simonsen, September 1998.

Record Transfer Fee Paid: £450,000 to Aston Villa for Shaun Teale, August 1995.

Football League Record: 1921 Original Member of Division 3 (N): 1938–39 Division 2; 1946–58 Division 3 (N); 1958–61 Division 3; 1961–67 Division 4; 1967–75 Division 3; 1975–76 Division 4; 1976–79 Division 3; 1979–89 Division 4; 1989–91 Division 3; 1991–92 Division 2; 1992–2001 Division 1; 2001– Division 2.

MANAGERS

Bert Cooke 1912–35
Jackie Carr 1935–36
Jim Knowles 1936–39
Bill Ridding 1939–45
Ernie Blackburn 1946–55
Noel Kelly 1955–57
Peter Farrell 1957–60
Walter Galbraith 1961
Dave Russell 1961–69
Jackie Wright 1969–72
Ron Yeats 1972–75
John King 1975–80
Bryan Hamilton 1980–85
Frank Worthington 1985–87
Ronnie Moore 1987
John King 1987–96
John Aldridge 1996–2001
Dave Watson 2001–02
Ray Mathias September 2002–

LATEST SEQUENCES

Longest Sequence of League Wins: 9, 9.2.1990 – 19.3.1990.

Longest Sequence of League Defeats: 8, 29.10.1938 – 17.12.1938.

Longest Sequence of League Draws: 5, 26.12.1997 – 31.1.1998.

Longest Sequence of Unbeaten League Matches: 18, 16.3.1970 – 4.9.1970.

Longest Sequence Without a League Win: 16, 8.11.1969 – 14.3.1970.

Successive Scoring Runs: 32 from 24.2.1934.

Successive Non-scoring Runs: 7 from 20.12.1997.

TEN YEAR LEAGUE RECORD

		P	*W*	*D*	*L*	*F*	*A*	*Pts*	*Pos*
1993-94	Div 1	46	21	9	16	69	53	72	5
1994-95	Div 1	46	22	10	14	67	58	76	5
1995-96	Div 1	46	14	17	15	64	60	59	13
1996-97	Div 1	46	17	14	15	63	56	65	11
1997-98	Div 1	46	14	14	18	54	57	56	14
1998-99	Div 1	46	12	20	14	63	61	56	15
1999-2000	Div 1	46	15	12	19	57	68	57	13
2000-01	Div 1	46	9	11	26	46	77	38	24
2001-02	Div 2	46	16	15	15	63	60	63	12
2002-03	Div 2	46	23	11	12	66	57	80	7

DID YOU KNOW ?

Tranmere Rovers won the Welsh Cup in 1935 beating another English club Chester 1-0 in the final having defeated Flint Town 5-0, Lovells Athletic 6-5 after a 1-1 draw and Shrewsbury Town 3-0 in the semi-final.

TRANMERE ROVERS 2002–03 LEAGUE RECORD

Match No.	*Date*	*Venue*	*Opponents*	*Result*		*H/T Score*	*Lg. Pos.*	*Goalscorers*	*Attendance*
1	Aug 10	A	Port Vale	W	4-1	2-1	—	Koumas [40], Haworth 2 [45, 81], Allen [47]	5629
2	13	H	Colchester U	D	1-1	1-0	—	Koumas [15]	7499
3	17	H	Cheltenham T	W	1-0	0-0	3	Barlow [60]	6807
4	24	A	Oldham Ath	L	0-2	0-0	8		5933
5	26	H	Huddersfield T	W	2-1	0-1	4	Price [71], Gray [77]	7534
6	31	A	Bristol C	L	0-2	0-0	7		9849
7	Sept 7	A	Blackpool	L	0-3	0-0	13		6834
8	14	H	Brentford	W	3-1	1-0	10	Haworth 2 [45, 66], Price [86]	6626
9	17	H	Wigan Ath	L	0-2	0-0	—		8153
10	21	A	Crewe Alex	L	0-2	0-0	13		6875
11	28	H	Stockport Co	W	1-0	1-0	10	Haworth [17]	7513
12	Oct 5	A	Mansfield T	L	1-6	1-0	13	Hay [13]	3668
13	12	A	Chesterfield	L	0-1	0-0	15		4111
14	19	H	Barnsley	W	1-0	1-0	12	Allen [3]	6855
15	26	A	Cardiff C	L	0-4	0-2	13		12,096
16	29	H	Peterborough U	D	1-1	0-0	—	Hume [53]	5980
17	Nov 2	H	Plymouth Arg	W	2-1	0-1	11	Roberts [87], Wotton (og) [90]	7083
18	9	A	Swindon T	D	1-1	0-1	11	Jones [80]	5077
19	23	A	Wycombe W	W	3-1	0-0	11	Barlow 2 [63, 90], Haworth [67]	5386
20	30	H	Luton T	L	1-3	1-0	11	Roberts [24]	8273
21	Dec 14	A	Northampton T	W	4-0	1-0	10	Haworth 2 [10, 66], Taylor [71], Hay [76]	4268
22	21	H	Notts Co	D	2-2	2-1	10	Allen [1], Haworth [11]	8275
23	26	A	Huddersfield T	W	2-1	0-0	8	Nicholson (pen) [58], Roberts [77]	11,002
24	28	H	QPR	W	3-0	0-0	7	Haworth [54], Jones 2 [60, 71]	8434
25	Jan 1	H	Oldham Ath	L	1-2	0-1	8	Haworth [59]	9795
26	4	A	Colchester U	D	2-2	1-1	7	Haworth [38], Mellon [60]	2846
27	18	H	Bristol C	D	1-1	0-1	9	Haworth [61]	7459
28	25	A	QPR	W	2-1	0-0	9	Robinson [80], Haworth [90]	12,249
29	Feb 1	H	Port Vale	W	1-0	1-0	7	McClare (og) [31]	7461
30	4	A	Cheltenham T	L	1-3	0-1	—	Sharps [50]	3936
31	8	H	Swindon T	L	0-1	0-0	10		7181
32	15	A	Plymouth Arg	W	1-0	0-0	9	Haworth [57]	8590
33	22	H	Blackpool	W	2-1	1-0	8	Hume 2 [14, 70]	9111
34	Mar 1	A	Brentford	W	2-1	1-0	8	Hume [20], Sharps [48]	5396
35	4	A	Wigan Ath	D	0-0	0-0	—		9021
36	8	H	Crewe Alex	W	2-1	1-0	7	Price [43], Sharps [88]	8670
37	14	H	Cardiff C	D	3-3	0-1	—	Haworth [47], Hume [78], Roberts [89]	9637
38	18	A	Barnsley	D	1-1	0-1	—	Nicholson (pen) [49]	8786
39	22	A	Peterborough U	D	0-0	0-0	7		4158
40	29	H	Chesterfield	W	2-1	1-0	7	Anderson [30], Hume [51]	8238
41	Apr 5	A	Luton T	D	0-0	0-0	7		6326
42	12	H	Wycombe W	W	1-0	0-0	7	Jones [90]	6814
43	19	A	Notts Co	W	1-0	0-0	7	Haworth [65]	5715
44	21	H	Northampton T	W	4-0	0-0	7	Nicholson (pen) [59], Haworth [60], Hay [89], Anderson [90]	7348
45	29	H	Mansfield T	W	3-1	1-0	—	Jones [15], Haworth [81], Price [90]	10,418
46	May 3	A	Stockport Co	W	3-2	0-2	7	Nicholson (pen) [48], Haworth [70], Jones [81]	7236

Final League Position: 7

GOALSCORERS

League (66): Haworth 20, Hume 6, Jones 6, Nicholson 4 (4 pens), Price 4, Roberts 4, Allen 3, Barlow 3, Hay 3, Sharps 3, Anderson 2, Koumas 2, Gray 1, Mellon 1, Robinson 1, Taylor 1, own goals 2.
Worthington Cup (3): Allen 1, Haworth 1, Taylor 1.
FA Cup (3): Barlow 1, Haworth 1, Mellon 1.
LDV Vans Trophy (7): Barlow 2, Jones 2, Harrison 1, Roberts 1, Taylor 1.

Welch K 2	Hinds R 6+2	Nicholson S 36+2	Sharps I 30	Allen G 40+1	Gray K 9+1	Navarro A 5	Mellon M 29+5	Haworth S 42	Price J 14+11	Koumas J 4	Harrison D 7+5	Barlow S 19+10	Nixon E —+2	Feuer I 2	McGibbon P 4	Hume I 22+13	Parkinson A 1+9	Achterberg J 38	Curtis T 8	Jones G 40	Roberts G 34+3	Taylor R 18+7	Edwards C 12	Whitehead P 2	Hay A 11+8	Olsen J 1+2	Connelly S 33	Proudlock A 5	Robinson M 1+5	Jackson M 6	Loran T 16+1	Howarth R 2+1	Anderson I 7	Match No.
1[G]	2	3	4	5	6	7	8[1]	9	10[2]	11	12	13	15																					1
		3	4[2]	2	6	7[1]	8	9	10[3]	11	12	14		1	5	13																		2
		3	4	2	6[1]	7[2]	8	9	10[3]		11	14		1	5	12	13																	3
		3	4[3]	2	6	7[1]	8	9	10[2]	11	12	13			5	14		1																4
		3	4[3]	2	6	7[2]	8	9[1]	12	11	13	10			5	14		1																5
	2	3[1]	4[3]	5	6		8	9	12			10				14	13	1	7[2]	11														6
	2		4[1]	5	6		8	9	10[2]			12				14	13	1	7[3]	11	3													7
			4	5	6[1]		8	9	10			12						1	11	7	3	2												8
			4	5			8	9■	11[2]			10				13	12	1	7[1]	6	3	2												9
1[G]				5			8	9	7[1]			10	15			13	12[2]		4	11	3	2	6											10
				5			8	9				10							7	4	3	2	6	1	11									11
		3		5			8	9■									10[1]		7	6		2	4	1	11	12								12
		3		5			8	9			7	12						1		11		2	6		10[1]		4							13
		3		5			8				7	9[2]					12	1	11	10	13	2[1]	4				6							14
		3		5			8[1]				7	12					13	1			6[2]	11	4			10	2	9						15
		3		5■							7	9[1]				12		1		6	11	8	4				2	10						16
		3[1]		5			8	9	13		11[2]					14		1		6	12	7[3]	4				2	10						17
		3[1]		5			8	9	7[2]			12						1		6	11	13	4				2	10						18
		3		5	12		8	9				10						1		6	11		4				2[1]	7						19
		3		5	6						7[2]	9[1]				12		1		8	11	2	4			13			10					20
		3		5			8	9				10[2]				11[1]		1		6		7	4		12		2		13					21
	12	3		5■			8	9				10[2]						1		6	13	11■			7[1]		2			4				22
	12	3		5			8	9				10						1		6	11				7[1]		2			4				23
		3	4				8	9				10[2]				12		1		6	11				7[1]		2		13	5				24
				5			8	9				10				12		1		6	3	11[1]			7[2]		2		13	4				25
							8	9				10[1]				11		1		6	3				7		2		12	5	4			26
		12	4				8	9	13			10[2]				11		1		6	3				7[1]		2			5				27
	5	11[3]	4				8	9	12			10[2]				7[1]		1		6	3				13		2		14					28
	5	11[1]	4				8	9				10				7		1		6[2]	3	12					2				13			29
	5[1]	11[2]	4	12			8	9				10				7		1[G]		6	3	13					2					15		30
		11[1]	4	5			8[2]	9	12		13					7		1		10	3	6					2							31
		11	4	5				9								10		1		8	3	7					2				6			32
		11[1]	4	5				9								10		1		8	3	7			12		2				6			33
			4	5				9	11							10		1		8	3				7		2				6			34
		12	4	5				9	11[3]							10[2]	13	1		8	3	14			7[1]		2				6			35
		11	4	5				9	7[2]			12				10[1]		1		8	3	13					2				6			36
		11	4	5				9	7[1]							10		1		8	3	12					2				6			37
		11	4	5				9	7[2]							10[1]		1		8	3	13			12		2				6			38
		11	4	5				9								10[1]	12	1		8	3	7[2]			13		2				6			39
		11	4	5				9								10		1		8	3				12		2				6		7[1]	40
		11[2]	4	5			12	9								10				8[1]	3				13		2				6	1	7	41
		11[2]	4	5			12	9	13							10				8	3						2				6[1]	1	7	42
		11	4	5				9	12							10[1]		1		8	3						2				6		7	43
		11[2]	4	5			12	9	13							10[3]		1		8	3				14		2				6[1]		7	44
		11[2]	4	5			12	9	13							10		1		8	3						2				6[1]		7	45
		11	4	5			12	9	13							10[2]		1		8	3						2				6[1]		7	46

Worthington Cup

First Round	Hartlepool U	(a)	2-1
Second Round	Southampton	(a)	1-6

LDV Vans Trophy

First Round	Hartlepool U	(h)	5-0
Second Round	Macclesfield T	(a)	2-1
Quarter-final	Bury	(a)	0-2

FA Cup

First Round	Cardiff C	(h)	2-2
		(a)	1-2

WALSALL Division 1

FOUNDATION

Two of the leading clubs around Walsall in the 1880s were Walsall Swifts (formed 1877) and Walsall Town (formed 1879). The Swifts were winners of the Birmingham Senior Cup in 1881, while the Town reached the 4th round (5th round modern equivalent) of the FA Cup in 1883. These clubs amalgamated as Walsall Town Swifts in 1888, becoming simply Walsall in 1895.

Bescot Stadium, Bescot Crescent, Walsall WS1 4SA.
Telephone: (01922) 622 791. ***Fax:*** (01922) 613 202.
ClubCall: 09068 555 800. ***Website:*** www.saddlers.co.uk
Email: info@walsallfc.co.uk (General Information), commercial@walsallfc.co.uk (Commercial), tickets @walsallfc.co.uk (Ticket Office), a.poole@walsallfc.co.uk (Matchday Programme/ Official Website)

Commercial Dept: (01922) 651 412.

Ground Capacity: 11,300.

Record Attendance: 11,037 v Wolverhampton W, Division 1, 11 January 2003.

Record Receipts: £98,828 v Leeds U, FA Cup 3rd rd, 7 January 1995.

Pitch Measurements: 110yd × 73yd.

Chairman: M. N. Lloyd.

Directors: J. W. Bonser, R. E. Tisdale, C. Welch, K. R. Whalley. ***Chief Executive:*** K. R. Whalley. ***Director of Finance:*** K. Avery. ***Director of Conference and Banqueting Services:*** C. Deakin.

Manager: Colin Lee. ***First Team Coach/Reserve Team Manager:*** Mick Halsall.
Physio: Kevin O'Leary. ***Chief Scout:*** Bob Rickwood. ***Youth Coaches:*** John Kerr, Mick Gooding.
Youth Liaison & Recruitment Officer: Bill Jones. ***Centre of Excellence Director:*** John Kerr.
Secretary/Commercial Director: Roy Whalley.

Year Formed: 1888. ***Turned Professional:*** 1888. ***Ltd Co.:*** 1921.

Previous Names: Walsall Swifts (founded 1877) and Walsall Town (founded 1879) amalgamated in 1888 and were known as Walsall Town Swifts until 1895.

Club Nickname: 'The Saddlers'.

Colours: Red shirts, red shorts, red stockings with white trim.

Change Colours: Sky/navy blue shirts, navy blue shorts, sky/navy blue stockings.

Previous Grounds: 1888, Fellows Park; 1990, Bescot Stadium.

First Football League Game: 3 September 1892, Division 2, v Darwen (h) L 1–2 – Hawkins; Withington, Pinches; Robinson, Whitrick, Forsyth; Marshall, Holmes, Turner, Gray (1), Pangbourn.

Record League Victory: 10–0 v Darwen, Division 2, 4 March 1899 – Tennent; E. Peers (1), Davies; Hickinbotham, Jenkyns, Taggart; Dean (3), Vail (2), Aston (4), Martin, Griffin.

Record Cup Victory: 7–0 v Macclesfield T (a), FA Cup 2nd rd, 6 December 1997 – Walker; Evans, Marsh, Viveash (1), Ryder, Peron, Boli (2 incl. 1p) (Ricketts), Porter (2), Keates, Watson (Platt), Hodge (2 incl. 1p).

HONOURS

Football League: Division 2: Runners-up, 1998–99, Promoted to Division 1 – 2000–01 (play-offs); Division 3 – Runners-up 1960–61, 1994–95; Division 4 – Champions 1959–60; Runners-up 1979–80.

FA Cup: best season: 5th rd, 1939, 1975, 1978, 1987, 2002, 2003 and last 16 1889.

Football League Cup: Semi-final 1984.

SKY SPORTS FACT FILE

On 25 January 1930 Walsall switched their FA Cup fourth round tie to Villa Park; gates closed and 74,600 crammed inside. Though Aston Villa won 3-1 they signed goalkeeper Fred Biddlestone from The Saddlers.

Record Defeat: 0–12 v Small Heath, 17 December 1892. 0–12 v Darwen, 26 December 1896, both Division 2.

Most League Points (2 for a win): 65, Division 4, 1959–60.

Most League Points (3 for a win): 87, Division 2, 1998–99.

Most League Goals: 102, Division 4, 1959–60.

Highest League Scorer in Season: Gilbert Alsop, 40, Division 3 (N), 1933–34 and 1934–35.

Most League Goals in Total Aggregate: Tony Richards, 184, 1954–63; Colin Taylor, 184, 1958–63, 1964–68, 1969–73.

Most League Goals in One Match: 5, Gilbert Alsop v Carlisle U, Division 3N, 2 February 1935; 5, Bill Evans v Mansfield T, Division 3N, 5 October 1935; 5, Johnny Devlin v Torquay U, Division 3S, 1 September 1949.

Most Capped Player: Mick Kearns, 15 (18), Republic of Ireland.

Most League Appearances: Colin Harrison, 467, 1964–82.

Youngest League Player: Geoff Morris, 16 years 218 days v Scunthorpe U, 14 September 1965.

Record Transfer Fee Received: £600,000 from West Ham U for David Kelly, July 1988.

Record Transfer Fee Paid: £175,000 to Birmingham C for Alan Buckley, June 1979.

Football League Record: 1892 Elected to Division 2; 1895 Failed re-election; 1896–1901 Division 2; 1901 Failed re-election; 1921 Original Member of Division 3 (N); 1927–31 Division 3 (S); 1931–36 Division 3 (N); 1936–58 Division 3 (S); 1958–60 Division 4; 1960–61 Division 3; 1961–63 Division 2; 1963–79 Division 3; 1979–80 Division 4; 1980–88 Division 3; 1988–89 Division 2; 1989–90 Division 3; 1990–92 Division 4; 1992–95 Division 3; 1995–99 Division 2; 1999–2000 Division 1; 2000–01 Division 2; 2001– Division 1.

LATEST SEQUENCES

Longest Sequence of League Wins: 7, 10.10.1959 – 21.11.1959.

Longest Sequence of League Defeats: 15, 29.10.1988 – 4.2.1989.

Longest Sequence of League Draws: 5, 7.5.1988 – 17.9.1988.

Longest Sequence of Unbeaten League Matches: 21, 6.11.1979 – 22.3.1980.

Longest Sequence Without a League Win: 18, 15.10.1988 – 4.2.1989.

Successive Scoring Runs: 27 from 9.2.1928.

Successive Non-scoring Runs: 5 from 8.10.1927.

MANAGERS

H. Smallwood 1888–91 *(Secretary-Manager)*
A. G. Burton 1891–93
J. H. Robinson 1893–95
C. H. Ailso 1895–96 *(Secretary-Manager)*
A. E. Parsloe 1896–97 *(Secretary-Manager)*
L. Ford 1897–98 *(Secretary-Manager)*
G. Hughes 1898–99 *(Secretary-Manager)*
L. Ford 1899–1901 *(Secretary-Manager)*
J. E. Shutt 1908–13 *(Secretary-Manager)*
Haydn Price 1914–20
Joe Burchell 1920–26
David Ashworth 1926–27
Jack Torrance 1927–28
James Kerr 1928–29
Sid Scholey 1929–30
Peter O'Rourke 1930–32
Bill Slade 1932–34
Andy Wilson 1934–37
Tommy Lowes 1937–44
Harry Hibbs 1944–51
Tony McPhee 1951
Brough Fletcher 1952–53
Major Frank Buckley 1953–55
John Love 1955–57
Billy Moore 1957–64
Alf Wood 1964
Reg Shaw 1964–68
Dick Graham 1968
Ron Lewin 1968–69
Billy Moore 1969–72
John Smith 1972–73
Doug Fraser 1973–77
Dave Mackay 1977–78
Alan Ashman 1978
Frank Sibley 1979
Alan Buckley 1979–86
Neil Martin *(Joint Manager with Buckley)* 1981–82
Tommy Coakley 1986–88
John Barnwell 1989–90
Kenny Hibbitt 1990–94
Chris Nicholl 1994–97
Jan Sorensen 1997–98
Ray Graydon 1998–2002
Colin Lee January 2002–

TEN YEAR LEAGUE RECORD

		P	W	D	L	F	A	Pts	Pos
1993-94	Div 3	42	17	9	16	48	53	60	10
1994-95	Div 3	42	24	11	7	75	40	83	2
1995-96	Div 2	46	19	12	15	60	45	69	11
1996-97	Div 2	46	19	10	17	54	53	67	12
1997-98	Div 2	46	14	12	20	43	52	54	19
1998-99	Div 2	46	26	9	11	63	47	87	2
1999-2000	Div 1	46	11	13	22	52	77	46	22
2000-01	Div 2	46	23	12	11	79	50	81	4
2001-02	Div 1	46	13	12	21	51	71	51	18
2002-03	Div 1	46	15	9	22	57	69	54	17

DID YOU KNOW 

The record number of goals scored in the FA Cup by a Walsall player is 23 by Sammy Holmes, the figure reached chiefly in qualifying rounds from 1892 to 1901. His 43 appearances in the same competition is another club record.

WALSALL 2002–03 LEAGUE RECORD

Match No.	*Date*	*Venue*	*Opponents*	*Result*		*H/T Score*	*Lg. Pos.*	*Goalscorers*	*Attendance*
1	Aug 10	H	Ipswich T	L	0-2	0-1	—		5253
2	14	A	Wolverhampton W	L	1-3	0-1	—	Herivelto ^{68}	27,904
3	17	A	Sheffield U	D	1-1	1-1	20	Corica ^{23}	14,011
4	24	H	Nottingham F	W	2-1	1-0	17	Sonner (pen) ^{25}, Wrack ^{90}	5096
5	26	A	Brighton & HA	W	2-0	2-0	10	Corica ^{6}, Leitao ^{7}	6519
6	31	H	Reading	L	0-2	0-0	16		5327
7	Sept 7	A	Watford	L	0-2	0-0	18		10,528
8	14	H	Bradford C	L	0-1	0-0	19		4678
9	17	H	Rotherham U	L	3-4	2-3	—	Zdrilic 2 $^{15, 45}$, Leitao ^{62}	4648
10	21	A	Millwall	W	3-0	2-0	17	Zdrilic ^{22}, Wrack ^{35}, Leitao ^{76}	7525
11	28	H	Sheffield W	W	1-0	1-0	15	Simpson ^{45}	6792
12	Oct 5	A	Derby Co	D	2-2	0-1	16	Corica ^{64}, Aranalde (pen) ^{90}	25,247
13	12	A	Burnley	L	1-2	0-1	17	Birch ^{79}	12,907
14	19	H	Preston NE	D	3-3	3-1	16	Leitao ^{21}, Junior ^{26}, Aranalde (pen) ^{45}	6832
15	26	A	Coventry C	D	0-0	0-0	18		14,544
16	29	H	Crystal Palace	L	3-4	2-1	—	Corica ^{2}, Junior 2 $^{5, 53}$	6368
17	Nov 2	H	Stoke C	W	4-2	0-0	16	Leitao 2 $^{51, 57}$, Junior ^{66}, Aranalde (pen) ^{84}	6391
18	9	A	Leicester C	L	0-2	0-0	18		25,243
19	16	A	Wimbledon	L	2-3	1-1	19	Junior ^{42}, Sonner (pen) ^{80}	1255
20	23	H	Gillingham	W	1-0	1-0	19	Junior ^{7}	6630
21	30	A	Portsmouth	L	2-3	1-1	19	Sonner 2 (2 pens) $^{31, 68}$	17,701
22	Dec 7	H	Grimsby T	W	3-1	1-1	18	Junior ^{27}, Leitao ^{66}, Wrack ^{87}	5888
23	14	H	Wimbledon	W	2-0	1-0	18	Wrack ^{11}, Junior ^{62}	6596
24	21	A	Norwich C	L	1-2	0-0	19	Easton (og) ^{50}	19,872
25	26	H	Sheffield U	L	0-1	0-0	19		10,459
26	28	A	Ipswich T	L	2-3	0-1	19	Wrack 2 $^{68, 89}$	26,550
27	Jan 1	A	Nottingham F	D	1-1	0-1	19	Ainsworth ^{63}	28,441
28	11	H	Wolverhampton W	L	0-1	0-0	19		11,037
29	18	A	Reading	D	0-0	0-0	19		11,786
30	Feb 1	H	Brighton & HA	W	1-0	1-0	20	Leitao ^{7}	8413
31	8	H	Leicester C	L	1-4	0-2	20	O'Connor ^{87}	8741
32	22	H	Watford	W	2-0	1-0	20	Junior ^{25}, Leitao ^{86}	7705
33	26	A	Stoke C	L	0-1	0-1	—		10,409
34	Mar 1	A	Bradford C	W	2-1	0-0	19	Robinson ^{49}, Matias ^{73}	10,893
35	4	A	Rotherham U	D	0-0	0-0	—		5792
36	8	H	Millwall	L	1-2	0-0	20	Junior ^{85}	6647
37	15	H	Burnley	W	3-2	2-0	19	Leitao ^{24}, Carbon ^{33}, Matias ^{66}	6327
38	18	A	Preston NE	L	0-5	0-2	—		11,170
39	22	A	Crystal Palace	L	0-2	0-1	19		19,102
40	Apr 5	H	Portsmouth	L	1-2	1-2	20	Junior ^{45}	7899
41	12	A	Gillingham	W	1-0	0-0	20	Leitao ^{49}	6972
42	15	H	Coventry C	D	0-0	0-0	—		7337
43	19	H	Norwich C	D	0-0	0-0	20		7018
44	21	A	Grimsby T	W	1-0	0-0	19	Junior ^{47}	4618
45	26	H	Derby Co	W	3-2	1-0	17	Junior 3 $^{3, 51, 70}$	8416
46	May 4	A	Sheffield W	L	1-2	0-0	17	Matias ^{56}	20,864

Final League Position: 17

GOALSCORERS

League (57): Junior 15, Leitao 11, Wrack 6, Corica 4, Sonner 4 (4 pens), Aranalde 3 (3 pens), Matias 3, Zdrilic 3, Ainsworth 1, Birch 1, Carbon 1, Herivelto 1, O'Connor 1, Robinson 1, Simpson 1, own goal 1.
Worthington Cup (5): Leitao 2, Aranalde 1 (pen), Junior 1, Zdrilic 1.
FA Cup (2): Wrack 1, Zdrilic 1.

Walker J 41	Bazeley D 41 + 2	Aranalde Z 38 + 1	Sonner D 20 + 4	Roper I 39 + 1	Carbon M 20 + 5	Wrack D 43	Birch G 6 + 13	Leitao J 43 + 1	Corica S 33 + 8	Matias P 8 + 15	Rodrigues D — + 1	Herivelto H — + 4	Wright M 2 + 3	Hay D 26 + 3	Martinez R 1 + 5	Barras T 14 + 5	Simpson F 16 + 9	Zdrilic D 9 + 15	Junior 28 + 8	O'Connor M 33 + 2	Ward G 5 + 2	Pollet L 5	Ainsworth G 2 + 3	Emblen N 3 + 2	Robinson C 10 + 1	Samways V 13	Shuker C 3 + 2	Lawrence J 4 + 1	Match No.
1	2	3	4	5	6	7	8	9[1]	10	11[2]	12	13																	1
1	2	3		5	6[2]	7	8	9[1]	10	11[3]		12	4	13	14■														2
1	2	3	4	5		7	8	9	10[1]			12	11[2]	6[3]	13	14													3
1	2	3	4	5		7	8[2]	9	10					6	12		11[1]	13											4
1	2	3	4	5		7	8[1]	9	10[2]	12				6			11	13											5
1	2	3	4	5		7	8[1]	9	10[2]	12				6	11■				13										6
1	2	3	7■	5	6	11[2]		9[1]	10[3]	12				4				13	14	8									7
1	2	3	4[1]		6	11	13	9[3]	8	12				5				10[2]	14	7									8
1	2	3	4[2]	12	6[1]	7		9	10					5			13	11	14	8[3]									9
1	2	3		5		7	12	9[3]	10				14	6[2]		13	11	8[1]		4									10
1	2	3		5		11	12	9	7				13	6	14		8[3]	10[1]		4[2]									11
1	2	3		5		7	12	9	8					6■		13	11[2]		10[1]	4									12
1	2	3		5		11	12	9	7					6	13		8		10[1]	4[2]									13
1■	2	3	12	5	6	7		9[2]	8								11[1]	13	10[3]	4	14								14
1	2	3		5	6	7		9	8								11	12	10[1]	4									15
1	2	3	12	5		7		9	8			13		6			11		10[2]	4[1]									16
	2	3	4	5		7		9[3]	8[2]	12				6		13	11	14	10[1]		1								17
1	2		4	5	3	7[1]	12	9[2]	11[3]				14	6				10	13	8									18
1	2		4		3	7		9	11[2]					6		12	13	14	10[3]	8		5[1]							19
1	2		4	3		7	12	9	11					6			13		10[1]	8[2]		5							20
1	2		7	5		3	12	9	11					6					10[1]	8		4							21
1	2	12	7	5		3		9	11[1]					6			13		10[2]	8		4[3]	14						22
1	2	3	4	5		7		9	11					6					10	8									23
1	2	3	4	5		7	12	9	11[2]					6					10[1]	8			13■						24
	2	3	4	5[1]	12	7		9	11[3]					6				13	10[2]	8	1		14						25
	2	3	12	5	13	8		9	10[3]					6[2]			11		14	4	1		7[1]						26
1	2	3	12	5	13	7		9		14							11		10[1]	4		6[2]	8[3]						27
1	2	3	4	5	6	7			12					11[1]			13	9[3]	10	8[2]				14					28
1	2	3			5[1]	7		9[2]	8	12				6			11	13	10					4					29
1	2	3	7	5[1]	12			9	11[3]					6		4	13	10		8[2]				14					30
1	2	3			6	7		9[2]	12							5	11	13	10	8				4[1]					31
1	2	3		5	13[3]	7		12	8	14				6[2]			11	9	10[1]						4				32
1	2	3		5		7[2]	12		8[1]	13						6	11[3]	9	10	14					4				33
1	2			5		3	12	9	13	11						6		14		8					4[1]	7[2]	10[3]		34
1	2			5		3	12	9[3]	13	11						6		14		8[2]					4	7	10[1]		35
1	2			5		3		9	12	11						6			13	8					4[1]	7	10[2]		36
1■	2	3			6		12	9[2]	7[1]	11						5		13	10[G]	8	15					4			37
1	2	3			6			9[1]	7[2]	11						5		12	10	8					13	4[3]	14		38
1	2	3[2]		5	6	7		9		11[1]									12	8■					10■	4	13		39
	2	3	7	5	6	11[1]		9[3]	8[2]	12				13				14	10		1					4			40
	13	3		5[1]	6	11		9						12[2]		4	14		10	8[3]	1					7		2	41
1	12	3		5	6[1]	2		9		13						4	14		10[3]	8						11		7[2]	42
1		3[2]		5	6	2		9	12	13						4			10[1]						8	11		7	43
1		3		5	6	2		9[2]	12	13						4			10[1]	14					8	11		7[3]	44
1	2	3		5		7[1]		9		12						4	13		10	8					6	11[2]			45
1		3		5		2		9[1]	14	12						4			10	8[2]				6	7	11		13[3]	46

Worthington Cup

First Round	Shrewsbury T	(h)	1-0
Second Round	Nottingham F	(a)	2-1
Third Round	Blackburn R	(a)	2-2

FA Cup

Third Round	Reading	(h)	0-0
		(a)	1-1
Fourth Round	Wimbledon	(h)	1-0
Fifth Round	Sheffield U	(a)	0-2

WATFORD Division 1

FOUNDATION

The club was formed as Watford Rovers in 1881. The name was changed to West Herts in 1893 and then the name Watford was adopted after rival club Watford St Mary's was absorbed in 1898.

Vicarage Road Stadium, Watford WD18 0ER.
Telephone: (01923) 496 000. ***Fax:*** (01923) 496 001.
Ticket Office: (01923) 496 010.
Ticket Office Fax: (01923) 351 145.
ClubCall: 09068 104 104. ***Club Shop:*** (01923) 496 005.
Club Shop Fax: (01923) 496 238. ***Catering:*** (01923) 496 002.
Football in the Community: (01923) 440 449.
Junior Hornets Club: (01923) 496 256.
Marketing: (01923) 496 006. ***Press Office:*** (01923) 496 396.

Ground Capacity: 20,800.

Record Attendance: 34,099 v Manchester U, FA Cup 4th rd (replay), 3 February 1969.

Record Receipts: £440,349 v Chelsea, FA Premier League, 18 September 1999.

Pitch Measurements: 113yd × 73yd.

Life Presidents: Sir Elton John CBE, Geoff Smith, Graham Taylor OBE.

Chairman: Graham Simpson.

Vice-chairman: Haig Oundjian.

Directors: B. Anderson, D. Meller, T. Shaw, D. Lester, C. Lissack, C. Norton, M. Sherwood, A. Wilson.

Chief Executive: Tim Shaw.

Football Secretary: Catherine Alexander.

Football Manager: Ray Lewington. ***First Team Coach:*** Terry Burton.
Reserve Team Coach: Nigel Gibbs. ***General Manager:*** Terry Byrne.

Academy Director: David Dodds. ***Academy Assistant Directors:*** Chris Cummins, David Hockaday.

Media Manager: Andrew French. ***Director of Marketing:*** Ed Coan.

Safety Officer: Paul Dumpleton. ***Stadium Manager:*** Paddy Flavin.

Colours: Yellow shirts, black shorts, black stockings with red and yellow turnover.

Change Colours: White shirts, shorts and stockings, all with yellow, red and black trim.

Year Formed: 1881.

Turned Professional: 1897.

Ltd Co.: 1909.

Club Nickname: 'The Hornets'.

Previous Names: 1881, Watford Rovers; 1893, West Herts; 1898, Watford.

Previous Grounds: 1883, Vicarage Meadow, Rose and Crown Meadow; 1889, Colney Butts; 1890, Cassio Road; 1922, Vicarage Road.

First Football League Game: 28 August 1920, Division 3, v QPR (a) W 2–1 – Williams; Horseman, F. Gregory; Bacon, Toone, Wilkinson; Bassett, Ronald (1), Hoddinott, White (1), Waterall.

HONOURS

Football League: Division 1 – Runners-up 1982–83, promoted from Division 1 1998–99 (play-offs); Division 2 – Champions 1997–98; Runners-up 1981–82; Division 3 – Champions 1968–69; Runners-up 1978–79; Division 4 – Champions 1977–78; Promoted 1959–60 (4th).

FA Cup: Runners-up 1984, semi-finals 1970, 1984, 1987, 2003.

Football League Cup: Semi-final 1979.

European Competitions: *UEFA Cup:* 1983–84.

SKY SPORTS FACT FILE

The only FA Premier League player to have appeared in first-class cricket was Steve Palmer of Watford. He once turned out for Cambridge University and actually dismissed England batsman Graeme Fowler.

Record League Victory: 8–0 v Sunderland, Division 1, 25 September 1982 – Sherwood; Rice, Rostron, Taylor, Terry, Bolton, Callaghan (2), Blissett (4), Jenkins (2), Jackett, Barnes.

Record Cup Victory: 10–1 v Lowestoft T, FA Cup 1st rd, 27 November 1926 – Yates; Prior, Fletcher (1); F. Smith, 'Bert' Smith, Strain; Stephenson, Warner (3), Edmonds (3), Swan (1), Daniels (1), (1 og).

Record Defeat: 0–10 v Wolverhampton W, FA Cup 1st rd (replay), 24 January 1912.

Most League Points (2 for a win): 71, Division 4, 1977–78.

Most League Points (3 for a win): 88, Division 2, 1997–98.

Most League Goals: 92, Division 4, 1959–60.

Highest League Scorer in Season: Cliff Holton, 42, Division 4, 1959–60.

Most League Goals in Total Aggregate: Luther Blissett, 148, 1976–83, 1984–88, 1991–92.

Most League Goals in One Match: 5, Eddie Mummery v Newport Co, Division 3S, 5 January 1924.

Most Capped Player: John Barnes, 31 (79), England and Kenny Jackett, 31, Wales.

Most League Appearances: Luther Blissett, 415, 1976–83, 1984–88, 1991–92.

Youngest League Player: Keith Mercer, 16 years 125 days v Tranmere R, 16 February 1973.

Record Transfer Fee Received: £2,300,000 from Chelsea for Paul Furlong, May 1994.

Record Transfer Fee Paid: £2,250,000 to Tottenham H for Allan Nielsen, August 2000.

Football League Record: 1920 Original Member of Division 3; 1921–58 Division 3 (S); 1958–60 Division 4; 1960–69 Division 3; 1969–72 Division 2; 1972–75 Division 3; 1975–78 Division 4; 1978–79 Division 3; 1979–82 Division 2; 1982–88 Division 1; 1988–92 Division 2; 1992–96 Division 1; 1996–98 Division 2; 1998–99 Division 1; 1999–2000 FA Premier League; 2000– Division 1.

MANAGERS

John Goodall 1903–10
Harry Kent 1910–26
Fred Pagnam 1926–29
Neil McBain 1929–37
Bill Findlay 1938–47
Jack Bray 1947–48
Eddie Hapgood 1948–50
Ron Gray 1950–51
Haydn Green 1951–52
Len Goulden 1952–55
(General Manager to 1956)
Johnny Paton 1955–56
Neil McBain 1956–59
Ron Burgess 1959–63
Bill McGarry 1963–64
Ken Furphy 1964–71
George Kirby 1971–73
Mike Keen 1973–77
Graham Taylor 1977–87
Dave Bassett 1987–88
Steve Harrison 1988–90
Colin Lee 1990
Steve Perryman 1990–93
Glenn Roeder 1993–96
Kenny Jackett 1996–97
Graham Taylor 1997–2001
Gianluca Vialli 2001–02
Ray Lewington July 2002–

LATEST SEQUENCES

Longest Sequence of League Wins: 7, 28.8.2000 – 14.10.2000.

Longest Sequence of League Defeats: 9, 26.12.1972 – 27.2.1973.

Longest Sequence of League Draws: 7, 30.11.1996 – 27.1.1997.

Longest Sequence of Unbeaten League Matches: 22, 1.10.1996 – 1.3.1997.

Longest Sequence Without a League Win: 19, 27.11.1971 – 8.4.1972.

Successive Scoring Runs: 22 from 20.8.1985.

Successive Non-scoring Runs: 7 from 18.12.1971.

TEN YEAR LEAGUE RECORD

		P	*W*	*D*	*L*	*F*	*A*	*Pts*	*Pos*
1993-94	Div 1	46	15	9	22	66	80	54	19
1994-95	Div 1	46	19	13	14	52	46	70	7
1995-96	Div 1	46	10	18	18	62	70	48	23
1996-97	Div 2	46	16	19	11	45	38	67	13
1997-98	Div 2	46	24	16	6	67	41	88	1
1998-99	Div 1	46	21	14	11	65	56	77	5
1999-2000	PR Lge	38	6	6	26	35	77	24	20
2000-01	Div 1	46	20	9	17	76	67	69	9
2001-02	Div 1	46	16	11	19	62	56	59	14
2002-03	Div 1	46	17	9	20	54	70	60	13

DID YOU KNOW ?

Watford's Vicarage Road ground once sported an ancient stationary car behind one of the goals. It was used to drag the hare round the greyhound track on a a steel wire attached to a specially fitted back wheel.

WATFORD 2002–03 LEAGUE RECORD

Match No.	Date	Venue	Opponents	Result		H/T Score	Lg. Pos.	Goalscorers	Attendance
1	Aug 10	A	Leicester C	L	0-2	0-0	—		31,022
2	13	H	Millwall	D	0-0	0-0	—		11,187
3	17	H	Wimbledon	W	3-2	2-1	14	Webber 31, Robinson 42, Nielsen 87	10,292
4	24	A	Portsmouth	L	0-3	0-2	18		17,901
5	26	H	Coventry C	W	5-2	3-0	9	Glass 5, Smith T 34, Webber 40, Nielsen 63, Robinson 71	11,136
6	31	A	Norwich C	L	0-4	0-1	17		20,563
7	Sept 7	H	Walsall	W	2-0	0-0	11	Smith T 72, Foley 90	10,528
8	14	A	Nottingham F	W	1-0	1-0	7	Cox 45	17,865
9	17	A	Preston NE	D	1-1	1-0	—	Robinson 31	12,408
10	21	H	Crystal Palace	D	3-3	2-3	8	Ardley 28, Hyde 40, Helguson 47	12,153
11	28	A	Sheffield U	W	2-1	2-1	8	Cox (pen) 36, Helguson 37	16,301
12	Oct 5	H	Brighton & HA	W	1-0	1-0	7	Helguson 40	15,305
13	12	H	Grimsby T	W	2-0	1-0	4	Foley 13, Smith T 90	13,821
14	19	A	Gillingham	L	0-3	0-2	6		8728
15	26	H	Sheffield W	W	1-0	1-0	5	Helguson 42	15,058
16	30	A	Stoke C	W	2-1	2-0	—	Helguson 18, Cox 37	11,215
17	Nov 2	H	Wolverhampton W	D	1-1	0-0	3	Cox 67	16,524
18	9	A	Rotherham U	L	1-2	0-1	4	Foley 60	6790
19	17	H	Ipswich T	L	0-2	0-0	5		16,184
20	23	A	Reading	L	0-1	0-0	8		17,465
21	30	H	Burnley	W	2-1	1-0	7	Helguson 40, Smith T (pen) 72	13,977
22	Dec 7	A	Derby Co	L	0-3	0-1	8		21,653
23	14	A	Ipswich T	L	2-4	0-2	9	Smith T 50, Cox 75	22,985
24	21	H	Bradford C	W	1-0	0-0	8	Cox (pen) 90	12,579
25	26	A	Wimbledon	D	0-0	0-0	8		2643
26	28	H	Leicester C	L	1-2	1-1	9	Helguson 29	16,017
27	Jan 1	H	Portsmouth	D	2-2	0-0	9	Hyde 51, Cox 81	15,048
28	11	A	Millwall	L	0-4	0-2	10		9030
29	19	H	Norwich C	W	2-1	1-0	10	Nielsen 45, Helguson 90	13,338
30	Feb 1	A	Coventry C	W	1-0	0-0	8	Hyde 60	17,393
31	8	H	Rotherham U	L	1-2	0-0	8	Smith T 62	15,025
32	22	A	Walsall	L	0-2	0-1	10		7705
33	25	A	Wolverhampton W	D	0-0	0-0	—		24,591
34	Mar 1	H	Nottingham F	D	1-1	1-0	12	Helguson 13	17,944
35	4	H	Preston NE	L	0-1	0-1	—		11,101
36	15	A	Grimsby T	L	0-1	0-0	16		4847
37	18	H	Gillingham	L	0-1	0-0	—		10,492
38	22	H	Stoke C	L	1-2	0-1	17	Helguson 67	12,570
39	29	A	Sheffield W	D	2-2	1-0	17	Smith T 33, Norville 82	17,086
40	Apr 5	A	Burnley	W	7-4	5-4	15	Brown 13, Hyde 16, Cox 26, Chopra 4 29, 40, 61, 90	10,208
41	8	A	Crystal Palace	W	1-0	1-0	—	Hunt (og) 45	14,051
42	19	A	Bradford C	L	1-2	1-2	16	Helguson 41	11,145
43	21	H	Derby Co	W	2-0	1-0	14	Chopra 18, Ardley 85	11,909
44	26	A	Brighton & HA	L	0-4	0-2	15		6841
45	30	H	Reading	L	0-3	0-1	—		11,814
46	May 4	H	Sheffield U	W	2-0	0-0	13	Cox 64, Fitzgerald 79	14,320

Final League Position: 13

GOALSCORERS

League (54): Helguson 11, Cox 9 (2 pens), Smith T 7 (1 pen), Chopra 5, Hyde 4, Foley 3, Nielsen 3, Robinson 3, Ardley 2, Webber 2, Brown 1, Fitzgerald 1, Glass 1, Norville 1, own goal 1.
Worthington Cup (1): Foley 1
FA Cup (7): Helguson 2, Smith T 2 (1 pen), Glass 1, Gayle 1, Pennant 1.

Chamberlain A 42	Doyley L 21 + 1	Robinson P 37	Cox N 40	Dyche S 23 + 1	Gayle M 30 + 1	Hyde M 37	Nielsen A 31 + 3	Foley D 6 + 9	Smith T 25 + 10	Hand J 20 + 3	Ardley N 42 + 1	Norville J 6 + 6	McNamee A 1 + 22	Glass S 26 + 7	Webber D 11 + 1	Vernazza P 13 + 10	Helguson H 28 + 2	Johnson R 5 + 7	Pennant J 12	Mahon G 13 + 4	Noel-Williams G 8 + 8	Brown W 12 + 1	Lee R 4	Fisken G 3 + 1	Godfrey E — + 1	Cook L 3 + 1	Chopra M 4 + 1	Ifil J 1	Swonnell S 1 + 1	Fitzgerald S 1 + 3	Smith J — + 1	*Match No.*
1	2^1	3	4	5	6	7	8	9^2	10	11^3	12	13	14																			1
1		3	4	5	6		8	9^2	10	11^3	2		12	7^1	13	14																2
1		3	4	5	6		8	12	10	11^3	2		13	7^2	9^1	14																3
1	12	3	4	5	6	7	8■		10^2	11^3	2^1			13	9	14																4
1		3	4	5	6	7	8		10		2			11	9																	5
1		3■	4	5	6	7	8	9■	10		2			11																		6
1	7	3	4	5	9^1	8		12	10	13	2		14	11^3		6^2																7
1	2		4	5		7	8		10^1	6	11			3	9		12															8
1	2	3	4	5		8	11		10^1	6	7			12	9																	9
1	2	3	4	5	12	8	11			6^2	7		13		9		10^1															10
1	2	3	4		5	8■	11^1			6	7			12	9^2		10	13														11
1	2	3	4	5	6^2	8	11^3	12			7			13	9		10^1	14														12
1	2		4	5			11^3	10^1	12	6	7		14	3	9	13		8^2														13
1	2	3^2	4	5		6	8^1		12		7		13	11^3	9		10	14														14
1	2	3	4	5		6	8^2		12		7			11	9^1	13	10															15
1	2	3	4	5		6	8	12	10^1		7			11^2			9	13														16
1	2	3	4^1	5		6	8	9			7			11			10	12														17
1	2	3^3	4	5		6	8^1	9	12		7^2			11		13	10	14														18
1	2	3	4		5	6	8		12		7^2			11^1			9	13	10													19
1	2	3	4		5	6^2	8^1		12	11^3	7		14	13			9		10													20
1	2	3	4		5	6		12	10^2	8^3	7			13			9^1		11	14												21
1	2	3	4		5	6		12	10	11^2	7		14	13			9^1		8^3													22
1		3^2	4		5	6	8^3	12	10		2			11		13	9		7^1	14												23
1		3	4		5	8	11	12	10^3		2		13			6^2	9^1		7		14											24
1		3	4		6	11	12		10		2						9^2		7^1	8	13	5										25
1		3	4		6	11		12	10^3		2		13			8^2	9^1		7		14	5										26
1		11^3	4		5	8	12		13		2		14			6^1	9		7^2		10	3										27
1			4		5	8^3	11^2		12		2		13			6	9^1		7	14	10	3										28
1		3	4		5	8	11^2		12		2		13			6^3	9		7	14	10^1											29
1		3	4		5	7	11		10^1	8	2					6	9				12											30
1		3	4	5		8	11^1		10		2		12			6^2	9		7		13											31
1	4^1				5	8	12			11^2	2	10^3	13	3			9			7	14	6										32
1			4		5	8	11				2	12		3		6	9			7	10^1											33
1		3	4		5	8	7			6	2	12		11			9				10^1											34
		3		5■						8	2	10	12	11^3		13				7^2	9	6	1	4^1	14							35
1		3	4	12	5	8			10^1	6^3	2			11^2		13	9			7	14											36
1		3	4		5	8^3			10^1		2		13	11		12	9			6	14			7^2								37
1			4		5^3	8^2			12		2		13	3			9			6	10	14		7^1		11						38
1		3^1	2	5					10	12	7	13		11		4				8		6					9^2					39
1			2			8	11		10^1		7	12		3		4				6		5					9					40
	2	3		5						8		12					13	7		6	10^2	4	1			11	9^1					41
1		3		5		8^1	7^3		10	12			13				9	6		2		4				11^2	14					42
	2	3			5					8	7	9	12	11^1		6^2							1				10^3	4	13	14		43
1		3	5						10^2		2	9		11^3				6		8		4		12					7^1	13	14	44
1				5	6	8	11		10^2		2	9	12	3		4^1				7										13		45
	2		4		5		11^1			7		9	8					6				3	1			12				10		46

Worthington Cup

First Round	Luton T	(h)	1-2

FA Cup

Third Round	Macclesfield T	(a)	2-0
Fourth Round	WBA	(h)	1-0
Fifth Round	Sunderland	(a)	1-0
Sixth Round	Burnley	(h)	2-0
Semi-final (at Villa Park)	Southampton		1-2

WEST BROMWICH ALBION Division 1

FOUNDATION

There is a well known story that when employees of Salter's Spring Works in West Bromwich decided to form a football club, they had to send someone to the nearby Association Football stronghold of Wednesbury to purchase a football. A weekly subscription of 2d (less than 1p) was imposed and the name of the new club was West Bromwich Strollers.

The Hawthorns, West Bromwich B71 4LF.

Telephone: (0121) 525 8888 (all Depts).
Fax: (0121) 524 3461.

Registered Office: The Hawthorns, West Bromwich, West Midlands B71 4LF.

Ground Capacity: 28,000 (all seated).

Record Attendance: 64,815 v Arsenal, FA Cup 6th rd, 6 March 1937.

Record Receipts: £375,272 v Cheltenham T, FA Cup 5th rd, 16 February 2002.

Pitch Measurements: 115yd × 72yd.

President: John G. Silk LL.B (Lond).
Chairman: J. R. Peace.

Directors: J. W. Brandrick, M. O'Leary (Chief Executive), B. Batson (Managing Director), M. J. Jenkins, J. J. Evans.

Manager: Gary Megson.

Assistant Manager: Frank Burrows.

Coach: Alan Crawford. ***Reserve Coach:*** Gary Shelton.

Youth Coach: Craig Shakespeare. ***Physio:*** Nick Worth.

Secretary: Dr John J. Evans BA, PHD. (Wales).

Club Statistician: Tony Matthews.

Colours: Navy blue and white striped shirts, blue shorts, blue stockings.

Change Colours: Yellow and green striped shirts, green shorts, yellow stockings.

Year Formed: 1878. ***Turned Professional:*** 1885.

Ltd Co.: 1892. ***Plc:*** 1996.

Previous Name: 1878, West Bromwich Strollers; 1881, West Bromwich Albion.

Club Nicknames: 'Throstles', 'Baggies', 'Albion'.

Previous Grounds: 1878, Coopers Hill; 1879, Dartmouth Park; 1881, Bunns Field, Walsall Street; 1882, Four Acres (Dartmouth Cricket Club); 1885, Stoney Lane; 1900, The Hawthorns.

First Football League Game: 8 September 1888, Football League, v Stoke (a) W 2–0 – Roberts; J. Horton, Green; E. Horton, Perry, Bayliss; Bassett, Woodhall (1), Hendry, Pearson, Wilson (1).

Record League Victory: 12–0 v Darwen, Division 1, 4 April 1892 – Reader; J. Horton, McCulloch; Reynolds (2), Perry, Groves; Bassett (3), McLeod, Nicholls (1), Pearson (4), Geddes (1), (1 og).

HONOURS

Football League: Division 1 – Champions 1919–20; Runners-up 1924–25, 1953–54, 2001–02; Division 2 – Champions 1901–02, 1910–11; Runners-up 1930–31, 1948–49; Promoted to Division 1 1975–76 (3rd); 1992–93 (play-offs); Promoted to FA Premier League 2001–02.

FA Cup: Winners 1888, 1892, 1931, 1954, 1968; Runners-up 1886, 1887, 1895, 1912, 1935.

Football League Cup: Winners 1966; Runners-up 1967, 1970.

European Competitions: *European Cup-Winners' Cup:* 1968–69. *European Fairs Cup:* 1966–67. *UEFA Cup:* 1978–79, 1979–80, 1981–82.

SKY SPORTS FACT FILE

West Bromwich Albion signed Billy (WG) Richardson, a bus inspector and centre-forward from Hartlepools United for £1,000 in June 1929. He was recommended to the club by Jack Manners who had left Albion for United in pre-war days.

Record Cup Victory: 10–1 v Chatham (away), FA Cup 3rd rd, 2 March 1889 – Roberts; J. Horton, Green; Timmins (1), Charles Perry, E. Horton; Bassett (2), Perry (1), Bayliss (2), Pearson, Wilson (3), (1 og).

Record Defeat: 3–10 v Stoke C, Division 1, 4 February 1937.

Most League Points (2 for a win): 60, Division 1, 1919–20.

Most League Points (3 for a win): 89, Division 1, 2001–02.

Most League Goals: 105, Division 2, 1929–30.

Highest League Scorer in Season: William 'Ginger' Richardson, 39, Division 1, 1935–36.

Most League Goals in Total Aggregate: Tony Brown, 218, 1963–79.

Most League Goals in One Match: 6, Jimmy Cookson v Blackpool, Division 2, 17 September 1927.

Most Capped Player: Stuart Williams, 33 (43), Wales.

Most League Appearances: Tony Brown, 574, 1963–80.

Youngest League Player: Charlie Wilson, 16 years 73 days v Oldham Ath, 1 October 1921.

Record Transfer Fee Received: £5,000,001 from Coventry C for Lee Hughes, July 2001.

Record Transfer Fee Paid: £2,500,000 to Coventry C for Lee Hughes, August 2002 and £2,500,000 to Tranmere R for Jason Koumas, August 2002.

Football League Record: 1888 Founder Member of Football League; 1901–02 Division 2; 1902–04 Division 1; 1904–11 Division 2; 1911–27 Division 1; 1927–31 Division 2; 1931–38 Division 1; 1938–49 Division 2; 1949–73 Division 1; 1973–76 Division 2; 1976–86 Division 1; 1986–91 Division 2; 1991–92 Division 3; 1992–93 Division 2; 1993–2002 Division 1; 2002–03 FA Premier League; 2003– Division 1.

MANAGERS

Louis Ford 1890–92
(Secretary-Manager)
Henry Jackson 1892–94
(Secretary-Manager)
Edward Stephenson 1894–95
(Secretary-Manager)
Clement Keys 1895–96
(Secretary-Manager)
Frank Heaven 1896–1902
(Secretary-Manager)
Fred Everiss 1902–48
Jack Smith 1948–52
Jesse Carver 1952
Vic Buckingham 1953–59
Gordon Clark 1959–61
Archie Macaulay 1961–63
Jimmy Hagan 1963–67
Alan Ashman 1967–71
Don Howe 1971–75
Johnny Giles 1975–77
Ronnie Allen 1977
Ron Atkinson 1978–81
Ronnie Allen 1981–82
Ron Wylie 1982–84
Johnny Giles 1984–85
Ron Saunders 1986–87
Ron Atkinson 1987–88
Brian Talbot 1988–91
Bobby Gould 1991–92
Ossie Ardiles 1992–93
Keith Burkinshaw 1993–94
Alan Buckley 1994–97
Ray Harford 1997
Denis Smith 1997–2000
Brian Little 2000
Gary Megson March 2000–

LATEST SEQUENCES

Longest Sequence of League Wins: 11, 5.4.1930 – 8.9.1930.

Longest Sequence of League Defeats: 11, 28.10.1995 – 26.12.1995.

Longest Sequence of League Draws: 5, 30.8.1999 – 3.10.1999.

Longest Sequence of Unbeaten League Matches: 17, 7.9.1957 – 7.12.1957.

Longest Sequence Without a League Win: 14, 28.10.1995 – 3.2.1996.

Successive Scoring Runs: 36 from 26.4.1958.

Successive Non-scoring Runs: 4 from 15.2.1913.

TEN YEAR LEAGUE RECORD

		P	*W*	*D*	*L*	*F*	*A*	*Pts*	*Pos*
1993-94	Div 1	46	13	12	21	60	69	51	21
1994-95	Div 1	46	16	10	20	51	57	58	19
1995-96	Div 1	46	16	12	18	60	68	60	11
1996-97	Div 1	46	14	15	17	68	72	57	16
1997-98	Div 1	46	16	12	17	50	56	61	10
1998-99	Div 1	46	16	11	19	69	76	59	12
1999-2000	Div 1	46	10	19	17	43	60	49	21
2000-01	Div 1	46	21	11	14	60	52	74	6
2001-02	Div 1	46	27	8	11	61	29	89	2
2002-03	PR Lge	38	6	8	24	29	65	26	19

DID YOU KNOW?

On 16 February 1935 at Edgeley Park, West Bromwich Albion defeated Stockport County 5-0 in a fifth round FA Cup tie played in a rain storm. Appropriately enough it was Arthur Gale who opened the Baggies' account.

WEST BROMWICH ALBION 2002–03 LEAGUE RECORD

Match No.	Date	Venue	Opponents	Result		H/T Score	Lg. Pos.	Goalscorers	Attendance
1	Aug 17	A	Manchester U	L	0-1	0-0	—		67,645
2	24	H	Leeds U	L	1-3	0-1	18	Marshall 90	26,598
3	27	A	Arsenal	L	2-5	0-3	—	Dobie 51, Roberts 87	37,920
4	31	H	Fulham	W	1-0	0-0	18	Moore 48	25,440
5	Sept 11	A	West Ham U	W	1-0	1-0	—	Roberts 28	34,927
6	14	H	Southampton	W	1-0	0-0	7	Gregan 79	26,377
7	21	A	Liverpool	L	0-2	0-0	11		43,830
8	30	H	Blackburn R	L	0-2	0-0	—		25,090
9	Oct 5	A	Newcastle U	L	1-2	1-1	15	Balis 27	52,142
10	19	H	Birmingham C	D	1-1	0-0	16	Roberts 87	26,914
11	26	A	Chelsea	L	0-2	0-1	18		40,893
12	Nov 2	H	Manchester C	L	1-2	0-0	19	Clement 62	26,907
13	9	A	Bolton W	D	1-1	1-0	19	Dobie 17	23,630
14	16	H	Aston Villa	D	0-0	0-0	20		26,973
15	23	A	Everton	L	0-1	0-1	19		40,113
16	30	H	Middlesbrough	W	1-0	0-0	17	Dichio 72	26,833
17	Dec 8	A	Tottenham H	L	1-3	0-2	17	Dobie 73	35,994
18	14	A	Aston Villa	L	1-2	1-1	18	Koumas 29	40,391
19	21	H	Sunderland	D	2-2	2-0	18	Dichio 27, Koumas 33	26,448
20	26	H	Arsenal	L	1-2	1-0	19	Dichio 3	26,782
21	28	A	Charlton Ath	L	0-1	0-1	19		26,156
22	Jan 11	H	Manchester U	L	1-3	1-2	20	Koumas 6	26,936
23	18	A	Leeds U	D	0-0	0-0	19		39,708
24	29	H	Charlton Ath	L	0-1	0-0	—		25,608
25	Feb 1	A	Manchester C	W	2-1	1-1	18	Clement 18, Moore 71	34,765
26	8	H	Bolton W	D	1-1	0-1	18	Johnson 90	26,627
27	19	A	Fulham	L	0-3	0-0	—		15,799
28	23	H	West Ham U	L	1-2	0-1	19	Dichio 50	26,739
29	Mar 1	A	Southampton	L	0-1	0-1	19		31,915
30	16	H	Chelsea	L	0-2	0-1	19		26,749
31	22	A	Birmingham C	L	0-1	0-0	19		29,449
32	Apr 5	A	Middlesbrough	L	0-3	0-1	19		30,187
33	12	H	Everton	L	1-2	1-2	19	Balis (pen) 18	26,713
34	19	A	Sunderland	W	2-1	2-0	19	McInnes 2 39, 42	36,025
35	21	H	Tottenham H	L	2-3	1-1	19	Dichio 24, Clement 61	26,569
36	26	H	Liverpool	L	0-6	0-1	19		26,852
37	May 3	A	Blackburn R	D	1-1	0-1	19	Koumas 54	27,470
38	11	H	Newcastle U	D	2-2	0-1	19	Dobie 2 57, 71	26,773

Final League Position: 19

GOALSCORERS

League (29): Dichio 5, Dobie 5, Koumas 4, Clement 3, Roberts 3, Balis 2 (1 pen), McInnes 2, Moore 2, Gregan 1, Johnson 1, Marshall 1.
Worthington Cup (1): Hughes 1.
FA Cup (3): Dichio 3.

Hoult R 37	Balis I 27 + 1	Clement N 34 + 2	Sigurdsson L 23 + 6	Moore D 29	Gilchrist P 22	Gregan S 36	McInnes D 28 + 1	Dichio D 19 + 9	Roberts J 31 + 1	Johnson A 30 + 2	Taylor B 2 + 2	Dobie S 10 + 21	Marshall L 4 + 5	Wallwork R 23 + 4	Hughes L 14 + 9	Chambers J 2 + 6	Koumas J 27 + 5	Murphy J 1 + 1	Chambers A 10 + 3	Udeze I 7 + 4	Jordao — + 3	Lyttle D 2 + 2	Match No.
1	2	3	4	5	6	7^{1}	8■	9^{2}	10^{3}	11	12	13	14										1
1	2	3	4	5^{1}	6	7	8^{3}	12	10	11^{2}		9	13	14									2
1	2	3	4	5	6	7	8^{1}		10	11		9	12										3
1	2	3		5	6	7			10^{3}	11	12		8^{2}	4	9^{1}	14	13						4
1	2	3	12	5	6	4			10^{3}	11		13		8	9^{2}	14	7^{1}						5
1	2	3	12	5	6	4		13	10	11		14		8^{1}	9^{3}		7^{2}						6
1■	2^{2}	3	4	5	6	7		12	10	8		9^{6}	13				11^{1}	15					7
1	2	3	4^{3}	5	6	7			10	8	9^{1}	12	13	14			11^{2}						8
	2	3		5	6	4	8		10	11		9^{2}	7^{1}		13		12	1					9
1	2	3		5	6	4			10	11		12	7	8	9^{1}								10
1	2	3	12	5	6	4^{1}	8		10	11		9	7^{2}		13								11
1	2	3		5	6	4	8		10	11		9^{1}			12		13		7^{2}				12
1	2	3	4	5		6	8		10	11		9^{1}					12		7				13
1	2	3	4	5	6^{1}	7^{2}	8	13	10	11		9^{3}			14				12				14
1	2^{2}	3	4	5		6	7		10	11		9^{1}		8	12		13						15
1	2	3	4	5^{3}		6	7	12	10^{2}	8		13			9^{1}	14	11						16
1	2	3	4			6	7	12	10^{1}	8^{3}		13		5	9^{2}		11		14				17
1	2	3	4	5		6	7	12	10^{2}	8		13			9^{1}		11						18
1	2^{2}	3	4	5		6	7	9	10^{1}	8		12					11		13				19
1		3	4	5		6		9	10	8		12		7^{2}		13	11		2^{1}				20
1		3	4	5		6		9	10	8		12		7	13		11^{2}		2^{1}				21
1	12	3	4^{2}	5	6			9	10	8		13		7			11		2^{1}				22
1	2^{3}	3	12	5	6	4	7	9		8■		10^{2}		14	13		11^{1}						23
1				5^{1}	6	4	12	9^{2}	10	8		13		7			11		2	3			24
1		3	12	5	6	4	8	13	10■					7	9^{2}		11^{1}		2				25
1		3		5	6^{3}	4	8^{1}	9	10^{2}	12				7	13		11		2	14			26
1		3^{2}		5	6	4	8	9^{3}				12		7	10^{1}		11		2	13	14		27
1			12	5	6	4	8^{2}	9				13		7^{1}	10		11		2	3			28
1		12	4	5	6	7	8^{3}	9				13		2^{2}	10		11			3^{1}	14		29
1	2	6	4	5^{3}		7	8^{2}	12	10					13	9	14	11			3^{1}			30
1	2	6	4			7	8	9	10					5	12		11^{1}			3			31
1	2^{3}	3	4		6	7	8^{2}	9	10^{1}	13		12		5			11					14	32
1	2	3^{2}	4			6	8^{1}	9		7		12		5	10		11			13			33
1	2	3	4			6	8	9	12	7				5	10^{1}		11						34
1	2	12	4			6	8	9^{2}	10	7		13		5			11			3^{1}			35
1	2	6				4^{2}	8	9	10	7				5^{1}		12	11			3^{3}	13	14	36
1		3				6	8	9^{1}	10	7		12		5		4	11					2	37
1		3	4				8	9		7	10^{1}	12		5		6^{2}	11			13		2	38

Worthington Cup
Second Round Wigan Ath (a) 1-3

FA Cup
Third Round Bradford C (h) 3-1
Fourth Round Watford (a) 0-1

WEST HAM UNITED Division 1

FOUNDATION

Thames Iron Works FC was formed by employees of this famous shipbuilding company in 1895 and entered the FA Cup in their initial season at Chatham and the London League in their second. The committee wanted to introduce professional players, so Thames Iron Works was wound up in June 1900 and relaunched a month later as West Ham United.

Boleyn Ground, Green Street, Upton Park, London E13 9AZ.

Telephone General Office: (020) 8548 2748.
Fax: (020) 8548 2758. ***Ticket Office:*** (020) 8548 2700.
Sportswear Stadium Store: (020) 8548 2794.
Membership Office: (020) 8548 2727.
Commercial: (020) 8548 2777.
Conference & Banqueting: (020) 8548 2775.

Football in the Community: (020) 8548 2707.

ClubCall: 09068 121 110.

Hammers Line: 09065 861 966.

Website: www.whufc.co.uk

Ground Capacity: 35,089.

Record Attendance: 42,322 v Tottenham H, Division 1, 17 October 1970.

Record Receipts: £910,500 v Chelsea, FA Cup 4th rd replay, 6 February 2002.

Pitch Measurements: 112yd × 72yd.

Chairman: T. W. Brown FCIS, AII, FCCA. ***Vice-chairman:*** M. W. Cearns ACIB.
Directors: C. J. Warner, N. Igoe, C. Manhire, T. Brooking CBE, P. Aldridge (Managing).

Manager: Glenn Roeder. ***Assistant Manager:*** Paul Goddard. ***Reserve Team Coach:*** Roger Cross.

Physio: John Green BSC (HONS), MCSP, SRP.

Football Secretary: Peter Barnes.

Stadium Manager: John Ball.

Press Officer: Peter Stewart.

Colours: Claret shirts with sky blue sleeves, white shorts and stockings.

Change Colours: All navy.

Year Formed: 1895.

Turned Professional: 1900.

Ltd Co.: 1900.

Previous Name: Thames Iron Works FC, 1895–1900.

Club Nicknames: 'The Hammers', 'The Irons'.

Previous Grounds: 1895, Memorial Recreation Ground, Canning Town; 1904, Boleyn Ground.

HONOURS

Football League: Division 1 best season: 3rd, 1985–86; Division 2 – Champions 1957–58, 1980–81; Runners-up 1922–23, 1990–91.

FA Cup: Winners 1964, 1975, 1980; Runners-up 1923.

Football League Cup: Runners-up 1966, 1981.

European Competitions: *European Cup-Winners' Cup:* 1964–65 (winners), 1965–66, 1975–76 (runners-up), 1980–81. *UEFA Cup:* 1999–2000. *Intertoto Cup:* 1999 (winners).

SKY SPORTS FACT FILE

West Ham United's 1966 World Cup trio of Bobby Moore, Geoff Hurst and Martin Peters won a total of 224 England international caps between them. In 37 of these matches all three played together in the same match.

MANAGERS

Syd King 1902–32
Charlie Paynter 1932–50
Ted Fenton 1950–61
Ron Greenwood 1961–74
(continued as General Manager to 1977)
John Lyall 1974–89
Lou Macari 1989–90
Billy Bonds 1990–94
Harry Redknapp 1994–2001
Glenn Roeder June 2001–

First Football League Game: 30 August 1919, Division 2, v Lincoln C (h) D 1–1 – Hufton; Cope, Lee; Lane, Fenwick, McCrae; D. Smith, Moyes (1), Puddefoot, Morris, Bradshaw.

Record League Victory: 8–0 v Rotherham U, Division 2, 8 March 1958 – Gregory; Bond, Wright; Malcolm, Brown, Lansdowne; Grice, Smith (2), Keeble (2), Dick (4), Musgrove. 8–0 v Sunderland, Division 1, 19 October 1968 – Ferguson; Bonds, Charles; Peters, Stephenson, Moore (1); Redknapp, Boyce, Brooking (1), Hurst (6), Sissons.

Record Cup Victory: 10–0 v Bury, League Cup 2nd rd (2nd leg), 25 October 1983 – Parkes; Stewart (1), Walford, Bonds (Orr), Martin (1), Devonshire (2), Allen, Cottee (4), Swindlehurst, Brooking (2), Pike.

Record Defeat: 2–8 v Blackburn R, Division 1, 26 December 1963.

Most League Points (2 for a win): 66, Division 2, 1980–81.

Most League Points (3 for a win): 88, Division 1, 1992–93.

Most League Goals: 101, Division 2, 1957–58.

Highest League Scorer in Season: Vic Watson, 42, Division 1, 1929–30.

Most League Goals in Total Aggregate: Vic Watson, 298, 1920–35.

Most League Goals in One Match: 6, Vic Watson v Leeds U, Division 1, 9 February 1929; 6, Geoff Hurst v Sunderland, Division 1, 19 October 1968.

Most Capped Player: Bobby Moore, 108, England.

Most League Appearances: Billy Bonds, 663, 1967–88.

Youngest League Player: Neil Finn, 17 years 3 days v Manchester C, 1 January 1996.

Record Transfer Fee Received: £18,000,000 from Leeds U for Rio Ferdinand, November 2000.

Record Transfer Fee Paid: £5,000,000 to Sunderland for Don Hutchison, August 2001 and £5,000,000 to Sparta Prague for Tomas Repka, September 2001.

Football League Record: 1919 Elected to Division 2; 1923–32 Division 1; 1932–58 Division 2; 1958–78 Division 1; 1978–81 Division 2; 1981–89 Division 1; 1989–91 Division 2; 1991–93 Division 1; 1993–2003 FA Premier League; 2003– Division 1.

LATEST SEQUENCES

Longest Sequence of League Wins: 9, 19.10.1985 – 14.12.1985.

Longest Sequence of League Defeats: 9, 28.3.1932 – 29.8.1932.

Longest Sequence of League Draws: 5, 7.9.1968 – 5.10.1968.

Longest Sequence of Unbeaten League Matches: 27, 27.12.80 – 10.10.81.

Longest Sequence Without a League Win: 17, 31.1.1976 – 21.8.1976.

Successive Scoring Runs: 27 from 5.10.1957.

Successive Non-scoring Runs: 5 from 1.5.1971.

TEN YEAR LEAGUE RECORD

		P	*W*	*D*	*L*	*F*	*A*	*Pts*	*Pos*
1993-94	PR Lge	42	13	13	16	47	58	52	13
1994-95	PR Lge	42	13	11	18	44	48	50	14
1995-96	PR Lge	38	14	9	15	43	52	51	10
1996-97	PR Lge	38	10	12	16	39	48	42	14
1997-98	PR Lge	38	16	8	14	56	57	56	8
1998-99	PR Lge	38	16	9	13	46	53	57	5
1999-2000	PR Lge	38	15	10	13	52	53	55	9
2000-01	PR Lge	38	10	12	16	45	50	42	15
2001-02	PR Lge	38	15	8	15	48	57	53	7
2002-03	PR Lge	38	10	12	16	42	59	42	18

DID YOU KNOW ?

On 9 May 2002 Her Majesty Queen Elizabeth II visited Upton Park as part of her Golden Jubilee celebrations. HM formally opened West Ham United's Dr Martens Stand as the club hosted a luncheon for neighbouring boroughs.

WEST HAM UNITED 2002–03 LEAGUE RECORD

Match No.	Date	Venue	Opponents	Result	H/T Score	Lg. Pos.	Goalscorers	Attendance
1	Aug 19	A	Newcastle U	L 0-4	0-0	—		51,072
2	24	H	Arsenal	D 2-2	1-0	16	Cole 44, Kanoute 53	35,046
3	31	H	Charlton Ath	L 0-2	0-2	20		32,424
4	Sept 11	H	WBA	L 0-1	0-1	—		34,927
5	15	A	Tottenham H	L 2-3	0-0	20	Kanoute 66, Sinclair 77	35,996
6	21	H	Manchester C	D 0-0	0-0	20		35,050
7	28	A	Chelsea	W 3-2	1-1	20	Defoe 40, Di Canio 2 48, 84	38,937
8	Oct 5	H	Birmingham C	L 1-2	1-2	20	Cole 17	35,010
9	19	A	Sunderland	W 1-0	1-0	17	Sinclair 23	44,352
10	23	A	Fulham	W 1-0	0-0	—	Di Canio (pen) 90	15,858
11	27	H	Everton	L 0-1	0-0	15		34,117
12	Nov 2	A	Liverpool	L 0-2	0-1	17		44,048
13	10	H	Leeds U	L 3-4	1-4	18	Di Canio 2 (1 pen) 21, 50 (p), Sinclair 74	33,297
14	17	H	Manchester U	D 1-1	0-1	19	Defoe 86	35,049
15	23	A	Aston Villa	L 1-4	0-1	20	Di Canio 70	33,279
16	Dec 2	H	Southampton	L 0-1	0-0	—		28,844
17	7	A	Middlesbrough	D 2-2	0-0	20	Cole 46, Pearce 76	28,283
18	14	A	Manchester U	L 0-3	0-2	20		67,555
19	21	H	Bolton W	D 1-1	1-0	20	Pearce 17	34,892
20	26	H	Fulham	D 1-1	0-0	20	Sinclair (pen) 65	35,025
21	28	A	Blackburn R	D 2-2	1-1	20	Taylor (og) 24, Defoe 86	24,998
22	Jan 11	H	Newcastle U	D 2-2	2-1	19	Cole 14, Defoe 45	35,048
23	19	A	Arsenal	L 1-3	1-1	20	Defoe 40	38,053
24	22	A	Charlton Ath	L 2-4	1-2	—	Rufus (og) 19, Fish (og) 62	26,327
25	29	H	Blackburn R	W 2-1	0-1	—	Di Canio (pen) 58, Defoe 89	34,743
26	Feb 2	H	Liverpool	L 0-3	0-2	19		35,033
27	8	A	Leeds U	L 0-1	0-1	19		40,126
28	23	A	WBA	W 2-1	1-0	18	Sinclair 2 45, 67	26,739
29	Mar 1	H	Tottenham H	W 2-0	1-0	18	Ferdinand 31, Carrick 47	35,049
30	15	A	Everton	D 0-0	0-0	18		40,158
31	22	H	Sunderland	W 2-0	1-0	17	Defoe 24, Kanoute 65	35,033
32	Apr 5	A	Southampton	D 1-1	0-1	18	Defoe 83	31,941
33	12	H	Aston Villa	D 2-2	1-1	18	Sinclair 15, Kanoute 65	35,029
34	19	A	Bolton W	L 0-1	0-1	18		27,160
35	21	H	Middlesbrough	W 1-0	0-0	18	Sinclair 77	35,019
36	27	A	Manchester C	W 1-0	0-0	18	Kanoute 81	34,815
37	May 3	H	Chelsea	W 1-0	0-0	18	Di Canio 71	35,042
38	11	A	Birmingham C	D 2-2	0-0	18	Ferdinand 66, Di Canio 89	29,449

Final League Position: 18

GOALSCORERS

League (42): Di Canio 9 (3 pens), Defoe 8, Sinclair 8 (1 pen), Kanoute 5, Cole 4, Ferdinand 2, Pearce 2, Carrick 1, own goals 3.
Worthington Cup (1): Defoe 1.
FA Cup (3): Defoe 2, Cole 1.

James D 38	Pearce I 26 + 4	Winterburn N 16 + 2	Schemmel S 15 + 1	Repka T 32	Dailly C 23 + 3	Sinclair T 36 + 2	Cisse E 18 + 7	Defoe J 29 + 9	Cole J 36	Carrick M 28 + 2	Labant V — + 1	Moncur J — + 7	Kanoute F 12 + 5	Breen G 9 + 5	Camara T — + 4	Lomas S 27 + 2	Di Canio P 16 + 2	Minto S 9 + 3	Hutchison D — + 10	Bowyer L 10	Ferdinand L 12 + 2	Johnson G 14 + 1	Brevett R 12 + 1	Match No.
1	2	3	4^{1}	5	6	7	8^{2}	9	10	11	12	13												1
1		3^{1}	2	5	6	7	4	10	8^{2}	11		13	9	12										2
1		3^{1}	2	5	6	7	4^{2}	10	8	11			9		12	13								3
1		3^{1}	2	5	12	7	4	13	8	11^{3}			9	6		14	10^{2}							4
1	2■	12		5^{1}	6	7	11	13	8	14			9^{2}	4		3	10^{3}							5
1	12		2	5		7	11^{3}	13	8^{1}	14			9	6		4	10^{2}	3						6
1			2	5		7	12	13	8	11			9^{2}	6		4	10^{1}	3						7
1	12		2^{1}	5		7		9	8^{2}	11				6	13	4	10	3						8
1	6^{1}			5	2	7^{2}	13	9	8	11				12		4	10	3						9
1	4			5	2	7	6	9	8	11							10	3						10
1	6			5	2	7	12	9	8	11					13	4^{1}	10	3^{2}						11
1	6			5	2	10	7	9^{1}	8	11					12	4		3						12
1	6	3	12	5^{1}	2	7	13	9	8	11						4^{2}	10							13
1	4	3	2		5	7	6	9	8	11							10							14
1	4	3	2		5	7	6	9	8	11							10							15
1	8	3	2	5	6	7		9	4	11		12					10^{1}							16
1	10^{2}	3	2	5	6	7	8^{1}	9	4	11		12		13										17
1	10		2	5	6	7		9	8	11		12		13		4^{1}		3^{2}						18
1	10^{1}	3	2	5	6	7		9	8	11						4			12					19
1	12	3	2	5■	6	7		10	8	11			9^{1}			4^{2}			13					20
1	9	3^{3}	2		6	7	8^{2}	12	10	11		13		5		4^{1}		14						21
1	12	3^{2}			6	10^{1}	4^{3}	9	8	11				5		2		13	14	7				22
1	4	3^{2}			6	7	8^{1}	9	10			12		5		2■		13		11				23
1		12			6	7	4^{2}	9		11				5		2		3^{1}		8	10	13		24
1	4	3^{1}		5		13		12	8	11			14			6	10^{2}			7	9^{3}	2		25
1		3^{3}		5	6	7^{1}		12	4	11			13				10			8	9^{2}	2	14	26
1	6			5		12		13	8	11^{3}			9■			4	10^{2}		14	7		2	3^{1}	27
1	6			5		7		12		11				13		4	10^{1}		14	8^{2}	9^{3}	2	3	28
1	6			5		7		10	4	11									12	8	9^{1}	2	3	29
1	6			5	13	7	12	10	8^{1}	11						4					9^{2}	2	3	30
1	6			5		7	12	10	8^{1}	11			13			4^{3}			14		9^{2}	2	3	31
1	6			5		11	12	10	8				13			4^{1}				7	9^{2}	2	3	32
1	6			5		11		10	8				9^{1}			4			12	7^{2}	13	2	3	33
1	6■			5		11	7^{1}	10	8				9			4					12	2	3	34
1	6			5		7	11	10	8							4					9	2	3	35
1	6^{1}			5	12	7	8^{2}	10	11				13			4			14		9^{3}	2	3	36
1				5	6	7		8	11				10			4	12				9^{1}	2	3	37
1				5	6	7		8	11^{2}				10			4	12		13		9	2	3^{1}	38

Worthington Cup

Second Round	Chesterfield	(a)	1-1
Third Round	Oldham Ath	(h)	0-1

FA Cup

Third Round	Nottingham F	(h)	3-2
Fourth Round	Manchester U	(a)	0-6

WIGAN ATHLETIC — Division 1

FOUNDATION

Following the demise of Wigan Borough and their resignation from the Football League in 1931, a public meeting was called in Wigan at the Queen's Hall in May 1932 at which a new club, Wigan Athletic, was founded in the hope of carrying on in the Football League. With this in mind, they bought Springfield Park for £2,250, but failed to gain admission to the Football League until 46 years later.

JJB Stadium, Robin Park Complex, Newtown, Wigan WN5 0UZ.

Telephone: (01942) 774 000.

Fax: (01942) 770 477.

Website: www.wiganathletic.tv

Ticket Office: (01942) 770 410.

Commercial Dept: (01942) 774 000.

Latics ClubCall: 09068 121 655.

Football in the Community: (01942) 824 599.

Ground Capacity: 25,000.

Record Attendance: 27,526 v Hereford U, 12 December 1953.

Record Receipts: £190,000 v Blackburn R, Worthington Cup quarter-final, 17 December 2002.

Pitch Measurements: 115yd × 75yd.

President: S. Jackson.

Chairman: David Whelan.

Directors: D. Whelan, J. Winstanley, P. Williams, B. Ashcroft, B. Spencer.

Chief Executive: Mrs Brenda Spencer.

Football Secretary: Stuart Hayton.

Manager: Paul Jewell.

Physio: Alex Cribley.

Safety Officer: Raymond Johnston.

Groundsman: Ian Forshaw.

Colours: Blue shirts, blue shorts, white stockings.

Change Colours: White shirts, navy shorts, white stockings.

Year Formed: 1932.

Club Nickname: 'The Latics'.

First Football League Game: 19 August 1978, Division 4, v Hereford U (a) D 0–0 – Brown; Hinnigan, Gore, Gillibrand, Ward, Davids, Corrigan, Purdie, Houghton, Wilkie, Wright.

HONOURS

Football League: Division 2 Champions, 2002–03; Division 3 Champions, 1996–97; Division 4 – Promoted (3rd) 1981–82.

FA Cup: best season: 6th rd, 1987.

Football League Cup: best season: 5th rd, 2003.

Freight Rover Trophy: Winners 1985.

Auto Windscreens Shield: Winners 1999.

SKY SPORTS FACT FILE

In 1965-66 Wigan Athletic drew 1-1 at Doncaster Rovers in the FA Cup first round, Harry Lyon scoring. In the replay he hit a hat-trick in the 3-0 win after suffering torn ligaments and going off the field for 15 minutes.

Record League Victory: 7–1 v Scarborough, Division 3, 11 March 1997 – Butler L, Butler J, Sharp (Morgan), Greenall, McGibbon (Biggins (1)), Martinez (1), Diaz (2), Jones (Lancashire (1)), Lowe (2), Rogers, Kilford.

Record Cup Victory: 6–0 v Carlisle U (away), FA Cup 1st rd, 24 November 1934 – Caunce; Robinson, Talbot; Paterson, Watson, Tufnell; Armes (2), Robson (1), Roberts (2), Felton, Scott (1).

Record Defeat: 1–6 v Bristol R, Division 3, 3 March 1990.

Most League Points (2 for a win): 55, Division 4, 1978–79 and 1979–80.

Most League Points (3 for a win): 100, Division 2, 2002–03.

Most League Goals: 84, Division 3, 1996–97.

Highest League Scorer in Season: Graeme Jones, 31, Division 3, 1996–97.

Most League Goals in Total Aggregate: David Lowe, 66, 1982–87 and 1995–99.

Most League Goals in One Match: Not more than three goals by one player.

Most Capped Player: Roy Carroll, 9 (13), Northern Ireland.

Most League Appearances: Kevin Langley, 317, 1981–86, 1990–94.

Youngest League Player: Steve Nugent, 16 years 132 days v Leyton Orient, 16 September 1989.

Record Transfer Fee Received: £2,500,000 from Manchester U for Roy Carroll, July 2001

Record Transfer Fee Paid: £1,200,000 to Bristol R for Nathan Ellington, March 2002.

Football League Record: 1978 Elected to Division 4; 1982–92 Division 3; 1992–93 Division 2; 1993–97 Division 3; 1997–2003 Division 2; 2003– Division 1.

MANAGERS

Charlie Spencer 1932–37
Jimmy Milne 1946–47
Bob Pryde 1949–52
Ted Goodier 1952–54
Walter Crook 1954–55
Ron Suart 1955–56
Billy Cooke 1956
Sam Barkas 1957
Trevor Hitchen 1957–58
Malcolm Barrass 1958–59
Jimmy Shirley 1959
Pat Murphy 1959–60
Allenby Chilton 1960
Johnny Ball 1961–63
Allan Brown 1963–66
Alf Craig 1966–67
Harry Leyland 1967–68
Alan Saunders 1968
Ian McNeill 1968–70
Gordon Milne 1970–72
Les Rigby 1972–74
Brian Tiler 1974–76
Ian McNeill 1976–81
Larry Lloyd 1981–83
Harry McNally 1983–85
Bryan Hamilton 1985–86
Ray Mathias 1986–89
Bryan Hamilton 1989–93
Dave Philpotts 1993
Kenny Swain 1993–94
Graham Barrow 1994–95
John Deehan 1995–98
Ray Mathias 1998–99
John Benson 1999–2000
Bruce Rioch 2000–01
Steve Bruce 2001
Paul Jewell June 2001–

LATEST SEQUENCES

Longest Sequence of League Wins: 11, 2.11.2002 – 18.1.2003.

Longest Sequence of League Defeats: 7, 6.4.1993 – 4.5.1993.

Longest Sequence of League Draws: 6, 11.12.2001 – 5.1.2002.

Longest Sequence of Unbeaten League Matches: 25, 8.5.1999 – 3.1.2000.

Longest Sequence Without a League Win: 14, 9.5.1989 – 17.10.1989.

Successive Scoring Runs: 24 from 27.4.1996.

Successive Non-scoring Runs: 4 from 15.4.1995.

TEN YEAR LEAGUE RECORD

		P	W	D	L	F	A	Pts	Pos
1993-94	Div 3	42	11	12	19	51	70	45	19
1994-95	Div 3	42	14	10	18	53	60	52	14
1995-96	Div 3	46	20	10	16	62	56	70	10
1996-97	Div 3	46	26	9	11	84	51	87	1
1997-98	Div 2	46	17	11	18	64	66	62	11
1998-99	Div 2	46	22	10	14	75	48	76	6
1999-2000	Div 2	46	22	17	7	72	38	83	4
2000-01	Div 2	46	19	18	9	53	42	75	6
2001-02	Div 2	46	16	16	14	66	51	64	10
2002-03	Div 2	46	29	13	4	68	25	100	1

DID YOU KNOW ?

On 17 December 1977 Wigan Athletic had the highest FA Cup second round attendance of the day when 13,871 watched Sheffield Wednesday lose 1-0. A free kick from Maurice Whittle settled the tie.

WIGAN ATHLETIC 2002–03 LEAGUE RECORD

Match No.	Date	Venue	Opponents	Result		H/T Score	Lg. Pos.	Goalscorers	Attendance
1	Aug 10	A	Cheltenham T	W	2-0	2-0	—	Liddell [6], McCulloch [25]	5138
2	13	H	Mansfield T	W	3-2	2-1	—	Ellington 2 [28, 32], De Vos [65]	5837
3	17	H	Bristol C	W	2-0	0-0	1	Green [75], McCulloch [90]	6548
4	24	A	Notts Co	W	2-0	0-0	1	Liddell 2 [64, 75]	6302
5	26	H	Port Vale	L	0-1	0-1	2		6532
6	31	A	Colchester U	L	0-1	0-1	3		2721
7	Sept 7	H	Wycombe W	W	3-0	2-0	1	McCulloch [3], Liddell 2 [36, 90]	5358
8	14	A	Chesterfield	D	0-0	0-0	1		4124
9	17	A	Tranmere R	W	2-0	0-0	—	Ellington 2 (1 pen) [54 (p), 67]	8153
10	21	H	Peterborough U	D	2-2	1-0	2	Liddell (pen) [40], Ellington [48]	5797
11	28	A	Barnsley	W	3-1	2-0	4	Liddell [2], Jackson [11], Green [65]	9977
12	Oct 5	H	Cardiff C	D	2-2	2-1	3	Dinning [26], Ellington [28]	8047
13	12	A	Plymouth Arg	W	3-1	1-1	2	Dinning 2 [25, 58], Ellington [90]	8746
14	19	H	Stockport Co	W	2-1	0-1	1	Ellington [50], Roberts [61]	7276
15	26	A	Luton T	D	1-1	0-1	1	De Vos [88]	7364
16	29	H	QPR	D	1-1	1-1	—	Liddell [29]	6241
17	Nov 2	H	Crewe Alex	W	2-0	2-0	3	Liddell (pen) [10], Foster (og) [45]	7086
18	9	A	Blackpool	W	2-0	1-0	1	Dinning [12], Flynn [86]	7676
19	23	A	Brentford	W	1-0	1-0	1	Roberts [45]	5454
20	30	H	Northampton T	W	1-0	1-0	1	Roberts [37]	6032
21	Dec 14	A	Oldham Ath	W	2-0	1-0	1	Ellington [36], De Vos [60]	8269
22	21	H	Huddersfield T	W	1-0	1-0	1	De Vos [45]	6013
23	26	A	Port Vale	W	1-0	0-0	1	De Vos [69]	6395
24	28	H	Swindon T	W	2-0	1-0	1	Teale [42], Ellington [90]	6114
25	Jan 1	H	Notts Co	W	3-1	1-0	1	Dinning [45], De Vos [57], Liddell [73]	6009
26	10	A	Bristol C	W	1-0	0-0	—	Kennedy [49]	13,151
27	18	H	Colchester U	W	2-1	1-0	1	De Vos [44], Liddell (pen) [74]	5792
28	25	A	Swindon T	L	1-2	0-2	1	McCulloch [55]	5238
29	28	A	Mansfield T	W	2-1	2-0	—	Ellington [39], Liddell [43]	5524
30	Feb 1	H	Cheltenham T	D	0-0	0-0	1		6171
31	8	H	Blackpool	D	1-1	1-0	1	Liddell [1]	10,546
32	22	A	Wycombe W	W	2-0	1-0	1	McCulloch [9], Liddell (pen) [89]	6052
33	25	A	Crewe Alex	W	1-0	1-0	—	Ellington [38]	8917
34	Mar 1	H	Chesterfield	W	3-1	2-0	1	Teale [25], Dinning [40], Liddell (pen) [74]	6384
35	4	H	Tranmere R	D	0-0	0-0	—		9021
36	8	A	Peterborough U	D	1-1	0-0	1	Arber (og) [82]	4970
37	15	H	Luton T	D	1-1	0-0	1	Roberts [75]	7087
38	18	A	Stockport Co	D	1-1	0-0	—	De Vos [63]	6719
39	22	A	QPR	W	1-0	0-0	1	Ellington [47]	14,703
40	29	H	Plymouth Arg	L	0-1	0-1	1		7203
41	Apr 4	A	Northampton T	W	2-0	2-0	—	Ellington [9], Liddell (pen) [43]	5822
42	12	H	Brentford	W	2-0	0-0	1	Ellington [57], McCulloch [90]	7204
43	19	A	Huddersfield T	D	0-0	0-0	1		13,769
44	21	H	Oldham Ath	W	3-1	1-1	1	Roberts 2 [9, 80], Bullard [71]	12,783
45	26	A	Cardiff C	D	0-0	0-0	1		14,702
46	May 3	H	Barnsley	W	1-0	1-0	1	Dinning [13]	12,537

Final League Position: 1

GOALSCORERS

League (68): Liddell 16 (6 pens), Ellington 15 (1 pen), De Vos 8, Dinning 7, McCulloch 6, Roberts 6, Green 2, Teale 2, Bullard 1, Flynn 1, Jackson 1, Kennedy 1, own goals 2.
Worthington Cup (7): Ellington 5, Jarrett 1, Roberts 1.
FA Cup (4): Ellington 2, Flynn 1, Green 1.
LDV Vans Trophy (3): Teale 2, Jarrett 1.

Filan J 46	Brannan G 6	Kennedy P 21 + 1	Dinning T 36 + 2	De Vos J 43	Jackson M 45	Teale G 28 + 10	Jarrett J 25 + 10	Ellington N 41 + 1	Liddell A 32 + 5	McCulloch L 33 + 5	Green S 14 + 3	McMillan S 28 + 4	Breckin I 7 + 2	Flynn M 3 + 14	Roberts N 25 + 12	Mitchell P 13 + 14	Eaden N 37	Baines L 6	Bullard J 17	*Match No.*
1	2	3	4	5	6	7¹	8	9	10	11²	12	13								1
1	2	3	4	5	6		8	9	10	11	7									2
1	2²	3	4	5	6		8¹	9	10	11	7		13	12						3
1			4	5	2	12	13	9³	10	11¹	7	3	6	8²	14					4
1			4²	5	2¹	12	13	9	10	11	7	3	6	8						5
1			4■	5	2¹	12	13	9	10	11	7	3³	6	8²	14					6
1	2¹			5	6	12	8	9	10	11	7	3				4				7
1	2			5	6	11¹	8	9	10		7	3		12		4				8
1	2¹			5	6		8	9	10■	11	7	3		12		4				9
1				5	6		8¹	9	10	11	7	3		12		4	2			10
1			4	5	6		8	9²	10	11	7¹	3		12	13		2			11
1			4	5	6	12	8	9		11	7¹	3			10		2			12
1			4	5	6	7¹	8²	9		11		3		12	10	13	2			13
1			4³	5	6	7¹	8	9²	12	11		3		13	10	14	2			14
1			4	5	6■	7¹	8	9	12	11		3			10		2			15
1			4	5	6		8	9	7	11		3			10		2			16
1		11	4	5	6	12	8	9¹	7			3			10²	13	2			17
1		11	4	5		7²	8	9			13		6	12	10¹	3	2			18
1		11	4	5	6		8	9			7¹	3			10	12	2			19
1		11²	4³	5	6	12	8	9			7¹	3		13	10	14	2			20
1		11	4	5	6	12	8	9			7¹			13	10²		2	3		21
1		11²	4	5	6	7	8³	9¹	12	13		3			10	14	2			22
1		11	4	5	6	7³	8	9	12	13		3²			10¹	14	2			23
1		11	4	5	6	7		9	12	8²				13	10¹	3	2			24
1		3	4	5	6	7		9	10²	11¹	12				13	8	2			25
1		3	4	5	6	7¹	12	9²	10	11					13	8	2			26
1		3	4	5	6	7		9¹	10	11					12	8	2			27
1		3	4	5	6	7		9	10	11						8	2			28
1		3	4	5	6	7¹	12	9	10³	11²		13			14	8	2			29
1		3	4	5	6	7		9	10²			12			13	8¹	2		11	30
1		3	4¹	5	6	7	12	9²	10	11					13		2		8	31
1			4	5	6	7¹	12	9²	10	11³		3			13	14	2		8	32
1			4	5	6	7¹	12	9	10³	11²		3			13	14	2		8	33
1			4²	5	6	7¹		9	11	12		3			10	13	2		8	34
1			4²	5	6	7¹		9	11	12		3			10	13	2		8	35
1			4	5	6	7		12	10	11		3			9¹		2		8	36
1				5	6	7²	12	9	10	11		3			13	4¹	2		8	37
1			4	5	6			9	7	11					10		2	3	8	38
1			4²	5	6	12	13	9¹	7³	11					10	14	2	3	8	39
1				5	6	12	4	9	7	11²			13		10¹		2	3	8	40
1				5	6	7¹	4	9	11					12	10		2	3	8	41
1				5	6	11	4	9	7¹	12		13			10	14	2	3²	8³	42
1		12	13	5	6	7	4		10¹	11		3			9		2		8²	43
1		11	12		6³	7	4¹			10²		3	5	13	9	14	2		8	44
1		11	4		6	7				10		3	5	12	9¹		2		8	45
1		11	4		6	7				10		3	5		9		2		8	46

Worthington Cup

First Round	Northampton T	(a)	1-0
Second Round	WBA	(h)	3-1
Third Round	Manchester C	(h)	1-0
Fourth Round	Fulham	(h)	2-1
Fifth Round	Blackburn R	(h)	0-2

FA Cup

First Round	Hereford U	(a)	1-0
Second Round	Luton T	(h)	3-0
Third Round	Stoke C	(a)	0-3

LDV Vans Trophy

First Round	Notts Co	(a)	3-2
Second Round	Doncaster R	(h)	0-1

WIMBLEDON Division 1

FOUNDATION

Old boys from Central School formed this club as Wimbledon Old Centrals in 1889. Their earliest successes were in the Clapham League before switching to the Southern Suburban League in 1902.

Selhurst Park, South Norwood, London SE25 6PY.

Telephone: (020) 8771 2233.

Fax: (020) 8768 0641.

Website: www.wimbledon-fc.co.uk

Box Office: (020) 8771 8841.

ClubCall: 09068 121 175.

Ground Capacity: 26,297.

Record Attendance: 30,115 v Manchester U, FA Premier League, 9 May 1993.

Record Receipts: £531,976 v Tottenham H, Worthington Cup semi-final, 2nd leg, 16 February 1999.

Pitch Measurements: 110yd × 74yd.

Chairman: Charles Koppel.

Deputy Chairman: Peter Lloyd-Cooper.

Directors: K. I. Røkke, B Gjelsten, J. H. Lelliott, P. E. Cork, P. J. B. Miller, M. Hauger, C. Stromberg.

Manager: Stuart Murdoch.

Club Secretary: Steve Rooke.

Director of Media and Communications: Graham Thorley.

Press Manager: Reg Davis.

Chief Scout: Terry Murphy.

Team Physio: Steve Allen.

Club Physio: John Clinkard.

Stadium Manager: Kevin Corner.

Colours: All navy blue with yellow trim.

Change Colours: All red with black trim.

Year Formed: 1889.

Turned Professional: 1964.

Ltd Co.: 1964.

Previous Name: Wimbledon Old Centrals, 1899–1905.

Previous Ground: 1899, Plough Lane; 1991, Selhurst Park.

HONOURS

FA Premier League: best season: 6th, 1993–94.

Football League: Division 3 – Runners-up 1983–84; Division 4 – Champions 1982–83.

FA Cup: Winners 1988.

Football League Cup: Semi-final 1996–97, 1998–99.

League Group Cup: Runners-up 1982.

Amateur Cup: Winners 1963; Runners-up 1935, 1947.

European Competitions: *Intertoto Cup:* 1995.

SKY SPORTS FACT FILE

Of the Wimbledon team which won the FA Amateur Cup in 1963, eight of the players either were or were to become amateur internationals. In addition to their cup success, three out of the club's four teams retained their league titles.

MANAGERS

Les Henley 1955–71
Mike Everitt 1971–73
Dick Graham 1973–74
Allen Batsford 1974–78
Dario Gradi 1978–81
Dave Bassett 1981–87
Bobby Gould 1987–90
Ray Harford 1990–91
Peter Withe 1991
Joe Kinnear 1992–99
Egil Olsen 1999–2000
Terry Burton 2000–02
Stuart Murdoch June 2002–

Club Nicknames: 'The Dons', 'The Crazy Gang'.

First Football League Game: 20 August 1977, Division 4, v Halifax T (h) D 3–3 – Guy; Bryant (1), Galvin, Donaldson, Aitken, Davies, Galliers, Smith, Connell (1), Holmes, Leslie (1).

Record League Victory: 6–0 v Newport Co, Division 3, 3 September 1983 – Beasant; Peters, Winterburn, Galliers, Morris, Hatter, Evans (2), Ketteridge (1), Cork (3 incl. 1p), Downes, Hodges (Driver).

Record Cup Victory: 7–2 v Windsor & Eton, FA Cup 1st rd, 22 November 1980 – Beasant; Jones, Armstrong, Galliers, Mick Smith (2), Cunningham (1), Ketteridge, Hodges, Leslie, Cork (1), Hubbick (3).

Record Defeat: 0–8 v Everton, League Cup 2nd rd, 29 August 1978.

Most League Points (2 for a win): 61, Division 4, 1978–79.

Most League Points (3 for a win): 98, Division 4, 1982–83.

Most League Goals: 97, Division 3, 1983–84.

Highest League Scorer in Season: Alan Cork, 29, 1983–84.

Most League Goals in Total Aggregate: Alan Cork, 145, 1977–92.

Most League Goals in One Match: 4, Alan Cork v Torquay U, Division 4, 28 February 1979.

Most Capped Player: Kenny Cunningham, 40 (48), Republic of Ireland.

Most League Appearances: Alan Cork, 430, 1977–92.

Youngest League Player: Kevin Gage, 17 years 15 days v Bury, 2 May 1981.

Record Transfer Fee Received: £7,000,000 from Newcastle U for Carl Cort, July 2000.

Record Transfer Fee Paid: £7,500,000 to West Ham U for John Hartson, January 1999.

Football League Record: 1977 Elected to Division 4; 1979–80 Division 3; 1980–81 Division 4; 1981–82 Division 3; 1982–83 Division 4; 1983–84 Division 3; 1984–86 Division 2; 1986–92 Division 1; 1992–2000 FA Premier League; 2000– Division 1.

LATEST SEQUENCES

Longest Sequence of League Wins: 7, 4.9.1996 – 19.10.1996.

Longest Sequence of League Defeats: 14, 19.3.2000 – 28.8.2000.

Longest Sequence of League Draws: 4, 24.4.2001 – 6.5.2001.

Longest Sequence of Unbeaten League Matches: 22, 15.1.1983 – 14.5.1983.

Longest Sequence Without a League Win: 14, 19.3.2000 – 28.8.2000.

Successive Scoring Runs: 23 from 18.2.1984.

Successive Non-scoring Runs: 5 from 13.4.1995.

TEN YEAR LEAGUE RECORD

		P	W	D	L	F	A	Pts	Pos
1993-94	PR Lge	42	18	11	13	56	53	65	6
1994-95	PR Lge	42	15	11	16	48	65	56	9
1995-96	PR Lge	38	10	11	17	55	70	41	14
1996-97	PR Lge	38	15	11	12	49	46	56	8
1997-98	PR Lge	38	10	14	14	34	46	44	15
1998-99	PR Lge	38	10	12	16	40	63	42	16
1999-2000	PR Lge	38	7	12	19	46	74	33	18
2000-01	Div 1	46	17	18	11	71	50	69	8
2001-02	Div 1	46	18	13	15	63	57	67	9
2002-03	Div 1	46	18	11	17	76	73	65	10

DID YOU KNOW ?

During the 1982–83 season, Wimbledon received £25,000 awarded by Capital Radio to the London-based Football League club which first reached 80 League goals. The Dons went on to score 96 in the term.

WIMBLEDON 2002–03 LEAGUE RECORD

Match No.	Date	Venue	Opponents	Result		H/T Score	Lg. Pos.	Goalscorers	Attendance
1	Aug 10	H	Gillingham	L	0-1	0-0	—		2476
2	13	A	Grimsby T	D	0-0	0-0	—		4625
3	17	A	Watford	L	2-3	1-2	19	Nowland [17], Francis [86]	10,292
4	24	H	Brighton & HA	W	1-0	0-0	15	Shipperley (pen) [73]	2522
5	28	A	Nottingham F	L	0-2	0-2	—		16,431
6	31	H	Wolverhampton W	W	3-2	1-1	15	Shipperley 2 [4, 77], Gray [54]	3223
7	Sept 7	H	Leicester C	L	2-3	2-2	17	Williams [11], Shipperley [16]	2165
8	14	A	Reading	W	1-0	0-0	13	McAnuff [90]	14,832
9	17	A	Portsmouth	L	1-4	1-3	—	Shipperley [11]	18,837
10	21	H	Coventry C	L	0-1	0-1	18		2077
11	28	A	Burnley	L	0-1	0-0	20		12,259
12	Oct 6	H	Ipswich T	L	0-1	0-0	21		3238
13	12	A	Millwall	D	1-1	0-0	21	Nethercott (og) [71]	8248
14	19	H	Crystal Palace	D	2-2	0-1	22	Shipperley [77], Agyemang [79]	6538
15	26	A	Sheffield U	D	1-1	1-0	21	Connolly [12]	17,372
16	29	H	Rotherham U	W	2-1	1-0	—	Shipperley [19], Connolly [60]	849
17	Nov 2	H	Norwich C	W	4-2	3-0	17	Shipperley [24], Connolly 3 (1 pen) [42, 45, 83 (p)]	3908
18	9	A	Bradford C	W	5-3	2-3	15	Connolly 4 [30, 45, 49, 61], Darlington [89]	10,615
19	16	H	Walsall	W	3-2	1-1	12	McAnuff [25], Shipperley (pen) [69], Francis [90]	1255
20	25	A	Derby Co	L	2-3	1-1	—	Shipperley [8], Connolly [88]	25,597
21	30	H	Sheffield W	W	3-0	1-0	13	Morgan [42], Connolly [63], Shipperley [89]	2131
22	Dec 7	A	Preston NE	W	5-3	1-2	11	Connolly 2 (1 pen) [40, 65 (p)], McAnuff 2 [72, 82], Reo-Coker [90]	12,415
23	14	A	Walsall	L	0-2	0-1	15		6596
24	21	H	Stoke C	D	1-1	0-0	14	Connolly [82]	1697
25	26	H	Watford	D	0-0	0-0	14		2643
26	Jan 11	H	Grimsby T	D	3-3	0-1	17	Agyemang [67], Darlington [69], Francis [73]	1336
27	18	A	Wolverhampton W	D	1-1	0-1	17	Francis [46]	23,716
28	Feb 1	H	Nottingham F	L	2-3	0-2	17	Gray [59], Francis [63]	3382
29	4	A	Brighton & HA	W	3-2	1-1	—	Connolly 2 [39, 79], Volz [48]	6111
30	8	H	Bradford C	D	2-2	0-1	16	Ainsworth [47], Shipperley [71]	1178
31	22	A	Leicester C	L	0-4	0-2	17		31,438
32	Mar 1	H	Reading	W	2-0	1-0	17	Francis [31], Tapp [85]	3869
33	4	H	Portsmouth	W	2-1	0-1	—	Agyemang [66], Ainsworth [87]	10,356
34	8	A	Coventry C	D	2-2	1-1	17	Connolly [12], Shipperley [76]	11,796
35	11	A	Gillingham	D	3-3	1-0	—	Connolly [4], Reo-Coker [79], Shipperley (pen) [87]	7884
36	15	H	Millwall	W	2-0	1-0	9	Shipperley [19], Agyemang [90]	2952
37	18	A	Crystal Palace	W	1-0	1-0	—	Andersen [45]	13,713
38	22	A	Rotherham U	L	1-2	0-1	9	Connolly [59]	5896
39	25	A	Norwich C	L	0-1	0-1	—		21,059
40	Apr 5	A	Sheffield W	L	2-4	0-1	11	Connolly [54], Agyemang [55]	17,649
41	7	H	Sheffield U	W	1-0	1-0	—	Shipperley [38]	1325
42	12	H	Derby Co	L	0-2	0-1	9		1934
43	19	A	Stoke C	L	1-2	0-2	12	Shipperley [51]	12,587
44	21	H	Preston NE	W	2-0	0-0	10	Shipperley 2 [60, 65]	1053
45	26	A	Ipswich T	W	5-1	1-0	10	Shipperley [28], Nowland [60], Connolly 2 [83, 85], Tapp [88]	25,564
46	May 4	H	Burnley	W	2-1	0-1	10	Connolly 2 [55, 81]	1972

Final League Position: 10

GOALSCORERS

League (76): Connolly 24 (2 pens), Shipperley 20 (3 pens), Francis 6, Agyemang 5, McAnuff 4, Ainsworth 2, Darlington 2, Gray 2, Nowland 2, Reo-Coker 2, Tapp 2, Andersen 1, Morgan 1, Volz 1, Williams 1, own goal 1.
Worthington Cup (8): Shipperley 3, Agyemang 1, Andersen 1, Leigertwood 1, McAnuff 1, Tapp 1.
FA Cup (3): McAnuff 1, Morgan 1, Shipperley 1.

Davis K 46	Darlington J 32 + 3	Hawkins P 43	Andersen T 34 + 4	Williams M 23	Willmott C 5	McAnuff J 29 + 2	Francis D 29 + 5	Shipperley N 46	Agyemang P 12 + 21	Nowland A 10 + 14	Gray W 12 + 18	Karlsson P 2 + 1	Ainsworth G 8 + 4	Gier R 27 + 2	Tapp A 23 + 1	Leigertwood M 27 + 1	Holloway D 14 + 2	Connolly D 28	Reo-Coker N 32	Morgan L 6 + 5	Volz M 10	Chorley B 8 + 2	Lewington D — + 1	Gordon M — + 1	Kamara M — + 2	Match No.
1	2	3	4	5	6	7	8	9	10	11[1]	12															1
1	2	3	4	5	6	7	8	9	10	11[1]	12															2
1	2	3	4	5	6	7	8	9	10[2]	11[1]	12	13														3
1	2	3	4	5	6	7	8	9		12	10[1]	11														4
1	2	3	4	5	6	7	8	9[1]		12	10	11[2]	13													5
1	2	3	4	5		7	8	9		12	10[1]			6	11											6
1	2	3		5		7	8	9		12	10[1]		13	6	11	4[2]										7
1	2	3	4	5		7	8	9		12	10[1]			6	11											8
1	2	3	4	5■		7	8	9[1]		10[2]	12		13	6[3]	11	14										9
1	2	3[3]	4	5		7	8	9		10[1]	12		13	6	11[2]		14									10
1		3	4	5		7	8	9[2]	13	12	10			6	11[1]		2									11
1		3	4			7	8	9		10[1]	12			6	11	5	2									12
1	4	3				7	8	9		12				6	11	5	2	10[1]								13
1	4	3[2]	12			7	8	9	13					6	11[1]	5	2	10								14
1	8	3	4			7[1]		9	13		12			6		5	2	10[2]	11							15
1	8	3	4			7	12	9	13					6		5	2	10[2]	11[1]							16
1	8	3	4			7[1]	12	9						6		5	2	10	11[2]	13						17
1	8	3	4			7[2]	12	9						6		5	2	10	11[1]	13						18
1	8[1]	3	4			7	12	9	13					6■		5	2	10[2]	11							19
1	8	3	4			7[2]	12	9	13		14			6		5	2[1]	10	11[3]							20
1	2	3		6		7	8	9	12		13					5		10[2]	11	4[1]						21
1	2	3	12	6		7	8	9								5		10	11	4[1]						22
1	2	3	4[1]	6		7	8[3]	9[2]	13	12	14					5		10	11							23
1	2[1]	3	4	6		7	8	9	12							5		10	11							24
1	2[1]	3	4	5		7	8	9	12							6		10	11							25
1	2	3	4	6		7	8	9	10[1]		12					5			11							26
1	2	3		6			8	9	10[1]	12	13			4	7	5			11[2]							27
1	2[1]	3	12	5			8	9[2]	10[3]	14	13		7	6		4			11							28
1	2		4				8	9			12		7	6		5		10[1]	11		3					29
1	2[1]		4	5			8	9	12				7			6		10	11		3					30
1	2[2]		8[1]	5				9	12		10		7	6		4			11	13	3					31
1	12	3	4	5			8	9	13		10[2]		2		14				11[1]	7[3]	6					32
1		3	4	5		12		9	13		10[2]		7		6				11	8[1]	2					33
1		3	4			12	8	9	13				7	5	6[1]			10[2]	11		2					34
1	12	3	4			7	6	9	13				8[1]	5				10[2]	11		2					35
1	2	3	4			7	8[2]	9[1]	12						6			10	11	13		5				36
1	12	3	4[1]			7[3]	8	9[2]	13						6			10	11	14	2	5				37
1	7[2]	3						9[3]	12	14	13			6	4[1]			10	11	8	2	5				38
1	4[2]	3						9	12	7				13	6[1]		14	10	11	8[3]	2	5				39
1		3	4[2]					9[1]	8	13	12			6	7[3]		2	10	11			5	14			40
1		3	4					9[1]	8	7■				12	6	5	2	10	11							41
1		3	4					9	8[3]	7[2]	12				6	5	2[1]	10	11			13		14		42
1		3						9	8[1]	7	12			6	4	5	2[2]	10	11			13				43
1		3						9	7[1]		8			2	4	5		10	11			6			12	44
1		3	12					9	7[2]	13	8[3]			2	4	5		10	11[1]			6			14	45
1		3	4					9	12	13	8[2]			2	7[1]	5		10	11			6				46

Worthington Cup

First Round	Southend U	(a)	4-1
Second Round	Portsmouth	(a)	3-1
Third Round	Rotherham U	(h)	1-3

FA Cup

Third Round	Rotherham U	(a)	3-0
Fourth Round	Walsall	(a)	0-1

WOLVERHAMPTON WANDERERS FA Premiership

FOUNDATION

Enthusiasts of the game at St Luke's School, Blakenhall formed a club in 1877. In the same neighbourhood a cricket club called Blakenhall Wanderers had a football section. Several St Luke's footballers played cricket for them and shortly before the start of the 1879–80 season the two amalgamated and Wolverhampton Wanderers FC was brought into being.

Molineux Stadium, Wolverhampton WV1 4QR.

Telephone: (01902) 655 000. ***Fax:*** (01902) 687 006. ***ClubCall:*** 09068 121 103.

Ground Capacity: 28,525.

Record Attendance: 61,315 v Liverpool, FA Cup 5th rd, 11 February 1939.

Record Receipts: £369,232 v Norwich C, Division 1 play-off semi-final, 1 May 2002.

Pitch Measurements: 110yd × 75yd.

President and Chairman: Sir Jack Hayward.

Deputy Chairman: Derek Harrington.

Directors: Jack Harris, John Harris, Rick Hayward, Rachael Heyhoe Flint, Michael Lister, Paul Manduca, Jez Moxey (Chief Executive).

Manager: Dave Jones.

Coach: Terry Connor. ***Physio:*** Barry Holmes.

Secretary: Richard Skirrow.

Stadium Manager: Steve Sutton.

Safety Officer: Bob Morrison.

Colours: Gold shirts, black shorts, black stockings.

Change Colours: All black with gold trim.

Year Formed: 1877* (*see Foundation*).

Turned Professional: 1888.

Ltd Co.: 1923 (but current club is WWFC (1986) Ltd).

Previous Names: 1879, St Luke's combined with Wanderers Cricket Club to become Wolverhampton Wanderers (1923) Ltd. New limited companies followed in 1982 and 1986 (current).

Club Nickname: 'Wolves'.

Previous Grounds: 1877, Windmill Field; 1879, John Harper's Field; 1881, Dudley Road; 1889, Molineux.

First Football League Game: 8 September 1888, Football League, v Aston Villa (h) D 1–1 – Baynton; Baugh, Mason; Fletcher, Allen, Lowder; Hunter, Cooper, Anderson, White, Cannon, (1 og).

Record League Victory: 10–1 v Leicester C, Division 1, 15 April 1938 – Sidlow; Morris, Dowen; Galley, Cullis, Gardiner; Maguire (1), Horace Wright, Westcott (4), Jones (1), Dorsett (4).

HONOURS

Football League: Division 1 – Champions 1953–54, 1957–58, 1958–59; Runners-up 1937–38, 1938–39, 1949–50, 1954–55, 1959–60; 2002–03 (play-offs). Division 2 – Champions 1931–32, 1976–77; Runners-up 1966–67, 1982–83; Division 3 (N) – Champions 1923–24; Division 3 – Champions 1988–89; Division 4 – Champions 1987–88.

FA Cup: Winners 1893, 1908, 1949, 1960; Runners-up 1889, 1896, 1921, 1939.

Football League Cup: Winners 1974, 1980.

Texaco Cup: Winners 1971.

Sherpa Van Trophy: Winners 1988.

European Competitions: *European Cup:* 1958–59, 1959–60. *European Cup-Winners' Cup:* 1960–61. *UEFA Cup:* 1971–72 (runners-up), 1973–74, 1974–75, 1980–81.

SKY SPORTS FACT FILE

Though his successful goalscoring career straddled the Second World War years, Wolverhampton Wanderers centre-forward Dennis Westcott began with Leasowe Road Brickworks in Wallasey before trials with Everton and West Ham and joining New Brighton.

Record Cup Victory: 14–0 v Crosswell's Brewery, FA Cup 2nd rd, 13 November 1886 – I. Griffiths; Baugh, Mason; Pearson, Allen (1), Lowder; Hunter (4), Knight (2), Brodie (4), B. Griffiths (2), Wood. Plus one goal 'scrambled through'.

Record Defeat: 1–10 v Newton Heath, Division 1, 15 October 1892.

Most League Points (2 for a win): 64, Division 1, 1957–58.

Most League Points (3 for a win): 92, Division 3, 1988–89.

Most League Goals: 115, Division 2, 1931–32.

Highest League Scorer in Season: Dennis Westcott, 38, Division 1, 1946–47.

Most League Goals in Total Aggregate: Steve Bull, 250, 1986–99.

Most League Goals in One Match: 5, Joe Butcher v Accrington, Division 1, 19 November 1892; 5, Tom Phillipson v Barnsley, Division 2, 26 April 1926; 5, Tom Phillipson v Bradford C, Division 2, 25 December 1926; 5, Billy Hartill v Notts Co, Division 2, 12 October 1929; 5, Billy Hartill v Aston Villa, Division 1, 3 September 1934.

Most Capped Player: Billy Wright, 105, England (70 consecutive).

Most League Appearances: Derek Parkin, 501, 1967–82.

Youngest League Player: Jimmy Mullen, 16 years 43 days v Leeds U, 18 February 1939.

Record Transfer Fee Received: £5,000,000 from Leicester C for Ade Akinbiyi, July 2000.

Record Transfer Fee Paid: £3,000,000 to Bristol C for Ade Akinbiyi, September 1999 and £3,000,000 to Rangers for Kenny Miller, December 2001.

Football League Record: 1888 Founder Member of Football League: 1906–23 Division 2; 1923–24 Division 3 (N); 1924–32 Division 2; 1932–65 Division 1; 1965–67 Division 2; 1967–76 Division 1; 1976–77 Division 2; 1977–82 Division 1; 1982–83 Division 2; 1983–84 Division 1; 1984–85 Division 2; 1985–86 Division 3; 1986–88 Division 4; 1988–89 Division 3; 1989–92 Division 2; 1992–2003 Division 1; 2003– FA Premier League.

MANAGERS

George Worrall 1877–85
(Secretary-Manager)
John Addenbrooke 1885–1922
George Jobey 1922–24
Albert Hoskins 1924–26
(had been Secretary since 1922)
Fred Scotchbrook 1926–27
Major Frank Buckley 1927–44
Ted Vizard 1944–48
Stan Cullis 1948–64
Andy Beattie 1964–65
Ronnie Allen 1966–68
Bill McGarry 1968–76
Sammy Chung 1976–78
John Barnwell 1978–81
Ian Greaves 1982
Graham Hawkins 1982–84
Tommy Docherty 1984–85
Bill McGarry 1985
Sammy Chapman 1985–86
Brian Little 1986
Graham Turner 1986–94
Graham Taylor 1994–95
Mark McGhee 1995–98
Colin Lee 1998–2000
Dave Jones January 2001–

LATEST SEQUENCES

Longest Sequence of League Wins: 8, 15.10.1988 – 26.11.1988.

Longest Sequence of League Defeats: 8, 5.12.1981 – 13.2.1982.

Longest Sequence of League Draws: 6, 22.4.1995 – 20.8.1995.

Longest Sequence of Unbeaten League Matches: 20, 24.11.1923 – 5.4.1924.

Longest Sequence Without a League Win: 19, 1.12.1984 – 6.4.1985.

Successive Scoring Runs: 41 from 20.12.1958.

Successive Non-scoring Runs: 7 from 2.2.1985.

TEN YEAR LEAGUE RECORD

		P	W	D	L	F	A	Pts	Pos
1993-94	Div 1	46	17	17	12	60	47	68	8
1994-95	Div 1	46	21	13	12	77	61	76	4
1995-96	Div 1	46	13	16	17	56	62	55	20
1996-97	Div 1	46	22	10	14	68	51	76	3
1997-98	Div 1	46	18	11	17	57	53	65	9
1998-99	Div 1	46	19	16	11	64	43	73	7
1999-2000	Div 1	46	21	11	14	64	48	74	7
2000-01	Div 1	46	14	13	19	45	48	55	12
2001-02	Div 1	46	25	11	10	76	43	86	3
2002-03	Div 1	46	20	16	10	81	44	76	5

DID YOU KNOW ?

When Wolverhampton Wanderers beat Den Haag in a UEFA Cup second round second leg tie 4-0 on 3 November 1971, three of the goals were contributed by Dutch players putting through their own goal. Wolves won 7-1 on aggregate.

WOLVERHAMPTON WANDERERS 2002–03 LEAGUE RECORD

Match No.	Date	Venue	Opponents	Result		H/T Score	Lg. Pos.	Goalscorers	Attendance
1	Aug 11	A	Bradford C	D	0-0	0-0	—		13,223
2	14	H	Walsall	W	3-1	1-0	—	Cameron 2 [11, 55], Newton [86]	27,904
3	17	H	Burnley	W	3-0	1-0	3	Blake [2], Irwin [49], Cooper [88]	25,031
4	24	A	Derby Co	W	4-1	1-1	1	Rae 2 [19, 88], Cooper [77], Miller [90]	29,954
5	27	H	Sheffield W	D	2-2	0-1	—	Blake [60], Sturridge [68]	27,096
6	31	A	Wimbledon	L	2-3	1-1	4	Ingimarsson [15], Gier (og) [70]	3223
7	Sept 14	A	Crystal Palace	L	2-4	1-2	10	Ingimarsson [31], Blake [71]	16,961
8	21	H	Reading	L	0-1	0-0	14		25,560
9	24	H	Preston NE	W	4-0	2-0	—	Blake 2 [23, 85], Sturridge [45], Miller [86]	23,695
10	28	A	Leicester C	L	0-1	0-1	11		32,082
11	Oct 5	H	Sheffield U	L	1-3	1-1	14	Ullathorne (og) [35]	24,625
12	19	A	Stoke C	W	2-0	0-0	13	Cameron [78], Blake [90]	16,885
13	26	H	Grimsby T	W	4-1	1-1	11	Irwin [30], Miller [66], Ndah [71], Sturridge [90]	23,875
14	29	A	Gillingham	W	4-0	2-0	—	Cameron (pen) [28], Blake 3 [45, 52, 59]	10,036
15	Nov 2	A	Watford	D	1-1	0-0	9	Cooper [90]	16,524
16	6	H	Portsmouth	D	1-1	0-0	—	Sturridge [62]	27,022
17	11	H	Brighton & HA	D	1-1	0-1	—	Miller [76]	23,016
18	16	A	Coventry C	W	2-0	1-0	6	Lescott [38], Rae [77]	18,998
19	23	H	Nottingham F	W	2-1	0-1	5	Miller [76], Sturridge [80]	27,953
20	30	A	Rotherham U	D	0-0	0-0	8		6736
21	Dec 7	H	Norwich C	W	1-0	1-0	6	Cole [37]	25,753
22	14	H	Coventry C	L	0-2	0-1	7		25,577
23	21	A	Millwall	D	1-1	1-1	7	Kennedy [5]	9091
24	26	A	Burnley	L	1-2	0-2	9	Butler [85]	18,641
25	28	H	Bradford C	L	1-2	0-0	10	Ndah [54]	25,812
26	Jan 1	H	Derby Co	D	1-1	0-1	10	Ince [66]	26,442
27	11	A	Walsall	W	1-0	0-0	8	Ndah [64]	11,037
28	18	H	Wimbledon	D	1-1	1-0	8	Miller [43]	23,716
29	Feb 1	A	Sheffield W	W	4-0	2-0	6	Proudlock 2 [24, 42], Miller [67], Sturridge [89]	21,381
30	8	A	Brighton & HA	L	1-4	0-2	7	Miller [65]	6754
31	19	A	Ipswich T	W	4-2	1-2	—	Miller 2 [11, 63], Naylor [74], Ndah [81]	27,700
32	22	A	Preston NE	W	2-0	0-0	6	Ndah [53], Miller [83]	16,070
33	25	H	Watford	D	0-0	0-0	—		24,591
34	Mar 1	H	Crystal Palace	W	4-0	1-0	4	Miller 3 (1 pen) [40, 83, 90 (p)], Sturridge [77]	26,010
35	5	H	Ipswich T	D	1-1	0-0	—	Ince [48]	26,901
36	12	A	Reading	W	1-0	1-0	—	Miller [44]	19,731
37	15	A	Portsmouth	L	0-1	0-1	6		19,558
38	18	H	Stoke C	D	0-0	0-0	—		25,235
39	22	H	Gillingham	W	6-0	5-0	6	Blake [16], Cameron [22], Kennedy 2 [37, 45], Miller 2 [44, 48]	25,171
40	Apr 5	H	Rotherham U	D	0-0	0-0	6		25,934
41	8	A	Grimsby T	W	1-0	1-0	—	Blake [13]	4983
42	11	A	Nottingham F	D	2-2	2-1	—	Blake [9], Cameron [26]	27,209
43	19	H	Millwall	W	3-0	1-0	5	Newton 2 [5, 80], Cameron [78]	27,015
44	21	A	Norwich C	W	3-0	0-0	4	Ndah [52], Sturridge [74], Miller [90]	20,843
45	26	A	Sheffield U	D	3-3	2-1	5	Ndah [10], Sturridge 2 (1 pen) [45, 62 (p)]	22,211
46	May 4	H	Leicester C	D	1-1	0-0	5	Miller [58]	28,190

Final League Position: 5

GOALSCORERS

League (81): Miller 19 (1 pen), Blake 12, Sturridge 10 (1 pen), Cameron 7 (1 pen), Ndah 7, Cooper 3, Kennedy 3, Newton 3, Rae 3, Ince 2, Ingimarsson 2, Irwin 2, Proudlock 2, Butler 1, Cole 1, Lescott 1, Naylor 1, own goals 2.
Worthington Cup (7): Rae 2, Blake 1, Miller 1, Newton 1 (pen), Pollet 1, own goal 1.
FA Cup (10): Ndah 4, Miller 3, Ince 1, Kennedy 1, Proudlock 1.
Play-offs (6): Blake 1, Kennedy 1, Miller 1, Naylor 1, Rae 1, own goal 1.

Oakes M 6	Irwin D 43	Naylor L 31 + 1	Ingimarsson I 10 + 3	Butler P 31 + 1	Lescott J 44	Newton S 29 + 4	Rae A 30 + 8	Blake N 22 + 1	Miller K 35 + 8	Cameron C 29 + 4	Ndah G 17 + 8	Proudlock A 2 + 15	Sturridge D 17 + 22	Cooper K 13 + 13	Ince P 35 + 2	Murray M 40	Edworthy M 18 + 4	Clyde M 15 + 2	Kennedy M 30 + 1	Andrews K 2 + 7	Melligan J — + 2	Cole C 5 + 2	Pollet L 2	*Match No.*
1	2	3	4	5	6	7	8	9	10^1	11	12													1
1	2	3	4	5	6	7	8	9^2	10^1	11		13	12											2
1	2	3	4	5	6	7	8^2	9	10^1	11^3			12	13	14									3
1	2	3	4	5	6	7^2	8	9	12			13	10^1	14	11^3									4
1	2	3	4	5	6	7^1	8	9	12				10	11										5
	2	3	4	5	6	7^1	8	9	12			13	10^2	11		1								6
1	2	3	4	5	6	7^1	8^3	9	13			12	10^2	14	11									7
	2	3	4	5^2	6	7	8	12			9^1		10	13	11	1								8
	2	3	12	5	6	7^3	8	9	13				10^2	11	4^1	1	14							9
	2	3		5	6	7	8	9	12		13		10^1	11^2	4	1								10
	3		4^2	5	6	7^1	8	9	10		11^3		12	14	13	1	2							11
	3				6	7^2	8	9	10^1	11	13		12		4	1	2	5						12
	3		12		6	7^2	8^1	9	10^3	11	13		14		4	1	2	5						13
	3	12	13		6			9	10^3	7^2	8^1		14	11	4	1	2	5						14
	3				6	12	13	9	10^3	7^2	8^1		14	11	4	1	2	5						15
	3				6	12	8	9^2	10		11^3		13	7^1	4	1	2	5	14					16
	3		4^2		6	12	8		10				9	7^1		1	2	5	11	13				17
	3				6	7	8^2		10^1				9		4	1	2	5	11	12	13			18
	3				6	7^1	8		10				9^2	12		1	2	5	11	4	13			19
	3				6		8		10^1				9	7	4	1	2	5	11			12		20
	3				6		8^2		10^1	13			12	7	4	1	2	5	11^3	14		9		21
	2				6		8		10^1	4			12	13		1	3	5	11	7^2		9		22
	3				6		8^2		12	13	14		10	7^1	4	1	2	5	11			9^3		23
	3^1			12	6		8^2			13	14		10	7^3	4	1	2	5	11			9		24
		3			6				12	8	7		10^2	13	4	1	2	5	11			9^1		25
	2	3		5	6	7			10	8	9^1				4	1			11			12		26
	2	3		5	6	7^1			10	8	9	12			4	1			11					27
	2	3		5	6	7^1			10^2	8	9	13		12	4	1			11					28
	2	3		5	6	7^2	12		10^1	8		9	13		4	1			11^3	14				29
		3^3		5	6	7	12		10	8		9^2	13		4	1	2^1	14	11					30
	2	3		5^2	6		8^3		10^1	7	9	12			4	1	13		11	14				31
	2	3		5	6		8^1		10	7^2	9	12			4	1			11	13				32
	2	3		5	6		8^1		10	7	9^2	12	13		4^3	1			11	14				33
	2	3		5	6	7^3	12		10	8^1	9^2	13	14		4	1			11					34
	2	3		5	6	7		9^1	10^2	8		12	13		4	1			11					35
	2	3		5	6	7	8	9^1	10^2	4^3		12	13			1		14	11					36
	3					12	8		10^2	7^1		13	9		4	1	2	5	11				6	37
	2	3		5	6	7^3	8^1		10	12		13	9^2	14	4	1			11					38
	2	3		5	6	7	12	9	10^3	8^1		13	14		4	1			11^2					39
	2	3		5	6	7^2	12	9^1	10^3	8	14		13		4^1	1			11					40
	2	3		5	6			9	10^1	8	7^2		12	13	4	1			11					41
	2^2	3		5	6		8	9	10^1	7	12				4	1	13		11					42
	2	3		5	6	7^3	12		10^2	8	9		13	14	4^1	1			11					43
	2	3		5	6	7^2			10	8	9^1		12	13	4	1			11					44
		3		5	6		8			4	9		10	7		1	2		11					45
	2	3^3		5		7	12	9	10^2	8			13		4^1	1	14		11				6	46

Worthington Cup

First Round	Swansea C	(a)	3-2
Second Round	Rotherham U	(a)	4-4

FA Cup

Third Round	Newcastle U	(h)	3-2
Fourth Round	Leicester C	(h)	4-1
Fifth Round	Rochdale	(h)	3-1
Sixth Round	Southampton	(a)	0-2

WREXHAM Division 2

FOUNDATION

The club was formed on 28 September 1872 by members of Wrexham Cricket Club, so they could continue playing a sport during the winter months. This meeting was held at the Turf Hotel, which although rebuilt since, still stands at one corner of the present ground. Their first game was a few weeks later and matches often included 17 players on either side! By 1875 team formations were reduced to 11 men and a year later the club was among the founder members of the Cambrian Football Association, which quickly changed its title to the Football Association of Wales.

Racecourse Ground, Mold Road, Wrexham LL11 2AH.

Telephone: (01978) 262 129. ***Fax:*** (01978) 357 821.
Commercial Dept: (01978) 352 536.
Community Office: (01978) 358 545.
ClubCall: 09068 121 642.

Ground Capacity: 15,500.

Record Attendance: 34,445 v Manchester U, FA Cup 4th rd, 26 January 1957.

Record Receipts: £126,012 v West Ham U, FA Cup 4th rd, 4 February 1992.

Pitch Measurements: 111yd × 71yd.

Chairman: M. Guterman.
Managing Director: D. L. Rhodes (Vice-chairman).
Directors: D. Griffiths, D. Bennett.

Manager: Denis Smith.
Assistant Manager: Kevin Russell.
Player-Coach: Joey Jones. ***Physio:*** Mel Pejic.

Secretary: D. L. Rhodes.

Commercial Director: W. Wingrove.

Colours: Red shirts, white shorts, red stockings.

Change Colours: Black and white hoops.

Year Formed: 1872 (oldest club in Wales). ***Turned Professional:*** 1912. ***Ltd Co.:*** 1912.

Club Nickname: 'Red Dragons'.

Previous Grounds: 1872, Racecourse Ground; 1883, Rhosddu Recreation Ground; 1887, Racecourse Ground.

First Football League Game: 27 August 1921, Division 3 (N), v Hartlepools U (h) L 0–2 – Godding; Ellis, Simpson; Matthias, Foster, Griffiths; Burton, Goode, Cotton, Edwards, Lloyd.

Record League Victory: 10–1 v Hartlepool U, Division 4, 3 March 1962 – Keelan; Peter Jones, McGavan; Tecwyn Jones, Fox, Ken Barnes; Ron Barnes (3), Bennion (1), Davies (3), Ambler (3), Ron Roberts.

HONOURS

Football League: Division 3 – Champions 1977–78; Runners-up 1992–93; Promoted (3rd) 2002–03; Division 3 (N) – Runners-up 1932–33; Division 4 – Runners-up 1969–70.

FA Cup: best season: 6th rd, 1974, 1978, 1997.

Football League Cup: best season: 5th rd, 1961, 1978.

Welsh Cup: Winners 22 times (joint record); Runners-up 22 times (record).

FAW Premier Cup: Winners 1998, 2000, 2001, 2003.

European Competition: *European Cup-Winners' Cup:* 1972–73, 1975–76, 1978–79, 1979–80, 1984–85, 1986–87, 1990–91, 1995–96.

SKY SPORTS FACT FILE

Wrexham's record FA Cup run to the sixth round in 1973–74, since equalled twice, saw them concede just two goals. Their victims included Middlesbrough, Crystal Palace and Southampton before losing 1-0 to Burnley.

Record Cup Victory: 11–1 v New Brighton, Football League Northern Section Cup 1st rd, 3 January 1934 – Foster; Alfred Jones, Hamilton, Bulling, McMahon, Lawrence, Bryant (3), Findlay (1), Bamford (5), Snow, Waller (1), (o.g. 1).

Record Defeat: 0–9 v Brentford, Division 3, 15 October 1963.

Most League Points (2 for a win): 61, Division 4, 1969–70 and Division 3, 1977–78.

Most League Points (3 for a win): 84, Division 3, 2002–03.

Most League Goals: 106, Division 3 (N), 1932–33.

Highest League Scorer in Season: Tom Bamford, 44, Division 3 (N), 1933–34.

Most League Goals in Total Aggregate: Tom Bamford, 175, 1928–34.

Most League Goals in One Match: 5, Tom Bamford v Carlisle U, Division 3N, 17 March 1934; 5, Lee Jones v Cambridge U, Division 2, 6 April 2002.

Most Capped Player: Joey Jones, 29 (72), Wales.

Most League Appearances: Arfon Griffiths, 592, 1959–61, 1962–79.

Youngest League Player: Ken Roberts, 15 years 158 days v Bradford PA, 1 September 1951.

Record Transfer Fee Received: £800,000 from Birmingham C for Bryan Hughes, March 1997.

Record Transfer Fee Paid: £210,000 to Liverpool for Joey Jones, October 1978.

MANAGERS

Selection Committee 1872–1924
Charlie Hewitt 1924–25
Selection Committee 1925–29
Jack Baynes 1929–31
Ernest Blackburn 1932–37
James Logan 1937–38
Arthur Cowell 1938
Tom Morgan 1938–42
Tom Williams 1942–49
Les McDowell 1949–50
Peter Jackson 1950–55
Cliff Lloyd 1955–57
John Love 1957–59
Cliff Lloyd 1959–60
Billy Morris 1960–61
Ken Barnes 1961–65
Billy Morris 1965
Jack Rowley 1966–67
Alvan Williams 1967–68
John Neal 1968–77
Arfon Griffiths 1977–81
Mel Sutton 1981–82
Bobby Roberts 1982–85
Dixie McNeil 1985–89
Brian Flynn 1989–2001
Denis Smith October 2001–

Football League Record: 1921 Original Member of Division 3 (N); 1958–60 Division 3; 1960–62 Division 4; 1962–64 Division 3; 1964–70 Division 4; 1970–78 Division 3; 1978–82 Division 2; 1982–83 Division 3; 1983–92 Division 4; 1992–93 Division 3; 1993–2002 Division 2; 2002–03 Division 3; 2003– Division 2.

LATEST SEQUENCES

Longest Sequence of League Wins: 8, 5.4.2003 – 3.5.2003.

Longest Sequence of League Defeats: 9, 2.10.1963 – 30.10.1963.

Longest Sequence of League Draws: 6, 12.11.1999 – 26.12.1999.

Longest Sequence of Unbeaten League Matches: 16, 3.9.1966 – 19.11.1966.

Longest Sequence Without a League Win: 16, 25.9.1999 – 3.1.2000.

Successive Scoring Runs: 25 from 5.5.1928.

Successive Non-scoring Runs: 6 from 12.9.1973.

TEN YEAR LEAGUE RECORD

		P	*W*	*D*	*L*	*F*	*A*	*Pts*	*Pos*
1993-94	Div 2	46	17	11	18	66	77	62	12
1994-95	Div 2	46	16	15	15	65	64	63	13
1995-96	Div 2	46	18	16	12	76	55	70	8
1996-97	Div 2	46	17	18	11	54	50	69	8
1997-98	Div 2	46	18	16	12	55	51	70	7
1998-99	Div 2	46	13	14	19	43	62	53	17
1999-2000	Div 2	46	17	11	18	52	61	62	11
2000-01	Div 2	46	17	12	17	65	71	63	10
2001-02	Div 2	46	11	10	25	56	89	43	23
2002-03	Div 3	46	23	15	8	84	50	84	3

DID YOU KNOW ?

In successive seasons in the 1930s, Wrexham had 8-1 wins. In 1932–33 they defeated Hartlepools United and in 1933–34 they recorded a similar success against Carlisle United on the occasion of Tom Bamford's five goals.

WREXHAM 2002–03 LEAGUE RECORD

Match No.	Date	Venue	Opponents	Result		H/T Score	Lg. Pos.	Goalscorers	Attendance
1	Aug 10	A	Scunthorpe U	D	1-1	0-1	—	Morrell [65]	3879
2	13	H	Oxford U	W	1-0	0-0	—	Sam [88]	3591
3	17	H	Boston U	D	1-1	1-0	9	Trundle [27]	3293
4	24	A	Macclesfield T	W	1-0	0-0	2	Sam [68]	2592
5	26	H	Rochdale	L	2-5	2-4	5	Thomas [13], Morrell [38]	4340
6	31	A	Torquay U	L	1-2	1-2	12	Morrell (pen) [15]	2283
7	Sept 14	H	Swansea C	W	4-0	3-0	9	Morrell 2 [10, 12], Sam [30], Edwards C [56]	3515
8	17	H	Exeter C	W	4-0	2-0	—	Morrell 3 (1 pen) [38, 40, 81 (p)], Ferguson [47]	2968
9	21	A	Rushden & D	D	2-2	1-1	7	Edwards C [10], Morrell [66]	4090
10	24	A	Darlington	W	1-0	1-0	—	Morrell [36]	2573
11	28	H	Bury	D	2-2	2-1	4	Morrell 2 (1 pen) [22, 25 (p)]	3941
12	Oct 5	A	Cambridge U	D	2-2	1-0	5	Whitley [26], Morgan [90]	6044
13	12	H	Leyton Orient	D	0-0	0-0	7		3495
14	19	A	Hartlepool U	L	3-4	1-3	10	Jones L [21], Trundle [68], Sam (pen) [88]	4506
15	26	H	Lincoln C	L	0-2	0-0	13		3312
16	29	A	York C	D	1-1	1-0	—	Roberts [8]	2970
17	Nov 2	A	Southend U	W	1-0	1-0	9	Thomas [41]	3727
18	9	H	Bournemouth	W	3-2	1-1	5	Trundle [5], Morrell [69], Edwards P [86]	3105
19	23	A	Bristol R	W	3-0	2-0	5	Morrell 2 [18, 43], Trundle [75]	6328
20	30	H	Hull C	D	0-0	0-0	7		4412
21	Dec 14	A	Carlisle U	W	2-1	1-1	5	Jones L [33], Sam [87]	4480
22	21	H	Kidderminster H	L	0-2	0-1	8		3734
23	26	A	Rochdale	D	2-2	1-2	7	Morrell 2 [23, 75]	3727
24	Jan 1	H	Macclesfield T	L	1-3	1-1	11	Trundle [29]	3445
25	18	H	Torquay U	W	2-1	1-1	9	Morrell [21], Edwards C [76]	3006
26	Feb 1	H	Scunthorpe U	W	2-1	1-0	9	Morrell (pen) [39], Trundle [80]	3129
27	4	A	Oxford U	W	2-0	0-0	—	Morrell [63], Lawrence [74]	5532
28	8	A	Bournemouth	L	0-2	0-0	10		5445
29	15	H	Southend U	W	3-0	1-0	7	Edwards C [15], Morrell [50], Edwards P [75]	3109
30	23	H	Darlington	D	0-0	0-0	6		4079
31	Mar 1	A	Swansea C	D	0-0	0-0	8		6463
32	4	A	Exeter C	L	0-1	0-0	—		2537
33	8	H	Rushden & D	W	3-0	1-0	6	Edwards C [15], Morrell 2 [62, 79]	3441
34	11	H	Shrewsbury T	D	3-3	1-2	—	Trundle [31], Morrell [58], Edwards P [72]	7024
35	15	A	Lincoln C	D	1-1	0-0	8	Morrell [58]	3916
36	18	H	Hartlepool U	W	2-0	1-0	—	Green 2 [3, 66]	4658
37	22	H	York C	D	1-1	0-1	6	Morrell [89]	4425
38	Apr 2	A	Boston U	D	3-3	1-1	—	Trundle 2 [12, 76], Carey [64]	1919
39	5	A	Hull C	W	2-1	0-0	4	Morrell 2 (1 pen) [67 (p), 80]	15,002
40	9	A	Shrewsbury T	W	2-1	1-0	—	Morrell [24], Jones L [90]	5451
41	12	H	Bristol R	W	3-2	2-1	3	Green [23], Morrell (pen) [43], Edwards C [88]	5330
42	19	A	Kidderminster H	W	2-0	1-0	3	Trundle 2 [37, 64]	3689
43	21	H	Carlisle U	W	6-1	3-0	3	Morrell 3 (1 pen) [22 (p), 32, 85], Carey 2 [39, 54], Edwards C [89]	6746
44	26	H	Cambridge U	W	5-0	3-0	3	Barrett [16], Carey [20], Roberts [23], Edwards P [60], Jones L [62]	9960
45	29	A	Leyton Orient	W	1-0	1-0	—	Morrell (pen) [25]	3766
46	May 3	A	Bury	W	3-0	1-0	3	Edwards C [7], Swailes (og) [57], Ferguson [61]	5186

Final League Position: 3

GOALSCORERS

League (84): Morrell 34 (8 pens), Trundle 11, Edwards C 8, Sam 5 (1 pen), Carey 4, Edwards P 4, Jones L 4, Green 3, Ferguson 2, Roberts 2, Thomas 2, Barrett 1, Lawrence 1, Morgan 1, Whitley 1, own goal 1.
Worthington Cup (2): Edwards C 1, Morrell 1.
FA Cup (0).
LDV Vans Trophy (6): Jones L 2 (1 pen), Edwards C 1, Roberts 1, Thomas 1, Trundle 1.

Rogers K 6 + 1	Whitley J 44	Edwards P 33 + 5	Carey B 31 + 2	Pejic S 23 + 4	Roberts S 39	Phillips W 1	Jones L 9 + 14	Morrell A 45	Trundle L 31 + 13	Russell K 1	Edwards C 43 + 1	Barrett P 22 + 4	Lawrence D 30 + 2	Holmes S 13 + 17	Thomas S 19 + 6	Sam H 8 + 18	Dibble A 33	Ferguson D 41	Bennett D 14 + 4	Jones M —+1	Whitfield P 7 + 1	Morgan C 1 + 5	Evans M —+1	Green S 12 + 3	*Match No.*
1	2	3	4^{3}	5	6	7^{1}	8	9	10	11^{2}	12	13	14												1
1	7	12		5	6		8^{2}	9	13		2	11	4	3^{1}	10^{3}	14									2
	2	12		5	6			9	10		7	8	4	3^{1}	11^{2}	13	1								3
	2			5	6			9^{1}	10		7^{2}		4	3	11	12	1	8	13						4
	2	12		5^{3}	6			9	10		7		4	3^{1}	11^{2}	13	1	8	14						5
	2	12		5	6^{3}			9	10		7		4	3^{1}	11^{2}	13	1	8	14						6
	2	3^{2}		5	6			9	12		7	11		13		10^{1}	1	8	4						7
	2^{3}	3^{2}		5	6			9	12		7	11		13		10^{1}	1	8	4	14					8
	2	3^{3}		5	6^{1}			9	13		7	11	12	14		10^{2}	1	8	4						9
	2			5	6			9	12		7	11		3		10^{1}	1	8	4						10
	2	3^{2}		5	6			9^{1}	12		7■	11		13	14	10^{3}	1	8	4						11
	2		4	5				9	12		7	11	6^{2}	3		10^{1}	1^{G}	8			15	13			12
	2	3^{3}		5	6		10^{2}	9	12			11			7^{1}	13	1	8	4				14		13
	2	3^{2}		5	6		10	9^{1}	12			11		14	7^{2}	13	1	8	4						14
	2^{2}		12	5	6		10^{3}	9	13		7	11		3		14		8	4^{1}		1				15
	2		4	5	6^{1}			9^{2}	10		7	11		3		13		8	12		1				16
	7		4	5				9	10		2	11^{1}		3	12			8	6		1				17
	11	12	4	5			13	9^{2}	10		2			3^{1}	7^{3}	14		8	6		1				18
	7	3	4		6			9	10		2	11						8	5		1				19
	7	3	4^{1}	12	6		13	9	10^{3}		2	11^{2}				14		8	5		1				20
	8	3^{2}		5	6		9		10		2	11	4	13	7^{1}	12					1				21
1	7	3^{1}	13	5^{2}	6		10^{3}	9			2	11	4		12	14		8■							22
1	7	3	4		6			9	10^{2}		2	11^{1}	5		13	12		8							23
	7^{1}	3	4	5				9	10		2	11^{2}			12	13	1	8	6						24
	8	3^{3}	5				12	9	13		2	11^{2}	4	14	7	10^{1}	1		6						25
	11	3^{1}	4		6			9	10		2		5	12	7		1	8							26
	11	3	4		6			9	10		2		5		7		1	8							27
	11	3	4		6		12	9^{2}	10		2		5		7^{1}	13	1	8							28
	11	3	4	12	6^{1}		13	9	10^{2}		2		5		7		1	8^{3}						14	29
	11		4		6			9	10^{1}		2		5	3	7^{2}	12	1	8						13	30
		3	4		6		12	9^{2}	13		2		5		7	10^{1}	1	8						11	31
		3	4		6		10^{2}	9	12		2		5	13	7		1	8						11^{1}	32
	11	3	4	12	6^{1}			9	10		2		5		7		1	8							33
	11	3	4	5	6			9	10		2				7^{1}		1	8						12	34
	7	3^{3}	4	12	6^{1}		13	9	10		2		5	14			1	8						11^{2}	35
	7^{1}	3^{2}	4	5^{3}				9	10		2	12	6	13			1	8				14		11	36
	7^{1}	3^{2}	4		6		12	9	10		2		5	13			1	8						11	37
	7	3^{1}	4		6			9	10		2		5	12			1	8						11	38
	7	3^{2}	4^{3}		6		12	9	10^{1}		2		5	13			1	8				14		11	39
	7		4				12	9	10^{1}		2		5	3			1	8				6		11	40
1	7	3^{2}	4		6		12	9	10		2		5	13				8						11^{1}	41
	7	3	4		6			9	10		2	12	5				1	8^{1}						11	42
	7	3^{3}	4		6		12	9	10		2	13	5	14			1	8^{1}						11^{2}	43
15	7	3	4		6		10	9			2	11^{1}	5			12	1^{G}	8							44
1	7	3	4^{2}		6		12	9	10^{1}		2	11^{3}	5		14			8				13			45
	7	3^{2}	4		6		12	9	10^{1}		2		5^{3}	13			1	8				14		11	46

Worthington Cup

First Round	Bradford C	(h)	2-1
Second Round	Everton	(h)	0-3

FA Cup

First Round	Darlington	(h)	0-2

LDV Vans Trophy

First Round	Huddersfield T	(h)	2-1
Second Round	Leigh RMI	(a)	4-3
Quarter-final	Carlisle U	(a)	0-2

WYCOMBE WANDERERS Division 2

FOUNDATION

In 1887 a group of young furniture trade workers called a meeting at the Steam Engine public house with the aim of forming a football club and entering junior football. It is thought that they were named after the famous FA Cup winners, The Wanderers who had visited the town in 1877 for a tie with the original High Wycombe club. It is also possible that they played informally before their formation, although there is no proof of this.

Adams Park, Hillbottom Road, Sands, High Wycombe HP12 4HJ.

Telephone: (01494) 472 100. ***Fax:*** (01494) 527 633.
Credit Card Hotline: (01494) 441 118.
Information Line: 09003 446 855.

Ground Capacity: 10,000; new stand now seats 7,350.

Record Attendance: 9,650 v Wimbledon, FA Cup 5th rd, 17 February 2001.

Pitch Measurements: 115yd × 75yd.

President: M. E. Seymour.

Chairman: I. L. Beeks JP.

Directors: G. Peart (Financial), R. Tomlin, A. Parry, A. Thibault, B. Kane, D. Vere.

Associate Directors: G. Cox, B. R. Lee, J. Goldsworthy. ***Secretary:*** Keith J. Allen.

Manager: Lawrie Sanchez. ***Assistant Manager:*** Terry Gibson.

Physio: David Jones.

Youth Team Manager: Micky Forsyth.

Youth Development Officer: Adrian Cole.

Youth Physio: Terry Evans.

Marketing Manager: Mark Austin.

Promotions Manager: Mike Phillips.

Press Officer: Alan Hutchinson.

Colours: Light and dark blue quartered shirts, navy shorts, light blue stockings.

Change Colours: All red and blue.

Year Formed: 1887.

Turned Professional: 1974.

Club Nicknames: 'Chairboys' (after High Wycombe's tradition of furniture making), 'The Blues'.

Previous Grounds: 1887, The Rye; 1893, Spring Meadow; 1895, Loakes Park; 1899, Daws Hill Park; 1901, Loakes Park; 1990, Adams Park.

HONOURS

Football League: Division 2 best season: 6th, 1994–95. Division 3 1993–94 (play-offs).

FA Amateur Cup: Winners 1931.

FA Trophy: Winners 1991, 1993.

GM Vauxhall Conference: Winners 1992–93.

FA Cup: semi-final 2001.

Football League Cup: never beyond 2nd rd.

SKY SPORTS FACT FILE

In 1908–09 Wycombe Wanderers joined the Great Western Suburban League. Any team in Middlesex, Berks or Bucks could enter providing their ground was within one mile of a GWR station. Wycombe finished third.

First Football League Game: 14 August 1993, Division 3 v Carlisle U (a) D 2–2: Hyde; Cousins, Horton (Langford), Kerr, Crossley, Ryan, Carroll, Stapleton, Thompson, Scott, Guppy (1) (Hutchinson), (1 og).

Record League Victory: 5–0 v Burnley, Division 2, 15 April 1997 – Parkin; Cousins, Bell, Kavanagh, McCarthy, Forsyth, Carroll (2p) (Simpson), Scott (Farrell), Stallard (1), McGavin (1) (Read (1)), Brown.

Record Cup Victory: 5–0 v Hitchin T (a), FA Cup 2nd rd, 3 December 1994 – Hyde; Cousins, Brown, Crossley, Evans, Ryan (1), Carroll, Bell (1), Thompson, Garner (3) (Hemmings), Stapleton (Langford).

Record Defeat: 0–5 v Walsall, Auto Windscreens Shield 1st rd, 7 November 1995.

Most League Points (3 for a win): 78, Division 2, 1994–95.

Most League Goals: 67, Division 3, 1993–94.

Highest League Goalscorer in Season: Sean Devine, 23, 1999–2000.

Most League Goals in Total Aggregate: Dave Carroll, 41, 1993–2002.

Most League Goals in One Match: 3, Miguel Desouza v Bradford C, Division 2, 26 March 1996; 3, Mark Stallard v Walsall, Division 2, 21 October 1997; 3, Sean Devine v Reading, Division 2, 2 October 1999; 3, Sean Divine v Bury, Division 2, 26 February 2000.

Most Capped Player: Mark Rogers, 5, Canada.

Most League Appearances: Steve Brown, 309, 1994–2002.

Youngest League Player: Roger Johnson, 17 years 8 days v Cambridge U, 6 May 2000.

Record Transfer Fee Received: £375,000 from Swindon T for Keith Scott, November 1993.

Record Transfer Fee Paid: £220,000 to Barnet for Sean Devine, 15 April 1999.

Football League Record: Promoted to Division 3 from GMVC in 1993; 1993–94 Division 3; 1994– Division 2.

MANAGERS

First coach appointed 1951.
Prior to Brian Lee's appointment in 1969 the team was selected by a Match Committee which met every Monday evening.

James McCormack 1951–52
Sid Cann 1952–61
Graham Adams 1961–62
Don Welsh 1962–64
Barry Darvill 1964–68
Brian Lee 1969–76
Ted Powell 1976–77
John Reardon 1977–78
Andy Williams 1978–80
Mike Keen 1980–84
Paul Bence 1984–86
Alan Gane 1986–87
Peter Suddaby 1987–88
Jim Kelman 1988–90
Martin O'Neill 1990–95
Alan Smith 1995–96
John Gregory 1996–98
Neil Smillie 1998–99
Lawrie Sanchez February 1999–

LATEST SEQUENCES

Longest Sequence of League Wins: 4, 26.2.1994 – 19.3.1994.

Longest Sequence of League Defeats: 4, 2.1.1999 – 30.1.1999.

Longest Sequence of League Draws: 4, 16.9.1995 – 7.10.1995.

Longest Sequence of Unbeaten League Matches: 14, 29.8.1995 – 18.11.1995.

Longest Sequence Without a League Win: 12, 8.8.1998 – 10.10.1998.

Successive Scoring Runs: 11 from 29.3.1994

Successive Non-scoring Runs: 5 from 15.10.1996

TEN YEAR LEAGUE RECORD

		P	*W*	*D*	*L*	*F*	*A*	*Pts*	*Pos*
1993-94	Div 3	42	19	13	10	67	53	70	4
1994-95	Div 2	46	21	15	10	60	46	78	6
1995-96	Div 2	46	15	15	16	63	59	60	12
1996-97	Div 2	46	15	10	21	51	56	55	18
1997-98	Div 2	46	14	18	14	51	53	60	14
1998-99	Div 2	46	13	12	21	52	58	51	19
1999-2000	Div 2	46	16	13	17	56	53	61	12
2000-01	Div 2	46	15	14	17	46	53	59	13
2001-02	Div 2	46	17	13	16	58	64	64	11
2002-03	Div 2	46	13	13	20	59	66	52	18

DID YOU KNOW?

Richard Harris played a leading role for 34 minutes for Wycombe Wanderers against Notts County on 1 February 2003 before being substituted with injury. He had scored twice and was voted player of the match which was won 3-1.

WYCOMBE WANDERERS 2002–03 LEAGUE RECORD

Match No.	Date	Venue	Opponents	Result	H/T Score	Lg. Pos.	Goalscorers	Attendance
1	Aug 10	A	Notts Co	D 1-1	0-0	—	Faulconbridge [89]	6012
2	13	H	Northampton T	D 1-1	0-0	—	Currie [48]	5993
3	17	H	Mansfield T	D 3-3	2-1	16	Devine [6], Faulconbridge [45], McCarthy [90]	5057
4	24	A	Bristol C	L 0-3	0-1	20		9597
5	26	H	QPR	W 4-1	1-1	14	Faulconbridge [35], Rammell [47], Devine [61], Simpson [84]	8383
6	31	A	Oldham Ath	W 2-0	1-0	9	Bulman [5], Harris [85]	5963
7	Sept 7	A	Wigan Ath	L 0-3	0-2	14		5358
8	14	H	Blackpool	L 1-2	1-2	15	Faulconbridge [20]	5815
9	17	H	Crewe Alex	L 1-2	1-2	—	Devine [3]	4909
10	21	A	Brentford	L 0-1	0-0	20		6172
11	28	H	Plymouth Arg	W 2-1	1-0	16	Currie 2 (1 pen) [28 (p), 68]	6708
12	Oct 5	A	Colchester U	W 1-0	1-0	15	Brown (pen) [4]	3252
13	12	A	Cardiff C	L 0-1	0-0	16		13,130
14	19	H	Peterborough U	W 3-2	2-1	13	Simpson [32], Brown (pen) [35], Senda [85]	5539
15	26	A	Barnsley	D 1-1	1-1	11	Ryan [44]	10,044
16	29	H	Chesterfield	W 2-0	0-0	—	Rammell 2 [72, 80]	4897
17	Nov 2	H	Swindon T	L 2-3	1-1	12	Faulconbridge [17], Rammell [72]	6021
18	9	A	Huddersfield T	D 0-0	0-0	12		8695
19	23	H	Tranmere R	L 1-3	0-0	14	Simpson [71]	5386
20	30	A	Stockport Co	L 1-2	0-2	17	Johnson [86]	4731
21	Dec 14	H	Port Vale	W 3-1	1-0	13	Thomson [40], Devine 2 (1 pen) [75 (p), 90]	5229
22	21	A	Cheltenham T	D 0-0	0-0	14		4303
23	26	A	QPR	L 1-2	0-2	14	Dixon [79]	14,874
24	28	H	Luton T	L 1-2	0-2	13	Dixon [65]	7740
25	Jan 1	H	Bristol C	W 2-1	0-0	13	Johnson [49], Brown (pen) [68]	6785
26	4	A	Northampton T	W 5-0	2-0	13	Dixon [8], Simpson [45], Roberts 3 [46, 78, 82]	4679
27	11	A	Mansfield T	D 0-0	0-0	13		4811
28	18	H	Oldham Ath	D 2-2	0-1	13	Harris [71], Brown (pen) [83]	6226
29	25	A	Luton T	L 0-1	0-0	14		7351
30	Feb 1	H	Notts Co	W 3-1	2-0	12	Harris 2 [15, 18], Roberts [59]	5690
31	8	H	Huddersfield T	D 0-0	0-0	12		5886
32	15	A	Swindon T	W 3-0	1-0	11	Ryan [25], Bulman [57], Faulconbridge [73]	6239
33	22	H	Wigan Ath	L 0-2	0-1	12		6052
34	Mar 1	A	Blackpool	L 0-1	0-1	13		7266
35	4	A	Crewe Alex	L 2-4	1-2	—	Dixon [9], Bulman [67]	5398
36	8	H	Brentford	W 4-0	2-0	12	Dixon [16], Senda [17], Holligan [80], Currie [87]	5930
37	15	H	Barnsley	D 2-2	1-0	11	McSporran [34], Johnson [82]	5931
38	18	A	Peterborough U	W 2-1	1-1	—	Rogers [37], Holligan [89]	3627
39	22	A	Chesterfield	L 0-4	0-1	12		3081
40	Apr 5	H	Stockport Co	L 1-4	0-0	15	Simpson [65]	5632
41	8	H	Cardiff C	L 0-4	0-1	—		5889
42	12	A	Tranmere R	L 0-1	0-0	15		6814
43	19	H	Cheltenham T	D 1-1	1-0	16	Brown (pen) [4]	6070
44	21	A	Port Vale	D 1-1	0-1	17	Harris [57]	3590
45	26	H	Colchester U	D 0-0	0-0	17		6283
46	May 3	A	Plymouth Arg	L 0-1	0-0	18		10,129

Final League Position: 18

GOALSCORERS

League (59): Faulconbridge 6, Brown 5 (5 pens), Devine 5 (1 pen), Dixon 5, Harris 5, Simpson 5, Currie 4 (1 pen), Rammell 4, Roberts 4, Bulman 3, Johnson 3, Holligan 2, Ryan 2, Senda 2, McCarthy 1, McSporran 1, Rogers 1, Thomson 1.
Worthington Cup (3): McCarthy 2, Harris 1.
FA Cup (2): Brown 1, Rammell 1.
LDV Vans Trophy (6): Devine 3, Bulman 1, Cook 1, Rogers 1.

Taylor M 11	Senda D 39 + 2	Vinnicombe C 25	Bulman D 42	Rogers M 31 + 5	McCarthy P 22 + 2	Brown S 33 + 4	Simpson M 42	Faulconbridge C 29 + 5	Devine S 13 + 5	Currie D 23 + 15	Johnson R 26 + 7	Roberts S 14 + 14	Thomson A 34 + 2	Dixon J 14 + 8	Cook L 4 + 13	Harris R 5 + 17	Talia F 35	Ryan K 33 + 3	Rammell A 17 + 4	Anderson I 5	Lee M 2 + 4	Holligan G 1 + 9	McSporran J 6 + 3	Oliver L — + 2	Simpemba I — + 1	*Match No.*
1	2	3	4^{1}	5	6	7^{2}	8	9	10	11	12	13														1
1	2	3	4	5^{1}	6	7^{2}	8		10	9	12	11^{3}	13	14												2
1	2	3	4	5	6	7^{1}	8	9	10^{2}	11					12	13										3
	2	3		5	6	7^{1}	8	9^{2}	10^{3}	11		12				13	1	4	14							4
	2■	3	4	12	6	13	8	9^{3}	10^{2}	7^{1}	5	14					1		11■							5
	2	3	4	12	6	13	8	9	10^{1}	7^{2}	5					14	1		11^{3}							6
	2	3	4		6		8	9	10^{3}	7^{2}	5	12				14	1	13	11^{1}							7
		3	4	5	6		8	9	10^{3}	11^{1}		7^{2}	2		14	13	1	12								8
		3	4	2	6	11^{3}	8	9	10^{1}	7^{2}		12	5	14		13	1									9
1	2	3	7		6	11^{2}	8	9^{1}	13	12	4^{3}	14	5						10							10
1	2	3	4		6		8	9^{3}	12	7	13	11^{2}	5			14			10^{1}							11
1	2	3	7		6	11^{2}	8	9^{1}			13		5			12		4	10							12
1	2	3			6	11^{1}	8	9^{3}	13	12		7^{2}	5			14		4	10							13
	2	3		12	6	11	8	9^{2}	13	7^{1}			5			14	1	4	10^{3}							14
	2	3	4	12	6	11^{1}	8	13	10^{3}				5			14	1	7	9^{2}							15
	2	3	4		6	12	8	9	10^{3}	13			5		11^{1}		1	7^{2}	14							16
	2	3	4^{1}	5		12	8	9		7^{2}	14		6		13		1	11	10^{3}							17
	2■	3	4	12	6	7^{2}	8	9^{3}		13			5			14	1	11	10^{1}							18
1				2	6	3^{1}	8		10	7			5	12	11			4	9							19
1			4	2	6^{2}	7		12	10^{1}		13		5	14	8			11	9^{3}	3						20
1			4	5			8	9^{1}	12	7		13	6					2	10	3	11^{2}					21
1	12		4	5	6		8	9^{3}		7^{1}		11^{2}		14				2	10	3	13					22
	12		4^{1}	5	6		8			11^{3}	13	7^{2}		9	14		1	2	10	3						23
	2		4	5	6	11	8	12				7^{2}		9	13		1		10^{1}	3						24
	2		7	5		11	8	9^{1}			6		4	10		12	1	3								25
	2		7	5		11^{1}	8	9^{3}		12	6	13	4	10^{2}		14	1	3								26
	2		7	5		11	8	9			6	10^{1}	4		12		1	3								27
	2		7	5^{3}		11	8	9		12	6	10^{2}	4		14	13	1	3^{1}								28
	2		7	5		11^{2}	8	9		12	6	13	4^{1}		14	10	1	3^{3}								29
	2		7	5	12	11^{1}	8	9		13	6	14	4			10^{3}	1	3^{2}								30
	2		7	5	12	11^{2}	8	9^{1}		13	6	10	4				1	3								31
	2		7	5		11^{1}	8	9^{2}		12	6	10^{3}	4				1	3				13	14			32
	2		7	5		11^{1}	8	9		12	6	10^{3}	4		13		1	3^{2}					14			33
	2^{2}		7	5		3^{1}	8	9^{3}		12	6		4	10	13		1					14	11			34
	2		7	5		11	8	9^{2}			6		4^{1}	10	12		1	3^{3}				13	14			35
	2		7	5		11^{2}	8	12		13	6		4	10^{1}			1	3				14	9^{3}			36
	2		7	5		11■		12		8^{2}	6		4	10^{1}			1	3			13	14	9^{3}			37
	2		7	5		11^{3}				8	6		4	10^{1}			1	3	12		14	13	9^{2}			38
	2		7	5		11^{3}				8^{1}	6		4	10			1	3^{2}	12		14	13	9			39
	2	3^{2}	7	5			8			12	6		4	13			1	14			11^{1}	10	9^{3}			40
	2	3	7	5		11^{1}	8			9	6	12		10^{2}	13		1	4^{3}				14				41
	2	3	4	5^{1}		11	8			9^{2}	6	12	13	10^{3}		14	1	7								42
	2	3	4			11^{1}	8			9^{3}	6	12	5	10^{2}		13	1	7						14		43
	2	3	4			11^{1}	8			12	6	10^{2}	5	13		9	1	7								44
	2	3	4				8			7^{1}	6	12	5	10	13	9^{3}	1	11^{2}							14	45
	2	3	4				8^{3}				6	10	5	12	11^{1}	9^{2}	1	7				13		14		46

Worthington Cup

First Round	Swindon T	(a)	2-1
Second Round	Sheffield U	(a)	1-4

FA Cup

First Round	Brentford	(h)	2-4

LDV Vans Trophy

First Round	Torquay U	(a)	4-0
Second Round	Cheltenham T	(a)	2-1
Quarter-final	Bristol C	(a)	0-3

YEOVIL TOWN — Division 3

FOUNDATION

One of the prime movers of Yeovil football was Ernest J. Sercombe. His association with the club began in 1895 as a playing member of Yeovil Casuals, of which team he became vice-captain and in his last season 1899–1900, he was chosen to play for Somerset against Devon. Upon the reorganisation of the club, he became secretary of the old Yeovil Town FC and with the amalgamation with Petters United in 1914, he continued to serve until his resignation in 1930.

Huish Park, Lufton Way, Yeovil, Somerset BA22 8YF.

Telephone: (01935) 423 662.

Fax: (01935) 473 956.

Website: www.ytfc.net

Ground Capacity: 9,107.

Record Attendance: 8,612 v Arsenal, F.A. Cup 3rd rd, 2 January 1993 (16,318 v Sunderland at Huish).

Chairman & Chief Executive: John R. Fry.

President: S. N. Burfield MBE.

Directors: S. Allinson, D. Cox, P. Sargent.

Company Secretary: Stephen Allinson/Jean Cotton

Manager: Gary Johnson.

First Team Coach: Steve Thompson.

Reserve Team Manager: Maurice O'Donnell.

Youth Team Coach: Stuart Housley.

Physio: Tony Farmer.

Colours: Green and white hooped shirts, white shorts, white stockings.

Change Colours: White shirts with green trim, green shorts, green stockings.

Year formed: 1895.

Turned Professional: 1921.

Ltd Co.: 1923.

Club Nickname: "Glovers".

HONOURS

Conference: Champions 2002–03.

Southern League: Champions 1954–55, 1963–64, 1970–71; Runners-up: 1923–24, 1931–32, 1934–35, 1969–70, 1972–73.

Southern League Cup: Winners 1948–49, 1954–55, 1960–61, 1965–66; Runners-up: 1946–47, 1955–56.

Isthmian League: Winners 1987–88; Runners-up*:* 1985–86, 1986–87, 1996–97.

AC Delco Cup: Winners 1987–88.

Bob Lord Trophy: Winners 1989–90.

FA Trophy: Winners 2002.

London Combination: Runners-up 1930–31, 1932–33.

SKY SPORTS FACT FILE

The outstanding team in terms of FA Cup giant-killing, Yeovil Town have reached the third round of the competition 13 times and recorded 20 victories over Football League teams during their history.

Previous names: 1895 Yeovil; 1907 Yeovil Town; 1914 Yeovil & Petters United; 1946 Yeovil Town.

Previous grounds: Pen Mill Ground 1895–1921; Huish 1921–1990; Huish Park 1990.

Record League Victory: 10–0 v Kidderminster H, Southern League, 27 December 1955. 10–0 v Bedford T, Southern League, 4 March 1961.

Record Cup Victory: 12–1 v Westbury United, FA Cup 1st qual rd, 1923–24.

Record Defeat: 0–8 v Manchester United, FA Cup 5th rd, 12 February 1949.

Most League Goals: Dave Taylor, 285, Southern League 1960–69.

Highest League Scorer in Season: Dave Taylor, 59, Southern League 1960–61 (in all competitions Cecil Pemberton, 69, 1931–32).

Most League Appearances: Len Harris, 691, 1958–1972.

Record Transfer Fee Received: £75,000 from Bristol C for Mark Shail.

Record Transfer Fee Paid: £20,000 to Stevenage Borough for Kirk Jackson, November 2002.

YEOVIL TOWN ROLL CALL 2002–03

Player	Position	Height	Weight	Birthdate	Birthplace	Source
Chris Weale	G	6 2	13 03	09.02.1982	Yeovil	Youth
Stephen Collis	G	6 3	12 05	18.03.1981	Harrow	Nottingham F
Adam Lockwood	D	6 0	12 07	26.10.1981	Wakefield	Reading
Terry Skiverton	D	6 1	13 06	26.06.1975	Mile End	Welling U
Roy O'Brien	D	6 0	12 02	23.11.1974	Cork	Dorchester T
Tom White	D	6 0	14 00	26.01.1976	Bristol	Bristol R
Colin Pluck	D	6 0	13 10	06.09.1978	Edmonton	Dover Ath
Nick Crittenden	M	5 10	11 07	11.11.1978	Ascot	Chelsea
Darren Way	M	5 6	10 00	21.11.1979	Plymouth	Norwich C
Lee Johnson	M	5 6	10 07	07.06.1981	Newmarket	Watford
Gavin Williams	M	5 10	11 05	20.06.1980	Merthyr	Hereford U
Steve Reed	D	5 8	12 02	18.06.1985	Barnstaple	Plymouth Arg
Michael McIndoe	M	5 10	11 05	02.12.1979	Edinburgh	Hereford U
Abdelhalim El Kholti	M	5 10	11 00	17.10.1980	Annewsse	Raja Morocco
Andy Lindegaard	F	5 8	11 04	10.09.1980	Taunton	Youth
Chris Giles	F	6 2	13 00	16.04.1982	Bridgend	Youth
Adam Stansfield	F	5 11	11 02	10.09.1978	Plymouth	Elmore
Kirk Jackson	F	6 0	13 00	16.10.1976	Doncaster	Stevenage B
Kevin Gall	F	5 9	10 08	04.02.1982	Merthyr	Bristol R

TEN YEAR LEAGUE RECORD

		P	W	D	L	F	A	Pts	Pos
1993–94	Conf.	42	14	9	19	49	62	51	19
1994–95	Conf.	42	8	14	20	50	71	37*	22
1995–96	Isth.	42	23	11	8	83	51	80	4
1996–97	Isth.	42	31	8	3	83	34	101	1
1997–98	Conf.	42	17	8	17	73	63	59	11
1998–99	Conf.	42	20	11	11	68	54	71	5
1999–2000	Conf.	42	18	10	14	60	63	64	7
2000–01	Conf.	42	24	8	10	73	50	80	2
2001–02	Conf.	42	19	13	10	66	53	70	3
2002–03	Conf.	42	28	11	3	100	37	95	1

*1 point deducted.

In 1946 Yeovil Town appointed Alec Stock at 29, then the youngest player-manager of a professional club in the country. On 29 January 1949 he scored the first goal in the 2-1 cup win over First Division Sunderland.

YORK CITY Division 3

FOUNDATION

Although there was a York City club formed in 1903 by a soccer enthusiast from Darlington, this has no connection with the modern club because it went out of existence during World War I. Unlike many others of that period who restarted in 1919, York City did not re-form until 1922 and the tendency now is to ignore the modern club's pre-1922 existence.

Bootham Crescent, York YO30 7AQ.

Telephone: (01904) 624 447.

Fax: (01904) 631 457.

ClubCall: 09068 121 643.

Ground Capacity: 9,496.

Record Attendance: 28,123 v Huddersfield T, FA Cup 6th rd, 5 March 1938.

Record Receipts: £63,680 v Manchester U, Coca-Cola Cup 2nd rd, 2nd leg, 3 October 1995.

Pitch Measurements: 115yd × 74yd.

Chairman: Steve Beck.

Directors: I. McAndrew, D. M. Craig, S. McGill, J. McGill.

Manager: Chris Brass.

First Team Coach: Adie Shaw.

Chief Executive: Keith Usher.

Commercial Manager: Peter Salter.

Physio: Jeff Miller.

Hon. Orthopaedic Surgeon: Mr Peter De Boer MA, FRCS.

Medical Officer: Dr R. Porter.

Colours: Red shirts, red shorts, red stockings.

Change Colours: All yellow.

Year Formed: 1922.

Turned Professional: 1922.

Ltd Co.: 1922.

Club Nickname: 'Minstermen'.

Previous Grounds: 1922, Fulfordgate; 1932, Bootham Crescent.

First Football League Game: 31 August 1929, Division 3 (N), v Wigan Borough (a) W 2–0 – Farmery; Archibald, Johnson; Beck, Davis, Thompson; Evans, Gardner, Cowie (1), Smailes, Stockill (1).

Record League Victory: 9–1 v Southport, Division 3 (N), 2 February 1957 – Forgan; Phillips, Howe; Brown (1), Cairney, Mollatt; Hill, Bottom (4 incl. 1p), Wilkinson (2), Wragg (1), Fenton (1).

HONOURS

Football League: Division 3 – Promoted 1973–74 (3rd); Division 4 – Champions 1983–84. 1992–93 (play-offs).

FA Cup: Semi-finals 1955, when in Division 3.

Football League Cup: best season: 5th rd, 1962.

SKY SPORTS FACT FILE

In 1937–38 York City's FA Cup run included a memorable fight-back against West Bromwich Albion in the fourth round. York were trailing 2-1 with six minutes left only for local hero Reg Baines to complete his hat-trick.

Record Cup Victory: 6–0 v South Shields (away), FA Cup 1st rd, 16 November 1968 – Widdowson; Baker (1p), Richardson; Carr, Jackson, Burrows; Taylor, Ross (3), MacDougall (2), Hodgson, Boyer.

Record Defeat: 0–12 v Chester, Division 3 (N), 1 February 1936.

Most League Points (2 for a win): 62, Division 4, 1964–65.

Most League Points (3 for a win): 101, Division 4, 1983–84.

Most League Goals: 96, Division 4, 1983–84.

Highest League Scorer in Season: Bill Fenton, 31, Division 3 (N), 1951–52; Arthur Bottom, 31, Division 3 (N), 1954–55 and 1955–56.

Most League Goals in Total Aggregate: Norman Wilkinson, 125, 1954–66.

Most League Goals in One Match: 5, Alf Patrick v Rotherham U, Division 3N, 20 November 1948.

Most Capped Player: Peter Scott, 7 (10), Northern Ireland.

Most League Appearances: Barry Jackson, 481, 1958–70.

Youngest League Player: Reg Stockill, 15 years 281 days v Wigan Borough, 31 August 1929.

Record Transfer Fee Received: £1,000,000 from Manchester U for Jonathan Greening, March 1998.

Record Transfer Fee Paid: £140,000 to Burnley for Adrian Randall, December 1995.

Football League Record: 1929 Elected to Division 3 (N); 1958–59 Division 4; 1959–60 Division 3; 1960–65 Division 4; 1965–66 Division 3; 1966–71 Division 4; 1971–74 Division 3; 1974–76 Division 2; 1976–77 Division 3; 1977–84 Division 4; 1984–88 Division 3; 1988–92 Division 4; 1992–93 Division 3; 1993–99 Division 2; 1999– Division 3.

MANAGERS

Bill Sherrington 1924–60
(was Secretary for most of this time but virtually Secretary-Manager for a long pre-war spell)
John Collier 1929–36
Tom Mitchell 1936–50
Dick Duckworth 1950–52
Charlie Spencer 1952–53
Jimmy McCormick 1953–54
Sam Bartram 1956–60
Tom Lockie 1960–67
Joe Shaw 1967–68
Tom Johnston 1968–75
Wilf McGuinness 1975–77
Charlie Wright 1977–80
Barry Lyons 1980–81
Denis Smith 1982–87
Bobby Saxton 1987–88
John Bird 1988–91
John Ward 1991–93
Alan Little 1993–99
Neil Thompson 1999–2000
Terry Dolan February 2000–2003
Chris Brass June 2003–

LATEST SEQUENCES

Longest Sequence of League Wins: 7, 31.10.1964 – 26.12.1964.

Longest Sequence of League Defeats: 8, 14.11.1966 – 31.12.1966.

Longest Sequence of League Draws: 6, 26.12.1992 – 22.1.1993.

Longest Sequence of Unbeaten League Matches: 21, 10.9.1973 – 12.1.1974.

Longest Sequence Without a League Win: 17, 4.5.1987 – 24.10.1987.

Successive Scoring Runs: 24 from 3.3.1984.

Successive Non-scoring Runs: 7 from 28.8.1972.

TEN YEAR LEAGUE RECORD

		P	W	D	L	F	A	Pts	Pos
1993-94	Div 2	46	21	12	13	64	40	75	5
1994-95	Div 2	46	21	9	16	67	51	72	9
1995-96	Div 2	46	13	13	20	58	73	52	20
1996-97	Div 2	46	13	13	20	47	68	52	20
1997-98	Div 2	46	14	17	15	52	58	59	16
1998-99	Div 2	46	13	11	22	56	80	50	21
1999-2000	Div 3	46	12	16	18	39	53	52	20
2000-01	Div 3	46	13	13	20	42	63	52	17
2001-02	Div 3	46	16	9	21	54	67	57	14
2002-03	Div 3	46	17	15	14	52	53	66	10

DID YOU KNOW ?

Albert Thompson made a two-goal scoring debut for York City on 31 October 1936 against Wrexham and went on to register exactly 24 goals in 24 League games. A centre-forward previously with Bradford Park Avenue he then joined Swansea Town.

YORK CITY 2002–03 LEAGUE RECORD

Match No.	Date	Venue	Opponents	Result		H/T Score	Lg. Pos.	Goalscorers	Attendance
1	Aug 10	A	Macclesfield T	D	1-1	0-1	—	Duffield [90]	2586
2	13	H	Shrewsbury T	W	2-1	0-1	—	Duffield [47], Parkin [73]	3463
3	17	H	Torquay U	W	4-3	1-0	2	Duffield [15], Nogan [49], Parkin 2 [53, 73]	3203
4	24	A	Scunthorpe U	L	1-2	1-2	4	Duffield [25]	3540
5	26	H	Boston U	W	2-0	1-0	3	Duffield [22], Nogan [52]	4228
6	31	A	Swansea C	W	2-1	1-0	2	Bullock [31], Duffield (pen) [81]	4086
7	Sept 6	A	Bury	L	1-2	0-2	—	Cowan [53]	3294
8	14	H	Rushden & D	D	0-0	0-0	5		4102
9	17	H	Darlington	W	1-0	0-0	—	Parkin [73]	4128
10	21	A	Cambridge U	L	0-3	0-1	5		4204
11	28	H	Oxford U	L	0-1	0-0	9		3962
12	Oct 5	A	Exeter C	W	1-0	1-0	7	Cook [43]	3178
13	12	A	Southend U	L	0-1	0-0	10		4411
14	19	H	Bristol R	D	2-2	1-2	12	Duffield (pen) [39], Brackstone [90]	3616
15	26	A	Bournemouth	L	0-1	0-0	14		5755
16	29	H	Wrexham	D	1-1	0-1	—	Duffield [75]	2970
17	Nov 1	A	Hartlepool U	D	0-0	0-0	—		5789
18	9	H	Leyton Orient	W	3-2	1-1	12	Brass [28], Parkin [80], Bullock [87]	3304
19	23	A	Rochdale	W	1-0	0-0	10	Duffield [71]	3056
20	30	H	Carlisle U	W	2-1	1-0	8	Reddy [44], Duffield [79]	4335
21	Dec 14	A	Kidderminster H	W	2-1	1-1	6	Brackstone [23], Nogan [86]	2304
22	20	H	Lincoln C	D	1-1	0-1	—	Cooper [81]	3411
23	26	A	Boston U	L	0-3	0-1	9		3864
24	28	H	Hull C	D	1-1	1-0	8	Edmondson [33]	7856
25	Jan 1	H	Scunthorpe U	L	1-3	1-2	9	Edmondson [26]	4554
26	11	A	Torquay U	L	1-3	1-3	10	Duffield (pen) [5]	2663
27	18	H	Swansea C	W	3-1	2-1	8	Duffield 2 (1 pen) [9 (p), 41], Reddy [82]	4611
28	25	A	Hull C	D	0-0	0-0	7		18,437
29	Feb 2	H	Macclesfield T	W	2-1	1-0	7	Parkin [5], Bullock [52]	4009
30	8	A	Leyton Orient	W	1-0	0-0	4	Shandran [70]	4260
31	11	A	Shrewsbury T	D	2-2	0-1	—	Potter [60], Parkin [62]	2599
32	15	H	Hartlepool U	D	0-0	0-0	6		5953
33	22	H	Bury	D	1-1	0-0	5	Parkin (pen) [53]	4115
34	Mar 1	A	Rushden & D	L	1-2	0-1	9	Bullock [90]	4463
35	4	A	Darlington	L	1-2	0-1	—	Bullock [48]	3434
36	8	H	Cambridge U	W	3-1	0-1	10	Parkin [48], Nogan [49], Shandran [90]	3394
37	15	H	Bournemouth	W	1-0	0-0	7	Parkin [49]	3642
38	18	A	Bristol R	W	1-0	1-0	—	Edmondson [42]	8248
39	22	A	Wrexham	D	1-1	1-0	5	Edmondson [6]	4425
40	29	H	Southend U	W	2-0	2-0	3	Nogan [18], Bullock [45]	4312
41	Apr 12	H	Rochdale	D	2-2	1-1	7	Graydon (pen) [35], Edmondson [63]	3966
42	15	A	Carlisle U	D	1-1	0-0	—	Shandran [75]	4935
43	19	A	Lincoln C	L	0-1	0-1	9		4653
44	21	H	Kidderminster H	D	0-0	0-0	8		4069
45	26	H	Exeter C	L	0-2	0-1	9		4840
46	May 3	A	Oxford U	L	0-2	0-1	10		6905

Final League Position: 10

GOALSCORERS

League (52): Duffield 13 (4 pens), Parkin 10 (1 pen), Bullock 6, Edmondson 5, Nogan 5, Shandran 3, Brackstone 2, Reddy 2, Brass 1, Cook 1, Cooper 1, Cowan 1, Graydon 1 (pen), Potter 1.
Worthington Cup (0).
FA Cup (3): Duffield 2, Bullock 1.
LDV Vans Trophy (3): Cook 1 (pen), Nogan 1, Parkin 1.

Beresford M 6	Okoli J 1 + 2	Cowan T 31 + 2	Jones S 19 + 1	Smith C 33 + 3	Hobson G 24 + 4	Brass C 40	Fox C 6 + 5	Nogan L 39 + 7	Duffield P 28	Brackstone S 22 + 4	Edmondson D 37 + 1	Parkin J 37 + 4	Mathie A 2 + 8	Wilding C 1 + 6	Wise S 3 + 5	Carvalho R — + 4	Bullock L 38 + 1	Potter G 37 + 2	Wood L 7 + 12	Fettis A 21	Yalcin L — + 5	Mazzina N — + 3	Cook L 7	Reddy M 10 + 1	McCarthy J 1	Cooper R 21 + 3	Ingham M 17	Shandran A 12 + 6	Graydon K 4 + 3	Whitehead P 2	Stockdale D — + 1	*Match No.*
1	2^{1}	3	4	5	6^{2}	7	8	9^{3}	10	11	12	13	14																			1
1		3	4	5	6	7		9	10^{1}	11	2	8^{2}	12	13																		2
1	12	3	4	5^{1}	6	7		9^{2}	10	11	2	8^{3}	13	14																		3
1		3	4^{1}	5	6	7		9	10	11^{3}	2	8			12^{2}	13	14															4
1		6		5	12	7^{1}		9	10	11	2^{3}	4^{2}				13	8	3	14													5
1		6		5	12	7		9	10^{2}	11	2	4^{3}	13				8	3^{1}	14													6
		6		5^{2}	12	7		9	10	11	2	4^{3}	13			14	8	3^{1}		1												7
		3		5	6	7		9^{1}	10	11	2		4^{2}			12	8			1	13											8
		3		5	6	4		9	10	11	2	12	7^{1}				8			1												9
		3^{1}		5	6	4		9	10	11	2	8^{2}		13			7	12		1												10
		11		5	6^{1}	4		9^{3}	10^{2}		2	8					7	3	12	1	13	14										11
				5	6	4		9^{1}	10^{2}	11	2	12					8	3	14	1		13	7^{3}									12
		3^{2}		5	6	4		9^{1}	10	11	2	12					8	13		1			7									13
				5		4		12	10	11	2	9^{2}					8^{3}	3	6^{1}	1	13	14	7									14
	12		4	5	6^{1}	7		13	10^{2}			9					8	3	2	1			11									15
			5^{1}	12		4		13	10		2	9		6^{2}			8^{3}	3	11	1	14		7									16
						4		9^{1}	10	11	2	5					8	3	6	1			7	12								17
						4		12	10	11	2^{1}	5					6	3		1			8	9	7							18
				5	6			9	10	11	2				4		8	3		1				7								19
					6	4	12	9^{1}	10	11^{2}	2	5					8	3	13	1				7								20
		12			6^{1}	4^{2}	14	9	10	11^{3}	2	5					8	3	13	1				7								21
		6					12	9	10	11^{1}	2	5			4^{2}		8	3		1				7		13						22
		6		12			11	9	10		2	5^{1}					8	3		1				7		4						23
		4		5^{1}	6		11	9^{1}	10^{2}		2			12			8	3	13	1				7								24
		4		5^{1}	6		7	9^{2}	10		2	11		13			8	3		1						12						25
		4^{1}	12		6		11	9	10		2^{2}	5^{3}			14		8	3		1				7		13						26
		4			6	7		9	10			5					8	3		1				11		2						27
		4	6			7		9	10^{1}			5					8	3			12			11		2	1					28
		4	6	5		7		9				10					8	3	12							2	1	11^{1}				29
		2	4	5		6		9				10					8	11								3	1	7				30
		4	6	5		7	12	9				10					8	3								2	1	11^{1}				31
		4	6^{3}	5		7	13	9^{1}				10	12		14		8	3								2	1	11^{2}				32
		4^{1}		5		7		9^{2}			2	10	13		6			3	12							11	1	8				33
			4	5		6		9			2	10					8	3								7	1	11				34
			5	6		4		9^{1}			2	10	13		14		8	3	12							7^{3}	1	11^{2}				35
		4	6	5		7		9^{1}			2	10					8	3								11	1	12				36
		4	5	6		7		9		12	2	10^{3}					8^{2}	3	13							11^{1}	1	14				37
		4	6	5	12	7^{1}		13			2	9^{2}						3	8							11	1	10				38
		4^{2}	6	5		7		12		13	2	9^{1}		14				3	8							11	1	10^{3}				39
				5	6	4		9		12	2	8^{3}					7^{1}	3	13							11^{2}	1	14	10			40
				5	6	4		9			2						8	3								7	1	11	10			41
		11		5	6	4		9			2						8	3								7		12	10^{1}	1		42
		11		5	6	4		9		12	2^{3}	10					8	3^{2}								7^{1}		13	14	1		43
		12	5		6	4		9		11	2	10						3^{1}								7	1	8^{2}	13			44
			5	12	6^{1}	4		9^{2}		11	2	10					8	3								7^{3}	1	13	14			45
		3				4	7	12		11		5			13		8		6							2	1^{G}	10^{2}	9^{1}		15	46

Worthington Cup
First Round | Sheffield U | (a) | 0-1

LDV Vans Trophy
First Round | Lincoln C | (a) | 3-4

FA Cup
First Round | Swansea C | (h) | 2-1
Second Round | Brentford | (h) | 1-2

ENGLISH LEAGUE PLAYERS DIRECTORY

*Free transfer, †Non-contract, ‡Registration cancelled, §Trainee/Scholar/Schoolboy
#Players over age 24, out of contract but who have been made an offer of re-engagement.
Players listed refer to the retain and transfer list May 2003.

ARSENAL

ALIADIERE, Jeremie (F) 4 1
H: 6 0 W: 11 00 b.Rambouillet 30-3-83
Source: Scholarship.

1999–2000	Arsenal	0	0		
2000-01	Arsenal	0	0		
2001-02	Arsenal	1	0		
2002-03	Arsenal	3	1	4	1

BAILEY, Alex (D) 0 0
H: 5 9 W: 10 07 b.Newham 21-9-83
Source: Scholar. *Honours:* England Youth.

2001-02	Arsenal	0	0		
2002-03	Arsenal	0	0		

BARRETT, Graham* (F) 56 5
H: 5 10 W: 11 07 b.Dublin 6-10-81
Source: Trainee. *Honours:* Eire Schools, Youth, Under-21, 1 full cap, 1 goal.

1998-99	Arsenal	0	0		
1999–2000	Arsenal	2	0		
2000-01	Arsenal	0	0		
2000-01	*Bristol R*	1	0	1	0
2001-02	Arsenal	0	0		
2001-02	*Crewe Alex*	3	0	3	0
2001-02	*Colchester U*	20	4	20	4
2002-03	Arsenal	0	0	2	0
2002-03	*Brighton & HA*	30	1	30	1

BENTLEY, David (F) 0 0
H: 5 10 W: 10 07 b.Peterborough 27-8-84
Source: Scholar. *Honours:* England Youth.

2001-02	Arsenal	0	0		
2002-03	Arsenal	0	0		

BERGKAMP, Dennis (F) 471 187
H: 6 0 W: 12 05 b.Amsterdam 18-5-69
Honours: Holland 79 full caps, 36 goals.

1986-87	Ajax	14	2		
1987-88	Ajax	25	5		
1988-89	Ajax	30	13		
1989-90	Ajax	25	8		
1990-91	Ajax	33	25		
1991-92	Ajax	30	24		
1992-93	Ajax	28	26	185	103
1993-94	Internazionale	31	8		
1994-95	Internazionale	21	3	52	11
1995-96	Arsenal	33	11		
1996-97	Arsenal	29	12		
1997-98	Arsenal	28	16		
1998-99	Arsenal	29	12		
1999–2000	Arsenal	28	6		
2000-01	Arsenal	25	3		
2001-02	Arsenal	33	9		
2002-03	Arsenal	29	4	234	73

BIRCHALL, Adam (F) 0 0
H: 5 7 W: 12 06 b.Maidstone 2-12-84
Source: Trainee. *Honours:* Wales Under-21.

2002-03	Arsenal	0	0		

BRADLEY, Stephen (M) 0 0
H: 5 8 W: 9 07 b.Dublin 19-11-84
Source: Scholar.

2001-02	Arsenal	0	0		
2002-03	Arsenal	0	0		

BROWN, Jermaine* (F) 0 0
H: 5 11 W: 11 00 b.Lambeth 12-1-83
Source: Scholar.

2001-02	Arsenal	0	0		
2002-03	Arsenal	0	0		

CAMPBELL, Sol (D) 319 14
H: 6 2 W: 14 02 b.Newham 18-9-74
Source: Trainee. *Honours:* England Youth, Under-21, 54 full caps, 1 goal.

1992-93	Tottenham H	1	1		
1993-94	Tottenham H	34	0		
1994-95	Tottenham H	30	0		
1995-96	Tottenham H	31	1		
1996-97	Tottenham H	38	0		
1997-98	Tottenham H	34	0		
1998-99	Tottenham H	37	6		
1999–2000	Tottenham H	29	0		
2000-01	Tottenham H	21	2	255	10
2001-02	Arsenal	31	2		
2002-03	Arsenal	33	2	64	4

CHILVERS, Liam (D) 22 1
H: 6 0 W: 12 04 b.Chelmsford 6-10-81
Source: Scholar.

2000-01	Arsenal	0	0		
2000-01	*Northampton T*	7	0	7	0
2001-02	Arsenal	0	0		
2001-02	*Notts Co*	9	1	9	1
2002-03	Arsenal	0	0		
2002-03	*Colchester U*	6	0	6	0

COLE, Ashley (D) 92 7
H: 5 8 W: 10 10 b.Stepney 20-12-80
Source: Trainee. *Honours:* England Youth, Under-21, 19 full caps.

1998-99	Arsenal	0	0		
1999–2000	Arsenal	1	0		
1999–2000	*Crystal Palace*	14	1	14	1
2000-01	Arsenal	17	3		
2001-02	Arsenal	29	2		
2002-03	Arsenal	31	1	78	6

CREGG, Patrick (M) 0 0
H: 5 7 W: 8 10 b.Dublin 21-2-86
Source: Trainee.

2002-03	Arsenal	0	0		

CYGAN, Pascal (D) 197 10
H: 6 3 W: 14 02 b.Lens 29-4-74
Source: Wasquehal.

1995-96	Lille	27	0		
1996-97	Lille	14	0		
1997-98	Lille	26	3		
1998-99	Lille	21	1		
1999–2000	Lille	33	2		
2000-01	Lille	29	2		
2001-02	Lille	29	1	179	9
2002-03	Arsenal	18	1	18	1

EDU (M) 65 3
H: 6 1 W: 12 04 b.Sao Paulo 15-5-78

1998	Corinthians	1	0		
1999	Corinthians	19	0		
2000	Corinthians	8	0	28	0
2000-01	Arsenal	5	0		
2001-02	Arsenal	14	1		
2002-03	Arsenal	18	2	37	3

FOWLER, Jordan (M) 0 0
H: 5 10 W: 11 00 b.Barking 1-10-84
Source: Trainee.

2002-03	Arsenal	0	0		

GARRY, Ryan (D) 1 0
H: 6 2 W: 13 00 b.Hornchurch 29-9-83
Source: Scholar. *Honours:* England Youth, Under-20.

2001-02	Arsenal	0	0		
2002-03	Arsenal	1	0	1	0

GRONDIN, David (D) 1 0
H: 5 9 W: 11 11 b.Paris 8-5-80
Source: St Etienne, France Youth.

1998-99	Arsenal	1	0		
1999–2000	Arsenal	0	0		
2000-01	Arsenal	0	0		
2001-02	Arsenal	0	0		
2002-03	Arsenal	0	0	1	0

HALLS, John (D) 6 0
H: 6 0 W: 11 00 b.Islington 14-2-82
Source: Scholar. *Honours:* England Youth, Under-20.

2000-01	Arsenal	0	0		
2001-02	Arsenal	0	0		
2001-02	*Colchester U*	6	0	6	0
2002-03	Arsenal	0	0		

HENRY, Thierry (F) 257 105
H: 6 2 W: 13 01 b.Paris 17-8-77
Honours: France 51 full caps, 22 goals.

1994-95	Monaco	8	3		
1995-96	Monaco	18	3		
1996-97	Monaco	36	9		
1997-98	Monaco	30	4		
1998-99	Monaco	13	1	105	20
1998-99	Juventus	16	3	16	3
1999–2000	Arsenal	31	17		
2000-01	Arsenal	35	17		
2001-02	Arsenal	33	24		
2002-03	Arsenal	37	24	136	82

HOJSTED, Ingi (M) 0 0
H: 5 9 W: 9 10 b.Torshavn 12-12-85
Source: Trainee.

2002-03	Arsenal	0	0		

HOLLOWAY, Craig (G) 0 0
b.Blackheath 10-8-84
Source: Trainee.

2002-03	Arsenal	0	0		

HOYTE, Justin (D) 1 0
H: 5 11 W: 10 09 b.Waltham Forest 20-11-84
Source: Scholar. *Honours:* England Youth, Under-20.

2002-03	Arsenal	1	0	1	0

JEFFERS, Francis (F) 71 22
H: 5 10 W: 10 07 b.Liverpool 25-1-81
Source: Trainee. *Honours:* England Schools, Youth, Under-21, 1 full cap, 1 goal.

1997-98	Everton	1	0		
1998-99	Everton	15	6		
1999–2000	Everton	21	6		
2000-01	Everton	12	6	49	18
2001-02	Arsenal	6	2		
2002-03	Arsenal	16	2	22	4

JUAN (D) 0 0
H: 5 6 W: 9 07 b.Sao Paulo 6-2-82
Source: Sao Paulo.

2001-02	Arsenal	0	0		
2002-03	Arsenal	0	0		

KANU, Nwankwo (F) 235 70
H: 6 5 W: 12 01 b.Owerri 1-8-76
Honours: Nigeria 39 full caps, 6 goals.

1991-92	Federation Works	30	9	30	9
1992-93	Iwanyanwu	30	6	30	6
1993-94	Ajax	6	2		
1994-95	Ajax	18	10		
1995-96	Ajax	30	13	54	25
1996-97	Internazionale	0	0		
1997-98	Internazionale	11	1		
1998-99	Internazionale	1	0	12	1
1998-99	Arsenal	12	6		
1999–2000	Arsenal	31	12		
2000-01	Arsenal	27	3		
2001-02	Arsenal	23	3		
2002-03	Arsenal	16	5	109	29

KEOWN, Martin (D) 553 8
H: 6 1 W: 12 04 b.Oxford 24-7-66
Source: Apprentice. *Honours:* England Youth, Under-21, B, 43 full caps, 2 goals.

1983-84	Arsenal	0	0		
1984-85	Arsenal	0	0		
1984-85	*Brighton & HA*	16	0		
1985-86	Arsenal	22	0		
1985-86	*Brighton & HA*	7	1	23	1
1986-87	Aston Villa	36	0		
1987-88	Aston Villa	42	3		
1988-89	Aston Villa	34	0	112	3
1989-90	Everton	20	0		
1990-91	Everton	24	0		
1991-92	Everton	39	0		
1992-93	Everton	13	0	96	0
1992-93	Arsenal	16	0		
1993-94	Arsenal	33	0		
1994-95	Arsenal	31	1		
1995-96	Arsenal	34	0		
1996-97	Arsenal	33	1		
1997-98	Arsenal	18	0		
1998-99	Arsenal	34	1		
1999–2000	Arsenal	27	1		
2000-01	Arsenal	28	0		
2001-02	Arsenal	22	0		
2002-03	Arsenal	24	0	322	4

LARSSON, Sebastian (M) 0 0
H: 5 9 W: 10 08 b.Eskiltuna 6-6-85
Source: Trainee.

2002-03	Arsenal	0	0		

LAUREN, Etame-Mayer (M) 215 23
H: 5 11 W: 11 03 b.Londi Keisi 19-1-77
Honours: Cameroon 25 full caps, 1 goal.

1995-96	Utrera	30	5	30	5
1996-97	Sevilla B	17	3	17	3
1997-98	Levante	34	6	34	6

1998–99 Mallorca 32 1
1999–2000 Mallorca 30 3 **62 4**
2000-01 Arsenal 18 2
2001-02 Arsenal 27 2
2002-03 Arsenal 27 1 **72 5**

LJUNGBERG, Frederik (M) 196 41
H: 5 9 W: 10 13 b.Halmstad 16-4-77
Honours: Sweden 38 full caps, 3 goals.
1994 Halmstad 1 0
1995 Halmstad 16 1
1996 Halmstad 20 2
1997 Halmstad 24 5
1998 Halmstad 18 2 **79 10**
1998–99 Arsenal 16 1
1999–2000 Arsenal 26 6
2000-01 Arsenal 30 6
2001-02 Arsenal 25 12
2002-03 Arsenal 20 6 **117 31**

LUZHNY, Oleg* (D) 315 11
H: 5 10 W: 12 01 b.Ukraine 5-8-68
Honours: USSR 8 full caps, Ukraine 50 full caps.
1989 Dynamo Kiev 27 0
1990 Dynamo Kiev 12 0
1991 Dynamo Kiev 28 0
1992–93 Dynamo Kiev 26 3
1993–94 Dynamo Kiev 34 1
1994–95 Dynamo Kiev 24 4
1995–96 Dynamo Kiev 24 1
1996–97 Dynamo Kiev 28 2
1997–98 Dynamo Kiev 16 0
1998–99 Dynamo Kiev 21 0 **240 11**
1999–2000 Arsenal 21 0
2000-01 Arsenal 19 0
2001-02 Arsenal 18 0
2002-03 Arsenal 17 0 **75 0**

NICOLAU, Nicky (D) 0 0
H: 5 8 W: 10 08 b.Camden 12-10-83
Source: Trainee.
2002-03 Arsenal 0 0

O'DONNELL, Steven (M) 0 0
H: 5 9 W: 9 02 b.Galway 15-1-86
Source: Trainee.
2002-03 Arsenal 0 0

PARLOUR, Ray (M) 314 22
H: 5 10 W: 11 12 b.Romford 7-3-73
Source: Trainee. *Honours:* England Under-21, B, 10 full caps.
1990–91 Arsenal 0 0
1991–92 Arsenal 6 1
1992–93 Arsenal 21 1
1993–94 Arsenal 27 2
1994–95 Arsenal 30 0
1995–96 Arsenal 22 0
1996–97 Arsenal 30 2
1997–98 Arsenal 34 5
1998–99 Arsenal 35 6
1999–2000 Arsenal 30 1
2000-01 Arsenal 33 4
2001-02 Arsenal 27 0
2002-03 Arsenal 19 0 **314 22**

PAULINHO (M) 0 0
H: 5 7 W: 10 04 b.Sao Paulo 2-3-83
Source: Sao Paulo.
2001-02 Arsenal 0 0
2002-03 Arsenal 0 0

PENNANT, Jermaine (M) 26 5
H: 5 8 W: 10 01 b.Nottingham 15-1-83
Honours: England Schools, Youth, England Under-21.
1998–99 Notts Co 0 0
1998–99 Arsenal 0 0
1999–2000 Arsenal 0 0
2000-01 Arsenal 0 0
2001-02 Arsenal 0 0
2001-02 *Watford* 9 2
2002-03 Arsenal 5 3 **5 3**
2002-03 *Watford* 12 0 **21 2**

PIRES, Robert (M) 315 78
H: 6 1 W: 11 09 b.Reims 29-10-73
Honours: France 61 full caps, 14 goals.
1992–93 Metz 2 0
1993–94 Metz 24 1
1994–95 Metz 35 9
1995–96 Metz 38 11
1996–97 Metz 32 11
1997–98 Metz 31 11 **162 43**
1998–99 Marseille 34 6
1999–2008 Marseille 32 2 **66 8**
2000-01 Arsenal 33 4
2001-02 Arsenal 28 9
2002-03 Arsenal 26 14 **87 27**

SEAMAN, David (G) 712 0
H: 6 4 W: 13 00 b.Rotherham 19-9-63
Source: Apprentice. *Honours:* England Under-21, B, 75 full caps.
1981–82 Leeds U 0 0
1982–83 Peterborough U 38 0
1983–84 Peterborough U 45 0
1984–85 Peterborough U 8 0 **91 0**
1984–85 Birmingham C 33 0
1985–86 Birmingham C 42 0 **75 0**
1986–87 QPR 41 0
1987–88 QPR 32 0
1988–89 QPR 35 0
1989–90 QPR 33 0 **141 0**
1990–91 Arsenal 38 0
1991–92 Arsenal 42 0
1992–93 Arsenal 39 0
1993–94 Arsenal 39 0
1994–95 Arsenal 31 0
1995–96 Arsenal 38 0
1996–97 Arsenal 22 0
1997–98 Arsenal 31 0
1998–99 Arsenal 32 0
1999–2000 Arsenal 24 0
2000-01 Arsenal 24 0
2001-02 Arsenal 17 0
2002-03 Arsenal 28 0 **405 0**

SHAABAN, Rami (G) 144 0
H: 6 4 W: 14 02 b.Sweden 30-6-75
1994 Saltsjobadens 26 0
1995 Saltsjobadens 13 0 **39 0**
1995–96 Zamalek 4 0 **4 0**
1995–96 Thadodosman 5 0 **5 0**
1997– Nacka 2 0
1998– Nacka 20 0
1999– Nacka 26 0 **48 0**
2000- Djurgaarden 29 0
2001- Djurgaarden 5 0
2001 Djurgaarden 5 0
2002 Djurgaarden 6 0 **45 0**
2002-03 Arsenal 3 0 **3 0**

SHIELS, Dean (F) 0 0
H: 5 11 W: 9 10 b.Magherfelt 1-2-85
Source: Trainee.
2002-03 Arsenal 0 0

SILVA, Gilberto (M) 62 3
H: 6 3 W: 13 10 b.Lagoa da Prata 7-10-76
Honours: Brazil 20 full caps, 3 goals.
2000 Atletico Mineiro 1 0
2001 Atletico Mineiro 26 3 **27 3**
2002-03 Arsenal 35 0 **35 0**

SIMEK, Franklin (D) 0 0
H: 6 0 W: 11 06 b.Missouri 13-10-84
Source: Trainee.
2002-03 Arsenal 0 0

SKULASON, Olafur-Ingi (M) 0 0
H: 6 0 W: 11 10 b.Reykjavik 1-4-83
Source: Fylkir.
2001-02 Arsenal 0 0
2002-03 Arsenal 0 0

SPICER, John (M) 0 0
H: 5 11 W: 11 07 b.Romford 13-9-83
Source: Scholar. *Honours:* England Youth, Under-20.
2001-02 Arsenal 0 0
2002-03 Arsenal 0 0

STACK, Graham (G) 0 0
H: 6 2 W: 12 06 b.Hampstead 26-9-81
Honours: Eire Under-21.
2000-01 Arsenal 0 0
2001-02 Arsenal 0 0
2002-03 Arsenal 0 0

STEPANOVS, Igor (D) 166 13
H: 6 4 W: 13 05 b.Ogre 21-1-76
Honours: Latvia 57 full caps, 2 goals.
1994 Interskonto 20 2 **20 2**
1995 Skonto Riga 23 1
1996 Skonto Riga 22 2
1997 Skonto Riga 22 2
1998 Skonto Riga 24 0
1999 Skonto Riga 20 4
2000 Skonto Riga 18 2 **129 11**
2000-01 Arsenal 9 0
2001-02 Arsenal 6 0
2002-03 Arsenal 2 0 **17 0**

SVARD, Sebastian (D) 0 0
H: 6 1 W: 12 02 b.Hvidovre 15-1-83
2000-01 Arsenal 0 0
2001-02 Arsenal 0 0
2002-03 Arsenal 0 0

TAVLARIDIS, Efstathios (D) 69 1
H: 6 2 W: 12 11 b.Serres 25-1-80
1996–97 Iraklis 0 0
1997–98 Iraklis 2 0
1998–99 Iraklis 12 1
1999–2000 Iraklis 23 0
2000-01 Iraklis 27 0 **64 1**
2001-02 Arsenal 0 0
2002-03 Arsenal 1 0 **1 0**
2002-03 *Portsmouth* 4 0 **4 0**

TAYLOR, Stuart (G) 38 0
H: 6 5 W: 13 06 b.Romford 28-11-80
Source: Trainee. *Honours:* FA Schools, England Youth, Under-21.
1998–99 Arsenal 0 0
1999–2000 Arsenal 0 0
1999–2000 *Bristol R* 4 0 **4 0**
2000-01 Arsenal 0 0
2000-01 *Crystal Palace* 10 0 **10 0**
2000-01 *Peterborough U* 6 0 **6 0**
2001-02 Arsenal 10 0
2002-03 Arsenal 8 0 **18 0**

THOMAS, Jerome (M) 10 3
H: 5 10 W: 11 10 b.Brent 23-3-83
Source: Scholar. *Honours:* England Youth, Under-20.
2001-02 Arsenal 0 0
2001-02 *QPR* 4 1
2002-03 Arsenal 0 0
2002-03 *QPR* 6 2 **10 3**

TOURE, Kolo (M) 26 2
H: 5 10 W: 11 09 b.Ivory Coast 19-3-81
Source: ASEC Mimosas. *Honours:* Ivory Coast full caps.
2001-02 Arsenal 0 0
2002-03 Arsenal 26 2 **26 2**

VAN BRONCKHORST, Giovanni (M) 229 39
H: 5 9 W: 11 03 b.Rotterdam 5-2-75
Source: LMO, SC Feyenoord. *Honours:* Holland 29 full caps, 3 goals.
1993–94 Feyenoord 0 0
1993–94 RKC 12 2 **12 2**
1994–95 Feyenoord 10 1
1995–96 Feyenoord 27 9
1996–97 Feyenoord 34 4
1997–98 Feyenoord 32 8 **103 22**
1998–99 Rangers 35 7
1999–2000 Rangers 27 4
2000-01 Rangers 11 2
2000-01 Rangers 0 0 **73 13**
2001-02 Arsenal 21 1
2002-03 Arsenal 20 1 **41 2**

VIEIRA, Patrick (M) 269 21
H: 6 4 W: 13 00 b.Dakar 23-6-76
Honours: France Under-21, 62 full caps, 4 goals.
1993–94 Cannes 5 0
1994–95 Cannes 31 2
1995–96 Cannes 13 0 **49 2**
1995–96 AC Milan 2 0 **2 0**
1996–97 Arsenal 31 2
1997–98 Arsenal 33 2
1998–99 Arsenal 34 3
1999–2000 Arsenal 30 2
2000-01 Arsenal 30 5
2001-02 Arsenal 36 2
2002-03 Arsenal 24 3 **218 19**

VOLZ, Moritz (D) 10 1
H: 5 10 W: 12 06 b.Siegen 21-1-83
1999–2000 Arsenal 0 0
2000-01 Arsenal 0 0
2001-02 Arsenal 0 0
2002-03 Arsenal 0 0
2002-03 *Wimbledon* 10 1 **10 1**

WARMUZ, Guillaume* (G) 419 0
H: 6 2 W: 12 10 b.Saint-Vallier 22-5-70
1989–90 Marseille 0 0
1990–91 Louhans 34 0
1991–92 Louhans 34 0 **68 0**
1992–93 Lens 38 0
1993–94 Lens 38 0
1994–95 Lens 38 0
1995–96 Lens 36 0
1996–97 Lens 17 0
1997–98 Lens 34 0
1998–99 Lens 34 0
1999–2000 Lens 32 0
2000-01 Lens 34 0
2001-02 Lens 34 0

2002-03 Lens 16 0 351 0
2002-03 Arsenal 0 0

WILTORD, Sylvain (F) 318 86
H: 5 9 W: 12 04 b.Neuilly-sur-Marne 10-5-74
Honours: France 55 full caps, 17 goals.
1991–92 Rennes 0 0
1992–93 Rennes 2 0
1993–94 Rennes 26 8
1994–95 La Coruna 0 0
1994–95 Rennes 25 5
1995–96 Rennes 37 15
1996–97 Rennes 35 5 125 33
1997–98 Bordeaux 34 10
1998–99 Bordeaux 33 2
1999–2000 Bordeaux 32 13 99 25
2000-01 Arsenal 27 8
2001-02 Arsenal 33 10
2002-03 Arsenal 34 10 94 28

Trainees
Artry, Marcus DR; Jordan, Michael W; Kanu, Samuel; Kilkenny, Neil M; McDonald, Dean L; Oji, Samuel U; Owusu-Abeyie, Quincy J; Probets, Ashley; Small, Dorian A; Sulaiman, Hassan O

ASTON VILLA

AARITALO, Mika (F) 0 0
b.Taivassalo 25-7-85
Source: TPS Turku.
2002-03 Aston Villa 0 0

ALLBACK, Marcus (F) 291 119
H: 5 9 W: 12 00 b.Stockholm 5-7-73
Honours: Sweden 32 full caps, 16 goals.
1992 Orgryte 24 10
1993 Orgryte 20 4
1994 Orgryte 25 19
1995 Orgryte 22 4
1996 Orgryte 24 8
1997 Orgryte 24 9
1997–98 Lyngby 4 1 4 1
1997–98 Bari 16 0 16 0
1998 Orgryte 12 3
1999 Orgryte 26 15
2000 Orgryte 26 16 203 88
2000-01 Heerenveen 16 10
2001-02 Heerenveen 32 15 48 25
2002-03 Aston Villa 20 5 20 5

ALPAY, Ozalan (D) 252 13
H: 6 2 W: 14 00 b.Izmir 29-5-73
Source: Soma Linyit. *Honours:* Turkey 80 full caps, 4 goals.
1992–93 Altay 23 1 23 1
1993–94 Besiktas 10 0
1994–95 Besiktas 29 3
1995–96 Besiktas 31 2
1996–97 Besiktas 25 3
1997–98 Besiktas 26 1
1998–99 Besiktas 27 0 148 9
1999–2000 Fenerbahce 29 3 29 3
2000-01 Aston Villa 33 0
2001-02 Aston Villa 14 0
2002-03 Aston Villa 5 0 52 0

AMOO, Ryan (M) 0 0
H: 5 10 W: 9 12 b.Leicester 11-10-83
Source: Scholar.
2001-02 Aston Villa 0 0
2002-03 Aston Villa 0 0

ANGEL, Juan Pablo (F) 144 59
H: 6 0 W: 12 10 b.Medellin 24-10-75
Source: Nacional. *Honours:* Colombia 22 full caps, 5 goals.
1997–98 River Plate 12 2
1998–99 River Plate 27 11
1999–2000 River Plate 34 19
2000-01 River Plate 18 13 91 45
2000-01 Aston Villa 9 1
2001-02 Aston Villa 29 12
2002-03 Aston Villa 15 1 53 14

BALABAN, Bosko (F) 130 35
H: 5 10 W: 11 10 b.Rijeka 15-10-78
Honours: Croatia 13 full caps, 6 goals.
1995–96 Rijeka 2 0
1996–97 Rijeka 17 1
1997–98 Rijeka 26 1
1998–99 Rijeka 23 4
1999–2000 Rijeka 29 15 97 21
2000-01 Dynamo Zagreb 25 14 25 14
2001-02 Aston Villa 8 0
2002-03 Aston Villa 0 0 8 0

BARRY, Gareth (D) 149 6
H: 5 11 W: 12 06 b.Hastings 23-2-81
Source: Trainee. *Honours:* England Youth, Under-21, 8 full caps.
1997–98 Aston Villa 2 0
1998–99 Aston Villa 32 2
1999–2000 Aston Villa 30 1
2000-01 Aston Villa 30 0
2001-02 Aston Villa 20 0
2002-03 Aston Villa 35 3 149 6

BEWERS, Jonathan (D) 1 0
H: 5 8 W: 9 13 b.Kettering 10-9-82
Source: Trainee. *Honours:* England Youth, Under-20.
1999–2000 Aston Villa 1 0
2000-01 Aston Villa 0 0
2001-02 Aston Villa 0 0
2002-03 Aston Villa 0 0 1 0

BRAZIL, Alan (M) 0 0
H: 5 7 W: 12 02 b.Edinburgh 5-7-85
Source: Trainee.
2002-03 Aston Villa 0 0

BRIDGES, Stuart (D) 0 0
b.Oxford 6-1-86
Source: Trainee. *Honours:* FA Schools, England Youth.
2002-03 Aston Villa 0 0

COOKE, Stephen (M) 10 0
H: 5 7 W: 9 00 b.Walsall 15-2-83
Honours: England Youth, Under-20.
1999–2000 Aston Villa 0 0
2000-01 Aston Villa 0 0
2001-02 Aston Villa 0 0
2001-02 *Bournemouth* 7 0 7 0
2002-03 Aston Villa 3 0 3 0

CROUCH, Peter (F) 100 30
H: 6 7 W: 11 12 b.Macclesfield 30-1-81
Source: Trainee. *Honours:* England Youth, Under-20, Under-21.
1998–99 Tottenham H 0 0
1999–2000 Tottenham H 0 0
2000-01 QPR 42 10 42 10
2001-02 Portsmouth 37 18 37 18
2001-02 Aston Villa 7 2
2002-03 Aston Villa 14 0 21 2

DAVIS, Steven (M) 0 0
H: 5 7 W: 9 07 b.Ballymena 1-1-85
Source: Scholar.
2001-02 Aston Villa 0 0
2002-03 Aston Villa 0 0

DE LA CRUZ, Ulises (D) 104 12
H: 5 8 W: 12 10 b.Bolivar 8-2-74
Source: Cruzeiro. *Honours:* Equador 61 full caps, 3 goals.
1999 LDU Quito 22 4
1999 LDU Quito 0 0
2000 LDU Quito 30 5 52 9
2001-02 Hibernian 32 2 32 2
2002-03 Aston Villa 20 1 20 1

DELANEY, Mark (D) 119 1
H: 6 1 W: 11 07 b.Haverfordwest 13-5-76
Source: Carmarthen T. *Honours:* Wales 19 full caps.
1998–99 Cardiff C 28 0 28 0
1998–99 Aston Villa 2 0
1999–2000 Aston Villa 28 1
2000-01 Aston Villa 19 0
2001-02 Aston Villa 30 0
2002-03 Aston Villa 12 0 91 1

DUBLIN, Dion (F) 450 162
H: 6 2 W: 12 04 b.Leicester 22-4-69
Source: Oakham U. *Honours:* England 4 full caps.
1987–88 Norwich C 0 0
1988–89 Cambridge U 21 6
1989–90 Cambridge U 46 15
1990–91 Cambridge U 46 16
1991–92 Cambridge U 43 15 156 52
1992–93 Manchester U 7 1
1993–94 Manchester U 5 1 12 2
1994–95 Coventry C 31 13
1995–96 Coventry C 34 14
1996–97 Coventry C 34 13
1997–98 Coventry C 36 18
1998–99 Coventry C 10 3 145 61
1998–99 Aston Villa 24 11
1999–2000 Aston Villa 26 12
2000-01 Aston Villa 33 8
2001-02 Aston Villa 21 4
2001-02 *Millwall* 5 2 5 2
2002-03 Aston Villa 28 10 132 45

EDWARDS, Rob (D) 8 0
H: 6 1 W: 11 10 b.Telford 25-12-82
Source: Trainee. *Honours:* Wales 1 full cap.
1999–2000 Aston Villa 0 0
2000-01 Aston Villa 0 0
2001-02 Aston Villa 0 0
2002-03 Aston Villa 8 0 8 0

ENCKELMAN, Peter (G) 131 0
H: 6 2 W: 12 05 b.Turku 10-3-77
Source: TPS Turku. *Honours:* Finland 6 full caps.
1995 TPS Turku 6 0
1996 TPS Turku 24 0
1997 TPS Turku 25 0
1998 TPS Turku 24 0 79 0
1998–99 Aston Villa 0 0
1999–2000 Aston Villa 10 0
2000-01 Aston Villa 0 0
2001-02 Aston Villa 9 0
2002-03 Aston Villa 33 0 52 0

ENNIS, Pierre (D) 0 0
H: 5 10 W: 12 03 b.Dublin 25-2-84
Source: Scholar.
2000-01 Aston Villa 0 0
2001-02 Aston Villa 0 0
2002-03 Aston Villa 0 0

FAHEY, Keith‡ (M) 0 0
H: 5 10 W: 12 07 b.Dublin 15-1-83
1999–2000 Aston Villa 0 0
2000-01 Aston Villa 0 0
2001-02 Aston Villa 0 0
2002-03 Aston Villa 0 0

FOLEY-SHERIDAN, Steven (M) 0 0
H: 5 4 W: 9 02 b.Dublin 10-2-86
Source: Trainee.
2002-03 Aston Villa 0 0

GUDJONSSON, Joey (M) 77 11
H: 5 8 W: 11 05 b.Akranes 25-5-80
Honours: Iceland 13 full caps, 1 goal.
1998–99 Genk 5 0 5 0
1999–2000 MVV 19 5 19 5
2000-01 RKC 31 4 31 4
2001-02 Betis 11 0 11 0
2002-03 Aston Villa 11 2 11 2

HADJI, Mustapha (M) 302 50
H: 5 11 W: 11 12 b.Ifrane 16-11-71
Honours: Morocco 60 full caps.
1992–93 Nancy 32 6
1993–94 Nancy 37 11
1994–95 Nancy 28 3
1995–96 Nancy 42 11 139 31
1996–97 Sporting 27 3
1997–98 Sporting 9 0 36 3
1997–98 La Coruna 10 0
1998–99 La Coruna 21 2 31 2
1999–2000 Coventry C 33 6
2000-01 Coventry C 29 6 62 12
2001-02 Aston Villa 23 2
2002-03 Aston Villa 11 0 34 2

HENDERSON, Wayne (G) 0 0
H: 5 11 W: 12 02 b.Dublin 16-9-83
Source: Scholar.
2000-01 Aston Villa 0 0
2001-02 Aston Villa 0 0
2002-03 Aston Villa 0 0

HENDRIE, Lee (M) 173 19
H: 5 10 W: 11 00 b.Birmingham 18-5-77
Source: Trainee. *Honours:* England Youth, Under-21, B, 1 full cap.
1993–94 Aston Villa 0 0
1994–95 Aston Villa 0 0
1995–96 Aston Villa 3 0
1996–97 Aston Villa 4 0
1997–98 Aston Villa 17 3
1998–99 Aston Villa 32 3
1999–2000 Aston Villa 29 1
2000-01 Aston Villa 32 6
2001-02 Aston Villa 29 2
2002-03 Aston Villa 27 4 173 19

HITZLSPERGER, Thomas (M) 44 3
H: 6 0 W: 11 12 b.Germany 5-4-82
Source: Bayern Munich. Germany Under-21.
2000-01 Aston Villa 1 0
2001-02 *Chesterfield* 5 0 5 0
2001-02 Aston Villa 12 1
2002-03 Aston Villa 26 2 39 3

HUSBANDS, Michael* (F) 0 0
H: 5 9 W: 9 13 b.Birmingham 13-11-83
Source: Scholar.
2001-02 Aston Villa 0 0
2002-03 Aston Villa 0 0

HYLTON, Leon* (D) 8 0
H: 5 9 W: 11 00 b.Birmingham 27-1-83
Honours: England Youth, Under-20.
1999–2000 Aston Villa 0 0
2000-01 Aston Villa 0 0
2001-02 Aston Villa 0 0
2002-03 Aston Villa 0 0
2002-03 *Swansea C* 8 0 **8 0**

HYNES, Peter (F) 0 0
H: 5 9 W: 11 12 b.Dublin 28-11-83
2000-01 Aston Villa 0 0
2001-02 Aston Villa 0 0
2002-03 Aston Villa 0 0

JACKMAN, Daniel (D) 7 1
H: 5 4 W: 9 08 b.Worcester 3-1-83
Source: Scholar.
2000-01 Aston Villa 0 0
2001-02 Aston Villa 0 0
2001-02 *Cambridge U* 7 1 **7 1**
2002-03 Aston Villa 0 0

JOHNSEN, Ronny (D) 201 19
H: 6 3 W: 13 00 b.Sandefjord 10-6-69
Honours: Norway 56 full caps, 3 goals.
1992 Lyn 12 1
1993 Lyn 19 6 **31 7**
1994 Lillestrom 10 3
1995 Lillestrom 13 1 **23 4**
1995–96 Besiktas 22 1 **22 1**
1996–97 Manchester U 31 0
1997–98 Manchester U 22 2
1998–99 Manchester U 22 3
1999–2000 Manchester U 3 0
2000-01 Manchester U 11 1
2001-02 Manchester U 10 1 **99 7**
2002-03 Aston Villa 26 0 **26 0**

KACHLOUL, Hassan (M) 245 48
H: 6 1 W: 12 01 b.Agadir 19-2-73
Honours: Morocco 12 full caps.
1992–93 Nimes 17 1
1993–94 Nimes 37 17
1994–95 Nimes 32 8 **86 26**
1995–96 Dunkerque 28 6 **28 6**
1996–97 Metz 7 0 **7 0**
1997–98 St Etienne 16 0 **16 0**
1998–99 Southampton 22 5
1999–2000 Southampton 32 5
2000-01 Southampton 32 4 **86 14**
2001-02 Aston Villa 22 2
2002-03 Aston Villa 0 0 **22 2**

KINSELLA, Mark (M) 407 46
H: 5 9 W: 10 09 b.Dublin 12-8-72
Source: Home Farm. *Honours:* Eire 41 full caps, 3 goals.
1989–90 Colchester U 6 0
1990–91 Colchester U 0 0
1991–92 Colchester U 0 0
1992–93 Colchester U 38 6
1993–94 Colchester U 42 8
1994–95 Colchester U 42 6
1995–96 Colchester U 45 5
1996–97 Colchester U 7 2 **180 27**
1996–97 Charlton Ath 37 6
1997–98 Charlton Ath 46 6
1998–99 Charlton Ath 38 2
1999–2000 Charlton Ath 38 3
2000-01 Charlton Ath 32 2
2001-02 Charlton Ath 17 0
2002-03 Charlton Ath 0 0 **208 19**
2002-03 Aston Villa 19 0 **19 0**

KOUMAN, Amadou (F) 0 0
b.Marcory 14-4-86
Source: Trainee.
2002-03 Aston Villa 0 0

LEONHARDSEN, Oyvind (M) 313 59
H: 5 10 W: 11 02 b.Kristiansund 17-8-70
Source: Clausenengen. *Honours:* Norway 86 full caps, 19 goals.
1989 Molde 22 5
1990 Molde 21 2
1991 Molde 21 2 **64 9**
1992 Rosenborg 22 6
1993 Rosenborg 19 6
1994 Rosenborg 22 8 **63 20**
1994–95 Wimbledon 20 4
1995–96 Wimbledon 29 4
1996–97 Wimbledon 27 5 **76 13**
1997–98 Liverpool 28 6
1998–99 Liverpool 9 1 **37 7**
1999–2000 Tottenham H 22 4
2000-01 Tottenham H 25 3
2001-02 Tottenham H 7 0 **54 7**
2002-03 Aston Villa 19 3 **19 3**

MASALIN, Jon (G) 0 0
b.Helsinki 29-1-86
2002-03 Aston Villa 0 0

McGRATH, John* (F) 3 0
H: 5 10 W: 10 04 b.Limerick 27-3-80
Source: Belvedere. *Honours:* Eire Under-21.
1999–2000 Aston Villa 0 0
2000-01 Aston Villa 3 0
2001-02 Aston Villa 0 0
2002-03 Aston Villa 0 0 **3 0**

MELLBERG, Olof (D) 232 1
H: 6 1 W: 12 10 b.Amncharad 3-9-77
Honours: Sweden 35 full caps.
1996 Degerfors 22 0
1997 Degerfors 25 0 **47 0**
1998 AIK Stockholm 17 0 **17 0**
1998–99 Santander 25 0
1999–2000 Santander 37 0
2000-01 Santander 36 0 **98 0**
2001-02 Aston Villa 32 0
2002-03 Aston Villa 38 1 **70 1**

MOORE, Luke (F) 0 0
b.Birmingham 13-2-86
Source: Trainee. *Honours:* FA Schools, England Youth.
2002-03 Aston Villa 0 0

MOORE, Stefan (F) 15 1
H: 5 10 W: 10 12 b.Birmingham 28-9-83
Source: Scholar. *Honours:* England Youth.
2000-01 Aston Villa 0 0
2001-02 Aston Villa 0 0
2001-02 *Chesterfield* 2 0 **2 0**
2002-03 Aston Villa 13 1 **13 1**

MULCAHY, Kevin (D) 0 0
b.Cork 2-3-86
Source: Trainee.
2002-03 Aston Villa 0 0

MYHILL, Boaz (G) 2 0
H: 6 3 W: 14 06 b.California 9-11-82
Source: Scholar. *Honours:* England Youth, Under-20.
2000-01 Aston Villa 0 0
2001-02 Aston Villa 0 0
2001-02 *Stoke C* 0 0
2002-03 Aston Villa 0 0
2002-03 *Bristol C* 0 0
2002-03 *Bradford C* 2 0 **2 0**

NIX, Kyle (F) 0 0
b.Sydney 21-1-86
Source: Manchester U Trainee. *Honours:* FA Schools, England Youth.
2002-03 Aston Villa 0 0

POSTMA, Stefan (G) 106 0
H: 6 4 W: 15 04 b.Utrecht 6-10-76
1995–96 Utrecht 5 0
1996–97 Utrecht 12 0
1997–98 Utrecht 13 0
1998–99 Utrecht 1 0
1999–2000 Utrecht 2 0 **33 0**
2000-01 De Graafschap 34 0
2001-02 De Graafschap 33 0 **67 0**
2002-03 Aston Villa 6 0 **6 0**

RIDGEWELL, Liam (D) 5 0
H: 5 10 W: 10 03 b.London 21-7-84
Source: Scholar. *Honours:* England Youth.
2001-02 Aston Villa 0 0
2002-03 Aston Villa 0 0
2002-03 *Bournemouth* 5 0 **5 0**

SAMUEL, J Lloyd (D) 81 0
H: 5 11 W: 11 04 b.Trinidad 29-3-81
Source: Charlton Ath Trainee. *Honours:* England Youth, Under-20, Under-21.
1998–99 Aston Villa 0 0
1999–2000 Aston Villa 9 0
2000-01 Aston Villa 3 0
2001-02 *Gillingham* 8 0 **8 0**
2001-02 Aston Villa 23 0
2002-03 Aston Villa 38 0 **73 0**

SCULLION, David (F) 8 2
H: 5 8 W: 10 03 b.Craigavon 27-4-84
2000-01 Portadown 8 2 **8 2**
2001-02 Aston Villa 0 0
2002-03 Aston Villa 0 0

STAUNTON, Steve (D) 404 17
H: 6 0 W: 12 12 b.Drogheda 19-1-69
Source: Dundalk. *Honours:* Eire Under-21, 102 full caps, 7 goals.
1986–87 Liverpool 0 0
1987–88 Liverpool 0 0
1987–88 *Bradford C* 8 0 **8 0**
1988–89 Liverpool 21 0
1989–90 Liverpool 20 0
1990–91 Liverpool 24 0
1991–92 Aston Villa 37 4
1992–93 Aston Villa 42 2
1993–94 Aston Villa 24 2
1994–95 Aston Villa 35 5
1995–96 Aston Villa 13 0
1996–97 Aston Villa 30 2
1997–98 Aston Villa 27 1
1998–99 Liverpool 31 0
1999–2000 Liverpool 12 0
2000-01 Liverpool 1 0 **109 0**
2000-01 *Crystal Palace* 6 1 **6 1**
2000-01 Aston Villa 14 0
2001-02 Aston Villa 33 0
2002-03 Aston Villa 26 0 **281 16**

STUART, Cameron* (D) 0 0
H: 5 6 W: 10 08 b.York 9-1-84
Source: Scholar.
2001-02 Aston Villa 0 0
2002-03 Aston Villa 0 0

TAYLOR, Ian* (M) 330 57
H: 6 1 W: 12 00 b.Birmingham 4-6-68
Source: Moor Green.
1992–93 Port Vale 41 15
1993–94 Port Vale 42 13 **83 28**
1994–95 Sheffield W 14 1 **14 1**
1994–95 Aston Villa 22 1
1995–96 Aston Villa 25 3
1996–97 Aston Villa 34 2
1997–98 Aston Villa 32 6
1998–99 Aston Villa 33 4
1999–2000 Aston Villa 29 5
2000-01 Aston Villa 29 4
2001-02 Aston Villa 16 3
2002-03 Aston Villa 13 0 **233 28**

VASSELL, Darius (F) 109 24
H: 5 7 W: 12 00 b.Birmingham 13-6-80
Source: Trainee. *Honours:* England Youth, Under-21, 14 full caps, 4 goals.
1998–99 Aston Villa 6 0
1999–2000 Aston Villa 11 0
2000-01 Aston Villa 23 4
2001-02 Aston Villa 36 12
2002-03 Aston Villa 33 8 **109 24**

WHITTINGHAM, Peter (D) 4 0
H: 5 10 W: 9 13 b.Nuneaton 8-9-84
Source: Trainee. *Honours:* England Youth.
2002-03 Aston Villa 4 0 **4 0**

WILLETTS, Ben‡ (D) 0 0
H: 5 9 W: 11 05 b.West Bromwich 10-2-83
Source: Scholar. *Honours:* England Youth.
1999–2000 Aston Villa 0 0
2000-01 Aston Villa 0 0
2001-02 Aston Villa 0 0
2002-03 Aston Villa 0 0

WRIGHT, Alan* (D) 432 6
H: 5 4 W: 9 09 b.Ashton-under-Lyme 28-9-71
Source: Trainee. *Honours:* England Schools, Youth, Under-21.
1987–88 Blackpool 1 0
1988–89 Blackpool 16 0
1989–90 Blackpool 24 0
1990–91 Blackpool 45 0
1991–92 Blackpool 12 0 **98 0**
1991–92 Blackburn R 33 1
1992–93 Blackburn R 24 0
1993–94 Blackburn R 12 0
1994–95 Blackburn R 5 0 **74 1**
1994–95 Aston Villa 8 0
1995–96 Aston Villa 38 2
1996–97 Aston Villa 38 1
1997–98 Aston Villa 37 0
1998–99 Aston Villa 38 0
1999–2000 Aston Villa 32 1
2000-01 Aston Villa 36 1
2001-02 Aston Villa 23 0
2002-03 Aston Villa 10 0 **260 5**

Trainees
Cahill, Gary J; Cormell, Scott; Grady, John MJ; Grant, Lee; Green, Nicholas J; Marshall, Colin J; O'Connor, James F; Pecora, Antoni; Ward, Jamie J; Yarnold, Andrew

BARNSLEY

AUSTIN, Neil (F) 34 0
H: 5 10 W: 11 09 b.Barnsley 26-4-83
Source: Trainee. *Honours:* England Youth, Under-20.
1999–2000 Barnsley 0 0
2000-01 Barnsley 0 0
2001-02 Barnsley 0 0
2002-03 Barnsley 34 0 **34 0**

BARROWCLOUGH, Carl (F) 12 0
H: 5 7 W: 9 08 b.Doncaster 25-9-81
Source: Scholar.
2000-01 Barnsley 7 0
2001-02 Barnsley 0 0
2002-03 Barnsley 5 0 **12 0**

BERTOS, Leo* (M) 12 1
H: 5 8 W: 12 08 b.Wellington 20-12-81
2000-01 Barnsley 2 0
2001-02 Barnsley 4 0
2002-03 Barnsley 6 1 **12 1**

BETSY, Kevin (M) 71 6
H: 6 1 W: 12 02 b.Seychelles 20-3-78
Source: Woking.
1998–99 Fulham 7 1
1999–2000 Fulham 2 0
1999–2000 *Bournemouth* 5 0 **5 0**
1999–2000 *Hull C* 2 0 **2 0**
2000-01 Fulham 5 0
2001-02 Fulham 1 0 **15 1**
2001-02 Barnsley 10 0
2002-03 Barnsley 39 5 **49 5**

CROOKS, Lee (D) 123 2
H: 6 2 W: 13 12 b.Wakefield 14-1-78
Source: Trainee. *Honours:* England Youth.
1994–95 Manchester C 0 0
1995–96 Manchester C 0 0
1996–97 Manchester C 15 0
1997–98 Manchester C 5 0
1998–99 Manchester C 34 1
1999–2000 Manchester C 20 1
2000-01 Manchester C 2 0 **76 2**
2000-01 *Northampton T* 3 0 **3 0**
2000-01 Barnsley 0 0
2001-02 Barnsley 26 0
2002-03 Barnsley 18 0 **44 0**

CYRUS, Andrew† (D) 0 0
H: 6 3 W: 11 09 b.Huddersfield 31-1-86
Source: Scholar.
2002-03 Barnsley 0 0

DIXON, Kevin (M) 3 0
H: 5 8 W: 12 08 b.Easington 27-6-80
Source: Trainee. *Honours:* England Youth.
1997–98 Leeds U 0 0
1998–99 Leeds U 0 0
1999–2000 Leeds U 0 0
1999–2000 *York C* 3 0 **3 0**
2000-01 Leeds U 0 0
2001-02 Barnsley 0 0
2002-03 Barnsley 0 0

DONOVAN, Kevin (M) 404 45
H: 5 10 W: 11 11 b.Halifax 17-12-71
Source: Trainee.
1989–90 Huddersfield T 1 0
1990–91 Huddersfield T 6 1
1991–92 Huddersfield T 10 0
1991–92 *Halifax T* 6 0 **6 0**
1992–93 Huddersfield T 3 0 **20 1**
1992–93 WBA 32 6
1993–94 WBA 37 8
1994–95 WBA 33 5
1995–96 WBA 34 0
1996–97 WBA 32 0 **168 19**
1997–98 Grimsby T 46 16
1998–99 Grimsby T 28 0
1999–2000 Grimsby T 41 3
2000-01 Grimsby T 41 5 **156 24**
2001-02 Barnsley 32 1
2002-03 Barnsley 22 0 **54 1**

DUDGEON, James* (D) 22 3
H: 6 2 W: 12 04 b.Newcastle 19-3-81
Source: Trainee. *Honours:* Scotland Youth.
1999–2000 Barnsley 0 0
2000-01 Barnsley 0 0
2000-01 *Lincoln C* 22 3 **22 3**
2001-02 Barnsley 0 0
2002-03 Barnsley 0 0

DYER, Bruce# (F) 348 102
H: 5 11 W: 12 08 b.Ilford 13-4-75
Source: Trainee. *Honours:* England Under-21.
1992–93 Watford 2 0
1993–94 Watford 29 6 **31 6**
1993–94 Crystal Palace 11 0
1994–95 Crystal Palace 16 1
1995–96 Crystal Palace 35 13
1996–97 Crystal Palace 43 17
1997–98 Crystal Palace 24 4
1998–99 Crystal Palace 6 2 **135 37**
1998–99 Barnsley 28 7
1999–2000 Barnsley 32 6
2000-01 Barnsley 38 15
2001-02 Barnsley 44 14
2002-03 Barnsley 40 17 **182 59**

FALLON, Rory (F) 47 7
H: 6 2 W: 12 02 b.Gisbourne 20-3-82
Source: North Shore U. *Honours:* England Youth.
1998–99 Barnsley 0 0
1999–2000 Barnsley 0 0
2000-01 Barnsley 1 0
2001-02 Barnsley 9 0
2001-02 *Shrewsbury T* 11 0 **11 0**
2002-03 Barnsley 26 7 **36 7**

GHENT, Matthew (G) 9 0
H: 6 3 W: 14 09 b.Burton 5-10-80
Source: Trainee. *Honours:* England Schools, Youth.
1997–98 Aston Villa 0 0
1998–99 Aston Villa 0 0
1999–2000 Aston Villa 0 0
2000-01 Aston Villa 0 0
2000-01 Lincoln C 1 0 **1 0**
2001-02 Barnsley 1 0
2002-03 Barnsley 7 0 **8 0**

GIBBS, Paul (D) 212 17
H: 5 11 W: 11 07 b.Great Yarmouth 26-10-72
Source: Diss T.
1994–95 Colchester U 9 0
1995–96 Colchester U 24 3
1996–97 Colchester U 20 0 **53 3**
1997–98 Torquay U 41 7 **41 7**
1998–99 Plymouth Arg 27 3
1999–2000 Plymouth Arg 7 0 **34 3**
2000-01 Brentford 27 1
2001-02 Brentford 27 2 **54 3**
2001-02 Barnsley 4 0
2002-03 Barnsley 26 1 **30 1**

GORRE, Dean (M) 297 44
H: 5 7 W: 11 09 b.Surinam 10-9-70
1991–92 SVV/Dordrecht 32 8 **32 8**
1992–93 Feyenoord 25 2
1993–94 Feyenoord 12 3
1994–95 Feyenoord 5 1 **42 6**
1994–95 Groningen 12 3
1995–96 Groningen 34 4
1996–97 Groningen 34 11 **80 18**
1997–98 Ajax 21 3
1998–99 Ajax 14 1 **35 4**
1999–2000 Huddersfield T 28 4
2000-01 Huddersfield T 34 2 **62 6**
2001-02 Barnsley 19 2
2002-03 Barnsley 27 0 **46 2**

HAYWARD, Steve (M) 247 22
H: 5 11 W: 12 13 b.Walsall 8-9-71
Source: Trainee. *Honours:* England Youth.
1988–89 Derby Co 0 0
1989–90 Derby Co 3 0
1990–91 Derby Co 1 0
1991–92 Derby Co 7 0
1992–93 Derby Co 7 1
1993–94 Derby Co 5 0
1994–95 Derby Co 3 0 **26 1**
1994–95 Carlisle U 9 2
1995–96 Carlisle U 38 4
1996–97 Carlisle U 43 7 **90 13**
1997–98 Fulham 35 4
1998–99 Fulham 42 3
1999–2000 Fulham 37 0
2000-01 Fulham 1 0 **115 7**
2000-01 Barnsley 10 1
2001-02 Barnsley 0 0
2002-03 Barnsley 6 0 **16 1**

JONES, Gary (M) 204 24
H: 5 11 W: 12 06 b.Birkenhead 3-6-77
1997–98 Swansea C 8 0 **8 0**
1997–98 Rochdale 17 2
1998–99 Rochdale 20 0
1999–2000 Rochdale 39 7
2000-01 Rochdale 44 8
2001-02 Rochdale 20 5 **140 22**
2001-02 Barnsley 25 1
2002-03 Barnsley 31 1 **56 2**

JONES, Griff (F) 2 0
H: 5 8 W: 12 02 b.Liverpool 22-6-84
Source: Scholar.
2002-03 Barnsley 2 0 **2 0**

KAY, Antony (F) 24 0
H: 5 11 W: 11 07 b.Barnsley 21-10-82
Source: Trainee. *Honours:* England Youth.
1999–2000 Barnsley 0 0
2000-01 Barnsley 7 0
2001-02 Barnsley 1 0
2002-03 Barnsley 16 0 **24 0**

LAIGHT, Ryan† (D) 0 0
H: 6 0 W: 11 09 b.Barnsley 16-11-85
Source: Scholar.
2002-03 Barnsley 0 0

LUMSDON, Chris (M) 81 11
H: 5 11 W: 10 02 b.Newcastle 15-12-79
Source: Trainee.
1997–98 Sunderland 1 0
1998–99 Sunderland 0 0
1999–2000 Sunderland 1 0
1999–2000 *Blackpool* 6 1 **6 1**
2000-01 Sunderland 0 0
2000-01 *Crewe Alex* 16 0 **16 0**
2001-02 Sunderland 0 0 **2 0**
2001-02 Barnsley 32 7
2002-03 Barnsley 25 3 **57 10**

MORGAN, Chris (D) 185 7
H: 6 1 W: 12 13 b.Barnsley 9-11-77
Source: Trainee.
1996–97 Barnsley 0 0
1997–98 Barnsley 11 0
1998–99 Barnsley 19 0
1999–2000 Barnsley 37 0
2000-01 Barnsley 40 1
2001-02 Barnsley 42 4
2002-03 Barnsley 36 2 **185 7**

MULLIGAN, David (M) 61 1
H: 5 5 W: 9 13 b.Fazakerley 24-3-82
Source: Scholar. New Zealand full caps.
2000-01 Barnsley 0 0
2001-02 Barnsley 28 0
2002-03 Barnsley 33 1 **61 1**

NEIL, Alex (M) 106 7
H: 5 9 W: 11 03 b.Bellshill 9-6-81
Source: Dunfermline Ath.
1999–2000 Airdrieonians 16 5 **16 5**
2000-01 Barnsley 32 0
2001-02 Barnsley 25 2
2002-03 Barnsley 33 0 **90 2**

O'CALLAGHAN, Brian (D) 46 1
H: 6 1 W: 12 02 b.Limerick 24-2-81
Source: Pike Rovers.
1998–99 Barnsley 0 0
1999–2000 Barnsley 0 0
2000-01 Barnsley 26 0
2001-02 Barnsley 6 0
2002-03 Barnsley 14 1 **46 1**

OLDHAM, Adam (D) 0 0
H: 6 0 W: 11 07 b.Sheffield 26-1-85
Honours: England Youth.
2001-02 Barnsley 0 0
2002-03 Barnsley 0 0

PADGETT, Greg† (M) 0 0
H: 5 9 W: 9 06 b.Barnsley 9-11-85
Source: Scholar.
2002-03 Barnsley 0 0

PARRY, Craig (G) 0 0
H: 5 11 W: 12 04 b.Barnsley 15-3-84
Source: Scholar.
2000-01 Barnsley 0 0
2001-02 Barnsley 0 0
2002-03 Barnsley 0 0

RANKIN, Isiah (F) 105 18
H: 5 10 W: 11 00 b.London 22-5-78
Source: Trainee.
1995–96 Arsenal 0 0
1996–97 Arsenal 0 0
1997–98 Arsenal 1 0 **1 0**

1997–98	*Colchester U*	11	5	**11**	**5**
1998–99	Bradford C	27	4		
1999–2000	Bradford C	9	0		
1999–2000	*Birmingham C*	13	4	**13**	**4**
2000-01	Bradford C	1	0	**37**	**4**
2000-01	*Bolton W*	16	2	**16**	**2**
2000-01	Barnsley	9	1		
2001-02	Barnsley	9	1		
2002-03	Barnsley	9	1	**27**	**3**

SCOTHERN, Ashley (F) 1 0
H: 6 0 W: 11 00 b.Pontefract 11-9-84
Source: Scholar. *Honours:* England Youth.

2001-02	Barnsley	1	0		
2002-03	Barnsley	0	0	**1**	**0**

SEED, Andrew† (M) 0 0
H: 5 6 W: 9 0 b.Pontefract 8-5-86
Source: Scholar.

2002-03	Barnsley	0	0

SHEARD, Daniel† (D) 0 0
H: 6 0 W: 10 08 b.Barnsley 3-10-85
Source: Scholar.

2002-03	Barnsley	0	0

SHERON, Mike* (F) 417 113
H: 5 10 W: 12 08 b.Liverpool 11-1-72
Source: Trainee. *Honours:* England Under-21.

1990–91	Manchester C	0	0		
1990–91	*Bury*	5	1	**5**	**1**
1991–92	Manchester C	29	7		
1992–93	Manchester C	38	11		
1993–94	Manchester C	33	6	**100**	**24**
1994–95	Norwich C	21	1		
1995–96	Norwich C	7	1	**28**	**2**
1995–96	Stoke C	28	15		
1996–97	Stoke C	41	19	**69**	**34**
1997–98	QPR	40	11		
1998–99	QPR	23	8	**63**	**19**
1998–99	Barnsley	15	2		
1999–2000	Barnsley	36	9		
2000-01	Barnsley	34	1		
2001-02	Barnsley	33	12		
2002-03	Barnsley	34	9	**152**	**33**

WARD, Mitch# (M) 259 12
H: 5 8 W: 11 07 b.Sheffield 19-6-71
Source: Trainee.

1989–90	Sheffield U	0	0		
1990–91	Sheffield U	4	0		
1990–91	*Crewe Alex*	4	1	**4**	**1**
1991–92	Sheffield U	6	2		
1992–93	Sheffield U	26	0		
1993–94	Sheffield U	22	1		
1994–95	Sheffield U	14	2		
1995–96	Sheffield U	42	1		
1996–97	Sheffield U	34	4		
1997–98	Sheffield U	6	1	**154**	**11**
1997–98	Everton	8	0		
1998–99	Everton	6	0		
1999–2000	Everton	10	0	**24**	**0**
2000-01	Barnsley	36	0		
2001-02	Barnsley	15	0		
2002-03	Barnsley	26	0	**77**	**0**

WILLIAMS, Robbie (D) 8 0
H: 5 10 W: 11 13 b.Pontefract 2-10-84
Source: Scholar.

2002-03	Barnsley	8	0	**8**	**0**

WROE, Nicky (M) 1 0
H: 5 11 W: 11 13 b.Sheffield 28-9-85
Source: Scholar.

2002-03	Barnsley	1	0	**1**	**0**

Scholars
Baker, Thomas; Black, Grant; Carrington, Richard J; Cox, Christopher D; Flinders, Scott; Greaves, Sean; Harban, Thomas; Jones, Griffith T; Joynes, Nathan; Scothern, Ashley; Selby, Callum S; Shackleton, Marc; Tonge, Dale; Williams, Robert I; Wordsworth, Dean; Wroe, Nicholas

Non-Contract
Cyrus, Andrew; Laight, Ryan; Padgett, Greg; Seed, Andrew; Sheard, Daniel

BIRMINGHAM C

BARROWMAN, Andrew (F) 0 0
H: 5 11 W: 11 06 b.Wishaw 27-11-84
Source: Scholar.

2001-02	Birmingham C	0	0
2002-03	Birmingham C	0	0

BENNETT, Ian (G) 353 0
H: 6 0 W: 13 01 b.Worksop 10-10-71
Source: Newcastle U Trainee.

1991–92	Peterborough U	7	0		
1992–93	Peterborough U	46	0		
1993–94	Peterborough U	19	0	**72**	**0**
1993–94	Birmingham C	22	0		
1994–95	Birmingham C	46	0		
1995–96	Birmingham C	24	0		
1996–97	Birmingham C	40	0		
1997–98	Birmingham C	45	0		
1998–99	Birmingham C	10	0		
1999–2000	Birmingham C	21	0		
2000-01	Birmingham C	45	0		
2001-02	Birmingham C	18	0		
2002-03	Birmingham C	10	0	**281**	**0**

CARTER, Darren (M) 25 1
H: 6 2 W: 12 11 b.Solihull 18-12-83
Source: Scholar. *Honours:* England Youth, Under-20.

2001-02	Birmingham C	13	1		
2002-03	Birmingham C	12	0	**25**	**1**

CISSE, Aliou (M) 87 2
H: 5 9 W: 12 02 b.Zinguichor 24-3-76
Honours: Senegal 23 full caps, 1 goal.

1994–95	Lille	6	0		
1995–96	Lille	0	0		
1996–97	Lille	0	0	**6**	**0**
From Sedan					
1998–99	Paris St Germain	8	0		
1999–2000	Paris St Germain	25	1		
2000-01	Paris St Germain	10	0	**43**	**1**
2001-02	Montpellier	17	1	**17**	**1**
2002-03	Birmingham C	21	0	**21**	**0**

CLAPHAM, Jamie (M) 235 10
H: 5 9 W: 11 09 b.Lincoln 7-12-75
Source: Trainee.

1994–95	Tottenham H	0	0		
1995–96	Tottenham H	0	0		
1996–97	Tottenham H	1	0		
1996–97	*Leyton Orient*	6	0	**6**	**0**
1996–97	*Bristol R*	5	0	**5**	**0**
1997–98	Tottenham H	0	0	**1**	**0**
1997–98	Ipswich T	22	0		
1998–99	Ipswich T	46	3		
1999–2000	Ipswich T	46	2		
2000-01	Ipswich T	35	2		
2001-02	Ipswich T	32	2		
2002-03	Ipswich T	26	1	**207**	**10**
2002-03	Birmingham C	16	0	**16**	**0**

CLEMENCE, Stephen (M) 105 4
H: 6 0 W: 12 09 b.Liverpool 31-3-78
Source: Trainee. *Honours:* England Schools, Youth, Under-21.

1994–95	Tottenham H	0	0		
1995–96	Tottenham H	0	0		
1996–97	Tottenham H	0	0		
1997–98	Tottenham H	17	0		
1998–99	Tottenham H	18	0		
1999–2000	Tottenham H	20	1		
2000-01	Tottenham H	29	1		
2001-02	Tottenham H	6	0		
2002-03	Tottenham H	0	0	**90**	**2**
2002-03	Birmingham C	15	2	**15**	**2**

COLY, Ferdinand* (D) 232 14
H: 5 9 W: 12 12 b.Dakar 10-9-73
Honours: Senegal 22 full caps.

1994–95	Poitiers	28	2		
1995–96	Poitiers	38	2	**66**	**4**
1996–97	Chateauroux	39	3		
1997–98	Chateauroux	19	3		
1998–99	Chateauroux	33	2	**91**	**8**
1999–2000	Lens	10	0		
2000-01	Lens	28	1		
2001-02	Lens	26	1		
2002-03	Lens	10	0	**74**	**2**
2002-03	Birmingham C	1	0	**1**	**0**

CUNNINGHAM, Kenny (D) 417 1
H: 5 11 W: 12 07 b.Dublin 28-6-71
Source: Tolka R. *Honours:* Eire Under-21, B, 48 full caps.

1989–90	Millwall	5	0		
1990–91	Millwall	23	0		
1991–92	Millwall	17	0		
1992–93	Millwall	37	0		
1993–94	Millwall	39	1		
1994–95	Millwall	15	0	**136**	**1**
1994–95	Wimbledon	28	0		
1995–96	Wimbledon	33	0		
1996–97	Wimbledon	36	0		
1997–98	Wimbledon	32	0		
1998–99	Wimbledon	35	0		
1999–2000	Wimbledon	37	0		
2000-01	Wimbledon	15	0		
2001-02	Wimbledon	34	0	**250**	**0**
2002-03	Birmingham C	31	0	**31**	**0**

DAVIES, Clint* (G) 0 0
H: 6 2 W: 11 09 b.Perth 24-4-83
Source: Scholar.

2002-03	Birmingham C	0	0

DEVLIN, Paul (M) 414 81
H: 5 7 W: 11 09 b.Birmingham 14-4-72
Source: Stafford R. *Honours:* Scotland 8 full caps.

1991–92	Notts Co	2	0		
1992–93	Notts Co	32	3		
1993–94	Notts Co	41	7		
1994–95	Notts Co	40	9		
1995–96	Notts Co	26	6		
1995–96	Birmingham C	16	7		
1996–97	Birmingham C	38	16		
1997–98	Birmingham C	22	5		
1997–98	Sheffield U	10	1		
1998–99	Sheffield U	33	5		
1998–99	*Notts Co*	5	0	**146**	**25**
1999–2000	Sheffield U	44	11		
2000-01	Sheffield U	41	5		
2001-02	Sheffield U	19	2	**147**	**24**
2001-02	Birmingham C	13	1		
2002-03	Birmingham C	32	3	**121**	**32**

DUGARRY, Christophe (F) 348 59
H: 6 1 W: 12 10 b.Bordeaux 24-3-72
Honours: France 55 full caps, 8 goals.

1988–89	Bordeaux	2	0		
1989–90	Bordeaux	0	0		
1990–91	Bordeaux	32	3		
1991–92	Bordeaux	27	4		
1992–93	Bordeaux	35	6		
1993–94	Bordeaux	35	8		
1994–95	Bordeaux	32	9		
1995–96	Bordeaux	24	2		
1996–97	AC Milan	21	5	**21**	**5**
1997–98	Barcelona	7	0	**7**	**0**
1997–98	Marseille	9	1		
1998–99	Marseille	28	4		
1999–2000	Marseille	15	3	**52**	**8**
1999–2000	Bordeaux	12	3		
2000-01	Bordeaux	22	5		
2001-02	Bordeaux	18	1		
2002-03	Bordeaux	13	0	**252**	**41**
2002-03	Birmingham C	16	5	**16**	**5**

FAGAN, Craig (F) 7 1
H: 5 11 W: 11 09 b.Birmingham 11-12-82
Source: Scholar.

2001-02	Birmingham C	0	0		
2002-03	Birmingham C	1	0	**1**	**0**
2002-03	*Bristol C*	6	1	**6**	**1**

GILBERT, Peter (D) 0 0
H: 5 9 W: 12 13 b.Newcastle 31-7-83
Source: Scholar.

2002-03	Birmingham C	0	0

GRAINGER, Martin (D) 369 43
H: 5 10 W: 12 11 b.Enfield 23-8-72
Source: Trainee.

1989–90	Colchester U	7	2		
1990–91	Colchester U	0	0		
1991–92	Colchester U	0	0		
1992–93	Colchester U	31	3		
1993–94	Colchester U	8	2	**46**	**7**
1993–94	Brentford	31	2		
1994–95	Brentford	37	7		
1995–96	Brentford	33	3	**101**	**12**
1995–96	Birmingham C	8	0		
1996–97	Birmingham C	23	3		
1997–98	Birmingham C	33	2		
1998–99	Birmingham C	40	4		
1999–2000	Birmingham C	34	5		
2000-01	Birmingham C	35	6		
2001-02	Birmingham C	40	4		
2002-03	Birmingham C	9	0	**222**	**24**

GRONDIN, Christophe‡ (M) 0 0
b.Toulouse 2-9-83
Source: Toulouse.

2000-01	Birmingham C	0	0
2001-02	Birmingham C	0	0
2002-03	Birmingham C	0	0

HORSFIELD, Geoff (F) 186 53
H: 6 0 W: 11 07 b.Barnsley 1-11-73

1992–93	Scarborough	6	1		
1993–94	Scarborough	6	0	**12**	**1**
From Witton Alb					
1998–99	Halifax T	10	7	**10**	**7**

1998–99	Fulham	28	15		
1999–2000	Fulham	31	7	**59**	**22**
2000-01	Birmingham C	34	7		
2001-02	Birmingham C	40	11		
2002-03	Birmingham C	31	5	**105**	**23**

HUGHES, Bryan (M) 316 43
H: 5 9 W: 11 03 b.Liverpool 19-6-76
Source: Trainee.

1993–94	Wrexham	11	0		
1994–95	Wrexham	38	9		
1995–96	Wrexham	22	0		
1996–97	Wrexham	23	3	**94**	**12**
1996–97	Birmingham C	11	0		
1997–98	Birmingham C	40	5		
1998–99	Birmingham C	28	3		
1999–2000	Birmingham C	45	10		
2000-01	Birmingham C	45	4		
2001-02	Birmingham C	31	7		
2002-03	Birmingham C	22	2	**222**	**31**

HUTCHINSON, Jonathan (D) 4 0
H: 5 11 W: 11 11 b.Middlesbrough 2-4-82
Source: Scholar.

2000-01	Birmingham C	0	0		
2001-02	Birmingham C	3	0		
2002-03	Birmingham C	1	0	**4**	**0**

JOHN, Stern (F) 172 74
H: 6 0 W: 12 11 b.Trinidad 30-10-76
Honours: Trinidad & Tobago 16 full caps, 8 goals.

1998	Columbus Crew	27	26		
1999	Columbus Crew	28	18	**55**	**44**
1999–2000	Nottingham F	17	3		
2000-01	Nottingham F	29	2		
2001-02	Nottingham F	26	13	**72**	**18**
2001-02	Birmingham C	15	7		
2002-03	Birmingham C	30	5	**45**	**12**

JOHNSON, Damien (M) 104 5
H: 5 9 W: 11 09 b.Lisburn 18-11-78
Source: Trainee. *Honours:* Northern Ireland Youth, Under-21, 24 full caps.

1995–96	Blackburn R	0	0		
1996–97	Blackburn R	0	0		
1997–98	Blackburn R	0	0		
1997–98	*Nottingham F*	6	0	**6**	**0**
1998–99	Blackburn R	21	1		
1999–2000	Blackburn R	16	1		
2000-01	Blackburn R	16	0		
2001-02	Blackburn R	7	1	**60**	**3**
2001-02	Birmingham C	8	1		
2002-03	Birmingham C	30	1	**38**	**2**

JOHNSON, Michael (D) 369 13
H: 5 11 W: 12 08 b.Nottingham 4-7-73
Source: Trainee. *Honours:* Jamaica 9 full caps.

1991–92	Notts Co	5	0		
1992–93	Notts Co	37	0		
1993–94	Notts Co	34	0		
1994–95	Notts Co	31	0		
1995–96	Notts Co	0	0	**107**	**0**
1995–96	Birmingham C	33	0		
1996–97	Birmingham C	35	0		
1997–98	Birmingham C	38	3		
1998–99	Birmingham C	45	5		
1999–2000	Birmingham C	34	2		
2000-01	Birmingham C	39	2		
2001-02	Birmingham C	32	1		
2002-03	Birmingham C	6	0	**262**	**13**

KENNA, Jeff (D) 344 7
H: 5 11 W: 12 04 b.Dublin 27-8-70
Source: Trainee. *Honours:* Eire Youth, Under-21, B, 27 full caps.

1988–89	Southampton	0	0		
1989–90	Southampton	0	0		
1990–91	Southampton	2	0		
1991–92	Southampton	14	0		
1992–93	Southampton	29	2		
1993–94	Southampton	41	2		
1994–95	Southampton	28	0	**114**	**4**
1994–95	Blackburn R	9	1		
1995–96	Blackburn R	32	0		
1996–97	Blackburn R	37	0		
1997–98	Blackburn R	37	0		
1998–99	Blackburn R	23	0		
1999–2000	Blackburn R	11	0		
2000-01	Blackburn R	6	0		
2000-01	*Tranmere R*	11	0	**11**	**0**
2001-02	Blackburn R	0	0	**155**	**1**
2001-02	*Wigan Ath*	6	1	**6**	**1**
2001-02	Birmingham C	21	0		
2002-03	Birmingham C	37	1	**58**	**1**

KIROVSKI, Jovan (F) 98 10
H: 6 1 W: 12 01 b.Escondido 18-3-76
Source: San Diego Nomads. *Honours:* USA 60 full caps, 8 goals.

1994–95	Manchester U	0	0		
1995–96	Borussia Dortmund	0	0		
1996–97	Borussia Dortmund	7	1		
1997–98	Borussia Dortmund	13	0		
1998–99	Fortuna Cologne	20	2	**20**	**2**
1999–2000	Borussia Dortmund	0	0	**20**	**1**
2000-01	Sporting Lisbon	5	0	**5**	**0**
2001-02	Crystal Palace	36	5	**36**	**5**
2002-03	Birmingham C	17	2	**17**	**2**

LAZARIDIS, Stan (M) 266 14
H: 5 9 W: 11 12 b.Perth 16-8-72
Honours: Australia Youth, Under-23, 45 full caps.

1992–93	Adelaide Sharks	28	2		
1993–94	Adelaide Sharks	23	3		
1994–95	Adelaide Sharks	22	0	**73**	**5**
1995–96	West Ham U	4	0		
1996–97	West Ham U	22	1		
1997–98	West Ham U	28	2		
1998–99	West Ham U	15	0	**69**	**3**
1999–2000	Birmingham C	31	2		
2000-01	Birmingham C	31	2		
2001-02	Birmingham C	32	0		
2002-03	*Portsmouth*	0	0		
2002-03	Birmingham C	30	2	**124**	**6**

LUNTALA, Tresor‡ (M) 15 0
H: 5 9 W: 10 11 b.Dreux 31-5-82

1999–2000	Birmingham C	0	0		
2000-01	Birmingham C	0	0		
2001-02	Birmingham C	15	0		
2002-03	Birmingham C	0	0	**15**	**0**

MARRIOTT, Andy* (G) 311 0
H: 6 0 W: 12 04 b.Sutton-in-Ashfield 11-10-70
Source: Trainee. *Honours:* England Schools, FA Schools, Youth, Under-21, Wales 5 full caps.

1988–89	Arsenal	0	0		
1989–90	Nottingham F	0	0		
1989–90	*WBA*	3	0	**3**	**0**
1989–90	*Blackburn R*	2	0	**2**	**0**
1989–90	*Colchester U*	10	0	**10**	**0**
1990–91	Nottingham F	0	0		
1991–92	Nottingham F	6	0		
1991–92	*Burnley*	15	0	**15**	**0**
1992–93	Nottingham F	5	0		
1993–94	Nottingham F	0	0	**11**	**0**
1993–94	Wrexham	36	0		
1994–95	Wrexham	46	0		
1995–96	Wrexham	46	0		
1996–97	Wrexham	43	0		
1997–98	Wrexham	42	0		
1998–99	Wrexham	0	0	**213**	**0**
1998–99	Sunderland	1	0		
1999–2000	Sunderland	1	0		
2000-01	Sunderland	0	0	**2**	**0**
2000-01	*Wigan Ath*	0	0		
2000-01	Barnsley	0	0		
2001-02	Barnsley	18	0		
2002-03	Barnsley	36	0	**54**	**0**
2002-03	Birmingham C	1	0	**1**	**0**

MOONEY, Tommy (F) 428 111
H: 5 11 W: 13 08 b.Teeside North 11-8-71
Source: Trainee.

1989–90	Aston Villa	0	0		
1990–91	Scarborough	27	13		
1991–92	Scarborough	40	8		
1992–93	Scarborough	40	9	**107**	**30**
1993–94	Southend U	14	5	**14**	**5**
1993–94	*Watford*	10	2		
1994–95	Watford	29	3		
1995–96	Watford	42	6		
1996–97	Watford	37	13		
1997–98	Watford	45	6		
1998–99	Watford	36	9		
1999–2000	Watford	12	2		
2000-01	Watford	39	19	**250**	**60**
2001-02	Birmingham C	33	13		
2002-03	Birmingham C	1	0	**34**	**13**
2002-03	*Stoke C*	12	3	**12**	**3**
2002-03	*Sheffield U*	3	0	**3**	**0**
2002-03	*Derby Co*	8	0	**8**	**0**

MORRISON, Clinton (F) 185 68
H: 6 1 W: 11 13 b.Tooting 14-5-79
Source: Trainee. *Honours:* Eire 10 full caps, 4 goals.

1996–97	Crystal Palace	0	0		
1997–98	Crystal Palace	1	1		
1998–99	Crystal Palace	37	12		
1999–2000	Crystal Palace	29	13		
2000-01	Crystal Palace	45	14		
2001-02	Crystal Palace	45	22	**157**	**62**
2002-03	Birmingham C	28	6	**28**	**6**

PURSE, Darren (D) 273 17
H: 6 2 W: 13 01 b.Stepney 14-2-76
Source: Trainee. *Honours:* England Under-21.

1993–94	Leyton Orient	5	0		
1994–95	Leyton Orient	38	3		
1995–96	Leyton Orient	12	0	**55**	**3**
1996–97	Oxford U	31	1		
1997–98	Oxford U	28	4	**59**	**5**
1997–98	Birmingham C	8	0		
1998–99	Birmingham C	20	0		
1999–2000	Birmingham C	38	2		
2000-01	Birmingham C	37	3		
2001-02	Birmingham C	36	3		
2002-03	Birmingham C	20	1	**159**	**9**

SADLER, Matthew (D) 2 0
H: 5 11 W: 11 08 b.Birmingham 26-2-85
Source: Scholar. *Honours:* England Youth.

2001-02	Birmingham C	0	0		
2002-03	Birmingham C	2	0	**2**	**0**

SAVAGE, Robbie (M) 282 22
H: 5 11 W: 11 00 b.Wrexham 18-10-74
Source: Trainee. *Honours:* Wales Schools, Youth, Under-21, 29 full caps, 2 goals.

1993–94	Manchester U	0	0		
1994–95	Crewe Alex	6	2		
1995–96	Crewe Alex	30	7		
1996–97	Crewe Alex	41	1	**77**	**10**
1997–98	Leicester C	35	2		
1998–99	Leicester C	34	1		
1999–2000	Leicester C	35	1		
2000-01	Leicester C	33	4		
2001-02	Leicester C	35	0	**172**	**8**
2002-03	Birmingham C	33	4	**33**	**4**

SWIERCZEWSKI, Pietr‡ (M) 380 19
H: 5 11 W: 12 06 b.Nowy-Sacz 8-4-72
Honours: Poland 92 full caps, 1 goal.

1988–89	Katowice	1	0		
1989–90	Katowice	15	1		
1990–91	Katowice	28	0		
1991=92	Katowice	30	2		
1992=93	Katowice	27	1	**101**	**4**
1993–94	St Etienne	31	1		
1994–05	St Etienne	30	1	**61**	**2**
1995–96	Bastia	35	1		
1996–97	Bastia	33	4		
1997–98	Bastia	31	2		
1998–99	Bastia	20	1		
1999	Gamba Osaka	0	0		
1999–2000	Bastia	30	1		
2000-01	Bastia	32	3	**181**	**12**
2001-02	Marseille	25	1		
2002-03	Marseille	11	0	**36**	**1**
2002-03	Birmingham C	1	0	**1**	**0**

TEBILY, Oliver (D) 76 1
H: 6 0 W: 13 05 b.Abidjan 19-12-75
Source: Chateauroux. *Honours:* Ivory Coast full caps.

1997–98	Chateauroux	11	1	**11**	**1**
1998–99	Sheffield U	8	0	**8**	**0**
1999–2000	Celtic	23	0		
2000-01	Celtic	4	0		
2001-02	Celtic	11	0	**38**	**0**
2001-02	Birmingham C	7	0		
2002-03	Birmingham C	12	0	**19**	**0**

UPSON, Matthew (D) 71 0
H: 6 1 W: 11 04 b.Hartismere 18-4-79
Source: Trainee. *Honours:* England Youth, Under-21, 3 full caps.

1995–96	Luton T	0	0		
1996–97	Luton T	1	0	**1**	**0**
1996–97	Arsenal	0	0		
1997–98	Arsenal	5	0		
1998–99	Arsenal	5	0		
1999–2000	Arsenal	8	0		
2000-01	Arsenal	2	0		
2000-01	*Nottingham F*	1	0	**1**	**0**
2000-01	*Crystal Palace*	7	0	**7**	**0**
2001-02	Arsenal	14	0		
2002-03	Arsenal	0	0	**34**	**0**
2002-03	*Reading*	14	0	**14**	**0**
2002-03	Birmingham C	14	0	**14**	**0**

VAESEN, Nico (G) **234 0**
H: 6 3 W: 12 13 b.Hasselt 28-9-69
Source: Tongeren.

1993–94	CS Brugge	13	0		
1994–95	CS Brugge	3	0	**16**	**0**
1995–96	Aalst	20	0		
1996–97	Aalst	0	0		
1997–98	Aalst	14	0	**34**	**0**
1998–99	Huddersfield T	43	0		
1999–2000	Huddersfield T	46	0		
2000-01	Huddersfield T	45	0	**134**	**0**
2001-02	Birmingham C	23	0		
2002-03	Birmingham C	27	0	**50**	**0**

VICKERS, Steve‡ (D) **595 20**
H: 6 2 W: 12 10 b.Bishop Auckland 13-10-67
Source: Spennymoor U.

1985–86	Tranmere R	3	0		
1986–87	Tranmere R	36	2		
1987–88	Tranmere R	46	1		
1988–89	Tranmere R	46	3		
1989–90	Tranmere R	42	3		
1990–91	Tranmere R	42	1		
1991–92	Tranmere R	43	1		
1992–93	Tranmere R	42	0		
1993–94	Tranmere R	11	0	**311**	**11**
1993–94	Middlesbrough	26	3		
1994–95	Middlesbrough	44	3		
1995–96	Middlesbrough	32	1		
1996–97	Middlesbrough	29	0		
1997–98	Middlesbrough	33	0		
1998–99	Middlesbrough	31	1		
1999–2000	Middlesbrough	32	0		
2000-01	Middlesbrough	30	0		
2001-02	Middlesbrough	2	0	**259**	**8**
2001-02	*Crystal Palace*	6	0	**6**	**0**
2001-02	Birmingham C	14	1		
2002-03	Birmingham C	5	0	**19**	**1**

WILLIAMS, Tom (M) **66 3**
H: 6 0 W: 11 13 b.Carshalton 8-7-80
Source: Walton & Hersham.

1999–2000	West Ham U	0	0		
2000-01	West Ham U	0	0		
2000-01	*Peterborough U*	2	0		
2001-02	Peterborough U	34	2	**36**	**2**
2001-02	Birmingham C	4	0		
2002-03	Birmingham C	0	0	**4**	**0**
2002-03	*QPR*	26	1	**26**	**1**

WOODHOUSE, Curtis (M) **163 8**
H: 5 7 W: 12 02 b.Driffield 17-4-80
Source: Trainee. *Honours:* England Youth, Under-21.

1997–98	Sheffield U	9	0		
1998–99	Sheffield U	33	3		
1999–2000	Sheffield U	37	3		
2000-01	Sheffield U	25	0	**104**	**6**
2000-01	Birmingham C	17	2		
2001-02	Birmingham C	28	0		
2002-03	Birmingham C	3	0	**48**	**2**
2002-03	*Rotherham U*	11	0	**11**	**0**

Trainees
Allen, Mark A; Alsop, Sam; Arrowsmith, David G; Birley, Matthew M; Cottrill, Christopher; Courtney, Duane; Curtis, Dean; Dormand, James; Doyle, Colin; Longthorn, Paul D; Luckett, Stephen P; Motteram, Carl; O'Brien, Paul; Painter, Marcos; Parratt, Tom; Sheppard, Chad; Till, Peter; Vaughan, Lee

BLACKBURN R

BELL, Andrew* (F) **0 0**
b.Blackburn 12-2-84
Source: Scholar. *Honours:* England Youth.

2000-01	Blackburn R	0	0		
2001-02	Blackburn R	0	0		
2002-03	Blackburn R	0	0		

BERG, Henning* (D) **358 10**
H: 6 0 W: 12 07 b.Eidsvoll 1-9-69
Source: Lillestrom. *Honours:* Norway Under-21, 95 full caps, 9 goals.

1990	Viking	22	0		
1991	Viking	0	0	**22**	**0**
1992	Lillestrom	20	1	**20**	**1**
1992–93	Blackburn R	4	0		
1993–94	Blackburn R	41	1		
1994–95	Blackburn R	40	1		
1995–96	Blackburn R	38	0		
1996–97	Blackburn R	36	2		
1997–98	Manchester U	27	1		
1998–99	Manchester U	16	0		
1999–2000	Manchester U	22	1		
2000-01	Manchester U	1	0	**66**	**2**
2000-01	Blackburn R	41	1		
2001-02	Blackburn R	34	1		
2002-03	Blackburn R	16	1	**250**	**7**

BLACK, Ian (M) **0 0**
b.Edinburgh 14-3-85
Source: Trainee.

2002-03	Blackburn R	0	0		

BRUCE, Alex (D) **0 0**
b.Norwich 28-9-84
Source: Trainee.

2002-03	Blackburn R	0	0		

COLE, Andy (F) **369 187**
H: 5 11 W: 12 04 b.Nottingham 15-10-71
Source: Trainee. *Honours:* England Schools, Youth, Under-21, B, 15 full caps, 1 goal. Football League.

1989–90	Arsenal	0	0		
1990–91	Arsenal	1	0		
1991–92	Arsenal	0	0	**1**	**0**
1991–92	*Fulham*	13	3	**13**	**3**
1991–92	*Bristol C*	12	8		
1992–93	Bristol C	29	12	**41**	**20**
1992–93	Newcastle U	12	12		
1993–94	Newcastle U	40	34		
1994–95	Newcastle U	18	9	**70**	**55**
1994–95	Manchester U	18	12		
1995–96	Manchester U	34	11		
1996–97	Manchester U	20	6		
1997–98	Manchester U	33	15		
1998–99	Manchester U	32	17		
1999–2000	Manchester U	28	19		
2000-01	Manchester U	19	9		
2001-02	Manchester U	11	4	**195**	**93**
2001-02	Blackburn R	15	9		
2002-03	Blackburn R	34	7	**49**	**16**

CORBETT, Jimmy* (F) **26 4**
H: 5 10 W: 12 00 b.Hackney 6-7-80
Source: Trainee.

1997–98	Gillingham	16	2	**16**	**2**
1998–99	Blackburn R	0	0		
1999–2000	Blackburn R	0	0		
2000-01	Blackburn R	0	0		
2001-02	Blackburn R	0	0		
2002-03	Blackburn R	0	0		
2002-03	*Darlington*	10	2	**10**	**2**

CUMMING, Stuart (D) **0 0**
b.Aberdeen 30-1-85

2001-02	Blackburn R	0	0		
2002-03	Blackburn R	0	0		

CURTIS, John (D) **114 2**
H: 5 10 W: 11 07 b.Nuneaton 3-9-78
Source: Trainee. *Honours:* England Schools, Youth, Under-21, B.

1995–96	Manchester U	0	0		
1996–97	Manchester U	0	0		
1997–98	Manchester U	8	0		
1998–99	Manchester U	4	0		
1999–2000	Manchester U	1	0	**13**	**0**
1999–2000	*Barnsley*	28	2	**28**	**2**
2000-01	Blackburn R	46	0		
2001-02	Blackburn R	10	0		
2002-03	Blackburn R	5	0	**61**	**0**
2002-03	*Sheffield U*	12	0	**12**	**0**

DANNS, Neil (F) **2 0**
b.Liverpool 23-11-82
Source: Scholar.

2000-01	Blackburn R	0	0		
2001-02	Blackburn R	0	0		
2002-03	Blackburn R	2	0	**2**	**0**

DONNELLY, Ciaran (M) **0 0**
b.Blackpool 2-4-84
Source: Scholar. *Honours:* England Youth.

2001-02	Blackburn R	0	0		
2002-03	Blackburn R	0	0		

DOUGLAS, Jonathan (M) **8 1**
H: 6 0 W: 12 07 b.Monaghan 22-11-81
Source: Trainee.

1999–2000	Blackburn R	0	0		
2000-01	Blackburn R	0	0		
2001-02	Blackburn R	0	0		
2002-03	Blackburn R	1	0	**1**	**0**
2002-03	*Chesterfield*	7	1	**7**	**1**

DRENCH, Steven (G) **0 0**
b.Salford 11-9-85
Source: Trainee.

2002-03	Blackburn R	0	0		

DUFF, Damien (F) **184 27**
H: 5 10 W: 12 00 b.Ballyboden 3-3-79
Source: Lourdes Celtic. *Honours:* Eire Youth, 37 full caps, 4 goals.

1995–96	Blackburn R	0	0		
1996–97	Blackburn R	1	0		
1997–98	Blackburn R	26	4		
1998–99	Blackburn R	28	1		
1999–2000	Blackburn R	39	5		
2000-01	Blackburn R	32	1		
2001-02	Blackburn R	32	7		
2002-03	Blackburn R	26	9	**184**	**27**

DUNN, David (M) **136 30**
H: 5 10 W: 12 05 b.Blackburn 27-12-79
Source: Trainee. *Honours:* England Youth, Under-21, 1 full cap.

1997–98	Blackburn R	0	0		
1998–99	Blackburn R	15	1		
1999–2000	Blackburn R	22	2		
2000-01	Blackburn R	42	12		
2001-02	Blackburn R	29	7		
2002-03	Blackburn R	28	8	**136**	**30**

DUNNING, Darren* (M) **44 1**
H: 5 7 W: 11 08 b.Scarborough 8-1-81
Source: Trainee.

1998–99	Blackburn R	0	0		
1999–2000	Blackburn R	0	0		
2000-01	Blackburn R	1	0		
2000-01	*Bristol C*	9	0	**9**	**0**
2001-02	Blackburn R	0	0		
2001-02	*Rochdale*	5	0	**5**	**0**
2001-02	*Blackpool*	5	0	**5**	**0**
2002-03	Blackburn R	0	0	**1**	**0**
2002-03	*Torquay U*	7	1	**7**	**1**
2002-03	*Macclesfield T*	17	0	**17**	**0**

FITZGERALD, John (D) **0 0**
b.Dublin 2-10-84
Source: Scholar.

2000-01	Blackburn R	0	0		
2001-02	Blackburn R	0	0		
2002-03	Blackburn R	0	0		

FLITCROFT, Garry (M) **321 24**
H: 6 1 W: 12 11 b.Bolton 6-11-72
Source: Trainee. *Honours:* England Schools, Under-21.

1991–92	Manchester C	0	0		
1991–92	*Bury*	12	0	**12**	**0**
1992–93	Manchester C	32	5		
1993–94	Manchester C	21	3		
1994–95	Manchester C	37	5		
1995–96	Manchester C	25	0	**115**	**13**
1995–96	Blackburn R	3	0		
1996–97	Blackburn R	28	3		
1997–98	Blackburn R	33	0		
1998–99	Blackburn R	8	2		
1999–2000	Blackburn R	19	0		
2000-01	Blackburn R	41	3		
2001-02	Blackburn R	29	1		
2002-03	Blackburn R	33	2	**194**	**11**

FRIEDEL, Brad (G) **163 0**
H: 6 3 W: 14 00 b.Lakewood 18-5-71
Honours: USA 81 full caps.

1996	Columbus Crew	9	0		
1997	Columbus Crew	29	0	**38**	**0**
1997–98	Liverpool	11	0		
1998–99	Liverpool	12	0		
1999–2000	Liverpool	2	0		
2000-01	Liverpool	0	0	**25**	**0**
2000-01	Blackburn R	27	0		
2001-02	Blackburn R	36	0		
2002-03	Blackburn R	37	0	**100**	**0**

GALLAGHER, Paul (F) **1 0**
b.Glasgow 9-8-84
Source: Trainee. *Honours:* Scotland Under-21.

2002-03	Blackburn R	1	0	**1**	**0**

GILLESPIE, Keith* (F) **248 21**
H: 5 10 W: 11 12 b.Larne 18-2-75
Source: Trainee. *Honours:* Northern Ireland Schools, Youth, Under-21, 47 full caps, 1 goal.

1992–93	Manchester U	0	0		
1993–94	Manchester U	0	0		
1993–94	*Wigan Ath*	8	4		
1994–95	Manchester U	9	1	**9**	**1**
1994–95	Newcastle U	17	2		
1995–96	Newcastle U	28	4		
1996–97	Newcastle U	32	1		
1997–98	Newcastle U	29	4		
1998–99	Newcastle U	7	0	**113**	**11**
1998–99	Blackburn R	16	1		
1999–2000	Blackburn R	22	2		

2000-01 Blackburn R 18 0
2000-01 *Wigan Ath* 5 0 **13 4**
2001-02 Blackburn R 32 2
2002-03 Blackburn R 25 0 **113 5**

GRABBI, Corrado (F) 219 78
H: 5 11 W: 12 13 b.Turin 29-7-75
1993–94 Spartta Novara 31 8 **31 8**
1994–95 Juventus 2 1 **2 1**
1995–96 Lucchese 8 1 **8 1**
1995–96 Chievo 18 2 **18 2**
1996–97 Modena 31 15
1997–98 Modena 27 14 **58 29**
1998–99 Ternana 14 2
1999–2000 Ravenna 29 13 **29 13**
2000-01 Ternana 34 20 **48 22**
2001-02 Blackburn R 14 1
2002-03 Blackburn R 11 1 **25 2**

GREER, Gordon (D) 35 1
H: 6 2 W: 12 05 b.Glasgow 14-12-80
Source: Port Glasgow.
2000-01 Clyde 30 0 **30 0**
2000-01 Blackburn R 0 0
2001-02 Blackburn R 0 0
2002-03 Blackburn R 0 0
2002-03 *Stockport Co* 5 1 **5 1**

GRESKO, Vratislav (M) 131 5
H: 6 0 W: 11 05 b.Pressburg 24-7-77
1995–96 Dukla Banska 1 0
1996–97 Dukla Banska 7 0 **8 0**
1997–98 Internazionale 22 0
1998–99 Internazionale 29 5
1999–2000 Leverkusen 9 0
2000-01 Leverkusen 7 0 **16 0**
2000-01 Internazionale 18 0
2001-02 Internazionale 23 0 **92 5**
2002-03 Parma 5 0 **5 0**
2002-03 Blackburn R 10 0 **10 0**

HIGNETT, Craig (M) 417 115
H: 5 9 W: 11 10 b.Whiston 12-1-70
Source: Liverpool Trainee.
1987–88 Crewe Alex 0 0
1988–89 Crewe Alex 1 0
1989–90 Crewe Alex 35 8
1990–91 Crewe Alex 38 13
1991–92 Crewe Alex 33 13
1992–93 Crewe Alex 14 8 **121 42**
1992–93 Middlesbrough 21 4
1993–94 Middlesbrough 29 5
1994–95 Middlesbrough 26 8
1995–96 Middlesbrough 22 5
1996–97 Middlesbrough 22 4
1997–98 Middlesbrough 36 7 **156 33**
1998–99 Aberdeen 13 2 **13 2**
1998–99 Barnsley 24 9
1999–2000 Barnsley 42 19 **66 28**
2000-01 Blackburn R 30 3
2001-02 Blackburn R 20 4
2002-03 Blackburn R 3 1 **53 8**
2002-03 *Coventry C* 8 2 **8 2**

HOCKENHULL, Darren* (M) 7 1
b.Knowsley 5-9-82
Source: Scholar.
2002-03 Blackburn R 0 0
2002-03 *Darlington* 0 0
2002-03 *Rochdale* 7 1 **7 1**

JANSEN, Matt (F) 200 61
H: 5 11 W: 12 04 b.Carlisle 20-10-77
Source: Trainee. *Honours:* England Under-21.
1995–96 Carlisle U 0 0
1996–97 Carlisle U 19 1
1997–98 Carlisle U 23 9 **42 10**
1997–98 Crystal Palace 8 3
1998–99 Crystal Palace 18 7 **26 10**
1998–99 Blackburn R 11 2
1999–2000 Blackburn R 30 4
2000-01 Blackburn R 40 23
2001-02 Blackburn R 35 10
2002-03 Blackburn R 7 0 **123 39**
2002-03 *Coventry C* 9 2 **9 2**

JOHANSSON, Nils-Eric (D) 60 0
H: 6 2 W: 13 03 b.Stockholm 13-1-80
Source: Viksjo, Brommapojkana. *Honours:* Sweden 4 full caps.
1998 AIK Stockholm 0 0
1998–99 Bayern Munich 2 0
1999–2000 Bayern Munich 0 0
2000-01 Bayern Munich 0 0 **2 0**
2001-02 Nuremberg 8 0 **8 0**
2001-02 Blackburn R 20 0
2002-03 Blackburn R 30 0 **50 0**

JOHNSON, Jemal (M) 0 0
b.New Jersey 3-5-84
2001-02 Blackburn R 0 0
2002-03 Blackburn R 0 0

KEBE, Yahia (M) 0 0
b.Mali 11-7-85
Source: Trainee.
2002-03 Blackburn R 0 0

KELLY, Alan (G) 406 0
H: 6 2 W: 14 05 b.Preston 1-8-68
Source: Trainee. *Honours:* Eire Youth, Under-21, Under-23, 34 full caps.
1985–86 Preston NE 13 0
1986–87 Preston NE 22 0
1987–88 Preston NE 19 0
1988–89 Preston NE 0 0
1989–90 Preston NE 42 0
1990–91 Preston NE 23 0
1991–92 Preston NE 23 0 **142 0**
1992–93 Sheffield U 33 0
1993–94 Sheffield U 30 0
1994–95 Sheffield U 38 0
1995–96 Sheffield U 35 0
1996–97 Sheffield U 39 0
1997–98 Sheffield U 19 0
1998–99 Sheffield U 22 0 **216 0**
1999–2000 Blackburn R 30 0
2000-01 Blackburn R 7 0
2000-01 *Stockport Co* 2 0 **2 0**
2001-02 Blackburn R 2 0
2001-02 *Birmingham C* 6 0 **6 0**
2002-03 Blackburn R 1 0 **40 0**

MAHON, Alan (M) 169 16
H: 5 8 W: 11 10 b.Dublin 4-4-78
Source: Crumplin U. *Honours:* Eire Under-21, 2 full caps.
1994–95 Tranmere R 0 0
1995–96 Tranmere R 2 0
1996–97 Tranmere R 25 2
1997–98 Tranmere R 18 1
1998–99 Tranmere R 39 6
1999–2000 Tranmere R 36 4 **120 13**
2000-01 Sporting Lisbon 1 0 **1 0**
2000-01 Blackburn R 18 0
2001-02 Blackburn R 13 1
2002-03 Blackburn R 2 0 **33 1**
2002-03 *Cardiff C* 15 2 **15 2**

MARTIN, Anthony* (M) 0 0
b.Dublin 20-9-83
Source: Scholar.
2000-01 Blackburn R 0 0
2001-02 Blackburn R 0 0
2002-03 Blackburn R 0 0

McEVELEY, James (D) 9 0
b.Liverpool 11-2-85
Source: Trainee. *Honours:* England Under-21.
2002-03 Blackburn R 9 0 **9 0**

McKAY, Ross (F) 0 0
b.North Shields 21-9-84
Source: Trainee.
2002-03 Blackburn R 0 0

MORGAN, Alan (M) 0 0
b.Edinburgh 27-11-83
Source: Scholar.
2000-01 Blackburn R 0 0
2001-02 Blackburn R 0 0
2002-03 Blackburn R 0 0

NEILL, Lucas (M) 217 14
H: 6 1 W: 12 07 b.Sydney 9-3-78
Source: NSW Soccer Academy. *Honours:* Australia Under-20, Under-23, 3 full caps.
1995–96 Millwall 13 0
1996–97 Millwall 39 3
1997–98 Millwall 6 0
1998–99 Millwall 35 6
1999–2000 Millwall 31 1
2000-01 Millwall 24 2
2001-02 Millwall 4 1 **152 13**
2001-02 Blackburn R 31 1
2002-03 Blackburn R 34 0 **65 1**

NELSON, Adam (M) 0 0
b.Edinburgh 24-7-84
Source: Trainee.
2002-03 Blackburn R 0 0

OSTENSTAD, Egil (F) 290 94
H: 6 0 W: 12 11 b.Haugesund 2-1-72
Honours: Norway 17 full caps, 6 goals.
1990 Viking 10 1
1991 Viking 10 1
1992 Viking 20 1
1993 Viking 22 10
1994 Viking 21 6
1995 Viking 21 12
1996 Viking 24 23 **128 54**
1996–97 Southampton 30 9
1997–98 Southampton 29 11
1998–99 Southampton 34 7
1999–2000 Southampton 3 1 **96 28**
1999–2000 Blackburn R 28 8
2000-01 Blackburn R 13 3
2000-01 *Manchester C* 4 0 **4 0**
2001-02 Blackburn R 4 0
2002-03 Blackburn R 17 1 **62 12**

PEERS, Gavin (D) 0 0
b.Dublin 10-11-85
Source: Trainee.
2002-03 Blackburn R 0 0

PELZER, Sebastian (M) 0 0
b.Trier 24-9-80
2002-03 Blackburn R 0 0

REID, Andrew (M) 0 0
b.Kilmarnock 26-9-85
2002-03 Blackburn R 0 0

RENTON, Keiron (G) 0 0
b.Edinburgh 13-2-84
Source: Scholar.
2001-02 Blackburn R 0 0
2002-03 Blackburn R 0 0

RICHARDS, Marc* (F) 31 7
H: 5 11 W: 12 12 b.Wolverhampton 8-7-82
Source: Trainee. *Honours:* England Youth, Under-20.
1999–2000 Blackburn R 0 0
2000-01 Blackburn R 0 0
2001-02 Blackburn R 0 0
2001-02 *Crewe Alex* 4 0 **4 0**
2001-02 *Oldham Ath* 5 0 **5 0**
2001-02 *Halifax T* 5 0 **5 0**
2002-03 Blackburn R 0 0
2002-03 *Swansea C* 17 7 **17 7**

ROBINSON, Ryan* (G) 0 0
H: 6 2 W: 13 02 b.Cumbria 13-10-82
Source: Scholar.
2001-02 Blackburn R 0 0
2002-03 Blackburn R 0 0

SAKALI, Abdeltareck (F) 0 0
b.Torcy 25-4-86
Source: Trainee.
2002-03 Blackburn R 0 0

SHORT, Craig (D) 509 28
H: 6 3 W: 13 12 b.Bridlington 25-6-68
Source: Pickering T. *Honours:* England Schools.
1987–88 Scarborough 21 2
1988–89 Scarborough 42 5 **63 7**
1989–90 Notts Co 44 2
1990–91 Notts Co 0 0
1990–91 Notts Co 43 0
1991–92 Notts Co 38 3
1992–93 Notts Co 3 1 **128 6**
1992–93 Derby Co 38 3
1993–94 Derby Co 43 3
1994–95 Derby Co 37 3 **118 9**
1995–96 Everton 23 2
1996–97 Everton 23 2
1997–98 Everton 31 0
1998–99 Everton 22 0 **99 4**
1999–2000 Blackburn R 17 0
2000-01 Blackburn R 35 1
2001-02 Blackburn R 22 0
2002-03 Blackburn R 27 1 **101 2**

SUKUR, Hakan* (F) 398 208
b.Sakarya 1-9-71
Honours: Turkey 84 full caps, 38 goals.
1987–88 Sakarya 6 4
1988–89 Sakarya 11 4
1989–90 Sakarya 27 5 **44 13**
1990–91 Bursa 27 4
1991–92 Bursa 27 7 **54 11**
1992–93 Galatasaray 30 19
1993–94 Galatasaray 28 16
1994–95 Galatasaray 33 19
1995–96 Torino 5 1 **5 1**
1995–96 Galatasaray 25 16
1996–97 Galatasaray 32 38
1997–98 Galatasaray 34 32
1998–99 Galatasaray 33 19
1999–2000 Galatasaray 32 14 **247 173**
2000-01 Internazionale 24 5 **24 5**

2001-02 Parma 15 3 **15 3**
2002-03 Blackburn R 9 2 **9 2**

TAYLOR, Martin (D) 88 5
H: 6 4 W: 15 00 b.Ashington 9-11-79
Source: Trainee. *Honours:* England Youth, Under-21.
1997–98 Blackburn R 0 0
1998–99 Blackburn R 3 0
1999–2000 Blackburn R 6 0
1999–2000 *Darlington* 4 0 **4 0**
1999–2000 *Stockport Co* 7 0 **7 0**
2000-01 Blackburn R 16 3
2001-02 Blackburn R 19 0
2002-03 Blackburn R 33 2 **77 5**

TAYLOR, Michael (M) 12 0
b.Liverpool 21-11-82
Source: Scholarship.
1999–2000 Blackburn R 0 0
2000-01 Blackburn R 0 0
2001-02 Blackburn R 0 0
2002-03 Blackburn R 0 0
2002-03 *Carlisle U* 10 0 **10 0**
2002-03 *Rochdale* 2 0 **2 0**

THOMPSON, David (M) 147 24
H: 5 7 W: 10 00 b.Birkenhead 12-9-77
Source: Trainee. *Honours:* England Youth, Under-21.
1994–95 Liverpool 0 0
1995–96 Liverpool 0 0
1996–97 Liverpool 2 0
1997–98 Liverpool 5 1
1997–98 *Swindon T* 10 0 **10 0**
1998–99 Liverpool 14 1
1999–2000 Liverpool 27 3 **48 5**
2000-01 Coventry C 25 3
2001-02 Coventry C 37 12
2002-03 Coventry C 4 0 **66 15**
2002-03 Blackburn R 23 4 **23 4**

TODD, Andy (D) 169 7
H: 5 11 W: 13 04 b.Derby 21-9-74
Source: Trainee.
1991–92 Middlesbrough 0 0
1992–93 Middlesbrough 0 0
1993–94 Middlesbrough 3 0
1994–95 Middlesbrough 5 0 **8 0**
1994–95 *Swindon T* 13 0 **13 0**
1995–96 Bolton W 12 2
1996–97 Bolton W 15 0
1997–98 Bolton W 25 0
1998–99 Bolton W 20 0
1999–2000 Bolton W 12 0 **84 2**
1999–2000 Charlton Ath 12 0
2000-01 Charlton Ath 23 1
2001-02 Charlton Ath 5 0 **40 1**
2001-02 *Grimsby T* 12 3 **12 3**
2002-03 Blackburn R 12 1 **12 1**

TUGAY, Kerimoglu (M) 387 42
H: 5 9 W: 11 00 b.Istanbul 24-8-70
Honours: Turkey 86 full caps, 2 goals.
1988–89 Galatasaray 16 0
1989–90 Galatasaray 23 0
1990–91 Galatasaray 12 0
1991–92 Galatasaray 26 3
1992–93 Galatasaray 25 6
1993–94 Galatasaray 25 12
1994–95 Galatasaray 23 1
1995–96 Galatasaray 30 3
1996–97 Galatasaray 33 4
1997–98 Galatasaray 30 2
1998–99 Galatasaray 22 2
1999–2000 Galatasaray 10 1 **275 34**
1999–2000 Rangers 16 1
2000-01 Rangers 26 3 **42 4**
2001-02 Blackburn R 33 3
2002-03 Blackburn R 37 1 **70 4**

WATT, Jerome (M) 0 0
b.Preston 20-10-84
Source: Scholar. *Honours:* England Youth.
2001-02 Blackburn R 0 0
2002-03 Blackburn R 0 0

WEAVER, Paul (M) 0 0
b.Irvine 27-2-86
Source: Trainee.
2002-03 Blackburn R 0 0

YORKE, Dwight (F) 360 129
H: 5 10 W: 12 03 b.Canaan 3-11-71
Source: St Clair's, Tobago. *Honours:* Trinidad & Tobago full caps.
1989–90 Aston Villa 2 0
1990–91 Aston Villa 18 2
1991–92 Aston Villa 32 11
1992–93 Aston Villa 27 6
1993–94 Aston Villa 12 2
1994–95 Aston Villa 37 6
1995–96 Aston Villa 35 17
1996–97 Aston Villa 37 17
1997–98 Aston Villa 30 12
1998–99 Aston Villa 1 0 **231 73**
1998–99 Manchester U 32 18
1999–2000 Manchester U 32 20
2000-01 Manchester U 22 9
2001-02 Manchester U 10 1 **96 48**
2002-03 Blackburn R 33 8 **33 8**

Trainees
Corvino, Peter; Harkins, Gary; Hoyle, James D; Humphreys, Luke J; Taylor, Andrew; Walsh, Clark; Whelan, Daniel

BLACKPOOL

BARNES, Phil (G) 124 0
H: 6 1 W: 11 01 b.Sheffield 2-3-79
Source: Trainee.
1996–97 Rotherham U 2 0 **2 0**
1997–98 Blackpool 1 0
1998–99 Blackpool 1 0
1999–2000 Blackpool 12 0
2000-01 Blackpool 34 0
2001-02 Blackpool 30 0
2002-03 Blackpool 44 0 **122 0**

BLINKHORN, Matthew§ (F) 10 2
H: 6 0 W: 10 10 b.Blackpool 2-3-85
Source: Scholar.
2001-02 Blackpool 3 0
2002-03 Blackpool 7 2 **10 2**

BULLOCK, Martin (M) 272 8
H: 5 5 W: 10 07 b.Derby 5-3-75
Source: Eastwood T. *Honours:* England Under-21.
1993–94 Barnsley 0 0
1994–95 Barnsley 29 0
1995–96 Barnsley 41 1
1996–97 Barnsley 28 0
1997–98 Barnsley 33 0
1998–99 Barnsley 32 2
1999–2000 Barnsley 4 0
1999–2000 *Port Vale* 6 1 **6 1**
2000-01 Barnsley 18 1
2001-02 Barnsley 0 0 **185 4**
2001-02 Blackpool 43 2
2002-03 Blackpool 38 1 **81 3**

BURNS, Jamie§ (M) 7 0
H: 5 9 W: 10 11 b.Blackpool 6-3-84
Source: Scholar.
2002-03 Blackpool 7 0 **7 0**

CLARKE, Chris (D) 79 2
H: 6 3 W: 12 10 b.Leeds 18-12-80
Source: Wolverhampton W Trainee.
1999–2000 Halifax T 1 0
2000-01 Halifax T 26 1
2001-02 Halifax T 24 0 **51 1**
2001-02 Blackpool 11 0
2002-03 Blackpool 17 1 **28 1**

COID, Danny (D) 131 6
H: 5 11 W: 11 07 b.Liverpool 3-10-81
Source: Trainee.
1998–99 Blackpool 1 0
1999–2000 Blackpool 21 1
2000-01 Blackpool 46 1
2001-02 Blackpool 27 3
2002-03 Blackpool 36 1 **131 6**

COLLINS, Lee (M) 174 5
H: 5 8 W: 11 06 b.Bellshill 3-2-74
Source: Possil U.
1993–94 Albion R 20 0
1994–95 Albion R 17 0
1995–96 Albion R 8 1 **45 1**
1995–96 Swindon T 5 0
1996–97 Swindon T 4 0
1997–98 Swindon T 26 1
1998–99 Swindon T 4 0
1999–2000 Swindon T 24 1 **63 2**
2000-01 Blackpool 28 0
2001-02 Blackpool 32 2
2002-03 Blackpool 6 0 **66 2**

DALGLISH, Paul* (F) 136 9
H: 5 10 W: 10 00 b.Glasgow 18-2-77
Honours: Scotland Under-21.
1995–96 Celtic 0 0
1996–97 Liverpool 0 0
1997–98 Liverpool 0 0
1997–98 Newcastle U 0 0
1997–98 *Bury* 12 0 **12 0**
1998–99 Newcastle U 11 1 **11 1**
1998–99 *Norwich C* 5 0
1999–2000 Norwich C 31 2
2000-01 Norwich C 7 0 **43 2**
2000-01 *Wigan Ath* 6 0
2001-02 Wigan Ath 29 2 **35 2**
2002-03 Blackpool 27 1 **27 1**
2002-03 *Scunthorpe U* 8 3 **8 3**

FENTON, Graham‡ (F) 161 26
H: 5 10 W: 12 10 b.Wallsend 22-5-74
Source: Trainee. *Honours:* England Under-21.
1991–92 Aston Villa 0 0
1992–93 Aston Villa 0 0
1993–94 Aston Villa 12 1
1993–94 *WBA* 7 3 **7 3**
1994–95 Aston Villa 17 2
1995–96 Aston Villa 3 0 **32 3**
1995–96 Blackburn R 14 6
1996–97 Blackburn R 13 1 **27 7**
1997–98 Leicester C 23 3
1998–99 Leicester C 9 0
1999–2000 Leicester C 2 0 **34 3**
1999–2000 Walsall 9 1 **9 1**
2000-01 Stoke C 5 1 **5 1**
2000-01 St Mirren 26 2 **26 2**
2001-02 Blackpool 15 5
2002-03 Blackpool 0 0 **15 5**
2002-03 *Darlington* 6 1 **6 1**

FLYNN, Mike (D) 618 24
H: 6 1 W: 13 05 b.Oldham 23-2-69
Source: Trainee.
1986–87 Oldham Ath 0 0
1987–88 Oldham Ath 31 1
1988–89 Oldham Ath 9 0 **40 1**
1988–89 Norwich C 0 0
1989–90 Norwich C 0 0
1989–90 Preston NE 23 1
1990–91 Preston NE 35 1
1991–92 Preston NE 43 3
1992–93 Preston NE 35 2 **136 7**
1992–93 Stockport Co 10 0
1993–94 Stockport Co 46 1
1994–95 Stockport Co 43 2
1995–96 Stockport Co 46 6
1996–97 Stockport Co 46 2
1997–98 Stockport Co 34 1
1998–99 Stockport Co 46 1
1999–2000 Stockport Co 46 1
2000-01 Stockport Co 44 0
2001-02 Stockport Co 26 2 **387 16**
2001-02 *Stoke C* 13 0 **13 0**
2001-02 Barnsley 7 0
2002-03 Barnsley 14 0 **21 0**
2002-03 Blackpool 21 0 **21 0**

GRAYSON, Simon (D) 352 8
H: 6 0 W: 13 07 b.Ripon 16-12-69
Source: Trainee.
1987–88 Leeds U 2 0
1988–89 Leeds U 0 0
1989–90 Leeds U 0 0
1990–91 Leeds U 0 0
1991–92 Leeds U 0 0 **2 0**
1991–92 Leicester C 13 0
1992–93 Leicester C 24 1
1993–94 Leicester C 40 1
1994–95 Leicester C 34 0
1995–96 Leicester C 41 2
1996–97 Leicester C 36 0 **188 4**
1997–98 Aston Villa 33 0
1998–99 Aston Villa 15 0 **48 0**
1999–2000 Blackburn R 34 0
2000-01 Blackburn R 0 0
2000-01 *Sheffield W* 5 0 **5 0**
2000-01 *Stockport Co* 13 0 **13 0**
2001-02 Blackburn R 0 0 **34 0**
2001-02 *Notts Co* 10 1 **10 1**
2001-02 *Bradford C* 7 0 **7 0**
2002-03 Blackpool 45 3 **45 3**

HERZIG, Denny (M) 0 0
b.Pobneck 13-11-84
2001-02 Wimbledon 0 0
2002-03 Wimbledon 0 0
2002-03 Blackpool 0 0

HILLS, John‡ (M) 183 17
H: 5 9 W: 11 02 b.St Annes-on-Sea 21-4-78
Source: Trainee.
1995–96 Blackpool 0 0
1995–96 Everton 0 0

1996–97 Everton 3 0
1996–97 *Swansea C* 11 0
1997–98 Everton 0 0 3 0
1997–98 *Swansea C* 7 1 18 1
1997–98 Blackpool 19 1
1998–99 Blackpool 28 1
1999–2000 Blackpool 33 2
2000–01 Blackpool 18 2
2001–02 Blackpool 37 5
2002–03 Blackpool 27 5 **162 16**

HUGHES, Ian‡ (D) 335 4
H: 5 10 W: 12 08 b.Bangor 2-8-74
Source: Trainee. *Honours:* Wales Youth, Under-21.
1991–92 Bury 17 0
1992–93 Bury 15 0
1992–93 Bury 15 0
1993–94 Bury 38 0
1994–95 Bury 23 1
1995–96 Bury 32 0
1996–97 Bury 22 0
1997–98 Bury 13 0 **175 1**
1997–98 Blackpool 21 0
1998–99 Blackpool 33 1
1999–2000 Blackpool 34 0
2000–01 Blackpool 34 1
2001–02 Blackpool 20 1
2002–03 Blackpool 18 0 **160 3**

JASZCZUN, Tommy (D) 115 0
H: 5 10 W: 10 10 b.Kettering 16-9-77
Source: Trainee.
1996–97 Aston Villa 0 0
1997–98 Aston Villa 0 0
1998–99 Aston Villa 0 0
1999–2000 Aston Villa 0 0
1999–2000 Blackpool 19 0
2000–01 Blackpool 35 0
2001–02 Blackpool 40 0
2002–03 Blackpool 21 0 **115 0**

McMAHON, Steve (M) 6 0
H: 5 9 W: 10 05 b.Southport 31-7-84
Source: Scholar.
2002–03 Blackpool 6 0 **6 0**

MILLIGAN, Jamie‡ (M) 34 1
H: 5 6 W: 9 12 b.Blackpool 3-1-80
Source: Trainee. *Honours:* England Youth.
1997–98 Everton 0 0
1998–99 Everton 3 0
1999–2000 Everton 1 0
2000–01 Everton 0 0 **4 0**
2000–01 Blackpool 6 0
2001–02 Blackpool 17 0
2002–03 Blackpool 7 1 **30 1**

MURPHY, John (F) 260 77
H: 6 2 W: 14 00 b.Whiston 18-10-76
Source: Trainee.
1994–95 Chester C 5 0
1995–96 Chester C 18 3
1996–97 Chester C 11 1
1997–98 Chester C 27 4
1998–99 Chester C 42 12 **103 20**
1999–2000 Blackpool 39 10
2000–01 Blackpool 46 18
2001–02 Blackpool 37 13
2002–03 Blackpool 35 16 **157 57**

O'KANE, John‡ (M) 134 9
H: 5 10 W: 12 02 b.Nottingham 15-11-74
Source: Trainee.
1992–93 Manchester U 0 0
1993–94 Manchester U 0 0
1994–95 Manchester U 0 0
1994–95 *Wimbledon* 0 0
1995–96 Manchester U 1 0
1996–97 Manchester U 1 0
1996–97 *Bury* 13 3 **13 3**
1997–98 Manchester U 0 0 **2 0**
1997–98 *Bradford C* 7 0 **7 0**
1997–98 Everton 12 0
1998–99 Everton 2 0
1998–99 *Burnley* 8 0 **8 0**
1999–2000 Everton 0 0 **14 0**
1999–2000 Bolton W 11 1
2000–01 Bolton W 27 1 **38 2**
2001–02 Blackpool 38 4
2002–03 Blackpool 14 0 **52 4**

REID, Brian‡ (D) 111 8
H: 6 2 W: 11 12 b.Paisley 15-6-70
1998–99 Burnley 31 3 **31 3**
1999–2000 Dunfermline Ath 23 3
2000–01 Dunfermline Ath 2 0 **25 3**
2000–01 Blackpool 29 2
2001–02 Blackpool 26 0
2002–03 Blackpool 0 0 **55 2**

ROBINSON, Paul† (F) 73 6
H: 5 11 W: 12 00 b.Sunderland 20-11-78
Source: Trainee.
1995–96 Darlington 4 0
1996–97 Darlington 3 0
1997–98 Darlington 19 3 **26 3**
1997–98 Newcastle U 0 0
1998–99 Newcastle U 0 0
1999–2000 Newcastle U 11 0 **11 0**
2000–01 Wimbledon 2 0
2000–01 *Burnley* 4 0 **4 0**
2001–02 Wimbledon 1 0 **3 0**
2001–02 *Grimsby T* 5 0
2002–03 Grimsby T 12 1 **17 1**
2002–03 *Carlisle U* 5 1 **5 1**
2002–03 Blackpool 7 1 **7 1**

SOUTHERN, Keith (M) 38 1
H: 5 10 W: 12 04 b.Gateshead 24-4-81
Source: Trainee.
1998–99 Everton 0 0
1999–2000 Everton 0 0
2000–01 Everton 0 0
2001–02 Everton 0 0
2002–03 Everton 0 0
2002–03 Blackpool 38 1 **38 1**

TAYLOR, Scott (F) 252 41
H: 5 10 W: 11 04 b.Chertsey 5-5-76
Source: Staines T.
1994–95 Millwall 6 0
1995–96 Millwall 22 0 **28 0**
1995–96 Bolton W 1 0
1996–97 Bolton W 11 1
1997–98 Bolton W 0 0
1997–98 *Rotherham U* 10 3 **10 3**
1997–98 *Blackpool* 5 1
1998–99 Bolton W 0 0 **12 1**
1998–99 Tranmere R 36 9
1999–2000 Tranmere R 35 3
2000–01 Tranmere R 37 5 **108 17**
2001–02 Stockport Co 28 4 **28 4**
2001–02 Blackpool 17 2
2002–03 Blackpool 44 13 **66 16**

THEOKLITOS, Michael* (G) 22 0
H: 6 2 W: 13 12 b.Melbourne 11-2-81
From Kingz
2001–02 Football Kingz 20 0 **20 0**
2002–03 Blackpool 2 0 **2 0**

THORNLEY, Ben* (F) 166 11
H: 5 9 W: 11 08 b.Bury 21-4-75
Source: Trainee. *Honours:* England Schools, Under-21.
1992–93 Manchester U 0 0
1993–94 Manchester U 1 0
1994–95 Manchester U 0 0
1995–96 Manchester U 1 0
1995–96 *Stockport Co* 10 1 **10 1**
1995–96 *Huddersfield T* 12 2
1996–97 Manchester U 2 0
1997–98 Manchester U 5 0 **9 0**
1998–99 Huddersfield T 35 4
1999–2000 Huddersfield T 28 1
2000–01 Huddersfield T 36 0 **111 7**
2001–02 Aberdeen 24 3 **24 3**
2002–03 Blackpool 12 0 **12 0**

WALKER, Richard (F) 110 23
H: 6 0 W: 12 00 b.Sutton Coldfield 8-11-77
Source: Trainee.
1995–96 Aston Villa 0 0
1996–97 Aston Villa 0 0
1997–98 Aston Villa 1 0
1998–99 Aston Villa 0 0
1998–99 *Cambridge U* 21 3 **21 3**
1999–2000 Aston Villa 5 2
2000–01 Aston Villa 0 0
2000–01 *Blackpool* 18 3
2001–02 Aston Villa 0 0 **6 2**
2001–02 *Wycombe W* 12 3 **12 3**
2001–02 Blackpool 21 8
2002–03 Blackpool 32 4 **71 15**

WELLENS, Richard (M) 119 10
H: 5 9 W: 11 06 b.Manchester 26-3-80
Source: Trainee. *Honours:* England Youth.
1996–97 Manchester U 0 0
1997–98 Manchester U 0 0
1998–99 Manchester U 0 0
1999–2000 Manchester U 0 0
1999–2000 Blackpool 8 0
2000–01 Blackpool 36 8
2001–02 Blackpool 36 1
2002–03 Blackpool 39 1 **119 10**

Scholars
Blinkhorn, Matthew D; Burns, Jamie D; Fenech, Jonathan; Gilston, Matthew; Gordon, William D; Heffernan, Guy; Lawlor, Sean P; Mangan, Andrew F; McInally, Garry; McMahon, Stephen J; Russell, Mark P; Swan, Mark L; Wiles, Simon
Non-Contract
Robinson, Paul D

BOLTON W

ANDRE, Pierre-Yves (F) 279 48
H: 6 2 W: 13 06 b.Lannion 14-5-74
1993–94 Rennes 26 5
1994–95 Rennes 33 5
1995–96 Rennes 36 6
1996–97 Rennes 30 1 **125 17**
1997–98 Bastia 29 1
1998–99 Bastia 22 9
1999–2000 Bastia 30 7
2000–01 Bastia 32 10 **113 27**
2001–02 Nantes 26 4
2002–03 Nantes 6 0 **32 4**
2002–03 Bolton W 9 0 **9 0**

ARMSTRONG, Chris* (F) 347 111
H: 6 0 W: 13 03 b.Newcastle 19-6-71
Source: Llay Welfare. *Honours:* England B.
1988–89 Wrexham 0 0
1989–90 Wrexham 22 3
1990–91 Wrexham 38 10 **60 13**
1991–92 Millwall 25 4
1992–93 Millwall 3 1 **28 5**
1992–93 Crystal Palace 35 15
1993–94 Crystal Palace 43 22
1994–95 Crystal Palace 40 8 **118 45**
1995–96 Tottenham H 36 15
1996–97 Tottenham H 12 5
1997–98 Tottenham H 19 5
1998–99 Tottenham H 34 7
1999–2000 Tottenham H 31 14
2000–01 Tottenham H 9 2
2001–02 Tottenham H 0 0 **141 48**
2002–03 Bolton W 0 0

BARNESS, Anthony* (D) 212 4
H: 5 10 W: 12 11 b.Lewisham 25-2-73
Source: Trainee.
1990–91 Charlton Ath 0 0
1991–92 Charlton Ath 22 1
1992–93 Charlton Ath 5 0
1992–93 Chelsea 2 0
1993–94 Chelsea 0 0
1993–94 *Middlesbrough* 0 0
1994–95 Chelsea 12 0
1995–96 Chelsea 0 0 **14 0**
1995–96 *Southend U* 5 0 **5 0**
1996–97 Charlton Ath 45 2
1997–98 Charlton Ath 29 1
1998–99 Charlton Ath 3 0
1999–2000 Charlton Ath 19 0 **123 4**
2000–01 Bolton W 20 0
2001–02 Bolton W 25 0
2002–03 Bolton W 25 0 **70 0**

BERGSSON, Gudni* (D) 341 25
H: 6 1 W: 12 03 b.Reykjavik 21-7-65
Source: Valur. *Honours:* Iceland Youth, Under-21, 80 full caps, 1 goal.
1988–89 Tottenham H 8 0
1989–90 Tottenham H 18 0
1990–91 Tottenham H 12 1
1991–92 Tottenham H 28 1
1992–93 Tottenham H 5 0
1993–94 Tottenham H 0 0 **71 2**
1994–95 Bolton W 8 0
1995–96 Bolton W 34 4
1996–97 Bolton W 33 3
1997–98 Bolton W 35 2
1998–99 Bolton W 17 0
1999–2000 Bolton W 38 4
2000–01 Bolton W 44 8
2001–02 Bolton W 30 1
2002–03 Bolton W 31 1 **270 23**

BON, Jeremy (G) 0 0
b.Begles 21-10-84
Source: Bordeaux.
2001–02 Bolton W 0 0
2002–03 Bolton W 0 0

BUCHANAN, Wayne (D) 3 0
H: 6 1 W: 13 02 b.Bambridge 12-1-82
Source: Scholar. *Honours:* Northern Ireland Under-21.

2001-02	Bolton W	0	0		
2001-02	*Chesterfield*	3	0	**3**	**0**
2002-03	Bolton W	0	0		

BULENT, Akin‡ (M) 1 0
H: 5 10 W: 12 02 b.Brussels 28-8-79

2002-03	Bolton W	1	0	**1**	**0**

CAMPO, Ivan (D) 200 9
H: 6 1 W: 12 12 b.San Sebastian 21-2-74
Honours: Spain 4 full caps.

1993–94	Alaves	11	1		
1994–95	Alaves	23	1		
1995–96	Alaves	11	0	**45**	**2**
1995–96	Valladolid	24	2	**24**	**2**
1996–97	Valencia	7	1	**7**	**1**
1997–98	Mallorca	33	1	**33**	**1**
1998–99	Real Madrid	27	1		
1999–2000	Real Madrid	20	0		
2000-01	Real Madrid	10	0		
2001-02	Real Madrid	3	0	**60**	**1**
2002-03	Bolton W	31	2	**31**	**2**

CHARLTON, Simon (D) 399 3
H: 5 8 W: 11 04 b.Huddersfield 25-10-71
Source: Trainee. *Honours:* FA Schools.

1989–90	Huddersfield T	3	0		
1990–91	Huddersfield T	30	0		
1991–92	Huddersfield T	45	0		
1992–93	Huddersfield T	46	1	**124**	**1**
1993–94	Southampton	33	1		
1994–95	Southampton	25	1		
1995–96	Southampton	26	0		
1996–97	Southampton	27	0		
1997–98	Southampton	3	0	**114**	**2**
1998–99	Birmingham C	28	0		
1997–98	Birmingham C	24	0		
1999–2000	Birmingham C	20	0	**72**	**0**
2000-01	Bolton W	22	0		
2001-02	Bolton W	36	0		
2002-03	Bolton W	31	0	**89**	**0**

DJORKAEFF, Youri (M) 496 176
H: 5 10 W: 11 02 b.Lyon 9-3-68
Honours: France 82 full caps, 28 goals.

1984–85	Grenoble	2	0		
1985–86	Grenoble	6	0		
1986–87	Grenoble	26	4		
1987–88	Grenoble	19	8		
1988–89	Grenoble	25	11		
1989–90	Grenoble	3	0	**81**	**23**
1989–90	Strasbourg	28	21		
1990–91	Strasbourg	7	4	**35**	**25**
1990–91	Monaco	20	5		
1991–92	Monaco	35	9		
1992–93	Monaco	32	12		
1993–94	Monaco	35	20		
1994–95	Monaco	33	14	**155**	**60**
1995–96	Paris St Germain	35	13	**35**	**13**
1996–97	Internazionale	33	14		
1997–98	Internazionale	29	8		
1998–99	Internazionale	25	8	**87**	**30**
1999–2000	Kaiserslautern	25	11		
2000-01	Kaiserslautern	26	3		
2001-02	Kaiserslautern	4	0	**55**	**14**
2001-02	Bolton W	12	4		
2002-03	Bolton W	36	7	**48**	**11**

DOWNEY, Chris* (F) 1 0
H: 5 10 W: 9 11 b.Warrington 19-4-83
Source: Scholar.

2000-01	Bolton W	1	0		
2001-02	Bolton W	0	0		
2002-03	Bolton W	0	0	**1**	**0**

FACEY, Delroy (F) 90 17
H: 6 0 W: 13 00 b.Huddersfield 22-4-80
Source: Trainee.

1996–97	Huddersfield T	3	0		
1997–98	Huddersfield T	3	0		
1998–99	Huddersfield T	20	3		
1999–2000	Huddersfield T	2	0		
2000-01	Huddersfield T	34	10		
2001-02	Huddersfield T	13	2		
2002-03	Huddersfield T	0	0	**75**	**15**
2002-03	*Bradford C*	6	1	**6**	**1**
2002-03	Bolton W	9	1	**9**	**1**

FARRELLY, Gareth (M) 129 8
H: 6 0 W: 12 07 b.Dublin 28-8-75
Source: Home Farm. *Honours:* Eire Under-21, 6 full caps.

1992–93	Aston Villa	0	0		
1993–94	Aston Villa	0	0		
1994–95	Aston Villa	0	0		
1994–95	*Rotherham U*	10	2		
1995–96	Aston Villa	5	0		
1996–97	Aston Villa	3	0	**8**	**0**
1997–98	Everton	26	1		
1998–99	Everton	1	0		
1999–2000	Everton	0	0	**27**	**1**
1999–2000	Bolton W	11	1		
2000-01	Bolton W	41	3		
2001-02	Bolton W	18	0		
2002-03	Bolton W	8	1	**78**	**5**
2002-03	*Rotherham U*	6	0	**16**	**2**

FORSCHELET, Gerald (M) 0 0
H: 6 1 W: 13 05 b.Papeete 19-9-81
Source: Cannes.

2001-02	Bolton W	0	0		
2002-03	Bolton W	0	0		

FRANDSEN, Per (M) 452 87
H: 6 1 W: 12 06 b.Copenhagen 6-2-70
Honours: Denmark 23 full caps.

1990	B 1903	25	15	**25**	**15**
1990–91	Lille	19	4		
1991–92	Lille	27	8		
1992–93	Lille	32	3		
1993–94	Lille	31	4	**109**	**19**
1994–95	FC Copenhagen	29	12		
1995–96	FC Copenhagen	26	7	**55**	**19**
1996–97	Bolton W	41	5		
1997–98	Bolton W	38	2		
1998–99	Bolton W	44	8		
1999–2000	Bolton W	7	2		
1999–2000	Blackburn R	31	5	**31**	**5**
2000-01	Bolton W	39	7		
2001-02	Bolton W	29	3		
2002-03	Bolton W	34	2	**232**	**29**

GARDNER, Ricardo (M) 154 15
H: 5 9 W: 11 00 b.St Andrews 25-9-78
Source: Harbour View. *Honours:* Jamaica 43 full caps, 5 goals.

1998–99	Bolton W	30	2		
1999–2000	Bolton W	29	5		
2000-01	Bolton W	32	3		
2001-02	Bolton W	31	3		
2002-03	Bolton W	32	2	**154**	**15**

HENDRY, Colin* (D) 511 44
H: 6 1 W: 12 07 b.Keith 7-12-65
Source: Islavale. *Honours:* Scotland B, 51 full caps, 3 goals.

1983–84	Dundee	4	0		
1984–85	Dundee	4	0		
1985–86	Dundee	20	0		
1986–87	Dundee	13	2	**41**	**2**
1986–87	Blackburn R	13	3		
1987–88	Blackburn R	44	12		
1988–89	Blackburn R	38	7		
1989–90	Blackburn R	7	0		
1989–90	Manchester C	25	3		
1990–91	Manchester C	32	1		
1991–92	Manchester C	6	1	**63**	**5**
1991–92	Blackburn R	30	4		
1992–93	Blackburn R	41	1		
1993–94	Blackburn R	23	0		
1994–95	Blackburn R	38	4		
1995–96	Blackburn R	33	1		
1996–97	Blackburn R	35	1		
1997–98	Blackburn R	34	1	**336**	**34**
1998–99	Rangers	19	0	**19**	**0**
1999–2000	Coventry C	9	0		
2000-01	Coventry C	2	0	**11**	**0**
2000-01	Bolton W	22	3		
2001-02	Bolton W	3	0		
2001-02	*Preston NE*	2	0	**2**	**0**
2002-03	Bolton W	0	0	**25**	**3**
2002-03	*Blackpool*	14	0	**14**	**0**

HOLDSWORTH, David‡ (D) 445 22
H: 6 1 W: 12 04 b.Walthamstow 8-11-68
Source: Trainee. *Honours:* England Youth, Under-21.

1986–87	Watford	0	0		
1987–88	Watford	0	0		
1988–89	Watford	33	1		
1989–90	Watford	44	3		
1990–91	Watford	15	2		
1991–92	Watford	33	2		
1992–93	Watford	39	0		
1993–94	Watford	28	0		
1994–95	Watford	39	1		
1995–96	Watford	27	1		
1996–97	Watford	0	0	**258**	**10**
1996–97	Sheffield U	37	1		
1997–98	Sheffield U	40	2		
1998–99	Sheffield U	16	1	**93**	**4**
1998–99	Birmingham C	8	1		
1999–2000	Birmingham C	44	5		
2000-01	Birmingham C	29	1		
2001-02	Birmingham C	4	0		
2001-02	*Walsall*	9	1	**9**	**1**
2002-03	Birmingham C	0	0	**85**	**7**
2002-03	Bolton W	0	0		

HUNT, Nicky (D) 1 0
H: 6 0 W: 11 00 b.Westhoughton 3-9-83
Source: Scholar.

2000-01	Bolton W	1	0		
2001-02	Bolton W	0	0		
2002-03	Bolton W	0	0	**1**	**0**

JAASKELAINEN, Jussi (G) 285 0
H: 6 4 W: 12 10 b.Mikkeli 19-4-75
Honours: Finland 14 full caps.

1992	MP	6	0		
1993	MP	6	0		
1994	MP	26	0		
1995	MP	26	0	**64**	**0**
1996	VPS	27	0		
1997	VPS	27	0	**54**	**0**
1997–98	Bolton W	0	0		
1998–99	Bolton W	34	0		
1999–2000	Bolton W	34	0		
2000-01	Bolton W	27	0		
2001-02	Bolton W	34	0		
2002-03	Bolton W	38	0	**167**	**0**

JOHNSON, Jermaine (M) 12 0
H: 5 11 W: 11 05 b.Kingston, Jamaica 25-6-80
Source: Tivoli Gardens.

2001-02	Bolton W	10	0		
2002-03	Bolton W	2	0	**12**	**0**

LAVILLE, Florent (D) 215 2
H: 6 2 W: 13 12 b.Valence 7-8-83

1993–94	Lyon	8	0		
1994–95	Lyon	28	0		
1995–96	Lyon	28	0		
1996–97	Lyon	27	1		
1997–98	Lyon	29	0		
1998–99	Lyon	29	0		
1999–2000	Lyon	29	0		
2000-01	Lyon	9	0		
2001-02	Lyon	13	0		
2002-03	Lyon	5	1	**205**	**2**
2002-03	Bolton W	10	0	**10**	**0**

LIVESEY, Danny (D) 2 0
H: 6 3 W: 12 10 b.Salford 31-12-84
Source: Trainee.

2002-03	Bolton W	2	0	**2**	**0**

MENDY, Bernard (D) 95 3
H: 5 11 W: 12 02 b.Evreux 20-8-81

1998–99	Caen	4	0		
1999–2000	Caen	30	2	**34**	**2**
2000-01	Paris St Germain	19	0		
2001-02	Paris St Germain	21	1	**40**	**1**
2002-03	Bolton W	21	0	**21**	**0**

N'GOTTY, Bruno (D) 416 22
H: 6 2 W: 13 05 b.Lyon 10-6-71
Honours: France 6 full caps.

1989–90	Lyon	27	0		
1990–91	Lyon	37	2		
1991–92	Lyon	36	1		
1992–93	Lyon	36	3		
1993–94	Lyon	36	3		
1994–95	Lyon	35	3	**207**	**12**
1995–96	Paris St Germain	24	1		
1996–97	Paris St Germain	30	4		
1997–98	Paris St Germain	26	2	**80**	**7**
1998–99	AC Milan	25	1		
1999–2000	AC Milan	9	0	**34**	**1**
1999–2000	Venezia	16	0	**16**	**0**
2000-01	Marseille	30	0	**30**	**0**
2001-02	Bolton W	26	1		
2002-03	Bolton W	23	1	**49**	**2**

NIVEN, Derek (M) 1 0
H: 6 1 W: 11 02 b.Falkirk 12-12-83
Source: Stenhousemuir.

2000-01	Raith R	1	0	**1**	**0**
2001-02	Bolton W	0	0		
2002-03	Bolton W	0	0		

NOLAN, Kevin (M) 103 10
H: 6 0 W: 14 00 b.Liverpool 24-6-82
Source: Scholar. *Honours:* England Youth, Under-20, Under-21.

1999–2000	Bolton W	4	0		
2000-01	Bolton W	31	1		
2001-02	Bolton W	35	8		
2002-03	Bolton W	33	1	**103**	**10**

OKOCHA, Jay-Jay (M) **267 66**
H: 5 7 W: 11 02 b.Enugu 14-8-73
Source: Enugu Rangers, Neunkirchen.
Honours: Nigeria 59 full caps, 8 goals.

1992–93	Eintracht Frankfurt	20	2		
1993–94	Eintracht Frankfurt	19	2		
1994–95	Eintracht Frankfurt	27	6		
1995–96	Eintracht Frankfurt	24	7	**90**	**17**
1996–97	Fenerbahce	33	16		
1997–98	Fenerbahce	30	14	**63**	**30**
1998–99	Paris St Germain	25	4		
1999–2000	Paris St Germain	23	2		
2000-01	Paris St Germain	15	2		
2001-02	Paris St Germain	20	4	**83**	**12**
2002-03	Bolton W	31	7	**31**	**7**

PEDERSEN, Henrik (F) **166 69**
H: 6 0 W: 12 05 b.Jutland 10-6-75
Honours: Denmark 2 full caps.

1995–96	Silkeborg	12	4		
1996–97	Silkeborg	2	0		
1997–98	Silkeborg	15	9		
1998–99	Silkeborg	33	16		
1999–2000	Silkeborg	28	13		
2000-01	Silkeborg	32	20	**122**	**62**
2001-02	Bolton W	11	0		
2002-03	Bolton W	33	7	**44**	**7**

POOLE, Kevin* (G) **299 0**
H: 5 11 W: 12 06 b.Bromsgrove 21-7-63
Source: Apprentice.

1981–82	Aston Villa	0	0		
1982–83	Aston Villa	0	0		
1983–84	Aston Villa	0	0		
1984–85	Aston Villa	7	0		
1984–85	*Northampton T*	3	0	**3**	**0**
1985–86	Aston Villa	11	0		
1986–87	Aston Villa	10	0	**28**	**0**
1987–88	Middlesbrough	1	0		
1988–89	Middlesbrough	12	0		
1989–90	Middlesbrough	21	0		
1990–91	Middlesbrough	0	0	**34**	**0**
1990–91	*Hartlepool U*	12	0	**12**	**0**
1991–92	Leicester C	42	0		
1992–93	Leicester C	19	0		
1993–94	Leicester C	14	0		
1994–95	Leicester C	36	0		
1995–96	Leicester C	45	0		
1996–97	Leicester C	7	0	**163**	**0**
1997–98	Birmingham C	1	0		
1998–99	Birmingham C	36	0		
1999–2000	Birmingham C	18	0		
2000-01	Birmingham C	1	0		
2001-02	Birmingham C	0	0	**56**	**0**
2001-02	Bolton W	3	0		
2002-03	Bolton W	0	0	**3**	**0**

RICHARDSON, Leam* (D) **54 0**
H: 5 9 W: 11 00 b.Leeds 19-11-79
Source: Trainee.

1997–98	Blackburn R	0	0		
1998–99	Blackburn R	0	0		
1999–2000	Blackburn R	0	0		
2000-01	Bolton W	12	0		
2001-02	Bolton W	1	0		
2001-02	*Notts Co*	21	0	**21**	**0**
2002-03	Bolton W	0	0	**13**	**0**
2002-03	*Blackpool*	20	0	**20**	**0**

RYAN, Ciaran‡ (D) **0 0**
b.Dublin 27-2-83
Source: Scholar.

2001-02	Bolton W	0	0
2002-03	Bolton W	0	0

SALVA, Ballesta (F) **216 85**
H: 6 0 W: 12 08 b.Zaragoza 22-5-75
Honours: Spain 3 full caps.

1994–95	Sevilla B	16	4		
1995–96	Sevilla B	19	6	**35**	**10**
1995–96	Sevilla	1	0		
1995–96	Ecija	17	6	**17**	**6**
1996–97	Sevilla	34	12		
1997–98	Sevilla	14	3	**49**	**15**
1998–99	Santander	16	2		
1999–2000	Santander	36	27	**52**	**29**
2000-01	Atletico Madrid	33	20	**33**	**20**
2001-02	Valencia	22	5		
2002-03	Valencia	2	0	**24**	**5**
2002-03	Bolton W	6	0	**6**	**0**

SMITH, Jeff (M) **13 2**
H: 5 10 W: 11 08 b.Middlesbrough 28-6-80
Source: Trainee.

1998–99	Hartlepool U	3	0		
1999–2000	Hartlepool U	0	0	**3**	**0**

From Bishop Auckland

2000-01	Bolton W	1	0		
2001-02	*Macclesfield T*	8	2	**8**	**2**
2001-02	Bolton W	1	0		
2002-03	Bolton W	0	0	**2**	**0**

TAYLOR, Cleveland (M) **3 0**
H: 5 8 W: 11 08 b.Leicester 9-9-83
Source: Scholar.

2001-02	Bolton W	0	0		
2002-03	Bolton W	0	0		
2002-03	*Exeter C*	3	0	**3**	**0**

TOFTING, Stig‡ (M) **315 37**
H: 5 10 W: 12 02 b.Aarhus 14-8-69
Honours: Denmark 41 full caps, 2 goals.

1990	Aarhus	22	2		
1990–91	Aarhus	18	0		
1991–92	Aarhus	24	2		
1992–93	Aarhus	30	7		
1993–94	Odense	12	3	**12**	**3**
1993–94	Hamburg	5	0		
1994–95	Hamburg	3	0		
1994–95	Aarhus	14	2		
1995–96	Aarhus	24	3		
1996–97	Aarhus	32	12	**164**	**28**
1997–98	Duisburg	12	0		
1998–99	Duisburg	28	2		
1999–2000	Duisburg	29	2	**69**	**4**
2000-01	Hamburg	28	2		
2001-02	Hamburg	20	0	**56**	**2**
2001-02	Bolton W	6	0		
2002-03	Bolton W	8	0	**14**	**0**

WALTERS, Jonathan (F) **15 5**
H: 6 0 W: 12 06 b.Wirral 20-9-83
Source: Blackburn R Scholar.

2001-02	Bolton W	0	0		
2002-03	Bolton W	4	0	**4**	**0**
2002-03	*Hull C*	11	5	**11**	**5**

WARHURST, Paul* (M) **313 17**
H: 6 0 W: 13 00 b.Stockport 26-9-69
Source: Trainee. *Honours:* England Under-21.

1987–88	Manchester C	0	0		
1988–89	Oldham Ath	4	0		
1989–90	Oldham Ath	30	1		
1990–91	Oldham Ath	33	1	**67**	**2**
1991–92	Sheffield W	33	0		
1992–93	Sheffield W	29	6		
1993–94	Sheffield W	4	0	**66**	**6**
1993–94	Blackburn R	9	0		
1994–95	Blackburn R	27	2		
1995–96	Blackburn R	10	0		
1996–97	Blackburn R	11	2	**57**	**4**
1997–98	Crystal Palace	22	3		
1998–99	Crystal Palace	5	1	**27**	**4**
1998–99	Bolton W	20	0		
1999–2000	Bolton W	19	0		
2000-01	Bolton W	20	0		
2001-02	Bolton W	25	0		
2002-03	Bolton W	7	0	**91**	**0**
2002-03	*Stoke C*	5	1	**5**	**1**

WHITLOW, Mike* (D) **356 14**
H: 6 0 W: 12 13 b.Northwich 13-1-68
Source: Witton Alb.

1988–89	Leeds U	20	1		
1989–90	Leeds U	29	1		
1990–91	Leeds U	18	1		
1991–92	Leeds U	10	1	**77**	**4**
1991–92	Leicester C	5	0		
1992–93	Leicester C	24	1		
1993–94	Leicester C	31	2		
1994–95	Leicester C	28	2		
1995–96	Leicester C	42	3		
1996–97	Leicester C	17	0		
1997–98	Leicester C	0	0	**147**	**8**
1997–98	Bolton W	13	0		
1998–99	Bolton W	28	0		
1999–2000	Bolton W	37	1		
2000-01	Bolton W	8	1		
2001-02	Bolton W	29	0		
2002-03	Bolton W	17	0	**132**	**2**

Trainees
Comyn-Platt, Charlie; Errington, Anthony; Gibb, Jamie A; Gillan, Michael A; Hamlin, Lewis; Howarth, Christopher; Jones, Reece L; Kribib, Reda; Moran, Martin R; O'Brien, Joseph M; Shakes, Ricky U; Talbot, Jason C; Thach, Duong

BOSTON U

ANGEL, Mark# (M) **139 11**
H: 5 8 W: 11 02 b.Newcastle 23-8-75
Source: Trainee.

1993–94	Sunderland	0	0		
1994–95	Sunderland	0	0		
1995–96	Oxford U	27	1		
1996–97	Oxford U	24	2		
1997–98	Oxford U	22	1	**73**	**4**
1998–99	WBA	22	1		
1999–2000	WBA	3	0	**25**	**1**
2000-01	Darlington	5	0	**5**	**0**
2000-01	*Q of S*	5	1	**5**	**1**
2002-03	Boston U	31	5	**31**	**5**

BALMER, Stuart (D) **391 18**
H: 6 1 W: 12 06 b.Falkirk 20-9-69
Source: Celtic BC. *Honours:* Scotland Schools, Youth.

1987–88	Celtic	0	0		
1988–89	Celtic	0	0		
1989–90	Celtic	0	0		
1990–91	Charlton Ath	24	0		
1991–92	Charlton Ath	18	0		
1992–93	Charlton Ath	45	2		
1993–94	Charlton Ath	31	1		
1994–95	Charlton Ath	29	2		
1995–96	Charlton Ath	32	1		
1996–97	Charlton Ath	32	2		
1997–98	Charlton Ath	16	0		
1998–99	Charlton Ath	0	0	**227**	**8**
1998–99	Wigan Ath	36	1		
1999–2000	Wigan Ath	41	2		
2000-01	Wigan Ath	24	1	**101**	**4**
2001-02	Oldham Ath	36	6		
2002-03	Oldham Ath	0	0	**36**	**6**
2002-03	*Scunthorpe U*	6	0	**6**	**0**
2002-03	Boston U	21	0	**21**	**0**

BASTOCK, Paul# (G) **58 0**
H: 5 8 W: 10 00 b.Leamington 19-5-70
Source: Trainee.

1986–87	Coventry C	0	0		
1987–88	Cambridge U	10	0		
1988–89	Cambridge U	2	0	**12**	**0**

From Fisher, Ketteri

2002-03	Boston U	46	0	**46**	**0**

BENNETT, Tom (M) **347 15**
H: 5 11 W: 11 08 b.Falkirk 12-12-69
Source: Trainee.

1987–88	Aston Villa	0	0		
1988–89	Wolverhampton W	2	0		
1989–90	Wolverhampton W	30	0		
1990–91	Wolverhampton W	26	0		
1991–92	Wolverhampton W	38	2		
1992–93	Wolverhampton W	1	0		
1993–94	Wolverhampton W	10	0		
1994–95	Wolverhampton W	8	0	**115**	**2**
1995–96	Stockport Co	24	1		
1996–97	Stockport Co	43	3		
1997–98	Stockport Co	27	1		
1998–99	Stockport Co	7	0		
1999–2000	Stockport Co	9	0	**110**	**5**
1999–2000	*Walsall*	11	3		
2000-01	Walsall	38	5		
2001-02	Walsall	40	0	**89**	**8**
2002-03	Boston U	33	0	**33**	**0**

CHAPMAN, Ben (D) **58 0**
H: 5 6 W: 11 05 b.Scunthorpe 2-3-79
Source: Trainee.

1997–98	Grimsby T	0	0		
1998–99	Grimsby T	1	0		
1999–2000	Grimsby T	1	0		
2000-01	Grimsby T	2	0		
2001-02	Grimsby T	17	0	**21**	**0**
2002-03	Boston U	37	0	**37**	**0**

CLARE, Daryl‡ (F) **104 13**
H: 5 9 W: 12 05 b.Jersey 1-8-78
Source: Trainee. *Honours:* Eire Under-21.

1995–96	Grimsby T	1	0		
1996–97	Grimsby T	0	0		
1997–98	Grimsby T	22	3		
1998–99	Grimsby T	22	3		
1999–2000	Grimsby T	17	3		
1999–2000	*Northampton T*	10	3		
2000-01	Grimsby T	17	0	**79**	**9**
2000-01	*Northampton T*	4	0	**14**	**3**
2000-01	*Cheltenham T*	4	0	**4**	**0**
2002-03	Boston U	7	1	**7**	**1**

CLIFFORD, Mark‡ (D)				**11**	**0**
H: 5 10 W: 10 10 b.Nottingham 11-9-77					
Source: Trainee.					
1994–95	Mansfield T	1	0		
1995–96	Mansfield T	0	0		
1996–97	Mansfield T	3	0	**4**	**0**
From Ilkeston T					
2002-03	Boston U	7	0	**7**	**0**

CONROY, Nick# (G)				**0**	**0**
b.Boston 9-4-76					
Source: Stamford.					
2002-03	Boston U	0	0		

COOK, Jamie‡ (F)				**93**	**9**
H: 5 10 W: 10 10 b.Oxford 2-8-79					
Source: Trainee.					
1997–98	Oxford U	20	2		
1998–99	Oxford U	19	1		
1999–2000	Oxford U	29	3		
2000-01	Oxford U	9	1	**77**	**7**
2002-03	Boston U	16	2	**16**	**2**

COSTELLO, Peter* (M)				**119**	**19**
H: 6 0 W: 11 07 b.Halifax 31-10-69					
1988–89	Bradford C	8	2		
1989–90	Bradford C	12	0	**20**	**2**
1990–91	Rochdale	34	10	**34**	**10**
1990–91	Peterborough U	5	0		
1991–92	Peterborough U	1	0	**6**	**0**
1991–92	*Lincoln C*	3	0		
1992–93	Lincoln C	27	7		
1993–94	Lincoln C	11	0	**41**	**7**
From Kettering T.					
2002-03	Boston U	18	0	**18**	**0**

DOUGLAS, Stuart (F)				**188**	**25**
H: 5 9 W: 12 05 b.London 9-4-78					
Source: Trainee.					
1995–96	Luton T	8	1		
1996–97	Luton T	9	0		
1997–98	Luton T	17	1		
1998–99	Luton T	42	9		
1999–2000	Luton T	40	3		
2000-01	Luton T	21	4		
2001-02	Luton T	9	0	**146**	**18**
2001-02	*Oxford U*	4	0	**4**	**0**
2001-02	*Rushden & D*	9	0	**9**	**0**
2002-03	Boston U	29	7	**29**	**7**

DUFFIELD, Peter (F)				**347**	**121**
H: 5 7 W: 10 13 b.Middlesbrough 4-2-69					
Source: Apprentice.					
1986–87	Middlesbrough	0	0		
1987–88	Sheffield U	11	1		
1987–88	*Halifax T*	12	6	**12**	**6**
1988–89	Sheffield U	38	11		
1989–90	Sheffield U	5	2		
1990–91	Sheffield U	2	0		
1990–91	*Rotherham U*	17	4	**17**	**4**
1991–92	Sheffield U	2	0		
1992–93	Sheffield U	0	0		
1992–93	*Blackpool*	5	1	**5**	**1**
1992–93	*Bournemouth*	0	0		
1992–93	*Stockport Co*	7	4	**7**	**4**
1992–93	*Crewe Alex*	2	0	**2**	**0**
1993–94	Sheffield U	0	0	**58**	**14**
1993–94	Hamilton A	36	19		
1994–95	Hamilton A	36	20	**72**	**39**
1995–96	Airdrieonians	24	6	**24**	**6**
1995–96	Raith R	9	5		
1996–97	Raith R	33	5		
1997–98	Raith R	0	0		
1998–99	Raith R	0	0	**42**	**10**
1998–99	Darlington	14	2		
1999–2000	Darlington	33	12	**47**	**14**
2000-01	York C	6	3		
2001-02	York C	11	3		
2002-03	York C	28	13	**45**	**19**
2002-03	Boston U	16	4	**16**	**4**

ELDING, Anthony‡ (F)				**8**	**0**
b.Boston 16-4-82					
Source: Trainee.					
2002-03	Boston U	8	0	**8**	**0**

ELLENDER, Paul# (D)				**26**	**0**
H: 6 1 W: 12 07 b.Scunthorpe 21-10-74					
Source: Trainee.					
1992–93	Scunthorpe U	0	0		
1993–94	Scunthorpe U	0	0		
From Altrincham, Sca					
2002-03	Boston U	26	0	**26**	**0**

GEORGE, Liam‡ (F)				**113**	**21**
H: 5 9 W: 11 04 b.Luton 2-2-79					
Source: Trainee. *Honours:* Eire Under-21.					
1996–97	Luton T	0	0		
1997–98	Luton T	1	0		
1998–99	Luton T	12	0		
1999–2000	Luton T	42	13		
2000-01	Luton T	43	7		
2001-02	Luton T	4	0	**102**	**20**
From Stevenage B.					
2002-03	Bury	8	1	**8**	**1**
2002-03	Boston U	3	0	**3**	**0**

GOULD, James* (M)				**21**	**2**
H: 5 8 W: 10 06 b.Rushden 15-1-82					
Source: Trainee.					
2000-01	Northampton T	1	0	**1**	**0**
2002-03	Boston U	20	2	**20**	**2**

GREAVES, Mark (D)				**203**	**11**
H: 6 1 W: 13 00 b.Hull 22-1-75					
Source: Brigg Town.					
1996–97	Hull C	30	2		
1997–98	Hull C	25	2		
1998–99	Hull C	25	0		
1999–2000	Hull C	38	3		
2000-01	Hull C	30	2		
2001-02	Hull C	26	1		
2002-03	Hull C	3	0	**177**	**10**
2002-03	Boston U	26	1	**26**	**1**

HIGGINS, Alex (M)				**14**	**0**
H: 5 9 W: 11 04 b.Sheffield 22-7-81					
Source: Trainee. *Honours:* England Schools.					
1998–99	Sheffield W	0	0		
1999–2000	Sheffield W	0	0		
2000-01	Sheffield W	0	0		
2000-01	QPR	1	0	**1**	**0**
From Chester C, Stalybridge C.					
2002-03	Boston U	13	0	**13**	**0**

HOCKING, Matt (D)				**199**	**5**
H: 6 0 W: 12 09 b.Boston 30-1-78					
Source: Trainee.					
1995–96	Sheffield U	0	0		
1996–97	Sheffield U	0	0		
1997–98	Sheffield U	0	0		
1997–98	Hull C	31	1		
1998–99	Hull C	26	1	**57**	**2**
1998–99	*York C*	6	0		
1999–2000	York C	32	2		
2000-01	York C	26	0		
2001-02	York C	33	0	**97**	**2**
2002-03	Boston U	45	1	**45**	**1**

JONES, Graeme (F)				**253**	**80**
H: 6 1 W: 13 06 b.Gateshead 13-3-70					
Source: Bridlington T.					
1993–94	Doncaster R	28	4		
1994–95	Doncaster R	32	12		
1995–96	Doncaster R	32	10	**92**	**26**
1996–97	Wigan Ath	40	31		
1997–98	Wigan Ath	33	9		
1998–99	Wigan Ath	20	3		
1999–2000	Wigan Ath	3	1	**96**	**44**
1999–2000	St Johnstone	19	3		
2000-01	St Johnstone	9	3		
2001-02	St Johnstone	13	1	**41**	**7**
2002-03	Southend U	21	2	**21**	**2**
2002-03	Boston U	3	1	**3**	**1**

LODGE, Andy‡ (D)				**2**	**0**
b.Peterborough 17-5-78					
Source: Stamford.					
2002-03	Boston U	2	0	**2**	**0**

LOGAN, Richard (F)				**51**	**15**
H: 6 0 W: 12 05 b.Bury St Edmunds 4-1-82					
Source: Trainee. *Honours:* England Youth.					
1998–99	Ipswich T	2	0		
1999–2000	Ipswich T	1	0		
2000-01	Ipswich T	0	0		
2000-01	*Cambridge U*	5	1	**5**	**1**
2001-02	Ipswich T	0	0		
2001-02	*Torquay U*	16	4	**16**	**4**
2002-03	Ipswich T	0	0	**3**	**0**
2002-03	Boston U	27	10	**27**	**10**

MONINGTON, Mark‡ (D)				**259**	**20**
H: 6 1 W: 13 07 b.Mansfield 21-10-70					
Source: School.					
1988–89	Burnley	8	1		
1989–90	Burnley	13	0		
1990–91	Burnley	0	0		
1991–92	Burnley	12	1		
1992–93	Burnley	31	2		
1993–94	Burnley	20	1		
1994–95	Burnley	0	0	**84**	**5**
1994–95	Rotherham U	25	2		
1995–96	Rotherham U	11	0		
1996–97	Rotherham U	28	0		
1997–98	Rotherham U	15	1	**79**	**3**
1998–99	Rochdale	37	3		
1999–2000	Rochdale	24	2		
2000-01	Rochdale	34	7		
2001-02	Rochdale	0	0	**95**	**12**
2002-03	Boston U	1	0	**1**	**0**

MORLEY, Ben‡ (D)				**28**	**0**
H: 5 9 W: 10 11 b.Hull 22-12-80					
Source: Trainee.					
1997–98	Hull C	8	0		
1998–99	Hull C	12	0		
1999–2000	Hull C	1	0		
2000-01	Hull C	2	0		
2001-02	Hull C	3	0	**26**	**0**
2002-03	Boston U	2	0	**2**	**0**

REDFEARN, Neil# (M)				**758**	**151**
H: 5 11 W: 13 01 b.Dewsbury 20-6-65					
Source: Nottingham F Apprentice.					
1982–83	Bolton W	10	0		
1983–84	Bolton W	25	1	**35**	**1**
1983–84	*Lincoln C*	10	1		
1984–85	Lincoln C	45	4		
1985–86	Lincoln C	45	8	**100**	**13**
1986–87	Doncaster R	46	14	**46**	**14**
1987–88	Crystal Palace	42	8		
1988–89	Crystal Palace	15	2	**57**	**10**
1988–89	Watford	12	2		
1989–90	Watford	12	1	**24**	**3**
1989–90	Oldham Ath	17	2		
1990–91	Oldham Ath	45	14	**62**	**16**
1991–92	Barnsley	36	4		
1992–93	Barnsley	46	3		
1993–94	Barnsley	46	12		
1994–95	Barnsley	39	11		
1995–96	Barnsley	45	14		
1996–97	Barnsley	43	17		
1997–98	Barnsley	37	10	**292**	**71**
1998–99	Charlton Ath	30	3	**30**	**3**
1999–2000	Bradford C	17	1	**17**	**1**
1999–2000	Wigan Ath	12	6		
2000-01	Wigan Ath	10	1	**22**	**7**
2000-01	Halifax T	12	0		
2001-02	Halifax T	30	6	**42**	**6**
2002-03	Boston U	31	6	**31**	**6**

RODWELL, Jim‡ (D)				**12**	**0**
H: 6 1 W: 14 02 b.Lincoln 20-11-70					
Source: Halesowen T.					
2001-02	Rushden & D	9	0	**9**	**0**
2002-03	Boston U	3	0	**3**	**0**

RUSK, Simon (M)				**18**	**2**
b.Peterborough 17-12-81					
Source: Peterborough U.					
2002-03	Boston U	18	2	**18**	**2**

THOMPSON, Lee (M)				**15**	**4**
H: 5 7 W: 10 10 b.Sheffield 25-3-83					
Honours: England Schools.					
2000-01	Sheffield U	0	0		
2001-02	Sheffield U	0	0		
2002-03	Sheffield U	0	0		
2002-03	Boston U	15	4	**15**	**4**

THOMPSON, Neil† (D)				**404**	**47**
H: 6 0 W: 13 08 b.Beverley 2-10-63					
Source: Nottingham F Apprentice.					
1981–82	Hull C	23	0		
1982–83	Hull C	8	0	**31**	**0**
From Scarborough					
1987–88	Scarborough	41	6		
1988–89	Scarborough	46	9	**87**	**15**
1989–90	Ipswich T	45	3		
1990–91	Ipswich T	38	6		
1991–92	Ipswich T	45	6		
1992–93	Ipswich T	31	3		
1993–94	Ipswich T	32	0		
1994–95	Ipswich T	10	0		
1995–96	Ipswich T	5	1	**206**	**19**
1996–97	Barnsley	24	5		
1997–98	Barnsley	3	0	**27**	**5**
1997–98	*Oldham Ath*	8	0	**8**	**0**
1997–98	York C	12	2		
1998–99	York C	24	6		
1999–2000	York C	6	0	**42**	**8**
From Scarborough.					
2002-03	Boston U	3	0	**3**	**0**

TOWN, David# (F)				**64**	**2**
H: 5 7 W: 11 13 b.Bournemouth 9-12-76					
Source: Trainee.					
1993–94	Bournemouth	1	0		
1994–95	Bournemouth	5	0		
1995–96	Bournemouth	7	0		
1996–97	Bournemouth	26	2		
1997–98	Bournemouth	7	0		
1998–99	Bournemouth	10	0	**56**	**2**
1999–2000	Rushden & D	0	0		

2000-01 Rushden & D 0 0
From Kettering T
2002-03 Boston U 8 0 **8 0**

WARBURTON, Ray‡ (D) 297 21
H: 6 0 W: 13 03 b.Rotherham 7-10-67
Source: Apprentice.
1984–85 Rotherham U 1 0
1985–86 Rotherham U 0 0
1986–87 Rotherham U 3 0
1987–88 Rotherham U 0 0
1988–89 Rotherham U 0 0 **4 0**
1989–90 York C 43 2
1990–91 York C 22 4
1991–92 York C 9 0
1992–93 York C 10 3
1993–94 York C 6 0 **90 9**
1993–94 *Northampton T* 17 1
1994–95 Northampton T 39 3
1995–96 Northampton T 44 3
1996–97 Northampton T 35 4
1997–98 Northampton T 39 0
1998–99 Northampton T 12 1
1999–2000 Northampton T 0 0
2000-01 Northampton T 0 0
2001-02 Northampton T 0 0 **186 12**
2001-02 Rushden & D 1 0 **1 0**
2002-03 Boston U 16 0 **16 0**

WEATHERSTONE, Ross‡ (M) 12 0
H: 5 11 W: 11 10 b.Reading 16-5-81
Source: Trainee.
1999–2000 Oxford U 3 0
2000-01 Oxford U 1 0
2001-02 Oxford U 0 0 **4 0**
2002-03 Boston U 8 0 **8 0**

WEATHERSTONE, Simon (F) 97 9
H: 5 10 W: 12 04 b.Reading 26-1-80
Source: Trainee.
1996–97 Oxford U 1 0
1997–98 Oxford U 11 1
1998–99 Oxford U 12 1
1999–2000 Oxford U 21 1
2000-01 Oxford U 7 0 **52 3**
2002-03 Boston U 45 6 **45 6**

Non-Contract
Thompson, Neil

BOURNEMOUTH

BERNARD, Narada* (M) 29 0
H: 5 7 W: 10 07 b.Bristol 30-1-81
Source: Trainee.
1999–2000 Arsenal 0 0
2000-01 Bournemouth 14 0
2001-02 Bournemouth 8 0
2002-03 Bournemouth 7 0 **29 0**

BLOOMFIELD, Danny‡ (F) 0 0
H: 5 8 W: 11 07 b.Ipswich 28-7-82
Source: Felixstowe & Walton U.
2000-01 Norwich C 0 0
2001-02 Norwich C 0 0
2002-03 Bournemouth 0 0

BROADHURST, Karl (D) 90 1
H: 6 1 W: 11 07 b.Portsmouth 18-3-80
Source: Trainee.
1998–99 Bournemouth 0 0
1999–2000 Bournemouth 16 0
2000-01 Bournemouth 30 0
2001-02 Bournemouth 23 0
2002-03 Bournemouth 21 1 **90 1**

BROWNING, Marcus (M) 335 22
H: 6 1 W: 12 12 b.Bristol 22-4-71
Source: Trainee. *Honours:* Wales 5 full caps.
1989–90 Bristol R 1 0
1990–91 Bristol R 0 0
1991–92 Bristol R 11 0
1992–93 Bristol R 19 1
1992–93 *Hereford U* 7 5 **7 5**
1993–94 Bristol R 31 4
1994–95 Bristol R 41 2
1995–96 Bristol R 45 4
1996–97 Bristol R 26 2 **174 13**
1996–97 Huddersfield T 13 0
1997–98 Huddersfield T 14 0
1998–99 Huddersfield T 6 0 **33 0**
1998–99 Gillingham 4 0
1999–2000 Gillingham 1 0
2000-01 Gillingham 31 0
2001-02 Gillingham 42 3 **78 3**
2002-03 Bournemouth 43 1 **43 1**

CONNELL, Alan (F) 13 6
H: 6 0 W: 10 10 b.London 5-2-83
Source: Ipswich T Trainee.
2002-03 Bournemouth 13 6 **13 6**

CUMMINGS, Warren (D) 47 1
H: 5 8 W: 11 05 b.Aberdeen 15-10-80
Source: Trainee. *Honours:* Scotland Under-21, 1 full cap.
1999–2000 Chelsea 0 0
2000-01 Chelsea 0 0
2000-01 *Bournemouth* 10 1
2000-01 *WBA* 3 0
2001-02 Chelsea 0 0
2001-02 *WBA* 14 0 **17 0**
2002-03 Chelsea 0 0
2002-03 Bournemouth 20 0 **30 1**

ELLIOTT, Wade (M) 138 24
H: 5 10 W: 11 01 b.Southampton 14-12-78
1999–2000 Bournemouth 12 3
2000-01 Bournemouth 36 9
2001-02 Bournemouth 46 8
2002-03 Bournemouth 44 4 **138 24**

ERIBENNE, Chukkie* (F) 47 1
H: 5 10 W: 11 12 b.London 2-11-80
Source: Trainee.
1997–98 Coventry C 0 0
1998–99 Coventry C 0 0
1999–2000 Coventry C 0 0
2000-01 Bournemouth 17 1
2001-02 Bournemouth 24 0
2002-03 Bournemouth 6 0 **47 1**

FEENEY, Warren (F) 68 24
H: 5 10 W: 11 05 b.Belfast 17-1-81
Source: Trainee. *Honours:* Northern Ireland Schools, Youth, Under-21, 3 full caps.
1997–98 Leeds U 0 0
1998–99 Leeds U 0 0
1999–2000 Leeds U 0 0
2000-01 Leeds U 0 0
2000-01 *Bournemouth* 10 4
2001-02 Bournemouth 37 13
2002-03 Bournemouth 21 7 **68 24**

FLETCHER, Carl (M) 147 15
H: 5 10 W: 11 07 b.Camberley 7-4-80
Source: Trainee.
1997–98 Bournemouth 1 0
1998–99 Bournemouth 1 0
1999–2000 Bournemouth 25 3
2000-01 Bournemouth 43 6
2001-02 Bournemouth 35 5
2002-03 Bournemouth 42 1 **147 15**

FLETCHER, Steve# (F) 380 69
H: 6 2 W: 14 09 b.Hartlepool 26-7-72
Source: Trainee.
1990–91 Hartlepool U 14 2
1991–92 Hartlepool U 18 2 **32 4**
1992–93 Bournemouth 31 4
1993–94 Bournemouth 36 6
1994–95 Bournemouth 40 6
1995–96 Bournemouth 7 1
1996–97 Bournemouth 35 7
1997–98 Bournemouth 42 12
1998–99 Bournemouth 39 8
1999–2000 Bournemouth 36 7
2000-01 Bournemouth 45 9
2001-02 Bournemouth 2 0
2002-03 Bournemouth 35 5 **348 65**

FOYEWA, Amos‡ (F) 9 0
H: 5 8 W: 12 00 b.Nigeria 26-12-81
2001-02 Bournemouth 8 0
2002-03 Bournemouth 1 0 **9 0**

GRANT, Peter# (M) 475 19
H: 5 8 W: 11 07 b.Bellshill 30-8-65
Source: Celtic BC. *Honours:* Scotland Schools, Youth, Under-21, B, 2 full caps.
1982–83 Celtic 0 0
1983–84 Celtic 3 0
1984–85 Celtic 20 4
1985–86 Celtic 30 1
1986–87 Celtic 37 1
1987–88 Celtic 37 2
1988–89 Celtic 21 0
1989–90 Celtic 26 0
1990–91 Celtic 27 0
1991–92 Celtic 22 0
1992–93 Celtic 31 2
1993–94 Celtic 28 0
1994–95 Celtic 28 2
1995–96 Celtic 30 3
1996–97 Celtic 23 0 **363 15**

1997–98 Norwich C 35 3
1998–99 Norwich C 33 0
1999–2000 Norwich C 0 0 **68 3**
1999–2000 Reading 29 1 **29 1**
2000-01 Bournemouth 15 0
2001-02 Bournemouth 0 0
2002-03 Bournemouth 0 0 **15 0**

HAYTER, James (F) 187 31
H: 5 9 W: 10 13 b.Newport (IW) 9-4-79
Source: Trainee.
1996–97 Bournemouth 2 0
1997–98 Bournemouth 5 0
1998–99 Bournemouth 20 2
1999–2000 Bournemouth 31 2
2000-01 Bournemouth 40 11
2001-02 Bournemouth 44 7
2002-03 Bournemouth 45 9 **187 31**

HOLMES, Derek (F) 112 26
H: 6 2 W: 13 07 b.Lanark 18-10-78
Source: Royal Albert.
1995–96 Hearts 0 0
1996–97 Hearts 1 0
1997–98 Hearts 1 1
1997–98 Cowdenbeath 13 5 **13 5**
1998–99 Hearts 6 0 **8 1**
1999–2000 Ross Co 25 8
2000-01 Ross Co 0 0 **25 8**
2001-02 Bournemouth 37 9
2002-03 Bournemouth 29 3 **66 12**

KANDOL, Tresor‡ (F) 33 3
H: 6 0 W: 13 07 b.Banga 30-8-81
Source: Trainee.
1998–99 Luton T 4 0
1999–2000 Luton T 4 0
2000-01 Luton T 13 3 **21 3**
2001-02 Bournemouth 12 0
2002-03 Bournemouth 0 0 **12 0**

MAHER, Shaun# (D) 105 4
H: 6 1 W: 13 02 b.Dublin 20-6-78
Source: Bohemians.
1996–97 Bohemians 2 0
1997–98 Fulham 0 0
1997–98 Bohemians 11 0
1998–99 Bohemians 25 1
1999–2000 Bohemians 28 1
2000-01 Bohemians 0 0 **66 2**
2001-02 Bournemouth 31 0
2002-03 Bournemouth 8 2 **39 2**

McDONALD, Scott (F) 25 2
H: 5 7 W: 12 07 b.Dandenorg 21-8-83
Honours: Australia Youth, Under-20, Under-23.
1998–99 Eastern Pride 3 0 **3 0**
1999–2000 Southampton 0 0
2000-01 Southampton 0 0
2001-02 Southampton 2 0
2002-03 Southampton 0 0 **2 0**
2002-03 *Huddersfield T* 13 1 **13 1**
2002-03 Bournemouth 7 1 **7 1**

MOSS, Neil (G) 89 0
H: 6 2 W: 12 03 b.New Milton 10-5-75
Source: Trainee.
1992–93 Bournemouth 1 0
1993–94 Bournemouth 6 0
1994–95 Bournemouth 8 0
1995–96 Bournemouth 7 0
1995–96 Southampton 0 0
1996–97 Southampton 3 0
1997–98 Southampton 0 0
1997–98 *Gillingham* 10 0 **10 0**
1998–99 Southampton 7 0
1999–2000 Southampton 9 0
2000-01 Southampton 3 0
2001-02 Southampton 2 0
2002-03 Southampton 0 0 **24 0**
2002-03 Bournemouth 33 0 **55 0**

O'CONNOR, Gareth# (F) 121 13
H: 5 10 W: 11 00 b.Dublin 10-11-78
Source: Bohemians.
1998–99 Shamrock R 8 0 **8 0**
1999–2000 Bohemians 22 4 **22 4**
2000-01 Bournemouth 22 1
2001-02 Bournemouth 28 0
2002-03 Bournemouth 41 8 **91 9**

PURCHES, John‡ (M) 0 0
b.Redbridge 12-3-83
2002-03 Bournemouth 0 0

PURCHES, Stephen (M) 119 5
H: 5 11 W: 11 09 b.Ilford 14-1-80
Source: Trainee.

1998–99	West Ham U	0	0		
1999–2000	West Ham U	0	0		
2000-01	Bournemouth	34	0		
2001-02	Bournemouth	41	2		
2002-03	Bournemouth	44	3	**119**	**5**

STEWART, Gareth (G) 84 0
H: 6 0 W: 12 08 b.Preston 3-2-80
Source: Trainee. *Honours:* England Schools, Youth.

1996–97	Blackburn R	0	0		
1997–98	Blackburn R	0	0		
1998–99	Blackburn R	0	0		
1999–2000	Bournemouth	3	0		
2000-01	Bournemouth	35	0		
2001-02	Bournemouth	45	0		
2002-03	Bournemouth	1	0	**84**	**0**

STOCK, Brian (M) 59 4
H: 5 11 W: 11 02 b.Winchester 24-12-81
Source: Trainee. *Honours:* Wales Under-21.

1999–2000	Bournemouth	5	0		
2000-01	Bournemouth	1	0		
2001-02	Bournemouth	26	2		
2002-03	Bournemouth	27	2	**59**	**4**

THOMAS, Danny (M) 52 2
H: 5 7 W: 10 10 b.Leamington Spa 1-5-81
Source: Trainee.

1997–98	Nottingham F	0	0		
1997–98	Leicester C	0	0		
1998–99	Leicester C	0	0		
1999–2000	Leicester C	3	0		
2000-01	Leicester C	0	0		
2001-02	Leicester C	0	0	**3**	**0**
2001-02	Bournemouth	12	0		
2002-03	Bournemouth	37	2	**49**	**2**

TINDALL, Jason# (M) 141 6
H: 6 1 W: 12 13 b.Stepney 15-11-77
Source: Trainee.

1996–97	Charlton Ath	0	0		
1997–98	Charlton Ath	0	0		
1998–99	Bournemouth	17	1		
1999–2000	Bournemouth	8	0		
2000-01	Bournemouth	45	1		
2001-02	Bournemouth	44	3		
2002-03	Bournemouth	27	1	**141**	**6**

YOUNG, Neil# (D) 292 4
H: 5 9 W: 12 00 b.Harlow 31-8-73
Source: Trainee.

1991–92	Tottenham H	0	0		
1992–93	Tottenham H	0	0		
1993–94	Tottenham H	0	0		
1994–95	Bournemouth	32	0		
1995–96	Bournemouth	41	0		
1996–97	Bournemouth	44	0		
1997–98	Bournemouth	44	2		
1998–99	Bournemouth	44	1		
1999–2000	Bournemouth	37	0		
2000-01	Bournemouth	7	0		
2001-02	Bournemouth	11	0		
2002-03	Bournemouth	32	1	**292**	**4**

BRADFORD C

ATHERTON, Peter* (D) 538 11
H: 5 11 W: 13 12 b.Wigan 6-4-70
Source: Trainee. *Honours:* England Schools, Under-21.

1987–88	Wigan Ath	16	0		
1988–89	Wigan Ath	40	1		
1989–90	Wigan Ath	46	0		
1990–91	Wigan Ath	46	0		
1991–92	Wigan Ath	1	0	**149**	**1**
1991–92	Coventry C	35	0		
1992–93	Coventry C	39	0		
1993–94	Coventry C	40	0	**114**	**0**
1994–95	Sheffield W	41	1		
1995–96	Sheffield W	36	0		
1996–97	Sheffield W	37	2		
1997–98	Sheffield W	27	3		
1998–99	Sheffield W	38	2		
1999–2000	Sheffield W	35	1	**214**	**9**
2000-01	Bradford C	25	0		
2000-01	*Birmingham C*	10	0	**10**	**0**
2001-02	Bradford C	1	0		
2002-03	Bradford C	25	1	**51**	**1**

BOWER, Mark (D) 86 4
H: 5 10 W: 11 00 b.Bradford 23-1-80
Source: Trainee.

1997–98	Bradford C	3	0		
1998–99	Bradford C	0	0		
1999–2000	Bradford C	0	0		
1999–2000	*York C*	15	1		
2000-01	Bradford C	0	0		
2000-01	*York C*	21	1	**36**	**2**
2001-02	Bradford C	10	2		
2002-03	Bradford C	37	0	**50**	**2**

CADAMARTERI, Danny (F) 132 16
H: 5 9 W: 12 10 b.Bradford 12-10-79
Source: Trainee. *Honours:* England Youth, Under-21.

1996–97	Everton	1	0		
1997–98	Everton	26	4		
1998–99	Everton	30	4		
1999–2000	Everton	17	1		
1999–2000	*Fulham*	5	1	**5**	**1**
2000-01	Everton	16	4		
2001-02	Everton	3	0	**93**	**13**
2001-02	Bradford C	14	2		
2002-03	Bradford C	20	0	**34**	**2**

DANKS, Mark‡ (F) 3 0
H: 5 9 W: 10 09 b.Worley 8-2-84
Source: Wolverhampton W Scholar.

2002-03	Wolverhampton W	0	0		
2002-03	Bradford C	3	0	**3**	**0**

DAVISON, Aidan* (G) 221 0
H: 6 1 W: 13 02 b.Sedgefield 11-5-68
Source: Billingham Synthonia. *Honours:* Northern Ireland B, 3 full caps.

1987–88	Notts Co	0	0		
1988–89	Notts Co	1	0		
1989–90	Notts Co	0	0	**1**	**0**
1989–90	*Leyton Orient*	0	0		
1989–90	Bury	0	0		
1989–90	*Chester C*	0	0		
1990–91	Bury	0	0		
1990–91	*Blackpool*	0	0		
1991–92	Millwall	33	0		
1992–93	Millwall	1	0	**34**	**0**
1993–94	Bolton W	31	0		
1994–95	Bolton W	4	0		
1995–96	Bolton W	2	0		
1996–97	Bolton W	0	0	**37**	**0**
1996–97	*Ipswich T*	0	0		
1996–97	*Hull C*	9	0	**9**	**0**
1996–97	Bradford C	10	0		
1997–98	Grimsby T	42	0		
1998–99	Grimsby T	35	0		
1999–2000	Grimsby T	0	0	**77**	**0**
1999–2000	Sheffield U	2	0	**2**	**0**
1999–2000	Bradford C	6	0		
2000-01	Bradford C	2	0		
2001-02	Bradford C	9	0		
2002-03	Bradford C	34	0	**61**	**0**

EMANUEL, Lewis (D) 38 0
H: 5 8 W: 12 01 b.Bradford 14-10-83
Source: Scholar. *Honours:* England Youth.

2001-02	Bradford C	9	0		
2002-03	Bradford C	29	0	**38**	**0**

EVANS, Paul (M) 357 60
H: 5 8 W: 12 06 b.Oswestry 1-9-74
Source: Trainee. *Honours:* Wales Youth, Under-21, 1 full cap.

1991–92	Shrewsbury T	2	0		
1992–93	Shrewsbury T	4	0		
1993–94	Shrewsbury T	13	0		
1994–95	Shrewsbury T	32	5		
1995–96	Shrewsbury T	34	3		
1996–97	Shrewsbury T	42	6		
1997–98	Shrewsbury T	39	6		
1998–99	Shrewsbury T	32	6	**198**	**26**
1998–99	Brentford	14	3		
1999–2000	Brentford	33	7		
2000-01	Brentford	43	7		
2001-02	Brentford	40	14	**130**	**31**
2002-03	Bradford C	19	2	**19**	**2**
2002-03	*Blackpool*	10	1	**10**	**1**

FISHLOCK, Craig* (M) 0 0
H: 5 10 W: 11 09 b.Middlesbrough 23-2-83
Source: Scholar.

2002-03	Bradford C	0	0		

FORREST, Danny (M) 17 3
b.Keighley 23-10-84
Source: Trainee. *Honours:* England Youth.

2002-03	Bradford C	17	3	**17**	**3**

FRANCIS, Simon (M) 25 1
b.Nottingham 16-2-85
Source: Scholar. *Honours:* England Youth.

2002-03	Bradford C	25	1	**25**	**1**

GRAY, Andy (M) 145 17
H: 6 2 W: 13 00 b.Harrogate 15-11-77
Source: Trainee. *Honours:* Scotland Youth, 2 full caps.

1995–96	Leeds U	15	0		
1996–97	Leeds U	7	0		
1997–98	Leeds U	0	0		
1997–98	*Bury*	6	1	**6**	**1**
1998–99	Leeds U	0	0	**22**	**0**
1998–99	Nottingham F	8	0		
1998–99	*Preston NE*	5	0	**5**	**0**
1998–99	*Oldham Ath*	4	0	**4**	**0**
1999–2000	Nottingham F	22	0		
2000-01	Nottingham F	18	0		
2001-02	Nottingham F	16	1	**64**	**1**
2002-03	Bradford C	44	15	**44**	**15**

JACOBS, Wayne (D) 468 18
H: 5 9 W: 11 02 b.Sheffield 3-2-69
Source: Apprentice.

1986–87	Sheffield W	0	0		
1987–88	Sheffield W	6	0	**6**	**0**
1987–88	Hull C	6	0		
1988–89	Hull C	33	0		
1989–90	Hull C	46	3		
1990–91	Hull C	19	1		
1991–92	Hull C	25	0		
1992–93	Hull C	0	0	**129**	**4**
1993–94	Rotherham U	42	2	**42**	**2**
1994–95	Bradford C	38	1		
1995–96	Bradford C	28	0		
1996–97	Bradford C	39	3		
1997–98	Bradford C	36	2		
1998–99	Bradford C	44	3		
1999–2000	Bradford C	24	0		
2000-01	Bradford C	21	2		
2001-02	Bradford C	38	1		
2002-03	Bradford C	23	0	**291**	**12**

JORGENSEN, Claus# (M) 137 26
H: 5 11 W: 11 00 b.Holstebro 27-4-76
Source: Resen-Humlum, Struer BK, Holstebro, Aarhus, AC Horsens.

1999–2000	Bournemouth	44	6		
2000-01	Bournemouth	43	8	**87**	**14**
2001-02	Bradford C	18	1		
2002-03	Bradford C	32	11	**50**	**12**

JUANJO* (F) 134 14
H: 5 9 W: 10 08 b.Barcelona 4-5-77

1997–98	Barcelona B	36	4	**36**	**4**
1998–99	Hearts	11	0		
1999–2000	Hearts	15	3		
2000-01	Hearts	37	4		
2001-02	Hearts	9	2	**72**	**9**
2001-02	Bradford C	17	1		
2002-03	Bradford C	9	0	**26**	**1**

KEARNEY, Tom (M) 9 0
H: 5 11 W: 10 08 b.Liverpool 7-10-81
Source: Trainee.

1999–2000	Everton	0	0		
2000-01	Everton	0	0		
2001-02	Everton	0	0		
2001-02	Bradford C	5	0		
2002-03	Bradford C	4	0	**9**	**0**

LEE, Andy* (M) 2 0
H: 5 8 W: 10 06 b.Bradford 18-8-82
Source: Scholar.

2001-02	Bradford C	1	0		
2002-03	Bradford C	1	0	**2**	**0**

MAGNUSSON, Stefan (G) 0 0
b.Iceland 5-9-80
From Farum

2002-03	Bradford C	0	0		

McHUGH, Frazer† (M) 21 0
H: 5 9 W: 12 05 b.Nottingham 14-7-81
Source: Trainee.

1998–99	Swindon T	1	0		
1999–2000	Swindon T	14	0		
2000-01	Swindon T	4	0		
2001-02	Swindon T	0	0	**19**	**0**

From Tamworth, Gainsborough T

2002-03	Bradford C	2	0	**2**	**0**

MOLENAAR, Robert* (D) 246 10
H: 6 2 W: 14 04 b.Zaandam 27-2-69

1992–93	Volendam	28	2		
1993–94	Volendam	27	1		
1994–95	Volendam	31	0		
1995–96	Volendam	21	0		

1996–97	Volendam	17	0	**124**	**3**
1996–97	Leeds U	12	1		
1997–98	Leeds U	22	2		
1998–99	Leeds U	17	2		
1999–2000	Leeds U	0	0		
2000–01	Leeds U	0	0	**51**	**5**
2000–01	Bradford C	21	1		
2001–02	Bradford C	21	0		
2002–03	Bradford C	29	1	**71**	**2**

MORGAN, Robert* (D) 0 0
H: 6 2 W: 12 07 b.Bradford 16-1-83
Source: Scholar.

2002–03	Bradford C	0	0		

MUIRHEAD, Ben (M) 8 0
H: 5 9 W: 11 02 b.Doncaster 5-1-83
Source: Trainee. *Honours:* England Youth.

1999–2000	Manchester U	0	0		
2000–01	Manchester U	0	0		
2001–02	Manchester U	0	0		
2002–03	Manchester U	0	0		
2002–03	Bradford C	8	0	**8**	**0**

MYERS, Andy* (D) 181 5
H: 5 10 W: 13 12 b.Hounslow 3-11-73
Source: Trainee. *Honours:* England Schools, Youth, Under-21.

1990–91	Chelsea	3	0		
1991–92	Chelsea	11	1		
1992–93	Chelsea	3	0		
1993–94	Chelsea	6	0		
1994–95	Chelsea	10	0		
1995–96	Chelsea	20	0		
1996–97	Chelsea	18	1		
1997–98	Chelsea	12	0		
1998–99	Chelsea	1	0	**84**	**2**
1999–2000	Bradford C	13	0		
1999–2000	*Portsmouth*	8	0	**8**	**0**
2000–01	Bradford C	20	1		
2001–02	Bradford C	32	2		
2002–03	Bradford C	24	0	**89**	**3**

PENFORD, Thomas§ (M) 3 0
b.Leeds 5-1-85
Source: Scholar.

2002–03	Bradford C	3	0	**3**	**0**

REID, Paul (M) 106 17
H: 5 10 W: 10 10 b.Sydney 6-7-79
Honours: Australia Under-20.

1998–99	Wollongong Wolves	22	2		
1999–2000	Wollongong Wolves	31	3		
2000–01	Wollongong Wolves	30	7		
2001–02	Wollongong Wolves	15	3	**98**	**15**
2002–03	Bradford C	8	2	**8**	**2**

SANASY, Kevin§ (M) 1 0
b.Leeds 2-11-84
Source: Scholar.

2002–03	Bradford C	1	0	**1**	**0**

STANDING, Michael (M) 24 2
H: 5 10 W: 10 05 b.Shoreham 20-3-81
Source: Trainee. *Honours:* England Schools.

1997–98	Aston Villa	0	0		
1998–99	Aston Villa	0	0		
1999–2000	Aston Villa	0	0		
2000–01	Aston Villa	0	0		
2001–02	Aston Villa	0	0		
2001–02	Bradford C	0	0		
2002–03	Bradford C	24	2	**24**	**2**

TOD, Andy (D) 275 43
H: 5 10 W: 11 13 b.Dunfermline 4-11-71
Source: Kelty Hearts.

1993–94	Dunfermline Ath	22	11		
1994–95	Dunfermline Ath	35	6		
1995–96	Dunfermline Ath	36	5		
1996–97	Dunfermline Ath	35	4		
1997–98	Dunfermline Ath	35	6		
1998–99	Dunfermline Ath	25	1		
1999–2000	Dunfermline Ath	30	1		
2000–01	Dunfermline Ath	8	0		
2000–01	*Stockport Co*	11	3	**11**	**3**
2001–02	Dunfermline Ath	0	0	**226**	**34**
2001–02	Bradford C	30	4		
2001–02	*Hearts*	3	1	**3**	**1**
2002–03	Bradford C	5	1	**35**	**5**

TOMLINSON, Graeme‡ (F) 136 20
H: 5 10 W: 12 00 b.Watford 10-12-75
Source: Trainee.

1993–94	Bradford C	17	6		
1994–95	Manchester U	0	0		
1995–96	Manchester U	0	0		
1995–96	*Luton T*	7	0	**7**	**0**
1996–97	Manchester U	0	0		
1997–98	Manchester U	0	0		
1997–98	*Bournemouth*	7	1	**7**	**1**
1997–98	*Millwall*	3	1	**3**	**1**
1998–99	Macclesfield T	28	4		
1999–2000	Macclesfield T	18	2	**46**	**6**
2000–01	Exeter C	24	1		
2001–02	Exeter C	32	5	**56**	**6**
2002–03	Bradford C	0	0	**17**	**6**

UHLENBEEK, Gus* (D) 289 9
H: 5 8 W: 11 11 b.Paramaribo 20-8-70

1990–91	Ajax	2	0		
1991–92	Ajax	0	0	**2**	**0**
1992–93	Cambuur	24	0		
1993–94	Cambuur	15	0	**39**	**0**
1994–95	TOPS SV	22	3	**22**	**3**
1995–96	Ipswich T	40	4		
1996–97	Ipswich T	38	0		
1997–98	Ipswich T	11	0	**89**	**4**
1998–99	Fulham	23	1		
1999–2000	Fulham	16	0	**39**	**1**
2000–01	Sheffield U	31	0		
2001–02	Sheffield U	20	0	**51**	**0**
2001–02	*Walsall*	5	0	**5**	**0**
2002–03	Bradford C	42	1	**42**	**1**

WALSH, Gary* (G) 238 0
H: 6 3 W: 14 03 b.Wigan 21-3-68
Source: Apprentice. *Honours:* England Under-21.

1984–85	Manchester U	0	0		
1985–86	Manchester U	0	0		
1986–87	Manchester U	14	0		
1987–88	Manchester U	16	0		
1988–89	Manchester U	0	0		
1988–89	*Airdrieonians*	3	0	**3**	**0**
1989–90	Manchester U	0	0		
1990–91	Manchester U	5	0		
1991–92	Manchester U	2	0		
1992–93	Manchester U	0	0		
1993–94	Manchester U	3	0		
1993–94	*Oldham Ath*	6	0	**6**	**0**
1994–95	Manchester U	10	0	**50**	**0**
1995–96	Middlesbrough	32	0		
1996–97	Middlesbrough	12	0		
1997–98	Middlesbrough	0	0		
1997–98	Bradford C	35	0		
1998–99	Bradford C	46	0		
1999–2000	Bradford C	11	0		
2000–01	Bradford C	19	0		
2000–01	*Middlesbrough*	3	0	**47**	**0**
2001–02	Bradford C	18	0		
2002–03	Bradford C	3	0	**132**	**0**

WARD, Ashley (F) 355 105
H: 6 0 W: 11 00 b.Manchester 24-11-70
Source: Trainee.

1989–90	Manchester C	1	0		
1990–91	Manchester C	0	0	**1**	**0**
1990–91	*Wrexham*	4	2	**4**	**2**
1991–92	Leicester C	10	0		
1992–93	Leicester C	0	0	**10**	**0**
1992–93	*Blackpool*	2	1	**2**	**1**
1992–93	Crewe Alex	20	4		
1993–94	Crewe Alex	25	13		
1994–95	Crewe Alex	16	8	**61**	**25**
1994–95	Norwich C	25	8		
1995–96	Norwich C	28	10	**53**	**18**
1995–96	Derby Co	7	1		
1996–97	Derby Co	30	8		
1997–98	Derby Co	3	0	**40**	**9**
1997–98	Barnsley	29	8		
1998–99	Barnsley	17	12	**46**	**20**
1998–99	Blackburn R	17	5		
1999–2000	Blackburn R	37	8	**54**	**13**
2000–01	Bradford C	33	4		
2001–02	Bradford C	27	10		
2002–03	Bradford C	24	3	**84**	**17**

WETHERALL, David (D) 294 17
H: 6 3 W: 13 12 b.Sheffield 14-3-71
Source: School. *Honours:* England Schools.

1989–90	Sheffield W	0	0		
1990–91	Sheffield W	0	0		
1991–92	Leeds U	1	0		
1992–93	Leeds U	13	1		
1993–94	Leeds U	32	1		
1994–95	Leeds U	38	3		
1995–96	Leeds U	34	4		
1996–97	Leeds U	29	0		
1997–98	Leeds U	34	3		
1998–99	Leeds U	21	0	**202**	**12**
1999–2000	Bradford C	38	2		
2000–01	Bradford C	18	1		
2001–02	Bradford C	19	2		
2002–03	Bradford C	17	0	**92**	**5**

Scholars
Beach, Nicholas; Bentham, Craig M; Brodie, Keith J; Denton, Sam; Doherty, Anthony PJ; Ekoku, Daniel C; Ellis, Daniel L; Flynn, Liam D; Forrest, Daniel PH; Keehan, Kevin FA; McGahey, Phillip M; Penford, Thomas J; Richardson, Luke C; Sanasy, Kevin R; Swift, John M; Wright, Jake M

Non-Contract
McHugh, Frazer

Players who do not hold a current contract but their registration has been retained by the club
Hutton, Peter; Tomlinson, Paul; Holmes, Richard

BRENTFORD

ALLEN-PAGE, Danny (M) 0 0
H: 5 8 W: 10 13 b.London 30-10-83
Source: Trainee.

2002–03	Brentford	0	0		

BLACKMAN, Lloyd (F) 1 0
H: 5 10 W: 12 03 b.London 24-9-83
Source: Trainee.

2002–03	Brentford	1	0	**1**	**0**

CONSTANTINE, Leon* (F) 30 3
H: 6 2 W: 11 10 b.Hackney 24-2-78
Source: Edgware T.

2000–01	Millwall	1	0		
2001–02	Millwall	0	0	**1**	**0**
2001–02	*Leyton Orient*	10	3	**10**	**3**
2001–02	*Partick T*	2	0	**2**	**0**
2002–03	Brentford	17	0	**17**	**0**

DOBSON, Michael (D) 111 1
H: 5 11 W: 12 04 b.Isleworth 9-4-81
Source: Trainee.

1999–2000	Brentford	0	0		
2000–01	Brentford	26	0		
2001–02	Brentford	39	0		
2002–03	Brentford	46	1	**111**	**1**

EVANS, Stephen (M) 33 3
H: 6 1 W: 11 06 b.Caerphilly 25-9-80
Source: Trainee. *Honours:* Wales Youth, Under-21.

1998–99	Crystal Palace	4	0		
1999–2000	Crystal Palace	1	0		
2000–01	Crystal Palace	1	0		
2001–02	Crystal Palace	0	0	**6**	**0**
2001–02	*Swansea C*	4	0	**4**	**0**
2001–02	Brentford	0	0		
2002–03	Brentford	23	3	**23**	**3**

FIELDWICK, Lee (D) 7 0
H: 5 11 W: 11 08 b.Croydon 6-9-82
Source: Trainee.

2001–02	Brentford	0	0		
2002–03	Brentford	7	0	**7**	**0**

FRAMPTON, Andrew (D) 43 0
H: 5 11 W: 10 10 b.Wimbledon 3-9-79
Source: Trainee.

1998–99	Crystal Palace	6	0		
1999–2000	Crystal Palace	9	0		
2000–01	Crystal Palace	10	0		
2001–02	Crystal Palace	2	0		
2002–03	Crystal Palace	1	0	**28**	**0**
2002–03	Brentford	15	0	**15**	**0**

FULLARTON, Jamie# (M) 210 5
H: 5 10 W: 10 06 b.Bellshill 20-7-75

1991–92	St Mirren	1	0		
1992–93	St Mirren	25	0		
1993–94	St Mirren	37	0		
1994–95	St Mirren	17	1		
1995–96	St Mirren	22	2	**102**	**3**
1996–97	Bastia	17	0	**17**	**0**
1997–98	Crystal Palace	25	1		
1998–99	Crystal Palace	7	0		
1998–99	*Bolton W*	1	0	**1**	**0**
1999–2000	Crystal Palace	13	0		
2000–01	Crystal Palace	2	0	**47**	**1**
2000–01	Dundee U	5	0		
2001–02	Dundee U	11	0	**16**	**0**
2002–03	Brentford	27	1	**27**	**1**

GOTTSKALKSSON, Olafur‡ (G) 304 0
H: 6 3 W: 13 12 b.Keflavik 12-3-68
Honours: Iceland 9 full caps.

1988	IA Akranes	18	0		
1989	IA Akranes	15	0	**33**	**0**
1990	KR	18	0		
1991	KR	18	0		

1992	KR	18	0		
1993	KR	17	0	**71**	**0**
1994	Keflavik	18	0		
1995	Keflavik	17	0		
1996	Keflavik	18	0		
1997	Keflavik	10	0	**63**	**0**
1997–98	Hibernian	16	0		
1998–99	Hibernian	36	0		
1999–2000	Hibernian	0	0		
2000-01	Hibernian	12	0	**64**	**0**
2000-01	Brentford	45	0		
2001-02	Brentford	28	0		
2002-03	Brentford	0	0	**73**	**0**

HUGHES, Stephen (F) **3** **0**
H: 6 1 W: 12 10 b.London 26-1-84
Source: Trainee.

2002-03	Brentford	3	0	**3**	**0**

HUNT, Steve (M) **80** **11**
H: 5 7 W: 12 06 b.Port Laoise 1-8-80
Source: Trainee.

1999–2000	Crystal Palace	3	0		
2000-01	Crystal Palace	0	0	**3**	**0**
2001-02	Brentford	35	4		
2002-03	Brentford	42	7	**77**	**11**

HUTCHINSON, Eddie (M) **39** **0**
H: 6 1 W: 12 07 b.Kingston 23-2-82
Source: Sutton U.

2000-01	Brentford	7	0		
2001-02	Brentford	9	0		
2002-03	Brentford	23	0	**39**	**0**

JULIAN, Alan (G) **3** **0**
H: 6 2 W: 13 07 b.Ashford 11-3-83
Source: Trainee.

2001-02	Brentford	0	0		
2002-03	Brentford	3	0	**3**	**0**

LOVETT, Jay* (D) **28** **0**
H: 6 2 W: 12 05 b.Brighton 22-1-78
Source: Crawley T.

2000-01	Brentford	25	0		
2001-02	Brentford	2	0		
2002-03	Brentford	1	0	**28**	**0**

MARSHALL, Scott* (D) **130** **5**
H: 6 1 W: 12 05 b.Edinburgh 1-5-73
Source: Trainee. *Honours:* Scotland Youth, Under-21.

1992–93	Arsenal	2	0		
1993–94	Arsenal	0	0		
1993–94	*Rotherham U*	10	1	**10**	**1**
1993–94	*Oxford U*	0	0		
1994–95	Arsenal	0	0		
1994–95	*Sheffield U*	17	0	**17**	**0**
1995–96	Arsenal	11	1		
1996–97	Arsenal	8	0		
1997–98	Arsenal	3	0	**24**	**1**
1998–99	Southampton	2	0		
1998–99	Celtic	2	0	**2**	**0**
1999–2000	Southampton	0	0	**2**	**0**
1999–2000	Brentford	22	2		
2000-01	Brentford	29	0		
2001-02	Brentford	0	0		
2002-03	Brentford	24	1	**75**	**3**

O'CONNOR, Kevin (F) **87** **6**
H: 5 11 W: 12 00 b.Blackburn 24-2-82
Source: Trainee. *Honours:* Eire Under-21.

1999–2000	Brentford	6	0		
2000-01	Brentford	11	1		
2001-02	Brentford	25	0		
2002-03	Brentford	45	5	**87**	**6**

PETERS, Mark (F) **11** **1**
H: 5 8 W: 10 10 b.Frimley 4-10-83
Source: Scholar.

2000-01	Southampton	0	0		
2001-02	Southampton	0	0		
2001-02	Brentford	0	0		
2002-03	Brentford	11	1	**11**	**1**

REHMAN, Riz* (M) **0** **0**
H: 5 8 W: 11 00 b.London 19-11-82
Source: Trainee.

2002-03	Brentford	0	0		

ROGET, Leo (D) **166** **8**
H: 6 1 W: 12 02 b.Ilford 1-8-77
Source: Trainee.

1995–96	Southend U	8	1		
1996–97	Southend U	25	0		
1997–98	Southend U	11	0		
1998–99	Southend U	14	0		
1999–2000	Southend U	36	2		
2000-01	Southend U	26	4	**120**	**7**
2000-01	Stockport Co	9	0		
2001-02	Stockport Co	22	1	**31**	**1**
2001-02	*Reading*	1	0	**1**	**0**
2002-03	Brentford	14	0	**14**	**0**

ROWLANDS, Martin* (M) **149** **20**
H: 5 9 W: 10 10 b.Hammersmith 8-2-79
Source: Farnborough T. *Honours:* Eire Under-21.

1998–99	Brentford	36	4		
1999–2000	Brentford	40	6		
2000-01	Brentford	32	2		
2001-02	Brentford	23	7		
2002-03	Brentford	18	1	**149**	**20**

SMITH, Jay (M) **29** **0**
H: 5 11 W: 11 07 b.Hammersmith 29-12-81
Source: Trainee.

2000-01	Brentford	3	0		
2001-02	Brentford	0	0		
2002-03	Brentford	26	0	**29**	**0**

SMITH, Paul (G) **63** **0**
H: 6 4 W: 14 02 b.Epsom 17-12-79

1998–99	Charlton Ath	0	0		
1998–99	*Brentford*	0	0		
1999–2000	Charlton Ath	0	0		
From Carshalton Ath.					
2000-01	Brentford	2	0		
2001-02	Brentford	18	0		
2002-03	Brentford	43	0	**63**	**0**

SOMNER, Matt (D) **43** **1**
H: 6 0 W: 13 00 b.Isleworth 8-12-82
Source: Trainee.

2000-01	Brentford	3	0		
2001-02	Brentford	0	0		
2002-03	Brentford	40	1	**43**	**1**

SONKO, Ibrahima (D) **37** **5**
H: 6 3 W: 13 07 b.Bignola 22-1-81

2002-03	Brentford	37	5	**37**	**5**

TABB, Jay (M) **10** **0**
H: 5 5 W: 9 07 b.Tooting 21-2-84
Source: Trainee.

2000-01	Brentford	2	0		
2001-02	Brentford	3	0		
2002-03	Brentford	5	0	**10**	**0**

THOMAS, Daniel (M) **0** **0**
b.Shrewsbury 16-6-84
Source: Trainee.

2002-03	Brentford	0	0		

TRAYNOR, Robert (M) **2** **0**
H: 5 9 W: 12 02 b.Burnham 1-11-83
Source: Trainee.

2002-03	Brentford	2	0	**2**	**0**

WILLIAMS, Mark* (F) **72** **4**
H: 5 9 W: 11 00 b.Chatham 19-10-81
Source: Scholar.

2000-01	Brentford	30	2		
2001-02	Brentford	20	1		
2002-03	Brentford	22	1	**72**	**4**

Scholars
Gauci, Dominique V; Hillier, Sean; Lake, Ryan M; Lennie, Joshua; Marchena, Barry J; Matharu, Harpal; McNamara, Steven; Morrison, James; Muldowney, Luke J; Palmer, Jamie; Paterson, Matthew J; Scotchford, Mark N; Wells, Dean T

BRIGHTON & HA

BEASANT, Dave* (G) **773** **0**
H: 6 4 W: 14 04 b.Willesden 20-3-59
Source: Edgware T. *Honours:* England B, 2 full caps.

1979–80	Wimbledon	2	0		
1980–81	Wimbledon	34	0		
1981–82	Wimbledon	46	0		
1982–83	Wimbledon	46	0		
1983–84	Wimbledon	46	0		
1984–85	Wimbledon	42	0		
1985–86	Wimbledon	42	0		
1986–87	Wimbledon	42	0		
1987–88	Wimbledon	40	0	**340**	**0**
1988–89	Newcastle U	20	0	**20**	**0**
1988–89	Chelsea	22	0		
1989–90	Chelsea	38	0		
1990–91	Chelsea	35	0		
1991–92	Chelsea	21	0		
1992–93	Chelsea	17	0		
1992–93	*Grimsby T*	6	0	**6**	**0**
1992–93	*Wolverhampton W*	4	0	**4**	**0**
1993–94	Chelsea	0	0	**133**	**0**
1993–94	Southampton	25	0		
1994–95	Southampton	13	0		
1995–96	Southampton	36	0		
1996–97	Southampton	14	0		
1997–98	Southampton	0	0	**88**	**0**
1997–98	Nottingham F	41	0		
1998–99	Nottingham F	26	0		
1999–2000	Nottingham F	27	0		
2000-01	Nottingham F	45	0	**139**	**0**
2001-02	Portsmouth	27	0	**27**	**0**
2002-03	Bradford C	0	0		
2002-03	Wigan Ath	0	0		
2002-03	Brighton & HA	16	0	**16**	**0**

BLACKWELL, Dean* (D) **233** **3**
H: 6 1 W: 12 09 b.Camden 5-12-69
Source: Trainee. *Honours:* England Under-21.

1988–89	Wimbledon	0	0		
1989–90	Wimbledon	3	0		
1989–90	*Plymouth Arg*	7	0	**7**	**0**
1990–91	Wimbledon	35	0		
1991–92	Wimbledon	4	1		
1992–93	Wimbledon	24	0		
1993–94	Wimbledon	18	0		
1994–95	Wimbledon	0	0		
1995–96	Wimbledon	8	0		
1996–97	Wimbledon	27	0		
1997–98	Wimbledon	35	0		
1998–99	Wimbledon	28	0		
1999–2000	Wimbledon	17	0		
2000-01	Wimbledon	6	0		
2001-02	Wimbledon	0	0		
2002-03	Wimbledon	0	0	**205**	**1**
2002-03	Brighton & HA	21	2	**21**	**2**

BROOKER, Paul# (F) **190** **19**
H: 5 8 W: 10 04 b.Hammersmith 25-11-76
Source: Trainee.

1995–96	Fulham	20	2		
1996–97	Fulham	26	2		
1997–98	Fulham	9	0		
1998–99	Fulham	1	0		
1999–2000	Fulham	0	0	**56**	**4**
1999–2000	*Brighton & HA*	15	2		
2000-01	Brighton & HA	41	3		
2001-02	Brighton & HA	41	4		
2002-03	Brighton & HA	37	6	**134**	**15**

BUTTERS, Guy (D) **373** **27**
H: 6 1 W: 15 09 b.Hillingdon 30-10-69
Source: Trainee. *Honours:* England Under-21.

1988–89	Tottenham H	28	1		
1989–90	Tottenham H	7	0	**35**	**1**
1989–90	*Southend U*	16	3	**16**	**3**
1990–91	Portsmouth	23	0		
1991–92	Portsmouth	33	2		
1992–93	Portsmouth	15	1		
1993–94	Portsmouth	15	1		
1994–95	Portsmouth	24	0		
1994–95	*Oxford U*	3	1	**3**	**1**
1995–96	Portsmouth	37	2		
1996–97	Portsmouth	7	0	**154**	**6**
1996–97	Gillingham	30	0		
1997–98	Gillingham	31	7		
1998–99	Gillingham	23	3		
1999–2000	Gillingham	40	2		
2000-01	Gillingham	12	3		
2001-02	Gillingham	23	1	**159**	**16**
2002-03	Brighton & HA	6	0	**6**	**0**

CARPENTER, Richard (M) **386** **24**
H: 6 0 W: 13 00 b.Sheppey 30-9-72
Source: Trainee.

1990–91	Gillingham	9	1		
1991–92	Gillingham	3	0		
1992–93	Gillingham	28	0		
1993–94	Gillingham	40	3		
1994–95	Gillingham	29	0		
1995–96	Gillingham	12	0		
1996–97	Gillingham	1	0	**122**	**4**
1996–97	Fulham	34	5		
1997–98	Fulham	24	2	**58**	**7**
1998–99	Cardiff C	42	1		
1999–2000	Cardiff C	33	1	**75**	**2**
2000-01	Brighton & HA	42	6		
2001-02	Brighton & HA	45	3		
2002-03	Brighton & HA	44	2	**131**	**11**

CULLIP, Danny (D) **224** **8**
H: 6 0 W: 13 04 b.Ascot 17-9-76
Source: Trainee.

1995–96	Oxford U	0	0		
1996–97	Fulham	29	1		
1997–98	Fulham	21	1	**50**	**2**
1997–98	Brentford	13	0		
1998–99	Brentford	2	0		

1999–2000	Brentford	0	0	**15**	**0**
1999–2000	Brighton & HA	33	2		
2000-01	Brighton & HA	38	2		
2001-02	Brighton & HA	44	0		
2002-03	Brighton & HA	44	2	**159**	**6**

HAMMOND, Dean (M) 4 0

H: 6 1 W: 11 02 b.Hastings 7-3-83

Source: Scholar.

2002-03	Brighton & HA	4	0	**4**	**0**

HARDING, Daniel§ (M) 1 0

b.Gloucester 23-12-83

Source: Scholar.

2002-03	Brighton & HA	1	0	**1**	**0**

HART, Gary (F) 207 36

H: 5 9 W: 12 07 b.Harlow 21-9-76

Source: Stansted.

1998-99	Brighton & HA	44	12		
1999–2000	Brighton & HA	43	9		
2000-01	Brighton & HA	45	7		
2001-02	Brighton & HA	39	4		
2002-03	Brighton & HA	36	4	**207**	**36**

HINSHELWOOD, Adam§ (D) 7 0

b.Oxford 8-1-84

Source: Scholar.

2002-03	Brighton & HA	7	0	**7**	**0**

JONES, Nathan (M) 212 9

H: 5 6 W: 10 10 b.Rhondda 28-5-73

Source: Cardiff C Trainee, Maesteg Park, Ton Pentre, Merthyr T.

1995-96	Luton T	0	0		
Badajoz, Numaicia					
1997-98	Southend U	39	0		
1998-99	Southend U	17	0		
1998-99	*Scarborough*	9	0	**9**	**0**
1999–2000	Southend U	43	2	**99**	**2**
2000-01	Brighton & HA	40	4		
2001-02	Brighton & HA	36	2		
2002-03	Brighton & HA	28	1	**104**	**7**

KITSON, Paul* (F) 274 73

H: 6 0 W: 13 00 b.Murton 9-1-71

Source: Trainee. *Honours:* England Under-21.

1988-89	Leicester C	0	0		
1989-90	Leicester C	13	0		
1990-91	Leicester C	7	0		
1991-92	Leicester C	30	6	**50**	**6**
1991-92	Derby Co	12	4		
1992-93	Derby Co	44	17		
1993-94	Derby Co	41	13		
1994-95	Derby Co	8	2	**105**	**36**
1994-95	Newcastle U	26	8		
1995-96	Newcastle U	7	2		
1996-97	Newcastle U	3	0	**36**	**10**
1996-97	West Ham U	14	8		
1997-98	West Ham U	13	4		
1998-99	West Ham U	17	3		
1999–2000	West Ham U	10	0		
1999–2000	*Charlton Ath*	6	1	**6**	**1**
2000-01	West Ham U	2	0		
2000-01	*Crystal Palace*	4	0	**4**	**0**
2001-02	West Ham U	7	3		
2002-03	West Ham U	0	0	**63**	**18**
2002-03	Brighton & HA	10	2	**10**	**2**

KUIPERS, Michels (G) 95 0

H: 6 2 W: 14 09 b.Amsterdam 26-6-74

1998-99	Bristol R	1	0		
1999–2000	Bristol R	0	0	**1**	**0**
2000-01	Brighton & HA	34	0		
2001-02	Brighton & HA	39	0		
2002-03	Brighton & HA	21	0	**94**	**0**

LEE, David (M) 60 9

H: 5 11 W: 12 12 b.Basildon 28-3-80

Source: Trainee.

1998-99	Tottenham H	0	0		
1999–2000	Tottenham H	0	0		
2000-01	Southend U	42	8	**42**	**8**
2001-02	Hull C	11	1	**11**	**1**
2001-02	Brighton & HA	2	0		
2002-03	Brighton & HA	0	0	**2**	**0**
2002-03	*Bristol R*	5	0	**5**	**0**

MARNEY, Daniel (F) 29 0

H: 5 9 W: 10 12 b.Sidcup 2-10-81

Source: Scholar.

2001-02	Brighton & HA	0	0		
2002-03	Brighton & HA	12	0	**12**	**0**
2002-03	*Southend U*	17	0	**17**	**0**

MAYO, Kerry (D) 243 10

H: 5 9 W: 13 05 b.Cuckfield 21-9-77

Source: Trainee.

1996-97	Brighton & HA	24	0		
1997-98	Brighton & HA	44	6		
1998-99	Brighton & HA	25	1		
1999–2000	Brighton & HA	31	1		
2000-01	Brighton & HA	45	1		
2001-02	Brighton & HA	33	0		
2002-03	Brighton & HA	41	1	**243**	**10**

McARTHUR, Duncan (M) 3 0

H: 5 9 W: 12 06 b.Brighton 6-5-81

Source: Trainee.

1998-99	Brighton & HA	3	0		
1999–2000	Brighton & HA	0	0		
2000-01	Brighton & HA	0	0		
2001-02	Brighton & HA	0	0		
2002-03	Brighton & HA	0	0	**3**	**0**

McPHEE, Christopher (M) 8 0

H: 5 11 W: 11 09 b.Eastbourne 20-3-83

Source: Scholarship.

1999–2000	Brighton & HA	4	0		
2000-01	Brighton & HA	0	0		
2001-02	Brighton & HA	2	0		
2002-03	Brighton & HA	2	0	**8**	**0**

OATWAY, Charlie (M) 300 7

H: 5 7 W: 11 11 b.Hammersmith 28-11-73

Source: Yeading.

1994-95	Cardiff C	30	0		
1995-96	Cardiff C	2	0	**32**	**0**
1995-96	Torquay U	24	0		
1996-97	Torquay U	41	1		
1997-98	Torquay U	2	0	**67**	**1**
1997-98	Brentford	33	0		
1998-99	Brentford	24	0	**57**	**0**
1998-99	*Lincoln C*	3	0	**3**	**0**
1999–2000	Brighton & HA	42	4		
2000-01	Brighton & HA	38	0		
2001-02	Brighton & HA	32	1		
2002-03	Brighton & HA	29	1	**141**	**6**

PACKHAM, Will* (G) 2 0

H: 6 2 W: 13 02 b.Brighton 13-1-81

Source: Trainee.

1999–2000	Brighton & HA	0	0		
2000-01	Brighton & HA	1	0		
2001-02	Brighton & HA	1	0		
2002-03	Brighton & HA	0	0	**2**	**0**

PETHICK, Robbie# (D) 302 5

H: 5 10 W: 12 02 b.Tavistock 8-9-70

Source: Weymouth.

1993-94	Portsmouth	18	0		
1994-95	Portsmouth	44	1		
1995-96	Portsmouth	38	0		
1996-97	Portsmouth	35	0		
1997-98	Portsmouth	44	2		
1998-99	Portsmouth	10	0	**189**	**3**
1998-99	Bristol R	9	0		
1999–2000	Bristol R	41	2		
2000-01	Bristol R	13	0	**63**	**2**
2001-02	Brighton & HA	24	0		
2002-03	Brighton & HA	26	0	**50**	**0**

PETTERSON, Andy‡ (G) 152 0

H: 6 2 W: 15 02 b.Fremantle 29-9-69

1988-89	Luton T	0	0		
1988-89	*Swindon T*	0	0		
1989-90	Luton T	0	0		
1990-91	Luton T	0	0		
1991-92	Luton T	0	0		
1991-92	*Ipswich T*	0	0		
1992-93	Luton T	14	0		
1992-93	*Ipswich T*	1	0		
1993-94	Luton T	5	0	**19**	**0**
1994-95	Charlton Ath	9	0		
1994-95	*Bradford C*	3	0	**3**	**0**
1995-96	Charlton Ath	9	0		
1995-96	*Ipswich T*	1	0	**2**	**0**
1995-96	*Plymouth Arg*	6	0	**6**	**0**
1995-96	*Colchester U*	5	0	**5**	**0**
1996-97	Charlton Ath	21	0		
1997-98	Charlton Ath	23	0		
1998-99	Charlton Ath	10	0	**72**	**0**
1998-99	Portsmouth	13	0		
1999–2000	Portsmouth	17	0		
1999–2000	*Wolverhampton W*	0	0		
2000-01	Portsmouth	2	0		
2000-01	*Torquay U*	6	0	**6**	**0**
2001-02	Portsmouth	0	0	**32**	**0**
2001-02	WBA	0	0		
2002-03	Bournemouth	0	0		
2002-03	Brighton & HA	7	0	**7**	**0**

PIERCY, John (M) 12 0

H: 5 9 W: 13 00 b.Forest Gate 18-9-79

Source: Trainee. *Honours:* England Youth.

1998-99	Tottenham H	0	0		
1999–2000	Tottenham H	3	0		
2000-01	Tottenham H	5	0		
2001-02	Tottenham H	0	0		
2002-03	Tottenham H	0	0	**8**	**0**
2002-03	Brighton & HA	4	0	**4**	**0**

PITCHER, Geoff (M) 24 2

H: 5 7 W: 11 11 b.Sutton 15-8-75

Source: Millwall Trainee.

1994-95	Watford	4	1		
1995-96	Watford	9	1	**13**	**2**
From Kingstonian.					
1996-97	Colchester U	1	0	**1**	**0**
From Kingstonian.					
2001-02	Brighton & HA	10	0		
2002-03	Brighton & HA	0	0	**10**	**0**

RODGER, Simon* (M) 318 14

H: 5 9 W: 11 05 b.Shoreham 3-10-71

Source: Trainee.

1989-90	Crystal Palace	0	0		
1990-91	Crystal Palace	0	0		
1991-92	Crystal Palace	22	0		
1992-93	Crystal Palace	23	2		
1993-94	Crystal Palace	42	3		
1994-95	Crystal Palace	4	0		
1995-96	Crystal Palace	24	0		
1996-97	Crystal Palace	11	0		
1996-97	*Manchester C*	8	1	**8**	**1**
1996-97	*Stoke C*	5	0	**5**	**0**
1997-98	Crystal Palace	29	2		
1998-99	Crystal Palace	18	1		
1999–2000	Crystal Palace	34	2		
2000-01	Crystal Palace	33	0		
2001-02	Crystal Palace	36	1	**276**	**11**
From Woking.					
2002-03	Brighton & HA	29	2	**29**	**2**

ROGERS, Paul* (M) 366 32

H: 6 0 W: 12 12 b.Portsmouth 21-3-65

Source: Sutton U.

1991-92	Sheffield U	13	0		
1992-93	Sheffield U	27	3		
1993-94	Sheffield U	25	3		
1994-95	Sheffield U	44	4		
1995-96	Sheffield U	16	0	**125**	**10**
1995-96	Notts Co	21	2		
1996-97	Notts Co	1	0	**22**	**2**
1996-97	Wigan Ath	20	3		
1997-98	Wigan Ath	38	0		
1998-99	Wigan Ath	42	2	**100**	**5**
1999–2000	Brighton & HA	45	8		
2000-01	Brighton & HA	45	6		
2001-02	Brighton & HA	25	1		
2002-03	Brighton & HA	4	0	**119**	**15**

VIRGO, Adam (D) 24 0

H: 6 2 W: 13 12 b.Brighton 25-1-83

2000-01	Brighton & HA	6	0		
2001-02	Brighton & HA	6	0		
2002-03	Brighton & HA	3	0	**15**	**0**
2002-03	*Exeter C*	9	0	**9**	**0**

WATSON, Paul (D) 327 20

H: 5 8 W: 11 05 b.Hastings 4-1-75

Source: Trainee.

1992-93	Gillingham	1	0		
1993-94	Gillingham	14	0		
1994-95	Gillingham	39	2		
1995-96	Gillingham	8	0	**62**	**2**
1996-97	Fulham	44	3		
1997-98	Fulham	6	1	**50**	**4**
1997-98	Brentford	25	0		
1998-99	Brentford	12	0	**37**	**0**
1999–2000	Brighton & HA	42	4		
2000-01	Brighton & HA	46	5		
2001-02	Brighton & HA	45	5		
2002-03	Brighton & HA	45	0	**178**	**14**

WILKINSON, Shaun (D) 16 0

H: 5 6 W: 10 08 b.Portsmouth 12-9-81

Source: Scholarship.

1999–2000	Brighton & HA	2	0		
2000-01	Brighton & HA	1	0		
2001-02	Brighton & HA	0	0		
2002-03	Brighton & HA	12	0	**15**	**0**
2002-03	*Chesterfield*	1	0	**1**	**0**

ZAMORA, Bobby (F) 129 76

H: 5 11 W: 11 11 b.Barking 16-1-81

Source: Trainee. *Honours:* England Under-21.

1999–2000	Bristol R	4	0	**4**	**0**
1999–2000	*Brighton & HA*	6	6		
2000-01	Brighton & HA	43	28		
2001-02	Brighton & HA	41	28		
2002-03	Brighton & HA	35	14	**125**	**76**

Scholars

Bartholomew, Philip O; Beck, Daniel G;

Breach, Christopher B; Bridle, Nicholas P; Budd, Darren L; El Abd, Adam; Elphick, Gary; Fillery, Ben M; Greatwich, Christopher R; Harding, Daniel A; Hinshelwood, Adam; May, Christopher; Piper, Matthew T; Watson, Ben C; Windsor, Mark L

Non-Contract

Keeley, John H

Players who do not hold a current contract but their registration has been retained by the club

McArthur, Duncan E

BRISTOL C

ALLEN, James* (F) 0 0
b.Kent 8-10-83
Source: Trainee.
2002-03 West Ham U 0 0
2002-03 Bristol C 0 0

AMANKWAAH, Kevin (D) 50 1
H: 6 0 W: 12 12 b.London 19-5-82
Source: Scholar. *Honours:* England Youth.
1999–2000 Bristol C 5 0
2000-01 Bristol C 14 0
2001-02 Bristol C 24 1
2002-03 Bristol C 1 0 **44 1**
2002-03 *Torquay U* 6 0 **6 0**

ANYINSAH, Joseph (M) 0 0
b.Bristol 8-10-84
Source: Scholar.
2001-02 Bristol C 0 0
2002-03 Bristol C 0 0

BEADLE, Peter* (F) 343 80
H: 6 1 W: 15 10 b.Lambeth 13-5-72
Source: Trainee.
1988–89 Gillingham 2 0
1989–90 Gillingham 10 2
1990–91 Gillingham 22 7
1991–92 Gillingham 33 5 **67 14**
1992–93 Tottenham H 0 0
1992–93 *Bournemouth* 9 2 **9 2**
1993–94 Tottenham H 0 0
1993–94 *Southend U* 8 1 **8 1**
1994–95 Tottenham H 0 0
1994–95 Watford 20 1
1995–96 Watford 3 0 **23 1**
1995–96 Bristol R 27 12
1996–97 Bristol R 42 12
1997–98 Bristol R 40 15 **109 39**
1998–99 Port Vale 23 6 **23 6**
1998–99 Notts Co 14 3
1999–2000 Notts Co 8 0 **22 3**
1999–2000 Bristol C 25 6
2000-01 Bristol C 33 4
2001-02 Bristol C 0 0
2002-03 Bristol C 24 4 **82 14**

BELL, Mickey (D) 505 49
H: 5 7 W: 12 09 b.Newcastle 15-11-71
Source: Trainee.
1989–90 Northampton T 6 0
1990–91 Northampton T 28 0
1991–92 Northampton T 30 4
1992–93 Northampton T 39 5
1993–94 Northampton T 38 0
1994–95 Northampton T 12 1 **153 10**
1994–95 Wycombe W 31 3
1995–96 Wycombe W 41 1
1996–97 Wycombe W 46 2 **118 6**
1997–98 Bristol C 44 10
1998–99 Bristol C 33 5
1999–2000 Bristol C 36 5
2000-01 Bristol C 41 4
2001-02 Bristol C 42 7
2002-03 Bristol C 38 2 **234 33**

BROWN, Aaron (M) 135 8
H: 5 11 W: 12 13 b.Bristol 14-3-80
Source: Trainee. *Honours:* England Schools.
1997–98 Bristol C 0 0
1998–99 Bristol C 14 0
1999–2000 Bristol C 13 2
1999–2000 *Exeter C* 5 1 **5 1**
2000-01 Bristol C 35 2
2001-02 Bristol C 36 1
2002-03 Bristol C 32 2 **130 7**

BROWN, Marvin (F) 36 2
H: 5 9 W: 11 12 b.Bristol 6-7-83
Honours: England Youth.
1999–2000 Bristol C 2 0
2000-01 Bristol C 5 0
2001-02 Bristol C 10 0
2002-03 Bristol C 0 0 **17 0**
2002-03 *Torquay U* 4 0 **4 0**
2002-03 *Cheltenham T* 15 2 **15 2**

BURKE, Andrew‡ (M) 0 0
b.Camden 9-1-83
2000-01 Bristol C 0 0
2001-02 Bristol C 0 0
2002-03 Bristol C 0 0

BURNELL, Joe (D) 114 0
H: 5 8 W: 12 00 b.Bristol 10-10-80
Source: Trainee.
1999–2000 Bristol C 17 0
2000-01 Bristol C 23 0
2001-02 Bristol C 30 0
2002-03 Bristol C 44 0 **114 0**

BUTLER, Tony (D) 374 7
H: 6 1 W: 13 07 b.Stockport 28-9-72
Source: Trainee.
1990–91 Gillingham 6 0
1991–92 Gillingham 5 0
1992–93 Gillingham 41 0
1993–94 Gillingham 27 1
1994–95 Gillingham 33 2
1995–96 Gillingham 36 2 **148 5**
1996–97 Blackpool 42 0
1997–98 Blackpool 37 0
1998–99 Blackpool 20 0 **99 0**
1998–99 Port Vale 4 0
1999–2000 Port Vale 15 0 **19 0**
1999–2000 WBA 7 0
2000-01 WBA 44 1
2001-02 WBA 19 0
2002-03 WBA 0 0 **70 1**
2002-03 Bristol C 38 1 **38 1**

CAREY, Louis (D) 271 4
H: 5 9 W: 12 09 b.Bristol 20-1-77
Source: Trainee. *Honours:* Scotland Under-21.
1995–96 Bristol C 23 0
1996–97 Bristol C 42 0
1997–98 Bristol C 38 0
1998–99 Bristol C 41 0
1999–2000 Bristol C 22 0
2000-01 Bristol C 46 3
2001-02 Bristol C 35 0
2002-03 Bristol C 24 1 **271 4**

CLEVERLEY, Benjamin* (M) 0 0
H: 5 7 W: 10 00 b.Bristol 12-9-81
Source: Scholar.
2001-02 Bristol C 0 0
2002-03 Bristol C 0 0

CLIST, Simon (M) 81 8
H: 5 8 W: 11 05 b.Bournemouth 13-6-81
Source: Tottenham H Trainee.
1999–2000 Bristol C 9 0
2000-01 Bristol C 38 4
2001-02 Bristol C 20 1
2002-03 Bristol C 3 1 **70 6**
2002-03 *Torquay U* 11 2 **11 2**

COLES, Daniel (D) 65 2
H: 6 0 W: 13 05 b.Bristol 31-10-81
Source: Scholarship.
1999–2000 Bristol C 1 0
2000-01 Bristol C 2 0
2001-02 Bristol C 23 0
2002-03 Bristol C 39 2 **65 2**

CORREIA, Albano‡ (F) 0 0
H: 6 2 W: 12 13 b.Guinea Bissau 18-10-81
2000-01 Bristol C 0 0
2001-02 Bristol C 0 0
2002-03 Bristol C 0 0

DOHERTY, Tom# (M) 126 4
H: 5 7 W: 11 12 b.Bristol 17-3-79
Source: Trainee. *Honours:* Northern Ireland 2 full caps.
1997–98 Bristol C 30 2
1998–99 Bristol C 23 1
1999–2000 Bristol C 1 0
2000-01 Bristol C 0 0
2001-02 Bristol C 34 1
2002-03 Bristol C 38 0 **126 4**

FORTUNE, Clayton (D) 11 0
H: 6 0 W: 14 04 b.Forest Gate 10-11-82
Source: Tottenham H Scholar.
2000-01 Bristol C 0 0
2001-02 Bristol C 1 0
2002-03 Bristol C 10 0 **11 0**

HEY, Antoine‡ (M) 0 0
H: 5 11 W: 12 02 b.Berlin 19-9-70
2002-03 Bristol C 0 0

HILL, Matt (D) 133 4
H: 5 7 W: 11 13 b.Bristol 26-3-81
Source: Trainee.
1998–99 Bristol C 3 0
1999–2000 Bristol C 14 0
2000-01 Bristol C 34 0
2001-02 Bristol C 40 1
2002-03 Bristol C 42 3 **133 4**

HULBERT, Robin (M) 75 0
H: 5 8 W: 11 10 b.Plymouth 14-3-80
Source: Trainee. *Honours:* England Youth.
1997–98 Swindon T 1 0
1997–98 *Newcastle U* 0 0
1998–99 Swindon T 16 0
1999–2000 Swindon T 12 0 **29 0**
1999–2000 Bristol C 2 0
2000-01 Bristol C 19 0
2001-02 Bristol C 11 0
2002-03 Bristol C 7 0 **39 0**
2002-03 *Shrewsbury T* 7 0 **7 0**

JONES, Darren (D) 2 0
H: 6 0 W: 14 12 b.Newport 28-8-83
Source: Scholar. *Honours:* Wales Schools, Youth.
2000-01 Bristol C 0 0
2001-02 Bristol C 2 0
2002-03 Bristol C 0 0 **2 0**

LITA, Leroy (F) 15 2
H: 5 7 W: 11 12 b.Congo 28-12-84
Source: Scholar.
2002-03 Bristol C 15 2 **15 2**

LOXTON, Craig (M) 0 0
b.Bath 14-9-84
Source: Scholar.
2001-02 Bristol C 0 0
2002-03 Bristol C 0 0

MATTHEWS, Lee (F) 48 7
H: 5 11 W: 14 08 b.Middlesbrough 16-1-79
Source: Trainee. *Honours:* England Youth.
1995–96 Leeds U 0 0
1996–97 Leeds U 0 0
1997–98 Leeds U 3 0
1998–99 Leeds U 0 0
1998–99 *Notts Co* 5 0 **5 0**
1999–2000 Leeds U 0 0
1999–2000 *Gillingham* 5 0 **5 0**
2000-01 Leeds U 0 0 **3 0**
2000-01 Bristol C 6 3
2001-02 Bristol C 22 3
2002-03 Bristol C 7 1 **35 7**

MERCER, Billy (G) 282 0
H: 6 1 W: 13 02 b.Liverpool 22-5-69
Source: Trainee.
1987–88 Liverpool 0 0
1988–89 Liverpool 0 0
1988–89 Rotherham U 0 0
1989–90 Rotherham U 2 0
1990–91 Rotherham U 13 0
1991–92 Rotherham U 35 0
1992–93 Rotherham U 36 0
1993–94 Rotherham U 17 0
1994–95 Rotherham U 1 0 **104 0**
1994–95 Sheffield U 3 0
1994–95 *Nottingham F* 0 0
1995–96 Sheffield U 1 0 **4 0**
1995–96 Chesterfield 34 0
1996–97 Chesterfield 35 0
1997–98 Chesterfield 36 0
1998–99 Chesterfield 44 0
1999–2000 Chesterfield 0 0 **149 0**
1999–2000 Bristol C 25 0
2000-01 Bristol C 0 0
2001-02 Bristol C 0 0
2002-03 Bristol C 0 0 **25 0**

MILLEN, Keith* (D) 530 26
H: 6 2 W: 13 03 b.Croydon 26-9-66
Source: Juniors.
1984–85 Brentford 17 0
1985–86 Brentford 32 2
1986–87 Brentford 39 2
1987–88 Brentford 40 3
1988–89 Brentford 36 3
1989–90 Brentford 32 0
1990–91 Brentford 32 2
1991–92 Brentford 34 1
1992–93 Brentford 43 4
1993–94 Brentford 0 0 **305 17**

1993–94	Watford	10	0		
1994–95	Watford	31	1		
1995–96	Watford	33	0		
1996–97	Watford	42	2		
1997–98	Watford	38	1		
1998–99	Watford	11	1		
1999–2000	Watford	0	0	**165**	**5**
1999–2000	Bristol C	28	2		
2000-01	Bristol C	29	2		
2001-02	Bristol C	0	0		
2002-03	Bristol C	3	0	**60**	**4**

MURRAY, Scott (M) 228 46

H: 5 7 W: 11 02 b.Aberdeen 26-5-74

Source: Fraserburgh.

1993–94	Aston Villa	0	0		
1994–95	Aston Villa	0	0		
1995–96	Aston Villa	3	0		
1996–97	Aston Villa	1	0		
1997–98	Aston Villa	0	0	**4**	**0**
1997–98	Bristol C	23	0		
1998–99	Bristol C	32	3		
1999–2000	Bristol C	41	6		
2000-01	Bristol C	46	10		
2001-02	Bristol C	37	8		
2002-03	Bristol C	45	19	**224**	**46**

PEACOCK, Lee (F) 276 80

H: 6 0 W: 13 13 b.Paisley 9-10-76

Source: Trainee. *Honours:* Scotland Youth, Under-21.

1993–94	Carlisle U	1	0		
1994–95	Carlisle U	7	0		
1995–96	Carlisle U	22	2		
1996–97	Carlisle U	44	9		
1997–98	Carlisle U	2	0	**76**	**11**
1997–98	Mansfield T	32	5		
1998–99	Mansfield T	45	17		
1999–2000	Mansfield T	12	7	**89**	**29**
1999–2000	Manchester C	8	0	**8**	**0**
2000-01	Bristol C	35	13		
2001-02	Bristol C	31	15		
2002-03	Bristol C	37	12	**103**	**40**

PHILLIPS, Steve (G) 146 0

H: 6 0 W: 13 06 b.Bath 6-5-78

Source: Paulton R.

1996–97	Bristol C	0	0		
1997–98	Bristol C	0	0		
1998–99	Bristol C	15	0		
1999–2000	Bristol C	21	0		
2000-01	Bristol C	42	0		
2001-02	Bristol C	22	0		
2002-03	Bristol C	46	0	**146**	**0**

ROBERTS, Chris (F) 150 35

H: 5 9 W: 13 02 b.Cardiff 22-10-79

Source: Trainee. *Honours:* Wales Youth, Under-21.

1997–98	Cardiff C	11	3		
1998–99	Cardiff C	4	0		
1999–2000	Cardiff C	8	0	**23**	**3**
2000-01	Exeter C	42	8		
2001-02	Exeter C	37	11	**79**	**19**
2001-02	Bristol C	4	0		
2002-03	Bristol C	44	13	**48**	**13**

ROSENIOR, Liam (M) 22 2

H: 5 9 W: 11 05 b.Wandsworth 9-7-84

Source: Scholar.

2001-02	Bristol C	1	0		
2002-03	Bristol C	21	2	**22**	**2**

SHANAHAN, Aaron‡ (M) 0 0

b.Coventry 10-9-82

Source: Coventry C Scholar.

2000-01	Bristol C	0	0		
2001-02	Bristol C	0	0		
2002-03	Bristol C	0	0		

SHEPPARD, Kyle* (D) 0 0

b.Cardiff 4-12-82

Source: Chelsea Scholar.

2000-01	Bristol C	0	0		
2001-02	Bristol C	0	0		
2002-03	Bristol C	0	0		

STOWELL, Mike# (G) 453 0

H: 6 2 W: 14 01 b.Preston 19-4-65

Source: Leyland Motors.

1984–85	Preston NE	0	0		
1985–86	Preston NE	0	0		
1985–86	Everton	0	0		
1986–87	Everton	0	0		
1987–88	*Chester C*	14	0	**14**	**0**
1987–88	*York C*	6	0	**6**	**0**
1987–88	*Manchester C*	14	0	**14**	**0**
1988–89	Everton	0	0		
1988–89	*Port Vale*	7	0	**7**	**0**
1988–89	*Wolverhampton W*	7	0		
1989–90	Everton	0	0		
1989–90	*Preston NE*	2	0	**2**	**0**
1990–91	Wolverhampton W	39	0		
1991–92	Wolverhampton W	46	0		
1992–93	Wolverhampton W	26	0		
1993–94	Wolverhampton W	46	0		
1994–95	Wolverhampton W	37	0		
1995–96	Wolverhampton W	38	0		
1996–97	Wolverhampton W	46	0		
1997–98	Wolverhampton W	35	0		
1998–99	Wolverhampton W	46	0		
1999–2000	Wolverhampton W	18	0		
2000-01	Wolverhampton W	1	0	**385**	**0**
2001-02	Bristol C	25	0		
2002-03	Bristol C	0	0	**25**	**0**

TINNION, Brian# (M) 568 57

H: 6 0 W: 13 05 b.Stanley 23-3-68

Source: Apprentice.

1985–86	Newcastle U	0	0		
1986–87	Newcastle U	3	0		
1987–88	Newcastle U	16	1		
1988–89	Newcastle U	13	1	**32**	**2**
1988–89	Bradford C	14	1		
1989–90	Bradford C	37	5		
1990–91	Bradford C	41	5		
1991–92	Bradford C	26	8		
1992–93	Bradford C	27	3	**145**	**22**
1992–93	Bristol C	11	2		
1993–94	Bristol C	41	5		
1994–95	Bristol C	35	2		
1995–96	Bristol C	30	3		
1996–97	Bristol C	32	1		
1997–98	Bristol C	44	3		
1998–99	Bristol C	35	1		
1999–2000	Bristol C	43	3		
2000-01	Bristol C	42	1		
2001-02	Bristol C	38	3		
2002-03	Bristol C	40	9	**391**	**33**

WOODMAN, Craig (D) 18 0

H: 5 8 W: 11 00 b.Tiverton 22-12-82

Source: Trainee.

1999–2000	Bristol C	0	0		
2000-01	Bristol C	2	0		
2001-02	Bristol C	6	0		
2002-03	Bristol C	10	0	**18**	**0**

Scholars

Allcock, Kyle K; Aubrey, Matthew D; Bailey, Sam; Clayton, Jonathan J; Davies, Christopher J; Donkor, Victor; Folkes, Peter; Gardner, Lee RJ; Gibbs, Stuart J; Harley, Ryan; Hart, Callum L; Hart, David TJ; Hawkins, Darren; Hodgson, Dean A; Jacobs, Thomas; Long, Joe; Lukeman, Daniel M; Metitiri, Kesiena A; Monelle, Grant; Moundi, Didier; Pollinger, Jordan; Simpson, Sekani; Skuse, Cole; Stabler, James N; Trace, Benjamin; Turnor, James M

BRISTOL R

ALLEN, Bradley* (F) 224 56

H: 5 8 W: 11 00 b.Harold Wood 13-9-71

Source: School. *Honours:* England Youth, Under-21.

1988–89	QPR	1	0		
1989–90	QPR	0	0		
1990–91	QPR	10	2		
1991–92	QPR	11	5		
1992–93	QPR	25	10		
1993–94	QPR	21	7		
1994–95	QPR	5	2		
1995–96	QPR	8	1	**81**	**27**
1995–96	Charlton Ath	10	3		
1996–97	Charlton Ath	18	4		
1997–98	Charlton Ath	12	2		
1998–99	Charlton Ath	0	0	**40**	**9**
1998–99	*Colchester U*	4	1	**4**	**1**
1999–2000	Grimsby T	31	8		
2000-01	Grimsby T	21	3		
2001-02	Grimsby T	28	4	**80**	**15**
2002-03	Peterborough U	11	3	**11**	**3**
2002-03	Bristol R	8	1	**8**	**1**

ANDERSON, Ijah (D) 221 4

H: 5 8 W: 10 06 b.Hackney 30-12-75

Source: Tottenham H Trainee.

1994–95	Southend U	0	0		
1995–96	Brentford	25	2		
1996–97	Brentford	46	1		
1997–98	Brentford	17	0		
1998–99	Brentford	38	1		
1999–2000	Brentford	31	0		
2000-01	Brentford	1	0		
2001-02	Brentford	35	0		
2002-03	Brentford	9	0	**202**	**4**
2002-03	*Wycombe W*	5	0	**5**	**0**
2002-03	Bristol R	14	0	**14**	**0**

ARNDALE, Neil§ (D) 2 0

H: 5 7 W: 10 07 b.Bristol 26-4-84

Source: Scholar. *Honours:* England Youth.

2001-02	Bristol R	1	0		
2002-03	Bristol R	1	0	**2**	**0**

ASTAFJEVS, Vitalijs# (M) 289 77

H: 5 11 W: 12 03 b.Riga 3-4-71

Honours: Latvia 93 full caps, 10 goals.

1992	Skonto Riga	21	0		
1993	Skonto Riga	11	5		
1994	Skonto Riga	21	7		
1995	Skonto Riga	28	19		
1996	Skonto Riga	18	12		
1996–97	*FK Austria*	26	1	**26**	**1**
1997	Skonto Riga	14	1		
1998	Skonto Riga	23	7		
1999	Skonto Riga	18	9	**154**	**60**
1999–2000	Bristol R	16	2		
2000-01	Bristol R	41	5		
2001-02	Bristol R	19	1		
2002-03	Bristol R	33	8	**109**	**16**

AUSTIN, Kevin# (D) 283 5

H: 6 0 W: 14 00 b.Hackney 12-2-73

Source: Saffron Walden. *Honours:* Trinidad & Tobago 1 full cap.

1993–94	Leyton Orient	30	0		
1994–95	Leyton Orient	39	2		
1995–96	Leyton Orient	40	1	**109**	**3**
1996–97	Lincoln C	44	1		
1997–98	Lincoln C	46	0		
1998–99	Lincoln C	39	1	**129**	**2**
1999–2000	Barnsley	3	0		
2000-01	Barnsley	0	0	**3**	**0**
2000-01	*Brentford*	3	0	**3**	**0**
2001-02	Cambridge U	6	0	**6**	**0**
2002-03	Bristol R	33	0	**33**	**0**

BARRETT, Adam (D) 134 5

H: 5 10 W: 12 00 b.Dagenham 29-11-79

Source: Leyton Orient Trainee.

1998–99	Plymouth Arg	1	0		
1999–2000	Plymouth Arg	42	3		
2000-01	Plymouth Arg	9	0	**52**	**3**
2000-01	Mansfield T	8	1		
2001-02	Mansfield T	29	0	**37**	**1**
2002-03	Bristol R	45	1	**45**	**1**

BOXALL, Danny (D) 133 1

H: 5 8 W: 11 05 b.Croydon 24-8-77

Source: Trainee. *Honours:* Eire Under-21.

1994–95	Crystal Palace	0	0		
1995–96	Crystal Palace	1	0		
1996–97	Crystal Palace	6	0		
1997–98	Crystal Palace	1	0	**8**	**0**
1997–98	*Oldham Ath*	18	0	**18**	**0**
1998–99	Brentford	38	1		
1999–2000	Brentford	25	0		
2000-01	Brentford	0	0		
2001-02	Brentford	5	0	**68**	**1**
2002-03	Bristol R	39	0	**39**	**0**

BRYANT, Simon (M) 75 2

H: 5 11 W: 13 04 b.Bristol 22-11-82

Source: Scholarship. *Honours:* England Youth.

1999–2000	Bristol R	15	0		
2000-01	Bristol R	30	1		
2001-02	Bristol R	8	0		
2002-03	Bristol R	22	1	**75**	**2**

CARLISLE, Wayne (M) 103 12

H: 5 11 W: 11 06 b.Lisburn 9-9-79

Source: Trainee. *Honours:* Northern Ireland Schools, Youth, Under-21.

1996–97	Crystal Palace	0	0		
1997–98	Crystal Palace	0	0		
1998–99	Crystal Palace	6	0		
1999–2000	Crystal Palace	26	3		
2000-01	Crystal Palace	14	0		
2001-02	Crystal Palace	0	0	**46**	**3**
2001-02	*Swindon T*	11	2	**11**	**2**
2001-02	Bristol R	5	0		
2002-03	Bristol R	41	7	**46**	**7**

CHALLIS, Trevor* (D) 158 1

H: 5 8 W: 11 13 b.Paddington 23-10-75

Source: Trainee. *Honours:* England Youth, Under-21.

1994–95	QPR	0	0		

1995–96 QPR 11 0
1996–97 QPR 2 0
1997–98 QPR 0 0 **13 0**
1998–99 Bristol R 38 0
1999–2000 Bristol R 40 1
2000-01 Bristol R 22 0
2001-02 Bristol R 29 0
2002-03 Bristol R 16 0 **145 1**

CLARKE, Ryan (G) 3 0
H: 6 3 W: 13 00 b.Bristol 30-4-82
Source: Scholar.
2001-02 Bristol R 1 0
2002-03 Bristol R 2 0 **3 0**

GALL, Kevin‡ (M) 50 5
H: 5 9 W: 10 13 b.Merthyr 4-2-82
Source: Trainee. *Honours:* Wales Schools, Youth, Under-21.
1998–99 Newcastle U 0 0
1999–2000 Newcastle U 0 0
2000-01 Newcastle U 0 0
2000-01 Bristol R 10 2
2001-02 Bristol R 31 3
2002-03 Bristol R 9 0 **50 5**

GILROY, David (F) 15 0
H: 5 11 W: 11 05 b.Yeovil 23-10-82
Source: Scholar.
2001-02 Bristol R 4 0
2002-03 Bristol R 11 0 **15 0**

GRAZIOLI, Giuliano (F) 153 45
H: 5 11 W: 12 11 b.Marylebone 23-3-75
Source: Wembley.
1995–96 Peterborough U 3 1
1996–97 Peterborough U 4 0
1997–98 Peterborough U 0 0
1998–99 Peterborough U 34 15 **41 16**
1999–2000 Swindon T 19 8
2000-01 Swindon T 28 2
2001-02 Swindon T 31 8 **78 18**
2002-03 Bristol R 34 11 **34 11**

HOGG, Lewis* (M) 74 3
H: 5 9 W: 11 11 b.Bristol 13-9-82
Source: Trainee.
1999–2000 Bristol R 0 0
2000-01 Bristol R 34 3
2001-02 Bristol R 23 0
2002-03 Bristol R 17 0 **74 3**

HOWIE, Scott* (G) 301 0
H: 6 3 W: 14 06 b.Motherwell 4-1-72
Source: Ferguslie U. *Honours:* Scotland Under-21.
1991–92 Clyde 15 0
1992–93 Clyde 39 0
1993–94 Clyde 1 0 **55 0**
1993–94 Norwich C 2 0 **2 0**
1994–95 Motherwell 3 0
1995–96 Motherwell 36 0
1996–97 Motherwell 30 0
1997–98 Motherwell 0 0 **69 0**
1997–98 Reading 7 0
1998–99 Reading 42 0
1999–2000 Reading 36 0
2000-01 Reading 0 0 **85 0**
2001-02 Bristol R 46 0
2002-03 Bristol R 44 0 **90 0**

HYDE, Graham (M) 263 14
H: 5 8 W: 11 11 b.Doncaster 10-11-70
Source: Trainee.
1988–89 Sheffield W 0 0
1989–90 Sheffield W 0 0
1990–91 Sheffield W 0 0
1991–92 Sheffield W 13 0
1992–93 Sheffield W 20 1
1993–94 Sheffield W 36 1
1994–95 Sheffield W 35 5
1995–96 Sheffield W 26 1
1996–97 Sheffield W 19 2
1997–98 Sheffield W 22 1
1998–99 Sheffield W 1 0 **172 11**
1998–99 Birmingham C 13 0
1999–2000 Birmingham C 31 1
2000-01 Birmingham C 3 0
2001-02 Birmingham C 5 0
2001-02 *Chesterfield* 9 1 **9 1**
2002-03 Birmingham C 0 0 **52 1**
2002-03 *Peterborough U* 9 0 **9 0**
2002-03 Bristol R 21 1 **21 1**

McKEEVER, Mark* (M) 58 2
H: 5 11 W: 11 08 b.Derry 16-11-78
Source: Trainee. *Honours:* Northern Ireland Youth. Eire Under-21.
1996–97 Peterborough U 3 0 **3 0**
1996–97 Sheffield W 0 0
1997–98 Sheffield W 0 0
1998–99 Sheffield W 3 0
1998–99 *Bristol R* 7 0
1998–99 *Reading* 7 2 **7 2**
1999–2000 Sheffield W 2 0
2000-01 Sheffield W 0 0 **5 0**
2000-01 Bristol R 12 0
2001-02 Bristol R 8 0
2002-03 Bristol R 16 0 **43 0**

PARKER, Sonny (D) 15 0
H: 5 11 W: 11 11 b.Middlesbrough 28-2-83
Source: Trainee. *Honours:* England Youth.
1999–2000 Birmingham C 0 0
2000-01 Birmingham C 0 0
2001-02 Birmingham C 0 0
2002-03 Birmingham C 0 0
2002-03 Bristol R 15 0 **15 0**

PLUMMER, Dwayne‡ (M) 49 1
H: 5 9 W: 11 00 b.Bristol 12-5-78
Source: Trainee.
1995–96 Bristol C 11 0
1996–97 Bristol C 2 0
1997–98 Bristol C 1 0
1998–99 Bristol C 0 0
1999–2000 Bristol C 0 0 **14 0**
From St'age, Cheshm
2000-01 Bristol R 20 1
2001-02 Bristol R 15 0
2002-03 Bristol R 0 0 **35 1**

QUINN, Robert (M) 205 7
H: 5 11 W: 11 02 b.Sidcup 8-11-76
Source: Trainee.
1994–95 Crystal Palace 0 0
1995–96 Crystal Palace 1 0
1996–97 Crystal Palace 21 1
1997–98 Crystal Palace 1 0 **23 1**
1998–99 Brentford 43 2
1999–2000 Brentford 44 0
2000-01 Brentford 22 0 **109 2**
2000-01 Oxford U 13 2
2001-02 Oxford U 16 0 **29 2**
2002-03 Bristol R 44 2 **44 2**

RAMMELL, Andy# (F) 404 109
H: 6 1 W: 13 12 b.Nuneaton 10-2-67
Source: Atherstone U.
1989–90 Manchester U 0 0
1990–91 Barnsley 40 12
1991–92 Barnsley 37 8
1992–93 Barnsley 30 7
1993–94 Barnsley 34 6
1994–95 Barnsley 24 7
1995–96 Barnsley 20 4 **185 44**
1995–96 Southend U 7 2
1996–97 Southend U 36 9
1997–98 Southend U 26 2 **69 13**
1998–99 Walsall 39 18
1999–2000 Walsall 30 5
2000-01 Walsall 0 0 **69 23**
2000-01 Wycombe W 26 10
2001-02 Wycombe W 27 11
2002-03 Wycombe W 21 4 **74 25**
2002-03 Bristol R 7 4 **7 4**

RICHARDS, Justin‡ (F) 19 0
H: 5 11 W: 11 00 b.Sandwell 16-10-80
Source: Trainee.
1998–99 WBA 1 0
1999–2000 WBA 0 0
2000-01 WBA 0 0 **1 0**
2000-01 Bristol R 7 0
2001-02 Bristol R 1 0
2002-03 Bristol R 8 0 **16 0**
2002-03 *Colchester U* 2 0 **2 0**

SCOTT, Robert‡ (D) 0 0
H: 5 11 W: 11 04 b.Oxford 24-9-82
Source: Scholar.
2002-03 Bristol R 0 0

SHORE, Drew‡ (M) 9 0
H: 5 11 W: 11 12 b.Poole 8-4-82
Source: Trainee.
2001-02 Bristol R 9 0
2002-03 Bristol R 0 0 **9 0**

SHORE, Jamie‡ (M) 24 2
H: 5 9 W: 12 05 b.Bristol 1-9-77
Source: Trainee. *Honours:* England Youth.
1994–95 Norwich C 0 0
1995–96 Norwich C 0 0
1996–97 Norwich C 0 0
1997–98 Norwich C 0 0
1998–99 Bristol R 24 2
1999–2000 Bristol R 0 0
2000-01 Bristol R 0 0
2001-02 Bristol R 0 0
2002-03 Bristol R 0 0 **24 2**

STREET, Kevin (M) 137 10
H: 5 10 W: 11 02 b.Crewe 25-11-77
Source: Trainee.
1996–97 Crewe Alex 0 0
1997–98 Crewe Alex 32 4
1998–99 Crewe Alex 23 2
1999–2000 Crewe Alex 28 1
2000-01 Crewe Alex 23 1
2001-02 *Luton T* 2 0 **2 0**
2001-02 Crewe Alex 9 1
2002-03 Crewe Alex 0 0 **115 9**
From Northwich Vic.
2002-03 Bristol R 20 1 **20 1**

TAIT, Paul (F) 111 13
H: 6 1 W: 11 10 b.Newcastle 24-10-74
Source: Trainee.
1993–94 Everton 0 0
1994–95 Wigan Ath 5 0
1995–96 Wigan Ath 0 0 **5 0**
From Northwich Vic.
1999–2000 Crewe Alex 33 6
2000-01 Crewe Alex 18 0
2001-02 *Hull C* 2 0 **2 0**
2001-02 Crewe Alex 12 0 **63 6**
2002-03 Bristol R 41 7 **41 7**

U'DDIN, Anwar (D) 18 1
H: 5 11 W: 11 10 b.Whitechapel 1-11-81
Source: West Ham U Scholar.
2001-02 West Ham U 0 0
2001-02 Sheffield W 0 0
2002-03 Bristol R 18 1 **18 1**

WARREN, Christer‡ (D) 163 14
H: 5 10 W: 11 10 b.Dorchester 10-10-74
Source: Cheltenham T.
1994–95 Southampton 0 0
1995–96 Southampton 7 0
1996–97 Southampton 1 0
1996–97 *Brighton & HA* 3 0 **3 0**
1996–97 *Fulham* 11 1 **11 1**
1997–98 Southampton 0 0 **8 0**
1997–98 Bournemouth 30 6
1998–99 Bournemouth 32 5
1999–2000 Bournemouth 41 2 **103 13**
2000-01 QPR 22 0
2001-02 QPR 14 0 **36 0**
2002-03 Bristol R 2 0 **2 0**

Scholars
Arndale, Neil D; Davis, Anthony S; Duharty, Marcus; Greaves, Daniel G; Guibarra, Daniel G; Haldane, Lewis O; Hill, Matthew P; Hobbs, Shane M; Jones, Samuel M; Nestor, Christopher J; O'Neill, Darren; Price, Graham; Webb, Victor; Weisberg, Ryan P; Wilson, Dene
Non-Contract
Jinadu, Tobi
Players who do not hold a current contract but their registration has been retained by the club
Pierre, Nigel N

BURNLEY

ARMSTRONG, Gordon* (D) 535 60
H: 6 0 W: 13 04 b.Newcastle 15-7-67
Source: Apprentice.
1984–85 Sunderland 4 0
1985–86 Sunderland 14 2
1986–87 Sunderland 41 5
1987–88 Sunderland 37 5
1988–89 Sunderland 45 8
1989–90 Sunderland 46 8
1990–91 Sunderland 35 6
1991–92 Sunderland 40 10
1992–93 Sunderland 45 3
1993–94 Sunderland 26 2
1994–95 Sunderland 15 1
1995–96 Sunderland 1 0 **349 50**
1995–96 *Bristol C* 6 0 **6 0**
1995–96 *Northampton T* 4 1 **4 1**
1996–97 Bury 32 2
1997–98 Bury 37 2
1998–99 Bury 2 0 **71 4**
1998–99 Burnley 40 2
1999–2000 Burnley 22 1
2000-01 Burnley 19 0

2001-02 Burnley 18 2
2002-03 Burnley 6 0 **105 5**

BERESFORD, Marlon‡ (G) 339 0
H: 6 1 W: 13 01 b.Lincoln 2-9-69
Source: Trainee.
1987–88 Sheffield W 0 0
1988–89 Sheffield W 0 0
1989–90 Sheffield W 0 0
1989–90 *Bury* 1 0 **1 0**
1989–90 *Ipswich T* 0 0
1990–91 Sheffield W 0 0
1990–91 *Northampton T* 13 0
1990–91 *Crewe Alex* 3 0 **3 0**
1991–92 Sheffield W 0 0
1991–92 *Northampton T* 15 0 **28 0**
1992–93 Burnley 44 0
1993–94 Burnley 46 0
1994–95 Burnley 40 0
1995–96 Burnley 36 0
1996–97 Burnley 40 0
1997–98 Burnley 34 0
1997–98 Middlesbrough 3 0
1998–99 Middlesbrough 4 0
1999–2000 Middlesbrough 1 0
2000-01 Middlesbrough 1 0
2000-01 *Sheffield W* 4 0 **4 0**
2001-02 Middlesbrough 1 0 **10 0**
2001-02 *Wolverhampton W* 0 0
2001-02 *Burnley* 13 0
2002-03 York C 6 0 **6 0**
2002-03 Burnley 34 0 **287 0**

BLAKE, Robbie (F) 283 75
H: 5 9 W: 12 06 b.Middlesbrough 4-3-76
Source: Trainee.
1994–95 Darlington 9 0
1995–96 Darlington 29 11
1996–97 Darlington 30 10 **68 21**
1996–97 Bradford C 5 0
1997–98 Bradford C 34 8
1998–99 Bradford C 39 16
1999–2000 Bradford C 28 2
2000-01 Bradford C 21 4
2000-01 *Nottingham F* 11 1 **11 1**
2001-02 Bradford C 26 10 **153 40**
2001-02 Burnley 10 0
2002-03 Burnley 41 13 **51 13**

BRANCH, Graham# (D) 264 23
H: 6 2 W: 12 02 b.Liverpool 12-2-72
Source: Heswall.
1991–92 Tranmere R 4 0
1992–93 Tranmere R 3 0
1992–93 *Bury* 4 1 **4 1**
1993–94 Tranmere R 13 0
1994–95 Tranmere R 1 0
1995–96 Tranmere R 21 2
1996–97 Tranmere R 35 5
1997–98 Tranmere R 25 3 **102 10**
1997–98 *Wigan Ath* 3 0 **3 0**
1998–99 Stockport Co 14 3 **14 3**
1998–99 Burnley 20 1
1999–2000 Burnley 44 3
2000-01 Burnley 35 5
2001-02 Burnley 10 0
2002-03 Burnley 32 0 **141 9**

BRISCOE, Lee* (D) 189 9
H: 5 11 W: 11 12 b.Pontefract 30-9-75
Source: Trainee. *Honours:* England Under-21.
1993–94 Sheffield W 1 0
1994–95 Sheffield W 6 0
1995–96 Sheffield W 26 0
1996–97 Sheffield W 6 0
1997–98 Sheffield W 7 0
1997–98 *Manchester C* 5 1 **5 1**
1998–99 Sheffield W 16 1
1999–2000 Sheffield W 16 0 **78 1**
2000-01 Burnley 29 0
2001-02 Burnley 44 5
2002-03 Burnley 33 2 **106 7**

CHAPLOW, Richard§ (M) 5 0
b.Bury 2-2-85
Source: Scholar.
2002-03 Burnley 5 0 **5 0**

COOK, Paul‡ (M) 581 55
H: 5 11 W: 11 00 b.Liverpool 22-6-67
Source: Marine.
1984–85 Wigan Ath 2 0
1985–86 Wigan Ath 13 2
1986–87 Wigan Ath 27 4
1987–88 Wigan Ath 41 8
1988–89 Norwich C 4 0
1989–90 Norwich C 2 0 **6 0**
1989–90 *Wolverhampton W* 28 2
1990–91 Wolverhampton W 42 6
1991–92 Wolverhampton W 43 8
1992–93 Wolverhampton W 44 1
1993–94 Wolverhampton W 36 2 **193 19**
1994–95 Coventry C 34 3
1995–96 Coventry C 3 0 **37 3**
1995–96 Tranmere R 15 1
1996–97 Tranmere R 36 3
1997–98 Tranmere R 9 0 **60 4**
1997–98 Stockport Co 25 3
1998–99 Stockport Co 24 0 **49 3**
1998–99 *Burnley* 12 1
1999–2000 Burnley 44 3
2000-01 Burnley 40 3
2001-02 Burnley 28 5
2001-02 *Wigan Ath* 6 0 **89 14**
2002-03 Burnley 23 0 **147 12**

COX, Ian* (D) 302 21
H: 6 0 W: 12 00 b.Croydon 25-3-71
Source: Carshalton Ath. *Honours:* Trinidad & Tobago 5 full caps.
1993–94 Crystal Palace 0 0
1994–95 Crystal Palace 11 0
1995–96 Crystal Palace 4 0 **15 0**
1995–96 Bournemouth 8 0
1996–97 Bournemouth 44 8
1997–98 Bournemouth 46 3
1998–99 Bournemouth 46 5
1999–2000 Bournemouth 28 0 **172 16**
1999–2000 Burnley 17 1
2000-01 Burnley 38 1
2001-02 Burnley 34 2
2002-03 Burnley 26 1 **115 5**

DAVIS, Earl (D) 0 0
H: 6 1 W: 13 02 b.Manchester 17-5-83
Source: Scholar.
2002-03 Burnley 0 0

DAVIS, Steve* (D) 474 63
H: 6 2 W: 14 07 b.Hexham 30-10-68
Source: Trainee.
1987–88 Southampton 0 0
1988–89 Southampton 0 0
1989–90 Southampton 4 0
1989–90 *Burnley* 9 0
1990–91 Southampton 3 0 **7 0**
1990–91 *Notts Co* 2 0 **2 0**
1991–92 Burnley 40 6
1992–93 Burnley 37 2
1993–94 Burnley 42 7
1994–95 Burnley 43 7
1995–96 Luton T 36 2
1996–97 Luton T 44 8
1997–98 Luton T 38 5
1998–99 Luton T 20 6 **138 21**
1998–99 Burnley 19 3
1999–2000 Burnley 42 7
2000-01 Burnley 44 5
2001-02 Burnley 23 1
2002-03 Burnley 28 4 **327 42**

DIALLO, Drissa‡ (D) 14 1
H: 6 1 W: 12 00 b.Mauritania 4-1-73
Honours: Guinea full caps.
2002-03 Burnley 14 1 **14 1**

GNOHERE, Arthur (D) 95 7
H: 6 0 W: 13 00 b.Yamoussoukro 20-11-78
2000-01 Caen 28 2 **28 2**
2001-02 Burnley 34 3
2002-03 Burnley 33 2 **67 5**

GRANT, Tony (M) 161 4
H: 5 11 W: 10 10 b.Liverpool 14-11-74
Source: Trainee. *Honours:* England Under-21.
1993–94 Everton 0 0
1994–95 Everton 5 0
1995–96 Everton 13 1
1995–96 *Swindon T* 3 1 **3 1**
1996–97 Everton 18 0
1997–98 Everton 7 1
1998–99 Everton 16 0
1999–2000 Everton 2 0 **61 2**
1999–2000 *Tranmere R* 9 0 **9 0**
1999–2000 Manchester C 8 0
2000-01 Manchester C 10 0
2000-01 *WBA* 5 0 **5 0**
2001-02 Manchester C 3 0 **21 0**
2001-02 Burnley 28 0
2002-03 Burnley 34 1 **62 1**

LEESON, Andrew* (D) 0 0
H: 5 10 W: 11 00 b.Capetown 27-9-82
Source: Scholar.
2002-03 Burnley 0 0

LITTLE, Glen (M) 224 32
H: 6 3 W: 13 00 b.Wimbledon 15-10-75
Source: Trainee.
1994–95 Crystal Palace 0 0
1995–96 Crystal Palace 0 0
1996–97 Glentoran 6 2 **6 2**
1996–97 Burnley 9 0
1997–98 Burnley 24 4
1998–99 Burnley 34 5
1999–2000 Burnley 41 3
2000-01 Burnley 34 3
2001-02 Burnley 37 9
2002-03 Burnley 33 5 **212 29**
2002-03 *Reading* 6 1 **6 1**

MAYLETT, Brad (M) 51 0
H: 5 8 W: 10 07 b.Manchester 24-12-80
Source: Trainee.
1998–99 Burnley 17 0
1999–2000 Burnley 0 0
2000-01 Burnley 12 0
2001-02 Burnley 10 0
2002-03 Burnley 6 0 **45 0**
2002-03 *Swansea C* 6 0 **6 0**

McGREGOR, Mark (D) 275 12
H: 5 9 W: 12 08 b.Chester 16-2-77
Source: Trainee.
1994–95 Wrexham 1 0
1995–96 Wrexham 32 1
1996–97 Wrexham 38 1
1997–98 Wrexham 42 2
1998–99 Wrexham 43 1
1999–2000 Wrexham 45 1
2000-01 Wrexham 43 5
2001-02 Wrexham 0 0 **244 11**
2001-02 Burnley 1 0
2002-03 Burnley 30 1 **31 1**

MICHOPOULOS, Nick* (G) 192 0
H: 6 3 W: 14 00 b.Karditsa 20-2-70
Honours: Greece 13 full caps.
1996–97 PAOK Salonika 34 0
1997–98 PAOK Salonika 32 0
1998–99 PAOK Salonika 19 0
1999–2000 PAOK Salonika 17 0 **102 0**
2000-01 Burnley 39 0
2001-02 Burnley 33 0
2002-03 Burnley 13 0 **85 0**
2002-03 *Crystal Palace* 5 0 **5 0**

MOORE, Alan (M) 179 18
H: 5 10 W: 11 11 b.Dublin 25-11-74
Source: Rivermount. *Honours:* Eire Under-21, 8 full caps.
1991–92 Middlesbrough 0 0
1992–93 Middlesbrough 2 0
1993–94 Middlesbrough 42 10
1994–95 Middlesbrough 37 4
1995–96 Middlesbrough 12 0
1996–97 Middlesbrough 17 0
1997–98 Middlesbrough 4 0
1998–99 Middlesbrough 4 0
1998–99 *Barnsley* 5 0 **5 0**
1999–2000 Middlesbrough 0 0
2000-01 Middlesbrough 0 0 **118 14**
2001-02 Burnley 29 3
2002-03 Burnley 27 1 **56 4**

MOORE, Ian (F) 290 57
H: 5 11 W: 12 02 b.Birkenhead 26-8-76
Source: Trainee. *Honours:* England Youth, Under-21.
1994–95 Tranmere R 1 0
1995–96 Tranmere R 36 9
1996–97 Tranmere R 21 3 **58 12**
1996–97 *Bradford C* 6 0 **6 0**
1996–97 Nottingham F 5 0
1997–98 Nottingham F 10 1 **15 1**
1997–98 *West Ham U* 1 0 **1 0**
1998–99 Stockport Co 38 3
1999–2000 Stockport Co 38 10
2000-01 Stockport Co 17 7 **93 20**
2000-01 Burnley 27 5
2001-02 Burnley 46 11
2002-03 Burnley 44 8 **117 24**

O'NEILL, Matt§ (M) 7 0
b.Blackburn 25-6-84
Source: Scholar.
2002-03 Burnley 7 0 **7 0**

PAPADOPOULOS, Dimitri (F) **40 3**
H: 5 8 W: 11 04 b.Kazakhstan 20-9-81
Source: Akratitos. *Honours:* Greece 1 full cap.

2001-02	Burnley	6	0		
2002-03	Burnley	34	3	**40**	**3**

PAYTON, Andy‡ (F) **509 200**
H: 5 9 W: 11 13 b.Whalley 23-10-67
Source: Apprentice.

1985–86	Hull C	0	0		
1986–87	Hull C	2	0		
1987–88	Hull C	21	2		
1988–89	Hull C	28	4		
1989–90	Hull C	39	17		
1990–91	Hull C	43	25		
1991–92	Hull C	10	7	**143**	**55**
1991–92	Middlesbrough	19	3	**19**	**3**
1992–93	Celtic	29	13		
1993–94	Celtic	7	2	**36**	**15**
1993–94	Barnsley	25	12		
1994–95	Barnsley	43	12		
1995–96	Barnsley	40	17	**108**	**41**
1996–97	Huddersfield T	38	17		
1997–98	Huddersfield T	5	0	**43**	**17**
1997–98	Burnley	19	9		
1998–99	Burnley	40	19		
1999–2000	Burnley	41	27		
2000-01	Burnley	40	9		
2001-02	Burnley	15	4		
2001-02	*Blackpool*	4	1	**4**	**1**
2002-03	Burnley	1	0	**156**	**68**

RASMUSSEN, Mark* (M) **2 0**
H: 5 6 W: 10 10 b.Newcastle 28-11-83

2001-02	Burnley	0	0		
2002-03	Burnley	2	0	**2**	**0**

SHANDRAN, Anthony* (F) **19 3**
H: 5 9 W: 12 10 b.North Shields 17-9-81
Source: Scholar.

2000-01	Burnley	1	0		
2001-02	Burnley	0	0		
2002-03	Burnley	0	0	**1**	**0**
2002-03	*York C*	18	3	**18**	**3**

TAYLOR, Gareth (F) **299 88**
H: 6 2 W: 13 07 b.Weston-Super-Mare 25-2-73
Source: Southampton Trainee. *Honours:* Wales Under-21, 12 full caps.

1991–92	Bristol R	1	0		
1992–93	Bristol R	0	0		
1993–94	Bristol R	0	0		
1994–95	Bristol R	39	12		
1995–96	Bristol R	7	4	**47**	**16**
1995–96	Crystal Palace	20	1	**20**	**1**
1995–96	Sheffield U	10	2		
1996–97	Sheffield U	34	12		
1997–98	Sheffield U	28	10		
1998–99	Sheffield U	12	1	**84**	**25**
1998–99	Manchester C	26	4		
1999–2000	Manchester C	17	5		
1999–2000	*Port Vale*	4	0	**4**	**0**
1999–2000	*QPR*	6	1	**6**	**1**
2000-01	Manchester C	0	0	**43**	**9**
2000-01	*Burnley*	15	4		
2001-02	Burnley	40	16		
2002-03	Burnley	40	16	**95**	**36**

WAINE, Andrew* (M) **2 0**
H: 5 9 W: 10 05 b.Manchester 24-2-83
Source: Scholar.

2002-03	Burnley	2	0	**2**	**0**

WELLER, Paul (M) **219 11**
H: 5 8 W: 11 02 b.Brighton 6-3-75
Source: Trainee.

1993–94	Burnley	0	0		
1994–95	Burnley	0	0		
1995–96	Burnley	25	1		
1996–97	Burnley	31	2		
1997–98	Burnley	39	2		
1998–99	Burnley	1	0		
1999–2000	Burnley	7	1		
2000-01	Burnley	44	3		
2001-02	Burnley	38	2		
2002-03	Burnley	34	0	**219**	**11**

WEST, Dean (D) **355 32**
H: 5 10 W: 11 07 b.Leeds 5-12-72
Source: Leeds U Schoolboy.

1990–91	Lincoln C	1	1		
1991–92	Lincoln C	32	3		
1992–93	Lincoln C	19	3		
1993–94	Lincoln C	18	6		
1994–95	Lincoln C	41	6		
1995–96	Lincoln C	8	1	**119**	**20**
1995–96	Bury	37	1		
1996–97	Bury	46	4		
1997–98	Bury	4	0		
1998–99	Bury	23	3	**110**	**8**
1999–2000	Burnley	34	0		
2000-01	Burnley	7	0		
2001-02	Burnley	44	0		
2002-03	Burnley	41	4	**126**	**4**

Scholars
Barrett, Paul J; Blakey, Sean; Carpenter, Rhys E; Carter, Gary P; Chaplow, Richard D; Eves, Liam J; Fogarty, Brian W; Hindle, Damien; Jones, Colin A; O'Neill, Matthew P; Pilkington, Joel T; Pitham, Daniel J; Richardson, Steven; Salisbury, James A; Scott, Paul D; Townsend, Ryan MG

BURY

BARRASS, Matt* (D) **53 1**
H: 5 10 W: 12 05 b.Bury 28-2-81
Source: Trainee.

1999–2000	Bury	25	1		
2000-01	Bury	5	0		
2001-02	Bury	7	0		
2002-03	Bury	16	0	**53**	**1**

BILLY, Chris* (M) **396 24**
H: 6 0 W: 12 13 b.Huddersfield 2-1-73
Source: Trainee.

1991–92	Huddersfield T	10	2		
1992–93	Huddersfield T	13	0		
1993–94	Huddersfield T	34	0		
1994–95	Huddersfield T	37	2	**94**	**4**
1995–96	Plymouth Arg	32	4		
1996–97	Plymouth Arg	45	3		
1997–98	Plymouth Arg	41	2	**118**	**9**
1998–99	Notts Co	6	0	**6**	**0**
1998–99	Bury	37	0		
1999–2000	Bury	36	4		
2000-01	Bury	46	0		
2001-02	Bury	21	3		
2002-03	Bury	38	4	**178**	**11**

BORLEY, David‡ (M) **21 3**
H: 5 9 W: 12 08 b.Newcastle 17-4-83
Source: Scholar. *Honours:* England Schools.

2001-02	Bury	21	3		
2002-03	Bury	0	0	**21**	**3**

BULLOCK, Darren (M) **253 23**
H: 5 9 W: 12 10 b.Worcester 12-2-69
Source: Nuneaton Bor.

1993–94	Huddersfield T	20	3		
1994–95	Huddersfield T	39	6		
1995–96	Huddersfield T	42	6		
1996–97	Huddersfield T	27	1	**128**	**16**
1996–97	Swindon T	13	1		
1997–98	Swindon T	31	0		
1998–99	Swindon T	22	1	**66**	**2**
1998–99	Bury	12	1		
1999–2000	Bury	27	2		
2000-01	Bury	10	2		
2000-01	*Sheffield U*	6	0	**6**	**0**
2001-02	Bury	4	0		
2002-03	Bury	0	0	**53**	**5**

CLEGG, George (M) **72 9**
H: 5 10 W: 12 00 b.Manchester 16-11-80
Source: Trainee.

1999–2000	Manchester U	0	0		
2000-01	Manchester U	0	0		
2000-01	*Wycombe W*	10	0	**10**	**0**
2001-02	Bury	31	4		
2002-03	Bury	31	5	**62**	**9**

CONNELL, Lee (D) **30 3**
H: 6 1 W: 13 01 b.Bury 24-6-81
Source: Trainee.

1999–2000	Bury	2	0		
2000-01	Bury	1	1		
2001-02	Bury	13	0		
2002-03	Bury	14	2	**30**	**3**

CRAMB, Colin# (F) **268 68**
H: 6 0 W: 12 09 b.Lanark 23-6-74
Source: Hamilton A BC.

1990–91	Hamilton A	3	2		
1991–92	Hamilton A	12	1		
1992–93	Hamilton A	33	7	**48**	**10**
1993–94	Southampton	1	0	**1**	**0**
1994–95	Falkirk	8	1	**8**	**1**
1994–95	Hearts	6	1	**6**	**1**
1995–96	Doncaster R	21	7		
1996–97	Doncaster R	41	18	**62**	**25**
1997–98	Bristol C	40	9		
1998–99	Bristol C	13	0		
1998–99	*Walsall*	4	4	**4**	**4**
1999–2000	Bristol C	0	0	**53**	**9**
1999–2000	Crewe Alex	37	6		
2000-01	Crewe Alex	13	4		
2000-01	*Notts Co*	3	0	**3**	**0**
2000-01	*Bury*	15	5		
2001-02	Crewe Alex	0	0		
2002-03	Crewe Alex	0	0	**50**	**10**
2002-03	Bury	18	3	**33**	**8**

DUNFIELD, Terry (M) **30 2**
H: 5 11 W: 12 04 b.Vancouver 20-2-82
Source: Trainee.

1998–99	Manchester C	0	0		
1999–2000	Manchester C	0	0		
2000-01	Manchester C	1	0		
2001-02	Manchester C	0	0		
2002-03	Manchester C	0	0	**1**	**0**
2002-03	Bury	29	2	**29**	**2**

EVANS, Gary‡ (D) **1 0**
H: 5 9 W: 12 03 b.Doncaster 13-9-82
Source: Scholar.

2001-02	Bury	1	0		
2002-03	Bury	0	0	**1**	**0**

FORREST, Martyn (M) **106 2**
H: 5 9 W: 11 07 b.Bury 2-1-79

1997–98	Bury	0	0		
1998–99	Bury	1	0		
1999–2000	Bury	15	0		
2000-01	Bury	27	0		
2001-02	Bury	34	1		
2002-03	Bury	29	1	**106**	**2**

GARNER, Glyn (G) **53 0**
H: 6 2 W: 13 04 b.Pontypool 9-12-76
Source: Llanelli.

2000-01	Bury	0	0		
2001-02	Bury	7	0		
2002-03	Bury	46	0	**53**	**0**

GUNBY, Stephen (M) **1 0**
H: 5 11 W: 13 03 b.Lincoln 14-4-84
Source: Scholar.

2001-02	Bury	1	0		
2002-03	Bury	0	0	**1**	**0**

HILL, Nicky* (D) **22 0**
H: 6 0 W: 13 07 b.Accrington 26-2-81
Source: Trainee.

1999–2000	Bury	5	0		
2000-01	Bury	10	0		
2001-02	Bury	5	0		
2002-03	Bury	2	0	**22**	**0**

KENNEDY, Thomas (M) **0 0**
b.Bury 24-6-85
Source: Scholar.

2002-03	Bury	0	0		

LAWSON, Ian (F) **132 30**
H: 5 11 W: 12 08 b.Huddersfield 4-11-77
Source: Trainee.

1994–95	Huddersfield T	0	0		
1995–96	Huddersfield T	0	0		
1996–97	Huddersfield T	18	3		
1997–98	Huddersfield T	18	0		
1998–99	Huddersfield T	6	2	**42**	**5**
1998–99	*Blackpool*	9	3	**9**	**3**
1999–2000	Bury	25	11		
1999–2000	Stockport Co	15	4		
2000-01	Stockport Co	10	0		
2001-02	Stockport Co	0	0	**25**	**4**
2001-02	Bury	24	4		
2002-03	Bury	7	3	**56**	**18**

NELSON, Michael (D) **72 8**
H: 6 2 W: 13 03 b.Gateshead 15-3-82

2000-01	Bury	2	1		
2001-02	Bury	31	2		
2002-03	Bury	39	5	**72**	**8**

NEWBY, Jon* (F) **129 21**
H: 5 11 W: 11 00 b.Warrington 28-11-78
Source: Trainee.

1998–99	Liverpool	0	0		
1999–2000	Liverpool	1	0		
1999–2000	*Crewe Alex*	6	0	**6**	**0**
2000-01	Liverpool	0	0	**1**	**0**
2000-01	*Sheffield U*	13	0	**13**	**0**
2000-01	Bury	17	5		
2001-02	Bury	46	6		
2002-03	Bury	46	10	**109**	**21**

NUGENT, Dave (F) **36** **4**
H: 5 11 W: 12 00 b.Liverpool 2-5-85
Source: Scholar.

2001-02	Bury	5	0		
2002-03	Bury	31	4	**36**	**4**

O'SHAUGHNESSY, Paul (M) **18** **0**
H: 5 10 W: 11 10 b.Bury 3-10-81
Source: Scholar.

2001-02	Bury	2	0		
2002-03	Bury	16	0	**18**	**0**

PORTER, Chris† (M) **2** **0**
b.Wigan 12-12-83

2002-03	Bury	2	0	**2**	**0**

PREECE, Andy (F) **449** **110**
H: 6 2 W: 13 06 b.Evesham 27-3-67
Source: Evesham U.

1988-89	Northampton T	1	0	**1**	**0**
From Worcester C					
1989-90	Wrexham	7	1		
1990-91	Wrexham	34	4		
1991-92	Wrexham	10	2	**51**	**7**
1991-92	Stockport Co	25	13		
1992-93	Stockport Co	29	8		
1993-94	Stockport Co	43	21	**97**	**42**
1994-95	Crystal Palace	20	4	**20**	**4**
1995-96	Blackpool	41	14		
1996-97	Blackpool	41	10		
1997-98	Blackpool	44	11	**126**	**35**
1998-99	Bury	39	3		
1999-2000	Bury	43	12		
2000-01	Bury	30	2		
2001-02	Bury	13	1		
2002-03	Bury	29	4	**154**	**22**

REDMOND, Steve# (D) **591** **17**
H: 5 11 W: 13 02 b.Liverpool 2-11-67
Source: Apprentice. *Honours:* England Youth, Under-21.

1984-85	Manchester C	0	0		
1985-86	Manchester C	9	0		
1986-87	Manchester C	30	2		
1987-88	Manchester C	44	0		
1988-89	Manchester C	46	1		
1989-90	Manchester C	38	0		
1990-91	Manchester C	37	3		
1991-92	Manchester C	31	1	**235**	**7**
1992-93	Oldham Ath	31	0		
1993-94	Oldham Ath	33	1		
1994-95	Oldham Ath	43	0		
1995-96	Oldham Ath	40	1		
1996-97	Oldham Ath	24	2		
1997-98	Oldham Ath	34	0	**205**	**4**
1998-99	Bury	26	0		
1999-2000	Bury	33	1		
2000-01	Bury	39	2		
2001-02	Bury	26	1		
2002-03	Bury	27	2	**151**	**6**

SEDDON, Gareth* (F) **39** **6**
H: 5 9 W: 12 04 b.Burnley 23-5-80
Source: Atherstone U.

2001-02	Bury	35	6		
2002-03	Bury	4	0	**39**	**6**

STUART, Jamie (D) **156** **4**
H: 5 10 W: 11 02 b.Southwark 5-10-76
Source: Trainee. *Honours:* England Youth, Under-21.

1994-95	Charlton Ath	12	0		
1995-96	Charlton Ath	27	2		
1996-97	Charlton Ath	10	1		
1997-98	Charlton Ath	1	0	**50**	**3**
1998-99	Millwall	35	0		
1999-2000	Millwall	9	0		
2000-01	Millwall	1	0		
2001-02	Millwall	0	0	**45**	**0**
2001-02	Bury	24	1		
2002-03	Bury	37	0	**61**	**1**

SWAILES, Danny (D) **102** **7**
H: 6 3 W: 13 03 b.Bolton 1-4-79
Source: Trainee.

1997-98	Bury	0	0		
1998-99	Bury	0	0		
1999-2000	Bury	24	3		
2000-01	Bury	11	0		
2001-02	Bury	28	1		
2002-03	Bury	39	3	**102**	**7**

TARSUS, Eddie* (D) **0** **0**
H: 5 9 W: 11 07 b.Leeds 3-11-82
Source: Doncaster R.

2001-02	Bury	0	0		
2002-03	Bury	0	0		

UNSWORTH, Lee (D) **211** **3**
H: 5 11 W: 11 09 b.Eccles 25-2-73
Source: Ashton U.

1994-95	Crewe Alex	0	0		
1995-96	Crewe Alex	29	0		
1996-97	Crewe Alex	29	0		
1997-98	Crewe Alex	36	0		
1998-99	Crewe Alex	24	0		
1999-2000	Crewe Alex	8	0	**126**	**0**
2000-01	Bury	15	0		
2001-02	Bury	35	1		
2002-03	Bury	35	2	**85**	**3**

WHALEY, Simon (F) **2** **0**
b.Bolton 7-6-85
Source: Scholar.

2002-03	Bury	2	0	**2**	**0**

WOODTHORPE, Colin# (D) **431** **12**
H: 6 0 W: 11 08 b.Ellesmere Pt 13-1-69
Source: Apprentice.

1986-87	Chester C	30	2		
1987-88	Chester C	35	0		
1988-89	Chester C	44	3		
1989-90	Chester C	46	1	**155**	**6**
1990-91	Norwich C	1	0		
1991-92	Norwich C	15	1		
1992-93	Norwich C	7	0		
1993-94	Norwich C	20	0	**43**	**1**
1994-95	Aberdeen	14	0		
1995-96	Aberdeen	15	1		
1996-97	Aberdeen	19	0	**48**	**1**
1997-98	Stockport Co	32	1		
1998-99	Stockport Co	37	2		
1999-2000	Stockport Co	26	0		
2000-01	Stockport Co	24	1		
2001-02	Stockport Co	34	0		
2002-03	Stockport Co	0	0	**153**	**4**
2002-03	Bury	32	0	**32**	**0**

Scholars
Bernard, Ryan AL; Buchanan, David TH; Buckley, Craig; Horrocks, Luke A; Kazim-Richards, Collin; Maden, Steven A; McDonald, Karl; Thompson, James; Winstanley, Richard A

Non-Contract
Porter, Christopher; Solly, Lewis A

Players who do not hold a current contract but their registration has been retained by the club
Bullock, Darren J

CAMBRIDGE U

ANGUS, Stevland (D) **90** **0**
H: 6 0 W: 12 00 b.Essex 16-9-80
Source: Trainee.

1999-2000	West Ham U	0	0		
2000-01	West Ham U	0	0		
2000-01	*Bournemouth*	9	0	**9**	**0**
2001-02	Cambridge U	41	0		
2002-03	Cambridge U	40	0	**81**	**0**

BOURGEOIS, Daryl‡ (D) **0** **0**
H: 5 11 W: 12 00 b.Newham 22-9-82
Source: Southend U Scholar.

2001-02	Cambridge U	0	0		
2002-03	Cambridge U	0	0		

BRENNAN, Martin† (G) **1** **0**
H: 6 1 W: 12 00 b.Whipps Cross 14-9-82

2000-01	Charlton Ath	0	0		
2001-02	Charlton Ath	0	0		
2002-03	Cambridge U	1	0	**1**	**0**

BRIDGES, David (M) **24** **3**
H: 6 0 W: 12 00 b.Huntingdon 22-9-82
Source: Scholar.

2001-02	Cambridge U	7	1		
2002-03	Cambridge U	17	2	**24**	**3**

CHILLINGWORTH, Daniel (F) **50** **3**
H: 6 0 W: 12 06 b.Cambridge 13-9-81
Source: Scholarship.

1999-2000	Cambridge U	3	0		
2000-01	Cambridge U	1	0		
2001-02	*Darlington*	4	1	**4**	**1**
2001-02	Cambridge U	12	2		
2002-03	Cambridge U	30	0	**46**	**2**

CLARK, George§ (G) **0** **0**
H: 6 4 W: 13 10 b.Cambridge 9-9-84
Source: Scholar.

2001-02	Cambridge U	0	0		
2002-03	Cambridge U	0	0		

DUNCAN, Andy (D) **163** **3**
H: 5 11 W: 14 03 b.Hexham 20-10-77
Source: Trainee. *Honours:* England Schools.

1996-97	Manchester U	0	0		
1997-98	Manchester U	0	0		
1997-98	Cambridge U	19	0		
1998-99	Cambridge U	45	1		
1999-2000	Cambridge U	13	1		
2000-01	Cambridge U	39	1		
2001-02	Cambridge U	24	0		
2002-03	Cambridge U	23	0	**163**	**3**

FLEMING, Terry (M) **363** **14**
H: 5 9 W: 10 01 b.Marston Green 1-5-73
Source: Trainee.

1990-91	Coventry C	2	0		
1991-92	Coventry C	0	0		
1992-93	Coventry C	11	0	**13**	**0**
1993-94	Northampton T	31	1	**31**	**1**
1994-95	Preston NE	27	2		
1995-96	Preston NE	5	0	**32**	**2**
1995-96	Lincoln C	22	0		
1996-97	Lincoln C	37	0		
1997-98	Lincoln C	40	3		
1998-99	Lincoln C	43	0		
1999-2000	Lincoln C	41	5	**183**	**8**
2000-01	Plymouth Arg	17	0	**17**	**0**
2000-01	Cambridge U	10	1		
2001-02	Cambridge U	34	0		
2002-03	Cambridge U	43	2	**87**	**3**

GOODHIND, Warren (D) **144** **3**
H: 5 11 W: 11 02 b.Johannesburg 16-8-77
Source: Trainee.

1996-97	Barnet	3	0		
1997-98	Barnet	35	1		
1998-99	Barnet	15	1		
1999-2000	Barnet	9	0		
2000-01	Barnet	31	1		
2001-02	Barnet	0	0	**93**	**3**
2001-02	Cambridge U	14	0		
2002-03	Cambridge U	37	0	**51**	**0**

GUTTRIDGE, Luke (M) **74** **6**
H: 5 5 W: 8 06 b.Barnstaple 27-3-82
Source: Trainee.

1999-2000	Torquay U	1	0		
2000-01	Torquay U	0	0	**1**	**0**
2000-01	Cambridge U	1	1		
2001-02	Cambridge U	29	2		
2002-03	Cambridge U	43	3	**73**	**6**

HEATHCOTE, Jon (M) **2** **0**
H: 5 10 W: 11 02 b.Camberley 10-11-83
Source: Scholar.

2002-03	Cambridge U	2	0	**2**	**0**

KITSON, Dave (F) **85** **30**
H: 6 3 W: 13 00 b.Hitchin 21-1-80
Source: Arlesey.

2000-01	Cambridge U	8	1		
2001-02	Cambridge U	33	9		
2002-03	Cambridge U	44	20	**85**	**30**

MARSHALL, Shaun (G) **109** **0**
H: 6 1 W: 13 03 b.Fakenham 3-10-78
Source: Trainee.

1996-97	Cambridge U	1	0		
1997-98	Cambridge U	2	0		
1998-99	Cambridge U	19	0		
1999-2000	Cambridge U	24	0		
2000-01	Cambridge U	11	0		
2001-02	Cambridge U	7	0		
2002-03	Cambridge U	45	0	**109**	**0**

MURRAY, Fred (D) **50** **0**
H: 5 10 W: 11 12 b.Tipperary 22-5-82
Source: Trainee.

1998-99	Blackburn R	0	0		
1999-2000	Blackburn R	0	0		
2000-01	Blackburn R	0	0		
2001-02	Blackburn R	0	0		
2001-02	Cambridge U	21	0		
2002-03	Cambridge U	29	0	**50**	**0**

NACCA, Franco (D) **17** **0**
H: 5 6 W: 10 00 b.Venezuela 9-11-82
Source: Scholar.

2000-01	Cambridge U	0	0		
2001-02	Cambridge U	0	0		
2002-03	Cambridge U	17	0	**17**	**0**

ONE, Armand‡ (F) **38** **5**
H: 6 4 W: 14 00 b.Paris 15-3-83
Source: Nantes.

2001-02	Cambridge U	32	4		
2002-03	Cambridge U	0	0	**32**	**4**
2002-03	*Northampton T*	6	1	**6**	**1**

OPARA, Lloyd (F) 8 0

H: 6 1 W: 13 00 b.Edmonton 6-1-84

Source: Scholar.

2001-02	Colchester U	1	0		
2002-03	Colchester U	5	0	**6**	**0**
2002-03	Cambridge U	2	0	**2**	**0**

PAYNTER, Owen‡ (F) 0 0

H: 5 8 W: 11 00 b.Newmarket 22-10-82

Source: Scholar.

2001-02	Cambridge U	0	0		
2002-03	Cambridge U	0	0		

REVELL, Alex (F) 37 2

H: 6 3 W: 13 00 b.Cambridge 7-7-83

Source: Scholar.

2000-01	Cambridge U	4	0		
2001-02	Cambridge U	24	2		
2002-03	Cambridge U	9	0	**37**	**2**

RIZA, Omer* (F) 68 18

H: 5 9 W: 11 00 b.Edmonton 8-11-79

Source: Trainee.

1998–99	Arsenal	0	0		
1999–2000	Arsenal	0	0		
1999–2000	West Ham U	0	0		
2000-01	West Ham U	0	0		
2000-01	*Barnet*	10	4	**10**	**4**
2000-01	*Cambridge U*	12	3		
2001-02	West Ham U	0	0		
2002-03	Cambridge U	46	11	**58**	**14**

SCULLY, Tony* (M) 125 4

H: 5 7 W: 11 06 b.Dublin 12-6-76

Source: Trainee. *Honours:* Eire Under-21.

1993–94	Crystal Palace	0	0		
1994–95	Crystal Palace	0	0		
1994–95	*Bournemouth*	10	0	**10**	**0**
1995–96	Crystal Palace	2	0		
1995–96	*Cardiff C*	14	0	**14**	**0**
1996–97	Crystal Palace	1	0		
1997–98	Crystal Palace	0	0	**3**	**0**
1997–98	Manchester C	9	0	**9**	**0**
1997–98	*Stoke C*	7	0	**7**	**0**
1997–98	QPR	7	0		
1998–99	QPR	23	2		
1999–2000	QPR	8	0		
2000-01	QPR	2	0	**40**	**2**
2001-02	Cambridge U	25	2		
2002-03	Cambridge U	6	0	**31**	**2**
2002-03	*Southend U*	8	0	**8**	**0**
2002-03	*Peterborough U*	3	0	**3**	**0**

TANN, Adam (D) 51 1

H: 6 0 W: 11 05 b.Fakenham 12-5-82

Source: Scholar. *Honours:* England Youth.

1999–2000	Cambridge U	0	0		
2000-01	Cambridge U	1	0		
2001-02	Cambridge U	25	0		
2002-03	Cambridge U	25	1	**51**	**1**

TAYLOR, John* (F) 507 151

H: 6 2 W: 15 00 b.Norwich 24-10-64

Source: Local.

1982–83	Colchester U	0	0		
1983–84	Colchester U	0	0		
1984–85	Colchester U	0	0		
From Sudbury T					
1988–89	Cambridge U	40	12		
1989–90	Cambridge U	45	15		
1990–91	Cambridge U	40	14		
1991–92	Cambridge U	35	5		
1991–92	Bristol R	8	7		
1992–93	Bristol R	42	14		
1993–94	Bristol R	45	23	**95**	**44**
1994–95	Bradford C	36	11	**36**	**11**
1994–95	Luton T	9	3		
1995–96	Luton T	28	0		
1996–97	Luton T	0	0	**37**	**3**
1996–97	*Lincoln C*	5	2	**5**	**2**
1996–97	*Colchester U*	8	5	**8**	**5**
1996–97	Cambridge U	21	4		
1997–98	Cambridge U	34	10		
1998–99	Cambridge U	40	17		
1999–2000	Cambridge U	40	6		
2000-01	Cambridge U	30	3		
2001-02	Cambridge U	0	0		
2002-03	Cambridge U	1	0	**326**	**86**

THEOBALD, David‡ (D) 45 0

H: 6 3 W: 12 08 b.Cambridge 15-12-78

Source: Trainee.

1997–98	Ipswich T	0	0		
1998–99	Ipswich T	0	0		
1999–2000	Brentford	10	0		
2000-01	Brentford	15	0		
2001-02	Brentford	6	0	**31**	**0**
2002-03	Swansea C	10	0	**10**	**0**
2002-03	Cambridge U	4	0	**4**	**0**

THORNTON, Rob§ (G) 0 0

H: 5 11 W: 12 06 b.Bedford 21-11-83

Source: Scholar.

2001-02	Cambridge U	0	0		
2002-03	Cambridge U	0	0		

TUDOR, Shane (M) 60 12

H: 5 7 W: 11 00 b.Wolverhampton 10-2-82

Source: Trainee.

1999–2000	Wolverhampton W	0	0		
2000-01	Wolverhampton W	1	0		
2001-02	Wolverhampton W	0	0	**1**	**0**
2001-02	Cambridge U	32	3		
2002-03	Cambridge U	27	9	**59**	**12**

TURNER, John§ (M) 1 1

H: 6 2 W: 11 00 b.Harrow 12-2-86

Source: Scholar.

2002-03	Cambridge U	1	1	**1**	**1**

WANLESS, Paul (M) 324 44

H: 6 1 W: 14 08 b.Banbury 14-12-73

Source: Trainee.

1991–92	Oxford U	6	0		
1992–93	Oxford U	7	0		
1993–94	Oxford U	9	0		
1994–95	Oxford U	10	0	**32**	**0**
1995–96	Lincoln C	8	0	**8**	**0**
1995–96	*Cambridge U*	14	1		
1996–97	Cambridge U	30	3		
1997–98	Cambridge U	42	8		
1998–99	Cambridge U	45	8		
1999–2000	Cambridge U	42	3		
2000-01	Cambridge U	43	10		
2001-02	Cambridge U	29	6		
2002-03	Cambridge U	39	5	**284**	**44**

WARNER, Phil‡ (D) 40 0

H: 5 10 W: 11 12 b.Southampton 2-2-79

Source: Trainee.

1997–98	Southampton	1	0		
1998–99	Southampton	5	0		
1999–2000	Southampton	0	0		
1999–2000	*Brentford*	14	0	**14**	**0**
2000-01	Southampton	0	0	**6**	**0**
2001-02	Cambridge U	12	0		
2002-03	Cambridge U	8	0	**20**	**0**

Scholars

Beech, Thomas PE; Bennett, Lee; Clark, George; Daniels, David W; George, Rikki; Gleeson, Daniel; Hammond, Daniel J; Meddows, Leigh J; Quinton, Darren J; Shinn, Michael J; Stephenson-Lowe, Jermaine J; Stone, Brady T; Thornton, Robert I; Turner, John AJ; Winkworth, Kevin P

Non-Contract

Brennan, Martin I

Players who do not hold a current contract but their registration jas been retained by the club

Millership, Jamie C; Okay, Erhan

CARDIFF C

AINSWORTH, Gareth* (M) 284 68

H: 5 10 W: 12 05 b.Blackburn 10-5-73

Source: Blackburn R Trainee.

1991–92	Preston NE	5	0		
1992–93	Cambridge U	4	1	**4**	**1**
1992–93	Preston NE	26	0		
1993–94	Preston NE	38	11		
1994–95	Preston NE	16	1		
1995–96	Preston NE	2	0		
1995–96	Lincoln C	31	12		
1996–97	Lincoln C	46	22		
1997–98	Lincoln C	6	3	**83**	**37**
1997–98	Port Vale	40	5		
1998–99	Port Vale	15	5	**55**	**10**
1998–99	Wimbledon	8	0		
1999–2000	Wimbledon	2	2		
2000-01	Wimbledon	12	2		
2001-02	Wimbledon	2	0		
2001-02	*Preston NE*	5	1	**92**	**13**
2002-03	Wimbledon	12	2	**36**	**6**
2002-03	*Walsall*	5	1	**5**	**1**
2002-03	Cardiff C	9	0	**9**	**0**

ALEXANDER, Neil (G) 194 0

H: 6 1 W: 11 07 b.Edinburgh 10-3-78

Source: Edina Hibs. *Honours:* Scotland Under-21.

1996–97	Stenhousemuir	12	0		
1997–98	Stenhousemuir	36	0	**48**	**0**
1998–99	Livingston	21	0		
1999–2000	Livingston	13	0		
2000-01	Livingston	26	0	**60**	**0**
2001-02	Cardiff C	46	0		
2002-03	Cardiff C	40	0	**86**	**0**

BARKER, Chris (D) 153 3

H: 6 2 W: 11 08 b.Sheffield 2-3-80

Source: Alfreton.

1998–99	Barnsley	0	0		
1999–2000	Barnsley	29	0		
2000-01	Barnsley	40	0		
2001-02	Barnsley	44	3	**113**	**3**
2002-03	Cardiff C	40	0	**40**	**0**

BOLAND, Willie (M) 199 3

H: 5 9 W: 11 02 b.Ennis 6-8-75

Source: Trainee. *Honours:* Eire Youth, Under-21.

1992–93	Coventry C	1	0		
1993–94	Coventry C	27	0		
1994–95	Coventry C	12	0		
1995–96	Coventry C	3	0		
1996–97	Coventry C	1	0		
1997–98	Coventry C	19	0		
1998–99	Coventry C	0	0	**63**	**0**
1999–2000	Cardiff C	28	1		
2000-01	Cardiff C	25	1		
2001-02	Cardiff C	42	1		
2002-03	Cardiff C	41	0	**136**	**3**

BONNER, Mark (M) 302 17

H: 5 10 W: 11 00 b.Ormskirk 7-6-74

Source: Trainee.

1991–92	Blackpool	3	0		
1992–93	Blackpool	15	0		
1993–94	Blackpool	40	7		
1994–95	Blackpool	17	0		
1995–96	Blackpool	42	3		
1996–97	Blackpool	29	1		
1997–98	Blackpool	32	3	**178**	**14**
1998–99	Cardiff C	25	1		
1998–99	*Hull C*	1	1	**1**	**1**
1999–2000	Cardiff C	31	0		
2000-01	Cardiff C	24	1		
2001-02	Cardiff C	29	0		
2002-03	Cardiff C	14	0	**123**	**2**

BOWEN, Jason (F) 322 68

H: 5 6 W: 8 10 b.Merthyr 24-8-72

Source: Trainee. *Honours:* Wales Schools, Youth, Under-21, 2 full caps.

1990–91	Swansea C	3	0		
1991–92	Swansea C	11	0		
1992–93	Swansea C	38	10		
1993–94	Swansea C	41	11		
1994–95	Swansea C	31	5	**124**	**26**
1995–96	Birmingham C	23	4		
1996–97	Birmingham C	25	3		
1997–98	Birmingham C	0	0	**48**	**7**
1997–98	*Southampton*	3	0	**3**	**0**
1997–98	Reading	14	1		
1998–99	Reading	1	0	**15**	**1**
1998–99	Cardiff C	17	2		
1999–2000	Cardiff C	39	12		
2000-01	Cardiff C	40	12		
2001-02	Cardiff C	25	5		
2002-03	Cardiff C	11	3	**132**	**34**

CAMPBELL, Andy (F) 109 17

H: 5 11 W: 11 07 b.Middlesbrough 18-4-79

Source: Trainee. *Honours:* England Youth, Under-21.

1995–96	Middlesbrough	2	0		
1996–97	Middlesbrough	3	0		
1997–98	Middlesbrough	7	0		
1998–99	Middlesbrough	8	0		
1998–99	*Sheffield U*	11	3	**11**	**3**
1999–2000	Middlesbrough	25	4		
2000-01	Middlesbrough	7	0		
2000-01	*Bolton W*	6	0	**6**	**0**
2001-02	Middlesbrough	4	0	**56**	**4**
2001-02	Cardiff C	8	7		
2002-03	Cardiff C	28	3	**36**	**10**

COLLINS, James (F) 12 1

H: 6 2 W: 13 00 b.Newport 23-8-83

Source: Scholar. *Honours:* Wales Youth, Under-21.

2000-01	Cardiff C	3	0		
2001-02	Cardiff C	7	1		
2002-03	Cardiff C	2	0	**12**	**1**

CROFT, Gary (D) **274 7**
H: 5 9 W: 11 08 b.Burton-on-Trent 17-2-74
Source: Trainee. *Honours:* England Under-21.

1990–91	Grimsby T	1	0		
1991–92	Grimsby T	0	0		
1992–93	Grimsby T	32	0		
1993–94	Grimsby T	36	1		
1994–95	Grimsby T	44	1		
1995–96	Grimsby T	36	1	**149**	**3**
1995–96	Blackburn R	0	0		
1996–97	Blackburn R	5	0		
1997–98	Blackburn R	23	1		
1998–99	Blackburn R	12	0		
1999–2000	Blackburn R	0	0	**40**	**1**
1999–2000	Ipswich T	21	1		
2000-01	Ipswich T	8	0		
2001-02	Ipswich T	0	0	**29**	**1**
2001-02	*Wigan Ath*	7	0	**7**	**0**
2001-02	*Cardiff C*	6	1		
2002-03	Cardiff C	43	1	**49**	**2**

DIMOND, Kristian‡ (M) **0 0**
b.Cardiff 1-2-83
Source: Trainee.

1999–2000	Crystal Palace	0	0
2000-01	Crystal Palace	0	0
2001-02	Crystal Palace	0	0
2001-02	Cardiff C	0	0
2002-03	Cardiff C	0	0

EARNSHAW, Robert (F) **131 65**
H: 5 6 W: 9 09 b.Zambia 6-4-81
Source: Trainee. *Honours:* Wales Youth, Under-21, 4 full caps, 2 goals.

1997–98	Cardiff C	5	0		
1998–99	Cardiff C	5	1		
1998–99	*Middlesbrough*	0	0		
1999–2000	Cardiff C	6	1		
1999–2000	*Morton*	3	2	**3**	**2**
2000-01	Cardiff C	36	19		
2001-02	Cardiff C	30	11		
2002-03	Cardiff C	46	31	**128**	**63**

FISH, Nicholas (M) **0 0**
b.Cardiff 15-9-84
Source: Scholar.

2001-02	Cardiff C	0	0
2002-03	Cardiff C	0	0

FORTUNE-WEST, Leo* (F) **248 72**
H: 6 4 W: 13 10 b.Stratford 9-4-71
Source: Tiptree, Dagenham, Dartford, Bishops Stortford, Stevenage Bor.

1995–96	Gillingham	40	12		
1996–97	Gillingham	7	2		
1996–97	*Leyton Orient*	5	0	**5**	**0**
1997–98	Gillingham	20	4	**67**	**18**
1998–99	Lincoln C	9	1	**9**	**1**
1998–99	Brentford	11	0	**11**	**0**
1998–99	Rotherham U	20	12		
1999–2000	Rotherham U	39	17		
2000-01	Rotherham U	5	1	**64**	**30**
2000-01	Cardiff C	37	12		
2001-02	Cardiff C	36	9		
2002-03	Cardiff C	19	2	**92**	**23**

GABBIDON, Daniel (D) **131 6**
H: 5 10 W: 11 02 b.Cwmbran 8-8-79
Source: Trainee. *Honours:* Wales Youth, Under-21, 4 full caps.

1998–99	WBA	2	0		
1999–2000	WBA	18	0		
2000-01	WBA	0	0	**20**	**0**
2000-01	Cardiff C	43	3		
2001-02	Cardiff C	44	3		
2002-03	Cardiff C	24	0	**111**	**6**

GILES, Martyn* (D) **5 0**
H: 6 0 W: 12 00 b.Cardiff 10-4-83
Source: Scholar. *Honours:* Wales Youth.

2000-01	Cardiff C	5	0		
2001-02	Cardiff C	0	0		
2002-03	Cardiff C	0	0	**5**	**0**

GORDON, Gavin (F) **178 42**
H: 6 1 W: 12 00 b.Manchester 24-6-79
Source: Trainee.

1995–96	Hull C	13	3		
1996–97	Hull C	20	4		
1997–98	Hull C	5	2	**38**	**9**
1997–98	Lincoln C	13	3		
1998–99	Lincoln C	27	5		
1999–2000	Lincoln C	41	11		
2000-01	Lincoln C	18	9	**99**	**28**
2000-01	Cardiff C	10	1		
2001-02	Cardiff C	15	1		
2002-03	Cardiff C	10	2	**35**	**4**
2002-03	*Oxford U*	6	1	**6**	**1**

HAMILTON, Des (M) **154 6**
H: 5 11 W: 12 09 b.Bradford 15-8-76
Source: Trainee. *Honours:* England Under-21.

1993–94	Bradford C	2	1		
1994–95	Bradford C	30	1		
1995–96	Bradford C	24	3		
1996–97	Bradford C	32	0	**88**	**5**
1996–97	Newcastle U	0	0		
1997–98	Newcastle U	12	0		
1998–99	Newcastle U	0	0		
1998–99	*Sheffield U*	6	0	**6**	**0**
1998–99	*Huddersfield T*	10	1	**10**	**1**
1999–2000	Newcastle U	0	0		
1999–2000	*Norwich C*	7	0	**7**	**0**
2000-01	Newcastle U	0	0	**12**	**0**
2000-01	*Tranmere R*	6	0	**6**	**0**
2001-02	Cardiff C	19	0		
2002-03	Cardiff C	6	0	**25**	**0**

HEAL, Simon* (M) **0 0**
b.Barnstaple 10-11-82
Source: Scholar.

2001-02	Cardiff C	0	0
2002-03	Cardiff C	0	0

HUGGINS, Kirk (M) **0 0**
b.Cardiff 4-6-85
Source: Scholar.

2002-03	Cardiff C	0	0

HUGHES, David‡ (D) **68 3**
H: 6 4 W: 14 02 b.Wrexham 1-2-78
Source: Trainee. *Honours:* Wales Youth, Under-21, B.

1996–97	Aston Villa	7	0		
1997–98	Aston Villa	0	0		
1997–98	*Carlisle U*	1	0	**1**	**0**
1998–99	Aston Villa	0	0		
1999–2000	Aston Villa	0	0	**7**	**0**
1999–2000	Shrewsbury T	22	1		
2000-01	Shrewsbury T	24	2	**46**	**3**
2000-01	Cardiff C	12	0		
2001-02	Cardiff C	2	0		
2002-03	Cardiff C	0	0	**14**	**0**

INGRAM, Richard (M) **0 0**
b.Merthyr 15-2-85
Source: Scholar.

2001-02	Cardiff C	0	0
2002-03	Cardiff C	0	0

JENKINS, Steve* (D) **430 5**
H: 5 11 W: 12 12 b.Merthyr 16-7-72
Source: Trainee. *Honours:* Wales Youth, Under-21, 16 full caps.

1990–91	Swansea C	1	0		
1991–92	Swansea C	34	0		
1992–93	Swansea C	33	0		
1993–94	Swansea C	40	1		
1994–95	Swansea C	42	0		
1995–96	Swansea C	15	0	**165**	**1**
1995–96	Huddersfield T	31	1		
1996–97	Huddersfield T	33	0		
1997–98	Huddersfield T	29	1		
1998–99	Huddersfield T	36	1		
1999–2000	Huddersfield T	33	0		
2000-01	Huddersfield T	30	0		
2000-01	*Birmingham C*	3	0	**3**	**0**
2001-02	Huddersfield T	40	1		
2002-03	Huddersfield T	26	0	**258**	**4**
2002-03	Cardiff C	4	0	**4**	**0**

JONES, Gethin* (D) **3 0**
H: 5 11 W: 12 04 b.Carmarthen 8-8-81
Source: Carmarthen T.

2000-01	Cardiff C	2	0		
2001-02	Cardiff C	1	0		
2002-03	Cardiff C	0	0	**3**	**0**

JORDAN, Andrew* (D) **16 0**
H: 6 2 W: 13 05 b.Manchester 14-12-79
Source: Trainee. *Honours:* Scotland Under-21.

1997–98	Bristol C	0	0		
1998–99	Bristol C	1	0		
1999–2000	Bristol C	8	0		
2000-01	Bristol C	2	0	**11**	**0**
2000-01	Cardiff C	5	0		
2001-02	Cardiff C	0	0		
2002-03	Cardiff C	0	0	**5**	**0**

KAVANAGH, Graham (M) **333 56**
H: 5 10 W: 12 08 b.Dublin 2-12-73
Source: Home Farm. *Honours:* Eire Under-21, 3 full caps, 1 goal.

1991–92	Middlesbrough	0	0		
1992–93	Middlesbrough	10	0		
1993–94	Middlesbrough	11	2		
1993–94	*Darlington*	5	0	**5**	**0**
1994–95	Middlesbrough	7	0		
1995–96	Middlesbrough	7	1		
1996–97	Middlesbrough	0	0	**35**	**3**
1996–97	Stoke C	38	4		
1997–98	Stoke C	44	5		
1998–99	Stoke C	36	11		
1999–2000	Stoke C	45	7		
2000-01	Stoke C	43	8	**206**	**35**
2001-02	Cardiff C	43	13		
2002-03	Cardiff C	44	5	**87**	**18**

LEE-BARRETT, Arran (M) **0 0**
b.Ipswich 28-2-84
Source: Norwich C Scholar.

2002-03	Cardiff C	0	0

LEGG, Andy# (M) **495 56**
H: 5 8 W: 10 07 b.Neath 28-7-66
Source: Briton Ferry. *Honours:* Wales 6 full caps.

1988–89	Swansea C	6	0		
1989–90	Swansea C	26	3		
1990–91	Swansea C	39	5		
1991–92	Swansea C	46	9		
1992–93	Swansea C	46	12	**163**	**29**
1993–94	Notts Co	30	2		
1994–95	Notts Co	34	3		
1995–96	Notts Co	25	4	**89**	**9**
1995–96	Birmingham C	12	1		
1996–97	Birmingham C	33	4		
1997–98	Birmingham C	0	0	**45**	**5**
1997–98	*Ipswich T*	6	1	**6**	**1**
1997–98	Reading	10	0		
1998–99	Reading	2	0	**12**	**0**
1998–99	*Peterborough U*	5	0	**5**	**0**
1998–99	Cardiff C	24	2		
1999–2000	Cardiff C	42	2		
2000-01	Cardiff C	39	3		
2001-02	Cardiff C	35	2		
2002-03	Cardiff C	35	3	**175**	**12**

MARGETSON, Martyn (G) **140 0**
H: 6 0 W: 13 12 b.West Neath 8-9-71
Source: Trainee. *Honours:* Wales Schools, Youth, Under-21, B.

1990–91	Manchester C	2	0		
1991–92	Manchester C	3	0		
1992–93	Manchester C	1	0		
1993–94	Manchester C	0	0		
1993–94	*Bristol R*	3	0	**3**	**0**
1993–94	*Bolton W*	0	0		
1994–95	Manchester C	0	0		
1994–95	*Luton T*	0	0		
1995–96	Manchester C	0	0		
1996–97	Manchester C	17	0		
1997–98	Manchester C	28	0	**51**	**0**
1998–99	Southend U	32	0	**32**	**0**
1999–2000	Huddersfield T	0	0		
2000-01	Huddersfield T	2	0		
2001-02	Huddersfield T	46	0	**48**	**0**
2002-03	Cardiff C	6	0	**6**	**0**

MAXWELL, Leyton (M) **53 3**
H: 5 8 W: 11 00 b.Rhyl 3-10-79
Source: Trainee. *Honours:* Wales Youth, Under-21.

1997–98	Liverpool	0	0		
1998–99	Liverpool	0	0		
1999–2000	Liverpool	0	0		
2000-01	Liverpool	0	0		
2000-01	*Stockport Co*	20	2	**20**	**2**
2001-02	Cardiff C	17	1		
2002-03	Cardiff C	16	0	**33**	**1**

PARKINS, Michael (M) **0 0**
b.Cardiff 12-1-85
Source: Scholar.

2001-02	Cardiff C	0	0
2002-03	Cardiff C	0	0

PRIOR, Spencer (D) **431 11**
H: 6 3 W: 13 00 b.Rochford 22-4-71
Source: Trainee.

1988–89	Southend U	14	1		
1989–90	Southend U	15	1		
1990–91	Southend U	19	0		
1991–92	Southend U	42	1		
1992–93	Southend U	45	0	**135**	**3**
1993–94	Norwich C	13	0		

1994–95 Norwich C 17 0
1995–96 Norwich C 44 1 **74 1**
1996–97 Leicester C 34 0
1997–98 Leicester C 30 0 **64 0**
1998–99 Derby Co 34 1
1999–2000 Derby Co 20 0 **54 1**
1999–2000 Manchester C 9 3
2000–01 Manchester C 21 1 **30 4**
2001–02 Cardiff C 37 2
2002–03 Cardiff C 37 0 **74 2**

SIMPKINS, Mike‡ (D) 50 0
H: 6 0 W: 11 11 b.Sheffield 28-11-78
Source: Trainee.
1997–98 Sheffield W 0 0
1997–98 Chesterfield 0 0
1998–99 Chesterfield 1 0
1999–2000 Chesterfield 9 0
2000–01 Chesterfield 16 0 **26 0**
2001–02 Cardiff C 17 0
2002–03 Cardiff C 0 0 **17 0**
2002–03 *Exeter C* 5 0 **5 0**
2002–03 *Cheltenham T* 2 0 **2 0**

THOMAS, Daniel (M) 0 0
b.Caerphilly 13-5-85
Source: Scholar.
2002–03 Cardiff C 0 0

THORNE, Peter (F) 318 113
H: 6 0 W: 12 10 b.Manchester 21-6-73
Source: Trainee.
1991–92 Blackburn R 0 0
1992–93 Blackburn R 0 0
1993–94 Blackburn R 0 0
1993–94 *Wigan Ath* 11 0 **11 0**
1994–95 Blackburn R 0 0
1994–95 Swindon T 20 9
1995–96 Swindon T 26 10
1996–97 Swindon T 31 8 **77 27**
1997–98 Stoke C 36 12
1998–99 Stoke C 34 9
1999–2000 Stoke C 45 24
2000–01 Stoke C 38 16
2001–02 Stoke C 5 4 **158 65**
2001–02 Cardiff C 26 8
2002–03 Cardiff C 46 13 **72 21**

WALLIS, Tony* (M) 0 0
b.Portsmouth 9-10-82
Source: Scholar.
2001–02 Cardiff C 0 0
2002–03 Cardiff C 0 0

WALTON, Mark* (G) 210 0
H: 6 4 W: 13 13 b.Merthyr 1-6-69
Source: Swansea C. *Honours:* Wales Under-21.
1986–87 Luton T 0 0
1987–88 Luton T 0 0
1987–88 Colchester U 17 0
1988–89 Colchester U 23 0 **40 0**
1989–90 Norwich C 1 0
1990–91 Norwich C 4 0
1991–92 Norwich C 17 0
1992–93 Norwich C 0 0
1993–94 Norwich C 0 0
1993–94 *Wrexham* 6 0 **6 0**
1993–94 Dundee 0 0
1993–94 Bolton W 3 0 **3 0**
From Fakenham T.
1996–97 Fulham 28 0
1997–98 Fulham 12 0 **40 0**
1997–98 *Gillingham* 1 0 **1 0**
1997–98 *Norwich C* 0 0 **22 0**
1998–99 Brighton & HA 19 0
1999–2000 Brighton & HA 39 0 **58 0**
2000–01 Cardiff C 40 0
2001–02 Cardiff C 0 0
2002–03 Cardiff C 0 0 **40 0**

WESTON, Rhys (D) 104 2
H: 6 1 W: 12 03 b.Kingston 27-10-80
Source: Trainee. *Honours:* Wales Schools, Youth, Under-21, 4 full caps.
1999–2000 Arsenal 1 0
2000–01 Arsenal 0 0 **1 0**
2000–01 Cardiff C 28 0
2001–02 Cardiff C 37 0
2002–03 Cardiff C 38 2 **103 2**

WHALLEY, Gareth (M) 309 12
H: 5 10 W: 11 00 b.Manchester 19-12-73
Source: Trainee.
1992–93 Crewe Alex 25 1
1993–94 Crewe Alex 15 1
1994–95 Crewe Alex 40 1
1995–96 Crewe Alex 44 2
1996–97 Crewe Alex 38 3
1997–98 Crewe Alex 18 1
1998–99 Bradford C 45 2
1999–2000 Bradford C 16 1
2000–01 Bradford C 19 0
2001–02 Bradford C 23 0 **103 3**
2001–02 *Crewe Alex* 7 0 **187 9**
2002–03 Cardiff C 19 0 **19 0**

YOUNG, Scott (D) 277 22
H: 6 1 W: 12 00 b.Tonypandy 14-1-76
Source: Trainee. *Honours:* Wales Under-21, B.
1993–94 Cardiff C 6 0
1994–95 Cardiff C 22 0
1995–96 Cardiff C 41 0
1996–97 Cardiff C 32 1
1997–98 Cardiff C 31 3
1998–99 Cardiff C 33 1
1999–2000 Cardiff C 22 2
2000–01 Cardiff C 45 10
2001–02 Cardiff C 33 4
2002–03 Cardiff C 12 1 **277 22**

ZHIYI, Fan# (M) 94 4
H: 6 2 W: 12 01 b.Shanghai 6-11-69
Source: Shanghai Shenhua. *Honours:* China 109 full caps, 16 goals.
1998–99 Crystal Palace 29 2
1999–2000 Crystal Palace 29 1
2000–01 Crystal Palace 28 1
2001–02 Crystal Palace 2 0 **88 4**
2002–03 Cardiff C 6 0 **6 0**

Scholars
Anthony, Byron; Bailey, John; Brimble, Daniel; Cronin, Sean A; Fleetwood, Stuart; Hartley, Michael, Hayward, Michael; Khalil, Tareq; Kift, Jonathan; Lippiett, Darren; Parslow, Daniel; Taylor, Anthony P; Williams, Steven P

CARLISLE U

ANDREWS, Lee (D) 62 0
H: 5 11 W: 12 00 b.Carlisle 23-4-83
Source: Scholar.
2001–02 Carlisle U 39 0
2002–03 Carlisle U 15 0 **54 0**
2002–03 *Rochdale* 8 0 **8 0**

BALDACCHINO, Ryan (M) 22 0
H: 5 10 W: 11 08 b.Leicester 13-1-81
Source: Trainee.
1998–99 Blackburn R 0 0
1999–2000 Blackburn R 0 0
2000–01 Blackburn R 0 0
2000–01 Bolton W 0 0
2001–02 Bolton W 0 0
2002–03 Carlisle U 22 0 **22 0**

BELL, Stuart‡ (M) 5 0
H: 5 9 W: 11 04 b.Carlisle 15-3-84
Source: Trainee.
2001–02 Carlisle U 5 0
2002–03 Carlisle U 0 0 **5 0**

BIRCH, Mark# (D) 110 1
H: 5 11 W: 12 08 b.Stoke 5-1-77
Source: Trainee.
1997–98 Stoke C 0 0
From Northwich V.
2000–01 Carlisle U 44 0
2001–02 Carlisle U 42 0
2002–03 Carlisle U 24 1 **110 1**

BURNS, John‡ (M) 19 0
H: 5 10 W: 11 04 b.Dublin 4-12-77
Source: Belvedere, Trainee.
1994–95 Nottingham F 0 0
1995–96 Nottingham F 0 0
1996–97 Nottingham F 0 0
1997–98 Nottingham F 0 0
1998–99 Nottingham F 0 0
1999–2000 Nottingham F 3 0 **3 0**
1999–2000 Bristol C 11 0
2000–01 Bristol C 0 0
2001–02 Bristol C 0 0 **11 0**
2002–03 Carlisle U 5 0 **5 0**

BYRNE, Dessie (D) 28 0
H: 5 10 W: 12 00 b.Dublin 10-4-81
Source: Trainee.
1998–99 Stockport Co 2 0 **2 0**
1999–2000 Sr Patrick's Ath 11 0 **11 0**
2000–01 Wimbledon 0 0
2001–02 *Cambridge U* 4 0 **4 0**
2001–02 Wimbledon 1 0
2002–03 Wimbledon 0 0 **1 0**
2002–03 Carlisle U 10 0 **10 0**

DICKINSON, Mike‡ (F) 1 0
H: 5 11 W: 11 06 b.Ashington 4-5-84
Source: Trainee.
2001–02 Carlisle U 1 0
2002–03 Carlisle U 0 0 **1 0**

DILLON, Dan‡ (M) 1 0
H: 5 9 W: 10 07 b.Huntingdon 6-9-86
2002–03 Carlisle U 1 0 **1 0**

FARRELL, Craig (F) 33 11
H: 6 0 W: 12 06 b.Middlesbrough 5-12-82
Source: Trainee.
1999–2000 Leeds U 0 0
2000–01 Leeds U 0 0
2001–02 Leeds U 0 0
2002–03 Leeds U 0 0
2002–03 Carlisle U 33 11 **33 11**

FORAN, Richie (F) 96 32
H: 6 1 W: 13 00 b.Dublin 16-6-80
2000–01 Shelbourne 28 11 **28 11**
2001–02 Carlisle U 37 14
2002–03 Carlisle U 31 7 **68 21**

FREEMAN, David‡ (F) 15 0
H: 5 10 W: 11 09 b.Dublin 25-11-79
Source: Cherry Orchard. *Honours:* Eire Under-21.
1996–97 Nottingham F 0 0
1997–98 Nottingham F 0 0
1998–99 Nottingham F 0 0
1999–2000 Nottingham F 3 0
2000–01 Nottingham F 5 0
2000–01 *Port Vale* 3 0 **3 0**
2001–02 Nottingham F 0 0 **8 0**
2002–03 Carlisle U 4 0 **4 0**

GALLOWAY, Mick‡ (M) 156 7
H: 5 11 W: 11 05 b.Nottingham 13-10-74
Source: Trainee.
1993–94 Notts Co 0 0
1994–95 Notts Co 7 0
1995–96 Notts Co 9 0
1996–97 Notts Co 5 0 **21 0**
1996–97 *Gillingham* 9 1
1997–98 Gillingham 39 1
1998–99 Gillingham 25 3
1999–2000 Gillingham 2 0 **75 5**
1999–2000 *Lincoln C* 5 0 **5 0**
1999–2000 Chesterfield 15 1
2000–01 Chesterfield 5 0 **20 1**
2000–01 Carlisle U 26 1
2001–02 Carlisle U 0 0
2002–03 Carlisle U 9 0 **35 1**

GLENNON, Matty (G) 97 0
H: 6 2 W: 14 08 b.Stockport 8-10-78
Source: Trainee.
1997–98 Bolton W 0 0
1998–99 Bolton W 0 0
1999–2000 Bolton W 0 0
1999–2000 *Port Vale* 0 0
1999–2000 *Stockport Co* 0 0
2000–01 Bolton W 0 0
2000–01 *Bristol R* 1 0 **1 0**
2000–01 *Carlisle U* 29 0
2001–02 Hull C 26 0
2002–03 Hull C 9 0 **35 0**
2002–03 Carlisle U 32 0 **61 0**

HEVICON, Ryan‡ (M) 1 0
H: 5 10 W: 11 02 b.Manchester 3-12-82
Source: Scholar.
2001–02 Blackburn R 0 0
2002–03 Carlisle U 1 0 **1 0**

JACK, Michael (M) 39 0
H: 5 10 W: 11 08 b.Carlisle 2-10-82
Source: Trainee.
2001–02 Carlisle U 32 0
2002–03 Carlisle U 7 0 **39 0**

KEEN, Peter (G) 65 1
H: 6 0 W: 13 00 b.Middlesbrough 16-11-76
Source: Trainee.
1995–96 Newcastle U 0 0
1996–97 Newcastle U 0 0
1997–98 Newcastle U 0 0
1998–99 Newcastle U 0 0
1999–2000 Carlisle U 6 0
2000–01 Carlisle U 3 1
2000–01 *Darlington* 7 0 **7 0**
2001–02 Carlisle U 36 0
2002–03 Carlisle U 13 0 **58 1**

KELLY, Darren (D)				**32**	**1**
H: 6 0 W: 13 00 b.Derry 30-6-79					
From Derry C.					
2002-03	Carlisle U	32	1	**32**	**1**

MADDISON, Lee# (D)				**266**	**2**
H: 5 11 W: 12 10 b.Bristol 5-10-72					
Source: Trainee.					
1991–92	Bristol R	10	0		
1992–93	Bristol R	12	0		
1993–94	Bristol R	37	0		
1994–95	Bristol R	14	0		
1995–96	Bristol R	0	0	**73**	**0**
1995–96	Northampton T	21	0		
1996–97	Northampton T	34	0	**55**	**0**
1997–98	Dundee	24	1		
1998–99	Dundee	21	0		
1999–2000	Dundee	20	0		
2000-01	Dundee	0	0	**65**	**1**
2000-01	Carlisle U	34	0		
2001-02	Carlisle U	7	0		
2001-02	*Oxford U*	11	0	**11**	**0**
2002-03	Carlisle U	21	1	**62**	**1**

MAGENNIS, Mark‡ (M)				**6**	**1**
H: 5 7 W: 10 02 b.Newtonards 15-3-83					
Source: Scholar.					
2000-01	Coventry C	0	0		
2001-02	Coventry C	0	0		
2002-03	Carlisle U	6	1	**6**	**1**

McCARTHY, Jon# (M)				**452**	**51**
H: 5 10 W: 11 08 b.Middlesbrough 18-8-70					
Honours: Northern Ireland B, 18 full caps.					
1987–88	Hartlepool U	1	0	**1**	**0**
From Shepshed					
1990–91	York C	27	2		
1991–92	York C	42	6		
1992–93	York C	42	7		
1993–94	York C	44	7		
1994–95	York C	44	9		
1995–96	Port Vale	45	7		
1996–97	Port Vale	45	4		
1997–98	Port Vale	4	0		
1997–98	Birmingham C	41	4		
1998–99	Birmingham C	43	0		
1999–2000	Birmingham C	21	4		
2000-01	Birmingham C	15	0		
2001-02	Birmingham C	4	0	**124**	**8**
2001-02	*Sheffield W*	4	0	**4**	**0**
2002-03	Port Vale	8	0	**102**	**11**
2002-03	York C	1	0	**200**	**31**
2002-03	Carlisle U	21	1	**21**	**1**

McDONAGH, Will (M)				**36**	**3**
H: 6 0 W: 12 06 b.Dublin 14-3-83					
Source: Bohemians.					
2001-02	Carlisle U	12	1		
2002-03	Carlisle U	24	2	**36**	**3**

McGILL, Brendan (M)				**62**	**5**
H: 5 7 W: 11 00 b.Dublin 22-3-81					
1998–99	Sunderland	0	0		
1999–2000	Sunderland	0	0		
2000-01	Sunderland	0	0		
2001-02	Sunderland	0	0		
2001-02	*Carlisle U*	28	2		
2002-03	Sunderland	0	0		
2002-03	Carlisle U	34	3	**62**	**5**

MOLLOY, Trevor‡ (F)				**7**	**1**
H: 5 10 W: 11 06 b.Dublin 14-4-77					
From Bohemians.					
2002-03	Carlisle U	7	1	**7**	**1**

MURPHY, Peter (D)				**101**	**3**
H: 5 11 W: 12 06 b.Dublin 27-10-80					
Source: Trainee. *Honours:* Eire Under-21.					
1998–99	Blackburn R	0	0		
1999–2000	Blackburn R	0	0		
2000-01	Blackburn R	0	0		
2000-01	*Halifax T*	21	1	**21**	**1**
2001-02	Blackburn R	0	0		
2001-02	Carlisle U	40	0		
2002-03	Carlisle U	40	2	**80**	**2**

NAISBITT, Danny‡ (G)				**24**	**0**
H: 6 1 W: 11 12 b.Bishop Auckland 25-11-78					
Source: Trainee.					
1997–98	Walsall	0	0		
1998–99	Walsall	0	0		
1999–2000	Barnet	4	0		
2000-01	Barnet	19	0		
2001-02	Barnet	0	0	**23**	**0**
2002-03	Carlisle U	1	0	**1**	**0**

NIXON, Marc (F)				**7**	**0**
H: 5 10 W: 12 00 b.Hexham 29-1-84					
Source: Trainee.					
2001-02	Carlisle U	0	0		
2002-03	Carlisle U	7	0	**7**	**0**

RAVEN, Paul‡ (D)				**371**	**21**
H: 6 1 W: 13 02 b.Salisbury 28-7-70					
Source: School. *Honours:* England Schools, Youth.					
1987–88	Doncaster R	17	3		
1988–89	Doncaster R	35	1		
1988–89	WBA	3	0		
1989–90	WBA	7	0		
1990–91	WBA	13	0		
1991–92	WBA	7	1		
1991–92	*Doncaster R*	7	0	**59**	**4**
1992–93	WBA	44	7		
1993–94	WBA	34	1		
1994–95	WBA	31	0		
1995–96	WBA	40	4		
1996–97	WBA	33	1		
1997–98	WBA	8	0		
1998–99	WBA	7	0		
1998–99	*Rotherham U*	11	2	**11**	**2**
1999–2000	WBA	32	1	**259**	**15**
2000-01	Grimsby T	15	0		
2001-02	Grimsby T	9	0		
2002-03	Grimsby T	7	0	**31**	**0**
2002-03	Carlisle U	11	0	**11**	**0**

RUNDLE, Adam (M)				**38**	**1**
H: 5 8 W: 11 00 b.Durham 8-7-84					
Source: Scholar.					
2001-02	Darlington	12	0		
2002-03	Darlington	5	0	**17**	**0**
2002-03	Carlisle U	21	1	**21**	**1**

RUSSELL, Craig# (F)				**260**	**40**
H: 5 10 W: 12 07 b.Jarrow 4-2-74					
Source: Trainee.					
1991–92	Sunderland	4	0		
1992–93	Sunderland	0	0		
1993–94	Sunderland	35	9		
1994–95	Sunderland	38	5		
1995–96	Sunderland	41	13		
1996–97	Sunderland	29	4		
1997–98	Sunderland	3	0	**150**	**31**
1997–98	Manchester C	24	1		
1998–99	Manchester C	7	1		
1998–99	*Tranmere R*	4	0	**4**	**0**
1998–99	*Port Vale*	8	1	**8**	**1**
1999–2000	Manchester C	0	0	**31**	**2**
1999–2000	*Darlington*	12	2	**12**	**2**
1999–2000	*Oxford U*	6	0	**6**	**0**
1999–2000	*St Johnstone*	1	1		
2000-01	St Johnstone	13	1		
2001-02	St Johnstone	14	1		
2002-03	St Johnstone	8	0	**36**	**3**
2002-03	Carlisle U	13	1	**13**	**1**

SHELLEY, Brian (D)				**35**	**1**
H: 6 0 W: 13 00 b.Dublin 15-11-81					
Honours: Eire Under-21.					
From Bohemians.					
2002-03	Carlisle U	35	1	**35**	**1**

SLAVEN, John (F)				**3**	**0**
H: 5 10 W: 11 00 b.Edinburgh 8-10-85					
2001-02	Carlisle U	2	0		
2002-03	Carlisle U	1	0	**3**	**0**

SUMMERBELL, Mark (M)				**100**	**2**
H: 5 9 W: 11 06 b.Durham 30-10-76					
Source: Trainee.					
1995–96	Middlesbrough	1	0		
1996–97	Middlesbrough	2	0		
1997–98	Middlesbrough	11	0		
1998–99	Middlesbrough	11	0		
1999–2000	Middlesbrough	19	0		
2000-01	Middlesbrough	7	1		
2001-02	Middlesbrough	0	0		
2001-02	*Bristol C*	5	0	**5**	**0**
2001-02	*Portsmouth*	5	0	**5**	**0**
2002-03	Middlesbrough	0	0	**51**	**1**
2002-03	Carlisle U	39	1	**39**	**1**

THWAITES, Adam* (D)				**1**	**0**
H: 5 10 W: 11 10 b.Carlisle 18-12-81					
Source: Trainee.					
2000-01	Carlisle U	0	0		
2001-02	Carlisle U	1	0		
2002-03	Carlisle U	0	0	**1**	**0**

WAKE, Brian (F)				**28**	**9**
H: 6 0 W: 12 00 b.Stockton 13-8-82					
Source: Tow Law T.					
2001-02	Carlisle U	0	0		
2002-03	Carlisle U	28	9	**28**	**9**

WEAVER, Luke* (G)				**68**	**0**
H: 6 4 W: 14 08 b.Woolwich 26-6-79					
Source: Trainee. *Honours:* England Schools, Youth.					
1996–97	Leyton Orient	9	0		
1996–97	*West Ham U*	0	0		
1997–98	Leyton Orient	0	0	**9**	**0**
1997–98	Sunderland	0	0		
1998–99	Sunderland	0	0		
1998–99	*Scarborough*	6	0	**6**	**0**
1999–2000	Sunderland	0	0		
1999–2000	Carlisle U	29	0		
2000-01	Carlisle U	14	0		
2001-02	Carlisle U	10	0		
2002-03	Carlisle U	0	0	**53**	**0**

Trainees
Bell, Lewis; Byrne, Robert; Hamilton, Lee; Hamilton, Paul; Hewitt, Steven E; Lynn, Charles D; Maybin, Jonathan NP; Percival, John; Reed, Michael T; Taylor, Tyran D; Wills, Andrew M; Wright, Anthony J

Non-Contract
Dalton, Neil J

CHARLTON ATH

BART-WILLIAMS, Chris (M)				**396**	**50**
H: 5 11 W: 12 07 b.Freetown 16-6-74					
Source: Trainee. *Honours:* England Youth, Under-21.					
1990–91	Leyton Orient	21	2		
1991–92	Leyton Orient	15	0	**36**	**2**
1991–92	Sheffield W	15	0		
1992–93	Sheffield W	34	6		
1993–94	Sheffield W	37	8		
1994–95	Sheffield W	38	2	**124**	**16**
1995–96	Nottingham F	33	0		
1996–97	Nottingham F	16	1		
1997–98	Nottingham F	33	4		
1998–99	Nottingham F	24	3		
1999–2000	Nottingham F	38	5		
2000-01	Nottingham F	46	14		
2001-02	Nottingham F	17	3	**207**	**30**
2001-02	Charlton Ath	16	1		
2002-03	Charlton Ath	13	1	**29**	**2**

BARTLETT, Shaun (F)				**197**	**54**
H: 6 2 W: 12 04 b.Cape Town 31-10-72					
Source: Cape Town Spurs. *Honours:* South Africa 64 full caps, 26 goals.					
1996	Colorado Rapids	26	8		
1996–97	Amazulu	0	0		
1997	New York/ New Jersey M	13	2	**13**	**2**
1997	Colorado Rapids	10	1	**36**	**9**
1998	Cape Town Spurs	18	8	**18**	**8**
1998–99	Zurich	27	13		
1999–2000	Zurich	20	2		
2000-01	Zurich	20	8	**67**	**23**
2000-01	Charlton Ath	18	7		
2001-02	Charlton Ath	14	1		
2002-03	Charlton Ath	31	4	**63**	**12**

BLOMQVIST, Jesper* (M)				**200**	**31**
H: 5 10 W: 11 06 b.Tavelsjo 5-2-74					
Honours: Sweden 30 full caps.					
1992	Umea	27	6		
1993	Umea	11	2	**38**	**8**
1993	IFK Gothenburg	6	1		
1994	IFK Gothenburg	24	8		
1995	IFK Gothenburg	18	3		
1996	IFK Gothenburg	23	7	**71**	**19**
1996–97	AC Milan	19	1		
1997–98	AC Milan	1	0	**20**	**1**
1997–98	Parma	28	1	**28**	**1**
1998–99	Manchester U	25	1		
1999–2000	Manchester U	0	0		
2000-01	Manchester U	0	0		
2001-02	Manchester U	0	0	**25**	**1**
2001-02	Everton	15	1	**15**	**1**
2002-03	Charlton Ath	3	0	**3**	**0**

CAMPBELL-RYCE, Jamal (F)				**18**	**2**
H: 5 7 W: 11 10 b.Lambeth 6-4-83					
Source: Scholar.					
2002-03	Charlton Ath	1	0	**1**	**0**
2002-03	*Leyton Orient*	17	2	**17**	**2**

DE BOLLA, Mark (F) **0 0**
H: 5 7 W: 11 09 b.London 1-1-83
Source: Trainee.

1999–2000	Aston Villa	0	0		
2000-01	Charlton Ath	0	0		
2001-02	Charlton Ath	0	0		
2002-03	Charlton Ath	0	0		

DEANE, Adrian (M) **0 0**
H: 5 10 W: 10 00 b.London 24-2-83

2001-02	Charlton Ath	0	0		
2002-03	Charlton Ath	0	0		

DINCER, Fatih* (D) **0 0**
H: 5 8 W: 11 00 b.Stockholm 13-7-83

2000-01	Charlton Ath	0	0		
2001-02	Charlton Ath	0	0		
2002-03	Charlton Ath	0	0		

EL KHALEJ, Tahar* (D) **176 21**
H: 6 2 W: 13 07 b.Marrakesh 16-6-68
Source: KAC Marrakesh. *Honours:* Morocco 69 full caps, 8 goals.

1994–95	Uniao Leiria	21	5		
1995–96	Uniao Leiria	22	3	**43**	**8**
1996–97	Benfica	25	1		
1997–98	Benfica	21	5		
1998–99	Benfica	22	4		
1999–2000	Benfica	4	0	**72**	**10**
1999–2000	Southampton	11	1		
2000-01	Southampton	32	1		
2001-02	Southampton	14	1		
2002-03	Southampton	1	0	**58**	**3**
2002-03	Charlton Ath	3	0	**3**	**0**

EUELL, Jason (F) **213 62**
H: 5 11 W: 11 02 b.Lambeth 6-2-77
Source: Trainee. *Honours:* England Youth, Under-21.

1995–96	Wimbledon	9	2		
1996–97	Wimbledon	7	2		
1997–98	Wimbledon	19	4		
1998–99	Wimbledon	33	10		
1999–2000	Wimbledon	37	4		
2000-01	Wimbledon	36	19	**141**	**41**
2001-02	Charlton Ath	36	11		
2002-03	Charlton Ath	36	10	**72**	**21**

FISH, Mark (D) **320 14**
H: 6 4 W: 12 11 b.Cape Town 14-3-74
Source: Arcadia Shepherds. *Honours:* South Africa 60 full caps, 2 goals.

1992	Jomo Cosmos	14	1		
1993	Jomo Cosmos	41	1	**55**	**2**
1994	Orlando Pirates	37	5		
1995	Orlando Pirates	38	1	**75**	**6**
1996–97	Lazio	15	1	**15**	**1**
1997–98	Bolton W	22	2		
1998–99	Bolton W	36	1		
1999–2000	Bolton W	31	0		
2000-01	Bolton W	14	0	**103**	**3**
2000-01	Charlton Ath	24	1		
2001-02	Charlton Ath	25	0		
2002-03	Charlton Ath	23	1	**72**	**2**

FORTUNE, Jon (D) **63 1**
H: 6 2 W: 12 12 b.Islington 23-8-80
Source: Trainee.

1998-99	Charlton Ath	0	0		
1999–2000	Charlton Ath	0	0		
1999–2000	*Mansfield T*	4	0		
2000-01	Charlton Ath	0	0		
2000-01	*Mansfield T*	14	0	**18**	**0**
2001-02	Charlton Ath	19	0		
2002-03	Charlton Ath	26	1	**45**	**1**

HREIDARSSON, Hermann (D) **270 16**
H: 6 3 W: 13 01 b.Iceland 11-7-74
Honours: Iceland 49 full caps, 3 goals.

1993	IBV	2	0		
1994	IBV	18	2		
1995	IBV	18	1		
1996	IBV	17	2		
1997	IBV	11	0	**66**	**5**
1997–98	Crystal Palace	30	2		
1998–99	Crystal Palace	7	0	**37**	**2**
1998–99	Brentford	33	4		
1999–2000	Brentford	8	2	**41**	**6**
1999–2000	Wimbledon	24	1	**24**	**1**
2000-01	Ipswich T	36	1		
2001-02	Ipswich T	38	1		
2002-03	Ipswich T	28	0	**102**	**2**
2002-03	Charlton Ath	0	0		

JENSEN, Claus (M) **243 34**
H: 5 11 W: 12 00 b.Nykobing 29-4-77
Source: Stubbekobing, Nykobing. *Honours:* Denmark Under-21, 23 full caps, 5 goals.

1995–96	Naestved	4	0	**4**	**0**
1996–97	Lyngby	31	3		
1997–98	Lyngby	31	11	**62**	**14**
1998–99	Bolton W	44	2		
1999–2000	Bolton W	42	6	**86**	**8**
2000-01	Charlton Ath	38	5		
2001-02	Charlton Ath	18	1		
2002-03	Charlton Ath	35	6	**91**	**12**

JOHANSSON, Jonatan (F) **180 48**
H: 6 2 W: 12 08 b.Stockholm 16-8-75
Source: Flora Tallinn. *Honours:* Finland 51 full caps, 10 goals.

1995	TPS Turku	9	0		
1996	TPS Turku	23	6	**32**	**6**
1996–97	Flora Tallinn	9	9	**9**	**9**
1997–98	Rangers	6	0		
1998–99	Rangers	25	8		
1999–2000	Rangers	16	6	**47**	**14**
2000-01	Charlton Ath	31	11		
2001-02	Charlton Ath	30	5		
2002-03	Charlton Ath	31	3	**92**	**19**

KIELY, Dean (G) **493 0**
H: 6 1 W: 13 10 b.Salford 10-10-70
Source: WBA School. *Honours:* England Schools, FA Schools, Youth, Eire 8 full caps.

1987–88	Coventry C	0	0		
1988–89	Coventry C	0	0		
1989–90	Coventry C	0	0		
1989–90	*Ipswich T*	0	0		
1989–90	*York C*	0	0		
1990–91	York C	17	0		
1991–92	York C	21	0		
1992–93	York C	40	0		
1993–94	York C	46	0		
1994–95	York C	46	0		
1995–96	York C	40	0	**210**	**0**
1996–97	Bury	46	0		
1997–98	Bury	46	0		
1998–99	Bury	45	0	**137**	**0**
1999–2000	Charlton Ath	45	0		
2000-01	Charlton Ath	25	0		
2001-02	Charlton Ath	38	0		
2002-03	Charlton Ath	38	0	**146**	**0**

KISHISHEV, Radostin (D) **257 19**
H: 5 11 W: 12 03 b.Bourgas 30-7-74
Honours: Bulgaria 50 full caps.

1991–92	Chernomorets	6	1		
1992–93	Chernomorets	23	2		
1993–94	Chernomorets	23	1	**52**	**4**
1994–95	Neftochimik	14	0		
1995–96	Neftochimik	30	0		
1996–97	Neftochimik	30	6		
1997–98	Neftochimik	1	0	**75**	**6**
1997–98	Bursaspor	20	3	**20**	**3**
1997–98	Litets Lovch	5	0	**5**	**0**
1998–99	Litets Lovech	26	2		
1999–2000	Litets Lovech	15	2	**41**	**4**
2000-01	Charlton Ath	27	0		
2001-02	Charlton Ath	3	0		
2002-03	Charlton Ath	34	2	**64**	**2**

KONCHESKY, Paul (D) **100 4**
H: 5 10 W: 11 07 b.Barking 15-5-81
Source: Trainee. *Honours:* England Youth, Under-20, Under-21, 1 full cap.

1997–98	Charlton Ath	3	0		
1998–99	Charlton Ath	2	0		
1999–2000	Charlton Ath	8	0		
2000-01	Charlton Ath	23	0		
2001-02	Charlton Ath	34	1		
2002-03	Charlton Ath	30	3	**100**	**4**

LISBIE, Kevin (F) **126 15**
H: 5 10 W: 11 06 b.Hackney 17-10-78
Source: Trainee. *Honours:* England Youth. Jamaica 6 full caps.

1996–97	Charlton Ath	25	1		
1997–98	Charlton Ath	17	1		
1998–99	Charlton Ath	1	0		
1998–99	*Gillingham*	7	4	**7**	**4**
1999–2000	Charlton Ath	0	0		
1999–2000	*Reading*	2	0	**2**	**0**
2000-01	Charlton Ath	18	0		
2000-01	*QPR*	2	0	**2**	**0**
2001-02	Charlton Ath	22	5		
2002-03	Charlton Ath	32	4	**115**	**11**

LONG, Stacy (F) **0 0**
H: 5 8 W: 10 00 b.Bromley 11-1-85
Source: Scholar. *Honours:* England Youth.

2001-02	Charlton Ath	0	0		
2002-03	Charlton Ath	0	0		

McCAFFERTY, Neil (M) **0 0**
H: 5 7 W: 10 00 b.Derry 19-7-84
Source: Scholar.

2001-02	Charlton Ath	0	0		
2002-03	Charlton Ath	0	0		

MUSTOE, Robbie‡ (M) **462 35**
H: 6 0 W: 12 03 b.Oxford 28-8-68

1986–87	Oxford U	3	0		
1987–88	Oxford U	17	0		
1988–89	Oxford U	33	3		
1989–90	Oxford U	38	7	**91**	**10**
1990–91	Middlesbrough	41	4		
1991–92	Middlesbrough	30	2		
1992–93	Middlesbrough	23	1		
1993–94	Middlesbrough	38	2		
1994–95	Middlesbrough	27	3		
1995–96	Middlesbrough	21	1		
1996–97	Middlesbrough	31	3		
1997–98	Middlesbrough	32	3		
1998–99	Middlesbrough	33	4		
1999–2000	Middlesbrough	28	0		
2000-01	Middlesbrough	25	0		
2001-02	Middlesbrough	36	2	**365**	**25**
2002-03	Charlton Ath	6	0	**6**	**0**

PARKER, Scott (M) **114 8**
H: 5 9 W: 10 10 b.Lambeth 13-10-80
Source: Trainee. *Honours:* England Schools, Youth, Under-21.

1997–98	Charlton Ath	3	0		
1998–99	Charlton Ath	4	0		
1999–2000	Charlton Ath	15	1		
2000-01	Charlton Ath	20	1		
2000-01	*Norwich C*	6	1	**6**	**1**
2001-02	Charlton Ath	38	1		
2002-03	Charlton Ath	28	4	**108**	**7**

POWELL, Chris (D) **537 5**
H: 5 11 W: 11 12 b.Lambeth 8-9-69
Source: Trainee. *Honours:* England 5 full caps.

1987–88	Crystal Palace	0	0		
1988–89	Crystal Palace	3	0		
1989–90	Crystal Palace	0	0	**3**	**0**
1989–90	*Aldershot*	11	0	**11**	**0**
1990–91	Southend U	45	1		
1991–92	Southend U	44	0		
1992–93	Southend U	42	2		
1993–94	Southend U	46	0		
1994–95	Southend U	44	0		
1995–96	Southend U	27	0	**248**	**3**
1995–96	Derby Co	19	0		
1996–97	Derby Co	35	0		
1997–98	Derby Co	37	1	**91**	**1**
1998–99	Charlton Ath	38	0		
1999–2000	Charlton Ath	40	0		
2000-01	Charlton Ath	33	0		
2001-02	Charlton Ath	36	1		
2002-03	Charlton Ath	37	0	**184**	**1**

RACHUBKA, Paul (G) **17 0**
H: 6 1 W: 13 01 b.San Luis Opispo 21-5-81
Source: Trainee. *Honours:* England Youth.

1999–2000	Manchester U	0	0		
2000-01	Manchester U	1	0		
2001-02	Manchester U	0	0	**1**	**0**
2001-02	*Oldham Ath*	16	0	**16**	**0**
2001-02	Charlton Ath	0	0		
2002-03	Charlton Ath	0	0		

ROBERTS, Ben* (G) **77 0**
H: 6 1 W: 12 11 b.Bishop Auckland 22-6-75
Source: Trainee. *Honours:* England Under-21.

1992–93	Middlesbrough	0	0		
1993–94	Middlesbrough	0	0		
1994–95	Middlesbrough	0	0		
1995–96	Middlesbrough	0	0		
1995–96	*Hartlepool U*	4	0	**4**	**0**
1995–96	*Wycombe W*	15	0	**15**	**0**
1996–97	Middlesbrough	10	0		
1996–97	*Bradford C*	2	0	**2**	**0**
1997–98	Middlesbrough	6	0		
1998–99	Middlesbrough	0	0		
1998–99	*Millwall*	11	0	**11**	**0**
1999–2000	Middlesbrough	0	0	**16**	**0**
1999–2000	*Luton T*	14	0		
2000-01	Charlton Ath	0	0		
2001-02	Charlton Ath	0	0		

2001-02 *Reading* 6 0 **6 0**
2002-03 Charlton Ath 1 0 **1 0**
2002-03 *Luton T* 5 0 **19 0**
2002-03 *Brighton & HA* 3 0 **3 0**

ROBINSON, John (M) 394 41
H: 5 9 W: 11 11 b.Bulawayo 29-8-71
Source: Apprentice. *Honours:* Wales Under-21, 30 full caps, 3 goals.
1989–90 Brighton & HA 5 0
1990–91 Brighton & HA 15 0
1991–92 Brighton & HA 36 6
1992–93 Brighton & HA 6 0 **62 6**
1992–93 Charlton Ath 15 2
1993–94 Charlton Ath 27 1
1994–95 Charlton Ath 21 3
1995–96 Charlton Ath 44 6
1996–97 Charlton Ath 42 3
1997–98 Charlton Ath 38 8
1998–99 Charlton Ath 30 2
1999–2000 Charlton Ath 45 7
2000-01 Charlton Ath 29 2
2001-02 Charlton Ath 28 1
2002-03 Charlton Ath 13 0 **332 35**

ROBSON, Paul* (D) 0 0
H: 5 9 W: 11 05 b.Hull 4-8-83
Source: Doncaster R.
2001-02 Charlton Ath 0 0
2002-03 Charlton Ath 0 0

ROWETT, Gary (D) 337 20
H: 6 0 W: 12 10 b.Bromsgrove 6-3-74
Source: Trainee.
1991–92 Cambridge U 13 2
1992–93 Cambridge U 21 2
1993–94 Cambridge U 29 5 **63 9**
1993–94 Everton 2 0
1994–95 Everton 2 0 **4 0**
1994–95 *Blackpool* 17 0 **17 0**
1995–96 Derby Co 35 0
1996–97 Derby Co 35 1
1997–98 Derby Co 35 1
1998–99 Derby Co 0 0 **105 2**
1998–99 Birmingham C 42 5
1999–2000 Birmingham C 45 1 **87 6**
2000-01 Leicester C 38 2
2001-02 Leicester C 11 0 **49 2**
2001-02 Charlton Ath 0 0
2002-03 Charlton Ath 12 1 **12 1**

RUFUS, Richard (D) 288 12
H: 6 1 W: 12 12 b.Lewisham 12-1-75
Source: Trainee. *Honours:* England Under-21.
1993–94 Charlton Ath 0 0
1994–95 Charlton Ath 28 0
1995–96 Charlton Ath 41 0
1996–97 Charlton Ath 34 0
1997–98 Charlton Ath 42 0
1998–99 Charlton Ath 27 1
1999–2000 Charlton Ath 44 6
2000-01 Charlton Ath 32 2
2001-02 Charlton Ath 10 1
2002-03 Charlton Ath 30 2 **288 12**

SAM, Lloyd (F) 0 0
H: 5 8 W: 10 00 b.Leeds 27-9-84
Honours: England Youth.
2002-03 Charlton Ath 0 0

SANKOFA, Osei (D) 1 0
H: 6 0 W: 12 04 b.London 19-3-85
Source: Scholar. *Honours:* England Youth.
2002-03 Charlton Ath 1 0 **1 0**

SHARLAND, Greg* (F) 0 0
H: 6 2 W: 12 08 b.Perth 23-1-83
2002-03 Charlton Ath 0 0

SNODIN, Lee (M) 0 0
H: 5 10 W: 11 10 b.Doncaster 19-6-83
Source: Doncaster R.
2001-02 Charlton Ath 0 0
2002-03 Charlton Ath 0 0

STUART, Graham (M) 392 66
H: 5 9 W: 12 01 b.Tooting 24-10-70
Source: Trainee. *Honours:* FA Schools, England Under-21.
1989–90 Chelsea 2 1
1990–91 Chelsea 19 4
1991–92 Chelsea 27 0
1992–93 Chelsea 39 9 **87 14**
1993–94 Everton 30 3
1994–95 Everton 28 3
1995–96 Everton 29 9
1996–97 Everton 35 5
1997–98 Everton 14 2 **136 22**
1997–98 Sheffield U 28 5
1998–99 Sheffield U 25 6 **53 11**
1998–99 Charlton Ath 9 4
1999–2000 Charlton Ath 37 7
2000-01 Charlton Ath 35 5
2001-02 Charlton Ath 31 3
2002-03 Charlton Ath 4 0 **116 19**

SVENSSON, Mathias (F) 172 43
H: 6 1 W: 12 08 b.Boras 24-9-74
Honours: Sweden 3 full caps.
1996 Elfsborg 22 15 **22 15**
1996–97 Portsmouth 19 6
1997–98 Portsmouth 26 4 **45 10**
1998–99 Innsbruck 6 1 **6 1**
1998–99 Crystal Palace 8 1
1999–2000 Crystal Palace 24 9 **32 10**
1999–2000 Charlton Ath 18 2
2000-01 Charlton Ath 22 5
2001-02 Charlton Ath 12 0
2002-03 Charlton Ath 15 0 **67 7**

TURNER, Michael (D) 7 1
H: 6 4 W: 12 06 b.Lewisham 9-11-83
Source: Scholar.
2001-02 Charlton Ath 0 0
2002-03 Charlton Ath 0 0
2002-03 *Leyton Orient* 7 1 **7 1**

WELLS, Andrew‡ (D) 0 0
H: 5 10 W: 11 00 b.Wordsley 20-12-83
2002-03 Charlton Ath 0 0

YOUNG, Luke (D) 124 0
H: 6 0 W: 12 04 b.Harlow 19-7-79
Source: Trainee. *Honours:* England Youth, Under-21.
1997–98 Tottenham H 0 0
1998–99 Tottenham H 15 0
1999–2000 Tottenham H 20 0
2000-01 Tottenham H 23 0 **58 0**
2001-02 Charlton Ath 34 0
2002-03 Charlton Ath 32 0 **66 0**

Trainees
Beckford, Karl L; Elliot, Robert; Fuller, Barry M; Gross, Adam C; Jackson, Simon P; Ndombe, Sebastian, Ricketts, Mark J; Thanda, Lekeladio B; Tucker, Stephen; Varney, Alexander; Wilson, Wayne

CHELSEA

AMBROSETTI, Gabriele (M) 230 44
H: 5 11 W: 11 05 b.Varese 7-8-73
1990–91 Varese 8 0
1991–92 Varese 16 2
1992–93 Varese 26 9 **50 11**
1993–94 Brescia 25 8
1994–95 Brescia 9 2
1994–95 Venezia 18 3 **18 3**
1995–96 Brescia 9 2 **43 12**
1995–96 Vicenza 24 3
1996–97 Vicenza 25 6
1996–97 Vicenza 0 0
1997–98 Vicenza 30 5
1998–99 Vicenza 24 4 **103 18**
1999–2000 Chelsea 16 0
2000-01 Chelsea 0 0
2001-02 Chelsea 0 0
2002-03 Chelsea 0 0 **16 0**

ANIS, Jean-Yves* (D) 0 0
H: 5 10 W: 11 11 b.Oume 30-11-80
2002-03 Chelsea 0 0

BABAYARO, Celestine (D) 197 12
H: 5 9 W: 11 09 b.Kaduna 29-8-78
Source: Plateau U. *Honours:* Nigeria 26 full caps.
1994–95 Anderlecht 22 0
1995–96 Anderlecht 28 5
1996–97 Anderlecht 25 3 **75 8**
1997–98 Chelsea 8 0
1998–99 Chelsea 28 3
1999–2000 Chelsea 25 0
2000-01 Chelsea 24 0
2001-02 Chelsea 18 0
2002-03 Chelsea 19 1 **122 4**

BOGARDE, Winston (D) 201 26
H: 6 3 W: 14 02 b.Rotterdam 22-10-70
Honours: Holland 20 full caps.
1988–89 SVV 9 1
1989–90 SVV 2 0
1989–90 Excelsior 10 1 **10 1**
1990–91 SVV 0 0 **11 1**
1991–92 Sparta 0 0
1992–93 Sparta 32 3
1993–94 Sparta 33 11 **65 14**
1994–95 Ajax 13 0
1995–96 Ajax 33 2
1996–97 Ajax 16 4 **62 6**
1997–98 AC Milan 3 0 **3 0**
1997–98 Barcelona 19 2
1998–99 Barcelona 1 0
1999–2000 Barcelona 21 2 **41 4**
2000-01 Chelsea 9 0
2001-02 Chelsea 0 0
2002-03 Chelsea 0 0 **9 0**

BOSNICH, Mark (G) 215 0
H: 6 2 W: 14 09 b.Fairfield 13-1-72
Honours: Australia Youth, Under-20, Under-23, 17 full caps, 1 goal.
1989–90 Manchester U 1 0
1990–91 Manchester U 2 0
1991–92 Sydney U 5 0 **5 0**
1991–92 Aston Villa 1 0
1992–93 Aston Villa 17 0
1993–94 Aston Villa 28 0
1994–95 Aston Villa 30 0
1995–96 Aston Villa 38 0
1996–97 Aston Villa 20 0
1997–98 Aston Villa 30 0
1998–99 Aston Villa 15 0 **179 0**
1999–2000 Manchester U 23 0
2000-01 Manchester U 0 0 **26 0**
2000-01 Chelsea 0 0
2001-02 Chelsea 5 0
2002-03 Chelsea 0 0 **5 0**

BOUSSOUFA, Mbark (F) 0 0
H: 5 5 W: 8 09 b.Amsterdam 15-8-84
2002-03 Chelsea 0 0

COLE, Carlton (F) 23 5
H: 6 3 W: 12 13 b.Surrey 12-11-83
Source: Scholar. *Honours:* England Youth, Under-20, Under-21.
2000-01 Chelsea 0 0
2001-02 Chelsea 3 1
2002-03 Chelsea 13 3 **16 4**
2002-03 *Wolverhampton W* 7 1 **7 1**

COUSINS, Scott* (D) 0 0
H: 5 10 W: 11 06 b.Edgware 12-7-83
2002-03 Chelsea 0 0

CUDICINI, Carlo (G) 172 0
H: 6 1 W: 12 02 b.Milan 6-9-73
1991–92 AC Milan 0 0
1992–93 AC Milan 0 0
1993–94 Como 6 0 **6 0**
1994–95 AC Milan 0 0
1995–96 AC Milan 0 0
1995–96 Prato 30 0 **30 0**
1996–97 Lazio 1 0 **1 0**
1997–98 Castel di Sangro 14 0
1998–99 Castel di Sangro 32 0 **46 0**
1999–2000 Chelsea 1 0
2000-01 Chelsea 24 0
2001-02 Chelsea 28 0
2002-03 Chelsea 36 0 **89 0**

DA SILVA, Mauro* (D) 0 0
H: 6 2 W: 11 13 b.Oporto 28-2-84
2002-03 Chelsea 0 0

DE GOEY, Ed* (G) 469 0
H: 6 6 W: 14 05 b.Gouda 20-12-66
Honours: Holland 31 full caps.
1985–86 Sparta 12 0
1986–87 Sparta 34 0
1987–88 Sparta 34 0
1988–89 Sparta 31 0
1989–90 Sparta 34 0 **145 0**
1990–91 Feyenoord 34 0
1991–92 Feyenoord 34 0
1992–93 Feyenoord 33 0
1993–94 Feyenoord 34 0
1994–95 Feyenoord 32 0
1995–96 Feyenoord 34 0 **201 0**
1997–98 Chelsea 28 0
1998–99 Chelsea 35 0
1999–2000 Chelsea 37 0
2000-01 Chelsea 15 0
2001-02 Chelsea 6 0
2002-03 Chelsea 2 0 **123 0**

DE LUCAS, Enrique (M) 189 41
H: 5 8 W: 11 11 b.LHospitalet Llobregat 17-8-78
1996–97 Espanyol B 27 5
1997–98 Espanyol B 28 13
1997–98 Espanyol 1 1

1998–99	Espanyol B	13	5	**68**	**23**
1998–99	Espanyol	20	6		
1999–2000	Espanyol	30	4		
2000-01	Espanyol	8	0		
2000-01	Paris St Germain	4	0	**4**	**0**
2001-02	Espanyol	33	7	**92**	**18**
2002-03	Chelsea	25	0	**25**	**0**

DESAILLY, Marcel (D) 490 17
H: 6 0 W: 13 05 b.Accra 7-9-68
Honours: France 108 full caps, 3 goals.

1986–87	Nantes	15	0		
1987–88	Nantes	11	0		
1988–89	Nantes	36	1		
1989–90	Nantes	36	1		
1990–91	Nantes	34	1		
1991–92	Nantes	32	2	**164**	**5**
1992–93	Marseille	31	1		
1993–94	Marseille	15	0	**46**	**1**
1993–94	AC Milan	21	1		
1994–95	AC Milan	22	1		
1995–96	AC Milan	32	2		
1996–97	AC Milan	29	1		
1997–98	AC Milan	33	0	**137**	**5**
1998–99	Chelsea	31	0		
1999–2000	Chelsea	23	1		
2000-01	Chelsea	34	2		
2001-02	Chelsea	24	1		
2002-03	Chelsea	31	2	**143**	**6**

DI CESARE, Valerio (D) 0 0
H: 6 1 W: 11 13 b.Rome 23-5-83

2000-01	Chelsea	0	0		
2001-02	Chelsea	0	0		
2002-03	Chelsea	0	0		

EVANS, Rhys* (G) 22 0
H: 6 1 W: 11 13 b.Swindon 27-1-82
Source: Trainee. *Honours:* England Schools, Youth, Under-20, Under-21.

1998–99	Chelsea	0	0		
1999–2000	Chelsea	0	0		
1999–2000	*Bristol R*	4	0	**4**	**0**
2000-01	Chelsea	0	0		
2001-02	Chelsea	0	0		
2001-02	*QPR*	11	0	**11**	**0**
2002-03	Chelsea	0	0		
2002-03	*Leyton Orient*	7	0	**7**	**0**

FERRER, Albert* (D) 298 1
H: 5 6 W: 12 02 b.Barcelona 6-6-70
Honours: Spain 36 full caps.

1989–90	Tenerife	17	0	**17**	**0**
1990–91	Barcelona	26	0		
1991–92	Barcelona	12	1		
1992–93	Barcelona	32	0		
1993–94	Barcelona	34	0		
1994–95	Barcelona	31	0		
1995–96	Barcelona	28	0		
1996–97	Barcelona	18	0		
1997–98	Barcelona	24	0	**205**	**1**
1998–99	Chelsea	30	0		
1999–2000	Chelsea	25	0		
2000-01	Chelsea	14	0		
2001-02	Chelsea	4	0		
2002-03	Chelsea	3	0	**76**	**0**

FORSSELL, Mikael (F) 117 29
H: 6 0 W: 12 10 b.Steinfurt 15-3-81
Honours: Finland 24 full caps, 9 goals.

1997	HJK Helsinki	1	0		
1998	HJK Helsinki	16	1	**17**	**1**
1998–99	Chelsea	10	1		
1999–2000	Chelsea	0	0		
1999–2000	*Crystal Palace*	13	3		
2000-01	Chelsea	0	0		
2000-01	*Crystal Palace*	39	13	**52**	**16**
2001-02	Chelsea	22	4		
2002-03	*Moenchengladbach*	16	7	**16**	**7**
2002-03	Chelsea	0	0	**32**	**5**

GALLACCIO, Michele (F) 0 0
H: 5 8 W: 10 12 b.Rome 3-3-86
Source: Lazio.

2002-03	Chelsea	0	0		

GALLAS, William (D) 171 7
H: 6 0 W: 11 13 b.Asnieres 17-8-77
Honours: France 10 caps.

1996–97	Caen	18	0	**18**	**0**
1997–98	Marseille	3	0		
1998–99	Marseille	30	0		
1999–2000	Marseille	22	0		
2000-01	Marseille	30	2	**85**	**2**
2001-02	Chelsea	30	1		
2002-03	Chelsea	38	4	**68**	**5**

GRONKJAER, Jesper (M) 199 26
H: 6 2 W: 13 03 b.Nuuk 12-8-77
Honours: Denmark 37 full caps, 3 goals.

1995–96	Aalborg	29	3		
1996–97	Aalborg	28	1		
1997–98	Aalborg	29	6	**86**	**10**
1998–99	Ajax	25	8		
1999–2000	Ajax	25	3		
2000-01	Ajax	6	0	**56**	**11**
2000-01	Chelsea	14	1		
2001-02	Chelsea	13	0		
2002-03	Chelsea	30	4	**57**	**5**

GUDJOHNSEN, Eidur (F) 188 62
H: 6 1 W: 14 00 b.Reykjavik 15-9-78
Honours: Iceland Youth, 24 full caps, 8 goals.

1994–95	Valur	17	7	**17**	**7**
1995–96	PSV Eindhoven	13	3		
1996–97	PSV Eindhoven	0	0	**13**	**3**
1998	KR	6	0	**6**	**0**
1998–99	Bolton W	14	5		
1999–2000	Bolton W	41	13	**55**	**18**
2000-01	Chelsea	30	10		
2001-02	Chelsea	32	14		
2002-03	Chelsea	35	10	**97**	**34**

HASSELBAINK, Jimmy Floyd (F) 269 147
H: 5 10 W: 13 10 b.Paramaribo 27-3-72
Honours: Holland 23 full caps, 9 goals.

1995–96	Campomairorense	31	12	**31**	**12**
1996–97	Boavista	29	20	**29**	**20**
1997–98	Leeds U	33	16		
1998–99	Leeds U	36	18	**69**	**34**
1999–2000	Atletico Madrid	34	24	**34**	**24**
2000-01	Chelsea	35	23		
2001-02	Chelsea	35	23		
2002-03	Chelsea	36	11	**106**	**57**

HUTH, Robert (D) 3 0
H: 6 3 W: 12 12 b.Berlin 18-8-84

2001-02	Chelsea	1	0		
2002-03	Chelsea	2	0	**3**	**0**

JEFFREYS, Danny (M) 0 0
H: 5 7 W: 9 03 b.Hammersmith 21-1-85
Source: Scholar. *Honours:* England Youth.

2001-02	Chelsea	0	0		
2002-03	Chelsea	0	0		

KEENAN, Joe (M) 2 0
H: 5 8 W: 9 12 b.Southampton 14-10-82
Source: Trainee. *Honours:* England Youth, Under-20.

1999–2000	Chelsea	0	0		
2000-01	Chelsea	0	0		
2001-02	Chelsea	1	0		
2002-03	Chelsea	1	0	**2**	**0**

KITAMIRIKE, Joel (D) 0 0
H: 5 10 W: 13 01 b.Kampala 5-4-84
Source: Scholar. *Honours:* England Youth.

2000-01	Chelsea	0	0		
2001-02	Chelsea	0	0		
2002-03	Chelsea	0	0		

KNEISSL, Sebastian (F) 0 0
H: 5 11 W: 11 05 b.Lindelfels 13-1-83

2000-01	Chelsea	0	0		
2001-02	Chelsea	0	0		
2002-03	Chelsea	0	0		

KNIGHT, Leon (F) 66 19
H: 5 4 W: 9 04 b.Mile End 16-9-82
Source: Trainee. *Honours:* England Youth, Under-20.

1999–2000	Chelsea	0	0		
2000-01	Chelsea	0	0		
2000-01	*QPR*	11	0	**11**	**0**
2001-02	Chelsea	0	0		
2001-02	*Huddersfield T*	31	16	**31**	**16**
2002-03	Chelsea	0	0		
2002-03	*Sheffield W*	24	3	**24**	**3**

LAMPARD, Frank (M) 232 35
H: 6 0 W: 14 00 b.Romford 20-6-78
Source: Trainee. *Honours:* England Youth, Under-21, B, 11 full caps.

1994–95	West Ham U	0	0		
1995–96	West Ham U	2	0		
1995–96	*Swansea C*	9	1	**9**	**1**
1996–97	West Ham U	13	0		
1997–98	West Ham U	31	4		
1998–99	West Ham U	38	5		
1999–2000	West Ham U	34	7		
2000-01	West Ham U	30	7	**148**	**23**
2001-02	Chelsea	37	5		
2002-03	Chelsea	38	6	**75**	**11**

LE SAUX, Graeme (D) 359 19
H: 5 10 W: 11 09 b.Jersey 17-10-68
Source: St Pauls. *Honours:* England Under-21, B, 36 full caps, 1 goal.

1987–88	Chelsea	0	0		
1988–89	Chelsea	1	0		
1989–90	Chelsea	7	1		
1990–91	Chelsea	28	4		
1991–92	Chelsea	40	3		
1992–93	Chelsea	14	0		
1992–93	Blackburn R	9	0		
1993–94	Blackburn R	41	2		
1994–95	Blackburn R	39	3		
1995–96	Blackburn R	14	1		
1996–97	Blackburn R	26	1	**129**	**7**
1997–98	Chelsea	26	1		
1998–99	Chelsea	31	0		
1999–2000	Chelsea	8	0		
2000-01	Chelsea	20	0		
2001-02	Chelsea	27	1		
2002-03	Chelsea	28	2	**230**	**12**

MELCHIOT, Mario (D) 180 3
H: 6 2 W: 11 11 b.Amsterdam 4-11-76
Honours: Holland 10 full caps.

1996–97	Ajax	23	0		
1997–98	Ajax	26	0		
1998–99	Ajax	24	1	**73**	**1**
1999–2000	Chelsea	5	0		
2000-01	Chelsea	31	0		
2001-02	Chelsea	37	2		
2002-03	Chelsea	34	0	**107**	**2**

MORRIS, Jody* (M) 124 5
H: 5 5 W: 10 05 b.Hammersmith 22-12-78
Source: Trainee. *Honours:* England Schools, Youth, Under-21.

1995–96	Chelsea	1	0		
1996–97	Chelsea	12	0		
1997–98	Chelsea	12	1		
1998–99	Chelsea	18	1		
1999–2000	Chelsea	30	3		
2000-01	Chelsea	21	0		
2001-02	Chelsea	5	0		
2002-03	Chelsea	25	0	**124**	**5**

NICOLAS, Alexis (M) 0 0
H: 5 10 W: 9 12 b.Westminster 13-2-83
Source: Scholar.

2000-01	Aston Villa	0	0		
2001-02	Aston Villa	0	0		
2001-02	Chelsea	0	0		
2002-03	Chelsea	0	0		

OLIVEIRA, Filipe (F) 3 0
H: 5 10 W: 10 12 b.Braga 27-5-84

2001-02	Chelsea	0	0		
2002-03	Chelsea	3	0	**3**	**0**

PETIT, Emmanuel (M) 381 16
H: 6 1 W: 13 03 b.Dieppe 22-9-70
Source: ES Arques. *Honours:* France 63 full caps, 6 goals.

1988–89	Monaco	9	0		
1989–90	Monaco	28	0		
1990–91	Monaco	27	1		
1991–92	Monaco	28	0		
1992–93	Monaco	25	1		
1993–94	Monaco	28	0		
1994–95	Monaco	25	1		
1995–96	Monaco	23	1		
1996–97	Monaco	29	0	**222**	**4**
1997–98	Arsenal	32	2		
1998–99	Arsenal	27	4		
1999–2000	Arsenal	26	3	**85**	**9**
2000-01	Barcelona	23	1	**23**	**1**
2001-02	Chelsea	27	1		
2002-03	Chelsea	24	1	**51**	**2**

ROSS, Andy* (M) 0 0
H: 5 11 W: 11 10 b.Irvine 18-9-82
Source: Trainee.

2002-03	Chelsea	0	0		

STANIC, Mario (M) 322 88
H: 6 2 W: 13 07 b.Sarajevo 10-4-72
Honours: Croatia 49 full caps, 7 goals.

1988–89	Zeljeznicar	14	0		
1989–90	Zeljeznicar	14	0		
1990–91	Zeljeznicar	28	1		
1991–92	Zeljeznicar	21	11	**77**	**12**
1992–93	Croatia Zagreb	26	11	**26**	**11**
1993–94	Gijon	34	7	**34**	**7**
1994–95	Benfica	14	5	**14**	**5**
1995–96	FC Brugge	30	20		
1996–97	FC Brugge	7	7	**37**	**27**
1996–97	Parma	13	3		
1997–98	Parma	23	4		

1998–99	Parma	18	7		
1999–2000	Parma	23	5	**77**	**19**
2000-01	Chelsea	12	2		
2001-02	Chelsea	27	1		
2002-03	Chelsea	18	4	**57**	**7**

TERRY, John (D) **87 5**
H: 6 1 W: 12 13 b.Barking 7-12-80
Source: Trainee. *Honours:* England Under-21, 1 full cap.

1997–98	Chelsea	0	0		
1998–99	Chelsea	2	0		
1999–2000	Chelsea	4	0		
1999–2000	*Nottingham F*	6	0	**6**	**0**
2000-01	Chelsea	22	1		
2001-02	Chelsea	33	1		
2002-03	Chelsea	20	3	**81**	**5**

THORNTON, Paul‡ (D) **0 0**
H: 5 8 W: 11 02 b.Frimley 7-1-83
Source: Trainee.

1999–2000	Chelsea	0	0
2000-01	Chelsea	0	0
2001-02	Chelsea	0	0
2002-03	Chelsea	0	0

TILLEN, Sam (D) **0 0**
H: 5 9 W: 10 05 b.Reading 16-4-85
Source: Trainee. *Honours:* England Youth.

2002-03	Chelsea	0	0

WATT, Steven (D) **0 0**
H: 6 2 W: 12 09 b.Aberdeen 1-5-85
Source: Trainee.

2002-03	Chelsea	0	0

WOLLEASTON, Robert* (M) **18 0**
H: 5 11 W: 11 07 b.Perivale 21-12-79
Source: Trainee.

1998–99	Chelsea	0	0		
1999–2000	Chelsea	1	0		
1999–2000	*Bristol R*	4	0	**4**	**0**
2000-01	Chelsea	0	0		
2000-01	*Portsmouth*	6	0	**6**	**0**
2001-02	Chelsea	0	0		
2001-02	*Northampton T*	7	0	**7**	**0**
2002-03	Chelsea	0	0	**1**	**0**

ZENDEN, Boudewijn (M) **218 30**
H: 5 8 W: 11 09 b.Maastricht 15-8-76
Honours: Holland 45 full caps, 6 goals.

1994–95	PSV Eindhoven	27	5		
1995–96	PSV Eindhoven	25	7		
1996–97	PSV Eindhoven	34	8		
1997–98	PSV Eindhoven	25	3	**111**	**23**
1998–99	Barcelona	25	0		
1999–2000	Barcelona	29	2		
2000-01	Barcelona	10	1	**64**	**3**
2001-02	Chelsea	22	3		
2002-03	Chelsea	21	1	**43**	**4**

ZOLA, Gianfranco (F) **555 171**
H: 5 6 W: 10 08 b.Oliena 5-7-66
Honours: Italy 35 full caps, 8 goals.

1984–85	Nuorese	4	0		
1985–86	Nuorese	27	10	**31**	**10**
1986–87	Torres	30	8		
1987–88	Torres	24	2		
1988–89	Torres	34	11	**88**	**21**
1989–90	Napoli	18	2		
1990–91	Napoli	20	6		
1991–92	Napoli	34	12		
1992–93	Napoli	33	12	**105**	**32**
1993–94	Parma	33	18		
1994–95	Parma	32	19		
1995–96	Parma	29	10		
1996–97	Parma	8	2	**102**	**49**
1996–97	Chelsea	23	8		
1997–98	Chelsea	27	8		
1998–99	Chelsea	37	13		
1999–2000	Chelsea	33	4		
2000-01	Chelsea	36	9		
2001-02	Chelsea	35	3		
2002-03	Chelsea	38	14	**229**	**59**

Trainees
Hollands, Daniel T; Hudell, Ben JC; McKinlay, Kevin; Morais, Filipe A; Pidgeley, Leonard J; Sentance, Billy; Smith, Dean FA; Woodards, Daniel M

CHELTENHAM T

ALSOP, Julian* (F) **240 55**
H: 6 5 W: 15 02 b.Nuneaton 28-5-73
Source: Nuneaton, VS Rugby, RC Warwick, Tamworth, Halesowen T.

1996–97	Bristol R	16	3		
1997–98	Bristol R	17	1	**33**	**4**
1997–98	Swansea C	12	3		
1998–99	Swansea C	41	10		
1999–2000	Swansea C	37	3	**90**	**16**
2000-01	Cheltenham T	39	5		
2001-02	Cheltenham T	41	20		
2002-03	Cheltenham T	37	10	**117**	**35**

BANKS, Chris‡ (D) **230 3**
H: 5 11 W: 12 05 b.Stone 12-11-65
Source: local.

1982–83	Port Vale	0	0		
1983–84	Port Vale	0	0		
1984–85	Port Vale	7	0		
1985–86	Port Vale	19	1		
1986–87	Port Vale	25	0		
1987–88	Port Vale	14	0	**65**	**1**
1988–89	Exeter C	45	1	**45**	**1**
From Bath C.					
1999–2000	Cheltenham T	42	0		
2000-01	Cheltenham T	40	1		
2001-02	Cheltenham T	38	0		
2002-03	Cheltenham T	0	0	**120**	**1**

BIRD, David (M) **14 0**
H: 5 8 W: 12 05 b.Gloucester 26-12-84
Source: Cinderford T.

2001-02	Cheltenham T	0	0		
2002-03	Cheltenham T	14	0	**14**	**0**

BOOK, Steve (G) **167 0**
H: 5 11 W: 11 11 b.Bournemouth 7-7-69

1997–98	Brighton & HA	0	0		
1998–99	Lincoln C	0	0		
From Forest Green R.					
1999–2000	Cheltenham T	46	0		
2000-01	Cheltenham T	46	0		
2001-02	Cheltenham T	39	0		
2002-03	Cheltenham T	36	0	**167**	**0**

BRAYSON, Paul (F) **156 26**
H: 5 4 W: 11 03 b.Newcastle 16-9-77
Source: Trainee. *Honours:* England Youth.

1995–96	Newcastle U	0	0		
1996–97	Newcastle U	0	0		
1996–97	*Swansea C*	11	5	**11**	**5**
1997–98	Newcastle U	0	0		
1997–98	Reading	6	1		
1998–99	Reading	28	0		
1999–2000	Reading	7	0	**41**	**1**
1999–2000	*Cardiff C*	9	1		
2000-01	Cardiff C	40	15		
2001-02	Cardiff C	35	3	**84**	**19**
2002-03	Cheltenham T	20	1	**20**	**1**

BROUGH, John# (D) **192 8**
H: 6 0 W: 13 10 b.Ilkeston 8-1-73

1991–92	Notts Co	0	0		
1992–93	Shrewsbury T	14	1		
1993–94	Shrewsbury T	2	0	**16**	**1**
From Telford U.					
1994–95	Hereford U	18	1		
1995–96	Hereford U	22	1		
1996–97	Hereford U	39	1	**79**	**3**
1999–2000	Cheltenham T	37	2		
2000-01	Cheltenham T	10	0		
2001-02	Cheltenham T	21	1		
2002-03	Cheltenham T	29	1	**97**	**4**

BRUTSCHIN, Christian‡ (M) **0 0**
b.Berlin 29-4-80
Source: SV Lichtenberg.

2002-03	Cheltenham T	0	0

BUTTERY, Luke (D) **0 0**
H: 5 11 W: 10 12 b.Wegberg 12-2-85

2002-03	Cheltenham T	0	0

CORBETT, Luke (F) **0 0**
H: 6 0 W: 11 02 b.Worcester 10-8-84

2002-03	Cheltenham T	0	0

DEVANEY, Martin (F) **125 23**
H: 5 11 W: 11 13 b.Cheltenham 1-6-80
Source: Trainee.

1997–98	Coventry C	0	0		
1998–99	Coventry C	0	0		
1999–2000	Cheltenham T	26	6		
2000-01	Cheltenham T	34	10		
2001-02	Cheltenham T	25	1		
2002-03	Cheltenham T	40	6	**125**	**23**

DUFF, Michael (D) **159 12**
H: 6 1 W: 12 01 b.Belfast 11-1-78
Source: Trainee. *Honours:* Northern Ireland 2 full caps.

1999–2000	Cheltenham T	31	2		
2000-01	Cheltenham T	39	5		
2001-02	Cheltenham T	45	3		
2002-03	Cheltenham T	44	2	**159**	**12**

DUFF, Shane (D) **18 0**
H: 6 1 W: 12 13 b.Wroughton 2-4-82
Honours: Northern Ireland Under-21.

2000-01	Cheltenham T	0	0		
2001-02	Cheltenham T	0	0		
2002-03	Cheltenham T	18	0	**18**	**0**

FINNIGAN, John (M) **192 6**
H: 5 8 W: 10 13 b.Wakefield 29-3-76
Source: Trainee.

1992–93	Nottingham F	0	0		
1993–94	Nottingham F	0	0		
1994–95	Nottingham F	0	0		
1995–96	Nottingham F	0	0		
1996–97	Nottingham F	0	0		
1997–98	Nottingham F	0	0		
1997–98	*Lincoln C*	6	0		
1998–99	Lincoln C	37	1		
1999–2000	Lincoln C	37	2		
2000-01	Lincoln C	40	0		
2001-02	Lincoln C	23	0	**143**	**3**
2001-02	Cheltenham T	12	2		
2002-03	Cheltenham T	37	1	**49**	**3**

FORSYTH, Richard (M) **216 23**
H: 5 11 W: 13 13 b.Dudley 3-10-70
Source: Kidderminster H.

1995–96	Birmingham C	26	2	**26**	**2**
1996–97	Stoke C	40	8		
1997–98	Stoke C	37	7		
1998–99	Stoke C	18	2	**95**	**17**
1999–2000	Blackpool	13	0	**13**	**0**
2000-01	Peterborough U	30	2		
2001-02	Peterborough U	32	0		
2002-03	Peterborough U	8	0	**70**	**2**
2002-03	Cheltenham T	12	2	**12**	**2**

GRIFFIN, Anthony (D) **87 1**
H: 5 11 W: 11 05 b.Bournemouth 22-3-79
Source: Trainee.

1997–98	Bournemouth	0	0		
1998–99	Bournemouth	6	0	**6**	**0**
1999–2000	Cheltenham T	24	0		
2000-01	Cheltenham T	22	1		
2001-02	Cheltenham T	24	0		
2002-03	Cheltenham T	11	0	**81**	**1**

HIGGS, Shane (G) **22 0**
H: 6 3 W: 14 06 b.Oxford 13-5-77
Source: Trainee.

1994–95	Bristol R	0	0		
1995–96	Bristol R	0	0		
1996–97	Bristol R	2	0		
1997–98	Bristol R	8	0	**10**	**0**
From Worcester C.					
1999–2000	Cheltenham T	0	0		
2000-01	Cheltenham T	1	0		
2001-02	Cheltenham T	1	0		
2002-03	Cheltenham T	10	0	**12**	**0**

HOWARTH, Neil* (D) **181 10**
H: 6 2 W: 13 01 b.Bolton 15-11-71
Source: Trainee.

1989–90	Burnley	1	0	**1**	**0**
From Macclesfield T.					
1997–98	Macclesfield T	41	3		
1998–99	Macclesfield T	19	0	**60**	**3**
1999–2000	Cheltenham T	44	2		
2000-01	Cheltenham T	23	3		
2001-02	Cheltenham T	26	1		
2002-03	Cheltenham T	27	1	**120**	**7**

HOWELLS, Lee (M) **112 6**
H: 5 11 W: 11 13 b.Fremantle 14-10-68
Source: Apprentice.

1986–87	Bristol R	0	0		
From Brisbane Lions.					
1999–2000	Cheltenham T	45	3		
2000-01	Cheltenham T	36	1		
2001-02	Cheltenham T	31	2		
2002-03	Cheltenham T	0	0	**112**	**6**

JONES, Steve* (D) **156 4**
H: 5 10 W: 12 06 b.Bristol 25-12-70
Source: Cheltenham T.

1995–96	Swansea C	17	0
1996–97	Swansea C	46	1
1997–98	Swansea C	0	0
1998–99	Swansea C	32	2

1999–2000 Swansea C 38 0
2000-01 Swansea C 13 1 **146 4**
2001-02 Cheltenham T 5 0
2002-03 Cheltenham T 5 0 **10 0**

KEAR, Richard* (F) 0 0
H: 5 9 W: 11 01 b.Gloucester 5-11-83
Source: Trainee.
2001-02 Cheltenham T 0 0
2002-03 Cheltenham T 0 0

McCANN, Grant (M) 63 9
H: 5 10 W: 12 09 b.Belfast 14-4-80
Source: Trainee. *Honours:* Northern Ireland Youth, Under-21, 7 full caps.
1998–99 West Ham U 0 0
1999–2000 West Ham U 0 0
2000-01 West Ham U 1 0
2000-01 *Notts Co* 2 0 **2 0**
2000-01 *Cheltenham T* 30 3
2001-02 West Ham U 3 0
2002-03 West Ham U 0 0 **4 0**
2002-03 Cheltenham T 27 6 **57 9**

MILTON, Russell* (M) 117 14
H: 5 8 W: 11 12 b.Folkestone 12-1-69
Source: Apprentice.
1986–87 Arsenal 0 0
1987–88 Arsenal 0 0
From Dover Ath.
1999–2000 Cheltenham T 38 9
2000-01 Cheltenham T 19 1
2001-02 Cheltenham T 39 2
2002-03 Cheltenham T 21 2 **117 14**

NAYLOR, Tony* (F) 449 134
H: 5 4 W: 11 04 b.Manchester 29-3-67
Source: Droylsden.
1989–90 Crewe Alex 2 0
1990–91 Crewe Alex 14 1
1991–92 Crewe Alex 34 15
1992–93 Crewe Alex 35 16
1993–94 Crewe Alex 37 13 **122 45**
1994–95 Port Vale 33 9
1995–96 Port Vale 39 11
1996–97 Port Vale 43 17
1997–98 Port Vale 38 10
1998–99 Port Vale 22 4
1999–2000 Port Vale 36 6
2000-01 Port Vale 42 14 **253 71**
2001-02 Cheltenham T 44 12
2002-03 Cheltenham T 30 6 **74 18**

SPENCER, Damien (F) 49 7
H: 6 0 W: 15 05 b.Ascot 19-9-81
Source: Scholarship.
1999–2000 Bristol C 9 1
2000-01 Bristol C 4 0
2000-01 *Exeter C* 6 0 **6 0**
2001-02 Bristol C 0 0 **13 1**
2002-03 Cheltenham T 30 6 **30 6**

VICTORY, Jamie (D) 156 15
H: 5 11 W: 12 12 b.London 14-11-75
Source: Trainee.
1994–95 West Ham U 0 0
1995–96 Bournemouth 16 1
1996–97 Bournemouth 0 0 **16 1**
1999–2000 Cheltenham T 46 4
2000-01 Cheltenham T 3 1
2001-02 Cheltenham T 46 7
2002-03 Cheltenham T 45 2 **140 14**

WALKER, Richard# (D) 141 5
H: 5 10 W: 13 03 b.Derby 9-11-71
Source: Trainee.
1991–92 Notts Co 0 0
1992–93 Notts Co 12 3
1993–94 Notts Co 21 1
1994–95 Notts Co 7 0
1994–95 *Mansfield T* 4 0 **4 0**
1995–96 Notts Co 11 0
1996–97 Notts Co 16 0 **67 4**
From Hereford U.
1999–2000 Cheltenham T 7 0
2000-01 Cheltenham T 36 0
2001-02 Cheltenham T 12 1
2002-03 Cheltenham T 15 0 **70 1**

WILLIAMS, Lee* (M) 322 13
H: 5 7 W: 12 11 b.Edgbaston 3-2-73
Source: Trainee.
1991–92 Aston Villa 0 0
1992–93 Aston Villa 0 0
1992–93 *Shrewsbury T* 3 0 **3 0**
1993–94 Aston Villa 0 0
1993–94 Peterborough U 18 0
1994–95 Peterborough U 40 1
1995–96 Peterborough U 33 0 **91 1**
1996–97 Tranmere R 0 0
1996–97 Mansfield T 6 0
1997–98 Mansfield T 38 3
1998–99 Mansfield T 44 2
1999–2000 Mansfield T 46 0
2000-01 Mansfield T 41 4
2001-02 Mansfield T 2 0 **177 9**
2001-02 Cheltenham T 38 3
2002-03 Cheltenham T 13 0 **51 3**

YATES, Mark (M) 293 28
H: 5 11 W: 13 08 b.Birmingham 24-1-70
1987–88 Birmingham C 3 0
1988–89 Birmingham C 20 3
1989–90 Birmingham C 20 2
1990–91 Birmingham C 9 1
1991–92 Birmingham C 2 0 **54 6**
1991–92 Burnley 17 1
1992–93 Burnley 1 0 **18 1**
1992–93 *Lincoln C* 14 0 **14 0**
1993–94 Doncaster R 34 4 **34 4**
From Kidderminster H
1999–2000 Cheltenham T 46 2
2000-01 Cheltenham T 45 6
2001-02 Cheltenham T 45 7
2002-03 Cheltenham T 37 2 **173 17**

Scholars
Connolly, Adam J; Davis, Lee M; Henry, Leon; Mazurek, Daniel; Thompson, Daniel P

CHESTERFIELD

ALLOTT, Mark (F) 208 35
H: 5 11 W: 10 12 b.Middleton 16-3-78
Source: Trainee.
1995–96 Oldham Ath 0 0
1996–97 Oldham Ath 5 1
1997–98 Oldham Ath 22 2
1998–99 Oldham Ath 41 7
1999–2000 Oldham Ath 32 10
2000-01 Oldham Ath 39 7
2001-02 Oldham Ath 15 4 **154 31**
2001-02 Chesterfield 21 4
2002-03 Chesterfield 33 0 **54 4**

BLATHERWICK, Steve (D) 177 3
H: 6 1 W: 15 00 b.Nottingham 20-9-73
Source: Notts Co.
1992–93 Nottingham F 0 0
1993–94 Nottingham F 3 0
1993–94 *Wycombe W* 2 0 **2 0**
1994–95 Nottingham F 0 0
1995–96 Nottingham F 0 0
1995–96 *Hereford U* 10 1 **10 1**
1996–97 Nottingham F 7 0 **10 0**
1996–97 *Reading* 7 0 **7 0**
1997–98 Burnley 21 0
1998–99 Burnley 3 0 **24 0**
1998–99 Chesterfield 14 1
1999–2000 Chesterfield 36 0
2000-01 Chesterfield 38 1
2001-02 Chesterfield 5 0
2002-03 Chesterfield 31 0 **124 2**

BOOTY, Martyn* (D) 323 8
H: 5 8 W: 12 03 b.Kirby Muxloe 30-5-71
Source: Trainee.
1991–92 Coventry C 3 0
1992–93 Coventry C 0 0
1993–94 Coventry C 2 0 **5 0**
1993–94 Crewe Alex 31 1
1994–95 Crewe Alex 44 2
1995–96 Crewe Alex 21 2 **96 5**
1995–96 Reading 17 1
1996–97 Reading 14 0
1997–98 Reading 25 0
1998–99 Reading 8 0 **64 1**
1998–99 Southend U 20 0
1999–2000 Southend U 28 0
2000-01 Southend U 32 0 **80 0**
2001-02 Chesterfield 40 2
2002-03 Chesterfield 38 0 **78 2**

BRADLEY, Shayne* (F) 73 14
H: 5 11 W: 13 02 b.Gloucester 8-12-79
Source: Trainee. *Honours:* England Schools.
1997–98 Southampton 0 0
1998–99 Southampton 3 0
1998–99 *Swindon T* 7 0 **7 0**
1999–2000 Southampton 1 0
1999–2000 *Exeter C* 8 1 **8 1**
2000-01 Southampton 0 0 **4 0**
2000-01 Mansfield T 26 7
2001-02 Mansfield T 16 3
2002-03 Mansfield T 0 0 **42 10**
2002-03 Chesterfield 9 2 **9 2**
2002-03 *Lincoln C* 3 1 **3 1**

BRANDON, Chris (M) 107 15
H: 5 8 W: 11 00 b.Bradford 7-4-76
Source: Bradford PA.
1999–2000 Torquay U 42 5
2000-01 Torquay U 2 0
2001-02 Torquay U 27 3 **71 8**
2002-03 Chesterfield 36 7 **36 7**

BURT, Jamie (F) 44 9
H: 5 10 W: 12 00 b.Ashington 29-9-79
Source: Whitby T.
2001-02 Chesterfield 24 7
2002-03 Chesterfield 16 1 **40 8**
2002-03 *Carlisle U* 4 1 **4 1**

DAVIES, Gareth (M) 34 1
H: 6 1 W: 12 00 b.Chesterfield 4-2-83
Source: Trainee.
2001-02 Chesterfield 0 0
2002-03 Chesterfield 34 1 **34 1**

DAWSON, Kevin (D) 42 1
H: 6 0 W: 12 06 b.Northallerton 18-6-81
Source: Trainee.
1998–99 Nottingham F 0 0
1999–2000 Nottingham F 7 0
2000-01 Nottingham F 1 0
2000-01 *Barnet* 5 0 **5 0**
2001-02 Nottingham F 3 0 **11 0**
2002-03 Chesterfield 26 1 **26 1**

EBDON, Marcus* (M) 339 28
H: 5 10 W: 11 02 b.Pontypool 17-10-70
Source: Trainee. *Honours:* Wales Youth, Under-21.
1988–89 Everton 0 0
1989–90 Everton 0 0
1990–91 Everton 0 0
1991–92 Peterborough U 15 2
1992–93 Peterborough U 28 4
1993–94 Peterborough U 10 0
1994–95 Peterborough U 35 6
1995–96 Peterborough U 39 2
1996–97 Peterborough U 20 1 **147 15**
1996–97 Chesterfield 12 1
1997–98 Chesterfield 33 2
1998–99 Chesterfield 40 1
1999–2000 Chesterfield 11 0
2000-01 Chesterfield 41 3
2001-02 Chesterfield 31 2
2002-03 Chesterfield 24 4 **192 13**

EDWARDS, Rob* (M) 387 65
H: 5 9 W: 12 04 b.Manchester 23-2-70
Source: Trainee.
1987–88 Crewe Alex 6 1
1988–89 Crewe Alex 4 0
1989–90 Crewe Alex 4 0
1990–91 Crewe Alex 29 11
1991–92 Crewe Alex 28 6
1992–93 Crewe Alex 23 7
1993–94 Crewe Alex 12 2
1994–95 Crewe Alex 17 2
1995–96 Crewe Alex 32 15 **155 44**
1995–96 Huddersfield T 13 7
1996–97 Huddersfield T 33 3
1997–98 Huddersfield T 38 1
1998–99 Huddersfield T 45 2
1999–2000 Huddersfield T 9 1
2000-01 Huddersfield T 0 0 **138 14**
2000-01 Chesterfield 34 4
2001-02 Chesterfield 31 1
2002-03 Chesterfield 29 2 **94 7**

FOLAN, Caleb (F) 20 1
H: 6 2 W: 14 02 b.Leeds 26-10-82
Source: Trainee.
1999–2000 Leeds U 0 0
2000-01 Leeds U 0 0
2001-02 Leeds U 0 0
2001-02 *Rushden & D* 6 0 **6 0**
2001-02 *Hull C* 1 0 **1 0**
2002-03 Leeds U 0 0
2002-03 Chesterfield 13 1 **13 1**

HOWARD, Jonathan* (F) 272 44
H: 5 11 W: 11 07 b.Sheffield 7-10-71
Source: Trainee.
1990–91 Rotherham U 1 0
1991–92 Rotherham U 10 3
1992–93 Rotherham U 17 2
1993–94 Rotherham U 8 0
1994–95 Rotherham U 0 0 **36 5**
1994–95 Chesterfield 12 1
1995–96 Chesterfield 30 2

1996–97 Chesterfield 35 9
1997–98 Chesterfield 35 6
1998–99 Chesterfield 37 9
1999–2000 Chesterfield 27 2
2000-01 Chesterfield 31 5
2001-02 Chesterfield 20 5
2002-03 Chesterfield 9 0 **236 39**

HOWSON, Stuart (M) 60 4
H: 6 1 W: 12 13 b.Chorley 30-9-81
Source: Trainee.
1999–2000 Blackburn R 0 0
2000-01 Blackburn R 0 0
2000-01 Northern Spirit 14 1 **14 1**
2001-02 Blackburn R 0 0
2001-02 Chesterfield 13 1
2002-03 Chesterfield 33 2 **46 3**

HUDSON, Mark (M) 44 4
H: 5 10 W: 11 03 b.Bishop Auckland 24-10-80
Source: Trainee.
1999–2000 Middlesbrough 0 0
2000-01 Middlesbrough 3 0
2001-02 Middlesbrough 2 0
2002-03 Middlesbrough 0 0 **5 0**
2002-03 *Carlisle U* 15 1 **15 1**
2002-03 Chesterfield 24 3 **24 3**

HURST, Glynn (F) 156 53
H: 5 10 W: 11 06 b.Barnsley 17-1-76
Source: Tottenham H Trainee.
1994–95 Barnsley 2 0
1995–96 Barnsley 5 0
1995–96 *Swansea C* 2 1 **2 1**
1996–97 Barnsley 1 0 **8 0**
1996–97 *Mansfield T* 6 0 **6 0**
1998–99 Ayr U 34 18
1999–2000 Ayr U 25 14 **59 32**
2000-01 Stockport Co 11 0
2001-02 Stockport Co 15 4 **26 4**
2001-02 Chesterfield 23 9
2002-03 Chesterfield 32 7 **55 16**

INNES, Mark (D) 106 3
H: 5 10 W: 12 04 b.Bellshill 27-9-78
Source: Trainee.
1995–96 Oldham Ath 0 0
1996–97 Oldham Ath 0 0
1997–98 Oldham Ath 4 0
1998–99 Oldham Ath 13 1
1999–2000 Oldham Ath 21 0
2000-01 Oldham Ath 30 0
2001-02 Oldham Ath 5 0 **73 1**
2001-02 Chesterfield 23 2
2002-03 Chesterfield 10 0 **33 2**

MUGGLETON, Carl (G) 308 0
H: 6 2 W: 13 00 b.Leicester 13-9-68
Source: Apprentice. *Honours:* England Under-21.
1986–87 Leicester C 0 0
1987–88 Leicester C 0 0
1987–88 *Chesterfield* 17 0
1987–88 *Blackpool* 2 0 **2 0**
1988–89 Leicester C 3 0
1988–89 *Hartlepool U* 8 0 **8 0**
1989–90 Leicester C 0 0
1989–90 *Stockport Co* 4 0 **4 0**
1990–91 Leicester C 22 0
1990–91 *Liverpool* 0 0
1991–92 Leicester C 4 0
1992–93 Leicester C 17 0
1993–94 Leicester C 0 0 **46 0**
1993–94 *Stoke C* 6 0
1993–94 *Sheffield U* 0 0
1993–94 Celtic 12 0 **12 0**
1994–95 Stoke C 24 0
1995–96 Stoke C 6 0
1995–96 *Rotherham U* 6 0 **6 0**
1995–96 *Sheffield U* 1 0 **1 0**
1996–97 Stoke C 33 0
1997–98 Stoke C 34 0
1998–99 Stoke C 40 0
1999–2000 Stoke C 0 0
1999–2000 *Mansfield T* 9 0 **9 0**
1999–2000 *Chesterfield* 5 0
2000-01 Stoke C 12 0 **155 0**
2000-01 *Cardiff C* 6 0 **6 0**
2001-02 Cheltenham T 7 0 **7 0**
2001-02 *Bradford C* 4 0 **4 0**
2002-03 Chesterfield 26 0 **48 0**

O'HARE, Alan (D) 41 0
H: 6 2 W: 12 02 b.Dundalk 31-7-82
Source: Scholar.
2001-02 Bolton W 0 0
2001-02 *Chesterfield* 19 0
2002-03 Bolton W 0 0
2002-03 Chesterfield 22 0 **41 0**

PAYNE, Steve (D) 208 9
H: 5 11 W: 12 05 b.Castleford 1-8-75
Source: Trainee.
1993–94 Huddersfield T 0 0
1994–95 Huddersfield T 0 0
1995–96 Huddersfield T 0 0
1996–97 Huddersfield T 0 0
1997–98 Macclesfield T 39 0
1998–99 Macclesfield T 38 2 **77 2**
1999–2000 Chesterfield 18 3
2000-01 Chesterfield 35 1
2001-02 Chesterfield 44 1
2002-03 Chesterfield 34 2 **131 7**

REEVES, David# (F) 585 164
H: 6 0 W: 12 06 b.Birkenhead 19-11-67
Source: Heswall.
1986–87 Sheffield W 0 0
1986–87 *Scunthorpe U* 4 2
1987–88 Sheffield W 0 0
1987–88 *Scunthorpe U* 6 4 **10 6**
1987–88 *Burnley* 16 8 **16 8**
1988–89 Sheffield W 17 2 **17 2**
1989–90 Bolton W 41 10
1990–91 Bolton W 44 10
1991–92 Bolton W 35 8
1992–93 Bolton W 14 1 **134 29**
1992–93 Notts Co 9 2
1993–94 Notts Co 4 0 **13 2**
1993–94 Carlisle U 34 11
1994–95 Carlisle U 42 21
1995–96 Carlisle U 43 13
1996–97 Carlisle U 8 3 **127 48**
1996–97 Preston NE 34 11
1997–98 Preston NE 13 1 **47 12**
1997–98 Chesterfield 26 5
1998–99 Chesterfield 40 10
1999–2000 Chesterfield 43 14
2000-01 Chesterfield 37 13
2001-02 Chesterfield 22 4
2001-02 Oldham Ath 13 3
2002-03 Oldham Ath 0 0 **13 3**
2002-03 Chesterfield 40 8 **208 54**

RICHARDSON, Lee J# (M) 402 38
H: 5 11 W: 10 06 b.Halifax 12-3-69
Source: Trainee.
1986–87 Halifax T 1 0
1987–88 Halifax T 30 1
1988–89 Halifax T 25 1 **56 2**
1988–89 Watford 9 0
1989–90 Watford 32 1 **41 1**
1990–91 Blackburn R 38 2
1991–92 Blackburn R 24 1
1992–93 Blackburn R 0 0 **62 3**
1992–93 Aberdeen 29 2
1993–94 Aberdeen 35 4 **64 6**
1994–95 Oldham Ath 30 6
1995–96 Oldham Ath 27 11
1996–97 Oldham Ath 31 4
1997–98 Oldham Ath 0 0 **88 21**
1997–98 *Stockport Co* 6 0 **6 0**
1997–98 Huddersfield T 21 3
1998–99 Huddersfield T 15 0
1999–2000 Huddersfield T 0 0 **36 3**
1999–2000 *Bury* 5 1 **5 1**
1999–2000 Livingston 0 0
2000-01 Chesterfield 30 0
2001-02 Chesterfield 14 1
2002-03 Chesterfield 0 0 **44 1**

RICHMOND, Andy (G) 7 0
H: 6 3 W: 12 10 b.Chesterfield 9-1-83
Source: Scholar.
2002-03 Chesterfield 7 0 **7 0**

ROWLAND, Keith‡ (M) 234 8
H: 5 10 W: 10 07 b.Portadown 1-9-71
Source: Trainee. *Honours:* Northern Ireland Youth, B, 19 full caps, 1 goal.
1990–91 Bournemouth 0 0
1991–92 Bournemouth 37 0
1992–93 Bournemouth 35 2 **72 2**
1992–93 *Coventry C* 2 0 **2 0**
1993–94 West Ham U 23 0
1994–95 West Ham U 12 0
1995–96 West Ham U 23 0
1996–97 West Ham U 15 1
1997–98 West Ham U 7 0 **80 1**
1997–98 QPR 7 0
1998–99 QPR 30 3
1999–2000 QPR 15 0
2000-01 QPR 4 0 **56 3**
2000-01 *Luton T* 12 2 **12 2**
2001-02 Chesterfield 9 0
2002-03 Chesterfield 3 0 **12 0**

RUSHBURY, Andy (M) 35 0
H: 5 10 W: 11 07 b.Carlisle 7-3-83
Source: Scholar.
2000-01 Chesterfield 2 0
2001-02 Chesterfield 3 0
2002-03 Chesterfield 30 0 **35 0**

WARNE, Stephen§ (M) 3 0
b.Sutton-in-Ashfield 27-2-84
Source: Scholar.
2002-03 Chesterfield 3 0 **3 0**

Scholars
Cooke, Nicholas J; Cressey, Ben; Di Gregorio, Adrian; Fox, Michael JS; Jenkinson, Simon; Jubb, Anthony; Lancaster, Samuel J; Lockwood, Daniel R; Mitchell, Adam T; Shaw, Craig P; Smith, Mark; Smith, Nathan A; Warne, Stephen J; Wharton, Lee

COLCHESTER U

ATANGANA, Simon‡ (F) 19 0
H: 5 8 W: 12 11 b.Yaounde 10-7-79
Source: Tonerre Kalara. *Honours:* Cameroon full caps.
2000-01 Dundee U 11 0
2001-02 *Port Vale* 2 0 **2 0**
2002-03 Dundee U 0 0 **11 0**
2002-03 Colchester U 6 0 **6 0**

BALDWIN, Pat (D) 19 0
H: 6 3 W: 11 07 b.London 12-11-82
Source: Chelsea Academy.
2002-03 Colchester U 19 0 **19 0**

BOWRY, Bobby# (M) 261 8
H: 5 10 W: 11 00 b.Hampstead 19-5-71
Honours: St. Kitts & Nevis full caps.
1990–91 QPR 0 0
From Carshalton Ath
1991–92 Crystal Palace 0 0
1992–93 Crystal Palace 11 1
1993–94 Crystal Palace 21 0
1994–95 Crystal Palace 18 0 **50 1**
1995–96 Millwall 38 2
1996–97 Millwall 28 1
1997–98 Millwall 43 2
1998–99 Millwall 25 0
1999–2000 Millwall 5 0
2000-01 Millwall 1 0 **140 5**
2001-02 Colchester U 36 1
2002-03 Colchester U 35 1 **71 2**

BROWN, Simon (G) 103 0
H: 6 2 W: 15 00 b.Chelmsford 3-12-76
Source: Trainee.
1995–96 Tottenham H 0 0
1996–97 Tottenham H 0 0
1997–98 Tottenham H 0 0
1997–98 *Lincoln C* 1 0 **1 0**
1998–99 Tottenham H 0 0
1998–99 *Fulham* 0 0
1999–2000 Colchester U 38 0
2000-01 Colchester U 18 0
2001-02 Colchester U 19 0
2002-03 Colchester U 27 0 **102 0**

CANHAM, Marc* (M) 4 0
H: 5 10 W: 12 03 b.Wegburg 11-9-82
Source: Scholar.
2001-02 Colchester U 1 0
2002-03 Colchester U 3 0 **4 0**

CHAMBERS, Triston‡ (F) 1 0
b.Enfield 25-12-82
Source: Scholar.
2001-02 Colchester U 1 0
2002-03 Colchester U 0 0 **1 0**

COOTE, Adrian (F) 94 8
H: 6 2 W: 13 00 b.Gt Yarmouth 30-9-78
Source: Trainee. *Honours:* Northern Ireland Under-21, B, 6 full caps.
1997–98 Norwich C 23 2
1998–99 Norwich C 6 0
1999–2000 Norwich C 11 1
2000-01 Norwich C 14 0
2001-02 Norwich C 0 0 **54 3**
2001-02 Colchester U 19 4
2002-03 Colchester U 16 0 **35 4**
2002-03 *Bristol R* 5 1 **5 1**

DUGUID, Karl (F) **240 35**
H: 5 11 W: 11 07 b.Hitchin 21-3-78
Source: Trainee.

1995–96	Colchester U	16	1		
1996–97	Colchester U	20	3		
1997–98	Colchester U	21	3		
1998–99	Colchester U	33	4		
1999–2000	Colchester U	41	12		
2000-01	Colchester U	41	5		
2001-02	Colchester U	41	4		
2002-03	Colchester U	27	3	**240**	**35**

DUNNE, Joe‡ (D) **278 7**
H: 5 9 W: 11 10 b.Dublin 25-5-73
Source: Trainee. *Honours:* Eire Youth, Under-21.

1990–91	Gillingham	26	0		
1991–92	Gillingham	11	0		
1992–93	Gillingham	4	0		
1993–94	Gillingham	37	0		
1994–95	Gillingham	35	1		
1995–96	Gillingham	2	0	**115**	**1**
1995–96	Colchester U	5	1		
1996–97	Colchester U	35	0		
1997–98	Colchester U	25	2		
1998–99	Colchester U	36	0		
From Dover Ath.					
1999–2000	Colchester U	20	0		
2000-01	Colchester U	34	1		
2001-02	Colchester U	8	2		
2002-03	Colchester U	0	0	**163**	**6**

EDWARDS, Mike (D) **183 6**
H: 6 0 W: 12 10 b.North Ferriby 25-4-80
Source: Trainee.

1997–98	Hull C	21	0		
1998–99	Hull C	30	0		
1999–2000	Hull C	40	1		
2000-01	Hull C	42	4		
2001-02	Hull C	39	1		
2002-03	Hull C	6	0	**178**	**6**
2002-03	Colchester U	5	0	**5**	**0**

FITZGERALD, Scott# (D) **294 2**
H: 6 1 W: 13 00 b.Westminster 13-8-69
Source: Trainee. *Honours:* Eire Under-21, B.

1988–89	Wimbledon	0	0		
1989–90	Wimbledon	1	0		
1990–91	Wimbledon	0	0		
1991–92	Wimbledon	36	1		
1992–93	Wimbledon	20	0		
1993–94	Wimbledon	28	0		
1994–95	Wimbledon	17	0		
1995–96	Wimbledon	4	0		
1995–96	*Sheffield U*	6	0	**6**	**0**
1996–97	Wimbledon	0	0	**106**	**1**
1996–97	*Millwall*	7	0		
1997–98	Millwall	18	0		
1998–99	Millwall	32	1		
1999–2000	Millwall	31	0		
2000-01	Millwall	1	0	**89**	**1**
2000-01	Colchester U	30	0		
2001-02	Colchester U	37	0		
2002-03	Colchester U	26	0	**93**	**0**

HALFORD, Greg§ (M) **1 0**
b.Chelmsford 8-12-84
Source: Scholar.

2002-03	Colchester U	1	0	**1**	**0**

IZZET, Kem (M) **91 12**
H: 5 7 W: 11 00 b.Mile End 29-9-80
Source: Trainee.

1998–99	Charlton Ath	0	0		
1999–2000	Charlton Ath	0	0		
2000-01	Charlton Ath	0	0		
2000-01	Colchester U	6	1		
2001-02	Colchester U	40	3		
2002-03	Colchester U	45	8	**91**	**12**

JOHNSON, Gavin# (M) **331 22**
H: 5 11 W: 12 13 b.Eye 10-10-70
Source: Trainee.

1988–89	Ipswich T	4	0		
1989–90	Ipswich T	6	0		
1990–91	Ipswich T	7	0		
1991–92	Ipswich T	42	5		
1992–93	Ipswich T	40	5		
1993–94	Ipswich T	16	1		
1994–95	Ipswich T	17	0	**132**	**11**
1995–96	Luton T	5	0	**5**	**0**
1995–96	Wigan Ath	27	3		
1996–97	Wigan Ath	37	3		
1997–98	Wigan Ath	20	2	**84**	**8**
1998–99	Dunfermline Ath	18	0	**18**	**0**
1999–2000	Colchester U	27	0		
2000-01	Colchester U	37	2		
2001-02	Colchester U	20	1		
2002-03	Colchester U	8	0	**92**	**3**

KEEBLE, Chris (M) **25 2**
H: 5 10 W: 10 12 b.Colchester 17-9-78
Source: Trainee.

1997–98	Ipswich T	1	0		
1998–99	Ipswich T	0	0		
1999–2000	Ipswich T	0	0	**1**	**0**
1999–2000	Colchester U	5	1		
2000-01	Colchester U	16	1		
2001-02	Colchester U	0	0		
2002-03	Colchester U	3	0	**24**	**2**

KEITH, Joe# (D) **149 17**
H: 5 7 W: 11 00 b.London 1-10-78
Source: Trainee.

1997–98	West Ham U	0	0		
1998–99	West Ham U	0	0		
1999–2000	Colchester U	45	1		
2000-01	Colchester U	27	3		
2001-02	Colchester U	41	4		
2002-03	Colchester U	36	9	**149**	**17**

McGLEISH, Scott# (F) **330 85**
H: 5 9 W: 11 12 b.Euston 10-2-74
Source: Edgware T.

1994–95	Charlton Ath	6	0	**6**	**0**
1994–95	*Leyton Orient*	6	1		
1995–96	Peterborough U	12	0		
1995–96	*Colchester U*	15	6		
1996–97	Peterborough U	1	0	**13**	**0**
1996–97	*Cambridge U*	10	7	**10**	**7**
1996–97	Leyton Orient	28	7		
1997–98	Leyton Orient	8	0	**42**	**8**
1997–98	Barnet	37	13		
1998–99	Barnet	36	8		
1999–2000	Barnet	42	10		
2000-01	Barnet	19	5	**134**	**36**
2000-01	Colchester U	21	5		
2001-02	Colchester U	46	15		
2002-03	Colchester U	43	8	**125**	**34**

McKINNEY, Richard# (G) **22 0**
H: 6 1 W: 14 04 b.Ballymoney 18-5-79
Source: Ballymena U.

1999–2000	Manchester C	0	0		
2000-01	Manchester C	0	0		
2001-02	Swindon T	1	0	**1**	**0**
2002-03	Colchester U	21	0	**21**	**0**

MORGAN, Dean (F) **71 6**
H: 6 0 W: 12 02 b.Enfield 3-10-83
Source: Scholar.

2000-01	Colchester U	4	0		
2001-02	Colchester U	30	0		
2002-03	Colchester U	37	6	**71**	**6**

PINAULT, Thomas (M) **93 5**
H: 5 9 W: 11 10 b.Grasse 4-12-81
Source: Cannes.

1999–2000	Colchester U	4	0		
2000-01	Colchester U	5	1		
2001-02	Colchester U	42	0		
2002-03	Colchester U	42	4	**93**	**5**

RAPLEY, Kevin* (F) **180 31**
H: 5 10 W: 12 02 b.Reading 21-9-77
Source: Trainee.

1996–97	Brentford	2	0		
1997–98	Brentford	37	9		
1998–99	Brentford	12	3	**51**	**12**
1998–99	*Southend U*	9	4	**9**	**4**
1998–99	Notts Co	16	2		
1999–2000	Notts Co	29	2		
2000-01	Notts Co	7	0	**52**	**4**
2000-01	*Exeter C*	7	0	**7**	**0**
2000-01	*Scunthorpe U*	5	0	**5**	**0**
2001-02	Colchester U	35	9		
2002-03	Colchester U	21	2	**56**	**11**

STEELE, Daniel‡ (M) **8 0**
b.London 11-10-82

2001-02	Millwall	0	0		
2002-03	Colchester U	8	0	**8**	**0**

STOCKLEY, Sam (M) **256 3**
H: 6 0 W: 12 11 b.Tiverton 5-9-77
Source: Trainee.

1996–97	Southampton	0	0		
1996–97	Barnet	21	0		
1997–98	Barnet	41	0		
1998–99	Barnet	41	0		
1999–2000	Barnet	34	1		
2000-01	Barnet	45	1	**182**	**2**
2001-02	Oxford U	41	0		
2002-03	Oxford U	0	0	**41**	**0**
2002-03	Colchester U	33	1	**33**	**1**

STOCKWELL, Micky* (M) **638 57**
H: 5 6 W: 12 00 b.Maldon 14-2-65
Source: Apprentice.

1982–83	Ipswich T	0	0		
1983–84	Ipswich T	0	0		
1984–85	Ipswich T	0	0		
1985–86	Ipswich T	8	0		
1986–87	Ipswich T	21	1		
1987–88	Ipswich T	43	1		
1988–89	Ipswich T	23	2		
1989–90	Ipswich T	34	3		
1990–91	Ipswich T	44	6		
1991–92	Ipswich T	46	2		
1992–93	Ipswich T	39	4		
1993–94	Ipswich T	42	1		
1994–95	Ipswich T	15	0		
1995–96	Ipswich T	37	1		
1996–97	Ipswich T	43	7		
1997–98	Ipswich T	46	3		
1998–99	Ipswich T	30	2		
1999–2000	Ipswich T	35	2	**506**	**35**
2000-01	Colchester U	46	11		
2001-02	Colchester U	46	9		
2002-03	Colchester U	40	2	**132**	**22**

WARREN, Mark# (D) **260 6**
H: 5 11 W: 13 02 b.Hackney 12-11-74
Source: Trainee.

1991–92	Leyton Orient	1	0		
1992–93	Leyton Orient	14	0		
1993–94	Leyton Orient	6	0		
1993–94	*West Ham U*	0	0		
1994–95	Leyton Orient	31	3		
1995–96	Leyton Orient	22	1		
1996–97	Leyton Orient	27	1		
1997–98	Leyton Orient	41	0		
1998–99	Leyton Orient	10	0	**152**	**5**
1998–99	*Oxford U*	4	0	**4**	**0**
1998–99	Notts Co	18	0		
1999–2000	Notts Co	33	1		
2000-01	Notts Co	16	0		
2001-02	Notts Co	17	0	**84**	**1**
2002-03	Colchester U	20	0	**20**	**0**

WHITE, Alan# (D) **190 6**
H: 6 2 W: 13 07 b.Darlington 22-3-76
Source: Derby Co Schoolboy.

1994–95	Middlesbrough	0	0		
1995–96	Middlesbrough	0	0		
1996–97	Middlesbrough	0	0		
1997–98	Middlesbrough	0	0		
1997–98	Luton T	28	1		
1998–99	Luton T	33	1		
1999–2000	Luton T	19	1	**80**	**3**
1999–2000	*Colchester U*	4	0		
2000-01	Colchester U	32	0		
2001-02	Colchester U	33	3		
2002-03	Colchester U	41	0	**110**	**3**

Scholars

Akpinar, Huseyin; Artun, Ergun C; Coleman, Liam P; Cranfield, Ben MD; Crouch, Ross A; Driver, Sherdan; Edwards, Dwayne W; Gerken, Dean J; Halford, Gregory; Hanna, Aaron J; Harrop, Angelo; Hearn, Matthew J; Irving, Daniel J; Johnston, Craig J; Redmond, Gary St C; Richards, Garry; Toney, Tristan; White, John A

Players who do not hold a current contract but their registration has been retained by the club

Launders, Brian T

COVENTRY C

BATES, Tom (M) **1 0**
H: 5 10 W: 12 00 b.Coventry 31-10-85

2002-03	Coventry C	1	0	**1**	**0**

BETTS, Robert* (D) **23 0**
H: 5 10 W: 11 00 b.Doncaster 21-12-81
Source: School.

1997–98	Doncaster R	3	0	**3**	**0**
1998–99	Coventry C	0	0		
1999–2000	Coventry C	2	0		
2000-01	Coventry C	1	0		
2000-01	*Plymouth Arg*	4	0	**4**	**0**
2001-02	*Lincoln C*	3	0	**3**	**0**
2001-02	Coventry C	9	0		
2002-03	Coventry C	1	0	**13**	**0**

BOTHROYD, Jay (F) **72 14**
H: 6 3 W: 13 00 b.Islington 7-5-82
Source: Trainee. *Honours:* England Youth, Under-20, Under-21.

1999–2000	Arsenal	0	0		
2000-01	Coventry C	8	0		
2001-02	Coventry C	31	6		
2002-03	Coventry C	33	8	**72**	**14**

BRANCATI, Marco‡ (M) **0 0**
H: 5 10 W: 11 05 b.Rome 16-4-83

2000-01	Coventry C	0	0		
2001-02	Coventry C	0	0		
2002-03	Coventry C	0	0		

BRISCOE, Michael (D) **0 0**
H: 5 11 W: 12 00 b.Northampton 4-7-83

2002-03	Coventry C	0	0		

BRUSH, Richard (G) **0 0**
H: 6 1 W: 12 00 b.Birmingham 26-11-84
Source: Scholar.

2002-03	Coventry C	0	0		

CHIPPO, Youssef (M) **152 8**
H: 5 11 W: 12 00 b.Rabat 10-5-73
Source: Al Arabi. *Honours:* Morocco 43 full caps.

1997–98	Porto	18	2		
1998–99	Porto	12	0	**30**	**2**
1999–2000	Coventry C	33	2		
2000-01	Coventry C	32	0		
2001-02	Coventry C	34	4		
2002-03	Coventry C	23	0	**122**	**6**

COONEY, Sean (D) **1 0**
H: 6 3 W: 13 00 b.Perth 31-10-83
Source: Scholar.

2002-03	Coventry C	1	0	**1**	**0**

DAHL, Andreas (M) **0 0**
H: 5 11 W: 12 10 b.Sweden 6-6-84
Source: IFK Hassleholm.

2001-02	Coventry C	0	0		
2002-03	Coventry C	0	0		

DAVENPORT, Calum (D) **36 3**
H: 6 4 W: 14 00 b.Bedford 1-1-83
Source: Trainee. *Honours:* England Youth, Under-20.

1999–2000	Coventry C	0	0		
2000-01	Coventry C	1	0		
2001-02	Coventry C	3	0		
2002-03	Coventry C	32	3	**36**	**3**

DEBEC, Fabien* (G) **30 0**
H: 6 1 W: 14 00 b.Lyon 18-1-76

1996–97	Lyon	0	0		
1997–98	Rennes	1	0		
1998–99	Rennes	0	0		
1999–2000	Rennes	8	0		
2000-01	Rennes	2	0		
2001-02	Rennes	8	0	**19**	**0**
2002-03	Coventry C	11	0	**11**	**0**

DELORGE, Laurent‡ (M) **40 9**
H: 5 10 W: 11 12 b.Leuven 21-7-79
Honours: .

1998–99	Gent	10	5	**10**	**5**
1998–99	Coventry C	0	0		
1999–2000	Coventry C	0	0		
2000-01	Coventry C	0	0		
2001-02	Coventry C	28	4		
2002-03	Coventry C	2	0	**30**	**4**

ENGONGA, Vicente* (D) **333 9**
H: 5 11 W: 13 03 b.Barcelona 20-10-65
Source: Mahones. *Honours:* Spain 14 full caps, 1 goal.

1991–92	Valladolid	36	3	**36**	**3**
1992–93	Celta Vigo	36	0		
1993–94	Celta Vigo	36	0	**72**	**0**
1994–95	Valencia	9	0		
1995–96	Valencia	25	0		
1996–97	Valencia	35	2	**69**	**2**
1997–98	Mallorca	34	0		
1998–99	Mallorca	32	0		
1999–2000	Mallorca	31	0		
2000-01	Mallorca	31	2		
2001-02	Mallorca	20	2	**148**	**4**
2002-03	Coventry C	8	0	**8**	**0**

EUSTACE, John (M) **98 8**
H: 5 11 W: 11 12 b.Solihull 3-11-79
Source: Trainee.

1996–97	Coventry C	0	0		
1997–98	Coventry C	0	0		
1998–99	Coventry C	0	0		
1998–99	Dundee U	11	1	**11**	**1**
1999–2000	Coventry C	16	1		
2000-01	Coventry C	32	2		
2001-02	Coventry C	6	0		
2002-03	Coventry C	32	4	**86**	**7**
2002-03	*Middlesbrough*	1	0	**1**	**0**

FORD, Brian* (D) **0 0**
H: 5 11 W: 12 00 b.Edinburgh 23-9-82
Source: Trainee.

1999–2000	Coventry C	0	0		
2000-01	Coventry C	0	0		
2001-02	Coventry C	0	0		
2002-03	Coventry C	0	0		

FOWLER, Lee (M) **14 0**
H: 5 7 W: 10 00 b.Cardiff 10-6-83
Source: Scholar. *Honours:* Wales Under-21.

2000-01	Coventry C	0	0		
2001-02	Coventry C	13	0		
2002-03	Coventry C	1	0	**14**	**0**

GALLIERI, Antonio‡ (F) **0 0**
H: 5 8 W: 11 00 b.Rome 5-7-83

2000-01	Coventry C	0	0		
2001-02	Coventry C	0	0		
2002-03	Coventry C	0	0		

GORDON, Dean (D) **301 27**
H: 5 11 W: 13 08 b.Thornton Heath 10-2-73
Source: Trainee. *Honours:* England Under-21.

1991–92	Crystal Palace	4	0		
1992–93	Crystal Palace	10	0		
1993–94	Crystal Palace	45	5		
1994–95	Crystal Palace	41	2		
1995–96	Crystal Palace	34	8		
1996–97	Crystal Palace	30	3		
1997–98	Crystal Palace	37	2	**201**	**20**
1998–99	Middlesbrough	38	3		
1999–2000	Middlesbrough	4	0		
2000-01	Middlesbrough	20	1		
2001-02	Middlesbrough	1	0	**63**	**4**
2001-02	*Cardiff C*	7	2	**7**	**2**
2002-03	Coventry C	30	1	**30**	**1**

GUERRERO, Ivan‡ (D) **7 0**
H: 5 7 W: 10 00 b.Comayagua 30-11-77
Source: Motagua. *Honours:* Honduras full caps.

2000-01	Coventry C	3	0		
2001-02	Coventry C	4	0		
2002-03	Coventry C	0	0	**7**	**0**

HIGGINS, Ruaidhri (M) **0 0**
H: 5 10 W: 12 00 b.Derry 23-10-84
Source: Scholar.

2001-02	Coventry C	0	0		
2002-03	Coventry C	0	0		

HYLDGAARD, Morten (G) **32 0**
H: 6 6 W: 14 00 b.Herning 26-1-78
Source: Ikast.

1999–2000	Coventry C	0	0		
1999–2000	*Scunthorpe U*	5	0	**5**	**0**
2000-01	Coventry C	0	0		
2000-01	*Grimsby T*	0	0		
2001-02	Coventry C	0	0		
2002-03	Coventry C	27	0	**27**	**0**

JEPHCOTT, Avun (F) **1 0**
H: 6 2 W: 14 00 b.Coventry 16-10-83
Source: Scholar.

2002-03	Coventry C	1	0	**1**	**0**

JOACHIM, Julian (F) **267 67**
H: 5 6 W: 12 00 b.Boston 20-9-74
Source: Trainee. *Honours:* England Youth, Under-21.

1992–93	Leicester C	26	10		
1993–94	Leicester C	36	11		
1994–95	Leicester C	15	3		
1995–96	Leicester C	22	1	**99**	**25**
1995–96	Aston Villa	11	1		
1996–97	Aston Villa	15	3		
1997–98	Aston Villa	26	8		
1998–99	Aston Villa	36	14		
1999–2000	Aston Villa	33	6		
2000-01	Aston Villa	20	7	**141**	**39**
2001-02	Coventry C	16	1		
2002-03	Coventry C	11	2	**27**	**3**

KENNA, Conor (D) **0 0**
H: 5 10 W: 12 00 b.Dublin 21-11-84
Source: Scholar.

2001-02	Coventry C	0	0		
2002-03	Coventry C	0	0		

KONJIC, Muhamed (D) **258 14**
H: 6 3 W: 13 00 b.Bosnia 14-5-70
Honours: Bosnia 31 full caps, 3 goals.

1990–91	Tuzla	3	0		
1991–92	Tuzla	5	0	**8**	**0**
1992–93	Belisce	18	0	**18**	**0**
1993–94	Zagreb	29	3		
1994–95	Zagreb	19	1		
1995–96	Zagreb	15	1	**63**	**5**
1996–97	Zurich	29	2		
1997–98	Zurich	7	3	**36**	**5**
1997–98	Monaco	19	0		
1998–99	Monaco	18	2	**37**	**2**
1998–99	Coventry C	4	0		
1999–2000	Coventry C	4	0		
2000-01	Coventry C	8	0		
2001-02	Coventry C	38	2		
2002-03	Coventry C	42	0	**96**	**2**

MACKEY, Ben‡ (M) **3 0**
H: 5 8 W: 11 09 b.Leamington 27-10-86

2002-03	Coventry C	3	0	**3**	**0**

MARTINEZ, Jairo‡ (F) **11 3**
H: 5 9 W: 11 08 b.Honduras 14-5-78
Honours: Honduras full caps.

2000-01	Coventry C	0	0		
2001-02	Coventry C	11	3		
2002-03	Coventry C	0	0	**11**	**3**

McALLISTER, Gary† (M) **706 116**
H: 6 1 W: 11 11 b.Motherwell 25-12-64
Source: Fir Park BC. *Honours:* Scotland Under-21, B, 57 full caps, 5 goals.

1981–82	Motherwell	1	0		
1982–83	Motherwell	1	0		
1983–84	Motherwell	21	0		
1984–85	Motherwell	35	6		
1985–86	Motherwell	1	0	**59**	**6**
1985–86	Leicester C	31	7		
1986–87	Leicester C	39	10		
1987–88	Leicester C	42	9		
1988–89	Leicester C	46	11		
1989–90	Leicester C	43	10	**201**	**47**
1990–91	Leeds U	38	2		
1991–92	Leeds U	42	5		
1992–93	Leeds U	32	5		
1993–94	Leeds U	42	8		
1994–95	Leeds U	41	6		
1995–96	Leeds U	36	5	**231**	**31**
1996–97	Coventry C	38	6		
1997–98	Coventry C	14	0		
1998–99	Coventry C	29	3		
1999–2000	Coventry C	38	11		
2000-01	Liverpool	30	5		
2001-02	Liverpool	25	0	**55**	**5**
2002-03	Coventry C	41	7	**160**	**27**

McSHEFFREY, Gary (F) **46 6**
H: 5 8 W: 10 06 b.Coventry 13-8-82
Source: Trainee. *Honours:* England Youth, Under-20.

1998–99	Coventry C	1	0		
1999–2000	Coventry C	3	0		
2000-01	Coventry C	0	0		
2001-02	*Stockport Co*	5	1	**5**	**1**
2001-02	Coventry C	8	1		
2002-03	Coventry C	29	4	**41**	**5**

MILLER, Kirk* (D) **0 0**
H: 5 10 W: 11 10 b.Coventry 15-9-83
Source: Scholar.

2000-01	Coventry C	0	0		
2001-02	Coventry C	0	0		
2002-03	Coventry C	0	0		

MONTGOMERY, Gary* (G) **10 0**
H: 6 1 W: 13 07 b.Leamington Spa 8-10-82
Source: Scholar.

2000-01	Coventry C	0	0		
2001-02	Coventry C	0	0		
2001-02	*Crewe Alex*	0	0		
2001-02	*Kidderminster H*	2	0	**2**	**0**
2002-03	Coventry C	8	0	**8**	**0**

NOON, Mark (M) **2 0**
H: 5 10 W: 12 00 b.Leamington Spa 23-9-83
Source: Scholar.

2001-02	Coventry C	0	0		
2002-03	Coventry C	2	0	**2**	**0**

NORMANN, Runar‡ (M) **54 7**
H: 5 11 W: 12 00 b.Harstad 1-3-78
Source: Harstad.

1997	Lillestrom	1	1		
1998	Lillestrom	23	2		
1999	Lillestrom	17	3	**41**	**6**

1999–2000 Coventry C 8 0
2000-01 Coventry C 0 0
2001-02 Coventry C 2 0
2002-03 Coventry C 3 1 **13 1**

O'DONOVAN, Roy (F) 0 0
H: 5 10 W: 11 07 b.Cork 10-8-85
Source: Scholar.
2002-03 Coventry C 0 0

O'NEILL, Keith (M) 121 9
H: 6 1 W: 13 03 b.Dublin 16-12-76
Source: Trainee. *Honours:* Eire 13 full caps, 4 goals.
1994–95 Norwich C 1 0
1995–96 Norwich C 19 1
1996–97 Norwich C 26 6
1997–98 Norwich C 9 1
1998–99 Norwich C 18 1 **73 9**
1998–99 Middlesbrough 6 0
1999–2000 Middlesbrough 16 0
2000-01 Middlesbrough 15 0 **37 0**
2001-02 Coventry C 11 0
2002-03 Coventry C 0 0 **11 0**

OSBOURNE, Isaac§ (M) 2 0
H: 5 10 W: 11 11 b.Birmingham 22-6-86
Source: Scholar.
2002-03 Coventry C 2 0 **2 0**

PEAD, Craig (M) 25 2
H: 5 9 W: 11 06 b.Bromsgrove 15-9-81
Source: Trainee. *Honours:* England Youth, Under-20.
1998–99 Coventry C 0 0
1999–2000 Coventry C 0 0
2000-01 Coventry C 0 0
2001-02 Coventry C 1 0
2002-03 Coventry C 24 2 **25 2**

PIPE, David (M) 21 1
H: 5 9 W: 12 01 b.Caerphilly 5-11-83
Source: Scholar. *Honours:* Wales Under-21, 1 full cap.
2000-01 Coventry C 0 0
2001-02 Coventry C 0 0
2002-03 Coventry C 21 1 **21 1**

QUIGLEY, Stephen‡ (D) 0 0
b.Dublin 13-1-85
Source: Scholar.
2001-02 Coventry C 0 0
2002-03 Coventry C 0 0

QUINN, Barry (M) 83 0
H: 6 0 W: 12 02 b.Dublin 9-5-79
Source: Trainee. *Honours:* Eire Under-21, 4 full caps.
1996–97 Coventry C 0 0
1997–98 Coventry C 0 0
1998–99 Coventry C 7 0
1999–2000 Coventry C 11 0
2000-01 Coventry C 25 0
2001-02 Coventry C 22 0
2002-03 Coventry C 18 0 **83 0**

REGAN, Martin (D) 0 0
H: 5 11 W: 12 00 b.Tralee 29-1-85
Source: Scholar.
2001-02 Coventry C 0 0
2002-03 Coventry C 0 0

RICE, Stephen‡ (M) 0 0
H: 5 9 W: 10 10 b.Dublin 6-10-84
Source: Scholar.
2001-02 Coventry C 0 0
2002-03 Coventry C 0 0

SAFRI, Youseff (M) 60 1
H: 5 8 W: 10 12 b.Casablanca 13-1-77
Source: Raja. *Honours:* Morocco full caps.
2001-02 Coventry C 33 1
2002-03 Coventry C 27 0 **60 1**

SARA, Juan (F) 91 33
H: 6 0 W: 11 07 b.Buenos Aires 13-10-76
2000 Cerro Porteno 10 4 **10 4**
2000-01 Dundee 31 15
2001-02 Dundee 28 11
2002-03 Dundee 19 2 **78 28**
2002-03 Coventry C 3 1 **3 1**

SHAW, Richard (D) 451 3
H: 5 9 W: 12 08 b.Brentford 11-9-68
Source: Apprentice.
1986–87 Crystal Palace 0 0
1987–88 Crystal Palace 3 0
1988–89 Crystal Palace 14 0
1989–90 Crystal Palace 21 0
1989–90 *Hull C* 4 0 **4 0**
1990–91 Crystal Palace 36 1
1991–92 Crystal Palace 10 0
1992–93 Crystal Palace 33 0
1993–94 Crystal Palace 34 2
1994–95 Crystal Palace 41 0
1995–96 Crystal Palace 15 0 **207 3**
1995–96 Coventry C 21 0
1996–97 Coventry C 35 0
1997–98 Coventry C 33 0
1998–99 Coventry C 37 0
1999–2000 Coventry C 29 0
2000-01 Coventry C 24 0
2001-02 Coventry C 32 0
2002-03 Coventry C 29 0 **240 0**

SPONG, Richard‡ (D) 0 0
H: 5 11 W: 11 09 b.Falun 23-9-83
Source: Scholar.
2000-01 Coventry C 0 0
2001-02 Coventry C 0 0
2002-03 Coventry C 0 0

STANFORD, Eddie§ (M) 1 0
H: 5 7 W: 10 05 b.Blackburn 4-2-85
Source: Scholar.
2002-03 Coventry C 1 0 **1 0**

THORNTON, Barry (F) 0 0
H: 6 1 W: 13 00 b.Dublin 21-1-85
Source: Scholar.
2001-02 Coventry C 0 0
2002-03 Coventry C 0 0

WALSH, Steve‡ (D) 501 57
H: 6 3 W: 15 02 b.Fulwood 3-11-64
Source: Local.
1982–83 Wigan Ath 31 0
1983–84 Wigan Ath 42 1
1984–85 Wigan Ath 40 2
1985–86 Wigan Ath 13 1 **126 4**
1986–87 Leicester C 21 0
1987–88 Leicester C 32 7
1988–89 Leicester C 30 2
1989–90 Leicester C 34 3
1990–91 Leicester C 35 3
1991–92 Leicester C 43 7
1992–93 Leicester C 40 15
1993–94 Leicester C 10 4
1994–95 Leicester C 5 0
1995–96 Leicester C 37 4
1996–97 Leicester C 22 2
1997–98 Leicester C 26 3
1998–99 Leicester C 22 3
1999–2000 Leicester C 11 0
2000-01 Leicester C 1 0 **369 53**
2000-01 Norwich C 4 0 **4 0**
From Tamworth
2002-03 Coventry C 2 0 **2 0**

WHING, Andrew (D) 14 0
H: 6 0 W: 12 00 b.Birmingham 20-9-84
Source: Scholar.
2002-03 Coventry C 14 0 **14 0**

YAZDANI, Hussain (M) 0 0
H: 5 9 W: 11 00 b.Dublin 6-1-85
Source: Scholar.
2001-02 Coventry C 0 0
2002-03 Coventry C 0 0

YULU, Christian (F) 3 0
H: 5 10 W: 12 00 b.Kinshasa 17-8-84
2002-03 Coventry C 3 0 **3 0**

Scholars
Giddings, Stuart J; Goodman, Mark I; Hall, Andrew; May, Rory J; Munn, Stephen W; Nelson, Daniel M; Newbold, Blake; Nicell, Liam; Oddy, Robert J; Osbourne, Isaac S; Stanford, Edward J; Thornton, Kevin
Non-Contract
McAllister, Gary

CREWE ALEX

ASHTON, Dean (F) 91 24
H: 6 2 W: 12 08 b.Crewe 24-11-83
Source: Schoolboy. *Honours:* England Youth, Under-20.
2000-01 Crewe Alex 21 8
2001-02 Crewe Alex 31 7
2002-03 Crewe Alex 39 9 **91 24**

BANKOLE, Ademola (G) 59 0
H: 6 3 W: 14 00 b.Lagos 9-9-69
Source: Leyton Orient.
1996–97 Crewe Alex 3 0
1997–98 Crewe Alex 3 0
1998–99 QPR 0 0
1998–99 *Grimsby T* 0 0
1999–2000 QPR 1 0 **1 0**
1999–2000 *Bradford C* 0 0
2000-01 Crewe Alex 21 0
2001-02 Crewe Alex 28 0
2002-03 Crewe Alex 3 0 **58 0**

BELL, Lee (M) 17 1
H: 5 11 W: 11 00 b.Crewe 26-1-83
Source: Scholar.
2000-01 Crewe Alex 0 0
2001-02 Crewe Alex 0 0
2002-03 Crewe Alex 17 1 **17 1**

BETTS, Tom (D) 0 0
H: 6 0 W: 12 00 b.Stone 3-12-82
Source: Scholar.
2000-01 Crewe Alex 0 0
2001-02 Crewe Alex 0 0
2002-03 Crewe Alex 0 0

BRAMMER, Dave (M) 281 18
H: 5 11 W: 12 00 b.Bromborough 28-2-75
Source: Trainee.
1992–93 Wrexham 2 0
1993–94 Wrexham 22 2
1994–95 Wrexham 14 1
1995–96 Wrexham 11 2
1996–97 Wrexham 21 1
1997–98 Wrexham 33 4
1998–99 Wrexham 34 2 **137 12**
1998–99 Port Vale 9 0
1999–2000 Port Vale 29 0
2000-01 Port Vale 35 3 **73 3**
2001-02 Crewe Alex 30 2
2002-03 Crewe Alex 41 1 **71 3**

COLLINS, Wayne‡ (M) 226 24
H: 5 11 W: 12 02 b.Manchester 4-3-69
Source: Winsford U.
1993–94 Crewe Alex 35 2
1994–95 Crewe Alex 40 11
1995–96 Crewe Alex 42 1
1996–97 Sheffield W 12 1
1997–98 Sheffield W 19 5 **31 6**
1997–98 Fulham 13 1
1998–99 Fulham 21 2
1999–2000 Fulham 19 1
2000-01 Fulham 5 0 **58 4**
2001-02 Crewe Alex 20 0
2002-03 Crewe Alex 0 0 **137 14**

COVERLEY, Neil‡ (D) 0 0
b.Colwyn Bay 20-1-83
Source: Scholar.
2002-03 Crewe Alex 0 0

EDWARDS, Paul (F) 2 0
H: 6 0 W: 11 07 b.Derby 10-11-82
Source: Scholar.
2000-01 Crewe Alex 0 0
2001-02 Crewe Alex 0 0
2002-03 Crewe Alex 2 0 **2 0**

FOSTER, Stephen (D) 100 9
H: 6 0 W: 11 05 b.Warrington 10-9-80
Source: Trainee. *Honours:* England Schools.
1998–99 Crewe Alex 1 0
1999–2000 Crewe Alex 0 0
2000-01 Crewe Alex 30 0
2001-02 Crewe Alex 34 5
2002-03 Crewe Alex 35 4 **100 9**

FROST, Carl (M) 0 0
H: 5 9 W: 10 07 b.Chester 19-7-83
Source: Scholar.
2000-01 Crewe Alex 0 0
2001-02 Crewe Alex 0 0
2002-03 Crewe Alex 0 0

HIGDON, Michael (M) 0 0
H: 6 1 W: 11 05 b.Liverpool 2-9-83
Source: School.
2000-01 Crewe Alex 0 0
2001-02 Crewe Alex 0 0
2002-03 Crewe Alex 0 0

HULSE, Rob (F) 116 46
H: 6 1 W: 12 05 b.Crewe 25-10-79
Source: Trainee.
1998–99 Crewe Alex 0 0
1999–2000 Crewe Alex 4 1
2000-01 Crewe Alex 33 11
2001-02 Crewe Alex 41 12
2002-03 Crewe Alex 38 22 **116 46**

INCE, Clayton (G) **64 0**
H: 6 3 W: 13 00 b.Trinidad 13-7-72
Source: Defence Force. *Honours:* Trinidad & Tobago 29 full caps.
1999–2000 Crewe Alex 1 0
2000-01 Crewe Alex 1 0
2001-02 Crewe Alex 19 0
2002-03 Crewe Alex 43 0 **64 0**

JACK, Rodney* (F) **250 57**
H: 5 7 W: 10 05 b.Kingston, Jamaica 28-9-72
Source: Lambada. *Honours:* St Vincent full caps.
1995–96 Torquay U 14 2
1996–97 Torquay U 33 10
1997–98 Torquay U 40 12 **87 24**
1998–99 Crewe Alex 39 9
1999–2000 Crewe Alex 23 4
2000-01 Crewe Alex 30 4
2001-02 Crewe Alex 33 7
2002-03 Crewe Alex 38 9 **163 33**

JEFFS, Ian (M) **0 0**
H: 5 7 W: 10 00 b.Chester 12-10-82
Source: Scholar.
2000-01 Crewe Alex 0 0
2001-02 Crewe Alex 0 0
2002-03 Crewe Alex 0 0

JONES, Steve (F) **46 10**
H: 5 10 W: 10 05 b.Derry 25-10-76
Source: Leigh RMI. *Honours:* Northern Ireland 2 full caps.
2001-02 *Rochdale* 9 1 **9 1**
2001-02 Crewe Alex 6 0
2002-03 Crewe Alex 31 9 **37 9**

LITTLE, Colin* (F) **204 34**
H: 5 10 W: 12 00 b.Wythenshaw 4-11-72
Source: Hyde U.
1995–96 Crewe Alex 12 1
1996–97 Crewe Alex 17 0
1997–98 Crewe Alex 40 13
1998–99 Crewe Alex 37 10
1999–2000 Crewe Alex 37 4
2000-01 Crewe Alex 27 4
2001-02 Crewe Alex 17 1
2002-03 Crewe Alex 6 0 **193 33**
2002-03 *Mansfield T* 5 0 **5 0**
2002-03 *Macclesfield T* 6 1 **6 1**

LUNT, Kenny (M) **239 19**
H: 5 10 W: 10 05 b.Runcorn 20-11-79
Source: Trainee. *Honours:* England Schools, Youth.
1997–98 Crewe Alex 41 2
1998–99 Crewe Alex 18 1
1999–2000 Crewe Alex 43 3
2000-01 Crewe Alex 46 1
2001-02 Crewe Alex 45 5
2002-03 Crewe Alex 46 7 **239 19**

McCREADY, Chris (D) **9 0**
H: 6 1 W: 12 05 b.Chester 5-9-81
Source: Scholar.
2000-01 Crewe Alex 0 0
2001-02 Crewe Alex 1 0
2002-03 Crewe Alex 8 0 **9 0**

MORRIS, Alexander (M) **0 0**
H: 6 0 W: 11 08 b.Stoke 5-10-82
Source: Scholar.
2000-01 Crewe Alex 0 0
2001-02 Crewe Alex 0 0
2002-03 Crewe Alex 0 0

PLATT, Matthew (F) **0 0**
H: 6 0 W: 11 03 b.Crewe 15-10-83
Source: Scholar.
2002-03 Crewe Alex 0 0

RIX, Ben (M) **44 0**
H: 5 9 W: 11 05 b.Wolverhampton 11-12-82
Source: Scholar.
2000-01 Crewe Alex 0 0
2001-02 Crewe Alex 21 0
2002-03 Crewe Alex 23 0 **44 0**

ROBERTS, Mark (D) **0 0**
H: 6 1 W: 12 00 b.Northwich 16-10-83
Source: Scholar.
2002-03 Crewe Alex 0 0

ROBINSON, James (M) **1 0**
H: 5 10 W: 11 03 b.Whiston 18-9-82
Source: Scholar.
2001-02 Crewe Alex 0 0
2002-03 Crewe Alex 1 0 **1 0**

SODJE, Efetobar (D) **193 9**
H: 6 1 W: 12 05 b.Greenwich 5-10-72
Source: Delta Steel Pioneer, Stevenage Bor. *Honours:* Nigeria 10 full caps, 1 goal.
1997–98 Macclesfield T 41 3
1998–99 Macclesfield T 42 3 **83 6**
1999–2000 Luton T 9 0 **9 0**
1999–2000 Colchester U 3 0 **3 0**
2000-01 Crewe Alex 32 0
2001-02 Crewe Alex 36 2
2002-03 Crewe Alex 30 1 **98 3**

SORVEL, Neil# (M) **268 17**
H: 6 0 W: 12 03 b.Widnes 2-3-73
Source: Trainee.
1991–92 Crewe Alex 9 0
1992–93 Crewe Alex 0 0
1997–98 Macclesfield T 45 3
1998–99 Macclesfield T 41 4 **86 7**
1999–2000 Crewe Alex 46 6
2000-01 Crewe Alex 46 1
2001-02 Crewe Alex 38 0
2002-03 Crewe Alex 43 3 **182 10**

TOMLINSON, Stuart§ (G) **1 0**
H: 6 0 W: 11 02 b.Chester 10-5-85
Source: Scholar.
2002-03 Crewe Alex 1 0 **1 0**

VARNEY, Luke (F) **0 0**
H: 5 11 W: 11 00 b.Leicester 28-9-82
Source: Quorn.
2002-03 Crewe Alex 0 0

VAUGHAN, David (M) **46 3**
H: 5 7 W: 11 00 b.St Asaph 18-2-83
Source: Scholar. *Honours:* Wales Under-21, 1 full cap.
2000-01 Crewe Alex 1 0
2001-02 Crewe Alex 13 0
2002-03 Crewe Alex 32 3 **46 3**

WALKER, Richard (D) **39 2**
H: 6 2 W: 12 08 b.Stafford 17-9-80
Source: Brook House.
1999–2000 Crewe Alex 0 0
2000-01 Crewe Alex 3 0
2001-02 Crewe Alex 1 0
2002-03 Crewe Alex 35 2 **39 2**

WALTON, David* (D) **283 13**
H: 6 2 W: 13 00 b.Bellingham 10-4-73
Source: Trainee.
1991–92 Sheffield U 0 0
1992–93 Sheffield U 0 0
1993–94 Sheffield U 0 0
1993–94 Shrewsbury T 27 5
1994–95 Shrewsbury T 36 3
1995–96 Shrewsbury T 35 0
1996–97 Shrewsbury T 24 1
1997–98 Shrewsbury T 6 1 **128 10**
1997–98 Crewe Alex 27 0
1998–99 Crewe Alex 38 1
1999–2000 Crewe Alex 11 0
2000-01 Crewe Alex 20 0
2001-02 Crewe Alex 31 1
2002-03 Crewe Alex 28 1 **155 3**

WRIGHT, David (D) **171 2**
H: 5 11 W: 11 00 b.Warrington 1-5-80
Source: Trainee. *Honours:* England Youth.
1997–98 Crewe Alex 3 0
1998–99 Crewe Alex 20 1
1999–2000 Crewe Alex 45 0
2000-01 Crewe Alex 42 0
2001-02 Crewe Alex 30 0
2002-03 Crewe Alex 31 1 **171 2**

YATES, Adam (D) **0 0**
H: 5 10 W: 10 07 b.Stoke 28-5-83
Source: Scholar.
2000-01 Crewe Alex 0 0
2001-02 Crewe Alex 0 0
2002-03 Crewe Alex 0 0

Scholars
Austin, Ryan; Ball, Craig; Bignot, Paul J; Bond, Andrew M; Booth, Martin T; Brown, Alexander JA; Clare, Craig G; Clark, James; Fletcher, James E; Garner, Matt NP; Hawthorne, Robert; Howard, Adam; Jenkins, Byron K; Lee, Jamie A; Lloyd, Robert F; Malbon, Craig D; McGowan, Lloyd E; Roberts, Mark A; Sutton, Ritchie A; Tomlinson, Stuart; White, Christopher J; Wilson, Kyle

CRYSTAL PALACE

ADEBOLA, Dele# (F) **297 75**
H: 6 3 W: 15 00 b.Lagos 23-6-75
Source: Trainee.
1992–93 Crewe Alex 6 0
1993–94 Crewe Alex 0 0
1994–95 Crewe Alex 30 8
1995–96 Crewe Alex 29 8
1996–97 Crewe Alex 32 16
1997–98 Crewe Alex 27 7 **124 39**
1997–98 Birmingham C 17 7
1998–99 Birmingham C 39 13
1999–2000 Birmingham C 42 5
2000-01 Birmingham C 31 6
2001-02 Birmingham C 0 0 **129 31**
2001-02 *Oldham Ath* 5 0 **5 0**
2002-03 Crystal Palace 39 5 **39 5**

AKINBIYI, Ade (F) **293 90**
H: 6 1 W: 12 08 b.Hackney 10-10-74
Source: Trainee. *Honours:* Nigeria full caps.
1992–93 Norwich C 0 0
1993–94 Norwich C 2 0
1993–94 *Hereford U* 4 2 **4 2**
1994–95 Norwich C 13 0
1994–95 *Brighton & HA* 7 4 **7 4**
1995–96 Norwich C 22 3
1996–97 Norwich C 12 0 **49 3**
1996–97 Gillingham 19 7
1997–98 Gillingham 44 21 **63 28**
1998–99 Bristol C 44 19
1999–2000 Bristol C 3 2 **47 21**
1999–2000 Wolverhampton W 37 16 **37 16**
2000-01 Leicester C 37 9
2001-02 Leicester C 21 2 **58 11**
2001-02 Crystal Palace 14 2
2002-03 Crystal Palace 10 1 **24 3**
2002-03 *Stoke C* 4 2 **4 2**

ANTWI, Will* (D) **4 0**
H: 6 2 W: 12 08 b.London 19-10-82
Source: Scholar.
2002-03 Crystal Palace 4 0 **4 0**

AUSTIN, Dean‡ (D) **362 8**
H: 5 11 W: 11 11 b.Hemel Hempstead 26-4-70
Source: St. Albans C.
1989–90 Southend U 7 0
1990–91 Southend U 44 0
1991–92 Southend U 45 2 **96 2**
1992–93 Tottenham H 34 0
1993–94 Tottenham H 23 0
1994–95 Tottenham H 24 0
1995–96 Tottenham H 28 0
1996–97 Tottenham H 15 0
1997–98 Tottenham H 0 0 **124 0**
1998–99 Crystal Palace 20 1
1999–2000 Crystal Palace 45 2
2000-01 Crystal Palace 39 3
2001-02 Crystal Palace 35 0
2002-03 Crystal Palace 3 0 **142 6**

BERTHELIN, Cedric# (G) **18 0**
H: 6 4 W: 15 00 b.Courrieres 25-12-76
2002-03 Luton T 9 0 **9 0**
2002-03 Crystal Palace 9 0 **9 0**

BLACK, Tommy (M) **111 11**
H: 5 7 W: 11 10 b.Chigwell 26-11-79
Source: Trainee.
1998–99 Arsenal 0 0
1999–2000 Arsenal 1 0 **1 0**
1999–2000 *Carlisle U* 5 1 **5 1**
1999–2000 *Bristol C* 4 0 **4 0**
2000-01 Crystal Palace 40 4
2001-02 Crystal Palace 25 0
2002-03 Crystal Palace 36 6 **101 10**

BORROWDALE, Gary (D) **13 0**
H: 6 0 W: 12 01 b.Sutton 16-7-85
Source: Scholar. *Honours:* England Youth.
2002-03 Crystal Palace 13 0 **13 0**

BUTTERFIELD, Danny (D) **170 4**
H: 5 10 W: 11 06 b.Boston 21-11-79
Source: Trainee. *Honours:* England Youth.
1997–98 Grimsby T 7 0
1998–99 Grimsby T 12 0
1999–2000 Grimsby T 29 0
2000-01 Grimsby T 30 1
2001-02 Grimsby T 46 2 **124 3**
2002-03 Crystal Palace 46 1 **46 1**

CLARKE, Matt (G) 208 0
H: 6 4 W: 13 08 b.Sheffield 3-11-73
Source: Trainee.
1992–93 Rotherham U 9 0
1993–94 Rotherham U 30 0
1994–95 Rotherham U 45 0
1995–96 Rotherham U 40 0 **124 0**
1996–97 Sheffield W 1 0
1997–98 Sheffield W 3 0
1998–99 Sheffield W 0 0 **4 0**
1999–2000 Bradford C 21 0
2000-01 Bradford C 17 0
2000-01 *Bolton W* 8 0 **8 0**
2001-02 Bradford C 0 0 **38 0**
2001-02 *Fulham* 0 0
2001-02 Crystal Palace 28 0
2002-03 Crystal Palace 6 0 **34 0**

CRONIN, Lance (G) 0 0
H: 6 1 W: 13 04 b.Brighton 11-9-85
Source: Scholar.
2002-03 Crystal Palace 0 0

DERRY, Shaun (M) 239 6
H: 5 10 W: 13 02 b.Nottingham 6-12-77
Source: Trainee.
1995–96 Notts Co 12 0
1996–97 Notts Co 39 2
1997–98 Notts Co 28 2 **79 4**
1997–98 Sheffield U 12 0
1998–99 Sheffield U 26 0
1999–2000 Sheffield U 34 0 **72 0**
1999–2000 Portsmouth 9 1
2000-01 Portsmouth 28 0
2001-02 Portsmouth 12 0 **49 1**
2002-03 Crystal Palace 39 1 **39 1**

FLEMING, Curtis (D) 300 3
H: 5 10 W: 12 09 b.Manchester 8-10-68
Source: St Patrick's Ath. *Honours:* Eire Youth, Under-21, B, 10 full caps.
1991–92 Middlesbrough 28 0
1992–93 Middlesbrough 24 0
1993–94 Middlesbrough 40 0
1994–95 Middlesbrough 21 0
1995–96 Middlesbrough 13 1
1996–97 Middlesbrough 30 0
1997–98 Middlesbrough 31 1
1998–99 Middlesbrough 14 1
1999–2000 Middlesbrough 27 0
2000-01 Middlesbrough 30 0
2001-02 Middlesbrough 8 0 **266 3**
2001-02 *Birmingham C* 6 0 **6 0**
2001-02 Crystal Palace 17 0
2002-03 Crystal Palace 11 0 **28 0**

FREEDMAN, Dougie (F) 331 126
H: 5 9 W: 12 05 b.Glasgow 21-1-74
Source: Trainee. *Honours:* Scotland Schools, Under-21, B, 2 full caps, 1 goal.
1991–92 QPR 0 0
1992–93 QPR 0 0
1993–94 QPR 0 0
1994–95 Barnet 42 24
1995–96 Barnet 5 3 **47 27**
1995–96 Crystal Palace 39 20
1996–97 Crystal Palace 44 11
1997–98 Crystal Palace 7 0
1997–98 Wolverhampton W 29 10 **29 10**
1998–99 Nottingham F 31 9
1999–2000 Nottingham F 34 9
2000-01 Nottingham F 5 0 **70 18**
2000-01 Crystal Palace 26 11
2001-02 Crystal Palace 40 20
2002-03 Crystal Palace 29 9 **185 71**

GRANVILLE, Danny (D) 253 13
H: 6 0 W: 12 00 b.Islington 19-1-75
Source: Trainee. *Honours:* England Under-21.
1993–94 Cambridge U 11 5
1994–95 Cambridge U 16 2
1995–96 Cambridge U 35 0
1996–97 Cambridge U 37 0 **99 7**
1996–97 Chelsea 5 0
1997–98 Chelsea 13 0 **18 0**
1998–99 Leeds U 9 0
1999–2000 Leeds U 0 0 **9 0**
1999–2000 Manchester C 35 2
2000-01 Manchester C 19 0
2000-01 *Norwich C* 6 0 **6 0**
2001-02 Manchester C 16 1 **70 3**
2001-02 Crystal Palace 16 0
2002-03 Crystal Palace 35 3 **51 3**

GRAY, Julian (M) 102 8
H: 6 1 W: 11 08 b.Lewisham 21-9-79
Source: Trainee.
1998–99 Arsenal 0 0
1999–2000 Arsenal 1 0 **1 0**
2000-01 Crystal Palace 23 1
2001-02 Crystal Palace 43 2
2002-03 Crystal Palace 35 5 **101 8**

HARRISON, Craig* (D) 68 0
H: 6 0 W: 11 08 b.Middlesbrough 10-11-77
Source: Trainee.
1996–97 Middlesbrough 0 0
1997–98 Middlesbrough 20 0
1998–99 Middlesbrough 4 0
1998–99 *Preston NE* 6 0 **6 0**
1999–2000 Middlesbrough 0 0
2000-01 Middlesbrough 0 0 **24 0**
2000-01 Crystal Palace 32 0
2001-02 Crystal Palace 6 0
2002-03 Crystal Palace 0 0 **38 0**

HEEROO, Gavin (M) 0 0
H: 5 11 W: 11 07 b.Harringey 2-9-84
2001-02 Crystal Palace 0 0
2002-03 Crystal Palace 0 0

HUNT, David (D) 2 0
H: 5 11 W: 11 09 b.Dulwich 10-9-82
Source: Scholar.
2002-03 Crystal Palace 2 0 **2 0**

JOHNSON, Andrew (F) 111 19
H: 5 7 W: 10 09 b.Bedford 10-2-81
Source: Trainee. *Honours:* England Youth, Under-20.
1997–98 Birmingham C 0 0
1998–99 Birmingham C 4 0
1999–2000 Birmingham C 22 1
2000-01 Birmingham C 34 4
2001-02 Birmingham C 23 3 **83 8**
2002-03 Crystal Palace 28 11 **28 11**

KOLINKO, Aleksandrs* (G) 190 0
H: 6 2 W: 14 02 b.Latvia 18-6-75
Honours: Latvia 38 full caps.
1994 Interskonto 22 0 **22 0**
1995 Skonto Metals 25 0 **25 0**
1996 Skonto Riga 9 0
1997 Skonto Riga 12 0
1998 Skonto Riga 5 0
1999 Skonto Riga 18 0
2000 Skonto Riga 17 0 **61 0**
2000-01 Crystal Palace 35 0
2001-02 Crystal Palace 19 0
2002-03 Crystal Palace 28 0 **82 0**

MULLINS, Hayden (D) 212 18
H: 6 0 W: 11 12 b.Reading 27-3-79
Source: Trainee. *Honours:* England Under-21.
1996–97 Crystal Palace 0 0
1997–98 Crystal Palace 0 0
1998–99 Crystal Palace 40 5
1999–2000 Crystal Palace 45 10
2000-01 Crystal Palace 41 1
2001-02 Crystal Palace 43 0
2002-03 Crystal Palace 43 2 **212 18**

POPOVIC, Tony (D) 305 33
H: 6 5 W: 13 01 b.Australia 7-4-73
Honours: Australia Youth, Under-20, Under-23, 40 full caps, 7 goals.
1989–90 Sydney U 13 0
1990–91 Sydney U 17 1
1991–92 Sydney U 20 1
1992–93 Sydney U 24 2
1993–94 Sydney U 27 2
1994–95 Sydney U 25 3
1995–96 Sydney U 29 4
1995–96 Wolverhampton W 0 0
1996–97 Wolverhampton W 0 0
1996–97 Sydney U 7 2 **162 15**
1997 Sanfrecce 11 0
1998 Sanfrecce 25 4
1999 Sanfrecce 23 6
2000 Sanfrecce 21 3
2001 Sanfrecce 7 0 **87 13**
2001-02 Crystal Palace 20 2
2002-03 Crystal Palace 36 3 **56 5**

POWELL, Darren (D) 167 7
H: 6 4 W: 13 03 b.Hammersmith 10-3-76
Source: Hampton.
1998–99 Brentford 33 2
1999–2000 Brentford 36 2
2000-01 Brentford 18 1
2001-02 Brentford 41 1 **128 6**
2002-03 Crystal Palace 39 1 **39 1**

RIIHILAHTI, Aki (M) 104 12
H: 5 11 W: 12 06 b.Helsinki 9-9-76
Honours: Finland 45 full caps, 7 goals.
1999 Valerenga 25 5 **25 5**
2000-01 Crystal Palace 9 1
2001-02 Crystal Palace 45 5
2002-03 Crystal Palace 25 1 **79 7**

ROUTLEDGE, Wayne (F) 28 4
H: 5 6 W: 10 07 b.Eltham 7-1-85
Source: Scholar. *Honours:* England Youth.
2001-02 Crystal Palace 2 0
2002-03 Crystal Palace 26 4 **28 4**

RUBINS, Andrejs‡ (M) 98 14
H: 5 8 W: 10 13 b.Latvia 26-11-78
Honours: Latvia 42 full caps, 5 goals.
1998 Skonto Riga 19 1
1999 Skonto Riga 25 6
2000 Skonto Riga 23 7 **67 14**
2000-01 Crystal Palace 22 0
2001-02 Crystal Palace 7 0
2002-03 Crystal Palace 2 0 **31 0**

SMITH, Jamie* (D) 230 5
H: 5 8 W: 11 02 b.Birmingham 17-9-74
Source: Trainee.
1993–94 Wolverhampton W 0 0
1994–95 Wolverhampton W 25 0
1995–96 Wolverhampton W 13 0
1996–97 Wolverhampton W 38 0
1997–98 Wolverhampton W 11 0 **87 0**
1997–98 Crystal Palace 18 0
1998–99 Crystal Palace 26 0
1998–99 *Fulham* 9 1 **9 1**
1999–2000 Crystal Palace 27 0
2000-01 Crystal Palace 29 0
2001-02 Crystal Palace 32 4
2002-03 Crystal Palace 2 0 **134 4**

SMITH, Robert (M) 0 0
H: 5 10 W: 11 09 b.Croydon 10-6-82
Source: Scholar.
2002-03 Crystal Palace 0 0

SUREY, Ben (M) 0 0
H: 5 10 W: 11 02 b.Camberley 18-12-82
Source: Scholar.
2002-03 Crystal Palace 0 0

SYMONS, Kit (D) 421 27
H: 6 1 W: 13 00 b.Basingstoke 8-3-71
Source: Trainee. *Honours:* Wales Youth, Under-21, B, 36 full caps, 2 goals.
1988–89 Portsmouth 2 0
1989–90 Portsmouth 1 0
1990–91 Portsmouth 1 0
1991–92 Portsmouth 46 1
1992–93 Portsmouth 41 2
1993–94 Portsmouth 29 3
1994–95 Portsmouth 40 4
1995–96 Portsmouth 1 0 **161 10**
1995–96 Manchester C 38 2
1996–97 Manchester C 44 0
1997–98 Manchester C 42 2 **124 4**
1998–99 Fulham 45 11
1999–2000 Fulham 29 2
2000-01 Fulham 24 0
2001-02 Fulham 4 0 **102 13**
2001-02 Crystal Palace 9 0
2002-03 Crystal Palace 25 0 **34 0**

TAYLOR, Charlie‡ (M) 0 0
b.Lewisham 28-12-85
2002-03 Crystal Palace 0 0

THOMSON, Steve* (M) 105 1
H: 5 8 W: 10 04 b.Glasgow 23-1-78
Source: Trainee. *Honours:* Scotland Youth.
1995–96 Crystal Palace 0 0
1996–97 Crystal Palace 0 0
1997–98 Crystal Palace 0 0
1998–99 Crystal Palace 16 0
1999–2000 Crystal Palace 21 0
2000-01 Crystal Palace 18 0
2001-02 Crystal Palace 23 0
2002-03 Crystal Palace 27 1 **105 1**

TOGWELL, Sam§ (D) 1 0
H: 5 11 W: 12 04 b.Beaconsfield 14-10-84
Source: Scholar.
2002-03 Crystal Palace 1 0 **1 0**

WATSON, Ben§ (M) 5 0
H: 5 10 W: 10 11 b.London 9-7-85
Source: Scholar.
2002-03 Crystal Palace 5 0 **5 0**

WILLIAMS, Gareth (F) 13 6
H: 5 10 W: 11 13 b.Germiston 10-9-82
Source: Scholar. *Honours:* Wales Under-21.

2002–03	Crystal Palace	5	0	**5**	**0**
2002–03	*Colchester U*	8	6	**8**	**6**

Scholars
Bashkal, Kerem; Conroy, Jay; Dobson, Craig G; Dolan, Ricci J; El-Salahi, Karim; Gibson, James D; Hay, Adam; Julius, Andrew; Nabil, Tariq; Prigent, Gary RD; Simpson, Nathaniel; Soares, Thomas J; Togwell, Samuel; Watson, Ben; Wilson, Glenn M

DARLINGTON

ALEXANDER, John§ (F) 1 0
H: 5 11 W: 12 00 b.Middlesbrough 24-9-85

2002–03	Darlington	1	0	**1**	**0**

BETTS, Simon* (M) 260 12
H: 5 8 W: 11 00 b.Middlesbrough 3-3-73
Source: Trainee.

1991–92	Ipswich T	0	0		
1992–93	Scarborough	0	0		
1992–93	Colchester U	23	0		
1993–94	Colchester U	33	1		
1994–95	Colchester U	35	2		
1995–96	Colchester U	45	5		
1996–97	Colchester U	10	1		
1997–98	Colchester U	17	0		
1998–99	Colchester U	28	2		
1999–2000	Colchester U	0	0		
2000–01	Colchester U	0	0	**191**	**11**
From Yeovil T.					
2001–02	Darlington	29	0		
2002–03	Darlington	40	1	**69**	**1**

BRIGHTWELL, David‡ (D) 257 8
H: 6 2 W: 12 09 b.Lutterworth 7-1-71
Source: Trainee.

1987–88	Manchester C	0	0		
1988–89	Manchester C	0	0		
1989–90	Manchester C	0	0		
1990–91	Manchester C	0	0		
1990–91	*Chester C*	6	0	**6**	**0**
1991–92	Manchester C	4	0		
1992–93	Manchester C	8	0		
1993–94	Manchester C	22	1		
1994–95	Manchester C	9	0		
1995–96	Manchester C	0	0	**43**	**1**
1995–96	*Lincoln C*	5	0	**5**	**0**
1995–96	*Stoke C*	1	0	**1**	**0**
1995–96	Bradford C	22	0		
1996–97	Bradford C	2	0	**24**	**0**
1996–97	*Blackpool*	2	0	**2**	**0**
1997–98	Northampton T	35	1	**35**	**1**
1998–99	Carlisle U	41	4		
1999–2000	Carlisle U	37	0	**78**	**4**
2000–01	Hull C	27	2	**27**	**2**
2000–01	Darlington	14	0		
2001–02	Darlington	22	0		
2002–03	Darlington	0	0	**36**	**0**

CAMPBELL, Paul* (M) 61 6
H: 6 0 W: 11 05 b.Middlesbrough 29-1-80
Source: Trainee.

1997–98	Darlington	6	1		
1998–99	Darlington	9	1		
1999–2000	Darlington	9	2		
2000–01	Darlington	16	1		
2001–02	Darlington	16	1		
2002–03	Darlington	5	0	**61**	**6**

CLARK, Ian (M) 244 40
H: 5 11 W: 11 07 b.Stockton 23-10-74
Source: Stockton.

1995–96	Doncaster R	23	1		
1996–97	Doncaster R	20	2		
1997–98	Doncaster R	2	0	**45**	**3**
1997–98	Hartlepool U	24	7		
1998–99	Hartlepool U	39	2		
1999–2000	Hartlepool U	44	6		
2000–01	Hartlepool U	24	0		
2001–02	Hartlepool U	7	2	**138**	**17**
2001–02	Darlington	28	13		
2002–03	Darlington	33	7	**61**	**20**

CLARKE, Matthew (F) 107 5
H: 6 3 W: 13 00 b.Leeds 18-12-80
Source: Wolverhampton W Trainee.

1999–2000	Halifax T	19	0		
2000–01	Halifax T	19	1		
2001–02	Halifax T	31	1	**69**	**2**
2002–03	Darlington	38	3	**38**	**3**

COLLETT, Andy (G) 225 0
H: 6 0 W: 12 01 b.Middlesbrough 28-10-73
Source: Trainee.

1991–92	Middlesbrough	0	0		
1992–93	Middlesbrough	2	0		
1993–94	Middlesbrough	0	0		
1994–95	Middlesbrough	0	0	**2**	**0**
1994–95	Bristol R	4	0		
1995–96	Bristol R	26	0		
1996–97	Bristol R	44	0		
1997–98	Bristol R	30	0		
1998–99	Bristol R	3	0	**107**	**0**
1999–2000	Darlington	13	0		
2000–01	Darlington	37	0		
2001–02	Darlington	28	0		
2002–03	Darlington	38	0	**116**	**0**

CONLON, Barry (F) 204 53
H: 6 3 W: 13 07 b.Drogheda 1-10-78
Source: QPR Trainee. *Honours:* Eire Under-21.

1997–98	Manchester C	7	0		
1997–98	*Plymouth Arg*	13	2	**13**	**2**
1998–99	Manchester C	0	0	**7**	**0**
1998–99	Southend U	34	7	**34**	**7**
1999–2000	York C	40	11		
2000–01	York C	8	0	**48**	**11**
2000–01	*Colchester U*	26	8	**26**	**8**
2001–02	Darlington	35	10		
2002–03	Darlington	41	15	**76**	**25**

CONVERY, Mark (M) 28 1
H: 5 6 W: 10 05 b.Newcastle 29-5-81
Source: Trainee.

1998–99	Sunderland	0	0		
1999–2000	Sunderland	0	0		
2000–01	Sunderland	0	0		
2000–01	Darlington	11	0		
2001–02	Darlington	17	1		
2002–03	Darlington	0	0	**28**	**1**

CULLEN, Jon‡ (M) 126 23
H: 6 0 W: 13 00 b.Durham 10-1-73
Source: Trainee.

1990–91	Doncaster R	1	0		
1991–92	Doncaster R	8	0		
1992–93	Doncaster R	0	0		
1993–94	Doncaster R	0	0	**9**	**0**
From Morpeth T					
1996–97	Hartlepool U	6	0		
1997–98	Hartlepool U	28	12	**34**	**12**
1997–98	Sheffield U	2	0		
1998–99	Sheffield U	2	0		
1999–2000	Sheffield U	0	0	**4**	**0**
1999–2000	*Shrewsbury T*	10	1	**10**	**1**
1999–2000	*Halifax T*	11	5	**11**	**5**
1999–2000	Peterborough U	13	3		
2000–01	Peterborough U	18	1		
2000–01	*Carlisle U*	11	0	**11**	**0**
2001–02	Peterborough U	13	1		
2002–03	Peterborough U	0	0	**44**	**5**
2002–03	Darlington	3	0	**3**	**0**

FORD, Mark* (M) 177 14
H: 5 8 W: 10 01 b.Pontefract 10-10-75
Source: Trainee. *Honours:* England Youth, Under-21.

1992–93	Leeds U	0	0		
1993–94	Leeds U	1	0		
1994–95	Leeds U	0	0		
1995–96	Leeds U	12	0		
1996–97	Leeds U	16	1	**29**	**1**
1997–98	Burnley	36	1		
1998–99	Burnley	12	0	**48**	**1**
1999–2000	Lommel	15	0	**15**	**0**
2000–01	Torquay U	28	3	**28**	**3**
2000–01	Darlington	11	2		
2001–02	Darlington	35	7		
2002–03	Darlington	11	0	**57**	**9**

HADLAND, Phil‡ (F) 49 4
H: 5 9 W: 11 05 b.Warrington 20-10-80
Source: Trainee.

1999–2000	Reading	0	0		
2000–01	Rochdale	32	2	**32**	**2**
2001–02	*Carlisle U*	4	1	**4**	**1**
2001–02	Leyton Orient	5	1	**5**	**1**
2001–02	Brighton & HA	2	0	**2**	**0**
2002–03	Darlington	6	0	**6**	**0**

HODGSON, Richard* (M) 99 6
H: 5 10 W: 11 08 b.Sunderland 1-10-79
Source: Trainee.

1996–97	Nottingham F	0	0		
1997–98	Nottingham F	0	0		
1998–99	Nottingham F	0	0		
1999–2000	Nottingham F	0	0		
1999–2000	Scunthorpe U	1	0	**1**	**0**
2000–01	Darlington	35	2		
2001–02	Darlington	36	2		
2002–03	Darlington	27	2	**98**	**6**

KELTIE, Clark (M) 31 3
H: 5 11 W: 11 05 b.Gateshead 31-8-83
Source: Shildon.

2001–02	Darlington	1	0		
2002–03	Darlington	30	3	**31**	**3**

KILTY, Mark (D) 23 1
H: 5 11 W: 12 05 b.Sunderland 24-6-81
Source: Trainee.

1998–99	Darlington	2	0		
1999–2000	Darlington	2	0		
2000–01	Darlington	18	1		
2001–02	Darlington	1	0		
2002–03	Darlington	0	0	**23**	**1**

LIDDLE, Craig (D) 247 12
H: 5 11 W: 12 07 b.Newcastle 21-10-71
Source: Blyth Spartans.

1994–95	Middlesbrough	1	0		
1995–96	Middlesbrough	13	0		
1996–97	Middlesbrough	5	0		
1997–98	Middlesbrough	6	0	**25**	**0**
1997–98	*Darlington*	15	0		
1998–99	Darlington	44	3		
1999–2000	Darlington	45	1		
2000–01	Darlington	45	2		
2001–02	Darlington	31	2		
2002–03	Darlington	42	4	**222**	**12**

MADDISON, Neil# (M) 293 26
H: 5 10 W: 12 00 b.Darlington 2-10-69
Source: Trainee.

1987–88	Southampton	0	0		
1988–89	Southampton	5	2		
1989–90	Southampton	2	0		
1990–91	Southampton	4	0		
1991–92	Southampton	6	0		
1992–93	Southampton	37	4		
1993–94	Southampton	41	7		
1994–95	Southampton	35	3		
1995–96	Southampton	15	1		
1996–97	Southampton	18	1		
1997–98	Southampton	6	1	**169**	**19**
1997–98	Middlesbrough	22	4		
1998–99	Middlesbrough	21	0		
1999–2000	Middlesbrough	13	0		
2000–01	Middlesbrough	0	0	**56**	**4**
2000–01	*Barnsley*	3	0	**3**	**0**
2000–01	*Bristol C*	7	1	**7**	**1**
2001–02	Darlington	30	1		
2002–03	Darlington	28	1	**58**	**2**

McGURK, David (D) 16 0
H: 6 0 W: 11 10 b.Middlesbrough 30-9-82
Source: Scholar.

2001–02	Darlington	12	0		
2002–03	Darlington	4	0	**16**	**0**

MELLANBY, Danny (F) 37 8
H: 5 10 W: 11 09 b.Bishop Auckland 17-7-79
Source: Bishop Auckland.

2001–02	Darlington	24	4		
2002–03	Darlington	13	4	**37**	**8**

NAYLOR, Glenn* (F) 324 77
H: 6 0 W: 11 08 b.Goole 11-8-72
Source: Trainee.

1989–90	York C	1	0		
1990–91	York C	20	5		
1991–92	York C	21	8		
1992–93	York C	4	0		
1993–94	York C	10	1		
1994–95	York C	29	9		
1995–96	York C	25	7		
1995–96	*Darlington*	4	1		
1996–97	York C	1	0	**111**	**30**
1996–97	Darlington	37	11		
1997–98	Darlington	42	8		
1998–99	Darlington	42	9		
1999–2000	Darlington	25	3		
2000–01	Darlington	44	11		
2001–02	Darlington	6	1		
2002–03	Darlington	13	3	**213**	**47**

NICHOLLS, Ashley (M) 41 6
H: 5 11 W: 11 11 b.Suffolk 30-10-81
Source: Ipswich W. *Honours:* England Schools.

2000–01	Ipswich T	0	0		
2001–02	Ipswich T	0	0		
2002–03	Darlington	41	6	**41**	**6**

PEARSON, Gary (D) 30 2
H: 6 0 W: 12 04 b.Easington 7-12-76
Source: Trainee.
1995–96 Sheffield U 0 0
1996–97 Sheffield U 0 0
1997–98 Sheffield U 0 0
1998–99 Sheffield U 0 0
From Durham C.
2001-02 Darlington 9 1
2002-03 Darlington 21 1 30 2

PORTER, Chris* (G) 10 0
H: 6 2 W: 12 03 b.Middlesbrough 17-7-79
Source: Trainee.
1998–99 Sunderland 0 0
1999–2000 Sunderland 0 0
2000-01 Darlington 0 0
2000-01 Hartlepool U 0 0
2000-01 Southend U 0 0
2001-02 Darlington 7 0
2002-03 Darlington 3 0 10 0

REED, Adam* (D) 170 3
H: 6 0 W: 12 00 b.Bishop Auckland 18-2-75
Source: Trainee.
1991–92 Darlington 1 0
1992–93 Darlington 0 0
1993–94 Darlington 13 0
1994–95 Darlington 38 1
1995–96 Blackburn R 0 0
1996–97 Blackburn R 0 0
1996–97 *Darlington* 14 0
1997–98 Blackburn R 0 0
1997–98 *Rochdale* 10 0 10 0
1998–99 Darlington 29 2
1999–2000 Darlington 23 0
2000-01 Darlington 34 0
2001-02 Darlington 7 0
2002-03 Darlington 1 0 160 3

SHEERAN, Mark (F) 26 6
H: 6 0 W: 11 10 b.Newcastle 9-9-82
Source: Scholar.
2001-02 Darlington 22 6
2002-03 Darlington 4 0 26 6

VALENTINE, Ryan (D) 43 1
H: 5 10 W: 11 07 b.Wrexham 19-8-82
Source: Trainee. *Honours:* Wales Under-21.
1999–2000 Everton 0 0
2000-01 Everton 0 0
2001-02 Everton 0 0
2002-03 Darlington 43 1 43 1

WAINWRIGHT, Neil (M) 111 12
H: 6 1 W: 12 00 b.Warrington 4-11-77
Source: Trainee.
1996–97 Wrexham 0 0
1997–98 Wrexham 11 3 11 3
1998–99 Sunderland 2 0
1999–2000 Sunderland 0 0
1999–2000 *Darlington* 17 4
2000-01 Sunderland 0 0
2000-01 *Halifax T* 13 0 13 0
2001-02 Sunderland 0 0 2 0
2001-02 Darlington 35 4
2002-03 Darlington 33 1 85 9

WALLER, Russell (M) 0 0
H: 5 10 W: 11 04 b.Adelaide 6-2-84
2001-02 Darlington 0 0
2002-03 Darlington 0 0

WHITEHEAD, Stuart# (D) 175 2
H: 6 0 W: 12 02 b.Bromsgrove 17-7-77
Source: Bromsgrove R.
1995–96 Bolton W 0 0
1996–97 Bolton W 0 0
1997–98 Bolton W 0 0
1998–99 Carlisle U 37 0
1999–2000 Carlisle U 29 0
2000-01 Carlisle U 45 1
2001-02 Carlisle U 32 1
2002-03 Carlisle U 9 0 152 2
2002-03 Darlington 23 0 23 0

Scholars
Addison, Richard C; Alexander, John D; Bond, Michael; Coghlan; Michael J; Collins, Paul; Graham, Stephen T; Hartley, Liam JM; Hughes; Christopher; Mason, Christopher; Matthewson, Graeme T; Maughan, Gavin; McGee, Paul; Mendum, Dale S; Morley; Steven; Paxton, Richard J; Smith, Martin M; Summers, Benjamin J; Thompson, David J

DERBY CO

BANNISTER, Patrick* (M) 0 0
b.Walsall 3-12-83
Source: Scholar.
2000-01 Derby Co 0 0
2001-02 Derby Co 0 0
2002-03 Derby Co 0 0

BARTON, Warren (D) 439 14
H: 6 3 W: 11 13 b.Islington 19-3-69
Source: Leytonstone/Ilford. *Honours:* England B, 3 full caps.
1989–90 Maidstone U 42 0 42 0
1990–91 Wimbledon 37 3
1991–92 Wimbledon 42 1
1992–93 Wimbledon 23 2
1993–94 Wimbledon 39 2
1994–95 Wimbledon 39 2 180 10
1995–96 Newcastle U 31 0
1996–97 Newcastle U 18 1
1997–98 Newcastle U 23 3
1998–99 Newcastle U 24 0
1999–2000 Newcastle U 34 0
2000-01 Newcastle U 29 0
2001-02 Newcastle U 5 0 164 4
2001-02 Derby Co 14 0
2002-03 Derby Co 39 0 53 0

BOERTIEN, Paul (D) 104 3
H: 5 11 W: 11 11 b.Carlisle 21-1-79
Source: Trainee.
1996–97 Carlisle U 0 0
1997–98 Carlisle U 9 0
1998–99 Carlisle U 8 1 17 1
1998–99 Derby Co 1 0
1999–2000 Derby Co 2 0
1999–2000 *Crewe Alex* 2 0 2 0
2000-01 Derby Co 8 1
2001-02 Derby Co 32 0
2002-03 Derby Co 42 1 85 2

BOLDER, Adam (M) 78 6
H: 5 8 W: 11 13 b.Hull 25-10-80
Source: Trainee.
1998–99 Hull C 1 0
1999–2000 Hull C 19 0 20 0
1999–2000 Derby Co 0 0
2000-01 Derby Co 2 0
2001-02 Derby Co 11 0
2002-03 Derby Co 45 6 58 6

BRAGSTAD, Bjorn‡ (D) 209 26
H: 6 3 W: 14 06 b.Trondheim 5-1-71
Honours: Norway 15 full caps.
1989 Rosenborg 1 0
1990 Rosenborg 9 0
1991 Rosenborg 6 1
1992 Rosenborg 16 4
1993 Rosenborg 20 4
1994 Rosenborg 21 3
1995 Rosenborg 25 6
1996 Rosenborg 8 2
1997 Rosenborg 22 0
1998 Rosenborg 25 4
1999 Rosenborg 25 1
2000 Rosenborg 16 1 194 26
2000-01 Derby Co 12 0
2001-02 Derby Co 0 0
2001-02 *Birmingham C* 3 0 3 0
2002-03 Derby Co 0 0 12 0

BURLEY, Craig* (M) 242 36
H: 6 1 W: 13 03 b.Ayr 24-9-71
Source: Trainee. *Honours:* Scotland Schools, Youth, Under-21, 46 full caps, 3 goals.
1989–90 Chelsea 0 0
1990–91 Chelsea 1 0
1991–92 Chelsea 8 0
1992–93 Chelsea 3 0
1993–94 Chelsea 23 3
1994–95 Chelsea 25 2
1995–96 Chelsea 22 0
1996–97 Chelsea 31 2 113 7
1997–98 Celtic 35 10
1998–99 Celtic 21 9
1999–2000 Celtic 0 0 56 19
1999–2000 Derby Co 18 5
2000-01 Derby Co 24 2
2001-02 Derby Co 11 0
2002-03 Derby Co 20 3 73 10

CAMP, Lee (G) 1 0
b.Derby 22-8-84
Source: Scholar. *Honours:* England Youth.
2002-03 Derby Co 1 0 1 0

CARBONARI, Horace Angel‡ (D) 230 35
H: 6 3 W: 14 08 b.Rosario 2-5-71
1993–94 Rosario Central 23 2
1994–95 Rosario Central 15 3
1995–96 Rosario Central 32 7
1996–97 Rosario Central 31 5
1997–98 Rosario Central 34 9 135 26
1998–99 Derby Co 29 5
1999–2000 Derby Co 29 2
2000-01 Derby Co 27 1
2001-02 Derby Co 3 0
2001-02 *Coventry C* 5 0 5 0
2002-03 Derby Co 2 1 90 9

DONNELLY, Sean* (M) 0 0
b.London 7-4-84
Source: Trainee.
2002-03 Derby Co 0 0

ELLIOTT, Steve (D) 69 1
H: 6 2 W: 14 08 b.Derby 29-10-78
Source: Trainee.
1996–97 Derby Co 0 0
1997–98 Derby Co 3 0
1998–99 Derby Co 11 0
1999–2000 Derby Co 20 0
2000-01 Derby Co 6 0
2001-02 Derby Co 6 0
2002-03 Derby Co 23 1 69 1

EVATT, Ian* (D) 45 0
H: 6 3 W: 14 04 b.Coventry 23-11-81
Source: Trainee.
1998–99 Derby Co 0 0
1999–2000 Derby Co 0 0
2000-01 Derby Co 1 0
2001-02 *Northampton T* 11 0 11 0
2001-02 Derby Co 3 0
2002-03 Derby Co 30 0 34 0

FLANAGAN, Martin* (M) 0 0
b.Omagh 13-1-84
Source: Scholar.
2000-01 Derby Co 0 0
2001-02 Derby Co 0 0
2002-03 Derby Co 0 0

GRANT, Lee (G) 29 0
H: 6 2 W: 13 00 b.Watford 27-1-83
Source: Scholar. *Honours:* England Youth, Under-21.
2000-01 Derby Co 0 0
2001-02 Derby Co 0 0
2002-03 Derby Co 29 0 29 0

GRENET, Francois‡ (D) 195 4
H: 5 10 W: 11 06 b.Bordeaux 8-3-75
1992–93 Bordeaux 1 0
1993–94 Bordeaux 3 0
1994–95 Bordeaux 5 1
1995–96 Bordeaux 26 0
1996–97 Bordeaux 27 1
1997–98 Bordeaux 24 2
1998–99 Bordeaux 23 0
1999–2000 Bordeaux 31 0
2000-01 Bordeaux 29 0
2001-02 Bordeaux 8 0 177 4
2001-02 Derby Co 15 0
2002-03 Derby Co 3 0 18 0

HOLMES, Lee‡ (M) 2 0
b.Mansfield 2-4-87
Honours: FA Schools, England Youth.
2002-03 Derby Co 2 0 2 0

HUNT, Lewis (D) 10 0
H: 5 11 W: 12 08 b.Birmingham 25-8-82
Source: Scholar.
2000-01 Derby Co 0 0
2001-02 Derby Co 0 0
2002-03 Derby Co 10 0 10 0

JACKSON, Richard (D) 54 0
H: 5 7 W: 11 02 b.Whitby 18-4-80
Source: Trainee.
1997–98 Scarborough 2 0
1998–99 Scarborough 20 0 22 0
1998–99 Derby Co 0 0
1999–2000 Derby Co 2 0
2000-01 Derby Co 2 0
2001-02 Derby Co 7 0
2002-03 Derby Co 21 0 32 0

KINKLADZE, Georgiou# (M) 367 86
H: 5 6 W: 11 05 b.Tbilisi 6-7-73
Source: Dynamo Tbilisi. *Honours:* Georgia 49 full caps, 8 goals.
1990 Mretebi 34 8
1991 Mretebi 16 1
1991–92 Mretebi 30 9 80 18

1992–93 Dynamo Tbilisi 30 14
1993–94 Dynamo Tbilisi 14 13
1993–94 Saarbrucken 11 0 **11 0**
1994–95 Dynamo Tbilisi 21 14 **65 41**
1995–96 Manchester C 37 4
1996–97 Manchester C 39 12
1997–98 Manchester C 30 4 **106 20**
1998–99 Ajax 12 0 **12 0**
1999–2000 Derby Co 17 1
2000-01 Derby Co 24 1
2001-02 Derby Co 24 1
2002-03 Derby Co 28 4 **93 7**

LEE, Robert* (M) 649 105
H: 5 10 W: 11 10 b.Plaistow 1-2-66
Source: Hornchurch. *Honours:* England Under-21, 21 full caps, 2 goals.
1983–84 Charlton Ath 11 4
1984–85 Charlton Ath 39 10
1985–86 Charlton Ath 35 8
1986–87 Charlton Ath 33 3
1987–88 Charlton Ath 23 2
1988–89 Charlton Ath 31 5
1989–90 Charlton Ath 37 1
1990–91 Charlton Ath 43 13
1991–92 Charlton Ath 39 12
1992–93 Charlton Ath 7 1 **298 59**
1992–93 Newcastle U 36 10
1993–94 Newcastle U 41 7
1994–95 Newcastle U 35 9
1995–96 Newcastle U 36 8
1996–97 Newcastle U 33 5
1997–98 Newcastle U 28 4
1998–99 Newcastle U 26 0
1999–2000 Newcastle U 30 0
2000-01 Newcastle U 22 0
2001-02 Newcastle U 16 1 **303 44**
2001-02 Derby Co 13 0
2002-03 Derby Co 35 2 **48 2**

MAWENE, Youl (D) 31 1
H: 6 1 W: 13 05 b.Caen 16-7-79
1999–2000 Lens 6 0 **6 0**
2000-01 Derby Co 8 0
2001-02 Derby Co 17 1
2002-03 Derby Co 0 0 **25 1**

McARDLE, Fiachra‡ (M) 0 0
b.Newry 18-8-83
Source: Scholar.
2000-01 Derby Co 0 0
2001-02 Derby Co 0 0
2002-03 Derby Co 0 0

McLEOD, Izale (F) 29 3
H: 6 0 W: 11 02 b.Perry Bar 15-10-84
Source: Scholar.
2002-03 Derby Co 29 3 **29 3**

MILLS, Pablo (M) 16 0
b.Birmingham 27-5-84
Source: Trainee. *Honours:* England Youth.
2002-03 Derby Co 16 0 **16 0**

MOLLOY, Barry (M) 0 0
b.Derry 28-11-83
Source: Trainee.
2002-03 Derby Co 0 0

MORRIS, Lee (F) 99 19
H: 5 9 W: 11 02 b.Driffield 30-4-80
Source: Trainee. *Honours:* England Youth.
1997–98 Sheffield U 5 0
1998–99 Sheffield U 20 6
1999–2000 Sheffield U 1 0 **26 6**
1999–2000 Derby Co 3 0
2000-01 Derby Co 20 0
2000-01 *Huddersfield T* 5 1 **5 1**
2001-02 Derby Co 15 4
2002-03 Derby Co 30 8 **68 12**

MURRAY, Adam (M) 69 7
H: 5 9 W: 11 11 b.Birmingham 30-9-81
Source: Trainee. *Honours:* England Youth, Under-20.
1998–99 Derby Co 4 0
1999–2000 Derby Co 8 0
2000-01 Derby Co 14 0
2001-02 Derby Co 6 0
2001-02 *Mansfield T* 13 7 **13 7**
2002-03 Derby Co 24 0 **56 0**

O'HALLORAN, Matthew* (M) 0 0
b.Nottingham 18-11-82
Source: Trainee.
2002-03 Derby Co 0 0

OAKES, Andy (G) 52 0
H: 6 1 W: 12 04 b.Crewe 11-1-77
1995–96 Bury 0 0
1996–97 Bury 0 0
1997–98 Bury 0 0
From Winsford U.
1998–99 Hull C 19 0 **19 0**
1999–2000 Derby Co 0 0
1999–2000 *Port Vale* 0 0
2000-01 Derby Co 6 0
2001-02 Derby Co 20 0
2002-03 Derby Co 7 0 **33 0**

RAVANELLI, Fabrizio* (F) 477 181
H: 6 2 W: 13 04 b.Perugia 11-12-68
Honours: Italy 21 full caps, 9 goals.
1986–87 Perugia 26 5
1987–88 Perugia 32 23
1988–89 Perugia 32 13 **90 41**
1989–90 Avellino 7 0
1989–90 *Casertana* 27 12 **27 12**
1990–91 Avellino 0 0 **7 0**
1990–91 Reggiana 34 16
1991–92 Reggiana 32 8 **66 24**
1992–93 Juventus 22 5
1993–94 Juventus 30 9
1994–95 Juventus 33 15
1995–96 Juventus 26 12 **111 41**
1996–97 Middlesbrough 33 16
1997–98 Middlesbrough 2 1 **35 17**
1997–98 Marseille 21 9
1998–99 Marseille 29 13
1999–2000 Marseille 14 6 **64 28**
1999–2000 Lazio 16 2
2000-01 Lazio 11 2 **27 4**
2001-02 Derby Co 31 9
2002-03 Derby Co 19 5 **50 14**

ROBINSON, Marvin* (F) 21 3
H: 6 0 W: 13 05 b.Crewe 11-4-80
Source: Trainee.
1998–99 Derby Co 1 0
1999–2000 Derby Co 8 0
2000-01 Derby Co 0 0
2000-01 *Stoke C* 3 1 **3 1**
2001-02 Derby Co 2 1
2002-03 Derby Co 1 0 **12 1**
2002-03 *Tranmere R* 6 1 **6 1**

STRUPAR, Branko* (F) 151 77
H: 6 3 W: 14 06 b.Zagreb 9-2-70
Source: Spansko. *Honours:* Belgium 17 full caps, 5 goals.
1996–97 Genk 31 12
1997–98 Genk 31 22
1998–99 Genk 33 18
1999–2000 Genk 15 9 **110 61**
1999–2000 Derby Co 15 5
2000-01 Derby Co 9 6
2001-02 Derby Co 12 4
2002-03 Derby Co 5 1 **41 16**

TUDGAY, Marcus (F) 8 0
b.Worthing 3-2-83
Source: Trainee.
2002-03 Derby Co 8 0 **8 0**

TWIGG, Gary (F) 9 0
H: 6 0 W: 11 02 b.Glasgow 19-3-84
Source: Scholar.
2000-01 Derby Co 0 0
2001-02 Derby Co 1 0
2002-03 Derby Co 8 0 **9 0**

VALAKARI, Simo (M) 178 8
H: 5 11 W: 12 08 b.Helsinki 24-4-73
Honours: Finland 30 full caps.
1995 Finn PA 22 3
1996 Finn PA 26 2 **48 5**
1996–97 Motherwell 11 0
1997–98 Motherwell 28 0
1998–99 Motherwell 35 0
1999–2000 Motherwell 30 0 **104 0**
2000-01 Derby Co 11 1
2001-02 Derby Co 9 0
2002-03 Derby Co 6 2 **26 3**

WECKSTROM, Kristoffer (F) 0 0
b.Helsinki 26-5-83
Source: IFK Mariehamn.
2000-01 Derby Co 0 0
2001-02 Derby Co 0 0
2002-03 Derby Co 0 0

ZAVAGNO, Luciano (D) 96 3
H: 5 11 W: 11 07 b.Rosario 6-8-77
1997–98 Strasbourg 5 0
1998–99 Strasbourg 9 1 **14 1**
1999–2000 Troyes 26 0
2000-01 Troyes 13 0
2001-02 Troyes 8 0 **47 0**
2001-02 Derby Co 26 0
2002-03 Derby Co 9 2 **35 2**

Scholars
Bradshaw, Luke P; Cassidy, David; Deans, Christopher; Francis, Carl S; Gibson-Cain, Stephen; Hamilton, Lewis E; Harmainen, Samu T; Keenan, Colin P; Kuduzovic, Fahrudin; MacAuley, Kyle D; Millar, Paul T; Palmer, Christopher L; Richardson, Liam; Sheard, Carl G; Short, John JM; Tosh, Bryan R; Turner, James J; Wilson, Lee T

EVERTON

ALEXANDERSSON, Niclas (M) 330 50
H: 5 9 W: 11 08 b.Halmstad 29-12-71
Honours: Sweden 68 full caps, 7 goals.
1989 Halmstad 4 0
1990 Halmstad 22 2
1991 Halmstad 16 3
1992 Halmstad 27 7
1993 Halmstad 25 4
1994 Halmstad 25 4
1995 Halmstad 26 5 **145 25**
1996 IFK Gothenburg 26 7
1997 IFK Gothenburg 26 6 **52 13**
1997–98 Sheffield W 6 0
1998–99 Sheffield W 32 3
1999–2000 Sheffield W 37 5 **75 8**
2000-01 Everton 20 2
2001-02 Everton 31 2
2002-03 Everton 7 0 **58 4**

BAARDSEN, Espen‡ (G) 65 0
H: 6 5 W: 13 03 b.San Rafael 7-12-77
Source: San Francisco All Blacks. *Honours:* USA Youth, Norway Under-21, 4 full caps.
1996–97 Tottenham H 2 0
1997–98 Tottenham H 9 0
1998–99 Tottenham H 12 0
1999–2000 Tottenham H 0 0 **23 0**
2000-01 Watford 27 0
2001-02 Watford 14 0
2002-03 Watford 0 0 **41 0**
2002-03 Everton 1 0 **1 0**

BECK, Steven* (M) 0 0
b.Liverpool 4-6-84
Source: Scholar. *Honours:* England Youth.
2001-02 Everton 0 0
2002-03 Everton 0 0

BROWN, Scott (M) 0 0
H: 5 7 W: 10 03 b.Chester 8-5-85
Source: Scholar. *Honours:* England Youth.
2001-02 Everton 0 0
2002-03 Everton 0 0

CAMPBELL, Kevin (F) 412 141
H: 6 0 W: 13 13 b.Lambeth 4-2-70
Source: Trainee. *Honours:* England Under-21, B.
1987–88 Arsenal 1 0
1988–89 Arsenal 0 0
1988–89 *Leyton Orient* 16 9 **16 9**
1989–90 Arsenal 15 2
1989–90 *Leicester C* 11 5 **11 5**
1990–91 Arsenal 22 9
1991–92 Arsenal 31 13
1992–93 Arsenal 37 4
1993–94 Arsenal 37 14
1994–95 Arsenal 23 4 **166 46**
1995–96 Nottingham F 21 3
1996–97 Nottingham F 17 6
1997–98 Nottingham F 42 23 **80 32**
1998–99 Trabzonspor 17 5 **17 5**
1998–99 Everton 8 9
1999–2000 Everton 26 12
2000-01 Everton 29 9
2001-02 Everton 23 4
2002-03 Everton 36 10 **122 44**

CARNEY, David* (M) 0 0
b.Sydney 30-11-83
Source: Scholar.
2000-01 Everton 0 0
2001-02 Everton 0 0
2002-03 Everton 0 0

CARSLEY, Lee (M) 263 23
H: 5 10 W: 12 04 b.Birmingham 28-2-74
Source: Trainee. *Honours:* Eire 28 full caps.
1992–93 Derby Co 0 0
1993–94 Derby Co 0 0
1994–95 Derby Co 23 2

1995–96 Derby Co 35 1
1996–97 Derby Co 24 0
1997–98 Derby Co 34 1
1998–99 Derby Co 22 1 **138 5**
1998–99 Blackburn R 8 0
1999–2000 Blackburn R 30 10
2000-01 Blackburn R 8 0 **46 10**
2000-01 Coventry C 21 2
2001-02 Coventry C 26 2 **47 4**
2001-02 Everton 8 1
2002-03 Everton 24 3 **32 4**

CHADWICK, Nick (F) 16 3
H: 5 11 W: 10 09 b.Stoke 26-10-82
1999–2000 Everton 0 0
2000-01 Everton 0 0
2001-02 Everton 9 3
2002-03 Everton 1 0 **10 3**
2002-03 *Derby Co* 6 0 **6 0**

CLARKE, Peter (D) 37 4
H: 6 0 W: 12 00 b.Southport 3-1-82
Source: Trainee. *Honours:* England Youth, Under-20, Under-21.
1998–99 Everton 0 0
1999–2000 Everton 0 0
2000-01 Everton 1 0
2001-02 Everton 7 0
2002-03 Everton 0 0 **8 0**
2002-03 *Blackpool* 16 3 **16 3**
2002-03 *Port Vale* 13 1 **13 1**

COLBECK, Franklyn* (M) 0 0
b.Liverpool 5-11-83
Source: Trainee.
2002-03 Everton 0 0

CROWDER, Martin* (D) 0 0
H: 5 8 W: 11 02 b.Liverpool 11-4-84
Source: Scholar.
2001-02 Everton 0 0
2002-03 Everton 0 0

FERGUSON, Duncan (F) 278 87
H: 6 4 W: 13 07 b.Stirling 27-12-71
Source: Carse T. *Honours:* Scotland Schools, Youth, Under-21, B, 7 full caps.
1990–91 Dundee U 9 1
1991–92 Dundee U 38 15
1992–93 Dundee U 30 12 **77 28**
1993–94 Rangers 10 1
1994–95 Rangers 4 1 **14 2**
1994–95 Everton 23 7
1995–96 Everton 18 5
1996–97 Everton 33 10
1997–98 Everton 29 11
1998–99 Everton 13 4
1998–99 Newcastle U 7 2
1999–2000 Newcastle U 23 6 **30 8**
2000-01 Everton 12 6
2001-02 Everton 22 6
2002-03 Everton 7 0 **157 49**

GARSIDE, Craig (D) 0 0
H: 5 11 W: 13 00 b.Chester 11-1-85
Source: Scholar.
2001-02 Everton 0 0
2002-03 Everton 0 0

GEMMILL, Scot (M) 342 26
H: 5 10 W: 11 08 b.Paisley 2-1-71
Source: School. *Honours:* Scotland Under-21, B, 26 full caps, 1 goal.
1989–90 Nottingham F 0 0
1990–91 Nottingham F 4 0
1991–92 Nottingham F 39 8
1992–93 Nottingham F 33 1
1993–94 Nottingham F 31 8
1994–95 Nottingham F 19 1
1995–96 Nottingham F 31 1
1996–97 Nottingham F 24 0
1997–98 Nottingham F 44 2
1998–99 Nottingham F 20 0 **245 21**
1998–99 Everton 7 1
1999–2000 Everton 14 1
2000-01 Everton 28 2
2001-02 Everton 32 1
2002-03 Everton 16 0 **97 5**

GERRARD, Paul (G) 230 1
H: 6 2 W: 13 11 b.Heywood 22-1-73
Source: Trainee. *Honours:* England Under-21.
1991–92 Oldham Ath 0 0
1992–93 Oldham Ath 25 0
1993–94 Oldham Ath 16 0
1994–95 Oldham Ath 42 0
1995–96 Oldham Ath 36 1 **119 1**
1996–97 Everton 5 0
1997–98 Everton 4 0
1998–99 Everton 0 0
1998–99 *Oxford U* 16 0 **16 0**
1999–2000 Everton 34 0
2000-01 Everton 32 0
2001-02 Everton 13 0
2002-03 Everton 2 0 **90 0**
2002-03 *Ipswich T* 5 0 **5 0**

GRAVESEN, Thomas (M) 222 21
H: 5 9 W: 13 06 b.Vejle 11-3-76
Honours: Denmark 37 full caps, 5 goals.
1995–96 Vejle 28 2
1996–97 Vejle 30 8 **58 10**
1997–98 Hamburg 26 2
1998–99 Hamburg 22 3
1999–2000 Hamburg 26 1 **74 6**
2000-01 Everton 32 2
2001-02 Everton 25 2
2002-03 Everton 33 1 **90 5**

HIBBERT, Tony (D) 37 0
H: 5 9 W: 11 05 b.Liverpool 20-2-81
Source: Trainee.
1998–99 Everton 0 0
1999–2000 Everton 0 0
2000-01 Everton 3 0
2001-02 Everton 10 0
2002-03 Everton 24 0 **37 0**

LI TIE (M) 29 0
H: 6 0 W: 11 10 b.China 18-9-77
Source: Liaoning Bodao. *Honours:* China 79 full caps, 5 goals.
2002-03 Everton 29 0 **29 0**

LI WEIFENG‡ (D) 1 0
H: 6 0 W: 11 05 b.China 26-1-78
Source: Shenzhen Pingan. *Honours:* China 57 full caps, 7 goals.
2002-03 Everton 1 0 **1 0**

LINDEROTH, Tobias (M) 138 13
H: 5 10 W: 11 08 b.Marseille 21-4-79
Honours: Sweden 25 full caps, 1 goal.
1996 Elfsborg 10 0
1997 Elfsborg 25 1
1998 Elfsborg 22 3 **57 4**
1999 Stabaek 23 3
2000 Stabaek 24 4
2001 Stabaek 21 2 **68 9**
2001-02 Everton 8 0
2002-03 Everton 5 0 **13 0**

McBRIDE, Brian‡ (F) 166 56
H: 6 1 W: 12 06 b.USA 17-8-72
Source: St Louis Univ. *Honours:* USA 68 full caps, 19 goals.
1994–95 Wolfsburg 12 1 **12 1**
1996 Columbus Crew 28 17
1997 Columbus Crew 13 6
1998 Columbus Crew 24 10
1999 Columbus Crew 25 5
2000 Columbus Crew 18 6
2000-01 Preston NE 9 1 **9 1**
2001 Columbus Crew 15 1
2002 Columbus Crew 14 5 **137 50**
2002-03 Everton 8 4 **8 4**

McLEOD, Kevin (M) 13 2
H: 5 11 W: 12 00 b.Liverpool 12-9-80
Source: Trainee.
1998–99 Everton 0 0
1999–2000 Everton 0 0
2000-01 Everton 5 0
2001-02 Everton 0 0
2002-03 Everton 0 0 **5 0**
2002-03 *QPR* 8 2 **8 2**

MOOGAN, Alan (M) 0 0
b.Liverpool 22-2-84
Source: Scholar. *Honours:* England Youth.
2000-01 Everton 0 0
2001-02 Everton 0 0
2002-03 Everton 0 0

MOOGAN, Brian (D) 0 0
b.Liverpool 22-2-84
Source: Scholar.
2001-02 Everton 0 0
2002-03 Everton 0 0

MOORE, Joe-Max‡ (F) 129 45
H: 5 8 W: 11 06 b.USA 23-2-71
Honours: USA 100 full caps, 24 goals.
1996 New England Rev 14 11
1997 New England Rev 13 4
1998 New England Rev 21 7
1999 New England Rev 29 15 **77 37**
1999–2000 Everton 15 6
2000-01 Everton 21 0
2001-02 Everton 16 2
2002-03 Everton 0 0 **52 8**

NAYSMITH, Gary (D) 169 6
H: 5 9 W: 12 01 b.Edinburgh 16-11-78
Source: Whitehill Welfare Colts. *Honours:* Scotland Schools, Under-21, 15 full caps, 1 goal.
1995–96 Hearts 1 0
1996–97 Hearts 10 0
1997–98 Hearts 16 2
1998–99 Hearts 26 0
1999–2000 Hearts 35 1
2000-01 Hearts 9 0 **97 3**
2000-01 Everton 20 2
2001-02 Everton 24 0
2002-03 Everton 28 1 **72 3**

NYARKO, Alex (M) 144 14
H: 6 0 W: 13 00 b.Accra 15-10-73
Source: Asanti Kotoko, Deawe Youngsters. *Honours:* Ghana full caps.
1994–95 Sportul 0 0
1995–96 Basle 26 3
1996–97 Basle 29 5 **55 8**
1997–98 Karlsruhe 22 1 **22 1**
1998–99 Lens 24 3
1999–2000 Lens 21 1 **45 4**
2000-01 Everton 22 1
2001-02 Everton 0 0
2002-03 Everton 0 0 **22 1**

O'HANLON, Sean (D) 0 0
H: 6 1 W: 12 05 b.Southport 2-1-83
Honours: England Youth, Under-20.
1999–2000 Everton 0 0
2000-01 Everton 0 0
2001-02 Everton 0 0
2002-03 Everton 0 0

OSMAN, Leon (F) 14 1
H: 5 8 W: 10 09 b.Billinge 17-5-81
Source: Trainee. *Honours:* England Schools, Youth.
1998–99 Everton 0 0
1999–2000 Everton 0 0
2000-01 Everton 0 0
2001-02 Everton 0 0
2002-03 Everton 2 0 **2 0**
2002-03 *Carlisle U* 12 1 **12 1**

PEMBRIDGE, Mark (M) 369 50
H: 5 7 W: 11 09 b.Merthyr 29-11-70
Source: Trainee. *Honours:* Wales Schools, Under-21, B, 48 full caps, 6 goals.
1989–90 Luton T 0 0
1990–91 Luton T 18 1
1991–92 Luton T 42 5 **60 6**
1992–93 Derby Co 42 8
1993–94 Derby Co 41 11
1994–95 Derby Co 27 9 **110 28**
1995–96 Sheffield W 25 1
1996–97 Sheffield W 34 6
1997–98 Sheffield W 34 4 **93 11**
1998–99 Benfica 19 1 **19 1**
1999–2000 Everton 31 2
2000-01 Everton 21 0
2001-02 Everton 14 1
2002-03 Everton 21 1 **87 4**

PILKINGTON, George* (D) 7 0
H: 5 11 W: 11 00 b.Rugeley 7-11-81
Source: Trainee. *Honours:* England Youth.
1998–99 Everton 0 0
1999–2000 Everton 0 0
2000-01 Everton 0 0
2001-02 Everton 0 0
2002-03 Everton 0 0
2002-03 *Exeter C* 7 0 **7 0**

PISTONE, Alessandro (D) 193 8
H: 5 11 W: 11 08 b.Milan 27-7-75
1992–93 Vicenza 0 0
1993–94 Solbiatese 20 1 **20 1**
1994–95 Crevalcore 29 4 **29 4**
1995–96 Vicenza 6 0 **6 0**
1995–96 Internazionale 19 1
1996–97 Internazionale 26 0 **45 1**
1997–98 Newcastle U 28 0
1998–99 Newcastle U 3 0
1999–2000 Newcastle U 15 1 **46 1**
2000-01 Everton 7 0
2001-02 Everton 25 1
2002-03 Everton 15 0 **47 1**

RADZINSKI, Tomasz (F) 239 111
H: 5 7 W: 11 10 b.Poznan 14-12-73
Source: Toronto Rockets, St Catherines Roma. *Honours:* Canada 16 full caps, 3 goals.

1994–95	Ekeren	28	6		
1995–96	Ekeren	22	9		
1996–97	Ekeren	23	8		
1997–98	Ekeren	31	19	**104**	**42**
1998–99	Anderlecht	22	15		
1999–2000	Anderlecht	25	14		
2000-01	Anderlecht	31	23	**78**	**52**
2001-02	Everton	27	6		
2002-03	Everton	30	11	**57**	**17**

RODRIGO (F) 64 19
H: 5 8 W: 11 07 b.Santos 7-8-76

1999	Botafogo	21	1		
2000	Botafogo	20	7		
2001	Botafogo	19	11	**60**	**19**
2002-03	Everton	4	0	**4**	**0**

ROONEY, Wayne (F) 33 6
H: 5 10 W: 12 04 b.Liverpool 24-10-85
Source: Scholar. *Honours:* FA Schools, England Youth, 5 full caps.

2002-03	Everton	33	6	**33**	**6**

SAID, Ibrahim (D) 0 0
b.Cairo 16-10-79
Source: Al-Ahly.

2002-03	Everton	0	0

SCHUMACHER, Steven (M) 0 0
b.Liverpool 30-4-84
Source: Scholar. *Honours:* England Youth.

2000-01	Everton	0	0
2001-02	Everton	0	0
2002-03	Everton	0	0

SIMONSEN, Steve (G) 64 0
H: 6 2 W: 14 00 b.South Shields 3-4-79
Source: Trainee. *Honours:* England Youth, Under-21.

1996–97	Tranmere R	0	0		
1997–98	Tranmere R	30	0		
1998–99	Tranmere R	5	0	**35**	**0**
1998–99	Everton	0	0		
1999–2000	Everton	1	0		
2000-01	Everton	1	0		
2001-02	Everton	25	0		
2002-03	Everton	2	0	**29**	**0**

SOUTHERN, Robert* (M) 0 0
b.Gateshead 24-9-83
Source: Scholar.

2000-01	Everton	0	0
2001-02	Everton	0	0
2002-03	Everton	0	0

STUBBS, Alan (D) 374 14
H: 6 2 W: 13 12 b.Kirkby 6-10-71
Source: Trainee.

1990–91	Bolton W	23	0		
1991–92	Bolton W	32	1		
1992–93	Bolton W	42	2		
1993–94	Bolton W	41	1		
1994–95	Bolton W	39	1		
1995–96	Bolton W	25	4	**202**	**9**
1996–97	Celtic	20	0		
1997–98	Celtic	29	1		
1998–99	Celtic	23	1		
1999–2000	Celtic	23	0		
2000-01	Celtic	11	1	**106**	**3**
2001-02	Everton	31	2		
2002-03	Everton	35	0	**66**	**2**

SYMES, Michael (F) 0 0
H: 6 3 W: 12 04 b.Gt Yarmouth 31-10-83
Source: Scholar.

2001-02	Everton	0	0
2002-03	Everton	0	0

TURNER, Ian (M) 0 0
b.Stirling 26-1-84
Source: Trainee.

2002-03	Everton	0	0

UNSWORTH, Dave (D) 310 33
H: 6 1 W: 15 02 b.Chorley 16-10-73
Source: Trainee. *Honours:* England Youth, Under-21, 1 full cap.

1991–92	Everton	2	1		
1992–93	Everton	3	0		
1993–94	Everton	8	0		
1994–95	Everton	38	3		
1995–96	Everton	31	2		
1996–97	Everton	34	5		
1997–98	West Ham U	32	2	**32**	**2**
1998–99	Aston Villa	0	0		
1998–99	Everton	34	1		
1999–2000	Everton	33	6		
2000-01	Everton	29	5		
2001-02	Everton	33	3		
2002-03	Everton	33	5	**278**	**31**

WATSON, Steve (D) 326 21
H: 6 0 W: 12 07 b.North Shields 1-4-74
Source: Trainee. *Honours:* England Youth, Under-21, B.

1990–91	Newcastle U	24	0		
1991–92	Newcastle U	28	1		
1992–93	Newcastle U	2	0		
1993–94	Newcastle U	32	2		
1994–95	Newcastle U	27	4		
1995–96	Newcastle U	23	3		
1996–97	Newcastle U	36	1		
1997–98	Newcastle U	29	1		
1998–99	Newcastle U	7	0	**208**	**12**
1998–99	Aston Villa	27	0		
1999–2000	Aston Villa	14	0	**41**	**0**
2000-01	Everton	34	0		
2001-02	Everton	25	4		
2002-03	Everton	18	5	**77**	**9**

WEIR, David (D) 378 23
H: 6 5 W: 14 03 b.Falkirk 10-5-70
Source: Celtic BC. *Honours:* Scotland 37 full caps, 1 goal.

1992–93	Falkirk	30	1		
1993–94	Falkirk	37	3		
1994–95	Falkirk	32	1		
1995–96	Falkirk	34	3	**133**	**8**
1996–97	Hearts	34	6		
1997–98	Hearts	35	1		
1998–99	Hearts	23	1	**92**	**8**
1998–99	Everton	14	0		
1999–2000	Everton	35	2		
2000-01	Everton	37	1		
2001-02	Everton	36	4		
2002-03	Everton	31	0	**153**	**7**

WRIGHT, Richard (G) 285 0
H: 6 2 W: 14 04 b.Ipswich 5-11-77
Source: Trainee. *Honours:* England Schools, Youth, Under-21, 2 full caps.

1994–95	Ipswich T	3	0		
1995–96	Ipswich T	23	0		
1996–97	Ipswich T	40	0		
1997–98	Ipswich T	46	0		
1998–99	Ipswich T	46	0		
1999–2000	Ipswich T	46	0		
2000-01	Ipswich T	36	0	**240**	**0**
2001-02	Arsenal	12	0	**12**	**0**
2002-03	Everton	33	0	**33**	**0**

YOBO, Joseph (D) 95 2
H: 6 1 W: 13 00 b.Kano 6-9-80
Source: Mechelen.

1998–99	Standard Liege	0	0		
1999–2000	Standard Liege	18	0		
2000-01	Standard Liege	30	2	**48**	**2**
2001-02	Marseille	23	0	**23**	**0**
2002-03	Everton	24	0	**24**	**0**

Trainees
Barry, Anthony; Booth, Robert; Flood, Jack; Fox, Daniel; Gerard, Anthony; Jones, Joseph; Jones, Morgan; Lynch, Gavin; Martland, Damon G; Potter, James; Thorbinson, Colin

EXETER C

AFFUL, Leslie (F) 2 0
H: 5 6 W: 10 00 b.Liverpool 4-2-84
Source: Scholar.

2001-02	Exeter C	2	0		
2002-03	Exeter C	0	0	**2**	**0**

ALCIDE, Colin‡ (F) 212 37
H: 6 2 W: 13 11 b.Huddersfield 14-4-72
Source: Emley.

1995–96	Lincoln C	27	6		
1996–97	Lincoln C	42	7		
1997–98	Lincoln C	29	12		
1998–99	Lincoln C	23	1	**121**	**26**
1998–99	Hull C	17	3		
1999–2000	Hull C	12	1	**29**	**4**
1999–2000	York C	15	2		
2000-01	York C	38	5	**53**	**7**
2001-02	Cambridge U	8	0		
2002-03	Cambridge U	0	0	**8**	**0**
2002-03	Exeter C	1	0	**1**	**0**

AMPADU, Kwame# (M) 371 18
H: 5 10 W: 11 08 b.Bradford 20-12-70
Source: Belvedere, Trainee. *Honours:* Eire Youth, Under-21.

1988–89	Arsenal	0	0		
1989–90	Arsenal	2	0		
1990–91	Arsenal	0	0	**2**	**0**
1990–91	*Plymouth Arg*	6	1	**6**	**1**
1990–91	*WBA*	7	1		
1991–92	WBA	21	3		
1992–93	WBA	10	0		
1993–94	WBA	11	0	**49**	**4**
1993–94	Swansea C	13	0		
1994–95	Swansea C	44	6		
1995–96	Swansea C	43	2		
1996–97	Swansea C	29	4		
1997–98	Swansea C	18	0	**147**	**12**
1998–99	Leyton Orient	29	1		
1999–2000	Leyton Orient	43	0	**72**	**1**
2000-01	Exeter C	36	0		
2001-02	Exeter C	36	0		
2002-03	Exeter C	23	0	**95**	**0**

BAKER, Phillip† (D) 6 0
H: 6 0 W: 11 10 b.Birkenhead 4-11-82
Source: Scholar.

2001-02	Tranmere R	0	0		
2002-03	Tranmere R	0	0		
2002-03	Exeter C	6	0	**6**	**0**

BRESLAN, Geoff* (M) 109 6
H: 5 9 W: 10 05 b.Torbay 4-6-80
Source: Trainee.

1997–98	Exeter C	1	0		
1998–99	Exeter C	34	4		
1999–2000	Exeter C	29	0		
2000-01	Exeter C	2	0		
2001-02	Exeter C	33	2		
2002-03	Exeter C	10	0	**109**	**6**

COPPINGER, James (F) 68 10
H: 5 7 W: 10 03 b.Middlesbrough 18-1-81
Source: Darlington Trainee. *Honours:* England Youth.

1997–98	Newcastle U	0	0		
1998–99	Newcastle U	0	0		
1999–2000	Newcastle U	0	0		
1999–2000	*Hartlepool U*	10	3		
2000-01	Newcastle U	1	0		
2001-02	Newcastle U	0	0	**1**	**0**
2001-02	*Hartlepool U*	14	2	**24**	**5**
2002-03	Exeter C	43	5	**43**	**5**

CRONIN, Glenn (M) 69 0
H: 5 8 W: 10 08 b.Dublin 14-9-81
Source: Trainee.

2000-01	Exeter C	0	0		
2001-02	Exeter C	30	0		
2002-03	Exeter C	39	0	**69**	**0**

CURRAN, Chris# (D) 339 10
H: 5 11 W: 12 12 b.Birmingham 17-9-71
Source: Trainee.

1989–90	Torquay U	1	0		
1990–91	Torquay U	13	0		
1991–92	Torquay U	17	0		
1992–93	Torquay U	34	0		
1993–94	Torquay U	41	1		
1994–95	Torquay U	27	2		
1995–96	Torquay U	19	1	**152**	**4**
1995–96	Plymouth Arg	8	0		
1996–97	Plymouth Arg	22	0	**30**	**0**
1997–98	Exeter C	9	0		
1998–99	Exeter C	34	4		
1999–2000	Exeter C	38	1		
2000-01	Exeter C	26	0		
2001-02	Exeter C	37	1		
2002-03	Exeter C	13	0	**157**	**6**

DEVINE, Sean (F) 238 96
H: 5 11 W: 13 00 b.Lewisham 6-9-72
Source: Omonia.

1995–96	Barnet	35	19		
1996–97	Barnet	31	11		
1997–98	Barnet	40	16		
1998–99	Barnet	20	1	**126**	**47**
1998–99	Wycombe W	12	8		
1999–2000	Wycombe W	39	23		
2000-01	Wycombe W	0	0		
2001-02	Wycombe W	20	5		
2002-03	Wycombe W	18	5	**89**	**41**
2002-03	Exeter C	23	8	**23**	**8**

FLACK, Steve (F) 279 64
H: 6 1 W: 14 04 b.Cambridge 29-5-71
Source: Cambridge C.

1995–96	Cardiff C	10	1		
1996–97	Cardiff C	1	0	**11**	**1**

1996–97 Exeter C 27 4
1997–98 Exeter C 41 14
1998–99 Exeter C 44 11
1999–2000 Exeter C 40 2
2000-01 Exeter C 40 13
2001-02 Exeter C 36 6
2002-03 Exeter C 40 13 **268 63**

FRASER, Stuart* (G) 20 0
H: 6 0 W: 12 00 b.Cheltenham 1-8-78
Source: Cheltenham T.
1996–97 Stoke C 0 0
1997–98 Stoke C 0 0
1998–99 Stoke C 1 0
1999–2000 Stoke C 0 0 **1 0**
2000-01 Exeter C 6 0
2001-02 Exeter C 12 0
2002-03 Exeter C 1 0 **19 0**

GAIA, Santos (D) 33 1
H: 6 1 W: 12 09 b.Brazil 8-9-79
From Agrimiacao.
2002-03 Exeter C 33 1 **33 1**

GOFF, Shaun* (D) 2 0
H: 5 10 W: 11 10 b.Tiverton 13-4-84
Source: Trainee.
2001-02 Exeter C 2 0
2002-03 Exeter C 0 0 **2 0**

GOODMAN, Don* (F) 580 162
H: 5 10 W: 12 12 b.Leeds 9-5-66
Source: School.
1983–84 Bradford C 2 0
1984–85 Bradford C 25 5
1985–86 Bradford C 20 4
1986–87 Bradford C 23 5 **70 14**
1986–87 WBA 10 2
1987–88 WBA 40 7
1988–89 WBA 36 15
1989–90 WBA 39 21
1990–91 WBA 22 8
1991–92 WBA 11 7 **158 60**
1991–92 Sunderland 22 11
1992–93 Sunderland 41 16
1993–94 Sunderland 35 10
1994–95 Sunderland 18 3 **116 40**
1994–95 Wolverhampton W 24 3
1995–96 Wolverhampton W 44 16
1996–97 Wolverhampton W 27 6
1997–98 Wolverhampton W 30 8 **125 33**
1998 Kashima Antlers 10 2 **10 2**
1998–99 *Barnsley* 8 0 **8 0**
1998–99 Motherwell 8 1
1999–2000 Motherwell 29 7
2000-01 Motherwell 18 1 **55 9**
2000-01 Walsall 8 2
2001-02 Walsall 17 1 **25 3**
2002-03 Exeter C 13 1 **13 1**

HARRIES, Paul‡ (F) 33 3
H: 6 1 W: 13 00 b.Sydney 19-11-77
Source: Wollongong Wolves 6 apps, 1 goal.
1997–98 Portsmouth 1 0 **1 0**
1998–99 Crystal Palace 0 0
1998–99 *Torquay U* 5 0 **5 0**
1999–2000 Carlisle U 20 2
2000-01 Wollongong Wolves6 1 **6 1**
2000-01 Carlisle U 0 0 **20 2**
2001-02 Macclesfield T 0 0
2002-03 Exeter C 1 0 **1 0**

HILEY, Scott# (D) 412 12
H: 5 8 W: 11 08 b.Plymouth 27-9-68
Source: Trainee.
1986–87 Exeter C 0 0
1987–88 Exeter C 15 1
1988–89 Exeter C 37 5
1989–90 Exeter C 46 0
1990–91 Exeter C 46 2
1991–92 Exeter C 33 1
1992–93 Exeter C 33 3
1992–93 Birmingham C 7 0
1993–94 Birmingham C 28 0
1994–95 Birmingham C 9 0
1995–96 Birmingham C 5 0 **49 0**
1995–96 Manchester C 6 0
1996–97 Manchester C 3 0
1997–98 Manchester C 0 0 **9 0**
1998–99 Southampton 29 0
1999–2000 Southampton 3 0 **32 0**
1999–2000 Portsmouth 8 0
2000-01 Portsmouth 34 0
2001-02 Portsmouth 33 0
2002-03 Portsmouth 0 0 **75 0**
2002-03 Exeter C 37 0 **247 12**

KILHEENEY, Ciaran (F) 4 0
H: 5 11 W: 11 09 b.Stockport 9-1-84
2001-02 Manchester C 0 0
2002-03 Manchester C 0 0
2002-03 Exeter C 4 0 **4 0**

LOCK, Matthew* (D) 3 0
H: 5 11 W: 10 12 b.Barnstaple 10-3-84
Source: Trainee.
2002-03 Exeter C 3 0 **3 0**

McCARTHY, Sean* (F) 547 172
H: 6 1 W: 12 05 b.Bridgend 12-9-67
Source: Bridgend. *Honours:* Wales B.
1985–86 Swansea C 22 3
1986–87 Swansea C 44 14
1987–88 Swansea C 25 8 **91 25**
1988–89 Plymouth Arg 38 8
1989–90 Plymouth Arg 32 11
1990–91 Bradford C 42 13
1991–92 Bradford C 29 16
1992–93 Bradford C 42 17
1993–94 Bradford C 18 14 **131 60**
1993–94 Oldham Ath 20 4
1994–95 Oldham Ath 39 18
1995–96 Oldham Ath 35 10
1996–97 Oldham Ath 21 3
1997–98 Oldham Ath 25 7 **140 42**
1997–98 *Bristol C* 7 1 **7 1**
1998–99 Plymouth Arg 16 3
1999–2000 Plymouth Arg 29 6
2000-01 Plymouth Arg 37 10 **152 38**
2001-02 Exeter C 26 6
2002-03 Exeter C 0 0 **26 6**

McCONNELL, Barry (D) 162 15
H: 5 11 W: 10 10 b.Exeter 1-1-77
Source: Trainee.
1995–96 Exeter C 8 0
1996–97 Exeter C 34 0
1997–98 Exeter C 16 6
1998–99 Exeter C 22 5
1999–2000 Exeter C 25 1
2000-01 Exeter C 4 0
2001-02 Exeter C 32 3
2002-03 Exeter C 21 0 **162 15**

MILLER, Kevin (G) 542 0
H: 6 1 W: 15 10 b.Falmouth 15-3-69
Source: Newquay.
1988–89 Exeter C 3 0
1989–90 Exeter C 28 0
1990–91 Exeter C 46 0
1991–92 Exeter C 42 0
1992–93 Exeter C 44 0
1993–94 Birmingham C 24 0 **24 0**
1994–95 Watford 44 0
1995–96 Watford 42 0
1996–97 Watford 42 0 **128 0**
1997–98 Crystal Palace 38 0
1998–99 Crystal Palace 28 0
1999–2000 Crystal Palace 0 0 **66 0**
1999–2000 Barnsley 41 0
2000-01 Barnsley 46 0
2001-02 Barnsley 28 0 **115 0**
2002-03 Exeter C 46 0 **209 0**

MOOR, Reinier (F) 19 3
H: 6 0 W: 11 10 b.The Hague 12-6-83
Source: Scholar.
2001-02 Exeter C 2 0
2002-03 Exeter C 17 3 **19 3**

MUDGE, James (F) 3 0
H: 5 11 W: 11 09 b.Exeter 25-3-83
Source: Scholar.
2000-01 Exeter C 3 0
2001-02 Exeter C 0 0
2002-03 Exeter C 0 0 **3 0**

POWER, Graeme* (D) 197 2
H: 5 11 W: 11 07 b.Northwick Park 7-8-77
Source: Trainee. *Honours:* England Schools, Youth.
1994–95 QPR 0 0
1995–96 QPR 0 0
1996–97 Bristol R 16 0
1997–98 Bristol R 10 0 **26 0**
1998–99 Exeter C 40 0
1999–2000 Exeter C 29 0
2000-01 Exeter C 35 1
2001-02 Exeter C 37 1
2002-03 Exeter C 30 0 **171 2**

ROSCOE, Andy* (M) 358 31
H: 5 9 W: 12 00 b.Liverpool 4-6-73
Source: Trainee.
1991–92 Liverpool 0 0
1992–93 Bolton W 0 0
1993–94 Bolton W 3 0
1994–95 Bolton W 0 0 **3 0**
1994–95 Rotherham U 31 4
1995–96 Rotherham U 45 2
1996–97 Rotherham U 43 0
1997–98 Rotherham U 45 7
1998–99 Rotherham U 38 5 **202 18**
1999–2000 Mansfield T 39 2 **39 2**
2000-01 Exeter C 43 1
2001-02 Exeter C 38 7
2002-03 Exeter C 33 3 **114 11**

RUSSELL, Matthew‡ (M) 0 0
b.Dewsbury 17-1-78
2002-03 Exeter C 0 0

SHARPE, Lee‡ (M) 317 34
H: 6 0 W: 12 13 b.Halesowen 27-5-71
Source: Trainee. *Honours:* England Under-21, B, 8 full caps.
1987–88 Torquay U 14 3 **14 3**
1988–89 Manchester U 22 0
1989–90 Manchester U 18 1
1990–91 Manchester U 23 2
1991–92 Manchester U 14 1
1992–93 Manchester U 27 1
1993–94 Manchester U 30 9
1994–95 Manchester U 28 3
1995–96 Manchester U 31 4 **193 21**
1996–97 Leeds U 26 5
1997–98 Leeds U 0 0
1998–99 Leeds U 4 0 **30 5**
1998–99 *Bradford C* 9 2
1998–99 Sampdoria 3 0 **3 0**
1999–2000 Bradford C 18 0
2000-01 Bradford C 11 0
2000-01 *Portsmouth* 17 0 **17 0**
2001-02 Bradford C 18 2 **56 4**
2002-03 Exeter C 4 1 **4 1**

SHELDON, Gareth (F) 106 7
H: 5 10 W: 12 08 b.Birmingham 31-1-80
Source: Trainee.
1997–98 Scunthorpe U 1 0
1998–99 Scunthorpe U 11 1
1999–2000 Scunthorpe U 22 2
2000-01 Scunthorpe U 39 1
2001-02 Scunthorpe U 14 2 **87 6**
2002-03 Exeter C 19 1 **19 1**

THOMAS, Martin (M) 234 23
H: 5 8 W: 11 04 b.Lyndhurst 12-9-73
Source: Trainee.
1992–93 Southampton 0 0
1993–94 Southampton 0 0
1993–94 Leyton Orient 5 2 **5 2**
1994–95 Fulham 23 3
1995–96 Fulham 37 5
1996–97 Fulham 26 0
1997–98 Fulham 4 0 **90 8**
1998–99 Swansea C 30 3
1999–2000 Swansea C 40 4
2000-01 Swansea C 21 1 **91 8**
2000-01 Brighton & HA 8 0 **8 0**
2001-02 Oxford U 14 2 **14 2**
2002-03 Exeter C 26 3 **26 3**

TODD, Chris (D) 55 4
H: 6 0 W: 12 09 b.Swansea 22-8-81
Source: Trainee.
2000-01 Swansea C 11 1
2001-02 Swansea C 32 3 **43 4**
2002-03 Exeter C 12 0 **12 0**

WALKER, Justin (M) 247 11
H: 5 11 W: 12 04 b.Nottingham 6-9-75
Source: Trainee. *Honours:* England Schools, Youth.
1992–93 Nottingham F 0 0
1993–94 Nottingham F 0 0
1994–95 Nottingham F 0 0
1995–96 Nottingham F 0 0
1996–97 Nottingham F 0 0
1996–97 Scunthorpe U 9 0
1997–98 Scunthorpe U 40 1
1998–99 Scunthorpe U 41 1
1999–2000 Scunthorpe U 42 0 **132 2**
2000-01 Lincoln C 45 1
2001-02 Lincoln C 31 3 **76 4**
2002-03 Exeter C 39 5 **39 5**

WATSON, Alex* (D) 418 15
H: 6 1 W: 12 00 b.Liverpool 5-4-68
Source: Apprentice. *Honours:* England Youth.
1984–85 Liverpool 0 0
1985–86 Liverpool 0 0

1986–87 Liverpool 0 0
1987–88 Liverpool 2 0
1988–89 Liverpool 2 0
1989–90 Liverpool 0 0
1990–91 Liverpool 0 0 **4 0**
1990–91 *Derby Co* 5 0 **5 0**
1990–91 Bournemouth 23 3
1991–92 Bournemouth 15 0
1992–93 Bournemouth 46 1
1993–94 Bournemouth 45 1
1994–95 Bournemouth 22 0
1995–96 Bournemouth 0 0 **151 5**
1995–96 *Gillingham* 10 1 **10 1**
1995–96 Torquay U 29 2
1996–97 Torquay U 46 1
1997–98 Torquay U 46 1
1998–99 Torquay U 8 0
1999–2000 Torquay U 43 4
2000–01 Torquay U 30 0 **202 8**
2001–02 Exeter C 43 1
2002–03 Exeter C 3 0 **46 1**

WHITWORTH, Neil* (D) 187 7
H: 6 0 W: 12 11 b.Ince 12-4-72
Source: Trainee. *Honours:* England Youth.
1989–90 Wigan Ath 2 0
1990–91 Manchester U 1 0
1991–92 Manchester U 0 0
1991–92 *Preston NE* 6 0 **6 0**
1991–92 *Barnsley* 11 0 **11 0**
1992–93 Manchester U 0 0
1993–94 Manchester U 0 0 **1 0**
1993–94 *Rotherham U* 8 1 **8 1**
1993–94 *Blackpool* 3 0 **3 0**
1994–95 Kilmarnock 30 3
1995–96 Kilmarnock 28 0
1996–97 Kilmarnock 7 0
1997–98 Kilmarnock 11 0 **76 3**
1997–98 Wigan Ath 4 0 **6 0**
1998–99 Hull C 18 2
1999–2000 Hull C 1 0 **19 2**
2000–01 Exeter C 34 1
2001–02 Exeter C 15 0
2002–03 Exeter C 8 0 **57 1**

Trainees
Alexander, James; Bowker, Scott; Canham, Sean; Clay, Daniel; Forbes, Edward J; Harris, Ben; Harris, Jonathan A; Kiely, James; McShane, Kevin JP; Moxey, Dean; O'Connor, David L; Parker, Lee; Reed, Lewis C; Rice, Martin; Rivans, Dominic; Tippett, Rhys J

Non-Contract
Baker, Phillip

Players who do not hold a current contract but their registration has been retained by the club
Mudge, James RM; Drake, David

FULHAM

BOA MORTE, Luis (F) 130 22
H: 5 10 W: 11 10 b.Lisbon 4-8-77
Source: Sporting Lisbon, Lourihanense (loan). *Honours:* Portugal Under-21, 5 full caps, 1 goal.
1997–98 Arsenal 15 0
1998–99 Arsenal 8 0
1999–2000 Arsenal 2 0 **25 0**
1999–2000 Southampton 14 1
2000–01 Southampton 0 0 **14 1**
2000–01 *Fulham* 39 18
2001–02 Fulham 23 1
2002–03 Fulham 29 2 **91 21**

CLARK, Lee (M) 375 56
H: 5 8 W: 11 10 b.Wallsend 27-10-72
Source: Trainee. *Honours:* England Schools, Youth, Under-21.
1989–90 Newcastle U 0 0
1990–91 Newcastle U 19 2
1991–92 Newcastle U 29 5
1992–93 Newcastle U 46 9
1993–94 Newcastle U 29 2
1994–95 Newcastle U 19 1
1995–96 Newcastle U 28 2
1996–97 Newcastle U 25 2 **195 23**
1997–98 Sunderland 46 13
1998–99 Sunderland 27 3 **73 16**
1999–2000 Fulham 42 8
2000–01 Fulham 45 7
2001–02 Fulham 9 0
2002–03 Fulham 11 2 **107 17**

COLEMAN, Chris‡ (D) 478 23
H: 6 2 W: 14 07 b.Swansea 10-6-70
Source: Apprentice. *Honours:* Wales Schools, Youth, Under-21, 32 full caps, 4 goals.
1987–88 Swansea C 30 0
1988–89 Swansea C 43 0
1989–90 Swansea C 46 2
1990–91 Swansea C 41 0 **160 2**
1991–92 Crystal Palace 18 4
1992–93 Crystal Palace 38 5
1993–94 Crystal Palace 46 3
1994–95 Crystal Palace 35 1
1995–96 Crystal Palace 17 0 **154 13**
1995–96 Blackburn R 20 0
1996–97 Blackburn R 8 0
1997–98 Blackburn R 0 0 **28 0**
1997–98 Fulham 26 1
1998–99 Fulham 45 4
1999–2000 Fulham 40 3
2000–01 Fulham 25 0
2001–02 Fulham 0 0
2002–03 Fulham 0 0 **136 8**

COLLINS, John* (M) 554 76
H: 5 8 W: 10 10 b.Galashiels 31-1-68
Source: Hutchison Vale BC. *Honours:* Scotland Youth, Under-21, 58 full caps, 12 goals.
1984–85 Hibernian 0 0
1985–86 Hibernian 19 1
1986–87 Hibernian 30 1
1987–88 Hibernian 44 6
1988–89 Hibernian 35 2
1989–90 Hibernian 35 6 **163 16**
1990–91 Celtic 35 1
1991–92 Celtic 38 11
1992–93 Celtic 43 8
1993–94 Celtic 38 8
1994–95 Celtic 34 8
1995–96 Celtic 29 11 **217 47**
1996–97 Monaco 28 6
1997–98 Monaco 25 1 **53 7**
1998–99 Everton 20 1
1999–2000 Everton 35 2 **55 3**
2000–01 Fulham 27 3
2001–02 Fulham 34 0
2002–03 Fulham 5 0 **66 3**

COLLINS, Matthew (M) 0 0
b.Merthyr 31-3-86
Source: Trainee.
2002–03 Fulham 0 0

CORNWALL, Luke* (F) 17 5
H: 5 10 W: 10 02 b.Lambeth 23-7-80
Source: Trainee.
1998–99 Fulham 4 1
1999–2000 Fulham 0 0
2000–01 Fulham 0 0
2000–01 *Grimsby T* 10 4 **10 4**
2001–02 Fulham 0 0
2002–03 Fulham 0 0 **4 1**
2002–03 *Lincoln C* 3 0 **3 0**

DAVIS, Sean (M) 131 9
H: 5 9 W: 12 09 b.Lambeth 20-9-79
Source: Trainee. *Honours:* England Under-21.
1996–97 Fulham 1 0
1997–98 Fulham 0 0
1998–99 Fulham 6 0
1999–2000 Fulham 26 0
2000–01 Fulham 40 6
2001–02 Fulham 30 0
2002–03 Fulham 28 3 **131 9**

DJETOU, Martin (M) 247 8
H: 5 11 W: 12 06 b.Brogohla 15-12-74
Honours: France 6 full caps.
1992–93 Strasbourg 28 0
1993–94 Strasbourg 4 0
1994–95 Strasbourg 21 0
1995–96 Strasbourg 30 1 **83 1**
1996–97 Monaco 26 0
1997–98 Monaco 24 3
1998–99 Monaco 15 0
1999–2000 Monaco 22 0
2000–01 Monaco 29 1 **116 4**
2001–02 Parma 23 2 **23 2**
2002–03 Fulham 25 1 **25 1**

DOHERTY, Sean (M) 0 0
H: 5 8 W: 10 00 b.Basingstoke 10-5-85
Source: Scholar. *Honours:* England Youth, Under-20.
2001–02 Fulham 0 0
2002–03 Fulham 0 0

FAZACKERLEY, Loui (M) 0 0
b.Winchester 24-7-84
2002–03 Fulham 0 0

FINNAN, Steve (D) 284 14
H: 5 10 W: 12 04 b.Limerick 20-4-76
Source: Welling U. *Honours:* Eire 22 full caps, 1 goal.
1995–96 Birmingham C 12 1
1995–96 *Notts Co* 17 2
1996–97 Birmingham C 3 0 **15 1**
1996–97 Notts Co 23 0
1997–98 Notts Co 44 5
1998–99 Notts Co 13 0 **97 7**
1998–99 Fulham 22 2
1999–2000 Fulham 35 2
2000–01 Fulham 45 2
2001–02 Fulham 38 0
2002–03 Fulham 32 0 **172 6**

GOLDBAEK, Bjarne* (M) 297 41
H: 5 10 W: 12 04 b.Denmark 6-10-68
Honours: Denmark 28 full caps.
1991–92 Kaiserslautern 24 2
1992–93 Kaiserslautern 28 5
1993–94 Kaiserslautern 3 0 **55 7**
1993–94 Tennis Borussia 24 5 **24 5**
1994–95 Cologne 14 0
1995–96 Cologne 16 2 **30 2**
1996–97 FC Copenhagen 32 7
1997–98 FC Copenhagen 30 6
1998–99 FC Copenhagen 12 3 **74 16**
1998–99 Chelsea 23 5
1999–2000 Chelsea 6 0 **29 5**
1999–2000 Fulham 18 3
2000–01 Fulham 44 2
2001–02 Fulham 13 1
2002–03 Fulham 10 0 **85 6**

GOMA, Alain (D) 294 5
H: 6 0 W: 13 05 b.Sault 15-10-72
Honours: France 2 full caps.
1990–91 Auxerre 1 0
1991–92 Auxerre 1 0
1992–93 Auxerre 15 1
1993–94 Auxerre 33 0
1994–95 Auxerre 28 0
1995–96 Auxerre 32 0
1996–97 Auxerre 34 2
1997–98 Auxerre 22 1 **166 4**
1998–99 Paris St Germain 30 0 **30 0**
1999–2000 Newcastle U 14 0
2000–01 Newcastle U 19 1 **33 1**
2000–01 Fulham 3 0
2001–02 Fulham 33 0
2002–03 Fulham 29 0 **65 0**

HAMMOND, Elvis (F) 17 0
H: 5 10 W: 11 06 b.Accra 6-10-80
Source: Trainee.
1999–2000 Fulham 0 0
2000–01 Fulham 0 0
2001–02 Fulham 0 0
2001–02 *Bristol R* 7 0 **7 0**
2002–03 Fulham 10 0 **10 0**

HARLEY, Jon (D) 66 6
H: 5 9 W: 11 05 b.Maidstone 26-9-79
Source: Trainee. *Honours:* England Under-21.
1996–97 Chelsea 0 0
1997–98 Chelsea 3 0
1998–99 Chelsea 0 0
1999–2000 Chelsea 17 2
2000–01 Chelsea 10 0 **30 2**
2000–01 *Wimbledon* 6 2 **6 2**
2001–02 Fulham 10 0
2002–03 Fulham 11 1 **21 1**
2002–03 *Sheffield U* 9 1 **9 1**

HAYLES, Barry (F) 211 72
H: 5 10 W: 12 11 b.Lambeth 17-5-72
Source: Stevenage Bor. *Honours:* Jamaica 9 full caps.
1997–98 Bristol R 45 23
1998–99 Bristol R 17 9 **62 32**
1998–99 Fulham 30 8
1999–2000 Fulham 35 5
2000–01 Fulham 35 18
2001–02 Fulham 35 8
2002–03 Fulham 14 1 **149 40**

HERRERA, Martin (G) 135 0
H: 6 0 W: 12 06 b.Argentina 13-9-70
1997–98 Toluca 5 0 **5 0**
1998–99 Ferro Carril 34 0 **34 0**
1999–2000 Alaves 38 0
2000–01 Alaves 36 0

2001-02	Alaves	20	0	**94**	**0**
2002-03	Fulham	2	0	**2**	**0**

HUDSON, Mark (D) **0 0**
H: 6 3 W: 12 06 b.Guildford 30-3-82
Source: Trainee.

1998–99	Fulham	0	0		
1999–2000	Fulham	0	0		
2000-01	Fulham	0	0		
2001-02	Fulham	0	0		
2002-03	Fulham	0	0		

INAMOTO, Junichi (M) **137 18**
H: 5 11 W: 11 11 b.Osaka 18-9-79
Honours: Japan 40 full caps, 4 goals.

1997	Gamba Osaka	27	3		
1998	Gamba Osaka	28	6		
1999	Gamba Osaka	22	1		
2000	Gamba Osaka	28	4		
2001	Gamba Osaka	13	2	**118**	**16**
2001-02	Arsenal	0	0		
2002-03	Fulham	19	2	**19**	**2**

KNIGHT, Zat (D) **35 0**
H: 6 6 W: 14 06 b.Solihull 2-5-80
Honours: England Under-21.

1998–99	Fulham	0	0		
1999–2000	Fulham	0	0		
1999–2000	*Peterborough U*	8	0	**8**	**0**
2000-01	Fulham	0	0		
2001-02	Fulham	10	0		
2002-03	Fulham	17	0	**27**	**0**

LEACOCK, Dean (D) **0 0**
H: 6 2 W: 12 04 b.Croydon 10-6-84
Source: Trainee. *Honours:* England Youth, Under-20.

2002-03	Fulham	0	0		

LEGWINSKI, Sylvain (M) **242 22**
H: 6 1 W: 11 10 b.Clermont-Ferrand 6-10-73

1992–93	Monaco	2	0		
1993–94	Monaco	0	0		
1994–95	Monaco	21	1		
1995–96	Monaco	29	2		
1996–97	Monaco	37	9		
1997–98	Monaco	22	0		
1998–99	Monaco	14	1	**125**	**13**
1999–2000	Bordeaux	13	1		
2000-01	Bordeaux	32	1		
2001-02	Bordeaux	4	0	**49**	**2**
2001-02	Fulham	33	3		
2002-03	Fulham	35	4	**68**	**7**

MALBRANQUE, Steed (M) **151 19**
H: 5 8 W: 11 10 b.Mouscron 6-1-80

1997–98	Lyon	2	0		
1998–99	Lyon	21	0		
1999–2000	Lyon	28	3		
2000-01	Lyon	26	2	**77**	**5**
2001-02	Fulham	37	8		
2002-03	Fulham	37	6	**74**	**14**

MARLET, Steve (F) **192 47**
H: 5 11 W: 11 10 b.Pithiviers 1-10-74
Honours: France 17 full caps, 4 goals.

1996–97	Auxerre	24	3		
1997–98	Auxerre	18	6		
1998–99	Auxerre	32	7		
1999–2000	Auxerre	33	9	**107**	**25**
2000-01	Lyon	31	12	**31**	**12**
2001-02	Fulham	26	6		
2002-03	Fulham	28	4	**54**	**10**

McDERMOTT, Neale (M) **0 0**
H: 5 9 W: 10 11 b.Newcastle 8-3-85
Source: Scholar. *Honours:* England Youth.

2001-02	Newcastle U	0	0		
2002-03	Newcastle U	0	0		
2002-03	Fulham	0	0		

MELVILLE, Andy (D) **664 54**
H: 6 1 W: 12 13 b.Swansea 29-11-68
Source: School. *Honours:* Wales Under-21, B, 58 full caps, 3 goals.

1985–86	Swansea C	5	0		
1986–87	Swansea C	42	3		
1987–88	Swansea C	37	4		
1988–89	Swansea C	45	10		
1989–90	Swansea C	46	5	**175**	**22**
1990–91	Oxford U	46	3		
1991–92	Oxford U	45	4		
1992–93	Oxford U	44	6	**135**	**13**
1993–94	Sunderland	44	2		
1994–95	Sunderland	36	3		
1995–96	Sunderland	40	4		
1996–97	Sunderland	30	2		
1997–98	Sunderland	10	1		
1997–98	*Bradford C*	6	1	**6**	**1**
1998–99	Sunderland	44	2	**204**	**14**
1999–2000	Fulham	40	3		
2000-01	Fulham	43	1		
2001-02	Fulham	35	0		
2002-03	Fulham	26	0	**144**	**4**

NOBLE, Stuart (M) **0 0**
b.Edinburgh 14-10-83
Source: Trainee.

2002-03	Fulham	0	0		

OUADDOU, Abdes (D) **68 0**
H: 6 4 W: 12 03 b.Ksar-Askour 1-11-78
Honours: Morocco full caps.

1999–2000	Nancy	16	0		
2000-01	Nancy	31	0	**47**	**0**
2001-02	Fulham	8	0		
2002-03	Fulham	13	0	**21**	**0**

PRATLEY, Darren (F) **0 0**
H: 6 0 W: 10 13 b.Barking 22-4-85
Source: Scholar.

2001-02	Fulham	0	0		
2002-03	Fulham	0	0		

REHMAN, Zesh (M) **0 0**
H: 6 2 W: 12 09 b.Birmingham 14-10-83
Source: Scholar. *Honours:* England Youth.

2001-02	Fulham	0	0		
2002-03	Fulham	0	0		

SAHA, Louis (F) **154 46**
H: 6 1 W: 12 06 b.Paris 8-8-78

1997–98	Metz	21	1		
1998–99	Metz	3	0		
1998–99	Newcastle U	11	1	**11**	**1**
1999–2000	Metz	23	4	**47**	**5**
2000-01	Fulham	43	27		
2001-02	Fulham	36	8		
2002-03	Fulham	17	5	**96**	**40**

SAVA, Facundo (F) **270 78**
H: 6 1 W: 13 03 b.Ituzaingo 7-3-74

1993–94	Ferro Carril	27	3		
1994–95	Ferro Carril	18	0		
1995–96	Ferro Carril	34	4		
1996–97	Ferro Carril	1	0	**80**	**7**
1996–97	Boca Juniors	7	0	**7**	**0**
1997–98	Gimnasia	32	8		
1998–99	Gimnasia	28	10		
1999–2000	Gimnasia	35	12		
2000-01	Gimnasia	34	13		
2001-02	Gimnasia	34	23	**163**	**66**
2002-03	Fulham	20	5	**20**	**5**

SHEVEL, David* (M) **0 0**
H: 5 8 W: 9 10 b.Croydon 14-9-83
Source: Scholar.

2000-01	Fulham	0	0		
2001-02	Fulham	0	0		
2002-03	Fulham	0	0		

STOLCERS, Andrejs (M) **135 36**
H: 5 11 W: 11 00 b.Latvia 8-7-74
Honours: Latvia 67 full caps, 7 goals.

1996	Skonto Riga	26	6		
1997	Skonto Riga	23	9	**49**	**15**
1997–98	Shakhtar Donetsk	13	4		
1998–99	Shakhtar Donetsk	21	6		
1999–2000	Shakhtar Donetsk	15	4	**49**	**14**
2000	Spartak Moscow	12	5	**12**	**5**
2000-01	Fulham	15	2		
2001-02	Fulham	5	0		
2002-03	Fulham	5	0	**25**	**2**

TAYLOR, Maik (G) **272 0**
H: 6 3 W: 14 02 b.Hildeshein 4-9-71
Source: Farnborough T. *Honours:* Northern Ireland Under-21, B, 29 full caps.

1995–96	Barnet	45	0		
1996–97	Barnet	25	0	**70**	**0**
1996–97	Southampton	18	0		
1997–98	Southampton	0	0	**18**	**0**
1997–98	Fulham	28	0		
1998–99	Fulham	46	0		
1999–2000	Fulham	46	0		
2000-01	Fulham	44	0		
2001-02	Fulham	1	0		
2002-03	Fulham	19	0	**184**	**0**

TIMLIN, Michael (M) **0 0**
b.London 19-3-85
Source: Trainee.

2002-03	Fulham	0	0		

VAN DER SAR, Edwin (G) **348 1**
H: 6 5 W: 14 08 b.Voorhout 29-10-70
Honours: Holland 72 full caps.

1990–91	Ajax	9	0		
1991–92	Ajax	0	0		
1992–93	Ajax	19	0		
1993–94	Ajax	32	0		
1994–95	Ajax	33	0		
1995–96	Ajax	33	0		
1996–97	Ajax	33	0		
1997–98	Ajax	33	1	**192**	**1**
1998–99	Juventus	34	0		
1999–2000	Juventus	32	0		
2000-01	Juventus	34	0	**100**	**0**
2001-02	Fulham	37	0		
2002-03	Fulham	19	0	**56**	**0**

WILLOCK, Calum (F) **8 0**
H: 6 0 W: 12 09 b.London 29-10-81
Source: Scholar. *Honours:* England Schools.

2000-01	Fulham	1	0		
2001-02	Fulham	2	0		
2002-03	Fulham	2	0	**5**	**0**
2002-03	*QPR*	3	0	**3**	**0**

WOME, Pierre* (D) **175 25**
H: 5 8 W: 11 11 b.Douala 26-3-79
Honours: Cameroon 55 full caps, 1 goal.

1993–94	Fogape	30	6	**30**	**6**
1994–95	Canon Yaounde	30	8		
1995–96	Canon Yaounde	21	5	**51**	**13**
1996–97	Vicenza	3	0	**3**	**0**
1997–98	Lucchese	24	2	**24**	**2**
1998–99	Roma	8	0	**8**	**0**
1999–2000	Bologna	14	1		
2000-01	Bologna	19	1		
2001-02	Bologna	12	1	**45**	**3**
2002-03	Fulham	14	1	**14**	**1**

Trainees
Buari, Malik; Davis, Thomas; Flitney, Ross; Fontaine, Liam VH; Green, Adam; McFrederick, William S; Nowacki, Aaron M; Stratford, Daniel J; Watkins, Robert J; White, Daniel R

GILLINGHAM

ASHBY, Barry (D) **463 13**
H: 6 1 W: 14 04 b.London 2-11-70
Source: Trainee.

1988–89	Watford	0	0		
1989–90	Watford	18	1		
1990–91	Watford	23	0		
1991–92	Watford	21	0		
1992–93	Watford	35	0		
1993–94	Watford	17	2	**114**	**3**
1993–94	Brentford	8	1		
1994–95	Brentford	40	1		
1995–96	Brentford	33	1		
1996–97	Brentford	40	1	**121**	**4**
1997–98	Gillingham	43	0		
1998–99	Gillingham	38	1		
1999–2000	Gillingham	41	3		
2000-01	Gillingham	40	1		
2001-02	Gillingham	28	1		
2002-03	Gillingham	38	0	**228**	**6**

AWUAH, Jones§ (M) **4 0**
H: 6 0 W: 11 07 b.Ghana 10-7-83
Source: Scholar.

2002-03	Gillingham	4	0	**4**	**0**

BARTRAM, Vince (G) **355 0**
H: 6 2 W: 15 04 b.Birmingham 7-8-68
Source: Local.

1985–86	Wolverhampton W	0	0		
1986–87	Wolverhampton W	1	0		
1987–88	Wolverhampton W	0	0		
1988–89	Wolverhampton W	0	0		
1989–90	Wolverhampton W	0	0		
1989–90	*Blackpool*	9	0	**9**	**0**
1990–91	Wolverhampton W	4	0		
1990–91	*WBA*	0	0		
1991–92	Bournemouth	46	0		
1992–93	Bournemouth	45	0		
1993–94	Bournemouth	41	0	**132**	**0**
1994–95	Arsenal	11	0		
1995–96	Arsenal	0	0		
1996–97	Arsenal	0	0		
1996–97	*Wolverhampton W*	0	0	**5**	**0**
1997–98	Arsenal	0	0	**11**	**0**
1997–98	*Huddersfield T*	12	0	**12**	**0**
1997–98	Gillingham	9	0		
1998–99	Gillingham	44	0		
1999–2000	Gillingham	43	0		
2000-01	Gillingham	46	0		
2001-02	Gillingham	36	0		
2002-03	Gillingham	8	0	**186**	**0**

BROWN, Jason (G)				**49**	**0**
H: 6 0 W: 15 05 b.Southwark 18-5-82					
Source: Charlton Ath Scholar. *Honours:* Wales Under-21.					
2000-01	Gillingham	0	0		
2001-02	Gillingham	10	0		
2002-03	Gillingham	39	0	**49**	**0**

CROFTS, Andrew§ (D)				**1**	**0**
H: 5 9 W: 10 02 b.Chatham 29-5-84					
Source: Trainee.					
2000-01	Gillingham	1	0		
2001-02	Gillingham	0	0		
2002-03	Gillingham	0	0	**1**	**0**

EDGE, Roland* (D)				**102**	**1**
H: 5 9 W: 12 09 b.Gillingham 25-11-78					
Source: Trainee.					
1997–98	Gillingham	0	0		
1998–99	Gillingham	8	0		
1999–2000	Gillingham	26	1		
2000-01	Gillingham	20	0		
2001-02	Gillingham	14	0		
2002-03	Gillingham	34	0	**102**	**1**

EDUSEI, Akwasi‡ (M)				**2**	**0**
H: 5 9 W: 11 00 b.London 12-9-86					
2002-03	Gillingham	2	0	**2**	**0**

GOODEN, Ty* (M)				**205**	**14**
H: 5 8 W: 12 08 b.Canvey Island 23-10-72					
Source: Arsenal, Wycombe W.					
1993–94	Swindon T	4	0		
1994–95	Swindon T	16	2		
1995–96	Swindon T	26	3		
1996–97	Swindon T	13	1		
1997–98	Swindon T	39	2		
1998–99	Swindon T	38	1		
1999–2000	Swindon T	10	0	**146**	**9**
1999–2000	Gillingham	16	4		
2000-01	Gillingham	18	0		
2001-02	Gillingham	25	1		
2002-03	Gillingham	0	0	**59**	**5**

HESSENTHALER, Andy (M)				**429**	**28**
H: 5 7 W: 11 10 b.Gravesend 17-6-65					
Source: Dartford, Redbridge Forest.					
1991–92	Watford	35	1		
1992–93	Watford	45	3		
1993–94	Watford	42	5		
1994–95	Watford	43	2		
1995–96	Watford	30	0	**195**	**11**
1996–97	Gillingham	38	2		
1997–98	Gillingham	42	0		
1998–99	Gillingham	39	7		
1999–2000	Gillingham	42	5		
2000-01	Gillingham	23	2		
2001-02	Gillingham	17	0		
2002-03	Gillingham	33	1	**234**	**17**

HOPE, Chris (D)				**425**	**26**
H: 6 1 W: 12 11 b.Sheffield 14-11-72					
Source: Darlington.					
1991–92	Nottingham F	0	0		
1992–93	Nottingham F	0	0		
1993–94	Scunthorpe U	41	0		
1994–95	Scunthorpe U	24	0		
1995–96	Scunthorpe U	40	3		
1996–97	Scunthorpe U	46	3		
1997–98	Scunthorpe U	46	5		
1998–99	Scunthorpe U	46	5		
1999–2000	Scunthorpe U	44	3	**287**	**19**
2000-01	Gillingham	46	2		
2001-02	Gillingham	46	4		
2002-03	Gillingham	46	1	**138**	**7**

IPOUA, Guy* (F)				**171**	**39**
H: 6 0 W: 13 13 b.Douala 14-1-76					
Source: Atletico Madrid, Novelda.					
1998–99	Bristol R	24	3	**24**	**3**
1999–2000	Scunthorpe U	40	9		
2000-01	Scunthorpe U	25	14	**65**	**23**
2000-01	Gillingham	9	0		
2001-02	Gillingham	40	8		
2002-03	Gillingham	33	5	**82**	**13**

JAMES, Kevin (F)				**32**	**3**
H: 5 7 W: 11 12 b.Southwark 3-1-80					
Source: Trainee.					
1998–99	Charlton Ath	0	0		
1999–2000	Charlton Ath	0	0		
2000-01	Gillingham	7	0		
2001-02	Gillingham	10	0		
2002-03	Gillingham	15	3	**32**	**3**

JOHNSON, Leon (M)				**66**	**3**
H: 6 0 W: 12 00 b.London 10-5-81					
Source: Scholarship.					
1999–2000	Southend U	0	0		
2000-01	Southend U	20	1		
2001-02	Southend U	28	2	**48**	**3**
2002-03	Gillingham	18	0	**18**	**0**

JOHNSON, Tommy (F)				**329**	**108**
H: 5 11 W: 12 07 b.Newcastle 15-1-71					
Source: Trainee. *Honours:* England Under-21.					
1988–89	Notts Co	10	4		
1989–90	Notts Co	40	18		
1990–91	Notts Co	37	16		
1991–92	Notts Co	31	9	**118**	**47**
1991–92	Derby Co	12	2		
1992–93	Derby Co	35	8		
1993–94	Derby Co	37	13		
1994–95	Derby Co	14	7	**98**	**30**
1994–95	Aston Villa	14	4		
1995–96	Aston Villa	23	5		
1996–97	Aston Villa	20	4	**57**	**13**
1996–97	Celtic	4	1		
1997–98	Celtic	2	0		
1998–99	Celtic	3	3		
1999–2000	Celtic	10	9		
1999–2000	*Everton*	3	0	**3**	**0**
2000-01	Celtic	0	0		
2001-02	Celtic	0	0	**19**	**13**
2001-02	Sheffield W	8	3	**8**	**3**
2002-03	Gillingham	26	2	**26**	**2**

KING, Marlon (F)				**143**	**50**
H: 6 0 W: 12 10 b.Dulwich 26-4-80					
Source: Trainee.					
1998–99	Barnet	22	6		
1999–2000	Barnet	31	8	**53**	**14**
2000-01	Gillingham	38	15		
2001-02	Gillingham	42	17		
2002-03	Gillingham	10	4	**90**	**36**

LATHAM, Stuart‡ (F)				**0**	**0**
H: 5 10 W: 15 00 b.Chalfont St Giles 2-4-65					
Source: Reading, Alloa, Wokingham T, Maidenhead U, Bracknell T, Cobham, Swindon Supermarine.					
2002-03	Gillingham	0	0		

NOSWORTHY, Nayron (D)				**110**	**3**
H: 6 1 W: 12 10 b.London 11-10-80					
Source: Trainee.					
1998–99	Gillingham	3	0		
1999–2000	Gillingham	29	1		
2000-01	Gillingham	10	0		
2001-02	Gillingham	29	0		
2002-03	Gillingham	39	2	**110**	**3**

OSBORN, Simon* (M)				**320**	**28**
H: 5 8 W: 11 08 b.New Addington 19-1-72					
Source: Apprentice.					
1989–90	Crystal Palace	0	0		
1990–91	Crystal Palace	4	0		
1991–92	Crystal Palace	14	2		
1992–93	Crystal Palace	31	2		
1993–94	Crystal Palace	6	1	**55**	**5**
1994–95	Reading	32	5	**32**	**5**
1995–96	QPR	9	1	**9**	**1**
1995–96	Wolverhampton W	21	2		
1996–97	Wolverhampton W	35	5		
1997–98	Wolverhampton W	24	2		
1998–99	Wolverhampton W	37	2		
1999–2000	Wolverhampton W	25	0		
2000-01	Wolverhampton W	20	0	**162**	**11**
2000-01	Tranmere R	9	1	**9**	**1**
2001-02	Port Vale	7	0	**7**	**0**
2001-02	Gillingham	28	4		
2002-03	Gillingham	18	1	**46**	**5**

PATTERSON, Mark‡ (D)				**331**	**8**
H: 5 8 W: 12 08 b.Leeds 13-9-68					
Source: Trainee.					
1986–87	Carlisle U	6	0		
1987–88	Carlisle U	16	0	**22**	**0**
1987–88	Derby Co	0	0		
1988–89	Derby Co	1	0		
1989–90	Derby Co	9	0		
1990–91	Derby Co	11	1		
1991–92	Derby Co	12	2		
1992–93	Derby Co	18	0	**51**	**3**
1993–94	Plymouth Arg	41	0		
1994–95	Plymouth Arg	38	3		
1995–96	Plymouth Arg	43	0		
1996–97	Plymouth Arg	12	0		
1997–98	Plymouth Arg	0	0	**134**	**3**
1997–98	Gillingham	23	0		
1998–99	Gillingham	42	2		
1999–2000	Gillingham	9	0		
2000-01	Gillingham	28	0		
2001-02	Gillingham	20	0		
2002-03	Gillingham	2	0	**124**	**2**

PENNOCK, Adrian‡ (D)				**300**	**11**
H: 6 1 W: 14 03 b.Ipswich 27-3-71					
Source: Trainee.					
1989–90	Norwich C	1	0		
1990–91	Norwich C	0	0		
1991–92	Norwich C	0	0	**1**	**0**
1992–93	Bournemouth	43	1		
1993–94	Bournemouth	40	3		
1994–95	Bournemouth	31	5		
1995–96	Bournemouth	17	0		
1996–97	Bournemouth	0	0	**131**	**9**
1996–97	Gillingham	26	2		
1997–98	Gillingham	20	0		
1998–99	Gillingham	40	0		
1999–2000	Gillingham	34	0		
2000-01	Gillingham	35	0		
2001-02	Gillingham	10	0		
2002-03	Gillingham	3	0	**168**	**2**

PERPETUINI, David (M)				**82**	**4**
H: 5 10 W: 12 01 b.Hitchin 26-9-79					
Source: Trainee.					
1997–98	Watford	0	0		
1998–99	Watford	1	0		
1999–2000	Watford	13	1		
2000-01	Watford	5	0	**19**	**1**
2001-02	Gillingham	34	1		
2002-03	Gillingham	29	2	**63**	**3**

PHILLIPS, Michael (M)				**1**	**0**
H: 5 10 W: 10 00 b.Camberwell 22-1-83					
Source: Trainee.					
2000-01	Gillingham	1	0		
2001-02	Gillingham	0	0		
2002-03	Gillingham	0	0	**1**	**0**

ROSE, Richard (D)				**18**	**0**
H: 6 0 W: 11 07 b.Pembury 8-9-82					
Source: Trainee.					
2000-01	Gillingham	4	0		
2001-02	Gillingham	3	0		
2002-03	Gillingham	2	0	**9**	**0**
2002-03	*Bristol R*	9	0	**9**	**0**

SAUNDERS, Mark (M)				**220**	**25**
H: 6 0 W: 12 07 b.Reading 23-7-71					
Source: Tiverton.					
1995–96	Plymouth Arg	10	1		
1996–97	Plymouth Arg	25	3		
1997–98	Plymouth Arg	37	7	**72**	**11**
1998–99	Gillingham	34	4		
1999–2000	Gillingham	26	1		
2000-01	Gillingham	35	5		
2001-02	Gillingham	19	1		
2002-03	Gillingham	34	3	**148**	**14**

SHAW, Paul (F)				**262**	**57**
H: 5 11 W: 13 03 b.Burnham 4-9-73					
Source: Trainee.					
1991–92	Arsenal	0	0		
1992–93	Arsenal	0	0		
1993–94	Arsenal	0	0		
1994–95	Arsenal	1	0		
1994–95	*Burnley*	9	4	**9**	**4**
1995–96	Arsenal	3	0		
1995–96	*Cardiff C*	6	0	**6**	**0**
1995–96	*Peterborough U*	12	5	**12**	**5**
1996–97	Arsenal	8	2		
1997–98	Arsenal	0	0	**12**	**2**
1997–98	Millwall	40	11		
1998–99	Millwall	34	10		
1999–2000	Millwall	35	5	**109**	**26**
2000-01	Gillingham	33	1		
2001-02	Gillingham	37	7		
2002-03	Gillingham	44	12	**114**	**20**

SIDIBE, Mamady (F)				**61**	**10**
H: 6 4 W: 12 02 b.Mali 18-12-79					
Source: CA Paris. *Honours:* Mali full caps.					
2001-02	Swansea C	31	7	**31**	**7**
2002-03	Gillingham	30	3	**30**	**3**

SMITH, Paul (M)				**447**	**30**
H: 6 0 W: 14 00 b.East Ham 18-9-71					
Source: Trainee.					
1989–90	Southend U	10	1		
1990–91	Southend U	2	0		
1991–92	Southend U	0	0		
1992–93	Southend U	8	0	**20**	**1**
1993–94	Brentford	32	3		
1994–95	Brentford	35	3		
1995–96	Brentford	46	4		
1996–97	Brentford	46	1	**159**	**11**
1997–98	Gillingham	46	3		
1998–99	Gillingham	45	6		
1999–2000	Gillingham	44	1		

2000-01	Gillingham	42	3		
2001-02	Gillingham	46	2		
2002-03	Gillingham	45	3	**268**	**18**

SOUTHALL, Nicky (M) **415** **48**
H: 5 10 W: 12 12 b.Stockton 28-1-72
Source: Trainee.

1990–91	Hartlepool U	0	0		
1991–92	Hartlepool U	22	3		
1992–93	Hartlepool U	39	6		
1993–94	Hartlepool U	40	9		
1994–95	Hartlepool U	37	6	**138**	**24**
1995–96	Grimsby T	33	2		
1996–97	Grimsby T	34	3		
1997–98	Grimsby T	5	0	**72**	**5**
1997–98	Gillingham	23	2		
1998–99	Gillingham	42	4		
1999–2000	Gillingham	45	9		
2000-01	Gillingham	44	2		
2001-02	Bolton W	18	1		
2002-03	Bolton W	0	0	**18**	**1**
2002-03	*Norwich C*	9	0	**9**	**0**
2002-03	Gillingham	24	1	**178**	**18**

SPILLER, Daniel (M) **11** **0**
H: 5 7 W: 11 01 b.Maidstone 10-10-81
Source: Trainee.

2000-01	Gillingham	0	0		
2001-02	Gillingham	1	0		
2002-03	Gillingham	10	0	**11**	**0**

WALLACE, Rod (F) **458** **151**
H: 5 7 W: 11 03 b.Lewisham 2-10-69
Source: Trainee. *Honours:* England Under-21, B.

1987–88	Southampton	15	1		
1988–89	Southampton	38	12		
1989–90	Southampton	38	18		
1990–91	Southampton	37	14	**128**	**45**
1991–92	Leeds U	34	11		
1992–93	Leeds U	32	7		
1993–94	Leeds U	37	17		
1994–95	Leeds U	32	4		
1995–96	Leeds U	24	1		
1996–97	Leeds U	22	3		
1997–98	Leeds U	31	10	**212**	**53**
1998–99	Rangers	34	18		
1999–2000	Rangers	28	16		
2000-01	Rangers	15	5	**77**	**39**
2001-02	Bolton W	19	3	**19**	**3**
2002-03	Gillingham	22	11	**22**	**11**

WHITE, Ben (D) **0** **0**
H: 6 0 W: 14 01 b.Hastings 2-6-82
Source: Trainee.

2000-01	Gillingham	0	0		
2001-02	Gillingham	0	0		
2002-03	Gillingham	0	0		

Scholars
Awuah, Jones; Beckwith, Dean S; Benjamin, Ronayne; Carew, Ashley; Crofts, Andrew L; Flaherty, Darren S; Green, Mark; Jarvis, Matthew T; Knowles, Daniel; Millar, James Stephen BM; Peters, Ryan J; Solomon, Leon; Vella, Daniel MT; Wallis, Jonathan

GRIMSBY T

BARNARD, Darren (D) **310** **47**
H: 5 9 W: 13 00 b.Rinteln 30-11-71
Source: Wokingham T. *Honours:* England Schools, Wales 18 full caps.

1990–91	Chelsea	0	0		
1991–92	Chelsea	4	0		
1992–93	Chelsea	13	1		
1993–94	Chelsea	12	1		
1994–95	Chelsea	0	0		
1994–95	*Reading*	4	0	**4**	**0**
1995–96	Chelsea	0	0	**29**	**2**
1995–96	Bristol C	34	4		
1996–97	Bristol C	44	11	**78**	**15**
1997–98	Barnsley	35	2		
1998–99	Barnsley	26	4		
1999–2000	Barnsley	41	13		
2000-01	Barnsley	30	2		
2001-02	Barnsley	38	7	**170**	**28**
2002-03	Grimsby T	29	2	**29**	**2**

BOLDER, Chris (M) **12** **0**
H: 5 11 W: 12 00 b.Hull 19-8-82
Source: Hull C scholar.

2001-02	Grimsby T	0	0		
2002-03	Grimsby T	12	0	**12**	**0**

BOULDING, Mick (F) **119** **27**
H: 5 9 W: 11 07 b.Sheffield 8-2-76

1999–2000	Mansfield T	33	6		
2000-01	Mansfield T	33	6		
2001-02	Mansfield T	0	0	**66**	**12**
2001-02	Grimsby T	35	11		
2002-03	Aston Villa	0	0		
2002-03	*Sheffield U*	6	0	**6**	**0**
2002-03	Grimsby T	12	4	**47**	**15**

CAMPBELL, Stuart (M) **155** **11**
H: 5 10 W: 12 00 b.Corby 9-12-77
Source: Trainee. *Honours:* Scotland Under-21.

1996–97	Leicester C	10	0		
1997–98	Leicester C	11	0		
1998–99	Leicester C	12	0		
1999–2000	Leicester C	4	0		
1999–2000	*Birmingham C*	2	0	**2**	**0**
2000-01	Leicester C	0	0	**37**	**0**
2000-01	*Grimsby T*	38	2		
2001-02	Grimsby T	33	3		
2002-03	Grimsby T	45	6	**116**	**11**

CHETTLE, Steve* (D) **533** **14**
H: 6 1 W: 12 09 b.Nottingham 27-9-68
Source: Apprentice. *Honours:* England Under-21.

1986–87	Nottingham F	0	0		
1987–88	Nottingham F	30	0		
1988–89	Nottingham F	28	2		
1989–90	Nottingham F	22	1		
1990–91	Nottingham F	37	2		
1991–92	Nottingham F	22	1		
1992–93	Nottingham F	30	0		
1993–94	Nottingham F	46	1		
1994–95	Nottingham F	41	0		
1995–96	Nottingham F	37	0		
1996–97	Nottingham F	32	0		
1997–98	Nottingham F	45	1		
1998–99	Nottingham F	34	2		
1999–2000	Nottingham F	11	1	**415**	**11**
1999–2000	Barnsley	25	2		
2000-01	Barnsley	35	0		
2001-02	Barnsley	32	0	**92**	**2**
2001-02	*Walsall*	6	0	**6**	**0**
2002-03	Grimsby T	20	1	**20**	**1**

COLDICOTT, Stacy# (M) **285** **6**
H: 5 8 W: 12 08 b.Worcester 29-4-74
Source: Trainee.

1991–92	WBA	0	0		
1992–93	WBA	14	0		
1993–94	WBA	5	0		
1994–95	WBA	11	0		
1995–96	WBA	33	0		
1996–97	WBA	19	3		
1996–97	*Cardiff C*	6	0	**6**	**0**
1997–98	WBA	22	0	**104**	**3**
1998–99	Grimsby T	37	0		
1999–2000	Grimsby T	44	2		
2000-01	Grimsby T	37	1		
2001-02	Grimsby T	26	0		
2002-03	Grimsby T	31	0	**175**	**3**

COOKE, Terry* (M) **113** **10**
H: 5 8 W: 12 08 b.Marston Green 5-8-76
Source: Trainee. *Honours:* England Youth, Under-21.

1994–95	Manchester U	0	0		
1995–96	Manchester U	4	0		
1995–96	*Sunderland*	6	0	**6**	**0**
1996–97	Manchester U	0	0		
1996–97	*Birmingham C*	4	0	**4**	**0**
1997–98	Manchester U	0	0		
1998–99	Manchester U	0	0	**4**	**0**
1998–99	*Wrexham*	10	0	**10**	**0**
1998–99	Manchester C	21	7		
1999–2000	Manchester C	13	0		
1999–2000	*Wigan Ath*	10	1	**10**	**1**
2000-01	Manchester C	0	0		
2000-01	*Sheffield W*	17	1	**17**	**1**
2001-02	Manchester C	0	0	**34**	**7**
2001-02	Grimsby T	3	1		
2002-03	Grimsby T	25	0	**28**	**1**

COYNE, Danny (G) **292** **0**
H: 6 0 W: 13 04 b.Prestatyn 27-8-73
Source: Trainee. *Honours:* Wales Schools, Youth, Under-21, B, 2 full caps.

1991–92	Tranmere R	0	0		
1992–93	Tranmere R	1	0		
1993–94	Tranmere R	5	0		
1994–95	Tranmere R	5	0		
1995–96	Tranmere R	46	0		
1996–97	Tranmere R	21	0		
1997–98	Tranmere R	16	0		
1998–99	Tranmere R	17	0	**111**	**0**
1999–2000	Grimsby T	44	0		
2000-01	Grimsby T	46	0		
2001-02	Grimsby T	45	0		
2002-03	Grimsby T	46	0	**181**	**0**

CROUDSON, Steve* (G) **10** **0**
H: 6 0 W: 11 12 b.Grimsby 14-9-79
Source: Trainee.

1998–99	Grimsby T	2	0		
1999–2000	Grimsby T	3	0		
2000-01	Grimsby T	0	0		
2001-02	*Scunthorpe U*	4	0	**4**	**0**
2001-02	Grimsby T	1	0		
2002-03	Grimsby T	0	0	**6**	**0**

DOWNES, Steven (M) **0** **0**
b.Leeds 12-11-81

2002-03	Grimsby T	0	0		

FORD, Simon (D) **52** **3**
H: 6 1 W: 12 04 b.Lincoln 17-11-81
Source: Charlton Ath scholar.

2001-02	Grimsby T	13	1		
2002-03	Grimsby T	39	2	**52**	**3**

GALLIMORE, Tony* (D) **424** **13**
H: 5 11 W: 13 04 b.Crewe 21-2-72
Source: Trainee.

1989–90	Stoke C	1	0		
1990–91	Stoke C	7	0		
1991–92	Stoke C	3	0		
1991–92	*Carlisle U*	16	0		
1992–93	Stoke C	0	0	**11**	**0**
1992–93	*Carlisle U*	8	1		
1993–94	Carlisle U	40	1		
1994–95	Carlisle U	40	5		
1995–96	Carlisle U	36	2	**140**	**9**
1995–96	Grimsby T	10	1		
1996–97	Grimsby T	42	1		
1997–98	Grimsby T	35	2		
1998–99	Grimsby T	43	0		
1999–2000	Grimsby T	39	0		
2000-01	Grimsby T	28	0		
2001-02	Grimsby T	38	0		
2002-03	Grimsby T	38	0	**273**	**4**

GEORGE, Kevin† (M) **0** **0**
H: 5 11 W: 12 04 b.London 21-11-82
Source: Scholar.

2000-01	Charlton Ath	0	0		
2001-02	Charlton Ath	0	0		
2002-03	Grimsby T	0	0		

GROVES, Paul (M) **603** **98**
H: 5 11 W: 13 04 b.Derby 28-2-66
Source: Burton Alb.

1987–88	Leicester C	1	1		
1988–89	Leicester C	15	0		
1989–90	Leicester C	0	0	**16**	**1**
1989–90	*Lincoln C*	8	1	**8**	**1**
1989–90	Blackpool	19	1		
1990–91	Blackpool	46	11		
1991–92	Blackpool	42	9	**107**	**21**
1992–93	Grimsby T	46	12		
1993–94	Grimsby T	46	11		
1994–95	Grimsby T	46	5		
1995–96	Grimsby T	46	10		
1996–97	WBA	29	4	**29**	**4**
1997–98	Grimsby T	46	7		
1998–99	Grimsby T	46	14		
1999–2000	Grimsby T	43	3		
2000-01	Grimsby T	45	4		
2001-02	Grimsby T	43	2		
2002-03	Grimsby T	36	3	**443**	**71**

HOCKLESS, Graham (M) **1** **0**
H: 5 7 W: 10 02 b.Hull 20-10-82

2001-02	Grimsby T	0	0		
2002-03	Grimsby T	1	0	**1**	**0**

JEVONS, Phil (F) **66** **9**
H: 5 10 W: 12 00 b.Liverpool 1-8-79
Source: Trainee.

1996–97	Everton	0	0		
1997–98	Everton	0	0		
1998–99	Everton	1	0		
1999–2000	Everton	3	0		
2000-01	Everton	4	0	**8**	**0**
2001-02	Grimsby T	31	6		
2002-03	Grimsby T	3	0	**34**	**6**
2002-03	*Hull C*	24	3	**24**	**3**

LIVINGSTONE, Steve* (F) **356** **58**
H: 6 1 W: 15 03 b.Middlesbrough 8-9-68
Source: Trainee.

1986–87	Coventry C	3	0		
1987–88	Coventry C	4	0		

1988–89 Coventry C 1 0
1989–90 Coventry C 13 3
1990–91 Coventry C 10 2 **31 5**
1990–91 Blackburn R 18 9
1991–92 Blackburn R 10 1
1992–93 Blackburn R 2 0 **30 10**
1992–93 Chelsea 1 0
1993–94 Chelsea 0 0 **1 0**
1993–94 *Port Vale* 5 0 **5 0**
1993–94 Grimsby T 27 3
1994–95 Grimsby T 34 8
1995–96 Grimsby T 38 11
1996–97 Grimsby T 32 6
1997–98 Grimsby T 41 5
1998–99 Grimsby T 23 0
1999–2000 Grimsby T 29 0
2000-01 Grimsby T 32 7
2001-02 Grimsby T 3 0
2002-03 Grimsby T 30 3 **289 43**

MANSARAM, Darren (F) 34 2
H: 6 1 W: 11 02 b.Doncaster 25-6-84
Source: Scholar.
2002-03 Grimsby T 34 2 **34 2**

McDERMOTT, John# (D) 532 7
H: 5 7 W: 10 13 b.Middlesbrough 3-2-69
Source: Trainee.
1986–87 Grimsby T 13 0
1987–88 Grimsby T 28 0
1988–89 Grimsby T 38 1
1989–90 Grimsby T 39 0
1990–91 Grimsby T 43 0
1991–92 Grimsby T 39 1
1992–93 Grimsby T 38 2
1993–94 Grimsby T 26 0
1994–95 Grimsby T 12 0
1995–96 Grimsby T 28 1
1996–97 Grimsby T 29 1
1997–98 Grimsby T 41 1
1998–99 Grimsby T 37 0
1999–2000 Grimsby T 26 0
2000-01 Grimsby T 36 0
2001-02 Grimsby T 24 0
2002-03 Grimsby T 35 0 **532 7**

PARKER, Wesley§ (D) 5 0
H: 5 8 W: 10 05 b.Boston 7-12-83
Source: Scholar.
2002-03 Grimsby T 5 0 **5 0**

PETTINGER, Andrew (G) 0 0
b.Scunthorpe 21-4-84
Source: Scunthorpe U.
2000-01 Everton 0 0
2001-02 Everton 0 0
2002-03 Everton 0 0
2002-03 Grimsby T 0 0

POUTON, Alan (M) 206 19
H: 6 0 W: 12 10 b.Newcastle 1-2-77
Source: Newcastle U Trainee.
1995–96 Oxford U 0 0
1995–96 York C 0 0
1996–97 York C 22 1
1997–98 York C 41 5
1998–99 York C 27 1
1999–2000 York C 0 0 **90 7**
1999–2000 Grimsby T 35 1
2000-01 Grimsby T 21 1
2001-02 Grimsby T 35 5
2002-03 Grimsby T 25 5 **116 12**

ROWAN, Jonathan (F) 38 4
H: 5 10 W: 11 06 b.Grimsby 29-11-81
2000-01 Grimsby T 5 0
2001-02 Grimsby T 24 4
2002-03 Grimsby T 9 0 **38 4**

SAGARE, Jake (M) 1 0
H: 5 11 W: 11 07 b.USA 5-4-80
Source: Portland T.
2002-03 Grimsby T 1 0 **1 0**

SANTOS, Georges# (M) 142 9
H: 6 3 W: 14 02 b.Marseille 15-8-70
Source: Toulon.
1998–99 Tranmere R 37 1
1999–2000 Tranmere R 10 1 **47 2**
1999–2000 WBA 8 0 **8 0**
2000-01 Sheffield U 31 4
2001-02 Sheffield U 30 2 **61 6**
2002-03 Grimsby T 26 1 **26 1**

SOAMES, David§ (F) 10 1
H: 5 5 W: 10 08 b.Grimsby 10-2-84
Source: Scholar.
2002-03 Grimsby T 10 1 **10 1**

THOMPSON, Chris (F) 14 1
H: 5 10 W: 11 12 b.Warrington 7-2-82
Source: Liverpool scholar.
2001-02 Grimsby T 8 0
2002-03 Grimsby T 6 1 **14 1**

WARD, Iain (D) 12 0
H: 6 0 W: 10 10 b.Cleethorpes 13-5-83
2000-01 Grimsby T 0 0
2001-02 Grimsby T 1 0
2002-03 Grimsby T 11 0 **12 0**

WHEELER, Kirk (M) 0 0
b.Grimsby 13-6-84
2002-03 Grimsby T 0 0

YOUNG, Greg (D) 1 0
H: 6 1 W: 12 03 b.Doncaster 25-4-83
2002-03 Grimsby T 1 0 **1 0**

Scholars
Beesley, Lee G; Carchedi, Giovanni R; Davey, James A; Haseley, Ashley; Hegarty, Nicholas I; Hildred, Ashley; Hughes, Bradley R; Hyam, Christopher; Lightowler, Joseph; Morfitt, Adrian J; Newton, Mark; Nimmo, Liam; Parker, Liam S; Parker, Wesley; Smith, Michael G; Soames, David M; Thorne, Sam; Wall, Christopher A
Non-Contract
George, Kevin C

HARTLEPOOL U

ARNISON, Paul# (D) 73 3
H: 5 9 W: 10 12 b.Hartlepool 18-9-77
Source: Trainee.
1995–96 Newcastle U 0 0
1996–97 Newcastle U 0 0
1997–98 Newcastle U 0 0
1998–99 Newcastle U 0 0
1999–2000 Newcastle U 0 0
1999–2000 Hartlepool U 8 1
2000-01 Hartlepool U 27 1
2001-02 Hartlepool U 19 0
2002-03 Hartlepool U 19 1 **73 3**

BARRON, Micky (D) 239 2
H: 5 11 W: 11 10 b.Lumley 22-12-74
Source: Trainee.
1992–93 Middlesbrough 0 0
1993–94 Middlesbrough 2 0
1994–95 Middlesbrough 0 0
1995–96 Middlesbrough 1 0
1996–97 Middlesbrough 0 0 **3 0**
1996–97 *Hartlepool U* 16 0
1997–98 Hartlepool U 33 0
1998–99 Hartlepool U 38 1
1999–2000 Hartlepool U 40 0
2000-01 Hartlepool U 28 0
2001-02 Hartlepool U 39 1
2002-03 Hartlepool U 42 0 **236 2**

BASS, Jonathan# (D) 102 1
H: 6 0 W: 12 02 b.Weston-Super-Mare 1-1-76
Source: Trainee. *Honours:* England Schools.
1994–95 Birmingham C 0 0
1995–96 Birmingham C 5 0
1996–97 Birmingham C 13 0
1996–97 *Carlisle U* 3 0 **3 0**
1997–98 Birmingham C 30 0
1998–99 Birmingham C 11 0
1999–2000 Birmingham C 8 0
1999–2000 *Gillingham* 7 0 **7 0**
2000-01 Birmingham C 1 0 **68 0**
2001-02 Hartlepool U 20 1
2002-03 Hartlepool U 4 0 **24 1**

BOYD, Adam (F) 60 15
H: 6 0 W: 10 12 b.Hartlepool 25-5-82
Source: Scholarship.
1999–2000 Hartlepool U 4 1
2000-01 Hartlepool U 5 0
2001-02 Hartlepool U 29 9
2002-03 Hartlepool U 22 5 **60 15**

CLARKE, Darrell (M) 239 38
H: 5 10 W: 11 06 b.Mansfield 16-12-77
Source: Trainee.
1995–96 Mansfield T 3 0
1996–97 Mansfield T 19 2
1997–98 Mansfield T 35 4
1998–99 Mansfield T 33 5
1999–2000 Mansfield T 39 7
2000-01 Mansfield T 32 6 **161 24**
2001-02 Hartlepool U 33 7
2002-03 Hartlepool U 45 7 **78 14**

EASTER, Jermaine (F) 24 2
H: 5 10 W: 12 03 b.Cardiff 15-1-82
Source: Trainee. *Honours:* Wales Youth.
2000-01 Wolverhampton W 0 0
2000-01 Hartlepool U 4 0
2001-02 Hartlepool U 12 2
2002-03 Hartlepool U 8 0 **24 2**

HENDERSON, Kevin (F) 142 30
H: 5 11 W: 13 02 b.Ashington 8-6-74
Source: Morpeth Town.
1997–98 Burnley 7 0
1998–99 Burnley 7 1 **14 1**
1999–2000 Hartlepool U 35 8
2000-01 Hartlepool U 40 17
2001-02 Hartlepool U 23 2
2002-03 Hartlepool U 30 2 **128 29**

HUMPHREYS, Richie (M) 181 27
H: 5 11 W: 12 07 b.Sheffield 30-11-77
Source: Trainee. *Honours:* England Youth, Under-21.
1995–96 Sheffield W 5 0
1996–97 Sheffield W 29 3
1997–98 Sheffield W 7 0
1998–99 Sheffield W 19 1
1999–2000 Sheffield W 0 0
1999–2000 *Scunthorpe U* 6 2 **6 2**
1999–2000 *Cardiff C* 9 2 **9 2**
2000-01 Sheffield W 7 0 **67 4**
2000-01 Cambridge U 7 3 **7 3**
2001-02 Hartlepool U 46 5
2002-03 Hartlepool U 46 11 **92 16**

ISTEAD, Steven§ (M) 6 0
H: 5 8 W: 11 04 b.South Shields 23-4-86
Source: Scholar.
2002-03 Hartlepool U 6 0 **6 0**

LEE, Graeme# (D) 219 19
H: 6 2 W: 13 08 b.Middlesbrough 31-5-78
Source: Trainee.
1995–96 Hartlepool U 6 0
1996–97 Hartlepool U 24 0
1997–98 Hartlepool U 37 3
1998–99 Hartlepool U 24 3
1999–2000 Hartlepool U 38 7
2000-01 Hartlepool U 6 0
2001-02 Hartlepool U 39 4
2002-03 Hartlepool U 45 2 **219 19**

McKENZIE, Colin (M) 0 0
H: 6 0 W: 12 05 b.North Shields 29-11-83
Source: Scholar.
2002-03 Hartlepool U 0 0

PROVETT, Jim (G) 0 0
H: 6 0 W: 13 04 b.Stockton 22-12-82
Source: Trainee.
1999–2000 Hartlepool U 0 0
2000-01 Hartlepool U 0 0
2001-02 Hartlepool U 0 0
2002-03 Hartlepool U 0 0

RICHARDSON, Marcus (F) 79 15
H: 6 3 W: 12 05 b.Reading 31-8-77
Source: Harrow B.
2000-01 Cambridge U 10 2
2001-02 Cambridge U 6 0 **16 2**
2001-02 Torquay U 30 6
2002-03 Torquay U 9 2 **39 8**
2002-03 Hartlepool U 24 5 **24 5**

ROBINSON, Mark (D) 81 0
H: 5 9 W: 11 00 b.Guisborough 24-7-81
Source: Trainee.
1999–2000 Hartlepool U 0 0
2000-01 Hartlepool U 6 0
2001-02 Hartlepool U 37 0
2002-03 Hartlepool U 38 0 **81 0**

ROBSON, Matty (M) 0 0
H: 5 10 W: 11 02 b.Durham 23-1-85
Source: Scholar.
2002-03 Hartlepool U 0 0

ROSS, Brian* (M) 0 0
H: 5 6 W: 10 02 b.Hartlepool 21-8-83
2001-02 Hartlepool U 0 0
2002-03 Hartlepool U 0 0

SHARP, James* (D) 49 2
H: 6 2 W: 14 06 b.Reading 2-1-76
Source: Reading, Florida Tech, Aldershot T, Wokingham, Andover T.
2000-01 Hartlepool U 34 2
2001-02 Hartlepool U 15 0
2002-03 Hartlepool U 0 0 **49 2**

SIMMS, Gordon* (D) 11 0
H: 6 3 W: 12 03 b.Larne 23-3-81
Source: Trainee. *Honours:* Northern Ireland Under-21.
1997–98 Wolverhampton W 0 0
1998–99 Wolverhampton W 0 0
1999–2000 Wolverhampton W 0 0
2000-01 Wolverhampton W 0 0
2000-01 Hartlepool U 0 0
2001-02 Hartlepool U 10 0
2002-03 Hartlepool U 1 0 **11 0**

SMITH, Paul# (M) 171 9
H: 6 0 W: 13 03 b.Easington 22-1-76
Source: Trainee.
1993–94 Burnley 1 0
1994–95 Burnley 0 0
1995–96 Burnley 10 0
1996–97 Burnley 37 4
1997–98 Burnley 14 0
1998–99 Burnley 12 0
1999–2000 Burnley 24 0
2000-01 Burnley 14 1 **112 5**
2000-01 *Oldham Ath* 4 0 **4 0**
2001-02 Torquay U 0 0
2001-02 Hartlepool U 31 4
2002-03 Hartlepool U 24 0 **55 4**

STEPHENSON, Paul* (M) 483 28
H: 5 10 W: 12 12 b.Wallsend 2-1-68
Source: Apprentice. *Honours:* England Youth.
1985–86 Newcastle U 22 1
1986–87 Newcastle U 24 0
1987–88 Newcastle U 7 0
1988–89 Newcastle U 8 0 **61 1**
1989–90 Millwall 12 1
1989–90 Millwall 23 2
1990–91 Millwall 30 1
1991–92 Millwall 28 2
1992–93 Millwall 5 0 **98 6**
1992–93 *Gillingham* 12 2 **12 2**
1992–93 Brentford 11 0
1993–94 Brentford 25 0
1994–95 Brentford 34 2 **70 2**
1995–96 York C 27 2
1996–97 York C 35 1
1997–98 York C 35 5 **97 8**
1997–98 Hartlepool U 3 0
1998–99 Hartlepool U 27 2
1999–2000 Hartlepool U 46 5
2000-01 Hartlepool U 40 2
2001-02 Hartlepool U 29 0
2002-03 Hartlepool U 0 0 **145 9**

SWEENEY, Anthony (M) 6 0
H: 6 0 W: 11 07 b.Stockton 5-9-83
Source: Scholar.
2001-02 Hartlepool U 2 0
2002-03 Hartlepool U 4 0 **6 0**

TINKLER, Mark (M) 284 34
H: 6 2 W: 12 00 b.Bishop Auckland 24-10-74
Source: Trainee. *Honours:* England Schools, Youth.
1991–92 Leeds U 0 0
1992–93 Leeds U 7 0
1993–94 Leeds U 3 0
1994–95 Leeds U 3 0
1995–96 Leeds U 9 0
1996–97 Leeds U 3 0 **25 0**
1996–97 York C 9 1
1997–98 York C 44 5
1998–99 York C 37 2
1999–2000 York C 0 0 **90 8**
1999–2000 Southend U 41 0
2000-01 Southend U 15 1 **56 1**
2000-01 Hartlepool U 28 3
2001-02 Hartlepool U 40 9
2002-03 Hartlepool U 45 13 **113 25**

WATSON, Gordon* (F) 225 58
H: 5 10 W: 12 08 b.Sidcup 20-3-71
Source: Trainee. *Honours:* England Under-21.
1988–89 Charlton Ath 0 0
1989–90 Charlton Ath 9 0
1990–91 Charlton Ath 22 7 **31 7**
1990–91 Sheffield W 5 0
1991–92 Sheffield W 4 0
1992–93 Sheffield W 11 1
1993–94 Sheffield W 23 12
1994–95 Sheffield W 23 2 **66 15**
1994–95 Southampton 12 3
1995–96 Southampton 25 3
1996–97 Southampton 15 2 **52 8**
1996–97 Bradford C 3 1
1997–98 Bradford C 0 0
1998–99 Bradford C 18 4 **21 5**
1999–2000 Bournemouth 6 0
2000-01 Bournemouth 0 0 **6 0**
2001-02 Hartlepool U 32 18
2002-03 Hartlepool U 17 5 **49 23**

WESTWOOD, Chris (D) 172 4
H: 5 11 W: 12 10 b.Dudley 13-2-77
Source: Trainee.
1995–96 Wolverhampton W 0 0
1996–97 Wolverhampton W 0 0
1997–98 Wolverhampton W 4 1
1998–99 Wolverhampton W 0 0 **4 1**
1998–99 Hartlepool U 4 0
1999–2000 Hartlepool U 37 0
2000-01 Hartlepool U 46 1
2001-02 Hartlepool U 35 1
2002-03 Hartlepool U 46 1 **168 3**

WIDDRINGTON, Tommy* (M) 308 24
H: 5 9 W: 11 12 b.Newcastle 1-10-71
Source: Trainee.
1989–90 Southampton 0 0
1990–91 Southampton 0 0
1991–92 Southampton 3 0
1991–92 *Wigan Ath* 6 0 **6 0**
1992–93 Southampton 12 0
1993–94 Southampton 11 1
1994–95 Southampton 28 0
1995–96 Southampton 21 2 **75 3**
1996–97 Grimsby T 42 4
1997–98 Grimsby T 21 3
1998–99 Grimsby T 26 1 **89 8**
1998–99 *Port Vale* 9 1
1999–2000 Port Vale 38 5
2000-01 Port Vale 35 2 **82 8**
2001-02 Hartlepool U 24 2
2002-03 Hartlepool U 32 3 **56 5**

WILLIAMS, Anthony (G) 156 0
H: 6 2 W: 13 08 b.Ogwr 20-9-77
Source: Trainee. *Honours:* Wales Youth, Under-21.
1996–97 Blackburn R 0 0
1997–98 Blackburn R 0 0
1997–98 *QPR* 0 0
1998–99 Blackburn R 0 0
1998–99 *Macclesfield T* 4 0
1998–99 *Huddersfield T* 0 0
1998–99 *Bristol R* 9 0 **9 0**
1999–2000 Blackburn R 0 0
1999–2000 *Gillingham* 2 0 **2 0**
1999–2000 *Macclesfield T* 11 0 **15 0**
2000-01 Hartlepool U 41 0
2001-02 Hartlepool U 43 0
2002-03 Hartlepool U 46 0 **130 0**

WILLIAMS, Eifion (F) 164 43
H: 5 11 W: 11 02 b.Bangor 15-11-75
Source: Barry T. *Honours:* Wales B.
1998–99 Torquay U 7 5
1999–2000 Torquay U 42 9
2000-01 Torquay U 37 9
2001-02 Torquay U 25 1 **111 24**
2001-02 Hartlepool U 8 4
2002-03 Hartlepool U 45 15 **53 19**

Scholars
Appleby, Andrew; Batey, Marc; Brackstone, John; Craddock, Darren; Duncan, Kevin M; Flockett, Stephen; Fox, Daniel J; Hill, Andrew S; Istead, Steven B; Manson, Stephen; McKenzie, Colin JF; Peachey, Lee G; Richards, Karl D; Robson, Matthew J; Watts, Andrew; Wilkinson, Neil S; Winter, James H

HUDDERSFIELD T

AUSTIN, Ben* (M) 0 0
H: 5 11 W: 11 09 b.Halifax 21-7-83
Source: Scholar.
2002-03 Huddersfield T 0 0

BALDRY, Simon* (M) 151 8
H: 5 10 W: 12 12 b.Huddersfield 12-2-76
Source: Trainee.
1993–94 Huddersfield T 10 2
1994–95 Huddersfield T 11 0
1995–96 Huddersfield T 14 0
1996–97 Huddersfield T 7 0
1997–98 Huddersfield T 11 1
1998–99 Huddersfield T 13 0
1998–99 *Bury* 5 0 **5 0**
1999–2000 Huddersfield T 19 1
2000-01 Huddersfield T 35 2
2001-02 Huddersfield T 4 0
2002-03 Huddersfield T 22 2 **146 8**

BOOTH, Andy (F) 337 102
H: 6 1 W: 13 00 b.Huddersfield 6-12-73
Source: Trainee. *Honours:* England Under-21.
1991–92 Huddersfield T 3 0
1992–93 Huddersfield T 5 2
1993–94 Huddersfield T 26 10
1994–95 Huddersfield T 46 26
1995–96 Huddersfield T 43 16
1996–97 Sheffield W 35 10
1997–98 Sheffield W 23 7
1998–99 Sheffield W 34 6
1999–2000 Sheffield W 23 2
2000-01 Sheffield W 18 3 **133 28**
2000-01 *Tottenham H* 4 0 **4 0**
2000-01 Huddersfield T 8 3
2001-02 Huddersfield T 36 11
2002-03 Huddersfield T 33 6 **200 74**

BROWN, Chris* (D) 0 0
H: 5 11 W: 13 00 b.Leeds 2-3-83
Source: Scholar.
2002-03 Huddersfield T 0 0

BROWN, Nathaniel (F) 38 0
H: 6 2 W: 12 06 b.Sheffield 15-6-81
Source: Trainee.
1999–2000 Huddersfield T 0 0
2000-01 Huddersfield T 0 0
2001-02 Huddersfield T 0 0
2002-03 Huddersfield T 38 0 **38 0**

CLARKE, Doni‡ (M) 0 0
H: 5 9 W: 11 00 b.Burnley 18-9-81
Source: Scholar.
2001-02 Huddersfield T 0 0
2002-03 Huddersfield T 0 0

CLARKE, Nathan (D) 39 1
H: 6 1 W: 11 11 b.Halifax 30-7-83
Source: Scholar.
2001-02 Huddersfield T 36 1
2002-03 Huddersfield T 3 0 **39 1**

DYSON, Jon‡ (D) 216 9
H: 5 10 W: 12 07 b.Mirfield 18-12-71
Source: School.
1991–92 Huddersfield T 0 0
1992–93 Huddersfield T 15 0
1993–94 Huddersfield T 22 0
1994–95 Huddersfield T 28 2
1995–96 Huddersfield T 17 0
1996–97 Huddersfield T 23 0
1997–98 Huddersfield T 36 1
1998–99 Huddersfield T 14 1
1999–2000 Huddersfield T 28 2
2000-01 Huddersfield T 30 3
2001-02 Huddersfield T 0 0
2002-03 Huddersfield T 3 0 **216 9**

EVANS, Gareth* (D) 36 0
H: 6 0 W: 12 09 b.Leeds 10-4-81
Source: Trainee. *Honours:* England Youth.
1997–98 Leeds U 0 0
1998–99 Leeds U 0 0
1999–2000 Leeds U 0 0
2000-01 Leeds U 1 0 **1 0**
2001-02 Huddersfield T 35 0
2002-03 Huddersfield T 0 0 **35 0**

FOWLER, Adam‡ (M) 0 0
H: 5 7 W: 11 02 b.Huddersfield 11-9-81
Source: Scholar.
2001-02 Huddersfield T 0 0
2002-03 Huddersfield T 0 0

GALLACHER, Kevin‡ (F) 430 106
H: 5 8 W: 10 10 b.Clydebank 23-11-66
Source: Duntocher BC. *Honours:* Scotland Youth, Under-21, B, 53 full caps, 9 goals.
1983–84 Dundee U 0 0
1984–85 Dundee U 0 0
1985–86 Dundee U 20 3
1986–87 Dundee U 37 10
1987–88 Dundee U 26 4
1988–89 Dundee U 31 9
1989–90 Dundee U 17 1 **131 27**
1989–90 Coventry C 15 3
1990–91 Coventry C 32 11
1991–92 Coventry C 33 8
1992–93 Coventry C 20 6 **100 28**
1992–93 Blackburn R 9 5
1993–94 Blackburn R 30 7

1994–95	Blackburn R	1	1		
1995–96	Blackburn R	16	2		
1996–97	Blackburn R	34	10		
1997–98	Blackburn R	33	16		
1998–99	Blackburn R	16	5		
1999–2000	Blackburn R	5	0	**144**	**46**
1999–2000	Newcastle U	20	2		
2000-01	Newcastle U	19	2	**39**	**4**
2001-02	Preston NE	5	1	**5**	**1**
2001-02	Sheffield W	4	0	**4**	**0**
2002-03	Huddersfield T	7	0	**7**	**0**

HAY, Nathan‡ (D) **0 0**
H: 5 8 W: 10 10 b.Leeds 5-10-81
Source: Scholar.

2001-02	Huddersfield T	0	0
2002-03	Huddersfield T	0	0

HEARY, Thomas* (D) **92 0**
H: 5 10 W: 13 02 b.Dublin 14-2-79
Source: Trainee. *Honours:* Eire Under-21.

1995–96	Huddersfield T	0	0		
1996–97	Huddersfield T	5	0		
1997–98	Huddersfield T	3	0		
1998–99	Huddersfield T	3	0		
1999–2000	Huddersfield T	1	0		
2000-01	Huddersfield T	28	0		
2001-02	Huddersfield T	32	0		
2002-03	Huddersfield T	20	0	**92**	**0**

HOLLAND, Chris# (M) **191 2**
H: 5 9 W: 12 13 b.Clitheroe 11-9-75
Source: Trainee. *Honours:* England Youth, Under-21.

1993–94	Preston NE	1	0	**1**	**0**
1993–94	Newcastle U	3	0		
1994–95	Newcastle U	0	0		
1995–96	Newcastle U	0	0		
1996–97	Newcastle U	0	0	**3**	**0**
1996–97	Birmingham C	32	0		
1997–98	Birmingham C	10	0		
1998–99	Birmingham C	14	0		
1999–2000	Birmingham C	14	0	**70**	**0**
1999–2000	Huddersfield T	17	1		
2000-01	Huddersfield T	29	0		
2001-02	Huddersfield T	37	1		
2002-03	Huddersfield T	34	0	**117**	**2**

IRONS, Kenny* (M) **500 65**
H: 5 9 W: 12 02 b.Liverpool 4-11-70
Source: Trainee.

1989–90	Tranmere R	3	0		
1990–91	Tranmere R	32	6		
1991–92	Tranmere R	43	7		
1992–93	Tranmere R	42	7		
1993–94	Tranmere R	34	3		
1994–95	Tranmere R	38	4		
1995–96	Tranmere R	32	3		
1996–97	Tranmere R	41	5		
1997–98	Tranmere R	43	4		
1998–99	Tranmere R	43	15	**351**	**54**
1999–2000	Huddersfield T	40	3		
2000-01	Huddersfield T	33	0		
2001-02	Huddersfield T	41	7		
2002-03	Huddersfield T	35	1	**149**	**11**

LABARTHE, Gianfranco‡ (M) **3 0**
H: 5 10 W: 10 07 b.Peru 20-9-84
Source: Sport Boys.

2002-03	Huddersfield T	3	0	**3**	**0**

MACARI, Paul (F) **14 0**
H: 5 8 W: 12 06 b.Manchester 23-8-76
Source: Trainee.

1993–94	Stoke C	0	0		
1994–95	Stoke C	0	0		
1995–96	Stoke C	0	0		
1996–97	Stoke C	0	0		
1997–98	Stoke C	3	0	**3**	**0**
1998–99	Sheffield U	0	0		
1999–2000	Sheffield U	0	0		
2000-01	Huddersfield T	0	0		
2001-02	Huddersfield T	6	0		
2002-03	Huddersfield T	5	0	**11**	**0**

MATTIS, Dwayne (M) **64 2**
H: 6 1 W: 11 00 b.Huddersfield 31-7-81
Source: Trainee. *Honours:* Eire Under-21.

1998–99	Huddersfield T	2	0		
1999–2000	Huddersfield T	0	0		
2000-01	Huddersfield T	0	0		
2001-02	Huddersfield T	29	1		
2002-03	Huddersfield T	33	1	**64**	**2**

McCOMBE, John§ (M) **1 0**
H: 6 2 W: 12 10 b.Pontefract 7-5-85
Source: Scholar.

2002-03	Huddersfield T	1	0	**1**	**0**

MIRFIN, David§ (M) **1 0**
H: 6 2 W: 14 05 b.Sheffield 18-4-85
Source: Scholar.

2002-03	Huddersfield T	1	0	**1**	**0**

MOSES, Adi# (D) **220 4**
H: 5 11 W: 13 01 b.Doncaster 4-5-75
Source: School. *Honours:* England Under-21.

1993–94	Barnsley	0	0		
1994–95	Barnsley	4	0		
1995–96	Barnsley	24	1		
1996–97	Barnsley	28	2		
1997–98	Barnsley	35	0		
1998–99	Barnsley	34	0		
1999–2000	Barnsley	12	0		
2000-01	Barnsley	14	0	**151**	**3**
2000-01	Huddersfield T	12	0		
2001-02	Huddersfield T	17	0		
2002-03	Huddersfield T	40	1	**69**	**1**

SCHOFIELD, Danny (F) **74 10**
H: 5 11 W: 11 04 b.Doncaster 10-4-80
Source: Brodsworth.

1998–99	Huddersfield T	1	0		
1999–2000	Huddersfield T	2	0		
2000-01	Huddersfield T	1	0		
2001-02	Huddersfield T	40	8		
2002-03	Huddersfield T	30	2	**74**	**10**

SCOTT, Paul (M) **13 0**
H: 6 0 W: 12 08 b.Wakefield 5-11-79
Source: Trainee.

1998–99	Huddersfield T	0	0		
1999–2000	Huddersfield T	0	0		
2000-01	Huddersfield T	0	0		
2001-02	Huddersfield T	0	0		
2002-03	Huddersfield T	13	0	**13**	**0**

SENIOR, Chris‡ (F) **0 0**
H: 5 5 W: 9 04 b.Huddersfield 18-11-81
Source: Scholar.

2001-02	Huddersfield T	0	0
2002-03	Huddersfield T	0	0

SENIOR, Michael‡ (M) **4 0**
H: 5 9 W: 10 11 b.Huddersfield 3-3-81
Source: Trainee.

1999–2000	Huddersfield T	0	0		
2000-01	Huddersfield T	4	0		
2001-02	Huddersfield T	0	0		
2002-03	Huddersfield T	0	0	**4**	**0**

SENIOR, Philip (G) **18 0**
H: 5 10 W: 11 01 b.Huddersfield 30-10-82
Source: Trainee.

1999–2000	Huddersfield T	0	0		
2000-01	Huddersfield T	0	0		
2001-02	Huddersfield T	0	0		
2002-03	Huddersfield T	18	0	**18**	**0**

SHARP, Kevin‡ (M) **249 10**
H: 5 7 W: 11 10 b.Ontario 19-9-74
Source: Auxerre. *Honours:* England Schools, Youth.

1992–93	Leeds U	4	0		
1993–94	Leeds U	10	0		
1994–95	Leeds U	2	0		
1995–96	Leeds U	1	0	**17**	**0**
1995–96	Wigan Ath	20	6		
1996–97	Wigan Ath	35	2		
1997–98	Wigan Ath	38	0		
1998–99	Wigan Ath	31	2		
1999–2000	Wigan Ath	21	0		
2000-01	Wigan Ath	31	0		
2001-02	Wigan Ath	2	0	**178**	**10**
2001-02	Wrexham	15	0	**15**	**0**
2002-03	Huddersfield T	39	0	**39**	**0**

SIMPSON, Neil‡ (M) **0 0**
H: 5 8 W: 9 09 b.Bradford 2-12-81
Source: Scholar.

2001-02	Huddersfield T	0	0
2002-03	Huddersfield T	0	0

SMITH, Martin# (F) **225 64**
H: 5 11 W: 12 03 b.Sunderland 13-11-74
Source: Trainee. *Honours:* England Schools, Under-21.

1992–93	Sunderland	0	0		
1993–94	Sunderland	29	8		
1994–95	Sunderland	35	10		
1995–96	Sunderland	20	2		
1996–97	Sunderland	11	0		
1997–98	Sunderland	16	2		
1998–99	Sunderland	8	3	**119**	**25**
1999–2000	Sheffield U	26	10	**26**	**10**
1999–2000	Huddersfield T	12	4		
2000-01	Huddersfield T	30	8		
2001-02	Huddersfield T	0	0		
2002-03	Huddersfield T	38	17	**80**	**29**

STEAD, Jon (M) **42 6**
H: 6 3 W: 12 02 b.Huddersfield 7-4-83
Source: Scholar.

2001-02	Huddersfield T	0	0		
2002-03	Huddersfield T	42	6	**42**	**6**

THORRINGTON, John (M) **62 7**
H: 5 8 W: 10 06 b.Johannesburg 10-7-79
Source: US College. *Honours:* USA 1 full cap.

1997–98	Manchester U	0	0		
1998–99	Manchester U	0	0		
1999–2000	Manchester U	0	0		
2000-01	Huddersfield T	0	0		
2001-02	Huddersfield T	31	6		
2002-03	Huddersfield T	31	1	**62**	**7**

WORTHINGTON, Jon (M) **22 0**
H: 5 9 W: 11 04 b.Dewsbury 16-4-83
Source: Scholar.

2001-02	Huddersfield T	0	0		
2002-03	Huddersfield T	22	0	**22**	**0**

YOUDS, Eddie* (D) **242 13**
H: 6 2 W: 14 10 b.Liverpool 3-5-70
Source: Trainee.

1988–89	Everton	0	0		
1989–90	Everton	0	0		
1989–90	*Cardiff C*	1	0	**1**	**0**
1989–90	*Wrexham*	20	2	**20**	**2**
1990–91	Everton	8	0		
1991–92	Everton	0	0	**8**	**0**
1991–92	Ipswich T	1	0		
1992–93	Ipswich T	16	0		
1993–94	Ipswich T	23	1		
1994–95	Ipswich T	10	0	**50**	**1**
1994–95	Bradford C	17	3		
1995–96	Bradford C	30	4		
1996–97	Bradford C	0	0		
1997–98	Bradford C	38	1	**85**	**8**
1997–98	Charlton Ath	8	0		
1998–99	Charlton Ath	22	2		
1999–2000	Charlton Ath	23	0		
2000-01	Charlton Ath	0	0		
2001-02	Charlton Ath	0	0	**53**	**2**
2002-03	Huddersfield T	25	0	**25**	**0**

Scholars
Ahmed, Adnan; Caulfield, Luke P; Clapham, Daniel D; Collins, Michael A; Giles, Jacob D; Hardy, Aaron; Holdsworth, Andrew; Kelly, Gregory; Kenworthy, Steven P; Lloyd, Anthony F; McAliskey, John J; McCombe, John P; Mirfin, David M; Padgett, Lee J; Sheridan, Mark; Tunnacliffe, Michael; Walsh, Joseph J; Washington, Joe; Young, Matthew G

HULL C

ALLSOPP, Danny (F) **182 56**
H: 6 1 W: 14 00 b.Melbourne 10-8-78
Honours: Australia Youth, Under-20, Under-23.

1995–96	South Melbourne	14	1		
1996–97	South Melbourne	6	1	**20**	**2**
1997–98	Carlton	16	3	**16**	**3**
1998–99	Manchester C	24	4		
1999–2000	Manchester C	4	0		
1999–2000	*Notts Co*	3	1		
1999–2000	*Wrexham*	3	4	**3**	**4**
2000-01	Manchester C	1	0	**29**	**4**
2000-01	*Bristol R*	6	0	**6**	**0**
2000-01	Notts Co	29	13		
2001-02	Notts Co	43	19		
2002-03	Notts Co	33	10	**108**	**43**
2002-03	Hull C	0	0		

ANDERSON, John (D) **289 32**
H: 6 2 W: 12 02 b.Greenock 2-10-72
Source: Gourock YAC.

1993–94	Morton	19	2		
1994–95	Morton	30	3		
1995–96	Morton	30	4		
1996–97	Morton	31	4		
1997–98	Morton	33	4		
1998–99	Morton	33	6		
1999–2000	Morton	29	5	**205**	**28**
2000-01	Livingston	30	3		
2001-02	Livingston	11	0	**41**	**3**
2002-03	Hull C	43	1	**43**	**1**

APPLEBY, Ritchie (M) 148 15
H: 5 9 W: 11 04 b.Stockton 18-9-75
Source: Trainee. *Honours:* England Youth.
1993–94 Newcastle U 0 0
1994–95 Newcastle U 0 0
1994–95 *Darlington* 0 0
1995–96 Ipswich T 3 0 **3 0**
1996–97 Swansea C 11 1
1997–98 Swansea C 35 3
1998–99 Swansea C 39 3
1999–2000 Swansea C 20 4
2000-01 Swansea C 5 0
2001-02 Swansea C 10 0 **120 11**
2001-02 Kidderminster H 19 4
2002-03 Kidderminster H 0 0 **19 4**
2002-03 Hull C 6 0 **6 0**

ASHBEE, Ian (M) 235 12
H: 6 1 W: 13 07 b.Birmingham 6-9-76
Source: Trainee. *Honours:* England Youth.
1994–95 Derby Co 1 0
1995–96 Derby Co 0 0
1996–97 Derby Co 0 0 **1 0**
1996–97 Cambridge U 18 0
1997–98 Cambridge U 27 1
1998–99 Cambridge U 31 4
1999–2000 Cambridge U 45 1
2000-01 Cambridge U 44 3
2001-02 Cambridge U 38 2 **203 11**
2002-03 Hull C 31 1 **31 1**

BRADSHAW, Gary‡ (M) 22 1
H: 5 6 W: 10 06 b.Hull 30-12-82
Source: Scholarship.
1999–2000 Hull C 12 0
2000-01 Hull C 2 0
2001-02 Hull C 3 1
2002-03 Hull C 5 0 **22 1**

BURGESS, Ben (F) 105 41
H: 6 3 W: 14 13 b.Buxton 9-11-81
Source: Trainee. *Honours:* Eire Under-21.
1998–99 Blackburn R 0 0
1999–2000 Blackburn R 2 0
2000-01 Blackburn R 0 0
2000-01 Northern Spirit 27 16 **27 16**
2001-02 Blackburn R 0 0 **2 0**
2001-02 *Brentford* 43 17 **43 17**
2002-03 Stockport Co 19 4 **19 4**
2002-03 *Oldham Ath* 7 0 **7 0**
2002-03 Hull C 7 4 **7 4**

BURTON, Steven (D) 11 0
H: 6 1 W: 11 05 b.Hull 10-10-82
Source: Scholar.
2002-03 Hull C 11 0 **11 0**

DELANEY, Damien (D) 59 2
H: 6 3 W: 13 10 b.Cork 20-7-81
Source: Cork C.
2000-01 Leicester C 5 0
2001-02 Leicester C 3 0
2001-02 *Stockport Co* 12 1 **12 1**
2001-02 *Huddersfield T* 2 0 **2 0**
2002-03 Leicester C 0 0 **8 0**
2002-03 *Mansfield T* 7 0 **7 0**
2002-03 Hull C 30 1 **30 1**

DONALDSON, Clayton (F) 2 0
H: 6 1 W: 11 07 b.Bradford 7-2-84
Source: Scholar.
2002-03 Hull C 2 0 **2 0**

ELLIOTT, Stuart (M) 202 61
H: 5 10 W: 11 09 b.Belfast 23-7-78
Honours: Northern Ireland Under-21, 16 full caps, 1 goal.
1994–95 Glentoran 0 0
1995–96 Glentoran 1 0
1996–97 Glentoran 8 1
1997–98 Glentoran 22 5
1998–99 Glentoran 31 7
1999–2000 Glentoran 34 16 **96 29**
2000-01 Motherwell 33 10
2001-02 Motherwell 37 10 **70 20**
2002-03 Hull C 36 12 **36 12**

FETTIS, Alan (G) 295 2
H: 6 1 W: 11 04 b.Newtownards 1-2-71
Source: Ards. *Honours:* Northern Ireland Schools, Youth, B, 25 full caps.
1991–92 Hull C 43 0
1992–93 Hull C 20 0
1993–94 Hull C 37 0
1994–95 Hull C 28 2
1995–96 Hull C 7 0
1995–96 *WBA* 3 0 **3 0**
1996–97 Nottingham F 4 0
1997–98 Nottingham F 0 0 **4 0**
1997–98 Blackburn R 8 0
1998–99 Blackburn R 2 0
1999–2000 Blackburn R 1 0 **11 0**
1999–2000 *Leicester C* 0 0
1999–2000 York C 13 0
2000-01 York C 46 0
2001-02 York C 45 0
2002-03 York C 21 0 **125 0**
2002-03 Hull C 17 0 **152 2**

FORRESTER, Jamie (F) 303 92
H: 5 6 W: 11 00 b.Bradford 1-11-74
Source: Auxerre. *Honours:* England Schools, Youth.
1992–93 Leeds U 6 0
1993–94 Leeds U 3 0
1994–95 Leeds U 0 0
1994–95 *Southend U* 5 0 **5 0**
1994–95 *Grimsby T* 9 1
1995–96 Leeds U 0 0 **9 0**
1995–96 Grimsby T 28 5
1996–97 Grimsby T 13 1 **50 7**
1996–97 Scunthorpe U 10 6
1997–98 Scunthorpe U 45 11
1998–99 Scunthorpe U 46 20 **101 37**
1999–2000 Utrecht 1 0 **1 0**
1999–2000 Walsall 5 0 **5 0**
1999–2000 *Northampton T* 10 6
2000-01 Northampton T 43 17
2001-02 Northampton T 43 17
2002-03 Northampton T 25 5 **121 45**
2002-03 Hull C 11 3 **11 3**

FRY, Russell (M) 0 0
b.Hull 4-12-85
Source: Scholar.
2002-03 Hull C 0 0

GREEN, Stuart (M) 54 11
H: 5 10 W: 11 00 b.Carlisle 15-6-81
Source: Trainee.
1999–2000 Newcastle U 0 0
2000-01 Newcastle U 0 0
2001-02 Newcastle U 0 0
2001-02 *Carlisle U* 16 3
2002-03 Newcastle U 0 0
2002-03 Hull C 28 6 **28 6**
2002-03 *Carlisle U* 10 2 **26 5**

HOLT, Andy (D) 186 12
H: 6 1 W: 12 06 b.Stockport 21-4-78
Source: Trainee.
1996–97 Oldham Ath 1 0
1997–98 Oldham Ath 14 1
1998–99 Oldham Ath 43 5
1999–2000 Oldham Ath 46 3
2000-01 Oldham Ath 20 1 **124 10**
2000-01 *Hull C* 10 2
2001-02 Hull C 30 0
2002-03 Hull C 6 0 **46 2**
2002-03 *Barnsley* 7 0 **7 0**
2002-03 *Shrewsbury T* 9 0 **9 0**

JOSEPH, Marc (D) 237 2
H: 6 2 W: 10 07 b.Leicester 10-11-76
Source: Trainee.
1995–96 Cambridge U 12 0
1996–97 Cambridge U 8 0
1997–98 Cambridge U 41 0
1998–99 Cambridge U 29 0
1999–2000 Cambridge U 33 0
2000-01 Cambridge U 30 0 **153 0**
2001-02 Peterborough U 44 2
2002-03 Peterborough U 17 0 **61 2**
2002-03 Hull C 23 0 **23 0**

KEATES, Dean (M) 195 13
H: 5 6 W: 10 10 b.Walsall 30-6-78
Source: Trainee.
1996–97 Walsall 2 0
1997–98 Walsall 33 1
1998–99 Walsall 43 2
1999–2000 Walsall 35 1
2000-01 Walsall 33 4
2001-02 Walsall 13 1 **159 9**
2002-03 Hull C 36 4 **36 4**

KERR, Scott‡ (M) 1 0
H: 5 8 W: 10 08 b.Leeds 11-12-81
Source: Scholar.
2000-01 Bradford C 1 0 **1 0**
2001-02 Hull C 0 0
2002-03 Hull C 0 0

MANN, Neil‡ (M) 175 9
H: 5 10 W: 12 01 b.Nottingham 19-11-72
Source: Notts Co, Spalding U, Grantham T.
1993–94 Hull C 5 0
1994–95 Hull C 31 2
1995–96 Hull C 38 1
1996–97 Hull C 32 2
1997–98 Hull C 34 3
1998–99 Hull C 20 1
1999–2000 Hull C 2 0
2000-01 Hull C 13 0
2001-02 Hull C 0 0
2002-03 Hull C 0 0 **175 9**

MELTON, Steve (M) 79 3
H: 5 11 W: 12 03 b.Lincoln 3-10-78
Source: Trainee.
1995–96 Nottingham F 0 0
1996–97 Nottingham F 0 0
1997–98 Nottingham F 0 0
1998–99 Nottingham F 1 0
1999–2000 Nottingham F 2 0 **3 0**
1999–2000 Stoke C 5 0 **5 0**
2000-01 Brighton & HA 28 1
2001-02 Brighton & HA 10 1
2002-03 Brighton & HA 8 1 **46 3**
2002-03 Hull C 25 0 **25 0**

MUSSELWHITE, Paul (G) 521 0
H: 6 2 W: 14 02 b.Portsmouth 22-12-68
Source: Apprentice.
1987–88 Portsmouth 0 0
1988–89 Scunthorpe U 41 0
1989–90 Scunthorpe U 29 0
1990–91 Scunthorpe U 38 0
1991–92 Scunthorpe U 24 0 **132 0**
1992–93 Port Vale 41 0
1993–94 Port Vale 46 0
1994–95 Port Vale 44 0
1995–96 Port Vale 39 0
1996–97 Port Vale 33 0
1997–98 Port Vale 41 0
1998–99 Port Vale 38 0
1999–2000 Port Vale 30 0 **312 0**
2000-01 Sheffield W 0 0
2000-01 Hull C 37 0
2001-02 Hull C 20 0
2002-03 Hull C 20 0 **77 0**

PEAT, Nathan (M) 1 0
H: 5 9 W: 10 09 b.Hull 19-9-82
Source: Scholar.
2002-03 Hull C 1 0 **1 0**

PETTY, Ben‡ (M) 75 0
H: 6 0 W: 12 05 b.Solihull 22-3-77
Source: Trainee.
1994–95 Aston Villa 0 0
1995–96 Aston Villa 0 0
1996–97 Aston Villa 0 0
1997–98 Aston Villa 0 0
1998–99 Aston Villa 0 0
1998–99 Stoke C 11 0
1999–2000 Stoke C 13 0
2000-01 Stoke C 22 0 **46 0**
2001-02 Hull C 27 0
2002-03 Hull C 2 0 **29 0**

PHILPOTT, Lee* (M) 385 30
H: 5 10 W: 11 08 b.Barnet 21-2-70
Source: Trainee.
1987–88 Peterborough U 1 0
1988–89 Peterborough U 3 0 **4 0**
1989–90 Cambridge U 42 5
1990–91 Cambridge U 45 5
1991–92 Cambridge U 31 5
1992–93 Cambridge U 16 2 **134 17**
1992–93 Leicester C 27 3
1993–94 Leicester C 19 0
1994–95 Leicester C 23 0
1995–96 Leicester C 6 0 **75 3**
1995–96 Blackpool 10 0
1996–97 Blackpool 26 3
1997–98 Blackpool 35 2 **71 5**
1998–99 Lincoln C 24 0
1999–2000 Lincoln C 23 3 **47 3**
2000-01 Hull C 42 1
2001-02 Hull C 11 1
2002-03 Hull C 1 0 **54 2**

PRICE, Mike‡ (D) 4 0
H: 5 8 W: 11 01 b.Wrexham 29-4-82
Source: Trainee. *Honours:* Wales Under-21.
1999–2000 Everton 0 0
2000-01 Everton 0 0
2001-02 Hull C 1 0
2002-03 Hull C 3 0 **4 0**

REGAN, Carl (D) 75 0
H: 6 0 W: 11 03 b.Liverpool 14-1-80
Source: Trainee. *Honours:* England Youth.
1997–98 Everton 0 0

1998–99	Everton	0	0		
1999–2000	Everton	0	0		
2000–01	Barnsley	27	0		
2001–02	Barnsley	10	0		
2002–03	Barnsley	0	0	**37**	**0**
2002–03	Hull C	38	0	**38**	**0**

RUSSELL, Simon§ (M) 1 0
b.Beverley 19-3-85
Source: Scholar.

2002–03	Hull C	1	0	**1**	**0**

SMITH, Shaun (D) 431 42
H: 5 10 W: 11 00 b.Leeds 9-4-71
Source: Trainee.

1988–89	Halifax T	1	0		
1989–90	Halifax T	6	0		
1990–91	Halifax T	0	0	**7**	**0**
1991–92	Crewe Alex	10	0		
1992–93	Crewe Alex	36	4		
1993–94	Crewe Alex	37	7		
1994–95	Crewe Alex	45	8		
1995–96	Crewe Alex	29	1		
1996–97	Crewe Alex	38	4		
1997–98	Crewe Alex	43	6		
1998–99	Crewe Alex	46	4		
1999–2000	Crewe Alex	31	2		
2000–01	Crewe Alex	45	4		
2001–02	Crewe Alex	42	1	**402**	**41**
2002–03	Hull C	22	1	**22**	**1**

STRONG, Greg (D) 151 9
H: 6 2 W: 11 12 b.Bolton 5-9-75
Source: Trainee. *Honours:* England Schools, Youth.

1992–93	Wigan Ath	0	0		
1993–94	Wigan Ath	18	1		
1994–95	Wigan Ath	17	2	**35**	**3**
1995–96	Bolton W	1	0		
1996–97	Bolton W	0	0		
1997–98	Bolton W	0	0		
1997–98	*Blackpool*	11	1	**11**	**1**
1998–99	Bolton W	5	1		
1998–99	*Stoke C*	5	1	**5**	**1**
1999–2000	Bolton W	6	0	**12**	**1**
1999–2000	*Motherwell*	10	0		
2000–01	Motherwell	32	1		
2001–02	Motherwell	32	2	**74**	**3**
2002–03	Hull C	3	0	**3**	**0**
2002–03	*Cheltenham T*	4	0	**4**	**0**
2002–03	*Scunthorpe U*	7	0	**7**	**0**

WEBB, Daniel (F) 63 5
H: 6 0 W: 12 08 b.Poole 2-7-83

2000–01	Southend U	15	1		
2001–02	Southend U	16	2		
2001–02	*Brighton & HA*	12	1		
2002–03	Southend U	0	0	**31**	**3**
2002–03	*Brighton & HA*	3	0	**15**	**1**
2002–03	Hull C	12	0	**12**	**0**
2002–03	*Lincoln C*	5	1	**5**	**1**

WHITTLE, Justin (D) 254 3
H: 6 1 W: 12 12 b.Derby 18-3-71
Source: Celtic.

1994–95	Stoke C	0	0		
1995–96	Stoke C	8	0		
1996–97	Stoke C	37	0		
1997–98	Stoke C	20	0		
1998–99	Stoke C	14	1	**79**	**1**
1998–99	Hull C	24	1		
1999–2000	Hull C	38	0		
2000–01	Hull C	38	0		
2001–02	Hull C	36	0		
2002–03	Hull C	39	1	**175**	**2**

WICKS, Matt‡ (D) 77 3
H: 6 2 W: 13 05 b.Reading 8-9-78
Source: Manchester U Trainee. *Honours:* England Youth.

1995–96	Arsenal	0	0		
1996–97	Arsenal	0	0		
1997–98	Arsenal	0	0		
1998–99	Crewe Alex	6	0	**6**	**0**
1998–99	Peterborough U	11	0		
1999–2000	Peterborough U	20	0		
2000–01	Peterborough U	0	0	**31**	**0**
2000–01	Brighton & HA	24	3		
2001–02	Brighton & HA	2	0	**26**	**3**
2001–02	Hull C	14	0		
2002–03	Hull C	0	0	**14**	**0**

WILLIAMS, Ryan (M) 158 18
H: 5 5 W: 11 04 b.Sutton-in-Ashfield 31-8-78
Source: Trainee. *Honours:* England Youth.

1995–96	Mansfield T	10	3		
1996–97	Mansfield T	16	0	**26**	**3**
1997–98	Tranmere R	0	0		
1998–99	Tranmere R	5	0		
1999–2000	Tranmere R	0	0	**5**	**0**
1999–2000	Chesterfield	30	5		
2000–01	Chesterfield	45	8	**75**	**13**
2001–02	Hull C	29	2		
2002–03	Hull C	23	0	**52**	**2**

Scholars
Benson, Alistair D; Chapman, Liam J; Cooper, Michael JN; Crutwell, Ian G; Harvey, Daniel; Heard, Jamie; Hudson, Christopher J; O'Neill, Edward; Russell, Simon C; Tomlinson, James; Turnbull, Peter E; Wiseman, Scott

Players who do not hold a current contact but their registration has been retained by the club
Johnson, Julian

IPSWICH T

ABIDALLAH, Nabil (M) 2 0
H: 5 7 W: 9 00 b.Amsterdam 5-8-82

2000–01	Ipswich T	2	0		
2001–02	Ipswich T	0	0		
2002–03	Ipswich T	0	0	**2**	**0**

ARMSTRONG, Alun (F) 266 69
H: 6 0 W: 13 08 b.Gateshead 22-2-75
Source: School.

1993–94	Newcastle U	0	0		
1994–95	Stockport Co	45	14		
1995–96	Stockport Co	46	13		
1996–97	Stockport Co	39	9		
1997–98	Stockport Co	29	12	**159**	**48**
1997–98	Middlesbrough	11	7		
1998–99	Middlesbrough	6	1		
1999–2000	Middlesbrough	12	1		
1999–2000	*Huddersfield T*	6	0	**6**	**0**
2000–01	Middlesbrough	0	0	**29**	**9**
2000–01	Ipswich T	21	7		
2001–02	Ipswich T	32	4		
2002–03	Ipswich T	19	1	**72**	**12**

ARTUN, Erdem* (D) 0 0
b.London 11-11-82
Source: Trainee.

1999–2000	Ipswich T	0	0		
2000–01	Ipswich T	0	0		
2001–02	Ipswich T	0	0		
2002–03	Ipswich T	0	0		

BEEVERS, Lee* (D) 1 0
H: 6 1 W: 13 00 b.Doncaster 4-12-83
Source: Scholar.

2000–01	Ipswich T	0	0		
2001–02	Ipswich T	0	0		
2002–03	Ipswich T	0	0		
2002–03	*Boston U*	1	0	**1**	**0**

BENT, Darren (F) 40 13
H: 5 11 W: 11 07 b.Tooting 6-2-84
Source: Scholar. *Honours:* England Youth, Under-21.

2001–02	Ipswich T	5	1		
2002–03	Ipswich T	35	12	**40**	**13**

BENT, Marcus (F) 263 62
H: 6 2 W: 12 04 b.Hammersmith 19-5-78
Source: Trainee. *Honours:* England Under-21.

1995–96	Brentford	12	1		
1996–97	Brentford	34	3		
1997–98	Brentford	24	4	**70**	**8**
1997–98	Crystal Palace	16	5		
1998–99	Crystal Palace	12	0	**28**	**5**
1998–99	Port Vale	15	0		
1999–2000	Port Vale	8	1	**23**	**1**
1999–2000	Sheffield U	32	15		
2000–01	Sheffield U	16	5	**48**	**20**
2000–01	Blackburn R	28	8		
2001–02	Blackburn R	9	0	**37**	**8**
2001–02	Ipswich T	25	9		
2002–03	Ipswich T	32	11	**57**	**20**

BLOOMFIELD, Matt (M) 0 0
H: 5 9 W: 11 00 b.Ipswich 8-2-84
Source: Scholar. *Honours:* England Youth, Under-20.

2001–02	Ipswich T	0	0		
2002–03	Ipswich T	0	0		

BOWDITCH, Dean§ (F) 5 0
H: 5 11 W: 10 08 b.Hertfordshire 15-6-86
Source: Trainee. *Honours:* FA Schools, England Youth.

2002–03	Ipswich T	5	0	**5**	**0**

BRANAGAN, Keith‡ (G) 376 0
H: 6 0 W: 14 00 b.Fulham 10-7-66
Honours: Eire B. 1 full cap.

1983–84	Cambridge U	1	0		
1984–85	Cambridge U	19	0		
1985–86	Cambridge U	9	0		
1986–87	Cambridge U	46	0		
1987–88	Cambridge U	35	0	**110**	**0**
1987–88	Millwall	0	0		
1988–89	Millwall	0	0		
1989–90	Millwall	16	0		
1989–90	*Brentford*	2	0	**2**	**0**
1990–91	Millwall	18	0		
1991–92	Millwall	12	0	**46**	**0**
1991–92	*Gillingham*	1	0	**1**	**0**
1991–92	*Fulham*	0	0		
1992–93	Bolton W	46	0		
1993–94	Bolton W	10	0		
1994–95	Bolton W	43	0		
1995–96	Bolton W	31	0		
1996–97	Bolton W	36	0		
1997–98	Bolton W	34	0		
1998–99	Bolton W	3	0		
1999–2000	Bolton W	11	0	**214**	**0**
1999–2000	Ipswich T	0	0		
2000–01	Ipswich T	2	0		
2001–02	Ipswich T	1	0		
2002–03	Ipswich T	0	0	**3**	**0**

BURTON, Steve‡ (F) 8 0
H: 6 1 W: 13 05 b.Doncaster 9-10-83
Source: Trainee.

2002–03	Ipswich T	0	0		
2002–03	*Boston U*	8	0	**8**	**0**

COLLINS, Aidan‡ (M) 1 0
H: 6 2 W: 11 10 b.Chelmsford 18-10-86

2002–03	Ipswich T	1	0	**1**	**0**

COUNAGO, Pablo (F) 100 22
H: 5 11 W: 11 06 b.Pontevedra 9-8-79

1998–99	Numancia	13	1	**13**	**1**
1998–99	Celta Vigo	1	0		
1999–2000	Huelva	26	4	**26**	**4**
2000–01	Celta Vigo	8	0	**9**	**0**
2001–02	Ipswich T	13	0		
2002–03	Ipswich T	39	17	**52**	**17**

DICKINSON, Robert* (M) 0 0
H: 5 9 W: 10 00 b.Leeds 27-11-83
Source: Scholar.

2000–01	Ipswich T	0	0		
2001–02	Ipswich T	0	0		
2002–03	Ipswich T	0	0		

GAARDSOE, Thomas (D) 103 10
H: 6 2 W: 12 06 b.Denmark 23-11-79

1996–97	Aalborg	1	0		
1997–98	Aalborg	6	1		
1998–99	Aalborg	17	2		
1999–2000	Aalborg	18	2		
2000–01	Aalborg	20	0	**62**	**5**
2001–02	Ipswich T	4	1		
2002–03	Ipswich T	37	4	**41**	**5**

GEORGE, Finidi (F) 282 68
H: 6 0 W: 12 04 b.Port Harcourt 15-4-71
Honours: Nigeria full caps.

1993–94	Ajax	27	4		
1994–95	Ajax	30	8		
1995–96	Ajax	29	6	**86**	**18**
1996–97	Betis	36	10		
1997–98	Betis	34	9		
1998–99	Betis	36	11		
1999–2000	Betis	24	8	**130**	**38**
2000–01	Mallorca	31	5	**31**	**5**
2001–02	Ipswich T	25	6		
2002–03	Ipswich T	10	1	**35**	**7**

HOGG, Chris (D) 0 0
H: 6 0 W: 12 07 b.Middlesbrough 12-3-85
Source: Trainee. *Honours:* England Youth.

2002–03	Ipswich T	0	0		

HOLLAND, Matt (M) 363 56
H: 5 9 W: 12 07 b.Bury 11-4-74
Source: Trainee. *Honours:* Eire 33 full caps, 4 goals.

1992–93	West Ham U	0	0		
1993–94	West Ham U	0	0		
1994–95	West Ham U	0	0		
1994–95	Bournemouth	16	1		
1995–96	Bournemouth	43	10		

1996–97 Bournemouth 45 7 **104 18**
1997–98 Ipswich T 46 10
1998–99 Ipswich T 46 5
1999–2000 Ipswich T 46 10
2000-01 Ipswich T 38 3
2001-02 Ipswich T 38 3
2002-03 Ipswich T 45 7 **259 38**

KARIC, Amir‡ (D) 186 28
H: 5 11 W: 12 08 b.Oramovica Ponja 31-12-73
Honours: Slovenia 46 full caps, 1 goal.
1991–92 Rudar 7 0
1992–93 Rudar 27 10 **34 10**
1993–94 Maribor 20 0
1994–95 Maribor 28 2
1995–96 Maribor 21 4
1996–97 Maribor 25 6
1997 Gamba Osaka 5 0
1998 Gamba Osaka 7 0 **12 0**
1998–99 Maribor 15 3
1999–2000 Maribor 25 3
2000-01 Maribor 3 0 **137 18**
2000-01 Ipswich T 0 0
2000-01 *Crystal Palace* 3 0 **3 0**
2001-02 Ipswich T 0 0
2002-03 Ipswich T 0 0

KELLY, Darren‡ (G) 0 0
b.Dublin 30-5-84
Source: Scholar.
2001-02 Ipswich T 0 0
2002-03 Ipswich T 0 0

LE PEN, Ulrich (M) 81 1
H: 5 7 W: 9 09 b.Auray 21-1-74
1994–95 Rennes 20 1
1995–96 Rennes 31 0
1996–97 Rennes 17 0 **68 1**
From Laval
2001-02 Lorient 12 0 **12 0**
2001-02 Ipswich T 1 0
2002-03 Ipswich T 0 0 **1 0**

MAGILTON, Jim# (M) 461 59
H: 6 0 W: 13 10 b.Belfast 6-5-69
Source: Apprentice. *Honours:* Northern Ireland Schools, Youth, Under-21, Under-23, 52 full caps, 5 goals. Football League.
1986–87 Liverpool 0 0
1987–88 Liverpool 0 0
1988–89 Liverpool 0 0
1989–90 Liverpool 0 0
1990–91 Liverpool 0 0
1990–91 Oxford U 37 6
1991–92 Oxford U 44 12
1992–93 Oxford U 40 11
1993–94 Oxford U 29 5 **150 34**
1993–94 Southampton 15 0
1994–95 Southampton 42 6
1995–96 Southampton 31 3
1996–97 Southampton 37 4
1997–98 Southampton 5 0 **130 13**
1997–98 Sheffield W 21 1
1998–99 Sheffield W 6 0 **27 1**
1998–99 Ipswich T 19 3
1999–2000 Ipswich T 38 4
2000-01 Ipswich T 33 1
2001-02 Ipswich T 24 0
2002-03 Ipswich T 40 3 **154 11**

MAKIN, Chris (D) 331 7
H: 5 10 W: 11 02 b.Manchester 8-5-73
Source: Trainee. *Honours:* England Schools, Under-21.
1991–92 Oldham Ath 0 0
1992–93 Oldham Ath 0 0
1992–93 *Wigan Ath* 15 2 **15 2**
1993–94 Oldham Ath 27 1
1994–95 Oldham Ath 28 1
1995–96 Oldham Ath 39 2 **94 4**
1996–97 Marseille 29 0 **29 0**
1997–98 Sunderland 25 0
1998–99 Sunderland 38 0
1999–2000 Sunderland 34 1
2000-01 Sunderland 23 0 **120 1**
2000-01 Ipswich T 10 0
2001-02 Ipswich T 30 0
2002-03 Ipswich T 33 0 **73 0**

MARSHALL, Andy (G) 264 0
H: 6 2 W: 13 07 b.Bury 14-4-75
Source: Trainee. *Honours:* England Under-21.
1993–94 Norwich C 0 0
1994–95 Norwich C 21 0
1995–96 Norwich C 3 0
1996–97 Norwich C 7 0
1996–97 *Bournemouth* 11 0 **11 0**
1996–97 *Gillingham* 5 0 **5 0**
1997–98 Norwich C 42 0
1998–99 Norwich C 37 0
1999–2000 Norwich C 44 0
2000-01 Norwich C 41 0 **195 0**
2001-02 Ipswich T 13 0
2002-03 Ipswich T 40 0 **53 0**

McGREAL, John (D) 300 4
H: 5 11 W: 13 00 b.Birkenhead 2-6-72
Source: Trainee.
1990–91 Tranmere R 3 0
1991–92 Tranmere R 0 0
1992–93 Tranmere R 0 0
1993–94 Tranmere R 15 1
1994–95 Tranmere R 43 0
1995–96 Tranmere R 32 0
1996–97 Tranmere R 24 0
1997–98 Tranmere R 42 0
1998–99 Tranmere R 36 0 **195 1**
1999–2000 Ipswich T 34 0
2000-01 Ipswich T 28 1
2001-02 Ipswich T 27 1
2002-03 Ipswich T 16 1 **105 3**

MILLER, Tommy (M) 175 41
H: 6 1 W: 11 12 b.Easington 8-1-79
Source: Trainee.
1997–98 Hartlepool U 13 1
1998–99 Hartlepool U 34 4
1999–2000 Hartlepool U 44 14
2000-01 Hartlepool U 46 16
2001-02 Hartlepool U 0 0 **137 35**
2001-02 Ipswich T 8 0
2002-03 Ipswich T 30 6 **38 6**

MORROW, Sam (F) 0 0
H: 6 0 W: 12 10 b.Derry 3-3-85
Source: Trainee.
2002-03 Ipswich T 0 0

MURRAY, Antonio§ (M) 1 0
b.Cambridge 15-9-84
Source: Scholar.
2002-03 Ipswich T 1 0 **1 0**

NAYLOR, Richard# (F) 153 23
H: 6 1 W: 13 07 b.Leeds 28-2-77
Source: Trainee.
1995–96 Ipswich T 0 0
1996–97 Ipswich T 27 4
1997–98 Ipswich T 5 2
1998–99 Ipswich T 30 5
1999–2000 Ipswich T 36 8
2000-01 Ipswich T 13 1
2001-02 Ipswich T 14 1
2001-02 *Millwall* 3 0 **3 0**
2001-02 *Barnsley* 8 0 **8 0**
2002-03 Ipswich T 17 2 **142 23**

PRICE, Lewis (G) 0 0
H: 6 3 W: 13 06 b.Bournemouth 19-7-84
Source: Academy.
2002-03 Ipswich T 0 0

PULLEN, James (G) 17 0
H: 6 2 W: 14 00 b.Chelmsford 18-3-82
Source: Heybridge S.
1999–2000 Ipswich T 0 0
2000-01 Ipswich T 0 0
2001-02 Ipswich T 0 0
2001-02 *Blackpool* 16 0 **16 0**
2002-03 Ipswich T 1 0 **1 0**

REUSER, Martijn (M) 172 31
H: 5 7 W: 12 10 b.Amsterdam 1-2-75
Honours: Holland 1 full cap.
1993–94 Ajax 2 0
1994–95 Ajax 2 0
1995–96 Ajax 18 3
1996–97 Ajax 19 3
1997–98 Ajax 1 0 **42 6**
1997–98 Vitesse 24 6
1998–99 Vitesse 32 8 **56 14**
1999–2000 Ipswich T 8 2
2000-01 Ipswich T 26 6
2001-02 Ipswich T 24 1
2002-03 Ipswich T 16 2 **74 11**

RICHARDS, Matthew (D) 13 0
H: 5 8 W: 10 10 b.Harlow 26-12-84
Source: Scholar.
2001-02 Ipswich T 0 0
2002-03 Ipswich T 13 0 **13 0**

VENUS, Mark* (D) 500 24
H: 6 0 W: 13 02 b.Hartlepool 6-4-67
1984–85 Hartlepool U 4 0 **4 0**
1985–86 Leicester C 1 0
1986–87 Leicester C 39 0
1987–88 Leicester C 21 1 **61 1**
1987–88 Wolverhampton W 4 0
1988–89 Wolverhampton W 35 0
1989–90 Wolverhampton W 44 2
1990–91 Wolverhampton W 6 0
1991–92 Wolverhampton W 46 1
1992–93 Wolverhampton W 12 0
1993–94 Wolverhampton W 39 1
1994–95 Wolverhampton W 39 3
1995–96 Wolverhampton W 22 0
1996–97 Wolverhampton W 40 0 **287 7**
1997–98 Ipswich T 14 1
1998–99 Ipswich T 44 9
1999–2000 Ipswich T 28 2
2000-01 Ipswich T 25 3
2001-02 Ipswich T 29 1
2002-03 Ipswich T 8 0 **148 16**

WESTLAKE, Ian (M) 4 0
H: 5 11 W: 11 00 b.Clacton 10-11-83
Source: Scholar.
2002-03 Ipswich T 4 0 **4 0**

WILNIS, Fabian# (D) 372 9
H: 5 8 W: 12 06 b.Paramaribo 23-8-70
Source: Het Noorden, NOC, De Zwervers, Sparta.
1990–91 NAC 7 3
1991–92 NAC 30 0
1992–93 NAC 32 0
1993–94 NAC 34 0
1994–95 NAC 31 0 **134 3**
1995–96 De Graafschap 32 0
1996–97 De Graafschap 23 0
1997–98 De Graafschap 33 1
1998–99 De Graafschap 19 0 **107 1**
1998–99 Ipswich T 18 1
1999–2000 Ipswich T 35 0
2000-01 Ipswich T 29 2
2001-02 Ipswich T 14 0
2002-03 Ipswich T 35 2 **131 5**

WRIGHT, Jermaine (M) 221 10
H: 5 10 W: 12 07 b.Greenwich 21-10-75
Source: Trainee. *Honours:* England Youth.
1992–93 Millwall 0 0
1993–94 Millwall 0 0
1994–95 Millwall 0 0
1994–95 Wolverhampton W 6 0
1995–96 Wolverhampton W 7 0
1995–96 *Doncaster R* 13 0 **13 0**
1996–97 Wolverhampton W 3 0
1997–98 Wolverhampton W 4 0 **20 0**
1997–98 Crewe Alex 5 0
1998–99 Crewe Alex 44 5 **49 5**
1999–2000 Ipswich T 34 1
2000-01 Ipswich T 37 2
2001-02 Ipswich T 29 1
2002-03 Ipswich T 39 1 **139 5**

Scholars
Barron, Scott; Boardley, Stuart J; Bowditch, Dean P; Chaffey, Lee; Flack, Daniel; Hill, Victor; Manning, Liam; Mitchell, Scott A; Murray, Antonio J; Nash, Gerard T; O'Connor, Gerard; Okay, Erkan; Peat, Scott M; Reid, Craig K; Robinson, Matthew A; Smith, Marc A; Sobolewski, Henry

KIDDERMINSTER H

AYRES, Lee (D) 35 2
H: 6 2 W: 12 06 b.Birmingham 28-8-82
2001-02 Kidderminster H 6 0
2002-03 Kidderminster H 29 2 **35 2**

BENNETT, Dean (M) 117 13
H: 6 0 W: 12 00 b.Wolverhampton 13-12-77
1996–97 WBA 1 0
1997–98 WBA 0 0 **1 0**
From Bromsgrove R
2000-01 Kidderminster H 42 4
2001-02 Kidderminster H 42 8
2002-03 Kidderminster H 32 1 **116 13**

BLAKE, Mark‡ (M) 266 24
H: 5 11 W: 13 05 b.Nottingham 16-12-70
Source: Trainee. *Honours:* England Schools, Youth, Under-21.
1989–90 Aston Villa 9 0
1990–91 Aston Villa 7 0
1990–91 *Wolverhampton W* 2 0 **2 0**
1991–92 Aston Villa 14 2

1992–93 Aston Villa 1 0 **31 2**
1993–94 Portsmouth 15 0 **15 0**
1993–94 Leicester C 11 1
1994–95 Leicester C 30 3
1995–96 Leicester C 8 0 **49 4**
1996–97 Walsall 38 4
1997–98 Walsall 23 1 **61 5**
1999–2000 Mansfield T 43 1
2000-01 Mansfield T 41 8 **84 9**
2001-02 Kidderminster H 24 4
2002-03 Kidderminster H 0 0 **24 4**

BROCK, Stuart (G) 98 0
H: 6 1 W: 14 00 b.Sandwell 26-9-76
Source: Trainee.
1994–95 Aston Villa 0 0
1995–96 Aston Villa 0 0
1996–97 Aston Villa 0 0
1996–97 Northampton T 0 0
1997–98 Northampton T 0 0
1998–99 Northampton T 0 0
1999–2000 Northampton T 0 0
2000-01 Kidderminster H 21 0
2001-02 Kidderminster H 42 0
2002-03 Kidderminster H 35 0 **98 0**

BROUGHTON, Drewe (F) 143 28
H: 6 3 W: 14 00 b.Hitchin 25-10-78
Source: Trainee.
1996–97 Norwich C 8 1
1997–98 Norwich C 1 0
1997–98 *Wigan Ath* 4 0 **4 0**
1998–99 Norwich C 0 0 **9 1**
1998–99 Brentford 1 0 **1 0**
1998–99 Peterborough U 25 7
1999–2000 Peterborough U 10 1
2000-01 Peterborough U 0 0 **35 8**
2000-01 Kidderminster H 19 7
2001-02 Kidderminster H 38 8
2002-03 Kidderminster H 37 4 **94 19**

CORBETT, Andy‡ (F) 8 0
H: 6 0 W: 11 07 b.Worcester 20-2-82
2000-01 Kidderminster H 6 0
2001-02 Kidderminster H 2 0
2002-03 Kidderminster H 0 0 **8 0**

DANBY, John (G) 2 0
H: 6 2 W: 14 06 b.Stoke 20-9-83
2001-02 Kidderminster H 2 0
2002-03 Kidderminster H 0 0 **2 0**

DIGBY, Fraser‡ (G) 506 0
H: 6 1 W: 12 12 b.Sheffield 23-4-67
Source: Apprentice. *Honours:* England Schools, Youth, Under-21.
1984–85 Manchester U 0 0
1985–86 Manchester U 0 0
1985–86 *Oldham Ath* 0 0
1985–86 *Swindon T* 0 0
1986–87 Manchester U 0 0
1986–87 Swindon T 39 0
1987–88 Swindon T 31 0
1988–89 Swindon T 46 0
1989–90 Swindon T 45 0
1990–91 Swindon T 41 0
1991–92 Swindon T 21 0
1992–93 Swindon T 33 0
1992–93 *Manchester U* 0 0
1993–94 Swindon T 28 0
1994–95 Swindon T 39 0
1995–96 Swindon T 25 0
1996–97 Swindon T 31 0
1997–98 Swindon T 38 0 **417 0**
1998–99 Crystal Palace 18 0
1999–2000 Crystal Palace 38 0
2000-01 Crystal Palace 0 0 **56 0**
2001-02 Huddersfield T 0 0
2001-02 QPR 19 0
2002-03 QPR 3 0 **22 0**
2002-03 Kidderminster H 11 0 **11 0**

DOYLE, Daire‡ (M) 21 0
H: 5 11 W: 11 13 b.Dublin 18-10-80
Source: Cherry Orchard.
1998–99 Coventry C 0 0
1999–2000 Coventry C 0 0
2000-01 Coventry C 0 0
2000-01 Kidderminster H 15 0
2001-02 Kidderminster H 1 0
2002-03 Kidderminster H 5 0 **21 0**

DUCROS, Andy‡ (M) 58 4
H: 5 7 W: 10 06 b.Evesham 16-9-77
Source: Trainee. *Honours:* England Schools, Youth.
1994–95 Coventry C 0 0
1995–96 Coventry C 0 0
1996–97 Coventry C 5 0
1997–98 Coventry C 3 0
1998–99 Coventry C 0 0 **8 0**
From Nuneaton B
2000-01 Kidderminster H 34 2
2001-02 Kidderminster H 14 2
2002-03 Kidderminster H 2 0 **50 4**

FLYNN, Sean (M) 381 28
H: 5 8 W: 11 09 b.Birmingham 13-3-68
Source: Halesowen T.
1991–92 Coventry C 22 2
1992–93 Coventry C 7 0
1993–94 Coventry C 36 3
1994–95 Coventry C 32 4 **97 9**
1995–96 Derby Co 42 2
1996–97 Derby Co 17 1 **59 3**
1996–97 *Stoke C* 5 0 **5 0**
1997–98 WBA 35 2
1998–99 WBA 38 2
1999–2000 WBA 36 4 **109 8**
2000-01 Tranmere R 35 1
2001-02 Tranmere R 31 5 **66 6**
2002-03 Kidderminster H 45 2 **45 2**

FOSTER, Ian* (F) 91 11
H: 5 7 W: 11 00 b.Merseyside 11-11-76
Source: Liverpool Schoolboy. *Honours:* England Schools.
1996–97 Hereford U 19 0 **19 0**
From Barrow
2000-01 Kidderminster H 10 2
2001-02 Kidderminster H 33 8
2002-03 Kidderminster H 29 1 **72 11**

HEATH, Nick† (M) 1 0
H: 5 9 W: 11 00 b.Sutton Coldfield 2-1-85
2002-03 Kidderminster H 1 0 **1 0**

HENRIKSEN, Bo (F) 178 62
H: 5 10 W: 11 00 b.Roskilde 7-2-75
1995–96 Odense 10 3
1996–97 Odense 23 8 **33 11**
1997–98 Aarhus 0 0
1997–98 Herfolge 15 6
1998–99 Herfolge 23 6
1999–2000 Herfolge 10 1
2000-01 Herfolge 21 1
2000-01 *Frem* 4 3 **4 3**
2001-02 Herfolge 10 6 **79 20**
2001-02 Kidderminster H 25 8
2002-03 Kidderminster H 37 20 **62 28**

HINTON, Craig (D) 131 2
H: 6 0 W: 12 06 b.Wolverhampton 26-11-77
Source: Trainee.
1996–97 Birmingham C 0 0
1997–98 Birmingham C 0 0
2000-01 Kidderminster H 46 2
2001-02 Kidderminster H 41 0
2002-03 Kidderminster H 44 0 **131 2**

JOY, Ian‡ (D) 47 2
H: 5 8 W: 11 00 b.San Diego 14-7-81
Source: Trainee.
1998–99 Tranmere R 0 0
1999–2000 Tranmere R 0 0
2000-01 Montrose 25 2 **25 2**
2001-02 Kidderminster H 16 0
2002-03 Kidderminster H 6 0 **22 0**

KHELA, Inderpaul† (M) 1 0
H: 6 0 W: 12 06 b.Coventry 6-10-83
2002-03 Kidderminster H 1 0 **1 0**

LEWIS, Matt (F) 4 0
H: 6 2 W: 12 02 b.Coventry 20-3-84
Source: Marconi.
2001-02 Kidderminster H 2 0
2002-03 Kidderminster H 2 0 **4 0**

McAULEY, Hugh‡ (M) 104 9
H: 5 10 W: 11 08 b.Plymouth 13-5-77
Source: Leek T.
1999–2000 Cheltenham T 39 4
2000-01 Cheltenham T 35 3
2001-02 Cheltenham T 7 0
2002-03 Cheltenham T 19 2 **100 9**
2002-03 Kidderminster H 4 0 **4 0**

MORTIMER, Alex‡ (M) 1 0
H: 5 10 W: 10 06 b.Manchester 28-11-82
Source: Trainee.
1999–2000 Leicester C 0 0
2000-01 Leicester C 0 0
2001-02 Leicester C 0 0
2002-03 Leicester C 0 0
2002-03 Shrewsbury T 1 0 **1 0**
2002-03 Kidderminster H 0 0

PARRISH, Sean (M) 262 37
H: 5 10 W: 12 00 b.Wrexham 14-3-72
Source: Trainee.
1989–90 Shrewsbury T 2 0
1990–91 Shrewsbury T 1 0 **3 0**
From Telford U
1994–95 Doncaster R 25 3
1995–96 Doncaster R 41 5 **66 8**
1996–97 Northampton T 39 8
1997–98 Northampton T 12 1
1998–99 Northampton T 33 1
1999–2000 Northampton T 25 3 **109 13**
2000-01 Chesterfield 35 10
2001-02 Chesterfield 20 1 **55 11**
2002-03 Kidderminster H 29 5 **29 5**

SALL, Abdou‡ (D) 32 2
H: 6 3 W: 12 13 b.Senegal 1-11-80
Source: Toulouse.
2001-02 Kidderminster H 27 2
2002-03 Kidderminster H 4 0 **31 2**
2002-03 *Oxford U* 1 0 **1 0**

SCOTT, Dion (D) 21 1
H: 5 11 W: 11 00 b.Bearwood 24-12-80
Source: Trainee.
1999–2000 Walsall 0 0
2000-01 Walsall 1 0
2001-02 Walsall 1 0 **2 0**
2002-03 Mansfield T 0 0
2002-03 Kidderminster H 19 1 **19 1**

SHILTON, Sam# (M) 129 12
H: 5 11 W: 13 00 b.Nottingham 21-7-78
Source: School.
1994–95 Plymouth Arg 2 0
1995–96 Plymouth Arg 1 0 **3 0**
1995–96 Coventry C 0 0
1996–97 Coventry C 0 0
1997–98 Coventry C 2 0
1998–99 Coventry C 5 0
1999–2000 Coventry C 0 0 **7 0**
1999–2000 Hartlepool U 21 3
2000-01 Hartlepool U 33 4 **54 7**
2001-02 Kidderminster H 24 0
2002-03 Kidderminster H 41 5 **65 5**

SMITH, Adie (D) 100 8
H: 5 10 W: 12 02 b.Birmingham 11-8-73
Source: Bromsgrove R.
2000-01 Kidderminster H 34 5
2001-02 Kidderminster H 36 2
2002-03 Kidderminster H 30 1 **100 8**

STAMPS, Scott (D) 236 6
H: 5 10 W: 12 03 b.Edgbaston 20-3-75
Source: Trainee.
1992–93 Torquay U 2 0
1993–94 Torquay U 6 0
1994–95 Torquay U 25 1
1995–96 Torquay U 23 1
1996–97 Torquay U 30 3 **86 5**
1996–97 Colchester U 8 0
1997–98 Colchester U 27 1
1998–99 Colchester U 21 0 **56 1**
2000-01 Kidderminster H 34 0
2001-02 Kidderminster H 37 0
2002-03 Kidderminster H 23 0 **94 0**

WILLIAMS, Danny (M) 122 6
H: 6 1 W: 13 06 b.Wrexham 12-7-79
Source: Trainee. *Honours:* Wales Under-21.
1996–97 Liverpool 0 0
1997–98 Liverpool 0 0
1998–99 Liverpool 0 0
1998–99 Wrexham 0 0
1999–2000 Wrexham 24 1
2000-01 Wrexham 15 2 **39 3**
2001-02 Kidderminster H 38 1
2002-03 Kidderminster H 45 2 **83 3**

Non-Contract
Heath, Nicholas A; Khela, Inderpaul

LEEDS U

ALLAWAY, Shaun (G) 0 0
H: 6 2 W: 13 00 b.Reading 16-2-83
Source: Trainee. *Honours:* England Youth, Under-20.
1999–2000 Reading 0 0
1999–2000 Leeds U 0 0
2000-01 Leeds U 0 0
2001-02 Leeds U 0 0
2002-03 *Grimsby T* 0 0
2002-03 Leeds U 0 0

ARMSTRONG, Chris (F) 0 0
H: 6 1 W: 13 07 b.Durham 8-11-84
Source: Scholar.
2001-02 Leeds U 0 0
2002-03 Leeds U 0 0

BAKKE, Eirik (M) 195 24
H: 6 2 W: 12 09 b.Sogndal 13-9-77
Honours: Norway 25 full caps.
1994 Sogndal 5 0
1995 Sogndal 0 0
1996 Sogndal 19 8
1997 Sogndal 25 4
1998 Sogndal 19 2
1999 Sogndal 8 3 **76 17**
1999–2000 Leeds U 29 2
2000-01 Leeds U 29 2
2001-02 Leeds U 27 2
2002-03 Leeds U 34 1 **119 7**

BARMBY, Nick (M) 296 52
H: 5 7 W: 10 08 b.Hull 11-2-74
Source: Trainee. *Honours:* England Schools, Youth, Under-21, B, 23 full caps, 4 goals.
1991–92 Tottenham H 0 0
1992–93 Tottenham H 22 6
1993–94 Tottenham H 27 5
1994–95 Tottenham H 38 9 **87 20**
1995–96 Middlesbrough 32 7
1996–97 Middlesbrough 10 1 **42 8**
1996–97 Everton 25 4
1997–98 Everton 30 2
1998–99 Everton 24 3
1999–2000 Everton 37 9 **116 18**
2000-01 Liverpool 26 2
2001-02 Liverpool 6 0 **32 2**
2002-03 Leeds U 19 4 **19 4**

BATTY, David (M) 426 8
H: 5 8 W: 12 12 b.Leeds 2-12-68
Source: Trainee. *Honours:* England Under-21, B, 42 full caps.
1987–88 Leeds U 23 1
1988–89 Leeds U 30 0
1989–90 Leeds U 42 0
1990–91 Leeds U 37 0
1991–92 Leeds U 40 2
1992–93 Leeds U 30 1
1993–94 Leeds U 9 0
1993–94 Blackburn R 26 0
1994–95 Blackburn R 5 0
1995–96 Blackburn R 23 1 **54 1**
1995–96 Newcastle U 11 1
1996–97 Newcastle U 32 1
1997–98 Newcastle U 32 1
1998–99 Newcastle U 8 0 **83 3**
1998–99 Leeds U 10 0
1999–2000 Leeds U 16 0
2000-01 Leeds U 16 0
2001-02 Leeds U 36 0
2002-03 Leeds U 0 0 **289 4**

BRAVO, Raul (D) 47 3
H: 5 9 W: 12 06 b.Valencia 14-4-81
Honours: Spain 7 full caps.
2001-02 Real Madrid B 34 2 **34 2**
2001-02 Real Madrid 6 0
2002-03 Real Madrid 2 1 **8 1**
2002-03 Leeds U 5 0 **5 0**

BREEN, Gerard‡ (M) 0 0
H: 5 9 W: 13 07 b.County Louth 29-3-84
Source: Scholar.
2000-01 Leeds U 0 0
2001-02 Leeds U 0 0
2002-03 Leeds U 0 0

BRIDGES, Michael (F) 125 35
H: 6 1 W: 12 06 b.North Shields 5-8-78
Source: Trainee. *Honours:* England Schools, Youth, Under-21.
1995–96 Sunderland 15 4
1996–97 Sunderland 25 3
1997–98 Sunderland 9 1
1998–99 Sunderland 30 8 **79 16**
1999–2000 Leeds U 34 19
2000-01 Leeds U 7 0
2001-02 Leeds U 0 0
2002-03 Leeds U 5 0 **46 19**

BURNS, Jacob* (M) 88 8
H: 5 10 W: 12 02 b.Sydney 21-4-78
Honours: Australia Under-23, 2 full caps.
1996–97 Sydney U 5 0
1997–98 Sydney U 25 2
1998–99 Sydney U 27 3 **57 5**
1999–2000 Parramatta Power 25 3 **25 3**
2000-01 Leeds U 4 0
2001-02 Leeds U 0 0
2002-03 Leeds U 2 0 **6 0**

BYRNE, Luke (M) 0 0
H: 5 6 W: 9 06 b.Castle Bar 2-9-85
Source: Scholar.
2002-03 Leeds U 0 0

CANSDELL-SHERIFF, Shane (D) 3 0
H: 5 11 W: 11 08 b.Sydney 10-11-82
Source: NSW Academy. *Honours:* Australia Youth, Under-23.
1999–2000 Leeds U 0 0
2000-01 Leeds U 0 0
2001-02 Leeds U 0 0
2002-03 Leeds U 0 0
2002-03 *Rochdale* 3 0 **3 0**

CARSON, Scott (G) 0 0
H: 6 3 W: 13 07 b.Whitehaven 3-9-85
Source: Scholar. *Honours:* England Youth.
2002-03 Leeds U 0 0

CONSTABLE, Robert (D) 0 0
H: 5 9 W: 12 00 b.Pontefract 26-1-86
Source: Trainee.
2002-03 Leeds U 0 0

CORR, Barry (F) 0 0
H: 6 3 W: 12 01 b.Co Wicklow 2-4-85
Source: Scholar.
2001-02 Leeds U 0 0
2002-03 Leeds U 0 0

COUSINS, Andrew (M) 0 0
H: 5 8 W: 10 12 b.Dublin 30-1-85
Source: Scholar.
2001-02 Leeds U 0 0
2002-03 Leeds U 0 0

COYLES, William (G) 0 0
H: 6 0 W: 12 01 b.Co Antrim 20-12-84
Source: Scholar.
2001-02 Leeds U 0 0
2002-03 Leeds U 0 0

CRONIN, Kevin (D) 0 0
H: 5 11 W: 11 13 b.Dublin 18-5-85
Source: Scholar.
2001-02 Leeds U 0 0
2002-03 Leeds U 0 0

DACOURT, Olivier (M) 240 11
H: 5 10 W: 11 07 b.Montreuil 25-9-74
Honours: France 9 full caps.
1992–93 Strasbourg 6 0
1993–94 Strasbourg 8 0
1994–95 Strasbourg 18 0
1995–96 Strasbourg 34 0
1996–97 Strasbourg 31 1
1997–98 Strasbourg 30 3 **127 4**
1998–99 Everton 30 2 **30 2**
1999–2000 Lens 26 2 **26 2**
2000-01 Leeds U 33 3
2001-02 Leeds U 17 0
2002-03 Leeds U 7 0 **57 3**

DUBERRY, Michael (D) 128 2
H: 6 1 W: 14 07 b.Enfield 14-10-75
Source: Trainee. *Honours:* England Under-21.
1993–94 Chelsea 1 0
1994–95 Chelsea 0 0
1995–96 Chelsea 22 0
1995–96 *Bournemouth* 7 0 **7 0**
1996–97 Chelsea 15 1
1997–98 Chelsea 23 0
1998–99 Chelsea 25 0 **86 1**
1999–2000 Leeds U 13 1
2000-01 Leeds U 5 0
2001-02 Leeds U 3 0
2002-03 Leeds U 14 0 **35 1**

EDWARDS, Stewart (D) 0 0
H: 5 11 W: 11 06 b.Swansea 1-10-84
Source: Scholar.
2001-02 Leeds U 0 0
2002-03 Leeds U 0 0

FARREN, Larry (D) 0 0
H: 6 0 W: 12 02 b.Donegal 29-7-83
Source: Scholar.
2000-01 Leeds U 0 0
2001-02 Leeds U 0 0
2002-03 Leeds U 0 0

FERGUSON, Steven‡ (M) 0 0
H: 5 7 W: 11 03 b.Newry 25-2-83
Source: St Andrew's.
1999–2000 Leeds U 0 0
2000-01 Leeds U 0 0
2001-02 Leeds U 0 0
2002-03 Leeds U 0 0

GRAY, Nicholas (M) 0 0
H: 6 0 W: 9 6 b.Harrogate 17-10-85
Source: Trainee.
2002-03 Leeds U 0 0

HARTE, Ian (D) 190 27
H: 5 11 W: 12 09 b.Drogheda 31-8-77
Source: Trainee. *Honours:* Eire 49 full caps, 8 goals.
1995–96 Leeds U 4 0
1996–97 Leeds U 14 2
1997–98 Leeds U 12 0
1998–99 Leeds U 35 4
1999–2000 Leeds U 33 6
2000-01 Leeds U 29 7
2001-02 Leeds U 36 5
2002-03 Leeds U 27 3 **190 27**

JOHNSON, Seth (M) 189 9
H: 5 10 W: 12 05 b.Birmingham 12-3-79
Source: Trainee. *Honours:* England Youth, Under-21, 1 full cap.
1996–97 Crewe Alex 11 1
1997–98 Crewe Alex 40 1
1998–99 Crewe Alex 42 4 **93 6**
1999–2000 Derby Co 36 1
2000-01 Derby Co 30 1
2001-02 Derby Co 7 0 **73 2**
2001-02 Leeds U 14 0
2002-03 Leeds U 9 1 **23 1**

JOHNSON, Simon (F) 16 2
H: 5 9 W: 11 09 b.West Bromwich 9-3-83
Source: Scholar. *Honours:* England Youth, Under-20.
2000-01 Leeds U 0 0
2001-02 Leeds U 0 0
2002-03 Leeds U 4 0 **4 0**
2002-03 *Hull C* 12 2 **12 2**

JONES, Christopher (M) 0 0
H: 5 6 W: 8 3 b.Bangor 9-10-85
Source: Trainee.
2002-03 Leeds U 0 0

KEEGAN, Paul (M) 0 0
H: 5 10 W: 11 07 b.Dublin 5-7-84
Source: Scholar.
2000-01 Leeds U 0 0
2001-02 Leeds U 0 0
2002-03 Leeds U 0 0

KELLY, Gary (D) 290 2
H: 5 10 W: 11 05 b.Drogheda 9-7-74
Source: Home Farm. *Honours:* Eire Youth, 52 full caps, 2 goals.
1991–92 Leeds U 2 0
1992–93 Leeds U 0 0
1993–94 Leeds U 42 0
1994–95 Leeds U 42 0
1995–96 Leeds U 34 0
1996–97 Leeds U 36 2
1997–98 Leeds U 34 0
1998–99 Leeds U 0 0
1999–2000 Leeds U 31 0
2000-01 Leeds U 24 0
2001-02 Leeds U 20 0
2002-03 Leeds U 25 0 **290 2**

KEWELL, Harry (F) 181 45
H: 5 11 W: 13 00 b.Sydney 22-9-78
Source: NSW Soccer Academy. *Honours:* Australia Youth, Under-20, 13 full caps, 4 goals.
1995–96 Leeds U 2 0
1996–97 Leeds U 1 0
1997–98 Leeds U 29 5
1998–99 Leeds U 38 6
1999–2000 Leeds U 36 10
2000-01 Leeds U 17 2
2001-02 Leeds U 27 8
2002-03 Leeds U 31 14 **181 45**

KEYES, Edward (D) 0 0
H: 5 9 W: 10 05 b.Dublin 2-5-85
Source: Scholar.
2001-02 Leeds U 0 0
2002-03 Leeds U 0 0

KILGALLON, Matthew (D) 2 0
H: 6 1 W: 12 13 b.York 8-1-84
Source: Scholar. *Honours:* England Youth.
2000-01 Leeds U 0 0
2001-02 Leeds U 0 0
2002-03 Leeds U 2 0 **2 0**

KINSELLA, Alan‡ (F) **0 0**
H: 5 8 W: 11 06 b.Dublin 2-2-84
Source: Scholar.
2000-01 Leeds U 0 0
2001-02 Leeds U 0 0
2002-03 Leeds U 0 0

KRIEF, Domonique (M) **0 0**
H: 5 9 W: 10 07 b.Leeds 15-9-83
Source: Scholar.
2000-01 Leeds U 0 0
2001-02 Leeds U 0 0
2002-03 Leeds U 0 0

LAVERY, Sean‡ (M) **0 0**
H: 5 7 W: 11 05 b.Lurgan 16-11-83
Source: Scholar.
2000-01 Leeds U 0 0
2001-02 Leeds U 0 0
2002-03 Leeds U 0 0

LEISTER, Brenton (D) **0 0**
H: 5 11 W: 11 13 b.Leeds 3-9-85
Source: Scholar.
2002-03 Leeds U 0 0

LUCIC, Teddy (D) **273 20**
H: 6 1 W: 11 08 b.Gothenburg 15-4-73
Honours: Sweden 52 full caps.
1989 Lundby 1 0
1990 Lundby 18 3
1991 Lundby 22 3
1992 Lundby 22 7 **63 13**
1993 Vastra Frolunda 17 0
1994 Vastra Frolunda 25 0
1995 Vastra Frolunda 26 0 **68 0**
1996 IFK Gothenburg 24 0
1997 IFK Gothenburg 11 2
1998 IFK Gothenburg 23 0 **58 2**
1998–99 Bologna 8 0
1999–2000 Bologna 1 0 **9 0**
2000 AIK Stockholm 22 3
2001 AIK Stockholm 20 0
2002 AIK Stockholm 16 1 **58 4**
2002-03 Leeds U 17 1 **17 1**

MARTYN, Nigel (G) **580 0**
H: 6 1 W: 14 09 b.St Austell 11-8-66
Source: St Blazey. *Honours:* England Under-21, B, 23 full caps.
1987–88 Bristol R 39 0
1988–89 Bristol R 46 0
1989–90 Bristol R 16 0 **101 0**
1989–90 Crystal Palace 25 0
1990–91 Crystal Palace 38 0
1991–92 Crystal Palace 38 0
1992–93 Crystal Palace 42 0
1993–94 Crystal Palace 46 0
1994–95 Crystal Palace 37 0
1995–96 Crystal Palace 46 0 **272 0**
1996–97 Leeds U 37 0
1997–98 Leeds U 37 0
1998–99 Leeds U 34 0
1999–2000 Leeds U 38 0
2000-01 Leeds U 23 0
2001-02 Leeds U 38 0
2002-03 Leeds U 0 0 **207 0**

MATTEO, Dominic (D) **210 1**
H: 6 1 W: 13 04 b.Dumfries 28-4-74
Source: Trainee. *Honours:* England Youth, Under-21, B, Scotland 6 full caps.
1992–93 Liverpool 0 0
1993–94 Liverpool 11 0
1994–95 Liverpool 7 0
1994–95 *Sunderland* 1 0 **1 0**
1995–96 Liverpool 5 0
1996–97 Liverpool 26 0
1997–98 Liverpool 26 0
1998–99 Liverpool 20 1
1999–2000 Liverpool 32 0
2000-01 Liverpool 0 0 **127 1**
2000-01 Leeds U 30 0
2001-02 Leeds U 32 0
2002-03 Leeds U 20 0 **82 0**

McDAID, Sean (D) **0 0**
H: 5 6 W: 9 8 b.Harrogate 6-3-86
Source: Trainee.
2002-03 Leeds U 0 0

McMASTER, Jamie (M) **6 0**
H: 5 10 W: 11 07 b.Sydney 29-11-82
Source: NSW Academy. *Honours:* England Youth, Under-20.
1999–2000 Leeds U 0 0
2000-01 Leeds U 0 0
2001-02 Leeds U 0 0
2002-03 Leeds U 4 0 **4 0**
2002-03 *Coventry C* 2 0 **2 0**

McPHAIL, Stephen (M) **69 2**
H: 5 9 W: 12 06 b.London 9-12-79
Source: Trainee. *Honours:* Eire Under-21, 7 full caps, 1 goal.
1996–97 Leeds U 0 0
1997–98 Leeds U 4 0
1998–99 Leeds U 17 0
1999–2000 Leeds U 24 2
2000-01 Leeds U 7 0
2001-02 Leeds U 1 0
2001-02 *Millwall* 3 0 **3 0**
2002-03 Leeds U 13 0 **66 2**

McSTAY, Henry (D) **0 0**
H: 6 0 W: 11 12 b.Co Armagh 6-3-85
Source: Scholar.
2001-02 Leeds U 0 0
2002-03 Leeds U 0 0

MILLS, Danny (D) **212 6**
H: 5 11 W: 12 06 b.Norwich 18-5-77
Source: Trainee. *Honours:* England Youth, Under-21, 17 full caps.
1994–95 Norwich C 0 0
1995–96 Norwich C 14 0
1996–97 Norwich C 32 0
1997–98 Norwich C 20 0 **66 0**
1997–98 Charlton Ath 9 1
1998–99 Charlton Ath 36 2 **45 3**
1999–2000 Leeds U 17 1
2000-01 Leeds U 23 0
2001-02 Leeds U 28 1
2002-03 Leeds U 33 1 **101 3**

MILNER, James (F) **18 2**
H: 5 7 W: 10 07 b.Leeds 4-1-86
Source: Trainee. *Honours:* FA Schools, England Youth.
2002-03 Leeds U 18 2 **18 2**

MILOSEVIC, Danny (G) **33 0**
H: 6 2 W: 14 08 b.Carlton 26-6-78
Honours: Australia Under-20, Under-23.
1995–96 Canberra Cosmos 3 0
1996–97 Canberra Cosmos 11 0 **14 0**
1997–98 Arminia Bielefeld 0 0
1997–98 Prussen Munster 0 0
1998–99 Perth Glory 17 0 **17 0**
1999–2000 Leeds U 0 0
2000-01 Leeds U 0 0
2001-02 Leeds U 0 0
2001-02 *Wolverhampton W* 0 0
2002-03 Leeds U 0 0
2002-03 *Plymouth Arg* 1 0 **1 0**
2002-03 *Crewe Alex* 1 0 **1 0**

MITCHELL, Peter‡ (D) **0 0**
H: 5 8 W: 11 00 b.Londonderry 10-4-84
Source: Scholar.
2000-01 Leeds U 0 0
2001-02 Leeds U 0 0
2002-03 Leeds U 0 0

NEWEY, Tom* (D) **13 1**
H: 5 10 W: 11 00 b.Sheffield 31-10-82
Source: Scholar.
2000-01 Leeds U 0 0
2001-02 Leeds U 0 0
2002-03 Leeds U 0 0
2002-03 *Cambridge U* 6 0 **6 0**
2002-03 *Darlington* 7 1 **7 1**

OKON, Paul (M) **209 5**
H: 5 11 W: 13 05 b.Sydney 5-4-72
Honours: Australia Under-20, Under-23, 26 full caps.
1989–90 Marconi Stallions 22 2
1990–91 Marconi Stallions 27 2 **49 4**
1991–92 FC Brugge 0 0
1992–93 FC Brugge 5 0
1993–94 FC Brugge 27 0
1994–95 FC Brugge 26 0
1995–96 FC Brugge 14 1 **72 1**
1996–97 Lazio 14 0
1997–98 Lazio 0 0
1998–99 Lazio 5 0 **19 0**
1999–2000 Fiorentina 11 0 **11 0**
2000-01 Middlesbrough 24 0
2001-02 Middlesbrough 4 0 **28 0**
2001-02 Watford 15 0 **15 0**
2002-03 Leeds U 15 0 **15 0**

RADEBE, Lucas (D) **183 0**
H: 6 0 W: 12 04 b.Johannesburg 12-4-69
Source: Kaizer Chiefs. *Honours:* South Africa 70 full caps, 2 goals.
1994–95 Leeds U 12 0
1995–96 Leeds U 13 0
1996–97 Leeds U 32 0
1997–98 Leeds U 27 0
1998–99 Leeds U 29 0
1999–2000 Leeds U 31 0
2000-01 Leeds U 20 0
2001-02 Leeds U 0 0
2002-03 Leeds U 19 0 **183 0**

REEVES, Damian (F) **0 0**
H: 5 8 W: 11 08 b.Doncaster 18-12-85
Source: Trainee.
2002-03 Leeds U 0 0

RICHARDSON, Frazer (D) **7 0**
H: 5 11 W: 12 03 b.Rotherham 29-10-82
Source: Trainee. *Honours:* England Youth, Under-20.
1999–2000 Leeds U 0 0
2000-01 Leeds U 0 0
2001-02 Leeds U 0 0
2002-03 Leeds U 0 0
2002-03 *Stoke C* 7 0 **7 0**

ROBINSON, Paul (G) **59 0**
H: 6 4 W: 15 07 b.Beverley 15-10-79
Source: Trainee. *Honours:* England Under-21, 2 full caps.
1996–97 Leeds U 0 0
1997–98 Leeds U 0 0
1998–99 Leeds U 5 0
1999–2000 Leeds U 0 0
2000-01 Leeds U 16 0
2001-02 Leeds U 0 0
2002-03 Leeds U 38 0 **59 0**

SHIELDS, Robbie (M) **0 0**
H: 5 6 W: 9 09 b.Dublin 1-5-84
Source: Scholar.
2000-01 Leeds U 0 0
2001-02 Leeds U 0 0
2002-03 Leeds U 0 0

SINGH, Harpal (F) **18 2**
H: 5 7 W: 10 02 b.Bradford 15-9-81
Source: Trainee.
1998–99 Leeds U 0 0
1999–2000 Leeds U 0 0
2000-01 Leeds U 0 0
2001-02 Leeds U 0 0
2001-02 *Bury* 12 2 **12 2**
2001-02 *Bristol C* 3 0 **3 0**
2002-03 Leeds U 0 0
2002-03 *Bradford C* 3 0 **3 0**

SMITH, Alan (F) **137 29**
H: 5 10 W: 11 05 b.Leeds 28-10-80
Source: Trainee. *Honours:* England Youth, Under-21, 6 full caps, 1 goal.
1997–98 Leeds U 0 0
1998–99 Leeds U 22 7
1999–2000 Leeds U 26 4
2000-01 Leeds U 33 11
2001-02 Leeds U 23 4
2002-03 Leeds U 33 3 **137 29**

STIENS, Craig (F) **3 0**
H: 5 8 W: 12 04 b.Swansea 31-7-84
Source: Scholar.
2000-01 Leeds U 0 0
2001-02 Leeds U 0 0
2002-03 Leeds U 0 0
2002-03 *Swansea C* 3 0 **3 0**

TYRRELL, Derek (D) **0 0**
H: 6 1 W: 11 09 b.Dublin 14-4-85
Source: Scholar.
2001-02 Leeds U 0 0
2002-03 Leeds U 0 0

VIDUKA, Mark (F) **269 158**
H: 6 2 W: 15 01 b.Melbourne 9-10-75
Honours: Australia Under-20, Under-23, 20 full caps, 2 goals.
1992–93 Melbourne Knights 4 2
1993–94 Melbourne Knights 20 17
1994–95 Melbourne Knights 24 21 **48 40**
1995–96 Croatia Zagreb 27 12
1996–97 Croatia Zagreb 25 18
1997–98 Croatia Zagreb 25 8
1998–99 Croatia Zagreb 7 2 **84 40**
1998–99 Celtic 9 5
1999–2000 Celtic 28 25 **37 30**
2000-01 Leeds U 34 17

2001-02 Leeds U 33 11
2002-03 Leeds U 33 20 **100 48**

WARD, Michael‡ (F) 0 0
H: 5 8 W: 11 05 b.Omagh 17-4-84
Source: Scholar.
2000-01 Leeds U 0 0
2001-02 Leeds U 0 0
2002-03 Leeds U 0 0

WILCOX, Jason (M) 344 35
H: 6 0 W: 11 07 b.Bolton 15-7-71
Source: Trainee. *Honours:* England B, 3 full caps.
1989–90 Blackburn R 1 0
1990–91 Blackburn R 18 0
1991–92 Blackburn R 38 4
1992–93 Blackburn R 33 4
1993–94 Blackburn R 33 6
1994–95 Blackburn R 27 5
1995–96 Blackburn R 10 3
1996–97 Blackburn R 28 2
1997–98 Blackburn R 31 4
1998–99 Blackburn R 30 3
1999–2000 Blackburn R 20 0 **269 31**
1999–2000 Leeds U 20 3
2000-01 Leeds U 17 0
2001-02 Leeds U 13 0
2002-03 Leeds U 25 1 **75 4**

WINTER, Jamie (F) 0 0
H: 5 10 W: 13 04 b.Dundee 4-8-85
Source: Scholar.
2002-03 Leeds U 0 0

WOODS, Martin (M) 0 0
H: 5 9 W: 10 09 b.Bellshill 1-1-86
Source: Trainee.
2002-03 Leeds U 0 0

Trainees
Bowler, Justin M; Keogh, Andrew D

LEICESTER C

ASHTON, Jon (D) 11 0
H: 6 2 W: 13 07 b.Nuneaton 4-10-82
Source: Scholar.
2000-01 Leicester C 0 0
2001-02 Leicester C 7 0 **7 0**
2002-03 *Notts Co* 4 0 **4 0**

BENJAMIN, Trevor (F) 205 46
H: 6 2 W: 14 04 b.Kettering 8-2-79
Source: Trainee. *Honours:* England Under-21. Jamaica 1 full cap
1995–96 Cambridge U 5 0
1996–97 Cambridge U 7 1
1997–98 Cambridge U 25 4
1998–99 Cambridge U 42 10
1999–2000 Cambridge U 44 20 **123 35**
2000-01 Leicester C 21 1
2001-02 Leicester C 11 0
2001-02 *Crystal Palace* 6 1 **6 1**
2001-02 *Norwich C* 6 0 **6 0**
2001-02 *WBA* 3 1 **3 1**
2002-03 Leicester C 35 8 **67 9**

DAVIDSON, Callum (D) 197 7
H: 5 10 W: 12 06 b.Stirling 25-6-76
Source: 'S' Form. *Honours:* Scotland Under-21, 17 full caps.
1994–95 St Johnstone 7 1
1995–96 St Johnstone 2 0
1996–97 St Johnstone 20 2
1997–98 St Johnstone 15 1 **44 4**
1997–98 Blackburn R 1 0
1998–99 Blackburn R 34 1
1999–2000 Blackburn R 30 0 **65 1**
2000-01 Leicester C 28 1
2001-02 Leicester C 30 0
2002-03 Leicester C 30 1 **88 2**

DEANE, Brian* (F) 577 181
H: 6 3 W: 14 05 b.Leeds 7-2-68
Source: Apprentice. *Honours:* England B, 3 full caps.
1985–86 Doncaster R 3 0
1986–87 Doncaster R 20 2
1987–88 Doncaster R 43 10 **66 12**
1988–89 Sheffield U 43 22
1989–90 Sheffield U 45 21
1990–91 Sheffield U 38 13
1991–92 Sheffield U 30 12
1992–93 Sheffield U 41 14
1993–94 Leeds U 41 11
1994–95 Leeds U 35 9
1995–96 Leeds U 34 7
1996–97 Leeds U 28 5 **138 32**
1997–98 Sheffield U 24 11 **221 93**
1997–98 Benfica 14 7
1998–99 Benfica 4 0 **18 7**
1998–99 Middlesbrough 26 6
1999–2000 Middlesbrough 29 9
2000-01 Middlesbrough 25 2
2001-02 Middlesbrough 7 1 **87 18**
2001-02 Leicester C 15 6
2002-03 Leicester C 32 13 **47 19**

DICKOV, Paul# (F) 254 63
H: 5 6 W: 10 09 b.Livingston 1-11-72
Source: Trainee. *Honours:* Scotland Schools, Youth, Under-21, 4 full caps.
1992–93 Arsenal 3 2
1993–94 Arsenal 1 0
1993–94 *Luton T* 15 1 **15 1**
1993–94 *Brighton & HA* 8 5 **8 5**
1994–95 Arsenal 9 0
1995–96 Arsenal 7 1
1996–97 Arsenal 1 0 **21 3**
1996–97 Manchester C 29 5
1997–98 Manchester C 30 9
1998–99 Manchester C 35 10
1999–2000 Manchester C 34 5
2000-01 Manchester C 21 4
2001-02 Manchester C 7 0 **156 33**
2001-02 Leicester C 12 4
2002-03 Leicester C 42 17 **54 21**

DOYLE, Jamie (M) 0 0
H: 5 8 W: 9 11 b.Glasgow 23-5-85
Source: Trainee.
2002-03 Leicester C 0 0

EADIE, Darren* (F) 208 37
H: 5 7 W: 10 12 b.Chippenham 10-6-75
Source: Trainee. *Honours:* England Youth, Under-21.
1992–93 Norwich C 0 0
1993–94 Norwich C 15 3
1994–95 Norwich C 26 2
1995–96 Norwich C 31 6
1996–97 Norwich C 42 17
1997–98 Norwich C 19 3
1998–99 Norwich C 22 3
1999–2000 Norwich C 13 1 **168 35**
1999–2000 Leicester C 16 0
2000-01 Leicester C 24 2
2001-02 Leicester C 0 0
2002-03 Leicester C 0 0 **40 2**

ELLIOTT, Matt (D) 569 70
H: 6 3 W: 14 10 b.Wandsworth 1-11-68
Source: Epsom & Ewell. *Honours:* Scotland 18 full caps, 1 goal.
1988–89 Charlton Ath 0 0
1988–89 Torquay U 13 2
1989–90 Torquay U 33 2
1990–91 Torquay U 45 6
1991–92 Torquay U 33 5 **124 15**
1991–92 *Scunthorpe U* 8 1
1992–93 Scunthorpe U 39 6
1993–94 Scunthorpe U 14 1 **61 8**
1993–94 Oxford U 32 5
1994–95 Oxford U 45 4
1995–96 Oxford U 45 8
1996–97 Oxford U 26 4 **148 21**
1996–97 Leicester C 16 4
1997–98 Leicester C 37 7
1998–99 Leicester C 37 2
1999–2000 Leicester C 37 6
2000-01 Leicester C 34 2
2001-02 Leicester C 31 0
2002-03 Leicester C 44 5 **236 26**

FLOWERS, Tim* (G) 504 0
H: 6 2 W: 14 08 b.Kenilworth 3-2-67
Source: Apprentice. *Honours:* England Youth, Under-21, 11 full caps.
1984–85 Wolverhampton W 38 0
1985–86 Wolverhampton W 25 0 **63 0**
1985–86 *Southampton* 0 0
1986–87 Southampton 9 0
1986–87 *Swindon T* 2 0
1987–88 Southampton 9 0
1987–88 *Swindon T* 5 0 **7 0**
1988–89 Southampton 7 0
1989–90 Southampton 35 0
1990–91 Southampton 37 0
1991–92 Southampton 41 0
1992–93 Southampton 42 0
1993–94 Southampton 12 0 **192 0**
1993–94 Blackburn R 29 0
1994–95 Blackburn R 39 0
1995–96 Blackburn R 37 0
1996–97 Blackburn R 36 0
1997–98 Blackburn R 25 0
1998–99 Blackburn R 11 0 **177 0**
1999–2000 Leicester C 29 0
2000-01 Leicester C 22 0
2001-02 Leicester C 4 0
2001-02 *Stockport Co* 4 0 **4 0**
2001-02 *Coventry C* 5 0 **5 0**
2002-03 Leicester C 1 0 **56 0**

HEATH, Matthew (D) 16 3
H: 6 4 W: 13 04 b.Leicester 1-11-81
Source: Scholar.
2000-01 Leicester C 0 0
2001-02 Leicester C 5 0
2002-03 Leicester C 11 3 **16 3**

IMPEY, Andrew (D) 353 14
H: 5 8 W: 11 11 b.Hammersmith 30-9-71
Source: Yeading. *Honours:* England Under-21.
1990–91 QPR 0 0
1991–92 QPR 13 0
1992–93 QPR 40 2
1993–94 QPR 33 3
1994–95 QPR 40 3
1995–96 QPR 29 3
1996–97 QPR 32 2 **187 13**
1997–98 West Ham U 19 0
1998–99 West Ham U 8 0 **27 0**
1998–99 Leicester C 18 0
1999–2000 Leicester C 29 1
2000-01 Leicester C 33 0
2001-02 Leicester C 27 0
2002-03 Leicester C 32 0 **139 1**

IZZET, Muzzy (M) 239 36
H: 5 10 W: 11 00 b.Mile End 31-10-74
Source: Trainee. *Honours:* Turkey 8 full caps.
1993–94 Chelsea 0 0
1994–95 Chelsea 0 0
1995–96 Chelsea 0 0
1995–96 *Leicester C* 9 1
1996–97 Leicester C 35 3
1997–98 Leicester C 36 4
1998–99 Leicester C 31 5
1999–2000 Leicester C 32 8
2000-01 Leicester C 27 7
2001-02 Leicester C 31 4
2002-03 Leicester C 38 4 **239 36**

JONES, Matthew (M) 50 1
H: 5 11 W: 12 09 b.Llanelli 1-9-80
Source: Trainee. *Honours:* Wales Youth, Under-21, B, 13 full caps.
1997–98 Leeds U 0 0
1998–99 Leeds U 8 0
1999–2000 Leeds U 11 0
2000-01 Leeds U 4 0 **23 0**
2000-01 Leicester C 11 0
2001-02 Leicester C 10 1
2002-03 Leicester C 6 0 **27 1**

LARVIN, Kevin (F) 0 0
H: 5 10 W: 11 05 b.Hull 4-9-84
Source: Trainee.
2002-03 Leicester C 0 0

LAURSEN, Jacob‡ (D) 372 15
H: 6 0 W: 12 13 b.Vejle 6-10-71
Honours: Denmark 22 full caps.
1990 Vejle 20 0
1990–91 Vejle 18 0
1991–92 Vejle 17 1 **55 1**
1992–93 Silkeborg 32 0
1993–94 Silkeborg 30 1
1994–95 Silkeborg 31 3
1995–96 Silkeborg 32 4 **125 8**
1996–97 Derby Co 36 1
1997–98 Derby Co 28 1
1998–99 Derby Co 37 0
1999–2000 Derby Co 36 1 **137 3**
2000-01 FC Copenhagen 28 3
2001-02 FC Copenhagen 17 0 **45 3**
2001-02 Leicester C 10 0
2001-02 *Wolverhampton W* 0 0
2002-03 Leicester C 0 0 **10 0**

LEWIS, Junior (M) 119 12
H: 6 5 W: 13 04 b.Wembley 9-10-73
Source: Trainee.
1992–93 Fulham 6 0 **6 0**
From Dover, Hendon
1999–2000 Gillingham 42 6
2000-01 Gillingham 17 2 **59 8**
2000-01 Leicester C 15 0
2001-02 Leicester C 6 0

2001-02 *Brighton & HA* 15 3 **15 3**
2002-03 Leicester C 9 1 **30 1**
2002-03 *Swindon T* 9 0 **9 0**

LYTH, Ashley‡ (D) 0 0
H: 5 11 W: 11 03 b.Whitby 14-6-83
2000-01 Leicester C 0 0
2001-02 Leicester C 0 0
2002-03 Leicester C 0 0

McKINLAY, Billy* (M) 368 27
H: 5 8 W: 11 06 b.Glasgow 22-4-69
Source: Hamilton Th. *Honours:* Scotland Under-21, B, 29 full caps, 4 goals.
1986–87 Dundee U 3 0
1987–88 Dundee U 12 1
1988–89 Dundee U 30 1
1989–90 Dundee U 13 0
1990–91 Dundee U 34 2
1991–92 Dundee U 22 1
1992–93 Dundee U 37 1
1993–94 Dundee U 39 9
1994–95 Dundee U 27 4
1995–96 Dundee U 5 4 **222 23**
1995–96 Blackburn R 19 2
1996–97 Blackburn R 25 1
1997–98 Blackburn R 30 0
1998–99 Blackburn R 16 0
1999–2000 Blackburn R 0 0
2000-01 Blackburn R 0 0 **90 3**
2000-01 *Leicester C* 0 0
2000-01 Bradford C 11 0 **11 0**
2001-02 Preston NE 0 0
2001-02 Clydebank 8 0 **8 0**
2002-03 Leicester C 37 1 **37 1**

McSWEENEY, Leon (F) 0 0
H: 5 10 W: 10 11 b.Cork 19-2-83
Source: Cork C.
2001-02 Leicester C 0 0
2002-03 Leicester C 0 0

MURPHY, Paul (G) 0 0
H: 6 0 W: 11 03 b.Dundalk 23-8-85
Source: Trainee.
2002-03 Leicester C 0 0

O'GRADY, Christopher§ (M) 1 0
b.Nottingham 25-1-86
Source: Trainee. *Honours:* England Youth.
2002-03 Leicester C 1 0 **1 0**

OAKES, Stefan* (M) 71 2
H: 6 1 W: 13 04 b.Leicester 6-9-78
Source: Trainee.
1997–98 Leicester C 0 0
1998–99 Leicester C 3 0
1999–2000 Leicester C 22 1
2000-01 Leicester C 13 0
2001-02 Leicester C 21 1
2002-03 Leicester C 5 0 **64 2**
2002-03 *Crewe Alex* 7 0 **7 0**

PETRESCU, Tomi§ (M) 1 0
b.Jyvaskyla 24-7-86
Source: Scholar.
2002-03 Leicester C 1 0 **1 0**

PRICE, Michael* (G) 0 0
H: 6 3 W: 13 10 b.Ashington 3-4-83
Source: Scholar.
2000-01 Leicester C 0 0
2001-02 Leicester C 0 0
2002-03 Leicester C 0 0

REEVES, Martin* (M) 16 1
H: 6 0 W: 12 01 b.Birmingham 7-9-81
Source: Scholar.
2000-01 Leicester C 0 0
2001-02 Leicester C 5 0
2002-03 Leicester C 3 0 **8 0**
2002-03 *Hull C* 8 1 **8 1**

ROGERS, Alan (D) 248 18
H: 5 9 W: 12 10 b.Liverpool 3-1-77
Source: Trainee.
1995–96 Tranmere R 26 2
1996–97 Tranmere R 31 0 **57 2**
1997–98 Nottingham F 46 1
1998–99 Nottingham F 34 3
1999–2000 Nottingham F 37 9
2000-01 Nottingham F 17 3
2001-02 Nottingham F 3 0 **137 16**
2001-02 Leicester C 13 0
2002-03 Leicester C 41 0 **54 0**

ROYCE, Simon (G) 198 0
H: 6 2 W: 13 02 b.Newham 9-9-71
Source: Heybridge Swifts.
1991–92 Southend U 1 0
1992–93 Southend U 3 0
1993–94 Southend U 6 0
1994–95 Southend U 13 0
1995–96 Southend U 46 0
1996–97 Southend U 43 0
1997–98 Southend U 37 0 **149 0**
1998–99 Charlton Ath 8 0
1999–2000 Charlton Ath 0 0 **8 0**
2000-01 Leicester C 19 0
2001-02 Leicester C 0 0
2001-02 *Brighton & HA* 6 0 **6 0**
2001-02 *Manchester C* 0 0
2002-03 Leicester C 0 0 **19 0**
2002-03 *QPR* 16 0 **16 0**

SCOWCROFT, James (F) 269 62
H: 6 1 W: 14 07 b.Bury St Edmunds 15-11-75
Source: Trainee. *Honours:* England Under-21.
1994–95 Ipswich T 0 0
1995–96 Ipswich T 23 2
1996–97 Ipswich T 41 9
1997–98 Ipswich T 31 6
1998–99 Ipswich T 32 13
1999–2000 Ipswich T 41 13
2000-01 Ipswich T 34 4 **202 47**
2001-02 Leicester C 24 5
2002-03 Leicester C 43 10 **67 15**

SINCLAIR, Frank (D) 325 10
H: 5 09 W: 12 02 b.Lambeth 3-12-71
Source: Trainee. *Honours:* Jamaica 22 full caps, 1 goal.
1989–90 Chelsea 0 0
1990–91 Chelsea 4 0
1991–92 Chelsea 8 1
1991–92 *WBA* 6 1 **6 1**
1992–93 Chelsea 32 0
1993–94 Chelsea 35 0
1994–95 Chelsea 35 3
1995–96 Chelsea 13 1
1996–97 Chelsea 20 1
1997–98 Chelsea 22 1 **169 7**
1998–99 Leicester C 31 1
1999–2000 Leicester C 34 0
2000-01 Leicester C 17 0
2001-02 Leicester C 35 0
2002-03 Leicester C 33 1 **150 2**

STEVENSON, Jon* (F) 12 2
H: 5 6 W: 11 08 b.Leicester 13-10-82
Source: Scholar.
2000-01 Leicester C 0 0
2001-02 Leicester C 6 1
2002-03 Leicester C 6 1 **12 2**

STEWART, Jordan (D) 54 4
H: 5 11 W: 12 05 b.Birmingham 3-3-82
Source: Trainee. *Honours:* England Youth, Under-21.
1999–2000 Leicester C 1 0
1999–2000 *Bristol R* 4 0 **4 0**
2000-01 Leicester C 0 0
2001-02 Leicester C 12 0
2002-03 Leicester C 37 4 **50 4**

SUMMERBEE, Nicky* (M) 394 22
H: 5 11 W: 12 03 b.Altrincham 26-8-71
Source: Trainee. *Honours:* England Under-21.
1989–90 Swindon T 1 0
1990–91 Swindon T 7 0
1991–92 Swindon T 27 0
1992–93 Swindon T 39 3
1993–94 Swindon T 38 3 **112 6**
1994–95 Manchester C 41 1
1995–96 Manchester C 37 1
1996–97 Manchester C 44 4
1997–98 Manchester C 9 0
1997–98 Sunderland 25 3
1998–99 Sunderland 36 3
1999–2000 Sunderland 32 1
2000-01 Sunderland 0 0 **93 7**
2000-01 Bolton W 12 1 **12 1**
2001-02 Manchester C 0 0 **131 6**
2001-02 Nottingham F 17 2 **17 2**
2002-03 Leicester C 29 0 **29 0**

TAGGART, Gerry* (D) 401 30
H: 6 1 W: 14 07 b.Belfast 18-10-70
Source: Trainee. *Honours:* Northern Ireland Schools, Youth, Under-23, 51 full caps, 7 goals.
1988–89 Manchester C 11 1
1989–90 Manchester C 1 0 **12 1**
1989–90 Barnsley 21 2
1990–91 Barnsley 30 2
1991–92 Barnsley 38 3
1992–93 Barnsley 44 4
1993–94 Barnsley 38 2
1994–95 Barnsley 41 3 **212 16**
1995–96 Bolton W 11 1
1996–97 Bolton W 43 3
1997–98 Bolton W 15 0 **69 4**
1998–99 Leicester C 15 0
1999–2000 Leicester C 31 6
2000-01 Leicester C 24 2
2001-02 Leicester C 1 0
2002-03 Leicester C 37 1 **108 9**

WALKER, Ian (G) 342 0
H: 6 2 W: 13 05 b.Watford 31-10-71
Source: Trainee. *Honours:* England Youth, Under-21, B, 3 full caps.
1989–90 Tottenham H 0 0
1990–91 Tottenham H 1 0
1990–91 *Oxford U* 2 0 **2 0**
1990–91 *Ipswich T* 0 0
1991–92 Tottenham H 18 0
1992–93 Tottenham H 17 0
1993–94 Tottenham H 11 0
1994–95 Tottenham H 41 0
1995–96 Tottenham H 38 0
1996–97 Tottenham H 37 0
1997–98 Tottenham H 29 0
1998–99 Tottenham H 25 0
1999–2000 Tottenham H 38 0
2000-01 Tottenham H 4 0 **259 0**
2001-02 Leicester C 35 0
2002-03 Leicester C 46 0 **81 0**

WILLIAMSON, Tom (M) 1 0
H: 5 9 W: 10 02 b.Leicester 24-12-84
Source: Scholar.
2001-02 Leicester C 1 0
2002-03 Leicester C 0 0 **1 0**

WRIGHT, Thomas§ (M) 14 2
H: 6 0 W: 11 12 b.Leicester 28-9-84
Source: Scholar. *Honours:* England Youth.
2001-02 Leicester C 1 0
2002-03 Leicester C 13 2 **14 2**

Scholars
Butcher, Aaron S; Campbell, Gareth; Dawson, Stephen J; Deen, Ahmead; Howard, Christopher; Logan, Conrad J; Matthews, Nicholas; McAlea, Daniel M; McAnallen, Conor P; McGavigan, Ryan; Mortimer, Benjamin; O'Grady, Christopher J; O'Shea, Colin G; Pearmain, Dominic C; Petrescu, Tomi; Powell, Liam; Tozer, Lewis; Wright, Thomas A

LEYTON ORIENT

ALEXANDER, Gary (F) 159 48
H: 6 0 W: 13 01 b.Lambeth 15-8-79
Source: Trainee.
1998–99 West Ham U 0 0
1999–2000 West Ham U 0 0
1999–2000 *Exeter C* 37 16 **37 16**
2000-01 Swindon T 37 7 **37 7**
2001-02 Hull C 43 17
2002-03 Hull C 25 6 **68 23**
2002-03 Leyton Orient 17 2 **17 2**

BARNARD, Donny (D) 39 0
H: 5 10 W: 11 05 b.Forest Gate 1-7-84
2001-02 Leyton Orient 10 0
2002-03 Leyton Orient 29 0 **39 0**

BARRETT, Scott‡ (G) 373 0
H: 5 11 W: 14 06 b.Ilkeston 2-4-63
Source: Ilkeston T.
1984–85 Wolverhampton W 4 0
1985–86 Wolverhampton W 21 0
1986–87 Wolverhampton W 5 0 **30 0**
1987–88 Stoke C 27 0
1988–89 Stoke C 17 0
1989–90 Stoke C 7 0 **51 0**
1989–90 *Colchester U* 13 0
1989–90 *Stockport Co* 10 0 **10 0**
1990–91 Colchester U 0 0
1991–92 Colchester U 0 0 **13 0**
1992–93 Gillingham 34 0
1993–94 Gillingham 13 0
1994–95 Gillingham 4 0 **51 0**
1995–96 Cambridge U 31 0
1996–97 Cambridge U 45 0
1997–98 Cambridge U 43 0
1998–99 Cambridge U 0 0 **119 0**

1998–99 Leyton Orient 20 0
1999–2000 Leyton Orient 29 0
2000-01 Leyton Orient 7 0
2001-02 Leyton Orient 32 0
2002-03 Leyton Orient 11 0 **99 0**

BRAZIER, Matt (M) 166 9
H: 5 10 W: 10 10 b.Whipps Cross 2-7-76
Source: Trainee.
1994–95 QPR 0 0
1995–96 QPR 11 0
1996–97 QPR 27 2
1997–98 QPR 11 0 **49 2**
1997–98 Fulham 7 1
1998–99 Fulham 2 0 **9 1**
1998–99 *Cardiff C* 11 2
1999–2000 Cardiff C 30 1
2000-01 Cardiff C 26 2
2001-02 Cardiff C 0 0 **67 5**
2001-02 Leyton Orient 8 0
2002-03 Leyton Orient 33 1 **41 1**

CANHAM, Scott‡ (M) 101 7
H: 5 8 W: 11 06 b.Newham 5-11-74
Source: Trainee.
1993–94 West Ham U 0 0
1994–95 West Ham U 0 0
1995–96 West Ham U 0 0
1995–96 *Torquay U* 3 0 **3 0**
1995–96 *Brentford* 14 0
1996–97 Brentford 13 1
1997–98 Brentford 22 0 **49 1**
1998–99 Leyton Orient 8 0
1999–2000 Leyton Orient 1 0
2000-01 Leyton Orient 0 0
2001-02 Leyton Orient 24 4
2002-03 Leyton Orient 16 2 **49 6**

DOWNER, Simon (D) 76 0
H: 6 1 W: 13 02 b.Romford 19-10-81
Source: Trainee.
1998–99 Leyton Orient 1 0
1999–2000 Leyton Orient 24 0
2000-01 Leyton Orient 31 0
2001-02 Leyton Orient 12 0
2002-03 Leyton Orient 8 0 **76 0**

FLETCHER, Gary (F) 26 1
H: 5 11 W: 12 06 b.Liverpool 4-6-81
Source: Northwich Vic. *Honours:* England Schools.
2000-01 Hull C 5 0 **5 0**
2001-02 Leyton Orient 9 0
2002-03 Leyton Orient 12 1 **21 1**

FORBES, Boniek§ (M) 3 0
b.Guinea Bissau 30-9-83
Source: Scholar.
2002-03 Leyton Orient 3 0 **3 0**

HARRIS, Andy‡ (D) 221 2
H: 5 11 W: 12 05 b.Springs 26-2-77
Source: Trainee.
1993–94 Liverpool 0 0
1994–95 Liverpool 0 0
1995–96 Liverpool 0 0
1996–97 Southend U 44 0
1997–98 Southend U 27 0
1998–99 Southend U 1 0 **72 0**
1999–2000 Leyton Orient 15 0
2000-01 Leyton Orient 44 0
2001-02 Leyton Orient 45 1
2002-03 Leyton Orient 45 1 **149 2**

HARRISON, Lee (G) 215 0
H: 6 2 W: 13 03 b.Billericay 12-9-71
Source: Trainee.
1990–91 Charlton Ath 0 0
1991–92 Charlton Ath 0 0
1991–92 *Fulham* 0 0
1991–92 *Gillingham* 2 0 **2 0**
1992–93 Charlton Ath 0 0
1992–93 *Fulham* 0 0
1993–94 Fulham 0 0
1994–95 Fulham 7 0
1995–96 Fulham 5 0 **12 0**
1996–97 Barnet 21 0
1997–98 Barnet 46 0
1998–99 Barnet 43 0
1999–2000 Barnet 43 0
2000-01 Barnet 30 0
2001-02 Barnet 0 0 **183 0**
2002-03 Peterborough U 12 0 **12 0**
2002-03 Leyton Orient 6 0 **6 0**

HATCHER, Daniel‡ (F) 16 0
H: 5 10 W: 11 00 b.Newport (IW) 24-12-83
Source: Scholar.
2000-01 Leyton Orient 2 0
2001-02 Leyton Orient 8 0
2002-03 Leyton Orient 6 0 **16 0**

HEALD, Greg (D) 251 20
H: 6 1 W: 12 10 b.Enfield 26-9-71
Source: Enfield. *Honours:* England Schools.
1994–95 Peterborough U 29 0
1995–96 Peterborough U 40 4
1996–97 Peterborough U 36 2 **105 6**
1997–98 Barnet 43 3
1998–99 Barnet 19 2
1999–2000 Barnet 40 5
2000-01 Barnet 39 3
2001-02 Barnet 0 0
2002-03 Barnet 0 0 **141 13**
2002-03 Leyton Orient 5 1 **5 1**

HUTCHINGS, Carl‡ (M) 295 16
H: 6 0 W: 11 06 b.Hammersmith 24-9-74
Source: Trainee.
1993–94 Brentford 29 0
1994–95 Brentford 39 0
1995–96 Brentford 23 0
1996–97 Brentford 28 2
1997–98 Brentford 43 5
1998–99 Bristol C 21 2
1999–2000 Bristol C 21 1
1999–2000 *Brentford* 8 0 **170 7**
2000-01 Bristol C 0 0 **42 3**
2000-01 *Exeter C* 2 0 **2 0**
2000-01 Southend U 14 0
2001-02 Southend U 29 4 **43 4**
2001-02 Leyton Orient 10 1
2002-03 Leyton Orient 28 1 **38 2**

IBEHRE, Jabo (F) 61 11
H: 6 2 W: 13 00 b.Islington 28-1-83
Source: Trainee.
1999–2000 Leyton Orient 3 0
2000-01 Leyton Orient 5 2
2001-02 Leyton Orient 28 4
2002-03 Leyton Orient 25 5 **61 11**

JONES, Billy (D) 41 0
H: 6 1 W: 11 04 b.Chatham 26-6-83
Source: Trainee.
2000-01 Leyton Orient 1 0
2001-02 Leyton Orient 16 0
2002-03 Leyton Orient 24 0 **41 0**

JOSEPH, Matt# (D) 359 8
H: 5 5 W: 10 07 b.Bethnal Green 30-9-72
Source: Trainee. *Honours:* Barbados 2 full caps.
1991–92 Arsenal 0 0
1992–93 Gillingham 0 0
1993–94 Cambridge U 27 2
1994–95 Cambridge U 39 2
1995–96 Cambridge U 42 2
1996–97 Cambridge U 44 0
1997–98 Cambridge U 7 0 **159 6**
1997–98 Leyton Orient 14 1
1998–99 Leyton Orient 34 0
1999–2000 Leyton Orient 41 0
2000-01 Leyton Orient 44 0
2001-02 Leyton Orient 30 1
2002-03 Leyton Orient 37 0 **200 2**

LOCKWOOD, Matt (D) 240 24
H: 5 10 W: 11 07 b.Rochford 17-10-76
Source: Trainee.
1994–95 QPR 0 0
1995–96 QPR 0 0
1996–97 Bristol R 39 1
1997–98 Bristol R 24 0 **63 1**
1998–99 Leyton Orient 37 3
1999–2000 Leyton Orient 41 6
2000-01 Leyton Orient 32 7
2001-02 Leyton Orient 24 2
2002-03 Leyton Orient 43 5 **177 23**

MARTIN, John‡ (M) 92 5
H: 5 8 W: 10 03 b.Bethnal Green 15-7-81
Source: Trainee.
1997–98 Leyton Orient 1 0
1998–99 Leyton Orient 1 0
1999–2000 Leyton Orient 8 0
2000-01 Leyton Orient 19 0
2001-02 Leyton Orient 31 2
2002-03 Leyton Orient 32 3 **92 5**

McGHEE, Dave (D) 222 14
H: 6 0 W: 13 07 b.Worthing 19-6-76
Source: Trainee.
1994–95 Brentford 7 1
1995–96 Brentford 36 5
1996–97 Brentford 45 1
1997–98 Brentford 29 1
1998–99 Brentford 0 0 **117 8**
From Stevenage Bor.
1999–2000 Leyton Orient 23 1
2000-01 Leyton Orient 39 3
2001-02 Leyton Orient 40 2
2002-03 Leyton Orient 3 0 **105 6**

McLEAN, Aaron‡ (F) 40 2
H: 5 9 W: 10 10 b.Hammersmith 25-5-83
Source: Trainee.
1999–2000 Leyton Orient 3 0
2000-01 Leyton Orient 2 1
2001-02 Leyton Orient 27 1
2002-03 Leyton Orient 8 0 **40 2**

MILLER, Justin (D) 19 0
H: 6 0 W: 11 04 b.Johannesburg 16-12-80
Source: Academy.
1999–2000 Ipswich T 0 0
2000-01 Ipswich T 0 0
2001-02 Ipswich T 0 0
2002-03 Ipswich T 0 0
2002-03 Leyton Orient 19 0 **19 0**

MORRIS, Glenn (G) 25 0
H: 5 11 W: 11 00 b.Woolwich 20-12-83
Source: Scholar.
2001-02 Leyton Orient 2 0
2002-03 Leyton Orient 23 0 **25 0**

PURSER, Wayne (F) 25 6
H: 5 8 W: 12 05 b.Basildon 13-4-80
Source: Trainee.
1996–97 QPR 0 0
1997–98 QPR 0 0
1998–99 QPR 0 0
1999–2000 QPR 0 0
2000-01 Barnet 18 3
2001-02 Barnet 0 0
2002-03 Barnet 0 0 **18 3**
2002-03 Leyton Orient 7 3 **7 3**

STEPHENS, Kevin§ (D) 3 0
b.Enfield 28-7-84
Source: Scholar.
2002-03 Leyton Orient 3 0 **3 0**

TATE, Chris (F) 119 26
H: 6 0 W: 12 08 b.York 27-12-77
Source: York C Trainee.
1996–97 Sunderland 0 0
1997–98 Scarborough 24 1
1998–99 Scarborough 25 12 **49 13**
1999–2000 Halifax T 18 4 **18 4**
From Scarborough.
2000-01 Leyton Orient 22 3
2001-02 Leyton Orient 7 0
2002-03 Leyton Orient 23 6 **52 9**

THORPE, Lee (F) 242 66
H: 6 1 W: 12 07 b.Wolverhampton 14-12-75
Source: Trainee.
1993–94 Blackpool 1 0
1994–95 Blackpool 1 0
1995–96 Blackpool 1 0
1996–97 Blackpool 9 0 **12 0**
1997–98 Lincoln C 44 14
1998–99 Lincoln C 38 8
1999–2000 Lincoln C 42 16
2000-01 Lincoln C 31 7
2001-02 Lincoln C 37 13 **192 58**
2001-02 Leyton Orient 0 0
2002-03 Leyton Orient 38 8 **38 8**

TONER, Ciaran (M) 37 1
H: 5 10 W: 12 10 b.Craigavon 30-6-81
Source: Trainee. *Honours:* Northern Ireland Under-21, 2 full caps.
1999–2000 Tottenham H 0 0
2000-01 Tottenham H 0 0
2001-02 Tottenham H 0 0
2001-02 *Peterborough U* 6 0 **6 0**
2001-02 Bristol R 6 0 **6 0**
2001-02 Leyton Orient 0 0
2002-03 Leyton Orient 25 1 **25 1**

ZAKUANI, Gaby§ (M) 1 0
H: 6 1 W: 10 10 b.Zaire 31-5-86
Source: Scholar.
2002-03 Leyton Orient 1 0 **1 0**

Scholars
Bray, Thomas J; Butler, Graeme KM; Forbes, Boniek MG; Game, Matthew; Holder, Philip; Jones, Paul; Laxton, Thomas; Levy, Adam H; Rodden, James C; Stephens, Kevin; Tiffin, Gregory; Toku, Prince K; Wareham, Ross; Wild, Christopher; Williams, Andre; Zakuani, Gabriel

LINCOLN C

BAILEY, Mark (D) 130 1
H: 5 8 W: 10 12 b.Stoke 12-8-76
Source: Trainee.
1994–95 Stoke C 0 0
1995–96 Stoke C 0 0
1996–97 Stoke C 0 0
1996–97 Rochdale 15 0
1997–98 Rochdale 33 0
1998–99 Rochdale 19 1
1999–2000 Rochdale 0 0
2000–01 Rochdale 0 0 **67 1**
From Northwich Vic.
2001–02 Lincoln C 18 0
2002–03 Lincoln C 45 0 **63 0**

BIMSON, Stuart# (D) 211 4
H: 5 9 W: 11 13 b.Liverpool 29-9-69
Source: Macclesfield T.
1994–95 Bury 19 0
1995–96 Bury 16 0
1996–97 Bury 1 0 **36 0**
1996–97 Lincoln C 15 1
1997–98 Lincoln C 12 0
1998–99 Lincoln C 31 2
1999–2000 Lincoln C 20 0
2000–01 Lincoln C 20 0
2001–02 Lincoln C 35 0
2002–03 Lincoln C 42 1 **175 4**

BLACK, Kingsley‡ (M) 417 56
H: 5 10 W: 12 00 b.Luton 22-6-68
Source: School. *Honours:* England Schools, Northern Ireland Under-21, 30 full caps, 1 goal.
1986–87 Luton T 0 0
1987–88 Luton T 13 0
1988–89 Luton T 37 8
1989–90 Luton T 36 11
1990–91 Luton T 37 7
1991–92 Luton T 4 0 **127 26**
1991–92 Nottingham F 25 4
1992–93 Nottingham F 24 5
1993–94 Nottingham F 37 3
1994–95 Nottingham F 10 2
1994–95 *Sheffield U* 11 2 **11 2**
1995–96 Nottingham F 2 0 **98 14**
1995–96 *Millwall* 3 1 **3 1**
1996–97 Grimsby T 24 0
1997–98 Grimsby T 39 2
1998–99 Grimsby T 42 4
1999–2000 Grimsby T 31 2
2000–01 Grimsby T 5 0 **141 8**
2000–01 *Lincoln C* 5 0
2001–02 Lincoln C 31 5
2002–03 Lincoln C 1 0 **37 5**

BLOOMER, Matt† (D) 33 1
H: 6 1 W: 13 11 b.Cleethorpes 3-11-78
Source: Trainee.
1997–98 Grimsby T 0 0
1998–99 Grimsby T 4 0
1999–2000 Grimsby T 2 0
2000–01 Grimsby T 6 0
2001–02 Grimsby T 0 0 **12 0**
2001–02 Hull C 3 0
2001–02 *Lincoln C* 5 0
2002–03 Hull C 0 0 **3 0**
2002–03 Lincoln C 13 1 **18 1**

BUCKLEY, Adam* (M) 49 0
H: 5 9 W: 11 07 b.Nottingham 2-8-79
Source: WBA schoolboy.
1997–98 Grimsby T 0 0
1998–99 Grimsby T 2 0
1999–2000 Grimsby T 13 0
2000–01 Grimsby T 0 0 **15 0**
2001–02 Lincoln C 31 0
2002–03 Lincoln C 3 0 **34 0**

BUTCHER, Richard (M) 26 3
b.Northampton 22-1-81
Source: Kettering T.
2002–03 Lincoln C 26 3 **26 3**

CAMM, Mark (D) 32 0
H: 5 7 W: 11 05 b.Mansfield 1-10-80
Source: Trainee.
1999–2000 Sheffield U 0 0
2000–01 Lincoln C 3 0
2001–02 Lincoln C 16 0
2002–03 Lincoln C 13 0 **32 0**

CORNELLY, Chris (F) 16 0
H: 5 7 W: 11 07 b.Huddersfield 7-7-76
Source: Leigh RMI, Ashton U.
2002–03 Lincoln C 16 0 **16 0**

CROPPER, Dean (F) 29 3
H: 6 2 W: 13 11 b.Chesterfield 5-1-83
Source: Sheffield W Scholar.
2002–03 Lincoln C 29 3 **29 3**

FUTCHER, Ben (D) 53 8
H: 6 7 W: 12 05 b.Bradford 4-6-81
Source: Trainee.
1999–2000 Oldham Ath 5 0
2000–01 Oldham Ath 5 0
2001–02 Oldham Ath 0 0 **10 0**
From Stalybridge C, Doncaster R.
2002–03 Lincoln C 43 8 **43 8**

GAIN, Peter (M) 145 14
H: 6 0 W: 11 07 b.Hammersmith 2-11-76
Source: Trainee.
1995–96 Tottenham H 0 0
1996–97 Tottenham H 0 0
1997–98 Tottenham H 0 0
1998–99 Tottenham H 0 0
1998–99 Lincoln C 4 0
1999–2000 Lincoln C 32 2
2000–01 Lincoln C 24 5
2001–02 Lincoln C 42 2
2002–03 Lincoln C 43 5 **145 14**

HAMILTON, Ian‡ (M) 520 46
H: 5 10 W: 12 07 b.Stevenage 14-12-67
Source: Apprentice.
1985–86 Southampton 0 0
1986–87 Southampton 0 0
1987–88 Southampton 0 0
1987–88 Cambridge U 9 1
1988–89 Cambridge U 15 0 **24 1**
1988–89 Scunthorpe U 27 1
1989–90 Scunthorpe U 43 6
1990–91 Scunthorpe U 34 2
1991–92 Scunthorpe U 41 9 **145 18**
1992–93 WBA 46 7
1993–94 WBA 42 3
1994–95 WBA 35 4
1995–96 WBA 41 3
1996–97 WBA 39 5
1997–98 WBA 37 1 **240 23**
1997–98 Sheffield U 8 1
1998–99 Sheffield U 30 2
1999–2000 Sheffield U 7 0
1999–2000 *Grimsby T* 6 1 **6 1**
2000–01 Sheffield U 0 0 **45 3**
2000–01 Notts Co 25 0
2001–02 Notts Co 9 0 **34 0**
2001–02 Lincoln C 26 0
2002–03 Lincoln C 0 0 **26 0**

HORRIGAN, Darren† (G) 1 0
H: 6 4 W: 13 07 b.Middlesbrough 2-6-83
Source: Scholar.
2001–02 Lincoln C 1 0
2002–03 Lincoln C 0 0 **1 0**

LOGAN, Richard* (D) 228 21
H: 6 0 W: 12 08 b.Barnsley 24-5-69
Source: Gainsborough T.
1993–94 Huddersfield T 16 0
1994–95 Huddersfield T 27 1
1995–96 Huddersfield T 2 0 **45 1**
1995–96 Plymouth Arg 31 4
1996–97 Plymouth Arg 28 4
1997–98 Plymouth Arg 27 4 **86 12**
1998–99 Scunthorpe U 41 6
1999–2000 Scunthorpe U 39 1 **80 7**
2000–01 Lincoln C 5 0
2001–02 Lincoln C 2 0
2002–03 Lincoln C 10 1 **17 1**

MARRIOTT, Alan# (G) 137 0
H: 6 0 W: 12 04 b.Bedford 3-9-78
Source: Trainee.
1997–98 Tottenham H 0 0
1998–99 Tottenham H 0 0
1999–2000 Lincoln C 18 0
2000–01 Lincoln C 30 0
2001–02 Lincoln C 43 0
2002–03 Lincoln C 46 0 **137 0**

MAYO, Paul (D) 75 0
H: 5 11 W: 11 13 b.Lincoln 13-10-81
Source: Scholarship.
1999–2000 Lincoln C 19 0
2000–01 Lincoln C 27 0
2001–02 Lincoln C 14 0
2002–03 Lincoln C 15 0 **75 0**

MIKE, Adie‡ (F) 103 11
H: 6 0 W: 12 10 b.Manchester 16-11-73
Source: Trainee. *Honours:* England Schools, Youth.
1991–92 Manchester C 2 1
1992–93 Manchester C 3 0
1992–93 *Bury* 7 1 **7 1**
1993–94 Manchester C 9 1
1994–95 Manchester C 2 0
1995–96 Manchester C 0 0 **16 2**
1995–96 Stockport Co 8 0
1996–97 Stockport Co 1 0 **9 0**
1996–97 *Hartlepool U* 7 1 **7 1**
1996–97 *Doncaster R* 5 1
1997–98 Doncaster R 42 4
1998–99 Doncaster R 0 0 **47 5**
From Northwich Vic.
2002–03 Lincoln C 17 2 **17 2**

MORGAN, Paul (D) 79 1
H: 6 0 W: 11 05 b.Belfast 23-10-78
Source: Trainee. *Honours:* Northern Ireland Under-21.
1997–98 Preston NE 0 0
1998–99 Preston NE 0 0
1999–2000 Preston NE 0 0
2000–01 Preston NE 0 0
2001–02 Lincoln C 34 1
2002–03 Lincoln C 45 0 **79 1**

PEARCE, Allan (F) 16 1
H: 5 10 W: 11 05 b.Wellington 7-4-83
Source: Barnsley Scholar.
2002–03 Lincoln C 16 1 **16 1**

PETTINGER, Paul‡ (G) 23 0
H: 6 0 W: 13 00 b.Sheffield 1-10-75
Source: Barnsley. *Honours:* England Schools, Youth.
1992–93 Leeds U 0 0
1993–94 Leeds U 0 0
1994–95 Leeds U 0 0
1994–95 *Torquay U* 3 0 **3 0**
1995–96 Leeds U 0 0
1995–96 *Rotherham U* 1 0
1995–96 Gillingham 0 0
1996–97 Carlisle U 0 0
1997–98 Rotherham U 3 0
1998–99 Rotherham U 0 0
1999–2000 Rotherham U 0 0
2000–01 Rotherham U 13 0 **17 0**
2001–02 Lincoln C 3 0
2002–03 Lincoln C 0 0 **3 0**

SEDGEMORE, Ben# (M) 277 17
H: 5 10 W: 12 13 b.Wolverhampton 5-8-75
Source: Trainee. *Honours:* England Schools.
1993–94 Birmingham C 0 0
1994–95 Birmingham C 0 0
1994–95 *Northampton T* 1 0 **1 0**
1995–96 Birmingham C 0 0
1995–96 *Mansfield T* 9 0
1995–96 Peterborough U 17 0
1996–97 Peterborough U 0 0 **17 0**
1996–97 Mansfield T 39 4
1997–98 Mansfield T 28 2 **76 6**
1997–98 Macclesfield T 5 0
1998–99 Macclesfield T 35 2
1999–2000 Macclesfield T 35 1
2000–01 Macclesfield T 27 3 **102 6**
2000–01 Lincoln C 10 1
2001–02 Lincoln C 43 2
2002–03 Lincoln C 28 2 **81 5**

SMITH, Paul# (M) 157 19
H: 5 10 W: 11 11 b.Hastings 25-1-76
Source: Hastings T.
1994–95 Nottingham F 0 0
1995–96 Nottingham F 0 0
1996–97 Nottingham F 0 0
1997–98 Nottingham F 0 0
1997–98 *Lincoln C* 17 3
1998–99 Lincoln C 28 2
1999–2000 Lincoln C 27 5
2000–01 Lincoln C 40 7
2001–02 Lincoln C 8 0
2002–03 Lincoln C 37 2 **157 19**

WARD, Chris* (M) 6 2
H: 6 1 W: 11 00 b.Preston 28-4-81
Source: Lancaster C.
2000–01 Birmingham C 0 0
2001–02 Birmingham C 0 0
From Barrow, Leigh RMI.
2002–03 Lincoln C 6 2 **6 2**

WARD, Mark‡ (F) 2 0
H: 6 1 W: 10 11 b.Sheffield 27-1-82
Source: Sheffield Colleges. *Honours:* England Schools.
2000-01 Sheffield U 1 0
2001-02 Sheffield U 1 0 **2 0**
From Belper T.
2002-03 Lincoln C 0 0

WEAVER, Simon (D) 46 3
H: 6 1 W: 10 07 b.Doncaster 20-12-77
Source: Trainee.
1996–97 Sheffield W 0 0
1996–97 *Doncaster R* 2 0 **2 0**
1997–98 Sheffield W 0 0
From Ilkeston T, Nuneaton B.
2002-03 Lincoln C 44 3 **44 3**

WILLIS, Scott (M) 31 3
H: 5 9 W: 11 07 b.Liverpool 20-2-82
Source: Wigan Ath Trainee.
1999–2000 Mansfield T 0 0
2000-01 Mansfield T 0 0
2001-02 Carlisle U 1 0 **1 0**
2002-03 Lincoln C 30 3 **30 3**

YEO, Simon (M) 37 5
H: 5 10 W: 11 08 b.Stockport 20-10-73
Source: Hyde U.
2002-03 Lincoln C 37 5 **37 5**

Scholars
Basker, Carl; Bell, Jonathan; Davies, Christopher M; Fisher, Daniel; Frecklington, Lee C; Garfoot, Stephen R; Gordon, Christopher; Holtham, Adam D; Jones, Gareth; Kerley, Adam L; Langley, Ricky; Ryan, Oliver; Smith, Samuel AH; Stant, Craig PA; Trout, Charlie JS; Wilkinson, Thomas
Non-Contract
Bloomer, Matthew B; Coulson, David W; Horrigan, Darren

LIVERPOOL

ARPHEXAD, Pegguy* (G) 29 0
H: 6 2 W: 13 07 b.Abymes 18-5-73
Source: Brest.
1994–95 Lens 0 0
1995–96 Lens 3 0
1996–97 Lens 0 0 **3 0**
1997–98 Leicester C 6 0
1998–99 Leicester C 4 0
1999–2000 Leicester C 11 0 **21 0**
2000-01 Liverpool 0 0
2001-02 *Stockport Co* 3 0 **3 0**
2001-02 Liverpool 2 0
2002-03 Liverpool 0 0 **2 0**

BABBEL, Markus (D) 284 13
H: 6 0 W: 13 03 b.Munich 8-9-72
Honours: Germany 51 full caps, 1 goal.
1991–92 Bayern Munich 12 0
1992–93 Hamburg 27 1
1993–94 Hamburg 33 0 **60 1**
1994–95 Bayern Munich 26 2
1995–96 Bayern Munich 30 2
1996–97 Bayern Munich 31 2
1997–98 Bayern Munich 30 1
1998–99 Bayern Munich 27 1
1999–2000 Bayern Munich 26 1 **182 9**
2000-01 Liverpool 38 3
2001-02 Liverpool 2 0
2002-03 Liverpool 2 0 **42 3**

BAROS, Milan (F) 88 20
H: 6 0 W: 13 02 b.Valassake Mezirici 28-10-81
Honours: Czech Republic 19 full caps, 10 goals.
1998–99 Banik Ostrava 6 0
1999–2000 Banik Ostrava 29 6
2000-01 Banik Ostrava 26 5 **61 11**
2001-02 Liverpool 0 0
2002-03 Liverpool 27 9 **27 9**

BERGER, Patrik* (M) 262 56
H: 6 1 W: 13 00 b.Prague 10-11-73
Honours: Czechoslovakia 2 full caps.Czech Republic 44 full caps, 18 goals.
1991–92 Slavia Prague 20 3
1992–93 Slavia Prague 29 10
1993–94 Slavia Prague 12 4
1994–95 Slavia Prague 28 7 **89 24**
1995–96 Borussia Dortmund25 4 **25 4**
1996–97 Liverpool 23 6
1997–98 Liverpool 22 3
1998–99 Liverpool 32 7
1999–2000 Liverpool 34 9
2000-01 Liverpool 14 2
2001-02 Liverpool 21 1
2002-03 Liverpool 2 0 **148 28**

BISCAN, Igor (M) 103 12
H: 6 3 W: 12 08 b.Zagreb 4-5-78
Honours: Croatia 15 full caps, 1 goal.
1997–98 Samobor 12 1 **12 1**
1997–98 Dynamo Zagreb 5 0
1998–99 Dynamo Zagreb 19 2
1998–99 Dynamo Zagreb 0 0
1999–2000 Dynamo Zagreb 29 6
2000-01 Dynamo Zagreb 14 3 **67 11**
2000-01 Liverpool 13 0
2001-02 Liverpool 5 0
2002-03 Liverpool 6 0 **24 0**

CARRAGHER, Jamie (M) 194 2
H: 6 1 W: 12 05 b.Liverpool 28-1-78
Source: Trainee. *Honours:* England Youth, Under-21, B, 9 full caps.
1995–96 Liverpool 0 0
1996–97 Liverpool 2 1
1997–98 Liverpool 20 0
1998–99 Liverpool 34 1
1999–2000 Liverpool 36 0
2000-01 Liverpool 34 0
2001-02 Liverpool 33 0
2002-03 Liverpool 35 0 **194 2**

CHEYROU, Bruno (M) 114 28
H: 6 1 W: 13 03 b.Suresnes 10-5-78
Source: Lens, Racing. *Honours:* France 2 full caps.
1998–99 Lille 20 6
1999–2000 Lille 21 5
2000-01 Lille 27 6
2001-02 Lille 27 11 **95 28**
2002-03 Liverpool 19 0 **19 0**

DIAO, Salif (M) 103 1
H: 6 1 W: 13 03 b.Kedougou 10-2-77
Honours: Senegal 23 full caps, 3 goals.
1996–97 Epinal 2 0 **2 0**
1996–97 Monaco 0 0
1997–98 Monaco 12 0
1998–99 Monaco 14 0
1999–2000 Monaco 1 0 **27 0**
2000-01 Sedan 26 0
2001-02 Sedan 22 0 **48 0**
2002-03 Liverpool 26 1 **26 1**

DIOMEDE, Bernard* (M) 178 30
H: 5 9 W: 12 04 b.Bourges 23-1-74
Honours: France 8 full caps.
1992–93 Auxerre 7 0
1993–94 Auxerre 2 0
1994–95 Auxerre 26 3
1995–96 Auxerre 33 9
1996–97 Auxerre 31 6
1997–98 Auxerre 31 4
1998–99 Auxerre 27 5
1999–2000 Auxerre 19 3 **176 30**
2000-01 Liverpool 2 0
2001-02 Liverpool 0 0
2002-03 Liverpool 0 0 **2 0**

DIOUF, El Hadji (F) 126 22
H: 5 9 W: 12 03 b.Dakar 15-1-81
Honours: Senegal 25 full caps, 12 goals.
1998–99 Sochaux 15 0 **15 0**
1999–2000 Rennes 28 1 **28 1**
2000-01 Lens 28 8
2001-02 Lens 26 10 **54 18**
2002-03 Liverpool 29 3 **29 3**

DUDEK, Jerzy (G) 216 0
H: 6 2 W: 12 08 b.Ribnek 23-3-73
Source: GKS Tychy. *Honours:* Poland 30 full caps.
1995–96 Sokol Tychy 15 0 **15 0**
1996–97 Feyenoord 0 0
1997–98 Feyenoord 34 0
1998–99 Feyenoord 34 0
1999–2000 Feyenoord 34 0
2000-01 Feyenoord 34 0 **136 0**
2001-02 Liverpool 35 0
2002-03 Liverpool 30 0 **65 0**

FOLEY-SHERIDAN, Michael (M) 0 0
H: 5 6 W: 11 01 b.Dublin 9-3-83
1999–2000 Liverpool 0 0
2000-01 Liverpool 0 0
2001-02 Liverpool 0 0
2002-03 Liverpool 0 0

FOY, Robert (F) 0 0
b.Edinburgh 29-10-85
Source: Trainee.
2002-03 Liverpool 0 0

GERRARD, Steven (M) 136 16
H: 6 1 W: 12 03 b.Whiston 30-5-80
Source: Trainee. *Honours:* England Youth, Under-21, 18 full caps, 3 goals.
1997–98 Liverpool 0 0
1998–99 Liverpool 12 0
1999–2000 Liverpool 29 1
2000-01 Liverpool 33 7
2001-02 Liverpool 28 3
2002-03 Liverpool 34 5 **136 16**

HAMANN, Dietmar (M) 247 16
H: 6 2 W: 12 01 b.Waldasson 27-8-73
Source: Wacker Munich. *Honours:* Germany 49 full caps, 4 goals.
1993–94 Bayern Munich 5 1
1994–95 Bayern Munich 30 0
1995–96 Bayern Munich 20 2
1996–97 Bayern Munich 22 1
1997–98 Bayern Munich 28 2 **105 6**
1998–99 Newcastle U 23 4 **23 4**
1999–2000 Liverpool 28 1
2000-01 Liverpool 30 2
2001-02 Liverpool 31 1
2002-03 Liverpool 30 2 **119 6**

HEGGEM, Vegard* (D) 111 8
H: 5 11 W: 12 04 b.Trondheim 13-7-75
Honours: Norway 21 full caps, 1 goal.
1995 Rosenborg 15 1
1996 Rosenborg 14 1
1997 Rosenborg 23 3
1998 Rosenborg 5 0 **57 5**
1998–99 Liverpool 29 2
1999–2000 Liverpool 22 1
2000-01 Liverpool 3 0
2001-02 Liverpool 0 0
2002-03 Liverpool 0 0 **54 3**

HENCHOZ, Stephane (D) 327 3
H: 6 1 W: 12 13 b.Billens 7-9-74
Source: Bulle. *Honours:* Switzerland 58 full caps.
1992–93 Neuchatel Xamax 35 0
1993–94 Neuchatel Xamax 21 1
1994–95 Neuchatel Xamax 35 0 **91 1**
1995–96 Hamburg 31 2
1996–97 Hamburg 18 0 **49 2**
1997–98 Blackburn R 36 0
1998–99 Blackburn R 34 0 **70 0**
1999–2000 Liverpool 29 0
2000-01 Liverpool 32 0
2001-02 Liverpool 37 0
2002-03 Liverpool 19 0 **117 0**

HESKEY, Emile (F) 269 72
H: 6 1 W: 14 04 b.Leicester 11-1-78
Source: Trainee. *Honours:* England Youth, Under-21, B, 34 full caps, 5 goals.
1994–95 Leicester C 1 0
1995–96 Leicester C 30 7
1996–97 Leicester C 35 10
1997–98 Leicester C 35 10
1998–99 Leicester C 30 6
1999–2000 Leicester C 23 7 **154 40**
1999–2000 Liverpool 12 3
2000-01 Liverpool 36 14
2001-02 Liverpool 35 9
2002-03 Liverpool 32 6 **115 32**

HYYPIA, Sami (D) 309 17
H: 6 4 W: 13 11 b.Porvoo 7-10-73
Source: KuMu. *Honours:* Finland 55 full caps, 4 goals.
1993 MyPa 47 12 0
1994 MyPa 47 25 0
1995 MyPa 47 26 3 **63 3**
1995–96 Willem II 14 0
1996–97 Willem II 30 1
1997–98 Willem II 30 0
1998–99 Willem II 26 2 **100 3**
1999–2000 Liverpool 38 2
2000-01 Liverpool 35 3
2001-02 Liverpool 37 3
2002-03 Liverpool 36 3 **146 11**

KIRKLAND, Christopher (G) 33 0
H: 6 6 W: 14 12 b.Leicester 2-5-81
Source: Trainee. *Honours:* England Youth, Under-21.
1997–98 Coventry C 0 0
1998–99 Coventry C 0 0
1999–2000 Coventry C 0 0

2000-01 Coventry C 23 0
2001-02 Coventry C 1 0 **24 0**
2001-02 Liverpool 1 0
2002-03 Liverpool 8 0 **9 0**

LUZI-BERNARDI, Patrice (G) 0 0
H: 6 2 W: 14 01 b.Ajaccio 8-7-80
2002-03 Liverpool 0 0

MASSIE, Jason§ (M) 0 0
b.Whiston 13-9-84
Honours: England Youth.
2001-02 Liverpool 0 0
2002-03 Liverpool 0 0

McNULTY, Stephen* (D) 0 0
b.Liverpool 26-9-83
Source: Scholar.
2001-02 Liverpool 0 0
2002-03 Liverpool 0 0

MELLOR, Neil (F) 3 0
H: 6 0 W: 13 07 b.Manchester 4-11-82
Source: Scholar.
2001-02 Liverpool 0 0
2002-03 Liverpool 3 0 **3 0**

MURPHY, Danny (M) 289 48
H: 5 9 W: 12 08 b.Chester 18-3-77
Source: Trainee. *Honours:* England Schools, Youth, Under-21, 7 full caps, 1 goal.
1993–94 Crewe Alex 12 2
1994–95 Crewe Alex 35 5
1995–96 Crewe Alex 42 10
1996–97 Crewe Alex 45 10
1997–98 Liverpool 16 0
1998–99 Liverpool 1 0
1998–99 *Crewe Alex* 16 1 **150 28**
1999–2000 Liverpool 23 3
2000-01 Liverpool 27 4
2001-02 Liverpool 36 6
2002-03 Liverpool 36 7 **139 20**

OTSEMOBOR, John (D) 9 3
H: 5 10 W: 12 00 b.Liverpool 23-3-83
Source: Trainee. *Honours:* England Youth, Under-20.
1999–2000 Liverpool 0 0
2000-01 Liverpool 0 0
2001-02 Liverpool 0 0
2002-03 Liverpool 0 0
2002-03 *Hull C* 9 3 **9 3**

OWEN, Michael (F) 187 102
H: 5 8 W: 10 13 b.Chester 14-12-79
Source: Trainee. *Honours:* England Schools, Youth, Under-21, 50 full caps, 22 goals.
1996–97 Liverpool 2 1
1997–98 Liverpool 36 18
1998–99 Liverpool 30 18
1999–2000 Liverpool 27 11
2000-01 Liverpool 28 16
2001-02 Liverpool 29 19
2002-03 Liverpool 35 19 **187 102**

PARTRIDGE, Richie (M) 33 5
H: 5 8 W: 10 07 b.Dublin 12-9-80
Source: Trainee. *Honours:* Eire Under-21.
1998–99 Liverpool 0 0
1999–2000 Liverpool 0 0
2000-01 Liverpool 0 0
2000-01 *Bristol R* 6 1 **6 1**
2001-02 Liverpool 0 0
2002-03 Liverpool 0 0
2002-03 *Coventry C* 27 4 **27 4**

PEERS, Mark* (F) 0 0
b.St Helens 14-5-84
Honours: England Youth.
2001-02 Liverpool 0 0
2002-03 Liverpool 0 0

POTTER, Darren (F) 0 0
b.Liverpool 21-12-84
Source: Scholar.
2001-02 Liverpool 0 0
2002-03 Liverpool 0 0

RAVEN, David (D) 0 0
b.Wirral 10-3-85
Source: Scholar. *Honours:* England Youth.
2001-02 Liverpool 0 0
2002-03 Liverpool 0 0

RIISE, John Arne (M) 119 17
H: 6 1 W: 12 08 b.Molde 24-9-80
Honours: Norway 25 full caps, 3 goals.
1998–99 Monaco 7 0
1999–2000 Monaco 21 1
2000-01 Monaco 16 3 **44 4**
2001-02 Liverpool 38 7
2002-03 Liverpool 37 6 **75 13**

SJOLUND, Danny (F) 0 0
H: 5 11 W: 12 00 b.Mariehamn 22-4-83
1999–2000 West Ham U 0 0
2000-01 West Ham U 0 0
2000-01 Liverpool 0 0
2001-02 Liverpool 0 0
2002-03 Liverpool 0 0

SMICER, Vladimir (M) 263 49
H: 5 10 W: 12 02 b.Degin 24-5-73
Honours: Czechoslovakia 1 full cap, Czech Republic 64 full caps, 23 goals.
1992–93 Slavia Prague 21 8
1993–94 Slavia Prague 17 6
1994–95 Slavia Prague 15 3
1995–96 Slavia Prague 28 9 **81 26**
1996–97 Lens 33 5
1997–98 Lens 28 7
1998–99 Lens 30 4 **91 16**
1999–2000 Liverpool 21 1
2000-01 Liverpool 27 2
2001-02 Liverpool 22 4
2002-03 Liverpool 21 0 **91 7**

SMYTH, Mark (M) 0 0
b.Liverpool 9-1-85
Source: Scholar. *Honours:* England Youth.
2001-02 Liverpool 0 0
2002-03 Liverpool 0 0

TRAORE, Djimi (D) 40 0
H: 6 1 W: 12 06 b.Saint-Ouen 1-3-80
Source: Laval.
1998–99 Liverpool 0 0
1999–2000 Liverpool 0 0
2000-01 Liverpool 8 0
2001-02 Liverpool 0 0
2002-03 Liverpool 32 0 **40 0**

VAUGHAN, Stephen (D) 0 0
b.Liverpool 22-1-85
Source: Scholar.
2001-02 Liverpool 0 0
2002-03 Liverpool 0 0

VIGNAL, Gregory (D) 11 0
H: 5 11 W: 12 03 b.Montpellier 19-7-81
2000-01 Liverpool 6 0
2001-02 Liverpool 4 0
2002-03 Liverpool 1 0 **11 0**

WARNOCK, Stephen (M) 12 1
H: 5 7 W: 12 01 b.Ormskirk 12-12-81
Source: Trainee. *Honours:* England Schools, Youth.
1998–99 Liverpool 0 0
1999–2000 Liverpool 0 0
2000-01 Liverpool 0 0
2001-02 Liverpool 0 0
2002-03 Liverpool 0 0
2002-03 *Bradford C* 12 1 **12 1**

WELSH, John (M) 0 0
H: 5 7 W: 11 06 b.Liverpool 10-1-84
Source: Scholar. *Honours:* England Youth, Under-20.
2000-01 Liverpool 0 0
2001-02 Liverpool 0 0
2002-03 Liverpool 0 0

WHITBREAD, Zak (M) 0 0
b.Liverpool 4-3-84
2002-03 Liverpool 0 0

WILKIE, Ryan (M) 0 0
b.Glasgow 11-12-85
Source: Trainee.
2002-03 Liverpool 0 0

WRIGHT, Andrew (M) 0 0
b.Southport 15-1-85
Source: Scholar.
2001-02 Liverpool 0 0
2002-03 Liverpool 0 0

XAVIER, Abel (D) 231 7
H: 6 3 W: 12 07 b.Mozambique 30-11-72
Honours: Portugal 19 full caps, 2 goals.
1990–91 Amadora 22 0
1991–92 Amadora 21 0
1992–93 Amadora 0 0 **43 0**
1993–94 Benfica 24 1
1994–95 Benfica 22 3 **46 4**
1995–96 Bari 8 0 **8 0**
1996–97 Oviedo 27 0
1997–98 Oviedo 31 0 **58 0**
1998–99 PSV Eindhoven 19 2 **19 2**
1999–2000 Everton 20 0
2000-01 Everton 11 0
2001-02 Everton 12 0 **43 0**
2001-02 Liverpool 10 1
2002-03 Liverpool 4 0 **14 1**

Trainees
Butler, Christopher W; Flynn, Adam J; Gillespie, Steven; Harrison, Paul A; Jones, Mark; Mannix, David C; Massie, Jason D; O'Donnell, Daniel; Smith, James; Spring, Christopher; Willis, Paul A; Wright, Andrew D

LUTON T

BAYLISS, Dave (D) 217 9
H: 6 0 W: 12 11 b.Liverpool 8-6-76
Source: Trainee.
1994–95 Rochdale 1 0
1995–96 Rochdale 28 0
1996–97 Rochdale 24 0
1997–98 Rochdale 29 2
1998–99 Rochdale 25 1
1999–2000 Rochdale 29 3
2000-01 Rochdale 41 3
2001-02 Rochdale 9 0 **186 9**
2001-02 Luton T 18 0
2002-03 Luton T 13 0 **31 0**

BECKWITH, Rob§ (G) 4 0
H: 6 2 W: 13 05 b.London 12-9-84
Source: Scholar.
2002-03 Luton T 4 0 **4 0**

BOYCE, Emmerson (D) 144 4
H: 6 0 W: 11 13 b.Aylesbury 24-9-79
Source: Trainee.
1997–98 Luton T 0 0
1998–99 Luton T 1 0
1999–2000 Luton T 30 1
2000-01 Luton T 42 3
2001-02 Luton T 37 0
2002-03 Luton T 34 0 **144 4**

BRKOVIC, Ahmet (M) 126 12
H: 5 8 W: 11 10 b.Dubrovnik 23-9-74
Source: Dubrovnik.
1999–2000 Leyton Orient 29 5
2000-01 Leyton Orient 40 3
2001-02 Leyton Orient 0 0 **69 8**
2001-02 Luton T 21 1
2002-03 Luton T 36 3 **57 4**

COYNE, Chris (D) 100 4
H: 6 2 W: 13 12 b.Brisbane 20-12-78
Source: Perth SC. *Honours:* Australia Youth, Under-20.
1995–96 West Ham U 0 0
1996–97 West Ham U 0 0
1997–98 West Ham U 0 0
1998–99 West Ham U 1 0 **1 0**
1998–99 *Brentford* 7 0 **7 0**
1998–99 *Southend U* 1 0 **1 0**
1999–2000 Dundee 2 0
2000-01 Dundee 18 0 **20 0**
2001-02 Luton T 31 3
2002-03 Luton T 40 1 **71 4**

CROWE, Dean (F) 138 31
H: 5 7 W: 11 08 b.Stockport 6-6-79
Source: Trainee.
1996–97 Stoke C 0 0
1997–98 Stoke C 16 4
1998–99 Stoke C 38 8
1999–2000 Stoke C 6 0
1999–2000 *Northampton T* 5 0 **5 0**
1999–2000 *Bury* 4 1
2000-01 Stoke C 0 0
2000-01 *Bury* 7 1 **11 2**
2001-02 Stoke C 0 0 **60 12**
2001-02 *Plymouth Arg* 1 0 **1 0**
2001-02 Luton T 34 15
2002-03 Luton T 27 2 **61 17**

DAVIS, Sol (D) 151 0
H: 5 8 W: 11 12 b.Cheltenham 4-9-79
Source: Trainee.
1997–98 Swindon T 6 0
1998–99 Swindon T 25 0
1999–2000 Swindon T 29 0
2000-01 Swindon T 36 0
2001-02 Swindon T 21 0
2002-03 Swindon T 0 0 **117 0**
2002-03 Luton T 34 0 **34 0**

EMBERSON, Carl* (G) 253 0
H: 6 2 W: 14 13 b.Epsom 13-7-73
Source: Trainee.

1991–92	Millwall	0	0		
1992–93	Millwall	0	0		
1992–93	*Colchester U*	13	0		
1993–94	Millwall	0	0		
1994–95	Colchester U	20	0		
1995–96	Colchester U	41	0		
1996–97	Colchester U	35	0		
1997–98	Colchester U	46	0		
1998–99	Colchester U	37	0	**192**	**0**
1999–2000	Walsall	5	0		
2000-01	Walsall	3	0	**8**	**0**
2001-02	Luton T	33	0		
2002-03	Luton T	20	0	**53**	**0**

FOLEY, Kevin§ (M) 2 0
H: 5 10 W: 11 03 b.London 1-11-84
Source: Scholar.

2002-03	Luton T	2	0	**2**	**0**

FORBES, Adrian (M) 157 13
H: 5 7 W: 12 02 b.Greenford 23-1-79
Source: Trainee. *Honours:* England Youth.

1996–97	Norwich C	10	0		
1997–98	Norwich C	33	4		
1998–99	Norwich C	15	0		
1999–2000	Norwich C	25	1		
2000-01	Norwich C	29	3	**112**	**8**
2001-02	Luton T	40	4		
2002-03	Luton T	5	1	**45**	**5**

GRIFFITHS, Carl* (F) 334 124
H: 5 11 W: 12 12 b.Oswestry 15-7-71
Source: Trainee. *Honours:* Wales Youth, Under-21, B.

1988–89	Shrewsbury T	28	6		
1989–90	Shrewsbury T	18	4		
1990–91	Shrewsbury T	19	4		
1991–92	Shrewsbury T	27	8		
1992–93	Shrewsbury T	42	27		
1993–94	Shrewsbury T	9	5	**143**	**54**
1993–94	Manchester C	16	4		
1994–95	Manchester C	2	0		
1995–96	Manchester C	0	0	**18**	**4**
1995–96	Portsmouth	14	2	**14**	**2**
1995–96	Peterborough U	4	1		
1996–97	Peterborough U	12	1	**16**	**2**
1996–97	Leyton Orient	13	6		
1997–98	Leyton Orient	33	18		
1998–99	Leyton Orient	24	8		
1998–99	*Wrexham*	4	3	**4**	**3**
1998–99	Port Vale	3	1		
1999–2000	Port Vale	5	0	**8**	**1**
1999–2000	Leyton Orient	11	4		
2000-01	Leyton Orient	37	14	**118**	**50**
2001-02	Luton T	10	7		
2002-03	Luton T	3	1	**13**	**8**

HILLIER, Ian (D) 45 1
H: 6 1 W: 12 01 b.Neath 26-12-79
Source: Trainee. *Honours:* Wales Schools, Youth, Under-21.

1998–99	Tottenham H	0	0		
1999–2000	Tottenham H	0	0		
2000-01	Tottenham H	0	0		
2001-02	Tottenham H	0	0		
2001-02	Luton T	23	1		
2002-03	Luton T	22	0	**45**	**1**

HOLMES, Peter* (M) 42 3
H: 5 11 W: 11 08 b.Bishop Auckland 18-11-80
Source: Trainee. *Honours:* England Schools.

1997–98	Sheffield W	0	0		
1998–99	Sheffield W	0	0		
1999–2000	Sheffield W	0	0		
2000-01	Luton T	18	1		
2001-02	Luton T	7	1		
2002-03	Luton T	17	1	**42**	**3**

HOWARD, Steve (F) 323 94
H: 6 3 W: 15 00 b.Durham 10-5-76
Source: Tow Law T.

1995–96	Hartlepool U	39	7		
1996–97	Hartlepool U	32	8		
1997–98	Hartlepool U	43	7		
1998–99	Hartlepool U	28	5	**142**	**27**
1998–99	Northampton T	12	0		
1999–2000	Northampton T	41	10		
2000-01	Northampton T	33	8	**86**	**18**
2000-01	Luton T	12	3		
2001-02	Luton T	42	24		
2002-03	Luton T	41	22	**95**	**49**

HUGHES, Paul (M) 89 8
H: 6 0 W: 12 05 b.Hammersmith 17-4-76
Source: Trainee. *Honours:* England Schools.

1994–95	Chelsea	0	0		
1995–96	Chelsea	0	0		
1996–97	Chelsea	12	2		
1997–98	Chelsea	9	0		
1998–99	Chelsea	0	0		
1998–99	*Stockport Co*	7	0	**7**	**0**
1998–99	*Norwich C*	4	1	**4**	**1**
1999–2000	Chelsea	0	0	**21**	**2**
1999–2000	*Crewe Alex*	0	0		
1999–2000	Southampton	0	0		
2000-01	Southampton	0	0		
2001-02	Southampton	0	0		
2001-02	Luton T	22	2		
2002-03	Luton T	35	3	**57**	**5**

JOHNSON, Marvin† (D) 373 7
H: 6 0 W: 13 05 b.Wembley 29-10-68
Source: Apprentice.

1986–87	Luton T	0	0		
1987–88	Luton T	9	0		
1988–89	Luton T	16	0		
1989–90	Luton T	12	0		
1990–91	Luton T	26	0		
1991–92	Luton T	0	0		
1992–93	Luton T	40	3		
1993–94	Luton T	17	0		
1994–95	Luton T	46	1		
1995–96	Luton T	36	0		
1996–97	Luton T	44	0		
1997–98	Luton T	14	2		
1998–99	Luton T	42	0		
1999–2000	Luton T	44	0		
2000-01	Luton T	9	0		
2001-02	Luton T	18	1		
2002-03	Luton T	0	0	**373**	**7**

JUDGE, Matthew§ (F) 1 0
H: 6 0 W: 11 07 b.Barking 18-1-85
Source: Scholar.

2002-03	Luton T	1	0	**1**	**0**

JUPP, Duncan‡ (D) 148 2
H: 6 0 W: 12 12 b.Guildford 25-1-75
Source: Trainee. *Honours:* Scotland Under-21.

1992–93	Fulham	3	0		
1993–94	Fulham	30	0		
1994–95	Fulham	36	2		
1995–96	Fulham	36	0	**105**	**2**
1996–97	Wimbledon	6	0		
1997–98	Wimbledon	3	0		
1998–99	Wimbledon	6	0		
1999–2000	Wimbledon	9	0		
2000-01	Wimbledon	4	0		
2001-02	Wimbledon	2	0		
2002-03	Wimbledon	0	0	**30**	**0**
2002-03	*Notts Co*	8	0	**8**	**0**
2002-03	Luton T	5	0	**5**	**0**

KIMBLE, Alan* (D) 536 24
H: 5 10 W: 12 08 b.Dagenham 6-8-66

1984–85	Charlton Ath	6	0		
1985–86	Charlton Ath	0	0	**6**	**0**
1985–86	*Exeter C*	1	0	**1**	**0**
1986–87	Cambridge U	35	0		
1987–88	Cambridge U	41	2		
1988–89	Cambridge U	45	6		
1989–90	Cambridge U	44	8		
1990–91	Cambridge U	43	4		
1991–92	Cambridge U	45	0		
1992–93	Cambridge U	46	4	**299**	**24**
1993–94	Wimbledon	14	0		
1994–95	Wimbledon	26	0		
1995–96	Wimbledon	31	0		
1996–97	Wimbledon	31	0		
1997–98	Wimbledon	25	0		
1998–99	Wimbledon	26	0		
1999–2000	Wimbledon	28	0		
2000-01	Wimbledon	25	0		
2001-02	Wimbledon	9	0	**215**	**0**
2001-02	*Peterborough U*	3	0	**3**	**0**
2002-03	Luton T	12	0	**12**	**0**

LEARY, Michael (M) 0 0
H: 5 11 W: 11 10 b.Ealing 17-4-83
Source: Scholar.

2001-02	Luton T	0	0		
2002-03	Luton T	0	0		

MANSELL, Lee (M) 30 6
H: 5 9 W: 11 00 b.Gloucester 28-10-82
Source: Scholar.

2000-01	Luton T	18	5		
2001-02	Luton T	11	1		
2002-03	Luton T	1	0	**30**	**6**

NEILSON, Alan (D) 170 3
H: 5 11 W: 12 12 b.Wegburg 26-9-72
Source: Trainee. *Honours:* Wales Under-21, B, 5 full caps.

1990–91	Newcastle U	3	0		
1991–92	Newcastle U	16	1		
1992–93	Newcastle U	3	0		
1993–94	Newcastle U	14	0		
1994–95	Newcastle U	6	0	**42**	**1**
1995–96	Southampton	18	0		
1996–97	Southampton	29	0		
1997–98	Southampton	8	0	**55**	**0**
1997–98	Fulham	17	0		
1998–99	Fulham	4	1		
1999–2000	Fulham	5	1		
2000-01	Fulham	3	0		
2001-02	Fulham	0	0	**29**	**2**
2001-02	*Grimsby T*	10	0	**10**	**0**
2001-02	Luton T	8	0		
2002-03	Luton T	26	0	**34**	**0**

NICHOLLS, Kevin (M) 122 14
H: 5 10 W: 12 04 b.Newham 2-1-79
Source: Trainee. *Honours:* England Youth.

1995–96	Charlton Ath	0	0		
1996–97	Charlton Ath	6	1		
1997–98	Charlton Ath	6	0		
1998–99	Charlton Ath	0	0	**12**	**1**
1998–99	*Brighton & HA*	4	1	**4**	**1**
1999–2000	Wigan Ath	8	0		
2000-01	Wigan Ath	20	0	**28**	**0**
2001-02	Luton T	42	7		
2002-03	Luton T	36	5	**78**	**12**

OVENDALE, Mark* (G) 140 0
H: 6 2 W: 14 04 b.Leicester 22-11-73
Source: Wisbech T.

1994–95	Northampton T	6	0	**6**	**0**

From Barry T.

1997–98	Bournemouth	0	0		
1998–99	Bournemouth	46	0		
1999–2000	Bournemouth	43	0	**89**	**0**
2000-01	Luton T	26	0		
2001-02	Luton T	13	0		
2002-03	Luton T	6	0	**45**	**0**

PERRETT, Russell (D) 161 8
H: 6 1 W: 12 04 b.Barton-on-Sea 18-6-73
Source: AFC Lymington.

1995–96	Portsmouth	9	0		
1996–97	Portsmouth	32	1		
1997–98	Portsmouth	16	1		
1998–99	Portsmouth	15	0	**72**	**2**
1999–2000	Cardiff C	27	1		
2000-01	Cardiff C	2	0	**29**	**1**
2001-02	Luton T	40	3		
2002-03	Luton T	20	2	**60**	**5**

ROBINSON, Steve (M) 301 54
H: 5 9 W: 11 02 b.Lisburn 10-12-74
Source: Trainee. *Honours:* Northern Ireland Schools, Youth, Under-21, B, 5 full caps.

1992–93	Tottenham H	0	0		
1993–94	Tottenham H	2	0		
1994–95	Tottenham H	0	0	**2**	**0**
1994–95	*Leyton Orient*	0	0		
1994–95	Bournemouth	32	5		
1995–96	Bournemouth	41	7		
1996–97	Bournemouth	40	7		
1997–98	Bournemouth	45	10		
1998–99	Bournemouth	42	13		
1999–2000	Bournemouth	40	9	**240**	**51**
2000-01	Preston NE	22	1		
2001-02	Preston NE	2	0	**24**	**1**
2001-02	*Bristol C*	6	1	**6**	**1**
2002-03	Luton T	29	1	**29**	**1**

SKELTON, Aaron* (M) 150 19
H: 5 11 W: 13 01 b.Welwyn 22-11-74
Source: Trainee.

1992–93	Luton T	0	0		
1993–94	Luton T	0	0		
1994–95	Luton T	5	0		
1995–96	Luton T	0	0		
1996–97	Luton T	3	0		
1997–98	Colchester U	39	7		
1998–99	Colchester U	9	0		
1999–2000	Colchester U	33	4		
2000-01	Colchester U	44	6	**125**	**17**
2001-02	Luton T	9	1		
2002-03	Luton T	8	1	**25**	**2**

SPRING, Matthew (M) 226 24
H: 6 0 W: 12 06 b.Harlow 17-11-79
Source: Trainee.

1997–98	Luton T	12	0		
1998–99	Luton T	45	3		
1999–2000	Luton T	45	6		
2000-01	Luton T	41	4		
2001-02	Luton T	42	6		
2002-03	Luton T	41	5	**226**	**24**

THORPE, Tony (F) 309 122
H: 5 9 W: 12 01 b.Leicester 10-4-74
Source: Leicester C.

1992–93	Luton T	0	0		
1993–94	Luton T	14	1		
1994–95	Luton T	4	0		
1995–96	Luton T	33	7		
1996–97	Luton T	41	28		
1997–98	Luton T	28	14		
1997–98	Fulham	13	3	**13**	**3**
1998–99	Bristol C	16	2		
1998–99	*Reading*	6	1	**6**	**1**
1998–99	*Luton T*	8	4		
1999–2000	Bristol C	31	13		
1999–2000	*Luton T*	4	1		
2000-01	Bristol C	39	19		
2001-02	Bristol C	42	16	**128**	**50**
2002-03	Luton T	30	13	**162**	**68**

WINTERS, Robert‡ (F) 250 67
H: 5 10 W: 11 06 b.East Kilbride 4-11-74
Source: Muirend Amateur. *Honours:* Scotland 1 full cap.

1993–94	Dundee U	0	0		
1994–95	Dundee U	13	2		
1995–96	Dundee U	35	7		
1996–97	Dundee U	36	8		
1997–98	Dundee U	30	8		
1998–99	Dundee U	3	1		
1998–99	Aberdeen	28	12		
1999–2000	Aberdeen	33	7		
2000-01	Aberdeen	37	9		
2001-02	Aberdeen	34	13	**132**	**41**
2001-02	Dundee U	0	0	**117**	**26**
2002-03	Luton T	1	0	**1**	**0**

Scholars
Barnett, Leon P; Beckwith, Robert; Brill, Dean M; Chatfield, Jonathan D; Davies, Curtis; Deeney, Joseph, E; Dillon, Christopher H; Foley, Kevin P; Gillman, Robert; Howell, Max; Jeffery, Marcus P; Judge, Matthew P; Mansell, Richard J; O'Leary, Stephen; Okai, Parys; Osborn, James

Non-Contract
Johnson, Marvin A

MACCLESFIELD T

ABBEY, Ben‡ (F) 34 8
H: 5 7 W: 11 00 b.London 13-5-78
Source: Crawley T. *Honours:* Nigeria 3 full caps.

1999–2000	Oxford U	10	0		
2000-01	Oxford U	0	0	**10**	**0**
2000-01	Southend U	24	8		
2001-02	Southend U	0	0	**24**	**8**

From Woking

2002-03	Macclesfield T	0	0		

ABBEY, George (D) 75 1
H: 5 10 W: 10 08 b.Port Harcourt 20-10-78
Source: Sharks.

1999–2000	Macclesfield T	18	0		
2000-01	Macclesfield T	18	0		
2001-02	Macclesfield T	17	0		
2002-03	Macclesfield T	22	1	**75**	**1**

ADAMS, Danny (D) 121 1
H: 5 8 W: 13 09 b.Manchester 3-1-76
Source: Altrincham.

2000-01	Macclesfield T	37	0		
2001-02	Macclesfield T	39	0		
2002-03	Macclesfield T	45	1	**121**	**1**

ALDRIDGE, Paul* (M) 7 0
H: 5 11 W: 12 04 b.Liverpool 2-12-81
Source: Scholarship.

1999–2000	Tranmere R	4	0		
2000-01	Tranmere R	2	0		
2001-02	Tranmere R	0	0	**6**	**0**
2001-02	Macclesfield T	0	0		
2002-03	Macclesfield T	1	0	**1**	**0**

ASKEY, John† (F) 181 31
H: 6 0 W: 12 02 b.Stoke 4-11-64
Source: Port Vale.

1997–98	Macclesfield T	39	6		
1998–99	Macclesfield T	38	4		
1999–2000	Macclesfield T	40	15		
2000-01	Macclesfield T	37	3		
2001-02	Macclesfield T	18	1		
2002-03	Macclesfield T	9	2	**181**	**31**

BRACKENRIDGE, Steve§ (M) 2 0
b.Rochdale 31-7-84
Source: Scholar.

2002-03	Macclesfield T	2	0	**2**	**0**

BYRNE, Chris‡ (M) 104 18
H: 5 10 W: 10 08 b.Manchester 9-2-75
Source: Crewe Alex, Macclesfield T.

1997–98	Sunderland	8	0	**8**	**0**
1997–98	Stockport Co	26	7		
1998–99	Stockport Co	11	2		
1999–2000	Stockport Co	18	2		
1999–2000	*Macclesfield T*	5	0		
2000-01	Stockport Co	1	0	**56**	**11**
2001-02	Macclesfield T	32	6		
2002-03	Macclesfield T	3	1	**40**	**7**

CAME, Shaun‡ (D) 9 0
H: 6 3 W: 11 10 b.Crewe 15-6-83
Source: Trainee.

2000-01	Macclesfield T	7	0		
2001-02	Macclesfield T	1	0		
2002-03	Macclesfield T	1	0	**9**	**0**

CARR, Michael§ (D) 4 0
b.Crewe 6-12-83
Source: Scholar.

2002-03	Macclesfield T	4	0	**4**	**0**

EATON, David* (F) 20 5
b.Liverpool 30-9-81
Source: Scholar.

2001-02	Everton	0	0		
2002-03	Macclesfield T	20	5	**20**	**5**

HADDRELL, Matt (D) 4 0
b.Staffordshire 19-3-81

2002-03	Macclesfield T	4	0	**4**	**0**

HARDY, Lee* (M) 17 0
H: 6 1 W: 12 06 b.Blackpool 26-11-81
Source: Scholar.

2000-01	Blackburn R	0	0		
2001-02	Oldham Ath	1	0	**1**	**0**
2002-03	Macclesfield T	16	0	**16**	**0**

HITCHEN, Steve (D) 142 1
H: 5 8 W: 11 07 b.Salford 28-11-76
Source: Trainee.

1995–96	Blackburn R	0	0		
1996–97	Blackburn R	0	0		
1997–98	Macclesfield T	2	0		
1998–99	Macclesfield T	35	0		
1999–2000	Macclesfield T	5	0		
2000-01	Macclesfield T	37	0		
2001-02	Macclesfield T	30	1		
2002-03	Macclesfield T	33	0	**142**	**1**

LIGHTBOURNE, Kyle* (F) 388 106
H: 6 2 W: 11 11 b.Bermuda 29-9-68
Honours: Bermuda 22 full caps.

1992–93	Scarborough	19	3		
1993–94	Scarborough	0	0	**19**	**3**
1993–94	Walsall	35	7		
1994–95	Walsall	42	23		
1995–96	Walsall	43	15		
1996–97	Walsall	45	20	**165**	**65**
1997–98	Coventry C	7	0	**7**	**0**
1997–98	*Fulham*	4	2	**4**	**2**
1997–98	Stoke C	13	2		
1998–99	Stoke C	36	7		
1999–2000	Stoke C	40	7		
2000-01	Stoke C	22	5	**111**	**21**
2000-01	*Swindon T*	2	0	**2**	**0**
2000-01	*Cardiff C*	3	0	**3**	**0**
2001-02	Macclesfield T	29	4		
2001-02	*Hull C*	4	0	**4**	**0**
2002-03	Macclesfield T	44	11	**73**	**15**

MACAULEY, Steve (D) 299 27
H: 6 1 W: 12 04 b.Lytham 4-3-69
Source: Fleetwood T.

1991–92	Crewe Alex	9	1		
1992–93	Crewe Alex	25	3		
1993–94	Crewe Alex	17	3		
1994–95	Crewe Alex	43	4		
1995–96	Crewe Alex	29	7		
1996–97	Crewe Alex	42	2		
1997–98	Crewe Alex	0	0		
1998–99	Crewe Alex	20	1		
1999–2000	Crewe Alex	37	4		
2000-01	Crewe Alex	30	1		
2001-02	Crewe Alex	9	0	**261**	**26**
2001-02	*Macclesfield T*	12	0		
2002-03	Rochdale	6	0	**6**	**0**
2002-03	Macclesfield T	20	1	**32**	**1**

MARTIN, Lee* (G) 242 0
H: 6 0 W: 13 07 b.Huddersfield 9-9-68
Source: Trainee. *Honours:* England Schools.

1987–88	Huddersfield T	18	0		
1988–89	Huddersfield T	0	0		
1989–90	Huddersfield T	25	0		
1990–91	Huddersfield T	4	0		
1991–92	Huddersfield T	7	0	**54**	**0**
1992–93	Blackpool	24	0		
1993–94	Blackpool	43	0		
1994–95	Blackpool	31	0		
1995–96	Blackpool	0	0		
1995–96	*Bradford C*	0	0		
1996–97	Blackpool	0	0	**98**	**0**
1996–97	Rochdale	0	0		
1997–98	Rochdale	0	0		
1998–99	Halifax T	37	0	**37**	**0**
1999–2000	Macclesfield T	21	0		
2000-01	Macclesfield T	21	0		
2001-02	Macclesfield T	9	0		
2002-03	Macclesfield T	2	0	**53**	**0**

MILES, John (F) 14 5
H: 5 10 W: 10 08 b.Fazackerley 28-9-81
Source: Trainee.

1998–99	Liverpool	0	0		
1999–2000	Liverpool	0	0		
2000-01	Liverpool	0	0		
2001-02	Liverpool	0	0		
2001-02	Stoke C	1	0	**1**	**0**
2002-03	Crewe Alex	5	1	**5**	**1**
2002-03	Macclesfield T	8	4	**8**	**4**

MUNROE, Karl (M) 84 1
H: 6 1 W: 11 00 b.Manchester 23-9-79
Source: Trainee.

1997–98	Swansea C	1	0		
1998–99	Swansea C	0	0		
1999–2000	Swansea C	0	0	**1**	**0**
1999–2000	Macclesfield T	5	0		
2000-01	Macclesfield T	23	1		
2001-02	Macclesfield T	30	0		
2002-03	Macclesfield T	25	0	**83**	**1**

NASH, Martin‡ (M) 32 0
H: 5 11 W: 12 03 b.Regina 27-12-75
Source: Regina. *Honours:* Canada 26 full caps, 2 goals.

1996–97	Stockport Co	3	0		
1997–98	Stockport Co	8	0	**11**	**0**

From Vancouver 89ers

1999–2000	Chester C	16	0	**16**	**0**

From Rochester.

2002-03	Macclesfield T	5	0	**5**	**0**

O'NEILL, Paul* (D) 36 0
H: 6 3 W: 12 04 b.Farnworth 17-6-82
Source: Trainee.

1999–2000	Macclesfield T	1	0		
2000-01	Macclesfield T	12	0		
2001-02	Macclesfield T	11	0		
2002-03	Macclesfield T	12	0	**36**	**0**

PRIEST, Chris (M) 288 37
H: 5 10 W: 12 00 b.Leigh 18-10-73
Source: Trainee.

1992–93	Everton	0	0		
1993–94	Everton	0	0		
1994–95	Everton	0	0		
1994–95	Chester C	24	1		
1995–96	Chester C	39	13		
1996–97	Chester C	32	2		
1997–98	Chester C	37	6		
1998–99	Chester C	35	4	**167**	**26**
1999–2000	Macclesfield T	36	4		
2000-01	Macclesfield T	15	4		
2001-02	Macclesfield T	33	1		
2002-03	Macclesfield T	37	2	**121**	**11**

RIDLER, Dave‡ (D) 172 1
H: 6 0 W: 12 01 b.Liverpool 12-3-76
Source: Prescot T.

1996–97	Wrexham	11	0		
1997–98	Wrexham	20	0		
1998–99	Wrexham	36	1		
1999–2000	Wrexham	25	0		
2000-01	Wrexham	24	0	**116**	**1**
2001-02	Macclesfield T	39	0		
2002-03	Macclesfield T	17	0	**56**	**0**

ROBINSON, Neil (F) **10 0**
H: 6 0 W: 12 12 b.Liverpool 18-11-79
Source: Prescot Cables.
2002-03 Macclesfield T 10 0 **10 0**

ROSS, Neil (F) **22 2**
H: 6 1 W: 12 02 b.West Bromwich 10-8-82
Source: Birmingham C Trainee, Leeds U Trainee.
1999–2000 Leeds U 0 0
1999–2000 Stockport Co 2 0
2000-01 Stockport Co 0 0
2001-02 *Bristol R* 5 0 **5 0**
2001-02 Stockport Co 3 1
2002-03 Stockport Co 4 1 **9 2**
2002-03 Macclesfield T 8 0 **8 0**

SMITH, David (M) **298 5**
H: 5 10 W: 12 11 b.Liverpool 26-12-70
Source: Trainee.
1989–90 Norwich C 1 0
1990–91 Norwich C 3 0
1991–92 Norwich C 1 0
1992–93 Norwich C 6 0
1993–94 Norwich C 7 0 **18 0**
1994–95 Oxford U 42 0
1995–96 Oxford U 45 1
1996–97 Oxford U 45 0
1997–98 Oxford U 44 1
1998–99 Oxford U 22 0 **198 2**
1998–99 Stockport Co 17 1
1999–2000 Stockport Co 9 1
2000-01 Stockport Co 34 1
2001-02 Stockport Co 11 0 **71 3**
2001-02 *Macclesfield T* 8 0
2002-03 Macclesfield T 3 0 **11 0**

TINSON, Darren (D) **263 5**
H: 6 0 W: 12 07 b.Birmingham 15-11-69
Source: Northwich V.
1997–98 Macclesfield T 44 0
1998–99 Macclesfield T 37 0
1999–2000 Macclesfield T 46 1
2000-01 Macclesfield T 45 3
2001-02 Macclesfield T 46 1
2002-03 Macclesfield T 45 0 **263 5**

TIPTON, Matt (F) **161 27**
H: 5 10 W: 13 10 b.Bangor 29-6-80
Source: Trainee. *Honours:* Wales Youth, Under-21.
1997–98 Oldham Ath 3 0
1998–99 Oldham Ath 28 2
1999–2000 Oldham Ath 29 3
2000-01 Oldham Ath 30 5
2001-02 Oldham Ath 22 5 **112 15**
2001-02 Macclesfield T 13 3
2002-03 Macclesfield T 36 9 **49 12**

WELCH, Michael (D) **45 3**
H: 6 3 W: 11 12 b.Crewe 11-1-82
Source: Barnsley Scholar.
2001-02 Macclesfield T 6 0
2002-03 Macclesfield T 39 3 **45 3**

WHITAKER, Danny (M) **57 12**
H: 5 10 W: 11 02 b.Manchester 14-11-80
2000-01 Macclesfield T 0 0
2001-02 Macclesfield T 16 2
2002-03 Macclesfield T 41 10 **57 12**

WILSON, Steve (G) **264 0**
H: 6 0 W: 11 02 b.Hull 24-4-74
Source: Trainee.
1990–91 Hull C 2 0
1991–92 Hull C 3 0
1992–93 Hull C 26 0
1993–94 Hull C 9 0
1994–95 Hull C 20 0
1995–96 Hull C 19 0
1996–97 Hull C 15 0
1997–98 Hull C 37 0
1998–99 Hull C 23 0
1999–2000 Hull C 27 0
2000-01 Hull C 0 0 **181 0**
2000-01 *Macclesfield T* 1 0
2001-02 Macclesfield T 38 0
2002-03 Macclesfield T 44 0 **83 0**

Scholars
Bayliss, Richard L; Brackenridge, Stephen J; Campbell, John R; Carr, Michael A; Deasy, Timothy; Drummond, Philip A; Goodeve, Jordan; Higgins, Matthew R; McDonald, Marvin M; Naylor, Adam R; Owens, Stephen P; Swann, Paul M; Teague, Andrew H; Vernon, Karl M

Non-Contract
Askey, John C

MANCHESTER C

ALMOND, James‡ (F) **0 0**
b.Northallerton 5-10-83
Source: Scholar. *Honours:* England Youth.
2000-01 Manchester C 0 0
2001-02 Manchester C 0 0
2002-03 Manchester C 0 0

ANELKA, Nicolas (F) **191 54**
H: 6 1 W: 13 03 b.Versailles 14-3-79
Honours: France Youth, Under-21, 28 full caps, 6 goals.
1995–96 Paris St Germain 2 0
1996–97 Paris St Germain 8 1
1996–97 Arsenal 4 0
1997–98 Arsenal 26 6
1998–99 Arsenal 35 17 **65 23**
1999–2000 Real Madrid 19 2 **19 2**
2000-01 Paris St Germain 27 8
2001-02 Paris St Germain 12 2 **49 11**
2001-02 Liverpool 20 4 **20 4**
2002-03 Manchester C 38 14 **38 14**

BARTON, Joey (M) **7 1**
H: 5 11 W: 11 06 b.Huyton 2-9-82
Source: Scholar.
2001-02 Manchester C 0 0
2002-03 Manchester C 7 1 **7 1**

BELMADI, Djamel (M) **139 23**
H: 5 8 W: 10 10 b.Champigny-sur-Marne 27-3-76
Honours: Algeria full caps.
1995–96 Paris St Germain 1 0 **1 0**
1996–97 Martigues 31 8 **31 8**
1997–98 Marseille 0 0
1998–99 Cannes 26 6 **26 6**
1999–2000 Marseille 9 1
1999–2000 Celta Vigo 10 0 **10 0**
2000-01 Marseille 29 8
2001-02 Marseille 10 0
2002-03 Marseille 15 0 **63 9**
2002-03 Manchester C 8 0 **8 0**

BENARBIA, Ali (M) **429 45**
H: 5 6 W: 11 04 b.Oran 8-10-68
Honours: Algeria full caps.
1988–89 Martigues 30 2
1989–90 Martigues 28 3
1990–91 Martigues 29 5
1991–92 Martigues 24 2
1992–93 Martigues 25 2
1993–94 Martigues 34 2
1994–95 Martigues 31 7 **201 23**
1995–96 Monaco 25 4
1996–97 Monaco 35 3
1997–98 Monaco 30 1 **90 8**
1998–99 Bordeaux 25 3 **25 3**
1999–2000 Paris St Germain 27 0
2000-01 Paris St Germain 14 0
2001-02 Paris St Germain 1 0 **42 0**
2001-02 Manchester C 38 8
2002-03 Manchester C 33 3 **71 11**

BERKOVIC, Eyal (M) **316 58**
H: 5 9 W: 10 13 b.Haifa 2-4-72
Honours: Israel 75 full caps, 9 goals.
1992–93 Maccabi Haifa 32 7
1993–94 Maccabi Haifa 38 10
1994–95 Maccabi Haifa 29 5
1995–96 Maccabi Haifa 29 3 **128 25**
1996–97 Southampton 28 4 **28 4**
1997–98 West Ham U 35 7
1998–99 West Ham U 30 3 **65 10**
1999–2000 Celtic 28 9
2000-01 Celtic 4 1 **32 10**
2000-01 Blackburn R 11 2 **11 2**
2001-02 Manchester C 25 6
2002-03 Manchester C 27 1 **52 7**

BERMINGHAM, Karl‡ (M) **0 0**
b.Dublin 6-10-85
Source: Scholar.
2002-03 Manchester C 0 0

BISCHOFF, Mikkel (D) **11 0**
H: 6 3 W: 13 12 b.Denmark 3-2-82
2001-02 AB Copenhagen 10 0 **10 0**
2002-03 Manchester C 1 0 **1 0**

BROWNE, Gary* (F) **0 0**
H: 5 10 W: 10 10 b.Dundonald 17-1-83
Source: Scholar. *Honours:* Northern Ireland Under-21.
2000-01 Manchester C 0 0
2001-02 Manchester C 0 0
2002-03 Manchester C 0 0

CHARVET, Laurent‡ (D) **173 22**
H: 5 11 W: 13 07 b.Beziers 8-5-73
1994–95 Cannes 19 4
1995–96 Cannes 31 8
1996–97 Cannes 38 6
1997–98 Cannes 11 1 **99 19**
1997–98 Chelsea 11 2 **11 2**
1998–99 Newcastle U 31 1
1999–2000 Newcastle U 2 0
2000-01 Newcastle U 7 0 **40 1**
2000-01 Manchester C 20 0
2001-02 Manchester C 3 0
2002-03 Manchester C 0 0 **23 0**

CROFT, Lee (F) **0 0**
b.Wigan 21-6-85
Source: Scholar. *Honours:* England Youth.
2002-03 Manchester C 0 0

DISTIN, Sylvain (D) **149 4**
H: 6 3 W: 14 04 b.Bagnolet 16-12-77
1998–99 Tours 26 3 **26 3**
1999–2000 Gueugnon 33 1 **33 1**
2000-01 Paris St Germain 28 0 **28 0**
2001-02 Newcastle U 28 0 **28 0**
2002-03 Manchester C 34 0 **34 0**

DUNNE, Richard (D) **153 1**
H: 6 2 W: 16 10 b.Dublin 21-9-79
Source: Trainee. *Honours:* Eire Under-21, 17 full caps, 3 goals.
1996–97 Everton 7 0
1997–98 Everton 3 0
1998–99 Everton 16 0
1999–2000 Everton 31 0
2000-01 Everton 3 0 **60 0**
2000-01 Manchester C 25 0
2001-02 Manchester C 43 1
2002-03 Manchester C 25 0 **93 1**

ELLEGAARD, Kevin Stuhr (G) **0 0**
H: 6 5 W: 14 13 b.Copenhagen 23-5-83
Source: Farum.
2001-02 Manchester C 0 0
2002-03 Manchester C 0 0

ELLIOTT, Stephen (F) **0 0**
b.Dublin 6-1-84
Source: School. *Honours:* Eire Under-21.
2000-01 Manchester C 0 0
2001-02 Manchester C 0 0
2002-03 Manchester C 0 0

FLOOD, William (M) **0 0**
b.Dublin 10-4-85
2001-02 Manchester C 0 0
2002-03 Manchester C 0 0

FOE, Marc Vivien (M) (Deceased) **201 24**
H: 6 2 W: 14 06 b.Yaounde 1-5-75
Source: Canon Yaounde. *Honours:* Cameroon 64 full caps, 8 goals.
1994–95 Lens 15 3
1995–96 Lens 19 2
1996–97 Lens 28 2
1997–98 Lens 18 2
1998–99 Lens 5 2 **85 11**
1998–99 West Ham U 13 0
1999–2000 West Ham U 25 1 **38 1**
2000-01 Lyon 25 1
2001-02 Lyon 18 2 **43 3**
2002-03 Manchester C 35 9 **35 9**

FOWLER, Robbie (F) **279 136**
H: 5 9 W: 12 04 b.Liverpool 9-4-75
Source: Trainee. *Honours:* England Youth, B, Under-21, 26 full caps, 7 goals.
1991–92 Liverpool 0 0
1992–93 Liverpool 0 0
1993–94 Liverpool 28 12
1994–95 Liverpool 42 25
1995–96 Liverpool 38 28
1996–97 Liverpool 32 18
1997–98 Liverpool 20 9
1998–99 Liverpool 25 14
1999–2000 Liverpool 14 3
2000-01 Liverpool 27 8
2001-02 Liverpool 10 3 **236 120**
2001-02 Leeds U 22 12
2002-03 Leeds U 8 2 **30 14**
2002-03 Manchester C 13 2 **13 2**

GILDER, Philip* (M) **0 0**
b.Manchester 5-11-83
Source: Scholar.
2002-03 Manchester C 0 0

GOATER, Shaun (F) **469 194**
H: 6 0 W: 12 02 b.Bermuda 25-2-70
Honours: Bermuda 19 full caps.

1988–89	Manchester U	0	0		
1989–90	Manchester U	0	0		
1989–90	Rotherham U	12	2		
1990–91	Rotherham U	22	2		
1991–92	Rotherham U	24	9		
1992–93	Rotherham U	23	7		
1993–94	Rotherham U	39	13		
1993–94	*Notts Co*	1	0	**1**	**0**
1994–95	Rotherham U	45	19		
1995–96	Rotherham U	44	18	**209**	**70**
1996–97	Bristol C	42	23		
1997–98	Bristol C	33	17	**75**	**40**
1997–98	Manchester C	7	3		
1998–99	Manchester C	43	17		
1999–2000	Manchester C	40	23		
2000–01	Manchester C	26	6		
2001–02	Manchester C	42	28		
2002–03	Manchester C	26	7	**184**	**84**

HAALAND, Alf-Inge (D) **187 18**
H: 6 1 W: 12 06 b.Bryne 23-11-72
Source: Bryne. *Honours:* Norway 34 full caps.

1993–94	Nottingham F	3	0		
1994–95	Nottingham F	20	1		
1995–96	Nottingham F	17	0		
1996–97	Nottingham F	35	6	**75**	**7**
1997–98	Leeds U	32	7		
1998–99	Leeds U	29	1		
1999–2000	Leeds U	13	0	**74**	**8**
2000–01	Manchester C	35	3		
2001–02	Manchester C	3	0		
2002–03	Manchester C	0	0	**38**	**3**

HORLOCK, Kevin (M) **367 59**
H: 6 0 W: 12 12 b.Erith 1-11-72
Source: Trainee. *Honours:* Northern Ireland B, 32 full caps.

1991–92	West Ham U	0	0		
1992–93	West Ham U	0	0		
1992–93	Swindon T	14	1		
1993–94	Swindon T	38	0		
1994–95	Swindon T	38	1		
1995–96	Swindon T	45	12		
1996–97	Swindon T	28	8	**163**	**22**
1996–97	Manchester C	18	4		
1997–98	Manchester C	25	5		
1998–99	Manchester C	37	9		
1999–2000	Manchester C	38	10		
2000–01	Manchester C	14	2		
2001–02	Manchester C	42	7		
2002–03	Manchester C	30	0	**204**	**37**

HOWEY, Steve (D) **285 17**
H: 6 2 W: 13 05 b.Sunderland 26-10-71
Source: Trainee. *Honours:* England 4 full caps.

1988–89	Newcastle U	1	0		
1989–90	Newcastle U	0	0		
1990–91	Newcastle U	11	0		
1991–92	Newcastle U	21	1		
1992–93	Newcastle U	41	2		
1993–94	Newcastle U	14	0		
1994–95	Newcastle U	30	1		
1995–96	Newcastle U	28	1		
1996–97	Newcastle U	8	1		
1997–98	Newcastle U	14	0		
1998–99	Newcastle U	14	0		
1999–2000	Newcastle U	9	0	**191**	**6**
2000–01	Manchester C	36	6		
2001–02	Manchester C	34	3		
2002–03	Manchester C	24	2	**94**	**11**

HUCKERBY, Darren (F) **247 65**
H: 5 10 W: 12 02 b.Nottingham 23-4-76
Source: Trainee. *Honours:* England Under-21, B.

1993–94	Lincoln C	6	1		
1994–95	Lincoln C	6	2		
1995–96	Lincoln C	16	2	**28**	**5**
1995–96	Newcastle U	1	0		
1996–97	Newcastle U	0	0	**1**	**0**
1996–97	*Millwall*	6	3	**6**	**3**
1996–97	Coventry C	25	5		
1997–98	Coventry C	34	14		
1998–99	Coventry C	34	9		
1999–2000	Coventry C	1	0	**94**	**28**
1999–2000	Leeds U	33	2		
2000–01	Leeds U	7	0	**40**	**2**
2000–01	Manchester C	13	1		
2001–02	Manchester C	40	20		
2002–03	Manchester C	16	1	**69**	**22**
2002–03	*Nottingham F*	9	5	**9**	**5**

JAMES, William* (M) **0 0**
b.Swansea 11-1-84
Source: Scholar.

2001–02	Manchester C	0	0		
2002–03	Manchester C	0	0		

JENSEN, Niclas (D) **269 16**
H: 5 9 W: 13 00 b.Copenhagen 17-8-74
Honours: Denmark 21 full caps.

1992–93	Lyngby	12	2		
1993–94	Lyngby	21	0		
1994–95	Lyngby	20	1		
1995–96	Lyngby	32	3		
1996–97	Lyngby	7	1	**92**	**7**
1996–97	PSV Eindhoven	2	0		
1997–98	PSV Eindhoven	2	0	**4**	**0**
1997–98	FC Copenhagen	10	0		
1998–99	FC Copenhagen	33	4		
1999–2000	FC Copenhagen	29	1		
2000–01	FC Copenhagen	32	1		
2001–02	FC Copenhagen	18	1	**122**	**7**
2001–02	Manchester C	18	1		
2002–03	Manchester C	33	1	**51**	**2**

JIHAI, Sun (D) **58 2**
H: 5 9 W: 12 04 b.Dalian 30-9-77
Source: Dalian Wanda. *Honours:* China 62 full caps, 8 goals.

1998–99	Crystal Palace	23	0	**23**	**0**
From Dalian Wanda.					
2001–02	Manchester C	7	0		
2002–03	Manchester C	28	2	**35**	**2**

JORDAN, Stephen (D) **12 0**
H: 6 1 W: 11 13 b.Warrington 6-3-82
Source: Scholarship.

1998–99	Manchester C	0	0		
1999–2000	Manchester C	0	0		
2000–01	Manchester C	0	0		
2001–02	Manchester C	0	0		
2002–03	Manchester C	1	0	**1**	**0**
2002–03	*Cambridge U*	11	0	**11**	**0**

JOYCE, Damien‡ (M) **0 0**
H: 5 8 W: 12 03 b.Dublin 8-3-83
Source: Scholarship.

1999–2000	Manchester C	0	0		
2000–01	Manchester C	0	0		
2001–02	Manchester C	0	0		
2002–03	Manchester C	0	0		

KERKAR, Karim‡ (M) **18 0**
H: 5 8 W: 10 12 b.Givors 3-1-77

2001–02	Le Havre	18	0	**18**	**0**
2002–03	Manchester C	0	0		

MACKEN, Jon (F) **197 68**
H: 5 11 W: 13 06 b.Manchester 7-9-77
Source: Trainee. *Honours:* England Youth.

1996–97	Manchester U	0	0		
1997–98	Preston NE	29	6		
1998–99	Preston NE	42	8		
1999–2000	Preston NE	44	22		
2000–01	Preston NE	38	19		
2001–02	Preston NE	31	8	**184**	**63**
2001–02	Manchester C	8	5		
2002–03	Manchester C	5	0	**13**	**5**

MATTHEWS, James (M) **0 0**
b.Dublin 2-2-85
Source: Scholar.

2002–03	Manchester C	0	0		

McCARTHY, Patrick (D) **18 0**
H: 6 2 W: 12 12 b.Dublin 31-5-83
Source: Scholar.

2000–01	Manchester C	0	0		
2001–02	Manchester C	0	0		
2002–03	Manchester C	0	0		
2002–03	*Boston U*	12	0	**12**	**0**
2002–03	*Notts Co*	6	0	**6**	**0**

McDOWALL, Ryan (M) **0 0**
b.Knowsley 30-3-84
Source: School.

2000–01	Manchester C	0	0		
2001–02	Manchester C	0	0		
2002–03	Manchester C	0	0		

METTOMO, Lucien (D) **108 10**
H: 6 0 W: 13 05 b.Douala 19-4-77
Source: Ocean Kribi. *Honours:* Cameroon 30 full caps, 1 goal.

1998–99	St Etienne	33	7		
1999–2000	St Etienne	26	1		
2000–01	St Etienne	17	1		
2001–02	St Etienne	5	0	**81**	**9**
2001–02	Manchester C	23	1		
2002–03	Manchester C	4	0	**27**	**1**

MURPHY, Brian* (G) **1 0**
H: 6 1 W: 13 08 b.Waterford 7-5-83

2000–01	Manchester C	0	0		
2001–02	Manchester C	0	0		
2002–03	Manchester C	0	0		
2002–03	*Oldham Ath*	0	0		
2002–03	*Peterborough U*	1	0	**1**	**0**

MURPHY, Paul (D) **0 0**
b.Wexford 12-4-85
Source: Scholar.

2002–03	Manchester C	0	0		

NASH, Carlo (G) **148 0**
H: 6 5 W: 15 03 b.Bolton 13-9-73
Source: Clitheroe.

1996–97	Crystal Palace	21	0		
1997–98	Crystal Palace	0	0	**21**	**0**
1998–99	Stockport Co	43	0		
1999–2000	Stockport Co	38	0		
2000–01	Stockport Co	8	0	**89**	**0**
2000–01	Manchester C	6	0		
2001–02	Manchester C	23	0		
2002–03	Manchester C	9	0	**38**	**0**

NEGOUAI, Christian (M) **50 7**
H: 6 4 W: 14 00 b.Fort-de-France 20-1-75

1999–2000	Charleroi	9	0		
2000–01	Charleroi	26	4		
2001–02	Charleroi	10	2	**45**	**6**
2001–02	Manchester C	5	1		
2002–03	Manchester C	0	0	**5**	**1**

ORR, Adrian* (F) **0 0**
b.Manchester 22-2-84
Source: Scholar.

2002–03	Manchester C	0	0		

PAISLEY, Stephen* (D) **0 0**
H: 6 1 W: 12 08 b.Dublin 28-7-83
Source: Scholar. *Honours:* Eire Under-21.

2000–01	Manchester C	0	0		
2001–02	Manchester C	0	0		
2002–03	Manchester C	0	0		

PEARSON, Sean (M) **0 0**
b.Manchester 7-3-85

2002–03	Manchester C	0	0		

PROFFITT, Darrly (M) **0 0**
b.Stoke 2-5-85
Source: Scholar. *Honours:* England Youth.

2002–03	Manchester C	0	0		

RITCHIE, Paul (D) **186 4**
H: 5 11 W: 12 10 b.Kirkcaldy 21-8-75
Source: Links U. *Honours:* Scotland Schools, Under-21, B, 6 full caps, 1 goal.

1992–93	Hearts	0	0		
1993–94	Hearts	0	0		
1994–95	Hearts	0	0		
1995–96	Hearts	28	1		
1996–97	Hearts	28	1		
1997–98	Hearts	34	0		
1998–99	Hearts	29	1		
1999–2000	Hearts	14	1	**133**	**4**
1999–2000	Bolton W	14	0	**14**	**0**
2000–01	Manchester C	12	0		
2001–02	Manchester C	8	0		
2002–03	Manchester C	0	0	**20**	**0**
2002–03	*Portsmouth*	12	0	**12**	**0**
2002–03	*Derby Co*	7	0	**7**	**0**

SCHMEICHEL, Peter* (G) **607 9**
H: 6 4 W: 16 12 b.Gladsaxe 18-11-63
Honours: Denmark 129 full caps, 1goal.

1984	Hvidovre	30	0		
1985	Hvidovre	28	6		
1986	Hvidovre	30	0	**88**	**6**
1987	Brondby	23	2		
1988	Brondby	26	0		
1989	Brondby	26	0		
1990	Brondby	26	0		
1991	Brondby	18	0	**119**	**2**
1991–92	Manchester U	40	0		
1992–93	Manchester U	42	0		
1993–94	Manchester U	40	0		
1994–95	Manchester U	32	0		
1995–96	Manchester U	36	0		
1996–97	Manchester U	36	0		
1997–98	Manchester U	32	0		
1998–99	Manchester U	34	0	**292**	**0**
1999–2000	Sporting Lisbon	28	0		
2000–01	Sporting Lisbon	22	0	**50**	**0**
2001–02	Aston Villa	29	1	**29**	**1**
2002–03	Manchester C	29	0	**29**	**0**

SHUKER, Chris (F) **19 1**
H: 5 5 W: 9 08 b.Liverpool 9-5-82
Source: Scholarship.

Season	Club	Apps	Gls	Total Apps	Total Gls
1999–2000	Manchester C	0	0		
2000–01	Manchester C	0	0		
2000–01	*Macclesfield T*	9	1	**9**	**1**
2001–02	Manchester C	2	0		
2002–03	Manchester C	3	0	**5**	**0**
2002–03	*Walsall*	5	0	**5**	**0**

SLACK, Leyton (M) **0 0**
b.Glasgow 25-7-85
Source: Scholar.

Season	Club	Apps	Gls	Total Apps	Total Gls
2002–03	Manchester C	0	0		

SOMMEIL, David (D) **273 4**
H: 5 9 W: 12 09 b.Ponte-a-Pitre 10-8-74

Season	Club	Apps	Gls	Total Apps	Total Gls
1993–94	Caen	1	0		
1994–95	Caen	25	0		
1995–96	Caen	30	0		
1996–97	Caen	25	0		
1997–98	Caen	38	1	**119**	**1**
1998–99-	Rennes	33	0		
1999–2000	Rennes	30	1	**63**	**1**
2000–01	Bordeaux	29	0		
2001–02	Bordeaux	31	0		
2002–03	Bordeaux	17	1	**77**	**1**
2002–03	Manchester C	14	1	**14**	**1**

TANDY, Jamie (M) **0 0**
b.Manchester 1-9-84
Source: Scholar.

Season	Club	Apps	Gls	Total Apps	Total Gls
2002–03	Manchester C	0	0		

TIATTO, Danny (M) **204 8**
H: 5 7 W: 11 07 b.Melbourne 22-5-73
Honours: Australia Under-23, 19 full caps, 1 goal.

Season	Club	Apps	Gls	Total Apps	Total Gls
1994–95	Melbourne Knights	25	3		
1995–96	Melbourne Knights	18	0	**43**	**3**
1996–97	Salernitana	11	1	**11**	**1**
1997–98	Stoke C	15	1	**15**	**1**
From Baden					
1998–99	Manchester C	17	0		
1999–2000	Manchester C	35	0		
2000–01	Manchester C	33	2		
2001–02	Manchester C	37	1		
2002–03	Manchester C	13	0	**135**	**3**

TICKLE, David* (M) **0 0**
b.Billinge 3-9-83

Season	Club	Apps	Gls	Total Apps	Total Gls
2001–02	Manchester C	0	0		
2002–03	Manchester C	0	0		

TIMMS, Ashley* (M) **0 0**
b.Manchester 6-11-85
Source: Scholar.

Season	Club	Apps	Gls	Total Apps	Total Gls
2002–03	Manchester C	0	0		

TOURE, Alioune‡ (F) **50 3**
H: 5 8 W: 11 05 b.Saint-Denis 9-9-78

Season	Club	Apps	Gls	Total Apps	Total Gls
1996–97	Nantes	2	0		
1997–98	Nantes	9	0		
1998–99	Nantes	17	2		
1999–2000	Nantes	6	1		
2000–01	Nantes	15	0	**49**	**3**
2001–02	Manchester C	1	0		
2002–03	Manchester C	0	0	**1**	**0**

VUOSO, Vicente (D) **65 8**
H: 5 9 W: 12 05 b.Mar del Plata 3-11-81

Season	Club	Apps	Gls	Total Apps	Total Gls
2000–01	Independiente	29	7		
2001–02	Independiente	36	1	**65**	**8**
2002–03	Manchester C	0	0		

WANCHOPE, Paulo (F) **149 56**
H: 6 3 W: 13 04 b.Heredia 31-7-76
Source: Herediano. *Honours:* Costa Rica 53 full caps, 37 goals.

Season	Club	Apps	Gls	Total Apps	Total Gls
1996–97	Derby Co	5	1		
1997–98	Derby Co	32	13		
1998–99	Derby Co	35	9	**72**	**23**
1999–2000	West Ham U	35	12	**35**	**12**
2000–01	Manchester C	27	9		
2001–02	Manchester C	15	12		
2002–03	Manchester C	0	0	**42**	**21**

WEAVER, Nick (G) **147 0**
H: 6 4 W: 14 08 b.Sheffield 2-3-79
Source: Trainee. *Honours:* England Under-21.

Season	Club	Apps	Gls	Total Apps	Total Gls
1995–96	Mansfield T	1	0		
1996–97	Mansfield T	0	0	**1**	**0**
1996–97	Manchester C	0	0		
1997–98	Manchester C	0	0		
1998–99	Manchester C	45	0		
1999–2000	Manchester C	45	0		
2000–01	Manchester C	31	0		
2001–02	Manchester C	25	0		
2002–03	Manchester C	0	0	**146**	**0**

WESTWOOD, Keiren (G) **0 0**
b.Manchester 23-10-84

Season	Club	Apps	Gls	Total Apps	Total Gls
2001–02	Manchester C	0	0		
2002–03	Manchester C	0	0		

WHELAN, Glenn (D) **0 0**
H: 6 0 W: 12 03 b.Dublin 13-1-84
Source: Scholar.

Season	Club	Apps	Gls	Total Apps	Total Gls
2000–01	Manchester C	0	0		
2001–02	Manchester C	0	0		
2002–03	Manchester C	0	0		

WHITLEY, Jeff‡ (M) **150 10**
H: 5 8 W: 11 04 b.Zambia 28-1-79
Source: Trainee. *Honours:* Northern Ireland Under-21, B, 7 full caps, 1 goal.

Season	Club	Apps	Gls	Total Apps	Total Gls
1995–96	Manchester C	0	0		
1996–97	Manchester C	23	1		
1997–98	Manchester C	17	1		
1998–99	Manchester C	8	1		
1998–99	*Wrexham*	9	2	**9**	**2**
1999–2000	Manchester C	42	4		
2000–01	Manchester C	31	1		
2001–02	Manchester C	2	0		
2001–02	*Notts Co*	6	0		
2002–03	Manchester C	0	0	**123**	**8**
2002–03	*Notts Co*	12	0	**18**	**0**

WIEKENS, Gerard (D) **215 11**
H: 5 9 W: 13 05 b.Tolhuiswyk 25-2-73

Season	Club	Apps	Gls	Total Apps	Total Gls
1996–97	Veendam	33	1	**33**	**1**
1997–98	Manchester C	37	5		
1998–99	Manchester C	42	2		
1999–2000	Manchester C	34	1		
2000–01	Manchester C	34	2		
2001–02	Manchester C	29	0		
2002–03	Manchester C	6	0	**182**	**10**

WRIGHT-PHILLIPS, Bradley (M) **0 0**
b.Lewisham 12-3-85
Source: Scholar.

Season	Club	Apps	Gls	Total Apps	Total Gls
2002–03	Manchester C	0	0		

WRIGHT-PHILLIPS, Shaun (M) **85 9**
H: 5 4 W: 9 13 b.London 25-10-81
Honours: England Under-21.

Season	Club	Apps	Gls	Total Apps	Total Gls
1998–99	Manchester C	0	0		
1999–2000	Manchester C	4	0		
2000–01	Manchester C	15	0		
2001–02	Manchester C	35	8		
2002–03	Manchester C	31	1	**85**	**9**

Trainees
Bennett, Ian JA; Brindle, Adam T; Collins, Paul J; D'Laryea, Jonathan A; D'Laryea, Nathan A; Davies, Craig M; Douglas-Pringle, Daniel F; Ireland, Stephen J; Laird, Marc JP; Logan, Carlos S; Reilly, Philip B; Smith, Craig C; Warrender, Daniel J

MANCHESTER U

BARTHEZ, Fabien (G) **367 0**
H: 5 11 W: 12 08 b.Lavelanet 28-6-71
Honours: France 59 full caps.

Season	Club	Apps	Gls	Total Apps	Total Gls
1991–92	Toulouse	26	0	**26**	**0**
1992–93	Marseille	30	0		
1993–94	Marseille	37	0		
1994–95	Marseille	39	0	**106**	**0**
1995–96	Monaco	21	0		
1996–97	Monaco	36	0		
1997–98	Monaco	30	0		
1998–99	Monaco	32	0		
1999–2000	Monaco	24	0	**143**	**0**
2000–01	Manchester U	30	0		
2001–02	Manchester U	32	0		
2002–03	Manchester U	30	0	**92**	**0**

BECKHAM, David (M) **270 64**
H: 6 0 W: 11 13 b.Leytonstone 2-5-75
Source: Trainee. *Honours:* England Youth, Under-21, 60 full caps, 11 goals.

Season	Club	Apps	Gls	Total Apps	Total Gls
1992–93	Manchester U	0	0		
1993–94	Manchester U	0	0		
1994–95	Manchester U	4	0		
1994–95	*Preston NE*	5	2	**5**	**2**
1995–96	Manchester U	33	7		
1996–97	Manchester U	36	8		
1997–98	Manchester U	37	9		
1998–99	Manchester U	34	6		
1999–2000	Manchester U	31	6		
2000–01	Manchester U	31	9		
2001–02	Manchester U	28	11		
2002–03	Manchester U	31	6	**265**	**62**

BLANC, Laurent* (D) **602 124**
H: 6 3 W: 13 10 b.Ales 19-11-65
Honours: France 97 full caps, 16 goals.

Season	Club	Apps	Gls	Total Apps	Total Gls
1983–84	Montpellier	15	0		
1984–85	Montpellier	32	5		
1985–86	Montpellier	29	6		
1986–87	Montpellier	34	18		
1987–88	Montpellier	24	6		
1988–89	Montpellier	35	15		
1989–90	Montpellier	36	12		
1990–91	Montpellier	38	14	**243**	**76**
1991–92	Napoli	31	6	**31**	**6**
1992–93	Nimes	29	1	**29**	**1**
1993–94	St Etienne	33	5		
1994–95	St Etienne	37	13	**70**	**18**
1995–96	Auxerre	23	2	**23**	**2**
1996–97	Barcelona	28	1	**28**	**1**
1997–98	Marseille	31	11		
1998–99	Marseille	32	2	**63**	**13**
1999–2000	Internazionale	34	3		
2000–01	Internazionale	33	3	**67**	**6**
2001–02	Manchester U	29	1		
2002–03	Manchester U	19	0	**48**	**1**

BROWN, Wes (D) **83 0**
H: 6 1 W: 13 11 b.Manchester 13-10-79
Source: Trainee. *Honours:* England Schools, Youth, Under-21, 7 full caps.

Season	Club	Apps	Gls	Total Apps	Total Gls
1996–97	Manchester U	0	0		
1997–98	Manchester U	2	0		
1998–99	Manchester U	14	0		
1999–2000	Manchester U	0	0		
2000–01	Manchester U	28	0		
2001–02	Manchester U	17	0		
2002–03	Manchester U	22	0	**83**	**0**

BUTT, Nicky (M) **249 20**
H: 5 10 W: 11 11 b.Manchester 21-1-75
Source: Trainee. *Honours:* England Schools, Youth, Under-21, 27 full caps.

Season	Club	Apps	Gls	Total Apps	Total Gls
1992–93	Manchester U	1	0		
1993–94	Manchester U	1	0		
1994–95	Manchester U	22	1		
1995–96	Manchester U	32	2		
1996–97	Manchester U	26	5		
1997–98	Manchester U	33	3		
1998–99	Manchester U	31	2		
1999–2000	Manchester U	32	3		
2000–01	Manchester U	28	3		
2001–02	Manchester U	25	1		
2002–03	Manchester U	18	0	**249**	**20**

CARROLL, Roy (G) **198 0**
H: 6 2 W: 13 12 b.Enniskillen 30-9-77
Source: Trainee. *Honours:* Northern Ireland Youth, Under-21, 13 full caps.

Season	Club	Apps	Gls	Total Apps	Total Gls
1995–96	Hull C	23	0		
1996–97	Hull C	23	0	**46**	**0**
1996–97	Wigan Ath	0	0		
1997–98	Wigan Ath	29	0		
1998–99	Wigan Ath	43	0		
1999–2000	Wigan Ath	34	0		
2000–01	Wigan Ath	29	0	**135**	**0**
2001–02	Manchester U	7	0		
2002–03	Manchester U	10	0	**17**	**0**

CHADWICK, Luke (F) **40 3**
H: 5 11 W: 11 08 b.Cambridge 18-11-80
Source: Trainee. *Honours:* England Youth, Under-21.

Season	Club	Apps	Gls	Total Apps	Total Gls
1998–99	Manchester U	0	0		
1999–2000	Manchester U	0	0		
2000–01	Manchester U	16	2		
2001–02	Manchester U	8	0		
2002–03	Manchester U	1	0	**25**	**2**
2002–03	*Reading*	15	1	**15**	**1**

COGGER, John‡ (D) **0 0**
H: 5 10 W: 13 05 b.Waltham Forest 12-9-83
Source: Scholar.

Season	Club	Apps	Gls	Total Apps	Total Gls
2001–02	Manchester U	0	0		
2002–03	Manchester U	0	0		

DAVIS, Jimmy (F) **13 2**
H: 5 8 W: 11 05 b.Bromsgrove 6-2-82
Source: Trainee. *Honours:* England Youth, Under-20.

Season	Club	Apps	Gls	Total Apps	Total Gls
1999–2000	Manchester U	0	0		
2000–01	Manchester U	0	0		
2001–02	Manchester U	0	0		
2002–03	Manchester U	0	0		
2002–03	*Swindon T*	13	2	**13**	**2**

DJORDJIC, Bojan (F) **6 0**
H: 5 10 W: 11 01 b.Belgrade 6-2-82
Source: On loan to Brommapojkarna.

Season	Club	Apps	Gls	Total Apps	Total Gls
1998–99	Manchester U	0	0		

1999–2000 Manchester U 0 0
2000-01 Manchester U 1 0
2001-02 Manchester U 0 0
2001-02 *Sheffield W* 5 0 **5 0**
2002-03 Manchester U 0 0 **1 0**

FERDINAND, Rio (D) 219 4
H: 6 2 W: 13 12 b.Peckham 7-11-78
Source: Trainee. *Honours:* England Youth, Under-21, 32 full caps, 1 goal.
1995–96 West Ham U 1 0
1996–97 West Ham U 15 2
1996–97 *Bournemouth* 10 0 **10 0**
1997–98 West Ham U 35 0
1998–99 West Ham U 31 0
1999–2000 West Ham U 33 0
2000-01 West Ham U 12 0 **127 2**
2000-01 Leeds U 23 2
2001-02 Leeds U 31 0 **54 2**
2002-03 Manchester U 28 0 **28 0**

FLETCHER, Darren (M) 0 0
H: 6 0 W: 13 01 b.Edinburgh 1-2-84
Source: Scholar. *Honours:* Scotland Under-21.
2000-01 Manchester U 0 0
2001-02 Manchester U 0 0
2002-03 Manchester U 0 0

FORLAN, Diego (F) 115 42
H: 5 8 W: 11 11 b.Montevideo 19-5-79
Honours: Uruguay 7 full caps, 3 goals.
1998–99 Independiente 2 0
1999–2000 Independiente 24 7
2000-01 Independiente 36 18
2001-02 Independiente 15 11 **77 36**
2001-02 Manchester U 13 0
2002-03 Manchester U 25 6 **38 6**

FORTUNE, Quinton (F) 132 13
H: 5 9 W: 11 09 b.Cape Town 21-5-77
Source: Kaizer Chiefs, Tottenham H schoolboy. *Honours:* South Africa 43 full caps, 1 goal.
1995–96 Mallorca 8 1 **8 1**
1995–96 Atletico Madrid 3 0
1996–97 Atletico Madrid B30 2
1996–97 Atletico Madrid 2 0
1997–98 Atletico Madrid B31 1
1997–98 Atletico Madrid 0 0
1998–99 Atletico Madrid 2 0
1998–99 Atletico Madrid B20 4 **7 0**
1999–2000 Manchester U 6 2
2000-01 Manchester U 7 2
2001-02 Manchester U 14 1
2002-03 Manchester U 9 0 **36 5**

FOX, David (M) 0 0
H: 5 9 W: 12 02 b.Stoke 13-12-83
Source: Scholar. *Honours:* England Youth, Under-20.
2000-01 Manchester U 0 0
2001-02 Manchester U 0 0
2002-03 Manchester U 0 0

GIGGS, Ryan (F) 382 79
H: 5 11 W: 11 00 b.Cardiff 29-11-73
Source: School. *Honours:* England Schools, Wales Youth, Under-21, 40 full caps, 8 goals.
1990–91 Manchester U 2 1
1991–92 Manchester U 38 4
1992–93 Manchester U 41 9
1993–94 Manchester U 38 13
1994–95 Manchester U 29 1
1995–96 Manchester U 33 11
1996–97 Manchester U 26 3
1997–98 Manchester U 29 8
1998–99 Manchester U 24 3
1999–2000 Manchester U 30 6
2000-01 Manchester U 31 5
2001-02 Manchester U 25 7
2002-03 Manchester U 36 8 **382 79**

HEATH, Colin (F) 0 0
H: 6 0 W: 13 01 b.Chesterfield 31-12-83
Source: Scholar.
2000-01 Manchester U 0 0
2001-02 Manchester U 0 0
2002-03 Manchester U 0 0

HILTON, Kirk* (D) 0 0
H: 5 7 W: 10 01 b.Flixton 2-4-81
Source: Trainee.
1999–2000 Manchester U 0 0
2000-01 Manchester U 0 0
2001-02 Manchester U 0 0
2002-03 Manchester U 0 0

HUMPHREYS, Chris‡ (F) 0 0
H: 5 9 W: 13 05 b.Manchester 22-9-83
Source: Scholar.
2001-02 Manchester U 0 0
2002-03 Manchester U 0 0

JOHNSON, Eddie (F) 0 0
H: 5 10 W: 13 05 b.Chester 20-9-84
Source: Scholar. *Honours:* England Youth.
2001-02 Manchester U 0 0
2002-03 Manchester U 0 0

JOWSEY, James (G) 0 0
H: 6 0 W: 12 04 b.Scarborough 24-11-83
Source: Scholar.
2000-01 Manchester U 0 0
2001-02 Manchester U 0 0
2002-03 Manchester U 0 0

KEANE, Roy (M) 376 51
H: 5 11 W: 11 10 b.Cork 10-8-71
Source: Cobh Ramb. *Honours:* Eire Youth, Under-21, 58 full caps, 9 goals.
1990–91 Nottingham F 35 8
1991–92 Nottingham F 39 8
1992–93 Nottingham F 40 6 **114 22**
1993–94 Manchester U 37 5
1994–95 Manchester U 25 2
1995–96 Manchester U 29 6
1996–97 Manchester U 21 2
1997–98 Manchester U 9 2
1998–99 Manchester U 35 2
1999–2000 Manchester U 29 5
2000-01 Manchester U 28 2
2001-02 Manchester U 28 3
2002-03 Manchester U 21 0 **262 29**

LAWRENCE, Lee (D) 0 0
b.Boston 1-12-84
Source: Trainee.
2002-03 Manchester U 0 0

LYNCH, Mark (D) 20 0
H: 5 11 W: 11 03 b.Manchester 2-9-81
Source: Trainee.
1999–2000 Manchester U 0 0
2000-01 Manchester U 0 0
2001-02 Manchester U 0 0
2001-02 *St Johnstone* 20 0 **20 0**
2002-03 Manchester U 0 0

MAY, David* (D) 209 9
H: 6 0 W: 13 05 b.Oldham 24-6-70
Source: Trainee.
1988–89 Blackburn R 1 0
1989–90 Blackburn R 17 0
1990–91 Blackburn R 19 1
1991–92 Blackburn R 12 0
1992–93 Blackburn R 34 1
1993–94 Blackburn R 40 1 **123 3**
1994–95 Manchester U 19 2
1995–96 Manchester U 16 1
1996–97 Manchester U 29 3
1997–98 Manchester U 9 0
1998–99 Manchester U 6 0
1999–2000 Manchester U 1 0
1999–2000 *Huddersfield T* 1 0 **1 0**
2000-01 Manchester U 2 0
2001-02 Manchester U 2 0
2002-03 Manchester U 1 0 **85 6**

McSHANE, Paul (D) 0 0
b.Wicklow 6-1-86
Source: Trainee.
2002-03 Manchester U 0 0

MOONIARUCK, Kalam* (F) 0 0
H: 5 8 W: 11 09 b.Yeovil 22-11-83
Source: Scholar. *Honours:* England Youth, Under-20.
2000-01 Manchester U 0 0
2001-02 Manchester U 0 0
2002-03 Manchester U 0 0

NARDIELLO, Daniel (F) 0 0
H: 5 11 W: 11 04 b.Coventry 22-10-82
Source: Trainee.
1999–2000 Manchester U 0 0
2000-01 Manchester U 0 0
2001-02 Manchester U 0 0
2002-03 Manchester U 0 0

NEVILLE, Gary (D) 263 3
H: 5 11 W: 12 04 b.Bury 18-2-75
Source: Trainee. *Honours:* England Youth, 57 full caps.
1992–93 Manchester U 0 0
1993–94 Manchester U 1 0
1994–95 Manchester U 18 0
1995–96 Manchester U 31 0
1996–97 Manchester U 31 1
1997–98 Manchester U 34 0
1998–99 Manchester U 34 1
1999–2000 Manchester U 22 0
2000-01 Manchester U 32 1
2001-02 Manchester U 34 0
2002-03 Manchester U 26 0 **263 3**

NEVILLE, Phil (D) 213 5
H: 5 11 W: 12 00 b.Bury 21-1-77
Source: Trainee. *Honours:* England Schools, Youth, Under-21, 40 full caps.
1994–95 Manchester U 2 0
1995–96 Manchester U 24 0
1996–97 Manchester U 18 0
1997–98 Manchester U 30 1
1998–99 Manchester U 28 0
1999–2000 Manchester U 29 0
2000-01 Manchester U 29 1
2001-02 Manchester U 28 2
2002-03 Manchester U 25 1 **213 5**

O'SHEA, John (D) 51 1
H: 6 3 W: 12 10 b.Waterford 30-4-81
Source: Waterford. *Honours:* Eire Under-21, 7 full caps.
1998–99 Manchester U 0 0
1999–2000 Manchester U 0 0
1999–2000 *Bournemouth* 10 1 **10 1**
2000-01 Manchester U 0 0
2001-02 Manchester U 9 0
2002-03 Manchester U 32 0 **41 0**

POOLE, David (F) 0 0
b.Manchester 12-11-84
Source: Trainee.
2002-03 Manchester U 0 0

PUGH, Danny (M) 1 0
H: 6 0 W: 12 10 b.Manchester 19-10-82
Source: Scholar.
2000-01 Manchester U 0 0
2001-02 Manchester U 0 0
2002-03 Manchester U 1 0 **1 0**

RANKIN, John‡ (M) 0 0
H: 5 8 W: 12 08 b.Bellshill 27-6-83
Source: Scholar.
2000-01 Manchester U 0 0
2001-02 Manchester U 0 0
2002-03 Manchester U 0 0

RICARDO (G) 119 0
H: 6 2 W: 13 12 b.Madrid 31-12-71
Honours: Spain 1 full cap.
1994–95 Atletico Madrid B29 0
1995–96 Atletico Madrid 0 0
1996–97 Atletico Madrid 1 0
1997–98 Atletico Madrid B35 0 **1 0**
1998–99 Valladolid 0 0
1999–2000 Valladolid 3 0
2000-01 Valladolid 12 0
2001-02 Valladolid 38 0 **53 0**
2002-03 Manchester U 1 0 **1 0**

RICHARDSON, Kieran§ (M) 2 0
b.Greenwich 21-10-84
Source: Scholar.
2002-03 Manchester U 2 0 **2 0**

ROCHE, Lee* (D) 42 0
H: 5 10 W: 10 10 b.Bolton 28-10-80
Source: Trainee. *Honours:* England Youth, Under-21.
1998–99 Manchester U 0 0
1999–2000 Manchester U 0 0
2000-01 Manchester U 0 0
2000-01 *Wrexham* 41 0 **41 0**
2001-02 Manchester U 0 0
2002-03 Manchester U 1 0 **1 0**

SCHOLES, Paul (M) 260 69
H: 5 7 W: 11 00 b.Salford 16-11-74
Source: Trainee. *Honours:* England Youth, 57 full caps, 13 goals.
1992–93 Manchester U 0 0
1993–94 Manchester U 0 0
1994–95 Manchester U 17 5
1995–96 Manchester U 26 10
1996–97 Manchester U 24 3
1997–98 Manchester U 31 8
1998–99 Manchester U 31 6
1999–2000 Manchester U 31 9
2000-01 Manchester U 32 6
2001-02 Manchester U 35 8
2002-03 Manchester U 33 14 **260 69**

SILVESTRE, Mikael (D) 197 3
H: 6 0 W: 13 01 b.Chambray les Tours 9-8-77
Honours: France 22 full caps, 2 goals.

1995–96	Rennes	1	0		
1996–97	Rennes	16	0		
1997–98	Rennes	32	0	**49**	**0**
1998–99	Internazionale	18	1	**18**	**1**
1999–2000	Manchester U	31	0		
2000-01	Manchester U	30	1		
2001-02	Manchester U	35	0		
2002-03	Manchester U	34	1	**130**	**2**

SIMS, Lee (D) 0 0
b.Manchester 6-9-84
Source: Trainee.

2002-03	Manchester U	0	0		

SOLSKJAER, Ole Gunnar (F) 242 114
H: 5 10 W: 11 11 b.Kristiansund 26-2-73
Honours: Norway Under-21, 58 full caps, 21 goals.

1995	Molde	26	20		
1996	Molde	16	11	**42**	**31**
1996–97	Manchester U	33	17		
1997–98	Manchester U	22	6		
1998–99	Manchester U	19	12		
1999–2000	Manchester U	28	12		
2000-01	Manchester U	31	10		
2001-02	Manchester U	30	17		
2002-03	Manchester U	37	9	**200**	**83**

STEELE, Luke (G) 2 0
H: 6 2 W: 12 00 b.Peterborough 24-9-84
Source: Scholar. *Honours:* England Youth.

2001-02	Peterborough U	2	0	**2**	**0**
2001-02	Manchester U	0	0		
2002-03	Manchester U	0	0		

STEWART, Michael (M) 7 0
H: 5 11 W: 11 11 b.Edinburgh 26-2-81
Source: Trainee. *Honours:* Scotland Schools, Under-21, 3 full caps.

1997–98	Manchester U	0	0		
1998–99	Manchester U	0	0		
1999–2000	Manchester U	0	0		
2000-01	Manchester U	3	0		
2001-02	Manchester U	3	0		
2002-03	Manchester U	1	0	**7**	**0**

TATE, Alan (D) 27 0
H: 6 1 W: 13 05 b.Easington 2-9-82
Source: Scholar.

2000-01	Manchester U	0	0		
2001-02	Manchester U	0	0		
2002-03	Manchester U	0	0		
2002-03	*Swansea C*	27	0	**27**	**0**

TIERNEY, Paul (M) 17 1
H: 5 10 W: 12 05 b.Salford 15-9-82
Source: Scholar. *Honours:* Eire Under-21.

2000-01	Manchester U	0	0		
2001-02	Manchester U	0	0		
2002-03	Manchester U	0	0		
2002-03	*Crewe Alex*	17	1	**17**	**1**

TIMM, Mads (F) 0 0
H: 5 9 W: 12 10 b.Odense 31-10-84
Source: Scholar.

2001-02	Manchester U	0	0		
2002-03	Manchester U	0	0		

VAN NISTELROOY, Ruud (F) 233 140
H: 6 2 W: 12 13 b.Oss 1-7-76
Source: Nooit Gedacht, Margriet. *Honours:* Holland 25 full caps, 11 goals.

1993–94	Den Bosch	2	0		
1994–95	Den Bosch	15	3		
1995–96	Den Bosch	21	2		
1996–97	Den Bosch	31	12	**69**	**17**
1997–98	Heerenveen	31	13	**31**	**13**
1998–99	PSV Eindhoven	34	31		
1999–2000	PSV Eindhoven	23	29		
2000-01	PSV Eindhoven	10	2	**67**	**62**
2001-02	Manchester U	32	23		
2002-03	Manchester U	34	25	**66**	**48**

VERON, Juan Sebastian (F) 268 37
H: 6 1 W: 12 08 b.Buenos Aires 9-3-75
Honours: Argentina 52 full caps, 8 goals.

1993–94	Estudiantes	7	0		
1994–95	Estudiantes	38	5		
1995–96	Estudiantes	15	2	**60**	**7**
1995–96	Boca Juniors	17	4	**17**	**4**
1996–97	Sampdoria	32	5		
1997–98	Sampdoria	29	2	**61**	**7**
1998–99	Parma	26	1	**26**	**1**
1999–2000	Lazio	31	8		
2000-01	Lazio	22	3	**53**	**11**
2001-02	Manchester U	26	5		
2002-03	Manchester U	25	2	**51**	**7**

WEBBER, Danny (F) 21 4
H: 5 9 W: 10 08 b.Manchester 28-12-81
Source: Trainee. *Honours:* England Youth, Under-20.

1998–99	Manchester U	0	0		
1999–2000	Manchester U	0	0		
2000-01	Manchester U	0	0		
2001-02	Manchester U	0	0		
2001-02	*Port Vale*	4	0	**4**	**0**
2001-02	*Watford*	5	2		
2002-03	Manchester U	0	0		
2002-03	*Watford*	12	2	**17**	**4**

WILLIAMS, Ben (G) 14 0
H: 6 0 W: 13 01 b.Manchester 27-8-82
Source: Scholar. *Honours:* England Schools.

2001-02	Manchester U	0	0		
2002-03	Manchester U	0	0		
2002-03	*Coventry C*	0	0		
2002-03	*Chesterfield*	14	0	**14**	**0**

WILLIAMS, Matthew (F) 0 0
H: 5 8 W: 9 11 b.St Asaph 5-11-82
Honours: Wales Under-21.

1999–2000	Manchester U	0	0		
2000-01	Manchester U	0	0		
2001-02	Manchester U	0	0		
2002-03	Manchester U	0	0		

WOOD, Neil (F) 0 0
H: 5 10 W: 13 02 b.Manchester 4-1-83
Source: Trainee. *Honours:* England Youth.

1999–2000	Manchester U	0	0		
2000-01	Manchester U	0	0		
2001-02	Manchester U	0	0		
2002-03	Manchester U	0	0		

Trainees
Bardsley, Phillip A; Byrne, Daniel T; Calliste, Ramon T; Collett, Benjamin; Eagles, Christopher M; Ebanks-Blake, Sylvan; Eckersley, Adam J; Flanagan, Callum; Heaton, Thomas D; Hogg, Steven R; Howard, Mark J; Jones, David FL; Lee, Thomas E; Nevins, Adrian C; Picken, Philip J; Port, Graeme R; Richardson, Kieran E

MANSFIELD T

BACON, Danny (F) 44 4
H: 5 10 W: 10 12 b.Mansfield 20-9-80
Source: Trainee.

1999–2000	Mansfield T	8	2		
2000-01	Mansfield T	22	1		
2001-02	Mansfield T	8	1		
2002-03	Mansfield T	6	0	**44**	**4**

BEARDSLEY, Christopher§ (M) 5 0
b.Derby 28-2-84
Source: Scholar.

2002-03	Mansfield T	5	0	**5**	**0**

BINGHAM, Michael‡ (G) 2 0
H: 6 0 W: 12 07 b.Preston 21-5-81
Source: Trainee. *Honours:* England Schools.

1998–99	Blackburn R	0	0		
1999–2000	Blackburn R	0	0		
2000-01	Blackburn R	0	0		
2001-02	Mansfield T	2	0		
2002-03	Mansfield T	0	0	**2**	**0**

BUXTON, Jake (D) 3 0
H: 6 0 W: 13 00 b.Sutton-in-Ashfield 4-3-85
Source: Scholar.

2002-03	Mansfield T	3	0	**3**	**0**

CHRISTIE, Iyseden (F) 189 48
H: 5 10 W: 12 02 b.Coventry 14-11-76
Source: Trainee.

1994–95	Coventry C	0	0		
1995–96	Coventry C	1	0		
1996–97	Coventry C	0	0	**1**	**0**
1996–97	*Bournemouth*	4	0	**4**	**0**
1996–97	*Mansfield T*	8	0		
1997–98	Mansfield T	39	10		
1998–99	Mansfield T	42	8		
1999–2000	Leyton Orient	36	7		
2000-01	Leyton Orient	7	2		
2001-02	Leyton Orient	15	3	**58**	**12**
2002-03	Mansfield T	37	18	**126**	**36**

CLARKE, Jamie (D) 22 1
H: 6 2 W: 12 09 b.Sunderland 18-9-82
Source: Scholar.

2001-02	Mansfield T	1	0		
2002-03	Mansfield T	21	1	**22**	**1**

CORDEN, Wayne (F) 190 25
H: 5 9 W: 11 03 b.Leek 1-11-75
Source: Trainee.

1994–95	Port Vale	1	0		
1995–96	Port Vale	2	0		
1996–97	Port Vale	12	0		
1997–98	Port Vale	33	1		
1998–99	Port Vale	16	0		
1999–2000	Port Vale	2	0	**66**	**1**
2000-01	Mansfield T	34	3		
2001-02	Mansfield T	46	8		
2002-03	Mansfield T	44	13	**124**	**24**

CURLE, Keith† (D) 705 34
H: 6 1 W: 12 05 b.Bristol 14-11-63
Source: Apprentice. *Honours:* England B, 3 full caps.

1981–82	Bristol R	20	2		
1982–83	Bristol R	12	2		
1983–84	Bristol R	0	0	**32**	**4**
1983–84	Torquay U	16	5	**16**	**5**
1983–84	Bristol C	6	0		
1984–85	Bristol C	40	0		
1985–86	Bristol C	44	1		
1986–87	Bristol C	28	0		
1987–88	Bristol C	3	0	**121**	**1**
1987–88	Reading	30	0		
1988–89	Reading	10	0	**40**	**0**
1988–89	Wimbledon	18	0		
1989–90	Wimbledon	38	2		
1990–91	Wimbledon	37	1	**93**	**3**
1991–92	Manchester C	40	5		
1992–93	Manchester C	39	3		
1993–94	Manchester C	29	1		
1994–95	Manchester C	31	2		
1995–96	Manchester C	32	0	**171**	**11**
1996–97	Wolverhampton W	21	2		
1997–98	Wolverhampton W	40	1		
1998–99	Wolverhampton W	44	4		
1999–2000	Wolverhampton W	45	2	**150**	**9**
2000-01	Sheffield U	25	0		
2001-02	Sheffield U	32	1	**57**	**1**
2002-03	Barnsley	11	0	**11**	**0**
2002-03	Mansfield T	14	0	**14**	**0**

CURTIS, Tom (M) 288 12
H: 5 10 W: 12 10 b.Exeter 1-3-73
Source: School.

1991–92	Derby Co	0	0		
1992–93	Derby Co	0	0		
1993–94	Chesterfield	36	3		
1994–95	Chesterfield	40	2		
1995–96	Chesterfield	46	0		
1996–97	Chesterfield	40	3		
1997–98	Chesterfield	36	1		
1998–99	Chesterfield	24	3		
1999–2000	Chesterfield	18	0	**240**	**12**
2000-01	Portsmouth	4	0		
2001-02	Portsmouth	9	0		
2001-02	*Walsall*	4	0	**4**	**0**
2002-03	Portsmouth	0	0	**13**	**0**
2002-03	*Tranmere R*	8	0	**8**	**0**
2002-03	Mansfield T	23	0	**23**	**0**

DAY, Rhys (D) 32 1
H: 6 2 W: 13 09 b.Bridgend 31-8-82
Source: Scholarship. *Honours:* Wales Under-21.

1999–2000	Manchester C	0	0		
2000-01	Manchester C	0	0		
2001-02	Manchester C	0	0		
2001-02	*Blackpool*	9	0	**9**	**0**
2002-03	Manchester C	0	0		
2002-03	Mansfield T	23	1	**23**	**1**

DISLEY, Craig (M) 107 11
H: 5 10 W: 11 00 b.Worksop 24-8-81
Source: Trainee.

1999–2000	Mansfield T	5	0		
2000-01	Mansfield T	24	0		
2001-02	Mansfield T	36	7		
2002-03	Mansfield T	42	4	**107**	**11**

EATON, Adam (D) 34 0
H: 5 9 W: 11 10 b.Liverpool 2-5-80
Source: Trainee.

1997–98	Everton	0	0		
1998–99	Everton	0	0		
1999–2000	Preston NE	0	0		
2000-01	Preston NE	1	0		
2001-02	Preston NE	12	0		

2002-03	Preston NE	1	0	**14**	**0**
2002-03	Mansfield T	20	0	**20**	**0**

GADSBY, Matt* (D) 57 0
H: 6 1 W: 11 12 b.Sutton Coldfield 6-9-79
Source: Trainee.

1997–98	Walsall	1	0		
1998–99	Walsall	6	0		
1999–2000	Walsall	3	0		
2000-01	Walsall	5	0		
2001-02	Walsall	22	0		
2002-03	Walsall	0	0	**37**	**0**
2002-03	Mansfield T	20	0	**20**	**0**

GLOVER, Lee‡ (F) 325 64
H: 5 11 W: 11 09 b.Kettering 24-4-70
Source: Trainee. *Honours:* Scotland Youth, Under-21.

1986–87	Nottingham F	0	0		
1987–88	Nottingham F	20	3		
1988–89	Nottingham F	0	0		
1989–90	Nottingham F	0	0		
1989–90	*Leicester C*	5	1	**5**	**1**
1989–90	*Barnsley*	8	0	**8**	**0**
1990–91	Nottingham F	8	1		
1991–92	Nottingham F	16	0		
1991–92	*Luton T*	1	0	**1**	**0**
1992–93	Nottingham F	14	0		
1993–94	Nottingham F	18	5	**76**	**9**
1994–95	Port Vale	28	4		
1995–96	Port Vale	24	3	**52**	**7**
1996–97	Rotherham U	22	1		
1996–97	*Huddersfield T*	11	0	**11**	**0**
1997–98	Rotherham U	37	17		
1998–99	Rotherham U	19	10		
1999–2000	Rotherham U	7	1	**85**	**29**
2000-01	Macclesfield T	37	8		
2001-02	Macclesfield T	43	9		
2002-03	Macclesfield T	5	1	**85**	**18**
2002-03	Mansfield T	2	0	**2**	**0**

HANKEY, Dean§ (M) 1 0
b.Sutton-in-Ashfield 23-8-86
Source: Scholar.

2002-03	Mansfield T	1	0	**1**	**0**

HASSELL, Bobby (D) 126 3
H: 5 9 W: 12 06 b.Derby 4-6-80
Source: Trainee.

1997–98	Mansfield T	9	0		
1998–99	Mansfield T	3	0		
1999–2000	Mansfield T	11	1		
2000-01	Mansfield T	40	1		
2001-02	Mansfield T	43	1		
2002-03	Mansfield T	20	0	**126**	**3**

HOLYOAK, Daniel‡ (M) 2 0
b.London 27-11-83
Source: Scholar.

2002-03	Mansfield T	2	0	**2**	**0**

HURST, Mark§ (D) 1 0
b.Mansfield 18-2-85
Source: Scholar.

2002-03	Mansfield T	1	0	**1**	**0**

JERVIS, David‡ (D) 30 0
H: 5 10 W: 11 00 b.Worksop 18-1-82
Source: Trainee.

2000-01	Mansfield T	22	0		
2001-02	Mansfield T	3	0		
2002-03	Mansfield T	5	0	**30**	**0**

JOHN-BAPTISTE, Alex (D) 4 0
H: 5 11 W: 11 07 b.Sutton-in-Ashfield 31-1-86
Source: Scholar.

2002-03	Mansfield T	4	0	**4**	**0**

JONES, Andy§ (M) 1 0
b.Sutton-in-Ashfield 12-2-86
Source: Scholar.

2002-03	Mansfield T	1	0	**1**	**0**

LARKIN, Colin (F) 58 13
H: 5 9 W: 10 02 b.Dundalk 27-4-82
Source: Trainee.

1998–99	Wolverhampton W	0	0		
1999–2000	Wolverhampton W	1	0		
2000-01	Wolverhampton W	2	0		
2001-02	Wolverhampton W	0	0	**3**	**0**
2001-02	*Kidderminster H*	33	6	**33**	**6**
2002-03	Mansfield T	22	7	**22**	**7**

LAWRENCE, Liam (M) 95 16
H: 5 10 W: 11 03 b.Retford 14-12-81
Source: Trainee.

1999–2000	Mansfield T	2	0		
2000-01	Mansfield T	18	4		
2001-02	Mansfield T	32	2		
2002-03	Mansfield T	43	10	**95**	**16**

LEVER, Mark‡ (D) 407 9
H: 6 3 W: 12 08 b.Beverley 29-3-70
Source: Trainee.

1987–88	Grimsby T	1	0		
1988–89	Grimsby T	37	2		
1989–90	Grimsby T	38	2		
1990–91	Grimsby T	40	2		
1991–92	Grimsby T	36	0		
1992–93	Grimsby T	14	1		
1993–94	Grimsby T	22	0		
1994–95	Grimsby T	31	0		
1995–96	Grimsby T	24	1		
1996–97	Grimsby T	21	0		
1997–98	Grimsby T	38	0		
1998–99	Grimsby T	24	0		
1999–2000	Grimsby T	35	0	**361**	**8**
2000-01	Bristol C	2	0		
2001-02	Bristol C	29	1		
2002-03	Bristol C	0	0	**31**	**1**
2002-03	Mansfield T	15	0	**15**	**0**

MACKENZIE, Neil (M) 135 7
H: 6 2 W: 12 05 b.Birmingham 15-4-76
Source: WBA schoolboy.

1996–97	Stoke C	22	1		
1997–98	Stoke C	12	0		
1998–99	Stoke C	6	0		
1998–99	*Cambridge U*	4	1		
1999–2000	Stoke C	2	0	**42**	**1**
1999–2000	Cambridge U	22	0		
2000-01	Cambridge U	6	0	**32**	**1**
2000-01	Kidderminster H	23	3	**23**	**3**
2001-02	Blackpool	14	1	**14**	**1**
2002-03	Mansfield T	24	1	**24**	**1**

MENDES, Junior (M) 63 12
H: 5 11 W: 12 04 b.Balham 15-9-76
Source: Trainee.

1995–96	Chelsea	0	0		
1996–97	Chelsea	0	0		
1997–98	Chelsea	0	0		
1998–99	St Mirren	22	4		
1998–99	*Carlisle U*	6	1		
1999–2000	Carlisle U	0	0		
2000-01	Carlisle U	0	0	**6**	**1**
2001-02	Rushden & D	0	0		
2002-03	St Mirren	17	6	**39**	**10**
2002-03	Mansfield T	18	1	**18**	**1**

MITCHELL, Craig§ (M) 15 1
b.Mansfield 6-5-85
Source: Scholar.

2002-03	Mansfield T	15	1	**15**	**1**

MOORE, Neil‡ (D) 128 5
H: 6 0 W: 12 00 b.Liverpool 21-9-72
Source: Trainee.

1991–92	Everton	0	0		
1992–93	Everton	1	0		
1993–94	Everton	4	0		
1994–95	Everton	0	0		
1994–95	*Blackpool*	7	0	**7**	**0**
1994–95	*Oldham Ath*	5	0	**5**	**0**
1995–96	Everton	0	0		
1995–96	*Carlisle U*	13	0	**13**	**0**
1995–96	*Rotherham U*	11	0	**11**	**0**
1996–97	Everton	0	0	**5**	**0**
1996–97	Norwich C	2	0	**2**	**0**
1997–98	Burnley	40	3		
1998–99	Burnley	12	0	**52**	**3**
1999–2000	Macclesfield T	15	2		
2000-01	Macclesfield T	0	0		
2001-02	Macclesfield T	0	0	**15**	**2**

From Telford U.

2002-03	Mansfield T	18	0	**18**	**0**

PILKINGTON, Kevin (G) 131 0
H: 6 2 W: 12 10 b.Hitchin 8-3-74
Source: Trainee. *Honours:* England Schools.

1992–93	Manchester U	0	0		
1993–94	Manchester U	0	0		
1994–95	Manchester U	1	0		
1995–96	Manchester U	3	0		
1995–96	*Rochdale*	6	0	**6**	**0**
1996–97	Manchester U	0	0		
1996–97	*Rotherham U*	17	0	**17**	**0**
1997–98	Manchester U	2	0		
1998–99	Manchester U	0	0	**6**	**0**
1998–99	Port Vale	8	0		
1999–2000	Port Vale	15	0	**23**	**0**
2000-01	Macclesfield T	0	0		
2000-01	Wigan Ath	0	0		
2000-01	Mansfield T	2	0		
2001-02	Mansfield T	45	0		
2002-03	Mansfield T	32	0	**79**	**0**

REDDINGTON, Stuart* (D) 54 1
H: 6 4 W: 13 07 b.Lincoln 21-2-78
Source: Lincoln U.

1999–2000	Chelsea	0	0		
2000-01	Chelsea	0	0		
2000-01	*Mansfield T*	9	0		
2001-02	Mansfield T	38	1		
2002-03	Mansfield T	7	0	**54**	**1**

SELLARS, Scott# (M) 545 72
H: 5 8 W: 10 00 b.Sheffield 27-11-65
Source: Apprentice. *Honours:* England Under-21.

1982–83	Leeds U	1	0		
1983–84	Leeds U	19	3		
1984–85	Leeds U	39	7		
1985–86	Leeds U	17	2		
1986–87	Blackburn R	32	4		
1987–88	Blackburn R	42	7		
1988–89	Blackburn R	46	2		
1989–90	Blackburn R	43	14		
1990–91	Blackburn R	9	1		
1991–92	Blackburn R	30	7	**202**	**35**
1992–93	Leeds U	7	0	**83**	**12**
1992–93	Newcastle U	13	2		
1993–94	Newcastle U	30	3		
1994–95	Newcastle U	12	0		
1995–96	Newcastle U	6	0	**61**	**5**
1995–96	Bolton W	22	3		
1996–97	Bolton W	42	8		
1997–98	Bolton W	22	2		
1998–99	Bolton W	25	2	**111**	**15**
1999–2000	Huddersfield T	34	1		
2000-01	Huddersfield T	14	0	**48**	**1**
2000-01	Aarhus	9	1		
2001-02	Aarhus	11	0	**20**	**1**
2001-02	Port Vale	0	0		
2001-02	Mansfield T	6	1		
2002-03	Mansfield T	14	2	**20**	**3**

SISSON, Michael‡ (M) 31 2
H: 5 9 W: 10 10 b.Sutton-in-Ashfield 24-11-78
Source: Trainee.

1997–98	Mansfield T	1	0		
1998–99	Mansfield T	1	0		
1999–2000	Mansfield T	25	2		
2000-01	Mansfield T	4	0		
2001-02	Mansfield T	0	0		
2002-03	Mansfield T	0	0	**31**	**2**

TANKARD, Allen‡ (D) 519 17
H: 5 10 W: 11 10 b.Fleet 21-5-69
Source: Trainee. *Honours:* England Youth.

1985–86	Southampton	3	0		
1986–87	Southampton	2	0		
1987–88	Southampton	0	0	**5**	**0**
1988–89	Wigan Ath	33	1		
1989–90	Wigan Ath	45	1		
1990–91	Wigan Ath	46	1		
1991–92	Wigan Ath	44	0		
1992–93	Wigan Ath	41	1	**209**	**4**
1993–94	Port Vale	26	0		
1994–95	Port Vale	39	1		
1995–96	Port Vale	29	0		
1996–97	Port Vale	37	1		
1997–98	Port Vale	39	0		
1998–99	Port Vale	37	4		
1999–2000	Port Vale	35	1		
2000-01	Port Vale	33	4	**275**	**11**
2001-02	Mansfield T	30	2		
2002-03	Mansfield T	0	0	**30**	**2**

WELCH, Keith# (G) 607 0
H: 6 2 W: 13 07 b.Bolton 3-10-68
Source: Trainee.

1986–87	Bolton W	0	0		
1986–87	Rochdale	24	0		
1987–88	Rochdale	46	0		
1988–89	Rochdale	46	0		
1989–90	Rochdale	46	0		
1990–91	Rochdale	43	0	**205**	**0**
1991–92	Bristol C	26	0		
1992–93	Bristol C	45	0		
1993–94	Bristol C	45	0		
1994–95	Bristol C	44	0		
1995–96	Bristol C	35	0		
1996–97	Bristol C	11	0		
1997–98	Bristol C	44	0		
1998–99	Bristol C	21	0	**271**	**0**
1999–2000	Northampton T	39	0		
2000-01	Northampton T	40	0		
2001-02	Northampton T	38	0	**117**	**0**
2002-03	Tranmere R	2	0	**2**	**0**

2002-03 Torquay U 3 0 **3 0**
2002-03 Mansfield T 9 0 **9 0**

WHITE, Andy (F) 56 10
H: 6 4 W: 14 03 b.Derby 6-11-81
Source: Hucknall T.
2000-01 Mansfield T 4 0
2001-02 Mansfield T 22 4
2002-03 Mansfield T 28 6 **54 10**
2002-03 *Crewe Alex* 2 0 **2 0**

WHITE, Jason (G) 1 0
H: 6 2 W: 12 01 b.Mansfield 28-1-83
Source: Trainee.
2002-03 Mansfield T 1 0 **1 0**

WILLIAMSON, Lee (M) 105 3
H: 5 10 W: 10 04 b.Derby 7-6-82
Source: Trainee.
1999–2000 Mansfield T 4 0
2000-01 Mansfield T 15 0
2001-02 Mansfield T 46 3
2002-03 Mansfield T 40 0 **105 3**

Scholars
Beardsley, Christopher K; Carter, Mark; Coates, James A; Davies, Andrew P; Hankey, Dean A; Hurst, Mark; Jones, Andrew S; Lloyd, Callum; Mitchell, Craig R; Mulligan, Lance M; Robinson, Mark; Ryalls, Peter; Sangra, Gavinder S
Non-Contract
Curle, Keith

MIDDLESBROUGH

BERNHARDT, Arthur* (F) 0 0
H: 6 1 W: 12 00 b.Santa Catarina 27-8-82
Source: Hamburg.
1999–2000 Middlesbrough 0 0
2000-01 Middlesbrough 0 0
2001-02 Middlesbrough 0 0
2002-03 Middlesbrough 0 0

BOATENG, George (M) 255 10
H: 5 9 W: 10 12 b.Nkawkaw 5-9-75
Honours: Holland 2 full caps.
1994–95 Excelsior 9 0 **9 0**
1995–96 Feyenoord 24 1
1996–97 Feyenoord 26 0
1997–98 Feyenoord 18 0 **68 1**
1997–98 Coventry C 14 1
1998–99 Coventry C 33 4 **47 5**
1999–2000 Aston Villa 33 2
2000-01 Aston Villa 33 1
2001-02 Aston Villa 37 1 **103 4**
2002-03 Middlesbrough 28 0 **28 0**

BOKSIC, Alen* (F) 350 109
H: 6 1 W: 14 01 b.Niakarska 21-1-70
Honours: Croatia 52 full caps, 10 goals.
1987–88 Hajduk Split 13 2
1988–89 Hajduk Split 26 7
1989–90 Hajduk Split 27 12
1990–91 Hajduk Split 29 6 **95 27**
1991–92 Cannes 1 0 **1 0**
1992–93 Marseille 37 23
1993–94 Marseille 12 3 **49 26**
1993–94 Lazio 21 4
1994–95 Lazio 23 9
1995–96 Lazio 23 4
1996–97 Juventus 22 3 **22 3**
1997–98 Lazio 26 10
1998–99 Lazio 3 0
1999–2000 Lazio 19 4 **115 31**
2000-01 Middlesbrough 28 12
2001-02 Middlesbrough 22 8
2002-03 Middlesbrough 18 2 **68 22**

BRUNT, Chris (M) 0 0
H: 6 1 W: 11 08 b.Northern Ireland 14-12-84
Source: Trainee.
2002-03 Middlesbrough 0 0

CADE, Jamie (F) 0 0
H: 5 8 W: 10 10 b.Durham 15-1-84
Source: Scholar. *Honours:* England Youth.
2001-02 Middlesbrough 0 0
2002-03 Middlesbrough 0 0

CHRISTIE, Malcolm (F) 128 34
H: 6 0 W: 12 06 b.Peterborough 11-4-79
Source: Nuneaton B. *Honours:* England Under-21.
1998–99 Derby Co 2 0
1999–2000 Derby Co 21 5
2000-01 Derby Co 34 8
2001-02 Derby Co 35 9
2002-03 Derby Co 24 8 **116 30**
2002-03 Middlesbrough 12 4 **12 4**

CLOSE, Brian (D) 8 1
H: 5 10 W: 12 03 b.Belfast 27-1-82
Honours: Northern Ireland Under-21.
1999–2000 Middlesbrough 0 0
2000-01 Middlesbrough 0 0
2001-02 Middlesbrough 0 0
2002-03 Middlesbrough 0 0
2002-03 *Chesterfield* 8 1 **8 1**

COOPER, Colin (D) 568 37
H: 5 11 W: 11 11 b.Sedgefield 28-2-67
Honours: England Under-21, 2 full caps.
1984–85 Middlesbrough 0 0
1985–86 Middlesbrough 11 0
1986–87 Middlesbrough 46 0
1987–88 Middlesbrough 43 2
1988–89 Middlesbrough 35 2
1989–90 Middlesbrough 21 2
1990–91 Middlesbrough 32 0
1991–92 Millwall 36 2
1992–93 Millwall 41 4 **77 6**
1993–94 Nottingham F 37 7
1994–95 Nottingham F 35 1
1995–96 Nottingham F 37 5
1996–97 Nottingham F 36 2
1997–98 Nottingham F 35 5
1998–99 Nottingham F 0 0 **180 20**
1998–99 Middlesbrough 32 1
1999–2000 Middlesbrough 26 0
2000-01 Middlesbrough 27 2
2001-02 Middlesbrough 18 2
2002-03 Middlesbrough 20 0 **311 11**

CROSSLEY, Mark (G) 351 0
H: 6 0 W: 15 09 b.Barnsley 16-6-69
Source: Trainee. *Honours:* England Under-21, Wales B, 6 full caps.
1987–88 Nottingham F 0 0
1988–89 Nottingham F 2 0
1989–90 Nottingham F 8 0
1989–90 *Manchester U* 0 0
1990–91 Nottingham F 38 0
1991–92 Nottingham F 36 0
1992–93 Nottingham F 37 0
1993–94 Nottingham F 37 0
1994–95 Nottingham F 42 0
1995–96 Nottingham F 38 0
1996–97 Nottingham F 33 0
1997–98 Nottingham F 0 0
1997–98 *Millwall* 13 0 **13 0**
1998–99 Nottingham F 12 0
1999–2000 Nottingham F 20 0 **303 0**
2000-01 Middlesbrough 5 0
2001-02 Middlesbrough 18 0
2002-03 Middlesbrough 0 0 **23 0**
2002-03 *Stoke C* 12 0 **12 0**

DAVIES, Andrew (D) 1 0
H: 6 3 W: 14 08 b.Stockton 17-12-84
Source: Scholar. *Honours:* England Youth, Under-20.
2002-03 Middlesbrough 1 0 **1 0**

DORIVA (M) 186 10
H: 5 7 W: 11 04 b.Mirasol 28-5-72
Honours: Brazil 12 full caps.
1993 Sao Paulo 12 0
1994 Sao Paulo 15 0 **27 0**
1995 Atletico Mineiro 11 1
1996 Atletico Mineiro 24 0
1997 Atletico Mineiro 24 0 **59 1**
1997–98 Porto 13 1
1998–99 Porto 17 4 **30 5**
1999–2000 Sampdoria 31 3 **31 3**
2000-01 Celta Vigo 17 1
2001-02 Celta Vigo 14 0
2002-03 Celta Vigo 3 0 **34 1**
2002-03 Middlesbrough 5 0 **5 0**

DOVE, Craig (M) 0 0
H: 5 8 W: 11 00 b.Hartlepool 16-8-83
Source: Scholar. *Honours:* England Youth, Under-20.
2000-01 Middlesbrough 0 0
2001-02 Middlesbrough 0 0
2002-03 Middlesbrough 0 0

DOWNING, Stewart (M) 5 0
H: 5 10 W: 10 04 b.Middlesbrough 22-7-84
Source: Scholar. *Honours:* England Youth.
2001-02 Middlesbrough 3 0
2002-03 Middlesbrough 2 0 **5 0**

EHIOGU, Ugo (D) 321 19
H: 6 2 W: 14 10 b.Hackney 3-11-72
Source: Trainee. *Honours:* England Under-21, B, 4 full caps, 1 goal.
1990–91 WBA 2 0 **2 0**
1991–92 Aston Villa 8 0
1992–93 Aston Villa 4 0
1993–94 Aston Villa 17 0
1994–95 Aston Villa 39 3
1995–96 Aston Villa 36 1
1996–97 Aston Villa 38 3
1997–98 Aston Villa 37 2
1998–99 Aston Villa 25 2
1999–2000 Aston Villa 31 1
2000-01 Aston Villa 2 0 **237 12**
2000-01 Middlesbrough 21 3
2001-02 Middlesbrough 29 1
2002-03 Middlesbrough 32 3 **82 7**

GAVIN, Jason (D) 51 1
H: 6 0 W: 11 12 b.Dublin 14-3-80
Source: Trainee. *Honours:* Eire Under-21.
1996–97 Middlesbrough 0 0
1997–98 Middlesbrough 0 0
1998–99 Middlesbrough 2 0
1999–2000 Middlesbrough 6 0
2000-01 Middlesbrough 14 0
2001-02 Middlesbrough 9 0
2002-03 Middlesbrough 0 0 **31 0**
2002-03 *Grimsby T* 10 0 **10 0**
2002-03 *Huddersfield T* 10 1 **10 1**

GEREMI (M) 141 16
H: 5 9 W: 13 03 b.Bafoussam 20-12-78
Source: Racing Bafousam. *Honours:* Cameroon 60 full caps.
1997 Cerro Porteno 6 0 **6 0**
1997–98 Genclerbirligi 28 4
1998–99 Genclerbirligi 29 5 **57 9**
1999–2000 Real Madrid 20 0
2000-01 Real Madrid 16 0
2001-02 Real Madrid 9 0 **45 0**
2002-03 Middlesbrough 33 7 **33 7**

GILROY, Keith‡ (F) 0 0
H: 5 10 W: 11 04 b.Sligo 8-7-83
2000-01 Middlesbrough 0 0
2001-02 Middlesbrough 0 0
2002-03 Middlesbrough 0 0

GREENING, Jonathan (M) 113 5
H: 6 0 W: 11 08 b.Scarborough 2-1-79
Source: Trainee. *Honours:* England Youth, Under-21.
1996–97 York C 5 0
1997–98 York C 20 2 **25 2**
1997–98 Manchester U 0 0
1998–99 Manchester U 3 0
1999–2000 Manchester U 4 0
2000-01 Manchester U 7 0 **14 0**
2001-02 Middlesbrough 36 1
2002-03 Middlesbrough 38 2 **74 3**

GULLIVER, Phil (D) 10 0
H: 6 2 W: 13 10 b.Bishop Auckland 12-9-82
Source: Scholar.
2000-01 Middlesbrough 0 0
2001-02 Middlesbrough 0 0
2002-03 Middlesbrough 0 0
2002-03 *Blackpool* 3 0 **3 0**
2002-03 *Carlisle U* 1 0 **1 0**
2002-03 *Bournemouth* 6 0 **6 0**

JOB, Joseph-Desire (F) 109 22
H: 5 11 W: 11 00 b.Venissieux 1-12-77
Honours: Cameroon 43 full caps, 6 goals.
1997–98 Lyon 22 5
1998–99 Lyon 19 6 **41 11**
1999–2000 Lens 24 4 **24 4**
2000-01 Middlesbrough 12 3
2001-02 Middlesbrough 4 0
2002-03 Middlesbrough 28 4 **44 7**

JOHNSTON, Allan (M) 264 39
H: 5 10 W: 11 04 b.Glasgow 14-12-73
Source: Tynecastle BC. *Honours:* Scotland Under-21, B, 18 full caps, 2 goals.
1991–92 Hearts 0 0
1992–93 Hearts 2 1
1993–94 Hearts 28 1
1994–95 Hearts 21 1
1995–96 Hearts 33 9 **84 12**
1996–97 Rennes 23 2 **23 2**
1996–97 Sunderland 6 1
1997–98 Sunderland 40 11
1998–99 Sunderland 40 7 **86 19**
1999–2000 Rangers 0 0

1999–2000 *Birmingham C* 9 0 **9 0**
1999–2000 Bolton W 19 3 **19 3**
2000-01 Rangers 13 0
2001-02 Rangers 1 0 **14 0**
2001-02 Middlesbrough 17 1
2002-03 Middlesbrough 0 0 **17 1**
2002-03 *Sheffield W* 12 2 **12 2**

JONES, Brad (G) 1 0
H: 6 3 W: 12 01 b.Armadale 19-3-82
Source: Trainee. *Honours:* Australia Under-20.
1998–99 Middlesbrough 0 0
1999–2000 Middlesbrough 0 0
2000-01 Middlesbrough 0 0
2001-02 Middlesbrough 0 0
2002-03 Middlesbrough 0 0
2002-03 *Stockport Co* 1 0 **1 0**

JUNINHO (F) 236 45
H: 5 5 W: 9 10 b.Sao Paulo 22-2-73
Source: Juventus, Corinthians, Ituano, Sao Paulo. *Honours:* Brazil 49 full caps, 5 goals.
1993 Sao Paulo 16 1
1994 Sao Paulo 19 0
1995 Sao Paulo 9 0 **44 1**
1995–96 Middlesbrough 21 2
1996–97 Middlesbrough 35 12
1997–98 Atletico Madrid 23 6
1998–99 Atletico Madrid 32 8 **55 14**
1999–2000 Middlesbrough 28 4
2000 Vasco da Gama 28 5
2001 Vasco da Gama 15 4 **43 9**
2002-03 Middlesbrough 10 3 **94 21**

MACCARONE, Massimo (F) 69 25
H: 5 10 W: 12 05 b.Galliate 6-9-79
Honours: Italy 2 full caps.
2000-01 Empoli 35 16
2001-02 Empoli 0 0 **35 16**
2002-03 Middlesbrough 34 9 **34 9**

MARINELLI, Carlos (M) 42 2
H: 5 8 W: 11 06 b.Buenos Aires 14-3-82
Source: Boca Juniors.
1999–2000 Middlesbrough 2 0
2000-01 Middlesbrough 13 0
2001-02 Middlesbrough 20 2
2002-03 Middlesbrough 7 0 **42 2**

MURPHY, David (D) 13 0
H: 6 1 W: 12 03 b.Hartlepool 1-3-84
Source: Scholar. *Honours:* England Youth.
2001-02 Middlesbrough 5 0
2002-03 Middlesbrough 8 0 **13 0**

NEMETH, Szilard (F) 205 94
H: 5 11 W: 11 04 b.Komarno 8-8-77
Honours: Slovakia 39 full caps, 16 goals.
1994–95 Slovan Bratislava 3 0
1995–96 Slovan Bratislava 28 12
1996–97 Slovan Bratislava 30 13 **61 25**
1997–98 Kosice 18 12
1998–99 Kosice 19 8 **37 20**
1999–2000 Inter Bratislava 26 16
2000-01 Inter Bratislava 32 23 **58 39**
2001-02 Middlesbrough 21 3
2002-03 Middlesbrough 28 7 **49 10**

NORDGREN, Niklas (M) 0 0
b.Sweden 1-4-85
Source: Trainee.
2002-03 Middlesbrough 0 0

PARNABY, Stuart (M) 27 0
H: 5 11 W: 11 00 b.Durham City 19-7-82
Source: Trainee. *Honours:* England Youth, Under-20, Under-21.
1999–2000 Middlesbrough 0 0
2000-01 Middlesbrough 0 0
2000-01 *Halifax T* 6 0 **6 0**
2001-02 Middlesbrough 0 0
2002-03 Middlesbrough 21 0 **21 0**

QUEUDRUE, Franck (D) 101 5
H: 6 1 W: 12 01 b.Paris 27-8-78
Source: Meaux.
1999–2000 Lens 16 1
2000-01 Lens 24 1
2001-02 Lens 2 0 **42 2**
2001-02 Middlesbrough 28 2
2002-03 Middlesbrough 31 1 **59 3**

RICKETTS, Michael (F) 183 52
H: 6 2 W: 11 12 b.Birmingham 4-12-78
Source: Trainee. *Honours:* England 1 full cap.
1995–96 Walsall 1 1
1996–97 Walsall 11 1
1997–98 Walsall 24 1
1998–99 Walsall 8 0
1999–2000 Walsall 32 11 **76 14**
2000-01 Bolton W 39 19
2001-02 Bolton W 37 12
2002-03 Bolton W 22 6 **98 37**
2002-03 Middlesbrough 9 1 **9 1**

RIGGOTT, Chris (D) 96 7
H: 6 2 W: 13 09 b.Derby 1-9-80
Source: Trainee. *Honours:* England Youth, Under-21.
1998–99 Derby Co 0 0
1999–2000 Derby Co 1 0
2000-01 Derby Co 31 3
2001-02 Derby Co 37 0
2002-03 Derby Co 22 2 **91 5**
2002-03 Middlesbrough 5 2 **5 2**

RUSSELL, Sam (G) 1 0
H: 6 0 W: 10 08 b.Middlesbrough 4-10-82
Source: Scholar.
2000-01 Middlesbrough 0 0
2001-02 Middlesbrough 0 0
2002-03 Middlesbrough 0 0
2002-03 *Darlington* 1 0 **1 0**

SCHWARZER, Mark (G) 280 0
H: 6 5 W: 15 01 b.Sydney 6-10-72
Honours: Australia Youth, Under-20, 17 full caps.
1990–91 Marconi Stallions 1 0
1991–92 Marconi Stallions 9 0
1992–93 Marconi Stallions 23 0
1993–94 Marconi Stallions 25 0 **58 0**
1994–95 Dynamo Dresden 2 0 **2 0**
1995–96 Kaiserslautern 4 0
1996–97 Kaiserslautern 0 0 **4 0**
1996–97 Bradford C 13 0 **13 0**
1996–97 Middlesbrough 7 0
1997–98 Middlesbrough 35 0
1998–99 Middlesbrough 34 0
1999–2000 Middlesbrough 37 0
2000-01 Middlesbrough 31 0
2001-02 Middlesbrough 21 0
2002-03 Middlesbrough 38 0 **203 0**

SMITH, Gary (M) 0 0
H: 5 8 W: 10 08 b.Middlesbrough 30-1-84
Source: Trainee.
2002-03 Middlesbrough 0 0

SOUTHGATE, Gareth (D) 416 25
H: 6 0 W: 12 03 b.Watford 3-9-70
Source: Trainee. *Honours:* England 55 full caps, 2 goals.
1988–89 Crystal Palace 0 0
1989–90 Crystal Palace 0 0
1990–91 Crystal Palace 1 0
1991–92 Crystal Palace 30 0
1992–93 Crystal Palace 33 3
1993–94 Crystal Palace 46 9
1994–95 Crystal Palace 42 3 **152 15**
1995–96 Aston Villa 31 1
1996–97 Aston Villa 28 1
1997–98 Aston Villa 32 0
1998–99 Aston Villa 38 1
1999–2000 Aston Villa 31 2
2000-01 Aston Villa 31 2 **191 7**
2001-02 Middlesbrough 37 1
2002-03 Middlesbrough 36 2 **73 3**

STOCKDALE, Robbie (D) 79 2
H: 6 0 W: 12 03 b.Redcar 30-11-79
Source: Trainee. *Honours:* England Under-21, Scotland 5 full caps.
1997–98 Middlesbrough 1 0
1998–99 Middlesbrough 19 0
1999–2000 Middlesbrough 11 1
2000-01 Middlesbrough 0 0
2000-01 *Sheffield W* 6 0 **6 0**
2001-02 Middlesbrough 28 1
2002-03 Middlesbrough 14 0 **73 2**

TURNBULL, Ross (G) 0 0
H: 6 4 W: 13 05 b.Bishop Auckland 4-1-85
Source: Trainee. *Honours:* England Youth.
2002-03 Middlesbrough 0 0

VAN KANTEN, Sergio* (M) 0 0
b.Miami 2-7-84
Source: AFC Schakel.
2002-03 Middlesbrough 0 0

VIDMAR, Tony* (D) 338 28
H: 6 0 W: 12 08 b.Adelaide 15-4-69
Honours: Australia Under-23, 54 full caps, 2 goals.
1989 Adelaide City 11 1
1989–90 Adelaide City 27 4
1990–91 Adelaide City 27 3
1991–92 Adelaide City 24 1
1992–93 Adelaide City 9 0
1992–93 Ekeren 9 1 **9 1**
1993–94 Adelaide City 27 4
1994–95 Adelaide City 24 1 **149 14**
1995–96 NAC 30 2
1996–97 NAC 31 2 **61 4**
1997–98 Rangers 12 0
1998–99 Rangers 28 1
1999–2000 Rangers 27 6
2000-01 Rangers 15 1
2001-02 Rangers 25 1 **107 9**
2002-03 Middlesbrough 12 0 **12 0**

WHELAN, Noel (F) 251 47
H: 6 2 W: 12 03 b.Leeds 30-12-74
Source: Trainee. *Honours:* England Under-21.
1992–93 Leeds U 1 0
1993–94 Leeds U 16 0
1994–95 Leeds U 23 7
1995–96 Leeds U 8 0 **48 7**
1995–96 Coventry C 21 8
1996–97 Coventry C 35 6
1997–98 Coventry C 21 6
1998–99 Coventry C 31 10
1999–2000 Coventry C 26 1 **134 31**
2000-01 Middlesbrough 27 1
2001-02 Middlesbrough 19 4
2002-03 Middlesbrough 15 1 **61 6**
2002-03 *Crystal Palace* 8 3 **8 3**

WILKSHIRE, Luke (M) 21 0
H: 5 8 W: 11 00 b.Wollongong 2-10-81
Honours: Australia Under-20, Under-23.
1998–99 Middlesbrough 0 0
1999–2000 Middlesbrough 0 0
2000-01 Middlesbrough 0 0
2001-02 Middlesbrough 7 0
2002-03 Middlesbrough 14 0 **21 0**

WILSON, Mark (M) 36 4
H: 5 10 W: 12 07 b.Scunthorpe 9-2-79
Source: Trainee. *Honours:* England Schools, Under-21.
1995–96 Manchester U 0 0
1996–97 Manchester U 0 0
1997–98 Manchester U 0 0
1997–98 *Wrexham* 13 4 **13 4**
1998–99 Manchester U 0 0
1999–2000 Manchester U 3 0
2000-01 Manchester U 0 0 **3 0**
2001-02 Middlesbrough 10 0
2002-03 Middlesbrough 6 0 **16 0**
2002-03 *Stoke C* 4 0 **4 0**

Trainees
Graham, Daniel AW; Harrison, Alan G; Liddle, Gary D; Masters, Peter A; McMahon, Anthony; Morrison, James C; Peacock, Anthony L; Taylor, Andrew D; Van Geele, Michael

MILLWALL

ASHIKODI, Moses‡ (M) 5 0
H: 6 0 W: 11 09 b.Lagos 27-6-87
Honours: FA Schools, England Youth.
2002-03 Millwall 5 0 **5 0**

BALTACHA, Sergei‡ (D) 2 0
H: 6 5 W: 12 07 b.Kiev 28-7-79
Source: Kinnoull Juniors.
2002-03 Millwall 2 0 **2 0**

BOOTH, Stuart* (M) 0 0
H: 5 11 W: 11 11 b.Roehampton 7-12-83
Source: School.
2000-01 Millwall 0 0
2001-02 Millwall 0 0
2002-03 Millwall 0 0

BRANIFF, Kevin (F) 16 0
H: 5 11 W: 10 13 b.Belfast 4-3-83
Source: Scholarship. *Honours:* Northern Ireland Schools, Youth, Under-21.
1999–2000 Millwall 0 0
2000-01 Millwall 5 0
2001-02 Millwall 1 0
2002-03 Millwall 10 0 **16 0**

BULL, Ronnie (D) 50 0
H: 5 7 W: 11 01 b.Hackney 26-12-80
Source: Trainee.
1998–99 Millwall 1 0
1999–2000 Millwall 9 0
2000-01 Millwall 2 0

2001-02	Millwall	26	0		
2002-03	Millwall	12	0	**50**	**0**

CAHILL, Tim (M) **177 43**
H: 5 10 W: 11 01 b.Sydney 6-12-79
Source: Sydney U.

1997–98	Millwall	1	0		
1998–99	Millwall	36	6		
1999–2000	Millwall	45	12		
2000-01	Millwall	41	9		
2001-02	Millwall	43	13		
2002-03	Millwall	11	3	**177**	**43**

CLANCY, Timothy (M) **0 0**
b.Trim 8-6-84

2002-03	Millwall	0	0		

CLARIDGE, Steve* (F) **578 184**
H: 6 0 W: 12 10 b.Portsmouth 10-4-66
Source: Portsmouth, Fareham T.

1984–85	Bournemouth	6	1		
1985–86	Bournemouth	1	0	**7**	**1**
From Weymouth					
1988–89	Crystal Palace	0	0		
1988–89	Aldershot	37	9		
1989–90	Aldershot	25	10	**62**	**19**
1989–90	Cambridge U	20	4		
1990–91	Cambridge U	30	12		
1991–92	Cambridge U	29	12		
1992–93	Luton T	16	2	**16**	**2**
1992–93	Cambridge U	29	7		
1993–94	Cambridge U	24	11	**132**	**46**
1993–94	Birmingham C	18	7		
1994–95	Birmingham C	42	20		
1995–96	Birmingham C	28	8	**88**	**35**
1995–96	Leicester C	14	5		
1996–97	Leicester C	32	11		
1997–98	Leicester C	17	0	**63**	**16**
1997–98	*Portsmouth*	10	2		
1997–98	Wolverhampton W	5	0	**5**	**0**
1998–99	Portsmouth	39	9		
1999–2000	Portsmouth	34	14		
2000-01	Portsmouth	31	11	**114**	**36**
2000-01	*Millwall*	6	3		
2001-02	Millwall	41	17		
2002-03	Millwall	44	9	**91**	**29**

COGAN, Barry (F) **0 0**
H: 5 9 W: 9 0 b.Sligo 4-11-84
Source: Scholar.

2001-02	Millwall	0	0		
2002-03	Millwall	0	0		

CRAIG, Tony (D) **2 1**
H: 6 0 W: 10 03 b.Greenwich 20-4-85
Source: Scholar.

2002-03	Millwall	2	1	**2**	**1**

DOLAN, Joe (D) **48 3**
H: 6 2 W: 13 10 b.Harrow 27-5-80
Source: Chelsea Trainee. *Honours:* Northern Ireland Youth, Under-21.

1998–99	Millwall	9	1		
1999–2000	Millwall	17	1		
2000-01	Millwall	20	1		
2001-02	Millwall	0	0		
2002-03	Millwall	2	0	**48**	**3**

DUNNE, Alan (D) **5 0**
H: 5 10 W: 11 01 b.Dublin 23-8-82

1999–2000	Millwall	0	0		
2000-01	Millwall	0	0		
2001-02	Millwall	1	0		
2002-03	Millwall	4	0	**5**	**0**

ELLIOTT, Marvin (M) **1 0**
H: 6 0 W: 12 02 b.Wandsworth 15-9-84
Source: Scholar.

2001-02	Millwall	0	0		
2002-03	Millwall	1	0	**1**	**0**

GROGAN, Kevin‡ (M) **0 0**
H: 5 10 W: 12 06 b.Dublin 15-11-81
Source: UCD.

2002-03	Millwall	0	0		

GUERET, Willy (G) **12 0**
H: 6 1 W: 13 05 b.Saint Claude 3-8-73

2000-01	Millwall	11	0		
2001-02	Millwall	1	0		
2002-03	Millwall	0	0	**12**	**0**

HARPUR, Chad* (G) **0 0**
H: 6 0 W: 12 11 b.Johannesburg 3-9-82

2000-01	Leeds U	0	0		
2001-02	Millwall	0	0		
2002-03	Millwall	0	0		

HARRIS, Neil (F) **183 83**
H: 5 11 W: 12 01 b.Orsett 12-7-77
Source: Cambridge C.

1997–98	Millwall	3	0		
1998–99	Millwall	39	15		
1999–2000	Millwall	38	25		
2000-01	Millwall	42	27		
2001-02	Millwall	21	4		
2002-03	Millwall	40	12	**183**	**83**

HEARN, Charley (M) **11 0**
H: 5 11 W: 11 13 b.Ashford 5-11-83
Source: School.

2000-01	Millwall	0	0		
2001-02	Millwall	2	0		
2002-03	Millwall	9	0	**11**	**0**

IFILL, Paul (M) **179 28**
H: 6 0 W: 12 10 b.Brighton 20-10-79
Source: Trainee.

1998–99	Millwall	15	1		
1999–2000	Millwall	44	11		
2000-01	Millwall	35	6		
2001-02	Millwall	40	4		
2002-03	Millwall	45	6	**179**	**28**

KINET, Christophe‡ (M) **132 13**
H: 5 6 W: 10 -8 b.Huy 31-12-74

1995–96	Ekeren	15	1		
1996–97	Ekeren	23	3	**38**	**4**
1997–98	Strasbourg	17	2		
1998–99	Strasbourg	10	0	**27**	**2**
1999–2000	Millwall	3	0		
2000-01	Millwall	27	2		
2001-02	Millwall	17	3		
2002-03	Millwall	20	2	**67**	**7**

LAMBU, Goma* (M) **0 0**
H: 5 3 W: 9 0 b.London 10-11-84
Source: Scholar. *Honours:* England Youth.

2001-02	Millwall	0	0		
2002-03	Millwall	0	0		

LAWRENCE, Matthew (D) **251 5**
H: 6 0 W: 12 07 b.Northampton 19-6-74
Source: Grays Ath. *Honours:* England Schools.

1995–96	Wycombe W	3	0		
1996–97	Wycombe W	13	1		
1996–97	Fulham	15	0		
1997–98	Fulham	43	0		
1998–99	Fulham	1	0	**59**	**0**
1998–99	Wycombe W	34	2		
1999–2000	Wycombe W	29	2	**79**	**5**
1999–2000	Millwall	9	0		
2000-01	Millwall	45	0		
2001-02	Millwall	26	0		
2002-03	Millwall	33	0	**113**	**0**

LIVERMORE, David (M) **155 7**
H: 6 0 W: 12 07 b.Edmonton 20-5-80
Source: Trainee.

1998–99	Arsenal	0	0		
1999–2000	Millwall	32	2		
2000-01	Millwall	39	3		
2001-02	Millwall	43	0		
2002-03	Millwall	41	2	**155**	**7**

MAY, Ben (F) **16 1**
H: 6 1 W: 12 12 b.Gravesend 10-3-84

2000-01	Millwall	0	0		
2001-02	Millwall	0	0		
2002-03	Millwall	10	1	**10**	**1**
2002-03	*Colchester U*	6	0	**6**	**0**

McCAMMON, Mark (F) **94 12**
H: 6 5 W: 14 05 b.Barnet 7-8-78
Source: Cambridge C.

1997–98	Cambridge U	2	0		
1998–99	Cambridge U	2	0	**4**	**0**
1998–99	Charlton Ath	0	0		
1999–2000	Charlton Ath	4	0	**4**	**0**
1999–2000	*Swindon T*	4	0	**4**	**0**
2000-01	Brentford	24	3		
2001-02	Brentford	14	0		
2002-03	Brentford	37	7	**75**	**10**
2002-03	Millwall	7	2	**7**	**2**

NETHERCOTT, Stuart (D) **271 10**
H: 6 0 W: 13 01 b.Ilford 21-3-73
Source: Trainee. *Honours:* England Under-21.

1991–92	Tottenham H	0	0		
1991–92	*Maidstone U*	13	1	**13**	**1**
1991–92	*Barnet*	3	0	**3**	**0**
1992–93	Tottenham H	5	0		
1993–94	Tottenham H	10	0		
1994–95	Tottenham H	17	0		
1995–96	Tottenham H	13	0		
1996–97	Tottenham H	9	0		
1997–98	Tottenham H	0	0	**54**	**0**
1997–98	Millwall	10	0		
1998–99	Millwall	37	2		
1999–2000	Millwall	37	0		
2000-01	Millwall	35	2		
2001-02	Millwall	46	3		
2002-03	Millwall	36	2	**201**	**9**

ODUNSI, Leke‡ (M) **23 0**
H: 5 9 W: 11 07 b.Walworth 5-12-80
Source: Trainee.

1998–99	Millwall	3	0		
1999–2000	Millwall	4	0		
2000-01	Millwall	8	0		
2001-02	Millwall	2	0		
2002-03	Millwall	0	0	**17**	**0**
2002-03	*Colchester U*	6	0	**6**	**0**

PHILLIPS, Mark (D) **8 0**
H: 6 2 W: 11 02 b.Lambeth 27-1-82
Source: Scholarship.

1999–2000	Millwall	0	0		
2000-01	Millwall	0	0		
2001-02	Millwall	1	0		
2002-03	Millwall	7	0	**8**	**0**

QUIGLEY, Mark (M) **0 0**
b. 26-10-85
Source: Scholar.

2002-03	Millwall	0	0		

REES, Matthew (D) **0 0**
H: 6 3 W: 13 02 b.Swansea 2-9-82
Source: Trainee. *Honours:* Wales Under-21.

1999–2000	Millwall	0	0		
2000-01	Millwall	0	0		
2001-02	Millwall	0	0		
2002-03	Millwall	0	0		

REID, Steven (M) **139 18**
H: 6 0 W: 12 07 b.Kingston 10-3-81
Source: Trainee. *Honours:* England Youth. Eire 9 full caps, 2 goals.

1997–98	Millwall	1	0		
1998–99	Millwall	25	0		
1999–2000	Millwall	21	0		
2000-01	Millwall	37	7		
2001-02	Millwall	35	5		
2002-03	Millwall	20	6	**139**	**18**

ROBERTS, Andy (M) **385 15**
H: 5 11 W: 14 05 b.Dartford 20-3-74
Source: Trainee. *Honours:* England Under-21.

1991–92	Millwall	7	0		
1992–93	Millwall	45	0		
1993–94	Millwall	42	2		
1994–95	Millwall	44	3		
1995–96	Crystal Palace	38	0		
1996–97	Crystal Palace	45	2		
1997–98	Crystal Palace	25	0	**108**	**2**
1997–98	Wimbledon	12	1		
1998–99	Wimbledon	28	2		
1999–2000	Wimbledon	16	0		
2000-01	Wimbledon	27	2		
2001-02	Wimbledon	18	1	**101**	**6**
2001-02	*Norwich C*	5	0	**5**	**0**
2002-03	Millwall	33	2	**171**	**7**

ROBINSON, Paul (D) **14 0**
H: 6 1 W: 11 08 b.Barnet 7-1-82
Source: Scholar.

2000-01	Millwall	0	0		
2001-02	Millwall	0	0		
2002-03	Millwall	14	0	**14**	**0**

RYAN, Robbie (D) **211 2**
H: 5 10 W: 12 05 b.Dublin 16-5-77
Source: Belvedere. *Honours:* Eire Youth, Under-21.

1994–95	Huddersfield T	0	0		
1995–96	Huddersfield T	0	0		
1996–97	Huddersfield T	5	0		
1997–98	Huddersfield T	10	0	**15**	**0**
1997–98	Millwall	16	0		
1998–99	Millwall	26	0		
1999–2000	Millwall	34	0		
2000-01	Millwall	42	0		
2001-02	Millwall	37	0		
2002-03	Millwall	41	2	**196**	**2**

SADLIER, Richard (F) **143 34**
H: 6 2 W: 13 07 b.Dublin 14-1-79
Source: Belvedere. *Honours:* Eire Youth, Under-21, 1 full cap.

1996–97	Millwall	10	0		
1997–98	Millwall	4	3		
1998–99	Millwall	31	5		

1999–2000	Millwall	27	5		
2000-01	Millwall	29	6		
2001-02	Millwall	37	14		
2002-03	Millwall	5	1	**143**	**34**

SAMBA, Cherno (M) **0** **0**
H: 5 10 W: 10 01 b.Gambia 10-1-85
Source: Scholar. *Honours:* England Youth.

2001-02	Millwall	0	0		
2002-03	Millwall	0	0		

SEVERINO, Daniel‡ (F) **0** **0**
b.Sydney 12-2-82
Source: Piacenza.

2002-03	Millwall	0	0		

SMITH, Michael‡ (M) **0** **0**
b.London 27-11-83
Source: Arsenal Scholar.

2002-03	Millwall	0	0		

SWEENEY, Peter (F) **6** **1**
H: 6 0 W: 12 01 b.Glasgow 25-9-84
Source: Scholar.

2001-02	Millwall	1	0		
2002-03	Millwall	5	1	**6**	**1**

TIESSE, Alex (M) **0** **0**
b.Ivory Coast 15-8-85
Source: Scholar.

2002-03	Millwall	0	0		

TUTTLE, David‡ (D) **203** **6**
H: 6 3 W: 14 06 b.Reading 6-2-72
Source: Trainee. *Honours:* England Youth.

1989–90	Tottenham H	0	0		
1990–91	Tottenham H	6	0		
1991–92	Tottenham H	2	0		
1992–93	Tottenham H	5	0	**13**	**0**
1992–93	*Peterborough U*	7	0	**7**	**0**
1993–94	Sheffield U	31	0		
1994–95	Sheffield U	6	0		
1995–96	Sheffield U	26	1	**63**	**1**
1995–96	Crystal Palace	10	1		
1996–97	Crystal Palace	39	2		
1997–98	Crystal Palace	9	0		
1998–99	Crystal Palace	22	2		
1998–99	*Charlton Ath*	0	0		
1999–2000	Crystal Palace	1	0	**81**	**5**
1999–2000	Barnsley	12	0	**12**	**0**
1999–2000	Millwall	8	0		
2000-01	Millwall	9	0		
2001-02	Millwall	5	0		
2001-02	*Wycombe W*	4	0	**4**	**0**
2002-03	Millwall	1	0	**23**	**0**

WARD, Darren (D) **126** **3**
H: 6 4 W: 11 04 b.Kenton 13-9-78
Source: Trainee.

1995–96	Watford	1	0		
1996–97	Watford	7	0		
1997–98	Watford	0	0		
1998–99	Watford	1	0		
1999–2000	Watford	9	1		
1999–2000	*QPR*	14	0	**14**	**0**
2000-01	Watford	40	1		
2001-02	Watford	1	0	**59**	**2**
2001-02	Millwall	14	0		
2002-03	Millwall	39	1	**53**	**1**

WARNER, Tony (G) **183** **0**
H: 6 4 W: 14 04 b.Liverpool 11-5-74
Source: School.

1993–94	Liverpool	0	0		
1994–95	Liverpool	0	0		
1995–96	Liverpool	0	0		
1996–97	Liverpool	0	0		
1997–98	Liverpool	0	0		
1997–98	*Swindon T*	2	0	**2**	**0**
1998–99	Liverpool	0	0		
1998–99	*Celtic*	3	0	**3**	**0**
1998–99	*Aberdeen*	6	0	**6**	**0**
1999–2000	Millwall	45	0		
2000-01	Millwall	35	0		
2001-02	Millwall	46	0		
2002-03	Millwall	46	0	**172**	**0**

WISE, Dennis (M) **513** **84**
H: 5 6 W: 10 10 b.Kensington 16-12-66
Source: Southampton Apprentice. *Honours:* England Under-21, B, 21 full caps, 1 goal.

1984–85	Wimbledon	1	0		
1985–86	Wimbledon	4	0		
1986–87	Wimbledon	28	4		
1987–88	Wimbledon	30	10		
1988–89	Wimbledon	37	5		
1989–90	Wimbledon	35	8	**135**	**27**
1990–91	Chelsea	33	10		
1991–92	Chelsea	38	10		
1992–93	Chelsea	27	3		
1993–94	Chelsea	35	4		
1994–95	Chelsea	19	6		
1995–96	Chelsea	35	7		
1996–97	Chelsea	31	3		
1997–98	Chelsea	26	3		
1998–99	Chelsea	22	0		
1999–2000	Chelsea	30	4		
2000-01	Chelsea	36	3	**332**	**53**
2001-02	Leicester C	17	1		
2002-03	Leicester C	0	0	**17**	**1**
2002-03	Millwall	29	3	**29**	**3**

Scholars
Cant, Steven; Donovan, James; Elliott, Jason; Harris, Daniel R; Hart, Edward M; Masterson, Terence P; McCartney, David J; Robinson, Anton D; Robinson, Trevor; Rose, Jason; Simpson, James W

NEWCASTLE U

ACUNA, Clarence (M) **217** **25**
H: 5 10 W: 12 00 b.Rancagua 8-2-75
Honours: Chile 58 full caps, 3 goals.

1994	O'Higgins	28	2		
1995	O'Higgins	26	3		
1996	O'Higgins	27	3	**81**	**8**
1997	Univ de Chile	27	3		
1998	Univ de Chile	27	3		
1999	Univ de Chile	36	5	**90**	**11**
2000-01	Newcastle U	26	3		
2001-02	Newcastle U	16	3		
2002-03	Newcastle U	4	0	**46**	**6**

AMBROSE, Darren (M) **31** **8**
H: 5 11 W: 10 05 b.Harlow 29-2-84
Source: Scholar. *Honours:* England Youth, Under-21.

2001-02	Ipswich T	1	0		
2002-03	Ipswich T	29	8	**30**	**8**
2002-03	Newcastle U	1	0	**1**	**0**

AMEOBI, Foluwashola (F) **63** **7**
H: 6 3 W: 12 03 b.Zaria 12-10-81
Source: Trainee. *Honours:* England Under-21.

1998–99	Newcastle U	0	0		
1999–2000	Newcastle U	0	0		
2000-01	Newcastle U	20	2		
2001-02	Newcastle U	15	0		
2002-03	Newcastle U	28	5	**63**	**7**

BASSEDAS, Christian‡ (M) **292** **22**
H: 5 8 W: 11 09 b.Buenos Aires 16-2-73
Honours: Argentina 22 full caps.

1990–91	Velez Sarsfield	12	1		
1991–92	Velez Sarsfield	36	4		
1992–93	Velez Sarsfield	32	1		
1993–94	Velez Sarsfield	26	1		
1994–95	Velez Sarsfield	21	2		
1995–96	Velez Sarsfield	32	2		
1996–97	Velez Sarsfield	23	4		
1997–98	Velez Sarsfield	31	2		
1998–99	Velez Sarsfield	28	2		
1999–2000	Velez Sarsfield	27	2	**268**	**21**
2000-01	Newcastle U	22	1		
2001-02	Newcastle U	2	0		
2002-03	Newcastle U	0	0	**24**	**1**

BEAUMONT, James (M) **0** **0**
H: 5 7 W: 10 10 b.Stockton 11-12-84
Source: Scholar.

2001-02	Newcastle U	0	0		
2002-03	Newcastle U	0	0		

BELLAMY, Craig (F) **174** **54**
H: 5 10 W: 11 00 b.Cardiff 13-7-79
Source: Trainee. *Honours:* Wales Schools, Youth, Under-21, 20 full caps, 6 goals.

1996–97	Norwich C	3	0		
1997–98	Norwich C	36	13		
1998–99	Norwich C	40	17		
1999–2000	Norwich C	4	2		
2000-01	Norwich C	1	0	**84**	**32**
2000-01	Coventry C	34	6	**34**	**6**
2001-02	Newcastle U	27	9		
2002-03	Newcastle U	29	7	**56**	**16**

BERNARD, Olivier (D) **56** **7**
H: 5 7 W: 10 11 b.Lyon 14-10-79

2000-01	Newcastle U	0	0		
2000-01	*Darlington*	10	2	**10**	**2**
2001-02	Newcastle U	16	3		
2002-03	Newcastle U	30	2	**46**	**5**

BRAMBLE, Titus (D) **66** **1**
H: 6 2 W: 14 10 b.Ipswich 31-7-81
Source: Trainee. *Honours:* England Under-21.

1998–99	Ipswich T	4	0		
1999–2000	Ipswich T	0	0		
1999–2000	*Colchester U*	2	0	**2**	**0**
2000-01	Ipswich T	26	1		
2001-02	Ipswich T	18	0	**48**	**1**
2002-03	Newcastle U	16	0	**16**	**0**

BRENNAN, Stephen (D) **0** **0**
H: 5 8 W: 11 10 b.Dublin 26-3-83
Honours: Eire Under-21.

1999–2000	Newcastle U	0	0		
2000-01	Newcastle U	0	0		
2001-02	Newcastle U	0	0		
2002-03	Newcastle U	0	0		

CAIG, Tony (G) **286** **0**
H: 6 0 W: 13 04 b.Whitehaven 11-4-74
Source: Trainee.

1992–93	Carlisle U	1	0		
1993–94	Carlisle U	20	0		
1994–95	Carlisle U	40	0		
1995–96	Carlisle U	33	0		
1996–97	Carlisle U	46	0		
1997–98	Carlisle U	46	0		
1998–99	Carlisle U	37	0	**223**	**0**
1998–99	Blackpool	10	0		
1999–2000	Blackpool	33	0		
2000-01	Blackpool	6	0	**49**	**0**
2000-01	Charlton Ath	1	0	**1**	**0**
2001-02	Hibernian	8	0		
2002-03	Hibernian	5	0	**13**	**0**
2002-03	Newcastle U	0	0		

CALDWELL, Gary (D) **51** **0**
H: 5 11 W: 11 10 b.Stirling 12-4-82
Source: Trainee. *Honours:* Scotland Under-21, 4 full caps.

1998–99	Newcastle U	0	0		
1999–2000	Newcastle U	0	0		
2000-01	Newcastle U	0	0		
2001-02	Newcastle U	0	0		
2001-02	*Darlington*	4	0	**4**	**0**
2001-02	*Hibernian*	11	0	**11**	**0**
2002-03	Newcastle U	0	0		
2002-03	*Coventry C*	36	0	**36**	**0**

CALDWELL, Steven (D) **38** **1**
H: 6 0 W: 11 05 b.Stirling 12-9-80
Source: Trainee. *Honours:* Scotland Youth, Under-21, 2 full caps.

1997–98	Newcastle U	0	0		
1998–99	Newcastle U	0	0		
1999–2000	Newcastle U	0	0		
2000-01	Newcastle U	9	0		
2001-02	Newcastle U	0	0		
2001-02	*Blackpool*	6	0	**6**	**0**
2001-02	*Bradford C*	9	0	**9**	**0**
2002-03	Newcastle U	14	1	**23**	**1**

CHOPRA, Michael (F) **6** **5**
H: 5 8 W: 9 06 b.Newcastle 23-12-83
Source: Scholar. *Honours:* England Youth, Under-20.

2000-01	Newcastle U	0	0		
2001-02	Newcastle U	0	0		
2002-03	Newcastle U	1	0	**1**	**0**
2002-03	*Watford*	5	5	**5**	**5**

CORT, Carl (F) **101** **24**
H: 6 4 W: 12 07 b.Southwark 1-11-77
Source: Trainee. *Honours:* England Under-21.

1996–97	Wimbledon	1	0		
1996–97	*Lincoln C*	6	1	**6**	**1**
1997–98	Wimbledon	22	4		
1998–99	Wimbledon	16	3		
1999–2000	Wimbledon	34	9	**73**	**16**
2000-01	Newcastle U	13	6		
2001-02	Newcastle U	8	1		
2002-03	Newcastle U	1	0	**22**	**7**

DABIZAS, Nikos (D) **234** **18**
H: 6 1 W: 12 07 b.Amindeo 3-8-73
Honours: Greece 61 full caps.

1994–95	Olympiakos	26	2		
1995–96	Olympiakos	27	1		
1996–97	Olympiakos	31	0		
1997–98	Olympiakos	20	5	**104**	**8**
1997–98	Newcastle U	11	1		
1998–99	Newcastle U	30	3		
1999–2000	Newcastle U	29	3		
2000-01	Newcastle U	9	0		
2001-02	Newcastle U	35	3		
2002-03	Newcastle U	16	0	**130**	**10**

DUNN, Paul* (M) 0 0
b.Ashington 10-11-82
Source: Trainee.
2002-03 Newcastle U 0 0

DYER, Kieron (M) 200 22
H: 5 7 W: 9 07 b.Ipswich 29-12-78
Source: Trainee. *Honours:* England Youth, Under-21, B, 16 full caps.
1996–97 Ipswich T 13 0
1997–98 Ipswich T 41 4
1998–99 Ipswich T 37 5 **91 9**
1999–2000 Newcastle U 30 3
2000-01 Newcastle U 26 5
2001-02 Newcastle U 18 3
2002-03 Newcastle U 35 2 **109 13**

ELLIOTT, Robbie (D) 194 15
H: 5 8 W: 12 03 b.Gosforth 25-12-73
Source: Trainee. *Honours:* England Under-21.
1990–91 Newcastle U 6 0
1991–92 Newcastle U 9 0
1992–93 Newcastle U 0 0
1993–94 Newcastle U 15 0
1994–95 Newcastle U 14 2
1995–96 Newcastle U 6 0
1996–97 Newcastle U 29 7
1997–98 Bolton W 4 0
1998–99 Bolton W 22 0
1999–2000 Bolton W 27 3
2000-01 Bolton W 33 2 **86 5**
2001-02 Newcastle U 27 1
2002-03 Newcastle U 2 0 **108 10**

FERRELL, Andrew (M) 0 0
b.Newcastle 9-1-84
Source: Trainee.
2002-03 Newcastle U 0 0

GARDNER, Ross (M) 0 0
H: 5 8 W: 10 06 b.South Shields 15-12-85
Source: Scholar. *Honours:* England Youth.
2001-02 Newcastle U 0 0
2002-03 Newcastle U 0 0

GAVILAN, Diego (M) 7 1
H: 5 8 W: 10 07 b.Asuncion 1-3-80
Source: Cerro Porteno. *Honours:* Paraguay 23 full caps.
1999–2000 Newcastle U 6 1
2000-01 Newcastle U 1 0
2001-02 Newcastle U 0 0
2002-03 Newcastle U 0 0 **7 1**

GIVEN, Shay (G) 203 0
H: 6 1 W: 13 04 b.Lifford 20-4-76
Source: Celtic. *Honours:* Eire Under-21, 52 full caps.
1994–95 Blackburn R 0 0
1994–95 *Swindon T* 0 0
1995–96 Blackburn R 0 0
1995–96 *Swindon T* 5 0 **5 0**
1995–96 *Sunderland* 17 0 **17 0**
1996–97 Blackburn R 2 0 **2 0**
1997–98 Newcastle U 24 0
1998–99 Newcastle U 31 0
1999–2000 Newcastle U 14 0
2000-01 Newcastle U 34 0
2001-02 Newcastle U 38 0
2002-03 Newcastle U 38 0 **179 0**

GRIFFIN, Andy (D) 128 4
H: 5 9 W: 10 10 b.Billinge 7-3-79
Source: Trainee. *Honours:* England Youth, Under-21.
1996–97 Stoke C 34 1
1997–98 Stoke C 23 1 **57 2**
1997–98 Newcastle U 4 0
1998–99 Newcastle U 14 0
1999–2000 Newcastle U 3 1
2000-01 Newcastle U 19 0
2001-02 Newcastle U 4 0
2002-03 Newcastle U 27 1 **71 2**

GUY, Lewis (M) 0 0
b.Penrith 22-8-85
Source: Trainee. *Honours:* England Youth.
2002-03 Newcastle U 0 0

HARPER, Steve (G) 71 0
H: 6 2 W: 13 00 b.Easington 14-3-75
Source: Seaham Red Star.
1993–94 Newcastle U 0 0
1994–95 Newcastle U 0 0
1995–96 Newcastle U 0 0
1995–96 *Bradford C* 1 0 **1 0**
1996–97 Newcastle U 0 0
1996–97 *Stockport Co* 0 0
1997–98 Newcastle U 0 0
1997–98 *Hartlepool U* 15 0 **15 0**
1997–98 *Huddersfield T* 24 0 **24 0**
1998–99 Newcastle U 8 0
1999–2000 Newcastle U 18 0
2000-01 Newcastle U 5 0
2001-02 Newcastle U 0 0
2002-03 Newcastle U 0 0 **31 0**

HOGG, Ryan* (D) 0 0
H: 6 2 W: 13 00 b.Ashington 20-11-82
Source: Scholar.
2001-02 Newcastle U 0 0
2002-03 Newcastle U 0 0

HUGHES, Aaron (D) 149 3
H: 6 1 W: 11 02 b.Cookstown 8-11-79
Source: Trainee. *Honours:* Northern Ireland Youth, B, 31 full caps.
1996–97 Newcastle U 0 0
1997–98 Newcastle U 4 0
1998–99 Newcastle U 14 0
1999–2000 Newcastle U 27 2
2000-01 Newcastle U 35 0
2001-02 Newcastle U 34 0
2002-03 Newcastle U 35 1 **149 3**

JENAS, Jermaine (M) 73 10
H: 5 10 W: 12 00 b.Nottingham 18-2-83
Source: Scholar. *Honours:* England Youth, Under-21, 3 full caps.
1999–2000 Nottingham F 0 0
2000-01 Nottingham F 1 0
2001-02 Nottingham F 28 4 **29 4**
2001-02 Newcastle U 12 0
2002-03 Newcastle U 32 6 **44 6**

KARELSE, John* (G) 385 0
H: 6 3 W: 13 07 b.Kapelle 17-5-70
1986–87 NAC Breda 8 0
1987–88 NAC Breda 13 0
1988–89 NAC Breda 36 0
1989–90 NAC Breda 34 0
1990–91 NAC Breda 38 0
1991–92 NAC Breda 37 0
1992–93 NAC Breda 33 0
1993–94 NAC Breda 34 0
1994–95 NAC Breda 32 0
1995–96 NAC Breda 29 0
1996–97 NAC Breda 27 0
1997–98 NAC Breda 33 0
1998–99 NAC Breda 28 0 **382 0**
1999–2000 Newcastle U 3 0
2000-01 Newcastle U 0 0
2001-02 Newcastle U 0 0
2002-03 Newcastle U 0 0 **3 0**

KENDRICK, Joseph* (D) 0 0
H: 6 0 W: 11 05 b.Dublin 26-6-83
Source: Scholar.
2000-01 Newcastle U 0 0
2001-02 Newcastle U 0 0
2002-03 Newcastle U 0 0

KERR, Brian (M) 12 0
H: 5 10 W: 10 11 b.Motherwell 12-10-81
Source: Trainee. *Honours:* Scotland Schools, Youth, Under-21, 1 full cap.
1998–99 Newcastle U 0 0
1999–2000 Newcastle U 0 0
2000-01 Newcastle U 1 0
2001-02 Newcastle U 0 0
2002-03 Newcastle U 8 0 **9 0**
2002-03 *Coventry C* 3 0 **3 0**

LUA-LUA, Lomano (F) 113 20
H: 5 8 W: 12 00 b.Kinshasa 28-12-80
Honours: DR Congo 4 full caps.
1998–99 Colchester U 13 1
1999–2000 Colchester U 41 12
2000-01 Colchester U 7 2 **61 15**
2000-01 Newcastle U 21 0
2001-02 Newcastle U 20 3
2002-03 Newcastle U 11 2 **52 5**

MAKONGO, Calvin (F) 0 0
H: 6 1 W: 12 00 b.Kinshasha 31-12-84
Source: Scholar.
2001-02 Newcastle U 0 0
2002-03 Newcastle U 0 0

MARCELINO, Elena‡ (D) 134 9
H: 6 2 W: 13 00 b.Gijon 26-9-71
Honours: Spain 5 full caps.
1993–94 Gijon 2 0
1994–95 Gijon 8 0
1995–96 Gijon 4 0 **14 0**
1996–97 Mallorca 33 4
1997–98 Mallorca 36 2
1998–99 Mallorca 34 3 **103 9**
1999–2000 Newcastle U 11 0
2000-01 Newcastle U 6 0
2001-02 Newcastle U 0 0
2002-03 Newcastle U 0 0 **17 0**

McCLEN, Jamie (M) 14 0
H: 5 8 W: 10 07 b.Newcastle 13-5-79
Source: Trainee.
1997–98 Newcastle U 0 0
1998–99 Newcastle U 1 0
1999–2000 Newcastle U 9 0
2000-01 Newcastle U 0 0
2001-02 Newcastle U 3 0
2002-03 Newcastle U 1 0 **14 0**

NORTON, Lee (M) 0 0
b.Newcastle 1-8-84
Source: Trainee.
2002-03 Newcastle U 0 0

O'BRIEN, Alan (M) 0 0
H: 5 9 W: 11 00 b.Dublin 20-2-85
Source: Scholar.
2001-02 Newcastle U 0 0
2002-03 Newcastle U 0 0

O'BRIEN, Andy (D) 202 6
H: 6 3 W: 11 05 b.Harrogate 29-6-79
Source: Trainee. *Honours:* England Youth, Under-21, Eire Under-21, 6 full caps.
1996–97 Bradford C 22 2
1997–98 Bradford C 26 0
1998–99 Bradford C 31 0
1999–2000 Bradford C 36 1
2000-01 Bradford C 18 0 **133 3**
2000-01 Newcastle U 9 1
2001-02 Newcastle U 34 2
2002-03 Newcastle U 26 0 **69 3**

OFFIONG, Richard (F) 7 2
H: 5 11 W: 12 00 b.South Shields 17-12-83
Source: Scholar. *Honours:* England Youth, Under-20.
2001-02 Newcastle U 0 0
2002-03 Newcastle U 0 0
2002-03 *Darlington* 7 2 **7 2**

ORR, Bradley (M) 0 0
H: 6 0 W: 11 11 b.Liverpool 1-11-82
Source: Scholar.
2001-02 Newcastle U 0 0
2002-03 Newcastle U 0 0

QUINN, Wayne (D) 160 6
H: 5 10 W: 11 12 b.Truro 19-11-76
Source: Trainee. *Honours:* England Under-21, B.
1994–95 Sheffield U 0 0
1995–96 Sheffield U 0 0
1996–97 Sheffield U 0 0
1997–98 Sheffield U 28 2
1998–99 Sheffield U 44 1
1999–2000 Sheffield U 43 1
2000-01 Sheffield U 24 2
2000-01 Newcastle U 15 0
2001-02 Newcastle U 0 0
2002-03 Newcastle U 0 0 **15 0**
2002-03 *Sheffield U* 6 0 **145 6**

ROBERT, Laurent (F) 248 55
H: 5 8 W: 10 13 b.Saint-Benoit 21-5-75
Honours: France 9 full caps, 1 goal.
1994–95 Montpellier 7 0
1995–96 Montpellier 21 5
1996–97 Nancy 38 1 **38 1**
1997–98 Montpellier 26 2
1998–99 Montpellier 32 11 **86 18**
1999–2000 Paris St Germain 28 9
2000-01 Paris St Germain 32 14
2001-02 Paris St Germain 1 0 **61 23**
2001-02 Newcastle U 36 8
2002-03 Newcastle U 27 5 **63 13**

ROBSON, Damon* (M) 0 0
H: 5 7 W: 13 06 b.Co Durham 19-9-83
Source: Scholar. *Honours:* England Youth.
2000-01 Newcastle U 0 0
2001-02 Newcastle U 0 0
2002-03 Newcastle U 0 0

SHEARER, Alan (F) 462 244
H: 6 0 W: 12 06 b.Newcastle 13-8-70
Source: Trainee. *Honours:* England Youth, Under-21, B, 63 full caps, 30 goals.
1987–88 Southampton 5 3
1988–89 Southampton 10 0
1989–90 Southampton 26 3
1990–91 Southampton 36 4
1991–92 Southampton 41 13 **118 23**

1992–93 Blackburn R 21 16
1993–94 Blackburn R 40 31
1994–95 Blackburn R 42 34
1995–96 Blackburn R 35 31 **138 112**
1996–97 Newcastle U 31 25
1997–98 Newcastle U 17 2
1998–99 Newcastle U 30 14
1999–2000 Newcastle U 37 23
2000–01 Newcastle U 19 5
2001–02 Newcastle U 37 23
2002–03 Newcastle U 35 17 **206 109**

SOLANO, Nolberto (M) 267 66
H: 5 9 W: 11 02 b.Callao 12-12-74
Honours: Peru 57 full caps, 11 goals.
1994–95 Sporting Cristal 38 12
1995–96 Sporting Cristal 26 13
1996–97 Sporting Cristal 11 7 **75 32**
1997–98 Boca Juniors 32 5 **32 5**
1998–99 Newcastle U 29 6
1999–2000 Newcastle U 30 3
2000–01 Newcastle U 33 6
2001–02 Newcastle U 37 7
2002–03 Newcastle U 31 7 **160 29**

SPEED, Gary (M) 481 81
H: 5 10 W: 10 12 b.Deeside 8-9-69
Source: Trainee. *Honours:* Wales Youth, Under-21, 73 full caps, 6 goals.
1988–89 Leeds U 1 0
1989–90 Leeds U 25 3
1990–91 Leeds U 38 7
1991–92 Leeds U 41 7
1992–93 Leeds U 39 7
1993–94 Leeds U 36 10
1994–95 Leeds U 39 3
1995–96 Leeds U 29 2 **248 39**
1996–97 Everton 37 9
1997–98 Everton 21 7 **58 16**
1997–98 Newcastle U 13 1
1998–99 Newcastle U 38 4
1999–2000 Newcastle U 36 9
2000–01 Newcastle U 35 5
2001–02 Newcastle U 29 5
2002–03 Newcastle U 24 2 **175 26**

TAYLOR, Steven (D) 0 0
b.Greenwich 23-1-86
Source: Trainee. *Honours:* FA Schools, England Youth.
2002–03 Newcastle U 0 0

VIANA, Hugo (M) 49 3
H: 5 9 W: 11 09 b.Barcelos 15-1-83
Honours: Portual 7 full caps.
2001–02 Sporting Lisbon 26 1 **26 1**
2002–03 Newcastle U 23 2 **23 2**

WOODGATE, Jonathan (D) 114 4
H: 6 2 W: 12 06 b.Middlesbrough 22-1-80
Source: Trainee. *Honours:* England Youth, Under-21, 4 full caps.
1996–97 Leeds U 0 0
1997–98 Leeds U 0 0
1998–99 Leeds U 25 2
1999–2000 Leeds U 34 1
2000–01 Leeds U 14 1
2001–02 Leeds U 13 0
2002–03 Leeds U 18 0 **104 4**
2002–03 Newcastle U 10 0 **10 0**

Trainees
Bartlett, Adam J; Bates, Guy L; Blair, Steven; Brittain, Martin; Carr, Christopher P; Collin, Adam J; Gate, Kristopher; Howe, Daniel; Jackson, Ben R; Ramage, Peter I; Smylie, Daryl; Webster, Benjamin G

NORTHAMPTON T

ABBEY, Nathan* (G) 106 0
H: 6 1 W: 11 13 b.Islington 11-7-78
Source: Trainee.
1995–96 Luton T 0 0
1996–97 Luton T 0 0
1997–98 Luton T 0 0
1998–99 Luton T 2 0
1999–2000 Luton T 33 0
2000–01 Luton T 20 0 **55 0**
2001–02 Chesterfield 46 0 **46 0**
2002–03 Northampton T 5 0 **5 0**

ASAMOAH, Derek (F) 82 7
H: 5 6 W: 10 12 b.Ghana 1-5-81
Source: Slough T.
2001–02 Northampton T 40 3
2002–03 Northampton T 42 4 **82 7**

BURGESS, Daryl* (D) 393 12
H: 5 11 W: 12 03 b.Birmingham 24-1-71
Source: Trainee.
1989–90 WBA 34 0
1990–91 WBA 25 0
1991–92 WBA 36 2
1992–93 WBA 18 1
1993–94 WBA 43 2
1994–95 WBA 22 0
1995–96 WBA 45 2
1996–97 WBA 33 1
1997–98 WBA 27 1
1998–99 WBA 20 0
1999–2000 WBA 26 1
2000–01 WBA 3 0 **332 10**
2001–02 Northampton T 36 1
2002–03 Northampton T 25 1 **61 2**

CARRUTHERS, Chris (D) 49 1
H: 5 10 W: 12 03 b.Kettering 19-8-83
Source: Scholar. *Honours:* England Under-20.
2000–01 Northampton T 3 0
2001–02 Northampton T 13 1
2002–03 Northampton T 33 0 **49 1**

CAVILL, Aaran§ (M) 1 0
b.Bedford 5-3-84
Source: Scholar.
2001–02 Northampton T 1 0
2002–03 Northampton T 0 0 **1 0**

CHAMBERS, Luke§ (M) 1 0
H: 5 11 W: 11 00 b.Kettering 28-9-85
Source: Scholar.
2002–03 Northampton T 1 0 **1 0**

DUDFIELD, Lawrie (F) 88 17
H: 6 1 W: 13 09 b.Southwark 7-5-80
Source: Kettering T.
1997–98 Leicester C 0 0
1998–99 Leicester C 0 0
1999–2000 Leicester C 2 0
2000–01 Leicester C 0 0 **2 0**
2000–01 *Lincoln C* 3 0 **3 0**
2000–01 *Chesterfield* 14 3 **14 3**
2001–02 Hull C 38 12
2002–03 Hull C 21 1 **59 13**
2002–03 Northampton T 10 1 **10 1**

FRAIN, John* (D) 481 27
H: 5 10 W: 12 04 b.Birmingham 8-10-68
Source: Apprentice.
1985–86 Birmingham C 3 0
1986–87 Birmingham C 3 1
1987–88 Birmingham C 14 2
1988–89 Birmingham C 28 3
1989–90 Birmingham C 38 1
1990–91 Birmingham C 42 3
1991–92 Birmingham C 44 5
1992–93 Birmingham C 45 6
1993–94 Birmingham C 26 2
1994–95 Birmingham C 7 0
1995–96 Birmingham C 23 0
1996–97 Birmingham C 1 0 **274 23**
1996–97 Northampton T 13 0
1997–98 Northampton T 45 1
1998–99 Northampton T 41 0
1999–2000 Northampton T 40 2
2000–01 Northampton T 27 1
2001–02 Northampton T 27 0
2002–03 Northampton T 14 0 **207 4**

GABBIADINI, Marco* (F) 644 217
H: 5 10 W: 13 04 b.Nottingham 20-1-68
Source: Apprentice. *Honours:* England Under-21, B.
1984–85 York C 1 0
1985–86 York C 22 4
1986–87 York C 29 9
1987–88 York C 8 1
1987–88 Sunderland 35 21
1988–89 Sunderland 36 18
1989–90 Sunderland 46 21
1990–91 Sunderland 31 9
1991–92 Sunderland 9 5 **157 74**
1991–92 Crystal Palace 15 5 **15 5**
1991–92 Derby Co 20 6
1992–93 Derby Co 44 9
1993–94 Derby Co 39 13
1994–95 Derby Co 32 11
1995–96 Derby Co 39 11
1996–97 Derby Co 14 0 **188 50**
1996–97 *Birmingham C* 2 0 **2 0**
1996–97 *Oxford U* 5 1 **5 1**
1997–98 Stoke C 8 0 **8 0**
1997–98 York C 7 1 **67 15**
1998–99 Darlington 40 23
1999–2000 Darlington 42 24 **82 47**
2000–01 Northampton T 44 6
2001–02 Northampton T 35 7
2002–03 Northampton T 41 12 **120 25**

GILL, Jeremy# (D) 101 0
H: 5 11 W: 12 00 b.Clevedon 8-9-70
Source: Yeovil T.
1997–98 Birmingham C 3 0
1998–99 Birmingham C 3 0
1999–2000 Birmingham C 11 0
2000–01 Birmingham C 29 0
2001–02 Birmingham C 14 0
2002–03 Birmingham C 0 0 **60 0**
2002–03 Northampton T 41 0 **41 0**

HARGREAVES, Chris (M) 350 19
H: 5 11 W: 13 04 b.Cleethorpes 12-5-72
Source: Trainee.
1989–90 Grimsby T 19 2
1990–91 Grimsby T 18 3
1991–92 Grimsby T 10 0
1992–93 Grimsby T 4 0
1992–93 *Scarborough* 3 0 **3 0**
1993–94 Grimsby T 0 0 **51 5**
1993–94 Hull C 28 0
1994–95 Hull C 21 0 **49 0**
1995–96 WBA 1 0 **1 0**
1995–96 *Hereford U* 17 2
1996–97 Hereford U 44 4
1997–98 Hereford U 0 0 **61 6**
From Hereford U.
1998–99 Plymouth Arg 32 2
1999–2000 Plymouth Arg 44 3 **76 5**
2000–01 Northampton T 31 0
2001–02 Northampton T 39 3
2002–03 Northampton T 39 0 **109 3**

HARPER, Lee (G) 153 0
H: 6 1 W: 13 11 b.Chelsea 30-10-71
Source: Sittingbourne.
1994–95 Arsenal 0 0
1995–96 Arsenal 0 0
1996–97 Arsenal 1 0 **1 0**
1997–98 QPR 36 0
1998–99 QPR 15 0
1999–2000 QPR 38 0
2000–01 QPR 29 0 **118 0**
2001–02 Walsall 3 0 **3 0**
2002–03 Northampton T 31 0 **31 0**

HARSLEY, Paul (M) 218 18
H: 5 8 W: 11 05 b.Scunthorpe 29-5-78
Source: Trainee.
1996–97 Grimsby T 0 0
1997–98 Scunthorpe U 15 1
1998–99 Scunthorpe U 34 0
1999–2000 Scunthorpe U 46 3
2000–01 Scunthorpe U 33 1 **128 5**
2001–02 Halifax T 45 11 **45 11**
2002–03 Northampton T 45 2 **45 2**

HOPE, Richard* (D) 198 8
H: 6 3 W: 13 05 b.Middlesbrough 22-6-78
Source: Trainee.
1995–96 Blackburn R 0 0
1996–97 Blackburn R 0 0
1996–97 Darlington 20 0
1997–98 Darlington 35 1
1998–99 Darlington 8 0 **63 1**
1998–99 Northampton T 19 0
1999–2000 Northampton T 17 0
2000–01 Northampton T 33 0
2001–02 Northampton T 43 6
2002–03 Northampton T 23 1 **135 7**

LAVIN, Gerard‡ (D) 226 3
H: 5 10 W: 11 10 b.Corby 5-2-74
Source: Trainee. *Honours:* Scotland Under-21.
1991–92 Watford 1 0
1992–93 Watford 28 0
1993–94 Watford 46 3
1994–95 Watford 35 0
1995–96 Watford 16 0 **126 3**
1995–96 Millwall 20 0
1996–97 Millwall 9 0
1997–98 Millwall 7 0
1998–99 Millwall 38 0 **74 0**
1999–2000 Bristol C 19 0
2000–01 Bristol C 3 0 **22 0**
2000–01 *Wycombe W* 2 0 **2 0**

2001-02 Northampton T 2 0
2002-03 Northampton T 0 0 **2 0**

LINCOLN, Greg (M) 12 0
H: 5 9 W: 10 01 b.Cheshunt 23-3-80
Source: Trainee. *Honours:* England Youth.
1998–99 Arsenal 0 0
1999–2000 Arsenal 0 0
2000-01 Arsenal 0 0
2001-02 Torquay U 0 0
2002-03 Northampton T 12 0 **12 0**

LOWE, Daniel§ (F) 4 0
H: 5 7 W: 10 05 b.Barnsley 12-1-84
Source: Scholar.
2000-01 Northampton T 4 0
2001-02 Northampton T 0 0
2002-03 Northampton T 0 0 **4 0**

MARSH, Chris* (D) 445 23
H: 5 11 W: 13 02 b.Sedgley 14-1-70
Source: Trainee.
1987–88 Walsall 3 0
1988–89 Walsall 13 0
1989–90 Walsall 9 0
1990–91 Walsall 23 2
1991–92 Walsall 37 1
1992–93 Walsall 33 3
1993–94 Walsall 39 4
1994–95 Walsall 38 9
1995–96 Walsall 41 2
1996–97 Walsall 30 0
1997–98 Walsall 36 0
1998–99 Walsall 43 2
1999–2000 Walsall 40 0
2000-01 Walsall 7 0 **392 23**
2000-01 Wycombe W 11 0
2001-02 Wycombe W 1 0 **12 0**
2001-02 Northampton T 26 0
2002-03 Northampton T 15 0 **41 0**

McGREGOR, Paul* (M) 183 30
H: 5 10 W: 11 06 b.Liverpool 17-12-74
Source: Trainee.
1991–92 Nottingham F 0 0
1992–93 Nottingham F 0 0
1993–94 Nottingham F 0 0
1994–95 Nottingham F 11 1
1995–96 Nottingham F 14 2
1996–97 Nottingham F 5 0
1997–98 Nottingham F 0 0
1998–99 Nottingham F 0 0 **30 3**
1998–99 *Carlisle U* 10 3 **10 3**
1998–99 Preston NE 4 0 **4 0**
1999–2000 Plymouth Arg 44 13
2000-01 Plymouth Arg 33 6 **77 19**
2001-02 Northampton T 39 3
2002-03 Northampton T 23 2 **62 5**

MORISON, Steven§ (F) 14 1
H: 6 2 W: 12 00 b.Enfield 29-8-83
Source: Scholar.
2001-02 Northampton T 1 0
2002-03 Northampton T 13 1 **14 1**

RAHIM, Brent# (M) 17 1
H: 5 8 W: 10 10 b.Trinidad 8-8-78
Honours: Trinidad & Tobago full caps.
2001-02 Levski 11 0 **11 0**
2002-03 West Ham United 0 0
2002-03 Northampton T 6 1 **6 1**

RICKERS, Paul (M) 272 20
H: 5 10 W: 11 04 b.Pontefract 9-5-75
Source: Trainee.
1993–94 Oldham Ath 0 0
1994–95 Oldham Ath 4 1
1995–96 Oldham Ath 23 0
1996–97 Oldham Ath 46 4
1997–98 Oldham Ath 40 4
1998–99 Oldham Ath 45 4
1999–2000 Oldham Ath 41 3
2000-01 Oldham Ath 38 2
2001-02 Oldham Ath 24 2 **261 20**
2002-03 Northampton T 11 0 **11 0**

SAMPSON, Ian (D) 370 25
H: 6 2 W: 13 05 b.Wakefield 14-11-68
Source: Goole T.
1990–91 Sunderland 0 0
1991–92 Sunderland 8 0
1992–93 Sunderland 5 1
1993–94 Sunderland 4 0 **17 1**
1993–94 *Northampton T* 8 0
1994–95 Northampton T 42 2
1995–96 Northampton T 33 4
1996–97 Northampton T 43 5
1997–98 Northampton T 39 3
1998–99 Northampton T 42 1
1999–2000 Northampton T 45 6
2000-01 Northampton T 41 2
2001-02 Northampton T 27 0
2002-03 Northampton T 33 1 **353 24**

SPEDDING, Duncan* (D) 130 2
H: 6 2 W: 12 01 b.Frimley 7-9-77
Source: Trainee.
1996–97 Southampton 0 0
1997–98 Southampton 7 0 **7 0**
1998–99 Northampton T 24 1
1999–2000 Northampton T 44 1
2000-01 Northampton T 21 0
2001-02 Northampton T 23 0
2002-03 Northampton T 11 0 **123 2**

STAMP, Darryn (F) 84 10
H: 6 2 W: 12 00 b.Beverley 21-9-78
1997–98 Scunthorpe U 10 1
1998–99 Scunthorpe U 25 4
1999–2000 Scunthorpe U 10 0
1999–2000 *Halifax T* 5 0 **5 0**
2000-01 Scunthorpe U 12 1 **57 6**
From Scarborough.
2002-03 Northampton T 22 4 **22 4**

THOMPSON, Chris (M) 0 0
b.Swindon 15-8-82
Source: Scholar.
2001-02 Northampton T 0 0
2002-03 Northampton T 0 0

THOMPSON, Glyn (G) 28 0
H: 6 2 W: 13 01 b.Telford 24-2-81
Source: Trainee.
1998–99 Shrewsbury T 1 0
1999–2000 Shrewsbury T 0 0
1999–2000 Fulham 0 0
1999–2000 *Mansfield T* 16 0 **16 0**
2000-01 Fulham 0 0
2000-01 *Shrewsbury T* 0 0 **1 0**
2001-02 Fulham 0 0
2002-03 Fulham 0 0
2002-03 Northampton T 11 0 **11 0**

TROLLOPE, Paul (M) 310 29
H: 6 0 W: 12 06 b.Swindon 3-6-72
Source: Trainee. *Honours:* Wales B, 9 full caps.
1989–90 Swindon T 0 0
1990–91 Swindon T 0 0
1991–92 Swindon T 0 0
1991–92 *Torquay U* 10 0
1992–93 Torquay U 36 2
1993–94 Torquay U 42 10
1994–95 Torquay U 18 4 **106 16**
1994–95 Derby Co 24 4
1995–96 Derby Co 17 0
1996–97 Derby Co 14 1
1996–97 *Grimsby T* 7 1 **7 1**
1996–97 *Crystal Palace* 9 0 **9 0**
1997–98 Derby Co 10 0 **65 5**
1997–98 Fulham 24 3
1998–99 Fulham 20 2
1999–2000 Fulham 22 0
2000-01 Fulham 10 0
2001-02 Fulham 0 0 **76 5**
2001-02 Coventry C 6 0 **6 0**
2002-03 Northampton T 41 2 **41 2**

TURNER, Andy‡ (M) 124 9
H: 5 10 W: 11 10 b.Woolwich 23-3-75
Source: Trainee. *Honours:* England Schools, Eire Under-21.
1991–92 Tottenham H 0 0
1992–93 Tottenham H 18 3
1993–94 Tottenham H 1 0
1994–95 Tottenham H 1 0
1994–95 *Wycombe W* 4 0 **4 0**
1994–95 *Doncaster R* 4 1 **4 1**
1995–96 Tottenham H 0 0
1995–96 *Huddersfield T* 5 1 **5 1**
1995–96 *Southend U* 6 0 **6 0**
1996–97 Tottenham H 0 0 **20 3**
1996–97 Portsmouth 24 2
1997–98 Portsmouth 16 1
1998–99 Portsmouth 0 0 **40 3**
1998–99 Crystal Palace 2 0 **2 0**
1998–99 Wolverhampton W 0 0
1999–2000 Rotherham U 32 1
2000-01 Rotherham U 4 0
2000-01 *Rochdale* 4 0 **4 0**
2001-02 Rotherham U 0 0 **36 1**
2002-03 Northampton T 3 0 **3 0**

YOUNGS, Tom (F) 155 43
H: 5 9 W: 11 01 b.Bury St Edmunds 31-8-79
Source: Trainee.
1997–98 Cambridge U 4 0
1998–99 Cambridge U 10 0
1999–2000 Cambridge U 21 8
2000-01 Cambridge U 38 14
2001-02 Cambridge U 42 11
2002-03 Cambridge U 35 10 **150 43**
2002-03 Northampton T 5 0 **5 0**

Scholars
Barradell, Adam L; Bridgeford, Adam; Bunn, Mark J; Cavill, Aaran; Chambers, Luke; Cracknell, Dean P; Daly, Ben AJ; Georcelin, Justin S; Graham, Luke W; Howard, Matthew A; Khan, Yakoob; Lowe, Daniel J; Morison, Steven; Stirling, James S; White, Robert

NORWICH C

ABBEY, Zema (F) 78 12
H: 6 1 W: 12 11 b.Luton 17-4-77
Source: Arlesey, Baldock T, Hitchin T.
1999–2000 Cambridge U 8 0
2000-01 Cambridge U 14 5 **22 5**
2000-01 Norwich C 20 1
2001-02 Norwich C 6 1
2002-03 Norwich C 30 5 **56 7**

BRIGGS, Keith (M) 60 2
H: 6 0 W: 11 00 b.Glossop 11-12-81
Source: Trainee.
1999–2000 Stockport Co 7 1
2000-01 Stockport Co 0 0
2001-02 Stockport Co 32 0
2002-03 Stockport Co 19 1 **58 2**
2002-03 Norwich C 2 0 **2 0**

CRICHTON, Paul (G) 418 0
H: 6 1 W: 13 02 b.Pontefract 3-10-68
Source: Apprentice.
1986–87 Nottingham F 0 0
1986–87 *Notts Co* 5 0 **5 0**
1986–87 *Darlington* 5 0
1986–87 *Peterborough U* 4 0
1987–88 Nottingham F 0 0
1987–88 *Darlington* 3 0 **8 0**
1987–88 *Swindon T* 4 0 **4 0**
1987–88 *Rotherham U* 6 0 **6 0**
1988–89 Nottingham F 0 0
1988–89 *Torquay U* 13 0 **13 0**
1988–89 Peterborough U 31 0
1989–90 Peterborough U 16 0 **51 0**
1990–91 Doncaster R 20 0
1991–92 Doncaster R 16 0
1992–93 Doncaster R 41 0 **77 0**
1993–94 Grimsby T 46 0
1994–95 Grimsby T 43 0
1995–96 Grimsby T 44 0
1996–97 Grimsby T 0 0 **133 0**
1996–97 WBA 30 0
1997–98 WBA 2 0
1997–98 *Aston Villa* 0 0
1998–99 WBA 0 0 **32 0**
1998–99 Burnley 29 0
1999–2000 Burnley 46 0
2000-01 Burnley 8 0 **83 0**
2001-02 Norwich C 6 0
2002-03 Norwich C 0 0 **6 0**

DRURY, Adam (D) 234 4
H: 5 10 W: 11 07 b.Cottenham 29-8-78
Source: Trainee.
1995–96 Peterborough U 1 0
1996–97 Peterborough U 5 1
1997–98 Peterborough U 31 0
1998–99 Peterborough U 40 0
1999–2000 Peterborough U 42 1
2000-01 Peterborough U 29 0 **148 2**
2000-01 Norwich C 6 0
2001-02 Norwich C 35 0
2002-03 Norwich C 45 2 **86 2**

EASTON, Clint (M) 104 4
H: 5 11 W: 10 11 b.Barking 1-10-77
Source: Trainee. *Honours:* England Youth.
1996–97 Watford 17 1
1997–98 Watford 12 0
1998–99 Watford 7 0
1999–2000 Watford 17 0
2000-01 Watford 11 0 **64 1**
2001-02 Norwich C 14 1
2002-03 Norwich C 26 2 **40 3**

FLEMING, Craig (D) **434 8**
H: 5 11 W: 12 07 b.Halifax 6-10-71
Source: Trainee.

1988–89	Halifax T	1	0		
1989–90	Halifax T	10	0		
1990–91	Halifax T	46	0	**57**	**0**
1991–92	Oldham Ath	32	1		
1992–93	Oldham Ath	24	0		
1993–94	Oldham Ath	37	0		
1994–95	Oldham Ath	5	0		
1995–96	Oldham Ath	22	0		
1996–97	Oldham Ath	44	0	**164**	**1**
1997–98	Norwich C	22	1		
1998–99	Norwich C	37	3		
1999–2000	Norwich C	39	3		
2000-01	Norwich C	39	0		
2001-02	Norwich C	46	0		
2002-03	Norwich C	30	0	**213**	**7**

GREEN, Robert (G) **97 0**
H: 6 3 W: 13 00 b.Chertsey 18-1-80
Source: Trainee. *Honours:* England Youth.

1997–98	Norwich C	0	0		
1998–99	Norwich C	2	0		
1999–2000	Norwich C	3	0		
2000-01	Norwich C	5	0		
2001-02	Norwich C	41	0		
2002-03	Norwich C	46	0	**97**	**0**

HECKINGBOTTOM, Paul (D) **164 6**
H: 6 0 W: 12 02 b.Barnsley 17-7-77
Source: Manchester U Trainee.

1995–96	Sunderland	0	0		
1996–97	Sunderland	0	0		
1997–98	Sunderland	0	0		
1997–98	*Scarborough*	29	0	**29**	**0**
1998–99	Sunderland	0	0		
1998–99	*Hartlepool U*	5	1	**5**	**1**
1998–99	*Darlington*	10	0		
1999–2000	Darlington	45	1		
2000-01	Darlington	18	1		
2001-02	Darlington	42	3	**115**	**5**
2002-03	Norwich C	15	0	**15**	**0**

HENDERSON, Ian (F) **20 1**
H: 5 9 W: 11 00 b.Thetford 24-1-85
Source: Scholar. *Honours:* England Youth.

2002-03	Norwich C	20	1	**20**	**1**

HOLT, Gary (M) **247 11**
H: 6 1 W: 12 01 b.Irvine 9-3-73
Source: Celtic. *Honours:* Scotland 3 full caps.

1994–95	Stoke C	0	0		
1995–96	Kilmarnock	26	0		
1996–97	Kilmarnock	12	1		
1997–98	Kilmarnock	27	2		
1998–99	Kilmarnock	33	3		
1999–2000	Kilmarnock	35	0		
2000-01	Kilmarnock	19	3	**152**	**9**
2000-01	Norwich C	4	0		
2001-02	Norwich C	46	2		
2002-03	Norwich C	45	0	**95**	**2**

JARVIS, Ryan§ (F) **3 0**
H: 6 0 W: 11 03 b.Norwich 11-7-86
Source: Scholar. *Honours:* FA Schools, England Youth.

2002-03	Norwich C	3	0	**3**	**0**

LLEWELLYN, Chris (M) **156 20**
H: 6 0 W: 11 09 b.Merthyr 29-8-79
Source: Trainee. *Honours:* Wales Youth, Under-21, B, 2 full caps.

1996–97	Norwich C	0	0		
1997–98	Norwich C	15	4		
1998–99	Norwich C	31	2		
1999–2000	Norwich C	36	3		
2000-01	Norwich C	42	8		
2001-02	Norwich C	13	0		
2002-03	Norwich C	5	0	**142**	**17**
2002-03	*Bristol R*	14	3	**14**	**3**

MACKAY, Malky (D) **274 21**
H: 6 3 W: 13 00 b.Bellshill 19-2-72
Source: Queen's Park Youth.

1990–91	Queen's Park	10	0		
1991–92	Queen's Park	27	3		
1992–93	Queen's Park	33	3	**70**	**6**
1993–94	Celtic	0	0		
1994–95	Celtic	1	0		
1995–96	Celtic	11	1		
1996–97	Celtic	20	1		
1997–98	Celtic	4	1		
1998–99	Celtic	1	1	**37**	**4**
1998–99	Norwich C	27	1		
1999–2000	Norwich C	21	0		
2000-01	Norwich C	38	1		
2001-02	Norwich C	44	3		
2002-03	Norwich C	37	6	**167**	**11**

McVEIGH, Paul (F) **101 24**
H: 5 6 W: 10 08 b.Belfast 6-12-77
Source: Trainee. *Honours:* Northern Ireland Schools, Youth, Under-21, 10 full caps.

1995–96	Tottenham H	0	0		
1996–97	Tottenham H	3	1		
1997–98	Tottenham H	0	0		
1998–99	Tottenham H	0	0		
1999–2000	Tottenham H	0	0	**3**	**1**
1999–2000	Norwich C	1	0		
2000-01	Norwich C	11	1		
2001-02	Norwich C	42	8		
2002-03	Norwich C	44	14	**98**	**23**

MULRYNE, Phil (M) **118 15**
H: 5 9 W: 11 02 b.Belfast 1-1-78
Source: Trainee. *Honours:* Northern Ireland Youth, Under-21, B, 18 full caps, 3 goals.

1994–95	Manchester U	0	0		
1995–96	Manchester U	0	0		
1996–97	Manchester U	0	0		
1997–98	Manchester U	1	0		
1998–99	Manchester U	0	0	**1**	**0**
1998–99	Norwich C	7	2		
1999–2000	Norwich C	9	0		
2000-01	Norwich C	28	1		
2001-02	Norwich C	40	6		
2002-03	Norwich C	33	6	**117**	**15**

NEDERGAARD, Steen‡ (D) **290 25**
H: 6 1 W: 11 10 b.Odense 25-2-70

1991–92	Odense	17	0		
1992–93	Odense	30	9		
1993–94	Odense	25	1		
1994–95	Odense	27	1		
1995–96	Odense	30	1		
1996–97	Odense	24	4		
1997–98	Odense	21	2		
1998–99	Odense	0	0		
1999–2000	Odense	26	2	**200**	**20**
2000-01	Norwich C	15	1		
2001-02	Norwich C	40	2		
2002-03	Norwich C	35	2	**90**	**5**

NIELSEN, David (F) **204 59**
H: 6 0 W: 12 00 b.Sonderborg 1-12-76

1996–97	FC Copenhagen	14	1		
1997–98	FC Copenhagen	31	11		
1998–99	FC Copenhagen	30	15		
1999–2000	FC Copenhagen	26	8		
2000-01	FC Copenhagen	7	1	**108**	**36**
2000-01	Grimsby T	17	5	**17**	**5**
2000-01	Wimbledon	11	2		
2001-02	Wimbledon	12	2	**23**	**4**
2001-02	Norwich C	23	8		
2002-03	Norwich C	33	6	**56**	**14**

NOTMAN, Alex (F) **65 4**
H: 5 7 W: 11 00 b.Edinburgh 10-12-79
Source: Trainee. *Honours:* Scotland Schools, Youth, Under-21.

1996–97	Manchester U	0	0		
1997–98	Manchester U	0	0		
1998–99	Manchester U	0	0		
1998–99	*Aberdeen*	2	0	**2**	**0**
1999–2000	Manchester U	0	0		
1999–2000	*Sheffield U*	10	3	**10**	**3**
2000-01	Manchester U	0	0		
2000-01	Norwich C	15	1		
2001-02	Norwich C	30	0		
2002-03	Norwich C	8	0	**53**	**1**

RIVERS, Mark (F) **265 49**
H: 5 10 W: 11 03 b.Crewe 26-11-75
Source: Trainee.

1993–94	Crewe Alex	0	0		
1994–95	Crewe Alex	0	0		
1995–96	Crewe Alex	33	10		
1996–97	Crewe Alex	27	6		
1997–98	Crewe Alex	35	6		
1998–99	Crewe Alex	43	7		
1999–2000	Crewe Alex	32	7		
2000-01	Crewe Alex	33	7	**203**	**43**
2001-02	Norwich C	32	2		
2002-03	Norwich C	30	4	**62**	**6**

ROBERTS, Iwan (F) **575 188**
H: 6 3 W: 13 00 b.Bangor 26-6-68
Source: Trainee. *Honours:* Wales Schools, Youth, B, 15 full caps.

1985–86	Watford	4	0		
1986–87	Watford	3	1		
1987–88	Watford	25	2		
1988–89	Watford	22	6		
1989–90	Watford	9	0	**63**	**9**
1990–91	Huddersfield T	44	13		
1991–92	Huddersfield T	46	24		
1992–93	Huddersfield T	37	9		
1993–94	Huddersfield T	15	4	**142**	**50**
1993–94	Leicester C	26	13		
1994–95	Leicester C	37	9		
1995–96	Leicester C	37	19	**100**	**41**
1996–97	Wolverhampton W	33	12	**33**	**12**
1997–98	Norwich C	31	5		
1998–99	Norwich C	45	19		
1999–2000	Norwich C	44	17		
2000-01	Norwich C	44	15		
2001-02	Norwich C	30	13		
2002-03	Norwich C	43	7	**237**	**76**

RUSSELL, Darel (M) **132 7**
H: 6 0 W: 12 01 b.Mile End 22-10-80
Source: Trainee. *Honours:* England Youth.

1997–98	Norwich C	1	0		
1998–99	Norwich C	13	1		
1999–2000	Norwich C	33	4		
2000-01	Norwich C	41	2		
2001-02	Norwich C	23	0		
2002-03	Norwich C	21	0	**132**	**7**

SHACKELL, Jason (D) **2 0**
H: 6 3 W: 12 04 b.Hitchin 27-9-83
Source: Scholar.

2002-03	Norwich C	2	0	**2**	**0**

SINCLAIR, Dean (M) **2 0**
H: 5 10 W: 11 02 b.St Albans 17-12-84
Source: Scholar.

2002-03	Norwich C	2	0	**2**	**0**

Scholars
Batt, Damien AN; Blackburn, Lee C; Chick, David R; Crane, Gregory W; Crow, Daniel S; Howell, Nicholas; Jarvis, Ryan R; Osborne, Aaron A; Self, Daniel G; Smith, Adam; Thompson, Ben; Tyrie, David L; Willis, Oliver D; Woodrow, Richard

NOTTINGHAM F

ANTOINE-CURIER, Mickael* (F) **11 3**
H: 6 0 W: 12 00 b.Orsay 5-3-83

2000-01	Preston NE	0	0		
2001-02	Nottingham F	0	0		
2002-03	Nottingham F	0	0		
2002-03	*Brentford*	11	3	**11**	**3**

BIGGINS, James (D) **0 0**
b.Nottingham 6-6-85
Source: Scholar. *Honours:* England Youth.

2002-03	Nottingham F	0	0		

BIRCH, Jay* (F) **0 0**
b.Barnsley 23-11-83
Source: Scholar.

2001-02	Nottingham F	0	0		
2002-03	Nottingham F	0	0		

BODKIN, Matt (F) **0 0**
b.Chatham 16-9-83
Source: Scholar.

2002-03	Nottingham F	0	0		

BOPP, Eugene (M) **32 3**
H: 5 11 W: 12 03 b.Kiev 5-9-83
Source: Bayern Munich.

2000-01	Nottingham F	0	0		
2001-02	Nottingham F	19	1		
2002-03	Nottingham F	13	2	**32**	**3**

BRENNAN, Jim# (D) **180 4**
H: 5 11 W: 13 01 b.Toronto 8-5-77
Source: Sora Lazio. *Honours:* Canada 33 full caps, 3 goals.

1994–95	Bristol C	0	0		
1995–96	Bristol C	0	0		
1996–97	Bristol C	8	0		
1997–98	Bristol C	6	0		
1998–99	Bristol C	29	1		
1999–2000	Bristol C	12	2	**55**	**3**
1999–2000	Nottingham F	25	0		
2000-01	Nottingham F	12	0		
2000-01	*Huddersfield T*	2	0	**2**	**0**
2001-02	Nottingham F	41	0		
2002-03	Nottingham F	45	1	**123**	**1**

CASH, Brian (M) **11 0**
H: 5 9 W: 11 01 b.Dublin 24-11-82
Source: Trainee.

1999–2000	Nottingham F	0	0		
2000-01	Nottingham F	0	0		
2001-02	Nottingham F	5	0		
2002-03	Nottingham F	1	0	**6**	**0**
2002-03	*Swansea C*	5	0	**5**	**0**

DAWSON, Michael (D) **39 5**
H: 6 2 W: 12 02 b.Northallerton 18-11-83
Source: School. *Honours:* England Youth, Under-21.
2000-01 Nottingham F 0 0
2001-02 Nottingham F 1 0
2002-03 Nottingham F 38 5 **39 5**

DOIG, Chris (D) **46 1**
H: 6 2 W: 13 07 b.Dumfries 13-2-81
Source: Trainee. *Honours:* Scotland Schools, Youth, Under-21.
1997–98 Nottingham F 0 0
1998–99 Nottingham F 2 0
1999–2000 Nottingham F 11 0
2000-01 Nottingham F 15 0
2001-02 Nottingham F 8 1
2002-03 Nottingham F 10 0 **46 1**

EDWARDS, Christian (D) **204 8**
H: 6 2 W: 12 03 b.Caerphilly 23-11-75
Source: Trainee. *Honours:* Wales Under-21, B, 1 full cap.
1994–95 Swansea C 9 0
1995–96 Swansea C 38 2
1996–97 Swansea C 36 0
1997–98 Swansea C 32 2 **115 4**
1997–98 Nottingham F 0 0
1998–99 Nottingham F 12 0
1998–99 *Bristol C* 3 0 **3 0**
1999–2000 Nottingham F 0 0
1999–2000 *Oxford U* 5 1
2000-01 Nottingham F 36 3
2001-02 Nottingham F 6 0
2001-02 *Crystal Palace* 9 0 **9 0**
2002-03 Nottingham F 0 0 **54 3**
2002-03 *Tranmere R* 12 0 **12 0**
2002-03 *Oxford U* 6 0 **11 1**

ERVIN, Robert (D) **0 0**
b.Belfast 5-6-85
Source: Scholar.
2002-03 Nottingham F 0 0

FORMANN, Pascal (G) **0 0**
H: 6 1 W: 11 07 b.Werne 16-11-82
2000-01 Nottingham F 0 0
2001-02 Nottingham F 0 0
2002-03 Nottingham F 0 0

FOY, Keith‡ (D) **22 1**
H: 5 10 W: 13 01 b.Crumlin 30-12-81
Source: Trainee.
1998–99 Nottingham F 0 0
1999–2000 Nottingham F 0 0
2000-01 Nottingham F 20 1
2001-02 Nottingham F 2 0
2002-03 Nottingham F 0 0 **22 1**

GAVANON, Benjamin* (M) **1 0**
H: 5 9 W: 9 10 b.Marseille 20-9-80
2000-01 Marseille 1 0
2001-02 Marseille 0 0
2002-03 Marseille 0 0 **1 0**
2002-03 Nottingham F 0 0

GROVES, Tom (D) **0 0**
b.Nottingham 18-7-85
Source: Scholar. *Honours:* England Youth.
2002-03 Nottingham F 0 0

HAREWOOD, Marlon (F) **169 40**
H: 6 1 W: 13 07 b.Hampstead 25-8-79
Source: Trainee.
1996–97 Nottingham F 0 0
1997–98 Nottingham F 1 0
1998–99 Nottingham F 23 1
1998–99 *Ipswich T* 6 1 **6 1**
1999–2000 Nottingham F 34 4
2000-01 Nottingham F 33 3
2001-02 Nottingham F 28 11
2002-03 Nottingham F 44 20 **163 39**

HASKINS, Andy (M) **0 0**
b.York 30-4-84
Source: School. *Honours:* England Youth.
2000-01 Nottingham F 0 0
2001-02 Nottingham F 0 0
2002-03 Nottingham F 0 0

HJELDE, Jon Olav* (D) **184 5**
H: 6 3 W: 13 07 b.Levanger 30-7-72
1994 Rosenborg 1 0
1995 Rosenborg 7 0
1996 Rosenborg 16 1
1997 Rosenborg 3 0 **27 1**
1997–98 Nottingham F 28 1
1998–99 Nottingham F 17 1
1999–2000 Nottingham F 33 0
2000-01 Nottingham F 11 2
2001-02 Nottingham F 42 0
2002-03 Nottingham F 26 0 **157 4**

JEFFREY, Richard (F) **0 0**
H: 5 9 W: 11 00 b.Derby 4-11-83
Source: Scholar.
2000-01 Nottingham F 0 0
2001-02 Nottingham F 0 0
2002-03 Nottingham F 0 0

JESS, Eoin (F) **430 99**
H: 5 10 W: 11 09 b.Aberdeen 13-12-70
Source: Rangers 'S' Form. *Honours:* Scotland Under-21, B, 18 full caps, 2 goals.
1987–88 Aberdeen 0 0
1988–89 Aberdeen 2 0
1989–90 Aberdeen 11 3
1990–91 Aberdeen 27 13
1991–92 Aberdeen 39 12
1992–93 Aberdeen 31 12
1993–94 Aberdeen 41 6
1994–95 Aberdeen 25 1
1995–96 Aberdeen 25 3
1995–96 Coventry C 12 1
1996–97 Coventry C 27 0 **39 1**
1997–98 Aberdeen 34 9
1998–99 Aberdeen 36 14
1999–2000 Aberdeen 26 5
2000-01 Aberdeen 0 0 **297 78**
2000-01 Bradford C 17 3
2001-02 Bradford C 45 14 **62 17**
2002-03 Nottingham F 32 3 **32 3**

JOHNSON, David (F) **326 110**
H: 5 6 W: 12 00 b.Kingston, Jamaica 15-8-76
Source: Trainee. *Honours:* England Schools, B. Jamaica 4 full caps.
1994–95 Manchester U 0 0
1995–96 Bury 36 5
1996–97 Bury 44 8
1997–98 Bury 17 5 **97 18**
1997–98 Ipswich T 31 20
1998–99 Ipswich T 42 13
1999–2000 Ipswich T 44 22
2000-01 Ipswich T 14 0 **131 55**
2000-01 Nottingham F 19 2
2001-02 Nottingham F 22 3
2001-02 *Sheffield W* 7 2 **7 2**
2001-02 *Burnley* 8 5 **8 5**
2002-03 Nottingham F 42 25 **83 30**

KEARNEY, Liam* (M) **0 0**
H: 5 7 W: 10 12 b.Dublin 10-1-83
Source: Scholarship.
1999–2000 Nottingham F 0 0
2000-01 Nottingham F 0 0
2001-02 Nottingham F 0 0
2002-03 Nottingham F 0 0

LESTER, Jack* (F) **243 39**
H: 5 11 W: 11 06 b.Sheffield 8-10-75
Source: Trainee. *Honours:* England Schools.
1994–95 Grimsby T 7 0
1995–96 Grimsby T 5 0
1996–97 Grimsby T 22 5
1996–97 *Doncaster R* 11 1 **11 1**
1997–98 Grimsby T 40 4
1998–99 Grimsby T 33 4
1999–2000 Grimsby T 26 4 **133 17**
1999–2000 Nottingham F 15 2
2000-01 Nottingham F 19 7
2001-02 Nottingham F 32 5
2002-03 Nottingham F 33 7 **99 21**

LORRIMER, Wayne (M) **0 0**
b.Belfast 27-10-84
Source: Scholar.
2002-03 Nottingham F 0 0

LOUIS-JEAN, Mathieu# (D) **213 2**
H: 5 9 W: 11 03 b.Mont-St-Aignan 22-2-76
1993–94 Le Havre 7 0
1994–95 Le Havre 9 0
1995–96 Le Havre 15 0
1996–97 Le Havre 31 0
1997–98 Le Havre 16 0 **78 0**
1998–99 Nottingham F 16 0
1999–2000 Nottingham F 27 0
2000-01 Nottingham F 13 0
2001-02 Nottingham F 38 1
2002-03 Nottingham F 41 1 **135 2**

LUKIC, John (M) **0 0**
b.Enfield 25-4-86
Source: Scholar.
2002-03 Nottingham F 0 0

McCLEAN, Craig (M) **0 0**
b.Belfast 6-7-85
Source: Scholar.
2002-03 Nottingham F 0 0

MORGAN, Wes (D) **5 1**
H: 6 2 W: 14 00 b.Nottingham 21-1-84
Source: Scholar.
2002-03 Nottingham F 0 0
2002-03 *Kidderminster H* 5 1 **5 1**

OYEN, Davy (D) **17 1**
H: 6 0 W: 12 02 b.Bilzen 17-7-75
Honours: Belgium 3 full caps.
1999–2000 Anderlecht 7 0
2000-01 Anderlecht 4 1
2001-02 Anderlecht 2 0
2002-03 Anderlecht 0 0 **13 1**
2002-03 Nottingham F 4 0 **4 0**

PERCH, James (D) **0 0**
b.Mansfield 29-9-85
Source: Scholar.
2002-03 Nottingham F 0 0

PEYTON, Emmet* (G) **0 0**
b.Castlebar 26-10-83
2000-01 Nottingham F 0 0
2001-02 Nottingham F 0 0
2002-03 Nottingham F 0 0

REID, Andrew‡ (G) **0 0**
b.Aberdeen 3-6-85
Source: Scholar.
2001-02 Nottingham F 0 0
2002-03 Nottingham F 0 0

REID, Andy (F) **73 3**
H: 5 8 W: 11 02 b.Dublin 29-7-82
Source: Trainee. *Honours:* Eire Under-21.
1999–2000 Nottingham F 0 0
2000-01 Nottingham F 14 2
2001-02 Nottingham F 29 0
2002-03 Nottingham F 30 1 **73 3**

ROBERTS, Justyn (D) **0 0**
b.Lewisham 12-2-86
Source: Scholar.
2002-03 Nottingham F 0 0

ROBERTSON, Gregor (D) **0 0**
b.Edinburgh 19-1-84
2000-01 Nottingham F 0 0
2001-02 Nottingham F 0 0
2002-03 Nottingham F 0 0

ROCHE, Barry (G) **3 0**
H: 6 5 W: 14 00 b.Dublin 6-4-82
Source: Trainee.
1999–2000 Nottingham F 0 0
2000-01 Nottingham F 2 0
2001-02 Nottingham F 0 0
2002-03 Nottingham F 1 0 **3 0**

SCIMECA, Riccardo# (D) **224 9**
H: 6 1 W: 13 05 b.Leamington Spa 13-6-75
Source: Trainee. *Honours:* England Under-21, B.
1993–94 Aston Villa 0 0
1994–95 Aston Villa 0 0
1995–96 Aston Villa 17 0
1996–97 Aston Villa 17 0
1997–98 Aston Villa 21 0
1998–99 Aston Villa 18 2 **73 2**
1999–2000 Nottingham F 38 0
2000-01 Nottingham F 36 4
2001-02 Nottingham F 37 0
2002-03 Nottingham F 40 3 **151 7**

STEVENSON, David (G) **0 0**
b.Blackpool 20-9-84
Source: Trainee.
2002-03 Blackburn R 0 0
2002-03 Nottingham F 0 0

THOMPSON, John (D) **28 3**
H: 6 0 W: 12 01 b.Dublin 12-10-81
Honours: Eire Under-21.
1999–2000 Nottingham F 0 0
2000-01 Nottingham F 0 0
2001-02 Nottingham F 8 0
2002-03 Nottingham F 20 3 **28 3**

TYNAN, Scott (M) **0 0**
b.Knowsley 27-11-83
Source: Wigan Ath Scholar.
2001-02 Nottingham F 0 0
2002-03 Nottingham F 0 0

VAUGHAN, Tony* (D) **191 6**
H: 6 1 W: 13 04 b.Manchester 11-10-75
Source: Trainee. *Honours:* England Schools.
1994–95 Ipswich T 10 0
1995–96 Ipswich T 25 1
1996–97 Ipswich T 32 2 **67 3**
1997–98 Manchester C 19 1
1998–99 Manchester C 38 1
1999–2000 Manchester C 1 0 **58 2**
1999–2000 *Cardiff C* 14 0 **14 0**
1999–2000 Nottingham F 10 0
2000-01 Nottingham F 25 1
2001-02 Nottingham F 8 0
2001-02 *Scunthorpe U* 5 0 **5 0**
2002-03 Nottingham F 0 0 **43 1**
2002-03 *Mansfield T* 4 0 **4 0**

WALKER, Des# (D) **632 1**
H: 5 11 W: 11 13 b.Enfield 26-11-65
Source: Apprentice. *Honours:* England Under-21, 59 full caps.
1983–84 Nottingham F 4 0
1984–85 Nottingham F 3 0
1985–86 Nottingham F 39 0
1986–87 Nottingham F 41 0
1987–88 Nottingham F 35 0
1988–89 Nottingham F 34 0
1989–90 Nottingham F 38 0
1990–91 Nottingham F 37 0
1991–92 Nottingham F 33 1
1992–93 Sampdoria 30 0 **30 0**
1993–94 Sheffield W 42 0
1994–95 Sheffield W 38 0
1995–96 Sheffield W 36 0
1996–97 Sheffield W 36 0
1997–98 Sheffield W 38 0
1998–99 Sheffield W 37 0
1999–2000 Sheffield W 37 0
2000-01 Sheffield W 43 0 **307 0**
2001-02 Nottingham F 0 0
2002-03 Nottingham F 31 0 **295 1**

WARD, Darren (G) **423 0**
H: 6 0 W: 13 02 b.Worksop 11-5-74
Source: Trainee. *Honours:* Wales Under-21, B, 4 full caps.
1992–93 Mansfield T 13 0
1993–94 Mansfield T 33 0
1994–95 Mansfield T 35 0 **81 0**
1995–96 Notts Co 46 0
1996–97 Notts Co 38 0
1997–98 Notts Co 44 0
1998–99 Notts Co 43 0
1999–2000 Notts Co 45 0
2000-01 Notts Co 35 0 **251 0**
2000-01 Nottingham F 0 0
2001-02 Nottingham F 46 0
2002-03 Nottingham F 45 0 **91 0**

WEBB, Steven (M) **0 0**
b.Macclesfield 13-9-84
Source: Academy.
2001-02 Nottingham F 0 0
2002-03 Nottingham F 0 0

WESTCARR, Craig (F) **19 1**
H: 5 11 W: 11 04 b.Nottingham 29-1-85
Source: Scholar. *Honours:* England Youth.
2001-02 Nottingham F 8 0
2002-03 Nottingham F 11 1 **19 1**

WILLIAMS, Gareth (M) **103 3**
H: 6 1 W: 12 03 b.Glasgow 16-12-81
Source: Trainee. *Honours:* Scotland Youth, Under-21, 5 full caps.
1998–99 Nottingham F 0 0
1999–2000 Nottingham F 2 0
2000-01 Nottingham F 17 0
2001-02 Nottingham F 44 0
2002-03 Nottingham F 40 3 **103 3**

Scholars
France, Aaron J; Freyne, David P; Hawkins, Nicholas C; Hurren, Gavin; Jones, Nathan C; Morgan, Neil; Munster, Darren; Plummer, Michael J; Swannick, Scott DW; Weir-Daley, Spencer

NOTTS CO

BARACLOUGH, Ian (D) **437 33**
H: 6 1 W: 12 11 b.Leicester 4-12-70
Source: Trainee.
1988–89 Leicester C 0 0
1989–90 Leicester C 0 0
1989–90 *Wigan Ath* 9 2 **9 2**
1990–91 Leicester C 0 0
1990–91 *Grimsby T* 4 0
1991–92 Grimsby T 0 0
1992–93 Grimsby T 1 0 **5 0**
1992–93 Lincoln C 36 5
1993–94 Lincoln C 37 5 **73 10**
1994–95 Mansfield T 36 3
1995–96 Mansfield T 11 2 **47 5**
1995–96 Notts Co 35 2
1996–97 Notts Co 38 2
1997–98 Notts Co 38 6
1997–98 QPR 8 0
1998–99 QPR 43 1
1999–2000 QPR 45 0
2000-01 QPR 29 0 **125 1**
2001-02 Notts Co 33 3
2002-03 Notts Co 34 2 **178 15**

BOLLAND, Paul (M) **105 4**
H: 6 0 W: 12 10 b.Bradford 23-12-79
Source: Trainee.
1997–98 Bradford C 10 0
1998–99 Bradford C 2 0 **12 0**
1998–99 Notts Co 13 0
1999–2000 Notts Co 25 1
2000-01 Notts Co 7 0
2001-02 Notts Co 19 0
2002-03 Notts Co 29 3 **93 4**

BROUGH, Michael (M) **79 2**
H: 5 9 W: 12 05 b.Nottingham 1-8-81
Source: Trainee. *Honours:* Wales Under-21.
1999–2000 Notts Co 11 0
2000-01 Notts Co 16 1
2001-02 Notts Co 21 0
2002-03 Notts Co 31 1 **79 2**

CASKEY, Darren (M) **321 48**
H: 5 8 W: 12 04 b.Basildon 21-8-74
Source: Trainee. *Honours:* England Schools, Youth.
1991–92 Tottenham H 0 0
1992–93 Tottenham H 0 0
1993–94 Tottenham H 25 4
1994–95 Tottenham H 4 0
1995–96 Tottenham H 3 0 **32 4**
1995–96 *Watford* 6 1 **6 1**
1995–96 Reading 15 2
1996–97 Reading 35 0
1997–98 Reading 23 0
1998–99 Reading 42 7
1999–2000 Reading 44 17
2000-01 Reading 43 9 **202 35**
2001-02 Notts Co 42 5
2002-03 Notts Co 39 3 **81 8**

DEENEY, Saul (G) **7 0**
H: 6 1 W: 12 07 b.Londonderry 12-3-83
Source: Scholar.
2000-01 Notts Co 0 0
2001-02 Notts Co 0 0
2002-03 Notts Co 7 0 **7 0**

FENTON, Nicky (D) **153 9**
H: 5 10 W: 12 04 b.Preston 23-11-79
Source: Trainee. *Honours:* England Youth.
1996–97 Manchester C 0 0
1997–98 Manchester C 0 0
1998–99 Manchester C 15 0
1999–2000 Manchester C 0 0
1999–2000 *Notts Co* 13 1
1999–2000 *Bournemouth* 8 0
2000-01 Manchester C 0 0 **15 0**
2000-01 *Bournemouth* 5 0 **13 0**
2000-01 Notts Co 30 2
2001-02 Notts Co 42 3
2002-03 Notts Co 40 3 **125 9**

FRANCIS, Willis§ (M) **10 0**
H: 5 5 W: 10 10 b.Nottingham 26-7-85
Source: Scholar.
2002-03 Notts Co 10 0 **10 0**

GARDEN, Stuart (G) **39 0**
H: 6 0 W: 12 06 b.Dundee 10-2-72
2001-02 Notts Co 21 0
2002-03 Notts Co 18 0 **39 0**

HACKWORTH, Tony (F) **42 1**
H: 6 2 W: 13 07 b.Durham 19-5-80
Source: Trainee. *Honours:* England Youth.
1997–98 Leeds U 0 0
1998–99 Leeds U 0 0
1999–2000 Leeds U 0 0
2000-01 Leeds U 0 0
2001-02 Notts Co 33 1
2002-03 Notts Co 9 0 **42 1**

HARRAD, Shaun§ (M) **5 0**
H: 5 10 W: 12 04 b.Nottingham 11-12-84
Source: Scholar.
2002-03 Notts Co 5 0 **5 0**

HEFFERNAN, Paul (F) **62 16**
H: 5 10 W: 11 05 b.Dublin 29-12-81
Source: Newton.
1999–2000 Notts Co 2 0
2000-01 Notts Co 1 0
2001-02 Notts Co 23 6
2002-03 Notts Co 36 10 **62 16**

HOLMES, Richard* (D) **59 0**
H: 5 11 W: 11 08 b.Grantham 7-11-80
Source: Trainee.
1998–99 Notts Co 8 0
1999–2000 Notts Co 41 0
2000-01 Notts Co 5 0
2001-02 Notts Co 1 0
2002-03 Notts Co 4 0 **59 0**

IRELAND, Craig* (D) **163 7**
H: 6 3 W: 13 09 b.Dundee 29-11-75
Source: Aberdeen Lads.
1994–95 Aberdeen 0 0
1995–96 Aberdeen 0 0
1995–96 Dunfermline Ath 10 0
1996–97 Dunfermline Ath 9 1
1997–98 Dunfermline Ath 12 1
1998–99 Dunfermline Ath 23 0
1999–2000 Dunfermline Ath 3 0 **57 2**
1999–2000 Dundee 14 1 **14 1**
2000-01 Airdrieonians 12 2 **12 2**
2000-01 *Notts Co* 16 0
2001-02 Notts Co 27 1
2002-03 Notts Co 37 1 **80 2**

LIBURD, Richard* (D) **282 13**
H: 5 9 W: 11 08 b.Nottingham 26-9-73
Source: Forest Ath.
1992–93 Middlesbrough 0 0
1993–94 Middlesbrough 41 1 **41 1**
1994–95 Bradford C 9 1
1995–96 Bradford C 33 1
1996–97 Bradford C 36 1
1997–98 Bradford C 0 0 **78 3**
1997–98 Carlisle U 9 0 **9 0**
1998–99 Notts Co 35 1
1999–2000 Notts Co 31 1
2000-01 Notts Co 31 3
2001-02 Notts Co 25 2
2002-03 Notts Co 32 2 **154 9**

MILDENHALL, Steve (G) **80 0**
H: 6 4 W: 15 01 b.Swindon 13-5-78
Source: Trainee.
1996–97 Swindon T 1 0
1997–98 Swindon T 4 0
1998–99 Swindon T 0 0
1999–2000 Swindon T 5 0
2000-01 Swindon T 23 0 **33 0**
2001-02 Notts Co 26 0
2002-03 Notts Co 21 0 **47 0**

NICHOLSON, Kevin (D) **80 3**
H: 5 8 W: 12 01 b.Derby 2-10-80
Source: Trainee. *Honours:* England Schools.
1997–98 Sheffield W 0 0
1998–99 Sheffield W 0 0
1999–2000 Sheffield W 0 0
2000-01 Sheffield W 1 0 **1 0**
From Forest Green R
2000-01 Northampton T 7 0 **7 0**
2000-01 Notts Co 11 2
2001-02 Notts Co 24 1
2002-03 Notts Co 37 0 **72 3**

RICHARDSON, Ian# (D) **210 18**
H: 6 0 W: 12 04 b.Barking 22-10-70
Source: Dagenham & Redbridge.
1995–96 Birmingham C 7 0 **7 0**
1995–96 Notts Co 15 0
1996–97 Notts Co 19 1
1997–98 Notts Co 30 2
1998–99 Notts Co 23 7
1999–2000 Notts Co 33 4
2000-01 Notts Co 25 1
2001-02 Notts Co 24 2
2002-03 Notts Co 34 1 **203 18**

RILEY, Paul (D) **9 0**
H: 5 9 W: 10 07 b.Nottingham 29-9-82
Source: Scholar.
2001-02 Notts Co 6 0
2002-03 Notts Co 3 0 **9 0**

STALLARD, Mark (F) **311 102**
H: 6 0 W: 13 09 b.Derby 24-10-74
Source: Trainee.
1991–92 Derby Co 3 0
1992–93 Derby Co 5 0
1993–94 Derby Co 0 0
1994–95 Derby Co 16 2
1994–95 *Fulham* 4 3 **4 3**
1995–96 Derby Co 3 0 **27 2**
1995–96 Bradford C 21 9
1996–97 Bradford C 22 1 **43 10**
1996–97 *Preston NE* 4 1 **4 1**
1996–97 Wycombe W 12 4
1997–98 Wycombe W 43 17
1998–99 Wycombe W 15 2 **70 23**
1998–99 Notts Co 14 4
1999–2000 Notts Co 36 14
2000–01 Notts Co 42 17
2001–02 Notts Co 26 4
2002–03 Notts Co 45 24 **163 63**

STONE, Danny* (D) **21 0**
H: 6 0 W: 12 03 b.Liverpool 14-9-82
Honours: Blackburn R Scholar.
2001–02 Notts Co 6 0
2002–03 Notts Co 15 0 **21 0**

Scholars
Appleby, Craig; Barcherini, Alessandro; Barrow; James G; Bostock, Daniel; Clarke, Ryan A; Commons, Spencer J; Francis, Willis D; Friars, Emmet C; Harrad, Shaun; McFaul, Shane; McIntyre, Edmond JJ; Nurse, Kristopher F; Richardson, Ben; Screaton, Iain P; Smith, Gregory M; Wilson, Kelvin

OLDHAM ATH

ANDREWS, Wayne# (F) **77 20**
H: 5 10 W: 11 09 b.Paddington 25-11-77
Source: Trainee.
1995–96 Watford 1 0
1996–97 Watford 25 4
1997–98 Watford 2 0
1998–99 Watford 0 0 **28 4**
1998–99 *Cambridge U* 2 0 **2 0**
1998–99 *Peterborough U* 10 5 **10 5**
From Chesham U
2001–02 Oldham Ath 0 0
2002–03 Oldham Ath 37 11 **37 11**

APPLEBY, Matty (M) **277 17**
H: 5 10 W: 11 04 b.Middlesbrough 16-4-72
Source: Trainee.
1989–90 Newcastle U 0 0
1990–91 Newcastle U 1 0
1991–92 Newcastle U 18 0
1992–93 Newcastle U 0 0
1993–94 Newcastle U 1 0 **20 0**
1993–94 *Darlington* 10 1
1994–95 Darlington 36 1
1995–96 Darlington 43 6 **89 8**
1996–97 Barnsley 35 0
1997–98 Barnsley 15 0
1998–99 Barnsley 34 0
1999–2000 Barnsley 36 5
2000–01 Barnsley 19 2
2001–02 Barnsley 0 0 **139 7**
2001–02 Oldham Ath 17 2
2002–03 Oldham Ath 12 0 **29 2**

ARMSTRONG, Chris (D) **98 2**
H: 5 9 W: 10 09 b.Newcastle 5-8-82
Source: Scholar. *Honours:* England Under-20.
2000–01 Bury 22 1
2001–02 Bury 11 0 **33 1**
2001–02 Oldham Ath 32 0
2002–03 Oldham Ath 33 1 **65 1**

BAUDET, Julien# (D) **44 3**
H: 6 3 W: 12 09 b.St Martin D'heres 13-1-79
Source: Toulouse.
2001–02 Oldham Ath 20 1
2002–03 Oldham Ath 24 2 **44 3**

BEHARALL, David (D) **70 1**
H: 6 0 W: 11 06 b.Newcastle 8-3-79
Source: Trainee.
1997–98 Newcastle U 0 0
1998–99 Newcastle U 4 0
1999–2000 Newcastle U 2 0
2000–01 Newcastle U 0 0 **6 0**
2001–02 Grimsby T 14 0 **14 0**
2001–02 Oldham Ath 18 1
2002–03 Oldham Ath 32 0 **50 1**

BOSHELL, Danny (M) **32 1**
H: 5 11 W: 11 08 b.Bradford 30-5-81
Source: Trainee.
1998–99 Oldham Ath 0 0
1999–2000 Oldham Ath 8 0
2000–01 Oldham Ath 18 1
2001–02 Oldham Ath 4 0
2002–03 Oldham Ath 2 0 **32 1**

CARSS, Tony# (M) **216 9**
H: 5 10 W: 11 07 b.Alnwick 31-3-76
Source: Bradford C Trainee.
1994–95 Blackburn R 0 0
1995–96 Darlington 28 2
1996–97 Darlington 29 0 **57 2**
1997–98 Cardiff C 42 1 **42 1**
1998–99 Chesterfield 4 0
1999–2000 Chesterfield 31 1 **35 1**
2000–01 Carlisle U 7 0 **7 0**
2000–01 Oldham Ath 35 2
2001–02 Oldham Ath 14 1
2002–03 Oldham Ath 26 2 **75 5**

CLEGG, Michael (D) **32 0**
H: 5 9 W: 11 07 b.Ashton-under-Lyne 3-7-77
Source: Trainee. *Honours:* England Under-21.
1995–96 Manchester U 0 0
1996–97 Manchester U 4 0
1997–98 Manchester U 3 0
1998–99 Manchester U 0 0
1999–2000 Manchester U 2 0
1999–2000 *Ipswich T* 3 0 **3 0**
1999–2000 *Wigan Ath* 6 0 **6 0**
2000–01 Manchester U 0 0
2001–02 Manchester U 0 0 **9 0**
2001–02 Oldham Ath 6 0
2002–03 Oldham Ath 8 0 **14 0**

CORAZZIN, Carlo* (F) **367 111**
H: 5 10 W: 12 07 b.Vancouver 25-12-71
Source: Vancouver 86ers. *Honours:* Canada 56 full caps, 10 goals.
1993–94 Cambridge U 28 10
1994–95 Cambridge U 46 19
1995–96 Cambridge U 31 10 **105 39**
1995–96 Plymouth Arg 6 1
1996–97 Plymouth Arg 30 5
1997–98 Plymouth Arg 38 16 **74 22**
1998–99 Northampton T 39 16
1999–2000 Northampton T 39 14 **78 30**
2000–01 Oldham Ath 38 7
2001–02 Oldham Ath 33 9
2002–03 Oldham Ath 39 4 **110 20**

DORAN, Joseph‡ (M) **0 0**
b.Liverpool 19-3-83
Source: Scholar.
2002–03 Oldham Ath 0 0

DUXBURY, Lee# (M) **559 66**
H: 5 10 W: 10 09 b.Keighley 7-10-69
Source: Trainee.
1988–89 Bradford C 1 0
1989–90 Bradford C 12 1
1989–90 *Rochdale* 10 0 **10 0**
1990–91 Bradford C 45 5
1991–92 Bradford C 46 5
1992–93 Bradford C 42 5
1993–94 Bradford C 43 9
1994–95 Bradford C 20 0
1994–95 Huddersfield T 26 2
1995–96 Huddersfield T 3 0 **29 2**
1995–96 Bradford C 30 4
1996–97 Bradford C 33 3 **272 32**
1996–97 Oldham Ath 12 1
1997–98 Oldham Ath 38 5
1998–99 Oldham Ath 41 6
1999–2000 Oldham Ath 43 4
2000–01 Oldham Ath 40 8
2001–02 Oldham Ath 40 4
2002–03 Oldham Ath 34 4 **248 32**

EYRE, John# (M) **286 72**
H: 6 0 W: 11 05 b.Hull 9-10-74
Source: Trainee.
1993–94 Oldham Ath 2 0
1994–95 Oldham Ath 8 1
1994–95 *Scunthorpe U* 9 8
1995–96 Scunthorpe U 39 10
1996–97 Scunthorpe U 42 8
1997–98 Scunthorpe U 42 10
1998–99 Scunthorpe U 41 15 **173 51**
1999–2000 Hull C 24 8
2000–01 Hull C 28 5 **52 13**
2001–02 Oldham Ath 20 5
2002–03 Oldham Ath 31 2 **61 8**

EYRES, David# (M) **556 119**
H: 5 11 W: 11 06 b.Liverpool 26-2-64
Source: Rhyl.
1989–90 Blackpool 35 7
1990–91 Blackpool 36 6
1991–92 Blackpool 41 9
1992–93 Blackpool 46 16 **158 38**
1993–94 Burnley 45 19
1994–95 Burnley 39 8
1995–96 Burnley 42 6
1996–97 Burnley 36 3
1997–98 Burnley 13 1 **175 37**
1997–98 Preston NE 28 4
1998–99 Preston NE 34 8
1999–2000 Preston NE 41 7
2000–01 Preston NE 5 0 **108 19**
2000–01 Oldham Ath 30 3
2001–02 Oldham Ath 45 9
2002–03 Oldham Ath 40 13 **115 25**

GARNETT, Shaun‡ (D) **332 17**
H: 6 2 W: 13 05 b.Wallasey 22-11-69
Source: Trainee.
1987–88 Tranmere R 1 0
1988–89 Tranmere R 0 0
1989–90 Tranmere R 4 0
1990–91 Tranmere R 16 1
1991–92 Tranmere R 8 0
1992–93 Tranmere R 5 1
1992–93 *Chester C* 9 0 **9 0**
1992–93 *Preston NE* 10 2 **10 2**
1992–93 *Wigan Ath* 13 1 **13 1**
1993–94 Tranmere R 26 2
1994–95 Tranmere R 34 1
1995–96 Tranmere R 18 0 **112 5**
1995–96 Swansea C 9 0
1996–97 Swansea C 6 0 **15 0**
1996–97 Oldham Ath 23 1
1997–98 Oldham Ath 34 3
1998–99 Oldham Ath 37 2
1999–2000 Oldham Ath 32 2
2000–01 Oldham Ath 39 1
2001–02 Oldham Ath 8 0
2002–03 Oldham Ath 0 0 **173 9**

GILL, Wayne* (M) **33 9**
H: 5 10 W: 11 04 b.Chorley 28-11-75
Source: Trainee.
1994–95 Blackburn R 0 0
1995–96 Blackburn R 0 0
1996–97 Blackburn R 0 0
1997–98 Blackburn R 0 0
1997–98 Dundee U 2 0 **2 0**
1998–99 Blackburn R 0 0
1999–2000 Blackburn R 0 0
1999–2000 Blackpool 12 7 **12 7**
2000–01 Tranmere R 16 2
2001–02 Tranmere R 0 0 **16 2**
2001–02 Oldham Ath 3 0
2002–03 Oldham Ath 0 0 **3 0**

GRIFFIN, Adam§ (M) **1 0**
H: 5 7 W: 10 03 b.Manchester 26-8-84
Source: Scholar.
2001–02 Oldham Ath 1 0
2002–03 Oldham Ath 0 0 **1 0**

HAINING, Will (D) **30 2**
H: 6 0 W: 11 00 b.Glasgow 2-10-82
Source: Scholar.
2001–02 Oldham Ath 4 0
2002–03 Oldham Ath 26 2 **30 2**

HALL, Danny§ (M) **2 0**
b.Tameside 14-11-83
Source: Scholar.
2002–03 Oldham Ath 2 0 **2 0**

HALL, Fitz (D) **44 5**
H: 6 5 W: 13 01 b.Walthamstow 20-12-80
Source: Barnet Trainee, Chesham U.
2001–02 Oldham Ath 4 1
2002–03 Oldham Ath 40 4 **44 5**

HILL, Clint (D) **157 17**
H: 6 1 W: 12 00 b.Liverpool 19-10-78
Source: Trainee.
1997–98 Tranmere R 14 0
1998–99 Tranmere R 33 4
1999–2000 Tranmere R 29 5
2000–01 Tranmere R 34 5
2001–02 Tranmere R 30 2 **140 16**
2002–03 Oldham Ath 17 1 **17 1**

HOLDEN, Dean (D) **42** **5**

H: 6 1 W: 12 05 b.Salford 15-9-79
Source: Trainee. *Honours:* England Youth.

1997–98	Bolton W	0	0		
1998–99	Bolton W	0	0		
1999–2000	Bolton W	12	0		
2000-01	Bolton W	1	1		
2001-02	Bolton W	0	0	**13**	**1**
2001-02	*Oldham Ath*	23	2		
2002-03	Oldham Ath	6	2	**29**	**4**

KILLEN, Chris (F) **51** **12**

H: 6 0 W: 11 05 b.Wellington 8-10-81
Source: Miramar R. *Honours:* New Zealand 4 full caps.

1998–99	Manchester C	0	0		
1999–2000	Manchester C	0	0		
2000-01	Manchester C	0	0		
2000-01	*Wrexham*	12	3	**12**	**3**
2001-02	*Port Vale*	9	6	**9**	**6**
2001-02	Manchester C	3	0	**3**	**0**
2002-03	Oldham Ath	27	3	**27**	**3**

LOURENCO (F) **10** **2**

H: 5 8 W: 11 05 b.Luanda 5-6-83
Source: Sporting Lisbon.

2000-01	Bristol C	3	1		
2001-02	Bristol C	0	0		
2002-03	Bristol C	0	0	**3**	**1**
2002-03	Oldham Ath	7	1	**7**	**1**

LOW, Josh (F) **123** **10**

H: 6 1 W: 12 00 b.Bristol 15-2-79
Source: Trainee. *Honours:* Wales Youth, Under-21.

1995–96	Bristol R	1	0		
1996–97	Bristol R	3	0		
1997–98	Bristol R	10	0		
1998–99	Bristol R	8	0	**22**	**0**
1999–2000	Leyton Orient	5	1	**5**	**1**
1999–2000	Cardiff C	17	2		
2000-01	Cardiff C	36	4		
2001-02	Cardiff C	22	0		
2002-03	Cardiff C	0	0	**75**	**6**
2002-03	Oldham Ath	21	3	**21**	**3**

MISKELLY, David* (G) **20** **0**

H: 6 1 W: 12 04 b.Ards 3-9-79
Source: Trainee. *Honours:* Northern Ireland Youth, Under-21.

1997–98	Oldham Ath	0	0		
1998–99	Oldham Ath	1	0		
1999–2000	Oldham Ath	2	0		
2000-01	Oldham Ath	2	0		
2001-02	Oldham Ath	4	0		
2002-03	Oldham Ath	11	0	**20**	**0**

MURRAY, Paul (M) **236** **14**

H: 5 8 W: 10 01 b.Carlisle 31-8-76
Source: Trainee. *Honours:* England Youth, Under-21, B.

1993–94	Carlisle U	8	0		
1994–95	Carlisle U	5	0		
1995–96	Carlisle U	28	1	**41**	**1**
1995–96	QPR	1	0		
1996–97	QPR	32	5		
1997–98	QPR	32	1		
1997–98	QPR	0	0		
1998–99	QPR	39	1		
1999–2000	QPR	30	0		
2000-01	QPR	6	0	**140**	**7**
2001-02	Southampton	1	0	**1**	**0**
2001-02	Oldham Ath	24	5		
2002-03	Oldham Ath	30	1	**54**	**6**

POGLIACOMI, Les (G) **142** **0**

H: 6 4 W: 14 05 b.Sydney 3-5-76
Honours: Australia Under-20.

1994–95	Marconi Stallions	11	0		
1995–96	Marconi Stallions	1	0		
1996–97	Marconi Stallions	10	0	**22**	**0**
1997–98	Adelaide City	0	0		
1998–99	Wollongong Wolves	22	0		
1999–2000	Wollongong Wolves	34	0	**56**	**0**
2000-01	Parramatta Power	8	0		
2001-02	Parramatta Power	19	0	**27**	**0**
2002-03	Oldham Ath	37	0	**37**	**0**

SHERIDAN, Darren (M) **290** **11**

H: 5 6 W: 10 10 b.Manchester 8-12-67
Source: Winsford U.

1993–94	Barnsley	3	0		
1994–95	Barnsley	35	2		
1995–96	Barnsley	41	0		
1996–97	Barnsley	41	2		
1997–98	Barnsley	26	0		
1998–99	Barnsley	25	1	**171**	**5**
1999–2000	Wigan Ath	31	3		
2000-01	Wigan Ath	27	0	**58**	**3**
2001-02	Oldham Ath	28	2		
2002-03	Oldham Ath	33	1	**61**	**3**

SHERIDAN, John* (M) **584** **83**

H: 5 10 W: 11 12 b.Stretford 1-10-64
Source: Local. *Honours:* Eire Youth, Under-21, Under-23, B, 34 full caps, 5 goals.

1981–82	Leeds U	0	0		
1982–83	Leeds U	27	2		
1983–84	Leeds U	11	1		
1984–85	Leeds U	42	6		
1985–86	Leeds U	32	4		
1986–87	Leeds U	40	15		
1987–88	Leeds U	38	12		
1988–89	Leeds U	40	7	**230**	**47**
1989–90	Nottingham F	0	0		
1989–90	Sheffield W	27	2		
1990–91	Sheffield W	46	10		
1991–92	Sheffield W	24	6		
1992–93	Sheffield W	25	3		
1993–94	Sheffield W	20	3		
1994–95	Sheffield W	36	1		
1995–96	Sheffield W	17	0		
1995–96	*Birmingham C*	2	0	**2**	**0**
1996–97	Sheffield W	2	0	**197**	**25**
1996–97	Bolton W	20	2		
1997–98	Bolton W	12	0	**32**	**2**
From Doncaster R					
1998–99	Oldham Ath	30	2		
1999–2000	Oldham Ath	36	1		
2000-01	Oldham Ath	25	4		
2001-02	Oldham Ath	27	2		
2002-03	Oldham Ath	5	0	**123**	**9**

SMITH, Ben‡ (D) **0** **0**

H: 5 9 W: 10 03 b.Oldham 16-6-86
Source: Scholar.

2001-02	Oldham Ath	0	0		
2002-03	Oldham Ath	0	0		

VERNON, Scott (F) **8** **1**

H: 6 0 W: 11 10 b.Manchester 8-7-84
Source: Scholar.

2002-03	Oldham Ath	8	1	**8**	**1**

WHITTLE, Tom‡ (G) **0** **0**

H: 6 3 W: 12 07 b.Cheshire 24-9-86
Source: Scholar.

2002-03	Oldham Ath	0	0		

WIJNHARD, Clyde# (F) **217** **69**

H: 5 11 W: 13 02 b.Paramaribo 1-11-73

1992–93	Ajax	4	2		
1993–94	Groningen	23	3	**23**	**3**
1994–95	Ajax	0	0	**4**	**2**
1995–96	RKC	33	8		
1996–97	RKC	17	10	**50**	**18**
1997–98	Willem II	29	14	**29**	**14**
1998–99	Leeds U	18	3	**18**	**3**
1999–2000	Huddersfield T	45	15		
2000-01	Huddersfield T	4	0		
2001-02	Huddersfield T	13	1	**62**	**16**
2001-02	Preston NE	6	3	**6**	**3**
2002-03	Oldham Ath	25	10	**25**	**10**

Scholars

Armstrong, Paul V; Davenport, Michael J; Fleming, Craig M; Grange, Christopher D; Griffin, Adam; Hall, Daniel A; Lavery, Karl A; Mee, Anthony; O'Grady, Paul JO; Roca, Carlos J; Schofield, Marc; Treacy, Charles; Walker, Robert S; Wilkinson, Paul A; Winn, Ashley; Yates, Daniel T

Non-Contract

Forde, Daniel A; Tierney, Marc

OXFORD U

ALEXIS, Michael (M) **0** **0**

H: 6 1 W: 12 02 b.Oxford 2-1-85

2001-02	Oxford U	0	0		
2002-03	Oxford U	0	0		

BASHAM, Steve# (F) **123** **24**

H: 5 11 W: 12 01 b.Southampton 2-12-77
Source: Trainee.

1996–97	Southampton	6	0		
1997–98	Southampton	9	0		
1997–98	*Wrexham*	5	0	**5**	**0**
1998–99	Southampton	4	1	**19**	**1**
1998–99	*Preston NE*	17	10		
1999–2000	Preston NE	24	2		
2000-01	Preston NE	11	2		
2001-02	Preston NE	16	1	**68**	**15**
2002-03	Oxford U	31	8	**31**	**8**

BOLLAND, Phil* (D) **20** **1**

H: 6 4 W: 13 12 b.Liverpool 26-8-76

2001-02	Oxford U	20	1		
2002-03	Oxford U	0	0	**20**	**1**

BOUND, Matt (D) **297** **16**

H: 6 2 W: 14 06 b.Bradford-on-Avon 9-11-72
Source: Trainee.

1990–91	Southampton	1	0		
1991–92	Southampton	0	0		
1992–93	Southampton	3	0		
1993–94	Southampton	1	0		
1993–94	*Hull C*	7	1	**7**	**1**
1994–95	Southampton	0	0	**5**	**0**
1994–95	Stockport Co	14	0		
1995–96	Stockport Co	26	5		
1995–96	*Lincoln C*	4	0	**4**	**0**
1996–97	Stockport Co	4	0		
1997–98	Stockport Co	0	0	**44**	**5**
1997–98	Swansea C	28	0		
1998–99	Swansea C	45	2		
1999–2000	Swansea C	43	2		
2000-01	Swansea C	40	3		
2001-02	Swansea C	18	2	**174**	**9**
2001-02	Oxford U	22	0		
2002-03	Oxford U	41	1	**63**	**1**

BROOKS, Jamie (M) **29** **11**

H: 5 9 W: 10 08 b.Oxford 12-8-83
Source: Scholar.

2000-01	Oxford U	4	1		
2001-02	Oxford U	25	10		
2002-03	Oxford U	0	0	**29**	**11**

CROSBY, Andy (D) **414** **19**

H: 6 2 W: 14 00 b.Rotherham 3-3-73
Source: Leeds U Trainee.

1991–92	Doncaster R	22	0		
1992–93	Doncaster R	29	0		
1993–94	Doncaster R	0	0	**51**	**0**
1993–94	Darlington	25	0		
1994–95	Darlington	35	0		
1995–96	Darlington	45	1		
1996–97	Darlington	42	1		
1997–98	Darlington	34	1	**181**	**3**
1998–99	Chester C	41	4	**41**	**4**
1999–2000	Brighton & HA	36	3		
2000-01	Brighton & HA	34	2		
2001-02	Brighton & HA	2	0	**72**	**5**
2001-02	Oxford U	23	1		
2002-03	Oxford U	46	6	**69**	**7**

FORD, Bobby# (M) **308** **14**

H: 5 9 W: 11 00 b.Bristol 22-9-74
Source: Trainee.

1992–93	Oxford U	0	0		
1993–94	Oxford U	14	0		
1994–95	Oxford U	23	2		
1995–96	Oxford U	28	3		
1996–97	Oxford U	33	0		
1997–98	Oxford U	18	2		
1997–98	Sheffield U	23	1		
1998–99	Sheffield U	30	0		
1999–2000	Sheffield U	41	2		
2000-01	Sheffield U	35	3		
2001-02	Sheffield U	26	0	**155**	**6**
2002-03	Oxford U	37	1	**153**	**8**

HACKETT, Chris (M) **45** **2**

H: 6 0 W: 11 09 b.Oxford 1-3-83
Source: Scholarship.

1999–2000	Oxford U	2	0		
2000-01	Oxford U	16	2		
2001-02	Oxford U	15	0		
2002-03	Oxford U	12	0	**45**	**2**

HUNT, James (M) **230** **10**

H: 5 11 W: 12 05 b.Derby 17-12-76
Source: Trainee.

1994–95	Notts Co	0	0		
1995–96	Notts Co	10	1		
1996–97	Notts Co	9	0	**19**	**1**
1997–98	Northampton T	21	0		
1998–99	Northampton T	35	2		
1999–2000	Northampton T	37	1		
2000-01	Northampton T	41	1		
2001-02	Northampton T	38	4	**172**	**8**
2002-03	Oxford U	39	1	**39**	**1**

HUNTER, Roy# (M) **203** **19**

H: 5 10 W: 12 08 b.Saltburn 29-10-73
Source: Trainee.

1991–92	WBA	6	1		
1992–93	WBA	1	0		
1993–94	WBA	2	0		
1994–95	WBA	0	0	**9**	**1**
1995–96	Northampton T	34	0		

1996–97 Northampton T 36 6
1997–98 Northampton T 28 3
1998–99 Northampton T 18 1
1999–2000 Northampton T 17 3
2000-01 Northampton T 4 0
2001-02 Northampton T 40 4
2002-03 Northampton T 0 0 **177 17**
From Nuneaton B.
2002-03 Oxford U 17 1 **17 1**

ITONGA, Carlin‡ (F) 0 0
H: 5 9 W: 11 09 b.Congo DR 11-12-82
Source: Scholar.
2001-02 Arsenal 0 0
2002-03 Oxford U 0 0

JUDGE, Alan‡ (G) 284 0
H: 5 11 W: 11 06 b.Kingsbury 14-5-60
Source: Amateur.
1977–78 Luton T 0 0
1978–79 Luton T 0 0
1979–80 Luton T 1 0
1980–81 Luton T 2 0
1981–82 Luton T 4 0
1982–83 Luton T 4 0 **11 0**
1982–83 *Reading* 33 0
1983–84 Reading 41 0
1984–85 Reading 3 0 **77 0**
1984–85 Oxford U 0 0
1985–86 Oxford U 19 0
1985–86 *Lincoln C* 2 0 **2 0**
1986–87 Oxford U 9 0
1987–88 Oxford U 9 0
1987–88 *Cardiff C* 8 0 **8 0**
1988–89 Oxford U 20 0
1989–90 Oxford U 17 0
1990–91 Oxford U 6 0
1991–92 Hereford U 24 0
1992–93 Hereford U 42 0
1993–94 Hereford U 39 0 **105 0**
1994–95 Chelsea 0 0
2002-03 Oxford U 1 0 **81 0**
From retirement
2002-03 Swindon T 0 0

KING, Simon (D) 4 0
H: 6 0 W: 12 09 b.Oxford 11-4-83
Source: Scholar.
2000-01 Oxford U 2 0
2001-02 Oxford U 2 0
2002-03 Oxford U 0 0 **4 0**

LOUIS, Jefferson (F) 35 6
H: 6 2 W: 14 13 b.Harrow 22-2-79
Source: Thame U.
2001-02 Oxford U 1 0
2002-03 Oxford U 34 6 **35 6**

McCALDON, Ian* (G) 108 0
H: 6 5 W: 16 00 b.Liverpool 14-9-74
Source: Glenafton Ath.
1996–97 Livingston 0 0
1997–98 Livingston 36 0
1998–99 Livingston 15 0
1999–2000 Livingston 23 0
2000-01 Livingston 6 0 **80 0**
2001-02 Oxford U 28 0
2002-03 Oxford U 0 0 **28 0**

McNIVEN, Scott (D) 266 4
H: 5 10 W: 12 07 b.Leeds 27-5-78
Source: Trainee. *Honours:* Scotland Youth, Under-21.
1994–95 Oldham Ath 1 0
1995–96 Oldham Ath 15 0
1996–97 Oldham Ath 12 0
1997–98 Oldham Ath 32 1
1998–99 Oldham Ath 37 1
1999–2000 Oldham Ath 45 1
2000-01 Oldham Ath 45 0
2001-02 Oldham Ath 35 0 **222 3**
2002-03 Oxford U 44 1 **44 1**

OLDFIELD, David‡ (F) 548 73
H: 6 1 W: 13 02 b.Perth (Aus) 30-5-68
Source: Apprentice. *Honours:* England Under-21.
1986–87 Luton T 0 0
1987–88 Luton T 8 3
1988–89 Luton T 21 1
1988–89 Manchester C 11 3
1989–90 Manchester C 15 3 **26 6**
1989–90 Leicester C 20 5
1990–91 Leicester C 42 7
1991–92 Leicester C 41 4
1992–93 Leicester C 44 5
1993–94 Leicester C 27 4
1994–95 Leicester C 14 1 **188 26**
1994–95 *Millwall* 17 6 **17 6**
1995–96 Luton T 34 2
1996–97 Luton T 38 6
1997–98 Luton T 45 10 **146 22**
1998–99 Stoke C 46 6
1999–2000 Stoke C 19 1 **65 7**
1999–2000 Peterborough U 9 0
2000-01 Peterborough U 39 3
2001-02 Peterborough U 30 1 **78 4**
2002-03 Oxford U 28 2 **28 2**

OMOYINMI, Manny (F) 109 16
H: 5 6 W: 10 08 b.Nigeria 28-12-77
Source: Trainee. *Honours:* England Schools.
1994–95 West Ham U 0 0
1995–96 West Ham U 0 0
1996–97 West Ham U 1 0
1996–97 *Bournemouth* 7 0 **7 0**
1997–98 West Ham U 5 2
1997–98 *Dundee U* 4 0 **4 0**
1998–99 West Ham U 3 0
1998–99 *Leyton Orient* 4 1 **4 1**
1999–2000 West Ham U 0 0 **9 2**
1999–2000 *Gillingham* 9 3 **9 3**
1999–2000 *Scunthorpe U* 6 1 **6 1**
1999–2000 *Barnet* 6 0 **6 0**
2000-01 Oxford U 24 3
2001-02 Oxford U 23 3
2002-03 Oxford U 17 3 **64 9**

POWELL, Paul* (D) 178 17
H: 5 8 W: 11 13 b.Wallingford 30-6-78
Source: Trainee.
1995–96 Oxford U 3 0
1996–97 Oxford U 0 0
1997–98 Oxford U 21 1
1998–99 Oxford U 44 3
1999–2000 Oxford U 40 6
2000-01 Oxford U 20 1
2001-02 Oxford U 36 4
2002-03 Oxford U 14 2 **178 17**

RICKETTS, Sam (D) 45 1
H: 6 1 W: 11 11 b.Wendover 11-10-81
Source: Trainee.
1999–2000 Oxford U 0 0
2000-01 Oxford U 14 0
2001-02 Oxford U 29 1
2002-03 Oxford U 2 0 **45 1**

ROBINSON, Matt (D) 190 2
H: 5 11 W: 11 09 b.Exeter 23-12-74
Source: Trainee.
1993–94 Southampton 0 0
1994–95 Southampton 1 0
1995–96 Southampton 5 0
1996–97 Southampton 7 0
1997–98 Southampton 1 0 **14 0**
1997–98 Portsmouth 15 0
1998–99 Portsmouth 29 1
1999–2000 Portsmouth 25 0 **69 1**
1999–2000 Reading 19 0
2000-01 Reading 32 0
2001-02 Reading 14 0 **65 0**
2002-03 Oxford U 42 1 **42 1**

SAVAGE, David* (M) 330 29
H: 6 2 W: 13 02 b.Dublin 30-7-73
Source: Longford T. *Honours:* Eire Under-21, 5 full caps.
1994–95 Millwall 37 2
1995–96 Millwall 27 0
1996–97 Millwall 35 3
1997–98 Millwall 31 1
1998–99 Millwall 2 0 **132 6**
1998–99 Northampton T 27 5
1999–2000 Northampton T 43 5
2000-01 Northampton T 43 8 **113 18**
2001-02 Oxford U 42 1
2002-03 Oxford U 43 4 **85 5**

SCOTT, Andy* (F) 295 61
H: 6 1 W: 12 04 b.Epsom 2-8-72
Source: Sutton U.
1992–93 Sheffield U 2 1
1993–94 Sheffield U 15 0
1994–95 Sheffield U 37 4
1995–96 Sheffield U 7 0
1996–97 Sheffield U 8 1
1996–97 *Chesterfield* 5 3 **5 3**
1996–97 *Bury* 8 0 **8 0**
1997–98 Sheffield U 6 0 **75 6**
1997–98 Brentford 26 5
1998–99 Brentford 34 7
1999–2000 Brentford 36 3
2000-01 Brentford 22 13 **118 28**
2000-01 Oxford U 21 5
2001-02 Oxford U 30 8
2002-03 Oxford U 38 11 **89 24**

STEELE, Lee (F) 183 51
H: 5 8 W: 12 05 b.Liverpool 2-12-73
Source: Bootle, Northwich V.
1997–98 Shrewsbury T 38 13
1998–99 Shrewsbury T 38 13
1999–2000 Shrewsbury T 37 11 **113 37**
2000-01 Brighton & HA 23 2
2001-02 Brighton & HA 37 9 **60 11**
2002-03 Oxford U 10 3 **10 3**

WATERMAN, David (M) 114 1
H: 5 11 W: 11 13 b.Guernsey 16-5-77
Source: Trainee. *Honours:* Northern Ireland Under-21.
1995–96 Portsmouth 0 0
1996–97 Portsmouth 4 0
1997–98 Portsmouth 15 0
1998–99 Portsmouth 10 0
1999–2000 Portsmouth 20 0
2000-01 Portsmouth 22 0
2001-02 Portsmouth 9 0 **80 0**
2001-02 Oxford U 5 0
2002-03 Oxford U 29 1 **34 1**

WHITEHEAD, Dean (M) 78 2
H: 6 0 W: 12 07 b.Oxford 12-1-82
Source: Trainee.
1999–2000 Oxford U 0 0
2000-01 Oxford U 20 0
2001-02 Oxford U 40 1
2002-03 Oxford U 18 1 **78 2**

WOODMAN, Andy (G) 361 0
H: 6 2 W: 14 00 b.Camberwell 11-8-71
Source: Apprentice.
1989–90 Crystal Palace 0 0
1990–91 Crystal Palace 0 0
1991–92 Crystal Palace 0 0
1992–93 Crystal Palace 0 0
1993–94 Crystal Palace 0 0
1994–95 Exeter C 6 0 **6 0**
1994–95 Northampton T 10 0
1995–96 Northampton T 44 0
1996–97 Northampton T 45 0
1997–98 Northampton T 46 0
1998–99 Northampton T 18 0 **163 0**
1998–99 Brentford 22 0
1999–2000 Brentford 39 0
1999–2000 *Peterborough U* 0 0
2000-01 Brentford 0 0 **61 0**
2000-01 *Southend U* 17 0 **17 0**
2000-01 Colchester U 28 0
2001-02 Colchester U 26 0 **54 0**
2001-02 Oxford U 15 0
2002-03 Oxford U 45 0 **60 0**

Scholars
Blackstock, Dexter A; Brandish, Matthew; Carbon, Josias; Ciampoli, Dwight M; Cox, Simon P; Garner, Adam R; Lovegrove, Robert T; Mackay, Angus R; O'Sullivan, Taurean J; Winters, Thomas R

PETERBOROUGH U

ARBER, Mark (D) 150 17
H: 6 1 W: 12 11 b.Johannesburg 8-10-77
Source: Trainee.
1995–96 Tottenham H 0 0
1996–97 Tottenham H 0 0
1997–98 Tottenham H 0 0
1998–99 Tottenham H 0 0
1998–99 Barnet 35 2
1999–2000 Barnet 45 6
2000-01 Barnet 45 7
2001-02 Barnet 0 0 **125 15**
2002-03 Peterborough U 25 2 **25 2**

BURTON, Sagi (D) 152 3
H: 6 2 W: 13 06 b.Birmingham 25-11-77
Source: Trainee.
1995–96 Crystal Palace 0 0
1996–97 Crystal Palace 0 0
1997–98 Crystal Palace 2 0
1998–99 Crystal Palace 23 1 **25 1**
1999–2000 Colchester U 9 0 **9 0**
1999–2000 Sheffield U 0 0
1999–2000 Port Vale 20 2
2000-01 Port Vale 29 0
2001-02 Port Vale 37 0 **86 2**
2002-03 Crewe Alex 1 0 **1 0**
2002-03 Peterborough U 31 0 **31 0**

CLARKE, Andy (F) 332 62
H: 5 10 W: 11 07 b.Islington 22-7-67
Source: Barnet.
1990–91 Wimbledon 12 3
1991–92 Wimbledon 34 3
1992–93 Wimbledon 33 5
1993–94 Wimbledon 23 2
1994–95 Wimbledon 25 1
1995–96 Wimbledon 18 2
1996–97 Wimbledon 11 1
1997–98 Wimbledon 14 0
1998–99 Wimbledon 0 0 **170 17**
1998–99 *Port Vale* 6 0 **6 0**
1998–99 *Northampton T* 4 0 **4 0**
1998–99 Peterborough U 0 0
1999–2000 Peterborough U 37 15
2000-01 Peterborough U 42 9
2001-02 Peterborough U 28 5
2002-03 Peterborough U 45 16 **152 45**

CLARKE, Lee (F) 2 0
H: 5 11 W: 10 08 b.Peterborough 28-7-83
Source: Yaxley. *Honours:* Northern Ireland Under-21.
2001-02 Peterborough U 1 0
2002-03 Peterborough U 1 0 **2 0**

CONNOR, Dan‡ (G) 8 0
H: 6 2 W: 13 04 b.Dublin 31-1-81
Source: Trainee.
1997–98 Peterborough U 0 0
1998–99 Peterborough U 2 0
1999–2000 Peterborough U 1 0
2000-01 Peterborough U 0 0
2001-02 Peterborough U 1 0
2002-03 Peterborough U 4 0 **8 0**

COULSON, Mark (M) 0 0
b.Huntingdon 11-2-86
Source: Scholar.
2002-03 Peterborough U 0 0

CRAIG, David‡ (F) 0 0
H: 5 8 W: 10 08 b.Glasgow 20-5-81
2002-03 Peterborough U 0 0

DANIELSSON, Helgi (M) 55 2
H: 6 0 W: 12 00 b.Reykjavik 13-7-81
Source: Fylkir. *Honours:* Iceland 1 full cap.
1998–99 Peterborough U 0 0
1999–2000 Peterborough U 0 0
2000-01 Peterborough U 6 0
2001-02 Peterborough U 31 2
2002-03 Peterborough U 18 0 **55 2**

FARRELL, Dave (M) 304 38
H: 5 11 W: 11 08 b.Birmingham 11-11-71
Source: Redditch U.
1992–93 Aston Villa 2 0
1992–93 *Scunthorpe U* 5 1 **5 1**
1993–94 Aston Villa 4 0
1994–95 Aston Villa 0 0
1995–96 Aston Villa 0 0 **6 0**
1995–96 Wycombe W 33 7
1996–97 Wycombe W 27 1 **60 8**
1997–98 Peterborough U 42 6
1998–99 Peterborough U 37 4
1999–2000 Peterborough U 35 3
2000-01 Peterborough U 44 7
2001-02 Peterborough U 38 6
2002-03 Peterborough U 37 3 **233 29**

FENN, Neale (F) 76 8
H: 5 9 W: 10 12 b.Edmonton 18-1-77
Source: Trainee. *Honours:* Eire Youth, Under-21.
1995–96 Tottenham H 0 0
1996–97 Tottenham H 4 0
1997–98 Tottenham H 4 0
1997–98 *Leyton Orient* 3 0 **3 0**
1997–98 *Norwich C* 7 1 **7 1**
1998–99 Tottenham H 0 0
1998–99 *Swindon T* 4 0 **4 0**
1998–99 *Lincoln C* 4 0 **4 0**
1999–2000 Tottenham H 0 0
2000-01 Tottenham H 0 0 **8 0**
2001-02 Peterborough U 36 6
2002-03 Peterborough U 14 1 **50 7**

FOTIADIS, Andrew (F) 134 20
H: 6 0 W: 12 13 b.Hitchin 6-9-77
Source: School. *Honours:* England Schools.
1996–97 Luton T 17 3
1997–98 Luton T 15 1
1998–99 Luton T 21 2
1999–2000 Luton T 23 2
2000-01 Luton T 22 3
2001-02 Luton T 8 1
2002-03 Luton T 17 6 **123 18**
2002-03 Peterborough U 11 2 **11 2**

FRENCH, Daniel‡ (M) 18 1
H: 5 11 W: 11 00 b.Peterborough 25-11-79
Source: Trainee.
1998–99 Peterborough U 0 0
1999–2000 Peterborough U 6 0
2000-01 Peterborough U 2 0
2001-02 Peterborough U 10 1
2002-03 Peterborough U 0 0 **18 1**

FRY, Adam (M) 0 0
H: 5 8 W: 10 07 b.Luton 9-2-85
Source: Scholar.
2002-03 Peterborough U 0 0

GILL, Matthew (M) 118 5
H: 5 11 W: 11 07 b.Cambridge 8-11-80
Source: Trainee.
1997–98 Peterborough U 2 0
1998–99 Peterborough U 26 0
1999–2000 Peterborough U 20 1
2000-01 Peterborough U 17 1
2001-02 Peterborough U 12 2
2002-03 Peterborough U 41 1 **118 5**

GREEN, Francis (F) 105 14
H: 5 9 W: 11 04 b.Derby 23-4-80
Source: Ilkeston T.
1997–98 Peterborough U 4 1
1998–99 Peterborough U 7 1
1999–2000 Peterborough U 20 1
2000-01 Peterborough U 32 6
2001-02 Peterborough U 23 3
2002-03 Peterborough U 19 2 **105 14**

HENDON, Ian# (D) 353 17
H: 6 1 W: 14 03 b.Ilford 5-12-71
Source: Trainee. *Honours:* England Youth, Under-21.
1989–90 Tottenham H 0 0
1990–91 Tottenham H 2 0
1991–92 Tottenham H 2 0
1991–92 *Portsmouth* 4 0 **4 0**
1991–92 *Leyton Orient* 6 0
1992–93 Tottenham H 0 0 **4 0**
1992–93 *Barnsley* 6 0 **6 0**
1993–94 Leyton Orient 36 2
1994–95 Leyton Orient 29 0
1994–95 *Birmingham C* 4 0 **4 0**
1995–96 Leyton Orient 38 2
1996–97 Leyton Orient 28 1 **137 5**
1996–97 Notts Co 12 0
1997–98 Notts Co 38 0
1998–99 Notts Co 32 6 **82 6**
1998–99 Northampton T 7 0
1999–2000 Northampton T 44 2
2000-01 Northampton T 9 1 **60 3**
2000-01 Sheffield W 31 2
2001-02 Sheffield W 9 0
2002-03 Sheffield W 9 0 **49 2**
2002-03 Peterborough U 7 1 **7 1**

JELLEYMAN, Gareth (D) 70 0
H: 5 10 W: 10 03 b.Holywell 14-11-80
Source: Trainee. *Honours:* Wales Youth, Under-21.
1998–99 Peterborough U 0 0
1999–2000 Peterborough U 20 0
2000-01 Peterborough U 8 0
2001-02 Peterborough U 10 0
2002-03 Peterborough U 32 0 **70 0**

LAURIE, Steve (D) 0 0
H: 6 3 W: 13 00 b.Melbourne 30-10-82
1999–2000 West Ham U 0 0
2000-01 West Ham U 0 0
2001-02 West Ham U 0 0
2001-02 Peterborough U 0 0
2002-03 Peterborough U 0 0

LEE, Jason* (F) 354 71
H: 6 3 W: 13 03 b.Newham 9-5-71
Source: Trainee.
1989–90 Charlton Ath 1 0
1990–91 Charlton Ath 0 0
1990–91 *Stockport Co* 2 0 **2 0**
1990–91 Lincoln C 17 3
1991–92 Lincoln C 35 6
1992–93 Lincoln C 41 12 **93 21**
1993–94 Southend U 24 3 **24 3**
1993–94 Nottingham F 13 2
1994–95 Nottingham F 22 3
1995–96 Nottingham F 28 8
1996–97 Nottingham F 13 1 **76 14**
1996–97 *Charlton Ath* 8 3 **9 3**
1996–97 *Grimsby T* 7 1 **7 1**
1997–98 Watford 36 10
1998–99 Watford 1 1 **37 11**
1998–99 Chesterfield 22 1
1999–2000 Chesterfield 6 0 **28 1**
1999–2000 Peterborough U 23 6
2000-01 Peterborough U 30 8
2001-02 Peterborough U 0 0
2002-03 Peterborough U 25 3 **78 17**

MACDONALD, Gary‡ (M) 17 1
H: 6 1 W: 12 00 b.Germany 25-10-79
1998–99 Portsmouth 0 0
1999–2000 Portsmouth 0 0
2000-01 Portsmouth 0 0
From Havant & W.
2000-01 Peterborough U 1 0
2001-02 Peterborough U 8 1
2002-03 Peterborough U 8 0 **17 1**

McGOVERN, Brian‡ (D) 28 1
H: 6 3 W: 12 06 b.Dublin 28-4-80
Source: Cherry Orchard. *Honours:* Eire Youth, Under-21.
1997–98 Arsenal 0 0
1998–99 Arsenal 0 0
1999–2000 Arsenal 1 0
1999–2000 *QPR* 5 0 **5 0**
2000-01 Arsenal 0 0 **1 0**
2000-01 Norwich C 12 1
2001-02 Norwich C 9 0
2002-03 Norwich C 0 0 **21 1**
2002-03 Peterborough U 1 0 **1 0**

McKENZIE, Leon (F) 173 51
H: 5 10 W: 10 03 b.Croydon 17-5-78
Source: Trainee.
1995–96 Crystal Palace 12 0
1996–97 Crystal Palace 21 2
1997–98 Crystal Palace 3 0
1997–98 *Fulham* 3 0 **3 0**
1998–99 Crystal Palace 16 1
1998–99 *Peterborough U* 14 8
1999–2000 Crystal Palace 25 4
2000-01 Crystal Palace 8 0 **85 7**
2000-01 Peterborough U 30 13
2001-02 Peterborough U 30 18
2002-03 Peterborough U 11 5 **85 44**

MURRAY, Dan‡ (D) 5 0
H: 6 2 W: 12 12 b.Cambridge 16-5-82
Source: Scholarship.
1999–2000 Peterborough U 2 0
2000-01 Peterborough U 3 0
2001-02 Peterborough U 0 0
2002-03 Peterborough U 0 0 **5 0**

NEWTON, Adam (M) 71 4
H: 5 10 W: 11 00 b.Ascot 4-12-80
Source: West Ham U Trainee. *Honours:* England Under-21.
1999–2000 West Ham U 2 0
1999–2000 *Portsmouth* 3 0 **3 0**
2000-01 West Ham U 0 0
2000-01 *Notts Co* 20 1 **20 1**
2001-02 West Ham U 0 0 **2 0**
2001-02 *Leyton Orient* 10 1 **10 1**
2002-03 Peterborough U 36 2 **36 2**

PEARCE, Dennis (D) 138 3
H: 6 0 W: 11 07 b.Wolverhampton 10-9-74
Source: Trainee.
1993–94 Aston Villa 0 0
1994–95 Aston Villa 0 0
1995–96 Wolverhampton W 5 0
1996–97 Wolverhampton W 4 0 **9 0**
1997–98 Notts Co 38 2
1998–99 Notts Co 33 1
1999–2000 Notts Co 20 0
2000-01 Notts Co 27 0 **118 3**
2000-01 Peterborough U 0 0
2001-02 Peterborough U 9 0
2002-03 Peterborough U 2 0 **11 0**

REA, Simon (D) 118 7
H: 6 1 W: 13 00 b.Coventry 20-9-76
Source: Trainee.
1994–95 Birmingham C 0 0
1995–96 Birmingham C 1 0
1996–97 Birmingham C 0 0
1997–98 Birmingham C 0 0
1998–99 Birmingham C 0 0
1999–2000 Birmingham C 0 0 **1 0**
1999–2000 Peterborough U 14 1
2000-01 Peterborough U 36 2
2001-02 Peterborough U 30 1
2002-03 Peterborough U 37 3 **117 7**

SCOTT, Richard‡ (M) **214 26**
H: 5 11 W: 12 08 b.Dudley 29-9-74
Source: Trainee.
1992–93 Birmingham C 1 0
1993–94 Birmingham C 6 0
1994–95 Birmingham C 5 0 **12 0**
1994–95 Shrewsbury T 8 1
1995–96 Shrewsbury T 36 6
1996–97 Shrewsbury T 27 1
1997–98 Shrewsbury T 34 10 **105 18**
1998–99 Peterborough U 27 4
1999–2000 Peterborough U 34 3
2000–01 Peterborough U 20 0
From Telford U, Stevenage B.
2002–03 Peterborough U 16 1 **97 8**

SEMPLE, Ryan (M) **3 0**
H: 5 11 W: 10 11 b.Belfast 4-7-85
Source: Scholar.
2002–03 Peterborough U 3 0 **3 0**

SHIELDS, Tony (M) **115 3**
H: 5 8 W: 10 01 b.Derry 4-6-80
Source: Trainee.
1997–98 Peterborough U 1 0
1998–99 Peterborough U 9 0
1999–2000 Peterborough U 24 1
2000–01 Peterborough U 33 1
2001–02 Peterborough U 15 0
2002–03 Peterborough U 33 1 **115 3**

SHOWLER, Paul (M) **186 33**
H: 5 10 W: 11 00 b.Doncaster 10-10-66
Source: Sheffield W, Sunderland, Colne Dynamoes, Altrincham.
1991–92 Barnet 39 7
1992–93 Barnet 32 5 **71 12**
1993–94 Bradford C 32 5
1994–95 Bradford C 23 2
1995–96 Bradford C 33 8 **88 15**
1996–97 Luton T 23 6
1997–98 Luton T 1 0
1998–99 Luton T 3 0 **27 6**
1999–2000 Peterborough U 0 0
2000–01 Peterborough U 0 0
2001–02 Peterborough U 0 0
2002–03 Peterborough U 0 0

ST LEDGER-HALL, Sean§ (M) **1 0**
b.Solihull 28-12-84
Source: Scholar.
2002–03 Peterborough U 1 0 **1 0**

TOLLEY, Shane (F) **0 0**
H: 5 7 W: 11 11 b.Barnstaple 18-2-85
Source: Scholar. *Honours:* England Youth.
2001–02 Peterborough U 0 0
2002–03 Peterborough U 0 0

TYLER, Mark (G) **226 0**
H: 5 11 W: 12 00 b.Norwich 2-4-77
Source: Trainee. *Honours:* England Youth.
1994–95 Peterborough U 5 0
1995–96 Peterborough U 0 0
1996–97 Peterborough U 3 0
1997–98 Peterborough U 46 0
1998–99 Peterborough U 27 0
1999–2000 Peterborough U 32 0
2000–01 Peterborough U 40 0
2001–02 Peterborough U 44 0
2002–03 Peterborough U 29 0 **226 0**

WILLIS, Roger‡ (M) **318 54**
H: 6 0 W: 12 00 b.Islington 17-6-67
Source: Dunkirk.
1989–90 Grimsby T 9 0 **9 0**
From Barnet
1991–92 Barnet 38 12
1992–93 Barnet 6 1 **44 13**
1992–93 Watford 32 2
1993–94 Watford 4 0 **36 2**
1993–94 Birmingham C 16 5
1994–95 Birmingham C 3 0 **19 5**
1994–95 Southend U 21 4
1995–96 Southend U 10 3 **31 7**
1996–97 Peterborough U 40 6
1997–98 Chesterfield 34 8
1998–99 Chesterfield 17 0
1999–2000 Chesterfield 28 4
2000–01 Chesterfield 32 5
2001–02 Chesterfield 24 4 **135 21**
2002–03 Peterborough U 4 0 **44 6**

Scholars
Bowater, Graham J; Brennan, Killian E; Burton, Paul D; Chapman, Simon MJ; Cobb, Stuart D; Day, Jamie; Frew, Michael A; Hutton, Rory N; Judge, Liam; Kennedy, Luke D; Last, Guy D; McShane, Luke; St Ledger-Hall, Sean P; Thomas, Bradley M; Thompson, Craig J

PLYMOUTH ARG

ADAMS, Steve (M) **101 4**
H: 6 0 W: 12 01 b.Plymouth 25-9-80
Source: Trainee.
1999–2000 Plymouth Arg 1 0
2000–01 Plymouth Arg 17 0
2001–02 Plymouth Arg 46 2
2002–03 Plymouth Arg 37 2 **101 4**

ALJOFREE, Hasney (D) **86 5**
H: 6 0 W: 12 03 b.Manchester 11-7-78
Source: Trainee.
1996–97 Bolton W 0 0
1997–98 Bolton W 2 0
1998–98 Bolton W 4 0
1999–2000 Bolton W 8 0 **14 0**
2000–01 Dundee U 26 2
2001–02 Dundee U 27 2 **53 4**
2002–03 Plymouth Arg 19 1 **19 1**

BASTOW, Darren (M) **42 3**
H: 5 11 W: 12 00 b.Torquay 22-12-81
Source: Trainee.
1998–99 Plymouth Arg 29 2
1999–2000 Plymouth Arg 13 1
2000–01 Plymouth Arg 0 0
2001–02 Plymouth Arg 0 0
2002–03 Plymouth Arg 0 0 **42 3**

BENT, Jason (M) **104 6**
H: 5 9 W: 11 11 b.Toronto 8-3-77
Honours: Canada 30 full caps.
1998 Colorado Rapids 14 0
1999 Colorado Rapids 20 0
2000 Colorado Rapids 24 2 **58 2**
2001–02 Plymouth Arg 21 3
2002–03 Plymouth Arg 25 1 **46 4**

BERESFORD, David (F) **170 6**
H: 5 8 W: 10 09 b.Middleton 11-11-76
Source: Trainee. *Honours:* England Schools, Youth.
1993–94 Oldham Ath 1 0
1994–95 Oldham Ath 2 0
1995–96 Oldham Ath 28 2
1995–96 *Swansea C* 6 0 **6 0**
1996–97 Oldham Ath 33 0 **64 2**
1996–97 Huddersfield T 6 1
1997–98 Huddersfield T 8 0
1998–99 Huddersfield T 19 2
1999–2000 Huddersfield T 0 0
1999–2000 *Preston NE* 4 0 **4 0**
2000–01 Huddersfield T 2 0 **35 3**
2000–01 *Port Vale* 4 0 **4 0**
2001–02 Hull C 41 1 **41 1**
2002–03 Plymouth Arg 16 0 **16 0**

BERNARD, Paul# (M) **221 24**
H: 6 0 W: 13 01 b.Edinburgh 30-12-72
Source: Trainee. *Honours:* Scotland Under-21, 2 full caps.
1990–91 Oldham Ath 2 1
1991–92 Oldham Ath 21 5
1992–93 Oldham Ath 33 4
1993–94 Oldham Ath 32 5
1994–95 Oldham Ath 17 2
1995–96 Oldham Ath 7 1 **112 18**
1995–96 Aberdeen 31 1
1996–97 Aberdeen 14 0
1997–98 Aberdeen 17 0
1998–99 Aberdeen 9 1
1999–2000 Aberdeen 25 4
2000–01 Aberdeen 3 0 **99 6**
2001–02 Barnsley 0 0
2002–03 Barnsley 0 0
2002–03 Plymouth Arg 10 0 **10 0**

BROAD, Joseph (M) **12 0**
H: 5 9 W: 12 00 b.Bristol 24-8-82
Source: Trainee.
2000–01 Plymouth Arg 0 0
2001–02 Plymouth Arg 7 0
2002–03 Plymouth Arg 5 0 **12 0**

CAPALDI, Tony (D) **1 0**
H: 6 0 W: 11 06 b.Porsgrunn 12-8-81
Source: Trainee. *Honours:* Northern Ireland Under-21.
1999–2000 Birmingham C 0 0
2000–01 Birmingham C 0 0
2001–02 Birmingham C 0 0
2002–03 Birmingham C 0 0
2002–03 Plymouth Arg 1 0 **1 0**

CONNOLLY, Paul (D) **3 0**
H: 6 0 W: 11 09 b.Liverpool 29-9-83
Source: Scholar.
2000–01 Plymouth Arg 1 0
2001–02 Plymouth Arg 0 0
2002–03 Plymouth Arg 2 0 **3 0**

COUGHLAN, Graham (D) **147 18**
H: 6 2 W: 13 04 b.Dublin 18-11-74
Source: Bray Wanderers.
1995–96 Blackburn R 0 0
1996–97 Blackburn R 0 0
1996–97 *Swindon T* 3 0 **3 0**
1997–98 Blackburn R 0 0
1998–99 Livingston 6 0
1999–2000 Livingston 29 0
2000–01 Livingston 21 2 **56 2**
2001–02 Plymouth Arg 46 11
2002–03 Plymouth Arg 42 5 **88 16**

EVANS, Micky (F) **359 67**
H: 6 0 W: 13 04 b.Plymouth 1-1-73
Source: Trainee. *Honours:* Eire 1 full cap.
1990–91 Plymouth Arg 4 0
1991–92 Plymouth Arg 13 0
1992–93 Plymouth Arg 23 1
1992–93 *Blackburn R* 0 0
1993–94 Plymouth Arg 22 9
1994–95 Plymouth Arg 23 4
1995–96 Plymouth Arg 45 12
1996–97 Plymouth Arg 33 12
1996–97 Southampton 12 4
1997–98 Southampton 10 0 **22 4**
1997–98 WBA 10 1
1998–99 WBA 20 2
1999–2000 WBA 33 3
2000–01 WBA 0 0 **63 6**
2000–01 Bristol R 21 4 **21 4**
2000–01 Plymouth Arg 10 4
2001–02 Plymouth Arg 38 7
2002–03 Plymouth Arg 42 4 **253 53**

FRIIO, David (M) **103 19**
H: 6 0 W: 11 07 b.Thionville 17-2-73
Source: Epinal, Nimes, ASOA Valence.
2000–01 Plymouth Arg 26 5
2001–02 Plymouth Arg 41 8
2002–03 Plymouth Arg 36 6 **103 19**

GOVIER, Piers‡ (M) **0 0**
b.Taunton 14-6-84
2002–03 Plymouth Arg 0 0

HEANEY, Neil‡ (F) **167 15**
H: 5 9 W: 11 06 b.Middlesbrough 3-11-71
Source: Trainee. *Honours:* England Youth, Under-21.
1989–90 Arsenal 0 0
1990–91 Arsenal 0 0
1990–91 *Hartlepool U* 3 0 **3 0**
1991–92 Arsenal 1 0
1991–92 *Cambridge U* 13 4 **13 4**
1992–93 Arsenal 5 0
1993–94 Arsenal 1 0 **7 0**
1993–94 Southampton 2 0
1994–95 Southampton 34 2
1995–96 Southampton 17 2
1996–97 Southampton 8 1 **61 5**
1996–97 Manchester C 15 1
1997–98 Manchester C 3 0
1997–98 *Charlton Ath* 6 0 **6 0**
1998–99 Manchester C 0 0 **18 1**
1998–99 *Bristol C* 3 0 **3 0**
1999–2000 Darlington 36 5 **36 5**
2000–01 Dundee U 12 0
2001–02 Dundee U 0 0 **12 0**
2001–02 Plymouth Arg 8 0
2002–03 Plymouth Arg 0 0 **8 0**

HODGES, Lee (M) **283 46**
H: 5 9 W: 11 06 b.Epping 4-9-73
Source: Trainee.
1991–92 Tottenham H 0 0
1992–93 Tottenham H 4 0
1992–93 *Plymouth Arg* 7 2
1993–94 Tottenham H 0 0 **4 0**
1993–94 *Wycombe W* 4 0 **4 0**
1994–95 Barnet 34 4
1995–96 Barnet 40 17
1996–97 Barnet 31 5 **105 26**
1997–98 Reading 24 6
1998–99 Reading 1 0
1999–2000 Reading 25 2
2000–01 Reading 29 2
2001–02 Reading 0 0 **79 10**

2001-02	Plymouth Arg	45	6		
2002-03	Plymouth Arg	39	2	**91**	**10**

KEITH, Marino (F) **147 54**
H: 5 10 W: 12 13 b.Fraserburgh 16-12-74
Source: Fraserburgh.

1995–96	Dundee U	4	0		
1996–97	Dundee U	0	0	**4**	**0**
1997–98	Falkirk	32	10		
1998–99	Falkirk	29	17	**61**	**27**
1999–2000	Livingston	9	4		
2000-01	Livingston	13	3	**22**	**7**
2001-02	Plymouth Arg	23	9		
2002-03	Plymouth Arg	37	11	**60**	**20**

LARRIEU, Romain (G) **103 0**
H: 6 2 W: 13 00 b.Mont-de-Marsan 31-8-76
Source: Montpellier, ASOA Valence.

2000-01	Plymouth Arg	15	0		
2001-02	Plymouth Arg	45	0		
2002-03	Plymouth Arg	43	0	**103**	**0**

LOPES, Osvaldo (M) **9 0**
H: 5 10 W: 11 07 b.France 6-4-80

2002-03	Plymouth Arg	9	0	**9**	**0**

LOWNDES, Nathan (F) **110 19**
H: 5 11 W: 10 04 b.Salford 2-6-77
Source: Trainee.

1994–95	Leeds U	0	0		
1995–96	Leeds U	0	0		
1995–96	Watford	0	0		
1996–97	Watford	3	0		
1997–98	Watford	4	0	**7**	**0**
1998–99	St Johnstone	29	2		
1999–2000	St Johnstone	25	10		
2000-01	St Johnstone	10	2	**64**	**14**
2001-02	Livingston	21	3	**21**	**3**
2001-02	*Rotherham U*	2	0	**2**	**0**
2002-03	Plymouth Arg	16	2	**16**	**2**

MALCOLM, Stuart (D) **8 0**
H: 6 0 W: 11 11 b.Edinburgh 28-8-79
Source: Hutchison Vale BC.

1998–99	St Johnstone	0	0		
1998–99	*Cowdenbeath*	4	0	**4**	**0**
1999–2000	St Johnstone	0	0		
2000-01	St Johnstone	1	0		
2001-02	St Johnstone	0	0	**1**	**0**
2002-03	Plymouth Arg	3	0	**3**	**0**

McANESPIE, Kieran‡ (D) **61 6**
H: 5 8 W: 11 06 b.Gosport 11-9-79
Source: St Johnstone BC. *Honours:* Scotland Under-17, Under-21.

1995–96	St Johnstone	0	0		
1996–97	St Johnstone	9	2		
1997–98	St Johnstone	3	0		
1998–99	St Johnstone	18	2		
1999–2000	St Johnstone	20	1	**50**	**5**
2000-01	Fulham	0	0		
2001-02	Fulham	0	0		
2001-02	*Bournemouth*	7	1	**7**	**1**
2002-03	Fulham	0	0		
2002-03	Plymouth Arg	4	0	**4**	**0**

McCORMICK, Luke (G) **4 0**
H: 6 0 W: 13 12 b.Coventry 15-8-83
Source: Scholar.

2000-01	Plymouth Arg	1	0		
2001-02	Plymouth Arg	0	0		
2002-03	Plymouth Arg	3	0	**4**	**0**

McGLINCHEY, Brian (M) **97 4**
H: 5 7 W: 10 02 b.Derry 26-10-77
Source: Trainee. *Honours:* Northern Ireland Youth, Under-21, B.

1995–96	Manchester C	0	0		
1996–97	Manchester C	0	0		
1997–98	Manchester C	0	0		
1998–99	Port Vale	15	1	**15**	**1**
1999–2000	Gillingham	13	1		
2000-01	Gillingham	1	0	**14**	**1**
2000-01	Plymouth Arg	20	0		
2001-02	Plymouth Arg	29	1		
2002-03	Plymouth Arg	19	1	**68**	**2**

NORRIS, David (M) **39 7**
H: 5 7 W: 11 06 b.Peterborough 22-2-81
Source: Boston U.

1999–2000	Bolton W	0	0		
2000-01	Bolton W	0	0		
2001-02	Bolton W	0	0		
2001-02	*Hull C*	6	1	**6**	**1**
2002-03	Bolton W	0	0		
2002-03	Plymouth Arg	33	6	**33**	**6**

PHILLIPS, Martin (M) **209 15**
H: 5 11 W: 12 08 b.Exeter 13-3-76
Source: Trainee.

1992–93	Exeter C	6	0		
1993–94	Exeter C	9	0		
1994–95	Exeter C	24	2		
1995–96	Exeter C	13	3		
1995–96	Manchester C	11	0		
1996–97	Manchester C	4	0		
1997–98	Manchester C	0	0		
1997–98	*Scunthorpe U*	3	0	**3**	**0**
1997–98	*Exeter C*	8	0	**60**	**5**
1998–99	Manchester C	0	0	**15**	**0**
1998–99	Portsmouth	17	1		
1998–99	*Bristol R*	2	0	**2**	**0**
1999–2000	Portsmouth	7	0	**24**	**1**
2000-01	Plymouth Arg	42	1		
2001-02	Plymouth Arg	39	6		
2002-03	Plymouth Arg	24	2	**105**	**9**

STONEBRIDGE, Ian (F) **141 33**
H: 6 0 W: 11 04 b.Lewisham 30-8-81
Source: Tottenham H Trainee. *Honours:* England Youth.

1999–2000	Plymouth Arg	31	9		
2000-01	Plymouth Arg	31	11		
2001-02	Plymouth Arg	42	8		
2002-03	Plymouth Arg	37	5	**141**	**33**

STURROCK, Blair (F) **66 8**
H: 5 11 W: 11 06 b.Dundee 25-8-81
Source: Dundee U.

2000-01	Brechin C	27	6	**27**	**6**
2001-02	Plymouth Arg	19	1		
2002-03	Plymouth Arg	20	1	**39**	**2**

TAYLOR, Craig (D) **148 9**
H: 6 1 W: 12 03 b.Plymouth 24-1-74
Source: Dorchester T.

1996–97	Swindon T	0	0		
1997–98	Swindon T	32	2		
1998–99	Swindon T	21	0		
1998–99	*Plymouth Arg*	6	1		
1999–2000	Swindon T	2	0	**55**	**2**
1999–2000	Plymouth Arg	41	3		
2000-01	Plymouth Arg	39	3		
2001-02	Plymouth Arg	1	0		
2002-03	Plymouth Arg	1	0	**88**	**7**
2002-03	*Torquay U*	5	0	**5**	**0**

TRUDGIAN, Ryan (M) **1 0**
H: 6 0 W: 12 01 b.Truro 15-9-83
Source: Scholar.

2000-01	Plymouth Arg	1	0		
2001-02	Plymouth Arg	0	0		
2002-03	Plymouth Arg	0	0	**1**	**0**

VILLIS, Matthew (M) **0 0**
b.Bridgwater 13-4-84

2002-03	Plymouth Arg	0	0		

WORRELL, David (D) **116 0**
H: 5 10 W: 11 08 b.Dublin 12-1-78
Source: Trainee. *Honours:* Eire Youth, Under-21.

1994–95	Blackburn R	0	0		
1995–96	Blackburn R	0	0		
1996–97	Blackburn R	0	0		
1997–98	Blackburn R	0	0		
1998–99	Blackburn R	0	0		
1998–99	Dundee U	4	0		
1999–2000	Dundee U	13	0	**17**	**0**
2000-01	Plymouth Arg	14	0		
2001-02	Plymouth Arg	42	0		
2002-03	Plymouth Arg	43	0	**99**	**0**

WOTTON, Paul (D) **241 20**
H: 5 11 W: 11 01 b.Plymouth 17-8-77
Source: Trainee.

1994–95	Plymouth Arg	7	0		
1995–96	Plymouth Arg	1	0		
1996–97	Plymouth Arg	9	1		
1997–98	Plymouth Arg	34	1		
1998–99	Plymouth Arg	36	1		
1999–2000	Plymouth Arg	23	0		
2000-01	Plymouth Arg	42	4		
2001-02	Plymouth Arg	46	5		
2002-03	Plymouth Arg	43	8	**241**	**20**

YETTON, Stuart§ (M) **1 0**
H: 5 8 W: 10 03 b.Plymouth 27-7-85
Source: Scholar.

2002-03	Plymouth Arg	1	0	**1**	**0**

Scholars
Bulley, Daniel SA; Coxon, Lee D; Entwisle, Thomas; Fice, Ryan P; Guppy, Robert A; Kerr, Scott S; Martin, Marcus AP; Parish, Darren L; Sawyer, Gary D; Schofield, Kenny S; Steward, Benjamin L; Trudgian, Ryan; Yetton, Stewart D

Non-Contract
Chapman, Jason

Players who do not hold a current contract but their registration has been retained by the club
Bastow, Darren J

PORTSMOUTH

ALLEN, Rory* (F) **44 11**
H: 5 11 W: 11 10 b.Beckenham 17-10-77
Source: Trainee. *Honours:* England Under-21.

1995–96	Tottenham H	0	0		
1996–97	Tottenham H	12	2		
1997–98	Tottenham H	4	0		
1997–98	*Luton T*	8	6	**8**	**6**
1998–99	Tottenham H	5	0	**21**	**2**
1999–2000	Portsmouth	15	3		
2000-01	Portsmouth	0	0		
2001-02	Portsmouth	0	0		
2002-03	Portsmouth	0	0	**15**	**3**

BARRETT, Neil (M) **26 2**
H: 5 10 W: 11 00 b.Tooting 24-12-81
Source: Chelsea. *Honours:* England Schools.

2001-02	Portsmouth	26	2		
2002-03	Portsmouth	0	0	**26**	**2**

BRADBURY, Lee (F) **257 67**
H: 6 0 W: 13 10 b.Isle of Wight 3-7-75
Source: Cowes. *Honours:* England Under-21.

1995–96	Portsmouth	12	0		
1995–96	*Exeter C*	14	5	**14**	**5**
1996–97	Portsmouth	42	15		
1997–98	Manchester C	27	7		
1998–99	Manchester C	13	3	**40**	**10**
1998–99	Crystal Palace	22	4		
1998–99	*Birmingham C*	7	0	**7**	**0**
1999–2000	Crystal Palace	10	2	**32**	**6**
1999–2000	Portsmouth	35	10		
2000-01	Portsmouth	39	10		
2001-02	Portsmouth	22	7		
2002-03	Portsmouth	3	1	**153**	**43**
2002-03	*Sheffield W*	11	3	**11**	**3**

BRADSHAW, Craig (M) **0 0**
b.Chertsey 31-7-84
Source: Scholar.

2001-02	Portsmouth	0	0		
2002-03	Portsmouth	0	0		

BURCHILL, Mark (F) **67 23**
H: 5 8 W: 11 09 b.Broxburn 18-8-80
Source: Celtic BC. *Honours:* Scotland Schools, Under-21, 6 full caps.

1997–98	Celtic	0	0		
1998–99	Celtic	21	9		
1999–2000	Celtic	0	0		
2000-01	Celtic	2	1	**23**	**10**
2000-01	*Birmingham C*	13	4	**13**	**4**
2000-01	*Ipswich T*	7	1		
2001-02	Ipswich T	0	0	**7**	**1**
2001-02	Portsmouth	6	4		
2002-03	Portsmouth	18	4	**24**	**8**

BURTON, Deon (F) **222 43**
H: 5 9 W: 11 09 b.Reading 25-10-77
Source: Trainee. *Honours:* Jamaica 44 full caps, 8 goals.

1993–94	Portsmouth	2	0		
1994–95	Portsmouth	7	2		
1995–96	Portsmouth	32	7		
1996–97	Portsmouth	21	1		
1996–97	*Cardiff C*	5	2	**5**	**2**
1997–98	Derby Co	29	3		
1998–99	Derby Co	21	9		
1998–99	*Barnsley*	3	0	**3**	**0**
1999–2000	Derby Co	19	4		
2000-01	Derby Co	32	5		
2001-02	Derby Co	17	1		
2001-02	*Stoke C*	12	2	**12**	**2**
2002-03	Derby Co	7	3	**125**	**25**
2002-03	Portsmouth	15	4	**77**	**14**

BUXTON, Lewis (D) **51 0**
H: 6 1 W: 13 10 b.Newport (IW) 10-12-83
Source: School.

2000-01	Portsmouth	0	0		
2001-02	Portsmouth	29	0		
2002-03	Portsmouth	1	0	**30**	**0**
2002-03	*Exeter C*	4	0	**4**	**0**
2002-03	*Bournemouth*	17	0	**17**	**0**

CASEY, Mark (M) **0 0**

b.Glasgow 9-10-82

2001-02	Portsmouth	0	0		
2002-03	Portsmouth	0	0		

CLARK, Christopher (M) **0 0**

b.Shoreham 9-6-84

Source: Scholar.

2002-03	Portsmouth	0	0		

COOPER, Shaun (D) **7 0**

H: 5 10 W: 10 07 b.Isle of Wight 5-10-83

Source: School.

2000-01	Portsmouth	0	0		
2001-02	Portsmouth	7	0		
2002-03	Portsmouth	0	0	**7**	**0**

CROWE, Jason* (D) **103 5**

H: 5 9 W: 11 02 b.Sidcup 30-9-78

Source: Trainee. *Honours:* England Schools, Youth.

1995–96	Arsenal	0	0		
1996–97	Arsenal	0	0		
1997–98	Arsenal	0	0		
1998–99	Arsenal	0	0		
1998–99	*Crystal Palace*	8	0	**8**	**0**
1999–2000	Portsmouth	25	0		
2000-01	Portsmouth	23	0		
2000-01	*Brentford*	9	0	**9**	**0**
2001-02	Portsmouth	22	1		
2002-03	Portsmouth	16	4	**86**	**5**

DE ZEEUW, Arjan (D) **404 19**

H: 6 0 W: 13 06 b.Castricum 16-4-70

Source: Vitesse 22.

1992–93	Telstar	30	1		
1993–94	Telstar	31	2		
1994–95	Telstar	29	1		
1995–96	Telstar	12	1	**102**	**5**
1995–96	Barnsley	31	1		
1996–97	Barnsley	43	2		
1997–98	Barnsley	26	0		
1998–99	Barnsley	38	4	**138**	**7**
1999–2000	Wigan Ath	39	3		
2000-01	Wigan Ath	45	1		
2001-02	Wigan Ath	42	2	**126**	**6**
2002-03	Portsmouth	38	1	**38**	**1**

DIABATE, Lassina* (M) **189 3**

H: 5 11 W: 11 11 b.Bouake 16-9-74

Source: Bourges. *Honours:* Ivory Coast full caps.

1995–96	Perpignan	24	0		
1996–97	Perpignan	26	1	**50**	**1**
1997–98	Bordeaux	21	1		
1998–99	Bordeaux	30	1		
1999–2000	Bordeaux	24	0		
2000-01	Bordeaux	16	0	**91**	**2**
2001-02	Auxerre	23	0	**23**	**0**
2002-03	Portsmouth	25	0	**25**	**0**

FESTA, Gianluca* (D) **434 17**

H: 5 11 W: 13 00 b.Cagliari 15-3-69

1986–87	Cagliari	3	0		
1987–88	*Fersuicis*	26	2	**26**	**2**
1988–89	Cagliari	27	0		
1989–90	Cagliari	36	0		
1990–91	Cagliari	28	0		
1991–92	Cagliari	31	0		
1992–93	Cagliari	31	0	**156**	**0**
1993–94	Internazionale	4	0		
1993–94	*Roma*	21	1	**21**	**1**
1994–95	Internazionale	26	2		
1995–96	Internazionale	31	1		
1996–97	Internazionale	5	0	**66**	**3**
1996–97	Middlesbrough	13	1		
1997–98	Middlesbrough	38	2		
1998–99	Middlesbrough	25	2		
1999–2000	Middlesbrough	29	2		
2000-01	Middlesbrough	25	2		
2001-02	Middlesbrough	8	1		
2002-03	Middlesbrough	0	0	**138**	**10**
2002-03	Portsmouth	27	1	**27**	**1**

FOXE, Hayden (D) **85 6**

H: 6 3 W: 13 05 b.Sydney 23-6-77

Honours: Australia Youth, Under-20, Under-23, 10 full caps, 2 goals.

1997–98	Arminia Bielefeld	1	0	**1**	**0**
1998	Sanfrecce	15	3		
1999	Sanfrecce	22	2	**37**	**5**
2000-01	Mechelen	4	0	**4**	**0**
2000-01	West Ham U	5	0		
2001-02	West Ham U	6	0	**11**	**0**
2002-03	Portsmouth	32	1	**32**	**1**

HARPER, Kevin (F) **249 26**

H: 5 6 W: 12 00 b.Oldham 15-1-76

Source: Hutcheson Vale BC. *Honours:* Scotland Schools, Under-21, B.

1993–94	Hibernian	2	0		
1994–95	Hibernian	23	5		
1995–96	Hibernian	16	3		
1996–97	Hibernian	26	5		
1997–98	Hibernian	27	1		
1998–99	Hibernian	2	1	**96**	**15**
1998–99	Derby Co	27	1		
1999–2000	Derby Co	5	0	**32**	**1**
1999–2000	*Walsall*	9	1	**9**	**1**
1999–2000	Portsmouth	12	2		
2000-01	Portsmouth	24	2		
2001-02	Portsmouth	39	1		
2002-03	Portsmouth	37	4	**112**	**9**

HEIKKINEN, Markus (D) **152 2**

H: 6 0 W: 12 13 b.Katrineholm 13-10-78

Honours: Finland 7 full caps.

1996	TPS Turku	0	0		
1997	TPS Turku	22	0	**22**	**0**
1998	MyPa	14	0		
1999	MyPa	29	1	**43**	**1**
2000	HJK Helsinki	32	0		
2001	HJK Helsinki	33	1		
2002	HJK Helsinki	20	0	**85**	**1**
2002-03	Portsmouth	2	0	**2**	**0**

HISLOP, Shaka (G) **308 0**

H: 6 4 W: 14 04 b.Hackney 22-2-69

Source: Howard Univ, USA. *Honours:* England Under-21. Trinidad & Tobago 7 full caps.

1992–93	Reading	12	0		
1993–94	Reading	46	0		
1994–95	Reading	46	0	**104**	**0**
1995–96	Newcastle U	24	0		
1996–97	Newcastle U	16	0		
1997–98	Newcastle U	13	0	**53**	**0**
1998–99	West Ham U	37	0		
1999–2000	West Ham U	22	0		
2000-01	West Ham U	34	0		
2001-02	West Ham U	12	0	**105**	**0**
2002-03	Portsmouth	46	0	**46**	**0**

HOWE, Eddie (D) **202 10**

H: 5 11 W: 11 07 b.Amersham 29-11-77

Source: Trainee.

1995–96	Bournemouth	5	0		
1996–97	Bournemouth	13	0		
1997–98	Bournemouth	40	1		
1998–99	Bournemouth	45	2		
1999–2000	Bournemouth	28	1		
2000-01	Bournemouth	31	2		
2001-02	Bournemouth	38	4	**200**	**10**
2001-02	Portsmouth	1	0		
2002-03	Portsmouth	1	0	**2**	**0**

HUGHES, Richard (M) **149 15**

H: 6 0 W: 13 03 b.Glasgow 25-6-79

Source: Atalanta. *Honours:* Scotland Youth, Under-21.

1997–98	Arsenal	0	0		
1998–99	Bournemouth	44	2		
1999–2000	Bournemouth	21	2		
2000-01	Bournemouth	44	8		
2001-02	Bournemouth	22	2	**131**	**14**
2002-03	Portsmouth	6	0	**6**	**0**
2002-03	*Grimsby T*	12	1	**12**	**1**

HUNT, Warren (M) **0 0**

b.Portsmouth 2-3-84

Source: Scholar.

2001-02	Portsmouth	0	0		
2002-03	Portsmouth	0	0		

ILIC, Sasa* (G) **59 0**

H: 6 4 W: 14 12 b.Melbourne 18-7-72

Source: Partizan Belgrade, Radnicki, Ringwood, Daewoo Royals, St Leonards Stamcroft. *Honours:* Yugoslavia 1 full cap.

1997–98	Charlton Ath	14	0		
1998–99	Charlton Ath	23	0		
1999–2000	Charlton Ath	1	0		
1999–2000	*West Ham U*	1	0	**1**	**0**
2000-01	Charlton Ath	13	0		
2001-02	Charlton Ath	0	0	**51**	**0**
2001-02	*Portsmouth*	7	0		
2002-03	Portsmouth	0	0	**7**	**0**

KAWAGUCHI, Yoshikatsu (G) **205 0**

H: 5 10 W: 12 03 b.Shizuoka 15-8-75

Honours: Japan 54 full caps.

1995	Yokohama Flugels	41	0		
1996	Yokohama Flugels	15	0		
1997	Yokohama Flugels	22	0		
1998	Yokohama Flugels	34	0	**112**	**0**
1999	Yokohama Marinos	28	0		
2000	Yokohama Marinos	28	0		
2001	Yokohama Marinos	25	0	**81**	**0**
2001-02	Portsmouth	11	0		
2002-03	Portsmouth	1	0	**12**	**0**

MERSON, Paul (F) **544 119**

H: 6 0 W: 13 02 b.Northolt 20-3-68

Source: Apprentice. *Honours:* England Youth, Under-21, B, 21 full caps, 3 goals.

1985–86	Arsenal	0	0		
1986–87	Arsenal	7	3		
1986–87	*Brentford*	7	0	**7**	**0**
1987–88	Arsenal	15	5		
1988–89	Arsenal	37	10		
1989–90	Arsenal	29	7		
1990–91	Arsenal	37	13		
1991–92	Arsenal	42	12		
1992–93	Arsenal	33	6		
1993–94	Arsenal	33	7		
1994–95	Arsenal	24	4		
1995–96	Arsenal	38	5		
1996–97	Arsenal	32	6	**327**	**78**
1997–98	Middlesbrough	45	11		
1998–99	Middlesbrough	3	0	**48**	**11**
1998–99	Aston Villa	26	5		
1999–2000	Aston Villa	32	5		
2000-01	Aston Villa	38	6		
2001-02	Aston Villa	21	2	**117**	**18**
2002-03	Portsmouth	45	12	**45**	**12**

MOLYNEAUX, Lee* (M) **0 0**

b.Portsmouth 16-1-83

Source: Scholar.

2001-02	Portsmouth	0	0		
2002-03	Portsmouth	0	0		

NIGHTINGALE, Luke* (F) **48 4**

H: 5 11 W: 11 07 b.Portsmouth 22-12-80

Source: Trainee.

1998–99	Portsmouth	19	3		
1999–2000	Portsmouth	7	0		
2000-01	Portsmouth	19	1		
2001-02	Portsmouth	0	0		
2002-03	Portsmouth	0	0	**45**	**4**
2002-03	*Swindon T*	3	0	**3**	**0**

O'NEIL, Gary (M) **75 5**

H: 5 10 W: 11 00 b.Beckenham 18-5-83

Source: Scholar. *Honours:* England Youth, Under-20.

1999–2000	Portsmouth	1	0		
2000-01	Portsmouth	10	1		
2001-02	Portsmouth	33	1		
2002-03	Portsmouth	31	3	**75**	**5**

PARKER, Terry (M) **0 0**

b.Southampton 20-12-83

Source: Scholar.

2002-03	Portsmouth	0	0		

PERICARD, Vincent de Paul* (F) **32 9**

H: 6 1 W: 13 08 b.Efko 3-10-82

From Juventus.

2002-03	Portsmouth	32	9	**32**	**9**

PETTEFER, Carl (M) **34 1**

H: 5 7 W: 10 02 b.Taplow 22-3-81

Source: Trainee.

1998–99	Portsmouth	0	0		
1999–2000	Portsmouth	0	0		
2000-01	Portsmouth	1	0		
2001-02	Portsmouth	2	0		
2002-03	Portsmouth	0	0	**3**	**0**
2002-03	*Exeter C*	31	1	**31**	**1**

PITT, Courtney (M) **39 3**

H: 5 7 W: 10 08 b.London 17-12-81

Source: Scholar.

2000-01	Chelsea	0	0		
2001-02	Portsmouth	39	3		
2002-03	Portsmouth	0	0	**39**	**3**

PRIMUS, Linvoy (D) **311 10**

H: 5 10 W: 12 04 b.Forest Gate 14-9-73

Source: Trainee.

1992–93	Charlton Ath	4	0		
1993–94	Charlton Ath	0	0	**4**	**0**
1994–95	Barnet	39	0		
1995–96	Barnet	42	4		
1996–97	Barnet	46	3	**127**	**7**
1997–98	Reading	36	1		
1998–99	Reading	31	0		
1999–2000	Reading	28	0	**95**	**1**
2000-01	Portsmouth	23	0		
2001-02	Portsmouth	22	2		
2002-03	Portsmouth	40	0	**85**	**2**

PULIS, Anthony (M) 0 0
b.Bristol 21-7-84
Source: Scholar.
2002-03 Portsmouth 0 0

QUASHIE, Nigel (M) 209 17
H: 5 9 W: 12 08 b.Nunhead 20-7-78
Source: Trainee. *Honours:* England Youth, Under-21, B.
1995–96 QPR 11 0
1996–97 QPR 13 0
1997–98 QPR 33 3
1998–99 QPR 0 0 **57 3**
1998–99 Nottingham F 16 0
1999–2000 Nottingham F 28 2 **44 2**
2000-01 Portsmouth 31 5
2001-02 Portsmouth 35 2
2002-03 Portsmouth 42 5 **108 12**

ROBINSON, Carl (M) 198 21
H: 5 10 W: 12 10 b.Llandrindod Wells 13-10-76
Source: Trainee. *Honours:* Wales Youth, Under-21, B, 12 full caps.
1995–96 Wolverhampton W 0 0
1995–96 *Shrewsbury T* 4 0 **4 0**
1996–97 Wolverhampton W 2 0
1997–98 Wolverhampton W 32 3
1998–99 Wolverhampton W 34 8
1999–2000 Wolverhampton W 33 3
2000-01 Wolverhampton W 40 3
2001-02 Wolverhampton W 23 2 **164 19**
2002-03 Portsmouth 15 0 **15 0**
2002-03 *Sheffield W* 4 1 **4 1**
2002-03 *Walsall* 11 1 **11 1**

SHERWOOD, Tim (M) 459 50
H: 6 0 W: 12 08 b.St Albans 2-2-69
Source: Trainee. *Honours:* England Under-21, B, 3 full caps.
1986–87 Watford 0 0
1987–88 Watford 13 0
1988–89 Watford 19 2 **32 2**
1989–90 Norwich C 27 3
1990–91 Norwich C 37 7
1991–92 Norwich C 7 0 **71 10**
1991–92 Blackburn R 11 0
1992–93 Blackburn R 39 3
1993–94 Blackburn R 38 2
1994–95 Blackburn R 38 6
1995–96 Blackburn R 33 3
1996–97 Blackburn R 37 3
1997–98 Blackburn R 31 5
1998–99 Blackburn R 19 3 **246 25**
1998–99 Tottenham H 14 2
1999–2000 Tottenham H 27 8
2000-01 Tottenham H 33 2
2001-02 Tottenham H 19 0
2002-03 Tottenham H 0 0 **93 12**
2002-03 Portsmouth 17 1 **17 1**

STONE, Steve (M) 301 31
H: 5 8 W: 12 07 b.Gateshead 20-8-71
Source: Trainee. *Honours:* England 9 full caps, 2 goals.
1989–90 Nottingham F 0 0
1990–91 Nottingham F 0 0
1991–92 Nottingham F 1 0
1992–93 Nottingham F 12 1
1993–94 Nottingham F 45 5
1994–95 Nottingham F 41 5
1995–96 Nottingham F 34 7
1996–97 Nottingham F 5 0
1997–98 Nottingham F 29 2
1998–99 Nottingham F 26 3 **193 23**
1998–99 Aston Villa 10 0
1999–2000 Aston Villa 24 1
2000-01 Aston Villa 34 2
2001-02 Aston Villa 22 1
2002-03 Aston Villa 0 0 **90 4**
2002-03 Portsmouth 18 4 **18 4**

TARDIF, Chris (G) 14 0
H: 6 1 W: 12 07 b.Guernsey 10-9-79
Source: Trainee.
1998–99 Portsmouth 0 0
1999–2000 Portsmouth 0 0
2000-01 Portsmouth 4 0
2001-02 Portsmouth 1 0
2002-03 Portsmouth 0 0 **5 0**
2002-03 *Bournemouth* 9 0 **9 0**

TAYLOR, Matthew (D) 164 23
H: 5 11 W: 12 03 b.Oxford 27-11-81
Source: Trainee. *Honours:* England Under-21.
1998–99 Luton T 0 0
1999–2000 Luton T 41 4
2000-01 Luton T 45 1
2001-02 Luton T 43 11 **129 16**
2002-03 Portsmouth 35 7 **35 7**

TILER, Carl* (D) 263 11
H: 6 2 W: 14 03 b.Sheffield 11-2-70
Source: Trainee. *Honours:* England Under-21.
1987–88 Barnsley 1 0
1988–89 Barnsley 4 0
1989–90 Barnsley 21 1
1990–91 Barnsley 45 2 **71 3**
1991–92 Nottingham F 26 1
1992–93 Nottingham F 37 0
1993–94 Nottingham F 3 0
1994–95 Nottingham F 3 0
1994–95 *Swindon T* 2 0 **2 0**
1995–96 Nottingham F 0 0 **69 1**
1995–96 Aston Villa 1 0
1996–97 Aston Villa 11 1 **12 1**
1996–97 Sheffield U 6 1
1997–98 Sheffield U 17 1 **23 2**
1997–98 Everton 19 1
1998–99 Everton 2 0 **21 1**
1998–99 Charlton Ath 27 1
1999–2000 Charlton Ath 11 1
2000-01 Charlton Ath 7 0 **45 2**
2000-01 *Birmingham C* 1 0 **1 0**
2000-01 Portsmouth 9 1
2001-02 Portsmouth 8 0
2002-03 Portsmouth 2 0 **19 1**

TODOROV, Svetoslav (F) 145 67
H: 6 0 W: 12 02 b.Dobrich 30-8-78
Honours: Bulgaria 29 full caps, 4 goals.
1996–97 Dobrudzha 12 2 **12 2**
1997–98 Litets Lovech 19 9
1998–99 Litets Lovech 11 2
1999–2000 Litets Lovech 26 19
2000-01 Litets Lovech 15 7 **71 37**
2000-01 West Ham U 8 1
2001-02 West Ham U 6 0 **14 1**
2001-02 Portsmouth 3 1
2002-03 Portsmouth 45 26 **48 27**

VINCENT, Jamie (D) 245 8
H: 5 10 W: 11 09 b.London 18-6-75
Source: Trainee.
1993–94 Crystal Palace 0 0
1994–95 Crystal Palace 0 0
1994–95 *Bournemouth* 8 0
1995–96 Crystal Palace 25 0
1996–97 Crystal Palace 0 0 **25 0**
1996–97 Bournemouth 29 0
1997–98 Bournemouth 44 3
1998–99 Bournemouth 32 2 **113 5**
1998–99 Huddersfield T 7 0
1999–2000 Huddersfield T 36 2
2000-01 Huddersfield T 16 0 **59 2**
2000-01 Portsmouth 14 0
2001-02 Portsmouth 34 1
2002-03 Portsmouth 0 0 **48 1**

VINE, Rowan (F) 55 10
H: 6 1 W: 11 12 b.Basingstoke 21-9-82
Source: Scholar.
2000-01 Portsmouth 2 0
2001-02 Portsmouth 11 0
2002-03 Portsmouth 0 0 **13 0**
2002-03 *Brentford* 42 10 **42 10**

WHITE, Tom* (M) 0 0
b.Chichester 30-10-81
Source: Trainee.
2000-01 Portsmouth 0 0
2001-02 Portsmouth 0 0
2002-03 Portsmouth 0 0

YAKUBU, Ayegbeni (F) 50 23
H: 6 0 W: 13 01 b.Nigeria 22-11-82
Source: Julius Berger. *Honours:* Nigeria full caps.
1999–2000 Gil Vicente 0 0
2000-01 Maccabi Haifa 14 3
2001-02 Maccabi Haifa 22 13 **36 16**
2002-03 Portsmouth 14 7 **14 7**

Scholars
Angus, Calum J; Crawford, James L; Hards, Alex; Harris, Scott G; Horsted, Liam A; Hughes, Ryan; Keene, James D; Moore, Ben; Roach, Jamie; Silk, Gary L; Whitley, Luke

PORT VALE

ARMSTRONG, Ian (M) 60 10
H: 5 8 W: 9 13 b.Liverpool 16-11-81
Source: Trainee. *Honours:* England Schools, Youth.
1998–99 Liverpool 0 0
1999–2000 Liverpool 0 0
2000-01 Liverpool 0 0
2001-02 Port Vale 31 3
2002-03 Port Vale 29 7 **60 10**

BIRCHALL, Chris§ (F) 3 0
H: 5 8 W: 13 00 b.Stafford 5-5-84
Source: Scholar.
2001-02 Port Vale 1 0
2002-03 Port Vale 2 0 **3 0**

BOYD, Mark (M) 20 3
H: 5 9 W: 12 03 b.Carlisle 22-10-81
Source: Trainee.
1998–99 Newcastle U 0 0
1999–2000 Newcastle U 0 0
2000-01 Newcastle U 0 0
2001-02 Newcastle U 0 0
2002-03 Port Vale 20 3 **20 3**

BRIDGE-WILKINSON, Marc (M) 100 24
H: 5 8 W: 11 05 b.Coventry 16-3-79
Source: Trainee.
1996–97 Derby Co 0 0
1997–98 Derby Co 0 0
1998–99 Derby Co 1 0
1998–99 *Carlisle U* 7 0 **7 0**
1999–2000 Derby Co 0 0 **1 0**
2000-01 Port Vale 42 9
2001-02 Port Vale 19 6
2002-03 Port Vale 31 9 **92 24**

BRIGHTWELL, Ian* (D) 441 18
H: 5 10 W: 12 10 b.Lutterworth 9-4-68
Source: Congleton T. *Honours:* England Schools, Youth, Under-21.
1986–87 Manchester C 16 1
1987–88 Manchester C 33 5
1988–89 Manchester C 26 6
1989–90 Manchester C 28 2
1990–91 Manchester C 33 0
1991–92 Manchester C 40 1
1992–93 Manchester C 21 1
1993–94 Manchester C 7 0
1994–95 Manchester C 30 0
1995–96 Manchester C 29 0
1996–97 Manchester C 37 2
1997–98 Manchester C 21 0 **321 18**
1998–99 Coventry C 0 0
1999–2000 Coventry C 0 0
1999–2000 Walsall 10 0
2000-01 Walsall 44 0
2001-02 Walsall 27 0 **81 0**
2001-02 Stoke C 4 0 **4 0**
2002-03 Port Vale 35 0 **35 0**

BRISCO, Neil (M) 91 2
H: 6 0 W: 13 05 b.Billinge 26-1-78
Source: Trainee.
1996–97 Manchester C 0 0
1997–98 Manchester C 0 0
1998–99 Port Vale 1 0
1999–2000 Port Vale 12 0
2000-01 Port Vale 17 1
2001-02 Port Vale 37 0
2002-03 Port Vale 24 1 **91 2**

BROOKER, Stephen (F) 91 23
H: 5 11 W: 14 00 b.Newport Pagnell 21-5-81
Source: Trainee.
1999–2000 Watford 1 0
2000-01 Watford 0 0 **1 0**
2000-01 Port Vale 23 9
2001-02 Port Vale 41 9
2002-03 Port Vale 26 5 **90 23**

BROWN, Ryan§ (D) 1 0
H: 5 9 W: 10 10 b.Stoke 15-3-85
Source: Scholar.
2002-03 Port Vale 1 0 **1 0**

BURNS, Liam (D) 91 0
H: 6 2 W: 13 05 b.Belfast 30-10-78
Source: Trainee. *Honours:* Northern Ireland Youth, Under-21.
1997–98 Port Vale 1 0
1998–99 Port Vale 4 0
1999–2000 Port Vale 24 0
2000-01 Port Vale 13 0

2001-02 Port Vale 33 0
2002-03 Port Vale 16 0 **91 0**

BYRNE, Paul* (D) 11 0
H: 5 8 W: 11 08 b.Natal 26-11-82
Source: Scholar.
2000-01 Port Vale 1 0
2001-02 Port Vale 2 0
2002-03 Port Vale 8 0 **11 0**

CARRAGHER, Matt* (D) 313 1
H: 5 8 W: 11 12 b.Liverpool 14-1-76
Source: Trainee.
1993–94 Wigan Ath 32 0
1994–95 Wigan Ath 41 0
1995–96 Wigan Ath 28 0
1996–97 Wigan Ath 18 0 **119 0**
1997–98 Port Vale 26 0
1998–99 Port Vale 10 0
1999–2000 Port Vale 37 1
2000-01 Port Vale 45 0
2001-02 Port Vale 41 0
2002-03 Port Vale 35 0 **194 1**

CHARNOCK, Phil* (M) 179 9
H: 5 11 W: 12 09 b.Southport 14-2-75
Source: Trainee.
1992–93 Liverpool 0 0
1993–94 Liverpool 0 0
1994–95 Liverpool 0 0
1995–96 Liverpool 0 0
1995–96 *Blackpool* 4 0 **4 0**
1996–97 Liverpool 0 0
1996–97 Crewe Alex 32 1
1997–98 Crewe Alex 33 3
1998–99 Crewe Alex 44 2
1999–2000 Crewe Alex 16 1
2000-01 Crewe Alex 9 0
2001-02 Crewe Alex 23 1 **157 8**
2002-03 Port Vale 18 1 **18 1**

COLLINS, Sam (D) 163 7
H: 6 3 W: 14 11 b.Pontefract 5-6-77
Source: Trainee.
1994–95 Huddersfield T 0 0
1995–96 Huddersfield T 0 0
1996–97 Huddersfield T 4 0
1997–98 Huddersfield T 10 0
1998–99 Huddersfield T 23 0 **37 0**
1999–2000 Bury 19 0
2000-01 Bury 34 2
2001-02 Bury 29 0 **82 2**
2002-03 Port Vale 44 5 **44 5**

CUMMINS, Michael (M) 135 15
H: 5 11 W: 12 12 b.Dublin 1-6-78
Source: Trainee. *Honours:* Eire Youth, Under-21.
1995–96 Middlesbrough 0 0
1996–97 Middlesbrough 0 0
1997–98 Middlesbrough 0 0
1998–99 Middlesbrough 1 0
1999–2000 Middlesbrough 1 0 **2 0**
1999–2000 Port Vale 12 1
2000-01 Port Vale 45 2
2001-02 Port Vale 46 8
2002-03 Port Vale 30 4 **133 15**

DELANY, Dean (G) 22 0
H: 6 2 W: 13 04 b.Dublin 15-9-80
Honours: Eire Under-21.
1997–98 Everton 0 0
1998–99 Everton 0 0
1999–2000 Everton 0 0
2000-01 Port Vale 8 0
2001-02 Port Vale 4 0
2002-03 Port Vale 10 0 **22 0**

DURNIN, John‡ (M) 452 91
H: 5 10 W: 12 05 b.Liverpool 18-8-65
Source: Waterloo Dock.
1985–86 Liverpool 0 0
1986–87 Liverpool 0 0
1987–88 Liverpool 0 0
1988–89 Liverpool 0 0
1988–89 *WBA* 5 2 **5 2**
1988–89 Oxford U 19 3
1989–90 Oxford U 42 13
1990–91 Oxford U 26 9
1991–92 Oxford U 37 8
1992–93 Oxford U 37 11 **161 44**
1993–94 Portsmouth 28 6
1994–95 Portsmouth 16 2
1995–96 Portsmouth 41 3
1996–97 Portsmouth 34 3
1997–98 Portsmouth 34 10
1998–99 Portsmouth 26 7
1999–2000 Portsmouth 2 0 **181 31**
1999–2000 Blackpool 5 1 **5 1**
1999–2000 Carlisle U 22 2
2000-01 Carlisle U 0 0 **22 2**
2000-01 Kidderminster H 31 9
2001-02 Kidderminster H 0 0 **31 9**
From Rhyl.
2001-02 Port Vale 19 1
2002-03 Port Vale 28 1 **47 2**

ELDERSHAW, Simon§ (F) 2 0
H: 5 9 W: 10 11 b.Stoke 2-12-83
Source: Scholar.
2002-03 Port Vale 2 0 **2 0**

GOODLAD, Mark (G) 124 0
H: 6 2 W: 14 03 b.Barnsley 9-9-79
Source: Trainee.
1996–97 Nottingham F 0 0
1997–98 Nottingham F 0 0
1998–99 Nottingham F 0 0
1998–99 *Scarborough* 3 0 **3 0**
1999–2000 Nottingham F 0 0
1999–2000 Port Vale 1 0
2000-01 Port Vale 40 0
2001-02 Port Vale 43 0
2002-03 Port Vale 37 0 **121 0**

INGRAM, Rae* (D) 154 1
H: 5 11 W: 12 09 b.Manchester 6-12-74
Source: Trainee.
1993–94 Manchester C 0 0
1994–95 Manchester C 0 0
1995–96 Manchester C 5 0
1996–97 Manchester C 18 0
1997–98 Manchester C 0 0 **23 0**
1997–98 *Macclesfield T* 5 0
1998–99 Macclesfield T 29 0
1999–2000 Macclesfield T 36 0
2000-01 Macclesfield T 33 1 **103 1**
2001-02 Port Vale 24 0
2002-03 Port Vale 4 0 **28 0**

LITTLEJOHN, Adrian† (M) 359 64
H: 5 10 W: 11 00 b.Wolverhampton 26-9-71
Source: WBA Trainee.
1989–90 Walsall 11 0
1990–91 Walsall 33 1 **44 1**
1991–92 Sheffield U 7 0
1992–93 Sheffield U 27 8
1993–94 Sheffield U 19 3
1994–95 Sheffield U 16 1
1995–96 Plymouth Arg 42 17
1996–97 Plymouth Arg 37 6
1997–98 Plymouth Arg 31 6 **110 29**
1997–98 Oldham Ath 5 3
1998–99 Oldham Ath 16 2 **21 5**
1998–99 Bury 20 1
1999–2000 Bury 42 9
2000-01 Bury 37 4 **99 14**
2001-02 Sheffield U 3 0
2002-03 Sheffield U 0 0 **72 12**
2002-03 Port Vale 13 3 **13 3**

McCLARE, Sean* (M) 99 7
H: 5 10 W: 12 02 b.Rotherham 12-1-78
Source: Trainee. *Honours:* Eire Under-21.
1996–97 Barnsley 0 0
1997–98 Barnsley 0 0
1998–99 Barnsley 30 3
1999–2000 Barnsley 10 2
1999–2000 *Rochdale* 9 0 **9 0**
2000-01 Barnsley 10 1
2001-02 Barnsley 0 0 **50 6**
2001-02 Port Vale 23 1
2002-03 Port Vale 17 0 **40 1**

McPHEE, Stephen (F) 84 14
H: 5 8 W: 11 10 b.Glasgow 5-6-81
Honours: Scotland Under-21.
1998–99 Coventry C 0 0
1999–2000 Coventry C 0 0
2000-01 Coventry C 0 0
2001-02 Port Vale 44 11
2002-03 Port Vale 40 3 **84 14**

PAYNTER, Billy (F) 39 5
H: 6 0 W: 12 11 b.Liverpool 13-7-84
Source: Schoolboy.
2000-01 Port Vale 1 0
2001-02 Port Vale 7 0
2002-03 Port Vale 31 5 **39 5**

REID, Levi§ (M) 1 0
H: 5 6 W: 11 04 b.Stafford 19-12-83
Source: Scholar.
2002-03 Port Vale 1 0 **1 0**

ROWLAND, Stephen (D) 50 1
H: 5 10 W: 11 11 b.Wrexham 2-11-81
Source: Scholar.
2001-02 Port Vale 25 1
2002-03 Port Vale 25 0 **50 1**

WALSH, Michael (D) 218 5
H: 6 0 W: 13 05 b.Rotherham 5-8-77
Source: Trainee.
1994–95 Scunthorpe U 3 0
1995–96 Scunthorpe U 25 0
1996–97 Scunthorpe U 36 0
1997–98 Scunthorpe U 39 1 **103 1**
1998–99 Port Vale 19 1
1999–2000 Port Vale 12 1
2000-01 Port Vale 39 1
2001-02 Port Vale 28 0
2002-03 Port Vale 17 1 **115 4**

Scholars
Birchall, Christopher; Booth, Edward AR; Brown, Ryan A; Doxey, Shaun G; Eldershaw, Simon; Gowland, Matthew J; Hibbert, David J; Mitchell, Craig J; Molloy, Joseph M; O'Reilly, Graham; Orpe, Mark; Reid, Ishmale M; Reid, Levi SJ; Robinson, Simon; Sly Benjamin P
Non-Contract
Littlejohn, Adrian S

PRESTON NE

ABBOTT, Pawel (F) 33 10
H: 5 7 W: 11 07 b.York 5-5-82
Source: LKS Lodz.
2000-01 Preston NE 0 0
2001-02 Preston NE 0 0
2002-03 Preston NE 16 4 **16 4**
2002-03 *Bury* 17 6 **17 6**

ALEXANDER, Graham (D) 489 60
H: 5 11 W: 12 04 b.Coventry 10-10-71
Source: Trainee. *Honours:* Scotland 12 full caps.
1989–90 Scunthorpe U 0 0
1990–91 Scunthorpe U 1 0
1991–92 Scunthorpe U 36 5
1992–93 Scunthorpe U 41 5
1993–94 Scunthorpe U 41 4
1994–95 Scunthorpe U 40 4 **159 18**
1995–96 Luton T 37 1
1996–97 Luton T 45 2
1997–98 Luton T 39 8
1998–99 Luton T 29 4 **150 15**
1998–99 Preston NE 10 0
1999–2000 Preston NE 46 6
2000-01 Preston NE 34 5
2001-02 Preston NE 45 6
2002-03 Preston NE 45 10 **180 27**

ANDERSON, Iain (M) 218 30
H: 5 5 W: 12 04 b.Glasgow 23-7-77
Source: X-Form. *Honours:* Scotland Under-21.
1994–95 Dundee 10 1
1995–96 Dundee 17 0
1996–97 Dundee 35 5
1997–98 Dundee 36 6
1998–99 Dundee 28 3 **126 15**
1999–2000 Toulouse 3 0 **3 0**
1999–2000 Preston NE 12 2
2000-01 Preston NE 31 6
2001-02 Preston NE 31 5
2002-03 Preston NE 8 0 **82 13**
2002-03 *Tranmere R* 7 2 **7 2**

BAILEY, John (M) 1 0
H: 5 8 W: 10 05 b.Manchester 2-7-84
Source: Scholar. *Honours:* England Youth.
2001-02 Preston NE 0 0
2002-03 Preston NE 1 0 **1 0**

BROOMES, Marlon (D) 110 2
H: 6 0 W: 12 12 b.Meriden 28-11-77
Source: Trainee. *Honours:* England Schools, Youth, Under-21.
1994–95 Blackburn R 0 0
1995–96 Blackburn R 0 0
1996–97 Blackburn R 0 0
1996–97 *Swindon T* 12 1 **12 1**
1997–98 Blackburn R 4 0
1998–99 Blackburn R 13 0
1999–2000 Blackburn R 13 1
2000-01 Blackburn R 1 0
2000-01 *QPR* 5 0 **5 0**

2001-02 Blackburn R 0 0 **31 1**
2001-02 *Grimsby T* 15 0 **15 0**
2001-02 Sheffield W 19 0 **19 0**
2002-03 Preston NE 28 0 **28 0**

CARTWRIGHT, Lee (M) 385 22
H: 5 8 W: 11 05 b.Rossendale 19-9-72
Source: Trainee.
1990–91 Preston NE 14 1
1991–92 Preston NE 33 3
1992–93 Preston NE 34 3
1993–94 Preston NE 39 1
1994–95 Preston NE 36 1
1995–96 Preston NE 26 3
1996–97 Preston NE 14 1
1997–98 Preston NE 36 2
1998–99 Preston NE 27 4
1999–2000 Preston NE 30 1
2000-01 Preston NE 38 0
2001-02 Preston NE 36 1
2002-03 Preston NE 22 1 **385 22**

CRESSWELL, Richard (F) 232 55
H: 6 1 W: 11 00 b.Bridlington 20-9-77
Source: Trainee. *Honours:* England Under-21.
1995–96 York C 16 1
1996–97 York C 17 0
1996–97 *Mansfield T* 5 1 **5 1**
1997–98 York C 26 4
1998–99 York C 36 16 **95 21**
1998–99 Sheffield W 7 1
1999–2000 Sheffield W 20 1
2000-01 Sheffield W 4 0 **31 2**
2000-01 Leicester C 8 0 **8 0**
2000-01 *Preston NE* 11 2
2001-02 Preston NE 40 13
2002-03 Preston NE 42 16 **93 31**

EDWARDS, Rob (D) 409 14
H: 6 0 W: 13 03 b.Carlisle 1-7-73
Source: Trainee. *Honours:* Wales Youth, Under-21, B, 4 full caps.
1989–90 Carlisle U 12 0
1990–91 Carlisle U 36 5 **48 5**
1990–91 Bristol C 0 0
1991–92 Bristol C 20 1
1992–93 Bristol C 18 0
1993–94 Bristol C 38 2
1994–95 Bristol C 30 0
1995–96 Bristol C 19 0
1996–97 Bristol C 31 0
1997–98 Bristol C 37 2
1998–99 Bristol C 23 0 **216 5**
1999–2000 Preston NE 41 2
2000-01 Preston NE 42 0
2001-02 Preston NE 36 2
2002-03 Preston NE 26 0 **145 4**

ELEBERT, David (D) 0 0
b.Dublin 21-3-86
Source: Scholar.
2002-03 Preston NE 0 0

ETUHU, Dixon (M) 67 9
H: 6 2 W: 13 00 b.Kano 8-6-82
Source: Scholarship.
1999–2000 Manchester C 0 0
2000-01 Manchester C 0 0
2001-02 Manchester C 12 0 **12 0**
2001-02 Preston NE 16 3
2002-03 Preston NE 39 6 **55 9**

FULLER, Ricardo (F) 53 17
H: 6 3 W: 13 03 b.Kingston, Jamaica 31-10-79
Source: Tivoli Gardens. *Honours:* Jamaica full caps.
2000-01 Crystal Palace 8 0 **8 0**
2001-02 Hearts 27 8 **27 8**
From Tivoli Gardens.
2002-03 Preston NE 18 9 **18 9**

GOULD, Jonathan (G) 173 0
H: 6 1 W: 12 07 b.Paddington 18-7-68
Source: Clevedon T. *Honours:* Scotland B, 2 full caps..
1990–91 Halifax T 23 0
1991–92 Halifax T 9 0 **32 0**
1991–92 WBA 0 0
1992–93 Coventry C 9 0
1993–94 Coventry C 9 0
1994–95 Coventry C 7 0
1995–96 Coventry C 0 0 **25 0**
1995–96 *Bradford C* 9 0
1996–97 Bradford C 9 0 **18 0**
1996–97 *Gillingham* 3 0 **3 0**
1997–98 Celtic 35 0
1998–99 Celtic 28 0
1999–2000 Celtic 0 0
2000-01 Celtic 15 0
2001-02 Celtic 1 0
2002-03 Celtic 2 0 **81 0**
2002-03 Preston NE 14 0 **14 0**

HALLAM, Tony‡ (D) 0 0
H: 6 1 W: 13 11 b.Ormskirk 12-3-83
Source: Scholar.
2002-03 Preston NE 0 0

HEALY, David (F) 120 29
H: 5 7 W: 11 05 b.Downpatrick 5-8-79
Source: Trainee. *Honours:* Northern Ireland Schools, Youth, Under-21, B, 26 full caps, 8 goals.
1997–98 Manchester U 0 0
1998–99 Manchester U 0 0
1999–2000 Manchester U 0 0
1999–2000 *Port Vale* 16 3 **16 3**
2000-01 Manchester U 1 0 **1 0**
2000-01 Preston NE 22 9
2001-02 Preston NE 44 10
2002-03 Preston NE 24 5 **90 24**
2002-03 *Norwich C* 13 2 **13 2**

JACKSON, Michael (D) 338 26
H: 6 0 W: 13 07 b.Chester 4-12-73
Source: Trainee.
1991–92 Crewe Alex 1 0
1992–93 Crewe Alex 4 0 **5 0**
1993–94 Bury 39 0
1994–95 Bury 24 2
1995–96 Bury 31 4
1996–97 Bury 31 3 **125 9**
1996–97 Preston NE 7 0
1997–98 Preston NE 40 2
1998–99 Preston NE 44 8
1999–2000 Preston NE 46 5
2000-01 Preston NE 30 1
2001-02 Preston NE 13 0
2002-03 Preston NE 22 1 **202 17**
2002-03 *Tranmere R* 6 0 **6 0**

KEANE, Michael (M) 34 4
H: 5 4 W: 13 07 b.Dublin 29-12-82
Source: Scholar. *Honours:* Eire Under-21.
2000-01 Preston NE 2 0
2001-02 Preston NE 20 2
2002-03 Preston NE 5 0 **27 2**
2002-03 *Grimsby T* 7 2 **7 2**

KOUMANTARAKIS, George# (F) 156 52
H: 6 3 W: 13 03 b.South Africa 27-3-74
Source: AmaZulu, Manning R, Supersport U. *Honours:* South Africa 11 full caps, 1 goal.
1997–98 Supersport U 35 14 **35 14**
1998–99 Lucerne 27 9 **27 9**
1999–2000 Basle 32 13
2000-01 Basle 13 3
2001-02 Basle 28 10
2002-03 Basle 11 0 **84 26**
2002-03 Preston NE 10 3 **10 3**

LEWIS, Eddie (M) 169 14
H: 5 10 W: 11 02 b.California 17-5-74
Honours: USA 49 full caps, 3 goals.
1996 San Jose Clash 25 0
1997 San Jose Clash 29 2
1998 San Jose Clash 32 3
1999 San Jose Clash 29 4 **115 9**
1999–2000 Fulham 8 0
2000-01 Fulham 7 0
2001-02 Fulham 1 0 **16 0**
2002-03 Preston NE 38 5 **38 5**

LONERGAN, Andrew (G) 3 0
H: 6 4 W: 13 10 b.Preston 19-10-83
Source: Scholar. *Honours:* England Youth, Under-20.
2000-01 Preston NE 1 0
2001-02 Preston NE 0 0
2002-03 Preston NE 0 0 **1 0**
2002-03 *Darlington* 2 0 **2 0**

LUCAS, David (G) 139 0
H: 6 0 W: 12 04 b.Preston 23-11-77
Source: Trainee. *Honours:* England Youth.
1995–96 Preston NE 1 0
1995–96 *Darlington* 6 0
1996–97 Preston NE 2 0
1996–97 *Darlington* 7 0 **13 0**
1996–97 *Scunthorpe U* 6 0 **6 0**
1997–98 Preston NE 6 0
1998–99 Preston NE 31 0
1999–2000 Preston NE 6 0
2000-01 Preston NE 29 0
2001-02 Preston NE 24 0
2002-03 Preston NE 21 0 **120 0**

LUCKETTI, Chris (D) 465 15
H: 6 0 W: 13 04 b.Littleborough 28-9-71
Source: Trainee.
1988–89 Rochdale 1 0
1989–90 Rochdale 0 0 **1 0**
1990–91 Stockport Co 0 0
1991–92 Halifax T 36 0
1992–93 Halifax T 42 2 **78 2**
1993–94 Bury 27 1
1994–95 Bury 39 3
1995–96 Bury 42 1
1996–97 Bury 38 0
1997–98 Bury 46 2
1998–99 Bury 43 1 **235 8**
1999–2000 Huddersfield T 26 0
2000-01 Huddersfield T 40 1
2001-02 Huddersfield T 2 0 **68 1**
2001-02 Preston NE 40 2
2002-03 Preston NE 43 2 **83 4**

LYNCH, Simon (M) 21 4
b.Montreal 19-5-82
Honours: Scotland Under-21.
1999–2000 Celtic 2 1
2000-01 Celtic 0 0
2001-02 Celtic 1 2
2002-03 Celtic 1 0 **4 3**
2002-03 Preston NE 17 1 **17 1**

McCORMICK, Alan (M) 0 0
b.Dublin 10-1-84
2002-03 Preston NE 0 0

McKENNA, Paul (M) 193 15
H: 5 5 W: 13 03 b.Eccleston 29-10-77
Source: Trainee.
1995–96 Preston NE 0 0
1996–97 Preston NE 5 1
1997–98 Preston NE 5 0
1998–99 Preston NE 36 0
1999–2000 Preston NE 24 2
2000-01 Preston NE 44 5
2001-02 Preston NE 38 4
2002-03 Preston NE 41 3 **193 15**

MEARS, Tyrone (D) 23 1
H: 5 10 W: 12 03 b.Stockport 18-2-83
2000-01 Manchester C 0 0
2001-02 Manchester C 1 0 **1 0**
2002-03 Preston NE 22 1 **22 1**

MOILANEN, Teuvo (G) 267 0
H: 6 5 W: 11 10 b.Oulu 12-12-73
Honours: Finland Under-21, 3 full caps.
1990 Ilves 3 0
1991 Ilves 7 0
1992 Ilves 29 0
1993 Ilves 5 0
1994 Ilves 19 0 **63 0**
1995 Jaro 26 0 **26 0**
1995–96 Preston NE 2 0
1996–97 Preston NE 4 0
1996–97 *Scarborough* 4 0 **4 0**
1996–97 *Darlington* 16 0 **16 0**
1997–98 Preston NE 40 0
1998–99 Preston NE 15 0
1999–2000 Preston NE 41 0
2000-01 Preston NE 17 0
2001-02 Preston NE 24 0
2002-03 Preston NE 15 0 **158 0**

MURDOCK, Colin* (D) 177 6
H: 6 3 W: 13 05 b.Belfast 12-7-76
Source: Trainee. *Honours:* Northern Ireland Schools, Youth, B, 17 full caps.
1992–93 Manchester U 0 0
1993–94 Manchester U 0 0
1994–95 Manchester U 0 0
1995–96 Manchester U 0 0
1996–97 Manchester U 0 0
1997–98 Preston NE 27 1
1998–99 Preston NE 33 1
1999–2000 Preston NE 33 2
2000-01 Preston NE 37 0
2001-02 Preston NE 23 2
2002-03 Preston NE 24 0 **177 6**

O'NEIL, Brian (M) 236 12
H: 6 0 W: 13 10 b.Paisley 6-9-72
Source: X Form. *Honours:* Scotland Schools, Youth, Under-21, 6 full caps.
1991–92 Celtic 28 1
1992–93 Celtic 17 3
1993–94 Celtic 28 2
1994–95 Celtic 26 0
1995–96 Celtic 5 0
1996–97 Celtic 16 2 **120 8**

1996–97 *Nottingham F* 5 0 **5 0**
1997–98 Aberdeen 29 1 **29 1**
1998–99 Wolfsburg 26 2
1999–2000 Wolfsburg 16 1
2000-01 Wolfsburg 8 0 **50 3**
2000-01 Derby Co 4 0
2001-02 Derby Co 10 0
2002-03 Derby Co 3 0 **17 0**
2002-03 Preston NE 15 0 **15 0**

O'NEILL, Joe (F) 0 0
H: 6 0 W: 10 05 b.Blackburn 28-10-82
Source: Scholar.
2001-02 Preston NE 0 0
2002-03 Preston NE 0 0

ONIBUJE, Folawiyo (M) 0 0
b.Lagos 25-9-84
2002-03 Preston NE 0 0

RANKINE, Mark (M) 535 33
H: 5 7 W: 12 01 b.Doncaster 30-9-69
Source: Trainee.
1987–88 Doncaster R 18 2
1988–89 Doncaster R 46 11
1989–90 Doncaster R 36 2
1990–91 Doncaster R 40 2
1991–92 Doncaster R 24 3 **164 20**
1991–92 Wolverhampton W 15 1
1992–93 Wolverhampton W 27 0
1993–94 Wolverhampton W 31 0
1994–95 Wolverhampton W 27 0
1995–96 Wolverhampton W 32 0
1996–97 Wolverhampton W 0 0 **132 1**
1996–97 Preston NE 23 0
1997–98 Preston NE 35 1
1998–99 Preston NE 42 3
1999–2000 Preston NE 44 0
2000-01 Preston NE 44 4
2001-02 Preston NE 26 4
2002-03 Preston NE 19 0 **233 12**
2002-03 *Sheffield U* 6 0 **6 0**

SKORA, Eric (M) 40 0
H: 5 10 W: 11 00 b.Metz 20-8-81
2001-02 Preston NE 4 0
2002-03 Preston NE 36 0 **40 0**

WRIGHT, Mark (F) 3 0
H: 5 10 W: 11 07 b.Chorley 4-9-81
Source: Schoolboy.
1998–99 Preston NE 1 0
1999–2000 Preston NE 2 0
2000-01 Preston NE 0 0
2001-02 Preston NE 0 0
2002-03 Preston NE 0 0 **3 0**

Scholars
Armstrong, Kyle; Brown, Michael; Carvill, Paul G; Clampitt, Carl E; Curwen, George E; Davies, John M; Forker, Paul J; Jackson, Mark P; Kempson, Darran K; Kewley, Michael; Kitchen, Benjamin; Langmead, Kelvin S; Lyng, Ciaran; Neal, Christopher M
Players who do not hold a current contract but their registration has been retained by the club
Wilkinson, Craig R

QPR

ANGELL, Brett# (F) 465 164
H: 6 2 W: 13 11 b.Marlborough 20-8-68
Source: Portsmouth, Cheltenham T.
1987–88 Derby Co 0 0
1988–89 Stockport Co 26 5
1989–90 Stockport Co 44 23
1990–91 Southend U 42 15
1991–92 Southend U 43 21
1992–93 Southend U 13 5
1993–94 Southend U 5 4
1993–94 *Everton* 1 0
1993–94 Southend U 12 2 **115 47**
1993–94 Everton 15 1
1994–95 Everton 4 0 **20 1**
1994–95 Sunderland 8 0
1995–96 Sunderland 2 0
1995–96 *Sheffield U* 6 2 **6 2**
1995–96 *WBA* 3 0 **3 0**
1996–97 Sunderland 0 0 **10 0**
1996–97 Stockport Co 34 15
1997–98 Stockport Co 45 18
1998–99 Stockport Co 42 17
1999–2000 Stockport Co 5 0 **196 78**
1999–2000 *Notts Co* 6 5 **6 5**
1999–2000 *Preston NE* 15 8 **15 8**
2000-01 Walsall 41 13
2001-02 Walsall 20 3 **61 16**
2001-02 Rushden & D 5 2 **5 2**
2002-03 Port Vale 15 5 **15 5**
2002-03 QPR 13 0 **13 0**

BEAN, Marcus§ (M) 7 0
H: 5 11 W: 11 06 b.Hammersmith 2-11-84
Source: Scholar.
2002-03 QPR 7 0 **7 0**

BIRCHAM, Marc (M) 140 5
H: 5 11 W: 11 06 b.Hammersmith 11-5-78
Source: Trainee. *Honours:* Canada 13 full caps, 1 goal.
1996–97 Millwall 6 0
1997–98 Millwall 4 0
1998–99 Millwall 28 0
1999–2000 Millwall 22 1
2000-01 Millwall 20 2
2001-02 Millwall 24 0 **104 3**
2002-03 QPR 36 2 **36 2**

BRADY, Richard‡ (F) 0 0
H: 5 8 W: 10 04 b.Dartford 17-9-82
Source: Trainee.
1999–2000 QPR 0 0
2000-01 QPR 0 0
2001-02 QPR 0 0
2002-03 QPR 0 0

BURGESS, Oliver§ (M) 10 1
H: 5 10 W: 11 07 b.Ascot 12-10-81
Source: Scholar.
2000-01 QPR 1 0
2001-02 QPR 4 1
2002-03 QPR 5 0 **10 1**

CARLISLE, Clarke (D) 156 12
H: 6 3 W: 12 07 b.Preston 14-10-79
Source: Trainee. *Honours:* England Under-21.
1997–98 Blackpool 11 2
1998–99 Blackpool 39 1
1999–2000 Blackpool 43 4 **93 7**
2000-01 QPR 27 3
2001-02 QPR 0 0
2002-03 QPR 36 2 **63 5**

CONNOLLY, Karl* (F) 430 100
H: 5 10 W: 11 08 b.Prescot 9-2-70
Source: Napoli (Liverpool Sunday League).
1990–91 Wrexham 0 0
1991–92 Wrexham 36 8
1992–93 Wrexham 42 9
1993–94 Wrexham 39 2
1994–95 Wrexham 45 10
1995–96 Wrexham 46 18
1996–97 Wrexham 30 14
1997–98 Wrexham 35 7
1998–99 Wrexham 44 11
1999–2000 Wrexham 41 9 **358 88**
2000-01 QPR 23 4
2001-02 QPR 33 4
2002-03 QPR 16 4 **72 12**

CULKIN, Nick (G) 88 0
H: 6 2 W: 13 07 b.York 6-7-78
Source: York C.
1995–96 Manchester U 0 0
1996–97 Manchester U 0 0
1997–98 Manchester U 0 0
1998–99 Manchester U 0 0
1999–2000 Manchester U 1 0
1999–2000 *Hull C* 4 0 **4 0**
2000-01 Manchester U 0 0
2000-01 *Bristol R* 45 0 **45 0**
2001-02 Manchester U 0 0 **1 0**
2001-02 *Livingston* 21 0 **21 0**
2002-03 QPR 17 0 **17 0**

D'AUSTIN, Ryan* (M) 0 0
H: 5 9 W: 10 13 b.Edgware 29-11-82
Source: Trainee.
1999–2000 QPR 0 0
2000-01 QPR 0 0
2001-02 QPR 0 0
2002-03 QPR 0 0

DALY, Wesley§ (M) 7 0
H: 5 9 W: 11 00 b.Hammersmith 7-3-84
Source: Scholar.
2001-02 QPR 1 0
2002-03 QPR 6 0 **7 0**

DAY, Chris# (G) 77 0
H: 6 2 W: 13 06 b.Whipps Cross 28-7-75
Source: Trainee. *Honours:* England Under-21.
1992–93 Tottenham H 0 0
1993–94 Tottenham H 0 0
1994–95 Tottenham H 0 0
1995–96 Tottenham H 0 0
1996–97 Crystal Palace 24 0 **24 0**
1997–98 Watford 0 0
1998–99 Watford 0 0
1999–2000 Watford 11 0
2000-01 Watford 0 0 **11 0**
2000-01 *Lincoln C* 14 0 **14 0**
2001-02 QPR 16 0
2002-03 QPR 12 0 **28 0**

DODOU, Ebeli M'bombo* (F) 46 3
H: 5 5 W: 9 11 b.Kinshasa 11-9-80
2001-02 QPR 36 3
2002-03 QPR 10 0 **46 3**

DUNCAN, Lyndon* (D) 0 0
H: 5 8 W: 11 02 b.Ealing 12-1-83
Source: Trainee. *Honours:* England Youth, Under-20.
1999–2000 QPR 0 0
2000-01 QPR 0 0
2001-02 QPR 0 0
2002-03 QPR 0 0

FITZGERALD, Brian* (M) 1 0
H: 5 9 W: 12 00 b.Perivale 23-10-83
Source: School.
2000-01 QPR 0 0
2001-02 QPR 1 0
2002-03 QPR 0 0 **1 0**

FORBES, Terrell (D) 84 0
H: 6 0 W: 12 05 b.Southwark 17-8-81
Source: Trainee.
1999–2000 West Ham U 0 0
1999–2000 *Bournemouth* 3 0 **3 0**
2000-01 West Ham U 0 0
2001-02 QPR 43 0
2002-03 QPR 38 0 **81 0**

FURLONG, Paul (F) 351 120
H: 6 0 W: 13 11 b.London 1-10-68
Source: Enfield.
1991–92 Coventry C 37 4 **37 4**
1992–93 Watford 41 19
1993–94 Watford 38 18 **79 37**
1994–95 Chelsea 36 10
1995–96 Chelsea 28 3 **64 13**
1996–97 Birmingham C 43 10
1997–98 Birmingham C 25 15
1998–99 Birmingham C 29 13
1999–2000 Birmingham C 19 11
2000-01 Birmingham C 4 0
2000-01 *QPR* 3 1
2001-02 Birmingham C 11 1
2001-02 *Sheffield U* 4 2 **4 2**
2002-03 Birmingham C 0 0 **131 50**
2002-03 QPR 33 13 **36 14**

GALLEN, Kevin (F) 285 68
H: 5 11 W: 13 05 b.Hammersmith 21-9-75
Source: Trainee. *Honours:* England Schools, Youth, Under-21.
1992–93 QPR 0 0
1993–94 QPR 0 0
1994–95 QPR 37 10
1995–96 QPR 30 8
1996–97 QPR 2 3
1997–98 QPR 27 3
1998–99 QPR 44 8
1999–2000 QPR 31 4
2000-01 Huddersfield T 38 10 **38 10**
2001-02 Barnsley 9 2 **9 2**
2001-02 QPR 25 7
2002-03 QPR 42 13 **238 56**

GRADLEY, Patrick* (M) 0 0
b.London 1-6-83
Source: Scholar.
2000-01 QPR 0 0
2001-02 QPR 0 0
2002-03 QPR 0 0

GRIFFITHS, Leroy (F) 36 3
H: 5 11 W: 13 05 b.London 30-12-76
Source: Hampton & Richmond B.
2000-01 QPR 0 0
2001-02 QPR 30 3
2002-03 QPR 6 0 **36 3**

LANGLEY, Richard (M) 132 17
H: 6 0 W: 12 06 b.London 27-12-79
Source: Trainee. *Honours:* England Youth. Jamaica 6 full caps.
1996–97 QPR 0 0
1997–98 QPR 0 0
1998–99 QPR 8 1
1999–2000 QPR 41 3

2000-01 QPR 26 1
2001-02 QPR 18 3
2002-03 QPR 39 9 **132 17**

MURPHY, Danny* (D) 23 0
H: 5 6 W: 10 04 b.London 4-12-82
Source: Trainee.
1999–2000 QPR 0 0
2000-01 QPR 0 0
2001-02 QPR 12 0
2002-03 QPR 11 0 **23 0**

OLI, Dennis (F) 20 0
H: 6 0 W: 12 00 b.Newham 28-1-84
2001-02 QPR 2 0
2002-03 QPR 18 0 **20 0**

PACQUETTE, Richard (F) 29 6
H: 5 11 W: 13 12 b.Paddington 28-1-83
Source: Trainee.
1999–2000 QPR 0 0
2000-01 QPR 2 0
2001-02 QPR 16 2
2002-03 QPR 11 4 **29 6**

PADULA, Gino# (D) 50 1
H: 5 9 W: 12 11 b.Buenos Aires 11-7-76
Source: Xerex.
1999–2000 Bristol R 0 0
1999–2000 Walsall 25 0 **25 0**
2000-01 Wigan Ath 4 0
2001-02 Wigan Ath 0 0 **4 0**
2002-03 QPR 21 1 **21 1**

PALMER, Steve# (D) 438 15
H: 6 1 W: 12 13 b.Brighton 31-3-68
Source: Cambridge Univ. *Honours:* England Schools.
1989–90 Ipswich T 5 0
1990–91 Ipswich T 23 1
1991–92 Ipswich T 23 0
1992–93 Ipswich T 7 0
1993–94 Ipswich T 36 1
1994–95 Ipswich T 12 0
1995–96 Ipswich T 5 0 **111 2**
1995–96 Watford 35 1
1996–97 Watford 41 2
1997–98 Watford 41 2
1998–99 Watford 41 2
1999–2000 Watford 38 0
2000-01 Watford 39 1 **235 8**
2001-02 QPR 46 4
2002-03 QPR 46 1 **92 5**

PLUMMER, Chris* (D) 64 2
H: 6 2 W: 13 08 b.Isleworth 12-10-76
Source: Trainee. *Honours:* England Youth, Under-21.
1994–95 QPR 0 0
1995–96 QPR 1 0
1996–97 QPR 5 0
1997–98 QPR 0 0
1998–99 QPR 10 0
1999–2000 QPR 18 0
2000-01 QPR 25 2
2001-02 QPR 1 0
2002-03 QPR 2 0 **62 2**
2002-03 *Bristol R* 2 0 **2 0**

ROSE, Matthew (D) 173 6
H: 5 11 W: 12 02 b.Dartford 24-9-75
Source: Trainee. *Honours:* England Under-21.
1994–95 Arsenal 0 0
1995–96 Arsenal 4 0
1996–97 Arsenal 1 0 **5 0**
1997–98 QPR 16 0
1998–99 QPR 29 0
1999–2000 QPR 29 1
2000-01 QPR 27 0
2001-02 QPR 39 3
2002-03 QPR 28 2 **168 6**

SHITTU, Dan (D) 87 11
H: 6 2 W: 16 03 b.Lagos 2-9-80
Honours: Nigeria 1 full cap.
1999–2000 Charlton Ath 0 0
2000-01 Charlton Ath 0 0
2000-01 *Blackpool* 17 2 **17 2**
2001-02 Charlton Ath 0 0
2001-02 QPR 27 2
2002-03 QPR 43 7 **70 9**

THOMSON, Andy (F) 454 170
H: 5 11 W: 11 11 b.Motherwell 1-4-71
Source: Jerviston BC.
1989–90 Q of S 26 6
1990–91 Q of S 37 11
1991–92 Q of S 39 26
1992–93 Q of S 38 21
1993–94 Q of S 35 29 **175 93**
1994–95 Southend U 39 11
1995–96 Southend U 33 6
1996–97 Southend U 17 5
1997–98 Southend U 33 6 **122 28**
1998–99 Oxford U 38 7 **38 7**
1999–2000 Gillingham 28 9
2000-01 Gillingham 24 5 **52 14**
2000-01 QPR 8 4
2001-02 QPR 38 21
2002-03 QPR 21 3 **67 28**

WALSHE, Ben (M) 2 0
H: 5 11 W: 12 12 b.Hammersmith 24-5-83
Source: Scholar.
2000-01 QPR 1 0
2001-02 QPR 0 0
2002-03 QPR 1 0 **2 0**

WATTLEY, David* (M) 0 0
b.Enfield 5-9-83
Source: School.
2000-01 QPR 0 0
2001-02 QPR 0 0
2002-03 QPR 0 0

Scholars
Bean, Marcus T; Burgess, Oliver D; Butler, Kerry RJ; Cole, Jake; Daly, Wesley JP; Herron, Christopher J; Ifura, Marien M; Lewis, Daniel G; Lodge, Dean; Mills, Christopher I; Ramsey, Matthew J; Scully, Samuel I; Stanp, Nathan; Williams, Martyn

READING

ALLAWAY, Ricky‡ (D) 0 0
H: 6 2 W: 12 05 b.Reading 16-2-83
Source: Trainee.
1999–2000 Reading 0 0
2000-01 Reading 0 0
2001-02 Reading 0 0
2002-03 Reading 0 0

ASHDOWN, Jamie (G) 5 0
H: 6 1 W: 12 05 b.Reading 30-11-80
1999–2000 Reading 0 0
2000-01 Reading 1 0
2001-02 Reading 1 0
2001-02 *Arsenal* 0 0
2002-03 Reading 1 0 **3 0**
2002-03 *Bournemouth* 2 0 **2 0**

BOUCAUD, Andre (M) 6 0
H: 5 10 W: 11 04 b.Enfield 9-10-84
Source: Scholar.
2001-02 Reading 0 0
2002-03 Reading 0 0
2002-03 *Peterborough U* 6 0 **6 0**

BROWN, Steve (D) 263 10
H: 6 1 W: 14 10 b.Brighton 13-5-72
Source: Trainee.
1990–91 Charlton Ath 0 0
1991–92 Charlton Ath 1 0
1992–93 Charlton Ath 0 0
1993–94 Charlton Ath 19 0
1994–95 Charlton Ath 42 3
1995–96 Charlton Ath 19 0
1996–97 Charlton Ath 27 0
1997–98 Charlton Ath 34 2
1998–99 Charlton Ath 18 0
1999–2000 Charlton Ath 40 2
2000-01 Charlton Ath 25 0
2001-02 Charlton Ath 14 2
2002-03 Charlton Ath 3 0 **242 9**
2002-03 Reading 21 1 **21 1**

BUTLER, Martin (F) 277 81
H: 5 11 W: 12 00 b.Wordsley 15-9-74
Source: Trainee.
1993–94 Walsall 15 3
1994–95 Walsall 8 0
1995–96 Walsall 28 4
1996–97 Walsall 23 1 **74 8**
1997–98 Cambridge U 31 10
1998–99 Cambridge U 46 17
1999–2000 Cambridge U 26 14 **103 41**
1999–2000 Reading 17 4
2000-01 Reading 45 24
2001-02 Reading 17 2
2002-03 Reading 21 2 **100 32**

CAMPBELL, Darren (M) 1 0
H: 5 8 W: 10 08 b.Huntingdon 16-4-86
Source: Scholar. *Honours:* England Youth.
2002-03 Reading 1 0 **1 0**

CASTLE, Peter‡ (D) 1 0
b.Southampton 12-3-87
Source: Scholar. *Honours:* FA Schools.
2002-03 Reading 1 0 **1 0**

CURETON, Jamie# (F) 316 128
H: 5 8 W: 12 08 b.Bristol 28-8-75
Source: Trainee. *Honours:* England Youth.
1992–93 Norwich C 0 0
1993–94 Norwich C 0 0
1994–95 Norwich C 17 4
1995–96 Norwich C 12 2
1995–96 *Bournemouth* 5 0 **5 0**
1996–97 Norwich C 0 0 **29 6**
1996–97 Bristol R 38 11
1997–98 Bristol R 43 13
1998–99 Bristol R 46 25
1999–2000 Bristol R 46 22
2000-01 Bristol R 1 1 **174 72**
2000-01 Reading 43 26
2001-02 Reading 38 15
2002-03 Reading 27 9 **108 50**

FORSTER, Nicky (F) 371 120
H: 5 8 W: 11 05 b.Caterham 8-9-73
Source: Horley T. *Honours:* England Under-21.
1992–93 Gillingham 26 6
1993–94 Gillingham 41 18 **67 24**
1994–95 Brentford 46 24
1995–96 Brentford 38 5
1996–97 Brentford 25 10 **109 39**
1996–97 Birmingham C 7 3
1997–98 Birmingham C 28 3
1998–99 Birmingham C 33 5 **68 11**
1999–2000 Reading 36 10
2000-01 Reading 9 1
2001-02 Reading 42 19
2002-03 Reading 40 16 **127 46**

GAMBLE, Joe (M) 7 0
H: 5 7 W: 11 00 b.Cork 14-1-82
Source: Cork C. *Honours:* Eire Under-21.
2000-01 Reading 1 0
2001-02 Reading 6 0
2002-03 Reading 0 0 **7 0**

HAHNEMANN, Marcus (G) 120 0
H: 6 3 W: 16 04 b.Seattle 15-6-72
Honours: USA 4 full caps.
1997 Colorado Rapids 25 0
1998 Colorado Rapids 28 0
1999 Colorado Rapids 13 0 **66 0**
1999–2000 Fulham 0 0
2000-01 Fulham 2 0
2001-02 Fulham 0 0 **2 0**
2001-02 *Rochdale* 5 0 **5 0**
2001-02 *Reading* 6 0
2002-03 Reading 41 0 **47 0**

HARPER, James (M) 77 4
H: 5 10 W: 11 02 b.Chelmsford 9-11-80
Source: Trainee.
1999–2000 Arsenal 0 0
2000-01 Arsenal 0 0
2000-01 *Cardiff C* 3 0 **3 0**
2000-01 Reading 12 1
2001-02 Reading 26 1
2002-03 Reading 36 2 **74 4**

HENDERSON, Darius (F) 70 11
H: 6 2 W: 13 02 b.Doncaster 7-9-81
Source: Trainee.
1999–2000 Reading 6 0
2000-01 Reading 4 0
2001-02 Reading 38 7
2002-03 Reading 22 4 **70 11**

HUGHES, Andy (M) 225 33
H: 5 11 W: 12 01 b.Manchester 2-1-78
Source: Trainee.
1995–96 Oldham Ath 15 1
1996–97 Oldham Ath 8 0
1997–98 Oldham Ath 10 0 **33 1**
1997–98 Notts Co 15 2
1998–99 Notts Co 30 3
1999–2000 Notts Co 35 7
2000-01 Notts Co 30 5 **110 17**
2001-02 Reading 39 6
2002-03 Reading 43 9 **82 15**

IGOE, Sammy* (M) **249 18**
H: 5 6 W: 9 07 b.Spelthorne 30-9-75
Source: Trainee.

1993–94	Portsmouth	0	0		
1994–95	Portsmouth	1	0		
1995–96	Portsmouth	22	0		
1996–97	Portsmouth	40	2		
1997–98	Portsmouth	31	3		
1998–99	Portsmouth	40	5		
1999–2000	Portsmouth	26	1	**160**	**11**
1999–2000	Reading	6	0		
2000-01	Reading	31	6		
2001-02	Reading	35	1		
2002-03	Reading	15	0	**87**	**7**
2002-03	*Luton T*	2	0	**2**	**0**

MACKIE, John (D) **62 2**
H: 6 1 W: 13 00 b.London 5-7-76
Source: Sutton U.

1999–2000	Reading	0	0		
2000-01	Reading	10	0		
2001-02	Reading	27	2		
2002-03	Reading	25	0	**62**	**2**

MURTY, Graeme (M) **253 8**
H: 5 10 W: 11 11 b.Saltburn 13-11-74
Source: Trainee.

1992–93	York C	0	0		
1993–94	York C	1	0		
1994–95	York C	20	2		
1995–96	York C	35	2		
1996–97	York C	27	2		
1997–98	York C	34	1	**117**	**7**
1998–99	Reading	9	0		
1999–2000	Reading	17	0		
2000-01	Reading	23	1		
2001-02	Reading	43	0		
2002-03	Reading	44	0	**136**	**1**

NEWMAN, Ricky# (D) **282 10**
H: 5 11 W: 12 03 b.Guildford 5-8-70
Source: Trainee.

1987–88	Crystal Palace	0	0		
1988–89	Crystal Palace	0	0		
1989–90	Crystal Palace	0	0		
1990–91	Crystal Palace	0	0		
1991–92	Crystal Palace	0	0		
1991–92	*Maidstone U*	10	1	**10**	**1**
1992–93	Crystal Palace	2	0		
1993–94	Crystal Palace	11	0		
1994–95	Crystal Palace	35	3	**48**	**3**
1995–96	Millwall	36	1		
1996–97	Millwall	41	3		
1997–98	Millwall	35	1		
1998–99	Millwall	24	0		
1999–2000	Millwall	14	0	**150**	**5**
1999–2000	*Reading*	7	1		
2000-01	Reading	39	0		
2001-02	Reading	0	0		
2002-03	Reading	28	0	**74**	**1**

PARKINSON, Phil‡ (M) **507 25**
H: 6 0 W: 12 09 b.Chorley 1-12-67
Source: Apprentice.

1985–86	Southampton	0	0		
1986–87	Southampton	0	0		
1987–88	Southampton	0	0		
1987–88	Bury	8	1		
1988–89	Bury	39	0		
1989–90	Bury	22	2		
1990–91	Bury	44	2		
1991–92	Bury	32	0	**145**	**5**
1992–93	Reading	39	4		
1993–94	Reading	42	3		
1994–95	Reading	31	0		
1995–96	Reading	42	0		
1996–97	Reading	24	1		
1997–98	Reading	37	0		
1998–99	Reading	42	5		
1999–2000	Reading	22	1		
2000-01	Reading	44	4		
2001-02	Reading	33	2		
2002-03	Reading	6	0	**362**	**20**

RIFAT, Ahmet (D) **0 0**
H: 6 1 W: 11 06 b.London 3-1-86
Source: Scholar. *Honours:* England Youth.

2002-03	Reading	0	0		

ROUGIER, Tony* (F) **232 22**
H: 6 0 W: 14 11 b.Trinidad 17-7-71
Source: Trinity Pros. *Honours:* Trinidad & Tobago full caps.

1994–95	Raith R	4	0		
1995–96	Raith R	22	1		
1996–97	Raith R	30	1	**56**	**2**
1997–98	Hibernian	20	3		
1998–99	Hibernian	15	1	**35**	**4**
1998–99	Port Vale	13	0		
1999–2000	Port Vale	38	8	**51**	**8**
2000-01	Reading	31	2		
2001-02	Reading	33	1		
2002-03	Reading	20	3	**84**	**6**
2002-03	*Brighton & HA*	6	2	**6**	**2**

SALAKO, John (M) **438 42**
H: 5 9 W: 12 03 b.Nigeria 11-2-69
Source: Trainee. *Honours:* England 5 full caps.

1986–87	Crystal Palace	4	0		
1987–88	Crystal Palace	31	0		
1988–89	Crystal Palace	28	0		
1989–90	Crystal Palace	17	2		
1989–90	*Swansea C*	13	3	**13**	**3**
1990–91	Crystal Palace	35	6		
1991–92	Crystal Palace	10	2		
1992–93	Crystal Palace	13	0		
1993–94	Crystal Palace	38	8		
1994–95	Crystal Palace	39	4	**215**	**22**
1995–96	Coventry C	37	3		
1996–97	Coventry C	24	1		
1997–98	Coventry C	11	0	**72**	**4**
1997–98	Bolton W	7	0	**7**	**0**
1998–99	Fulham	10	1		
1999–2000	Fulham	0	0	**10**	**1**
1999–2000	Charlton Ath	27	2		
2000-01	Charlton Ath	17	0		
2001-02	Charlton Ath	3	0	**47**	**2**
2001-02	Reading	31	6		
2002-03	Reading	43	4	**74**	**10**

SAVAGE, Bas (F) **1 0**
H: 6 4 W: 13 08 b.London 7-1-82
Source: Walton & Hersham.

2001-02	Reading	1	0		
2002-03	Reading	0	0	**1**	**0**

SHOREY, Nicky (D) **90 2**
H: 5 8 W: 10 05 b.Romford 19-2-81
Source: Trainee.

1999–2000	Leyton Orient	7	0		
2000-01	Leyton Orient	8	0	**15**	**0**
2000-01	Reading	0	0		
2001-02	Reading	32	0		
2002-03	Reading	43	2	**75**	**2**

SIDWELL, Steven (M) **55 11**
H: 5 10 W: 11 02 b.Wandsworth 14-12-82
Source: Scholar. *Honours:* England Under-20, Under-21.

2001-02	Arsenal	0	0		
2001-02	*Brentford*	30	4	**30**	**4**
2002-03	Arsenal	0	0		
2002-03	*Brighton & HA*	12	5	**12**	**5**
2002-03	Reading	13	2	**13**	**2**

SMITH, Alex* (M) **154 7**
H: 5 9 W: 10 06 b.Liverpool 15-2-76
Source: Trainee.

1994–95	Everton	0	0		
1995–96	Everton	0	0		
1995–96	Swindon T	8	0		
1996–97	Swindon T	18	1		
1997–98	Swindon T	5	0	**31**	**1**
1997–98	Huddersfield T	6	0	**6**	**0**
1998–99	Chester C	32	2	**32**	**2**
1998–99	Port Vale	8	0		
1999–2000	Port Vale	13	0		
2000-01	Port Vale	37	2	**58**	**2**
2001-02	Reading	13	2		
2002-03	Reading	1	0	**14**	**2**
2002-03	*Shrewsbury T*	13	0	**13**	**0**

TYSON, Nathan (F) **44 3**
H: 5 10 W: 10 02 b.Reading 4-5-82
Source: Trainee. *Honours:* England Under-20.

1999–2000	Reading	1	0		
2000-01	Reading	0	0		
2001-02	Reading	1	0		
2001-02	*Swansea C*	11	1	**11**	**1**
2001-02	*Cheltenham T*	8	1	**8**	**1**
2002-03	Reading	23	1	**25**	**1**

VIVEASH, Adrian# (D) **343 19**
H: 6 2 W: 12 12 b.Swindon 30-9-69
Source: Trainee.

1988–89	Swindon T	0	0		
1989–90	Swindon T	0	0		
1990–91	Swindon T	25	1		
1991–92	Swindon T	10	0		
1992–93	Swindon T	5	0		
1992–93	*Reading*	5	0		
1993–94	Swindon T	0	0		
1994–95	Swindon T	14	1		
1994–95	*Reading*	6	0		
1995–96	Swindon T	0	0	**54**	**2**
1995–96	*Barnsley*	2	1	**2**	**1**
1995–96	Walsall	31	0		
1996–97	Walsall	46	9		
1997–98	Walsall	42	3		
1998–99	Walsall	40	0		
1999–2000	Walsall	43	1	**202**	**13**
2000-01	Reading	40	2		
2001-02	Reading	18	1		
2002-03	Reading	5	0	**74**	**3**
2002-03	*Oxford U*	11	0	**11**	**0**

WARREN, Steven* (M) **0 0**
H: 5 11 W: 12 11 b.Slough 27-9-83

2000-01	Crystal Palace	0	0		
2001-02	Crystal Palace	0	0		
2001-02	Reading	0	0		
2002-03	Reading	0	0		

WATSON, Kevin (M) **239 10**
H: 6 0 W: 12 06 b.Hackney 3-1-74
Source: Trainee.

1991–92	Tottenham H	0	0		
1992–93	Tottenham H	5	0		
1993–94	Tottenham H	0	0		
1993–94	*Brentford*	3	0	**3**	**0**
1994–95	Tottenham H	0	0		
1994–95	*Bristol C*	2	0	**2**	**0**
1994–95	*Barnet*	13	0	**13**	**0**
1995–96	Tottenham H	0	0	**5**	**0**
1996–97	Swindon T	27	1		
1997–98	Swindon T	18	0		
1998–99	Swindon T	18	0	**63**	**1**
1999–2000	Rotherham U	44	1		
2000-01	Rotherham U	46	5		
2001-02	Rotherham U	19	1	**109**	**7**
2001-02	Reading	12	1		
2002-03	Reading	32	1	**44**	**2**

WHITBREAD, Adrian‡ (D) **367 5**
H: 6 1 W: 13 05 b.Epping 22-10-71
Source: Trainee.

1989–90	Leyton Orient	8	0		
1990–91	Leyton Orient	38	0		
1991–92	Leyton Orient	43	1		
1992–93	Leyton Orient	36	1	**125**	**2**
1993–94	Swindon T	35	1		
1994–95	Swindon T	1	0	**36**	**1**
1994–95	West Ham U	8	0		
1995–96	West Ham U	2	0		
1995–96	*Portsmouth*	13	0		
1996–97	West Ham U	0	0	**10**	**0**
1996–97	Portsmouth	24	0		
1997–98	Portsmouth	38	1		
1998–99	Portsmouth	33	0		
1999–2000	Portsmouth	39	1		
2000-01	Portsmouth	0	0	**147**	**2**
2000-01	*Luton T*	9	0	**9**	**0**
2000-01	*Reading*	19	0		
2001-02	Reading	14	0		
2002-03	Reading	0	0	**33**	**0**
2002-03	*Exeter C*	7	0	**7**	**0**

WHITEHEAD, Phil‡ (G) **420 0**
H: 6 3 W: 13 07 b.Halifax 17-12-69
Source: Trainee.

1986–87	Halifax T	12	0		
1987–88	Halifax T	0	0		
1988–89	Halifax T	11	0		
1989–90	Halifax T	19	0		
1989–90	Barnsley	0	0		
1990–91	Barnsley	0	0		
1990–91	*Halifax T*	9	0	**51**	**0**
1991–92	Barnsley	3	0		
1991–92	*Scunthorpe U*	8	0		
1992–93	Barnsley	13	0		
1992–93	*Scunthorpe U*	8	0	**16**	**0**
1992–93	*Bradford C*	6	0	**6**	**0**
1993–94	Barnsley	0	0	**16**	**0**
1993–94	Oxford U	39	0		
1994–95	Oxford U	38	0		
1995–96	Oxford U	34	0		
1996–97	Oxford U	43	0		
1997–98	Oxford U	32	0		
1998–99	Oxford U	21	0	**207**	**0**
1998–99	WBA	26	0		
1999–2000	WBA	0	0	**26**	**0**
1999–2000	Reading	11	0		
2000-01	Reading	46	0		
2001-02	Reading	33	0		
2002-03	Reading	4	0	**94**	**0**
2002-03	*Tranmere R*	2	0	**2**	**0**
2002-03	*York C*	2	0	**2**	**0**

WILLIAMS, Adrian (D) **316 17**
H: 6 2 W: 12 06 b.Reading 16-8-71
Source: Trainee. *Honours:* Wales 13 full caps, 1 goal.

1988–89	Reading	8	0		
1989–90	Reading	16	2		
1990–91	Reading	7	0		
1991–92	Reading	40	4		
1992–93	Reading	31	4		
1993–94	Reading	41	0		
1994–95	Reading	22	1		
1995–96	Reading	31	3		
1996–97	Wolverhampton W	6	0		
1997–98	Wolverhampton W	20	0		
1998–99	Wolverhampton W	0	0		
1999–2000	Wolverhampton W	1	0	**27**	**0**
1999–2000	*Reading*	15	1		
2000-01	Reading	5	0		
2001-02	Reading	35	1		
2002-03	Reading	38	1	**289**	**17**

Scholars
Awbery, Jason S; Bailey, Nathan; Bird, Leon; Boddy, Mark S; Bouton, Richard LM; Clarke, Bradie J; Davies, Christopher; Earl, Callum T; Fashanu, Andre; Howell, Simieon; Laidler, Stephen T; Middleton, Gary; Mullins, John C; Noto, Mario; Soares, Louie; Theophanides, Adam; Young, Jamie I

ROCHDALE

BAKER, John* (G) **0 0**
H: 6 0 W: 11 03 b.Kent 23-11-82
Source: Scholar.

2002-03	Rochdale	0	0		

BEECH, Chris (M) **265 39**
H: 5 11 W: 11 12 b.Blackpool 16-9-74
Source: Trainee.

1992–93	Blackpool	1	0		
1993–94	Blackpool	35	2		
1994–95	Blackpool	28	2		
1995–96	Blackpool	18	0	**82**	**4**
1996–97	Hartlepool U	42	7		
1997–98	Hartlepool U	36	6		
1998–99	Hartlepool U	16	9	**94**	**22**
1998–99	Huddersfield T	17	2		
1999–2000	Huddersfield T	35	9		
2000-01	Huddersfield T	10	0		
2001-02	Huddersfield T	9	1	**71**	**12**
2002-03	Rochdale	18	1	**18**	**1**

BENNETT, Neil‡ (G) **12 0**
H: 6 0 W: 12 02 b.Dewsbury 29-10-80
Source: Trainee.

2001-02	Airdrieonians	11	0	**11**	**0**
2002-03	Bradford C	0	0		
2002-03	Rochdale	1	0	**1**	**0**

BISHOP, Ian‡ (M) **540 32**
H: 5 10 W: 12 07 b.Liverpool 29-5-65
Source: Apprentice. *Honours:* England B.

1983–84	Everton	1	0		
1983–84	*Crewe Alex*	4	0	**4**	**0**
1984–85	Everton	0	0	**1**	**0**
1984–85	Carlisle U	30	2		
1985–86	Carlisle U	36	6		
1986–87	Carlisle U	42	3		
1987–88	Carlisle U	24	3	**132**	**14**
1988–89	Bournemouth	44	2	**44**	**2**
1989–90	Manchester C	19	2		
1989–90	West Ham U	17	2		
1990–91	West Ham U	40	4		
1991–92	West Ham U	41	1		
1992–93	West Ham U	22	1		
1993–94	West Ham U	36	1		
1994–95	West Ham U	31	1		
1995–96	West Ham U	35	1		
1996–97	West Ham U	29	1		
1997–98	West Ham U	3	0	**254**	**12**
1997–98	Manchester C	6	0		
1998–99	Manchester C	25	0		
1999–2000	Manchester C	37	2		
2000-01	Manchester C	10	0	**97**	**4**
From Barry T.					
2002-03	Rochdale	8	0	**8**	**0**

CONNOR, Paul (F) **124 35**
H: 6 2 W: 11 08 b.Bishop Auckland 12-1-79
Source: Trainee.

1996–97	Middlesbrough	0	0		
1997–98	Middlesbrough	0	0		
1997–98	*Hartlepool U*	5	0	**5**	**0**
1998–99	Middlesbrough	0	0		
1998–99	*Stoke C*	3	2		
1999–2000	Stoke C	26	5		
2000-01	Stoke C	7	0	**36**	**7**
2000-01	*Cambridge U*	13	5	**13**	**5**
2000-01	Rochdale	14	10		
2001-02	Rochdale	17	1		
2002-03	Rochdale	39	12	**70**	**23**

DOUGHTY, Matt* (D) **110 2**
H: 5 8 W: 12 00 b.Warrington 2-11-81
Source: Scholarship.

1999–2000	Chester C	33	1	**33**	**1**
2001-02	Rochdale	36	1		
2002-03	Rochdale	41	0	**77**	**1**

DUFFY, Lee (D) **28 0**
H: 5 5 W: 9 04 b.Oldham 24-7-82
Source: Scholar.

2001-02	Rochdale	6	0		
2002-03	Rochdale	22	0	**28**	**0**

EDWARDS, Neil (G) **353 0**
H: 5 8 W: 11 02 b.Aberdare 5-12-70
Source: Trainee.

1988–89	Leeds U	0	0		
1989–90	Leeds U	0	0		
1990–91	Leeds U	0	0		
1990–91	*Huddersfield T*	0	0		
1991–92	Stockport Co	39	0		
1992–93	Stockport Co	35	0		
1993–94	Stockport Co	26	0		
1994–95	Stockport Co	19	0		
1995–96	Stockport Co	45	0		
1996–97	Stockport Co	0	0		
1997–98	Stockport Co	0	0	**164**	**0**
1997–98	Rochdale	27	0		
1998–99	Rochdale	45	0		
1999–2000	Rochdale	40	0		
2000-01	Rochdale	44	0		
2001-02	Rochdale	7	0		
2002-03	Rochdale	26	0	**189**	**0**

EVANS, Wayne (D) **357 4**
H: 5 10 W: 12 01 b.Abermule 25-8-71
Source: Welshpool.

1993–94	Walsall	41	0		
1994–95	Walsall	36	0		
1995–96	Walsall	24	0		
1996–97	Walsall	28	0		
1997–98	Walsall	43	1		
1998–99	Walsall	11	0	**183**	**1**
1999–2000	Rochdale	46	1		
2000-01	Rochdale	45	2		
2001-02	Rochdale	43	0		
2002-03	Rochdale	40	0	**174**	**3**

FLITCROFT, David* (M) **337 24**
H: 5 10 W: 13 05 b.Bolton 14-1-74
Source: Trainee.

1991–92	Preston NE	0	0		
1992–93	Preston NE	8	2		
1993–94	Preston NE	0	0	**8**	**2**
1993–94	*Lincoln C*	2	0	**2**	**0**
1993–94	Chester C	8	1		
1994–95	Chester C	32	0		
1995–96	Chester C	9	1		
1996–97	Chester C	32	6		
1997–98	Chester C	44	4		
1998–99	Chester C	42	6	**167**	**18**
1999–2000	Rochdale	43	2		
2000-01	Rochdale	41	0		
2001-02	Rochdale	35	0		
2002-03	Rochdale	41	2	**160**	**4**

GILKS, Matthew (G) **42 0**
H: 6 1 W: 11 06 b.Rochdale 4-6-82
Source: Scholar.

2000-01	Rochdale	3	0		
2001-02	Rochdale	19	0		
2002-03	Rochdale	20	0	**42**	**0**

GRAND, Simon (D) **23 2**
H: 6 1 W: 10 12 b.Chorley 23-2-84
Source: Scholar.

2002-03	Rochdale	23	2	**23**	**2**

GRIFFITHS, Gareth# (D) **236 16**
H: 6 4 W: 12 12 b.Winsford 10-4-70
Source: Rhyl.

1992–93	Port Vale	0	0		
1993–94	Port Vale	4	2		
1994–95	Port Vale	20	0		
1995–96	Port Vale	41	2		
1996–97	Port Vale	26	0		
1997–98	Port Vale	3	0	**94**	**4**
1997–98	*Shrewsbury T*	6	0	**6**	**0**
1998–99	Wigan Ath	20	0		
1999–2000	Wigan Ath	16	1		
2000-01	Wigan Ath	17	1	**53**	**2**
2001-02	Rochdale	41	4		
2002-03	Rochdale	42	6	**83**	**10**

HILL, Stephen (D) **10 0**
H: 5 10 W: 11 02 b.Prescot 12-11-82
Source: Scholar.

2002-03	Rochdale	10	0	**10**	**0**

HODGES, Lee‡ (M) **174 21**
H: 5 5 W: 9 06 b.Newham 2-3-78
Source: Trainee. *Honours:* England Schools.

1994–95	West Ham U	0	0		
1995–96	West Ham U	0	0		
1996–97	West Ham U	0	0		
1996–97	*Exeter C*	17	0	**17**	**0**
1996–97	*Leyton Orient*	3	0	**3**	**0**
1997–98	West Ham U	2	0		
1997–98	*Plymouth Arg*	9	0	**9**	**0**
1998–99	West Ham U	1	0	**3**	**0**
1998–99	*Ipswich T*	4	0	**4**	**0**
1998–99	*Southend U*	10	1	**10**	**1**
1999–2000	Scunthorpe U	40	6		
2000-01	Scunthorpe U	38	8		
2001-02	Scunthorpe U	35	6	**113**	**20**
2002-03	Rochdale	7	0	**7**	**0**
2002-03	*Bristol R*	8	0	**8**	**0**

JOBSON, Richard* (D) **588 40**
H: 6 1 W: 13 05 b.Hull 9-5-63
Source: Burton Alb. *Honours:* England B.

1982–83	Watford	13	1		
1983–84	Watford	13	2		
1984–85	Watford	2	1		
1984–85	Hull C	8	0		
1985–86	Hull C	36	7		
1986–87	Hull C	40	5		
1987–88	Hull C	44	2		
1988–89	Hull C	46	1		
1989–90	Hull C	45	2		
1990–91	Hull C	2	0	**221**	**17**
1990–91	Oldham Ath	44	1		
1991–92	Oldham Ath	36	2		
1992–93	Oldham Ath	40	2		
1993–94	Oldham Ath	37	5		
1994–95	Oldham Ath	20	0		
1995–96	Oldham Ath	12	0	**189**	**10**
1995–96	Leeds U	12	1		
1996–97	Leeds U	10	0		
1997–98	Leeds U	0	0	**22**	**1**
1997–98	*Southend U*	8	1	**8**	**1**
1997–98	Manchester C	6	1		
1998–99	Manchester C	0	0		
1999–2000	Manchester C	44	3		
2000-01	Manchester C	0	0	**50**	**4**
2000-01	*Watford*	2	0	**30**	**4**
2000-01	Tranmere R	16	0		
2001-02	Tranmere R	1	0	**17**	**0**
2001-02	Rochdale	35	3		
2002-03	Rochdale	16	0	**51**	**3**

McCOURT, Patrick (M) **49 6**
H: 5 11 W: 10 12 b.Derry 16-12-83
Source: Scholar. *Honours:* Northern Ireland Under-21, 1 full cap.

2001-02	Rochdale	23	4		
2002-03	Rochdale	26	2	**49**	**6**

McEVILLY, Lee (F) **55 19**
H: 6 0 W: 12 08 b.Liverpool 15-4-82
Source: Burscough. *Honours:* Northern Ireland Under-21, 1 full cap.

2001-02	Rochdale	18	4		
2002-03	Rochdale	37	15	**55**	**19**

MELAUGH, Gavin (M) **19 1**
H: 5 7 W: 9 07 b.Derry 9-7-81
Source: Trainee. *Honours:* Northern Ireland Under-21.

1998–99	Aston Villa	0	0		
1999–2000	Aston Villa	0	0		
2000-01	Aston Villa	0	0		
2001-02	Aston Villa	0	0		
2002-03	Aston Villa	0	0		
2002-03	Rochdale	19	1	**19**	**1**

OLIVER, Michael* (M) **276 24**
H: 5 10 W: 12 04 b.Middlesbrough 2-8-75
Source: Trainee.

1992–93	Middlesbrough	0	0		
1993–94	Middlesbrough	0	0		
1994–95	Stockport Co	13	0		
1995–96	Stockport Co	9	1	**22**	**1**
1996–97	Darlington	39	9		
1997–98	Darlington	39	2		
1998–99	Darlington	36	1		
1999–2000	Darlington	37	2	**151**	**14**
2000-01	Rochdale	38	0		

2001-02 Rochdale 45 7
2002-03 Rochdale 20 2 **103 9**

PATTERSON, Rory§ (M) 8 0
b.Derry 16-7-84
Source: Scholar.
2002-03 Rochdale 8 0 **8 0**

PLATT, Clive# (F) 201 34
H: 6 4 W: 12 07 b.Wolverhampton 27-10-77
Source: Trainee.
1995–96 Walsall 4 2
1996–97 Walsall 1 0
1997–98 Walsall 20 1
1998–99 Walsall 7 1
1999–2000 Walsall 0 0 **32 4**
1999–2000 Rochdale 41 9
2000-01 Rochdale 43 8
2001-02 Rochdale 43 7
2002-03 Rochdale 42 6 **169 30**

SIMPSON, Paul* (M) 637 144
H: 5 7 W: 12 03 b.Carlisle 26-7-66
Source: Apprentice. *Honours:* England Youth, Under-21.
1982–83 Manchester C 3 0
1983–84 Manchester C 0 0
1984–85 Manchester C 10 6
1985–86 Manchester C 37 8
1986–87 Manchester C 32 3
1987–88 Manchester C 38 1
1988–89 Manchester C 1 0 **121 18**
1988–89 Oxford U 25 8
1989–90 Oxford U 42 9
1990–91 Oxford U 46 17
1991–92 Oxford U 31 9 **144 43**
1991–92 Derby Co 16 7
1992–93 Derby Co 35 12
1993–94 Derby Co 34 9
1994–95 Derby Co 42 8
1995–96 Derby Co 39 10
1996–97 Derby Co 19 2
1996–97 *Sheffield U* 6 0 **6 0**
1997–98 Derby Co 1 0 **186 48**
1997–98 Wolverhampton W 28 4
1998–99 Wolverhampton W 11 2
1998–99 *Walsall* 10 1 **10 1**
1999–2000 Wolverhampton W 13 0
2000-01 Wolverhampton W 0 0 **52 6**
2000-01 Blackpool 44 12
2001-02 Blackpool 32 1 **76 13**
2001-02 Rochdale 7 5
2002-03 Rochdale 35 10 **42 15**

TOWNSON, Kevin (F) 68 15
H: 5 5 W: 10 11 b.Kirby 19-4-83
Honours: England Youth.
2000-01 Rochdale 3 0
2001-02 Rochdale 41 14
2002-03 Rochdale 24 1 **68 15**

WARNER, Scott§ (M) 7 0
b.Rochdale 3-12-83
Source: Scholar.
2002-03 Rochdale 7 0 **7 0**

Scholars
Allen, Nicholas; Brown, Gary; Crowther, Dean; Doherty, Eoin; Gartside, Karl; Gibbins, Kevin P; Gibbons, Joseph; Hamilton, Kiel; Mann, James; Patterson, Rory C; Semmens, Christopher; Smith, Steven K; Warner, Scott

ROTHERHAM U

ARTELL, David* (D) 65 5
H: 6 3 W: 13 13 b.Rotherham 22-11-80
Source: Trainee.
1999–2000 Rotherham U 1 0
2000-01 Rotherham U 36 4
2001-02 Rotherham U 0 0
2002-03 Rotherham U 0 0 **37 4**
2002-03 *Shrewsbury T* 28 1 **28 1**

BARKER, Richard (F) 215 46
H: 6 1 W: 14 00 b.Sheffield 30-5-75
Source: Trainee. *Honours:* England Schools.
1993–94 Sheffield W 0 0
1994–95 Sheffield W 0 0
1995–96 Sheffield W 0 0
1995–96 *Doncaster R* 6 0 **6 0**
1996–97 Sheffield W 0 0
From Linfield
1997–98 Brighton & HA 17 2
1998–99 Brighton & HA 43 10 **60 12**
1999–2000 Macclesfield T 35 16
2000-01 Macclesfield T 23 7 **58 23**
2000-01 Rotherham U 19 1
2001-02 Rotherham U 35 3
2002-03 Rotherham U 37 7 **91 11**

BARKER, Shaun (D) 11 0
H: 6 2 W: 12 08 b.Nottingham 19-9-82
Source: Scholar.
2002-03 Rotherham U 11 0 **11 0**

BEECH, Chris‡ (D) 101 2
H: 5 9 W: 11 08 b.Congleton 5-11-75
Source: Trainee. *Honours:* England Schools, Youth.
1992–93 Manchester C 0 0
1993–94 Manchester C 0 0
1994–95 Manchester C 0 0
1995–96 Manchester C 0 0
1996–97 Manchester C 0 0
1997–98 Cardiff C 46 1 **46 1**
1998–99 Rotherham U 24 0
1999–2000 Rotherham U 6 0
2000-01 Rotherham U 15 0
2001-02 Rotherham U 8 1
2002-03 Rotherham U 2 0 **55 1**

BRANSTON, Guy (D) 120 15
H: 6 1 W: 15 02 b.Leicester 9-1-79
Source: Trainee.
1997–98 Leicester C 0 0
1997–98 *Colchester U* 12 1
1998–99 Leicester C 0 0
1998–99 *Colchester U* 1 0 **13 1**
1998–99 *Plymouth Arg* 7 1 **7 1**
1999–2000 Leicester C 0 0
1999–2000 *Lincoln C* 4 0 **4 0**
1999–2000 Rotherham U 30 4
2000-01 Rotherham U 41 6
2001-02 Rotherham U 10 1
2002-03 Rotherham U 15 2 **96 13**

BRYAN, Marvin* (D) 259 5
H: 5 11 W: 12 11 b.Paddington 2-8-75
Source: Trainee.
1992–93 QPR 0 0
1993–94 QPR 0 0
1994–95 QPR 0 0
1994–95 *Doncaster R* 5 1 **5 1**
1995–96 Blackpool 46 1
1996–97 Blackpool 34 1
1997–98 Blackpool 43 1
1998–99 Blackpool 41 1
1999–2000 Blackpool 18 0 **182 4**
1999–2000 Bury 9 0 **9 0**
2000-01 Rotherham U 28 0
2001-02 Rotherham U 19 0
2002-03 Rotherham U 16 0 **63 0**

BYFIELD, Darren (F) 142 30
H: 5 11 W: 12 00 b.Sutton Coldfield 29-9-76
Source: Trainee. *Honours:* Jamaica 2 full caps.
1993–94 Aston Villa 0 0
1994–95 Aston Villa 0 0
1995–96 Aston Villa 0 0
1996–97 Aston Villa 0 0
1997–98 Aston Villa 7 0
1998–99 Aston Villa 0 0
1998–99 *Preston NE* 5 1 **5 1**
1999–2000 Aston Villa 0 0 **7 0**
1999–2000 *Northampton T* 6 1 **6 1**
1999–2000 *Cambridge U* 4 0 **4 0**
1999–2000 *Blackpool* 3 0 **3 0**
2000-01 Walsall 40 9
2001-02 Walsall 37 4 **77 13**
2001-02 Rotherham U 3 2
2002-03 Rotherham U 37 13 **40 15**

DAWS, Nick (M) 437 18
H: 5 11 W: 13 09 b.Salford 15-3-70
Source: Altrincham.
1992–93 Bury 36 1
1993–94 Bury 37 1
1994–95 Bury 34 2
1995–96 Bury 37 1
1996–97 Bury 46 2
1997–98 Bury 46 2
1998–99 Bury 46 2
1999–2000 Bury 43 2
2000-01 Bury 44 3 **369 16**
2001-02 Rotherham U 35 1
2002-03 Rotherham U 33 1 **68 2**

GARNER, Darren (M) 260 24
H: 5 10 W: 12 02 b.Plymouth 10-12-71
Source: Trainee.
1988–89 Plymouth Arg 1 0
1989–90 Plymouth Arg 1 0
1990–91 Plymouth Arg 5 1
1991–92 Plymouth Arg 10 0
1992–93 Plymouth Arg 10 0
1993–94 Plymouth Arg 0 0 **27 1**
From Dorchester T.
1995–96 Rotherham U 31 1
1996–97 Rotherham U 30 2
1997–98 Rotherham U 40 3
1998–99 Rotherham U 40 4
1999–2000 Rotherham U 35 9
2000-01 Rotherham U 31 1
2001-02 Rotherham U 0 0
2002-03 Rotherham U 26 3 **233 23**

GRAY, Ian* (G) 134 0
H: 6 2 W: 14 00 b.Manchester 25-2-75
Source: Trainee.
1993–94 Oldham Ath 0 0
1994–95 Oldham Ath 0 0
1994–95 *Rochdale* 12 0
1995–96 Rochdale 20 0
1996–97 Rochdale 46 0 **78 0**
1997–98 Stockport Co 3 0
1998–99 Stockport Co 3 0
1999–2000 Stockport Co 10 0 **16 0**
2000-01 Rotherham U 33 0
2001-02 Rotherham U 1 0
2002-03 Rotherham U 6 0 **40 0**

HUDSON, Danny* (M) 48 5
H: 5 9 W: 11 07 b.Mexborough 25-6-79
Source: Trainee.
1997–98 Rotherham U 10 0
1998–99 Rotherham U 26 4
1999–2000 Rotherham U 7 1
2000-01 Rotherham U 5 0
2001-02 Rotherham U 0 0
2002-03 Rotherham U 0 0 **48 5**

HURST, Paul (D) 312 12
H: 5 5 W: 10 04 b.Sheffield 25-9-74
Source: Trainee.
1993–94 Rotherham U 4 0
1994–95 Rotherham U 13 0
1995–96 Rotherham U 40 1
1996–97 Rotherham U 30 3
1997–98 Rotherham U 30 0
1998–99 Rotherham U 32 2
1999–2000 Rotherham U 30 2
2000-01 Rotherham U 44 3
2001-02 Rotherham U 45 0
2002-03 Rotherham U 44 1 **312 12**

JONES, Rhodri‡ (D) 0 0
H: 6 0 W: 12 07 b.Cardiff 19-1-82
Source: Trainee.
1999–2000 Manchester U 0 0
2000-01 Manchester U 0 0
2001-02 Rotherham U 0 0
2002-03 Rotherham U 0 0

LEE, Alan (F) 143 41
H: 6 2 W: 14 03 b.Galway 21-8-78
Source: Trainee. *Honours:* Eire Under-21, 2 full caps.
1995–96 Aston Villa 0 0
1996–97 Aston Villa 0 0
1997–98 Aston Villa 0 0
1998–99 Aston Villa 0 0
1998–99 *Torquay U* 7 2 **7 2**
1998–99 *Port Vale* 11 2 **11 2**
1999–2000 Burnley 15 0
2000-01 Burnley 0 0 **15 0**
2000-01 Rotherham U 31 13
2001-02 Rotherham U 38 9
2002-03 Rotherham U 41 15 **110 37**

McINTOSH, Martin (D) 357 36
H: 6 2 W: 12 13 b.East Kilbride 19-3-71
Honours: Scotland B.
1988–89 St Mirren 2 0
1989–90 St Mirren 2 0
1990–91 St Mirren 0 0 **4 0**
1991–92 Clydebank 28 5
1992–93 Clydebank 33 4
1993–94 Clydebank 4 1 **65 10**
1993–94 Hamilton A 13 2
1994–95 Hamilton A 30 2
1995–96 Hamilton A 23 1
1996–97 Hamilton A 33 7 **99 12**
1997–98 Stockport Co 38 2
1998–99 Stockport Co 41 3

1999–2000	Stockport Co	20	0	**99**	**5**
1999–2000	Hibernian	9	0		
2000-01	Hibernian	0	0		
2001-02	Hibernian	0	0	**9**	**0**
2001-02	Rotherham U	39	4		
2002-03	Rotherham U	42	5	**81**	**9**

MIRANDA, Jose‡ (F) 2 0

H: 5 7 W: 9 13 b.Lisbon 20-4-74

2001-02	Rotherham U	2	0		
2002-03	Rotherham U	0	0	**2**	**0**

MONKHOUSE, Andy (M) 75 3

H: 6 2 W: 12 10 b.Leeds 23-10-80

Source: Trainee.

1998–99	Rotherham U	5	1		
1999–2000	Rotherham U	0	0		
2000-01	Rotherham U	12	0		
2001-02	Rotherham U	38	2		
2002-03	Rotherham U	20	0	**75**	**3**

MULLIN, John (M) 211 19

H: 6 1 W: 12 09 b.Bury 11-8-75

Source: School.

1992–93	Burnley	0	0		
1993–94	Burnley	6	1		
1994–95	Burnley	12	1		
1995–96	Sunderland	10	1		
1996–97	Sunderland	10	1		
1997–98	Sunderland	6	0		
1997–98	*Preston NE*	7	0	**7**	**0**
1997–98	*Burnley*	6	0		
1998–99	Sunderland	9	2	**35**	**4**
1999–2000	Burnley	37	5		
2000-01	Burnley	36	3		
2001-02	Burnley	4	0	**101**	**10**
2001-02	Rotherham U	34	2		
2002-03	Rotherham U	34	3	**68**	**5**

POLLITT, Mike (G) 374 0

H: 6 4 W: 15 00 b.Farnworth 29-2-72

Source: Trainee.

1990–91	Manchester U	0	0		
1990–91	*Oldham Ath*	0	0		
1991–92	Bury	0	0		
1992–93	Lincoln C	27	0		
1993–94	Lincoln C	30	0	**57**	**0**
1994–95	Darlington	40	0		
1995–96	Darlington	15	0	**55**	**0**
1995–96	Notts Co	0	0		
1996–97	Notts Co	8	0		
1997–98	Notts Co	2	0	**10**	**0**
1997–98	*Oldham Ath*	16	0	**16**	**0**
1997–98	*Gillingham*	6	0	**6**	**0**
1997–98	*Brentford*	5	0	**5**	**0**
1997–98	Sunderland	0	0		
1998–99	Rotherham U	46	0		
1999–2000	Rotherham U	46	0		
2000-01	Chesterfield	46	0	**46**	**0**
2001-02	Rotherham U	46	0		
2002-03	Rotherham U	41	0	**179**	**0**

ROBINS, Mark (F) 323 97

H: 5 8 W: 11 12 b.Ashton-under-Lyne 22-12-69

Source: Apprentice. *Honours:* England Under-21.

1986–87	Manchester U	0	0		
1987–88	Manchester U	0	0		
1988–89	Manchester U	10	0		
1989–90	Manchester U	17	7		
1990–91	Manchester U	19	4		
1991–92	Manchester U	2	0	**48**	**11**
1992–93	Norwich C	37	15		
1993–94	Norwich C	13	1		
1994–95	Norwich C	17	4	**67**	**20**
1994–95	Leicester C	17	5		
1995–96	Leicester C	31	6		
1996–97	Leicester C	8	1		
1997–98	Leicester C	0	0	**56**	**12**
1997–98	*Reading*	5	0	**5**	**0**
From Panionios.					
1998–99	Manchester C	2	0	**2**	**0**
1999–2000	Walsall	40	6	**40**	**6**
2000-01	Rotherham U	42	24		
2001-02	Rotherham U	41	15		
2002-03	Rotherham U	16	5	**99**	**44**
2002-03	*Bristol C*	6	4	**6**	**4**

SCOTT, Rob (D) 250 31

H: 6 1 W: 12 03 b.Epsom 15-8-73

Source: Sutton U.

1993–94	Sheffield U	0	0		
1994–95	Sheffield U	1	0		
1994–95	*Scarborough*	8	3	**8**	**3**
1995–96	Sheffield U	5	1	**6**	**1**
1995–96	*Northampton T*	5	0	**5**	**0**
1995–96	Fulham	21	5		
1996–97	Fulham	43	9		
1997–98	Fulham	17	3		
1998–99	Fulham	3	0	**84**	**17**
1998–99	*Carlisle U*	7	3	**7**	**3**
1998–99	Rotherham U	6	1		
1999–2000	Rotherham U	34	1		
2000-01	Rotherham U	39	2		
2001-02	Rotherham U	38	3		
2002-03	Rotherham U	23	0	**140**	**7**

SEDGWICK, Chris (M) 183 13

H: 6 1 W: 12 02 b.Sheffield 28-4-80

Source: Trainee.

1997–98	Rotherham U	4	0		
1998–99	Rotherham U	33	4		
1999–2000	Rotherham U	38	5		
2000-01	Rotherham U	21	2		
2001-02	Rotherham U	44	1		
2002-03	Rotherham U	43	1	**183**	**13**

SWAILES, Chris (D) 295 20

H: 6 2 W: 12 12 b.Gateshead 19-10-70

Source: Ipswich T Trainee, Peterborough U, Boston U, Birmingham C, Bridlington T.

1993–94	Doncaster R	17	0		
1994–95	Doncaster R	32	0	**49**	**0**
1995–96	Ipswich T	5	0		
1996–97	Ipswich T	23	1		
1997–98	Ipswich T	5	0	**33**	**1**
1997–98	Bury	13	1		
1998–99	Bury	43	3		
1999–2000	Bury	27	2		
2000-01	Bury	43	4	**126**	**10**
2001-02	Rotherham U	44	6		
2002-03	Rotherham U	43	3	**87**	**9**

TALBOT, Stuart (M) 233 17

H: 6 0 W: 13 12 b.Birmingham 14-6-73

Source: Doncaster R, Moor Green.

1994–95	Port Vale	2	0		
1995–96	Port Vale	20	0		
1996–97	Port Vale	34	4		
1997–98	Port Vale	42	6		
1998–99	Port Vale	33	0		
1999–2000	Port Vale	6	0	**137**	**10**
2000-01	Rotherham U	38	5		
2001-02	Rotherham U	38	1		
2002-03	Rotherham U	15	1	**91**	**7**
2002-03	*Shrewsbury T*	5	0	**5**	**0**

WARNE, Paul (F) 207 29

H: 5 10 W: 11 02 b.Norwich 8-5-73

Source: Wroxham.

1997–98	Wigan Ath	25	2		
1998–99	Wigan Ath	11	1	**36**	**3**
1998–99	Rotherham U	19	8		
1999–2000	Rotherham U	43	10		
2000-01	Rotherham U	44	7		
2001-02	Rotherham U	25	0		
2002-03	Rotherham U	40	1	**171**	**26**

Scholars

Bowler, Kris PM; Clarke, Leon K; Clayton, Gareth N; Fells, Daniel D; Fletcher, Thomas M; Gregory, Benjamin D; Hoskins, William R; Jones, Andrew S; Kay, Liam J; Letts, Scott D; Ludlam, Stuart J; Middlebrook, Andrew; Mudd, Craig R; Page, Nicholas A; Pritchard, Luke J; Smith, Thomas; Waite, Jamie; Wright, Mark J

RUSHDEN & D

BATTERSBY, Tony‡ (F) 254 41

H: 6 0 W: 13 07 b.Doncaster 30-8-75

Source: Trainee.

1993–94	Sheffield U	0	0		
1994–95	Sheffield U	0	0		
1994–95	*Southend U*	8	1	**8**	**1**
1995–96	Sheffield U	10	1	**10**	**1**
1995–96	Notts Co	21	7		
1996–97	Notts Co	18	1	**39**	**8**
1996–97	*Bury*	11	2		
1997–98	Bury	37	6		
1998–99	Bury	0	0	**48**	**8**
1998–99	Lincoln C	39	7		
1999–2000	Lincoln C	16	3		
1999–2000	*Northampton T*	3	1	**3**	**1**
2000-01	Lincoln C	35	6		
2001-02	Lincoln C	39	5		
2002-03	Lincoln C	1	0	**130**	**21**
2002-03	Boston U	11	1	**11**	**1**
2002-03	Rushden & D	5	0	**5**	**0**

BELL JNR, David† (M) 1 0

H: 5 10 W: 11 01 b.Buncrana 13-5-85

Source: Institute.

2001-02	Rushden & D	1	0		
2002-03	Rushden & D	0	0	**1**	**0**

BELL, David (M) 30 3

H: 5 10 W: 12 01 b.Kettering 21-1-84

Source: Trainee.

2001-02	Rushden & D	0	0		
2002-03	Rushden & D	30	3	**30**	**3**

BIGNOT, Marcus (D) 208 2

H: 5 7 W: 11 04 b.Birmingham 22-8-74

Source: Kidderminster H.

1997–98	Crewe Alex	42	0		
1998–99	Crewe Alex	26	0		
1999–2000	Crewe Alex	27	0	**95**	**0**
2000-01	Bristol R	26	1	**26**	**1**
2000-01	QPR	9	1		
2001-02	QPR	45	0	**54**	**1**
2002-03	Rushden & D	33	0	**33**	**0**

BURGESS, Andy (M) 59 5

H: 6 2 W: 11 12 b.Bedford 10-8-81

2001-02	Rushden & D	32	4		
2002-03	Rushden & D	27	1	**59**	**5**

DARBY, Duane# (F) 306 83

H: 5 11 W: 13 12 b.Birmingham 17-10-73

Source: Trainee.

1991–92	Torquay U	14	2		
1992–93	Torquay U	34	12		
1993–94	Torquay U	36	8		
1994–95	Torquay U	24	4	**108**	**26**
1995–96	Doncaster R	17	4	**17**	**4**
1995–96	Hull C	8	1		
1996–97	Hull C	41	13		
1997–98	Hull C	29	13		
1998–99	Notts Co	0	0		
1998–99	*Hull C*	8	0	**86**	**27**
1999–2000	Notts Co	28	5		
2000-01	Notts Co	0	0	**28**	**5**
2001-02	Rushden & D	30	7		
2002-03	Rushden & D	37	14	**67**	**21**

DEMPSTER, John (D) 18 1

H: 6 0 W: 12 05 b.Kettering 1-4-83

Source: Trainee.

2001-02	Rushden & D	2	0		
2002-03	Rushden & D	16	1	**18**	**1**

DUFFY, Robert (F) 20 1

H: 6 1 W: 13 01 b.Swansea 2-12-82

Honours: Wales Under-18.

2001-02	Rushden & D	8	1		
2002-03	Rushden & D	12	0	**20**	**1**

EDWARDS, Andy (D) 465 17

H: 6 2 W: 12 13 b.Epping 17-9-71

Source: Trainee.

1988–89	Southend U	1	0		
1989–90	Southend U	8	0		
1990–91	Southend U	2	1		
1991–92	Southend U	9	0		
1992–93	Southend U	41	0		
1993–94	Southend U	42	1		
1994–95	Southend U	44	3	**147**	**5**
1995–96	Birmingham C	37	1		
1996–97	Birmingham C	3	0	**40**	**1**
1996–97	Peterborough U	25	0		
1997–98	Peterborough U	46	2		
1998–99	Peterborough U	41	2		
1999–2000	Peterborough U	44	2		
2000-01	Peterborough U	43	1		
2001-02	Peterborough U	44	2		
2002-03	Peterborough U	23	1	**266**	**10**
2002-03	Rushden & D	12	1	**12**	**1**

GRAY, Stuart# (D) 130 10

H: 5 10 W: 13 07 b.Harrogate 18-12-73

Source: Giffnock N. *Honours:* Scotland Under-21.

1992–93	Celtic	1	0		
1993–94	Celtic	0	0		
1994–95	Celtic	11	0		
1995–96	Celtic	5	1		
1996–97	Celtic	11	0		
1997–98	Celtic	0	0	**28**	**1**
1997–98	Reading	7	0		
1998–99	Reading	27	2		
1999–2000	Reading	15	0		
2000-01	Reading	3	0	**52**	**2**
2001-02	Rushden & D	12	0		
2002-03	Rushden & D	38	7	**50**	**7**

HALL, Paul (M) **437 73**
H: 5 8 W: 12 06 b.Manchester 3-7-72
Source: Trainee. *Honours:* Jamaica 41 full caps, 9 goals.
1989–90 Torquay U 10 0
1990–91 Torquay U 17 0
1991–92 Torquay U 38 1
1992–93 Torquay U 28 0 **93 1**
1992–93 Portsmouth 0 0
1993–94 Portsmouth 28 4
1994–95 Portsmouth 43 5
1995–96 Portsmouth 46 10
1996–97 Portsmouth 42 13
1997–98 Portsmouth 29 5 **188 37**
1998–99 Coventry C 9 0
1998–99 *Bury* 7 0 **7 0**
1999–2000 Coventry C 1 0 **10 0**
1999–2000 *Sheffield U* 4 1 **4 1**
1999–2000 *WBA* 4 0 **4 0**
1999–2000 Walsall 10 4
2000–01 Walsall 42 6
2001–02 Walsall 0 0 **52 10**
2001–02 Rushden & D 34 8
2002–03 Rushden & D 45 16 **79 24**

HANLON, Ritchie (M) **84 9**
H: 6 1 W: 13 09 b.Kenton 25-5-78
Source: Chelsea Trainee.
1996–97 Southend U 2 0
1997–98 Southend U 0 0 **2 0**
From Rushden & D.
1998–99 Peterborough U 4 1
From Welling U.
1999–2000 Peterborough U 16 1
2000–01 Peterborough U 26 1
2001–02 Peterborough U 1 0 **47 3**
2001–02 Rushden & D 35 6
2002–03 Rushden & D 0 0 **35 6**

HOLDSWORTH, Dean† (F) **499 160**
H: 5 11 W: 11 13 b.Walthamstow 8-11-68
Source: Trainee.
1986–87 Watford 2 0
1987–88 *Carlisle U* 4 1 **4 1**
1987–88 *Port Vale* 6 2 **6 2**
1988–89 Watford 10 2
1988–89 *Swansea C* 5 1 **5 1**
1988–89 *Brentford* 7 1
1989–90 Watford 4 1 **16 3**
1989–90 Brentford 39 24
1990–91 Brentford 30 5
1991–92 Brentford 41 24 **117 54**
1992–93 Wimbledon 36 19
1993–94 Wimbledon 42 17
1994–95 Wimbledon 28 7
1995–96 Wimbledon 33 10
1996–97 Wimbledon 25 5
1997–98 Wimbledon 5 0 **169 58**
1997–98 Bolton W 20 3
1998–99 Bolton W 32 12
1999–2000 Bolton W 35 11
2000–01 Bolton W 31 11
2001–02 Bolton W 31 2
2002–03 Bolton W 9 0 **158 39**
2002–03 Coventry C 17 0 **17 0**
2002–03 Rushden & D 7 2 **7 2**

HUNTER, Barry# (D) **243 12**
H: 6 4 W: 12 06 b.Coleraine 18-11-68
Source: Crusaders. *Honours:* Northern Ireland Youth, B, 15 full caps, 1 goal.
1993–94 Wrexham 23 1
1994–95 Wrexham 37 0
1995–96 Wrexham 31 3 **91 4**
1996–97 Reading 27 2
1997–98 Reading 0 0
1998–99 Reading 3 0
1998–99 *Southend U* 5 2 **5 2**
1999–2000 Reading 31 1
2000–01 Reading 23 1
2001–02 Reading 0 0 **84 4**
2001–02 Rushden & D 23 1
2002–03 Rushden & D 40 1 **63 2**

LOWE, Onandi (F) **69 35**
H: 6 3 W: 14 12 b.Kingston, Jamaica 2-12-74
Honours: Jamaica full caps.
2000–01 Port Vale 5 1 **5 1**
From Kansas City W.
2001–02 Rushden & D 25 19
2002–03 Rushden & D 39 15 **64 34**

MILLS, Gary (M) **39 0**
H: 5 9 W: 11 11 b.Sheppey 20-5-81
2001–02 Rushden & D 9 0
2002–03 Rushden & D 30 0 **39 0**

MUSTAFA, Tarkan‡ (D) **45 1**
H: 5 11 W: 11 11 b.Islington 28-8-73
Source: Kettering T.
1997–98 Barnet 11 0 **11 0**
From Kingstonian.
2001–02 Rushden & D 23 1
2002–03 Rushden & D 11 0 **34 1**

PETERS, Mark (D) **194 10**
H: 6 0 W: 13 04 b.St Asaph 6-7-72
Source: Trainee. *Honours:* Wales Under-21.
1991–92 Manchester C 0 0
1992–93 Norwich C 0 0
1993–94 Peterborough U 19 0
1994–95 Peterborough U 0 0 **19 0**
1994–95 Mansfield T 26 4
1995–96 Mansfield T 21 2
1996–97 Mansfield T 0 0
1997–98 Mansfield T 24 2
1998–99 Mansfield T 37 1 **108 9**
2001–02 Rushden & D 40 0
2002–03 Rushden & D 27 1 **67 1**

SAMBROOK, Andrew (D) **42 0**
H: 5 10 W: 11 09 b.Chatham 13-7-79
Source: Trainee.
1996–97 Gillingham 1 0
1997–98 Gillingham 0 0
1998–99 Gillingham 0 0 **1 0**
2001–02 Rushden & D 26 0
2002–03 Rushden & D 15 0 **41 0**

SETCHELL, Gary* (D) **33 1**
H: 6 0 W: 14 01 b.Kings Lynn 8-5-75
2001–02 Rushden & D 22 1
2002–03 Rushden & D 11 0 **33 1**

SOLKHON, Brett‡ (D) **2 0**
H: 5 11 W: 12 06 b.Canvey Island 12-9-82
2001–02 Rushden & D 1 0
2002–03 Rushden & D 1 0 **2 0**

SOLLITT, Adam* (G) **19 0**
H: 6 0 W: 13 06 b.Sheffield 22-6-77
Source: Gainsborough Tr, Kettering T. *Honours:* England semi-pro.
1995–96 Barnsley 0 0
1996–97 Barnsley 0 0
2000–01 Northampton T 6 0
2001–02 Northampton T 10 0 **16 0**
2002–03 Rushden & D 3 0 **3 0**

TALBOT, Daniel (D) **16 0**
H: 5 9 W: 11 00 b.Enfield 30-1-84
2001–02 Rushden & D 3 0
2002–03 Rushden & D 13 0 **16 0**

TILLSON, Andy‡ (D) **461 20**
H: 6 2 W: 13 05 b.Huntingdon 30-6-66
Source: Kettering T.
1988–89 Grimsby T 45 2
1989–90 Grimsby T 42 3
1990–91 Grimsby T 18 0
1990–91 QPR 19 2
1991–92 QPR 10 0
1992–93 QPR 0 0 **29 2**
1992–93 *Grimsby T* 4 0 **109 5**
1992–93 Bristol R 29 0
1993–94 Bristol R 13 0
1994–95 Bristol R 40 2
1995–96 Bristol R 38 1
1996–97 Bristol R 38 2
1997–98 Bristol R 33 3
1998–99 Bristol R 19 2
1999–2000 Bristol R 43 1 **253 11**
2000–01 Walsall 42 1
2001–02 Walsall 9 1 **51 2**
2001–02 Rushden & D 14 0
2002–03 Rushden & D 5 0 **19 0**

TURLEY, Billy (G) **129 0**
H: 6 3 W: 15 11 b.Wolverhampton 15-7-73
Source: Evesham U.
1995–96 Northampton T 2 0
1996–97 Northampton T 1 0
1997–98 Northampton T 0 0
1997–98 *Leyton Orient* 14 0 **14 0**
1998–99 Northampton T 25 0 **28 0**
2001–02 Rushden & D 43 0
2002–03 Rushden & D 44 0 **87 0**

UNDERWOOD, Paul (D) **80 1**
H: 5 11 W: 12 11 b.Wimbledon 16-8-73
Source: Enfield.
2001–02 Rushden & D 40 0
2002–03 Rushden & D 40 1 **80 1**

WARDLEY, Stuart (M) **144 24**
H: 5 11 W: 13 12 b.Cambridge 10-9-75
Source: Saffron Walden T.
1999–2000 QPR 43 11
2000–01 QPR 34 3
2001–02 QPR 10 0 **87 14**
2001–02 Rushden & D 18 4
2002–03 Rushden & D 39 6 **57 10**

Scholars
Daniels, Karl; Gahan, Stephen; Manangu, Eric M; Okuonghae, Magnus; Story, Owen G; Taylor, Jason L
Non-Contract
Bell, David J; Holdsworth, Dean C

SCUNTHORPE U

BARWICK, Terry (M) **16 0**
H: 5 10 W: 10 12 b.Doncaster 11-1-83
Source: Scholarship.
1999–2000 Scunthorpe U 1 0
2000–01 Scunthorpe U 0 0
2001–02 Scunthorpe U 10 0
2002–03 Scunthorpe U 5 0 **16 0**

BEAGRIE, Peter# (M) **563 72**
H: 5 9 W: 12 04 b.Middlesbrough 28-11-65
Source: Local. *Honours:* England Under-21, B.
1983–84 Middlesbrough 0 0
1984–85 Middlesbrough 7 1
1985–86 Middlesbrough 26 1 **33 2**
1986–87 Sheffield U 41 9
1987–88 Sheffield U 43 2 **84 11**
1988–89 Stoke C 41 7
1989–90 Stoke C 13 0 **54 7**
1989–90 Everton 19 0
1990–91 Everton 17 2
1991–92 Everton 27 3
1991–92 *Sunderland* 5 1 **5 1**
1992–93 Everton 22 3
1993–94 Everton 29 3
1993–94 Manchester C 9 1
1994–95 Manchester C 37 2
1995–96 Manchester C 5 0
1996–97 Manchester C 1 0 **52 3**
1997–98 Bradford C 34 0
1997–98 *Everton* 6 0 **120 11**
1998–99 Bradford C 43 12
1999–2000 Bradford C 35 7
2000–01 Bradford C 19 1 **131 20**
2000–01 Wigan Ath 10 1 **10 1**
2001–02 Scunthorpe U 40 11
2002–03 Scunthorpe U 34 5 **74 16**

BROUGH, Scott‡ (M) **46 3**
H: 5 5 W: 9 11 b.Doncaster 10-2-83
2000–01 Scunthorpe U 4 0
2001–02 Scunthorpe U 19 1
2002–03 Scunthorpe U 23 2 **46 3**

CALVO-GARCIA, Alex (M) **221 30**
H: 5 9 W: 12 03 b.Ordizia 1-1-72
Source: Eibar.
1996–97 Scunthorpe U 13 1
1997–98 Scunthorpe U 44 6
1998–99 Scunthorpe U 43 9
1999–2000 Scunthorpe U 18 1
2000–01 Scunthorpe U 34 4
2001–02 Scunthorpe U 34 6
2002–03 Scunthorpe U 35 3 **221 30**

CARRUTHERS, Martin# (F) **354 102**
H: 5 10 W: 11 13 b.Nottingham 7-8-72
Source: Trainee.
1990–91 Aston Villa 0 0
1991–92 Aston Villa 3 0
1992–93 Aston Villa 1 0 **4 0**
1992–93 *Hull C* 13 6 **13 6**
1993–94 Stoke C 34 5
1994–95 Stoke C 32 5
1995–96 Stoke C 24 3
1996–97 Stoke C 1 0 **91 13**
1996–97 Peterborough U 14 4
1997–98 Peterborough U 39 15
1998–99 Peterborough U 14 2 **67 21**
1998–99 *York C* 6 0 **6 0**
1998–99 Darlington 11 2
1999–2000 Darlington 6 0 **17 2**
1999–2000 Southend U 38 19
2000–01 Southend U 32 7 **70 26**
2000–01 Scunthorpe U 8 1
2001–02 Scunthorpe U 33 13
2002–03 Scunthorpe U 45 20 **86 34**

COLLINS, Neil§ (G) 0 0
H: 6 0 W: 12 02 b.Pontypridd 12-4-84
Source: Scholar.
2001-02 Scunthorpe U 0 0
2002-03 Scunthorpe U 0 0

COTTERILL, James* (D) 23 0
H: 5 11 W: 12 04 b.Barnsley 3-8-82
Source: Scholar.
2000-01 Scunthorpe U 4 0
2001-02 Scunthorpe U 10 0
2002-03 Scunthorpe U 9 0 **23 0**

DAWSON, Andy# (D) 195 8
H: 5 9 W: 11 12 b.Northallerton 20-10-78
Source: Trainee.
1995–96 Nottingham F 0 0
1996–97 Nottingham F 0 0
1997–98 Nottingham F 0 0
1998–99 Nottingham F 0 0
1998–99 Scunthorpe U 24 0
1999–2000 Scunthorpe U 43 2
2000-01 Scunthorpe U 41 4
2001-02 Scunthorpe U 44 0
2002-03 Scunthorpe U 43 2 **195 8**

EVANS, Tom (G) 191 0
H: 6 1 W: 13 11 b.Doncaster 31-12-76
Source: Trainee. *Honours:* Northern Ireland Youth.
1995–96 Sheffield U 0 0
1996–97 Crystal Palace 0 0
1996–97 *Coventry C* 0 0
1997–98 Scunthorpe U 5 0
1998–99 Scunthorpe U 24 0
1999–2000 Scunthorpe U 28 0
2000-01 Scunthorpe U 46 0
2001-02 Scunthorpe U 42 0
2002-03 Scunthorpe U 46 0 **191 0**

FEATHERSTONE, Lee (M) 20 0
b.Chesterfield 20-7-83
Source: Scholar.
2001-02 Sheffield U 0 0
2002-03 Sheffield U 0 0
2002-03 Scunthorpe U 20 0 **20 0**

GRAVES, Wayne (M) 114 6
H: 5 7 W: 11 01 b.Scunthorpe 18-9-80
Source: Trainee.
1997–98 Scunthorpe U 3 0
1998–99 Scunthorpe U 0 0
1999–2000 Scunthorpe U 19 0
2000-01 Scunthorpe U 34 2
2001-02 Scunthorpe U 17 3
2002-03 Scunthorpe U 41 1 **114 6**

HAYES, Paul (F) 18 8
H: 6 0 W: 12 12 b.Dagenham 20-9-83
Source: Norwich C Scholar.
2002-03 Scunthorpe U 18 8 **18 8**

JACKSON, Mark (D) 141 4
H: 5 11 W: 12 13 b.Leeds 30-9-77
Source: Trainee. *Honours:* England Youth.
1995–96 Leeds U 1 0
1996–97 Leeds U 17 0
1997–98 Leeds U 1 0
1998–99 Leeds U 0 0
1998–99 *Huddersfield T* 5 0 **5 0**
1999–2000 Leeds U 0 0 **19 0**
1999–2000 *Barnsley* 1 0 **1 0**
1999–2000 Scunthorpe U 6 0
2000-01 Scunthorpe U 32 1
2001-02 Scunthorpe U 45 3
2002-03 Scunthorpe U 33 0 **116 4**

KELL, Richard* (M) 31 4
H: 6 1 W: 10 13 b.Bishop Auckland 15-9-79
Source: Trainee.
1998–99 Middlesbrough 0 0
1999–2000 Middlesbrough 0 0
2000-01 Middlesbrough 0 0
2000-01 Torquay U 15 3
2001-02 Torquay U 0 0 **15 3**
2001-02 Scunthorpe U 16 1
2002-03 Scunthorpe U 0 0 **16 1**

KILFORD, Ian# (M) 250 35
H: 5 10 W: 11 06 b.Bristol 6-10-73
Source: Trainee.
1991–92 Nottingham F 0 0
1992–93 Nottingham F 0 0
1993–94 Nottingham F 1 0 **1 0**
1993–94 *Wigan Ath* 8 3
1994–95 Wigan Ath 35 5
1995–96 Wigan Ath 25 3
1996–97 Wigan Ath 35 8
1997–98 Wigan Ath 30 10
1998–99 Wigan Ath 23 0
1999–2000 Wigan Ath 21 1
2000-01 Wigan Ath 24 2
2001-02 Wigan Ath 20 0 **221 32**
2002-03 Bury 0 0
2002-03 Scunthorpe U 28 3 **28 3**

McCOMBE, Jamie (D) 48 1
H: 6 5 W: 12 05 b.Pontefract 1-1-83
Source: Scholar.
2001-02 Scunthorpe U 17 0
2002-03 Scunthorpe U 31 1 **48 1**

O'CONNOR, Aaron‡ (F) 3 0
H: 5 10 W: 12 00 b.Nottingham 9-8-83
Source: Ilkeston T.
2002-03 Scunthorpe U 3 0 **3 0**

PARTON, Andy§ (M) 9 0
H: 5 10 W: 12 00 b.Doncaster 29-9-83
Source: Scholar.
2001-02 Scunthorpe U 1 0
2002-03 Scunthorpe U 8 0 **9 0**

RIDLEY, Lee (D) 17 0
H: 5 9 W: 11 10 b.Scunthorpe 5-12-81
Source: Scholar.
2000-01 Scunthorpe U 2 0
2001-02 Scunthorpe U 4 0
2002-03 Scunthorpe U 11 0 **17 0**

RYAN, Leon‡ (F) 2 0
b.Sunderland 8-11-82
2002-03 Scunthorpe U 2 0 **2 0**

SPARROW, Matthew (M) 88 14
H: 5 11 W: 10 06 b.London 3-10-81
Source: Scholarship.
1999–2000 Scunthorpe U 11 0
2000-01 Scunthorpe U 11 4
2001-02 Scunthorpe U 24 1
2002-03 Scunthorpe U 42 9 **88 14**

STANTON, Nathan (D) 161 0
H: 5 9 W: 12 07 b.Nottingham 6-5-81
Source: Trainee. *Honours:* England Youth.
1997–98 Scunthorpe U 1 0
1998–99 Scunthorpe U 4 0
1999–2000 Scunthorpe U 34 0
2000-01 Scunthorpe U 38 0
2001-02 Scunthorpe U 42 0
2002-03 Scunthorpe U 42 0 **161 0**

TAYLOR, Robert‡ (F) 360 114
H: 6 1 W: 13 08 b.Norwich 30-4-71
Source: Trainee.
1989–90 Norwich C 0 0
1990–91 Norwich C 0 0
1990–91 *Leyton Orient* 3 1
1991–92 Birmingham C 0 0
1991–92 Leyton Orient 11 1
1992–93 Leyton Orient 39 18
1993–94 Leyton Orient 23 1 **76 21**
1993–94 Brentford 5 2
1994–95 Brentford 43 23
1995–96 Brentford 42 11
1996–97 Brentford 43 7
1997–98 Brentford 40 13 **173 56**
1998–99 Gillingham 43 16
1999–2000 Gillingham 15 15
1999–2000 Manchester C 16 5 **16 5**
2000-01 Wolverhampton W 9 0
2001-02 Wolverhampton W 0 0 **9 0**
2001-02 *QPR* 4 0 **4 0**
2001-02 *Gillingham* 11 0 **69 31**
2001-02 Grimsby T 4 1
2002-03 Grimsby T 1 0 **5 1**
2002-03 Scunthorpe U 8 0 **8 0**

TORPEY, Steve (F) 463 114
H: 6 3 W: 13 06 b.Islington 8-12-70
Source: Trainee.
1988–89 Millwall 0 0
1989–90 Millwall 7 0
1990–91 Millwall 0 0 **7 0**
1990–91 Bradford C 29 7
1991–92 Bradford C 43 10
1992–93 Bradford C 24 5 **96 22**
1993–94 Swansea C 40 9
1994–95 Swansea C 41 11
1995–96 Swansea C 42 15
1996–97 Swansea C 39 9 **162 44**
1997–98 Bristol C 29 8
1998–99 Bristol C 21 4
1998–99 *Notts Co* 6 1 **6 1**
1999–2000 Bristol C 20 1 **70 13**
1999–2000 Scunthorpe U 15 1
2000-01 Scunthorpe U 40 10
2001-02 Scunthorpe U 39 13
2002-03 Scunthorpe U 28 10 **122 34**

WHEATCROFT, Paul‡ (F) 12 3
H: 5 9 W: 9 11 b.Manchester 22-11-80
Source: Trainee. *Honours:* England Schools, Youth.
1998–99 Manchester U 0 0
1999–2000 Manchester U 0 0
2000-01 Bolton W 0 0
2001-02 Bolton W 0 0
2001-02 *Rochdale* 6 3 **6 3**
2001-02 *Mansfield T* 2 0 **2 0**
2002-03 Scunthorpe U 4 0 **4 0**

WILCOX, Russ‡ (D) 500 27
H: 6 0 W: 13 01 b.Hemsworth 25-3-64
Source: Apprentice.
1980–81 Doncaster R 1 0
From Cambridge U, Frickley Ath
1986–87 Northampton
1987–88 Northampton T 46 4
1988–89 Northampton T 11 1
1989–90 Northampton T 46 3 **138 9**
1990–91 Hull C 31 1
1991–92 Hull C 40 4
1992–93 Hull C 29 2 **100 7**
1993–94 Doncaster R 40 2
1994–95 Doncaster R 37 4
1995–96 Doncaster R 4 0 **82 6**
1995–96 Preston NE 27 1
1996–97 Preston NE 35 0 **62 1**
1997–98 Scunthorpe U 31 2
1998–99 Scunthorpe U 28 1
1999–2000 Scunthorpe U 14 0
2000-01 Scunthorpe U 36 1
2001-02 Scunthorpe U 9 0
2002-03 Scunthorpe U 0 0 **118 4**

WRIGHT, Stephen‡ (D) 181 2
H: 5 10 W: 11 09 b.Bellshill 27-8-71
Source: Aberdeen Lads. *Honours:* Scotland Under-21, 2 full caps.
1987–88 Aberdeen 0 0
1988–89 Aberdeen 0 0
1989–90 Aberdeen 1 0
1990–91 Aberdeen 17 1
1991–92 Aberdeen 23 0
1992–93 Aberdeen 36 0
1993–94 Aberdeen 36 0
1994–95 Aberdeen 34 1 **147 2**
1995–96 Rangers 6 0
1996–97 Rangers 1 0
1997–98 Rangers 0 0 **7 0**
1997–98 *Wolverhampton W* 3 0 **3 0**
1998–99 Bradford C 22 0
1999–2000 Bradford C 0 0
2000-01 Bradford C 0 0
2001-02 Bradford C 0 0 **22 0**
2002-03 Scunthorpe U 2 0 **2 0**

Scholars
Baxter, Matthew; Brown, Andrew D; Butler, Andrew P; Capp, Adam; Collins, Neil J; Hawcroft, Richard C; Hunt, Jonathan M; Johnston, Bradley D; Morley, Craig C; Parton, Andrew; Penn, Russell; Ridout, Aaron J; Roughley, Jason; Singh, Sean; Smith, Fabian SM; Williams, Marcus V

SHEFFIELD U

ALLISON, Wayne (F) 598 149
H: 6 1 W: 15 07 b.Huddersfield 16-10-68
Source: Trainee.
1986–87 Halifax T 8 4
1987–88 Halifax T 35 4
1988–89 Halifax T 41 15 **84 23**
1989–90 Watford 7 0 **7 0**
1990–91 Bristol C 37 6
1991–92 Bristol C 43 10
1992–93 Bristol C 39 4
1993–94 Bristol C 39 15
1994–95 Bristol C 37 13 **195 48**
1995–96 Swindon T 44 17
1996–97 Swindon T 41 11
1997–98 Swindon T 16 3 **101 31**
1997–98 Huddersfield T 27 6
1998–99 Huddersfield T 44 9
1999–2000 Huddersfield T 3 0 **74 15**
1999–2000 Tranmere R 40 16
2000-01 Tranmere R 36 6
2001-02 Tranmere R 27 4 **103 26**
2002-03 Sheffield U 34 6 **34 6**

ASABA, Carl (F) **243 94**
H: 6 1 W: 14 02 b.London 28-1-73
Source: Dulwich Hamlet.
1994–95 Brentford 0 0
1994–95 *Colchester U* 12 2 **12 2**
1995–96 Brentford 10 2
1996–97 Brentford 44 23 **54 25**
1997–98 Reading 32 8
1998–99 Reading 1 0 **33 8**
1998–99 Gillingham 41 20
1999–2000 Gillingham 11 6
2000–01 Gillingham 25 10 **77 36**
2000–01 Sheffield U 10 5
2001–02 Sheffield U 29 7
2002–03 Sheffield U 28 11 **67 23**

BAUM, Adam* (D) **0 0**
H: 5 7 W: 10 02 b.Nottingham 14-10-82
Source: Scholar.
2002–03 Sheffield U 0 0

BROWN, Michael R (M) **235 28**
H: 5 9 W: 12 04 b.Hartlepool 25-1-77
Source: Trainee. *Honours:* England Under-21.
1994–95 Manchester C 0 0
1995–96 Manchester C 21 0
1996–97 Manchester C 11 0
1996–97 *Hartlepool U* 6 1 **6 1**
1997–98 Manchester C 26 0
1998–99 Manchester C 31 2
1999–2000 Manchester C 0 0 **89 2**
1999–2000 *Portsmouth* 4 0 **4 0**
1999–2000 Sheffield U 24 3
2000–01 Sheffield U 36 1
2001–02 Sheffield U 36 5
2002–03 Sheffield U 40 16 **136 25**

CAS, Marcel† (M) **130 14**
H: 6 1 W: 12 08 b.Breda 30-4-72
1997–98 RBC 27 3
1998–99 RBC 9 1
1999–2000 RBC 30 2 **66 6**
2001–02 Notts Co 40 6
2002–03 Notts Co 18 2 **58 8**
2002–03 Sheffield U 6 0 **6 0**

COLLEY, Karl (D) **0 0**
H: 6 1 W: 12 06 b.Sheffield 13-10-83
Source: Scholar.
2000–01 Sheffield W 0 0
2001–02 Sheffield W 0 0
2001–02 Newcastle U 0 0
2002–03 Sheffield U 0 0

CROISSANT, Benoit (D) **0 0**
H: 6 0 W: 12 05 b.Vitriy le Francois 9-8-80
Source: Troyes.
2001–02 Sheffield U 0 0
2002–03 Sheffield U 0 0

CRYAN, Colin (D) **4 0**
H: 5 11 W: 13 00 b.Dublin 23-3-81
Source: Scholar. *Honours:* Eire Under-21.
1999–2000 Sheffield U 0 0
2000–01 Sheffield U 1 0
2001–02 Sheffield U 1 0
2002–03 Sheffield U 2 0 **4 0**

DE VOGT, Wilko‡ (G) **21 0**
H: 6 1 W: 12 08 b.Breda 17-9-75
1996–97 NAC Breda 1 0
1997–98 NAC Breda 1 0
1998–99 NAC Breda 7 0
1999–2000 NAC Breda 6 0
2000–01 NAC Breda 0 0 **15 0**
2001–02 Sheffield U 6 0
2002–03 Sheffield U 0 0 **6 0**

DOANE, Ben‡ (D) **34 1**
H: 5 9 W: 11 06 b.Sheffield 22-12-79
Source: Trainee.
1998–99 Sheffield U 0 0
1999–2000 Sheffield U 1 0
2000–01 Sheffield U 3 0
2001–02 Sheffield U 14 1
2002–03 Sheffield U 5 0 **23 1**
2002–03 *Mansfield T* 11 0 **11 0**

EDGHILL, Richard‡ (D) **185 1**
H: 5 9 W: 12 01 b.Oldham 23-9-74
Source: Trainee. *Honours:* England Under-21.
1992–93 Manchester C 0 0
1993–94 Manchester C 22 0
1994–95 Manchester C 14 0
1995–96 Manchester C 13 0
1996–97 Manchester C 0 0
1997–98 Manchester C 36 0
1998–99 Manchester C 38 0
1999–2000 Manchester C 41 1
2000–01 Manchester C 6 0
2000–01 *Birmingham C* 3 0 **3 0**
2001–02 Manchester C 11 0 **181 1**
2002–03 Wigan Ath 0 0
2002–03 Sheffield U 1 0 **1 0**

HOWARTH, Ricky* (M) **0 0**
H: 5 9 W: 11 08 b.Johannesburg 10-4-85
2002–03 Sheffield U 0 0

JAGIELKA, Phil (M) **81 3**
H: 5 11 W: 13 05 b.Manchester 17-8-82
Source: Scholar. *Honours:* England Youth, Under-20, Under-21.
1999–2000 Sheffield U 1 0
2000–01 Sheffield U 15 0
2001–02 Sheffield U 23 3
2002–03 Sheffield U 42 0 **81 3**

JAVARY, Jean-Philippe (M) **44 1**
H: 6 0 W: 12 07 b.Montpellier 10-1-78
1995–96 Montpellier 3 0
1996–97 Montpellier 7 0
1997–98 Montpellier 0 0 **10 0**
1998–99 Espanyol 0 0
1999–2000 Raith R 11 0 **11 0**
2000–01 Brentford 6 0 **6 0**
2000–01 Plymouth Arg 4 0
2001–02 Plymouth Arg 0 0 **4 0**
2001–02 Sheffield U 7 1
2002–03 Sheffield U 6 0 **13 1**

KABBA, Steven (F) **51 14**
H: 5 10 W: 11 12 b.Lambeth 7-3-81
Source: Trainee.
1999–2000 Crystal Palace 1 0
2000–01 Crystal Palace 1 0
2001–02 Crystal Palace 4 0
2001–02 *Luton T* 3 0 **3 0**
2002–03 Crystal Palace 4 1 **10 1**
2002–03 *Grimsby T* 13 6 **13 6**
2002–03 Sheffield U 25 7 **25 7**

KELLY, Gary (G) **520 0**
H: 5 11 W: 13 06 b.Fulwood 3-8-66
Source: Apprentice. *Honours:* Eire Under-21, B.
1984–85 Newcastle U 0 0
1985–86 Newcastle U 0 0
1986–87 Newcastle U 3 0
1987–88 Newcastle U 37 0
1988–89 Newcastle U 9 0
1988–89 *Blackpool* 5 0 **5 0**
1989–90 Newcastle U 4 0 **53 0**
1989–90 Bury 38 0
1990–91 Bury 46 0
1991–92 Bury 46 0
1992–93 Bury 42 0
1993–94 Bury 1 0
1993–94 *West Ham U* 0 0
1994–95 Bury 38 0
1995–96 Bury 25 0 **236 0**
1996–97 Oldham Ath 42 0
1997–98 Oldham Ath 26 0
1998–99 Oldham Ath 45 0
1999–2000 Oldham Ath 44 0
2000–01 Oldham Ath 45 0
2001–02 Oldham Ath 23 0
2002–03 Oldham Ath 0 0 **225 0**
From Northwich Vic.
2002–03 Sheffield U 1 0 **1 0**

KENNY, Paddy (G) **178 0**
H: 6 0 W: 15 00 b.Halifax 15-5-78
Source: Bradford PA.
1998–99 Bury 0 0
1999–2000 Bury 46 0
2000–01 Bury 46 0
2001–02 Bury 41 0
2002–03 Bury 0 0 **133 0**
2002–03 Sheffield U 45 0 **45 0**

KILLEEN, Lewis* (F) **1 0**
H: 5 9 W: 10 07 b.Peterborough 23-9-82
Source: Scholar.
2001–02 Sheffield U 1 0
2002–03 Sheffield U 0 0 **1 0**

KOZLUK, Rob# (D) **146 1**
H: 5 8 W: 11 08 b.Sutton-in-Ashfield 5-7-77
Source: Trainee. *Honours:* England Under-21.
1995–96 Derby Co 0 0
1996–97 Derby Co 0 0
1997–98 Derby Co 9 0
1998–99 Derby Co 7 0 **16 0**
1998–99 Sheffield U 10 0
1999–2000 Sheffield U 39 0
2000–01 Sheffield U 27 0
2000–01 *Huddersfield T* 14 0 **14 0**
2001–02 Sheffield U 8 0
2002–03 Sheffield U 32 1 **116 1**

LONGMORE, Danny* (M) **0 0**
b.London 10-1-85
2002–03 Sheffield U 0 0

MALLON, Ryan* (F) **1 0**
H: 5 7 W: 11 10 b.Sheffield 22-3-83
Source: Schoolboy.
2001–02 Sheffield U 1 0
2002–03 Sheffield U 0 0 **1 0**

McCALL, Stuart# (M) **726 65**
H: 5 8 W: 10 02 b.Leeds 10-6-64
Source: Apprentice. *Honours:* Scotland Under-21, 40 full caps, 1 goal.
1982–83 Bradford C 28 4
1983–84 Bradford C 46 5
1984–85 Bradford C 46 8
1985–86 Bradford C 38 4
1986–87 Bradford C 36 7
1987–88 Bradford C 44 9
1988–89 Everton 33 0
1989–90 Everton 37 3
1990–91 Everton 33 3 **103 6**
1991–92 Rangers 36 1
1992–93 Rangers 36 5
1993–94 Rangers 34 3
1994–95 Rangers 30 2
1995–96 Rangers 21 3
1996–97 Rangers 7 0
1997–98 Rangers 30 0 **194 14**
1998–99 Bradford C 43 3
1999–2000 Bradford C 34 1
2000–01 Bradford C 37 1
2001–02 Bradford C 43 3 **395 45**
2002–03 Sheffield U 34 0 **34 0**

MONTGOMERY, Nick (M) **81 2**
H: 5 9 W: 12 06 b.Leeds 28-10-81
Source: Scholar. *Honours:* Scotland Under-21.
2000–01 Sheffield U 27 0
2001–02 Sheffield U 31 2
2002–03 Sheffield U 23 0 **81 2**

MORRISON, Owen (M) **66 8**
H: 5 8 W: 11 12 b.Derry 8-12-81
Source: Trainee. *Honours:* Northern Ireland Schools, Youth, Under-21.
1998–99 Sheffield W 1 0
1999–2000 Sheffield W 0 0
2000–01 Sheffield W 30 6
2001–02 Sheffield W 24 2
2002–03 Sheffield W 1 0 **56 8**
2002–03 *Hull C* 2 0 **2 0**
2002–03 Sheffield U 8 0 **8 0**

MURPHY, Kevin* (M) **0 0**
b.Perth (Australia) 4-9-80
2002–03 Sheffield U 0 0

MURPHY, Shaun (D) **368 23**
H: 6 1 W: 13 13 b.Sydney 5-11-70
Honours: Australia Under-20, Under-23, 18 full caps, 3 goals.
1989–90 Blacktown City 10 1
1990–91 Blacktown City 0 0 **10 1**
1991–92 Heidelberg 9 0 **9 0**
1992–93 Notts Co 8 1
1993–94 Notts Co 11 1
1994–95 Notts Co 35 0
1995–96 Notts Co 39 3
1996–97 Notts Co 16 0 **109 5**
1996–97 WBA 17 2
1997–98 WBA 17 1
1998–99 WBA 37 4 **71 7**
1999–2000 Sheffield U 42 3
2000–01 Sheffield U 46 5
2001–02 Sheffield U 27 0
2001–02 *Crystal Palace* 11 0 **11 0**
2002–03 Sheffield U 43 2 **158 10**

NDLOVU, Peter# (F) **389 79**
H: 5 7 W: 10 02 b.Bulawayo 25-2-73
Source: Highlanders. *Honours:* Zimbabwe full caps.
1991–92 Coventry C 23 2
1992–93 Coventry C 32 7
1993–94 Coventry C 40 11
1994–95 Coventry C 30 11
1995–96 Coventry C 32 5
1996–97 Coventry C 20 1 **177 37**
1997–98 Birmingham C 39 9

1998–99 Birmingham C 43 10
1999–2000 Birmingham C 13 1
2000-01 Birmingham C 12 2 **107 22**
2000-01 *Huddersfield T* 6 4 **6 4**
2000-01 Sheffield U 15 4
2001-02 Sheffield U 45 4
2002-03 Sheffield U 39 8 **99 16**

NUGENT, Rob* (D) 0 0
H: 6 0 W: 12 04 b.Manchester 27-12-82
Source: Scholar.
2001-02 Sheffield U 0 0
2002-03 Sheffield U 0 0

ONUORA, Iffy (F) 421 113
H: 6 2 W: 13 13 b.Glasgow 28-7-67
Source: British Univ.
1989–90 Huddersfield T 20 3
1990–91 Huddersfield T 43 7
1991–92 Huddersfield T 41 8
1992–93 Huddersfield T 39 6
1993–94 Huddersfield T 22 6 **165 30**
1994–95 Mansfield T 14 7
1995–96 Mansfield T 14 1 **28 8**
1996–97 Gillingham 40 21
1997–98 Gillingham 22 2
1997–98 Swindon T 6 1
1998–99 Swindon T 43 20
1999–2000 Swindon T 24 4 **73 25**
1999–2000 Gillingham 22 6
2000-01 Gillingham 31 9
2001-02 Gillingham 33 11 **148 49**
2002-03 Sheffield U 7 1 **7 1**

PAGE, Robert (D) 293 2
H: 5 11 W: 13 12 b.Tylorstown 3-9-74
Source: Trainee. *Honours:* Wales Schools, Youth, Under-21, B, 28 full caps.
1992–93 Watford 0 0
1993–94 Watford 4 0
1994–95 Watford 5 0
1995–96 Watford 19 0
1996–97 Watford 36 0
1997–98 Watford 41 0
1998–99 Watford 39 0
1999–2000 Watford 36 1
2000-01 Watford 36 1
2001-02 Watford 0 0 **216 2**
2001-02 Sheffield U 43 0
2002-03 Sheffield U 34 0 **77 0**

PESCHISOLIDO, Paul (F) 325 90
H: 5 7 W: 11 08 b.Canada 25-5-71
Source: Toronto Blizzard. *Honours:* Canada 45 full caps, 9 goals.
1992–93 Birmingham C 19 7
1993–94 Birmingham C 24 9
1994–95 Stoke C 40 13
1995–96 Stoke C 26 6 **66 19**
1995–96 Birmingham C 9 1 **52 17**
1996–97 WBA 37 15
1997–98 WBA 8 3 **45 18**
1997–98 Fulham 32 13
1998–99 Fulham 33 7
1999–2000 Fulham 30 4
2000-01 Fulham 0 0 **95 24**
2000-01 *QPR* 5 1 **5 1**
2000-01 *Sheffield U* 5 2
2000-01 *Norwich C* 5 0 **5 0**
2001-02 Sheffield U 29 6
2002-03 Sheffield U 23 3 **57 11**

PURKISS, Ben* (D) 0 0
b.Sheffield 1-4-84
2001-02 Sheffield U 0 0
2002-03 Sheffield U 0 0

QUINN, Gerry‡ (M) 0 0
b.Dublin 16-9-83
2000-01 Sheffield U 0 0
2001-02 Sheffield U 0 0
2002-03 Sheffield U 0 0

SCOTT, Ben† (G) 0 0
b.Doncaster 16-11-83
Source: Schoolboy.
2001-02 Sheffield U 0 0
2002-03 Sheffield U 0 0

SESTANOVICH, Ashley (M) 0 0
H: 6 3 W: 13 00 b.London 18-9-81
Source: Hampton & Richmond B.
2002-03 Sheffield U 0 0

SMITH, Grant* (M) 26 1
H: 6 0 W: 13 09 b.Irvine 5-5-80
1998–99 Reading 0 0
1999–2000 Reading 0 0
2000-01 Reading 0 0
2001-02 *Halifax T* 11 0 **11 0**
2001-02 Sheffield U 7 0
2002-03 Sheffield U 3 0 **10 0**
2002-03 *Plymouth Arg* 5 1 **5 1**

TANSLEY, Anthony† (F) 0 0
b.Derby 17-1-84
Source: Scholar.
2002-03 Sheffield U 0 0

TEN HEUVEL, Laurens (F) 20 0
H: 6 2 W: 12 03 b.Duivendrecht 6-6-76
Source: Den Bosch.
1995–96 Den Bosch 3 0 **3 0**
1995–96 Barnsley 2 0
1996–97 Barnsley 3 0
1997–98 Barnsley 2 0 **7 0**
1997–98 *Northampton T* 0 0
From First Vienna, DCG.
2001-02 Telstar 0 0
2002-03 Sheffield U 5 0 **5 0**
2002-03 *Bradford C* 5 0 **5 0**

THOMPSON, Tyrone* (F) 1 0
H: 5 8 W: 11 05 b.Sheffield 8-5-82
Source: Scholar.
2000-01 Sheffield U 0 0
2001-02 Sheffield U 0 0
2002-03 Sheffield U 0 0
2002-03 *Lincoln C* 1 0 **1 0**

TONGE, Michael (M) 76 9
H: 6 0 W: 13 02 b.Manchester 7-4-83
Source: Scholar. *Honours:* England Under-20.
2000-01 Sheffield U 2 0
2001-02 Sheffield U 30 3
2002-03 Sheffield U 44 6 **76 9**

TRACEY, Simon* (G) 338 0
H: 6 1 W: 14 09 b.Woolwich 9-12-67
Source: Apprentice.
1985–86 Wimbledon 0 0
1986–87 Wimbledon 0 0
1987–88 Wimbledon 0 0
1988–89 Wimbledon 1 0
1988–89 Sheffield U 7 0
1989–90 Sheffield U 46 0
1990–91 Sheffield U 31 0
1991–92 Sheffield U 29 0
1992–93 Sheffield U 10 0
1993–94 Sheffield U 15 0
1994–95 Sheffield U 5 0
1994–95 *Manchester C* 3 0 **3 0**
1994–95 *Norwich C* 1 0 **1 0**
1995–96 Sheffield U 11 0
1995–96 *Wimbledon* 1 0 **2 0**
1996–97 Sheffield U 7 0
1997–98 Sheffield U 27 0
1998–99 Sheffield U 18 0
1999–2000 Sheffield U 45 0
2000-01 Sheffield U 40 0
2001-02 Sheffield U 41 0
2002-03 Sheffield U 0 0 **332 0**

ULLATHORNE, Robert‡ (D) 183 8
H: 5 7 W: 12 00 b.Wakefield 11-10-71
Source: Trainee.
1989–90 Norwich C 0 0
1990–91 Norwich C 2 0
1991–92 Norwich C 20 3
1992–93 Norwich C 0 0
1993–94 Norwich C 16 2
1994–95 Norwich C 27 2
1995–96 Norwich C 29 0 **94 7**
1996–97 Osasuna 18 0 **18 0**
1996–97 Leicester C 0 0
1997–98 Leicester C 6 1
1998–99 Leicester C 25 0
1999–2000 Leicester C 0 0 **31 1**
2000-01 Sheffield U 14 0
2001-02 Sheffield U 14 0
2002-03 Sheffield U 12 0 **40 0**

WINDASS, Dean (F) 415 118
H: 5 10 W: 12 06 b.North Ferriby 1-4-69
Source: N Ferriby U.
1991–92 Hull C 32 6
1992–93 Hull C 41 7
1993–94 Hull C 43 23
1994–95 Hull C 44 17
1995–96 Hull C 16 4 **176 57**
1995–96 Aberdeen 20 6
1996–97 Aberdeen 29 10
1997–98 Aberdeen 24 5 **73 21**
1998–99 Oxford U 33 15 **33 15**
1998–99 Bradford C 12 3
1999–2000 Bradford C 38 10
2000-01 Bradford C 24 3 **74 16**
2000-01 Middlesbrough 8 2
2001-02 Middlesbrough 27 1
2001-02 *Sheffield W* 2 0 **2 0**
2002-03 Middlesbrough 2 0 **37 3**
2002-03 Sheffield U 20 6 **20 6**

YATES, Steve (D) 456 9
H: 5 10 W: 12 03 b.Bristol 29-1-70
Source: Trainee.
1986–87 Bristol R 2 0
1987–88 Bristol R 0 0
1988–89 Bristol R 35 0
1989–90 Bristol R 42 0
1990–91 Bristol R 34 0
1991–92 Bristol R 39 0
1992–93 Bristol R 44 0
1993–94 Bristol R 1 0 **197 0**
1993–94 QPR 29 0
1994–95 QPR 23 1
1995–96 QPR 30 0
1996–97 QPR 16 1
1997–98 QPR 30 0
1998–99 QPR 6 0 **134 2**
1999–2000 Tranmere R 33 2
2000-01 Tranmere R 43 2
2001-02 Tranmere R 37 3 **113 7**
2002-03 Sheffield U 12 0 **12 0**

Scholars
Ashmore, James C; Ellis, Nicky; Forte, Jonathan RJ; Glarvey, Christopher; Gyaki, Ryan; Harper, Adrian; Hazell, Rohan J; Horwood, Evan D; Hurrell, Paul J; Hurst, Kevan; Lindley, Thomas; Marrison, Colin I; McGuiness, Craig; Platel, Daniel; Roma, Dominic M; Ross, Ian; Sharp, Billy L; Sloane, Daniel; Wood, Daniel J

Non-Contract
Blackwell, Kevin P; Cas, Marcel; Scott, Benjamin T; Tansley, Anthony D

SHEFFIELD W

ARMSTRONG, Craig (D) 215 6
H: 5 11 W: 13 02 b.South Shields 23-5-75
Source: Trainee.
1992–93 Nottingham F 0 0
1993–94 Nottingham F 0 0
1994–95 Nottingham F 0 0
1994–95 *Burnley* 4 0 **4 0**
1995–96 Nottingham F 0 0
1995–96 *Bristol R* 14 0 **14 0**
1996–97 Nottingham F 0 0
1996–97 *Gillingham* 10 0 **10 0**
1996–97 *Watford* 15 0 **15 0**
1997–98 Nottingham F 18 0
1998–99 Nottingham F 22 0 **40 0**
1998–99 Huddersfield T 13 1
1999–2000 Huddersfield T 39 0
2000-01 Huddersfield T 44 3
2001-02 Huddersfield T 11 1 **107 5**
2001-02 Sheffield W 8 0
2002-03 Sheffield W 17 1 **25 1**

BARRY-MURPHY, Brian (M) 133 3
H: 5 11 W: 13 03 b.Cork 27-7-78
Honours: Eire Under-21.
1995–96 Cork City 13 0
1996–97 Cork City 25 0
1997–98 Cork City 15 1
1998–99 Cork City 27 1 **80 2**
1999–2000 Preston NE 1 0
2000-01 Preston NE 14 0
2001-02 Preston NE 4 0
2001-02 *Southend U* 8 1 **8 1**
2002-03 Preston NE 2 0 **21 0**
2002-03 *Hartlepool U* 7 0 **7 0**
2002-03 Sheffield W 17 0 **17 0**

BESWETHERICK, John (D) 155 0
H: 6 0 W: 12 07 b.Liverpool 15-1-78
Source: Trainee.
1996–97 Plymouth Arg 0 0
1997–98 Plymouth Arg 2 0
1998–99 Plymouth Arg 22 0
1999–2000 Plymouth Arg 45 0
2000-01 Plymouth Arg 45 0
2001-02 Plymouth Arg 32 0 **146 0**
2002-03 Sheffield W 6 0 **6 0**
2002-03 *Swindon T* 3 0 **3 0**

BROMBY, Leigh (D) 86 2
H: 5 11 W: 11 12 b.Dewsbury 2-6-80
Honours: England Schools.
1998–99 Sheffield W 0 0
1999–2000 Sheffield W 0 0

1999–2000 *Mansfield T* 10 1 **10 1**
2000-01 Sheffield W 18 0
2001-02 Sheffield W 26 1
2002-03 Sheffield W 27 0 **71 1**
2002-03 *Norwich C* 5 0 **5 0**

BURROWS, David‡ (D) 397 5
H: 5 11 W: 12 04 b.Dudley 25-10-68
Source: Apprentice. *Honours:* England Under-21, B.
1985–86 WBA 1 0
1986–87 WBA 15 1
1987–88 WBA 21 0
1988–89 WBA 9 0 **46 1**
1988–89 Liverpool 21 0
1989–90 Liverpool 26 0
1990–91 Liverpool 35 0
1991–92 Liverpool 30 1
1992–93 Liverpool 30 2
1993–94 Liverpool 4 0 **146 3**
1993–94 West Ham U 25 1
1994–95 West Ham U 4 0 **29 1**
1994–95 Everton 19 0 **19 0**
1994–95 Coventry C 11 0
1995–96 Coventry C 11 0
1996–97 Coventry C 18 0
1997–98 Coventry C 33 0
1998–99 Coventry C 23 0
1999–2000 Coventry C 15 0 **111 0**
2000-01 Birmingham C 13 0
2001-02 Birmingham C 12 0 **25 0**
2001-02 Sheffield W 8 0
2002-03 Sheffield W 13 0 **21 0**

CONNOLLY, Calem* (D) 0 0
H: 5 9 W: 11 12 b.Leeds 12-2-82
2000-01 Sheffield W 0 0
2001-02 Sheffield W 0 0
2002-03 Sheffield W 0 0

CRANE, Tony* (D) 49 4
H: 6 5 W: 15 05 b.Liverpool 8-9-82
Source: Trainee. *Honours:* England Youth.
1999–2000 Sheffield W 0 0
2000-01 Sheffield W 15 2
2001-02 Sheffield W 15 0
2002-03 Sheffield W 19 2 **49 4**

DI PIEDI, Michaelli‡ (F) 44 5
H: 6 0 W: 13 00 b.Palermo 4-12-80
2000-01 Sheffield W 25 4
2001-02 Sheffield W 12 1
2002-03 Sheffield W 2 0 **39 5**
2002-03 *Bristol R* 5 0 **5 0**

DONNELLY, Simon* (M) 199 38
H: 5 9 W: 11 11 b.Glasgow 1-12-74
Source: Celtic BC. *Honours:* Scotland Under-21, 10 full caps.
1993–94 Celtic 12 5
1994–95 Celtic 17 0
1995–96 Celtic 35 6
1996–97 Celtic 29 4
1997–98 Celtic 30 10
1998–99 Celtic 23 5 **146 30**
1999–2000 Sheffield W 12 1
2000-01 Sheffield W 3 1
2001-02 Sheffield W 23 4
2002-03 Sheffield W 15 2 **53 8**

EKOKU, Efan (F) 309 106
H: 6 1 W: 13 00 b.Manchester 8-6-67
Source: Sutton U. *Honours:* Nigeria 5 full caps.
1990–91 Bournemouth 20 3
1991–92 Bournemouth 28 11
1992–93 Bournemouth 14 7 **62 21**
1992–93 Norwich C 4 3
1993–94 Norwich C 27 12
1994–95 Norwich C 6 0 **37 15**
1994–95 Wimbledon 24 9
1995–96 Wimbledon 31 7
1996–97 Wimbledon 30 11
1997–98 Wimbledon 16 4
1998–99 Wimbledon 22 6 **123 37**
1999–2000 Grasshoppers 21 16
2000-01 Grasshoppers 7 3 **28 19**
2000-01 Sheffield W 32 7
2001-02 Sheffield W 27 7
2002-03 Sheffield W 0 0 **59 14**

EVANS, Paul* (G) 7 0
H: 6 4 W: 15 00 b.Newcastle, SA 28-12-73
Source: Witts Univ.
1995–96 Leeds U 0 0
1995–96 *Crystal Palace* 0 0
1996–97 Leeds U 0 0
1996–97 *Bradford C* 0 0
From Jomo Cosmos.
2001-02 Huddersfield T 0 0
2002-03 Sheffield W 7 0 **7 0**

EVANS, Richard (M) 4 1
H: 5 8 W: 11 08 b.Cardiff 19-6-83
Source: Scholar.
2002-03 Birmingham C 0 0
2002-03 Sheffield W 4 1 **4 1**

GEARY, Derek (D) 63 0
H: 5 7 W: 12 03 b.Dublin 19-6-80
1997–98 Sheffield W 0 0
1998–99 Sheffield W 0 0
1999–2000 Sheffield W 0 0
2000-01 Sheffield W 5 0
2001-02 Sheffield W 32 0
2002-03 Sheffield W 26 0 **63 0**

GREEN, Ryan (M) 35 0
H: 5 7 W: 10 10 b.Cardiff 20-10-80
Source: Danes Court. *Honours:* Wales Youth, Under-21, 2 full caps.
1997–98 Wolverhampton W 0 0
1998–99 Wolverhampton W 1 0
1999–2000 Wolverhampton W 0 0
2000-01 Wolverhampton W 7 0
2000-01 *Torquay U* 10 0 **10 0**
2001-02 Wolverhampton W 0 0 **8 0**
2001-02 Millwall 13 0 **13 0**
2002-03 Cardiff C 0 0
2002-03 Sheffield W 4 0 **4 0**

HAMSHAW, Matthew (M) 54 1
H: 5 9 W: 13 00 b.Rotherham 1-1-82
Source: Trainee. *Honours:* England Youth, Under-20.
1998–99 Sheffield W 0 0
1999–2000 Sheffield W 0 0
2000-01 Sheffield W 18 0
2001-02 Sheffield W 21 0
2002-03 Sheffield W 15 1 **54 1**

HASLAM, Steven (D) 119 2
H: 5 11 W: 11 03 b.Sheffield 6-9-79
Source: Trainee. *Honours:* England Schools, Youth.
1996–97 Sheffield W 0 0
1997–98 Sheffield W 0 0
1998–99 Sheffield W 2 0
1999–2000 Sheffield W 23 0
2000-01 Sheffield W 27 1
2001-02 Sheffield W 41 0
2002-03 Sheffield W 26 1 **119 2**

HOLT, Grant (M) 13 1
H: 6 0 W: 12 06 b.Carlisle 12-4-81
Source: Workington.
1999–2000 Halifax T 4 0
2000-01 Halifax T 2 0 **6 0**
From Sengkang,Barrow
2002-03 Sheffield W 7 1 **7 1**

KUQI, Shefki (F) 214 53
H: 6 1 W: 14 00 b.Kosovo 11-11-76
Source: Trepka, Miki. *Honours:* Albania 8 full caps, 1 goal; Finland 31 full caps, 4 goals.
1995 MP 24 3
1996 MP 26 7 **50 10**
1997 HJK Helsinki 25 6
1998 HJK Helsinki 22 1
1999 HJK Helsinki 25 11 **72 18**
From Jokerit
2000-01 Stockport Co 17 6
2001-02 Stockport Co 18 5 **35 11**
2001-02 Sheffield W 17 6
2002-03 Sheffield W 40 8 **57 14**

MADDIX, Danny* (D) 355 15
H: 5 11 W: 12 11 b.Ashford 11-10-67
Source: Apprentice. *Honours:* Jamaica 2 full caps.
1985–86 Tottenham H 0 0
1986–87 Tottenham H 0 0
1986–87 *Southend U* 2 0 **2 0**
1987–88 QPR 9 0
1988–89 QPR 33 2
1989–90 QPR 32 3
1990–91 QPR 32 1
1991–92 QPR 19 0
1992–93 QPR 14 0
1993–94 QPR 0 0
1994–95 QPR 27 1
1995–96 QPR 22 0
1996–97 QPR 25 0
1997–98 QPR 25 1
1998–99 QPR 37 4
1999–2000 QPR 17 1
2000-01 QPR 2 0 **294 13**
2001-02 Sheffield W 36 1
2002-03 Sheffield W 23 1 **59 2**

McLAREN, Paul (M) 238 10
H: 6 1 W: 13 04 b.High Wycombe 17-11-76
Source: Trainee.
1993–94 Luton T 1 0
1994–95 Luton T 0 0
1995–96 Luton T 12 1
1996–97 Luton T 24 0
1997–98 Luton T 43 0
1998–99 Luton T 23 0
1999–2000 Luton T 29 1
2000-01 Luton T 35 2 **167 4**
2001-02 Sheffield W 35 2
2002-03 Sheffield W 36 4 **71 6**

O'DONNELL, Phil* (M) 234 30
H: 5 11 W: 12 08 b.Bellshill 25-3-72
Source: X Form. *Honours:* Scotland Under-21, 1 full cap.
1990–91 Motherwell 12 0
1991–92 Motherwell 42 4
1992–93 Motherwell 32 4
1993–94 Motherwell 35 7
1994–95 Motherwell 3 0 **124 15**
1994–95 Celtic 27 6
1995–96 Celtic 15 3
1996–97 Celtic 19 2
1997–98 Celtic 14 2
1998–99 Celtic 15 2 **90 15**
1999–2000 Sheffield W 1 0
2000-01 Sheffield W 11 0
2001-02 Sheffield W 8 0
2002-03 Sheffield W 0 0 **20 0**

OWUSU, Lloyd (F) 196 68
H: 6 1 W: 13 07 b.Slough 12-12-76
Source: Slough T.
1998–99 Brentford 46 22
1999–2000 Brentford 41 12
2000-01 Brentford 33 10
2001-02 Brentford 44 20 **164 64**
2002-03 Sheffield W 32 4 **32 4**

POWELL, Darryl (M) 358 26
H: 6 1 W: 13 03 b.Lambeth 15-11-71
Source: Trainee. *Honours:* Jamaica full caps.
1988–89 Portsmouth 3 0
1989–90 Portsmouth 0 0
1990–91 Portsmouth 8 0
1991–92 Portsmouth 36 6
1992–93 Portsmouth 23 0
1993–94 Portsmouth 28 5
1994–95 Portsmouth 34 5 **132 16**
1995–96 Derby Co 37 5
1996–97 Derby Co 33 1
1997–98 Derby Co 23 0
1998–99 Derby Co 33 0
1999–2000 Derby Co 31 2
2000-01 Derby Co 27 1
2001-02 Derby Co 23 1
2002-03 Derby Co 0 0 **207 10**
2002-03 Birmingham C 11 0 **11 0**
2002-03 Sheffield W 8 0 **8 0**

PRESSMAN, Kevin (G) 387 0
H: 6 1 W: 15 02 b.Fareham 6-11-67
Source: Apprentice. *Honours:* England Schools, Youth, Under-21, B.
1985–86 Sheffield W 0 0
1986–87 Sheffield W 0 0
1987–88 Sheffield W 11 0
1988–89 Sheffield W 9 0
1989–90 Sheffield W 15 0
1990–91 Sheffield W 23 0
1991–92 Sheffield W 1 0
1991–92 *Stoke C* 4 0 **4 0**
1992–93 Sheffield W 3 0
1993–94 Sheffield W 32 0
1994–95 Sheffield W 34 0
1995–96 Sheffield W 30 0
1996–97 Sheffield W 38 0
1997–98 Sheffield W 36 0
1998–99 Sheffield W 15 0
1999–2000 Sheffield W 19 0
2000-01 Sheffield W 39 0
2001-02 Sheffield W 40 0
2002-03 Sheffield W 38 0 **383 0**

QUINN, Alan (M) 133 12
H: 5 9 W: 11 03 b.Dublin 13-6-79
Source: Cherry Orchard. *Honours:* Eire Under-21, 1 full cap.
1997–98 Sheffield W 1 0
1998–99 Sheffield W 1 0
1999–2000 Sheffield W 19 3

2000-01 Sheffield W 37 2
2001-02 Sheffield W 38 2
2002-03 Sheffield W 37 5 **133 12**

SHAW, Jon§ (M) 1 0
b.Sheffield 10-11-83
Source: Scholar.
2002-03 Sheffield W 1 0 **1 0**

SHAW, Matthew (F) 0 0
H: 6 1 W: 11 09 b.Blackpool 17-5-84
2001-02 Sheffield W 0 0
2002-03 Sheffield W 0 0

SIBON, Gerald‡ (F) 242 87
H: 6 5 W: 14 05 b.Emmen 19-4-74
1993–94 Twente 3 0 **3 0**
1994–95 VVV 30 20
1995–96 VVV 23 14 **53 34**
1996–97 Roda 34 13 **34 13**
1997–98 Ajax 12 2
1998–99 Ajax 11 2 **23 4**
1999–2000 Sheffield W 28 5
2000-01 Sheffield W 41 13
2001-02 Sheffield W 35 12
2002-03 Sheffield W 25 6 **129 36**

SMITH, Dean (D) 512 53
H: 6 0 W: 13 03 b.West Bromwich 19-3-71
Source: Trainee.
1988–89 Walsall 15 0
1989–90 Walsall 7 0
1990–91 Walsall 33 0
1991–92 Walsall 9 0
1992–93 Walsall 42 1
1993–94 Walsall 36 1 **142 2**
1994–95 Hereford U 35 3
1995–96 Hereford U 40 8
1996–97 Hereford U 42 8 **117 19**
1997–98 Leyton Orient 43 9
1998–99 Leyton Orient 37 9
1999–2000 Leyton Orient 44 4
2000-01 Leyton Orient 43 5
2001-02 Leyton Orient 45 2
2002-03 Leyton Orient 27 3 **239 32**
2002-03 Sheffield W 14 0 **14 0**

SOLTVEDT, Trond Egil* (M) 350 69
H: 6 1 W: 12 09 b.Voss 15-2-67
Source: Dale, Ny-Krohnborg. *Honours:* Norway 4 full caps.
1988 Viking 21 3
1989 Viking 11 3
1990 Viking 20 3
1991 Viking 13 1 **65 10**
1992 Brann 22 6
1993 Brann 21 16
1994 Brann 21 12 **64 34**
1995 Rosenborg 25 4
1996 Rosenborg 26 10
1997 Rosenborg 9 4 **60 18**
1997–98 Coventry C 30 1
1998–99 Coventry C 27 2
1999–2000 Coventry C 0 0 **57 3**
1999–2000 Southampton 24 1
2000-01 Southampton 6 1 **30 2**
2000-01 Sheffield W 15 1
2001-02 Sheffield W 38 1
2002-03 Sheffield W 21 0 **74 2**

STRINGER, Chris (G) 9 0
H: 6 2 W: 12 09 b.Grimsby 16-6-83
Source: Scholar.
2000-01 Sheffield W 5 0
2001-02 Sheffield W 1 0
2002-03 Sheffield W 3 0 **9 0**

WESTWOOD, Ashley* (D) 204 16
H: 6 0 W: 12 09 b.Bridgnorth 31-8-76
Source: Trainee. *Honours:* England Youth.
1994–95 Manchester U 0 0
1995–96 Crewe Alex 33 4
1996–97 Crewe Alex 44 2
1997–98 Crewe Alex 21 3 **98 9**
1998–99 Bradford C 19 2
1999–2000 Bradford C 5 0
2000-01 Bradford C 0 0 **24 2**
2000-01 Sheffield W 33 2
2001-02 Sheffield W 26 1
2002-03 Sheffield W 23 2 **82 5**

WOOD, Richard (D) 3 1
b.Yorkshire 5-7-85
Source: Scholar.
2002-03 Sheffield W 3 1 **3 1**

Scholars
Beadsley, Scott M; Callaghan, Aaron C; Docker, Jonathon M; Doherty, Michael F; Douglas, Ian M; Foster, Luke J; Greenwood, Ross M; Hill, Matthew J; Knowles, Alexander S; Lowe, Scott; Marsden, Thomas; McMahon, Lewis J; Needham, Liam P; Ogden, Adam J; Orlik, Marcus J; Palmieri, Mason J; Poulter, Robert J; Shaw, Jon S; Smith, Jason K; Stevenson, Lee C; Stone, Keeron J; Taylor, Robert J; Wilson, Laurie J; Wood, Daniel G

SHREWSBURY T

AISTON, Sam* (F) 159 6
H: 6 1 W: 12 00 b.Newcastle 21-11-76
Source: Newcastle U Trainee. *Honours:* England Schools.
1995–96 Sunderland 14 0
1996–97 Sunderland 2 0
1996–97 *Chester C* 14 0
1997–98 Sunderland 3 0
1998–99 Sunderland 1 0
1998–99 *Chester C* 11 0 **25 0**
1999–2000 Sunderland 0 0 **20 0**
1999–2000 *Stoke C* 6 0 **6 0**
1999–2000 *Shrewsbury T* 10 0
2000-01 Shrewsbury T 42 2
2001-02 Shrewsbury T 35 2
2002-03 Shrewsbury T 21 2 **108 6**

ATKINS, Mark* (M) 521 51
H: 6 0 W: 12 05 b.Doncaster 14-8-68
Honours: England Schools.
1986–87 Scunthorpe U 26 0
1987–88 Scunthorpe U 22 2 **48 2**
1988–89 Blackburn R 46 6
1989–90 Blackburn R 41 7
1990–91 Blackburn R 42 4
1991–92 Blackburn R 44 6
1992–93 Blackburn R 31 5
1993–94 Blackburn R 15 1
1994–95 Blackburn R 34 6
1995–96 Blackburn R 4 0 **257 35**
1995–96 Wolverhampton W 32 3
1996–97 Wolverhampton W 45 4
1997–98 Wolverhampton W 34 2
1998–99 Wolverhampton W 15 0 **126 9**
1999–2000 York C 10 2 **10 2**
2000-01 Doncaster R 0 0
2000-01 Hull C 8 0 **8 0**
2001-02 Shrewsbury T 42 2
2002-03 Shrewsbury T 30 1 **72 3**

BRYNGELSSON, Fredrik‡ (D) 78 2
H: 6 2 W: 11 13 b.Sweden 10-4-75
1996 Norrby 13 0
1997 Norrby 23 1 **36 1**
1998 Hacken 2 0
1999 Hacken 24 1
2000 Hacken 8 0 **34 1**
2000-01 Stockport Co 5 0
2001-02 Stockport Co 3 0 **8 0**
2002-03 Shrewsbury T 0 0

CARTWRIGHT, Mark (G) 77 0
H: 6 2 W: 13 00 b.Chester 13-1-73
Source: York C.
1994–95 Wrexham 0 0
1995–96 Wrexham 0 0
1996–97 Wrexham 3 0
1997–98 Wrexham 4 0
1998–99 Wrexham 30 0
1999–2000 Wrexham 0 0
2000-01 Wrexham 0 0 **37 0**
2000-01 Brighton & HA 13 0 **13 0**
2001-02 Shrewsbury T 14 0
2002-03 Shrewsbury T 13 0 **27 0**

DRYSDALE, Leon* (D) 65 1
H: 5 9 W: 10 12 b.Walsall 3-2-81
Source: Trainee.
1998–99 Shrewsbury T 2 0
1999–2000 Shrewsbury T 0 0
2000-01 Shrewsbury T 18 0
2001-02 Shrewsbury T 26 0
2002-03 Shrewsbury T 19 1 **65 1**

DUNBAVIN, Ian (G) 96 0
H: 6 1 W: 12 10 b.Knowsley 27-5-80
Source: Trainee.
1998–99 Liverpool 0 0
1999–2000 Liverpool 0 0
1999–2000 Shrewsbury T 7 0
2000-01 Shrewsbury T 22 0
2001-02 Shrewsbury T 34 0
2002-03 Shrewsbury T 33 0 **96 0**

EDWARDS, David§ (M) 1 0
b.Shrewsbury 3-2-86
Source: Scholar.
2002-03 Shrewsbury T 1 0 **1 0**

HARRIS, Richard‡ (M) 0 0
b.Shrewsbury 14-9-84
2001-02 Manchester C 0 0
2002-03 Shrewsbury T 0 0

HEATHCOTE, Mickey‡ (D) 430 35
H: 6 2 W: 12 05 b.Kelloe 10-9-65
Source: Middlesbrough, Spennymoor U.
1987–88 Sunderland 1 0
1987–88 *Halifax T* 7 1 **7 1**
1988–89 Sunderland 0 0
1989–90 Sunderland 8 0 **9 0**
1989–90 *York C* 3 0 **3 0**
1990–91 Shrewsbury T 39 6
1991–92 Shrewsbury T 5 0
1991–92 Cambridge U 22 5
1992–93 Cambridge U 42 2
1993–94 Cambridge U 40 5
1994–95 Cambridge U 24 1 **128 13**
1995–96 Plymouth Arg 44 4
1996–97 Plymouth Arg 42 1
1997–98 Plymouth Arg 36 4
1998–99 Plymouth Arg 43 3
1999–2000 Plymouth Arg 29 1
2000-01 Plymouth Arg 5 0 **199 13**
2001-02 Shrewsbury T 34 2
2002-03 Shrewsbury T 6 0 **84 8**

JAGIELKA, Steve (F) 165 17
H: 5 8 W: 11 03 b.Manchester 10-3-78
Source: Trainee.
1996–97 Stoke C 0 0
1997–98 Shrewsbury T 16 1
1998–99 Shrewsbury T 31 1
1999–2000 Shrewsbury T 33 1
2000-01 Shrewsbury T 31 6
2001-02 Shrewsbury T 31 5
2002-03 Shrewsbury T 23 3 **165 17**

JEMSON, Nigel* (M) 420 109
H: 5 11 W: 13 00 b.Preston 10-8-69
Source: Trainee. *Honours:* England Under-21.
1985–86 Preston NE 1 0
1986–87 Preston NE 4 3
1987–88 Preston NE 27 5
1987–88 Nottingham F 0 0
1988–89 Nottingham F 0 0
1988–89 *Bolton W* 5 0 **5 0**
1988–89 *Preston NE* 9 2 **41 10**
1989–90 Nottingham F 18 4
1990–91 Nottingham F 23 8
1991–92 Nottingham F 6 1 **47 13**
1991–92 Sheffield W 20 4
1992–93 Sheffield W 13 0
1993–94 Sheffield W 18 5 **51 9**
1993–94 *Grimsby T* 6 2 **6 2**
1994–95 Notts Co 11 1
1994–95 *Watford* 4 0 **4 0**
1994–95 *Coventry C* 0 0
1995–96 Notts Co 3 0 **14 1**
1995–96 *Rotherham U* 16 5 **16 5**
1996–97 Oxford U 44 18
1997–98 Oxford U 24 9
1997–98 Bury 15 1
1998–99 Bury 14 0 **29 1**
1999–2000 Ayr U 12 5 **12 5**
1999–2000 Oxford U 18 0 **86 27**
2000-01 Shrewsbury T 41 15
2001-02 Shrewsbury T 28 10
2002-03 Shrewsbury T 40 11 **109 36**

KENDALL, Lee‡ (G) 0 0
H: 6 0 W: 13 00 b.Newport 8-1-81
Source: Trainee. *Honours:* Wales Under-21.
1997–98 Crystal Palace 0 0
1998–99 Crystal Palace 0 0
1999–2000 Crystal Palace 0 0
2000-01 Crystal Palace 0 0
2000-01 Cardiff C 0 0
2001-02 Cardiff C 0 0
2002-03 Shrewsbury T 0 0

LOWE, Ryan (F) 107 20
H: 5 11 W: 11 05 b.Liverpool 18-9-78
Source: Burscough.
2000-01 Shrewsbury T 30 4
2001-02 Shrewsbury T 38 7
2002-03 Shrewsbury T 39 9 **107 20**

MOSS, Darren (D) **113 4**
H: 5 10 W: 11 00 b.Wrexham 24-5-81
Source: Trainee. *Honours:* Wales Under-21.

1998–99	Chester C	7	0		
1999–2000	Chester C	35	0		
2000-01	Chester C	0	0	**42**	**0**
2001-02	Shrewsbury T	31	2		
2002-03	Shrewsbury T	40	2	**71**	**4**

MURPHY, Chris* (F) **8 0**
H: 5 8 W: 10 05 b.Leamington Spa 8-3-83
Source: Scholar.

2000-01	Shrewsbury T	1	0		
2001-02	Shrewsbury T	4	0		
2002-03	Shrewsbury T	3	0	**8**	**0**

MURRAY, Karl (M) **109 5**
H: 5 10 W: 12 00 b.Islington 24-6-82
Source: Trainee.

1999–2000	Shrewsbury T	12	1		
2000-01	Shrewsbury T	35	0		
2001-02	Shrewsbury T	34	2		
2002-03	Shrewsbury T	28	2	**109**	**5**

PARTRIDGE, Scott# (F) **296 53**
H: 5 9 W: 11 00 b.Leicester 13-10-74
Source: Trainee.

1992–93	Bradford C	4	0		
1993–94	Bradford C	1	0	**5**	**0**
1993–94	Bristol C	9	4		
1994–95	Bristol C	33	2		
1995–96	Bristol C	9	1		
1995–96	*Torquay U*	5	2		
1995–96	*Plymouth Arg*	7	2	**7**	**2**
1995–96	*Scarborough*	7	0	**7**	**0**
1996–97	Bristol C	6	0	**57**	**7**
1996–97	Cardiff C	15	0		
1997–98	Cardiff C	22	2	**37**	**2**
1997–98	Torquay U	5	0		
1998–99	Torquay U	29	12	**39**	**14**
1998–99	Brentford	14	7		
1999–2000	Brentford	41	6		
2000-01	Brentford	36	8		
2001-02	Brentford	1	0	**92**	**21**
2001-02	Rushden & D	37	5		
2002-03	Rushden & D	7	0	**44**	**5**
2002-03	Exeter C	4	2	**4**	**2**
2002-03	Shrewsbury T	4	0	**4**	**0**

REDMILE, Matt* (D) **254 13**
H: 6 3 W: 14 10 b.Nottingham 12-11-76
Source: Trainee.

1995–96	Notts Co	0	0		
1996–97	Notts Co	23	2		
1997–98	Notts Co	34	3		
1998–99	Notts Co	41	1		
1999–2000	Notts Co	41	1		
2000-01	Notts Co	8	0	**147**	**7**
2000-01	Shrewsbury T	24	3		
2001-02	Shrewsbury T	44	2		
2002-03	Shrewsbury T	39	1	**107**	**6**

RODGERS, Luke (F) **106 46**
H: 5 8 W: 11 00 b.Birmingham 1-1-82
Source: Trainee.

1999–2000	Shrewsbury T	6	1		
2000-01	Shrewsbury T	26	7		
2001-02	Shrewsbury T	38	22		
2002-03	Shrewsbury T	36	16	**106**	**46**

STEPHENS, Ross§ (M) **1 0**
H: 5 7 W: 8 06 b.Llandidloes 28-5-85
Source: Scholar.

2002-03	Shrewsbury T	1	0	**1**	**0**

STEVENS, Ian* (F) **461 136**
H: 5 9 W: 12 06 b.Malta 21-10-66
Source: Trainee.

1984–85	Preston NE	4	1		
1985–86	Preston NE	7	1	**11**	**2**
1986–87	Stockport Co	2	0	**2**	**0**
From Lancaster C					
1986–87	Bolton W	8	2		
1987–88	Bolton W	9	0		
1988–89	Bolton W	21	5		
1989–90	Bolton W	4	0		
1990–91	Bolton W	5	0	**47**	**7**
1991–92	Bury	45	17		
1992–93	Bury	32	14		
1993–94	Bury	33	7	**110**	**38**
1994–95	Shrewsbury T	38	8		
1995–96	Shrewsbury T	32	12		
1996–97	Shrewsbury T	41	17		
1996–97	Carlisle U	0	0		
1997–98	Carlisle U	37	17		
1998–99	Carlisle U	41	9		
1999–2000	Wrexham	16	4	**16**	**4**
1999–2000	*Cheltenham T*	1	0	**1**	**0**
2000-01	Carlisle U	41	12		
2001-02	Carlisle U	26	8	**145**	**46**
2002-03	Shrewsbury T	18	2	**129**	**39**

THOMPSON, Andy* (D) **533 48**
H: 5 4 W: 10 11 b.Cannock 9-11-67
Source: Apprentice.

1985–86	WBA	15	1		
1986–87	WBA	9	0	**24**	**1**
1986–87	Wolverhampton W	29	8		
1987–88	Wolverhampton W	42	2		
1988–89	Wolverhampton W	46	6		
1989–90	Wolverhampton W	33	4		
1990–91	Wolverhampton W	44	3		
1991–92	Wolverhampton W	17	0		
1992–93	Wolverhampton W	20	0		
1993–94	Wolverhampton W	37	3		
1994–95	Wolverhampton W	31	9		
1995–96	Wolverhampton W	45	6		
1996–97	Wolverhampton W	32	2	**376**	**43**
1997–98	Tranmere R	44	3		
1998–99	Tranmere R	37	1		
1999–2000	Tranmere R	15	0	**96**	**4**
2000-01	Cardiff C	7	0		
2001-02	Cardiff C	0	0	**7**	**0**
2001-02	Shrewsbury T	14	0		
2002-03	Shrewsbury T	16	0	**30**	**0**

TOLLEY, Glenn§ (M) **1 0**
b.Shrewsbury 24-9-83
Source: Scholar.

2002-03	Shrewsbury T	1	0	**1**	**0**

TOLLEY, Jamie (M) **88 6**
H: 6 1 W: 10 08 b.Ludlow 12-5-83
Source: Scholarship. *Honours:* Wales Under-21.

1999–2000	Shrewsbury T	2	0		
2000-01	Shrewsbury T	24	2		
2001-02	Shrewsbury T	23	1		
2002-03	Shrewsbury T	39	3	**88**	**6**

VAN BLERK, Jason* (D) **381 22**
H: 6 1 W: 13 00 b.Sydney 16-3-68
Honours: Australia Under-20, 27 full caps, 1 goal.

1989	Blackdown City	24	3	**24**	**3**
1989–90	Leichhardt	25	1		
1990–91	St Truiden	23	2	**23**	**2**
1991–92	Leichhardt	14	4	**39**	**5**
1992–93	Go Ahead	18	1		
1993–94	Go Ahead	30	4	**48**	**5**
1994–95	Millwall	27	1		
1995–96	Millwall	42	1		
1996–97	Millwall	4	0	**73**	**2**
1997–98	Manchester C	19	0	**19**	**0**
1997–98	WBA	8	0		
1998–99	WBA	30	0		
1999–2000	WBA	35	1		
2000-01	WBA	36	2	**109**	**3**
2001-02	Stockport Co	13	0	**13**	**0**
2001-02	Hull C	10	1	**10**	**1**
2002-03	Shrewsbury T	23	1	**23**	**1**

WATTS, Steve (F) **144 30**
H: 6 0 W: 14 02 b.Lambeth 11-7-76
Source: Fisher Ath.

1998–99	Leyton Orient	28	6		
1999–2000	Leyton Orient	32	6		
2000-01	Leyton Orient	36	8		
2001-02	Leyton Orient	30	9		
2002-03	Leyton Orient	6	0	**132**	**29**
2002-03	*Lincoln C*	5	1	**5**	**1**
2002-03	Shrewsbury T	7	0	**7**	**0**

WILDING, Peter* (D) **193 7**
H: 6 1 W: 12 09 b.Shrewsbury 28-11-68
Source: Telford U.

1997–98	Shrewsbury T	34	1		
1998–99	Shrewsbury T	42	0		
1999–2000	Shrewsbury T	41	2		
2000-01	Shrewsbury T	21	1		
2001-02	Shrewsbury T	22	0		
2002-03	Shrewsbury T	33	3	**193**	**7**

WOAN, Ian* (F) **296 41**
H: 5 10 W: 12 04 b.Heswall 14-12-67
Source: Runcorn.

1989–90	Nottingham F	0	0		
1990–91	Nottingham F	12	3		
1991–92	Nottingham F	21	5		
1992–93	Nottingham F	28	3		
1993–94	Nottingham F	24	5		
1994–95	Nottingham F	37	5		
1995–96	Nottingham F	33	8		
1996–97	Nottingham F	32	1		
1997–98	Nottingham F	21	1		
1998–99	Nottingham F	2	0		
1999–2000	Nottingham F	11	0	**221**	**31**
2000-01	Barnsley	3	0	**3**	**0**
2000-01	Swindon T	22	3	**22**	**3**
2001-02	Shrewsbury T	14	3		
2002-03	Shrewsbury T	36	4	**50**	**7**

Scholars
Bragoli, Daniele; Brooks-Courtney, Christian D; Edwards, David A; Evans, Nicholas J; Griffin, Thomas B; Harris, Carl D; March, Daniel S; McCann, Neal; Morgan, Stephen J; Murray, Liam J; Packer, Christopher; Smith, Benjamin; Stephens, Ross; Thompson, Neville E; Tolley, Glenn A; Walker, Richard

SOUTHAMPTON

ARIAS, Frederico (M) **73 5**
H: 5 8 W: 11 07 b.Rosario 24-4-79

1998–99	Rosario Central	2	0		
1999–2000	Rosario Central	6	0		
2000-01	Rosario Central	21	1		
2001-02	Rosario Central	34	4	**63**	**5**
2002-03	Velez Sarsfield	10	0	**10**	**0**
2002-03	Southampton	0	0		

BAIRD, Chris (D) **3 0**
H: 5 10 W: 11 11 b.Ballymoney 25-2-82
Source: Scholar. *Honours:* Northern Ireland Under-21, 2 full caps..

2000-01	Southampton	0	0		
2001-02	Southampton	0	0		
2002-03	Southampton	3	0	**3**	**0**

BEATTIE, James (F) **160 51**
H: 6 1 W: 13 06 b.Lancaster 27-2-78
Source: Trainee. *Honours:* England Under-21, 2 full caps.

1994–95	Blackburn R	0	0		
1995–96	Blackburn R	0	0		
1996–97	Blackburn R	1	0		
1997–98	Blackburn R	3	0	**4**	**0**
1998–99	Southampton	35	5		
1999–2000	Southampton	18	0		
2000-01	Southampton	37	11		
2001-02	Southampton	28	12		
2002-03	Southampton	38	23	**156**	**51**

BENALI, Francis* (D) **326 1**
H: 5 9 W: 11 04 b.Southampton 30-12-68
Source: Apprentice. *Honours:* England Schools.

1986–87	Southampton	0	0		
1987–88	Southampton	0	0		
1988–89	Southampton	7	0		
1989–90	Southampton	27	0		
1990–91	Southampton	12	0		
1991–92	Southampton	22	0		
1992–93	Southampton	33	0		
1993–94	Southampton	37	0		
1994–95	Southampton	35	0		
1995–96	Southampton	29	0		
1996–97	Southampton	18	0		
1997–98	Southampton	33	1		
1998–99	Southampton	23	0		
1999–2000	Southampton	26	0		
2000-01	Southampton	4	0		
2000-01	*Nottingham F*	15	0	**15**	**0**
2001-02	Southampton	3	0		
2002-03	Southampton	2	0	**311**	**1**

BEVAN, Scott (G) **30 0**
H: 6 6 W: 15 10 b.Southampton 16-9-79
Source: Trainee.

1997–98	Southampton	0	0		
1998–99	Southampton	0	0		
1999–2000	Southampton	0	0		
2000-01	Southampton	0	0		
2001-02	Southampton	0	0		
2001-02	*Stoke C*	0	0		
2002-03	Southampton	0	0		
2002-03	*Huddersfield T*	30	0	**30**	**0**

BLAYNEY, Alan (G) **4 0**
H: 6 2 W: 13 12 b.Belfast 9-10-81
Source: Scholar. *Honours:* Northern Ireland Under-21.

2001-02	Southampton	0	0		
2002-03	Southampton	0	0		
2002-03	*Stockport Co*	2	0	**2**	**0**
2002-03	*Bournemouth*	2	0	**2**	**0**

BLEIDELIS, Imants‡ (M) **131 25**
H: 5 10 W: 12 01 b.Latvia 16-8-75
Honours: Latvia 68 full caps, 7 goals.

1994	Interskonto Riga	11	1	**11**	**1**

1994 Skonto Riga 11 0
1995 Skonto Riga 24 1
1996 Skonto Riga 20 3
1997 Skonto Riga 20 8
1998 Skonto Riga 24 8
1999 Skonto Riga 19 4 **118 24**
1999–2000 Southampton 0 0
2000-01 Southampton 1 0
2001-02 Southampton 1 0
2002-03 Southampton 0 0 **2 0**

BRIDGE, Wayne (D) 152 2
H: 5 10 W: 12 05 b.Southampton 5-8-80
Source: Trainee. *Honours:* England Youth, Under-21, 12 full caps.
1997–98 Southampton 0 0
1998–99 Southampton 23 0
1999–2000 Southampton 19 1
2000-01 Southampton 38 0
2001-02 Southampton 38 0
2002-03 Southampton 34 1 **152 2**

BYLES, Luke (D) 0 0
H: 5 11 W: 12 00 b.Southampton 8-1-84
Source: Scholar.
2001-02 Southampton 0 0
2002-03 Southampton 0 0

CHALA, Kleber‡ (M) 0 0
H: 5 10 W: 12 07 b.Ibarra 29-6-71
Source: Nacional. *Honours:* Ecuador 69 full caps, 6 goals.
2001-02 Southampton 0 0
2002-03 Southampton 0 0

CROWELL, Matt (M) 0 0
H: 5 9 W: 10 09 b.Bridgend 3-7-84
Source: Scholar.
2001-02 Southampton 0 0
2002-03 Southampton 0 0

DAVIES, Arron (M) 0 0
H: 5 9 W: 10 00 b.Cardiff 22-6-84
Source: Trainee.
2002-03 Southampton 0 0

DAVIES, Kevin* (F) 268 45
H: 6 1 W: 13 11 b.Sheffield 26-3-77
Source: Trainee. *Honours:* England Youth, Under-21.
1993–94 Chesterfield 24 4
1994–95 Chesterfield 41 11
1995–96 Chesterfield 30 4
1996–97 Chesterfield 34 3 **129 22**
1996–97 Southampton 0 0
1997–98 Southampton 25 9
1998–99 Blackburn R 21 1
1999–2000 Blackburn R 2 0 **23 1**
1999–2000 Southampton 23 6
2000-01 Southampton 27 1
2001-02 Southampton 23 2
2002-03 Southampton 9 1 **107 19**
2002-03 *Millwall* 9 3 **9 3**

DELAP, Rory (M) 220 20
H: 6 3 W: 13 00 b.Sutton Coldfield 6-7-76
Source: Trainee. *Honours:* Eire 9 full caps.
1992–93 Carlisle U 1 0
1993–94 Carlisle U 1 0
1994–95 Carlisle U 3 0
1995–96 Carlisle U 19 3
1996–97 Carlisle U 32 4
1997–98 Carlisle U 9 0 **65 7**
1997–98 Derby Co 13 0
1998–99 Derby Co 23 0
1999–2000 Derby Co 34 8
2000-01 Derby Co 33 3 **103 11**
2001-02 Southampton 28 2
2002-03 Southampton 24 0 **52 2**

DELGADO, Agustin (F) 161 73
H: 6 3 W: 13 08 b.Ibarra 23-12-74
Honours: Ecuador 49 full caps, 22 goals.
1996 Nacional 30 18 **30 18**
1997 Barcelona 25 12
1998 Barcelona 9 3 **34 15**
1998–99 Cruz Azul 8 2 **8 2**
1998–99 Necaxa 15 5
1999–2000 Necaxa 33 25
2000-01 Necaxa 34 8 **82 38**
2001-02 Southampton 1 0
2002-03 Southampton 6 0 **7 0**

DODD, Jason (D) 365 9
H: 5 10 W: 12 11 b.Bath 2-11-70
Source: Bath C. *Honours:* England Under-21.
1988–89 Southampton 0 0
1989–90 Southampton 22 0
1990–91 Southampton 19 0
1991–92 Southampton 28 0
1992–93 Southampton 30 1
1993–94 Southampton 10 0
1994–95 Southampton 26 2
1995–96 Southampton 37 2
1996–97 Southampton 23 1
1997–98 Southampton 36 1
1998–99 Southampton 28 1
1999–2000 Southampton 31 0
2000-01 Southampton 31 1
2001-02 Southampton 29 0
2002-03 Southampton 15 0 **365 9**

DRAPER, Mark (M) 405 53
H: 5 10 W: 11 04 b.Long Eaton 11-11-70
Source: Trainee. *Honours:* England Under-21.
1988–89 Notts Co 20 3
1989–90 Notts Co 34 3
1990–91 Notts Co 45 9
1991–92 Notts Co 35 1
1992–93 Notts Co 44 11
1993–94 Notts Co 44 13 **222 40**
1994–95 Leicester C 39 5 **39 5**
1995–96 Aston Villa 36 2
1996–97 Aston Villa 29 0
1997–98 Aston Villa 31 3
1998–99 Aston Villa 23 2
1999–2000 Aston Villa 1 0 **120 7**
2000-01 Southampton 22 1
2001-02 Southampton 2 0
2002-03 Southampton 0 0 **24 1**

ELA-EYENE, Jacinto (M) 31 5
H: 5 7 W: 10 02 b.Equatorial Guinea 2-5-82
2000-01 Espanyol B 31 5 **31 5**
2001-02 Southampton 0 0
2002-03 Southampton 0 0

FERNANDES, Fabrice (M) 118 10
H: 5 8 W: 10 07 b.Aubervilliers 29-10-79
1998–99 Rennes 15 2
1999–2000 Rennes 17 1
2000-01 Fulham 29 2 **29 2**
2000-01 Rangers 4 1 **4 1**
2001-02 Marseille 4 0 **4 0**
2001-02 Southampton 11 1
2001-02 Rennes 1 0 **33 3**
2002-03 Southampton 37 3 **48 4**

GLEESON, Jamie (F) 0 0
H: 6 0 W: 12 03 b.Poole 15-1-85
Source: Trainee.
2002-03 Southampton 0 0

GREEN, Michael (D) 0 0
H: 5 9 W: 11 04 b.Gloucester 18-12-84
Source: Trainee.
2002-03 Southampton 0 0

HIGGINBOTHAM, Danny (D) 99 3
H: 6 2 W: 12 03 b.Manchester 29-12-78
Source: Trainee.
1997–98 Manchester U 1 0
1998–99 Manchester U 0 0
1999–2000 Manchester U 3 0 **4 0**
2000-01 Derby Co 26 0
2001-02 Derby Co 37 1
2002-03 Derby Co 23 2 **86 3**
2002-03 Southampton 9 0 **9 0**

HOWARD, Brian‡ (M) 0 0
H: 5 8 W: 11 01 b.Winchester 23-1-83
Source: Trainee. *Honours:* England Youth, Under-20.
1999–2000 Southampton 0 0
2000-01 Southampton 0 0
2001-02 Southampton 0 0
2002-03 Southampton 0 0

JONES, Paul (G) 264 0
H: 6 3 W: 15 02 b.Chirk 18-4-67
Source: Bridgnorth, Kidderminster H.
Honours: Wales 31 full caps.
1991–92 Wolverhampton W 0 0
1992–93 Wolverhampton W 16 0
1993–94 Wolverhampton W 0 0
1994–95 Wolverhampton W 9 0
1995–96 Wolverhampton W 8 0 **33 0**
1996–97 Stockport Co 46 0 **46 0**
1997–98 Southampton 38 0
1998–99 Southampton 31 0
1999–2000 Southampton 31 0
2000-01 Southampton 35 0
2001-02 Southampton 36 0
2002-03 Southampton 14 0 **185 0**

JONES, Richard (M) 0 0
H: 5 10 W: 10 01 b.Swansea 6-1-85
Source: Scholar.
2001-02 Southampton 0 0
2002-03 Southampton 0 0

KANCHELSKIS, Andrei‡ (M) 330 68
H: 5 10 W: 11 12 b.Kirovograd 23-1-69
Honours: USSR/CIS 23 full caps, 3 goals; Russia 36 full caps, 5 goals.
1988 Dynamo Kiev 7 1
1989 Dynamo Kiev 15 0 **22 1**
1990 Donetsk 16 2
1991 Donetsk 5 1 **21 3**
1990–91 Manchester U 1 0
1991–92 Manchester U 34 5
1992–93 Manchester U 27 3
1993–94 Manchester U 31 6
1994–95 Manchester U 30 14 **123 28**
1995–96 Everton 32 16
1996–97 Everton 20 4 **52 20**
1996–97 Fiorentina 9 0
1997–98 Fiorentina 17 2 **26 2**
1998–99 Rangers 30 8
1999–2000 Rangers 28 4
2000-01 Rangers 7 1
2000-01 *Manchester C* 10 0 **10 0**
2001-02 Rangers 10 1 **75 14**
2002-03 Southampton 1 0 **1 0**

KENTON, Darren (D) 158 9
H: 5 11 W: 12 02 b.Wandsworth 13-9-78
Source: Trainee.
1997–98 Norwich C 11 0
1998–99 Norwich C 22 1
1999–2000 Norwich C 26 1
2000-01 Norwich C 29 2
2001-02 Norwich C 33 4
2002-03 Norwich C 37 1 **158 9**
2002-03 Southampton 0 0

LUCAS, Jay (M) 7 0
H: 6 1 W: 13 03 b.Wollongong 14-1-85
Source: Scholar.
2000-01 Wollongong Wolves 7 0 **7 0**
2001-02 Southampton 0 0
2002-03 Southampton 0 0

LUNDEKVAM, Claus (D) 278 1
H: 6 3 W: 13 05 b.Necare 22-2-73
Honours: Norway 20 full caps, 1 goal.
1993 Brann 3 0
1994 Brann 20 0
1995 Brann 14 0
1996 Brann 16 1 **53 1**
1996–97 Southampton 29 0
1997–98 Southampton 31 0
1998–99 Southampton 33 0
1999–2000 Southampton 27 0
2000-01 Southampton 38 0
2001-02 Southampton 34 0
2002-03 Southampton 33 0 **225 0**

MARSDEN, Chris (M) 395 22
H: 5 11 W: 12 08 b.Sheffield 3-1-69
Source: Trainee.
1986–87 Sheffield U 0 0
1987–88 Sheffield U 16 1 **16 1**
1988–89 Huddersfield T 14 1
1989–90 Huddersfield T 32 2
1990–91 Huddersfield T 43 5
1991–92 Huddersfield T 23 1
1992–93 Huddersfield T 7 0
1993–94 Huddersfield T 2 0 **121 9**
1993–94 *Coventry C* 7 0 **7 0**
1993–94 Wolverhampton W 8 0
1994–95 Wolverhampton W 0 0 **8 0**
1994–95 Notts Co 7 0
1995–96 Notts Co 3 0 **10 0**
1995–96 Stockport Co 20 1
1996–97 Stockport Co 35 2
1997–98 Stockport Co 10 0 **65 3**
1997–98 Birmingham C 32 1
1998–99 Birmingham C 20 2 **52 3**
1998–99 Southampton 14 2
1999–2000 Southampton 21 0
2000-01 Southampton 23 0
2001-02 Southampton 28 3
2002-03 Southampton 30 1 **116 6**

McDONALD, Chris (D) 0 0
H: 6 1 W: 13 00 b.Wycombe 28-12-85
Source: Trainee.
2002-03 Southampton 0 0

MILLS, Jonathan‡ (M) **0 0**
H: 5 9 W: 11 03 b.Swindon 8-9-83
Source: Oxford U.
2000-01 Southampton 0 0
2001-02 Southampton 0 0
2002-03 Southampton 0 0

MONK, Garry (D) **44 0**
H: 6 1 W: 13 10 b.Bedford 6-3-79
Source: Trainee.
1995–96 Torquay U 5 0
1996–97 Southampton 0 0
1997–98 Southampton 0 0
1998–99 Southampton 4 0
1998–99 *Torquay U* 6 0 **11 0**
1999–2000 Southampton 2 0
1999–2000 *Stockport Co* 2 0 **2 0**
2000-01 Southampton 2 0
2000-01 *Oxford U* 5 0 **5 0**
2001-02 Southampton 2 0
2002-03 Southampton 1 0 **11 0**
2002-03 *Sheffield W* 15 0 **15 0**

NIEMI, Antti (G) **276 0**
H: 6 1 W: 12 04 b.Oulu 31-5-72
Honours: Finland 56 full caps.
1991 HJK Helsinki 2 0
1992 HJK Helsinki 28 0
1993 HJK Helsinki 24 0
1994 HJK Helsinki 24 0
1995 HJK Helsinki 24 0 **102 0**
1995–96 FC Copenhagen 17 0
1996–97 FC Copenhagen 30 0 **47 0**
1997–98 Rangers 5 0
1998–99 Rangers 7 0
1999–2000 Rangers 1 0 **13 0**
1999–2000 Hearts 17 0
2000-01 Hearts 37 0
2001-02 Hearts 32 0
2002-03 Hearts 3 0 **89 0**
2002-03 Southampton 25 0 **25 0**

OAKLEY, Matthew (M) **218 11**
H: 5 10 W: 12 06 b.Peterborough 17-8-77
Source: Trainee. *Honours:* England Under-21.
1994–95 Southampton 1 0
1995–96 Southampton 10 0
1996–97 Southampton 28 3
1997–98 Southampton 33 1
1998–99 Southampton 22 2
1999–2000 Southampton 31 3
2000-01 Southampton 35 1
2001-02 Southampton 27 1
2002-03 Southampton 31 0 **218 11**

ORMEROD, Brett (F) **177 51**
H: 5 11 W: 11 12 b.Blackburn 18-10-76
Source: Blackburn R Trainee, Accrington S.
1996–97 Blackpool 4 0
1997–98 Blackpool 9 2
1998–99 Blackpool 40 8
1999–2000 Blackpool 13 5
2000-01 Blackpool 41 17
2001-02 Blackpool 21 13 **128 45**
2001-02 Southampton 18 1
2002-03 Southampton 31 5 **49 6**

PAHARS, Marian (F) **233 91**
H: 5 8 W: 10 08 b.Latvia 5-8-76
Honours: Latvia 56 full caps, 14 goals.
1994 Pardaugava Riga 17 3 **17 3**
1995 Skonto/Metals Riga 16 4 **16 4**
1995 Skonto Riga 9 8
1996 Skonto Riga 28 12
1997 Skonto Riga 22 5
1998 Skonto Riga 26 19 **85 44**
1998–99 Southampton 6 3
1999–2000 Southampton 33 13
2000-01 Southampton 31 9
2001-02 Southampton 36 14
2002-03 Southampton 9 1 **115 40**

POATE, Brett‡ (D) **0 0**
b.Portsmouth 30-9-83
Source: Trainee.
2002-03 Southampton 0 0

PRUTTON, David (M) **155 7**
H: 5 10 W: 12 03 b.Hull 12-9-81
Source: Trainee. *Honours:* England Youth, Under-21.
1998–99 Nottingham F 0 0
1999–2000 Nottingham F 34 2
2000-01 Nottingham F 42 1
2001-02 Nottingham F 43 3
2002-03 Nottingham F 24 1 **143 7**
2002-03 Southampton 12 0 **12 0**

ROCHE, Jermaine (F) **0 0**
H: 5 8 W: 9 00 b.High Wycombe 4-9-85
Source: Trainee.
2002-03 Southampton 0 0

SVENSSON, Anders (M) **224 44**
H: 5 10 W: 12 10 b.Gothenburg 17-7-76
Honours: Sweden 38 full caps, 9 goals.
1992 Hestrafors 2 0 **2 0**
1993 Elfsborg 0 0
1994 Elfsborg 1 0
1995 Elfsborg 26 3
1996 Elfsborg 24 9
1997 Elfsborg 26 3
1998 Elfsborg 26 5
1999 Elfsborg 20 3
2000 Elfsborg 24 10
2001 Elfsborg 8 5 **155 38**
2001-02 Southampton 34 4
2002-03 Southampton 33 2 **67 6**

SVENSSON, Michael (D) **212 9**
H: 6 2 W: 13 07 b.Sweden 25-11-75
Honours: Sweden 20 full caps.
1992 Skillingaryds 21 0 **21 0**
1993 Varnamo 20 0
1994 Varnamo 20 0
1995 Varnamo 17 1
1996 Varnamo 0 0 **57 1**
1997 Halmstad 0 0
1998 Halmstad 14 2
1999 Halmstad 20 0
2000 Halmstad 25 2
2001 Halmstad 18 1 **77 5**
2001-02 Troyes 23 1 **23 1**
2002-03 Southampton 34 2 **34 2**

TELFER, Paul (M) **396 26**
H: 5 10 W: 11 13 b.Edinburgh 21-10-71
Source: Trainee. *Honours:* Scotland Under-21, B, 1 full cap.
1988–89 Luton T 0 0
1989–90 Luton T 0 0
1990–91 Luton T 1 0
1991–92 Luton T 20 1
1992–93 Luton T 32 2
1993–94 Luton T 45 7
1994–95 Luton T 46 9 **144 19**
1995–96 Coventry C 31 1
1996–97 Coventry C 34 0
1997–98 Coventry C 33 3
1998–99 Coventry C 32 2
1999–2000 Coventry C 30 0
2000-01 Coventry C 31 0
2001-02 Coventry C 0 0 **191 6**
2001-02 Southampton 28 1
2002-03 Southampton 33 0 **61 1**

TESSEM, Jo (M) **207 49**
H: 6 2 W: 13 01 b.Orlandet 28-2-72
Honours: Norway 8 full caps.
1996 Lyn 22 15
1997 Lyn 26 8 **48 23**
1998 Molde 26 8
1999 Molde 26 6 **52 14**
1999–2000 Southampton 25 4
2000-01 Southampton 33 4
2001-02 Southampton 22 2
2002-03 Southampton 27 2 **107 12**

WILLIAMS, Gareth (G) **0 0**
H: 6 1 W: 12 05 b.Pontypool 18-3-85
Source: Scholar.
2001-02 Southampton 0 0
2002-03 Southampton 0 0

WILLIAMS, Paul (D) **371 31**
H: 5 11 W: 14 04 b.Burton 26-3-71
Source: Trainee. *Honours:* England Under-21.
1989–90 Derby Co 10 1
1989–90 *Lincoln C* 3 0 **3 0**
1990–91 Derby Co 19 4
1991–92 Derby Co 41 13
1992–93 Derby Co 19 4
1993–94 Derby Co 34 1
1994–95 Derby Co 37 3 **160 26**
1995–96 Coventry C 32 2
1996–97 Coventry C 32 2
1997–98 Coventry C 20 0
1998–99 Coventry C 22 0
1999–2000 Coventry C 28 1
2000-01 Coventry C 30 0
2001-02 Coventry C 5 0 **169 5**
2001-02 Southampton 28 0
2002-03 Southampton 11 0 **39 0**

WILLIAMSON, Mike (D) **3 0**
H: 6 4 W: 13 03 b.Stoke 8-11-83
Source: Trainee.
2001-02 Torquay U 3 0 **3 0**
2001-02 Southampton 0 0
2002-03 Southampton 0 0

Trainees
Anaclet, Edward BO; Anderson, Stuart; Christensen, Matthew S; Gillett, Simon J; Hunt, Stephen J; Mills, Matthew C; Poke, Michael H; Surman, Andrew RE

SOUTHEND U

BEARD, Mark# (D) **219 3**
H: 5 6 W: 10 09 b.Roehampton 8-10-74
Source: Trainee.
1992–93 Millwall 0 0
1993–94 Millwall 14 1
1994–95 Millwall 31 1 **45 2**
1995–96 Sheffield U 20 0
1996–97 Sheffield U 16 0
1997–98 Sheffield U 2 0 **38 0**
1997–98 *Southend U* 8 0
1998–99 Southend U 37 0
1999–2000 Southend U 41 1
2000-01 Southend U 0 0
2001-02 Southend U 14 0
2002-03 Southend U 36 0 **136 1**

BELGRAVE, Barrington* (F) **70 8**
H: 5 8 W: 13 03 b.Bedford 16-9-80
Source: Norwich C Trainee.
1999–2000 Plymouth Arg 15 0
2000-01 Plymouth Arg 0 0 **15 0**
2001-02 Southend U 34 5
2002-03 Southend U 21 3 **55 8**

BRAMBLE, Tesfaye (F) **85 24**
H: 6 2 W: 13 13 b.Ipswich 20-7-80
Source: Cambridge C.
2000-01 Southend U 16 6
2001-02 Southend U 35 9
2002-03 Southend U 34 9 **85 24**

BROAD, Stephen* (D) **59 3**
H: 6 0 W: 12 05 b.Epsom 10-6-80
Source: Trainee.
1997–98 Chelsea 0 0
1998–99 Chelsea 0 0
1999–2000 Chelsea 0 0
2000-01 Chelsea 0 0
2000-01 *Southend U* 10 0
2001-02 Southend U 32 2
2002-03 Southend U 17 1 **59 3**

BYRNE, Paul (M) **125 11**
H: 5 11 W: 13 00 b.Dublin 30-6-72
Source: Trainee. *Honours:* Eire Youth.
1989–90 Oxford U 3 0
1990–91 Oxford U 2 0
1991–92 Oxford U 1 0 **6 0**
From Bangor
1993–94 Celtic 22 2
1994–95 Celtic 6 2 **28 4**
1994–95 *Brighton & HA* 8 1 **8 1**
1995–96 Southend U 41 5
1996–97 Southend U 32 1
1997–98 Southend U 10 0
1998–99 Southend U 0 0
1999–2000 Southend U 0 0
2000-01 Southend U 0 0
2001-02 Southend U 0 0
2002-03 Southend U 0 0 **83 6**

CLARK, Anthony§ (M) **2 0**
H: 5 10 W: 8 10 b.Camden 5-10-84
Source: Scholar.
2001-02 Southend U 2 0
2002-03 Southend U 0 0 **2 0**

CLARK, Steve (M) **45 1**
H: 5 11 W: 12 04 b.Mile End 10-2-82
Source: Scholar.
2001-02 West Ham U 0 0
2001-02 Southend U 12 1
2002-03 Southend U 33 0 **45 1**

CORT, Leon (D) **91 10**
H: 6 4 W: 12 07 b.Southwark 11-9-79
Source: Dulwich H.
1997–98 Millwall 0 0
1998–99 Millwall 0 0
1999–2000 Millwall 0 0
2000-01 Millwall 0 0

2001-02 Southend U 45 4
2002-03 Southend U 46 6 **91 10**

DARBY, Brett‡ (F) 10 0
H: 5 8 W: 11 09 b.Leicester 10-11-83
Source: Scholar.
2000-01 Leicester C 0 0
2001-02 Leicester C 0 0
2002-03 Leicester C 0 0
2002-03 Southend U 10 0 **10 0**

FLAHAVAN, Darryl* (G) 111 0
H: 5 11 W: 12 06 b.Southampton 28-11-78
Source: Trainee.
From Woking.
2000-01 Southend U 29 0
2001-02 Southend U 41 0
2002-03 Southend U 41 0 **111 0**

GAY, Daniel* (G) 11 0
H: 6 0 W: 13 07 b.Kings Lynn 5-8-82
Source: Norwich C Scholar.
2001-02 Southend U 6 0
2002-03 Southend U 5 0 **11 0**

JENKINS, Neil (M) 34 7
H: 5 6 W: 10 05 b.Carshalton 6-1-82
Source: Scholar. *Honours:* England Youth, Under-20.
2000-01 Wimbledon 0 0
2001-02 Wimbledon 0 0
2002-03 Southend U 34 7 **34 7**

JORDAN, Thomas‡ (D) 1 0
H: 6 3 W: 12 04 b.Manchester 24-5-81
Source: School.
2000-01 Bristol C 0 0
2001-02 Bristol C 0 0
2002-03 Southend U 1 0 **1 0**

KIGHTLY, Michael§ (M) 1 0
H: 5 9 W: 9 11 b.Basildon 24-1-86
Source: Scholar.
2002-03 Southend U 1 0 **1 0**

LUNAN, Daniel§ (D) 1 0
H: 6 0 W: 13 00 b.Farnborough 14-3-84
Source: Scholar.
2001-02 Southend U 1 0
2002-03 Southend U 0 0 **1 0**

MAHER, Kevin (M) 195 14
H: 6 0 W: 13 01 b.Ilford 17-10-76
Source: Trainee.
1995–96 Tottenham H 0 0
1996–97 Tottenham H 0 0
1997–98 Tottenham H 0 0
1997–98 Southend U 18 1
1998–99 Southend U 34 4
1999–2000 Southend U 24 0
2000-01 Southend U 41 2
2001-02 Southend U 36 5
2002-03 Southend U 42 2 **195 14**

MAYE, Daniel‡ (M) 4 0
H: 5 6 W: 11 00 b.Leicester 14-7-82
Source: Scholar.
2001-02 Port Vale 2 0 **2 0**
2002-03 Southend U 2 0 **2 0**

McSWEENEY, Dave (D) 49 0
H: 5 9 W: 11 11 b.Basildon 28-12-81
Source: Scholar.
2000-01 Southend U 11 0
2001-02 Southend U 21 0
2002-03 Southend U 17 0 **49 0**

NEWMAN, Rob‡ (D) 690 77
H: 6 2 W: 13 01 b.Bradford-on-Avon 13-12-63
Source: Apprentice.
1981–82 Bristol C 21 3
1982–83 Bristol C 43 3
1983–84 Bristol C 30 1
1984–85 Bristol C 34 3
1985–86 Bristol C 39 3
1986–87 Bristol C 45 6
1987–88 Bristol C 44 11
1988–89 Bristol C 46 6
1989–90 Bristol C 46 8
1990–91 Bristol C 46 8 **394 52**
1991–92 Norwich C 41 7
1992–93 Norwich C 18 2
1993–94 Norwich C 32 2
1994–95 Norwich C 32 1
1995–96 Norwich C 23 1
1996–97 Norwich C 44 1
1997–98 Norwich C 15 0 **205 14**
1997–98 *Motherwell* 11 0 **11 0**
1997–98 *Wigan Ath* 8 0 **8 0**
1998–99 Southend U 36 7
1999–2000 Southend U 19 0
2000-01 Southend U 6 2
2001-02 Southend U 11 2
2002-03 Southend U 0 0 **72 11**

RAWLE, Mark# (F) 78 15
H: 6 0 W: 12 02 b.Leicester 27-4-79
Source: Boston U.
2000-01 Southend U 14 1
2001-02 Southend U 30 5
2002-03 Southend U 34 9 **78 15**

SALTER, Mark* (F) 13 1
H: 6 1 W: 11 06 b.Oxford 16-3-80
Source: Frome T.
2002-03 Southend U 13 1 **13 1**

SEARLE, Damon* (D) 488 9
H: 5 9 W: 12 00 b.Cardiff 26-10-71
Source: Trainee. *Honours:* Wales Schools, Youth, Under-21, B.
1990–91 Cardiff C 35 0
1991–92 Cardiff C 42 1
1992–93 Cardiff C 42 1
1993–94 Cardiff C 42 0
1994–95 Cardiff C 32 0
1995–96 Cardiff C 41 1 **234 3**
1996–97 Stockport Co 10 0
1997–98 Stockport Co 31 0 **41 0**
1998–99 Carlisle U 45 2
1999–2000 Carlisle U 21 1 **66 3**
1999–2000 *Rochdale* 14 0 **14 0**
2000-01 Southend U 46 1
2001-02 Southend U 43 1
2002-03 Southend U 44 1 **133 3**

SMITH, Jay (M) 31 5
H: 5 7 W: 10 00 b.London 24-9-81
Source: Scholar.
2000-01 Aston Villa 0 0
2001-02 Aston Villa 0 0
2002-03 Aston Villa 0 0
2002-03 Southend U 31 5 **31 5**

STRACHAN, Gavin‡ (M) 31 0
H: 5 10 W: 11 07 b.Aberdeen 23-12-78
Source: Trainee. *Honours:* Scotland Youth, Under-21.
1996–97 Coventry C 0 0
1997–98 Coventry C 9 0
1998–99 Coventry C 0 0
1998–99 *Dundee* 6 0 **6 0**
1999–2000 Coventry C 3 0
2000-01 Coventry C 2 0
2001-02 Coventry C 1 0
2002-03 Coventry C 1 0 **16 0**
2002-03 *Peterborough U* 2 0 **2 0**
2002-03 Southend U 7 0 **7 0**

SUTCH, Daryl# (D) 321 10
H: 5 11 W: 12 02 b.Lowestoft 11-9-71
Source: Trainee. *Honours:* England Youth, Under-21.
1989–90 Norwich C 0 0
1990–91 Norwich C 4 0
1991–92 Norwich C 9 0
1992–93 Norwich C 22 2
1993–94 Norwich C 3 0
1994–95 Norwich C 30 1
1995–96 Norwich C 13 0
1996–97 Norwich C 44 3
1997–98 Norwich C 40 1
1998–99 Norwich C 36 0
1999–2000 Norwich C 45 2
2000-01 Norwich C 40 0
2001-02 Norwich C 19 0
2002-03 Norwich C 0 0 **305 9**
2002-03 Southend U 16 1 **16 1**

THURGOOD, Stuart (M) 79 1
H: 5 8 W: 12 03 b.Enfield 4-11-81
From Shimizu S-Pulse
2000-01 Southend U 13 1
2001-02 Southend U 39 0
2002-03 Southend U 27 0 **79 1**

TILSON, Steve† (M) 244 26
H: 5 11 W: 13 00 b.Wickford 27-7-66
Source: Burnham Ramb.
1988–89 Southend U 16 2
1989–90 Southend U 16 0
1990–91 Southend U 38 8
1991–92 Southend U 46 7
1992–93 Southend U 31 3
1993–94 Southend U 10 0
1993–94 *Brentford* 2 0 **2 0**
1994–95 Southend U 26 2
1995–96 Southend U 28 3
1996–97 Southend U 28 1
1997–98 Southend U 0 0
1998–99 Southend U 0 0
From Canvey Island
2002-03 Southend U 3 0 **242 26**

WHELAN, Phil* (D) 271 15
H: 6 4 W: 14 09 b.Stockport 7-3-72
Honours: England Under-21.
1989–90 Ipswich T 0 0
1990–91 Ipswich T 0 0
1991–92 Ipswich T 8 2
1992–93 Ipswich T 32 0
1993–94 Ipswich T 29 0
1994–95 Ipswich T 13 0 **82 2**
1994–95 Middlesbrough 0 0
1995–96 Middlesbrough 13 1
1996–97 Middlesbrough 9 0 **22 1**
1997–98 Oxford U 8 0
1998–99 Oxford U 15 0
1998–99 *Rotherham U* 13 4 **13 4**
1999–2000 Oxford U 31 2 **54 2**
2000-01 Southend U 42 1
2001-02 Southend U 44 5
2002-03 Southend U 14 0 **100 6**

Scholars
Bourne, Steven P; Brown, Jonathan P; Bryan, David; Clark, Anthony C; Cleverly, Gareth FJ; Coburn, Sean; England, Gerald L; Gray, Jamie; Ilett, Joseph P; Kawu-Zinga, Flory; Kightly, Michael J; Lunan, Daniel D; Moore, Luke; Plummer, Daryl O; Price, Benjamin M; Smith, Liam K; Williams, Stuart

Non-Contract
Tilson, Stephen B

Players who do not hold a current contract but their registration has been retained by the club
Byrne, Paul P

STOCKPORT CO

BECKETT, Luke (F) 197 81
H: 5 11 W: 13 01 b.Sheffield 25-11-76
Source: Trainee.
1995–96 Barnsley 0 0
1996–97 Barnsley 0 0
1997–98 Barnsley 0 0
1998–99 Chester C 28 11
1999–2000 Chester C 46 14 **74 25**
2000-01 Chesterfield 41 16
2001-02 Chesterfield 21 6 **62 22**
2001-02 Stockport Co 19 7
2002-03 Stockport Co 42 27 **61 34**

BYRNE, Mark‡ (F) 5 0
H: 5 9 W: 11 00 b.Billinge 8-5-83
Source: Blackburn R Scholar.
2001-02 Stockport Co 5 0
2002-03 Stockport Co 0 0 **5 0**

CARRIGAN, Brian* (F) 125 26
H: 5 8 W: 10 07 b.Glasgow 26-9-79
Source: Kilsyth R. *Honours:* Scotland Under-21.
1996–97 Clyde 14 1
1997–98 Clyde 34 3
1998–99 Clyde 31 3
1999–2000 Clyde 33 18 **112 25**
2000-01 Stockport Co 13 1
2001-02 Stockport Co 0 0
2002-03 Stockport Co 0 0 **13 1**

CHALLINOR, Dave (D) 204 7
H: 6 1 W: 14 00 b.Chester 2-10-75
Source: Bromborough Pool. *Honours:* England Schools.
1994–95 Tranmere R 0 0
1995–96 Tranmere R 0 0
1996–97 Tranmere R 5 0
1997–98 Tranmere R 32 1
1998–99 Tranmere R 34 2
1999–2000 Tranmere R 41 3
2000-01 Tranmere R 22 0
2001-02 Tranmere R 6 0 **140 6**
2001-02 Stockport Co 18 0
2002-03 Stockport Co 46 1 **64 1**

CLARE, Rob (D) 81 0
H: 6 1 W: 11 00 b.Belper 28-2-83
Source: Trainee. *Honours:* England Under-20.
1999–2000 Stockport Co 0 0
2000-01 Stockport Co 22 0
2001-02 Stockport Co 23 0
2002-03 Stockport Co 36 0 **81 0**

CLARK, Peter (D) **154 4**

H: 6 1 W: 12 04 b.Romford 10-12-79

Source: Arsenal Trainee.

1998–99	Carlisle U	36	0		
1999–2000	Carlisle U	43	1	**79**	**1**
2000-01	Stockport Co	37	2		
2001-02	Stockport Co	14	0		
2002-03	Stockport Co	21	1	**72**	**3**
2002-03	*Mansfield T*	3	0	**3**	**0**

DALY, Jon (F) **52 8**

H: 6 3 W: 12 00 b.Dublin 8-1-83

Source: Trainee. *Honours:* Eire Under-21.

1999–2000	Stockport Co	4	0		
2000-01	Stockport Co	0	0		
2001-02	Stockport Co	13	1		
2002-03	Stockport Co	35	7	**52**	**8**

EAMES, Haydn* (M) **0 0**

H: 5 9 W: 11 00 b.Stockport 13-10-83

Source: Trainee.

2002-03	Stockport Co	0	0		

ELDERTON, Ryan* (M) **0 0**

H: 5 10 W: 12 07 b.Morecambe 3-11-83

Source: Trainee.

2002-03	Stockport Co	0	0		

ELLISON, Kevin (F) **35 1**

H: 6 1 W: 12 08 b.Liverpool 23-2-79

Source: Altrincham.

2000-01	Leicester C	1	0		
2001-02	Leicester C	0	0	**1**	**0**
2001-02	Stockport Co	11	0		
2002-03	Stockport Co	23	1	**34**	**1**

FRADIN, Karim‡ (M) **262 13**

H: 5 11 W: 12 00 b.Ste Martin d'Hyeres 2-2-72

1993–94	Niort	36	1		
1994–95	Niort	37	0		
1995–96	Niort	39	1		
1996–97	Niort	37	1		
1997–98	Niort	25	1	**174**	**4**
1998–99	Nice	7	0	**7**	**0**
1999–2000	Stockport Co	21	1		
2000-01	Stockport Co	31	6		
2001-02	Stockport Co	20	2		
2002-03	Stockport Co	9	0	**81**	**9**

GIBB, Ali (M) **270 5**

H: 5 9 W: 11 07 b.Salisbury 17-2-76

Source: Trainee.

1994–95	Norwich C	0	0		
1995–96	Norwich C	0	0		
1995–96	Northampton T	23	2		
1996–97	Northampton T	18	1		
1997–98	Northampton T	35	1		
1998–99	Northampton T	41	0		
1999–2000	Northampton T	14	0	**131**	**4**
1999–2000	Stockport Co	14	0		
2000-01	Stockport Co	39	0		
2001-02	Stockport Co	41	0		
2002-03	Stockport Co	45	1	**139**	**1**

GOODWIN, Jim (D) **33 3**

H: 5 9 W: 12 02 b.Waterford 20-11-81

Source: Tramore. *Honours:* Eire Under-21, 1 full cap.

2001-02	Celtic	0	0		
2002-03	Stockport Co	33	3	**33**	**3**

HANCOCK, Glynn* (D) **3 0**

H: 6 0 W: 12 02 b.Biddulph 24-5-82

Source: Trainee.

1999–2000	Stockport Co	0	0		
2000-01	Stockport Co	2	0		
2001-02	Stockport Co	1	0		
2002-03	Stockport Co	0	0	**3**	**0**

HARDIKER, John (D) **35 3**

H: 6 0 W: 11 01 b.Preston 7-7-82

Source: Morecambe.

2001-02	Stockport Co	12	3		
2002-03	Stockport Co	23	0	**35**	**3**

HOLT, David (F) **1 0**

b.Gorton 18-11-84

Source: Trainee.

2001-02	Stockport Co	1	0		
2002-03	Stockport Co	0	0	**1**	**0**

JONES, Lee (G) **157 0**

H: 6 3 W: 14 10 b.Pontypridd 9-8-70

Source: Porth.

1993–94	Swansea C	0	0		
1994–95	Swansea C	2	0		
1995–96	Swansea C	1	0		
1995–96	*Crewe Alex*	0	0		
1996–97	Swansea C	1	0		
1997–98	Swansea C	2	0	**6**	**0**
1997–98	Bristol R	8	0		
1998–99	Bristol R	32	0		
1999–2000	Bristol R	36	0	**76**	**0**
2000-01	Stockport Co	27	0		
2001-02	Stockport Co	24	0		
2002-03	Stockport Co	24	0	**75**	**0**

JONES, Robert (M) **0 0**

b.Stockton 30-11-79

2002-03	Stockport Co	0	0		

KIELTY, Anthony* (D) **0 0**

H: 6 0 W: 12 07 b.Manchester 6-4-83

Source: Trainee.

2001-02	Stockport Co	0	0		
2002-03	Stockport Co	0	0		

LAMBERT, Ricky (M) **76 10**

H: 6 2 W: 12 07 b.Liverpool 16-2-82

Source: Trainee.

1999–2000	Blackpool	3	0		
2000-01	Blackpool	0	0	**3**	**0**
2000-01	Macclesfield T	9	0		
2001-02	Macclesfield T	35	8	**44**	**8**
2001-02	Stockport Co	0	0		
2002-03	Stockport Co	29	2	**29**	**2**

LESCOTT, Aaron (M) **100 1**

H: 5 8 W: 10 09 b.Birmingham 2-12-78

Source: Trainee. *Honours:* England Schools.

1996–97	Aston Villa	0	0		
1997–98	Aston Villa	0	0		
1998–99	Aston Villa	0	0		
1999–2000	Aston Villa	0	0		
1999–2000	*Lincoln C*	5	0	**5**	**0**
2000-01	Aston Villa	0	0		
2000-01	Sheffield W	30	0		
2001-02	Sheffield W	7	0	**37**	**0**
2001-02	Stockport Co	17	0		
2002-03	Stockport Co	41	1	**58**	**1**

McLACHLAN, Fraser (M) **33 1**

H: 5 11 W: 12 07 b.Knutsford 9-11-82

Source: Scholar.

2001-02	Stockport Co	11	1		
2002-03	Stockport Co	22	0	**33**	**1**

OGDEN, Michael* (M) **0 0**

H: 5 10 W: 12 02 b.Worsley 28-4-82

Source: Trainee.

2002-03	Stockport Co	0	0		

PALMER, Carlton† (M) **589 32**

H: 6 2 W: 12 04 b.West Bromwich 5-12-65

Source: Trainee. *Honours:* England Under-21, B, 18 full caps, 1 goal.

1984–85	WBA	0	0		
1985–86	WBA	20	0		
1986–87	WBA	37	1		
1987–88	WBA	38	3		
1988–89	WBA	26	0	**121**	**4**
1988–89	Sheffield W	13	1		
1989–90	Sheffield W	34	0		
1990–91	Sheffield W	45	2		
1991–92	Sheffield W	42	5		
1992–93	Sheffield W	34	1		
1993–94	Sheffield W	37	5		
1994–95	Leeds U	39	3		
1995–96	Leeds U	35	2		
1996–97	Leeds U	28	0		
1997–98	Leeds U	0	0	**102**	**5**
1997–98	Southampton	26	3		
1998–99	Southampton	19	0	**45**	**3**
1998–99	Nottingham F	13	0		
1999–2000	Nottingham F	3	1	**16**	**1**
1999–2000	Coventry C	15	1		
2000-01	Coventry C	15	0		
2000-01	*Watford*	5	0	**5**	**0**
2000-01	*Sheffield W*	12	0		
2001-02	Coventry C	0	0	**30**	**1**
2001-02	*Sheffield W*	10	0	**227**	**14**
2001-02	Stockport Co	21	3		
2002-03	Stockport Co	22	1	**43**	**4**

PEMBERTON, Martin (M) **126 7**

H: 5 11 W: 11 08 b.Bradford 1-2-76

Source: Trainee.

1994–95	Oldham Ath	0	0		
1995–96	Oldham Ath	2	0		
1996–97	Oldham Ath	3	0	**5**	**0**
1996–97	Doncaster R	9	1		
1997–98	Doncaster R	26	1	**35**	**2**
1997–98	Scunthorpe U	6	0	**6**	**0**
1998–99	Hartlepool U	4	0		
1999–2000	Hartlepool U	0	0	**4**	**0**

From Bradford PA.

2000-01	Mansfield T	18	1		
2001-02	Mansfield T	38	4	**56**	**5**
2001-02	Stockport Co	0	0		
2002-03	Stockport Co	20	0	**20**	**0**

SCRAGG, Jonathan‡ (D) **0 0**

H: 6 0 W: 11 10 b.Macclesfield 30-10-83

Source: Trainee.

2002-03	Stockport Co	0	0		

SPENCER, James (G) **3 0**

H: 6 5 W: 15 04 b.Stockport 11-4-85

Source: Trainee.

2001-02	Stockport Co	2	0		
2002-03	Stockport Co	1	0	**3**	**0**

THOMAS, Andy* (D) **12 0**

H: 5 8 W: 10 00 b.Stockport 2-12-82

Source: Trainee.

2001-02	Stockport Co	10	0		
2002-03	Stockport Co	2	0	**12**	**0**

TIDMAN, Ola# (G) **24 0**

b.Malmo 11-5-79

2001-02	La Louviere	6	0	**6**	**0**
2002-03	Stockport Co	18	0	**18**	**0**

TONKIN, Anthony (D) **24 0**

H: 5 11 W: 12 02 b.Cornwall 19-1-80

Source: Yeovil T.

2002-03	Stockport Co	24	0	**24**	**0**

WALSH, Gareth* (D) **0 0**

H: 6 2 W: 11 07 b.Walkden 6-10-83

Source: Trainee.

2002-03	Stockport Co	0	0		

WELSH, Andy (M) **34 4**

H: 5 8 W: 9 06 b.Manchester 24-11-83

Source: Scholar.

2001-02	Stockport Co	15	0		
2002-03	Stockport Co	13	2	**28**	**2**
2002-03	*Macclesfield T*	6	2	**6**	**2**

WILBRAHAM, Aaron (F) **131 27**

H: 6 3 W: 12 04 b.Knutsford 21-10-79

Source: Trainee.

1997–98	Stockport Co	7	1		
1998–99	Stockport Co	26	0		
1999–2000	Stockport Co	26	4		
2000-01	Stockport Co	36	12		
2001-02	Stockport Co	21	3		
2002-03	Stockport Co	15	7	**131**	**27**

WILD, Peter* (F) **4 1**

H: 5 9 W: 11 10 b.Stockport 12-10-82

Source: Trainee.

2001-02	Stockport Co	1	0		
2002-03	Stockport Co	3	1	**4**	**1**

WILLIAMS, Chris (F) **6 0**

H: 5 8 W: 9 00 b.Manchester 2-2-85

Source: Scholar.

2001-02	Stockport Co	5	0		
2002-03	Stockport Co	1	0	**6**	**0**

Trainees

Allen, Damien S; Baguley, Jamie C; Bailey, Mathew J; Brolly, Sean; Campbell, Danny; Cartner, Michael D; Coppinger, Ben; Davies, Matthew L; Dillon, John; Gollop, Wesley A; Hilton, Oliver; Jones, Matthew P; Lord, Alexander P; McCabe, Lee D; Meadowcroft, Daniel B; Newby, Daniel J; Paterson, Daniel; Warrender, Oliver J; Wonfor, James

Non-Contract

Palmer, Carlton L

STOKE C

ALBRIGTSEN, Ole‡ (F) **0 0**

H: 5 9 W: 12 00 b.Sortland 21-4-75

Source: Vestealen.

2001-02	Stoke C	0	0		
2002-03	Stoke C	0	0		

ALCOCK, Danny§ (G) **0 0**

H: 5 11 W: 11 03 b.Staffordshire 15-2-84

Source: Scholar.

2001-02	Stoke C	0	0		
2002-03	Stoke C	0	0		

BANKS, Steve* (G) **276 0**

H: 6 0 W: 13 12 b.Hillingdon 9-2-72

Source: Trainee.

1991–92	West Ham U	0	0		
1992–93	West Ham U	0	0		
1993–94	Gillingham	29	0		
1994–95	Gillingham	38	0	**67**	**0**
1995–96	Blackpool	24	0		
1996–97	Blackpool	46	0		
1997–98	Blackpool	45	0		

1998–99	Blackpool	35	0	**150**	**0**
1998–99	Bolton W	9	0		
1999–2000	Bolton W	2	0		
2000-01	Bolton W	9	0		
2001-02	Bolton W	1	0		
2001-02	*Rochdale*	15	0	**15**	**0**
2002-03	Bolton W	0	0	**21**	**0**
2002-03	*Bradford C*	9	0	**9**	**0**
2002-03	Stoke C	14	0	**14**	**0**

CARTWRIGHT, Shaun (M) **0** **0**
b.Stoke-on-Trent 15-4-86
Source: Scholar.

2002-03	Stoke C	0	0		

CLARKE, Clive (D) **139** **5**
H: 6 1 W: 12 02 b.Dublin 14-1-80
Source: Trainee. *Honours:* Eire Under-21.

1996–97	Stoke C	0	0		
1997–98	Stoke C	0	0		
1998–99	Stoke C	2	0		
1999–2000	Stoke C	42	1		
2000-01	Stoke C	21	0		
2001-02	Stoke C	43	1		
2002-03	Stoke C	31	3	**139**	**5**

COMMONS, Kris (D) **8** **1**
H: 5 6 W: 9 08 b.Nottingham 30-8-83
Source: Scholar.

2000-01	Stoke C	0	0		
2001-02	Stoke C	0	0		
2002-03	Stoke C	8	1	**8**	**1**

COOKE, Andy (F) **259** **73**
H: 6 0 W: 12 07 b.Shrewsbury 20-1-74
Source: Newtown.

1994–95	Burnley	0	0		
1995–96	Burnley	23	5		
1996–97	Burnley	31	13		
1997–98	Burnley	34	16		
1998–99	Burnley	36	9		
1999–2000	Burnley	36	7		
2000-01	Burnley	11	2	**171**	**52**
2000-01	Stoke C	22	6		
2001-02	Stoke C	35	9		
2002-03	Stoke C	31	6	**88**	**21**

CUTLER, Neil (G) **110** **0**
H: 6 1 W: 12 00 b.Birmingham 3-9-76
Source: Trainee. *Honours:* England Schools, Youth.

1993–94	WBA	0	0		
1994–95	WBA	0	0		
1995–96	WBA	0	0		
1995–96	*Coventry C*	0	0		
1995–96	*Chester C*	1	0		
1996–97	Crewe Alex	0	0		
1996–97	*Chester C*	5	0		
1997–98	Crewe Alex	0	0		
1998–99	Chester C	23	0		
1999–2000	Chester C	0	0	**29**	**0**
1999–2000	Aston Villa	1	0		
2000-01	Aston Villa	0	0		
2000-01	*Oxford U*	11	0	**11**	**0**
2001-02	Aston Villa	0	0	**1**	**0**
2001-02	Stoke C	36	0		
2002-03	Stoke C	20	0	**56**	**0**
2002-03	*Swansea C*	13	0	**13**	**0**

FOSTER, Ben (G) **0** **0**
H: 6 0 W: 12 06 b.Leamington Spa 3-4-83
Source: Racing Club Warwick.

2000-01	Stoke C	0	0		
2001-02	Stoke C	0	0		
2002-03	Stoke C	0	0		

GOODFELLOW, Marc (F) **50** **6**
H: 5 10 W: 11 00 b.Swadlincote 20-9-81

1998–99	Stoke C	0	0		
1999–2000	Stoke C	0	0		
2000-01	Stoke C	7	0		
2001-02	Stoke C	23	5		
2002-03	Stoke C	20	1	**50**	**6**

GREENACRE, Chris (F) **186** **58**
H: 5 11 W: 12 08 b.Halifax 23-12-77
Source: Trainee.

1995–96	Manchester C	0	0		
1996–97	Manchester C	4	0		
1997–98	Manchester C	3	1		
1997–98	*Cardiff C*	11	2	**11**	**2**
1997–98	*Blackpool*	4	0	**4**	**0**
1998–99	Manchester C	1	0		
1998–99	*Scarborough*	12	2	**12**	**2**
1999–2000	Manchester C	0	0	**8**	**1**
1999–2000	Mansfield T	31	9		
2000-01	Mansfield T	46	19		
2001-02	Mansfield T	44	21	**121**	**49**
2002-03	Stoke C	30	4	**30**	**4**

GUDJONSSON, Bjarni* (M) **171** **26**
H: 5 8 W: 11 02 b.Reykjavik 26-2-79
Honours: Iceland Under-21, 12 full caps, 1 goal.

1995	IA Akranes	2	0		
1996	IA Akranes	17	13		
1997	IA Akranes	6	2	**25**	**15**
1997–98	Newcastle U	0	0		
1998–99	Newcastle U	0	0		
1999–2000	Genk	14	0	**14**	**0**
1999–2000	Stoke C	8	1		
2000-01	Stoke C	42	6		
2001-02	Stoke C	46	3		
2002-03	Stoke C	36	1	**132**	**11**

GUNNARSSON, Brynjar# (D) **186** **19**
H: 6 1 W: 12 01 b.Reykjavik 16-10-75
Honours: Iceland 37 full caps, 3 goals.

1995	KR	16	1		
1996	KR	18	0		
1997	KR	16	0	**50**	**1**
1998	Moss	5	2	**5**	**2**
1999–2000	Stoke C	22	1		
2000-01	Stoke C	46	5		
2001-02	Stoke C	23	5		
2002-03	Stoke C	40	5	**131**	**16**

HALL, Laurence (F) **0** **0**
H: 6 0 W: 12 00 b.Nottingham 26-3-84
Source: Scholar.

2001-02	Stoke C	0	0		
2002-03	Stoke C	0	0		

HALL, Marcus# (D) **157** **2**
H: 6 1 W: 12 02 b.Coventry 24-3-76
Source: Trainee. *Honours:* England Under-21, B.

1994–95	Coventry C	5	0		
1995–96	Coventry C	25	0		
1996–97	Coventry C	13	0		
1997–98	Coventry C	25	1		
1998–99	Coventry C	5	0		
1999–2000	Coventry C	9	0		
2000-01	Coventry C	21	0		
2001-02	Coventry C	29	1	**132**	**2**
2002-03	Nottingham F	1	0	**1**	**0**
2002-03	Stoke C	24	0	**24**	**0**

HANDYSIDE, Peter (D) **268** **4**
H: 6 2 W: 13 09 b.Dumfries 31-7-74
Source: Trainee. *Honours:* Scotland Under-21.

1992–93	Grimsby T	11	0		
1993–94	Grimsby T	13	0		
1994–95	Grimsby T	35	0		
1995–96	Grimsby T	30	0		
1996–97	Grimsby T	9	1		
1997–98	Grimsby T	42	0		
1998–99	Grimsby T	31	2		
1999–2000	Grimsby T	0	0		
2000-01	Grimsby T	19	1	**190**	**4**
2001-02	Stoke C	34	0		
2002-03	Stoke C	44	0	**78**	**0**

HENRY, Karl (M) **42** **1**
H: 6 0 W: 11 04 b.Wolverhampton 26-11-82
Source: Trainee. *Honours:* England Youth, Under-20.

1999–2000	Stoke C	0	0		
2000-01	Stoke C	0	0		
2001-02	Stoke C	24	0		
2002-03	Stoke C	18	1	**42**	**1**

HOEKSTRA, Peter# (M) **226** **43**
H: 6 3 W: 12 03 b.Asser 4-4-73
Source: ACV. *Honours:* Holland 5 full caps.

1991–92	PSV Eindhoven	14	3		
1992–93	PSV Eindhoven	19	0		
1993–94	PSV Eindhoven	23	6		
1994–95	PSV Eindhoven	19	6		
1995–96	PSV Eindhoven	15	6	**90**	**21**
1995–96	Ajax	16	5		
1996–97	Ajax	8	0		
1997–98	Ajax	23	3		
1998–99	Ajax	21	6		
1999–2000	Ajax	0	0	**68**	**14**
2000-01	Groningen	14	1	**14**	**1**
2001-02	Stoke C	24	3		
2002-03	Stoke C	30	4	**54**	**7**

IWELUMO, Chris (F) **144** **23**
H: 6 4 W: 13 00 b.Coatbridge 1-8-79

1996–97	St Mirren	14	0		
1997–98	St Mirren	12	0	**26**	**0**
1998–99	Aarhus Fremad	27	4	**27**	**4**
1999–2000	Stoke C	3	0		
2000-01	Stoke C	2	1		
2000-01	*York C*	12	2	**12**	**2**
2000-01	*Cheltenham T*	4	1	**4**	**1**
2001-02	Stoke C	38	10		
2002-03	Stoke C	32	5	**75**	**16**

MARTEINSSON, Petur (M) **180** **10**
H: 6 1 W: 12 02 b.Reykjavik 14-7-73
Honours: Iceland 24 full caps.

1994	Fram	16	0		
1995	Fram	16	0	**32**	**0**
1996	Hammarby	23	0		
1997	Hammarby	23	2		
1998	Hammarby	24	2		
1999	Hammarby	0	0	**70**	**4**
1999	Stabaek	18	0		
2000	Stabaek	21	2		
2001	Stabaek	24	2	**63**	**4**
2001-02	Stoke C	3	0		
2002-03	Stoke C	12	2	**15**	**2**

MILLS, Lee* (F) **293** **85**
H: 6 4 W: 12 09 b.Mexborough 10-7-70
Source: Stocksbridge PS.

1992–93	Wolverhampton W	0	0		
1993–94	Wolverhampton W	14	1		
1994–95	Wolverhampton W	11	1	**25**	**2**
1994–95	Derby Co	16	7	**16**	**7**
1995–96	Port Vale	32	8		
1996–97	Port Vale	35	13		
1997–98	Port Vale	42	14	**109**	**35**
1998–99	Bradford C	44	23		
1999–2000	Bradford C	21	5	**65**	**28**
1999–2000	*Manchester C*	3	0	**3**	**0**
2000-01	Portsmouth	24	4		
2001-02	Portsmouth	2	0	**26**	**4**
2001-02	Coventry C	20	5		
2002-03	Coventry C	18	2	**38**	**7**
2002-03	Stoke C	11	2	**11**	**2**

NEAL, Lewis (M) **28** **0**
H: 5 11 W: 10 11 b.Leicester 14-7-81

1998–99	Stoke C	0	0		
1999–2000	Stoke C	0	0		
2000-01	Stoke C	1	0		
2001-02	Stoke C	11	0		
2002-03	Stoke C	16	0	**28**	**0**

O'CONNOR, James (M) **176** **16**
H: 5 8 W: 11 00 b.Dublin 1-9-79
Source: Trainee. *Honours:* Eire Under-21.

1996–97	Stoke C	0	0		
1997–98	Stoke C	0	0		
1998–99	Stoke C	4	0		
1999–2000	Stoke C	42	6		
2000-01	Stoke C	44	8		
2001-02	Stoke C	43	2		
2002-03	Stoke C	43	0	**176**	**16**

OWEN, Gareth (D) **0** **0**
H: 6 1 W: 11 07 b.Staffordshire 21-9-82
Source: Scholar.

2001-02	Stoke C	0	0		
2002-03	Stoke C	0	0		

ROWSON, David‡ (M) **108** **7**
H: 5 10 W: 11 09 b.Aberdeen 14-9-76
Source: FC Stoneywood. *Honours:* Scotland Under-21.

1994–95	Aberdeen	0	0		
1995–96	Aberdeen	9	0		
1996–97	Aberdeen	34	2		
1997–98	Aberdeen	30	5		
1998–99	Aberdeen	22	0		
1999–2000	Aberdeen	0	0		
2000-01	Aberdeen	0	0	**95**	**7**
2001-02	Stoke C	13	0		
2002-03	Stoke C	0	0	**13**	**0**

SHTANYUK, Sergei (D) **282** **18**
H: 6 3 W: 12 12 b.Minsk 11-1-72
Honours: Belarus 42 full caps, 1 goal.

1992–93	Belarus Minsk	30	3	**30**	**3**
1993–94	Dynamo 93 Minsk	30	0	**30**	**0**
1994–95	Dynamo Minsk	13	1		
1995	Dynamo Minsk	11	0	**24**	**1**
1996	Moscow Dynamo	28	3		
1997	Moscow Dynamo	33	2		
1998	Moscow Dynamo	27	2		
1999	Moscow Dynamo	2	0		
2000	Moscow Dynamo	24	2	**114**	**9**
2001-02	Stoke C	40	2		
2002-03	Stoke C	44	3	**84**	**5**

THOMAS, Wayne (D) **238** **7**
H: 5 11 W: 11 02 b.Gloucester 17-5-79
Source: Trainee.

1995–96	Torquay U	6	0		
1996–97	Torquay U	12	0		
1997–98	Torquay U	21	1		

1998–99 Torquay U 44 1
1999–2000 Torquay U 40 3 **123 5**
2000-01 Stoke C 34 0
2001-02 Stoke C 40 2
2002-03 Stoke C 41 0 **115 2**

VAN DEURZEN, Jurgen‡ (M) 52 5
H: 5 7 W: 11 00 b.Genk 26-1-74
Source: Turnhout.
2001-02 Stoke C 40 4
2002-03 Stoke C 12 1 **52 5**

VIANDER, Jani (G) 157 0
H: 6 4 W: 13 04 b.Tuusula 18-8-75
Honours: Finland 11 full caps.
1994 FinnPa 25 0
1995 FinnPa 14 0 **39 0**
1995 Ilves 6 0 **6 0**
1996 Jaro 27 0 **27 0**
1997 Jazz 2 0 **2 0**
From Kortrijk
1998 HJK Helsinki 8 0
1999 HJK Helsinki 27 0
2000 HJK Helsinki 32 0
2001 HJK Helsinki 16 0 **83 0**
2001-02 Stoke C 0 0
2002-03 Stoke C 0 0

WILKINSON, Andy (D) 0 0
H: 5 11 W: 11 00 b.Stone 6-8-84
Source: Scholar.
2001-02 Stoke C 0 0
2002-03 Stoke C 0 0

WILLIAMS, Mark* (D) 368 23
H: 6 0 W: 13 00 b.Stalybridge 28-9-70
Source: Newtown. *Honours:* Northern Ireland B, 25 full caps, 1 goal.
1991–92 Shrewsbury T 3 0
1992–93 Shrewsbury T 28 1
1993–94 Shrewsbury T 36 1
1994–95 Shrewsbury T 35 1 **102 3**
1995–96 Chesterfield 42 3
1996–97 Chesterfield 42 3
1997–98 Chesterfield 44 3
1998–99 Chesterfield 40 3 **168 12**
1999–2000 Watford 22 1 **22 1**
2000-01 Wimbledon 42 6
2001-02 Wimbledon 5 0
2002-03 Wimbledon 23 1 **70 7**
2002-03 Stoke C 6 0 **6 0**

WILSON, Brian (D) 4 0
H: 5 10 W: 11 00 b.Manchester 9-5-83
Source: Scholar.
2001-02 Stoke C 1 0
2002-03 Stoke C 3 0 **4 0**

Scholars
Alcock, Daniel J; Armstrong, Matthew; Denny, Jay; Hall, Laurence W; Humphreys, Shaun J; Hutchinson, Ryan C; Jones, Steven D; Keogh, Richard J; Palmer, Jermaine AC; Parsons, Lee A; Rees, Oliver HW; Swift, Christopher; Teague, Wayne R; Warwick, Michael
Players who do not hold a current contract but their registration has been retained by the club
Beardsley, Gary J; Robinson, Martin P

SUNDERLAND

ARCA, Julio (M) 98 4
H: 6 2 W: 11 00 b.Quilmes 31-1-81
1999–2000 Argentinos Juniors 19 0
2000-01 Argentinos Juniors 17 1 **36 1**
2000-01 Sunderland 27 2
2001-02 Sunderland 22 1
2002-03 Sunderland 13 0 **62 3**

BABB, Phil (D) 326 18
H: 6 0 W: 12 03 b.Lambeth 30-11-70
Source: Trainee. *Honours:* Eire B, 35 full caps.
1988–89 Millwall 0 0
1989–90 Millwall 0 0
1990–91 Bradford C 34 10
1991–92 Bradford C 46 4 **80 14**
1992–93 Coventry C 34 0
1993–94 Coventry C 40 3
1994–95 Coventry C 3 0 **77 3**
1994–95 Liverpool 34 0
1995–96 Liverpool 28 0
1996–97 Liverpool 22 1
1997–98 Liverpool 19 0
1998–99 Liverpool 25 0
1999–2000 Liverpool 0 0 **128 1**
1999–2000 *Tranmere R* 4 0 **4 0**
2000-01 Sporting Lisbon 11 0
2001-02 Sporting Lisbon 0 0 **11 0**
2002-03 Sunderland 26 0 **26 0**

BELLION, David (F) 20 1
H: 6 0 W: 11 09 b.Paris 27-11-82
Source: Cannes.
2001-02 Sunderland 9 0
2002-03 Sunderland 11 1 **20 1**

BJORKLUND, Joachim (D) 307 1
H: 6 0 W: 12 06 b.Vaxjo 12-2-71
Honours: Sweden 78 full caps.
1988 Osters 6 0
1989 Osters 0 0 **6 0**
1990 Brann 21 0
1991 Brann 22 0
1992 Brann 13 0 **56 0**
1993 IFK Gothenburg 19 0
1994 IFK Gothenburg 16 0
1995 IFK Gothenburg 11 0 **46 0**
1995–96 Vicenza 33 0 **33 0**
1996–97 Rangers 28 0
1997–98 Rangers 31 0 **59 0**
1998–99 Valencia 24 1
1999–2000 Valencia 23 0
2000-01 Valencia 10 0 **57 1**
2001-02 Venezia 18 0 **18 0**
2001-02 Sunderland 12 0
2002-03 Sunderland 20 0 **32 0**

BLACK, Chris (M) 2 0
H: 6 0 W: 12 00 b.Ashington 7-9-82
Source: Scholar.
2000-01 Sunderland 0 0
2001-02 Sunderland 0 0
2002-03 Sunderland 2 0 **2 0**

BROWN, Chris (M) 0 0
b.Doncaster 11-12-84
Source: Trainee. *Honours:* England Youth.
2002-03 Sunderland 0 0

BUTLER, Thomas (M) 27 0
H: 5 7 W: 10 06 b.Ballymena 25-4-81
Source: Trainee. *Honours:* Eire Under-21, 2 full caps.
1998–99 Sunderland 0 0
1999–2000 Sunderland 1 0
2000-01 Sunderland 4 0
2000-01 *Darlington* 8 0 **8 0**
2001-02 Sunderland 7 0
2002-03 Sunderland 7 0 **19 0**

BYRNE, Cliff* (D) 13 0
H: 6 0 W: 12 11 b.Dublin 27-4-82
Honours: Eire Under-21.
1999–2000 Sunderland 0 0
2000-01 Sunderland 0 0
2001-02 Sunderland 0 0
2002-03 Sunderland 0 0
2002-03 *Scunthorpe U* 13 0 **13 0**

CAPPER, Stephen* (D) 0 0
H: 5 8 W: 10 09 b.Dublin 28-2-83
Source: Scholar. *Honours:* Eire Under-21.
2001-02 Sunderland 0 0
2002-03 Sunderland 0 0

CLARK, Ben (D) 1 0
H: 6 2 W: 12 06 b.Shotley Bridge 24-1-83
Source: Manchester U Trainee. *Honours:* England Youth, Under-20.
2000-01 Sunderland 0 0
2001-02 Sunderland 0 0
2002-03 Sunderland 1 0 **1 0**

COLLINS, Patrick (D) 0 0
H: 6 1 W: 11 10 b.Oman 4-2-85
Source: Scholar. *Honours:* England Youth.
2001-02 Sunderland 0 0
2002-03 Sunderland 0 0

CRADDOCK, Jody (D) 301 6
H: 6 2 W: 12 00 b.Bromsgrove 25-7-75
Source: Christchurch.
1993–94 Cambridge U 20 0
1994–95 Cambridge U 38 0
1995–96 Cambridge U 46 3
1996–97 Cambridge U 41 1 **145 4**
1997–98 Sunderland 32 0
1998–99 Sunderland 6 0
1999–2000 Sunderland 19 0
1999–2000 *Sheffield U* 10 0 **10 0**
2000-01 Sunderland 34 0
2001-02 Sunderland 30 1
2002-03 Sunderland 25 1 **146 2**

DICKMAN, Jonjo (M) 1 0
H: 5 8 W: 10 05 b.Hexham 22-9-81
1998–99 Sunderland 0 0
1999–2000 Sunderland 0 0
2000-01 Sunderland 0 0
2001-02 Sunderland 0 0
2002-03 Sunderland 1 0 **1 0**

DODDS, Lewis (M) 0 0
b.Dublin 14-12-85
Source: Trainee. *Honours:* England Youth.
2002-03 Sunderland 0 0

EL KARKOURI, Talal (D) 56 0
H: 6 2 W: 12 10 b.Casablanca 8-7-76
Source: Casablanca School of Sportsmen.
Honours: Morroco full caps.
1999–2000 Paris St Germain 10 0
2000-01 Paris St Germain 11 0
2000-01 Aris Salonika 11 0 **11 0**
2001-02 Paris St Germain 16 0 **37 0**
2002-03 Sunderland 8 0 **8 0**

EMERSON (D) 126 3
H: 6 2 W: 13 04 b.Porto Alegre 30-3-72
Source: Benfica.
1997–98 Sheffield W 6 0
1998–99 Sheffield W 38 1
1999–2000 Sheffield W 17 0 **61 1**
1999–2000 Chelsea 20 0
2000-01 Chelsea 1 0 **21 0**
2000-01 Sunderland 31 1
2001-02 Sunderland 12 1
2002-03 Sunderland 1 0 **44 2**

FLO, Tore Andre (F) 282 117
H: 6 4 W: 13 08 b.Strin 15-6-73
Honours: Norway 68 full caps, 22 goals.
1994 Sogndal 22 5 **22 5**
1995 Tromso 26 18 **26 18**
1996 Brann 24 19
1997 Brann 16 9 **40 28**
1997–98 Chelsea 34 11
1998–99 Chelsea 30 10
1999–2000 Chelsea 34 10
2000-01 Chelsea 14 3 **112 34**
2000-01 Rangers 19 11
2001-02 Rangers 30 17
2002-03 Rangers 4 0 **53 28**
2002-03 Sunderland 29 4 **29 4**

FLYNN, Niall (M) 0 0
b.Dublin 22-1-86
Source: Trainee.
2002-03 Sunderland 0 0

GEORGE, Lee (F) 0 0
b.Ashington 20-4-85
Source: Trainee.
2002-03 Sunderland 0 0

GRAY, Michael (D) 362 16
H: 5 9 W: 10 07 b.Sunderland 3-8-74
Source: Trainee. *Honours:* England 3 full caps.
1992–93 Sunderland 27 2
1993–94 Sunderland 22 1
1994–95 Sunderland 16 0
1995–96 Sunderland 46 4
1996–97 Sunderland 34 3
1997–98 Sunderland 44 2
1998–99 Sunderland 37 2
1999–2000 Sunderland 33 0
2000-01 Sunderland 36 1
2001-02 Sunderland 35 0
2002-03 Sunderland 32 1 **362 16**

GRAYDON, Keith* (F) 7 1
H: 5 11 W: 12 00 b.Dublin 10-2-83
1999–2000 Sunderland 0 0
2000-01 Sunderland 0 0
2001-02 Sunderland 0 0
2002-03 Sunderland 0 0
2002-03 *York C* 7 1 **7 1**

HAAS, Bernt (D) 187 6
H: 6 1 W: 12 08 b.Vienna 8-4-78
Honours: Switzerland 14 full caps, 1 goal.
1994–95 Grasshoppers 2 0
1995–96 Grasshoppers 20 0
1996–97 Grasshoppers 29 1
1997–98 Grasshoppers 27 2
1998–99 Grasshoppers 28 1
1999–2000 Grasshoppers 29 1
2000-01 Grasshoppers 25 1 **160 6**
2001-02 Sunderland 27 0
2002-03 Sunderland 0 0 **27 0**

HUNTLEY, Robert (M) **0 0**
b.Easington 27-9-84
2002-03 Sunderland 0 0

INGHAM, Michael (G) **45 0**
H: 6 4 W: 13 10 b.Preston 7-9-80
Source: Malachians. *Honours:* Northern Ireland Under-21.
1998–99 Cliftonville 18 0 **18 0**
1999–2000 Sunderland 0 0
1999–2000 *Carlisle U* 7 0 **7 0**
2000-01 Sunderland 0 0
2001-02 Sunderland 0 0
2001-02 *Stoke C* 0 0
2002-03 Sunderland 0 0
2002-03 *Darlington* 3 0 **3 0**
2002-03 *York C* 17 0 **17 0**

JAMES, Craig (D) **0 0**
H: 6 2 W: 12 10 b.Middlesbrough 15-11-82
Source: Scholar.
2000-01 Sunderland 0 0
2001-02 Sunderland 0 0
2002-03 Sunderland 0 0

KENNEDY, Jon* (G) **6 0**
H: 6 1 W: 14 03 b.Rotherham 30-11-80
Source: Worksop T.
1999–2000 Sunderland 0 0
2000-01 Sunderland 0 0
2000-01 *Blackpool* 6 0 **6 0**
2001-02 Sunderland 0 0
2002-03 Sunderland 0 0

KILBANE, Kevin (M) **261 26**
H: 6 0 W: 12 07 b.Preston 1-2-77
Source: Trainee. *Honours:* Eire Under-21, 46 full caps, 4 goals.
1993–94 Preston NE 0 0
1994–95 Preston NE 0 0
1995–96 Preston NE 11 1
1996–97 Preston NE 36 2 **47 3**
1997–98 WBA 43 4
1998–99 WBA 44 6
1999–2000 WBA 19 5 **106 15**
1999–2000 Sunderland 20 1
2000-01 Sunderland 30 4
2001-02 Sunderland 28 2
2002-03 Sunderland 30 1 **108 8**

KINGSBERRY, Chris (M) **0 0**
b.Lisburn 10-9-85
Source: Trainee.
2002-03 Sunderland 0 0

KYLE, Kevin (F) **41 1**
H: 6 3 W: 13 00 b.Stranraer 7-6-81
Honours: Scotland Under-21, 8 full caps, 1 goal.
1998–99 Sunderland 0 0
1999–2000 Sunderland 0 0
2000-01 Sunderland 3 0
2000-01 *Huddersfield T* 4 0 **4 0**
2000-01 *Darlington* 5 1 **5 1**
2000-01 *Rochdale* 6 0 **6 0**
2001-02 Sunderland 6 0
2002-03 Sunderland 17 0 **26 0**

LASLANDES, Lilian (F) **289 104**
H: 6 1 W: 13 05 b.Pauillac 4-9-71
Honours: France 7 full caps, 3 goals.
1991–92 Saint-Seurin 33 10 **33 10**
1992–93 Auxerre 19 9
1993–94 Auxerre 19 5
1994–95 Auxerre 26 11
1995–96 Auxerre 34 12
1996–97 Auxerre 27 10 **125 47**
1997–98 Bordeaux 33 14
1998–99 Bordeaux 33 15
1999–2000 Bordeaux 31 14
2000-01 Bordeaux 22 4 **119 47**
2001-02 Sunderland 12 0
2002-03 Sunderland 0 0 **12 0**

LEADBITTER, Grant (M) **0 0**
b.Sunderland 7-1-86
Source: Trainee. *Honours:* FA Schools, England Youth.
2002-03 Sunderland 0 0

MACHO, Jurgen* (G) **22 0**
H: 6 4 W: 13 12 b.Vienna 24-8-77
Source: Honda Havelka, First Vienna.
2000-01 Sunderland 5 0
2001-02 Sunderland 4 0
2002-03 Sunderland 13 0 **22 0**

MALEY, Mark‡ (D) **17 0**
H: 6 0 W: 13 00 b.Newcastle 26-1-81
Source: Trainee. *Honours:* England Schools, Youth.
1997–98 Sunderland 0 0
1998–99 Sunderland 0 0
1999–2000 Sunderland 0 0
2000-01 Sunderland 0 0
2000-01 *Blackpool* 2 0 **2 0**
2000-01 *Northampton T* 2 0 **2 0**
2001-02 Sunderland 0 0
2001-02 *York C* 13 0 **13 0**
2002-03 Sunderland 0 0

McATEER, Jason (M) **321 18**
H: 5 10 W: 11 12 b.Birkenhead 18-6-71
Source: Marine. *Honours:* Eire B, 51 full caps, 3 goals.
1991–92 Bolton W 0 0
1992–93 Bolton W 21 0
1993–94 Bolton W 46 3
1994–95 Bolton W 43 5
1995–96 Bolton W 4 0 **114 8**
1995–96 Liverpool 29 0
1996–97 Liverpool 37 1
1997–98 Liverpool 21 2
1998–99 Liverpool 13 0 **100 3**
1998–99 Blackburn R 13 1
1999–2000 Blackburn R 28 2
2000-01 Blackburn R 27 1
2001-02 Blackburn R 4 0 **72 4**
2001-02 Sunderland 26 2
2002-03 Sunderland 9 1 **35 3**

McCANN, Gavin (M) **127 8**
H: 6 1 W: 12 08 b.Blackpool 10-1-78
Source: Trainee. *Honours:* England 1 full cap.
1995–96 Everton 0 0
1996–97 Everton 0 0
1997–98 Everton 11 0
1998–99 Everton 0 0 **11 0**
1998–99 Sunderland 11 0
1999–2000 Sunderland 24 4
2000-01 Sunderland 22 3
2001-02 Sunderland 29 0
2002-03 Sunderland 30 1 **116 8**

McCARTNEY, George (D) **44 0**
H: 5 11 W: 10 10 b.Belfast 29-4-81
Source: Trainee. *Honours:* Northern Ireland Schools, Youth, Under-21, 12 full caps, 1 goal.
1998–99 Sunderland 0 0
1999–2000 Sunderland 0 0
2000-01 Sunderland 2 0
2001-02 Sunderland 18 0
2002-03 Sunderland 24 0 **44 0**

MEDINA, Nicolas (M) **47 1**
H: 5 9 W: 10 04 b.Buenos Aires 17-2-82
1999–2000 Argentinos Jun 26 0
2000-01 Argentinos Jun 21 1 **47 1**
2001-02 Sunderland 0 0
2002-03 Sunderland 0 0

MERCIMEK, Baki (D) **0 0**
H: 6 1 W: 11 11 b.Amsterdam 17-9-82
Source: Haarlem.
2001-02 Sunderland 0 0
2002-03 Sunderland 0 0

MYHRE, Thomas (G) **203 0**
H: 6 3 W: 13 13 b.Sarpsborg 16-10-73
Honours: Norway 29 full caps.
1993 Viking 22 0
1994 Viking 22 0
1995 Viking 24 0
1996 Viking 0 0
1997 Viking 26 0 **94 0**
1997–98 Everton 22 0
1998–99 Everton 38 0
1999–2000 Everton 4 0
1999–2000 *Birmingham C* 7 0 **7 0**
2000-01 Everton 6 0
2000-01 *Tranmere R* 3 0 **3 0**
2000-01 FC Copenhagen 14 0 **14 0**
2001-02 Everton 0 0 **70 0**
2001-02 Besiktas 13 0 **13 0**
2002-03 Sunderland 2 0 **2 0**

OSTER, John (M) **104 10**
H: 5 9 W: 10 09 b.Boston 8-12-78
Source: Trainee. *Honours:* Wales Youth, Under-21, B, 7 full caps.
1996–97 Grimsby T 24 3
1997–98 Everton 31 1
1998–99 Everton 9 0 **40 1**
1999–2000 Sunderland 10 0
2000-01 Sunderland 8 0
2001-02 Sunderland 0 0
2001-02 *Barnsley* 2 0 **2 0**
2002-03 Sunderland 3 0 **21 0**
2002-03 *Grimsby T* 17 6 **41 9**

PEETERS, Tom (M) **33 1**
H: 5 10 W: 11 00 b.Bornem 25-9-78
Source: Ekeren.
1999–2000 Mechelen 33 1 **33 1**
2000-01 Sunderland 0 0
2001-02 Sunderland 0 0
2002-03 Sunderland 0 0

PHILLIPS, Kevin (F) **267 137**
H: 5 8 W: 11 05 b.Hitchin 25-7-73
Source: Baldock T. *Honours:* England B, 8 full caps.
1994–95 Watford 16 9
1995–96 Watford 27 11
1996–97 Watford 16 4 **59 24**
1997–98 Sunderland 43 29
1998–99 Sunderland 26 23
1999–2000 Sunderland 36 30
2000-01 Sunderland 34 14
2001-02 Sunderland 37 11
2002-03 Sunderland 32 6 **208 113**

PIPER, Matt (F) **37 2**
H: 6 1 W: 12 09 b.Leicester 29-9-81
Source: Trainee.
1999–2000 Leicester C 0 0
2000-01 Leicester C 0 0
2001-02 *Mansfield T* 8 1 **8 1**
2001-02 Leicester C 16 1
2002-03 Leicester C 0 0 **16 1**
2002-03 Sunderland 13 0 **13 0**

POOM, Mart (G) **195 0**
H: 6 4 W: 14 03 b.Tallinn 3-2-72
Honours: Estonia 92 full caps.
1992–93 Flora Tallinn 11 0
1993–94 Flora Tallinn 11 0
1994–95 Portsmouth 0 0
1995–96 Portsmouth 4 0
1995–96 Flora Tallinn 7 0
1996–97 Portsmouth 0 0 **4 0**
1996–97 Flora Tallinn 12 0 **41 0**
1996–97 Derby Co 4 0
1997–98 Derby Co 36 0
1998–99 Derby Co 17 0
1999–2000 Derby Co 28 0
2000-01 Derby Co 33 0
2001-02 Derby Co 15 0
2002-03 Derby Co 13 0 **146 0**
2002-03 Sunderland 4 0 **4 0**

PROCTOR, Michael (F) **86 24**
H: 6 0 W: 11 08 b.Sunderland 3-10-80
Source: Trainee.
1997–98 Sunderland 0 0
1998–99 Sunderland 0 0
1999–2000 Sunderland 0 0
2000-01 Sunderland 0 0
2000-01 *Halifax T* 12 4 **12 4**
2001-02 Sunderland 0 0
2001-02 *York C* 41 14 **41 14**
2002-03 Sunderland 21 2 **21 2**
2002-03 *Bradford C* 12 4 **12 4**

QUINN, Niall (F) **473 141**
H: 6 5 W: 14 08 b.Dublin 6-10-66
Honours: Eire Youth, Under-21, Under-23, B, 91 full caps, 21 goals.
1983–84 Arsenal 0 0
1984–85 Arsenal 0 0
1985–86 Arsenal 12 1
1986–87 Arsenal 35 8
1987–88 Arsenal 11 2
1988–89 Arsenal 3 1
1989–90 Arsenal 6 2 **67 14**
1989–90 Manchester C 9 4
1990–91 Manchester C 38 20
1991–92 Manchester C 35 12
1992–93 Manchester C 39 9
1993–94 Manchester C 15 5
1994–95 Manchester C 35 8
1995–96 Manchester C 32 8 **203 66**
1996–97 Sunderland 12 2
1997–98 Sunderland 35 14
1998–99 Sunderland 39 18
1999–2000 Sunderland 37 14
2000-01 Sunderland 34 7
2001-02 Sunderland 38 6
2002-03 Sunderland 8 0 **203 61**

RAMSDEN, Simon (D) **32 0**
H: 6 0 W: 12 04 b.Bishop Auckland 17-12-81
Source: Scholar.
2000-01 Sunderland 0 0
2001-02 Sunderland 0 0
2002-03 Sunderland 0 0
2002-03 *Notts Co* 32 0 **32 0**

REDDY, Michael (F) **59 14**
H: 6 1 W: 11 07 b.Graignamanagh 24-3-80
Source: Kilkenny C. *Honours:* Eire Under-21.
1999–2000 Sunderland 8 1
2000-01 Sunderland 2 0
2000-01 *Swindon T* 18 4 **18 4**
2001-02 Sunderland 0 0
2001-02 *Hull C* 5 4 **5 4**
2001-02 *Barnsley* 0 0
2002-03 Sunderland 0 0 **10 1**
2002-03 *York C* 11 2 **11 2**
2002-03 *Sheffield W* 15 3 **15 3**

REYNA, Claudio (M) **144 17**
H: 5 9 W: 11 09 b.New Jersey 20-7-73
Source: Union County SC, Univ Virginia. *Honours:* USA 93 full caps, 8 goals.
1996–97 Leverkusen 5 0 **5 0**
1997–98 Wolfsburg 28 4
1998–99 Wolfsburg 20 2 **48 6**
1998–99 Rangers 6 0
1999–2000 Rangers 29 5
2000-01 Rangers 18 2
2001-02 Rangers 10 1 **63 8**
2001-02 Sunderland 17 3
2002-03 Sunderland 11 0 **28 3**

ROSSITER, Mark (D) **0 0**
H: 5 11 W: 12 06 b.Sligo 27-5-83
Source: Scholar. *Honours:* Eire Under-21.
2000-01 Sunderland 0 0
2001-02 Sunderland 0 0
2002-03 Sunderland 0 0

RYAN, Ritchie (M) **2 0**
H: 5 10 W: 11 03 b.Kilkenny 27-5-83
Source: Scholar.
2001-02 Sunderland 0 0
2002-03 Sunderland 2 0 **2 0**

SCHWARZ, Stefan* (M) **318 18**
H: 6 0 W: 12 00 b.Malmo 18-4-69
Honours: Sweden 69 full caps, 6 goals.
1987 Malmo 0 0
1988 Malmo 10 0
1989 Malmo 15 0
1990 Malmo 7 0 **32 0**
1990–91 Benfica 9 3
1991–92 Benfica 16 0
1992–93 Benfica 29 3
1993–94 Benfica 23 1 **77 7**
1994–95 Arsenal 34 2 **34 2**
1995–96 Fiorentina 32 0
1996–97 Fiorentina 24 0
1997–98 Fiorentina 22 2 **78 2**
1998–99 Valencia 30 4 **30 4**
1999–2000 Sunderland 27 1
2000-01 Sunderland 20 1
2001-02 Sunderland 20 1
2002-03 Sunderland 0 0 **67 3**

SCOTT, Chris (D) **0 0**
b.South Shields 11-1-85
Source: Trainee.
2002-03 Sunderland 0 0

SHIELDS, Dene‡ (F) **7 1**
H: 5 9 W: 12 00 b.Edinburgh 16-9-82
Source: Granton BC.
1999–2000 Raith R 0 0
2000-01 Raith R 7 1 **7 1**
2000-01 Sunderland 0 0
2001-02 Sunderland 0 0
2002-03 Sunderland 0 0

SHIPPEN, Carl* (M) **0 0**
H: 5 10 W: 12 02 b.Bishop Auckland 2-3-84
Source: Scholar.
2001-02 Sunderland 0 0
2002-03 Sunderland 0 0

SORENSEN, Thomas (G) **171 0**
H: 6 4 W: 13 08 b.Odense 12-6-76
Source: Odense. *Honours:* Denmark 27 full caps.
1998–99 Sunderland 45 0
1999–2000 Sunderland 37 0
2000-01 Sunderland 34 0
2001-02 Sunderland 34 0
2002-03 Sunderland 21 0 **171 0**

STEWART, Marcus (F) **398 143**
H: 5 10 W: 11 08 b.Bristol 7-11-72
Source: Trainee. *Honours:* England Schools, Football League.
1991–92 Bristol R 33 5
1992–93 Bristol R 38 11
1993–94 Bristol R 29 5
1994–95 Bristol R 27 15
1995–96 Bristol R 44 21 **171 57**
1996–97 Huddersfield T 20 7
1997–98 Huddersfield T 41 15
1998–99 Huddersfield T 43 22
1999–2000 Huddersfield T 29 14 **133 58**
1999–2000 Ipswich T 10 2
2000-01 Ipswich T 34 19
2001-02 Ipswich T 28 6
2002-03 Ipswich T 3 0 **75 27**
2002-03 Sunderland 19 1 **19 1**

STRAKER, Phil* (G) **0 0**
H: 6 3 W: 12 00 b.Middlesbrough 9-11-83
Source: Scholar.
2001-02 Sunderland 0 0
2002-03 Sunderland 0 0

SULLIVAN, David* (D) **0 0**
H: 5 10 W: 11 10 b.Glasgow 7-9-76
2001-02 Sunderland 0 0
2002-03 Sunderland 0 0

TAYLOR, Sean (M) **0 0**
b.Wansbeck 9-12-85
Source: Trainee.
2002-03 Sunderland 0 0

TEGGART, Neil (F) **0 0**
H: 6 2 W: 12 01 b.Downpatrick 16-9-84
Source: Scholar.
2001-02 Sunderland 0 0
2002-03 Sunderland 0 0

THIRLWELL, Paul (M) **60 0**
H: 5 11 W: 11 04 b.Springwell Village 13-2-79
Source: Trainee. *Honours:* England Under-21.
1996–97 Sunderland 0 0
1997–98 Sunderland 0 0
1998–99 Sunderland 2 0
1999–2000 Sunderland 8 0
1999–2000 *Swindon T* 12 0 **12 0**
2000-01 Sunderland 5 0
2001-02 Sunderland 14 0
2002-03 Sunderland 19 0 **48 0**

THORNTON, Sean (M) **25 2**
H: 5 10 W: 11 00 b.Drogheda 18-5-83
Source: Scholar. *Honours:* Eire Under-21.
2001-02 Tranmere R 11 1 **11 1**
2002-03 Sunderland 11 1 **11 1**
2002-03 *Blackpool* 3 0 **3 0**

TURNS, Craig‡ (G) **0 0**
H: 6 1 W: 11 09 b.Easington 4-11-82
Source: Scholar.
2000-01 Sunderland 0 0
2001-02 Sunderland 0 0
2002-03 Sunderland 0 0

VARGA, Stanislav‡ (D) **187 23**
H: 6 5 W: 14 09 b.Lipany 8-10-72
Honours: Slovakia 40 full caps.
1993–94 Tatran Presov 12 2
1994–95 Tatran Presov 25 2
1995–96 Tatran Presov 21 2
1996–97 Tatran Presov 22 3
1997–98 Tatran Presov 26 1 **106 10**
1998–99 Slovan Bratislava 28 3
1999–2000 Slovan Bratislava 28 9 **56 12**
2000-01 Sunderland 12 1
2001-02 Sunderland 9 0
2001-02 *WBA* 4 0 **4 0**
2002-03 Sunderland 0 0 **21 1**

WHITE, Robert§ (M) **0 0**
b.Sunderland 1-10-85
2002-03 Sunderland 0 0

WILLIAMS, Darren (D) **189 4**
H: 5 11 W: 12 00 b.Middlebrough 28-4-77
Source: Trainee. *Honours:* England Under-21, B.
1994–95 York C 1 0
1995–96 York C 18 0
1996–97 York C 1 0 **20 0**
1996–97 Sunderland 11 2
1997–98 Sunderland 36 2
1998–99 Sunderland 25 0
1999–2000 Sunderland 25 0
2000-01 Sunderland 28 0
2001-02 Sunderland 28 0
2002-03 Sunderland 16 0 **169 4**

WRIGHT, Stephen (D) **63 0**
H: 6 0 W: 11 11 b.Liverpool 8-2-80
Source: Trainee. *Honours:* England Youth, Under-21.
1997–98 Liverpool 0 0
1998–99 Liverpool 0 0
1999–2000 Liverpool 0 0
1999–2000 *Crewe Alex* 23 0 **23 0**
2000-01 Liverpool 2 0
2001-02 Liverpool 12 0 **14 0**
2002-03 Sunderland 26 0 **26 0**

Trainees
Bell, Ryan; McLean, Euan; Smith, Adam; Toft, John; Wanless, Jack; White, Robert J

SWANSEA C

COATES, Jonathan† (M) **253 23**
H: 5 8 W: 10 04 b.Swansea 27-6-75
Source: Trainee. *Honours:* Wales Youth, B, Under-21.
1993–94 Swansea C 4 1
1994–95 Swansea C 5 0
1995–96 Swansea C 18 0
1996–97 Swansea C 40 3
1997–98 Swansea C 44 7
1998–99 Swansea C 33 0
1999–2000 Swansea C 42 6
2000-01 Swansea C 19 1
2001-02 Swansea C 45 5
2001-02 Cheltenham T 0 0
From Woking.
2002-03 Swansea C 3 0 **253 23**

CUSACK, Nick‡ (M) **537 71**
H: 6 0 W: 11 13 b.Maltby 24-12-65
Source: Alvechurch.
1987–88 Leicester C 16 1 **16 1**
1988–89 Peterborough U 44 10 **44 10**
1989–90 Motherwell 31 11
1990–91 Motherwell 29 4
1991–92 Motherwell 17 2 **77 17**
1991–92 Darlington 21 6 **21 6**
1992–93 Oxford U 39 4
1993–94 Oxford U 20 6
1993–94 *Wycombe W* 4 0 **4 0**
1994–95 Oxford U 2 0 **61 10**
1994–95 Fulham 27 7
1995–96 Fulham 42 5
1996–97 Fulham 45 2
1997–98 Fulham 2 0 **116 14**
1997–98 Swansea C 32 0
1998–99 Swansea C 43 1
1999–2000 Swansea C 43 7
2000-01 Swansea C 40 2
2001-02 Swansea C 35 2
2002-03 Swansea C 5 1 **198 13**

DE-VULGT, Leigh* (M) **23 0**
H: 5 9 W: 11 02 b.Swansea 17-3-81
Source: Trainee. *Honours:* Wales Youth, Under-21.
1999–2000 Swansea C 2 0
2000-01 Swansea C 7 0
2001-02 Swansea C 10 0
2002-03 Swansea C 4 0 **23 0**

DUFFY, Richard (M) **0 0**
b.Swansea 30-8-85
Source: Scholar.
2002-03 Swansea C 0 0

DURKAN, Kieron# (M) **260 21**
H: 5 10 W: 11 09 b.Chester 1-12-73
Source: Trainee. *Honours:* Eire Under-21.
1991–92 Wrexham 1 0
1992–93 Wrexham 1 0
1993–94 Wrexham 10 1
1994–95 Wrexham 30 2
1995–96 Wrexham 8 0 **50 3**
1995–96 Stockport Co 16 0
1996–97 Stockport Co 41 3
1997–98 Stockport Co 7 1 **64 4**
1997–98 Macclesfield T 4 0
1998–99 Macclesfield T 26 3
1999–2000 Macclesfield T 42 6
2000-01 Macclesfield T 31 4 **103 13**
2000-01 *York C* 7 0 **7 0**
2001-02 Rochdale 30 1

2002-03	Rochdale	0	0	**30**	**1**
2002-03	Swansea C	6	0	**6**	**0**

EVANS, Terry* (D) **57 0**
H: 5 7 W: 11 08 b.Pontypridd 8-1-76
Source: Trainee. *Honours:* Wales Under-21.

1993–94	Cardiff C	5	0		
1994–95	Cardiff C	7	0		
1995–96	Cardiff C	2	0		
1996–97	Cardiff C	0	0		
1997–98	Cardiff C	0	0		
1998–99	Cardiff C	0	0	**14**	**0**
From Barry Town.					
2001-02	Swansea C	16	0		
2002-03	Swansea C	27	0	**43**	**0**

FREESTONE, Roger# (G) **592 3**
H: 6 2 W: 12 02 b.Newport 19-8-68
Source: Trainee. *Honours:* Wales Schools, Youth, Under-21, 1 full cap.

1986–87	Newport Co	13	0	**13**	**0**
1986–87	Chelsea	6	0		
1987–88	Chelsea	15	0		
1988–89	Chelsea	21	0		
1989–90	Chelsea	0	0		
1989–90	*Swansea C*	14	0		
1989–90	*Hereford U*	8	0	**8**	**0**
1990–91	Chelsea	0	0	**42**	**0**
1991–92	Swansea C	42	0		
1992–93	Swansea C	46	0		
1993–94	Swansea C	46	0		
1994–95	Swansea C	45	1		
1995–96	Swansea C	45	2		
1996–97	Swansea C	45	0		
1997–98	Swansea C	43	0		
1998–99	Swansea C	38	0		
1999–2000	Swansea C	46	0		
2000-01	Swansea C	43	0		
2001-02	Swansea C	43	0		
2002-03	Swansea C	33	0	**529**	**3**

HOWARD, Mike# (D) **203 2**
H: 5 7 W: 10 07 b.Birkenhead 2-12-78
Source: Tranmere R Trainee.

1997–98	Swansea C	3	0		
1998–99	Swansea C	39	1		
1999–2000	Swansea C	40	0		
2000-01	Swansea C	41	0		
2001-02	Swansea C	42	1		
2002-03	Swansea C	38	0	**203**	**2**

JACKSON, Michael D‡ (M) **10 0**
H: 5 7 W: 11 00 b.Cheltenham 26-6-80
Source: Trainee.

1999–2000	Cheltenham T	2	0		
2000-01	Cheltenham T	6	0		
2001-02	Cheltenham T	1	0	**9**	**0**
2002-03	Swansea C	1	0	**1**	**0**

JENKINS, Lee# (M) **158 3**
H: 5 9 W: 11 00 b.Pontypool 28-6-79
Source: Trainee. *Honours:* Wales Schools, Youth, Under-21.

1996–97	Swansea C	23	2		
1997–98	Swansea C	21	0		
1998–99	Swansea C	12	0		
1999–2000	Swansea C	16	0		
2000-01	Swansea C	39	0		
2001-02	Swansea C	15	1		
2002-03	Swansea C	32	0	**158**	**3**

JOHNROSE, Lenny† (M) **398 49**
H: 5 11 W: 12 06 b.Preston 27-11-69
Source: Trainee.

1987–88	Blackburn R	1	0		
1988–89	Blackburn R	0	0		
1989–90	Blackburn R	8	3		
1990–91	Blackburn R	26	7		
1991–92	Blackburn R	7	1	**42**	**11**
1991–92	*Preston NE*	3	1	**3**	**1**
1991–92	Hartlepool U	15	2		
1992–93	Hartlepool U	38	6		
1993–94	Hartlepool U	13	3	**66**	**11**
1993–94	Bury	14	0		
1994–95	Bury	26	4		
1995–96	Bury	34	6		
1996–97	Bury	43	4		
1997–98	Bury	44	3		
1998–99	Bury	27	2		
1998–99	Burnley	12	1		
1999–2000	Burnley	35	2		
2000-01	Burnley	19	1		
2001-02	Burnley	6	0		
2002-03	Burnley	6	0	**78**	**4**
2002-03	Bury	6	0	**194**	**19**
2002-03	Swansea C	15	3	**15**	**3**

JONES, Stuart§ (D) **6 0**
H: 6 0 W: 11 08 b.Aberystwyth 14-3-84
Source: Scholar.

2002-03	Swansea C	6	0	**6**	**0**

KEAVENY, Jonathan‡ (F) **9 0**
H: 5 10 W: 11 00 b.Swansea 24-5-81
Source: Carmarthen T.

2002-03	Swansea C	9	0	**9**	**0**

LACEY, Damien* (M) **104 2**
H: 5 9 W: 11 03 b.Bridgend 3-8-77
Source: Trainee.

1996–97	Swansea C	10	0		
1997–98	Swansea C	22	1		
1998–99	Swansea C	12	0		
1999–2000	Swansea C	16	0		
2000-01	Swansea C	18	0		
2001-02	Swansea C	16	1		
2002-03	Swansea C	10	0	**104**	**2**

MARSH, Andrew‡ (G) **0 0**
b.Swansea 21-2-84
Source: Pontardawe.

2002-03	Swansea C	0	0		

MARTINEZ, Roberto† (M) **229 19**
H: 5 09 W: 12 02 b.Balaguer 13-7-73
Source: Balaguer.

1995–96	Wigan Ath	42	9		
1996–97	Wigan Ath	43	4		
1997–98	Wigan Ath	33	1		
1998–99	Wigan Ath	10	0		
1999–2000	Wigan Ath	25	3		
2000-01	Wigan Ath	34	0	**187**	**17**
2001-02	Motherwell	17	0	**17**	**0**
2002-03	Walsall	6	0	**6**	**0**
2002-03	Swansea C	19	2	**19**	**2**

MOSS, David‡ (M) **242 67**
H: 6 0 W: 13 07 b.Doncaster 15-11-68
Source: Boston U.

1992–93	Doncaster R	9	3		
1993–94	Doncaster R	9	2	**18**	**5**
1993–94	Chesterfield	26	6		
1994–95	Chesterfield	32	10		
1995–96	Chesterfield	13	0	**71**	**16**
1996–97	Scunthorpe U	4	0	**4**	**0**
1996–97	Partick T	31	11	**31**	**11**
1997–98	Falkirk	30	12		
1998–99	Falkirk	17	5		
1999–2000	Falkirk	4	3		
1999–2000	Dunfermline Ath	24	6		
2000-01	Dunfermline Ath	26	6		
2001-02	Dunfermline Ath	0	0	**50**	**12**
2001-02	*Ayr U*	5	1	**5**	**1**
2001-02	Falkirk	3	0	**54**	**20**
2002-03	Swansea C	9	2	**9**	**2**

MUMFORD, Andrew (M) **62 6**
H: 6 1 W: 12 03 b.Neath 18-6-81
Source: Llanelli. *Honours:* Wales Schools, Youth, Under-21.

2000-01	Swansea C	6	0		
2001-02	Swansea C	32	5		
2002-03	Swansea C	24	1	**62**	**6**

MURPHY, Matt* (M) **270 40**
H: 6 1 W: 12 12 b.Northampton 20-8-71
Source: Corby T.

1992–93	Oxford U	2	0		
1993–94	Oxford U	0	0		
1994–95	Oxford U	22	7		
1995–96	Oxford U	34	5		
1996–97	Oxford U	30	3		
1997–98	Oxford U	29	2		
1997–98	*Scunthorpe U*	3	0	**3**	**0**
1998–99	Oxford U	43	4		
1999–2000	Oxford U	46	11		
2000-01	Oxford U	40	6	**246**	**38**
2001-02	Bury	9	0	**9**	**0**
2002-03	Swansea C	12	2	**12**	**2**

NUGENT, Kevin# (F) **437 104**
H: 6 1 W: 13 07 b.Edmonton 10-4-69
Source: Trainee. *Honours:* Eire Youth.

1987–88	Leyton Orient	11	3		
1988–89	Leyton Orient	3	0		
1989–90	Leyton Orient	11	0		
1990–91	Leyton Orient	33	5		
1991–92	Leyton Orient	36	12		
1991–92	Plymouth Arg	4	0		
1992–93	Plymouth Arg	45	11		
1993–94	Plymouth Arg	39	14		
1994–95	Plymouth Arg	37	7		
1995–96	Plymouth Arg	6	0	**131**	**32**
1995–96	Bristol C	34	8		
1996–97	Bristol C	36	6	**70**	**14**
1997–98	Cardiff C	4	0		
1998–99	Cardiff C	41	15		
1999–2000	Cardiff C	39	10		
2000-01	Cardiff C	14	4		
2001-02	Cardiff C	1	0	**99**	**29**
2001-02	Leyton Orient	9	1		
2002-03	Leyton Orient	19	3	**122**	**24**
2002-03	Swansea C	15	5	**15**	**5**

O'LEARY, Kristian# (D) **169 7**
H: 5 11 W: 12 09 b.Port Talbot 30-8-77
Source: Trainee. *Honours:* Wales Youth.

1995–96	Swansea C	1	0		
1996–97	Swansea C	12	1		
1997–98	Swansea C	29	0		
1998–99	Swansea C	19	2		
1999–2000	Swansea C	20	0		
2000-01	Swansea C	24	2		
2001-02	Swansea C	31	2		
2002-03	Swansea C	33	0	**169**	**7**

PHILLIPS, Gareth* (M) **88 2**
H: 5 8 W: 9 08 b.Pontypridd 19-8-79
Source: Trainee. *Honours:* Wales Schools, Youth, Under-21.

1996–97	Swansea C	1	0		
1997–98	Swansea C	6	0		
1998–99	Swansea C	1	0		
1999–2000	Swansea C	3	0		
2000-01	Swansea C	15	0		
2001-02	Swansea C	35	2		
2002-03	Swansea C	27	0	**88**	**2**

REID, Paul‡ (M) **551 58**
H: 5 8 W: 12 03 b.Oldbury 19-1-68
Source: Apprentice.

1985–86	Leicester C	0	0		
1986–87	Leicester C	6	0		
1987–88	Leicester C	26	5		
1988–89	Leicester C	45	6		
1989–90	Leicester C	40	8		
1990–91	Leicester C	33	2		
1991–92	Leicester C	12	0	**162**	**21**
1991–92	*Bradford C*	7	0		
1992–93	Bradford C	44	6		
1993–94	Bradford C	38	9	**89**	**15**
1994–95	Huddersfield T	42	6		
1995–96	Huddersfield T	13	0		
1996–97	Huddersfield T	22	0	**77**	**6**
1996–97	Oldham Ath	9	1		
1997–98	Oldham Ath	44	4		
1998–99	Oldham Ath	40	1	**93**	**6**
1999–2000	Bury	39	2		
2000-01	Bury	43	4		
2001-02	Bury	28	3	**110**	**9**
2002-03	Swansea C	20	1	**20**	**1**

SHARP, Neil* (D) **32 1**
H: 6 1 W: 12 08 b.Hemel Hempstead 19-1-78
Source: Merthyr T.

2001-02	Swansea C	25	1		
2002-03	Swansea C	7	0	**32**	**1**

SMITH, David‡ (D) **411 34**
H: 5 7 W: 11 11 b.Gloucester 29-5-68
Source: Apprentice. *Honours:* England Under-21.

1986–87	Coventry C	0	0		
1987–88	Coventry C	16	4		
1988–89	Coventry C	35	3		
1989–90	Coventry C	37	6		
1990–91	Coventry C	36	1		
1991–92	Coventry C	24	4		
1992–93	Coventry C	6	1	**154**	**19**
1992–93	*Bournemouth*	1	0	**1**	**0**
1992–93	Birmingham C	13	1		
1993–94	Birmingham C	25	2	**38**	**3**
1993–94	WBA	18	0		
1994–95	WBA	22	0		
1995–96	WBA	16	0		
1996–97	WBA	24	2		
1997–98	WBA	22	0	**102**	**2**
1997–98	Grimsby T	17	1		
1998–99	Grimsby T	31	5		
1999–2000	Grimsby T	36	1		
2000-01	Grimsby T	24	1		
2001-02	Grimsby T	4	1	**112**	**9**
2002-03	Swansea C	4	1	**4**	**1**

SMITH, Jason# (D) **142 8**
H: 6 3 W: 14 00 b.Bromsgrove 6-9-74
Source: Tiverton. *Honours:* England Schools.

1993–94	Coventry C	0	0		
1994–95	Coventry C	0	0		
1995–96	Coventry C	0	0		
1996–97	Coventry C	0	0		

1997–98	Coventry C	0	0		
From Tiverton T					
1998–99	Swansea C	42	4		
1999–2000	Swansea C	43	1		
2000–01	Swansea C	22	0		
2001–02	Swansea C	8	0		
2002–03	Swansea C	27	3	**142**	**8**

THOMAS, James# (F) **72** **18**
H: 6 1 W: 13 05 b.Swansea 16-1-79
Source: Trainee. *Honours:* Wales Under-21.

1996–97	Blackburn R	0	0		
1997–98	Blackburn R	0	0		
1997–98	*WBA*	3	0	**3**	**0**
1998–99	Blackburn R	0	0		
1999–2000	Blackburn R	0	0		
1999–2000	*Blackpool*	9	2	**9**	**2**
2000–01	Blackburn R	4	1		
2000–01	*Sheffield U*	10	1	**10**	**1**
2001–02	Blackburn R	0	0	**4**	**1**
2001–02	*Bristol R*	7	1	**7**	**1**
2002–03	Swansea C	39	13	**39**	**13**

WATKIN, Steve* (F) **406** **99**
H: 5 10 W: 11 10 b.Wrexham 16-6-71
Source: School. *Honours:* Wales Schools, B.

1989–90	Wrexham	0	0		
1990–91	Wrexham	9	1		
1991–92	Wrexham	28	8		
1992–93	Wrexham	33	18		
1993–94	Wrexham	40	9		
1994–95	Wrexham	32	4		
1995–96	Wrexham	29	7		
1996–97	Wrexham	26	7		
1997–98	Wrexham	3	1	**200**	**55**
1997–98	Swansea C	32	3		
1998–99	Swansea C	43	17		
1999–2000	Swansea C	39	7		
2000–01	Swansea C	35	7		
2001–02	Swansea C	31	8		
2002–03	Swansea C	26	2	**206**	**44**

WILLIAMS, John* (F) **408** **67**
H: 6 1 W: 13 12 b.Birmingham 11-5-68
Source: Cradley T.

1991–92	Swansea C	39	11		
1992–93	Coventry C	41	8		
1993–94	Coventry C	32	3		
1994–95	Coventry C	7	0		
1994–95	*Notts Co*	5	2	**5**	**2**
1994–95	*Stoke C*	4	0	**4**	**0**
1994–95	*Swansea C*	7	2		
1995–96	Coventry C	0	0	**80**	**11**
1995–96	Wycombe W	29	8		
1996–97	Wycombe W	19	1	**48**	**9**
1996–97	Hereford U	11	3	**11**	**3**
1997–98	Walsall	1	0	**1**	**0**
1997–98	Exeter C	36	4	**36**	**4**
1998–99	Cardiff C	43	12		
1999–2000	Cardiff C	0	0	**43**	**12**
1999–2000	York C	36	3		
2000–01	York C	6	0	**42**	**3**
2000–01	Darlington	24	5	**24**	**5**
2001–02	Swansea C	41	4		
2002–03	Swansea C	27	1	**114**	**18**

WOOD, Jamie* (F) **80** **8**
H: 5 10 W: 12 10 b.Salford 21-9-78
Source: Trainee. *Honours:* Cayman Islands 2 full caps.

1997–98	Manchester U	0	0		
1998–99	Manchester U	0	0		
1999–2000	Hull C	32	6		
2000–01	Hull C	15	0	**47**	**6**
2001–02	Halifax T	16	0	**16**	**0**
2002–03	Swansea C	17	2	**17**	**2**

Scholars
Cole, Simon D; Corbisiero, Antonio; Cunnah, Robert R; Davies, Kevin R; Davies, Peter B; Eames, Jonathan J; Frowen, Geraint; Harrison, Ryan-Lee; Jones, Stuart J; King, Jack A; Pritchard, Mark O; Rewbury, Jamie; Roberts, Matthew N; Surman, Lee B; Thompson, Jay K; Waters, Michael
Non-Contract
Coates, Jonathan S; Johnrose, Leonard; Martinez, Roberto

SWINDON T

BAMPTON, David§ (M) **3** **0**
b.Swindon 5-5-85

2002–03	Swindon T	3	0	**3**	**0**

COBIAN, Juan‡ (D) **16** **0**
H: 5 6 W: 10 10 b.Buenos Aires 11-9-75
Source: Boca Juniors.

1998–99	Sheffield W	9	0	**9**	**0**
1999–2000	Charlton Ath	0	0		
1999–2000	Aberdeen	3	0	**3**	**0**
2000–01	Swindon T	3	0		
2001–02	Swindon T	1	0		
2002–03	Swindon T	0	0	**4**	**0**

COLLINS, Christopher‡ (M) **0** **0**
b.Merthyr 6-8-83
Source: Scholar.

2001–02	Swindon T	0	0		
2002–03	Swindon T	0	0		

DUKE, David (M) **118** **5**
H: 5 10 W: 11 01 b.Inverness 7-11-78
Source: Redby CA.

1997–98	Sunderland	0	0		
1998–99	Sunderland	0	0		
1999–2000	Sunderland	0	0		
2000–01	Swindon T	32	1		
2001–02	Swindon T	42	2		
2002–03	Swindon T	44	2	**118**	**5**

DYKES, Darren‡ (F) **5** **0**
b.Aylesbury 28-4-81
Source: Buckingham T.

2002–03	Swindon T	2	0	**2**	**0**
2002–03	*Lincoln C*	3	0	**3**	**0**

EDDS, Gareth* (M) **30** **1**
H: 6 0 W: 12 00 b.Sydney 3-2-81
Source: Trainee. *Honours:* Australia Under-20, Under-23.

1997–98	Nottingham F	0	0		
1998–99	Nottingham F	0	0		
1999–2000	Nottingham F	2	0		
2000–01	Nottingham F	13	1		
2001–02	Nottingham F	1	0	**16**	**1**
2002–03	Swindon T	14	0	**14**	**0**

EDWARDS, Nathan* (M) **10** **0**
H: 5 11 W: 12 10 b.Lincoln 8-4-83
Source: Scholar.

2001–02	Swindon T	7	0		
2002–03	Swindon T	3	0	**10**	**0**

FARR, Craig (G) **2** **0**
b.Newbury 27-6-84
Source: Scholar.

2002–03	Swindon T	2	0	**2**	**0**

GARRARD, Luke† (M) **1** **0**
b.Barnet 22-9-85

2002–03	Swindon T	1	0	**1**	**0**

GRIEMINK, Bart (G) **196** **0**
H: 6 3 W: 15 02 b.Holland 29-3-72
Source: WKE.

1995–96	Birmingham C	20	0		
1996–97	Birmingham C	0	0	**20**	**0**
1996–97	*Barnsley*	0	0		
1996–97	Peterborough U	27	0		
1997–98	Peterborough U	0	0		
1998–99	Peterborough U	17	0		
1999–2000	Peterborough U	14	0	**58**	**0**
1999–2000	*Swindon T*	4	0		
2000–01	Swindon T	25	0		
2001–02	Swindon T	45	0		
2002–03	Swindon T	44	0	**118**	**0**

GURNEY, Andy (D) **323** **36**
H: 5 8 W: 10 08 b.Bristol 25-1-74
Source: Trainee.

1992–93	Bristol R	0	0		
1993–94	Bristol R	3	0		
1994–95	Bristol R	38	1		
1995–96	Bristol R	43	6		
1996–97	Bristol R	24	2	**108**	**9**
1997–98	Torquay U	44	9		
1998–99	Torquay U	20	1	**64**	**10**
1998–99	Reading	8	0		
1999–2000	Reading	38	2		
2000–01	Reading	21	1	**67**	**3**
2001–02	Swindon T	43	6		
2002–03	Swindon T	41	8	**84**	**14**

HALLIDAY, Kevin* (M) **0** **0**
b.Swindon 8-7-83
Source: Scholar.

2002–03	Swindon T	0	0		

HERRING, Ian§ (M) **5** **0**
H: 6 1 W: 11 12 b.Swindon 14-2-84
Source: Scholar.

2001–02	Swindon T	1	0		
2002–03	Swindon T	4	0	**5**	**0**

HEWLETT, Matt (M) **234** **11**
H: 6 2 W: 12 12 b.Bristol 25-2-76
Source: Trainee. *Honours:* England Youth.

1993–94	Bristol C	12	0		
1994–95	Bristol C	1	0		
1995–96	Bristol C	27	2		
1996–97	Bristol C	36	2		
1997–98	Bristol C	34	4		
1998–99	Bristol C	10	1		
1998–99	*Burnley*	2	0	**2**	**0**
1999–2000	Bristol C	7	0	**127**	**9**
2000–01	Swindon T	26	0		
2001–02	Swindon T	39	1		
2002–03	Swindon T	40	1	**105**	**2**

HEYWOOD, Matthew (D) **124** **6**
H: 6 3 W: 14 00 b.Chatham 26-8-79
Source: Trainee.

1998–99	Burnley	13	0		
1999–2000	Burnley	0	0		
2000–01	Burnley	0	0	**13**	**0**
2000–01	Swindon T	21	2		
2001–02	Swindon T	44	3		
2002–03	Swindon T	46	1	**111**	**6**

INVINCIBILE, Danny* (M) **172** **25**
H: 6 0 W: 12 02 b.Australia 31-3-79
Honours: Australia Under-20.

1997–98	Brisbane Strikers	5	1	**5**	**1**
1998–99	Marconi Stallions	7	0		
1999–2000	Marconi Stallions	32	2	**39**	**2**
2000–01	West Ham U	0	0		
2000–01	Swindon T	42	9		
2001–02	Swindon T	44	6		
2002–03	Swindon T	42	7	**128**	**22**

MIGLIORANZI, Stefani (M) **76** **5**
H: 6 1 W: 12 12 b.Pacos de Caldas 20-9-77
Source: St Johns Univ.

1998–99	Portsmouth	7	0		
1999–2000	Portsmouth	13	2		
2000–01	Portsmouth	12	0		
2001–02	Portsmouth	3	0	**35**	**2**
2002–03	Swindon T	41	3	**41**	**3**

O'HALLORAN, Keith* (D) **108** **9**
H: 5 9 W: 11 06 b.Ireland 10-11-75
Source: Cherry Orchard.

1994–95	Middlesbrough	1	0		
1995–96	Middlesbrough	3	0		
1995–96	*Scunthorpe U*	7	0	**7**	**0**
1996–97	Middlesbrough	0	0	**4**	**0**
1996–97	*Cardiff C*	8	0	**8**	**0**
1996–97	St Johnstone	5	0		
1997–98	St Johnstone	22	1		
1998–99	St Johnstone	16	1		
1999–2000	St Johnstone	0	0	**43**	**2**
2000–01	Swindon T	40	5		
2001–02	Swindon T	6	2		
2002–03	Swindon T	0	0	**46**	**7**

PARKIN, Sam (F) **105** **37**
H: 6 2 W: 13 03 b.Roehampton 14-3-81
Honours: England Schools.

1998–99	Chelsea	0	0		
1999–2000	Chelsea	0	0		
2000–01	Chelsea	0	0		
2000–01	*Millwall*	7	4	**7**	**4**
2000–01	*Wycombe W*	8	1	**8**	**1**
2000–01	*Oldham Ath*	7	3	**7**	**3**
2001–02	Chelsea	0	0		
2001–02	*Northampton T*	40	4	**40**	**4**
2002–03	Swindon T	43	25	**43**	**25**

REEVES, Alan# (D) **408** **26**
H: 6 0 W: 12 00 b.Birkenhead 19-11-67
Source: Heswall.

1988–89	Norwich C	0	0		
1988–89	*Gillingham*	18	0	**18**	**0**
1989–90	Chester C	30	2		
1990–91	Chester C	10	0	**40**	**2**
1991–92	Rochdale	34	3		
1992–93	Rochdale	41	3		
1993–94	Rochdale	41	3		
1994–95	Rochdale	5	0	**121**	**9**
1994–95	Wimbledon	31	3		
1995–96	Wimbledon	24	1		
1996–97	Wimbledon	2	0		
1997–98	Wimbledon	0	0	**57**	**4**
1998–99	Swindon T	24	2		
1999–2000	Swindon T	43	1		
2000–01	Swindon T	44	3		
2001–02	Swindon T	25	2		
2002–03	Swindon T	36	3	**172**	**11**

ROBINSON, Steve# (M) **188 4**
H: 5 9 W: 11 00 b.Nottingham 17-10-75
Source: Trainee.

1993–94	Birmingham C	0	0		
1994–95	Birmingham C	6	0		
1995–96	Birmingham C	0	0		
1995–96	*Peterborough U*	5	0	**5**	**0**
1996–97	Birmingham C	9	0		
1997–98	Birmingham C	25	0		
1998–99	Birmingham C	31	0		
1999–2000	Birmingham C	6	0		
2000-01	Birmingham C	4	0	**81**	**0**
2000-01	Swindon T	18	2		
2001-02	Swindon T	40	0		
2002-03	Swindon T	44	2	**102**	**4**

RUDDOCK, Neil‡ (D) **355 29**
H: 6 2 W: 12 12 b.Wandsworth 9-5-68
Source: Apprentice. *Honours:* England Youth, Under-21, B, 1 full cap.

1985–86	Millwall	0	0		
1985–86	Tottenham H	0	0		
1986–87	Tottenham H	4	0		
1987–88	Tottenham H	5	0		
1988–89	Millwall	2	1	**2**	**1**
1988–89	Southampton	13	3		
1989–90	Southampton	29	3		
1990–91	Southampton	35	3		
1991–92	Southampton	30	0	**107**	**9**
1992–93	Tottenham H	38	3	**47**	**3**
1993–94	Liverpool	39	3		
1994–95	Liverpool	37	2		
1995–96	Liverpool	20	5		
1996–97	Liverpool	17	1		
1997–98	Liverpool	2	0	**115**	**11**
1997–98	*QPR*	7	0	**7**	**0**
1998–99	West Ham U	27	2		
1999–2000	West Ham U	15	0	**42**	**2**
2000-01	Crystal Palace	20	2	**20**	**2**
2001-02	Swindon T	15	1		
2002-03	Swindon T	0	0	**15**	**1**

SABIN, Eric* (F) **101 12**
H: 6 0 W: 12 00 b.Sarcelles 22-1-75

2000-01	Wasquehal	28	3	**28**	**3**
2001-02	Swindon T	34	5		
2002-03	Swindon T	39	4	**73**	**9**

SUTTON, John‡ (F) **8 1**
H: 6 0 W: 14 02 b.Norwich 26-12-83
Source: Scholar. *Honours:* England Youth.

2001-02	Tottenham H	0	0		
2002-03	Tottenham H	0	0		
2002-03	*Carlisle U*	7	1	**7**	**1**
2002-03	Swindon T	1	0	**1**	**0**

TAYLOR, Chris§ (D) **4 0**
H: 5 8 W: 10 05 b.Swindon 30-10-85
Source: Scholar.

2002-03	Swindon T	4	0	**4**	**0**

WILLIS, Adam* (D) **102 1**
H: 6 1 W: 12 02 b.Nuneaton 21-9-76
Source: Trainee.

1995–96	Coventry C	0	0		
1996–97	Coventry C	0	0		
1997–98	Coventry C	0	0		
1997–98	Swindon T	0	0		
1998–99	Swindon T	11	0		
1998–99	*Mansfield T*	10	0	**10**	**0**
1999–2000	Swindon T	23	0		
2000-01	Swindon T	21	0		
2001-02	Swindon T	22	1		
2002-03	Swindon T	15	0	**92**	**1**

YOUNG, Alan (F) **29 1**
H: 5 6 W: 10 00 b.Swindon 12-8-83
Source: Scholar. *Honours:* England Youth.

2000-01	Swindon T	4	0		
2001-02	Swindon T	14	1		
2002-03	Swindon T	11	0	**29**	**1**

Scholars
Bampton, David P; Cheeseman, James; Draycott, Mark R; Fenwick, Mark T; Hambidge, James H; Herring, Ian; Lapham, Kyle; Oliver, Ian A; Pook, Michael D; Salter, Aaron J; Smith, Steven A; Taylor, Christopher J; Taylor, Daniel S
Non-Contract
Bulman, Matthew; Garrard, Luke E

TORQUAY U

ASHINGTON, Ryan‡ (F) **16 0**
H: 5 10 W: 12 06 b.Torbay 28-3-83
Source: Scholar.

2000-01	Torquay U	14	0		
2001-02	Torquay U	0	0		
2002-03	Torquay U	2	0	**16**	**0**

ATTWELL, Jamie‡ (G) **4 0**
H: 6 4 W: 15 00 b.Bristol 8-6-82
Source: Tottenham H scholar.

2001-02	Bristol C	0	0		
2002-03	Torquay U	4	0	**4**	**0**

BEDEAU, Anthony (F) **218 46**
H: 5 10 W: 12 03 b.Hammersmith 24-3-79
Source: Trainee.

1995–96	Torquay U	4	0		
1996–97	Torquay U	8	1		
1997–98	Torquay U	34	5		
1998–99	Torquay U	36	9		
1999–2000	Torquay U	38	16		
2000-01	Torquay U	34	5		
2001-02	Torquay U	21	4		
2001-02	*Barnsley*	3	0	**3**	**0**
2002-03	Torquay U	40	6	**215**	**46**

BENEFIELD, Jimmy (F) **17 0**
H: 5 11 W: 11 05 b.Bristol 6-5-83
Source: Scholar.

2000-01	Torquay U	1	0		
2001-02	Torquay U	8	0		
2002-03	Torquay U	8	0	**17**	**0**

BOND, Kain§ (F) **1 0**
H: 5 8 W: 10 10 b.Torquay 19-6-85
Source: Scholar.

2002-03	Torquay U	1	0	**1**	**0**

CAMARA, Ben§ (F) **2 0**
H: 6 2 W: 12 05 b.Bonn 20-8-84
Source: Trainee.

2002-03	Torquay U	2	0	**2**	**0**

CANOVILLE, Lee (F) **50 1**
H: 6 0 W: 11 04 b.Ealing 14-3-81
Source: Trainee. *Honours:* FA Schools, England Youth.

1998–99	Arsenal	0	0		
1999–2000	Arsenal	0	0		
2000-01	Arsenal	0	0		
2000-01	*Northampton T*	2	0	**2**	**0**
2001-02	Torquay U	12	1		
2002-03	Torquay U	36	0	**48**	**1**

DEARDEN, Kevin# (G) **411 0**
H: 5 11 W: 14 02 b.Luton 8-3-70
Source: Trainee.

1988–89	Tottenham H	0	0		
1988–89	*Cambridge U*	15	0	**15**	**0**
1989–90	Tottenham H	0	0		
1989–90	*Hartlepool U*	10	0	**10**	**0**
1989–90	*Oxford U*	0	0		
1989–90	*Swindon T*	1	0	**1**	**0**
1990–91	Tottenham H	0	0		
1990–91	*Peterborough U*	7	0	**7**	**0**
1990–91	*Hull C*	3	0	**3**	**0**
1991–92	Tottenham H	0	0		
1991–92	*Rochdale*	2	0	**2**	**0**
1991–92	*Birmingham C*	12	0	**12**	**0**
1992–93	Tottenham H	1	0		
1992–93	*Portsmouth*	0	0		
1993–94	Tottenham H	0	0	**1**	**0**
1993–94	Brentford	35	0		
1994–95	Brentford	43	0		
1995–96	Brentford	41	0		
1996–97	Brentford	44	0		
1997–98	Brentford	35	0		
1998–99	Brentford	7	0	**205**	**0**
1998–99	*Barnet*	1	0	**1**	**0**
1998–99	*Huddersfield T*	0	0		
1999–2000	Wrexham	45	0		
2000-01	Wrexham	36	0	**81**	**0**
2001-02	Torquay U	46	0		
2002-03	Torquay U	27	0	**73**	**0**

DOUGLIN, Troy‡ (D) **14 0**
H: 6 0 W: 12 03 b.Coventry 7-5-82
Source: Trainee.

2000-01	Torquay U	3	0		
2001-02	Torquay U	6	0		
2002-03	Torquay U	5	0	**14**	**0**

FORINTON, Howard‡ (F) **65 14**
H: 5 11 W: 12 04 b.Boston 18-9-75
Source: Yeovil T.

1997–98	Birmingham C	1	0		
1998–99	Birmingham C	3	1		
1998–99	*Plymouth Arg*	9	3	**9**	**3**
1999–2000	Birmingham C	1	0	**5**	**1**
1999–2000	Peterborough U	25	7		
2000-01	Peterborough U	8	1		
2001-02	Peterborough U	17	2		
2002-03	Peterborough U	0	0	**50**	**10**
2002-03	Torquay U	1	0	**1**	**0**

FOWLER, Jason (M) **224 19**
H: 6 3 W: 12 01 b.Bristol 20-8-74
Source: Trainee.

1992–93	Bristol C	1	0		
1993–94	Bristol C	1	0		
1994–95	Bristol C	13	0		
1995–96	Bristol C	10	0	**25**	**0**
1996–97	Cardiff C	37	5		
1997–98	Cardiff C	38	5		
1998–99	Cardiff C	37	3		
1999–2000	Cardiff C	28	1		
2000-01	Cardiff C	5	0		
2001-02	Cardiff C	0	0	**145**	**14**
2001-02	Torquay U	14	1		
2002-03	Torquay U	40	4	**54**	**5**

GRAHAM, David (F) **99 27**
H: 5 11 W: 12 01 b.Edinburgh 6-10-78
Source: Rangers SABC. *Honours:* Scotland Under-21.

1995–96	Rangers	0	0		
1996–97	Rangers	0	0		
1997–98	Rangers	0	0		
1998–99	Rangers	3	0	**3**	**0**
1998–99	Dunfermline Ath	21	2		
1999–2000	Dunfermline Ath	0	0		
2000-01	Dunfermline Ath	0	0	**21**	**2**
2000-01	Torquay U	5	2		
2001-02	Torquay U	36	8		
2002-03	Torquay U	34	15	**75**	**25**

GRITTON, Martin (F) **87 20**
H: 6 1 W: 12 02 b.Glasgow 1-6-78
Source: Porthleven.

1998–99	Plymouth Arg	2	0		
1999–2000	Plymouth Arg	30	6		
2000-01	Plymouth Arg	10	1		
2001-02	Plymouth Arg	2	0		
2002-03	Plymouth Arg	0	0	**44**	**7**
2002-03	Torquay U	43	13	**43**	**13**

HANKIN, Sean (M) **47 1**
H: 5 11 W: 12 04 b.Camberley 28-2-81
Source: Trainee.

1999–2000	Crystal Palace	1	0		
2000-01	Crystal Palace	0	0		
2001-02	Crystal Palace	0	0	**1**	**0**
2001-02	Torquay U	27	0		
2002-03	Torquay U	19	1	**46**	**1**

HAZELL, Reuben (D) **107 2**
H: 5 9 W: 11 07 b.Birmingham 24-4-79
Source: Trainee.

1996–97	Aston Villa	0	0		
1997–98	Aston Villa	0	0		
1998–99	Aston Villa	0	0		
1999–2000	Tranmere R	23	1		
2000-01	Tranmere R	13	0		
2001-02	Tranmere R	6	0	**42**	**1**
2001-02	Torquay U	19	0		
2002-03	Torquay U	46	1	**65**	**1**

HILL, Kevin (M) **242 29**
H: 5 8 W: 10 06 b.Exeter 6-3-76
Source: Torrington.

1997–98	Torquay U	37	7		
1998–99	Torquay U	35	5		
1999–2000	Torquay U	43	2		
2000-01	Torquay U	44	9		
2001-02	Torquay U	44	2		
2002-03	Torquay U	39	4	**242**	**29**

HOCKLEY, Matthew (D) **58 3**
H: 5 10 W: 11 11 b.Paignton 5-6-82
Source: Trainee.

2000-01	Torquay U	6	1		
2001-02	Torquay U	12	0		
2002-03	Torquay U	40	2	**58**	**3**

HOLMES, Paul* (D) **408 8**
H: 5 10 W: 12 05 b.Stocksbridge 18-2-68
Source: Apprentice.

1985–86	Doncaster R	5	1		
1986–87	Doncaster R	16	0		
1987–88	Doncaster R	26	0	**47**	**1**
1988–89	Torquay U	25	0		
1989–90	Torquay U	44	2		
1990–91	Torquay U	33	1		
1991–92	Torquay U	36	1		
1992–93	Birmingham C	12	0	**12**	**0**

1992–93	Everton	4	0		
1993–94	Everton	15	0		
1994–95	Everton	1	0		
1995–96	Everton	1	0	**21**	**0**
1995–96	WBA	18	0		
1996–97	WBA	38	1		
1997–98	WBA	30	0		
1998–99	WBA	17	0		
1999–2000	WBA	0	0	**103**	**1**
1999–2000	Torquay U	30	0		
2000-01	Torquay U	32	2		
2001-02	Torquay U	18	0		
2002-03	Torquay U	7	0	**225**	**6**

KILLOUGHERY, Graham§ (M) **3 0**
H: 5 10 W: 11 07 b.London 22-7-84
Source: Trainee.

2002-03	Torquay U	3	0	**3**	**0**

MORRIS, Jason‡ (D) **0 0**
H: 6 0 W: 12 07 b.Torquay 7-5-83
Source: Buckland Ath.

2001-02	Torquay U	0	0		
2002-03	Torquay U	0	0		

OSEI-KUFFOUR, Jo (F) **41 7**
H: 5 7 W: 10 03 b.Edmonton 17-11-81
Source: Scholar.

2000-01	Arsenal	0	0		
2001-02	Arsenal	0	0		
2001-02	*Swindon T*	11	2	**11**	**2**
2002-03	Torquay U	30	5	**30**	**5**

PRINCE, Neil‡ (M) **7 0**
H: 5 11 W: 10 07 b.Liverpool 17-3-83
Source: Liverpool Scholar.

2002-03	Torquay U	7	0	**7**	**0**

RUSSELL, Alex (M) **255 38**
H: 5 10 W: 12 00 b.Crosby 17-3-73
Source: Burscough.

1994–95	Rochdale	7	1		
1995–96	Rochdale	25	0		
1996–97	Rochdale	39	9		
1997–98	Rochdale	31	4	**102**	**14**
1998–99	Cambridge U	37	6		
1999–2000	Cambridge U	15	0		
2000-01	Cambridge U	29	2	**81**	**8**
2001-02	Torquay U	33	7		
2002-03	Torquay U	39	9	**72**	**16**

STEPHENS, Nicholas‡ (M) **0 0**
H: 6 2 W: 12 00 b.Plymouth 30-5-83
Source: Scholar.

2001-02	Torquay U	0	0		
2002-03	Torquay U	0	0		

STEVENS, Dean§ (F) **3 0**
H: 5 10 W: 12 00 b.Torbay 7-2-86

2002-03	Torquay U	3	0	**3**	**0**

VAN HEUSDEN, Arjan (G) **174 0**
H: 6 4 W: 14 05 b.Alphen 11-12-72
Source: Noordwijk.

1994–95	Port Vale	2	0		
1995–96	Port Vale	7	0		
1996–97	Port Vale	13	0		
1997–98	Port Vale	5	0	**27**	**0**
1997–98	*Oxford U*	11	0	**11**	**0**
1998–99	Cambridge U	27	0		
1999–2000	Cambridge U	15	0	**42**	**0**
2000-01	Exeter C	41	0		
2001-02	Exeter C	33	0	**74**	**0**
2002-03	Mansfield T	5	0	**5**	**0**
2002-03	Torquay U	15	0	**15**	**0**

WILLS, Kevin (M) **52 2**
H: 5 9 W: 10 04 b.Torbay 15-10-80
Source: Trainee.

1998–99	Plymouth Arg	2	0		
1999–2000	Plymouth Arg	2	0		
2000-01	Plymouth Arg	10	1		
2001-02	Plymouth Arg	18	0		
2002-03	Plymouth Arg	0	0	**32**	**1**
2002-03	Torquay U	20	1	**20**	**1**

WOODS, Steve# (D) **111 2**
H: 6 0 W: 13 00 b.Northwich 15-12-76
Source: Trainee.

1995–96	Stoke C	0	0		
1996–97	Stoke C	0	0		
1997–98	Stoke C	1	0		
1997–98	*Plymouth Arg*	5	0	**5**	**0**
1998–99	Stoke C	33	0	**34**	**0**
1999–2000	Chesterfield	25	0		
2000-01	Chesterfield	0	0	**25**	**0**
2001-02	Torquay U	38	2		
2002-03	Torquay U	9	0	**47**	**2**

WOOZLEY, David (D) **98 3**
H: 6 0 W: 12 10 b.Berkshire 6-12-79
Source: Trainee.

1997–98	Crystal Palace	0	0		
1998–99	Crystal Palace	7	0		
1999–2000	Crystal Palace	23	0		
2000-01	Crystal Palace	0	0		
2000-01	*Bournemouth*	6	0	**6**	**0**
2001-02	Crystal Palace	0	0	**30**	**0**
2001-02	Torquay U	16	0		
2002-03	Torquay U	46	3	**62**	**3**

Trainees
Bond, Kain; Brimming, Robert G; Burgess, Lucas; Camara, Ben I; Carns, David; Clark, Thomas; Corderoy, Scott PJ; Crush, Jake R; Johnson, Matthew S; Killoughery, Graham A; Kironde, Biju S; Lamacraft, Richard; McAdam, Paul MJ; Redhead, Daniel; Skinner, Nicholas; Small, Michael S; Stevens, Dean W

Non-Contract
Hancox, Richard C

TOTTENHAM H

ACIMOVIC, Milenko (M) **153 41**
H: 6 2 W: 12 08 b.Ljubljana 15-2-77
Honours: Slovenia 46 full caps, 10 goals.

1996–97	Olimpija	18	3		
1997–98	Olimpija	16	4	**34**	**7**
1997–98	Red Star Belgrade	9	1		
1998–99	Red Star Belgrade	22	8		
1999–2000	Red Star Belgrade	21	4		
2000-01	Red Star Belgrade	28	14		
2001-02	Red Star Belgrade	22	7	**102**	**34**
2001-02	Tottenham H	0	0		
2002-03	Tottenham H	17	0	**17**	**0**

ANDERTON, Darren (M) **341 40**
H: 6 1 W: 12 11 b.Southampton 3-3-72
Source: Trainee. *Honours:* England Youth, Under-21, B, 30 full caps, 7 goals.

1989–90	Portsmouth	0	0		
1990–91	Portsmouth	20	0		
1991–92	Portsmouth	42	7	**62**	**7**
1992–93	Tottenham H	34	6		
1993–94	Tottenham H	37	6		
1994–95	Tottenham H	37	5		
1995–96	Tottenham H	8	2		
1996–97	Tottenham H	16	3		
1997–98	Tottenham H	15	0		
1998–99	Tottenham H	32	3		
1999–2000	Tottenham H	22	3		
2000-01	Tottenham H	23	2		
2001-02	Tottenham H	35	3		
2002-03	Tottenham H	20	0	**279**	**33**

BARNARD, Lee (F) **3 0**
H: 5 10 W: 10 10 b.Romford 18-7-84
Source: Trainee.

2002-03	Tottenham H	0	0		
2002-03	*Exeter C*	3	0	**3**	**0**

BLACK, Jonathan (M) **0 0**
b.Larne 7-5-85
Source: Trainee. *Honours:* Northern Ireland Under-21.

2002-03	Tottenham H	0	0		

BLONDEL, Jonathan (M) **19 0**
H: 5 8 W: 10 12 b.Ypres 3-3-84
Honours: Belgium 1 full cap.

2001-02	Mouscron	18	0	**18**	**0**
2002-03	Tottenham H	1	0	**1**	**0**

BORTOLOZZO, Diego‡ (M) **0 0**
b.Brazil 29-9-82
Source: Treviso.

2002-03	Tottenham H	0	0		

BOWDITCH, Ben (D) **0 0**
b.Harlow 19-2-84
Source: Scholar. *Honours:* England Youth, Under-20.

2000-01	Tottenham H	0	0		
2001-02	Tottenham H	0	0		
2002-03	Tottenham H	0	0		

BUNJEVCEVIC, Goran (D) **226 21**
H: 6 3 W: 12 02 b.Karlovac 17-2-73
Honours: Yugoslavia 14 full caps.

1994–95	Rad	17	0		
1995–96	Rad	13	2		
1996–97	Rad	30	3	**60**	**5**
1997–98	Red Star Belgrade	30	5		
1998–99	Red Star Belgrade	22	4		
1999–2000	Red Star Belgrade	40	7		
2000-01	Red Star Belgrade	33	0	**125**	**16**
2001-02	Tottenham H	6	0		
2002-03	Tottenham H	35	0	**41**	**0**

BURCH, Rob (G) **0 0**
b.Yeovil 18-10-83
Source: Trainee. *Honours:* England Under-20.

2002-03	Tottenham H	0	0		

CARR, Stephen (D) **194 6**
H: 5 9 W: 12 04 b.Dublin 29-8-76
Source: Trainee. *Honours:* Eire Under-21, 24 full caps.

1993–94	Tottenham H	1	0		
1994–95	Tottenham H	0	0		
1995–96	Tottenham H	0	0		
1996–97	Tottenham H	26	0		
1997–98	Tottenham H	38	0		
1998–99	Tottenham H	37	0		
1999–2000	Tottenham H	34	3		
2000-01	Tottenham H	28	3		
2001-02	Tottenham H	0	0		
2002-03	Tottenham H	30	0	**194**	**6**

DAVIES, Simon (M) **148 17**
H: 5 10 W: 11 07 b.Haverfordwest 23-10-79
Source: Trainee. *Honours:* Wales Youth, Under-21, B, 15 full caps, 3 goals.

1997–98	Peterborough U	6	0		
1998–99	Peterborough U	43	4		
1999–2000	Peterborough U	16	2	**65**	**6**
1999–2000	Tottenham H	3	0		
2000-01	Tottenham H	13	2		
2001-02	Tottenham H	31	4		
2002-03	Tottenham H	36	5	**83**	**11**

DOHERTY, Gary (D) **116 16**
H: 6 2 W: 13 01 b.Carndonagh 31-1-80
Source: Trainee. *Honours:* Eire Under-21, 18 full caps, 4 goals.

1997–98	Luton T	10	0		
1998–99	Luton T	20	6		
1999–2000	Luton T	40	6	**70**	**12**
1999–2000	Tottenham H	2	0		
2000-01	Tottenham H	22	3		
2001-02	Tottenham H	7	0		
2002-03	Tottenham H	15	1	**46**	**4**

ETHERINGTON, Matthew (F) **109 8**
H: 5 9 W: 10 12 b.Truro 14-8-81
Source: School. *Honours:* England Youth, Under-21.

1996–97	Peterborough U	1	0		
1997–98	Peterborough U	2	0		
1998–99	Peterborough U	29	3		
1999–2000	Peterborough U	19	3	**51**	**6**
1999–2000	Tottenham H	5	0		
2000-01	Tottenham H	6	0		
2001-02	*Bradford C*	13	1	**13**	**1**
2001-02	Tottenham H	11	0		
2002-03	Tottenham H	23	1	**45**	**1**

EYRE, Nicky (G) **0 0**
b.Braintree 7-9-85
Source: Trainee.

2002-03	Tottenham H	0	0		

FERGUSON, Steven‡ (F) **11 6**
H: 5 11 W: 11 02 b.Dunfermline 1-4-82

2000-01	East Fife	11	6	**11**	**6**
2000-01	Tottenham H	0	0		
2001-02	Tottenham H	0	0		
2002-03	Tottenham H	0	0		

FOSTER, Danny (D) **0 0**
b.Enfield 23-9-84
Source: Trainee.

2002-03	Tottenham H	0	0		

FREUND, Steffen* (M) **303 9**
H: 5 10 W: 12 08 b.Brandenburg 19-1-70
Source: Motor Sud, Stahl Brandenburg.
Honours: Germany 21 full caps.

1989–90	Brandenburg	9	0		
1990–91	Brandenburg	22	0	**31**	**0**
1991–92	Schalke	33	1		
1992–93	Schalke	20	2	**53**	**3**
1993–94	Borussia Dortmund	19	0		
1994–95	Borussia Dortmund	28	2		
1995–96	Borussia Dortmund	30	2		
1996–97	Borussia Dortmund	2	0		
1997–98	Borussia Dortmund	25	2		
1998–99	Borussia Dortmund	13	0	**117**	**6**
1998–99	Tottenham H	17	0		
1999–2000	Tottenham H	27	0		
2000-01	Tottenham H	21	0		

2001-02 Tottenham H 20 0
2002-03 Tottenham H 17 0 **102 0**

GARDNER, Anthony (D) 76 5
H: 6 3 W: 14 00 b.Stafford 19-9-80
Source: Trainee. *Honours:* England Under-21.
1998–99 Port Vale 15 1
1999–2000 Port Vale 26 3 **41 4**
1999–2000 Tottenham H 0 0
2000-01 Tottenham H 8 0
2001-02 Tottenham H 15 0
2002-03 Tottenham H 12 1 **35 1**

HENRY, Ronnie (D) 3 0
H: 5 11 W: 11 10 b.Hemel Hempstead 2-1-84
Source: Trainee.
2002-03 Tottenham H 0 0
2002-03 *Southend U* 3 0 **3 0**

HIRSCHFELD, Lars (G) 5 0
H: 6 4 W: 13 08 b.Edmonton 17-10-78
Honours: Canada 12 full caps.
2002-03 Tottenham H 0 0
2002-03 *Luton T* 5 0 **5 0**

HUGHES, Mark (M) 0 0
b.Dungannon 16-9-83
Source: Scholar. *Honours:* Northern Ireland Under-21.
2001-02 Tottenham H 0 0
2002-03 Tottenham H 0 0

IVERSEN, Steffen (F) 168 45
H: 6 1 W: 12 07 b.Oslo 10-11-76
Honours: Norway 39 full caps, 7 goals.
1996 Rosenborg 25 10 **25 10**
1996–97 Tottenham H 16 6
1997–98 Tottenham H 13 0
1998–99 Tottenham H 27 8
1999–2000 Tottenham H 36 14
2000-01 Tottenham H 14 2
2001-02 Tottenham H 18 4
2002-03 Tottenham H 19 1 **143 35**

JACKSON, Johnnie (M) 21 1
H: 6 1 W: 12 00 b.Camden 15-8-82
Source: Trainee. *Honours:* England Youth, Under-20.
1999–2000 Tottenham H 0 0
2000-01 Tottenham H 0 0
2001-02 Tottenham H 0 0
2002-03 Tottenham H 0 0
2002-03 *Swindon T* 13 1 **13 1**
2002-03 *Colchester U* 8 0 **8 0**

JALAL, Shwan (G) 0 0
H: 6 2 W: 14 02 b.Baghdad 14-8-83
Source: Hastings T.
2001-02 Tottenham H 0 0
2002-03 Tottenham H 0 0

KEANE, Robbie (F) 185 62
H: 5 9 W: 12 06 b.Dublin 8-7-80
Source: Trainee. *Honours:* Eire 44 full caps, 16 goals.
1997–98 Wolverhampton W 38 11
1998–99 Wolverhampton W 33 11
1999–2000 Wolverhampton W 2 2 **73 24**
1999–2000 Coventry C 31 12 **31 12**
2000-01 Internazionale 6 0 **6 0**
2000-01 Leeds U 18 9
2001-02 Leeds U 25 3
2002-03 Leeds U 3 1 **46 13**
2002-03 Tottenham H 29 13 **29 13**

KELLER, Kasey (G) 373 0
H: 6 1 W: 13 08 b.Washington 27-11-69
Source: Portland Univ. *Honours:* USA 62 full caps.
1991–92 Millwall 1 0
1992–93 Millwall 45 0
1993–94 Millwall 44 0
1994–95 Millwall 44 0
1995–96 Millwall 42 0 **176 0**
1996–97 Leicester C 31 0
1997–98 Leicester C 32 0
1998–99 Leicester C 36 0 **99 0**
1999–2000 Rayo Vallecano 28 0
2000-01 Rayo Vallecano 23 0 **51 0**
2001-02 Tottenham H 9 0
2002-03 Tottenham H 38 0 **47 0**

KELLY, Gavin* (G) 0 0
H: 6 0 W: 13 07 b.Hammersmith 3-6-81
Source: Trainee.
1999–2000 Tottenham H 0 0
2000-01 Tottenham H 0 0
2001-02 Tottenham H 0 0
2002-03 Tottenham H 0 0

KELLY, Stephen (D) 17 0
H: 5 11 W: 12 04 b.Dublin 6-9-83
Honours: Eire Under-21.
2000-01 Tottenham H 0 0
2001-02 Tottenham H 0 0
2002-03 Tottenham H 0 0
2002-03 *Southend U* 10 0 **10 0**
2002-03 *QPR* 7 0 **7 0**

KING, Ledley (D) 79 1
H: 6 2 W: 14 05 b.Bow 12-10-80
Source: Trainee. *Honours:* England Youth, Under-21, 2 full caps.
1998–99 Tottenham H 1 0
1999–2000 Tottenham H 3 0
2000-01 Tottenham H 18 1
2001-02 Tottenham H 32 0
2002-03 Tottenham H 25 0 **79 1**

MALCOLM, Michael (F) 0 0
b.Harrow 13-10-85
Source: Trainee. *Honours:* England Youth.
2002-03 Tottenham H 0 0

MARNEY, Dean (M) 9 0
H: 5 9 W: 11 04 b.Barking 31-1-84
Source: Scholar.
2002-03 Tottenham H 0 0
2002-03 *Swindon T* 9 0 **9 0**

McKIE, Marcel (D) 0 0
b.Edmonton 22-9-84
Source: Scholar. *Honours:* England Youth.
2001-02 Tottenham H 0 0
2002-03 Tottenham H 0 0

O'DONOGHUE, Paul (D) 0 0
b.Lewisham 14-12-83
Source: Scholar.
2001-02 Tottenham H 0 0
2002-03 Tottenham H 0 0

PERRY, Chris (D) 287 5
H: 5 8 W: 10 12 b.Carshalton 26-4-73
Source: Trainee.
1991–92 Wimbledon 0 0
1992–93 Wimbledon 0 0
1993–94 Wimbledon 2 0
1994–95 Wimbledon 22 0
1995–96 Wimbledon 37 0
1996–97 Wimbledon 37 1
1997–98 Wimbledon 35 1
1998–99 Wimbledon 34 0 **167 2**
1999–2000 Tottenham H 37 1
2000-01 Tottenham H 32 1
2001-02 Tottenham H 33 0
2002-03 Tottenham H 18 1 **120 3**

POYET, Gustavo (M) 406 114
H: 6 2 W: 13 00 b.Montevideo 15-11-67
Source: River Plate, Grenoble, Bella Vista. *Honours:* Uruguay 25 full caps, 3 goals.
1990–91 Zaragoza 31 7
1991–92 Zaragoza 33 3
1992–93 Zaragoza 33 6
1993–94 Zaragoza 34 11
1994–95 Zaragoza 34 11
1995–96 Zaragoza 36 11
1996–97 Zaragoza 38 14 **239 63**
1997–98 Chelsea 14 4
1998–99 Chelsea 28 11
1999–2000 Chelsea 33 10
2000-01 Chelsea 30 11 **105 36**
2001-02 Tottenham H 34 10
2002-03 Tottenham H 28 5 **62 15**

REBROV, Sergei (F) 275 115
H: 5 8 W: 11 00 b.Gorlovka 3-6-74
Honours: Ukraine 49 full caps, 13 goals.
1991 Shakhtor Donetsk 7 2
1991–92 Shakhtor Donetsk 19 10 **26 12**
1992–93 Dynamo Kiev 23 5
1993–94 Dynamo Kiev 10 2
1994–95 Dynamo Kiev 25 8
1995–96 Dynamo Kiev 31 9
1996–97 Dynamo Kiev 30 20
1997–98 Dynamo Kiev 29 22
1998–99 Dynamo Kiev 22 9
1999–2000 Dynamo Kiev 20 18 **190 93**
2000-01 Tottenham H 29 9
2001-02 Tottenham H 30 1
2002-03 Tottenham H 0 0 **59 10**

REDKNAPP, Jamie (M) 267 33
H: 6 0 W: 13 03 b.Barton-on-Sea 25-6-73
Source: Tottenham H Schoolboy, Bournemouth Trainee. *Honours:* England Schools, Youth, B, Under-21, 17 full caps, 1 goal.
1989–90 Bournemouth 4 0
1990–91 Bournemouth 9 0 **13 0**
1990–91 Liverpool 0 0
1991–92 Liverpool 6 1
1992–93 Liverpool 29 2
1993–94 Liverpool 35 4
1994–95 Liverpool 41 3
1995–96 Liverpool 23 3
1996–97 Liverpool 23 2
1997–98 Liverpool 20 3
1998–99 Liverpool 34 8
1999–2000 Liverpool 22 3
2000-01 Liverpool 0 0
2001-02 Liverpool 4 1 **237 30**
2001-02 Tottenham H 0 0
2002-03 Tottenham H 17 3 **17 3**

RICHARDS, Dean (D) 325 18
H: 6 2 W: 13 01 b.Bradford 9-6-74
Source: Trainee. *Honours:* England Under-21.
1991–92 Bradford C 7 1
1992–93 Bradford C 3 0
1993–94 Bradford C 46 2
1994–95 Bradford C 30 1 **86 4**
1994–95 *Wolverhampton W* 10 2
1995–96 Wolverhampton W 37 1
1996–97 Wolverhampton W 21 1
1997–98 Wolverhampton W 13 0
1998–99 Wolverhampton W 41 3 **122 7**
1999–2000 Southampton 35 2
2000-01 Southampton 28 1
2001-02 Southampton 4 0 **67 3**
2001-02 Tottenham H 24 2
2002-03 Tottenham H 26 2 **50 4**

RICKETTS, Rohan (M) 0 0
H: 5 8 W: 11 05 b.Clapham 22-12-82
Source: Scholar. *Honours:* England Youth, Under-20.
2001-02 Arsenal 0 0
2002-03 Tottenham H 0 0

SHERINGHAM, Teddy* (F) 607 235
H: 5 11 W: 12 05 b.Highams Park 2-4-66
Source: Apprentice. *Honours:* England Youth, 51 full caps, 11 goals.
1983–84 Millwall 7 1
1984–85 Millwall 0 0
1984–85 *Aldershot* 5 0 **5 0**
1985–86 Millwall 18 4
1986–87 Millwall 42 13
1987–88 Millwall 43 22
1988–89 Millwall 33 11
1989–90 Millwall 31 9
1990–91 Millwall 46 33 **220 93**
1991–92 Nottingham F 39 13
1992–93 Nottingham F 3 1 **42 14**
1992–93 Tottenham H 38 21
1993–94 Tottenham H 19 13
1994–95 Tottenham H 42 18
1995–96 Tottenham H 38 16
1996–97 Tottenham H 29 7
1997–98 Manchester U 31 9
1998–99 Manchester U 17 2
1999–2000 Manchester U 27 5
2000-01 Manchester U 29 15 **104 31**
2001-02 Tottenham H 34 10
2002-03 Tottenham H 36 12 **236 97**

SLABBER, Jamie (F) 1 0
H: 6 2 W: 11 10 b.Enfield 31-12-84
Source: Scholar. *Honours:* England Youth.
2001-02 Tottenham H 0 0
2002-03 Tottenham H 1 0 **1 0**

SNEE, George* (F) 0 0
H: 5 9 W: 11 11 b.Dublin 26-1-83
Source: Scholar.
2000-01 Tottenham H 0 0
2001-02 Tottenham H 0 0
2002-03 Tottenham H 0 0

SULLIVAN, Neil (G) 246 0
H: 6 2 W: 15 03 b.Sutton 24-2-70
Source: Trainee. *Honours:* Scotland 28 full caps.
1988–89 Wimbledon 0 0
1989–90 Wimbledon 0 0
1990–91 Wimbledon 1 0
1991–92 Wimbledon 1 0

1991–92 *Crystal Palace* 1 0 **1 0**
1992–93 Wimbledon 1 0
1993–94 Wimbledon 2 0
1994–95 Wimbledon 11 0
1995–96 Wimbledon 16 0
1996–97 Wimbledon 36 0
1997–98 Wimbledon 38 0
1998–99 Wimbledon 38 0
1999–2000 Wimbledon 37 0 **181 0**
2000-01 Tottenham H 35 0
2001-02 Tottenham H 29 0
2002-03 Tottenham H 0 0 **64 0**

TARICCO, Mauricio (D) 256 5
H: 5 8 W: 11 07 b.Buenos Aires 10-3-73
Honours: Argentina Under-23.
1993–94 Argentinos Juniors 21 0 **21 0**
1994–95 Ipswich T 0 0
1995–96 Ipswich T 39 0
1996–97 Ipswich T 41 3
1997–98 Ipswich T 41 0
1998–99 Ipswich T 16 1 **137 4**
1998–99 Tottenham H 13 0
1999–2000 Tottenham H 29 0
2000-01 Tottenham H 5 0
2001-02 Tottenham H 30 0
2002-03 Tottenham H 21 1 **98 1**

THATCHER, Ben (D) 212 1
H: 5 10 W: 12 06 b.Swindon 30-11-75
Source: Trainee. *Honours:* England Youth, Under-21.
1992–93 Millwall 0 0
1993–94 Millwall 8 0
1994–95 Millwall 40 1
1995–96 Millwall 42 0 **90 1**
1996–97 Wimbledon 9 0
1997–98 Wimbledon 26 0
1998–99 Wimbledon 31 0
1999–2000 Wimbledon 20 0 **86 0**
2000-01 Tottenham H 12 0
2001-02 Tottenham H 12 0
2002-03 Tottenham H 12 0 **36 0**

THELWELL, Alton* (D) 18 0
H: 5 10 W: 12 02 b.Holloway 5-9-80
Source: Trainee.
1998–99 Tottenham H 0 0
1999–2000 Tottenham H 0 0
2000-01 Tottenham H 16 0
2001-02 Tottenham H 2 0
2002-03 Tottenham H 0 0 **18 0**

THOMAS, Walter‡ (M) 0 0
b.Sierra Leone 19-11-83
Source: Scholar.
2001-02 Tottenham H 0 0
2002-03 Tottenham H 0 0

TODA, Kazuyuki (M) 167 7
H: 5 10 W: 10 11 b.Japan 30-12-77
Honours: Japan 15 full caps, 1 goal.
1994 Shimizu S-Pulse 0 0
1995 Shimizu S-Pulse 0 0
1996 Shimizu S-Pulse 5 0
1997 Shimizu S-Pulse 20 5
1998 Shimizu S-Pulse 34 0
1999 Shimizu S-Pulse 28 0
2000 Shimizu S-Pulse 27 1
2001 Shimizu S-Pulse 27 0
2002 Shimizu S-Pulse 22 1 **163 7**
2002-03 Tottenham H 4 0 **4 0**

YEATES, Mark (F) 0 0
b.Dublin 11-1-85
Source: Trainee.
2002-03 Tottenham H 0 0

ZIEGE, Christian (D) 295 59
H: 6 1 W: 12 13 b.Berlin 1-2-72
Honours: Germany 71 full caps, 9 goals.
1990–91 Bayern Munich 13 1
1991–92 Bayern Munich 26 2
1992–93 Bayern Munich 28 9
1993–94 Bayern Munich 29 3
1994–95 Bayern Munich 29 10
1995–96 Bayern Munich 20 9
1996–97 Bayern Munich 27 7 **172 41**
1997–98 AC Milan 22 2
1998–99 AC Milan 17 2 **39 4**
1999–2000 Middlesbrough 29 6
2000-01 Middlesbrough 0 0 **29 6**
2000-01 Liverpool 16 1 **16 1**
2001-02 Tottenham H 27 5
2002-03 Tottenham H 12 2 **39 7**

Trainees
Barnett, Lee J; Dobson, Ricky M; Francis, Liam D; Galbraith, David J; Hicks, David C; Hodges, Andrew R; Jenkins, Gareth M; McKenna, Kieran; Price, Owen; Watson, Joe D; Wettner, Nicholas T

TRANMERE R

ACHTERBERG, John# (G) 179 0
H: 6 1 W: 13 00 b.Utrecht 8-7-71
Source: VV RUC, Utrecht.
1993–94 NAC 1 0
1994–95 NAC 2 0
1995–96 NAC 6 0 **9 0**
1996–97 Eindhoven 32 0 **32 0**
From Utrecht.
1998–99 Tranmere R 24 0
1999–2000 Tranmere R 26 0
2000-01 Tranmere R 25 0
2001-02 Tranmere R 25 0
2002-03 Tranmere R 38 0 **138 0**

ALLEN, Graham# (D) 165 9
H: 6 1 W: 12 00 b.Bolton 8-4-77
Source: Trainee. *Honours:* England Youth.
1994–95 Everton 0 0
1995–96 Everton 0 0
1996–97 Everton 1 0
1997–98 Everton 5 0
1998–99 Everton 0 0 **6 0**
1998–99 Tranmere R 41 5
1999–2000 Tranmere R 24 0
2000-01 Tranmere R 22 0
2001-02 Tranmere R 31 1
2002-03 Tranmere R 41 3 **159 9**

ASHTON, Neil (M) 0 0
b.Liverpool 15-1-85
Source: Scholar.
2002-03 Tranmere R 0 0

BARLOW, Stuart‡ (F) 341 100
H: 5 10 W: 11 02 b.Liverpool 16-7-68
Source: School.
1990–91 Everton 2 0
1991–92 Everton 7 0
1991–92 *Rotherham U* 0 0
1992–93 Everton 26 5
1993–94 Everton 22 3
1994–95 Everton 11 2
1995–96 Everton 3 0 **71 10**
1995–96 Oldham Ath 26 7
1996–97 Oldham Ath 35 12
1997–98 Oldham Ath 32 12 **93 31**
1997–98 Wigan Ath 9 3
1998–99 Wigan Ath 41 19
1999–2000 Wigan Ath 33 18 **83 40**
2000-01 Tranmere R 27 2
2001-02 Tranmere R 38 14
2002-03 Tranmere R 29 3 **94 19**

CONNELLY, Sean (D) 349 6
H: 5 10 W: 11 01 b.Sheffield 26-6-70
Source: Hallam.
1991–92 Stockport Co 0 0
1992–93 Stockport Co 7 0
1993–94 Stockport Co 32 0
1994–95 Stockport Co 39 0
1995–96 Stockport Co 43 0
1996–97 Stockport Co 45 0
1997–98 Stockport Co 45 2
1998–99 Stockport Co 35 1
1999–2000 Stockport Co 43 3
2000-01 Stockport Co 13 0 **302 6**
2000-01 *Wolverhampton W* 6 0
2001-02 Wolverhampton W 8 0
2002-03 Wolverhampton W 0 0 **14 0**
2002-03 Tranmere R 33 0 **33 0**

FEUER, Ian‡ (G) 169 0
H: 6 7 W: 14 00 b.Las Vegas 20-5-71
Source: Los Angeles Salsa. *Honours:* USA full caps.
1993–94 West Ham U 0 0
1994–95 West Ham U 0 0
1994–95 *Peterborough U* 16 0 **16 0**
1995–96 West Ham U 0 0
1995–96 Luton T 38 0
1996–97 Luton T 46 0
1997–98 Luton T 13 0 **97 0**
1998 New England Rev 26 0 **26 0**
1999 Colorado Rapids 19 0 **19 0**
1999–2000 Cardiff C 0 0
1999–2000 West Ham U 3 0 **3 0**
2000-01 Wimbledon 0 0
2001-02 Wimbledon 4 0 **4 0**
2001-02 *Derby Co* 2 0 **2 0**
2002-03 Tranmere R 2 0 **2 0**

GRAY, Kevin (D) 382 10
H: 6 0 W: 13 00 b.Sheffield 7-1-72
Source: Trainee.
1988–89 Mansfield T 1 0
1989–90 Mansfield T 16 0
1990–91 Mansfield T 31 1
1991–92 Mansfield T 18 0
1992–93 Mansfield T 33 0
1993–94 Mansfield T 42 2 **141 3**
1994–95 Huddersfield T 5 0
1995–96 Huddersfield T 38 0
1996–97 Huddersfield T 39 1
1997–98 Huddersfield T 35 1
1998–99 Huddersfield T 34 1
1999–2000 Huddersfield T 18 2
2000-01 *Stockport Co* 1 0 **1 0**
2000-01 Huddersfield T 17 0
2001-02 Huddersfield T 44 1 **230 6**
2002-03 Tranmere R 10 1 **10 1**

HARRISON, Danny (M) 13 0
H: 5 11 W: 12 04 b.Liverpool 4-11-82
Source: Scholar.
2001-02 Tranmere R 1 0
2002-03 Tranmere R 12 0 **13 0**

HAWORTH, Simon (F) 219 78
H: 6 3 W: 13 08 b.Cardiff 30-3-77
Source: Trainee. *Honours:* Wales Youth, Under-21, B, 5 full caps.
1995–96 Cardiff C 13 0
1996–97 Cardiff C 24 9 **37 9**
1997–98 Coventry C 10 0
1998–99 Coventry C 1 0 **11 0**
1998–99 Wigan Ath 20 10
1999–2000 Wigan Ath 40 13
2000-01 Wigan Ath 30 11
2001-02 Wigan Ath 27 10 **117 44**
2001-02 Tranmere R 12 5
2002-03 Tranmere R 42 20 **54 25**

HAY, Alex (F) 22 3
H: 5 10 W: 11 05 b.Birkenhead 14-10-81
Source: Scholarship.
1999–2000 Tranmere R 0 0
2000-01 Tranmere R 0 0
2001-02 Tranmere R 3 0
2002-03 Tranmere R 19 3 **22 3**

HINDS, Richard* (D) 55 0
H: 6 2 W: 12 02 b.Sheffield 22-8-80
Source: Schoolboy.
1998–99 Tranmere R 2 0
1999–2000 Tranmere R 6 0
2000-01 Tranmere R 29 0
2001-02 Tranmere R 10 0
2002-03 Tranmere R 8 0 **55 0**

HOWARTH, Russell (G) 11 0
H: 6 2 W: 14 07 b.York 27-3-82
Source: Scholar. *Honours:* England Youth, Under-20.
1999–2000 York C 6 0
2000-01 York C 0 0
2001-02 York C 2 0
2002-03 York C 0 0 **8 0**
2002-03 Tranmere R 3 0 **3 0**

HUME, Iain (F) 62 6
H: 5 7 W: 11 02 b.Edinburgh 31-10-83
Honours: Canada 1 full cap.
1999–2000 Tranmere R 3 0
2000-01 Tranmere R 10 0
2001-02 Tranmere R 14 0
2002-03 Tranmere R 35 6 **62 6**

JENNINGS, Steven (M) 0 0
b.Liverpool 28-10-84
Source: Scholar.
2002-03 Tranmere R 0 0

JONES, Gary (M) 254 36
H: 6 3 W: 14 00 b.Chester 10-5-75
Source: Trainee.
1993–94 Tranmere R 6 2
1994–95 Tranmere R 19 3
1995–96 Tranmere R 23 1
1996–97 Tranmere R 30 6
1997–98 Tranmere R 43 8
1998–99 Tranmere R 26 5
1999–2000 Tranmere R 31 3
2000-01 Nottingham F 31 1
2001-02 Nottingham F 5 1
2002-03 Nottingham F 0 0 **36 2**
2002-03 Tranmere R 40 6 **218 34**

LINWOOD, Paul (D) **0 0**
b.Birkenhead 24-10-83
Source: Scholar.
2001-02 Tranmere R 0 0
2002-03 Tranmere R 0 0

LORAN, Tyrone (D) **17 0**
H: 6 2 W: 13 11 b.Amsterdam 29-6-81
2002-03 Manchester C 0 0
2002-03 Tranmere R 17 0 **17 0**

McGIBBON, Pat‡ (D) **184 11**
H: 6 2 W: 12 11 b.Lurgan 6-9-73
Source: Portadown. *Honours:* Northern Ireland Schools, Under-21, B, 7 full caps.
1992–93 Manchester U 0 0
1993–94 Manchester U 0 0
1994–95 Manchester U 0 0
1995–96 Manchester U 0 0
1996–97 Manchester U 0 0
1996–97 *Swansea C* 1 0 **1 0**
1996–97 *Wigan Ath* 10 1
1997–98 Wigan Ath 35 0
1998–99 Wigan Ath 36 5
1999–2000 Wigan Ath 34 2
2000-01 Wigan Ath 40 2
2001-02 Wigan Ath 18 1 **173 11**
2001-02 *Scunthorpe U* 6 0 **6 0**
2002-03 Tranmere R 4 0 **4 0**

McGUIRE, Jamie (M) **0 0**
H: 5 7 W: 10 00 b.Birkenhead 13-11-83
Source: Scholar.
2001-02 Tranmere R 0 0
2002-03 Tranmere R 0 0

MELLON, Micky (M) **419 32**
H: 5 9 W: 11 03 b.Paisley 18-3-72
Source: Trainee.
1989–90 Bristol C 9 0
1990–91 Bristol C 0 0
1991–92 Bristol C 16 0
1992–93 Bristol C 10 1 **35 1**
1992–93 WBA 17 3
1993–94 WBA 21 2
1994–95 WBA 7 1 **45 6**
1994–95 Blackpool 26 4
1995–96 Blackpool 45 6
1996–97 Blackpool 43 4
1997–98 Blackpool 10 0 **124 14**
1997–98 Tranmere R 33 2
1998–99 Tranmere R 24 1
1998–99 Burnley 20 2
1999–2000 Burnley 42 3
2000-01 Burnley 22 0 **84 5**
2000-01 Tranmere R 13 1
2001-02 Tranmere R 27 1
2002-03 Tranmere R 34 1 **131 6**

NAVARRO, Alan (D) **41 2**
H: 5 10 W: 11 07 b.Liverpool 31-5-81
Source: Trainee.
1998–99 Liverpool 0 0
1999–2000 Liverpool 0 0
2000-01 Liverpool 0 0
2000-01 *Crewe Alex* 8 1
2001-02 Liverpool 0 0
2001-02 *Crewe Alex* 7 0 **15 1**
2001-02 Tranmere R 21 1
2002-03 Tranmere R 5 0 **26 1**

NICHOLSON, Shane (D) **423 17**
H: 5 10 W: 12 02 b.Newark 3-6-70
Source: Trainee.
1986–87 Lincoln C 7 0
1987–88 Lincoln C 0 0
1988–89 Lincoln C 34 1
1989–90 Lincoln C 23 0
1990–91 Lincoln C 40 4
1991–92 Lincoln C 29 1 **133 6**
1991–92 Derby Co 0 0
1992–93 Derby Co 17 0
1993–94 Derby Co 22 1
1994–95 Derby Co 15 0
1995–96 Derby Co 20 0 **74 1**
1995–96 WBA 18 0
1996–97 WBA 18 0
1997–98 WBA 16 0 **52 0**
1998–99 Chesterfield 24 0 **24 0**
1999–2000 Stockport Co 42 1
2000-01 Stockport Co 35 2 **77 3**
2001-02 Sheffield U 25 3 **25 3**
2002-03 Tranmere R 38 4 **38 4**

NIXON, Eric‡ (G) **523 0**
H: 6 4 W: 15 07 b.Manchester 4-10-62
Source: Curzon Ashton.
1983–84 Manchester C 0 0
1984–85 Manchester C 0 0
1985–86 Manchester C 28 0
1986–87 Manchester C 5 0
1986–87 *Wolverhampton W* 16 0 **16 0**
1986–87 *Bradford C* 3 0
1986–87 *Southampton* 4 0 **4 0**
1986–87 *Carlisle U* 16 0 **16 0**
1987–88 Manchester C 25 0 **58 0**
1987–88 *Tranmere R* 8 0
1988–89 Tranmere R 45 0
1989–90 Tranmere R 46 0
1990–91 Tranmere R 43 0
1991–92 Tranmere R 46 0
1992–93 Tranmere R 45 0
1993–94 Tranmere R 42 0
1994–95 Tranmere R 41 0
1995–96 Tranmere R 0 0
1995–96 *Blackpool* 20 0 **20 0**
1996–97 Tranmere R 25 0
1996–97 *Bradford C* 12 0 **15 0**
1997–98 Stockport Co 43 0
1998–99 Stockport Co 0 0 **43 0**
1998–99 Wigan Ath 3 0 **3 0**
1999–2000 Tranmere R 2 0
2000-01 Tranmere R 0 0
2001-02 Kidderminster H 2 0 **2 0**
2001-02 Tranmere R 1 0
2002-03 Tranmere R 2 0 **346 0**

OLSEN, James (D) **4 0**
H: 6 2 W: 11 00 b.Bootle 23-10-81
Source: Liverpool scholar.
2000-01 Tranmere R 1 0
2001-02 Tranmere R 0 0
2002-03 Tranmere R 3 0 **4 0**

PARKINSON, Andy‡ (F) **164 18**
H: 5 8 W: 10 02 b.Liverpool 27-5-79
Source: Liverpool Trainee.
1996–97 Tranmere R 0 0
1997–98 Tranmere R 18 1
1998–99 Tranmere R 29 2
1999–2000 Tranmere R 37 7
2000-01 Tranmere R 39 6
2001-02 Tranmere R 31 2
2002-03 Tranmere R 10 0 **164 18**

PRICE, Jason# (M) **208 29**
H: 6 2 W: 11 05 b.Pontypridd 12-4-77
Source: Aberaman Ath. *Honours:* Wales Under-21.
1995–96 Swansea C 0 0
1996–97 Swansea C 2 0
1997–98 Swansea C 34 3
1998–99 Swansea C 28 4
1999–2000 Swansea C 39 6
2000-01 Swansea C 41 4 **144 17**
2001-02 Brentford 15 1 **15 1**
2001-02 Tranmere R 24 7
2002-03 Tranmere R 25 4 **49 11**

ROBERTS, Gareth (D) **153 7**
H: 5 8 W: 11 00 b.Wrexham 6-2-78
Source: Trainee. *Honours:* Wales Under-21, B, 4 full caps.
1995–96 Liverpool 0 0
1996–97 Liverpool 0 0
1997–98 Liverpool 0 0
1998–99 Liverpool 0 0
1999–2000 Tranmere R 37 1
2000-01 Tranmere R 34 0
2001-02 Tranmere R 45 2
2002-03 Tranmere R 37 4 **153 7**

ROBINSON, Andy (F) **0 0**
b.Birkenhead 3-11-79
Source: Cammell Laird.
2002-03 Tranmere R 0 0

ROBINSON, Paul (F) **0 0**
H: 6 0 W: 12 00 b.Newcastle 28-5-84
Source: Scholar.
2002-03 Tranmere R 0 0

SHARPS, Ian (D) **60 3**
H: 6 3 W: 13 05 b.Warrington 23-10-80
Source: Trainee.
1998–99 Tranmere R 1 0
1999–2000 Tranmere R 0 0
2000-01 Tranmere R 0 0
2001-02 Tranmere R 29 0
2002-03 Tranmere R 30 3 **60 3**

TAYLOR, Ryan (D) **25 1**
H: 5 8 W: 10 00 b.Liverpool 19-8-84
Source: Scholar. *Honours:* England Youth.
2001-02 Tranmere R 0 0
2002-03 Tranmere R 25 1 **25 1**

Scholars
Brown, Paul; Carroll, Thomas; Dagnall, Christopher; Dunbar, Karl A; Fowler, Joseph A; Griffiths, Alan T; Hooper, Gareth P; Martin, Paul A; Pinch, Gary; Rooney, Thomas; Scott, Gerard; Tremarco, Carl

WALSALL

ARANALDE, Zigor (D) **129 5**
H: 6 1 W: 13 03 b.Ibarra 28-2-73
Source: Logrones.
2000-01 Walsall 45 0
2001-02 Walsall 45 2
2002-03 Walsall 39 3 **129 5**

BARRAS, Tony# (D) **402 27**
H: 6 0 W: 13 00 b.Billingham 29-3-71
Source: Trainee.
1988–89 Hartlepool U 3 0
1989–90 Hartlepool U 9 0 **12 0**
1990–91 Stockport Co 40 0
1991–92 Stockport Co 42 5
1992–93 Stockport Co 14 0
1993–94 Stockport Co 3 0 **99 5**
1993–94 *Rotherham U* 5 1 **5 1**
1994–95 York C 31 1
1995–96 York C 32 3
1996–97 York C 46 1
1997–98 York C 38 6
1998–99 York C 24 0 **171 11**
1998–99 Reading 6 1 **6 1**
1999–2000 Walsall 24 4
2000-01 Walsall 36 1
2001-02 Walsall 26 4
2002-03 Walsall 19 0 **105 9**
2002-03 *Plymouth Arg* 4 0 **4 0**

BAZELEY, Darren (D) **353 25**
H: 5 11 W: 11 09 b.Northampton 5-10-72
Source: Trainee. *Honours:* England Under-21.
1989–90 Watford 1 0
1990–91 Watford 7 0
1991–92 Watford 34 6
1992–93 Watford 22 1
1993–94 Watford 10 1
1994–95 Watford 28 4
1995–96 Watford 41 1
1996–97 Watford 41 3
1997–98 Watford 16 3
1998–99 Watford 40 2 **240 21**
1999–2000 Wolverhampton W 46 3
2000-01 Wolverhampton W 24 1
2001-02 Wolverhampton W 0 0 **70 4**
2002-03 Walsall 43 0 **43 0**

BIRCH, Gary (F) **44 3**
H: 6 0 W: 12 03 b.Birmingham 8-10-81
Source: Trainee.
1998–99 Walsall 0 0
1999–2000 Walsall 0 0
2000-01 Walsall 0 0
2000-01 *Exeter C* 9 2
2001-02 *Exeter C* 15 0 **24 2**
2001-02 Walsall 1 0
2002-03 Walsall 19 1 **20 1**

BISHOP, Andy (F) **29 5**
H: 6 0 W: 10 10 b.Stone 19-10-82
Source: Scholar.
2002-03 Walsall 0 0
2002-03 *Kidderminster H* 29 5 **29 5**

CARBON, Matt# (D) **249 17**
H: 6 2 W: 12 05 b.Nottingham 8-6-75
Source: Trainee. *Honours:* England Under-21.
1992–93 Lincoln C 1 0
1993–94 Lincoln C 9 0
1994–95 Lincoln C 33 7
1995–96 Lincoln C 26 3 **69 10**
1995–96 Derby Co 6 0
1996–97 Derby Co 10 0
1997–98 Derby Co 4 0 **20 0**
1997–98 WBA 16 1
1998–99 WBA 39 2
1999–2000 WBA 34 2
2000-01 WBA 24 0 **113 5**
2001-02 Walsall 22 1
2002-03 Walsall 25 1 **47 2**

CORICA, Steve# (F) 316 42
H: 5 8 W: 10 10 b.Cairns 24-3-73
Honours: Australia Youth, Under-20, Under-23, 31 full caps, 5 goals.

1990–91	Marconi Stallions	17	0		
1991–92	Marconi Stallions	17	2		
1992–93	Marconi Stallions	27	4		
1993–94	Marconi Stallions	24	5		
1994–95	Marconi Stallions	18	3	**103**	**14**
1995–96	Leicester C	16	2	**16**	**2**
1995–96	Wolverhampton W	17	0		
1996–97	Wolverhampton W	36	2		
1997–98	Wolverhampton W	1	0		
1998–99	Wolverhampton W	31	2		
1999–2000	Wolverhampton W	15	1	**100**	**5**
2000	Sanfrecce	21	3		
2001	Sanfrecce	22	11	**43**	**14**
2001-02	Walsall	13	3		
2002-03	Walsall	41	4	**54**	**7**

EMBLEN, Neil‡ (M) 246 16
H: 6 1 W: 13 08 b.Bromley 19-6-71
Source: Tonbridge, Sittingbourne.

1993–94	Millwall	12	0	**12**	**0**
1994–95	Wolverhampton W	27	7		
1995–96	Wolverhampton W	33	2		
1996–97	Wolverhampton W	28	0		
1997–98	Wolverhampton W	7	0		
1997–98	Crystal Palace	13	0	**13**	**0**
1998–99	Wolverhampton W	33	2		
1999–2000	Wolverhampton W	46	5		
2000-01	Wolverhampton W	28	0	**202**	**16**
2001-02	Norwich C	2	0		
2002-03	Norwich C	12	0	**14**	**0**
2002-03	Walsall	5	0	**5**	**0**

FRYATT, Matthew (M) 0 0
b.Nuneaton 5-3-86
Source: Scholar.

2002-03	Walsall	0	0		

HAWLEY, Karl (F) 1 0
H: 5 8 W: 12 02 b.Walsall 6-12-81
Source: Scholar.

2000-01	Walsall	0	0		
2001-02	Walsall	1	0		
2002-03	Walsall	0	0	**1**	**0**

HAY, Danny# (D) 81 2
H: 6 3 W: 14 11 b.Auckland 15-5-75
Source: Waitakere, Central Utd. *Honours:* New Zealand 11 full caps.

1997–98	Perth Glory	24	1		
1998–99	Perth Glory	24	1	**48**	**2**
1999–2000	Leeds U	0	0		
2000-01	Leeds U	4	0		
2001-02	Leeds U	0	0	**4**	**0**
2002-03	Walsall	29	0	**29**	**0**

HERIVELTO, Harry‡ (M) 28 5
H: 5 10 W: 11 06 b.Brazil 23-8-75
Source: Flamengo, Maritimo, Cruzeiro.

2001-02	Walsall	24	4		
2002-03	Walsall	4	1	**28**	**5**

JUNIOR# (F) 36 15
H: 6 0 W: 13 00 b.Brazil 20-7-76
Source: Trezze.

2002-03	Walsall	36	15	**36**	**15**

LAWRENCE, Jamie (M) 236 16
H: 5 9 W: 12 10 b.Balham 8-3-70
Source: Cowes. *Honours:* Jamaica 12 full caps.

1993–94	Sunderland	4	0	**4**	**0**
1993–94	Doncaster R	9	1		
1994–95	Doncaster R	16	2	**25**	**3**
1994–95	Leicester C	17	1		
1995–96	Leicester C	15	0		
1996–97	Leicester C	15	0	**47**	**1**
1997–98	Bradford C	43	3		
1998–99	Bradford C	35	2		
1999–2000	Bradford C	23	3		
2000-01	Bradford C	17	1		
2001-02	Bradford C	21	2		
2002-03	Bradford C	16	1	**155**	**12**
2002-03	Walsall	5	0	**5**	**0**

LEITAO, Jorge (F) 126 37
H: 5 11 W: 13 06 b.Oporto 14-1-74
Source: Feirense.

2000-01	Walsall	44	18		
2001-02	Walsall	38	8		
2002-03	Walsall	44	11	**126**	**37**

MATIAS, Pedro (M) 164 25
H: 6 0 W: 12 00 b.Madrid 11-10-73

1998–99	Logrones	12	0	**12**	**0**
1998–99	Macclesfield T	22	2	**22**	**2**
1999–2000	Tranmere R	4	0	**4**	**0**
1999–2000	Walsall	33	6		
2000-01	Walsall	40	9		
2001-02	Walsall	30	5		
2002-03	Walsall	23	3	**126**	**23**

O'CONNOR, Martin# (M) 359 43
H: 5 8 W: 11 08 b.Walsall 10-12-67
Source: Bromsgrove R. *Honours:* Cayman Islands 2 full caps.

1992–93	Crystal Palace	0	0		
1992–93	*Walsall*	10	1		
1993–94	Crystal Palace	2	0	**2**	**0**
1993–94	Walsall	14	2		
1994–95	Walsall	39	10		
1995–96	Walsall	41	9		
1996–97	Peterborough U	18	3	**18**	**3**
1996–97	Birmingham C	24	4		
1997–98	Birmingham C	33	1		
1998–99	Birmingham C	37	4		
1999–2000	Birmingham C	39	2		
2000-01	Birmingham C	30	5		
2001-02	Birmingham C	24	0	**187**	**16**
2001-02	Walsall	13	1		
2002-03	Walsall	35	1	**152**	**24**

RODRIGUES, Dani‡ (F) 16 0
H: 5 11 W: 11 05 b.Madeira 3-3-80
Source: Farense.

1998–99	Bournemouth	5	0	**5**	**0**
1998–99	Southampton	0	0		
1999–2000	Southampton	2	0		
2000-01	Southampton	0	0		
2000-01	*Bristol C*	4	0		
2001-02	Southampton	0	0	**2**	**0**
2001-02	*Bristol C*	4	0	**8**	**0**
2002-03	Walsall	1	0	**1**	**0**

ROPER, Ian (D) 195 2
H: 6 2 W: 14 00 b.Nuneaton 20-6-77
Source: Trainee.

1994–95	Walsall	0	0		
1995–96	Walsall	5	0		
1996–97	Walsall	11	0		
1997–98	Walsall	21	0		
1998–99	Walsall	32	1		
1999–2000	Walsall	34	1		
2000-01	Walsall	25	0		
2001-02	Walsall	27	0		
2002-03	Walsall	40	0	**195**	**2**

SAMWAYS, Vinny# (M) 433 19
H: 5 8 W: 11 02 b.Bethnal Green 27-10-68
Source: Apprentice. *Honours:* England Youth, Under-21.

1985–86	Tottenham H	0	0		
1986–87	Tottenham H	2	0		
1987–88	Tottenham H	26	0		
1988–89	Tottenham H	19	3		
1989–90	Tottenham H	23	3		
1990–91	Tottenham H	23	1		
1991–92	Tottenham H	27	1		
1992–93	Tottenham H	34	0		
1993–94	Tottenham H	39	3	**193**	**11**
1994–95	Everton	19	1		
1995–96	Everton	4	1		
1995–96	*Wolverhampton W*	3	0	**3**	**0**
1995–96	*Birmingham C*	12	0	**12**	**0**
1996–97	Las Palmas	20	0		
1997–98	Las Palmas	32	2		
1998–99	Las Palmas	35	1		
1999–2000	Las Palmas	38	2		
2000-01	Las Palmas	31	0		
2001-02	Las Palmas	33	1	**189**	**6**
2002-03	Sevilla	0	0		
1997–98	Everton	0	0		
1998–99	Everton	0	0	**23**	**2**
2002-03	Walsall	13	0	**13**	**0**

SIMPSON, Fitzroy# (M) 408 27
H: 5 8 W: 12 00 b.Trowbridge 26-2-70
Source: Trainee. *Honours:* Jamaica 39 full caps, 3 goals.

1988–89	Swindon T	7	0		
1989–90	Swindon T	30	2		
1990–91	Swindon T	38	3		
1991–92	Swindon T	30	4	**105**	**9**
1991–92	Manchester C	11	1		
1992–93	Manchester C	29	1		
1993–94	Manchester C	15	0		
1994–95	Manchester C	16	2		
1994–95	*Bristol C*	4	0	**4**	**0**
1995–96	Manchester C	0	0	**71**	**4**
1995–96	Portsmouth	30	5		
1996–97	Portsmouth	41	4		
1997–98	Portsmouth	19	0		
1998–99	Portsmouth	41	1		
1999–2000	Portsmouth	17	0	**148**	**10**
1999–2000	Hearts	11	0		
2000-01	Hearts	6	0	**17**	**0**
2000-01	*Walsall*	10	1		
2001-02	Walsall	28	2		
2002-03	Walsall	25	1	**63**	**4**

SMITH, Nick (M) 0 0
H: 5 10 W: 10 08 b.Bloxwich 5-10-82
Source: Scholar.

2002-03	Walsall	0	0		

SONNER, Danny* (M) 185 15
H: 5 11 W: 12 08 b.Wigan 9-1-72
Source: Wigan Ath. *Honours:* Northern Ireland B, 7 full caps.

1990–91	Burnley	2	0		
1991–92	Burnley	3	0		
1992–93	Burnley	1	0	**6**	**0**
1992–93	*Bury*	5	3	**5**	**3**
From Erzgebirge Aue					
1996–97	Ipswich T	29	2		
1997–98	Ipswich T	23	1		
1998–99	Ipswich T	4	0	**56**	**3**
1998–99	Sheffield W	26	3		
1999–2000	Sheffield W	27	0	**53**	**3**
2000-01	Birmingham C	26	1		
2001-02	Birmingham C	15	1	**41**	**2**
2002-03	Walsall	24	4	**24**	**4**

STANLEY, Craig (M) 0 0
H: 5 8 W: 10 08 b.Bedworth 3-3-83
Source: Scholar.

2002-03	Walsall	0	0		

TAYLOR, Kris (M) 0 0
H: 5 9 W: 13 05 b.Stafford 12-1-84
Source: Scholar. *Honours:* England Youth.

2000-01	Manchester U	0	0		
2001-02	Manchester U	0	0		
2002-03	Manchester U	0	0		
2002-03	Walsall	0	0		

WALKER, James (G) 360 0
H: 5 11 W: 13 04 b.Sutton-in-Ashfield 9-7-73
Source: Trainee.

1991–92	Notts Co	0	0		
1992–93	Notts Co	0	0		
1993–94	Walsall	31	0		
1994–95	Walsall	4	0		
1995–96	Walsall	26	0		
1996–97	Walsall	36	0		
1997–98	Walsall	46	0		
1998–99	Walsall	46	0		
1999–2000	Walsall	43	0		
2000-01	Walsall	44	0		
2001-02	Walsall	43	0		
2002-03	Walsall	41	0	**360**	**0**

WARD, Gavin* (G) 258 0
H: 6 3 W: 12 12 b.Sutton Coldfield 30-6-70
Source: Aston Villa Trainee.

1988–89	Shrewsbury T	0	0		
1989–90	WBA	0	0		
1989–90	Cardiff C	2	0		
1990–91	Cardiff C	1	0		
1991–92	Cardiff C	24	0		
1992–93	Cardiff C	32	0	**59**	**0**
1993–94	Leicester C	32	0		
1994–95	Leicester C	6	0	**38**	**0**
1995–96	Bradford C	36	0	**36**	**0**
1995–96	Bolton W	5	0		
1996–97	Bolton W	11	0		
1997–98	Bolton W	6	0		
1998–99	Bolton W	0	0	**22**	**0**
1998–99	*Burnley*	17	0	**17**	**0**
1998–99	Stoke C	6	0		
1999–2000	Stoke C	46	0		
2000-01	Stoke C	17	0		
2001-02	Stoke C	10	0	**79**	**0**
2002-03	Walsall	7	0	**7**	**0**

WRACK, Darren# (M) 247 33
H: 5 9 W: 12 03 b.Cleethorpes 5-5-76
Source: Trainee.

1994–95	Derby Co	16	1		
1995–96	Derby Co	10	0	**26**	**1**
1996–97	Grimsby T	12	1		
1996–97	*Shrewsbury T*	4	0	**4**	**0**
1997–98	Grimsby T	1	0	**13**	**1**
1998–99	Walsall	46	13		
1999–2000	Walsall	44	4		
2000-01	Walsall	28	4		
2001-02	Walsall	43	4		
2002-03	Walsall	43	6	**204**	**31**

WRIGHT, Mark (M) 9 0
H: 5 11 W: 11 00 b.Wolverhampton 24-2-82
Source: Scholar.

2000-01	Walsall	4	0		
2001-02	Walsall	0	0		
2002-03	Walsall	5	0	**9**	**0**

ZDRILIC, David* (F) 241 53
H: 6 0 W: 12 07 b.Sydney 13-4-74
Honours: Australia 22 full caps, 18 goals.

1993–94	Sydney United	26	1		
1994–95	Sydney United	23	7		
1995–96	Sydney United	35	10		
1996–97	Sydney United	30	21	**114**	**39**
1997–98	Aarau	25	2	**25**	**2**
1998–99	Ulm	33	2		
1999–2000	Ulm	22	6	**55**	**8**
2000-01	Unterhaching	16	1		
2001-02	Unterhaching	7	0	**23**	**1**
2002-03	Walsall	24	3	**24**	**3**

Scholars
Atieno, Taiwo L; Bennett, Julian; Branch, Mark L; Caines, Gavin L; Churchill, Lewis A; Harkness, Jonathan; Harris, Andrew; Joseph, Andre P; Lloyd, Arron SD; Paschalis, Eliot D; Perry, Kyle B; Platt, Sean D; Taylor, Daryl S; Wheeler, Bruce J; Willetts, Ryan J; Worley, Andrew I
Non-Contract
Coleman, Dean S

WATFORD

ARDLEY, Neal (M) 288 20
H: 5 11 W: 11 09 b.Epsom 1-9-72
Source: Trainee. *Honours:* England Under-21.

1990–91	Wimbledon	1	0		
1991–92	Wimbledon	8	0		
1992–93	Wimbledon	26	4		
1993–94	Wimbledon	16	1		
1994–95	Wimbledon	14	1		
1995–96	Wimbledon	6	0		
1996–97	Wimbledon	34	2		
1997–98	Wimbledon	34	2		
1998–99	Wimbledon	23	0		
1999–2000	Wimbledon	17	2		
2000-01	Wimbledon	37	3		
2001-02	Wimbledon	29	3	**245**	**18**
2002-03	Watford	43	2	**43**	**2**

BLIZZARD, Dominic (M) 0 0
H: 6 2 W: 11 11 b.High Wycombe 2-9-83
Source: Scholar.

2001-02	Watford	0	0		
2002-03	Watford	0	0		

BROWN, Wayne (D) 85 5
H: 6 0 W: 12 06 b.Barking 20-8-77
Source: Trainee.

1995–96	Ipswich T	0	0		
1996–97	Ipswich T	0	0		
1997–98	Ipswich T	1	0		
1997–98	*Colchester U*	2	0	**2**	**0**
1998–99	Ipswich T	1	0		
1999–2000	Ipswich T	25	0		
2000-01	Ipswich T	4	0		
2000-01	*QPR*	2	0	**2**	**0**
2001-02	Ipswich T	0	0		
2001-02	*Wimbledon*	17	1	**17**	**1**
2001-02	*Watford*	11	3		
2002-03	Ipswich T	9	0	**40**	**0**
2002-03	Watford	13	1	**24**	**4**

CHAMBERLAIN, Alec (G) 645 0
H: 6 2 W: 13 10 b.March 20-6-64
Source: Ramsey T.

1981–82	Ipswich T	0	0		
1982–83	Colchester U	0	0		
1983–84	Colchester U	46	0		
1984–85	Colchester U	46	0		
1985–86	Colchester U	46	0		
1986–87	Colchester U	46	0	**184**	**0**
1987–88	Everton	0	0		
1987–88	*Tranmere R*	15	0	**15**	**0**
1988–89	Luton T	6	0		
1989–90	Luton T	38	0		
1990–91	Luton T	38	0		
1991–92	Luton T	24	0		
1992–93	Luton T	32	0	**138**	**0**
1992–93	*Chelsea*	0	0		
1993–94	Sunderland	43	0		
1994–95	Sunderland	18	0		
1994–95	*Liverpool*	0	0		
1995–96	Sunderland	29	0	**90**	**0**
1996–97	Watford	4	0		
1997–98	Watford	46	0		
1998–99	Watford	46	0		
1999–2000	Watford	27	0		
2000-01	Watford	21	0		
2001-02	Watford	32	0		
2002-03	Watford	42	0	**218**	**0**

COHEN, Gary‡ (F) 0 0
H: 5 10 W: 10 05 b.Leyton 20-1-84
Source: Academy.

2002-03	Watford	0	0		

COOK, Lee (M) 38 2
H: 5 9 W: 11 04 b.Hammersmith 3-8-82
Source: Aylesbury U.

1999–2000	Watford	0	0		
2000-01	Watford	4	0		
2001-02	Watford	10	0		
2002-03	Watford	4	0	**18**	**0**
2002-03	*York C*	7	1	**7**	**1**
2002-03	*QPR*	13	1	**13**	**1**

COX, Neil# (D) 390 30
H: 6 0 W: 12 01 b.Scunthorpe 8-10-71
Source: Trainee. *Honours:* England Under-21.

1989–90	Scunthorpe U	0	0		
1990–91	Scunthorpe U	17	1	**17**	**1**
1990–91	Aston Villa	0	0		
1991–92	Aston Villa	7	0		
1992–93	Aston Villa	15	1		
1993–94	Aston Villa	20	2	**42**	**3**
1994–95	Middlesbrough	40	1		
1995–96	Middlesbrough	35	2		
1996–97	Middlesbrough	31	0	**106**	**3**
1997–98	Bolton W	21	1		
1998–99	Bolton W	44	4		
1999–2000	Bolton W	15	2	**80**	**7**
1999–2000	Watford	21	0		
2000-01	Watford	44	5		
2001-02	Watford	40	2		
2002-03	Watford	40	9	**145**	**16**

DOYLEY, Lloyd (D) 42 0
H: 5 10 W: 11 04 b.London 1-12-82
Source: Scholar.

2000-01	Watford	0	0		
2001-02	Watford	20	0		
2002-03	Watford	22	0	**42**	**0**

DYCHE, Sean (D) 355 12
H: 6 1 W: 13 09 b.Kettering 28-6-71
Source: Trainee.

1988–89	Nottingham F	0	0		
1989–90	Nottingham F	0	0		
1989–90	Chesterfield	22	2		
1990–91	Chesterfield	28	2		
1991–92	Chesterfield	42	3		
1992–93	Chesterfield	20	1		
1993–94	Chesterfield	20	0		
1994–95	Chesterfield	22	0		
1995–96	Chesterfield	41	0		
1996–97	Chesterfield	36	0	**231**	**8**
1997–98	Bristol C	11	0		
1998–99	Bristol C	6	0	**17**	**0**
1998–99	*Luton T*	14	1	**14**	**1**
1999–2000	Millwall	1	0		
2000-01	Millwall	33	0		
2001-02	Millwall	35	3	**69**	**3**
2002-03	Watford	24	0	**24**	**0**

FISKEN, Gary (M) 21 1
H: 5 10 W: 12 08 b.Watford 27-10-81
Source: Scholarship.

1999–2000	Watford	0	0		
2000-01	Watford	0	0		
2001-02	Watford	17	1		
2002-03	Watford	4	0	**21**	**1**

FITZGERALD, Scott (F) 4 1
H: 6 1 W: 12 08 b.Hillingdon 20-1-84
Source: Northwood.

2002-03	Watford	4	1	**4**	**1**

FOLEY, Dominic* (F) 86 11
H: 6 1 W: 12 08 b.Cork 7-7-76
Source: St James Gate. *Honours:* Eire 6 full caps, 2 goals.

1995–96	Wolverhampton W	5	0		
1996–97	Wolverhampton W	5	1		
1997–98	Wolverhampton W	5	0		
1997–98	*Watford*	8	1		
1998–99	Wolverhampton W	5	2	**20**	**3**
1998–99	*Notts Co*	2	0	**2**	**0**
1999–2000	Watford	12	1		
2000-01	Watford	5	1		
2001-02	Watford	1	0		
2001-02	*Swindon T*	7	1	**7**	**1**
2001-02	*QPR*	5	1	**5**	**1**
2002-03	Watford	15	3	**41**	**6**
2002-03	*Southend U*	5	0	**5**	**0**
2002-03	*Oxford U*	6	0	**6**	**0**

FORDE, Fabian* (F) 1 0
H: 5 11 W: 12 10 b.London 26-10-81
Source: Scholar.

2000-01	Watford	1	0		
2001-02	Watford	0	0		
2002-03	Watford	0	0	**1**	**0**

GAYLE, Marcus (F) 463 63
H: 6 3 W: 13 12 b.Hammersmith 28-9-70
Source: Trainee. *Honours:* England Youth. Jamaica 14 full caps, 3 goals.

1988–89	Brentford	3	0		
1989–90	Brentford	9	0		
1990–91	Brentford	33	6		
1991–92	Brentford	38	6		
1992–93	Brentford	38	4		
1993–94	Brentford	35	6	**156**	**22**
1993–94	Wimbledon	10	0		
1994–95	Wimbledon	23	2		
1995–96	Wimbledon	34	5		
1996–97	Wimbledon	36	8		
1997–98	Wimbledon	30	2		
1998–99	Wimbledon	35	10		
1999–2000	Wimbledon	36	7		
2000-01	Wimbledon	32	3	**236**	**37**
2000-01	Rangers	4	0	**4**	**0**
2001-02	Watford	36	4		
2002-03	Watford	31	0	**67**	**4**

GIBBS, Nigel† (D) 408 5
H: 5 7 W: 11 06 b.St Albans 20-11-65
Source: Apprentice. *Honours:* England Youth, Under-21.

1983–84	Watford	3	0		
1984–85	Watford	12	0		
1985–86	Watford	40	1		
1986–87	Watford	15	0		
1987–88	Watford	30	0		
1988–89	Watford	46	1		
1989–90	Watford	41	0		
1990–91	Watford	34	0		
1991–92	Watford	43	1		
1992–93	Watford	7	0		
1993–94	Watford	0	0		
1994–95	Watford	11	0		
1995–96	Watford	9	0		
1996–97	Watford	45	1		
1997–98	Watford	38	1		
1998–99	Watford	10	0		
1999–2000	Watford	17	0		
2000-01	Watford	6	0		
2001-02	Watford	1	0		
2002-03	Watford	0	0	**408**	**5**

GLASS, Stephen* (M) 213 18
H: 5 9 W: 10 11 b.Dundee 23-5-76
Source: Crombie Sports. *Honours:* Scotland Schools, Under-21, B, 1 full cap.

1994–95	Aberdeen	19	1		
1995–96	Aberdeen	32	3		
1996–97	Aberdeen	24	1		
1997–98	Aberdeen	31	2	**106**	**7**
1998–99	Newcastle U	22	3		
1999–2000	Newcastle U	7	1		
2000-01	Newcastle U	14	3	**43**	**7**
2001-02	Watford	31	3		
2002-03	Watford	33	1	**64**	**4**

GODFREY, Elliott (F) 1 0
H: 5 9 W: 10 02 b.Toronto 22-2-83
Source: Scholar.

2000-01	Watford	0	0		
2001-02	Watford	0	0		
2002-03	Watford	1	0	**1**	**0**

HAND, Jamie (M) 33 0
H: 6 0 W: 11 08 b.Uxbridge 7-2-84
Source: Scholar. *Honours:* England Youth.

2001-02	Watford	10	0		
2002-03	Watford	23	0	**33**	**0**

HELGUSON, Heidar (F) 157 49
H: 5 10 W: 12 04 b.Akureyri 22-8-77
Source: Throttur. *Honours:* Iceland 23 full caps, 2 goals.

1998	Lillestrom	19	2		
1999	Lillestrom	25	16	**44**	**18**
1999–2000	Watford	16	6		
2000-01	Watford	33	8		
2001-02	Watford	34	6		
2002-03	Watford	30	11	**113**	**31**

HERD, Ben (D) **0 0**
b.Welwyn 21-6-85
Source: Scholar.

2002-03	Watford	0	0		

HUGHES, Stephen‡ (M) **96 5**
H: 6 0 W: 12 12 b.Wokingham 18-9-76
Source: Trainee. *Honours:* England Schools, Youth, Under-21.

1994–95	Arsenal	1	0		
1995–96	Arsenal	1	0		
1996–97	Arsenal	14	1		
1997–98	Arsenal	17	2		
1998–99	Arsenal	14	1		
1999–2000	Fulham	3	0	**3**	**0**
1999–2000	Arsenal	2	0	**49**	**4**
1999–2000	Everton	11	1		
2000-01	Everton	18	0	**29**	**1**
2001-02	Watford	15	0		
2002-03	Watford	0	0	**15**	**0**

HYDE, Micah (M) **327 36**
H: 5 10 W: 11 07 b.Newham 10-11-74
Source: Trainee. *Honours:* Jamaica 8 full caps.

1993–94	Cambridge U	18	2		
1994–95	Cambridge U	27	0		
1995–96	Cambridge U	24	4		
1996–97	Cambridge U	38	7	**107**	**13**
1997–98	Watford	40	4		
1998–99	Watford	44	2		
1999–2000	Watford	34	3		
2000-01	Watford	26	6		
2001-02	Watford	39	4		
2002-03	Watford	37	4	**220**	**23**

IFIL, Jerel (D) **12 0**
H: 6 1 W: 12 11 b.London 27-6-82
Source: Academy.

1999–2000	Watford	0	0		
2000-01	Watford	0	0		
2001-02	Watford	0	0		
2001-02	*Huddersfield T*	2	0	**2**	**0**
2002-03	Watford	1	0	**1**	**0**
2002-03	*Swindon T*	9	0	**9**	**0**

JOHNSON, Richard (M) **248 21**
H: 5 10 W: 11 13 b.Kurri Kurri 27-4-74
Source: Trainee. *Honours:* Australia 1 full cap.

1991–92	Watford	2	0		
1992–93	Watford	1	0		
1993–94	Watford	27	0		
1994–95	Watford	35	3		
1995–96	Watford	20	1		
1996–97	Watford	37	2		
1997–98	Watford	42	7		
1998–99	Watford	40	4		
1999–2000	Watford	23	3		
2000-01	Watford	3	0		
2001-02	Watford	0	0		
2002-03	Watford	12	0	**242**	**20**
2002-03	*Northampton T*	6	1	**6**	**1**

KOO-BOOTHE, Nathan (M) **0 0**
b.London 18-7-85

2002-03	Watford	0	0		

LANGSTON, Matt* (D) **0 0**
H: 6 2 W: 12 04 b.Brighton 2-4-81
Source: Trainee.

1998–99	Watford	0	0		
1999–2000	Watford	0	0		
2000-01	Watford	0	0		
2001-02	Watford	0	0		
2002-03	Watford	0	0		

LEE, Richard (G) **4 0**
H: 6 0 W: 12 07 b.Oxford 5-10-82
Source: Scholar. *Honours:* England Under-20.

2000-01	Watford	0	0		
2001-02	Watford	0	0		
2002-03	Watford	4	0	**4**	**0**

MAHON, Gavin (M) **175 9**
H: 6 0 W: 13 02 b.Birmingham 2-1-77
Source: Trainee.

1995–96	Wolverhampton W	0	0		
1996–97	Hereford U	11	1		
1997–98	Hereford U	0	0		
1998–99	Hereford U	0	0	**11**	**1**
1998–99	Brentford	29	4		
1999–2000	Brentford	37	3		
2000-01	Brentford	40	1		
2001-02	Brentford	35	0	**141**	**8**
2001-02	Watford	6	0		
2002-03	Watford	17	0	**23**	**0**

MATTHEWS, Barrie* (D) **0 0**
H: 5 9 W: 10 10 b.Cinderford 1-2-83
Source: Scholar.

2000-01	Watford	0	0		
2001-02	Watford	0	0		
2002-03	Watford	0	0		

McNAMEE, Anthony (F) **30 1**
H: 5 5 W: 9 06 b.Lambeth 13-7-83
Source: Scholar. *Honours:* England Youth, Under-20.

2001-02	Watford	7	1		
2002-03	Watford	23	0	**30**	**1**

MEAD, Daniel* (M) **0 0**
b.Luton 19-9-84
Source: Scholar.

2001-02	Watford	0	0		
2002-03	Watford	0	0		

NIELSEN, Allan* (M) **329 56**
H: 5 8 W: 11 02 b.Esbjerg 13-3-71
Source: Esbjerg. *Honours:* Denmark Under-21, 45 full caps, 7 goals.

1988–89	Bayern Munich	0	0		
1989–90	Bayern Munich	0	0		
1990–91	Bayern Munich	1	0	**1**	**0**
1991–92	Sion	0	0		
1991–92	Odense	8	2		
1992–93	Odense	30	4		
1993–94	Odense	17	3	**55**	**9**
1993–94	FC Copenhagen	8	0		
1994–95	FC Copenhagen	18	3	**26**	**3**
1994–95	Brondby	10	3		
1995–96	Brondby	28	6		
1996–97	Brondby	4	2	**42**	**11**
1996–97	Tottenham H	29	6		
1997–98	Tottenham H	26	3		
1998–99	Tottenham H	28	3		
1999–2000	Tottenham H	14	0	**97**	**12**
1999–2000	*Wolverhampton W*	7	2	**7**	**2**
2000-01	Watford	45	10		
2001-02	Watford	22	6		
2002-03	Watford	34	3	**101**	**19**

NOEL-WILLIAMS, Gifton* (F) **169 33**
H: 6 4 W: 14 00 b.Islington 21-1-80
Source: Trainee. *Honours:* England Youth.

1996–97	Watford	25	2		
1997–98	Watford	38	7		
1998–99	Watford	26	10		
1999–2000	Watford	3	0		
2000-01	Watford	32	8		
2001-02	Watford	29	6		
2002-03	Watford	16	0	**169**	**33**

NORVILLE, Jason (F) **14 1**
H: 5 11 W: 10 07 b.Trinidad & Tobago 9-9-83
Source: Scholar.

2001-02	Watford	2	0		
2002-03	Watford	12	1	**14**	**1**

PATTERSON, Simon (F) **0 0**
H: 6 4 W: 13 01 b.Northwick Park 4-9-82

2000-01	Watford	0	0		
2001-02	Watford	0	0		
2002-03	Watford	0	0		

ROBINSON, Paul (D) **209 8**
H: 5 9 W: 11 11 b.Watford 14-12-78
Source: Trainee. *Honours:* England Under-21.

1996–97	Watford	12	0		
1997–98	Watford	22	2		
1998–99	Watford	29	0		
1999–2000	Watford	32	0		
2000-01	Watford	39	0		
2001-02	Watford	38	3		
2002-03	Watford	37	3	**209**	**8**

SAUNDERS, Neil* (M) **0 0**
H: 5 11 W: 11 02 b.Dagenham 7-5-83
Source: Scholar.

2001-02	Watford	0	0		
2002-03	Watford	0	0		

SMITH, Jack (D) **1 0**
H: 6 0 W: 11 05 b.Hemel Hempstead 14-10-83
Source: Scholar.

2001-02	Watford	0	0		
2002-03	Watford	1	0	**1**	**0**

SMITH, Tommy (F) **149 33**
H: 5 9 W: 10 00 b.Hemel Hempstead 22-5-80
Source: Trainee. *Honours:* England Youth, Under-21.

1997–98	Watford	1	0		
1998–99	Watford	8	2		
1999–2000	Watford	22	2		
2000-01	Watford	43	11		
2001-02	Watford	40	11		
2002-03	Watford	35	7	**149**	**33**

SWONNELL, Sam (M) **2 0**
H: 5 10 W: 11 10 b.Brentwood 13-9-82
Source: Scholar.

2000-01	Watford	0	0		
2001-02	Watford	0	0		
2002-03	Watford	2	0	**2**	**0**

VERNAZZA, Paulo (M) **81 3**
H: 5 10 W: 10 13 b.Islington 1-11-79
Source: Trainee. *Honours:* England Youth, Under-21.

1997–98	Arsenal	1	0		
1998–99	Arsenal	0	0		
1998–99	*Ipswich T*	2	0	**2**	**0**
1999–2000	Arsenal	2	0		
1999–2000	*Portsmouth*	7	0	**7**	**0**
2000-01	Arsenal	2	1	**5**	**1**
2000-01	Watford	23	2		
2001-02	Watford	21	0		
2002-03	Watford	23	0	**67**	**2**

WILLIAMS, Nick* (D) **0 0**
H: 6 1 W: 12 10 b.Cheltenham 16-2-83

2000-01	Watford	0	0		
2001-02	Watford	0	0		
2002-03	Watford	0	0		

WRIGHT, Nick‡ (F) **62 11**
H: 5 10 W: 11 08 b.Derby 15-10-75
Source: Trainee.

1994–95	Derby Co	0	0		
1995–96	Derby Co	0	0		
1996–97	Derby Co	0	0		
1997–98	Derby Co	0	0		
1997–98	Carlisle U	25	5	**25**	**5**
1998–99	Watford	33	6		
1999–2000	Watford	4	0		
2000-01	Watford	0	0		
2001-02	Watford	0	0		
2002-03	Watford	0	0	**37**	**6**

YOUNG, Ashley (M) **0 0**
b.Stevenage 9-7-85

2002-03	Watford	0	0		

Scholars
Ainon, Michael; Bouazza, Hameur; Buxton, Nicholas J; Catchpole, Lee A; Chase, Christopher; Collins, James E; Cowen, Joseph W; Coyne, Paul; Dean, Peter AE; Elliott, James; Fisher, Leon ML; Hammond, Benjamin I; Hopton, Matthew A; Martin Robert; Mawer, Cameron; Newing, Lee; Tinkler, Liam; Walsh, Liam S; Watson, Liam J
Non-Contract
Gibbs, Nigel J; Hitchcock, Kevin

WBA

ADAMS, Ross (D) **0 0**
H: 5 11 W: 12 04 b.Birmingham 11-3-83
Source: Scholar.

2001-02	WBA	0	0		
2002-03	WBA	0	0		

ADAMSON, Chris‡ (G) **22 0**
H: 6 0 W: 11 07 b.Ashington 4-11-78
Source: Trainee.

1997–98	WBA	3	0		
1998–99	WBA	0	0		
1998–99	*Mansfield T*	2	0	**2**	**0**
1999–2000	WBA	9	0		
1999–2000	*Halifax T*	7	0	**7**	**0**
2000-01	WBA	0	0		
2001-02	WBA	0	0		
2001-02	*Plymouth Arg*	1	0	**1**	**0**
2002-03	WBA	0	0	**12**	**0**

APPLETON, Michael (M) **162 15**
H: 5 8 W: 11 00 b.Salford 4-12-75
Source: Trainee.

1994–95	Manchester U	0	0		
1995–96	Manchester U	0	0		
1995–96	*Lincoln C*	4	0	**4**	**0**
1996–97	Manchester U	0	0		
1996–97	*Grimsby T*	10	3	**10**	**3**
1997–98	Preston NE	38	2		
1998–99	Preston NE	25	2		
1999–2000	Preston NE	26	3		
2000-01	Preston NE	26	5	**115**	**12**

2000-01 WBA 15 0
2001-02 WBA 18 0
2002-03 WBA 0 0 **33 0**

BALIS, Igor (D) 205 9
H: 5 11 W: 11 02 b.Czech Republic 5-1-70
Honours: Slovakia 41 full caps, 1 goal.
1995–96 Spartak Trnava 32 0
1996–97 Spartak Trnava 26 4
1997–98 Spartak Trnava 28 0
1998–99 Spartak Trnava 26 1
1999–2000 Spartak Trnava 24 0 **136 5**
2000-01 WBA 7 0
2001-02 WBA 34 2
2002-03 WBA 28 2 **69 4**

BRIGGS, Mark‡ (M) 0 0
H: 6 0 W: 11 07 b.Wolverhampton 16-2-82
Source: Scholar.
2000-01 WBA 0 0
2001-02 WBA 0 0
2002-03 WBA 0 0

CHAMBERS, Adam (M) 56 1
H: 5 10 W: 10 10 b.Sandwell 20-11-80
Source: Trainee. *Honours:* England Youth.
1998–99 WBA 0 0
1999–2000 WBA 0 0
2000-01 WBA 11 1
2001-02 WBA 32 0
2002-03 WBA 13 0 **56 1**

CHAMBERS, James (D) 56 0
H: 5 10 W: 10 10 b.Sandwell 20-11-80
Source: Trainee. *Honours:* England Youth.
1998–99 WBA 0 0
1999–2000 WBA 12 0
2000-01 WBA 31 0
2001-02 WBA 5 0
2002-03 WBA 8 0 **56 0**

CLEMENT, Neil (D) 158 15
H: 6 0 W: 13 00 b.Reading 3-10-78
Source: Trainee. *Honours:* England Schools, Youth.
1995–96 Chelsea 0 0
1996–97 Chelsea 1 0
1997–98 Chelsea 0 0
1998–99 Chelsea 0 0
1998–99 *Reading* 11 1 **11 1**
1998–99 *Preston NE* 4 0 **4 0**
1999–2000 Chelsea 0 0 **1 0**
1999–2000 *Brentford* 8 0 **8 0**
1999–2000 *WBA* 8 0
2000-01 WBA 45 5
2001-02 WBA 45 6
2002-03 WBA 36 3 **134 14**

COLLINS, Matt* (M) 0 0
H: 5 10 W: 12 00 b.Hitchin 10-2-82
Source: Scholar.
2000-01 WBA 0 0
2001-02 WBA 0 0
2002-03 WBA 0 0

DICHIO, Danny (F) 219 48
H: 6 4 W: 13 10 b.Hammersmith 19-10-74
Source: Trainee. *Honours:* England Schools, Under-21.
1993–94 QPR 0 0
1993–94 *Barnet* 9 2 **9 2**
1994–95 QPR 9 3
1995–96 QPR 29 10
1996–97 QPR 37 7 **75 20**
1997–98 Sampdoria 0 0
1997–98 Lecce 4 1 **4 1**
1997–98 Sunderland 13 0
1998–99 Sunderland 36 10
1999–2000 Sunderland 12 0
2000-01 Sunderland 15 1
2001-02 Sunderland 0 0 **76 11**
2001-02 WBA 27 9
2002-03 WBA 28 5 **55 14**

DOBIE, Scott (F) 216 39
H: 6 2 W: 12 09 b.Workington 10-10-78
Source: Trainee. *Honours:* Scotland 6 full caps, 1 goal.
1996–97 Carlisle U 2 1
1997–98 Carlisle U 23 0
1998–99 Carlisle U 33 6
1998–99 *Clydebank* 6 0 **6 0**
1999–2000 Carlisle U 34 7
2000-01 Carlisle U 44 10 **136 24**
2001-02 WBA 43 10
2002-03 WBA 31 5 **74 15**

DYER, Lloyd (D) 0 0
H: 5 9 W: 10 02 b.Birmingham 13-9-82
2001-02 WBA 0 0
2002-03 WBA 0 0

GILCHRIST, Phil (D) 371 11
H: 5 11 W: 12 00 b.Stockton 25-8-73
Source: Trainee.
1990–91 Nottingham F 0 0
1991–92 Middlesbrough 0 0
1992–93 Hartlepool U 24 0
1993–94 Hartlepool U 35 0
1994–95 Hartlepool U 23 0 **82 0**
1994–95 Oxford U 18 1
1995–96 Oxford U 42 3
1996–97 Oxford U 38 2
1997–98 Oxford U 39 2
1998–99 Oxford U 39 2
1999–2000 Oxford U 1 0 **177 10**
1999–2000 Leicester C 27 1
2000-01 Leicester C 12 0 **39 1**
2000-01 WBA 8 0
2001-02 WBA 43 0
2002-03 WBA 22 0 **73 0**

GREGAN, Sean (M) 384 17
H: 6 2 W: 14 00 b.Middlesbrough 29-3-74
Source: Trainee.
1991–92 Darlington 17 0
1992–93 Darlington 17 1
1993–94 Darlington 23 1
1994–95 Darlington 25 2
1995–96 Darlington 38 0
1996–97 Darlington 16 0 **136 4**
1996–97 Preston NE 21 1
1997–98 Preston NE 35 2
1998–99 Preston NE 41 3
1999–2000 Preston NE 33 3
2000-01 Preston NE 41 2
2001-02 Preston NE 41 1 **212 12**
2002-03 WBA 36 1 **36 1**

HOULT, Russell (G) 289 0
H: 6 3 W: 13 08 b.Ashby 22-11-72
Source: Trainee.
1990–91 Leicester C 0 0
1991–92 Leicester C 0 0
1991–92 *Lincoln C* 2 0
1991–92 *Blackpool* 0 0
1992–93 Leicester C 10 0
1993–94 Leicester C 0 0
1993–94 *Bolton W* 4 0 **4 0**
1994–95 Leicester C 0 0 **10 0**
1994–95 *Lincoln C* 15 0 **17 0**
1994–95 *Derby Co* 15 0
1995–96 Derby Co 41 0
1996–97 Derby Co 32 0
1997–98 Derby Co 2 0
1998–99 Derby Co 23 0
1999–2000 Derby Co 10 0 **123 0**
1999–2000 Portsmouth 18 0
2000-01 Portsmouth 22 0 **40 0**
2000-01 WBA 13 0
2001-02 WBA 45 0
2002-03 WBA 37 0 **95 0**

HUGHES, Lee (F) 221 93
H: 5 11 W: 11 07 b.Smethwick 22-5-76
Source: Kidderminster H.
1997–98 WBA 37 14
1998–99 WBA 42 31
1999–2000 WBA 36 12
2000-01 WBA 41 21
2001-02 Coventry C 38 14
2002-03 Coventry C 4 1 **42 15**
2002-03 WBA 23 0 **179 78**

JENSEN, Brian* (G) 47 0
H: 6 3 W: 12 04 b.Copenhagen 8-6-75
1997–98 AZ 0 0
1998–99 AZ 1 0 **1 0**
1999–2000 WBA 12 0
2000-01 WBA 33 0
2001-02 WBA 1 0
2002-03 WBA 0 0 **46 0**

JOHNSON, Andy (M) 249 27
H: 6 0 W: 12 06 b.Bristol 2-5-74
Source: Trainee. *Honours:* Wales 10 full caps.
1991–92 Norwich C 2 0
1992–93 Norwich C 2 1
1993–94 Norwich C 2 0
1994–95 Norwich C 7 0
1995–96 Norwich C 26 7
1996–97 Norwich C 27 5 **66 13**
1997–98 Nottingham F 34 4
1998–99 Nottingham F 28 0
1999–2000 Nottingham F 25 2
2000-01 Nottingham F 31 3
2001-02 Nottingham F 1 0 **119 9**
2001-02 WBA 32 4
2002-03 WBA 32 1 **64 5**

JORDAO* (M) 250 18
H: 6 2 W: 12 08 b.Malanje 30-8-71
1990–91 Amadora 0 0
1991–92 Amadora 17 3
1992–93 Amadora 3 0
1993–94 Campomaiorense 9 0 **9 0**
1994–95 Leca 26 3 **26 3**
1995–96 Amadora 30 1
1996–97 Amadora 31 3 **81 7**
1997–98 Benfica 6 0 **6 0**
1997–98 Braga 14 1
1998–99 Braga 29 1
1999–2000 Braga 22 0 **65 2**
2000-01 WBA 35 1
2001-02 WBA 25 5
2002-03 WBA 3 0 **63 6**

KOUMAS, Jason (M) 159 29
H: 5 10 W: 11 06 b.Wrexham 25-9-79
Source: Trainee. *Honours:* Wales 4 full caps.
1997–98 Tranmere R 0 0
1998–99 Tranmere R 23 3
1999–2000 Tranmere R 23 2
2000-01 Tranmere R 39 10
2001-02 Tranmere R 38 8
2002-03 Tranmere R 4 2 **127 25**
2002-03 WBA 32 4 **32 4**

LYTTLE, Des* (D) 325 5
H: 5 8 W: 11 05 b.Wolverhampton 24-9-71
Source: Worcester C.
1992–93 Swansea C 46 1 **46 1**
1993–94 Nottingham F 37 1
1994–95 Nottingham F 38 0
1995–96 Nottingham F 33 1
1996–97 Nottingham F 32 1
1997–98 Nottingham F 35 0
1998–99 Nottingham F 10 0 **185 3**
1998–99 *Port Vale* 7 0 **7 0**
1999–2000 Watford 11 0 **11 0**
1999–2000 *WBA* 9 0
2000-01 WBA 40 1
2001-02 WBA 23 0
2002-03 WBA 4 0 **76 1**

MARSHALL, Lee (M) 171 12
H: 6 0 W: 11 11 b.Islington 21-1-79
Source: Enfield. *Honours:* England Under-21.
1996–97 Norwich C 0 0
1997–98 Norwich C 4 0
1998–99 Norwich C 44 3
1999–2000 Norwich C 33 5
2000-01 Norwich C 36 3 **117 11**
2000-01 Leicester C 9 0
2001-02 Leicester C 35 0
2002-03 Leicester C 1 0 **45 0**
2002-03 WBA 9 1 **9 1**

McINNES, Derek (M) 359 26
H: 5 8 W: 11 05 b.Paisley 5-7-71
Source: Gleniffer Th. *Honours:* Scotland 2 full caps.
1987–88 Greenock Morton 2 0
1988–89 Greenock Morton 29 1
1989–90 Greenock Morton 23 1
1990–91 Greenock Morton 31 3
1991–92 Greenock Morton 42 7
1992–93 Greenock Morton 40 2
1993–94 Greenock Morton 16 1
1994–95 Greenock Morton 26 3
1995–96 Greenock Morton 12 1 **221 19**
1995–96 Rangers 6 0
1996–97 Rangers 21 1
1997–98 Rangers 0 0
1998–99 Rangers 7 0 **34 1**
1998–99 *Stockport Co* 13 0 **13 0**
1999–2000 Toulouse 3 0 **3 0**
2000-01 WBA 14 1
2001-02 WBA 45 3
2002-03 WBA 29 2 **88 6**

MKANDAWIRE, Tamika (D) 0 0
H: 6 1 W: 12 03 b.Malawi 28-5-83
Source: Scholar.
2002-03 WBA 0 0

MOORE, Darren (D) 361 24
H: 6 3 W: 15 08 b.Birmingham 22-4-74
Source: Trainee. *Honours:* Jamaica 3 full caps.
1991–92 Torquay U 5 1
1992–93 Torquay U 31 2
1993–94 Torquay U 37 2

1994–95	Torquay U	30	3	**103**	**8**
1995–96	Doncaster R	35	2		
1996–97	Doncaster R	41	5	**76**	**7**
1997–98	Bradford C	18	0		
1998–99	Bradford C	44	3		
1999–2000	Bradford C	0	0	**62**	**3**
1999–2000	Portsmouth	25	1		
2000-01	Portsmouth	32	1		
2001-02	Portsmouth	2	0	**59**	**2**
2001-02	WBA	32	2		
2002-03	WBA	29	2	**61**	**4**

MURPHY, Joe (G) **65** **0**

H: 6 2 W: 13 07 b.Dublin 21-8-81

Source: Trainee. *Honours:* Eire Under-21.

1999–2000	Tranmere R	21	0		
2000-01	Tranmere R	20	0		
2001-02	Tranmere R	22	0	**63**	**0**
2002-03	WBA	2	0	**2**	**0**

OLIVER, Adam‡ (M) **23** **1**

H: 5 9 W: 11 02 b.Sandwell 25-10-80

Source: Trainee. *Honours:* England Youth.

1998–99	WBA	1	0		
1999–2000	WBA	15	1		
2000-01	WBA	7	0		
2001-02	WBA	0	0		
2002-03	WBA	0	0	**23**	**1**

ROBERTS, Jason (F) **184** **69**

H: 6 0 W: 12 06 b.Park Royal 25-1-78

Source: Hayes. *Honours:* Grenada 6 full caps.

1997–98	Wolverhampton W	0	0		
1997–98	*Torquay U*	14	6	**14**	**6**
1997–98	*Bristol C*	3	1	**3**	**1**
1998–99	Bristol R	37	16		
1999–2000	Bristol R	41	22	**78**	**38**
2000-01	WBA	43	14		
2001-02	WBA	14	7		
2002-03	WBA	32	3	**89**	**24**

SCOTT, Mark‡ (F) **0** **0**

H: 6 1 W: 12 02 b.Sandwell 16-7-82

Source: Scholar.

2000-01	WBA	0	0		
2001-02	WBA	0	0		
2002-03	WBA	0	0		

SIGURDSSON, Larus (D) **311** **8**

H: 6 0 W: 12 04 b.Akureyri 4-6-73

Source: Thor. *Honours:* Iceland 41 full caps, 2 goals.

1994–95	Stoke C	23	1		
1995–96	Stoke C	46	0		
1996–97	Stoke C	45	0		
1997–98	Stoke C	43	1		
1998–99	Stoke C	38	4		
1999–2000	Stoke C	5	1	**200**	**7**
1999–2000	WBA	27	0		
2000-01	WBA	12	0		
2001-02	WBA	43	1		
2002-03	WBA	29	0	**111**	**1**

TAYLOR, Bob* (F) **549** **193**

H: 5 10 W: 12 04 b.Easington 3-2-67

Source: Horden CW.

1985–86	Leeds U	2	0		
1986–87	Leeds U	2	0		
1987–88	Leeds U	32	9		
1988–89	Leeds U	6	0	**42**	**9**
1988–89	Bristol C	12	8		
1989–90	Bristol C	37	27		
1990–91	Bristol C	39	11		
1991–92	Bristol C	18	4	**106**	**50**
1991–92	WBA	19	8		
1992–93	WBA	46	30		
1993–94	WBA	42	18		
1994–95	WBA	42	11		
1995–96	WBA	42	17		
1996–97	WBA	32	10		
1997–98	WBA	15	2		
1997–98	*Bolton W*	12	3		
1998–99	Bolton W	38	15		
1999–2000	Bolton W	27	3	**77**	**21**
1999–2000	WBA	8	5		
2000-01	WBA	40	5		
2001-02	WBA	34	7		
2002-03	WBA	4	0	**324**	**113**

TURNER, Matt‡ (M) **0** **0**

H: 5 6 W: 10 03 b.Nottingham 29-12-81

Source: Trainee. *Honours:* England Youth.

1998–99	Nottingham F	0	0		
1999–2000	Nottingham F	0	0		
2000-01	Nottingham F	0	0		
2000-01	WBA	0	0		
2001-02	WBA	0	0		
2002-03	WBA	0	0		

UDEZE, Ifeanyi (D) **100** **0**

H: 5 9 W: 11 07 b.Nigeria 21-7-80

Source: Benden Insurance. *Honours:* Nigeria 16 full caps.

1997–98	Kavala	22	0		
1998–99	Kavala	14	0		
1999–2000	Kavala	23	0	**59**	**0**
2000-01	PAOK Salonika	16	0		
2001-02	PAOK Salonika	14	0	**30**	**0**
2002-03	WBA	11	0	**11**	**0**

WALLWORK, Ronnie (M) **63** **1**

H: 5 10 W: 12 00 b.Manchester 10-9-77

Source: Trainee. *Honours:* England Youth.

1994–95	Manchester U	0	0		
1995–96	Manchester U	0	0		
1996–97	Manchester U	0	0		
1997–98	Manchester U	1	0		
1997–98	*Carlisle U*	10	1	**10**	**1**
1997–98	*Stockport Co*	7	0	**7**	**0**
1998–99	Manchester U	0	0		
1999–2000	Manchester U	5	0		
2000-01	Manchester U	12	0		
2001-02	Manchester U	1	0	**19**	**0**
2002-03	WBA	27	0	**27**	**0**

Trainees

Brown, Simon; Clarke, Ross; Crane, Daniel; Cudworth, Jack R; Holmes, James; Midworth, Philip; Patterson, Kyle; Sherwood, Lee G; Smikle, Brian J; Tomlinson, Ezekiel J; Warmer, Thomas E

WEST HAM U

BOWYER, Lee* (M) **259** **46**

H: 5 8 W: 10 04 b.London 3-1-77

Source: Trainee. *Honours:* England Youth, Under-21, 1 full cap.

1993–94	Charlton Ath	0	0		
1994–95	Charlton Ath	5	0		
1995–96	Charlton Ath	41	8	**46**	**8**
1996–97	Leeds U	32	4		
1997–98	Leeds U	25	3		
1998–99	Leeds U	35	9		
1999–2000	Leeds U	33	5		
2000-01	Leeds U	38	9		
2001-02	Leeds U	25	5		
2002-03	Leeds U	15	3	**203**	**38**
2002-03	West Ham U	10	0	**10**	**0**

BREEN, Gary* (D) **339** **5**

H: 6 1 W: 11 12 b.London 12-12-73

Source: Charlton Ath. *Honours:* Eire Under-21, 56 full caps, 6 goals.

1991–92	Maidstone U	19	0	**19**	**0**
1992–93	Gillingham	29	0		
1993–94	Gillingham	22	0	**51**	**0**
1994–95	Peterborough U	44	1		
1995–96	Peterborough U	25	0	**69**	**1**
1995–96	Birmingham C	18	1		
1996–97	Birmingham C	22	1	**40**	**2**
1996–97	Coventry C	9	0		
1997–98	Coventry C	30	1		
1998–99	Coventry C	25	0		
1999–2000	Coventry C	21	0		
2000-01	Coventry C	31	1		
2001-02	Coventry C	30	0	**146**	**2**
2002-03	West Ham U	14	0	**14**	**0**

BREVETT, Rufus (D) **447** **5**

H: 5 8 W: 11 13 b.Derby 24-9-69

Source: Trainee.

1987–88	Doncaster R	17	0		
1988–89	Doncaster R	23	0		
1989–90	Doncaster R	42	0		
1990–91	Doncaster R	27	3	**109**	**3**
1990–91	QPR	10	0		
1991–92	QPR	7	0		
1992–93	QPR	15	0		
1993–94	QPR	7	0		
1994–95	QPR	19	0		
1995–96	QPR	27	1		
1996–97	QPR	44	0		
1997–98	QPR	23	0	**152**	**1**
1997–98	Fulham	11	0		
1998–99	Fulham	45	1		
1999–2000	Fulham	23	0		
2000-01	Fulham	39	0		
2001-02	Fulham	35	0		
2002-03	Fulham	20	0	**173**	**1**
2002-03	West Ham U	13	0	**13**	**0**

BRITTON, Leon (M) **25** **0**

H: 5 5 W: 9 09 b.Merton 16-9-82

Source: Trainee. *Honours:* England Youth.

1999–2000	West Ham U	0	0		
2000-01	West Ham U	0	0		
2001-02	West Ham U	0	0		
2002-03	West Ham U	0	0		
2002-03	*Swansea C*	25	0	**25**	**0**

BYRNE, Shaun (D) **4** **0**

H: 5 9 W: 11 08 b.Taplow 21-1-81

Source: Trainee. *Honours:* Eire Under-21.

1999–2000	West Ham U	1	0		
1999–2000	*Bristol R*	2	0	**2**	**0**
2000-01	West Ham U	0	0		
2001-02	West Ham U	1	0		
2002-03	West Ham U	0	0	**2**	**0**

BYWATER, Steve (G) **11** **0**

H: 6 2 W: 12 00 b.Manchester 7-6-81

Source: Trainee. *Honours:* England Youth, Under-20, Under-21.

1997–98	Rochdale	0	0		
1998–99	West Ham U	0	0		
1999–2000	West Ham U	4	0		
1999–2000	*Wycombe W*	2	0	**2**	**0**
1999–2000	*Hull C*	4	0	**4**	**0**
2000-01	West Ham U	1	0		
2001-02	West Ham U	0	0		
2001-02	*Wolverhampton W*	0	0		
2001-02	*Cardiff C*	0	0		
2002-03	West Ham U	0	0	**5**	**0**

CAMARA, Titi (F) **262** **47**

H: 6 0 W: 13 00 b.Conakry 17-11-72

Honours: Guinea full caps.

1990–91	St Etienne	4	0		
1991–92	St Etienne	15	3		
1992–93	St Etienne	16	2		
1993–94	St Etienne	26	4		
1994–95	St Etienne	33	7	**94**	**16**
1995–96	Lens	36	8		
1996–97	Lens	27	6	**63**	**14**
1997–98	Marseille	31	2		
1998–99	Marseille	30	6	**61**	**8**
1999–2000	Liverpool	33	9		
2000-01	Liverpool	0	0	**33**	**9**
2000-01	West Ham U	6	0		
2001-02	West Ham U	1	0		
2002-03	West Ham U	4	0	**11**	**0**

CARRICK, Michael (M) **109** **7**

H: 6 1 W: 11 10 b.Wallsend 28-7-81

Source: Trainee. *Honours:* England Youth, Under-21, 2 full caps.

1998–99	West Ham U	0	0		
1999–2000	West Ham U	8	1		
1999–2000	*Swindon T*	6	2	**6**	**2**
1999–2000	*Birmingham C*	2	0	**2**	**0**
2000-01	West Ham U	33	1		
2001-02	West Ham U	30	2		
2002-03	West Ham U	30	1	**101**	**5**

CISSE, Edouard (M) **143** **5**

H: 6 2 W: 11 13 b.Pau 30-3-78

Source: Pau.

1997–98	Paris St Germain	11	0		
1998–99	Rennes	28	2	**28**	**2**
1999–2000	Paris St Germain	28	0		
2000-01	Paris St Germain	26	2		
2001-02	Paris St Germain	25	1	**90**	**3**
2002-03	West Ham U	25	0	**25**	**0**

COLE, Joe (M) **126** **10**

H: 5 7 W: 9 08 b.Islington 8-11-81

Source: Trainee. *Honours:* England Schools, Youth, Under-21, 10 full caps, 1 goal.

1998–99	West Ham U	8	0		
1999–2000	West Ham U	22	1		
2000-01	West Ham U	30	5		
2001-02	West Ham U	30	0		
2002-03	West Ham U	36	4	**126**	**10**

COLE, Mitchell (M) **0** **0**

b.London 6-10-85

Source: Trainee. *Honours:* England Youth.

2002-03	West Ham U	0	0		

COURTOIS, Laurent‡ (M) **30** **0**

H: 5 7 W: 10 11 b.Lyon 11-9-78

Source: Lyon.

1998–99	Ajaccio	0	0		
1999–2000	Toulouse	0	0		
2000-01	Toulouse	23	0	**23**	**0**
2001-02	West Ham U	7	0		
2002-03	West Ham U	0	0	**7**	**0**

DAILLY, Christian (D) **354 26**
H: 6 0 W: 12 10 b.Dundee 23-10-73
Source: 'S' Form. *Honours:* Scotland Schools, Youth, B, Under-21, 46 full caps, 4 goals.

1990–91	Dundee U	18	5		
1991–92	Dundee U	8	0		
1992–93	Dundee U	14	4		
1993–94	Dundee U	38	4		
1994–95	Dundee U	33	4		
1995–96	Dundee U	30	1	**141**	**18**
1996–97	Derby Co	36	3		
1997–98	Derby Co	30	1		
1998–99	Derby Co	1	0	**67**	**4**
1998–99	Blackburn R	17	0		
1999–2000	Blackburn R	43	4		
2000–01	Blackburn R	10	0	**70**	**4**
2000–01	West Ham U	12	0		
2001–02	West Ham U	38	0		
2002–03	West Ham U	26	0	**76**	**0**

DEFOE, Jermain (F) **103 36**
H: 5 7 W: 10 04 b.Beckton 7-10-82
Source: Charlton Ath. *Honours:* England Youth, Under-21.

1999–2000	West Ham U	0	0		
2000–01	West Ham U	1	0		
2000–01	*Bournemouth*	29	18	**29**	**18**
2001–02	West Ham U	35	10		
2002–03	West Ham U	38	8	**74**	**18**

DELANEY, Craig* (D) **0 0**
H: 6 6 W: 14 00 b.Dublin 2-1-80
Source: UCD.

2002–03	West Ham U	0	0		

DI CANIO, Paolo* (F) **407 96**
H: 5 9 W: 11 09 b.Rome 9-7-68
Source: Milan AC.

1985–86	Lazio	0	0		
1986–87	Ternana	27	2	**27**	**2**
1987–88	Lazio	0	0		
1988–89	Lazio	30	1		
1989–90	Lazio	24	3	**54**	**4**
1990–91	Juventus	23	3		
1991–92	Juventus	24	0		
1992–93	Juventus	31	3		
1993–94	Napoli	26	5	**26**	**5**
1994–95	Juventus	0	0	**78**	**6**
1994–95	AC Milan	15	1		
1995–96	AC Milan	22	5	**37**	**6**
1996–97	Celtic	26	12	**26**	**12**
1997–98	Sheffield W	35	12		
1998–99	Sheffield W	6	3	**41**	**15**
1998–99	West Ham U	13	3		
1999–2000	West Ham U	30	16		
2000–01	West Ham U	31	9		
2001–02	West Ham U	26	9		
2002–03	West Ham U	18	9	**118**	**46**

FERDINAND, Anton (D) **0 0**
b.Peckham 18-2-85
Source: Trainee. *Honours:* England Youth.

2002–03	West Ham U	0	0		

FERDINAND, Les* (F) **390 170**
H: 5 11 W: 13 02 b.Paddington 8-12-66
Source: Hayes. *Honours:* England B, 17 full caps, 5 goals.

1986–87	QPR	2	0		
1987–88	QPR	1	0		
1987–88	*Brentford*	3	0	**3**	**0**
1988–89	QPR	0	0		
1988–89	*Besiktas*	24	14	**24**	**14**
1989–90	QPR	9	2		
1990–91	QPR	18	8		
1991–92	QPR	23	10		
1992–93	QPR	37	20		
1993–94	QPR	36	16		
1994–95	QPR	37	24	**163**	**80**
1995–96	Newcastle U	37	25		
1996–97	Newcastle U	31	16	**68**	**41**
1997–98	Tottenham H	21	5		
1998–99	Tottenham H	24	5		
1999–2000	Tottenham H	9	2		
2000–01	Tottenham H	28	10		
2001–02	Tottenham H	25	9		
2002–03	Tottenham H	11	2	**118**	**33**
2002–03	West Ham U	14	2	**14**	**2**

FORDE, David (G) **0 0**
H: 6 3 W: 13 06 b.Galway 20-12-79
Source: Barry T.

2001–02	West Ham U	0	0		
2002–03	West Ham U	0	0		

GARCIA, Richard (F) **26 4**
H: 5 11 W: 12 00 b.Perth 9-4-81
Source: Trainee. *Honours:* Australia Under-23.

1998–99	West Ham U	0	0		
1999–2000	West Ham U	0	0		
2000–01	West Ham U	0	0		
2000–01	*Leyton Orient*	18	4	**18**	**4**
2001–02	West Ham U	8	0		
2002–03	West Ham U	0	0	**8**	**0**

HUTCHISON, Don (M) **325 44**
H: 6 1 W: 11 08 b.Gateshead 9-5-71
Source: Trainee. *Honours:* Scotland B, 23 full caps, 6 goals.

1989–90	Hartlepool U	13	2		
1990–91	Hartlepool U	11	0	**24**	**2**
1990–91	Liverpool	0	0		
1991–92	Liverpool	3	0		
1992–93	Liverpool	31	7		
1993–94	Liverpool	11	0	**45**	**7**
1994–95	West Ham U	23	9		
1995–96	West Ham U	12	2		
1995–96	Sheffield U	19	2		
1996–97	Sheffield U	41	3		
1997–98	Sheffield U	18	0	**78**	**5**
1997–98	Everton	11	1		
1998–99	Everton	33	3		
1999–2000	Everton	31	6	**75**	**10**
2000–01	Sunderland	32	8		
2001–02	Sunderland	2	0	**34**	**8**
2001–02	West Ham U	24	1		
2002–03	West Ham U	10	0	**69**	**12**

IRIEKPEN, Ezomo* (D) **18 2**
H: 6 2 W: 12 02 b.East London 14-5-82
Source: Trainee. *Honours:* England Youth.

1998–99	West Ham U	0	0		
1999–2000	West Ham U	0	0		
2000–01	West Ham U	0	0		
2001–02	West Ham U	0	0		
2002–03	West Ham U	0	0		
2002–03	*Leyton Orient*	5	1	**5**	**1**
2002–03	*Cambridge U*	13	1	**13**	**1**

JAMES, David (G) **434 0**
H: 6 5 W: 14 02 b.Welwyn 1-8-70
Source: Trainee. *Honours:* England Youth, Under-21, B, 16 full caps.

1988–89	Watford	0	0		
1989–90	Watford	0	0		
1990–91	Watford	46	0		
1991–92	Watford	43	0	**89**	**0**
1992–93	Liverpool	29	0		
1993–94	Liverpool	14	0		
1994–95	Liverpool	42	0		
1995–96	Liverpool	38	0		
1996–97	Liverpool	38	0		
1997–98	Liverpool	27	0		
1998–99	Liverpool	26	0	**214**	**0**
1999–2000	Aston Villa	29	0		
2000–01	Aston Villa	38	0	**67**	**0**
2001–02	West Ham U	26	0		
2002–03	West Ham U	38	0	**64**	**0**

JOHNSON, Glen (D) **23 0**
H: 6 0 W: 12 00 b.London 23-8-84
Source: Scholar. *Honours:* England Youth, Under-20, Under-21.

2001–02	West Ham U	0	0		
2002–03	West Ham U	15	0	**15**	**0**
2002–03	*Millwall*	8	0	**8**	**0**

KANOUTE, Frederic (F) **124 38**
H: 6 3 W: 13 08 b.Ste. Foy-Les-Lyon 2-9-77

1997–98	Lyon	18	6		
1998–99	Lyon	9	2		
1999–2000	Lyon	13	1	**40**	**9**
1999–2000	West Ham U	8	2		
2000–01	West Ham U	32	11		
2001–02	West Ham U	27	11		
2002–03	West Ham U	17	5	**84**	**29**

LABANT, Vladimir (D) **142 8**
H: 6 0 W: 13 00 b.Zilina 8-6-74
Honours: Slovakia 24 full caps, 2 goals.

1996–97	Bystrica	28	3	**28**	**3**
1997–98	Slavia Prague	23	0		
1998–99	Slavia Prague	26	1	**49**	**1**
1999–2000	Sparta Prague	12	2		
2000–01	Sparta Prague	24	1		
2001–02	Sparta Prague	16	1	**52**	**4**
2001–02	West Ham U	12	0		
2002–03	West Ham U	1	0	**13**	**0**

LOMAS, Steve (M) **270 17**
H: 6 0 W: 12 08 b.Hanover 14-3-72
Source: Trainee. *Honours:* Northern Ireland Schools, Youth, B, 45 full caps, 3 goals.

1991–92	Manchester C	0	0		
1992–93	Manchester C	0	0		
1993–94	Manchester C	23	0		
1994–95	Manchester C	20	2		
1995–96	Manchester C	33	3		
1996–97	Manchester C	35	3	**111**	**8**
1996–97	West Ham U	7	0		
1997–98	West Ham U	33	2		
1998–99	West Ham U	30	1		
1999–2000	West Ham U	25	1		
2000–01	West Ham U	20	1		
2001–02	West Ham U	15	4		
2002–03	West Ham U	29	0	**159**	**9**

McMAHON, Daryl (M) **0 0**
b.Dublin 10-10-83

2000–01	West Ham U	0	0		
2001–02	West Ham U	0	0		
2002–03	West Ham U	0	0		

MINTO, Scott* (D) **316 11**
H: 5 10 W: 10 00 b.Wirral 6-8-71
Source: Trainee. *Honours:* England Youth, Under-21.

1988–89	Charlton Ath	3	0		
1989–90	Charlton Ath	23	2		
1990–91	Charlton Ath	43	1		
1991–92	Charlton Ath	33	1		
1992–93	Charlton Ath	36	1		
1993–94	Charlton Ath	42	2	**180**	**7**
1994–95	Chelsea	19	0		
1995–96	Chelsea	10	0		
1996–97	Chelsea	25	4	**54**	**4**
1997–98	Benfica	21	0		
1998–99	Benfica	10	0	**31**	**0**
1998–99	West Ham U	15	0		
1999–2000	West Ham U	18	0		
2000–01	West Ham U	1	0		
2001–02	West Ham U	5	0		
2002–03	West Ham U	12	0	**51**	**0**

MONCUR, John* (M) **280 13**
H: 5 8 W: 9 10 b.Mile End 22-9-66
Source: Apprentice.

1984–85	Tottenham H	0	0		
1985–86	Tottenham H	0	0		
1986–87	Tottenham H	1	0		
1986–87	*Cambridge U*	4	0	**4**	**0**
1986–87	*Doncaster R*	4	0	**4**	**0**
1987–88	Tottenham H	5	0		
1988–89	Tottenham H	1	0		
1988–89	*Portsmouth*	7	0	**7**	**0**
1989–90	Tottenham H	5	1		
1989–90	*Brentford*	5	1	**5**	**1**
1990–91	Tottenham H	9	0	**21**	**1**
1991–92	*Ipswich T*	6	0	**6**	**0**
1991–92	*Nottingham F*	0	0		
1991–92	Swindon T	3	0		
1992–93	Swindon T	14	1		
1993–94	Swindon T	41	4	**58**	**5**
1994–95	West Ham U	30	2		
1995–96	West Ham U	20	0		
1996–97	West Ham U	27	2		
1997–98	West Ham U	20	1		
1998–99	West Ham U	14	0		
1999–2000	West Ham U	22	1		
2000–01	West Ham U	16	0		
2001–02	West Ham U	19	0		
2002–03	West Ham U	7	0	**175**	**6**

NOBLE, David* (M) **15 1**
H: 6 0 W: 12 04 b.Hitchin 2-2-82
Source: Scholar. *Honours:* England Youth, Under-20, Scotland Under-21.

2000–01	Arsenal	0	0		
2001–02	Arsenal	0	0		
2001–02	*Watford*	15	1	**15**	**1**
2002–03	Arsenal	0	0		
2002–03	West Ham U	0	0		

PEARCE, Ian (D) **184 10**
H: 6 3 W: 14 04 b.Bury St Edmunds 7-5-74
Source: School. *Honours:* England Youth, Under-21.

1990–91	Chelsea	1	0		
1991–92	Chelsea	2	0		
1992–93	Chelsea	1	0		
1993–94	Chelsea	0	0	**4**	**0**
1993–94	Blackburn R	5	1		
1994–95	Blackburn R	28	0		
1995–96	Blackburn R	12	1		
1996–97	Blackburn R	12	0		

1997–98	Blackburn R	5	0	**62**	**2**
1997–98	West Ham U	30	1		
1998–99	West Ham U	33	2		
1999–2000	West Ham U	1	0		
2000–01	West Ham U	15	1		
2001–02	West Ham U	9	2		
2002–03	West Ham U	30	2	**118**	**8**

REPKA, Tomas (D) **310 9**
H: 6 0 W: 12 04 b.Slavicin Zlin 2-1-74
Honours: Czechoslovakia 1 full cap.Czech Republic 46 full caps, 1 goal.

1991–92	Banik Ostrava	16	1		
1992–93	Banik Ostrava	19	0		
1993–94	Banik Ostrava	26	2		
1994–95	Banik Ostrava	16	0	**77**	**3**
1995–96	Sparta Prague	29	3		
1996–97	Sparta Prague	25	1		
1997–98	Sparta Prague	28	2	**82**	**6**
1998–99	Fiorentina	31	0		
1999–2000	Fiorentina	29	0		
2000–01	Fiorentina	28	0	**88**	**0**
2001–02	West Ham U	31	0		
2002–03	West Ham U	32	0	**63**	**0**

RIDDLE, Louis‡ (M) **0 0**
H: 5 11 W: 12 00 b.Harlow 26-9-82
Source: Trainee.

2002–03	West Ham U	0	0		

SCHEMMEL, Sebastian (D) **269 4**
H: 5 8 W: 11 13 b.Nancy 2-6-75

1993–94	Nancy	6	0		
1994–95	Nancy	35	0		
1995–96	Nancy	33	0		
1996–97	Nancy	32	0		
1997–98	Nancy	40	1	**146**	**1**
1998–99	Metz	20	1		
1999–2000	Metz	21	1		
2000–01	Metz	19	0	**60**	**2**
2000–01	West Ham U	12	0		
2001–02	West Ham U	35	1		
2002–03	West Ham U	16	0	**63**	**1**

SINCLAIR, Trevor (M) **456 68**
H: 5 10 W: 12 05 b.Dulwich 2-3-73
Source: Trainee. *Honours:* England Youth, Under-21, B, 11 full caps.

1989–90	Blackpool	9	0		
1990–91	Blackpool	31	1		
1991–92	Blackpool	27	3		
1992–93	Blackpool	45	11	**112**	**15**
1993–94	QPR	32	4		
1994–95	QPR	33	4		
1995–96	QPR	37	2		
1996–97	QPR	39	3		
1997–98	QPR	26	3	**167**	**16**
1997–98	West Ham U	14	7		
1998–99	West Ham U	36	7		
1999–2000	West Ham U	36	7		
2000–01	West Ham U	19	3		
2001–02	West Ham U	34	5		
2002–03	West Ham U	38	8	**177**	**37**

SOFIANE, Youssef (F) **0 0**
H: 5 8 W: 11 00 b.Lyon 8-7-84

2001–02	Auxerre	0	0		
2002–03	West Ham U	0	0		

VAN DER GOUW, Raimond* (G) **392 0**
H: 6 3 W: 13 09 b.Oldenzaal 24-3-63

1985–86	Go Ahead	28	0		
1986–87	Go Ahead	34	0		
1987–88	Go Ahead	35	0	**97**	**0**
1988–89	Vitesse	36	0		
1989–90	Vitesse	34	0		
1990–91	Vitesse	31	0		
1991–92	Vitesse	34	0		
1992–93	Vitesse	34	0		
1993–94	Vitesse	34	0		
1994–95	Vitesse	34	0		
1995–96	Vitesse	21	0	**258**	**0**
1996–97	Manchester U	2	0		
1997–98	Manchester U	5	0		
1998–99	Manchester U	5	0		
1999–2000	Manchester U	14	0		
2000–01	Manchester U	10	0		
2001–02	Manchester U	1	0	**37**	**0**
2002–03	West Ham U	0	0		

WARD, Elliott (D) **0 0**
b.Harrow 19-1-85
Source: Scholar.

2001–02	West Ham U	0	0		
2002–03	West Ham U	0	0		

WINTERBURN, Nigel* (D) **687 17**
H: 5 8 W: 11 04 b.Coventry 11-12-63
Source: Local. *Honours:* England Youth, Under-21, B, 2 full caps.

1981–82	Birmingham C	0	0		
1982–83	Birmingham C	0	0		
1983–84	Oxford U	0	0		
1983–84	Wimbledon	43	1		
1984–85	Wimbledon	41	4		
1985–86	Wimbledon	39	1		
1986–87	Wimbledon	42	2	**165**	**8**
1987–88	Arsenal	17	0		
1988–89	Arsenal	38	3		
1989–90	Arsenal	36	0		
1990–91	Arsenal	38	0		
1991–92	Arsenal	41	1		
1992–93	Arsenal	29	1		
1993–94	Arsenal	34	0		
1994–95	Arsenal	39	0		
1995–96	Arsenal	36	2		
1996–97	Arsenal	38	0		
1997–98	Arsenal	36	1		
1998–99	Arsenal	30	0		
1999–2000	Arsenal	28	0	**440**	**8**
2000–01	West Ham U	33	1		
2001–02	West Ham U	31	0		
2002–03	West Ham U	18	0	**82**	**1**

Trainees
Blewitt, Darren L; Bunce, Daniel C; Carrick, Graeme; Collington, Marce D; Laws, Thomas S; Lee, San; Lumsden, Philip; McClenahan, Trent J; Parrington, Liam W; Pearson, Gregory; Sealey, George B; Tattam, Brent S; Tucker, Ian MC; Wright, Sam A
Non-Contract
Keen, Kevin I; Miklosko, Ludek

WIGAN ATH

ASHCROFT, Lee‡ (F) **365 75**
H: 5 9 W: 12 10 b.Preston 7-9-72
Source: Trainee. *Honours:* England Under-21.

1990–91	Preston NE	14	1		
1991–92	Preston NE	38	5		
1992–93	Preston NE	39	7		
1993–94	WBA	21	3		
1994–95	WBA	38	10		
1995–96	WBA	26	4		
1995–96	*Notts Co*	6	0	**6**	**0**
1996–97	WBA	5	0	**90**	**17**
1996–97	Preston NE	27	8		
1997–98	Preston NE	37	14		
1998–99	Preston NE	0	0	**155**	**35**
1998–99	Grimsby T	27	3		
1999–2000	Grimsby T	34	12	**61**	**15**
2000–01	Wigan Ath	30	5		
2001–02	Wigan Ath	16	3		
2002–03	Wigan Ath	0	0	**46**	**8**
2002–03	*Port Vale*	3	0	**3**	**0**
2002–03	*Huddersfield T*	4	0	**4**	**0**

BAINES, Leighton (D) **6 0**
H: 5 8 W: 11 10 b.Liverpool 11-12-84

2002–03	Wigan Ath	6	0	**6**	**0**

BRANNAN, Ged (M) **402 35**
H: 6 0 W: 12 08 b.Liverpool 15-1-72
Source: Trainee.

1990–91	Tranmere R	18	1		
1991–92	Tranmere R	18	1		
1992–93	Tranmere R	38	1		
1993–94	Tranmere R	45	9		
1994–95	Tranmere R	41	2		
1995–96	Tranmere R	44	0		
1996–97	Tranmere R	34	6	**238**	**20**
1996–97	Manchester C	11	1		
1997–98	Manchester C	32	3		
1998–99	Manchester C	0	0	**43**	**4**
1998–99	*Norwich C*	11	1	**11**	**1**
1998–99	Motherwell	25	5		
1999–2000	Motherwell	33	5	**58**	**10**
2000–01	Wigan Ath	13	0		
2001–02	Wigan Ath	33	0		
2002–03	Wigan Ath	6	0	**52**	**0**

BRECKIN, Ian (D) **353 14**
H: 6 2 W: 13 05 b.Rotherham 24-2-75
Source: Trainee.

1993–94	Rotherham U	10	0		
1994–95	Rotherham U	41	2		
1995–96	Rotherham U	39	1		
1996–97	Rotherham U	42	3	**132**	**6**
1997–98	Chesterfield	43	1		
1998–99	Chesterfield	44	2		
1999–2000	Chesterfield	38	1		
2000–01	Chesterfield	45	3		
2001–02	Chesterfield	42	1	**212**	**8**
2002–03	Wigan Ath	9	0	**9**	**0**

BULLARD, Jimmy (M) **83 12**
H: 5 9 W: 10 00 b.Newham 23-10-78
Source: Corinthian, Dartford, Gravesend & N.

1998–99	West Ham U	0	0		
1999–2000	West Ham U	0	0		
2000–01	West Ham U	0	0		
2001–02	Peterborough U	40	8		
2002–03	Peterborough U	26	3	**66**	**11**
2002–03	Wigan Ath	17	1	**17**	**1**

CHARNOCK, Kieran‡ (D) **0 0**
H: 6 1 W: 13 07 b.Preston 3-8-84
Source: Scholar.

2002–03	Wigan Ath	0	0		

DE VOS, Jason (D) **200 20**
H: 6 4 W: 14 10 b.London, Canada 2-1-74
Source: Montreal Impact. *Honours:* Canada 39 full caps.

1996–97	Darlington	8	0		
1997–98	Darlington	24	3		
1998–99	Darlington	12	2	**44**	**5**
1998–99	Dundee U	25	0		
1999–2000	Dundee U	35	2		
2000–01	Dundee U	33	0	**93**	**2**
2001–02	Wigan Ath	20	5		
2002–03	Wigan Ath	43	8	**63**	**13**

DINNING, Tony (M) **302 43**
H: 6 0 W: 13 00 b.Wallsend 12-4-75
Source: Trainee.

1993–94	Newcastle U	0	0		
1994–95	Stockport Co	40	1		
1995–96	Stockport Co	10	1		
1996–97	Stockport Co	20	2		
1997–98	Stockport Co	30	4		
1998–99	Stockport Co	41	5		
1999–2000	Stockport Co	44	12		
2000–01	Stockport Co	6	0	**191**	**25**
2000–01	Wolverhampton W	31	6		
2001–02	Wolverhampton W	4	0	**35**	**6**
2001–02	Wigan Ath	33	5		
2001–02	*Stoke C*	5	0	**5**	**0**
2002–03	Wigan Ath	38	7	**71**	**12**

EADEN, Nicky (D) **404 13**
H: 5 9 W: 12 04 b.Sheffield 12-12-72
Source: Trainee.

1991–92	Barnsley	0	0		
1992–93	Barnsley	2	0		
1993–94	Barnsley	37	2		
1994–95	Barnsley	45	1		
1995–96	Barnsley	46	2		
1996–97	Barnsley	46	3		
1997–98	Barnsley	35	0		
1998–99	Barnsley	40	1		
1999–2000	Barnsley	42	1	**293**	**10**
2000–01	Birmingham C	45	2		
2001–02	Birmingham C	29	1		
2002–03	Birmingham C	0	0	**74**	**3**
2002–03	Wigan Ath	37	0	**37**	**0**

ELLINGTON, Nathan (F) **161 52**
H: 5 10 W: 13 01 b.Bradford 2-7-81
Source: Walton & Hersham.

1998–99	Bristol R	10	1		
1999–2000	Bristol R	37	4		
2000–01	Bristol R	42	15		
2001–02	Bristol R	27	15	**116**	**35**
2001–02	Wigan Ath	3	2		
2002–03	Wigan Ath	42	15	**45**	**17**

FILAN, John (G) **298 0**
H: 6 2 W: 14 06 b.Sydney 8-2-70
Honours: Australia Under-20, Under-23, 2 full caps.

1989–90	St George	26	0		
1990–91	St George	26	0	**52**	**0**
1991–92	Wollongong Wolves	23	0		
1992–93	Wollongong Wolves	6	0	**29**	**0**
1992–93	Cambridge U	6	0		
1993–94	Cambridge U	46	0		
1994–95	Cambridge U	16	0	**68**	**0**
1994–95	*Nottingham F*	0	0		
1994–95	Coventry C	2	0		
1995–96	Coventry C	13	0		
1996–97	Coventry C	1	0	**16**	**0**
1997–98	Blackburn R	7	0		
1998–99	Blackburn R	26	0		
1999–2000	Blackburn R	16	0		

2000-01 Blackburn R 13 0
2001-02 Blackburn R 0 0 **62 0**
2001-02 Wigan Ath 25 0
2002-03 Wigan Ath 46 0 **71 0**

FLYNN, Mike (M) 17 1
H: 5 10 W: 12 10 b.Newport 17-10-80
Source: Barry T.
2002-03 Wigan Ath 17 1 **17 1**

JACKSON, Matt (D) 408 11
H: 6 1 W: 14 00 b.Leeds 19-10-71
Source: School. *Honours:* England Schools, Under-21.
1990–91 Luton T 0 0
1990–91 *Preston NE* 4 0 **4 0**
1991–92 Luton T 9 0 **9 0**
1991–92 Everton 30 1
1992–93 Everton 27 3
1993–94 Everton 38 0
1994–95 Everton 29 0
1995–96 Everton 14 0
1995–96 *Charlton Ath* 8 0 **8 0**
1996–97 Everton 0 0 **138 4**
1996–97 *QPR* 7 0 **7 0**
1996–97 *Birmingham C* 10 0 **10 0**
1996–97 Norwich C 19 2
1997–98 Norwich C 41 3
1998–99 Norwich C 37 1
1999–2000 Norwich C 38 0
2000-01 Norwich C 26 0
2001-02 Norwich C 0 0 **161 6**
2001-02 Wigan Ath 26 0
2002-03 Wigan Ath 45 1 **71 1**

JARRETT, Jason (M) 105 4
H: 6 1 W: 13 01 b.Bury 14-9-79
Source: Trainee.
1998–99 Blackpool 2 0
1999–2000 Blackpool 0 0 **2 0**
1999–2000 Wrexham 1 0 **1 0**
2000-01 Bury 25 2
2001-02 Bury 37 2 **62 4**
2001-02 Wigan Ath 5 0
2002-03 Wigan Ath 35 0 **40 0**

KENNEDY, Peter (M) 190 19
H: 5 10 W: 11 11 b.Lisburn 10-9-73
Source: Portadown. *Honours:* Northern Ireland B, 17 full caps.
1996–97 Notts Co 22 0 **22 0**
1997–98 Watford 34 11
1998–99 Watford 46 6
1999–2000 Watford 18 1
2000-01 Watford 17 0 **115 18**
2001-02 Wigan Ath 31 0
2002-03 Wigan Ath 22 1 **53 1**

LIDDELL, Andy (F) 375 95
H: 5 9 W: 11 07 b.Leeds 28-6-73
Source: Trainee. *Honours:* Scotland Under-21.
1990–91 Barnsley 0 0
1991–92 Barnsley 1 0
1992–93 Barnsley 21 2
1993–94 Barnsley 22 1
1994–95 Barnsley 39 13
1995–96 Barnsley 43 9
1996–97 Barnsley 38 8
1997–98 Barnsley 26 1
1998–99 Barnsley 8 0 **198 34**
1998–99 Wigan Ath 28 10
1999–2000 Wigan Ath 41 8
2000-01 Wigan Ath 37 9
2001-02 Wigan Ath 34 18
2002-03 Wigan Ath 37 16 **177 61**

McCULLOCH, Lee (F) 204 37
H: 6 1 W: 13 00 b.Bellshill 14-5-78
Source: Cumbernauld U. *Honours:* Scotland Under-18, Under-21.
1995–96 Motherwell 1 0
1996–97 Motherwell 15 0
1997–98 Motherwell 25 2
1998–99 Motherwell 26 3
1999–2000 Motherwell 29 9
2000-01 Motherwell 26 8 **122 22**
2000-01 Wigan Ath 10 3
2001-02 Wigan Ath 34 6
2002-03 Wigan Ath 38 6 **82 15**

McMILLAN, Steve (D) 219 6
H: 5 9 W: 11 12 b.Edinburgh 19-1-76
Source: Troon Juniors. *Honours:* Scotland Under-21.
1993–94 Motherwell 1 0
1994–95 Motherwell 3 0
1995–96 Motherwell 12 0
1996–97 Motherwell 16 0
1997–98 Motherwell 34 1
1998–99 Motherwell 30 2
1999–2000 Motherwell 31 3
2000-01 Motherwell 25 0 **152 6**
2000-01 Wigan Ath 6 0
2001-02 Wigan Ath 29 0
2002-03 Wigan Ath 32 0 **67 0**

MITCHELL, Paul (D) 62 0
H: 5 9 W: 11 12 b.Manchester 26-8-81
Source: Trainee.
2000-01 Wigan Ath 1 0
2000-01 *Halifax T* 11 0 **11 0**
2001-02 Wigan Ath 23 0
2002-03 Wigan Ath 27 0 **51 0**

PENDLEBURY, Ian‡ (D) 4 0
H: 5 7 W: 11 03 b.Bolton 3-9-83
Source: Trainee.
2001-02 Wigan Ath 4 0
2002-03 Wigan Ath 0 0 **4 0**

ROBERTS, Neil (F) 178 34
H: 5 10 W: 12 08 b.Wrexham 7-4-78
Source: Trainee. *Honours:* Wales Youth, Under-21, B, 3 full caps.
1996–97 Wrexham 0 0
1997–98 Wrexham 34 8
1998–99 Wrexham 22 3
1999–2000 Wrexham 19 6 **75 17**
1999–2000 Wigan Ath 9 1
2000-01 Wigan Ath 34 6
2001-02 *Hull C* 6 0 **6 0**
2001-02 Wigan Ath 17 4
2002-03 Wigan Ath 37 6 **97 17**

SANTUS, Paul* (M) 1 0
H: 5 10 W: 11 06 b.Billinge 8-9-83
Source: Trainee.
2001-02 Wigan Ath 1 0
2002-03 Wigan Ath 0 0 **1 0**

TEALE, Gary (F) 205 24
H: 5 11 W: 12 00 b.Glasgow 21-7-78
Source: Ayr U.
1996–97 Clydebank 33 6
1997–98 Clydebank 27 6 **60 12**
1998–99 Ayr U 23 4
1999–2000 Ayr U 32 0
2000-01 Ayr U 29 5 **84 9**
2001-02 Wigan Ath 23 1
2002-03 Wigan Ath 38 2 **61 3**

TRAYNOR, Greg§ (M) 1 0
b.Salford 17-10-84
Source: Scholar.
2001-02 Wigan Ath 1 0
2002-03 Wigan Ath 0 0 **1 0**

YEOMANS, Ryan (G) 0 0
H: 6 0 W: 12 10 b.Blackpool 20-11-85
Source: Scholar.
2002-03 Wigan Ath 0 0

Scholars
Dixon, Philip T; Edwards, Philip L; Foulkes, Michael G; Jones, Christopher; Kay, Robert P; Lee, Kevin; Lynch, Christopher; Moore, David L; Owens, Lee T; Roberts, J; Thompson, Jonathan; Traynor, Greg

WIMBLEDON

AGYEMANG, Patrick (F) 107 13
H: 6 1 W: 12 00 b.Walthamstow 20-9-80
Source: Trainee.
1998–99 Wimbledon 0 0
1999–2000 Wimbledon 0 0
1999–2000 *Brentford* 12 0 **12 0**
2000-01 Wimbledon 29 4
2001-02 Wimbledon 33 4
2002-03 Wimbledon 33 5 **95 13**

ANDERSEN, Trond (M) 251 10
H: 6 1 W: 13 01 b.Kristiansund 6-1-75
Source: Clausenengen. *Honours:* Norway 29 full caps.
1995 Molde 18 1
1996 Molde 21 0
1997 Molde 25 0
1998 Molde 24 2
1999 Molde 17 1 **105 4**
1999–2000 Wimbledon 36 0
2000-01 Wimbledon 42 5
2001-02 Wimbledon 30 0
2002-03 Wimbledon 38 1 **146 6**

BERNI, Tommaso* (G) 0 0
H: 6 3 W: 14 00 b.Florence 6-3-83
Source: Internazionale.
2000-01 Wimbledon 0 0
2001-02 Wimbledon 0 0
2002-03 Wimbledon 0 0

CHORLEY, Ben (D) 12 0
H: 6 3 W: 13 02 b.Sidcup 30-9-82
Source: Scholar.
2001-02 Arsenal 0 0
2002-03 Arsenal 0 0
2002-03 *Brentford* 2 0 **2 0**
2002-03 Wimbledon 10 0 **10 0**

CONNOLLY, David (F) 178 94
H: 5 8 W: 10 09 b.Willesden 6-6-77
Source: Trainee. *Honours:* Eire 37 full caps, 8 goals.
1994–95 Watford 2 0
1995–96 Watford 11 8
1996–97 Watford 13 2 **26 10**
1997–98 Feyenoord 10 2
1998–99 Wolverhampton W 32 6 **32 6**
1999–2000 Excelsior 32 29 **32 29**
2000-01 Feyenoord 15 5 **25 7**
2001-02 Wimbledon 35 18
2002-03 Wimbledon 28 24 **63 42**

DARLINGTON, Jermaine (D) 135 4
H: 5 9 W: 13 00 b.Hackney 11-4-74
Source: Aylesbury U.
1998–99 QPR 4 0
1999–2000 QPR 34 2
2000-01 QPR 33 0 **71 2**
2001-02 Wimbledon 29 0
2002-03 Wimbledon 35 2 **64 2**

DAVIS, Kelvin (G) 227 0
H: 6 1 W: 13 06 b.Bedford 29-9-76
Source: Trainee. *Honours:* England Youth, Under-21.
1993–94 Luton T 1 0
1994–95 Luton T 9 0
1994–95 *Torquay U* 2 0 **2 0**
1995–96 Luton T 6 0
1996–97 Luton T 0 0
1997–98 Luton T 32 0
1997–98 *Hartlepool U* 2 0 **2 0**
1998–99 Luton T 44 0 **92 0**
1999–2000 Wimbledon 0 0
2000-01 Wimbledon 45 0
2001-02 Wimbledon 40 0
2002-03 Wimbledon 46 0 **131 0**

FRANCIS, Damien (M) 97 15
H: 6 0 W: 10 10 b.Wandsworth 27-2-79
Source: Trainee.
1996–97 Wimbledon 0 0
1997–98 Wimbledon 2 0
1998–99 Wimbledon 0 0
1999–2000 Wimbledon 9 0
2000-01 Wimbledon 29 8
2001-02 Wimbledon 23 1
2002-03 Wimbledon 34 6 **97 15**

GIER, Rob (D) 46 0
H: 5 9 W: 11 07 b.Ascot 6-1-80
Source: Trainee.
1998–99 Wimbledon 0 0
1999–2000 Wimbledon 0 0
2000-01 Wimbledon 14 0
2001-02 Wimbledon 3 0
2002-03 Wimbledon 29 0 **46 0**

GORDON, Michael (M) 1 0
H: 5 6 W: 10 04 b.Wandsworth 11-10-84
Source: Arsenal Trainee.
2002-03 Wimbledon 1 0 **1 0**

GORE, Shane (G) 1 0
H: 6 1 W: 12 01 b.Ashford 28-10-81
Source: Scholar.
2001-02 Wimbledon 1 0
2002-03 Wimbledon 0 0 **1 0**

GRAY, Wayne (F) 76 10
H: 5 10 W: 12 07 b.South London 7-11-80
Source: Trainee.
1998–99 Wimbledon 0 0
1999–2000 Wimbledon 1 0
1999–2000 *Swindon T* 12 2 **12 2**
2000-01 Wimbledon 11 0
2000-01 *Port Vale* 3 0 **3 0**
2001-02 Wimbledon 0 0
2001-02 *Leyton Orient* 15 5 **15 5**
2001-02 *Brighton & HA* 4 1 **4 1**
2002-03 Wimbledon 30 2 **42 2**

HAARA, Heikki‡ (D) **0 0**
H: 6 1 W: 11 04 b.Lahti 20-11-82
2000-01 Wimbledon 0 0
2001-02 Wimbledon 0 0
2002-03 Wimbledon 0 0

HARDING, Ben (M) **0 0**
H: 5 10 W: 11 02 b.Carshalton 6-9-84
Source: Scholar. *Honours:* England Youth.
2001-02 Wimbledon 0 0
2002-03 Wimbledon 0 0

HAWKINS, Peter (D) **116 0**
H: 6 0 W: 11 04 b.Maidstone 19-9-78
Source: Trainee.
1996–97 Wimbledon 0 0
1997–98 Wimbledon 0 0
1998–99 Wimbledon 0 0
1999–2000 Wimbledon 0 0
1999–2000 *York C* 14 0 **14 0**
2000-01 Wimbledon 30 0
2001-02 Wimbledon 29 0
2002-03 Wimbledon 43 0 **102 0**

HEALD, Paul* (G) **213 0**
H: 6 2 W: 14 00 b.Wath-on-Dearne 20-9-68
Source: Trainee.
1987–88 Sheffield U 0 0
1988–89 Sheffield U 0 0
1988–89 Leyton Orient 28 0
1989–90 Leyton Orient 37 0
1990–91 Leyton Orient 38 0
1991–92 Leyton Orient 2 0
1991–92 *Coventry C* 2 0 **2 0**
1992–93 Leyton Orient 26 0
1992–93 *Crystal Palace* 0 0
1993–94 Leyton Orient 0 0
1993–94 *Swindon T* 2 0 **2 0**
1994–95 Leyton Orient 45 0 **176 0**
1995–96 Wimbledon 18 0
1996–97 Wimbledon 2 0
1997–98 Wimbledon 0 0
1998–99 Wimbledon 0 0
1999–2000 Wimbledon 1 0
2000-01 Wimbledon 3 0
2001-02 Wimbledon 4 0
2001-02 *Sheffield W* 5 0 **5 0**
2002-03 Wimbledon 0 0 **28 0**

HERZIG, Nico (M) **0 0**
H: 5 10 W: 11 00 b.Pobneck 10-12-83
Source: Carl Zeiss Jena.
2001-02 Wimbledon 0 0
2002-03 Wimbledon 0 0

HOLLOWAY, Darren (D) **146 0**
H: 6 0 W: 12 05 b.Crook 3-10-77
Source: Trainee. *Honours:* England Under-21.
1995–96 Sunderland 0 0
1996–97 Sunderland 0 0
1997–98 Sunderland 32 0
1997–98 *Carlisle U* 5 0 **5 0**
1998–99 Sunderland 6 0
1999–2000 Sunderland 15 0
1999–2000 *Bolton W* 4 0 **4 0**
2000-01 Sunderland 5 0 **58 0**
2000-01 Wimbledon 31 0
2001-02 Wimbledon 32 0
2002-03 Wimbledon 16 0 **79 0**

HUGHES, Michael* (M) **310 28**
H: 5 6 W: 10 08 b.Larne 2-8-71
Source: Carrick R. *Honours:* Northern Ireland Schools, Youth, Under-21, Under-23, 65 full caps, 5 goals.
1988–89 Manchester C 1 0
1989–90 Manchester C 0 0
1990–91 Manchester C 1 0
1991–92 Manchester C 24 1 **26 1**
1992–93 Strasbourg 36 2
1993–94 Strasbourg 34 7
1994–95 Strasbourg 13 0 **83 9**
1994–95 *West Ham U* 17 2
1995–96 *West Ham U* 28 0
1996–97 West Ham U 33 3
1997–98 West Ham U 5 0 **83 5**
1997–98 Wimbledon 29 4
1998–99 Wimbledon 30 2
1999–2000 Wimbledon 20 2
2000-01 Wimbledon 10 1
2001-02 Wimbledon 26 4
2001-02 *Birmingham C* 3 0 **3 0**
2002-03 Wimbledon 0 0 **115 13**

JARRETT, Albert (M) **0 0**
H: 5 11 W: 11 02 b.Sierra Leone 23-10-84
Source: Dulwich Hamlet.
2002-03 Wimbledon 0 0

KAMARA, Malvin§ (M) **2 0**
H: 5 11 W: 13 07 b.London 17-11-83
Source: Scholar.
2002-03 Wimbledon 2 0 **2 0**

KARLSSON, Par‡ (M) **90 6**
H: 5 8 W: 10 11 b.Gothenburg 29-5-78
Source: Karlskoga.
1997 IFK Gothenburg 10 3
1998 IFK Gothenburg 13 0
1999 IFK Gothenburg 25 1
2000 IFK Gothenburg 16 2 **64 6**
2000-01 Wimbledon 16 0
2001-02 Wimbledon 7 0
2002-03 Wimbledon 3 0 **26 0**

LEIGERTWOOD, Mikele (D) **37 0**
H: 6 1 W: 13 13 b.Enfield 12-1-82
Source: Scholar.
2001-02 Wimbledon 1 0
2001-02 *Leyton Orient* 8 0 **8 0**
2002-03 Wimbledon 28 0 **29 0**

LEWINGTON, Dean§ (M) **1 0**
b.London 18-5-84
Source: Scholar.
2002-03 Wimbledon 1 0 **1 0**

McANUFF, Jobi (M) **69 8**
H: 5 9 W: 10 07 b.Edmonton 9-11-81
Source: Scholar. *Honours:* Jamaica 1 full cap.
2000-01 Wimbledon 0 0
2001-02 Wimbledon 38 4
2002-03 Wimbledon 31 4 **69 8**

MORGAN, Lionel (F) **27 2**
H: 6 0 W: 12 03 b.Tottenham 17-2-83
Source: Scholar. *Honours:* England Youth, Under-20.
2000-01 Wimbledon 5 0
2001-02 Wimbledon 11 1
2002-03 Wimbledon 11 1 **27 2**

MOUTER, Ryan (M) **0 0**
H: 5 11 W: 11 01 b.Sunderland 2-7-85
Source: Redheugh BC.
2002-03 Wimbledon 0 0

NOWLAND, Adam (F) **100 7**
H: 5 11 W: 11 06 b.Preston 6-7-81
Source: Trainee.
1997–98 Blackpool 1 0
1998–99 Blackpool 37 2
1999–2000 Blackpool 21 3
2000-01 Blackpool 10 0 **69 5**
2001-02 Wimbledon 7 0
2002-03 Wimbledon 24 2 **31 2**

REO-COKER, Nigel (M) **33 2**
H: 5 9 W: 12 03 b.Southwark 14-5-84
Source: Scholar. *Honours:* England Youth.
2001-02 Wimbledon 1 0
2002-03 Wimbledon 32 2 **33 2**

SELLEY, Ian* (M) **77 0**
H: 5 10 W: 10 11 b.Chertsey 14-6-74
Source: Trainee. *Honours:* England Youth, Under-21.
1992–93 Arsenal 9 0
1993–94 Arsenal 18 0
1994–95 Arsenal 13 0
1995–96 Arsenal 0 0
1996–97 Arsenal 1 0
1996–97 *Southend U* 4 0
1997–98 Arsenal 0 0 **41 0**
1997–98 Fulham 3 0
1998–99 Fulham 0 0
1999–2000 Fulham 0 0 **3 0**
2000-01 Wimbledon 4 0
2001-02 Wimbledon 0 0
2001-02 *Southend U* 14 0
2002-03 Wimbledon 0 0 **4 0**
2002-03 *Southend U* 11 0 **29 0**

SHIPPERLEY, Neil (F) **355 100**
H: 6 1 W: 13 12 b.Chatham 30-10-74
Source: Trainee. *Honours:* England Under-21.
1992–93 Chelsea 3 1
1993–94 Chelsea 24 4
1994–95 Chelsea 10 2 **37 7**
1994–95 *Watford* 6 1 **6 1**
1994–95 Southampton 19 4
1995–96 Southampton 37 7
1996–97 Southampton 10 1 **66 12**
1996–97 Crystal Palace 32 12
1997–98 Crystal Palace 26 7
1998–99 Crystal Palace 3 1 **61 20**
1998–99 Nottingham F 20 1 **20 1**
1999–2000 Barnsley 39 13
2000-01 Barnsley 39 14 **78 27**
2001-02 Wimbledon 41 12
2002-03 Wimbledon 46 20 **87 32**

TAPP, Alex (M) **24 2**
H: 5 8 W: 10 13 b.Redhill 7-6-82
Source: Trainee.
1999–2000 Wimbledon 0 0
2000-01 Wimbledon 0 0
2001-02 Wimbledon 0 0
2002-03 Wimbledon 24 2 **24 2**

WAEHLER, Kjetil‡ (M) **88 6**
H: 5 10 W: 11 04 b.Oslo 16-3-76
1992 Lyn 8 0
1993 Lyn 20 2
1994 Lyn 0 0
1995 Lyn 0 0
1996 Lyn 12 0
1997 Lyn 26 3
1998 Lyn 0 0
1999 Lyn 22 1 **88 6**
1999–2000 Wimbledon 0 0
2000-01 Wimbledon 0 0
2001-02 Wimbledon 0 0
2002-03 Wimbledon 0 0

WILLMOTT, Chris* (D) **80 2**
H: 6 2 W: 11 05 b.Bedford 30-9-77
Source: Trainee.
1995–96 Luton T 0 0
1996–97 Luton T 0 0
1997–98 Luton T 0 0
1998–99 Luton T 14 0
1999–2000 Wimbledon 7 0
2000-01 Wimbledon 14 1
2001-02 Wimbledon 27 1
2002-03 Wimbledon 5 0 **53 2**
2002-03 *Luton T* 13 0 **27 0**

Scholars
Ahmed, Shahed; Boyce, Jerome; Crooks, Leon EG; Deacons, James T; E'Beyer, Mark E; Hallett, David JN; Holmes, Antony I; Jerwood, Ryan; Kamara, Malvin G; Lewington, Dean S; MacLean-Daley, Kingslee J; Martin, David E; Morgan, Daniel F; Nolan, Robert D; Oyedele, Shola; Puncheon, Jason DI; Sikora, Christopher J; Slater, Jamie R; Small, Wade K; Suleymanoglu, Ahmet; Wildy, Luke; Worgan, Lee J

WOLVERHAMPTON W

ANDREWS, Keith (M) **48 1**
H: 6 0 W: 13 05 b.Dublin 13-9-80
Source: Trainee.
1997–98 Wolverhampton W 0 0
1998–99 Wolverhampton W 0 0
1999–2000 Wolverhampton W 2 0
2000-01 Wolverhampton W 22 0
2000-01 *Oxford U* 4 1 **4 1**
2001-02 Wolverhampton W 11 0
2002-03 Wolverhampton W 9 0 **44 0**

BLAKE, Nathan (F) **423 143**
H: 5 11 W: 13 12 b.Cardiff 27-1-72
Source: Chelsea Trainee. *Honours:* Wales Youth, B, Under-21, 23 full caps, 4 goals.
1989–90 Cardiff C 6 0
1990–91 Cardiff C 40 4
1991–92 Cardiff C 31 6
1992–93 Cardiff C 34 11
1993–94 Cardiff C 20 14 **131 35**
1993–94 Sheffield U 12 5
1994–95 Sheffield U 35 17
1995–96 Sheffield U 22 12 **69 34**
1995–96 Bolton W 18 1
1996–97 Bolton W 42 19
1997–98 Bolton W 35 12
1998–99 Bolton W 12 6 **107 38**
1998–99 Blackburn R 11 3
1999–2000 Blackburn R 28 3
2000-01 Blackburn R 12 6
2001-02 Blackburn R 3 1 **54 13**
2001-02 Wolverhampton W 39 11
2002-03 Wolverhampton W 23 12 **62 23**

BRANCH, Michael* (F) **126 16**
H: 5 10 W: 11 07 b.Liverpool 18-10-78
Source: Trainee. *Honours:* England Schools, Youth, Under-21.

1995–96	Everton	3	0		
1996–97	Everton	25	3		
1997–98	Everton	6	0		
1998–99	Everton	7	0		
1998–99	*Manchester C*	4	0	**4**	**0**
1999–2000	Everton	0	0	**41**	**3**
2000-01	Wolverhampton W	38	4		
1999–2000	Wolverhampton W	27	6		
2001-02	Wolverhampton W	7	0		
2001-02	*Reading*	2	0	**2**	**0**
2002-03	Wolverhampton W	0	0	**72**	**10**
2002-03	*Hull C*	7	3	**7**	**3**

BUTLER, Paul (D) **408 19**
H: 6 0 W: 14 09 b.Manchester 2-11-72
Source: Trainee. *Honours:* Eire 1 full cap.

1990–91	Rochdale	2	0		
1991–92	Rochdale	25	0		
1992–93	Rochdale	16	2		
1993–94	Rochdale	38	2		
1994–95	Rochdale	39	3		
1995–96	Rochdale	38	3	**158**	**10**
1996–97	Bury	41	2		
1997–98	Bury	43	2	**84**	**4**
1998–99	Sunderland	44	2		
1999–2000	Sunderland	32	1		
2000-01	Sunderland	3	0	**79**	**3**
2000-01	Wolverhampton W	12	0		
2001-02	Wolverhampton W	43	1		
2002-03	Wolverhampton W	32	1	**87**	**2**

CAMARA, Mohammed* (D) **162 2**
H: 5 11 W: 11 09 b.Conakry 25-6-75

1993–94	Beauvais	19	0		
1994–95	Beauvais	0	0		
1995–96	Troyes	13	0	**13**	**0**
1996–97	Beauvais	35	0	**54**	**0**
1997–98	Le Havre	14	0		
1998–99	Lille	34	2	**34**	**2**
1999–2000	Le Havre	2	0	**16**	**0**
2000-01	Wolverhampton W	18	0		
2001-02	Wolverhampton W	27	0		
2002-03	Wolverhampton W	0	0	**45**	**0**

CAMERON, Colin (M) **351 80**
H: 5 8 W: 11 00 b.Kirkcaldy 23-10-72
Source: Lochore Welfare. *Honours:* Scotland B, 19 full caps, 2 goals.

1990–91	Raith R	0	0		
1991–92	*Sligo R*	0	0		
1992–93	Raith R	16	1		
1993–94	Raith R	41	6		
1994–95	Raith R	35	7		
1995–96	Raith R	30	9	**122**	**23**
1995–96	Hearts	4	2		
1996–97	Hearts	36	7		
1997–98	Hearts	31	8		
1998–99	Hearts	11	6		
1999–2000	Hearts	32	8		
2000-01	Hearts	37	12		
2001-02	Hearts	4	3	**155**	**46**
2001-02	Wolverhampton W	41	4		
2002-03	Wolverhampton W	33	7	**74**	**11**

CLINGAN, Sammy (M) **0 0**
H: 5 11 W: 11 06 b.Belfast 13-1-84
Source: Scholar.

2001-02	Wolverhampton W	0	0
2002-03	Wolverhampton W	0	0

CLYDE, Mark (D) **21 0**
H: 6 2 W: 12 04 b.Limavady 27-12-82
Source: Scholar. *Honours:* Northern Ireland Under-21.

2001-02	Wolverhampton W	0	0		
2002-03	Wolverhampton W	17	0	**17**	**0**
2002-03	*Kidderminster H*	4	0	**4**	**0**

COLEMAN, Kenny* (D) **15 0**
H: 6 0 W: 13 07 b.Cork 20-9-82
Source: Scholar.

2000-01	Wolverhampton W	0	0		
2001-02	Wolverhampton W	0	0		
2002-03	Wolverhampton W	0	0		
2002-03	*Kidderminster H*	15	0	**15**	**0**

COOPER, Kevin (M) **252 37**
H: 5 8 W: 10 04 b.Derby 8-2-75
Source: Trainee.

1993–94	Derby Co	0	0		
1994–95	Derby Co	1	0		
1995–96	Derby Co	1	0		
1996–97	Derby Co	0	0	**2**	**0**
1996–97	*Stockport Co*	12	3		
1997–98	Stockport Co	38	8		
1998–99	Stockport Co	38	1		
1999–2000	Stockport Co	46	4		
2000-01	Stockport Co	34	5	**168**	**21**
2000-01	Wimbledon	11	3		
2001-02	Wimbledon	40	10	**51**	**13**
2001-02	Wolverhampton W	5	0		
2002-03	Wolverhampton W	26	3	**31**	**3**

EDWORTHY, Marc* (D) **293 2**
H: 5 7 W: 9 06 b.Barnstaple 24-12-72
Source: Trainee.

1990–91	Plymouth Arg	0	0		
1991–92	Plymouth Arg	15	0		
1992–93	Plymouth Arg	15	0		
1993–94	Plymouth Arg	12	0		
1994–95	Plymouth Arg	27	1	**69**	**1**
1995–96	Crystal Palace	44	0		
1996–97	Crystal Palace	45	0		
1997–98	Crystal Palace	34	0		
1998–99	Crystal Palace	3	0	**126**	**0**
1998–99	Coventry C	22	0		
1999–2000	Coventry C	10	0		
2000-01	Coventry C	24	1		
2001-02	Coventry C	20	0	**76**	**1**
2002-03	Wolverhampton W	22	0	**22**	**0**

FLYNN, Patrick (M) **0 0**
b.Dublin 13-1-85
Source: Scholar.

2002-03	Wolverhampton W	0	0

INCE, Paul* (M) **527 63**
H: 5 10 W: 12 04 b.Ilford 21-10-67
Source: Trainee. *Honours:* England Youth, Under-21, B, 53 full caps, 2 goals.

1985–86	West Ham U	0	0		
1986–87	West Ham U	10	1		
1987–88	West Ham U	28	3		
1988–89	West Ham U	33	3		
1989–90	West Ham U	1	0	**72**	**7**
1989–90	Manchester U	26	0		
1990–91	Manchester U	31	3		
1991–92	Manchester U	33	3		
1992–93	Manchester U	41	5		
1993–94	Manchester U	39	8		
1994–95	Manchester U	36	5	**206**	**24**
1995–96	Internazionale	30	3		
1996–97	Internazionale	24	6	**54**	**9**
1997–98	Liverpool	31	8		
1998–99	Liverpool	34	6	**65**	**14**
1999–2000	Middlesbrough	32	3		
2000-01	Middlesbrough	30	2		
2001-02	Middlesbrough	31	2	**93**	**7**
2002-03	Wolverhampton W	37	2	**37**	**2**

INGIMARSSON, Ivar (D) **226 23**
H: 6 0 W: 12 07 b.Reykjavik 20-8-77
Honours: Iceland 11 full caps.

1995	Valur	12	0		
1996	Valur	17	2		
1997	Valur	16	3	**45**	**5**
1998	IBV	18	1		
1999	IBV	18	4	**36**	**5**
1999–2000	Torquay U	4	1	**4**	**1**
1999–2000	Brentford	25	1		
2000-01	Brentford	42	3		
2001-02	Brentford	46	6	**113**	**10**
2002-03	Wolverhampton W	13	2	**13**	**2**
2002-03	*Brighton & HA*	15	0	**15**	**0**

IRWIN, Denis# (D) **650 29**
H: 5 8 W: 10 10 b.Cork 31-10-65
Source: Apprentice. *Honours:* Eire Schools, Youth, Under-21, B, 56 full caps, 4 goals.

1983–84	Leeds U	12	0		
1984–85	Leeds U	41	1		
1985–86	Leeds U	19	0	**72**	**1**
1986–87	Oldham Ath	41	1		
1987–88	Oldham Ath	43	0		
1988–89	Oldham Ath	41	2		
1989–90	Oldham Ath	42	1	**167**	**4**
1990–91	Manchester U	34	0		
1991–92	Manchester U	38	4		
1992–93	Manchester U	40	5		
1993–94	Manchester U	42	2		
1994–95	Manchester U	40	2		
1995–96	Manchester U	31	1		
1996–97	Manchester U	31	1		
1997–98	Manchester U	25	2		
1998–99	Manchester U	29	2		
1999–2000	Manchester U	25	3		
2000-01	Manchester U	21	0		
2001-02	Manchester U	12	0	**368**	**22**
2002-03	Wolverhampton W	43	2	**43**	**2**

JONES, Jimmi (M) **0 0**
b.Wolverhampton 11-11-83
Source: Scholar.

2002-03	Wolverhampton W	0	0

KENNEDY, Mark (M) **220 27**
H: 5 11 W: 11 09 b.Dublin 15-5-76
Source: Belvedere, Trainee. *Honours:* Eire Under-21, 34 full caps, 3 goals.

1992–93	Millwall	1	0		
1993–94	Millwall	12	4		
1994–95	Millwall	30	5	**43**	**9**
1994–95	Liverpool	6	0		
1995–96	Liverpool	4	0		
1996–97	Liverpool	5	0		
1997–98	Liverpool	1	0	**16**	**0**
1997–98	*QPR*	8	2	**8**	**2**
1997–98	Wimbledon	4	0		
1998–99	Wimbledon	17	0	**21**	**0**
1999–2000	Manchester C	41	8		
2000-01	Manchester C	25	0	**66**	**8**
2001-02	Wolverhampton W	35	5		
2002-03	Wolverhampton W	31	3	**66**	**8**

LESCOTT, Jolean (D) **125 8**
H: 6 2 W: 14 00 b.Birmingham 16-8-82
Source: Trainee. *Honours:* England Youth, Under-20, Under-21.

1999–2000	Wolverhampton W	0	0		
2000-01	Wolverhampton W	37	2		
2001-02	Wolverhampton W	44	5		
2002-03	Wolverhampton W	44	1	**125**	**8**

McCHRYSTAL, Mark‡ (D) **0 0**
H: 6 1 W: 13 07 b.Derry 25-6-84
Source: Scholar.

2001-02	Wolverhampton W	0	0
2002-03	Wolverhampton W	0	0

McGRANE, Ian (M) **0 0**
H: 5 10 W: 12 00 b.Dublin 4-8-84
Source: Scholar.

2001-02	Wolverhampton W	0	0
2002-03	Wolverhampton W	0	0

MELLIGAN, John (M) **39 10**
H: 5 9 W: 11 02 b.Dublin 11-2-82
Source: Trainee. *Honours:* Eire Under-21.

2000-01	Wolverhampton W	0	0		
2001-02	Wolverhampton W	0	0		
2001-02	*Bournemouth*	8	0	**8**	**0**
2002-03	Wolverhampton W	2	0	**2**	**0**
2002-03	*Kidderminster H*	29	10	**29**	**10**

MILLER, Kenny (F) **138 41**
H: 5 10 W: 11 04 b.Edinburgh 23-12-79
Source: Hutchison Vale. *Honours:* Scotland Under-21, 5 full caps, 2 goals..

1996–97	Hibernian	0	0		
1997–98	Hibernian	7	0		
1998–99	Hibernian	7	1		
1999–2000	Hibernian	31	11	**45**	**12**
2000-01	Rangers	27	8		
2001-02	Rangers	3	0	**30**	**8**
2001-02	Wolverhampton W	20	2		
2002-03	Wolverhampton W	43	19	**63**	**21**

MULLIGAN, Gary (M) **0 0**
b.Dublin 23-4-85
Source: Scholar.

2002-03	Wolverhampton W	0	0

MURRAY, Matt (G) **40 0**
H: 6 4 W: 13 10 b.Solihull 2-5-81
Source: Trainee. *Honours:* England Youth, Under-21.

1997–98	Wolverhampton W	0	0		
1998–99	Wolverhampton W	0	0		
1999–2000	Wolverhampton W	0	0		
2000-01	Wolverhampton W	0	0		
2001-02	Wolverhampton W	0	0		
2002-03	Wolverhampton W	40	0	**40**	**0**

NAYLOR, Lee (D) **174 5**
H: 5 10 W: 12 00 b.Bloxwich 19-3-80
Source: Trainee. *Honours:* England Youth, Under-21.

1997–98	Wolverhampton W	16	0		
1998–99	Wolverhampton W	23	1		
1999–2000	Wolverhampton W	30	2		
2000-01	Wolverhampton W	46	1		
2001-02	Wolverhampton W	27	0		
2002-03	Wolverhampton W	32	1	**174**	**5**

NDAH, George (F) **234 38**
H: 6 1 W: 12 06 b.Dulwich 23-12-74
Source: Trainee.

1992–93	Crystal Palace	13	0
1993–94	Crystal Palace	1	0
1994–95	Crystal Palace	12	1

1995–96 Crystal Palace 23 4
1995–96 *Bournemouth* 12 2 **12 2**
1996–97 Crystal Palace 26 3
1997–98 Crystal Palace 3 0 **78 8**
1997–98 *Gillingham* 4 0 **4 0**
1997–98 Swindon T 14 2
1998–99 Swindon T 41 11
1999–2000 Swindon T 12 1 **67 14**
1999–2000 Wolverhampton W 4 0
2000-01 Wolverhampton W 29 6
2001-02 Wolverhampton W 15 1
2002-03 Wolverhampton W 25 7 **73 14**

NEWTON, Shaun (M) 318 31
H: 5 8 W: 11 00 b.Camberwell 20-8-75
Source: Trainee. *Honours:* England Under-21.
1992–93 Charlton Ath 2 0
1993–94 Charlton Ath 19 2
1994–95 Charlton Ath 26 0
1995–96 Charlton Ath 41 5
1996–97 Charlton Ath 43 3
1997–98 Charlton Ath 41 5
1998–99 Charlton Ath 16 0
1999–2000 Charlton Ath 42 5
2000-01 Charlton Ath 10 0 **240 20**
2001-02 Wolverhampton W 45 8
2002-03 Wolverhampton W 33 3 **78 11**

OAKES, Michael (G) 178 0
H: 6 2 W: 14 00 b.Northwich 30-10-73
Source: Trainee. *Honours:* England Under-21.
1991–92 Aston Villa 0 0
1992–93 Aston Villa 0 0
1993–94 Aston Villa 0 0
1993–94 *Scarborough* 1 0 **1 0**
1993–94 *Tranmere R* 0 0
1994–95 Aston Villa 0 0
1995–96 Aston Villa 0 0
1996–97 Aston Villa 20 0
1997–98 Aston Villa 8 0
1998–99 Aston Villa 23 0
1999–2000 Aston Villa 0 0 **51 0**
1999–2000 Wolverhampton W 28 0
2000-01 Wolverhampton W 46 0
2001-02 Wolverhampton W 46 0
2002-03 Wolverhampton W 6 0 **126 0**

POLLET, Ludovic* (D) 223 10
H: 5 11 W: 11 07 b.Vieux-conde 18-6-70
1991–92 Cannes 9 0
1992–93 Cannes 6 0
1993–94 Cannes 8 1
1994–95 Cannes 15 2 **38 3**
1995–96 Le Havre 26 0
1996–97 Le Havre 21 0
1997–98 Le Havre 34 0
1998–99 Le Havre 21 0 **102 0**
1999–2000 Wolverhampton W 39 5
2000-01 Wolverhampton W 29 2
2001-02 Wolverhampton W 8 0
2002-03 Wolverhampton W 2 0 **78 7**
2002-03 *Walsall* 5 0 **5 0**

PROUDLOCK, Adam (F) 88 19
H: 6 0 W: 13 07 b.Wellington 9-5-81
Source: Trainee.
1999–2000 Wolverhampton W 0 0
2000-01 *Clyde* 4 4 **4 4**
2000-01 Wolverhampton W 35 8
2001-02 Wolverhampton W 19 3
2001-02 *Nottingham F* 3 0 **3 0**
2002-03 Wolverhampton W 17 2 **71 13**
2002-03 *Tranmere R* 5 0 **5 0**
2002-03 *Sheffield W* 5 2 **5 2**

RAE, Alex (M) 489 105
H: 5 10 W: 11 09 b.Glasgow 30-9-69
Source: Bishopbriggs. *Honours:* Scotland Under-21, B.
1987–88 Falkirk 12 0
1988–89 Falkirk 37 12
1989–90 Falkirk 34 8 **83 20**
1990–91 Millwall 39 10
1991–92 Millwall 38 11
1992–93 Millwall 30 6
1993–94 Millwall 36 13
1994–95 Millwall 38 10
1995–96 Millwall 37 13 **218 63**
1996–97 Sunderland 23 2
1997–98 Sunderland 29 3
1998–99 Sunderland 15 2
1999–2000 Sunderland 26 3
2000-01 Sunderland 18 2
2001-02 Sunderland 3 0 **114 12**
2001-02 Wolverhampton W 36 7
2002-03 Wolverhampton W 38 3 **74 10**

ROUSSEL, Cedric (F) 100 21
H: 6 3 W: 13 12 b.Mons 6-1-78
Honours: La Louviere.
1998–99 Gent 31 8
1999–2000 Gent 4 3 **35 11**
1999–2000 Coventry C 22 6
2000-01 Coventry C 17 2 **39 8**
2000-01 Wolverhampton W 9 0
2001-02 Wolverhampton W 17 2
2002-03 Wolverhampton W 0 0 **26 2**

STURRIDGE, Dean (F) 288 94
H: 5 8 W: 12 02 b.Birmingham 27-7-73
Source: Trainee.
1991–92 Derby Co 1 0
1992–93 Derby Co 10 0
1993–94 Derby Co 0 0
1994–95 Derby Co 12 1
1994–95 *Torquay U* 10 5 **10 5**
1995–96 Derby Co 39 20
1996–97 Derby Co 30 11
1997–98 Derby Co 30 9
1998–99 Derby Co 29 5
1999–2000 Derby Co 25 6
2000-01 Derby Co 14 1 **190 53**
2000-01 Leicester C 13 3
2001-02 Leicester C 9 3 **22 6**
2001-02 Wolverhampton W 27 20
2002-03 Wolverhampton W 39 10 **66 30**

WARD, Graham* (M) 0 0
H: 5 8 W: 11 09 b.Dublin 25-2-83
Source: Scholar. *Honours:* Eire Under-21.
2000-01 Wolverhampton W 0 0
2001-02 Wolverhampton W 0 0
2002-03 Wolverhampton W 0 0

Scholars
Barnes-Homer, Matt; Bonnar, Thomas; Bradley, Luke D; Brown, Scott; Clarke, Leon M; Fitter, John A; Gobern, Lewis; Goodhead, Mark; Ikeme, Carl; Lowe, Keith S; Mahon, Ryan; O'Connor, Kevin JA; Steele, Jonathan; Talbott, Nathan; Townsend, Michael J; Vincent, Ashley D; Walters, Marlon J; Watson, Matthew G
Associated Schoolboys
Clark, David; Rollins, Mark

WREXHAM

BARRETT, Paul# (M) 93 3
H: 5 10 W: 11 04 b.Newcastle 13-4-78
Source: Trainee.
1996–97 Newcastle U 0 0
1997–98 Newcastle U 0 0
1998–99 Newcastle U 0 0
1998–99 Wrexham 10 0
1999–2000 Wrexham 18 2
2000-01 Wrexham 24 0
2001-02 Wrexham 15 0
2002-03 Wrexham 26 1 **93 3**

BENNETT, Dan* (D) 24 0
H: 6 1 W: 12 05 b.Great Yarmouth 7-1-78
Source: Balestier Central, Tanjong Pagar. *Honours:* Singapore full caps.
2001-02 Wrexham 6 0
2002-03 Wrexham 18 0 **24 0**

CAREY, Brian# (D) 318 15
H: 6 3 W: 13 02 b.Cork 31-5-68
Source: Cork C. *Honours:* Eire 3 full caps.
1989–90 Manchester U 0 0
1990–91 Manchester U 0 0
1990–91 *Wrexham* 3 0
1991–92 Manchester U 0 0
1991–92 *Wrexham* 13 1
1992–93 Manchester U 0 0
1993–94 Leicester C 27 0
1994–95 Leicester C 12 0
1995–96 Leicester C 19 1 **58 1**
1996–97 Wrexham 38 0
1997–98 Wrexham 43 1
1998–99 Wrexham 36 2
1999–2000 Wrexham 43 1
2000-01 Wrexham 33 3
2001-02 Wrexham 18 2
2002-03 Wrexham 33 4 **260 14**

DIBBLE, Andy# (G) 344 0
H: 6 2 W: 16 07 b.Cwmbran 8-5-65
Source: Apprentice. *Honours:* Wales Schools, Youth, Under-21, 3 full caps.
1981–82 Cardiff C 1 0
1982–83 Cardiff C 20 0
1983–84 Cardiff C 41 0 **62 0**
1984–85 Luton T 13 0
1985–86 Luton T 7 0
1985–86 *Sunderland* 12 0 **12 0**
1986–87 Luton T 1 0
1986–87 *Huddersfield T* 5 0 **5 0**
1987–88 Luton T 9 0
1988–89 Manchester C 38 0
1989–90 Manchester C 31 0
1990–91 Manchester C 3 0
1990–91 *Aberdeen* 5 0 **5 0**
1990–91 *Middlesbrough* 19 0
1991–92 Manchester C 2 0
1991–92 *Bolton W* 13 0 **13 0**
1991–92 *WBA* 9 0 **9 0**
1992–93 Manchester C 2 0
1992–93 *Oldham Ath* 0 0
1993–94 Manchester C 11 0
1994–95 Manchester C 15 0
1995–96 Manchester C 0 0
1996–97 Manchester C 13 0 **115 0**
1996–97 Rangers 7 0 **7 0**
1997–98 Luton T 1 0 **31 0**
1997–98 Middlesbrough 2 0
1998–99 Middlesbrough 0 0 **21 0**
From Altrincham
1998–99 Hartlepool U 0 0
1999–2000 Hartlepool U 6 0 **6 0**
1999–2000 *Carlisle U* 2 0 **2 0**
2000-01 Stockport Co 10 0
2001-02 Stockport Co 13 0 **23 0**
2002-03 Wrexham 33 0 **33 0**

EDWARDS, Carlos (F) 106 17
H: 5 11 W: 11 01 b.Trinidad 24-10-78
Honours: Trinidad & Tobago 2 full caps.
2000-01 Wrexham 36 4
2001-02 Wrexham 26 5
2002-03 Wrexham 44 8 **106 17**

EDWARDS, Paul (M) 58 4
H: 5 11 W: 10 12 b.Manchester 1-1-80
Source: Altrincham. *Honours:* Trinidad 2 full caps.
2001-02 Swindon T 20 0 **20 0**
2002-03 Wrexham 38 4 **38 4**

EVANS, Mark§ (F) 5 0
H: 6 1 W: 11 02 b.Chester 16-9-82
Source: Scholar.
2001-02 Wrexham 4 0
2002-03 Wrexham 1 0 **5 0**

FERGUSON, Darren (M) 303 22
H: 5 10 W: 11 10 b.Glasgow 9-2-72
Source: Trainee. *Honours:* Scotland Youth, Under-21.
1990–91 Manchester U 5 0
1991–92 Manchester U 4 0
1992–93 Manchester U 15 0
1993–94 Manchester U 3 0 **27 0**
1993–94 Wolverhampton W 14 0
1994–95 Wolverhampton W 24 0
1995–96 Wolverhampton W 33 1
1996–97 Wolverhampton W 16 3
1997–98 Wolverhampton W 26 0
1998–99 Wolverhampton W 4 0
1999–2000 Wolverhampton W 0 0 **117 4**
1999–2000 Wrexham 37 4
2000-01 Wrexham 43 9
2001-02 Wrexham 38 3
2002-03 Wrexham 41 2 **159 18**

GREEN, Scott# (D) 434 38
H: 5 10 W: 12 05 b.Walsall 15-1-70
Source: Trainee.
1988–89 Derby Co 0 0
1989–90 Derby Co 0 0
1989–90 Bolton W 5 2
1990–91 Bolton W 41 6
1991–92 Bolton W 37 2
1992–93 Bolton W 41 6
1993–94 Bolton W 22 4
1994–95 Bolton W 31 1
1995–96 Bolton W 31 3
1996–97 Bolton W 12 1 **220 25**
1997–98 Wigan Ath 38 1
1998–99 Wigan Ath 37 0
1999–2000 Wigan Ath 33 2
2000-01 Wigan Ath 35 2

2001-02 Wigan Ath 39 3
2002-03 Wigan Ath 17 2 **199 10**
2002-03 Wrexham 15 3 **15 3**

HOLMES, Shaun (D) 70 0
H: 5 9 W: 10 07 b.Derry 27-12-80
Source: Trainee. *Honours:* Northern Ireland Under-21, 1 full cap.
1997–98 Manchester C 0 0
1998–99 Manchester C 0 0
1999–2000 Manchester C 0 0
2000-01 Manchester C 0 0
2001-02 Wrexham 40 0
2002-03 Wrexham 30 0 **70 0**

JONES, Lee (F) 229 50
H: 5 8 W: 10 06 b.Wrexham 29-5-73
Source: Trainee. *Honours:* Wales Youth, Under-21, B, 2 full caps.
1990–91 Wrexham 18 5
1991–92 Wrexham 21 5
1991–92 Liverpool 0 0
1992–93 Liverpool 0 0
1993–94 Liverpool 0 0
1993–94 *Crewe Alex* 8 1 **8 1**
1994–95 Liverpool 1 0
1995–96 Liverpool 0 0
1995–96 *Wrexham* 20 9
1996–97 Liverpool 2 0 **3 0**
1996–97 *Wrexham* 6 0
1996–97 *Tranmere R* 8 5
1997–98 Tranmere R 34 9
1998–99 Tranmere R 30 2
1999–2000 Tranmere R 14 0 **86 16**
2000-01 Barnsley 27 5
2001-02 Barnsley 13 0 **40 5**
From Oswestry T
2001-02 Wrexham 4 5
2002-03 Wrexham 23 4 **92 28**

JONES, Mark§ (M) 1 0
H: 5 11 W: 12 00 b.Wrexham 15-8-83
Source: Scholar.
2002-03 Wrexham 1 0 **1 0**

LAWRENCE, Dennis (D) 67 3
H: 6 7 W: 11 13 b.Trinidad 1-8-74
Source: Defence Force. *Honours:* Trinidad & Tobago 34 full caps.
2000-01 Wrexham 3 0
2001-02 Wrexham 32 2
2002-03 Wrexham 32 1 **67 3**

MORGAN, Craig§ (D) 8 1
H: 6 0 W: 11 06 b.St Asaph 16-6-85
Source: Scholar.
2001-02 Wrexham 2 0
2002-03 Wrexham 6 1 **8 1**

MORRELL, Andy# (F) 110 40
H: 5 11 W: 11 06 b.Doncaster 28-9-74
Source: Newcastle Blue Star.
1998–99 Wrexham 7 0
1999–2000 Wrexham 13 1
2000-01 Wrexham 20 3
2001-02 Wrexham 25 2
2002-03 Wrexham 45 34 **110 40**

PEJIC, Shaun (D) 40 0
H: 6 0 W: 11 07 b.Hereford 16-11-82
Honours: Wales Under-21.
2000-01 Wrexham 1 0
2001-02 Wrexham 12 0
2002-03 Wrexham 27 0 **40 0**

PHILLIPS, Wayne‡ (M) 267 18
H: 5 11 W: 11 00 b.Bangor 15-12-70
Source: Trainee. *Honours:* Wales B.
1989–90 Wrexham 5 0
1990–91 Wrexham 28 0
1991–92 Wrexham 30 3
1992–93 Wrexham 15 0
1993–94 Wrexham 21 1
1994–95 Wrexham 18 1
1995–96 Wrexham 44 5
1996–97 Wrexham 26 5
1997–98 Wrexham 20 1
1997–98 Stockport Co 13 0
1998–99 Stockport Co 9 0 **22 0**
1999–2000 Wrexham 3 0
2000-01 Wrexham 7 1
2001-02 Wrexham 27 1
2002-03 Wrexham 1 0 **245 18**

ROBERTS, Steve (D) 89 3
H: 6 2 W: 11 06 b.Wrexham 24-2-80
Source: Trainee. *Honours:* Wales Youth, Under-21.
1997–98 Wrexham 0 0
1998–99 Wrexham 0 0
1999–2000 Wrexham 19 0
2000-01 Wrexham 7 0
2001-02 Wrexham 24 1
2002-03 Wrexham 39 2 **89 3**

ROGERS, Kristian* (G) 40 0
H: 6 0 W: 11 12 b.Chester 2-10-80
Honours: England Schools.
1999–2000 Wrexham 1 0
2000-01 Wrexham 5 0
2001-02 Wrexham 27 0
2002-03 Wrexham 7 0 **40 0**

RUSSELL, Kevin‡ (M) 456 88
H: 5 9 W: 10 12 b.Portsmouth 6-12-66
Source: Brighton & HA Apprentice. *Honours:* England Youth.
1984–85 Portsmouth 0 0
1985–86 Portsmouth 1 0
1986–87 Portsmouth 3 1 **4 1**
1987–88 Wrexham 38 21
1988–89 Wrexham 46 22
1989–90 Leicester C 10 0
1990–91 Leicester C 13 5
1990–91 *Peterborough U* 7 3 **7 3**
1990–91 *Cardiff C* 3 0 **3 0**
1991–92 Leicester C 20 5 **43 10**
1991–92 *Hereford U* 3 1 **3 1**
1991–92 *Stoke C* 5 1
1992–93 Stoke C 40 5 **45 6**
1993–94 Burnley 28 6 **28 6**
1993–94 Bournemouth 17 1
1994–95 Bournemouth 13 0 **30 1**
1994–95 Notts Co 11 0 **11 0**
1995–96 Wrexham 40 7
1996–97 Wrexham 41 0
1997–98 Wrexham 16 0
1998–99 Wrexham 31 2
1999–2000 Wrexham 33 4
2000-01 Wrexham 26 4
2001-02 Wrexham 10 0
2002-03 Wrexham 1 0 **282 60**

SAM, Hector (F) 75 16
H: 5 9 W: 11 05 b.Trinidad 25-2-78
Source: San Juan Jabloteh. *Honours:* Trinidad & Tobago 14 full caps, 1 goal.
2000-01 Wrexham 20 6
2001-02 Wrexham 29 5
2002-03 Wrexham 26 5 **75 16**

THOMAS, Steve (M) 75 5
H: 5 10 W: 11 07 b.Hartlepool 23-6-79
Source: Trainee. *Honours:* Wales Youth, Under-21.
1997–98 Wrexham 0 0
1998–99 Wrexham 4 0
1999–2000 Wrexham 2 0
2000-01 Wrexham 6 0
2001-02 Wrexham 38 3
2002-03 Wrexham 25 2 **75 5**

TRUNDLE, Lee# (F) 94 27
H: 6 0 W: 11 11 b.Liverpool 10-10-76
Source: Rhyl.
2000-01 Wrexham 14 8
2001-02 Wrexham 36 8
2002-03 Wrexham 44 11 **94 27**

WHITFIELD, Paul (G) 8 0
H: 6 0 W: 12 00 b.St Asaph 6-5-82
Source: Scholar. *Honours:* wales Under-21.
2001-02 Wrexham 0 0
2002-03 Wrexham 8 0 **8 0**

WHITLEY, Jim# (D) 147 2
H: 5 9 W: 10 12 b.Zambia 14-4-75
Source: Trainee. *Honours:* Northern Ireland B, 3 full caps.
1993–94 Manchester C 0 0
1994–95 Manchester C 0 0
1995–96 Manchester C 0 0
1996–97 Manchester C 0 0
1997–98 Manchester C 19 0
1998–99 Manchester C 18 0
1999–2000 Manchester C 1 0
1999–2000 *Blackpool* 8 0 **8 0**
2000-01 Manchester C 0 0 **38 0**
2000-01 *Norwich C* 8 1 **8 1**
2000-01 *Swindon T* 2 0 **2 0**
2000-01 *Northampton T* 13 0 **13 0**
2000-01 *Nottingham F* 0 0
2001-02 Wrexham 34 0
2002-03 Wrexham 44 1 **78 1**

Scholars
Dabbs, Matthew S; Evans, Daniel; Jones, Mark A; Jones, Osian L; Leather, Wayne M; Mackin, Levi; McNulty, Jimmy; Morgan, Craig; Owen, Dylan; Parry, Christopher D; Quinn, Kieran F; Spender, Simon; Stacey, Alec J; Sudlow, Gareth GL

WYCOMBE W

BROWN, Steve# (M) 504 53
H: 5 10 W: 11 12 b.Northampton 6-7-66
1985–86 Northampton T 0 0
From Irthlingborough D
1989–90 Northampton T 21 1
1990–91 Northampton T 40 2
1991–92 Northampton T 35 3
1992–93 Northampton T 38 9
1993–94 Northampton T 24 4 **158 19**
1993–94 Wycombe W 9 2
1994–95 Wycombe W 40 1
1995–96 Wycombe W 38 0
1996–97 Wycombe W 34 5
1997–98 Wycombe W 40 3
1998–99 Wycombe W 38 3
1999–2000 Wycombe W 39 3
2000-01 Wycombe W 32 4
2001-02 Wycombe W 39 8
2002-03 Wycombe W 37 5 **346 34**

BULMAN, Dannie (M) 164 14
H: 5 9 W: 11 12 b.Ashford 24-1-79
Source: Ashford T.
1998–99 Wycombe W 11 1
1999–2000 Wycombe W 29 1
2000-01 Wycombe W 36 4
2001-02 Wycombe W 46 5
2002-03 Wycombe W 42 3 **164 14**

COOK, Lewis (M) 17 0
H: 5 7 W: 11 01 b.High Wycombe 28-12-83
Source: Scholar.
2002-03 Wycombe W 17 0 **17 0**

CURRIE, Darren (M) 311 36
H: 5 10 W: 12 07 b.Hampstead 29-11-74
Source: Trainee.
1993–94 West Ham U 0 0
1994–95 West Ham U 0 0
1994–95 *Shrewsbury T* 17 2
1995–96 West Ham U 0 0
1995–96 *Leyton Orient* 10 0 **10 0**
1995–96 Shrewsbury T 13 2
1996–97 Shrewsbury T 37 2
1997–98 Shrewsbury T 16 4 **83 10**
1997–98 Plymouth Arg 7 0 **7 0**
1998–99 Barnet 38 4
1999–2000 Barnet 44 5
2000-01 Barnet 45 10 **127 19**
2001-02 Wycombe W 46 3
2002-03 Wycombe W 38 4 **84 7**

DIXON, Jonny (F) 22 5
H: 5 9 W: 11 01 b.Murcia 16-1-84
Source: Scholar.
2002-03 Wycombe W 22 5 **22 5**

FAULCONBRIDGE, Craig (F) 168 38
H: 6 1 W: 13 00 b.Nuneaton 20-4-78
Source: Trainee.
1996–97 Coventry C 0 0
1997–98 Coventry C 0 0
1997–98 Dunfermline Ath 7 1
1998–99 Dunfermline Ath 6 0 **13 1**
1998–99 *Hull C* 10 0 **10 0**
1999–2000 Wrexham 35 8
2000-01 Wrexham 39 10
2001-02 Wrexham 37 13 **111 31**
2002-03 Wycombe W 34 6 **34 6**

HARRIS, Richard (F) 40 5
H: 5 11 W: 10 09 b.Croydon 23-10-80
Source: Trainee.
1997–98 Crystal Palace 0 0
1998–99 Crystal Palace 1 0
1999–2000 Crystal Palace 6 0
2000-01 Crystal Palace 2 0
2001-02 Crystal Palace 0 0 **9 0**
2001-02 *Mansfield T* 6 0 **6 0**
2001-02 Wycombe W 3 0
2002-03 Wycombe W 22 5 **25 5**

HOLLIGAN, Gavin (F) 35 6
H: 5 10 W: 13 00 b.Lambeth 30-6-80
Source: Kingstonian.
1998–99 West Ham U 1 0

1999–2000 West Ham U 0 0
1999–2000 *Leyton Orient* 1 0 **1 0**
2000-01 West Ham U 0 0 **1 0**
2000-01 *Exeter C* 3 0 **3 0**
2001-02 Wycombe W 20 4
2002-03 Wycombe W 10 2 **30 6**

JOHNSON, Roger (D) 42 4
H: 6 3 W: 11 00 b.Ashford 28-4-83
Source: Trainee.
1999–2000 Wycombe W 1 0
2000-01 Wycombe W 1 0
2001-02 Wycombe W 7 1
2002-03 Wycombe W 33 3 **42 4**

LEE, Martyn‡ (M) 46 3
H: 5 6 W: 9 00 b.Guildford 10-8-80
Source: Trainee.
1998–99 Wycombe W 3 0
1999–2000 Wycombe W 4 0
2000-01 Wycombe W 21 3
2001-02 Wycombe W 7 0
2001-02 *Cheltenham T* 5 0 **5 0**
2002-03 Wycombe W 6 0 **41 3**

McCARTHY, Paul* (D) 399 16
H: 5 10 W: 13 10 b.Cork 4-8-71
Source: Trainee. *Honours:* Eire Youth, Under-21.
1989–90 Brighton & HA 3 0
1990–91 Brighton & HA 21 0
1991–92 Brighton & HA 20 0
1992–93 Brighton & HA 30 0
1993–94 Brighton & HA 37 3
1994–95 Brighton & HA 37 2
1995–96 Brighton & HA 33 1 **181 6**
1996–97 Wycombe W 40 0
1997–98 Wycombe W 31 1
1998–99 Wycombe W 29 1
1999–2000 Wycombe W 22 1
2000-01 Wycombe W 38 2
2001-02 Wycombe W 28 3
2002-03 Wycombe W 24 1 **212 9**
2002-03 *Oxford U* 6 1 **6 1**

McCLURG, James (M) 0 0
b.Ascot 10-10-85
2002-03 Wycombe W 0 0

McSPORRAN, Jermaine (M) 125 23
H: 5 10 W: 10 12 b.Manchester 1-1-77
Source: Oxford C.
1998–99 Wycombe W 26 4
1999–2000 Wycombe W 38 9
2000-01 Wycombe W 20 2
2001-02 Wycombe W 32 7
2002-03 Wycombe W 9 1 **125 23**

OLIVER, Luke (M) 2 0
H: 6 6 W: 14 05 b.Hammersmith 1-5-84
2002-03 Wycombe W 2 0 **2 0**

OSBORN, Mark‡ (G) 1 0
H: 6 0 W: 14 01 b.Bletchley 19-6-81
Source: Trainee.
1998–99 Wycombe W 0 0
1999–2000 Wycombe W 1 0
2000-01 Wycombe W 0 0
2001-02 Wycombe W 0 0
2002-03 Wycombe W 0 0 **1 0**

ROBERTS, Stuart (F) 146 18
H: 5 6 W: 9 08 b.Carmarthen 22-7-80
Source: Trainee. *Honours:* Wales Under-21.
1998–99 Swansea C 32 3
1999–2000 Swansea C 11 1
2000-01 Swansea C 36 5
2001-02 Swansea C 13 5 **92 14**
2001-02 Wycombe W 26 0
2002-03 Wycombe W 28 4 **54 4**

ROGERS, Mark (D) 124 4
H: 5 11 W: 12 12 b.Geulph 3-11-78
Honours: Canada 5 full caps.
1998–99 Wycombe W 0 0
1999–2000 Wycombe W 25 0
2000-01 Wycombe W 22 1
2001-02 Wycombe W 41 2
2002-03 Wycombe W 36 1 **124 4**

RYAN, Keith# (M) 296 26
H: 5 10 W: 12 06 b.Northampton 25-6-70
Source: Berkhamsted T.
1993–94 Wycombe W 42 1
1994–95 Wycombe W 24 4
1995–96 Wycombe W 23 4
1996–97 Wycombe W 0 0
1997–98 Wycombe W 40 3
1998–99 Wycombe W 28 1
1999–2000 Wycombe W 38 6
2000-01 Wycombe W 30 4
2001-02 Wycombe W 35 1
2002-03 Wycombe W 36 2 **296 26**

SENDA, Danny (D) 148 5
H: 5 10 W: 10 02 b.Harrow 17-4-81
Source: Southampton Trainee. *Honours:* England Youth.
1998–99 Wycombe W 6 0
1999–2000 Wycombe W 27 1
2000-01 Wycombe W 31 2
2001-02 Wycombe W 43 0
2002-03 Wycombe W 41 2 **148 5**

SIMPEMBA, Ian (M) 1 0
H: 6 2 W: 12 08 b.Dublin 28-3-83
Source: Scholar.
2001-02 Wycombe W 0 0
2002-03 Wycombe W 1 0 **1 0**

SIMPSON, Michael (M) 308 17
H: 5 8 W: 11 07 b.Nottingham 28-2-74
Source: Trainee.
1992–93 Notts Co 0 0
1993–94 Notts Co 6 1
1994–95 Notts Co 19 2
1995–96 Notts Co 23 0
1996–97 Notts Co 1 0 **49 3**
1996–97 *Plymouth Arg* 12 0 **12 0**
1996–97 Wycombe W 20 1
1997–98 Wycombe W 21 0
1998–99 Wycombe W 33 4
1999–2000 Wycombe W 43 0
2000-01 Wycombe W 45 3
2001-02 Wycombe W 43 1
2002-03 Wycombe W 42 5 **247 14**

TALIA, Frank (G) 176 0
H: 6 1 W: 13 06 b.Melbourne 20-7-72
Honours: Australia Under-20.
1990–91 Sunshine 11 0
1991–92 Sunshine 0 0 **11 0**
1992–93 Blackburn R 0 0
1992–93 *Hartlepool U* 14 0 **14 0**
1993–94 Blackburn R 0 0
1994–95 Blackburn R 0 0
1995–96 Blackburn R 0 0
1995–96 Swindon T 16 0
1996–97 Swindon T 15 0
1997–98 Swindon T 2 0
1998–99 Swindon T 43 0
1999–2000 Swindon T 31 0 **107 0**
2000-01 Wolverhampton W 0 0
2000-01 Sheffield U 6 0 **6 0**
2001-02 Antwerp 3 0 **3 0**
2001-02 Reading 0 0
2002-03 Wycombe W 35 0 **35 0**

TAYLOR, Martin (G) 362 0
H: 6 0 W: 13 11 b.Tamworth 9-12-66
Source: Mile Oak R.
1986–87 Derby Co 0 0
1987–88 Derby Co 0 0
1987–88 *Carlisle U* 10 0 **10 0**
1987–88 *Scunthorpe U* 8 0 **8 0**
1988–89 Derby Co 0 0
1989–90 Derby Co 3 0
1990–91 Derby Co 7 0
1991–92 Derby Co 5 0
1992–93 Derby Co 21 0
1993–94 Derby Co 46 0
1994–95 Derby Co 12 0
1995–96 Derby Co 0 0
1996–97 Derby Co 3 0 **97 0**
1996–97 *Crewe Alex* 6 0 **6 0**
1996–97 *Wycombe W* 4 0
1997–98 Wycombe W 45 0
1998–99 Wycombe W 44 0
1999–2000 Wycombe W 42 0
2000-01 Wycombe W 46 0
2001-02 Wycombe W 46 0
2002-03 Wycombe W 11 0 **238 0**
2002-03 *Barnsley* 3 0 **3 0**

THOMSON, Andy (D) 281 10
H: 6 3 W: 14 03 b.Swindon 28-3-74
Source: Trainee.
1992–93 Swindon T 0 0
1993–94 Swindon T 1 0
1994–95 Swindon T 21 0
1995–96 Swindon T 0 0 **22 0**
1995–96 Portsmouth 16 0
1996–97 Portsmouth 28 1
1997–98 Portsmouth 35 2
1998–99 Portsmouth 14 0 **93 3**
1998–99 Bristol R 21 1
1999–2000 Bristol R 43 3
2000-01 Bristol R 32 1
2001-02 Bristol R 31 1 **127 6**
2001-02 Wycombe W 3 0
2002-03 Wycombe W 36 1 **39 1**

TOWNSEND, Ben‡ (D) 13 0
H: 5 10 W: 11 03 b.Reading 8-10-81
Source: Scholar.
1999–2000 Wycombe W 1 0
2000-01 Wycombe W 10 0
2001-02 Wycombe W 2 0
2002-03 Wycombe W 0 0 **13 0**

VINNICOMBE, Chris (D) 342 7
H: 5 9 W: 10 12 b.Exeter 20-10-70
Source: Trainee. *Honours:* England Under-21.
1988–89 Exeter C 25 0
1989–90 Exeter C 14 1 **39 1**
1989–90 Rangers 7 0
1990–91 Rangers 10 1
1991–92 Rangers 2 0
1992–93 Rangers 0 0
1993–94 Rangers 4 0 **23 1**
1994–95 Burnley 29 1
1995–96 Burnley 35 2
1996–97 Burnley 8 0
1997–98 Burnley 23 0 **95 3**
1998–99 Wycombe W 41 0
1999–2000 Wycombe W 35 0
2000-01 Wycombe W 42 1
2001-02 Wycombe W 42 1
2002-03 Wycombe W 25 0 **185 2**

WILLIAMS, Steve (G) 0 0
b.Oxford 21-4-83
Source: Scholar.
2001-02 Wycombe W 0 0
2002-03 Wycombe W 0 0

Scholars
Boland, Mark L; Fox, Matthew W; Gordon, Leon; Gott, Tom P; Griffiths, Nathaniel R; Harding, Billy; Heggie, Matthew; Hole, Stuart M; Kelly, John P; Lynott, Patrick J; Parsons, Ryan D; Philo, Mark; Reilly, Andrew; Rogers, James P; Smillie, Jack; Sudheimer, Kai; Tungatt, Robert P; Warner, Matthew J

YORK C

BASHAM, Mike‡ (D) 160 7
H: 6 0 W: 13 09 b.Barking 27-9-73
Source: Trainee. *Honours:* England Schools.
1992–93 West Ham U 0 0
1993–94 West Ham U 0 0
1993–94 *Colchester U* 1 0 **1 0**
1993–94 Swansea C 5 0
1994–95 Swansea C 13 0
1995–96 Swansea C 11 1 **29 1**
1995–96 Peterborough U 14 1
1996–97 Peterborough U 5 0 **19 1**
1997–98 Barnet 20 1
1998–99 Barnet 32 1
1999–2000 Barnet 15 0
2000-01 Barnet 8 0 **75 2**
2000-01 York C 7 1
2001-02 York C 29 2
2002-03 York C 0 0 **36 3**

BRACKSTONE, Stephen (M) 35 2
H: 5 11 W: 10 06 b.Hartlepool 19-9-82
Source: Scholar. *Honours:* England Youth.
2000-01 Middlesbrough 0 0
2001-02 Middlesbrough 0 0
2001-02 York C 9 0
2002-03 York C 26 2 **35 2**

BRASS, Chris (M) 238 5
H: 5 10 W: 11 11 b.Easington 24-7-75
Source: Trainee.
1993–94 Burnley 0 0
1994–95 Burnley 5 0
1994–95 *Torquay U* 7 0 **7 0**
1995–96 Burnley 9 0
1996–97 Burnley 39 0
1997–98 Burnley 40 1
1998–99 Burnley 34 0
1999–2000 Burnley 7 0
2000-01 Burnley 0 0 **134 1**
2000-01 *Halifax T* 6 0 **6 0**
2000-01 York C 10 1
2001-02 York C 41 2
2002-03 York C 40 1 **91 4**

BULLOCK, Lee (M) **136 17**
H: 6 0 W: 12 12 b.Stockton 22-5-81
Source: Trainee.

1999–2000	York C	24	0		
2000-01	York C	33	3		
2001-02	York C	40	8		
2002-03	York C	39	6	**136**	**17**

CARVALHO, Rogerio‡ (F) **4 0**
H: 6 4 W: 15 05 b.Brazil 28-5-80
Source: Ituano.

2002-03	York C	4	0	**4**	**0**

COLLINSON, John‡ (G) **0 0**
H: 5 11 W: 12 07 b.Middlesbrough 4-3-83
Source: Scholar.

2002-03	York C	0	0		

COOPER, Richard (M) **66 2**
H: 5 8 W: 11 01 b.Nottingham 27-9-79
Source: Trainee. *Honours:* England Schools, Youth.

1996–97	Nottingham F	0	0		
1997–98	Nottingham F	0	0		
1998–99	Nottingham F	0	0		
1999–2000	Nottingham F	1	0		
2000-01	Nottingham F	2	0	**3**	**0**
2000-01	York C	14	0		
2001-02	York C	25	1		
2002-03	York C	24	1	**63**	**2**

COWAN, Tom* (D) **332 16**
H: 5 6 W: 11 10 b.Bellshill 28-8-69
Source: Netherdale BC.

1988–89	Clyde	16	2	**16**	**2**
1988–89	Rangers	4	0		
1989–90	Rangers	3	0		
1990–91	Rangers	5	0	**12**	**0**
1991–92	Sheffield U	20	0		
1992–93	Sheffield U	21	0		
1993–94	Sheffield U	4	0	**45**	**0**
1993–94	*Stoke C*	14	0	**14**	**0**
1993–94	*Huddersfield T*	10	0		
1994–95	Huddersfield T	37	2		
1995–96	Huddersfield T	43	2		
1996–97	Huddersfield T	42	4		
1997–98	Huddersfield T	0	0		
1998–99	Huddersfield T	5	0	**137**	**8**
1998–99	Burnley	12	1		
1999–2000	Burnley	8	0	**20**	**1**
1999–2000	*Cambridge U*	4	0		
2000-01	Cambridge U	41	2		
2001-02	Cambridge U	5	1	**50**	**3**
2001-02	*Peterborough U*	5	1	**5**	**1**
2002-03	York C	33	1	**33**	**1**

EDMONDSON, Darren (D) **359 14**
H: 6 0 W: 12 07 b.Ulverston 4-11-71
Source: Trainee.

1990–91	Carlisle U	31	0		
1991–92	Carlisle U	27	2		
1992–93	Carlisle U	34	0		
1993–94	Carlisle U	22	3		
1994–95	Carlisle U	38	2		
1995–96	Carlisle U	42	1		
1996–97	Carlisle U	20	1	**214**	**9**
1996–97	Huddersfield T	10	0		
1997–98	Huddersfield T	19	0		
1998–99	Huddersfield T	3	0		
1998–99	*Plymouth Arg*	4	0	**4**	**0**
1999–2000	Huddersfield T	5	0	**37**	**0**
1999–2000	York C	7	0		
2000-01	York C	23	0		
2001-02	York C	36	0		
2002-03	York C	38	5	**104**	**5**

FOX, Christian* (M) **65 1**
H: 5 10 W: 11 12 b.Auchenbrae 11-4-81
Source: Trainee.

1999–2000	York C	34	1		
2000-01	York C	8	0		
2001-02	York C	12	0		
2002-03	York C	11	0	**65**	**1**

HOBSON, Gary* (D) **315 1**
H: 6 1 W: 13 04 b.North Ferriby 12-11-72
Source: Trainee.

1990–91	Hull C	4	0		
1991–92	Hull C	16	0		
1992–93	Hull C	21	0		
1993–94	Hull C	36	0		
1994–95	Hull C	36	0		
1995–96	Hull C	29	0	**142**	**0**
1995–96	Brighton & HA	9	0		
1996–97	Brighton & HA	37	1		
1997–98	Brighton & HA	33	0		
1998–99	Brighton & HA	13	0		
1999–2000	Brighton & HA	6	0	**98**	**1**
1999–2000	Chester C	20	0	**20**	**0**
2000-01	York C	11	0		
2001-02	York C	16	0		
2002-03	York C	28	0	**55**	**0**

JONES, Scott (D) **175 8**
H: 5 8 W: 12 09 b.Sheffield 1-5-75
Source: Trainee.

1993–94	Barnsley	0	0		
1994–95	Barnsley	0	0		
1995–96	Barnsley	4	0		
1996–97	Barnsley	18	0		
1997–98	Barnsley	12	1		
1997–98	*Mansfield T*	6	0	**6**	**0**
1997–98	*Notts Co*	0	0		
1998–99	Barnsley	29	3		
1999–2000	Barnsley	20	0		
2000-01	Barnsley	0	0	**83**	**4**
2000-01	Bristol R	39	3		
2001-02	Bristol R	19	0	**58**	**3**
2001-02	*York C*	8	1		
2002-03	York C	20	0	**28**	**1**

MATHIE, Alex‡ (F) **320 82**
H: 5 10 W: 12 00 b.Bathgate 20-12-68
Source: Celtic BC. *Honours:* Scotland Youth.

1987–88	Celtic	0	0		
1988–89	Celtic	1	0		
1989–90	Celtic	6	0		
1990–91	Celtic	4	0	**11**	**0**
1991–92	Morton	42	18		
1992–93	Morton	32	13	**74**	**31**
1992–93	*Port Vale*	3	0	**3**	**0**
1993–94	Newcastle U	16	3		
1994–95	Newcastle U	9	1	**25**	**4**
1994–95	Ipswich T	13	2		
1995–96	Ipswich T	39	18		
1996–97	Ipswich T	12	4		
1997–98	Ipswich T	37	13		
1998–99	Ipswich T	8	1	**109**	**38**
1998–99	Dundee U	22	1		
1999–2000	Dundee U	12	3	**34**	**4**
1999–2000	Preston NE	12	2	**12**	**2**
2000-01	York C	19	1		
2001-02	York C	23	2		
2002-03	York C	10	0	**52**	**3**

MAZZINA, Nicolas‡ (M) **6 0**
H: 5 8 W: 11 01 b.Buenos Aires 31-1-79
Source: AC Kimberley.

2001-02	Swansea C	3	0	**3**	**0**
2002-03	York C	3	0	**3**	**0**

NOGAN, Lee* (F) **522 106**
H: 5 10 W: 11 09 b.Cardiff 21-5-69
Source: Apprentice. *Honours:* Wales Under-21, B, 2 full caps.

1986–87	Oxford U	0	0		
1986–87	*Brentford*	11	2	**11**	**2**
1987–88	Oxford U	3	0		
1987–88	*Southend U*	6	1		
1988–89	Oxford U	3	0		
1989–90	Oxford U	4	0		
1990–91	Oxford U	32	5		
1991–92	Oxford U	22	5	**64**	**10**
1991–92	Watford	23	5		
1992–93	Watford	42	11		
1993–94	Watford	26	3		
1993–94	*Southend U*	5	0	**11**	**1**
1994–95	Watford	14	7	**105**	**26**
1994–95	Reading	20	10		
1995–96	Reading	39	10		
1996–97	Reading	32	6	**91**	**26**
1996–97	*Notts Co*	6	0	**6**	**0**
1997–98	Grimsby T	36	8		
1998–99	Grimsby T	38	2	**74**	**10**
1999–2000	Darlington	31	2		
2000-01	Darlington	18	4	**49**	**6**
2000-01	*Luton T*	7	1	**7**	**1**
2000-01	York C	16	6		
2001-02	York C	42	13		
2002-03	York C	46	5	**104**	**24**

O'KANE, Aiden‡ (M) **40 6**
H: 5 9 W: 11 03 b.Belfast 24-11-79

2000-01	Cliftonville	28	6	**28**	**6**
2001-02	York C	12	0		
2002-03	York C	0	0	**12**	**0**

OKOLI, James‡ (D) **3 0**
H: 6 1 W: 12 02 b.Nigeria 11-1-76

2002-03	York C	3	0	**3**	**0**

PARKIN, Jonathan (D) **70 12**
H: 6 1 W: 15 00 b.Barnsley 30-12-81
Source: Scholarship.

1998–99	Barnsley	2	0		
1999–2000	Barnsley	0	0		
2000-01	Barnsley	4	0		
2001-02	Barnsley	4	0	**10**	**0**
2001-02	*Hartlepool U*	1	0	**1**	**0**
2001-02	York C	18	2		
2002-03	York C	41	10	**59**	**12**

POTTER, Graham* (D) **246 8**
H: 5 11 W: 11 13 b.Solihull 20-5-75
Source: Trainee. *Honours:* England Youth, Under-21.

1992–93	Birmingham C	18	2		
1993–94	Birmingham C	7	0	**25**	**2**
1993–94	*Wycombe W*	3	0	**3**	**0**
1993–94	Stoke C	3	0		
1994–95	Stoke C	1	0		
1995–96	Stoke C	41	1	**45**	**1**
1996–97	Southampton	8	0	**8**	**0**
1996–97	WBA	6	0		
1997–98	WBA	5	0		
1997–98	*Northampton T*	4	0	**4**	**0**
1998–99	WBA	22	0		
1999–2000	WBA	10	0	**43**	**0**
1999–2000	*Reading*	4	0	**4**	**0**
2000-01	York C	38	2		
2001-02	York C	37	2		
2002-03	York C	39	1	**114**	**5**

SMITH, Christopher* (D) **51 0**
H: 5 11 W: 13 01 b.Derby 30-6-81
Source: Trainee.

1999–2000	Reading	0	0		
2000-01	Reading	0	0		
2001-02	York C	15	0		
2002-03	York C	36	0	**51**	**0**

STOCKDALE, David§ (G) **1 0**
b.Leeds 20-9-85
Source: Scholar.

2002-03	York C	1	0	**1**	**0**

WILDING, Craig* (F) **7 0**
H: 5 11 W: 12 00 b.Birmingham 30-10-81
Source: Scholar.

2001-02	Chesterfield	0	0		
2002-03	York C	7	0	**7**	**0**

WISE, Stuart§ (M) **14 0**
b.Middlesbrough 4-4-84
Source: Scholar.

2001-02	York C	6	0		
2002-03	York C	8	0	**14**	**0**

WOOD, Leigh (M) **38 0**
H: 5 11 W: 11 10 b.Selby 21-5-83
Source: Scholar.

2000-01	York C	5	0		
2001-02	York C	14	0		
2002-03	York C	19	0	**38**	**0**

YALCIN, Levent§ (M) **5 0**
b.Middlesbrough 25-3-85
Source: Scholar.

2002-03	York C	5	0	**5**	**0**

Scholars
Anderson, Gary D; Arthur, Adam J; Ashcroft, Kane J; Barry, Daniel; Baynes, Steven; Boyce, Marvin; Coad, Matthew P; Davies, Sean G; Hampshire, Mark; Ibbetson, Luke G; Law, Graeme; MacKenzie, Michael; McCabe, Matthew D; Stewart, Bryan W; Stockdale, David A; Wise, Stuart; Yalcin, Levent

TRANSFERS 2002–03

	From	To	Fee in £
MAY 2002			
31 Dawson, Kevin E.	Nottingham Forest	Chesterfield	Free
8 Devlin, Paul J.	Sheffield United	Birmingham City	200,000
20 Rachubka, Paul S.	Manchester United	Charlton Athletic	200,000
14 Rowett, Gary	Leicester City	Charlton Athletic	2,500,000
30 Savage, Robert W.	Leicester City	Birmingham City	2,500,000
17 Steele, Luke	Peterborough United	Manchester United	500,000
6 Thorpe, Lee A.	Lincoln City	Leyton Orient	Free
31 Todd, Andrew J.J.	Charlton Athletic	Blackburn Rovers	750,000
16 Toner, Ciaran	Bristol Rovers	Leyton Orient	Free
TEMPORARY TRANSFERS			
7 Devlin, Paul J.	Sheffield United	Birmingham City	
3 Evers, Sean A.	Plymouth Argyle	Stevenage Borough	
1 Lee, Martyn J.	Wycombe Wanderers	Cheltenham Town	
1 Liddle, Gareth J.C.	Crewe Alexandra	Leek Town	
1 Tyson, Nathan	Reading	Cheltenham Town	
JUNE 2002			
6 Beswetherick, Jonathan B.	Plymouth Argyle	Sheffield Wednesday	Free
25 Breckin, Ian	Chesterfield	Wigan Athletic	150,000
6 Foxe, Hayden	West Ham United	Portsmouth	400,000
21 Holden, Dean T.J.	Bolton Wanderers	Oldham Athletic	Free
13 Hughes, Richard D.	AFC Bournemouth	Portsmouth	100,000
20 Robinson, Stephen	Preston North End	Luton Town	50,000
JULY 2002			
12 Barker, Christopher A.	Barnsley	Cardiff City	600,000
23 Beresford, David	Hull City	Plymouth Argyle	Free
12 Bramble, Titus M.	Ipswich Town	Newcastle United	5,000,000
20 Burgess, Benjamin K.	Blackburn Rovers	Stockport County	450,000
5 Colley, Karl P.	Newcastle United	Sheffield United	undisclosed
18 Cunningham, Kenneth E.	Wimbledon	Birmingham City	600,000
12 Edwards, Paul	Swindon Town	Wrexham	Free
12 Elliott, Stuart	Motherwell	Hull City	230,000
24 Faulconbridge, Craig M.	Wrexham	Wycombe Wanderers	Free
4 Hardy, Lee	Oldham Athletic	Macclesfield Town	Free
16 Hill, Clinton S.	Tranmere Rovers	Oldham Athletic	200,000
30 Jones, Graeme A.	St Johnstone	Southend United	35,000
31 Killen, Christopher J.	Manchester City	Oldham Athletic	200,000
23 Lowndes, Nathan P.	Livingston	Plymouth Argyle	Free
10 Mears, Tyrone	Manchester City	Preston North End	175,000
3 Taylor, Matthew S.	Luton Town	Portsmouth	400,000
19 Woods, Danny	Bournemouth	Eastleigh	undisclosed
26 Wright, Richard I.	Arsenal	Everton	3,500,000
26 Yorke, Dwight E.	Manchester United	Blackburn Rovers	2,000,000
TEMPORARY TRANSFERS			
27 Bevan, Scott	Southampton	Huddersfield Town	
3 Caldwell, Gary	Newcastle United	Coventry City	
4 Green, Stuart	Newcastle United	Hull City	
26 Kenny, Patrick J.	Bury	Sheffield United	
8 Knight, Leon L.	Chelsea	Sheffield Wednesday	
27 McDonald, Scott	Southampton	Huddersfield Town	
AUGUST 2002			
16 Baldacchino, Ryan L.	Bolton Wanderers	Carlisle United	Free
8 Barmby, Nicholas J.	Liverpool	Leeds United	2,750,000
8 Boateng, George	Aston Villa	Middlesbrough	5,000,000
29 Butters, Guy	Gillingham	Brighton & Hove Albion	Free
16 Davis, Sol S.	Swindon Town	Luton Town	undisclosed
6 Derry, Shaun P.	Portsmouth	Crystal Palace	600,000
29 Dudley, Craig B.	Oldham Athletic	Burton Albion	Free
27 Festa, Gianluca	Middlesbrough	Portsmouth	undisclosed
29 Greaves, Mark A.	Hull City	Boston United	Free
6 Gregan, Sean M.	Preston North End	West Bromwich Albion	1,500,000
13 Harewood, Jermaine L.	Ipswich Wanderers	AFC Sudbury	undisclosed
1 Hedman, Magnus C.	Coventry City	Celtic	1,500,000
30 Hughes, Lee	Coventry City	West Bromwich Albion	2,500,000
8 Jones, Scott	Bristol Rovers	York City	Free
31 Keane, Robert D.	Leeds United	Tottenham Hotspur	7,000,000
23 Kinsella, Mark	Charlton Athletic	Aston Villa	750,000
29 Koumas, Jason	Tranmere Rovers	West Bromwich Albion	2,500,000
9 Larkin, Colin	Wolverhampton Wanderers	Mansfield Town	120,000
6 Locke, Gary	Bradford City	Kilmarnock	Free
12 Low, Joshua D.	Cardiff City	Oldham Athletic	Free
6 MacKenzie, Neil D.	Blackpool	Mansfield Town	Free
14 Marshall, Lee K.	Leicester City	West Bromwich Albion	700,000
15 McGill, Brendan	Sunderland	Carlisle United	Free
8 Merson, Paul C.	Aston Villa	Portsmouth	Free
3 Morrison, Clinton	Crystal Palace	Birmingham City	4,250,000
8 Parkin, Sam	Chelsea	Swindon Town	50,000
23 Piper, Matthew J.	Leicester City	Sunderland	3,500,000
8 Powell, Darren D.	Brentford	Crystal Palace	400,000
30 Stewart, Marcus P.	Ipswich Town	Sunderland	3,250,000
28 Thompson, David A.	Coventry City	Blackburn Rovers	1,500,000
15 Wright, Stephen J.	Liverpool	Sunderland	3,000,000

TEMPORARY TRANSFERS

9 Abbott, Pawel T.H.	Preston North End	Bury
31 Alcide, Colin J.	Cambridge United	Gainsborough Trinity
16 Allaway, Ricky	Reading	Basingstoke Town
30 Allaway, Shaun	Leeds United	Grimsby Town
23 Ashdown, Jamie L.	Reading	AFC Bournemouth
30 Banks, Steven	Bolton Wanderers	Bradford City
29 Barrett, Graham	Arsenal	Brighton & Hove Albion
12 Bloomer, Matthew B.	Hull City	Telford United
9 Burton, Deon J.	Derby County	Portsmouth
15 Burton, Steven P.	Ipswich Town	Boston United
30 Butler, Philip A.	West Bromwich Albion	Bristol City
10 Campbell-Ryce, Jamal J.	Charlton Athletic	Leyton Orient
14 Chorley, Benjamin F.	Arsenal	Brentford
8 Clarke, Peter M.	Everton	Blackpool
19 Collins, Daniel L.	Chester City	Vauxhall Motors
30 Curtis, Thomas D.	Portsmouth	Tranmere Rovers
9 Davis, James R.W.	Manchester United	Swindon Town
16 Dickinson, Michael J.	Carlisle United	Workington
16 Dunfield, Terry	Manchester City	Bury
10 Evans, Rhys K.	Chelsea	Leyton Orient
23 Festa, Gianluca	Middlesbrough	Portsmouth
16 Flowers, Timothy D.	Leicester City	Manchester City
8 Furlong, Paul A.	Birmingham City	Queens Park Rangers
9 Gill, Jeremy M.	Birmingham City	Northampton Town
12 Griffiths, Leroy	Queens Park Rangers	Farnborough Town
8 Gritton, Martin	Plymouth Argyle	Torquay United
16 Heal, Simon A.F.	Cardiff City	Haverfordwest
15 Holt, Andrew	Hull City	Barnsley
12 Horrigan, Darren	Lincoln City	Stamford
13 Hudson, Mark	Middlesbrough	Chesterfield
23 Ingham, Michael G.	Sunderland	Stockport County
12 Johnson, Simon A.	Leeds United	Hull City
29 Jones, Gary S.	Nottingham Forest	Tranmere Rovers
23 Kabba, Steven	Crystal Palace	Grimsby Town
9 Lazaridis, Stan	Birmingham City	Portsmouth
9 Lovell, Stephen W.H.	Portsmouth	Queens Park Rangers
16 Mallon, Ryan	Sheffield United	Halifax Town
16 Mann, Neil	Hull City	Gainsborough Trinity
13 McGovern, Jon P.	Celtic	Sheffield United
23 Morrison, John O.	Sheffield Wednesday	Hull City
9 Myhill, Glyn O.	Aston Villa	Bristol City
23 Naisbitt, Daniel J.	Barnet	Carlisle United
12 O'Brien, Christopher T.	Chester City	Droylsden
16 Odunsi, Leke	Millwall	Colchester United
1 Osborn, Mark	Wycombe Wanderers	Farnborough Town
30 Poate, Brett	Southampton	Havant & Waterlooville
23 Proctor, Michael A.	Sunderland	Bradford City
16 Ramsden, Simon	Sunderland	Notts County
16 Reeves, David	Oldham Athletic	Chesterfield
15 Regan, Carl A.	Barnsley	Hull City
24 Roberts, Ben J.	Charlton Athletic	Luton Town
9 Robinson, Paul D.	Wimbledon	Grimsby Town
29 Ross, Brian S.	Hartlepool United	Whitby Town
24 Royce, Simon E.	Leicester City	Queens Park Rangers
9 Selley, Ian	Wimbledon	Southend United
30 Shields, Dene	Sunderland	Doncaster Rovers
19 Smith, Jay A.	Aston Villa	Southend United
8 Southern, Keith W.	Everton	Blackpool
30 Stockley, Sam J.	Oxford United	Colchester United
9 Tardif, Christopher L.	Portsmouth	AFC Bournemouth
9 Taylor, Cleveland K.W.	Bolton Wanderers	Exeter City
29 Thomas, Jerome W.	Arsenal	Queens Park Rangers
29 Thomas, Walter A.	Tottenham Hotspur	Wingate & Finchley
30 Thwaites, Adam	Carlisle United	Gretna
23 Town, David	Boston United	Kettering Town
7 Vine, Rowan L.	Portsmouth	Brentford
16 Wallis, Tony	Cardiff City	Haverfordwest
13 Webber, Daniel V.	Manchester United	Watford
30 Welsh, Andrew	Stockport County	Macclesfield Town
16 White, Thomas J.C.	Portsmouth	Bognor Regis Town
8 Williams, Thomas A.	Birmingham City	Queens Park Rangers

SEPTEMBER 2002

6 Gritton, Martin	Plymouth Argyle	Torquay United	Free
27 Jones, Gary S.	Nottingham Forest	Tranmere Rovers	Free
5 Lewis, Edward J.	Fulham	Preston North End	undisclosed
26 Tonkin, Anthony	Yeovil Town	Stockport County	50,000
27 Villis, Matthew	Bridgwater Town	Plymouth Argyle	undisclosed

TEMPORARY TRANSFERS

26 Artell, David J.	Rotherham United	Shrewsbury Town
16 Artun, Erdem K.	Ipswich Town	Doncaster Rovers
27 Boulding, Michael T.	Aston Villa	Sheffield United
18 Brady, Richard	Queens Park Rangers	Molesey
26 Brown, Marvin R.	Bristol City	Torquay United
7 Burton, Steven P.G.	Hull City	Ilkeston Town
29 Butler, Philip A.	West Bromwich Albion	Bristol City
7 Campbell, Paul A.	Darlington	Whitby Town
13 Chambers, Triston G.	Colchester United	Harlow Town
6 Clark, Peter J.	Stockport County	Mansfield Town
13 Clyde, Mark G.	Wolverhampton Wanderers	Kidderminster Harriers
30 Curtis, Thomas D.	Portsmouth	Tranmere Rovers

10 D'Austin, Ryan A.	Queens Park Rangers	Chertsey Town	
13 Davies, Kevin C.	Southampton	Millwall	
6 Delaney, Damien	Leicester City	Mansfield Town	
18 Dunfield, Terry	Manchester City	Bury	
20 Eaden, Nicholas J.	Birmingham City	Wigan Athletic	
17 Edwards, Christian N.H.	Nottingham Forest	Tranmere Rovers	
9 Edwards, Paul	Crewe Alexandra	Stafford Rangers	
17 Fenton, Graham A.	Blackpool	Darlington	
9 Garnett, Shaun M.	Oldham Athletic	Halifax Town	
9 Gill, Jeremy M.	Birmingham City	Northampton Town	
20 Hiley, Scott P.	Portsmouth	Exeter City	
27 Hudson, Mark	Middlesbrough	Chesterfield	
20 Hyde, Graham	Birmingham City	Peterborough United	
25 Ingham, Michael	Sunderland	Stockport County	
13 Jackson, Johnnie	Tottenham Hotspur	Swindon Town	
6 Jevons, Philip	Grimsby Town	Hull City	
12 Johnson, Simon A.	Leeds United	Hull City	
23 Jones, Darren L.	Bristol City	Forest Green Rovers	
20 Jones, Thomas G.	Cardiff City	Weymouth	
16 Kerr, Scott	Hull City	Frickley Athletic	
4 Mallon, Ryan	Sheffield United	Halifax Town	
20 McLean, Aaron	Leyton Orient	Grays Athletic	
13 Melligan, John J.	Wolverhampton Wanderers	Kidderminster Harriers	
27 Michopoulos, Nikalaos	Burnley	Crystal Palace	
13 Miller, Justin J.	Ipswich Town	Leyton Orient	
13 Mooney, Thomas J.	Birmingham City	Stoke City	
13 Moss, Neil G.	Southampton	AFC Bournemouth	
10 One, Armand	Cambridge United	Northampton Town	
16 Osborn, Mark	Wycombe Wanderers	Farnborough Town	
27 Partridge, Richard J.	Liverpool	Coventry City	
6 Petty, Ben J.	Hull City	Moor Green	
20 Ritchie, Paul M.	Manchester City	Portsmouth	
23 Royce, Simon E.	Leicester City	Queens Park Rangers	
27 Russell, Matthew L.	Exeter City	Forest Green Rovers	
6 Shanahan, Aaron M.	Bristol City	Halesowen Town	
20 Simpkins, Michael J.	Cardiff City	Exeter City	
27 Southall, Leslie N.	Bolton Wanderers	Norwich City	
6 Tardif, Christopher L.	Portsmouth	AFC Bournemouth	
27 Taylor, Michael J.	Blackburn Rovers	Carlisle United	
27 Thomas, Walter A.	Tottenham Hotspur	Wingate & Finchley	
6 Upson, Matthew J.	Arsenal	Reading	
6 Viveash, Adrian L.	Reading	Oxford United	
13 Warnock, Stephen	Liverpool	Bradford City	
13 Watts, Steven	Leyton Orient	Margate	
30 Welsh, Andrew	Stockport County	Macclesfield Town	
27 Whitehead, Philip M.	Reading	Tranmere Rovers	
OCTOBER 2002			
25 Byrne, Desmond	Wimbledon	Carlisle United	Free
18 Delaney, Damien	Leicester City	Hull City	Free
21 Eaden, Nicholas J.	Birmingham City	Wigan Athletic	Free
18 Glennon, Matthew W.	Hull City	Carlisle United	Free
16 Kenny, Patrick J.	Bury	Sheffield United	Free
3 Whitehead, Stuart D.	Carlisle United	Darlington	Free
TEMPORARY TRANSFERS			
25 Artell, David J.	Rotherham United	Shrewsbury Town	
11 Ashcroft, Lee	Wigan Athletic	Port Vale	
10 Balmer, Stuart M.	Oldham Athletic	Scunthorpe United	
15 Barrett, Graham	Arsenal	Brighton & Hove Albion	
30 Barry-Murphy, Brian	Preston North End	Hartlepool United	
29 Blayney, Alan	Southampton	Stockport County	
28 Boulding, Michael	Aston Villa	Sheffield United	
18 Bourgeois, Daryl T.A.	Cambridge United	Ford United	
22 Brady, Richard L.	Queens Park Rangers	Molesey	
4 Branch, Paul M.	Wolverhampton Wanderers	Hull City	
21 Buxton, Lewis E.	Portsmouth	Exeter City	
19 Cash, Brian D.	Nottingham Forest	Swansea City	
11 Coleman, Kenneth J.	Wolverhampton Wanderers	Kidderminster Harriers	
2 Cook, Lee	Watford	York City	
21 Coote, Adrian	Colchester United	Bristol Rovers	
12 Cryan, Colin	Sheffield United	Scarborough	
14 Davies, Kevin C.	Southampton	Millwall	
16 Day, Christopher N.	Queens Park Rangers	Aylesbury United	
24 Deeney, Saul	Notts County	Hull City	
7 Delaney, Damien	Leicester City	Mansfield Town	
22 Dunfield, Terry	Manchester City	Bury	
17 Edwards, Christian	Nottingham Forest	Tranmere Rovers	
10 Edwards, Paul	Crewe Alexandra	Stafford Rangers	
18 Eribenne, Chukwunyeaka O.	AFC Bournemouth	Hereford United	
4 Farrell, Craig W.	Leeds United	Carlisle United	
24 Farren, Larry T.	Leeds United	Hyde United	
11 Featherstone, Lee	Sheffield United	Scunthorpe United	
17 Fenton, Graham A.	Blackpool	Darlington	
12 Fletcher, Gary	Leyton Orient	Dagenham & Redbridge	
1 Forde, Fabian W.	Watford	Enfield	
11 Forsyth, Richard M.	Peterborough United	Cheltenham Town	
11 Frost, Carl R.	Crewe Alexandra	Witton Albion	
3 Galloway, Michael A.	Carlisle United	Hereford United	
7 Garnett, Shaun M.	Oldham Athletic	Halifax Town	
9 Gill, Jeremy M.	Birmingham City	Northampton Town	
30 Harley, Jonathon	Fulham	Sheffield United	
21 Hiley, Scott	Portsmouth	Exeter City	

16 Hudson, Daniel R.	Rotherham United	Doncaster Rovers	
28 Hudson, Mark	Middlesbrough	Chesterfield	
25 Hyde, Graham	Birmingham City	Peterborough United	
22 Iriekpen, Ezomo	West Ham United	Leyton Orient	
15 Jackson, Johnnie	Tottenham Hotspur	Swindon Town	
31 Jalal, Shwan	Tottenham Hotspur	Woking	
17 Johnson, Glen M.C.	West Ham United	Millwall	
31 Jones, Darren L.	Bristol City	Forest Green Rovers	
4 Jordan, Stephen	Manchester City	Cambridge United	
4 Kear, Richard S.	Cheltenham Town	Weston-Super-Mare	
11 Kelly, Gavin R.	Tottenham Hotspur	Kettering Town	
24 Kerr, Brian	Newcastle United	Coventry City	
25 Lee, Andrew J.	Bradford City	Farsley Celtic	
16 Lee, David J.F.	Brighton & Hove Albion	Bristol Rovers	
28 Lewis, Matthew T.	Kidderminster Harriers	EveshamUnited	
24 Little, Colin C.	Crewe Alexandra	Mansfield Town	
15 Mallon, Ryan	Sheffield United	Halifax Town	
12 Mayo, Paul	Lincoln City	Dagenham & Redbridge	
12 McCaldon, Ian	Oxford United	Chester City	
4 McCann, Grant S.	West Ham United	Cheltenham Town	
21 McLean, Aaron	Leyton Orient	Grays Athletic	
13 Melligan, John J.	Wolverhampton Wanderers	Kidderminster Harriers	
25 Michopoulos, Nicolaos	Burnley	Crystal Palace	
14 Miller, Justin J.	Ipswich Town	Leyton Orient	
24 Mills, Jonathan P.	Southampton	Basingstoke Town	
25 Morgan, Robert D.	Bradford City	Farsley Celtic	
14 Moss, Neil G.	Southampton	AFC Bournemouth	
10 Muirhead, Ben R.	Manchester United	Doncaster Rovers	
8 Norris, David M.	Bolton Wanderers	Plymouth Argyle	
9 O'Hare, Alan P.J.	Bolton Wanderers	Chesterfield	
10 One, Armand	Cambridge United	Northampton Town	
4 Osman, Leon	Everton	Carlisle United	
18 Pacquette, Richard F.	Queens Park Rangers	Stevenage Borough	
27 Partridge, Richard J.	Liverpool	Coventry City	
14 Patterson, Simon	Watford	Slough Town	
21 Pettefer, Carl J.	Portsmouth	Exeter City	
6 Petty, Ben J.	Hull City	Moor Green	
25 Proudlock, Adam D.	Wolverhampton Wanderers	Tranmere Rovers	
2 Reddington, Stuart	Mansfield Town	Burton Albion	
21 Richards, Justin	Bristol Rovers	Colchester United	
18 Ricketts, Sam D.	Oxford United	Nuneaton Borough	
11 Ridgewell, Liam M.	Aston Villa	AFC Bournemouth	
14 Royce, Simon E.	Leicester City	Queens Park Rangers	
28 Russell, Matthew L.	Exeter City	Forest Green Rovers	
4 Simpemba, Ian	Wycombe Wanderers	Woking	
1 Stockley, Sam J.	Oxford United	Colchester United	
24 Stone, Steven B.	Aston Villa	Portsmouth	
4 Sutton, John W.M.	Tottenham Hotspur	Carlisle United	
11 Tardif, Christopher L.	Portsmouth	AFC Bournemouth	
24 Tate, Christopher D.	Leyton Orient	Chester City	
4 Thompson, Lee J.	Sheffield United	Boston United	
18 Thompson, Tyrone	Sheffield United	Lincoln City	
25 Vaughan, Anthony J.	Nottingham Forest	Mansfield Town	
18 Viveash, Adrian L.	Reading	Oxford United	
14 Warnock, Stephen	Liverpool	Bradford City	
18 Warren, Stephen R.	Reading	Walton & Hersham	
24 White, Andrew	Mansfield Town	Crewe Alexandra	
18 Whitley, Jeffrey	Manchester City	Notts County	
NOVEMBER 2002			
7 Butler, Philip A.	West Bromwich Albion	Bristol City	Free
1 Clare, Daryl A.	Boston United	Chester City	undisclosed
15 Forsyth, Richard M.	Peterborough United	Cheltenham Town	15,000
8 Gadsby, Matthew J.	Walsall	Mansfield Town	Free
5 Howarth, Russell M.	York City	Tranmere Rovers	Free
22 Joseph, Marc E.	Peterborough United	Hull City	40,000
15 Kabba, Steven	Crystal Palace	Sheffield United	250,000
11 O'Hare, Alan P.J.	Bolton Wanderers	Chesterfield	Free
6 Reddington, Stuart	Mansfield Town	Burton Albion	undisclosed
4 Regan, Carl A.	Barnsley	Hull City	undisclosed
20 Smith, Jay A.	Aston Villa	Southend United	Free
8 Southern, Keith W.	Everton	Blackpool	Free
8 Stockley, Sam J.	Oxford United	Colchester United	Free
7 Thompson, Lee J.	Sheffield United	Boston United	Free
TEMPORARY TRANSFERS			
22 Allaway, Shaun	Leeds United	Grimsby Town	
27 Anderson, Ijah M.	Brentford	Wycombe Wanderers	
28 Artell, David J.	Rotherham United	Shrewsbury Town	
8 Ashton, Jonathan J.	Leicester City	Notts County	
1 Barnard, Lee J.	Tottenham Hotspur	Exeter City	
22 Barras, Anthony	Walsall	Plymouth Argyle	
25 Bishop, Andrew J.	Walsall	Kidderminster Harriers	
8 Blayney, Alan	Southampton	Stockport County	
18 Bourgeois, Daryl T.A.	Cambridge United	Ford United	
15 Brady, Richard	Queens Park Rangers	Molesey	
5 Branch, Paul M.	Wolverhampton Wanderers	Hull City	
21 Byrne, Clifford	Sunderland	Scunthorpe United	
8 Cansdell-Sheriff, Shane L.	Leeds United	Rochdale	
28 Cole, Carlton	Chelsea	Wolverhampton Wanderers	
11 Coleman, Kenneth J.	Wolverhampton Wanderers	Kidderminster Harriers	
29 Connell, Darren S.	Scarborough	Barrow	
29 Cook, Lee	Watford	York City	

29 Crossley, Mark G.	Middlesbrough	Stoke City
22 Davis, Earl A.	Burnley	Stalybridge Celtic
14 Day, Christopher N.	Queens Park Rangers	Aylesbury United
29 Day, Rhys	Manchester City	Mansfield Town
23 Deane, Saul	Notts County	Hull City
5 Dickinson, Michael J.	Carlisle United	Gateshead
7 Dunning, Darren	Blackburn Rovers	Torquay United
19 Edwards, Christian	Nottingham Forest	Tranmere Rovers
10 Edwards, Paul	Crewe Alexandra	Stafford Rangers
8 Facey, Delroy M.	Bolton Wanderers	Bradford City
4 Farrell, Craig W.	Leeds United	Carlisle United
12 Featherstone, Lee	Sheffield United	Scunthorpe United
4 Ferguson, Steven	Leeds United	Hyde United
14 Fletcher, Gary	Leyton Orient	Dagenham & Redbridge
8 Forsyth, Richard	Peterborough United	Cheltenham Town
13 Foster, Benjamin	Stoke City	Bristol City
8 French, Daniel J.	Peterborough United	Cambridge City
12 Frost, Carl R.	Crewe Alexandra	Witton Albion
5 Galloway, Michael A.	Carlisle United	Hereford United
1 Gavin, Jason J.	Middlesbrough	Grimsby Town
16 Gerrard, Paul W.	Everton	Ipswich Town
8 Griffiths, Leroy	Queens Park Rangers	Margate
29 Gulliver, Philip S.	Middlesbrough	Blackpool
27 Harley, Jon	Fulham	Sheffield United
1 Hignett, Craig J.	Blackburn Rovers	Coventry City
29 Holdsworth, Dean C.	Bolton Wanderers	Coventry City
15 Hudson, Daniel R.	Rotherham United	Doncaster Rovers
22 Ingham, Michael G.	Sunderland	Darlington
12 Jackson, Johnnie	Tottenham Hotspur	Swindon Town
17 Johnson, Glen M.C.	West Ham United	Millwall
6 Jordan, Stephen	Manchester City	Cambridge United
8 Jupp, Duncan A.	Wimbledon	Notts County
9 Kelly, Gavin R.	Tottenham Hotspur	Kettering Town
2 Kerrigan, Steven P.	Halifax Town	Telford United
22 Killeen, Lewis K.	Sheffield United	Halifax Town
8 Krief, Dominique	Leeds United	Sheffield Wednesday
24 Little, Colin C.	Crewe Alexandra	Mansfield Town
8 Logan, Richard A.	Lincoln City	Gainsborough Trinity
30 Logan, Richard J.	Ipswich Town	Boston United
22 Macauley, Steven R.	Rochdale	Macclesfield Town
6 MacDonald, Gary	Peterborough United	Stevenage Borough
29 McCann, Grant S.	West Ham United	Cheltenham Town
22 McCarthy, Patrick	Manchester City	Boston United
29 McGrath, John M.	Aston Villa	Dagenham & Redbridge
22 McMaster, Jamie	Leeds United	Coventry City
22 Mallon, Ryan	Sheffield United	Scarborough
7 Melaugh, Gavin M.J.	Aston Villa	Rochdale
20 Melton, Stephen	Brighton & Hove Albion	Hull City
11 Miller, Justin J.	Ipswich Town	Leyton Orient
5 Milosevic, Dejan	Leeds United	Plymouth Argyle
23 Monington, Mark D.	Boston United	Halifax Town
15 Morris, Alexander S.	Crewe Alexandra	Kidsgrove Athletic
14 Moss, Neil G.	Southampton	AFC Bournemouth
8 Muirhead, Ben R.	Manchester United	Doncaster Rovers
22 Myhill, Glyn O.	Aston Villa	Bradford City
5 Norris, David M.	Bolton Wanderers	Plymouth Argyle
29 Offiong, Richard	Newcastle United	Darlington
4 Osman, Leon	Everton	Carlisle United
1 Oster, John M.	Sunderland	Grimsby Town
15 Pennant, Jermaine	Arsenal	Watford
1 Pilkington, George E.	Everton	Exeter City
30 Pitcher, Geoffrey	Brighton & Hove Albion	Dagenham & Redbridge
7 Plummer, Christopher S.	Queens Park Rangers	Bristol Rovers
15 Pollet, Ludovic	Wolverhampton Wanderers	Walsall
23 Poom, Mart A.	Derby County	Sunderland
20 Price, Michael D.	Hull City	Barnet
1 Reddy, Michael	Sunderland	York City
22 Richards, Marc J.	Blackburn Rovers	Swansea City
19 Ricketts, Sam D.	Oxford United	Nuneaton Borough
29 Robinson, James G.	Crewe Alexandra	Altrincham
29 Robinson, Marvin L.S.C.	Derby County	Tranmere Rovers
22 Robinson, Paul D.	Wimbledon	Carlisle United
14 Royce, Simon E.	Leicester City	Queens Park Rangers
29 Sall, Abdou H.	Kidderminster Harriers	Oxford United
1 Scully, Anthony D.T.	Cambridge United	Southend United
9 Sidwell, Steven J.	Arsenal	Brighton & Hove Albion
5 Simpemba, Ian	Wycombe Wanderers	Woking
8 Singh, Harpal	Leeds United	Bradford City
5 Sutton, John W.M.	Tottenham Hotspur	Carlisle United
22 Tate, Alan	Manchester United	Swansea City
29 Thompson, Glyn W.	Fulham	Northampton Town
7 Thornton, Sean	Sunderland	Blackpool
8 Tierney, Paul T.	Manchester United	Crewe Alexandra
29 Virgo, Adam J.	Brighton & Hove Albion	Exeter City
13 Warnock, Stephen	Liverpool	Bradford City
22 Warren, Stephen R.	Reading	Walton & Hersham
8 Webb, Daniel J.	Southend United	Brighton & Hove Albion
24 White, Andrew	Mansfield Town	Crewe Alexandra
25 Whitley, Jeffrey	Manchester City	Notts County
8 Whittle, Thomas J.	Oldham Athletic	Hinckley United
27 Wilkinson, Shaun F.	Brighton & Hove Albion	Chesterfield
29 Williams, Benjamin P.	Manchester United	Coventry City
7 Willock, Calum D.	Fulham	Queens Park Rangers

29 Wills, Kevin M.	Plymouth Argyle	Torquay United	
14 Windass, Dean	Middlesbrough	Sheffield United	

DECEMBER 2002

13 Burton, Dion J.	Derby County	Portsmouth	75,000
20 Dunfield, Terry	Manchester City	Bury	Free
9 Farrell, Craig W.	Leeds United	Carlisle United	undisclosed
18 Featherstone, Lee	Sheffield United	Scunthorpe United	Free
30 Green, Stuart	Newcastle United	Hull City	150,000
31 Holdsworth, Dean C.	Bolton Wanderers	Coventry City	Free
13 MacDonald, Gary	Peterborough United	Stevenage Borough	10,000
24 Melton, Stephen	Brighton & Hove Albion	Hull City	Free
19 Norris, David M.	Bolton Wanderers	Plymouth Argyle	Free
24 Pettinger, Andrew R.	Everton	Grimsby Town	Free
13 Webb, Daniel J.	Southend United	Hull City	Free
31 Wills, Kevin M.	Plymouth Argyle	Torquay United	Free

TEMPORARY TRANSFERS

13 Adamson, Chris	West Bromwich Albion	Halesowen Town
5 Ainsworth, Gareth	Wimbledon	Walsall
27 Artell, David J.	Rotherham United	Shrewsbury Town
13 Ashcroft, Lee	Wigan Athletic	Huddersfield Town
4 Ashington, Ryan D.	Torquay United	Newport County
6 Banks, Steven	Bolton Wanderers	Stoke City
6 Barrett, Graham	Arsenal	Brighton & Hove Albion
20 Bishop, Andrew	Walsall	Kidderminster Harriers
24 Blayney, Alan	Southampton	AFC Bournemouth
13 Bracken, James	Woking	Burnham
24 Bradbury, Lee M.	Portsmouth	Sheffield Wednesday
13 Britton, Leon	West Ham United	Swansea City
31 Burt, Jamie P.	Chesterfield	Carlisle United
22 Byrne, Clifford	Sunderland	Scunthorpe United
13 Carvalho, Rogerio	York City	Harrogate Town
21 Cleverley, Benjamin R.	Bristol City	Forest Green Rovers
13 Coleman, Kenneth J.	Wolverhampton Wanderers	Kidderminster Harriers
23 Collins, Christopher J.	Swindon Town	Newport County
20 Cook, Lee	Watford	Queens Park Rangers
27 Curran, Christopher	Exeter City	Tiverton Town
27 Day, Rhys	Manchester City	Mansfield Town
26 Deeney, Saul	Notts County	Hull City
4 Dickinson, Michael J.	Carlisle United	Gateshead
20 Ducros, Andrew J.	Kidderminster Harriers	Nuneaton Borough
20 Dykes, Darren	Swindon Town	Lincoln City
10 Eaton, Adam P.	Preston North End	Mansfield Town
13 Edwards, Paul	Crewe Alexandra	Southport
6 Evans, Richard G.	Birmingham City	Moor Green
14 Fletcher, Gary	Leyton Orient	Dagenham & Redbridge
18 Foster, Benjamin	Stoke City	Tiverton Town
7 Frost, Carl R.	Crewe Alexandra	Witton Albion
3 Gavin, Jason J.	Middlesbrough	Grimsby Town
31 Gulliver, Philip S.	Middlesbrough	Carlisle United
13 Harrison, Lee D.	Barnet	Peterborough United
23 Hendon, Ian M.	Sheffield Wednesday	Barnet
20 Hendry, Edward C.J.	Bolton Wanderers	Blackpool
21 Hill, Nicholas D.	Bury	Leigh RMI
10 Hudson, Mark	Middlesbrough	Carlisle United
24 Husbands, Michael P.	Aston Villa	Hereford United
18 Jackson, Michael J.	Preston North End	Tranmere Rovers
23 Jeffs, Ian D.	Crewe Alexandra	Kidsgrove Athletic
15 Johnson, Glen M.C.	West Ham United	Millwall
13 Johnston, Allan	Middlesbrough	Sheffield Wednesday
13 Jones, Bradley	Middlesbrough	Stockport County
3 Jones, Darren L.	Bristol City	Forest Green Rovers
5 Jordan, Stephen	Manchester City	Cambridge United
9 Jupp, Duncan A.	Wimbledon	Notts County
24 Kennedy, Jon	Sunderland	Gateshead
23 Killeen, Lewis	Sheffield United	Halifax Town
6 Langston, Matthew J.	Watford	Aldershot Town
5 Lewis, Matthew T.	Kidderminster Harriers	Bath City
13 Little, Colin C.	Crewe Alexandra	Macclesfield Town
30 Logan, Richard J.	Ipswich Town	Boston United
9 Logan, Richard	Lincoln City	Gainsborough Trinity
20 Lonergan, Andrew	Preston North End	Darlington
31 Loran, Tyrone	Manchester City	Tranmere Rovers
24 Mallon, Ryan	Sheffield United	Scarborough
19 Marney, Daniel G.	Brighton & Hove Albion	Southend United
24 Marney, Dean E.	Tottenham Hotspur	Swindon Town
23 McCarthy, Patrick	Manchester City	Boston United
30 McGrath, John M.	Aston Villa	Dagenham & Redbridge
7 Melaugh, Gavin M.J.	Aston Villa	Rochdale
5 Melligan, John J.	Wolverhampton Wanderers	Kidderminster Harriers
13 Monk, Garry A.	Southampton	Sheffield Wednesday
18 Moore, Neil	Mansfield Town	Southport
13 Morris, Alexander S.	Crewe Alexandra	Kidsgrove Athletic
1 Murphy, Brian B.	Preston North End	Hartlepool United
19 Mustafa, Tarkan	Rushden & Diamonds	Doncaster Rovers
24 Nightingale, Luke R.	Portsmouth	Swindon Town
3 Norris, David M.	Bolton Wanderers	Plymouth Arygle
27 Offiong, Richard	Newcastle United	Darlington
24 O'Halloran, Matthew V.	Derby County	Burton Albion
2 Oster, John	Sunderland	Grimsby Town
31 Partridge, Scott	Rushden & Diamonds	Exeter City
30 Pettinger, Paul A.	Lincoln City	Telford United

13 Proudlock, Adam D.	Wolverhampton Wanderers	Sheffield Wednesday	
2 Reddy, Michael	Sunderland	York City	
13 Richards, Justin	Bristol Rovers	Stevenage Borough	
20 Richardson, Leam N.	Bolton Wanderers	Blackpool	
24 Ricketts, Sam D.	Oxford United	Nuneaton Borough	
1 Robinson, James G.	Crewe Alexandra	Altrincham	
30 Robinson, Marvin L.S.C.	Derby County	Tranmere Rovers	
13 Rose, Richard A.	Gillingham	Bristol Rovers	
28 Russell, Samuel I.	Middlesbrough	Darlington	
31 Sall, Abdou H.	Kidderminster Harriers	Oxford United	
14 Shanahan, Aaron M.	Bristol City	Halesowen Town	
6 Sidwell, Steven J.	Arsenal	Brighton & Hove Albion	
13 Simpemba, Ian	Wycombe Wanderers	Woking	
23 Simpkins, Michael J.	Cardiff City	Cheltenham Town	
13 Smith, Alex P.	Reading	Shrewsbury Town	
6 Southall, Nicholas L.	Bolton Wanderers	Gillingham	
20 Tarsuslugil, Edward J.M.	Bury	Wakefield & Emley	
27 Thompson, Glyn	Fulham	Northampton Town	
9 Tierney, Paul T.	Manchester United	Crewe Alexandra	
24 Turns, Craig A.	Sunderland	Harrogate Town	
29 Virgo, Adam J.	Brighton & Hove Albion	Exeter City	
6 Walshe, Benjamin M.	Queens Park Rangers	Aldershot Town	
12 Watts, Stephen	Leyton Orient	Lincoln City	
30 Williams, Benjamin P.	Manchester United	Chesterfield	
7 Williams, Steven	Wycombe Wanderers	Windsor & Eton	
JANUARY 2003			
29 Alexander, Gary G.	Hull City	Leyton Orient	undisclosed
31 Barry-Murphy, Brian	Preston North End	Sheffield Wednesday	Free
14 Boulding, Michael	Aston Villa	Grimsby Town	Free
8 Bowyer, Lee D.	Leeds United	West Ham United	100,000
31 Brevett, Rufus E.	Fulham	West Ham United	undisclosed
16 Briggs, Keith	Stockport County	Norwich City	65,000
31 Bullard, James R.	Peterborough United	Wigan Athletic	275,000
31 Christie, Malcolm N.	Derby County	Middlesbrough	3,000,000 combined
10 Clapham, James R.	Ipswich Town	Birmingham City	1,000,000
10 Clemence, Stephen N.	Tottenham Hotspur	Birmingham City	250,000
17 Day, Rhys	Manchester City	Mansfield Town	Free
8 Devine, Sean T.	Wycombe Wanderers	Exeter City	undisclosed
21 Ferdinand, Leslie	Tottenham Hotspur	West Ham United	200,000
22 Forrester, Jamie	Northampton Town	Hull City	undisclosed
30 Fowler, Robert B.	Leeds United	Manchester City	3,000,000
27 Logan, Richard J.	Ipswich Town	Boston United	Free
8 Lynch, Simon	Celtic	Preston North End	130,000
29 McCann, Grant S.	West Ham United	Cheltenham Town	50,000
31 McDermott, Neale T.	Newcastle United	Fulham	undisclosed
30 Mendes, Junior	St Mirren	Mansfield Town	undisclosed
31 Miller, Justin J.	Ipswich Town	Leyton Orient	Free
22 Poom, Mart A.	Derby County	Sunderland	2,500,000
31 Prutton, David T.	Nottingham Forest	Southampton	2,500,000
31 Ricketts, Michael B.	Bolton Wanderers	Middlesbrough	2,500,000
10 Ross, Neil J.	Stockport County	Macclesfield Town	30,000
29 Sherwood, Timothy A.	Tottenham Hotspur	Portsmouth	Free
24 Sidwell, Steven J.	Arsenal	Reading	250,000
8 Southall, Nicholas L.	Bolton Wanderers	Gillingham	Free
23 Upson, Matthew J.	Arsenal	Birmingham City	1,000,000
16 Windass, Dean	Middlesbrough	Sheffield United	undisclosed
31 Woodgate, Jonathan S.	Leeds United	Newcastle United	9,000,000
TEMPORARY TRANSFERS			
27 Alexander, Gary G.	Hull City	Leyton Orient	
25 Amankwaah, Kevin	Bristol City	Torquay United	
13 Balmer, Stuart M.	Oldham Athletic	Boston United	
16 Banks, Steven	Bolton Wanderers	Stoke City	
25 Basham, Michael	York City	Chelmsford City	
10 Boulding, Michael	Aston Villa	Grimsby Town	
17 Bourgeois, Daryl T.A.	Cambridge United	Ford United	
31 Brannan, Gerald D.	Wigan Athletic	Dunfermline Athletic	
30 Brown, Marvin R.	Bristol City	Cheltenham Town	
31 Burchill, Mark J.	Portsmouth	Dundee	
10 Burgess, Benjamin K.	Stockport County	Oldham Athletic	
10 Buxton, Lewis E.	Portsmouth	AFC Bournemouth	
22 Byrne, Clifford	Sunderland	Scunthorpe United	
31 Camp, Lee M.J.	Derby County	Burton Albion	
24 Chilvers, Liam C.	Arsenal	Colchester United	
29 Cleverley, Benjamin R.	Bristol City	Forest Green Rovers	
17 Clifford, Mark R.	Boston United	Chester City	
4 Coleman, Kenneth J.	Wolverhampton Wanderers	Kidderminster Harriers	
20 Cook, Lee	Watford	Queens Park Rangers	
17 Cornwall, Lucas C.C.	Fulham	Lincoln City	
27 Curran, Christopher	Exeter City	Tiverton Town	
14 Davies, Clint	Birmingham City	Tamworth	
6 Dickinson, Michael J.	Carlisle United	Gateshead	
16 Doane, Ben N.D.	Sheffield United	Mansfield Town	
17 Doyle, Daire M.	Kidderminster Harriers	Nuneaton Borough	
16 Dunning, Darren	Blackburn Rovers	Macclesfield Town	
17 Edwards, Christian N.H.	Nottingham Forest	Oxford United	
10 Emblen, Neil R.	Norwich City	Walsall	
17 Eustace, John M.	Coventry City	Middlesbrough	
17 Evans, Paul S.	Bradford City	Blackpool	
20 Evans, Richard G.	Birmingham City	Moor Green	
16 Fagan, Craig	Birmingham City	Bristol City	
10 Flynn, Michael A.	Barnsley	Blackpool	

3 Forde, Fabian W.	Watford	Chesham United	
19 Foster, Benjamin	Stoke City	Tiverton Town	
3 Gunby, Stephen R.	Bury	Hyde United	
12 Harrison, Lee D.	Barnet	Peterborough United	
31 Heal, Simon A.F.	Cardiff City	Total Network Solutions	
30 Healy, David J.	Preston North End	Norwich City	
31 Higginbotham, Daniel J.	Derby County	Southampton	
10 Hill, Nicholas D.	Bury	Leigh RMI	
9 Hudson, Mark	Middlesbrough	Carlisle United	
27 Husbands, Michael P.	Aston Villa	Hereford United	
30 Ifil, Jerel C.	Watford	Swindon Town	
24 Ingham, Michael G.	Sunderland	York City	
17 Javary, Jean P.	Sheffield United	Walsall	
24 Jeffs, Ian D.	Crewe Alexandra	Kidsgrove Athletic	
14 Johnston, Allan	Middlesbrough	Sheffield Wednesday	
1 Jones, Darren L.	Bristol City	Forest Green Rovers	
16 Jupp, Duncan A.	Wimbledon	Notts County	
30 Kelly, Stephen M.	Tottenham Hotspur	Southend United	
27 Kennedy, Jon	Sunderland	Gateshead	
20 Killeen, Lewis	Sheffield United	Halifax Town	
24 Lewis, Matthew T.	Kidderminster Harriers	Solihull Borough	
24 Lovett, Jay	Brentford	Hereford United	
16 Macauley, Steven R.	Rochdale	Macclesfield Town	
24 Mahon, Alan J.	Blackburn Rovers	Cardiff City	
20 Marney, Daniel G.	Brighton & Hove Albion	Southend United	
28 Marney, Dean E.	Tottenham Hotspur	Swindon Town	
24 McCarthy, Patrick	Manchester City	Boston United	
7 Melaugh, Gavin M.J.	Aston Villa	Rochdale	
4 Melligan, John J.	Wolverhampton Wanderers	Kidderminster Harriers	
17 Mills, Rowan L.	Coventry City	Stoke City	
20 Milosevic, Dejan	Leeds United	Crewe Alexandra	
24 Moilanen, Teuvo J.	Preston North End	Heart of Midlothian	
14 Monk, Garry	Southampton	Sheffield Wednesday	
17 Mooney, Thomas J.	Birmingham City	Sheffield United	
30 Murphy, Brian	Manchester City	Oldham Athletic	
17 Nugent, Kevin P.	Leyton Orient	Swansea City	
3 Pilkington, George E.	Everton	Exeter City	
7 Quinn, Wayne R.	Newcastle United	Sheffield United	
30 Reddy, Michael	Sunderland	Sheffield Wednesday	
12 Richards, Justin	Bristol Rovers	Stevenage Borough	
10 Richardson, Frazer	Leeds United	Stoke City	
18 Ricketts, Sam D.	Oxford United	Nuneaton Borough	
31 Riggott, Christopher M.	Derby County	Middlesbrough	
17 Roberts, Ben J.	Charlton Athletic	Brighton & Hove Albion	
17 Robinson, Carl P.	Portsmouth	Sheffield Wednesday	
13 Rose, Richard	Gillingham	Bristol Rovers	
31 Ross, Brian S.	Hartlepool United	Bishop Auckland	
10 Sara, Juan M.	Dundee	Coventry City	
3 Seddon, Gareth J.	Bury	Northwich Victoria	
31 Shandran, Anthony M.	Burnley	York City	
14 Smith, Alexander P.	Reading	Shrewsbury Town	
17 Straker, Philip	Sunderland	Farsley Celtic	
2 Tavlaridis, Efstathios	Arsenal	Portsmouth	
30 Thompson, Glyn	Fulham	Northampton Town	
28 Tod, Andrew	Bradford City	Dundee United	
16 Townsend, Ben	Wycombe Wanderers	Woking	
31 Vaughan, Anthony J.	Nottingham Forest	Motherwell	
31 Virgo, Adam J.	Brighton & Hove Albion	Exeter City	
24 Whitbread, Adrian R.	Reading	Exeter City	
3 Whitley, Jeffrey	Manchester City	Notts County	
31 Williams, Benjamin W.	Manchester United	Chesterfield	
24 Williams, Gareth A.	Crystal Palace	Colchester United	
31 Willmott, Christopher A.	Wimbledon	Luton Town	
31 Woodhouse, Curtis	Birmingham City	Rotherham United	

FEBRUARY 2003

12 Elding, Anthony L.	Boston United	Stevenage Borough	Free
24 Folan, Caleb C.	Leeds United	Chesterfield	Free
11 Fotiadis, Andrew	Luton Town	Peterborough United	Free
27 Sestanovich, Ashley	Hampton & Richmond Borough	Sheffield United	20,000

TEMPORARY TRANSFERS

12 Anderson, Ijah M.	Brentford	Bristol Rovers
25 Andrews, Lee D.	Carlisle United	Rochdale
9 Banks, Steven	Bolton Wanderers	Stoke City
28 Basham, Michael	York City	Chelmsford City
21 Beswetherick, Jonathan B.	Sheffield Wednesday	Swindon Town
21 Bourgeois, Daryl T.A.	Cambridge United	Heybridge Swifts
24 Bromby, Leigh	Sheffield Wednesday	Norwich City
14 Burch, Robert K.	Tottenham Hotspur	Woking
10 Buxton, Lewis E.	Portsmouth	AFC Bournemouth
7 Camm, Mark L.	Lincoln City	Gainsborough Trinity
7 Chadwick, Luke H.	Manchester United	Reading
28 Chadwick, Nicholas G.	Everton	Derby County
26 Chilvers, Liam C.	Arsenal	Colchester United
20 Clarke, Peter M.	Everton	Port Vale
26 Cleverley, Benjamin R.	Bristol City	Forest Green Rovers
19 Clifford, Mark R.	Boston United	Ilkeston Town
22 Clist, Simon J.	Bristol City	Torquay United
28 Corbett, James J.	Blackburn Rovers	Darlington
3 Cummings, Warren	Chelsea	AFC Bournemouth
28 Cutler, Neil	Stoke City	Swansea City
7 Danby, John R.	Kidderminster Harriers	Stourport Swifts

28 Danks, Mark J.	Bradford City	Halesowen Town
14 Davies, Clint	Birmingham City	Nuneaton Borough
21 Di Piedi, Michele	Sheffield Wednesday	Bristol Rovers
16 Doane, Ben N.D.C.	Sheffield United	Mansfield Town
17 Dunning, Darren	Blackburn Rovers	Macclesfield Town
11 Eaton, Adam P.	Preston North End	Mansfield Town
7 Elding, Anthony L.	Boston United	Gainsborough Trinity
17 Evans, Gary L.	Bury	Hyde United
17 Evans, Paul S.	Bradford City	Blackpool
21 Evans, Richard G.	Birmingham City	Moor Green
14 Folan, Caleb C.	Leeds United	Chesterfield
10 Foley, Dominic	Watford	Southend United
14 Ford, Mark S.	Darlington	Leigh RMI
7 Foster, Benjamin	Stoke City	Tiverton Town
7 Fotiadis, Andrew	Luton Town	Peterborough United
19 Green, Stuart	Hull City	Carlisle United
3 Gunby, Stephen	Bury	Hyde United
7 Hallam, Anthony	Preston North End	Morecambe
7 Harpur, Chad L.	Millwall	Basingstoke Town
22 Hirschfeld, Lars	Tottenham Hotspur	Luton Town
28 Hockenhull, Darren	Blackburn Rovers	Darlington
24 Huckerby, Darren C.	Manchester City	Nottingham Forest
21 Hughes, Richard D.	Portsmouth	Grimsby Town
7 Hylton, Leon D.	Aston Villa	Swansea City
21 Ingham, Michael	Sunderland	York City
10 Ingimarsson, Ivar	Wolverhampton Wanderers	Brighton & Hove Albion
28 Iriekpen, Ezomo	West Ham United	Cambridge United
13 Jansen, Matthew B.	Blackburn Rovers	Coventry City
7 Johnson, Richard M.	Watford	Northampton Town
18 Johnston, Allan	Middlesbrough	Sheffield Wednesday
26 Kennedy, Jon	Sunderland	Gateshead
28 Lewis, Matthew T.	Kidderminster Harriers	Solihull Borough
21 Llewellyn, Christopher M.	Norwich City	Bristol Rovers
7 Lonergan, Andrew	Preston North End	Blackpool
17 Lovett, Jay	Brentford	Hereford United
16 Macauley, Steven R.	Rochdale	Macclesfield Town
20 Marney, Daniel G.	Brighton & Hove Albion	Southend United
20 Monk, Garry	Southampton	Sheffield Wednesday
27 Morgan, Westley N.	Nottingham Forest	Kidderminster Harriers
14 Newey, Thomas	Leeds United	Cambridge United
21 Oster, John M.	Sunderland	Grimsby Town
8 Pitcher, Geoffrey	Brighton & Hove Albion	Farnborough Town
18 Price, Michael	Leicester City	Boston United
10 Quinn, Wayne	Newcastle United	Sheffield United
28 Reddy, Michael	Sunderland	Sheffield Wednesday
9 Richards, Justin	Bristol Rovers	Stevenage Borough
9 Richardson, Frazer	Leeds United	Stoke City
18 Robins, Mark G.	Rotherham United	Bristol City
20 Robinson, Carl P.	Portsmouth	Walsall
13 Robinson, Paul	Tranmere Rovers	Vauxhall Motors
20 Rougier, Anthony L.	Reading	Brighton & Hove Albion
26 Shuker, Christopher A.	Manchester City	Walsall
14 Smith, Alexander P.	Reading	Shrewsbury Town
15 Straker, Philip	Sunderland	Farsley Celtic
4 Strong, Greg	Hull City	Cheltenham Town
10 Tabb, Jay A.	Brentford	Crawley Town
11 Talbot, Stewart D.	Rotherham United	Shrewsbury Town
3 Tavlaridis, Efstathios	Arsenal	Portsmouth
24 Taylor, Craig	Plymouth Argyle	Torquay United
3 Volz, Moritz	Arsenal	Wimbledon
27 Walters, Jonathan R.	Bolton Wanderers	Hull City
10 Watts, Stephen	Leyton Orient	Dagenham & Redbridge
26 Williams, Gareth A.	Crystal Palace	Colchester United
7 Williams, Lee	Cheltenham Town	Halesowen Town
1 Willmott, Christopher A.	Wimbledon	Luton Town
1 Woodhouse, Curtis	Birmingham City	Rotherham United

MARCH 2003

17 Ainsworth, Gareth	Wimbledon	Cardiff City	50,000
25 Ambrose, Darren P.F.	Ipswich Town	Newcastle United	1,000,000
27 Burgess, Benjamin K.	Stockport County	Hull City	100,000
7 Eaton, Adam P.	Preston North End	Mansfield Town	undisclosed
27 Evans, Richard G.	Birmingham City	Sheffield Wednesday	undisclosed
27 Heald, Greg J.	Barnet	Leyton Orient	18,000 combined
27 Holt, Grant	Barrow	Sheffield Wednesday	Free
27 Hreidarsson, Hermann	Ipswich Town	Charlton Athletic	800,000
28 Lawrence, James H.	Bradford City	Walsall	Free
19 Macauley, Steven R.	Rochdale	Macclesfield Town	Free
13 Marriott, Andrew	Barnsley	Birmingham City	nominal
27 Purser, Wayne M.	Barnet	Leyton Orient	18,000 combined
26 Thompson, Glyn W.	Fulham	Northampton Town	Free
25 Varney, Luke I.	Quorn	Crewe Alexandra	nominal
27 Youngs, Thomas A.J.	Cambridge United	Northampton Town	50,000

TEMPORARY TRANSFERS

18 Abbott, Pawel T.H.	Preston North End	Bury
27 Akinbiyi, Adeola P.	Crystal Palace	Stoke City
27 Anderson, Iain	Preston North End	Tranmere Rovers
10 Antoine-Curier, Mackael	Nottingham Forest	Brentford
7 Bacon, Daniel S.	Mansfield Town	Hucknall Town
27 Beevers, Lee J.	Ipswich Town	Boston United
27 Boucaud, Andre	Reading	Peterborough United
1 Bradbury, Lee M.	Portsmouth	Sheffield Wednesday

4 Bradley, Shayne	Chesterfield	Lincoln City
27 Brown, Marvin R.	Bristol City	Cheltenham Town
18 Butters, Guy	Brighton & Hove Albion	Barnet
10 Buxton, Lewis E.	Portsmouth	AFC Bournemouth
10 Camm, Mark	Lincoln City	Gainsborough Trinity
6 Canham, Scott W.	Leyton Orient	Woking
27 Chadwick, Luke H.	Manchester United	Reading
25 Chopra, Michael	Newcastle United	Watford
21 Clarke, Lee	Peterborough United	Kettering Town
25 Clarke, Peter M.	Everton	Port Vale
23 Clist, Simon J.	Bristol City	Torquay United
7 Close, Brian A.	Middlesbrough	Chesterfield
27 Collins, Lee	Blackpool	Morecambe
28 Corbett, James J.	Blackburn Rovers	Darlington
31 Corbett, Luke J.	Cheltenham Town	Hednesford Town
6 Crossley, Mark G.	Middlesbrough	Stoke City
3 Curtis, John C.K.	Blackburn Rovers	Sheffield United
14 D'Austin, Ryan A.	Queens Park Rangers	Molesey
20 Dalglish, Paul	Blackpool	Scunthorpe United
4 Danby, John	Kidderminster Harriers	Stourport Swifts
27 Danks, Mark J.	Bradford City	Halesowen Town
21 Davies, Clint	Birmingham City	Woking
7 Davis, Earl A.	Burnley	Southport
27 Dickinson, Robert D.	Ipswich Town	Boston United
16 Doane, Ben N.D.C.	Sheffield United	Mansfield Town
26 Douglas, Jonathan	Blackburn Rovers	Chesterfield
27 Dudfield, Lawrie G.	Hull City	Northampton Town
19 Dunning, Darren	Blackburn Rovers	Macclesfield Town
27 Evans, Richard G.	Birmingham City	Sheffield Wednesday
14 Farrelly, Gareth	Bolton Wanderers	Rotherham United
25 Foley, Dominic	Watford	Oxford United
16 Ford, Mark	Darlington	Leigh RMI
18 Foster, Benjamin	Stoke City	Tiverton Town
17 Fowler, Lee A.	Coventry City	Cardiff City
19 Frost, Carl R.	Crewe Alexandra	Kidsgrove Athletic
14 Gavin, Jason J.	Middlesbrough	Huddersfield Town
10 Goodman, Donald R.	Exeter City	Doncaster Rovers
27 Graydon, Keith	Sunderland	York City
27 Greer, Gordon	Blackburn Rovers	Stockport County
27 Gulliver, Philip S.	Middlesbrough	AFC Bournemouth
4 Gunby, Stephen	Bury	Hyde United
14 Harrison, Lee D.	Barnet	Leyton Orient
27 Hawley, Karl L.	Walsall	Hereford United
13 Healy, David J.	Preston North End	Norwich City
27 Henry, Ronnie S.	Tottenham Hotspur	Southend United
27 Hockenhull, Darren	Blackburn Rovers	Rochdale
21 Hodges, Lee L.	Rochdale	Bristol Rovers
27 Holt, Andrew	Hull City	Shrewsbury Town
7 Howard, Jonathan	Chesterfield	Burton Albion
25 Hughes, Richard D.	Portsmouth	Grimsby Town
27 Hulbert, Robin J.	Bristol City	Shrewsbury Town
27 Igoe, Samuel G.	Reading	Luton Town
27 Ingham, Michael	Sunderland	York City
10 Ingimarsson, Ivar	Wolverhampton Wanderers	Brighton & Hove Albion
28 Iriekpen, Ezomo	West Ham United	Cambridge United
27 Jackson, Johnnie	Tottenham Hotspur	Colchester United
27 Keane, Michael T.	Preston North End	Grimsby Town
26 Kear, Richard S.	Cheltenham Town	Chippenham Town
13 Kelly, Stephen M.	Tottenham Hotspur	Southend United
27 Kelly, Stephen M.	Tottenham Hotspur	Queens Park Rangers
21 Langston, Matthew J.	Watford	Barnet
19 Lewis, Karl J.	Leicester City	Swindon Town
27 Little, Colin C.	Crewe Alexandra	Macclesfield Town
27 Little, Glen M.	Burnley	Reading
25 Llewellyn, Christopher M.	Norwich City	Bristol Rovers
19 Lovett, Jay	Brentford	Gravesend & Northfleet
27 Mansell, Lee R.S.	Luton Town	Nuneaton Borough
27 Matthews, Barrie J.	Watford	Swindon Supermarine
27 May, Ben S.	Millwall	Colchester United
14 Maylett, Bradley	Burnley	Swansea City
27 McCarthy, Patrick	Manchester City	Notts County
27 McCarthy, Paul J.	Wycombe Wanderers	Oxford United
27 McGuire, Jamie A.	Tranmere Rovers	Northwich Victoria
21 McLeod, Kevin A.	Everton	Queens Park Rangers
27 Miles, John F.	Crewe Alexandra	Macclesfield Town
19 Mooney, Thomas J.	Birmingham City	Derby County
7 Murphy, Christopher	Shrewsbury Town	Stafford Rangers
27 Newey, Thomas	Leeds United	Darlington
21 Nixon, Marc S.	Carlisle United	Workington
17 Oakes, Stefan T.	Leicester City	Crewe Alexandra
13 Otsemobor, John	Liverpool	Hull City
9 Pitcher, Geoffrey	Brighton & Hove Albion	Farnborough Town
20 Price, Michael	Leicester City	Boston United
27 Rankine, Simon M.	Preston North End	Sheffield United
7 Reeves, Martin L.	Leicester City	Hull City
17 Revell, Alexander D.	Cambridge United	Kettering Town
27 Ritchie, Paul M.	Manchester City	Derby County
7 Ross, Brian S.	Hartlepool United	Bishop Auckland
26 Scully, Anthony D.T.	Cambridge United	Peterborough United
31 Shandran, Anthony	Burnley	York City
10 Smith, Grant G.	Sheffield United	Plymouth Argyle
25 Strong, Greg	Hull City	Scunthorpe United
27 Taylor, Cleveland	Bolton Wanderers	Scarborough

21 Taylor, Martin J.	Wycombe Wanderers	Barnsley	
27 Taylor, Michael J.	Blackburn Rovers	Rochdale	
27 Ten Heuvel, Laurens	Sheffield United	Bradford City	
27 Thompson, Tyrone	Sheffield United	Doncaster Rovers	
26 Turner, Michael T.	Charlton Athletic	Leyton Orient	
10 Volz, Moritz	Arsenal	Wimbledon	
24 Walters, Jonathan R.	Bolton Wanderers	Hull City	
27 Warhurst, Paul	Bolton Wanderers	Stoke City	
18 Weaver, Luke D.S.	Carlisle United	Barrow	
14 Webb, Daniel J.	Hull City	Lincoln City	
7 Whelan, Noel D.	Middlesbrough	Crystal Palace	
3 Williams, Benjamin W.	Manchester United	Chesterfield	
14 Williams, Lee	Cheltenham Town	Halesowen Town	
20 Williams, Nicholas C.	Watford	Swindon Supermarine	
13 Willmott, Christopher A.	Wimbledon	Luton Town	
14 Wilson, Mark A.	Middlesbrough	Stoke City	

APRIL 2003

15 Cummings, Warren	Chelsea	AFC Bournemouth	undisclosed
8 Evans, Richard G.	Birmingham City	Sheffield Wednesday	undisclosed
4 Harrison, Lee D.	Barnet	Leyton Orient	undisclosed
30 Higginbotham, Daniel J.	Derby County	Southampton	undisclosed
30 Riggott, Christopher M.	Derby County	Middlesbrough	undisclosed

TEMPORARY TRANSFERS

28 Anderson, Iain	Preston North End	Tranmere Rovers
9 Antoine-Curier, Michael	Nottingham Forest	Brentford
20 Butters, Guy	Brighton & Hove Albion	Barnet
11 Camm, Mark	Lincoln City	Gainsborough Trinity
6 Canham, Scott W.	Leyton Orient	Woking
24 Clarke, Peter M.	Everton	Port Vale
7 Close, Brian A.	Middlesbrough	Chesterfield
7 Crossley, Mark G.	Middlesbrough	Stoke City
20 Dalglish, Paul	Blackpool	Scunthorpe United
8 Davis, Earl A.	Burnley	Southport
23 Foley, Dominic	Watford	Oxford United
28 Gavin, Jason J.	Middlesbrough	Huddersfield Town
7 Howard, Jonathan	Chesterfield	Burton Albion
28 Hulbert, Robin J.	Bristol City	Shrewsbury Town
14 Ingimarsson, Ivar	Wolverhampton Wandereres	Brighton & Hove Albion
17 Kear, Richard S.	Cheltenham Town	Chippenham Town
27 Kelly, Stephen M.	Tottenham Hotspur	Queens Park Rangers
20 Langston, Matthew J.	Watford	Barnet
22 Lewis, Karl J.	Leicester City	Swindon Town
23 Matthews, Barrie J.	Watford	Swindon Supermarine
30 McCarthy, Paul J.	Wycombe Wanderers	Oxford United
22 McLeod, Kevin A.	Everton	Queens Park Rangers
22 Mooney, Thomas J.	Birmingham City	Derby County
8 Murphy, Christopher P.	Shrewsbury Town	Stafford Rangers
17 Oakes, Stefan T.	Leicester City	Crewe Alexandra
15 Otsemobor, Jon	Liverpool	Hull City
1 Reddy, Michael	Sunderland	Sheffield Wednesday
6 Ross, Brian S.	Hartlepool United	Bishop Auckland
25 Strong, Greg	Hull City	Scunthorpe United
3 Weaver, Luke D.S.	Carlisle United	Barrow
15 Whitehead, Philip M.	Reading	York City
8 Willmott, Christopher A.	Wimbledon	Luton Town

MAY 2003

7 Allsopp, Daniel	Notts County	Hull City	nominal
3 Miles, John F.	Crewe Alexandra	Macclesfield Town	undisclosed

TEMPORARY TRANSFERS

6 Chadwick, Luke H.	Manchester United	Reading
6 Gulliver, Philip S.	Middlesbrough	AFC Bournemouth
22 McLeod, Kevin A.	Everton	Queens Park Rangers
2 Murphy, Brian	Manchester City	Peterborough United

THE NEW FOREIGN LEGION 2002–03

	From	To	Fee in £
MAY 2002			
30 Allback, Marcus	Heerenveen	Aston Villa	2,000,000
28 Postma, Stefan	De Graafschap	Aston Villa	1,500,000
JUNE 2002			
25 Sava, Facundo	Gimnasia	Fulham	2,000,000
26 Sofiane, Youssef	Auxerre	West Ham United	Free
JULY 2002			
16 Anelka, Nicolas	Paris St Germain	Manchester City	13,000,000
2 Bischoff, Mikkel	FC Copenhagen	Manchester City	750,000
16 Blondel, Jonathan	Mouscron	Tottenham Hotspur	900,000
12 Cheyrou, Bruno	Lille	Liverpool	4,000,000
26 Cisse, Aliou	Paris St Germain	Birmingham City	1,500,000
19 De Lucas, Enrique	Espanyol	Chelsea	Free
17 Diouf, El Hadji	Lens	Liverpool	10,000,000
4 Distin, Sylvain	Paris St Germain	Manchester City	4,000,000
24 Djetou, Martin	Parma	Fulham	loan
22 Djorkaeff, Youri	Kaiserslautern	Bolton Wanderers	Free
5 Foe, Marc-Vivien	Lyon	Manchester City	loan
5 Herrera, Martin	Alaves	Fulham	Free
16 Loran, Tyrone	Volendam	Manchester City	60,000
20 Maccarone, Massimo	Empoli	Middlesbrough	8,150,000
22 Mendy, Bernard	Paris St Germain	Bolton Wanderers	loan
31 Geremi	Real Madrid	Middlesbrough	loan
30 Pelzer, Sebastian	Kaiserslautern	Blackburn Rovers	370,000
6 Queudrue, Franck	Lens	Middlesbrough	2,500,000
12 Svensson, Michael	Troyes	Southampton	2,000,000
19 Viana, Hugo	Sporting Lisbon	Newcastle United	8,500,000
6 Vuoso, Vicente	Independiente	Manchester City	3,500,000
AUGUST 2002			
31 Anis, Jean-Yves	Rennes	Chelsea	Free
21 Bortolozzo, Diego	Treviso	Tottenham Hotspur	Free
30 Boussoufa, Mbark	Ajax	Chelsea	undisclosed
30 Bulent, Akin	Galatasaray	Bolton Wanderers	Free
31 Campo, Ivan	Real Madrid	Bolton Wanderers	loan
8 Cisse, Edouard	Paris St Germain	West Ham United	loan
8 Cygan, Pascal	Lille	Arsenal	2,100,000
30 Da Silva, Mauro	Porto	Chelsea	undisclosed
2 De la Cruz, Ulises	Hibernian	Aston Villa	1,500,000
9 Diao, Salif	Sedan	Liverpool	5,000,000
30 Flo, Tore Andre	Rangers	Sunderland	8,000,000
31 Hirschfeld, Lars	Calgary Storm	Tottenham Hotspur	undisclosed
14 Juninho	Atletico Madrid	Middlesbrough	6,000,000
31 Kanchelskis, Andrei	Rangers	Southampton	Free
22 Kerkar, Karim	Le Havre	Manchester City	Free
31 Lucic, Teddy	AIK Stockholm	Leeds United	loan
5 Luzi, Patrice	Monaco	Liverpool	Free
8 Myhre, Thomas	Besiktas	Sunderland	Free
28 Niemi, Antti	Heart of Midlothian	Southampton	2,000,000
3 Okocha, Jay-Jay	Paris St Germain	Bolton Wanderers	Free
30 Rahim, Brent	Levski	West Ham United	loan
30 Ricardo	Valladolid	Manchester United	1,500,000
2 Rodrigo	Botafogo	Everton	loan
30 Shaaban, Rami	Djurgaarden	Arsenal	undisclosed
9 Silva, Gilberto	Atletico Mineiro	Arsenal	4,500,000
8 Tie, Li	Lialong Bodao	Everton	loan
16 Weifeng, Li	Shenzen Pingan	Everton	loan
23 Wome, Pierre	Bologna	Fulham	loan
6 Yobo, Joseph	Marseille	Everton	5,000,000
DECEMBER 2002			
6 Sukur, Hakan	unattached	Blackburn Rovers	Free
JANUARY 2003			
13 Aaritalo, Mika	TPS Turku	Aston Villa	undisclosed
31 Andre, Pierre-Yves	Nantes	Bolton Wanderers	Free
13 Arias, Federico	Velez Sarsfield	Southampton	500,000
31 Salva, Ballesta	Valencia	Bolton Wanderers	loan
3 Belmadi, Djamel	Marseille	Manchester City	loan
1 Coly, Ferdinand	Lens	Birmingham City	loan
3 Dugarry, Christophe	Bordeaux	Birmingham City	loan
31 El Karkouri, Talal	Paris St Germain	Sunderland	loan
31 Gresko, Vratislav	Parma	Blackburn Rovers	loan
27 Gudjonsson, Joey	Betis	Aston Villa	loan
27 Sommeil, David	Bordeaux	Manchester City	3,500,000
23 Swierczewski, Piotr	Marseille	Birmingham City	loan
28 Toda, Kazu	Shimizu S-Pulse	Tottenham Hotspur	loan
17 Udeze, Ifeanyi	PAOK Salonika	West Bromwich Albion	loan
31 Warmuz, Guillaume	Lens	Arsenal	Free
FEBRUARY 2003			
3 Bravo, Raul	Real Madrid	Leeds United	loan
3 Doriva	Celta Vigo	Middlesbrough	loan
1 Laville, Florent	Lyon	Bolton Wanderers	500,000
5 McBride, Brian	Columbus Crew	Everton	loan

Summer transfers to be found in Stop Press on page 991.

REFEREEING AND THE REFEREES

After several years of considerable change, the International Board has made few alterations to the Laws over the last two seasons. This is carried over for the forthcoming season where the changes which have been made are mainly cosmetic. Thus in Law 4 relating to players' equipment, shirts, or jerseys must have sleeves to avoid teams playing in vest-like tops as occurred in the last World Cup Finals. Also players may not reveal undershirts which contain political slogans or advertising. As an afterthought and some months following the intended changes FIFA have outlawed the removal of shirts to celebrate goal scoring as it has been getting excessive.

Further responsibility has been given to the Fourth Official where one is appointed. Now they are required to point out to the Referee, cases where the Referee has made a mistake on cautioning or dismissal owing to mistaken identity; or where a player has received two cautions but has not been dismissed. Added to that, violent conduct seen by the Fourth Official but missed by any of the other three Officials must be brought to the Referee's attention. He nonetheless remains an assistant and not an 'insistent'.

Another change, which occurs only in penalty shoot-outs, is that the captain winning the toss can now choose whether his side takes the initial kick or requires his opponents to do so. Previously the winner of the toss was required to take the first kick. Dealing with all forms of penalties, Referees are reminded to ensure that goalkeepers do not move before the kick is taken or that there is no encroachment. Owing in part to FIFA's previous tampering with the penalty Laws by allowing more latitude to goalkeepers, yet at the same time encouraging attackers to receive a greater chance to score, something has got to be done to resolve the conflict between these two concepts. This was highlighted by the farce, which occurred in the penalty shoot-out in the Champions League Final. Most Referees appear to be reluctant to ever enforce a retake, and since this occurs in match play, as well as shoot-outs, it must be remembered that a penalty is awarded for a breach of the Laws and is therefore a punishment. In order to redress the current balance and to overcome cheating at penalties, it would seem a reasonable solution to move the penalty spot forward so that as with any other free kick it is 9.15 metres (10 yards) from the nearest defender, in this case the goalkeeper. This gives the kicker his rightful chance and by leaving the penalty arc (the D) where it is, it will also frustrate encroachment by both sides.

Those who have advocated a 'sin bin' have again been knocked back by FIFA's reiteration that temporary expulsions are not permitted at ANY level. They are however prepared to reconsider looking into the future use of artificial surfaces.

Domestically the FA's own refereeing organisation, the Match Officials Association has continued to grow in strength and now has numerous meetings, roadshows and conferences. The Referees Association will be looking to its laurels to remain the prime mover in the refereeing domain.

The new Referees appointed to the National List for this season are Messrs Atkinson, Friend, Kettle, Marriner, Miller, Probert, Tanner and Wright. The new Assistant Referees to that list are Messrs Beck, Beevor, Benton, Bramley, Brown, Brumwell, Duncan, Evans, Ganfield, Hendley, Holdsworth, John, Law, McDermid, Mort, Moss, Phillips, Pickavance, Shoebridge, Simpson, Turner, Vaughan, Waring and Yeo.

The National List of both sets of Officials is set out below, and includes the select group of 21 Referees and 40 Assistant Referees.

KEN GOLDMAN

NATIONAL LIST OF REFEREES FOR SEASON 2003–04

**Indicates Select Group Referees*

Armstrong, P (Paul) Berkshire
Atkinson, M (Martin) W. Yorkshire
Barber, GP (Graham) Hertfordshire*
Barry, NS (Neale) N. Lincolnshire*
Bates, A (Tony) Staffordshire
Beeby, RJ (Richard) Northamptonshire
Bennett, SG (Steve) Kent*
Boyeson, C (Carl) E. Yorkshire
Butler, AN (Alan) Nottinghamshire
Cable, LE (Lee) Surrey
Cain, G (George) Merseyside
Clattenburg, M (Mark) Co. Durham
Cooper, MA (Mark) W. Midlands
Cowburn, MG (Mark) Lancashire
Crick, DR (David) Surrey
Crossley, PT (Phil) Kent
Curson, B (Brian) Leicestershire
Danson, PS (Paul) Leicestershire
Dean, ML (Mike) Wirral*
Dowd, P (Phil) Staffordshire*
Dunn, SW (Steve) Gloucestershire*
Durkin, PA (Paul) Dorset*
D'Urso, AP (Andy) Essex*
Evans, EM (Eddie) Greater Manchester
Fletcher, M (Mick) Worcestershire
Foy, CJ (Chris) Merseyside*
Friend, KA (Kevin) Leicestershire
Gallagher, DJ (Dermot) Oxfordshire*
Hall, AR (Andy) W. Midlands
Halsey, MR (Mark) Lancashire*
Hegley, GK (Grant) Hertfordshire
Hill, KD (Keith) Hertfordshire
Ilderton, EL (Eddie) Tyne & Wear
Jones, MJ (Michael) Cheshire
Joslin, PJ (Phil) Nottinghamshire
Kaye, A (Alan) W. Yorkshire
Kettle, TM (Trevor) Berkshire
Knight, B (Barry) Kent*
Laws, G (Graham) Tyne & Wear
Leake, AR (Tony) Lancashire
Marriner, AM (Andre) Warwickshire
Mason, LS (Lee) Lancashire
Mathieson, SW (Scott) Cheshire
Messias, MD (Matt) S. Yorkshire*
Miller, NS (Nigel) Co. Durham
Olivier, RJ (Ray) W. Midlands
Parkes, TA (Trevor) W. Midlands
Pearson, R (Roy) Co. Durham
Penn, AM (Andy) W. Midlands
Penton, C (Clive) Sussex
Pike, MS (Mike) Cumbria
Poll, G (Graham) Hertfordshire*
Probert, LW (Lee) Avon
Prosser, PJ (Phil) W. Yorkshire
Pugh, D (David) Merseyside
Rennie, UD (Uriah) S. Yorkshire*
Riley, MA (Mike) W. Yorkshire*
Robinson, JP (Paul) E. Yorkshire
Ross, JJ (Joe) London
Ryan, M (Michael) Lancashire
Salisbury, G (Graham) Lancashire
Stretton, FG (Frazer) Nottinghamshire
Styles, R (Rob) Hampshire*
Tanner, SJ (Steve) Avon
Taylor, P (Paul) Hertfordshire
Thorpe, M (Mike) Suffolk
Tomlin, SG (Steve) E. Sussex
Walton, P (Peter) Northamptonshire*
Warren, MR (Mark) W. Midlands
Webb, HM (Howard) S. Yorkshire*
Webster, CH (Colin) Tyne & Wear
Wiley, AG (Alan) Staffordshire*
Williamson, IG (Iain) Berkshire
Winter, JT (Jeff) Cleveland*
Wright, KK (Kevin) Cambridgeshire

ASSISTANT REFEREES

**Indicates Select Group Assistant Referees*

Ansell, I (Ian) Devon
Appleby, ND (Norman) Hertfordshire
Artis, SG (Stephen) Norfolk
Astley, MA (Mark) Greater Manchester
Aston, GA (Glenn) W. Midlands
Atkins, G (Graeme) W. Yorkshire*
Babski, DS (Dave) Lincolnshire*
Baker, BD (Bernard) Hampshire*
Bannister, N (Nigel) E. Yorkshire*
Barker, C (Craig) W. Yorkshire
Barnes, KG (Kevin) Wiltshire
Barnes, PW (Paul) Cambridgeshire*
Bassindale, C (Carl) S. Yorkshire
Beadle, J (Jon) Kent
Beale, GA (Guy) Somerset*
Beck, SP (Simon) Essex
Beevor, R (Richard) Norfolk
Bentley, IF (Ian) Kent
Benton, DK (David) S. Yorkshire
Birkett, DJ (Dave) Lincolnshire
Bone, R (Ralph) Kent*
Booth, RJ (Russell) Nottinghamshire*
Bramley, P (Philip) S. Yorkshire
Brand, SR (Steve) Cheshire*
Bratt, SJ (Steve) W. Midlands
Brittain, GM (Gary) S. Yorkshire*
Brown, M (Mark) E. Yorkshire
Brumwell, CA (Chris) Cumbria
Bryan, DS (Dave) Lincolnshire*
Buller, KR (Keith) Somerset
Burton, R (Roy) Staffordshire*
Butler, AN (Andrew) Lancashire*
Cairns, MJ (Mike) Northamptonshire*
Canadine, P (Paul) S. Yorkshire*
Cann, DJ (Darren) Norfolk
Carter, JE (John) Tyne & Wear
Cassidy, MT (Martin) Avon
Castle, S (Steve) W. Midlands
Chapman, GJ (Gary) Gloucestershire
Chittenden, S (Steve) Hertfordshire
Clyde, AL (Alec) S. Yorkshire
Conn, AJ (Tony) Hertfordshire
Cooke, DG (Dave) W. Midlands
Cordy, JN (Jon) Avon
Coulson, DH (Des) N. Yorkshire
Couzens, C (Carl) Hertfordshire
Darlow, M (Martin) Bedfordshire
Deadman, D (Darren) Hertfordshire
Desmond, RP (Bob) Gloucestershire
Devine, JP (Jim) Cleveland*
Dewfield, A (Adam) Leicestershire
Dexter, MC (Martin) Leicestershire
Dorr, SJ (Steve) Worcestershire
Drysdale, D (Darren) Lincolnshire*
Duncan, SAJ (Scott) Tyne & Wear
East, R (Roger) Wiltshire
Eastwood, P (Peter) Greater Manchester
Ebbage, M (Martin) Hampshire
Evans, C (Craig) Lincolnshire
Evans, IA (Ian) W. Midlands
Evetts, GS (Gary) Hertfordshire
Faulkner, IL (Ian) Merseyside
Flynn, J (John) Wiltshire
Foster, D (Dave) Tyne & Wear
Foulkes, GW (Gary) Merseyside
Francis, CJ (Chris) Cambridgeshire
Gagen, SL (Simon) Surrey*
Ganfield, RS (Ron) Somerset
Garratt, AM (Andy) W. Midlands*
Gate, S (Stan) Tyne & Wear
Gibbs, PN (Phil) W. Midlands
Gosling, IJ (Ian) Kent
Gould, R (Ray) Derbyshire*
Graham, F (Fred) Essex
Greaves, AJ (Alan) S. Yorkshire
Green, AJ (Tony) Leicestershire*
Green, RC (Russell) Gloucestershire
Grove, PJ (Peter) W. Midlands
Habgood, SD (Steve) Wiltshire
Haines, A (Andy) Tyne & Wear
Halliday, A (Andy) N. Yorkshire
Hambling, GS (Glenn) Norfolk
Hancox, N (Neil) W. Midlands
Harris, IR (Ian) Cornwall
Harris, MA (Martin) Lincolnshire
Harwood, CN (Colin) Greater Manchester
Hawken, MA (Mike) Cornwall
Hawkes, KJ (Kevin) Gloucestershire
Hayto, JM (John) Essex
Haywood, M (Mark) W. Yorkshire
Hendley, AR (Andy) W. Midlands
Hewitt, RT (Richard) N. Yorkshire
Hilton, G (Gary) Lancashire
Hine, DJ (David) Worcestershire
Hogg, AS (Andy) S. Yorkshire
Holbrook, JH (John) Worcestershire*
Holdsworth, RJ (Richard) W. Yorkshire
Hollick, S (Simon) Devon
Horton, AJ (Tony) W. Midlands
Horwood, GD (Graham) Bedfordshire
Howes, TP (Tim) Norfolk
Hubbard, JR (Jim) Leicestershire
Hutchinson, AD (Andrew) Cheshire
Hutchinson, SM (Mark) Nottinghamshire
Ingram, KR (Kevin) W. Midlands
Ives, GL (Gary) Essex
Ives, M (Mark) Bedfordshire
James, RG (Ron) Buckinghamshire
John, MA (Mark) Surrey
Jones, NL (Neil) Devon
Keane, PJ (Patrick) W. Midlands
Kellett, DG (Gary) W. Yorkshire
King, EA (Eddie) Northumberland
Kinseley, N (Nick) Essex
Kirkup, PJ (Peter) Northamptonshire
Knight, MT (Matthew) Sussex
Law, GC (Geoff) Leicestershire
Lawson, KD (Keith) Lincolnshire
Lee, R (Ray) Essex
Lewis, GJ (Gary) Cambridgeshire
Lewis, RL (Robert) Shropshire*
Lockhart, R (Bob) Tyne & Wear
Lomas, WD (Wayne) S. Yorkshire
McCallum, DA (Dave) Tyne & Wear
McCoy, MT (Michael) Kent
McDermid, DS (Danny) Hampshire
McGee, A (Tony) Merseyside
McIntosh, WA (Wayne) Lincolnshire
McPherson, MW (Michael) Cambridgeshire
Mackrell, EB (Eric) Hampshire
Malone, B (Brendan) Wiltshire
Martin, AJ (Andy) Staffordshire*
Martin, EAC (Edward) Somerset
Martin, PC (Paul) Northamptonshire
Martin, RW (Rob) S. Yorkshire*
Massey, T (Trevor) Cheshire*
Matadar, M (Mo) Lancashire
Mattocks, KJ (Kevin) Lancashire
Melin, PW (Paul) Surrey*
Mellor, G (Glyn) Derbyshire
Mellor, GS (Gary) S. Yorkshire
Merchant, K (Kevin) Surrey
Miller, P (Patrick) Bedfordshire
Morrison, DP (Des) Derbyshire*
Mort, DF (David) Lancashire
Moss, J (Jonathon) W. Yorkshire
Mullarkey, M (Mike) Devon
Murphy, ME (Michael) W. Yorkshire
Murphy, N (Nigel) Nottinghamshire
Naylor, D (Dave) Nottinghamshire
Nicholson, AR (Andy) W. Yorkshire
Nicholson, PW (Paul) Co. Durham
Nolan, I (Ian) Lancashire
Norman, PV (Paul) Dorset*
Oliver, CW (Clive) Northumberland
Page, A (Andy) Derbyshire
Palmer, R (Richard) Somerset
Parker, AR (Alan) Derbyshire
Parry, B (Brian) Co. Durham
Peacock, D (David) Cleveland
Pearce, JE (John) Essex
Perkin, NF (Neil) Kent
Perlejewski, AJ (Andy) Dorset
Phillips, D (David) Sussex
Pickavance, SD (Stephen) S. Yorkshire
Pike, K (Kevin) Dorset*
Pollard, TJ (Trevor) Suffolk
Pollock, RM (Bob) Merseyside
Powell, K (Ken) Co. Durham
Procter-Green, SRM (Shaun) Lincolnshire*
Pryme, GD (Greg) Essex
Ramsay, W (William) W. Midlands
Rawcliffe, A (Allan) Greater Manchester
Reeves, CL (Christopher) E. Yorkshire
Richards, DC (Ceri) Carmarthenshire*
Richardson, D (David) W. Yorkshire
Robinson, MG (Martin) Co. Durham
Rubery, SP (Steve) Essex
Russell, GR (Geoff) Buckinghamshire
Russell, MP (Mike) Hertfordshire
Sainsbury, A (Andrew) Wiltshire
Sarginson, CD (Christopher) Staffordshire
Scarr, IK (Ian) W. Midlands
Scholes, MS (Mark) Buckinghamshire
Sharp, PR (Phil) Hertfordshire*
Sheffield, JA (Alan) W. Midlands
Shoebridge, RL (Robert) Derbyshire
Short, M (Michael) S. Yorkshire
Short, ML (Martyn) Lincolnshire*
Sim, TJ (Tom) Staffordshire
Simpson, GH (George) N. Yorkshire
Simpson, P (Paul) Co. Durham
Singh, J (Jarnail) Middlesex
Smith, AN (Andrew) W. Yorkshire
Smith, RG (Robert) Essex
Smith, RH (Richard) W. Midlands
Snartt, SP (Simon) S. Gloucestershire
Spicer, DR (Darren) Hampshire
Steans, RJ (Rob) Leicestershire
Stokes, JD (John) Merseyside
Storrie, D (David) W. Yorkshire
Stott, GT (Gary) Greater Manchester
Stroud, KP (Keith) Dorset*
Sutton, GJ (Gary) Lincolnshire
Swarbrick, ND (Neil) Lancashire
Sygmuta, BC (Barry) N. Yorkshire
Tarry, EJ (Eddie) Greater Manchester
Tattan, JF (James) Merseyside*
Taylor, JT (Joe) Lancashire
Thiarra, SS (Sukhdev) Bedfordshire
Tiffin, R (Russell) Co. Durham
Tilling, MR (Mark) Cleveland
Tincknell, SW (Steve) Hertfordshire
Tingey, M (Mike) Buckinghamshire*
Tomlinson, SD (Stephen) Hampshire
Townsend, KN (Keith) W. Midlands
Turner, A (Andrew) Devon
Turner, GB (Glenn) Derbyshire*
Unsworth, D (David) Lancashire
Vaughan, RG (Roger) Somerset
Wallace, G (Gary) Tyne & Wear
Ward, GL (Gavin) Kent
Waring, J (Jim) Lancashire
Weaver, M (Mark) W. Midlands
West, MG (Malcolm) Cornwall
Whitby, D (Dave) Merseyside
Whitestone, D (Dean) Northamptonshire
Wilkinson, K (Keith) Northumberland
Williams, MA (Andy) Herefordshire
Wilson, SM (Stuart) W. Yorkshire
Wood, PM (Paul) Lancashire
Woodward, IJ (Irvine) E. Sussex
Woolmer, KA (Andy) Northamptonshire*
Yates, NA (Neil) Lancashire
Yeo, KG (Keith) Essex
Yerby, MS (Martin) Kent*
Young, GR (Gary) Bedfordshire

THE THINGS THEY SAID . . .

Jason McAteer of Sunderland when asked about Roy Keane's autobiography:
"I'd rather buy a Bob the Builder CD for my two-year-old son."

Arsenal manager Arsene Wenger:
"A football team is like a beautiful woman. When you do not tell her so, she forgets she is beautiful. It is the same with a team."

Monsieur Wenger commenting on Sir Alex Ferguson's reference to Manchester United playing more attractive football than Arsenal:
"What do you want me to say? Everyone thinks he has the prettiest wife at home."

Ronaldo on why Real Madrid always do their best to entertain:
"The supporters are like a woman who you have to keep happy every day."

Mick McCarthy on his appointment as Sunderland manager:
"Yee-haah! I've looked like I've had a coat-hanger in my mouth ever since."

Previous encumbent at the Stadium of Light, Howard Wilkinson on being given the job:
"I'm very, very excited, like a kid on Christmas Eve. I still believe that Sunderland is a club with enormous potential, but it will take time and there will be difficult and unpleasant decisions."

And later deliberating to a long-suffering supporter: "You can't give a team confidence. You can't put it in a pill, or a suppository."

Ron Atkinson's thoughts on Manchester City:
"If they blow millions chasing the dream but end up missing the boat, they're not even back at square one – they're right in it, with the future of the club up in the air."

Simon Jordan, Crystal Palace chairman on some of his players:
"They're earning £8,000 a week and they have a big-time Charlie attitude. At times we have been a disgrace."

Theo Paphitis, the Millwall chairman with his thoughts on Football League chief executive David Burns:
"He couldn't run a kebab shop,"

Darlington chairman George Reynolds on the chances of signing Paul Gascoigne:
"I'll give him a fresh start if he's prepared to take £1,000 a week."

Neil Warnock, Sheffield United manager, replying to the scenario if he was appointed boss of Sheffield Wednesday:
"I would buy some bad players, get the sack and then retire to Cornwall."

Keith Harris on stepping down as Football League chairman:
"I'm leaving the asylum to the lunatics."

Sir Bobby Robson in Sarajevo for the Champions League qualifier:
"Our hotel's fine. The food's OK, the people are nice, but it isn't Hawaii."

Glenn Roeder discussing the impending return of Paolo Di Canio to West Ham United from injury:
"Have we missed him? No comment."

Leroy Rosenior, Torquay United boss, on Lincoln City's game:
"Their approach was negative – it's closer to rugby than football."

Terry Venables talking about his appointment at Leeds United:
"For the first time I am at a club where I believe I've got a chance to win it (The Premiership title)."

Before signing for Middlesbrough, Italy's Massimo Maccarone:
"It is too soon to go to England. I am ready for Serie A even as a fourth striker."

One-time Everton manager Howard Kendall:
"I've never perceived any wisdom in this new-fangled rotation system."

Kevin Ratcliffe prior to being relieved of his managerial role at Shrewsbury Town:
"Any manager who says he does not take the pressures home is a liar."

Terry Butcher to a crowd of yobs at the England v Turkey game at Sunderland:
"If you're so brave go and enlist to fight in Iraq. Now get out of here."

Ray Wilkins summing up a Chelsea v Arsenal clash:
"Chelsea signed me, sold me and also sacked me, but I've still got a soft spot for them. Even so, I've got to go for Arsenal."

Claudio Ranieri on the cabbage patch of a Chelsea pitch:
"Stamford Bridge is fantastic – for potatoes."

Ex-Chelsea defender Ron "Chopper" Harris discussing Roy Keane:
"He's a tough character, but I wouldn't put him in the same mould as Peter Storey, Dave Mackay or Tommy Smith. Football is like a non-contact sport now."

Robbie Savage, the Birmingham City and Wales midfield player:
"In the previous three Wales games, I've clattered somebody in the first 30 seconds and I'm not going to change – if I get booked I get booked."

Middlesbrough manager Steve McClaren on the scarcity of penalty awards for his team:
"It's been so long since we have had a penalty nobody knew who was taking it. We had forgotten where the spot was."

Welsh manager Mark Hughes on speculation linking him with Manchester United:
"Football being what it is, the manager invariably gets linked with other jobs!"

Mark Palios, new chief executive of the Football Association, getting back to basics:
"As a former player and a fan of the game, I'm in no doubt the FA must at all times put football first."

David Beckham revealing a real secret:
"I always bring Brooklyn a strip home from every country I visit and he has been wearing the Madrid one for some time. At least he can go out in public in it now!"

David O'Leary talking about his time at Leeds United:
"It was a tough job and I made mistakes. The biggest one is that I became too opinionated in newspapers and you won't hear that from David O'Leary again."

Ruud Van Nistelrooy:
"I can see myself staying at Manchester United for the rest of my career. What I really want is to score 150 goals."

Martin O'Neill on his style of coaching from the touchline:
"I will calm down when I retire or die."

Middlesbrough's Dean Windass on his refusal to join his father-in-law's team North Ferriby United:
"I may be desperate but not that desperate."

Rotherham United manager Ronnie Moore on viewing the fixture list last season:
"If we can take 11 points from the first six matches, it'll be like we've swum the channel."

The then Stoke City manager Steve Cotterill after the first match of the season:
"We had a lesson today about life in the First Division. That's one game over and 45 headaches to come."

Jimmy Greaves on the old days:
"Back then unless you took a machete out on the pitch you wouldn't get booked. The whole game was much tougher."

After finding themselves bottom of the First Division following a 3-0 defeat by Reading, Burnley manager Stan Ternent said:
"We were woeful and I am embarrassed to be the manager."

Gary Neville on Wayne Rooney:
"Wayne is only 17 but Sachin Tendulkar didn't become an Indian cricket legend by him being kept back because of his age."

Sven Goran Eriksson on the same subject:
"I can't see any reason to leave him out and if he goes on playing like that I won't leave him out."

Sir Alex Ferguson after the dressing-room bust-up with David Beckham:
"I'm looking for another goalkeeper, a full-back, a centre-half, a midfielder, a winger and a centre-forward."

Gary Pallister on the same theme:
"It's amazing. People were saying he should have retired, but the whole boot incident with David Beckham showed the passion is still there and he wants to be a winner."

Leeds United chairman Professor John McKenzie dealing with the club's financial problems:
"It's like an oil tanker that was heading for the rocks and the shareholders have put someone else on board to turn it around. The trouble with oil tankers is they're two miles long and they don't turn around in two minutes."

Peter Schmeichel before his last game for Manchester City:
"I made a decision that this is going to be my last season and I'm not going to be too emotional about that on Sunday. If it comes, it will be at the start of next season when everyone is going back to training and I'm not part of it."

Teddy Sheringham on his hopes of returning to Tottenham Hotspur(?):
"If I become a manager, having played for this great club, I would love to manage it one day."

Norwich City manager Nigel Worthington on missing out on the play-offs:
"Over the course of two seasons, players have given blood for this football club and it's a case of how much blood you can get out of the stone. Now we need to add some quality."

Gordon Strachan the Southampton manager on what he said to Fulham fans at Loftus Road after he raced out of the dugout:
"I just told them – it's not your pitch anyway!"

Aston Villa manager Graham Taylor on the derby with West Bromwich Albion:
"We will have a police escort from Villa Park to the Hawthorns for obvious reasons. If we lose we will need an escort coming back – from our own supporters!"

Hugo Gatti, reporter from the Spanish newspaper *Marca* on Fabien Barthez's performance for Manchester United against Real Madrid:
"(Like) A woman on her wedding day – nervous, out of position and hoping everything would soon be over so she could go up to the bedroom."

Ipswich Town chairman David Sheepshanks on life after relegation:
"I wouldn't wish relegation on my worst enemy. It doesn't seem right that the price of going down is near bankruptcy. You accept there should be some financial hardship, but the penalty is too great."

Paul Gascoigne on the China experience:
"China feels great. I've tried chicken's head, chicken's feet and bats and hopefully if I keep that up, I'll be flying."

Paul Rideout, man of many clubs and seasons:
"China is so far behind the rest of the world that you need to have a different mentality to live there."

Terry Fenwick on his 48 days as Northampton Town manager:
"Northampton are currently making payments to four managers, but not paying any bills."

Everton's David Unsworth talking about his colleague Wayne Rooney:
"He can go all the way to the top providing he keeps his head firmly on the ground."

Mark Lawrenson, TV pundit:
"All strikers go through what they call a glut, where they don't score goals."

Rangers manager Alex McLeish on the dramatic end to the Scottish Premier League season:
"It feels absolutely wonderful. But the dividing line between success and failure is so thin. One minute we looked out of it but then I was told it was over at Rugby Park. It was brilliant."

Paolo Maldini, the AC Milan captain on emulating his father Cesare in taking a European Cup trophy:
"To do something my father did all those years ago was a dream but our victory proves they happen sometimes."

Steve McManaman laying it on the line at Real Madrid:
"We'll have to win the League now after failing in Europe or we will all be shot."

Mick Wadsworth the Huddersfield Town manager after the 3-3 draw with Cheltenham Town:
"We attacked like Real Madrid, but defended like a team from the Dog and Duck."

Barry Venison TV pundit:
"Terry Venables has literally had his legs cut off from underneath him three times while he's been manager."

Sir Bobby Robson on his preference, Portuguese-wise:
"That's easy. On Saturday afternoon Viana, Saturday night Viagra."

Mike Parry, the 'Seeker of Truth and Justice' from talkSPORT, the UK's most successful commercial radio station, endlessly asks:
"Did you know that I once scored a penalty at Old Trafford?"

THE FA CHARITY SHIELD WINNERS 1908–2002

Year	Match	Score
1908	Manchester U v QPR	4-0 after 1-1 draw
1909	Newcastle U v Northampton T	2-0
1910	Brighton v Aston Villa	1-0
1911	Manchester U v Swindon T	8-4
1912	Blackburn R v QPR	2-1
1913	Professionals v Amateurs	7-2
1920	WBA v Tottenham H	2-0
1921	Tottenham H v Burnley	2-0
1922	Huddersfield T v Liverpool	1-0
1923	Professionals v Amateurs	2-0
1924	Professionals v Amateurs	3-1
1925	Amateurs v Professionals	6-1
1926	Amateurs v Professionals	6-3
1927	Cardiff C v Corinthians	2-1
1928	Everton v Blackburn R	2-1
1929	Professionals v Amateurs	3-0
1930	Arsenal v Sheffield W	2-1
1931	Arsenal v WBA	1-0
1932	Everton v Newcastle U	5-3
1933	Arsenal v Everton	3-0
1934	Arsenal v Manchester C	4-0
1935	Sheffield W v Arsenal	1-0
1936	Sunderland v Arsenal	2-1
1937	Manchester C v Sunderland	2-0
1938	Arsenal v Preston NE	2-1
1948	Arsenal v Manchester U	4-3
1949	Portsmouth v Wolverhampton W	1-1*
1950	World Cup Team v Canadian Touring Team	4-2
1951	Tottenham H v Newcastle U	2-1
1952	Manchester U v Newcastle U	4-2
1953	Arsenal v Blackpool	3-1
1954	Wolverhampton W v WBA	4-4*
1955	Chelsea v Newcastle U	3-0
1956	Manchester U v Manchester C	1-0
1957	Manchester U v Aston Villa	4-0
1958	Bolton W v Wolverhampton W	4-1
1959	Wolverhampton W v Nottingham F	3-1
1960	Burnley v Wolverhampton W	2-2*
1961	Tottenham H v FA XI	3-2
1962	Tottenham H v Ipswich T	5-1
1963	Everton v Manchester U	4-0
1964	Liverpool v West Ham U	2-2*
1965	Manchester U v Liverpool	2-2*
1966	Liverpool v Everton	1-0
1967	Manchester U v Tottenham H	3-3*
1968	Manchester C v WBA	6-1
1969	Leeds U v Manchester C	2-1
1970	Everton v Chelsea	2-1
1971	Leicester C v Liverpool	1-0
1972	Manchester C v Aston Villa	1-0
1973	Burnley v Manchester C	1-0
1974	Liverpool† v Leeds U	1-1
1975	Derby Co v West Ham U	2-0
1976	Liverpool v Southampton	1-0
1977	Liverpool v Manchester U	0-0*
1978	Nottingham F v Ipswich T	5-0
1979	Liverpool v Arsenal	3-1
1980	Liverpool v West Ham U	1-0
1981	Aston Villa v Tottenham H	2-2*
1982	Liverpool v Tottenham H	1-0
1983	Manchester U v Liverpool	2-0
1984	Everton v Liverpool	1-0
1985	Everton v Manchester U	2-0
1986	Everton v Liverpool	1-1*
1987	Everton v Coventry C	1-0
1988	Liverpool v Wimbledon	2-1
1989	Liverpool v Arsenal	1-0
1990	Liverpool v Manchester U	1-1*
1991	Arsenal v Tottenham H	0-0*
1992	Leeds U v Liverpool	4-3
1993	Manchester U† v Arsenal	1-1
1994	Manchester U v Blackburn R	2-0
1995	Everton v Blackburn R	1-0
1996	Manchester U v Newcastle U	4-0
1997	Manchester U† v Chelsea	1-1
1998	Arsenal v Manchester U	3-0
1999	Arsenal v Manchester U	2-1
2000	Chelsea v Manchester U	2-0
2001	Liverpool v Manchester U	2-1
2002	Arsenal v Liverpool	1-0

** Each club retained shield for six months.* *† Won on penalties.*

THE FA COMMUNITY SHIELD 2002

Arsenal (0) 1, Liverpool (0) 0

At Millennium Stadium, 11 August 2002, attendance 67,337

Arsenal: Seaman; Lauren, Cole, Vieira, Campbell, Keown, Parlour, Edu (Silva), Henry, Bergkamp (Toure), Wiltord.

Scorer: Silva 69.

Liverpool: Dudek; Xavier (Babbel), Traore (Cheyrou), Hamann (Murphy), Henchoz, Hyypia, Gerrard, Diouf, Heskey (Baros), Owen (Smicer), Riise.

Referee: A. Wiley (Burntwood).

ENGLISH LEAGUE HONOURS 1888 TO 2003

FA PREMIER LEAGUE

Maximum points: a 126; b 114.

**Won or placed on goal average (ratio), goal difference or most goals scored.*
††Not promoted after play-offs.

	First	*Pts*	*Second*	*Pts*	*Third*	*Pts*
1992–93*a*	Manchester U	84	Aston Villa	74	Norwich C	72
1993–94*a*	Manchester U	92	Blackburn R	84	Newcastle U	77
1994–95*a*	Blackburn R	89	Manchester U	88	Nottingham F	77
1995–96*a*	Manchester U	82	Newcastle U	78	Liverpool	71
1996–97*b*	Manchester U	75	Newcastle U*	68	Arsenal*	68
1997–98*b*	Arsenal	78	Manchester U	77	Liverpool	65
1998–99*b*	Manchester U	79	Arsenal	78	Chelsea	75
1999–2000*b*	Manchester U	91	Arsenal	73	Leeds U	69
2000–01	Manchester U	80	Arsenal	70	Liverpool	69
2001–02	Arsenal	87	Liverpool	80	Manchester U	77
2002-03	Manchester U	83	Arsenal	78	Newcastle U	69

FIRST DIVISION

Maximum points: 138

1992–93	Newcastle U	96	West Ham U*	88	Portsmouth††	88
1993–94	Crystal Palace	90	Nottingham F	83	Millwall††	74
1994–95	Middlesbrough	82	Reading††	79	Bolton W	77
1995–96	Sunderland	83	Derby Co	79	Crystal Palace††	75
1996–97	Bolton W	98	Barnsley	80	Wolverhampton W††	76
1997–98	Nottingham F	94	Middlesbrough	91	Sunderland††	90
1998–99	Sunderland	105	Bradford C	87	Ipswich T††	86
1999–2000	Charlton Ath	91	Manchester C	89	Ipswich T	87
2000–01	Fulham	101	Blackburn R	91	Bolton W	87
2001–02	Manchester C	99	WBA	89	Wolverhampton W††	86
2002-03	Portsmouth	98	Leicester C	92	Sheffield U††	80

SECOND DIVISION

Maximum points: 138

1992–93	Stoke C	93	Bolton W	90	Port Vale††	89
1993–94	Reading	89	Port Vale	88	Plymouth Arg*††	85
1994–95	Birmingham C	89	Brentford††	85	Crewe Alex††	83
1995–96	Swindon T	92	Oxford U	83	Blackpool††	82
1996–97	Bury	84	Stockport Co	82	Luton T††	78
1997–98	Watford	88	Bristol C	85	Grimsby T	72
1998–99	Fulham	101	Walsall	87	Manchester C	82
1999–2000	Preston NE	95	Burnley	88	Gillingham	85
2000–01	Millwall	93	Rotherham U	91	Reading††	86
2001–02	Brighton & HA	90	Reading	84	Brentford*††	83
2002-03	Wigan Ath	100	Crewe Alex	86	Bristol C††	83

THIRD DIVISION

Maximum points: a 126; b 138.

1992–93*a*	Cardiff C	83	Wrexham	80	Barnet	79
1993–94*a*	Shrewsbury T	79	Chester C	74	Crewe Alex	73
1994–95*a*	Carlisle U	91	Walsall	83	Chesterfield	81
1995–96*b*	Preston NE	86	Gillingham	83	Bury	79
1996–97*b*	Wigan Ath*	87	Fulham	87	Carlisle U	84
1997–98*b*	Notts Co	99	Macclesfield T	82	Lincoln C	72
1998–99*b*	Brentford	85	Cambridge U	81	Cardiff C	80
1999–2000*b*	Swansea C	85	Rotherham U	84	Northampton T	82
2000–01	Brighton & HA	92	Cardiff C	82	Chesterfield¶	80
2001–02	Plymouth Arg	102	Luton T	97	Mansfield T	79
2002-03	Rushden & D	87	Hartlepool U	85	Wrexham	84

¶9pts deducted for irregularities.

FOOTBALL LEAGUE

Maximum points: a 44; b 60

	First	*Pts*	*Second*	*Pts*	*Third*	*Pts*
1888–89*a*	Preston NE	40	Aston Villa	29	Wolverhampton W	28
1889–90*a*	Preston NE	33	Everton	31	Blackburn R	27
1890–91*a*	Everton	29	Preston NE	27	Notts Co	26
1891–92*b*	Sunderland	42	Preston NE	37	Bolton W	36

FIRST DIVISION to 1991–92

Maximum points: a 44; b 52; c 60; d 68; e 76; f 84; g 126; h 120; k 114.

1892–93*c*	Sunderland	48	Preston NE	37	Everton	36
1893–94*c*	Aston Villa	44	Sunderland	38	Derby Co	36
1894–95*c*	Sunderland	47	Everton	42	Aston Villa	39
1895–96*c*	Aston Villa	45	Derby Co	41	Everton	39
1896–97*c*	Aston Villa	47	Sheffield U*	36	Derby Co	36
1897–98*c*	Sheffield U	42	Sunderland	37	Wolverhampton W*	35

	First	*Pts*	*Second*	*Pts*	*Third*	*Pts*
1898–99*d*	Aston Villa	45	Liverpool	43	Burnley	39
1899–1900*d*	Aston Villa	50	Sheffield U	48	Sunderland	41
1900–01*d*	Liverpool	45	Sunderland	43	Notts Co	40
1901–02*d*	Sunderland	44	Everton	41	Newcastle U	37
1902–03*d*	The Wednesday	42	Aston Villa*	41	Sunderland	41
1903–04*d*	The Wednesday	47	Manchester C	44	Everton	43
1904–05*d*	Newcastle U	48	Everton	47	Manchester C	46
1905–06*e*	Liverpool	51	Preston NE	47	The Wednesday	44
1906–07*e*	Newcastle U	51	Bristol C	48	Everton*	45
1907–08*e*	Manchester U	52	Aston Villa*	43	Manchester C	43
1908–09*e*	Newcastle U	53	Everton	46	Sunderland	44
1909–10*e*	Aston Villa	53	Liverpool	48	Blackburn R*	45
1910–11*e*	Manchester U	52	Aston Villa	51	Sunderland*	45
1911–12*e*	Blackburn R	49	Everton	46	Newcastle U	44
1912–13*e*	Sunderland	54	Aston Villa	50	Sheffield W	49
1913–14*e*	Blackburn R	51	Aston Villa	44	Middlesbrough*	43
1914–15*e*	Everton	46	Oldham Ath	45	Blackburn R*	43
1919–20*f*	WBA	60	Burnley	51	Chelsea	49
1920–21*f*	Burnley	59	Manchester C	54	Bolton W	52
1921–22*f*	Liverpool	57	Tottenham H	51	Burnley	49
1922–23*f*	Liverpool	60	Sunderland	54	Huddersfield T	53
1923–24*f*	Huddersfield T*	57	Cardiff C	57	Sunderland	53
1924–25*f*	Huddersfield T	58	WBA	56	Bolton W	55
1925–26*f*	Huddersfield T	57	Arsenal	52	Sunderland	48
1926–27*f*	Newcastle U	56	Huddersfield T	51	Sunderland	49
1927–28*f*	Everton	53	Huddersfield T	51	Leicester C	48
1928–29*f*	Sheffield W	52	Leicester C	51	Aston Villa	50
1929–30*f*	Sheffield W	60	Derby Co	50	Manchester C*	47
1930–31*f*	Arsenal	66	Aston Villa	59	Sheffield W	52
1931–32*f*	Everton	56	Arsenal	54	Sheffield W	50
1932–33*f*	Arsenal	58	Aston Villa	54	Sheffield W	51
1933–34*f*	Arsenal	59	Huddersfield T	56	Tottenham H	49
1934–35*f*	Arsenal	58	Sunderland	54	Sheffield W	49
1935–36*f*	Sunderland	56	Derby Co*	48	Huddersfield T	48
1936–37*f*	Manchester C	57	Charlton Ath	54	Arsenal	52
1937–38*f*	Arsenal	52	Wolverhampton W	51	Preston NE	49
1938–39*f*	Everton	59	Wolverhampton W	55	Charlton Ath	50
1946–47*f*	Liverpool	57	Manchester U*	56	Wolverhampton W	56
1947–48*f*	Arsenal	59	Manchester U*	52	Burnley	52
1948–49*f*	Portsmouth	58	Manchester U*	53	Derby Co	53
1949–50*f*	Portsmouth*	53	Wolverhampton W	53	Sunderland	52
1950–51*f*	Tottenham H	60	Manchester U	56	Blackpool	50
1951–52*f*	Manchester U	57	Tottenham H*	53	Arsenal	53
1952–53*f*	Arsenal*	54	Preston NE	54	Wolverhampton W	51
1953–54*f*	Wolverhampton W	57	WBA	53	Huddersfield T	51
1954–55*f*	Chelsea	52	Wolverhampton W*	48	Portsmouth*	48
1955–56*f*	Manchester U	60	Blackpool*	49	Wolverhampton W	49
1956–57*f*	Manchester U	64	Tottenham H*	56	Preston NE	56
1957–58*f*	Wolverhampton W	64	Preston NE	59	Tottenham H	51
1958–59*f*	Wolverhampton W	61	Manchester U	55	Arsenal*	50
1959–60*f*	Burnley	55	Wolverhampton W	54	Tottenham H	53
1960–61*f*	Tottenham H	66	Sheffield W	58	Wolverhampton W	57
1961–62*f*	Ipswich T	56	Burnley	53	Tottenham H	52
1962–63*f*	Everton	61	Tottenham H	55	Burnley	54
1963–64*f*	Liverpool	57	Manchester U	53	Everton	52
1964–65*f*	Manchester U*	61	Leeds U	61	Chelsea	56
1965–66*f*	Liverpool	61	Leeds U*	55	Burnley	55
1966–67*f*	Manchester U	60	Nottingham F*	56	Tottenham H	56
1967–68*f*	Manchester C	58	Manchester U	56	Liverpool	55
1968–69*f*	Leeds U	67	Liverpool	61	Everton	57
1969–70*f*	Everton	66	Leeds U	57	Chelsea	55
1970–71*f*	Arsenal	65	Leeds U	64	Tottenham H*	52
1971–72*f*	Derby Co	58	Leeds U*	57	Liverpool*	57
1972–73*f*	Liverpool	60	Arsenal	57	Leeds U	53
1973–74*f*	Leeds U	62	Liverpool	57	Derby Co	48
1974–75*f*	Derby Co	53	Liverpool*	51	Ipswich T	51
1975–76*f*	Liverpool	60	QPR	59	Manchester U	56
1976–77*f*	Liverpool	57	Manchester C	56	Ipswich T	52
1977–78*f*	Nottingham F	64	Liverpool	57	Everton	55
1978–79*f*	Liverpool	68	Nottingham F	60	WBA	59
1979–80*f*	Liverpool	60	Manchester U	58	Ipswich T	52
1980–81*f*	Aston Villa	60	Ipswich T	56	Arsenal	53
1981–82*g*	Liverpool	87	Ipswich T	83	Manchester U	78
1982–83*g*	Liverpool	82	Watford	71	Manchester U	70
1983–84*g*	Liverpool	80	Southampton	77	Nottingham F*	74
1984–85*g*	Everton	90	Liverpool*	77	Tottenham H	77
1985–86*g*	Liverpool	88	Everton	86	West Ham U	84
1986–87*g*	Everton	86	Liverpool	77	Tottenham H	71
1987–88*h*	Liverpool	90	Manchester U	81	Nottingham F	73
1988–89*k*	Arsenal*	76	Liverpool	76	Nottingham F	64
1989–90*k*	Liverpool	79	Aston Villa	70	Tottenham H	63
1990–91*k*	Arsenal†	83	Liverpool	76	Crystal Palace	69
1991–92*g*	Leeds U	82	Manchester U	78	Sheffield W	75

No official competition during 1915–19 and 1939–46; Regional Leagues operated.
†2 pts deducted

SECOND DIVISION to 1991–92

Maximum points: a 44; b 56; c 60; d 68; e 76; f 84; g 126; h 132; k 138.

	First	*Pts*	*Second*	*Pts*	*Third*	*Pts*
1892–93*a*	Small Heath	36	Sheffield U	35	Darwen	30
1893–94*b*	Liverpool	50	Small Heath	42	Notts Co	39
1894–95*c*	Bury	48	Notts Co	39	Newton Heath*	38
1895–96*c*	Liverpool*	46	Manchester C	46	Grimsby T*	42
1896–97*c*	Notts Co	42	Newton Heath	39	Grimsby T	38
1897–98*c*	Burnley	48	Newcastle U	45	Manchester C	39
1898–99*d*	Manchester C	52	Glossop NE	46	Leicester Fosse	45
1899–1900*d*	The Wednesday	54	Bolton W	52	Small Heath	46
1900–01*d*	Grimsby T	49	Small Heath	48	Burnley	44
1901–02*d*	WBA	55	Middlesbrough	51	Preston NE*	42
1902–03*d*	Manchester C	54	Small Heath	51	Woolwich A	48
1903–04*d*	Preston NE	50	Woolwich A	49	Manchester U	48
1904–05*d*	Liverpool	58	Bolton W	56	Manchester U	53
1905–06*e*	Bristol C	66	Manchester U	62	Chelsea	53
1906–07*e*	Nottingham F	60	Chelsea	57	Leicester Fosse	48
1907–08*e*	Bradford C	54	Leicester Fosse	52	Oldham Ath	50
1908–09*e*	Bolton W	52	Tottenham H*	51	WBA	51
1909–10*e*	Manchester C	54	Oldham Ath*	53	Hull C*	53
1910–11*e*	WBA	53	Bolton W	51	Chelsea	49
1911–12*e*	Derby Co*	54	Chelsea	54	Burnley	52
1912–13*e*	Preston NE	53	Burnley	50	Birmingham	46
1913–14*e*	Notts Co	53	Bradford PA*	49	Woolwich A	49
1914–15*e*	Derby Co	53	Preston NE	50	Barnsley	47
1919–20*f*	Tottenham H	70	Huddersfield T	64	Birmingham	56
1920–21*f*	Birmingham*	58	Cardiff C	58	Bristol C	51
1921–22*f*	Nottingham F	56	Stoke C*	52	Barnsley	52
1922–23*f*	Notts Co	53	West Ham U*	51	Leicester C	51
1923–24*f*	Leeds U	54	Bury*	51	Derby Co	51
1924–25*f*	Leicester C	59	Manchester U	57	Derby Co	55
1925–26*f*	Sheffield W	60	Derby Co	57	Chelsea	52
1926–27*f*	Middlesbrough	62	Portsmouth*	54	Manchester C	54
1927–28*f*	Manchester C	59	Leeds U	57	Chelsea	54
1928–29*f*	Middlesbrough	55	Grimsby T	53	Bradford PA*	48
1929–30*f*	Blackpool	58	Chelsea	55	Oldham Ath	53
1930–31*f*	Everton	61	WBA	54	Tottenham H	51
1931–32*f*	Wolverhampton W	56	Leeds U	54	Stoke C	52
1932–33*f*	Stoke C	56	Tottenham H	55	Fulham	50
1933–34*f*	Grimsby T	59	Preston NE	52	Bolton W*	51
1934–35*f*	Brentford	61	Bolton W*	56	West Ham U	56
1935–36*f*	Manchester U	56	Charlton Ath	55	Sheffield U*	52
1936–37*f*	Leicester C	56	Blackpool	55	Bury	52
1937–38*f*	Aston Villa	57	Manchester U*	53	Sheffield U	53
1938–39*f*	Blackburn R	55	Sheffield U	54	Sheffield W	53
1946–47*f*	Manchester C	62	Burnley	58	Birmingham C	55
1947–48*f*	Birmingham C	59	Newcastle U	56	Southampton	52
1948–49*f*	Fulham	57	WBA	56	Southampton	55
1949–50*f*	Tottenham H	61	Sheffield W*	52	Sheffield U*	52
1950–51*f*	Preston NE	57	Manchester C	52	Cardiff C	50
1951–52*f*	Sheffield W	53	Cardiff C*	51	Birmingham C	51
1952–53*f*	Sheffield U	60	Huddersfield T	58	Luton T	52
1953–54*f*	Leicester C*	56	Everton	56	Blackburn R	55
1954–55*f*	Birmingham C*	54	Luton T*	54	Rotherham U	54
1955–56*f*	Sheffield W	55	Leeds U	52	Liverpool*	48
1956–57*f*	Leicester C	61	Nottingham F	54	Liverpool	53
1957–58*f*	West Ham U	57	Blackburn R	56	Charlton Ath	55
1958–59*f*	Sheffield W	62	Fulham	60	Sheffield U*	53
1959–60*f*	Aston Villa	59	Cardiff C	58	Liverpool*	50
1960–61*f*	Ipswich T	59	Sheffield U	58	Liverpool	52
1961–62*f*	Liverpool	62	Leyton Orient	54	Sunderland	53
1962–63*f*	Stoke C	53	Chelsea*	52	Sunderland	52
1963–64*f*	Leeds U	63	Sunderland	61	Preston NE	56
1964–65*f*	Newcastle U	57	Northampton T	56	Bolton W	50
1965–66*f*	Manchester C	59	Southampton	54	Coventry C	53
1966–67*f*	Coventry C	59	Wolverhampton W	58	Carlisle U	52
1967–68*f*	Ipswich T	59	QPR*	58	Blackpool	58
1968–69*f*	Derby Co	63	Crystal Palace	56	Charlton Ath	50
1969–70*f*	Huddersfield T	60	Blackpool	53	Leicester C	51
1970–71*f*	Leicester C	59	Sheffield U	56	Cardiff C*	53
1971–72*f*	Norwich C	57	Birmingham C	56	Millwall	55
1972–73*f*	Burnley	62	QPR	61	Aston Villa	50
1973–74*f*	Middlesbrough	65	Luton T	50	Carlisle U	49
1974–75*f*	Manchester U	61	Aston Villa	58	Norwich C	53
1975–76*f*	Sunderland	56	Bristol C*	53	WBA	53
1976–77*f*	Wolverhampton W	57	Chelsea	55	Nottingham F	52
1977–78*f*	Bolton W	58	Southampton	57	Tottenham H*	56
1978–79*f*	Crystal Palace	57	Brighton & HA*	56	Stoke C	56
1979–80*f*	Leicester C	55	Sunderland	54	Birmingham C*	53
1980–81*f*	West Ham U	66	Notts Co	53	Swansea C*	50
1981–82*g*	Luton T	88	Watford	80	Norwich C	71
1982–83*g*	QPR	85	Wolverhampton W	75	Leicester C	70
1983–84*g*	Chelsea*	88	Sheffield W	88	Newcastle U	80

	First	*Pts*	*Second*	*Pts*	*Third*	*Pts*
1984–85*g*	Oxford U	84	Birmingham C	82	Manchester C	74
1985–86*g*	Norwich C	84	Charlton Ath	77	Wimbledon	76
1986–87*g*	Derby Co	84	Portsmouth	78	Oldham Ath††	75
1987–88*h*	Millwall	82	Aston Villa*	78	Middlesbrough	78
1988–89*k*	Chelsea	99	Manchester C	82	Crystal Palace	81
1989–90*k*	Leeds U*	85	Sheffield U	85	Newcastle U††	80
1990–91*k*	Oldham Ath	88	West Ham U	87	Sheffield W	82
1991–92*k*	Ipswich T	84	Middlesbrough	80	Derby Co	78

No official competition during 1915–19 and 1939–46; Regional Leagues operated.

THIRD DIVISION to 1991–92

Maximum points: 92; 138 from 1981–82.

	First	*Pts*	*Second*	*Pts*	*Third*	*Pts*
1958–59	Plymouth Arg	62	Hull C	61	Brentford*	57
1959–60	Southampton	61	Norwich C	59	Shrewsbury T*	52
1960–61	Bury	68	Walsall	62	QPR	60
1961–62	Portsmouth	65	Grimsby T	62	Bournemouth*	59
1962–63	Northampton T	62	Swindon T	58	Port Vale	54
1963–64	Coventry C*	60	Crystal Palace	60	Watford	58
1964–65	Carlisle U	60	Bristol C*	59	Mansfield T	59
1965–66	Hull C	69	Millwall	65	QPR	57
1966–67	QPR	67	Middlesbrough	55	Watford	54
1967–68	Oxford U	57	Bury	56	Shrewsbury T	55
1968–69	Watford*	64	Swindon T	64	Luton T	61
1969–70	Orient	62	Luton T	60	Bristol R	56
1970–71	Preston NE	61	Fulham	60	Halifax T	56
1971–72	Aston Villa	70	Brighton & HA	65	Bournemouth*	62
1972–73	Bolton W	61	Notts Co	57	Blackburn R	55
1973–74	Oldham Ath	62	Bristol R*	61	York C	61
1974–75	Blackburn R	60	Plymouth Arg	59	Charlton Ath	55
1975–76	Hereford U	63	Cardiff C	57	Millwall	56
1976–77	Mansfield T	64	Brighton & HA	61	Crystal Palace*	59
1977–78	Wrexham	61	Cambridge U	58	Preston NE*	56
1978–79	Shrewsbury T	61	Watford*	60	Swansea C	60
1979–80	Grimsby T	62	Blackburn R	59	Sheffield W	58
1980–81	Rotherham U	61	Barnsley*	59	Charlton Ath	59
1981–82	Burnley*	80	Carlisle U	80	Fulham	78
1982–83	Portsmouth	91	Cardiff C	86	Huddersfield T	82
1983–84	Oxford U	95	Wimbledon	87	Sheffield U*	83
1984–85	Bradford C	94	Millwall	90	Hull C	87
1985–86	Reading	94	Plymouth Arg	87	Derby Co	84
1986–87	Bournemouth	97	Middlesbrough	94	Swindon T	87
1987–88	Sunderland	93	Brighton & HA	84	Walsall	82
1988–89	Wolverhampton W	92	Sheffield U*	84	Port Vale	84
1989–90	Bristol R	93	Bristol C	91	Notts Co	87
1990–91	Cambridge U	86	Southend U	85	Grimsby T*	83
1991–92	Brentford	82	Birmingham C	81	Huddersfield T	78

FOURTH DIVISION (1958–1992)

Maximum points: 92; 138 from 1981–82.

	First	*Pts*	*Second*	*Pts*	*Third*	*Pts*	*Fourth*	*Pts*
1958–59	Port Vale	64	Coventry C*	60	York C	60	Shrewsbury T	58
1959–60	Walsall	65	Notts Co*	60	Torquay U	60	Watford	57
1960–61	Peterborough U	66	Crystal Palace	64	Northampton T*	60	Bradford PA	60
1961–62†	Millwall	56	Colchester U	55	Wrexham	53	Carlisle U	52
1962–63	Brentford	62	Oldham Ath*	59	Crewe Alex	59	Mansfield T*	57
1963–64	Gillingham*	60	Carlisle U	60	Workington	59	Exeter C	58
1964–65	Brighton & HA	63	Millwall*	62	York C	62	Oxford U	61
1965–66	Doncaster R*	59	Darlington	59	Torquay U	58	Colchester U*	56
1966–67	Stockport Co	64	Southport*	59	Barrow	59	Tranmere R	58
1967–68	Luton T	66	Barnsley	61	Hartlepools U	60	Crewe Alex	58
1968–69	Doncaster R	59	Halifax T	57	Rochdale*	56	Bradford C	56
1969–70	Chesterfield	64	Wrexham	61	Swansea C	60	Port Vale	59
1970–71	Notts Co	69	Bournemouth	60	Oldham Ath	59	York C	56
1971–72	Grimsby T	63	Southend U	60	Brentford	59	Scunthorpe U	57
1972–73	Southport	62	Hereford U	58	Cambridge U	57	Aldershot*	56
1973–74	Peterborough U	65	Gillingham	62	Colchester U	60	Bury	59
1974–75	Mansfield T	68	Shrewsbury T	62	Rotherham U	59	Chester*	57
1975–76	Lincoln C	74	Northampton T	68	Reading	60	Tranmere R	58
1976–77	Cambridge U	65	Exeter C	62	Colchester U*	59	Bradford C	59
1977–78	Watford	71	Southend U	60	Swansea C*	56	Brentford	56
1978–79	Reading	65	Grimsby T*	61	Wimbledon*	61	Barnsley	61
1979–80	Huddersfield T	66	Walsall	64	Newport Co	61	Portsmouth*	60
1980–81	Southend U	67	Lincoln C	65	Doncaster R	56	Wimbledon	55
1981–82	Sheffield U	96	Bradford C*	91	Wigan Ath	91	Bournemouth	88
1982–83	Wimbledon	98	Hull C	90	Port Vale	88	Scunthorpe U	83
1983–84	York C	101	Doncaster R	85	Reading*	82	Bristol C	82
1984–85	Chesterfield	91	Blackpool	86	Darlington	85	Bury	84
1985–86	Swindon T	102	Chester C	84	Mansfield T	81	Port Vale	79
1986–87	Northampton T	99	Preston NE	90	Southend U	80	Wolverhampton W††	79
1987–88	Wolverhampton W	90	Cardiff C	85	Bolton W	78	Scunthorpe U††	77
1988–89	Rotherham U	82	Tranmere R	80	Crewe Alex	78	Scunthorpe U††	77

	First	Pts	Second	Pts	Third	Pts	Fourth	Pts
1989–90	Exeter C	89	Grimsby T	79	Southend U	75	Stockport Co††	74
1990–91	Darlington	83	Stockport Co*	82	Hartlepool U	82	Peterborough U	80
1991–92†*	Burnley	83	Rotherham U*	77	Mansfield T	77	Blackpool	76

†*Maximum points:* 88 owing to Accrington Stanley's resignation.
†**Maximum points:* 126 owing to Aldershot being expelled (and only 23 teams started the competition).

THIRD DIVISION—SOUTH (1920–1958)

1920–21 season as Third Division. Maximum points: a 84; b 92.

	First	Pts	Second	Pts	Third	Pts
1920–21*a*	Crystal Palace	59	Southampton	54	QPR	53
1921–22*a*	Southampton*	61	Plymouth Arg	61	Portsmouth	53
1922–23*a*	Bristol C	59	Plymouth Arg*	53	Swansea T	53
1923–24*a*	Portsmouth	59	Plymouth Arg	55	Millwall	54
1924–25*a*	Swansea T	57	Plymouth Arg	56	Bristol C	53
1925–26*a*	Reading	57	Plymouth Arg	56	Millwall	53
1926–27*a*	Bristol C	62	Plymouth Arg	60	Millwall	56
1927–28*a*	Millwall	65	Northampton T	55	Plymouth Arg	53
1928–29*a*	Charlton Ath*	54	Crystal Palace	54	Northampton T*	52
1929–30*a*	Plymouth Arg	68	Brentford	61	QPR	51
1930–31*a*	Notts Co	59	Crystal Palace	51	Brentford	50
1931–32*a*	Fulham	57	Reading	55	Southend U	53
1932–33*a*	Brentford	62	Exeter C	58	Norwich C	57
1933–34*a*	Norwich C	61	Coventry C*	54	Reading*	54
1934–35*a*	Charlton Ath	61	Reading	53	Coventry C	51
1935–36*a*	Coventry C	57	Luton T	56	Reading	54
1936–37*a*	Luton T	58	Notts Co	56	Brighton & HA	53
1937–38*a*	Millwall	56	Bristol C	55	QPR*	53
1938–39*a*	Newport Co	55	Crystal Palace	52	Brighton & HA	49
1939–46	Competition cancelled owing to war. Regional Leagues operated.					
1946–47*a*	Cardiff C	66	QPR	57	Bristol C	51
1947–48*a*	QPR	61	Bournemouth	57	Walsall	51
1948–49*a*	Swansea T	62	Reading	55	Bournemouth	52
1949–50*a*	Notts Co	58	Northampton T*	51	Southend U	51
1950–51*b*	Nottingham F	70	Norwich C	64	Reading*	57
1951–52*b*	Plymouth Arg	66	Reading*	61	Norwich C	61
1952–53*b*	Bristol R	64	Millwall*	62	Northampton T	62
1953–54*b*	Ipswich T	64	Brighton & HA	61	Bristol C	56
1954–55*b*	Bristol C	70	Leyton Orient	61	Southampton	59
1955–56*b*	Leyton Orient	66	Brighton & HA	65	Ipswich T	64
1956–57*b*	Ipswich T*	59	Torquay U	59	Colchester U	58
1957–58*b*	Brighton & HA	60	Brentford*	58	Plymouth Arg	58

THIRD DIVISION—NORTH (1921–1958)

Maximum points: a 76; b 84; c 80; d 92.

	First	Pts	Second	Pts	Third	Pts
1921–22*a*	Stockport Co	56	Darlington*	50	Grimsby T	50
1922–23*a*	Nelson	51	Bradford PA	47	Walsall	46
1923–24*b*	Wolverhampton W	63	Rochdale	62	Chesterfield	54
1924–25*b*	Darlington	58	Nelson*	53	New Brighton	53
1925–26*b*	Grimsby T	61	Bradford PA	60	Rochdale	59
1926–27*b*	Stoke C	63	Rochdale	58	Bradford PA	55
1927–28*b*	Bradford PA	63	Lincoln C	55	Stockport Co	54
1928–29*b*	Bradford C	63	Stockport Co	62	Wrexham	52
1929–30*b*	Port Vale	67	Stockport Co	63	Darlington*	50
1930–31*b*	Chesterfield	58	Lincoln C	57	Wrexham*	54
1931–32*c*	Lincoln C*	57	Gateshead	57	Chester	50
1932–33*b*	Hull C	59	Wrexham	57	Stockport Co	54
1933–34*b*	Barnsley	62	Chesterfield	61	Stockport Co	59
1934–35*b*	Doncaster R	57	Halifax T	55	Chester	54
1935–36*b*	Chesterfield	60	Chester*	55	Tranmere R	55
1936–37*b*	Stockport Co	60	Lincoln C	57	Chester	53
1937–38*b*	Tranmere R	56	Doncaster R	54	Hull C	53
1938–39*b*	Barnsley	67	Doncaster R	56	Bradford C	52
1939–46	Competition cancelled owing to war. Regional Leagues operated.					
1946–47*b*	Doncaster R	72	Rotherham U	60	Chester	56
1947–48*b*	Lincoln C	60	Rotherham U	59	Wrexham	50
1948–49*b*	Hull C	65	Rotherham U	62	Doncaster R	50
1949–50*b*	Doncaster R	55	Gateshead	53	Rochdale*	51
1950–51*d*	Rotherham U	71	Mansfield T	64	Carlisle U	62
1951–52*d*	Lincoln C	69	Grimsby T	66	Stockport Co	59
1952–53*d*	Oldham Ath	59	Port Vale	58	Wrexham	56
1953–54*d*	Port Vale	69	Barnsley	58	Scunthorpe U	57
1954–55*d*	Barnsley	65	Accrington S	61	Scunthorpe U*	58
1955–56*d*	Grimsby T	68	Derby Co	63	Accrington S	59
1956–57*d*	Derby Co	63	Hartlepools U	59	Accrington S*	58
1957–58*d*	Scunthorpe U	66	Accrington S	59	Bradford C	57

PROMOTED AFTER PLAY-OFFS

(Not accounted for in previous section)

1986–87 Aldershot to Division 3.
1987–88 Swansea C to Division 3.
1988–89 Leyton Orient to Division 3.
1989–90 Cambridge U to Division 3; Notts Co to Division 2; Sunderland to Division 1.
1990–91 Notts Co to Division 1; Tranmere R to Division 2; Torquay U to Division 3.
1991–92 Blackburn R to Premier League; Peterborough U to Division 1.
1992–93 Swindon T to Premier League; WBA to Division 1; York C to Division 2.
1993–94 Leicester C to Premier League; Burnley to Division 1; Wycombe W to Division 2.
1994–95 Huddersfield T to Division 1.
1995–96 Leicester C to Premier League; Bradford C to Division 1; Plymouth Arg to Division 2.
1996–97 Crystal Palace to Premier League; Crewe Alex to Division 1; Northampton T to Division 2.
1997–98 Charlton Ath to Premier League; Colchester U to Division 2.
1998–99 Watford to Premier League; Scunthorpe U to Division 2.
1999–2000 Peterborough U to Division 2
2000–01 Walsall to Division 1; Blackpool to Division 2
2001–02 Birmingham C to Premier League; Stoke C to Division 1; Cheltenham T to Division 2
2002–03 Wolverhampton W to Premier League; Cardiff C to Division 1; Bournemouth to Division 2

LEAGUE TITLE WINS

FA PREMIER LEAGUE – Manchester U 8, Arsenal 2, Blackburn R 1.

LEAGUE DIVISION 1 – Liverpool 18, Arsenal 10, Everton 9, Sunderland 8, Aston Villa 7, Manchester U 7, Newcastle U 5, Sheffield W 4, Huddersfield T 3, Leeds U 3, Manchester C 3, Portsmouth 3, Wolverhampton W 3, Blackburn R 2, Burnley 2, Derby Co 2, Nottingham F 2, Preston NE 2, Tottenham H 2; Bolton W, Charlton Ath, Chelsea, Crystal Palace, Fulham, Ipswich T, Middlesbrough, Sheffield U, WBA 1 each.

LEAGUE DIVISION 2 – Leicester C 6, Manchester C 6, Birmingham C (one as Small Heath) 5, Sheffield W 5, Derby Co 4, Liverpool 4, Preston NE 4, Ipswich T 3, Leeds U 3, Middlesbrough 3, Notts Co 3, Stoke C 3, Aston Villa 2, Bolton W 2, Burnley 2, Bury 2, Chelsea 2, Fulham 2, Grimsby T 2, Manchester U 2, Millwall 2, Norwich C 2, Nottingham F 2, Tottenham H 2, WBA 2, West Ham U 2, Wolverhampton W 2; Blackburn R, Blackpool, Bradford C, Brentford, Brighton & HA, Bristol C, Coventry C, Crystal Palace, Everton, Huddersfield T, Luton T, Newcastle U, QPR, Oldham Ath, Oxford U, Reading, Sheffield U, Sunderland, Swindon T, Watford, Wigan Ath 1 each.

LEAGUE DIVISION 3 – Brentford 2, Carlisle U 2, Oxford U 2, Plymouth Arg 2, Portsmouth 2, Preston NE 2, Shrewsbury T 2; Aston Villa, Blackburn R, Bolton W, Bournemouth, Bradford C, Brighton & HA, Bristol R, Burnley, Bury, Cambridge U, Cardiff C, Coventry C, Grimsby T, Hereford U, Hull C, Leyton Orient, Mansfield T, Northampton T, Notts Co, Oldham Ath, QPR, Reading, Rotherham U, Rushden & D Southampton, Sunderland, Swansea C, Watford, Wigan Ath, Wolverhampton W, Wrexham 1 each.

LEAGUE DIVISION 4 – Chesterfield 2, Doncaster R 2, Peterborough U 2; Brentford, Brighton & HA, Burnley, Cambridge U, Darlington, Exeter C, Gillingham, Grimsby T, Huddersfield T, Lincoln C, Luton T, Mansfield T, Millwall, Northampton T, Notts Co, Port Vale, Reading, Rotherham U, Sheffield U, Southend U, Southport, Stockport Co, Swindon T, Walsall, Watford, Wimbledon, Wolverhampton W, York C 1 each.

To 1957–58

DIVISION 3 (South) – Bristol C 3, Charlton Ath 2, Ipswich T 2, Millwall 2, Notts Co 2, Plymouth Arg 2, Swansea T 2; Brentford, Brighton & HA, Bristol R, Cardiff C, Coventry C, Crystal Palace, Fulham, Leyton Orient, Luton T, Newport Co, Norwich C, Nottingham F, Portsmouth, QPR, Reading, Southampton 1 each.

DIVISION 3 (North) – Barnsley 3, Doncaster R 3, Lincoln C 3, Chesterfield 2, Grimsby T 2, Hull C 2, Port Vale 2, Stockport Co 2; Bradford C, Bradford PA, Darlington, Derby Co, Nelson, Oldham Ath, Rotherham U, Scunthorpe U, Stoke C, Tranmere R, Wolverhampton W 1 each.

RELEGATED CLUBS

1891–92 League extended. Newton Heath, Sheffield W and Nottingham F admitted. *Second Division formed* including Darwen.
1892–93 In Test matches, Sheffield U and Darwen won promotion in place of Notts Co and Accrington S.
1893–94 In Tests, Liverpool and Small Heath won promotion. Newton Heath and Darwen relegated.
1894–95 After Tests, Bury promoted, Liverpool relegated.
1895–96 After Tests, Liverpool promoted, Small Heath relegated.
1896–97 After Tests, Notts Co promoted, Burnley relegated.
1897–98 Test system abolished after success of Stoke C and Burnley. League extended. Blackburn R and Newcastle U elected to First Division. *Automatic promotion and relegation introduced.*

FA PREMIER LEAGUE TO DIVISION 1

1992–93 Crystal Palace, Middlesbrough, Nottingham F
1993–94 Sheffield U, Oldham Ath, Swindon T
1994–95 Crystal Palace, Norwich C, Leicester C, Ipswich T
1995–96 Manchester C, QPR, Bolton W
1996–97 Sunderland, Middlesbrough, Nottingham F
1997–98 Bolton W, Barnsley, Crystal Palace
1998–99 Charlton Ath, Blackburn R, Nottingham F
1999–2000 Wimbledon, Sheffield W, Watford
2000–01 Manchester C, Coventry C, Bradford C
2001–02 Ipswich T, Derby Co, Leicester C
2002-03 West Ham U, WBA, Sunderland

DIVISION 1 TO DIVISION 2

1898–99 Bolton W and Sheffield W
1899–1900 Burnley and Glossop
1900–01 Preston NE and WBA
1901–02 Small Heath and Manchester C
1902–03 Grimsby T and Bolton W
1903–04 Liverpool and WBA
1904–05 League extended. Bury and Notts Co, two bottom clubs in First Division, re-elected.
1905–06 Nottingham F and Wolverhampton W
1906–07 Derby Co and Stoke C
1907–08 Bolton W and Birmingham C
1908–09 Manchester C and Leicester Fosse
1909–10 Bolton W and Chelsea
1910–11 Bristol C and Nottingham F
1911–12 Preston NE and Bury
1912–13 Notts Co and Woolwich Arsenal
1913–14 Preston NE and Derby Co
1914–15 Tottenham H and Chelsea*
1919–20 Notts Co and Sheffield W
1920–21 Derby Co and Bradford PA

1921–22 Bradford C and Manchester U
1922–23 Stoke C and Oldham Ath
1923–24 Chelsea and Middlesbrough
1924–25 Preston NE and Nottingham F
1925–26 Manchester C and Notts Co
1926–27 Leeds U and WBA
1927–28 Tottenham H and Middlesbrough
1928–29 Bury and Cardiff C
1929–30 Burnley and Everton
1930–31 Leeds U and Manchester U
1931–32 Grimsby T and West Ham U
1932–33 Bolton W and Blackpool
1933–34 Newcastle U and Sheffield U
1934–35 Leicester C and Tottenham H
1935–36 Aston Villa and Blackburn R
1936–37 Manchester U and Sheffield W
1937–38 Manchester C and WBA
1938–39 Birmingham C and Leicester C
1946–47 Brentford and Leeds U
1947–48 Blackburn R and Grimsby T
1948–49 Preston NE and Sheffield U
1949–50 Manchester C and Birmingham C
1950–51 Sheffield W and Everton
1951–52 Huddersfield T and Fulham
1952–53 Stoke C and Derby Co
1953–54 Middlesbrough and Liverpool
1954–55 Leicester C and Sheffield W
1955–56 Huddersfield T and Sheffield U
1956–57 Charlton Ath and Cardiff C
1957–58 Sheffield W and Sunderland
1958–59 Portsmouth and Aston Villa
1959–60 Luton T and Leeds U
1960–61 Preston NE and Newcastle U
1961–62 Chelsea and Cardiff C
1962–63 Manchester C and Leyton Orient
1963–64 Bolton W and Ipswich T
1964–65 Wolverhampton W and Birmingham C
1965–66 Northampton T and Blackburn R
1966–67 Aston Villa and Blackpool
1967–68 Fulham and Sheffield U
1968–69 Leicester C and QPR
1969–70 Sunderland and Sheffield W
1970–71 Burnley and Blackpool
1971–72 Huddersfield T and Nottingham F
1972–73 Crystal Palace and WBA
1973–74 Southampton, Manchester U, Norwich C
1974–75 Luton T, Chelsea, Carlisle U
1975–76 Wolverhampton W, Burnley, Sheffield U
1976–77 Sunderland, Stoke C, Tottenham H
1977–78 West Ham U, Newcastle U, Leicester C
1978–79 QPR, Birmingham C, Chelsea
1979–80 Bristol C, Derby Co, Bolton W
1980–81 Norwich C, Leicester C, Crystal Palace
1981–82 Leeds U, Wolverhampton W, Middlesbrough
1982–83 Manchester C, Swansea C, Brighton & HA
1983–84 Birmingham C, Notts Co, Wolverhampton W
1984–85 Norwich C, Sunderland, Stoke C
1985–86 Ipswich T, Birmingham C, WBA
1986–87 Leicester C, Manchester C, Aston Villa
1987–88 Chelsea**, Portsmouth, Watford, Oxford U
1988–89 Middlesbrough, West Ham U, Newcastle U
1989–90 Sheffield W, Charlton Ath, Millwall
1990–91 Sunderland and Derby Co
1991–92 Luton T, Notts Co, West Ham U
1992–93 Brentford, Cambridge U, Bristol R
1993–94 Birmingham C, Oxford U, Peterborough U
1994–95 Swindon T, Burnley, Bristol C, Notts Co
1995–96 Millwall, Watford, Luton T
1996–97 Grimsby T, Oldham Ath, Southend U
1997–98 Manchester C, Stoke C, Reading
1998–99 Bury, Oxford U, Bristol C
1999–2000 Walsall, Port Vale, Swindon T
2000–01 Huddersfield T, QPR, Tranmere R
2001–02 Crewe Alex, Barnsley, Stockport Co
2002–03 Sheffield W, Brighton & HA, Grimsby T

***Relegated after play-offs.*

**Subsequently re-elected to Division 1 when League was extended after the War.*

DIVISION 2 TO DIVISION 3

1920–21 Stockport Co
1921–22 Bradford PA and Bristol C
1922–23 Rotherham Co and Wolverhampton W
1923–24 Nelson and Bristol C
1924–25 Crystal Palace and Coventry C
1925–26 Stoke C and Stockport Co
1926–27 Darlington and Bradford C
1927–28 Fulham and South Shields
1928–29 Port Vale and Clapton Orient
1929–30 Hull C and Notts Co
1930–31 Reading and Cardiff C
1931–32 Barnsley and Bristol C
1932–33 Chesterfield and Charlton Ath
1933–34 Millwall and Lincoln C
1934–35 Oldham Ath and Notts Co
1935–36 Port Vale and Hull C
1936–37 Doncaster R and Bradford C
1937–38 Barnsley and Stockport Co
1938–39 Norwich C and Tranmere R
1946–47 Swansea T and Newport Co
1947–48 Doncaster R and Millwall
1948–49 Nottingham F and Lincoln C
1949–50 Plymouth Arg and Bradford PA
1950–51 Grimsby T and Chesterfield
1951–52 Coventry C and QPR
1952–53 Southampton and Barnsley
1953–54 Brentford and Oldham Ath
1954–55 Ipswich T and Derby Co
1955–56 Plymouth Arg and Hull C
1956–57 Port Vale and Bury
1957–58 Doncaster R and Notts Co
1958–59 Barnsley and Grimsby T
1959–60 Bristol C and Hull C
1960–61 Lincoln C and Portsmouth
1961–62 Brighton & HA and Bristol R
1962–63 Walsall and Luton T
1963–64 Grimsby T and Scunthorpe U
1964–65 Swindon T and Swansea T
1965–66 Middlesbrough and Leyton Orient
1966–67 Northampton T and Bury
1967–68 Plymouth Arg and Rotherham U
1968–69 Fulham and Bury
1969–70 Preston NE and Aston Villa
1970–71 Blackburn R and Bolton W
1971–72 Charlton Ath and Watford
1972–73 Huddersfield T and Brighton & HA
1973–74 Crystal Palace, Preston NE, Swindon T
1974–75 Millwall, Cardiff C, Sheffield W
1975–76 Oxford U, York C, Portsmouth
1976–77 Carlisle U, Plymouth Arg, Hereford U
1977–78 Blackpool, Mansfield T, Hull C
1978–79 Sheffield U, Millwall, Blackburn R
1979–80 Fulham, Burnley, Charlton Ath
1980–81 Preston NE, Bristol C, Bristol R
1981–82 Cardiff C, Wrexham, Orient
1982–83 Rotherham U, Burnley, Bolton W
1983–84 Derby Co, Swansea C, Cambridge U
1984–85 Notts Co, Cardiff C, Wolverhampton W
1985–86 Carlisle U, Middlesbrough, Fulham
1986–87 Sunderland**, Grimsby T, Brighton & HA
1987–88 Huddersfield T, Reading, Sheffield U**
1988–89 Shrewsbury T, Birmingham C, Walsall
1989–90 Bournemouth, Bradford C, Stoke C
1990–91 WBA and Hull C
1991–92 Plymouth Arg, Brighton & HA, Port Vale
1992–93 Preston NE, Mansfield T, Wigan Ath, Chester C
1993–94 Fulham, Exeter C, Hartlepool U, Barnet
1994–95 Cambridge U, Plymouth Arg, Cardiff C, Chester C, Leyton Orient
1995–96 Carlisle U, Swansea C, Brighton & HA, Hull C
1996–97 Peterborough U, Shrewsbury T, Rotherham U, Notts Co
1997–98 Brentford, Plymouth Arg, Carlisle U, Southend U
1998–99 York C, Northampton T, Lincoln C, Macclesfield T
1999–2000 Cardiff C, Blackpool, Scunthorpe U, Chesterfield
2000–01 Bristol R, Luton T, Swansea C, Oxford U
2001–02 Bournemouth, Bury, Wrexham, Cambridge U
2002–03 Cheltenham T, Huddersfield T, Mansfield T Northampton T

DIVISION 3 TO DIVISION 4

1958–59 Rochdale, Notts Co, Doncaster R, Stockport Co
1959–60 Accrington S, Wrexham, Mansfield T, York C
1960–61 Chesterfield, Colchester U, Bradford C, Tranmere R
1961–62 Newport Co, Brentford, Lincoln C, Torquay U
1962–63 Bradford PA, Brighton & HA, Carlisle U, Halifax T
1963–64 Millwall, Crewe Alex, Wrexham, Notts Co
1964–65 Luton T, Port Vale, Colchester U, Barnsley
1965–66 Southend U, Exeter C, Brentford, York C
1966–67 Doncaster R, Workington, Darlington, Swansea T
1967–68 Scunthorpe U, Colchester U, Grimsby T, Peterborough U (demoted)
1968–69 Oldham Ath, Crewe Alex, Hartlepool, Northampton T
1969–70 Bournemouth, Southport, Barrow, Stockport Co
1970–71 Reading, Bury, Doncaster R, Gillingham
1971–72 Mansfield T, Barnsley, Torquay U, Bradford C
1972–73 Rotherham U, Brentford, Swansea C, Scunthorpe U
1973–74 Cambridge U, Shrewsbury T, Southport, Rochdale
1974–75 Bournemouth, Tranmere R, Watford, Huddersfield T
1975–76 Aldershot, Colchester U, Southend U, Halifax T
1976–77 Reading, Northampton T, Grimsby T, York C
1977–78 Port Vale, Bradford C, Hereford U, Portsmouth
1978–79 Peterborough U, Walsall, Tranmere R, Lincoln C
1979–80 Bury, Southend U, Mansfield T, Wimbledon
1980–81 Sheffield U, Colchester U, Blackpool, Hull C
1981–82 Wimbledon, Swindon T, Bristol C, Chester
1982–83 Reading, Wrexham, Doncaster R, Chesterfield
1983–84 Scunthorpe U, Southend U, Port Vale, Exeter C
1984–85 Burnley, Orient, Preston NE, Cambridge U
1985–86 Lincoln C, Cardiff C, Wolverhampton W, Swansea C
1986–87 Bolton W**, Carlisle U, Darlington, Newport Co
1987–88 Doncaster R, York C, Grimsby T, Rotherham U**
1988–89 Southend U, Chesterfield, Gillingham, Aldershot
1989–90 Cardiff C, Northampton T, Blackpool, Walsall
1990–91 Crewe Alex, Rotherham U, Mansfield T
1991–92 Bury, Shrewsbury T, Torquay U, Darlington

*** Relegated after play-offs. N.B. Relegated clubs not featured in exact order of finishing.*

APPLICATIONS FOR RE-ELECTION

FOURTH DIVISION

Eleven: Hartlepool U.
Seven: Crewe Alex.
Six: Barrow (lost League place to Hereford U 1972), Halifax T, Rochdale, Southport (lost League place to Wigan Ath 1978), York C.
Five: Chester C, Darlington, Lincoln C, Stockport Co, Workington (lost League place to Wimbledon 1977).
Four: Bradford PA (lost League place to Cambridge U 1970), Newport Co, Northampton T.
Three: Doncaster R, Hereford U.
Two: Bradford C, Exeter C, Oldham Ath, Scunthorpe U, Torquay U.
One: Aldershot, Colchester U, Gateshead (lost League place to Peterborough U 1960), Grimsby T, Swansea C, Tranmere R, Wrexham, Blackpool, Cambridge U, Preston NE.
Accrington S resigned and Oxford U were elected 1962.
Port Vale were forced to re-apply following expulsion in 1968.
Aldershot expelled March 1992. Maidstone U resigned August 1992.

THIRD DIVISIONS NORTH & SOUTH

Seven: Walsall.
Six: Exeter C, Halifax T, Newport Co.
Five: Accrington S, Barrow, Gillingham, New Brighton, Southport.
Four: Rochdale, Norwich C.
Three: Crystal Palace, Crewe Alex, Darlington, Hartlepool U, Merthyr T, Swindon T.
Two: Aberdare Ath, Aldershot, Ashington, Bournemouth, Brentford, Chester, Colchester U, Durham C, Millwall, Nelson, QPR, Rotherham U, Southend U, Tranmere R, Watford, Workington.
One: Bradford C, Bradford PA, Brighton & HA, Bristol R, Cardiff C, Carlisle U, Charlton Ath, Gateshead, Grimsby T, Mansfield T, Shrewsbury T, Torquay U, York C.

LEAGUE STATUS FROM 1986–87

	RELEGATED FROM LEAGUE	*PROMOTED TO LEAGUE*
1986–87	Lincoln C	Scarborough
1987–88	Newport Co	Lincoln C
1988–89	Darlington	Maidstone U
1989–90	Colchester U	Darlington
1990–91	—	Barnet
1991–92	—	Colchester U
1992–93	Halifax T	Wycombe W
1993–94	—	—
1994–95	—	—
1995–96	—	—
1996–97	Hereford U	Macclesfield T
1997–98	Doncaster R	Halifax T
1998–99	Scarborough	Cheltenham T
1999–2000	Chester C	Kidderminster H
2000–01	Barnet	Rushden & D
2001–02	Halifax T	Boston U
2002–03	Shrewsbury T, Exeter C	Yeovil T, Doncaster R

FOOTBALL AWARDS 2003

FOOTBALLER OF THE YEAR

The Football Writers' Association Sir Stanley Matthews Trophy for the Footballer of the Year went to Thierry Henry of Arsenal and France.

THE PFA AWARDS 2003

Player of the Year: Thierry Henry, Arsenal and France.
Young Player of the Year: Jermaine Jenas, Newcastle United and England.
Merit Award: Sir Bobby Robson.
Player of the Decade: Alan Shearer, Newcastle United and England.

SCOTTISH FOOTBALL WRITERS ASSOCIATION

Player of the Year: Barry Ferguson, Rangers and Scotland.

SCOTTISH PFA AWARDS 2003

Player of the Year: Barry Ferguson, Rangers.
Young Player of the Year: James McFadden, Motherwell.
First Division: Dennis Wyness, Inverness CT.
Second Division: Chris Templeman, Brechin C.
Third Division: Alex Williams, Morton.

EUROPEAN FOOTBALLER OF THE YEAR 2003

Ronaldo, Real Madrid and Brazil.

WORLD PLAYER OF THE YEAR 2003

Ronaldo, Real Madrid and Brazil.

WOMENS PLAYER OF THE YEAR 2003

Mia Hamm, United States.

Thierry Henry holds the PFA award aloft, a piece of silverware to accompany one as the Football Writers choice for the 2002–03 season. (Colorsport)

Ronaldo picked up the European Player of the Year trophy and coupled it with the World Player Award. (Associated Sports Photography)

LEAGUE ATTENDANCES SINCE 1946–47

Season	*Matches*	*Total*	*Div. 1*	*Div. 2*	*Div. 3 (S)*	*Div. 3 (N)*
1946–47	1848	35,604,606	15,005,316	11,071,572	5,664,004	3,863,714
1947–48	1848	40,259,130	16,732,341	12,286,350	6,653,610	4,586,829
1948–49	1848	41,271,414	17,914,667	11,353,237	6,998,429	5,005,081
1949–50	1848	40,517,865	17,278,625	11,694,158	7,104,155	4,440,927
1950–51	2028	39,584,967	16,679,454	10,780,580	7,367,884	4,757,109
1951–52	2028	39,015,866	16,110,322	11,066,189	6,958,927	4,880,428
1952–53	2028	37,149,966	16,050,278	9,686,654	6,704,299	4,708,735
1953–54	2028	36,174,590	16,154,915	9,510,053	6,311,508	4,198,114
1954–55	2028	34,133,103	15,087,221	8,988,794	5,996,017	4,051,071
1955–56	2028	33,150,809	14,108,961	9,080,002	5,692,479	4,269,367
1956–57	2028	32,744,405	13,803,037	8,718,162	5,622,189	4,601,017
1957–58	2028	33,562,208	14,468,652	8,663,712	6,097,183	4,332,661
					Div. 3	*Div. 4*
1958–59	2028	33,610,985	14,727,691	8,641,997	5,946,600	4,276,697
1959–60	2028	32,538,611	14,391,227	8,399,627	5,739,707	4,008,050
1960–61	2028	28,619,754	12,926,948	7,033,936	4,784,256	3,874,614
1961–62	2015	27,979,902	12,061,194	7,453,089	5,199,106	3,266,513
1962–63	2028	28,885,852	12,490,239	7,792,770	5,341,362	3,261,481
1963–64	2028	28,535,022	12,486,626	7,594,158	5,419,157	3,035,081
1964–65	2028	27,641,168	12,708,752	6,984,104	4,436,245	3,512,067
1965–66	2028	27,206,980	12,480,644	6,914,757	4,779,150	3,032,429
1966–67	2028	28,902,596	14,242,957	7,253,819	4,421,172	2,984,648
1967–68	2028	30,107,298	15,289,410	7,450,410	4,013,087	3,354,391
1968–69	2028	29,382,172	14,584,851	7,382,390	4,339,656	3,075,275
1969–70	2028	29,600,972	14,868,754	7,581,728	4,223,761	2,926,729
1970–71	2028	28,194,146	13,954,337	7,098,265	4,377,213	2,764,331
1971–72	2028	28,700,729	14,484,603	6,769,308	4,697,392	2,749,426
1972–73	2028	25,448,642	13,998,154	5,631,730	3,737,252	2,081,506
1973–74	2027	24,982,203	13,070,991	6,326,108	3,421,624	2,163,480
1974–75	2028	25,577,977	12,613,178	6,955,970	4,086,145	1,992,684
1975–76	2028	24,896,053	13,089,861	5,798,405	3,948,449	2,059,338
1976–77	2028	26,182,800	13,647,585	6,250,597	4,152,218	2,132,400
1977–78	2028	25,392,872	13,255,677	6,474,763	3,332,042	2,330,390
1978–79	2028	24,540,627	12,704,549	6,153,223	3,374,558	2,308,297
1979–80	2028	24,623,975	12,163,002	6,112,025	3,999,328	2,349,620
1980–81	2028	21,907,569	11,392,894	5,175,442	3,637,854	1,701,379
1981–82	2028	20,006,961	10,420,793	4,750,463	2,836,915	1,998,790
1982–83	2028	18,766,158	9,295,613	4,974,937	2,943,568	1,552,040
1983–84	2028	18,358,631	8,711,448	5,359,757	2,729,942	1,557,484
1984–85	2028	17,849,835	9,761,404	4,030,823	2,667,008	1,390,600
1985–86	2028	16,488,577	9,037,854	3,551,968	2,490,481	1,408,274
1986–87	2028	17,379,218	9,144,676	4,168,131	2,350,970	1,715,441
1987–88	2030	17,959,732	8,094,571	5,341,599	2,751,275	1,772,287
1988–89	2036	18,464,192	7,809,993	5,887,805	3,035,327	1,791,067
1989–90	2036	19,445,442	7,883,039	6,867,674	2,803,551	1,891,178
1990–91	2036	19,508,202	8,618,709	6,285,068	2,835,759	1,768,666
1991–92	2064*	20,487,273	9,989,160	5,809,787	2,993,352	1,694,974
		Total	*FA Premier*	*Div. 1*	*Div. 2*	*Div. 3*
1992–93	2028	20,657,327	9,759,809	5,874,017	3,483,073	1,540,428
1993–94	2028	21,683,381	10,644,551	6,487,104	2,972,702	1,579,024
1994–95	2028	21,856,020	11,213,168	6,044,293	3,037,752	1,560,807
1995–96	2036	21,844,416	10,469,107	6,566,349	2,843,652	1,965,308
1996–97	2036	22,783,163	10,804,762	6,931,539	3,195,223	1,851,639
1997–98	2036	24,692,608	11,092,106	8,330,018	3,503,264	1,767,220
1998–99	2036	25,435,542	11,620,326	7,543,369	4,169,697	2,102,150
1999-2000	2036	25,341,090	11,668,497	7,810,208	3,700,433	2,161,952
2000–01	2036	26,030,167	12,472,094	7,909,512	3,488,166	2,160,395
2001–02	2036	27,756,977	13,043,118	8,352,128	3,963,153	2,398,578
2002–03	2036	28,343,386	13,468,965	8,521,017	3,892,469	2,460,935

**Figures include matches played by Aldershot.*
Football League official total for their three divisions in 2001–02 was 14,716,162.

ENGLISH LEAGUE ATTENDANCES 2002–03

FA BARCLAYCARD PREMIERSHIP ATTENDANCES

	Average Gate			*Season 2002/03*	
	2001/02	2002/03	+/–%	Highest	Lowest
Arsenal	38,054	38,040	–0.04	38,164	37,878
Aston Villa	35,012	35,081	+0.20	42,602	25,817
Birmingham City	21,854	28,813	+31.84	29,505	26,164
Blackburn Rovers	25,984	26,228	+0.94	30,475	21,096
Bolton Wanderers	25,098	24,965	–0.53	27,409	21,753
Charlton Athletic	24,135	26,235	+8.70	26,704	25,615
Chelsea	39,033	39,799	+1.96	41,436	35,227
Everton	34,004	38,468	+13.13	40,168	32,440
Fulham	19,545	16,685	–14.63	18,385	14,019
Leeds United	39,789	39,127	–1.66	40,205	35,547
Liverpool	43,389	43,243	–0.34	44,250	41,462
Manchester City	33,059	34,451	+4.21	35,131	32,661
Manchester United	67,586	67,630	+0.07	67,721	67,508
Middlesbrough	28,450	31,005	+8.98	34,814	27,443
Newcastle United	51,373	51,920	+1.06	52,181	51,072
Southampton	30,633	30,680	+0.15	32,104	25,714
Sunderland	44,108	39,698	–10.00	47,586	34,102
Tottenham Hotspur	34,878	35,899	+2.93	36,084	34,701
West Bromwich Albion	20,691	26,523	+28.18	26,973	25,090
West Ham United	31,359	34,404	+9.71	35,050	28,844

TOTAL ATTENDANCES: 13,468,965 (380 games)
Average 35,445 (+3.03%)
HIGHEST: 67,721 Manchester United v Charlton Athletic
LOWEST: 14,019 Fulham v Blackburn Rovers
HIGHEST AVERAGE: 67,630 Manchester United
LOWEST AVERAGE: 16,685 Fulham

NATIONWIDE FOOTBALL LEAGUE: DIVISION ONE ATTENDANCES

	Average Gate			*Season 2002/03*	
	2001/02	2002/03	+/–%	Highest	Lowest
Bradford City	15,489	12,501	–19.3	19,088	10,615
Brighton & Hove Albion	6,559	6,651	+1.4	6,928	6,111
Burnley	15,252	13,977	–8.4	18,641	10,208
Coventry City	15,436	14,813	–4.0	19,526	11,796
Crystal Palace	17,177	16,867	–1.8	21,796	13,713
Derby County	29,818	25,470	–14.6	33,016	21,014
Gillingham	8,569	8,082	–5.7	10,036	6,281
Grimsby Town	6,430	5,884	–8.5	8,306	4,618
Ipswich Town	24,396	25,455	+4.3	29,503	22,736
Leicester City	19,835	29,219	+47.3	32,082	22,978
Millwall	13,253	8,512	–35.8	10,947	6,045
Norwich City	18,738	20,353	+8.6	21,335	18,536
Nottingham Forest	21,701	24,437	+12.6	29,725	16,073
Portsmouth	15,117	18,934	+25.2	19,558	17,201
Preston North End	14,883	13,853	–6.9	16,665	11,170
Reading	14,115	16,011	+13.4	23,462	11,030
Rotherham United	7,488	7,522	+0.5	11,480	5,792
Sheffield United	18,020	18,113	+0.5	29,179	13,024
Sheffield Wednesday	20,864	20,327	–2.6	27,075	16,112
Stoke City	13,966	14,588	+4.5	21,023	10,409
Walsall	6,816	6,978	+2.4	11,037	4,648
Watford	14,896	13,405	–10.0	17,944	10,292
Wimbledon	6,958	2,786	–60.0	10,356	849
Wolverhampton Wanderers	23,796	25,745	+8.2	28,190	23,016

TOTAL ATTENDANCES: 8,521,017 (552 games)
Average 15,437 (+2.0%)
HIGHEST: 33,016 Derby County v Reading
LOWEST: 849 Wimbledon v Rotherham United
HIGHEST AVERAGE: 29,219 Leicester City
LOWEST AVERAGE: 2,786 Wimbledon

Premiership attendance averages and highest crowd figures for 2002–03 are offical. Other attendances unofficial.

NATIONWIDE FOOTBALL LEAGUE: DIVISION TWO ATTENDANCES

	Average Gate			Season 2002/03	
	2001/02	2002/03	+/–%	Highest	Lowest
Barnsley	13,292	9,758	–26.6	12,474	8,661
Blackpool	5,682	6,991	+23.0	8,772	5,068
Brentford	6,729	5,759	–14.4	9,168	3,990
Bristol City	11,241	11,890	+5.8	18,085	9,084
Cardiff City	12,523	13,050	+4.2	15,245	11,389
Cheltenham Town	4,052	4,655	+14.9	6,382	3,568
Chesterfield	4,305	4,108	–4.6	6,813	3,081
Colchester United	3,822	3,387	–11.4	5,047	2,721
Crewe Alexandra	7,113	6,761	–4.9	9,562	5,138
Huddersfield Town	10,880	9,506	–12.6	13,769	7,294
Luton Town	7,413	6,747	–9.0	9,477	5,890
Mansfield Town	4,896	4,887	–0.2	8,134	3,414
Northampton Town	5,246	5,211	–0.7	5,906	3,663
Notts County	5,956	6,154	+3.3	10,302	3,875
Oldham Athletic	5,812	6,699	+15.3	9,415	5,039
Peterborough United	5,420	4,955	–8.6	7,767	3,627
Plymouth Argyle	8,788	8,981	+2.2	11,922	6,835
Port Vale	5,214	4,436	–14.9	6,395	3,039
Queens Park Rangers	11,750	13,206	+12.4	16,921	10,387
Stockport County	6,244	5,489	–12.1	8,168	4,011
Swindon Town	5,840	5,440	–6.8	8,629	4,136
Tranmere Rovers	8,656	7,877	–9.0	10,418	5,980
Wigan Athletic	5,651	7,288	+29.0	12,783	5,358
Wycombe Wanderers	6,681	6,002	–10.2	8,383	4,897

TOTAL ATTENDANCES: 3,892,469 (552 games)
Average 7,052 (–1.8%)

HIGHEST: 18,085 Bristol City v Plymouth Argyle
LOWEST: 2,721 Colchester United v Wigan Athletic
HIGHEST AVERAGE: 13,206 Queens Park Rangers
LOWEST AVERAGE: 3,387 Colchester United

NATIONWIDE FOOTBALL LEAGUE: DIVISION THREE ATTENDANCES

	Average Gate			Season 2002/03	
	2001/02	2002/03	+/–%	Highest	Lowest
AFC Bournemouth	5,062	5,829	+15.2	7,578	4,315
Boston United	2,435	3,049	+25.2	5,159	1,919
Bristol Rovers	6,565	6,934	+5.6	9,835	5,493
Bury	3,914	3,226	–17.6	5,827	2,039
Cambridge United	3,505	4,173	+19.1	6,237	2,586
Carlisle United	3,214	4,776	+48.6	10,684	3,124
Darlington	3,842	3,312	–13.8	5,832	2,076
Exeter City	3,313	3,763	+13.6	9,036	1,957
Hartlepool United	3,566	4,943	+38.6	6,360	3,889
Hull City	9,506	12,843	+35.1	22,319	7,684
Kidderminster Harriers	2,984	2,895	–3.0	3,872	2,006
Leyton Orient	4,550	4,257	–6.4	5,622	2,633
Lincoln City	2,673	3,924	+46.8	7,906	2,444
Macclesfield Town	2,128	2,110	–0.8	2,920	1,576
Oxford United	6,258	5,862	–6.3	8,732	4,547
Rochdale	3,412	2,740	–19.7	4,513	1,658
Rushden & Diamonds	4,404	4,330	–1.7	6,291	3,329
Scunthorpe United	3,800	3,692	–2.8	6,284	2,342
Shrewsbury Town	3,849	3,656	–5.0	7,236	2,599
Southend United	3,986	3,951	–0.9	6,453	2,832
Swansea City	3,693	5,160	+39.7	9,585	3,370
Torquay United	2,534	3,132	+23.6	5,761	2,244
Wrexham	3,782	4,263	+12.7	9,960	2,968
York City	3,143	4,176	+32.9	7,856	2,970

TOTAL ATTENDANCES: 2,460,935 (552 games)
Average 4,458 (+2.6%)

HIGHEST: 22,319 Hull City v Hartlepool United
LOWEST: 1,576 Macclesfield Town v Hartlepool United
HIGHEST AVERAGE: 12,843 Hull City
LOWEST AVERAGE: 2,110 Macclesfield Town

LEAGUE CUP FINALISTS 1961–2003

Played as a two-leg final until 1966. All subsequent finals at Wembley until 2000, then at Millennium Stadium, Cardiff.

Year	*Winners*	*Runners-up*	*Score*
1961	Aston Villa	Rotherham U	0-2, 3-0 (aet)
1962	Norwich C	Rochdale	3-0, 1-0
1963	Birmingham C	Aston Villa	3-1, 0-0
1964	Leicester C	Stoke C	1-1, 3-2
1965	Chelsea	Leicester C	3-2, 0-0
1966	WBA	West Ham U	1-2, 4-1
1967	QPR	WBA	3-2
1968	Leeds U	Arsenal	1-0
1969	Swindon T	Arsenal	3-1 (aet)
1970	Manchester C	WBA	2-1 (aet)
1971	Tottenham H	Aston Villa	2-0
1972	Stoke C	Chelsea	2-1
1973	Tottenham H	Norwich C	1-0
1974	Wolverhampton W	Manchester C	2-1
1975	Aston Villa	Norwich C	1-0
1976	Manchester C	Newcastle U	2-1
1977	Aston Villa	Everton	0-0, 1-1 (aet), 3-2 (aet)
1978	Nottingham F	Liverpool	0-0 (aet), 1-0
1979	Nottingham F	Southampton	3-2
1980	Wolverhampton W	Nottingham F	1-0
1981	Liverpool	West Ham U	1-1 (aet), 2-1

MILK CUP

1982	Liverpool	Tottenham H	3-1 (aet)
1983	Liverpool	Manchester U	2-1 (aet)
1984	Liverpool	Everton	0-0 (aet), 1-0
1985	Norwich C	Sunderland	1-0
1986	Oxford U	QPR	3-0

LITTLEWOODS CUP

1987	Arsenal	Liverpool	2-1
1988	Luton T	Arsenal	3-2
1989	Nottingham F	Luton T	3-1
1990	Nottingham F	Oldham Ath	1-0

RUMBELOWS LEAGUE CUP

1991	Sheffield W	Manchester U	1-0
1992	Manchester U	Nottingham F	1-0

COCA-COLA CUP

1993	Arsenal	Sheffield W	2-1
1994	Aston Villa	Manchester U	3-1
1995	Liverpool	Bolton W	2-1
1996	Aston Villa	Leeds U	3-0
1997	Leicester C	Middlesbrough	1-1 (aet), 1-0 (aet)
1998	Chelsea	Middlesbrough	2-0 (aet)

WORTHINGTON CUP

1999	Tottenham H	Leicester C	1-0
2000	Leicester C	Tranmere R	2-1
2001	Liverpool	Birmingham C	1-1 (aet)
Liverpool won 5-4 on penalties			
2002	Blackburn R	Tottenham H	2-1
2003	Liverpool	Manchester U	2-0

LEAGUE CUP WINS

Liverpool 7, Aston Villa 5, Nottingham F 4, Leicester C 3, Tottenham H 3, Arsenal 2, Chelsea 2, Manchester C 2, Norwich C 2, Wolverhampton W 2, Birmingham C 1, Blackburn R 1, Leeds U 1, Luton T 1, Manchester U 1, Oxford U 1, QPR 1, Sheffield W 1, Stoke C 1, Swindon T 1, WBA 1.

APPEARANCES IN FINALS

Liverpool 9, Aston Villa 7, Nottingham F 6, Arsenal 5, Leicester C 5, Manchester U 5, Tottenham H 5, Norwich C 4, Chelsea 3, Manchester C 3, WBA 3, Birmingham C 2, Everton 2, Leeds U 2, Luton T 2, Middlesbrough 2, QPR 2, Sheffield W 2, Stoke C 2, West Ham U 2, Wolverhampton W 2, Blackburn R 1, Bolton W 1, Newcastle U 1, Oldham Ath 1, Oxford U 1, Rochdale 1, Rotherham U 1, Southampton 1, Sunderland 1, Swindon T 1, Tranmere R 1.

APPEARANCES IN SEMI-FINALS

Liverpool 12, Aston Villa 11, Tottenham H 10, Arsenal 9, Manchester U 8, Chelsea 7, West Ham U 7, Nottingham F 6, Leeds U 5, Leicester C 5, Manchester C 5, Norwich C 5, Birmingham C 4, Blackburn R 4, Middlesbrough 4, Sheffield W 4, WBA 4, Bolton W 3, Burnley 3, Crystal Palace 3, Everton 3, Ipswich T 3, QPR 3, Sunderland 3, Swindon T 3, Wolverhampton W 3, Bristol C 2, Coventry C 2, Luton T 2, Oxford U 2, Plymouth Arg 2, Southampton 2, Stoke C 2, Tranmere R 2, Wimbledon 2, Blackpool 1, Bury 1, Cardiff C 1, Carlisle U 1, Chester C 1, Derby Co 1, Huddersfield T 1, Newcastle U 1, Oldham Ath 1, Peterborough U 1, Rochdale 1, Rotherham U 1, Sheffield U 1, Shrewsbury T 1, Stockport Co 1, Walsall 1, Watford 1.

WORTHINGTON CUP 2002–03

▪ *Denotes player sent off.*

PRELIMINARY ROUND

Tuesday, 20 August 2002

Bristol R (0) 0

Boston U (0) 2 *(Burton 52, Weatherstone S 72)* 4555

Bristol R: Howie; Boxall, Challis, Uddin, Barrett, Quinn, Carlisle, Hogg, Tait, Grazioli, McKeever.
Boston U: Bastock; Rusk, Thompson N, Hocking, Warburton, Ellender, Bennett, Weatherstone S, Clare, Burton, Angel.

FIRST ROUND

Tuesday, 10 September 2002

Bournemouth (3) 3 *(Thomas 3, 40, Connell 15)*

Brentford (1) 3 *(O'Connor 6 (pen), 57 (pen), Vine 72)* 3302

Bournemouth: Tardif (O'Connor); Broadhurst (Young), Purches S, Browning, Tindall, Maher, Thomas, Fletcher C, Holmes, Connell (Hayter), Elliott.
Brentford: Smith P; Dobson, Anderson, Chorley (Vine), Sonko, Marshall (Somner), Fullarton, Evans (Hunt), Constantine, O'Connor, Hutchinson.
aet; Brentford won 4-2 on penalties.

Bristol C (0) 0

Oxford U (1) 1 *(Hunt 17)* 4065

Bristol C: Phillips; Burnell, Woodman, Hulbert (Clist), Butler, Hill, Murray, Doherty (Beadle), Peacock, Roberts (Matthews), Tinnion.
Oxford U: Woodman; McNiven, Robinson (Powell), Crosby, Bound, Viveash, Ford, Hunt, Scott▪, Oldfield, Savage.

Burnley (1) 3 *(West 13, Papadopoulos 63, 75)*

Blackpool (0) 0 7448

Burnley: Beresford; West, Briscoe, McGregor, Cox, Gnohere, Little (Taylor), Weller, Moore I (Papadopoulos), Blake (Moore A), Grant.
Blackpool: Barnes; Grayson, Jaszczun, Southern, O'Kane, Collins (Bullock), Coid, Wellens (Walker), Taylor, Dalglish (Murphy J), Hills.

Bury (0) 1 *(Stuart 56)*

Stoke C (0) 0 2581

Bury: Garner; Unsworth (Billy), Stuart (Redmond), Nelson, Swailes, Woodthorpe, Forrest, Dunfield, Newby, Abbott (Preece), Clegg.
Stoke C: Cutler; Thomas, Clarke (Henry), Gunnarsson▪, Handyside, Shtanyuk, Gudjonsson (Goodfellow), O'Connor, Cooke (Hoekstra), Iwelumo, Commons.

Cambridge U (2) 3 *(Duncan 24, Kitson 39, Tudor 71)*

Reading (0) 1 *(Upson 89)* 2696

Cambridge U: Marshall; Warner, Murray (Nacca), Duncan, Angus, Fleming, Bridges, Tudor, Kitson, Youngs (Scully), Riza.
Reading: Hahnemann; Newman (Williams), Shorey (Rougier), Mackie, Upson, Parkinson, Forster, Hughes, Butler, Cureton (Igoe), Salako.

Crystal Palace (1) 2 *(Powell 22, Johnson 113)*

Plymouth Arg (1) 1 *(Sturrock 39)* 6385

Crystal Palace: Kolinko; Fleming, Granville, Mullins, Austin (Butterfield), Powell, Thomson, Johnson (Frampton), Freedman, Adebola (Black), Routledge.
Plymouth Arg: Larrieu; Worrell, Aljofree, Hodges, Wotton, Coughlan, Phillips (Friio), Sturrock (Evans), Lowndes (Stonebridge), Lopes, Adams.
aet.

Grimsby T (0) 0

Chesterfield (0) 1 *(Allott 91)* 3248

Grimsby T: Coyne; McDermott, Gallimore (Ward), Groves, Chettle, Coldicott, Cooke (Rowan), Pouton, Robinson (Mansaram), Kabba, Campbell.
Chesterfield: Muggleton; Booty, Davies, Dawson, Payne, Howson, Brandon, Ebdon (Richardson), Reeves (Allott), Burt, Rushbury.
aet.

Hartlepool U (0) 1 *(Williams E 79)*

Tranmere R (1) 2 *(Haworth 37, Taylor 83)* 2778

Hartlepool U: Williams A; Barron, Robinson, Lee, Westwood, Clarke, Arnison, Tinkler, Williams E (Henderson), Boyd, Humphreys.
Tranmere R: Achterberg; Curtis, Roberts, Sharps, Allen, Gray, Jones, Mellon, Haworth, Barlow (Hume), Taylor.

Huddersfield T (2) 2 *(Baldry 3, Clarke 16 (og))*

Darlington (0) 0 3810

Huddersfield T: Bevan; Jenkins, Sharp, Irons (Mattis), Moses, Dyson, Baldry (Smith), Holland, Gallacher (McDonald), Stead, Schofield.
Darlington: Collett; McGurk, Valentine, Liddle, Clarke, Maddison, Hadland (Nicholls), Cullen (Wainwright), Conlon, Ford, Clark (Naylor).

Hull C (1) 2 *(Alexander 31, Ashbee 118)*

Leicester C (1) 4 *(Rogers 18, 97, Dickov 91, Scowcroft 99)* 7061

Hull C: Glennon; Regan, Smith, Ashbee, Anderson, Whittle, Williams, Appleby (Johnson), Alexander, Jevons, Keates (Price).
Leicester C: Walker; Impey, Rogers, Elliott, Sinclair, Davidson (Stewart), Lewis, Izzet (Reeves), Dickov, Benjamin (McKinlay), Scowcroft.
aet.

Leyton Orient (2) 3 *(Campbell-Ryce 33, Thorpe 44, Fletcher 76)*

QPR (0) 2 *(Thomson 71 (pen), Gallen 89)* 4981

Leyton Orient: Morris; Joseph, Jones, Smith, McGhee (Martin), Harris, Hutchings, Campbell-Ryce, Fletcher (Barnard), Thorpe, Brazier.
QPR: Digby; Forbes, Williams, Palmer, Shittu, Carlisle (Dodou), Rose, Langley, Thomson, Pacquette (Gallen), Connolly (Oli).

Lincoln C (0) 1 *(Mike 58)*

Stockport Co (1) 3 *(Palmer 21, Beckett 54, Clare 83)* 2084

Lincoln C: Marriott; Bailey, Bimson, Mayo (Buckley), Morgan, Logan, Sedgemore (Mike), Willis▪, Cropper, Smith (Camm), Gain.
Stockport Co: Ingham; Gibb, Briggs, Challinor, Palmer, Clare, Hardiker, Lescott, Ross (Burgess), Beckett, Pemberton.

Mansfield T (1) 1 *(Moore 8)*

Derby Co (1) 3 *(Morris 10, Christie 71, Evatt 79)* 5788

Mansfield T: Pilkington; Reddington (White A), Disley, Williamson▪, Moore, Clark, Corden (Hurst), MacKenzie, Christie (Bacon), Clarke, Lawrence.
Derby Co: Poom; Barton (Hunt), Boertien, Riggott, Higginbotham, Bolder (Kinkladze), O'Neil, Lee, Christie, Strupar (Evatt), Morris.

Northampton T (0) 0

Wigan Ath (1) 1 *(Jarrett 31)* 2336

Northampton T: Abbey; Gill, Spedding, Harsley, Burgess (Rickers), Carruthers, McGregor, Trollope, Forrester (Asamoah), Gabbiadini (One), Hargreaves.
Wigan Ath: Filan; Green, McMillan, Mitchell, De Vos, Jackson, Teale, Jarrett, Ellington, Liddell, McCulloch (Roberts).

Norwich C (0) 0

Cheltenham T (2) 3 *(Naylor 30, 45, McAuley 83)* 13,285

Norwich C: Green; Nedergaard, Drury, Kenton, Mackay, Holt, Notman, Mulryne (Emblen), Roberts, Nielsen (Llewellyn), Easton (Heckingbottom).
Cheltenham T: Book; Howarth, Victory, Finnigan, Walker, Duff M, Milton, McAuley, Alsop, Naylor, Yates.

Oldham Ath (2) 3 *(Killen 10, Carss 45, Wijnhard 81)*

Notts Co (1) 2 *(Stallard 16, Heffernan 75)* 4205

Oldham Ath: Miskelly; Carss, Eyres, Beharall (Sheridan D), Hall F, Baudet, Low, Sheridan J, Wijnhard, Killen (Corazzin), Hill.
Notts Co: Garden; Ramsden, Baraclough, Caskey, Fenton, Ireland, Cas, Liburd, Stallard (Heffernan), Allsopp, Richardson (Hackworth).

Port Vale (0) 0

Crewe Alex (2) 2 *(Jack 17, 20)* 3765

Port Vale: Goodlad; Cummins, Brightwell, Carragher, Walsh, Collins, McCarthy (Angell), Boyd (Armstrong), McPhee, Brooker, Bridge-Wilkinson.
Crewe Alex: Ince; McCready, Sodje, Brammer, Walker, Vaughan, Little, Lunt, Jack, Miles, Sorvel.

Portsmouth (1) 2 *(Quashie 27, Primus 74)*

Peterborough U (0) 0 8581

Portsmouth: Hislop; Crowe (Harper), Taylor, Festa, Primus, De Zeeuw, Hughes (Robinson), Merson, Todorov, Burchill (Pericard), Quashie.
Peterborough U: Tyler; Joseph, Pearce, Shields (Gill), Rea, Burton■, Bullard, Danielsson, Green (Clarke A), Fenn (MacDonald), Newton.

Rotherham U (0) 3 *(Monkhouse 50, Robins 69, Warne 90)*

Carlisle U (0) 1 *(McGill 83)* 2902

Rotherham U: Pollitt; Scott, Beech, Sedgwick, Swailes, McIntosh, Mullin, Monkhouse (Warne), Barker R, Robins, Daws.
Carlisle U: Naisbitt; Birch, Murphy, Whitehead, Kelly (Andrews), Summerbell, Galloway (Jack), McGill, Wake, Molloy, Nixon.

Rushden & D (0) 0

Millwall (0) 0 2731

Rushden & D: Turley; Underwood, Mustafa, Dempster, Peters, Gray, Hall, Wardley, Darby, Mills (Burgess), Partridge.
Millwall: Warner; Lawrence, Ryan (Bull), Phillips (Claridge), Nethercott, Ward, Ifill, Livermore, May, Roberts, Kinet (Hearn).
aet; Rushden & D won 5-3 on penalties.

Sheffield U (1) 1 *(McGovern 13)*

York C (0) 0 4675

Sheffield U: Kenny; Kozluk, Ullathorne, McCall, Jagielka, Murphy, McGovern, Montgomery (Brown), Onuora, Peschisolido (Asaba), Tonge (Doane).
York C: Fettis; Edmondson, Potter (Yalcin), Cowan, Smith, Hobson, Brass, Bullock, Nogan (Carvalho), Duffield, Brackstone.

Southend U (0) 1 *(Rawle 82)*

Wimbledon (1) 4 *(Andersen 45, Tapp 65, Shipperley 68, 90)* 2634

Southend U: Flahavan; Beard, Searle (Maye), Maher, Cort, Broad (Whelan), Bramble (Clark S), Smith, Rawle, Jones, Jenkins.
Wimbledon: Davis; Holloway, Hawkins, Andersen (Reo-Coker), Leigertwood, Gier, Ainsworth (Darlington), Francis, Shipperley, Gray (Nowland), Tapp.

Torquay U (0) 0

Gillingham (0) 1 *(Hessenthaler 70)* 1981

Torquay U: Dearden; Hazell, Canoville, Hankin (Richardson), Woozley, Russell (Prince), Graham, Gritton, Bedeau, Fowler, Hill.
Gillingham: Brown; Patterson, Edge, Hope, Ashby, Saunders, Smith, Hessenthaler (Perpetuini), James, Ipoua, Shaw.

Walsall (1) 1 *(Leitao 23)*

Shrewsbury T (0) 0 3847

Walsall: Walker; Bazeley, Aranalde, Carbon, Roper, Hay, O'Connor (Wrack), Sonner, Leitao, Corica (Matias), Junior (Zdrilic).
Shrewsbury T: Dunbavin; Drysdale, Thompson (Wilding), Redmile, Murray, Tolley J, Lowe (Stevens), Atkins, Rodgers (Moss), Jemson, Van Blerk.

Watford (0) 1 *(Foley 75)*

Luton T (2) 2 *(Spring 31, Howard 41)* 14,171

Watford: Chamberlain; Ardley, Robinson, Doyley, Dyche, Cox, Hyde, Hand (Norville), Foley, Smith T, Glass (McNamee).
Luton T: Emberson; Boyce, Davis, Spring, Perrett, Bayliss, Nicholls, Brkovic (Robinson), Howard, Crowe, Hughes (Neilson).

Wrexham (0) 2 *(Morrell 89, Edwards C 90)*

Bradford C (0) 1 *(Cadamarteri 83)* 4340

Wrexham: Dibble; Edwards C, Edwards P (Holmes), Bennett, Pejic, Roberts, Whitley (Trundle), Ferguson, Morrell, Sam, Barrett.
Bradford C: Davison; Uhlenbeek, Myers, Bower, Molenaar, Evans, Gray, Forrest (Juanjo), Ward, Cadamarteri, Standing (Jorgensen).

Wednesday, 11 September 2002

Boston U (0) 1 *(Ellender 52)*

Cardiff C (4) 5 *(Earnshaw 25, 36, 42, Bennett 45 (og), Thorne 67)* 2280

Boston U: Bastock; Clifford, Thompson N, Redfearn, Warburton, Greaves, Bennett (Hocking), Weatherstone S, Douglas, Ellender (Burton), Angel (Cook).
Cardiff C: Margetson; Weston (Legg), Croft, Boland (Hamilton), Prior, Barker, Maxwell, Kavanagh, Fortune-West, Thorne (Campbell), Earnshaw.

Brighton & HA (1) 2 *(Wilkinson 34, Cullip 103)*

Exeter C (1) 1 *(McConnell 6 (pen))* 5200

Brighton & HA: Petterson; Watson, Pethick, Cullip, Butters, Carpenter, Melton, Oatway, Wilkinson, Marney (McPhee), Brooker (Jones).
Exeter C: Miller; McConnell, Power, Gaia, Curran, Walker (Ampadu), Thomas (Breslan), Cronin, Coppinger, Goodman (Harries), Roscoe.
aet.

Coventry C (2) 3 *(McSheffrey 1, McAllister 15, Mills 83)*

Colchester U (0) 0 6075

Coventry C: Debec; Caldwell, Gordon, Eustace, Konjic, Shaw, Delorge (Pipe), McAllister, Mills, McSheffrey (Bothroyd), Chippo (Normann).
Colchester U: McKinney; Baldwin, Keith, Pinault (Odunsi), Johnson, White, Izzet, Bowry, Morgan (Opara), McGleish, Stockwell (Rapley).

Macclesfield T (1) 4 *(Lightbourne 30, Whitaker 106, 107, 120)*

Barnsley (0) 1 *(Rankin 84)* 1720

Macclesfield T: Wilson; Hitchen, Adams, Welch, Tinson, Ridler, Byrne (Munroe), Priest, Tipton, Lightbourne (Askey), Whitaker.
Barnsley: Marriott; Mulligan, Holt, O'Callaghan, Curle, Ward, Lumsdon, Betsy, Rankin, Dyer (Fallon), Gary Jones (Sheron).
aet.

Nottingham F (2) 4 *(Lester 24, 71 (pen), Scimeca 45, Johnson 51)*

Kidderminster H (0) 0 4498

Nottingham F: Ward; Louis-Jean (Thompson), Brennan, Bopp, Dawson, Doig, Prutton, Scimeca (Reid Andy), Johnson (Jess), Lester, Westcarr.
Kidderminster H: Brock; Ayres, Stamps, Williams, Hinton, Flynn, Ducros (Doyle), Foster (Lower), Broughton, Henriksen (Shilton), Parrish.

Preston NE (1) 2 *(Alexander 23 (pen), Fuller 118)*
Scunthorpe U (1) 1 *(Torpey 10)* 5594
Preston NE: Lucas; Alexander, Edwards, Keane, Lucketti, Broomes, McKenna, Etuhu (Rankine), Cresswell, Healy (Fuller), Lewis (Cartwright).
Scunthorpe U: Evans; Wright, Stanton, Dawson, Sparrow (Parton), Jackson, Brough, Graves, Carruthers, Torpey, Calvo-Garcia (Barwick).
aet.

Sheffield W (1) 1 *(Sibon 2)*
Rochdale (0) 0 8815
Sheffield W: Pressman; Hendon (Geary), Burrows, Armstrong, Bromby, Maddix, McLaren, Sibon, Knight, Kuqi (Owusu) (Hamshaw), Quinn.
Rochdale: Edwards; Evans (McCourt), Doughty, Duffy, Jobson, Griffiths, Flitcroft, Oliver, Platt (Townson), Connor, Simpson.

Swansea C (2) 2 *(Thomas 8, Wood 22)*
Wolverhampton W (2) 3 *(Blake 16, Pollett 34, Rae 78)* 4799
Swansea C: Freestone; Jenkins, Howard, Cusack, O'Leary, Evans, Phillips, Thomas (Williams), Moss, Wood, Reid (Lacey).
Wolverhampton W: Oakes; Irwin, Naylor, Ingimarsson, Butler, Pollett, Newton (Proudlock), Rae, Blake, Sturridge (Miller), Ince.

Swindon T (0) 1 *(Willis 100)*
Wycombe W (0) 2 *(Harris 91, McCarthy 109)* 2993
Swindon T: Griemink; Gurney, Duke, Miglioranzi (Edds), Heywood, Willis (Reeves), Robinson, Parkin, Sabin, Hewlett, Davis J (Dykes).
Wycombe W: Talia; Rogers, Vinnicombe, Bulman, McCarthy, Thomson, Currie (Brown), Simpson, Faulconbridge, Devine (Ryan), Roberts (Harris).
aet.

SECOND ROUND

Tuesday, 24 September 2002

Ipswich T (3) 3 *(Bent D 13, Counago 22, Ambrose 45)*
Brighton & HA (1) 1 *(Hammond 8)* 13,266
Ipswich T: Marshall; Wilnis, Hreidarsson, Brown, McGreal, Magilton, Wright, Ambrose (George), Counago (Bent M), Bent D, Clapham.
Brighton & HA: Petterson; Watson, Mayo, Cullip, Virgo, Carpenter, Piercy (McPhee), Oatway (Melton), Hart, Hammond, Brooker (Rogers).

Tuesday, 1 October 2002

Brentford (0) 1 *(Sonko 90)*
Middlesbrough (2) 4 *(Marinelli 18, Whelan 20, Wilson 75, Downing 76)* 7558
Brentford: Smith P; Dobson, Anderson, Sonko, Roget, Hutchinson, Fullarton, O'Connor (Williams), McCammon (Constantine), Vine, Hunt (Evans).
Middlesbrough: Crossley; Parnaby, Cooper, Wilkshire, Gavin, Vidmar, Windass (Downing), Marinelli, Whelan (Dove), Wilson, Johnston.

Cambridge U (0) 0
Sunderland (2) 7 *(Reyna 21, McCann 25, Arca 54, Stewart 63, 65, Flo 75, 83)* 8175
Cambridge U: Marshall; Goodhind, Warner, Fleming (Nacca), Angus, Wanless (Guttridge), Bridges, Tudor, Kitson (Chillingworth), Youngs, Riza.
Sunderland: Myhre; Williams, Kilbane (McCartney), McCann, Babb, Craddock, Bellion, Reyna (Thirlwell), Stewart, Flo, Arca (Butler).

Charlton Ath (0) 0
Oxford U (0) 0 9494
Charlton Ath: Kiely; Kishishev, Konchesky, Fish (Brown), Rufus, Fortune, Mustoe (Robinson), Jensen, Euell, Johansson, Bartlett (Svensson).
Oxford U: Woodman; McNiven, Robinson, Crosby, Bound, Viveash, Ford, Hunt, Scott (Omoyinmi) (Powell), Oldfield (Louis), Savage.
aet; Oxford U won 6-5 on penalties.

Chesterfield (0) 1 *(Brandon 52)*
West Ham U (1) 1 *(Defoe 13)* 7102
Chesterfield: Muggleton; Davies, Rushbury (Edwards), Dawson, Blatherwick, Howson, Booty (Brandon), Hudson, Allott, Reeves (Burt), Ebdon.
West Ham U: James; Schemmel, Minto, Lomas, Repka, Breen, Sinclair, Cole, Defoe, Di Canio, Carrick.
aet; West Ham U won 5-4 on penalties.

Huddersfield T (0) 0
Burnley (0) 1 *(Papadopoulos 104)* 5887
Huddersfield T: Bevan; Sharp, Jenkins, Holland (Scott), Brown, Dyson, Baldry (Thorrington), Mattis, Stead, Smith (Macari), Schofield.
Burnley: Beresford; McGregor, Briscoe, Cox, Davis, Gnohere, Grant (Cook), Blake (Papadopoulos), Moore I, Taylor, Moore A (Branch).
aet.

Macclesfield T (1) 1 *(Tipton 8)*
Preston NE (1) 2 *(Skora 31, Jackson 90)* 2036
Macclesfield T: Wilson; Hitchen, Adams, Welch, Tinson, O'Neill, Hardy, Priest, Tipton, Lightbourne (Robinson), Whitaker.
Preston NE: Lucas (Moilanen); Alexander, Broomes, Jackson, Lucketti, Skora, Rankine (Lewis), Etuhu, Cresswell, Healy, Anderson.

Manchester C (0) 3 *(Berkovic 69, Walker 84 (og), Huckerby 87)*
Crewe Alex (1) 2 *(Jack 1, Hulse 86)* 21,820
Manchester C: Schmeichel; Jihai, Jensen, Mettomo (Wright-Phillips), Howey, Horlock, Benarbia, Berkovic, Anelka, Goater (Huckerby), Foe.
Crewe Alex: Ince; Wright, Sodje (Walton), Brammer, Foster, Walker, Hulse, Lunt, Jack (Jones), Ashton, Sorvel.

Portsmouth (1) 1 *(Pericard 6)*
Wimbledon (2) 3 *(McAnuff 7, Leigertwood 16, Shipperley 59)* 11,754
Portsmouth: Hislop; Harper, Taylor, Festa, Primus, Ritchie, Robinson, Merson, Pericard, Todorov (Burchill), O'Neil.
Wimbledon: Davis; Holloway, Hawkins, Andersen, Leigertwood, Gier, McAnuff, Francis, Shipperley, Nowland (Gray), Tapp.

Rotherham U (1) 4 *(Monkhouse 5, Robins 79 (pen), Swailes 86, Barker R 93)*
Wolverhampton W (1) 4 *(Newton 45 (pen), Miller 58, Rae 70, Scott 120 (og))* 5064
Rotherham U: Pollitt; Scott, Hurst, Garner (Daws), Swailes, Branston, Mullin, Monkhouse, Barker R, Robins, Warne (Bryan).
Wolverhampton W: Murray; Edworthy, Naylor, Ingimarsson, Butler, Lescott, Newton, Rae (Irwin), Blake, Miller (Ince), Ndah (Sturridge).
aet; Rotherham U won 4-2 on penalties.

Sheffield U (1) 4 *(Boulding 14, Brown 48, 87, Montgomery 86)*
Wycombe W (0) 1 *(McCarthy 90)* 4389
Sheffield U: Kenny; Doane, Ullathorne, Jagielka (Montgomery), Murphy, Page, McGovern (Ten Heuvel), Brown, Boulding (Ndlovu), Allison, Tonge.
Wycombe W: Taylor■; Senda, Vinnicombe, Thomson, McCarthy, Johnson (Harris), Bulman, Simpson, Faulconbridge, Currie (Brown), Roberts (Devine).

Stockport Co (1) 1 *(Daly 8)*
Gillingham (1) 2 *(Ipoua 25, Johnson T 112)* 2396
Stockport Co: Jones; Briggs, Tonkin, Challinor, Palmer, Goodwin, Gibb, Hardiker (Pemberton), Daly, Beckett (Ross), Lambert (Lescott).
Gillingham: Bartram; Nosworthy, Johnson L, Hope, Ashby, Spiller, Smith, Shaw (Crofts), Wallace (Rose), Ipoua (Johnson T), Perpetuini.
aet.

Tottenham H (1) 1 *(Sheringham 30)*

Cardiff C (0) 0 23,723

Tottenham H: Keller; Taricco (Doherty), Thatcher, Freund (Iversen), Richards, Bunjevcevic, Davies, Acimovic, Keane (Ferdinand), Sheringham, Etherington.
Cardiff C: Alexander; Weston, Croft, Gabbidon, Prior, Whalley, Boland (Maxwell), Kavanagh, Earnshaw, Campbell, Legg (Fortune-West).

Wrexham (0) 0

Everton (1) 3 *(Campbell 25, Rooney 83, 89)* 13,428

Wrexham: Whitfield; Edwards C, Edwards P (Holmes), Carey, Pejic, Lawrence, Whitley (Thomas), Ferguson, Morrell, Sam (Trundle), Barrett.
Everton: Wright; Hibbert, Naysmith, Carsley, Yobo, Unsworth, Li Tie (Stubbs), Li Weifeng, Campbell (Ferguson), Radzinski (Rooney), Gemmill.

Wednesday, 2 October 2002

Aston Villa (2) 3 *(De la Cruz 9, Dublin 25, 48)*

Luton T (0) 0 20,833

Aston Villa: Enckelman; De la Cruz, Samuel, Mellberg, Johnsen, Staunton (Leonhardsen), Kinsella, Hendrie, Dublin (Allback), Vassell (Moore), Barry.
Luton T: Emberson; Boyce, Davis, Spring, Perrett (Hillier), Coyne, Robinson, Holmes (Neilson), Howard, Fotiadis (Crowe), Hughes.

Bolton W (0) 0

Bury (0) 1 *(Mendy 48 (og))* 12,621

Bolton W: Poole; Mendy, Livesey, Campo, David Holdsworth, Bulent■, Smith, Tofting, Walters (Dean Holdsworth), Johnson (Nolan), Armstrong (Pedersen).
Bury: Garner; Barrass, Woodthorpe, Unsworth, Swailes, Nelson, Billy, Dunfield (Stuart), Newby, Abbott (Preece), Clegg (Forrest).

Coventry C (4) 8 *(McSheffrey 10, 36, 51, Mills 24, 45, Bothroyd 62, 85, Betts 81 (pen))*

Rushden & D (0) 0 8570

Coventry C: Debec; Caldwell, Quinn, Betts, Konjic (Shaw), Davenport, Pipe, Safri (Stanford), Mills (Bothroyd), McSheffrey, Partridge.
Rushden & D: Turley; Mustafa, Setchell, Bell (Dempster■), Hunter■, Peters, Hall (Partridge), Wardley, Mills, Talbot (Bignot), Gray.

Crystal Palace (1) 7 *(Adebola 21, 74, Mullins 47, Popovic 53, Freedman 55, 90, Walker 75 (og))*

Cheltenham T (0) 0 4901

Crystal Palace: Michopoulos; Butterfield, Granville, Mullins, Popovic (Antwi), Powell (Austin), Black (Gray), Derry, Freedman, Adebola, Routledge.
Cheltenham T: Book; Griffin, Victory, Finnigan, Walker, Duff M, Milton, McAuley (Williams), Alsop, Naylor, Yates.

Derby Co (1) 1 *(Higginbotham 17 (pen))*

Oldham Ath (1) 2 *(Eyres 18, Wijnhard 95 (pen))* 9029

Derby Co: Poom■; Barton (Hunt), Boertien (Morris), Riggott, Higginbotham, Carbonari, Murray, Lee (Evatt), Christie, McLeod, Bolder.
Oldham Ath: Miskelly; Duxbury (Andrews), Eyres, Beharall, Hall F, Hill, Lourenco (Haining), Carss, Wijnhard, Corazzin, Eyre (Holden).
aet.

Leyton Orient (0) 2 *(Nugent 60, Ibehre 82)*

Birmingham C (2) 3 *(John 16, 27, 77)* 3615

Leyton Orient: Morris; Smith, Lockwood, Harris, Miller, Campbell-Ryce (Ibehre), Hutchings (Martin), Toner (Barnard), Nugent, Thorpe, Brazier.
Birmingham C: Bennett; Kenna, Woodhouse, Vickers, Purse, Powell, Kirovski (Johnson D), Sadler, Horsfield, John (Fagan), Lazaridis.

Nottingham F (0) 1 *(Johnson 79)*

Walsall (2) 2 *(Leitao 21, Junior 24)* 6343

Nottingham F: Ward; Thompson, Doig, Williams, Dawson (Westcarr), Hjelde, Bopp (Cash), Scimeca, Johnson, Harewood, Reid Andy.
Walsall: Walker; Bazeley, Aranalde, O'Connor, Roper (Barras), Hay, Wrack, Corica (Matias), Leitao, Junior (Birch), Simpson.

Sheffield W (1) 1 *(Sibon 32)*

Leicester C (0) 2 *(Izzet 90, Benjamin 98)* 10,472

Sheffield W: Pressman; Burrows (Westwood), Quinn, Geary, Bromby, Maddix, Armstrong, Sibon (Hamshaw), Owusu, Kuqi, Knight (Donnelly).
Leicester C: Walker; Heath, Davidson, Elliott, Reeves (Stevenson), Izzet, Summerbee (Oakes), Lewis (Ashton), Benjamin, Scowcroft, Rogers.
aet.

Southampton (3) 6 *(Marsden 1, Ormerod 25, 43, 68, Fernandes 52, Svensson M 66)*

Tranmere R (1) 1 *(Allen 22)* 16,603

Southampton: Niemi; Dodd, Bridge, Marsden (Kanchelskis), Lundekvam, Svensson M, Fernandes, Oakley, Beattie (Tessem), Ormerod (Delap), Svensson A.
Tranmere R: Whitehead; Taylor, Roberts (Hinds), Jones, Allen, Edwards, Curtis, Mellon, Hay (Olsen), Barlow (Parkinson), Harrison.

Wigan Ath (1) 3 *(Ellington 31, 61, 80)*

WBA (0) 1 *(Hughes 89)* 6558

Wigan Ath: Filan; Eaden, McMillan, Dinning (Flynn), De Vos, Jackson, Teale, Jarrett, Ellington (Ashcroft), Roberts (Baines), McCulloch.
WBA: Murphy; Lyttle, Chambers J (Clement), Sigurdsson, Wallwork, Marshall, Dyer, Jordao, Dichio (Dobie), Hughes, Koumas.

THIRD ROUND

Tuesday, 5 November 2002

Birmingham C (0) 0

Preston NE (0) 2 *(Fuller 59, Lewis 80)* 12,241

Birmingham C: Bennett; Tebily, Sadler (Fagan), Hughes, Cunningham, Hutchinson, Powell, Carter (Kirovski), Morrison, Horsfield■, Lazaridis.
Preston NE: Lucas; Alexander, Edwards, Mears (Cresswell), Lucketti (Murdock), Broomes, McKenna, Etuhu, Healy, Fuller (Rankine), Lewis.

Manchester U (0) 2 *(Beckham 80 (pen), Richardson 90)*

Leicester C (0) 0 47,848

Manchester U: Carroll; Neville G, O'Shea, Ferdinand, Neville P (Scholes), May, Beckham, Forlan, Solskjaer, Nardiello (Richardson), Fortune (Veron).
Leicester C: Walker; Sinclair, Davidson, Elliott (Summerbee), Heath, Stewart, Impey, Izzet, Dickov (Benjamin), Scowcroft, Rogers (Stevenson).

Wigan Ath (1) 1 *(Roberts 35)*

Manchester C (0) 0 15,007

Wigan Ath: Filan; Eaden, McMillan (Mitchell), Dinning, De Vos, Jackson, Liddell (Teale), Jarrett, Ellington (Green), Roberts, Kennedy.
Manchester C: Nash; Jihai, Jensen, Dunne, Howey (Wiekens), Distin (Horlock), Wright-Phillips, Foe, Anelka, Goater (Huckerby), Benarbia.

Wimbledon (1) 1 *(Agyemang 35)*

Rotherham U (0) 3 *(Monkhouse 51, Barker R 75, Lee 85)* 664

Wimbledon: Davis; Holloway, Morgan (Ainsworth), Andersen (Francis), Leigertwood, Gier, McAnuff, Darlington, Shipperley, Agyemang, Reo-Coker.
Rotherham U: Pollitt; Scott, Hurst, Sedgwick (Bryan), Swailes, Branston, Daws, Monkhouse (Byfield), Lee, Barker R (Warne), Garner.

Wednesday, 6 November 2002

Arsenal (2) 2 *(Pires 12, Jeffers 32)*

Sunderland (0) 3 *(Kyle 56, Stewart 70, 72)* 19,059

Arsenal: Taylor; Luzhny, Tavlaridis, Svard (Garry), Stepanovs, Toure, Van Bronckhorst, Pennant (Volz), Kanu, Jeffers, Pires.
Sunderland: Macho; Williams, McCartney, Thirlwell, Varga, Emerson, Rossiter, Schwarz (Piper), Kyle, Stewart, Proctor.

Blackburn R (1) 2 *(Grabbi 45 (pen), Roper 105 (og))*

Walsall (0) 2 *(Aranalde 67 (pen), Zdrilic 98)* 9486

Blackburn R: Kelly; Pelzer (McEveley), Curtis, Todd, Johansson, Dunn, Gillespie, Danns (Douglas), Grabbi, Jansen (Richards), Mahon.
Walsall: Walker; Bazeley, Aranalde, Sonner, Roper, Hay (Barras), Wrack, Corica (Herivelto), Leitao, Junior (Zdrilic), Simpson.
aet; Blackburn R won 5-4 on penalties.

Burnley (0) 2 *(Blake 57, Davis 61)*

Tottenham H (1) 1 *(Poyet 17)* 13,512

Burnley: Beresford; West, Branch, McGregor (Little), Davis, Gnohere, Weller, Grant, Blake (Papadopoulos), Taylor, Briscoe (Cook).
Tottenham H: Keller; Carr, Bunjevcevic, Gardner, Perry, Clemence, Davies, Poyet, Iversen (Doherty), Ferdinand (Keane), Etherington (Anderton).

Chelsea (1) 2 *(Cole 20, 52)*

Gillingham (0) 1 *(King 90)* 28,033

Chelsea: Cudicini; Ferrer, Babayaro, Morris, Gallas, Terry, De Lucas (Bogarde), Lampard, Cole (Gronkjaer), Zola, Le Saux (De Oliveira).
Gillingham: Brown; Nosworthy, Perpetuini, Hope, Ashby, Saunders, Smith, Hessenthaler (Spiller), Sidibe (Johnson T), Ipoua (King), Shaw.

Crystal Palace (1) 3 *(Johnson 20, 75, Gray 89)*

Coventry C (0) 0 8102

Crystal Palace: Kolinko (Michopoulos); Butterfield, Granville, Mullins, Popovic, Powell, Riihilahti (Thomson), Derry, Freedman (Gray), Adebola, Johnson.
Coventry C: Hyldgaard; Caldwell (Eustace), Gordon, McAllister, Konjic, Davenport, Kerr (Chippo), Safri, Mills (Bothroyd), Hignett, Partridge.

Fulham (1) 3 *(Stolcers 40, 53, Clark 73)*

Bury (0) 1 *(Newby 90)* 6700

Fulham: Taylor; Finnan (Djetou), Wome, Melville (Hudson), Ouaddou, Clark, Goldbaek, Collins, Hayles, Inamoto (Sava), Stolcers.
Bury: Garner; Barrass (O'Shaughnessy), Stuart, Unsworth, Swailes, Nelson, Billy, Dunfield (Woodthorpe), Newby, Preece (Nugent), Forrest.

Ipswich T (3) 3 *(Gaardsoe 2, Clapham 40, Bent D 44)*

Middlesbrough (0) 1 *(Queudrue 88)* 14,417

Ipswich T: Pullen; Makin, Hreidarsson, Venus, Gaardsoe (Richards), Wilnis, Wright, Miller, Bent D, George (Logan), Clapham (Westlake).
Middlesbrough: Crossley; Stockdale (Dove), Vidmar, Davies, Cooper, Wilkshire, Wilson, Marinelli (Cade), Nemeth (Close), Johnston, Queudrue.

Liverpool (1) 3 *(Berger 45, Diouf 57, Baros 60)*

Southampton (0) 1 *(Delgado 55)* 35,870

Liverpool: Kirkland; Vignal, Otsemobor (Traore), Babbel, Biscan, Cheyrou, Gerrard, Smicer (Diao), Baros (Heskey), Diouf, Berger.
Southampton: Niemi; Dodd, Bridge, Marsden, Lundekvam, Svensson M, Delap, Oakley (Pahars), Beattie, Delgado, Telfer.

Newcastle U (0) 3 *(Dyer 77, 78, Pistone 100 (og))*

Everton (1) 3 *(Campbell 11, Watson 85, Unsworth 112 (pen))* 34,584

Newcastle U: Harper; Griffin, Elliott, Dabizas, Caldwell■, Acuna (Solano), Viana, Dyer, Cort, Lua-Lua (Chopra), Bernard (Robert).
Everton: Wright; Pistone, Naysmith, Stubbs, Weir, Linderoth (Watson), Carsley, Li Tie (Radzinski), Campbell, Rooney, Unsworth.
aet; Everton won 3-2 on penalties.

Oxford U (0) 0

Aston Villa (0) 3 *(Taylor 74, Barry 77, Dublin 86)* 12,177

Oxford U: Woodman; McNiven, Robinson, Crosby, Bound (Hackett), Viveash, Whitehead, Hunt, Basham (Omoyinmi), Louis (Gordon), Savage.
Aston Villa: Postma; Delaney, Samuel, Johnsen, Staunton, Taylor, Leonhardsen (Angel), Kinsella (Hitzlsperger), Dublin, Moore (Allback), Barry.

Sheffield U (0) 2 *(Jagielka 89, Ndlovu 90)*

Leeds U (1) 1 *(Yates 24 (og))* 26,663

Sheffield U: Kenny; Jagielka, Montgomery (Ndlovu), Yates, Murphy, Page, Brown, McCall (Ten Heuvel), Asaba (Peschisolido), Allison, Tonge.
Leeds U: Robinson; Mills, Harte, Bakke (McPhail), Woodgate (Duberry), Lucic, Barmby, Bowyer, Viduka, Kewell, Wilcox (Bridges).

West Ham U (0) 0

Oldham Ath (1) 1 *(Corazzin 42)* 21,919

West Ham U: James; Dailly, Minto (Schemmel), Lomas, Breen (Winterburn), Pearce, Camara, Cole, Defoe, Cisse (Garcia), Carrick.
Oldham Ath: Pogliacomi; Low, Eyres, Beharall, Hall F, Hill, Murray, Armstrong, Andrews (Killen), Corazzin, Eyre.

FOURTH ROUND

Tuesday, 3 December 2002

Burnley (0) 0

Manchester U (1) 2 *(Forlan 35, Solskjaer 65)* 22,034

Burnley: Beresford; West, Branch, Cook (Grant), Davis, Gnohere (Moore A), Little, Weller, Blake, Taylor, Briscoe (Papadopoulos).
Manchester U: Carroll; Neville P, Silvestre, Brown, O'Shea, May, Chadwick, Pugh, Van Nistelrooy (Solskjaer), Forlan (Giggs), Stewart (Scholes).

Crystal Palace (1) 2 *(Black 11, 74)*

Oldham Ath (0) 0 7431

Crystal Palace: Kolinko; Butterfield, Granville■, Symons (Antwi), Popovic, Powell, Mullins, Williams (Borrowdale), Black (Hunt), Adebola, Riihilahti.
Oldham Ath: Pogliacomi; Armstrong, Clegg (Lourenco), Beharall, Hall F, Hill (Andrews), Baudet, Sheridan D, Wijnhard (Corazzin), Killen, Eyres.

Sheffield U (0) 2 *(Murphy 54, Allison 56)*

Sunderland (0) 0 27,068

Sheffield U: Kenny; Jagielka, Harley, McCall, Murphy, Page, Ndlovu (Kozluk), Brown, Asaba (Peschisolido), Allison, Tonge.
Sunderland: Macho; Rossiter, McCartney, McCann, Varga, Emerson, Proctor, Williams, Stewart, Kyle (Schwarz), Bellion.

Wednesday, 4 December 2002

Aston Villa (1) 5 *(Vassell 44, 55, Dublin 80, Angel 84, Hitzlsperger 87)*

Preston NE (0) 0 23,042

Aston Villa: Enckelman; Samuel (De la Cruz), Barry, Johnsen, Staunton, Taylor (Kinsella), Leonhardsen, Hitzlsperger, Dublin, Vassell (Angel), Hendrie.
Preston NE: Lucas; Alexander, Eaton, Murdock, Lucketti, Skora (Mears), McKenna (Rankine), Etuhu (Cartwright), Cresswell, Healy, Lewis.

Blackburn R (4) 4 *(Yorke 12, 39, Cole 16, Duff 43)*
Rotherham U (0) 0 11,220
Blackburn R: Kelly; Neill, McEveley, Todd, Johansson, Tugay (Flitcroft), Thompson, Danns, Cole (Grabbi), Yorke (Ostenstad), Duff.
Rotherham U: Pollitt; Scott, Hurst, Sedgwick (Robins), Swailes, McIntosh, Daws, Monkhouse (Bryan), Lee, Barker R (Warne), Garner.

Chelsea (2) 4 *(Hasselbaink 26, 75, Petit 44, Stanic 69)*
Everton (0) 1 *(Naysmith 80)* 32,322
Chelsea: Cudicini; Melchiot, Babayaro, Petit, Gallas, Terry, Gronkjaer (De Lucas), Lampard, Hasselbaink, Zola (Gudjohnsen), Stanic (Morris).
Everton: Wright; Pistone, Unsworth, Weir, Yobo, Li Tie (Gemmill), Rooney, Gravesen, Campbell, Radzinski, Pembridge (Naysmith).

Liverpool (0) 1 *(Diouf 54 (pen))*
Ipswich T (1) 1 *(Miller 14)* 26,305
Liverpool: Dudek; Xavier, Riise, Biscan, Babbel (Carragher), Vignal, Gerrard, Smicer (Welsh), Mellor (Baros), Diouf, Diao.
Ipswich T: Marshall; Wright, Clapham, Venus, Gaardsoe, Hreidarsson, Miller, Holland, Bent D (Naylor), Counago (Armstrong), Ambrose (Magilton).
aet; Liverpool won 5-4 on penalties.

Wigan Ath (2) 2 *(Ellington 20, 28)*
Fulham (0) 1 *(Boa Morte 86)* 7615
Wigan Ath: Filan; Eaden, McMillan, Dinning, De Vos, Jackson, Green (Mitchell), Jarrett, Ellington, Roberts (Flynn), Kennedy.
Fulham: Taylor; Leacock, Wome, Ouaddou, Knight (Davis), Clark, Inamoto, Collins, Sava (Boa Morte), Djetou, Stolcers.

FIFTH ROUND

Tuesday, 17 December 2002

Manchester U (0) 1 *(Forlan 80)*
Chelsea (0) 0 57,985
Manchester U: Barthez; Neville G, O'Shea, Brown, Neville P, Silvestre, Beckham, Veron, Forlan, Scholes, Giggs.
Chelsea: Cudicini; Melchiot, Le Saux, Morris, Gallas, Terry, De Lucas (Zenden), Lampard, Hasselbaink (Gudjohnsen), Zola, Stanic.

Sheffield U (1) 3 *(Asaba 35, Peschisolido 86, 88)*
Crystal Palace (0) 1 *(Page 82 (og))* 22,211
Sheffield U: Kenny; Jagielka, Harley, McCall (Montgomery), Murphy, Page, Ndlovu, Brown, Asaba (Peschisolido), Allison, Tonge.
Crystal Palace: Kolinko; Butterfield, Gray, Symons, Powell, Antwi (Borrowdale), Mullins, Black, Johnson, Adebola (Williams), Riihilahti.

Wigan Ath (0) 0
Blackburn R (1) 2 *(Cole 16, 80)* 16,922
Wigan Ath: Filan; Eaden, Baines, Dinning, De Vos, Jackson, Green (Flynn), Jarrett, Ellington, Roberts, Kennedy (Teale).
Blackburn R: Friedel; Neill, Bjornebye (Johansson), Short, Taylor, Tugay, Gillespie, Flitcroft, Cole (Jansen), Yorke (Ostenstad), Thompson.

Wednesday, 18 December 2002

Aston Villa (1) 3 *(Vassell 23 (pen), Hitzlsperger 72, Henchoz 88 (og))*
Liverpool (1) 4 *(Murphy 27, 90, Baros 54, Gerrard 67)* 38,530
Aston Villa: Enckelman; De la Cruz (Angel), Barry, Mellberg, Samuel, Hendrie (Kinsella), Leonhardsen, Hitzlsperger, Dublin, Vassell, Hadji.
Liverpool: Kirkland; Babbel (Carragher), Traore, Diao, Henchoz, Hyypia, Murphy, Gerrard, Baros, Owen (Heskey), Riise.

SEMI-FINAL FIRST LEG

Tuesday, 7 January 2003

Manchester U (0) 1 *(Scholes 58)*
Blackburn R (0) 1 *(Thompson 61)* 62,740
Manchester U: Barthez; Neville G, Silvestre, Brown, Neville P (Forlan), Ferdinand, Beckham, Veron, Van Nistelrooy, Scholes, Giggs (Solskjaer).
Blackburn R: Friedel; Neill, McEveley, Todd, Taylor, Tugay, Thompson (Jansen), Flitcroft, Cole, Yorke, Dunn (Gillespie).

Wednesday, 8 January 2003

Sheffield U (0) 2 *(Tonge 76, 82)*
Liverpool (1) 1 *(Mellor 35)* 30,095
Sheffield U: Kenny; Jagielka, Quinn, McCall, Murphy, Page, Ndlovu, Brown, Asaba (Montgomery), Allison, Tonge.
Liverpool: Kirkland; Carragher, Traore, Diao, Henchoz, Hyypia, Murphy, Gerrard, Mellor (Owen), Diouf, Smicer (Heskey).

SEMI-FINAL SECOND LEG

Tuesday, 21 January 2003

Liverpool (1) 2 *(Diouf 9, Owen 107)*
Sheffield U (0) 0 43,837
Liverpool: Kirkland; Carragher, Riise, Gerrard, Henchoz, Hyypia, Murphy, Diouf, Heskey, Owen, Smicer (Cheyrou).
Sheffield U: Kenny; Jagielka, Quinn (Ten-Heuvel), McCall, Murphy, Page, Ndlovu, Brown, Tonge, Allison (Peschisolido), Montgomery (Mooney).
aet.

Wednesday, 22 January 2003

Blackburn R (1) 1 *(Cole 12)*
Manchester U (2) 3 *(Scholes 30, 42, Van Nistelrooy 77 (pen))* 29,048
Blackburn R: Friedel; Neill, McEveley, Todd, Taylor, Tugay, Thompson, Flitcroft, Cole, Yorke, Duff (Gillespie).
Manchester U: Barthez; Neville G, Silvestre, Brown, Keane, Ferdinand, Beckham, Veron, Van Nistelrooy (Forlan), Scholes (Butt), Giggs.

WORTHINGTON CUP FINAL

Sunday, 2 March 2003
(at Millennium Stadium, Cardiff)

Liverpool (1) 2 *(Gerrard 38, Owen 86)*
Manchester U (0) 0 74,500
Liverpool: Dudek; Carragher, Riise, Hamann, Henchoz, Hyypia, Gerrard, Diouf (Biscan), Heskey (Baros) (Smicer), Owen, Murphy.
Manchester U: Barthez; Neville G, Silvestre, Brown (Solskjaer), Keane, Ferdinand, Beckham, Veron, Van Nistelrooy, Scholes, Giggs.
Referee: P. Durkin (Portland).

FOOTBALL LEAGUE COMPETITION ATTENDANCES

LEAGUE CUP ATTENDANCES

Season	*Attendances*	*Games*	*Average*
1960–61	1,204,580	112	10,755
1961–62	1,030,534	104	9,909
1962–63	1,029,893	102	10,097
1963–64	945,265	104	9,089
1964–65	962,802	98	9,825
1965–66	1,205,876	106	11,376
1966–67	1,394,553	118	11,818
1967–68	1,671,326	110	15,194
1968–69	2,064,647	118	17,497
1969–70	2,299,819	122	18,851
1970–71	2,035,315	116	17,546
1971–72	2,397,154	123	19,489
1972–73	1,935,474	120	16,129
1973–74	1,722,629	132	13,050
1974–75	1,901,094	127	14,969
1975–76	1,841,735	140	13,155
1976–77	2,236,636	147	15,215
1977–78	2,038,295	148	13,772
1978–79	1,825,643	139	13,134
1979–80	2,322,866	169	13,745
1980–81	2,051,576	161	12,743
1981–82	1,880,682	161	11,681
1982–83	1,679,756	160	10,498
1983–84	1,900,491	168	11,312
1984–85	1,876,429	167	11,236
1985–86	1,579,916	163	9,693
1986–87	1,531,498	157	9,755
1987–88	1,539,253	158	9,742
1988–89	1,552,780	162	9,585
1989–90	1,836,916	168	10,934
1990–91	1,675,496	159	10,538
1991–92	1,622,337	164	9,892
1992–93	1,558,031	161	9,677
1993–94	1,744,120	163	10,700
1994–95	1,530,478	157	9,748
1995–96	1,776,060	162	10,963
1996–97	1,529,321	163	9,382
1997–98	1,484,297	153	9,701
1998–99	1,555,856	153	10,169
1999–2000	1,354,233	153	8,851
2000–01	1,501,304	154	9,749
2001–02	1,076,390	93	11,574

WORTHINGTON CUP 2002–03

Round	*Aggregate*	*Games*	*Average*
One	167,654	35	4,790
Two	235,637	24	9,818
Three	306,282	16	19,143
Four	157,037	8	19,630
Five	135,648	4	33,912
Semi-finals	165,720	4	41,430
Final	74,500	1	74,500
Total	1,242,478	92	13,505

LDV VANS TROPHY 2002–03

Round	*Aggregate*	*Games*	*Average*
One	48,726	28	1,740
Two	30,591	16	1,912
Area Quarter-finals	20,095	8	2,512
Area Semi-finals	15,242	4	3,811
Area finals	22,565	4	5,641
Final	50,913	1	50,913
Total	188,132	61	3,084

FA CUP ATTENDANCES 1967–2003

	1st Round	*2nd Round*	*3rd Round*	*4th Round*	*5th Round*	*6th Round*	*Semi-finals & Final*	*Total*	*No. of matches*	*Average per match*
2002–03	189,905	104,103	577,494	404,599	242,483	156,244	175,498	1,850,326	150	12,336
2001–02	198,369	119,781	566,284	330,434	249,190	173,757	171,278	1,809,093	148	12,224
2000–01	171,689	122,061	577,204	398,241	256,899	100,663	177,778	1,804,535	151	11,951
1999–2000	181,485	127,728	514,030	374,795	182,511	105,443	214,921	1,700,913	158	10,765
1998–99	191,954	132,341	609,486	431,613	359,398	181,005	202,150	2,107,947	155	13,599
1997–98	204,803	130,261	629,127	455,557	341,290	192,651	172,007	2,125,696	165	12,883
1996–97	209,521	122,324	651,139	402,293	199,873	67,035	191,813	1,843,998	151	12,211
1995–96	185,538	115,669	748,997	391,218	274,055	174,142	156,500	2,046,199	167	12,252
1994–95	219,511	125,629	640,017	438,596	257,650	159,787	174,059	2,015,249	161	12,517
1993–94	190,683	118,031	691,064	430,234	172,196	134,705	228,233	1,965,146	159	12,359
1992–93	241,968	174,702	612,494	377,211	198,379	149,675	293,241	2,047,670	161	12,718
1991–92	231,940	117,078	586,014	372,576	270,537	155,603	201,592	1,935,340	160	12,095
1990–91	194,195	121,450	594,592	530,279	276,112	124,826	196,434	2,038,518	162	12,583
1989–90	209,542	133,483	683,047	412,483	351,423	123,065	277,420	2,190,463	170	12,885
1988–89	212,775	121,326	690,199	421,255	206,781	176,629	167,353	1,966,318	164	12,173
1987–88	204,411	104,561	720,121	443,133	281,461	119,313	177,585	2,050,585	155	13,229
1986–87	209,290	146,761	593,520	349,342	263,550	119,396	195,533	1,877,400	165	11,378
1985–86	171,142	130,034	486,838	495,526	311,833	184,262	192,316	1,971,951	168	11,738
1984–85	174,604	137,078	616,229	320,772	269,232	148,690	242,754	1,909,359	157	12,162
1983–84	192,276	151,647	625,965	417,298	181,832	185,382	187,000	1,941,400	166	11,695
1982–83	191,312	150,046	670,503	452,688	260,069	193,845	291,162	2,209,625	154	14,348
1981–82	236,220	127,300	513,185	356,987	203,334	124,308	279,621	1,840,955	160	11,506
1980–81	246,824	194,502	832,578	534,402	320,530	288,714	339,250	2,756,800	169	16,312
1979–80	267,121	204,759	804,701	507,725	364,039	157,530	355,541	2,661,416	163	16,328
1978–79	243,773	185,343	880,345	537,748	243,683	263,213	249,897	2,604,002	166	15,687
1977–78	258,248	178,930	881,406	540,164	400,751	137,059	198,020	2,594,578	160	16,216
1976–77	379,230	192,159	942,523	631,265	373,330	205,379	258,216	2,982,102	174	17,139
1975–76	255,533	178,099	867,880	573,843	471,925	206,851	205,810	2,759,941	161	17,142
1974–75	283,956	170,466	914,994	646,434	393,323	268,361	291,369	2,968,903	172	17,261
1973–74	214,236	125,295	840,142	747,909	346,012	233,307	273,051	2,779,952	167	16,646
1972–73	259,432	169,114	938,741	735,825	357,386	241,934	226,543	2,928,975	160	18,306
1971–72	277,726	236,127	986,094	711,399	486,378	230,292	248,546	3,158,562	160	19,741
1970–71	329,687	230,942	956,683	757,852	360,687	304,937	279,644	3,220,432	162	19,879
1969–70	345,229	195,102	925,930	651,374	319,893	198,537	390,700	3,026,765	170	17,805
1968–69	331,858	252,710	1,094,043	883,675	464,915	188,121	216,232	3,431,554	157	21,857
1967–68	322,121	236,195	1,229,519	771,284	563,779	240,095	223,831	3,586,824	160	22,418

LDV VANS TROPHY 2002–03

■ *Denotes player sent off.*

NORTHERN SECTION FIRST ROUND

Tuesday, 22 October 2002

Chesterfield (1) 2 *(Allott 10, Brandon 90)*
Halifax T (0) 0 1382
Chesterfield: Muggleton; O'Hare, Edwards (Ebdon), Dawson, Payne, Howson, Brandon, Burt, Allott, Richardson (Hudson), Davies (Howard).
Halifax T: Morgan; Asher (Ibbotson), Grayston (Heinemann), Herbert, Garnett, Haigh, Mallon, Farrell■, Ryan (Parke), Senior, Fitzpatrick.

Lincoln C (1) 4 *(Yeo 42, 89, Futcher 80, Brass 90 (og))*
York C (0) 3 *(Cook 52 (pen), Nogan 58, Parkin 81)* 1275
Lincoln C: Pettinger; Camm, Bimson, Weaver (Smith), Morgan, Futcher, Willis, Sedgemore, Mike (Buckley), Yeo, Thompson (Cropper).
York C: Howarth; Okoli (Brass), Edmondson, Wilding, Smith, Jones, Cook, Wood, Nogan, Parkin, Potter.

Mansfield T (0) 0
Crewe Alex (2) 4 *(Hulse 4, 14, 59, Jack 62)* 1874
Mansfield T: Pilkington; Clarke, Hurst, Holyoak, Moore, Williamson (Buxton), Corden, MacKenzie, Christie (Bacon), Larkin (White A), Lawrence.
Crewe Alex: Bankole; Wright, Sodje, Brammer, Foster, Walker, Jack (Miles), Lunt (Bell), Hulse (Rix), Jones, Sorvel.

Notts Co (0) 2 *(Richardson 64, Bolland 80)*
Wigan Ath (3) 3 *(Teale 9, 22, Jarrett 36)* 1020
Notts Co: Mildenhall; Stone (Holmes), Nicholson, Brough (Bolland), Fenton, Richardson, Cas, Whitley, Stallard, Heffernan (Allsopp), Liburd.
Wigan Ath: Filan; Edghill, Baines, Flynn, Jackson, Mitchell, Green, Jarrett, Teale, Liddell, Kennedy.

Oldham Ath (1) 3 *(Andrews 19, Vernon 77, 79)*
Carlisle U (1) 4 *(Osman 25, 59, Farrell 63, 97)* 2821
Oldham Ath: Miskelly; Haining (Hall F), Carss (Eyre), Hill, Baudet (Clegg), Armstrong, Sheridan D, Vernon, Killen, Andrews, Lourenco.
Carlisle U: Glennon; Shelley, Murphy, Magennis (Farrell), Kelly, Taylor, McGill, Summerbell, Sutton (Wake), McDonagh (Baldacchino), Osman.
aet; Carlisle U won on sudden death.

Port Vale (2) 3 *(Angell 9, 34, Carragher 79)*
Hull C (0) 1 *(Donaldson 72)* 2621
Port Vale: Goodlad; Cummins, Charnock (McClare), Collins, Carragher, Brightwell, Ashcroft, McPhee, Paynter, Angell (Armstrong), Rowland.
Hull C: Musselwhite; Heard, Price, Chapman, Burton, Kerr (Fry), Peat, Williams (Russell), Alexander (Donaldson), Bradshaw, Philpott.

Rochdale (0) 0
Bury (0) 1 *(Woodthorpe 72)* 2486
Rochdale: Gilks; Duffy, Doughty, Bishop, Macauley, Griffiths (Patterson), Hodges (McCourt), Oliver, McEvilly (Connor), Townson, Simpson.
Bury: Garner; Unsworth, Woodthorpe, Hill, Swailes, Redmond, O'Shaughnessy, Johnrose, Nugent, Abbott (Preece), George (Whaley).

Scarborough (1) 1 *(Scott 45)*
Doncaster R (0) 2 *(Hudson 78, 113)* 1206
Scarborough: Walker; Cryan, Shepherd, Hotte, Ormerod, Stoker, Brassart (Henry), Pounder, Scott (Blunt), Campbell, Fatokun (Raw).
Doncaster R: Warrington; Price, Ryan, Owen, Foster (Barrick), Albrighton, Green (Morley), Hudson, Whitman, Gill (Bent), Paterson.
aet; Doncaster R won on sudden death.

Scunthorpe U (1) 2 *(Torpey 14, Dawson 46)*
Blackpool (0) 3 *(Milligan 63 (pen), Murphy 68, Taylor 81)* 1475
Scunthorpe U: Evans; Stanton, Dawson, Sparrow, Balmer, McCombe, Brough (Parton), Graves, Carruthers (Featherstone), Torpey, Beagrie.
Blackpool: Barnes; O'Kane, Jaszczun, Collins (Taylor), Hughes, Reid, Milligan, McMahon (Wellens), Walker, Blinkhorn (Murphy), Coid.

Shrewsbury T (1) 3 *(Rodgers 7, Atkins 56 (pen), Lowe 87)*
Morecambe (0) 0 1602
Shrewsbury T: Dunbavin; Moss, Van Blerk, Redmile, Artell, Murray (Wilding), Woan, Atkins, Rodgers (Murphy), Jemson (Stevens), Lowe.
Morecambe: Mawson; McKearney, Swan, Hill, Colkin, Elam, Rigoglioso, Drummond, Black, Bentley (Rogan), Curtis (Carlton).

Southport (1) 3 *(Whitehall 9, 70, 77)*
Leigh RMI (1) 4 *(Kielty 42, Howell 54 (og), Salt 66, Tolson 88)* 481
Southport: Dickinson; Connolly, Jones B, Winstanley (Lane), Nolan, Jones S, Soley (Howell), Gibson, Pickford, Thomson (Lloyd-Williams), Whitehall.
Leigh RMI: Coburn; Maden, Durkin, Fitzhenry, Williams (Monk), Salt, Kielty, Fisher, Heald, Courtney (Tolson), Maamria.

Stockport Co (1) 1 *(Briggs 39)*
Darlington (0) 0 1190
Stockport Co: Spencer; Lescott, Hardiker (Palmer), Challinor, Goodwin, Fradin, Briggs, Lambert (Welsh), Burgess, Ross, Ellison.
Darlington: Collett; Betts, Valentine, McGurk, Clarke, Kilty, Campbell (Convery), Nicholls, Conlon (Sheeran), Mellanby (Naylor), Hodgson.

Tranmere R (2) 5 *(Harrison 32, Jones 45, 75, Roberts 68, Taylor 79)*
Hartlepool U (0) 0 3387
Tranmere R: Achterberg; Connelly, Nicholson, Taylor, Allen, Edwards (Gray), Harrison, Mellon, Jones, Curtis (Olsen), Roberts (Hume).
Hartlepool U: Provett; Bass, Robson, Widdrington, Simms, Sharp, Arnison, McKenzie, Henderson (Easter), Boyd, Sweeney.

Wrexham (0) 2 *(Roberts 63, Thomas 88)*
Huddersfield T (0) 1 *(Mattis 77)* 1350
Wrexham: Dibble (Whitfield); Whitley, Holmes, Bennett, Pejic, Roberts, Thomas, Ferguson, Jones L (Sam), Trundle, Barrett.
Huddersfield T: Bevan; Heary, Sharp, Holland, Moses, Brown, Baldry (Irons), Mattis, Stead, Smith, Thorrington (Schofield).

SOUTHERN SECTION FIRST ROUND

Tuesday, 22 October 2002

Cambridge U (1) 4 *(Wanless 5, Tann 71, Tudor 80, Riza 87)*
Rushden & D (0) 0 2116
Cambridge U: Marshall (Brennan); Goodhind, Jordan, Nacca, Angus, Tann, Wanless (Fleming), Tudor, Scully (Kitson), Chillingworth, Riza.
Rushden & D: Sollitt; Bignot, Gray (Hall), Setchell, Peters, Tillson, Bell, Mills, Duffy, Lowe (Darby), Talbot (Wardley).

Cheltenham T (1) 4 *(Brayson 45 (pen), 78, McCann 63, Alsop 68)*
Colchester U (0) 1 *(McGleish 57)* 1369
Cheltenham T: Book; Howarth, Victory, Forsyth, Walker (Griffin), Duff M, Coates (Yates), Devaney, Alsop (Spencer), Brayson, McCann.
Colchester U: McKinney■; Stockley, Keith, Pinault, Steele, White, Izzet, Bowry (Odunsi), Rapley (Richards), McGleish, Stockwell (Brown).

Chester C (1) 1 *(Guyett 29)*

Plymouth Arg (1) 2 *(Keith 34, Evans 85)* 1126

Chester C: McCaldon; Guyett, McIntyre, Davies, Hatswell, Bolland, Carden, Brady (Woodyatt), Blackburn (Brown M), Twiss, Beesley (Sugden).
Plymouth Arg: McCormick; Connolly, McGlinchey, Lopes, Malcolm, Adams, Phillips, Broad, Lowndes (Evans), Keith, Beresford.

Dagenham & R (0) 1 *(Janney 71)*

Kidderminster H (2) 3 *(Melligan 21, Shilton 39, Bennett 49)* 742

Dagenham & R: Gothard; Cole (Lewis), Smith, Vickers, Rooney, Janney, Shipp, Perkins (Murat), Mayo, Fletcher (West), McDougald.
Kidderminster H: Brock; Williams (Parrish), Shilton, Ayres, Hinton, Smith (Bennett), Melligan, Flynn, Broughton, Henriksen (Foster), Coleman.

Exeter C (0) 1 *(Sheldon 66)*

Bristol R (0) 0 1613

Exeter C: Miller; Hiley, Power (Thomas), Gaia, Buxton, Walker, Sheldon (McConnell), Cronin, Flack, Coppinger, Pettefer.
Bristol R: Clarke; Arndale, Boxall, U'ddin (Gall), Barrett, Quinn, McKeever (Gilroy), Hogg, Lee, Coote, Bryant.

Hereford U (2) 3 *(Eribenne 6, 32, Parry 82)*

Northampton T (2) 4 *(Forrester 1, 96 (pen), Rickers 11, Asamoah 89)* 1087

Hereford U: Baker; Clarke (Sawyers), Tretton, Pitman, Teesdale, James, Rose, Williams, Eribenne, Parry (Guinan), Galloway.
Northampton T: Abbey; Gill (Harsley), Frain (Morison), Sampson, Hope, Rickers, Asamoah, Trollope, Forrester, Gabbiadini (Carruthers), Hargreaves.
aet; Northampton T won on sudden death.

Leyton Orient (3) 3 *(Iriekpen 11, Barnard 19, Lockwood 31)*

Peterborough U (2) 2 *(Clarke A 28, 32)* 953

Leyton Orient: Morris; Barnard, Lockwood, Smith, Miller, Iriekpen, Canham, Martin, Ibehre (Hatcher), Thorpe (Watts), Toner (Harris).
Peterborough U: Tyler; Joseph, Jelleyman (Danielsson), Shields (Lee), Rea, Edwards, Newton (Green), Bullard, Clarke A, Allen, Farrell.

Oxford U (0) 2 *(Waterman 61, Crosby 87 (pen))*

Bournemouth (3) 3 *(Fletcher S 24, Hayter 34, Purches S 38)* 4663

Oxford U: Woodman; Hackett, Powell, Crosby, Bound (Robinson), Viveash, Waterman, Hunter, Basham (Oldfield), Louis, Savage (Whitehead).
Bournemouth: Moss; Bernard, Purches S, Broadhurst, Fletcher C, Browning, Stock, O'Connor, Hayter, Fletcher S (Feeney), Thomas (Elliott).

QPR (0) 0

Bristol C (0) 0 4722

QPR: Royce; Forbes, Williams, Palmer, Rose, Burgess (Padula), Daly (Bean), Langley■, Thomson, Oli (Doudou), Connolly.
Bristol C: Phillips; Coles, Fortune, Burnell, Butler, Hill, Hulbert (Rosenior), Brown A, Beadle (Correia), Roberts, Tinnion (Doherty).
aet; Bristol C won 5-4 on penalties.

Stevenage B (0) 2 *(Jackson 64, Pacquette 67)*

Swansea C (1) 1 *(Thomas 45)* 746

Stevenage B: Westhead (Wilson); Travis, Fraser, Riddle, Trott, Stirling, Howell, Wormull, Blackwood, Jackson, Pacquette.
Swansea C: Freestone; Jenkins, Howard, Jones, O'Leary, Theobald, Lacey (Jackson), Cash, Thomas, Wood (Murphy), Reid.

Swindon T (3) 6 *(Jackson 10, Davis J 25, Heywood 45, Invincibile 49, Miglioranzi 89, Parkin 90)*

Southend U (1) 1 *(Jones 23)* 1747

Swindon T: Griemink (Farr); Edds, Duke, Gurney, Willis, Heywood, Miglioranzi, Jackson, Parkin, Invincibile (Dykes), Davis J (Sabin).
Southend U: Flahavan; Clark■, Searle, Jordan (Beard), Cort, Whelan, Thurgood (McSweeney), Smith, Belgrave (Salter), Jones, Tilson.

Torquay U (0) 0

Wycombe W (3) 4 *(Devine 24, 31, 77, Rogers 35)* 1133

Torquay U: Attwell; Hazell, Canoville, Holmes (Douglin), Woozley, Russell (Ashington), Hockley, Osei-Kuffour, Graham, Gritton (Fowler), Hill.
Wycombe W: Talia; Senda, Vinnicombe, Bulman, Rogers, Thomson (Johnson), Currie, Simpson, Faulconbridge (Dixon), Devine, Cook (Townsend).

Woking (0) 0

Luton T (1) 2 *(Holmes 26, Deeney 57)* 1216

Woking: Jalal; Piper, Boardman, Smith S (Reeks), Simpemba (Allman), Hamilton (Sharpling), Patmore, Banger, Payne, Smith N, Kember.
Luton T: Ovendale; Hillier, Kimble, Leary, Deeney, Johnson (Barnett), Holmes, Brkovic, Mansell, Osborn (Okai), Judge (Foley).

Wednesday, 23 October 2002

Boston U (0) 4 *(Battersby 59, Thompson L 71, Angel 89 (pen), Weatherstone S 90)*

Yeovil T (0) 2 *(Lockwood 73, Alford 80)* 1323

Boston U: Bastock; Clifford, Chapman, Bennett, Greaves (Warburton), Hocking, Thompson L, Higgins, Battersby (Elding), Weatherstone S, Angel.
Yeovil T: Sheffield; Lockwood, Skiverton, O'Brien (Alford), Lindegaard (Elkholti), Johnson■, Way, McIndoe, Williams, Crittenden, Demba (Grant).

NORTHERN SECTION SECOND ROUND

Tuesday, 12 November 2002

Bury (1) 1 *(Lawson 28)*

Barnsley (0) 0 1366

Bury: Garner; Unsworth, Woodthorpe, Nelson, Hill, Redmond, Billy, O'Shaughnessy, Nugent, Lawson (Swailes), George (Whaley).
Barnsley: Ghent; Mulligan, Gibbs, Morgan, Kay, Neil, Lumsdon, Betsy, Sheron (Griff Jones), Fallon, Gorre (Williams).

Carlisle U (0) 1 *(McDonagh 109)*

Stockport Co (0) 0 1918

Carlisle U: Glennon; Shelley, Byrne (Maddison), Summerbell, Kelly, Murphy, Baldacchino (McDonagh), McGill, Sutton (Foran), Farrell, Osman.
Stockport Co: Blayney; Hardiker, Gibb, Challinor, Clare (Wild), Fradin, Briggs, Lambert, Burgess (Ross), Beckett (Daly), Goodwin.
aet; Carlisle U won on sudden death.

Crewe Alex (0) 2 *(Ashton 60, Jack 71)*

Blackpool (0) 0 2600

Crewe Alex: Bankole; Wright, Tierney, Bell, Foster, Walker, Jones, Lunt, Ashton, Jack, Sorvel (Collins).
Blackpool: Barnes; Grayson, Coid, Southern (Dalglish), Clarke C, Jaszczun (Taylor), Thornton, Bullock, Murphy (Wellens), Walker, Hills.

Leigh RMI (2) 3 *(Kielty 6, 75, Maamria 36)*

Wrexham (2) 4 *(Trundle 40, Jones L 44 (pen), 92, Edwards C 78)* 703

Leigh RMI: Coburn; Maden, Harrison, Kielty, Durkin, Fitzhenry, Salt, Williams, Maamria, Whittaker, Fisher.
Wrexham: Whitfield; Edwards C, Edwards P, Morgan (Carey), Bennett, Lawrence, Thomas, Ferguson, Jones L, Trundle, Barrett (Sam).
aet; Wrexham won on sudden death.

Lincoln C (1) 1 *(Buckley 39)*
Shrewsbury T (1) 2 *(Rodgers 45, Moss 94)* 1390
Lincoln C: Pettinger; Camm, Bimson, Weaver, Morgan, Futcher, Smith, Thompson (Gain), Ward (Yeo), Mike, Buckley (Willis).
Shrewsbury T: Dunbavin; Moss, Drysdale, Redmile, Artell, Tolley J, Lowe (Jagielka), Atkins (Murray), Rodgers, Jemson (Stevens), Van Blerk.
aet; Shrewsbury T won on sudden death.

Macclesfield T (1) 1 *(Tipton 4)*
Tranmere R (0) 2 *(Barlow 67, 116)* 1145
Macclesfield T: Wilson; Hitchen, Adams, Welch (O'Neill), Tinson, Ridler, Munroe, Eaton (Hardy), Tipton, Lightbourne, Whitaker.
Tranmere R: Achterberg; Connelly, Nicholson, Edwards, Gray, Jones, Taylor (Barlow), Mellon (Harrison), Haworth, Proudlock, Roberts.
aet; Tranmere R won on sudden death.

Port Vale (1) 1 *(Armstrong 29)*
Chesterfield (1) 1 *(Brandon 8)* 2222
Port Vale: Goodlad; Carragher, Charnock, Collins, Burns, Rowland (McClare), Cummins, Boyd, McPhee, Armstrong (Durnin), Bridge-Wilkinson (Brooker).
Chesterfield: Muggleton; O'Hare, Rowland (Rushbury■), Dawson, Payne, Howson, Davies, Howard, Allott (Warne), Burt (Smith), Brandon.
aet; Port Vale won 4-3 on penalties.

Wigan Ath (0) 0
Doncaster R (0) 1 *(Albrighton 67)* 2030
Wigan Ath: Beasant; Eaden, Brannan (Jarrett), Mitchell, Jackson, Breckin, Teale, Flynn (Ellington), Roberts (Baines), Green, Kennedy.
Doncaster R: Warrington; Marples, Price, Owen, Ryan, Morley, Muirhead (Green), Albrighton, Jackson, Barnes, Paterson (Ravenhill).

SOUTHERN SECTION SECOND ROUND

Tuesday, 12 November 2002

Bournemouth (0) 1 *(Feeney 90)*
Leyton Orient (0) 0 2724
Bournemouth: Moss; Bernard (Fletcher S), Purches S, Broadhurst, Fletcher C, O'Connor, Thomas, Feeney, Hayter, Holmes, Elliott.
Leyton Orient: Morris; Barnard, Lockwood, Smith, Miller, Iriekpen, Harris, Martin (Brazier), Nugent, Hatcher (Watts), Toner.

Cheltenham T (0) 1 *(Forsyth 90)*
Wycombe W (0) 2 *(Bulman 79, Cook 99)* 1740
Cheltenham T: Higgs; Howarth, Yates, Forsyth, Brough, Duff M, Devaney, McAuley (Milton), Spencer (Alsop), Brayson, McCann.
Wycombe W: Taylor; Senda, Vinnicombe, Bulman, Thomson, McCarthy (Rogers), Currie, Simpson, Faulconbridge, Harris, Cook.
aet; Wycombe W won on sudden death.

Exeter C (0) 0
Cardiff C (0) 3 *(Bowen 49, Campbell 61 (pen), Fortune-West 90)* 1360
Exeter C: Miller; McConnell, Hiley, Cronin, Buxton, Pilkington, Barnard, Ampadu (Curran), Flack, Coppinger (Moor), Pettefer.
Cardiff C: Margetson; Green, Barker, Collins, Simpkins, Hamilton, Bowen, Bonner, Fortune-West, Campbell, Legg.

Kidderminster H (0) 3 *(Melligan 47, Broughton 49, Sall 105)*
Swindon T (1) 2 *(Invincibile 39, Young 47)* 1322
Kidderminster H: Brock; Stamps (Ayres), Shilton, Sall, Hinton, Coleman, Melligan, Flynn, Broughton, Foster (Henriksen), Parrish (Williams).
Swindon T: Farr; Edds (Gurney), Dykes (Parkin), Willis, Reeves, Heywood, Miglioranzi, Robinson, Young, Invincibile, Jackson (Duke).
aet; Kidderminster H won on sudden death.

Northampton T (2) 2 *(Hargreaves 17, Gabbiadini 27)*
Cambridge U (2) 4 *(Burgess 37 (og), Riza 45, 50, Youngs 72)* 2497
Northampton T: Abbey■; Rickers (Hope), Gill, Sampson, Burgess, Harsley, Asamoah, Trollope, Forrester (Morison), Gabbiadini (Harper), Hargreaves.
Cambridge U: Marshall; Tann, Jordan, Duncan, Angus, Fleming, Wanless, Nacca (Guttridge), Bridges (Paynter), Youngs, Riza (Chillingworth).

Plymouth Arg (0) 0
Brentford (0) 1 *(Hunt 89)* 3565
Plymouth Arg: McCormick; Worrell, McGlinchey, Malcolm, Aljofree, Broad, Beresford (Adams), Lopes (Keith), Lowndes (Stonebridge), Sturrock, Phillips.
Brentford: Julian; Dobson, Frampton (Smith J), Sonko, Marshall, Evans, Fullarton (Hutchinson), Tabb, Vine, Rowlands, Hunt.

Stevenage B (2) 3 *(Nicholls 6 (og), Pacquette 45, Scott 71)*
Luton T (1) 4 *(Thorpe 33, Brkovic 55, 57, 61)* 2601
Stevenage B: Westhead; Travis, Riddle, Howell (Blackwood), Stirling, MacDonald, Scott, Fraser, Midson (Sigere), Pacquette, Wormull (Jackson).
Luton T: Emberson; Foley (Johnson), Kimble, Mansell (Judge), Skelton, Deeney, Holmes, Nicholls (Leary), Brkovic, Thorpe, Hughes.

Wednesday, 13 November 2002

Boston U (1) 1 *(Thompson L 44)*
Bristol C (1) 2 *(Murray 33, Coles 111)* 1408
Boston U: Bastock; Rusk, Chapman, Hocking, Greaves (Weatherstone R), Bennett, Thompson L, Higgins, Battersby, Weatherstone S (Douglas), Angel.
Bristol C: Phillips; Murray, Woodman, Coles, Butler, Hill, Hulbert (Roberts) (Correia), Doherty, Peacock, Rosenior, Brown A (Tinnion).
aet; Bristol C won on sudden death.

NORTHERN QUARTER-FINALS

Tuesday, 10 December 2002

Bury (1) 2 *(Newby 15, Nugent 54)*
Tranmere R (0) 0 1656
Bury: Garner; Barrass, Unsworth, O'Shaughnessy, Swailes, Hill, Lawson (Forrest), Johnrose, Newby (Whaley), Nugent, Woodthorpe.
Tranmere R: Achterberg; Connelly, Nicholson (Robinson A), Sharps (Robinson M), Allen, Jones, Taylor (Hume), Mellon, Haworth, Barlow, Roberts.

Carlisle U (1) 2 *(McCarthy 41, Robinson 88)*
Wrexham (0) 0 2413
Carlisle U: Glennon; Shelley (Baldacchino), Maddison, McDonagh, Kelly, Murphy, McCarthy, McGill, Farrell (Foran), Summerbell, Osman (Robinson).
Wrexham: Whitfield; Edwards C, Edwards P (Holmes), Lawrence, Pejic, Roberts, Whitley, Ferguson, Morrell, Trundle (Sam), Barrett (Jones L).

Crewe Alex (3) 8 *(Vaughan 13, Ashton 19, 24, 76, Jack 54, 64, Jones 83, Lunt 86)*
Doncaster R (0) 0 2189
Crewe Alex: Bankole; Wright, Tierney, Brammer, Foster, Walker, Vaughan (Bell), Lunt, Jack (Jones), Ashton (Miles), Sorvel.
Doncaster R: Warrington; Marples, Barrick (Green), Ravenhill, Ryan (Foster), Morley, Whitman, Hudson, Barnes (Albrighton), Gill, Beech.

Shrewsbury T (1) 2 *(Rogers 3, Lowe 110)*
Port Vale (0) 1 *(Boyd 61)* 2597
Shrewsbury T: Dunbavin; Moss, Drysdale, Redmile, Artell, Tolley J, Lowe, Atkins (Murray), Rodgers, Jemson (Stevens), Van Blerk (Jagielka).
Port Vale: Goodlad; Cummins (McClare), Charnock, Collins, Burns, Carragher, Boyd, Durnin■, McPhee (Byrne), Paynter (Brooker), Armstrong.
aet; Shrewsbury T won on sudden death.

SOUTHERN QUARTER-FINALS

Tuesday, 10 December 2002

Bournemouth (0) 2 *(Elliott 79, Hayter 114)*

Cardiff C (0) 1 *(Gordon 81)* 3615

Bournemouth: Moss; Bernard (Tindall), Purches S, Broadhurst, Fletcher C, Browning, Thomas, O'Connor, Hayter, Fletcher S (Feeney), Elliott.
Cardiff C: Margetson; Weston, Hamilton, Collins, Zhiyi, Simpkins, Bonner, Campbell, Fortune-West (Gordon), Thorne (Bowen), Maxwell.
aet; Bournemouth won on sudden death.

Brentford (2) 2 *(Marshall 5, O'Connor 25)*

Kidderminster H (0) 1 *(Broughton 52)* 1541

Brentford: Smith P; Somner, Frampton, Sonko, Marshall, Evans, Fullarton, Smith J, O'Connor, Vine (Tabb), Rowlands.
Kidderminster H: Brock; Williams (Foster), Joy (Bishop), Coleman, Hinton, Ayres, Parrish, Flynn, Broughton, Melligan, Shilton (Bennett).

Luton T (1) 1 *(Thorpe 14)*

Cambridge U (0) 2 *(Fleming 58, Guttridge 113)* 2578

Luton T: Ovendale; Hillier, Davis (Kimble), Spring, Boyce, Coyne, Robinson, Brkovic, Crowe (Holmes), Thorpe (Fotiadis), Hughes.
Cambridge U: Marshall; Tann, Jordan, Duncan, Angus, Fleming, Guttridge, Tudor (Chillingworth), Bridges (Nacca), Youngs, Riza.
aet; Cambridge U won on sudden death.

Wednesday, 11 December 2002

Bristol C (1) 3 *(Murray 41, Peacock 64, 71)*

Wycombe W (0) 0 3506

Bristol C: Phillips; Murray (Beadle), Woodman (Fortune), Carey, Butler, Hill, Burnell, Doherty (Tinnion), Peacock, Rosenior, Brown A.
Wycombe W: Taylor; Rogers, Ryan, Bulman, Thomson, McCarthy, Cook (Roberts), Simpson, Faulconbridge, Harris (Dixon), Brown.

NORTHERN SEMI-FINALS

Tuesday, 21 January 2003

Carlisle U (1) 3 *(Foran 20, McDonagh 86, 118)*

Bury (0) 2 *(Dunfield 60, Clegg 70)* 2593

Carlisle U: Glennon; Shelley, Maddison (Birch), McDonagh, Kelly, Murphy, McCarthy (McGill), Russell (Baldacchino), Foran, Farrell, Rundle.
Bury: Garner; Unsworth, Stuart, Woodthorpe, Swailes, Redmond, Billy■, Dunfield, Newby, Lawson (Nugent), Clegg.
aet; Carlisle U won on sudden death.

Wednesday, 29 January 2003

Shrewsbury T (1) 4 *(Jemson 27, Lowe 47, 70, Rodgers 75)*

Crewe Alex (0) 2 *(Hulse 57, Ashton 81)* 4646

Shrewsbury T: Dunbavin; Moss, Smith, Redmile, Artell, Tolley J, Woan, Murray (Wilding), Rodgers, Jemson (Jagielka), Lowe (Aiston).
Crewe Alex: Bankole; Sodje (Wright), Tierney, Vaughan, Foster (Bell), Walker, Rix (Jones), Lunt, Hulse, Ashton, Sorvel.

SOUTHERN SEMI-FINALS

Tuesday, 21 January 2003

Bournemouth (1) 1 *(Fletcher C 15)*

Bristol C (0) 3 *(Bell 68, 77, Murray 90)* 5125

Bournemouth: Tardif; Bernard (Thomas), Purches S, Tindall, Fletcher C, Browning■, Feeney, O'Connor, Holmes (Fletcher S), Stock (Hayter), Elliott.
Bristol C: Phillips; Carey, Bell, Coles, Butler■, Fortune, Murray, Doherty, Fagan, Roberts (Lita), Tinnion (Brown A).

Brentford (1) 1 *(McCammon 43)*

Cambridge U (0) 2 *(Kitson 90, Riza 98)* 2878

Brentford: Smith P; Dobson, Frampton, Williams (Traynor), Marshall, Roget, Smith J, O'Connor, McCammon, Vine, Hunt (Hughes).
Cambridge U: Marshall; Goodhind, Murray, Duncan, Tann, Fleming, Guttridge (Nacca), Wanless, Kitson, Chillingworth (Riza), Youngs (Revell).
aet; Cambridge U won on sudden death.

NORTHERN FINAL FIRST LEG

Tuesday, 25 February 2003

Carlisle U (1) 1 *(Rundle 23)*

Shrewsbury T (0) 0 5163

Carlisle U: Glennon; Birch, Murphy, McDonagh, Kelly, Raven, Green, Russell (McGill), Foran, Farrell, Rundle.
Shrewsbury T: Dunbavin; Moss, Smith, Redmile, Artell (Drysdale), Tolley J, Woan, Talbot, Rodgers (Aiston), Jemson, Van Blerk.

NORTHERN FINAL SECOND LEG

Tuesday, 4 March 2003

Shrewsbury T (0) 0

Carlisle U (0) 0 6273

Shrewsbury T: Dunbavin; Moss, Smith, Redmile, Wilding, Talbot (Tolley J), Jagielka, Lowe (Aiston), Rodgers, Jemson (Stevens), Woan.
Carlisle U: Glennon; Birch, Murphy, Summerbell, Kelly, Raven, McCarthy, Russell, Foran (Wake), Farrell (Rundle), Green.

SOUTHERN FINAL FIRST LEG

Tuesday, 18 February 2003

Bristol C (1) 4 *(Doherty 21, Burnell 64, Murray 67, Robins 77)*

Cambridge U (1) 2 *(Kitson 34, 54)* 7173

Bristol C: Phillips; Carey, Bell, Burnell, Butler, Hill, Murray, Doherty, Peacock (Beadle), Roberts (Robins), Tinnion.
Cambridge U: Marshall; Goodhind, Newey, Murray, Tann, Wanless, Guttridge (Bridges), Tudor, Kitson, Youngs, Fleming.

SOUTHERN FINAL SECOND LEG

Tuesday, 25 February 2003

Cambridge U (0) 0

Bristol C (2) 3 *(Carey 11, Murray 45, Roberts 80)* 3956

Cambridge U: Marshall; Goodhind (Nacca), Murray, Fleming, Tann, Wanless (Chillingworth), Guttridge, Tudor, Kitson (Revell), Youngs, Riza.
Bristol C: Phillips; Carey, Bell, Burnell, Butler, Hill, Murray, Doherty, Peacock (Beadle), Robins (Roberts), Tinnion (Brown A).

LDV VANS TROPHY FINAL

Sunday, 6 April 2003
(at Millennium Stadium, Cardiff)

Bristol C (0) 2 *(Peacock 77, Rosenior 89)*

Carlisle U (0) 0 50,913

Bristol C: Phillips; Carey, Bell (Hill), Burnell, Butler, Coles, Murray, Doherty, Peacock, Roberts (Rosenior), Tinnion (Brown A).
Carlisle U: Glennon; Shelley, Murphy, Summerbell (McDonagh), Kelly (Maddison), Raven, McCarthy, Green, Foran, Farrell (Wake), Rundle.
Referee: P. Walton.

FA CUP FINALS 1872–2003

1872 and 1874–92	Kennington Oval	1910	Replay at Everton
1873	Lillie Bridge	1911	Replay at Old Trafford
1886	Replay at Derby (Racecourse Ground)	1912	Replay at Bramall Lane
1893	Fallowfield, Manchester	1915	Old Trafford, Manchester
1894	Everton	1920–22	Stamford Bridge
1895–1914	Crystal Palace	1923 to 2000	Wembley
1901	Replay at Bolton	1970	Replay at Old Trafford
		2001 to date	Millennium Stadium, Cardiff

Year	*Winners*	*Runners-up*	*Score*
1872	Wanderers	Royal Engineers	1-0
1873	Wanderers	Oxford University	2-0
1874	Oxford University	Royal Engineers	2-0
1875	Royal Engineers	Old Etonians	2-0 (after 1-1 draw aet)
1876	Wanderers	Old Etonians	3-0 (after 1-1 draw aet)
1877	Wanderers	Oxford University	2-1 (aet)
1878	Wanderers*	Royal Engineers	3-1
1879	Old Etonians	Clapham R	1-0
1880	Clapham R	Oxford University	1-0
1881	Old Carthusians	Old Etonians	3-0
1882	Old Etonians	Blackburn R	1-0
1883	Blackburn Olympic	Old Etonians	2-1 (aet)
1884	Blackburn R	Queen's Park, Glasgow	2-1
1885	Blackburn R	Queen's Park, Glasgow	2-0
1886	Blackburn R†	WBA	2-0 (after 0-0 draw)
1887	Aston Villa	WBA	2-0
1888	WBA	Preston NE	2-1
1889	Preston NE	Wolverhampton W	3-0
1890	Blackburn R	Sheffield W	6-1
1891	Blackburn R	Notts Co	3-1
1892	WBA	Aston Villa	3-0
1893	Wolverhampton W	Everton	1-0
1894	Notts Co	Bolton W	4-1
1895	Aston Villa	WBA	1-0
1896	Sheffield W	Wolverhampton W	2-1
1897	Aston Villa	Everton	3-2
1898	Nottingham F	Derby Co	3-1
1899	Sheffield U	Derby Co	4-1
1900	Bury	Southampton	4-0
1901	Tottenham H	Sheffield U	3-1 (after 2-2 draw)
1902	Sheffield U	Southampton	2-1 (after 1-1 draw)
1903	Bury	Derby Co	6-0
1904	Manchester C	Bolton W	1-0
1905	Aston Villa	Newcastle U	2-0
1906	Everton	Newcastle U	1-0
1907	Sheffield W	Everton	2-1
1908	Wolverhampton W	Newcastle U	3-1
1909	Manchester U	Bristol C	1-0
1910	Newcastle U	Barnsley	2-0 (after 1-1 draw)
1911	Bradford C	Newcastle U	1-0 (after 0-0 draw)
1912	Barnsley	WBA	1-0 (aet, after 0-0 draw)
1913	Aston Villa	Sunderland	1-0
1914	Burnley	Liverpool	1-0
1915	Sheffield U	Chelsea	3-0
1920	Aston Villa	Huddersfield T	1-0 (aet)
1921	Tottenham H	Wolverhampton W	1-0
1922	Huddersfield T	Preston NE	1-0
1923	Bolton W	West Ham U	2-0
1924	Newcastle U	Aston Villa	2-0
1925	Sheffield U	Cardiff C	1-0
1926	Bolton W	Manchester C	1-0
1927	Cardiff C	Arsenal	1-0
1928	Blackburn R	Huddersfield T	3-1
1929	Bolton W	Portsmouth	2-0
1930	Arsenal	Huddersfield T	2-0
1931	WBA	Birmingham	2-1
1932	Newcastle U	Arsenal	2-1
1933	Everton	Manchester C	3-0
1934	Manchester C	Portsmouth	2-1
1935	Sheffield W	WBA	4-2
1936	Arsenal	Sheffield U	1-0
1937	Sunderland	Preston NE	3-1
1938	Preston NE	Huddersfield T	1-0 (aet)
1939	Portsmouth	Wolverhampton W	4-1
1946	Derby Co	Charlton Ath	4-1 (aet)
1947	Charlton Ath	Burnley	1-0 (aet)
1948	Manchester U	Blackpool	4-2
1949	Wolverhampton W	Leicester C	3-1
1950	Arsenal	Liverpool	2-0
1951	Newcastle U	Blackpool	2-0
1952	Newcastle U	Arsenal	1-0
1953	Blackpool	Bolton W	4-3
1954	WBA	Preston NE	3-2
1955	Newcastle U	Manchester C	3-1
1956	Manchester C	Birmingham C	3-1

Year	Winners	Runners-up	Score
1957	Aston Villa	Manchester U	2-1
1958	Bolton W	Manchester U	2-0
1959	Nottingham F	Luton T	2-1
1960	Wolverhampton W	Blackburn R	3-0
1961	Tottenham H	Leicester C	2-0
1962	Tottenham H	Burnley	3-1
1963	Manchester U	Leicester C	3-1
1964	West Ham U	Preston NE	3-2
1965	Liverpool	Leeds U	2-1 (aet)
1966	Everton	Sheffield W	3-2
1967	Tottenham H	Chelsea	2-1
1968	WBA	Everton	1-0 (aet)
1969	Manchester C	Leicester C	1-0
1970	Chelsea	Leeds U	2-1 (aet)
	(after 2-2 draw,	*after extra time)*	
1971	Arsenal	Liverpool	2-1 (aet)
1972	Leeds U	Arsenal	1-0
1973	Sunderland	Leeds U	1-0
1974	Liverpool	Newcastle U	3-0
1975	West Ham U	Fulham	2-0
1976	Southampton	Manchester U	1-0
1977	Manchester U	Liverpool	2-1
1978	Ipswich T	Arsenal	1-0
1979	Arsenal	Manchester U	3-2
1980	West Ham U	Arsenal	1-0
1981	Tottenham H	Manchester C	3-2
	(after 1-1 draw,	*after extra time)*	
1982	Tottenham H	QPR	1-0
	(after 1-1 draw,	*after extra time)*	
1983	Manchester U	Brighton & HA	4-0
	(after 2-2 draw,	*after extra time)*	
1984	Everton	Watford	2-0
1985	Manchester U	Everton	1-0 (aet)
1986	Liverpool	Everton	3-1
1987	Coventry C	Tottenham H	3-2 (aet)
1988	Wimbledon	Liverpool	1-0
1989	Liverpool	Everton	3-2 (aet)
1990	Manchester U	Crystal Palace	1-0
	(after 3-3 draw,	*after extra time)*	
1991	Tottenham H	Nottingham F	2-1 (aet)
1992	Liverpool	Sunderland	2-0
1993	Arsenal	Sheffield W	2-1 (aet)
	(after 1-1 draw,	*after extra time)*	
1994	Manchester U	Chelsea	4-0
1995	Everton	Manchester U	1-0
1996	Manchester U	Liverpool	1-0
1997	Chelsea	Middlesbrough	2-0
1998	Arsenal	Newcastle U	2-0
1999	Manchester U	Newcastle U	2-0
2000	Chelsea	Aston Villa	1-0
2001	Liverpool	Arsenal	2-1
2002	Arsenal	Chelsea	2-0
2003	Arsenal	Southampton	1-0

** Won outright, but restored to the Football Association.*
† A special trophy was awarded for third consecutive win.

FA CUP WINS

Manchester U 10, Arsenal 9, Tottenham H 8, Aston Villa 7, Blackburn R 6, Liverpool 6, Newcastle U 6, Everton 5, The Wanderers 5, WBA 5, Bolton W 4, Manchester C 4, Sheffield U 4, Wolverhampton W 4, Chelsea 3, Sheffield W 3, West Ham U 3, Bury 2, Nottingham F 2, Old Etonians 2, Preston NE 2, Sunderland 2, Barnsley 1, Blackburn Olympic 1, Blackpool 1, Bradford C 1, Burnley 1, Cardiff C 1, Charlton Ath 1, Clapham R 1, Coventry C 1, Derby Co 1, Huddersfield T 1, Ipswich T 1, Leeds U 1, Notts Co 1, Old Carthusians 1, Oxford University 1, Portsmouth 1, Royal Engineers 1, Southampton 1, Wimbledon 1.

APPEARANCES IN FINALS

Arsenal 16, Manchester U 15, Newcastle U 13, Everton 12, Liverpool 12, Newcastle U 12, Aston Villa 10, WBA 10, Tottenham H 9, Blackburn R 8, Manchester C 8, Wolverhampton W 8, Bolton W 7, Chelsea 7, Preston NE 7, Old Etonians 6, Sheffield U 6, Sheffield W 6, Huddersfield T 5, *The Wanderers 5, Derby Co 4, Leeds U 4, Leicester C 4, Oxford University 4, Royal Engineers 4, Southampton 4, Sunderland 4, West Ham U 4, Blackpool 3, Burnley 3, Nottingham F 3, Portsmouth 3, Barnsley 2, Birmingham C 2, *Bury 2, Cardiff C 2, Charlton Ath 2, Clapham R 2, Notts Co 2, Queen's Park (Glasgow) 2, *Blackburn Olympic 1, *Bradford C 1, Brighton & HA 1, Bristol C 1, *Coventry C 1, Crystal Palace 1, Fulham 1, *Ipswich T 1, Luton T 4, Middlesbrough 1, *Old Carthusians 1, QPR 1, Watford 1, *Wimbledon 1.
** Denotes undefeated.*

APPEARANCES IN SEMI-FINALS

Arsenal 23, Everton 23, Manchester U 22, Liverpool 21, Aston Villa 19, WBA 19, Tottenham H 17, Blackburn R 16, Newcastle U 16, Sheffield W 16, Chelsea 15, Wolverhampton W 14, Bolton W 13, Derby Co 13, Sheffield U 13, Nottingham F 12, Southampton 11, Sunderland 11, Manchester C 10, Preston NE 10, Birmingham C 9, Burnley 8, Leeds U 8, Leicester C 8, Huddersfield T 7, Old Etonians 6, Fulham 6, Oxford University 6, West Ham U 6, Notts Co 5, Portsmouth 5, The Wanderers 5, Luton T 4, Queen's Park (Glasgow) 4, Royal Engineers 4, Watford 4, Blackpool 3, Cardiff C 3, Clapham R 3, Crystal Palace (professional club) 3, Ipswich T 3, Millwall 3, Norwich C 3, Old Carthusians 3, Oldham Ath 3, Stoke C 3, The Swifts 3, Barnsley 2, Blackburn Olympic 2, Bristol C 2, Bury 2, Charlton Ath 2, Grimsby T 2, Middlesbrough 2, Swansea T 2, Swindon T 2, Wimbledon 2, Bradford C 1, Brighton & HA 1, Cambridge University 1, Chesterfield 1, Coventry C 1, Crewe Alex 1, Crystal Palace (amateur club) 1, Darwen 1, Derby Junction 1, Glasgow R 1, Hull C 1, Marlow 1, Old Harrovians 1, Orient 1, Plymouth Arg 1, Port Vale 1, QPR 1, Reading 1, Shropshire W 1, Wycombe W 1, York C 1.

THE FA CUP 2002–03

PRELIMINARY AND QUALIFYING ROUNDS

EXTRA PRELIMINARY ROUND

Flixton v Goole 1-1, 0-0
Goole won 5-4 on penalties.
Holker Old Boys v Bridlington Town 0-2
West Auckland Town v Winsford United 2-1
Penrith v Brandon United 3-2
Marske United v Salford City 1-4
Maltby Main v Billingham Synthonia 0-6
Consett v Pontefract Collieries 4-1
Chester-Le-Street Town v Northallerton Town 3-1
Morpeth Town v Curzon Ashton 3-2
Nelson v Norton & Stockton Ancients 0-0, 2-1
Ramsbottom United v Thackley 1-0
Horden CW v Armthorpe Welfare 2-1
Bridgnorth Town v Gedling Town 4-2
Stratford Town v Stourbridge 4-1
Mickleover Sports v Shirebrook Town 3-1
Leek CSOB v Nantwich Town 0-3
Grosvenor Park v Stafford Town 2-0
Newmarket Town v Ely City 2-3
Newmarket Town awarded tie; Ely City fielded an ineligible player.
Dereham Town v AFC Wallingford 1-3
Saffron Walden Town v Hullbridge Sports 0-1
Bedford United & Valerio v Brook House 0-1
Potters Bar Town v Milton Keynes City 1-2
Sawbridgeworth Town v Harwich & Parkeston 2-0
Raunds Town v Ruislip Manor 1-0
Stotfold v Broxbourne Borough V&E 0-0, 5-1
Tiptree United v Ipswich Wanderers 1-1, 3-3
Ipswich Wanderers won 7-6 on penalties.
Ilford v Kempston Rovers 3-0
Walton Casuals v Whitehawk 0-4
Littlehampton Town v Godalming & Guildford 0-6
Greenwich Borough v Three Bridges 1-4
Deal Town v Chichester City United 2-2, 3-2
Lymington & New Milton v East Preston 2-2, 2-1
Moneyfields v Burgess Hill Town 1-0
Alton Town v Didcot Town 1-1, 0-1
Horsham YMCA v Eastleigh 1-3
AFC Totton v Southwick 3-2
Ramsgate v Maidstone United 1-1, 0-1
Chessington United v Ringmer 0-1
Reading Town v Farnham Town 3-1
Paulton Rovers v Downton 5-1
Highworth Town v Fareford Town 2-2, 4-1
Street v Keynsham Town 3-1
Portland United v Welton Rovers 6-2
Bishop Sutton v Melksham Town 2-1
Christchurch v Willand Rovers 3-0

PRELIMINARY ROUND

Shildon v Salford City 2-4
Morpeth Town v Woodleigh Sports 1-0
Hatfield Main v Shotton Comrades 0-1
Selby Town v Newcastle Blue Star 0-0, 4-2
Fleetwood Town v Workington 1-1, 0-1
Skelmersdale United v Penrith 1-3
Brigg Town v Kendal Town 2-4
Whitley Bay v Harrogate Railway 2-2, 4-5
Guisborough Town v Blackpool Mechanics 2-0
Farsley Celtic v Seaham Red Star 4-4, 6-1
Glasshoughton Welfare v Jarrow Roofing Boldon CA 1-3
Goole v Mossley 0-3
Nelson v Bishop Auckland 2-3
Ossett Town v Worsborough Bridge MW 0-2
Great Harwood Town v Winterton Rangers 0-0, 0-0
Great Harwood Town won 5-3 on penalties.
Horden CW v Trafford 2-1
Evenwood Town v Durham City 1-4
Prescot Cables v Witton Albion 3-6
Parkgate v St Helens Town 2-2, 1-3
Squires Gate v Lincoln United 1-2
Tow Law Town v Tadcaster Albion 2-1
Abbey Hey v Bamber Bridge 0-0, 2-2
Abbey Hey won 4-2 on penalties.
Louth United v Cheadle Town 4-1
Ramsbottom United v Chadderton 3-0
Matlock Town v Pickering Town 2-2, 1-0
Maine Road v Guiseley 1-2
Spennymoor United v Consett 4-0
Chester-Le-Street Town v Hall Road Rangers 2-0
Atherton LR v Rossington Main 0-2
Ashington v Colne 7-0
Willington v Atherton Collieries 0-0, 1-5
Chorley v Liversedge 5-0
Warrington Town v Esh Winning 2-2, 1-3
Bacup Borough v Bridlington Town 1-2
Bedlington Terriers v Brodsworth MW 3-0
Alnwick Town v Crook Town 1-2
Garforth Town v Yorkshire Amateur 3-1
Stocksbridge Park Steels v Oldham Town 17-1
Rossendale United v Ossett Albion 0-1
Thornaby v Dunston FB 1-1, 1-2
Clitheroe v Radcliffe Borough 1-3
Sheffield v West Auckland Town 0-4
South Shields v Hallam 1-2
Easington Colliery v Hebburn Town 1-3
Washington v North Ferriby United 0-2
Peterlee Newtown v Billingham Synthonia 2-1
Billingham Town w.o. v Gretna withdrew
Darwen v Eccleshill United 1-3
Stourport Swifts v Alfreton Town 1-4
Rocester v Congleton Town 3-0
Kidsgrove Athletic v Buxton 4-1
Rushall Olympic v Sutton Coldfield Town 1-4
Staveley MW v Boston Town 0-1
Halesowen Harriers v Shepshed Dynamo 1-3
Newcastle Town v Leek Town 0-1
Belper Town v Gresley Rovers 0-1
Mickleover Sports v Cradley Town 2-1
Redditch United v Grosvenor Park 2-1
Bourne Town v Eastwood Town 1-1, 1-3
Bedworth United v Causeway United 1-1, 2-1
Histon v Quorn 2-3
Oadby Town v Rugby United 2-2, 3-2
Atherstone United v Studley 3-0
Stratford Town v Ludlow Town 3-1
Biddulph Victoria v Bridgnorth Town 2-0
Nantwich Town v Holbech United 4-0
Chasetown v Spalding United 0-1
Corby Town v Stamford 0-6
Arnold Town v Racing Club Warwick 1-0
King's Lynn v Deeping Rangers 1-0
Willenhall Town v Glapwell 1-0
Pelsall Villa v Borrowash Victoria 1-1, 4-1
Shifnal Town v Blackstones 1-4
Glossop North End v Boldmere St Michaels 1-0
Solihull Borough v Oldbury United 2-0
Barwell v Bromsgrove Rovers 1-1, 3-4
Long Buckby v Marlow 0-2
Newmarket Town v Ilford 1-3
Barking & East Ham United v Soham Town Rangers 4-3
Hullbridge Sports v Edgware Town 2-5
Great Yarmouth Town v Holmer Green 2-1
Desborough Town v Romford 1-2
Southall Town v Wroxham 1-6
Northampton Spencer v Yaxley 1-1, 1-5
Banbury United v Berkhamsted Town 1-1, 4-1
Hoddesdon Town v AFC Sudbury 0-2
Cheshunt v Wembley 3-0
Maldon Town v Flackwell Heath 1-1, 0-1
Leighton Town v Royston Town 2-2, 0-3
Chalfont St Peter v Hemel Hempstead Town 0-3
Clacton Town v Sawbridgeworth Town 3-1
Wealdstone v Leyton 1-3
Cogenhoe United v Diss Town 0-2
Bowers United v Arlesey Town 1-4
Wivenhoe Town v Yeading 0-3
Stotfold v Hornchurch 1-1, 4-4
Stotfold won 5-4 on penalties.
St Neots Town v Stansted 6-0
Bury Town v Barton Rovers 2-3
Lowestoft Town v Uxbridge 0-2
Raunds Town v Burnham Ramblers 5-1
Wootton Blue Cross v Brackley Town 3-1
Stewarts & Lloyds v Ford Sports Daventry 1-0
Harlow Town v Aveley 0-1
Stowmarket Town v Southall 1-6
Wisbech Town v Woodbridge Town 3-1
Brook House v Burnham 2-3
Hanwell Town v Great Wakering Rovers 0-3
Mildenhall Town v London Colney 0-0, 0-1
Tilbury v Gorleston 4-3
Concord Rangers v Hertford Town 2-3
Ware v Milton Keynes City 5-1

Harringey Borough v Northwood	0-1
Ipswich Wanderers v Leyton Pennant	2-3
Letchworth v Staines Town	1-1, 0-1
Clapton v Beaconsfield SYCOB	0-3
Witham Town v Wingate & Finchley	0-5
St Margaretsbury v Dunstable Town	2-0
East Thurrock United v Harefield United	1-2
Buckingham Town v Tring Town	3-0
Rothwell Town v Kingsbury Town	3-1
Brentwood v AFC Wallingford	2-2, 1-4
Fakenham Town v Southend Manor	1-3
Wick v Abingdon United	1-4
Merstham v St Leonards	3-4
Three Bridges v Didcot Town	3-1
Erith Town v Ringmer	0-3
North Leigh v Cowes Sports	0-5
Bromley v Abingdon Town	3-2
Lymington & New Milton v Dulwich Hamlet	1-1, 3-1
Redhill v Peacehaven & Telscombe	1-3
Gosport Borough v Wantage Town	2-1
Oxford City v Cray Wanderers	0-1
Deal Town v Hythe Town	4-2
Eastleigh v Erith & Belvedere	5-0
Fisher Athletic v Wokingham Town	7-0
Whyteleafe v Reading Town	1-0
Whitstable Town v Chipstead	1-2
Croydon Athletic v Eastbourne Borough	0-0, 1-4
AFC Totton v Thamesmead Town	2-0
Molesey v Hassocks	3-0
Bedfont v Whitehawk	3-1
Saltdean United v VCD Athletic	0-3
Beckenham Town v Croydon	1-2
Brockenhurst v Fleet Town	3-2
Newport (IW) v Blackfield & Langley	1-1, 3-0
Moneyfields v BAT Sports	0-2
Chertsey Town v Arundel	4-1
Tunbridge Wells v Ashford Town (Middlesex)	2-1
Fareham Town v Tooting & Mitcham United	1-1, 0-1
Eastbourne Town v Windsor & Eton	1-1, 2-4
Godalming & Guildford v Whitchurch United	3-0
Thame United v Slough Town	1-2
Pagham v Bracknell Town	3-2
Sandhurst Town v Herne Bay	2-6
Sittingbourne v Slade Green	2-2, 1-3
Metropolitan Police v Lancing	4-0
Camberley Town v Cove	0-1
Horsham v Lordswood	2-2, 2-1
Lewes v Thatcham Town	1-0
Chatham Town v Egham Town	0-0, 1-0
Bognor Regis Town v Worthing	1-0
Banstead Athletic v Leatherhead	1-4
Westfield v Dorking	1-2
Tonbridge Angels v Maidstone United	2-3
Hillingdon Borough v Chessington & Hook United	2-2, 3-1
Corinthian Casuals v Epsom & Ewell	1-1, 2-1
Walton & Hersham v Andover	2-1
Ashford Town v Carshalton Athletic	1-3
AFC Newbury v Hailsham Town	2-1
Selsey v Ash United	3-0
Eastbourne United v Cobham	0-3
Dartford v Carterton Town	2-2, 0-1
Chard Town v Swindon Supermarine	2-0
Frome Town v Shortwood United	0-1
Bishop Sutton v Cinderford Town	1-3
Torrington v Westbury United	2-1
Odd Down v Paulton Rovers	0-2
Clevedon Town v Bitton	2-2, 2-1
Highworth Town v Cirencester Town	3-0
Hungerford Town v Shepton Mallet	2-0
Bridport v Taunton Town	2-3
Elmore v Backwell United	1-2
Bashley v Mangotsfield United	2-2, 1-0
Salisbury City v Bideford	1-2
Barnstaple Town v Team Bath	0-4
Corsham Town v Portland United	3-1
Devizes Town v Ilfracombe Town	5-2
Bournemouth v Bridgwater Town	3-0
Falmouth Town v Bristol Manor Farm	2-0
Merthyr Tydfil v Christchurch	5-0
Portleven v Dorchester Town	0-5
Tuffley Rovers v St Blazey	0-1
Minehead Town v Gloucester City	0-2
Weston-Super-Mare v Calne Town	4-0
Yate Town v Hallen	4-2
Dawlish Town v Wimborne Town	0-3
Brislington v Evesham United	2-2, 2-3
Street v Bemerton Heath Harlequins	1-3

FIRST QUALIFYING ROUND

Eccleshill United v St Helens Town	3-2
Bedlington Terriers v Ossett Albion	1-0
Radcliffe Borough v Abbey Hey	4-1
Esh Winning v Harrogate Railway	1-2
Horden CW v Shotton Comrades	4-1
Dunston FB v Selby Town	2-0
Kendal Town v North Ferriby United	2-1
Workington v Mossley	2-1
Hallam v Stocksbridge Park Steels	2-3
Bishop Auckland v Rossington Main	3-3, 1-1
Rossington Main won 4-1 on penalties.	
Jarrow Roofing Boldon CA v Billingham Town	2-4
Morpeth Town v Guisborough Town	0-1
West Auckland Town v Chorley	6-3
Chester-Le-Street Town v Penrith	2-0
Great Harwood Town v Crook Town	1-1, 1-1
Great Harwood Town won 8-7 on penalties.	
Bridlington Town v Garforth Town	1-0
Tow Law Town v Matlock Town	5-4
Witton Albion v Ramsbottom United	1-1, 3-2
Farsley Celtic v Lincoln United	3-1
Durham City v Worsbrough Bridge MW	5-1
Guiseley v Hebburn Town	3-0
Peterlee Newtown v Louth United	4-0
Spennymoor United v Ashington	1-1, 2-1
Atherton Collieries v Salford City	1-0
Alfreton Town v Kidsgrove Athletic	0-1
Nantwich Town v Rocester	2-0
Eastwood Town v Redditch United	1-2
Stamford v Oadby Town	3-1
Boston Town v Sutton Coldfield Town	1-1, 0-2
King's Lynn v Quorn	4-1
Blackstones v Pelsall Villa	2-2, 2-3
Bromsgrove Rovers v Gresley Rovers	5-0
Solihull Borough v Glossop North End	9-0
Willenhall Town v Atherstone United	0-2
Mickleover Sports v Shepshed Dynamo	0-1
Arnold Town v Biddulph Victoria	1-1, 2-1
Leek Town v Spalding United	2-1
Stratford Town v Bedworth United	1-2
Stewarts & Lloyds v Burnham	0-1
Rothwell Town v Southend Manor	3-2
Cheshunt v Edgware Town	4-0
Hertford Town v AFC Wallingford	1-4
Royston Town v London Colney	3-2
Hemel Hempstead Town v St Neots Town	7-1
Ilford v Clacton Town	2-3
Wootton Blue Cross v Wroxham	2-1
Raunds Town v AFC Sudbury	1-3
Barking & East Ham United v Banbury United	1-0
Leyton Pennant v Great Yarmouth Town	3-3, 1-5
Staines Town v Uxbridge	1-2
Harefield United v Barton Rovers	2-1
Tilbury v Yeading	0-2
Beaconsfield SYCOB v Great Wakering Rovers	5-0
Northwood v Wisbech Town	1-2
Aveley v Stotfold	2-2, 2-0
Diss Town v Romford	3-0
St Margaretsbury v Arlesey Town	1-2
Southall v Yaxley	2-3
Flackwell Heath v Buckingham Town	2-1
Leyton v Marlow	0-1
Wingate & Finchley v Ware	2-0
Bromley v BAT Sports	2-1
Herne Bay v Cowes Sports	3-2
Peacehaven & Telscombe v Carterton Town	1-2
Walton & Hersham v Cove	3-0
Horsham v Slade Green	3-0
Lewes v Brockenhurst	2-1
Eastleigh v Croydon	2-0
Abingdon United v Leatherhead	2-3
Chatham Town v Godalming & Guildford	2-3
Molesey v Fisher Athletic	3-0
Bognor Regis Town v Windsor & Eton	4-1
VCD Athletic v Bedfont	2-1
Tunbridge Wells v Selsey	2-2, 1-2
Newport (IoW) v Maidstone United	0-4
Metropolitan Police v Corinthian Casuals	1-0
Hillingdon Borough v Lymington & New Milton	2-3
Gosport Borough v Deal Town	2-1
Eastbourne Borough v AFC Newbury	6-2
St Leonards v Slough Town	1-2
Tooting & Mitcham United v Cobham	0-0, 3-0
AFC Totton v Pagham	3-1
Carshalton Athletic v Dorking	4-0
Cray Wanderers v Whyteleafe	1-0
Ringmer v Chertsey Town	1-2
Chipstead v Three Bridges	1-3
St Blazey v Bournemouth	1-0

Team Bath v Backwell United	3-1
Torrington v Hungerford Town	0-1
Yate Town v Bideford	0-4
Bemerton Heath Harlequins v Shortwood United	2-1
Merthyr Tydfil v Chard Town	2-0
Weston-Super-Mare v Wimborne Town	3-1
Clevedon Town v Dorchester Town	2-0
Gloucester City v Bashley	3-0
Devizes Town v Taunton Town	0-1
Falmouth Town v Evesham United	1-2
Highworth Town v Cinderford Town	2-3
Paulton Rovers v Corsham Town	2-1

SECOND QUALIFYING ROUND

Chester-Le-Street Town v Harrogate Railway	5-5, 2-7
Colwyn Bay v West Auckland Town	4-0
Hyde United v Tow Law Town	7-3
Guisborough Town v Guiseley	3-3, 0-1
Stocksbridge Park Steels v Ashton United	0-2
Stalybridge Celtic v Workington	2-2, 1-3
Bedlington Terriers v Vauxhall Motors	1-2
Durham City v Peterlee Newtown	3-0
Gainsborough Trinity v Frickley Athletic	3-2
Whitby Town v Bradford (Park Avenue)	0-4
Harrogate Town v Great Harwood Town	2-0
Marine v Eccleshill United	2-2, 3-2
Runcorn FC Halton v Wakefield & Emley	2-0
Bridlington Town v Witton Albion	3-1
Droylsden v Farsley Celtic	4-3
Altrincham v Kendal Town	1-0
Accrington Stanley v Billingham Town	2-0
Spennymoor United v Atherton Collieries	5-0
Horden CW v Worksop Town	0-4
Rossington Main v Radcliffe Borough	0-7
Lancaster City v Blyth Spartans	2-4
Dunston FB v Burscough	2-0
Gateshead v Barrow	3-4
Shepshed Dynamo v Stafford Rangers	0-2
Bedford Town v Pelsall Villa	6-1
King's Lynn v Cambridge City	1-0
Bromsgrove Rovers v Tamworth	1-2
Bedworth United v Moor Green	1-4
Ilkeston Town v Atherstone United	7-0
Sutton Coldfield Town v Halesowen Town	0-2
Hednesford Town v Hucknall Town	0-0, 3-3
Hucknall Town won 6-5 on penalties.	
Redditch United v Leek Town	1-1, 2-1
Nantwich Town v Arnold Town	0-3
Solihull Borough v Grantham Town	0-2
Worcester City v Stamford	3-3, 2-1
Hinckley United v Kidsgrove Athletic	3-0
Walton & Hersham v Chesham United	1-0
Harefield United v AFC Sudbury	4-4, 0-5
Grays Athletic v Marlow	1-0
Molesey v Hitchin Town	3-1
Hendon v Tooting & Mitcham United	3-0
Leatherhead v Bromley	1-1, 4-2
Godalming & Guildford v Hampton & Richmond Borough	0-1
AFC Wallingford v Eastbourne Borough	0-1
Clacton Town v Kingstonian	2-3
Billericay Town v Yeading	3-1
Hayes v Bognor Regis Town	6-0
AFC Totton v Slough Town	2-2, 0-2
Rothwell Town v Barking & East Ham United	1-0
Maidenhead United v Welling United	1-2
Lewes v Eastleigh	0-0, 4-2
Horsham v Yaxley	2-0
Havant & Waterlooville v Harrow Borough	2-1
Diss Town v Chertsey Town	2-3
Canvey Island v Folkestone Invicta	2-1
Carshalton Athletic v Chelmsford City	1-1, 0-1
Maidstone United v Boreham Wood	2-5
Heybridge Swifts v Sutton United	1-1, 2-1
Uxbridge v Braintree Town	1-2
Hastings United v Selsey	4-1
Flackwell Heath v Royston Town	2-2, 0-0
Flackwell Heath won 5-3 on penalties.	
Hemel Hempstead Town v Cray Wanderers	3-1
Enfield v Bishop's Stortford	1-5
Beaconsfield SYCOB v Gosport Borough	1-2
Burnham v Herne Bay	0-1
Aldershot Town v Aylesbury United	3-1
Dover Athletic v Basingstoke Town	2-0
Lymington & New Milton v Cheshunt	3-1
Carterton Town v Arlesey Town	0-6
Crawley Town v Great Yarmouth Town	3-0
Wisbech Town v VCD Athletic	6-1
Wootton Blue Cross v Purfleet	0-4
Three Bridges v Aveley	1-3
Ford United v Metropolitan Police	4-2
St Albans City v Wingate & Finchley	2-0
Tiverton Town v Taunton Town	1-1, 2-0
Bath City v Merthyr Tydfil	5-0
Weston-Super-Mare v Clevedon Town	2-0
Gloucester City v Newport County	1-1, 0-4
Team Bath v Bemerton Heath Harlequins	6-1
Bideford v St Blazey	3-1
Hungerford Town v Paulton Rovers	2-1
Evesham United v Cinderford Town	1-1, 5-0
Chippenham Town v Weymouth	1-4

THIRD QUALIFYING ROUND

Harrogate Railway v Workington	4-0
Droylsden v Spennymoor United	0-0, 2-3
Accrington Stanley v Harrogate Town	0-0, 2-3
Bradford (Park Avenue) v Bridlington Town	3-5
Vauxhall Motors v Gainsborough Trinity	6-1
Durham City v Blyth Spartans	1-1, 1-3
Barrow v Hyde United	3-1
Ashton United v Runcorn FC Halton	0-3
Dunston FB v Marine	0-1
Colwyn Bay v Radcliffe Borough	1-2
Guiseley v Altrincham	2-1
Ilkeston Town v King's Lynn	6-1
Redditch United v Arnold Town	0-1
Hinckley United v Tamworth	1-3
Moor Green v Halesowen Town	3-1
Wisbech Town v Bedford Town	1-0
Hucknall Town v Worcester City	1-0
Grantham Town v Worksop Town	1-0
Stafford Rangers v Rothwell Town	3-0
Canvey Island v Aveley	2-0
Billericay Town v Braintree Town	4-0
Heybridge Swifts v Herne Bay	1-0
Hemel Hempstead Town v Arlesey Town	1-2
Dover Athletic v Welling United	2-2, 3-1
Molesey v Chertsey Town	3-1
Bishop's Stortford v Eastbourne Borough	1-0
Flackwell Heath v Purfleet	1-0
Grays Athletic v Hayes	2-1
AFC Sudbury v Walton & Hersham	2-0
Hastings United v Hendon	2-1
Slough Town v Hampton & Richmond Borough	4-2
St Albans City v Chelmsford City	1-0
Boreham Wood v Kingstonian	2-0
Leatherhead v Ford United	1-2
Horsham v Hungerford Town	1-0
Havant & Waterlooville v Evesham United	4-0
Weston-Super-Mare v Bath City	0-5
Bideford v Gosport Borough	3-1
Aldershot Town v Lewes	2-0
Newport County v Team Bath	0-3
Lymington & New Milton v Crawley Town	0-2
Tiverton Town v Weymouth	4-2

FOURTH QUALIFYING ROUND

Wisbech Town v Harrogate Town	0-2
Blyth Spartans v Runcorn FC Halton	1-3
Morecambe v Grantham Town	3-1
Telford United v Doncaster Rovers	0-2
Ilkeston Town v Stafford Rangers	0-5
Burton Albion v Halifax Town	2-1
Moor Green v Leigh RMI	2-1
Harrogate Railway v Marine	4-2
Arnold Town v Scarborough	0-2
Northwich Victoria v Spennymoor United	3-1
Hucknall Town v Vauxhall Motors	1-1, 1-5
Guiseley v Tamworth	3-3, 3-2
Southport v Bridlington Town	4-1
Radcliffe Borough v Chester City	2-4
Nuneaton Borough v Barrow	1-1, 3-4
AFC Sudbury v St Albans City	1-2
Bishop's Stortford v Boreham Wood	1-1, 1-4
Heybridge Swifts v Bideford	2-0
Bath City v Yeovil Town	1-1, 1-3
Slough Town v Canvey Island	3-2
Aldershot Town v Dagenham & Redbridge	0-4
Hastings United v Kettering Town	0-0, 5-0
Havant & Waterlooville v Billericay Town	3-1
Hereford United v Arlesey Town	1-0
Horsham v Team Bath	0-0, 1-1
Team Bath won 4-3 on penalties.	
Gravesend & Northfleet v Margate	1-2
Forest Green Rovers v Ford United	2-1
Flackwell Heath v Crawley Town	1-4
Dover Athletic v Woking	1-1, 2-1
Barnet v Tiverton Town	0-2
Grays Athletic v Stevenage Borough	1-2
Molesey v Farnborough Town	0-6

THE FA CUP 2002–03

COMPETITION PROPER

▪ *Denotes player sent off.*

FIRST ROUND

Saturday, 16 November 2002

Barnsley (1) 1 *(Dyer 17)*
Blackpool (1) 4 *(Hills 37, Murphy 49, Dalglish 50, Taylor 70)* 6857
Barnsley: Marriott (Ghent); Mulligan, Williams, Morgan, Austin, Neil, Lumsdon, Betsy, Fallon (Sheron), Dyer, Gibbs.
Blackpool: Barnes; Grayson, Jaszczun, Southern, Clarke C, Coid, Wellens, Bullock, Murphy (Walker), Dalglish (Taylor), Hills (O'Kane).

Barrow (1) 2 *(Holt 16, Salmon 49)*
Moor Green (0) 0 2650
Barrow: Bishop; Shaw, Maxfield, Housham, Salmon, Hume, Anthony▪, Rogers, Arnold (Dawson), Holt, Warren.
Moor Green: Rachel; Hughes, Robinson, Woodley (Evans), Gillard, Sanders, Stanley (Faulds), Gayle (Blake), Martin, Myers, Lamey.

Bournemouth (1) 2 *(Thomas 38, Elliott 73)*
Doncaster R (0) 1 *(Gill 71)* 5371
Bournemouth: Moss; Young, Purches S, Broadhurst, Fletcher C, O'Connor, Thomas (Browning), Feeney (Foyewa), Hayter, Fletcher S, Elliott.
Doncaster R: Warrington; Marples, Price, Owen (Watson), Ryan, Morley, Hudson, Albrighton (Barrick), Barnes, Jackson▪, Paterson (Gill).

Bristol R (0) 0
Runcorn (0) 0 4135
Bristol R: Howie; Boxall, Challis (Austin), Plummer, Barrett, Quinn, Carlisle, Astafjevs, Tait, Grazioli, McKeever (Bryant).
Runcorn: McMillan; Parle, Ness, Lightfoot, Tomlinson, Ellis, Lunt (Gamble), Morley, McNeil (Watson), Kinney, Leadbetter.

Bury (0) 0
Plymouth Arg (2) 3 *(Evans 19, Nelson 32 (og), Wotton 86)* 2987
Bury: Garner; Unsworth, Stuart, Nelson, Barras (Preece), Swailes, Billy, O'Shaughnessy, Newby, Lawson (Nugent), Woodthorpe.
Plymouth Arg: Larrieu; Worrell, Hodges, Friio, Wotton, Coughlan, Lopes (McGlinchey), Keith (Sturrock), Stonebridge, Evans, Adams.

Carlisle U (0) 2 *(Foran 56, Farrell 67)*
Lincoln C (0) 1 *(Futcher 87)* 4388
Carlisle U: Glennon; Shelley, Maddison, McDonagh, Kelly▪, Murphy, Baldacchino, Birch, Sutton (McGill), Farrell, Foran (Andrews).
Lincoln C: Marriott; Bailey (Smith), Bimson, Weaver, Morgan, Futcher, Willis, Sedgemore (Mike), Cropper, Yeo (Ward), Gain.

Chesterfield (0) 1 *(Davies 74)*
Morecambe (1) 2 *(Elam 43, Thompson 90)* 3703
Chesterfield: Muggleton; Davies▪, Rushbury (Hurst), Dawson, Payne, Howson, Booty (Hudson), Edwards, Allott, Burt (Howard), Brandon.
Morecambe: Mawson; Swan, Colkin, McKearney, Bentley, Hill, Stringfellow, Drummond, Carlton (Perkins), Rigoglioso (Thompson), Elam (Black).

Colchester U (0) 0
Chester C (0) 1 *(Tate 83)* 2901
Colchester U: Brown; Stockley (Morgan), Keith, Pinault, Baldwin, Warren, Izzet (Atangana), Bowry, Rapley, McGleish, Stockwell.
Chester C: Brown W; Brady (Brown M), McIntyre, Guyett, Bolland, Hatswell, Carey, Clare (Blackburn), Tate (Ruffer), Carden, Davies.

Dagenham & R (3) 3 *(McDougald 14, Shipp 18, 24)*
Havant & W (2) 2 *(Haughton 21, 27)* 1546
Dagenham & R: Roberts; Smith, Potts (Vickers), Terry (Hill), Heffer, Matthews, Janney, Bruce, McDougald, West (Perkins), Shipp.
Havant & W: Kerr; Masson, Hall, Wood, Ferrett, Hale, Hanson, Hambley, Taylor, Haughton, Howe.

Dover Ath (0) 0
Oxford U (1) 1 *(Oldfield 22)* 4186
Dover Ath: Hyde; Browne, Norman, Chapman, Arnott, Readings, Day, Spiller, Tyne, Bent, Dyer (Glover).
Oxford U: Woodman; McNiven, Whitehead, Crosby, Bound, Waterman, Robinson, Hunt, Basham (Omoyinmi), Oldfield (Louis), Savage.

Farnborough T (5) 5 *(Baptiste 2, 35, Taggart 6, Charlery 13, Piper L 21)*
Harrogate T (1) 1 *(Hunter 11)* 1090
Farnborough T: Pennock; Warner, Gregory, Taggart (Annon), Bunce, Laker, Piper C, Piper L (Butterworth), Charlery (Green), Baptiste, Carroll.
Harrogate T: Connor; Richardson, Sykes (Aspin), Bonsall, McNaughton, Merris (Turley), Donaldson (Kerr), Sturpy, Marcelle, Whellans, Hunter.

Hereford U (0) 0
Wigan Ath (0) 1 *(Green 90)* 4005
Hereford U: Baker; Clarke, Rose, Parry, Tretton, James, Galloway, Williams D, Guinan, Eribenne, Pitman (Wright).
Wigan Ath: Filan; Eaden, Baines (Flynn), Dinning, De Vos, Jackson, Green, Jarrett, Ellington, Roberts, Kennedy.

Heybridge S (0) 0
Bristol C (4) 7 *(Roberts 16, 40, Tinnion 41 (pen), Murray 45, 61, Lita 66, 82)* 2046
Heybridge S: Banks; Blackwell, Barber, Tomlinson (Hunter), Pollard, Culverhouse, Abrahams, Baillie, Windows (Payne), Rainford, Budge (Cobb).
Bristol C: Phillips; Murray, Bell, Coles (Brown A), Butler, Hill, Burnell, Doherty, Peacock (Beadle), Roberts (Lita), Tinnion.

Hull C (0) 0
Macclesfield T (2) 3 *(Tipton 12, Lightbourne 27, Whitaker 76)* 7803
Hull C: Musselwhite; Regan, Burton (Smith), Ashbee, Anderson, Whittle (Peat), Green, Delaney, Alexander, Jevons (Elliott), Williams.
Macclesfield T: Wilson; Hitchen, Adams, Welch, Tinson, Ridler, Munroe, Eaton (Abbey), Tipton, Lightbourne, Whitaker.

Kidderminster H (0) 2 *(Setchell 58 (og), Broughton 77)*
Rushden & D (1) 2 *(Duffy 45, 71)* 3079
Kidderminster H: Brock; Foster (Bennett), Shilton, Ayres, Hinton, Coleman, Williams, Flynn, Broughton, Henriksen, Parrish.
Rushden & D: Turley; Bignot, Underwood, Peters, Hunter, Gray, Bell, Wardley, Darby (Hall), Duffy (Partridge), Setchell.

Leyton Orient (1) 1 *(Martin 25)*
Margate (1) 1 *(Keister 42)* 3605
Leyton Orient: Morris (Barrett); Barnard (Hatcher), Lockwood, Smith, Miller, Iriekpen, Canham, Martin, Nugent, Fletcher (Watts), Toner.
Margate: Mitten; Shearer, McFlynn, Oates, Lamb, Edwards, Porter, Keister (Munday), Sodje, Collins, Saunders.

Luton T (3) 4 *(Spring 3, Thorpe 44, Brkovic 45, 65)*
Guiseley (0) 0 5248
Luton T: Emberson; Boyce (Holmes), Davis, Spring, Perrett (Neilson), Coyne, Nicholls, Robinson, Howard, Thorpe, Brkovic.
Guiseley: Hill; Atkinson, Shaw, Henry, Freeman, Trevitt, Nettleton (Reilly), Sumner, Senior (Newhouse), Cooke, Stuart (Chattoe).

Northampton T (2) 3 *(Harsley 10, Gabbiadini 35, Asamoah 68)*
Boston U (0) 2 *(Battersby 56 (pen), Higgins 82)* 4373
Northampton T: Harper; Rickers (Hope), Carruthers, Sampson, Burgess, Harsley, Asamoah, Trollope, Forrester (McGregor), Gabbiadini, Hargreaves.
Boston U: Bastock; Rusk, Chapman, Hocking (Weatherstone R), Warburton, Bennett (Douglas), Thompson L, Higgins, Battersby, Cook (Elding), Angel.

Northwich Vic (0) 0
Scunthorpe U (1) 3 *(Torpey 38, 48, 72 (pen))* 1724
Northwich Vic: Parry; Sedgemore, Street, Cane, Ingram, Walsh (Quinn), Devlin, Owen, Allan (Garvey), Blundell, Norris.
Scunthorpe U: Evans; Wright, Stanton, Featherstone, Dawson, McCombe, Calvo-Garcia (Kilford), Graves, Carruthers, Torpey, Brough.

Oldham Ath (1) 2 *(Low 18, Hall F 90)*
Burton Alb (1) 2 *(Webster 42 (pen), Dudley 59)* 5802
Oldham Ath: Pogliacomi; Low, Eyres, Beharall, Hall F, Hill (Killen), Sheridan D, Armstrong, Andrews (Vernon), Corazzin, Eyre (Duxbury).
Burton Alb: Duke; Henshaw, Talbot, Kirkwood, Reddington, Hoyle■, Dudley (Kavanagh), Clough, Moore (Anderson), Glasser, Webster.

Port Vale (0) 0
Crewe Alex (0) 1 *(Ashton 85)* 5507
Port Vale: Goodlad; Carragher, Charnock, Collins, Burns, Brightwell (McClare), Cummins, Durnin (Armstrong), McPhee, Brooker (Paynter), Boyd.
Crewe Alex: Ince; Wright, Vaughan, Brammer, Foster, Walton, Rix (Jones), Lunt, Hulse, Jack (Sodje), Sorvel (Ashton).

Rochdale (2) 3 *(Connor 3, Platt 12, Beech 61)*
Peterborough U (0) 2 *(Fenn 83, Clarke A 88)* 2566
Rochdale: Edwards; Evans (Flitcroft), Doughty, Beech, Cansdell-Sheriff, Griffiths, Duffy, Melaugh, Platt, Connor, Simpson.
Peterborough U: Tyler; Gill, Jelleyman (Farrell), Joseph, Edwards, Burton, Bullard, Danielsson (Fenn), Clarke A, Lee, Shields (Newton).

Scarborough (0) 0
Cambridge U (0) 0 2084
Scarborough: Woods; Ormerod, Pounder, Sheppherd, Holdsworth, Hotte, Henry (Sillah), Stoker, Scott, Raw (Fatokun), Campbell (Blunt).
Cambridge U: Marshall (Brennan); Tann, Goodhind, Duncan, Angus, Fleming■, Wanless, Tudor (Guttridge), Kitson, Youngs, Riza (Nacca).

Shrewsbury T (2) 4 *(Jemson 32, Wilding 39, 74, Tolley J 89)*
Stafford R (0) 0 5114
Shrewsbury T: Dunbavin; Drysdale, Thompson, Redmile, Tolley J, Wilding, Lowe (Jagielka), Atkins, Rodgers, Jemson, Van Blerk.
Stafford R: Price; Gibson A, Daniel, Robinson (McAughtrie), Carter, Barrow, Lovatt, Heath (Downes), Davidson, Gibson R, Edwards (Bailey).

Slough T (1) 1 *(Bubb B 30)*
Harrogate R (0) 2 *(Smith 53, Davey 68)* 1687
Slough T: McCann; Howard, Brown, Spencer, Barrowcliff, Palmer, Bubb B, Metcalfe, Winston, Boot (Deaner), Bubb A (Wilkinson 77).
Harrogate R: Neale; Watkinson, McLean (Constable), Ames, Danby, Wilson, Walker, Stansfield, Smith (Hart), Flynn (Davey), Gore.

Southend U (1) 1 *(Lee 3 (og))*
Hartlepool U (1) 1 *(Barron 23)* 4984
Southend U: Flahavan; Beard, Searle, Maher, Cort, McSweeney, Clark, Smith, Bramble, Rawle, Scully (Jenkins).
Hartlepool U: Williams A; Barron, Barry-Murphy, Lee, Westwood, Tinkler, Clarke (Arnison), Humphreys, Williams E, Richardson, Smith (Widdrington).

Southport (1) 4 *(Pickford 43, 60, Thomson 75, Lane 90)*
Notts Co (2) 2 *(Allsopp 8, 41)* 3519
Southport: Welsby; Lane, Howell (Jones S), Jones B, Clark, Winstanley, Pickford, Soley, Lloyd-Williams (Thomson), Whitehall, Gibson.
Notts Co: Garden; Stone (Jupp), Ramsden, Caskey■, Fenton, Ireland (Heffernan), Cas, Whitley, Stallard (Baraclough), Allsopp, Brough.

Stevenage B (1) 1 *(Howell 6)*
Hastings U (0) 0 1821
Stevenage B: Westhead; Travis (Wormull), Fraser, Trott, MacDonald G, Stirling, Howell, Blackwood, Midson (MacDonald C), Jackson, Scott (Campbell J).
Hastings U: King; Yates, Hegley, Burt, Osborne, Flanagan■, McArthur, Playford, Honey (Webb), Zahana-Oni■, Simmonds (Ruddy).

Stockport Co (2) 4 *(Beckett 24, Fradin 42, Burgess 57 (pen), 80)*
St Albans C (0) 1 *(Browne D 68)* 3303
Stockport Co: Jones; Hardiker, Tonkin, Challinor, Goodwin, Fradin (Lescott), Gibb, McLachlan, Burgess, Beckett, Briggs.
St Albans C: Wilmot; Smith, Gould■, Castle, Campbell (Moran), Browne D, Kean (Mackail-Smith), Challinor, De Souza (Crawshaw), Browne S, Oakes.

Swindon T (0) 1 *(Gurney 85)*
Huddersfield T (0) 0 4210
Swindon T: Griemink; Gurney, Duke, Heywood, Reeves, Jackson, Robinson, Parkin, Sabin, Invincibile, Hewlett.
Huddersfield T: Bevan; Sharp, Jenkins, Brown, Moses, Holland, Worthington (Thorrington), Mattis, Stead, Smith, Schofield.

Team Bath (0) 2 *(Heiniger 71, Kamara-Taylor 83)*
Mansfield T (3) 4 *(Lawrence 19, 36, Tisdale 43 (og), Christie 56)* 5469
Team Bath: Northmore; Watson, Wisson, Nichols, Ball, Tisdale, Lewis M (Fullam), Cozic (Heiniger), Lavety, Sorbara (Kamara-Taylor), Prince.
Mansfield T: Pilkington; MacKenzie, Lawrence, Clarke, Moore, Gadsby, Williamson, Disley, Christie, Larkin (Bacon), Corden.

Tiverton T (1) 1 *(Pears 18)*
Crawley T (1) 1 *(McDonnell 36)* 1840
Tiverton T: Edwards; Winter, Haines, Rees, Rudge, Peters, Rogers, Cousins, Mudge (Ovens), Pears (Everett), Holloway (Nancekivell).
Crawley T: Little; Judge, Pullan, Holmes, Cooksey, Hooper, Fear (Hemsley), Harkin, Stevens, McDonnell, Le Bihan.

Torquay U (2) 5 *(Russell 6 (pen), Gritton 43, 62, Osei-Kuffour 76, Fowler 89)*
Boreham Wood (0) 0 2739
Torquay U: Van Heusden; Hockley, Canoville, Fowler, Woozley, Russell (Ashington), Bedeau■, Osei-Kuffour, Graham (Bond), Gritton (Benefield), Hill.
Boreham Wood: Imber; Grime, Honeyball■, Wotton, Harvey, Howard (Wall), Meah (Raymond), Browne, Forrester, Kodra (Walker), Boyle-Renner.

Tranmere R (1) 2 *(Barlow 7, Haworth 62)*
Cardiff C (2) 2 *(Collins 34, Kavanagh 44)* 5592
Tranmere R: Achterberg; Connelly (Gray), Nicholson (Harrison), Edwards, Allen, Jones, Taylor (Hay), Mellon, Haworth, Barlow, Roberts.
Cardiff C: Alexander; Weston, Barker, Collins, Prior, Maxwell, Bowen (Fortune-West), Kavanagh, Campbell (Earnshaw), Thorne, Legg (Hamilton).

Vauxhall M (0) 0
QPR (0) 0 3507
Vauxhall M: Ralph; Collins, Haddrell, Aspinall, McDermott, Brazier, Lawton, Nesbitt (Lynch), Fearns, Cumiskey, Young.
QPR: Digby; Rose (Forbes), Williams, Palmer, Shittu, Carlisle, Bircham, Burgess, Thomson, Oli (Gallen), Connolly (Padula).

Wrexham (0) 0
Darlington (0) 2 *(Conlon 59, Liddle 70)* 3442
Wrexham: Whitfield; Edwards C, Holmes (Edwards P), Carey, Pejic, Roberts, Thomas (Sam), Ferguson, Morrell, Trundle (Jones L), Whitley.
Darlington: Collett; Betts (Pearson), Valentine, Liddle, Clarke, Keltie, Wainwright, Nicholls, Conlon, Clark, Hodgson.

Wycombe W (2) 2 *(Rammell 12, Brown 26)*
Brentford (3) 4 *(O'Connor 3, Somner 9, Vine 42, 52)* 5673
Wycombe W: Talia; Senda, Vinnicombe, Bulman (Ryan), Thomson, McCarthy, Brown (Cook), Simpson, Faulconbridge (Currie), Rammell, Harris.
Brentford: Smith P; Dobson, Somner, Sonko, Marshall, Evans, Fullarton, O'Connor, McCammon, Vine (Tabb), Hunt.

Yeovil T (0) 0
Cheltenham T (1) 2 *(Alsop 8, Devaney 64)* 6455
Yeovil T: Weale; Lindegaard (Demba), Elkholti, Skiverton, Pluck (Grant), O'Brien, Way, Crittenden, Giles, Forinton (Alford), McIndoe.
Cheltenham T: Book; Howarth, Victory, Forsyth, Brough, Duff M, Finnigan, Devaney, Alsop, Brayson (Yates), McAuley.

Sunday, 17 November 2002

Forest Green R (0) 0
Exeter C (0) 0 2147
Forest Green R: Perrin; Coupe, Russell L, Richardson, Jones D, Foster, Russell M (Grayson), Owers (Allen), Meechan, Odejayi, Sykes.
Exeter C: Miller; Hiley, McConnell (Walker), Gaia, Pilkington, Cronin, Thomas, Pettefer, Flack, Moor, Roscoe.

Tuesday, 26 November 2002

York C (1) 2 *(Duffield 21, 88)*
Swansea C (0) 1 *(Murphy 80)* 2948
York C: Fettis; Edmondson, Potter, Brass, Smith, Hobson, Parkin, Bullock, Nogan, Duffield, Brackstone.
Swansea C: Freestone; Howard, Jenkins, Smith J, Theobald, Evans (Watkin), Phillips, Mumford, Thomas (Williams), Murphy, Wood.

FIRST ROUND REPLAYS

Tuesday, 26 November 2002

Cambridge U (1) 2 *(Wanless 31, Hotte 97 (og))*
Scarborough (0) 1 *(Jordan 90)* 3373
Cambridge U: Marshall; Goodhind, Tann, Duncan, Angus, Fleming, Wanless, Tudor, Kitson, Youngs (Chillingworth), Riza (Nacca).
Scarborough: Woods; Hotte, Ormerod, Jordan, Holdsworth, Sheppherd, Stoker, Pounder (Blunt), Scott, Raw (Fatokun), Campbell (Rose).
aet.

Cardiff C (0) 2 *(Campbell 60, Collins 68)*
Tranmere R (1) 1 *(Mellon 45)* 6853
Cardiff C: Margetson; Weston, Barker, Collins, Prior (Croft), Hamilton, Boland (Legg), Kavanagh, Campbell, Fortune-West, Bowen (Maxwell).
Tranmere R: Achterberg■; Taylor (Howarth), Nicholson (Hay), Edwards, Allen, Gray, Jones, Mellon, Haworth (Hume), Barlow, Roberts.

Crawley T (0) 3 *(McDonnell 66, 80, Bagnall 87)*
Tiverton T (1) 2 *(Pears 8, 64)* 3907
Crawley T: Little; Judge, Pullan, Holmes, Cooksey, Hooper (Bagnall), Fear, Harkin (Hemsley), McDonnell, Stevens, Le Bihan.
Tiverton T: Edwards; Peters, Winter (Mudge), Haines (Steele), Rudge, Cousins, Nancekivell, Rees, Everett, Pears, Rogers.

Exeter C (1) 2 *(Sheldon 25, Lock 85)*
Forest Green R (1) 1 *(Richardson 20)* 2951
Exeter C: Miller; Hiley, Roscoe, Gaia, Pilkington, Walker (Lock), Sheldon, Cronin, Flack, Coppinger (Moor), Pettefer.
Forest Green R: Perrin; Russell L, Jenkins, Russell M, Jones D, Richardson, Owers, Foster, Odejayi, Meechan, Sykes (Grayson).

Hartlepool U (0) 1 *(Richardson 63)*
Southend U (0) 2 *(Bramble 88, Cort 89)* 4080
Hartlepool U: Williams A; Barron, Barry-Murphy, Lee, Westwood, Tinkler, Arnison (Istead), Humphreys, Williams E (Boyd), Richardson, Smith.
Southend U: Flahavan; Beard (Jones), Searle, Maher, Cort, McSweeney, Scully, Smith, Bramble, Belgrave (Thurgood), Jenkins (Clark).

Margate (0) 1 *(Keister 51 (pen))*
Leyton Orient (0) 0 2048
Margate: Mitten; Shearer, Oates, Saunders (Munday), Edwards, Porter, Lamb, Sodje, Collins, Keister, McFlynn.
Leyton Orient: Barrett; Joseph, Lockwood, Smith (Brazier), Miller, Harris, Hatcher (Forbes), Martin, Nugent, Fletcher (Ibehre), Canham.
at Dover Ath.

QPR (1) 1 *(Thomson 18)*
Vauxhall Motors (1) 1 *(Brazier 22)* 5336
QPR: Digby; Forbes, Padula (Connolly), Palmer, Carlisle, Burgess (Oli), Bircham, Langley, Thomson, Furlong, Williams (Murphy).
Vauxhall Motors: Ralph; Lawton (Thompson), McDermott, Aspinall (Lynch), Brazier, Collins, Nesbitt, Cumiskey, Fearns, Young (Welton), Haddrell.
aet; Vauxhall Motors won 4-3 on penalties.

Runcorn (1) 1 *(Barrett 19 (og))* 2444
Bristol R (1) 3 *(Grazioli 17, Carlisle 108, Gilroy 119)*
Runcorn: McMillan; Carragher, Ness, Lunt, Ellis, Tomlinson, Parle■, Morley, Leadbetter, McNeil (Watson), Gamble.
Bristol R: Howie; Boxall, Challis, Austin, Barrett, Quinn, Carlisle, Bryant (Hogg), Tait, Grazioli (Gilroy), Astafjevs.
aet.

Rushden & D (1) 2 *(Duffy 36, Wardley 67)*
Kidderminster H (0) 1 *(Broughton 73)* 3391
Rushden & D: Turley; Bignot, Underwood, Peters, Hunter, Gray (Bell), Hall, Wardley, Darby (Lowe), Duffy, Mills.
Kidderminster H: Brock; Smith, Shilton (Joy), Ayres, Hinton, Coleman, Bennett (Foster), Williams (Doyle), Broughton, Henriksen, Parrish.

Wednesday, 27 November 2002

Burton Alb (0) 2 *(Moore 84, 110)*
Oldham Ath (0) 2 *(Wijnhard 50, Eyres 116)* 3416
Burton Alb: Duke; Henshaw, Talbot (Sinton), Glasser, Reddington, Hoyle, Kirkwood (Anderson), Clough, Webster, Moore (Blount), Stride.
Oldham Ath: Pogliacomi; Low (Corazzin), Eyres, Beharall, Hall F, Hill, Armstrong, Sheridan D, Wijnhard, Andrews (Duxbury), Eyre (Killen).
aet; Oldham Ath won 5-4 on penalties.

SECOND ROUND

Saturday, 7 December 2002

Blackpool (1) 3 *(Hazell 21 (og), Taylor 56, Murphy 90)*
Torquay U (1) 1 *(Gritton 8)* 5014

Blackpool: Theoklitos; Grayson, Coid, Collins, Clarke C, Gulliver, Wellens, Bullock (Walker), Murphy, Taylor (Doughty), Dalglish (O'Kane).
Torquay U: Welch; Hazell, Hankin, Woods, Woozley, Russell■, Bedeau, Fowler, Graham■, Gritton (Osei-Kuffour), Dunning (Wills).

Bristol R (0) 1 *(Allen 73)*
Rochdale (1) 1 *(Platt 6)* 4369

Bristol R: Howie; Boxall, Austin, Plummer, Barrett, Quinn (Gall), Astafjevs, Hyde, Tait, Grazioli (Allen), Carlisle.
Rochdale: Edwards; Duffy, Doughty, Evans, Jobson, Grand, McEvilly (Townson), Flitcroft, Platt, Connor, Melaugh.

Cambridge U (2) 2 *(Tann 5, 45)*
Northampton T (0) 2 *(Stamp 55, Hargreaves 83)* 5076

Cambridge U: Marshall; Tann, Fleming, Duncan, Angus, Wanless (Bridges), Guttridge, Tudor, Kitson, Youngs (Chillingworth), Riza.
Northampton T: Harper; Gill, Carruthers (Spedding), Sampson, Burgess, Harsley, Stamp (Hope), Trollope, Forrester (Asamoah), Gabbiadini, Hargreaves.

Crawley T (1) 1 *(McDonnell 3)*
Dagenham & R (1) 2 *(McDougald 26, Janney 88)* 4516

Crawley T: Little; Judge, Pullan, Holmes (Hemsley), Cooksey, Hooper■, Fear, Harkin (Payne), McDonnell (Hockton), Stevens, Le Bihan.
Dagenham & R: Roberts; Shipp, Heffer, Matthews, Potts, Smith (Vickers), McGrath, Terry, McDougald, West (Stein), Janney.

Crewe Alex (1) 3 *(Rix 6, Brammer 63 (pen), Ashton 78)*
Mansfield T (0) 0 4563

Crewe Alex: Ince; Wright, Vaughan, Brammer, Foster (Walker), Walton, Rix, Lunt, Jack, Ashton, Sorvel.
Mansfield T: Pilkington; Clarke, Gadsby (Moore), Lever, Day, MacKenzie, Corden, Disley, Christie, Larkin, Bacon (Jervis).

Darlington (2) 4 *(Hodgson 2, Offiong 38, 63, Conlon 46)*
Stevenage B (1) 1 *(Howell 4)* 3351

Darlington: Porter; Betts, Valentine, Liddle, Clarke, Keltie, Wainwright (Whitehead), Nicholls, Conlon, Offiong, Hodgson (Clark).
Stevenage B: Westhead; Wormull, Travis, Trott (Stirling), Campbell J, MacDonald G, Howell (Midson), Scott, MacDonald C, Sigere (McMahon), Riddle.

Exeter C (1) 3 *(McConnell 20, Walker 62 (pen), Moor 85)*
Rushden & D (0) 1 *(Lowe 71)* 2277

Exeter C: Fraser; Hiley, Roscoe, Gaia, Pilkington, Walker, McConnell, Ampadu (Lock), Flack, Coppinger (Moor), Pettefer.
Rushden & D: Sollitt; Bignot, Underwood, Peters, Dempster, Gray, Hall (Bell), Wardley, Duffy (Darby), Lowe, Mills.

Macclesfield T (0) 2 *(Lightbourne 82, Tipton 90)*
Vauxhall Motors (0) 0 2972

Macclesfield T: Wilson; Hitchen, Adams, Hardy (Askey), Tinson, Macauley, Munroe (Eaton), Priest, Tipton, Lightbourne, Whitaker.
Vauxhall Motors: Ralph; Lawton, Collins, McDermott, Brazier, Haddrell, Aspinall, Nesbitt (Lynch), Young, Fearns, Cumiskey (Welton).

Margate (0) 0
Cardiff C (2) 3 *(Thorne 28, Boland 34, Fortune-West 88)* 1362

Margate: Mitten; Oates, Lamb (Clarke), Edwards, Shearer, Porter (Munday), Saunders, Sodje, Collins, Keister, McFlynn (Beard).
Cardiff C: Alexander; Weston, Croft, Prior, Barker, Hamilton (Maxwell), Boland, Bowen, Earnshaw (Campbell), Thorne (Fortune-West), Legg.
at Dover Ath.

Morecambe (2) 3 *(Bentley 28, 45, Rigoglioso 57)*
Chester C (2) 2 *(Bolland 25, Clare 42)* 4293

Morecambe: Mawson; McKearney, Colkin, Bentley, Swan, Drummond, Rigoglioso, Stringfellow, Thompson (Black), Carlton (Curtis), Elam (Murphy).
Chester C: Brown W; Brady (Ruffer), McIntyre, Guyett, Hatswell, Bolland, Carey (Kelly), Carden, Clare, Sugden■, Davies (Brown M).

Oldham Ath (0) 1 *(Haining 83)*
Cheltenham T (2) 2 *(Yates 17, Brayson 20)* 4416

Oldham Ath: Pogliacomi; Eyre (Haining), Eyres, Baudet, Hall F, Beharall (Corazzin), Murray, Sheridan D, Wijnhard, Killen (Andrews), Armstrong.
Cheltenham T: Book; Howarth, Victory, Forsyth, Brough, Duff M, Finnigan, McAuley (Williams), Alsop (Spencer), Brayson, Yates.

Scunthorpe U (0) 0
Carlisle U (0) 0 3590

Scunthorpe U: Evans; Stanton, Dawson, Sparrow, Byrne, McCombe, Kilford, Brough, Carruthers, Torpey, Featherstone (Graves).
Carlisle U: Glennon; Shelley, Maddison, Summerbell, Taylor, Murphy, McCarthy (Baldacchino), Birch, Foran, Robinson (Nixon), McGill.

Shrewsbury T (2) 3 *(Van Blerk 7, Jemson 19, 76)*
Barrow (0) 1 *(Housham 60)* 4210

Shrewsbury T: Dunbavin; Moss, Drysdale, Redmile, Artell, Murray, Lowe, Atkins, Rodgers (Murphy), Jemson, Van Blerk.
Barrow: Bishop; Shaw, Maxfield, Salmon, Hume, Warren, Housham (Tearney), Gaughan, Bullimore, Holt, Arnold (Robinson).

Southend U (0) 1 *(Rawle 53)*
Bournemouth (1) 1 *(Broadhurst 41)* 5721

Southend U: Flahavan; Beard, Searle, Maher, Cort, McSweeney, Scully (Tilson), Smith, Bramble, Jones, Rawle (Clark).
Bournemouth: Moss; Young, Purches S, Broadhurst, Fletcher C, Browning, Thomas (Tindall), O'Connor, Hayter, Fletcher S, Elliott.

Southport (0) 0
Farnborough T (2) 3 *(Piper L 26, Carroll 39, Green 76)* 2534

Southport: Dickinson; Lane■, Howell (Sullivan), Jones B, Clark, Winstanley, Soley, Jones S, Thomson, Whitehall, Gibson.
Farnborough T: Pennock; Warner, Gregory, Watson, Bunce, Laker, Carroll, Piper L (Holloway), Charlery, Baptiste (Green), Piper C.

Stockport Co (0) 0
Plymouth Arg (2) 3 *(Stonebridge 9, Friio 14, Wotton 72 (pen))* 3571

Stockport Co: Jones; Gibb, Tonkin, Goodwin, Palmer, Fradin, McLachlan (Burgess), Lescott, Ross, Beckett, Briggs.
Plymouth Arg: Larrieu; Worrell, Hodges, Friio (McGlinchey), Wotton, Coughlan, Norris, Keith, Stonebridge, Evans, Adams.

Wigan Ath (1) 3 *(Ellington 37, 64, Flynn 86)*
Luton T (0) 0 4544

Wigan Ath: Filan; Eaden, Baines, Dinning, Breckin, Jackson, Green (Mitchell), Jarrett, Ellington, Roberts (Flynn), Kennedy (Teale).
Luton T: Emberson; Neilson, Kimble, Spring, Boyce, Coyne, Hughes, Robinson, Brkovic, Fotiadis (Judge), Holmes (Hillier).

York C (0) 1 *(Bullock 63)*

Brentford (1) 2 *(McCammon 35, Hunt 87)* 3517

York C: Fettis; Edmondson, Potter, Brass, Parkin, Hobson, Fox, Bullock, Nogan, Duffield, Brackstone.
Brentford: Smith P; Dobson, Frampton■, Sonko, Marshall, Evans, Rowlands, Smith J, McCammon (Somner), O'Connor, Hunt.

Sunday, 8 December 2002

Harrogate R (0) 1 *(Davey 78)*

Bristol C (1) 3 *(Walker 20 (og), Murray 53, Roberts 90)* 3500

Harrogate R: Neale; Walker, Watkinson (Constable), Ames, Danby, Wilson, McLean, Gore, Stansfield (Hart), Flynn (Davey), Smith.
Bristol C: Phillips; Murray, Bell, Coles (Carey), Butler, Hill, Burnell, Doherty, Peacock, Roberts, Tinnion.

Oxford U (0) 1 *(Louis 65)*

Swindon T (0) 0 11,645

Oxford U: Woodman; McNiven, Robinson, Crosby, Bound, Waterman, Ford (Whitehead), Hunt, Basham (Sall), Louis, Savage.
Swindon T: Griemink; Edds (Willis), Duke, Heywood, Reeves, Jackson (Bampton), Miglioranzi, Parkin, Sabin (Young), Invincibile, Hewlett.

SECOND ROUND REPLAYS

Tuesday, 17 December 2002

Bournemouth (1) 3 *(Fletcher S 39, Holmes 80, Browning 89)*

Southend U (2) 2 *(Bramble 42, Rawle 45)* 5456

Bournemouth: Stewart (Tardif); Young (Holmes), Purches S, Broadhurst, Fletcher C, Browning, Thomas, O'Connor (Feeney), Hayter, Fletcher S, Elliott.
Southend U: Flahavan; Beard, Searle, Maher, Cort, McSweeney, Scully (Smith), Thurgood, Rawle (Tilson), Jones (Clark), Bramble.

Northampton T (0) 0

Cambridge U (0) 1 *(Riza 79)* 4591

Northampton T: Thompson; Gill, Carruthers, Sampson, Hope, Harsley, Asamoah, Trollope, Forrester (Stamp), Gabbiadini (McGregor), Hargreaves.
Cambridge U: Marshall; Goodhind, Tann, Duncan, Angus, Fleming, Guttridge (Bridges), Wanless, Kitson, Youngs, Chillingworth (Riza).

Rochdale (1) 3 *(Platt 34, Connor 48, McCourt 80)*

Bristol R (1) 2 *(Barrett 19, Tait 51)* 2206

Rochdale: Edwards; Duffy, Doughty, Evans, Jobson, Grand, Flitcroft, Melaugh, Platt, Connor (McCourt), McEvilly.
Bristol R: Howie; Boxall, Parker, Austin, Barrett, Quinn, Bryant (Carlisle), Hyde, Tait, Allen, Astafjevs (Hogg).

Monday, 23 December 2002

Carlisle U (0) 0

Scunthorpe U (1) 1 *(Carruthers 25)* 6809

Carlisle U: Glennon; Shelley, Maddison (Byrne), Summerbell■, Kelly, Murphy, McCarthy, McDonagh (Baldacchino), Foran, Robinson (Wake), McGill.
Scunthorpe U: Evans; Stanton, Dawson, Sparrow, Jackson, Byrne, Brough, Graves (Parton), Carruthers, Torpey, Kilford (Calvo-Garcia).

THIRD ROUND

Saturday, 4 January 2003

Arsenal (1) 2 *(Bergkamp 15, McNiven 67 (og))*

Oxford U (0) 0 35,432

Arsenal: Seaman; Luzhny, Van Bronckhorst, Svard (Silva), Upson, Keown, Toure (Bentley), Edu, Jeffers, Bergkamp (Wiltord), Pires.
Oxford U: Woodman; McNiven, Robinson, Crosby, Bound, Waterman, Ford, Hunter, Basham (Steele), Oldfield (Louis), Savage (Scott).

Aston Villa (1) 1 *(Angel 41)*

Blackburn R (1) 4 *(Jansen 17, 60, Yorke 52, 71)* 23,884

Aston Villa: Postma; Edwards (Ridgewell), Wright, Mellberg, Samuel, Kinsella (Taylor), De La Cruz, Hendrie, Dublin, Angel (Vassell), Barry.
Blackburn R: Friedel; Neill, McEveley, Todd, Taylor, Dunn, Danns (Tugay), Jansen, Ostenstad (Gillespie), Yorke (Douglas), Flitcroft.

Blackpool (1) 1 *(Popovic 10 (og))*

Crystal Palace (0) 2 *(Black 56, 64)* 9062

Blackpool: Barnes; Richardson, Hills, Southern, Grayson, Clarke C (O'Kane), Coid (Bullock), Wellens, Murphy, Walker, Thornley (Collins).
Crystal Palace: Kolinko (Berthelin); Butterfield, Granville (Akinbiyi), Symons, Popovic, Mullins, Gray, Derry, Adebola (Borrowdale), Black, Riihilahti.

Bolton W (1) 1 *(Ricketts 18)*

Sunderland (0) 1 *(Phillips 63)* 10,123

Bolton W: Poole; Hunt, Smith, Campo, Barness, Livesey (Whitlow), Bulent (Okocha), Tofting (Nolan), Facey, Ricketts, Farrelly.
Sunderland: Macho; Wright (Rossiter) (Bjorklund), McCartney, Williams, Babb, Craddock, Proctor, Thirlwell, Kyle (Flo), Phillips, Oster.

Bournemouth (0) 0

Crewe Alex (0) 0 7252

Bournemouth: Tardif; Young (Bernard), Purches S, Tindall, Fletcher C, Browning, Thomas, O'Connor, Hayter (Holmes), Fletcher S (Feeney), Elliott.
Crewe Alex: Ince; Wright, Tierney (Sodje), Brammer, Foster, Walton, Vaughan, Lunt (Rix), Jones, Miles (Bell), Sorvel.

Brentford (1) 1 *(Hunt 36)*

Derby Co (0) 0 8709

Brentford: Smith P; Dobson, Frampton, Sonko, Marshall, Evans■, Rowlands, O'Connor, McCammon (Hughes), Vine, Hunt.
Derby Co: Grant; Barton, Mills (Zvagano), Elliott, Evatt, Bolder (Kinkladze), Murray (Holmes), Morris, Christie, Tudgay, Boertien.

Cambridge U (0) 1 *(Youngs 49)*

Millwall (0) 1 *(Claridge 60)* 6864

Cambridge U: Marshall; Goodhind, Tann, Duncan (Chillingworth) (Murray), Angus, Wanless, Nacca, Tudor, Kitson, Youngs, Bridges.
Millwall: Warner; Lawrence, Ryan, Livermore, Nethercott (Robinson), Ward, Kinet (Hearn), Ifill, Harris, Claridge, Reid.

Cardiff C (0) 2 *(Earnshaw 76, Campbell 90)*

Coventry C (1) 2 *(Mills 27, McAllister 55 (pen))* 16,013

Cardiff C: Alexander; Weston, Croft, Prior (Young), Barker, Boland, Bowen, Kavanagh, Earnshaw, Thorne (Fortune-West), Legg (Campbell).
Coventry C: Hyldgaard; Caldwell, Gordon, Eustace, Konjic, Davenport, Betts, McAllister, Bothroyd (Pipe), Holdsworth, Mills (McSheffrey).

Charlton Ath (1) 3 *(Johansson 25, 61, Euell 72 (pen))*

Exeter C (0) 1 *(Gaia 49)* 18,107

Charlton Ath: Kiely; Young, Konchesky, Bart-Williams, Rufus, Fortune, Kishishev, Euell, Bartlett, Johansson (Svensson), Blomqvist (Lisbie).
Exeter C: Miller; Sheldon (McConnell), Hiley, Gaia, Pilkington, Walker (Moor), Thomas, Cronin, Flack, Coppinger, Pettefer.

Chelsea (1) 1 *(Stanic 39)*

Middlesbrough (0) 0 29,796

Chelsea: Cudicini■; Gallas, Babayaro, Petit, Terry, Desailly, Gronkjaer (Melchiot), Lampard, Hasselbaink, Gudjohnsen (De Goey), Stanic (Zenden).
Middlesbrough: Schwarzer; Parnaby, Queudrue, Southgate, Vidmar, Wilson (Cooper), Geremi, Job (Whelan), Windass (Boksic), Nemeth, Greening.

Darlington (2) 2 *(Nicholls 13, Clark 37)*
Farnborough T (2) 3 *(Baptiste 10, Carroll 19, 60)* 4260
Darlington: Porter; Betts, Valentine, Liddle, Whitehead, Keltie, Wainwright, Nicholls, Clark, Offiong, Hodgson (Mellanby).
Farnborough T: Pennock; Warner, Gregory, Bunce, Laker, Watson, Holloway, Carroll, Charlery (Vansittart), Baptiste, Butterworth (Annon).

Grimsby T (0) 2 *(Cooke 57 (pen), Mansaram 87)*
Burnley (2) 2 *(Moore A 14, Weller 18)* 5350
Grimsby T: Coyne; McDermott (Rowan), Gallimore, Santos (Chettle), Ford, Coldicott, Cooke, Groves, Soames (Thompson), Mansaram, Campbell.
Burnley: Beresford; McGregor, Branch, Grant, Cox, Gnohere, Weller (Cook), Moore I, Blake, Papadopoulos (Armstrong), Moore A.

Ipswich T (1) 4 *(Clapham 2, Bent D 65, 77, Ambrose 75)*
Morecambe (0) 0 18,529
Ipswich T: Marshall; Wilnis, Clapham (Abidallah), Holland, Hreidarsson, Richards, Bent M, Ambrose, Counago (Reuser), Naylor (Bent D), Wright.
Morecambe: Mawson; McKearney, Colkin (Ubershar), Drummond, Bentley■, Swan, Rigoglioso (Talbot), Stringfellow, Carlton, Thompson (Murphy), Elam.

Leicester C (1) 2 *(Elliott 45, Dickov 74)*
Bristol C (0) 0 25,868
Leicester C: Walker; Impey, Rogers, Elliott, Sinclair, McKinlay, Summerbee (Heath), Lewis (Jones), Dickov, Deane, Stewart (Benjamin).
Bristol C: Phillips; Coles, Bell, Burnell, Butler, Hill, Murray, Doherty, Peacock, Roberts (Rosenior), Tinnion (Beadle).

Macclesfield T (0) 0
Watford (1) 2 *(Helguson 24, Pennant 61)* 4244
Macclesfield T: Wilson; Hitchen, Adams, Welch, Tinson, Whitaker, Munroe, Priest (Abbey), Tipton, Lightbourne, Hardy (Eaton).
Watford: Chamberlain; Ardley, Gayle, Brown, Cox, Mahon, Pennant, Vernazza, Helguson, Noel-Williams (Smith T), Nielsen.

Manchester U (2) 4 *(Van Nistelrooy 5 (pen), 81 (pen), Beckham 17, Scholes 90)*
Portsmouth (1) 1 *(Stone 39)* 67,222
Manchester U: Carroll; Neville G, Silvestre (Brown), Ferdinand, Keane (Stewart), Blanc, Beckham, Neville P, Van Nistelrooy, Richardson (Scholes), Giggs.
Portsmouth: Hislop; Harper, Taylor, Foxe, Primus, Tavlaridis, Stone (Burton), Diabate (O'Neil), Todorov, Merson (Pericard), Quashie.

Plymouth Arg (1) 2 *(Stonebridge 44, Wotton 61)*
Dagenham & R (1) 2 *(Terry 13, McDougald 67)* 11,885
Plymouth Arg: Larrieu; Worrell, Aljofree, Bent (Sturrock), Wotton, Coughlan, Norris, Adams, Stonebridge (Keith), Evans, Phillips (Friio).
Dagenham & R: Roberts; Heffer, Vickers, Terry, Smith, Matthews, Janney, Shipp, West (Hill), McDougald (Rooney), McGrath.

Preston NE (0) 1 *(Anderson 48)*
Rochdale (1) 2 *(McEvilly 39, Simpson 54)* 8762
Preston NE: Moilanen; Alexander, Broomes, Murdock, Lucketti, Skora (Cartwright), McKenna, Etuhu (Mears), Abbott, Healy, Lewis (Anderson).
Rochdale: Edwards; Warner, Doughty, Evans, Jobson, Grand, Oliver, Flitcroft, Platt (Simpson), Connor, McEvilly.

Rotherham U (0) 0
Wimbledon (1) 3 *(Shipperley 36, McAnuff 85, Morgan 90)* 4527
Rotherham U: Pollitt; Bryan, Hurst, Sedgwick, Swailes, McIntosh, Mullin, Warne (Garner), Barker R (Robins), Lee, Daws.
Wimbledon: Davis; Darlington, Hawkins, Andersen, Leigertwood, Williams, McAnuff, Francis, Shipperley, Connolly (Agyemang), Reo-Coker (Morgan).

Scunthorpe U (0) 0
Leeds U (1) 2 *(Viduka 32 (pen), Bakke 68)* 8329
Scunthorpe U: Evans; Stanton, Dawson, Sparrow, Jackson, Byrne, Kilford (Calvo-Garcia), Graves, Carruthers (Parton), Torpey, Featherstone (Brough).
Leeds U: Robinson; Kelly, Matteo, Bakke (Milner), Mills, Woodgate, Okon, Smith, Viduka, Kewell (Fowler), Wilcox (Johnson Seth).

Sheffield U (2) 4 *(Murphy 9, McGovern 20, Kabba 62, 84)*
Cheltenham T (0) 0 9166
Sheffield U: Kenny; Jagielka, Kozluk, McCall (Javary), Murphy, Page, McGovern, Tonge (Smith), Kabba, Peschisolido (Ten Heuvel), Montgomery.
Cheltenham T: Book; Howarth, Victory, Forsyth, Brough, Duff M, McAuley (Alsop), Devaney, Finnigan (Simpkins), Spencer (Brayson), Yates.

Shrewsbury T (1) 2 *(Jemson 38, 89)*
Everton (0) 1 *(Alexandersson 60)* 7800
Shrewsbury T: Dunbavin; Moss, Smith, Wilding, Artell, Tolley J, Lowe (Aiston), Atkins, Rodgers (Jagielka), Jemson (Drysdale), Woan.
Everton: Wright; Clarke, Unsworth (McLeod), Stubbs, Weir, Carsley, Gemmill (Li Tie), Gravesen (Alexandersson), Rooney, Radzinski, Naysmith.

Southampton (1) 4 *(Svensson M 13, Tessem 50, Svensson A 56, Beattie 80)*
Tottenham H (0) 0 25,589
Southampton: Niemi; Telfer, Bridge, Marsden (Svensson A), Lundekvam, Svensson M, Fernandes, Delap, Beattie (Ormerod), Tessem (Davies), Oakley.
Tottenham H: Keller; Carr, Taricco, King, Perry (Anderton), Thatcher, Davies (Doherty), Freund (Iversen), Keane, Sheringham, Poyet.

Stoke C (2) 3 *(Greenacre 20, 67, Iwelumo 31)*
Wigan Ath (0) 0 9618
Stoke C: Cutler; Thomas, Hall, Gunnarsson, Handyside, Shantyuk, Gudjonsson (Neal), O'Connor (Henry), Iwelumo, Greenacre (Goodfellow), Hoekstra.
Wigan Ath: Filan; Eaden, Kennedy, Mitchell, Jackson, Breckin, Teale, Jarrett, Roberts (Ellington), Liddell, Green (McCulloch).

WBA (3) 3 *(Dichio 4, 11, 19)*
Bradford C (0) 1 *(Danks 79)* 19,909
WBA: Hoult; Chambers A, Clement, Sigurdsson, Moore, Gregan (Gilchrist), Wallwork (Balis), Johnson, Dichio, Roberts (Dobie), Koumas.
Bradford C: Davison; Uhlenbeek, Jacobs, Emanuel, Molenaar, Bower, Francis, Standing, Juanjo (Danks), Gray, Jorgensen.

Walsall (0) 0
Reading (0) 0 5987
Walsall: Walker; Bazeley, Aranalde, O'Connor, Roper, Carbon, Wrack, Corica (Matias), Leitao, Junior (Zdrilic), Simpson.
Reading: Hahnemann; Murty, Shorey, Brown, Mackie, Newman, Igoe, Harper, Butler (Henderson), Cureton (Forster), Tyson (Salako).

West Ham U (1) 3 *(Defoe 26, 83, Cole 61)*
Nottingham F (1) 2 *(Harewood 17, Reid Andy 50)* 29,612
West Ham U: James; Schemmel, Winterburn (Repka), Cisse, Breen, Dailly, Sinclair, Cole, Defoe, Pearce (Camara), Carrick.
Nottingham F: Ward; Louis-Jean, Brennan, Thompson, Dawson, Doig, Prutton, Scimeca, Johnson, Harewood, Reid Andy.

Sunday, 5 January 2003
Fulham (2) 3 *(Sava 11, Goldbaek 23, Saha 46)*
Birmingham C (0) 1 *(John 90)* 9203
Fulham: Taylor; Finnan, Harley, Djetou, Goma, Davis, Goldbaek, Legwinski (Collins), Saha, Sava, Malbranque.
Birmingham C: Vaesen; Coly, Grainger, Hutchinson, Kenna, Powell, Devlin (Hughes), Savage, Morrison (Fagan), Kirovski (John), Johnson D.

Manchester C (0) 0

Liverpool (0) 1 *(Murphy 47 (pen))* 28,586

Manchester C: Schmeichel; Jihai (Goater), Jensen, Mettomo (Berkovic), Wiekens, Distin, Benarbia (Huckerby), Foe, Anelka, Wright-Phillips, Horlock.
Liverpool: Kirkland; Carragher, Traore, Diao, Henchoz, Hyypia, Murphy, Gerrard, Mellor (Heskey), Diouf, Smicer (Riise).

Wolverhampton W (2) 3 *(Ince 6, Kennedy 28, Ndah 49)*

Newcastle U (2) 2 *(Jenas 40, Shearer 43 (pen))* 27,316

Wolverhampton W: Murray; Irwin, Naylor, Ince, Butler (Clyde), Lescott, Newton (Cooper), Cameron, Ndah, Miller, Kennedy.
Newcastle U: Given; Griffin, Bernard, O'Brien (Dabizas), Hughes, Solano (Lua-Lua), Jenas, Acuna (Ameobi), Shearer, Bellamy, Robert.

Tuesday, 7 January 2003

Gillingham (3) 4 *(King 12, 18 (pen), Ipoua 41, Hope 75)*

Sheffield W (1) 1 *(Sibon 4)* 6434

Gillingham: Brown; Southall, Nosworthy, Hope, Ashby, Saunders, Smith, Hessenthaler (Spiller), Ipoua (Sidibe), King, Shaw.
Sheffield W: Stringer; Haslam, Beswetherick, Soltvedt, Westwood, Crane, Morrison (Knight), Bromby, Sibon (Shaw J), Kuqi, Quinn.

Tuesday, 14 January 2003

Norwich C (0) 3 *(Mulryne 51, 81, McVeigh 71)*

Brighton & HA (0) 1 *(Pethick 49)* 17,205

Norwich C: Green; Russell, Drury, Fleming, Mackay, Holt, Rivers (Henderson), Mulryne, Abbey (Roberts), Nielsen, McVeigh.
Brighton & HA: Kuipers (Packham); Watson (Blackwell), Mayo, Cullip, Pethick, Carpenter, Brooker, Oatway, Barrett, Zamora, Jones (Piercy).

THIRD ROUND REPLAYS

Tuesday, 14 January 2003

Burnley (1) 4 *(Moore I 25, 90, Little 79, Blake 86 (pen))*

Grimsby T (0) 0 5436

Burnley: Michopoulos; West (Cox), Branch, Grant, McGregor, Gnohere, Little, Cook, Moore I, Blake (Payton), Moore A (Papadopoulos).
Grimsby T: Coyne; Parker (Ward), Gallimore, Groves (Bolder), Chettle (Thompson), Soames, Cooke, Campbell, Livingstone, Mansaram, Barnard.

Crewe Alex (1) 2 *(Jones 29, Sodje 120)*

Bournemouth (1) 2 *(Hayter 38, Fletcher S 98)* 4540

Crewe Alex: Ince (Bankole); Wright, Tierney, Brammer, Walker (Sodje), Walton, Vaughan, Lunt, Miles (Bell), Jones, Sorvel.
Bournemouth: Tardif; Bernard (Holmes), Purches S, Tindall, Fletcher C, Stock, Thomas (Foyewa), O'Connor (Feeney), Hayter, Fletcher S, Elliott.
aet; Bournemouth won 3-1 on penalties.

Dagenham & R (1) 2 *(Shipp 20, McDougald 85)*

Plymouth Arg (0) 0 4530

Dagenham & R: Roberts; Smith, Janney, Heffer, Matthews, Vickers, Terry, Shipp, McGrath, McDougald, West (Rooney).
Plymouth Arg: Larrieu; Worrell, Hodges, Friio, Wotton, Coughlan, Norris, Keith, Stonebridge (Sturrock), Evans (Phillips), Adams (Bent).

Millwall (0) 3 *(Claridge 60 (pen), Robinson 70, Ifill 77)*

Cambridge U (0) 2 *(Kitson 58, Youngs 61)* 7031

Millwall: Warner; Lawrence, Ryan (Hearn), Livermore, Robinson, Ward, Ifill, Wise, Braniff (Sweeney), Claridge, Reid.
Cambridge U: Marshall; Goodhind, Tann (Chillingworth), Duncan, Angus, Wanless, Murray (Nacca), Tudor, Kitson (Riza), Youngs, Fleming.

Reading (1) 1 *(Aranalde 32 (og))*

Walsall (1) 1 *(Wrack 7)* 8767

Reading: Hahnemann; Murty, Shorey, Brown, Mackie, Newman (Hughes), Igoe, Harper, Butler, Forster (Cureton), Tyson (Salako).
Walsall: Walker; Bazeley, Aranalde, Hay, Roper, Carbon, Sonner (Simpson), O'Connor (Corica), Leitao, Junior (Zdrilic), Wrack.
aet; Walsall won 4-1 on penalties.

Sunderland (0) 2 *(Arca 99, Proctor 100)*

Bolton W (0) 0 14,550

Sunderland: Sorensen; Williams, Gray (Proctor), McCann, Emerson, Bjorklund (Varga), Medina (McCartney), Arca, Kyle, Stewart, Thornton.
Bolton W: Poole; Smith, Whitlow, Campo, N'Gotty, Nolan, Mendy (Hunt), Tofting, Facey (Warhurst), Djorkaeff, Farrelly (Walters).
aet.

Wednesday, 15 January 2003

Coventry C (1) 3 *(Fowler 21, Holdsworth 57, Bothroyd 89)*

Cardiff C (0) 0 11,997

Coventry C: Hyldgaard; Fowler, Gordon, Shaw, Konjic, Davenport, Pead, McAllister, Bothroyd, Holdsworth, Partridge (Betts).
Cardiff C: Alexander; Weston, Croft (Campbell), Kavanagh, Barker, Young (Collins), Boland, Bowen, Earnshaw, Thorne (Fortune-West), Legg.

FOURTH ROUND

Saturday, 25 January 2003

Blackburn R (1) 3 *(Cole 14, 73, Yorke 90)* 14.315

Sunderland (1) 3 *(Stewart 2, Proctor 52, Phillips 70)*

Blackburn R: Friedel; Douglas (Ostenstad), Neill, Todd, Taylor, Tugay, Thompson, Jansen (Gillespie), Cole, Yorke, Dunn (Johansson).
Sunderland: Sorensen; Clark, Gray, McCann, Babb, Craddock, Kilbane, Arca, Proctor, Phillips, Stewart.

Brentford (0) 0

Burnley (0) 3 *(Blake 52, Cook 86, Little 89)* 9563

Brentford: Smith P; Dobson, Frampton, Sonko, Marshall, Roget (Williams), Smith J, Hughes, O'Connor (Somner), Vine, Hunt.
Burnley: Beresford; West, Branch, Grant, Diallo, Gnohere, Taylor, Cook, Moore I (Moore A), Blake (Little), Briscoe.

Farnborough T (0) 1 *(Baptiste 71)*

Arsenal (2) 5 *(Campbell 19, Jeffers 23, 68, Bergkamp 74, Lauren 79)* 35,108

Farnborough T: Pennock; Warner, Gregory, Watson, Bunce, Annon, Lee■, Carroll (Piper L), Charlery (Butterworth), Baptiste, Holloway (Piper C).
Arsenal: Taylor; Lauren, Van Bronckhorst, Vieira, Campbell, Cygan, Parlour, Toure (Wiltord), Kanu (Edu), Jeffers, Pires (Bergkamp).
at Highbury.

Gillingham (0) 1 *(Sidibe 82)*

Leeds U (0) 1 *(Smith 49)* 11,093

Gillingham: Brown; Southall, Edge, Hope, Ashby, Saunders, Smith, Hessenthaler, Sidibe, Ipoua (Wallace), Shaw.
Leeds U: Robinson; Kelly, Lukic, Bakke, Radebe, Matteo, Okon, Smith, Viduka■, Kewell, Wilcox.

Norwich C (0) 1 *(Abbey 90)*

Dagenham & R (0) 0 21,164

Norwich C: Green; Russell, Drury, Fleming, Mackay, Holt, Rivers, Mulryne, Roberts, Nielsen (Abbey), McVeigh.
Dagenham & R: Roberts; Heffer, Vickers, Terry, Matthews, Smith, Janney, Shipp, West (Stein), McDougald, McGrath (Rooney).

Rochdale (1) 2 *(Connor 33, Griffiths 47)*

Coventry C (0) 0 9156

Rochdale: Edwards; Evans, Hill, Melaugh, Griffiths, Grand, Flitcroft, Oliver, Platt, Connor (Townson), Simpson (McEvilly).
Coventry C: Hyldgaard; Caldwell, Gordon (Fowler), McAllister, Konjic, Shaw, Pead, Bothroyd (Sara), McSheffrey, Holdsworth, Partridge (Davenport).

Sheffield U (2) 4 *(Brown 19, 64, Jagielka 31, Peschisolido 89)*

Ipswich T (0) 3 *(Gaardsoe 66, Miller T 68 (pen), Bent D 70)* 12,757

Sheffield U: De Vogt; Kozluk, Quinn, McCall, Jagielka, Page, Ndlovu, Thompson, Kabba (Allison), Mooney (Peschisolido), Brown.
Ipswich T: Marshall; Wilnis (Ambrose), Hreidarsson, Makin, Gaardsoe, Holland, Magilton (Bent D), Miller T, Counago, Bent M, Wright.

Southampton (0) 1 *(Davies 88)*

Millwall (1) 1 *(Claridge 17)* 23,809

Southampton: Niemi; Telfer, Benali, Oakley, Williams, Svensson M, Fernandes (Davies), Delap, Beattie (Marsden), Ormerod (Tessem), Svensson A.
Millwall: Warner; Lawrence, Ryan, Livermore, Robinson, Ward, Hearn, Wise, Ifill, Claridge (Braniff), Reid.

Walsall (0) 1 *(Zdrilic 75)*

Wimbledon (0) 0 6693

Walsall: Walker; Bazeley, Aranalde, Barras, Roper, Hay, Wrack, Sonner, Leitao, Zdrilic, Simpson (Matias).
Wimbledon: Davis; Leigertwood, Hawkins, Andersen (Reo-Coker), Williams, Gier, Tapp (Gray), Francis, Shipperley, Connolly, Agyemang (Ainsworth).

Watford (0) 1 *(Helguson 80)*

WBA (0) 0 16,975

Watford: Chamberlain; Ardley (Mahon), Robinson, Cox, Gayle, Vernazza, Pennant, Hyde, Helguson (Noel-Williams), Smith T, Nielsen.
WBA: Hoult; Wallwork, Clement, Gregan, Moore (Chambers A), Gilchrist, McInnes (Sigurdsson), Johnson, Dichio, Roberts (Dobie), Koumas.

Wolverhampton W (2) 4 *(Ndah 5, 45, Miller 51, 71)*

Leicester C (1) 1 *(Dickov 29 (pen))* 28,164

Wolverhampton W: Murray; Irwin, Naylor, Ince, Butler, Lescott, Newton, Cameron, Ndah (Proudlock), Miller, Kennedy.
Leicester C: Walker; Sinclair, Davidson, Elliott (Stewart), Heath, McKinlay (Jones), Summerbee, Izzet, Dickov, Scowcroft, Rogers (Wright).

Sunday, 26 January 2003

Crystal Palace (0) 0

Liverpool (0) 0 26,054

Crystal Palace: Kolinko; Fleming, Gray (Granville), Symons, Popovic, Mullins, Butterfield, Derry, Adebola (Akinbiyi), Black (Routledge), Johnson.
Liverpool: Kirkland (Dudek); Carragher, Riise, Gerrard, Traore, Hyypia, Murphy, Diouf (Biscan), Heskey, Owen, Cheyrou (Diao).

Fulham (0) 3 *(Malbranque 59, 66 (pen), 87 (pen))*

Charlton Ath (0) 0 12,203

Fulham: Taylor; Djetou (Knight), Harley, Melville, Goma, Davis, Malbranque (Goldbaek), Legwinski, Marlet, Sava, Boa Morte.
Charlton Ath: Kiely; Kishishev, Konchesky, Young (Fortune), Rufus, Fish■, Jensen (Bart-Williams), Euell, Bartlett, Johansson, Parker (Svensson).

Manchester U (2) 6 *(Giggs 8, 29, Van Nistelrooy 49, 58, Neville P 50, Solskjaer 69)*

West Ham U (0) 0 67,181

Manchester U: Barthez; Neville G, Neville P, O'Shea, Keane, Ferdinand, Beckham (Solskjaer), Veron (Butt), Van Nistelrooy, Scholes (Forlan), Giggs.
West Ham U: James; Lomas, Minto, Pearce, Breen (Dailly), Cisse (Garcia), Sinclair (Johnson), Bowyer, Defoe, Cole, Carrick.

Shrewsbury T (0) 0

Chelsea (1) 4 *(Zola 40, 75, Cole 53, Morris 80)* 7950

Shrewsbury T: Dunbavin; Moss (Drysdale), Smith, Wilding, Artell, Tolley J, Woan, Atkins (Murray), Rodgers, Jemson, Jagielka (Lowe).
Chelsea: Cudicini; Melchiot, Babayaro (Cole), Petit, Gallas, Terry, Zenden, Lampard (Morris), Gudjohnsen (Gronkjaer), Zola, Le Saux.

Stoke C (1) 3 *(Iwelumo 45 (pen), 51, Hoekstra 84)*

Bournemouth (0) 0 12,004

Stoke C: Banks (Cutler); Henry, Hall, Gunnarsson, Marteinsson, Thomas, Gudjonsson (Neal), O'Connor, Iwelumo, Greenacre, Hoekstra (Goodfellow).
Bournemouth: Tardif■; Buxton, Purches S, Tindall, Fletcher C, Stock, Thomas (Stewart), O'Connor, Hayter (Holmes), Fletcher S (Feeney), Elliott.

FOURTH ROUND REPLAYS

Tuesday, 4 February 2003

Leeds U (1) 2 *(Viduka 11, Bakke 58)*

Gillingham (0) 1 *(Ipoua 86)* 29,359

Leeds U: Robinson; Mills, Harte, Bakke, Radebe (Duberry), Matteo (Milner), Kelly, Okon, Viduka, Seth Johnson, Wilcox.
Gillingham: Brown; Nosworthy, Edge, James, Hope, Johnson L, Southall, Hessenthaler, Sidibe, Wallace (Johnson T), Perpetuini (Ipoua).

Wednesday, 5 February 2003

Liverpool (0) 0

Crystal Palace (0) 2 *(Gray 55, Henchoz 79 (og))* 35,109

Liverpool: Dudek; Carragher, Riise, Hamann, Henchoz, Hyypia, Murphy (Baros), Diouf, Heskey, Owen, Cheyrou.
Crystal Palace: Berthelin; Butterfield, Granville (Freedman■), Symons, Popovic, Powell, Mullins, Derry, Adebola (Akinbiyi), Johnson (Thomson), Gray.

Millwall (1) 1 *(Reid 37)*

Southampton (1) 2 *(Oakley 21, 102)* 10,197

Millwall: Warner; Lawrence (Baltacha), Ryan, Livermore, Robinson, Ward, Ifill, Hearn (Kinet), Claridge, Wise (May), Reid.
Southampton: Niemi; Telfer, Benali, Marsden, Lundekvam, Svensson M, Fernandes (Ormerod), Oakley, Beattie, Tessem (Davies), Svensson A.
aet.

Sunderland (1) 2 *(Phillips 10, McCann 79)*

Blackburn R (0) 2 *(Flitcroft 50, 90)* 15,745

Sunderland: Sorensen; Wright, Gray (Oster), McCann, Emerson, Craddock, Thornton, Arca (McCartney), Proctor (Kyle), Phillips, Kilbane.
Blackburn R: Friedel; Neill, McEveley (Douglas), Johansson (Grabbi), Berg, Taylor, Tugay, Flitcroft, Cole, Yorke (Ostenstad), Thompson.
aet; Sunderland won 3-0 on penalties.

FIFTH ROUND

Saturday, 15 February 2003

Manchester U (0) 0

Arsenal (1) 2 *(Edu 34, Wiltord 52)* 67,209

Manchester U: Barthez; Neville G, Silvestre, Brown, Keane, Ferdinand, Beckham (Butt), Scholes, Van Nistelrooy, Giggs (Forlan), Solskjaer.
Arsenal: Seaman; Lauren, Cole, Vieira, Campbell, Keown, Parlour, Edu, Wiltord (Toure), Jeffers (Henry), Pires (Van Bronckhorst).

Sheffield U (1) 2 *(Mooney 37, Ndlovu 56)*
Walsall (0) 0 17,510
Sheffield U: Kenny; Jagielka, Quinn, McCall, Murphy, Page, Ndlovu, Brown, Mooney (Allison), Kabba (Peschisolido), Tonge.
Walsall: Walker; Bazeley, Aranalde, O'Connor (Matias), Carbon (Roper), Hay, Wrack, Corica, Leitao, Junior, Simpson.

Southampton (0) 2 *(Svensson A 71, Tessem 74)*
Norwich C (0) 0 31,103
Southampton: Niemi; Telfer, Higginbotham, Marsden, Lundekvam, Svensson M, Svensson A, Delap (Fernandes), Beattie (Tessem), Ormerod, Oakley (Dodd).
Norwich C: Green; Nedergaard, Drury, Fleming, Mackay■, Holt, Russell, Mulryne (Abbey), Roberts, Nielsen (Henderson), McVeigh (Easton).

Sunderland (0) 0
Watford (0) 1 *(Smith T 65 (pen))* 26,916
Sunderland: Sorensen; Wright, Gray, McAteer, Babb (Proctor), Craddock, Thornton, Arca (El Karkouri), Flo (Bellion), Phillips, Kilbane.
Watford: Chamberlain; Ardley, Robinson, Cox, Gayle, Vernazza, Mahon, Hyde, Helguson, Smith T (Doyley), Nielsen.

Sunday, 16 February 2003

Crystal Palace (1) 1 *(Gray 35)*
Leeds U (1) 2 *(Kelly 33, Kewell 73)* 24,512
Crystal Palace: Berthelin; Butterfield (Freedman), Gray, Symons (Granville), Mullins, Powell (Akinbiyi), Black, Derry, Adebola, Johnson, Riihilahti.
Leeds U: Robinson; Mills, Harte, Seth Johnson, Radebe, Duberry, Kelly, Okon (Milner), Smith (Lucic), Kewell (Barmby), Wilcox.

Fulham (1) 1 *(Malbranque 45)*
Burnley (1) 1 *(Moore A 4)* 13,062
Fulham: Taylor; Finnan, Harley, Melville, Goma, Davis, Goldbaek (Marlet), Djetou, Saha, Sava (Inamoto), Malbranque.
Burnley: Beresford; West, Branch, Grant, Diallo, Cox, Briscoe, Cook (McGregor), Moore I, Taylor, Moore A (Weller).

Stoke C (0) 0
Chelsea (0) 2 *(Hasselbaink 52, Gronkjaer 76)* 26,615
Stoke C: Banks; Thomas, Hall, Gunnarsson, Handyside, Shtanyuk, Henry (Gudjonsson), O'Connor, Iwelumo, Greenacre (Goodfellow), Neal (Marteinsson).
Chelsea: Cudicini; Melchiot, Le Saux, Petit (Huth), Gallas, Terry, De Lucas (Gronkjaer), Lampard, Hasselbaink, Gudjohnsen, Stanic (Cole).

Wolverhampton W (1) 3 *(Ndah 32, Miller 79, Proudlock 90)*
Rochdale (0) 1 *(Melaugh 52)* 23,921
Wolverhampton W: Murray; Irwin, Naylor, Ince, Butler, Lescott, Newton (Rae), Cameron, Ndah, Miller (Proudlock), Kennedy.
Rochdale: Gilks; Warner, Hill, Evans (McCourt), Griffiths, Grand, Flitcroft, Melaugh, Platt, McEvilly, Simpson.

FIFTH ROUND REPLAY

Wednesday, 26 February 2003

Burnley (2) 3 *(Taylor 27, Moore I 35, Diallo 52)*
Fulham (0) 0 11,635
Burnley: Beresford; West, Branch, Grant (McGregor), Diallo, Cox, Briscoe, Cook (Weller), Moore I, Taylor, Moore A (Little).
Fulham: Taylor; Finnan, Harley, Melville, Djetou, Davis■, Malbranque (Wome), Legwinski, Saha (Ouaddou), Inamoto, Boa Morte (Sava).

SIXTH ROUND

Saturday, 8 March 2003

Arsenal (2) 2 *(Jeffers 37, Henry 45)*
Chelsea (1) 2 *(Terry 3, Lampard 84)* 38,104
Arsenal: Seaman; Lauren, Van Bronckhorst, Vieira, Campbell, Keown, Parlour, Edu, Henry (Toure), Jeffers (Wiltord), Ljungberg (Pires).
Chelsea: Cudicini; Melchiot, Babayaro, Petit (De Lucas), Gallas, Terry, Gronkjaer (Gudjohnsen), Lampard, Hasselbaink, Zola (Zenden), Morris.

Sunday, 9 March 2003

Sheffield U (0) 1 *(Kabba 78)*
Leeds U (0) 0 24,633
Sheffield U: Kenny; Jagielka, Kozluk, McCall, Murphy, Page, Montgomery, Brown, Kabba, Allison, Tonge.
Leeds U: Robinson; Mills, Harte (Milner), Okon (Barmby), Radebe, Lucic, Smith, Seth Johnson, Viduka, Kewell (Bakke), Bravo.

Southampton (0) 2 *(Marsden 56, Butler 81 (og))*
Wolverhampton W (0) 0 31,715
Southampton: Niemi; Dodd, Bridge, Marsden, Lundekvam, Svensson M, Fernandes, Oakley, Beattie (Davies), Ormerod, Svensson A (Tessem).
Wolverhampton W: Murray; Irwin, Naylor, Andrews (Rae), Butler, Lescott, Newton (Sturridge), Cameron, Blake (Proudlock), Miller, Kennedy.

Watford (0) 2 *(Smith T 64, Glass 80)*
Burnley (0) 0 20,336
Watford: Chamberlain; Ardley, Robinson, Cox, Gayle, Vernazza (Hand), Mahon, Hyde, Helguson, Smith T (Noel-Williams), Glass.
Burnley: Beresford; West, Branch, Grant (Blake), Diallo, Cox, Briscoe, Cook (Davis), Moore I, Taylor, Moore A (Little).

SIXTH ROUND REPLAY

Tuesday, 25 March 2003

Chelsea (0) 1 *(Terry 79)*
Arsenal (2) 3 *(Terry 25 (og), Wiltord 34, Lauren 82)* 41,456
Chelsea: Cudicini; Melchiot, Le Saux, Petit (Gudjohnsen), Gallas, Terry, Stanic (Gronkjaer), Lampard, Hasselbaink, Zola, Morris (Zenden).
Arsenal: Taylor; Lauren, Toure, Vieira, Campbell, Cygan■, Parlour, Edu, Wiltord (Henry), Jeffers (Van Bronckhorst), Pires (Ljungberg).

SEMI-FINALS

Sunday, 13 April 2003

Arsenal (1) 1 *(Ljungberg 34)*
Sheffield U (0) 0 59,170
Arsenal: Seaman; Lauren, Cole, Vieira (Silva), Campbell, Keown, Parlour, Edu, Wiltord (Bergkamp), Jeffers (Henry), Ljungberg.
Sheffield U: Kenny; Curtis, Kozluk, McCall (Montgomery), Jagielka, Page, Ndlovu, Brown, Kabba (Peschisolido), Allison (Asaba), Tonge.
at Old Trafford.

Watford (0) 1 *(Gayle 88)*
Southampton (1) 2 *(Ormerod 33, Robinson 80 (og))* 42,602
Watford: Chamberlain; Mahon, Robinson, Cox, Gayle, Vernazza (Nielsen), Ardley, Hyde, Chopra (Smith T), Helguson, Glass (Cook).
Southampton: Jones; Telfer, Bridge, Marsden, Lundekvam, Svensson M, Fernandes, Oakley, Beattie, Ormerod (Tessem), Svensson A (Delap).
at Villa Park.

THE FA CUP FINAL

Saturday, 17 May 2003

(at Millennium Stadium, Cardiff, attendance 73,726)

Arsenal (1) 1 *(Pires 38)* **Southampton (0) 0**

Arsenal: Seaman; Lauren, Cole, Silva, Luzhny, Keown, Ljungberg, Parlour, Henry, Bergkamp (Wiltord), Pires.

Southampton: Niemi (Jones); Baird (Fernandez), Bridge, Marsden, Lundekvam, Svensson M, Telfer, Oakley, Beattie, Ormerod, Svensson A (Tessem).

Referee: G. Barber (Hertfordshire).

Robert Pires takes full advantage of the deflection which enabled him to score the only goal of the FA Cup Final for Arsenal against Southampton. (Colorsport)

NATIONWIDE CONFERENCE 2002–03

Yeovil Town finally made it after 105 years, winning the Nationwide Conference in style to gain promotion to the Football League. The scourge of so many League clubs in the FA Cup during their history, they were joined by Doncaster Rovers who lost their Football League status in 1998, as another chapter in the comparatively short life of the competition began, with two clubs promoted.

With the play-offs enabling the competition to retain interest for virtually half its complement, it was ironic that the relegation issues generated even more in the closing weeks of the season, culminating in the last day drama.

Yet it had been Chester City who had emerged as the early front runners and were still the only unbeaten team when Yeovil overtook them on 28 September. But on 8 October Chester lost 2-1 at home to Nuneaton Borough, were then held to a 1-1 draw by Gravesend & Northfleet and lost 1-0 at Woking who had been top themselves after four games.

Fourth place was where Southport were placed on 4 November and by the turn of the year Halifax Town had made third spot, while both Hereford United and Scarborough were in contention for the play-offs.

By March, Dagenham & Redbridge, who had had a Conference record-breaking run of ten consecutive wins beating Macclesfield Town's record of nine years earlier, were fifth and moving up. A week later the top five were Yeovil, Doncaster, Dagenham, Morecambe and Chester and this was how it stayed.

On 12 April Yeovil won 4-0 at Doncaster, while Chester were held 2-2 by Woking, but the excitement was growing at the other end of the table with three matches left and nine clubs in jeopardy for the two remaining relegation berths as Kettering Town, bottom as early as 28 September were already doomed.

On the last day Gravesend beat Halifax 1-0, Nuneaton failed 2-0 at home to Farnborough Town and plunging Southport crashed 3-0 at Stevenage Borough whose escape had been bankrolled when Graham Westley left Farnborough after their FA Cup run. Woking defeated Telford United 3-0 and Leigh RMI won 1-0 at Kettering, leaving Nuneaton and Southport as the other demoted teams.

That evening Yeovil drew 1-1 with Chester in a Sky Sports TV match watched by a best crowd of the season at Huish Park of 8,111. The champions' ground had been a fortress with no defeats in the Conference and Morecambe lost only once at home.

In the play-offs Dagenham took a slender 2-1 lead over Morecambe, but Doncaster needed a last-minute goal to hold Chester 1-1 at Belle Vue. But second legs left stalemate, decided by penalty kicks, Doncaster and Dagenham being successful.

In the final at Stoke, Doncaster were seemingly coasting at 2-0 when Dagenham levelled the scores and forced extra time before Rovers clinched it in the extra period in front of 13,092 spectators.

Plans are well in hand for a regionalised Second Division and in 2003–04 there will be ten clubs in the Nationwide Conference with previous Football League connections.

NATIONWIDE CONFERENCE PLAY-OFFS 2002–03

SEMI-FINALS FIRST LEG

Thursday, 1 May 2003

Dagenham & R (1) 2 *(Stein 7, 66 (pen))*
Morecambe (1) 1 *(Shipp 29 (og))* 3447

Dagenham & R: Roberts; Mustafa, Goodwin, Terry, Cole, Matthews, Janney, Shipp, Stein, West, McGrath (Broom).
Morecambe: Mawson; McKearney, Perkins, Drummond, Bentley, Swan (Murphy), Thompson, Collins (Stringfellow), Curtis, Rigoglioso (Carlton), Elam.

Doncaster R (0) 1 *(Whitman 90)*
Chester C (1) 1 *(McIntyre 37)* 6857

Doncaster R: Warrington; Marples, Beech, Ravenhill, Foster (Morley), Ryan T, Paterson, Doolan (Green), Barnes, Whitman, Watson (Blundell).
Chester C: Brown W; Brady, McIntyre, Guyett, Bolland, Hatswell, Collins, Carden, Clare (Quayle), Sugden (Cameron), Davies.

SEMI-FINALS SECOND LEG

Monday, 5 May 2003

Chester C (1) 1 *(Hatswell 31)*
Doncaster R (0) 1 *(Barnes 57)* 5702

Chester C: Brown W; Brady (Quayle), McIntyre, Guyett, Bolland, Hatswell, Collins, Carden, Clare, Sugden (Cameron), Davies.
Doncaster R: Warrington; Paterson, Beech (Blunt), Morley, Foster, Ryan T, Green, Ravenhill, Barnes (Watson), Whitman, Tierney (Blundell).
aet; Doncaster R won 4-3 on penalties.

Morecambe (0) 2 *(West 50 (og), Rigoglioso 86)*
Dagenham & R (0) 1 *(Terry 89)* 5405

Morecambe: Mawson; McKearney, Perkins (Ubershar), Drummond, Bentley, Murphy, Thompson, Stringfellow, Curtis (Carlton), Rigoglioso (Talbot), Elam.
Dagenham & R: Roberts; Mustafa, Goodwin, Terry, Cole, Matthews, Janney (Heffer), Shipp, Stein, West (Smith), McGrath (Broom).
aet; Dagenham & R won 3-2 on penalties.

FINAL

Saturday, 10 May 2003
(at Britannia Stadium, Stoke)

Dagenham & R (0) 2 *(Stein 63, Mustafa 78)*
Doncaster R (1) 3 *(Green 39, Morley 55, Tierney 110)* 13,092

Dagenham & R: Roberts; Goodwin (Smith), Mustafa, Terry (Heffer), Matthews, Cole, McGrath (Vickers), Shipp, Stein, West, Janney.
Doncaster R: Warrington; Marples, Ryan T, Ravenhill, Morley, Foster, Paterson (Blunt), Green, Barnes, Whitman (Blundell), Tierney.
aet; Doncaster R won on sudden death.

NATIONWIDE CONFERENCE 2002–03 FINAL LEAGUE TABLE

			Home			Goals		Away			Goals			
		P	W	D	L	F	A	W	D	L	F	A	GD	Pts
1	Yeovil Town	42	16	5	0	54	13	12	6	3	46	24	63	95
2	Morecambe	42	17	3	1	52	13	6	6	9	34	29	44	78
3	Doncaster Rovers	42	11	6	4	28	17	11	6	4	45	30	26	78
4	Chester City	42	10	6	5	36	21	11	6	4	23	10	28	75
5	Dagenham & Redbridge	42	12	5	4	38	23	9	4	8	33	36	12	72
6	Hereford United	42	9	5	7	36	22	10	2	9	28	29	13	64
7	Scarborough	42	12	3	6	41	28	6	7	8	22	26	9	64
8	Halifax Town	42	11	5	5	34	28	7	5	9	16	23	–1	64
9	Forest Green Rovers	42	12	3	6	41	29	5	5	11	20	33	–1	59
10	Margate	42	8	9	4	32	24	7	2	12	28	42	–6	56
11	Barnet	42	9	4	8	32	28	4	10	7	33	40	–3	53
12	Stevenage Borough	42	7	6	8	31	25	7	4	10	30	30	6	52
13	Farnborough Town	42	8	6	7	37	29	5	6	10	20	27	1	51
14	Northwich Victoria	42	6	5	10	26	34	7	7	7	40	38	–6	51
15	Telford United	42	7	2	12	20	33	7	5	9	34	36	–15	49
16	Burton Albion	42	6	6	9	25	31	7	4	10	27	46	–25	49
17	Gravesend & Northfleet	42	8	5	8	37	35	4	7	10	25	38	–11	48
18	Leigh RMI	42	8	5	8	26	34	6	1	14	18	37	–27	48
19	Woking	42	8	7	6	30	35	3	7	11	22	46	–29	47
20	Nuneaton Borough	42	9	4	8	27	32	4	3	14	24	46	–27	46
21	Southport	42	6	8	7	31	32	5	4	12	23	37	–15	45
22	Kettering Town	42	4	3	14	23	39	4	4	13	14	34	–36	31

NATIONWIDE CONFERENCE LEADING GOALSCORERS 2002–03

	League	*P-offs*	*FA Cup*	*LDV*	*Trophy*	*Total*
Paul Barnes *(Doncaster R)*	25	1	2	0	0	28
Kirk Jackson *(Yeovil T)*	24	0	1	1	1	27
(Including 5 League goals, 1 FA Cup and 1 LDV Vans Trophy for Stevenage B)						
Gregg Blundell *(Doncaster R)*	20	0	0	0	2	22
(Including 19 League goals and 2 Trophy for Northwich Vic)						
Junior Agogo *(Barnet)*	20	0	0	0	0	20
Wayne Curtis *(Morecambe)*	18	0	0	0	0	18
Dino Maamria *(Stevenage B)*	17	0	1	0	0	18
(Including 12 League goals and 1 FA Cup for Leigh RMI)						
Daryl Clare *(Chester C)*	17	0	0	0	0	17
Mark Stein *(Dagenham & R)*	16	3	0	0	2	21
Christian Moore *(Burton Albion)*	16	0	2	0	0	18
Steve West *(Dagenham & R)*	16	0	0	0	1	17
David Brown *(Telford U)*	16	0	0	0	1	17
Nigel Grayson *(Forest Green R)*	15	0	0	0	5	20
Mark Quayle *(Chester C)*	15	0	1	0	0	16
(Including 14 League goals and 1 FA Cup for Nuneaton B)						
Warren Patmore *(Woking)*	14	0	0	0	2	16
Paul Moore *(Telford U)*	14	0	0	0	1	15
Kayode Odejayi *(Forest Green R)*	13	0	1	0	2	16
Lee Elam *(Morecambe)*	13	0	1	0	1	15
Kevin Gall *(Yeovil T)*	13	0	0	0	1	14
Steve Guinan *(Hereford U)*	13	0	0	0	0	13

ATTENDANCES BY CLUB 2002–03

	Aggregate 2002–03	*Average 2002–03*	*Highest Attendance 2002–03*
Yeovil Town	99,561	4,741	8,111 v Chester City
Doncaster Rovers	74,340	3,540	5,344 v Yeovil Town
Chester City	50,525	2,406	3,821 v Yeovil Town
Hereford United	42,795	2,038	3,271 v Forest Green Rovers
Woking	41,706	1,986	3,332 v Yeovil Town
Stevenage Borough	39,853	1,898	2,801 v Woking
Halifax Town	36,803	1,753	3,082 v Doncaster Rovers
Burton Albion	36,682	1,747	2,523 v Nuneaton Borough
Dagenham & Redbridge	33,582	1,599	2,588 v Yeovil Town
Morecambe	30,704	1,462	2,239 v Burton Albion
Scarborough	29,005	1,381	3,435 v Doncaster Rovers
Kettering Town	28,570	1,360	2,068 v Stevenage Borough
Barnet	28,194	1,343	1,909 v Stevenage Borough
Nuneaton Borough	26,406	1,257	2,337 v Burton Albion
Gravesend & Northfleet	25,800	1,229	2,036 v Dagenham & Redbridge
Southport	24,380	1,161	2,447 v Chester City
Telford United	20,694	985	2,047 v Hereford United
Farnborough Town	18,505	881	2,114 v Yeovil Town
Forest Green Rovers	18,016	858	1,836 v Yeovil Town
Northwich Victoria	15,777	751	2,305 v Chester City
Margate	14,380	685	1,415 v Gravesend & Northfleet
Leigh RMI	10,159	484	864 v Doncaster Rovers

NATIONWIDE CONFERENCE 2002–03

	Barnet	Burton Albion	Chester City	Dagenham & Redbridge	Doncaster Rovers	Farnborough Town	Forest Green Rovers	Gravesend & Northfleet	Halifax Town	Hereford United	Kettering Town	Leigh RMI	Margate	Morecambe	Northwich Victoria	Nuneaton Borough	Scarborough	Southport	Stevenage Borough	Telford United	Woking	Yeovil Town
Barnet	—	2-2	0-3	2-1	1-2	1-2	2-0	1-4	0-0	2-1	0-2	4-0	0-1	1-1	3-4	2-1	3-0	3-1	0-2	3-0	0-0	2-1
Burton Albion	0-3	—	2-0	0-0	1-2	2-0	2-3	1-1	2-2	2-0	2-0	0-1	0-1	1-4	1-1	1-0	1-1	1-0	1-2	4-7	0-2	1-1
Chester City	1-1	2-1	—	5-2	1-0	0-2	0-1	1-1	2-0	0-1	0-0	2-1	5-0	2-1	2-3	1-2	0-0	2-0	2-0	4-1	2-2	2-2
Dagenham & Redbridge	5-1	1-2	1-0	—	3-3	1-0	3-1	4-0	0-0	1-0	3-1	3-1	3-0	1-1	2-0	1-2	1-0	0-3	3-2	1-1	1-1	0-4
Doncaster Rovers	2-1	1-0	0-0	5-1	—	1-0	1-0	4-1	0-0	2-0	1-0	1-0	3-1	1-1	1-2	1-1	0-1	0-0	0-0	1-3	3-1	0-4
Farnborough Town	2-2	5-1	1-2	1-0	0-0	—	0-3	1-1	3-0	2-2	0-1	1-0	4-1	2-3	3-2	0-2	1-1	2-1	0-1	2-2	5-0	2-4
Forest Green Rovers	4-4	2-0	0-2	5-2	1-2	3-1	—	2-1	0-2	1-3	1-0	4-1	4-1	1-0	1-0	6-1	0-0	0-2	0-3	1-1	3-2	2-1
Gravesend & Northfleet	2-2	3-2	0-1	1-2	2-2	0-0	1-1	—	1-0	3-0	0-2	1-3	1-2	3-2	1-1	4-1	5-2	1-3	2-1	0-2	4-2	2-4
Halifax Town	2-4	0-1	0-0	3-3	2-1	1-0	1-1	2-1	—	1-0	4-0	1-0	2-2	1-0	0-5	3-1	2-1	3-4	1-0	2-0	1-1	2-3
Hereford United	4-0	4-0	0-0	2-1	2-4	2-1	1-1	3-0	1-1	—	2-0	0-1	2-3	1-2	1-2	2-1	0-1	0-2	2-2	2-0	5-0	0-0
Kettering Town	1-2	1-2	0-1	1-3	0-2	1-4	2-3	1-1	0-1	2-3	—	0-1	1-1	3-2	2-2	3-0	1-3	1-0	1-0	2-4	0-3	0-1
Leigh RMI	4-2	4-2	0-4	1-3	0-2	3-2	1-0	0-0	0-2	0-2	2-2	—	2-0	1-0	1-1	1-1	0-2	1-1	2-1	0-3	1-0	2-4
Margate	2-2	0-0	0-1	0-1	2-1	0-0	3-0	4-2	2-1	0-2	2-2	2-0	—	1-1	4-4	1-1	3-1	1-0	1-1	1-1	2-1	1-2
Morecambe	1-1	5-0	1-1	2-1	3-0	1-1	4-0	2-0	2-0	3-1	1-0	2-1	3-0	—	3-1	3-2	3-1	3-0	3-1	1-0	5-0	1-2
Northwich Victoria	1-1	1-3	1-1	0-2	1-2	2-2	2-1	1-2	0-2	2-2	1-2	0-1	1-0	3-2	—	3-1	0-2	2-1	1-1	2-1	1-3	1-2
Nuneaton Borough	3-2	1-2	1-0	1-3	0-3	0-2	3-2	0-1	2-0	0-3	1-0	0-1	3-2	1-1	1-4	—	1-1	3-2	3-0	1-0	1-1	1-1
Scarborough	1-1	4-1	0-1	0-1	2-5	1-0	3-0	3-2	0-1	2-1	4-1	2-0	3-2	1-0	4-1	4-1	—	2-2	1-2	1-4	1-1	2-1
Southport	2-1	2-2	1-3	2-3	0-4	0-0	2-2	1-1	2-0	1-2	0-0	4-2	0-2	2-3	1-1	1-0	1-1	—	3-2	1-1	5-1	0-1
Stevenage Borough	1-2	0-1	0-1	2-0	2-3	5-0	0-0	1-0	0-1	0-2	2-0	3-1	1-3	1-1	2-2	3-1	1-1	3-0	—	1-3	1-1	2-2
Telford United	2-1	0-2	0-1	1-2	4-4	0-2	0-1	2-1	1-2	0-1	2-0	1-1	1-0	0-3	1-0	1-2	0-2	2-0	1-3	—	1-0	0-5
Woking	0-0	2-2	1-0	0-0	2-2	1-1	1-0	2-3	2-1	1-2	2-1	3-0	1-5	0-6	2-3	2-1	2-1	1-1	1-5	3-0	—	1-1
Yeovil Town	0-0	6-1	1-1	2-2	1-1	2-0	1-0	2-2	3-0	4-0	4-0	3-1	2-1	2-0	2-1	3-2	1-0	6-0	2-1	3-0	4-0	—

NATIONWIDE CONFERENCE APPEARANCES AND GOALSCORERS 2002–03

BARNET

League Appearances: Agogo, 36+4; Arber, 12; Baimass, 0+7; Bell, 3+7; Brown, 12+2; Butters, 7; Cashman, 0+2; Doolan, 31; Flynn, 23+1; Gledhill, 10+2; Gower, 41; Harrison, 14; Heald, 23; Hendon, 4; Hillier, 6; Langston, 3+2; Lopez, 4+1; Midgley, 30+6; Millard, 2+1; Naisbitt, 26; Niven, 0+1; Oshitola, 3+18; Pluck, 36+2; Pope, 22+5; Price, 4; Purser, 20+6; Rowland, 6+2; Soloman, 18+3; Strevens, 21+2; Toms, 16+8; Wiper, 0+1; Yakabu, 29+7.

Goals: *League (65):* Agogo 20 (3 pens), Gower 9, Strevens 9 (1 pen), Midgley 5, Purser 4, Doolan 3, Heald 3, Brown 2, Oshitola 2, Soloman 2, Arber 1, Hendon 1, Pope 1, Toms 1, Wiper 1, Yakabu 1.
Trophy (2): Midgley 1, Purser 1.

BURTON ALBION

League Appearances: Anderson, 12+14; Blount, 19+2; Burns, 7+1; Camp, 5; Clough, 27+7; Ducros, 10+1; Dudley, 24+6; Duke, 36; Evans, 6+5; Farrell, 1+12; Glasser, 19+1; Glover, 6+3; Gough, 0+4; Gummer, 1+2; Henshaw, 33+3; Howard, 8; Hoyle, 28+2; Johnson, 0+1; Kavanagh, 13+3; Kirkwood, 20+5; Moore, 34+2; O'Halloran, 5+1; Petty, 3+6; Reddington, 25; Robinson, 1; Sinton, 27+6; Stride, 29+4; Swinscoe, 0+1; Talbot, 21+10; Wassall, 7; Webster, 34+6; Wraith, 1.

Goals: *League (52):* Moore 16, Anderson 5 (1 pen), Stride 5, Webster 4, Kavanagh 3 (3 pens), Reddington 3, Evans 2, Glover 2, Howard 2, Kirkwood 2, Clough 1, Ducros 1, Dudley 1 (pen), Farrell 1, Gummer 1, O'Halloran 1, Sinton 1, Talbot 1.
FA Cup (6): Dudley 2, Moore 2, Kirkwood 1, Webster 1 (pen).

CHESTER CITY

League Appearances: Beesley, 10+9; Blackburn, 15+4; Bolland, 30; Brady, 15+4; Brodie, 3+1; Brown, M, 6+17; Brown, W, 39; Cameron, 7+8; Carden, 31; Carey, 15+3; Clare, 23; Clifford, 1; Collins, 10; Davies, 24+5; Griffin, 0+1; Guyett, 32; Harkness, 10; Hatswell, 27+2; Joy, 3; Kelly, 29+3; Lancaster, 2+1; McCaldon, 2; McIntyre, 39+1; Quayle, 6+3; Ruffer, 24+7; Sugden, 26+7; Tate, 0+2; Twiss, 21+16; Woodyatt, 11+2; Worsnop, 1.

Goals: *League (59):* Clare 17 (2 pens), Sugden 12, Beesley 6 (1 pen), Twiss 6, Cameron 2 (1 pen), Carden 2, Davies 2, Guyett 2, Ruffer 2, Bolland 1, Brady 1, Carey 1, Hatswell 1, Kelly 1 (pen), McIntyre 1, Quayle 1, own goal 1.
Play-offs (2): Hatswell 1, McIntyre 1.
LDV Vans Trophy (1): Guyett 1.
Trophy (1): Twiss 1.

DAGENHAM & REDBRIDGE

League Appearances: Broom, 3+4; Bruce, 13+2; Cole, 10+4; Fletcher, 7+1; Goodwin, 12+2; Gothard, 5+2; Hayzelden, 2+3; Heffer, 28+3; Hill, 20+12; Janney, 14+11; Johnson, 7; Keeling, 2; Matthews, 32; Mayo, 2+1; McDougald, 27+9; McGavin, 4+3; McGrath, 21+1; Mustafa, 13+3; Opara, 0+1; Perkins, 10+3; Pitcher, 1; Potts, 19+2; Roberts, 37; Rooney, 9+11; Shipp, 32+9; Smith, 15+3; Stein, 28+3; Terry, 32+2; Vaughan, 0+1; Vickers, 29+4; Watts, 5+1; West, 23+14.

Goals: *League (71):* Stein 16, West 16, McDougald 11 (4 pens), Shipp 7, Terry 5, Hill 3, Janney 2, McGrath 2 (1 pen), Watts 2, Bruce 1, Fletcher 1, Matthews 1, Mayo 1, McGavin 1, Mustafa 1, own goal 1.
Play-offs (5): Stein 3 (1 pen), Mustafa 1, Terry 1.
FA Cup (13): McDougald 5, Shipp 3, Bruce 1, Hill 1, Janney 1, Matthews 1, Terry 1.
LDV Vans Trophy (1): Janney 1.
Trophy (7): Stein 2, Cole 1, Fletcher 1, Matthews 1, Terry 1, West 1.

DONCASTER ROVERS

League Appearances: Albrighton, 22+3; Barnes, 41; Barrick, 28; Beech, 17; Bent, 0+1; Blundell, 0+1; Blunt, 12+1; Burton, 1; Doolan, 7; Erdem Artum, 1+1; Foster, 19+2; Foy, 1; Gill, 21+9; Goodman, 2+4; Green, 16+14; Hudson, 9; Jackson, 16+6; Marples, 29+3; McCarthy, 1; Morgan, 2+1; Morley, 25+5; Muirhead, 3+3; Mustafa, 5; Nelson, 2; Owen, 20+3; Paterson, 20+1; Peyton, 4+2; Price, 2+2; Quailey, 0+2; Ravenhill, 16+10; Ryan, J, 0+1; Ryan, T, 37+1; Sandwith, 1+1; Shields, 1+3; Thompson, 1; Tierney, 15+3; Warrington, 40; Watson, 22+4; Whitman, 3+18.

Goals: *League (73):* Barnes 25 (4 pens), Gill 8, Paterson 7 (1 pen), Morley 5, Green 4, Tierney 4, Watson 4, Blunt 3, Jackson 2, Whitman 2, Albrighton 1, Barrick 1, Blundell 1, Burton 1, Foster 1, Hudson 1, Owen 1, own goals 2.
Play-offs (5): Barnes 1, Green 1, Morley 1, Tierney 1, Whitman 1.
FA Cup (3): Barnes 2 (1 pen), Gill 1.
LDV Vans Trophy (3): Hudson 2, Albrighton 1.
Trophy (1): Green 1.

FARNBOROUGH TOWN

League Appearances: Annon, 27+4; Ayres, 0+1; Baptiste, 26+3; Bunce, 13; Butterworth, 25+2; Carroll, 13+5; Charlery, 30+7; Green, 17+11; Gregory, 20; Griffiths, 1+4; Gwillem, 0+1; Harkness, 6+3; Holloway, 20+5; Laker, 18+1; Lee, 16+7; O'Shea, 3+1; Osborn, 1+2; Patterson, 13+3; Pennock, 41; Piper, C, 31+6; Piper, L, 34+4; Pitcher, 10; Potter, 1+7; Reeks, 5; Rodwell, 18+1; Taggart, 27+9; Vansittart, 10+11; Warner, 21; Watson, 15+1.

Goals: *League (57):* Charlery 12, Baptiste 11, Piper L 10 (1 pen), Vansittart 5, Pitcher 4, Green 3, Carroll 2, Butterworth 1, Harkness 1, Holloway 1, Laker 1, Lee 1, Patterson 1, Piper C 1, Rodwell 1, Taggart 1, Watson 1.
FA Cup (18): Baptiste 7, Carroll 3, Piper L 3, Butterworth 1, Charlery 1, Green 1, Holloway 1, Taggart 1.
Trophy (7): Piper L 3, Baptiste 2, Bunce 1, Vansittart 1.

FOREST GREEN ROVERS

League Appearances: Adams, 1+5; Allen, 6+6; Cleverley, 6+2; Cook, 3+16; Coupe, 18+1; Cowe, 9+8; Foster, 38; Futcher, 2+6; Glassup, 0+1; Grayson, 30+8; Heggs, 4+5; Impey, 3; Jenkins, 36+1; Jones, D, 27; Jones, L, 0+1; Langan, 28+3; McCloughlin, 10+2; Meechan, 27+7; Odejayi, 37+1; Owers, 35+1; Perrin, 40; Pritchard, 0+1; Richardson, 34+1; Russell, L, 14; Russell, M, 20; Shuttlewood, 2; Sykes, 31+2; Tearney, 1+3; Tweddle, 0+4.

Goals: *League (61):* Grayson 15 (4 pens), Odejayi 13, Meechan 12 (1 pen), Sykes 5, Richardson 4, Cowe 3, Jones D 2, Cook 1, Foster 1, Heggs 1, Tweddle 1, own goals 3.
FA Cup (3): Richardson 2, Odejayi 1.
Trophy (10): Grayson 5 (2 pens), Odejayi 2, Owers 2, Foster 1.

GRAVESEND & NORTHFLEET

League Appearances: Abbott, 4; Barnett, 10+2; Barr, 6; Bentley, 27; Berkley, 0+3; Booth, 7+6; Budge, 7+3; Burton, 29+2; Carter, 0+2; Cole, 5; Coyle, 3+1; Duku, 7; Evans, 7+8; Gedling, 0+1; Giles, 11; Grace, 0+3; Hatch, 17+6; Jackson, 41; Kwashi, 18+16; Lee, 23; Lovett, 5; Lye, 5; McKimm, 22+2; Nutter, 3+1; Owen, 15+6; Parker, 2+7; Pennock, 10; Plummer, 0+1; Skinner, 23+1; Sodje, 4+3; Stadhart, 29+5; Strouts, 31+3; Sturgess, 8; Turner, 2; Watts, 13+2; White, 9; Wilkerson, 40; Wilkins, 19+6.

Goals: *League (62):* Stadhart 12 (2 pens), Bentley 7, Hatch 7, Jackson 7, Kwashi 5, Burton 3, Strouts 3, Booth 2 (1 pen), Duku 2, Giles 2, Sodje 2, Wilkins 2, Barnett 1, Budge 1, Cole 1, Evans 1, Lye 1, McKimm 1, own goals 2.
FA Cup (1): Stadhart 1.

HALIFAX TOWN

League Appearances: Asher, 34+1; Bushell, 34; Butler, 37; Clarkson, 38; Elliott, 9+3; Farrell, 13+17; Fitzpatrick, 29+9; Garnett, 29; Gedman, 0+2; Grayston, 23+9; Haigh, 9+2; Hartfield, 2; Herbert, 0+3; Ingledow, 0+1; Kerrigan, 4+5; Killeen, 13; Mallon, 16+2; McAuley, 6+4; Midgley, 35+3; Monington, 16; Morgan, 5; Parke, 18+14; Quailey, 26+8; Quinn, 20+5; Ryan, 0+5; Sandwith, 20; Senior, 9+4; Stoneman, 15; Tolson, 2+1.

Goals: *League (50):* Mallon 8 (1 pen), Fitzpatrick 5, Parke 5, Clarkson 4, Farrell 4, Killeen 4, Midgley 4 (1 pen), Quailey 4, Stoneman 3, Hartfield 2, Monington 2, Garnett 1, Kerrigan 1, Sandwith 1, own goals 2.
FA Cup (1): Quailey 1.
Trophy (7): Killeen 2, Quailey 2, Clarkson 1, Fitzpatrick 1, Midgley 1 (pen).

HEREFORD UNITED

League Appearances: Baker, 42; Clarke, 32+2; Correia, 4+2; Eribenne, 3; Fox, 0+4; Galloway, 9; Grant, 23+3; Guinan, 37+2; Hawley, 5+1; Husbands, 0+5; James, 38+1; Lovett, 8+2; Martin, 0+1; Parry, 37; Pitman, 37+1; Purdey, 12+21; Rose, 41; Sawyers, 8+2; Smith, 22+2; Teesdale, 7+8; Tretton, 35+1; Voice, 0+4; Williams, 35+1; Wright, 27+2.

Goals: *League (64):* Guinan 13, Parry 10, Pitman 6, Smith 5, Williams 5, Clarke 4, Grant 4, Rose 4, Correia 3, Wright 2, Hawley 1, James 1, Lovett 1, Purdey 1, Sawyers 1, own goals 3.
FA Cup (1): Parry 1.
LDV Vans Trophy (3): Eribenne 2, Parry 1.
Trophy (1): Smith 1.

KETTERING TOWN
League Appearances: Asombang, 12+10; Bowling, 32; Boyle-Chong, 7+4; Butcher, 14+4; Clarke, 8+1; Colley, 2+2; Curtis, 2+1; Dancy, 1+5; Diuk, 28+6; Edwards, 0+3; Goodwin, 29+1; Gordon, 8+2; Gourley, 2; Haran, 30+3; Holyoak, 1; Howarth, 24+1; Hughes, 7+1; Inman, 31+5; Itonga, 1+1; Kelly, 7; Matthews, 42; McKenzie, 6+12; Murphy, 19+1; Murray, 26+4; Norman, 33; Parker, 11+3; Pepper, 0+1; Perkins, 3+5; Piercewright, 19+3; Revell, 7; Shutt, 8+17; Small, 7; Solkhon, 12; Tolson, 1; Town, 4+2; Walsh, 7+3; Ward, 1+1; Watkins, 8+3; Williamson, 0+2; Willis, 2.
Goals: *League (37):* Norman 6 (3 pens), Inman 5 (1 pen), Butcher 4, Parker 4, Murphy 3, Asombang 2, Howarth 2, Murray 2 (1 pen), Clarke 1, Goodwin 1, McKenzie 1, Revell 1, Solkhon 1, Town 1, Walsh 1, own goals 2.
Trophy (1): Shutt 1.

LEIGH RMI
League Appearances: Bent, 3; Black, 9; Blakeman, 0+3; Campbell, 11+1; Coburn, 42; Cornelly, 1+2; Courtney, 8+18; Durkin, 41; Fisher, 8+7; Fitzhenry, 34+3; Ford, 12+1; Harrison, 26+4; Heald, 20+10; Heffernan, 1+3; Hill, 3; Kielty, 25+4; Lancaster, 13; Ludden, 5; Maamria, 25; Maden, 32+3; McGill, 0+3; Monk, 37; Pendlebury, 6+1; Prince, 6; Robertson, 4; Salt, 38+2; Scott, 9+2; Spooner, 0+1; Tolson, 5+5; Ward, C, 3+2; Ward, M, 0+1; Whitaker, 18+1; Whitehead, 2+7; Williams, 14+9; Wilson, 1+2.
Goals: *League (44):* Maamria 12 (1 pen), Monk 6, Heald 4 (1 pen), Kielty 4, Salt 3, Scott 3, Courtney 2, Maden 2, Whitaker 2, Black 1, Harrison 1, Lancaster 1, Tolson 1, Ward C 1, own goal 1.
FA Cup (1): Maamria 1.
LDV Vans Trophy (5): Kielty 3, Salt 1, own goal 1.
Trophy (1): Robertson 1.

MARGATE
League Appearances: Beard, 10+1; Braithwaite, 28+5; Clarke, 19+3; Collins, 23+5; Edwards, 35+1; Griffiths, 1+2; Keister, 29+5; Lamb, 28+3; Leberl, 32+2; MacDonald, 5; McFlynn, 18+11; Mitten, 20; Munday, 2+5; O'Connell, 7+3; Oates, 39; Porter, 29+4; Pullman, 0+3; Saunders, 38+1; Shearer, 17+8; Sigere, 13+8; Smith, 22; Sodje, 40; Watts, 7; Webster, 0+1.
Goals: *League (60):* Braithwaite 10 (1 pen), Collins 7, Sodje 6, Saunders 5, Sigere 5, Beard 4, Keister 4 (1 pen), Watts 4 (1 pen), McFlynn 3, Oates 3, Lamb 1, Leberl 1, MacDonald 1, Munday 1, Porter 1, Shearer 1, own goals 3.
FA Cup (4): Keister 3 (1 pen), Collins 1.
Trophy (4): Beard 1, Braithwaite 1 (pen), Leberl 1, Sigere 1.

MORECAMBE
League Appearances: Bentley, 23; Black, 13+16; Carlton, 7+19; Colkin, 24+1; Collins, 6; Curtis, 30+7; Drummond, 42; Elam, 37+3; Gouck, 4+10; Hallam, 0+1; Hill, 19+1; Knowles, 6+1; Mawson, 42; McKearney, 37+1; Morgan, 2+4; Murphy, 8+11; Perkins, 17+4; Rigoglioso, 32+4; Rogan, 0+10; Stringfellow, 30+5; Swan, 39+2; Talbot, 6+11; Taylor, 0+1; Thompson, 31+4; Ubershar, 7+6.
Goals: *League (86):* Curtis 18 (1 pen), Elam 13, Drummond 11 (3 pens), Rigoglioso 10, Carlton 7, Black 5 (1 pen), Thompson 5, Bentley 3, Talbot 3, Stringfellow 2, Gouck 1, McKearney 1, Murphy 1, Swan 1, own goals 5.
Play-offs (3): Rigoglioso 1, own goals 2.
FA Cup (8): Bentley 2, Rogan 2, Drummond 1, Elam 1, Rigolioso 1, Thompson 1.
Trophy (2): Black 1, Elam 1.

NORTHWICH VICTORIA
League Appearances: Allan, 26+3; Blundell, 34; Cane, 10+2; Connett, 4; Davis, 9; Devlin, 41; Garvey, 25+13; Gibson, 12; Griggs, 5+10; Ingram, 35; Jarrett, 0+1; Kelly, 7; Matthews, 3+3; McGuire, 3+1; McNiven, 17+7; Norris, 28+9; Owen, 20+1; Parry, 19; Quinn, 8+12; Rioch, 34; Royle, 35; Seddon, 1; Sedgemore, 33+3; Street, 12+1; Taylor, 15+16; Tether, 3+4; Turner, 0+2; Walsh, 13+1; Whitehead, 3+2; Woodward, 7+1.
Goals: *League (66):* Blundell 19 (3 pens), Allan 10, Devlin 6, McNiven 6 (1 pen), Street 6, Garvey 4, Norris 4, Owen 2, Quinn 2 (1 pen), Rioch 1, Taylor 1, Tether 1, Turner 1, own goals 3.
Trophy (7): Blundell 2, Quinn 2, Norris 1, Woodward 1, own goal 1.

NUNEATON BOROUGH
League Appearances: Alford, 7+2; Angus, 32; Barrick, 11; Brodie, 11; Brown, 10; Clarkson, 10+2; Clifford, 4; Cooper, 11+4; Davis, 4; Doyle, 7+3; Ducros, 10; Dyson, 10; Harris, 1+9; Hodgson, 1+2; Holmes, 0+1; Howey, 7; Hunter, 3; Jones, 13+2; Lavery, 24+4; Lenton, 11+5; Love, 35+3; MacKenzie, 37; Mansell, 5; McGregor, 13+12; Murphy, 10; Paschalis, 3; Peake, 14+1; Peyton, 6+5; Quayle, 29; Ricketts, 11; Sall, 3; Squires, 19; Thackeray, 27+2; Turner, 15+10; Walling, 1; Weatherstone, 9; Whittaker, 2+2; Williams, B, 27+2; Williams, D, 1+19; Woodley, 8+1.
Goals: *League (51):* Quayle 14, Brodie 4, Jones 4, McGregor 3, Murphy 3 (1 pen), Williams B 3, Woodley 3, Alford 2 (1 pen), Brown 2, Mansell 2, Angus 1, Ducros 1, Harris 1, Lavery 1, Paschalis 1, Ricketts 1, Squires 1, Thackeray 1, Turner 1, Walling 1, own goal 1.
FA Cup (4): Love 1, McGregor 1, Quayle 1, own goal 1.

SCARBOROUGH
League Appearances: Baker, 3+1; Blunt, 7+8; Bradshaw, 2; Brassart, 27+4; Campbell, 12+11; Cohen, 7+1; Connell, 0+5; Crawford, 0+1; Cryan, 2; Dempsey, 11+2; Dryden, 20+2; Fatokun, 16+9; Gilroy, 7; Hall, 1; Henry, 13+1; Holdsworth, 16; Hotte, 29+4; Jordan, 8+4; Kerr, 9; Mallon, 6+1; Ormerod, 24+6; Patterson, 3+1; Pounder, 30+10; Price, 8; Raw, 3+1; Rennison, 12; Ridler, 7; Rose, 15+8; Scott, 27+1; Shepherd, 35+1; Sillah, 14+1; Stoker, 35+4; Taylor, 11+1; Walker, 4+1; Woods, 38.
Goals: *League (63):* Pounder 9, Scott 9, Fatokun 8, Shepherd 6 (5 pens), Campbell 4, Sillah 4, Taylor 4, Blunt 2, Cohen 2, Ormerod 2, Rose 2, Brassart 1, Dryden 1, Gilroy 1 (pen), Henry 1, Holdsworth 1, Mallon 1, Raw 1, own goals 4.
FA Cup (3): Scott 2, Jordan 1.
LDV Vans Trophy (1): Scott 1.
Trophy (4): Pounder 1, Raw 1, Sillah 1, own goal 1.

SOUTHPORT
League Appearances: Ashcroft, 11; Bauress, 1+4; Carden, 0+1; Charnock, 2+1; Clark, 32+3; Connolly, 1+3; Davis, 8; Dickinson, 31; Edwards, 4+1; Gibson, 24+4; Hogan, 0+1; Hornby, 2; Howell, 34+6; Jones, B, 40; Jones, S, 33+5; Lamb, 1+1; Lane, 36; Lloyd-Williams, 15+3; McGuire, 12+1; Moore, 16+1; Mulvaney, 8+4; Nolan, 8+1; O'Donnell, 0+1; Pell, 7+4; Pickford, 30+1; Prince, 0+1; Scott, 16+12; Soley, 18+2; Spearitt, 0+1; Sullivan, 2+11; Thomson, 25+5; Welsby, 11; Wheatcroft, 6+2; Whitehall, 5+12; Winstanley, 23.
Goals: *League (54):* Thomson 12 (2 pens), Soley 7 (1 pen), Mulvaney 4, Pickford 4, Whitehall 4, Howell 3, Lloyd-Williams 3, Pell 3, Ashcroft 2, Jones S 2, Bauress 1, Connolly 1, Edwards 1, Gibson 1, Lane 1, Nolan 1, Sullivan 1, Wheatcroft 1, Winstanley 1, own goal 1.
FA Cup (8): Pickford 2, Whitehall 2, Lane 1, Lloyd-Williams 1, Thomson 1, Winstanley 1.
Trophy (6): Thomson 2, Hazell 1, Jones B 1, Pickford 1, Scott 1.

STEVENAGE BOROUGH
League Appearances: Battersby, 4+2; Bell, 2+2; Blackwood, 17+1; Boyd, 1; Bunce, 11; Campbell, D, 0+2; Campbell, J, 25; Carroll, 15; Clarke, 3+1; Cook, 7+6; Dreyer, 2; Elding, 12+2; Fisher, 15; Flack, 0+1; Fraser, 12+5; Furness, 0+1; Goodliffe, 31+3; Gray, 0+2; Gregory, 4; Holloway, 6+3; Houghton, 3+3; Howell, 3+4; Jackson, 16+3; Laker, 14; Maamria, 8+3; MacDonald, C, 14+4; MacDonald, G, 4+3; McMahon, 21+2; Midson, 0+6; Mustoe, 0+2; Opara, 0+1; Pacquette, 6+1; Perez, 4+1; Richards, 12+7; Riddle, 6+1; Scott, 4+1; Sigere, 7+9; Smith, 4+4; Stirling, 9+1; Tomlinson, 2+8; Travis, 37+3; Trott, 19; Warner, 10+1; Watson, 15; Westhead, 37; Williams, 15; Wills, 1; Wilson, 1+2; Wormull, 23+7.
Goals: *League (61):* Elding 7, Richards 6 (1 pen), Carroll 5, Jackson 5, Maamria 5, Goodliffe 4 (2 pens), Wormull 4, Battersby 3 (1 pen), MacDonald C 3, Sigere 3, Blackwood 2, McMahon 2, Pacquette 2, Williams 2, Bunce 1, Campbell J 1, Cook 1, Fraser 1, Houghton 1 (pen), Laker 1, Midson 1, Trott 1.
FA Cup (4): Howell 2, Jackson 1, Trott 1.
LDV Vans Trophy (5): Pacquette 2, Jackson 1, Scott 1, own goal 1.
Trophy (2): Campbell J 1, own goal 1.

TELFORD UNITED
League Appearances: Barlow, 31; Bloomer, 14; Brown, D, 34+2; Brown, G, 37; Cameron, 6; Davies, 29+5; Edwards, 39; Fitzpatrick, 39; Foran, 39; Hanmer, 38+3; Jobling, 9+7; Jones, 0+2; Kerrigan, 4; King, 15+14; Lormor, 3+2; Moore, 34+4; Morley, 5; Palmer, 32+2; Pettinger, 3; Sayer, 3+4; Scott, 2+1; Smith, 26+13; Spink, 3; Wooliscroft, 17+1.
Goals: *League (54):* Brown D 16 (1 pen), Moore 14, Smith 6, Foran 5, Fitzpatrick 3, Barlow 2, King 2, Palmer 2, Davies 1, Hanmer 1, Jobling 1, Sayer 1.
Trophy (4): Barlow 1, Brown D 1, Foran 1, Moore 1.

WOKING

League Appearances: Abbey, 16+10; Allman, 15+4; Austin, 17; Banger, 11+9; Bayes, 5; Boardman, 38+1; Brady, 12; Burch, 6; Burnett, 3; Campbell, 13; Canham, 10; Clark, 2+4; Coates, 14+2; Cockerill, 1; Collins, 18+1; Da Costa, 0+2; Davies, 2; Evers, 5+1; Farrelly, 11+1; Foyewa, 3+4; Hamilton, 18+1; Jalal, 16; Kember, 25+2; Moore, 12+1; Nade, 24; Patmore, 31+7; Payne, 2+11; Piper, 13+5; Reeks, 9+3; Rodger, 1; Sandford, 12; Sharpling, 23+8; Simpemba, 14; Smith, N, 19+1; Smith, S, 11+6; Steele, S, 5+6; Townsend, 16; Tucker, 2; White, 2; Williams, 5+6.

Goals: *League (52):* Patmore 14 (4 pens), Abbey 7 (1 pen), Sharpling 5, Banger 4, Foyewa 3, Nade 3, Austin 2 (2 pens), Canham 2, Moore 2, Payne 2, Boardman 1, Brady 1, Coates 1, Collins 1, Kember 1, Townsend 1, Williams 1, own goal 1.
FA Cup (2): Abbey 1, Moore 1.
Trophy (3): Patmore 2, Abbey 1.

YEOVIL TOWN

League Appearances: Aggrey, 2+6; Alford, 3+11; Blunt, 0+1; Collis, 1; Crittenden, 30+5; Demba, 11+6; Elkholti, 15+12; Forinton, 11+3; Gall, 11+2; Giles, 0+7; Grant, 6+7; Jackson, 23; Johnson, 41; Lindegaard, 13+14; Lockwood, 37+4; McIndoe, 41; Mustoe, 2+1; O'Brien, 20+13; Pluck, 32+5; Reed, 0+1; Sheffield, 7+1; Skiverton, 34+3; Stansfield, 1; Tonkin, 7; Way, 40; Weale, 34; White, 2; Williams, 38.

Goals: *League (100):* Jackson 19, Gall 13, McIndoe 12 (3 pens), Crittenden 9 (4 pens), Demba 6, Lindegaard 6, Skiverton 6, Williams 6, Forinton 4, Johnson 4, Elkholti 3, Lockwood 3, Alford 2, Pluck 2, Giles 1, Grant 1, Way 1, own goals 2.
FA Cup (4): Demba 2, Lockwood 1, McIndoe 1.
LDV Vans Trophy (2): Alford 1, Lockwood 1.
Trophy (6): Lockwood 2, Gall 1, Jackson 1, Pluck 1, Skiverton 1.

NATIONWIDE CONFERENCE: MEMBERS CLUBS SEASON 2003–2004

ACCRINGTON STANLEY

Colours: Red shirts, white shorts, red stockings.
Ground: The Crown Ground, Livingstone Road, Accrington, Lancashire.
Tel: 01254 397869.
Year Formed: 1968 (formerly 1893).
Record Gate: 2,270 (1992 v Gateshead FA Cup First Round) (in Football League 17,634).
Nickname: Stanley.
Manager: John Coleman.
Secretary: Philip Terry.

ALDERSHOT TOWN

Colours: Red shirts with blue trim, red shorts, red stockings with blue trim.
Ground: Recreation Ground, High Street, Aldershot, Hampshire GU11 1TW.
Tel: (01252) 320211.
Year Formed: 1992 (formerly 1926).
Record Gate: 7,500 (2000 v Brighton & Hove Albion FA Cup First Round) (in Football League 19,138).
Nickname: Shots.
Manager: Terry Brown.
Secretary: Andy Morgan.

BARNET

Colours: Amber shirts with black trim, amber shorts, amber stockings.
Ground: Underhill Stadium, Barnet Lane, Barnet, Hertfordshire EN5 2BE.
Tel: (0208) 4416932.
Year Formed: 1888.
Record Gate: 11,026 (1952 v Wycombe Wanderers FA Amateur Cup Fourth Round).
Nickname: The Bees.
Manager: Martin Allen.
Secretary: Andrew Adie.

BURTON ALBION

Colours: All yellow with black trim.
Ground: Eton Park, Princess Way, Burton-on-Trent, DE14 2RU.
Tel: (01283) 565938.
Year Formed: 1950.
Record Gate: 5,860 (1964 v Weymouth Southern League Cup Final).
Nickname: Brewers.
Manager: Nigel Clough.
Secretary: Tony Kirkland.

CHESTER CITY

Colours: Blue and white striped shirts, blue shorts, white stockings.
Ground: Deva Stadium, Bumpers Lane, Chester CH1 4LT.
Tel: (01244) 371809.
Year Formed: 1884.
Record Gate: 5,538 (1994 v Preston North End Football League Division 3) (formerly at Sealand Road, 20,500 1952 v Chelsea FA Cup First Round).
Nickname: The Blues.
Manager: Mark Wright.
Secretary: Michael Beech.

DAGENHAM & REDBRIDGE

Colours: Red shirts, white shorts, red stockings.
Ground: Victoria Road, Dagenham, Essex RM10 7XL.
Tel: (0208) 5927194.
Year Formed: 1992.
Record Gate: 5,500 (1992 v Leyton Orient FA Cup First Round).
Nickname: Daggers.
Manager: Garry Hill.
Secretary: Derek Almond.

FARNBOROUGH TOWN

Colours: All red and white.
Ground: Cherrywood Road, Farnborough, Hampshire GU14 8UD.
Tel: (01252) 541469.
Year Formed: 1967.
Record Gate: 3,581 (1995 v Brentford FA Cup First Round).
Nickname: The Boro.
Manager: Tommy Taylor.
Secretary: Vince Williams.

FOREST GREEN ROVERS

Colours: Black and white striped shirts, black shorts, red stockings.
Ground: The Lawn, Nympsfield Road, Forest Green, Nailsworth GL6 0ET.
Tel: (01453) 834860.
Year Formed: 1890.
Record Gate: 3,002 (1999 v St Albans City FA Umbro Trophy).
Nickname: Rovers.
Manager: Colin Addison.
Secretary: David Honeybill.

GRAVESEND & NORTHFLEET

Colours: Red shirts, white shorts, red stockings.
Ground: Stonebridge Road, Northfleet, Kent DA11 9BA.
Tel: (01474) 533796.
Year Formed: 1946.
Record Gate: 12,036 (1963 v Sunderland FA Cup Fourth Round).
Nickname: The Fleet.
Manager: Andy Ford.
Secretary: Roly Edwards.

HALIFAX TOWN

Colours: All blue.
Ground: The Shay Stadium, Shay Syke, Halifax, West Yorkshire HX1 2YS.
Tel: (01422) 341222.
Year Formed: 1911.
Record Gate: 36,885 (1953 v Tottenham Hotspur FA Cup Fifth Round).
Nickname: The Shaymen.
Manager: Chris Wilder
Secretary: Jenna Helliwell.

HEREFORD UNITED

Colours: White and black shirts, black shorts, white stockings.
Ground: Edgar Street, Hereford, Herefordshire HR4 9JU.
Tel: (01432) 276666.
Year Formed: 1924.
Record Gate: 18,114 (1958 v Sheffield Wednesday FA Cup Third Round).
Nickname: The Bulls.
Manager: Graham Turner.
Secretary: Joan Fennessy.

LEIGH RMI
Colours: Red and white shirts, black shorts, white stockings.
Ground: Hilton Park, Kirkhall Lane, Leigh, Lancashire WN7 1RN.
Tel: (01942) 743743.
Year Formed: 1896.
Record Gate: 7,125 (1999 v Fulham FA Cup Third Round) (at Horwich 8,500 1954 v Wigan Athletic).
Nickname: Railwaymen.
Manager: Mark Patterson.
Secretary: Alan Robinson.

MARGATE
Colours: Royal blue shirts, royal blue shorts, white stockings.
Ground: Hartsdown Park, Hartsdown Road, Margate, Kent CT9 5OZ.
Tel: (01843) 221769.
Year Formed: 1896.
Record Gate: 14,500 (1973 v Tottenham Hotspur FA Cup Third Round).
Nickname: The Gate.
Manager: Chris Kinnear.
Secretary: Kenneth Tomlinson.

MORECAMBE
Colours: Red shirts, white shorts, black stockings.
Ground: Christie Park, Lancaster Road, Morecambe, Lancashire LA4 5TJ.
Tel: (01524) 411797.
Year Formed: 1920.
Record Gate: 9,326 (1962 v Weymouth FA Cup Third Round).
Nickname: The Shrimps.
Manager: Jim Harvey.
Secretary: Neil Marsdin.

NORTHWICH VICTORIA
Colours: Green shirts with white trim, white shorts, black stockings.
Ground: Witton Albion FC, Wincham Park, Chapel Street, Northwich, Cheshire.
Tel: (01606) 43008.
Year Formed: 1874.
Record Gate: 12,000 (1977 v Watford FA Cup Fourth Round).
Nickname: The Vics.
Manager: Steve Davis.
Secretary: Derek Nuttall.

SCARBOROUGH
Colours: All red.
Ground: McCain Stadium, Seamer Road, Scarborough, Yorkshire YO12 4HF.
Tel: (01723) 375094.
Year Formed: 1879.
Record Gate: 11,130 (1987 v Luton Town FA Cup Third Round).
Nickname: The Boro.
Manager: Russell Slade.
Secretary: Kevin Philliskirk.

STEVENAGE BOROUGH
Colours: Red and white shirts, black shorts, white stockings.
Ground: Broadhall Way Stadium, Broadhall Way, Stevenage, Hertfordshire SG2 8RH.
Tel: (01438) 223223.
Year Formed: 1976.
Record Gate: 6,489 (1997 v Kidderminster Harriers Conference).
Nickname: The Boro.
Manager: Graham Westley.
Secretary: Roger Austin.

TAMWORTH
Colours: Red shirts with white sleeves, black shorts, red stockings.
Ground: The Lamb Ground, Kettlebrook, Tamworth, Staffordshire B77 1AA.
Tel: (01827) 65798.
Year Formed: 1933.
Record Gate: 4,920 (1948 v Atherstone Town Birmingham Combination).
Nickname: Lambs.
Manager: Darron Gee.
Secretary: Russell Moore.

TELFORD UNITED
Colours; Red shirts, blue shorts, red stockings.
Ground: New Bucks Head Stadium, The Bucks Way, Telford, Shropshire TF1 2NT.
Tel: (01952) 640064.
Year Formed: 1876.
Record Gate: 13,000 (1935 v Shrewsbury Town Birmingham League).
Nickname: The Bucks.
Manager: Mick Jones.
Secretary: Mike Ferriday.

WOKING
Colours: Red and white shirts, black shorts, red stockings.
Ground: Kingfield Sports Ground, Kingfield, Woking, Surrey GU22 9AA.
Tel: (01483) 772470.
Year Formed: 1889.
Record Gate: 6,084 (1997 v Coventry City, FA Cup Third Round).
Nickname: The Cards.
Manager: Glenn Cockerill.
Secretary: Phil Ledger.

N.B. For **EXCETER CITY** *and* **SHREWSBURY TOWN** *see under Football League.*

NATIONWIDE CONFERENCE PREVIOUS WINNERS

Year	*Winners*
ALLIANCE PREMIER	
1980	Altrincham
1981	Altrincham
1982	Runcorn
1983	Enfield
1984	Maidstone United
GOLA LEAGUE	
1985	Wealdstone
1986	Enfield
GM VAUXHALL CONFERENCE	
1987	Scarborough
1988	Lincoln City
1989	Maidstone United
1990	Darlington
1991	Barnet
VAUXHALL CONFERENCE	
1992	Colchester United
1993	Wycombe Wanderers
1994	Kidderminster Harriers
1995	Macclesfield Town
1996	Stevenage Borough
1997	Macclesfield Town
1998	Halifax Town
FOOTBALL CONFERENCE	
1999	Cheltenham Town
NATIONWIDE CONFERENCE	
2000	Kidderminster Harriers
2001	Rushden & Diamonds
2002	Boston United

SHIELD

Year	*Winners*
1981	Northwich Victoria
1982	Altrincham
1983	Runcorn
1984	Enfield
1985	Maidstone United
1986	Runcorn
1987	Stafford Rangers
1988	Kidderminster Harriers
1989	Lincoln City
1990	Maidstone United
1991	Darlington
1992	Wycombe Wanderers
1993	Wycombe Wanderers
1994	Wycombe Wanderers
1995	Woking
1996	Macclesfield Town
1997	Macclesfield Town
1998	Macclesfield Town
1999	Halifax Town
2000	Kingstonian
2001	Kingstonian

REVIEW OF THE SCOTTISH SEASON 2002–03

May 10th proved to be a big day in the League. There were many outstanding questions to be answered:

In the First Division, the champions were Falkirk, well ahead of the rest, and only wondering if they could be admitted to the Premier League. They had failed once before, but only remained in this division for this season as Airdrieonians had departed. Inverness Caley Thistle had mounted a mid-term challenge, but it had foundered; St Johnstone never really looked like achieving their aim of bouncing back, but it was Clyde who finished strongly, and swept into second place. At the other end the season finished in much doubt: Arbroath were down for sure, but Alloa and Ross County fought to avoid joining them. The former, with the stalwart Terry Christie on the bridge, had moved steadily towards safety, whilst Ross County had not been firing on all cylinders for a while. The teams were on the same points for the last game, but the northerners had a far superior goal difference. At half time Alloa were demolishing St Mirren, whilst Ross County had no score against Ayr. Soon after half time, Ross County scored twice, and then twice more after a single response. That settled that issue.

The Second Division had doubts at top and bottom. In the lead were Raith. They had an unassailable lead by the end of March, but managed only one win and two draws in their last eight games. However, their lead did prove sufficient. Just. Berwick had been in second place for a while, but they had to give way to Brechin, whilst the new Airdrie United hovered dangerously and for the last match, they could take second if they won and Brechin lost. Both had games against opposition seriously interested in relegation. Airdrie came back to win after being a goal down at Stranraer, and thus doomed that club; after ninety minutes, things looked good for Airdrie. A last ditch equaliser from Brechin against Hamilton proved enough to elevate the Angus side, and the point was enough to ensure safety to their opposition. So it was Stranraer who joined Cowdenbeath in the drop. Dumbarton and Stenhousemuir – both of them candidates for relegation at the start of the day – did enough to survive.

If those two divisions did not provide sufficient excitement, they were as nothing compared with the Third Division. As the last matches started, any two of the top four clubs could go up. Two of these, Morton and Peterhead, were in head on collision, and the winner would be up. East Fife, for much of the season leaders in the race, had to win against Queen's Park, so often their bogey team. Albion Rovers had to win, and hope for Fife to lose. Albion Rovers were playing East Stirling, who had had a poor season, and they made no mistake. They then had an anxious time waiting for the results from the other two games, both of which had started late. Morton, at home in front of an eight-and-a-half thousand crowd, scored shortly after half time, and that was the only score. Fife and Queen's Park were level at no score as the minutes ticked away. Right on the stroke of time, the goal came to Fife, and the Rovers hopes were dashed.

Meantime, in the Premier League, things were by no means all over. With three games to go, Celtic had taken a minimal lead against Rangers – same points, and a one goal lead on goal difference! At the other end, Dundee United and Motherwell tried to avoid the last place, which might well lead to relegation and perhaps oblivion. Celtic managed a one goal win against Hearts. Dundee United won, with a priceless late goal, whilst Motherwell lost. What could Rangers do on the following day? Well enough, was the answer; and they took over again at the top – by an odd goal. It came to the last day with the two still locked, and a play-off for the title a distinct possibility. Such was the interest that the BBC took an unprecedented decision, and both the Rangers and Celtic matches were screened simultaneously, the one on BBC1, the other on BBC2 – a decision which must have caused tremors on this side of the Border with important golf due to be shown. Both teams won, but, although Celtic were in the catbird seat for a while, Rangers swept into a goalstorm; and that was that. Hard though their opponents tried, there was no stemming the flood.

The relegation position in the Premier League went to Motherwell after Dundee United had drawn clear with two wins in the last three games; even a very convincing last-game win at Fir Park was not enough.

Would Falkirk join the Premier League? The rules of this league were clear, but several meetings of the interested parties tried to see if there were a loophole for Falkirk's ground difficulties. A final meeting of the representatives of all the clubs in the league at last took the decision, and Motherwell were reprieved and remain in the top flight.

The national team moved rapidly from one disappointment to another; rays of light occasionally penetrated the dismal gloom. Gradually things started to improve, and it was good to see teams in which many home-based Scots were selected. It began to look as if we might qualify for the European finals, and a draw at Hampden against Germany gave the fans a chance to cheer. It was distinctly encouraging. Above all, the home team were seen to be giving their all, and there was in particular a majestic performance from Paul Lambert. We can look forward hopefully to the remaining games in the autumn.

The Scots Ladies were doing well. It is not often that a Scots team takes eight goals from foreign opposition. Good luck to them.

The Tennent's Scottish Cup and the CIS Insurance League Cup were both won by Rangers, not without some of the frequent surprises. Celtic, having suffered in the past in the north, dismissed Caley Thistle in the League Cup. That, we thought, is that. Well, that was not that: in the Scottish Cup the northerners again won, and continued their run into the semi-finals – for the first time. Meantime Falkirk had caught Hearts straight after the winter break, and won most convincingly. Subsequently they lost to Dundee only after a replay, whilst Dunfermline also earned a replay against Rangers. Stranraer reached the quarter finals, but they had had trouble defeating non-league Whitehill Welfare in Round 1. Deveronvale very nearly held Morton in a high scoring match, and Threave Rovers defeated league opposition to reach the second round. It was much as usual. However, Rangers won in the end against a Dundee team which held out manfully, and with a little luck could have caused a shock.

The Bell's League Challenge Cup added some interest to the early season, and the final was contested by Brechin City and Queen of the South, with the Doonhamers taking the trophy.

The Old Firm, with their legions of fanatical supporters, are rarely challenged. We can see the extent of the support, and perhaps understand how the two teams dominate the scene. It is usual for the home crowd at Parkhead or Ibrox each week to exceed the total of crowds at all the other games.

If Rangers collared all the silverware this season in the home market, it would perhaps appear that Celtic were left out in the cold. How near they were in the Premier League has already been seen, and they were finalists in the CIS Cup. However, they made magnificent progress in Europe, and brought back many old memories. Perhaps a shade unlucky to be dismissed in the first league stage of the Champions Cup, they set to in the UEFA Cup, and a series of fine wins (in which the opposition always announced that *they* had been the better team – even after losing!) took them to a final in Seville, and so nearly a success there. It had been a campaign which thrilled the fans at home. After many years of disappointment it was so good to see a Scottish team getting so far. Celtic may not have won anything tangible, but they certainly won respect.

Now we have that short spell between the end of one season and the beginning of the next. It is a time for meditation. Soon we are thrown into the new maelstrom, and are carried along – what will next season bring us?

ALAN ELLIOTT

ABERDEEN

Premier League

Year Formed: 1903. *Ground & Address:* Pittodrie Stadium, Pittodrie St, Aberdeen AB24 5QH. *Telephone:* 01224 650400. *Fax:* 01224 644173.
Ground Capacity: all seated: 21,487. *Size of Pitch:* 110yd × 72yd.
Chairman: Stewart Milne. *Chief Executive:* Keith Wyness. *Secretary:* Duncan Fraser. *Operations Manager:* John Morgan.
Manager: Steve Paterson. *Assistant Manager:* Duncan Shearer. *Coach:* Oshor Williams. *Physios:* David Wylie, John Sharp.
Managers since 1975: Ally MacLeod, Billy McNeill, Alex Ferguson, Ian Porterfield, Alex Smith and Jocky Scott, Willie Miller, Roy Aitken, Alex Miller, Paul Hegarty, Ebbe Skovdahl. *Club Nicknames(s):* The Dons. *Previous Grounds:* None.
Record Attendance: 45,061 v Hearts, Scottish Cup 4th rd; 13 Mar, 1954.
Record Transfer Fee received: £1.75 million for Eoin Jess to Coventry City (February 1996).
Record Transfer Fee paid: £1m+ for Paul Bernard from Oldham Athletic (September 1995).
Record Victory: 13-0 v Peterhead, Scottish Cup; 9 Feb, 1923.
Record Defeat: 0-8 v Celtic, Division 1; 30 Jan, 1965.
Most Capped Players: Alex McLeish, 77, Scotland.
Most League Appearances: 556: Willie Miller, 1973-90.
Most League Goals in Season (Individual): 38: Benny Yorston, Division I; 1929-30.
Most Goals Overall (Individual): 199: Joe Harper.

ABERDEEN 2002–03 LEAGUE RECORD

Match No.	*Date*	*Venue*	*Opponents*	*Result*		*H/T Score*	*Lg. Pos.*	*Goalscorers*	*Attendance*
1	Aug 3	A	Hibernian	W	2-1	0-1	—	Mackie 64, Clark 90	13,340
2	10	H	Celtic	L	0-4	0-2	7		17,314
3	18	H	Hearts	D	1-1	0-0	8	D'Jaffo 72	12,825
4	25	A	Rangers	L	0-2	0-1	8		49,219
5	Sept 1	H	Partick Th	L	0-1	0-1	10		12,591
6	11	H	Dundee U	L	1-2	1-2	—	Mackie 3	10,724
7	14	A	Kilmarnock	D	2-2	0-0	10	D'Jaffo 63, Young Darren 81	6538
8	22	A	Livingston	W	2-1	1-0	8	Anderson 1, McNaughton 73	5852
9	28	H	Dunfermline Ath	W	3-1	1-1	6	Billio 44, D'Jaffo 53, Young Derek 60	11,678
10	Oct 5	A	Motherwell	W	2-1	0-1	5	Young Derek 46, Deloumeaux 78	6014
11	19	H	Dundee	D	0-0	0-0	6		14,003
12	27	H	Hibernian	L	0-1	0-0	7		12,321
13	Nov 3	A	Celtic	L	0-7	0-3	7		57,797
14	9	A	Hearts	D	0-0	0-0	7		11,920
15	16	H	Rangers	D	2-2	0-1	8	Mike 56, Mackie 74	14,915
16	23	A	Partick Th	L	1-2	0-1	8	Mike 84	6182
17	30	A	Dundee U	D	1-1	1-1	9	McGuire (pen) 27	8261
18	Dec 3	H	Kilmarnock	L	0-1	0-0	—		8816
19	7	H	Motherwell	D	1-1	1-0	9	Young Derek 29	9569
20	15	A	Dunfermline Ath	L	0-3	0-1	9		4835
21	21	H	Livingston	D	0-0	0-0	9		11,253
22	26	A	Dundee	W	2-1	0-0	—	McGuire 50, Smith (og) 63	8574
23	29	A	Hibernian	L	0-2	0-0	10		11,604
24	Jan 2	H	Celtic	D	1-1	0-1	9	Anderson 50	16,331
25	28	H	Hearts	L	0-1	0-0	—		9322
26	Feb 1	A	Rangers	L	1-2	0-1	10	Tosh 74	49,667
27	8	H	Partick Th	L	0-1	0-1	10		11,332
28	16	H	Dundee U	W	3-0	1-0	10	Sheerin 2 37, 70, McGuire 73	9146
29	Mar 1	A	Kilmarnock	L	0-2	0-0	9		5769
30	8	A	Motherwell	W	1-0	1-0	8	Sheerin 6	5636
31	15	H	Dundee	D	3-3	0-2	9	Sheerin 2 56, 64, McGuire 79	12,119
32	Apr 5	A	Livingston	W	2-1	2-1	8	Young Derek 28, Sheerin 30	4994
33	12	H	Dunfermline Ath	W	1-0	1-0	8	Sheerin 10	10,030
34	26	H	Livingston	W	1-0	1-0	8	Hinds 24	8912
35	May 3	A	Hibernian	L	1-3	0-1	8	Tiernan 89	7904
36	10	H	Partick Th	W	2-1	0-1	8	Hinds 46, McGuire 58	9960
37	17	A	Motherwell	W	3-2	3-1	8	Hinds 19, Deloumeaux 27, Sheerin 33	4731
38	24	A	Dundee U	W	2-0	0-0	8	Mackie 51, Tosh 55	8516

Final League Position: 8

Honours
League Champions: Division I 1954-55. Premier Division 1979-80, 1983-84, 1984-85; *Runners-up:* Division I 1910-11, 1936-37, 1955-56, 1970-71, 1971-72. Premier Division 1977-78, 1980-81, 1981-82, 1988-89, 1989-90, 1990-91, 1992-93, 1993-94.
Scottish Cup Winners: 1947, 1970, 1982, 1983, 1984, 1986, 1990; *Runners-up:* 1937, 1953, 1954, 1959, 1967, 1978, 1993, 2000.
League Cup Winners: 1955-56, 1976-77, 1985-86, 1989-90, (Coca Cola cup) 1995-96; *Runners-up:* 1946-47, 1978-79, 1979-80, 1987-88, 1988-89, 1992-93, 1999-2000.
Drybrough Cup Winners: 1971, 1980.

European: *European Cup:* 12 matches (1980-81, 1984-85, 1985-86); *Cup Winners' Cup:* 39 matches (1967-68, 1970-71, 1978-79, 1982-83 winners, 1983-84 semi-finals, 1986-87, 1990-91, 1993-94); *UEFA Cup:* 48 matches (*Fairs Cup:* 1968-69. *UEFA Cup:* 1971-72, 1972-73, 1973-74, 1977-78, 1979-80, 1981-82, 1987-88, 1988-89, 1989-90, 1991-92, 1994-95, 1996-97, 2000-01, 2002-03).

Club colours: Shirt, Shorts, Stockings: Red with white trim.

Goalscorers: *League* (41): Sheerin 8, McGuire 5 (1 pen), Mackie 4, Derek Young 4, D'Jaffo 3, Hinds 3, Anderson 2, Deloumeaux 2, Mike 2, Tosh 2, Billio 1, Clark 1, McNaughton 1, Tiernan 1, Darren Young 1, own goal 1
Scottish Cup (4): D'Jaffo 2, Anderson 1, Tosh 1
CIS Cup (3): Deloumeaux 1, Michie 1, Mike 1

Kjaer P 23	McGuire P 36	McNaughton K 18 + 4	Anderson R 33	McAllister J 27 + 2	Young Darren 23 + 1	Bisconti R 11	Deloumeaux E 32	Thornley B 2 + 4	Young Derek 25 + 4	Mackie D 22 + 7	Mike L 13 + 12	Clark C 20 + 5	Tiernan F 15 + 6	D'Jaffo L 16 + 2	Fabiano N 8 + 4	Michie S 5 + 16	O'Donoghue R 1 + 4	Billio P 5 + 5	Preece D 15	Rutkiewcz K 18 + 2	Muirhead S — + 2	Payne S 3 + 5	Tosh S 14	Sheerin P 14	Hinds L 9 + 3	Hart M 8	Morrison S 2	Foster R — + 2	Diamond A — + 1	Soutar K — + 1	*Match No.*
1	2^{3}	3^{2}	4	5	6	7	8^{1}	9	10	11	12	13	14																		1
1	2	3	4	5	6	7	8			11	9^{1}	10^{2}	13	12																	2
1	2^{3}	3■	4	12	6^{2}	7	5^{1}		10	11	14	9	13	8																	3
1	2	3	4	5	6^{2}		7		10^{1}	11	12	13	8	9																	4
1	2		4	5	6		3	9^{2}			8^{1}	11		7	10	12	13														5
1	2	3	4	5	6^{3}		7	13	10^{2}	11	9^{1}	14				12		8													6
	2	3	4	5	12	7^{1}	6	13		11				9	10^{2}	14		8^{3}	1												7
1	2	3^{3}	4	5	6		7		10	11	9^{2}				13	12	14	8^{1}													8
1	2		4	5^{2}	6	7^{3}	3		10	11	12			9^{1}	14			8		13											9
1	2		4	5	6^{2}	8	7		10	11^{1}	9^{3}				13	12		14		3											10
1	2		4	5	6	8	7		10^{2}		11^{1}	13			9	12				3											11
1	2		4	5	6	8^{2}	7		10^{1}		11				9	12		13		3											12
	2		4	5	6	8^{1}	7		10^{2}		13		12		9	11		14	1	3^{3}											13
1	2			5	6	8	4	12			10		7		9^{1}	11				3											14
	2		4	5	6	8^{1}	7		10	11	9^{2}		12			13			1	3											15
1	2				6		4	13	10^{2}	11	9		5		8^{1}	12		7		3											16
	2		4		6		5		10^{1}	11	14		7	8^{3}		9^{2}		13	1	3	12										17
	2		4	5	6		7			11	12		8^{2}	10^{1}		9^{3}		14	1	3	13										18
	2	12	4	5^{1}	6		7		10	11	13		8	9^{2}					1	3■											19
	2	3	4	5	6		7^{3}		10	11^{1}	12	13	8	9^{2}		14			1												20
	2	8	4	5	6^{3}		7		10^{2}	13		11	14	9^{1}		12			1	3											21
	2	8	4	5^{2}			7		10^{1}	13	14	11	6	9^{3}		12			1	3											22
	2	8^{2}	4	5			7		10	13		11	6^{1}	9		12			1	3											23
	2	6	4	5^{1}			7		10	11		8		9^{2}		13			1	3		12									24
	2		4	5					13	11^{2}	9^{1}	8				12			1	3		6	7	10							25
	2	6^{2}	4	5					13	11^{1}	9	8							1	3			7	10	12						26
	2	6	4	5■					14	11^{2}	9^{3}	8					12		1	3^{1}			7	10	13						27
	2		4				3		13	14		8		11^{2}	12		5^{1}		1			6	7	10	9^{3}						28
1			4	5			2■		10	13		8		9^{1}	6^{2}					12			7	11		3					29
1	2		4	5	6				10^{2}	13		8		9^{1}									7	11	12	3					30
1	2			5^{2}	6				10^{1}		12	8								3		13	7	11	9	4					31
1	2	13	4		6		3		10		12	8^{2}											7	11	9^{1}	5					32
1	2	12	4				3		10			8	6									13	7^{1}	11	9	5^{2}					33
1	2	14	4				3		10^{1}			8^{3}	6	12		13							7	11	9^{2}	5					34
1	2	5^{2}	4				3			12		8	6			10^{1}						13	7	11	9						35
1	2	5	4^{1}				3			10^{2}			6									12	7	11	9		8	13			36
1		5		12			3			10		8^{1}	6				13					2	7^{2}	11	9	4					37
1	2^{1}	3								10^{3}		8	6										7^{2}	11	9	4	5	13	12	14	38

AIRDRIE UNITED — Second Division

Year Formed: 2002. *Ground & Address:* Shyberry Excelsior Stadium, Broomfield Park, Craigneuk Avenue, Airdrie ML6 8QZ.
Ground Capacity: all seated: 10,000. *Size of Pitch:* 112yd × 76yd.
Chairman: James Ballantyne. *Secretary:* Ann Marie Balantyne.
Manager: Sandy Stewart.
Record Attendance: 2285 v Forfar Ath, Second Division, 3 Aug, 2002.
Record Victory: 5-1 v Brechin C, Second Division, 23 Nov, 2002
Record Defeat: 1-5 v Forfar Ath, Second Division, 26 Oct, 2002
Most League Appearances: 35, M McGeown, 2002-03.
Most League Goals in Season (Individual): 18, Jerome Vareille, 2002-03.
Most Goals Overall (Individual): 19, Jerome Vareille, 2002-03.

AIRDRIE UNITED 2002–03 LEAGUE RECORD

Match No.	Date	Venue	Opponents	Result		H/T Score	Lg. Pos.	Goalscorers	Attendance
1	Aug 3	H	Forfar Ath	W	1-0	0-0	—	Docherty [78]	2285
2	10	A	Hamilton A	L	0-1	0-0	4		2366
3	17	H	Stranraer	W	2-1	0-1	2	Armstrong [50], Ronald [75]	1518
4	24	A	Dumbarton	L	1-3	0-1	6	Armstrong [64]	1417
5	31	H	Cowdenbeath	D	0-0	0-0	7		1486
6	Sept 14	A	Raith R	D	0-0	0-0	6		1962
7	21	H	Brechin C	L	2-4	1-2	9	Gow [20], Glancy [85]	1373
8	28	A	Stenhousemuir	L	3-4	0-3	9	Vareille [62], McKeown S 2 [75, 76]	842
9	Oct 5	H	Berwick R	W	2-1	1-1	7	McGuire [31], Vareille [63]	1349
10	19	H	Hamilton A	D	0-0	0-0	7		1593
11	26	A	Forfar Ath	L	1-5	0-1	9	Docherty [63]	666
12	Nov 2	A	Cowdenbeath	W	1-0	0-0	6	Vareille [63]	603
13	9	H	Dumbarton	L	0-1	0-0	8		1323
14	16	H	Raith R	D	0-0	0-0	8		1717
15	23	A	Brechin C	W	5-1	2-0	8	McKeown S 3 [23, 56, 83], Wilson M [32], Vareille [68]	557
16	30	A	Berwick R	D	2-2	2-0	7	McKeown S [18], Vareille [25]	647
17	Dec 14	H	Stenhousemuir	W	2-0	0-0	5	Vareille [60], Gow [73]	1228
18	28	A	Stranraer	L	0-2	0-2	6		695
19	Jan 1	A	Dumbarton	L	1-2	0-2	—	Vareille [88]	1024
20	18	A	Raith R	L	0-1	0-0	8		2247
21	Feb 1	H	Brechin C	W	3-0	1-0	8	Vareille [28], Ronald 2 [58, 74]	1275
22	8	A	Stenhousemuir	D	3-3	2-2	8	Armstrong [44], McKeown S (pen) [44], Dunn [46]	954
23	11	H	Cowdenbeath	D	1-1	0-1	—	McAuley [80]	1070
24	25	H	Forfar Ath	D	0-0	0-0	—		921
25	Mar 1	H	Stranraer	D	3-3	1-1	8	McKeown S [30], Vareille 2 [73, 77]	1187
26	8	H	Dumbarton	W	2-1	2-0	6	Gow [2], Dunn [16]	1136
27	11	A	Hamilton A	L	1-2	1-1	—	McVey [23]	1620
28	15	A	Cowdenbeath	W	2-1	1-0	4	McVey [15], Wilson S [84]	585
29	22	A	Brechin C	W	1-0	0-0	4	McKeown S [66]	672
30	28	H	Berwick R	W	2-0	0-0	—	Vareille [61], Glancy [84]	1276
31	Apr 5	H	Raith R	D	1-1	1-1	3	Gow [39]	1788
32	12	A	Berwick R	W	3-0	0-0	3	Vareille 3 [57, 64, 80]	631
33	19	H	Stenhousemuir	W	1-0	0-0	3	Vareille [79]	1468
34	26	A	Forfar Ath	D	1-1	1-1	3	Vareille [43]	884
35	May 3	H	Hamilton A	D	2-2	1-1	3	Vareille 2 [21, 49]	1960
36	10	A	Stranraer	W	2-1	1-1	3	McKeown S [36], Gow [75]	1343

Final League Position: 3

Club colours: Shirt: White with red diamond. Shorts: White with two red horizontal stripes. Stockings: White with red hoops.

Goalscorers: *League* (51): Vareille 18, McKeown S 10 (1 pen), Gow 5, Armstrong 3, Ronald 3, Docherty 2, Dunn 2, Glancy 2, McVey 2, McAuley 1, McGuire 1, Wilson M 1, Wilson S 1
Scottish Cup (3): Gow 1, McGuire 1, Vareille 1
CIS Cup (2): Gow 1, Vella 1
Challenge Cup (3): Docherty 1, Glancy 1, McGuire 1

McGeown M 35	Boyle J 7 + 2	McVey W 15 + 2	Stewart A 25	Brannigan K 16	Vella S 15	Gardner L 16 + 9	Wilson M 28	Ronald P 15 + 14	Docherty S 32	Glancy M 10 + 10	Armstrong P 32 + 3	McGuire D 11 + 8	Harvey P 7 + 6	Wilson W 19 + 5	Miller D — + 2	McGowan N 24 + 1	Gow A 18 + 9	Vareille J 30	Cherrie P 1 + 1	McKeown S 21 + 7	Wilson S 11 + 1	Risser O 1	McAuley S — + 3	Dunn D 6 + 7	Black K 1	*Match No.*
1	2^1	3	4	5	6	7	8	9^2	10	11	12	13														1
1	2^1	3	4	5	6^2	7^3	8▮	13	10	11	12	9	14													2
1	2^1	3	4	5	6	12		9	10^2	11	7		8^3	13	14											3
1	14	3▮	4^3	5	6^2	7	8^1	9	10	11	2	13		12												4
1			4	5	6^2	7	8	9^1	10	11^3	2	12	13			3	14									5
1	13	3^2	4	5		7			10	12	2	11^1	8			6	9									6
1▮			4	5		7^1			10	12	2	13	8^2	3		6	9	11^3	14							7
	7		4^1	5		12			10	8	2		13			3	9	11^3	1	14	6^2					8
1	3			5^1		7^2	8	9	4	10	2	12	13			6		11^3		14						9
1	2						8	11	4	7^1	3	12	6	14		5	10^3	9^2		13						10
1	2^3						8^1	9	4	10^2	3	7	6	14		5	12	11		13						11
1			4^1	5	6			9	10		8	7		2		3	12	11^2		13						12
1		12		5	6			9^2	4▮	14	8	7		2		3^1	10	11^3		13						13
1			4	5	6			12			3	7	10^1	2				9		11		8				14
1			4	5	6		10	13	8^3		3	7^1	14	2			12	11^2		9						15
1			4	5	6		8		10^1		3	7^2	12	2			13	11		9						16
1			4	5▮	6	13	8	14			10	7^1		2		3	12	11^3		9^2						17
1			4		5	13	8	12			3		10^1	2		6	7^2	11		9						18
1			4	5^2	6^1	7	8			13	12			2		3	11	9		10						19
1		3^3	4			14	8	10^2	5		2	12				6	11^1	9		7			13			20
1		3	4			13	8	9	5		2	11^1				6		7		10^2				12		21
1		3					8	9	4		2					6		7		10	5▮			11		22
1		3^1				13	8	9^2	5	12	2					6	10^3	7		4			14	11		23
1^1					5	7^3	8	14	4		2	11^2		12		6^1	13	10		9				3		24
1		3^1			6^3		8	13	4		5			2			12	7		9	14			11	10^2	25
1		12	4				8		10		2					6	11	7		9	5			3^1		26
1		3	4				8		10		2	12				6▮		7		9	5			11^1		27
1		3	4			12	8	13	10^3		5			2	14		11^1	7		9^2	6					28
1		3^1	4			13	8	14	10		5			2		12	11^2	7		9^3	6					29
1		3^2	4			10^3	8	14	6	12	5			2			11	7		9^1				13		30
1		3^2	4^1			8		12	10	14	6			2			11	7		9^3	5			13		31
1						10^2	8	12	4	13	2			3^3		6	11	7		9^1	5			14		32
1			4			10	8	14	2^1	13				3		6	11^3	7		9^2	5			12		33
1						10^2	8	11^1	4		2			3		6	9	7			5		13	12		34
1						10	8	13	4	9^3	2			3		6^1	11^2	7		14	5▮			12		35
1			4			10^1	8	11	5	13	2			3		6	12	7		9^2						36

ALBION ROVERS Third Division

Year Formed: 1882. *Ground & Address:* Cliftonhill Stadium, Main St, Coatbridge ML5 3RB. *Telephone/Fax:* 01236 606334.
Ground capacity: total: 2496, seated: 538. *Size of Pitch:* 110yd × 72yd.
Chairman: Andrew Dick, *Company Secretary:* David Shanks BSc. *General Manager:* John Reynolds.
Commercial Manager: Chris Fahey.
Manager: Peter Hetherston. *Assistant Manager:* Jock McStay. *Youth Development:* Jimmy Lindsay. *Physio:* Dan Young.
Managers since 1975: G. Caldwell, S. Goodwin, H. Hood, J. Baker, D. Whiteford, M. Ferguson, W. Wilson, B. Rooney, A. Ritchie, T. Gemmell, D. Provan, M. Oliver, B. McLaren, T. Gemmell, T Spence, J. Crease, V. Moore, B. McLaren, J. McVeigh.
Club Nickname(s): The Wee Rovers. *Previous Grounds:* Cowheath Park, Meadow Park, Whifflet.
Record Attendance: 27,381 v Rangers, Scottish Cup 2nd rd; 8 Feb, 1936.
Record Transfer Fee received: £40,000 from Motherwell for Bruce Cleland.
Record Transfer Fee paid: £7000 for Gerry McTeague to Stirling Albion, September 1989.
Record Victory: 12-0 v Airdriehill, Scottish Cup; 3 Sept, 1887.
Record Defeat: 1-11 v Partick T, League Cup, 11 August 1993.
Most Capped Player: Jock White, 1 (2), Scotland.
Most League Appearances: 399, Murdy Walls, 1921-36.
Most League Goals in Season (Individual): 41: Jim Renwick, Division II; 1932-33.
Most Goals Overall (Individual): 105: Bunty Weir, 1928-31.

ALBION ROVERS 2002–03 LEAGUE RECORD

Match No.	Date	Venue	Opponents	Result	H/T Score	Lg. Pos.	Goalscorers	Attendance
1	Aug 3	A	Stirling A	W 1-0	1-0	—	Dick J [13]	579
2	10	H	Peterhead	W 3-0	1-0	—	Cormack [12], Diack I [50], Carr [83]	440
3	17	A	East Stirling	W 3-0	0-0	1	Lumsden [46], Bradford 2 [79, 89]	321
4	24	A	Gretna	L 0-2	0-0	3		443
5	31	H	East Fife	L 1-5	1-2	3	Bradford [23]	451
6	Sept 14	A	Morton	W 1-0	1-0	2	Lumsden [10]	1739
7	21	H	Elgin C	D 1-1	0-0	3	McLean [72]	303
8	28	A	Queen's Park	W 4-2	2-0	1	Stirling 2 (2 pens) [6, 26], Diack I [82], Bradford [90]	506
9	Oct 5	H	Montrose	D 1-1	0-0	4	Diack I [54]	380
10	19	A	Peterhead	L 0-2	0-0	4		543
11	26	H	Stirling A	L 1-3	1-1	5	McLean [7]	489
12	Nov 2	A	East Fife	W 4-0	2-0	5	Mercer [21], Stirling (pen) [26], McCaig [69], McLean [85]	575
13	9	H	Gretna	W 2-1	0-0	3	Duncan [50], McLean [63]	332
14	16	H	Morton	W 2-1	0-1	2	Smith [82], Diack I [90]	843
15	23	H	Elgin C	D 1-1	0-0	2	Duncan [49]	253
16	30	A	Montrose	W 1-0	0-0	2	McLean [78]	271
17	Dec 7	A	Gretna	W 2-1	0-1	1	Silvestro [61], Mercer [74]	289
18	14	H	Queen's Park	L 0-2	0-2	2		442
19	28	H	East Stirling	W 6-0	3-0	1	Bradford 2 [15, 20], Diack I 3 [42, 72, 81], Lumsden [51]	326
20	Jan 18	A	Morton	L 1-2	1-1	3	Mercer [29]	2405
21	25	H	East Fife	D 0-0	0-0	3		475
22	Feb 8	A	Queen's Park	D 1-1	0-0	4	Dick J [90]	671
23	26	A	Stirling A	W 4-3	3-0	—	Diack I [10], Lumsden [19], Yardley [31], Rowe (og) [72]	466
24	Mar 1	A	East Stirling	W 4-0	2-0	4	Mercer 2 [5, 50], Yardley [35], McLean [85]	273
25	4	H	Montrose	W 3-0	1-0	—	Smith [35], Silvestro [53], Bradford [71]	224
26	8	H	Gretna	D 1-1	0-1	3	Lumsden [74]	327
27	11	H	Peterhead	D 0-0	0-0	—		389
28	15	A	East Fife	D 1-1	1-0	4	Mercer [15]	780
29	22	A	Elgin C	W 1-0	0-0	4	Yardley [65]	333
30	29	A	Elgin C	W 2-1	0-1	4	McLean [78], Yardley [79]	280
31	Apr 5	H	Morton	W 2-1	1-0	3	Mercer [24], Yardley [90]	1381
32	12	A	Montrose	D 1-1	1-1	4	Bradford [40]	282
33	19	H	Queen's Park	W 2-1	1-0	4	Yardley [35], McLean [68]	581
34	26	H	Stirling A	W 2-1	2-0	3	Yardley 2 [24, 27]	533
35	May 3	A	Peterhead	D 0-0	0-0	4		1693
36	10	H	East Stirling	W 3-1	3-1	3	Mercer 3 [15, 22, 36]	682

Final League Position: 3

Honours
League Champions: Division II 1933-34, Second Division 1988-89; *Runners-up:* Division II 1913-14, 1937-38, 1947-48.
Scottish Cup Runners-up: 1920.

Club colours: Shirt: Scarlet and yellow. Shorts: Scarlet. Stockings: Yellow.

Goalscorers: *League* (62): Mercer 10, Bradford 8, Diack I 8, McLean 8, Yardley 8, Lumsden 5, Stirling 3 (3 pens), Dick J 2, Duncan 2, Silvestro 2, Carr 1, Cormack 1, McCaig 1, Smith J 1, own goals 2
Scottish Cup (1): Diack I 1
CIS Cup (0)
Challenge Cup (0)

Shearer S 36	Paterson A 24 + 5	Stirling J 30	Smith J 35	Cormack P 32	Lumsden T 34	Dick J 16 + 7	Silvestro C 28 + 1	Bradford J 24 + 10	Diack I 16 + 18	Mercer J 30 + 2	McKinnon C — + 2	Coulter J 5 + 9	McLean C 13 + 19	McAllister K 33 + 1	Carr D — + 4	Duncan L 8 + 3	McCaig J 17 + 4	McCaul G — + 4	Weir M — + 5	Yardley M 15	McKenzie M — + 1	*Match No.*
1	2^{2}	3	4	5	6	7^{1}	8	9	10^{3}	11	12	13	14									1
1	2	3	4	5	6		8	9	10^{1}	11^{3}	14		12	7^{2}	13							2
1	2	3	4	5	6	12	8^{1}	9	10^{2}	11		14	13	7^{3}								3
1	2	3	4	5	6	8		9	10^{1}	11^{2}		13	12	7^{3}	14							4
1	2■	3	4	5	6	8■		9		11^{3}		12	14	7^{1}		10^{2}	13					5
1	2	3	4	5	6			9^{2}	13			8	10	7^{1}	12		11					6
1	2	3	4	5	6	13	12	9	14			8^{2}	10	7^{3}			11^{1}					7
1	2	3	4	5	6	8^{3}	11	9	12			13	10^{2}	7^{1}			14					8
1	2	3	4	5	6	8	11	9	10^{1}	13				7^{2}		12						9
1	2	3	4	5^{3}	6		8	9^{2}	10	11		14	12	7^{1}		13						10
1	2	3	4	5	6		8^{1}	9		11^{3}		12	10	7^{2}	14	13						11
1	2	3^{2}	4		6		8^{3}	13	12	11		14	10	7^{1}		9	5					12
1	2		4		6		8	14	12	11		3^{1}	10^{3}	7^{2}		9	5	13				13
1	2^{1}		4	5	6		8	13	12			11	10	7		9^{2}	3					14
1	2^{1}		4	5	6^{2}		8	14	12	11		13	10^{3}	7		9	3					15
1			4	5	6	13		12	8	11		2	10^{2}	7^{1}		9^{3}	3		14			16
1	2		4	5	6		8	7	12	11			10^{1}			9^{2}	3		13			17
1	2		4	5	6	14	8		12	11			10^{1}	7^{3}		9^{2}	3		13			18
1	2	3	4		6	11^{2}	8	9	10^{3}	13			14	7^{1}			5		12			19
1	2^{3}	3	4		6	12	8	9^{2}	10	11			13	7^{1}			5		14			20
1	2	3	4	5	6		8	9	10	11			12	7^{1}								21
1	2	3	4	5	6	12	8^{1}	7^{2}	10^{3}	11			14	13						9		22
1	12	3	4	5	6	2^{1}	8	13	10^{2}	11				7^{3}			14			9		23
1	14	3	4	5	6	2	8	12	10^{1}	11			13	7^{3}						9^{2}		24
1		3	4	5	6	14	8	12	10^{1}	11			13	7^{3}			2			9^{2}		25
1		3	4	5	6		8	10	12	11				7^{1}			2			9		26
1		3	4	5	6	2	8	10^{1}	12	11			13	7						9^{2}		27
1		3	4	5		2	8	10	12	11			13	7^{2}			6			9^{1}		28
1	13	3	4	5		2	8^{2}	10^{1}	12	11			14	7			6			9^{3}		29
1		3	4	5	6	2^{2}	8	12	10	11			13	7^{1}						9		30
1	13	3	4	5	6	2^{2}	8	10	12	11				7^{1}			14			9^{3}		31
1	2	3	4	5	6		8	10^{2}	12	11			13	7^{1}						9		32
1	13	3	4	5	6	2■	8^{2}	10^{1}	12	11			14	7^{3}						9		33
1		3	4	5	6				8^{1}	11			10	7^{2}			2	12		9	13	34
1	2	3		5	6	8^{3}		13	12	11			10^{1}	7^{2}			4	14		9		35
1	2^{2}	3	4	5^{3}	6	8^{1}		10	14	11			13	7				12		9		36

ALLOA ATHLETIC Second Division

Year Formed: 1878. *Ground & Address:* Recreation Park, Clackmannan Rd, Alloa FK10 1RY. *Telephone:* 01259 722695.
Ground Capacity: total: 3100, seated: 400. *Size of Pitch:* 110yd × 75yd.
Chairman: David Murray. *Secretary:* Ewen G. Cameron. *Commercial Director:* Willie McKie.
Manager: Terry Christie. *Assistant Manager:* Graeme Armstrong. *Physio:* Jim Law.
Managers since 1975: H. Wilson, A. Totten, W. Garner, J. Thomson, D. Sullivan, G. Abel, B. Little, H. McCann, W. Lamont, P. McAuley, T. Hendrie. *Club Nickname(s):* The Wasps. *Previous Grounds:* None.
Record Attendance: 13,000 v Dunfermline Athletic, Scottish Cup 3rd rd replay; 26 Feb, 1939.
Record Transfer Fee received: £100,000 for Martin Cameron to Bristol Rovers.
Record Transfer Fee paid: £26,000 for Ross Hamilton from Stenhousemuir.
Record Victory: 9-2 v Forfar Ath, Division II; 18 Mar, 1933.
Record Defeat: 0-10 v Dundee, Division II; 8 Mar, 1947: v Third Lanark, League Cup, 8 Aug, 1953.
Most Capped Player: Jock Hepburn, 1, Scotland.
Most League Goals in Season (Individual): 49: 'Wee' Willie Crilley, Division II; 1921-22.

ALLOA ATHLETIC 2002–03 LEAGUE RECORD

Match No.	*Date*	*Venue*	*Opponents*	*Result*		*H/T Score*	*Lg. Pos.*	*Goalscorers*	*Attendance*
1	Aug 3	A	Inverness CT	D	0-0	0-0	—		1623
2	10	H	Arbroath	L	0-3	0-1	8		518
3	17	A	St Mirren	L	1-3	1-1	10	Crabbe (pen) 36	3104
4	24	H	Falkirk	L	1-6	1-2	10	Ferguson B 5	2613
5	31	A	St Johnstone	L	0-2	0-2	10		2274
6	Sept 14	A	Clyde	D	0-0	0-0	10		973
7	21	H	Ayr U	L	0-1	0-0	10		619
8	28	A	Ross Co	W	1-0	0-0	10	Evans G 72	1921
9	Oct 5	H	Queen of the S	L	0-1	0-1	10		658
10	19	H	Inverness CT	L	0-6	0-4	10		531
11	26	A	Arbroath	W	1-0	0-0	10	Hamilton 54	687
12	Nov 2	H	St Johnstone	L	1-3	1-1	10	Seaton (pen) 27	952
13	9	A	Falkirk	L	0-3	0-1	10		3390
14	16	H	Clyde	L	1-4	1-2	10	Cowan 43	736
15	23	A	Ayr U	L	1-3	0-1	10	Cowan 87	1632
16	30	H	Ross Co	D	1-1	0-1	10	Little 63	445
17	Dec 7	A	Queen of the S	D	1-1	1-0	10	Hutchison 27	2111
18	14	H	St Mirren	L	2-3	1-0	10	Crabbe 10, Thomson 60	783
19	21	A	Inverness CT	D	1-1	1-1	10	Hutchison 45	1639
20	28	A	St Johnstone	L	0-3	0-0	10		2090
21	Jan 18	H	Queen of the S	D	3-3	2-2	10	Seaton 2 (2 pens) 12, 43, Thomson 75	561
22	Feb 1	A	Ross Co	W	2-1	2-0	9	Sloan 2 4, 9	2096
23	8	A	St Mirren	D	1-1	1-0	9	Hamilton 44	2105
24	25	H	Arbroath	W	3-2	1-0	—	Little 13, Watson 50, Hutchison 89	340
25	Mar 1	H	St Johnstone	L	1-2	1-1	9	Sloan 28	884
26	8	A	Falkirk	L	1-3	0-1	9	Hughes (og) 79	3320
27	11	A	Clyde	D	2-2	1-0	—	Sloan 11, Mensing (og) 86	665
28	15	A	Ayr U	W	1-0	0-0	9	Crabbe 66	1363
29	25	H	Ayr U	L	2-3	1-1	—	Little 2, Davidson 85	454
30	29	H	Falkirk	L	1-3	1-2	9	Hamilton 10	1686
31	Apr 5	H	Clyde	L	1-2	1-1	9	Hamilton 25	687
32	12	H	Ross Co	W	2-1	1-1	9	Hamilton 12, Sloan 72	876
33	19	A	Queen of the S	W	1-0	0-0	9	Thomson 67	1873
34	26	H	Inverness CT	L	1-5	0-2	9	Sloan 60	485
35	May 3	A	Arbroath	W	1-0	1-0	9	Ferguson B 44	405
36	10	H	St Mirren	W	4-0	2-0	9	Sloan 2 8, 30, Seaton 50, Hutchison 86	1084

Final League Position: 9

Honours
League Champions: Division II 1921-22; Third Division 1997-98. *Runners-up:* Division II 1938-39. Second Division 1976-77, 1981-82, 1984-85, 1988-89, 1999-2000, 2001-02.
Bell's League Challenge Winners: 1999-2000. *Runners-up:* 2001-02.

Club colours: Shirt: Gold with black trim. Shorts: Black with gold stripe. Stockings: Gold, black hoop on top.

Goalscorers: *League* (39): Sloan 8 (2 pens), Hamilton 5, Hutchison 4, Seaton 4 (3 pens), Crabbe 3 (1 pen), Little 3, Thomson 3, Cowan 2, Ferguson B 2, Davidson 1, Evans G 1, Watson 1, own goals 2
Scottish Cup (3): Crabbe 2, Thomson 1
CIS Cup (3): Hamilton 1, Hutchison 1, Little 1
Challenge Cup (0)

Hogarth M 8	Valentine C 34	Watson G 22 + 2	Ferguson D 25 + 2	Thomson S 35	Christie M 26 + 1	Hamilton R 35	Macdonald W 5 + 2	Crabbe S 18 + 10	Hutchison G 24 + 12	Little I 27 + 1	Evans G 2 + 12	Cowan M 7 + 2	Ferguson B 5 + 1	Fisher J 11 + 5	Seaton A 32 + 1	Evans J 16	Knox K 4 + 5	Walker R 25 + 3	Gillan G 1 + 5	Elliot R — + 5	Stevenson J 2	Sloan R 16	Davidson R 4 + 9	Soutar D 12	Match No.
1	2	3	4	5	6	7	8■	9	10	11[1]	12														1
1	2		4	5	6	7		9	10		13	3[1]	8[2]	11	12										2
	2			5		7	6	9[1]	10		13		8	11	3	1	4	12[2]							3
1	2		12	5		7	6	9[2]	10[1]	11		4	8	13	3										4
	2	4	10[2]	5		7		9[3]	13	11			8	12	3[1]	1			6	14					5
	2	4		5	6[2]	7	8		10	9	12	3		11[1]		1	13								6
	2[3]	4	13	5		7		9[1]	10	11	12	6		8[2]	3	1	14								7
	2	4	8	5	6[2]	7		9[1]	10	11	12			13	3	1									8
	2	4	8	5	6	7	14		10[2]	11	9[1]			12	3[3]	1		13							9
	2	4[1]	8	5	6[3]	9	7		10						3	1	12	13	14		11[2]				10
	2		8[1]	5	6	9			10		12			11	3	1	4	7							11
	2	8		5	6[1]	9	12		10		13			11	3	1	4[2]	7							12
	2	4		5		9[3]			10		8[1]	6		11	3	1	12	7[2]	13	14					13
	2			5	8■	9[1]			10			6[2]		11	3	1	4	7	13	12					14
1				5		7		8[2]	10	11	13	4		6	3			2		12	9[1]				15
1	2		4[1]	5	6	8		12	10	9[2]				11	3		13	7							16
	4	13	8[1]	5	6	7		9[3]	10	11	14				3[2]	1		2	12						17
	4		8	5	6	7		9	10	11					3	1		2							18
1	4	12	8	5		7		9[2]	10	11	13			6[1]	3			2							19
1	4		8	5	6	7[2]		9[1]	10	11	13			12	3			2							20
1	4			5	6	7		12	10	11					3			2				8[1]	9		21
	2	4	8[1]	5	6	10		9[2]	12						3			7				11	13	1	22
	4		8	5	6	7		9[1]	13	10[2]					3			2				11	12	1	23
	4	5	8		14	7[1]		9[2]	13	11[3]		12			3			2				6	10	1	24
	2	4	8	5	6[1]			13	14	11					3			7	12			10[3]	9[2]	1	25
	4			5	6	7		9	10	11					3			2				8[1]	12	1	26
	2	4	8[1]	5	6■	9[3]		14	12	11					3			7				10[2]	13	1	27
	2	4	8[1]	5		9		12	6[2]	11					3			7				10	13	1	28
		2		5	6	8		9[1]	4	11					3	1		7[2]		13		10	12		29
	2	4	8[2]	5	6	7		12	13	11[1]					3	1						10	9		30
	2	4[1]	8	5	6	9			14	11		12			3			7[2]				10[3]	13	1	31
	2	4	8	5	6[2]	9		12	13	11					3			7[1]				10		1	32
	2	4	8	5	6[2]	9		12	13	11[1]					3	1		7				10			33
	2	4	8	5	6	9[3]		14	12	11[2]					3[1]			7				10	13	1	34
	2	3	4	5	6[1]	9		13	8	11[2]			12					7				10		1	35
	2	6	4[1]	5		9		10[3]	14	12			8[2]		3			7				11	13	1	36

ARBROATH Second Division

Year Formed: 1878. *Ground & Address:* Gayfield Park, Arbroath DD11 1QB. *Telephone and Fax:* 01241 431125.
Ground Capacity: 4020, seated: 715. *Size of Pitch:* 115yd × 71yd.
President: John D. Christison. *Secretary:* Charles Kinnear. *Administrator:* Mike Cargill. *Commercial Manager:* M. Fairweather.
Manager: John Brownlie. *Assistant Manager:* Steve Kirk. *Coach:* Jake Ferrier. *Physio:* Jim Crosby.
Managers since 1975: A. Henderson, I. J. Stewart, G. Fleming, J. Bone, J. Young, W. Borthwick, M. Lawson, D. McGrain MBE, J. Scott, J. Brogan, T. Campbell, G. Mackie, D. Baikie.
Club Nickname(s): The Red Lichties. *Previous Grounds:* None.
Record Attendance: 13,510 v Rangers, Scottish Cup 3rd rd; 23 Feb, 1952.
Record Transfer Fee received: £120,000 for Paul Tosh to Dundee (Aug 1993).
Record Transfer Fee paid: £20,000 for Douglas Robb from Montrose (1981).
Record Victory: 36-0 v Bon Accord, Scottish Cup 1st rd; 12 Sept, 1885.
Record Defeat: 1-9 v Celtic, League Cup 3rd rd; 25 Aug 1993.
Most Capped Player: Ned Doig, 2 (5), Scotland.
Most League Appearances: 445: Tom Cargill, 1966-81.
Most League Goals in Season (Individual): 45: Dave Easson, Division II; 1958-59.
Most Goals Overall (Individual): 120: Jimmy Jack; 1966-71.

ARBROATH 2002–03 LEAGUE RECORD

Match No.	Date	Venue	Opponents	Result		H/T Score	Lg. Pos.	Goalscorers	Attendance
1	Aug 3	H	Ross Co	L	0-3	0-1	—		761
2	10	A	Alloa Ath	W	3-0	1-0	4	McDowell 25, Ritchie 67, Spink 89	518
3	17	H	Clyde	D	1-1	0-1	4	McDowell (pen) 80	744
4	24	H	St Johnstone	L	0-1	0-1	8		1467
5	31	A	Ayr U	L	0-1	0-1	8		1732
6	Sept 14	H	St Mirren	D	2-2	1-1	8	Feroz 8, Cusick (pen) 89	1008
7	21	A	Inverness CT	L	0-5	0-1	8		1686
8	28	A	Queen of the S	D	2-2	1-1	8	Currie 8, Cargill 53	1733
9	Oct 5	H	Falkirk	W	2-0	0-0	8	Cusick 83, Feroz (pen) 86	1730
10	19	A	Ross Co	L	0-4	0-3	8		2065
11	26	H	Alloa Ath	L	0-1	0-0	9		687
12	Nov 5	H	Ayr U	D	1-1	0-1	—	McDowell 77	381
13	9	A	St Johnstone	L	0-2	0-1	9		1994
14	16	A	St Mirren	L	0-2	0-2	9		3021
15	23	H	Inverness CT	L	1-2	0-1	9	Tait 75	653
16	30	H	Queen of the S	L	1-2	0-1	9	McDowell 65	630
17	Dec 7	A	Falkirk	L	1-2	0-1	9	Spink 53	2673
18	14	A	Clyde	L	0-3	0-3	9		861
19	21	H	Ross Co	W	2-1	2-0	9	Swankie 2 15, 43	580
20	28	A	Ayr U	L	0-4	0-1	9		1664
21	Jan 1	H	St Johnstone	L	2-3	1-0	—	Brownlie 20, McGlashan 87	1252
22	18	H	Falkirk	L	1-4	0-3	9	McGlashan 86	1950
23	Feb 8	H	Clyde	L	1-2	0-1	10	Dow 80	686
24	25	A	Alloa Ath	L	2-3	0-1	—	Cusick 48, Henslee 76	340
25	Mar 1	H	Ayr U	L	1-2	1-0	10	Forrest 42	505
26	4	A	Inverness CT	L	0-2	0-1	—		1396
27	8	A	St Johnstone	L	1-2	1-1	10	Swankie 20	1938
28	15	H	Inverness CT	L	1-3	1-0	10	Heenan 43	550
29	18	A	Queen of the S	L	0-3	0-2	—		1108
30	29	H	St Mirren	D	1-1	0-1	10	Dow 50	509
31	Apr 5	A	St Mirren	L	0-1	0-1	10		2122
32	12	H	Queen of the S	D	0-0	0-0	10		502
33	19	A	Falkirk	L	1-4	0-1	10	Cusick 74	4950
34	26	A	Ross Co	L	1-3	1-2	10	Brownlie 17	2206
35	May 3	H	Alloa Ath	L	0-1	0-1	10		405
36	10	A	Clyde	L	2-4	1-3	10	McInally 14, Henslee 81	1002

Final League Position: 10

Honours
League Champions Runners-up: Division II 1934-35, 1958-59, 1967-68, 1971-72; Second Division 2000-01; Third Division 1997-98.
Scottish Cup: Quarter-finals: 1993.

Club colours: Shirt: Maroon with white trim. Shorts: White. Stockings: Maroon.

Goalscorers: *League* (30): Cusick 4 (1 pen), McDowell 4 (1 pen), Swankie 3, Brownlie 2, Dow 2, Feroz 2 (1 pen), Henslee 2, McGlashan 2, Spink 2, Cargill 1, Currie 1, Forrest 1, Heenan 1, McInally 1, Ritchie 1, Tait 1
Scottish Cup (0)
CIS Cup (2): Feroz 2
Challenge Cup (0)

Hinchcliffe C 36	Tait J 17	McInally D 4 + 6	Currie R 28 + 3	Ritchie I 33	Cusick J 18	Heenan K 17 + 12	Cargill A 21 + 1	McDowell M 14 + 5	McGlashan J 14 + 2	Swankie G 16 + 13	Feroz C 20 + 3	Spink D 7 + 13	Brownlie P 22 + 5	Florence S 26	McCaig J 3	McAulay J 9 + 16	Henslee G 23 + 8	Graham E 4 + 6	Browne P 16	Bowman G 11 + 3	Durno P 2 + 6	McMullen K 10 + 1	Dow A 13	Forrest E 10	McDermott A 2	McMillan K — + 1	Farquharson P — + 2	*Match No.*
1	2	3^{3}	4	5	6^{1}	7	8	9	10	11^{2}	12	13	14															1
1	2			5	6	14		9^{2}		13	11^{3}	12	7	3^{1}	4	8	10											2
1	2^{1}		12	5	6^{3}			9		13	11	8^{2}	7		4	10	3	14										3
1			2	4		12	8^{3}	9	10	13	11	14	7^{1}		5	6^{2}	3											4
1			2	5		14	8^{3}	9^{1}	10	13	11		12^{2}			7	3		4	6								5
1		13	10	4	6	8	7^{1}	9^{3}	12	14	11						2		5	3^{2}								6
1		13	10	4	6^{1}	7^{3}		9	8		11	14				12	2^{2}		5	3								7
1	2	10	8^{1}	4	6	14	7	13		9^{3}	11^{2}			3			12		5									8
1	2	13		5	6^{3}	12	7	9^{1}	10		11			3		14			4	8^{2}								9
1	2	11^{2}		5	6^{1}	7	8^{3}		10	13	9			3		12	14		4									10
1	2		6^{1}	5		7^{3}		8^{2}	10	13	9			3		12	14		4	11								11
1	2					7^{1}	8^{3}	12	10		9^{2}	4		3		6	14		5	11	13							12
1	2	12				14	8^{3}	9	10	7^{2}	13	4		3		6			5	11^{1}								13
1	2		12	5			11^{3}		10	7^{2}	9	8	13	3		6^{1}			4	14								14
1	2		8^{2}	5	6		11	9	10		12	14	7^{1}	3^{3}			13		4									15
1	2		8^{1}	5	6	7^{2}		9		14			10	3		12	13		4	11^{3}								16
1	2		8^{2}	5		14		9		12		6	10^{1}	3		13	7		4	11^{3}								17
1	2		10	5	6^{3}	13		9^{2}		7		8^{1}	11	3		12		14	4									18
1	2		6	5			8^{2}	12		10^{1}	9^{3}	14	11	3		13	7		4									19
1	2		6^{3}	5			8	12		10^{1}	9	14	11	3^{2}			7		4	13								20
1			2	5		7^{1}	8	13	10	14	9^{3}		11^{2}	3		12	4	6										21
1	2		6^{2}	5			7		10	14	9	12	11^{3}	3		13	8	4^{1}										22
1			6	5		7			10^{1}	8^{3}	9	14	11^{2}			13	12					2	3	4				23
1			8	5	4^{2}	7				12	9^{1}		11				10				13	2	3	6				24
1		13	2	5	4^{1}	7				9^{3}			11^{2}			12	8	3			14		10	6				25
1			8	5	4	7							11^{2}	3			9^{1}	12			13	2	10	6				26
1		14	8^{1}	5		11^{3}				9		12	4	3		13	7					2	10	6^{2}				27
1			8	5		10				9		12^{3}	11^{2}	3		14	7			13		2^{1}	6		4			28
1			6	5						10^{2}	9	2	8^{3}	3			7	12			13		11		4^{1}	14		29
1			6^{3}	5		8	13			9^{2}		12	14	3			7			10		2	11	4^{1}				30
1			6	5	4	12	8^{3}			13			9^{1}	3			7			10^{2}		2	11				14	31
1			6	5	4	9	8^{3}		14	10				3^{1}			7	13				2^{2}	11				12	32
1			4^{2}	5	8	14	10^{3}			11^{1}	9		12			13	7					2	3	6				33
1			13		4^{3}	14	8						11	3		12	7	6^{2}			9	2^{1}	10	5				34
1			4^{2}	5		7^{1}	8			9^{3}		13	11	3		2	12				14		10	6				35
1		11^{1}	6^{2}	5		12	8						7	3^{3}		2	9	14			10	13		4				36

AYR UNITED

First Division

Year Formed: 1910. *Ground & Address:* Somerset Park, Tryfield Place, Ayr KA8 9NB. *Telephone:* 01292 263435.
Ground Capacity: 10,185, seated: 1549. *Size of Pitch:* 110yd × 72yd.
Chairman: W. J. Barr. *Administrator:* Brian Caldwell. *Secretary:* J. E. Eyley. *Lottery Manager:* Andrew Downie.
Commercial Manager: Louis Jardine.
Director of Football: Campbell Money. *Physio:* John Kerr.
Managers since 1975: Alex Stuart, Ally MacLeod, Willie McLean, George Caldwell, Ally MacLeod, George Burley, Simon Stainrod, Gordon Dalziel. *Club Nickname(s):* The Honest Men. *Previous Grounds:* None.
Record Attendance: 25,225 v Rangers, Division I; 13 Sept, 1969.
Record Transfer Fee received: £300,000 for Steven Nicol to Liverpool (Oct 1981).
Record Transfer Fee paid: £90,000 for Mark Campbell from Stranraer (March 1999).
Record Victory: 11-1 v Dumbarton, League Cup; 13 Aug, 1952.
Record Defeat: 0-9 in Division I v Rangers (1929); v Hearts (1931); B Division v Third Lanark (1954).
Most Capped Player: Jim Nisbet, 3, Scotland.
Most League Appearances: 459, John Murphy, 1963-78.
Most League League and Cup Goals in Season (Individual): 66, Jimmy Smith, 1927-28.
Most League and Cup Goals Overall (Individual): 213, Peter Price, 1955-61.

AYR UNITED 2002–03 LEAGUE RECORD

Match No.	Date	Venue	Opponents	Result		H/T Score	Lg. Pos.	Goalscorers	Attendance
1	Aug 3	H	Falkirk	L	1-3	0-2	—	Kean 66	3030
2	10	A	Clyde	L	0-1	0-0	9		1123
3	17	H	Ross Co	W	2-1	2-0	7	Perry (og) 10, Grady 17	1692
4	24	A	Queen of the S	W	2-1	1-0	5	Campbell 44, Grady 54	2803
5	31	H	Arbroath	W	1-0	1-0	3	Sheerin 44	1732
6	Sept 14	H	St Johnstone	D	0-0	0-0	4		2320
7	21	A	Alloa Ath	W	1-0	0-0	4	Chaplain 52	619
8	28	H	St Mirren	D	1-1	1-0	3	Grady 26	2489
9	Oct 5	A	Inverness CT	L	0-2	0-1	4		1803
10	19	A	Falkirk	L	0-3	0-0	5		3441
11	26	H	Clyde	D	1-1	1-1	5	Annand 22	1989
12	Nov 5	A	Arbroath	D	1-1	1-0	—	Annand 16	381
13	9	H	Queen of the S	L	0-1	0-0	5		2234
14	16	A	St Johnstone	W	2-0	1-0	5	Craig 2 33, 67	1943
15	23	H	Alloa Ath	W	3-1	1-0	5	Sheerin 26, Chaplain 47, Little (og) 87	1632
16	30	A	St Mirren	L	0-1	0-1	5		2426
17	Dec 7	H	Inverness CT	D	3-3	1-0	5	Chaplain 21, Annand 48, Lovering 52	1663
18	14	A	Ross Co	L	0-1	0-0	6		2352
19	28	H	Arbroath	W	4-0	1-0	5	Campbell 3, Kean 59, McColl 70, Ferguson 89	1664
20	Jan 1	A	Queen of the S	D	1-1	0-0	—	Kean 69	2921
21	18	A	Inverness CT	W	1-0	1-0	5	Kean 3	2021
22	Feb 1	H	St Mirren	D	0-0	0-0	5		2738
23	8	H	Ross Co	D	1-1	1-0	5	Whalen 37	1486
24	25	H	Falkirk	W	1-0	1-0	—	Chaplain 30	1783
25	Mar 1	A	Arbroath	W	2-1	0-1	5	Kean 2 88, 89	505
26	4	H	St Johnstone	L	0-1	0-0	—		1690
27	8	H	Queen of the S	L	0-1	0-0	5		1730
28	15	H	Alloa Ath	L	0-1	0-0	5		1363
29	22	A	Clyde	L	0-3	0-1	6		1015
30	25	A	Alloa Ath	W	3-2	1-1	—	Whalen 3 9, 69, 82	454
31	Apr 5	A	St Johnstone	L	0-1	0-1	5		2123
32	12	A	St Mirren	D	1-1	1-0	5	Chaplain 35	2248
33	26	A	Falkirk	L	0-3	0-2	6		4042
34	29	H	Inverness CT	W	1-0	1-0	—	Kean 19	1114
35	May 3	H	Clyde	L	0-3	0-2	6		1795
36	10	A	Ross Co	L	1-4	0-0	6	Whalen 50	3449

Final League Position: 6

Honours
League Champions: Division II 1911-12, 1912-13, 1927-28, 1936-37, 1958-59, 1965-66. Second Division 1987-88, 1996-97;
Runners-up: Division II 1910-11, 1955-56, 1968-69.
Scottish Cup: Semi-final 2002.
League Cup: (CIS) Runners-up: 2001-02.
B&Q Cup Runners-up: 1990-91, 1991-92.

Club colours: Shirt: White with black trim. Shorts: Black. Stockings: White with black.

Goalscorers: *League* (34): Kean 7, Chaplain 5, Whalen 5, Annand 3, Grady 3, Campbell 2, Craig 2, Sheerin 2, Ferguson 1, Lovering 1, McColl 1, own goals 2
Scottish Cup (2): Black 1, Grady 1
CIS Cup (0)
Challenge Cup (2): Annand 1, Grady 1

Nelson C 31	Bossy F 2	Lovering P 21 + 1	McManus A 25 + 1	Campbell M 29	Craig D 29 + 2	Chaplain S 33 + 2	Nicolson I 21 + 4	Annand E 18 + 1	Grady J 29 + 2	Sheerin P 19	Lyle W 29 + 5	Kean S 11 + 22	Black A 6 + 13	Smyth M 31 + 1	Dunlop M 11 + 13	McDermott A 1 + 1	Murray N 21 + 3	Dodds J 5	McColl M 6 + 4	Ferguson A 1 + 1	Mullen B 2 + 2	Whalen S 10 + 3	Latta J 3 + 2	McVeigh A — + 2	Burgess R — + 1	McGrady S 1 + 1	Conway C — + 1	Ferry M 1	*Match No.*
1	2	3[2]	4	5[1]	6	7[3]	8	9	10	11	12	13	14																1
1	4	3	5		6	8	7[1]	9	10	11	2	12																	2
1		3[1]		5	6[2]	8	7	9[3]	10	11	2	14		4	12	13													3
1				5		7	3	9[2]	10	11	2	13		4	12	6[1]	8												4
1			6[1]	5	12	7	3[2]	9[3]	10	11	2	14		4	13		8												5
1				5[1]	6	7[3]	3	9[2]	10	11	2	13	14	4	12		8												6
1		3■		5	6	7[3]	13	9[1]	10[2]	11	2	12		4	14		8												7
1				5		7	6	9	10	11	2	12		4	3		8[1]												8
1		3	12	5	6	7[2]	14	9	10	11	2[1]	13		4[3]			8												9
1		3	6■	5	12		7	9[2]	10	11	2[1]	13		4			8												10
1		3		5	6	7[2]	2[1]	9	10	11	12		13	4			8■												11
1		3	5		6	7	8	9[1]	10	11■	2[2]		13	4■	12														12
1		3[2]	4	5	6	7	8[1]	9	10		2	12	14		13		11[3]												13
		3[1]	4	5	6	7	2	9[2]	10	11		13		8	12			1											14
		3	5		6	7[1]	4	9[2]	10[3]	11	2	14	12	8				1	13										15
		3	4	5	6[3]	7	2[1]	9[2]	10	11	12	13		8				1	14										16
		3	4	5	6	7	2[1]	9[2]	10■	11	12	13					8	1											17
		3	4	5	6	7		9[1]		11	2	10		8				1	12										18
1			4	5	6	7[3]	3[1]			11	2	9		8			12		10[2]	13	14								19
1			4	5	6	7[3]	3[1]	13		11	2	9	14	8			12		10[2]										20
1		3■	4	5[1]	6	7			10[2]		2	9[3]	12	8	14		11					13							21
1			4	5	6	7			10[1]		2	9	11[2]	8	3		13					12							22
1			4	5	6	7			12		2	9[1]		8	3		11[2]					10	13						23
1		3[1]	4	5	6	7			10[2]		2	13		8	12		11					9							24
1			4	5[2]	6	7	13		10		2[3]	12	14	8	3		11[1]					9							25
1			4	5	6	7	3[1]		10[2]		2	13	14	8[3]	12							9	11						26
1			4	5	6	7			12		2	10[2]	14	8[3]	3							9	11[1]	13					27
1		3[2]	4	5	6	7			10		2	14	8[1]	12	13				11	9[3]									28
1		3	4■		6[1]	7			10		2■	9[2]	8	5	12		11		13										29
1		3		5		7	2		10			12	11	4	8		6					9[1]							30
1		6[2]		5[1]		7	2		10		13		14	4	3		11					9	8[3]		12				31
1		6		5		7	12		10		2[3]	9[2]		4	3		8		11[1]					13		14			32
1			4	5	6	7	11[1]				2[2]	13	12	8	3				10			9							33
1			4		6	12			10[3]		2	9[2]	11	5	3		8				7[1]	13					14		34
1		13	4		6	12			10[3]		2	14	11	5			8				7[1]	9				3[2]			35
1					6	7					2	9		4	3		8[2]		11[1]		13	10	12					5	36

BERWICK RANGERS Second Division

Year Formed: 1881. *Ground & Address:* Shielfield Park, Tweedmouth, Berwick-upon-Tweed TD15 2EF. *Telephone:* 01289 307424. *Fax:* 01289 309424. Club 24 hour hotline 09068 800697. *Ground Capacity:* 4131, seated: 1366. *Size of Pitch:* 110yd × 70yd.
Chairman: Robert L. Wilson. *Vice-chairman:* Moray McLaren. *Club Secretary:* Dennis McCleary. *Treasurer:* J. N. Simpson.
Manager: Paul Smith. *Assistant Manager:* Greg Shaw. *Coaches:* Ian Smith, Henry Smith. *Physio:* Rev. Glyn Jones. *Ground/Kit:* Ian Oliver.
Managers since 1975: H. Melrose, G. Haig, W. Galbraith, D. Smith, F. Connor, J. McSherry, E. Tait, J. Thomson, J. Jefferies, R. Callachan, J. Anderson, J. Crease, T. Hendrie, I. Ross, J. Thomson.
Club Nickname(s): The Borderers. *Previous Grounds:* Bull Stob Close, Pier Field, Meadow Field, Union Park, Old Shielfield.
Record Attendance: 13,365 v Rangers, Scottish Cup 1st rd; 28 Jan, 1967.
Record Victory: 8-1 v Forfar Ath. Division II; 25 Dec, 1965: v Vale of Leithen, Scottish Cup; Dec, 1966.
Record Defeat: 1-9 v Hamilton A, First Division; 9 Aug, 1980.
Most League Appearances: 435: Eric Tait, 1970-87.
Most League Goals in Season (Individual): 38: Ken Bowron, Division II; 1963-64.
Most Goals Overall (Individual): 115: Eric Tait, 1970-87.

BERWICK RANGERS 2002–03 LEAGUE RECORD

Match No.	Date	Venue	Opponents	Result		H/T Score	Lg. Pos.	Goalscorers	Attendance
1	Aug 3	A	Brechin C	W	4-2	2-2	—	Wood 3 [16, 36, 84], Smith J (og) [74]	501
2	10	H	Raith R	D	1-1	1-1	2	Wood [3]	804
3	17	A	Stenhousemuir	L	0-2	0-1	5		379
4	24	A	Hamilton A	W	2-1	1-1	4	Bonnar (og) [12], Wood [72]	1486
5	31	H	Dumbarton	L	1-2	0-2	6	Burke [46]	509
6	Sept 14	H	Stranraer	L	3-4	2-3	8	Smith D 2 [29, 52], Wood [31]	388
7	21	A	Forfar Ath	W	2-0	2-0	3	Neil M [8], Smith D [36]	483
8	28	H	Cowdenbeath	W	2-1	1-1	2	Smith D [45], Forrest G [78]	458
9	Oct 5	A	Airdrie U	L	1-2	1-1	4	Forrest G [9]	1349
10	19	A	Raith R	W	2-1	0-0	3	Wood [51], Smith D [69]	1906
11	26	H	Brechin C	L	0-3	0-3	4		410
12	Nov 2	A	Dumbarton	W	2-1	0-1	4	Burke [52], Wood [90]	763
13	9	H	Hamilton A	W	2-1	1-0	3	Burke 2 [44, 84]	461
14	16	A	Stranraer	L	0-1	0-1	4		412
15	23	H	Forfar Ath	W	2-1	1-1	3	Burke [9], Forrest G [53]	387
16	30	H	Airdrie U	D	2-2	0-2	3	Wood 2 [55, 57]	647
17	Dec 14	A	Cowdenbeath	W	2-1	1-1	2	Smith D [11], Burke [90]	306
18	28	H	Stenhousemuir	D	2-2	0-0	2	Neill A [80], Burke [89]	543
19	Jan 11	H	Dumbarton	L	0-1	0-0	2		580
20	18	H	Stranraer	W	1-0	0-0	2	Smith D [80]	422
21	25	A	Brechin C	D	2-2	2-0	2	McNicoll [8], Burke [20]	402
22	Feb 8	H	Cowdenbeath	L	1-2	0-0	2	Smith D [61]	530
23	22	H	Raith R	D	1-1	1-1	2	Burke [1]	820
24	25	A	Hamilton A	L	0-3	0-1	—		626
25	Mar 1	A	Stenhousemuir	L	0-1	0-0	4		684
26	4	A	Forfar Ath	D	2-2	1-1	—	Brown [41], Burke [79]	420
27	8	H	Hamilton A	W	1-0	0-0	3	Burke [73]	406
28	15	A	Dumbarton	D	2-2	0-1	3	Burke [71], McEwan (og) [90]	916
29	22	H	Forfar Ath	D	0-0	0-0	3		389
30	28	A	Airdrie U	L	0-2	0-0	—		1276
31	Apr 5	A	Stranraer	D	0-0	0-0	5		354
32	12	H	Airdrie U	L	0-3	0-0	6		631
33	19	A	Cowdenbeath	W	1-0	1-0	6	Forrest G [9]	256
34	26	H	Brechin C	W	2-0	1-0	4	Wood 2 [28, 89]	442
35	May 3	A	Raith R	L	0-1	0-0	5		2746
36	10	H	Stenhousemuir	D	0-0	0-0	5		579

Final League Position: 5

Honours
League Champions: Second Division 1978-79; *Runners-up:* Second Division 1993-94. Third Division 1999-2000.
Scottish Cup: Quarter-finals: 1953-54, 1979-80.
League Cup: Semi-finals: 1963-64.

Club colours: Shirt: Black with broad gold vertical stripes. Shorts: Black with white trim. Stockings: Gold with black and white trim.

Goalscorers: *League* (43): Burke 12, Wood 12, Smith D 8, Forrest G 4, Brown 1, McNicoll 1, Neil M 1, Neill A 1, own goals 3
Scottish Cup (1): Burke 1
CIS Cup (4): Wood 2, Burke 1, Forrest G 1
Challenge Cup (4): Burke 2, Bennett 1 (pen), Murie 1

Godfrey R 25 + 1	Murie D 28	Smith A 22 + 1	Forrest E 11	Neill A 19 + 4	Bennett N 10 + 5	Connolly G 34 + 1	Connell G 11 + 8	Wood G 26 + 1	Burke A 36	Smith D 31 + 3	Gray D 16 + 2	Bradley M 18 + 8	Ferguson I 2 + 7	Inglis N 10 + 1	Neil M 14 + 1	Forrest G 27 + 3	McCormick M — + 5	McNicoll G 23	Smith H 1	Brown K 17 + 2	Blackley D 1 + 4	McDowell M 11 + 4	Robertson J 3 + 7	*Match No.*
1	2^{1}	3^{2}	4	5	6	7	8	9	10^{3}	11	12	13	14											1
			4	5	3	7	8	9	10^{1}	11	2	6	12	1										2
			4	5	3	7^{3}	6^{2}	9	10	11^{1}	2	13		1	8	12	14							3
	2		5^{1}	3	11	7^{3}	8	9	10^{2}	12		6		1		14	13	4						4
1	2			5	3	7	8^{1}	9	10	11		6^{2}			12	13		4						5
	2	3		12		7		9	10	11	5				8	6		4^{1}	1					6
1	2	3		5	12	7		9	10^{2}	11^{1}	4				8	6	13							7
1	2	3		5	13	7^{3}	14	9	10^{1}	11	4				8	6	12^{2}							8
1	2	3		5	12■	7		9	10	11^{1}	4				8	6								9
1	2	3	4			7		9	10^{1}	11^{2}		12	13		8	6				5				10
1	2	3^{1}	4	12		7^{2}		9	10	11			13		8	6^{3}				5	14			11
15	2	3	4			7		9	10	11				1^{6}	8	6				5				12
1	2	3	4		12	7		9	10^{1}	11					8	6				5				13
1	2^{1}	3^{2}	4	12		7		9	10	11		14	13		8	6^{3}				5				14
1	2	3	4			7		9	10	11^{1}		12			8	6				5				15
1	2	3	4			7		9	10^{1}	11			12		8	6				5				16
1		3		5		12			10	11^{1}	2	7	9		8	6		4						17
1		3		5		7	12		10	11	2	6	9		8^{1}			4						18
1■	2^{3}	3		5		7^{1}	13	9	10	11		8^{2}	14	12		6		4						19
	2	3		5^{1}		7		9	10	11		8		1		6		4		12				20
	2	3				7		9	10	11^{1}		6		1		5		4				8	12	21
	2	3^{1}				7	13	9	10^{3}	11	12	6^{2}		1		5		4				8	14	22
	2					7	8		10	11	3			1		6		4		5		9		23
	2■			14		7	8		10^{3}	11^{1}	3	13		1		6^{2}		4		5		9	12	24
1		12		5^{1}		7	8		10	13	2					6■		4		3		9	11^{2}	25
1	3				12	7	8^{2}		10	11	2	6						5		4	13	9^{1}		26
1	3					7	12	9^{1}	10	11^{2}	2	6				8		4		5			13	27
1		3^{2}				7	8^{1}		10	12	2	6						4		5	13	9	11	28
1		3				7			10	11	2	6^{1}				8		4		5	12	9		29
1		3^{2}				7		12	10	11	2	6				8		4		5		9^{1}	13	30
1	2			3		7		9	10^{2}	11^{1}		6				8		4		5		13	12	31
1	2			3	8^{1}	7			10	11		12				6		4		5		9		32
1	2	3^{1}		5	11	7	13	9	10^{3}			8				6^{2}		4		12		14		33
1	2			5	3	7^{1}	12	9	10^{2}	11		8				6		4				13		34
1	2			5	3	7^{3}	13	9	10	11^{1}		8^{2}				6		4				14	12	35
	2			5	3		8	9	10			13		1			12	4			6^{2}	7	11^{1}	36

BRECHIN CITY

First Division

Year Formed: 1906. *Ground & Address:* Glebe Park, Trinity Rd, Brechin, Angus DD9 6BJ. *Telephone:* 01356 622856. *Fax (to Secretary):* 01356 625524.
Ground Capacity: total: 3060, seated: 1518. *Size of Pitch:* 110yd × 67yd.
Chairman: David Birse. *Vice-Chairman:* Hugh Campbell Adamson. *Secretary:* Ken Ferguson.
Manager: Dick Campbell. *Assistant Manager:* Ian Campbell. *Youth Coach:* Paul Martin. *Physio:* Tom Gilmartin.
Managers since 1975: C. Dunn, I. Stewart, D. Houston, I. Fleming, J. Ritchie, I. Redford, J. Young.
Club Nickname(s): The City. *Previous Grounds:* Nursery Park.
Record Attendance: 8122 v Aberdeen, Scottish Cup 3rd rd; 3 Feb, 1973.
Record Transfer Fee received: £100,000 for Scott Thomson to Aberdeen (1991).
Record Transfer Fee paid: £16,000 for Sandy Ross from Berwick Rangers (1991).
Record Victory: 12-1 v Thornhill, Scottish Cup 1st rd; 28 Jan, 1926.
Record Defeat: 0-10 v Airdrieonians, Albion R and Cowdenbeath, all in Division II; 1937-38.
Most League Appearances: 459: David Watt, 1975-89.
Most League Goals in Season (Individual): 26: W. McIntosh, Division II; 1959-60.
Most Goals Overall (Individual): 131: Ian Campbell.

BRECHIN CITY 2002–03 LEAGUE RECORD

Match No.	*Date*	*Venue*	*Opponents*	*Result*		*H/T Score*	*Lg. Pos.*	*Goalscorers*	*Attendance*
1	Aug 3	H	Berwick R	L	2-4	2-2	—	Gibson 2 [20, 33]	501
2	10	A	Dumbarton	L	0-1	0-1	10		735
3	17	H	Hamilton A	W	1-0	1-0	9	Fotheringham K [4]	498
4	24	H	Forfar Ath	W	1-0	0-0	7	Grant [79]	761
5	31	A	Stranraer	L	1-3	0-1	8	Fotheringham K (pen) [70]	348
6	Sept 14	H	Cowdenbeath	D	0-0	0-0	10		453
7	21	A	Airdrie U	W	4-2	2-1	6	Templeman [8], Grant 3 (1 pen) [41, 70 (p), 83]	1373
8	28	A	Raith R	L	1-3	0-0	8	Smith J [68]	2007
9	Oct 5	H	Stenhousemuir	W	1-0	1-0	5	King Charles [2]	489
10	26	A	Berwick R	W	3-0	3-0	3	Templeman 2 [19, 31], Grant [29]	410
11	29	H	Dumbarton	D	1-1	0-1	—	Templeman [53]	377
12	Nov 2	H	Stranraer	W	3-1	2-0	3	Grant [7], Clark [25], King Charles [86]	426
13	9	A	Forfar Ath	L	1-2	0-1	4	Templeman [70]	868
14	16	A	Cowdenbeath	W	1-0	1-0	3	Fotheringham K [19]	267
15	23	H	Airdrie U	L	1-5	0-2	4	King Charles [83]	557
16	30	A	Stenhousemuir	D	1-1	0-0	4	King Charles [63]	331
17	Dec 14	H	Raith R	L	1-2	0-2	4	King Charles [68]	746
18	28	A	Hamilton A	W	2-1	1-1	4	Smith D [22], Clark [61]	1418
19	Jan 1	H	Forfar Ath	L	3-4	1-1	—	Templeman 2 [2, 64], Black [63]	743
20	18	H	Cowdenbeath	L	5-7	2-2	5	Clark [9], Templeman 2 [23, 86], Fotheringham M (pen) [47], Smith J [70]	452
21	25	H	Berwick R	D	2-2	0-2	6	Templeman [50], Cairney [52]	402
22	Feb 1	A	Airdrie U	L	0-3	0-1	7		1275
23	8	A	Raith R	W	2-1	0-1	5	Grant [62], Templeman [71]	1776
24	25	A	Stranraer	W	3-2	3-1	—	King Charles [4], Templeman 2 [42, 44]	371
25	Mar 1	H	Hamilton A	W	4-1	3-0	2	Templeman [1], Fotheringham K [6], Gibson 2 [40, 80]	441
26	8	A	Forfar Ath	W	5-1	2-1	2	King Charles [9], Fotheringham K 2 [12, 74], Black [66], Rattray (og) [72]	774
27	11	A	Dumbarton	W	3-1	1-1	—	Templeman 3 [40, 60, 78]	513
28	15	H	Stranraer	W	3-1	1-0	2	King Charles [24], Black [57], Fotheringham K [86]	488
29	22	H	Airdrie U	L	0-1	0-0	2		672
30	29	H	Stenhousemuir	W	2-1	2-0	2	Templeman 2 [14, 32]	435
31	Apr 5	A	Cowdenbeath	L	0-1	0-0	2		274
32	12	A	Stenhousemuir	D	2-2	0-1	2	Grant [52], Coulston [81]	510
33	19	H	Raith R	W	1-0	1-0	2	Templeman [18]	1819
34	26	A	Berwick R	L	0-2	0-1	2		442
35	May 3	H	Dumbarton	D	1-1	1-1	2	King Charles [32]	895
36	10	A	Hamilton A	D	2-2	0-0	2	Fotheringham K [71], Templeman [90]	1644

Final League Position: 2

Honours
League Champions: C Division 1953-54. Second Division 1982-83, 1989-90. Third Division 2001-02. *Runners-up:* Second Division 1992-93, 2002-03. Third Division 1995-96.
Bell's League Challenge: Finalists 2002-03. Semi-finalists 2001-02.

Club colours: Shirt, Shorts, Stockings: Red with white trimmings.

Goalscorers: *League* (63): Templeman 21, Fotheringham K 9 (2 pens), Charles King 9, Grant 8 (1 pen), Gibson 4, Black 3, Clark 3, Smith J 2, Cairney 1, Coulston 1, Smith D 1, own goal 1
Scottish Cup (1): Riley 1
CIS Cup (1): Skinner 1
Challenge Cup (12): Grant 3, Fotheringham K 2, Millar M 2, Templeman 2, Gibson 1, Jackson 1, Charles King 1

Cairns M 11	Miller G 28 + 6	Black R 22 + 7	Smith J 30 + 1	Cairney H 29	Fotheringham K 31	King Charles 29 + 4	Millar M 7 + 1	Gibson G 13 + 20	Templeman C 34 + 1	Jackson C 32	Smith D 4 + 5	Campbell P — + 5	Riley P 2 + 6	McCulloch C 14 + 3	Grant R 22 + 5	Hay D 11	Skinner J 20	McKechnie G 1	Clark D 11 + 8	Donachie B 2 + 1	McDonald C 1 + 1	King Chris — + 2	Boyle S 3 + 9	Fotheringham M 6 + 7	Deas P 15	Thomson S 14	Coulston D 4 + 2	*Match No.*
1	2^{1}	3^{3}	4	5	6	7^{2}	8	9	10	11	12	13	14															1
1	3^{1}	12	4	5	6	7	10	11	9^{2}	8^{3}		14		2	13													2
	2	3	4	5	6		10	12	7	11					9^{1}	1	8											3
	2	3^{2}	4	5	6	13	11	12	10^{1}	8^{3}			14		9	1	7											4
	14		4	5	6	7	11	13	10^{2}	3		12	8		9^{3}	1	2^{1}											5
	13	3^{2}	4	5	6	7	8^{3}	12		2	14				9	1	10	11^{1}										6
	13	3	4	5		7■		12	10^{1}	8				2^{3}	9^{2}	1	6		11	14								7
		3	4	5	6^{2}		7^{3}	12	11^{1}	10		14		2	9	1	8		13									8
		3	4	5	6	11	14	12	13	10			8^{3}	2	9^{2}	1			7^{1}									9
1	7	12	4	5	6	13			11	10^{3}			14	2	9^{1}		8		3^{2}									10
1	7^{3}	3	4	5	6	13		14	11	10				2^{1}	9		8				12^{2}							11
1	7	3	4	5	6	12		14	11^{2}	10			13		9^{3}		8		2^{1}									12
1	7	3	4	5^{1}	6	2		12	11	10	14				9^{3}		8^{2}		13									13
1	10	12	4■	5	6	2^{1}		13	8	11					9^{2}				3	7								14
1	10			5	6	7		12	8^{3}	11		14			9^{1}				3^{2}	4■	2	13						15
1	7	3	4	5		2		11	8	10					9		6											16
	12	14	4	5	6	7		10^{3}	9	11	2^{1}					1	8		3^{2}			13						17
	10	12	4		6	7		9^{1}	8	11	2^{2}		13			1	5		3									18
1	2	13	4		6	7		10^{1}	9	11	8^{3}		14				5		3^{2}				12					19
	12	3	13	5	6^{2}	7		14	9	8						1	4		10				11^{3}	2^{1}				20
1	2	11^{2}		5	6	7			8	10					9^{1}		4		13				12		3			21
	2^{1}	13	4		8	7^{3}			9	10	14				12	1	5						3^{2}	11	6			22
	12	3		5	10	7		13	11	8	2^{1}				9^{2}		4								6	1		23
	7	3			6	11^{1}		12	10	8				2	9^{2}		4		13						5	1		24
	7	3			6			10	9^{2}	8				2			4^{1}		12				11^{3}	13	5	1	14	25
	8^{2}	3	4		6	7		9^{1}	10	11^{3}				2					12				14	13	5	1		26
	8	3	4^{3}	5	6	7^{2}		11^{1}	9	10				2					13				14	12		1		27
	10	3^{1}	4		6	7		11^{2}	9	8				2					13					12	5	1		28
	11^{3}	3^{2}	2	4	6	7		10^{1}	9	8					12								13	14	5	1		29
	8	3	11	4	6	7		10^{1}	9					2	12										5	1		30
	2^{2}	3	4	5	6	7		10^{1}	9					8	12									13	11	1		31
	11		8	5	6^{3}■	7		13	10					2	9^{2}				3^{1}					14	4	1	12	32
	2		4	5		7^{3}		12	11^{1}	8				13	9^{2}								14	10	6	1	3	33
	2^{3}		4	5		7		12	10	11	13				9^{1}								14	8	6	1	3^{2}	34
	2		4	5		7		12	10^{1}	11				14	9								13	8^{2}	6	1	3^{3}	35
	2		4	5	6	7		13	10					14	9^{2}								12	8^{3}	3	1	11^{1}	36

CELTIC — Premier League

Year Formed: 1888. *Ground & Address:* Celtic Park, Glasgow G40 3RE. *Telephone:* 0141 556 2611. *Fax:* 0141 551 8106.
Ground Capacity: all seated: 60,355. *Size of Pitch:* 105m × 68m.
Chairman: Brian Quinn. *Chief Executive:* To be appointed. *Secretary:* Robert Howat.
Manager: Martin O'Neill. *Assistant Manager:* John Robertson. *First Team Coach:* Steve Walford. *Youth Development Manager:* Tommy Burns. *Head Youth Coach:* Willie McStay. *Physio:* Brian Scott. *Assistant Physio:* Neil McLeod. *Kit Manager:* John Clark.
Managers since 1975: Jock Stein, Billy McNeill, David Hay, Billy McNeill, Liam Brady, Lou Macari, Tommy Burns, Wim Jansen, Dr Jozef Venglos, John Barnes (Head Coach). *Club Nickname(s):* The Bhoys. *Previous Grounds:* None.
Record Attendance: 92,000 v Rangers, Division I; 1 Jan, 1938.
Record Transfer Fee received: £4,700,000 for Paolo Di Canio to Sheffield W (August 1997).
Record Transfer Fee paid: £6,000,000 for Chris Sutton from Chelsea (July 2000).
Record Victory: 11-0 Dundee, Division I; 26 Oct, 1895.
Record Defeat: 0-8 v Motherwell, Division I; 30 Apr, 1937.
Most Capped Player: Pat Bonner 80, Republic of Ireland.
Most League Appearances: 486: Billy McNeill 1957-75.
Most League Goals in Season (Individual): 50: James McGrory, Division I; 1935-36.
Most Goals Overall (Individual): 397: James McGrory; 1922-39.

Honours
League Champions: (38 times) Division I 1892-93, 1893-94, 1895-96, 1897-98, 1904-05, 1905-06, 1906-07, 1907-08, 1908-09, 1909-10, 1913-14, 1914-15, 1915-16, 1916-17, 1918-19, 1921-22, 1925-26, 1935-36, 1937-38, 1953-54, 1965-66, 1966-67,

CELTIC 2002–03 LEAGUE RECORD

Match No.	Date	Venue	Opponents	Result		H/T Score	Lg. Pos.	Goalscorers	Attendance
1	Aug 3	H	Dunfermline Ath	W	2-1	1-0	—	Larsson 2 [41, 65]	56,438
2	10	A	Aberdeen	W	4-0	2-0	1	Mjällby [4], Sutton [33], Sylla [52], Lambert [65]	17,314
3	17	H	Dundee U	W	5-0	3-0	1	McNamara [24], Sutton [25], Petrov [32], Hartson [77], Larsson [79]	56,247
4	24	A	Partick Th	W	1-0	0-0	1	Larsson [71]	8053
5	Sept 1	H	Livingston	W	2-0	2-0	1	Larsson [25], Balde [38]	55,334
6	10	A	Motherwell	L	1-2	0-0	—	Hartson [87]	8448
7	14	H	Hibernian	W	1-0	1-0	2	Hartson [31]	56,462
8	22	A	Dundee	W	1-0	1-0	2	Larsson [17]	9483
9	28	H	Kilmarnock	W	5-0	3-0	2	Larsson 3 (1 pen) [10, 20, 90 (p)], Sutton 2 [15, 63]	57,070
10	Oct 6	H	Rangers	D	3-3	1-1	2	Larsson 2 [39, 52], Sutton [78]	58,939
11	20	A	Hearts	W	4-1	4-0	2	Sutton [3], Petrov [9], Larsson 2 [36, 41]	13,911
12	27	A	Dunfermline Ath	W	4-1	2-0	2	Larsson [24], Thompson [31], Petrov [73], Sutton [83]	9139
13	Nov 3	H	Aberdeen	W	7-0	3-0	2	Hartson 4 [26, 35, 47, 80], Larsson [42], Balde [70], Maloney [85]	57,797
14	10	A	Dundee U	W	2-0	1-0	2	Hartson [13], Sutton [87]	10,664
15	17	H	Partick Th	W	4-0	2-0	2	Sutton [10], Petrov 2 [33, 68], Larsson [90]	57,231
16	24	A	Livingston	W	2-0	1-0	1	Larsson 2 (1 pen) [5 (p), 82]	8320
17	Dec 1	H	Motherwell	W	3-1	0-0	1	Larsson [52], Leitch (og) [60], Valgaeren [71]	56,610
18	4	A	Hibernian	W	1-0	0-0	—	Petrov [76]	12,042
19	7	A	Rangers	L	2-3	1-3	2	Sutton [1], Hartson [61]	49,874
20	15	A	Kilmarnock	D	1-1	0-1	5	Valgaeren [66]	9225
21	21	H	Dundee	W	2-0	1-0	2	Hartson [37], Larsson [53]	56,162
22	26	H	Hearts	W	4-2	2-1	—	Hartson 3 [22, 44, 68], Larsson [72]	58,480
23	29	H	Dunfermline Ath	W	1-0	1-0	2	Larsson [18]	58,387
24	Jan 2	A	Aberdeen	D	1-1	1-0	2	Larsson [29]	16,331
25	29	H	Dundee U	W	2-0	2-0	—	Hartson [25], Larsson [29]	54,912
26	Feb 2	A	Partick Th	W	2-0	2-0	2	Sutton 2 [7, 32]	7119
27	9	H	Livingston	W	2-1	0-0	2	Sylla [77], Sutton [85]	56,982
28	Mar 2	H	Hibernian	W	3-2	2-1	2	Hartson 2 [2, 24], Mjällby [90]	57,096
29	8	H	Rangers	W	1-0	0-0	2	Hartson [58]	58,336
30	Apr 6	A	Dundee	D	1-1	1-1	2	Thompson [9]	9013
31	13	H	Kilmarnock	W	2-0	1-0	2	Larsson [19], Petrov [72]	56,736
32	19	A	Hearts	L	1-2	0-0	2	Larsson [59]	15,855
33	27	A	Rangers	W	2-1	2-0	2	Thompson (pen) [27], Hartson [41]	49,740
34	May 3	A	Dunfermline Ath	W	4-1	3-0	1	Larsson [21], Petrov 2 [29, 32], Thompson (pen) [59]	8923
35	7	A	Motherwell	W	4-0	1-0	—	Petrov 2 [36, 56], Lambert 2 [61, 65]	12,037
36	10	H	Hearts	W	1-0	1-0	2	Thompson [28]	58,906
37	14	H	Dundee	W	6-2	3-1	2	Larsson [14], Thompson 2 [27, 30], Maloney 2 [52, 63], Mjällby [77]	59,500
38	25	A	Kilmarnock	W	4-0	2-0	2	Sutton 2 [16, 42], Thompson [54], Petrov [83]	16,722

Final League Position: 2

1967-68, 1968-69, 1969-70, 1970-71, 1971-72, 1972-73, 1973-74. Premier Division 1976-77, 1978-79, 1980-81, 1981-82, 1985-86, 1987-88, 1997-98, 2000-01, 2001-02. *Runners-up:* 26 times.
Scottish Cup Winners: (31 times) 1892, 1899, 1900, 1904, 1907, 1908, 1911, 1912, 1914, 1923, 1925, 1927, 1931, 1933, 1937, 1951, 1954, 1965, 1967, 1969, 1971, 1972, 1974, 1975, 1977, 1980, 1985, 1988, 1989, 1995, 2001. *Runners-up:* 18 times.
League Cup Winners: (12 times) 1956-57, 1957-58, 1965-66, 1966-67, 1967-68, 1968-69, 1969-70, 1974-75, 1982-83, 1997-98, 1999-2000, 2000-01. *Runners-up:* 11 times.

European: *European Cup:* 92 matches (1966-67 winners, 1967-68, 1968-69, 1969-70 runners-up, 1970-71, 1971-72 semi-finals, 1972-73, 1973-74 semi-finals, 1974-75, 1977-78, 1979-80, 1981-82, 1982-83, 1986-87, 1988-89, 1998-99, 2001-02, 2002-03). *Cup Winners' Cup:* 39 matches (1963-64 semi-finals, 1965-66 semi-finals, 1975-76, 1980-81, 1984-85, 1985-86, 1989-90, 1995-96). *UEFA Cup:* 69 matches (*Fairs Cup:* 1962-63, 1964-65. *UEFA Cup:* 1976-77, 1983-84, 1987-88, 1991-92, 1992-93, 1993-94, 1996-97, 1997-98, 1998-99, 1999-2000, 2000-01, 2001-02, 2002-03 runners-up).

Club colours: Shirt: Emerald green and white hoops. Shorts: White with emerald trim. Stockings: White.

Goalscorers: *League* (98): Larsson 28 (2 pens), Hartson 18, Sutton 14, Petrov 12, Thompson 8, Lambert 3, Maloney 3, Mjällby 3, Balde 2, Sylla 2, Valgaeren 2, Laursen 1, McNamara 1, own goal 1
Scottish Cup (6): Larsson 2, Hartson 2 (1 pen), Smith 1, Sylla 1
CIS Cup (9): Balde 2, Hartson 2, Larsson 2, Lambert 1, Maloney 1, Thompson 1

Douglas R 21	Mjällby J 14	Valgaeren J 35	Balde D 36	Lennon N 28	Petrov S 33 + 1	Sylla M 13 + 5	Lambert P 27 + 3	Petta B 2	Larsson H 35	Sutton C 28	Fernandez D 3 + 7	Crainey S 3 + 10	Maloney S 5 + 15	Hedman M 8	Laursen U 22	McNamara J 12 + 7	Guppy S 12 + 4	Hartson J 18 + 9	Agathe D 24 + 3	Thompson A 26 + 3	Gould J 2	Lynch S — + 1	Smith J 3 + 9	Healy C — + 1	Broto J 7 + 1	Varga S 1	*Match No.*
1	2	3	4	5	6	7	8	9^{2}	10^{1}	11	12	13															1
1	2^{3}	3	4	5	6^{2}	7	8	9^{1}	10	11	12	14	13														2
	2^{3}	3		8^{2}	6	7			10	11^{1}	13	14		1	4	5	9	12									3
1		3	4	6^{1}			8		10	11^{2}		13			2	5	9	12	7								4
		3	4		6				10^{1}	11^{2}	9^{3}		13	1	2	5	8	12	7	14							5
1		3	4		6		8		10	11			13		2		9	12	7^{2}	5^{1}							6
		3	4	8		7			10				12		2	6	9	11		5^{1}	1						7
1		3	4	5	6	7^{2}	8		10	11^{1}		13			2		9	12									8
1		3	4^{3}	5	6^{1}	7^{2}	8		10	11			14		2		9	12	13								9
1		3	4	9	6^{2}	7^{1}	8^{3}		10	11			14		2			13	12	5							10
1		3^{2}	4	5	6^{1}		8		10	11		13			2		9^{3}	14	7	12							11
		3	4	9	6^{3}	13	8^{1}		10	11			14		2			12	7^{2}	5	1						12
1		3	4		6^{3}	7			10	8	12	13	14		2^{2}		9	11		5^{1}							13
1		3	4	6		7^{1}	13		10	8					2		9	11^{2}	12	5							14
1		3	4^{1}	9^{2}	6^{3}		8		10	11	12	14	13			5			7	2							15
1		3	4	9	6^{1}	7	8		10	11					2	12				5							16
1		3	4			13	8		10^{1}		9	2	12			14	6^{3}	11	7^{2}	5							17
1		3	4	9	6	7^{3}	8				10^{2}		13		2	14	12	11		5^{1}							18
1		3	4	5	6				10	9					2		8^{1}	11	7	12							19
1		3	4		6^{1}		8		10	9						5	12	11	7	2							20
1		3	4		6		8		10	9					2			11^{1}	7	5		12					21
		3	4		6		8		10	9				1	2			11	7	5							22
	2	3	4		6^{1}		8		10	9				1		13	12	11^{2}	7	5							23
	2	3	4		6^{2}		8		10^{1}	9	12^{3}		14	1		7		11		5			13				24
	2^{1}	3	4		6		8		10	9		13		1		12		11^{2}	7				5				25
		3	4	8^{1}	6				10	11				1	2	7			9				5	12			26
		3	4	8	6	7			10^{1}	11			12	1	2	9							5				27
	2	3		7	6^{2}	13	8^{1}					4	10				12	11	9	5					1		28
1	2	3	4	6	7^{2}	12	8			10						13		11	9^{1}	5							29
	2		4	6	7	9^{1}	8		10			3						11		5			12		1		30
1	2	3	4	6	7^{2}		8		10				13					11	9^{1}	5			12				31
1	2	3	4	6	7^{1}		8^{2}		10				12					11	9	5			13				32
1^{6}		3	4	6	12				10	9					2	7		11^{1}	8	5					15		33
		3^{1}	4	8^{3}	7		12		10		13		11		2	6			9^{2}	5			14		1		34
			4	6	7	13	8		10			14	11^{1}		2	3			9^{2}	5^{3}			12		1		35
	2	3	4	6	7^{2}		8		10	11						13			9	5^{1}			12		1		36
	2	3	4	6	7		8		10				11^{1}						9	5			12		1		37
	2		4	6	7		12		10	11			9^{1}						8^{2}	5			13		1	3	38

CLYDE First Division

Year Formed: 1877. *Ground & Address:* Broadwood Stadium, Cumbernauld, G68 9NE. *Telephone:* 01236 451511.
Ground Capacity: all seated: 8200. *Size of Pitch:* 112yd × 76yd.
Chairman: W. B. Carmichael. *Secretary:* John D. Taylor.
Manager: Alan Kernaghan. *Assistant Manager:* Billy Reid. *First Team Coach:* Denis McDaid. *Physio:* Ian McKinlay.
Managers since 1975: S. Anderson, C. Brown, J. Clark, A. Smith, G. Speirs, A. Maitland.
Club Nickname(s): The Bully Wee. *Previous Grounds:* Barrowfield Park 1877-97, Shawfield Stadium 1897-1994.
Record Attendance: 52,000 v Rangers, Division I; 21 Nov, 1908.
Record Transfer Fee received: £175,000 for Scott Howie to Norwich City (Aug 1993).
Record Transfer Fee paid: £14,000 for Harry Hood from Sunderland (1966).
Record Victory: 11-1 v Cowdenbeath, Division II; 6 Oct, 1951.
Record Defeat: 0-11 v Dumbarton, Scottish Cup 4th rd, 22 Nov, 1879; v Rangers, Scottish Cup 4th rd, 13 Nov, 1880.
Most Capped Player: Tommy Ring, 12, Scotland.
Most League Appearances: 428: Brian Ahern.
Most League Goals in Season (Individual): 32: Bill Boyd, 1932-33.

CLYDE 2002–03 LEAGUE RECORD

Match No.	Date	Venue	Opponents	Result		H/T Score	Lg. Pos.	Goalscorers	Attendance
1	Aug 3	A	Queen of the S	L	1-2	0-1	—	Millen 83	3206
2	10	H	Ayr U	W	1-0	0-0	5	Hinds 53	1123
3	17	A	Arbroath	D	1-1	1-0	5	Fraser 23	744
4	24	H	St Mirren	L	2-3	0-2	7	Keogh 2 53, 79	1814
5	31	A	Ross Co	D	1-1	0-0	7	Ross 84	2059
6	Sept 14	H	Alloa Ath	D	0-0	0-0	7		973
7	21	A	Falkirk	L	1-2	0-0	7	Kane P 89	3595
8	28	H	Inverness CT	W	3-0	2-0	6	Nish 2 30, 45, Convery 80	936
9	Oct 5	A	St Johnstone	W	1-0	1-0	5	Hinds (pen) 18	2037
10	12	H	Queen of the S	W	2-1	0-1	4	Kernaghan 51, Keogh 52	1026
11	26	A	Ayr U	D	1-1	1-1	4	Keogh 19	1989
12	Nov 2	H	Ross Co	W	2-1	2-1	4	Keogh 6, Ross 37	1047
13	9	A	St Mirren	W	4-1	0-1	4	Millen 62, Nish 2 74, 90, Ross 80	2703
14	16	A	Alloa Ath	W	4-1	2-1	3	Mensing 15, Nish 17, Fraser 47, Potter 64	736
15	23	H	Falkirk	W	2-0	2-0	3	Hinds 2 21, 27	3415
16	30	A	Inverness CT	L	0-1	0-0	3		2829
17	Dec 7	H	St Johnstone	L	1-2	0-1	3	Hinds 66	1367
18	14	H	Arbroath	W	3-0	3-0	3	Hinds 3, Mensing 21, Keogh 43	861
19	28	A	Ross Co	D	1-1	0-1	3	Cosgrove 66	2534
20	Jan 1	H	St Mirren	W	3-2	2-1	—	Falconer 2 19, 24, Keogh 69	1553
21	18	A	St Johnstone	W	2-1	1-1	3	Fraser 29, Mensing 55	2455
22	Feb 8	A	Arbroath	W	2-1	1-0	4	Falconer 12, Hagen 64	686
23	25	A	Queen of the S	D	1-1	0-1	—	Hagen 70	1375
24	Mar 1	H	Ross Co	W	1-0	1-0	4	Convery 35	980
25	4	A	Falkirk	L	0-3	0-3	—		3706
26	8	A	St Mirren	W	2-1	0-0	4	Kernaghan 82, Gilhaney 85	2683
27	11	H	Alloa Ath	D	2-2	0-1	—	Keogh 74, Gilhaney 77	665
28	15	H	Falkirk	D	0-0	0-0	4		3002
29	18	H	Inverness CT	W	4-1	3-1	—	McConalogue 1, Millen 7, Gilhaney 16, Shields 86	703
30	22	H	Ayr U	W	3-0	1-0	4	Millen 2 (2 pens) 25, 67, Falconer 88	1015
31	Apr 5	A	Alloa Ath	W	2-1	1-1	4	McConalogue 28, Keogh 63	687
32	12	A	Inverness CT	W	2-1	1-0	3	Mensing 28, McConalogue 61	1682
33	19	H	St Johnstone	W	2-1	2-1	2	Potter 23, Millen 43	1143
34	26	H	Queen of the S	D	2-2	2-1	2	Keogh 2, Gilhaney 24	960
35	May 3	A	Ayr U	W	3-0	2-0	2	McConalogue 2 18, 50, Hagen 33	1795
36	10	H	Arbroath	W	4-2	3-1	2	Keogh 2 4, 42, Hagen 30, Millen 66	1002

Final League Position: 2

Honours
League Champions: Division II 1904-05, 1951-52, 1956-57, 1961-62, 1972-73. Second Division 1977-78, 1981-82, 1992-93, 1999-2000.
Runners-up: Division II 1903-04, 1905-06, 1925-26, 1963-64.
Scottish Cup Winners: 1939, 1955, 1958; *Runners-up:* 1910, 1912, 1949.

Club colours: Shirt: White with red and black trim. Shorts: Black. Stockings: white.

Goalscorers: *League* (66): Keogh 12, Millen 7 (2 pens), Hinds 6 (1 pen), McConalogue 5, Nish 5, Falconer 4, Gilhaney 4, Hagen 4, Mensing 4, Fraser 3, Ross 3, Convery 2, Kernaghan 2, Potter 2, Cosgrove 1, Kane P 1, Shields 1
Scottish Cup (2): Hinds 1, Millen 1
CIS Cup (0)
Challenge Cup (1): Hinds 1

McEwan D 1	Mensing S 35	Potter J 32 + 1	Smith B 5	Kane P 14 + 1	Ross J 33	Millen A 30	Fraser J 28 + 6	Keogh P 24 + 4	Falconer W 10 + 8	Dunn D 3	Kane A — + 2	Convery S 3 + 21	Hinds L 19 + 1	Halliwell B 34	McClay A 2 + 2	Hagen D 30 + 1	Cosgrove S 9 + 11	Bossy F 11 + 4	McConalogue S 11 + 5	Nish C 13 + 2	McLaughlin M 7	Kernaghan A 26	Shields P 8 + 5	Morrison J 2	Gilhaney M 6 + 5	Reid W — + 1	Baird J — + 1	Doyle P — + 1	*Match No.*
1	2	3	4	5	6	7	8	9¹	10²	11³	12	14	13																1
	2	3	4		6	5	7	12	9¹			13	10²	1	8	11													2
	2	3	4		6	5	8			11	12	9¹	10	1	7²		13												3
	2	3	4³		6	5	8²	12		11		13	9¹	1			14	7	10										4
	2	3	4		6	5	8	9				14		1	13		12	7¹	11²	10³									5
	2	3			6	5	8³	7				14	9	1	13	11¹	12	4		10²									6
	2	4■		5	6	7	13	8				14	10³	1		11²		12		9	3¹								7
	3			5¹	6	8	12	10				13	11²	1		7		2		9		4							8
	3	2		5²	6¹	8	13	10				12	11	1		7				9		4							9
	3	2		5	6	8■	12	10				13	11¹	1		7				9²		4							10
	3	2		5	6		8	10				12	11²	1		7			13	9¹		4							11
	3	2		5	6		8	10				13	11²	1		7	12			9¹		4							12
	3	2		5¹	6	10	8					12	11	1		7				9		4							13
	3	2		5¹	6	10	8³		14			13	11	1		7²	12	4		9									14
	3	2			6	8²	5	10¹				12	11	1		7		13		9		4							15
	3	2			6		5	10				12	11	1		7		8¹		9		4							16
	3				6	8	5	10	12				11	1		7	13	2²		9¹		4							17
	3	2			6²	8■	5	10	9¹			13	11	1		7			12			4							18
	3	2³			6		5	10	9²			12	11	1		7	8¹	14		13		4							19
	3				6	8	5	10	9¹				11	1		7		2		12		4							20
	3	2			6²	8	5		9¹			12	11	1		7		10	13			4							21
	3	2		5	6	8			9¹			12		1		7	10		11²			4	13						22
	2	14		5²	6	8	13		9¹			12				7	10				3	4³	11	1					23
		2		5¹	6	8	10²					9		1		7	12		13		3	4	11						24
	6²	2		5		8	10		12			9¹		1		7	13				3	4	11						25
	3	2		14		8	5³	13	9					1		7¹	10	6				4	11²		12				26
	3	2		5¹		8	12	14	9³					1		7	10	6				4	11²		13				27
	3	2			6	8	5²	9³	14					1		7	10		13			4	11¹		12				28
	3	2			6	8	5	9	13					1		7³	14		10²			4	12		11¹				29
	3	2			6	8		9³	13					1		7¹	5		10			4	12	11²	14				30
	3	2			6		5	9						1			8		10			4	7		11				31
	3	2			6		5	9	13					1		12	8		10			4	7²		11¹				32
	3	2			6	8	5	9²	13					1		7			10¹		11	4³	12		14				33
	3	2			6	8	5	9						1		7	13		10²			4	12		11¹				34
	3	2			6	8	5²	9						1		7		13	10		4				11¹		12		35
	3²	2			6	8	5³	9				12		1		7¹			10		4				11	14		13	36

COWDENBEATH

Third Division

Year Formed: 1881. *Ground & Address:* Central Park, Cowdenbeath KY4 9EY. *Telephone:* 01383 610166. *Fax:* 01383 512132.
Ground Capacity: total: 5268, seated: 1622. *Size of Pitch:* 107yd × 66yd.
Chairman: Gordon McDougall. *Secretary:* Tom Ogilvie. *General Manager:* Joe McNamara.
Manager: Keith Wright. *Assistant Manager:* Mickey Weir. *Physio:* Neil Bryson.
Managers since 1975: D. McLindon, F. Connor, P. Wilson, A. Rolland, H. Wilson, W. McCulloch, J. Clark, J. Craig, R. Campbell, J. Blackley, J. Brownlie, A. Harrow, J. Reilly, P Dolan, T. Steven, S. Conn, C. Levein, G. Kirk. *Previous Grounds:* North End Park, Cowdenbeath.
Record Attendance: 25,586 v Rangers, League Cup quarter-final; 21 Sept, 1949.
Record Transfer Fee received: £30,000 for Nicky Henderson to Falkirk (March 1994).
Record Victory: 12-0 v Johnstone, Scottish Cup 1st rd; 21 Jan, 1928.
Record Defeat: 1-11 v Clyde, Division II; 6 Oct, 1951.
Most Capped Player: Jim Paterson, 3, Scotland.
Most League and Cup Appearances: 491 Ray Allan 1972-75, 1979-89.
Most League Goals in Season (Individual): 54, Rab Walls, Division II, 1938-39.
Most Goals Overall (Individual): 127, Willie Devlin, 1922-26, 1929-30.

COWDENBEATH 2002–03 LEAGUE RECORD

Match No.	Date	Venue	Opponents	Result		H/T Score	Lg. Pos.	Goalscorers	Attendance
1	Aug 3	H	Hamilton A	L	1-3	1-1	—	Gordon 7	427
2	10	A	Stranraer	W	3-2	2-1	6	Gordon 11, French 23, White 67	349
3	17	H	Forfar Ath	D	1-1	1-0	8	Brown G 24	347
4	24	H	Raith R	W	3-1	2-1	3	Gordon (pen) 33, Dair 34, Brown G 74	1678
5	31	A	Airdrie U	D	0-0	0-0	2		1486
6	Sept 14	A	Brechin C	D	0-0	0-0	3		453
7	21	H	Stenhousemuir	W	1-0	1-0	2	Brown G 6	340
8	28	A	Berwick R	L	1-2	1-1	4	Dixon 32	458
9	Oct 5	H	Dumbarton	W	3-1	1-1	3	Brown G 21, Winter 74, Gordon 85	363
10	19	H	Stranraer	L	0-1	0-0	4		358
11	26	A	Hamilton A	L	0-1	0-0	5		1052
12	Nov 2	H	Airdrie U	L	0-1	0-0	5		603
13	9	A	Raith R	L	1-4	0-1	7	Wright 90	2428
14	16	H	Brechin C	L	0-1	0-1	9		267
15	23	A	Stenhousemuir	L	1-4	1-1	10	Gordon 35	377
16	30	A	Dumbarton	D	1-1	1-1	10	Brown G 6	754
17	Dec 14	H	Berwick R	L	1-2	1-1	10	Brown G 12	306
18	28	A	Forfar Ath	L	1-2	1-0	10	Gordon 32	596
19	Jan 1	H	Raith R	D	1-1	0-1	—	Brown G 79	1875
20	18	A	Brechin C	W	7-5	2-2	10	White 20, Riordan 3 41, 46, 76, Gordon 55, Hilland 63, Mauchlen 73	452
21	Feb 8	A	Berwick R	W	2-1	0-0	10	Brown G 49, Buchanan 88	530
22	11	A	Airdrie U	D	1-1	1-0	—	Gordon 32	1070
23	25	H	Stenhousemuir	D	3-3	0-1	—	Mauchlen 62, Webster 64, Brown G 79	258
24	Mar 1	H	Forfar Ath	D	2-2	1-0	10	Mauchlen (pen) 27, Rattray (og) 49	323
25	4	H	Hamilton A	L	0-1	0-0	—		281
26	8	A	Raith R	L	1-2	1-2	10	Wilson 39	1900
27	11	A	Stranraer	D	4-4	2-2	—	Webster 2, Brown G 30, Elliott 2 46, 64	363
28	15	H	Airdrie U	L	1-2	0-1	10	Buchanan 73	585
29	18	H	Dumbarton	W	2-0	1-0	—	Mauchlen 18, Elliott 79	184
30	22	A	Stenhousemuir	D	1-1	0-0	10	Gordon 77	488
31	Apr 5	H	Brechin C	W	1-0	0-0	10	Mauchlen (pen) 72	274
32	12	A	Dumbarton	L	1-3	0-2	10	Gordon (pen) 85	1203
33	19	H	Berwick R	L	0-1	0-1	10		256
34	26	A	Hamilton A	L	0-2	0-2	10		1055
35	May 3	H	Stranraer	D	0-0	0-0	10		229
36	10	A	Forfar Ath	D	1-1	0-0	10	Mowat 48	465

Final League Position: 10

Honours
League Champions: Division II 1913-14, 1914-15, 1938-39; *Runners-up:* Division II 1921-22, 1923-24, 1969-70. Second Division 1991-92. *Runners-up:* Third Division 2000-01.
Scottish Cup: Quarter-finals: 1931.
League Cup: Semi-finals: 1959-60, 1970-71.

Club colours: Shirt: Royal blue with white cuffs and collar. Shorts: White. Stockings: White.

Goalscorers: *League* (46): Brown G 10, Gordon 10 (2 pens), Mauchlen 5 (2 pens), Elliott 3, Riordan 3, Buchanan 2, Webster 2, White 2, French 1, Dair 1, Dixon 1, Hilland 1, Mowat 1, Wilson 1, Winter 1, Wright 1, own goal 1
Scottish Cup (9): Gordon 2, Brown 1, Buchanan 1, Elliott 1, Gilfillan 1, O'Connor 1, Riordan 1, Winter 1
CIS Cup (4): Brown 1, Elliott 1, French 1, Wilson 1
Challenge Cup (0)

O'Connor G 26	Miller W 19	Campbell A 30 + 2	White D 30 + 1	Wilson K 28 + 1	Renwick M 33 + 3	French H 8	Winter C 30	Brown G 34	Gordon K 35 + 1	Mauchlen I 22 + 3	Elliott J 14 + 14	Gilfillan G — + 6	Dair L 9 + 4	Munro K 2 + 1	Dixon J 2 + 2	Gibb S — + 2	Wright K — + 6	Byle K 4 + 5	McDonald I 10 + 2	Risser O 1	Obidille E 2 + 1	Fusco G 3 + 4	Crabbe G — + 1	Graham M 10	Riordan D 2	Hilland P 2	Buchanan L 2 + 10	Webster C 12 + 4	Smith E 11 + 2	Mowat D 15 + 1	Bain J — + 1	Myles J — + 1	*Match No.*
1	2	3	4	5	6	7	8¹	9	10	11²	12	13																					1
1	2	3	4	5	6	11¹	8	9²	10	7	12		13																				2
1	2	3	4	5	6	11¹	8	9	10	7²	13		12																				3
1	2	3	4	5	6²	11	8	9	10		12	13	7¹																				4
1	2	3	4	5	6	11	8	9	10²		12	13	7¹																				5
1	2	3	4	5	6	11	8	9	10¹			12	7																				6
1	2	3	4	5	6	11	8	9	10		12		7¹																				7
1		3	4	5	6	11¹	8		10		9		7²	2	12	13																	8
1		3	4	5	6		8	9	12	13	11²		7	2	10¹																		9
1	2	3	4	5	6		8	9	11	7¹	13		12		10²																		10
1	2	3	4	5	6		8²	9	10	11	12		7¹		13																		11
1	2	3	4	5▮	6		8	9	10	11²	12		7¹				13																12
1	2¹	3	4		5			9	10	7	11		8²	12		13	14	6³															13
1	2	3	4	5	6			9¹	10²	7	8		13				12		11														14
1	2	3³	4	5	6				10	7	9	12						13	11¹	8²	14												15
1	2	3	4		5		8²	9¹	10	12	7							6			11	13											16
1		3	4	5	2		8	9	10	7		12						6²			11¹	13											17
1		3	4	5	2		8	9	10		7							6¹				11	12										18
		3	4	5	2		8	9	10²	6	12													1	7	11¹	13						19
		3	4	5	2		8	9	10²	6								13						1	7	11¹		12					20
		3	4	5¹	6		8	9	10³	7	13													1			14	11²	2	12			21
		3³	4		6		8	9	10	7²								13	14					1			12	11¹	2	5			22
		3	4		6		8	9	10¹	7	13													1			12	11²	2	5			23
		3³	5		6		8	9	10¹	7	13								14					1			12	11²	2	4			24
		12	4	5¹	6		8	9	10	7²	13													1				11	2	3			25
		12	4	5	6²		8	9	10³		7							14						1			13	11	2	3¹			26
		6	4	5¹	12		8	9	10	13	7													1				11²	2	3			27
		3▮	4	14	12		8	9	10	6	7²													1			13	11³	2¹	5			28
1				5	2		8	9²	10	6	7						13		3								11¹	12		4			29
1				5	6		8	9	10	11	7¹						13		3								12		2²	4			30
1	2	4			6		8	9	10¹	7									3								12	11		5			31
1	2¹	4	13		6		8	9	10	7▮									3²								14	11³	12	5			32
1		4		5²	2		8	9	10³		7						14		3¹			13						12	11	6			33
1	2	4²		5	12			9	10		7¹							14	3³			8						11	13	6			34
1	2		4	5²	8			9	10										3			7						11¹		6	12	13	35
1	2		4	5▮	8			9	10										3			12					11¹	13	7²	6			36

DUMBARTON

Second Division

Year Formed: 1872. *Ground:* Strathclyde Homes Stadium, Dumbarton G82 1JJ. *Telephone:* 01389 762569/767864. *Fax:* 01389 762629
Ground Capacity: total: 2050. *Size of Pitch:* 110yd × 75yd.
Chairman: Ian MacFarlane. *Club Secretary:* David Prophet. *Company Secretary:* John Benn.
Manager: Brian Fairley. *Assistant Manager:* Allan McGonigal. *Physio:* Linda McIllwraith.
Managers since 1975: A. Wright, D. Wilson, S. Fallon, W. Lamont, D. Wilson, D. Whiteford, A. Totten, M. Clougherty, R. Auld, J. George, W. Lamont, M. MacLeod, J. Fallon, I. Wallace, T. Carson, D. Winnie. *Club Nickname(s):* The Sons.
Previous Grounds: Broadmeadow, Ropework Lane, Townend Ground, Boghead Park.
Record Attendance: 18,000 v Raith Rovers, Scottish Cup; 2 Mar, 1957.
Record Transfer Fee received: £125,000 for Graeme Sharp to Everton (March 1982).
Record Transfer Fee paid: £50,000 for Charlie Gibson from Stirling Albion (1989).
Record Victory: 13-1 v Kirkintilloch Central. 1st rd; 1 Sept, 1888.
Record Defeat: 1-11 v Albion Rovers, Division II; 30 Jan, 1926: v Ayr United, League Cup; 13 Aug, 1952.
Most Capped Player: James McAulay, 9, Scotland.
Most League Appearances: 297: Andy Jardine, 1957-67.
Most Goals in Season (Individual): 38: Kenny Wilson, Division II; 1971-72. *(League and Cup):* 46 Hughie Gallacher, 1955-56.
Most Goals Overall (Individual): 169: Hughie Gallacher, 1954-62 (including C Division 1954-55). *(League and Cup):* 202 Hughie Gallacher, 1954-62

DUMBARTON 2002–03 LEAGUE RECORD

Match No.	Date	Venue	Opponents	Result		H/T Score	Lg. Pos.	Goalscorers	Attendance
1	Aug 3	A	Stenhousemuir	D	2-2	0-0	—	Bonar [78], Flannery [90]	437
2	10	H	Brechin C	W	1-0	1-0	3	Collins [19]	735
3	17	A	Raith R	L	0-1	0-0	6		1866
4	24	H	Airdrie U	W	3-1	1-0	2	Brown A [29], Dillon [51], Collins [61]	1417
5	31	A	Berwick R	W	2-1	2-0	1	McCutcheon 2 [1, 15]	509
6	Sept 14	H	Forfar Ath	L	1-2	1-0	1	McCutcheon [28]	827
7	21	A	Stranraer	L	0-1	0-1	4		455
8	28	H	Hamilton A	D	1-1	1-1	5	Brown A [29]	1202
9	Oct 5	A	Cowdenbeath	L	1-3	1-1	6	McCutcheon [42]	363
10	26	H	Stenhousemuir	D	0-0	0-0	9		815
11	29	A	Brechin C	D	1-1	1-0	—	Brown T [28]	377
12	Nov 2	H	Berwick R	L	1-2	1-0	10	Lynes [43]	763
13	9	A	Airdrie U	W	1-0	0-0	6	Flannery (pen) [67]	1323
14	16	A	Forfar Ath	L	0-2	0-0	7		556
15	23	H	Stranraer	W	3-0	1-0	7	Flannery (pen) [30], McCutcheon [74], Bonar [88]	772
16	30	H	Cowdenbeath	D	1-1	1-1	6	McCutcheon [36]	754
17	Dec 14	A	Hamilton A	L	0-1	0-1	8		1062
18	28	H	Raith R	L	0-3	0-1	9		1300
19	Jan 1	H	Airdrie U	W	2-1	2-0	—	Obidele [23], Dillon [42]	1024
20	11	A	Berwick R	W	1-0	0-0	6	Dillon [72]	580
21	18	H	Forfar Ath	L	1-2	1-1	7	Dillon [8]	867
22	25	A	Stenhousemuir	L	1-2	0-1	7	Dillon (pen) [53]	460
23	Feb 1	A	Stranraer	W	2-1	1-1	6	McCutcheon [5], Scally [62]	408
24	8	H	Hamilton A	W	3-1	0-1	4	Scally [50], Collins [60], McCutcheon [88]	1108
25	Mar 1	A	Raith R	L	1-2	0-2	7	Scally [70]	1790
26	8	A	Airdrie U	L	1-2	0-2	8	Flannery [80]	1136
27	11	H	Brechin C	L	1-3	1-1	—	Flannery [25]	513
28	15	H	Berwick R	D	2-2	1-0	9	Brown A [20], Bonar [70]	916
29	18	A	Cowdenbeath	L	0-2	0-1	—		184
30	Apr 1	H	Stranraer	D	1-1	0-1	—	Donald [64]	596
31	5	A	Forfar Ath	W	1-0	0-0	9	Scally [44]	485
32	12	H	Cowdenbeath	W	3-1	2-0	9	Flannery (pen) [28], Dillon [41], Obidele [88]	1203
33	19	A	Hamilton A	D	2-2	0-1	8	Flannery [60], Brown A [86]	1270
34	26	H	Stenhousemuir	W	3-1	2-1	8	Flannery [8], Russell [34], Scally [89]	906
35	May 3	A	Brechin C	D	1-1	1-1	8	Obidele [40]	895
36	10	H	Raith R	W	4-1	2-1	6	Russell 3 [27, 30, 51], Dillon [33]	1501

Final League Position: 6

Honours
League Champions: Division I 1890-91 (shared with Rangers), 1891-92. Division II 1910-11, 1971-72. Second Division 1991-92; *Runners-up:* First Division 1983-84. Division II 1907-08. Third Division 2001-02.
Scottish Cup Winners: 1883; *Runners-up:* 1881, 1882, 1887, 1891, 1897.

Club colours: Shirt: Yellow with black facing. Shorts: Yellow with black stripe. Stockings: Yellow.

Goalscorers: *League* (48): Flannery 8 (3 pens), McCutcheon 8, Dillon 7 (1 pen), Scally 5, Brown A 4, Russell 4, Bonar 3, Collins 3, Obidele 3, Brown T 1, Donald 1, Lynes 1
Scottish Cup (0)
CIS Cup (0)
Challenge Cup (4): Dillon 2, Brown T 1, Duffy 1

Wight J 3 + 1	McEwan C 21 + 2	Stewart D 16 + 4	Dillon J 34 + 1	Duffy N 23	Collins N 33	McCann K 2 + 3	Bonar S 26 + 9	Brown T 23 + 4	Brown A 19 + 10	Robertson J 4 + 9	Flannery P 18 + 9	Lynes C 4 + 10	McKeown J 12 + 4	Grindlay S 33	McKelvie D 1 + 3	Dickie M 20 + 3	Crilly M 12 + 2	McCutcheon G 23 + 8	Scally N 23 + 4	Brittain C 26	Obidele E 9 + 5	Russell I 8 + 3	Donald B 3 + 4	Match No.
1	2	3	4^{3}	5	6	7	8	9^{2}	10^{1}	11	12	13	14											1
	2	3	11	5	6	7^{3}		4	10		9^{1}	8^{2}		1	12	13	14							2
		3	11	5	6	12	8	4^{2}	10		9^{1}	13		1		2	7							3
	2	3	11	5^{1}	6	13	8	4^{3}	10	14			12	1			7^{2}	9						4
	2	3	11		6		8	4^{1}	10^{2}			13	5	1			7	9	12					5
	2	3	11	5	6		8	4^{1}	10^{3}		13	14		1			7	9^{2}	12					6
15	2	3	11^{2}	5	6		8^{1}		10	13	12			1^{6}			7	9	4■					7
1		3	11^{2}	5	6		8	4	10^{3}	13	12		14			2	7	9^{1}						8
1		3	11^{1}	5	6	13	8	4	10	12	14					2	7^{2}	9^{3}						9
		6	11^{1}	5			8	4^{2}	10	12			14	1		2	7	9^{3}	13	3				10
		6	11^{2}	5			8^{1}	4	10	13	14	12		1		2	7	9^{3}		3				11
		6	11	5			13	4^{1}		12	10	8^{2}		1		2	7	9		3				12
			11	5	6		12		14	4	9	8^{1}		1		2	7^{2}	10^{3}	13	3				13
			11	5	6		8^{1}		13	7	9	12		1		2	14	10^{2}	4^{3}	3				14
	8		11^{3}	5	6		12		10^{1}	14	9^{2}			1		2	7■	13	4	3				15
	8^{2}		11^{3}	5	6		13		10^{1}	7	9			1	14	2		12	4	3				16
	8	7^{2}	11^{3}	5	6		13		9^{1}		12	14		1		2		10	4	3				17
	12		11^{2}		6		8	7^{1}		13	14		5	1	10^{3}	2		9	4	3				18
	8^{3}	14	10		6		12	7^{1}			9^{2}		5	1	13	2			4	3	11			19
	8^{2}		10		6		12	7^{1}	13				5	1		2		9	4	3	11			20
			10^{1}		6		12	7	8				5	1		2		9	4	3	11			21
		14	10^{1}		6		13	4	8			12	5	1		2^{3}		9	7	3	11^{2}			22
		14	10^{2}		6		11	7^{3}	12		9^{1}		5	1		2		8	4	3	13			23
			11^{3}		6		8	7	14		9^{1}		5	1		2		10^{2}	4	3	12	13		24
	13		10		6		8^{1}	7^{3}	12				5	1		2		9	4	3	11^{2}		14	25
	2	12	11		6		8^{2}	7^{3}			9		5	1				10	4	3^{1}		13	14	26
	2	5			6		8^{1}	7			9	11		1				12	4	3		10		27
	2		11^{2}		6		8	7^{1}	10				5	1				9	4	3		13	12	28
	2		11^{2}		6		8	7■	10^{1}		12	13	5	1				9	4	3^{3}			14	29
	2	6	13	5	4		7		9^{1}			14		1				10^{3}		3^{2}	12	11	8	30
	2		11	5	4		7				9^{3}			1		13		14	6^{2}	3	12	10^{1}	8	31
	2		11	5	4		7				9^{3}			1		14		13	6	3	12	10^{2}	8^{1}	32
			11^{2}	5	4		8^{3}	13	14		9			1		2		12	6	3	7	10^{1}		33
	2		11^{2}	5	4		8	13	14		9^{3}			1				12	6	3	7	10^{1}		34
	2	3	11	5	4		8	13	12		9^{2}			1					6		7	10^{1}		35
	2		11	5	4		8	14	12		9^{1}			1				13	6	3	7^{3}	10^{2}		36

DUNDEE

Premier League

Year Formed: 1893. *Ground & Address:* Dens Park Stadium, Sandeman St, Dundee DD3 7JY. *Telephone:* 01382 889966. *Fax:* 01382 832284.
Ground Capacity: all seated: 11,760. *Size of Pitch:* 101m × 66m.
Chairman: Jim Marr. *Chief Executive:* Peter Marr.
Manager: Jim Duffy. *Goalkeeping Coach:* Paul Mathers. *Under 21 Coach:* Ray Farningham. *Under 18 Coach:* Steve Campbell. *Youth Development Coach:* Kenny Cameron. *Community Coach:* Kevin Lee. *Physio:* Jim Law.
Managers since 1975: David White, Tommy Gemmell, Donald Mackay, Archie Knox, Jocky Scott, Dave Smith, Gordon Wallace, Iain Munro, Simon Stainrod, Jim Duffy, John McCormack, John Scott, Ivano Bonetti.
Club Nickname(s): The Dark Blues or The Dee. *Previous Grounds:* Carolina Port 1893-98.
Record Attendance: 43,024 v Rangers, Scottish Cup; 1953.
Record Transfer Fee received: £500,000 for Tommy Coyne to Celtic (March 1989).
Record Transfer Fee paid: £200,000 for Jim Leighton (Feb 1992).
Record Victory: 10-0 Division II v Alloa; 9 Mar, 1947 and v Dunfermline Ath; 22 Mar, 1947.
Record Defeat: 0-11 v Celtic, Division I; 26 Oct, 1895.
Most Capped Player: Alex Hamilton, 24, Scotland. *Most League Appearances:* 341: Doug Cowie 1945-61.
Most League Goals in Season (Individual): 52: Alan Gilzean, 1963-64.
Most Goals Overall (Individual): 113: Alan Gilzean.

DUNDEE 2002–03 LEAGUE RECORD

Match No.	Date	Venue	Opponents	Result		H/T Score	Lg. Pos.	Goalscorers	Attendance
1	Aug 3	H	Hearts	D	1-1	0-1	—	Caballero 64	7705
2	10	A	Rangers	L	0-3	0-1	11		46,774
3	17	A	Dunfermline Ath	L	2-4	1-1	10	Novo 2 22, 58	5852
4	24	H	Hibernian	W	2-1	0-1	9	Caballero 78, Lovell 90	6411
5	31	A	Dundee U	D	0-0	0-0	8		12,402
6	Sept 11	H	Livingston	W	2-1	0-1	—	Novo 51, Rae 77	5391
7	14	A	Partick Th	D	1-1	0-1	6	Rae 49	4552
8	22	H	Celtic	L	0-1	0-1	6		9483
9	28	A	Motherwell	D	1-1	1-0	7	Lovell 13	4025
10	Oct 5	H	Kilmarnock	W	2-1	0-0	7	Rae 76, Caballero 90	5567
11	19	A	Aberdeen	D	0-0	0-0	7		14,003
12	26	A	Hearts	W	2-1	1-0	6	Lovell 2 25, 67	10,169
13	Nov 2	H	Rangers	L	0-3	0-1	6		10,124
14	12	H	Dunfermline Ath	L	2-3	2-1	—	Nicholson (og) 7, Lovell 19	5475
15	16	A	Hibernian	L	1-2	0-1	7	Novo 89	8870
16	23	H	Dundee U	W	3-2	2-0	6	Caballero 11, Lovell 29, Hernandez 54	11,593
17	30	A	Livingston	D	1-1	0-1	6	Novo (pen) 71	4151
18	Dec 4	H	Partick Th	W	4-1	1-0	—	Brady 38, Sara 51, Lovell 2 67, 74	5363
19	7	A	Kilmarnock	L	0-2	0-0	7		4806
20	14	H	Motherwell	D	1-1	1-1	7	Sara 39	5527
21	21	A	Celtic	L	0-2	0-1	7		56,162
22	26	H	Aberdeen	L	1-2	0-0	—	Milne 87	8574
23	29	H	Hearts	L	1-2	0-1	7	Milne 56	7340
24	Jan 2	A	Rangers	L	1-3	1-2	7	Lovell 23	49,112
25	28	A	Dunfermline Ath	W	1-0	1-0	—	Nicholson (og) 12	4237
26	Feb 9	A	Dundee U	D	1-1	1-1	7	Novo 30	10,547
27	25	H	Hibernian	W	3-0	1-0	—	Rae 9, Milne 85, Murray (og) 90	8414
28	Mar 1	A	Partick Th	W	3-1	2-1	6	Milne 15, Mackay 26, Novo 77	4599
29	5	H	Livingston	D	0-0	0-0	—		7554
30	8	H	Kilmarnock	D	2-2	2-0	6	Wilkie 38, Milne 40	6531
31	15	A	Aberdeen	D	3-3	2-0	6	Lovell (pen) 15, Caballero 24, Wilkie 80	12,119
32	Apr 6	H	Celtic	D	1-1	1-1	6	Burchill 19	9013
33	12	A	Motherwell	W	2-1	2-0	6	Burchill 1, Milne 23	4693
34	27	H	Kilmarnock	L	0-1	0-0	6		5964
35	May 4	H	Rangers	D	2-2	2-1	6	Caballero 2 17, 28	9204
36	10	H	Dunfermline Ath	D	2-2	1-0	6	Lovell 2 15, 57	9195
37	14	A	Celtic	L	2-6	1-3	6	Smith 26, Mair 90	59,500
38	25	A	Hearts	L	0-1	0-0	6		12,205

Final League Position: 6

Honours
League Champions: Division I 1961-62. First Division 1978-79, 1991-92, 1997-98. Division II 1946-47; *Runners-up:* Division I 1902-03, 1906-07, 1908-09, 1948-49, 1980-81.
Scottish Cup Winners: 1910; *Runners-up:* 1925, 1952, 1964, 2003.
League Cup Winners: 1951-52, 1952-53, 1973-74; *Runners-up:* 1967-68, 1980-81. *(Coca-Cola Cup):* 1995-96.
B&Q (Centenary) Cup Winners: 1990-91; *Runners-up:* 1994-95.

European: *European Cup:* 8 matches (1962-63 semi-finals). *Cup Winners' Cup:* 2 matches: (1964-65).
UEFA Cup: 18 matches: (*Fairs Cup:* 1967-68 semi-finals. *UEFA Cup:* 1971-72, 1973-74, 1974-75).

Club colours: Shirt: Navy with white and red shoulder and sleeve flashes. Shorts: White with navy/red piping. Stockings: Navy, top with two white hoops.

Goalscorers: *League* (50): Lovell 13 (1 pen), Caballero 7, Novo 7 (1 pen), Milne 6, Rae 3, Burchill 2, Sara 2, Wilkie 2, Brady 1, Hernandez 1, Mackay 1, Mair 1, Smith 1, own goals 3
Scottish Cup (10): Lovell 3, Nemsadze 2, Novo 2, Burchell 1, Caballero 1, Rae 1
CIS Cup (3): Sara 2, Caballero 1

Speroni J 38	Mackay D 35	Hernandez J 30 + 1	Mair L 23 + 6	Wilkie L 35	Smith B 37	Nemsadze G 24	Rae G 35 + 2	Novo I 26 + 10	Caballero F 34 + 2	Sara J 10 + 9	Milne S 11 + 14	Robb S 1 + 8	Forbes B 1 + 3	Beith G 1	Jablonski N — + 2	Lovell S 23 + 5	Hutchinson T 11	Brady G 19 + 8	Khizanishvili Z 16 + 3	Robertson M — + 5	Burchill M 7 + 4	Carranza B 1 + 4	*Match No.*
1	2	3	4	5	6	7	8	9	10	11													1
1	2	3	4^{1}	5	6	7	8	9^{2}	13	11	10	12											2
1	2	3	4^{1}	5	6	7	8	9■	10^{2}	11	13		12										3
1	2	3		5	6	7	8		10	11^{2}	13		9^{3}	4^{1}	12	14							4
1	2	3	13	5	6	7	8	9	10	12						11^{1}	4^{2}						5
1	2	3	13	5	6	7	8	9	10^{3}	12						11^{1}	4^{2}	14					6
1	2	3		5	6		8	9	10^{1}	12						11	4	7					7
1	2	3		5	6	7	8	9	10	11						12	4^{1}						8
1	2	3	7	5	6		8	12	10	11						9^{1}	4						9
1	2	3		5	4	7^{1}	8	9	10	11^{2}	12	13						6					10
1	2	3		5	6	7^{1}	8	9^{2}	10	13	11						4		12				11
1	2	3		5	6		8	9	10							11	4	7					12
1	2	3	12	5	6	7^{1}	8	11^{2}	10	13								9^{3}	4■	14			13
1	2	3	12	5■	6		8	9^{1}	10	13						11^{2}	4	7					14
1	2	3			6	7	8	12	10	11		13				9^{2}	4^{1}		5				15
1	2	3		5	6	7	8	9^{3}	10^{1}	13	14					11^{2}	4		12				16
1	2^{1}	3		5	6	7	8^{2}	9	10	12	14					11^{3}	4	13					17
1	2	3	4	5	6		12	9^{3}	10^{2}	11^{1}	13		14			8		7					18
1	2^{1}	3	4	5	6		8	9	10	12						11		7					19
1	2	3	4	5	6		12	9	10	11	13	8^{1}						7^{2}					20
1	2	3	4	5	6		8	9	10^{2}		13	14				11^{3}		12	7^{1}				21
1		3■	4	5■	6		8	9^{1}	10^{3}		12	14				11^{2}		7	2	13			22
1	2		3		6		8	9	10		7	13				11^{2}		5^{1}	4	12			23
1	2	3	4		6		8	12	10		9					11^{2}		7^{1}	5	13			24
1	2		4	5	6	7	8	13	10^{1}		11^{2}							9	3	12			25
1	2		4	5	6	7^{1}	8	11^{2}	10							12		9	3		13		26
1	2		4	5	6	7	8	9^{3}	10^{1}		13					12		14	3		11^{2}		27
1	2		4	5	6	7^{3}	8	13	12		9					11^{1}		14	3		10^{2}		28
1	2		3	5	6	7^{1}	8	9^{2}	10		14					11^{3}		12	4		13		29
1	2	13	3	5		7^{2}	8	12	10		9^{1}					11		6	4				30
1	2		3	5	6		8	12	10^{2}		9	13				11^{1}		7	4				31
1	2	4	3	5	6	7	8	12	10^{3}		13					11^{2}		14			9^{1}		32
1		4	3	5	6	7	8	12^{3}	10		11	13						2^{2}	14		9^{1}		33
1	2	4	3	5	6^{3}		8	9^{1}	10		13					12		7			11^{2}	14	34
1	2	3	14	5	6	7^{3}	8		10		12					11^{1}			4		13	9^{2}	35
1	2	3	12	5^{1}	6	7		13			9^{2}					10^{3}		8	4		11	14	36
1	2	3	7	5^{3}	6		8	9			10		12					14	4^{1}		11^{2}	13	37
1		3^{3}	2	4	6	7^{1}	8	9	10						12	11^{2}		5			13	14	38

DUNDEE UNITED

Premier League

Year Formed: 1909 (1923). *Ground & Address:* Tannadice Park, Tannadice St, Dundee DD3 7JW. *Telephone:* 01382 833166. *Fax:* 01382 889398. *Ground Capacity:* total: 14,223 all seated: stands: east 2868, west 2096, south 2201, Fair Play 1601, George Fox 5151, executive boxes 292.
Size of Pitch: 110yd × 72yd.
Chairman: Eddie Thomson. *Secretary:* Spence Anderson. *General Manager:* Bill Campbell. *Community Development Officer:* Gavin Levey.
Manager: Ian McCall. *Assistant Team Manager:* Gordon Chisholm. *Coaches:* Tony Docherty, Graeme Liveston. *Physio:* David Rankine.
Managers since 1975: J. McLean, I. Golac, W. Kirkwood, T. McLean, P. Sturrock, A. Smith. *Club Nickname(s):* The Terrors.
Previous Grounds: None.
Record Attendance: 28,000 v Barcelona, Fairs Cup; 16 Nov, 1966.
Record Transfer Fee received: £4,000,000 for Duncan Ferguson from Rangers (July 1993).
Record Transfer Fee paid: £750,000 for Steven Pressley from Coventry C (July 1995).
Record Victory: 14-0 v Nithsdale Wanderers, Scottish Cup 1st rd; 17 Jan, 1931.
Record Defeat: 1-12 v Motherwell, Division II; 23 Jan, 1954.
Most Capped Player: Maurice Malpas, 55, Scotland.
Most League Appearances: 612, Dave Narey; 1973-94.
Most Appearances in European Matches: 76, Dave Narey (record for Scottish player).
Most League Goals in Season (Individual): 41: John Coyle, Division II; 1955-56.
Most Goals Overall (Individual): 158: Peter McKay.

DUNDEE UNITED 2002–03 LEAGUE RECORD

Match No.	Date	Venue	Opponents	Result		H/T Score	Lg. Pos.	Goalscorers	Attendance
1	Aug 3	A	Partick Th	D	0-0	0-0	—		6375
2	10	H	Kilmarnock	L	1-2	0-0	10	Thompson [70]	6366
3	17	A	Celtic	L	0-5	0-3	11		56,247
4	25	H	Motherwell	D	1-1	0-1	11	McIntyre [46]	5795
5	31	H	Dundee	D	0-0	0-0	12		12,402
6	Sept 11	A	Aberdeen	W	2-1	2-1	—	Thompson 2 [17, 39]	10,724
7	14	H	Dunfermline Ath	L	1-2	0-2	9	Lilley [49]	6041
8	21	A	Hearts	L	0-2	0-1	11		11,532
9	28	H	Rangers	L	0-3	0-2	11		10,013
10	Oct 5	A	Hibernian	L	1-2	0-1	11	Thompson [75]	9175
11	19	H	Livingston	L	2-3	1-0	12	Lilley [44], McIntyre [58]	5572
12	26	H	Partick Th	D	1-1	1-0	12	Thompson [12]	6349
13	Nov 2	A	Kilmarnock	W	2-1	1-1	11	Thompson [7], McIntyre [90]	5411
14	10	H	Celtic	L	0-2	0-1	11		10,664
15	16	A	Motherwell	W	2-1	2-0	10	Hamilton 2 [1, 23]	5381
16	23	A	Dundee	L	2-3	0-2	11	Hamilton [86], McIntyre [83]	11,593
17	30	H	Aberdeen	D	1-1	1-1	11	Hamilton (pen) [37]	8261
18	Dec 4	A	Dunfermline Ath	L	1-4	0-3	—	McIntyre [60]	4342
19	7	H	Hibernian	D	1-1	1-1	11	Wilson [3]	5673
20	14	A	Rangers	L	0-3	0-1	11		47,639
21	21	H	Hearts	L	0-3	0-2	11		6025
22	26	A	Livingston	L	0-3	0-1	—		3969
23	29	A	Partick Th	D	0-0	0-0	12		5109
24	Jan 2	H	Kilmarnock	D	2-2	1-1	12	Dodds [31], McIntyre [90]	7183
25	29	A	Celtic	L	0-2	0-2	—		54,912
26	Feb 1	H	Motherwell	W	2-1	1-1	11	Tod [5], Miller [68]	6672
27	9	H	Dundee	D	1-1	1-1	12	Mackay (og) [19]	10,547
28	16	A	Aberdeen	L	0-3	0-1	12		9146
29	Mar 1	H	Dunfermline Ath	W	3-0	1-0	12	Easton [39], Tod [47], Ogunmade [88]	6004
30	9	A	Hibernian	D	1-1	0-1	11	McIntyre [69]	7518
31	15	H	Livingston	L	0-1	0-0	11		6247
32	Apr 5	A	Hearts	L	1-2	1-0	11	Griffin [39]	10,747
33	13	H	Rangers	L	1-4	0-3	11	Dodds [71]	10,271
34	26	H	Hibernian	L	1-2	1-0	11	McCracken [32]	6758
35	May 3	A	Motherwell	D	2-2	0-1	11	Miller [49], McIntyre [81]	9056
36	10	A	Livingston	W	2-1	1-0	11	McIntyre [1], Miller [89]	5462
37	17	A	Partick Th	W	1-0	0-0	11	Paterson [59]	6357
38	24	H	Aberdeen	L	0-2	0-0	11		8516

Final League Position: 11

Honours
League Champions: Premier Division 1982-83. Division II 1924-25, 1928-29; *Runners-up:* Division II 1930-31, 1959-60. First Division Runners-up 1995-96.
Scottish Cup Winners: 1994; *Runners-up:* 1974, 1981, 1985, 1987, 1988, 1991.
League Cup Winners: 1979-80, 1980-81; *Runners-up:* 1981-82, 1984-85, 1997-98.
Summer Cup Runners-up: 1964-65. *Scottish War Cup Runners-up:* 1939-40.

European: *European Cup:* 8 matches (1983-84, semi-finals). *Cup Winners' Cup:* 10 matches (1974-75, 1988-89, 1994-95). *UEFA Cup:* 84 matches (*Fairs Cup:* 1966-67, 1969-70, 1970-71. *UEFA Cup:* 1975-76, 1977-78, 1978-79, 1979-80, 1980-81, 1981-82, 1982-83, 1984-85, 1985-86, 1986-87 runners-up, 1987-88, 1989-90, 1990-91, 1993-94, 1997-98).

Club colours: Shirts: Tangerine. Shorts: Tangerine. Stockings: Tangerine.

Goalscorers: *League* (35): McIntyre 9, Thompson 6, Hamilton 4 (1 pen), Miller 3, Dodds 2, Lilley 2, Tod 2, Easton 1, Griffin 1, McCracken 1, Ogunmade 1, Paterson 1, Wilson 1,own goal 1
Scottish Cup (2): Hamilton 1, O'Donnell 1
CIS Cup (8): O'Donnell 3, Thompson 3, Lilley 2

Gallacher P 33 + 1	McGowne K 12	Lauchlan J 20 + 4	McCunnie J 16 + 2	Griffin D 16 + 1	Duff S 32 + 2	Easton C 35 + 1	Miller C 32 + 2	Venetis A 1 + 1	McIntyre J 30 + 3	Thompson S 19 + 1	Gunnlaugsson A 1 + 5	Paterson J 23 + 10	Lilley D 29 + 4	Smart A 2 + 16	Aljofree H 1	Cummings W 7 + 4	Winters D — + 1	Wilson M 22 + 4	O'Donnell S 6 + 5	McCracken D 25	Carson S 2 + 5	Hamilton J 9 + 4	Ogunmade D 1 + 4	Dodds W 6 + 8	Bollan G 13	Chiarini D 2 + 2	Tod A 12 + 1	Combe A 5	Latapy R 6 + 1	McGowan S — + 1	Conway A — + 1	*Match No.*
1	2	3	4	5	6	7	8[3]	9[1]	10[2]	11	12	13	14																			1
1	2	3	4	5	6	7	8[2]		9[3]	10	12	14	11[1]	13																		2
1	2	3	4[3]	5	6	7[2]	8[1]	13	11	10		14		12	9																	3
1	2	3	4[1]	5	6	7	13		9	10	14		11[2]	8[3]		12																4
1	2	3		5	6	7	8[3]		9[2]	10	11[1]	13		12		4	14															5
1	2	3		5	7	9	8			10		12	11			6		4[1]														6
1	2	3		5	7	9[3]	8		13	10		12	11[2]			6		4[1]	14													7
1	2	3		5	7	9	8[1]		14	10		12	11[2]	13		6		4[3]														8
1		3		5	7	9	8[1]			10	14	13	12			6		4[2]	11[3]	2												9
1	3	12			7	8	13			10		5[1]	11			6		4[3]	9[2]	2	14											10
1	2	3	13		5	6	8[2]		9	10		14	11[1]			4			7[3]			12										11
1	2		4		5	7	8		9	10[1]			11						6	3		12										12
1			2		5[1]	7	8		6	10		13	11	12				4		3		9[2]										13
1		3	2			7	8		9	10		6[1]	11	12				4		5												14
1		3	2		13	7	8[1]		9		12[2]	6	11					4		5		10										15
1		3	2[1]			7	8		9	10		6	11[2]	13				4		5		12										16
1		3				6	8		9	10		2	11					4		5		7										17
1		3[1]			12	6	8		9	10		2	11[2]	14				4		5	13	7[3]										18
1			2		6	7	8		9	13		3[1]	11[2]			12		4		5		10										19
1			2			7	8		9■	10[1]		3	11[2]	12				4		5	13	6										20
1	4	3	2[2]		6	7	8					5[1]	11	14		12			13		9	10[3]										21
1			2		5	7	8		9				11					4	13	3	6[1]	10[2]	12									22
1		3			6	7	8			10		2[1]	11			12		4	9	5												23
1		3			6	7	8[1]		12			2	11[2]					4	9	5		13		10								24
1					7[1]		8		9			2[2]	11					4	13	5				10	3	6	12					25
12					6	9	8		11				14	7[1]				13		5[2]				10	3	2	4[3]	1				26
1					6	7	8■		9			2[2]	13	14				4		5		11[1]		10[3]	3	12						27
1					6[3]	8			9			7[1]	11[2]	13				2		5	12			10	3	14	4					28
1			2		6	8			10[3]			7	11[2]	14						5			13	12	3		4		9[1]			29
1			2[1]		6	8			10			7	11							5	12			13	3		4		9[2]			30
1			2[1]	14	6	9	8		10			7[2]	11[3]							5			13	12	3		4					31
1			12	5[2]	6	9	8		11			7[3]		13						2			14		3		4		10[1]			32
1		13		5	6	9[1]	8		11			7		14				2[2]						12	3		4		10[3]			33
1		13		5	6		8		10			7	11[3]	14				2[2]		3				12			4		9[1]			34
		12		5[3]	6	9	8		10			7	11[2]					14		3[1]				13	2		4	1				35
		3		5	6	12	8		10			7[2]	11[3]					13						14	2		4	1	9[1]			36
		3		5	6	9[1]	8		10[3]			7[2]	11					13						14	2		4	1	12			37
				5[3]	6	9			11									7[2]	13	3			8	10[1]	2		4	1		12	14	38

DUNFERMLINE ATHLETIC Premier League

Year Formed: 1885. *Ground & Address:* East End Park, Halbeath Rd, Dunfermline KY12 7RB. *Telephone:* 01383 724295. *Fax:* 01383 723468. *Ticket office telephone:* 0870 300 1201. *e-mail:* pars@dunfermline-ath.com
Ground Capacity: all seated: 12,500. *Size of Pitch:* 115yd × 71yd.
Chairman: John Yorkston. *Secretary:* Mrs Elaine Cromwell. *Commercial Manager:* Karen McNeil.
Manager: Jim Calderwood. *Assistant Manager:* Jimmy Nichol. *Physio:* Philip Yeates, MCSP.
Coach and Youth Development Officer: John Ritchie.
Managers since 1975: G. Miller, H. Melrose, P. Stanton, T. Forsyth, J. Leishman, I. Munro, J. Scott, B. Paton, R. Campbell. *Club Nickname(s):* The Pars. *Previous Grounds:* None.
Record Attendance: 27,816 v Celtic, Division I, 30 April, 1968.
Record Transfer Fee received: £650,000 for Jackie McNamara to Celtic (Oct 1995).
Record Transfer Fee paid: £540,000 for Istvan Kozma from Bordeaux (Sept 1989).
Record Victory: 11-2 v Stenhousemuir, Division II, 27 Sept, 1930.
Record Defeat: 1-11 v Hibernian, Scottish Cup, 3rd rd replay, 26 Oct, 1889.
Most Capped Player: Colin Miller 16(61), Canada.
Most League Appearances: 497: Norrie McCathie, 1981-96.
Most League Goals in Season (Individual): 53: Bobby Skinner, Division II, 1925-26.
Most Goals Overall (Individual): 154: Charles Dickson.

DUNFERMLINE ATHLETIC 2002–03 LEAGUE RECORD

Match No.	*Date*	*Venue*	*Opponents*	*Result*		*H/T Score*	*Lg. Pos.*	*Goalscorers*	*Attendance*
1	Aug 3	A	Celtic	L	1-2	0-1	—	Dempsey 74	56,438
2	10	H	Livingston	W	2-1	1-0	6	Crawford 28, Brewster 50	4751
3	17	H	Dundee	W	4-2	1-1	3	Crawford 3 33, 80, 85, Brewster 68	5852
4	24	A	Hearts	L	0-2	0-0	5		11,367
5	Sept 1	H	Rangers	L	0-6	0-3	5		8950
6	11	A	Hibernian	W	4-1	3-1	—	Walker 10, Brewster 2 24, 56, Crawford 32	9837
7	14	A	Dundee U	W	2-1	2-0	5	Dempsey 9, Crawford 16	6041
8	21	H	Motherwell	W	1-0	0-0	4	Bullen 73	4987
9	28	A	Aberdeen	L	1-3	1-1	4	Bullen 40	11,678
10	Oct 5	H	Partick Th	W	4-1	1-0	3	Thomson SM 27, Nicholson 67, Crawford 2 78, 89	5522
11	19	A	Kilmarnock	D	2-2	1-0	3	Brewster 42, Bullen 57	5515
12	27	H	Celtic	L	1-4	0-2	3	Brewster 55	9139
13	Nov 2	A	Livingston	D	1-1	0-0	4	Brewster 47	5578
14	12	A	Dundee	W	3-2	1-2	—	Brewster 24, Crawford 73, Dair 84	5475
15	17	H	Hearts	W	3-1	0-0	3	Nicholson 64, Bullen 75, Crawford 90	5683
16	23	A	Rangers	L	0-3	0-0	3		48,431
17	30	H	Hibernian	D	1-1	0-0	3	Crawford 66	7506
18	Dec 4	H	Dundee U	W	4-1	3-0	—	Brewster 2 4, 37, Walker 40, Nicholson 50	4342
19	7	A	Partick Th	L	0-4	0-2	3		4110
20	15	H	Aberdeen	W	3-0	1-0	3	Crawford 38, McAllister (og) 46, Brewster (pen) 64	4835
21	26	H	Kilmarnock	L	0-2	0-0	—		5847
22	29	A	Celtic	L	0-1	0-1	5		58,387
23	Jan 2	H	Livingston	W	2-0	1-0	4	Crawford 2 44, 56	5218
24	28	H	Dundee	L	0-1	0-1	—		4237
25	Feb 1	A	Hearts	L	0-3	0-1	5		11,281
26	8	H	Rangers	L	1-3	0-1	5	Brewster 49	8754
27	15	A	Hibernian	W	3-1	2-0	4	Nicholson 20, Crawford 2 40, 56	9175
28	19	A	Motherwell	L	1-2	0-1	—	Crawford 51	3741
29	Mar 1	A	Dundee U	L	0-3	0-1	5		6004
30	9	H	Partick Th	D	0-0	0-0	5		4746
31	16	A	Kilmarnock	D	1-1	0-0	5	Shields (og) 59	4021
32	Apr 5	H	Motherwell	W	3-0	1-0	5	Hampshire 17, Nicholson 50, Hunt 76	4086
33	12	A	Aberdeen	L	0-1	0-1	5		10,030
34	26	H	Hearts	L	0-1	0-0	5		6968
35	May 3	H	Celtic	L	1-4	0-3	5	McNicol 80	8923
36	10	A	Dundee	D	2-2	0-1	5	Crawford 53, Bullen 89	9195
37	17	H	Kilmarnock	D	2-2	2-1	5	Crawford 5, Mason 11	6896
38	25	A	Rangers	L	1-6	1-3	5	Dair 10	49,731

Final League Position: 5

Honours
League Champions: First Division 1988-89, 1995-96. Division II 1925-26. Second Division 1985-86; *Runners-up:* First Division 1986-87, 1993-94, 1994-95, 1999-2000. Division II 1912-13, 1933-34, 1954-55, 1957-58, 1972-73. Second Division 1978-79.
Scottish Cup Winners: 1961, 1968; *Runners-up:* 1965.
League Cup Runners-up: 1949-50, 1991-92.

European: *Cup Winners' Cup:* 14 matches (1961-62, 1968-69 semi-finals). *UEFA Cup:* 28 matches (*Fairs Cup:* 1962-63, 1964-65, 1965-66, 1966-67, 1969-70).

Club colours: Shirt: Black and white vertical stripes. Shorts: White. Stockings: White.

Goalscorers: *League* (54): Crawford 19, Brewster 12 (1 pen), Bullen 5, Nicholson 5, Dair 2, Dempsey 2, Walker 2, Hampshire 1, Hunt 1, McNicol 1, Mason 1, Thomson SM 1, own goals 2
Scottish Cup (7): Brewster 2, Crawford 2, Grondin 1, Nicholson 1, Wilson 1
CIS Cup (4): Crawford 2, Bullen 1, Thomson SM 1

Ruitenbeek M 17	Bullen L 35	Thomson SM 22	Skerla A 32	Dair J 22 + 10	Mason G 24 + 3	Nicholson B 38	Kilgannon S 15 + 13	Hampshire S 9 + 13	Crawford S 37	Brewster C 37	Walker S 12 + 8	Dempsey G 17 + 14	McGroarty C 8 + 13	Petrie S — + 2	Wilson S 28 + 1	MacPherson A 17 + 1	Nicholls D 2 + 1	Karnebeek A 1 + 1	Stillie D 21	McLeish K — + 1	McGarty M 2 + 6	Hunt N 2 + 10	Brannan G 8	Grondin D 12 + 1	Hamilton J — + 2	McNicol S — + 2	*Match No.*
1	2	3	4	5	6	7	8^1	9^2	10	11	12	13															1
1	2	3	4	5		7	8^2	9	10	11^3	12	6^1	13	14													2
1	2	3	4	5^1		7	8	9^2	10	11		6	13		12												3
1	5	3	4	9^3	8	7	13	14	10	11		6^2	12			2^1											4
1	5^2	3	4	12	6	7^1	8^3	9	10	11		13	14		2												5
1	6	3	4	14	8	7	12	13	10^3	11^2	2^1	9			5												6
1	6	3	4	14	8	7	13	12	10^3	11^1	2	9^2			5												7
1	5	3	4	12	6	7	8^2		10	11^1	14	9^3	13		2												8
1	6	3	4		9	7	8	12^2	10	11▮	2^3	13	14		5^1												9
1	5	3	4	12	8	7	11		10			9^1	13	14		2^3	6^2										10
1	6		4^1	13	8	7			10	11		9^2	3		5	2	12										11
1	6	3	4			7		13	10	11	2	9^2	12		5			8^1									12
1	6	3	4		12	7			10	11		9^1			5	2	8										13
1	2	3	4	6	8	7	12		10	11^2	13	9^1			5												14
	6	3^1	4	8	12	7	9^3		10	11	14	13	2^2		5				1								15
	6	3	4	8^2		7	12	14	10	11		9^1	13		5	2^3			1								16
	6	3	4	8		7		12	10	11	2^1	9^2			5				1	13							17
	6	3	4	8^1		7	9^2	14	10	11	2	13^3	12		5				1								18
	5	3	4	8^2	6^3	7	9	13	10	11	2^1	14	12						1								19
	2	3	4	8	6	7^1		9	10	11^2		12			5				1		13						20
	6	3	4	8^1	9^3	7	12	13	10	11		14	2^2		5				1								21
	6	3	4	13	9^1	7		14	10	11^3	8^2	12	2		5				1								22
	6	3	4	8	12	7	14		10	11^2	13	9^3	2^1		5				1								23
	3		4	6		7	12	9^3	10	11		8^2			5	2^1			1		14	13					24
	3		4	6		7^3	13	9^1	10	11	2^2	14			5▮				1			12	8				25
	3		4	6^2		7	14	12	10	11						2^3		13	1			9^1	8	5			26
	3^1		4	12	9	7			10^2	11					5	2			1			13	8▮	6			27
			4	8^2	9	7		12	10	11		3^1			5	2^3			1		14	13		6			28
			4	8^1	9	7	13		10	11					5	2^2			1			12	6	3			29
			4	13		7	14		10	11		12			5	2			1		6^2	9^1	8	3^3			30
	6^2					7	9		10	11^3	4	13	12		5	2			1			14	8	3^1			31
	4^1				6	7	9	10^3		11^2			14		5	2			1			12	8	3	13		32
	6		4		9	7			10	11^3			5			2^2			1		13	12	8▮	3^1	14		33
1	2		4	6^3	8	7	13	9	10	11^1	14										5	12		3^2			34
1	2			5^1	8	7	9		10	11^3	4	6				13						12		3^2		14	35
1	6			12	8	7	9		10	11	4				5	2^2								3^1		13	36
	3			6	8	7	9^1		10	11		12	4^3		5	2^2			1		13			14			37
	6			9	8	7			10	11	13	12	4^3		5	2^2			1		14			3^1			38

EAST FIFE

Second Division

Year Formed: 1903. *Ground & Address:* Bayview Stadium, Harbour View, Methil, Fife KY8 3RW. *Telephone:* 01333 426323. *Fax:* 01333 426376.
Ground Capacity: all seated: 2000. *Size of Pitch:* 115yd × 75yd.
Chairman and Secretary: Derrick Brown.
Manager: James Moffat. *Assistant Manager:* Craig Robertson.
Managers since 1975: Frank Christie, Roy Barry, David Clarke, Gavin Murray, Alex Totten, Steve Archibald, James Bone, Steve Kirk, Rab Shannon, David Clarke. *Club Nickname(s):* The Fifers. *Previous Ground:* Bayview Park.
Record Attendance: 22,515 v Raith Rovers, Division I; 2 Jan, 1950.
Record Transfer Fee received: £150,000 for Paul Hunter from Hull C (March 1990).
Record Transfer Fee paid: £70,000 for John Sludden from Kilmarnock (July 1991).
Record Victory: 13-2 v Edinburgh City, Division II; 11 Dec, 1937.
Record Defeat: 0-9 v Hearts, Division I; 5 Oct, 1957.
Most Capped Player: George Aitken, 5 (8), Scotland.
Most League Appearances: 517: David Clarke, 1968-86.
Most League Goals in Season (Individual): 41: Jock Wood, Division II; 1926-27 and Henry Morris, Division II; 1947-48.
Most Goals Overall (Individual): 225: Phil Weir (215 in League).

EAST FIFE 2002–03 LEAGUE RECORD

Match No.	Date	Venue	Opponents	Result	H/T Score	Lg. Pos.	Goalscorers	Attendance
1	Aug 3	A	Peterhead	W 2-0	1-0	—	Graham 2 1, 55	510
2	10	H	East Stirling	W 4-1	3-1	—	Gilbert 11, Ovenstone 2 43, 75, Love 44	494
3	17	A	Queen's Park	D 0-0	0-0	3		537
4	24	H	Montrose	W 2-0	0-0	2	Deuchar 2 46, 68	578
5	31	A	Albion R	W 5-1	2-1	1	Gilbert 2, Nairn 5, Herkes 63, Love 75, Donaldson 79	451
6	Sept 14	A	Elgin C	D 1-1	0-0	1	Gilbert 49	599
7	21	H	Stirling A	D 1-1	0-1	1	Deuchar 59	588
8	28	A	Morton	L 1-2	0-2	2	Graham 47	1821
9	Oct 5	H	Gretna	W 3-2	1-2	1	Graham 3 11, 51, 68	462
10	19	A	East Stirling	W 4-1	1-1	1	Hall 13, Gilbert 59, Deuchar 2 67, 73	315
11	26	H	Peterhead	D 3-3	1-0	1	Allison 1, Gilbert 72, Herkes 85	847
12	Nov 2	H	Albion R	L 0-4	0-2	1		575
13	9	A	Montrose	W 5-0	0-0	1	Farnan 54, Cunningham 58, Deuchar 77, Herkes 2 79, 89	373
14	16	H	Elgin C	W 4-0	2-0	1	Herkes 2 8, 49, Deuchar 2 20, 48	525
15	23	A	Stirling A	D 0-0	0-0	1		808
16	30	A	Gretna	W 3-2	0-0	1	Ovenstone 57, Mortimer 89, Deuchar 90	352
17	Dec 14	H	Morton	L 1-4	0-2	4	Deuchar 59	1005
18	21	A	Peterhead	D 2-2	0-2	2	Hall 62, Deuchar 76	717
19	28	H	Queen's Park	D 1-1	0-0	3	Deuchar (pen) 74	808
20	Jan 1	H	Montrose	W 2-0	0-0	—	Deuchar 73, McMillan 75	519
21	18	A	Elgin C	W 1-0	0-0	1	McMillan 69	435
22	25	A	Albion R	D 0-0	0-0	1		475
23	Feb 8	A	Morton	D 1-1	1-1	1	McLean 45	2953
24	11	H	Stirling A	W 2-1	1-1	—	Herkes 5, Graham 69	602
25	22	H	East Stirling	W 3-0	1-0	1	Graham 44, Donaldson 78, Farnan 84	525
26	Mar 1	A	Queen's Park	W 2-1	1-0	1	Miller 32, Graham 60	697
27	4	H	Gretna	W 2-1	1-1	—	Deuchar 38, Hall 55	503
28	8	A	Montrose	W 2-0	1-0	1	Donaldson 10, Herkes 46	455
29	15	H	Albion R	D 1-1	0-1	1	Love 84	780
30	22	A	Stirling A	W 2-1	0-0	1	Farnan 51, McLean 89	866
31	Apr 5	H	Elgin C	W 5-0	4-0	1	McLean 5, Deuchar 4 (1 pen) 20, 33 (p), 69, 74	514
32	12	A	Gretna	D 3-3	1-2	1	Herkes 27, Graham 2 (1 pen) 70, 89 (p)	409
33	19	H	Morton	L 0-1	0-0	1		1991
34	26	H	Peterhead	L 0-2	0-0	4		1071
35	May 3	A	East Stirling	W 4-0	2-0	3	Farnan 38, Hall 45, Herkes 62, Deuchar 85	511
36	10	H	Queen's Park	W 1-0	0-0	2	Deuchar 90	1996

Final League Position: 2

Honours
League Champions: Division II 1947-48; *Runners-up:* Division II 1929-30, 1970-71. Second Division 1983-84, 1995-96. Third Division 2002-03
Scottish Cup Winners: 1938; *Runners-up:* 1927, 1950.
League Cup Winners: 1947-48, 1949-50, 1953-54.

Club colours: Shirt: Gold and black. Shorts: White. Stockings: Black.

Goalscorers: *League* (73): Deuchar 20 (2 pens), Graham 11 (1 pen), Herkes 10, Gilbert 5, Farnan 4, Hall 4, Donaldson 3, Love 3, McLean 3, Ovenstone 3, McMillan 2, Allison 1, Cunningham 1, Miller 1, Mortimer 1, Nairn 1
Scottish Cup (3): Deuchar 1, Graham 1, Herkes 1
CIS Cup (2): Deuchar 2
Challenge Cup (0)

Butter J 36	Allison J 23 + 4	Ovenstone J 10 + 3	Farnan C 27 + 5	Hall M 36	Graham R 26 + 3	Russell G 36	Mortimer P 30	McMillan C 19 + 6	Deuchar K 30 + 2	Donaldson E 29 + 2	Gilbert G 15 + 16	Cunningham G 5 + 5	Nairn J 4 + 5	Love G 11 + 19	Kerr B — + 1	Herkes J 30 + 1	Walker D — + 3	Lumsden C 5 + 1	Rollo A 2 + 4	McLean B 8 + 7	Miller C 14	McDonald G — + 1	*Match No.*
1	2	3	4	5	6^{3}	7	8	9^{2}	10^{1}	11	12	13	14										1
1	2^{1}	3	8	5	9^{3}	4	6	14	13	11	10^{2}			7	12								2
1	2^{3}	3	4■	5	9	6	8	13	12	11	10^{2}	14		7^{1}									3
1	2	5^{2}		3	9	4	6	13	10	8	11^{1}		14	7^{3}		12							4
1		3^{1}	4	5		7	6		10	2	11		8	12		9^{2}	13						5
1	12		4	5	8	2	6		10	3	9		7^{1}	13		11^{2}							6
1		3^{1}	2	5	9	4	6		8	11	12			10		7							7
1	12		8	5	9	4	6	2^{1}	10	11	3			13		7^{2}							8
1	6^{1}	14	8	5	10	4		13	9	3	11^{3}	12		7^{2}				2					9
1			4^{3}	5		2	6	7^{1}	9^{2}	3	11	8		12		10	13		14				10
1	8	12^{3}	6	5	9^{1}	2	4	3		11	10^{2}		14	13		7							11
1	10	11	8^{1}	5		6	4	2^{2}		3		12		7		9	13						12
1	8^{3}		6	5	9^{1}	2	4	13	10^{2}	3		11	14	12		7							13
1	8	12		5		2	4		9	3		11	6	7^{1}		10							14
1	8	3	12	5		2	4		9		13	11^{2}	6^{1}	7		10							15
1	8	3	6	5	12	2	4		9		11^{2}		13	7^{1}		10							16
1	8	3■	6	5	10^{1}	2	4		9		11			12		7							17
1	8		6^{2}	3	13	4	5	11	9	2	10^{1}			12		7							18
1	8		10^{3}	5	14	4^{1}	6	11	9	3	13			2^{2}		7		12					19
1	6		14	5	8^{2}	2	4	7	9	3	11^{1}	13		12		10^{3}							20
1	8		14	5	6^{3}	2	4	11	9	3	13			7^{1}		10^{2}				12			21
1	6			5	8	2	4	7^{2}	9	3	12	11^{1}		13		10							22
1	7^{2}			6	11	4	5^{1}	2	9	3	14					10			13	12	8^{3}		23
1	6		12	5	9^{3}	2		10		11^{2}	13					7		4	8^{1}	14	3		24
1	6^{2}		13	5	10	4		7^{3}	9	11	14							2	8^{1}	12	3		25
1			6	5	10	2		11^{1}	9	3	13					7^{2}		4		12	8		26
1			6	5	8	4		7	9	11	13					10^{2}		2^{1}		12	3		27
1			4	5	8^{2}	2		7	9	3				12		11			13	10^{1}	6		28
1			6	5	8	2	4		9	11^{2}	13			12		10				7^{1}	3		29
1	14		6	5	8^{3}	2	4	7^{2}	9	11^{1}				13		10				12	3		30
1	8^{1}		6	5		2	4	11^{3}	9		14			13		10			12	7^{2}	3		31
1	8		6	5	10	2	4	11^{1}			12			13		7				9^{2}	3		32
1	13		6	5	8	2	4		9^{1}	11	12^{2}			14		7				10^{3}	3		33
1			6	5	8■	2	4		9	11^{2}	13			12		7				10^{1}	3		34
1	8^{1}		6	5		2	4		9	14	11^{3}			13		10				7^{2}	3	12	35
1			6	5	8	2	4	14	9	13	11^{2}			12		10				7^{1}	3^{3}		36

EAST STIRLINGSHIRE Third Division

Year Formed: 1880. *Ground & Address:* Firs Park, Firs St, Falkirk FK2 7AY. *Telephone:* 01324 623583. *Fax:* 01324 637 862
Ground Capacity: total: 1880, seated: 200. *Size of Pitch:* 112yd × 72yd.
Chairman: A. Mackin. *Vice Chairman:* Douglas Morrison. *Chief Executive/Secretary:* Leslie G. Thomson.
Head Coach: Stephen Morrison. *Assistant Coach:* Alex Cleland. *Physio:* Laura Gillogley.
Managers since 1975: I. Ure, D. McLinden, W. P. Lamont, A. Ferguson, W. Little, D. Whiteford, D. Lawson, J. D. Connell, A. Mackin, D. Sullivan, B. McCulley, B. Little, J. Brownlie, H. McCann, G. Fairley, B. Ross, D. Diver.
Club Nickname(s): The Shire. *Previous Grounds:* Burnhouse, Randyford Park, Merchiston Park, New Kilbowie Park.
Record Attendance: 12,000 v Partick T, Scottish Cup 3rd rd; 21 Feb 1921.
Record Transfer Fee received: £35,000 for Jim Docherty to Chelsea (1978).
Record Transfer Fee paid: £6,000 for Colin McKinnon from Falkirk (March 1991).
Record Victory: 11-2 v Vale of Bannock, Scottish Cup 2nd rd; 22 Sept, 1888.
Record Defeat: 1-12 v Dundee United, Division II; 13 Apr, 1936.
Most Capped Player: Humphrey Jones, 5 (14), Wales.
Most League Appearances: 415: Gordon Russell, 1983-2001.
Most League Goals in Season (Individual): 36: Malcolm Morrison, Division II; 1938-39.

EAST STIRLINGSHIRE 2002–03 LEAGUE RECORD

Match No.	Date	Venue	Opponents	Result		H/T Score	Lg. Pos.	Goalscorers	Attendance
1	Aug 3	H	Montrose	D	1-1	1-1	—	Leishman 38	287
2	10	A	East Fife	L	1-4	1-3	—	Ure 23	494
3	17	H	Albion R	L	0-3	0-0	10		321
4	24	A	Stirling A	L	0-3	0-0	10		434
5	31	H	Morton	D	1-1	0-1	10	Livingstone 80	748
6	Sept 14	A	Queen's Park	W	2-0	1-0	9	Ormiston 4, Boyle 90	443
7	21	H	Gretna	L	0-4	0-0	9		190
8	28	H	Elgin C	L	1-2	1-1	9	Ormiston 9	195
9	Oct 5	A	Peterhead	L	0-5	0-1	9		558
10	19	H	East Fife	L	1-4	1-1	9	McAuley Sean 11	315
11	26	A	Montrose	D	2-2	0-0	9	Boyle 73, McAuley Sean 76	346
12	Nov 2	A	Morton	L	1-4	0-2	10	Leishman 86	1640
13	9	H	Stirling A	D	1-1	0-0	10	Ure 72	548
14	16	H	Queen's Park	L	0-4	0-2	10		315
15	23	A	Gretna	D	2-2	0-2	10	Leishman 75, Ure 85	221
16	30	H	Peterhead	L	1-4	1-2	10	Fairbairn 16	207
17	Dec 17	A	Elgin C	L	1-3	1-0	—	Ure 36	218
18	28	A	Albion R	L	0-6	0-3	10		326
19	Jan 1	A	Stirling A	L	1-2	1-2	—	Leishman 44	593
20	18	A	Queen's Park	W	4-3	1-3	10	Kerr 2 16, 85, Leishman 56, McAuley Sean 62	693
21	Feb 8	H	Elgin C	D	2-2	1-1	10	Maughan 26, McAuley Sean 54	178
22	12	H	Morton	L	0-1	0-1	—		627
23	15	A	Peterhead	L	0-6	0-2	10		584
24	22	A	East Fife	L	0-3	0-1	10		525
25	26	H	Gretna	L	1-2	0-1	—	McCulloch 57	146
26	Mar 1	H	Albion R	L	0-4	0-2	10		273
27	8	H	Stirling A	L	1-3	0-2	10	McLaren 62	302
28	12	H	Montrose	L	0-3	0-1	—		167
29	15	A	Morton	L	1-2	0-1	10	McLaren 51	2039
30	22	A	Gretna	L	1-3	0-1	10	Kelly 47	244
31	Apr 5	H	Queen's Park	L	0-2	0-1	10		281
32	12	H	Peterhead	D	1-1	0-0	10	McGhee 56	218
33	19	A	Elgin C	L	0-3	0-2	10		429
34	26	A	Montrose	L	4-5	2-3	10	Kelly 2 (1 pen) 13, 64 (p), Livingstone 2 34, 69	235
35	May 3	H	East Fife	L	0-4	0-2	10		511
36	10	A	Albion R	L	1-3	1-3	10	Ure 45	682

Final League Position: 10

Honours
League Champions: Division II 1931-32; C Division 1947-48. *Runners-up:* Division II 1962-63. Second Division 1979-80. Division Three 1923-24.

Club colours: Shirt: Black with white. Shorts: Black with white. Stockings: Black with white hoops.

Goalscorers: *League* (32): Leishman 5, Ure 5, Sean McAuley 4, Kelly 3 (1 pen), Livingstone 3, Boyle 2, Kerr 2, McLaren 2, Ormiston 2, Fairbairn 1, McCulloch 1, McGhee 1, Maughan 1
Scottish Cup (2): Leishman 1, McLaren 1
CIS Cup (0)
Challenge Cup (0)

Todd C 19 + 1	Maughan R 30 + 1	McLaren G 27 + 4	Bowman G 2	McGhee G 32	Leishman J 24 + 7	McAuley Sean 32	Boyle G 9 + 16	Ure D 15 + 16	Carmichael D 3	Morrison K 3	Donnelly D — + 1	Walker L — + 3	Struthers W 9 + 4	Findlay S 17 + 1	Slyth M — + 1	Drummond J 6	Reid C 7	Mackay J 24 + 2	Diver D — + 1	Miller C 1	McAuley Scott 1 + 1	Grant D 10 + 1	Ormiston D 4	Fairbairn B 13	Livingstone S 14 + 8	Oates S 9 + 1	Baldwin C 5 + 1	Sorbie S — + 2	Penman C 9	Clark P 14	Allison S 16	Lukowieci M 5	Kerr D 1	Kelly S 16	McCann K 8 + 2	Campbell M 7 + 7	McCulloch G 3 + 5	Skinner J 1	*Match No.*
1	2	3	4	5	6	7	8^{2}	9^{1}	10	11		12	13																										1
	6	3	4	5	8	7	12	10^{3}	9^{2}	11^{1}		14	2	1	13																								2
	2	11		5	6	8		9^{3}	10^{2}			13	7^{1}	1		3	4	12	14																				3
1	2	13		5	6	7	10^{1}	12		11^{2}			8				4			3	9																		4
	2	3		5	6^{1}	7	12								1				8				4	9	10	11														5
				5	7^{1}	8	12	13				2	1			3	6				4	10	9^{2}	11														6
				5	7^{1}	8	12	13				2^{2}	1			3	6				4	10	9	11														7
		3^{3}		5	7^{1}		6^{2}	13						1				8			14	4	9	10	11	2	12												8
14		3		5■	8^{1}	7	13	10^{2}				12	1■				6				4		9	11^{3}	2■														9
1	2	4				7	13	10				8			3		6				5^{1}		9^{2}	12		11												10
	2			5	7^{1}	8	10^{2}	13				12	1		3		6						9	11	4														11
	2	12		5	8	7	10	14					1		3^{1}		6				13		9	11^{3}	4^{2}														12
	2	12		5	8^{3}	7	10^{2}	13					1		3		6						9	11^{1}	4		14											13
	2	14		5	13	8	12	9				7^{3}	1		3^{1}		4						10		6	11^{2}													14
	2	3		6	11^{1}	10	7	12					1				8				5		9		4														15
	2	3		4	11^{2}	7	10	12					1				8				6		9		5^{1}		13											16
1	2	3		4	11			10^{1}				7					8■				6		9	12	5														17
1	2	3		5^{2}	11	10	7	9				13				6						4^{1}			14	12			8^{3}										18
	2	3			11	7	12	9				8^{1}	1			6									10					4	5								19
1	2	3			9	8	12											4	10												6	5	7^{1}	11						20
	2	3^{2}		6	10^{3}	7	13								1				8												11^{1}	4	5			9	12	14			21
	2			3		7■		12						1				8													4	5	11		9	6■	10^{1}			22
	2			3	11		14								1				8^{2}							13				4	6	5^{1}	7		9		10^{3}	12		23
1	2	3		6^{1}	12^{3}	7		14																		11					4^{2}		8		9	5	10	13		24
1	2^{3}	6			10^{2}		14	13											8											7	4	5	11^{1}		9		12	3		25
1		3^{3}		6	12	7		14											8^{2}							13					4	5			9		10	2	11^{1}	26
1	12	3		6		7		14			13							8^{1}							11^{3}					4	5			9		10	2^{2}		27
1	2	3		6	14	7		10^{2}										11											8^{1}	4	5			9^{3}	12	13			28
1	2	3		8	9^{1}	7		12										11												4	5			10	6				29
1	2^{3}	3		11	13	7		10										8^{1}							12					4^{2}	5			9	6	14			30
1	2^{3}	3		11^{2}	13	8	14	10^{1}									7■												4	5			9	6	12			31
1	2	11		3	7^{1}	8	13																				12				4^{2}		5			9	6	10			32
1	2	11		3	7^{1}	8	14	13																	12				4^{2}		5			9	6	10^{3}			33
1	2	3		6		8	14	10^{1}																	7		11^{3}		4^{2}		5			9		12	13		34
1	2	3^{3}		6	14	8		10^{2}																	7		11		4		5^{1}			9		13	12		35
1^{6}	2	3■		6		8		10^{2}					15■				13							7		11^{1}			4				9	5		12		36

ELGIN CITY — Third Division

Year Formed: 1893. *Ground and Address:* Borough Briggs, Borough Briggs Road, Elgin IV30 1AP.
Telephone: 01343 551114. *Fax:* 01343 547921.
Ground Capacity: 3927, seated 478, standing 3449. *Size of pitch:* 111yd × 72yd.
Chairman: Dennis J. Miller. *Secretary:* John A. Milton. *Commercial Manager:* Michael Teasdale.
Manager: David Robertson. *Coach:* Neil MacLennan. *Physio:* Maurice O'Donnell.
Managers since 1975: McHardy, Wilson, McHardy, Dickson, Shewan, Tedcastle, Grant, Cochran, Cumming, Cowie, Paterson, Winton, Black, Teasdale, Fleming, McHardy, Tatters, Caldwell.
Previous names: 1893-1900 Elgin City, 1900-03 Elgin City United, 1903- Elgin City.
Club Nickname(s): City or Black & Whites. *Previous Grounds:* Association Park 1893-95; Milnfield Park 1895-1909; Station Park 1909-19; Cooper Park 1919-21.
Record Attendance: 12,608 v Arbroath, Scottish Cup, 17 Feb 1968.
Record Transfer Fee received: £32,000 for Michael Teasdale to Dundee (Jan 1994).
Record Transfer Fee paid: £10,000 to Fraserburgh for Russell McBride (July 2001).
Record Victory: 18-1 v Brora Rangers, North of Scotland Cup, 6 Feb 1960.
Record Defeat: 1-14 v Hearts, Scottish Cup, 4 Feb 1939.
Most League Appearances: 97: Martin Pirie, 2000-03.
Most League Goals in Season (Individual): 12, Ian Gilzean, 2001-02.
Most Goals Overall (Individual): David Ross, 14, 2000-03.

ELGIN CITY 2002–03 LEAGUE RECORD

Match No.	Date	Venue	Opponents	Result		H/T Score	Lg. Pos.	Goalscorers	Attendance
1	Aug 3	A	Queen's Park	W	2-1	1-0	—	McMullan 10, Steele 50	585
2	10	H	Gretna	L	0-2	0-2	—		587
3	17	A	Stirling A	D	1-1	1-1	5	Sanderson 20	428
4	24	H	Peterhead	W	3-0	1-0	5	Ross 45, Sanderson 83, James 90	697
5	31	A	Montrose	L	0-1	0-1	5		417
6	Sept 14	H	East Fife	D	1-1	0-0	6	Craig 62	599
7	21	A	Albion R	D	1-1	0-0	6	McMullan 52	303
8	28	A	East Stirling	W	2-1	1-1	6	Steele (pen) 29, Ross 54	195
9	Oct 5	H	Morton	L	0-1	0-0	6		895
10	19	A	Gretna	D	0-0	0-0	7		323
11	26	H	Queen's Park	D	2-2	2-1	7	Love 17, Tully 25	567
12	Nov 2	H	Montrose	D	0-0	0-0	7		503
13	9	A	Peterhead	D	2-2	2-1	7	Craig 31, Campbell 33	728
14	16	A	East Fife	L	0-4	0-2	7		525
15	23	A	Albion R	D	1-1	0-0	7	McMullan 83	253
16	30	A	Morton	L	0-4	0-3	7		1658
17	Dec 7	H	Peterhead	L	0-4	0-2	7		457
18	17	H	East Stirling	W	3-1	0-1	—	McMullan 72, Sanderson 84, Ross 86	218
19	21	A	Queen's Park	L	2-3	1-1	8	Tully 2 29, 54	648
20	28	H	Stirling A	L	0-3	0-2	8		556
21	Jan 18	H	East Fife	L	0-1	0-0	8		435
22	25	A	Montrose	L	0-2	0-1	8		211
23	Feb 8	A	East Stirling	D	2-2	1-1	8	Ross 8, James 50	178
24	15	H	Morton	D	0-0	0-0	8		701
25	22	H	Gretna	D	2-2	1-1	8	Steele 39, Ross 73	383
26	Mar 1	A	Stirling A	L	0-4	0-3	8		407
27	8	A	Peterhead	L	2-3	1-1	8	Steele 34, Tully 90	854
28	15	H	Montrose	L	0-2	0-1	9		377
29	22	H	Albion R	L	0-1	0-0	9		333
30	29	H	Albion R	L	1-2	1-0	9	Steele 38	280
31	Apr 5	A	East Fife	L	0-5	0-4	8		514
32	12	A	Morton	L	0-2	0-0	9		1662
33	19	H	East Stirling	W	3-0	2-0	9	Bremner 22, Teasdale 2 45, 63	429
34	26	H	Queen's Park	D	0-0	0-0	9		444
35	May 3	A	Gretna	L	1-2	1-2	9	McMullan 19	250
36	10	H	Stirling A	D	2-2	1-1	9	Steele 45, Teasdale 78	386

Final League Position: 9

Honours
Scottish Cup, Quarter Finals 1968.
Highland League Champions: winners 15 times.
Scottish Qualifying Cup (North): winners 7 times.
North of Scotland Cup: winners 17 times.
Highland League Cup: winners 5 times.
Inverness Cup: winners twice.

Club colours: Shirt: Black and white vertical stripes. Shorts: Black. Stockings: Red.

Goalscorers: *League* (33): Steele 6 (1 pen), McMullan 5, Ross 5, Tully 4, Sanderson 3, Teasdale 3, Craig 2, James 2, Bremner 1, Campbell 1, Love 1
Scottish Cup (0)
CIS Cup (0)
Challenge Cup (1): Ross

Pirie M 30	MacDonald S 17 + 1	McBride R 19 + 7	Hind D 28 + 5	Mackay D 33	Tully C 34	Ross D 25	Love C 21 + 5	McMullan R 33	Steele K 32 + 1	Craig D 14 + 3	Sanderson M 23 + 9	James R 7 + 16	Campbell C 11 + 6	Smith A 3	Grant G 17 + 7	Hosie W — + 1	Teasdale M 18 + 3	Taylor R 1	Bremner F 7 + 5	Gallagher J 15	Rattray S 3 + 3	Allan S — + 1	Hamilton P 5	Tatters G — + 1	Macgregor M — + 4	*Match No.*
1	2	3	4^{2}	5	6	7	8	9	10	11^{1}	12	13														1
1	2	3^{1}	12	5	6	4	10	9	8^{2}	11^{3}	13	14	7													2
1	2	12	4	5	6	7	8	9^{2}	10		11	13		3^{1}												3
1	2	12	4	5	6	7	8	9^{2}	10^{3}		11	14	13	3^{1}												4
1	2		4^{2}	5	6	7	8	9	10^{3}		11	14	13	3^{1}	12											5
1	2	3	8^{1}	5	6	7		9	10^{2}	12	11	13	14		4^{3}											6
1	2	3		5	6	7^{2}		9	10^{1}	11	4		8		12	13										7
1	2	3		5	6	7	12	9^{3}	10	11^{1}	4	14	8^{2}		13											8
1	2	3		5	6	7	4	9	10	12	11^{1}		8													9
1	2		12	5	6	8	4	9	10	11			7^{2}		3^{1}		13									10
	2		13	5	6		4	9	10	11^{1}	12		7		3		8^{2}	1								11
1	2		12	5	6	7	10	9	13	11^{3}	14		8^{2}		3		4^{1}									12
1		3	13	5	6	7	8		10	11^{1}	12		9		2		4^{2}									13
1	13	3	4	5	6	7	8		10^{1}	11^{3}	14		9		2^{2}		12									14
1	2	3^{1}	4	5^{2}	6	7	8	9	10	11					13		12									15
1	2^{1}	13	4	3	6	7^{3}	8	9	10■	11		14			12		5^{2}									16
1		3	4	5	6	7^{2}	8	9^{1}		11	10	12			2				13							17
1	2	11	4	5^{1}	6	7	10^{2}	9		13	14	8^{3}			12		3									18
1	2	11	4		6	7	10^{2}	9	8	3^{1}		12			5				13							19
1	5	3	4^{1}		6	7	8	9	10^{3}	11^{2}	12	13			2				14							20
1		8	6				12	9	10		11	7^{2}			2		5			3	4^{1}	13				21
1		8^{2}	4	5		7	12	9	10		11^{1}	13			2^{3}		6			3	14					22
			2	5	6	7	12	9	10^{2}		11	8^{1}	13				4			3			1			23
			4	5	6	7		9	10		11	8^{1}	12				2			3			1			24
		12	4^{3}	5	6	7		9	10		11^{2}	8^{1}	13				2			3	14		1			25
1		8	4	5	6	7^{3}	14	9^{1}	10		11	12					2^{2}			3	13					26
1		12	4	5	6	7			10		11	9^{1}					2			3	8					27
1		2	4	5	6			9	10		11	12					3^{2}		7^{1}		8^{3}			13	14	28
			4	5	6			9	10^{1}		11	12	8		2				7	3			1			29
			4	5	6			9	10		11	12	8^{1}		2				7	3			1			30
1		13	4	5	6		8	7^{2}	10■		11	9^{1}			2				12	3						31
1			4	5	6		8	9			11^{1}				2		10		7	3					12	32
1		13	4	5	6		8	9^{1}	10		12				2^{2}		11^{3}		7	3					14	33
1			4	5	6		8	9^{2}	10		7^{1}				2		11		12	3					13	34
1		2	4	5	6			9	10		11				12		8^{1}		7	3						35
1		2	4	5	6			9	10		11						8		7	3						36

FALKIRK

First Division

Year Formed: 1876. *Ground & Address:* Ochilview Park, Gladstone Rd, Stenhousemuir FK5 5QL. *Telephone:* 01324 666808. *Fax:* 01324 664539.
Ground Capacity: total: 2374, seated: 626. *Size of Pitch:* 110yd × 72yd.
Chairman: Campbell Christie. *Secretary:* Alex Blackwood. *General Manager:* Crawford Baptie.
Head Coach: John Hughes. *Assistant Coach:* Brian Rice. *Director of Football:* Alex Totten. *Youth Co-ordinator:* Ian McIntyre.
Managers since 1975: J. Prentice, G. Miller, W. Little, J. Hagart, A. Totten, G. Abel, W. Lamont, D. Clarke, J. Duffy, W. Lamont, J. Jefferies, J. Lambie E. Bannon, A. Totten, I. McCall. *Club Nickname(s):* The Bairns. *Previous Grounds:* Randyford 1876-81; Blinkbonny Grounds 1881-83; Brockville Park 1883-2003.
Record Attendance: 23,100 v Celtic, Scottish Cup 3rd rd; 21 Feb, 1953.
Record Transfer Fee received: £380,000 for John Hughes to Celtic (Aug 1995).
Record Transfer Fee paid: £225,000 to Chelsea for Kevin McAllister (Aug 1991).
Record Victory: 12-1 v Laurieston, Scottish Cup 2nd rd; 23 Sept, 1893.
Record Defeat: 1-11 v Airdrieonians, Division I; 28 Apr, 1951.
Most Capped Player: Alex Parker, 14 (15), Scotland.
Most League Appearances: (post-war): 353, George Watson, 1975-87.
Most League Goals in Season (Individual): 43: Evelyn Morrison, Division I; 1928-29.
Most Goals Overall (Individual): Dougie Moran, 86, 1957-61 and 1964-67.

FALKIRK 2002–03 LEAGUE RECORD

Match No.	*Date*	*Venue*	*Opponents*	*Result*	*H/T Score*	*Lg. Pos.*	*Goalscorers*	*Attendance*
1	Aug 3	A	Ayr U	W 3-1	2-0	—	McQuilken [1], Coyle [23], James [75]	3030
2	10	H	St Mirren	W 2-0	2-0	2	Coyle [15], Lawrie [24]	4360
3	17	A	Inverness CT	W 2-1	0-1	1	Miller [81], Tosh [90]	2267
4	24	A	Alloa Ath	W 6-1	2-1	1	McPherson [11], Lawrie 2 [27, 53], Samuel 2 [70, 75], Coyle [77]	2613
5	31	H	Queen of the S	W 3-0	1-0	1	Lawrie [28], Allen (og) [76], Samuel [83]	4091
6	Sept 14	A	Ross Co	D 1-1	0-0	1	Coyle [68]	2729
7	21	H	Clyde	W 2-1	0-0	1	Coyle [57], McQuilken [68]	3595
8	28	H	St Johnstone	W 1-0	0-0	1	James [87]	5872
9	Oct 5	A	Arbroath	L 0-2	0-0	1		1730
10	19	H	Ayr U	W 3-0	0-0	1	Miller [60], Coyle 2 [77, 86]	3441
11	26	A	St Mirren	D 4-4	3-0	1	Kerr [12], Miller 3 [18, 34, 74]	3661
12	Nov 2	A	Queen of the S	D 1-1	0-1	1	Henry [52]	3017
13	9	H	Alloa Ath	W 3-0	1-0	1	Henry [10], Coyle [50], James [77]	3390
14	16	H	Ross Co	W 2-0	1-0	1	Miller 2 [24, 89]	3255
15	23	A	Clyde	L 0-2	0-2	2		3415
16	30	A	St Johnstone	W 1-0	0-0	2	James [61]	3696
17	Dec 7	H	Arbroath	W 2-1	1-0	1	Samuel [44], Coyle [60]	2673
18	14	H	Inverness CT	D 1-1	1-1	1	Hughes [17]	4671
19	28	H	Queen of the S	W 5-0	3-0	2	Miller [19], Henry [25], Coyle [36], Samuel 2 [47, 56]	3858
20	Jan 18	A	Arbroath	W 4-1	3-0	1	Samuel 3 [7, 16, 34], Coyle [48]	1950
21	Feb 1	H	St Johnstone	D 1-1	0-1	1	Henry [62]	4694
22	8	A	Inverness CT	W 4-3	2-2	1	Coyle 3 [30, 72, 85], Samuel [33]	3322
23	15	H	St Mirren	W 3-1	1-0	1	Coyle [16], Henry [58], Samuel [78]	4094
24	25	A	Ayr U	L 0-1	0-1	—		1783
25	Mar 1	A	Queen of the S	L 1-2	0-0	1	Miller [57]	2555
26	4	H	Clyde	W 3-0	3-0	—	McLaughlin (og) [6], Halliwell (og) [23], Miller [40]	3706
27	8	H	Alloa Ath	W 3-1	1-0	1	Miller (pen) [45], Rodgers [77], Taylor [90]	3320
28	11	A	Ross Co	W 1-0	1-0	—	Miller (pen) [18]	2161
29	15	A	Clyde	D 0-0	0-0	1		3002
30	29	A	Alloa Ath	W 3-1	2-1	1	Coyle [38], Miller [44], Taylor [54]	1686
31	Apr 5	H	Ross Co	W 3-0	1-0	1	Miller 2 [15, 68], Coyle [85]	3523
32	12	A	St Johnstone	W 1-0	0-0	1	Henry [54]	6579
33	19	H	Arbroath	W 4-1	1-0	1	Coyle 3 [25, 60, 89], Kerr [65]	4950
34	26	H	Ayr U	W 3-0	2-0	1	Miller [10], Taylor [39], Mackenzie (pen) [87]	4042
35	May 3	A	St Mirren	W 2-1	1-0	1	Taylor [18], Miller [49]	3062
36	10	H	Inverness CT	L 2-3	1-0	1	Taylor 2 [6, 50]	7300

Final League Position: 1

Honours
League Champions: Division II 1935-36, 1969-70, 1974-75. First Division 1990-91, 1993-94, 2002-03. Second Division 1979-80; *Runners-up:* Division I 1907-08, 1909-10. First Division 1985-86, 1988-89. Division II 1904-05, 1951-52, 1960-61. *Scottish Cup Winners:* 1913, 1957; *Runners-up:* 1997. *League Cup Runners-up:* 1947-48. *B&Q Cup Winners:* 1993-94. *League Challenge Cup Winners:* 1997-98.

Club colours: Shirt: Navy blue with white seams. Shorts: Navy. Stockings: Navy with two white hoops.

Goalscorers: *League* (80): Coyle 20, Miller 17 (2 pens), Samuel 11, Henry 6, Taylor 6, James 4, Lawrie 4, Kerr 2, McQuilken 2, Hughes 1, McKenzie 1 (pen), McPherson 1, Rodgers 1, Tosh 1, own goals 3
Scottish Cup (8): Samuel 4, Coyle 3, Taylor 1
CIS Cup (4): Coyle 1, Lawrie 1, Miller 1, Samuel 1
Challenge Cup (4): Miller 2, James 1, McPherson 1

Ferguson A 32	Lawrie A 7	McQuilken J 35	Rennie S 14 + 5	Hughes J 31	James K 13	Kerr M 32 + 4	Miller L 34	Coyle O 36	McPherson C 35	Tosh S 16	Henry J 27 + 6	Rodgers A — + 16	Samuel C 17 + 17	MacSween I 1 + 8	May E — + 1	Mackenzie S 32	Christie K 1 + 2	Cringean S 1 + 7	Craig S — + 4	Hill D 4	Nichols D 17	Taylor S 7 + 7	Reid B 4 + 4	Creaney P — + 1	*Match No.*
1	2	3	4	5	6	7	8^{2}	9	10^{1}	11	12	13													1
1	2	3	4	5	6	7^{1}	8^{2}	9		11	10		12	13											2
1	2	3	4^{1}	5	6	13	8	9^{3}	10	11	7^{2}		14		12										3
1	2	3		5	6^{3}	12	8	9	10^{2}	11	7^{1}		13			4	14								4
1	2	3		5	6^{3}	13	8	9^{1}	10	11^{2}	7		12			4		14							5
1	2	3	14	5	6^{3}	7	8	9^{2}	10^{1}	11	12		13			4									6
1	2^{1}	3	6	5^{3}		12	8	9	10	11	7^{2}		13			4		14							7
1		3	5		6	7	8	9	10^{2}	11	12	13	2^{1}			4									8
1		3	5		6■	7	8	9^{2}	10^{1}	11	12	13	2^{3}	14		4									9
1		3	6	5		7	8^{1}	9	10^{2}	11		12	2^{3}			4		13	14						10
1		3	2^{2}	5	6	7	8	9^{1}	10	11	13		12			4									11
		3		5	6	7	8	9	10	2	11^{1}		12			4				1					12
1		3^{1}	14	5^{3}	6	7	8^{2}	9	10	11	2		12			4			13						13
1		3	12	5	6^{1}	7	8	9	10^{2}	11	2^{3}		13	14		4									14
1		3	6^{3}	5		7	8■	9	10^{1}	11	2^{2}		12			4		13	14						15
1		3	13	5	6	7		9	10^{2}	11■	2^{1}		8			4		12							16
1		3		5		7		9	10		2		8	11^{1}		4		6	12						17
1		3	6	5		7	8	9	10		2		11			4									18
		3	6^{2}	5^{1}		7	8	9^{3}	10		2	14	11	13		4		12		1					19
1		3^{1}	12	5		7	8^{2}	9	10		2		11	13		4					6				20
1		3		5		7	8	9	10		2		11			4					6				21
1		3		5		7	8	9	10		2^{1}	13	11^{2}			4					6	12			22
		3		5		7	8^{1}	9^{2}	10		2	13	11			4				1	6	12			23
1		3		5		7	8	9	10		2^{1}	13	11			4^{2}					6	12			24
1		3		5		7	8	9	10		2^{1}		11			4					6		12		25
1		3		5		7	8^{3}	9^{2}	10		2	13	11^{1}	14		4					6	12			26
1		3		5		7	8^{3}	9	10		2^{2}	12	11^{1}	14		4					6	13			27
1		3^{1}		5		7	8	9^{3}	10		2	14	11^{2}			4					6	13	12		28
1				5		7	8	9^{1}	10		2	13	11^{2}			4					6	12	3		29
1		3		5		7	8^{2}	9^{1}	10		2	12		13		4					6	11			30
1^{3}		3		5		7	8	9	10		2^{1}		12			4	14				6^{2}	11	13		31
1		3		5		7	8	9^{1}	10		2^{2}		12			4					6	11	13		32
1		3		5		7	8^{2}	9^{3}	10		13	14	12			4					6	11	2^{1}		33
		3^{1}	5			7	8^{2}	9	10			13	12			4				1	6	11	2		34
1		3^{3}	5			7	8	9	10^{2}			12	13			4					6	11^{1}	2	14	35
1		3^{1}	5			7	8	9	10		2^{2}		13				4	12			6	11			36

FORFAR ATHLETIC — Second Division

Year Formed: 1885. *Ground & Address:* Station Park, Carseview Road, Forfar. *Telephone:* 01307 463576/462259. *Fax:* 01307 466956.
Ground Capacity: total: 4640, seated: 739. *Size of Pitch:* 115yd × 69yd.
Chairman and Secretary: David McGregor.
Manager: Raymond Stewart. *Assistant Manager:* Ian Miller. *Coaches:* Peter Castle, Derek Mitchell, Donald Ritchie. *Physio:* Brian McNeil.
Managers since 1975: Jerry Kerr, Archie Knox, Alex Rae, Doug Houston, Henry Hall, Bobby Glennie, Paul Hegarty, Tommy Campbell, Neil Cooper. *Club Nickname(s):* Loons. *Previous Grounds:* None.
Record Attendance: 10,780 v Rangers, Scottish Cup 2nd rd; 2 Feb, 1970.
Record Transfer Fee received: £65,000 for David Bingham to Dunfermline Ath (September 1995).
Record Transfer Fee paid: £50,000 for Ian McPhee from Airdrieonians (1991).
Record Victory: 14-1 v Lindertis, Scottish Cup 1st rd; 1 Sept 1988.
Record Defeat: 2-12 v King's Park, Division II; 2 Jan, 1930.
Most League Appearances: 484: Ian McPhee, 1978-88 and 1991-98.
Most League Goals in Season (Individual): 45: Dave Kilgour, Division II; 1929-30.
Most Goals Overall (Individual): 124, John Clark.

FORFAR ATHLETIC 2002–03 LEAGUE RECORD

Match No.	Date	Venue	Opponents	Result		H/T Score	Lg. Pos.	Goalscorers	Attendance
1	Aug 3	A	Airdrie U	L	0-1	0-0	—		2285
2	10	H	Stenhousemuir	W	1-0	0-0	5	Sellars 81	492
3	17	A	Cowdenbeath	D	1-1	0-1	7	Henderson 90	347
4	24	A	Brechin C	L	0-1	0-0	9		761
5	31	H	Hamilton A	D	1-1	1-1	9	Bavidge 30	486
6	Sept 14	A	Dumbarton	W	2-1	0-1	5	Bavidge 51, Byers 89	827
7	21	H	Berwick R	L	0-2	0-2	8		483
8	28	A	Stranraer	L	0-2	0-1	10		385
9	Oct 5	H	Raith R	L	1-2	1-1	10	Byers 26	1054
10	19	A	Stenhousemuir	L	1-2	1-1	10	Byers 13	295
11	26	H	Airdrie U	W	5-1	1-0	10	Tosh 2 39, 52, Bavidge 55, Sellars 60, Lunan 66	666
12	Nov 2	A	Hamilton A	W	2-1	0-0	9	Tosh 61, Sellars 82	960
13	9	H	Brechin C	W	2-1	1-0	5	Bavidge 2 14, 72	868
14	16	H	Dumbarton	W	2-0	0-0	5	Bavidge 2 53, 72	556
15	23	A	Berwick R	L	1-2	1-1	6	Tosh 32	387
16	30	A	Raith R	L	1-5	1-3	8	Byers 13	1779
17	Dec 28	H	Cowdenbeath	W	2-1	0-1	5	Byers 2 76, 87	596
18	Jan 1	A	Brechin C	W	4-3	1-1	—	Tosh 2 45, 51, Sellars 46, Bavidge 76	743
19	18	A	Dumbarton	W	2-1	1-1	4	Rattray 32, Byers 90	867
20	Feb 8	A	Stranraer	L	2-3	1-2	7	Milne 2, Byers 65	362
21	22	H	Stenhousemuir	D	3-3	1-1	7	Tosh 3 1, 83, 84	449
22	25	A	Airdrie U	D	0-0	0-0	—		921
23	Mar 1	A	Cowdenbeath	D	2-2	0-1	6	Hodge 67, Tosh 90	323
24	4	H	Berwick R	D	2-2	1-1	—	Williams 43, Bavidge 62	420
25	8	H	Brechin C	L	1-5	1-2	7	Tosh 31	774
26	11	H	Raith R	W	4-2	2-1	—	Anthony 9, Bavidge 2 25, 62, Stewart 90	688
27	15	A	Hamilton A	L	0-2	0-1	5		934
28	22	A	Berwick R	D	0-0	0-0	6		389
29	25	H	Hamilton A	L	0-1	0-0	—		453
30	30	H	Stranraer	W	2-1	1-0	7	Finlayson (og) 3, Tosh 86	394
31	Apr 5	H	Dumbarton	L	0-1	0-0	6		485
32	12	A	Raith R	W	1-0	1-0	5	Bavidge 39	2036
33	19	H	Stranraer	W	4-0	0-0	5	Sellars 55, Grecan 58, McCulloch 68, Bavidge 69	391
34	26	H	Airdrie U	D	1-1	1-1	5	Bavidge 34	884
35	May 3	A	Stenhousemuir	W	4-1	2-0	4	Sellars 13, Bavidge 28, Byers 58, Stewart 78	497
36	10	H	Cowdenbeath	D	1-1	0-0	4	Tosh 88	465

Final League Position: 4

Honours
League Champions: Second Division 1983-84. Third Division 1994-95; *Runners-up:* 1996-97. C Division 1948-49.
Scottish Cup: Semi-finals 1982; Quarter-finals 2002.
League Cup: Semi-finals 1977-78.

Club colours: Shirt: Sky blue with navy flashes. Shorts: Navy. Stockings: Navy.

Goalscorers: *League* (55): Bavidge 15, Tosh 13, Byers 9, Sellars 6, Stewart 2, Anthony 1, Greacen 1, Henderson 1, Hodge 1, Lunan 1, McCulloch 1, Milne 1, Rattray 1, Williams 1, own goal 1
Scottish Cup (8): Bavidge 3, Byers 2, Tosh 2, Lunan 1
CIS Cup (0)
Challenge Cup (4): Tosh 3, Bavidge 1

Brown M 31	Rattray A 28	McCulloch S 33 + 2	McCloy B 12 + 2	Good I 24 + 1	Byers K 36	Shaw G 6 + 7	Sellars B 29	Tosh P 31	Bavidge M 36	Henderson D 21 + 3	Milne K 11 + 7	Stewart W 10 + 18	Lunan P 28 + 4	Horn R 15	Anthony M 13 + 14	Williams D 5 + 5	Ferrie N 5 + 1	Greacan S 17	Hodge C — + 6	Cocozza M 2	Taylor S 3 + 4	Bannon M — + 1	*Match No.*
1	2	3[1]	4	5	6	7[2]	8	9	10	11	12	13											1
1	2	12	4	5	6	7[1]	3	9	10	11■		13	8[2]										2
1	2	3	4	5	8[2]	7[1]	6	9	10	11		12	13										3
1		3		5	2		8	9	10	11		12	6[1]	4	7								4
1		3		5	8		2	9■	10	11	12		6[1]	4	7								5
1	2	3[3]		5	7	13		9	10	11[2]	14	12	6	4	8[1]								6
1	2[3]	12	4[1]	5	8	7[2]		9	10	3	14	11	6		13								7
1		3		5	6	7		9	10	11■		2	12	4	8[1]								8
1		3	14	5	7	12	6[3]	9	10		11[1]	2	13	4	8[2]								9
1	2[2]	3		5	7		8		10		11	9[1]	6	4	12	13							10
1	2[2]	3		5	7		8	9	10		11[1]	12	6	4	13								11
1	2	3		5	7		8	9	10	12	11[1]		6	4									12
1	2	3		5	7		8	9	10		11		6	4									13
1	2	3		5	7		8	9	10		11	12	6[1]	4									14
1[G]	2	3		5	7		8	9	10		11		6[1]	4	12		15						15
	2	3		5	7[2]		8	9■	10		11	12	6[1]	4	13		1						16
	2	3		5	6		8	9[2]	10		11[1]	7	12	4	13		1						17
	2	3		5	7		8	9	10	13		12	6[1]	4	11[2]		1						18
	2	3		5	8			9	10	11[2]	12	7[1]	6	4	13		1						19
	2	3[2]		5	8	9[3]			10	11	7		6[1]		12	13	1	4	14				20
1	2	5	14		6	13	8	9	10	11[1]	3[2]		7[3]		12			4					21
1	2	3	4		6		7	9	10	11[1]					8	12		5					22
1	2■	3	4		6	12	7	9	10						8[1]	11[2]		5	13				23
1		3	4		6		7	9	10			12			8[2]	11[1]		5	13	2			24
1	2		4		6	12	7	9[1]	10			11	8					5	13	3[2]			25
1	2	3	4		6		7	9	10[1]			12	8		11			5					26
1		3	4[1]		6		7	9	10	2[3]	12	14	8		11[2]			5	13				27
1	2	3	4		6		7[1]		10	13	12[2]	14	8		11			5			9[3]		28
1	2	3	4	6	8[2]			9	10	11[1]		13	7		12			5					29
1	2	3		6	8[1]		4	9	10[2]	11[3]		12	7			14		5			13		30
1		3		5	8		2	9	10[2]	11[1]		7[3]	6		14	12		4			13		31
1		3		5	6		2		9	10[1]		7	8		13	11[2]		4			12		32
1	5[3]	3			6[2]		2		9	10[1]		7	8		13	11		4			12	14	33
1	5	3[2]		13	6		2	7	9	10		12	8			11[1]		4					34
1	5	3			6[2]	14	2	7	9[3]	10		12	8		13			4			11[1]		35
1	5	3			6	13		9	10[1]	8		12	2		7[3]			4	14		11[2]		36

GRETNA — Third Division

Year Formed: 1946. *Ground & Address:* Raydale Park, Dominion Rd, Gretna DG16 5AP. *Telephone:* 01461 337602. *Fax:* 01461 338047. *e-mail:* info@gretnafootballclub.co.uk.
Ground Capacity: 2200.
Club Shop: Alan Watson, 01387 251550.
President: Brian Fulton. *Chairman:* Ron MacGregor. *Secretary:* Helen MacGregor. *Commercial Director:* Stephen Barker.
Manager: Rowan Alexander. *Assistant Manager:* Derek Frye. *Physio:* William Bentley.
Record Attendance: 2307 v Rochdale, FA Cup; 16 Nov 1991.
Record Victory: 20-0 v Silloth, 1962.
Record Defeat: 0-6 v Worksop Town, 1994-95 and 0-6 v Bradford (Park Avenue) 1999-2000.
Most League Appearances: 36, David Irons, 2002-03.
Most League Goals in Season (Individual): 10, Mark Dobie, 2002-03.
Most Goals Overall (Individual): 13, Mark Dobie, 2002-03.

GRETNA 2002–03 LEAGUE RECORD

Match No.	Date	Venue	Opponents	Result		H/T Score	Lg. Pos.	Goalscorers	Attendance
1	Aug 3	H	Morton	D	1-1	1-1	—	Henney [1]	1566
2	10	A	Elgin C	W	2-0	2-0	—	Dobie [13], Skinner [31]	587
3	17	H	Montrose	W	4-1	2-1	2	Irons [25], Dobie [41], Hore 2 [62, 82]	373
4	24	H	Albion R	W	2-0	0-0	1	McGuffie [66], Hore [82]	443
5	31	A	Queen's Park	L	0-1	0-1	2		607
6	Sept 14	H	Peterhead	L	1-4	0-1	3	Benjamin [48]	357
7	21	A	East Stirling	W	4-0	0-0	2	Henney [57], Benjamin 2 [59, 82], Skinner [76]	190
8	28	H	Stirling A	L	0-2	0-2	5		402
9	Oct 5	A	East Fife	L	2-3	2-1	5	Henney [6], Hore [44]	462
10	19	H	Elgin C	D	0-0	0-0	6		323
11	26	A	Morton	D	2-2	0-1	6	May [52], Eeles [55]	1705
12	Nov 2	H	Queen's Park	D	2-2	1-1	6	Eeles [33], Dobie (pen) [88]	319
13	9	A	Albion R	L	1-2	0-0	6	McGuffie [47]	332
14	16	A	Peterhead	D	1-1	1-1	6	Henney [26]	496
15	23	H	East Stirling	D	2-2	2-0	6	Skinner 2 [6, 12]	221
16	30	H	East Fife	L	2-3	0-0	6	Dobie [46], Cleeland [48]	352
17	Dec 7	H	Albion R	L	1-2	1-0	6	Henney [17]	289
18	14	A	Stirling A	W	1-0	1-0	6	Dobie [7]	412
19	28	A	Montrose	W	2-0	1-0	6	Hore [5], Hewson [90]	381
20	Jan 11	A	Queen's Park	W	2-1	2-0	6	Dobie 2 (1 pen) [17, 26 (p)]	934
21	18	H	Peterhead	D	1-1	1-0	6	Dobie (pen) [44]	360
22	Feb 8	H	Stirling A	D	0-0	0-0	6		292
23	22	A	Elgin C	D	2-2	1-1	6	Dobie [35], Galloway [59]	383
24	26	A	East Stirling	W	2-1	1-0	—	Dobie [36], Ormiston [69]	146
25	Mar 1	H	Montrose	D	2-2	2-0	6	Galloway [3], Fairbairn [22]	227
26	4	A	East Fife	L	1-2	1-1	—	Hore [34]	503
27	8	A	Albion R	D	1-1	1-0	6	Hore [27]	327
28	15	H	Queen's Park	L	0-1	0-0	6		320
29	22	H	East Stirling	W	3-1	1-0	6	Hore [45], McGuffie [89], Gordon [90]	244
30	29	H	Morton	L	0-1	0-0	6		601
31	Apr 5	A	Peterhead	L	0-1	0-0	6		598
32	12	H	East Fife	D	3-3	2-1	6	Knox [1], May [25], Skelton [82]	409
33	19	A	Stirling A	L	0-1	0-1	6		376
34	26	A	Morton	L	0-5	0-1	6		2422
35	May 3	H	Elgin C	W	2-1	2-1	6	Skinner [40], Alexander [41]	250
36	10	A	Montrose	W	1-0	1-0	6	Fairbairn [32]	376

Final League Position: 6

Club colours: Shirt: Black with white hoops. Shorts: Black with white piping. Stockings: White topped with black hoops.

Goalscorers: *League* (50): Dobie 10 (3 pens), Hore 8, Henney 5, Skinner 5, Benjamin 3, McGuffie 3, Eeles 2, Fairbairn 2, Galloway 2, May 2, Alexander 1, Cleeland 1, Gordon 1, Hewson 1, Irons 1, Knox 1, Ormiston 1, Skelton 1
Scottish Cup (4): Dobie 2, Hore 1, Skinner 1
CIS Cup (1): Irons 1
Challenge Cup (1): Dobie 1

Mathieson D 35	McGuffie R 27 + 4	Skelton G 23 + 7	Turner T 19 + 1	Hewson D 20 + 4	Henney M 21	Skinner S 22 + 5	Irons D 36	Dobie M 25 + 3	Hore J 18 + 4	Gordon W 9	Alexander R 1 + 1	May K 27	Eeles S 4 + 1	Smart C 1 + 3	Cumersky I 5 + 7	Rooke S 2 + 2	Thwaites A 5 + 2	Benjamin A 2 + 4	McQuilter R 15 + 1	Cleeland M 17	Bell M 8 + 3	Harding G — + 1	Grainger D 7 + 1	Barr W 4	Milligan S 1 + 1	Wylie D 1 + 1	Fairbairn B 9 + 5	Galloway M 15 + 1	Knox K 12 + 1	Thurstan M 3 + 2	Ormiston D 1 + 4	Errington R 1 + 1	*Match No.*
1	2	3	4	5	6	7	8	9	10	11^{1}	12																						1
1	12	3	4	2	6	7^{2}	8	9	10^{3}			5	11^{1}	13	14																		2
1	11	3	4	2	6	7	8^{1}	9	10			5			12																		3
1	11	3	4	2^{1}	6	7	8	9	10			5				12																	4
1	11	3	4	2	6^{1}	7^{2}	8	9	10			5					12	13															5
1	11^{1}		4	2	6	7^{3}	8	9	14			5^{2}				12	3	10	13														6
1	7^{2}	14		11	6	13	8	9	10^{1}			4				2	3^{3}	12	5														7
1	11^{1}		14	2	6	12	8	9	13			4				7^{3}	3	10^{2}	5														8
1		3	4	2	6	7^{1}	8	9	10			5					11	12															9
1	12	3	4	2^{3}	10	7^{2}	8		9			6			14		11	13	5^{1}														10
1	2	3	4	6	10		8	13				5■	9	12	11^{1}					7^{2}													11
1	2	3^{1}	4	7^{2}	10		6	13					9		11^{3}		12			8	5	14											12
1	2		4		10		8	12				5	9^{1}		11					7			3	6									13
1	11	3		2	10	7	8	9				5								6	4												14
1	11	3	4	2	10	7^{2}	8	9				5			12					6^{1}					13								15
1	2		4	12	10	7	8	9	13			5		11^{1}						6^{2}				3									16
1	2		4		10	7	8	9				5	12						6	11					3^{1}								17
1	2	12	4		11	7^{2}	8	9	10			3		13					5	6^{1}													18
1^{G}	2	13		12	6^{1}	7	8	9	10^{2}			4							5	11				3		15							19
1		3	4		11^{2}	7	8	9	10^{1}			2							5	6							12	13					20
1			4			7	11	9	10^{1}			2							5	6								8	3	12			21
1		13	4			7	6	9				2							5	3^{1}							10^{3}	8	11^{2}	14	12		22
1	12	13				7^{1}	6	9				3							5	11^{2}							10	8	2	4			23
1		13	4			7^{2}	11	9											5	3■							10^{1}	8	2	6	12		24
1	13	3				12■	7^{2}	9	14										5		6						11^{1}	8	2	4	10^{3}		25
1	7	3					6	9	10			4							5	11^{1}								8	2		12		26
1	11	3				12	4	9	10										5	6	2							8	7^{1}				27
1	11	3			2^{1}		6	9	10						7				5		4						12	8					28
1	6	11		13			5	9■	10^{2}	7					8^{1}						2		3	4			12						29
1	6	11		7			4		9	10^{2}		5									2		3^{1}				12	8			13		30
1	6	11		2^{2}			4		9^{1}	7		5			13								3				10	8	12				31
1	6	11		7^{1}			4			10		5									12		3				9	8	2				32
1	6	11^{1}		7^{3}		12	4			10		5^{2}			14						13		3				9	8	2				33
1	6	3^{1}		11		7	4			10		5^{2}			13								12				9	8	2				34
1	6	13		5		11	4			9	10^{1}									3^{2}	14						12	8	2			7^{3}	35
	6	11^{2}		12		7	5			10^{1}											2		3			1	9	8	4			13	36

HAMILTON ACADEMICAL Second Division

Year Formed: 1874. *Ground:* New Douglas Park, Cadzow Avenue, Hamilton ML3 0FT. *Telephone:* 01698 368650. *Fax:* 01698 285422. *Ground Capacity:* 5474. *Size of Pitch:* 115yd × 75yd.
Chairman: Ronnie MacDonald. *Secretary:* Scott A. Struthers BA. *Commercial Director:* Arthur Lynch. *Commercial Manager:* Brian McPhee.
Manager: Allan Maitland. *Assistant Managers:* Jimmy McCade, Denis McDaid. *Physio:* Michael Valentine.
Managers since 1975: J. Eric Smith, Dave McParland, John Blackley, Bertie Auld, John Lambie, Jim Dempsey, John Lambie, Billy McLaren, Iain Munro, Sandy Clark, Colin Miller, Ally Dawson, Chris Hillcoat. *Club Nickname(s):* The Accies. *Previous Grounds:* Bent Farm, South Avenue, South Haugh, Douglas Park, Cliftonhill Stadium, Firhill Stadium.
Record Attendance: 28,690 v Hearts, Scottish Cup 3rd rd; 3 Mar, 1937.
Record Transfer Fee received: £380,000 for Paul Hartley to Millwall (July 1996).
Record Transfer Fee paid: £60,000 for Paul Martin from Kilmarnock (Oct 1988) and for John McQuade from Dumbarton (Aug 1993).
Record Victory: 11-1 v Chryston, Lanarkshire Cup; 28 Nov, 1885.
Record Defeat: 1-11 v Hibernian, Division I; 6 Nov, 1965.
Most Capped Player: Colin Miller, 29, Canada, 1988-94.
Most League Appearances: 452: Rikki Ferguson, 1974-88.
Most League Goals in Season (Individual): 35: David Wilson, Division I; 1936-37.
Most Goals Overall (Individual): 246: David Wilson, 1928-39.

HAMILTON ACADEMICAL 2002–03 LEAGUE RECORD

Match No.	Date	Venue	Opponents	Result		H/T Score	Lg. Pos.	Goalscorers	Attendance
1	Aug 3	A	Cowdenbeath	W	3-1	1-1	—	Graham Alastair S 2 [38, 76], Armstrong [80]	427
2	10	H	Airdrie U	W	1-0	0-0	1	Armstrong [46]	2366
3	17	A	Brechin C	L	0-1	0-1	1		498
4	24	H	Berwick R	L	1-2	1-1	5	Armstrong [2]	1486
5	31	A	Forfar Ath	D	1-1	1-1	5	Graham Alisdair [13]	486
6	Sept 14	A	Stenhousemuir	W	2-1	1-1	2	McPhee 2 [25, 78]	463
7	21	H	Raith R	L	0-4	0-2	7		1961
8	28	A	Dumbarton	D	1-1	1-1	6	Dobbins [20]	1202
9	Oct 5	H	Stranraer	L	1-5	0-3	8	Graham Alisdair [64]	1175
10	19	A	Airdrie U	D	0-0	0-0	8		1593
11	26	H	Cowdenbeath	W	1-0	0-0	6	McPhee [80]	1052
12	Nov 2	H	Forfar Ath	L	1-2	0-0	7	McPhee [83]	960
13	9	A	Berwick R	L	1-2	0-1	9	Callaghan (pen) [88]	461
14	16	H	Stenhousemuir	L	2-3	2-1	10	McPhee 2 [31, 45]	1226
15	23	A	Raith R	D	1-1	1-0	9	McPhee [19]	1897
16	30	A	Stranraer	W	2-1	1-1	9	Callaghan [1], Russell [66]	397
17	Dec 14	H	Dumbarton	W	1-0	1-0	6	Russell [1]	1062
18	28	H	Brechin C	L	1-2	1-1	8	McPhee [23]	1418
19	Jan 18	A	Stenhousemuir	D	2-2	1-1	84	Bonnar [23], Gribben [84]	581
20	Feb 1	H	Raith R	D	0-0	0-0	9		1292
21	8	A	Dumbarton	L	1-3	1-0	9	Armstrong [40]	1108
22	25	H	Berwick R	W	3-0	1-0	—	Graham Alastair S 2 [7, 61], Russell [70]	626
23	Mar 1	A	Brechin C	L	1-4	0-3	9	Russell [89]	441
24	4	A	Cowdenbeath	W	1-0	0-0	—	Armstrong [87]	281
25	8	A	Berwick R	L	0-1	0-0	9		406
26	11	H	Airdrie U	W	2-1	1-1	—	Armstrong 2 [23, 63]	1620
27	15	H	Forfar Ath	W	2-0	1-0	6	Armstrong 2 [24, 85]	934
28	18	H	Stranraer	L	1-2	1-2	—	Graham Alastair S [10]	743
29	22	A	Raith R	D	1-1	0-1	7	Dennis (og) [46]	1762
30	25	A	Forfar Ath	W	1-0	0-0	—	McPhee [87]	453
31	Apr 5	H	Stenhousemuir	L	0-1	0-0	7		1247
32	12	A	Stranraer	D	0-0	0-0	7		402
33	19	H	Dumbarton	D	2-2	1-0	7	Dobbins [41], Callaghan [67]	1270
34	26	H	Cowdenbeath	W	2-0	2-0	7	McPhee [9], Bonnar [15]	1055
35	May 3	A	Airdrie U	D	2-2	1-1	7	Russell 2 [34, 83]	1960
36	10	H	Brechin C	D	2-2	0-0	8	Callaghan [53], McPhee [54]	1644

Final League Position: 8

Honours
League Champions: First Division 1985-86, 1987-88; Third Division 2000-01. *Runners-up:* Division II 1903-04, 1952-53, 1964-65; Second Division 1996-97.
Scottish Cup Runners-up: 1911, 1935. *League Cup:* Semi-finalists three times.
B&Q Cup Winners: 1991-92, 1992-93.

Club colours: Shirt: Red and white hoops. Shorts: White. Stockings: White.

Goalscorers: *League* (43): McPhee 11, Armstrong 9, Russell 6, Alastair S Graham 5, Callaghan 4, Bonnar 2, Dobbins 2, Alisdair Graham 2, Gribben 1, own goal 1
Scottish Cup (10): McPhee 3, Bonnar 2, Armstrong 1, Callaghan 1 (pen), McDonald 1, Russell 1, own goal 1
CIS Cup (1): Callaghan 1 (pen)
Challenge Cup (0)

Macfarlane I 13	Nelson M 11 + 1	McDonald P 21 + 5	Dobbins I 30 + 3	Sweeney S 24 + 2	Paterson N 3 + 1	Bonnar M 28 + 1	Walker J 13 + 1	Armstrong G 21 + 4	Graham Alastair S 19 + 9	Graham Alisdair 34	Potter G 23 + 3	Elfallah M 9 + 10	McCreadie I 2 + 4	Davidson S — + 1	Callaghan S 32 + 1	McPhee B 24 + 3	Sherry J 21 + 3	Smillie C 6 + 1	Hillcoat C 3 + 4	Keegans M 6 + 5	Cunnington E 11 + 5	Russell A 15 + 8	Arbuckle A 3 + 2	Thomson S 1	Gribben D 1 + 3	Kerr D 16	Flynn P 4 + 3	McDermott A 2	*Match No.*
1^{G}	2	3	4	5	6^{1}	7^{2}	8	9	10	11	15	12	13																1
1	2	12	4	5	3^{1}	7	8^{3}	9	10	11		13	6^{2}	14															2
1^{G}	2	3	4	5	13	7	8^{2}	9	10	11	15	12	6^{1}																3
1	2	14	4	5	3	7	8^{3}	9^{2}	10^{1}	6					11	12	13												4
			4^{2}	5		7	8	9^{1}	12	2	1				11	10	3	6	13										5
		3	4	5			8^{1}	9^{2}	7	2	1		12		11	10			6	13									6
		3	4	5			8^{2}	9^{3}	7	2	1	14			11	10	13	12	6^{1}										7
			4	5		7		12	9	2^{1}	1	3			11	10	8	6											8
		13	4	5		7^{3}		9^{1}		2	1	3^{2}	14		11	10	8	6		12									9
1		3	4	5		7^{2}	8	9^{1}		2		6	13		11	10				12									10
1	14	3	4	5		7	8^{1}	9^{2}		2		6			11	10^{3}				13	12								11
1		3^{3}	4	5		7	8^{1}	9^{2}		2		6			11	10				13	12	14							12
1^{G}	2		4	5		7^{1}	13		9	6	15				11	10	8^{2}				3	12							13
	2^{1}	14	4	5		7		13	9^{2}	6	1				11	10	8				3^{3}	12							14
	2		4	5					9^{1}	6	1	12			11	10	8			7^{2}	3	13							15
	2	7^{1}	4	5		14			13	6^{3}	1	12			11		8			10^{2}	3	9							16
	2		4							6	1	12			11	10	8	5		9^{1}	3	7							17
	2		4			7^{2}			12	6	1				11	10		5		8^{1}	3	9	13						18
	2			5		7	8^{3}		13	6	1	14			11	10					3	9^{1}		4^{2}	12				19
				5		7	8^{2}	2	14	6	1				11	10^{3}	13	4				9^{1}			12	3			20
			4	5		7^{1}	8	2	13	6	1	12			11							9			10^{2}	3			21
		3	14	5^{3}		7		9	10^{2}	2	1				11		8					12	13			4	6^{1}		22
		3	13	5		7		9	10	2^{1}	1				11^{2}		8					12				4	6		23
		3		5		7		12	10	2	1				11		8					9				4	6^{1}		24
		3	13	5		7		12	10		1				11		8					9	2^{2}			4	6^{1}		25
		3	5			7		6	10^{1}	2	1				11	12	8					9				4			26
		3	5			7		6	10	2	1				11^{1}	12	8					9^{2}				4	13		27
		3	5^{2}					6	10^{1}	2	1				11	7	8		12			9				4	13		28
		3^{1}	5					6		2	1				11	10	8				12	9^{2}				4	13	7	29
		3	5			7		6^{1}	10^{3}	2	1				11	9	8		13		14	12				4^{2}			30
		3^{2}	4			7		11	9^{3}	2^{1}	1				13	10	8		5		14	12						6	31
1		12	4			7				2^{1}		6			11	10	8				3	9				5			32
1		8^{1}	5			7			13	2		6			11	10			12	9^{2}	3					4			33
1		8	5	14		7			12	2		6^{1}			11	10				9^{2}	3^{3}				13	4			34
1			5^{1}	13		7■				2^{2}		12			11	10	8				3	9	6			4			35
1		7	5	3					12			2^{1}			11	10	8					9	6			4			36

HEART OF MIDLOTHIAN Premier League

Year Formed: 1874. *Ground & Address:* Tynecastle Stadium, Gorgie Rd, Edinburgh EH11 2NL. *Telephone:* 0131 200 7200. *Fax:* 0131 200 7222. *Website:* www.heartsfc.co.uk
Ground Capacity: 18,000. *Size of Pitch:* 108yd × 73yd.
Chairman: Douglas Smith. *Chief Executive:* Christopher Robinson. *Sales and Marketing Manager:* Kenny Wittmann.
Manager: Craig Levein. *Assistant Coach:* Peter Houston. *Coach:* John McGlynn. *Physio:* Alan Rae.
Managers since 1975: J. Hagart, W. Ormond, R. Moncur, T. Ford, A. MacDonald, A. MacDonald & W. Jardine, A. MacDonald, J. Jordan, S. Clark, T. McLean, J. Jefferies.
Club Nickname(s): Hearts, Jambo's. *Previous Grounds:* The Meadows 1874, Powderhall 1878, Old Tynecastle 1881, (Tynecastle Park, 1886).
Record Attendance: 53,396 v Rangers, Scottish Cup 3rd rd; 13 Feb, 1932.
Record Transfer Fee received: £2,100,000 for Alan McLaren from Rangers (October 1994).
Record of Transfer paid: £750,000 for Derek Ferguson to Rangers (July 1990).
Record Victory: 21-0 v Anchor, EFA Cup 30th October 1880.
Record Defeat: 1-8 v Vale of Leven, Scottish Cup, 1888.
Most Capped Player: Bobby Walker, 29, Scotland.
Most League Appearances: 515: Gary Mackay, 1980-97.
Most League Goals in Season (Individual): 44: Barney Battles.
Most Goals Overall (Individual): 214: John Robertson, 1983-98.

HEART OF MIDLOTHIAN 2002–03 LEAGUE RECORD

Match No.	*Date*	*Venue*	*Opponents*	*Result*		*H/T Score*	*Lg. Pos.*	*Goalscorers*	*Attendance*
1	Aug 3	A	Dundee	D	1-1	1-0	—	Wales [33]	7705
2	11	H	Hibernian	W	5-1	2-0	2	Kirk [18], De Vries 4 [37, 65, 89, 90]	15,245
3	18	A	Aberdeen	D	1-1	0-0	4	De Vries [78]	12,825
4	24	H	Dunfermline Ath	W	2-0	0-0	3	Weir [53], De Vries [58]	11,367
5	31	H	Kilmarnock	D	1-1	1-1	3	McMullan [30]	11,912
6	Sept 11	A	Rangers	L	0-2	0-1	—		48,581
7	15	H	Motherwell	W	4-2	1-2	3	De Vries [34], Kirk 2 [63, 77], Boyack [74]	8759
8	21	H	Dundee U	W	2-0	1-0	3	Valois [25], De Vries [55]	11,532
9	28	A	Partick Th	D	2-2	1-1	3	Valois [37], Severin [80]	6111
10	Oct 6	A	Livingston	D	1-1	0-1	4	Stamp [46]	6492
11	20	H	Celtic	L	1-4	0-4	4	Wales [89]	13,911
12	26	H	Dundee	L	1-2	0-1	5	McKenna [60]	10,169
13	Nov 3	A	Hibernian	W	2-1	0-1	3	McKenna [85], Stamp [89]	15,560
14	9	H	Aberdeen	D	0-0	0-0	3		11,920
15	17	A	Dunfermline Ath	L	1-3	0-0	4	Severin [53]	5683
16	23	A	Kilmarnock	W	1-0	0-0	4	De Vries [48]	6511
17	Dec 1	H	Rangers	L	0-4	0-0	5		12,156
18	4	A	Motherwell	L	1-6	0-4	—	Valois [50]	4114
19	7	H	Livingston	W	2-1	1-0	4	Kirk 2 (1 pen) [5, 70 (p)]	8074
20	14	H	Partick Th	W	1-0	0-0	4	Maybury [90]	9734
21	21	A	Dundee U	W	3-0	2-0	3	De Vries [25], Kirk 2 [40, 50]	6025
22	26	A	Celtic	L	2-4	1-2	—	De Vries 2 [4, 66]	58,480
23	29	A	Dundee	W	2-1	1-0	3	Kirk [41], Weir [73]	7340
24	Jan 2	H	Hibernian	D	4-4	1-2	3	Pressley [29], De Vries [61], Weir 2 [88, 89]	17,732
25	28	A	Aberdeen	W	1-0	0-0	—	Wales [89]	9322
26	Feb 1	H	Dunfermline Ath	W	3-0	1-0	3	Severin [45], Wales [49], McKenna [90]	11,281
27	8	H	Kilmarnock	W	3-0	0-0	3	Maybury [50], De Vries [53], McKenna [77]	10,426
28	15	A	Rangers	L	0-1	0-1	3		49,459
29	Mar 1	H	Motherwell	W	2-1	1-0	3	McKenna [30], Simmons [71]	11,704
30	8	A	Livingston	D	1-1	1-0	3	Stamp [7]	6448
31	Apr 5	H	Dundee U	W	2-1	0-1	3	Webster [68], Kirk [78]	10,747
32	12	A	Partick Th	D	1-1	0-0	3	Pressley [78]	5288
33	19	H	Celtic	W	2-1	0-0	3	Stamp [72], McCann [89]	15,855
34	26	A	Dunfermline Ath	W	1-0	0-0	3	Pressley [56]	6968
35	May 3	A	Kilmarnock	L	0-1	0-1	3		9091
36	10	A	Celtic	L	0-1	0-1	3		58,906
37	18	H	Rangers	L	0-2	0-0	3		15,632
38	25	H	Dundee	W	1-0	0-0	3	De Vries [77]	12,205

Final League Position: 3

Honours
League Champions: Division I 1894-95, 1896-97, 1957-58, 1959-60. First Division 1979-80; *Runners-up:* Division I 1893-94, 1898-99, 1903-04, 1905-06, 1914-15, 1937-38, 1953-54, 1956-57, 1958-59, 1964-65. Premier Division 1985-86, 1987-88, 1991-92. First Division 1977-78, 1982-83.
Scottish Cup Winners: 1891, 1896, 1901, 1906, 1956, 1998; *Runners-up:* 1903, 1907, 1968, 1976, 1986, 1996.
League Cup Winners: 1954-55, 1958-59, 1959-60, 1962-63; *Runners-up:* 1961-62, 1996-97.

European: *European Cup:* 4 matches (1958-59, 1960-61). *Cup Winners' Cup:* 10 matches (1976-77, 1996-97, 1998-99). *UEFA Cup:* 37 matches (*Fairs Cup:* 1961-62, 1963-64, 1965-66. *UEFA Cup:* 1984-85, 1986-87, 1988-89, 1990-91, 1992-93, 1993-94, 2000-01).

Club colours: Shirt: Maroon. Shorts: White. Stockings: Maroon.

Goalscorers: *League* (57): De Vries 15, Kirk 9 (1 pen), McKenna 5, Stamp 4, Wales 4, Weir 4, Pressley 3, Severin 3, Valois 3, Maybury 2, Boyack 1, McCann 1, McMullan 1, Simmons 1, Webster 1
Scottish Cup (0)
CIS Cup (7): Pressley 2, Valois 2, Kirk 1, McKenna 1, Simmons 1

Niemi A 3	Pressley S 33	McCann A 15 + 2	Maybury A 35	McKenna K 30 + 6	Valois J 37 + 1	Severin S 37	Boyack S 19 + 7	Simmons S 9 + 14	Kirk A 17 + 12	Wales G 12 + 14	De Vries M 29 + 3	Twaddle K 1 + 7	McMullan P 13 + 3	Mahe S 8 + 3	Weir G 12 + 8	Janczyk N 1 + 7	McKenzie R 20	Stamp P 22 + 2	Gordon C 1	McGeown D 1	Webster A 19 + 2	Sloan R — + 1	Macfarlane N 20 + 1	Oueifio W 3	Dunn D 1	Knox J — + 1	Hamill J 1 + 3	Moilanen T 14	Neilson R 5	Match No.
1	2	3	4	5	6³	7	8	9	10²	11¹	12	13	14																	1
1	2		4	5	6	7	8	9¹	10³	14	11	12	13	3²																2
1	2		4	5	6	7	8	9²		10¹	11		3		12	13														3
	2		4	5	6	7	8	9¹			11	12	3		10		1													4
	2		4	5	6	7	8²		12		11	13	3		10¹		1	9												5
	2		4	5	6	7	8²		10¹	12	11	13	3				1	9												6
	2		4	5	6	7	8		10¹	12	11		3				1	9												7
	2		4	5	6	7	8		10	12	11¹		3				1	9												8
	2		4	5	6	7	8¹	12		13	11		3		10²		1	9												9
	2		4	5	6³	7²	8	13	10¹	12	11		3		14			9	1											10
	2		4	5	6	7		13	10³	14	11		3				1	9¹		8²	12									11
	2		4	5²	6	7		9¹	14	10	11³	12	3			13	1	8												12
	2		4	5	8	7³		10²	11¹			13	6		12	14	1	9■			3									13
	2		4	5	8	7		10¹		14		9²	6		11³	12	1				3	13								14
	2		4	5	8	7			10¹	11	12		6³		14	13	1	9²			3									15
	2¹	3	4	5	6³	7		13	10²		11		14				1				12		8	9						16
		3	4■	5	6	7		12	13	14	11²						1	8¹			2		10	9³						17
		3²		5	6	7		8	10		11			13	14		1				2			9¹	4³	12				18
		3	4	5	6	7			10³	9²	11				14	12	1				2¹		8				13			19
			4	5	6	7	12	3	10	9¹	11			2			1						8							20
	2	3	4	5	6	7³	8²	14	10		11						1	12					9¹				13			21
	2	3³	4	5	6		8¹	12			11			14	10		1	7					9²				13			22
	2		4	5	6	7	8²	13	10¹		11			3	12		1						9							23
	2		4	5	6	7	8²	13	10³		11			3	14		1	12					9¹							24
	2	12	4	13	6	7	8			14	11²			3¹	10³						5		9					1		25
	2	12	4	5	8	7				11				3¹				9			6		10					1		26
	2	3	4	13	6	7¹	14	12		10	11²							8³			5		9					1		27
	2		4	12	6³	7	8¹	13	14	10	11			3							5		9²					1		28
	2		4	5	8³	7	14	12	13	11²				3				9			6		10¹					1		29
	2	3	4	5²	8	7	12		13	11³	14							9			6		10¹					1		30
		3		5	8	7¹	12		13	11²	10					6		9			2							1	4	31
	2	3		13	6¹	7	8²		11³	14	10							9			5		12					1	4	32
	2	3	4		6³	7	12		14	13	10				11²			8			5		9¹					1		33
	2	3	4	12	6	7			13		10¹				11²			8			5		9					1		34
	2	3■	4	5	8²	7	13		12	14					11¹			9			6■		10³					1		35
	2		4	5²	6	7	8	13	14						11³	12		9¹					10					1	3	36
	2²		4	12	6³	7	8	13	14		10				11¹						5		9					1	3	37
	2	3³	4		13	7				12	10			14	11¹						5		9				8²	1	6	38

HIBERNIAN

Premier League

Year Formed: 1875. *Ground & Address:* Easter Road Stadium, Albion Rd, Edinburgh EH7 5QG. *Telephone:* 0131 661 2159. *Fax:* 0131 659 6488.
Ground Capacity: total: 17,500. *Size of Pitch:* 112yd × 74yd.
Chairman: Ken Lewandowski. *Managing Director:* Rod Petrie. *Commercial Director:* Steven Powell.
Manager: Bobby Williamson. *Assistant Managers:* Gerry McCabe, Jim Clarke.
Physio: Malcolm Colquhoun.
Managers since 1975: Eddie Turnbull, Willie Ormond, Bertie Auld, Pat Stanton, John Blackley, Alex Miller, Jim Duffy, Alex McLeish, Frank Sauzee. *Club Nickname(s):* Hibees. *Previous Grounds:* Meadows 1875-78, Powderhall 1878-79, Mayfield 1879-80, First Easter Road 1880-92, Second Easter Road 1892-.
Record Attendance: 65,860 v Hearts, Division I; 2 Jan, 1950.
Record Victory: 22-1 v 42nd Highlanders; 3 Sept, 1881.
Record Defeat: 0-10 v Rangers; 24 Dec, 1898.
Most Capped Player: Lawrie Reilly, 38, Scotland.
Most League Appearances: 446: Arthur Duncan.
Most League Goals in Season (Individual): 42: Joe Baker.
Most Goals Overall (Individual): 364: Gordon Smith.

HIBERNIAN 2002–03 LEAGUE RECORD

Match No.	Date	Venue	Opponents	Result		H/T Score	Lg. Pos.	Goalscorers	Attendance
1	Aug 3	H	Aberdeen	L	1-2	1-0	—	Luna [31]	13,340
2	11	A	Hearts	L	1-5	0-2	12	Murray [52]	15,245
3	18	H	Rangers	L	2-4	1-2	12	Townsley [35], O'Connor [88]	11,633
4	24	A	Dundee	L	1-2	1-0	12	O'Connor [8]	6411
5	31	A	Motherwell	W	2-0	1-0	11	Townsley 2 [16, 71]	5888
6	Sept 11	H	Dunfermline Ath	L	1-4	1-3	—	Paatelainen [42]	9837
7	14	A	Celtic	L	0-1	0-1	12		56,462
8	21	H	Kilmarnock	W	2-0	2-0	10	Murray [7], McManus [10]	8680
9	28	H	Livingston	W	1-0	1-0	9	Murray [44]	9451
10	Oct 5	H	Dundee U	W	2-1	1-0	7	O'Connor [27], Murray [50]	9175
11	19	A	Partick Th	W	3-0	1-0	5	O'Connor 2 [42, 87], Paatelainen [81]	5946
12	27	A	Aberdeen	W	1-0	0-0	4	Brebner [70]	12,321
13	Nov 3	H	Hearts	L	1-2	1-0	5	Paatelainen [35]	15,560
14	10	A	Rangers	L	1-2	1-2	5	McManus [44]	49,032
15	16	H	Dundee	W	2-1	1-0	5	Paatelainen 2 [12, 48]	8870
16	23	H	Motherwell	W	3-1	0-0	5	Paatelainen [58], McManus [64], O'Neil (pen) [89]	8859
17	30	A	Dunfermline Ath	D	1-1	0-0	4	McManus [57]	7506
18	Dec 4	H	Celtic	L	0-1	0-0	—		12,042
19	7	A	Dundee U	D	1-1	1-1	5	Murray [7]	5673
20	14	A	Livingston	W	2-1	0-0	5	Murray [55], James [66]	5501
21	21	A	Kilmarnock	L	1-2	0-0	5	Luna [82]	5814
22	26	H	Partick Th	D	1-1	0-0	—	O'Neil [88]	10,317
23	29	H	Aberdeen	W	2-0	0-0	4	Paatelainen [69], McManus [84]	11,604
24	Jan 2	A	Hearts	D	4-4	2-1	5	Townsley [11], McManus [17], James [88], Brebner [89]	17,732
25	29	H	Rangers	L	0-2	0-0	—		13,686
26	Feb 8	A	Motherwell	L	1-2	0-2	6	O'Connor [70]	4999
27	15	H	Dunfermline Ath	L	1-3	0-2	6	McManus [67]	9175
28	25	A	Dundee	L	0-3	0-1	—		8414
29	Mar 2	A	Celtic	L	2-3	1-2	7	McManus 2 [37, 60]	57,096
30	9	H	Dundee U	D	1-1	1-0	7	McManus [2]	7518
31	15	A	Partick Th	W	1-0	1-0	7	McManus [15]	4551
32	Apr 5	A	Kilmarnock	L	2-6	1-3	7	Murray [17], Jack [82]	5558
33	12	H	Livingston	D	2-2	1-0	7	Orman [43], Riordan [52]	8150
34	26	A	Dundee U	W	2-1	0-1	7	McManus (pen) [58], Murray [89]	6758
35	May 3	H	Aberdeen	W	3-1	1-0	7	Jack [40], Riordan 2 [61, 72]	7904
36	10	H	Motherwell	W	1-0	0-0	7	Brebner (pen) [65]	7809
37	17	A	Livingston	W	2-1	1-0	7	Brown 2 [38, 68]	5243
38	24	H	Partick Th	L	2-3	2-1	7	Jack [8], Brown [34]	8986

Final League Position: 7

Honours
League Champions: Division I 1902-03, 1947-48, 1950-51, 1951-52. First Division 1980-81, 1998-99. Division II 1893-94, 1894-95, 1932-33; *Runners-up:* Division I 1896-97, 1946-47, 1949-50, 1952-53, 1973-74, 1974-75.
Scottish Cup Winners: 1887, 1902; *Runners-up:* 1896, 1914, 1923, 1924, 1947, 1958, 1972, 1979, 2001.
League Cup Winners: 1972-73, 1991-92; *Runners-up:* 1950-51, 1968-69, 1974-75, 1993-94.

European: *European Cup:* 6 matches (1955-56 semi-finals). *Cup Winners' Cup:* 6 matches (1972-73). *UEFA Cup:* 61 matches (*Fairs Cup:* 1960-61 semi-finals, 1961-62, 1962-63, 1965-66, 1967-68, 1968-69, 1970-71. *UEFA Cup:* 1973-74, 1974-75, 1975-76, 1976-77, 1978-79, 1989-90, 1992-93, 2001-02).

Club colours: Shirt: Green with white sleeves and collar. Shorts: White with green stripe. Stockings: White with green trim.

Goalscorers: *League* (56): McManus 12 (1 pen), Murray 8, Paatelainen 7, O'Connor 6, Townsley 4, Brebner 3 (1 pen), Brown 3, Jack 3, Riordan 3, James 2, Luna 2, O'Neil 2 (1 pen), Orman 1
Scottish Cup (4): Brebner 3, Murray 1
CIS Cup (4): O'Connor 2, Brebner 1, Murray 1

Caig A 5	Orman A 25	Smith G 30 + 2	Dempsie M 2	Townsley D 15 + 9	Murray I 35 + 1	Arpinon F 3 + 5	Brebner G 25 + 7	O'Neil J 17 + 4	O'Connor G 17 + 7	Luna P 12 + 5	Wiss J 21 + 3	McManus T 20 + 14	Whittaker S 5 + 1	Jack M 17 + 2	Paatelainen M 21 + 3	Colgan N 30	Fenwick P 30 + 1	Doumbe M 11 + 1	Daquin F 1 + 1	Zambernardi Y 28	Dempsie A 2 + 1	Matyus J 14	James C 20 + 2	Reid A — + 6	Riordan D 4 + 6	Andersson D 3	Brown S 3 + 1	Thomson D 2	Nicol K — + 1	*Match No.*
1	2	3	4	5	6	7[2]	8	9[1]	10	11[3]	12	13	14																	1
1	2	3	4	8[3]	6	7	12	9[1]	10[2]	11		14		5	13															2
		3		12	6	7[1]	8		13	11■		10[3]		5	14	1	2	4	9[2]											3
		3		7[2]	6		8		11		13	9[1]		5	10	1	2		12	4										4
				7	6				11[1]			12	8	5	10	1	2			4	9	3								5
1				7	6		13			11[3]		14	8[1]	5[2]	10		2			4	9	3	12							6
1	9	3			6		8		12	11[2]	7	10[1]			13		2			4		5								7
	9	3		13	6		8		12	11[2]	7	10[1]				1	2			4		5								8
	9	3			6		8		10[2]	11	7	13				1	2			4[1]	12	5								9
	3			9	6		8		10	11[1]	7	12				1	2			4		5								10
	3	12		9[1]	6		8[2]		11		7	13			10	1	2			4			5							11
	3	12		9[1]	6		8[2]		11	14	7	13			10[3]	1	2			4			5							12
	9	3			6		8		11[2]	12	7	13			10[1]	1	2			4			5							13
	6[2]	3					8	13	11[1]	12	7	9			10	1	2			4			5							14
	8[1]	3			6			9		11	7			13	10	1	2[2]	12		4			5							15
	8[2]	3		13	6		14■	9		11[1]	7[3]	12			10	1	2			4			5							16
	8	3		12	6[1]			9			7	11			10[2]	1	2			4			5	13						17
	10[3]	3		8	6[1]		12	9			7[2]	11		13		1	2			4			5	14						18
	8	3		13	6			9[2]			7	11[1]			10	1	2			4			5	12						19
	8	3			6			9			7	11			10	1	2			4			5							20
	8[1]	3		12	6		14	9[3]		13	7	11[2]			10	1	2			4			5							21
	8	3			6			9		11	7				10	1	2			4			5							22
1	2	3■		6[3]	14		12	9		11[2]	7[1]	13			10			8		4			5							23
	8	3		9[1]	6		12			13	7	11[2]			10	1	2			4			5							24
	5	3		9	6		8	12	10		7	11				1	2[1]			4										25
	3			7	6	13	8	9	11[3]					5[2]	10	1	2			4[1]			12	14						26
	3[1]			7	6	13	8	9[2]	11[3]			12			10	1	2			4			5		14					27
	2	3		13	6	14	8	9[2]	12			11		4[1]	10[3]	1		7					5							28
		3		9[2]	6	13	8	12	10[3]			11[1]		4			2	7					5		14	1				29
		3			6		8	13	12			11[1]		7	10	1		9		4		2	5[2]							30
		3			6		8	9	12			11[2]		2	10[1]	1		7				4	5		13					31
		3			6	13	8[3]	9	14			11		2		1	12	7				4[2]	5[1]		10					32
	5			12	6		8	9	10[3]			11[2]		3		1	2[1]	7		4				14	13					33
		3			6		8		10[1]			11		7		1	2	9		4		5			12					34
		3		14	6		8		10[2]			11[1]		7		1	2	9		4[3]		5			12		13			35
		3			6		8				12		4	7[1]			2	9				5		13	10	1	11[2]			36
		3					8				6	12	4	7			2					5			10[1]	1	11	9		37
		3			6		8				7[2]	12	4[1]	2		1						5			10		11	9	13	38

INVERNESS CALEDONIAN THISTLE

First Division

Year Formed: 1994. *Ground & Address:* Caledonian Stadium, East Longman, Inverness IV1 1FF. *Telephone:* 01463 222880. *Fax:* 01463 715816
Ground Capacity: 6500, seated: 2200. *Size of Pitch:* 115yd × 75yd.
Chairman: Kenneth Mackie. *President:* John MacDonald. *Secretary:* Jim Falconer. *Commercial Manager:* Debbie Ross.
Youth Administrator: Charlie Christie. *Football and Community Development Manager:* Danny MacDonald.
Manager: John Robertson. *Head Coach:* Donald Park. *First Team Coach:* John Docherty. *Physio:* Emily Goodlad.
Managers since 1995: Steven Paterson.
Record Attendance: 6290 v Aberdeen, Scottish Cup, 20 February 2000.
Record Victory: 8-1, v Annan Ath, Scottish Cup 3rd rd, 24 January 1998.
Record Defeat: 1-5, v Morton, First Division, 12 November 1999 and v Airdrieonians, First Division, 15 April 2000.
Most League Appearances: 308, Charlie Christie, 1995-2003.
Most League Goals in Season: 27, Iain Stewart, 1996-97; Denis Wyness 2002-03.
Most Goals Overall (Individual): 82, Iain Stewart, 1995-2001.

INVERNESS CALEDONIAN THISTLE 2002–03 LEAGUE RECORD

Match No.	Date	Venue	Opponents	Result		H/T Score	Lg. Pos.	Goalscorers	Attendance
1	Aug 3	H	Alloa Ath	D	0-0	0-0	—		1623
2	10	A	St Johnstone	L	0-1	0-0	7		3770
3	17	H	Falkirk	L	1-2	1-0	9	Tokely [26]	2267
4	24	H	Ross Co	W	2-0	2-0	6	Wyness 2 [7, 33]	3699
5	31	A	St Mirren	W	4-0	3-0	4	Robson 2 [9, 21], Hart [24], Christie [72]	2485
6	Sept 14	A	Queen of the S	W	3-1	2-0	3	Mann [7], Wyness 2 [24, 48]	1611
7	21	H	Arbroath	W	5-0	1-0	3	Tokely 2 [6, 68], Hart [47], Wyness [51], Ritchie [85]	1686
8	28	A	Clyde	L	0-3	0-2	4		936
9	Oct 5	H	Ayr U	W	2-0	1-0	2	Ritchie [19], Wyness [76]	1803
10	19	A	Alloa Ath	W	6-0	4-0	2	Wyness 3 [6, 19, 27], Ritchie 3 [36, 71, 79]	531
11	26	H	St Johnstone	W	2-1	1-0	2	Wyness [45], Hart [61]	2541
12	Nov 2	H	St Mirren	W	4-1	2-0	2	Wyness 2 [7, 25], Hart [58], Robson [84]	2023
13	9	A	Ross Co	W	2-0	2-0	2	Robson [1], McCulloch (og) [8]	5449
14	16	H	Queen of the S	W	5-3	2-1	2	Ritchie 3 [6, 59, 89], Robson 2 (1 pen) [43 (p), 49]	1855
15	23	A	Arbroath	W	2-1	1-0	1	Wyness [23], Hart [71]	653
16	30	H	Clyde	W	1-0	0-0	1	Robson [80]	2829
17	Dec 7	A	Ayr U	D	3-3	0-1	2	Mann [54], Ritchie [70], Wyness [72]	1663
18	14	A	Falkirk	D	1-1	1-1	2	Mackenzie (og) [1]	4671
19	21	H	Alloa Ath	D	1-1	1-1	1	Mann [5]	1639
20	28	A	St Mirren	W	4-1	3-0	1	Wyness [14], Tokely [22], Stewart [29], Ritchie [51]	3054
21	Jan 18	H	Ayr U	L	0-1	0-1	2		2021
22	Feb 8	H	Falkirk	L	3-4	2-2	2	Robson [8], Wyness [28], Ritchie [56]	3322
23	15	A	St Johnstone	L	0-2	0-0	3		2631
24	25	H	Ross Co	L	1-5	0-3	—	Wyness [87]	3443
25	Mar 1	H	St Mirren	W	3-1	1-1	3	Ritchie 3 [25, 49, 55]	1973
26	4	H	Arbroath	W	2-0	1-0	—	Ritchie [42], Low [90]	1396
27	8	A	Ross Co	W	2-0	0-0	3	Hart [60], Robson [87]	4621
28	11	A	Queen of the S	D	0-0	0-0	—		1405
29	15	A	Arbroath	W	3-1	0-1	3	Hislop [67], Wyness 2 [68, 84]	550
30	18	A	Clyde	L	1-4	1-3	—	Robson [26]	703
31	Apr 5	H	Queen of the S	W	1-0	1-0	3	Tokely [43]	1656
32	12	H	Clyde	L	1-2	0-1	4	Hislop [63]	1682
33	26	A	Alloa Ath	W	5-1	2-0	4	Mann [19], Ritchie 3 [28, 50, 71], Golabek [84]	485
34	29	A	Ayr U	L	0-1	0-1	—		1114
35	May 3	H	St Johnstone	L	1-2	1-1	4	Hart [7]	1814
36	10	A	Falkirk	W	3-2	0-1	4	Nichols (og) [47], Mann [79], Christie [82]	7300

Final League Position: 4

Honours
Scottish Cup: Semi-finals 2003; Quarter-finals 1996.
League Champions: Third Division 1996-97; *Runners-up:* Second Division 1998-99.
Bell's League Challenge Cup runners-up: 1999-2000.

Club colours: Shirts: Royal blue with red stripes. Shorts: Royal blue. Stockings: Royal blue.

Goalscorers: *League* (74): Wyness 19, Ritchie 18, Robson 10 (1 pen), Hart 7, Mann 5, Tokely 5, Christie 2, Hislop 2, Golabek 1, Low 1, Stewart 1, own goals 3
Scottish Cup (9): Wyness 4, Robson 3 (1 pen), McCaffrey 1, Ritchie 1
CIS Cup (7): Wyness 4, Ritchie 2, Hart 1
Challenge Cup (0)

Brown M 36	Tokely R 34	Golabek S 34	Mann R 31	McCaffrey S 21 + 1	Munro G 30 + 2	Duncan R 25 + 2	Wyness D 35 + 1	Ritchie P 28 + 7	Christie C 13 + 9	Robson B 34	Keogh L 3 + 21	Hart R 27 + 3	McBain R 32 + 2	Low A 2 + 13	Gilfillan B — + 2	Miller C — + 1	Stewart G 3 + 6	Bagan D 3 + 10	Hislop S 5 + 9	Match No.
1	2	3	4	5	6	7^{2}	8	9^{1}	10	11^{3}	12	13	14							1
1	2	3	4	5	6	7	8	12	10	11	9^{1}									2
1	2^{1}	3	4	5	6	7	8^{3}	13	10	11	9^{2}		12	14						3
1	2^{1}	3	4	5		7	8	14	10^{3}	11		9^{2}	6	12	13					4
1	2	3	4		5	7	8	12	10^{2}	11^{3}		9^{1}	6	13		14				5
1	2	3	4		5	7	8	9^{2}		11	12	10^{1}	6	13						6
1	2	3	4		5^{1}	7^{3}	8	9		11		10	6^{2}	12	14		13			7
1		3	4		5	7	8	9		11^{1}		10	6	2			12			8
1		3	4		5	7	8	9		11		10	6	2						9
1	2	3	4		5	7	8^{2}	9	12	11^{3}	13	10	6^{1}	14						10
1	2	3	4		5	7	8	9^{2}	12	11	13	10^{1}	6							11
1	2^{2}	3	4		5	7	8^{3}	9	12	11	14	10^{1}	6	13						12
1	2	3	4		5	7	8^{2}	9^{3}	12	11	13	10^{1}	6	14						13
1	2^{3}	3	4		5^{1}	7^{2}	8	9	12	11	13	10	6	14						14
1	2	3	4		5	7	8	9^{1}		11	12	10	6							15
1	2	3	4		5	7	8	9^{2}	12	11	13	10^{1}	6							16
1	2	3	4		5	7■	8	9		11		10	6							17
1	2	3	4	13	5		8	9^{3}	7^{2}	11	12	10^{1}	6	14						18
1	2	3	4		5■		8	9^{1}	7	11	12	10^{2}	6					13		19
1	2	3	4	5			8	9^{2}	10^{1}	11	13		6	14			7^{3}	12		20
1	2^{1}	3	4	5		12	8	9^{3}	10	11	14	13	6				7^{2}			21
1	2	3	4	5		7	8	9^{1}	13	11		10^{2}	6						12	22
1	2	3	4	6	5	7^{3}	8	9^{1}	10^{2}		14		11					13	12	23
1	2	3	4^{2}	5	13	7^{3}	8	9^{1}	10	11			6					14	12	24
1	2	3^{1}		5	4		8	9^{2}		11	14	7	6				12	10^{3}	13	25
1	2	3		5	4		8^{1}	9^{2}		11^{3}	13	7	6	14				10	12	26
1	2	3		5	4		8^{3}	9^{2}	10^{1}	11		7	6				14	12	13	27
1	2	3		5	4		8^{2}	9^{1}		11	13	7	6					10	12	28
1	7	3	4	2^{1}	5		8	12		11	14	10^{2}	6				13		9^{3}	29
1	7	3	4	2^{1}	5		8	12		11^{2}	13	10^{3}	6				14		9	30
1	7	3	4	2	5	13	8^{3}	9	14		12	10	6^{2}						11^{1}	31
1	2		4	5	3	6	13		10^{1}	11	8^{2}	7						12	9	32
1	2	3	4	5	6	7^{1}	8^{3}	9^{2}		11			10	14				12	13	33
1	2	3		4	5	6	8	13		11^{3}		14	10				7^{1}	12	9^{2}	34
1	2^{2}	3	4	5	13	6^{1}	8	9		11^{3}	14	7	10					12		35
1	2		4	5	3	6	8^{1}	9^{2}	12	11^{3}		7	10					14	13	36

KILMARNOCK

Premier League

Year Formed: 1869. *Ground & Address:* Rugby Park, Kilmarnock KA1 2DP. *Telephone:* 01563 545300. *Fax:* 01563 522181. *Website:* www.kilmarnockfc.co.uk
Ground Capacity: all seated: 18,128. *Size of Pitch:* 114yd × 72yd.
Chairman: Sir John Orr. *Secretary:* Angela Burnett.
Manager: Jim Jefferies. *Assistant Manager:* Billy Brown. *Physio:* A. MacQueen.
Managers since 1975: W. Fernie, D. Sneddon, J. Clunie, E. Morrison, J. Fleeting, T. Burns, A. Totten, B. Brown.
Club Nickname(s): Killie. *Previous Grounds:* Rugby Park (Dundonald Road); The Grange; Holm Quarry; Present ground since 1899.
Record Attendance: 35,995 v Rangers, Scottish Cup; 10 March, 1962.
Record Transfer Fee received: £300,000 for Shaun McSkimming to Motherwell (1995).
Record Transfer Fee paid: £300,000 for Paul Wright from St Johnstone (1995).
Record Victory: 11-1 v Paisley Academical, Scottish Cup; 18 Jan, 1930 (15-0 v Lanemark, Ayrshire Cup; 15 Nov, 1890).
Record Defeat: 1-9 v Celtic, Division I; 13 Aug, 1938.
Most Capped Player: Joe Nibloe, 11, Scotland.
Most League Appearances: 481: Alan Robertson, 1972-88.
Most League Goals in Season (Individual): 34: Harry 'Peerie' Cunningham 1927-28 and Andy Kerr 1960-61.
Most Goals Overall (Individual): 148: W. Culley; 1912-23.

KILMARNOCK 2002–03 LEAGUE RECORD

Match No.	Date	Venue	Opponents	Result	H/T Score	Lg. Pos.	Goalscorers	Attendance
1	Aug 3	H	Rangers	D 1-1	0-1	—	McLaren [80]	13,972
2	10	A	Dundee U	W 2-1	0-0	4	Dargo [77], Boyd [82]	6366
3	17	H	Motherwell	L 0-3	0-0	7		6164
4	25	A	Livingston	W 1-0	1-0	4	Boyd [42]	5852
5	31	A	Hearts	D 1-1	1-1	4	Boyd [43]	11,912
6	Sept 11	H	Partick Th	W 1-0	1-0	—	Canero [41]	6848
7	14	H	Aberdeen	D 2-2	0-0	4	McLaughlin [56], Mahood [90]	6538
8	21	A	Hibernian	L 0-2	0-2	5		8680
9	28	A	Celtic	L 0-5	0-3	5		57,070
10	Oct 5	A	Dundee	L 1-2	0-0	8	Boutal [66]	5567
11	19	H	Dunfermline Ath	D 2-2	0-1	8	Shields [49], Boyd [75]	5515
12	27	A	Rangers	L 1-6	1-4	8	Fulton [44]	48,368
13	Nov 2	H	Dundee U	L 1-2	1-1	8	Fulton [24]	5411
14	9	A	Motherwell	W 1-0	0-0	8	Boyd [88]	4439
15	16	H	Livingston	W 2-0	0-0	6	Di Giacomo [63], McSwegan [89]	5270
16	23	H	Hearts	L 0-1	0-0	7		6511
17	30	A	Partick Th	L 0-3	0-0	7		5055
18	Dec 3	A	Aberdeen	W 1-0	0-0	—	McSwegan [66]	8816
19	7	H	Dundee	W 2-0	0-0	6	Fulton [56], Boyd [90]	4806
20	15	H	Celtic	D 1-1	1-0	6	McLaren [18]	9225
21	21	H	Hibernian	W 2-1	0-0	6	McSwegan [62], Fulton [86]	5814
22	26	A	Dunfermline Ath	W 2-0	0-0	—	McSwegan [70], Boyd [88]	5847
23	29	H	Rangers	L 0-1	0-1	6		13,396
24	Jan 2	A	Dundee U	D 2-2	1-1	6	Canero [20], McLaren [66]	7183
25	29	H	Motherwell	W 1-0	0-0	—	Boyd (pen) [81]	4457
26	Feb 1	A	Livingston	W 4-0	2-0	4	McLaren 2 [21, 70], Canero [33], Boyd [49]	4144
27	8	A	Hearts	L 0-3	0-0	4		10,426
28	23	H	Partick Th	W 1-0	1-0	4	Canero [45]	8651
29	Mar 1	H	Aberdeen	W 2-0	0-0	4	McSwegan [58], Canero [62]	5769
30	8	A	Dundee	D 2-2	0-2	4	Canero [50], McSwegan [85]	6531
31	16	H	Dunfermline Ath	D 1-1	0-0	4	Boyd [80]	4021
32	Apr 5	H	Hibernian	W 6-2	3-1	4	McDonald [10], McSwegan 4 [23, 41, 46, 61], Boyd [89]	5558
33	13	A	Celtic	L 0-2	0-1	4		56,736
34	27	A	Dundee	W 1-0	0-0	4	Innes [75]	5964
35	May 3	H	Hearts	W 1-0	1-0	4	McSwegan [29]	9091
36	11	A	Rangers	L 0-4	0-2	4		49,036
37	17	A	Dunfermline Ath	D 2-2	1-2	4	McDonald [25], Boyd [88]	6896
38	25	H	Celtic	L 0-4	0-2	4		16,722

Final League Position: 4

Honours
League Champions: Division I 1964-65. Division II 1897-98, 1898-99; *Runners-up:* Division I 1959-60, 1960-61, 1962-63, 1963-64. First Division 1975-76, 1978-79, 1981-82, 1992-93. Division II 1953-54, 1973-74. Second Division 1989-90.
Scottish Cup Winners: 1920, 1929, 1997; *Runners-up:* 1898, 1932, 1938, 1957, 1960.
League Cup Runners-up: 1952-53, 1960-61, 1962-63, 2000-01.

European: *European Cup:* 4 matches (1965-66). *Cup Winners' Cup:* 4 matches (1997-98). *UEFA Cup:* 24 matches (*Fairs Cup:* 1964-65, 1966-67, 1969-70, 1970-71, *UEFA Cup:* 1998-99, 1999-2000, 2001-02).

Club colours: Shirt: Blue and white vertical stripes. Shorts: Blue. Stockings: Blue.

Goalscorers: *League* (47): Boyd 12 (1 pen), McSwegan 11, Canero 6, McLaren 5, Fulton 4, McDonald 2, Boutal 1, Dargo 1, Di Giacomo 1, Innes 1, McLaughlin 1, Mahood 1, Shields 1
Scottish Cup (0)
CIS Cup (0)

Marshall G 30	Shields G 34	Dindeleux F 27	Hessey S 5	Hay G 12 + 9	Fulton S 36	Mahood A 35	Mitchell A 4 + 6	Sanjuan J 5 + 3	Dargo C 10 + 5	McSwegan G 25 + 7	McLaren A 23 + 2	Boyd K 17 + 21	McLaughlin B 17 + 3	Locke G 15 + 7	Canero P 31 + 2	Fowler J 25 + 7	Quitongo J 4 + 4	Di Giacomo P 6 + 14	Murray S 4 + 5	Innes C 19 + 1	Boutal S 3	McDonald G 10 + 2	Dillon S 13 + 1	Meldrum C 7	Canning M — + 1	Stewart1	Match No.
1	2	3	4	5	6	7	8[2]	9	10[1]	11[3]	12	13	14														1
1	2	3	4	5[1]	6	7		9	12	11[3]	10	13	14	8[2]													2
1	2	3	4	5[1]	6	7[3]		9■	13	11[2]	10■	14		8■	12												3
1	2	3	4		6	7	9[2]		10			11	5		8[1]	12	13										4
1	2	3	4■		6	7			10[2]	13	9[1]	11	5	8	12												5
1	2	3			6	7				11[3]	9[1]	10	5	8[2]	4	12	13	14									6
1	2	3			6	7[3]				11[2]		10	5	8[1]	4	12	9	14	13								7
1	2	3		14	6	7[3]	13			11[1]		10	5	8[2]	4	12	9										8
1	2			13	6	7	12	11[2]				14	5		4[1]	8	10[3]	9		3							9
1	2	3		4[1]	6	7[3]	14	12				10[2]	5	8		9		13			11						10
1	2	3[1]		5	7					10[3]		14	6	8			13		12	4	11	9[2]					11
1	2	3			7			6		14		10	5[1]	8	4	13	9[3]			12	11[2]						12
1	2	3			8	7				12		10			4		13	11[1]	9[2]	5			6				13
1	2			14	8[2]	7		13		12		10			4	6		11[1]	9[3]	5			3				14
1	2	3		14	8	7				12		10[2]		13	4	6		11[1]	9[3]				5				15
1	2	3			8	7			12	13		10		14	4	6[3]		11[2]	9[1]				5				16
1	2	3			8	7			10	11	9[2]	12			4	6[1]		13					5				17
1	2			3	8	7			10[1]	11[2]	9[3]	14		6	4	12		13					5				18
1	2				8	7			10[2]	11	9[3]	12		6[1]	4	14			13	3			5				19
1	2				8	7	9[1]	12	14	11[2]	10[3]	13			4	6				3			5				20
1	2			14	8	7	12		10[1]	11[3]	9[2]	13			4	6				3			5				21
1	2			14	8	7	12		10[2]	11[3]	9[1]	13			4	6				3			5				22
1	2				8	7	9[1]		12	11[2]	10	13			4	6				3			5				23
1	2				8	7	12		11[1]		9	10			4	6				3			5				24
	2	3		5	8	7			11[1]			10	4			6		12				9		1			25
	2	3		14	8	7					11[1]	10	5	13	4[3]	6		12				9[2]		1			26
	2■				8					13	11[1]	10[2]	5	7[3]	4	6		12		3		9		1	14		27
		3[1]			8	7				11[2]	10[3]	13	5	12	4	6		14		2		9		1			28
	2	3		8		7				11[1]	10[2]	12			4	6		13		5		9		1			29
	2	3		9	8[2]	7				11	10[1]	12		13	4	6				5				1			30
	2	3[1]		9[2]	8	7				11	10	12			4	6			13	5				1			31
	2	3			8[2]	7				11[1]	10[3]	12		13	4	6			14	5		9				1	32
1	2				8	7				11[2]	10	13	12	6	4	5				3		9[1]					33
1		3		9		7				11[3]	10[2]	12	6	8[1]	4	5		14		2			13				34
1		3		6	8	7				11[2]	10[1]	13			4	5		12		2		9					35
1	2	3			8[3]	7				11[2]	9[1]	13	6	12	4	5		10				14					36
1	2[1]	3		12	8	7				11	14	10	6		4	5[3]		13				9[2]					37
1		3		14	8[3]	7				11		10[2]	6	9[1]	4	5		13				12	2				38

LIVINGSTON

Premier League

Year Formed: 1974. *Ground:* West Lothian Courier Stadium, Alderton Road, Livingston EH54 7DN. *Telephone:* 01506 417000. *Fax:* 01506 418888. *Email:* info@livingstonfc.co.uk
Ground Capacity: 10,024 (all seated). *Size of Pitch:* 105yd × 72yd.
Chairman: Dominic Keane. *Chief Executive:* Jim Leishman. *General Manager:* David Hay. *Secretary:* J. R. S. Renton.
Head Coach: Marcio Maximo Barcellos. *Assistant Coach:* Allan Preston. *Physios:* Michael McBride, Arthur Duncan.
Managers since 1975: Jim Leishman, John Bain, Alec Ness, Willie MacFarlane, Terry Christie, Michael Lawson. *Club Nickname:* Livi Lions. *Previous Grounds:* None.
Record Attendance: 10,024 v Celtic, Premier League; 18 Aug, 2001.
Record Transfer Fee received: £1,000,000 for D. Fernandez to Celtic (June 2002).
Record Transfer Fee paid: £60,000 for Barry Wilson from Inverness CT (May 2000).
Record Victory: 7-0 v Queen of the South, Scottish Cup; 29 Jan, 2000.
Record Defeat: 0-8 v Hamilton A. Division II; 14 Dec, 1974.
Most Capped Player (under 18): I. Little.
Most League Appearances: 446: Walter Boyd, 1979-89.
Most League Goals in Season (Individual): 21: John McGachie, 1986-87. *(Team):* 69; Second Division, 1986-87.
Most Goals Overall (Individual): 64: David Roseburgh, 1986-93.

LIVINGSTON 2002–03 LEAGUE RECORD

Match No.	*Date*	*Venue*	*Opponents*	*Result*		*H/T Score*	*Lg. Pos.*	*Goalscorers*	*Attendance*
1	Aug 3	H	Motherwell	W	3-2	2-0	—	Rubio 8, Zarate 2 34, 46	5567
2	10	A	Dunfermline Ath	L	1-2	0-1	5	Xausa 89	4751
3	17	A	Partick Th	D	2-2	1-1	6	Rubio 2 31, 75	4255
4	25	H	Kilmarnock	L	0-1	0-1	7		5852
5	Sept 1	A	Celtic	L	0-2	0-2	9		55,334
6	11	A	Dundee	L	1-2	1-0	—	Nemsadze (og) 30	5391
7	14	H	Rangers	L	0-2	0-0	11		8787
8	22	H	Aberdeen	L	1-2	0-1	12	Xausa 55	5852
9	28	A	Hibernian	L	0-1	0-1	12		9451
10	Oct 6	H	Hearts	D	1-1	1-0	12	Wilson 40	6492
11	19	A	Dundee U	W	3-2	0-1	10	Bollan 67, Wilson 74, Dadi 77	5572
12	26	A	Motherwell	W	5-1	1-0	9	Makel 1, Toure-Maman 2 47, 57, Bingham 80, Xausa 90	4342
13	Nov 2	H	Dunfermline Ath	D	1-1	0-0	9	Toure-Maman 78	5578
14	9	H	Partick Th	W	3-0	0-0	9	Dadi 47, Andrews 50, Bingham 58	5426
15	16	A	Kilmarnock	L	0-2	0-0	9		5270
16	24	H	Celtic	L	0-2	0-1	9		8320
17	30	H	Dundee	D	1-1	1-0	10	Camacho 2	4151
18	Dec 4	A	Rangers	L	3-4	0-3	—	Zarate 2 50, 86, Wilson 71	45,992
19	7	A	Hearts	L	1-2	0-1	10	Zarate 62	8074
20	14	H	Hibernian	L	1-2	0-0	10	Brinquin 89	5501
21	21	A	Aberdeen	D	0-0	0-0	10		11,253
22	26	H	Dundee U	W	3-0	1-0	—	Camacho 8, Andrews 51, Bingham 86	3969
23	29	H	Motherwell	W	1-0	0-0	8	Zarate 86	5558
24	Jan 2	A	Dunfermline Ath	L	0-2	0-1	10		5218
25	28	A	Partick Th	W	3-1	1-1	—	Andrews 31, Zarate 68, McMenamin 79	3541
26	Feb 1	H	Kilmarnock	L	0-4	0-2	8		4144
27	9	A	Celtic	L	1-2	0-0	9	Zarate 51	56,982
28	Mar 2	H	Rangers	L	1-2	0-2	10	Dadi 90	8439
29	5	A	Dundee	D	0-0	0-0	—		7554
30	8	H	Hearts	D	1-1	0-1	9	Rubio 61	6448
31	15	A	Dundee U	W	1-0	0-0	8	Andrews 86	6247
32	Apr 5	H	Aberdeen	L	1-2	1-2	9	Lovell 2	4994
33	12	A	Hibernian	D	2-2	0-1	9	Wilson 87, O'Brien 89	8150
34	26	A	Aberdeen	L	0-1	0-1	9		8912
35	May 3	H	Partick Th	W	3-1	2-1	9	Xausa 25, Zarate 43, Camacho 50	4438
36	10	H	Dundee U	L	1-2	0-1	9	Bingham 77	5462
37	17	H	Hibernian	L	1-2	0-1	9	Pasquinelli 86	5243
38	24	A	Motherwell	L	2-6	1-1	9	Makel 16, McMenamin 54	4790

Final League Position: 9

Honours
League Champions: First Division: Champions: 2000-01. Second Division 1986-87, 1998-99. Third Division 1995-96; *Runners-up:* Second Division 1982-83. First Division 1987-88.
Scottish Cup: —. *League Cup:* Semi-finals 1984-85. *B&Q Cup:* Semi-finals 1992-93, 1993-94, 2001.
Bell's League Challenge Runners-up: 2000-01.

European: *UEFA Cup:* 4 matches (2002-03).

Club colours: Shirt: Gold. Shorts: Black. Stockings: Gold.

Goalscorers: *League* (48): Zarate 9, Andrews 4, Bingham 4, Rubio 4, Wilson 4, Xausa 4, Camacho 3, Dadi 3, Toure-Maman 3, McMenamin 2, Makel 2, Bollan 1, Brinquin 1, Lovell 1, O'Brien 1, Pasquinelli 1, own goal 1
Scottish Cup (1): Bollan 1
CIS Cup (1): Dadi 1

Broto J 24	Brinquin P 30	Bollan G 20 + 2	Rubio O 23 + 3	Andrews M 33	Quino F 27 + 7	Lovell S 15	Makel L 29 + 2	Dadi E 16 + 7	Camacho J 16 + 8	Zarate R 22 + 11	Bingham D 23 + 10	Toure-Maman C 12 + 11	Xausa D 13 + 17	Wilson B 17 + 8	Bahoken G 15	Dorado E 2	Hart M 10 + 1	O'Brien B 22 + 6	McNamee D 11 + 1	McMenamin C 3 + 11	McEwan D 2 + 1	Amor G 1 + 2	Main A 12	Maidana J 12	Pasquinelli F 6	Brittain R 1 + 2	McLaughlin S 1	Match No.
1	2^3	3	4	5	6	7^2	8	9	10^1	11	12	13	14															1
1	2	3	4	5	6		8^2	9^1	10	11	13	7^3	12	14														2
1	2	3	4		6	7		13	12	10^3	11^2	9	14	8^1	5													3
1	2	3	4	5	6	7	14	9^2	12	10^1	11	8^3	13															4
1	2^3	14	4	5	6	7^1	8	10		13	11	12			3	9^2												5
1			4	5	6		8^1	9^3		14	11		10		3^2	7	2	12	13									6
1		3	4	5	6	7^2		14	10^1	11	12	9■		8^3				13	2									7
1	2	3	4	5	6^3			9^1	13	10	11		12	8				7^2		14								8
1		12	4	5	6				13		11		10^3	8	3^2		7^1	9	2	14								9
1		3	4	5	6				14	10^3	11^1	13	12	8			7	9^2	2									10
1	2	3	4	5	6^2		14	12		13	11		10^1	8			7^3	9										11
1	2	3	4	5	6		7	10^3			11	12	14	8^2			13	9^1										12
1	2	3	4	5	6		7	10		12	11^2	14	13	8^1				9^3										13
1		3	4	5	6^1		7	10^2		13	11^3	8	14	12				9	2									14
1	2	3		5	6^1		7	9^2	11^3		13	8	10	12	4			14										15
1	2	3	4	5	6^1		9	12		13	11	8		10^2	7													16
1	2	3	4	5	12		7^1	9^2	10^3	13	11	8	14					6										17
1	2■	3■	4	5	14		7	9^2	10^1	13	11	8		12				6^3										18
1			4	5	6		7^2		14	10	11^3	13	12	9	3		2	8^1										19
1	2	3		5	6^1		7			10	11^2	12	13	9			4	8										20
1	2	3	14	5	6		7	9^2		10^1	11		13	8			4^3			12								21
1	2	3		5	6^3		7^2		9	10	11	14	12	8^1			4			13								22
1	2^1	3	12	5	6		7		9^2	10	11		8^3				4	13		14								23
1^6		3	4	5	6^1		7		9	10	11	13	8^2				2			12	15							24
	2		4	5	6^1		7			10	11		9^2		3			8		13	1	12						25
	2^2		4	5			7^1			10	11	12	9	13	3			8		14	1	6^3						26
	2		4	5	6	9^2		11		10^1	14			12	3			8				13	1	7^3				27
	2			5	6^1	9	7^3	12		10		14	13	11^2	3			8					1	4				28
	2			5		9	7	11^2	14	10^3		6^1	13	12	3			8					1	4				29
	2		13	5	6	9	7	11^2		10^3		8	12		3^1					14			1	4				30
	2		4	5	13	9	7		14	12			11^1		3			8^2		10^3			1	6				31
	2				12	9	7		6	13	14		11		3^1			8^2	5	10^3			1	4				32
	2^2			5	14	9	7^3	13	6				11^1	12				8	3				1	4	10			33
				3	12	9	7^2	14	5	10	13			8■				6	2^1				1	4	11^3			34
	2			5	12	9			6	10^3	14		8^1					7	3	13			1	4	11^2			35
	2					9	7^1		5	10^2	13		8^3					6	3	14			1	4	11	12		36
	2				6^2		7		5	14	11	8^1		9^3				12	3				1	4	10	13		37
	2						7		5^2		13			9				12	3	10			1	4	11	8^1	6	38

MONTROSE

Third Division

Year Formed: 1879. *Ground & Address:* Links Park, Wellington St, Montrose DD10 8QD. *Telephone:* 01674 673200.
Ground Capacity: total: 3292, seated: 1338. *Size of Pitch:* 113yd × 70yd.
Chairman: John F. Paton. *Secretary:* Malcolm J. Watters.
Manager: John Sheran.
Managers since 1975: A. Stuart, K. Cameron, R. Livingstone, S. Murray, D. D'Arcy, I. Stewart, C. McLelland, D. Rougvie, J. Leishman, J Holt, A. Dornan, D. Smith, T. Campbell, K. Drinkell.
Club Nickname(s): The Gable Endies. *Previous Grounds:* None.
Record Attendance: 8983 v Dundee, Scottish Cup 3rd rd; 17 Mar, 1973.
Record Transfer Fee received: £50,000 for Gary Murray to Hibernian (Dec 1980).
Record Transfer Fee paid: £17,500 for Jim Smith from Airdrieonians (Feb 1992).
Record Victory: 12-0 v Vale of Leithen, Scottish Cup 2nd rd; 4 Jan, 1975.
Record Defeat: 0-13 v Aberdeen; 17 Mar, 1951.
Most Capped Player: Alexander Keillor, 2 (6), Scotland.
Most League Appearances: 426: David Larter, 1987-98.
Most League Goals in Season (Individual): 28: Brian Third, Division II; 1972-73.

MONTROSE 2002–03 LEAGUE RECORD

Match No.	*Date*	*Venue*	*Opponents*	*Result*	*H/T Score*	*Lg. Pos.*	*Goalscorers*	*Attendance*
1	Aug 3	A	East Stirling	D 1-1	1-1	—	McDonald [44]	287
2	10	H	Queen's Park	W 1-0	1-0	—	Webster K [27]	402
3	17	A	Gretna	L 1-4	1-2	7	Webster C [6]	373
4	24	A	East Fife	L 0-2	0-0	7		578
5	31	H	Elgin C	W 1-0	1-0	6	Gibson [9]	417
6	Sept 14	A	Stirling A	D 1-1	0-0	7	Kerrigan [60]	439
7	21	H	Morton	L 2-5	1-2	7	Kerrigan [7], Webster C [62]	543
8	28	H	Peterhead	L 0-3	0-1	8		433
9	Oct 5	A	Albion R	D 1-1	0-0	8	Kerrigan [48]	380
10	19	A	Queen's Park	W 1-0	1-0	8	Henderson [16]	492
11	26	H	East Stirling	D 2-2	0-0	8	Kerrigan [47], Johnson [84]	346
12	Nov 2	A	Elgin C	D 0-0	0-0	8		503
13	9	H	East Fife	L 0-5	0-0	8		373
14	16	H	Stirling A	D 1-1	1-1	8	Webster K [7]	364
15	23	A	Morton	L 2-4	0-2	8	Henderson 2 [85, 88]	1748
16	30	H	Albion R	L 0-1	0-0	8		271
17	Dec 14	A	Peterhead	L 2-4	2-0	9	Gibson 2 [11, 15]	550
18	28	H	Gretna	L 0-2	0-1	9		381
19	Jan 1	A	East Fife	L 0-2	0-0	—		519
20	18	A	Stirling A	D 1-1	0-0	9	Johnson [46]	524
21	25	H	Elgin C	W 2-0	1-0	9	Henderson [44], Kerrigan [78]	211
22	Feb 8	H	Peterhead	L 1-2	0-1	9	Johnson [77]	442
23	22	H	Queen's Park	D 1-1	1-0	9	McKechnie [34]	315
24	25	H	Morton	D 0-0	0-0	—		343
25	Mar 1	A	Gretna	D 2-2	0-2	9	McKechnie [48], McCheyne [90]	227
26	4	A	Albion R	L 0-3	0-1	—		224
27	8	H	East Fife	L 0-2	0-1	9		455
28	12	A	East Stirling	W 3-0	1-0	—	Christie 2 [25, 63], Kerrigan [82]	167
29	15	A	Elgin C	W 2-0	1-0	7	Mackay (og) [34], Henderson [65]	377
30	22	A	Morton	L 0-1	0-1	7		2047
31	Apr 5	H	Stirling A	L 0-1	0-1	8		385
32	12	H	Albion R	D 1-1	1-1	8	Kerrigan [13]	282
33	19	A	Peterhead	L 0-3	0-3	8		709
34	26	H	East Stirling	W 5-4	3-2	7	McCheyne 2 [3, 43], Webster K [31], Kerrigan [77], Henderson [81]	235
35	May 3	A	Queen's Park	D 1-1	1-0	7	Johnson [4]	556
36	10	H	Gretna	L 0-1	0-1	7		376

Final League Position: 7

Honours
League Champions: Second Division 1984-85; *Runners-up:* 1990-91. Third Division, *Runners-up:* 1994-95.
Scottish Cup: Quarter-finals 1973, 1976.
League Cup: Semi-finals 1975-76.
B&Q Cup: Semi-finals 1992-93.
League Challenge Cup: Semi-finals: 1996-97.

Club colours: Shirt: Royal blue. Shorts: Royal blue. Stockings: White.

Goalscorers: *League* (35): Kerrigan 8, Henderson 6, Johnson 4, Gibson 3, McCheyne 3, Webster K 3, Christie 2, McKechnie 2, Webster C 2, McDonald 1, own goal 1
Scottish Cup (3): Gilzean 1, Johnson 1, Webster K 1
CIS Cup (2): McDonald 1, Robertson 1
Challenge Cup (1): Johnson 1

McGlynn G 28	McCheyne G 21 + 1	Robertson D 7	Gibson K 31 + 2	Conway F 15 + 4	McQuillan J 35	Webster K 25 + 7	Johnson G 29 + 1	McDonald C 12 + 6	Webster C 9 + 7	McKinnon R 11 + 2	Brand R 5 + 14	Mitchell J — + 2	Leask M — + 3	Ferguson S 29 + 1	Sharp G 4 + 7	Christie G 23	Kerrigan S 25 + 5	Henderson R 13 + 12	Camara L — + 1	Gilzean I 6 + 8	Craig D 9 + 4	Campbell J 7	Thomson G 12 + 3	Budd A 4 + 5	Hankinson M 1 + 1	Donachie B 14 + 2	McKechnie G 7	Riley P 14	Munro K — + 1	Match No.
1	2	3	4^{1}	5	6	7^{2}	8	9	10^{3}	11	12	13	14																	1
1	2	3	4	5	6	7^{3}	8	9^{2}	10^{1}	11	14	13	12																	2
1	2	3	4		6	7	8	9^{2}	10^{3}	11^{1}	12		14	5	13															3
1	2	3		6	4	7	8		10^{1}		9^{3}			11		5^{2}	12	13	14											4
1		3	4	6	2	7^{2}	8	9	14					11	13	5^{3}	12			10^{1}										5
1	7	6	4	5	2	13	8	9^{1}	11^{3}					3			12			10^{2}	14									6
1	6	3^{1}	4	5	2	12	8		11						13		9			10^{2}	7									7
	5		4^{1}		6	12	8		13	11	7			3			9			10^{2}	2	1								8
	6				2	9^{1}	8		11	4				3		5	10^{2}	13		12	7	1								9
	2		4		6	7^{3}	8	12	11					3		5	9^{2}	10^{1}		13	14	1								10
	2		4^{3}		6	7	8	12	11^{2}	13				3		5	9	10^{1}		14		1								11
	2		4	5	6	14	8	9^{2}	12	11^{3}				3			10^{1}			13	7	1								12
			4	5■	6	12	8	9^{2}		11^{1}				3		2■	10^{3}	13		14	7	1								13
1			4		6	7^{3}	8	9^{2}	13	12				3			10	14			2^{1}		5	11						14
1			4^{3}	2	6	7	8^{1}		13	10				3			9	12		14			5	11^{2}						15
1			2	4	6	7	8		13	11				3		5^{2}	9^{1}	10		12^{3}				14						16
1■			2	4	6	7^{1}	8		12	11	13			3		5	10^{3}	9^{2}							14					17
			2	4	6	13	8			11^{1}	10^{3}			3	7^{2}		9	12		14		1	5							18
1			4^{3}	6	2	7^{1}	8				13			3	12	5	10	11^{2}		9				14						19
1			4		6		8							3		5	12			9^{1}				11^{2}		2	7■	10	13	20
1			4^{1}	12	6		8	9						3		5	10	7^{2}					13			2		11		21
1	3^{1}		12		6		8	10						11^{3}		5	9^{2}	13					14			2	7	4		22
1			12	4^{1}	6	13	8				14			3		5	10^{3}				7^{2}					2	9	11		23
1			4		6	7^{2}	8				10^{1}					5					12		3	13		2	9	11		24
1	5		4^{2}		6	7^{3}	8							13			12	14			10^{1}		3			2	9	11		25
1	12		4		6	7^{2}	8^{1}				14			3		5	10^{3}	13								2	9	11		26
1	2^{3}		4		6						14			3^{2}	12	5	10	13			7		11^{1}				9■	8		27
1	2^{1}		4		6	7^{2}		13			14				11	5	10^{3}	9					3			12		8		28
1	2		4		6	7		14			12				11^{2}	5	10^{3}	9^{1}					3			13		8		29
1	2				6	7		13			10^{2}			4	11^{1}	5		9			12			14		3^{3}		8		30
1	2		10		6	7^{2}		13						3		5	9	11					12			4^{1}		8		31
1	5		4^{2}	12	6	7		9^{3}			13			3			10	14					11^{1}			2		8		32
1	5		4	13	6	7	14	10^{1}			12			3				9					11^{3}			2		8^{2}		33
	10		4^{1}	12	6	7	8							11		5	9	13					3^{3}	14	1	2^{2}				34
1			4		6	7^{1}	8				13			3	12	5	9	10^{2}					11			2				35
1			4	6		7	8				12			3	13	5	10	9^{1}						11^{2}		2				36

MORTON

Second Division

Year Formed: 1874. *Ground & Address:* Cappielow Park, Sinclair St, Greenock. *Telephone:* 01475 723571. *Fax:* 01475 781084
Ground Capacity: total: 11,612, seated: 6062. *Size of Pitch:* 110yd × 71yd.
Commercial Manager: Chris Norris.
Manager: John McCormack. *Managers since 1975:* Joe Gilroy, Benny Rooney, Alex Miller, Tommy McLean, Willie McLean, Allan McGraw, Billy Stark, Ian McCall, Allan Evans, Peter Cormack, Dave McPherson.
Club Nickname(s): The Ton. *Previous Grounds:* Grant Street 1874, Garvel Park 1875, Cappielow Park 1879, Ladyburn Park 1882, (Cappielow Park 1883).
Record Attendance: 23,500 v Celtic; 29 April, 1922.
Record Transfer Fee received: £350,000 for Neil Orr to West Ham U.
Record Transfer Fee paid: £150,000 for Allan Mahood from Nottingham Forest.
Record Victory: 11-0 v Carfin Shamrock, Scottish Cup 1st rd; 13 Nov, 1886.
Record Defeat: 1-10 v Port Glasgow Ath, Division II; 5 May, 1894 and v St Bernards, Division II; 14 Oct, 1933.
Most Capped Player: Jimmy Cowan, 25, Scotland.
Most League Appearances: 358: David Hayes, 1969-84.
Most League Goals in Season (Individual): 58: Allan McGraw, Division II; 1963-64.

MORTON 2002–03 LEAGUE RECORD

Match No.	Date	Venue	Opponents	Result		H/T Score	Lg. Pos.	Goalscorers	Attendance
1	Aug 3	A	Gretna	D	1-1	1-1	—	Hawke [6]	1566
2	10	H	Stirling A	W	5-1	3-1	—	Williams 2 [6, 40], Uotinen [33], Hawke [56], Gaughan [83]	1757
3	17	A	Peterhead	L	2-4	0-4	4	Uotinen [84], Maisano J (pen) [86]	729
4	24	H	Queen's Park	W	3-0	3-0	4	Duncan [11], Williams 2 [24, 35]	2001
5	31	A	East Stirling	D	1-1	1-0	4	Williams (pen) [9]	748
6	Sept 14	H	Albion R	L	0-1	0-1	5		1739
7	21	A	Montrose	W	5-2	2-1	5	MacDonald [11], Hawke [24], Uotinen 2 [46, 75], Maisano M [47]	543
8	28	H	East Fife	W	2-1	2-0	4	Williams [9], Uotinen [45]	1821
9	Oct 5	A	Elgin C	W	1-0	0-0	3	Williams [79]	895
10	19	A	Stirling A	L	0-2	0-0	3		1089
11	26	H	Gretna	D	2-2	1-0	3	Williams [17], Hopkin [47]	1705
12	Nov 2	H	East Stirling	W	4-1	2-0	3	Williams 3 [7, 71, 78], Cannie [14]	1640
13	9	A	Queen's Park	D	1-1	0-0	4	McGregor [70]	1775
14	16	A	Albion R	L	1-2	1-0	5	Cannie [37]	843
15	23	H	Montrose	W	4-2	2-0	3	Williams 2 [8, 90], Conway (og) [10], Hawke [77]	1748
16	30	H	Elgin C	W	4-0	3-0	3	Williams (pen) [18], Uotinen [42], Maisano J 2 [44, 54]	1658
17	Dec 7	H	Queen's Park	D	1-1	0-0	4	Williams [58]	1669
18	14	A	East Fife	W	4-1	2-0	3	Maisano J [28], Williams 2 [36, 53], Uotinen [47]	1005
19	28	H	Peterhead	W	1-0	1-0	2	Williams [6]	2640
20	Jan 18	H	Albion R	W	2-1	1-1	2	Williams [10], McGregor [86]	2405
21	Feb 8	H	East Fife	D	1-1	1-1	2	MacDonald [19]	2953
22	12	A	East Stirling	W	1-0	1-0	—	Maisano J [22]	627
23	15	A	Elgin C	D	0-0	0-0	2		701
24	25	A	Montrose	D	0-0	0-0	—		343
25	Mar 1	A	Peterhead	L	1-3	0-2	3	Hawke [53]	1086
26	8	A	Queen's Park	W	1-0	0-0	4	Adam [55]	1361
27	11	H	Stirling A	D	2-2	1-0	—	Annand 2 [34, 84]	1617
28	15	H	East Stirling	W	2-1	1-0	3	Annand [5], Bannerman [78]	2039
29	22	H	Montrose	W	1-0	1-0	3	Gaughan [16]	2047
30	29	A	Gretna	W	1-0	0-0	3	Annand [56]	601
31	Apr 5	A	Albion R	L	1-2	0-1	4	McGregor [47]	1381
32	12	H	Elgin C	W	2-0	0-0	3	Hawke [80], Bannerman (pen) [87]	1662
33	19	A	East Fife	W	1-0	0-0	3	Hawke [71]	1991
34	26	H	Gretna	W	5-0	1-0	2	Williams 2 [37, 78], Bottiglieri [65], Annand [67], Hawke [75]	2422
35	May 3	A	Stirling A	W	3-0	2-0	1	Williams 2 [12, 37], Uotinen [90]	2039
36	10	H	Peterhead	W	1-0	0-0	1	Bannerman [54]	8497

Final League Position: 1

Honours
League Champions: First Division 1977-78, 1983-84, 1986-87. Division II 1949-50, 1963-64, 1966-67. Second Division 1994-95. Third Division 2002-03. *Runners-up:* Division 1 1916-17, Division II 1899-1900, 1928-29, 1936-37.
Scottish Cup Winners: 1922; *Runners-up:* 1948. *League Cup Runners-up:* 1963-64.
B&Q Cup Runners-up: 1992-93.

European: *UEFA Cup:* 2 matches (*Fairs Cup:* 1968-69).

Club colours: Shirt: Royal blue with 3½ inch white hoops. Shorts: White with royal blue panel down side. Stockings: Royal blue with white tops.

Goalscorers: *League* (67): Williams 23 (2 pens), Hawke 8, Uotinen 8, Annand 5, Maisano J 5 (1 pen), Bannerman 3 (1 pen), MacGregor 3, Cannie 2, Gaughan 2, MacDonald 2, Adam 1, Bottiglieri 1, Duncan 1, Hopkin 1, Maisano M 1, own goal 1
Scottish Cup (6): Williams 3, MacGregor 1, Uotinen 1, own goal 1
CIS Cup (2): Bannerman 1, Hopkin 1
Challenge Cup (3): Williams 2, Hawke 1

Coyle C 36	Collins D 36	Bottiglieri E 31	McGregor D 30	Gaughan P 27 + 2	Maisano M 32	Uotinen J 23 + 10	Hawke W 14 + 13	Williams A 31	Maisano J 31 + 3	Riley C 2 + 4	Cannie P 12 + 16	MacDonald S 12 + 12	Bannerman S 17 + 10	Smith A 7 + 1	Curran S — + 2	Duncan L 1	Hopkin D 6	Struthers K — + 1	McAlister J 2 + 5	Henderson R 11	Robertson L 1 + 1	Miller C 13	Annand E 11	Adam J 4 + 1	Dale G 6	*Match No.*
1	2	3	4	5	6	7	8[1]	9	10	11[2]	12	13														1
1	2	3	4	5	6	7[1]	8[2]	9	10[3]		13	14	11■	12												2
1	2	3	4		6[1]	7	8	9	10		12		11[2]	5	13											3
1	2	3	4		5	7[3]		9	10[1]	12	13	14	8	6		11[2]										4
1	2	3	4		6[1]	7		9	10[2]		13	12	11	5			8									5
1	2	3	4	14		7	8	9	10[2]		13	12	11	5[3]			6[1]									6
1	2	3	4	5	6	7	11[1]		10		9	8	12													7
1	2	3	4	5	6	7	11	9	10[1]			8	12													8
1	2	3	4	6		7	13	9	10[3]	14	11[2]	5[1]	12	8												9
1	2	3	4	6	11		13	9	10[3]	7[1]	14		12	5			8[2]									10
1	2	3	4	6		7	11	9			12		10	5			8[1]									11
1	2[1]	3	4	5	6	11		9	10		7[2]	13	12				8									12
1	2	3	4	5	6[2]	11	13	9	10[1]		7[3]	14	12				8									13
1	2	3	4	5	6	8	10	9	7[1]		11■	12														14
1	2	3	4	5	6	11[2]	10	9	8	13		7[1]			12											15
1	2	3	4	5	6[2]	11		9	8		10[1]	7	12					13								16
1	2	3	4	5	6	11	10	9	8			7[1]	12													17
1	2	3	4	5	6	11	10[2]	9	8	13		12	7[1]													18
1	2	3	4	5	6[1]	11	10	9	8			7							12							19
1	2	3	4		6	11	10[1]	9[2]	8		12								13	5	7					20
1	2	3	4		6	11[1]	12	9	8		10[2]	7							13	5						21
1	2	3	4		6	11	12	9	8		10[1]	7								5						22
1	2	3	4		6	12	10[2]		8		9[1]	7	13						11	5						23
1	2	3	4[2]	13	6		12	9	14			7	8						10[1]	5		11[3]				24
1	2	3		4	6	13	12				9[2]	7	8[3]							5	14	11	10[1]			25
1	2	3	4	5	6	13			8[1]		9								12			7		10[2]	11	26
1	2		4	5	6	12		9	8[1]		13											7	11	10	3[2]	27
1	2		4	5[2]	6	9			8		12		13						14			7	11[3]	10[1]	3	28
1	2		4	5	6	12		9	14		10[1]	13	8[2]									7[3]	11		3	29
1	2		4	5	6[3]	10[2]	12	9[1]	13				8									7	11	14	3	30
1	2		4	5		13		9[2]	6[1]		12		8									7	11	10	3	31
1	2	3		5	6	14	13	9[1]	10[3]		12		8							4		7	11[2]			32
1	2	3		5	6		13	9[1]	10		12	14	8							4		7[3]	11[2]			33
1	2	3		5	6[3]	14	12	9	10[2]		13		8							4		7	11[1]			34
1	2	3		5	6	12	14	9[2]	10[1]		13		8							4		7	11[3]			35
1	2	3		5[1]	6[2]	14	13	9	10[3]			12	8							4		7	11			36

MOTHERWELL

Premier League

Year Formed: 1886. *Ground & Address:* Fir Park Stadium, Motherwell ML1 2QN. *Telephone:* 01698 333333. *Fax:* 01698 338001.
Ground Capacity: all seated: 13,742. *Size of Pitch:* 110yd × 75yd.
Chairman: John Boyle. *Secretary:* Stewart Robertson.
Manager: Terry Butcher. *Coach:* Maurice Malpas. *Physio:* John Porteous.
Managers since 1975: Ian St. John, Willie McLean, Rodger Hynd, Ally MacLeod, David Hay, Jock Wallace, Bobby Watson, Tommy McLean, Alex McLeish, Harri Kampman, Billy Davies, Eric Black.
Club Nickname(s): The Well. *Previous Grounds:* Roman Road, Dalziel Park.
Record Attendance: 35,632 v Rangers, Scottish Cup 4th rd replay; 12 Mar, 1952.
Record Transfer Fee received: £1,750,000 for Phil O'Donnell to Celtic (September 1994).
Record Transfer Fee paid: £500,000 for John Spencer from Everton (Jan 1999).
Record Victory: 12-1 v Dundee U, Division II; 23 Jan, 1954.
Record Defeat: 0-8 v Aberdeen, Premier Division; 26 Mar, 1979.
Most Capped Player: Tommy Coyne, 13, Republic of Ireland.
Most League Appearances: 626: Bobby Ferrier, 1918-37.
Most League Goals in Season (Individual): 52: Willie McFadyen, Division I; 1931-32.
Most Goals Overall (Individual): 283: Hugh Ferguson, 1916-25.

MOTHERWELL 2002–03 LEAGUE RECORD

Match No.	Date	Venue	Opponents	Result		H/T Score	Lg. Pos.	Goalscorers	Attendance
1	Aug 3	A	Livingston	L	2-3	0-2	—	Leitch 49, Lehmann 63	5567
2	10	H	Partick Th	D	1-1	0-0	9	Pearson 83	5788
3	17	A	Kilmarnock	W	3-0	0-0	5	Ramsay 66, Pearson 83, McFadden 85	6164
4	25	A	Dundee U	D	1-1	1-0	6	Pearson 3	5795
5	31	H	Hibernian	L	0-2	0-1	7		5888
6	Sept 10	H	Celtic	W	2-1	0-0	—	Fagan 76, McFadden (pen) 80	8448
7	15	A	Hearts	L	2-4	2-1	7	Lehmann 12, McFadden 27	8759
8	21	A	Dunfermline Ath	L	0-1	0-0	7		4987
9	28	H	Dundee	D	1-1	0-1	8	McFadden 55	4025
10	Oct 5	H	Aberdeen	L	1-2	1-0	9	McFadden 41	6014
11	19	A	Rangers	L	0-3	0-1	9		49,376
12	26	H	Livingston	L	1-5	0-1	10	Kemas 79	4342
13	Nov 2	A	Partick Th	L	0-2	0-1	12		5405
14	9	H	Kilmarnock	L	0-1	0-0	12		4439
15	16	H	Dundee U	L	1-2	0-2	12	Lehmann 81	5381
16	23	A	Hibernian	L	1-3	0-0	12	Ferguson 47	8859
17	Dec 1	A	Celtic	L	1-3	0-0	12	Lehmann 75	56,610
18	4	H	Hearts	W	6-1	4-0	—	Pearson 15, McFadden 2 18, 25, Adams 35, Corrigan 68, Ferguson 90	4114
19	7	A	Aberdeen	D	1-1	0-1	12	Kinniburgh 58	9569
20	14	A	Dundee	D	1-1	1-1	12	Lehmann 25	5527
21	26	H	Rangers	W	1-0	0-0	—	McFadden 64	11,234
22	29	A	Livingston	L	0-1	0-0	11		5558
23	Jan 2	H	Partick Th	D	2-2	1-1	11	Clarkson 8, Partridge 76	6262
24	29	A	Kilmarnock	L	0-1	0-0	—		4457
25	Feb 1	A	Dundee U	L	1-2	1-1	12	Adams (pen) 19	6672
26	8	H	Hibernian	W	2-1	2-0	11	Clarkson 30, Fagan 40	4999
27	19	H	Dunfermline Ath	W	2-1	1-0	—	Pearson 18, Craig 49	3741
28	Mar 1	A	Hearts	L	1-2	0-1	11	Lasley 53	11,704
29	8	H	Aberdeen	L	0-1	0-1	12		5636
30	19	A	Rangers	L	0-2	0-1	—		49,420
31	Apr 5	A	Dunfermline Ath	L	0-3	0-1	12		4086
32	12	H	Dundee	L	1-2	0-2	12	McFadden 77	4693
33	26	A	Partick Th	L	0-3	0-1	12		4870
34	May 3	H	Dundee U	D	2-2	1-0	12	Pearson 10, Vaughan 84	9056
35	7	H	Celtic	L	0-4	0-1	—		12,037
36	10	A	Hibernian	L	0-1	0-0	12		7809
37	17	H	Aberdeen	L	2-3	1-3	12	Clarkson 16, McFadden (pen) 82	4731
38	24	H	Livingston	W	6-2	1-1	12	Lasley 2 30, 89, Craig 57, McFadden 3 (1 pen) 63, 73 (p), 74	4790

Final League Position: 12

Honours
League Champions: Division I 1931-32. First Division 1981-82, 1984-85. Division II 1953-54, 1968-69; *Runners-up:* Premier Division 1994-95. Division I 1926-27, 1929-30, 1932-33, 1933-34. Division II 1894-95, 1902-03. *Scottish Cup:* 1952, 1991; *Runners-up:* 1931, 1933, 1939, 1951.
League Cup: 1950-51. *Runners-up:* 1954-55. *Scottish Summer Cup:* 1944, 1965.

Club colours: Shirt: Amber with claret hoop and trimmings. Shorts: Amber. Stockings: Amber with claret trim.

European: *Cup Winners' Cup:* 2 matches (1991-92). *UEFA Cup:* 6 matches (1994-95, 1995-96).

Goalscorers: *League* (45): McFadden 13 (3 pens), Pearson 6, Lehmann 5, Clarkson 3, Lasley 3, Adams 2 (1 pen), Craig 2, Fagan 2, Ferguson 2, Corrigan 1, Kemas 1, Kinniburgh 1, Leitch 1, Partridge 1, Ramsay 1, Vaughan 1
Scottish Cup (10): McFadden 5, Adams 2, Craig 1, Lehmann 1, own goal 1
CIS Cup (3): Adams 1, Lehmann 1, McFadden 1

Woods S 16 + 1	Corrigan M 38	Partridge D 32	Hammell S 37	Ramsay D 16 + 4	Lasley K 21 + 3	Pearson S 29	Leitch S 26	MacDonald K 4 + 4	McFadden J 29 + 1	Lehmann D 27 + 5	Clarke D — + 1	Kinniburgh W 11 + 4	Adams D 31	Fagan S 9 + 10	Ferguson S 8 + 11	Sengewald D 6 + 1	Russell I — + 5	Cowan D 15 + 1	Jack D — + 2	Kemas K 4 + 2	Dubourdeau F 22	Dempsie B 1	Quinn P 3 + 1	Clarkson C 13 + 6	Craig S 8 + 5	Vaughan A 12	Offiong R — + 9	Ballantyne R — + 1	Wright K — + 1	Scott A — + 1	*Match No.*
1	2	3	4	5	6	7	8	9^1	10	11	12																				1
1	2	3	4	5	6	7	8	9^1	10	11		12																			2
1	2	3	4^1	5	6	7	8^2		10	11		12	9	13																	3
1	2	3	4	5	6^1	7	8^3	14	10^2	11		13	9		12																4
1	2	3	4	5	6	7	8		10^2	11			9^1	13	12																5
1	2	3	4	12	6	7^1	8^2		10^3	11			9	13	14	5															6
1	2	3	4^3	5	6			12	10	11			9^2	8^1	13	7	14														7
1	2	3	4	12	6^3	7^2	8		10	11			9	13	14	5^1															8
1	2	3	4	5	6	7			10	11			9		8																9
1	2	3	4	5	6		8^1		10	11			9		7^2	12	13														10
1	2	3■	4	5	6	7^2				11^1			10		9		12	8	13												11
1	2		4	3	6^1	7^2	8			11			10		12			5	13	9											12
1	2		4		13	7	8■		10	12		3^3	11		14	5^1		6		9^2											13
	2	3	4	5		7		8		11			10		12		13	6^2		9^1	1										14
	2	3	4	5^2		7				11			10	12	8		13	6		9^1	1										15
	2	3■	4			7■			12	11			10	8^1	9	5■		6			1										16
	2		4				8^3	14	10	11		3	9	6■	7^1					12	1	5^2	13								17
	2	3	4			7	8		10	11		5	9		12	6^1					1										18
	2		4				8	12	10	11		3	9	6^1	7^2						1		5	13							19
	2		4				8		10	11		3	9	6	7^1						1		5	12							20
	2	3	4			7	8		10	11		5	9					6			1										21
	2	3	4			7	8		10	11		5^2	9		12			6^1			1			13							22
	2	3	4	14		7	8^1		10■	11^3		5	9	12	13						1			6^2							23
13	2	3			6	7	8					5	9^1	12				4			1			10	11^2						24
1	2	3	4		14	7	8^3					6	9^2	13										10	11^1	5	12				25
	2	3	4			7	8^1						9	12				6		13	1			10	11^2	5					26
	2	3	4	12	13	7							9	8				6^1			1			10^2	11	5					27
	2	3	4	6	9	7			10	13				8^2							1			11^1		5	12				28
	2	3	4	6^3	8^1	7■			10	12				9							1			11^2	14	5	13				29
	2	3	4	6^1	7				10	9^3				8				12			1			11^2	14	5	13				30
	2	3	4		6^2		8^3		10^1	11			9	14				7			1			12	13	5■					31
	2	3	4		6^1		7		10	11^2			9					5			1			12	8		13				32
	2	3	4						10	11			9					6			1			7	8^1	5	12				33
1	2	3	4			7	8		10	13			9											11^2	6^1	5	12				34
1	2	3	4			7	8		10^2	14		12	9■					6^1						11^3		5	13				35
	2	3	4	6	7^1	9	8		10	11											1			12	13	5^2					36
	2	3	4		6	7	8		10				9^2								1			11	12	5^1	13				37
	2^1		4		6	7		9	10			3									1		5	11^3	8^2			12	13	14	38

PARTICK THISTLE

Premier League

Year Formed: 1876. *Ground & Address:* Firhill Stadium, 80 Firhill Rd, Glasgow G20 7AL. *Telephone:* 0141 579 1971. *Fax:* 0141 945 1525
Ground Capacity: total: 13,141, seated: 10,921. *Size of Pitch:* 110yd × 75yd.
Chairman: Thomas Hughes. *Chief Executive Secretary:* Alan C. Dick. *Commercial Manager:* Amanda Barrie.
Manager: Gerry Collins. *Assistant Manager:* Bobby McCulley. *Physio:* George Hannah.
Managers since 1975: R. Auld, P. Cormack, B. Rooney, R. Auld, D. Johnstone, W. Lamont, S. Clark, J. Lambie, M. MacLeod, J. McVeigh, T. Bryce, J. Lambie. *Club Nickname(s):* The Jags. *Previous Grounds:* Jordanvale Park; Muirpark; Inchview; Meadowside Park.
Record Attendance: 49,838 v Rangers, Division I; 18 Feb, 1922. *Ground Record:* 54,728, Scotland v Ireland, 25 Feb 1928.
Record Transfer Fee received: £200,000 for Mo Johnston to Watford.
Record Transfer Fee paid: £85,000 for Andy Murdoch from Celtic (Feb 1991).
Record Victory: 16-0 v Royal Albert, Scottish Cup 1st rd; 17 Jan, 1931.
Record Defeat: 0-10 v Queen's Park, Scottish Cup; 3 Dec, 1881.
Most Capped Player: Alan Rough, 51 (53), Scotland.
Most League Appearances: 410: Alan Rough, 1969-82.
Most League Goals in Season (Individual): 41: Alex Hair, Division I; 1926-27.

PARTICK THISTLE 2002–03 LEAGUE RECORD

Match No.	Date	Venue	Opponents	Result		H/T Score	Lg. Pos.	Goalscorers	Attendance
1	Aug 3	H	Dundee U	D	0-0	0-0	—		6375
2	10	A	Motherwell	D	1-1	0-0	8	Burns 81	5788
3	17	H	Livingston	D	2-2	1-1	9	Mitchell 2 (1 pen) 34, 63 (p)	4255
4	24	H	Celtic	L	0-1	0-0	10		8053
5	Sept 1	A	Aberdeen	W	1-0	1-0	6	Lilley 30	12,591
6	11	A	Kilmarnock	L	0-1	0-1	—		6848
7	14	H	Dundee	D	1-1	1-0	8	Mitchell 40	4552
8	21	A	Rangers	L	0-3	0-2	9		48,696
9	28	H	Hearts	D	2-2	1-1	10	Archibald 2 27, 78	6111
10	Oct 5	A	Dunfermline Ath	L	1-4	0-1	10	Mitchell (pen) 60	5522
11	19	H	Hibernian	L	0-3	0-1	11		5946
12	26	A	Dundee U	D	1-1	0-1	11	Waddell 85	6349
13	Nov 2	H	Motherwell	W	2-0	1-0	10	Hardie 29, Burns 51	5405
14	9	A	Livingston	L	0-3	0-0	10		5426
15	17	A	Celtic	L	0-4	0-2	11		57,231
16	23	H	Aberdeen	W	2-1	1-0	10	Lilley 31, Hardie 79	6182
17	30	H	Kilmarnock	W	3-0	0-0	8	Burns 3 54, 77, 86	5055
18	Dec 4	A	Dundee	L	1-4	0-1	—	Britton 69	5363
19	7	H	Dunfermline Ath	W	4-0	2-0	8	Britton 4, Burns 2 44, 51, McLean 69	4110
20	14	A	Hearts	L	0-1	0-0	8		9734
21	22	H	Rangers	L	1-2	1-0	8	Burns 7	8022
22	26	A	Hibernian	D	1-1	0-0	—	Burns 77	10,317
23	29	H	Dundee U	D	0-0	0-0	9		5109
24	Jan 2	A	Motherwell	D	2-2	1-1	8	Burns 2 18, 48	6262
25	28	H	Livingston	L	1-3	1-1	—	Burns 39	3541
26	Feb 2	H	Celtic	L	0-2	0-2	9		7119
27	8	A	Aberdeen	W	1-0	1-0	8	Burns 12	11,332
28	23	A	Kilmarnock	L	0-1	0-1	8		8651
29	Mar 1	H	Dundee	L	1-3	1-2	8	Buchan 31	4599
30	9	A	Dunfermline Ath	D	0-0	0-0	10		4746
31	15	H	Hibernian	L	0-1	0-1	10		4551
32	Apr 5	A	Rangers	L	0-2	0-0	10		49,472
33	12	H	Hearts	D	1-1	0-0	10	Mitchell 72	5288
34	26	H	Motherwell	W	3-0	1-0	10	Burns 29, Britton 2 67, 89	4870
35	May 3	A	Livingston	L	1-3	1-2	10	Hardie 45	4438
36	10	A	Aberdeen	L	1-2	1-0	10	Burns (pen) 16	9960
37	17	H	Dundee U	L	0-1	0-0	10		6357
38	24	A	Hibernian	W	3-2	1-2	10	Britton 28, Rowson 52, Burns 85	8986

Final League Position: 10

Honours
League Champions: First Division 1975-76, 2001-02. Division II 1896-97, 1899-1900, 1970-71; Second Division 2000-01;
Runners-up: First Division 1991-92. Division II 1901-02.
Scottish Cup Winners: 1921; *Runners-up:* 1930; *Semi-finals:* 2002.
League Cup Winners: 1971-72; *Runners-up:* 1953-54, 1956-57, 1958-59.

European: *Fairs Cup:* 4 matches (1963-64). *UEFA Cup:* 2 matches (1972-73). *Intertoto Cup:* 4 matches 1995-96.

Club colours: Shirt: Red and yellow stripes. Shorts: Red. Stockings: Red with yellow hoops.

Goalscorers: *League* (37): Burns 16 (1 pen), Britton 5, Mitchell 5 (2 pens), Hardie 3, Archibald 2, Lilley 2, Buchan 1, McLean 1, Rowson 1, Waddell 1
Scottish Cup (0)
CIS Cup (5): Hardie 3, Buchan 1, Burns 1

Budinauckas K 3	Paterson S 32	Archibald A 36	Craigan S 36	Whyte D 22 + 3	McKinstry J 3 + 3	Mitchell J 27 + 4	Buchan J 23 + 5	Hardie M 35 + 2	McLean S 6 + 6	Burns A 38	Walker P 1 + 12	Lennon D 2 + 9	Britton G 28 + 5	Gibson A 1 + 11	Arthur K 35	Lilley D 34	Waddell R 5 + 11	Milne K 8 + 4	Charnley J — + 2	Morris I — + 1	Chiarini D 12	McGowne K 7	Rowson D 13	Ross I 6	Fleming D 4 + 4	Elliot B 1 + 2	Rushford G — + 1	Shields M — + 1	Match No.
1	2	3	4	5	6	7²	8	9	10¹	11	12	13																	1
1	2	3	4	5	6	7²	8	9	10¹	11			12	13															2
	2	3	4	5		7	8	9¹		11	13	12	10²	14	1	6³													3
	2	3	4	5		7³	8	9		11	12	13		10¹	1	6²	14												4
	2	3	4	5		7¹	8	9²		11		13	14	12³	1	6	10												5
	2	3	4	5			8	9	12	11			10¹		1	6	7²	13											6
	2	3	4	5		7²	8¹	9		11	13	12			1	6	10³		14										7
	2	3	4	5		7	8	9³		11		12²	13		1	6	10¹	14											8
	2	3	4	5		7	8	9	10¹	11			12		1	6													9
	2	3	4	5		7²	8³	10		11	9¹		12		1	6¹	13			14									10
	2	3	4	5	6²	7	8	9	10¹	11	12				1		13												11
	2	3	4	5		7¹	8³	9		11	12²		10	13	1		14				6								12
	2	3	4	5			13	8³	9¹	11			10²	14	1	6	12				7								13
	2¹		4	3	14		8	9		11			10²	13	1	6	12	5³			7								14
	2²	3	4	5	13	7³		9		11	12		10¹	14	1	6					8								15
	2	3	4	5		12	13	8²	9¹	11			10		1	6					7								16
	2	3	4	5		7		9		11	12		10¹		1	6					8								17
	2	3	4	5¹		7²	12	9³	13	11			10	14	1	6					8								18
	2	3	4			7		9	12	11¹			10²		1	6	13	8			5								19
	2	3	4			7		9		11			10		1	6		8			5								20
	2	3	4			7²		9	12	11		13	10		1	6		8¹			5								21
	2	3	4			7		9	12	11		13	10¹		1	6		8²			5								22
	2¹	3	4			7	8	9		11		12	10		1	6					5								23
	2	3	4		14	7¹	8³	9		11	12	5	10²		1	6	13												24
	2	3	4					9	13	11			10²		1	6	12					5	7	8¹					25
	2¹	3	4				13	9³		11	12		10	14	1	6		8²				5	7						26
	2	3	4¹			13	8	9		11			10²		1	6						5	7		12				27
	2	3	4			12	8²	9		11					1	6						5	7		13	10¹			28
	2	3				6	8	9		11	12		10		1	4						5	7¹						29
	2	3	4				8	9		11²			10¹	13	1	6							7		5	12			30
	2	3	4				8¹	9		11			10		1	6							7		5	12			31
	2¹	3	4	12		9	8			11	14		10³		1	6	13						7		5²				32
		3	4	2		9	8	12		11			10¹		1	6							7	5					33
		3	4	2		8	12	9		11¹			10		1	6		14					7²	5³			13		34
		3	4	2		8		9		11²			10	13	1	6		12					7	5¹					35
		3	4	2		9	8	12		11			10¹		1	6	14						7²	5³	13				36
1		3	4	14		12		9		11		7²	10			6³		8				2			5¹			13	37
				13		8		9³		11			10		1	6	3¹	5	14			2	7	4	12²				38

PETERHEAD

Third Division

Year Formed: 1891. *Ground and Address:* Balmoor Stadium, Lord Catto Park, Peterhead AB42 1EU.
Telephone: 01779 478256. *Fax:* 01779 490682. *Ground Capacity:* 3250, seated 1000.
Chairman: Roger Taylor. *General Manager:* Dave Watson. *Secretary:* George Moore.
Manager: Ian Wilson. *Assistant Manager:* Alan Lyons. *Physio:* Jennifer Johnson.
Managers since 1975: C. Grant, D. Darcy, I. Taylor, J. Harper, D. Smith, J. Hamilton, G. Adams, J. Guyan, I. Wilson, D. Watson, R. Brown, D. Watson, I. Wilson. *Club Nickname(s):* Blue Toon. *Previous Ground:* Recreation Park.
Record Attendance: 6310 friendly v Celtic, 1948.
Record Victory: 17-0 v Fort William, 1998-99 (in Highland League).
Record Defeat: 0-13 v Aberdeen, Scottish Cup 1923-24.
Most League Appearances: 97, Martin Johnston, 2000-03.
Most League Goals in Season (Individual): 21, Iain Stewart, 2002-03.
Most Goals Overall (Individual): 51, Iain Stewart, 2000-03.

PETERHEAD 2002–03 LEAGUE RECORD

Match No.	Date	Venue	Opponents	Result	H/T Score	Lg. Pos.	Goalscorers	Attendance
1	Aug 3	H	East Fife	L 0-2	0-1	—		510
2	10	A	Albion R	L 0-3	0-1	—		440
3	17	H	Morton	W 4-2	4-0	7	Roddie [8], Stewart 2 [22, 43], Johnston [41]	729
4	24	A	Elgin C	L 0-3	0-1	8		697
5	31	H	Stirling A	W 1-0	0-0	7	Stewart [54]	500
6	Sept 14	A	Gretna	W 4-1	1-0	4	Tindal [4], Roddie 2 [54, 79], Camara [84]	357
7	21	H	Queen's Park	W 3-0	1-0	4	Stewart 3 [3, 80, 83]	597
8	28	A	Montrose	W 3-0	1-0	3	Roddie [12], Bain (pen) [65], Camara [80]	433
9	Oct 5	H	East Stirling	W 5-0	1-0	2	Roddie [36], Johnston 3 [48, 50, 70], Kidd [82]	558
10	19	H	Albion R	W 2-0	0-0	2	Roddie [75], Tindal [80]	543
11	26	A	East Fife	D 3-3	0-1	2	Stewart 2 [60, 80], Tindal [70]	847
12	Nov 2	A	Stirling A	L 0-1	0-1	2		686
13	9	H	Elgin C	D 2-2	1-2	2	Stewart [7], Johnston [59]	728
14	16	H	Gretna	D 1-1	1-1	3	Johnston [3]	496
15	23	A	Queen's Park	L 0-2	0-1	4		495
16	30	A	East Stirling	W 4-1	2-1	4	Johnston 4 [6, 44, 52, 88]	207
17	Dec 7	A	Elgin C	W 4-0	2-0	3	Stewart 2 [1, 80], Johnston [8], Roddie [58]	457
18	14	H	Montrose	W 4-2	0-2	1	Roddie [48], Johnston 2 (1 pen) [80 (p), 88], Stewart [82]	550
19	21	H	East Fife	D 2-2	2-0	1	Johnston 2 [38, 40]	717
20	28	A	Morton	L 0-1	0-1	4		2640
21	Jan 18	A	Gretna	D 1-1	0-1	4	Robertson [82]	360
22	Feb 8	A	Montrose	W 2-1	1-0	3	Cameron [28], Bone (pen) [71]	442
23	15	H	East Stirling	W 6-0	2-0	3	Bone 2 [8, 16], Stewart 3 [47, 72, 85], Macdonald [49]	584
24	Mar 1	H	Morton	W 3-1	2-0	2	Stewart 3 [32, 44, 82]	1086
25	4	H	Stirling A	W 6-0	3-0	—	Roddie [16], Macdonald [35], Robertson [44], Tindal [52], Bone [70], McLean [79]	613
26	8	H	Elgin C	W 3-2	1-1	2	Bone 2 (1 pen) [39, 69 (p)], McLean [79]	854
27	11	A	Albion R	D 0-0	0-0	—		389
28	15	A	Stirling A	L 1-2	1-2	2	McLean [3]	564
29	22	A	Queen's Park	W 2-1	2-0	2	Roddie 2 [25, 35]	575
30	29	H	Queen's Park	W 3-1	2-0	2	Stewart [24], Mackay [39], Johnston [50]	589
31	Apr 5	H	Gretna	W 1-0	0-0	2	Stewart [55]	598
32	12	A	East Stirling	D 1-1	0-0	2	Raeside [89]	218
33	19	H	Montrose	W 3-0	3-0	2	Stewart [5], Macdonald [43], Bone [44]	709
34	26	A	East Fife	W 2-0	0-0	1	Bone 2 [60, 86]	1071
35	May 3	H	Albion R	D 0-0	0-0	2		1693
36	10	A	Morton	L 0-1	0-0	4		8497

Final League Position: 4

Honours
Scottish Cup: Quarter Finals 2001.
Highland League Champions: winners 5 times.
Scottish Qualifying Cup (North): winners 6 times.
North of Scotland Cup: winners 5 times.
Aberdeenshire Cup: winners: 20 times.

Club colours: Shirt: Royal blue with white; Shorts: Royal blue; Stockings: Royal blue tops with white hoops.

Goalscorers: *League* (76): Stewart 21, Johnston 16 (1 pen), Roddie 11, Bone 9 (2 pens), Tindal 4, MacDonald 3, McLean 3, Camara 2, Robertson 2, Bain 1 (pen), Cameron 1, Kidd 1, Mackay 1, Raeside 1
Scottish Cup (1): Cooper 1 (pen)
CIS Cup (0)
Challenge Cup (0)

Mathers P 36	McSkimming S 31 + 1	Burns G 12 + 4	Bain K 28	Simpson M 24 + 1	Tindal K 36	Cooper C 4 + 10	Stewart I 30 + 1	Mackay S 17 + 5	Johnston M 26 + 1	Livingstone R 2 + 1	Robertson K 2 + 11	Kidd A — + 4	Bissett K — + 4	Raeside R 32	Roddie A 31	Slater M 1	Macdonald C 29	Cameron D 21 + 6	Camara L — + 16	Clark S 4 + 2	McLean D 4 + 7	Perry M 13	Bone A 13 + 1	*Match No.*
1	2	3	4	5	6	7^{1}	8	9^{2}	10^{3}	11	12	13	14											1
1	3	2	4^{2}	5	9	7	8^{3}	11^{1}	10	12	14	13		6										2
1	3	2	4	5	9		8	7	10					6■	11■									3
1	3	14	6	5	9	12	8	7^{1}	10	11	13					2^{3}	4^{2}							4
1	3	2	6^{1}	5	9	7	8		10^{2}		13			4	11			12						5
1	3^{3}	2	6^{1}	5	7	12	8	9	10^{2}				14	4	11				13					6
1		2^{1}	6	5	7	12	8^{3}	9^{2}	10					4	11		3	13	14					7
1		2	6^{3}	5	7	13	8^{1}		10			14		4	11		3	9^{2}	12					8
1		2	6^{2}	5	7^{1}	12	8		10^{3}			13		4	11		3	9	14					9
1	13	2^{1}	6	5	7	12	8		10^{3}					4	11		3	9^{2}	14					10
1	9	2^{2}	6	5	7	13	8		10					4	11^{1}		3	12						11
1	11		6^{2}	5	7	2^{1}	8	12	10					4			3	9■	13					12
1	3		6^{1}	5	7	12	8	9	10^{2}					4	11		2		13					13
1	6	2		5	9	13	8	7^{1}	10					4	11^{2}		3		12					14
1	6			5	9^{2}	12	8	7	10				13	4	11		3^{3}		14	2^{1}				15
1	3		6	5	7		8^{1}	9	10					4	11		2		12					16
1	3		6	5	9^{2}		8^{1}	7	10^{3}		12			4	11		2	13	14					17
1			6^{2}	5	7		8	9^{1}	10		13			4	11		2	12		3				18
1	3		6	5	7		8^{3}	9^{2}	10					4	11^{1}		2	12	14	13				19
1	3		6^{2}	5^{1}	7		8	9	10		13			4			2	11	12					20
1	3		6	5	4			9^{2}	10		12		13		11		2	7			8^{1}			21
1	3		6^{2}		7		8^{3}		10^{1}					4	11		2	9		14	13	5	12	22
1	3		6		7		8^{1}							4	11		2	9			12	5	10	23
1	3		6		7		8							4	11		2	9				5	10	24
1	3		6	12	7						8			4	11^{2}		2	10			13	5^{1}	9	25
1	3		6	5	7						8^{1}			4	11		2	9			12		10	26
1	3	12	6	5	7									4^{1}	11			9	13	2	8^{2}		10	27
1	3	2^{1}		5	7			12							11			9	13	6^{2}	8	4	10	28
1	3		6^{1}		7		13	12			14			4	11^{2}		2	9			10^{3}	5	8	29
1	3	13			7		8	6	10^{1}					4	11^{2}		2	9	12			5		30
1	3				7		8	12	10^{1}					4	11		2	9				5	6	31
1	3				7		8	6^{1}			13			4	11		2	9			12	5	10^{2}	32
1	3				7		8		6^{1}		13			4	11		2	9			12	5	10^{2}	33
1	3	12	6^{1}		7		8							4	11^{2}		2	9			13	5	10	34
1	3				7		8	12	6					4	11		2	9^{1}				5	10	35
1	3		6^{1}		7		8		12					4	11		2	9				5	10■	36

QUEEN OF THE SOUTH First Division

Year Formed: 1919. *Ground & Address:* Palmerston Park, Dumfries DG2 9BA. *Telephone and Fax:* 01387 254853.
Ground Capacity: total: 8352, seated: 3549. *Size of Pitch:* 112yd × 73yd.
Vice-Chairman: Thomas Harkness. *Secretary:* Richard Shaw MBE. *Commercial Manager:* Margaret Heuchan.
Manager: John Connolly. *Assistant Manager:* Ian Scott.
Managers since 1975: M. Jackson, W. Hunter, B. Little, G. Herd, H. Hood, A. Busby, R. Clark, M. Jackson, D. Wilson, W. McLaren, F. McGarvey, A. MacLeod, D. Frye, W. McLaren, M. Shanks, R. Alexander. *Club Nickname(s):* The Doonhamers. *Previous Grounds:* None.
Record Attendance: 24,500 v Hearts, Scottish Cup 3rd rd; 23 Feb, 1952.
Record Transfer Fee received: £250,000 for Andy Thomson to Southend U (1994).
Record Transfer Fee paid: £30,000 for Jim Butter from Alloa Athletic (1995).
Record Victory: 11-1 v Stranraer, Scottish Cup 1st rd; 16 Jan, 1932.
Record Defeat: 2-10 v Dundee, Division I; 1 Dec, 1962.
Most Capped Player: Billy Houliston, 3, Scotland.
Most League Appearances: 731: Allan Ball, 1963-82.
Most League Goals in Season (Individual): 37: Jimmy Gray, Division II; 1927-28.
Most Goals in Season: 41: Jimmy Rutherford, 1931-32.
Most Goals Overall (Individual): 250: Jim Patterson, 1949-63.

QUEEN OF THE SOUTH 2002–03 LEAGUE RECORD

Match No.	*Date*	*Venue*	*Opponents*	*Result*		*H/T Score*	*Lg. Pos.*	*Goalscorers*	*Attendance*
1	Aug 3	H	Clyde	W	2-1	1-0	—	O'Connor 12, Paton 72	3206
2	10	A	Ross Co	L	0-2	0-1	6		2894
3	17	H	St Johnstone	D	0-0	0-0	6		3137
4	24	H	Ayr U	L	1-2	0-1	9	Bowey 84	2803
5	31	A	Falkirk	L	0-3	0-1	9		4091
6	Sept 14	H	Inverness CT	L	1-3	0-2	—	Weatherson 68	1611
7	21	A	St Mirren	L	1-2	1-1	9	Shields 8	2492
8	28	H	Arbroath	D	2-2	1-1	9	Lyle 2 5, 56	1733
9	Oct 5	A	Alloa Ath	W	1-0	1-0	9	O'Neil 43	658
10	12	A	Clyde	L	1-2	1-0	9	Thomson 21	1026
11	26	H	Ross Co	W	2-0	1-0	8	Lyle 2 11, 49	1533
12	Nov 2	H	Falkirk	D	1-1	1-0	8	McColligan 12	3017
13	9	A	Ayr U	W	1-0	0-0	6	McLaughlin 58	2234
14	16	A	Inverness CT	L	3-5	1-2	7	O'Connor 2 37, 53, O'Neil 73	1855
15	23	H	St Mirren	W	3-0	2-0	6	O'Connor 35, Paton 41, O'Neil 61	2663
16	30	A	Arbroath	W	2-1	1-0	6	Bowey 15, Lyle 46	630
17	Dec 7	H	Alloa Ath	D	1-1	0-1	6	McColligan 80	2111
18	14	A	St Johnstone	D	2-2	1-0	5	Paton 12, Bowey 73	1948
19	28	A	Falkirk	L	0-5	0-3	6		3858
20	Jan 1	H	Ayr U	D	1-1	0-0	—	Weatherson 62	2921
21	18	A	Alloa Ath	D	3-3	2-2	6	O'Neil 8, Weatherson 2 21, 62	561
22	Feb 8	H	St Johnstone	L	1-2	1-0	7	McLaughlin 41	1862
23	22	A	St Mirren	D	2-2	0-1	—	O'Neil 50, Bowey 59	1888
24	25	H	Clyde	D	1-1	1-0	—	McAlpine 16	1375
25	Mar 1	H	Falkirk	W	2-1	0-0	6	O'Neil (pen) 63, Weatherson 88	2555
26	8	A	Ayr U	W	1-0	0-0	6	Thomson 26	1730
27	11	H	Inverness CT	D	0-0	0-0	—		1405
28	15	H	St Mirren	L	0-2	0-1	6		1911
29	18	H	Arbroath	W	3-0	2-0	—	O'Neil 2 13, 79, O'Connor 41	1108
30	22	A	Ross Co	W	3-0	1-0	5	O'Neil 40, O'Connor 73, Macklay (og) 80	1976
31	Apr 5	A	Inverness CT	L	0-1	0-1	6		1656
32	12	A	Arbroath	D	0-0	0-0	6		502
33	19	H	Alloa Ath	L	0-1	0-0	6		1873
34	26	A	Clyde	D	2-2	1-2	5	Thomson 15, Weatherson 74	960
35	May 3	H	Ross Co	W	1-0	1-0	5	O'Connor 31	1810
36	10	A	St Johnstone	W	1-0	0-0	5	Lyle 66	1796

Final League Position: 5

Honours
League Champions: Division II 1950-51. Second Division 2001-02. *Runners-up:* Division II 1932-33, 1961-62, 1974-75. Second Division 1980-81, 1985-86.
Scottish Cup: semi-finalists 1949-50.
League Cup: semi-finalists 1950-51, 1960-61.
B&Q Cup: semi-finalists 1991-92. *League Challenge Cup:* winners 2002-03; runners-up 1997-98.

Club colours: Shirt: Royal blue with white sleeves. Shorts: White with blue piping. Stockings: Royal blue.

Goalscorers: *League* (45): O'Neil 9 (1 pen), O'Connor 7, Lyle 6, Weatherson 6, Bowey 4, Paton 3, Thomson 3, McColligan 2, McLaughlin 2, McAlpine 1, Shields 1, own goal 1
Scottish Cup (1): Weatherson 1
CIS Cup (3): O'Neil 2, Weatherson 1
Challenge Cup (12): Lyle 3, O'Neil 3, Shields 2, Weatherson 2, Bowey 1, O'Connor 1

Goram A 19	Atkinson P 7 + 1	Anderson D 23	Allan D 16 + 1	Aitken A 36	Paton E 17 + 7	Gray A 5 + 5	Bowey S 34	O'Connor S 17 + 5	Weatherson P 29 + 4	McAlpine J 21 + 7	Lyle D 27 + 6	McLaughlin B 20 + 13	O'Neil J 19 + 12	McColligan B 22 + 4	Shields P 9 + 4	Neilson R 13	Crawford J 5 + 1	Henderson R 2	Scott C 16 + 1	Thomson J 29 + 1	Renicks S 4 + 1	Dawson B 3	Burns P 1 + 3	Gibson W 1 + 2	Campbell J 1	Match No.
1	2	3	4	5	6	7	8	9^{1}	10^{2}	11	12	13														1
1	2^{2}	3	4	5	6^{1}	7	8	10	14	11^{3}	9	13	12													2
1		3	4	5	7	2^{1}	8		10	12	9^{2}	11	13	6												3
1	2	3	4	5	7^{3}		8		13	12	9	11^{2}	14	6^{1}	10											4
1		3	4	5			8		6	11^{1}	9^{2}	12	7		10	2■	13									5
1^{6}		3		5	11^{2}	2	8		9	12		13	7		10		4^{1}	6	15							6
				5	14		8		4	11	9^{2}	13	7		10	2	6^{3}	3^{1}	1	12						7
1		3		5			8		4	11	10	12	7		9^{1}	2				6						8
1		3		5	14		8		4	11	10^{2}	12	7^{3}	13	9^{1}	2				6						9
1		3^{1}		5		13	8		4	11	10	12	7		9^{2}	2				6						10
1		3		5			8	12	9	11	10^{1}	13	7^{2}	4		2				6						11
1		3		5			8	12	9		10	11	7^{1}	4		2				6						12
1		3		5			8	9^{1}	11		10^{2}	7	13	4	12	2				6						13
1	11^{3}	3		5			8	9^{1}	4■		10^{2}	14	13	7■	12	2				6						14
1		3		5	4	14	8	9^{3}		13	12	11^{2}	7		10^{1}	2				6						15
1				5	7^{1}		8	9	4		10^{2}	11	13	12		2	3			6						16
1		3		5	7		8^{3}	9	4		10^{1}	11	12	13	14	2^{2}				6						17
1				5	7		8	9^{1}	10^{2}		12	11	13	4		2	3			6						18
1	12			5	4	13			9	11^{2}	10^{3}	8	7^{1}	2	14		3			6						19
1		3		5	12	2	8		7		10^{1}	11	13	4	9^{2}					6						20
		3		5	9		8		10			11	7	4					1	6	2					21
		3		5	10		8	9^{1}	12	13		11^{2}	7	4					1	6	2					22
			4	5	10^{2}	14	8		9	12	13	11^{1}	7	3					1	6	2^{3}					23
		3	4	5	12		8		9^{1}	11	10		7	2					1	6						24
		3	4	5			8		9	11	10	12	7^{1}	2					1	6						25
		3^{1}	4	5			8	13	9^{2}	11	10	7		2					1	6	12					26
		3	4	5			8	12	9	11	10		7^{1}	2					1	6						27
		3^{3}	4	5	13	14	8	9		11	10^{1}	7	12	2^{2}					1	6						28
	3			5	10^{3}		8	9^{1}		13	12	11^{2}	7						1	6	2	4	14			29
	3		4	5	13		8	12	9	11	10^{2}		7^{1}	2					1	6						30
	3^{1}		4	5	13		8	7	9^{2}	11	10	12		2					1	6						31
			4	5	10^{2}		8	9^{1}	12	3	13	11	7	2^{3}					1	6			14			32
			4	5			8	7	9^{1}	3	10^{3}	11	12	2^{2}					1	6			13	14		33
			4	5			8	7^{1}	9	3	10	11	12						1	6		2				34
				5	4		8	7	9	3	10	11^{2}		12					1	6		2^{1}		13		35
			13	5	4			7^{1}	9	3	10^{2}	12		2						6			8	11	1	36

QUEEN'S PARK

Third Division

Year Formed: 1867. *Ground & Address:* Hampden Park, Mount Florida, Glasgow G42 9BA. *Telephone:* 0141 632 1275. *Fax:* 0141 636 1612.
Ground Capacity: all seated: 52,000. *Size of Pitch:* 115yd × 75yd.
President: David Gordon. *Secretary:* Alistair Mackay. *Treasurer:* Ross Caven.
Coach: Kenneth Brannigan. *Physio:* R. C. Findlay.
Coaches since 1975: D. McParland, J. Gilroy, E. Hunter, H. McCann, J. McCormack. *Club Nickname(s):* The Spiders.
Previous Grounds: 1st Hampden (Recreation Ground); (Titwood Park was used as an interim measure between 1st & 2nd Hampdens); 2nd Hampden (Cathkin); 3rd Hampden.
Record Attendance: 95,772 v Rangers, Scottish Cup, 18 Jan, 1930.
Record for Ground: 149,547 Scotland v England, 1937.
Record Transfer Fee received: Not applicable due to amateur status.
Record Transfer Fee paid: Not applicable due to amateur status.
Record Victory: 16-0 v St. Peters, Scottish Cup 1st rd; 29 Aug, 1885.
Record Defeat: 0-9 v Motherwell, Division I; 26 Apr, 1930.
Most Capped Player: Walter Arnott, 14, Scotland.
Most League Appearances: 532: Ross Caven.
Most League Goals in Season (Individual): 30: William Martin, Division I; 1937-38.
Most Goals Overall (Individual): 163: J. B. McAlpine.

QUEEN'S PARK 2002–03 LEAGUE RECORD

Match No.	Date	Venue	Opponents	Result		H/T Score	Lg. Pos.	Goalscorers	Atten-dance
1	Aug 3	H	Elgin C	L	1-2	0-1	—	Canning 75	585
2	10	A	Montrose	L	0-1	0-1	—		402
3	17	H	East Fife	D	0-0	0-0	8		537
4	24	A	Morton	L	0-3	0-3	9		2001
5	31	H	Gretna	W	1-0	1-0	9	Ferry 14	607
6	Sept 14	H	East Stirling	L	0-2	0-1	10		443
7	21	A	Peterhead	L	0-3	0-1	10		597
8	28	H	Albion R	L	2-4	0-2	10	Jack 57, Moffat 81	506
9	Oct 5	A	Stirling A	L	0-1	0-1	10		579
10	19	H	Montrose	L	0-1	0-1	10		492
11	26	A	Elgin C	D	2-2	1-2	10	Moffat 28, Whelan 83	567
12	Nov 2	A	Gretna	D	2-2	1-1	9	Moffat (pen) 14, Gallagher P 69	319
13	9	H	Morton	D	1-1	0-0	9	Canning 83	1775
14	16	A	East Stirling	W	4-0	2-0	9	Allan 2 14, 64, Whelan 32, Dunning 52	315
15	23	H	Peterhead	W	2-0	1-0	9	Allan 7, Clark 49	495
16	30	H	Stirling A	L	0-1	0-1	9		657
17	Dec 7	A	Morton	D	1-1	0-0	9	Moffat (pen) 82	1669
18	14	A	Albion R	W	2-0	2-0	7	Martin 13, Sinclair 45	442
19	21	H	Elgin C	W	3-2	1-1	7	Gemmell 3 15, 55, 58	648
20	28	A	East Fife	D	1-1	0-0	7	Moffat 71	808
21	Jan 11	H	Gretna	L	1-2	0-2	7	Whelan 79	934
22	18	H	East Stirling	L	3-4	3-1	7	Gemmell 2 3, 4, Allan 26	693
23	Feb 8	H	Albion R	D	1-1	0-0	7	Gemmell 60	671
24	22	A	Montrose	D	1-1	0-1	7	Whelan 50	315
25	Mar 1	H	East Fife	L	1-2	0-1	7	McCallum 76	697
26	8	H	Morton	L	0-1	0-0	7		1361
27	15	A	Gretna	W	1-0	0-0	8	McCallum 88	320
28	19	A	Stirling A	L	0-1	0-1	—		465
29	22	H	Peterhead	L	1-2	0-2	8	Martin 67	575
30	29	A	Peterhead	L	1-3	0-2	8	Gemmell 68	589
31	Apr 5	A	East Stirling	W	2-0	1-0	7	Menelaws 38, Martin 80	281
32	12	H	Stirling A	D	3-3	1-2	7	Sinclair 35, Whelan 82, Gemmell 89	714
33	19	A	Albion R	L	1-2	0-1	7	Menelaws 62	581
34	26	A	Elgin C	D	0-0	0-0	8		444
35	May 3	H	Montrose	D	1-1	0-1	8	Gallagher P 74	556
36	10	A	East Fife	L	0-1	0-0	8		1996

Final League Position: 8

Honours
League Champions: Division II 1922-23. B Division 1955-56. Second Division 1980-81. Third Division 1999-2000.
Scottish Cup Winners: 1874, 1875, 1876, 1880, 1881, 1882, 1884, 1886, 1890, 1893; *Runners-up:* 1892, 1900.
League Cup: —.
FA Cup runners-up: 1884, 1885.

Club colours: Shirt: White and black hoops. Shorts: White. Stockings: Black with white tops.

Goalscorers: *League* (39): Gemmell 8, Moffat 5 (1 pen), Whelan 5, Allen 4, Martin 3, Canning 2, Gallagher P 2, McCallum 2, Menelaws 2, Sinclair 2, Clark 1, Dunning 1, Ferry 1, Jack 1
Scottish Cup (7): Gemmell 3, Allen 1, Martin 1, Menelaws 1, Whelan 1
CIS Cup (2): Canning 1, Martin 1
Challenge Cup (9): Allen 2, Gemmell 2, Moffat 2, Whelan 2, Canning 1

Mitchell A 7	Ferry D 33 + 1	Gallagher J 11 + 2	Moffat S 21	Agostini D 34	Quinn A 18	Lappin G 3 + 1	Jack S 4 + 5	Gemmell J 31 + 2	Canning S 17 + 7	Allan J 25 + 1	Fisher C 1 + 9	Jackson R — + 1	Whelan J 31 + 1	Lejman K — + 1	Gallagher P 2 + 15	Martin W 18 + 9	Taggart C 4 + 4	Stewart C 16	Crozier B 4 + 3	Sinclair R 18 + 4	Fallon S 30	White J 5 + 4	Dunning A 7 + 7	Clark R 16 + 7	Menelaws D 6 + 5	Kettlewell S 9 + 2	Cairns M 13	McCallum D 11	Conlin R 1	*Match No.*
1	2^{2}	3	4	5	6	7	8^{1}	9	10	11	12	13																		1
1	2	3	4	5	6^{1}		7^{2}	9	10	11^{3}			8	12	13	14														2
1	2	3^{2}	4	5	6		12	9	10^{3}	11			8		14	7^{1}	13													3
1	2	3	4	5	6		14	9^{3}	10^{1}	11^{2}	13		8			12	7													4
	2	3	4	5	6			9	12	11^{3}	13		8				7^{2}	1	10^{1}	14										5
	2	11	4^{1}	5	6			9	13				8^{3}			10	14	1	7^{2}	12	3									6
	7	3^{2}		5	10		12	9^{1}	14				8^{3}			11	13	1		6	2	4								7
	7		4		5	2	11			12			8			13	6	1	10^{1}		3		9^{2}							8
	7	3	4	5	6		10^{1}	12		11			8^{3}		13	9^{2}	14	1			2									9
	2	3	4	5	10		12		7^{1}	11			8			9^{2}		1			6		13							10
	2	3	4	5	10^{3}		13		7^{2}	11			8			9^{1}		1			6		12	14						11
	2		4	5	10			9^{1}	3	11^{3}			8		12			1	13		6		7^{2}	14						12
	2		4	5	10^{2}			9	3	11^{3}			8		12			1	14		6		7^{1}	13						13
	2		4	5	10^{1}			9^{2}	3	11			8		13			1	14		6		7^{3}	12						14
	2		5	4	10			9^{2}	3	11^{3}			8		14	13		1	7^{1}		6			12						15
			4	5	10^{3}			9	3	11			8^{1}		14	12		1		13	6		7^{2}	2						16
			5	4	10			9^{1}	3	11			8			7		1		2	6		12							17
	13	14	4	5	10^{1}			9	3^{3}	11^{2}			8			7		1		2	6			12						18
	3	12	4	5				9^{3}		11^{2}	13		8			7		1		2^{1}	6		14	10						19
	3		4	5		12		9		11			8			7^{2}		1		2^{1}	6		13	10						20
1	3	11^{2}	4	5				9^{1}			13		8			7^{3}				2	6		12	10	14					21
1	3		4^{1}	5		2^{2}		9		11			8			7^{3}				12	6			10	14	13				22
	2			5				9	3^{1}	11			8		12					4■	6	14		7^{2}		13	1	10^{3}		23
	2			5				9	3^{2}	11^{3}	12		8		14						6	4		13	7^{1}		1	10		24
	2			5				9		11	12		8		13					3^{2}	6	4		7^{1}			1	10		25
1	2							9^{3}	13	11			8^{1}		12					5	6	4■		3	14	7^{2}		10		26
	2			5				9		11			8			10				4	6					7	1	3		27
	2			5				9		11^{2}	13				12	10				4	6			8		7^{1}	1	3		28
	2			5				9^{2}		11	13		14■			10				4^{1}	6	12		8		7	1	3^{3}		29
	2			5				12	14		11^{2}				7^{3}	9^{1}				4	6			10	13	8	1	3		30
	2^{2}			5				9					8^{3}		14	12				4	6		13	7	11^{1}	10	1	3		31
	2			5				9					8			12				4	6		3^{1}	7	11	10	1			32
	2			5				9	14				8^{1}			12				4^{2}	6	13		7	11	10■	1	3^{3}		33
	2			5				9	3				8			10				4	6■			7	11		1			34
	2			5				9	7				8		14	13	10^{3}			4^{1}		12			11^{2}		1	3	6	35
	8			5^{2}				9■	12						3	11					6	4	2^{1}	7	13	10■	1			36

RAITH ROVERS

First Division

Year Formed: 1883. *Ground & Address:* Stark's Park, Pratt St, Kirkcaldy KY1 1SA. *Telephone:* 01592 263514. *Fax:* 01592 642833.
Ground Capacity: all seated: 10,104. *Size of Pitch:* 113yd × 70yd.
Chairman: Danny Smith. *Office Manager:* Bob Mullen.
Manager: Antonio Calderon. *Assistant Manager:* Francisco Ortez Rivas.
Managers since 1975: R. Paton, A. Matthew, W. McLean, G. Wallace, R. Wilson, F. Connor, J. Nicholl, J. Thomson, T. McLean, I. Munro, J. Nicholl, J. McVeigh, P. Hetherston, J. Scott.
Club Nickname: Rovers. *Previous Grounds:* Robbie's Park.
Record Attendance: 31,306 v Hearts, Scottish Cup 2nd rd; 7 Feb, 1953.
Record Transfer Fee received: £900,000 for S. McAnespie to Bolton Wanderers (Sept 1995).
Record Transfer Fee paid: £225,000 for Paul Harvey from Airdrieonians (1996).
Record Victory: 10-1 v Coldstream, Scottish Cup 2nd rd; 13 Feb, 1954.
Record Defeat: 2-11 v Morton, Division II; 18 Mar, 1936.
Most Capped Player: David Morris, 6, Scotland.
Most League Appearances: 430: Willie McNaught.
Most League Goals in Season (Individual): 38: Norman Haywood, Division II; 1937-38.
Most Goals Overall (Individual): 154: Gordon Dalziel (League), 1987-94.

RAITH ROVERS 2002–03 LEAGUE RECORD

Match No.	Date	Venue	Opponents	Result		H/T Score	Lg. Pos.	Goalscorers	Attendance
1	Aug 3	H	Stranraer	D	1-1	1-0	—	Carrigan [35]	1790
2	10	A	Berwick R	D	1-1	1-1	7	Boylan [15]	804
3	17	H	Dumbarton	W	1-0	0-0	3	Hawley [89]	1866
4	24	A	Cowdenbeath	L	1-3	1-2	8	Boylan [42]	1678
5	31	H	Stenhousemuir	W	1-0	0-0	3	Smith [52]	1661
6	Sept 14	H	Airdrie U	D	0-0	0-0	4		1962
7	21	A	Hamilton A	W	4-0	2-0	1	Carrigan 2 (1 pen) [12, 84 (p)], Nanou [30], Boylan [52]	1961
8	28	H	Brechin C	W	3-1	0-0	1	Boylan [52], Hawley 2 [59, 70]	2007
9	Oct 5	A	Forfar Ath	W	2-1	1-1	1	Blackadder [34], Brady [56]	1054
10	19	H	Berwick R	L	1-2	0-0	2	Hawley [73]	1906
11	26	A	Stranraer	D	2-2	2-2	2	Carrigan [8], Rivas [17]	608
12	Nov 2	A	Stenhousemuir	W	1-0	0-0	1	Nanou [70]	1066
13	9	H	Cowdenbeath	W	4-1	1-0	1	Rivas [43], Blackadder 2 [55, 62], Hawley [81]	2428
14	16	A	Airdrie U	D	0-0	0-0	1		1717
15	23	H	Hamilton A	D	1-1	0-1	1	Boylan [63]	1897
16	30	H	Forfar Ath	W	5-1	3-1	1	McManus 2 [8, 74], Blackadder (pen) [35], Dennis [45], Rivas [50]	1779
17	Dec 14	A	Brechin C	W	2-1	2-0	1	McManus 2 [20, 43]	746
18	28	A	Dumbarton	W	3-0	1-0	1	Hawley [41], Smith 2 [81, 89]	1300
19	Jan 1	A	Cowdenbeath	D	1-1	1-0	—	Hawley [20]	1875
20	18	H	Airdrie U	W	1-0	0-0	1	Smith [84]	2247
21	Feb 1	A	Hamilton A	D	0-0	0-0	1		1292
22	8	H	Brechin C	L	1-2	1-0	1	McKinnon [43]	1776
23	22	A	Berwick R	D	1-1	1-1	1	Shields [13]	820
24	Mar 1	H	Dumbarton	W	2-1	2-0	1	Dennis [15], Prest [18]	1790
25	4	H	Stranraer	W	3-0	0-0	—	Fyfe [63], Nanou [77], Prest [83]	1448
26	8	H	Cowdenbeath	W	2-1	2-1	1	Patino [25], McManus [34]	1900
27	11	A	Forfar Ath	L	2-4	1-2	—	Prest 2 [23, 49]	688
28	15	A	Stenhousemuir	W	3-1	1-1	1	McKinnon [34], Rivas [45], Shields [90]	929
29	22	H	Hamilton A	D	1-1	1-0	1	Patino [17]	1762
30	26	H	Stenhousemuir	L	0-1	0-1	—		1627
31	Apr 5	A	Airdrie U	D	1-1	1-1	1	Smith [28]	1788
32	12	H	Forfar Ath	L	0-1	0-1	1		2036
33	19	A	Brechin C	L	0-1	0-1	1		1819
34	26	A	Stranraer	L	0-1	0-0	1		617
35	May 3	H	Berwick R	W	1-0	0-0	1	Smith [82]	2746
36	10	A	Dumbarton	L	1-4	1-2	1	Blackadder (pen) [17]	1501

Final League Position: 1

Honours
League Champions: First Division: 1992-93, 1994-95. Division II 1907-08, 1909-10 (shared), 1937-38, 1948-49;
Runners-up: Division II 1908-09, 1926-27, 1966-67. Second Division 1975-76, 1977-78, 1986-87.
Scottish Cup Runners-up: 1913. *League Cup Winners: (Coca-Cola Cup):* 1994-95. *Runners-up:* 1948-49.

European: *UEFA Cup:* 6 matches (1995-96).

Club colours: Shirt: Navy blue with white sleeves. Shorts: White with navy and red trim. Stockings: Navy blue with white turnover.

Goalscorers: *League* (53): Hawley 7, Smith 6, Blackadder 5 (2 pens), Boylan 5, McManus 5, Carrigan 4 (1 pen), Prest 4, Rivas 4, Nanou 3, Dennis 2, McKinnon 2, Patino 2, Shields 2, Brady 1, Fyfe 1
Scottish Cup (4): Blackadder 1, Carrigan 1, Hawley 1, Smith 1
CIS Cup (2): Carrigan 1, Prest 1
Challenge Cup (0)

Ojeda R 28	Ross D 3	Parkin P 9 + 1	Brady D 32 + 2	Browne P 2	Nanou W 25 + 5	Carrigan B 10 + 12	Rivas F 35	Smith A 23 + 2	Hampshire P 17 + 7	Prest M 14 + 11	Palicza S — + 2	Blackadder R 21 + 8	Moffat A 4	Matheson R 3 + 1	Boylan C 9 + 5	Brown I 6	Dennis S 29	Calderon A 16 + 6	Hawley K 15 + 2	Ellis L 28	Miller S — + 1	McManus P 7 + 13	Patino C 24	Monin S 1 + 1	Fyfe G 8 + 4	McKinnon R 10 + 2	Shields D 6 + 9	Sweeney J 1	Khebir 2	Gonzales R 6	Valdes A 2	Davidson A — + 1	*Match No.*
1	2	3	4	5	6	7^1	8	9^2	10	11■	12	13																					1
1	2	3	4	5		12	8	9	10			13	6	7^1	11^2																		2
1		3^2	6				8	9	10	13			4^3	7^1	11	2	5	12	14														3
1			4^3		14		8	9^2	10	13		12	6^1		7	2■	5		11	3													4
1			13		4		8	9^1	3	11		12			7^3		5	6^2	10	2	14												5
1			4		6	12	8	9^1		11^2		14			13	2	5	10^3	7	3													6
1			4		6	7^3	8		12			10^1			11^2	2	5	13	9	3		14											7
1			4		6	7^2	8					10			11^1	2	5	12	9	3		13											8
1			4		6	7	8		12			10			11^1		5		9^2	3		13	2										9
1		3^2	4^1		6	7	8	14				10			11			12	9	2^3		13	5										10
1			4^2		6^1	7	8		10	12		11			13			3	9	2			5										11
1			4		6		8	14	11	12		7			13		5	10^2	9^3	3			2^1										12
1			4		6		8	9^1	11			10^2			13		5		7	3		12	2										13
1		3	2		6^1		8	9^2	7^3	14		10			12		5		11	4		13											14
1■		3	4^2				8	9^3	10	12		6^1			7		5		11	2		13		14									15
		3	14		6^3	12	8	9^2	4			7^1					5	10	13	2		11		1									16
1			4		6		8	9	12	13		7					5	10^1		3		11^2	2										17
1			4		6	13	8	9^3	12	14		7^2					5	10	11	3^1			2										18
1			4		6	14	8	9^3	12	13		7					5		11	3^2			2		10^1								19
1			4		6	7^2	8	9	10^1			13					5	3	11^3			14	2		12								20
1		14	4		6^1	12	8	9				7					5			3^3		11^2	2			10	13						21
1			4				8	9		12		7					5	3				13	2		10^2	6	11^1						22
1					6	12	8	9				7					5	13		3			2		10^2	4	11^1						23
1			4		7^2	13	8			9^1							5	14		3		12	2		10	6	11^3						24
1			4		7	13	8		12	9^3							5			3		14	2		10	6^1	11^2						25
1			4		7	12	8		6	11^3							5			3		9^1	2		10^2	13	14						26
			4		7	12	8		6	11							5			3^2		9^3	2		10^1	14	13	1					27
1			6		12	9^2	8			11		7					5	3					4			10^1	13		2				28
1			6			7^1	8			9		11^2					5	3					4		12	10	13		2				29
1			6^3		2	7	8			9^1		13					5			3		14	4		12	10^2	11						30
			4		12	13	8	9^2	6	11		7				5^1		10		3			2							1			31
		3^2	6		12		8	9		11^3		7^1						10		5			2		13	4	14			1			32
			4^3		12		8	9	3	11^2		13					5	10					2			6^1	14			1	7■		33
			4		7		8	9	6^1	13				12			5	10^3		3		14	2^2				11			1			34
			4		6		8	9^2	13	11							5	10		3		7^1	2				12			1			35
	4	3						9^3			14	10	6	8						5^2		7			11^1		13			1	2	12	36

RANGERS

Premier League

Year Formed: 1873. *Ground & Address:* Ibrox Stadium, 150 Edmiston Drive, Glasgow G51 2XD.
Telephone: 0870 600 1972. *Fax:* 0870 600 1978. *Website:* www.rangers.co.uk
Ground Capacity: all seated: 50,444. *Size of Pitch:* 114.5m × 81.5m.
Chairman: John McClelland. *Hon. Chairman:* David Murray. *General Secretary/Director:* R. C. Ogilvie. *Director of Football Business:* Martin Bain.
Manager: Alex McLeish. *Assistant Manager:* Andy Watson. *First Team Coach:* Jan Wouters. *Physios:* David Henders, Stuart Collie. *Reserve team coaches:* John Brown, Tommy McLean.
Managers since 1975: Jock Wallace, John Greig, Jock Wallace, Graeme Souness, Walter Smith, Dick Advocaat.
Club Nickname(s): The Gers. *Previous Grounds:* Flesher's Haugh, Burnbank, Kinning Park, Old Ibrox.
Record Attendance: 118,567 v Celtic, Division I; 2 Jan, 1939.
Record Transfer Fee received: £8,500,000 for G. Van Bronckhorst to Arsenal (2001).
Record Transfer Fee paid: £12 million for Tore Andre Flo from Chelsea (November 2000).
Record Victory: 14-2 v Blairgowrie, Scottish Cup 1st rd; 20 Jan, 1934. *Record Defeat:* 2-10 v Airdrieonians; 1886.
Most Capped Player: Ally McCoist, 60, Scotland. *Most League Appearances:* 496: John Greig, 1962-78.
Most League Goals in Season (Individual): 44: Sam English, Division I; 1931-32.
Most Goals Overall (Individual): 355: Ally McCoist; 1985-98.

Honours
League Champions: (50 times) Division I 1890-91 (shared), 1898-99, 1899-1900, 1900-01, 1901-02, 1910-11, 1911-12, 1912-13, 1917-18, 1919-20, 1920-21, 1922-23, 1923-24, 1924-25, 1926-27, 1927-28, 1928-29, 1929-30, 1930-31, 1932-33, 1933-34, 1934-35, 1936-37, 1938-39, 1946-47, 1948-49, 1949-50, 1952-53, 1955-56, 1956-57, 1958-59, 1960-61, 1962-63, 1963-64, 1974-75. Premier Division: 1975-76, 1977-78, 1986-87, 1988-89, 1989-90, 1990-91, 1991-92, 1992-93, 1993-94, 1994-95, 1995-96, 1996-97, 1998-99, 1999-2000, 2002-03; *Runners-up:* 24 times.

RANGERS 2002–03 LEAGUE RECORD

Match No.	Date	Venue	Opponents	Result	H/T Score	Lg. Pos.	Goalscorers	Atten-dance
1	Aug 3	A	Kilmarnock	D 1-1	1-0	—	Arveladze ^{31}	13,972
2	10	H	Dundee	W 3-0	1-0	3	de Boer ^{2}, Arveladze ^{66}, Lovenkrands ^{87}	46,774
3	18	A	Hibernian	W 4-2	2-1	2	de Boer ^{6}, Ferguson ^{44}, Lovenkrands 2 $^{64, 86}$	11,633
4	25	H	Aberdeen	W 2-0	1-0	2	de Boer ^{29}, Ferguson (pen) ^{77}	49,219
5	Sept 1	A	Dunfermline Ath	W 6-0	3-0	2	Caniggia 3 $^{11, 51, 67}$, Arteta ^{27}, Ricksen ^{41}, Ferguson (pen) ^{56}	8950
6	11	H	Hearts	W 2-0	1-0	—	Caniggia ^{40}, Arveladze ^{78}	48,581
7	14	A	Livingston	W 2-0	0-0	1	Ross ^{46}, Ferguson (pen) ^{87}	8787
8	21	H	Partick Th	W 3-0	2-0	1	Lovenkrands ^{3}, de Boer 2 $^{27, 69}$	48,696
9	28	A	Dundee U	W 3-0	2-0	1	Amoruso ^{21}, Ferguson ^{45}, Arveladze ^{72}	10,013
10	Oct 6	A	Celtic	D 3-3	1-1	1	Arteta ^{6}, de Boer ^{54}, Arveladze ^{77}	58,939
11	19	H	Motherwell	W 3-0	1-0	1	Amoruso ^{2}, Lovenkrands ^{72}, de Boer ^{90}	49,376
12	27	H	Kilmarnock	W 6-1	4-1	1	Mols 2 $^{5, 15}$, de Boer ^{26}, Ferguson 2 (1 pen) $^{34 (p), 70}$, Moore ^{67}	48,368
13	Nov 2	A	Dundee	W 3-0	1-0	1	Malcolm ^{30}, Lovenkrands ^{50}, Moore ^{79}	10,124
14	10	H	Hibernian	W 2-1	2-1	1	Mols ^{10}, Arveladze ^{34}	49,032
15	16	A	Aberdeen	D 2-2	1-0	1	Numan ^{24}, Ferguson (pen) ^{77}	14,915
16	23	H	Dunfermline Ath	W 3-0	0-0	2	McCann ^{59}, Mols ^{81}, Arveladze ^{82}	48,431
17	Dec 1	A	Hearts	W 4-0	0-0	2	Ricksen 2 $^{52, 81}$, Ferguson (pen) ^{78}, Hughes ^{89}	12,156
18	4	H	Livingston	W 4-3	3-0	—	Ferguson ^{7}, Arveladze 3 $^{10, 17, 46}$	45,992
19	7	H	Celtic	W 3-2	3-1	1	Moore ^{10}, de Boer ^{35}, Mols ^{40}	49,874
20	14	H	Dundee U	W 3-0	1-0	1	Ferguson 3 (1 pen) $^{26, 56, 84 (p)}$	47,639
21	22	A	Partick Th	W 2-1	0-1	1	Mols ^{69}, de Boer ^{78}	8022
22	26	A	Motherwell	L 0-1	0-0	—		11,234
23	29	A	Kilmarnock	W 1-0	1-0	1	Lovenkrands ^{23}	13,396
24	Jan 2	H	Dundee	W 3-1	2-1	1	Ferguson ^{21}, de Boer ^{44}, Thompson ^{82}	49,112
25	29	A	Hibernian	W 2-0	0-0	—	McCann ^{52}, Caniggia ^{86}	13,686
26	Feb 1	H	Aberdeen	W 2-1	1-0	1	Mols 2 $^{36, 76}$	49,667
27	8	A	Dunfermline Ath	W 3-1	1-0	1	McCann ^{37}, Amoruso ^{71}, Caniggia ^{90}	8754
28	15	H	Hearts	W 1-0	1-0	1	Severin (og) ^{40}	49,459
29	Mar 2	A	Livingston	W 2-1	2-0	1	Amoruso ^{8}, Arveladze ^{15}	8439
30	8	A	Celtic	L 0-1	0-0	1		58,336
31	19	H	Motherwell	W 2-0	1-0	—	Ferguson ^{17}, Lovenkrands ^{46}	49,420
32	Apr 5	H	Partick Th	W 2-0	0-0	1	Mols 2 $^{70, 74}$	49,472
33	13	A	Dundee U	W 4-1	3-0	1	de Boer 2 $^{12, 45}$, Arveladze 2 $^{17, 68}$	10,271
34	27	H	Celtic	L 1-2	0-2	1	de Boer ^{57}	49,740
35	May 4	A	Dundee	D 2-2	1-2	2	Wilkie (og) ^{1}, Arteta (pen) ^{85}	9204
36	11	H	Kilmarnock	W 4-0	2-0	1	Mols 2 $^{5, 6}$, Arveladze ^{59}, Caniggia ^{80}	49,036
37	18	A	Hearts	W 2-0	0-0	1	de Boer ^{64}, Lovenkrands ^{72}	15,632
38	25	H	Dunfermline Ath	W 6-1	3-1	1	Mols ^{3}, Caniggia ^{16}, Arveladze ^{30}, McCann ^{64}, Thompson ^{67}, Arteta (pen) ^{90}	49,731

Final League Position: 1

Scottish Cup Winners: (31 times) 1894, 1897, 1898, 1903, 1928, 1930, 1932, 1934, 1935, 1936, 1948, 1949, 1950, 1953, 1960, 1962, 1963, 1964, 1966, 1973, 1976, 1978, 1979, 1981, 1992, 1993, 1996, 1999, 2000, 2002, 2003; *Runners-up:* 17 times.
League Cup Winners: (23 times) 1946-47, 1948-49, 1960-61, 1961-62, 1963-64, 1964-65, 1970-71, 1975-76, 1977-78, 1978-79, 1981-82, 1983-84, 1984-85, 1986-87, 1987-88, 1988-89, 1990-91, 1992-93, 1993-94, 1996-97, 1998-99, 2001-02, 2002-03; *Runners-up:* 6 times.

European: *European Cup:* 109 matches (1956-57, 1957-58, 1959-60 semi-finals, 1961-62, 1963-64, 1964-65, 1975-76, 1976-77, 1978-79, 1987-88, 1989-90, 1990-91, 1991-92, 1992-93 final pool, 1993-94, 1994-95, 1995-96; 1996-97, 1997-98, 1999-2000, 2000-01).
Cup Winners' Cup: 54 matches (1960-61 runners-up, 1962-63, 1966-67 runners-up, 1969-70, 1971-72 winners, 1973-74, 1977-78, 1979-80, 1981-82, 1983-84). *UEFA Cup:* 56 matches (*Fairs Cup:* 1967-68, 1968-69 semi-finals, 1970-71. *UEFA Cup:* 1982-83, 1984-85, 1985-86, 1986-87, 1988-89, 1997-98, 1998-99, 1999-2000, 2000-01, 2002-03).

Club colours: Shirt: Royal blue; red chevrons at neck, white collar, red trim at cuffs. Shorts: White with royal blue side panels and red trim. Stockings: Black with red tops; or Royal blue with white tops.

Goalscorers: *League* (101): de Boer 16, Ferguson 16 (7 pens), Arveladze 15, Mols 13, Lovenkrands 9, Caniggia 8, Amoruso 4, Arteta 4 (2 pens), Moore 3, Ricksen 3, McCann 2, Thompson 2, Hughes 1, Malcolm 1, Numan 1, Ross 1, own goals 2
Scottish Cup (13): Amoruso 2, Ferguson 2, Arteta 1, Arveladze 1, Caniggia 1, de Boer 1, Konterman 1, Lovenkrands 1, Mols 1, Moore 1, own goal 1
CIS Cup (7): Caniggia 3, Lovenkrands 2, de Boer 1, own goal 1

Klos S 38	Ricksen F 35	Moore C 35	Amoruso L 24	Numan A 26	Arteta M 26 + 1	Ferguson B 36	McCann N 10 + 8	de Boer R 33	Arveladze S 25 + 5	Lovenkrands P 21 + 5	Latapy R 2 + 5	Konterman B 4 + 12	Flo T 1 + 3	Muscat K 22 + 1	Malcolm R 19 + 5	Ross M 17 + 3	Caniggia C 10 + 15	Hughes S 6 + 7	Dodds W 1 + 5	Mols M 23 + 4	Nerlinger C — + 3	Hutton A 1	McLean S — + 3	Thompson S 1 + 7	Bonnissel J 2 + 1	*Match No.*
1	2	3	4	5	6[2]	7	8[3]	9[1]	10	11	12	13	14													1
1	2	3	4	5	8	7		9[1]	10	12			11	6												2
1	2	3	4	5	8	7		9[1]	10	11			12	6												3
1	2	3		5	8[3]	7		9	10	11[1]	14		12	6[2]	4	13										4
1	2	3		5	8[1]	7[3]		9[2]	10			14		6	4		11	12	13							5
1	2	3		5[2]	8	7		9[1]	10			14		6	4	13	11[3]		12							6
1	2	3			8	7			10	12	13			6	4	5	11[2]		9[1]							7
1	2	3[1]	4		8	7[2]		9	10[3]	11	14	12		6		5				13						8
1	2	3	4		8	7		9[1]	10	11		13		6[2]		5	12									9
1	2	3[1]	4	5	8	7	13	9[3]	10	11[2]		12				6	14									10
1	2	3[3]	4	5	8	7[2]		9		11		14				6	10[1]	13		12						11
1	2	3		5		7[3]		9[1]		11		14		12	4	6		8	13	10[2]						12
1	2	3		5[1]	8	7[2]		9		11		13		6	4			12		10						13
1	2		4[1]	5	8[2]	7			10		14	12			3	6	9[3]	13		11						14
1	2			5		7	12	9	10		8	3			4	6				11[1]						15
1	2	3		5	8	7	9[1]		10					6	4		12		13	11[2]						16
1	2	3	4[3]	5	8[1]	7	11[2]	9	10					6	14			12		13						17
1	2	3	4	5[3]		7[2]	8	9[1]	10	12				6		14				11	13					18
1	2	3	4	5		7	8	9	10[2]						12	6[1]	14	13		11[3]						19
1	2[1]	3	4			7		9[1]	10	11				6	12			5		8[2]	13					20
1		3	4			7		9		11	8[1]			6	13		12	5[3]		10		2[2]	14			21
1	2	3	4			7		9		11				6	5		8[1]		12	10						22
1		3	4			7		9	10[1]	11				6	5	2	12			8						23
1		3	4			7		9		11[3]				6	5	2	8[1]			10[2]	14		13	12		24
1	2	3		5		7	8	9	10						4	6	12			11[1]						25
1	2	3		5	8[1]	7	11[2]	9							4	6	12			10[3]			14		13	26
1	2	3	4	5	8[2]	7	11	9	10[3]						12	6[1]	13			14						27
1	2		4	5	8	7		9	13	12				6	3		11[1]			10[2]						28
1	2	3	4		8	7	9		10[2]					6			12			11[1]				13	5	29
1	2	3	4		8[2]	7	9		10	11		14				6[3]	13							12	5[1]	30
1	2	3				7	14	9[1]	13	11[3]		12		6	4	5				10[2]				8		31
1	2	3			8[2]		12	9	14	11[3]		5			4	6[1]	13	7		10						32
1	2	3		5	8[1]		14	9[2]	10	11[3]		6		7	4		12							13		33
1	2	3	4	5	12	7	13	9		11[3]		6[1]					8[2]			10				14		34
1	2	3		5	8	7		9[1]	12	11[2]				6[3]	4		13	14		10						35
1	2	3	4	5	8	7	14	9[3]	12	11[1]							13	6		10[2]						36
1	2	3	4	5	8[1]	7		9	11	12								6		10[2]				13		37
1	2	3	4	5	6	7	12	9	11								8[1]			10[2]				13		38

ROSS COUNTY

First Division

Year Formed: 1929. *Ground & Address:* Victoria Park, Dingwall IV15 9QW. *Telephone:* 01349 860860. *Fax:* 01349 866277.
Website: www.rosscountyfootballclub.co.uk
Ground Capacity: 6700. *Size of Ground:* 110×75yd.
Chairman: Roy McGregor. *Secretary:* Donnie MacBean.
Manager: Alex Smith. *Physio:* Douglas Sim.
Managers since 1994: Neale Cooper.
Record Attendance: 6600, benefit match v Celtic, 31 August 1970.
Record Transfer Fee Received: £200,000 for Neil Tarrant to Aston Villa (April 1999).
Record Transfer Fee Paid: £25,000 for Barry Wilson from Southampton (Oct. 1992).
Record Victory: 11-0 v St Cuthbert Wanderers, Scottish Cup, Dec. 1993.
Record Defeat: 1-10 v Inverness Thistle, Highland League.
Most League Appearances: 157: David Mackay, 1995-2001.
Most League Goals in Season: 22: D. Adams, 1996-97.
Most League Goals (Overall): 44: Steven Ferguson, 1996-2002.

ROSS COUNTY 2002–03 LEAGUE RECORD

Match No.	Date	Venue	Opponents	Result		H/T Score	Lg. Pos.	Goalscorers	Attendance
1	Aug 3	A	Arbroath	W	3-0	1-0	—	Bone [43], Cowie [63], Ferguson [69]	761
2	10	H	Queen of the S	W	2-0	1-0	1	Ferguson [40], Wood [90]	2894
3	17	A	Ayr U	L	1-2	0-2	3	Gethins [85]	1692
4	24	A	Inverness CT	L	0-2	0-2	3		3699
5	31	H	Clyde	D	1-1	0-0	5	Canning [87]	2059
6	Sept 14	H	Falkirk	D	1-1	0-0	5	Gilbert [88]	2729
7	21	A	St Johnstone	D	1-1	0-1	6	Bayne [60]	2434
8	28	H	Alloa Ath	L	0-1	0-0	7		1921
9	Oct 5	A	St Mirren	D	1-1	1-1	7	Irvine [42]	3737
10	19	H	Arbroath	W	4-0	3-0	6	Mackay [2], Hislop 2 [3, 41], Robertson [75]	2065
11	26	A	Queen of the S	L	0-2	0-1	6		1533
12	Nov 2	A	Clyde	L	1-2	1-2	6	Canning [39]	1047
13	9	H	Inverness CT	L	0-2	0-2	7		5449
14	16	A	Falkirk	L	0-2	0-1	8		3255
15	23	H	St Johnstone	D	0-0	0-0	8		2614
16	30	A	Alloa Ath	D	1-1	1-0	8	Irvine [38]	445
17	Dec 7	H	St Mirren	W	4-0	1-0	8	Bayne 3 [45, 51, 81], Mackay [90]	2429
18	14	H	Ayr U	W	1-0	0-0	8	Bone [59]	2352
19	21	A	Arbroath	L	1-2	0-2	7	Hislop [86]	580
20	28	H	Clyde	D	1-1	1-0	7	Mackay [37]	2534
21	Jan 11	A	St Johnstone	L	0-2	0-1	7		2400
22	18	A	St Mirren	L	0-1	0-0	8		2366
23	Feb 1	H	Alloa Ath	L	1-2	0-2	8	Irvine [88]	2096
24	8	A	Ayr U	D	1-1	0-1	8	Robertson [53]	1486
25	25	A	Inverness CT	W	5-1	3-0	—	McLeish [13], Ferguson (pen) [19], Venetis [39], Robertson [48], Gethins [88]	3443
26	Mar 1	A	Clyde	L	0-1	0-1	8		980
27	8	H	Inverness CT	L	0-2	0-0	8		4621
28	11	H	Falkirk	L	0-1	0-1	—		2161
29	15	H	St Johnstone	L	2-3	0-2	8	Bayne [78], Ferguson [81]	2689
30	22	H	Queen of the S	L	0-3	0-1	8		1976
31	Apr 5	A	Falkirk	L	0-3	0-1	8		3523
32	12	A	Alloa Ath	L	1-2	1-1	8	Ferguson (pen) [27]	876
33	19	H	St Mirren	W	2-0	0-0	8	Ferguson [57], McGarry [78]	1967
34	26	H	Arbroath	W	3-1	2-1	8	Robertson [16], Winters [21], Bayne [75]	2206
35	May 3	A	Queen of the S	L	0-1	0-1	8		1810
36	10	H	Ayr U	W	4-1	0-0	8	McGarry 2 [47, 50], Higgins [59], Mackay [79]	3449

Final League Position: 8

Honours
League Champions: Third Division: 1998-99.

Club colours: Shirt: Navy blue, white and red pin stripe on collar and sleeves. Shorts: White with navy and red side stripe. Stockings: Navy.

Goalscorers: *League* (42): Bayne 6, Ferguson 6 (2 pens), Mackay 4, Robertson 4, Hislop 3, Irvine 3, McGarry 3, Bone 2, Canning 2, Gethins 2, Cowie 1, Gilbert 1, Higgins 1, McLeish 1, Venetis 1, Winters 1, Wood 1
Scottish Cup (1): Winters 1
CIS Cup (4): Bone 1,Cowie 1, McCulloch 1, own goal 1
Challenge Cup (4): Gethins 2, Webb 1, own goal 1

Bullock A 36	McCulloch M 34	Deas P 11 + 3	Perry M 19 + 1	Irvine B 31	Gilbert K 22 + 1	McGarry S 21 + 8	Ferguson S 18 + 3	Bone A 9 + 3	Cowie D 20 + 10	Mackay S 18 + 10	Bayne G 21 + 9	Wood M 7 + 4	Webb S 16 + 1	Gethins C 5 + 12	Canning B 23 + 2	Robertson H 30 + 2	Campbell C 3 + 3	Hislop S 9 + 5	Higgins S 5 + 3	Davidson G — + 2	Lynch P — + 1	McLeish K 10 + 2	Winters D 6 + 6	Venetis T 7 + 2	Tait J 9 + 1	Hannah D 6	Bolochoweckyj M — + 1	Match No.
1	2	3	4	5	6	7^{2}	8	9	10	11^{1}	12	13																1
1	2	12	4	5	6	7	8	14	10	11^{2}		13	3^{1}	9^{3}														2
1	2	3^{1}	4	5^{3}	6	7	8	14	10^{2}	12		9		13	11													3
1	2		4		6■	14	8^{2}		13	7	9^{3}	12	3^{1}	10	5	11												4
1	6		4	5		7^{2}		9	10	3^{1}	13	8		12	2	11												5
1	8		4	5	6	11		9			7	10^{1}		12	2	3												6
1	8		4	5	6	11^{2}	12	9		14	7^{3}	10^{1}		13	2	3												7
1	8		4	5	6	13		9^{3}	10		7^{2}	11^{1}		14	2	3	12											8
1	8	12	4	5	6	7^{2}			10	3^{1}				13	2	11		9										9
1	8	13	4	5	6	9				3	7^{3}			14	2	11^{2}		10^{1}	12									10
1	8	4		5	6	7^{2}			11^{3}	12					2	3		10	9^{1}	13	14							11
1	6	5	4			13	8^{2}		11		7	9			2	3		10^{1}		12								12
1	6	5	4			12	8		10	11		7^{1}			2	3		9										13
1	6	3^{3}	4	5		7^{2}	8	12	10	11	13				2	14		9^{1}										14
1	6		4	5		7^{2}	8^{1}	9	10	3	13				2	11		12										15
1	6		4	5		7	8		10^{1}	3	9				2	11		12										16
1	8	3	6	5	4^{1}	7		10^{2}	12	14	9				2	11^{3}		13										17
1	8^{3}	3		5	4	7		10^{2}	13	14	9^{1}		6		2	11		12										18
1	8^{1}	3	6	5	4	7^{2}	14	10	12		9				2	11^{3}		13										19
1		3	8	5	4	12			7^{1}	11	9		6		2			10										20
1		3	8^{2}	5	4				14	11^{1}	9		6		2	12		10				7^{3}	13					21
1	8		12	5	4				13		9^{3}		6■		2^{1}	3		10				11	14	7^{2}				22
1	8^{1}			5	4	9			12	13					6	3			14			7	11^{3}	10^{2}	2			23
1	4			5	2	7^{1}			10^{3}	14	9		6			3						11^{2}	12	13	8			24
1	4			5		12	8^{3}		10	14	9^{1}		6	13		3						11		7^{2}	2			25
1	4			5	14		8^{3}		10	12	9		6	13		3^{1}						11		7^{2}	2			26
1	4			5	2^{1}	7^{2}			10		9		6	13	12	3			14			11^{3}			8			27
1	4			5	8				14	10^{3}	9		6	13	12	3						11^{1}	7^{2}		2■			28
1	4			5	7^{2}	12	8		10	13	14		6	9^{3}	2	3								11^{1}				29
1	4			5	7^{1}	10^{2}	8^{3}		12	11	9				6	3							13	14	2			30
1	6			5			13		8		9^{3}		4^{2}			3	12					11	14	7	2^{1}	10		31
1	4			5		7^{2}	8		10^{3}		9	12	2	13		3							14	11^{1}		6		32
1	4			5		12	8^{2}			3	14			10^{3}		11	2		9^{1}			13	7			6		33
1	4						8^{3}			3	13		5	10^{1}		11	2		9^{2}			12	7			6	14	34
1	4			5^{1}			8			3	14		13			11	2		9^{3}			10^{2}	7		12	6		35
1	4					10^{3}	8		14	3	13		5			11	12		9^{2}				7^{1}		2	6		36

ST JOHNSTONE First Division

Year Formed: 1884. *Ground & Address:* McDiarmid Park, Crieff Road, Perth PH1 2SJ. *Telephone:* 01738 459090. *Fax:* 01738 625 771. *Clubcall:* 0898 121559. *Website:* www.stjohnstonefc.co.uk
Ground Capacity: all seated: 10,673. *Size of Pitch:* 115yd × 75yd.
Chairman: G.S. Brown. *Secretary and Managing Director:* Stewart Duff. *Sales Executive:* Susan Weir.
Manager: Billy Stark. *Coach:* Mixu Paatelainen. *Physio:* Nick Summersgill. *Youth Development Officer:* Alistair Stevenson. *Youth Co-ordinator:* Tommy Campbell.
Managers since 1975: J. Stewart, J. Storrie, A. Stuart, A. Rennie, I. Gibson, A. Totten, J. McClelland, P. Sturrock, S. Clark.
Club Nickname(s): Saints. *Previous Grounds:* Recreation Grounds, Muirton Park.
Record Attendance: (McDiarmid Park): 10,545 v Dundee, Premier Division; 23 May, 1999.
Record Transfer Fee received: £1,750,000 for Calum Davidson to Blackburn R (March 1998).
Record Transfer Fee paid: £300,000 for Billy Dodds from Dundee (1994).
Record Victory: 9-0 v Albion R, League Cup; 9 March, 1946.
Record Defeat: 1-10 v Third Lanark, Scottish Cup; 24 January, 1903.
Most Capped Player: Nick Dasovic, 17, Canada.
Most League Appearances: 298: Drew Rutherford.
Most League Goals in Season (Individual): 36: Jimmy Benson, Division II; 1931-32.
Most Goals Overall (Individual): 140: John Brogan, 1977-83.

ST JOHNSTONE 2002–03 LEAGUE RECORD

Match No.	Date	Venue	Opponents	Result		H/T Score	Lg. Pos.	Goalscorers	Attendance
1	Aug 3	A	St Mirren	W	2-0	1-0	—	Parker 17, Hartley 53	3376
2	10	H	Inverness CT	W	1-0	0-0	3	McCaffrey (og) 82	3770
3	17	A	Queen of the S	D	0-0	0-0	2		3137
4	24	A	Arbroath	W	1-0	1-0	2	Hartley 29	1467
5	31	H	Alloa Ath	W	2-0	2-0	2	McCann 13, Connolly 41	2274
6	Sept 14	A	Ayr U	D	0-0	0-0	2		2320
7	21	H	Ross Co	D	1-1	1-0	2	McCann 30	2434
8	28	A	Falkirk	L	0-1	0-0	2		5872
9	Oct 5	H	Clyde	L	0-1	0-1	3		2037
10	19	H	St Mirren	W	2-0	2-0	3	Hartley 40, Hay 41	2457
11	26	A	Inverness CT	L	1-2	0-1	3	Hay (pen) 87	2541
12	Nov 2	A	Alloa Ath	W	3-1	1-1	3	Hay 2 25, 71, Connolly 47	952
13	9	H	Arbroath	W	2-0	1-0	3	Hay 2, Hartley 89	1994
14	16	H	Ayr U	L	0-2	0-1	4		1943
15	23	A	Ross Co	D	0-0	0-0	4		2614
16	30	H	Falkirk	L	0-1	0-0	4		3696
17	Dec 7	A	Clyde	W	2-1	1-0	4	Hay 13, Lovenkrands 75	1367
18	14	H	Queen of the S	D	2-2	0-1	4	McCann 88, Reilly 90	1948
19	28	H	Alloa Ath	W	3-0	0-0	4	Seaton (og) 76, Forsyth 82, Lovenkrands 84	2090
20	Jan 1	A	Arbroath	W	3-2	0-1	—	Maxwell 61, Lovenkrands 71, Connolly 79	1252
21	11	H	Ross Co	W	2-0	1-0	3	Hay 32, Forsyth 51	2400
22	18	H	Clyde	L	1-2	1-1	4	Connolly 5	2455
23	Feb 1	A	Falkirk	D	1-1	1-0	3	Hartley 25	4694
24	8	A	Queen of the S	W	2-1	0-1	3	Robertson M 77, Noble 87	1862
25	15	H	Inverness CT	W	2-0	0-0	2	Hay 2 86, 90	2631
26	Mar 1	A	Alloa Ath	W	2-1	1-1	2	Dods 25, Connolly 66	884
27	4	A	Ayr U	W	1-0	0-0	—	Dods 75	1690
28	8	H	Arbroath	W	2-1	1-1	2	MacDonald 22, Murray 90	1938
29	15	A	Ross Co	W	3-2	2-0	2	Noble 2 16, 38, Hartley 67	2689
30	22	A	St Mirren	W	3-1	2-0	2	Maxwell 12, MacDonald 20, Dods 75	2369
31	Apr 5	H	Ayr U	W	1-0	1-0	2	MacDonald 5	2123
32	12	H	Falkirk	L	0-1	0-0	2		6579
33	19	A	Clyde	L	1-2	1-2	3	MacDonald 30	1143
34	26	H	St Mirren	D	1-1	0-1	3	Noble 72	1819
35	May 3	A	Inverness CT	W	2-1	1-1	3	Maxwell 15, Reilly 57	1814
36	10	H	Queen of the S	L	0-1	0-0	3		1796

Final League Position: 3

Honours
League Champions: First Division 1982-83, 1989-90, 1996-97. Division II 1923-24, 1959-60, 1962-63; *Runners-up:* Division II 1931-32. Second Division 1987-88.
Scottish Cup: Semi-finals 1934, 1968, 1989, 1991.
League Cup Runners-up: 1969, 1998.
League Challenge Cup Runners-up: 1996-97.

European: *UEFA Cup:* 10 matches (1971-72, 1999-2000).

Club colours: Shirt: Royal blue with white trim. Shorts: White. Stockings: Royal blue with white hoops.

Goalscorers: *League* (49): Hay 9 (1 pen), Hartley 6, Connolly 5, MacDonald 4, Noble 4, Dods 3, Lovenkrands 3, McCann 3, Maxwell 3, Forsyth 2, Reilly 2, Murray 1, Parker 1, Robertson M 1, own goals 2
Scottish Cup (2): Baxter 1, Connolly 1
CIS Cup (3): Hay 2, McCulloch 1
Challenge Cup (5): MacDonald 2, McCann 1, Murray 1, Stevenson 1

Cuthbert K 22	Robertson J 26	McCulloch M 14 + 4	McCluskey S 15	Murray G 33	Maxwell I 34	McCann R 13 + 4	Reilly M 32	Hartley P 33	Connolly P 27 + 8	Parker K 17 + 14	Russell C 2 + 6	Stevenson R 2 + 12	Dods D 20 + 2	MacDonald P 9 + 4	Lovenkrands T 16 + 3	Hay C 13 + 11	Main A 14	Ferry M 4 + 4	McClune D 3 + 3	Weir J 2	Baxter M 15 + 3	Panther E 3 + 1	Forsyth R 7 + 5	Robertson M 10	Noble S 8 + 5	Malone E 2 + 1	Maher M — + 2	*Match No.*
1	2	3	4	5	6	7^{2}	8	9^{3}	10^{1}	11	12	13	14															1
1	2	3^{1}	4	5	6	7^{3}	8	9	10^{2}	11	12	14		13														2
1	2		4	5	6	7^{1}	8	9	10^{2}	11^{3}	14	12		13	3													3
1	2		4	5	6	7^{2}	8	9	10	11^{1}	14	13		12	3^{3}													4
1	2		4^{3}	5	6	7	8^{2}	9	10	14	12	13		11	3^{1}													5
1	2	14	4	5	6	7^{2}	8	9	10	12	11^{1}	13			3^{3}													6
1	2	3	4	5	6	7^{1}	8	9	10^{2}	12	11^{3}	14				13												7
1	2	3	4	5	6	7^{1}	8	9^{3}	10	12	13	14				11^{2}												8
	2	3	4	5	6	7^{1}	8	9^{3}	10^{2}	13		12				11	1	14										9
	2	3	4	5	6		8	9	13	11		7^{2}				10^{1}	1	12										10
	2	3^{3}	4	7	6	14	8^{1}	9	13	11		10^{2}	5			12	1											11
	2			3	6	4	8	9	10^{1}	11^{2}		12	5			7	1	13										12
	2^{2}			3	6	4^{1}	8	9	10^{3}	14			5		12	7	1	11	13									13
			5	3	6	4^{1}	8	9■		11		13			12	7	1	10^{2}	2									14
				3	6		8		12	9			4		11	7	1	10^{1}	2	5								15
				3		4^{2}	8		12	9^{1}		14	6		11	7	1			5■	2	10^{3}	13					16
				5	6	13	8	9	12				4		11	7^{1}	1				2	10^{2}	3					17
	2			4	6	13	8^{3}	9	14	12			5^{2}		11	7	1					10^{1}	3					18
	2^{3}	4		5	6	13	8^{1}	9	12	10					11^{2}	7	1				14		3					19
	2	4		5	6		8	9	12	10					11	7^{1}	1						3					20
	2	4		5	6^{2}		8	9	7^{1}	10^{3}			13		11	12	1				14		3					21
	2	4^{2}		5	6		8^{3}	9	7^{1}	10					11	12	1				14	13	3					22
1	2			3	6		8	9	10^{2}	12			5		11^{1}						7			4	13			23
1	3	12		5	6		8^{1}	9	10	14					11^{3}	7^{2}					2			4	13			24
1	3			8	6			9	10	12^{2}			5		11^{1}	13					2			4	7			25
1		3		4	6			9	10				5	12	11^{1}				7		2			8				26
1		3		4	6			9	10	11^{1}			5	7^{2}					13		2			8	12			27
1		3^{1}		4	6			9	10	14			5	7		13					2		12	8^{3}	11^{2}			28
1				3	6		8^{1}	9	10				5	7^{2}		13			12		2			4	11			29
1		13		3	6		8	9^{2}	10				5	7^{1}	12	14					2			4	11^{3}			30
1				3	6		8	9	10	13			5	7^{2}		12					2			4	11^{1}			31
1	11^{1}	14		3	6		8^{2}	9	10				5	7		13					2			4^{3}	12			32
1	3^{3}			4	6		8	9^{2}	10	13			5	7		12					2		14		11^{1}			33
1	2^{3}		4		6		8		10	12			5^{2}	9^{1}				11			7		3		14	13		34
1	2		4		6		8	9	10^{2}	7			5										12		11	3^{1}	13	35
1	6^{2}		4				8^{3}	9	10^{1}	7			5					14			2		12		11	3	13	36

ST MIRREN

First Division

Year Formed: 1877. *Ground & Address:* St Mirren Park, Love St, Paisley PA3 2EJ. *Telephone:* 0141 889 2558/0141 840 1337. *Fax:* 0141 848 6444.
Ground Capacity: 10,866 (all seated). *Size of Pitch:* 112yd × 73yd.
Chairman: Stewart Gilmour. *Vice-Chairman:* George Campbell. *Secretary:* Allan Marshall.
Manager: John Coughlin. *Assistant Manager:* Gus MacPherson. *Youth Development Officer:* Arthur Bell.
Managers since 1975: Alex Ferguson, Jim Clunie, Rikki MacFarlane, Alex Miller, Alex Smith, Tony Fitzpatrick, David Hay, Jimmy Bone, Tony Fitzpatrick, Tom Hendrie. *Club Nickname(s):* The Buddies. *Previous Grounds:* Short Roods 1877-79, Thistle Park Greenhill 1879-83, Westmarch 1883-94.
Record Attendance: 47,438 v Celtic, League Cup, 20 Aug, 1949.
Record Transfer Fee received: £850,000 for Ian Ferguson to Rangers (1988).
Record Transfer Fee paid: £400,000 for Thomas Stickroth from Bayer Uerdingen (1990).
Record Victory: 15-0 v Glasgow University, Scottish Cup 1st rd; 30 Jan, 1960.
Record Defeat: 0-9 v Rangers, Division I; 4 Dec, 1897.
Most Capped Player: Godmundor Torfason, 29, Iceland.
Most League Appearances: 351: Tony Fitzpatrick, 1973-88.
Most League Goals in Season (Individual): 45: Dunky Walker, Division I; 1921-22.
Most Goals Overall (Individual): 221: David McCrae, 1923-34.

ST MIRREN 2002–03 LEAGUE RECORD

Match No.	Date	Venue	Opponents	Result		H/T Score	Lg. Pos.	Goalscorers	Attendance
1	Aug 3	H	St Johnstone	L	0-2	0-1	—		3376
2	10	A	Falkirk	L	0-2	0-2	10		4360
3	17	H	Alloa Ath	W	3-1	1-1	8	Gillies 8, Cameron 81, Mackenzie 90	3104
4	24	A	Clyde	W	3-2	2-0	6	Mendes 3 25, 29, 90	1814
5	31	H	Inverness CT	L	0-4	0-3	6		2485
6	Sept 14	A	Arbroath	D	2-2	1-1	6	Cameron 45, Gillies 65	1008
7	21	H	Queen of the S	W	2-1	1-1	5	Cameron 19, Weatherson (og) 84	2492
8	28	A	Ayr U	D	1-1	0-1	5	Cameron 60	2489
9	Oct 5	H	Ross Co	D	1-1	1-1	6	Mendes 39	3737
10	19	A	St Johnstone	L	0-2	0-2	7		2457
11	26	H	Falkirk	D	4-4	0-3	7	Robb 53, Cameron 3 (1 pen) 58, 66, 86 (p)	3661
12	Nov 2	A	Inverness CT	L	1-4	0-2	7	Gillies 84	2023
13	9	H	Clyde	L	1-4	1-0	8	Robb 25	2703
14	16	H	Arbroath	W	2-0	2-0	6	Robb 18, Mendes 21	3021
15	23	A	Queen of the S	L	0-3	0-2	7		2663
16	30	H	Ayr U	W	1-0	1-0	7	Mendes 38	2426
17	Dec 7	A	Ross Co	L	0-4	0-1	7		2429
18	14	A	Alloa Ath	W	3-2	0-1	7	Gillies (pen) 71, Cameron 2 73, 84	783
19	28	H	Inverness CT	L	1-4	0-3	8	Cameron 86	3054
20	Jan 1	A	Clyde	L	2-3	1-2	—	Gillies 14, Broadfoot 47	1553
21	18	H	Ross Co	W	1-0	0-0	7	Cameron 60	2366
22	Feb 1	A	Ayr U	D	0-0	0-0	6		2738
23	8	H	Alloa Ath	D	1-1	0-1	6	Roberts 80	2105
24	15	A	Falkirk	L	1-3	0-1	6	Denham 55	4094
25	22	H	Queen of the S	D	2-2	1-0	6	McLean 16, Gillies 53	1888
26	Mar 1	A	Inverness CT	L	1-3	1-1	7	McHale 13	1973
27	8	H	Clyde	L	1-2	0-0	7	Roberts 20	2683
28	15	A	Queen of the S	W	2-0	1-0	7	Gillies 4, Denham 87	1911
29	22	H	St Johnstone	L	1-3	0-2	7	Gillies 60	2369
30	29	A	Arbroath	D	1-1	1-0	7	Roberts 4	509
31	Apr 5	H	Arbroath	W	1-0	1-0	7	Cameron 13	2122
32	12	H	Ayr U	D	1-1	0-1	7	McKenna 84	2248
33	19	A	Ross Co	L	0-2	0-0	7		1967
34	26	A	St Johnstone	D	1-1	1-0	7	Gillies (pen) 26	1819
35	May 3	H	Falkirk	L	1-2	0-1	7	McGinty 63	3062
36	10	A	Alloa Ath	L	0-4	0-2	7		1084

Final League Position: 7

Honours
League Champions: First Division 1976-77, 1999-2000. Division II 1967-68; *Runners-up:* 1935-36.
Scottish Cup Winners: 1926, 1959, 1987. *Runners-up:* 1908, 1934, 1962.
League Cup Runners-up: 1955-56.
B&Q Cup Runners-up: 1993-94. *Victory Cup:* 1919-20. *Summer Cup:* 1943-44. *Anglo-Scottish Cup:* 1979-80.

European: *Cup Winners' Cup:* 4 matches (1987-88). *UEFA Cup:* 10 matches (1980-81, 1983-84, 1985-86).

Club colours: Shirt: Black and white vertical stripes. Shorts: White with black trim. Stockings: White with 2 black hoops. Change colours: Predominantly red.

Goalscorers: *League* (42): Cameron 12 (1 pen), Gillies 9 (2 pens), Mendes 6, Robb 3, Roberts 3, Denham 2, Broadfoot 1, McGinty 1, McHale 1, McKenna 1, Mackenzie 1, McLean 1, own goal 1
Scottish Cup (0)
CIS Cup (4): Cameron 2, Lappin 1, Yardley 1
Challenge Cup (13): Cameron 5, Gillies 3, Baltacha 1, Fellner 1, Guy 1, McGinty 1, Ross 1

Roy L 21	Rudden P 11 + 5	Kerr C 9 + 11	McGowan J 13 + 1	Robb R 18 + 1	Dow A 5 + 5	Gillies R 33	Mackenzie S 1 + 1	McGinty B 23 + 2	Cameron M 28	Ross I 20	Lappin S 27 + 7	Guy G 15 + 6	Yardley M 5 + 7	Baltacha S 5	Mendes J 15 + 2	Murray H 13 + 2	Fellner G 1	Lowing D 14 + 9	Robertson K 14	Dietrich K 1	Dunbar J 7 + 16	Broadfoot K 21 + 2	Jack D — + 1	Baker M 10	Denham G 15	Dempsie M 9	Mitchell A 10 + 2	McHale P 12 + 1	McLean S 6 + 1	Roberts M 12 + 2	Ferguson J — + 2	Muir A 1 + 2	McKenna D — + 4	Bald W 1	McWilliam G — + 1	Match No.
1	2^2	3	4	5	6^1	7	8	9	10^3	11	12	13	14																							1
1		12	4	5^1	3	7		9^3	10	6	11^2	8	14	2	13																					2
1		3	5		6^2	7■	13	9^1	10	11	12	4		2	8																					3
1	13	3		7^2	6^1			9	10^3	11			14	2	8	4	5	12																		4
		3		12		4		9^1	10	11		7^3	14	2	8	6		13	1	5^2																5
1		6		5		8		9	10^1	11	3^2	2	12	4	13	7																				6
1	4	6		5		8			9	10	3^2	2^1	11			7		13			12															7
1	5^1	14		4		8		13	9	10	3^3	12	11^2			7■		6			2															8
1	4					7^2		11	9	8	3	13	12		10^1			6			2	5														9
1	4	14		5^1		7		11^3	9	8	3				10	13		6			2^2	12														10
1	4	13		5	14	7^3		11^2	9	8	3	12			10			6			2^1															11
	4	13		5	12	7		11	9	8	3^2	2^1			10^3			6	1		14															12
1		14		5	12	7		11	9^2	8	3	2^1			10^3			6			13	4														13
1	13			4^2		7		11	9	8	3	2			10^1			6			12	5														14
		6			10	7		11^1	9	8	3^2	2						5	1		12	4	13													15
				4		7			9	6	12	2	11^1		10	8^2		3	1		13	5														16
	13	12		4		7				6	9^1	2	11		10	8^2		3	1			5														17
		13	4		14	7			9^3	6	12	2	11^1		10^2	8		3■	1			5														18
1		14	4^1	2^2		7			9	6	11^3	8			10						13	12		3	5											19
1	2^1				13	7			9	11	6^2	8^3	12		10			14				4		3	5											20
1		12				7			9		11^1	2			10^2	8					13			3	5	4	6									21
1				2				9			11					8								3	5	4	6	7	10^1	12						22
1				2		7		11^1			13					8		14						3^3	5	4	6^2	12	9	10						23
	3					7		12			11^3							14	1		13	6			5	4	2^2	8	9	10^1						24
	2^1					7		11			3							13	1		12	6			5	4		8	9	10^2						25
			14			7		11			12							3^1	1		13	6			5^3	4	2	8	9^2	10						26
			2			7		9^1			11								1		12	4		3	5		6	8		10						27
1			2			7		11	9^1		13										14	4		3	5		6^2	8	12	10^3						28
1			2			7			9^1		11	14				13					12	4		3^3	5		6^2	8		10						29
1			2			7					11					6		12			9^2	4		3^1	5			8		10	13					30
1		3	2			7			9		11	14				6^2					12	4			5		13	8^3		10^1						31
	12	3				7^2		6^3	9		11								1		10^1	4			5	2		8				13	14			32
	14	13	2					7	9		11								1			4			5^2	3	6	8^3	10^1	12						33
			2			7		6^2	9		11							14	1			4		3		5	12	8^3		10^1			13			34
			5	2		7		8	9		11							3^2	1		12	4					6^3			10^1		14	13			35
	2			5		7			9^1		11							3^2			8	4^3								10	13	6	12	1	14	36

STENHOUSEMUIR Second Division

Year Formed: 1884. *Ground & Address:* Ochilview Park, Gladstone Rd, Stenhousemuir FK5 5QL. *Telephone:* 01324 562992. *Fax:* 01324 562980.
Ground Capacity: total: 2374, seated: 626. *Size of Pitch:* 110yd × 72yd.
Chairman: Mike Laing. *Secretary:* David O. Reid. *Commercial Manager:* Jock Rolland.
Manager: John McVeigh. *Assistant Manager:* Andy Smith. *Physio:* Alain Davidson.
Managers since 1975: H. Glasgow, J. Black, A. Rose, W. Henderson, A. Rennie, J. Meakin, D. Lawson, T. Christie, G. Armstrong, Brian Fairley.
Club Nickname(s): The Warriors. *Previous Grounds:* Tryst Ground 1884-86, Goschen Park 1886-90.
Record Attendance: 12,500 v East Fife, Scottish Cup 4th rd; 11 Mar, 1950.
Record Transfer Fee received: £70,000 for Euan Donaldson to St Johnstone (May 1995).
Record Transfer Fee paid: £20,000 to Livingston for Ian Little (June 1995).
Record Victory: 9-2 v Dundee U, Division II; 19 Apr, 1937.
Record Defeat: 2-11 v Dunfermline Ath. Division II; 27 Sept, 1930.
Most League Appearances: 360: Archie Rose.
Most League Goals in Season (Individual): 32: Robert Taylor, Division II; 1925-26.

STENHOUSEMUIR 2002–03 LEAGUE RECORD

Match No.	Date	Venue	Opponents	Result		H/T Score	Lg. Pos.	Goalscorers	Attendance
1	Aug 3	H	Dumbarton	D	2-2	0-0	—	Booth 2 (1 pen) [55, 72 (p)]	437
2	10	A	Forfar Ath	L	0-1	0-0	9		492
3	17	H	Berwick R	W	2-0	1-0	4	Sandison [34], McFarlane [73]	379
4	24	H	Stranraer	W	2-0	1-0	1	McFarlane [39], McKenzie [72]	295
5	31	A	Raith R	L	0-1	0-0	4		1661
6	Sept 14	H	Hamilton A	L	1-2	1-1	7	McCormick [22]	463
7	21	A	Cowdenbeath	L	0-1	0-1	10		340
8	28	H	Airdrie U	W	4-3	3-0	7	Donnelly [6], Graham [21], Waldie [26], Murphy S [81]	842
9	Oct 5	A	Brechin C	L	0-1	0-1	9		489
10	19	H	Forfar Ath	W	2-1	1-1	5	Crawford [33], McFarlane [64]	295
11	26	A	Dumbarton	D	0-0	0-0	7		815
12	Nov 2	H	Raith R	L	0-1	0-0	8		1066
13	9	A	Stranraer	L	1-2	1-2	10	Graham [34]	411
14	16	A	Hamilton A	W	3-2	1-2	6	Booth [21], Harty [51], Coulter [76]	1226
15	23	H	Cowdenbeath	W	4-1	1-1	5	Booth 2 [31, 61], Coulter [60], Crawford [87]	377
16	30	H	Brechin C	D	1-1	0-0	5	Murphy S [78]	331
17	Dec 14	A	Airdrie U	L	0-2	0-0	7		1228
18	28	A	Berwick R	D	2-2	0-0	7	Booth [66], Wilson [85]	543
19	Jan 1	H	Stranraer	W	1-0	0-0	—	Booth [87]	356
20	18	H	Hamilton A	D	2-2	1-1	6	Booth [33], McCormick [63]	581
21	25	H	Dumbarton	W	2-1	1-0	3	Booth [1], McFarlane [67]	460
22	Feb 8	H	Airdrie U	D	3-3	2-2	6	McCormick [21], McFarlane [28], Coulter [65]	954
23	22	A	Forfar Ath	D	3-3	1-1	6	Wilson [34], McFarlane [80], Waldie [90]	449
24	25	A	Cowdenbeath	D	3-3	1-0	—	McKenzie (pen) [34], McFarlane [50], McCormick [51]	258
25	Mar 1	H	Berwick R	W	1-0	0-0	3	Crawford [85]	684
26	15	H	Raith R	L	1-3	1-1	7	McFarlane [1]	929
27	22	H	Cowdenbeath	D	1-1	0-0	8	Donnelly [82]	488
28	26	A	Raith R	W	1-0	1-0	—	Stein [32]	1627
29	29	A	Brechin C	L	1-2	0-2	6	Crawford [62]	435
30	Apr 5	A	Hamilton A	W	1-0	0-0	4	Crawford [66]	1247
31	8	A	Stranraer	W	1-0	0-0	—	Harty [83]	321
32	12	H	Brechin C	D	2-2	1-0	4	Harty [4], Crawford [57]	510
33	19	A	Airdrie U	L	0-1	0-0	4		1468
34	26	A	Dumbarton	L	1-3	1-2	6	Crawford [16]	906
35	May 3	H	Forfar Ath	L	1-4	0-2	6	Graham [88]	497
36	10	A	Berwick R	D	0-0	0-0	7		579

Final League Position: 7

Honours

League Champions: Third Division runners-up: 1998-99. *Scottish Cup:* Semi-finals 1902-03. Quarter-finals 1948-49, 1949-50, 1994-95. *League Cup:* Quarter-finals 1947-48, 1960-61, 1975-76. *League Challenge Cup:* Winners 1995-96.

Club colours: Shirt: Maroon. Shorts: White. Stockings: Maroon.

Goalscorers: *League* (49): Booth 9 (1 pen), McFarlane 8, Crawford 7, McCormick 4, Coulter 3, Graham 3, Harty 3, Donnelly 2, McKenzie 2 (1 pen), Murphy S 2, Waldie 2, Wilson 2, Sandison 1, Stein 1
Scottish Cup (5): Coulter 1, Crawford 1, Graham 1, McCormick 1, McFarlane 1
CIS Cup (3): Crawford 1, McCormick 1, Waldie 1
Challenge Cup (1): Wilson 1

Gillespie A 1	Forrest F 5	Easton S 34	Hamilton S 26 + 5	McKenzie J 21 + 6	Booth M 28 + 1	Waldie C 28 + 2	Donnelly K 7 + 5	McCormick S 29 + 4	McFarlane D 23 + 4	Stein J 34 + 2	Harty M 8 + 12	Graham D 11 + 19	Smith G 32	McMillan A 1	McKenna G 30 + 1	Wilson M 18 + 3	Crawford B 16 + 10	Sandison J 8	Murphy S 6 + 13	Stone M 6 + 2	Coulter R 14 + 5	Armstrong M 1	Martin C 3 + 1	Carlin A 3	Carr D 1 + 3	McGowan M 2	*Match No.*
1	2	3	4	5	6	7	8^{1}	9^{2}	10	11	12	13															1
		8	4	5	6		14	9^{1}	10^{3}	11	13		1	2	3	7^{2}	12										2
		2	4	5	6	7		9^{2}	10	11			1		3		13	8^{1}	12								3
		8	4	5	6^{2}	7		9^{1}	10^{3}	11		14	1		3		12		13	2							4
		8^{1}	4	5	6^{3}	7		9	10^{2}	11		14	1		3		13		12	2							5
		8	4	5^{3}	6	7^{1}		10	13	11			1		3	12	9^{2}			2	14						6
		6^{1}	4	5^{2}		7		9	10^{3}	12	11	14	1		3	8			13	2							7
		5	4	14		7^{3}	6^{1}	9	13	11		10^{2}	1		3	8			12		2						8
		6	4	5		7			10^{2}	11^{3}		9	1		3	8^{1}	13		12	14	2						9
		2	4	5	6^{2}	7			10^{3}	11	13	14	1		3^{1}		9		8		12						10
		2	4	5	6	7		12	10^{1}	11	13	14	1		3		9^{3}		8^{2}								11
		3		5■	8	7		10^{3}		11	14	13	1		4		9^{2}		12		2	6^{1}					12
		5	4^{3}		6	7		10^{1}		11	13	8	1		3		9^{2}		12	14	2						13
		5	4^{3}		6^{2}	7		10	12	11	13	8^{1}	1		3					9	2		14				14
		5	4		6	7		9^{1}	10	11	12	8^{2}	1				13			3	2						15
		5	4		6		13		10	11	7	8^{2}	1		3		9^{1}		12		2						16
		5	4^{3}	14	6	7		12	10	11		8^{2}	1		3		9^{1}		13		2						17
		2	12	14	6	7		9^{3}	10	11	8^{2}				3	13			5				4^{1}	1			18
		5	4	14	6		12	9^{3}	10^{2}	11		8^{1}	1		3	7	13				2						19
	2	3	4	5	6	7		9^{2}	10^{1}	11		12	1			8									13		20
	2	3	4	5	6^{1}		8^{2}	9	10	11	13	14	1			7			12^{3}								21
	2^{1}	3	4	5				9	10	11		13	1			8			6^{2}		12					7	22
	2		4	5	6^{2}	12		9	10	11^{3}		14	1		3	8			13							7^{1}	23
				5	6	7		9	10	11		12	1		3	8^{2}		4^{1}	13		2						24
		5		12	6	7		9^{1}	10^{2}	11		8			3	4	13				2			1			25
		5	12		6	7		9^{2}	10	11		8^{1}			3	4^{3}	13				2■			1	14		26
		2			6^{2}	7	12	9		11^{3}	14	13	1		3	8	10	4	5^{1}								27
		2	5		6^{1}	7	8^{2}	9		11	13	14	1		3	12	10^{3}	4									28
		2	5^{3}			7	6^{1}	9		11^{2}	13	14	1		3	8	10	4			12						29
		2	14	5^{2}		7		9	10^{1}	11	6		1		3	8	12	4^{3}			13						30
		2	13	5^{3}		7		9^{1}	12	11	6	14	1		3	8	10	4^{2}									31
		2	4		6	7		12	10^{1}	11^{2}	8	13	1		3	5	9										32
		2		13	6	7		10^{3}		12	11	8^{1}	1		3	5^{2}	9						4		14		33
		2	4	5	12		6^{2}	14		11	7■		1		13		9				3		8^{1}		10^{3}		34
		8	4	5	6	7^{2}	13	10		11		12	1		3		9^{1}				2						35
		2^{3}	14	7	6	13	8^{2}	10^{1}		11		12	1		3		9	4	5								36

STIRLING ALBION Third Division

Year Formed: 1945. *Ground & Address:* Forthbank Stadium, Springkerse Industrial Estate, Stirling FK7 7UJ. *Telephone:* 01786 450399. *Fax:* 01786 448592.
Ground Capacity: 3808, seated: 2508. *Size of Pitch:* 110yd × 74yd.
Chairman: Peter McKenzie. *Secretary:* Mrs Marlyn Hallam.
Player/Coach: Allan Moore. *Physio:* Michael McLaughlan.
Managers since 1975: A. Smith, G. Peebles, J. Fleeting, J. Brogan, K. Drinkell, J. Philliben. *Club Nickname(s):* The Binos.
Previous Grounds: Annfield 1945-92.
Record Attendance: 26,400 (at Annfield) v Celtic, Scottish Cup 4th rd; 14 Mar, 1959. 3808 v Aberdeen, Scottish Cup 4th rd, 15 February 1996 (Forthbank).
Record Transfer Fee received: £70,000 for John Philliben to Doncaster R (Mar 1984).
Record Transfer Fee paid: £25,000 for Craig Taggart from Falkirk (Aug 1994).
Record Victory: 20-0 v Selkirk, Scottish Cup 1st rd; 8 Dec, 1984.
Record Defeat: 0-9 v Dundee U, Division I; 30 Dec, 1967.
Most League Appearances: 504: Matt McPhee, 1967-81.
Most League Goals in Season (Individual): 27: Joe Hughes, Division II; 1969-70.
Most Goals Overall (Individual): 129: Billy Steele, 1971-83.

STIRLING ALBION 2002–03 LEAGUE RECORD

Match No.	Date	Venue	Opponents	Result		H/T Score	Lg. Pos.	Goalscorers	Attendance
1	Aug 3	H	Albion R	L	0-1	0-1	—		579
2	10	A	Morton	L	1-5	1-3	—	Reilly 7	1757
3	17	H	Elgin C	D	1-1	1-1	9	Mallan 27	428
4	24	H	East Stirling	W	3-0	0-0	6	Mallan 2 (1 pen) 54 (p), 69, Rowe 68	434
5	31	A	Peterhead	L	0-1	0-0	8		500
6	Sept 14	H	Montrose	D	1-1	0-0	8	Nicholas 82	439
7	21	A	East Fife	D	1-1	1-0	8	Mallan 15	588
8	28	A	Gretna	W	2-0	2-0	7	McKinnon 14, Nicholas 34	402
9	Oct 5	H	Queen's Park	W	1-0	1-0	7	McKinnon 34	579
10	19	H	Morton	W	2-0	0-0	5	O'Brien 65, Nicholas 86	1089
11	26	A	Albion R	W	3-1	1-1	4	Nicholas (pen) 22, O'Brien 78, Mallan 79	489
12	Nov 2	H	Peterhead	W	1-0	1-0	4	O'Brien 11	686
13	9	A	East Stirling	D	1-1	0-0	5	Nicholas (pen) 51	548
14	16	A	Montrose	D	1-1	1-1	4	Johnson (og) 27	364
15	23	H	East Fife	D	0-0	0-0	5		808
16	30	A	Queen's Park	W	1-0	1-0	5	McKinnon 44	657
17	Dec 14	H	Gretna	L	0-1	0-1	5		412
18	28	A	Elgin C	W	3-0	2-0	5	Dunn 18, O'Brien 20, Reilly S 81	556
19	Jan 1	H	East Stirling	W	2-1	2-1	—	Dunn 3, Hay 23	593
20	18	H	Montrose	D	1-1	0-0	5	McLellan 85	524
21	Feb 8	A	Gretna	D	0-0	0-0	5		292
22	11	A	East Fife	L	1-2	1-1	—	O'Brien 2	602
23	26	H	Albion R	L	3-4	0-3	—	Kerrigan 50, Nicholas 85, Morris 90	466
24	Mar 1	H	Elgin C	W	4-0	3-0	5	O'Brien 17, Morris 25, Nicholas 2 (1 pen) 44 (p), 59	407
25	4	A	Peterhead	L	0-6	0-3	—		613
26	8	A	East Stirling	W	3-1	2-0	5	Morris 3, Rowe 29, Kerrigan 71	302
27	11	A	Morton	D	2-2	0-1	—	Mallan 50, Dunn 75	1617
28	15	H	Peterhead	W	2-1	2-1	5	Nicholas 2 (1 pen) 3, 42 (p)	564
29	19	H	Queen's Park	W	1-0	1-0	—	O'Brien 63	465
30	22	H	East Fife	L	1-2	0-0	5	O'Brien 75	866
31	Apr 5	A	Montrose	W	1-0	1-0	5	Crilly 39	385
32	12	A	Queen's Park	D	3-3	2-1	5	Kerrigan 4, Morris 19, Dunn 63	714
33	19	H	Gretna	W	1-0	1-0	5	Nicholas (pen) 11	376
34	26	A	Albion R	L	1-2	0-2	5	Morris 64	533
35	May 3	H	Morton	L	0-3	0-2	5		2039
36	10	A	Elgin C	D	2-2	1-1	5	Crilly 15, Rowe 86	386

Final League Position: 5

Honours
League Champions: Division II 1952-53, 1957-58, 1960-61, 1964-65. Second Division 1976-77, 1990-91, 1995-96; *Runners-up:* Division II 1948-49, 1950-51.

Club colours: Shirt: Red and white halves. Shorts: Red with white piping. Stockings: Red with 2 white hoops at top.

Goalscorers: *League* (50): Nicholas 11 (5 pens), O'Brien 8, Mallan 6 (1 pen), Morris 5, Dunn 4, Kerrigan 3, McKinnon 3, Rowe 3, Crilly 2, Reilly 2, Hay 1, McLellan 1, own goal 1
Scottish Cup (1): McKinnon 1
CIS Cup (5): Nicholas 2, Dunn 1, Mallan 1, Munro 1
Challenge Cup (2): Munro 1, Nicholas 1

Reid C 9	Nugent P 36	McCole D 4 + 1	McNally M 30	Rowe G 34	Duncan F 13 + 3	Moore A 2 + 4	Hay P 31 + 4	Munro G 6 + 6	Nicholas S 29 + 2	O'Brien D 26 + 2	Stuart W 1 + 1	Beveridge R 1 + 5	Butler D — + 2	Turner I 14	Reilly S 5 + 6	Wilson L 1 + 1	Davidson H 12 + 4	Mallan S 27 + 4	McLellan K — + 10	Dunn R 30 + 1	McKinnon C 20 + 2	Cummings D 1 + 3	Devine S — + 1	Wilson D 2 + 10	McGeown D 4 + 3	Morris I 14 + 1	Crilly M 12	Kerrigan S 9 + 5	Smith A 10	Nugent A 3 + 1	Hogarth M 10	Scotland C — + 1	*Match No.*
1	2	3	4	5	6	7^{1}	8	9^{2}	10	11^{3}	12	13	14																				1
	2		4■	5	3		11^{1}	7^{2}	10		6	13	12	1	8	9																	2
	2	3		4	5	12	11	7^{1}	10^{3}					1	6^{2}	14	8	9	13														3
	2	3	4	5	11^{3}		6	13	7	14				1			8^{1}	9		10^{2}	12												4
	2	3		4	5		11	13	7^{1}					1	6^{2}		8	9		10	12												5
1	2			5	4	14	11	12	7						6^{2}		8^{1}	9	13	10^{3}	3												6
1	2		4	5	6		3	11^{1}	10								12	9		7	8												7
1	2		4	5	6^{1}		3		10	7							12	9		11	8												8
1	2		4	5	6^{1}	13	3			11					14		12	9		7	8^{3}	10^{2}											9
	2		4	5	6^{1}	13	3		10^{2}	11				1			12	9		7	8												10
	2		4	5^{1}	12		3		10	11				1			6	9		7	8												11
	2		4	5			3		10	11				1			6	9		7	8												12
	2		4	5■			3		10^{1}	11		12		1			6	9		7	8												13
	2		4^{3}		5		3^{1}			11		10^{2}		1	13		6	9	14	7	8		12										14
	2		4	5		7^{1}	3	12	10	11				1			6	9			8												15
	2		4	5			3	10^{2}		11		13		1			6	9		7^{1}	8			12									16
	2		4		5		3^{2}	12		11		14		1	13		6	9		10^{3}	8			7^{1}									17
	2		5	4			3		10	11				1	12		8	9^{2}		7^{3}	6^{1}	13		14									18
	2		4	5			3		10	11				1	6^{2}			9	13	7^{1}	8			12									19
1	2		4	5			3	9^{1}	10^{3}	11								12	13	7	6			14	8^{2}								20
1	2		4	5					12	11								9^{1}		7	3					6	8■	10					21
1	2		4	5			8		9^{3}	11^{1}								12	13	7	3^{2}			14		6		10					22
1^{6}	2		4	5			12		10	11^{1}									13	7					6	8		9^{2}	3	15			23
	2		4	5	14		3		10	11^{2}									13	7^{1}	8^{3}			12	6	9				1			24
	2		4	5	11^{3}		3		10	12								13	14	7^{2}	6^{1}				8	9				1			25
	2^{1}		4	5			3		10^{3}	11								9	12						13	8	6	14	7^{2}	1			26
	2		4	5			12		10	11								9^{2}		7						8	6	13	3^{1}		1		27
	2			5			4		10^{3}	11								9^{2}		7^{1}				14	12	8	6	13	3		1		28
	2			5			3		10^{2}	11								9^{1}		7				13		8	6	12	4		1		29
	2			5	12		3^{2}		10	11								9		7^{3}	8^{1}			14			6	13	4		1		30
	2	13	4	5			3			11^{2}								10^{1}		7^{3}		12				14	8	9	6		1		31
	2		4	5			6		12									9^{1}		7		13				11	8	10^{2}	3		1		32
	2		4^{1}	5			12		10	11										7^{2}				13		6	8	9	3		1		33
	2		4	5			12	14	10^{2}	11								13		7^{3}						8	6	9	3^{1}		1		34
	2		4	5			3		11						12			9^{1}		7				13		8^{2}	6	10			1		35
	2		4	5			3		11^{3}						12			10		13				7		8^{1}	6	9^{2}			1	14	36

STRANRAER

Third Division

Year Formed: 1870. *Ground & Address:* Stair Park, London Rd, Stranraer DG9 8BS. *Telephone:* 01776 703271.
Ground Capacity: 5600. *Size of Pitch:* 110yd × 70yd.
Chairman: R. J. Clanachan. *Secretary:* Graham Rodgers. *Commercial Manager:* T. L. Sutherland.
Manager: Neil Watt. *Assistant Manager:* Stuart Millar. *Physio:* Walter Cannon.
Managers since 1975: J. Hughes, N. Hood, G. Hamilton, D. Sneddon, J. Clark, R. Clark, A. McAnespie, C. Money, W. McLaren. *Club Nickname(s):* The Blues. *Previous Grounds:* None.
Record Attendance: 6500 v Rangers, Scottish Cup 1st rd; 24 Jan, 1948.
Record Transfer Fee received: £90,000 for Mark Campbell to Ayr Utd, 1999.
Record Transfer Fee paid: £15,000 for Colin Harkness from Kilmarnock (Aug 1989).
Record Victory: 7-0 v Brechin C, Division II; 6 Feb, 1965.
Record Defeat: 1-11 v Queen of the South, Scottish Cup 1st rd; 16 Jan, 1932.
Most League Appearances: 301, Keith Knox, 1986-90; 1999-2001.
Most League Goals in Season (Individual): 59, Tommy Sloan.

STRANRAER 2002–03 LEAGUE RECORD

Match No.	Date	Venue	Opponents	Result		H/T Score	Lg. Pos.	Goalscorers	Attendance
1	Aug 3	A	Raith R	D	1-1	0-1	—	Lurinsky 85	1790
2	10	H	Cowdenbeath	L	2-3	1-2	8	Finlayson 40, Moore 73	349
3	17	A	Airdrie U	L	1-2	1-0	10	Lurinsky 44	1518
4	24	A	Stenhousemuir	L	0-2	0-1	10		295
5	31	H	Brechin C	W	3-1	1-0	10	Harty 2 (1 pen) 37, 60 (p), Moore 46	348
6	Sept 14	A	Berwick R	W	4-3	3-2	9	Kerr 22, Sharp 23, Harty 40, Jenkins 59	388
7	21	H	Dumbarton	W	1-0	1-0	5	Kerr 43	455
8	28	H	Forfar Ath	W	2-0	1-0	3	Sharp 43, Harty (pen) 77	385
9	Oct 5	A	Hamilton A	W	5-1	3-0	2	Sharp 6, Harty 2 33, 68, Jenkins 41, Finlayson 61	1175
10	19	A	Cowdenbeath	W	1-0	0-0	1	Hodge 61	358
11	26	H	Raith R	D	2-2	2-2	1	Jenkins 32, Harty 37	608
12	Nov 2	A	Brechin C	L	1-3	0-2	2	Smith J (og) 57	426
13	9	H	Stenhousemuir	W	2-1	2-1	2	Moore 2 10, 17	411
14	16	H	Berwick R	W	1-0	1-0	2	Moore 21	412
15	23	A	Dumbarton	L	0-3	0-1	2		772
16	30	H	Hamilton A	L	1-2	1-1	2	Moore 36	397
17	Dec 28	H	Airdrie U	W	2-0	2-0	3	Moore 15, Harty (pen) 17	695
18	Jan 1	A	Stenhousemuir	L	0-1	0-0	—		356
19	18	A	Berwick R	L	0-1	0-0	3		422
20	Feb 1	H	Dumbarton	L	1-2	1-1	4	Moore 14	408
21	8	H	Forfar Ath	W	3-2	2-1	3	Kerr 13, Jenkins 28, Finlayson 47	362
22	25	H	Brechin C	L	2-3	1-3	—	Crawford 16, Kerr 62	371
23	Mar 1	A	Airdrie U	D	3-3	1-1	5	Wright 45, Harty 50, Kerr 79	1187
24	4	A	Raith R	L	0-3	0-0	—		1448
25	11	H	Cowdenbeath	D	4-4	2-2	—	Harty 2 5, 56, Jenkins 39, Kane 53	363
26	15	A	Brechin C	L	1-3	0-1	8	Moore 53	488
27	18	A	Hamilton A	W	2-1	2-1	—	Moore 13, Harty 18	743
28	30	A	Forfar Ath	L	1-2	0-1	8	Moore 57	394
29	Apr 1	A	Dumbarton	D	1-1	1-0	—	Wingate 18	596
30	5	H	Berwick R	D	0-0	0-0	8		354
31	8	H	Stenhousemuir	L	0-1	0-0	—		321
32	12	H	Hamilton A	D	0-0	0-0	8		402
33	19	A	Forfar Ath	L	0-4	0-0	9		391
34	26	H	Raith R	W	1-0	0-0	9	Finlayson 64	617
35	May 3	A	Cowdenbeath	D	0-0	0-0	9		229
36	10	H	Airdrie U	L	1-2	1-1	9	Sharp 28	1343

Final League Position: 9

Honours
League Champions: Second Division 1993-94, 1997-98.
Qualifying Cup Winners: 1937.
Scottish Cup: Quarter-finals 2003
League Challenge Cup Winners: 1996-97.

Club colours: Shirt: Blue with white side panels. Shorts: Blue with white side panels. Stockings: Blue with two white hoops.

Goalscorers: *League* (49): Harty 12 (3 pens), Moore 11, Jenkins 5, Kerr 5, Finlayson 4, Sharp 4, Lurinsky 2, Crawford 1, Hodge 1, Kane 1, Wingate 1, Wright 1, own goal 1
Scottish Cup (13): Kerr 4, Harty 3 (1 pen), Sharp 2, Gaughan 1, Jenkins 1, Moore 1, Wingate 1
CIS Cup (7): Harty 3, Jenkins 1, Moore 1, Sharp 1, own goal 1
Challenge Cup (1): Fallon 1

McCulloch W 9	Gaughan K 26 + 1	Wright F 32	Wingate D 34	Jenkins A 33 + 2	Aitken S 35	Renicks S 2	Marshall S 6 + 1	Harty I 31 + 1	Sharp L 28 + 5	Finlayson K 29 + 4	Grace A 2 + 3	Fallon J 4 + 10	Lurinsky A 3 + 7	Hodge A 16 + 8	Moore M 30	Hillcoat J 27	Kerr P 15 + 6	Curran H 7 + 9	Kane A 4 + 10	Farrell D 15 + 2	McLaren R — + 3	Crawford J 3	Scott A 5 + 1	*Match No.*
1	2	3	4	5^{2}	6	7	8^{1}	9	10	11^{3}	12	13	14											1
1	2	3	4	14	6			9^{1}	11	7	8^{3}	12	13	5^{2}	10									2
	2	3	4	12	8		6^{1}		5^{3}	7	14	13	11^{2}	10	9■	1								3
	5	3	4		6	2		13	11^{3}	12	8	9^{2}	7^{1}	14		1	10							4
	2	3		4	6^{3}			9	5^{1}	7	14			13	10	1	11^{2}	8	12					5
		3	2	5	6			9	11	7			12		8	1	10^{1}			4				6
		3	2	5	6			9	11	7					8■	1	10			4				7
		3	2	5	6			9	11	7				12	8	1	10^{1}			4				8
		3	2	8	6			9^{2}	11	7		10		5^{1}		1		12	13	4				9
		3	2	8	6			9	11	7		12		5^{1}		1	10			4				10
		3	2	5	6			9	11	7		14	8^{2}	13		1	10^{3}	12		4^{1}				11
	2	3	4	8	6			9	11	7		13		5^{1}	10^{2}	1			12					12
	2	3	4	5	6^{2}		13	9	11	7		14		12	8^{3}	1	10^{1}							13
	2	3^{2}	4	5	6			9	11^{1}	7				12	10	1	8^{3}	14			13			14
	2	3^{1}	4^{2}	5	6			9	11	7		13			10	1		8			12			15
	2	4	5	8	6^{1}			9	3^{2}	7		13		11	10	1		12						16
	2	3	4	6	7^{2}			9	11					5	8	1	10^{1}	13			12			17
	2	3	4	8	6			9	11			7^{1}	12	5		1	10							18
	2	6	4	11	8			9	7	12				5^{1}	10	1						3		19
	2	3	4	11	8				12	7				5	9^{1}	1	10	6^{2}	13					20
		3	2	5	8			9	12	7				6	10	1	11^{1}					4		21
	2		4	8			7	9	11^{1}			12		5	10	1	13	6^{2}				3		22
	2	3	4	6	8			9	12	7				5	11	1	10^{1}							23
	2	3	4	8	6^{3}			9	11^{2}	7				5^{1}	10	1	12	14		13				24
	14	3	2	5	8			9		7^{1}				13	10^{3}	1	11^{2}		6	4			12	25
	2	3	5^{2}	8	6^{1}			9		7				12	10	1	13		11	4				26
	2	3		8	6		10^{1}	9^{2}		7			13	5	11^{3}	1		14	12	4				27
		5	2	8	6			9	12	7			13	3^{1}	10	1			11	4^{2}				28
		3	2	5	8			9	13	7		10^{1}			11	1	12		6^{2}	4				29
1	2^{2}	3	6	5	8			9	11	12					10				13	4			7^{1}	30
1	2		3	5	6		8^{1}	9	11	12					10		13			4			7^{2}	31
1	2		3	5	6^{2}			9^{1}	11	8			14		10^{3}			13	12	4			7■	32
1	2		4	5	6		8^{1}	9^{2}	11	7					10			12	13	3				33
1	2	3	4	9	5				11	8					10			6^{1}	12				7	34
1	2	3	4	5^{1}	6				11	9					10		13	8	12				7^{2}	35
1	2	3	4	5	8			9	11	7					10			6^{1}		12				36

SCOTTISH LEAGUE TABLES 2002–03

PREMIER DIVISION

		Home			Goals		Away			Goals			
	P	W	D	L	F	A	W	D	L	F	A	GD	Pts
Rangers	38	18	0	1	55	12	13	4	2	46	16	73	97
Celtic	38	18	1	0	56	12	13	3	3	42	14	72	97
Hearts	38	12	3	4	36	24	6	6	7	21	27	6	63
Kilmarnock	38	9	5	5	26	21	7	4	8	21	35	–9	57
Dunfermline Ath	38	9	3	7	32	30	4	4	11	22	41	–17	46
Dundee	38	6	7	6	29	27	4	7	8	21	33	–10	44
Hibernian	38	8	3	8	28	29	7	3	9	28	35	–8	51
Aberdeen	38	5	7	7	19	21	8	3	8	22	33	–13	49
Livingston	38	5	4	10	23	28	4	4	11	25	34	–14	35
Partick T	38	5	6	8	23	23	3	5	11	14	35	–21	35
Dundee U	38	2	7	10	18	32	5	4	10	17	36	–33	32
Motherwell	38	6	4	9	31	34	1	3	15	14	37	–26	28

FIRST DIVISION

		Home			Goals		Away			Goals			
	P	W	D	L	F	A	W	D	L	F	A	GD	Pts
Falkirk	36	15	2	1	46	10	10	4	4	34	22	48	81
Clyde	36	12	4	2	37	17	9	5	4	29	20	29	72
St Johnstone	36	9	3	6	22	13	11	4	3	27	16	20	67
Inverness CT	36	10	2	6	35	23	10	3	5	39	22	29	65
Queen of the S	36	6	7	5	22	18	6	5	7	23	30	–3	48
Ayr U	36	6	6	6	19	18	6	3	9	15	26	–10	45
St Mirren	36	6	5	7	24	32	3	5	10	18	39	–29	37
Ross Co	36	7	4	7	26	19	2	4	12	16	27	–4	35
Alloa Ath	36	3	2	13	24	49	6	6	6	15	23	–33	35
Arbroath	36	2	5	11	17	30	1	1	16	13	47	–47	15

SECOND DIVISION

		Home			Goals		Away			Goals			
	P	W	D	L	F	A	W	D	L	F	A	GD	Pts
Raith R	36	10	4	4	28	14	6	7	5	25	22	17	59
Brechin C	36	8	4	6	32	31	8	3	7	31	28	4	55
Airdrie U	36	8	8	2	24	15	6	4	8	27	29	7	54
Forfar Ath	36	8	5	5	32	25	6	4	8	23	28	2	51
Berwick R	36	6	6	6	21	24	7	4	7	22	24	–5	49
Dumbarton	36	8	5	5	31	23	5	4	9	17	24	1	48
Stenhousemuir	36	8	6	4	32	27	4	5	9	17	24	–2	47
Hamilton A	36	7	3	8	23	26	5	8	5	20	22	–5	47
Stranraer	36	8	4	6	28	23	4	4	10	21	34	–8	44
Cowdenbeath	36	5	5	8	20	21	3	7	8	26	36	–11	36

THIRD DIVISION

		Home			Goals		Away			Goals			
	P	W	D	L	F	A	W	D	L	F	A	GD	Pts
Morton	36	13	4	1	42	14	8	5	5	25	19	34	72
East Fife	36	10	4	4	35	22	10	7	1	38	15	36	71
Albion R	36	9	6	3	31	20	11	4	3	31	16	26	70
Peterhead	36	13	4	1	49	15	7	4	7	27	22	39	68
Stirling Albion	36	9	4	5	24	16	6	7	5	26	28	6	56
Gretna	36	4	8	6	26	27	7	4	7	24	23	0	45
Montrose	36	4	5	9	17	31	3	7	8	18	30	–26	33
Queen's Park	36	3	5	10	21	29	4	6	8	18	22	–12	32
Elgin C	36	3	7	8	17	24	2	6	10	16	39	–30	28
East Stirlingshire	36	0	5	13	11	46	2	2	14	21	59	–73	13

SCOTTISH LEAGUE ATTENDANCES 2002–03

PREMIER LEAGUE

	Average	Highest	Lowest
Aberdeen	11,745	17,314	8816
Celtic	57,243	59,500	54,912
Dundee	7601	11,593	5363
Dundee U	7650	12,402	5572
Dunfermline Ath	6171	9139	4086
Hearts	12,124	17,732	8074
Hibernian	10,137	15,560	7518
Kilmarnock	7565	16,722	4021
Livingston	5801	8787	3969
Motherwell	6085	12,037	3741
Partick T	5553	8053	3541
Rangers	48,822	49,874	45,992

FIRST DIVISION

	Average	Highest	Lowest
Alloa Ath	828	2613	340
Arbroath	833	1950	381
Ayr U	1897	3030	1114
Clyde	1310	3415	665
Falkirk	4158	7300	2673
Inverness CT	2182	3699	1396
Queen of the S	2146	3206	1108
Ross Co	2678	5449	1921
St Johnstone	2577	6579	1796
St Mirren	2717	3737	1888

SECOND DIVISION

	Average	Highest	Lowest
Airdrie U	1442	2285	921
Berwick R	523	820	387
Brechin C	620	1819	377
Cowdenbeath	497	1875	184
Dumbarton	957	1501	513
Forfar Ath	589	1054	391
Hamilton A	1285	2366	626
Raith R	1924	2746	1448
Stenhousemuir	552	1066	295
Stranraer	478	1343	321

THIRD DIVISION

	Average	Highest	Lowest
Albion R	492	1381	224
East Fife	799	1996	462
East Stirlingshire	324	748	146
Elgin C	492	895	218
Gretna	408	1566	221
Montrose	365	543	211
Morton	2334	8497	1617
Peterhead	703	1693	496
Queen's Park	719	1775	443
Stirling Albion	653	2039	376

Barry Ferguson the Rangers captain received both writers and players union awards in Scotland. Here he is in a tussle with Celtic's Henrik Larsson. (Actionimages)

SCOTTISH LEAGUE HONOURS 1890 to 2003

*On goal average (ratio)/difference. †Held jointly after indecisive play-off. ‡Won on deciding match. ††Held jointly. ¶Two points deducted for fielding ineligible player. Competition suspended 1940–45 during war; Regional Leagues operating. ‡‡Two points deducted for registration irregularities.

PREMIER LEAGUE

	First	Pts	Second	Pts	Third	Pts
			Maximum points: 108			
1998–99	Rangers	77	Celtic	71	St Johnstone	57
1999–2000	Rangers	90	Celtic	69	Hearts	54
			Maximum points: 114			
2000–01	Celtic	97	Rangers	82	Hibernian	66
2001–02	Celtic	103	Rangers	85	Livingston	58
2002–03	Rangers*	97	Celtic	97	Hearts	63

PREMIER DIVISION

	First	Pts	Second	Pts	Third	Pts
			Maximum points: 72			
1975–76	Rangers	54	Celtic	48	Hibernian	43
1976–77	Celtic	55	Rangers	46	Aberdeen	43
1977–78	Rangers	55	Aberdeen	53	Dundee U	40
1978–79	Celtic	48	Rangers	45	Dundee U	44
1979–80	Aberdeen	48	Celtic	47	St Mirren	42
1980–81	Celtic	56	Aberdeen	49	Rangers*	44
1981–82	Celtic	55	Aberdeen	53	Rangers	43
1982–83	Dundee U	56	Celtic*	55	Aberdeen	55
1983–84	Aberdeen	57	Celtic	50	Dundee U	47
1984–85	Aberdeen	59	Celtic	52	Dundee U	47
1985–86	Celtic*	50	Hearts	50	Dundee U	47
			Maximum points: 88			
1986–87	Rangers	69	Celtic	63	Dundee U	60
1987–88	Celtic	72	Hearts	62	Rangers	60
			Maximum points: 72			
1988–89	Rangers	56	Aberdeen	50	Celtic	46
1989–90	Rangers	51	Aberdeen*	44	Hearts	44
1990–91	Rangers	55	Aberdeen	53	Celtic*	41
			Maximum points: 88			
1991–92	Rangers	72	Hearts	63	Celtic	62
1992–93	Rangers	73	Aberdeen	64	Celtic	60
1993–94	Rangers	58	Aberdeen	55	Motherwell	54
			Maximum points: 108			
1994–95	Rangers	69	Motherwell	54	Hibernian	53
1995–96	Rangers	87	Celtic	83	Aberdeen*	55
1996–97	Rangers	80	Celtic	75	Dundee U	60
1997–98	Celtic	74	Rangers	72	Hearts	67

FIRST DIVISION

	First	Pts	Second	Pts	Third	Pts
			Maximum points: 52			
1975–76	Partick T	41	Kilmarnock	35	Montrose	30
			Maximum points: 78			
1976–77	St Mirren	62	Clydebank	58	Dundee	51
1977–78	Morton*	58	Hearts	58	Dundee	57
1978–79	Dundee	55	Kilmarnock*	54	Clydebank	54
1979–80	Hearts	53	Airdrieonians	51	Ayr U*	44
1980–81	Hibernian	57	Dundee	52	St Johnstone	51
1981–82	Motherwell	61	Kilmarnock	51	Hearts	50
1982–83	St Johnstone	55	Hearts	54	Clydebank	50
1983–84	Morton	54	Dumbarton	51	Partick T	46
1984–85	Motherwell	50	Clydebank	48	Falkirk	45
1985–86	Hamilton A	56	Falkirk	45	Kilmarnock	44
			Maximum points: 88			
1986–87	Morton	57	Dunfermline Ath	56	Dumbarton	53
1987–88	Hamilton A	56	Meadowbank T	52	Clydebank	49
			Maximum points: 78			
1988–89	Dunfermline Ath	54	Falkirk	52	Clydebank	48
1989–90	St Johnstone	58	Airdrieonians	54	Clydebank	44
1990–91	Falkirk	54	Airdrieonians	53	Dundee	52
			Maximum points: 88			
1991–92	Dundee	58	Partick T*	57	Hamilton A	57
1992–93	Raith R	65	Kilmarnock	54	Dunfermline Ath	52
1993–94	Falkirk	66	Dunfermline Ath	65	Airdrieonians	54
			Maximum points: 108			
1994–95	Raith R	69	Dunfermline Ath*	68	Dundee	68
1995–96	Dunfermline Ath	71	Dundee U*	67	Morton	67
1996–97	St Johnstone	80	Airdieonians	60	Dundee*	58
1997–98	Dundee	70	Falkirk	65	Raith R*	60
1998–99	Hibernian	89	Falkirk	66	Ayr U	62
1999–2000	St Mirren	76	Dunfermline Ath	71	Falkirk	68
2000–01	Livingston	76	Ayr U	69	Falkirk	56
2001–02	Partick T	66	Airdrieonians	56	Ayr U	52
2002–03	Falkirk	81	Clyde	72	St Johnstone	67

SECOND DIVISION

	First	*Pts*	*Second*	*Pts*	*Third*	*Pts*
			Maximum points: 52			
1975–76	Clydebank*	40	Raith R	40	Alloa	35
			Maximum points: 78			
1976–77	Stirling A	55	Alloa	51	Dunfermline Ath	50
1977–78	Clyde*	53	Raith R	53	Dunfermline Ath	48
1978–79	Berwick R	54	Dunfermline Ath	52	Falkirk	50
1979–80	Falkirk	50	East Stirling	49	Forfar Ath	46
1980–81	Queen's Park	50	Queen of the S	46	Cowdenbeath	45
1981–82	Clyde	59	Alloa*	50	Arbroath	50
1982–83	Brechin C	55	Meadowbank T	54	Arbroath	49
1983–84	Forfar Ath	63	East Fife	47	Berwick R	43
1984–85	Montrose	53	Alloa	50	Dunfermline Ath	49
1985–86	Dunfermline Ath	57	Queen of the S	55	Meadowbank T	49
1986–87	Meadowbank T	55	Raith R*	52	Stirling A*	52
1987–88	Ayr U	61	St Johnstone	59	Queen's Park	51
1988–89	Albion R	50	Alloa	45	Brechin C	43
1989–90	Brechin C	49	Kilmarnock	48	Stirling A	47
1990–91	Stirling A	54	Montrose	46	Cowdenbeath	45
1991–92	Dumbarton	52	Cowdenbeath	51	Alloa	50
1992–93	Clyde	54	Brechin C*	53	Stranraer	53
1993–94	Stranraer	56	Berwick R	48	Stenhousemuir*	47
			Maximum points: 108			
1994–95	Morton	64	Dumbarton	60	Stirling A	58
1995–96	Stirling A	81	East Fife	67	Berwick R	60
1996–97	Ayr U	77	Hamilton A	74	Livingston	64
1997–98	Stranraer	61	Clydebank	60	Livingston	59
1998–99	Livingston	77	Inverness CT	72	Clyde	53
1999–2000	Clyde	65	Alloa Ath	64	Ross Co	62
2000–01	Partick T	75	Arbroath	58	Berwick R*	54
2001–02	Queen of the S	67	Alloa	59	Forfar Ath	53
2002–03	Raith R	59	Brechin C	55	Airdrie U	54

THIRD DIVISION

			Maximum points: 108			
1994–95	Forfar Ath	80	Montrose	67	Ross Co	60
1995–96	Livingston	72	Brechin C	63	Caledonian T	57
1996–97	Inverness CT	76	Forfar Ath*	67	Ross Co	67
1997–98	Alloa Ath	76	Arbroath	68	Ross Co*	67
1998–99	Ross Co	77	Stenhousemuir	64	Brechin C	59
1999–2000	Queen's Park	69	Berwick R	66	Forfar Ath	61
2000–01	Hamilton A*	76	Cowdenbeath	76	Brechin C	72
2001–02	Brechin C	73	Dumbarton	61	Albion R	59
2002–03	Morton	72	East Fife	71	Albion R	70

FIRST DIVISION to 1974–75

Maximum points: a 36; *b* 44; *c* 40; *d* 52; *e* 60; *f* 68; g 76; *h* 84.

1890–91*a*	Dumbarton††	29	Rangers††	29	Celtic	21
1891–92*b*	Dumbarton	37	Celtic	35	Hearts	34
1892–93*a*	Celtic	29	Rangers	28	St Mirren	20
1893–94*a*	Celtic	29	Hearts	26	St Bernard's	23
1894–95*a*	Hearts	31	Celtic	26	Rangers	22
1895–96*a*	Celtic	30	Rangers	26	Hibernian	24
1896–97*a*	Hearts	28	Hibernian	26	Rangers	25
1897–98*a*	Celtic	33	Rangers	29	Hibernian	22
1898–99*a*	Rangers	36	Hearts	26	Celtic	24
1899–1900*a*	Rangers	32	Celtic	25	Hibernian	24
1900–01*c*	Rangers	35	Celtic	29	Hibernian	25
1901–02*a*	Rangers	28	Celtic	26	Hearts	22
1902–03*b*	Hibernian	37	Dundee	31	Rangers	29
1903–04*d*	Third Lanark	43	Hearts	39	Celtic*	38
1904–05*d*	Celtic‡	41	Rangers	41	Third Lanark	35
1905–06*e*	Celtic	49	Hearts	43	Airdrieonians	38
1906–07*f*	Celtic	55	Dundee	48	Rangers	45
1907–08*f*	Celtic	55	Falkirk	51	Rangers	50
1908–09*f*	Celtic	51	Dundee	50	Clyde	48
1909–10*f*	Celtic	54	Falkirk	52	Rangers	46
1910–11*f*	Rangers	52	Aberdeen	48	Falkirk	44
1911–12*f*	Rangers	51	Celtic	45	Clyde	42
1912–13*f*	Rangers	53	Celtic	49	Hearts*	41
1913–14*g*	Celtic	65	Rangers	59	Hearts*	54
1914–15*g*	Celtic	65	Hearts	61	Rangers	50
1915–16*g*	Celtic	67	Rangers	56	Morton	51
1916–17*g*	Celtic	64	Morton	54	Rangers	53
1917–18*f*	Rangers	56	Celtic	55	Kilmarnock*	43
1918–19*f*	Celtic	58	Rangers	57	Morton	47
1919–20*h*	Rangers	71	Celtic	68	Motherwell	57
1920–21*h*	Rangers	76	Celtic	66	Hearts	50
1921–22*h*	Celtic	67	Rangers	66	Raith R	51
1922–23*g*	Rangers	55	Airdrieonians	50	Celtic	46

	First	*Pts*	*Second*	*Pts*	*Third*	*Pts*
1923–24*g*	Rangers	59	Airdrieonians	50	Celtic	46
1924–25*g*	Rangers	60	Airdrieonians	57	Hibernian	52
1925–26*g*	Celtic	58	Airdrieonians*	50	Hearts	50
1926–27*g*	Rangers	56	Motherwell	51	Celtic	49
1927–28*g*	Rangers	60	Celtic*	55	Motherwell	55
1928–29*g*	Rangers	67	Celtic	51	Motherwell	50
1929–30*g*	Rangers	60	Motherwell	55	Aberdeen	53
1930–31*g*	Rangers	60	Celtic	58	Motherwell	56
1931–32*g*	Motherwell	66	Rangers	61	Celtic	48
1932–33*g*	Rangers	62	Motherwell	59	Hearts	50
1933–34*g*	Rangers	66	Motherwell	62	Celtic	47
1934–35*g*	Rangers	55	Celtic	52	Hearts	50
1935–36*g*	Celtic	66	Rangers*	61	Aberdeen	61
1936–37*g*	Rangers	61	Aberdeen	54	Celtic	52
1937–38*g*	Celtic	61	Hearts	58	Rangers	49
1938–39*g*	Rangers	59	Celtic	48	Aberdeen	46
1946–47*e*	Rangers	46	Hibernian	44	Aberdeen	39
1947–48*e*	Hibernian	48	Rangers	46	Partick T	36
1948–49*e*	Rangers	46	Dundee	45	Hibernian	39
1949–50*e*	Rangers	50	Hibernian	49	Hearts	43
1950–51*e*	Hibernian	48	Rangers*	38	Dundee	38
1951–52*e*	Hibernian	45	Rangers	41	East Fife	37
1952–53*e*	Rangers*	43	Hibernian	43	East Fife	39
1953–54*e*	Celtic	43	Hearts	38	Partick T	35
1954–55*e*	Aberdeen	49	Celtic	46	Rangers	41
1955–56*f*	Rangers	52	Aberdeen	46	Hearts*	45
1956–57*f*	Rangers	55	Hearts	53	Kilmarnock	42
1957–58*f*	Hearts	62	Rangers	49	Celtic	46
1958–59*f*	Rangers	50	Hearts	48	Motherwell	44
1959–60*f*	Hearts	54	Kilmarnock	50	Rangers*	42
1960–61*f*	Rangers	51	Kilmarnock	50	Third Lanark	42
1961–62*f*	Dundee	54	Rangers	51	Celtic	46
1962–63*f*	Rangers	57	Kilmarnock	48	Partick T	46
1963–64*f*	Rangers	55	Kilmarnock	49	Celtic*	47
1964–65*f*	Kilmarnock*	50	Hearts	50	Dunfermline Ath	49
1965–66*f*	Celtic	57	Rangers	55	Kilmarnock	45
1966–67*f*	Celtic	58	Rangers	55	Clyde	46
1967–68*f*	Celtic	63	Rangers	61	Hibernian	45
1968–69*f*	Celtic	54	Rangers	49	Dunfermline Ath	45
1969–70*f*	Celtic	57	Rangers	45	Hibernian	44
1970–71*f*	Celtic	56	Aberdeen	54	St Johnstone	44
1971–72*f*	Celtic	60	Aberdeen	50	Rangers	44
1972–73*f*	Celtic	57	Rangers	56	Hibernian	45
1973–74*f*	Celtic	53	Hibernian	49	Rangers	48
1974–75*f*	Rangers	56	Hibernian	49	Celtic	45

SECOND DIVISION to 1974–75

Maximum points: a 76; *b* 72; *c* 68; *d* 52; *e* 60; *f* 36; *g* 44.

1893–94*f*	Hibernian	29	Cowlairs	27	Clyde	24
1894–95*f*	Hibernian	30	Motherwell	22	Port Glasgow	20
1895–96*f*	Abercorn	27	Leith Ath	23	Renton	21
1896–97*f*	Partick T	31	Leith Ath	27	Kilmarnock*	21
1897–98*f*	Kilmarnock	29	Port Glasgow	25	Morton	22
1898–99*f*	Kilmarnock	32	Leith Ath	27	Port Glasgow	25
1899–1900*f*	Partick T	29	Morton	28	Port Glasgow	20
1900–01*f*	St Bernard's	25	Airdrieonians	23	Abercorn	21
1901–02*g*	Port Glasgow	32	Partick T	31	Motherwell	26
1902–03*g*	Airdrieonians	35	Motherwell	28	Ayr U*	27
1903–04*g*	Hamilton A	37	Clyde	29	Ayr U	28
1904–05*g*	Clyde	32	Falkirk	28	Hamilton A	27
1905–06*g*	Leith Ath	34	Clyde	31	Albion R	27
1906–07*g*	St Bernard's	32	Vale of Leven*	27	Arthurlie	27
1907–08*g*	Raith R	30	Dumbarton*‡‡	27	Ayr U	27
1908–09*g*	Abercorn	31	Raith R*	28	Vale of Leven	28
1909–10*g*	Leith Ath‡	33	Raith R	33	St Bernard's	27
1910–11*g*	Dumbarton	31	Ayr U	27	Albion R	25
1911–12*g*	Ayr U	35	Abercorn	30	Dumbarton	27
1912–13*d*	Ayr U	34	Dunfermline Ath	33	East Stirling	32
1913–14*g*	Cowdenbeath	31	Albion R	27	Dunfermline Ath*	26
1914–15*d*	Cowdenbeath*	37	St Bernard's*	37	Leith Ath	37
1921–22*a*	Alloa	60	Cowdenbeath	47	Armadale	45
1922–23*a*	Queen's Park	57	Clydebank¶	50	St Johnstone¶	45
1923–24*a*	St Johnstone	56	Cowdenbeath	55	Bathgate	44
1924–25*a*	Dundee U	50	Clydebank	48	Clyde	47
1925–26*a*	Dunfermline Ath	59	Clyde	53	Ayr U	52
1926–27*a*	Bo'ness	56	Raith R	49	Clydebank	45
1927–28*a*	Ayr U	54	Third Lanark	45	King's Park	44
1928–29*b*	Dundee U	51	Morton	50	Arbroath	47
1929–30*a*	Leith Ath*	57	East Fife	57	Albion R	54
1930–31*a*	Third Lanark	61	Dundee U	50	Dunfermline Ath	47
1931–32*a*	East Stirling*	55	St Johnstone	55	Raith R*	46

	First	*Pts*	*Second*	*Pts*	*Third*	*Pts*
1932–33*c*	Hibernian	54	Queen of the S	49	Dunfermline Ath	47
1933–34*c*	Albion R	45	Dunfermline Ath*	44	Arbroath	44
1934–35*c*	Third Lanark	52	Arbroath	50	St Bernard's	47
1935–36*c*	Falkirk	59	St Mirren	52	Morton	48
1936–37*c*	Ayr U	54	Morton	51	St Bernard's	48
1937–38*c*	Raith R	59	Albion R	48	Airdrieonians	47
1938–39*c*	Cowdenbeath	60	Alloa*	48	East Fife	48
1946–47*d*	Dundee	45	Airdrieonians	42	East Fife	31
1947–48*e*	East Fife	53	Albion R	42	Hamilton A	40
1948–49*e*	Raith R*	42	Stirling A	42	Airdrieonians*	41
1949–50*e*	Morton	47	Airdrieonians	44	Dunfermline Ath*	36
1950–51*e*	Queen of the S*	45	Stirling A	45	Ayr U*	36
1951–52*e*	Clyde	44	Falkirk	43	Ayr U	39
1952–53*e*	Stirling A	44	Hamilton A	43	Queen's Park	37
1953–54*e*	Motherwell	45	Kilmarnock	42	Third Lanark*	36
1954–55*e*	Airdrieonians	46	Dunfermline Ath	42	Hamilton A	39
1955–56*b*	Queen's Park	54	Ayr U	51	St Johnstone	49
1956–57*b*	Clyde	64	Third Lanark	51	Cowdenbeath	45
1957–58*b*	Stirling A	55	Dunfermline Ath	53	Arbroath	47
1958–59*b*	Ayr U	60	Arbroath	51	Stenhousemuir	46
1959–60*b*	St Johnstone	53	Dundee U	50	Queen of the S	49
1960–61*b*	Stirling A	55	Falkirk	54	Stenhousemuir	50
1961–62*b*	Clyde	54	Queen of the S	53	Morton	44
1962–63*b*	St Johnstone	55	East Stirling	49	Morton	48
1963–64*b*	Morton	67	Clyde	53	Arbroath	46
1964–65*b*	Stirling A	59	Hamilton A	50	Queen of the S	45
1965–66*b*	Ayr U	53	Airdrieonians	50	Queen of the S	47
1966–67*a*	Morton	69	Raith R	58	Arbroath	57
1967–68*b*	St Mirren	62	Arbroath	53	East Fife	49
1968–69*b*	Motherwell	64	Ayr U	53	East Fife*	48
1969–70*b*	Falkirk	56	Cowdenbeath	55	Queen of the S	50
1970–71*b*	Partick T	56	East Fife	51	Arbroath	46
1971–72*b*	Dumbarton*	52	Arbroath	52	Stirling A	50
1972–73*b*	Clyde	56	Dumfermline Ath	52	Raith R*	47
1973–74*b*	Airdrieonians	60	Kilmarnock	58	Hamilton A	55
1974–75*a*	Falkirk	54	Queen of the S*	53	Montrose	53

Elected to First Division: 1894 Clyde; 1895 Hibernian; 1896 Abercorn; 1897 Partick T; 1899 Kilmarnock; 1900 Morton and Partick T; 1902 Port Glasgow and Partick T; 1903 Airdrieonians and Motherwell; 1905 Falkirk and Aberdeen; 1906 Clyde and Hamilton A; 1910 Raith R; 1913 Ayr U and Dumbarton.

RELEGATED FROM PREMIER LEAGUE

1998–99 Dunfermline Ath
1999–2000 *No relegation due to League reorganization*
2000–01 St Mirren
2001–02 St Johnstone
2002–03 *No relegated team*

RELEGATED FROM PREMIER DIVISION

1974–75 *No relegation due to League reorganization*
1975–76 Dundee, St Johnstone
1976–77 Hearts, Kilmarnock
1977–78 Ayr U, Clydebank
1978–79 Hearts, Motherwell
1979–80 Dundee, Hibernian
1980–81 Kilmarnock, Hearts
1981–82 Partick T, Airdrieonians
1982–83 Morton, Kilmarnock
1983–84 St Johnstone, Motherwell
1984–85 Dumbarton, Morton
1985–86 *No relegation due to League reorganization*
1986–87 Clydebank, Hamilton A
1987–88 Falkirk, Dunfermline Ath, Morton
1988–89 Hamilton A
1989–90 Dundee
1990–91 *None*
1991–92 St Mirren, Dunfermline Ath
1992–93 Falkirk, Airdrieonians
1993–94 *See footnote*
1994–95 Dundee U
1995–96 Partick T, Falkirk
1996–97 Raith R
1997–98 Hibernian

RELEGATED FROM DIVISION 1

1974–75 *No relegation due to League reorganization*
1975–76 Dunfermline Ath, Clyde
1976–77 Raith R, Falkirk
1977–78 Alloa Ath, East Fife
1978–79 Montrose, Queen of the S
1979–80 Arbroath, Clyde
1980–81 Stirling A, Berwick R
1981–82 East Stirling, Queen of the S
1982–83 Dunfermline Ath, Queen's Park
1983–84 Raith R, Alloa
1984–85 Meadowbank T, St Johnstone
1985–86 Ayr U, Alloa
1986–87 Brechin C, Montrose
1987–88 East Fife, Dumbarton
1988–89 Kilmarnock, Queen of the S
1989–90 Albion R, Alloa
1990–91 Clyde, Brechin C
1991–92 Montrose, Forfar Ath
1992–93 Meadowbank T, Cowdenbeath
1993–94 *See footnote*
1994–95 Ayr U, Stranraer
1995–96 Hamilton A, Dumbarton
1996–97 Clydebank, East Fife
1997–98 Partick T, Stirling A
1998–99 Hamilton A, Stranraer
1999–2000 Clydebank
2000–01 Morton, Alloa
2001–02 Raith R
2002–03 Alloa, Arbroath

RELEGATED FROM DIVISION 2

1994–95 Meadowbank T, Brechin C
1995–96 Forfar Ath, Montrose
1996–97 Dumbarton, Berwick R
1997–98 Stenhousemuir, Brechin C
1998–99 East Fife, Forfar Ath
1999–2000 Hamilton A**
2000–01 Queen's Park, Stirling A
2001–02 Morton
2002–03 Stranraer, Cowdenbeath

RELEGATED FROM DIVISION 1 (TO 1973–74)

1921–22 *Queen's Park, Dumbarton, Clydebank
1922–23 Albion R, Alloa Ath
1923–24 Clyde, Clydebank
1924–25 Third Lanark, Ayr U
1925–26 Raith R, Clydebank
1926–27 Morton, Dundee U
1927–28 Dunfermline Ath, Bo'ness
1928–29 Third Lanark, Raith R
1929–30 St Johnstone, Dundee U
1930–31 Hibernian, East Fife
1931–32 Dundee U, Leith Ath
1932–33 Morton, East Stirling
1933–34 Third Lanark, Cowdenbeath
1934–35 St Mirren, Falkirk
1935–36 Airdrieonians, Ayr U
1936–37 Dunfermline Ath, Albion R
1937–38 Dundee, Morton
1938–39 Queen's Park, Raith R
1946–47 Kilmarnock, Hamilton A
1947–48 Airdrieonians, Queen's Park
1948–49 Morton, Albion R
1949–50 Queen of the S, Stirling A
1950–51 Clyde, Falkirk
1951–52 Morton, Stirling A
1952–53 Motherwell, Third Lanark
1953–54 Airdrieonians, Hamilton A
1954–55 *No clubs relegated*
1955–56 Stirling A, Clyde
1956–57 Dunfermline Ath, Ayr U
1957–58 East Fife, Queen's Park
1958–59 Queen of the S, Falkirk
1959–60 Arbroath, Stirling A
1960–61 Ayr U, Clyde
1961–62 St Johnstone, Stirling A
1962–63 Clyde, Raith R
1963–64 Queen of the S, East Stirling
1964–65 Airdrieonians, Third Lanark
1965–66 Morton, Hamilton A
1966–67 St Mirren, Ayr U
1967–68 Motherwell, Stirling A
1968–69 Falkirk, Arbroath
1969–70 Raith R, Partick T
1970–71 St Mirren, Cowdenbeath
1971–72 Clyde, Dunfermline Ath
1972–73 Kilmarnock, Airdrieonians
1973–74 East Fife, Falkirk

*Season 1921–22 – only 1 club promoted, 3 clubs relegated. ***15pts deducted for failing to field a team.*

Scottish League championship wins: Rangers 50, Celtic 38, Aberdeen 4, Hearts 4, Hibernian 4, Dumbarton 2, Dundee 1, Dundee U 1, Kilmarnock 1, Motherwell 1, Third Lanark 1.

At the end of the 1993–94 season four divisions were created assisted by the admission of two new clubs Ross County and Caledonian Thistle. Only one club was promoted from Division 1 and Division 2. The three relegated from the Premier joined with teams finishing second to seventh in Division 1 to form the new Division 1. Five relegated from Division 1 combined with those who finished second to sixth to form a new Division 2 and the bottom eight in Division 2 linked with the two newcomers to form a new Division 3. At the end of the 1997–98 season the nine clubs remaining in the Premier Division plus the promoted team from Division 1 formed a breakaway Premier League. At the end of the 1999–2000 season two teams were added to the Scottish League. There was no relegation from the Premier League but two promoted from the First Division and three from each of the Second and Third Divisions. One team was relegated from the First Division and one from the Second Division, leaving 12 teams in each division. In season 2002–03, Falkirk were not promoted to the Premier League due to the failure of their ground to meet League Standards.

Rangers players celebrate the Scottish Premier League title after beating Dunfermline Athletic 6-1 and edging Celtic out of it. Another generation of Rangers fans help out. (Actionimages)

SCOTTISH LEAGUE CUP FINALS 1946–2003

Season	*Winners*	*Runners-up*	*Score*
1946–47	Rangers	Aberdeen	4-0
1947–48	East Fife	Falkirk	4-1 after 0-0 draw
1948–49	Rangers	Raith R	2-0
1949–50	East Fife	Dunfermline Ath	3-0
1950–51	Motherwell	Hibernian	3-0
1951–52	Dundee	Rangers	3-2
1952–53	Dundee	Kilmarnock	2-0
1953–54	East Fife	Partick T	3-2
1954–55	Hearts	Motherwell	4-2
1955–56	Aberdeen	St Mirren	2-1
1956–57	Celtic	Partick T	3-0 after 0-0 draw
1957–58	Celtic	Rangers	7-1
1958–59	Hearts	Partick T	5-1
1959–60	Hearts	Third Lanark	2-1
1960–61	Rangers	Kilmarnock	2-0
1961–62	Rangers	Hearts	3-1 after 1-1 draw
1962–63	Hearts	Kilmarnock	1-0
1963–64	Rangers	Morton	5-0
1964–65	Rangers	Celtic	2-1
1965–66	Celtic	Rangers	2-1
1966–67	Celtic	Rangers	1-0
1967–68	Celtic	Dundee	5-3
1968–69	Celtic	Hibernian	6-2
1969–70	Celtic	St Johnstone	1-0
1970–71	Rangers	Celtic	1-0
1971–72	Partick T	Celtic	4-1
1972–73	Hibernian	Celtic	2-1
1973–74	Dundee	Celtic	1-0
1974–75	Celtic	Hibernian	6-3
1975–76	Rangers	Celtic	1-0
1976–77	Aberdeen	Celtic	2-1
1977–78	Rangers	Celtic	2-1
1978–79	Rangers	Aberdeen	2-1
1979–80	Dundee U	Aberdeen	3-0 after 0-0 draw
1980–81	Dundee U	Dundee	3-0
1981–82	Rangers	Dundee U	2-1
1982–83	Celtic	Rangers	2-1
1983–84	Rangers	Celtic	3-2
1984–85	Rangers	Dundee U	1-0
1985–86	Aberdeen	Hibernian	3-0
1986–87	Rangers	Celtic	2-1
1987–88	Rangers	Aberdeen	3-3
		(Rangers won 5-3 on penalties)	
1988–89	Rangers	Aberdeen	3-2
1989–90	Aberdeen	Rangers	2-1
1990–91	Rangers	Celtic	2-1
1991–92	Hibernian	Dunfermline Ath	2-0
1992–93	Rangers	Aberdeen	2-1
1993–94	Rangers	Hibernian	2-1
1994–95	Raith R	Celtic	2-2
		(Raith R won 6-5 on penalties)	
1995–96	Aberdeen	Dundee	2-0
1996–97	Rangers	Hearts	4-3
1997–98	Celtic	Dundee U	3-0
1998–99	Rangers	St Johnstone	2-1
1999–2000	Celtic	Aberdeen	2-0
2000–01	Celtic	Kilmarnock	3-0
2001–02	Rangers	Ayr U	4-0
2002–03	Rangers	Celtic	2-1

SCOTTISH LEAGUE CUP WINS

Rangers 23, Celtic 12, Aberdeen 5, Hearts 4, Dundee 3, East Fife 3, Dundee U 2, Hibernian 2, Motherwell 1, Partick T 1, Raith R 1.

APPEARANCES IN FINALS

Rangers 29, Celtic 25, Aberdeen 12, Hibernian 7, Dundee 6, Hearts 6, Dundee U 5, Kilmarnock 4, Partick T 4, East Fife 3, Dunfermline Ath 2, Motherwell 2, Raith R 2, St Johnstone 2, Ayr U 1, Falkirk 1, Morton 1, St Mirren 1, Third Lanark 1.

CIS SCOTTISH LEAGUE CUP 2002–03

■ *Denotes player sent off.*

FIRST ROUND

Saturday, 7 September 2002

Airdrie U (0) 1 *(Gow 87)*
Elgin C (0) 0 1120
Airdrie U: McGeown; Armstrong, McGowan, Stewart, Brannigan, Vella (McVey), Gardner, Wilson M (Harvey), Ronald (Gow), Docherty, McGuire.
Elgin C: Pirie; Grant, McBride, Hind, Mackay, Tully■, Ross, Steele (Sanderson), McMullan (MacDonald), Love■, Craig.

Albion R (0) 0
Hamilton A (0) 1 *(Callaghan 66 (pen))* 420
Albion R: Shearer; Stevenson (Carr), McCaig, Smith J, Cormack, Lumsden, McAllister (Duncan), Silvestro■, Bradford, McLean (Dick), Mercer■.
Hamilton A: Potter (Macfarlane); Alisdair Graham, Sherry, Dobbins, Sweeney, Smillie, Bonnar■, Walker (Keegans), Armstrong (McDonald), McPhee, Callaghan.

Berwick R (3) 4 *(Forrest G 6, Wood 34, 84, Burke 40)*
Arbroath (0) 2 *(Feroz 51, 89)* 263
Berwick R: Godfrey; Murie, Smith A (Neill A), McNicoll, Gray, Forrest G, Connelly, Neil M, Wood, Burke (Blackley), Smith D (Bennett N).
Arbroath: Gow; Currie, Henslee, Browne, Ritchie, Bowman, McAulay (Cusick), Cargill, McDowell (Heenen), McGlashan (McInally), Feroz.

Gretna (0) 1 *(Irons 77)*
East Fife (2) 2 *(Deuchar 6, 44)* 428
Gretna: Mathieson; Hewson, Skelton (Thwaites), Turner, May, Henney, Skinner, Irons, Dobie, Hore (Benjamin), McGuffie.
East Fife: Butter; Russell, Donaldson, Farnan, Hall, Mortimer, Nairn, Graham (Allison), Gilbert, Deuchar, Herkes (Ovenstone).

Morton (2) 2 *(Bannerman 18, Hopkin 28)*
St Mirren (0) 3 *(Cameron 56, Lappin 78, Yardley 115)* 4276
Morton: Coyle; Collins, Bottiglieri, MacGregor, Smith, Hopkin (Cannie), Uotinen, Maisano M■, Williams, Maisano J, Bannerman.
St Mirren: Robertson; Guy, Kerr, Gillies, Denham (Robb), Dow (Lowing), Murray, Cameron (Yardley), McGinty■, Mendes, Lappin.
aet.

Queen of the S (1) 2 *(O'Neil 25, 60)*
Forfar Ath (0) 0 1155
Queen of the S: Scott; Neilson, Crawford, Allan, Aitken, McAlpine (McLaughlin), O'Neil (Paton), McColligan (Anderson), Lyle, Shields, Weatherson.
Forfar Ath: Brown; Rattray, McCulloch, Horn, Good, Sellars (Stewart), Byers, Anthony, Shaw (Williams), Bavidge, Henderson.

Queen's Park (0) 1 *(Martin 90)*
East Stirling (0) 0 457
Queen's Park: Stewart; Ferry, Fallon, Moffat, Agostini, Quinn, Fisher (Martin), Whelan, Gemmell (Jackson), Lappin (Canning), Allan.
East Stirling: Findlay; Maughan (Struthers), McLaren, Grant, McGhee, Leishman (Boyle), Sean McAuley, Mackay, Fairbairn, Ormiston, Livingstone.

Stranraer (5) 6 *(Jenkins 5, Harty 17, 26, 41, Moore 37, Sharp 65)*
Brechin C (0) 1 *(Skinner 63)* 211
Stranraer: Hillcoat; Gaughan, Wright, Wingate (Farrell), Jenkins, Aitken, Finlayson, Moore, Harty, Kerr (Lurinsky), Sharp.
Brechin C: Hay; Miller G, Donachie (Riley), Smith J, Cairney, Fotheringham K, Charles King (Black), Skinner, Gibson (Grant), Jackson, Millar M.

Tuesday, 10 September 2002

Clyde (0) 0
Ross Co (1) 1 *(Bone 26)* 604
Clyde: Halliwell; Mensing, Potter, Smith (Convery), Millen, Ross, Bossy (Hagen), Fraser, Keogh, Nish, McConalogue (Hinds).
Ross Co: Bullock; Canning, Mackay (Gilbert), Perry, Irvine, McCulloch, McGarry (Gethins), Wood (Cowie), Bone, Bayne, Robertson.

Cowdenbeath (0) 3 *(Wilson 49, Brown 58, French 60)*
Montrose (0) 2 *(Robertson 55, McDonald 69)* 173
Cowdenbeath: O'Connor; Miller, Campbell, White, Wilson, Renwick, Dair, Winter, Brown, Gordon (Elliott), French.
Montrose: McGlynn; McQuillan, Ferguson, Gibson■, Conway, Robertson, Webster K (Henderson), Johnson, McDonald (Sharp), Gilzean, Webster C.

Falkirk (1) 2 *(Lawrie 45, Coyle 52)*
Peterhead (0) 0 2157
Falkirk: Ferguson; Lawrie, McQuilken, MacKenzie, Hughes, James, Kerr, Miller (McSween), Coyle, McPherson, Tosh (Samuel).
Peterhead: Mathers; Burns (Camara), McSkimming, Raeside (MacDonald), Simpson, Bain, Tindal, Stewart, Cameron (Mackay), Johnston, Roddie.

Inverness CT (1) 2 *(Wyness 25, Ritchie 71)*
Dumbarton (0) 0 667
Inverness CT: Brown; Tokely (Low), Golabek, Mann, Munro, McBain, Duncan, Wyness, Hart (Keogh), Christie (Ritchie), Robson.
Dumbarton: Grindlay; Dickie, Stewart, Scally, McKeown, Collins, Crilly (Lynes), McEwan, McCutcheon, Brown A (McCann), Dillon (Robertson).

Raith R (0) 2 *(Prest 76, Carrigan 83)*
Alloa Ath (1) 3 *(Hutchison 40, Little 65, Hamilton 107)* 1261
Raith R: Monin; Ross (Calderon), Hampshire, Ellis, Dennis, Nanou, Boylan (Blackadder), Rivas, Smith (Carrigan), Hawley, Prest.
Alloa Ath: Evans J; Valentine, Cowan, Watson, Thomson, Ferguson B (Knox) (Seaton), Hamilton, Macdonald, Crabbe (Evans G), Hutchison, Little.
aet.

Wednesday, 11 September 2002

Stirling Albion (0) 3 *(Dunn 79, Munro 90, Nicholas 120)*
Stenhousemuir (2) 3 *(McCormick 35, Crawford 42, Waldie 100)* 478
Stirling Albion: Reid; Nugent P, McCole (Moore), Duncan, Rowe, Davidson (McLellan), Hay, Reilly S■, Mallan (Munro), Dunn, Nicholas.
Stenhousemuir: Smith; Easton, Stone, McMillan, McKenzie (Murphy), Hamilton, Waldie, Wilson, McCormick (Graham), Crawford (Harty), Stein.
aet; Stirling Albion won 4-2 on penalties.

SECOND ROUND

Tuesday, 24 September 2002

Alloa Ath (0) 0
Hibernian (0) 2 *(Brebner 59, O'Connor 72)* 1824
Alloa Ath: Evans J; Valentine, Seaton (Knox), Watson, Thomson, Cowan, Hamilton, Ferguson (Macdonald), Crabbe, Hutchison (Evans G), Little.
Hibernian: Colgan; Fenwick, Smith, Zambernardi, Matyus, Townsley, Wiss, Brebner, Orman, O'Connor (Paatelainen), Luna (Riordan).

Ayr U (0) 0
Falkirk (1) 2 *(Samuel 23, Miller 53)* 2022
Ayr U: Nelson; Lyle (Nicolson), Lovering, Smyth, Campbell, Craig, Chaplain, Murray (Annand), Kean, Grady, Sheerin.
Falkirk: Ferguson; Samuel (McSween), McQuilken, McKenzie, Rennie, James (Cringean), Kerr, Miller, Coyle (Henry), McPherson, Tosh.

Berwick R (0) 0
Partick T (3) 3 *(Hardie 18, 32, Buchan 35)* 563
Berwick R: Godfrey; Murie, Smith A, Gray, Neill A, Forrest G (Connell), Connelly, Neil M (Bennett N), Wood, Burke (McCormick), Smith D.
Partick T: Arthur; Paterson, Archibald, Craigan, Whyte, Lilley, Mitchell (Waddell), Buchan (Morris), Walker (Charnley), Hardie, Burns.

Cowdenbeath (1) 1 *(Elliott 10)* 2988
Dunfermline Ath (0) 2 *(Thomson SM 80, Bullen 101)*
Cowdenbeath: O'Connor; Miller (Munro), Campbell, White, Wilson, Renwick, Dair (Gilfillan), Winter, Brown, Gordon, Elliott (Gibb).
Dunfermline Ath: Stillie; McGroarty, Thomson SM, Skerla, Wilson, Bullen, Nicholson, Mason (Dair), Dempsey (Walker), Crawford (Nicholls), Kilgannon.
aet.

Dundee U (2) 4 *(O'Donnell 8, 37, 68, Thompson 72)*
Queen's Park (1) 1 *(Canning 43)* 3600
Dundee U: Gallacher; McCracken, Lauchlan, Wilson, Cummings, Paterson (Winters), Duff, O'Donnell, McIntyre (Gunnlaugsson), Thompson, Lilley (Easton).
Queen's Park: Stewart; Fallon, Gallagher J, Moffat, Agostini, Quinn (Whelan), Ferry, Lappin, Martin (Gemmell), Taggart (Jack), Canning.

East Fife (0) 0
Motherwell (1) 2 *(Lehmann 37, McFadden 65)* 970
East Fife: Butter; Russell, Donaldson, Mortimer, Hall, McMillan, Love (Ovenstone), Farnan, Graham (Allison), Gilbert (Deuchar), Herkes.
Motherwell: Woods; Corrigan, Partridge, Hammell, Ramsay (Cowan), Lasley, Ferguson (Russell), Leitch (MacDonald), Adams, McFadden, Lehmann.

Inverness CT (1) 3 *(Hart 13, Wyness 73, 86)*
St Mirren (1) 1 *(Cameron 24)* 1194
Inverness CT: Brown; Tokely, Golabek, Mann, Munro, McBain, Duncan, Wyness, Ritchie, Hart, Robson.
St Mirren: Roy; Murray, Lowing (Lappin), Rudden, Robb (Broadfoot), Kerr, Dow (Dunbar), Gillies, Cameron, Ross, Yardley.

Kilmarnock (0) 0
Airdrie U (0) 0 4150
Kilmarnock: Marshall; Hay, Innes, Fowler (McDonald), McLaughlin, Fulton, DiGiacomo (Murray), Mitchell (Mahood), Quitongo, Boyd, Sanjuan.
Airdrie U: McGeown; Armstrong, McGowan, Stewart, Brannigan, Vella, Boyle (Wilson M), Glancy (Harvey), Gow, Docherty, Vareille (McKeown).
aet; Airdrie U won 4-3 on penalties.

Ross Co (1) 3 *(McCulloch 26, Cowie 76, Alisdair Graham (og) 87)*
Hamilton A (0) 0 902
Ross Co: Bullock; Canning, Robertson, Perry, Irvine, Gilbert, Bayne, McCulloch, Bone (McGarry), Ferguson (Cowie), Gethins (Wood).
Hamilton A: Potter; Alisdair Graham, Elfallah (McDonald), Dobbins (Walker), Sweeney, Smillie, Bonnar (Armstrong), Sherry, Alastair Graham, McPhee, Callaghan.

Stranraer (1) 1 *(McCulloch (og) 27)*
St Johnstone (1) 3 *(McCulloch 16, Hay 98, 119)* 422
Stranraer: Hillcoat; Wingate, Wright, Farrell (Scott), Hodge (Fallon), Aitken, Finlayson, Jenkins, Harty, Kerr (Kane), Sharp.
St Johnstone: Cuthbert; Robertson, McCulloch, McCluskey, Murray, Maxwell, McCann, Reilly, Hartley, Stevenson (Parker), Russell (Hay).
aet.

Wednesday, 25 September 2002

Dundee (3) 3 *(Sara 16, 37, Caballero 20)*
Queen of the S (1) 1 *(Weatherson 28)* 2190
Dundee: Speroni; Mackay, Hernandez, Hutchinson (Beith), Wilkie, Brady, Nemsadze, Rae, Lovell, Caballero (Milne), Sara.
Queen of the S: Robertson; Nielson, Henderson (Thomson), McColligan, Aitken, Anderson, McLaughlin (Lyle), Bowey, Weatherson (Paton), Shields, McAlpine.

Stirling Albion (1) 2 *(Mallan 2, Nicholas 49)*
Hearts (2) 3 *(Kirk 11, Valois 35, Pressley 68)* 2801
Stirling Albion: Reid; Nugent P, Hay, McNally, Rowe, Duncan (Davidson), Dunn, McKinnon, Mallan (Moore), Nicholas, O'Brien.
Hearts: McKenzie; Pressley, McMullan, Maybury, McKenna, Valois, Severin, Boyack, Stamp (Simmons), Kirk (Wales), De Vries.

THIRD ROUND

Tuesday, 22 October 2002

Dunfermline Ath (1) 2 *(Crawford 1, 78)*
Falkirk (0) 0 6933
Dunfermline Ath: Ruitenbeek; MacPherson (Dair), Thomson SM, McGroarty (Walker), Wilson, Bullen, Nicholson, Mason, Dempsey (Nicholls), Crawford, Brewster.
Falkirk: Ferguson; Rennie, McQuilken, McKenzie, Hughes, James, Kerr, Miller (McPherson), Coyle, Samuel, Tosh (Rodgers).

Partick T (0) 1 *(Hardie 82)*
Dundee (0) 0 2652
Partick T: Arthur; Paterson, Archibald, Craigan, Whyte, Lilley, Mitchell, Buchan (Britton), Chiarini, Hardie, Burns.
Dundee: Speroni; Mackay, Hernandez, Khizanishvili (Smith), Wilkie, Hutchinson, Brady, Robb (Novo), Robertson (Lovell), Milne, Sara.

Wednesday, 23 October 2002

Celtic (3) 4 *(Maloney 4, Hartson 19, 60, Thompson 43)*
Inverness CT (1) 2 *(Ritchie 10, Wyness 72)* 32,122
Celtic: Douglas; Boyd (Miller), Crainey, Balde (Kennedy), Thompson, Smith, Healy, Agathe (Walker), Fernandez, Maloney, Hartson.
Inverness CT: Brown; Tokely (Keogh), Golabek, Mann, Munro, McBain, Duncan, Wyness, Ritchie (Low), Hart, Robson (Christie).

Hearts (0) 3 *(Pressley 56 (pen), Simmons 59, Valois 80)*
Ross Co (0) 0 6454
Hearts: McKenzie; Pressley, McMullan, Maybury, McKenna, Valois, Webster, Jancyzk (McGeown), Simmons (Twaddle), Wales (Kirk), De Vries.
Ross Co: Bullock; Canning, Mackay (Cowie), Deas, Irvine, Gilbert, Bayne (Gethins), McCulloch, McGarry (Higgins), Hislop, Robertson.

Thursday, 24 October 2002

Hibernian (1) 2 *(Murray 6, O'Connor 72)*
Rangers (2) 3 *(Townsley (og) 21, Caniggia 24, Lovenkrands 78)* 8016
Hibernian: Colgan; Fenwick, Orman (Smith■), Zambernardi, James, Murray, Wiss, Brebner, Townsley (McManus), Paatelainen (Luna), O'Connor.
Rangers: Klos; Ricksen, Konterman, Amoruso, Numan, Ross, Ferguson, Arteta (Hughes), de Boer, Caniggia, Lovenkrands.

Tuesday, 29 October 2002

Airdrie U (0) 1 *(Vella 90)*
Dundee U (0) 2 *(Thompson 61, 68)* 1768
Airdrie U: McGeown; Wilson W, McGowan (Millar), Stewart, Brannigan, Vella, McGuire, Armstrong, Ronald (Glancy), Docherty, Vareille (Gow).
Dundee U: Gallacher; McCracken, McGowne, McCunnie, Wilson, Duff, Easton, Miller, McIntyre, Thompson, Lilley (Paterson).

Tuesday, 5 November 2002

St Johnstone (0) 0
Livingston (0) 1 *(Dadi 58)* 1806
St Johnstone: Main; Robertson, Murray, McCann, Dods, Maxwell, Hay, Reilly (Ferry), Hartley, Connolly (Stevenson), Parker.
Livingston: Broto; Brinquin (McNamee), Bollan, Rubio, Andrews, Quino, Makel, Wilson, Toure-Maman, Xausa (Bingham), Dadi (Zarate).

Wednesday, 6 November 2002

Aberdeen (3) 3 *(Mike 23, Deloumeaux 24, Michie 42)*
Motherwell (1) 1 *(Adams 41)* 6557

Aberdeen: Kjaer; McGuire, Rutkiewicz, Anderson (Tiernan), McAllister, Fabiano, Deloumeaux, Bisconti, Mike (Billio), Derek Young (Darren Young), Michie.
Motherwell: Woods; Corrigan, Partridge, Hammell, Lasley (Ramsay), Cowan, Pearson, Leitch, Kemas (Ferguson), Adams, Lehmann.

Wednesday, 13 November 2002

Livingston (0) 0
Dundee U (1) 2 *(Lilley 38, 70)* 3592

Livingston: Broto; McNamee, Bollan, Rubio■■, Andrews, Makel, Wilson (Zarate), Toure-Maman, O'Brien (Quino), Dadi, Bingham (Xausa).
Dundee U: Gallacher; McCracken, Lauchlan, McCunnie, Wilson, Easton, Paterson (Smart■), Miller, McIntyre, Thompson (Hamilton), Lilley (Duff).

QUARTER-FINALS

Wednesday, 6 November 2002

Celtic (1) 1 *(Lambert 42)*
Partick T (0) 1 *(Burns 54)* 26,795

Celtic: Douglas; Laursen, Crainey, Boyd, Smith, Lennon, Petta (Sylla), Lambert, Fernandez (Petrov), Maloney, Hartson.
Partick T: Arthur; Paterson, Archibald (Milne), Craigan, Whyte, Lilley, Chiarini, Walker (McKinstry), Hardie, Britton (McLean), Burns.
aet; Celtic won 5-4 on penalties.

Thursday, 7 November 2002

Dunfermline Ath (0) 0
Rangers (0) 1 *(Caniggia 79)* 8415

Dunfermline Ath: Ruitenbeek; MacPherson (Kilgannon), Bullen, Skerla, Wilson, Dair, Nicholson, Mason (Hampshire), Dempsey, Crawford, Brewster.
Rangers: Klos; Ricksen, Konterman, Malcolm, Numan, Ross, Ferguson, Arteta, Hughes (Arveladze), Mols (Caniggia), Lovenkrands.

Tuesday, 12 November 2002

Aberdeen (0) 0
Hearts (0) 1 *(McKenna 65)* 4576

Aberdeen: Kjaer; McGuire, Rutkiewicz, Anderson, McAllister, Tiernan, Deloumeaux, Bisconti (Darren Young), Mike (Michie), Derek Young (Thornley), Mackie.
Hearts: McKenzie; Pressley, McMullan, Maybury, McKenna, Webster, Severin, Janczyk (Macfarlane), Stamp, Kirk (McCann), Wales (Weir).

SEMI-FINALS

Tuesday, 4 February 2003
(at Hampden Park)

Hearts (0) 0
Rangers (1) 1 *(de Boer 27)* 31,609

Hearts: Moilanen; Pressley, Mahe (Kirk), Maybury, Webster, Valois, Severin, Macfarlane, Stamp (McKenna), Wales, De Vries.
Rangers: Klos; Ricksen, Moore, Amoruso, Numan, Ross, Ferguson, Arteta, de Boer, Mols (Caniggia), McCann.

Thursday, 6 February 2003
(at Hampden Park)

Dundee U (0) 0
Celtic (0) 3 *(Balde 52, 90, Larsson 80)* 18,856

Dundee U: Combe; McCracken, Lauchlan■, Wilson, Duff, Paterson (McCunnie), Easton, Miller (O'Donnell), McIntyre, Dodds (Hamilton), Lilley.
Celtic: Hedman; Laursen, Valgaeren, Balde, Smith (Thompson), Lennon, Agathe (Sylla), Lambert, Sutton, Larsson, Hartson (Fernandez).

FINAL

Sunday, 16 March 2003
(at Hampden Park)

Celtic (0) 1 *(Larsson 56)*
Rangers (2) 2 *(Caniggia 23, Lovenkrands 35)* 52,000

Celtic: Douglas; Mjälby (Petrov), Valgaeren, Balde, Thompson, Lennon■, Smith (Sylla), Lambert, Sutton (Maloney), Larsson, Hartson.
Rangers: Klos; Ricksen, Moore, Amoruso, Bonnisel (Ross), Arteta (Konterman), Ferguson, Caniggia, de Boer (Arveladze), Mols, Lovenkrands.
Referee: Kenny Clark (Paisley).

One-third of the treble for Rangers, the CIS Insurance Cup after beating eternal rivals Celtic 2-1 at Hampden Park in March. (Actionimages)

BELL'S LEAGUE CHALLENGE 2002–03

▪ *Denotes player sent off.*

FIRST ROUND

Tuesday, 6 August 2002

Airdrie U (2) 3 *(Glancy 11, McGuire 31, Docherty 86)*
Raith R (0) 0 1649
Airdrie U: McGeown; Boyle (Armstrong), McVey, Stewart, Brannigan, Vella, Gardner (Wilson W), Wilson M, McGuire (Ronald), Docherty, Glancy.
Raith R: Ojeda; Brown I (Mas), Ellis (Carrigan), Brady, Browne P, Nanou, Matheson, Rivas, Smith (Paliczka), Hampshire, Prest.

Arbroath (0) 0
Forfar Ath (2) 2 *(Tosh 25, 44)* 618
Arbroath: Hinchcliffe; Tait, Henslee, Currie (McAulay), Ritchie, Cargill (Spink), Heenan (Brownlie), McInally, McDowell, McGlashan, Feroz.
Forfar Ath: Brown; Rattray, Sellars, McCloy, Good, Byers (Williams), Shaw (Stewart), Lunan, Tosh (Horn), Bavidge, Henderson.

Berwick R (0) 1 *(Bennett 67 (pen))*
Inverness CT (0) 0 338
Berwick R: Inglis; Gray, Bennett N, Forrest E, Neill A, Bradley, Forrest G, Neil M, Wood, Ferguson (Connell), Smith D (Burke).
Inverness CT: Brown; Tokely (Low), Golabek, Mann, McCaffrey, Munro, Duncan (Christie), Keogh, Ritchie (Wyness), Hart, Robson.

Cowdenbeath (0) 0
Ross Co (0) 2 *(Webb 118, Gethin 119)* 193
Cowdenbeath: Graham; Miller, Campbell, White, Wilson, Renwick, Mauchlen (Crabbe), Winter, Brown (Gilfillan▪), Gordon (Elliott), French.
Ross Co: Bullock; McCulloch, Deas, Perry, Irvine (Bayne), Gilbert, McGarry, Ferguson, Bone (Webb), Cowie, Mackay (Gethin).
aet.

Dumbarton (1) 1 *(Duffy 12)*
East Fife (0) 0 452
Dumbarton: Grindlay; McEwan, Stewart, Brown T, Duffy, Collins, McCann, Bonar (Lynes), Flannery (McKelvie), Brown A, Dillon.
East Fife: Butter; Russell, Gilbert, Farnan, Hall, Cunningham, McMillan (Love), Mortimer, Graham (Ovenstone), Deuchar (Walker), Donaldson.

Elgin C (1) 1 *(Ross 31)*
Brechin C (1) 4 *(Templeman 41, 53, Millar M 51, King 90)* 505
Elgin C: Pirie; MacDonald, McBride, Ross, Mackay, Tully▪, Campbell, Love, McMullan, Steele (James), Sanderson (Craig).
Brechin C: Cairns; Miller G, Black (Riley), Smith J, Cairney, Fotheringham K, Charles King, Millar M, Templeman, Gibson (Grant), Jackson (Campbell).

Montrose (0) 1 *(Johnson 78)*
Albion R (0) 0 320
Montrose: McGlynn; McCheyne, Robertson, Gibson, Conway, McQuillan, Webster K (Leask), Johnson, McDonald, Webster C (Ferguson), McKinnon (Brand).
Albion R: Fahey; Paterson, Stirling, Smith J, Cormack, Lumsden, McKinnon, Coulter (Diack), McLean (Bradford), Carr, Mercer (Silvestro).

Morton (1) 3 *(Williams 11, 84, Hawke 48)*
Stirling Albion (1) 2 *(Munro 28, Nicholas 81)* 1287
Morton: Coyle; Collins, Bottiglieri, MacGregor, Gaughan, Maisano M (MacDonald), Uotinen (Bannerman), Hawke, Williams, Maisano J, Reilly.
Stirling Albion: Reid; Nugent, McCole (Beveridge), McNally, Rowe, Reilly S (Stuart), Nicholas, Duncan (Butler), Mallan, Munro, Hay.

Peterhead (0) 0
Queen of the S (0) 2 *(O'Neil 74, Weatherson 78)* 557
Peterhead: Mathers; Burns, McSkimming, Bain, Simpson, Tindal, Cooper, Stewart, Mackay, Robertson (Bisset), Livingstone (Kidd).
Queen of the S: Scott; Gray, Anderson, McLaughlin, Aitken, Crawford, O'Neil, McColligan, Lyle, Weatherson (O'Connor), McAlpine.

Queen's Park (1) 2 *(Canning 20, Gemmell 81)*
Gretna (0) 1 *(Dobie 65)* 602
Queen's Park: Mitchell; Lappin (Ferry), Gallagher J, Moffat, Agostini, Quinn, Jack (Fisher), Whelan, Gemmell, Canning, Allan (Martin).
Gretna: Mathieson; McGuffie (Alexander▪), Skelton, Turner, Hewson, Henney, Skinner, Irons, Dobie, Hore, Gordon (Smart).

St Johnstone (1) 3 *(Stevenson 35, McCann 65, MacDonald 85)*
Hamilton A (0) 0 1538
St Johnstone: Cuthbert; Robertson, Russell (Maher), McCluskey, Dods, Maxwell, McCann (Fotheringham), Murray, Hartley, Stevenson, Parker (MacDonald).
Hamilton A: Macfarlane; Nelson (Smillie), McDonald (Paterson), Dobbin, Sweeney, Alisdair Graham, Bonnar, Walker, Armstrong, Alastair Graham (McCreadie), Callaghan.

St Mirren (4) 7 *(Cameron 16, 29, 35, 43, Guy 50, Ross 77, Gillies 84)*
East Stirling (0) 0 1403
St Mirren: Roy; Baltacha, Dow, McGowan, Robb, Ross, Gillies, Guy (MacKenzie), McGinty (Yardley), Cameron (Kerr), Lappin.
East Stirling: Finlay; Dunbar (Struthers), Maughan, McGhee, McLaren, Leishman, McAuley, Boyle, Ure (Walker), Carmichael, Morrison (Reid).

Stenhousemuir (0) 1 *(Wilson 74)*
Falkirk (0) 1 *(Miller 56)* 1525
Stenhousemuir: Carlin; Forrest, McKenna, Hamilton, McKenzie, Booth, Waldie (Wilson), Easton, McCormick (Harty), McFarlane, Stein.
Falkirk: Ferguson; Lawrie, McQuilken, Rennie, Hughes, James, Kerr, Miller (Rodgers), Coyle, McPherson (Henry), Tosh (McSween).
aet; Falkirk won 3-2 on penalties.

Stranraer (0) 1 *(Fallon 78)*
Ayr U (1) 2 *(Annand 25, Grady 55)* 725
Stranraer: McCulloch; Gaughan, Wright, Wingate, Jenkins (Fallon), Grace (Lurinsky), Renicks (Hodge), Aitken, Harty, Moore, Sharp.
Ayr U: Nelson; Lyle, Lovering, Nicolson, McManus, Craig, Kean, Black (Dunlop), Annand, Grady, Sheerin.

SECOND ROUND

Tuesday, 13 August 2002

Alloa Ath (0) 0
Ross Co (0) 1 *(Ferguson B (og) 48)* 416
Alloa Ath: Evans J; Valentine, Seaton (Fisher), Knox, Thomson, Christie, Hamilton, Ferguson B, Crabbe (Evans G), Hutchison, Little.
Ross Co: Bullock; McCulloch, Deas, Perry, Canning, Gilbert, McGarry (Bone), Ferguson, Gethins (Mackay), Cowie (Campbell), Wood.

Berwick R (1) 2 *(Burke 11, 89)*
Airdrie U (0) 0 560
Berwick R: Godfrey; McNicoll, Bennett N, Forrest E, Neill A, Forrest G, Connelly (Connell), Neil M, Wood, Ferguson (Smith D), Burke.
Airdrie U: McGeown; Boyle, McVey (Miller D), Armstrong, Brannigan, Vella, Gardner (Wilson W), Wilson M, Ronald, Docherty, Glancy.

Clyde (0) 1 *(Hinds 48)*
St Mirren (2) 2 *(Baltacha 2, Gillies 34)* 1284
Clyde: Halliwell; Mensing, Potter, Smith, Millen, Ross, McLay (Cosgrove), Fraser, Keogh (Kane A), Hinds, Dunn (Convery).
St Mirren: Roy; Baltacha, Kerr, Guy, McGowan, Dow, Gillies, Mendes, McGinty, Cameron (Yardley), Ross.

Dumbarton (1) 3 *(Brown T 42, Dillon 50, 82)*
Ayr U (0) 0 983
Dumbarton: Grindlay; McEwan, Stewart, Brown T, Duffy, Collins, Crilly, Bonar (Dickie), Flannery (McKelvie), Brown A, Dillon.
Ayr U: Nelson; Lyle (Latta), Lovering, Chaplain, McManus (Ferry), Craig, Nicolson■, Black■, Annand (Kean), Grady, Sheerin.

Forfar Ath (0) 2 *(Bavidge 65, Tosh 111)*
Queen's Park (0) 2 *(Moffat 48, 104)* 384
Forfar Ath: Brown■; Rattray, McCulloch■, McCloy, Good, Byers (Ferrie), Shaw (Williams), Lunan (Stewart), Tosh, Bavidge, Sellars.
Queen's Park: Mitchell; Ferry, Gallagher J■, Moffat, Agostini, Quinn, Gallagher P (Fisher (Sinclair)), Whelan, Gemmell■, Canning, Allan (Martin).
aet; Queen's Park won 6-5 on penalties.

Montrose (0) 0
Falkirk (2) 2 *(Miller 16, James 44)* 805
Montrose: McGlynn; McCheyne, Robertson, Gibson, Conway, McQuillan, Webster K (Sharp), Johnson, Webster C (Leask), McKinnon, Ferguson.
Falkirk: Ferguson; Lawrie, McQuilken, Rennie, Hughes, James, Kerr, Miller, Coyle (Samuel), Henry, McPherson (MacSween).

Queen of the S (0) 1 *(O'Connor 83)*
Morton (0) 0 1982
Queen of the S: Scott; Atkinson, Anderson, McColligan, Aitken, Crawford, O'Neil, Gray (Paton), O'Connor, Weatherson (Lyle), McAlpine (McLaughlin).
Morton: Coyle; Collins, Bottiglieri, MacGregor, Gaughan, Smith, Uotinen, Hawke (Cannie), Williams■, MacDonald (Keenan■), Reilly■.

Wednesday, 14 August 2002

Brechin C (1) 3 *(Grant 35, 84, Gibson 50)*
St Johnstone (2) 2 *(Cuthbert 1, 2)* 1007
Brechin C: Hay; McCulloch (Miller G), Black (Charles King), Smith J, Cairney, Fotheringham K, Templeman, Jackson, Grant, Millar M, Gibson.
St Johnstone: Cuthbert; Murray (Ferry), Lovenkrands, McCluskey, Dods, Maxwell, Maher (McClune), Fotheringham, Stevenson, Russell (Parker), MacDonald.

QUARTER-FINALS

Tuesday, 20 August 2002

Berwick R (1) 1 *(Murie 39)*
Queen's Park (0) 2 *(Whelan 50, Allan 64)* 407
Berwick R: Godfrey; Murie, Smith A, McNicoll, Neill A, Bradley, Forrest G, Connell (Neil M), Wood, McCormick, Bennett N (Burke).
Queen's Park: Mitchell; Ferry, White (Sinclair), Moffat, Agostini, Quinn, Taggart (Fisher), Whelan, Martin (Jackson), Canning, Allan.

Brechin C (0) 1 *(Fotheringham 88)*
Falkirk (0) 1 *(McPherson 82)* 844
Brechin C: Hay; Miller G, Black (Charles King), Smith J, Cairney, Fotheringham K, Skinner (Gibson), Jackson (Riley), Grant, Templeman, Millar M.
Falkirk: Ferguson; Lawrie (Rodgers), McQuilken■, Rennie, Hughes, James, Kerr (Henry), Miller, Coyle (Samuel), McPherson, Tosh.
aet; Brechin C won 5-3 on penalties.

Queen of the S (1) 2 *(O'Neil 25, Lyle 90)*
Dumbarton (0) 0 1722
Queen of the S: Scott; Gray, Anderson, Paton, Aitken, Crawford, O'Neil, McColligan (Bowey), Lyle, Weatherson (Shields), McAlpine (McLaughlin).
Dumbarton: Grindlay; Dickie (Lynes), Stewart, Brown T, Duffy, Collins, Crilly, Bonar (McEwan), Flannery (McKelvie), Brown A, Dillon.

Ross Co (1) 1 *(Gethins 43)*
St Mirren (0) 1 *(Gillies 64)* 1128
Ross Co: Bullock; McCulloch, Mackay, Perry, Canning, Gilbert, McGarry (Bayne), Ferguson, Bone (Webb), Gethins, Robertson (Wood).
St Mirren: Robertson; McGowan, Kerr, Guy (Dow), Fellner, MacKenzie, Gillies, Mendes (Lappin), McGinty (Yardley), Cameron, Ross.
aet; St Mirren won 6-5 on penalties.

SEMI-FINALS

Tuesday, 27 August 2002

Queen's Park (1) 3 *(Allan 27, Gemmell 72, Whelan 75)*
Brechin C (1) 4 *(Millar M 35, Jackson 64, Fotheringham 69, Grant 73)* 1214
Queen's Park: Mitchell; Ferry, Gallagher J, Moffat, Agostini, Quinn, Taggart (Sinclair), Whelan, Gemmell, Canning (Fisher), Allan (Martin).
Brechin C: Hay; Miller G, Black (Charles King), Smith J, Cairney, Fotheringham K, Skinner, Millar M (Campbell), Grant, Gibson, Templeman (Jackson).

St Mirren (2) 3 *(McGinty 14, Cameron 43, Fellner 81)*
Queen of the S (2) 5 *(Shields 7, 89, Lyle 38, Bowey 50, Weatherson 88)* 2528
St Mirren: Roy; McGowan (Baltacha), Kerr, Murray, Fellner, Dow, Gillies, Mendes, McGinty (Yardley), Cameron (Kristo), Ross.
Queen of the S: Scott; Nielson, Atkinson (Anderson), McAlpine, Aitken, Crawford, O'Neil, Bowey, Lyle (McLaughlin), Shields (Allan), Weatherson.

FINAL

Sunday, 20 October 2002
(at Broadwood Stadium)

Brechin C (0) 0
Queen of the S (1) 2 *(O'Neil 23, Lyle 47)* 6428
Brechin C: Hay; McCulloch, Black, Smith J, Cairney, Fotheringham K, Charles King (Clark), Riley (Miller G), Grant, Jackson, Gibson (Templeman).
Queen of the S: Goram; Neilson, Anderson, McColligan, Aitken, Thomson, O'Neil, Bowey, Weatherson (O'Connor), Lyle (McLaughlin), McAlpine.
Referee: John Underhill (Edinburgh).

SCOTTISH CUP FINALS 1874–2003

Year	*Winners*	*Runners-up*	*Score*
1874	Queen's Park	Clydesdale	2-0
1875	Queen's Park	Renton	3-0
1876	Queen's Park	Third Lanark	2-0 after 1-1 draw
1877	Vale of Leven	Rangers	3-2 after 0-0 and 1-1 draws
1878	Vale of Leven	Third Lanark	1-0
1879	Vale of Leven*	Rangers	
1880	Queen's Park	Thornlibank	3-0
1881	Queen's Park†	Dumbarton	3-1
1882	Queen's Park	Dumbarton	4-1 after 2-2 draw
1883	Dumbarton	Vale of Leven	2-1 after 2-2 draw
1884	Queen's Park‡	Vale of Leven	
1885	Renton	Vale of Leven	3-1 after 0-0 draw
1886	Queen's Park	Renton	3-1
1887	Hibernian	Dumbarton	2-1
1888	Renton	Cambuslang	6-1
1889	Third Lanark§	Celtic	2-1
1890	Queen's Park	Vale of Leven	2-1 after 1-1 draw
1891	Hearts	Dumbarton	1-0
1892	Celtic¶	Queen's Park	5-1
1893	Queen's Park	Celtic	2-1
1894	Rangers	Celtic	3-1
1895	St Bernard's	Renton	2-1
1896	Hearts	Hibernian	3-1
1897	Rangers	Dumbarton	5-1
1898	Rangers	Kilmarnock	2-0
1899	Celtic	Rangers	2-0
1900	Celtic	Queen's Park	4-3
1901	Hearts	Celtic	4-3
1902	Hibernian	Celtic	1-0
1903	Rangers	Hearts	2-0 after 1-1 and 0-0 draws
1904	Celtic	Rangers	3-2
1905	Third Lanark	Rangers	3-1 after 0-0 draw
1906	Hearts	Third Lanark	1-0
1907	Celtic	Hearts	3-0
1908	Celtic	St Mirren	5-1
1909	••		
1910	Dundee	Clyde	2-1 after 2-2 and 0-0 draws
1911	Celtic	Hamilton A	2-0 after 0-0 draw
1912	Celtic	Clyde	2-0
1913	Falkirk	Raith R	2-0
1914	Celtic	Hibernian	4-1 after 0-0 draw
1920	Kilmarnock	Albion R	3-2
1921	Partick T	Rangers	1-0
1922	Morton	Rangers	1-0
1923	Celtic	Hibernian	1-0
1924	Airdrieonians	Hibernian	2-0
1925	Celtic	Dundee	2-1
1926	St Mirren	Celtic	2-0
1927	Celtic	East Fife	3-1
1928	Rangers	Celtic	4-0
1929	Kilmarnock	Rangers	2-0
1930	Rangers	Partick T	2-1 after 0-0 draw
1931	Celtic	Motherwell	4-2 after 2-2 draw
1932	Rangers	Kilmarnock	3-0 after 1-1 draw
1933	Celtic	Motherwell	1-0
1934	Rangers	St Mirren	5-0
1935	Rangers	Hamilton A	2-1
1936	Rangers	Third Lanark	1-0
1937	Celtic	Aberdeen	2-1
1938	East Fife	Kilmarnock	4-2 after 1-1 draw
1939	Clyde	Motherwell	4-0
1947	Aberdeen	Hibernian	2-1
1948	Rangers	Morton	1-0 after 1-1 draw
1949	Rangers	Clyde	4-1
1950	Rangers	East Fife	3-0
1951	Celtic	Motherwell	1-0
1952	Motherwell	Dundee	4-0
1953	Rangers	Aberdeen	1-0 after 1-1 draw
1954	Celtic	Aberdeen	2-1
1955	Clyde	Celtic	1-0 after 1-1 draw
1956	Hearts	Celtic	3-1
1957	Falkirk	Kilmarnock	2-1 after 1-1 draw
1958	Clyde	Hibernian	1-0
1959	St Mirren	Aberdeen	3-1
1960	Rangers	Kilmarnock	2-0
1961	Dunfermline Ath	Celtic	2-0 after 0-0 draw
1962	Rangers	St Mirren	2-0
1963	Rangers	Celtic	3-0 after 1-1 draw
1964	Rangers	Dundee	3-1
1965	Celtic	Dunfermline Ath	3-2
1966	Rangers	Celtic	1-0 after 0-0 draw
1967	Celtic	Aberdeen	2-0
1968	Dunfermline Ath	Hearts	3-1
1969	Celtic	Rangers	4-0
1970	Aberdeen	Celtic	3-1

Year	Winners	Runners-up	Score
1971	Celtic	Rangers	2-1 after 1-1 draw
1972	Celtic	Hibernian	6-1
1973	Rangers	Celtic	3-2
1974	Celtic	Dundee U	3-0
1975	Celtic	Airdrieonians	3-1
1976	Rangers	Hearts	3-1
1977	Celtic	Rangers	1-0
1978	Rangers	Aberdeen	2-1
1979	Rangers	Hibernian	3-2 after 0-0 and 0-0 draws
1980	Celtic	Rangers	1-0
1981	Rangers	Dundee U	4-1 after 0-0 draw
1982	Aberdeen	Rangers	4-1 (aet)
1983	Aberdeen	Rangers	1-0 (aet)
1984	Aberdeen	Celtic	2-1 (aet)
1985	Celtic	Dundee U	2-1
1986	Aberdeen	Hearts	3-0
1987	St Mirren	Dundee U	1-0 (aet)
1988	Celtic	Dundee U	2-1
1989	Celtic	Rangers	1-0
1990	Aberdeen	Celtic	0-0 (aet)
		(Aberdeen won 9-8 on penalties)	
1991	Motherwell	Dundee U	4-3 (aet)
1992	Rangers	Airdrieonians	2-1
1993	Rangers	Aberdeen	2-1
1994	Dundee U	Rangers	1-0
1995	Celtic	Airdrieonians	1-0
1996	Rangers	Hearts	5-1
1997	Kilmarnock	Falkirk	1-0
1998	Hearts	Rangers	2-1
1999	Rangers	Celtic	1-0
2000	Rangers	Aberdeen	4-0
2001	Celtic	Hibernian	3-0
2002	Rangers	Celtic	3-2
2003	Rangers	Dundee	1-0

*Vale of Leven awarded cup, Rangers failing to appear for replay after 1-1 draw.
†After Dumbarton protested the first game, which Queen's Park won 2-1.
‡Queen's Park awarded cup, Vale of Leven failing to appear.
§Replay by order of Scottish FA because of playing conditions in first match, won 3-0 by Third Lanark.
¶After mutually protested game which Celtic won 1-0.
••Owing to riot, the cup was withheld after two drawn games – between Celtic and Rangers 2-2 and 1-1.

SCOTTISH CUP WINS

Celtic 31, Rangers 31, Queen's Park 10, Aberdeen 7, Hearts 6, Clyde 3, Kilmarnock 3, St Mirren 3, Vale of Leven 3, Dunfermline Ath 2, Falkirk 2, Hibernian 2, Motherwell 2, Renton 2, Third Lanark 2, Airdrieonians 1, Dumbarton 1, Dundee 1, Dundee U 1, East Fife 1, Morton 1, Partick T 1, St Bernard's 1.

APPEARANCES IN FINAL

Celtic 50, Rangers 48, Aberdeen 15, Queen's Park 12, Hearts 12, Hibernian 11, Kilmarnock 8, Vale of Leven 7, Clyde 6, Dumbarton 6, Dundee U 7, Motherwell 6, St Mirren 6, Third Lanark 6, Dundee 5, Renton 5, Airdrieonians 4, Dunfermline Ath 3, East Fife 3, Falkirk 3, Hamilton A 2, Morton 2, Partick T 2, Albion R 1, Cambuslang 1, Clydesdale 1, Raith R 1, St Bernard's 1, Thornlibank 1.

LEAGUE CHALLENGE CUP FINALS 1991–2003

Year	Winners	Runners-up	Score
1991	Dundee	Ayr U	3-2
1992	Hamilton A	Ayr U	1-0
1993	Hamilton A	Morton	3-2
1994	St Mirren	Falkirk	9-3
1995	Airdrieonians	Dundee	3-2
1996	Stenhousemuir	Dundee U	0-0
	(Stenhousemuir won 5-4 on penalties)		
1997	Stranraer	St Johnstone	1-0
1998	Falkirk 1 Qeeen of the South 0		
1999	no competition		
2000	Alloa	Inverness CT	4-4
	(Alloa won 5-4 on penalties)		
2001	Airdrieonians	Livingston	2-2
	(Airdrieonians won 3-2 on penalties)		
2002	Airdrieonians	Alloa	2-1
2003	Queen of the S	Brechin C	2-0

TENNENT'S SCOTTISH CUP 2002–03

▪ *Denotes player sent off.*

FIRST ROUND

Saturday, 7 December 2002

East Stirling (1) 1 *(Leishman 15)*

Threave Rovers (1) 1 *(Parker 26)* 130

East Stirling: Findlay; Maughan, McLaren, McGhee, Grant, Oates, McAuley, Mackay, Fairbairn, Boyle (Ure), Leishman (Livingstone).
Threave Rovers: Gall; Smith, Kirkpatrick, Wilson, McGinley P, Cochrane, Budrys (Armstrong), McGinley A, Adams, Parker, Baker (Hudson).

Forfar Ath (0) 3 *(Bavidge 46, 49, Byers 58)*

Huntly (0) 1 *(De Barros 58)* 544

Forfar Ath: Ferrie; Rattray, McCulloch, Horn, Good, Lunan, Byers, Sellars, Stewart, Bavidge, Milne (Henderson).
Huntly: Bremner; Campbell, Henderson D, Guild, Small, Copland (Henderson C), De Barros, McGowan (Gillies), Stewart, Addicoat (Thomson), Farmer.

Montrose (2) 2 *(Johnson 32, Webster K 44)*

Berwick R (0) 1 *(Burke 89)* 290

Montrose: McGlynn; Gibson, Ferguson, Conway, Christie, McQuillan, Webster K (Gilzean), Johnson, Henderson (Webster C), Kerrigan (Budd), McKinnon.
Berwick R: Godfrey; Murie, Smith A, Forrest E▪, Brown▪, Forrest G, Connelly (Neill A), Bradley, Wood, Burke, Ferguson (Connell).

Preston Ath (0) 0

Hamilton A (1) 1 *(McPhee 4)* 973

Preston Ath: Lennie; Thomson, Brown, Wojyowycz, Scott, Nisbett, Houston, Moffat (Ballantyne M sr), McCall, Dixon, Ballantyne M jr.
Hamilton A: Potter; Nelson, Cunnington, Dobbins, Sweeney (Elfallah), Alisdair Graham, Russell, Sherry, Alastair Graham (Keegans), McPhee, Callaghan.

Raith R (0) 1 *(Blackadder 72)*

Dumbarton (0) 0 1639

Raith R: Monin; Ellis, Parkin, Brady, Dennis, Nanou (Miller), Blackadder, Rivas, Smith (Hawley), Calderon, McManus (Boylan).
Dumbarton: Grindlay; Dickie (Stewart), Brittain, Scally, Duffy, Collins, Robertson (McKelvie), McEwan (Bonar), Flannery, Lynes, Dillon.

Selkirk (1) 1 *(Kerr D 33).*

Cowdenbeath (1) 4 *(Winter 43, Gordon 64, Gilfillan 76, Buchanan 84)* 405

Selkirk: Lumsden; Biggs, Weir, Kerr D, Hume, Kayser, Potts, Edwards (Ross), Hastie, Whitehead (Linton), Kerr A (Wilson).
Cowdenbeath: O'Connor; Renwick, Campbell, White, Wilson, Byle, Mauchlen (Fusco), Winter, Gilfillan (Buchanan), Gordon, Elliott (Crabbe).

Stenhousemuir (3) 4 *(Coulter 14, Crawford 28, Graham 34, McFarlane 54)*

Brechin C (1) 1 *(Riley 8)* 309

Stenhousemuir: Smith; Coulter, McKenna, Hamilton, Easton, Booth, Waldie, Graham (McKenzie), Crawford, McFarlane (Murphy), Stein (Donnelly).
Brechin C: Cairns; Riley, Black, Smith J, Cairney, Fotheringham K (Smith D), Charles King, Templeman, Miller (Gibson), Jackson, Clark (Chris King).

Stranraer (1) 1 *(Moore 41)*

Whitehill Welfare (1) 1 *(Bennett 24)* 282

Stranraer: Hillcoat; Gaughan, Wright, Wingate, Marshall (Sharp), Aitken, Finlayson, Jenkins, Harty, Moore (Kerr), Scott.
Whitehill Welfare: Cantley; Johnstone, Lee, Lynes, Ewart, Martin, Cocker, Bennett, O'Donnell, Ronaldson, Hope.

FIRST ROUND REPLAYS

Saturday, 14 December 2002

Threave Rovers (0) 2 *(Smith 72 (pen), Adams 78)*

East Stirling (0) 1 *(McLaren 49)* 391

Threave Rovers: Gall; Smith, Kirkpatrick, Wilson, McGinlay, Baker, Parker, Adams, Budrys (Hudson), McGinley, Cochrane.
East Stirling: Findlay; Maughan, McLaren, McGhee, Grant, Mackay, Sean McAuley, Struthers (Ure), Fairbairn, Boyle (Diver), Leishman.

Whitehill Welfare (1) 2 *(Bennett 10, Ewart 89)*

Stranraer (2) 3 *(Kerr 5, 33, Gaughan 78)* 482

Whitehill Welfare: Cantley; Archibald (Price), Lee, Lynes (Hunter), Ewart, Martin, Cocker, Bennett, O'Donnell, Ronaldson, Hope.
Stranraer: Hillcoat; Gaughan, Wright, Wingate, Hodge (Fallon), Jenkins, Finlayson, Aitken (Curran), Kerr (Harty), Moore, Sharp.

SECOND ROUND

Saturday, 4 January 2003

Gretna (1) 3 *(Dobie 4, 75, Hore 55)*

Cove Rangers (0) 0 468

Gretna: Mathieson; May, Skelton, Turner, McQuilter, Cleeland, Skinner, Irons (McGuffie), Dobie, Hore (Milligan), Henney.
Cove Rangers: Coull M; Summers (Pilichos), McGinlay, Allan, Murphy, Yeats (McCraw), Clark (Greig), Smith, Coull K, Beattie, Brown.

Keith (0) 1 *(Nicol 50)*

Cowdenbeath (0) 3 *(Brown 54, Elliott 58, O'Connor 70)* 402

Keith: Shearer; Morrison B, Brown, Robertson (Calder), McKenzie (Gibson), King, Still, Smith, Cadger, Nicol (Donaldson), Reid.
Cowdenbeath: Graham; Renwick, Campbell, White, Wilson, Mauchlen, Elliott, Winter, Brown, Gordon, Buchanan (Byle).

Morton (3) 4 *(Uotinen 4, Chisholm (og) 35, MacGregor 41, Williams 81 (pen))*

Deveronvale (0) 3 *(Taylor 67, Dlugonski 84, Gaughan (og) 85)* 1772

Morton: Coyle; Collins, Bottiglieri, MacGregor, Gaughan, Maisano M (Bannerman), MacDonald, Maisano J, Williams, Hawke, Uotinen (Cannie).
Deveronvale: Thompson; Dolan, Kinghorn, Chisholm (Taylor), Dlugonski, Anderson, McAllister (Stephen B), Stephen L, McKenzie, Murray, Montgomery (Brown).

Queen's Park (0) 1 *(Whelan 63)*

Albion R (1) 1 *(Diack 2)* 1117

Queen's Park: Mitchell; Sinclair, Ferry, Moffat, Agostini, Fallon, Martin, Whelan, Dunning (Menelaws), Clark, Allan.
Albion R: Shearer; Paterson, Stirling, Smith J, McCaig, Cormack, McAllister (Mercer), Silvestro, Bradford, Diack, Dick (McLean).

Saturday, 11 January 2003

Peterhead (0) 1 *(Cooper 89 (pen))*

Elgin C (0) 0 1184

Peterhead: Mathers; MacDonald, McSkimming, Raeside, Simpson, Bain (Cooper), Tindal, Stewart (Robertson), Mackay (Cameron), Johnston, Roddie.
Elgin C: Pirie; Grant, Teasdale, Hind, Mackay▪, Tully, Ross, McBride, McMullan, Steele, Sanderson (James).

Monday, 13 January 2003

Forfar Ath (2) 3 *(Lunan 10, Tosh 22, Bavidge 89)*

Stenhousemuir (1) 1 *(McCormick 12)* 598

Forfar Ath: Ferrie; Rattray, McCulloch, Horn, Good, Lunan, Stewart, Byers, Tosh, Bavidge, Henderson.
Stenhousemuir: Smith; Coulter, McKenna, Hamilton, Easton (McKenzie), Booth■, Waldie (Donnelly), Wilson, Crawford (Graham), McCormick, Stein.

Raith R (3) 3 *(Hawley 24, Smith 27, Carrigan 33)*

Montrose (0) 1 *(Gilzean 63)* 1515

Raith R: Ojeda; Patino, Calderon (Moffat), Brady, Dennis, Nanou, Carrigan (McManus), Rivas, Smith, Hampshire, Hawley (Prest).
Montrose: McGlynn; McQuillan, Thomson (Kerrigan), Gibson, Christie, Conway, Webster K (Henderson), Johnson, Gilzean, Webster C (Brand), Ferguson.

Stranraer (0) 4 *(Wingate 62, Sharp 68, 86, Harty 82)*

Stirling Albion (0) 1 *(McKinnon 80)* 350

Stranraer: Hillcoat; Gaughan, Wright, Wingate, Hodge, Jenkins, Sharp, Aitken (Curran), Harty, Kerr (Finlayson), Moore.
Stirling Albion: Reid; Nugent P, Hay (Munro), McNally, Rowe, Reilly (Duncan), Dunn, McKinnon, Mallan, Nicholas, O'Brien.

Tuesday, 14 January 2003

Airdrie U (1) 1 *(Gow 18)*

Threave R (0) 0 1155

Airdrie U: McGeown; Wilson W, Armstrong, Stewart, Brannigan (McGuire), McGowan, Gow, Gardner (Ronald), McKeown, Docherty, Vareille.
Threave R: Gall; Smith, Kirkpatrick, Wilson, McGinley P, Cochrane, Budrys (Armstrong), McGinley A, Parker, Adams, Baker (Struthers).

Wednesday, 15 January 2003

Hamilton A (0) 1 *(McPhee 77)*

East Fife (0) 1 *(Deuchar 89)* 684

Hamilton A: Potter; Nelson, Cunnington, Dobbins, Sweeney, Alisdair Graham (Elfallah), Bonnar, Walker, Russell■, McPhee, Callaghan.
East Fife: Butter; Russell, Donaldson, Mortimer, Hall, Allison, McMillan (Farnan), Graham, Deuchar, Herkes, Gilbert (Love).

SECOND ROUND REPLAYS

Tuesday, 14 January 2003

Albion R (0) 0

Queen's Park (1) 2 *(Allan 18, Martin 85)* 404

Albion R: Shearer; Paterson, Stirling (McLean), Smith J (McAllister), Cormack (Dick), Lumsden, Mercer, Silvestro, Bradford, Diack, McCaig.
Queen's Park: Mitchell; Lappin, Ferry, Moffat, Agostini, Fallon, Martin (Menelaws), Whelan, Gemmell, Clark, Allan (Fisher).

Monday, 20 January 2003

East Fife (0) 2 *(Herkes 68, Graham 88)*

Hamilton A (1) 2 *(McPhee 34, Callaghan 90)* 737

East Fife: Butter; Russell, Donaldson, Mortimer, Hall, Allison, McMillan (Love), Graham (Rollo), Deuchar, Herkes, Cunningham (Gilbert).
Hamilton A: Potter; Nelson (McDonald), Cunnington, Dobbins, Sweeney, Alisdair Graham (Gribben), Bonnar, Walker, Armstrong (Elfallah), McPhee, Callaghan.
aet; Hamilton A won 5-3 on penalties.

THIRD ROUND

Saturday, 25 January 2003

Airdrie U (1) 1 *(McGuire 45)*

St Johnstone (0) 1 *(Baxter 88)* 2073

Airdrie U: McGeown; Armstrong, McVey, Stewart, Docherty, McGowan, Wilson M, McKeown, Ronald, Vareille (Wilson W), McGuire (Gardner).
St Johnstone: Main; Robertson, Forsyth (Hay), McCulloch, Murray, Maxwell, Connolly, Reilly (Dods), Hartley, Parker, Lovenkrands (Baxter).

Arbroath (0) 0

Rangers (2) 3 *(Ferguson 22, Moore 31, Arveladze 57)* 4153

Arbroath: Hinchcliffe; Tait, Florence, Cusick (Spink), Ritchie, Currie, Brownlie (Swankie), Cargill, Feroz, McGlashan, Hanslee (Heenan).
Rangers: Klos; Ricksen, Moore, Amoruso (Malcolm), Numan, Ross, Ferguson, McCann (Caniggia), de Boer, Mols, Arveladze (McLean).

Ayr U (1) 2 *(Black 9, Grady 76 (pen))*

Peterhead (0) 0 1966

Ayr U: Nelson; Lyle, Lovering (Dunlop), McManus, Campbell, Craig, Chaplain (Latta), Smyth, Kean, Grady, Black.
Peterhead: Mathers; MacDonald, McSkimming, Raeside, Simpson, Bain, Tindal, Stewart, Cameron, Johnston (Robertson), Roddie (McLean).

Celtic (0) 3 *(Larsson 47, 57, Sylla 70)*

St Mirren (0) 0 29,703

Celtic: Hedman; Mjällby, Valgaeren (Crainey), Laursen, Thompson (Maloney), McNamara, Sylla, Smith, Healy, Larsson, Sutton (Fernandez).
St Mirren: Roy; Guy, Baker, Broadfoot, Denham, McGinty (Lowing), Gillies, Murray, Cameron (Dunbar), Mendes, Lapin (Robb).

Cowdenbeath (0) 2 *(Riordan 58, Gordon 80)*

Alloa Ath (0) 3 *(Crabbe 53, 74, Thomson 72)* 529

Cowdenbeath: Graham; Renwick, Campbell, White, Wilson, Mauchlen, Riordan, Winter, Brown, Gordon, Hilland (Buchanan).
Alloa Ath: Hogarth; Valentine, Seaton, Watson, Thomson, Christie, Walker, Ferguson (Cowan), Davidson (Crabbe), Hutchison (Hamilton), Little.

Dundee U (0) 2 *(O'Donnell 70, Hamilton 79)*

Hibernian (2) 3 *(Brebner 9, 28, 86)* 8986

Dundee U: Gallacher; McCunnie (Hamilton), Lauchlan, Wilson, McCracken, Paterson, Chiarini, Miller, Easton (O'Donnell), Dodds, McIntyre.
Hibernian: Colgan; Fenwick, Smith, Zambernardi, Orman, Murray, Wiss, Brebner, Townsley (O'Neil), Paatelainen, McManus (O'Connor).

Falkirk (4) 4 *(Samuel 3, 15, 30, Coyle 13)*

Hearts (0) 0 7244

Falkirk: Ferguson; Henry, Rennie, MacKenzie, Hughes, Nicholls, Kerr, Miller, Coyle, McPherson, Samuel (McSween).
Hearts: Gordon; Pressley, Mahe, Maybury, McKenna, Valois, Stamp, Boyack (Webster), Macfarlane (Severin), Weir (Wales), De Vries.

Forfar Ath (1) 2 *(Byers 10, Tosh 77)*

Stranraer (1) 2 *(Kerr 34, Jenkins 51)* 661

Forfar Ath: Ferrie; Rattray, McCulloch, Horn, Good, Lunan (Williams), Milne (Anthony), Byers, Tosh, Bavidge, Henderson.
Stranraer: Hillcoat; Gaughan, Wright, Wingate, Hodge, Aitken, Finlayson, Curran, Moore, Kerr, Jenkins.

Gretna (1) 1 *(Skinner 3)*

Clyde (1) 2 *(Millen 29, Hinds 62)* 973

Gretna: Mathieson; Knox, Skelton (Hore), Turner, McQuilter, Irons, Skinner, Galloway, Dobie, Henney, Cleeland (McGuffie).
Clyde: Halliwell; Potter, McLaughlin, Kernaghan, Kane, Ross, Convery, Millen, Falconer (McConalogue), Cosgrove, Hinds (Reid).

Inverness CT (0) 2 *(Robson 66, Wyness 70)*
Raith R (0) 0 2293
Inverness CT: Brown; Tokely, Golabek, Mann, McCaffrey, McBain, Duncan, Wyness, Ritchie (Christie), Hart, Robson.
Raith R: Ojeda; Patino (Fyfe), Ellis, Brady, (Carrigan), Dennis, Nanou (Hawley), Blackadder, Rivas, Smith, Calderon, McManus.

Kilmarnock (0) 0
Motherwell (1) 1 *(McFadden 34)* 6882
Kilmarnock: Marshall; Shields, Innes■, Dillon, Fowler, DiGiacomo (Murray), Mahood, Fulton, McLaren (McSwegan), Dargo (McLaughlin), Boyd.
Motherwell: Dubourdeau; Corrigan, Partridge, Hammell (Cowan), Kinniburgh, Lasley (Fagan), Pearson, Leitch, Adams, McFadden, Clarkson.

Livingston (1) 1 *(Bollan 26)*
Dunfermline Ath (0) 1 *(Crawford 61)* 4334
Livingston: McEwan; Brinquin, Bollan, Rubio, Andrews, Quino, Makel, O'Brien (Toure-Maman), Wilson (Xausa), Zarate (McMenamin), Bingham.
Dunfermline Ath: Stillie; McGroarty (Hampshire), Dempsey, Skerla, Wilson, Bullen, Nicholson, Dair, Karnebeek (Kilgannon), Crawford, Brewster.

Partick T (0) 0
Dundeee (1) 2 *(Nemsadze 13, Rae 81)* 4825
Partick T: Arthur; Paterson, Archibald, Craigan, Lennon, Lilley, Mitchell (Walker), Buchan (McKinstry), Hardie, Britton, Burns.
Dundeee: Speroni; Mackay, Khizanishvili, Mair, Wilkie, Smith, Nemsadze, Rae, Brady, Novo, Milne.

Queen of the S (0) 0
Aberdeen (0) 0 5716
Queen of the S: Goram; Renicks, Anderson, McColligan (O'Connor), Aitken, Thomson, O'Neil, Bowey, Paton, Weatherson, McLaughlin.
Aberdeen: Preece; McGuire, Rutkiewicz, Anderson, McAllister (O'Donoghue), McNaughton (Sheerin), Tosh, Clark, D'Jaffo (Mike), Derek Young, Mackie.

Queen's Park (1) 2 *(Gemmell 31, 54)*
Hamilton A (1) 2 *(Bonnar 5, Russell 84)* 1362
Queen's Park: Mitchell; Ferry, Allan (Menelaws), Fallon, Agostini, Sinclair, Clark, Gallagher P, Gemmell, Whelan, Canning.
Hamilton A: Potter; Nelson, McDonald (Gribben), Dobbins, Sweeney, Alasdair Graham, Bonnar (Alistair Graham), Walker (Elfallah), Russell, McPhee, Callaghan.

Ross Co (1) 1 *(Winters 43)*
Morton (1) 2 *(Williams 20, 62)* 1822
Ross Co: Bullock; Perry, Robertson, Gilbert, Irvine, McCulloch (Webb), Hislop (McGarry), Cowie, Bayne, McLeish (Wood), Winters.
Morton: Coyle; Collins, Bottiglieri, MacGregor, Henderson, Maisano M, MacDonald, Maisano J (Bannerman), Williams, Cannie (McAlister), Uotinen.

THIRD ROUND REPLAYS

Tuesday, 4 February 2003

Dunfermline Ath (0) 2 *(Brewster 67, 90)*
Livingston (0) 0 3158
Dunfermline Ath: Stillie; Bullen, Dempsey, Skerla, Wilson, Dair, Nicholson, Kilgannon (MacPherson), Hampshire, Crawford, Brewster.
Livingston: McEwan; Brinquin, Bahoken, Rubio (McMenamin), Andrews, Quino, Toure-Maman (Bingham), O'Brien, Lovell, Zarate, Wilson (Camacho).

St Johnstone (1) 1 *(Connolly 34)*
Airdrie U (0) 1 *(Vareille 51)* 2105
St Johnstone: Cuthbert; Baxter (Ferry), Robertson, McCulloch, Murray, Maxwell, Hay (Parker), Reilly, Hartley, Connolly, Lovenkrands.
Airdrie U: McGeown; Armstrong, McVey, Stewart (Wilson W), Docherty, McGowan, Vareille, Wilson M, Ronald, McKeown (Gardner), McGuire (Gow).
aet; St Johnstone won 4-2 on penalties.

Monday, 10 February 2003

Hamilton A (2) 3 *(McDonald 9, Agostini (og) 26, Armstrong 48)*
Queen's Park (1) 2 *(Gemmell 15, Menelaws 82)* 807
Hamilton A: Potter; Arbuckle, McDonald, Dobbins, Sweeney, Alisdair Graham, Bonnar, Walker (Russell), Armstrong, McPhee, Callaghan.
Queen's Park: Mitchell; Ferry, Canning, Sinclair, Agostini, Fallon, Clark (Menelaws), Whelan, Gemmell, Gallagher, Allan.

Monday, 17 February 2003

Stranraer (0) 1 *(Harty 75)*
Forfar Ath (0) 0 425
Stranraer: Hillcoat; Gaughan (Sharp), Hodge, Crawford, Wingate, Wright, Finlayson, Aitken, Harty, Moore, Kerr (Lurinsky).
Forfar Ath: Brown; Rattray (Cocozza), McCulloch, Milne, Good (McCloy), Byers, Williams (Hodge), Anthony, Shaw, Bavidge, Henderson.

Tuesday, 18 February 2003

Aberdeen (3) 4 *(Tosh 16, D'Jaffo 22, 88, Anderson 25)*
Queen of the S (0) 1 *(Weatherson 85 (pen))* 6068
Aberdeen: Preece; McGuire (McAllister), Deloumeaux (Rutkiewicz), Anderson, O'Donoghue, Payne, Tosh (Fabiano), Clark, Sheerin, Derek Young, D'Jaffo.
Queen of the S: Scott; Renicks, Anderson, McColligan, Aitken, Thomson, O'Neil (Weatherson), Bowie, O'Connor (Lyle), Paton (McAlpine), McLaughlin.

FOURTH ROUND

Saturday, 22 February 2003

Alloa Ath (0) 0
Falkirk (0) 2 *(Coyle 52, Samuel 64)* 3059
Alloa Ath: Soutar; Walker, Seaton, Valentine, Thomson, Christie, Hamilton, Ferguson, Crabbe (Davidson), Sloan (Hutchison), Little (Evans G).
Falkirk: Ferguson; Henry (McSween), McQuilken, MacKenzie, Hughes, Nicholls, Kerr, Miller, Coyle (Taylor), McPherson, Samuel (Rodgers).

Ayr U (0) 0
Rangers (0) 1 *(de Boer 79)* 9608
Ayr U: Nelson; Lyle, Lovering, McManus, Campbell, Craig, Chaplain, Smyth, Whalen (Kean), Grady, Murray.
Rangers: Klos; Malcolm (Thompson), Moore, Amoruso, Numan, Muscat, Ferguson, Arteta (Hughes), de Boer, Arveladze, McCann (Caniggia).

Clyde (0) 0
Motherwell (1) 2 *(McFadden 41, 76)* 5032
Clyde: Halliwell (Morrison); Potter, Mensing, Kernaghan, Kane, Ross, Hagen, Millen, Falconer (Convery), Cosgrove, McConalogue (Shields).
Motherwell: Dubourdeau; Corrigan, Partridge, Hammell, Vaughan, Ramsay, Pearson, Fagan (Lasley), Adams, McFadden (Lehman), Craig (Clarkson).

Dundee (2) 2 *(Lovell 22, Novo 41)*
Aberdeen (0) 0 7549
Dundee: Speroni; Mackay, Khizanishvili, Mair, Wilkie, Smith, Nemsadze, Rae, Lovell (Burchill), Novo, Caballero (Milne).
Aberdeen: Preece; McGuire, Deloumeaux (McAllister), Anderson, Hart, O'Donoghue (Fabiano), Tosh, Clark (Payne), Sheerin, Derek Young, D'Jaffo.

Dunfermline Ath (0) 1 *(Nicholson 58)*
Hibernian (1) 1 *(Murray 41)* 6619
Dunfermline Ath: Stillie; MacPherson (Hunt), Grondin (Walker), Skerla, Wilson, Dair, Nicholson, Brannan, Mason, Crawford, Brewster.
Hibernian: Colgan; Fenwick, Smith, James, Doumbe, Murray, Townsley (Jack), Brebner, O'Neil, Paatelainen, McManus (O'Connor).

Inverness CT (2) 6 *(Wyness 8, 69, Robson 31, 51, Ritchie 49, McCaffrey 75)*
Hamilton A (1) 1 *(Bonnar 2)* 1917
Inverness CT: Brown; Tokely, Golabek, Mann (Munro), McCaffrey, McBain, Duncan, Wyness (Keogh), Ritchie, Christie, Robson (Bagan).
Hamilton A: Potter; Arbuckle (Sherry), McDonald (Dobbins), Kerr, Sweeney, Alisdair Graham, Bonnar, Walker, Armstrong, McPhee (Russell), Callaghan.

Morton (0) 0
Stranraer (1) 2 *(Kerr 33, Harty 52)* 3679
Morton: Coyle; Collins, Bottiglieri, MacGregor, Henderson, Maisano M, MacDonald, Maisano J (Bannerman), Williams, Hawke (Cannie), Uotinen (McAlister).
Stranraer: Hillcoat; Gaughan, Wright, Wingate, Hodge, Aitken, Finlayson (Sharp), Marshall (Crawford), Harty, Kerr (Lurinsky), Jenkins.

Sunday, 23 February 2003

Celtic (1) 3 *(Hartson 31 (pen), 85 (pen), Smith 76)*
St Johnstone (0) 0 26,205
Celtic: Broto (Marshall); Mjällby, Crainey, Laursen, Sylla, Smith, Healy, Lambert (Maloney), Guppy, Hartson, Fernandez.
St Johnstone: Cuthbert; Baxter, Robertson, McClune (Hay), Dods, Maxwell, Noble (Panther), Parker, Hartley, Connolly, Lovenkrands.

FOURTH ROUND REPLAY

Thursday, 6 March 2003

Hibernian (0) 0
Dunfermline Ath (0) 2 *(Crawford 56, Wilson 78)* 5851
Hibernian: Colgan; Fenwick (Arpinon), Smith, James, Jack, Murray, Doumbe, Brebner, Townsley (O'Neil), O'Connor (Paatelainen), McManus.
Dunfermline Ath: Stillie; MacPherson, Grondin (Walker), Skerla, Wilson, McGarty, Nicholson, Brannan, Mason (Dempsey), Crawford, Brewster (Hunt).

QUARTER-FINALS

Saturday, 22 March 2003

Falkirk (0) 1 *(Coyle 57)*
Dundee (0) 1 *(Novo 66)* 7403
Falkirk: Ferguson; Henry, McQuilken (Reid), MacKenzie, Hughes, Nicholls, Kerr, Miller, Coyle (Rodgers), McPherson, Samuel (Taylor).
Dundee: Speroni; Mackay, Khizanishvili, Hernandez, Wilkie, Smith, Nemsadze, Rae, Lovell (Milne), Novo (Burchill), Caballero.

Stranraer (0) 0
Motherwell (1) 4 *(Wright (og) 31, McFadden 54, Adams 59, Lehmann 86)* 4500
Stranraer: Hillcoat; Gaughan, Wright, Wingate, Farrell, Aitken (Curran), Finlayson, Jenkins, Harty, Moore (Kerr), Hodge (Kane).
Motherwell: Dubourdeau; Corrigan, Partridge (Cowan), Hammell, Vaughan, Lasley, Pearson, Leitch (Fagan), Adams, McFadden (Clarkson), Lehmann.

Lorenzo Amoruso with a flying header brings the third trophy for Rangers against Dundee with the Tennent's Scottish Cup. (Actionimages)

Ticker tape swamps jubilant Rangers players after the Scottish Cup victory. They retained the trophy which they had won the previous year. (Actionimages)

Sunday, 23 March 2003

Dunfermline Ath (1) 1 *(Grondin 23)*

Rangers (1) 1 *(Caniggia 30)* 9875

Dunfermline Ath: Stillie; MacPherson, McGroarty, Grondin (Kilgannon), Wilson, McGarty, Nicholson (Hunt), Brannan, Mason, Crawford, Brewster.
Rangers: Klos; Ricksen, Moore, Malcolm, Konterman, Muscat, Ferguson■, Arteta, de Boer, Caniggia, McCann (Arveladze).

Inverness CT (1) 1 *(Wyness 45)*

Celtic (0) 0 6050

Inverness CT: Brown; McCaffrey, Golabek, Mann, Munro, McBain, Tokely, Wyness, Ritchie (Keogh), Hart, Robson (Christie).
Celtic: Broto; Laursen, Valgaeren, McNamara, Lennon, Smith, Varga, Guppy, Maloney (Hartson), Larsson, Fernandez.

QUARTER-FINAL REPLAYS

Wednesday, 9 April 2003

Dundee (1) 4 *(Caballero 44, Burchill 93, Lovell 98, 108)*

Falkirk (1) 1 *(Taylor 31)* 9562

Dundee: Speroni; Mackay, Hernandez, Mair, Wilkie, Smith, Nemsadze, Rae (Brady), Novo (Burchill), Caballero, Milne (Lovell).
Falkirk: Ferguson; Henry, McQuilken, MacKenzie, Hughes (Christie), Reid, Kerr■, Miller (Rodgers), Coyle (Samuel), McPherson, Taylor.
aet.

Rangers (2) 3 *(Lovenkrands 4, Ferguson 19, Arteta 54)*

Dunfermline Ath (0) 0 24,752

Rangers: Klos; Ricksen, Konterman, Amoruso, Numan (McCann), Malcolm, Ferguson (Arveladze), Arteta, de Boer (Caniggia), Mols, Lovenkrands.
Dunfermline Ath: Stillie; MacPherson (Kilgannon), McGroarty, Skerla, Bullen, Mason, Nicholson, Brannan (Grondin), Hampshire, Crawford, Brewster (Hunt).

SEMI-FINALS

Saturday, 19 April 2003

(at Hampden Park)

Rangers (1) 4 *(Konterman 2, Mols 56, Amoruso 59, Partridge (og) 72)* 29,352

Motherwell (2) 3 *(Craig 15, McFadden 28, Adams 90)*

Rangers: Klos; Ricksen (Hughes), Moore (Malcolm), Amoruso, Numan, Konterman, Ferguson, Muscat, McCann, Mols, Arveladze (Thompson).
Motherwell: Dubourdeau; Corrigan, Partridge, Hammell (Cowan), Vaughan, Craig (Offiong), Pearson, Leitch (Lehmann), Adams, McFadden, Clarkson.

Sunday, 20 April 2003

(at Hampden Park)

Inverness CT (0) 0

Dundee (0) 1 *(Nemsadze 78)* 14,429

Inverness CT: Brown; Tokely, Golabek, Mann, McCaffrey (Christie), McBain, Duncan (Bagan), Wyness, Ritchie, Hart, Robson.
Dundee: Speroni; Mackay, Hernandez, Khizanishvili, Wilkie, Brady, Nemsadze, Rae, Lovell (Mair), Caballero, Milne (Novo).

FINAL

Saturday, 31 May 2003

(at Hampden Park)

Dundee (0) 0

Rangers (0) 1 *(Amoruso 66)* 47,136

Dundee: Speroni; Mackay (Milne), Hernandez, Khizanishvili, Mair, Smith, Nemsadze, Rae (Brady), Lovell, Caballero, Burchill (Novo).
Rangers: Klos; Ricksen, Moore, Amoruso, Numan (Muscat), Malcolm, Ferguson, McCann, de Boer, Mols (Ross), Arveladze (Thompson).
Referee: Kenny Clark (Paisley).

WELSH FOOTBALL 2002–03

There can rarely have been a season like it. Two promotions, a last-day escape from relegation and, most important of all, the national team giving themselves a wonderful opportunity of reaching the finals of a major tournament for the first time since the 1958 World Cup.

After forty-five years of frustration, Wales are desperately close to losing their reputation as the 'nearly men' of international football. With four games left, they lead their Euro 2004 qualifying group by two points from Italy and are virtually guaranteed at least a place in the play-offs.

All the hard work put in by manager Mark Hughes and his players began to bear fruit once the qualifying tournament got underway. A surprise 2-0 win in Finland was followed by the morale-boosting defeat of Italy at the Millennium Stadium with Newcastle's Craig Bellamy popping in a late winner. Wales then completed the double over humble Azerbaijan – winning 2-0 in Baku and 4-0 in Cardiff – to round off a fantastic first half of the campaign. A depleted team lost 2-0 to the United States in the close season to end a 20-month, 10-match unbeaten run but the result and the statistics were irrelevant. Another round of qualifiers in June made it clear that Wales and Italy were involved in a two-horse race for Group Nine's top spot. The Welsh performances were all the more impressive in the light of the various problems they encountered while trying to gain the release of key players before games.

After the previous season's disappointments, Cardiff and Wrexham both gave their supporters something to shout about. Automatic promotion behind Wigan was there for the taking but the Bluebirds lost form at precisely the wrong time and only just managed to scrape into the Second Division play-offs by a point. Having overcome their bogey team, Bristol City, in the semi-finals, Cardiff were struggling to beat QPR at the Millennium Stadium until a sublime volley by substitute Andy Campbell in extra-time sealed a place in the First Division. Equally pleasing was the absence of any crowd trouble throughout the season as owner Sam Hammam's plea for good behaviour was finally heeded.

Wrexham bounced back up to the Second Division at the first attempt with manager Denis Smith celebrating the fifth promotion of his career. Style and substance – and in particular a fondness for good old-fashioned hard work – were the ingredients of his classy side as Andy Morrell's 34 goals helped him secure a move to First Division Coventry in the summer. A 14-match unbeaten run enabled Wrexham to finish as the division's top scorers and take the third automatic promotion place behind Rushden and Hartlepool. They later went on to win the FAW Premier Cup by completely outclassing Newport County 6-1 in the final.

Swansea City endured another season of struggle and their Football League swansong was avoided only by a fairytale finale – courtesy of local boy James Thomas who scored a stunning hat-trick to beat Hull at the Vetch Field on the last day of the season. Having taken over from player/manager Nick Cusack in September, director of football Brian Flynn and his assistant Kevin Reeves more than justified their appointments and were rightly rewarded with two-year contracts.

Once again, it was a mixed season for the three sides who ply their trade in the English pyramid. Merthyr, revitalised under Andy Beattie and John Relish, immediately returned as Western Division champions to the Premier Division of the Dr Martens League where Newport County experienced an anti-climactic season while Colwyn Bay, after flirting with relegation from the Unibond League's Premier Division for the last three years, finally succumbed.

It was business as usual for those clubs who played in Europe. After losing 2-0 in the first leg against FC Marek in Bulgaria, Caersws almost became the first League of Wales side to win a match in the Intertoto Cup but were held 1-1 in the return leg. Barry went out of the Champions League to Latvia's Skonto Riga after never recovering from a 5-0 first-leg defeat, TNS Llantsantfffraid were overwhelmed 12-2 on aggregate by Amica Wronki of Poland while Bangor City beat FK Sartid 1-0 at the Racecourse in Wrexham before losing 2-0 in Yugoslavia. The results prompted the normally mild-mannered Welsh Premier secretary, John Deakin, to describe the clubs as 'cannon fodder' and their performances as 'just not good enough'. Better preparation, in his view, is the way forward.

As the club declared their opposition to the FAW's plan to reduce the Welsh Premier from 16 to 14 clubs over the next three years, Barry completed a terrific hat-trick of 'doubles' when they pipped TNS to the title and then beat Cwmbran Town in a penalty shoot-out to win the Welsh Cup. They will represent Wales again in the Champions League with Cwmbran taking their place in the UEFA Cup along with TNS and Bangor City playing in the Intertoto Cup.

The whole of Welsh football was shocked by the death of Cwmbran's manager Tony Wilcox in April. Under him, the Crows were the first team to win the League of Wales and then play in the Champions League in 1993 but it was as a thoroughly nice man that he will be remembered.

While not wishing to tempt fate, Wales will surely never have a better chance of qualifying for one of the two biggest football tournaments in the world. After their re-arranged game against Serbia and Montenegro in August, they have three crucial matches in 22 days in September and October – Italy (away) and Finland (home) before rounding off their campaign against Serbia in Cardiff.

There's still some way to go, but Wales could have done no more than reach the halfway stage with a 100 per cent record. As Welsh football fans know only too well, there's many a slip between cup and lip and although Mark Hughes won't be ordering the champagne just yet, he knows that his team's destiny lies in their own hands – and you can't ask for anything more than that.

GRAHAME LLOYD

JT HUGHES/MITSUBISHI WELSH PREMIER LEAGUE 2002–03

	Aberystwyth Town	Afan Lido	Bangor City	Barry Town	Caernarfon Town	Caersws	Carmarthen Town	Connah's Quay Nomads	Cwmbran Town	Flexsys Cefn Druids	Haverfordwest County	Llanelli	Newtown	Oswestry Town	Port Talbot Town	Rhyl	Total Network Solutions	Welshpool Town
Aberystwyth Town	—	0-0	0-1	3-1	1-1	1-3	2-0	3-1	1-1	3-0	2-1	2-0	3-1	5-1	1-0	1-1	2-2	0-0
Afan Lido	1-1	—	1-2	0-1	0-1	1-0	2-0	3-0	1-2	0-3	0-0	2-2	1-2	0-0	2-0	1-1	0-6	2-0
Bangor City	0-1	2-1	—	1-1	3-1	5-0	3-2	2-1	2-1	2-0	2-1	8-0	0-1	2-2	3-0	1-0	0-2	3-1
Barry Town	5-1	1-0	3-0	—	3-2	3-2	3-0	3-1	2-1	6-0	3-0	1-0	2-2	4-0	0-1	4-1	0-0	2-1
Caernarfon Town	0-3	1-1	2-2	1-4	—	1-2	2-1	2-0	3-1	3-3	0-1	1-1	1-2	1-1	2-1	0-2	1-1	0-0
Caersws	2-2	1-2	1-1	0-1	2-1	—	4-1	1-0	1-1	2-1	1-1	4-0	1-0	2-3	4-1	2-2	0-4	3-1
Carmarthen Town	0-2	0-2	0-6	2-2	0-3	3-1	—	1-1	0-4	0-1	0-2	2-1	1-4	2-1	0-2	0-3	1-1	5-1
Connah's Quay Nomads	2-1	2-1	2-1	0-2	1-1	1-3	1-0	—	1-1	4-1	3-1	3-0	1-0	2-4	2-2	2-1	0-1	4-0
Cwmbran Town	2-1	0-2	0-0	2-3	1-0	3-2	4-0	0-2	—	0-0	3-1	3-2	2-1	0-0	1-1	2-0	0-0	4-0
Flexsys Cefn Druids	3-0	0-1	0-2	0-3	2-1	0-1	0-1	0-0	1-0	—	0-1	4-0	3-0	0-0	3-2	0-2	0-1	0-2
Haverfordwest County	0-3	1-4	0-4	2-4	3-1	3-2	0-2	1-3	4-0	2-4	—	2-3	2-2	0-2	2-1	1-5	0-3	0-0
Llanelli	2-3	1-3	2-5	2-3	3-3	3-2	1-2	3-5	0-3	3-1	1-3	—	2-3	3-1	0-2	0-3	2-3	0-1
Newtown	3-1	1-2	2-1	0-0	0-3	0-2	2-2	1-2	4-1	1-2	4-0	2-1	—	1-3	2-4	0-2	2-4	0-2
Oswestry Town	0-1	0-3	1-2	0-4	3-0	0-2	1-2	2-3	0-5	0-1	1-1	3-1	0-0	—	0-0	2-3	0-3	1-1
Port Talbot Town	0-1	0-2	0-2	0-5	3-2	0-0	0-2	0-1	1-0	2-1	3-0	1-1	0-2	4-1	—	0-3	1-1	1-0
Rhyl	0-0	2-2	0-1	0-1	1-0	4-0	1-0	1-2	2-1	1-0	1-0	1-1	1-2	1-1	3-0	—	0-1	2-0
Total Network Solutions	3-0	1-1	4-2	1-0	0-2	2-1	2-0	2-0	1-0	2-0	1-2	3-1	1-1	2-1	1-0	5-0	—	2-0
Welshpool Town	1-3	0-0	1-4	0-4	1-0	0-4	1-1	1-2	1-2	3-3	0-2	1-0	1-0	6-1	2-3	0-2	1-2	—

JT HUGHES/MITSUBISHI WELSH PREMIER LEAGUE

			Home			Goals		Away			Goals			
		P	W	D	L	F	A	W	D	L	F	A	GD	Pts
1	Barry Town	34	14	2	1	45	12	12	3	2	39	14	58	83
2	Total Network Solutions	34	13	2	2	33	11	11	6	0	35	10	47	80
3	Bangor City	34	12	2	3	39	15	10	3	4	36	19	41	71
4	Aberystwyth Town	34	9	6	2	30	14	8	3	6	24	24	16	60
5	Connah's Quay Nomads	34	10	3	4	31	20	8	2	7	24	26	9	59
6	Rhyl	34	8	4	5	21	12	9	3	5	31	21	19	58
7	Afan Lido	34	5	5	7	17	21	9	5	3	27	13	10	52
8	Caersws	34	8	5	4	30	22	7	1	9	27	30	5	51
9	Cwmbran Town	34	9	5	3	27	15	5	3	8	24	24	12	50
10	Newtown	34	5	2	10	25	32	7	4	6	23	22	–6	42
11	Flexsys Cefn Druids	34	6	2	9	16	17	5	3	9	21	34	–14	38
12	Port Talbot Town	34	5	3	8	15	24	5	3	9	20	27	–16	36
13	Haverfordwest County	34	4	2	11	23	43	6	3	8	17	25	–28	35
14	Caernarfon Town	34	4	7	6	21	26	4	3	10	22	27	–10	34
15	Carmarthen Town	34	4	3	10	17	37	5	2	10	16	29	–33	32
16	Oswestry Town	34	2	4	11	14	32	4	6	7	22	35	–31	28
17	Welshpool Town	34	4	3	10	20	33	3	4	10	10	29	–32	28
18	Llanelli	34	3	1	13	28	46	1	4	12	14	43	–47	17

WELSH CUP 2002–03

PRELIMINARY ROUND

Caerau Ely v RTB Ebbw Vale 5-2
Caerwys v Rhos Aelwyd 2-0
Cwmaman United v Pontlottyn Blast Furnace 2-1
Glantraeth v Bala Town 10-2

FIRST ROUND

AFC Llwydcoed v Newport YMCA 1-0
AFC Rhondda v Porthcawl Town 4-1
Airbus UK v Ruthin Town 2-0
Amlwch Town v Buckley Town 0-3
Glantraeth v Corwen Amateurs 7-0
Bettws v Caerau Ely 2-3
Briton Ferry Athletic v Blaenrhondda 2-6 *(pens)*
Brymbo Broughton v Conwy United 3-2
Caerwys v Brickfield Rangers 5-6 *(pens)*
Caldicot Town v Morriston Town 2-1
Cardiff Civil Service v Tredegar Town 2-1
Cemaes Bay v Llandyrnog United 2-1
Cwmaman United v Newcastle Emlyn 3-2 *(aet)*
Denbigh Town v Porthmadog 0-3
Ely Rangers v Aberaman Athletic 1-2
Garden Village v Merthyr Saints 5-3
Garw Athletic v Seven Sisters 4-3
Goytre United v Milford United 2-1
Gresford Athletic v Holywell Town 6-0
Gwynfi United w.o. v Penrhiwceiber Rangers withdrew
Halkyn United v Flint Town United 3-0
Holyhead Hotspur v Castell Alun Colts 3-1
Llandudno v Mold Alexandra 4-0
Llanfairpwll v Chirk AAA 3-0
Llanrhaeadr v Llanidloes Town 4-1
Maesteg Park Athletic v Risca & Gelli United 3-0
Meifod withdrew v Presteigne St Andrews w.o.
Neath v Dinas Powys 2-1
Penrhyncoch v Guilsfield 4-0
Pontyclun v Treowen Stars 0-2
Pontypridd Town v Grange Harlequins 6-7 *(pens)*
Porth Tywyn Suburbs v Caerleon 3-0
Prestatyn Town v Lex XI 1-3 *(aet)*
Taffs Well v Cardiff Corinthians 4-0
Troedyrhiw v Fields Park Pontllanfraith 4-2

SECOND ROUND

Goytre United v Haverfordwest County 0-1
Aberystwyth Town v Welshpool Town 2-0
AFC Rhondda v AFC Llwydcoed 3-2
Airbus UK v Buckley Town 2-0
Blaenrhondda v Cwmaman United 0-1
Brymbo Broughton v Caernarfon Town 2-1
Caerau Ely v Grange Harlequins 3-0
Caldicot Town v Garw Athletic 1-3
Cardiff Civil Service v UWIC Inter Cardiff 0-1
Carmarthen Town v Gwynfi United 4-1
Cemaes Bay v Lex XI 4-6
Connah's Quay Nomads v Brickfield Rangers 3-0
Glantraeth v Porthmadog 4-3
Llandudno v Gresford Athletic 3-1
Llanelli v Cwmbran Town 1-4
Llanfairpwll v Halkyn United 5-6
Llangefni & Glantraeth v Pontardawe Town 3-5
Neath v Afan Lido 5-4
Newtown v Llanrhaeadr 6-1
Oswestry Town v Presteigne St Andrews 2-1
Porth Tywyn Suburbs v Garden Village 3-0
Port Talbot Town v Taffs Well 1-0
Rhayader Town v Penrhyncoch 0-5
Rhyl v Holyhead Hotspur 5-0
Treowen Stars v Maesteg Park Athletic 2-0
Troedyrhiw v Aberaman Athletic 0-2

THIRD ROUND

Aberaman Athletic v Barry Town 0-4
Aberystwyth Town v Lex XI 6-0
AFC Rhondda v Pontardawe Town 0-5
Bangor City v Halkyn United 6-0
Brymbo Broughton v Llandudno 0-1
Caersws v Total Network Solutions 1-0
Connah's Quay Nomads v Newtown 1-0
Cwmbran Town v Cwmaman United 3-1
Garw Athletc v Haverfordwest County 1-3
Flexsys Cefn Druids v Airbus UK 4-3
Glantraeth v Oswestry Town 1-2
Porth Tywn Suburbs v Ton Pentre 1-2
Port Talbot Town v Neath 2-1
Rhyl v Penrhyncoch 2-1
Treowen Stars v Carmarthen Town 0-4
UWIC Inter Cardiff v Caerau Ely 3-0

FOURTH ROUND

Barry Town v Pontardawe Town 4-1
Caersws v Bangor City 0-3
Carmarthen Town v Cwmbran Town 0-1
Llandudno v Connah's Quay Nomads 1-3
Oswestry Town v Haverfordwest County 2-1
Port Talbot Town v Aberystwyth Town 2-3
Ton Pentre v Flexys Cefn Druids 2-1
UWIC Inter Cardiff v Rhyl 0-1

FIFTH ROUND

Aberystwyth Town v Barry Town 2-3
Bangor City v Cwmbran Town 3-5 *(pens)*
Ton Pentre v Oswestry Town 3-0
Rhyl v Connah's Quay Nomads 1-0

SEMI-FINALS

Rhyl v Barry Town 0-1
(at Aberystwyth)
Ton Pentre v Cwmbran Town 1-2
(at Barry)

WELSH CUP FINAL

(at Stebonheath Park, Llanelli)

Barry Town (1) 2 Cwmbran Town (2) 2

(aet; Barry Town won 4-3 on penalties).

Barry Town: Baruwa; Brown (York), Lloyd, Kennedy, Morgan (Burke), Phillips, Jenkins (Cotterrall), French, Moralee, Ramasut, Akinfenwa.
Scorers: Ramasut 28 (pen), Phillips 86.

Cwmbran Town: Ellacott; Carter, Smothers (David), Wigg, Warton, Jones, Morris (Davies), Moore, Welsh, Watkins (Dunn), Hurlin.
Scorers: Welsh 34, Moore 39.

Referee: B. Bevan (Wrexham).

Attendance: 852

FAW PREMIER CUP

Group A	*P*	*W*	*D*	*L*	*F*	*A*	*GD*	*Pts*
Afan Lido	6	4	0	2	10	9	1	12
Rhyl	6	3	2	1	13	8	5	11
Cwmbran Town	6	2	0	4	9	12	–3	6
Caersws	6	1	2	3	8	11	–3	5

Group B	*P*	*W*	*D*	*L*	*F*	*A*	*GD*	*Pts*
TNS	6	4	1	1	16	3	13	13
Newport County	6	1	4	1	5	7	–2	7
Bangor City	6	1	3	2	7	12	–5	6
Connah's Quay Nomads	6	1	2	3	7	13	–6	5

QUARTER-FINALS

Afan Lido v Wrexham 0-4
Rhyl v Barry Town 1-1
(Rhyl won on penalties)
Newport County v Swansea City 3-1
TNS v Cardiff City 1-3

SEMI-FINALS

Newport County v Cardiff City 0-0
(Newport County won on penalties).
Wrexham v Rhyl 4-0

FINAL

Wrexham v Newport County 6-1

C.C. SPORTS WELSH LEAGUE

DIVISION ONE

	P	*W*	*D*	*L*	*F*	*A*	*GD*	*Pts*
Bettws	34	24	5	5	89	30	59	77
Neath	34	24	5	5	71	29	42	77
UWIC	34	23	7	4	67	33	34	76
Ton Pentre	34	22	3	9	86	35	51	69
Goytre United	34	19	3	12	56	39	17	60
Garw	34	16	5	13	61	57	4	53
Briton Ferry	34	14	4	16	50	53	–3	46
Cardiff Civil Service	34	12	9	13	45	52	–7	45
Maesteg Park	34	13	6	15	44	57	–13	45
Pontardawe	34	12	7	15	51	49	2	43
Cardiff Corries	34	12	6	16	40	59	–19	42
Caerleon	34	10	10	14	49	48	1	40
Llanwern	34	11	5	18	44	64	–20	38
Gwynfi United	34	10	7	17	56	57	–1	37
Ely Rangers	34	10	6	18	46	52	–6	36
Garden Village	34	9	7	18	39	65	–26	34
Penrhiwceiber	34	9	7	18	48	81	–33	34
Milford United	34	1	8	25	26	108	–82	11

HUWS GRAY – FITLOCK CYMRU ALLIANCE LEAGUE

	P	*W*	*D*	*L*	*F*	*A*	*GD*	*Pts*
Porthmadog	32	28	2	2	106	19	87	86
Llandudno	32	20	7	5	81	41	40	67
Buckley Town	32	19	7	6	85	34	51	64
Llangefni Glantraeth	32	21	1	10	78	39	39	64
Airbus UK	32	17	5	10	70	50	20	56
Ruthin Town	32	17	3	12	79	45	34	54
Halkyn United	32	14	9	9	56	57	–1	51
Amlwch Town	32	11	9	12	45	55	–10	42
Lex XI*	32	13	5	14	83	72	11	41
Holyhead Hotspur	32	11	8	13	60	62	–2	41
Flint Town United	32	11	7	14	50	61	–11	40
Mold Alexandra	32	8	7	17	35	56	–21	31
Gresford Athletic	32	8	6	18	52	64	–12	30
Llanfairpwll	32	8	5	19	35	66	–31	29
Guilsfield	32	7	7	18	43	86	–43	28
Cemaes Bay	32	7	3	22	41	129	–88	24
Holywell Town***	32	4	5	23	33	96	–63	8

**3 points deducted for non-fulfilment of fixture.*
****9 points deducted for fielding an ineligible player in 3 games.*

PREVIOUS WELSH LEAGUE WINNERS

1993	Cwmbran Town
1994	Bangor City
1995	Bangor City
1996	Barry Town
1997	Barry Town
1998	Barry Town
1999	Barry Town
2000	TNS
2001	Barry Town
2002	Barry Town
2003	Barry Town

PREVIOUS WELSH CUP WINNERS

1878	Wrexham Town
1879	White Star Newtown
1880	Druids
1881	Druids
1882	Druids
1883	Wrexham
1884	Oswestry United
1885	Druids
1886	Druids
1887	Chirk
1888	Chirk
1889	Bangor
1890	Druids
1891	Shrewsbury Town
1892	Chirk
1893	Wrexham
1894	Chirk
1895	Newtown
1896	Bangor
1897	Wrexham
1898	Druids
1899	Druids
1900	Aberystwyth
1901	Oswestry United
1902	Wellington Town
1903	Wrexham
1904	Druids
1905	Wrexham
1906	Wellington Town
1907	Oswestry United
1908	Chester
1909	Wrexham
1910	Wrexham
1911	Wrexham
1912	Cardiff City
1913	Swansea Town
1914	Wrexham
1915	Wrexham
1920	Cardiff City
1921	Wrexham
1922	Cardiff City
1923	Cardiff City
1924	Wrexham
1925	Wrexham
1926	Ebbw Vale
1927	Cardiff City
1928	Cardiff City
1929	Connah's Quay
1930	Cardiff City
1931	Wrexham
1932	Swansea Town
1933	Chester
1934	Bristol City
1935	Tranmere Rovers
1936	Crewe Alexandra
1937	Crewe Alexandra
1938	Shrewsbury Town
1939	South Liverpool
1940	Wellington Town
1947	Chester
1948	Lovell's Athletic
1949	Merthyr Tydfil
1950	Swansea Town
1951	Merthyr Tydfil
1952	Rhyl
1953	Rhyl
1954	Flint Town United
1955	Barry Town
1956	Cardiff City
1957	Wrexham
1958	Wrexham
1959	Cardiff City
1960	Wrexham
1961	Swansea Town
1962	Bangor City
1963	Borough United
1964	Cardiff City
1965	Cardiff City
1966	Swansea Town
1967	Cardiff City
1968	Cardiff City
1969	Cardiff City
1970	Cardiff City
1971	Cardiff City
1972	Wrexham
1973	Cardiff City
1974	Cardiff City
1975	Wrexham
1976	Cardiff City
1977	Shrewsbury Town
1978	Wrexham
1979	Shrewsbury Town
1980	Newport County
1981	Swansea City
1982	Swansea City
1983	Swansea City
1984	Shrewsbury Town
1985	Shrewsbury Town
1986	Wrexham
1987	Merthyr Tydfil
1988	Cardiff City
1989	Swansea City
1990	Hereford United
1991	Swansea City
1992	Cardiff City
1993	Cardiff City
1994	Barry Town
1995	Wrexham
1996	TNS
1997	Barry Town
1998	Bangor City
1999	Inter Cable-Tel
2000	Bangor City
2001	Barry Town
2002	Barry Town
2003	Barry Town

NORTHERN IRISH FOOTBALL 2002–03

It has been a somewhat traumatic season in Northern Ireland both off and on the pitch – a planned constitutional and administrative change in the Irish Football Association and a long, at times difficult, rebuilding process for the national side, but climaxed by a magnificent scoreless European championship qualifying draw against Spain at Windsor Park in June.

After almost two years of negotiations the Irish FA agreed with the Government's Task Force recommendations on a 'Way Forward Plan' for the game.

Consequently, the Government will release £8m over three years to be used primarily for ground improvements and development purposes. Clubs will, of course, have to fund 15 per cent of any project which may prove a hardship to some who advocate 100 per cent grants.

Basically, the new format means the Irish FA will be run by a 17-member Executive Committee, including two independent nominees, and a Premier League Committee looking after the affairs of senior clubs.

In other words, the Irish League comes under the IFA banner but will still have its own secretariat. Chairman of the Executive Committee is Jim Boyce, the IFA President, and David Bowen, the secretary, as the Chief Executive. The Council will meet only four times a year but the real business will be conducted by the new committee which has executive powers.

The changes to be implemented for the 2004–05 season will operate for two years when a review of its effectiveness is scheduled. There are many ifs and buts about the revolutionary project and only time can provide the answers.

Already the Irish League has been increased for the coming season to 16 clubs and the others divided into Intermediate Division One and Two with promotion and relegation operated. Here again it is a case of waiting to see how it all works out.

Internationally, the results have been disappointing with only two points from the European Championship Group Six qualifying series. Manager Sammy McIlroy, who has a limited supply of players, is, however, engaged in a long-term rebuilding process.

He took over from Lawrie McMenemy and Joe Jordan four years ago, but has not been able to parade his original selections in any game due to withdrawals through injuries and suspension as well as the premature international retirement of players such as Jim Magilton, Neil Lennon, Kevin Horlock and the prolonged absence of Leicester City's Gerry Taggart and Michael Hughes, who spent a year sidelined while Birmingham City and Wimbledon sorted out a contractual dispute.

Gradually, a silver lining has appeared as McIlroy persisted with what he calls his 'Young Lions'. A 'B' international with Scotland at Firhull Park and a friendly against Italy for the Italian Earthquake Disaster Fund proved, despite losing 2-0 on each occasion, more than useful exercises culminating with that scoreless draw against the Spaniards – one of the most refreshing performances for years, creating a major boost for players and public.

McIlroy, who has brought pride and passion to the squad reminiscent of the halcyon World Cup days of Sweden 1958, Spain '82 and Mexico '86, is almost certain to be given a two-year contract extension covering the World Cup 2006 qualifying series. He realises there is no chance now of obtaining even a play-off from Group Six but believes his squad will have a decisive say in who does automatically reach the finals in Portugal next summer. 'I believe Italy remain the favourites but it will be tight for them. Obtaining maximum points in the three remaining fixtures is vital', said McIlroy.

Domestically, it has, unquestionably, been Glentoran's year. They won the Daily Mirror Irish League Premier Division, CIS Insurance Cup and the TFG Sport County Antrim Shield, but missed out on a four-trophy clean sweep when Coleraine defeated them 1-0 in the Nationwide Irish Cup Final.

Gary Smyth, the centre-back, won the Northern Ireland Football Writers' Association Player of the Year award and the Ulster Footballer of the Year trophy, inaugurated in 1951 and judged by a distinguished panel of ex-players and other football officials. Roy Coyle, who has collected 46 trophies in a distinguished managerial career, was named Manager of the Year, while centre-forward Andy Smith made his debut against Italy and followed it up with a superb performance in the Spanish game.

For Linfield it was a disastrous nine months without a trophy, almost unknown at Windsor Park, and the annual meeting saw Billy McCoubrey, the chairman, voted off the management committee and succeeded as the chairman by David Crawford.

A chronic shortage of revenue haunts many clubs who are deep in debt and struggling to make ends meet. The next 12 months could be crucial for them, especially with sponsorship so difficult to obtain. Northern Ireland football remains at the crossroads.

DR MALCOLM BRODIE

DAILY MIRROR IRISH LEAGUE PREMIER DIVISION

	P	W	D	L	F	A	GD	Pts
Glentoran	38	28	6	4	78	22	+56	90
Portadown	38	24	8	6	89	36	+53	80
Coleraine	38	21	10	7	66	38	+28	73
Linfield	38	17	12	9	70	41	+29	63
Omagh Town	38	15	6	17	47	57	−10	51
Institute	38	12	6	20	44	75	−31	42
Ards	38	12	10	16	27	39	−12	46
Lisburn Distillery	38	12	6	20	39	49	−10	42
Cliftonville	38	9	14	15	37	43	−6	41
Glenavon	38	8	12	18	41	67	−26	36
Crusaders	38	9	9	20	26	61	−35	36
Newry Town	38	8	7	23	33	69	−36	31

PROMOTION/RELEGATION PLAY-OFF

First Leg

Bangor 0, Newry Town 0 *(at Clandeboye Road)*

Second Leg

Newry Town 2, Bangor 1 *(at The Showgrounds)*

Leading goalscorer: Vinny Arkins (Portadown) 39.

DAILY MIRROR FIRST DIVISION

	P	W	D	L	F	A	GD	Pts
Dungannon Swifts*	28	18	6	4	61	32	+29	60
Ballymena United*	28	16	6	6	71	40	+31	54
Limavady United*	28	15	5	8	53	37	+16	50
Larne*	28	13	4	11	35	30	+5	43
Bangor	28	12	5	11	40	39	+1	41
Carrick Rangers	28	8	4	16	44	76	−32	28
Ballyclare Comrades	28	6	4	18	36	65	−29	22
Armagh City	28	4	6	18	37	58	−21	18

*Promoted.

Leading goalscorer: Shea Campbell (Ballymena United) 36.

SECOND DIVISION

	P	W	D	L	F	A	GD	Pts
Ballinamallard United*	30	18	6	6	65	32	+33	60
H&W Welders*	30	16	9	5	71	35	+36	57
Lurgan Celtic*	30	17	6	7	65	39	+26	57
Brantwood*	30	16	6	8	48	34	+14	54
Ballymoney United*	30	16	5	9	58	41	+17	53
Donegal Celtic*	30	14	10	6	62	27	+35	52
Loughgall*	30	15	6	9	64	43	+21	51
Moyola Park*	30	14	7	9	44	28	+16	49
Banbridge Town	30	12	10	8	58	43	+15	46
Tobermore United	30	13	7	10	56	53	+3	46
Dundela	30	11	6	13	62	52	+10	39
Portstewart	30	10	5	15	43	54	−11	35
Chimney Corner	30	8	5	17	47	74	−27	29
Coagh United	30	5	8	17	47	78	−31	23
PSNI	30	3	3	27	33	95	−62	12
Crewe United	30	2	1	27	19	114	−95	7

*Promoted.

For the 2003–04 season there will be a Premier Division, Intermediate League Division One and Division Two, the last named also including Annagh United, Dergview, Queen's University and Wakehurst.

IFL RESERVE LEAGUE NORTH

	P	W	D	L	F	A	GD	Pts
Cliftonville Olympic	21	12	6	3	36	21	+15	42
Institute II	21	11	3	7	49	35	+14	36
Crusaders Reserves	21	11	3	7	51	38	+13	36
Larne Olympic	21	11	1	9	42	41	+1	34
Ballymena United Reserves	21	8	6	7	41	34	+7	30
Carrick Rangers Reserves	21	8	2	11	36	53	−17	26
Coleraine Reserves	21	7	1	13	47	56	−9	22
Limavady United Reserves	21	3	4	14	20	44	−24	13

Omagh Town Reserves resigned and record expunged.

IFL RESERVE LEAGUE SOUTH

	P	W	D	L	F	A	GD	Pts
Glentoran II	27	22	5	0	120	23	+97	71
Linfield Swifts	27	21	4	2	89	29	+60	67
Dungannon Swifts Reserves	27	17	2	8	67	39	+28	53
Lisburn Distillery II	27	11	4	12	48	50	−2	37
Newry Town Reserves	27	9	7	11	54	64	−10	34
Bangor Reserves	27	9	4	14	37	63	−26	31
Portadown Reserves	27	7	5	15	25	44	−19	26
Glenavon Reserves	27	6	7	14	37	60	−23	25
Ards II	27	7	2	18	31	77	−46	23
Armagh City Reserves	27	4	4	19	33	92	−59	16

FINAL

Cliftonville Olympic 0, Glentoran II 0
(Glentoran II won 5-2 on penalties).

IFL YOUTH LEAGUE

	P	W	D	L	F	A	GD	Pts
Cliftonville Strollers	30	23	2	5	130	47	+83	71
Linfield Rangers	30	21	4	5	95	35	+60	67
Glenavon III	30	19	4	7	83	34	+49	61
Limavady United III	30	15	7	8	54	55	−1	52
Glentoran Colts	30	13	8	9	59	46	+13	47
Lisburn Distillery III	30	12	6	12	60	56	+4	42
Institute Academy	30	12	6	12	53	50	+3	42
Ballymena United III	30	12	6	12	74	78	−4	42
Coleraine Colts	30	13	2	15	62	78	−16	41
Ballyclare Comrades Colts	30	9	11	10	58	62	−4	38
Newry Town Wanderers	30	11	4	15	42	59	−17	37
Crusaders Colts	30	10	6	14	67	71	−4	36
Ballinamallard Youth	30	8	10	12	55	66	−11	34
Portadown III	30	7	5	18	51	75	−24	26
Ards Colts	30	7	2	21	43	120	−77	23
Bangor Colts	30	3	6	21	35	89	−54	15

ULSTER CUP

(For First Division clubs)

	P	W	D	L	F	A	GD	Pts
Dungannon Swifts	7	6	1	0	14	3	+11	19
Ballymena United	7	4	2	1	16	6	+10	14
Larne	7	4	1	2	12	6	+6	13
Limavady United	7	3	1	3	12	8	+4	10
Bangor	7	3	0	4	8	13	−5	9
Carrick Rangers	7	1	3	3	5	10	−5	6
Ballyclare Comrades	7	1	2	4	13	22	−9	5
Armagh City	7	0	2	5	8	21	−13	2

ULSTER CUP WINNERS

1949 Linfield
1950 Larne
1951 Glentoran
1952
1953 Glentoran
1954 Crusaders
1955 Glenavon
1956 Linfield
1957 Linfield
1958 Distillery
1959 Glenavon
1960 Linfield
1961 Ballymena U
1962 Linfield
1963 Crusaders
1964 Linfield
1965 Coleraine
1966 Glentoran
1967 Linfield
1968 Coleraine
1969 Coleraine
1970 Linfield
1971 Linfield
1972 Coleraine
1973 Ards
1974 Linfield
1975 Coleraine
1976 Glentoran
1977 Linfield
1978 Linfield
1979 Linfield
1980 Ballymena U
1981 Glentoran
1982 Glentoran
1983 Glentoran
1984 Linfield
1985 Coleraine
1986 Coleraine
1987 Larne
1988 Glentoran
1989 Glentoran
1990 Portadown
1991 Bangor
1992 Linfield
1993 Crusaders
1994 Bangor
1995 Portadown
1996 Portadown
1997 Coleraine
1998 Ballyclare Comrades
1999 Distillery
2000 *No competition*
2001 *No competition*
2002 *No competition*
2003 Dungannon Swifts *(Confined to First Division clubs)*

IRISH LEAGUE CHAMPIONSHIP WINNERS

1891	Linfield	1911	Linfield	1936	Belfast Celtic	1964	Glentoran	1985	Linfield
1892	Linfield	1912	Glentoran	1937	Belfast Celtic	1965	Derry City	1986	Linfield
1893	Linfield	1913	Glentoran	1938	Belfast Celtic	1966	Linfield	1987	Linfield
1894	Glentoran	1914	Linfield	1939	Belfast Celtic	1967	Glentoran	1988	Glentoran
1895	Linfield	1915	Belfast Celtic	1940	Belfast Celtic	1968	Glentoran	1989	Linfield
1896	Distillery	1920	Belfast Celtic	1948	Belfast Celtic	1969	Linfield	1990	Portadown
1897	Glentoran	1921	Glentoran	1949	Linfield	1970	Glentoran	1991	Portadown
1898	Linfield	1922	Linfield	1950	Linfield	1971	Linfield	1992	Glentoran
1899	Distillery	1923	Linfield	1951	Glentoran	1972	Glentoran	1993	Linfield
1900	Belfast Celtic	1924	Queen's Island	1952	Glenavon	1973	Crusaders	1994	Linfield
1901	Distillery	1925	Glentoran	1953	Glentoran	1974	Coleraine	1995	Crusaders
1902	Linfield	1926	Belfast Celtic	1954	Linfield	1975	Linfield	1996	Portadown
1903	Distillery	1927	Belfast Celtic	1955	Linfield	1976	Crusaders	1997	Crusaders
1904	Linfield	1928	Belfast Celtic	1956	Linfield	1977	Glentoran	1998	Cliftonville
1905	Glentoran	1929	Belfast Celtic	1957	Glentoran	1978	Linfield	1999	Glentoran
1906	Cliftonville	1930	Linfield	1958	Ards	1979	Linfield	2000	Linfield
	Distillery	1931	Glentoran	1959	Linfield	1980	Linfield	2001	Linfield
1907	Linfield	1932	Linfield	1960	Glenavon	1981	Glentoran	2002	Portadown
1908	Linfield	1933	Belfast Celtic	1961	Linfield	1982	Linfield	2003	Glentoran
1909	Linfield	1934	Linfield	1962	Linfield	1983	Linfield		
1910	Cliftonville	1935	Linfield	1963	Distillery	1984	Linfield		

FIRST DIVISION

1996	Coleraine	1999	Distillery	2002	Lisburn Distillery
1997	Ballymena United	2000	Omagh Town	2003	Dungannon Swifts
1998	Newry Town	2001	Ards		

NATIONWIDE IRISH CUP 2002–03

FIFTH ROUND

Armagh City v Ballyclare Comrades	1-2
Ballymure Old Boys v Limavady	0-3
H&W Welders v Bangor	2-1
Carrick Rangers v Omagh Town	2-6
Crusaders v Lurgan Celtic	2-0
Dungannon Swifts v Institute	1-0
Glenavon v Loughgall United	4-0
Glentoran v Oxford United Stars	11-0
Killyleagh YC v Banbridge	2-1
Linfield v Cliftonville	1-0
Lisburn Distillery v Coleraine	0-2
Moyola Park v Ards	1-2
Newry Town v Knockbreda Parish	1-1, 1-2
Tobermore United v Brantwood	2-0
Portadown v Ballymena United	1-1, 6-0
Larne v Malachians	4-1

SIXTH ROUND

Tobermore United v Linfield	0-2
Ballyclare Comrades v Glentoran	0-3
Limavady v Glenavon	0-3
Coleraine v Larne	2-0
Ards v Killyleagh YC	1-0
Crusaders v H&W Welders	1-1, 2-1
Omagh Town v Dungannon Swifts	1-0
Portadown v Knockbreda Parish	2-0

QUARTER-FINALS

Ards v Glentoran	0-1
Coleraine v Crusaders	2-0
Omagh Town v Linfield	1-0
Portadown v Glenavon	5-0

SEMI-FINALS

Glentoran v Portadown *(at Mourneview Park, Lurgan)*	6-1
Omagh Town v Coleraine *(at The Showgrounds)*	2-5

NATIONWIDE IRISH CUP FINAL

(at Windsor Park)

Coleraine 1 Glentoran 0

Coleraine: O'Hare; Clanachan, Flynn, McAuley, Gaston, Gorman, Beatty, McAllister (Armstrong), McCoosh, Hamill, Tolan.
Scorer: Tolan.
Glentoran: Morris; Nixon, Glendinning, Smyth G, Leeman, Tim McCann I, Young, Tim McCann II (Walker), Lockhardt (O'Neill), Smith A, Armour (Halliday).
Referee: L. Irvine (Limavady).
Attendance: 8000.
Man of the Match: Pat McAllister (Coleraine).
Player of the Tournament: Marty Quinn (Coleraine Manager).
NB: Glentoran failed to make it a four trophy clean sweep, having already won the Irish Premier Division, League Cup and Antrim Shield.

IRISH CUP FINALS (from 1946–47)

1946–47 Belfast Celtic 1, Glentoran 0
1947–48 Linfield 3, Coleraine 0
1948–49 Derry City 3, Glentoran 1
1949–50 Linfield 2, Distillery 1
1950–51 Glentoran 3, Ballymena U 1
1951–52 Ards 1, Glentoran 0
1952–53 Linfield 5, Coleraine 0
1953–54 Derry City 1, Glentoran 0
1954–55 Dundela 3, Glenavon 0
1955–56 Distillery 1, Glentoran 0
1956–57 Glenavon 2, Derry City 0
1957–58 Ballymena U 2, Linfield 0
1958–59 Glenavon 2, Ballymena U 0
1959–60 Linfield 5, Ards 1
1960–61 Glenavon 5, Linfield 1
1961–62 Linfield 4, Portadown 0
1962–63 Linfield 2, Distillery 1
1963–64 Derry City 2, Glentoran 0
1964–65 Coleraine 2, Glenavon 1
1965–66 Glentoran 2, Linfield 0
1966–67 Crusaders 3, Glentoran 1
1967–68 Crusaders 2, Linfield 0
1968–69 Ards 4, Distillery 2
1969–70 Linfield 2, Ballymena U 1
1970–71 Distillery 3, Derry City
1971–72 Coleraine 2, Portadown 1
1972–73 Glentoran 3, Linfield 2
1973–74 Ards 2, Ballymena U 1
1974–75 Coleraine 1:0:1, Linfield 1:0:0
1975–76 Carrick Rangers 2, Linfield 1
1976–77 Coleraine 4, Linfield 1
1977–78 Linfield 3, Ballymena U 1
1978–79 Cliftonville 3, Portadown 2
1979–80 Linfield 2, Crusaders 0
1980–81 Ballymena U 1, Glenavon 0
1981–82 Linfield 2, Coleraine 1
1982–83 Glentoran 1:2, Linfield 1:1
1983–84 Ballymena U 4, Carrick Rangers 1
1984–85 Glentoran 1:1, Linfield 1:0
1985–86 Glentoran 2, Coleraine 1
1986–87 Glentoran 1, Larne 0
1987–88 Glentoran 1, Glenavon 0
1988–89 Ballymena U 1, Larne 0
1989–90 Glentoran 3, Portadown 0
1990–91 Portadown 2, Glenavon 1
1991–92 Glenavon 2, Linfield 1
1992–93 Bangor 1:1:1, Ards 1:1:0
1993–94 Linfield 2, Bangor 0
1994–95 Linfield 3, Carrick Rangers 1
1995–96 Glentoran 1, Glenavon 0
1996–97 Glenavon 1, Cliftonville 0
1997–98 Glentoran 1, Glenavon 0
1998–99 *Portadown awarded trophy after Cliftonville were eliminated for using an ineligible player in semi-final.*
1999–2000 Glentoran 1, Portadown 0
2000–01 Glentoran 1, Linfield 0
2001–02 Linfield 2, Portadown 1
2002–03 Coleraine 1 Glentoran 0

TFG SPORTS COUNTY ANTRIM SHIELD

SEMI-FINAL

Ballymena United v Chimney Corner	3-1
(at The Showgrounds)	
Glentoran v Linfield	1-0
(at Windsor Park)	

TFG SPORTS COUNTY ANTRIM SHIELD FINAL

(at The Oval)

Ballymena United 0 Glentoran 3

Ballymena United: Robinson; Carlisle, Boyd, McMullan (Stewart), Kearney G, Byrne, O'Loughlin, Kearney O, Campbell, McLernon (Gregg), Evans.
Glentoran: Morris; Nixon, Leeman, Walker, Young, Smyth G, Lockhardt, O'Neill, Smith A (Armour), Tim McCann I, Halliday, Riches.
Scorers: Armour, Smith A, Young.
Referee: A. Snoddy (Carryduff).
Attendance: 1577.

CIS INSURANCE IRISH LEAGUE CUP

FIRST PHASE NORTHERN

	P	*W*	*D*	*L*	*F*	*A*	*Pts*
Ballymena United	4	3	1	0	15	3	10
Omagh Town	4	3	1	0	6	2	10
Coleraine	4	2	0	2	11	10	6
Institute	4	1	0	3	5	10	3
Limavady United	4	0	0	4	3	15	0

SOUTHERN	*P*	*W*	*D*	*L*	*F*	*A*	*Pts*
Portadown	4	3	0	1	13	4	9
Glenavon	4	2	0	2	5	4	6
Dungannon Swifts	4	2	0	2	7	7	6
Newry Town	4	2	0	2	4	6	6
Armagh City	4	1	0	3	3	11	3

EASTERN	*P*	*W*	*D*	*L*	*F*	*A*	*Pts*
Cliftonville	4	2	2	0	6	3	8
Crusaders	4	2	2	0	4	2	8
Carrick Rangers	4	1	3	0	4	2	6
Larne	4	1	0	3	5	7	3
Ballyclare Comrades	4	0	1	3	2	7	1

GREATER BELFAST	*P*	*W*	*D*	*L*	*F*	*A*	*Pts*
Linfield	4	3	1	0	10	5	10
Glentoran	4	2	2	0	6	3	8
Lisburn Distillery	4	1	1	2	5	5	4
Ards	4	0	2	2	5	8	2
Bangor	4	0	2	2	0	5	2

Winners and runners-up qualified for quarter-finals.

QUARTER-FINALS

Linfield v Glenavon	2-0
Ballymena United v Crusaders	2-0
Cliftonville v Omagh Town	0-5
Portadown v Glentoran	1-2

SEMI-FINALS

Omagh Town v Linfield	2-3
Glentoran v Ballymena United	5-3

CIS INSURANCE IRISH LEAGUE CUP FINAL

(at Windsor Park)

Linfield 0 Glentoran 2

Linfield: Shannon; Collier, McShane, Wall, Murphy W, King (McCann), McBride, Feeney, Ferguson, Morgan (Larmour), Bailie.

Glentoran: Morris; Nixon, Leeman, Walker, Young, Smyth G, Tim McCann I, O'Neill, Smith A, Halliday (Armour), Lockhardt.

Scorers: Halliday, Smyth G.

Referee: A. Snoddy (Carryduff).

Attendance: 3600.

WHERE THE TROPHIES WENT

Daily Mirror Irish Premier League	*Winners*	*Runners-up*
Premier Division	Glentoran	Portadown
First Division	Dungannon Swifts	Ballymena United
Irish League Second Division	Ballinamallard United	H&W Welders
Irish Reserve League	Glentoran II	Cliftonville Olympic
Ulster Cup	Dungannon Swifts	Ballymena United
Irish League Youth Cup	Cliftonville III	Limavady United
Irish Youth League	Cliftonville Strollers	Linfield Rangers
Nationwide Irish Cup	Coleraine	Glentoran
CIS Insurance Irish League Cup	Glentoran	Linfield
TFG Sport County Antrim Shield	Glentoran	Ballymena United
TFG Sport Steel and Sons Cup	Killyleagh YC	Chimney Corner
TFG Sport County Antrim Junior Shield	Sir Oliver Plunkett	Ardoyne WMC
Belfast Telegraph Intermediate Cup	H&W Welders	Ballinamallard United
T Mobile Irish Junior Cup Final	Windmill Stars	Ardoyne WMC
Mid Ulster Cup Final (2002–03)	Portadown	Dungannon Swifts
Mid Ulster Cup Final (2001–02)	Portadown	Lurgan Celtic
Village Windows North West Senior Cup	Institute	Omagh Town
Harry Cavan Youth Cup	Coleraine Youth	Linfield Rangers
George Wilson Memorial Cup	Glentoran II	Coleraine Reserves

CHAMPIONS LEAGUE REVIEW 2002–03

The Champions League came into being retrospectively. In 1991–92 an experiment saw the quarter-finalists in the European Champion Clubs' Cup split into two groups, the winners contesting the final. Judged a success, the formula was repeated for 1992–93.

It was not until the draw for the second round in October 1992 that, to quote UEFA, 'a new name was coined for the final round – the Champions League'.

Since then there have been many changes in the format of the competition, not least being the increased entry and expansion of the league system, though this will be reduced for 2003–04. But ten years ago only such latter stages were referred to as the Champions League though the final remained as the Champion Clubs' Cup Final.

From the 1997–98 season onwards, clubs who were not champions of their country were included and there were six not four groups. Of course during its initial 1955–56 season some clubs had entered by invitation as countries were slow to react to the concept of such a European tournament.

At the end of the 1997–98 season there was little or no reference to the Champion Clubs' Cup and when it was announced in October 1998 that the Cup-Winners' Cup was to be merged with the UEFA Cup, that seemed to mark the end of the old title.

From 1997–98 teams eliminated in the second qualifying round qualified for the UEFA Cup and from 1999–2000 third placed teams in the initial group stage also went on to the UEFA Cup.

However UEFA do not consider matches played in the qualifying stages prior to the league system as worthy of mentioning in a statistical way. Any player appearing prior to the league stage is not listed in individual records, a quite bizarre situation, but doubtless one designed to restrict publicity for lesser clubs at the expense of the elite.

Even this idea has been of little consolation for Manchester United's Ruud Van Nistelrooy, who had his two goals in the qualifying stages in 2002–03 disregarded which robbed him of equalling Jose Altafini's 14 goal record achieved for AC Milan 40 years earlier.

The 11th Champions League final played at Old Trafford, was an all-Italian affair and – predictably some might say – decided on penalties with AC Milan edging Juventus, the conquerors of favourites Real Madrid, 3-2 in the shoot-out.

For 2003–04 the format will still involve 32 clubs over eight groups, but then reverts to the knock-out system with 16 teams, thus abolishing the second group stage.

Places in the Champions League are decided by performances over the previous five seasons and the resulting coefficients determine the number of entries per country. As holders, AC Milan will not have to play in the third qualifying round even though they were only third in the Italian League.

This move has enabled Grasshoppers of Switzerland to move up from the second qualifying round to the third and with the ban on Azerbaijan clubs, Rapid Bucharest (Romania), MTK (Hungary) and Maribor (Slovenia) are excused the first qualifying round.

For countries whose record allows four entries, their domestic champions and runners-up are exempt until the group stage, the third and fourth placed teams enter at the third qualifying round.

Spain, Italy and England are ranked in order at the top with four partcipants each, while with three teams are Germany 4th, France 5th and Greece 6th. Italy will have AC Milan, Juventus and Internazionale in the group stage and Lazio in the third qualifying round. But Holland have dropped down to just two entries.

Zinedine Zidane hurdles the fallen figures of Manchester United players Ole Gunnar Solksjaer and Nicky Butt as Real Madrid succeed in reaching the semi-final of the Champions League, 6-5 on aggregate. (Associated Sports Photography)

EUROPEAN CUP

EUROPEAN CUP FINALS 1956–1992

Year	Winners	Runners-up	Venue	Attendance	Referee
1956	Real Madrid 4	Reims 3	Paris	38,000	Ellis (E)
1957	Real Madrid 2	Fiorentina 0	Madrid	124,000	Horn (Ho)
1958	Real Madrid 3	AC Milan 2 *(aet)*	Brussels	67,000	Alsteen (Bel)
1959	Real Madrid 2	Reims 0	Stuttgart	80,000	Dutsch (WG)
1960	Real Madrid 7	Eintracht Frankfurt 3	Glasgow	135,000	Mowat (S)
1961	Benfica 3	Barcelona 2	Berne	28,000	Dienst (Sw)
1962	Benfica 5	Real Madrid 3	Amsterdam	65,000	Horn (Ho)
1963	AC Milan 2	Benfica 1	Wembley	45,000	Holland (E)
1964	Internazionale 3	Real Madrid 1	Vienna	74,000	Stoll (A)
1965	Internazionale 1	Benfica 0	Milan	80,000	Dienst (Sw)
1966	Real Madrid 2	Partizan Belgrade 1	Brussels	55,000	Kreitlein (WG)
1967	Celtic 2	Internazionale 1	Lisbon	56,000	Tschenscher (WG)
1968	Manchester U 4	Benfica 1 *(aet)*	Wembley	100,000	Lo Bello (I)
1969	AC Milan 4	Ajax 1	Madrid	50,000	Ortiz (Sp)
1970	Feyenoord 2	Celtic 1 *(aet)*	Milan	50,000	Lo Bello (I)
1971	Ajax 2	Panathinaikos 0	Wembley	90,000	Taylor (E)
1972	Ajax 2	Internazionale 0	Rotterdam	67,000	Helies (F)
1973	Ajax 1	Juventus 0	Belgrade	93,500	Guglovic (Y)
1974	Bayern Munich 1	Atletico Madrid 1	Brussels	49,000	Loraux (Bel)
Replay	Bayern Munich 4	Atletico Madrid 0	Brussels	23,000	Delcourt (Bel)
1975	Bayern Munich 2	Leeds U 0	Paris	50,000	Kitabdjian (F)
1976	Bayern Munich 1	St Etienne 0	Glasgow	54,864	Palotai (H)
1977	Liverpool 3	Moenchengladbach 1	Rome	57,000	Wurtz (F)
1978	Liverpool 1	FC Brugge 0	Wembley	92,000	Corver (Ho)
1979	Nottingham F 1	Malmo 0	Munich	57,500	Linemayr (A)
1980	Nottingham F 1	Hamburg 0	Madrid	50,000	Garrido (P)
1981	Liverpool 1	Real Madrid 0	Paris	48,360	Palotai (H)
1982	Aston Villa 1	Bayern Munich 0	Rotterdam	46,000	Konrath (F)
1983	Hamburg 1	Juventus 0	Athens	80,000	Rainea (R)
1984	Liverpool 1	Roma 1	Rome	69,693	Fredriksson (Se)
	(aet; Liverpool won 4-2 on penalties)				
1985	Juventus 1	Liverpool 0	Brussels	58,000	Daina (Sw)
1986	Steaua Bucharest 0	Barcelona 0	Seville	70,000	Vautrot (F)
	(aet; Steaua won 2-0 on penalties)				
1987	Porto 2	Bayern Munich 1	Vienna	59,000	Ponnet (Bel)
1988	PSV Eindhoven 0	Benfica 0	Stuttgart	70,000	Agnolin (I)
	(aet; PSV won 6-5 on penalties)				
1989	AC Milan 4	Steaua Bucharest 0	Barcelona	97,000	Tritschler (WG)
1990	AC Milan 1	Benfica 0	Vienna	57,500	Kohl (A)
1991	Red Star Belgrade 0	Marseille 0	Bari	56,000	Lanese (I)
	(aet; Red Star won 5-3 on penalties)				
1992	Barcelona 1	Sampdoria 0 *(aet)*	Wembley	70,827	Schmidhuber (G)

UEFA CHAMPIONS LEAGUE FINALS 1993–2003

Year	Winners	Runners-up	Venue	Attendance	Referee
1993	Marseille* 1	AC Milan 0	Munich	64,400	Rothlisberger (Sw)
1994	AC Milan 4	Barcelona 0	Athens	70,000	Don (E)
1995	Ajax 1	AC Milan 0	Vienna	49,730	Craciunescu (Ro)
1996	Juventus 1	Ajax 1	Rome	67,000	Vega (Sp)
	(aet; Juventus won 4-2 on penalties)				
1997	Borussia Dortmund 3	Juventus 1	Munich	59,000	Puhl (H)
1998	Real Madrid 1	Juventus 0	Amsterdam	47,500	Krug (G)
1999	Manchester U 2	Bayern Munich 1	Barcelona	90,000	Collina (I)
2000	Real Madrid 3	Valencia 0	Paris	78,759	Braschi (I)
2001	Bayern Munich 1	Valencia 1	Milan	71,500	Jol (Ho)
	(aet; Bayern Munich won 5-4 on penalties)				
2002	Real Madrid 2	Leverkusen 1	Glasgow	52,000	Meier (Sw)
2003	AC Milan 0	Juventus 0	Manchester	63,215	Merk (G)
	(aet; AC Milan won 3-2 on penalties)				

**Subsequently stripped of title.*

UEFA CHAMPIONS LEAGUE 2002–03

QUALIFYING COMPETITION

■ *Denotes player sent off.*

FIRST QUALIFYING ROUND, FIRST LEG

F91 Dudelange (0) 1 *(Remy 54)*, Vardar (0) 1 *(Georgievski 68)* 1200
Flora Tallinn (0) 0, Apoel (0) 0 1000
Kaunas (2) 2 *(Velicka 38, 42 (pen))*, Dinamo Tirana (0) 3 *(Ahmataj 55, Pisha 56, Qorri 76)* 3000
Serif (0) 2 *(Priganiuc 57, Tarkhnishvili 85 (pen))*, Zhenis (1) 1 *(Lovtchev 8)* 5000
Tampere United (0) 0, Pyunik (1) 4 *(Arm Karamian 32, 67, Art Karamian 47, Mkrchian 72)* 3007
Torpedo Kutaisi (2) 5 *(Asatiani 15, 46, Ionanidze 33, Kvetenadze 67, Poroshyn 71)*, B36 Torshavn (0) 2 *(Lakjuni 53, Mortansson 74)* 10,000
Zeljeznicar (2) 3 *(Guvo 4, 56, Gredic 38)*, IA Akranes (0) 0 5000

Wednesday, 17 July 2002

Skonto Riga (1) 5 *(Kolesnichenko 13, Zemlinsky 61, Korgalidze 66, Ksanavicius 87, Yeliseyev 90)*
Barry Town (0) 0 3500

Skonto Riga: Pavlov; Isakov, Zemlinsky, Samusevas, Moroz, Blagonadezhdin, Dedura, Menteshashvili (Korgalidze 46), Verpakovsky (Ksanavicius 78), Kolesnichenko, Mikholap (Yeliseyev 66).
Barry Town: Rayner; Lloyd, Kennedy, Morgan, Phillips, French, Moralee, Ramasut (Cotterrall 74), Brown (Jarman 82), York (Toomey 66), Bishop.

Portadown (0) 0
Belshina (0) 0 750

Portadown: Keenan; McCann, O'Hara, Fitzgerald, Clarke, Hamilton, Arkins, Neill, McAreavey, Ogden, Craig.
Belshina: Sinitsyn; Siadniou, Harbachou (Shahioka 46), Klimovich, Kukar, Harmash, Trukhov, Strypeikis, Karolik, Maliavko (Gradoboyev 73), Boltrouchevitch.

Hibernians (2) 2 *(Chukunyere 8, Pulis 37)*
Shelbourne (1) 2 *(Byrne 7, Gannon 66)* 2000

Hibernians: Muscat; Cassar (Zahra 74), Nisevic, Vella, Ciantar, Mbong, Mifsud A, Chukunyere, Pullicino, Pulis, Baldacchino (Mifsud M 80).
Shelbourne: Williams; Heary, Crawley, McCarthy, Doherty (Prenderville 61), Gannon, Cahill, Byrne, Molloy, Baker, Roberts.

FIRST QUALIFYING ROUND, SECOND LEG

Apoel (0) 1 *(Georgiou 51)*, Flora Tallinn (0) 0 *Piiroja*■ 1000
B36 Torshavn (0) 0, Torpedo Kutaisi (0) 1 *(Janashia 76)* 500
Dinamo Tirana (0) 0, Kaunas (0) 0 2000
IA Akranes (0) 0, Zeljeznicar (1) 1 *(Gredic 33)* 750
Pyunik (0) 2 *(Diawara 53, Cisterna 90)*, Tampere United (0) 0 15,000
Vardar (0) 3 *(Spasovski 70, 75, Petkov 84)*, F91 Dudelange (0) 0 5000
Zhenis (2) 3 *(Tlekhougov 32, Lovtchev 41, Klisjin 52)*, Serif (0) 2 *(Boret 58, Nesteruk 59)* 12,000

Wednesday, 24 July 2002

Barry Town (0) 0
Skonto Riga (0) 1 *(Kolesnichenko 52)* 1507

Barry Town: Rayner; Jarman, Lloyd, Kennedy (Ramasut 68), Phillips, Toomey (York 74), French, Moralee (Burke 63), Cotterrall, Pratt, Bishop.
Skonto Riga: Pavlov; Izakov, Zemlinsky, Samusevas, Dedura, Blagonadezhdin, Moroz, Menteshashvili (Korgalidze 46), Verpakovsky (Ksanavicius 57), Kolesnichenko, Mikholap (Yeliseyev 68).

Belshina (2) 3 *(Strypeikis 6, Karolik 22, 59)*
Portadown (1) 2 *(Hamilton 39, Fitzgerald 74)* 2000

Belshina: Sinitsyn; Siadniou, Harbachou, Klimovich, Kukar, Harmash (Gradoboyev 46), Trukhov, Strypeikis (Ostrikov 72), Karolik, Shahoika (Maliavko 74), Boltrouchevitch.
Portadown: Keenan; McCann, O'Hara, Fitzgerald, Hamilton, Arkins, Neill, McAreavey, Ogden, Craig, Alderdice (Hamilton 76).

Shelbourne (0) 0
Hibernians (0) 1 *(Chukunyere 90)* 4500

Shelbourne: Williams; Heary, Crawley (Houlihan 90), McCarthy, Gannon, Cahill, Byrne, Molloy, Baker, Prenderville, Roberts.
Hibernians: Muscat; Nisevic, Vella, Xuereb, Ciantar, Mbong, Mifsud A, Chukunyere, Pullicino (Zahra 70), Pulis, Baldacchino.

SECOND QUALIFYING ROUND, FIRST LEG

Boavista (3) 4 *(Silva 16, 29, Goulart 17, Avalos 89)*, Hibernians (0) 0 3500
Brondby (0) 1 *(Bagger 90)*, Dinamo Tirana (0) 0 13,047
FC Brugge (2) 3 *(Lange 24, 44, Mendoza 85)*, Dinamo Bucharest (1) 1 *(Alexa 43) Danciu*■ 10,837
Dynamo Kiev (1) 4 *(Cernat 15, Shatskikh 65, Machado 84, Bodnar 90)*, Pyunik (0) 0 *Bilibio*■ 15,000
Hammarby (1) 1 *(Winsnes 17)*, Partizan Belgrade (1) 1 *(Lazovic 37)* 19,417
Lillestrom (0) 0, Zeljeznicar (0) 1 *(Gredic 49)* 3532
Maccabi Haifa (3) 4 *(Cohen 19, 22, Rosso 45, Abiodun 86)*, Belshina (0) 0 200 *(in Nicosia)*.
Maribor (1) 2 *(Corovic 45, 64)*, Apoel (0) 1 *(Sirakov 90)* 5000
Serif (0) 1 *(Tarkhnishvili 51 (pen))*, Graz (2) 4 *(Bazina 3, 50, Aufhauser 45, Hastings 71)* 13,000
Skonto Riga (0) 0, Levski (0) 0 4354
Sparta Prague (2) 3 *(Baranek 7, 20, Pospisil 75)*, Torpedo Kutaisi (0) 0 9690
Vardar (0) 1 *(Ristovski 63)*, Legia (2) 3 *(Kucharski 3, Yahaya 37, Svitlica 89)* 7000
Zalaegerszeg (1) 1 *(Ljubojevic 17)*, Zagreb (0) 0 3000
Zilina (1) 1 *(Barcik 30)*, Basle (1) 1 *(Klago 39 (og))* 2500

SECOND QUALIFYING ROUND, SECOND LEG

Apoel (2) 4 *(Malekos 33 (pen), Elia 45, Charalambides 51, Daskalakis 69) Agathocleous*■, Maribor (1) 2 *(Duro 32 (pen), 82)* 3000
Basle (2) 3 *(Gimenez 12, 50, Yakin M 23)*, Zilina (0) 0 16,562
Belshina (0) 0, Maccabi Haifa (1) 1 *(Pralija 7 (pen))* 2500
Dinamo Bucharest (0) 0, FC Brugge (1) 1 *(Lange 19)* 4000
Dinamo Tirana (0) 0, Brondby (0) 4 *(Madsen 47, Bagger 50, 87, Skarbalius 90 (pen))* 7000
Graz (0) 2 *(Poetscher 58, Bazima 89 (pen))*, Serif (0) 0 4350
Hibernians (1) 3 *(Mifsud 32, 58 (pen), Chukunyere 55)*, Boavista (3) 3 *(Jocivalter 28, Luiz Claudio 38, Paulo Turra 40)* 2000
Legia (1) 1 *(Kucharski 33)*, Vardar (0) 1 *(Oliveira 51)* 5000
Levski (2) 2 *(Chilikov 12, Simonovic 31)*, Skonto Riga (0) 0 17,000
Partizan Belgrade (0) 4 *(Ivic 49, Lazovic 54, Iliev 64, Ilic 75)*, Hammarby (0) 0 15,000
Pyunik (1) 2 *(Art Karamian 30, Arm Karamian 60)*, Dynamo Kiev (2) 2 *(Shatskikh 8, Melashchenko 28)* 5000
Torpedo Kutaisi (1) 1 *(Ionanidze 33)*, Sparta Prague (1) 2 *(Zelenka 41, Novotny 57)* 7000
Zagreb (2) 2 *(Milinovic 2, Lovrek 28)*, Zalaegerszeg (0) 1 *(Urban 89 (pen)) Kocsardi*■ 7000
Zeljeznicar (0) 1 *(Biscevic 90)*, Lillestrom (0) 0 5500

THIRD QUALIFYING ROUND, FIRST LEG

Apoel (1) 2 *(Ouzounides 22, Malekos 89 (pen))*, AEK Athens (1) 3 *(Borbokis 43, 47, Nikolaidis 90)* 15,000
Barcelona (1) 3 *(De Boer 8, Riquelme 80, Cocu 90)*, Legia (0) 0 67,078
Boavista (0) 0, Auxerre (0) 1 *(Cisse 71)* 9000
Feyenoord (0) 1 *(Ono 64)*, Fenerbahce (0) 0 33,000
Graz (0) 0, Lokomotiv Moscow (2) 2 *(Lekgetho 6, Loskov 42)* 5271
Genk (2) 2 *(Thijs 34, Beslija 40)*, Sparta Prague (0) 0 10,000
Levski (0) 0, Dynamo Kiev (0) 1 *(Cernat 60)* 18,000
Maccabi Haifa (1) 2 *(Ayegbeni 17, 90)*, Sturm Graz (0) 0 600 *(in Sofia)*.
AC Milan (0) 1 *(Inzaghi 68)*, Slovan Liberec (0) 0 35,000
Partizan Belgrade (0) 0 *Duljaj*■, Bayern Munich (1) 3 *(Tarnat 22, Jeremies 71, Pizarro 78)* 30,000
Rosenborg (0) 1 *(Brattbakk 53)*, Brondby (0) 0 18,800
Shakhtjor Donetsk (0) 1 *(Aghahowa 49)*, FC Brugge (0) 1 *(Simons 87 (pen)) Van der Heyden*■ 27,982
Sporting Lisbon (0) 0, Internazionale (0) 0 50,000

Wednesday, 14 August 2002

Celtic (1) 3 *(Larsson 4 (pen), Sutton 52, Sylla 88)*

Basle (1) 1 *(Gimenez 2)* 58,520

Celtic: Douglas; Sylla, Petta (Guppy 56), Mjallby, Balde, Valgaeren, Lambert, Lennon, Sutton, Larsson, Petrov.
Basle: Zuberbuhler; Barberis, Duruz, Cantaluppi, Zwyssig (Quennoz 42), Yakin M, Ergic (Varela 60), Yakin H, Rossi (Tum 67), Gimenez, Esposito.

Zalaegerszeg (0) 1 *(Koplarovics 89)*

Manchester United (0) 0 40,000

Zalaegerszeg: Ilic; Babati, Szamosi, Csoka, Urban, Budisa, Farago (Balog 75), Ljubojevic, Kenesei (Koplarovics 83), Egressy (Molnar 65), Vincze.
Manchester United: Carroll; Brown (Neville P 6), Silvestre, O'Shea, Keane, Blanc, Beckham, Veron, Van Nistelrooy, Solskjaer (Forlan 80), Giggs.

Zeljeznicar (0) 0

Newcastle United (0) 1 *(Dyer 55)* 36,000

Zeljeznicar: Hasagic; Jahic (Alagic 72), Mulaosmanovic, Mesic (Mucrinic 83), Mulalic, Alihodzic, Karic, Gredic, Cosic (Radonja 88), Guvo, Seferovic.
Newcastle United: Given; Hughes, Bernard (Quinn 89), Dabizas, Bramble, Solano, Dyer, Jenas, Shearer, Lua-Lua (Ameobi 82), Viana (Elliott 89).

THIRD QUALIFYING ROUND, SECOND LEG

AEK Athens (0) 1 *(Nikolaidis 56)*, Apoel (0) 0 9500
Auxerre (0) 0, Boavista (0) 0 18,000
Bayern Munich (1) 3 *(Ballack 26, Elber 71, Salihamidzic 73 (pen))*, Partizan Belgrade (0) 1 *(Cakar 72)* 40,000
Brondby (0) 2 *(Jonson 82, Jorgensen 84)*, Rosenborg (1) 3 *(Johnsen F 28, 71, Brattbakk 79)* 20,935
FC Brugge (0) 1 *(Ceh 75)*, Shakhtjor Donetsk (1) 1 *(Vorobei 13)* 18,000
(aet; FC Brugge won 4-1 on penalties).
Dynamo Kiev (1) 1 *(Cernat 40)*, Levski (0) 0 19,000
Fenerbahce (0) 0, Feyenoord (0) 2 *(Ono 48, Buffel 88)* 43,000
Internazionale (2) 2 *(Di Biagio 32, Recoba 45)*, Sporting Lisbon (0) 0 50,000
Legia (0) 0 *Magiera*■, Barcelona (0) 1 *(Mendieta 67 (pen))* 13,000
Lokomotiv Moscow (3) 3 *(Ignachevitch 6, Yevseyev 32, Julio Cesar 45)*, Graz (1) 3 *(Naumoski 38, Bazina 47, Aufhauser 69)* 12,000
Slovan Liberec (0) 2 *(Slepicka 46, Langer 88) Langer*■, AC Milan (1) 1 *(Inzaghi 20)* 8740
Sparta Prague (0) 4 *(Poborsky 56, Jarosík 59, 64, Mares 84)*, Genk (1) 2 *(Dagano 25, Sonck 57)* 12,856
Sturm Graz (1) 3 *(Bosnar 11, Szabics 58, Neukirchner 71) Bosnar*■, *Pregelj*■, Maccabi Haifa (1) 3 *(Rosso 27, Keisi 77, Badir 90) Ayegbeni*■ 8000

Tuesday, 27 August 2002

Manchester United (3) 5 *(Van Nistelrooy 6, 76 (pen), Beckham 15, Scholes 21, Solskjaer 84)*

Zalaegerszeg (0) 0 66,814

Manchester United: Carroll; Neville P, Silvestre, Ferdinand (O'Shea 68), Keane, Blanc, Beckham (Forlan 72), Veron, Van Nistelrooy, Scholes (Solskjaer 49), Giggs.
Zalaegerszeg: Ilic■; Babati (Turi 76), Szamosi, Csoka, Urban, Budisa, Molnar, Vincze (Balog 64), Kenesei, Egressy, Ljubojevic (Farago 59).

Wednesday, 28 August 2002

Basle (2) 2 *(Gimenez 18, Yakin H 22)*

Celtic (0) 0 30,000

Basle: Zuberbuhler; Barberis, Duruz, Cantaluppi, Quennoz, Yakin M, Varela (Degen 62), Yakin H, Gimenez (Koumantarakis 85), Rossi (Tum 71), Ergic.
Celtic: Douglas; Valgaeren, Laursen (Agathe 46), Sylla (Hartson 71), Balde, Mjallby, Lambert (Guppy 46), Lennon, Sutton, Larsson, Petrov.

Newcastle United (2) 4 *(Dyer 23, Lua-Lua 37, Viana 74, Shearer 80)*

Zeljeznicar (0) 0 34,067

Newcastle United: Given; Hughes, Bernard, Dabizas, Bramble, Solano (Kerr 75), Dyer, Speed, Shearer, Lua-Lua (Ameobi 51), Viana.
Zeljeznicar: Hasagic; Jahic, Mulaosmanovic, Karic (Tica 64), Mulalic, Alihodzic, Cosic (Mucrinic 75), Biscevic, Guvo (Alagic 46), Radonja, Seferovic.

FIRST GROUP STAGE

▪ *Denotes player sent off.*

FIRST GROUP STAGE – GROUP A

Tuesday, 17 September 2002

Arsenal (0) 2 *(Bergkamp 62, Ljungberg 77)*

Borussia Dortmund (0) 0 34,907

Arsenal: Seaman; Luzhny (Lauren 73), Cole, Vieira, Campbell, Keown, Bergkamp, Silva, Wiltord (Toure 89), Henry, Ljungberg (Cygan 84).
Borussia Dortmund: Lehmann; Evanilson, Dede, Heinrich, Metzelder, Madouni, Ewerthon (Reina 72), Kehl, Koller, Frings, Fernandez (Herrlich 72).

Auxerre (0) 0

PSV Eindhoven (0) 0 21,000

Auxerre: Cool; Radet, Jaures, Faye, Boumsong, Mexes, Tainio, Lachuer, Kapo, Mwaruwari (Gonzalez 84), Fadiga.
PSV Eindhoven: Ten Rouwelaar; Bogelund, Heintze, Vogel, Ooijer, Hofland, Rommedahl, Van der Schaaf (Lucius 40), Bruggink (Leandro 86), Kezman, Bouma.

Wednesday, 25 September 2002

Borussia Dortmund (1) 2 *(Koller 6, Amoroso 78)*

Auxerre (0) 1 *(Mwaruwari 83)* 46,500

Borussia Dortmund: Lehmann; Evanilson, Heinrich, Frings (Ricken 74), Metzelder, Worns, Reuter, Rosicky (Amoroso 66), Ewerthon (Dede 84), Koller, Kehl.
Auxerre: Cool; Radet, Jaures, Faye, Boumsong, Mexes, Tainio, Lachuer, Kapo, Mwaruwari, Fadiga.

PSV Eindhoven (0) 0

Arsenal (1) 4 *(Silva 1, Ljungberg 66, Henry 81, 90)* 29,000

PSV Eindhoven: Waterreus; Bogelund, Heintze (Lucius 61), Van Bommel, Hofland (Vennegoor of Hesselink 46), Ooijer, Rommedahl, Vogel (Leandro 27), Bruggink, Kezman, Bouma.
Arsenal: Seaman; Lauren, Cole, Vieira, Campbell, Keown (Cygan 10), Wiltord, Silva, Henry, Bergkamp (Kanu 80), Ljungberg (Toure 86).

Wednesday, 2 October 2002

Auxerre (0) 0

Arsenal (0) 1 *(Silva 47)* 21,000

Auxerre: Cool; Radet, Jaures, Faye, Mexes, Boumsong, Lachuer (Gonzalez 73), Tainio (Sirieix 90), Benjani, Kapo, Fadiga.
Arsenal: Seaman; Lauren, Cole, Vieira, Campbell, Cygan, Wiltord (Luzhny 84), Silva, Kanu, Henry (Pennant 58), Toure (Edu 59).

PSV Eindhoven (0) 1 *(Van der Schaaf 73)*

Borussia Dortmund (1) 3 *(Koller 21, Rosicky 69, Amoroso 90)* 33,000

PSV Eindhoven: Waterreus; Bogelund, Bouma, Van Bommel, Faber, Ooijer, Rommedahl, Vogel, Kezman (Vennegoor of Hesselink 75), Leandro (Robben 55), Van der Schaaf.
Borussia Dortmund: Lehmann; Madouni, Dede, Frings, Metzelder, Worns, Reuter (Ricken 90), Rosicky (Kehl 79), Koller, Ewerthon (Amoroso 65), Henrich.

Tuesday, 22 October 2002

Arsenal (0) 1 *(Kanu 53)*

Auxerre (2) 2 *(Kapo 8, Fadiga 27)* 35,206

Arsenal: Seaman; Lauren (Toure 76), Cole, Vieira, Campbell, Cygan, Wiltord, Silva (Pires 70), Kanu, Henry, Ljungberg.
Auxerre: Cool; Radet, Jaures, Faye, Mexes, Boumsong, Lachuer, Tainio, Benjani, Kapo, Fadiga.

Borussia Dortmund (1) 1 *(Koller 10)*

PSV Eindhoven (0) 1 *(Bruggnik 47)* 47,000

Borussia Dortmund: Lehmann; Evanilson, Dede, Kehl, Worns, Madouni, Reuter (Frings 78), Ewerthon, Koller, Ricken (Amoroso 72), Rosicky.
PSV Eindhoven: Waterreus; Bogelund, Heintze (Robben 46), Van Bommel, Ooijer, Faber, Rommedahl, Bouma, Bruggnik (Ramzi 80), Kezman (Vennegoor of Hesselink 85), Vogel.

Wednesday, 30 October 2002

Borussia Dortmund (1) 2 *(Silva 38 (og), Rosicky 63 (pen))*

Arsenal (1) 1 *(Henry 18)* 51,200

Borussia Dortmund: Lehmann; Worns, Evanilson, Frings, Metzelder, Dede, Rosicky (Madouni 90), Ricken (Heinrich 84), Koller, Ewerthon, Kehl (Reuter 69).
Arsenal: Seaman; Lauren, Cole, Vieira, Campbell, Cygan, Wiltord (Kanu 79), Silva (Edu 80), Ljungberg, Henry, Pires (Toure 67).

PSV Eindhoven (1) 3 *(Bruggink 34, Rommedahl 48, Robben 64)*

Auxerre (0) 0 27,500

PSV Eindhoven: Waterreus; Bogelund, Bouma, Vogel (Lucius 78), Faber, Hofland, Van Bommel (Van der Schaaf 65), Rommedahl, Kezman, Bruggink, Robben (Ramzi 70).
Auxerre: Cool; Radet, Jaures, Faye, Mexes▪, Boumsong, Lachuer (Sirieix 81), Kapo▪, Mwaruwari (Grichting 28), Mathis, Fadiga (Gonzalez 87).

Tuesday, 12 November 2002

Arsenal (0) 0

PSV Eindhoven (0) 0 35,274

Arsenal: Shaaban; Luzhny, Toure▪, Vieira (Silva 76), Stepanovs, Cygan, Pires, Edu, Henry (Bergkamp 63), Jeffers (Wiltord 68), Van Bronckhorst.
PSV Eindhoven: Waterreus; Bogelund, Bouma, Van Bommel, Ooijer (Vennegoor of Hesselink 79), Hofland, Rommedahl, Vogel (Lucius 41), Kezman, Bruggink (Van der Schaaf 70), Robben.

Auxerre (0) 1 *(Mwaruwari 75)*

Borussia Dortmund (0) 0 19,000

Auxerre: Cool; Radet, Jaures, Faye, Boumsong, Grichting, Tainio (Mwaruwari 46), Mathis, Cisse, Lachuer, Fadiga.
Borussia Dortmund: Lehmann; Heinrich (Demel 26), Dede, Frings, Madouni, Kehl, Reuter, Ewerthon (Amoroso 65), Koller, Leandro (Reina 81), Ricken.

Group A Final Table	*P*	*W*	*D*	*L*	*F*	*A*	*Pts*
Arsenal	6	3	1	2	9	4	10
Borussia Dortmund	6	3	1	2	8	7	10
Auxerre	6	2	1	3	4	7	7
PSV Eindhoven	6	1	3	2	5	8	6

FIRST GROUP STAGE – GROUP B

Tuesday, 17 September 2002

Basle (0) 2 *(Yakin H 50, Rossi 55)*

Spartak Moscow (0) 0 29,500

Basle: Zuberbuhler; Haas, Esposito, Cantaluppi, Yakin M, Quennoz, Barberis, Yakin H (Savic 87), Gimenez, Rossi (Tum 75), Atouba.
Spartak Moscow: Cherchesov; Tchuisse, Kebe, Koudriachov, Moises, Kovtun, Baranov (Marcelo Silva 56), Khlestov, Bestchastnykh, Danishevski (Essien 46), Kalynychenko (Mitrevski 72).

Valencia (2) 2 *(Aimar 20, Baraja 39)*

Liverpool (0) 0 38,000

Valencia: Canizares; Curro Torres, Carboni, Albelda (De los Santos 84), Ayala, Pellegrino, Rufete (Angulo 74), Baraja, Aimar (Mista 71), Carew, Vicente.
Liverpool: Dudek; Carragher, Traore, Hamann▪, Diao (Cheyrou 46), Hyypia, Murphy (Baros 76), Gerrard, Diouf (Owen 46), Heskey, Riise.

Wednesday, 25 September 2002

Liverpool (1) 1 *(Baros 34)*

Basle (1) 1 *(Rossi 43)* 37,634

Liverpool: Dudek; Carragher, Riise, Cheyrou, Henchoz, Hyypia, Murphy, Gerrard, Baros, Owen (Berger 79), Heskey (Diouf 71).

Basle: Zuberbuhler; Haas, Esposito, Cantaluppi, Yakin M, Quennoz, Barberis, Yakin H (Duruz 67), Gimenez, Rossi (Tum 74), Atouba.

Spartak Moscow (0) 0

Valencia (1) 3 *(Angulo 6, Mista 70, Juan Sanchez 85)* 15,000

Spartak Moscow: Cherchesov; Kalynychenko, Moises, Koudriachov, Kovtun (Baranov 46), Tchuisse, Mitrevski, Khlestov, Bestchastnykh, Danishevski (Essien 54), Kebe.

Valencia: Canizares; Curro Torres, Carboni, Albelda, Ayala, Pellegrino, Angulo (Juan Sanchez 74), Baraja, Vicente (Rufete 67), Carew (Mista 58), Aimar.

Wednesday, 2 October 2002

Liverpool (3) 5 *(Heskey 7, 89, Cheyrou 14, Hyypia 28, Diao 81)*

Spartak Moscow (0) 0 40,812

Liverpool: Dudek; Carragher, Riise, Hamann, Henchoz (Traore 67), Hyypia, Murphy, Gerrard (Diao 76), Heskey, Owen, Cheyrou (Diouf 82).

Spartak Moscow: Cherchesov; Mitrevski, Khlestov (Bezrodny 25), Koudriachov (Marcelo Silva 50), Moises, Kovtun (Abramidze 63), Kalynychenko, Pavlenko, Bestchastnykh, Danishevski, Kebe.

Valencia (4) 6 *(Carew 10, 12, Fabio Aurelio 17, Baraja 27, Aimar 58, Mista 60)*

Basle (0) 2 *(Rossi 46, Yakin H 89)* 20,000

Valencia: Canizares; Curro Torres, Fabio Aurelio, Albelda, Ayala, Pellegrino, Angulo, Baraja (Mista 46), Carew, Aimar (Juan Sanchez 71), Vicente (Garrido 60).

Basle: Zuberbuhler; Haas, Esposito (Duruz 79), Cantaluppi, Yakin M, Quennoz (Ergic 62), Barberis, Yakin H, Gimenez (Varela 46), Rossi, Atouba.

Tuesday, 22 October 2002

Basle (1) 2 *(Ergic 32, 90)*

Valencia (1) 2 *(Baraja 35, Curro Torres 72)* 29,503

Basle: Zuberbuhler; Haas, Duruz, Cantaluppi, Yakin M, Zwyssig, Varela (Rossi 65), Ergic, Gimenez (Tum 60), Yakin H, Esposito (Koumantarakis 85).

Valencia: Canizares; Pellegrino, Curro Torres, Rufete (Angulo 71), Ayala■, Fabio Aurelio, De los Santos, Baraja (Marchena 76), Mista, Juan Sanchez (Carew 80), Kily Gonzalez.

Spartak Moscow (1) 1 *(Danishevski 23)*

Liverpool (1) 3 *(Owen 29, 70, 90)* 15,000

Spartak Moscow: Levitsky, Khlestov, Kovtun (Kebe 36), Bezrodny, Mitreski (Koudriachov 82), Abramidze, Pavlenko, Bestchastnykh, Danishevski, Sonin (Torbinsky 60), Kalynychenko.

Liverpool: Dudek; Carragher, Riise, Hamann, Traore, Hyypia, Murphy, Diao, Baros (Diouf 70), Owen, Heskey (Vignal 56) (Biscan 76).

Wednesday, 30 October 2002

Liverpool (0) 0

Valencia (1) 1 *(Rufete 34)* 41,831

Liverpool: Dudek; Carragher (Cheyrou 82), Riise, Hamann, Traore, Hyypia, Gerrard, Diao, Heskey (Baros 61), Owen, Murphy (Smicer 61).

Valencia: Canizares; Curro Torres, Carboni, Albelda, Marchena, Pellegrino, Rufete, Baraja, Aimar (Angulo 68), Carew (Mista 79), Kily Gonzalez (Vicente 87).

Tuesday, 5 November 2002

Spartak Moscow (0) 0

Basle (1) 2 *(Rossi 18, Gimenez 89)* 5500

Spartak Moscow: Levitsky; Khlestov, Kovtun, Moises, Abramidze, Pavlenko, Bezrodny (Koudriachov 46), Bestchastnykh, Kalynychenko (Torbinsky 71), Danishevski, Kebe (Mitreski 77).

Basle: Zuberbuhler; Haas, Duruz, Cantaluppi, Yakin M, Zwyssig, Esposito (Atouba 16), Yakin H, Rossi (Gimenez 67), Tum, Ergic.

Tuesday, 12 November 2002

Basle (3) 3 *(Rossi 2, Gimenez 22, Atouba 29)*

Liverpool (0) 3 *(Murphy 61, Smicer 64, Owen 85)* 29,534

Basle: Zuberbuhler; Haas, Atouba, Cantaluppi, Yakin M, Zwyssig, Ergic, Yakin H (Koumantarakis 90), Gimenez (Barberis 66), Rossi (Tum 76), Esposito.

Liverpool: Dudek; Carragher (Diouf 79), Riise, Hamann, Traore, Hyypia, Gerrard (Diao 46), Smicer, Heskey (Baros 61), Owen, Murphy.

Valencia (1) 3 *(Juan Sanchez 37, 46, Fabio Aurelio 76)*

Spartak Moscow (0) 0 22,000

Valencia: Palop; Garrido, Fabio Aurelio, De los Santos (Sanchez Ridaura 87), Marchena, Djukic, Angulo, Mista, Juan Sanchez (Fernando 88), Salva (Albiol 71), Kily Gonzalez.

Spartak Moscow: Levitsky; Abramidze, Kovtun, Koudriachov (Sonin 62), Moises, Mitrevski (Ogunsanya 77), Pavlenko, Bezrodny (Marcelo Silva 46), Bestchastnykh, Danishevski, Kalynychenko.

Group B Final Table	P	W	D	L	F	A	Pts
Valencia	6	5	1	0	17	4	16
Basle	6	2	3	1	12	12	9
Liverpool	6	2	2	2	12	8	8
Spartak Moscow	6	0	0	6	1	18	0

FIRST GROUP STAGE – GROUP C

Tuesday, 17 September 2002

Genk (0) 0

AEK Athens (0) 0 23,500

Genk: Moons; Vanbeuren, Ingrao, Thijs, Tomasic, Zokora, Beslija, Skoko, Sonck, Dagano, Daerden.

AEK Athens: Hiotis; Borbokis (Petkov 53), Kassapis, Kapsis, Kostenoglou, Wright, Katsouranis, Zagorakis, Nikolaidis, Tsartas (Maladenis 90), Nalitzis (Lakis 64).

Roma (0) 0

Real Madrid (1) 3 *(Guti 40, 75, Raul 56)* 71,130

Roma: Antonioli; Dellas, Panucci, Tommasi, Samuel, Cufre (Guardiola 46), Cafu, Emerson, Montella, Cassano (Delvecchio 64), Candela.

Real Madrid: Casillas; Michel Salgado, Roberto Carlos, Makelele (McManaman 78), Hierro, Helguera, Figo, Zidane (Solari 70), Raul, Guti, Cambiasso.

Wednesday, 25 September 2002

AEK Athens (0) 0

Roma (0) 0 18,000

AEK Athens: Hiotis; Lakis, Kassapis (Georgatos 46), Kapsis, Kostenoglou, Wright, Katsouranis, Zagorakis, Ivic (Nalitzis 63), Nikolaidis, Tsartas (Petkov 85).

Roma: Antonioli; Panucci, Cufre, Lima, Samuel, Emerson, Cafu, Tommasi, Batistuta (Cassano 90), Montella, Candela.

Real Madrid (2) 6 *(Zokora 44 (og), Michel Salgado 45, Figo 54 (pen), Guti 64, Celades 73, Raul 76)*

Genk (0) 0 65,000

Real Madrid: Casillas; Michel Salgado, Roberto Carlos (Raul Bravo 70), Celades, Hierro, Helguera, Figo, Cambiasso (Morientes 67), Raul (Portillo 76), Guti, Solari.

Genk: Moons; Vanbeuren (Seyfo 61), Roumani, Skoko, Tomasic, Zokora, Beslija (Suzuki 83), Wamfor, Sonck, Dagano (De Camargo 79), Daerden.

Wednesday, 2 October 2002

AEK Athens (3) 3 *(Tsartas 6, Maladenis 25, Nikolaidis 28)*

Real Madrid (2) 3 *(Zidane 15, 39, Guti 60)* 12,900

AEK Athens: Hiotis; Lakis, Kassapis, Kapsis, Kostenoglou, Wright, Katsouranis, Zagorakis (Centeno 84), Nikolaidis, Tsartas (Ivic 84), Petkov (Maladenis 16).
Real Madrid: Casillas; Michel Salgado, Roberto Carlos, Makelele, Helguera, Pavon, Figo, Cambiasso, Raul (Morientes 81), Guti (McManaman 87), Zidane (Portillo 84).

Genk (0) 0

Roma (0) 1 *(Cassano 81)* 22,600

Genk: Moons■; Wamfor, Roumani (Ingrao 85), Thijs, Tomasic, Zokora, Beslija (Schollen 12), Skoko, Sonck, Dagano, Daerden (Seyfo 68).
Roma: Antonioli; Zebina, Panucci, Tommasi (Tomic 53), Samuel, Emerson, Cafu (Cassano 46), Lima, Batistuta (Montella 68), Totti, Candela.

Tuesday, 22 October 2002

Real Madrid (2) 2 *(McManaman 23, 43)*

AEK Athens (0) 2 *(Katsouranis 74, Centeno 86)* 61,040

Real Madrid: Casillas; Michel Salgado, Roberto Carlos (Raul Bravo 75), Celades, Hierro, Helguera, Cambiasso, Guti, Ronaldo, Zidane (Solari 61), McManaman (Minambres 82).
AEK Athens: Hiotis; Kostenoglou, Georgatos (Centeno 69), Katsouranis, Wright, Kapsis, Lakis, Tsartas (Maladenis 54), Nikolaidis (Ivic 54), Zagorakis, Kasapis.

Roma (0) 0

Genk (0) 0 25,592

Roma: Antonioli; Cafu (Bombardini 84), Candela, Zebina, Samuel, Panucci, Tommasi (Guigou 60), Emerson, Batistuta, Cassano (Montella 46), Lima.
Genk: Schollen; Wamfor, Roumani, Thijs, Zokora, Tomasic, Beslija, Skoko, Sonck, Dagano, Daerden (Suzuki 77).

Wednesday, 30 October 2002

AEK Athens (1) 1 *(Lakis 30)*

Genk (1) 1 *(Sonck 22)* 24,000

AEK Athens: Hiotis; Borbokis (Ivic 66), Georgatos (Maladenis 78), Wright, Kapsis, Kostenoglou, Lakis, Katsouranis, Tsartas (Centeno 66), Nikolaidis, Kasapis.
Genk: Moons; Wamfor, Roumani, Thijs, Zokora, Tomasic, Beslija (Chatelle 90), Skoko, Sonck, Suzuki (Seyfo 90), Daerden.

Real Madrid (0) 0

Roma (1) 1 *(Totti 26)* 70,000

Real Madrid: Casillas; Michel Salgado, Roberto Carlos, Cambiasso (Guti 86), Hierro, Helguera, Figo, Makelele, Ronaldo (Morientes 78), Zidane (Solari 78), Raul.
Roma: Antonioli; Cafu, Candela, Aldair (Zebina 90), Samuel, Panucci, Tommasi, Emerson, Montella (Batistuta 72), Totti, Delvecchio (Lima 88).

Tuesday, 12 November 2002

Genk (0) 1 *(Sonck 85)*

Real Madrid (1) 1 *(Tote 21)* 22,500

Genk: Moons; Tomasic, Roumani, Thijs, Soley, Zokora, Beslija, Skoko, Vandenbergh (Chatelle 69), Sonck, Ingrao (Suzuki 60).
Real Madrid: Cesar; Minambres, Roberto Carlos, Flavio Conceicao, Hierro (Helguera 30), Pavon, Celades, Figo (McManaman 67), Morientes (Solari 77), Guti, Tote.

Roma (1) 1 *(Delvecchio 40)*

AEK Athens (0) 1 *(Centeno 90)* 32,734

Roma: Antonioli; Cafu (Bombardini 90), Lima (Guigou 81), Zebina, Samuel, Panucci, Tommasi, Emerson, Montella, Delvecchio, Cassano (Cufre 65).
AEK Athens: Hiotis; Lakis (Tsartas 61), Georgatos, Borbokis, Wright, Kapsis (Kostenoglou 46), Katsouranis, Zagorakis, Nikolaidis, Nalitzis (Ivic 46), Centeno.

Group C Final Table	*P*	*W*	*D*	*L*	*F*	*A*	*Pts*
Real Madrid	6	2	3	1	15	7	9
Roma	6	2	3	1	3	4	9
AEK Athens	6	0	6	0	7	7	6
Genk	6	0	4	2	2	9	4

FIRST GROUP STAGE – GROUP D

Tuesday, 17 September 2002

Ajax (2) 2 *(Ibrahimovic 11, 44)*

Lyon (0) 1 *(Anderson 84)* 37,455

Ajax: Stekelenburg; Trabelsi, O'Brien, Maxwell, Chivu, Yakubu■, Galasek (Van Halst 57), Litmanen, Ibrahimovic (Bergdolmo 81), Ver der Meyde, Sikora (Pienaar 68).
Lyon: Coupet; Chanelet (Diarra 79), Brechet, Carriere, Cacapa, Edmilson, Dhorasoo, Violeau (Laville 46), Anderson, Govou (Vairelles 41), Juninho Pernambucano.

Rosenborg (0) 2 *(Karadas 52, 65)*

Internazionale (1) 2 *(Crespo 33, 79)* 21,040

Rosenborg: Arason; Strand (Stensaas 75), Saarinen, Berg, Hoftun, Basma, Olsen, Karadas, Brattbakk, Johnsen F, Skammelsrud.
Internazionale: Toldo; Cannavaro■, Coco, Almeyda, Materazzi, Cordoba, Dalmat (Emre B 63), Zanetti J, Crespo (Adani 88), Vieri, Morfeo (Recoba 77).

Wednesday, 25 September 2002

Internazionale (0) 1 *(Crespo 74)*

Ajax (0) 0 45,784

Internazionale: Toldo; Zanetti J, Pasquale, Emre B (Recoba 52), Cordoba, Materazzi, Okan (Sergio Conceicao 69), Di Biagio (Almeyda 65), Crespo, Vieri, Dalmat.
Ajax: Stekelenburg (Timmer 23); Trabelsi, Van Damme, Galasek, Pasanen (Hossam 80), Chivu, Maxwell, Litmanen, Ibrahimovic, Sikora, Van der Meyde (Pienaar 76).

Lyon (4) 5 *(Carriere 5, Vairelles 25, 45, Anderson 34, Luyindula 75)*

Rosenborg (0) 0 37,505

Lyon: Coupet; Deflandre, Brechet, Carriere, Muller, Cacapa, Dhorasoo (Delmotte 78), Violeau, Anderson (Juninho Pernambucano 67), Vairelles (Luyindula 72), Diarra.
Rosenborg: Arason; Olsen (Sibaya 65), Saarinen (Blixt 83), Stensaas (Ludvigsen 72), Hoftun, Basma, Berg, Skammelsrud, Brattbakk, Johnsen F, Karadas.

Wednesday, 2 October 2002

Internazionale (0) 1 *(Cannavaro 72)*

Lyon (1) 2 *(Govou 21, Anderson 59)* 31,448

Internazionale: Toldo; Cannavaro, Coco (Pasquale 86), Almeyda, Materazzi, Cordoba, Zanetti J, Di Biagio (Sergio Conceicao 69), Crespo, Recoba, Dalmat (Morfeo 61).
Lyon: Coupet; Muller, Brechet, Violeau, Cacapa, Edmilson, Dhorasoo, Carriere (Juninho Pernambucano 88), Anderson (Laville 77), Govou (Vairelles 90), Diarra.

Rosenborg (0) 0

Ajax (0) 0 20,948

Rosenborg: Arason; Olsen, Saarinen, Berg, Hoftun, Basma, Strand, Skammelsrud, Brattbakk (George 40), Johnsen F (Enerly 35), Karadas.
Ajax: Didulica; Trabelsi, Van Damme, Van Halst (Winter 69), Bergdolmo, Chivu, Galasek, Wamberto, Ibrahimovic (Van der Meyde 69), Hossam, Witschge (Maxwell 79).

Tuesday, 22 October 2002

Ajax (1) 1 *(Ibrahimovic 41)*

Rosenborg (0) 1 *(Enerly 85 (pen))* 42,026

Ajax: Timmer; Trabelski, Van Damme■, Witschge (De Jong 83), Bergdolmo, Chivu, Galasek, Litmanen, Ibrahimovic (Hossam 71), Boukhari, Van der Meyde.
Rosenborg: Arason; Strand, Saarinen, Skammelsrud (Olsen 39), Basma, Hoftun, Berg, Brattbakk (Ludvigsen 74), Enerly, Johnsen F, Karadas.

Lyon (2) 3 *(Anderson 21, 74, Carriere 43)*

Internazionale (1) 3 *(Cacapa 31 (og), Crespo 56, 65)* 37,770

Lyon: Coupet; Muller, Brechet, Voileau (Vairelles 69), Edmilson, Cacapa, Diarra, Juninho Pernambucano (Laville 58), Carriere, Anderson, Dhorasoo.
Internazionale: Toldo; Zanetti J, Coco, Di Biagio (Almeyda 24), Materazzi, Cordoba, Sergio Conceicao (Adani 72), Emre B, Crespo (Recoba 78), Vieri, Morfeo.

Wednesday, 30 October 2002

Internazionale (1) 3 *(Recoba 30, Saarinen 52 (og), Crespo 72)*

Rosenborg (0) 0 33,686

Internazionale: Toldo; Zanetti J, Coco (Pasquale 87), Emre B, Materazzi, Cannavaro, Sergio Conceicao, Di Biagio, Vieri, Crespo (Almeyda 75), Recoba.
Rosenborg: Arason; Strand, Saarinen, Skammelsrud, Basma, Hoftun, Berg, Brattbakk (Olsen 57), Johnsen F, Karadas, Enerly (Ludvigsen 88).

Lyon (0) 0

Ajax (1) 2 *(Pienaar 7, Van der Vaart 90)* 38,134

Lyon: Coupet; Muller, Brechet, Carriere (Luyindula 80), Edmilson, Cacapa, Juninho Pernambucano, Violeau (Vairelles 59), Anderson, Govou, Dhorasoo.
Ajax: Didulica; Trabelsi, Maxwell, Pienaar, Bergdolmo, Chivu■, Galasek, De Jong, Ibrahimovic (Van der Meyde 77), Hossam (Van der Vaart 55), Sikora (Yakubu 65).

Tuesday, 12 November 2002

Ajax (0) 1 *(Van der Vaart 90)*

Internazionale (0) 2 *(Crespo 50, 52)* 50,272

Ajax: Didulica; Trabelsi, Van Damme (Witschge 58), Pienaar (Wamberto 58), De Jong, Bergdolmo, Galasek (Yakubu 71), Van der Meyde, Van der Vaart, Hossam, Maxwell.
Internazionale: Toldo; Zanetti J, Coco, Almeyda, Cordoba, Materazzi, Sergio Conceicao (Adani 72), Di Biagio, Crespo (Recoba 65), Vieri, Morfeo (Emre B 90).

Rosenborg (0) 1 *(Brattbakk 68)*

Lyon (0) 1 *(Govou 83)* 21,008

Rosenborg: Arason; Strand, Saarinen, Berg, Basma, Hoftun, Johnsen F, Skammelsrud, Karadas, Brattbakk, Enerly (Ludvigsen 79).
Lyon: Coupet; Muller, Brechet, Violeau (Juninho Pernambucano 66), Cacapa, Edmilson, Dhorasoo (Delmotte 72), Carriere (Luyindula 72), Govou, Anderson, Diarra.

Group D Final Table	P	W	D	L	F	A	Pts
Internazionale	6	3	2	1	12	8	11
Ajax	6	2	2	2	6	5	8
Lyon	6	2	2	2	12	9	8
Rosenborg	6	0	4	2	4	12	4

FIRST GROUP STAGE – GROUP E

Wednesday, 18 September 2002

Dynamo Kiev (1) 2 *(Shatskikh 16, Khatskevich 62)*

Newcastle United (0) 0 42,500

Dynamo Kiev: Reva; Peev, Nesmachni, Leko, Ghioane, Sablic, Gusin, Cernat, Leandro Machado (Melashchenko 56), Shatskikh, Khatskevich (Gavrancic 73).
Newcastle United: Given; Griffin, Bernard (Robert 89), Dabizas, O'Brien, Hughes (Solano 69), Dyer, Speed, Shearer (Ameobi 79), Bellamy, Viana.

Feyenoord (0) 1 *(Van Hooijdonk 74)*

Juventus (1) 1 *(Camoranesi 31)* 45,000

Feyenoord: Zoetebier; Gyan (Bombarda 70), Van Haaren, Emerton, Paauwe, Van Wonderen, Song, Ono, Buffel, Van Hooijdonk, Pardo (Kalou 55).
Juventus: Buffon; Thuram, Birindelli, Davids (Fresi 65), Montero, Ferrara, Camoranesi (Baiocco 81), Tacchinardi, Del Piero (Salas 76), Di Vaio, Nedved.

Tuesday, 24 September 2002

Juventus (2) 5 *(Di Vaio 14, 52, Del Piero 22, Davids 67, Nedved 79)*

Dynamo Kiev (0) 0 26,876

Juventus: Buffon; Thuram, Moretti, Tacchinardi (Tudor 68), Montero (Baiocco 76), Ferrara, Camoranesi, Davids, Del Piero, Di Vaio (Trezeguet 72), Nedved.
Dynamo Kiev: Reva; Peev, Nesmachni, Leko, Ghioane, Sablic, Gusin, Cernat, Shatskikh, Khatskevich (Melashchenko 71), Gavrancic.

Newcastle United (0) 0

Feyenoord (1) 1 *(Pardo 4)* 40,540

Newcastle United: Given; Griffin, Hughes, Dabizas, O'Brien, Solano, Dyer, Speed, Shearer, Bellamy (Lua-Lua 76), Robert.
Feyenoord: Zoetebier; Emerton, Rzasa, Bosvelt, Paauwe, Van Wonderen, Song, Ono, Buffel, Van Hooijdonk, Pardo (Lurling 82).

Tuesday, 1 October 2002

Feyenoord (0) 0

Dynamo Kiev (0) 0 41,200

Feyenoord: Zoetebier; Emerton, Rzasa, Bosvelt, Paauwe, De Haan, Song, Ono, Van Hooijdonk, Buffel (Kalou 66), Pardo (Van Persie 55).
Dynamo Kiev: Reva; Bodnar, Nesmachni, Gusin, Gavrancic, Ghioane, Peev, Cernat (Rincon 84), Melashchenko, Khatskevich (Leko 63), Shatskikh.

Juventus (0) 2 *(Del Piero 66, 81)*

Newcastle U (0) 0 41,424

Juventus: Buffon; Thuram, Moretti, Davids, Iuliano, Montero, Baiocco (Fresi 85), Nedved, Del Piero, Di Vaio (Trezeguet 17), Tudor (Birindelli 83).
Newcastle U: Given; Griffin (Ameobi 79), Hughes, Dabizas, O'Brien, Solano (Viana 70), Dyer, Speed, Shearer, Jenas (Lua-Lua 79), Robert.

Wednesday, 23 October 2002

Dynamo Kiev (1) 2 *(Khatskevich 16, Belkevich 47)*

Feyenoord (0) 0 73,000

Dynamo Kiev: Reva; Peev, Dmitrulin (Sablic 77), Gusin, Gavrancic, Ghioane, Belkevich, El Kaddouri, Khatskevich, Rincon (Nesmachni 57), Shatskikh.
Feyenoord: Zoetebier; Song, Van Haaren (Rzasa 56), Van Wonderen, Paauwe, Emerton (Bombarda 62), Loovens, Ono, Buffel, Kalou, Van Persie (Lurling 39).

Newcastle United (0) 1 *(Buffon 62 (og))*

Juventus (0) 0 48,370

Newcastle United: Harper; Griffin, Hughes, Bramble, O'Brien, Solano, Jenas, Speed, Shearer, Lua-Lua (Ameobi 85), Robert (Viana 85).
Juventus: Buffon; Thuram, Birindelli, Tacchinardi, Iuliano, Ferrara, Camoranesi (Zambrotta 69), Davids (Conte 46), Di Vaio (Zalayeta 57), Del Piero, Nedved.

Tuesday, 29 October 2002

Juventus (1) 2 *(Di Vaio 4, 69)*

Feyenoord (0) 0 35,789

Juventus: Buffon; Thuram (Iuliano 71), Birindelli, Tacchinardi, Ferrara, Tudor (Zambrotta 89), Camoranesi, Davids, Del Piero, Di Vaio, Nedved (Moretti 82).
Feyenoord: Zoetebier (Lodewijks 46); Song, Rzasa, Buffel, Van Wonderen, Paauwe, Emerton, Bosvelt, Bombarda, Lurling, Ono.

Newcastle United (0) 2 *(Speed 58, Shearer 69 (pen))*

Dynamo Kiev (0) 1 *(Shatskikh 47)* 40,185

Newcastle United: Harper; Griffin, Hughes, Bramble (Dabizas 27), O'Brien (Bernard 46), Solano (Dyer 82), Jenas, Speed, Shearer, Ameobi, Robert.
Dynamo Kiev: Reva; Gusin, Peev, Leko (Rincon 71), Ghioane, Gavrancic, Belkevich, El Kaddouri (Cernat 77), Shatskikh, Nesmachni, Dmitrulin.

Wednesday, 13 November 2002

Dynamo Kiev (0) 1 *(Shatskikh 50)*

Juventus (0) 2 *(Salas 53, Zalayeta 60)* 78,000

Dynamo Kiev: Reva; Bodnar, Nesmachni, Gusin, Gavrancic, Ghioane, Dmitrulin, Khatskevich (Leko 59), Belkevich, Rincon (Cernat 67), Shatskikh.
Juventus: Chimenti; Birindelli, Pessotto, Conte (Paro 27), Fresi, Iuliano, Zambrotta, Baiocco, Salas (Cassani 90), Zalayeta, Olivera (Davids 76).

Feyenoord (0) 2 *(Bombarda 65, Lurling 71)*

Newcastle United (1) 3 *(Bellamy 45, 90, Viana 49)* 45,000

Feyenoord: Lodewijks; Gyan, Rzasa, Bosvelt, Van Wonderen, Paauwe, Song (Bombarda 51), Emerton, Kalou, Buffel, Lurling.
Newcastle United: Given; Griffin, Hughes, Dabizas, O'Brien, Jenas, Dyer, Speed, Shearer, Bellamy, Viana (Bernard 82).

Group E Final Table	P	W	D	L	F	A	Pts
Juventus	6	4	1	1	12	3	13
Newcastle United	6	3	0	3	6	8	9
Dynamo Kiev	6	2	1	3	6	9	7
Feyenoord	6	1	2	3	4	8	5

FIRST GROUP STAGE – GROUP F

Wednesday, 18 September 2002

Manchester United (2) 5 *(Giggs 10, Solskjaer 35, Veron 46, Van Nistelrooy 54, Forlan 89 (pen))*

Maccabi Haifa (1) 2 *(Katan 8, Cohen 85)* 63,439

Manchester United: Barthez (Ricardo 67); O'Shea, Silvestre, Ferdinand, Neville P, Blanc, Beckham, Veron, Van Nistelrooy (Pugh 75), Solskjaer, Giggs (Forlan 56).
Maccabi Haifa: Awat; Harazi (Cohen 73), Keisi, Badir, Benado, Almoshnino (Zano 56), Katan, Ejifoor, Rosso, Zandberg (Israelevic 65), Pralija.

Olympiakos (3) 6 *(Giannakopoulos 38, Djordjevic 44, 64 (pen), 73, Zetterberg 87, Kleine 27 (og))*

Leverkusen (1) 2 *(Schneider 22, 78 (pen))* 15,000

Olympiakos: Eleftheropoulos; Patsatzoglou, Venetidis, Ze Elias, Anatolakis, Antzas, Giannakopoulos (Ofori-Quaye 83), Karembeu, Djordjevic (Edu Drassena 90), Giovanni (Alexandris 86), Zetterberg.
Leverkusen: Juric; Balitsch (Ojigwe 71), Zivkovic, Ramelow, Lucio, Kleine (Brdaric 51), Schneider, Basturk, Neuville, Simak, Vranjes.

Tuesday, 24 September 2002

Leverkusen (0) 1 *(Berbatov 52)*

Manchester United (2) 2 *(Van Nistelrooy 31, 44)* 22,500

Leverkusen: Juric; Balitsch (Franca 82), Zivkovic, Ramelow, Lucio, Ojigwe (Simak 64), Schneider, Basturk, Neuville (Berbatov 22), Brdaric, Babic.
Manchester United: Barthez; O'Shea (Neville G 46), Silvestre, Ferdinand, Neville P, Blanc, Beckham, Butt, Van Nistelrooy (Forlan 46), Veron (Solskjaer 87), Giggs.

Maccabi Haifa (1) 3 *(Yakubu 27 (pen), 60, 85)*

Olympiakos (0) 0 17,000

Maccabi Haifa: Awat; Keisi, Harazi (Zano 52), Badir, Benado, Zutautas, Katan (Zandberg 79), Ejifoor, Rosso, Yakubu, Pralija (Israelevich 87).
Olympiakos: Eleftheropoulos; Patsatzoglou, Venetidis, Ze Elias (Alexandris 55), Anatolakis, Antzas, Giannakopoulos (Ofori-Quaye 80), Karembeu, Djordjevic, Giovanni, Zetterberg (Niniadis 71).
(in Nicosia).

Tuesday, 1 October 2002

Maccabi Haifa (0) 0

Leverkusen (1) 2 *(Babic 31, 63)* 4500

Maccabi Haifa: Awat; Keisi, Zano, Badir (Zandberg 60), Benado, Zutautas, Katan (Cohen 60), Ejifoor, Rosso, Yakubu, Pralija (Israelevich 70).
Leverkusen: Butt; Zivkovic, Ojigwe, Balitsch, Lucio, Ramelow, Schneider (Bierofka 85), Basturk, Neuville, Brdaric (Berbatov 70), Babic (Vranjes 77).
(in Nicosia).

Manchester United (2) 4 *(Giggs 19, 67, Veron 26, Solskjaer 77)*

Olympiakos (0) 0 66,902

Manchester United: Barthez; Neville G, Silvestre, Ferdinand, Butt, Blanc (O'Shea 69), Beckham, Veron, Solskjaer, Scholes (Forlan 78), Giggs (Fortune 69).
Olympiakos: Eleftheropoulos; Amanatidis (Patsatzoglou 73), Venetidis, Zetterberg, Antzas, Anatolakis, Giannakopoulos (Edu Drassena 46), Karembeu, Ofori-Quaye (Alexandris 59), Ze Elias■, Djordjevic.

Wednesday, 23 October 2002

Leverkusen (1) 2 *(Babic 45, Juan 67)*

Maccabi Haifa (0) 1 *(Pralija 53)* 22,500

Leverkusen: Butt; Sebescen, Placente, Ramelow, Lucio, Juan, Schneider, Basturk, Franca (Simak 60), Brdaric (Neuville 46), Babic.
Maccabi Haifa: Awat; Zano (Sivilia 80), Keisi, Zutautas, Harazi, Benado, Badir, Rosso, Yakubu, Zandberg (Katan 74), Pralija (Israelevich 74).

Olympiakos (0) 2 *(Chotos 70, Djordjevic 74)*

Manchester United (1) 3 *(Blanc 21, Veron 59, Scholes 84)* 14,000

Olympiakos: Eleftheropoulos; Patsatzoglou, Venetidis, Edu Drassena, Anatolakis, Antzas, Giannakopoulos (Mavrogenidis 87), Zetterberg (Olori-Quaye 70), Giovanni (Chotos 46), Karembeu, Djordjevic.
Manchester United: Barthez; Neville G, Silvestre, O'Shea, Neville P, Blanc, Beckham (Chadwick 63), Veron (Richardson 87), Forlan, Scholes, Giggs (Fortune 63).

Tuesday, 29 October 2002

Leverkusen (1) 2 *(Juan 14, Schneider 89 (pen))*

Olympiakos (0) 0 22,500

Leverkusen: Butt; Zivkovic, Placente, Balitsch, Lucio, Juan (Ojigwe 45), Schneider, Basturk, Berbatov (Brdaric 90), Neuville (Simak 62), Babic.
Olympiakos: Eleftheropoulos; Mavrogenidis, Venetidis, Patsatzoglou, Antzas (Ofori-Quaye 63), Edu Drassena, Giannakopoulos, Anatolakis (Zetterberg 46), Choutos (Giovanni 24), Karembeu, Djordjevic.

Maccabi Haifa (1) 3 *(Katan 40, Zutautas 56, Yakubu 77 (pen))*

Manchester United (0) 0 23,000

Maccabi Haifa: Awat; Zano, Keisi, Badir, Harazi, Benado, Zutautas (Zandberg 81), Rosso, Yakubu (Almoshnino 84), Katan, Pralija.
Manchester United: Ricardo; Neville G, Silvestre, Ferdinand, Neville P, O'Shea, Richardson (Nardiello 61), Scholes, Forlan (Timm 78), Solskjaer, Fortune.
(in Nicosia).

Wednesday, 13 November 2002

Manchester United (1) 2 *(Veron 42, Van Nistelrooy 69)*

Leverkusen (0) 0 66,185

Manchester United: Ricardo; O'Shea, Silvestre, Ferdinand, Veron, Blanc (Neville G 78), Beckham (Solskjaer 78), Fortune, Van Nistelrooy, Scholes, Giggs (Chadwick 81).
Leverkusen: Butt; Sebescen, Zivkovic, Balitsch (Preuss 81), Ramelow, Kleine, Simak, Babic, Brdaric, Berbatov (Franca 61), Bierofka (Dogan 78).

Olympiakos (1) 3 *(Alexandris 36, Niniadis 50, Antzas 79)*
Maccabi Haifa (3) 3 *(Badir 9, Yakubu 10, Katan 41)* 12,500

Olympiakos: Eleftheropoulos; Patsatzoglou, Venetidis, Djordjevic, Antzas, Edu Drassena, Giannakopoulos, Zetterberg (Niniadis 46), Giovanni (Ofori-Quaye 71), Alexandris, Karembeu.
Maccabi Haifa: Awat; Zano, Keisi, Rosso, Harazi, Benado, Badir, Ejifoor, Yakubu, Katan (Zandberg 68), Pralija (Almoshnino 79).

Group F Final Table	P	W	D	L	F	A	Pts
Manchester United	6	5	0	1	16	8	15
Leverkusen	6	3	0	3	9	11	9
Maccabi Haifa	6	2	1	3	12	12	7
Olympiakos	6	1	1	4	11	17	4

FIRST GROUP STAGE – GROUP G

Wednesday, 18 September 2002

AC Milan (0) 2 *(Inzaghi 58, 61)*
Lens (0) 1 *(Moreira 75)* 70,259

AC Milan: Dida; Simic, Kaladze, Pirlo, Nesta, Maldini, Gattuso, Rui Costa (Tomasson 82), Inzaghi (Laursen 85), Rivaldo (Ambrosini 77), Seedorf.
Lens: Warmuz; Coly, Coulibaly, Blanchard (Bakari 84), Bak J, Song, Sibierski, Diop PB, Diagne-Faye (Keita 64), Moreira, Thomert (Utaka 64).

Bayern Munich (0) 2 *(Salihamidzic 59, Elber 64)*
La Coruna (2) 3 *(Makaay 12, 45, 77)* 40,000

Bayern Munich: Kahn; Sagnol (Hargreaves 46), Tarnat, Jeremies (Kovac N 78), Kuffour, Linke, Salihamidzic, Ballack, Elber, Pizarro, Ze Roberto (Zickler 84).
La Coruna: Juanmi; Hector, Romero, Mauro Silva, Naybet, Donato, Victor (Acuna 71), Valeron, Makaay (Luque 86), Sergio, Fran (Capdevila 67).

Tuesday, 24 September 2002

La Coruna (0) 0
AC Milan (2) 4 *(Seedorf 17, Inzaghi 32, 54, 61)* 32,000

La Coruna: Juanmi; Scaloni, Romero, Mauro Silva (Donato 79), Naybet, Cesar, Victor, Acuna (Duscher 62), Makaay, Sergio, Fran (Diego Tristan 62).
AC Milan: Dida; Simic, Kaladze, Pirlo (Ambrosini 64), Nesta, Maldini, Gattuso, Rui Costa (Dalla Bona 83), Inzaghi (Tomasson 80), Rivaldo, Seedorf.

Lens (0) 1 *(Utaka 76)*
Bayern Munich (1) 1 *(Linke 23)* 35,000

Lens: Warmuz; Coly, Rool, Blanchard (Bakari 68), Song, Bak J, Sibierski, Keita, Moreira, Diop PB, Utaka.
Bayern Munich: Kahn; Linke, Tarnat (Kuffour 77), Jeremies, Kovac R, Pizarro, Salihamidzic, Ballack, Elber (Zickler 73), Ze Roberto, Hargreaves.

Tuesday, 1 October 2002

Bayern Munich (0) 1 *(Pizarro 54)*
AC Milan (0) 2 *(Inzaghi 52, 84)* 60,000

Bayern Munich: Kahn; Kovac R, Tarnat (Zickler 87), Jeremies, Linke, Hargreaves, Salihamidzic, Ballack, Elber, Pizarro, Ze Roberto.
AC Milan: Dida; Simic, Kaladze, Pirlo (Serginho 77), Nesta, Maldini, Gattuso, Rui Costa (Laursen 87), Inzaghi, Rivaldo (Ambrosini 66), Seedorf.

La Coruna (0) 3 *(Makaay 49, Capdevila 78, Cesar 83)*
Lens (1) 1 *(Moreira 10)* 28,000

La Coruna: Juanmi; Hector (Sergio 46), Romero, Mauro Silva, Naybet, Cesar, Scaloni, Duscher (Capdevila 70), Makaay, Diego Tristan (Luque 76), Fran.
Lens: Warmuz; Coly, Rool, Blanchard, Song, Bak J (Coulibaly 65), Sibierski (Bakari 84), Coridon, Moreira, Pedron (Diagne-Faye 76), Utaka.

Wednesday, 23 October 2002

AC Milan (1) 2 *(Serginho 11, Inzaghi 64)*
Bayern Munich (1) 1 *(Tarnat 23)* 75,611

AC Milan: Dida; Simic, Kaladze, Pirlo, Nesta, Maldini, Ambrosini (Gattuso 46), Rui Costa (Laursen 85), Inzaghi, Seedorf, Serginho (Dalla Bona 79).
Bayern Munich: Kahn (Wessels 51); Sagnol, Tarnat, Jeremies, Kovac R, Kuffour, Salihamidzic (Scholl 71), Ballack, Elber, Pizarro (Santa Cruz 72), Ze Roberto.

Lens (0) 3 *(Coulibaly 60, Moreira 79, Thomert 85)*
La Coruna (1) 1 *(Makaay 14)* 38,000

Lens: Warmuz; Coulibaly, Rool, Diop PB (Coridon 73), Bak J, Song, Keita, Utaka, Moreira, Sibierski (Bakari 73), Thomert (Fanni 86).
La Coruna: Juanmi; Hector, Romero, Mauro Silva, Donato, Naybet, Sergio, Victor (Scaloni 65), Makaay (Diego Tristan 70), Capdevila (Luque 84), Fran.

Tuesday, 29 October 2002

La Coruna (0) 2 *(Victor 54, Makaay 89)*
Bayern Munich (0) 1 *(Santa Cruz 76)* 33,000

La Coruna: Juanmi; Scaloni, Romero, Mauro Silva, Naybet, Cesar, Sergio, Victor (Diego Tristan 84), Fran (Acuna 66), Makaay (Donato 90), Capdevila.
Bayern Munich: Wessels; Sagnol, Tarnat (Lizarazu 60), Jeremies, Kovac R, Kuffour, Salihamidzic (Santa Cruz 46), Ballack (Fink 52), Elber, Scholl, Ze Roberto.

Lens (1) 2 *(Moreira 41, Utaka 49)*
AC Milan (1) 1 *(Shevchenko 32)* 39,474

Lens: Warmuz; Coulibaly, Rool, Diop PB (Coly 57), Bak J, Song, Coridon, Sibierski (Diagne-Faye 87), Moreira (Thomert 90), Utaka, Keita.
AC Milan: Abbiati; Helveg, Maldini (Kaladze 65), Pirlo, Costacurta, Laursen, Dalla Bona, Ambrosini, Tomasson, Shevchenko (Borriello 46), Serginho (Seedorf 65).

Wednesday, 13 November 2002

AC Milan (1) 1 *(Tomasson 34)*
La Coruna (0) 2 *(Diego Tristan 58, Makaay 70)* 60,262

AC Milan: Abbiati; Helveg, Kaladze (Aubameyang 85), Pirlo, Simic, Maldini, Dalla Bona, Rui Costa (Inzaghi 75), Shevchenko, Tomasson, Serginho.
La Coruna: Juanmi; Scaloni, Capdevila, Mauro Silva, Romero, Hector, Sergio, Makaay (Duscher 78), Fran (Acuna 65), Luque (Amavisca 56), Diego Tristan.

Bayern Munich (2) 3 *(Kovac N 6, Salihamidzic 18, Feulner 86)*
Lens (1) 3 *(Fink 20 (og), Bakari 54, Blanchard 90)* 22,000

Bayern Munich: Wessels; Salihamidzic, Lizarazu, Scholl (Schweinsteiger 76), Kovac R, Linke, Kovac N, Feulner (Lahm 90), Pizarro (Elber 46), Zickler, Fink.
Lens: Warmuz; Coulibaly, Rool (Keita 69), Sibierski, Bak J, Song, Coridon (Diagne-Faye 29), Utaka, Bakari (Thomert 76), Blanchard, Moreira.

Group G Final Table	P	W	D	L	F	A	Pts
AC Milan	6	4	0	2	12	7	12
La Coruna	6	4	0	2	11	12	12
Lens	6	2	2	2	11	11	8
Bayern Munich	6	0	2	4	9	13	2

FIRST GROUP STAGE – GROUP H

Wednesday, 18 September 2002

Barcelona (3) 3 *(Luis Enrique 5, Mendieta 40, Saviola 43)*
FC Brugge (1) 2 *(Simons 22 (pen), Englebert 85)* 83,300

Barcelona: Victor Valdes; Puyol, Fernando, Xavi, De Boer, Cocu, Mendieta (Rochemback 76), Motta, Saviola, Kluivert, Luis Enrique (Riquelme 73).
FC Brugge: Verlinden; De Cock, Van der Heyden (Stoica 56), Simons, Spilar, Maertens, Englebert, Serebrennikov (Lesnjak 46), Verheyen, Mendoza, Martens (Ceh 71).

Lokomotiv Moscow (0) 0

Galatasaray (0) 2 *(Sarr 71, Arif 80)* 20,000

Lokomotiv Moscow: Ovchinnikov; Nizhegorodov, Pashinin (Sennikov 60), Maminov, Ignachevitch, Drozdov, Loskov, Bouznikin (Pimenov 46), Julio Cesar (Adamu 74), Yevseyev, Lekgetho.
Galatasaray: Mondragon; Umit D, Hakan Unsal, Ayhan (Fabio Pinto 46), Bulent K, Almagueira, Felipe, Batista, Arif (Emre A 84), Hasan Sas (Sarr 70), Ergun.

Tuesday, 24 September 2002

FC Brugge (0) 0

Lokomotiv Moscow (0) 0 17,000

FC Brugge: Verlinden; De Cock, Van der Heyden, Simons, Spilar (Clement 61), Maertens, Englebert, Serebrennikov, Mendoza (Stoica 66), Lange, Verheyen.
Lokomotiv Moscow: Ovchinnikov; Sennikov, Pimenov, Maminov (Obradovic 46), Ignachevitch, Nizhegorodov, Lekgetho, Loskov■, Bouznikin (Sirkhajev 46), Julio Cesar (Obiorah 74), Yevseyev.

Galatasaray (0) 0

Barcelona (1) 2 *(Kluivert 26, Luis Enrique 58)* 24,250

Galatasaray: Mondragon; Sarr (Hasan Sas 46), Hakan Unsal, Felipe, Bulent K, Almagueira, Umit D, Batista, Christian (Suat 70), Arif, Ergun (Umit K 80).
Barcelona: Victor Valdes; Puyol, Fernando, Xavi, De Boer, Cocu, Mendieta, Saviola (Geovanni 83), Kluivert (Gerard 90), Luis Enrique, Motta.

Tuesday, 1 October 2002

Galatasaray (0) 0

FC Brugge (0) 0 24,350

Galatasaray: Mondragon; Umit D, Hakan Unsal, Felipe (Ayhan 70), Bulent K (Vedat 83), Emre A, Batista, Arif, Umit K, Suat, Hasan Sas (Baljic 46).
FC Brugge: Verlinden; De Cock, Van der Heyden, Clement, Simons, Maertens, Englebert, Stoica (Ceh 87), Lange (Mendoza 54), Serebrennikov, Verheyen (Martens 90).

Lokomotiv Moscow (0) 1 *(Obiorah 56)*

Barcelona (2) 3 *(Kluivert 29, Saviola 32, 49)* 24,550

Lokomotiv Moscow: Ovchinnikov; Sennikov, Nizhegorodov, Maminov, Ignachevitch, Lekgetho, Obradovic, Drozdov, Obiorah (Bouznikin 66), Pimenov, Yevseyev.
Barcelona: Victor Valdes; Puyol, Fernando, Cocu, De Boer, Xavi, Mendieta, Motta, Kluivert (Gerard 75), Saviola (Rochemback 86), Luis Enrique (Geovanni 61).

Wednesday, 23 October 2002

Barcelona (0) 1 *(De Boer 75)*

Lokomotiv Moscow (0) 0 62,000

Barcelona: Bonano; Puyol, Xavi, De Boer, Fernando, Gabri, Mendieta (Rochemback 66), Saviola, Kluivert, Riquelme, Cocu.
Lokomotiv Moscow: Ovchinnikov; Pashinin, Ignachevitch, Sennikov, Obradovic, Maminov, Julio Cesar (Bouznikin 84), Loskov, Yevseyev, Pimenov, Obiorah.

FC Brugge (1) 3 *(Martens 45, Verheyen 71, Saeternes 90)*

Galatasaray (0) 1 *(Fabio Pinto 55)* 27,000

FC Brugge: Verlinden; De Cock, Van der Heyden (Smolders 90), Maertens, Simons, Clement, Englebert, Ceh (Saeternes 64), Stoica (Spilar 84), Verheyen, Martens.
Galatasaray: Mondragon; Mehmet P (Felipe 46), Hakan Unsal, Umit D, Emre A (Christian 82), Bulent K, Cihan, Ergun, Arif (Ayhan 55), Fabio Pinto, Baljic.

Tuesday, 29 October 2002

FC Brugge (0) 0

Barcelona (0) 1 *(Riquelme 63)* 27,000

FC Brugge: Verlinden; Maertens, Lesnjak (Saeternes 80), Englebert, Simons, Clement (Spilar 68), De Cock, Van der Heyden (Ristic 68), Verheyen, Martens, Stoica.
Barcelona: Enke; Puyol, Gabri (Sanchez 89), Gerard, Tortolero, Fernando, Rochemback, Iniesta, Geovanni (Garcia De la Fuente 62), Dani, Riquelme.

Galatasaray (0) 1 *(Hasan Sas 72)*

Lokomotiv Moscow (0) 2 *(Loskov 70, Yevseyev 75)* 21,575

Galatasaray: Mondragon; Umit D, Hakan Unsal, Cihan (Felipe 70), Emre A, Bulent K, Fabio Pinto, Ergun, Christian, Arif (Batista 46), Baljic (Hasan Sas 46).
Lokomotiv Moscow: Ovchinnikov; Nizhegorodov, Lekgetho, Ignachevitch, Pashinin, Sennikov, Yevseyev, Maminov, Pimenov, Obiorah (Julio Cesar 78), Loskov.

Wednesday, 13 November 2002

Barcelona (2) 3 *(Dani 10, Gerard 44, Geovanni 56)*

Galatasaray (1) 1 *(Cihan 20)* 42,928

Barcelona: Enke; Reiziger, Fernando, Gerard, Puyol (Tortolero 61), De Boer (Oleguer 86), Mendieta, Saviola, Dani, Geovanni (Kluivert 79), Motta.
Galatasaray: Mondragon; Sarr, Hakan Unsal, Batista (Ayhan 61), Bulent K, Almagueira, Cihan (Suat 46), Ergun, Fabio Pinto, Baljic (Christian 75), Hasan Sas.

Lokomotiv Moscow (1) 2 *(Julio Cesar 44, Loskov 90)*

FC Brugge (0) 0 19,700

Lokomotiv Moscow: Ovchinnikov; Nizhegorodov, Pashinin, Ignachevitch, Sennikov, Yevseyev, Loskov, Bouznikin (Obiorah 66), Julio Cesar (Adamu 90), Maminov, Lekgetho.
FC Brugge: Verlinden; De Cock, Van der Heyden, Simons, Maertens, Clement, Englebert, Martens, Verheyen, Mendoza (Lesnjak 72), Stoica (Ceh 84).

Group H Final Table	*P*	*W*	*D*	*L*	*F*	*A*	*Pts*
Barcelona	6	6	0	0	13	4	18
Lokomotiv Moscow	6	2	1	3	5	7	7
FC Brugge	6	1	2	3	5	7	5
Galatasaray	6	1	1	4	5	10	4

SECOND GROUP STAGE

SECOND GROUP STAGE – GROUP A

Wednesday, 27 November 2002

Leverkusen (1) 1 *(Berbatov 39)*

Barcelona (0) 2 *(Saviola 48, Overmars 88)* 25,500

Leverkusen: Butt; Zivkovic, Placente, Balitsch, Lucio, Ramelow, Schneider, Basturk, Berbatov (Simak 83), Brdaric (Neuville 55), Babic (Bierofka 66).
Barcelona: Bonano; Puyol, Fernando, Xavi, Reiziger, Cocu, Mendieta (Saviola 46), Gabri (Riquelme 46), Rochemback, Kluivert, Motta (Overmars 75).

Newcastle United (0) 1 *(Solano 72)*

Internazionale (3) 4 *(Morfeo 2, Almeyda 35, Crespo 45, Recoba 81)* 50,108

Newcastle United: Given; Griffin, Hughes (Caldwell S), Dabizas, O'Brien, Solano, Dyer, Speed, Shearer, Bellamy■, Viana (Robert 46).
Internazionale: Toldo; Zanetti J, Pasquale, Emre B, Cannavaro, Materazzi (Cordoba 15), Okan (Dalmat 66), Almeyda, Crespo (Recoba), Vieri, Morfeo.

Tuesday, 10 December 2002

Internazionale (2) 3 *(Di Biagio 14, 27, Butt 80 (og))*

Leverkusen (0) 2 *(Zivkovic 62, Franca 90)* 36,342

Internazionale: Toldo; Zanetti J, Pasquale, Emre B, Cordoba, Gamarra, Almeyda, Di Biagio (Beati 71), Crespo (Kallon 88), Vieri (Sergio Conceicao 74), Recoba.
Leverkusen: Butt; Zivkovic, Juan, Balitsch (Bierofka 78), Ramelow, Kleine, Schneider, Basturk (Simak 83), Neuville, Berbatov (Franca 75), Placente.

Wednesday, 11 December 2002

Barcelona (2) 3 *(Dani 7, Kluivert 35, Motta 58)*

Newcastle United (1) 1 *(Ameobi 24)* 45,100

Barcelona: Bonano; Puyol, Motta, Reiziger (Christanval 14), De Boer, Cocu (Mendieta 17), Dani (Saviola 77), Riquelme, Kluivert, Xavi, Overmars.
Newcastle United: Given; Griffin, Bernard, Hughes, O'Brien, Solano, Dyer, Speed, Lua-Lua (Chopra 83), Ameobi, Robert.

Tuesday, 18 February 2003

Barcelona (2) 3 *(Saviola 7, Cocu 29, Kluivert 66)*

Internazionale (0) 0 82,717

Barcelona: Bonano; Gabri, Reiziger, Cocu, Puyol, De Boer, Overmars (Rochemback 71), Xavi, Kluivert, Saviola (Luis Enrique 81), Motta (Mendieta 73).
Internazionale: Toldo; Zanetti J, Cordoba, Zanetti C, Cannavaro, Gamarra, Dalmat, Morfeo (Kallon 66), Di Biagio (Okan 59), Vieri, Recoba■.

Leverkusen (1) 1 *(Franca 25)*

Newcastle United (3) 3 *(Ameobi 5, 15, Lua-Lua 32)* 22,500

Leverkusen: Butt; Preuss (Schneider 46), Ojigwe, Simak, Kleine, Cris (Callsen-Bracher 72), Balitsch (Kaluzny 79), Basturk, Franca, Neuville, Brdaric.
Newcastle United: Given; Hughes, Bernard, O'Brien, Bramble, Jenas, Dyer, Speed, Ameobi (Cort 88), Lua-Lua (Chopra 83), Robert.

Wednesday, 26 February 2003

Internazionale (0) 0

Barcelona (0) 0 71,740

Internazionale: Toldo; Zanetti J, Pasquale, Dalmat (Martins Obaferni 61), Cannavaro, Gamarra, Guly (Sergio Conceicao 78), Zanetti C, Kallon (Di Biagio 34), Vieri, Morfeo.
Barcelona: Bonano; Reiziger, Gabri, Xavi, Puyol (Andersson 78), De Boer, Rochemback (Riquelme 67), Saviola, Cocu (Mendieta 59), Kluivert, Motta.

Newcastle United (3) 3 *(Shearer 5, 11, 36 (pen))*

Leverkusen (0) 1 *(Babic 73)* 40,508

Newcastle United: Given; Griffin, Bernard, Caldwell S, Bramble, Kerr (Viana 83), Dyer (Solano 70), Speed, Shearer (Lua-Lua 81), Ameobi, Robert.
Leverkusen: Butt; Preuss, Placente, Ramelow (Babic 46), Kleine, Cris (Zivkovic 29), Kaluzny, Basturk, Franca, Neuville (Brdaric 62), Simak.

Tuesday, 11 March 2003

Barcelona (1) 2 *(Saviola 16, De Boer 49)*

Leverkusen (0) 0 62,228

Barcelona: Bonano; Gabri, Reiziger, Riquelme, De Boer (Oleguer 62), Andersson, Overmars (Iniesta 68), Mendieta, Kluivert, Saviola (Motta 46), Xavi.
Leverkusen: Butt; Ojigwe, Kaluzny, Balitsch, Kleine, Cris, Simak, Basturk (Schneider 74), Berbatov (Brdaric 58), Franca, Babic (Dogan 33).

Internazionale (0) 2 *(Vieri 46, Cordoba 60)*

Newcastle U (1) 2 *(Shearer 42, 49)* 53,459

Internazionale: Toldo; Zanetti J, Coco, Okan, Cordoba, Cannavaro, Sergio Conceicao, Di Biagio, Emre B (Pasquale 77), Vieri, Guly (Martins Obaferni 46).
Newcastle U: Given; Griffin, Bernard, O'Brien (Hughes 59), Bramble, Solano (Lua-Lua 83), Jenas, Speed, Shearer, Bellamy, Robert (Viana 83).

Wednesday, 19 March 2003

Leverkusen (0) 0

Internazionale (1) 2 *(Martins 36, Emre B 90)* 22,070

Leverkusen: Butt; Ojigwe, Placente, Ramelow, Kaluzny, Kleine, Brdaric (Neuville 46), Basturk (Schneider 46), Franca, Bierofka, Simak (Cris 62).
Internazionale: Toldo; Zanetti J, Coco, Okan (Zanetti C 19), Cannavaro, Cordoba, Sergio Conceicao (Guglielminpietro 83), Di Biagio, Morfeo (Pasquale 75), Martins, Emre B.

Newcastle United (0) 0

Barcelona (0) 2 *(Kluivert 60, Motta 74)* 51,883

Newcastle United: Given; Griffin, Bernard, O'Brien, Bramble, Solano (Ameobi 67), Dyer, Jenas, Shearer, Bellamy, Robert (Viana 67).
Barcelona: Victor Valdes; Gabri, Reiziger, Xavi (Gerard 46), Andersson, De Boer, Rochemback, Motta, Kluivert (Sergio 70), Riquelme, Mendieta (Iniesta 66).

Group A Final Table	*P*	*W*	*D*	*L*	*F*	*A*	*Pts*
Barcelona	6	5	1	0	12	2	16
Internazionale	6	3	2	1	11	8	11
Newcastle United	6	2	1	3	10	13	7
Leverkusen	6	0	0	6	5	15	0

SECOND GROUP STAGE – GROUP B

Wednesday, 27 November 2002

Roma (1) 1 *(Cassano 4)*

Arsenal (1) 3 *(Henry 6, 70, 75)* 49,860

Roma: Antonioli; Cafu, Candela, Panucci, Zebina, Samuel, Emerson, Lima (Batistuta 72), Cassano (Montella 64), Delvecchio (Guigou 56), Totti.
Arsenal: Shaaban; Luzhny, Cole, Vieira, Campbell, Cygan, Ljungberg (Edu 90), Silva, Wiltord (Keown 84), Henry, Pires (Van Bronckhorst 78).

Valencia (0) 1 *(Angulo 90)*

Ajax (0) 1 *(Ibrahimovic 89)* 40,000

Valencia: Canizares; Curro Torres, Carboni (Fabio Aurelio 74), Albelda (De los Santos 84), Ayala, Pellegrino, Angulo, Baraja, Mista (Juan Sanchez 67), Carew, Vicente.
Ajax: Didulica; Trabelsi, Maxwell, Pienaar (De Jong 71), Bergdolmo, Chivu, Galasek, Van der Vaart, Van der Meyde, Hossam (Boukhari 85), Litmanen (Ibrahimovic 59).

Tuesday, 10 December 2002

Ajax (1) 2 *(Ibrahimovic 11, Litmanen 66)*

Roma (0) 1 *(Batistuta 89)* 50,148

Ajax: Stekelenburg; Trabelsi (Yakubu 33), Maxwell, Pienaar, Bergdolmo, Pasanen, Van der Meyde (Boukhari 80), De Jong, Ibrahimovic, Hossam (Litmanen 57), Witschge.
Roma: Antonioli; Zebina, Panucci, Emerson, Samuel, Dellas (Montella 61), Cafu, Lima, Totti, Cassano (Batistuta 72), Candela.

Arsenal (0) 0

Valencia (0) 0 34,793

Arsenal: Seaman; Lauren, Cole, Vieira (Parlour 38), Campbell, Cygan, Ljungberg (Wiltord 78), Silva, Henry, Bergkamp, Pires (Kanu 82).
Valencia: Palop; Curro Torres, Carboni, Albelda, Ayala, Pellegrino, Angulo■, Baraja (Fabio Aurelio 87), Aimar (Marchena 80), Carew, Vicente (Rufete 68).

Tuesday, 18 February 2003

Arsenal (1) 1 *(Wiltord 5)*

Ajax (1) 1 *(De Jong 17)* 35,427

Arsenal: Seaman (Taylor 46); Lauren, Cole, Vieira, Campbell, Cygan, Wiltord, Silva (Jeffers 72), Henry, Bergkamp (Kanu 84), Pires.
Ajax: Lobont; Trabelsi, Van Damme (Witschge 76), Galasek, Chivu, Pasanen, De Jong, Pienaar (Yakubu 90), Ibrahimovic (Boukhari 78), Van der Meyde, Maxwell.

Roma (0) 0

Valencia (0) 1 *(Carew 78)* 30,599

Roma: Pelizzoli; Zebina, Panucci, Tommasi, Dellas (Cufre 54), Aldair, Cafu, Lima, Montella (Cassano 46), Delvecchio (Bombardini 54), Guigou.
Valencia: Canizares; Reveillere, Carboni, Albelda, Ayala, Pellegrino, Baraja, Rufete (Mista 73), Aimar (Marchena 89), Vicente (Kily Gonzalez 63), Carew.

Wednesday, 26 February 2003

Ajax (0) 0

Arsenal (0) 0 51,500

Ajax: Lobont; Trabelsi, Maxwell, Galasek (Yakubu 70), Chivu, Pasanen, De Jong, Pienaar (Sneijder 90), Ibrahimovic (Hossam 86), Van der Meyde, Witschge.
Arsenal: Seaman; Lauren, Cole, Vieira, Campbell, Keown, Wiltord (Parlour 78), Silva, Henry, Bergkamp (Jeffers 78), Pires (Van Bronckhorst 86).

Valencia (0) 0

Roma (3) 3 *(Totti 24, 30, Emerson 36)* 35,000

Valencia: Canizares; Reveillere, Fabio Aurelio, Albelda, Ayala, Pellegrino (Carboni 77), Rufete (Aimar 64), Baraja, Juan Sanchez, Carew, Vicente (Kily Gonzalez 52).
Roma: Antonioli; Samuel, Candela, Emerson, Aldair, Zebina (Cufre 63), Cafu, Tommasi, Totti (Fuser 88), Cassano (Guigou 90), Lima.

Tuesday, 11 March 2003

Ajax (0) 1 *(Pasanen 56)*

Valencia (1) 1 *(Kily Gonzalez 28 (pen))* 48,633

Ajax: Lobont; Trabelsi, O'Brien, Galasek, Pasanen, Chivu, De Jong (Van der Meyde 46), Pienaar, Van der Vaart, Ibrahimovic, Maxwell.
Valencia: Canizares; Reveillere, Carboni, Albelda, Ayala (Marchena 88), Pellegrino, Rufete, Aimar (Juan Sanchez 84), Carew (Mista 64), Baraja, Kily Gonzalez.

Arsenal (1) 1 *(Vieira 12)*

Roma (1) 1 *(Cassano 45)* 35,472

Arsenal: Seaman; Lauren (Kanu 87), Van Bronckhorst, Vieira, Cygan, Keown, Wiltord (Ljungberg), Silva, Henry, Bergkamp (Jeffers 73), Pires.
Roma: Pelizzoli; Panucci, Candela, Tommasi, Aldair, Samuel, Cafu, Emerson, Cassano (Montella 62), Totti■, Lima.

Wednesday, 19 March 2003

Roma (1) 1 *(Cassano 23)*

Ajax (1) 1 *(Van der Meyde 1)* 54,502

Roma: Pelizzoli; Cufre, Candela, Tommasi (Guigou 80), Panucci, Aldair, Cafu (Fuser 80), Emerson, Delvecchio, Cassano, Lima (Montella 60).
Ajax: Lobont; Trabelsi, O'Brien (Van Damme 90), Galasek, Pasanen, Chivu, Pienaar, Van der Vaart, Ibrahimovic (Witschge 89), Van der Meyde (Sikora 72), Maxwell.

Valencia (1) 2 *(Carew 34, 57)*

Arsenal (0) 1 *(Henry 49)* 50,000

Valencia: Canizares (Palop 71); Rufete, Vicente, Albelda, Ayala, Pellegrino, Carboni, Juan Sanchez (Angulo 68), Carew (Marchena 88), Aimar, Reveillere.
Arsenal: Taylor; Lauren, Toure (Kanu 86), Vieira, Campbell, Cygan, Wiltord (Jeffers 76), Silva, Henry, Ljungberg, Pires.

Group B Final Table	P	W	D	L	F	A	Pts
Valencia	6	2	3	1	5	6	9
Ajax	6	1	5	0	6	5	8
Arsenal	6	1	4	1	6	5	7
Roma	6	1	2	3	7	8	5

SECOND GROUP STAGE – GROUP C

Tuesday, 26 November 2002

AC Milan (1) 1 *(Shevchenko 39)*

Real Madrid (0) 0 75,777

AC Milan: Dida; Simic (Chamot 89), Kaladze, Ambrosini, Costacurta, Maldini, Gattuso, Rui Costa (Serginho 76), Shevchenko (Tomasson 82), Rivaldo, Seedorf.
Real Madrid: Casillas; Michel Salgado, Roberto Carlos, Cambiasso (Solari 76), Pavon, Helguera, Celades, Figo, Morientes (Portillo 61), Zidane, Raul.

Lokomotiv Moscow (1) 1 *(Ignachevitch 31)*

Borussia Dortmund (2) 2 *(Frings 33, Koller 43)* 17,000

Lokomotiv Moscow: Ovchinnikov; Nizhegorodov, Ignachevitch, Pashinin, Sennikov, Loskov, Yevseyev, Lekgetho, Pimenov (Adamu 74), Obiorah (Bouznikin 65), Maminov (Obradovic 46).
Borussia Dortmund: Lehmann; Heinrich, Dede, Frings, Worns, Metzelder, Reuter, Rosicky (Reina 90), Ewerthon (Ricken 82), Koller, Kehl (Madouni 89).

Wednesday, 11 December 2002

Borussia Dortmund (0) 0

AC Milan (0) 1 *(Inzaghi 49)* 52,000

Borussia Dortmund: Lehmann; Heinrich (Evanilson 73), Dede, Kehl (Reina 83), Metzelder, Worns, Ewerthon (Ricken 64), Rosicky, Amoroso, Koller, Frings.
AC Milan: Dida; Simic, Kaladze, Pirlo, Maldini, Nesta, Seedorf, Rui Costa (Serginho 78), Inzaghi (Rivaldo 86), Shevchenko (Laursen 90), Ambrosini.

Real Madrid (1) 2 *(Raul 21, 75)*

Lokomotiv Moscow (0) 2 *(Obiorah 47, Mnguni 74)* 40,000

Real Madrid: Casillas; Michel Salgado, Roberto Carlos, Makelele (Flavio Conceicao 32), Hierro, Pavon, Figo, Cambiasso (Morientes 77), Ronaldo (Guti 46), Zidane, Raul.
Lokomotiv Moscow: Ovchinnikov; Yevseyev, Nizhegorodov, Mnguni, Ignachevitch, Pashinin, Lekgetho, Maminov, Pimenov (Drozdov 81), Julio Cesar (Obiorah 46), Loskov.

Wednesday, 19 February 2003

AC Milan (0) 1 *(Tomasson 62)*

Lokomotiv Moscow (0) 0 72,028

AC Milan: Dida; Brocchi (Simic 79), Maldini, Pirlo, Nesta, Costacurta, Gattuso, Tomasson (Seedorf 68), Inzaghi, Rui Costa (Serginho 63), Rivaldo.
Lokomotiv Moscow: Ovchinnikov; Nizhegorodov, Pashinin, Maminov, Ignachevitch (Parks 83), Sennikov, Loskov, Bouznikin (Izmailov 46), Obradovic, Pimenov, Lekgetho.

Real Madrid (1) 2 *(Raul 43, Ronaldo 55)*
Borussia Dortmund (1) 1 *(Koller 30)* 50,000
Real Madrid: Casillas; Michel Salgado, Roberto Carlos, Flavio Conceicao, Pavon, Helguera, Figo, Makelele, Ronaldo (Guti 74), Zidane (Solari 81), Raul.
Borussia Dortmund: Lehmann; Evanilson (Ricken 83), Dede, Frings, Metzelder, Worns, Ewerthon, Reuter (Kehl 76), Koller, Amoroso (Reina 67), Rosicky.

Tuesday, 25 February 2003

Borussia Dortmund (1) 1 *(Koller 21)*
Real Madrid (0) 1 *(Portillo 90)* 52,400
Borussia Dortmund: Lehmann; Metzelder, Dede (Amoroso 90), Frings, Worns, Madouni, Reuter, Evanilson (Ricken 80), Ewerthon (Reina 87), Koller, Kehl.
Real Madrid: Casillas; Michel Salgado, Roberto Carlos, Flavio Conceicao (Guti 68), Helguera, Pavon (Portillo 90), Figo (Minambres 72), Makelele, Ronaldo, Zidane, Raul.

Lokomotiv Moscow (0) 0
AC Milan (1) 1 *(Rivaldo 33 (pen))* 30,000
Lokomotiv Moscow: Ovchinnikov; Nizhegorodov, Ignachevitch, Sennikov, Yevseyev, Maminov, Izmailov, Mnguni, Julio Cesar (Parks 82), Loskov, Sirkhayev (Pimenov 58).
AC Milan: Dida; Costacurta, Kaladze, Redondo (Brocchi 76), Nesta, Maldini, Gattuso, Serginho (Rui Costa 87), Inzaghi (Tomasson 84), Rivaldo, Seedorf.

Wednesday, 12 March 2003

Borussia Dortmund (1) 3 *(Frings 39, Koller 58, Amoroso 66)*
Lokomotiv Moscow (0) 0 48,000
Borussia Dortmund: Lehmann; Evanilson, Dede (Madouni 20), Frings, Metzelder, Worns, Reuter, Ewerthon, Koller (Ricken 70), Amoroso (Herrlich 83), Kehl.
Lokomotiv Moscow: Ovchinnikov; Obradovic (Julio Cesar 46), Sennikov, Pashinin, Ignachevitch, Maminov, Mnguni, Yevseyev, Pimenov, Izmailov, Lekgetho.

Real Madrid (1) 3 *(Raul 12, 56, Guti 85)*
AC Milan (0) 1 *(Rivaldo 81)* 78,000
Real Madrid: Casillas; Michel Salgado, Roberto Carlos, Flavio Conceicao, Helguera, Pavon, Figo, Makelele, Ronaldo (Guti 67), Zidane (Solari 88), Raul (Portillo 90).
AC Milan: Abbiati; Simic (Nesta 62), Maldini, Redondo (Pirlo 79), Costacurta, Laursen, Brocchi, Seedorf, Shevchenko, Rivaldo, Dalla Bona (Rui Costa 46).

Tuesday, 18 March 2003

AC Milan (0) 0
Borussia Dortmund (0) 1 *(Koller 80)* 70,500
AC Milan: Abbiati; Simic, Maldini (Costacurta 46), Redondo, Nesta, Laursen, Gattuso, Rui Costa (Inzaghi 62), Tomasson, Rivaldo, Brocchi (Pirlo 82).
Borussia Dortmund: Lehmann; Evanilson, Dede (Madouni 83), Reuter (Ricken 50), Worns, Metzelder, Kehl, Ewerthon (Odonkor 74), Koller, Amoroso, Frings.

Lokomotiv Moscow (0) 0
Real Madrid (1) 1 *(Ronaldo 35)* 24,000
Lokomotiv Moscow: Ovchinnikov; Pashinin, Loskov, Ignachevitch, Nizhegorodov, Yevseyev, Maminov (Sirkhayev 81), Sennikov, Pimenov, Izmailov, Mnguni (Julio Cesar 72).
Real Madrid: Casillas; Michel Salgado, Solari, Flavio Conceicao, Helguera, Pavon, Figo, Makelele, Ronaldo (Guti 81), Zidane (Cambiasso 90), Raul.

Group C Final Table	P	W	D	L	F	A	Pts
AC Milan	6	4	0	2	5	4	12
Real Madrid	6	3	2	1	9	6	11
Borussia Dortmund	6	3	1	2	8	5	10
Lokomotiv Moscow	6	0	1	5	3	10	1

SECOND GROUP STAGE – GROUP D

Tuesday, 26 November 2002

Basle (1) 1 *(Gimenez 1)*
Manchester United (0) 3 *(Van Nistelrooy 61, 63, Solskjaer 68)* 29,501
Basle: Zuberbuhler; Haas, Atouba, Cantaluppi, Yakin M, Zwyssig, Ergic (Barberis 85), Yakin H, Gimenez, Rossi (Duruz 85), Chipperfield (Tum 73).
Manchester United: Barthez; Neville P, Silvestre, Brown, Fortune, O'Shea, Solskjaer (Chadwick 90), Veron (May 90), Van Nistelrooy (Forlan 75), Scholes, Giggs.

La Coruna (2) 2 *(Diego Tristan 9, Makaay 11)*
Juventus (1) 2 *(Birindelli 37, Nedved 56)* 30,000
La Coruna: Juanmi; Scaloni, Capdevila, Mauro Silva, Cesar, Romero, Sergio, Duscher, Makaay (Victor 62), Diego Tristan (Luque 65), Fran (Amavisca 77).
Juventus: Buffon; Thuram, Birindelli, Tacchinardi, Iuliano, Montero, Camoranesi (Zambrotta 75), Davids, Del Piero, Di Vaio (Zalayeta 75), Nedved.

Wednesday, 11 December 2002

Juventus (3) 4 *(Trezeguet 3, Montero 34, Tacchinardi 43, Del Piero 51 (pen))*
Basle (0) 0 22,639
Juventus: Buffon; Thuram (Ferrara 59), Birindelli, Tacchinardi, Montero, Iuliano, Zambrotta, Nedved, Trezeguet (Zalayeta 64), Del Piero (Conte 72), Davids.
Basle: Zuberbuhler; Barberis, Atouba, Cantaluppi, Yakin M, Zwyssig, Esposito, Yakin H (Tum 77), Gimenez (Varela 46), Rossi, Chipperfield (Duruz 65).

Manchester United (1) 2 *(Van Nistelrooy 7, 55)*
La Coruna (0) 0 67,014
Manchester United: Barthez; Neville G, O'Shea (Beckham 81), Brown, Neville P (Forlan 81), Silvestre, Solskjaer, Veron, Van Nistelrooy (Richardson 89), Scholes, Giggs.
La Coruna: Juanmi; Scaloni, Capdevila, Mauro Silva, Cesar, Romero, Victor (Luque 75), Sergio, Makaay, Valeron (Acuna 65), Amavisca (Diego Tristan 46).

Wednesday, 19 February 2003

Basle (1) 1 *(Yakin H 30)*
La Coruna (0) 0 29,031
Basle: Zuberbuhler; Haas, Atouba, Cantaluppi, Zwyssig, Yakin M, Barberis, Chipperfield (Duruz 70), Yakin H (Varela 85), Gimenez, Rossi (Huggel 51).
La Coruna: Juanmi; Hector, Romero, Duscher, Naybet, Jorge Andrade, Scaloni, Donato (Diego Tristan 46), Luque (Amavisca 64), Makaay, Sergio (Acuna 81).

Manchester United (1) 2 *(Brown 3, Van Nistelrooy 85)*
Juventus (0) 1 *(Nedved 90)* 66,703
Manchester United: Barthez; Neville G, Silvestre (O'Shea 52), Brown, Keane, Ferdinand, Beckham, Butt, Van Nistelrooy, Scholes (Solskjaer 79), Giggs (Forlan 90).
Juventus: Chimenti; Pessotto, Zenoni, Tacchinardi, Ferrara, Montero, Davids, Zalayeta, Nedved, Trezeguet (Olivera 66), Camoranesi.

Tuesday, 25 February 2003

Juventus (0) 0
Manchester United (2) 3 *(Giggs 15, 41, Van Nistelrooy 63)* 59,111
Juventus: Buffon; Thuram, Zambrotta (Pessotto 67), Camoranesi, Ferrara, Montero, Conte (Tudor 46), Nedved, Trezeguet, Di Vaio (Salas 46), Davids.
Manchester United: Barthez; Neville G, O'Shea (Pugh 60), Neville P, Keane, Ferdinand, Beckham, Butt, Solskjaer, Forlan (Giggs 8) (Van Nistelrooy 48), Veron.

La Coruna (1) 1 *(Diego Tristan 5)*
Basle (0) 0 21,000
La Coruna: Juanmi; Hector, Romero, Sergio, Naybet, Jorge Andrade, Scaloni, Duscher, Makaay (Luque 79), Diego Tristan (Valeron 69), Fran (Amavisca 59).
Basle: Zuberbuhler; Haas, Atouba, Huggel, Zwyssig, Quennoz, Barberis (Tum 73), Varela (Rossi 57), Yakin H, Chipperfield, Gimenez.

Wednesday, 12 March 2003

Juventus (1) 3 *(Ferrara 12, Trezeguet 63, Tudor 90)*

La Coruna (1) 2 *(Diego Tristan 34, Makaay 51)* 25,070

Juventus: Buffon; Thuram, Zambrotta, Tacchinardi (Tudor 77), Montero, Ferrara, Camoranesi (Pessotto 46), Davids, Trezeguet, Di Vaio (Zalayeta 46), Nedved.
La Coruna: Juanmi; Hector, Romero, Mauro Silva, Naybet, Cesar (Jorge Andrade 71), Scaloni, Duscher, Makaay, Diego Tristan (Valeron 66), Fran (Capdevila 46).

Manchester United (0) 1 *(Neville G 53)*

Basle (1) 1 *(Gimenez 14)* 66,870

Manchester United: Carroll; Neville G, O'Shea, Ferdinand, Neville P, Blanc (Scholes 73), Solskjaer, Butt, Forlan, Fletcher (Beckham 73), Richardson (Giggs 46).
Basle: Zuberbuhler; Haas, Atouba, Cantaluppi, Yakin M, Zwyssig, Barberis, Yakin H, Gimenez (Tum 77), Rossi (Huggel 62), Chipperfield.

Tuesday, 18 March 2003

Basle (1) 2 *(Cantaluppi 38, Gimenez 90)*

Juventus (1) 1 *(Tacchinardi 10)* 30,501

Basle: Zuberbuhler; Haas, Atouba, Cantaluppi, Yakin M, Zwyssig, Barberis (Huggel 56), Yakin H (Varela 79), Gimenez, Rossi (Tum 72), Chipperfield.
Juventus: Buffon; Thuram (Del Piero 70), Birindelli, Tacchinardi, Montero, Iuliano, Zenoni, Tudor (Pessotto 46), Trezeguet (Salas 30), Nedved, Zambrotta.

La Coruna (1) 2 *(Victor 32, Lynch 47 (og))*

Manchester United (0) 0 25,000

La Coruna: Dani Mallo; Manuel Pablo, Capdevila, Acuna, Cesar, Jorge Andrade (Djorovic 64), Victor (Hector 78), Duscher, Valeron, Luque, Fran (Scaloni 52).
Manchester United: Ricardo; Lynch, Pugh, Roche (Stewart 46), O'Shea, Blanc, Fletcher, Neville P, Forlan (Webber 72), Giggs (Richardson 72), Butt.

Group D Final Table	P	W	D	L	F	A	Pts
Manchester United	6	4	1	1	11	5	13
Juventus	6	2	1	3	11	11	7
Basle	6	2	1	3	5	10	7
La Coruna	6	2	1	3	7	8	7

QUARTER-FINALS, FIRST LEG

Tuesday, 8 April 2003

Ajax (0) 0

AC Milan (0) 0 51,000

Ajax: Lobont; Trabelsi, O'Brien, Galasek (Sneijder 67), Pasanen (De Jong 74), Chivu, Pienaar, Yakubu, Ibrahimovic (Litmanen 73), Van der Vaart, Maxwell.
AC Milan: Dida; Simic, Costacurta, Gattuso, Nesta, Maldini, Rui Costa, Ambrosini, Shevchenko (Rivaldo 79), Inzaghi (Tomasson 73), Seedorf (Serginho 26).

Real Madrid (2) 3 *(Figo 12, Raul 28, 49)*

Manchester United (0) 1 *(Van Nistelrooy 52)* 75,000

Real Madrid: Casillas; Michel Salgado, Roberto Carlos, Flavio Conceicao, Helguera, Hierro, Figo, Makelele, Ronaldo (Guti 83), Zidane, Raul.
Manchester United: Barthez; Neville G (Solskjaer 86), Silvestre (O'Shea 59), Brown, Keane, Ferdinand, Beckham, Butt, Van Nistelrooy, Scholes, Giggs.

Wednesday, 9 April 2003

Internazionale (1) 1 *(Vieri 14)*

Valencia (0) 0 52,623

Internazionale: Toldo; Zanetti J, Coco (Pasquale 31), Zanetti C, Cordoba, Materazzi, Sergio Conceicao (Okan 65), Di Biagio, Crespo (Cannavaro 83), Vieri, Emre B■.
Valencia: Canizares; Reveillere, Carboni, Albelda■, Ayala, Marchena, Rufete (Mista 80), Baraja, Carew (Angulo 66), Aimar, Vicente (Fabio Aurelio 85).

Juventus (1) 1 *(Montero 16)*

Barcelona (0) 1 *(Saviola 77)* 48,783

Juventus: Buffon; Thuram, Zambrotta (Zalayeta 67), Tacchinardi, Montero, Ferrara, Camoranesi, Tudor (Birindelli 60), Del Piero (Di Vaio 82), Nedved, Davids.
Barcelona: Bonano; Gabri, Reiziger, Xavi (Gerard 74), Puyol, De Boer, Overmars (Luis Enrique 83), Motta, Kluivert, Saviola, Riquelme (Mendieta 63).

QUARTER-FINALS, SECOND LEG

Tuesday, 22 April 2003

Barcelona (0) 1 *(Xavi 66)*

Juventus (0) 2 *(Nedved 53, Zalayeta 114)* 95,000

Barcelona: Bonano; Puyol, Reiziger (Gerard 90), Xavi, De Boer, Andersson (Mendieta 61), Overmars (Riquelme 85), Motta, Kluivert, Saviola, Luis Enrique.
Juventus: Buffon; Thuram, Zambrotta, Tacchinardi, Montero, Ferrara, Camoranesi (Birindelli 46), Davids■, Del Piero (Tudor 83), Di Vaio (Zalayeta 46), Nedved.
aet.

Valencia (1) 2 *(Aimar 6, Baraja 51)*

Internazionale (1) 1 *(Vieri 4)* 48,000

Valencia: Canizares; Reveillere, Carboni (Fabio Aurelio 80), Baraja, Ayala, Marchena, Angulo, Aimar (Mista 84), Juan Sanchez, Carew (Rufete 73), Vicente.
Internazionale: Toldo; Cordoba, Pasquale (Adani 46), Zanetti C, Materazzi, Gamarra, Zanetti J, Di Biagio (Okan 75), Crespo, Vieri (Recoba 32), Dalmat.

Wednesday, 23 April 2003

AC Milan (1) 3 *(Inzaghi 30, Shevchenko 64, Tomasson 90)*

Ajax (0) 2 *(Litmanen 63, Pienaar 78)* 76,079

AC Milan: Dida; Simic (Tomasson 83), Costacurta, Ambrosini, Maldini, Nesta, Brocchi, Rui Costa (Redondo 85), Inzaghi, Shevchenko, Kaladze (Rivaldo 80).
Ajax: Lobont; Trabelsi, Van Damme (Litmanen 46), Sneijder, Chivu, Pasanen, Pienaar (De Jong 84), Yakubu, Van der Meyde (Bergdolmo 89), Ibrahimovic, O'Brien.

Manchester United (1) 4 *(Van Nistelrooy 43, Helguera 52 (og), Beckham 71, 84)*

Real Madrid (1) 3 *(Ronaldo 12, 50, 59)* 66,708

Manchester United: Barthez; Brown, O'Shea, Ferdinand, Keane (Fortune 82), Silvestre (Neville P 78), Solskjaer, Butt, Van Nistelrooy, Veron (Beckham 63), Giggs.
Real Madrid: Casillas; Michel Salgado, Roberto Carlos, Guti, Hierro, Helguera, Figo (Pavon 87), Makelele, Ronaldo (Solari 67), Zidane, McManaman (Portillo 69).

SEMI-FINALS, FIRST LEG

Tuesday, 6 May 2003

Real Madrid (1) 2 *(Ronaldo 23, Roberto Carlos 73)*

Juventus (1) 1 *(Trezeguet 45)* 74,000

Real Madrid: Casillas; Michel Salgado, Roberto Carlos, Guti, Hierro, Helguera, Figo, Makelele, Ronaldo (Portillo 50), Zidane, Morientes (Solari 79).
Juventus: Buffon; Thuram, Birindelli, Conte, Ferrara, Iuliano (Pessotto 46), Zambrotta, Tudor (Comoranesi 80), Trezeguet, Del Piero, Nedved (Di Vaio 82).

Wednesday, 7 May 2003

AC Milan (0) 0

Internazionale (0) 0 78,175

AC Milan: Dida; Costacurta, Kaladze, Brocchi (Serginho 73), Nesta, Maldini, Gattuso (Redondo 78), Rui Costa, Inzaghi, Shevchenko (Rivaldo 81), Seedorf.
Internazionale: Toldo; Zanetti J, Coco (Pasquale 84), Cordoba, Materazzi, Cannavaro, Sergio Conceicao (Guglielminpietro 66), Di Biagio, Crespo, Recoba (Kallon 72), Emre B.

SEMI-FINALS, SECOND LEG

Tuesday, 13 May 2003

Internazionale (0) 1 *(Martins 83)*

AC Milan (1) 1 *(Shevchenko 45)* 76,854

Internazionale: Toldo; Zanetti J, Sergio Conceicao, Cordoba, Materazzi, Cannavaro, Zanetti C, Di Biagio (Dalmat 46), Crespo (Kallon 71), Recoba (Martins 46), Emre B.

AC Milan: Abbiati; Costacurta, Kaladze, Pirlo (Brocchi 88), Nesta, Maldini, Gattuso, Rui Costa (Ambrosini 65), Inzaghi (Serginho 80), Shevchenko, Seedorf.

Wednesday, 14 May 2003

Juventus (2) 3 *(Trezeguet 12, Del Piero 42, Nedved 73)*

Real Madrid (0) 1 *(Zidane 89)* 67,299

Juventus: Buffon; Thuram, Birindelli (Pessotto 60), Tacchinardi, Tudor, Montero, Zambrotta, Davids (Conte 90), Trezeguet (Camoranesi 77), Del Piero, Nedved.

Real Madrid: Casillas; Michel Salgado, Roberto Carlos, Guti, Hierro, Helguera, Figo, Flavio Conceicao (Ronaldo 53), Raul, Zidane, Cambiasso (McManaman 77).

UEFA CHAMPIONS LEAGUE FINAL 2003

AC Milan (0) 0 Juventus (0) 0

Wednesday, 28 May 2003

(at Old Trafford, Manchester, 63,215)

AC Milan: Dida; Costacurta (Roque Junior 70), Kaladze, Pirlo (Serginho 76), Nesta, Maldini, Gattuso, Rui Costa (Ambrosini 87), Inzaghi, Shevchenko, Seedorf.

Juventus: Buffon; Thuram, Montero, Tacchinardi, Tudor (Birindelli 42), Ferrara, Camoranesi (Conte 46), Davids (Zalayeta 70), Trezeguet, Del Piero, Zambrotta.

aet; AC Milan won 3-2 on penalties. Trezeguet (saved), Serginho (scored), Birindelli (scored), Seedorf (saved), Zalayeta (saved), Kaladze (saved), Montero (saved), Nesta (scored), Del Piero (scored), Shevchenko (scored).

Referee: M. Merk (Germany).

Andrei Shevchenko puts away the decisive penalty kick in the shoot-out to win the Champions League trophy for AC Milan against fellow Italians Juventus. (Colorsport)

EUROPEAN CUP-WINNERS' CUP FINALS 1961–99

Year	Winners	Runners-up	Venue	Attendance	Referee
1961	Fiorentina 2	Rangers 0 *(1st Leg)*	Glasgow	80,000	Steiner (A)
	Fiorentina 2	Rangers 1 *(2nd Leg)*	Florence	50,000	Hernadi (H)
1962	Atletico Madrid 1	Fiorentina 1	Glasgow	27,389	Wharton (S)
Replay	Atletico Madrid 3	Fiorentina 0	Stuttgart	38,000	Tschenscher (WG)
1963	Tottenham Hotspur 5	Atletico Madrid 1	Rotterdam	49,000	Van Leuwen (Ho)
1964	Sporting Lisbon 3	MTK Budapest 3 *(aet)*	Brussels	3000	Van Nuffel (Bel)
Replay	Sporting Lisbon 1	MTK Budapest 0	Antwerp	19,000	Versyp (Bel)
1965	West Ham U 2	Munich 1860 0	Wembley	100,000	Szolt (H)
1966	Borussia Dortmund 2	Liverpool 1 *(aet)*	Glasgow	41,657	Schwinte (F)
1967	Bayern Munich 1	Rangers 0 *(aet)*	Nuremberg	69,480	Lo Bello (I)
1968	AC Milan 2	Hamburg 0	Rotterdam	53,000	Ortiz (Sp)
1969	Slovan Bratislava 3	Barcelona 2	Basle	19,000	Van Ravens (Ho)
1970	Manchester C 2	Gornik Zabrze 1	Vienna	8,000	Schiller (A)
1971	Chelsea 1	Real Madrid 1 *(aet)*	Athens	42,000	Scheurer (Sw)
Replay	Chelsea 2	Real Madrid 1 *(aet)*	Athens	35,000	Bucheli (Sw)
1972	Rangers 3	Moscow Dynamo 2	Barcelona	24,000	Ortiz (Sp)
1973	AC Milan 1	Leeds U 0	Salonika	45,000	Mihas (Gr)
1974	Magdeburg 2	AC Milan 0	Rotterdam	4000	Van Gemert (Ho)
1975	Dynamo Kiev 3	Ferencvaros 0	Basle	13,000	Davidson (S)
1976	Anderlecht 4	West Ham U 2	Brussels	58,000	Wurtz (F)
1977	Hamburg 2	Anderlecht 0	Amsterdam	65,000	Partridge (E)
1978	Anderlecht 4	Austria/WAC 0	Paris	48,679	Adlinger (WG)
1979	Barcelona 4	Fortuna Dusseldorf 3 *(aet)*	Basle	58,000	Palotai (H)
1980	Valencia 0	Arsenal 0	Brussels	36,000	Christov (Cz)
	(aet; Valencia won 5-4 on penalties)				
1981	Dynamo Tbilisi 2	Carl Zeiss Jena 1	Dusseldorf	9000	Lattanzi (I)
1982	Barcelona 2	Standard Liege 1	Barcelona	100,000	Eschweiler (WG)
1983	Aberdeen 2	Real Madrid 1 *(aet)*	Gothenburg	17,804	Menegali (I)
1984	Juventus 2	Porto 1	Basle	60,000	Prokop (EG)
1985	Everton 3	Rapid Vienna 1	Rotterdam	50,000	Casarin (I)
1986	Dynamo Kiev 3	Atletico Madrid 0	Lyon	39,300	Wohrer (A)
1987	Ajax 1	Lokomotiv Leipzig 0	Athens	35,000	Agnolin (I)
1988	Mechelen 1	Ajax 0	Strasbourg	39,446	Pauly (WG)
1989	Barcelona 2	Sampdoria 0	Berne	45,000	Courtney (E)
1990	Sampdoria 2	Anderlecht 0	Gothenburg	20,103	Galler (Sw)
1991	Manchester U 2	Barcelona 1	Rotterdam	42,000	Karlsson (Se)
1992	Werder Bremen 2	Monaco 0	Lisbon	16,000	D'Elia (I)
1993	Parma 3	Antwerp 1	Wembley	37,393	Assenmacher (G)
1994	Arsenal 1	Parma 0	Copenhagen	33,765	Krondl (Czr)
1995	Zaragoza 2	Arsenal 1	Paris	42,424	Ceccarini (I)
1996	Paris St Germain 1	Rapid Vienna 0	Brussels	37,500	Pairetto (I)
1997	Barcelona 1	Paris St Germain 0	Rotterdam	45,000	Merk (G)
1998	Chelsea 1	Stuttgart 0	Stockholm	30,216	Braschi (I)
1999	Lazio 2	Mallorca 1	Villa Park	33,021	Benko (A)

INTER-CITIES FAIRS CUP FINALS 1958–71

(Winners in italics)

Year	First Leg	Attendance	Second Leg	Attendance
1958	London 2 Barcelona 2	45,466	*Barcelona* 6 London 0	62,000
1960	Birmingham C 0 Barcelona 0	40,500	*Barcelona* 4 Birmingham C 1	70,000
1961	Birmingham C 2 Roma 2	21,005	*Roma* 2 Birmingham C 0	60,000
1962	Valencia 6 Barcelona 2	65,000	Barcelona 1 *Valencia* 1	60,000
1963	Dynamo Zagreb 1 Valencia 2	40,000	*Valencia* 2 Dynamo Zagreb 0	55,000
1964	*Zaragoza* 2 Valencia 1	50,000	(in Barcelona)	
1965	*Ferencvaros* 1 Juventus 0	25,000	(in Turin)	
1966	Barcelona 0 Zaragoza 1	70,000	Zaragoza 2 *Barcelona* 4	70,000
1967	Dynamo Zagreb 2 Leeds U 0	40,000	Leeds U 0 *Dynamo Zagreb* 0	35,604
1968	Leeds U 1 Ferencvaros 0	25,368	Ferencvaros 0 *Leeds U* 0	70,000
1969	Newcastle U 3 Ujpest Dozsa 0	60,000	Ujpest Dozsa 2 *Newcastle U* 3	37,000
1970	Anderlecht 3 Arsenal 1	37,000	*Arsenal* 3 Anderlecht 0	51,612
1971	Juventus 0 Leeds U 0 *(abandoned 51 minutes)*	42,000		
	Juventus 2 Leeds U 2	42,000	*Leeds U* 1* Juventus 1	42,483

UEFA CUP FINALS 1972–97

(Winners in italics)

Year	First Leg	Attendance	Second Leg	Attendance
1972	Wolverhampton W 1 Tottenham H 2	45,000	*Tottenham H* 1 Wolverhampton W 1	48,000
1973	Liverpool 0 Moenchengladbach 0 *(abandoned 27 minutes)*	44,967		
	Liverpool 3 Moenchengladbach 0	41,169	Moenchengladbach 2 *Liverpool* 0	35,000
1974	Tottenham H 2 Feyenoord 2	46,281	*Feyenoord* 2 Tottenham H 0	68,000
1975	Moenchengladbach 0 Twente 0	45,000	Twente 1 *Moenchengladbach* 5	24,500
1976	Liverpool 3 FC Brugge 2	56,000	FC Brugge 1 *Liverpool* 1	32,000
1977	Juventus 1 Athletic Bilbao 0	75,000	Athletic Bilbao 2 *Juventus* 1*	43,000
1978	Bastia 0 PSV Eindhoven 0	15,000	*PSV Eindhoven* 3 Bastia 0	27,000
1979	Red Star Belgrade 1 Moenchengladbach 1	87,500	*Moenchengladbach* 1 Red Star Belgrade 0	45,000
1980	Moenchengladbach 3 Eintracht Frankfurt 2	25,000	*Eintracht Frankfurt* 1* Moenchengladbach 0	60,000
1981	Ipswich T 3 AZ 67 Alkmaar 0	27,532	AZ 67 Alkmaar 4 *Ipswich T* 2	28,500
1982	Gothenburg 1 Hamburg 0	42,548	Hamburg 0 *Gothenburg* 3	60,000
1983	Anderlecht 1 Benfica 0	45,000	Benfica 1 *Anderlecht* 1	80,000
1984	Anderlecht 1 Tottenham H 1	40,000	*Tottenham H* 1[1] Anderlecht 1	46,258
1985	Videoton 0 Real Madrid 3	30,000	*Real Madrid* 0 Videoton 1	98,300
1986	Real Madrid 5 Cologne 1	80,000	Cologne 2 *Real Madrid* 0	15,000
1987	Gothenburg 1 Dundee U 0	50,023	Dundee U 1 *Gothenburg* 1	20,911
1988	Espanol 3 Bayer Leverkusen 0	42,000	*Bayer Leverkusen* 3[2] Espanol 0	22,000
1989	Napoli 2 Stuttgart 1	83,000	Stuttgart 3 *Napoli* 3	67,000
1990	Juventus 3 Fiorentina 1	45,000	Fiorentina 0 *Juventus* 0	32,000
1991	Internazionale 2 Roma 0	68,887	Roma 1 *Internazionale* 0	70,901
1992	Torino 2 Ajax 2	65,377	*Ajax* 0* Torino 0	40,000
1993	Borussia Dortmund 1 Juventus 3	37,000	*Juventus* 3 Borussia Dortmund 0	62,781
1994	Salzburg 0 Internazionale 1	47,500	*Internazionale* 1 Salzburg 0	80,326
1995	Parma 1 Juventus 0	23,000	Juventus 1 *Parma* 1	80,750
1996	Bayern Munich 2 Bordeaux 0	62,000	Bordeaux 1 *Bayern Munich* 3	36,000
1997	Schalke 1 Internazionale 0	56,824	Internazionale 1 *Schalke* 0[3]	81,670

**won on away goals* [1]*aet; Tottenham H won 4-3 on penalties* [2]*aet; Bayer Leverkusen won 3-2 on penalties*
[3]*aet; Schalke won 4-1 on penalties*

UEFA CUP FINALS 1998–2003

Year	Winners	Runners-up	Venue	Attendance	Referee
1998	Internazionale 3	Lazio 0	Paris	42,938	Nieto (Sp)
1999	Parma 3	Marseille 0	Moscow	61,000	Dallas (S)
2000	Galatasaray 0 *(aet; Galatasaray won 4-1 on penalties).*	Arsenal 0	Copenhagen	38,919	Nieto (Sp)
2001	Liverpool 5¶ *(aet; Liverpool won on sudden death).*	Alaves 4	Dortmund	65,000	Veissiere (F)
2002	Feyenoord 3	Borussia Dortmund 2	Rotterdam	45,000	Pereira (P)
2003	Porto 3 *(aet).*	Celtic 2	Seville	52,972	Michel (Slv)

UEFA CUP 2002–03

▪ *Denotes player sent off.*

QUALIFYING ROUND, FIRST LEG

AIK Stockholm (1) 2 *(Hoch 26, Nordin 90)*, IBV (0) 0 6983

Anorthosis (2) 3 *(Piekarski 21, Kowalczyk 43, Xiourouppas 80 (pen))*, Grevenmacher (0) 0 6000

Atyrau (0) 0, Matador (0) 0 10,000

Brann (1) 2 *(Knudsen 45, Olsen 58)*, Sudova (3) 3 *(Zitinskas 8, 20, Radzinevicius 18)* 1761

FC Copenhagen (1) 3 *(Jonsson 42, 54, Larsen 46)*, Lokomotiv Tbilisi (1) 1 *(Janashia 9)* 10,692

Domagnano (0) 0, Viktoria Zizkov (1) 2 *(Sabou 27, Straceny 80) Pikl*▪ 1000

Dynamo Minsk (0) 1 *(Tsyhalka 66)*, CSKA Sofia (3) 4 *(Mukasi 18, Dimitrov 28, 47, Brito 31)* 5000

Dynamo Tbilisi (3) 4 *(Da Rosha 6, Daraselia 14, Shashiashvili 43, 49)*, VMK (0) 1 *(Leetma 75)* 6000

Encamp (0) 0, Zenit (1) 5 *(Arsjavin 2, 51, Spivak 59 (pen), Makarov 65, Ossipov 71)* 2000

Ferencvaros (2) 4 *(Tokoli 10, 11, Gera 55, Szukukalek 58)*, AEL (0) 0 12,000

Fylkir (0) 1 *(Sverrisson 59 (pen))*, Mouscron (1) 1 *(Gregoire 26)* 1500

Gomel (0) 1 *(Barel 60)*, HJK Helsinki (0) 0 3500

Hajduk Split (1) 3 *(Dolonga 22, Pletikosa 60 (pen), Deranja 84)*, GI Gotu (0) 0 5000

Hapoel Tel Aviv (0) 1 *(Abuksis 49)*, Partizani (0) 0 90 *(in Sofia)*.

Kairat (0) 0 *Shayakhmetov*▪, Red Star Belgrade (1) 2 *(Bogdanovic 43, Mrda 66)* 15,000

KI Klaksvik (1) 2 *(Morkore 45, 53)*, Ujpest (1) 2 *(Juhar 14, Farkas 68)* 200

Koba (1) 1 *(Juska 11)*, Siroki (1) 2 *(Katic 30, 70)* 2000

Leixoes (0) 2 *(Antchouet 60, Brito 75) Sergio*▪, Belasica (0) 2 *(Ahmetovic 53, 55)* 4000

Levadia (0) 0, Maccabi Tel Aviv (2) 2 *(Prohorenkovs 4, Strool 23)* 1500

Litets (1) 5 *(Nikolov 28, Stoilov 58, Yovov 70, 75, Roussev 79)*, Atlantas (0) 0 *Maciulevicius*▪ 3500

Metalurgs Liepaya (0) 0 *Klava*▪, Karnten (0) 2 *(Maric 57, Bubalo 77)* 1500

Metalurg Zapor (1) 3 *(Akopyan 17, Ivanov 58, Brdanin 68)*, Birkirkara (0) 0 4000

MyPa (1) 1 *(Manso 16)*, Odense (0) 0 2000

Pobeda (1) 2 *(Nielsen 35 (og), Krstev 70) Nikolaevski*▪, Midtjylland (0) 0 *Jorgensen*▪ 4000

Primorje (1) 6 *(Gregoric 31, Zatkovic 49, 72, 74, 89, Ranic 68)*, Zvartnorts (0) 1 *(Davityan 82)* 1000

Rapid Bucharest (1) 2 *(Schumacher 17, 72 (pen))*, Gorica (0) 0 8000

Sigma Olomouc (1) 2 *(Putik 45, Ekwueme 75)*, Sarajevo (1) 1 *(Osmanhodzic 30)* 5343

Sliema Wanderers (0) 1 *(Do Nascimento 90) Garcia*▪, Polonia (0) 3 *(Bartczak 54, Bak 71, Udenkwor 86)* 3000

Spartak Erevan (0) 0, Servette (0) 2 *(Coubadja Toure 72, 84)* 2500

SK Tirana (0) 0, National (1) 1 *(Radu 33 (pen))* 4000

Ventspils (1) 3 *(Landyrev 40, 67, Rimkus 58)*, Lugano (0) 0 2000

Zimbru Chisinau (3) 3 *(Frunza 22, 37, Gvazava 28)*, IFK Gothenburg (1) 1 *(Henriksson 36)* 7000

Tuesday, 13 August 2002

Vaduz (0) 1 *(Burgmeier 61)*

Livingston (0) 1 *(Rubio 51)* 1322

Vaduz: Peiser; Stocklasa, Brugnoli, Slekys, Obhafuoso, Perez (Gerser 90), Burgmeier (Beck 81), Zarn, Telser, Niederhauser, Merenda (Polverino 90).
Livingston: Broto; Brinquin, Bollan, Rubio, Wilson (Hart 75), Camacho Barnola (Bingham 46), Zarate, Quinovert, Makel, Bahoken, Dadi (Xausa 72).

Thursday, 15 August 2002

Aberdeen (0) 1 *(Mackie 59)*

Otaci (0) 0 9894

Aberdeen: Kjaer; McNaughton, Anderson, McGuire, Bisconti, Darren Young, Derek Young, Mackie, Clark (McAnespie 65), Deloumeaux, Djaffo (Mike 57).
Otaci: Dinov; Lupascu (Matiura 88), Lascencov, Kovalkov, Pidhayetskyy, Bursuc, Popescu (Kopystyanskyy 66), Pogreban, Grosev, Blajco (Yanchuk 75), Mincev.

Amica (1) 5 *(Bieniuk 35, Dembinski 57, Krol 64, Dawidowski 81, 85)*

TNS (0) 0 1200

Amica: Strozynski; Djokovic, Bieniuk, Bajor, Skrzypek, Gesior (Kucharski 66), Jikia, Burkhardt (Sobocinski 81), Zienczuk (Krol 59), Dawidowski, Dembinski.
TNS: Williams; Taylor, Ward, Holmes, Evans R (Evans S 63), Alexander, Ruscoe, Toner, Leah, Anthrobus (Bridgewater 76), Brabin.

Avenir Beggen (0) 0

Ipswich Town (0) 1 *(Stewart 90)* 2971

Avenir Beggen: Hartert; Lariccia, Picard (Gomes 67), Molitor, Miedico, Ney, Calvaruso, Da Luz, Martin, Schmit (Pace 46), Hamdaoui (Lopes 85).
Ipswich Town: Marshall; Wilnis, Richards, Miller T, Gaardsoe, Venus, Bent D, Wright (Magilton 46), Stewart, Armstrong (Holland 46), Clapham (Le Pen 67).

Bangor City (0) 1 *(Roberts 69)*

Sartid (0) 0 967

Bangor City: Priestley; Owain Jones (Darren Jones 88), Goodall, Eifion Jones, Rowlands, Griffiths, Williams (Couper 24), Blackmore, Roberts (Hunt 85), Davies, Burgess.
Sartid: Zilic; Damjanovic, Kekezovic (Djurkovic 66), Kizic, Spasic, Socanac, Bogdanovic, Vaskovic, Mirosavljevic, Kulic (Ramovic 79), Zecevic (Branezac 60).
(at Wrexham).

Glentoran (0) 0 4000

Wisla (0) 2 *(Zurawski 73 (pen), Dubicki 88)*

Glentoran: Morris; Nixon, Glendinning (Tim McCann I 90), Walker, Leeman, Smyth, Kilmartin, Lockhart, Halliday (Smith 62), Fitzgerald, Keegan (Riches 78).
Wisla: Hugues; Stolarczyk, Glowacki, Baszczynski, Jop, Moskal, Paszulewicz (Strak 72), Uche (Pater 62), Kosowski, Kuzba (Dubicki 82), Zurawski.

Shamrock Rovers (0) 1 *(McGuiness 49)* 4850

Djurgaarden (1) 3 *(Wowoah 24, 52, Kallstrom 70)*

Shamrock Rovers: Horgan; O'Keeffe, Doyle, Colwell (Grant S 75), McGuiness, Scully, Francis (Robinson 64), Grant T (Keddy 46), Hunt, Costello, Byrne.
Djurgaarden: Isaksson; Olsson, Dorsin, Johansson (Bergtoft 83), Karlsson, Stefanidis, Kallstrom, Wowoah (Bapupa-Ngabu 75), Rasck, Rehn, Chanko.

Stabaek (2) 4 *(Finstad 12, Gudmundsson 18, 90, Baldvinsson 75)*

Linfield (0) 0 1145

Stabaek: Knudsen; Stenvoll, Kjolo, Muri, Holter, Michelsen, Andresen, Sand (Olsen 53), Stenersen, Gudmundsson, Finstad (Baldvinsson 53).
Linfield: Mannus; Collier, McShane, Hunter, Murphy (King 72), Kelly, McBride, Dickson, Ferguson, Feeney (Shaw 45), Scates (Picking 35).

Varteks (2) 5 *(Huljev 28, Hrman 32, Mumlek 55 (pen), Karic 69, Sklepic 90)*

Dundalk (0) 0 4500

Varteks: Rumbak; Furnic, Hrman (Jancevski 61), Kristic, Karic, Mumlek, Huljev, Vuckevic, Safaric (Halimi 69), Sabolcki, Halilovic (Sklepic 66).
Dundalk: Connolly; Whyte, Brunton, Melvin (Haylock 35), McCrystal, Flanagan, Hoey, Reilly, Lawless (Chris Malone 73), Kavanagh, Ward (Cormac Malone 81).

QUALIFYING ROUND, SECOND LEG

AEL (1) 2 *(Kyriakou 29, Sebok 86)*, Ferencvaros (0) 1 *(Lipcsei 90)* 2000
Atlantas (1) 1 *(Tamosauskas 12)*, Litets (0) 3 *(Roussev 50, Hidiouad 62 (pen), Jelenkovic 66)* 1700
Belasica (0) 1 *(Baldovaljev 80)*, Leixoes (1) 2 *(Brito 34, Nene 73)* 2000
Birkirkara (0) 0, Metalurg Zapor (0) 0 3500
CSKA Sofia (0) 1 *(Sakiri 64 (pen)) Joao Carlos*▪, Dynamo Minsk (0) 0 *Dobrovolski*▪ 6000
GI Gotu (0) 0 *Eliassen*▪, Hajduk Split (5) 8 *(Erceg 12, 16, 78, Andric 23, 35, Pletikosa 45 (pen), Carevic 46, 85)* 600
Gorica (0) 1 *(Perja 85 (og))*, Rapid Bucharest (2) 3 *(Godfroid 3, Schumacher 14, 56)* 2500
IFK Gothenburg (2) 2 *(Rosenkvist 29, 39)*, Zimbru Chisinau (2) 2 *(Gvazava 34, Cibotari 36) Balasa*▪ 2109
Grevenmacher (1) 2 *(Manzangala 34, Albrecht 87)*, Anorthosis (0) 0 1000
HJK Helsinki (0) 0, Gomel (1) 4 *(Nazarov 32, Bliznioek 55, 90, Razumau 62)* 5000
IBV (1) 1 *(Thorvaldsson 3)*, AIK Stockholm (2) 3 *(Rubarth 9, Hoch 45, 66)* 540
Karnten (1) 4 *(Ambrosius 11, 53, 72, Bubalo 62)*, Metalurgs Liepaya (1) 2 *(Katasonov 18, Ivanovs 83)* 3400
Lokomotiv Tbilisi (1) 1 *(Janashia 9)*, FC Copenhagen (1) 4 *(Zuma 23, Pettersson 68, 72, Jonsson 80)* 4000
Lugano (0) 1 *(Andreoli 55)*, Ventspils (0) 0 3500
Maccabi Tel Aviv (0) 2 *(Pasins 74 (og), Prohorenkovs 84)*, Levadia (0) 0 250 *(in Sofia)*.
Matador (0) 2 *(Breska 51, Strba 90)*, Atyrau (0) 0 2500
Midtjylland (0) 3 *(Pimpong 59, Kristensen 79, Jessen 115)*, Pobeda (0) 0 *Georgieski*▪ *(aet)* 1244
Mouscron (1) 3 *(Dugardein 36, Bakadal 47, Gregoire 56)*, Fylkir (1) 1 *(Asbjornsson 45)* 6400
National (1) 2 *(Ilie 30, Radu 60)*, SK Tirana (1) 2 *(Merkoci 8, Zaccanti 68)* 5000
Odense (0) 2 *(Miti 63, 90)*, MyPa (0) 0 5616
Partizani (1) 1 *(Brachini 35) Brachini*▪, Hapoel Tel Aviv (1) 4 *(Afek 28, Balili 73, 84, Udi 87)* 3000
Polonia (2) 2 *(Bak 4, Bartczak 39)*, Sliema Wanderers (0) 0 2500
Red Star Belgrade (2) 3 *(Gvozdenovic 19, Pjanovic 44, Krivokapic 73)*, Kairat (0) 0 *Aliyev*▪ 10,000
Sarajevo (0) 2 *(Obuca 53, Osmanhodzic 78)*, Sigma Olomouc (1) 1 *(Putik 9)* 15,000
(aet; Sarajevo won 5-3 on penalties).
Servette (2) 3 *(Diogo Cruz 38, 43, Frei 77)*, Spartak Erevan (0) 0 2217
Siroki (1) 3 *(Erceg 13, Hrgovic 49, 73)*, Koba (0) 0 2500
Sudova (3) 3 *(Radzinevicius 3, 30, 39)*, Brann (1) 2 *(Nhleko 16, 44)* 1500
Ujpest (1) 1 *(Horvath 37)*, KI Klaksvik (0) 0 4035
Viktoria Zizkov (2) 3 *(Chihuri 2, Janousek 43, Kroty 69)*, Domagnano (0) 0 640
VMK (0) 0 *Mokolenko*▪, Dynamo Tbilisi (0) 1 *(Akhalaia 74)* 2000
Zvartnots (0) 2 *(Nazaryan 53 (pen), Avanesyan 78)*, Primorje (0) 0 2000
Zenit (2) 8 *(Ossipov 14, 69, Randjelovic 21, 71, 73, Spivak 57, Miceika 86, Nikolajev 89)*, Encamp (0) 0 16,000

Thursday, 29 August 2002

Djurgaarden (2) 2 *(Wowoah 19, Chanko 21)*
Shamrock Rovers (0) 0 7273
Djurgaarden: Isaksson; Olsson, Dorsin, Johansson, Karlsson, Stefanidis (Barlin 64), Kallstrom, Wowoah, Rasck, Rehn (Mattiasson 55), Chanko (Bapupa-Ngabu 78).
Shamrock Rovers: Horgan; O'Keeffe (Deans 46), Doyle, Byrne, McGuinness, Scully, Keddy, Hunt (Grant S 68), Francis (Colwell 46), Costello, Grant.

Dundalk (0)0 3000
Varteks (1) 4 *(Kristic 21, Halilovic 50, Huljev 69, Furnic 79)*
Dundalk: Connolly; Whyte, Brunton, D'Arcy, McCrystal▪, Kavanagh (Lawless 68), Hoey, Reilly (Chris Malone 72), Haylock (Cormac Malone 58), Flanagan, Ward.
Varteks: Rumbak; Toplak, Furnic, Kristic, Karic (Halilovic 46), Mumlek (Huljev 46), Granic, Jancevski (Safaric 66), Petricevic, Sklepic, Halimi.

Ipswich Town (5) 8 *(Miller T 3, 19, Counago 18, 21, 74, Brown 42, McGreal 61, Ambrose 79)*
Avenir Beggen (0) 1 *(Molitor 56)* 17,462
Ipswich Town: Marshall; Wilnis, Clapham, Holland, McGreal, Brown, Miller T (Ambrose 62), Magilton (George 72), Counago, Bent M, Reuser (Richards 51).
Avenir Beggen: Hartert; Miedico, Lariccia, Ney (Diallo 75), Calvaruso (Picard 77), Gomes, Da Silva, Molitor, Martin, Da Luz, Pace (Lopes 62).

Linfield (1) 1 *(Ferguson 44)*
Stabaek (0) 1 *(Gudmundsson 81)* 2000
Linfield: Mannus; Collier, McShane, Murphy, Hunter (King 81), Dickson, Picking, Shaw, Ferguson▪, Kelly, McBride.
Stabaek: Knudsen; Stenvoll, Kjolo, Muri (Flem▪ 25), Holter, Wilhelmsson, Andresen▪, Stenersen (Olsen 68), Michelsen, Gudmundsson, Finstad.

Livingston (0) 0
Vaduz (0) 0 7219
Livingston: Broto; Brinquin, Bahoken, Andrews, Rubio, Toure-Maman (Makel 57), Lovell, Quinovert, Bingham (Dadi 81), Zarate, Camacho Barnola (Wilson 61).
Vaduz: Peiser; Niederhauser, Obhafuoso (Polverino 81), Stocklasa, Brugnoli, Slekys, Merenda (Buchel 64), Perez, Burgmeier (Beck 57), Zarn, Telser▪.

Otaci (0) 0
Aberdeen (0) 0 4000
Otaci: Dinov; Lupascu, Lascencov, Kovalkov, Pidhayetskyy, Bursuc, Popescu (Matiura 54), Kopystyanskyy (Malitschi 77), Grosev, Yanchuk, Blajco (Pogreban 69).
Aberdeen: Kjaer; Deloumeaux, McAllister, Anderson, McGuire, Darren Young, Derek Young, McNaughton, Tiernan (Mackie 46) Bisconti (Clark 60), D'Jaffo.

Sartid (1) 2 *(Zecevic 14, Mirosavljevic 58)*
Bangor City (0) 0 9000
Sartid: Zilic; Djurkovic, Radosavljevic, Damjanovic▪, Spasic, Socanac, Kekezovic, Vaskovic, Mirosavljevic (Kizic 90), Kulic (Savic 83), Zecevic (Kocic 90).
Bangor City: Priestley; Goodall, Eifion Jones, Rowlands (Short 88), Griffiths, Blackmore, Roberts (Darren Jones 72), Davies, Burgess, Brett (Hunt 47), Couper.

TNS (2) 2 *(Anthrobus 20, Toner 28)*
Amica (2) 7 *(Krol 26, 71, 85, Burkhardt 34, 75, Sobocinski 66, Ludzinski 87)* 250
TNS: Doherty; Chris Taylor, Ward, Taylor (Leah 50), Evans, Alexander, Ruscoe, Toner (Wilde 82), Anthrobus (Perry 65), Brabin, Bridgewater.
Amica: Strozynski; Bajor, Bieniuk, Djokovic, Dawidowski (Sobocinski 56), Krol, Gesior (Ludzinski 76), Zienczuk, Sokolowski, Jikia (Sawala 69), Burkhardt. *(in Newtown)*.

Wisla (1) 4 *(Kuzba 19, 59, Uche 74, 80)*
Glentoran (0) 0 5000
Wisla: Hugues; Stolarczyk, Glowacki (Baszczynski 29), Moskal, Zurawski (Pater 71), Uche, Strak, Jop, Brozek, Kaliciak, Kuzba (Cantoro 62).
Glentoran: Morris; Nixon, Tim McCann II, Walker, Leeman, Smyth, Kilmartin (Lockhart 46), Halliday (Fitzgerald 65), Smith, O'Neill, Keegan (Tim McCann I 83).

FIRST ROUND, FIRST LEG

AIK Stockholm (1) 3 *(Nordin 19, Andersson A 67, Rubarth 75)*, Fenerbahce (3) 3 *(Revivo 15, Johnson 24, Stevic 38)* 17,839
Anderlecht (0) 0, Stabaek (1) 1 *(Michelsen 11)* 15,000
Ankaragucu (1) 1 *(Niculescu 30)*, Alaves (1) 2 *(Astudillo 43, Ruben Navarro 81)* 10,000
Apoel (1) 2 *(Sztipanovics 34, Khachatrian 70)*, Graz (0) 0 2500
FK Austria (3) 5 *(Janocko 33, 35, Feitoza 44 (pen), Helstad 85, 87)*, Shakhtjor Donetsk (1) 1 *(Bielik 16) Zubov*▪ 13,100

Besiktas (2) 2 *(Pancu 30, Ahmet Dursun 32)*, Sarajevo (0) 2 *(Obuca 62, Osmanhodzic 78)* 21,000
Bordeaux (2) 6 *(Sommeil 23, Dugarry 36, Feindouno 61, Pauleta 67 (pen), Vavrik 78 (og), Darcheville 89)*, Matador (0) 0 12,700
Celta Vigo (0) 2 *(Catanha 70, McCarthy 76)*, Odense (0) 0 9800
FC Copenhagen (0) 0, Djurgaarden (0) 0 18,152
CSKA Moscow (0) 1 *(Popov 68)*, Parma (0) 1 *(Mutu 53)* 18,500
Denizli (1) 2 *(Ozkan M 11, 68 (pen))*, Lorient (0) 0 8000
Dynamo Zagreb (2) 6 *(Maric 9, Mitu 19, Olic 47, Polovanec 76, Petrovic 83, 85)*, Zalaegerszeg (0) 0 10,000
Ferencvaros (2) 4 *(Tokoli 10, 90, Lipcsei 30, Dragoner 76)*, Kocaeli (0) 0 6176
Gomel (0) 1 *(Ivanov 61)*, Schalke (0) 4 *(Sand 58, 72, Poulsen 67, Rodriguez 73)* 5000
Grasshoppers (2) 3 *(Baturina 6, Barijho 44, Nunez 53)*, Zenit (1) 1 *(Kerzhakov 33)* 2300
Iraklis (1) 4 *(Mieciel 44, Stoltidis 50, Gonias 51, 88)*, Anorthosis (0) 2 *(Neophytou 61, 90 (pen))* 6000
Karnten (0) 0, Hapoel Tel Aviv (1) 4 *(Halmai 36, Welton 68, Gershon 76, Udi 88)* 3500
Lazio (1) 4 *(Manfredini 45, Claudio Lopez 52, Inzaghi 68, Cesar 69)*, Xanthi (0) 0 13,343
Legia (2) 4 *(Zielinski 20, Vukovic 28, Schut 59 (og), Svitlica 70)*, Utrecht (0) 1 *(Kuijt 48) Vreven*■ 12,000
Leixoes (1) 2 *(Brito 4, Detinho 52)*, PAOK Salonika (1) 1 *(Kukielka 25)* 10,000
Levski (2) 4 *(Simonovic 5, 35, Telkijski 51, 57)*, Brondby (1) 1 *(Madsen 18) Madsen*■ 7000
Litets (0) 0, Panathinaikos (0) 1 *(Jelenkovic 66 (og))* 4000
Maccabi Tel Aviv (1) 1 *(Dago 33)*, Boavista (0) 0 500 *(in Sofia)*.
Metalurg Donetsk (1) 2 *(Tchoutang 39, 52)*, Werder Bremen (2) 2 *(Lisztes 12, Verlaat 14)* 18,000
Midtjylland (0) 1 *(Laursen 89)*, Varteks (0) 0 4000
Mouscron (0) 2 *(Mpenza 72, 90 (pen))*, Slavia Prague (1) 2 *(Vachousek 41, Petrous 48) Bejbl*■ 5000
National (2) 3 *(Curt 6, Ilie 28 (pen), Olah 60)*, Heerenveen (0) 0 9000
Paris St Germain (3) 3 *(Ronaldinho Gaucho 13, Pochettino 24, Cardetti 44)*, Ujpest (0) 0 26,000
Porto (2) 6 *(Jankauskas 20, 56, Derlei 37, Ribeiro 55, Helder Postiga 69, 89)*, Polonia (0) 0 21,209
Primorje (0) 0, Wisla (1) 2 *(Uche 12, Kuzba 55)* 2500
Red Star Belgrade (0) 0, Chievo (0) 0 35,000
Servette (1) 2 *(Obradovic 26, Frei 59)*, Amica (0) 3 *(Krol 62, 85, Zienczuk 70)* 2641
Slovan Liberec (2) 3 *(Nezmar 18, Zboncak 25, Gyan 60)*, Dynamo Tbilisi (0) 2 *(Daraselia 48, Anchabadze 66)* 5100
Sparta Prague (1) 3 *(Pospisil 41, Baranek 63, Poborsky 76)*, Siroki (0) 0 5243
Sporting Lisbon (1) 1 *(Tonito 27)*, Partizan Belgrade (2) 3 *(Hugo 12 (og), Delibasic 37, Iliev 79)* 15,000
Stuttgart (3) 4 *(Amanatidis 22, Kuranyi 33, 40, Hleb 59 (pen))*, Ventspils (0) 1 *(Rimkus 66)* 6000
Vitesse (0) 1 *(Peeters 61)*, Rapid Bucharest (0) 1 *(Lencsi 90)* 10,850
Zeljeznicar (0) 0, Malaga (0) 0 12,000
Zimbru Chisinau (0) 0, Betis (2) 2 *(Alfonso 31, Dinu 45 (og))* 2500

Tuesday, 17 September 2002

Aberdeen (0) 0

Hertha Berlin (0) 0 10,180

Aberdeen: Kjaer; McNaughton, McAllister (Fabiano 74), Anderson, McGuire, Bisconti, Darren Young, Derek Young (Mike 82), Mackie (Michie 69), Deloumeaux, D'Jaffo.
Hertha Berlin: Kiraly; Friedrich, Sverrisson, Goor, Luizao, Marcelinho, Dardai, Neuendorf (Mladenov 88), Hartmann, Tretschok (Marx 63), Madlung.

Viktoria Zizkov (1) 2 *(Pikl 7, Straceny 60)*

Rangers (0) 0 3427

Viktoria Zizkov: Kucera; Buryan, Mlejnsky, Klimpl, Janousek (Kroty 83), Smarda, Sabou, Scasny, Pikl, Straceny (Licka 88), Chihuri (Sebesta 27).
Rangers: Klos; Ricksen, Moore (Konterman 62), Ferguson, Malcolm, Muscat, Ross, De Boer (Mols 84), Caniggia (Latapy 85), Arveladze, Lovenkrands.

Thursday, 19 September 2002

Blackburn Rovers (1) 1 *(Grabbi 27)*

CSKA Sofia (1) 1 *(Dimitrov 23)* 18,300

Blackburn Rovers: Friedel; Neill, Johansson, Todd, Taylor, Tugay, Hignett, Danns (Berg 68), Grabbi (Ostenstad 62), Yorke (Gillespie 11), Dunn.
CSKA Sofia: Petrov; Georgiev, Varbanov, Yanchev, Gueye, Galin, Stefanov, Brito (Gargorov 69), Mukasi (Sakiri 90), Dimitrov (Pavlov 82), Tomovski■.

Celtic (5) 8 *(Larsson 16, 24, 29, Petrov 27, Sutton 35, Lambert 50, Hartson 72, Valgaeren 83)*

Suduva (0) 1 *(Radzinevicius 90)* 36,824

Celtic: Douglas; Sylla, Balde, Petrov, Valgaeren, Laursen (Crainey 61), Lambert, Lennon (Fernandez 61), Sutton, Larsson (Hartson 61), Guppy.
Suduva: Padimanskas; Sendzikas, Suliaskas, Sidlauskas (Maciulis 46), Grigas, Devetinas, Kunevicius, Adomaitus (Krapavicius 77), Zitinskas (Stankevicius 82), Slavickas, Radzinevicius.

Chelsea (1) 2 *(Hasselbaink 43, De Lucas 69)*

Viking (0) 1 *(Wright 90)* 15,772

Chelsea: Cudicini; Gallas, Stanic, Morris, Huth, Desailly, De Lucas, Zola (Oliveira 86), Hasselbaink, Gudjohnsen (Lampard 46), Gronkjaer.
Viking: Olsen; Dahl, Periera, Sanne, Kuivasto, Hangeland, Nevland (Berland 86), Nygaard, Berre (Wright 61), Fuglestad, Kopteff.

Hajduk Split (0) 0

Fulham (0) 1 *(Malbranque 50)* 25,000

Hajduk Split: Pletikosa; Vukovic (Piric 83), Dolonga, Andric, Vejic, Neretljak, Miladin, Srna (Brgles 82), Carevic, Deranja, Radunica (Bule 70).
Fulham: Van der Sar; Ouaddou, Brevett (Wome 63), Melville, Goma, Davis, Legwinski, Inamoto (Clark 78), Marlet (Sava 82), Hayles, Malbranque.

Ipswich Town (0) 1 *(Armstrong 56)*

Sartid (1) 1 *(Mirosavljevic 32)* 16,933

Ipswich Town: Marshall; Wilnis, Hreidarsson, Miller T, McGreal, Venus, Ambrose (George 64), Holland, Counago, Armstrong (Bent M 72), Clapham.
Sartid: Zilic; Ramovic, Radosavljevic (Savic 67), Socanac, Spasic, Paunovic, Bogdanovic (Kizic 50), Vaskovic, Mirosavljevic, Zecevic, Kekezovic■.

Leeds United (0) 1 *(Smith 80)*

Metalurg Zapor (0) 0 30,000

Leeds United: Robinson; Kelly, Harte, Bakke, Radebe, Woodgate, Bowyer, Dacourt (McPhail 65), Smith, Viduka (Bridges 65), Kewell.
Metalurg Zapor: Glushchenko; Valuta, Visevic, Akopyan, Dodic, Raty, Vasconcios, Milosavljevic, Smirnov (Zayats 90), Modebadze (Brdanin 59) (Rodri 90), Klyuchyk.

Sturm Graz (1) 5 *(Wetl 37, Szabics 50, Dag 51, Mujiri 57, 58)*

Livingston (0) 2 *(Zarate 89, Lovell 90)* 2785

Sturm Graz: Hoffmann; Neukirchner, Mahlich, Strafner, Brzeczek (Kursos 77), Golemac, Wetl, Masudi (Kienzl 81), Mujiri, Szabics (Heldt 52), Dag.
Livingston: Broto; Brinquin, Bollan, Rubio, Andrews, Lovell, Quinovert, Bahoken (Toure-Maman 46), Camacho Barnola (Bingham 75), Zarate, Wilson (Dadi 66).

FIRST ROUND, SECOND LEG

Alaves (1) 3 *(Dursun 6 (og), Turiel 49, 75)*, Ankaragucu (0) 0 9476
Amica (0) 1 *(Burkhadt 60)*, Servette (1) 2 *(Frei 35, 88)* 2500
Anorthosis (1) 3 *(Ketsbaia 10, Majak 57, Xiouroupas 82)*, Iraklis (1) 1 *(Fofonka 32)* 10,000
Betis (2) 2 *(Tais 3, Casas 29)*, Zimbru Chisinau (1) 1 *(Cabotari 31 (pen))* 10,000

Boavista (2) 4 *(Strool 6 (og), Jocivalter 31, 90, Serginho 53)*, Maccabi Tel Aviv (0) 1 *(Torjman 76) Strool*▪ 5000
Brondby (0) 1 *(Jonson 73)*, Levski (1) 1 *(Ivankov 9 (pen))* 9456
Chievo (0) 0, Red Star Belgrade (0) 2 *(Gvozdenovic 70, Milovanovic 86)* 14,087
Djurgaarden (2) 3 *(Albrechtsen 13 (og), Elmander 45, Kallstrom 90 (pen))*, FC Copenhagen (0) 1 *(Zivkovic 88)* 13,459
Dynamo Tbilisi (0) 0, Slovan Liberec (0) 1 *(Zboncak 64)* 40,000
Fenerbahce (1) 3 *(Ali 29, Johnson 74, Serhat 90)*, AIK Stockholm (1) 1 *(Hoch 30)* 40,000
Graz (1) 1 *(Ehmann 43)*, Apoel (0) 1 *(Daskalakis 84)* 12,000
Hapoel Tel Aviv (0) 0, Karnten (1) 1 *(Oberleitner 44)* 200 *(in Sofia)*.
Heerenveen (0) 2 *(Hansson 54, Denneboom 65)*, National (0) 0 12,000
Kocaeli (0) 0, Ferencvaros (1) 1 *(Lipcsei 31)* 4000
Lorient (1) 3 *(Kroupi 44, Guel 47, Gauvin 88) Cavalli*▪, Denizli (1) 1 *(Martini 20 (og))* 8500
Malaga (1) 1 *(Dely Valdes 5 (pen))*, Zeljeznicar (0) 0 *Karic*▪ 8500
Matador (1) 1 *(Muzlay 45)*, Bordeaux (2) 4 *(Savio 14, Darcheville 42, 88, Feindouno 67)* 2700
Odense (0) 1 *(Derveld 62) Derveld*▪, Celta Vigo (0) 0 7051
Panathinaikos (0) 2 *(Waryzcha 110, 120)*, Litets (0) 1 *(Graf 90) Zagorcic*▪ *(aet)*. 15,000
PAOK Salonika (2) 4 *(Salpingidis 14, Okkas 16, 80, Koutsopoulos 56)*, Leixoes (0) 1 *(Pedras 81)* 7500
Parma (1) 3 *(Adriano 8, Mutu 66, 90)*, CSKA Moscow (2) 2 *(Semak 37, 43)* 8800
Partizan Belgrade (0) 3 *(Delibasic 78, Zivkovic 110, Cakar 117) Zivkovic*▪, Sporting Lisbon (1) 3 *(Tonito 13, Kutuzov 55, Contreras 82)* *(aet; played behind closed doors)*.
Polonia (0) 2 *(Lukasiewicz 67, Kus 80)*, Porto (0) 0 5000
Rapid Bucharest (0) 0, Vitesse (0) 1 *(Peeters 62)* 12,000
Sarajevo (0) 0, Besiktas (2) 5 *(Pancu 5, Uzulmez 42, Dursun 70 (pen), Sulun 83, Begecarslan 84)* 20,000
Schalke (1) 4 *(Wilmots 10, Hanke 63, 72, Kmetsch 67)*, Gomel (0) 0 52,441
Shakhtjor Donetsk (0) 1 *(Levandovski 78)*, FK Austria (0) 0 32,000
Siroki (0) 0, Sparta Prague (1) 1 *(Jarosik 28)* 4200
Slavia Prague (3) 5 *(Dosek 3, 40, Gedeon 8, Vachousek 53, Adauto 80)*, Mouscron (0) 1 *(Muller 83 (og))* 4000
Stabaek (1) 1 *(Wilhelmsson 4) Stenvoll*▪, Anderlecht (1) 2 *(De Bilde 12, McDonald 55)* 5990
Ujpest (0) 0, Paris St Germain (0) 1 *(Benachour 60)* 5964
Utrecht (1) 1 *(Omelyanchuk 42 (og))*, Legia (1) 3 *(Kucharski 7, Svitlica 62, 68 (pen))* 14,000
Varteks (0) 1 *(Mumiek 86)*, Midtjylland (0) 1 *(Pimpong 67)* 5000
Ventspils (1) 1 *(Landijev 16)*, Stuttgart (1) 4 *(Tiffert 22, 90, Ganea 52, Amanatidis 87)* 2000
Werder Bremen (3) 8 *(Verlaat 14, Micoud 43, 46, Borowski 45, 78, Charisteas 51, Klasnic 66, 90)*, Metalurg Donetsk (0) 0 16,300
Wisla (1) 6 *(Zurawski 16 (pen), 73, Uche 51, Jop 55, Brozek 74, Stolarczyk 84)*, Primorje (1) 1 *(Zatkovic 12)* 7000
Xanthi (0) 0, Lazio (0) 0 *Colonnese*▪ 8000
Zalaegerszeg (0) 1 *(Sabo 90)*, Dynamo Zagreb (2) 3 *(Mitu 13, Olic 41 (pen), Mucjin 75)* 10,000
Zenit (2) 2 *(Kerzhakov 1, 19)*, Grasshoppers (0) 1 *(Baturina 89)* 17,500

Tueday, 1 October 2002

Hertha Berlin (0) 1 *(Preetz 89)*

Aberdeen (0) 0 30,770

Hertha Berlin: Kiraly; Friedrich, Van Burik, Goor, Luizao (Preetz 86), Marcelinho, Roberto Pinto, Neuendorf▪, Hartmann, Marx (Dardai 57), Rehmer (Lapaczinski 80).
Aberdeen: Kjaer; McAllister, Anderson, McGuire, Bisconti (Billio 90), Darren Young, Derek Young (Fabiano 80), Mackie, Rutkiewicz, Deloumeaux▪, D'Jaffo (Mike 60).

Thurday, 3 October 2002

CSKA Sofia (0) 3 *(Gargorov 66, 88 (pen), Agnaldo 71)*

Blackburn Rovers (1) 3 *(Thompson 31, Ostenstad 56, Duff 57)* 21,000

CSKA Sofia: Petrov; Stefanov, Carlos, Yanchev, Gueye, Ivanov (Yanev 83), Georgiev, Brito (Gargorov 61), Mukasi (Agnaldo 61), Dimitrov▪, Charras.
Blackburn Rovers: Friedel; Neill, Johansson, Taylor, Berg, Tugay (Gillespie 62), Thompson, Dunn, Cole (Mahon 85), Ostenstad (Grabbi 60), Duff.

Fulham (2) 2 *(Marlet 20, Malbranque 44 (pen))*

Hajduk Split (2) 2 *(Dolonga 6, Vejic 40)* 18,500

Fulham: Van der Sar; Ouaddou, Brevett, Melville, Knight, Davis, Legwinski, Malbranque, Marlet, Sava (Hayles 74), Boa Morte (Inamoto 67).
Hajduk Split: Pletikosa; Vukovic, Dolonga, Bule, Vejic, Neretljak, Miladin, Srna, Deranja (Radunica 71), Andric, Carevic (Mise 84).

Livingston (1) 4 *(Wilson 32 (pen), 90, Xausa 56, Andrews 77)*

Sturm Graz (1) 3 *(Szabics 45, 54, Mujiri 48)* 5208

Livingston: Broto; McNamee, Bollan, Rubio, Andrews, Quinovert (Toure-Marman 82), Hart, O'Brien (Camacho Barnola 55), Wilson, Xausa (Zarate 63), Bingham.
Sturm Graz: Hoffmann; Neukirchner, Mahlich, Strafner, Brzeczek, Golemac, Wetl, Masudi (Heldt 71), Szabics (Korsos 64), Mujiri, Dag.

Metalurg Zapor (1) 1 *(Modebadze 24)*

Leeds United (0) 1 *(Barmby 77)* 7000

Metalurg Zapor: Glushchenko; Valuta, Visevic, Akopyan, Dodic, Raty, Vasconcios, Milosavljevic▪, Modebadze, Lapko, Klyuchyk.
Leeds United: Robinson; Kelly, Harte, Bakke, Mills, Matteo (Duberry 90), Bowyer, McPhail, Smith, Kewell, Barmby.

Rangers (1) 3 *(De Boer 43, 59, McCann 97)*

Viktoria Zizkov (0) 1 *(Licka 100)* 47,646

Rangers: Klos; Ricksen, Moore, Amoruso, Numan, Ferguson, Arteta, Konterman (Muscat 67), Lovenkrands (McCann 91), Arveladze (Ross 25), De Boer (Caniggia 99).
Viktoria Zizkov: Kucera; Buryan▪, Mlejnsky, Klimpl, Janousek (Kroty 67), Smarda, Sabou, Scasny, Pikl, Straceny, Chihuri (Licka 98).
aet.

Sartid (0) 0

Ipswich Town (1) 1 *(Bent M 9 (pen))* 16,500

Sartid: Zilic; Bogdanovic (Djokic 25), Savic (Kocic 56), Paunovic, Spasic, Socanac, Vaskovic, Radosavljevic, Mirosavljevic, Zecevic, Kizic (Kulic 46).
Ipswich Town: Marshall; Makin, Clapham, Brown, McGreal, Magilton, Wright, Holland, Counago (Bent D 84), Bent M, George (Miller T 64).

Suduva (0) 0

Celtic (2) 2 *(Fernandez 12, Thompson 34)* 1200

Suduva: Padimanskas; Sendzikas (Krapavicius 46), Devetinas, Kunevicius, Grigas, Adomaitus (Maciulis 68), Suliaskas (Sidlauskas 81), Zitinskas, Larcenka, Slavickas, Radzinevicius.
Celtic: Gould; McNamara (Miller 55), Thompson, Hartson, Fernandez, Petta (Lynch 79), Agathe, Healy, Maloney, Crainey, Kennedy (Smith 66).

Viking (2) 4 *(Berre 9, Kopteff 34, Nevland 60, 87)*

Chelsea (1) 2 *(Lampard 45, Terry 62)* 5500

Viking: Olsen; Dahl, Periera, Sanne, Kuivasto, Hangeland, Nygaard, Fuglestad, Berre, Nevland, Kopteff (Wright 82).
Chelsea: Cudicini; Gallas, Le Saux, Petit (Morris 60), Terry, Huth, Gronkjaer, Lampard, Hasselbaink (Gudjohnsen 80), Zola, Stanic (Zenden 89).

SECOND ROUND, FIRST LEG

Alaves (0) 1 *(Abelardo 90)*, Besiktas (1) 1 *(Karmona 31 (og))* 11,000
Anderlecht (0) 3 *(Jestrovic 55, 60 (pen), From 71 (og))*, Midtjylland (0) 1 *(Kristensen 80)* 16,000
Apoel (0) 0, Hertha Berlin (0) 1 *(Karwan 90)* 4178
FK Austria (0) 0, Porto (0) 1 *(Derlei 70)* 29,200
Boavista (1) 2 *(Pereira Silva 30, Eder 49)*, Anorthosis (0) 1 *(Michalski 87)* 3000
Celta Vigo (2) 3 *(Ignacio 33, Edu 37, McCarthy 77)*, Viking (0) 0 22,000
Djurgaarden (0) 0, Bordeaux (0) 1 *(Feindouno 64)* 13,558
Fenerbahce (1) 1 *(Washington 43)*, Panathinaikos (1) 1 *(Basinas 15)* 50,000
Ferencvaros (0) 0, Stuttgart (0) 0 14,000
Lazio (1) 1 *(Fiore 7)*, Red Star Belgrade (0) 0 16,511
Legia (0) 2 *(Dudek 58, Svitlica 63 (pen))*, Schalke (0) 3 *(Varela 50, 54, Sand 90)* 13,000
Malaga (1) 2 *(Romero 39, Dely Valdes 66)*, Amica (1) 1 *(Krol 1)* 18,000
National (0) 0, Paris St Germain (1) 2 *(Leroy 6, Luiz 67)* *J Leroy*■ 14,000
PAOK Salonika (1) 2 *(Chasiotis 3, Yiasoumi 47)*, Grasshoppers (0) 1 *(Nunez 63 (pen))* 19,000
Parma (1) 2 *(Donati 25, Mutu 73)*, Wisla (0) 1 *(Zurawski 46)* 6936
Partizan Belgrade (2) 3 *(Lazovic 4, Ilic 32, Vukic 69)*, Slavia Prague (0) 1 *(Dostalek 56)* 18,000
Sparta Prague (1) 1 *(Jarosik 20)*, Denizli (0) 0 5778
Sturm Graz (1) 1 *(Szabics 10)*, Levski (0) 0 *Vieira*■ 5400
Viktoria Zizkov (0) 0, Betis (1) 1 *(Denilson 45)* 4500
Vitesse (1) 2 *(Amoah 37, Verlaat 63 (og))*, Werder Bremen (1) 1 *(Verlaat 43)* 19,300

Thursday, 31 October 2002

Celtic (0) 1 *(Larsson 85)*

Blackburn Rovers (0) 0 59,553

Celtic: Douglas; Agathe (Sylla 80), Thompson, Valgaeren, Balde, Laursen, Lambert (Hartson 75), Lennon, Sutton, Larsson, Petrov.
Blackburn Rovers: Friedel; Neill, Johansson, Short, Taylor, Tugay, Thompson, Flitcroft, Ostenstad (Cole 46), Yorke, Duff (Dunn 67).

Dynamo Zagreb (0) 0

Fulham (1) 3 *(Boa Morte 35, Marlet 59, Hayles 77)* 30,000

Dynamo Zagreb: Butina; Mikic, Krznar, Sedloski, Smoje, Polovanec■, Maric, Agic, Balaban (Petrovic 64), Olic, Mitu.
Fulham: Van der Sar; Ouaddou, Brevett, Melville, Goma, Djetou (Inamoto 59), Finnan, Legwinski, Marlet (Hayles 65), Boa Morte (Stolcers 71), Malbranque.

Ipswich Town (0) 1 *(Bent D 69)*

Slovan Liberec (0) 0 16,138

Ipswich Town: Marshall; Makin, Hreidarsson, Brown, McGreal (Gaardso 36), Holland, Magilton, Ambrose (George 78), Counago (Bent D 64), Armstrong, Clapham.
Slovan Liberec: Kinsky; Zapotocny, Janu, Polak, Holenak, Lukas, Capek (Slovak 74), Hodur (Ancic 78), Slepicka (Gyan 57), Nezmar, Zboncak.

Leeds United (0) 1 *(Kewell 82)*

Hapoel Tel Aviv (0) 0 31,867

Leeds United: Robinson; Kelly, Harte, Bakke, Radebe, Woodgate, Dacourt (McPhail 65), Smith, Viduka (Mills 90), Kewell, Barmby (Bridges 70).
Hapoel Tel Aviv: Elimelech; Helis, Antebi, Halmai (Abutbul 65), Domb, Gershon, Affek, Abuksis, Welton (Clescenco 59), Balili (Udi 84), Tuaama.

SECOND ROUND, SECOND LEG

Amica (1) 1 *(Gesior 16)*, Malaga (1) 2 *(Silva 20, Musampa 72)* 3000
Anorthosis (0) 0, Boavista (0) 1 *(Silva 90 (pen)) Ico*■ 7000
Besiktas (1) 1 *(Ilhan 7) Ilhan*■, Alaves (0) 0 *Tellez*■ 28,500
Betis (1) 3 *(Casas 45, Joaquin 56 (pen), Tomas 86)*, Viktoria Zizkov (0) 0 10,000
Bordeaux (1) 2 *(Feindouno 36, 50)*, Djurgaarden (0) 1 *(Elmander 72)* 10,650
Denizli (1) 2 *(Ozkan 23, 54 (pen))*, Sparta Prague (0) 0 14,000
Grasshoppers (1) 1 *(Cabanas 45)*, PAOK Salonika (0) 1 *(Markos 90)* 6600
Hertha Berlin (2) 4 *(Preetz 7, Marcelinho 13, Beinlich 61, Luizao 67)*, Apoel (0) 0 10,483
Levski (1) 1 *(Simonovic 6)*, Sturm Graz (0) 0 *Rojas*■ *(aet; Sturm Graz won 8-7 on penalties)*. 30,000
Midtjylland (0) 0, Anderlecht (1) 3 *(Seol 11, Jestrovic 83, Dindane 90)* 4464
Panathinaikos (3) 4 *(Liberopoulos 24, Goumas 31, Michaelsen 43, Warzycha 90)*, Fenerbahce (1) 1 *(Sanli 37)* 12,000
Paris St Germain (0) 1 *(Leroy 56)*, National (0) 0 15,000
Porto (1) 2 *(Helder Postiga 29, Derlei 86)*, FK Austria (0) 0 15,000
Red Star Belgrade (0) 1 *(Boskovic 70)*, Lazio (0) 1 *(Chiesa 78)* 60,000
Schalke (0) 0, Legia (0) 0 52,260
Slavia Prague (2) 5 *(Vachousek 11, 41, Petrous 87 (pen), Gedeon 94, Adauto 110)*, Partizan Belgrade (0) 1 *(Ivic 90) Bajic*■ *(aet)*. 8563
Stuttgart (0) 2 *(Amanatidis 65, Meira 90 (pen))*, Ferencvaros (0) 0 *Lipcsei*■ 15,000
Viking (0) 1 *(Sigurdsson 84)*, Celta Vigo (0) 1 *(Mostovoi 75)* 5555
Werder Bremen (1) 3 *(Baumann 24, Krstajic 49, Charisteas 77)*, Vitesse (0) 3 *(Levchenko 50 (pen), Peeters 73, Mbamba 90) Rankovic*■ 19,300
Wisla (0) 4 *(Kosowski 71, Zurawski 80, 94, Dubicki 107)*, Parma (1) 1 *(Adriano 6) (aet)*. 9500

Thursday, 14 November 2002

Blackburn Rovers (0) 0

Celtic (1) 2 *(Larsson 15, Sutton 68)* 29,698

Blackburn Rovers: Friedel; Neill, Curtis (Gillespie 46), Short, Johansson, Tugay, Thompson, Dunn, Cole, Yorke (Jansen 64), Duff.
Celtic: Douglas; Agathe (Sylla 83), Guppy, Valgaeren, Balde, Laursen, Petrov (Thompson 77), Lennon, Hartson (Lambert 68), Larsson, Sutton.

Fulham (0) 2 *(Malbranque 89, Boa Morte 90)*

Dynamo Zagreb (0) 1 *(Olic 52)* 7700

Fulham: Van der Sar; Finnan, Brevett, Melville, Goma, Clark (Djetou 73), Goldbaek, Legwinski, Sava (Marlet 60), Boa Morte, Inamoto (Malbranque 64).
Dynamo Zagreb: Turina; Mikic, Krznar, Sedloski, Smoje, Cesar, Kranjcar (Juric 76), Balaban, Agic, Olic, Mitu.

Hapoel Tel Aviv (1) 1 *(Abuksis 2)* 3000

Leeds United (1) 4 *(Smith 30, 54, 62, 83)*

Hapoel Tel Aviv: Elimelech; Helis, Hilel, Halmai, Domb, Gershon, Affek (Luz 46), Abuksis■, Clescenco (Udi 46), Knafo (Balili 62), Tuaama.
Leeds United: Robinson; Kelly (Richardson 65), Harte, Bakke (McPhail 55), Radebe (Kilgallon 62), Duberry, Barmby, Bowyer, Smith, Kewell, Wilcox.
(in Florence).

Slovan Liberec (0) 1 *(Gyan 88)*

Ipswich Town (0) 0 6509

Slovan Liberec: Kinsky; Johana, Janu, Polak (Blaha 81), Holenak, Lukas, Papousek, Hodur, Nezmar (Slovak 56), Baffour, Zboncak (Ancic 63).
Ipswich Town: Marshall; Wilnis, Hreidarsson, Makin, McGreal, Gaardsoe, Wright, Ambrose (Holland 61), Counago (Bent D 51), Armstrong (George 81), Clapham.
(aet; Slovan Liberec won 4-2 on penalties).

THIRD ROUND, FIRST LEG

AEK Athens (4) 4 *(Georgatos 13, Nikolaidis 23, Petkov 30, Zagorakis 37)*, Maccabi Haifa (0) 0 19,000
Besiktas (1) 3 *(Pancu 30, Gularo 71, Nouma 83)*, Dynamo Kiev (1) 1 *(Rincon 29)* 28,000
Betis (1) 1 *(Alfonso 9 (pen))*, Auxerre (0) 0 28,000
Bordeaux (0) 0, Anderlecht (1) 2 *(Jestrovic 9, Hasi 90)* 12,180
FC Brugge (1) 1 *(Van der Heyden 42) Maertens*■, Stuttgart (0) 2 *(Balakov 71, Kuranyi 89)* 18,500
Denizli (0) 0, Lyon (0) 0 15,000
PAOK Salonika (0) 1 *(Georgiadis 51)*, Slavia Prague (0) 0 10,000
Paris St Germain (2) 2 *(Nyarko 17, Florese 45) Dehu*■, Boavista (0) 1 *(Barros 75)* 20,000
Porto (2) 3 *(Helder Postiga 36, 45, Jankauskas 87)*, Lens (0) 0 40,000

Slovan Liberec (1) 2 *(Zboncak 44, Slovak 85 (pen))*, Panathinaikos (1) 2 *(Basinas 13 (pen), Olisadebe 53)* 5805
Sturm Graz (1) 1 *(Amoah 44)*, Lazio (0) 3 *(Chiesa 46, Inzaghi 57, 87)* 15,360
Wisla (1) 1 *(Poulsen 39 (og))*, Schalke (0) 1 *(Mpenza 80)* 10,300

Tuesday, 26 November 2002

Hertha Berlin (0) 2 *(Beinlich 26, Sava 68 (og))*

Fulham (0) 1 *(Marlet 53)* 14,477

Hertha Berlin: Schmidt (Simunic 59); Hartmann, Friedrich, Van Burik, Nene, Beinlich (Roberto Pinto 90), Marcelinho, Goor, Alves (Preetz 59), Dardai.
Fulham: Van der Sar; Finnan, Brevett, Melville, Goma, Davis, Goldbaek (Boa Morte 46), Djetou, Marlet, Sava, Malbranque (Inamoto 79).

Thursday, 28 November 2002

Celtic (0) 1 *(Larsson 52)*

Celta Vigo (0) 0 53,726

Celtic: Douglas; Valgaeren, Guppy (Thompson 83), Agathe (Sylla 85), Balde, Laursen, Sutton, Lennon, Hartson, Larsson, Petrov.
Celta Vigo: Pinto; Silvinho, Berizzo, Mostovoi, Gustavo Lopez (McCarthy 83), Juanfran, Jose Ignacio, Mendez Pardifias, Sergio, Luccin, Catanha (Edu 49).

Malaga (0) 0

Leeds United (0) 0 35,000

Malaga: Contreras; Josemi, Valcarce, Marcelo Romero, Fernando Sanz, Roteta, Manu (Edgar 62), Sandro, Dely Valdes, Musampa, Iznata (Koke 62).
Leeds United: Robinson; Kelly, Harte, Bakke, Woodgate, Duberry, Bowyer, McPhail, Smith, Kewell, Wilcox.

Vitesse (0) 0

Liverpool (1) 1 *(Owen 26)* 28,000

Vitesse: Jevric; Cornelisse, Frankel (Sone 78), Levchenko, Zeman, Stefanovic, Mustapha, Janssen T, Amoah, Mbamba (Rojer 78), Claessens.
Liverpool: Dudek; Babbel, Traore, Gerrard, Henchoz, Hyypia, Murphy, Diao, Baros (Heskey 74), Owen, Cheyrou (Smicer 9).

THIRD ROUND, SECOND LEG

Anderlecht (1) 2 *(Dindane 28, Jestrovic 67)*, Bordeaux (0) 2 *(Darcheville 83, 89)* 17,721
Auxerre (1) 2 *(Tainio 18, Lachuer 48)*, Betis (0) 0 12,000
Boavista (0) 1 *(Elpidio 54 (pen)) Claudio*■, Paris St Germain (0) 0 5500
Dynamo Kiev (0) 0, Besiktas (0) 0 22,000
Lazio (0) 0, Sturm Graz (0) 1 *(Szabics 86)* 3958
Lens (1) 1 *(Song 28)*, Porto (0) 0 35,026
Lyon (0) 0, Denizli (1) 1 *(Ozkan 3)* 29,000
Maccabi Haifa (1) 1 *(Badir 5 (pen))*, AEK Athens (0) 4 *(Katsouranis 56, Lakis 79, 89, Nalitzis 90)* 3000
(in Nicosia).
Panathinaikos (1) 1 *(Fyssas 2)*, Slovan Liberec (0) 0 11,000
Schalke (1) 1 *(Hajto 42)*, Wisla (1) 4 *(Zurawski 40, 85, Uche 51, Kosowski 90)* 50,830
Slavia Prague (1) 4 *(Skacel 13, Vachousek 51, Kuka 89, 90)*, PAOK Salonika (0) 0 8563
Stuttgart (0) 1 *(Hleb 90)*, FC Brugge (0) 0 34,000

Thursday, 12 December 2002

Celta Vigo (1) 2 *(Jesuli 24, McCarthy 54)*

Celtic (1) 1 *(Hartson 37)* 17,000

Celta Vigo: Pinto; Mendez (Cavallero 59), Juanfran, Jose Ignacio, Caceres, Berizzo (Vagner 84), Jesuli, Luccin, McCarthy, Edu, Gustavo Lopez.
Celtic: Douglas; Agathe, Thompson, Valgaeren, Balde, Laursen, Lennon (Lambert 53), Sutton, Hartson (McNamara 61), Larsson, Petrov.

Fulham (0) 0

Hertha Berlin (0) 0 15,161

Fulham: Taylor; Finnan, Brevett (Goldbaek 71), Melville, Goma, Davis (Inamoto 62), Malbranque, Djetou (Legwinski 46), Marlet, Boa Morte, Wome.
Hertha Berlin: Kiraly; Rehmer, Nene, Dardai, Friedrich, Simunic (Van Burik 8), Goor, Neuendorf (Schmidt 73), Luizao (Preetz 81), Marcelinho, Hartmann.

Leeds United (1) 1 *(Bakke 23)*

Malaga (1) 2 *(Dely Valdes 14, 80)* 34,123

Leeds United: Robinson; Mills, Kelly, Bakke, Woodgate, Duberry, Bowyer, Okon, Smith, Bridges (Fowler 9), Wilcox.
Malaga: Contreras; Josemi, Valcarce, Marcelo Romero, Fernando Sanz, Roteta, Manu (Sandro 57), Gerardo, Dario Silva, Dely Valdes (Litos 90), Musampa (Miguel Angel 78).

Liverpool (1) 1 *(Owen 21)*

Vitesse (0) 0 23,576

Liverpool: Kirkland; Carragher, Traore, Diao (Hamann 68), Henchoz, Hyypia, Murphy, Gerrard, Diouf (Riise 78), Owen, Smicer (Baros 88).
Vitesse: Jevric; Cornelisse, Frankel (Mustapha 35), Janssen T, Jansen M, Stefanovic, Levchenko, Amoah (Dingsdag 68), Mbamba, Peeters, Claessens.

FOURTH ROUND, FIRST LEG

Hertha Berlin (2) 3 *(Alves 15, 42, Van Burik 90)*, Boavista (1) 2 *(Rui Oscar 37, Goulart 80)* 15,559
Lazio (2) 3 *(Lazetic 22, Jop 45 (og), Chiesa 70)*, Wisla (1) 3 *(Uche 39, Zurawski 49 (pen), 63)* 16,004
Malaga (0) 0, AEK Athens (0) 0 9700
Panathinaikos (1) 3 *(Olisadebe 12, 73, Liberopoulos 63)*, Anderlecht (0) 0 16,000
Porto (0) 6 *(Capucho 49, Derlei 53, Ricardo Costa 67, Jankauskas 69, Deco 72, Alenichev 82)*, Denizli (0) 1 *(Kratochvil 78)* 21,500
Slavia Prague (0) 1 *(Dosek T 62)*, Besiktas (0) 0 *Zago*■ 12,357

Thursday, 20 February 2003

Auxerre (0) 0

Liverpool (0) 1 *(Hyypia 73)* 20,452

Auxerre: Cool; Radet, Jaures, Tainio, Mexes, Boumsong, Mathis, Faye, Mwaruwari, Lachuer, Fadiga.
Liverpool: Dudek; Carragher, Traore, Gerrard, Henchoz (Diao 69), Hyypia, Murphy, Diouf, Heskey, Owen (Baros 90), Riise.

Celtic (2) 3 *(Lambert 36, Maloney 45, Petrov 68)*

Stuttgart (1) 1 *(Kuranyi 27)* 60,832

Celtic: Douglas; Agathe, Thompson (Smith 69), McNamara, Balde (Laursen 87), Valgaeren, Lambert, Lennon, Sutton, Maloney, Petrov.
Stuttgart: Hildebrand; Hinkel, Gerber, Soldo, Meira, Bordon■, Meissner (Rundio 75), Hleb (Carnell 51), Kuranyi, Amanatidis (Dangelmayr 19), Balakov.

FOURTH ROUND, SECOND LEG

AEK Athens (0) 0, Malaga (1) 1 *(Manu 28)* 18,000
Anderlecht (0) 2 *(Jestrovic 71, 81)*, Panathinaikos (0) 0 *Vokolos*■, *Konstantinidis*■ 14,000
Besiktas (1) 4 *(Pancu 42, Ronaldo 61, Ahmet Dursun 66, Ilhan 69)*, Slavia Prague (0) 2 *(Dostalek 77 (pen), Hrdlicka 84)* 27,500
Boavista (0) 1 *(Avalos 86) Anunciacao*■, Hertha Berlin (0) 0 *Dardai*■ 5500
Denizli (0) 2 *(Martin 52, Ozkan 58)*, Porto (1) 2 *(Derlei 43, Clayton 87)* 4300
Wisla (1) 1 *(Kuzba 4)*, Lazio (1) 2 *(Fernando Couto 21, Chiesa 54)* 10,000

Thursday, 27 February 2003

Liverpool (0) 2 *(Owen 67, Murphy 73)*

Auxerre (0) 0 34,252

Liverpool: Dudek; Carragher, Traore (Smicer 46), Gerrard, Henchoz (Biscan 77), Hyypia, Murphy, Diouf (Hamann 62), Heskey, Owen, Riise.
Auxerre: Cool; Radet, Jaures, Lachuer, Mexes, Boumsong, Mathis, Tainio, Cisse (Mwaruwari 77), Faye, Fadiga (Akale 77).

Stuttgart (1) 3 *(Tiffert 37, Hleb 75, Mutzel 87)*

Celtic (2) 2 *(Thompson 12, Sutton 14)* 50,348

Stuggart: Hildebrand; Hinkel, Gerber (Seitz 80), Soldo, Wenzel, Dangelmayr (Ganea 46), Tiffert (Mutzel 65), Balakov, Kuranyi, Amanatidis, Hleb.
Celtic: Douglas; Agathe, Thompson, Valgaeren, Balde, Laursen, Lambert (Maloney 82), Lennon, Hartson, Sutton (McNamara 86), Petrov.

QUARTER-FINALS, FIRST LEG

Lazio (0) 1 *(Inzaghi 55)*, Besiktas (0) 0 17,133
Malaga (1) 1 *(Dely Valdes 17)*, Boavista (0) 0 13,000
Porto (0) 0, Panathinaikos (0) 1 *(Olisadebe 72)* 44,310

Thursday, 13 March 2003

Celtic (1) 1 *(Larsson 3)*

Liverpool (1) 1 *(Heskey 17)* 59,759

Celtic: Douglas; Smith, Thompson (Guppy 26), Mjallby, Balde, Valgaeren, Lennon, Sutton, Hartson, Larsson (Lambert 76), Petrov.
Liverpool: Dudek; Carragher, Riise, Hamann, Traore, Hyypia, Gerrard, Diouf (Biscan 90), Heskey, Owen, Murphy.

QUARTER-FINALS, SECOND LEG

Besiktas (0) 1 *(Sergen 83)*, Lazio (2) 2 *(Fiore 5, Castroman 9)* 28,000
Boavista (0) 1 *(Luiz Claudio 83)*, Malaga (0) 0 *Sandro*▪ *(aet; Boavista won 4-1 on penalties).* 8500
Panathinaikos (0) 0, Porto (1) 2 *(Derlei 16, 103) (aet)* 15,000

Thursday, 20 March 2003

Liverpool (0) 0

Celtic (1) 2 *(Thompson 45, Hartson 81)* 44,238

Liverpool: Dudek; Carragher, Riise, Hamann, Traore, Hyypia, Murphy, Gerrard, Heskey, Owen, Smicer (Baros 56).
Celtic: Douglas; Sylla (Smith 86), Thompson, Mjallby, Balde, Valgaeren, Lennon, Lambert (McNamara 73), Hartson, Larsson, Petrov.

SEMI-FINALS, FIRST LEG

Porto (2) 4 *(Maniche 10, Derlei 27, 50, Helder Postiga 56)*, Lazio (1) 1 *(Lopez 5)* 45,518

Thursday, 10 April 2003

Celtic (0) 1 *(Larsson 50)*

Boavista (0) 1 *(Valgaeren 49 (og))* 60,000

Celtic: Douglas; Agathe (Sylla 74), Thompson, Mjallby, Balde, Valgaeren, Lambert, Lennon, Hartson, Larsson, Petrov (Fernandez 77).
Boavista: Ricardo; Martelinho, Loja, Pedrosa (Jorge Couto 89), Paulo Turra, Eder, Avalos, Anunciacao, Duda, Claudio (Cafu 46) (Bosingwa 81), Erivan.

SEMI-FINALS, SECOND LEG

Lazio (0) 0, *Cesar*▪ Porto (0) 0 *Helder Postiga*▪ 69,873

Thursday, 24 April 2003

Boavista (0) 0

Celtic (0) 1 *(Larsson 80)* 11,000

Boavista: Ricardo; Martelinho, Loja, Pedrosa (Yuri 84), Santos, Eder, Avalos, Erivan (Jocivalter 80), Duda, Silva (Claudio 68), Anunciacao.
Celtic: Douglas; Agathe, Thompson, Mjallby, Balde, Valgaeren (Smith 74), Lambert (Sutton 34), Lennon, Hartson, Larsson, Petrov.

UEFA CUP FINAL 2003

Wednesday, 21 May 2003

(in Seville, 52,972)

Celtic (0) 2

Porto (1) 3 *(aet)*

Celtic: Douglas; Agathe, Thompson, Mjallby, Balde▪, Valgaeren (Laursen 64), Lambert (McNamara 76), Lennon, Sutton, Larsson, Petrov (Maloney 104).
Scorers: Larsson 47, 57.
Porto: Vitor Baia; Ferreira P, Valente▪, Costinha (Ricardo Costa 9), Jorge Costa (Emanuel 71), Deco, Alenichev, Capucho (Ferreira M 98), Derlei, Maniche.
Scorers: Derlei 45, 115, Alenichev 54.
Referee: Michel (Slovakia).

Henrik Larsson gives Celtic some real hope in the UEFA Cup final against Porto with his team's and his own second goal, towering above the opposition. But the Portuguese snatched victory in extra time. (Colorsport)

UEFA CHAMPIONS LEAGUE 2003–04 DRAW

LIST OF PARTICIPATING TEAMS

IOC	*Stage*	*Club*
–	Grp	AC Milan – holders
ESP	Grp	Real Sociedad
ESP	Grp	Real Madrid CF
ESP	Q3	RC Deportivo La Coruña
ESP	Q3	RC Celta de Vigo
ITA	Grp	Juventus FC
ITA	Grp	Internazionale FC
ITA	Q3	S.S. Lazio
ENG	Grp	Manchester United FC
ENG	Grp	Arsenal FC
ENG	Q3	Newcastle United FC
ENG	Q3	Chelsea FC
GER	Grp	FC Bayern München
GER	Grp	VfB Stuttgart
GER	Q3	BV Borussia Dortmund
FRA	Grp	Olympique Lyonnais
FRA	Grp	AS Monaco FC
FRA	Q3	Olympique de Marseille
GRE	Grp	Olympiakos Piraeus FC
GRE	Grp	Panathinaikos FC
GRE	Q3	AEK Athens FC
HOL	Grp	PSV Eindhoven FC
HOL	Q3	AFC Ajax
TUR	Grp	Besiktas JK
TUR	Q3	Galatasaray SK
POR	Grp	FC Porto
POR	Q3	SL Benfica
RUS	Q3	FC Lokomotiv Moskva
RUS	Q2	PFC CSKA Moskva
CZE	Q3	AC Sparta Praha
CZE	Q2	SK Slavia Praha
SCO	Q3	Rangers FC
SCO	Q2	Celtic FC
UKR	Q3	FC Dynamo Kyiv
UKR	Q2	FC Shakhtar Donetsk
BEL	Q3	Club Brugge KV
BEL	Q2	RSC Anderlecht
AUT	Q3	FK Austria Wien
AUT	Q2	Grazer AK
SUI	Q3	Grasshopper-Club
NOR	Q2	Rosenborg BK
ISR	Q2	Maccabi Tel-Aviv
CRO	Q2	NK Dinamo Zagreb
POL	Q2	Wisla Kraków
DEN	Q2	FC København
SWE	Q2	Djurgårdens IF
SMN	Q2	FK Partizan
SVK	Q2	Zilina
BUL	Q2	PFC CSKA Sofia
ROM	Q2	FC Rapid Bucuresti
HUN	Q2	MTK Hungária FC
SLO	Q2	NK Maribor
CYP	Q1	Omonia Nicosia FC
FIN	Q1	HJK Helsinki
LAT	Q1	FC Skonto
GEO	Q1	FC Dinamo Tbilisi
MOL	Q1	FC Sheriff Tiraspol
ISL	Q1	KR Reykjavík
BLS	Q1	FC BATE Borisov
LIT	Q1	FBK Kaunas
IRL	Q1	Bohemians FC
MKD	Q1	FK Vardar
MLT	Q1	Sliema Wanderers FC
WAL	Q1	Barry Town AFC
EST	Q1	FC Flora
BHZ	Q1	FK Leotar
ARM	Q1	FC Pyunik
NIR	Q1	Glentoran FC
ALB	Q1	SK Tirana
FAR	Q1	HB Tórshavn
LUX	Q1	CS Grevenmacher
KAZ	Q1	FC Irtysh Pavlodar

UEFA CHAMPIONS LEAGUE FIRST QUALIFYING ROUND DRAW

First-leg matches: 16 July
Second-leg matches: 23 July

Match
1 FC Pyunik (ARM) v KR Reykjavík (ISL)
2 FC Sheriff (MOL) v FC Flora (EST)
3 HB Tórshavn (FAR) v FBK Kaunas (LIT)
4 FC BATE Borisov (BLS) v Bohemians FC (IRL)
5 FK Vardar (MKD) v Barry Town AFC (WAL)
6 CS Grevenmacher (LUX) v FK Leotar (BHZ)
7 HJK Helsinki (FIN) v Glentoran FC (NIR)
8 Sliema Wanderers FC (MLT) v FC Skonto (LAT)
9 Omonia AC (CYP) v FC Irtysh Pavlodar (KAZ)
10 FC Dinamo Tbilisi (GEO) v SK Tirana (ALB)

UEFA CHAMPIONS LEAGUE SECOND QUALIFYING ROUND DRAW

First-leg matches: 30 July 2003
Second-leg matches: 6 August 2003

MTK Hungária FC (HUN) v Winners match 7
Winners match 1 v PFC CSKA Sofia (BUL)
Winners match 3 v Celtic FC (SCO)
Winners match 6 v SK Slavia Praha (CZE)
Winners match 2 v FC Shakhtar Donetsk (UKR)
Zilina (SVK) v Maccabi Tel-Aviv FC (ISR)
Winners match 4 v Rosenborg BK (NOR)
NK Maribor (SLO) v NK Dinamo Zagreb (CRO)
PFC CSKA Moskva (RUS) v Winners match 5
AFC Rapid Bucuresti (ROM) v RSC Anderlecht (BEL)
FK Partizan (YUG) v Djurgårdens IF (SWE)
Wisla Kraków (POL) v Winners match 9
FC København v Winners match 8
Winners match 10 v Grazer AK (AUT)

UEFA CUP 2003–04 DRAW

LIST OF BRITISH & IRISH PARTICIPATING TEAMS

Southampton, Liverpool, Blackburn Rovers, Manchester City (Fair Play), Derry City, Shelbourne, Coleraine, Portadown, Dundee (beaten finalists), Heart of Midlothian, Cwmbran Town, TNS Llansantffraid.

UEFA CUP QUALIFYING ROUND

First leg: 14 August
Second leg: 28 August

AIK Solna (SWE) v Fylkir (ISL)
KS Vllaznia (ALB) v Dundee FC (SCO)
FC Levadia Maardu (EST) v NK Varteks (CRO)
FC Santa Coloma (AND) v Esbjerg fB (DEN)*
NK Zeljeznicar (NHZ) v Anorthosis Famagusta FC (CYP)
FC Banants (ARM) v Hapoel Tel-Aviv FC (ISR)
Brøndby IF (DEN)* v FC Dinamo Minsk (BLS)
Malmö FF (SWE) v Portadown FC (NIR)
FC Dinamo Bucuresti (ROM) v FHK Liepajas Metalurgs (LAT)
Valletta FC (MLT) v Neuchâtel Xamax FC (SUI)
FC Kärnten (AUT) v Grindavík (ISL)
FK Viktoria Zizkov (CZE) v FC Zhenis Astana (KAZ)
FK Sarajevo (BHZ) v FK Sartid (SMN)
APOEL Nicosia FC (CYP) v Derry City FC (IRL)
PFC Litex Lovech (BUL) v CSF Zimbru Chisinau (MOL)
FC Neman Grodno (BLS) v FC Steaua Bucuresti (ROM)
FC Etzella Ettelbrück (LUX) v NK Kamen Ingrad (CRO)
Manchester City FC v Total Network Solutions FC (WAL)
Molde FK (NOR) v KÍ Klaksvík (FAR)
Odense BK (DEN)* v FC TVMK Tallinn (EST)
FK Ventspils (LAT) v Wisla Plock (POL)
Myllykosken Pallo-47 (FIN) v BSC Young Boys (SUI)
FC Vaduz (LIE) v FC Dnipro Dnipropetrovsk (UKR)
Coleraine FC (NIR) v UD Leiria (POR)
Groclin Grodzisk Wielkopolski (POL) v FK Atlantas (LIT)
KS Dinamo Tirana (ALB) v K. Sporting Lokeren OV (BEL)
Cwmbran Town FC (WAL) v Maccabi Haifa FC (ISR)
NK Publikum (SLO) v FK Belasica GC (MKD)
FK Cementarnica 55 (MKD) v GKS Katowice (POL)
Púchov (SVK) v FC Sioni Bolnisi (GEO)
FK Crvena Zvezda (SMN) v FC Nistru Otaci (MOL)
FK Ekranas (LIT) v Debreceni VSC (HUN)
Birkirkara FC (MLT) v Ferencvárosi TC (HUN)
FC Haka (FIN) v HNK Hajduk Split (CRO)
FC Torpedo Moskva (RUS) v SP Domagnano (SMR)
FK Atyrau (KAZ) v PFC Levski Sofia (BUL)
NK Olimpija Ljubljana (SLO) v Shelbourne FC (IRL)
RC Lens (FRA) v FC Torpedo Kutaisi (GEO)
Farum (DEN) v FC Shirak (ARM)
FC Artmedia Petrzalka (SVK) v F91 Dudelange (LUX)
NSÍ Runavík (FAR) v SFK Lyn (NOR)

SUMMARY OF APPEARANCES

EUROPEAN CUP AND CHAMPIONS LEAGUE (1955–2003)

ENGLISH CLUBS
14 Liverpool, Manchester U
7 Arsenal
4 Leeds U
3 Nottingham F
2 Derby Co, Wolverhampton W, Everton, Aston Villa, Newcastle U
1 Burnley, Tottenham H, Ipswich T, Manchester C, Blackburn R, Chelsea

SCOTTISH CLUBS
22 Rangers
18 Celtic
3 Aberdeen
2 Hearts
1 Dundee, Dundee U, Kilmarnock, Hibernian

WELSH CLUBS
5 Barry T
1 Cwmbran T, TNS

NORTHERN IRELAND CLUBS
20 Linfield
9 Glentoran
3 Crusaders, Portadown
1 Glenavon, Ards, Distillery, Derry C, Coleraine, Cliftonville

EIRE CLUBS
7 Shamrock R, Dundalk
6 Waterford
4 Shelbourne
3 Bohemians, Drumcondra, St Patrick's Ath,
2 Sligo R, Limerick, Athlone T, Derry C*
1 Cork Hibs, Cork Celtic, Cork City

Winners: Celtic 1966–67; Manchester U 1967–68, 1998–99; Liverpool 1976–77, 1977–78, 1980–81, 1983–84; Nottingham F 1978–79, 1979–80; Aston Villa 1981–82

Finalists: Celtic 1969–70; Leeds U 1974–75; Liverpool 1984–85

EUROPEAN CUP-WINNERS' CUP (1960–99)

ENGLISH CLUBS
6 Tottenham H
5 Manchester U, Liverpool, Chelsea
4 West Ham U
3 Arsenal, Everton
2 Manchester C
1 Wolverhampton W, Leicester C, WBA, Leeds U, Sunderland, Southampton, Ipswich T, Newcastle U

SCOTTISH CLUBS
10 Rangers
8 Aberdeen, Celtic
3 Hearts
2 Dunfermline Ath, Dundee U
1 Dundee, Hibernian, St Mirren, Motherwell, Airdrieonians, Kilmarnock

WELSH CLUBS
14 Cardiff C
8 Wrexham
7 Swansea C
3 Bangor C
1 Borough U, Newport Co, Merthyr Tydfil, Barry T, Llansantfraid, Cwmbran T

NORTHERN IRELAND CLUBS
9 Glentoran
5 Glenavon
4 Ballymena U, Coleraine
3 Crusaders, Linfield
2 Ards, Bangor
1 Derry C, Distillery, Portadown, Carrick Rangers, Cliftonville

EIRE CLUBS
6 Shamrock R
4 Shelbourne
3 Limerick, Waterford, Dundalk, Bohemians
2 Cork Hibs, Galway U, Derry C*, Cork City
1 Cork Celtic, St Patrick's Ath, Finn Harps, Home Farm, University College Dublin, Bray W, Sligo R

Winners: Tottenham H 1962–63; West Ham U 1964–65; Manchester C 1969–70; Chelsea 1970–71, 1997–98; Rangers 1971–72; Aberdeen 1982–83; Everton 1984–85; Manchester U 1990–91; Arsenal 1993–94

Finalists: Rangers 1960–61, 1966–67; Liverpool 1965–66; Leeds U 1972–73; West Ham U 1975–76; Arsenal 1979–80, 1994–95

EUROPEAN FAIRS CUP & UEFA CUP (1955–2003)

ENGLISH CLUBS
13 Leeds U
11 Liverpool
10 Aston Villa, Ipswich T
9 Arsenal
7 Manchester U, Newcastle U
6 Everton, Tottenham H, Chelsea
5 Southampton, Nottingham F
4 Manchester C, Birmingham C, Wolverhampton W, WBA
3 Sheffield W, Blackburn R
2 Stoke C, Derby Co, QPR, Leicester C
1 Burnley, Coventry C, Norwich C, London Rep XI, Watford, West Ham U, Fulham

SCOTTISH CLUBS
18 Dundee U
15 Hibernian, Aberdeen, Celtic
13 Rangers
10 Hearts
7 Kilmarnock
5 Dunfermline Ath
4 Dundee
3 St Mirren
2 Partick T, Motherwell, St Johnstone
1 Morton, Raith R, Livingston

WELSH CLUBS
4 Bangor C
3 Inter Cardiff (formerly Inter Cable-Tel)
2 Newtown, Barry T, Cwmbran T, TNS
1 Afan Lido

NORTHERN IRELAND CLUBS
14 Glentoran
8 Coleraine, Linfield
5 Portadown, Glenavon
3 Crusaders
1 Ards, Ballymena U, Bangor

EIRE CLUBS
11 Bohemians
6 Dundalk
5 Shelbourne, Shamrock R
4 Cork City
3 Finn Harps, St Patrick's Ath
2 Drumcondra, Derry C*
1 Cork Hibs, Athlone T, Limerick, Drogheda U, Galway U, Bray Wanderers, Longford T

Winners: Leeds U 1967–68, 1970–71; Newcastle U 1968–69; Arsenal 1969–70; Tottenham H 1971–72, 1983–84; Liverpool 1972–73, 1975–76, 2000–01; Ipswich T 1980–81

Finalists: London 1955–58, Birmingham C 1958–60, 1960–61; Leeds U 1966–67; Wolverhampton W 1971–72; Tottenham H 1973–74; Dundee U 1986–87

** Now play in League of Ireland*

INTERTOTO CUP 2002

▪ *Denotes player sent off.*

FIRST ROUND
Lokeren v WIT 3-1, 2-3
BATE Borisov v Akademisk 1-0, 2-0
Zurich v Brotnjo 7-0, 1-2
Trencin v Slaven Belupo 3-1, 0-5
Kispest v Zalgiris 0-1, 0-0
St Gallen v B68 5-1, 6-0
Enosis v Bregenz 0-2, 1-3
Leiria v Levadia 0-3, 2-1
Valletta v Teuta 1-2, 0-0
Coleraine v Saint Julia 5-0, 2-2
Marek v Caersws 2-0, 1-1
Cement v FH 1-3, 2-1
Rijeka v St Patrick's Ath 3-2, 0-1
Tiraspol v Synot 0-0, 0-4
St Clara v Shirak 2-0, 3-3
Helsingborg v Koper 1-0, 0-0
Gloria v US Luxembourg 2-0, 0-0
Brno v Ashdod 0-5, 1-1
Zagliebie Lubin v Dinaburg 1-1, 0-1
Obilic v Haka 1-2, 1-1

SECOND ROUND
Coleraine v Troyes 1-2, 1-2
Villarreal v FH 2-0, 2-2
Gent v St Patrick's Ath 2-0, 1-3
Krilia v Dinaburg 3-0, 1-0
Willem II v St Gallen 1-0, 1-1
Zurich v Levadia 1-0, 0-0
Gloria v Teuta 3-0, 0-1
Ashdod v Marek 1-1, 0-1
Slaven Belupo v Belenenses 2-0, 1-0
Fulham v Haka 0-0, 1-1
Sochaux v Zalgiris 2-0, 2-1
Teplice v St Clara 5-1, 4-1
Stuttgart v Lokeren 2-0, 1-0
Torino v Bregenz 1-0, 1-1
1860 Munich v BATE Borisov 0-1, 0-4
Synot v Helsingborg 4-0, 0-2

THIRD ROUND
NAC Breda v Troyes 1-1, 0-0
Stuttgart v Perugia 3-1, 1-2
Fulham v Egaleo 1-0, 1-1
Gloria v Lille 0-2, 0-1
Bologna v BATE Borisov 2-0, 0-0
Malaga v Gent 3-0, 1-1
Marek v Slaven Belupo 0-3, 1-3
Synot v Sochaux 0-3, 0-0
Torino v Villarreal 2-0, 0-2
(Villarreal won on penalties)
Zurich v Aston Villa 2-0, 0-3
Kaiserslautern v Teplice 2-1, 0-4
Krilia v Willem II 3-1, 0-2

SEMI-FINALS
Fulham v Sochaux 1-0, 2-0
Lille v Aston Villa 1-1, 2-0
Stuttgart v Slaven Belupo 2-1, 1-0
Villarreal v Troyes 0-0, 3-0
(match forfeited)
Malaga v Willem II 2-1, 1-0
Bologna v Teplice 5-1, 3-1

FINALS
Villarreal v Malaga 0-1, 1-1
Bologna v Fulham 2-2, 1-3
Lille v Stuttgart 1-0, 0-2

Fulham (0) (0)
Haka (0) 0 7908
Fulham: Taylor; Ouaddou, Harley, Melville, Goma, Davis, Marlet (Boa Morte 70), Saha, Sava (Hayles 60), Collins, Malbranque (Goldbaek 79).

Haka (0) 1 *(Ristila 66)*
Fulham (0) 1 *(Marlet 47)* 3500
Fulham: Taylor; Ouaddou, Harley, Melville, Goma, Davis, Legwinski (Boa Morte 57), Marlet, Saha, Collins (Knight 79), Malbranque (Goldbaek 90).

Fulham (0) 1 *(Saha 77)*
Egaleo (0) 0 5199
Fulham: Van der Sar; Ouaddou (Legwinski 46), Harley, Knight, Goma, Davis, Malbranque (Hayles 66), Marlet, Sava (Saha 46), Collins, Boa Morte.

Egaleo (1) 1 *(Chloros 24)*
Fulham (1) 1 *(Marlet 34)* 2000
Fulham: Van der Sar; Ouaddou, Harley, Melville, Goma, Davis, Legwinski (Goldbaek 71), Marlet (Hayles 71), Saha, Boa Morte, Malbranque (Stolcers 85).

Zurich (1) 2 *(Keita 32, Yasar 83)*
Aston Villa (0) 0 4500
Aston Villa: Enckelman; Delaney, Wright, Samuel▪, Dublin, Boateng, Stone, Hitzlsperger (Hendrie 73), Crouch, Boulding (Hadji 58), Barry (Kachloul 81).

Aston Villa (1) 3 *(Boulding 32, Allback 48, Staunton 77)*
Zurich (0) 0 18,349
Aston Villa: Enckelman; Delaney, Barry, Mellberg, Staunton, Taylor, Boulding (Merson 46), Hitzlsperger, Crouch, Allback (Moore 71), Hendrie.

Lille (0) 1 *(D'Amico 90)*
Aston Villa (0) 1 *(Taylor 83)* 12,000
Aston Villa: Postma; Delaney, Samuel, Mellberg, Staunton, Taylor, Hadji (Vassell 70), Hitzlsperger, Crouch, Allback (Stone 83), Barry.

Aston Villa (0) 0
Lille (1) 2 *(Fahmi 45, Bonnal 46)* 25,000
Aston Villa: Enckelman; Delaney, Barry, Mellberg, Dublin (Hendrie 46), Staunton, Taylor (Hadji 57), Hitzlsperger, Crouch (Moore 82), Vassell, Allback.

Fulham (0) 1 *(Davis 90)*
Sochaux (0) 0 4717
Fulham: Van der Sar; Ouaddou (Knight 63), Brevett, Melville, Goma, Davis, Legwinski (Inamoto 46), Marlet, Saha, Boa Morte, Malbranque (Hayles 68).

Sochaux (0) 0 Pedrettij▪
Fulham (0) 2 *(Legwinski 64, Hayles 72)* 11,000
Fulham: Van der Sar; Ouaddou, Brevett, Melville, Goma, Davis, Legwinski, Marlet, Saha (Hayles 68), Boa Morte (Collins 72), Malbranque (Inamoto 60).

Bologna (0) 2 *(Signori 56 (pen), 75 (pen))*
Fulham (0) 2 *(Inamoto 62, Legwinski 85)* 23,620
Fulham: Van der Sar; Ouaddou, Brevett, Melville, Goma, Davis, Legwinski, Malbranque (Inamoto 60), Marlet, Hayles (Saha 60), Boa Morte.

Fulham (1) 3 *(Inamoto 12, 47, 50)*
Bologna (1) 1 *(Locatelli 34)* 13,756
Fulham: Van der Sar; Finnan, Brevett, Knight, Goma, Davis (Collins 74), Legwinski, Inamoto (Malbranque 72), Marlet (Saha 72), Sava, Boa Morte.

INTERTOTO CUP – PREVIOUS WINNERS

Year	*Winners*	*Runners-up*	*Score*
1995	Karlsruhe	Bursa	3-3
	Karlsruhe won 6-5 on penalties.		
	Strasbourg	Metz	2-0
	Bordeaux	Heerenveen	2-0
	Tirol	Leverkusen	2-2
	Tirol won 5-3 on penalties.		
1996	Silkeborg	Segesta	2-1, 0-1
	Guingamp	Volgograd	1-2, 1-0
	Karlsruhe	Standard Liege	0-1, 3-1
1997	Bastia	Halmstad	1-0, 1-1
	Auxerre	Duisburg	0-0, 2-0
	Lyon	Montpellier	1-0, 3-2
1998	Valencia	Salzburg	2-0, 2-1
	Werder Bremen	Vojvodina	1-0, 1-1
	Bologna	Ruch	1-0, 2-0
1999	Montpellier	Hamburg	1-1, 1-1
	Montpellier won 3-0 on penalties.		
	West Ham U	Metz	0-1, 3-1
	Juventus	Rennes	2-0, 2-2
2000	Stuttgart	Auxerre	2-0, 1-1
	Udinese	Sigma	2-2, 4-2
	Celta Vigo	Zenit	2-1, 2-2
2001	Aston Villa	Basle	1-1, 4-1
	Troyes	Newcastle U	0-0, 4-4
	Paris St Germain	Brescia	0-0, 1-1

INTERTOTO CUP 2003–04 RESULTS

FIRST ROUND

Home Team First Leg	*Away Team First Leg*	*1st Leg Score*	*2nd LegScore*	*Aggregate Score*
Partizani*	M. Netanya	2-0	1-3	3-3
Brno*	Kotayk	1-0	2-3	3-3
Györ*	Achnas	1-1	2-2	3-3
Bangor	Gloria	0-1	2-5	2-6
Dubnica	Olympiakos	3-0	4-1	7-1
Dacia	GÍ	4-1	1-0	5-1
Sloboda	KA	1-1	1-1	2-2
aet: Slobodo won 3-2 on penalties.				
Shakhtyor	Omagh	1-0	7-1	8-1
OFK	Trans	6-1	5-3	11-4
Dinaburg	Wil	1-0	0-2	1-2
Odra	Shamrock Rovers	1-2	0-1	1-3
Spartak	Pobeda	1-5	1-2	2-7
Allianssi	Hibernians	1-0	1-1	2-1
Pasching*	WIT	1-0	1-2	2-2
Koper	Zagreb	1-0	2-2	3-2
Zalgiris	Örgryte	1-1	0-3	1-4
Encamp	Lierse	0-3	1-4	1-7
Videoton	Marek	2-2	2-3	4-5
Polonia	Tobol	0-3	1-2	1-5
Tampere*	Ceahlaul	1-0	1-2	2-2
Sutjeska	US Luxembourg	3-0	1-1	4-1

SECOND ROUND

Home Team First Leg	*Away Team First Leg*	*1st Leg Score*	*2nd LegScore*	*Aggregate Score*
Örgryte	Nice*	3-2	1-2	4-4
Thun	Brno	2-3	1-1	3-4
Brescia	Gloria	2-1	1-1	3-2
Marek	Wolfsburg	1-1	0-2	1-3
Shakhtyor	Cibalia	1-1	2-4	3-5
Willem II	Wil	2-1	1-3	3-4
Pobeda	Pasching	1-1	1-2	2-3
Sloboda	Lierse	1-0	1-5	2-5
Dacia	Partizani	2-0	3-0	5-0
Koper*	Dubnica	1-0	2-3	3-3
Sint-Truiden	Tobol	0-2	0-1	0-3
Synot	OFK	1-0	3-3	4-3
Racing*	Györ	1-0	1-2	2-2
Liberec	Shamrock Rovers	2-0	2-0	4-0
Akratitos	Allianssi	0-1	0-0	0-1
Tampere	Sutjeska	0-0	1-0	1-0

** Won on away goals rule.*

WORLD CLUB CHAMPIONSHIP

Played annually up to 1974 and intermittently since then between the winners of the European Cup and the winners of the South American Champions Cup — known as the Copa Libertadores. In 1980 the winners were decided by one match arranged in Tokyo in February 1981 and the venue has been the same since. AC Milan replaced Marseille who had been stripped of their European Cup title in 1993.

1960 Real Madrid beat Penarol 0-0, 5-1
1961 Penarol beat Benfica 0-1, 5-0, 2-1
1962 Santos beat Benfica 3-2, 5-2
1963 Santos beat AC Milan 2-4, 4-2, 1-0
1964 Inter-Milan beat Independiente 0-1, 2-0, 1-0
1965 Inter-Milan beat Independiente 3-0, 0-0
1966 Penarol beat Real Madrid 2-0, 2-0
1967 Racing Club beat Celtic 0-1, 2-1, 1-0
1968 Estudiantes beat Manchester United 1-0, 1-1
1969 AC Milan beat Estudiantes 3-0, 1-2
1970 Feyenoord beat Estudiantes 2-2, 1-0
1971 Nacional beat Panathinaikos* 1-1, 2-1
1972 Ajax beat Independiente 1-1, 3-0
1973 Independiente beat Juventus* 1-0
1974 Atlético Madrid* beat Independiente 0-1, 2-0
1975 Independiente and Bayern Munich could not agree dates; no matches.
1976 Bayern Munich beat Cruzeiro 2-0, 0-0
1977 Boca Juniors beat Borussia Moenchengladbach* 2-2, 3-0
1978 Not contested
1979 Olimpia beat Malmö* 1-0, 2-1
1980 Nacional beat Nottingham Forest 1-0
1981 Flamengo beat Liverpool 3-0
1982 Penarol beat Aston Villa 2-0
1983 Gremio Porto Alegre beat SV Hamburg 2-1
1984 Independiente beat Liverpool 1-0
1985 Juventus beat Argentinos Juniors 4-2 on penalties after a 2-2 draw
1986 River Plate beat Steaua Bucharest 1-0
1987 FC Porto beat Penarol 2-1 after extra time
1988 Nacional (Uru) beat PSV Eindhoven 7-6 on penalties after 1-1 draw
1989 AC Milan beat Atletico Nacional (Col) 1-0 after extra time
1990 AC Milan beat Olimpia 3-0
1991 Red Star Belgrade beat Colo Colo 3-0
1992 Sao Paulo beat Barcelona 2-1
1993 Sao Paulo beat AC Milan 3-2
1994 Velez Sarsfield beat AC Milan 2-0
1995 Ajax beat Gremio Porto Alegre 4-3 on penalties after 0-0 draw
1996 Juventus beat River Plate 1-0
1997 Borussia Dortmund beat Cruzeiro 2-0
1998 Real Madrid beat Vasco da Gama 2-1
1999 Manchester U beat Palmeiras 1-0
2000 Boca Juniors beat Real Madrid 2-1
2001 Bayern Munich beat Boca Juniors 1-0 after extra time

*European Cup runners-up; winners declined to take part.

2002

3 December 2002, in Yokohama

Real Madrid (1) 2 *(Ronaldo 14, Guti 84)*

Olimpia (0) 0 72,370

Real Madrid: Casillas; Michel Salgado, Roberto Carlos, Cambiasso (Pavon 90), Hierro, Helguera, Figo, Makelele, Ronaldo (Guti 82), Zidane (Solari 86), Raul.

Olimpia: Tavarelli; Isasi, Jara, Caceres, Zelaya, Benitez P, Orteman, Enciso, Benitez M (Caballero 80), Cordoba (Baez 66), Lopez.

Referee: Simon (Brazil).

EUROPEAN SUPER CUP

Played annually between the winners of the European Champions' Cup and the European Cup-Winners' Cup (UEFA Cup from 2000). AC Milan replaced Marseille in 1993–94.

1972 Ajax beat Rangers 3-1, 3-2
1973 Ajax beat AC Milan 0-1, 6-0
1974 Not contested
1975 Dynamo Kiev beat Bayern Munich 1-0, 2-0
1976 Anderlecht beat Bayern Munich 4-1, 1-2
1977 Liverpool beat Hamburg 1-1, 6-0
1978 Anderlecht beat Liverpool 3-1, 1-2
1979 Nottingham F beat Barcelona 1-0, 1-1
1980 Valencia beat Nottingham F 1-0, 1-2
1981 Not contested
1982 Aston Villa beat Barcelona 0-1, 3-0
1983 Aberdeen beat Hamburg 0-0, 2-0
1984 Juventus beat Liverpool 2-0
1985 Juventus v Everton not contested due to UEFA ban on English clubs
1986 Steaua Bucharest beat Dynamo Kiev 1-0
1987 FC Porto beat Ajax 1-0, 1-0
1988 KV Mechelen beat PSV Eindhoven 3-0, 0-1
1989 AC Milan beat Barcelona 1-1, 1-0
1990 AC Milan beat Sampdoria 1-1, 2-0
1991 Manchester U beat Red Star Belgrade 1-0
1992 Barcelona beat Werder Bremen 1-1, 2-1
1993 Parma beat AC Milan 0-1, 2-0
1994 AC Milan beat Arsenal 0-0, 2-0
1995 Ajax beat Zaragoza 1-1, 4-0
1996 Juventus beat Paris St Germain 6-1, 3-1
1997 Barcelona beat Borussia Dortmund 2-0, 1-1
1998 Chelsea beat Real Madrid 1-0
1999 Lazio beat Manchester U 1-0
2000 Galatasaray beat Real Madrid 2-1
2001 Liverpool beat Bayern Munich 3-2

2002

30 August 2002, in Monaco

Real Madrid (2) 3 *(Paauwe 15 (og), Roberto Carlos 21, Guti 60)*

Feyenoord (0) 1 *(Van Hooijdonk 56)* 17,000

Real Madrid: Casillas; Michel Salgado, Roberto Carlos, Cambiasso (Pavon 88), Hierro, Helguera, Figo, Makelele, Guti (Portillo 71), Zidane (Solari 86), Raul.

Feyenoord: Zoetebier; Gyan (Buffel 72), Rzasa, Bosvelt, Van Wonderen, Paauwe, Emerton, Ono, Kalou, Van Hooijdonk, Lurling.

Referee: Dallas (Scotland).

INTERNATIONAL DIRECTORY

The latest available information has been given regarding numbers of clubs and players registered with FIFA, the world governing body. Where known, official colours are listed. With European countries, League tables show a number of signs. * indicates relegated teams, + play-offs, *+ relegated after play-offs, ++ promoted.

There are 197 member associations and one provisional member, Palestine. The four home countries, England, Scotland, Northern Ireland and Wales, are dealt with elsewhere in the Yearbook; but basic details appear in this directory.

EUROPE

ALBANIA

The Football Association of Albania, Rruga Dervish Hima Nr. 31, Tirana.
Founded: 1930; *Number of Clubs:* 49; *Number of Players:* 5,192; *National Colours:* All red.
Telephone: 00-355-42 27 877; *Cable:* ALBSPORT TIRANA; *Telex:* 2228 bfssh ab. *Fax:* 00-355-42 50 275.

International matches 2002
Macedonia (a) 0-0, Finland (h) 1-1, Bahrain (a) 0-3, Luxembourg (a) 0-0, Mexico (a) 0-4, Azerbaijan (h) 1-0, Andorra (a) 0-2, Switzerland (h) 1-1, Russia (a) 1-4.

League Championship wins (1930–37; 1945–2003)
SK Tirana 20 (including 17 Nentori 8); Dinamo Tirana 16; Partizani Tirana 15; Vllaznia 9; Flamurtari 1; Elbasan 2 (including Labinoti 1); Skenderbeu 1; Teuta 1.

Cup wins (1948–2003)
Partizani Tirana 14; Dinamo Tirana 13; SK Tirana 10 (including 17 Nentori 6); Vllaznia 5; Teuta 3; Elbasan 3 (including Labintoti 1); Flamurtari 2; Apolonia 1.

Final League Table 2002–03

	P	W	D	L	F	A	Pts
SK Tirana	26	19	3	4	57	18	60
Vllaznia	26	15	4	7	51	32	49
Partizani	26	12	10	4	41	27	46
Teuta	26	12	4	10	38	27	40
Shkumbini	26	11	7	8	33	23	40
Dinamo	26	10	8	8	29	24	38
Flamurtari	26	10	6	10	27	28	36
Elbasan	26	10	6	10	33	35	36
Besa	26	9	9	8	29	37	36
Lushnja	26	9	8	9	27	27	35
Apolonia*	26	10	5	11	27	33	35
Erzeni*	26	6	6	14	23	37	24
Bylis*	26	3	7	16	19	61	16
Beselidhja*	26	4	1	21	22	47	13

Relegation Play-off
Lushnja 3, Apolonia 1.
No promotions; championship reduced to ten clubs.
Top scorer: Halili (SK Tirana) 20.
Cup Final: Dinamo Tirana 1, Teuta 0.

ANDORRA

Federacio Andorrana de Futbol, C/Sant Salvador, 10-2-5, Edifici Galerias Plaza, Andorra la Vella, Principat d'Andorra.
Founded: 1994; *Number of Clubs:* 12; *Number of Players:* 300; *National Colours:* Yellow shirts, red shorts, yellow stockings.
Telephone: 00376 862003; *Fax:* 00376 862006.

International matches 2002
Malta (a) 1-1, Albania (h) 2-0, Armenia (h) 0-2, Iceland (a) 0-3, Belgium (h) 0-1, Bulgaria (a) 1-2.

League Championship wins (1996–2003)
Principat 3; Dicoansa 1; Constelacio 1; St Julia 1; Encamp 1; Santa Coloma 1.

Cup wins (1996–2003)
Principat 4; Santa Coloma 2; Constelacio 1; Lusitanos 1.

Qualifying League Table 2002–03

	P	W	D	L	F	A	Pts
Santa Coloma	16	13	3	0	51	8	42
Encamp	16	10	4	2	48	10	34
St Julia	16	9	3	4	57	17	30
Inter	16	8	2	6	30	33	26
Principat	16	6	5	5	32	25	23
Lusitanos	16	7	1	8	44	33	22
Rangers	16	6	3	7	39	38	21
Cerni	16	2	1	13	17	63	7
Sporting*	16	0	0	16	10	101	0

Final League Table 2002–03

	P	W	D	L	F	A	Pts
Santa Coloma	6	1	4	1	59	14	49
Encamp	6	4	2	0	62	16	48
St Julia	6	2	2	2	73	28	38
Inter	6	1	0	5	37	55	29

Relegation Table 2002–03

	P	W	D	L	F	A	Pts
Principat	6	5	0	1	63	40	37
Lusitanos	6	4	0	2	57	47	33
Rangers	6	3	0	3	39	35	32
Cerni*	6	0	0	6	21	85	7

Cup Final: Santa Coloma 5, St Julia 3.

ARMENIA

Football Federation of Armenia, 9, Abovian Str. 375001 Erevan, Armenia.
Founded: 1992; *Number of Clubs:* 32; *Number of Players:* 15,000; *National Colours:* Red shirts, blue shorts, orange stockings.
Telephone: 00374 2/589480; *Telex:* 243337 minor su; *Fax:* 00374 2/151573.

International matches 2002
Andorra (a) 2-0, Ukraine (h) 2-2, Greece (a) 0-2.

League Championship wins (1992–2002)
Shirak Gyumri 4*; Pyunik 4; Ararat Erevan 2*; Homenmen 1; FC Erevan 1; Tsement 1; Araks 1.
*Includes one unofficial title.

Cup wins (1992–2003)
Ararat Erevan 5; Tsement 2; Pyunik 2; Mika 2; Banants 1.

Final League Table 2002

	P	W	D	L	F	A	Pts
Pyunik	22	19	2	1	85	14	59
Shirak	22	16	3	3	49	15	51
Banants	22	16	2	4	43	15	50
Spartak	22	15	4	3	58	16	49
Ararat	22	9	6	7	39	22	33
Mika	22	9	6	7	35	28	33
Zvartnorts	22	10	2	10	57	29	32
Lemagorts	22	6	5	11	21	43	23
Lemayin**	22	5	2	15	21	52	17
Dinamo	22	3	3	16	19	63	12
Kotaik	22	2	5	15	17	62	11
Lori*	22	1	2	19	15	100	5

**Formerly Karabach.
Top scorer: Arm Karamian (Pyunik) 36.
Cup Final: Mika 1, Banants 0.

AUSTRIA

Oesterreichischer Fussball-Bund, Ernst-Happel Stadion, Postfach 340, Meierestrasse, A-1021 Wien.
Founded: 1904; *Number of Clubs:* 2,081; *Number of Players:* 253,576; *National Colours:* White shirts, black shorts, white stockings.
Telephone: 0043 1 727 180; *Cable:* FOOTBALL WIEN; *Telex:* 111919 oefb a; *Fax:* 0043 1 728 1632.

International matches 2002
Slovakia (h) 2-0, Cameroon (h) 0-0, Germany (a) 2-6, Switzerland (a) 2-3, Moldova (h) 2-0, Belarus (a) 2-0, Holland (h) 0-3, Norway (h) 0-1.

League Championship wins (1912–2003)
Rapid Vienna 30; FK Austria 23; Tirol-Svarowski-Innsbruck 10; Admira-Energie-Wacker 9; First Vienna 6; Wiener Sportklub 3; Austria Salzburg 3; Sturm Graz 2; FAC 1; Hakoah 1; Linz ASK 1; WAF 1; Voest Linz 1.

Cup wins (1919–2003)
FK Austria 26; Rapid Vienna 14; TS Innsbruck (formerly Wacker Innsbruck) 7; Admira-Energie-Wacker (formerly Sportklub Admira & Admira-Energie) 5; First Vienna 3; Sturm Graz 3; Graz 3; Linz ASK 1; Wacker Vienna 1; WAF 1; Wiener Sportklub 1; Stockerau 1; Ried 1; Karnten 1.

Final League Table 2002–03

	P	*W*	*D*	*L*	*F*	*A*	*Pts*
FK Austria	36	21	7	8	59	28	70
Graz	36	15	12	9	56	39	57
Salzburg	36	15	11	10	51	46	56
Rapid	36	13	12	11	40	38	51
Pasching	36	13	10	13	41	37	49
Sturm Graz	36	14	5	17	50	62	47
Admira	36	11	11	14	36	46	44
Carinthie	36	11	8	17	45	57	41
Bregenz	36	9	12	15	48	58	39
Ried*	36	10	8	18	41	56	38

Top scorer: Lawaree (Bregenz) 21.
Cup Final: FK Austria 3, Carinthie 0.

AZERBAIJAN

Association of Football Federations of Azerbaijan, Husu Haciyev kuc., 42, 370009 Baku, Azerbaijan.
Founded: 1992; *Number of Clubs:* 1,500; *Number of Players:* 95,000; *National Colours:* White shirts with blue stripes, blue shorts, white stockings.
Telephone: 00994 12 94 49 16; *Cable:* FOOTBALL ASSOCIATION, AZ; *Fax:* 00994 12 98 93 93.

International matches 2002
Albania (a) 0-1, Malta (a) 0-1, Estonia (a) 0-0, Latvia (a) 0-0, Iran (a) 1-1, Uzbekistan (h) 2-0, Italy (h) 0-2, Finland (a) 0-3, Wales (h) 0-2.

League Championship wins (1992–2002)
Kapaz 3; Shamkir 3; Karabakh 2; Neftchi 2; Turan 1.
Includes one unoffical title for Shamkir in 2002.

Cup wins (1992–2001)
Kapaz 4; Neftchi 3; Karabakh 1; Inshatchi 1; Shafa 1.

Following the continuing conflict between almost all clubs and the President of the Azerbaijan FA, no League Championship was played during 2002-03. At the start of December 2002, a Neftchi-65 tournament was organised devoted to the 65th anniversary of FC Neftchi, the first tournament since the last championship. All matches were played at the Ismet Gaibov Stadium.

Group A	*P*	*W*	*D*	*L*	*F*	*A*	*Pts*
Neftchi	3	2	1	0	10	3	7
Dinamo Baku	3	2	1	0	8	3	7
Ulduz	3	1	0	2	6	8	3
Shahdagh	3	0	0	3	5	15	0

Group B	*P*	*W*	*D*	*L*	*F*	*A*	*Pts*
Karabakh	3	3	0	0	4	0	9
OIK	3	1	1	1	1	1	4
Turan	3	0	2	1	2	4	2
Xazar	3	0	1	2	2	4	1

Third Place match
Dinamo Baku 3, OIK 1

Final
Neftchi 1, Karabakh 1
Karabakh won 5-4 on penalties.

BELARUS

Belarus Football Association, 8–2 Kyrov Str. 220600 Minsk, Belarus.
Founded: 1989; *Number of Clubs:* 455; *Number of Players:* 120,000; *National Colours:* All green.
Telephone: 007 0172 375 272325; *Telex:* 252175 athlet su; *Fax:* 007 0172 27 29 20.

International matches 2002
Hungary (a) 5-2, Russia (n) 1-1, Ukraine (n) 2-0, Latvia (a) 4-2, Holland (a) 0-3, Austria (h) 0-2, Czech Republic (a) 0-2.

League Championship wins (1992–2002)
Dynamo Minsk 6; Slavia Mozyr (formerly MPKC Mozyr) 2; BATE Borisov 2; Dnepr Mogilev 1; Belshina 1.

Cup wins (1992–2003)
Belshina 3; Dynamo Minsk 3; Slavia Mozyr (formerly MPKC Mozyr) 2; Neman 1; Dynamo 93 Minsk 1; Lokomotiv 96 1; Gomel 1.

Final League Table 2002

	P	*W*	*D*	*L*	*F*	*A*	*Pts*
BATE Borisov	26	18	2	6	51	20	56
Neman	26	17	5	4	47	20	56
Shakhter	26	15	6	5	41	23	51
Torpedo Minsk	26	15	6	5	30	16	51
Torpedo Zhodino	26	13	4	9	38	27	43
Gomel	26	13	4	9	46	33	43
Dynamo Minsk	26	12	6	8	44	28	42
Belshina**	26	12	4	10	44	38	37
Dnepr	26	10	6	10	38	37	36
Dynamo Brest	26	8	8	10	25	26	32
Slavia	26	6	6	14	38	61	24
Zvezda	26	4	6	16	28	48	18
Molodechno	26	3	3	20	23	59	12
Lokomotiv 96*	26	3	0	23	20	77	9

Championship play-off: BATE Borisov 1, Neman 0.
** Three points deducted for non-payment of transfer fees.
Top scorer: Stripiekis (Belshina) 18.
Cup Final: Dynamo Minsk 2, Lokomotiv 96 0.

BELGIUM

Union Royale Belge Des Societes De Football Association, 145 Avenue Houba de Strooper, B-1020 Bruxelles.
Founded: 1895; *Number of Clubs:* 2,120; *Number of Players:* 390,468; *National Colours:* All red.
Telephone: 0032 2 477 12 11; *Cable:* URBSFA BRUXELLES; *Telex:* 23257 bvbfbf b; *Fax:* 0032 2 478 23 91.

International matches 2002
Norway (h) 1-0, Greece (a) 2-3, Slovakia (h) 1-1, Algeria (h) 0-0, France (a) 2-1, Costa Rica (h) 1-0, Japan (n) 2-2, Tunisia (n) 1-1, Russia (n) 3-2, Brazil (n) 0-2, Poland (a) 1-1, Bulgaria (h) 0-2, Andorra (a) 1-0, Estonia (a) 1-0.

League Championship wins (1896–2003)
Anderlecht 26; FC Brugge 12; Union St Gilloise 11; Standard Liege 8; Beerschot 7; RC Brussels 6; FC Liege 5; Daring Brussels 5; Antwerp 4; Mechelen 4; Lierse SK 4; SV Brugge 3; Beveren 2; Genk 2; RWD Molenbeek 1.

Cup wins (1954–2003)
Anderlecht 8; FC Brugge 8; Standard Liege 5; Beerschot 2; Waterschei 2; Beveren 2; Gent 2; Antwerp 2; Lierse SK 2; Genk 2; Racing Doornik 1; Waregem 1; SV Brugge 1; Mechelen 1; FC Liege 1; Ekeren 1; Westerlo 1; La Louviere 1.

Final League Table 2002–03

	P	*W*	*D*	*L*	*F*	*A*	*Pts*
FC Brugge	32	25	4	3	96	33	79
Anderlecht	32	23	2	7	72	31	71
Lokeren	32	18	6	8	69	51	60
St Truiden	32	16	8	8	63	44	56
Lierse	32	16	8	8	51	41	56
Genk	32	16	7	9	73	52	55
Standard Liege	32	14	8	10	53	39	50
Gent	32	15	2	15	49	55	47
Mons	32	13	4	15	45	45	43
Westerlo	32	12	4	16	39	46	40
Beveren	32	12	2	18	50	69	38
Royal Antwerp	32	9	7	16	44	55	34
Mouscron	32	9	5	18	42	72	32
Antwerp	32	8	7	17	49	57	31
La Louviere	32	7	9	16	34	44	30
Charleroi	32	6	9	17	39	66	27
Mechelen*	32	4	6	22	18	86	18
Lommel**	0	0	0	0	0	0	0

***Relegated for financial problems, results annulled.*
Top scorer: Sonck (Genk) 24.
Cup Final: La Louviere 3, St Truiden 1.

BOSNIA HERZEGOVINA

Bosnia & Herzegovina Football Federation, Sime Milutinovico, 12/1 71000 Sarajevo.
Founded: 1992; *National Colours:* White shirts, blue shorts, white stockings.
Telephone: 00387 71/213881; *Fax:* 00387 71/444332.

International matches 2002
Macedonia (h) 4-4, Croatia (a) 0-2, Yugoslavia (h) 0-2, Romania (h) 0-3, Germany (h) 1-1, Norway (a) 0-2.

League Championship wins (1996–2003)
Zeljeznicar 3; Brotnjo 1; Leotar 1.

Cup wins (1996–2003)
Zeljeznicar 3; Sarajevo 2; Bosna 1; Celik 1.

Final League Table 2002–03

	P	W	D	L	F	A	Pts
Leotar	38	26	7	5	82	27	85
Zeljeznicar	38	24	10	4	66	24	82
Sarajevo	38	19	12	7	83	39	69
Siroki	38	21	5	12	69	45	68
Celik	38	16	10	12	61	33	58
Sloboda	38	16	6	16	51	38	54
Borac	38	15	9	14	50	49	54
Orasje	38	16	6	16	50	57	54
Posusje	38	14	11	13	42	55	53
Zovko	38	17	2	19	49	50	53
Zrinjski	38	16	4	18	46	65	52
Rudar	38	15	7	16	61	57	52
Brotnjo	38	16	4	18	47	55	52
Glasinac	38	15	6	17	37	54	51
Kozara*	38	15	6	17	55	62	51
Jedinstvo*	38	15	5	18	59	63	50
Velez*	38	14	3	21	47	59	45
Mladost*	38	11	6	21	40	65	39
Buducnost*	38	10	8	20	48	67	38
Bosna*	38	5	1	32	28	107	16

Top scorer: Obuca (Sarajevo) 23.
Cup Final: Leotar 0, 0, Zeljeznicar 0, 2.

BULGARIA

Bulgarian Football Union, Karnigradska 19, BG-1000 Sofia.
Founded: 1923; *Number of Clubs:* 376; *Number of Players:* 48,240; *National Colours:* White shirts, green shorts, white stockings.
Telephone: 00359 2 987 74 90; *Cable:* BULFUTBOL SOFIA; *Telex:* 23145 bfs bg; *Fax:* 00359 2 986 2538.

International matches 2002
Croatia (a) 0-0, Ecuador (a) 0-3, Mexico (a) 0-1, Germany (h) 2-2, Belgium (a) 2-0, Croatia (h) 2-0, Andorra (h) 2-1, Spain (a) 0-1.

League Championship wins (1925–2003)
CSKA Sofia 29; Levski Sofia 22; Slavia Sofia 7; Vladislav Varna 3; Lokomotiv Sofia 3; Litets 2; Trakia Plovdiv 2; AC 23 Sofia 1; Botev Plovdiv 1; SC Sofia 1; Sokol Varna 1; Spartak Plovdiv 1; Tichka Varna 1; JSZ Sofia 1; Beroe Stara Zagora 1; Etur 1.

Cup wins (1946–2003)
Levski Sofia 22; CSKA Sofia 16; Slavia Sofia 7; Lokomotiv Sofia 4; Botev Plovdiv 1; Spartak Plovdiv 1; Spartak Sofia 1; Marek Stanke 1; Trakia Plovdiv 1; Spartak Varna 1; Sliven 1; Litets 1.

Qualifying League Table 2002–03

	P	W	D	L	F	A	Pts
CSKA Sofia	26	21	3	2	67	16	66
Levski Sofia	26	19	3	4	61	19	60
Litets	26	17	4	5	49	22	55
Slavia Sofia	26	16	3	7	57	30	51
Cherno Varna	26	14	6	6	42	21	48
Lokomotiv Plovdiv	26	16	2	8	56	33	47
Spartak Varna	26	10	4	12	25	34	34
Naftex	26	10	3	13	31	36	33
Marek	26	8	6	12	35	42	30
Lokomotiv Sofia	26	7	4	15	23	37	25
Chernomorets	26	7	3	16	32	56	24
Botev Plovdiv	26	6	3	17	26	61	21
Dobroudja*	26	4	2	20	19	73	14
Ritski*	26	1	6	19	20	63	9

Next season 16 clubs.
Top scorer: Chiklikov (Levski Sofia), 22.
Cup Final: Levski Sofia 2, Litets 1.

CROATIA

Croatian Football Federation, Illica 31, CRO-10000 Zagreb, Croatia.
Founded: 1912; *Number of Clubs:* 1,221; *Number of Players:* 78,127; *National Colours:* Red/white shirts, white shorts, blue stockings.
Telephone: 00385 1/4554100. *Fax:* 00385 1 42 46 39.

International matches 2002
Bulgaria (h) 0-0, Slovenia (h) 0-0, Bosnia (h) 2-0, Hungary (a) 2-0, Mexico (n) 0-1, Italy (n) 2-1, Ecuador (n) 0-1, Wales (h) 1-1, Estonia (h) 0-0, Bulgaria (a) 0-2, Romania (a) 1-0.

League Championship wins (1941–44; 1992–2003)
Dynamo Zagreb (formerly Croatia Zagreb) 7; Hajduk Split 4; Gradanski 3; Concordia 1; Zagreb 1.

Cup wins (1993–2003)
Dynamo Zagreb (formerly Croatia Zagreb) 6; Hajduk Split 4; Osijek 1.

Qualifying Table 2002–03

	P	W	D	L	F	A	Pts
Dynamo Zagreb	22	18	3	1	51	17	57
Hajduk Split	22	16	2	4	42	14	50
Varteks	22	15	0	7	40	21	45
Cibalia	22	9	5	8	28	28	32
Kamen	22	7	9	6	23	22	30
Zagreb	22	8	6	8	28	30	30
Slaven	22	9	2	11	24	26	29
Osijek	22	6	5	11	21	39	23
Zadar	22	5	6	11	21	40	21
Rijeka	22	5	3	14	23	33	18
Pomorac	22	3	8	11	26	41	17
Sibenik	22	4	5	13	23	39	17

Championship Table 2002-03

	P	W	D	L	F	A	Pts
Dynamo Zagreb	32	25	3	4	76	27	78
Hajduk Split	32	22	4	6	56	22	70
Varteks	32	18	3	11	52	38	57
Kamen	32	11	11	10	34	34	44
Cibalia	32	12	7	13	39	44	43
Zagreb	32	9	9	14	40	52	36

Relegation Table 2002-03

	P	W	D	L	F	A	Pts
Slaven	32	12	4	16	37	36	40
Osijek	32	10	9	13	32	51	39
Rijeka	32	9	6	17	40	41	33
Zadar	32	9	6	17	36	71	33
Pomorac	32	7	11	14	42	52	32
Sibenik*	32	8	7	17	37	53	31

Top scorer: Olic (Dynamo Zagreb) 16.
Cup Final: Uljnik 0, 0, Hajduk Split 1, 4.

CYPRUS

Cyprus Football Association, 1 Stasinos Str., Engomi, P.O. Box 5071, CY-2404 Nicosia.
Founded: 1934; *Number of Clubs:* 85; *Number of Players:* 6,000; *National Colours:* Blue shirts, white shorts, blue stockings.
Telephone: 00357 2 /352341; *Cable:* FOOTBALL CYPRUS; *Telex:* 3880 football cy; *Fax:* 00357 2/590544.

International matches 2002
Switzerland (h) 1-1, Czech Republic (h) 3-4, Greece (a) 1-3, N Ireland (a) 0-0, France (h) 1-2, Malta (h) 2-1.

League Championship wins (1935–2003)
Omonia 19; Apoel 17; Anorthosis 11; AEL 5; EPA 3; Olympiakos 3; Apollon 2; Pezoporikos 2; Chetin Kayal 1; Trast 1.

Cup wins (1935–2003)
Apoel 17; Omonia 11; Anorthosis 7; AEL 6; EPA 5; Apollon 5; Trast 3; Chetin Kayal 2; Olympiakos 1; Pezoporikos 1; Salamina 1.

Final League Table 2002–03

	P	W	D	L	F	A	Pts
Omonia	26	18	6	2	68	22	60
Anorthosis	26	19	2	5	65	30	59
Apoel	26	16	7	3	55	24	55
Olympiakos	26	16	4	6	56	29	52
AEL	26	11	6	9	56	45	39
Ethnikos Ahnas	26	10	7	9	35	32	37
AEP	26	11	4	11	38	45	37
AEK	26	9	5	12	43	50	32
Digenis	26	9	4	13	40	40	31
Paralimni	26	8	7	11	39	40	31
Apollon	26	8	7	11	42	46	31
NEA*	26	6	11	9	39	40	29
Aris*	26	2	3	21	31	92	9
Alki*	26	1	3	22	21	93	6

Top scorer: Neophytou (Anorthosis) 33.
Cup Final: Anorthosis 0, AEL 0.
Anorthosis won 5-3 on penalties.

CZECH REPUBLIC

Football Association of Czech Republic, Diskarska 100, 169 00 Prague 6 - Strahov, Czech Republic.
Founded: 1901; *Number of Clubs:* 3,836; *Number of Players:* 319,500; *National Colours:* Red shirts, white shorts, blue stockings.
Telephone: 00422 20513575; *Cable:* SPORTSVAZ PRAHA; *Telex:* 122650 cstv c; *Fax:* 004202 3335 3107.

International matches 2002
Hungary (n) 2-0, Cyprus (n) 4-3, Wales (a) 0-0, Greece (a) 0-0, Italy (h) 1-0, Slovakia (h) 4-1, Yugoslavia (h) 5-0, Moldova (a) 2-0, Belarus (h) 2-0, Sweden (h) 3-3.

League Championship wins (1926–93)
Sparta Prague 19; Slavia Prague 12; Dukla Prague (prev. UDA) 11; Slovan Bratislava 7; Spartak Trnava 5; Banik Ostrava 3; Inter-Bratislava 1; Spartak Hradec Kralove 1; Viktoria Zizkov 1; Zbrojovka Brno 1; Bohemians 1; Vitkovice 1.

Cup wins (1961–93)
Dukla Prague 8; Sparta Prague 8; Slovan Bratislava 5; Spartak Trnava 4; Banik Ostrava 3; Lokomotiv Kosice 3; TJ Gottwaldov 1; Dunajska Streda 1.
From 1993–94, there were two separate countries; the Czech Republic and Slovakia.

League Championship wins (1994–2003)
Sparta Prague 8; Slavia Prague 1; Slovan Liberec 1.

Cup wins (1994–2003)
Slavia Prague 3; Viktoria Zizkov 2; Spartak Hradec Kralove 1; Sparta Prague 1; Jablonec 1; Slovan Liberec 1; Teplice 1.

Final League Table 2002–03

	P	W	D	L	F	A	Pts
Sparta Prague	30	20	5	5	51	17	65
Slavia Prague	30	18	10	2	65	19	64
Viktoria Zizkov	30	14	8	8	38	33	50
Slovan Liberec	30	14	8	8	43	36	50
Banik Ostrava	30	13	6	11	41	38	45
Teplice	30	13	6	11	33	32	45
Zlin	30	11	9	10	34	41	42
Synot	30	11	7	12	39	40	40
Artikel Brno	30	10	9	11	35	31	39
Marila Pribram	30	9	12	9	34	30	39
Sigma Olomouc	30	8	10	12	29	33	34
Jablonec	30	7	13	10	29	39	34
Ceske	30	8	6	16	36	54	30
Chmel Blsany	30	7	7	16	28	39	28
Bohemians*	30	5	9	16	34	56	24
Hredec Kralove*	30	3	13	14	23	54	22

Top scorer: Kowalik (Synot) 16.
Cup Final: Teplice 1, Jablonec 0.

DENMARK

Danish Football Association, Idraettens Hus, Brondby Stadion 20, DK-2605, Brondby.
Founded: 1889; *Number of Clubs:* 1,555; *Number of Players:* 268,517; *National Colours:* Red shirts, white shorts, red stockings.
Telephone: 0045 43/262222; *Cable:* DANSKBOLDSPIL COPENHAGEN; *Telex:* 15545 dbu dk; *Fax:* 0045 43/262245.

International matches 2002
Saudi Arabia (a) 1-0, Eire (a) 0-3, Israel (h) 3-1, Cameroon (h) 2-1, Tunisia (h) 2-1, Uruguay (n) 2-1, Senegal (n) 1-1, France (n) 2-0, England (n) 0-3, Scotland (a) 1-0, Norway (a) 2-2, Luxembourg (h) 2-0, Poland (h) 2-0.

League Championship wins (1913–2003)
KB Copenhagen 15; B 93 Copenhagen 10; AB (Akademisk) 9; Brondby 9; B 1903 Copenhagen 7; Frem 6; Esbjerg BK 5; Vejle BK 5; AGF Aarhus 5; Hvidovre 3; Odense BK 3; AaB Aalborg 2; B 1909 Odense 2; Koge BK 2; Lyngby 2; FC Copenhagen 3; Silkeborg 1; Herfolge 1.

Cup wins (1955–2003)
Aarhus GF 9; Vejle BK 6; OB Odense 4; Brondby 4; Randers Freja 3; Lyngby 3; B1909 Odense 2; Aalborg BK 2; Esbjerg BK 2; Frem 2; B 1903 Copenhagen 2; FC Copenhagen 2; B 93 Copenhagen 1; KB Copenhagen 1; Vanlose 1; Hvidovre 1; B1913 Odense 1, AB Copenhagen 1, Viborg 1; Silkeborg 1.

Final League Table 2002–03

	P	W	D	L	F	A	Pts
FC Copenhagen	33	17	10	6	51	32	61
Brondby	33	15	11	7	61	35	56
Farum	33	16	3	14	49	58	51
Odense	33	12	12	9	55	50	48
Esbjerg	33	12	11	10	65	57	47
Aalborg	33	14	4	15	42	45	46
Midtjylland	33	11	11	11	49	45	44
Viborg	33	11	10	12	58	55	43
AB Copenhagen	33	10	12	11	44	48	42
Aarhus	33	10	10	13	49	59	40
Silkeborg*	33	9	9	15	52	54	36
Koge*	33	8	3	22	45	82	27

Top scorers: Frederiksen (Viborg) 18, Kristiansen (Esbjerg) 18.
Cup Final: Brondby 3, Midtjylland 0.

ENGLAND

The Football Association, 25 Soho Square, London W1D 4FA.
Founded: 1863; *Number of Clubs:* 42,000; *Number of Players:* 2,250,000; *National Colours:* White shirts with vertical red stripe, navy shorts, white stockings.
Telephone: 020 7745 4545, 020 7402 7151; *Fax:* 020 7745 4546; *Website:* www.the-fa.org

ESTONIA

Estonian Football Association, Voidu 16, Tallinn EE 0012.
Founded: 1921; *Number of Clubs:* 40; *Number of Players:* 12,000; *National Colours:* Blue shirts, black shorts, white stockings.
Telephone: 00372 6/542715, 542716, 542717; *Fax:* 00372 6/542719.

International matches 2002
Saudi Arabia (a) 2-0, Russia (h) 2-1, Poland (a) 0-1, San Marino (a) 1-0, Azerbaijan (h) 0-0, Kazakhstan (a) 1-1, Moldova (h) 1-0, Croatia (a) 0-0, New Zealand (h) 3-2, Belgium (h) 0-1, Iceland (h) 2-0.

League Championship wins (1922–40; 1992–2002)
Flora Tallinn 6; Sport 8; Estonia 5; Norma Tallinn 2; Tallinn JK 2; Kalev 2; Levadia 2; LFLS 1; Olimpia 1; Lantana 1.

Cup wins (1992–2002)
Levadia (merged with Sadam) 4; VMV Tallinn 1; Nikol Tallinn 1; Norma Tallinn 1; Lantana 1; Flora Tallinn 1; Trans 1; Levadia Tallinn 1.

Final League Table 2002

	P	W	D	L	F	A	Pts
Flora	28	20	4	4	79	25	64
Levadia	28	18	8	2	70	25	62
VMK	28	16	5	7	90	35	53
Trans	28	14	5	9	54	49	47
Tulevik	28	10	6	12	51	52	36
Levadia Tallinn	28	6	5	17	32	70	23
Lootus*	28	5	6	17	24	67	21
Parnu*	28	1	5	22	19	96	8

Top scorer: Krovov (VMK) 37.
Cup Final: Levadia Tallinn 2, Levadia 0.

FAEROE ISLANDS

Fotboltssamband Foroya, The Faeroes' Football Assn., Gundalur, P.O. Box 3028, FR-110, Torshavn.
Founded: 1979; *Number of Clubs:* 16; *Number of Players:* 1,014; *National Colours:* White shirts, blue shorts, white stockings.
Telephone: 00298 31 6707/457607; *Telex:* 81328 nspkkl fa; *Fax:* 00298 31 9079.

International matches 2002
Poland (h) 1-2, Liechtenstein (a) 1-0, Liechtenstein (h) 3-1, Scotland (h) 2-2, Lithuania (a) 0-2, Germany (a) 1-2.

League Championship wins (1942–2002)
KI Klaksvik 16; HB Torshavn 16; TB Tvoroyri 7; GI Gotu 7; B36 Torshavn 7; B68 Toftir 3; SI Sorvag 1; IF Fuglafjordur 1; B71 Sandur 1; VB 1.

Cup wins (1955–2002)
HB Torshavn 25; KI Klaksvik 5; GI Gotu 5; TB Tvoroyri 4; B36 Torshavn 2; NSI Runavik 2; VB Vagur 1; B71 Sandur 1.

Final League Table 2002

	P	W	D	L	F	A	Pts
HB	18	13	2	3	52	19	41
NSI	18	11	3	4	38	21	36
KI	18	10	3	5	45	25	33
B36	18	9	5	4	55	27	32
GI	18	10	2	6	33	30	32
B68	18	7	5	6	28	28	26
VB	18	6	4	8	18	24	22
Skala	18	3	4	11	23	41	13
EB/Streymur	18	3	3	12	19	42	12
TB*	18	1	3	14	18	72	6

Top scorer: Flotum (HB) 18.
Cup Final: NSI 2, HB 1.

FINLAND

Suomen Palloliitto Finlands Bollfoerbund, Lantinen Brahenkatu 2, P.O. Box 179, SF-00511 Helsinki.
Founded: 1907; *Number of Clubs:* 1,135; *Number of Players:* 66,100; *National Colours:* White shirts, blue shorts, white stockings.
Telephone: 00358 0 9701 01 01; *Cable:* SUOMIFOTBOLL HELSINKI; *Telex:* 126033 spl sf; *Fax:* 00358 0 9701 01 099.

International matches 2002
Bahrain (a) 2-0, Albania (a) 1-1, Macedonia (h) 3-0, South Korea (h) 0-2, Portugal (a) 4-1, Macedonia (a) 0-1, Latvia (h) 2-1, Eire (h) 0-3, Wales (h) 0-2, Azerbaijan (h) 3-0, Yugoslavia (a) 0-2.

League Championship wins (1949–2002)
HJK Helsinki 11; Valkeakosken Haka 8; Turun Palloseura 5; Kuopion Palloseura 5; Kuusysi 4; Lahden Reipas 3; IF Kamraterna 3; Ilves-Kissat 2; Jazz Pori 2; Kotkan TP 2; OPS Oulu 2; Torun Pyrkiva 1; IF Kronohagens 1; Helsinki PS 1; Kokkolan PV 1; Vasa 1; TPV Tampere 1; Tampere U 1.

Cup wins (1955–2002)
Valkeakosken Haka 11; Lahden Reipas 7; HJK Helsinki 7; Kotkan TP 4; Mikkeli 2; Kuusysi 2; Kuopion Palloseura 2; Ilves Tampere 2; TPS Turku 2; MyPa 2; IFK Abo 1; Drott 1; Helsinki PS 1; Pallo-Peikot 1; Rovaniemi PS 1; Jokerit 1 (formerly PK-35); Atlantis 1.

Qualifying League Table 2002

	P	W	D	L	F	A	Pts
HJK Helsinki	22	15	3	4	36	16	48
MyPa	22	12	7	3	43	20	43
Haka	22	11	5	6	31	18	38
Allianssi**	22	10	4	6	35	36	34
Inter	22	8	8	6	28	17	32
Tampere U	22	7	11	4	23	15	32
Lahti	22	9	5	8	23	26	32
Jaro	22	7	5	10	23	36	26
KuPS	22	6	6	10	26	30	24
Hameenlinna	22	3	9	10	23	34	18
Vaasa	22	4	5	13	21	39	17
Jazz Pori	22	4	4	14	17	42	16

***Formerly Atlantis.*

Final League Table 2002

	P	W	D	L	F	A	Pts
HJK Helsinki	29	20	5	4	51	21	65
MyPa	29	17	9	3	57	25	60
Haka	29	15	7	7	51	30	52
Allianssi	29	12	5	12	39	44	41
Tampere U	29	8	15	6	31	24	39
Inter	29	9	9	11	33	29	36
Jaro	29	10	6	13	34	46	36
Lahti	29	9	6	14	25	44	33

Relegation Table 2002

	P	W	D	L	F	A	Pts
KuPS	7	4	1	2	14	4	16
Turku++	7	4	2	1	10	9	15
Hameenlinna	7	3	0	4	8	8	11
Jokerit++	7	3	1	3	13	13	10
Jazz Pori	7	2	3	2	6	5	9
Kotka++	7	2	2	3	8	11	9
Vaasa*	7	2	2	3	6	12	9
TP 47	7	2	1	4	6	9	7

Top scorer: Kottila (HJK Helsinki) 18.
Cup Final: Haka 4, Lahti 1.

FRANCE

Federation Francaise De Football, 60 Bis Avenue D'Iena, F-75783 Paris, Cedex 16.
Founded: 1919; *Number of Clubs:* 21,629; *Number of Players:* 1,692,205; *National Colours:* Blue shirts, white shorts, red stockings.
Telephone: 0033 1 44 31 73 00; *Cable:* CEFI PARIS 034; *Telex:* 640000 fedfoot f; *Fax:* 0033 1 47 20 82 96.

International matches 2002
Romania (h) 2-1, Scotland (h) 5-0, Russia (h) 0-0, South Korea (a) 3-2, Senegal (n) 0-1, Uruguay (n) 0-0, Denmark (n) 0-2, Tunisia (a) 1-1, Cyprus (a) 2-1, Slovenia (h) 5-0, Malta (a) 4-0, Yugoslavia (h) 3-0.

League Championship wins (1933–2003)
Saint Etienne 10; Olympique Marseille 8; Nantes 8; AS Monaco 7; Stade de Reims 6; Girondins Bordeaux 5; OGC Nice 4; Lille OSC 3; Paris St Germain 2; FC Sete 2; Sochaux 2; Lyon 2; Racing Club Paris 1; Roubaix-Tourcoing 1; Strasbourg 1; Auxerre 1; Lens 1.

Cup wins (1918–2003)
Olympique Marseille 10; Saint Etienne 6; AS Monaco 6; Lille OSC 5; Racing Club Paris 5; Red Star 5; Paris St Germain 4; Olympique Lyon 3; Girondins Bordeaux 3; OGC Nice 3; Nantes 3; Racing Club Strasbourg 3; Auxerre 3; CAS Genereaux 2; Nancy 2; Sedan 2; FC Sete 2; Stade de Reims 2; SO Montpellier 2; Stade Rennes 2; AS Cannes 1; Club Français 1; Excelsior Roubaix 1; Le Havre 1; Olympique de Pantin 1; CA Paris 1; Sochaux 1; Toulouse 1; Bastia 1; Metz 1; Lorient 1.

Final League Table 2002–03

	P	W	D	L	F	A	Pts
Lyon	38	19	11	8	63	41	68
Monaco	38	19	10	9	66	33	67
Marseille	38	19	8	11	41	36	65
Bordeaux	38	18	10	10	57	36	64
Sochaux	38	17	13	8	46	31	64
Auxerre	38	18	10	10	38	29	64
Guingamp	38	19	5	14	59	46	62
Lens	38	14	15	9	43	31	57
Nantes	38	16	8	14	37	39	56
Nice	38	13	16	9	39	31	55
Paris St Germain	38	14	12	12	47	36	54
Bastia	38	12	11	15	40	48	47
Strasbourg	38	11	12	15	40	54	45
Lille	38	10	12	16	29	44	42
Rennes	38	10	10	18	35	45	40
Montpellier	38	10	10	18	37	54	40
Ajaccio	38	9	12	17	29	49	39
Le Havre*	38	10	8	20	27	47	38
Sedan*	38	9	9	20	41	59	36
Troyes*	38	7	10	21	23	48	31

Top scorer: Nonda (Monaco) 26.
Cup Final: Auxerre 2, Paris St Germain 1.

GEORGIA

Georgian Football Federation, 5 Shota Iamanidze Str, Tbillisi 380012, Georgia.
Founded: 1990; *Number of Clubs:* 4050. *Number of Players:* 115,000; *National Colours:* White shirts, black shorts, cherry stockings.
Telephone: 00995 32/960750; *Fax:* 00995 32/001128.

International matches 2002
South Africa (h) 4-1, Ukraine (a) 1-2, Turkey (a) 0-3, Switzerland (a) 1-4, Russia (h) 0-0.

League Championship wins (1990–2003)
Dynamo Tbilisi 11; Torpedo Kutaisi 3.

Cup wins (1990–2003)
Dynamo Tbilisi 7; Torpedo Kutaisi 2; Lokomotivi 2; Dynamo Batumi 1; Guria 1.

Qualifying League Table 2002–03

	P	W	D	L	F	A	Pts
Dynamo Tbilisi	22	18	2	2	50	8	56
Torpedo Kutaisi	22	16	4	2	50	15	52
Lokomotivi	22	16	2	4	35	10	50
WIT	22	16	1	5	40	15	49
Sioni	22	9	3	10	26	27	30
Kolkheti	22	9	3	10	28	33	30
Merani 91	22	6	5	11	25	37	23
Dila Gori	22	6	3	13	17	29	21
Dynamo Batumi	22	5	5	12	16	27	20
Metalurgi	22	6	1	15	17	50	19
Gorda	22	4	1	17	22	45	13
Milani	22	3	4	15	11	47	13

Top scorer: Ionanidze (Torpedo Kutaisi) 17.

Championship Table 2002–03

	P	W	D	L	F	A	Pts
Dynamo Tbilisi	10	6	2	2	17	7	48
Torpedo Kutaisi	10	6	2	2	15	5	46
WIT	10	4	4	2	10	7	41
Lokomotivi	10	4	1	5	16	10	38
Sioni	10	2	2	6	9	20	23
Kolkheti	10	0	5	5	5	23	20

Relegation Table 2002–03

	P	W	D	L	F	A	Pts
Dila Gori	10	5	3	2	15	8	29
Dynamo Batumi	10	5	3	2	12	5	28
Merani**	10	4	3	3	15	5	27
Gorda+	10	5	3	2	8	3	25
Milani*	10	3	4	3	7	7	20
Metalurgi*	10	0	0	10	0	29	10

***Merani renamed Merani Olimpi.*
Top scorer: Ionanidze (Torpedo Kutaisi) 26.
Cup Final: Dynamo Tbilisi 3, Sioni 1.

GERMANY

Deutscher Fussball-Bund, Postfach 710265, D-60492, Frankfurt Am Main.
Founded: 1900; *Number of Clubs:* 26,760; *Number of Players:* 5,260,320; *National Colours:* White shirts, black shorts, white stockings.
Telephone: 0049 69 678 80; *Telex:* 416815 dfb d; *Fax:* 0049 69 678 82 66.

International matches 2002

Israel (h) 7-1, USA (h) 4-2, Argentina (h) 0-1, Kuwait (h) 7-0, Wales (a) 0-1, Austria (h) 6-2, Saudi Arabia (n) 8-0, Eire (n) 1-1, Cameroon (n) 2-0, Paraguay (n) 1-0, USA (n) 1-0, South Korea (n) 1-0, Brazil (n) 0-2, Bulgaria (a) 2-2, Lithuania (a) 2-0, Bosnia (a) 1-1, Faeroes (h) 2-1, Holland (h) 1-3.

League Championship wins (1903–2003)

Bayern Munich 18; IFC Nuremberg 9; Schalke 04 7; Borussia Dortmund 6; SV Hamburg 6; Borussia Moenchengladbach 5; VfB Stuttgart 4; IFC Kaiserslautern 4; VfB Leipzig 3; SpVgg Furth 3; IFC Cologne 3; Werder Bremen 3; Viktoria Berlin 2; Hertha Berlin 2; Hanover 96 2; Dresden SC 2; Munich 1860 1; Union Berlin 1; FC Freiburg 1; Phoenix Karlsruhe 1; Karlsruher FV 1; Holstein Kiel 1; Fortuna Dusseldorf 1; Rapid Vienna 1; VfR Mannheim 1; Rot-Weiss Essen 1; Eintracht Frankfurt 1; Eintracht Brunswick 1.

Cup wins (1935–2003)

Bayern Munich 11; IFC Cologne 4; Eintracht Frankfurt 4; Werder Bremen 4; Schalke 04 4; IFC Nuremberg 3; SV Hamburg 3; Moenchengladbach 3; VfB Stuttgart 3; Dresden SC 2; Fortuna Dusseldorf 2; Karlsruhe SC 2; Munich 1860 2; Borussia Dortmund 2; Kaiserslautern 2; First Vienna 1; VfB Leipzig 1; Kickers Offenbach 1; Rapid Vienna 1; Rot-Weiss Essen 1; SW Essen 1; Bayer Uerdingen 1; Hannover 96 1; Leverkusen 1.

Final League Table 2002–03

	P	W	D	L	F	A	Pts
Bayern Munich	34	23	6	5	70	25	71
Stuttgart	34	17	8	9	53	39	59
Borussia Dortmund	34	15	13	6	51	27	58
Hamburg	34	15	11	8	46	36	56
Hertha	34	16	6	12	52	43	54
Werder Bremen	34	16	4	14	51	50	52
Schalke	34	12	13	9	46	40	49
Wolfsburg	34	13	7	14	39	42	46
Bochum	34	12	9	13	55	56	45
Munich 1860	34	12	9	13	44	52	45
Hanover	34	12	7	15	47	57	43
Moenchengladbach	34	11	9	14	43	45	42
Hansa Rostock	34	11	8	15	35	41	41
Kaiserslautern	34	10	10	14	40	42	40
Leverkusen	34	11	7	16	47	56	40
Arminia*	34	8	12	14	35	46	36
Nuremberg*	34	8	6	20	33	60	30
Cottbus*	34	7	9	18	34	64	30

Top scorers: Christiansen (Bochum) 21, Elber (Bayern Munich 21).
Cup Final: Bayern Munich 3, Kaiserslautern 1.

GREECE

Federation Hellenique De Football, Singrou Avenue 137, 17121 Athens.
Founded: 1926; *Number of Clubs:* 4,050; *Number of Players:* 180,000; *National Colours:* White shirts, blue shorts, white stockings.
Telephone: 0030 1 933 88 50; *Cable:* FOOTBALL ATHENS; *Telex:* 215328 epo gr; *Fax:* 0030 1 935 96 66.

International matches 2002

Sweden (h) 2-2, Belgium (h) 3-2, Czech Republic (h) 0-0, Romania (h) 3-2, Cyprus (h) 3-1, Romania (a) 1-0, Spain (h) 0-2, Ukraine (a) 0-2, Armenia (h) 2-0, Eire (h) 0-0.

League Championship wins (1928–2003)

Olympiakos 32; Panathinaikos 18; AEK Athens 11; Aris Salonika 3; PAOK Salonika 2; Larissa 1.

Cup wins (1932–2003)

Olympiakos 21; Panathinaikos 16; AEK Athens 13; PAOK Salonika 4; Panionios 2; Aris Salonika 1; Ethnikos 1; Iraklis 1; Kastoria 1; Larissa 1; Ofi Crete 1.

Final League Table 2002–03

	P	W	D	L	F	A	Pts
Olympiakos	30	21	7	2	75	21	70
Panathinaikos	30	22	4	4	50	19	70
AEK Athens	30	21	5	4	74	29	68
PAOK Salonika	30	16	5	9	59	38	53
Panionios	30	15	8	7	35	25	53
Aris Salonika	30	15	6	9	37	34	51
Iraklis	30	15	4	11	44	37	49
Ofi Crete	30	12	8	10	39	34	44
Xanthi	30	8	11	11	31	33	35
Aigaleo	30	7	10	13	28	44	31
Proodeftiki	30	7	9	14	25	38	30
Kalithea	30	6	8	16	29	46	26
Akratitos	30	7	5	18	33	62	26
Ionikos+	30	5	9	16	22	42	24
Panachaiki*	30	1	6	23	11	71	9
PAS Giannina**	30	6	7	17	25	44	-65

***Suspended for non payment of salary; each incident resulting in three points deducted.*
Top scorer: Liberopoulos (Panathinaikos) 16.
Cup Final: PAOK Salonika 1, Aris Salonika 0.

HOLLAND

Koninklijke Nederlandsche Voetbalbond, Woudenbergseweg 56-58, Postbus 515, NL-3700 AM, Zeist.
Founded: 1889; *Number of Clubs:* 3,097; *Number of Players:* 962,397; *National Colours:* Orange shirts, white shorts, orange stockings.
Telephone: 0031343 499211; *Cable:* VOETBAL ZEIST; *Telex:* 40497 knvb nl; *Fax:* 0031343 499189.

International matches 2002

England (h) 1-1, Spain (h) 1-0, USA (a) 2-0, Norway (a) 1-0, Belarus (h) 3-0, Austria (a) 3-0, Germany (a) 3-1.

League Championship wins (1898–2003)

Ajax Amsterdam 28; PSV Eindhoven 17; Feyenoord 14; HVV The Hague 8; Sparta Rotterdam 6; Go Ahead Deventer 4; HBS The Hague 3; Willem II Tilburg 3; RAP 2; Heracles 2; ADO The Hague 2; Quick The Hague 1; BVV Den Bosch 2; NAC Breda 1; Eindhoven 1; Enschede 1; Volewijckers Amsterdam 1; Limburgia 1; Rapid JC Heerlen 3; DOS Utrecht 1; DWS Amsterdam 1; Haarlem 1; Be Quick Groningen 1; AZ 67 Alkmaar 1.

Cup wins (1899–2003)

Ajax Amsterdam 15; Feyenoord 10; PSV Eindhoven 7; Quick The Hague 4; AZ 67 Alkmaar 3; Rotterdam 3; DFC 2; Fortuna Geleen 2; Haarlem 2; HBS The Hague 2; RCH Haarlem 2; Roda 2; VOC 2; Wageningen 2; Willem II Tilburg 2; FC Den Haag 2; Twente Enschede 2; ; Utrecht 2; Concordia Rotterdam 1; CVV 1; Eindhoven 1; HVV The Hague 1; Longa 1; Quick Nijmegen 1; RAP 1; Roermond 1; Schoten 1; Velocitas Breda 1; Velocitas Groningen 1; VSV 1; VUC 1; VVV Groningen 1; ZFC 1; NAC Breda 1.

Final League Table 2002–03

	P	W	D	L	F	A	Pts
PSV Eindhoven	34	26	6	2	87	20	84
Ajax	34	26	5	3	96	32	83
Feyenoord	34	25	5	4	89	39	80
NAC Breda	34	13	13	8	42	31	52

NEC Nijmegen	34	14	9	11	41	40	51
Roda JC	34	14	8	12	58	54	50
Heerenveen	34	13	8	13	61	55	47
Utrecht	34	12	11	11	49	49	47
RKC Waalwijk	34	14	4	16	44	51	46
AZ	34	12	8	14	50	69	44
Willem II	34	11	9	14	48	51	42
Twente	34	10	11	13	36	45	41
Roosendaal	34	10	6	18	33	54	36
Vitesse	34	8	9	17	37	51	33
Groningen	34	7	11	16	28	44	32
Zwolle+	34	8	8	18	31	62	32
Excelsior+	34	5	8	21	38	72	23
De Graafschap*	34	6	5	23	35	84	23

Top scorer: Kezman (PSV Eindhoven) 35.
Cup Final: Utrecht 4, Feyenoord 1.

HUNGARY

Hungarian Football Federation, Magyar Labdarugo Szovetseg, Istvanmezei ut. 3-5, Nepstadion (Toronyepulet), H-1146 Budapest. For correspondence: Pf. 106H-1581 Budapest.
Founded: 1901; *Number of Clubs:* 1944; *Number of Players:* 95,986; *National Colours:* Red shirts, white shorts, green stockings.
Telephone: 0036 1 222 0343; *Telex:* 225782 misz h; *Fax:* 0036 1 222 0324/222 0344.

International matches 2002
Czech Republic (a) 0-2, Switzerland (a) 1-2, Moldova (a) 2-0, Belarus (h) 2-5, Croatia (h) 0-2, Spain (h) 1-1, Iceland (a) 2-0, Sweden (a) 1-1, San Marino (h) 3-0, Moldova (h) 1-1.

League Championship wins (1901–2003)
Ferencvaros 26; MTK-VM Budapest 22; Ujpest Dozsa 20; Honved 13; Vasas Budapest 6; Csepel 4; Raba Gyor 3; BTC 2; Nagyvarad 1; Vac 1; Dunaferr 1; Zalaegerszeg 1.

Cup wins (1910–2003)
Ferencvaros 18; MTK-VM Budapest 12; Ujpest Dozsa 9; Raba Gyor 4; Kispest Honved 4; Vasas Budapest 3; Diösgyör 2; ; Debrecen 2; Bocskai 1; III Ker 1; Kispesti AC 1; Soroksar 1; Szolnoki MAV 1; Siofok Banyasz 1; Bekescsaba 1; Pecs 1.
Cup not regularly held until 1964.

Qualifying League Table 2002–03

	P	W	D	L	F	A	Pts
Ferencvaros	22	15	3	4	41	17	48
MTK	22	14	5	3	42	21	47
Ujpest	22	12	4	6	45	29	40
Debrecen	22	10	9	3	44	30	39
Siofok	22	8	8	6	28	27	32
Gyor	22	9	5	8	35	35	32
Zalaegerszeg	22	8	6	8	37	36	30
Videoton	22	7	6	9	29	30	27
Matav	22	6	5	11	33	36	23
Dunaferr	22	4	6	12	28	43	18
Kispest Honved	22	4	3	15	27	51	15
Bekescsaba	22	4	2	16	25	59	14

Final Championship Table 2002–03

	P	W	D	L	F	A	Pts
MTK	32	20	6	59	34	66	66
Ferencvaros	32	19	7	6	50	24	64
Ujpest	32	13	14	5	57	38	53
Debrecen	32	15	7	10	54	41	52
Siofok	32	12	11	9	46	44	47
Gyor	32	9	9	14	41	50	36

Promotion/Relegation Table 2002–03

	P	W	D	L	F	A	Pts
Zalaegerszeg	32	15	8	9	62	49	53
Videoton	32	11	7	14	46	41	40
Matav	32	9	9	14	47	54	36
Bekescsaba	32	9	5	18	42	71	32
Kispest Honved*	32	8	5	19	43	66	29
Dunaferr*	32	4	8	20	37	72	20

Top scorer: Kenesei (Zalaegerszeg) 23.
Cup Final: Ferencvaros 2, Debrecen 1.

ICELAND

Knattspyrnusamband Island, Laugardal, 104 Reykjavik.
Founded: 1929; *Number of Clubs:* 73; *Number of Players:* 23,673; *National Colours:* All blue.
Telephone: 00354 5102900; *Cable* KSI REYKJAVIK; *Telex:* 2314 isi is; *Fax:* 00354 75689793.

International matches 2002
Kuwait (a) 0-0, Saudi Arabia (a) 0-1, Brazil (a) 1-6, Norway (a) 1-1, Andorra (h) 3-0, Hungary (h) 0-2, Scotland (h) 0-2, Lithuania (h) 3-0, Estonia (a) 0-2.

League Championship wins (1912–2002)
KR 23; Valur 19; Fram 18; IA Akranes 18; Vikingur 5; IBV Vestmann 4; IBK Keflavik 3; KA Akureyri 1.

Cup wins (1960–2002)
KR 10; Valur 8; Fram 7; IA Akranes 7; IBV Vestmann 4; IBK Keflavik 2; Fylkir 2; IBA Akureyri 1; Vikingur 1.

Final League Table 2002

	P	W	D	L	F	A	Pts
KR	18	10	6	2	32	18	36
Fylkir	18	10	4	4	30	22	34
Grindavik	18	8	5	5	32	26	29
KA	18	6	7	5	18	19	25
IA	18	6	5	7	29	26	23
FH	18	5	7	6	29	30	22
IBV	18	5	5	8	23	22	20
Fram	18	5	5	8	29	33	20
Keflavik*	18	4	8	6	25	30	20
Thor*	18	3	4	11	22	43	13

Top scorer: Hjartarson (Grindavik) 13.
Cup Final: Fylkir 3, Fram 1.

REPUBLIC OF IRELAND

The Football Association of Ireland (Cumann Peile Na H-Eireann), 80 Merrion Square, South Dublin 2.
Founded: 1921; *Number of Clubs:* 3,190; *Number of Players:* 124,615; *National Colours:* Green shirts, white shorts, green and white stockings.
Telephone: 00353 1 676 68 64; *Telex:* 91397 fai ei; *Fax:* 00353 1 661 09 31.

League Championship wins (1922–2003)
Shamrock Rovers 15; Shelbourne 10; Dundalk 9; Bohemians 9; St Patrick's Athletic 8; Waterford 6; Cork United 5; Drumcondra 5; St James's Gate 2; Cork Athletic 2; Sligo Rovers 2; Limerick 2; Athlone Town 2; Derry City 2; Dolphin 1; Cork Hibernians 1; Cork Celtic 1; Cork City 1.

Cup wins (1922–2003)
Shamrock Rovers 24; Dundalk 9; Shelbourne 6; Bohemians 6; Drumcondra 5; Derry City 3; Cork Athletic 2; Cork United 2; St James's Gate 2; St Patrick's Athletic 2; Cork Hibernians 2; Limerick 2; Waterford 2; Athlone Town 2; Sligo 2; Bray Wanderers 2; Alton United 1; Cork 1; Fordsons 1; Transport 1; Finn Harps 1; Home Farm 1; UCD 1; Galway United 1; Cork City 1.

Final League Table 2002–03

	P	W	D	L	F	A	Pts
Bohemians	27	15	9	3	47	27	54
Shelbourne	27	15	4	8	43	26	49
Shamrock Rovers	27	12	7	8	42	29	43
Cork City	27	11	6	10	37	34	39
Longford Town	27	8	11	8	25	29	35
UCD	27	8	9	10	23	25	33
St Patrick's Athletic	27	8	9	10	27	32	33
Derry City	27	8	7	12	31	37	31
Drogheda+	27	8	6	13	26	40	30
Bray Wanderers*	27	4	8	15	31	53	20

Top scorer: Crowe (Bohemians) 18.
Cup Final: Derry City 1, Shamrock Rovers 0.

ISRAEL

Israel Football Association, Ramat-Gan Stadium, 299 Aba Hilell Street, Ramat-Gan 52594.
Founded: 1948; *Number of Clubs:* 544; *Number of Players:* 30,449; *National Colours:* Blue shirts, white shorts, blue stockings.
Telephone: 00972 3 570 59 99; *Cable:* CADUREGEL RAMAT-GAN; *Telex:* 361353 fa; *Fax:* 00972 3 570 20 44.

International matches 2002
Germany (a) 1-7, Denmark (a) 1-3, Lithuania (a) 4-2, Luxembourg (a) 5-0, Malta (a) 2-0, Macedonia (a) 3-2.

League Championship wins (1932–2003)
Maccabi Tel Aviv 19; Hapoel Tel Aviv 13; Maccabi Haifa 7; Hapoel Petah Tikva 6; Maccabi Netanya 5; Beitar

Jerusalem 4; Hakoah Ramat Gan 2; Hapoel Beersheba 2; Bnei Yehouda 1; British Police 1; Hapoel Kfar Sava 1; Hapoel Ramat Gan 1; Hapoel Haifa 1 .

Cup wins (1928–2003)
Maccabi Tel Aviv 21; Hapoel Tel Aviv 11; Beitar Jerusalem 5; Maccabi Haifa 5; Hapoel Haifa 3; Hapoel Kfar Sava 3; Beitar Tel Aviv 2; Bnei Yehouda 2; Hakoah Ramat Gan 2; Hapoel Petah Tikva 2; Maccabi Petah Tikva 2; British Police 1; Hapoel Jerusalem 1; Hapoel Lod 1; Maccabi Netanya 1; Hapoel Beersheba 1; Hapoel Ramat Gan 1.

Final League Table 2002–03

	P	*W*	*D*	*L*	*F*	*A*	*Pts*
Maccabi Tel Aviv	33	23	3	8	66	31	69
Maccabi Haifa	33	21	6	6	75	42	69
Hapoel Tel Aviv	33	19	10	4	53	22	67
Maccabi Netanya	33	15	9	9	47	36	54
Hapoel Beersheba	33	15	6	12	56	41	51
Maccabi Petah Tikva	33	13	11	9	45	37	50
Ashdod	33	11	7	15	35	49	40
Hapoel Petah Tikva	33	11	6	16	41	53	39
Beitar Jerusalem	33	10	6	17	46	59	36
Bnei Yehouda	33	9	7	17	39	63	34
Hapoel Kfar Sava*	33	7	5	21	43	81	23
Ironi Rishon*	33	4	6	23	35	67	18

Hapoel Kfar Sava three points deducted for financial irregularities.
Top scorer: Abargil (Hapoel Kfar Sava) 14.
Cup Final: Hapoel Ramat Gan 1, Hapoel Beersheba 1.
Hapoel Ramat Gan won 5-4 on penalties.

ITALY

Federazione Italiana Giuoco Calcio, Via Gregorio Allegri 14, C.P. 2450, 1-00198, Roma.
Founded: 1898; *Number of Clubs:* 20,961; *Number of Players:* 1,420,160; *National Colours:* Blue shirts, white shorts, blue stockings with white trim.
Telephone: 0039 6 849 11; *Cable:* FEDERCALCIO ROMA; *Telex:* 624132 calcio i; *Fax:* 0039 6 849 12 526.

International matches 2002
USA (h) 1-0, England (a) 2-1, Uruguay (h) 1-1, Czech Republic (a) 0-1, Ecuador (n) 2-0, Croatia (n) 1-2, Mexico (n) 1-1, South Korea (n) 1-2, Slovenia (h) 0-1, Azerbaijan (a) 2-0, Yugoslavia (h) 1-1, Wales (a) 1-2, Turkey (h) 1-1.

League Championship wins (1898–2003)
Juventus 27; AC Milan 16; Inter-Milan 13; Genoa 9; Torino 8; Pro Vercelli 7; Bologna 7; AS Roma 3; Fiorentina 2; Lazio 2; Napoli 2; Casale 1; Novese 1; Cagliari 1; Verona 1; Sampdoria 1.

Cup wins (1922–2003)
Juventus 9; AS Roma 8; Fiorentina 6; AC Milan 5; Torino 4; Sampdoria 4; Lazio 3; Inter-Milan 3; Napoli 3; Parma 3; Bologna 2; Atalanta 1; Genoa 1; Vado 1; Venezia 1; Vicenza 1.

Final League Table 2002–03

	P	*W*	*D*	*L*	*F*	*A*	*Pts*
Juventus	34	21	9	4	64	29	72
Internazionale	34	19	8	7	64	38	65
AC Milan	34	18	7	9	55	30	61
Lazio	34	15	15	4	57	32	60
Parma	34	15	11	8	55	36	56
Udinese	34	16	8	10	38	35	56
Chievo	34	16	7	11	51	39	55
Roma	34	13	10	11	55	46	49
Brescia	34	9	15	10	36	38	42
Perugia	34	10	12	12	40	48	42
Bologna	34	10	11	13	39	47	41
Empoli	34	9	11	14	36	46	38
Modina	34	9	11	14	30	48	38
Atalanta*	34	8	14	12	35	47	38
Reggina+	34	10	8	16	38	53	38
Piacenza*	34	8	6	20	44	62	30
Como*	34	4	12	18	29	57	24
Torino*	34	4	9	21	23	58	21

Top scorer: Vieri (Internazionale) 24.
Cup Final: AC Milan 4, 2, Roma 1, 2.

KAZAKHSTAN

The Football Association of the Republic of Kazakhstan, 44 Abai Street, 480072 Almaty, Kazakhstan.
Founded: 1914; *Number of Clubs:* 5,793; *Number of Players:* 260,000.
Telephone: 0073272 671885; *Telex:* 251347 TREK SU; *Fax:* 0073272 671885.

International matches 2002
Latvia (a) 1-2, Estonia (h) 1-1.

League Championship wins (1992-2002)
Irtysh 4; Yelimai 3; Zhenis 2; Kairat 1; Taraz 1.

Cup wins (1992–2002)
Kairat 4; Zhenis 2; Dostyk 1; Vostok 1; Yelimai 1; Irtysh 1; Kaisar 1.

Final League Table 2002

	P	*W*	*D*	*L*	*F*	*A*	*Pts*
Irtysh	32	21	8	3	63	14	71
Atyrau	32	19	6	7	43	22	63
Tobol	32	15	7	10	45	43	52
Zhenis	32	14	10	8	40	23	52
Atobe	32	13	7	12	37	40	46
Shakhter	32	11	10	11	45	39	43
Kairat++	32	13	7	12	41	36	46
Yelimai	32	11	6	15	33	51	39
Yesil Bogatyr	32	10	7	15	31	35	37
Kaisar	32	10	2	20	31	55	32
Vostok	32	10	2	20	27	47	32
Yesil Kokshetau	32	6	6	20	25	56	24

Top scorer: Lunev (Shakhter) 16.
Cup Final: Zhenis 1, Irtysh 0.

LATVIA

Latvian Football Federation, Augsiela, 1, LV-1009, Riga.
Founded: 1921; *Number of Clubs:* 50; *Number of Players:* 12,000; *National Colours:* Carmine red shirts, white shorts, carmine red stockings.
Telephone: 00371 2 29 29 88; *Fax:* 00371 7828331.

International matches 2002
Luxembourg (a) 3-0, Kazakhstan (h) 2-1, Finland (a) 1-2, Azerbaijan (h) 0-0, Belarus (h) 2-4, Sweden (h) 0-0, Poland (a) 1-0, San Marino (a) 1-0.

League Championship wins (1922–2002)
Skonto Riga 12; ASK Riga 9; RFK Riga 8; Olympia Liepaya 7; Sarkanais Metalurgs Liepaya 7; VEF Riga 6; Energija Riga 4; Elektrons Riga 3; Torpedo Riga 3; Daugava Liepaya 2; ODO Riga 2; Khimikis Daugavpils 2; RAF Yelgava 2; Keisermezhs Riga 2; Dinamo Riga 1; Zhmilyeva Team 1; Darba Rezervi 1; REZ Riga 1; Start Brotseni 1; Venta Ventspils 1; Yurnieks Riga 1; Alfa Riga 1; Gauya Valmiera 1.

Cup wins (1937–2002)
Elektrons Riga 7; Skonto Riga 7; Sarkanais Metalurgs Liepaya 5; ODO Riga 3; VEF Riga 3; ASK Riga 3; Tseltnieks Riga 3; RAF Yelgava 3; RFK Riga 2; Daugava Liepaya 2; Start Brotseni 2; Selmash Liepaya 2; Yurnieks Riga 2; Khimikis Daugavpils 2; Rigas Vilki 1; Dinamo Liepaya 1; Dinamo Riga 1; REZ Riga 1; Voulkan Kouldiga 1; Baltija Liepaya 1; Venta Ventspils 1; Pilot Riga 1; Lielupe Yurmala 1; Energija Riga 1; Torpedo Riga 1; Daugava SKIF Riga 1; Tseltnieks Daugavpils 1; Olympia Riga 1; FK Riga 1.

Final League Table 2002

	P	*W*	*D*	*L*	*F*	*A*	*Pts*
Skonto Riga	28	23	4	1	95	19	73
FK Ventspils	28	22	5	1	77	20	71
Metalurgs Liepaya	28	15	6	7	56	31	51
Dinaburg Daugavpils	28	12	4	12	37	35	40
FK Valmiera	28	6	6	16	26	54	24
PFK/Daugava	28	6	5	17	29	60	23
FK Riga	28	6	2	20	24	75	20
Auda*	28	5	2	21	23	73	17

Top scorer: Mikholap (Skonto Riga) 23.
Cup Final: Skonto Riga 3, Metalurgs Liepaya 0.

LIECHTENSTEIN

Liechtensteiner Fussball-Verband, Malbuner Huus Altenbach 11, Postfach 165, 9490 Vaduz.
Founded: 1934; *Number of Clubs:* 7; *Number of Players:* 1,247; *National Colours:* Blue shirts, red shorts, blue stockings.

Telephone: 004175 237 4747; *Cable:* FUSSBALLVERBAND VADUZ; *Fax:* 004175 237 4748.

International matches 2002
Faeroes (h) 0-1, N Ireland (h) 0-0, Luxembourg (a) 3-3, Faeroes (a) 1-3, Macedonia (h) 1-1, Turkey (a) 0-5.
Liechtenstein has no national league. Teams compete in Swiss regional leagues.

Cup wins (1946–2003)
Vaduz 32; Balzers 11; Triesen 8; Eschen/Mauren 4; Schaan 3.
Cup Winners: Vaduz.

LITHUANIA

Lithuanian Football Federation, Seimyniskiu str. 15, 2005 Vilnius.
Founded: 1922; *Number of Clubs:* 152; *Number of Players:* 16,600; *National Colours:* Yellow shirts, green shorts, yellow stockings.
Telephone: 00370 2/723654; *Fax:* 00370 2/723651.

International matches 2002
Moldova (n) 1-0, Malta (n) 1-1, Jordan (n) 0-3, Yugoslavia (a) 1-4, Israel (h) 2-4, Germany (h) 0-2, Faeroes (h) 2-0, Iceland (a) 0-3.

League Championship wins (1922–2002)
Kovas Kaunas 6; KSS Klaipeda 6; LFLS Kaunas 4; Zalgiris Vilnius 4; FBK Kaunas 4; LGSF Kaunas 2; Kareda 2; MSK Kaunas 1; Ekranas Panevezys 1; Romar Mazeikiai 1; Inkaras Grifas 1.

Cup wins (1992–2003)
Zalgiris Vilnius 3; Kareda 2; Ekranas 2; Atlantas 2; Inkaras 1; Kaunas 1.

Final League Table 2002

	P	*W*	*D*	*L*	*F*	*A*	*Pts*
FBK Kaunas	32	24	6	2	85	20	78
Atlantas	32	20	7	5	58	23	67
Ekranas	32	16	7	9	43	25	55
Zalgiris	32	12	11	9	46	37	47
Inkaras	32	13	7	12	34	29	46
Suduva	32	11	8	13	44	50	41
Sakalas	32	8	10	14	30	56	34
Gelezinis*	32	4	6	22	26	75	18
Nevezis*	32	2	6	24	19	70	12

Cup Final: Atlantas 1, Vetra 1.
Atlantas won 3-1 on penalties.

LUXEMBOURG

Federation Luxembourgeoise De Football (F.L.F.), 50, Rue De Strasbourg, L-2560, Luxembourg.
Founded: 1908; *Number of Clubs:* 126; *Number of Players:* 21,684; *National Colours:* All red.
Telephone: 00352 48 86 65; *Cable:* FOOTBALL LUXEMBOURG; *Telex:* 2426 flf l; *Fax:* 00352 40 02 01.

International matches 2002
Albania (h) 0-0, Latvia (h) 0-3, Liechtenstein (h) 3-3, Morocco (h) 0-2, Israel (h) 0-5, Denmark (a) 0-2, Romania (h) 0-7, Cape Verde (h) 0-0.

League Championship wins (1910–2003)
Jeunesse Esch 26; Spora Luxembourg 11; Stade Dudelange 10; Avenir Beggen 7; Red Boys Differdange 6; US Hollerich-Bonnevoie 5; Fola Esch 5; US Luxembourg 5; Aris Bonnevoie 3; Progres Niedercorn 3; F91 Dudelange 3; Grevenmacher 1.

Cup wins (1922–2003)
Red Boys Differdange 16; Jeunesse Esch 12; US Luxembourg 10; Spora Luxembourg 8; Avenir Beggen 7; Stade Dudelange 4; Progres Niedercorn 4; Fola Esch 3; Grevenmacher 3; Alliance Dudelange 2; US Rumelange 2; Aris Bonnevoie 1; US Dudelange 1; Jeunesse Hautcharage 1; National Schiffige 1; Racing Luxembourg 1; SC Tetange 1; Hesperange 1; Etzella 1.

Qualifying Table 2002–03

	P	*W*	*D*	*L*	*F*	*A*	*Pts*
F91 Dudelange	22	14	3	5	60	27	45
Grevenmacher	22	13	5	4	56	21	44
Union Luxembourg	22	11	6	5	40	28	39
Jeunesse Esch	22	10	8	4	42	23	38
Hesperange	22	10	7	5	53	32	37
Mondercange	22	11	2	9	51	44	35
Rumelange	22	10	3	9	45	49	33
FC Wiltz 71	22	7	4	11	30	42	25
Victoria Rosport	22	6	7	9	32	50	25
Avenir Beggen	22	7	3	12	44	56	24
Niedercom	22	5	0	17	22	68	15
Sporting Mertzig	22	4	0	18	23	58	12

Championship Table 2002–03

	P	*W*	*D*	*L*	*F*	*A*	*Pts*
Grevenmacher	6	5	0	1	68	28	59
F91 Dudelange	6	2	1	3	66	34	52
Jeunesse Esch	6	3	1	2	54	30	48
Union	6	1	0	5	43	40	42

Promotion/Relegation Table 2002–03

Group A

	P	*W*	*D*	*L*	*F*	*A*	*Pts*
Hesperange	6	4	2	0	66	37	51
Victoria Rosport	6	4	1	1	44	55	38
Rumelange	6	1	1	4	51	63	37
Niedercom*	6	1	0	5	29	82	18

Group B

	P	*W*	*D*	*L*	*F*	*A*	*Pts*
Mondercange	6	1	1	4	60	59	39
Avenir Beggen	6	4	1	1	57	64	37
FC Wiltz 71	6	3	2	1	43	49	36
Sporting Mertzig*	6	2	0	4	36	76	18

Top scorer: Huss (Grevenmacher) 22.
Cup Final: Grevenmacher 1, Etzella 0.

MACEDONIA

Football Association of the Former Yugoslav Republic of Macedonia, VIII-ma Udarna Brigada 31A, PO Box 84, MAC-91000 Skopje.
Founded: 1948; *Number of Clubs:* 598; *Number of Players:* 15,165; *National Colours:* All red.
Telephone: 00389 1 22 90 42; *Fax:* 00389 1 23 54 48.

International matches 2002
Albania (h) 0-0, Bahrain (a) 1-1, Finland (a) 0-3, Bosnia (a) 4-4, Finland (h) 1-0, Malta (h) 5-0, Israel (h) 2-3, Liechtenstein (a) 1-1, Turkey (h) 1-2, England (a) 2-2.

League Championship wins (1993–2003)
Vardar 5; Sileks 3; Sloga 3.

Cup wins (1993–2003)
Vardar 4; Sileks 1; Sloga 1; Pellister 1; Pobeda 1; Cement 1.

Final League Table 2002–03

	P	*W*	*D*	*L*	*F*	*A*	*Pts*
Vardar	33	22	6	5	73	37	72
Belasica	33	20	9	4	50	32	69
Pobeda	33	20	5	8	55	33	65
Rabotnicki	33	16	6	11	41	35	54
Sloga	33	15	6	12	62	50	51
Sileks	33	14	4	15	40	35	46
Napredak	33	13	3	17	39	41	42
Cement	33	11	9	13	45	39	42
Tikves	33	11	4	18	37	58	37
Delcevo	33	10	6	17	44	49	36
Pelister*	33	7	7	19	30	60	28
Kumanovo*	33	4	5	24	24	71	17

Top scorer: Savic (Delcevo/Sloga) 25.
Cup Final: Cement 4, Sloga 4.
Cement won 3-2 on penalties.

MALTA

Malta Football Association, 280 St. Paul Street, Valletta VLT07.
Founded: 1900; *Number of Clubs:* 252; *Number of Players:* 5,544; *National Colours:* Red shirts, white shorts, red stockings.
Telephone: 00356 22 26 97; *Cable:* FOOTBALL MALTA VALLETTA; *Fax:* 00356 24 51 36.

International matches 2002
Jordan (h) 2-1, Lithuania (h) 1-1, Moldova (h) 3-0, Andorra (h) 1-1, Azerbaijan (h) 1-0, Macedonia (a) 0-5, Slovania (a) 0-3, Israel (h) 0-2, France (h) 0-4, Cyprus (a) 1-2.

League Championship wins (1910–2003)
Floriana 25; Sliema Wanderers 24; Valletta 18; Hibernians 9; Hamrun Spartans 7; Rabat Ajax 2; St George's 1; KOMR 1; Birkirkara 1.

Cup wins (1935–2003)
Floriana 18; Sliema Wanderers 18; Valletta 10; Hamrun Spartans 6; Hibernians 6; Birkirkara 2; Gzira United 1; Melita 1; Zurrieq 1; Rabat Ajax 1.

Qualifying League Table 2002–03

	P	W	D	L	F	A	Pts
Sliema Wanderers	18	14	2	2	51	16	44
Birkirkara	18	13	1	4	46	24	40
Valletta	18	12	1	5	42	18	37
Hibernians	18	9	3	6	35	26	30
Pieta Hotspurs	18	6	5	7	19	22	23
Marsaxlokk	18	7	0	11	27	38	21
Hamrun Spartans	18	6	2	10	22	31	20
Floriana	18	5	2	11	25	40	17
Marsa	18	4	4	10	25	45	16
Mosta	18	2	4	12	14	46	10

Championship Table 2002–03

	P	W	D	L	F	A	Pts
Sliema Wanderers	28	20	4	4	28	42	42
Birkirkara	28	18	3	7	34	37	37
Valletta	28	16	5	7	31	35	35
Hibernians	28	14	5	9	36	32	32
Pieta Hotspurs	28	7	9	2	43	19	19
Marsaxlokk	28	8	2	8	57	16	16

Promotion/Relegation Table 2002–03

	P	W	D	L	F	A	Pts
Hamrun Spartans	24	8	5	11	32	43	21
Floriana	24	8	6	10	32	34	20
Marsa*	24	8	6	12	33	53	16
Mosta*	24	2	5	17	17	60	6

Top scorers: Doncic (Sliema Wanderers) 18, Galea (Birkirkara) 18, Mifsud (Hibernians) 18.
Cup Final: Birkirkara 1, Sliema Wanderers 0.

MOLDOVA

Moldavian Football Federation, 39 Tricolorului Str, 2012, Chisinau.
Founded: 1990; *Number of Clubs:* 143; *Number of Players:* 75,000; *National Colours:* Blue shirts, red shorts, yellow stockings.
Telephone: 00373 2 247878. *Fax:* 00373 2 247890.

International matches 2002
Lithuania (n) 0-1, Jordan (n) 2-0, Malta (n) 0-3, Hungary (h) 0-2, Estonia (a) 0-1, Austria (a) 0-2, Czech Republic (h) 0-2, Hungary (a) 1-1.

League Championship wins (1992–2003)
Zimbru Chisinau 8; Serif 3; Constructorul 1.

Cup wins (1992–2003)
Tiligul 4; Serif 3; Zimbru Chisinau 3; Combat 1; Constructorul 1.

Final League Table 2002–03

	P	W	D	L	F	A	Pts
Serif	24	19	3	2	64	15	60
Zimbru Chisinau	24	15	5	4	47	20	50
Otaci	24	13	3	8	33	24	42
Dacia	24	8	8	8	24	28	32
Tiraspol**	24	7	5	12	27	38	26
Agro	24	4	8	12	13	33	22
Politehnica*	24	1	2	21	8	58	5
Hincesti	14	0	0	14	4	36	0

Hincesti withdrew during winter break; results expunged.
***Formerly Constructorul.*
Top scorer: Dadu (Tiraspol/Serif) 19.
Cup Final: Zimbru Chisinau 0, Otaci 0.
Zimbru Chisinau won 4-2 on penalties.

NORTHERN IRELAND

Irish Football Association Ltd, 20 Windsor Avenue, Belfast BT9 6EG.
Founded: 1880; *Number of Clubs:* 1,555; *Number of Players:* 24,558; *National Colours:* Green shirts, white shorts, green stockings.
Telephone: 01232 66 94 58; *Cable:* FOOTBALL BELFAST; *Telex:* 747317 ifa ni g; *Fax:* 01232 66 76 20.

NORWAY

Norges Fotballforbund, Ullevaal Stadion, Postboks 3823, Ulleval Hageby, 0805 Oslo 8.
Founded: 1902; *Number of Clubs:* 1,810; *Number of Players:* 300,000; *National Colours:* Red shirts, white shorts, blue stockings.
Telephone: 0047 22/024500; *Cable* FOTBALLFORBUND OSLO; *Telex:* 71722 nff n; *Fax:* 0047 22 95 10 10.

International matches 2002
Belgium (a) 0-1, Tunisia (a) 0-0, Sweden (h) 0-0, Japan (h) 3-0, Iceland (h) 1-1, Holland (h) 0-1, Denmark (h) 2-2, Romania (a) 1-0, Bosnia (h) 2-0, Austria (a) 1-0.

League Championship wins (1938–2002)
Rosenborg Trondheim 16; Fredrikstad 9; Viking Stavanger 8; Lillestroem 6; Vaalerenga 4; Larvik Turn 3; Brann Bergen 2; Lyn Oslo 2; IK Start 2; Friedig 1; Skeid Oslo 1; Strömsgodset Drammen 1; Moss 1.

Cup wins (1902–2002)
Odds Bk Skien 11; Fredrikstad 10; Lyn Oslo 8; Skeid Oslo 8; Rosenborg Trondheim 7; Sarpsborg FK 6; Brann Bergen 5; Viking Stavanger 5; Orn F Horten 4; Lillestroem 4; Strömsgodset Drammen 4; Frigg 3; Mjondalens F 3; Vaalerenga 3; Bodo-Glimt 2; Mercantile 2; Tromso 2; Grane Nordstrand 1; Kvik Halden 1; Sparta 1; Gjovik 1; Moss 1; Byrne 1; Molde 1; Stabaek 1; Odd Grenland 1.
(Known as the Norwegian Championship for HM The King's Trophy).

Final League Table 2002

	P	W	D	L	F	A	Pts
Rosenborg	26	17	5	4	57	30	56
Molde	26	15	5	6	48	26	50
Lyn	26	14	5	7	36	29	47
Viking	26	11	11	4	44	31	44
Stabaek	26	12	6	8	48	34	42
Odd	26	12	5	9	36	30	41
Lillestrom	26	10	6	10	37	30	36
Vaalerenga	26	7	12	7	38	31	33
Bryne	26	8	7	11	38	39	31
Bodo-Glimt	26	9	4	13	38	41	31
Sogndal	26	8	6	12	37	51	30
Brann+	26	8	3	15	35	52	27
Moss*	26	6	6	14	32	49	24
Start*	26	2	5	19	21	72	11

Top scorer: Brattbakk (Rosenborg) 17.
Cup Final: Valerenga 1, Odd 0.

POLAND

Federation Polonaise De Foot-Ball, Al. Ujazdowskie 22, 00-478 Warszawa.
Founded: 1919; *Number of Clubs:* 5,881; *Number of Players:* 317,442; *National Colours:* White shirts, red shorts, white and red stockings.
Telephone: 0048 22 6223398; *Cable:* PEZETPEEN WARSZAWA; *Telex:* 825320 pzpn pl; *Fax:* 0048 22 629 24 89.

International matches 2002
Faeroes (a) 2-1, N Ireland (h) 4-1, Japan (h) 0-2, Romania (h) 1-2, Estonia (h) 1-0, South Korea (n) 0-2, Portugal (n) 0-4, USA (n) 3-1, Belgium (h) 1-1, San Marino (a) 2-0, Latvia (h) 0-1, New Zealand (h) 2-0, Denmark (a) 0-2.

League Championship wins (1921–2003)
Gornik Zabrze 14; Ruch Chorzow 13; Wisla Krakow 9; Legia Warsaw 7; Widzew Lodz 6; Lech Poznan 5; Pogon Lwow 4; Cracovia 3; Warta Poznan 2; Polonia Bytom 2; Stal Mielec 2; LKS Lodz 2; Polonia Warsaw 2; Garbarnia Krakow 1; Slask Wroclaw 1; Szombierki Bytom 1; Zaglebie Lubin 1.

Cup wins (1951–2003)
Legia Warsaw 12; Gornik Zabrze 6; Zaglebie Sosnowiec 4; Lech Poznan 3; GKS Katowice 3; Ruch Chorzow 3; Amica Wronki 3; Wisla Krakow 3; Slask Wroclaw 2; Polonia Warsaw 2; Gwardia Warsaw 1; LKS Lodz 1; Stal Rzeszow 1; Arka Gdynia 1; Lechia Gdansk 1; Widzew Lodz 1; Miedz Legnica 1.

Final League Table 2002–03

	P	W	D	L	F	A	Pts
Wisla	30	21	5	4	75	28	68
Groclin	30	18	8	4	56	26	62
Katowice	30	19	4	7	39	21	61
Legia	30	17	9	4	59	29	60
Odra	30	17	5	8	55	42	56

Amica	30	11	10	9	43	34	43
Gornik Zabrze	30	10	11	9	46	32	41
Polonia	30	11	8	11	37	45	41
Wisla Plock	30	10	7	13	29	36	37
Widzew	30	10	7	13	29	39	37
Lech	30	8	11	11	41	38	35
Zaglebie Lubin	30	8	8	14	34	44	32
Ruch	30	7	11	12	29	39	32
Garbania*	30	8	8	14	40	54	32
KSZO*	30	4	3	23	21	63	15
Pogon*	30	2	3	25	14	77	9

Next season first division consisting of 14 clubs.
Top scorer: Svitlica (Legia) 24.
Cup Final: Wisla 3, Wisla Plock 0.

PORTUGAL

Federacao Portuguesa De Futebol, Praca De Alegria N.25, Apartado 21.100, P-1127, Lisboa Codex.
Founded: 1914; *Number of Clubs:* 204; *Number of Players:* 79,235; *National Colours:* Red shirts, green shorts, red stockings.
Telephone: 00351 1 342 8207/8/9/0; *Cable:* FUTEBOL LISBOA; *Telex:* 13489 fpf p; *Fax:* 00351 1 346 72 31.

International matches 2002

Spain (a) 1-1, Finland (h) 1-4, Brazil (h) 1-1, China (a) 2-0, USA (n) 2-3, Poland (n) 4-0, South Korea (n) 0-1, England (a) 1-1, Tunisia (h) 1-1, Sweden (a) 3-2, Scotland (h) 2-0.

League Championship wins (1935–2003)

Benfica 30; FC Porto 19; Sporting Lisbon 18; Belenenses 1; Boavista 1.

Cup wins (1939–2003)

Benfica 23; Sporting Lisbon 13; FC Porto 12; Boavista 5; Belenenses 3; Vitoria Setubal 2; Academica Coimbra 1; Leixoes Porto 1; Sporting Braga 1; Amadora 1; Beira Mar 1.

Final League Table 2002–03

	P	W	D	L	F	A	Pts
Porto	34	27	5	2	73	26	86
Benfica	34	23	6	5	74	27	75
Sporting Lisbon	34	17	8	9	52	38	59
Guimaraes	34	14	8	12	47	46	50
Uniao Leiria	34	13	10	11	49	47	49
Pacos	34	12	9	13	40	47	45
Gil Vicente	34	13	5	16	42	53	44
Maritimo	34	13	5	16	36	48	44
Boavista	34	10	13	11	32	31	43
Belenenses	34	11	10	13	47	48	43
Nacional	34	9	13	12	40	46	40
Moreirense	34	9	12	13	42	46	39
Beira Mar	34	10	9	15	43	50	39
Braga	34	8	14	12	34	47	38
Academica	34	8	13	13	38	48	37
Varzin*	34	10	6	18	38	51	36
Santa Clara*	34	8	11	15	39	54	35
Setubal*	34	6	13	15	40	53	31

Top scorers: Fary (Beira Mar) 18, Sabrosa (Benfica) 18 .
Cup Final: Porto 1, Uniao Leiria 0.

ROMANIA

Federatia Romana De Fotbal, Str. Poligrafiei 3, Sector 1, 71556 Bucharest.
Founded: 1909; *Number of Clubs:* 414; *Number of Players:* 22,920; *National Colours:* All yellow.
Telephone: 0040 1 224 1993/224 2983; *Cable:* SPORTROM BUCURESTI-FOTBAL; *Telex:* 10097 frf r; *Fax:* 0040 1 224 0661.

International matches 2002

Kuwait (a) 1-1, Saudi Arabia (a) 0-2, Oman (a) 2-1, France (a) 1-2, Ukraine (h) 4-1, Poland (a) 2-1, Greece (a) 2-3, Greece (h) 0-1, Bosnia (a) 3-0, Norway (h) 0-1, Luxembourg (a) 7-0, Croatia (h) 0-1.

League Championship wins (1910–2003)

Steaua Bucharest 21; Dinamo Bucharest 16; Venus Bucharest 8; Chinezul Timisoara 6; UT Arad 6; Ripensia Temesvar 4; Uni Craiova 4; Petrolul Ploesti 3; Rapid Bucharest 3; Olimpia Bucharest 2; Colentina Bucharest 2; Arges Pitesti 2; ICO Oradea 2; Soc RA Bucharest 1; Prahova Ploesti 1; Coltea Brasov 1; Juventus Bucharest 1; Metalochimia Resita 1; Ploesti United 1; Unirea Tricolor 1.

Cup wins (1934–2003)

Steaua Bucharest 20; Rapid Bucharest 11; Dinamo Bucharest 10; Uni Craiova 6; UT Arad 2; Ripensia Temesvar 2; Politehnica Timisoara 2; Petrolul Ploesti 2; ICO Oradeo 1; Metalochimia Resita 1; Stinta Cluj 1; CFR Turnu Severin 1; Chimia Ramnicu Vilcea 1; Jiul Petroseni 1; Progresul Bucharest 1; Progresul Oradea 1; Gloria Bistrita 1.

Final League Table 2002–03

	P	W	D	L	F	A	Pts
Rapid	30	20	3	7	59	25	63
Steaua	30	16	8	6	42	27	56
Gloria	30	13	6	11	32	33	45
Brasov	30	13	6	11	37	33	45
Ceahlaul	30	12	8	10	43	33	44
Dinamo	30	13	5	12	49	46	44
Uni Craiova	30	12	8	10	36	37	44
National	30	12	7	11	41	36	43
Astra	30	13	3	14	42	42	42
Farul	30	12	4	14	35	47	40
Arges	30	11	5	14	37	41	38
Bacau	30	10	8	12	31	31	38
Otelul	30	9	9	12	25	37	36
Timisoara	30	11	2	17	37	52	35
Sportul*	30	9	4	17	44	55	31
UT Arad*	30	8	6	16	37	52	30

Top scorer: Raducanu (Steaua) 21.
Cup Final: Dinamo 1, National 0.

RUSSIA

Football Union of Russia; Luzhnetskaya Naberezyhnaja, 8. SU-119871 Moscow.
Founded: 1912; *Number of Clubs:* 43,700; *Number of Players:* 785,000; *National Colours:* White shirts, blue shorts, red stockings.
Telephone: 0070 95 2011637; *Telex:* 411287 priz su; *Fax:* 0070 95 2011303.

International matches 2002

Eire (a) 0-2, Estonia (a) 1-2, France (a) 0-0, Belarus (h) 1-1, Yugoslavia (h) 1-1, Tunisia (n) 2-0, Japan (n) 0-1, Belgium (n) 2-3, Sweden (h) 1-1, Eire (h) 4-2, Georgia (a) 0-0, Albania (h) 4-1.

League Championship wins (1945–2002)

Spartak Moscow 20; Dynamo Kiev 13; Dynamo Moscow 11; CSKA Moscow 7; Torpedo Moscow 3; Dynamo Tbilisi 2; Dnepr Dnepropetrovsk 2; Saria Voroshilovgrad 1; Ararat Erevan 1; Dynamo Minsk 1; Zenit Leningrad 1; Spartak Vladikavkaz 1; Lokomotiv Moscow 1.

Cup wins (1936–2003)

Spartak Moscow 13; Dynamo Kiev 10; Torpedo Moscow 7; Dynamo Moscow 7; Lokomotiv Moscow 6; CSKA Moscow 6; Shakhtjor Donetsk 4; Dynamo Tbilisi 2; Ararat Erevan 2; Zenit Leningrad 2; Karpaty Lvov 1; SKA Rostov 1; Metallist Kharkov 1; Dnepr 1.

Final League Table 2002

	P	W	D	L	F	A	Pts
Lokomotiv Moscow	30	19	9	2	46	14	66
CSKA Moscow	30	21	3	6	60	26	66
Spartak Moscow	30	16	7	7	49	36	55
Torpedo Moscow	30	14	8	8	47	32	50
Krylia Sovetov	30	15	4	11	39	32	49
Shinnik	30	13	8	9	42	37	47
Saturn	30	13	8	9	41	37	47
Dynamo Moscow	30	12	6	12	38	33	42
Volgograd	30	11	5	14	27	34	38
Zenit	30	8	9	13	36	42	33
Rostselmash Rostov	30	7	10	13	29	49	31
Vladikavkaz	30	8	6	16	31	42	30
Uralan	30	6	11	13	32	42	29
Torpedo ZIL	30	6	10	14	20	39	28
Anzhi*	30	5	10	15	22	43	25
Sokol*	30	5	8	17	24	45	23

Championship Play-off: Lokomotiv Moscow 1, CSKA Moscow 0.
Top scorers: Gusev (CSKA Moscow) 15, Kirichenko (CSKA Moscow) 15.
Cup Final: Spartak Moscow 1, Rostselmash Rostov 0.

SAN MARINO

Federazione Sammarinese Giuoco Calcio, Viale Campo dei Giudei, 14; 47031-Rep. San Marino.
Founded: 1931; *Number of Clubs:* 17; *Number of Players:* 1,033; *National Colours:* All light blue.
Telephone: 00378 9990515; *Telex:* 0505284 cosmar so; *Fax:* 00378 9992348.

International matches 2002

Estonia (h) 0-1, Poland (h) 0-2, Hungary (a) 0-3, Latvia (h) 0-1.

League Championship wins (1986–2003)

Tre Fiori 4; Faetano 3; Folgore 3; Domagnano 3; Fiorita 2; Montevito 1; Libertas 1; Cosmos 1.

Cup wins (1986–2003)

Domagnano 7; Libertas 3; Faetano 3; Cosmos 2; Fiorita 1; Tre Penne 1; Murata 1.

Qualifying League Table 2002–03

Group A

	P	*W*	*D*	*L*	*F*	*A*	*Pts*
Pennarossa	20	12	4	4	48	22	40
Murata	20	11	6	3	41	25	39
Cailungo	20	10	8	2	40	19	38
Faetano	20	10	6	4	31	19	36
Folgore/Falciano	20	6	7	7	24	27	25
Montevito	20	1	6	13	21	48	9
La Fiorita	20	2	1	17	11	54	7

Group B

	P	*W*	*D*	*L*	*F*	*A*	*Pts*
Domagnano	21	11	6	4	32	18	39
Libertas	21	10	4	7	32	22	34
Virtus	21	8	8	5	32	27	32
Tre Penne	21	7	9	5	30	27	30
Cosmos	21	5	10	6	29	38	25
Juvenes/Dogana	21	4	11	6	23	28	23
Tre Fiore	21	4	8	9	25	32	20
San Giovanni	21	4	4	13	24	37	16

Play-offs: Murata 3, Virtus 2; Libertas 2, Cailungo 1; Domagnano 4, Murata 1; Pennarossa 3, Libertas 2; Cailungo 2, Murata 4; Virtus 0, Libertas 1; Domagnano 0, Pennarossa 0 *(Pennarossa won 5-4 on penalties)*; Murata 3, Libertas 3 *(Libertas won 4-3 on penalties)*.
Semi-final: Domagnano 5, Libertas 1.
Final: Domagnano 2, Pennarossa 1.
Cup Final: Domagnano 1, Pennarossa 0.

SCOTLAND

The Scottish Football Association Ltd, Hampden Park, Glasgow G42 9AY.
Founded: 1873; *Number of Clubs:* 6,148; *Number of Players:* 135,474; *National Colours:* Dark blue shirts, white shorts, red stockings with dark blue tops.
Telephone: 0141 616 6000; *Cable:* EXECUTIVE GLASGOW; *Telex:* 778904 sfa g; *Fax:* 0141 616 6001.

SERBIA-MONTENEGRO

Yugoslav Football Association, P.O. Box 263, Terazije 35, 11000 Beograd.
Founded: 1919; *Number of Clubs:* 6,532; *Number of Players:* 229,024; *National Colours:* Blue shirts, white shorts, red stockings.
Telephone: 00381 11 323 3447; *Cable:* JUGOFUDBAL BEOGRAD; *Telex:* 11666 fsj yu; *Fax:* 00381 11 323 3433.

International matches 2002

Mexico (a) 2-1, Brazil (a) 0-1, Lithuania (h) 4-1, Ecuador (a) 0-1, Ukraine (n) 0-2, Russia (n) 1-1, Bosnia (a) 2-0, Czech Republic (a) 0-5, Italy (a) 1-1, Finland (h) 2-0, France (a) 0-3.

League Championship wins (1923–2003)

Red Star Belgrade 22; Partizan Belgrade 18; Hajduk Split 9; Gradjanski Zagreb 5; BSK Belgrade 5; Dynamo Zagreb 4; Jugoslavija Belgrade 2; Concordia Zagreb 2; FC Sarajevo 2; Vojvodina Novi Sad 2; HASK Zagreb 1; Zeljeznicar 1; Obilic 1.

Cup wins (1947–2003)

Red Star Belgrade 19; Hajduk Split 9; Partizan Belgrade 9; Dynamo Zagreb 8; BSK Belgrade 2; OFK Belgrade 2; Rijeka 2; Velez Mostar 2; Vardar Skopje 1; Borac Banjaluka 1; Sartid 1.

Final League Table 2002–03

	P	*W*	*D*	*L*	*F*	*A*	*Pts*
Partizan Belgrade	34	29	2	3	88	36	89
Red Star Belgrade	34	21	7	6	68	26	70
OFK Belgrade	34	19	6	9	57	36	63
Niksic	34	19	5	10	43	32	62
Zeleznik	34	18	8	8	56	37	62
Vojvodina	34	17	5	12	48	36	56
Golubovci	34	15	6	13	51	43	51
Obilic	34	14	9	11	45	35	51
Hajduk Kula	34	13	9	12	39	29	48
Zemun	34	13	8	13	42	39	47
Sartid	34	10	15	9	44	44	45
Oblenovac	34	11	11	12	35	41	44
Rad*	34	11	10	13	39	43	43
Cukaricki*	34	10	7	17	42	56	37
Ivanjica*	34	9	7	18	21	44	34
Budva*	34	5	6	23	33	76	21
Pljevlja*	34	4	6	24	19	62	18
Radnicki Nis*	34	2	5	27	23	78	11

Next season first division reduced to 16.
Top scorer: Fukic (Partizan Belgrade) 22.
Cup Final: Sartid 1, Red Star Belgrade 0.

SLOVAKIA

Slovak Football Association, Junacka 6, 83280 Bratislava, Slovakia.
Founded: 1993; *Number of Clubs:* 2,140; *Number of Players:* 141,000; *National Colours:* All blue.
Telephone: 00421 75049151/5; *Fax:* 00421 75 049554.

International matches 2002

Iran (a) 3-2, Austria (a) 0-2, Belgium (a) 1-1, Japan (a) 0-1, Uzbekistan (h) 4-1, Czech Republic (a) 1-4, Turkey (a) 0-3, England (h) 1-2, Ukraine (h) 1-1.

League Championship wins (1939–44; 1994–2003)

Slovan Bratislava 8; Kosice 2; Inter 2; Zilina 2; Bystrica 1; OAP Bratislava 1.

Cup wins (1994–2003)

Inter 3; Slovan Bratislava 2; Tatran Presov 1; Humenne 1; Spartak Trnava 1; Koba 1; Matador 1.

Final League Table 2002–03

	P	*W*	*D*	*L*	*F*	*A*	*Pts*
Zilina	36	21	7	8	69	31	70
Petrzalka	36	20	7	9	49	32	67
Slovan Bratislava	36	19	6	11	60	42	63
Spartak Trnava	36	15	11	10	55	47	56
Matador	36	14	8	14	46	47	50
Inter	36	12	7	17	48	58	43
Dubnica	36	12	7	17	41	52	43
Ruzomberok	36	12	6	18	45	60	42
Trencin	36	11	5	20	48	69	38
Kosice*	36	6	12	18	41	64	30

Top scorers: Fabus (Trencin/Zilina) 20, Mintai (Zilina) 20.
Cup Final: Matador 2, Slovan Bratislava 1.

SLOVENIA

Football Association of Slovenia, P.P. 3986, 1001 Ljubljana, Slovenia.
Founded: 1920; *Number of Clubs:* 375; *Number of Players:* 20,117; *National Colours:* White shirts, green shorts, white stockings.
Telephone: 00386 1 5300400; *Fax:* 00386 1 5300410.

International matches 2002

Honduras (h) 1-5, China (a) 0-0, Croatia (a) 0-0, Tunisia (h) 1-0, Ghana (h) 2-0, Spain (n) 1-3, South Africa (n) 0-1, Paraguay (n) 1-3, Italy (a) 1-0, Malta (h) 3-0, France (a) 0-5.

League Championship wins (1992–2003)

Maribor 7; SCT Olimpija 4; Gorica 1.

Cup wins (1992–2003)

Maribor 4; SCT Olimpija 4; Gorica 2; Mura 1; Rudar 1.

Final League Table 2002–03

	P	*W*	*D*	*L*	*F*	*A*	*Pts*
Maribor	31	18	8	5	57	32	62
Publikum	31	15	10	6	57	38	55
Olimpija	31	14	12	5	54	32	54

Era	31	12	10	9	46	42	46
Koper	31	12	9	10	41	41	45
Primorje	31	13	5	13	47	44	44
Dravograd	31	9	9	13	40	43	36
Gorica	31	7	13	11	34	43	34
Mura	31	9	7	15	38	48	34
Ljubljana	31	9	6	16	41	66	30
Rudar	31	6	7	18	32	51	25
Korotan*	11	2	4	5	7	14	3

Korotan did not complete the season.
Top scorer: Krnetic (Olimpija) 23.
Cup Final: Olimpija 1, 2, Publikum 1, 2.

SPAIN

Real Federacion Espanola De Futbol, Calle Alberto Bosch 13, Apartado Postal 347, E-28014 Madrid.
Founded: 1913; *Number of Clubs:* 10,240; *Number of Players:* 408,135; *National Colours:* Red shirts, blue shorts, blue stockings with red, blue and yellow border.
Telephone: 0034 91 420 1362; *Cable:* FUTBOL MADRID; *Fax:* 0034 91 420 2094.

International matches 2002

Portugal (h) 1-1, Holland (a) 0-1, N Ireland (a) 5-0, Slovenia (n) 3-1, Paraguay (n) 3-1, South Africa (n) 3-2, Eire (n) 1-1, South Korea (n) 0-0, Hungary (a) 1-1, Greece (a) 2-0, N Ireland (h) 3-0, Paraguay (h) 0-0, Bulgaria (h) 1-0.

League Championship wins (1929–36; 1940–2003)

Real Madrid 29; Barcelona 16; Atletico Madrid 9; Athletic Bilbao 8; Valencia 5; Real Sociedad 2; Real Betis 1; Seville 1; La Coruna 1.

Cup wins (1902–2003)

Barcelona 24; Athletic Bilbao 23; Real Madrid 17; Atletico Madrid 9; Valencia 6; Real Zaragoza 5; Real Union de Irun 3; Seville 3; Espanyol 3; La Coruna 2; Arenas 1; Ciclista Sebastian 1; Racing de Irun 1; Vizcaya Bilbao 1; Real Betis 1; Real Sociedad 1; Mallorca 1.

Final League Table 2002–03

	P	*W*	*D*	*L*	*F*	*A*	*Pts*
Real Madrid	38	22	12	4	86	42	78
Real Sociedad	38	22	10	6	71	45	76
La Coruna	38	22	6	10	67	47	72
Celta	38	17	10	11	45	36	61
Valencia	38	17	9	12	56	35	60
Barcelona	38	15	11	12	63	47	56
Athletic Bilbao	38	15	10	13	63	61	55
Betis	38	14	12	12	56	53	54
Mallorca	38	14	10	14	49	56	52
Sevilla	38	13	11	14	38	39	50
Osasuna	38	12	11	15	40	48	47
Atletico Madrid	38	12	11	15	51	56	47
Malaga	38	11	13	14	44	49	46
Valladolid	38	12	10	16	37	40	46
Villarreal	38	11	12	15	44	53	55
Santander	38	13	5	20	54	64	44
Espanyol	38	10	13	15	48	54	43
Huelva*	38	8	12	18	35	61	36
Alaves*	38	8	11	19	38	68	35
Rayo Vallecano*	38	7	11	20	31	62	32

Top scorer: Makaay (La Coruna) 29.
Cup Final: Mallorca 3, Huelva 0.

SWEDEN

Svenska Fotbollfoerbundet, Box 1216, S-17123 Solna.
Founded: 1904; *Number of Clubs:* 3,250; *Number of Players:* 485,000; *National Colours:* Yellow shirts, blue shorts, yellow stockings.
Telephone: 0046 8 735 09 00; *Cable:* FOOTBALL-S; *Fax:* 0046 8 27 51 47.

International matches 2002

Greece (a) 2-2, Switzerland (h) 1-1, Norway (a) 0-0, Paraguay (h) 1-2, Japan (a) 1-1, England (n) 1-1, Nigeria (n) 2-1, Argentina (n) 1-1, Senegal (n) 1-2, Russia (a) 1-1, Latvia (a) 0-0, Hungary (h) 1-1, Portugal (h) 2-3, Czech Republic (a) 3-3.

League Championship wins (1896–2002)

IFK Gothenburg 18; Oergryte IS Gothenburg 14; Malmo FF 14; IFK Norrköping 11; AIK Stockholm 10; Djurgaarden 9; GAIS Gothenburg 6; IF Helsingborg 6; Boras IF Elfsborg 4; Oster Vaxjo 4; Halmstad 4; Atvidaberg 2; IFK Ekilstune 1; IF Gavic Brynas 1; IF Gothenburg 1; Fassbergs 1; Norrköping IK Sleipner 1; Hammarby 1.

Cup wins (1941–2002)

Malmo FF 13; AIK Stockholm 8; IFK Norrköping 6; IFK Gothenburg 4; Atvidaberg 2; Kalmar 2; Helsingborg 2; Djurgaarden 2; GAIS Gothenburg 1; IF Raa 1; Landskrona 1; Oster Vaxjo 1; Degerfors 1; Halmstad 1; Orgryte 1.

Final League Table 2002

	P	*W*	*D*	*L*	*F*	*A*	*Pts*
Djurgaarden	26	16	4	6	51	33	52
Malmo	26	14	4	8	52	32	46
Orgryte	26	12	8	6	49	38	44
Helsingborg	26	10	8	8	38	38	38
AIK	26	9	10	7	35	38	37
Halmstad	26	8	12	6	35	28	36
Orebro	26	9	8	9	32	39	35
Sundsvall	26	8	9	9	29	35	33
Hammarby	26	8	8	10	43	42	32
Elfsborg	26	8	8	10	25	31	32
Landskrona	26	8	6	12	41	39	30
IFK Gothenburg	26	8	4	14	25	39	28
Norrköping*	26	6	9	11	37	40	27
Kalmar*	26	6	6	14	20	40	24

Top scorer: Ijeh (Malmo) 24.
Cup Final: Djurgaarden 1, AIK 0.

SWITZERLAND

Schweizerisher Fussballverband, Postfach 3000 Berne 15.
Founded: 1895; *Number of Clubs:* 1,473; *Number of Players:* 185,286; *National Colours:* Red shirts, white shorts, red stockings.
Telephone: 0041 31 950 81 11; *Cable:* SWISSFOOT BERNE; *Fax:* 0041 31 950 81 81.

International matches 2002

Cyprus (n) 1-1, Hungary (n) 2-1, Sweden (a) 1-1, Canada (h) 1-3, Austria (h) 3-2, Georgia (h) 4-1, Albania (a) 1-1, Eire (a) 2-1.

League Championship wins (1898–2003)

Grasshoppers 26; Servette 17; Young Boys Berne 11; FC Zurich 9; FC Basle 9; Lausanne 7; La Chaux-de-Fonds 3; FC Lugano 3; Winterthur 3; FX Aarau 3; Neuchatel Xamax 3; Sion 2; St Gallen 2; FC Anglo-American 1; FC Brühl 1; Cantonal-Neuchatel 1; Biel 1; Bellinzona 1; FC Etoile La Chaux-de-Fonds 1; Lucerne 1.

Cup wins (1926–2003)

Grasshoppers 18; FC Sion 9; Lausanne 9; Servette 7; FC Basle 7; La Chaux-de-Fonds 6; Young Boys Berne 6; FC Zurich 6; Lucerne 2; FC Lugano 2; FC Granges 1; St Gallen 1; Urania Geneva 1; Young Fellows Zurich 1; Aarau 1.

Qualifying League Table 2002–03

	P	*W*	*D*	*L*	*F*	*A*	*Pts*
Grasshoppers	22	15	4	3	58	26	49
Basle	22	14	5	3	57	25	47
Thun	22	9	4	9	33	33	31
Wil	22	8	7	7	43	45	31
Zurich	22	9	4	9	35	37	31
Neuchatel Xamax	22	8	7	7	30	33	31
Young Boys	22	8	6	8	41	41	30
Servette	22	8	5	9	45	37	29
Lucerne**	22	7	5	10	31	38	24
St Gallen	22	6	6	10	31	48	24
Delemont	22	6	2	14	24	44	20
Aarau	22	5	3	14	19	40	18

Final League Table 2002-03

	P	*W*	*D*	*L*	*F*	*A*	*Pts*
Grasshoppers	14	9	5	0	37	15	57
Basle	14	10	2	2	38	17	56
Neuchatel Xamax	14	5	4	5	18	17	35
Young Boys	14	6	1	7	21	29	34
Zurich	14	4	3	7	20	23	31
Servette	14	4	4	6	16	26	31
Thun	14	3	3	8	18	30	28
Wil	14	2	4	8	19	30	26

Promotion/Relegation Table 2002-03

	P	W	D	L	F	A	Pts
Aarau	12	9	1	2	30	13	28
St Gallen	12	7	3	2	25	9	24
Lucerne	12	4	4	4	24	22	16
Vaduz	12	3	4	5	17	23	13
Sion	12	3	3	6	13	18	12
Delemont	12	3	3	6	13	24	12
Kriens	12	3	2	7	14	27	11

Lugano results annulled.
**Four points reduced to two deducted for licence irregularities.
Top scorer: Nunez (Grasshoppers) 27.
Cup Final: Basle 6, Neuchatel Xamax 0.

TURKEY

Turkiye Futbol Federasyonu, Konaklar Mah. Ihlamurlu Sok. 9, 80620 4 Levent, Istanbul.
Founded: 1923; *Number of Clubs:* 230; *Number of Players:* 64,521; *National Colours:* White shirts, white shorts, red and white stockings.
Telephone: 0090 212 282 70 10; *Cable:* ISTANBUL FUTBOL SPOR; *Telex:* 46308 btff tr; *Fax:* 0090 212 282 70 15.

International matches 2002
Ecuador (h) 0-1, South Korea (a) 0-0, Chile (h) 2-0, South Africa (h) 0-2, Brazil (n) 1-2, Costa Rica (n) 1-1, China (n) 3-0, Japan (n) 1-0, Senegal (n) 1-0, Brazil (n) 0-1, South Korea (n) 3-2, Georgia (h) 3-0, Slovakia (h) 3-0, Macedonia (a) 2-1, Liechtenstein (h) 5-0, Italy (a) 1-1.

League Championship wins (1960–2003)
Galatasaray 15; Fenerbahce 14; Besiktas 11; Trabzonspor 6.

Cup wins (1963–2003)
Galatasaray 13; Besiktas 6; Trabzonspor 6; Fenerbahce 4; Goztepe Izmir 2; Altay Izmir 2; Ankaragucu 2; Genclerbirligi 2; Kocaeli 2; Eskisehirspor 1; Bursapor 1; Sakaryaspor 1.

Final League Table 2002–03

	P	W	D	L	F	A	Pts
Besiktas	34	26	7	1	63	21	85
Galatasaray	34	24	5	5	61	27	77
Genclerbirligi	34	19	9	6	76	40	66
Gaziantep	34	16	9	9	62	42	57
Malatya	34	14	10	10	56	45	52
Fenerbahce	34	13	12	9	55	42	51
Trabzonspor	34	13	12	9	44	33	51
Ankaragucu	34	15	4	15	44	42	49
Istanbul	34	12	7	15	42	47	43
Denizli	34	10	10	14	38	43	40
Adana	34	10	10	14	44	54	40
Samsun	34	10	9	15	42	59	39
Elazig	34	10	7	17	40	59	37
Diyarbakir	34	9	9	16	34	47	36
Bursa	34	9	9	16	42	62	36
Altay*	34	9	8	17	48	69	35
Goztepe*	34	5	11	18	32	57	26
Kocaeli*	34	6	4	24	32	66	22

Top scorer: Okan (Bursa) 24.
Cup Final: Trabzonspor 3, Genclerbirligi 1.

UKRAINE

Football Federation of Ukraine, Ulianovyh Street 1, P.O. Box 503, 252150 Kiev, Ukraine.
Founded: 1991; *Number of Clubs:* 1500; *Number of Players:* 759,500; *National Colours:* Yellow and blue shirts, blue shorts, yellow stockings.
Telephone: 00380 44 2528498; *Fax:* 00380 44 2528513 (or) 2692550; *Telex:* 631461 uff ux.

International matches 2002
Japan (a) 0-1, Romania (a) 1-4, Georgia (h) 2-1, Yugoslavia (h) 2-0, Belarus (h) 0-2, Iran (h) 0-1, Armenia (a) 2-2, Greece (h) 2-0, N Ireland (a) 0-0, Slovakia (a) 1-1.

League Championship wins (1992–2003)
Dynamo Kiev 9; Tavriya Simferopol 1; Shakhtjor Donetsk 1.

Cup wins (1992–2003)
Dynamo Kiev 6; Shakhtjor Donetsk 4; Chernomorets 2.

Final League Table 2002–03

	P	W	D	L	F	A	Pts
Dynamo Kiev	30	23	4	3	66	20	73
Shakhtjor Donetsk	30	22	4	4	61	24	70
Metalurg Donetsk	30	18	6	6	44	26	60
Dnepr	30	18	5	7	48	27	59
Arsenal	30	16	8	6	49	24	56
Volyn	30	12	5	13	37	44	41
Karpaty	30	9	9	12	29	37	36
Chernomorets	30	10	4	16	31	45	34
Tavriya	30	9	7	14	36	50	34
Mariupol	30	8	10	12	34	38	34
Vorskla	30	8	8	14	26	41	32
Krivbas	30	8	7	15	25	37	31
Olexandriya	30	7	9	14	26	43	30
Obolon	30	7	7	16	32	45	28
Metalurg Zapor*	30	6	8	16	22	41	26
Metallist Charkov*	30	6	5	19	19	43	23

Top scorer: Shatskikh (Dynamo Kiev) 21.
Cup Final: Dynamo Kiev 2, Shakhtjor Donetsk 1.

WALES

The Football Association of Wales Limited, Plymouth Chambers, 3 Westgate Street, Cardiff, South Glamorgan CF1 1DD.
Founded: 1876; *Number of Clubs:* 2,326; *Number of Players:* 53,926; *National Colours:* All red.
Telephone: 01222 372325; *Telex:* 497 363 faw g; *Cable:* WELSOCCER CARDIFF; *Fax:* 01222 343961.

SOUTH AMERICA

ARGENTINA

Asociacion Del Futbol Argentina, Viamonte 1366/76, 1053 Buenos Aires.
Founded: 1893; *Number of Clubs:* 3,035; *Number of Players:* 306,365; *National Colours:* Light blue and white striped shirts, black shorts, white stockings.
Telephone: 00541 371 4276; *Cable:* FUTBOL BUENOS AIRES; *Telex:* 17848 AFA AR; *Fax:* 00541 375 4410.
International matches 2002
Holland (a) 1-1, Cameroon (h) 2-2, Germany (a) 1-0, Nigeria (n) 1-0, England (n) 0-1, Sweden (n) 1-1, Japan (a) 2-0.

BOLIVIA

Federacion Boliviana De Futbol, Av. Libertador Bolivar No. 1168, Casilla de Correo 484, Cochabamba, Bolivia.
Founded: 1925; *Number of Clubs:* 305; *Number of Players:* 15,290; *National Colours:* Green shirts with white borders, white shorts with green borders, green stockings.
Telephone: 0059142 44982; *Cable:* FEDFUTBOL COCHABAMBA; *Telex:* 6239 FEDBOL; *Fax:* 0059142 82132.
International matches 2002
Brazil (a) 0-6, Paraguay (a) 2-2, Senegal (a) 1-2, Mexico (a) 0-1, Venezuela (a) 0-2.

BRAZIL

Confederacao Brasileira De Futebol, Rua Da Alfandega, 70, P.O. Box 1078, 20.070 Rio De Janeiro.
Founded: 1914; *Number of Clubs:* 12,987; *Number of Players:* 551,358; *National Colours:* Yellow shirts with green collar/cuffs, blue shorts, white stockings with green-yellow border.
Telephone: 005521 509 5937; *Cable:* DESPORTOS RIO DE JANEIRO; *Telex:* 21509 CBDS BR; *Fax:* 005521 252 9294.
International matches 2002
Bolivia (h) 6-0, Saudi Arabia (a) 1-0, Iceland (h) 6-1, Yugoslavia (h) 1-0, Portugal (a) 1-1, Malaysia (a) 4-0, Turkey (n) 2-1, China (n) 4-0, Costa Rica (n) 5-2, Belgium (n) 2-0, England (n) 2-1, Turkey (n) 1-0, Germany (n) 2-0, Paraguay (h) 0-1, South Korea (a) 3-2.

CHILE

Federacion De Futbol De Chile, Avda. Quillin No. 5635, Casilla postal 3733, Correo Central, Santiago de Chile.
Founded: 1895; *Number of Clubs:* 4,598; *Number of Players:* 609,724; *National Colours:* Red shirts with white collar and cuffs, blue shorts, white stockings.
Telephone: 00562 2849000; *Cable:* FEDFUTBOL SANTIAGO DE CHILE; *Fax:* 00562 2843510.
International matches 2002
Turkey (a) 0-2.

COLOMBIA

Federacion Colombiana De Futbol, Avenida 32, No. 16-22 piso 40. Apartado Aereo 17602, Santafe de Bogota.
Founded: 1924; *Number of Clubs:* 3,685; *Number of Players:* 188,050; *National Colours:* Yellow shirts with tricolour borders, blue shorts, red stockings with tricolour borders.
Telephone: 00571 2853320; *Cable:* COLFUTBOL BOGOTA; *Fax:* 00571 2889740.
International matches 2002
Venezuela (a) 0-0, Costa Rica (a) 2-1, Mexico (a) 1-2, Honduras (a) 0-1.

ECUADOR

Federacion Ecuatoriana del Futbol, km 4 via a la Costa (Avda. del Bombero), Guayaquil.
Founded: 1925; *Number of Clubs:* 170; *Number of Players:* 15,700; *National Colours:* Yellow shirts with blue and red fringes, blue shorts, red stockings.
Telephone: 005934 352 372/3; *Cable:* ECUAFUTBOL GUAYAQUIL; *Fax:* 005934 352 116.
International matches 2002
Guatemala (h) 1-0, Haiti (n) 0-2, Canada (n) 2-0, Turkey (a) 1-0, USA (a) 0-1, Bulgaria (h) 3-0, South Africa (a) 0-0, Yugoslavia (h) 1-0, Senegal (h) 0-1, Italy (n) 0-2, Mexico (n) 1-2, Croatia (n) 1-0, Costa Rica (a) 1-1, Venezuela (a) 0-2, Costa Rica (h) 2-2.

PARAGUAY

Asociacion Paraguaya de Futbol, Estadio De Sajonia, Calles Mayor Martinez Y Alejo Garcia, Asuncion.
Founded: 1906; *Number of Clubs:* 1,500; *Number of Players:* 140,000; *National Colours:* Red and white shirts, blue shorts, blue stockings.
Telephone: 0059521 480120; *Telex:* 38009 PY FUTBOL; *Fax:* 0059521 480124.
International matches 2002
Bolivia (h) 2-2, Nigeria (a) 1-1, England (a) 0-4, Sweden (a) 2-1, South Africa (n) 2-2, Spain (n) 1-3, Slovenia (n) 3-1, Germany (n) 0-1, Brazil (a) 1-0, South Africa (h) 2-0, Iran (a) 1-1, Spain (a) 0-0.

PERU

Federacion Peruana De Futbol, Av. Aviacion Cdra. 20 s/n, San Luis, Lima.
Founded: 1922; *Number of Clubs:* 10,000; *Number of Players:* 325,650; *National Colours:* White shirts with red stripe, white shorts with red lines, white stockings with red line.
Telephone: 00511 2258236-9; *Cable* FEPEFUTBOL LIMA; *Fax:* 00511 2258240; *Telex:* 20066 FEPEFUT PE.
No International matches for 2002

URUGUAY

Asociacion Uruguaya De Futbol, Guayabo 1531, 11200 Montevideo.
Founded: 1900; *Number of Clubs:* 1,091; *Number of Players:* 134,310; *National Colours:* Sky blue shirts with white collar/cuffs, black shorts, black stockings with sky blue borders.
Telephone: 005982 4007101/06; *Cable:* FOOTBALL MONTEVIDEO; *Fax:* 005982 4090550; *Telex:* AUF UY 22607.
International matches 2002
South Korea (h) 2-1, Saudi Arabia (a) 2-3, Italy (a) 1-1, USA (a) 1-2, China (a) 2-0, Singapore (a) 2-1, Denmark (n) 1-2, France (n) 0-0, Senegal (n) 3-3, Venezuela (a) 0-1.

VENEZUELA

Federacion Venezolana De Futbol, Avda S. Erminy, Torre Mega II Pent House B, e/Sabana Gr. y la Solano, Parroquia el Recreo, Caracas.
Founded: 1926; *Number of Clubs:* 1,753; *Number of Players:* 63,175; *National Colours:* Dark red shirts, white shorts, white stockings with black border.
Telephone: 00582 7620362; *Cable:* FEVEFUTBOL CARACAS; *Telex:* 26140 FVFCS VC; *Fax:* 00582 7620596.
International matches 2002
Iran (a) 0-1, Colombia (h) 0-0, Bolivia (h) 2-0, Ecuador (h) 2-0, Uruguay (h) 1-0.

ASIA

AFGHANISTAN

Afghanistan Football Federation, c/o Afghanistan Olympic Committee, P.O. Box 1824, Kabul.
Founded: 1933; *Number of Clubs:* 30; *Number of Players:* 3,300; *National Colours:* All white with red lines.
Telephone: 0093 11420579; *Cable:* OLYMPIC KABUL.

BAHRAIN

Bahrain Football Association, P.O. Box 5464, Manama.
Founded: 1957; *Number of Clubs:* 25; *Number of Players:* 2,030; *National Colours:* All red.
Telephone: 00973 252929; *Cable:* BAHKORA BAHRAIN; *Telex:* 9040 FAB BN; *Fax:* 00973 255560.

BANGLADESH

Bangladesh Football Federation, National Stadium-1, Dhaka 1000.
Founded: 1972; *Number of Clubs:* 1,265; *Number of Players:* 30,385; *National Colours:* Orange shirts, white shorts, green stockings.
Telephone: 008802 9556072; *Cable:* FOOTBALFED DHAKA; *Fax:* 008802 9563419.

BHUTAN

Bhutan Football Federation, P.O. Box 365, Thimphu.
Telephone: 009752 322350; *Fax:* 009752 321131.

BRUNEI

The Football Association of Brunei Darussalam, P.O. Box 2010, 1920 Bandar Seri Begawan.
Founded: 1959; *Number of Clubs:* 22; *Number of Players:* 830; *National Colours:* Yellow shirts, black shorts, yellow stockings.
Telephone: 006732 383883; *Cable:* BAFA BRUNEI; *Telex:* BU 2575 Attn: BAFA; *Fax:* 006732 382900.

CAMBODIA

Cambodian Football Federation, PO Box 2327 PTT, Phnom-Penh 3.
Founded: 1933; *Number of Clubs:* 30; *Number of Players:* 650; *National Colours:* Blue, red and white shirts, white and blue shorts, red, white and blue stockings.
Telephone: 0085523 364889; *Cable:* CFF PHNOM PENH; *Fax:* 0088523 367191.

CHINA PR

Football Association of The People's Republic of China, 9 Tiyuguan Road, Beijing 100763.
Founded: 1924; *Number of Clubs:* 1,045; *Number of Players:* 2,250,000; *National Colours:* All white.
Telephone: 008610 67117019; *Cable:* SPORTSCHINE BEIJING; *Telex:* 22034 ACSF CN; *Fax:* 008610 67142533.

CHINA TAIPEI

Chinese Taipei Football Association, 100, Kuang-Fu South Road, Taipei, Taiwan.
Founded: 1936; *Number of Players:* 17,000; *National Colours:* Blue shirts, white shorts, red stockings.
Telephone: 008862 27117710; *Cable:* CTFA Taipei; *Fax:* 008862 27117713.

GUAM

Guam Soccer Association, P.O.Box 5093, Agana, Guam 96932.
Founded: 1975; *National Colours:* Blue shirts, white shorts, blue stockings.
Telephone: 00671 472 1824, 646 9609; *Fax:* 00671 4775424.

HONG KONG

The Hong Kong Football Association Ltd, 55 Fat Kwong Street, Homantin, Kowloon, Hong Kong.
Founded: 1914; *Number of Clubs:* 69; *Number of Players:* 3,274; *National Colours:* All red.
Telephone: 00852 27129122; *Cable:* FOOTBALL HONG KONG; *Telex:* 40518 FAHKG HX; *Fax:* 00852 27604303.

INDIA

All India Football Federation , Mr KN Mour, Gen. Secretary, Youth Hostel Complex, Paltan Bazar, Guwahati - 781 008, Assam.

Founded: 1937; *Number of Clubs:* 2,000; *Number of Players:* 56,000; *National Colours:* Orange shirts, white shorts, green stockings.
Telephone: 0091361 525109; *Fax:* 0091 361525110.

INDONESIA

All Indonesia Football Federation, Wisma Karsa Pemuda, Jl.Gerbang Pemuda No. 3, PO Box 2305, Jakarta 10023.
Founded: 1930; *Number of Clubs:* 2,880; *Number of Players:* 97,000; *National Colours:* Red shirts, white shorts, red and white stockings.
Telephone: 006221 5722948; *Cable:* PSSI JAKARTA; *Telex:* 65739 PSSI IA; *Fax:* 006221 5734386.

IRAN

IR Iran Football Federation, Shahid Keshvari Sports Complex, Mirdamad Ave., Razan Jonoobi Str., PO Box 15875-6967 Tehran 15875.
Founded: 1920; *Number of Clubs:* 6,326; *Number of Players:* 306,000; *National Colours:* All white.
Telephone: 009821 2258116; *Cable:* FOOTBALL IRAN - TEHRAN; *Telex:* 212691 NOC IR; *Fax:* 009821 2258123.

IRAQ

Iraqi Football Association, Olympic Committee Building, Palestine Street, PO Box 484, Baghdad.
Founded: 1948; *Number of Clubs:* 155; *Number of Players:* 4,400; *National Colours:* All black.
Telephone: 009641 7729990; *Cable:* BALL BAGHDAD; *Telex:* 213409 IRFA IK; *Fax:* 009641 7744475.

JAPAN

Japan Football Association, 2nd Floor, Gotoh Ikueikai Bldg, 1-10-7 Dogenzaka, Shibuya-Ku, Tokyo 150, Japan.
Founded: 1921; *Number of Clubs:* 13,047; *Number of Players:* 358,989; *National Colours:* Blue shirts, white shorts, blue stockings.
Telephone: 00813 34762011; *Cable:* SOCCERJAPAN TOKYO; *Telex:* 2422975 FOTJPN J; *Fax:* 00813 34762291.

JORDAN

Jordan Football Association, P.O. Box 962024 Al. Hussein Sports City, 11196 Amman.
Founded: 1949; *Number of Clubs:* 98; *Number of Players:* 4,305; *National Colours:* All white and red.
Telephone: 009626 5657662/3/4/5; *Cable:* JORDAN FOOTBALL ASSN AMMAN; *Fax:* 009626 5657660.

KOREA, NORTH

Football Association of The Democratic People's Rep. of Korea, Kumsong-dong 2, Mangyongdae Distr, Pyongyang.
Founded: 1945; *Number of Clubs:* 90; *Number of Players:* 3,420; *National Colours:* All white.
Telephone: 008502 3814164; *Cable:* DPR KOREA FOOTBALL PYONGYANG; *Telex:* 5472 KP; *Fax:* 008502 3814403.

KOREA, SOUTH

Korea Football Association, 110-39, Kyeonji-Dong, Chongro-Ku, Seoul.
Founded: 1928; *Number of Clubs:* 476; *Number of Players:* 2,047; *National Colours:* Red shirts, black shorts, red stockings.
Telephone: 00822 7336764; *Cable:* FOOTBALLKOREA SEOUL; *Telex:* KFASEL K 25373; *Fax:* 00822 7352755.

KUWAIT

Kuwait Football Association, P.O. Box 2029 Safat, 13021 Safat.
Founded: 1952; *Number of Clubs:* 14 (senior); *Number of Players:* 1,526; *National Colours:* Blue shirts, white shorts, blue stockings.
Telephone: 00965 2555851; *Cable:* FOOT KUWAIT; *Fax:* 00965 2549955.

KYRGYZSTAN

Football Association of Kyrgyz Republic, Frunze Street, 503 Bishkek 720040, Kyrgyzstan.
Founded: 1992; *Number of Players:* 20,000; *National Colours:* Red shirts, white shorts, red stockings.
Telephone: 00331 2223507; *Fax:* 00331 2225492.

LAOS

Federation Lao de Football, National Stadium, Vientiane, Laos.
Founded: 1951; *Number of Clubs:* 76; *Number of Players:* 2,060; *National Colours:* Red shirts, white shorts, blue stockings.
Telephone: 0085621 216008/9; *Cable:* FOOTBALL VIENTIANE; *Fax:* 0085621 216008.

LEBANON

Federation Libanaise De Football-Association, P.O. Box 4732, Verdun Street, Bristol, Radwan Centre Building, Beirut.
Founded: 1933; *Number of Clubs:* 105; *Number of Players:* 8,125; *National Colours:* Red shirts, white shorts, red stockings.
Telephone: 009611 347157; *Cable:* FOOTBALL BEIRUT; *Telex:* 21404 LIBALL; *Fax:* 009611 349529; Internet: http://www.lebanon-online.com/lfa; E-mail: lfa@lebanon-online.com.lb.

MACAO

Associacao De Futebol De Macau (AFM), P.O. Box 920, Macau.
Founded: 1939; *Number of Clubs:* 52; *Number of Players:* 800; *National Colours:* Green shirts, black shorts, green stockings.
Telephone: 00853 71996; *Cable:* FOOTBALL MACAU; *Fax:* 00853 260148.

MALAYSIA

Football Association of Malaysia, Wisma Fam, Tingkat 3, Jalan SS5A/9, Kelana Jaya, 47301 Petaling Jaya, Selangor.
Founded: 1933; *Number of Clubs:* 450; *Number of Players:* 11,250; *National Colours:* All yellow and black.
Telephone: 00603 7763766; *Cable:* FOOTB. PETALING JAYA SELANGO; *Telex:* FAM PJ MA 36701; *Fax:* 00603 7757984.

MALDIVES REPUBLIC

Football Association of Maldives, National Stadium Ghalolhu, Male 20-04.
Founded: 1982; *National Colours:* Green shirts, white shorts, red stockings.
Telephone: 0096031 7006; *Fax:* 0096031 7005.

MONGOLIA

Mongolia Football Federation, R413, Mongolia Youth Association Building, Baga Toiruu 10, Ulaanbaatar 10.
Telephone & fax: 009761 313145.

MYANMAR

Myanmar Football Federation, Attn Maj. Naw Tawng, Gen. Secr. Youth Training Centre, Thuwunna, Yangon.
Founded: 1947; *Number of Clubs:* 600; *Number of Players:* 21,000; *National Colours:* Red shirts, white shorts, red stockings.
Telephone: 00951 577366; *Cable:* FOOTBALL YANGON; *Telex:* 21253 SPED BM; *Fax:* 00951 571253.

NEPAL

All-Nepal Football Association, Dasharath Rangashala, Tripureshwor, PO Box 2090, Kathmandu.
Founded: 1951; *Number of Clubs:* 85; *Number of Players:* 2,550; *National Colours:* All red.
Telephone: 009771 241367; *Cable:* ANFA KATHMANDU; *Telex:* 2390 NSC NP; *Fax:* 009771 241365.

OMAN

Oman Football Association, P.O. Box 3462, Ruwi Postal Code 112.
Founded: 1978; *Number of Clubs:* 47; *Number of Players:* 2,340; *National Colours:* Red shirts with white sleeves, red/white shorts and stockings.
Telephone: 00968 787638/9; *Cable:* FOOTBALL MUSCAT; *Telex:* FOOTBALL 3223 ON; *Fax:* 00968 787632/33.

PAKISTAN

Pakistan Football Federation, 183, Abu Bakar Block, New Garden Town, Lahore, Pakistan.
Founded: 1948; *Number of Clubs:* 882; *Number of Players:* 21,000; *National Colours:* Green shirts, white shorts, green stockings.

Telephone: 009242 5832786; *Cable:* FOOTBALL LAHORE; *Telex:* 47643 PFF PK; *Fax:* 009242 7281541.

PALESTINE

Palestinian Football Federation, Al-Yarmouk, Gaza.
Telephone: 009727 829433; *Fax:* 009727 857020.

PHILIPPINES

Philippine Football Federation, Room 207 PSC, Administration Building, Rizal Memorial Sports Complex, P. Ocampo Street, Manila.
Founded: 1907; *Number of Clubs:* 650; *Number of Players:* 45,000; *National Colours:* Blue and red shirts, blue shorts, white stockings.
Telephone: 00632 5256502; *Cable:* FOOTBALL MANILA; *Telex:* 65014 POC PACA PN; *Fax:* 00632 5233741.

QATAR

Qatar Football Association, P.O. Box 5333, Doha.
Founded: 1960; *Number of Clubs:* 8 (senior); *Number of Players:* 1,380; *National Colours:* All white.
Telephone: 00974 434455; *Cable:* FOOTQATAR DOHA; *Telex:* 4749 QATFOT DH; *Fax:* 00974 411660.

SAUDI ARABIA

Saudi Arabian Football Federation, Al Mather Quarter (Olympic Complex), P.O. Box 5844, Riyadh 11432.
Founded: 1959; *Number of Clubs:* 120; *Number of Players:* 9,600; *National Colours:* White shirts, green shorts, white stockings.
Telephone: 009661 4822240; *Cable:* KURA RIYADH; *Telex:* 404300 SAFOTB SJ; *Fax:* 009661 4821215.

SINGAPORE

Football Association of Singapore, Jalan Besar Stadium, Tyrwhitt Road, Singapore 207542.
Founded: 1892; *Number of Clubs:* 250; *Number of Players:* 8,000; *National Colours:* All red.
Telephone: 0065 2931477; *Fax:* 0065 2933728.

SRI LANKA

Football Federation of Sri Lanka, No. 2, Old Grand Stand, Race Course, Reid Avenue, Colombo 7.
Founded: 1939; *Number of Clubs:* 600; *Number of Players:* 18,825; *National Colours:* Maroon and gold shirts, white shorts and stockings.
Telephone: 00941 696179; *Cable:* SOCCER COLOMBO; *Telex:* 21537 METALIX CE; *Fax:* 00941 682471.

SYRIA

Syrian Football Federation, Maysaloon St., PO Box 421, Damascus.
Founded: 1936; *Number of Clubs:* 102; *Number of Players:* 30,600; *National Colours:* All white.
Telephone: 0096311 3335866; *Cable:* FOOTBALL DAMASCUS; *Telex:* 411578 SPOFED SY; *Fax:* 0096311 3331511.

TAJIKISTAN

Tajikistan National Football Federation, 44, Rudaki Ave., PO Box 26, 734025 Dushanbe, Tajikistan.
Founded: 1991; *Number of Clubs:* 1,804; *Number of Players:* 71,400; *National Colours:* Green shirts, white shorts, green stockings.
Telephone: 0073772 212363; *Telex:* 116286 SHAKH; *Fax:* 00992 372212447 (or) 212953.

THAILAND

The Football Association of Thailand, National Stadium, Rama I Road, Bangkok.
Founded: 1916; *Number of Clubs:* 168; *Number of Players:* 15,000; *National Colours:* All red.
Telephone: 00662 2141058; *Cable:* FOOTBALL BANGKOK; *Telex:* 20211 FAT TH; *Fax:* 00662 2154494.

TURKMENISTAN

Turkmenistan Football Federation, 10 Turkmenbashi Avenue, 744005 Ashgabat, Turkmenistan.
Founded: 1992; *Number of Players:* 75,000; *National Colours:* Green shirts, white shorts, green stockings.
Telephone: 00363 2353739; *Fax:* 00363 2355327; *Telex:* 116175 TINTO SU.

UNITED ARAB EMIRATES

United Arab Emirates Football Association, P.O. Box 916, Abu Dhabi.
Founded: 1971; *Number of Clubs:* 23 (senior); *Number of Players:* 1,787; *National Colours:* All white.
Telephone: 00971 2444 5600; *Cable:* FOOTBALL EMIRATES ABU DHABI; *Telex:* 22121 UAEFA EM; *Fax:* 00971 2444 8558.

UZBEKISTAN

Uzbekistan Football Federation, Massiv Almazar Furkat Street 15/1, 700003 Tashkent, Uzbekistan.
Founded: 1946; *Number of Clubs:* 15,000; *Number of Players:* 217,000; *National Colours:* Blue shirts, white shorts, green stockings.
Telephone: 0073712 457106; *Telex:* 116108 PTB SU; *Fax:* 0073712 454948.

VIETNAM

Vietnam Football Federation, 141 Nguyen Thai Hoc Str., Dis Dongda, Hanoi.
Founded: 1962; *Number of Clubs:* 55 (senior); *Number of Players:* 16,000; *National Colours:* All red.
Telephone: 008448 452480; *Cable:* AFBVN, 141 NGUYEN THAI HOC STR.; *Fax:* 008448 233119.

YEMEN

Yemen Football Association, P.O. Box 908, Sana'a.
Founded: 1962; *Number of Clubs:* 26; *Number of Players:* 1750; *National Colours:* All green.
Telephone: 009671 269066. *Cable:* SANA'A FOOTBALL; *Telex:* 2710 YOUTH YE; *Fax:* 009671 276067.

CONCACAF

ANGUILLA

Anguilla Football Association, P.O. Box 608, The Valley, Anguilla, BWI.
National Colours: All blue.
Telephone: 001264 4975214/4972416; *Fax:* 001264 4972326.

ANTIGUA & BARBUDA

The Antigua Football Association, P.O. Box 773, St John's.
Founded: 1928; *Number of Clubs:* 60; *Number of Players:* 1,008; *National Colours:* Gold shirts, black shorts and stockings.
Telephone: 001268 4624863; *Cable:* AFA ANTIGUA; *Fax:* 001268 4624864.

ARUBA

Arubaanse Voetbal Bond, P.O. Box 376, Oranjestad, Aruba.
Founded: 1932; *Number of Clubs:* 50; *Number of Players:* 1,000; *National Colours:* Yellow shirts, blue shorts, yellow and blue stockings.
Telephone: 00297 829550; *Cable:* AVB ARUBA; *Fax:* 00297 820624.

BAHAMAS

Bahamas Football Association, P.O. Box N 8434, Nassau, NP.
Founded: 1967; *Number of Clubs:* 14; *Number of Players:* 700; *National Colours:* Yellow shirts, black shorts, yellow stockings.
Telephone: 001809 3233426; *Cable:* BAHSOCA NASSAU; *Fax:* 001809 3288006.

BARBADOS

Barbados Football Association, P.O. Box 1362, Bridgetown, Barbados.
Physical address: Hadley Court, Upper Collymore Rock, St Michael.
Founded: 1910; *Number of Clubs:* 92; *Number of Players:* 1,100; *National Colours:* Royal blue and gold shirts, gold shorts, white, gold and blue stockings.
Tel: 001246 2281707; *Cable:* FOOTBALL BRIDGETOWN; *Fax:* 001246 2286484.

BELIZE

Belize National Football Association, P.O. Box 1742, Belize City.
Founded: 1980; *National Colours:* Red, white and blue shirts and shorts, red stockings.
Telephone: 005012 36563; *Fax:* 005012 36564.

BERMUDA

The Bermuda Football Association, P.O. Box HM 745, Hamilton HM CX.
Founded: 1928; *Number of Clubs:* 30; *Number of Players:* 1,947; *National Colours:* Royal blue shirts, white shorts and stockings.
Telephone: 001809 2952199; *Cable:* FOOTBALL BERMUDA; *Telex:* 3441 BFA BA; *Fax:* 001809 2950773.

BRITISH VIRGIN ISLANDS

British Virgin Islands Football Association, P.O. Box 29, Road Town, Tortola, BVI.
Telephone: 001284 4945655; *Fax:* 001284 4948968.

US VIRGIN ISLANDS

V.I. Soccer Federation, P.O. Box 2618, Kingshill, St Croix, USVI 00851-2618.
Telephone: 001 340 7737216; *Fax:* 001 340 7739686.

CANADA

The Canadian Soccer Association, Place Soccer Canada, 237 Metcalfe Street, Ottawa, ONT K2P 1R2.
Founded: 1912; *Number of Clubs:* 1,600; *Number of Players:* 224,290; *National Colours:* All red.
Telephone: 001613 2377678; *Cable:* SOCCANADA OTTAWA; *Fax:* 001613 2371516.

CAYMAN ISLANDS

Cayman Islands Football Association, PO Box 178 GT, George Town, Grand Cayman, Cayman Islands WI.
Founded: 1966; *Number of Clubs:* 25; *Number of Players:* 875; *National Colours:* Red shirts, blue shorts, white stockings.
Telephone: 001345 9497822328. *Fax:* 001345 945 7673.

COSTA RICA

Federacion Costarricense De Futbol, Apartado 670-1000, Calle 40, Avda CTL & I, San Jose.
Founded: 1921; *Number of Clubs:* 431; *Number of Players:* 12,429; *National Colours:* Red and white shirts, blue shorts, white stockings.
Telephone: 00506 2221544; *Cable:* FEDEFUTBOL SAN JOSE; *Telex:* 3394 DIDER CR; *Fax:* 00506 2552674.

CUBA

Federacion Cubana De Futbol, c/o Comite Olimpico Cubano, Calle 13 No. 601, Esq. C. Vedado, La Habana, ZP 4.
Founded: 1924; *Number of Clubs:* 70; *Number of Players:* 12,900; *National Colours:* White shirts with red collar and cuffs, dark blue shorts, white and red stockings.
Telephone: 00537 403581; *Cable:* FOOTBALL HABANA; *Telex:* 511332 INDER CU; *Fax:* 00537 409037.

DOMINICA

Dominica Football Association, P.O. Box 372, Roseau, Commonwealth of Dominica.
Founded: 1970; *Number of Clubs:* 30; *Number of Players:* 500; *National Colours:* Emerald green shirts, green shorts, yellow stockings.
Telephone & fax: 001767 4492173.

DOMINICAN REPUBLIC

Federacion Dominicana De Futbol, Apartado De Correos No. 1953, Santo Domingo.
Founded: 1953; *Number of Clubs:* 128; *Number of Players:* 10,706; *National Colours:* Navy blue shirts, white shorts, red stockings.
Telephone: 001809542 6923. *Cable:* FEDOFUTBOL SANTO DOMINGO; *Telex:* 817240; *Fax:* 001809547 5363.

EL SALVADOR

Federacion Salvadorena De Futbol, Av. J.M. Delgado, Col. Escalon, Frente Ctro Espanol, Apartado 1029, San Salvador.
Founded: 1935; *Number of Clubs:* 944; *Number of Players:* 21,294; *National Colours:* Blue shirts, white shorts, blue stockings.
Telephone: 00503 2637525/6; *Cable:* FESFUT SAN SALVADOR; *Fax:* 00503 2637583.

GRENADA

Grenada Football Association, P.O. Box 326, St Juilles Street, St George's, Grenada, West Indies.
Founded: 1924; *Number of Clubs:* 15; *Number of Players:* 200; *National Colours:* Green and yellow striped shirts, red shorts, yellow stockings.
Telephone & fax: 001473 4404850; *Cable:* GRENBALL GRENADA; *Telex:* 3431 CW BUR.

GUATEMALA

Federacion Nacional de Futbol de Guatemala, 7a Avenida 12-23 Zona 9, Edificio Etisa 6. Nivel, Guatemala City.
Founded: 1946; *Number of Clubs:* 1,611; *Number of Players:* 43,516; *National Colours:* Blue shirts, white shorts, blue stockings.
Telephone: 005023 322424; *Cable:* FEDFUTBOL GUATEMALA C.A.; *Fax:* 005023 320406.

GUYANA

Guyana Football Association, Lot 65 King Street, P.O. Box 10727, Georgetown.
Founded: 1902; *Number of Clubs:* 103; *Number of Players:* 1,665; *National Colours:* Green shirts and shorts, yellow stockings.
Telephone: 0059222 78758, 63226;*Telex:* 2266 RICEBRD GY; *Fax:* 0059222 52096, 62641.

HAITI

Federation Haitienne De Football, P.O. Box 2258, Port-Au-Prince.
Founded: 1904; *Number of Clubs:* 40; *Number of Players:* 4,000; *National Colours:* Blue and red shirts, blue shorts, blue and red stockings.
Telephone: 00509 464509; *Cable:* FEDHAFOOB PORT-AU-PRINCE; *Fax:* 00509 573001.

HONDURAS

Federacion Nacional Autonoma De Futbol De Honduras, Apartado Postal 827, Costa Oeste Del Est. Nac, Tegucigalpa, D.C.
Founded: 1951; *Number of Clubs:* 1,050; *Number of Players:* 15,300; *National Colours:* Blue shirts, white shorts, blue stockings.
Telephone: 00504 235 4236 (or) 235 4246; *Cable* FENAFUTH TEGUCIGALPA; *Fax:* 00504 235 4237.

JAMAICA

Jamaica Football Federation, General Secretariat, Room 8, Nat. Arena, Institue of Sports, Independence Park, Kingston 6.
Founded: 1910; *Number of Clubs:* 266; *Number of Players:* 45,200; *National Colours:* Gold shirts, black shorts, gold stockings.
Telephone: 001809 9290484; *Cable:* FOOTBALL JAMAICA KINGSTON; *Telex:* 2224 FEDLASCO JA; *Fax:* 001809 9290483.

MEXICO

Federacion Mexicana De Futbol Asociacion, A.C., Abraham Gonzales 74, Col. Juarez, C.P. 06600, Mexico 6, D.F.
Founded: 1927; *Number of Clubs:* 77 (senior); *Number of Players:* 1,402,270; *National Colours:* Green shirts with white collar, white shorts, red stockings.
Telephone: 00525 5662155; *Cable:* MEXFUTBOL MEXICO; *Fax:* 00525 5667580.

MONSERRAT

Monserrat Football Association, P.O. Box 46, Church Road, Plymouth, Monserrat.
Telephone: 001664 4912346; *Fax:* 001664 4912719.

NETHERLANDS ANTILLES

Nederlands Antiliaanse Voetbal Unie, P.O. Box 341, Curacao, NA.
Founded: 1921; *Number of Clubs:* 85; *Number of Players:* 4,500; *National Colours:* white shirts with red and blue stripes, white shorts, red, white and blue stockings.
Telephone: 005999 4627222/4343862; *Cable:* NAVU CURACAO; *Telex:* 1046 ENNIA NA; *Fax:* 005999 4627087/4343837.

NICARAGUA

Federacion Nicaraguense De Futbol, Estadio Futbol Camilo Ortega (Cranshaw), Apdo Postal 976, Managua.
Founded: 1931; *Number of Clubs:* 31; *Number of Players:* 160 (senior); *National Colours:* Blue and white striped shirts, blue shorts, blue and white striped stockings.
Telephone: 005052 680006/7/8; *Cable:* FENIFUT MANAGUA; *Fax:* 005052 664134.

PANAMA

Federacion Panamena De Futbol, Apartado Postal 8-391, Zona 8, Panama.
Founded: 1937; *Number of Clubs:* 65; *Number of Players:* 4,225; *National Colours:* Red shirts, blue shorts, white stockings.
Telephone & fax: 00507 2282238.

PUERTO RICO

Federacion Puertorriquena De Futbol, Coliseo Roberto Clemente, P.O. Box 1944355, Hato Rey, P.R. 00919-4355.
Founded: 1940; *Number of Clubs:* 175; *Number of Players:* 4,200; *National Colours:* Blue shirts, blue and white shorts and stockings.
Telephone & fax: 001787 7642025.

SAINT LUCIA

St Lucia National Football Association, PO Box 255, Castries, St Lucia.
Founded: 1979; *Number of Clubs:* 100; *Number of Players:* 4,000; *National Colours:* Blue and white shirts, black shorts, blue stockings.
Telephone: 001758 0689; *Cable:* NFU ST. LUCIA; *Telex:* 6394 FOR AFF LC; *Fax:* 001758 2506.

SAINT KITTS & NEVIS

St Kitts-Nevis Football Association, P.O. Box 465, Basseterre, St Kitts, WI.
Founded: 1932; *Number of Clubs:* 36; *Number of Players:* 600; *National Colours:* Green and yellow shirts, red shorts, yellow stockings.
Telephone: 001869 465 6809; *Cable:* HORSFORD ST. KITTS; *Telex:* 6822 HORSFDSKB KC; *Fax:* 001869 465 1190; Internet: www.skbee.com/sknfa; E-mail: sknfa@skbee.com.

SAINT VINCENT & THE GRENADINES

St Vincent & The Grenadines Football Federation, PO Box 1278, Kingstown, St Vincent, WI.
Founded: 1979; *Number of Clubs:* 500; *Number of Players:* 5,000; *National Colours:* Green shirts with yellow border, blue shorts, yellow stockings.
Telephone: 001784 4561659; *Fax:* 001784 4571659.

SURINAM

Surinaamse Voetbal Bond, Letitia Vriesde Laan 7, P.O. Box 1223, Paramaribo.
Founded: 1920; *Number of Clubs:* 168; *Number of Players:* 4,430; *National Colours:* Red green and white shirts, white or green shorts and stockings.
Telephone: 00597 473112; *Cable:* SVB Paramaribo; *Fax:* 00597 479718.

TRINIDAD & TOBAGO

Trinidad & Tobago Football Federation, Petrotrin Savannah Building, 9 Queen's Park West, P.O. Box 400, Port of Spain.
Founded: 1908; *Number of Clubs:* 124; *Number of Players:* 5,050; *National Colours:* Red shirts, black shorts, white stockings.
Telephone: 001809 6271011; *Fax:* 001809 6271007.

TURKS & CAICOS

Turks & Caicos Football Association, P.O. Box 180, Providenciales, Turks & Caicos Islands, BWI.
Telephone: 001649 9464650; *Fax:* 001649 9464663.

USA

US Soccer, Soccer House, 1801-1811 S. Prairie Avenue, Chicago, Illinois 60616.
Founded: 1913; *Number of Clubs:* 7,000; *Number of Players:* 1,411,500; *National Colours:* All white.
Telephone: 001312 8081300; *Telex:* 450024 US SOCCER FED; *Fax:* 001312 8081301.

OCEANIA

AMERICAN SAMOA

American Samoa Football Association, P.O. Box 282, Pago Pago.
Telephone: 00684 6882290; *Fax:* 00684 6882291.

AUSTRALIA

Soccer Australia, Sydney Football Stadium, Driver Avenue, P.O. Box 175, Paddington NSW 2021.
Founded: 1961; *Number of Clubs:* 6,816; *Number of Players:* 433,957; *National Colours:* Gold shirts with green trim, gold shorts, gold and green stockings.
Telephone: 0061 293806099; *Cable:* FOOTBALL SYDNEY; *Fax:* 0061 293806155.

COOK ISLANDS

Cook Islands Football Federation, P.O. Box 29, Avarua, Rarotonga, Cook Islands.
Founded: 1971; *Number of Clubs:* 9; *National Colours:* Green shirts and shorts with gold stripes, gold and green stockings.
Telephone: 00682 21231; *Fax:* 00682 25912.

FIJI

Fiji Football Association, Bob S. Kumar, Hon. Secretary, Government Bldgs, P.O.Box 2514, Suva.
Founded: 1938; *Number of Clubs:* 140; *Number of Players:* 21,300; *National Colours:* White shirts, blue shorts and stockings.
Telephone: 00679 300453; *Fax:* 00679 304642.

NEW ZEALAND

Soccer New Zealand, 51 O'Rorke Road, Penrose, Auckland, New Zealand.
Founded: 1891; *Number of Clubs:* 312; *Number of Players:* 52,969; *National Colours:* White shirts with black trim, white shorts and stockings.
Telephone: 00649 5256120; *Fax:* 00649 5256123.

PAPUA NEW GUINEA

Papua New Guinea Football (Soccer) Association, c/o National Sports Institute, P.O. Box 337, Goroka, EHP 441.
Founded: 1962; *Number of Clubs:* 350; *Number of Players:* 8,250; *National Colours:* Red shirts, black shorts, red stockings.
Telephone: 00675 7321699; *Telex:* TOTOTRA NE 23436; *Fax:* 00675 7321941.

SOLOMON ISLANDS

Solomon Islands Football Federation, PO Box 854, Honiara, Solomon Islands.
Founded: 1978; *Number of Players:* 4,000; *National Colours:* Green, yellow and blue shirts and shorts, white stockings.
Telephone: 00677 26496; *Telex:* HQ 66349; *Fax:* 00677 26497.

TAHITI

Federation Tahitienne de Football (F.T.F.), B.P.50 358, Pirae, Tahiti, French Polynesia.
Founded: 1989; *National Colours:* White shirts, red shorts, white stockings.
Telephone: 00689 540954; *Cable:* FOOTBALL TAHITI; *Fax:* 00689 419629.

TONGA

Tonga Football Association, P.O. Box 852, Nuku'Alofa, Tonga.
Founded: 1965; *Number of Clubs:* 23; *Number of Players:* 350; *National Colours:* Red shirts, white shorts, red and white stockings.
Telephone: 00676 24442; *Cable:* SOCCER NUKU'ALOFA; *Fax:* 00676 23340; E-mail: tfa@kalianet.to.

VANUATU

Vanuatu Football Federation, P.O. Box 226, Port Vila, Vanuatu.
Founded: 1934; *National Colours:* Gold and black shirts, black shorts, gold and black stockings.
Telephone: 00678 25236; *Cable:* FUTBOL BLONG VANUATU; *Fax:* 00678 25236.

WESTERN SAMOA

Samoa Football (Soccer) Association, P.O. Box 960, Apia.
Founded: 1968; *National Colours:* Royal blue shirts, white shorts, royal blue and white stockings.
Telephone: 00685 22822; *Telex:* 233 TREASURY SX; *Fax:* 00685 21312.

AFRICA

ALGERIA

Federation Algerienne De Foot-ball, Chemin Ahmed Ouaked, Boite Postale No. 39, Dely-Ibrahim-Alger.
Founded: 1962; *Number of Clubs:* 780; *Number of Players:* 58,567; *National Colours:* Green shirts, white shorts, green stockings.
Telephone: 002132 365938; *Cable:* FAFOOT ALGER; *Telex:* 61378. *Fax:* 002132 365949.

ANGOLA

Federation Angolaise De Football, Compl. da Cidadela Desportiva, B.P. 3449, Luanda.
Founded: 1979; *Number of Clubs:* 276; *Number of Players:* 4,269; *National Colours:* Red shirts, black shorts, red stockings.
Telephone: 002442 261331, 264948, 265936; *Cable:* FUTANGOLA; *Telex:* 2580 PALANCA AN; *Fax:* 002442 260566.

BENIN

Federation Beninoise De Football, B.P. 965, Cotonou.
Founded: 1962; *Number of Clubs:* 117; *Number of Players:* 6,700; *National Colours:* Yellow shirts, green shorts, red stockings.
Telephone & fax: 00229 330537; *Cable:* FEBEFOOT COTONOU; *Telex:* 5245 SONACOP COTONOU.

BOTSWANA

Botswana Football Association, P.O. Box 1396, Gabarone.
Founded: 1970; *National Colours:* Blue and white shirts, blue, white and black shorts, blue, white and black striped stockings.
Telephone: 00267 300279; *Cable:* BOTSBALL GABARONE; *Telex:* 2977 BD; *Fax:* 00267 300280.

BURKINA FASO

Federation Burkinabe De Foot-Ball, 01 B.P. 57, Ouagadougou 01.
Founded: 1960; *Number of Clubs:* 57; *Number of Players:* 4,672; *National Colours:* Red shirts, green shorts with yellow star, red stockings.
Telephone: 00226 318815; *Cable:* FEDEFOOT OUAGADOUGOU; *Fax:* 00226 318843.

BURUNDI

Federation De Football Du Burundi, B.P. 3426, Bujumbura.
Founded: 1948; *Number of Clubs:* 132; *Number of Players:* 3,930; *National Colours:* Red shirts, white shorts, green stockings.
Telephone & fax: 00257 212891; *Cable:* FFB BUJA.

CAMEROON

Federation Camerounaise De Football, B.P. 1116, Yaounde.
Founded: 1959; *Number of Clubs:* 200; *Number of Players:* 9,328; *National Colours:* Green shirts, red shorts, yellow stockings.
Telephone: 00237 216662; *Cable:* FECAFOOT YAOUNDE; *Telex:* 8568 JEUNESPO KN; *Fax:* 00237 210012.

CAPE VERDE ISLANDS

Federacao Cabo-Verdiana De Futebol, P.O. Box 234, Praia.
Founded: 1982; *National Colours:* All green.
Telephone & fax: 00238 611362; *Cable:* FUTEBOL PRAIA CV; *Telex:* 6005 ACAS CV.

CENTRAL AFRICAN REPUBLIC

Federation Centrafricaine De Football Amateur, B.P. 344, Bangui.
Founded: 1937; *Number of Clubs:* 256; *Number of Players:* 7,200; *National Colours:* Grey and blue shirts with national emblem and star, white shorts, red stockings with yellow trim.
Telephone: 00236 612433; *Cable:* FOOTBANGUI BANGUI; *Fax:* 00236 615660.

CHAD

Federation Tchadienne de Football, B.P. 886, N'Djamena.
Founded: 1962; *National Colours:* Blue shirts, yellow shorts, red stockings.
Telephone: 00235/519204; *Telex:* 5248 kd; *Fax:* 00235/518648.

CONGO

Federation Congolaise De Football, B.P. 4041, Brazzaville.
Founded: 1962; *Number of Clubs:* 250; *Number of Players:* 5,940; *National Colours:* All red.
Telephone: 00242 834885; *Cable:* FECOFOOT BRAZZAVILLE; *Telex:* 5210 KG; *Fax:* 00242 836199.

CONGO DR

Federation Congolaise De Football-Association (FECOFA), P.O. Box 1284, Av. De L'Enseignem. 210, Z/Kasa-Vubu, Kinshasa 1.
Founded: 1919; *Number of Clubs:* 3,800; *Number of Players:* 64,627; *National Colours:* Green shirts, yellow shorts, red stockings.
Telephone & fax: 001212 3769411; *Cable:* FECOFA KINSHASA.

DJIBOUTI

Federation Djiboutienne de Football, B.P. 2694, Djibouti.
Founded: 1977; *Number of Players:* 2,000; *National Colours:* Green shirts, white shorts, blue stockings.
Telephone: 00253 342049; *Fax:* 00253 356793.

EGYPT

Egyptian Football Association, 5, Shareh Gabalaya, Guezira, Al Borg Post Office, Cairo.
Founded: 1921; *Number of Clubs:* 247; *Number of Players:* 19,735; *National Colours:* Red shirts, white shorts, black stockings.
Telephone: 00202 3401793; *Cable:* KORA CAIRO; *Telex:* 93506 KORA UN; *Fax:* 00202 3417817.

ERITREA

The Eritrean National Football Federation, P.O. Box 3665, Asmara.
Telephone & fax: 002911 126821.

ETHIOPIA

Ethiopia Football Federation, Addis Ababa Stadium, P.O. Box 1080, Addis Ababa.
Founded: 1943; *Number of Clubs:* 767; *Number of Players:* 20,594; *National Colours:* Green shirts, yellow shorts, red stockings.
Telephone: 002511 514453; *Cable:* FOOTBALL ADDIS ABABA; *Telex:* 21377 NESCO ET; *Fax:* 002511 513345.

GABON

Federation Gabonaise De Football, B.P. 181, Libreville.
Founded: 1962; *Number of Clubs:* 320; *Number of Players:* 10,000; *National Colours:* Green, yellow and blue shirts, blue and yellow shorts, white stockings with tri-colour trims.
Telephone: 00241 730460; *Cable:* FEGAFOOT LIBREVILLE; *Telex:* 5526 GO; *Fax:* 00241 746047.

GAMBIA

Gambia Football Association, Independence Stadium, Bakau, P.O. Box 523, Banjul.
Founded: 1952; *Number of Clubs:* 30; *Number of Players:* 860; *National Colours:* White shirts with striped band, white shorts, white stockings with red tops.
Telephone: 00220 496980; *Cable:* SPORTS GAMBIA BANJUL; *Telex:* 2262 FISCO GV.

GHANA

Ghana Football Association, P.O. Box 1272, Accra.
Founded: 1957; *Number of Clubs:* 347; *Number of Players:* 11,275; *National Colours:* All yellow.
Telephone: 0023321 666697; *Cable:* GFA ACCRA; *Telex:* 2519 SPORTS GH; *Fax:* 0023321 668590.

GUINEA

Federation Guineenne De Football, P.O. Box 3645, Conakry.
Founded: 1959; *Number of Clubs:* 351; *Number of Players:* 10,000; *National Colours:* Red shirts, yellow shorts, green stockings.
Telephone: 00224 461159; *Cable:* GUINEFOOT CONAKRY; *Telex:* 22302 MJ GE; *Fax:* 00224 411926.

GUINEA-BISSAU

Federacao De Football Da Guinea-Bissau, Rua 4 No. 10-C, Apartado 375, 1035 Bissau- Codex.
Founded: 1974; *National Colours:* All red.
Telephone & fax: 00245 201918; *Cable:* FUTEBOL BISSAU.

GUINEA, EQUATORIAL

Federacion Ecuatoguineana De Futbol, Malabo.
Founded: 1986; *National Colours:* All red.
Telephone: 002409 2392; *Cable:* FEGUIFUT MALABO; *Telex:* 9991111 EG; *Fax:* 002409 3353.

IVORY COAST

Federation Ivoirienne De Football, Av. 1 Treichville, 01 B.P. 1202, Abidjan 01.
Founded: 1960; *Number of Clubs:* 84 (senior); *Number of Players:* 3,655; *National Colours:* Orange shirts, white shorts, green stockings.
Telephone: 00225 242301; *Cable:* FIF ABIDJAN; *Telex:* 42344 FIF CI; *Fax:* 00225 257111.

KENYA

Kenya Football Federation, Nyayo National Stadium, P.O. Box 40234, Nairobi.
Founded: 1960; *Number of Clubs:* 351; *Number of Players:* 8,880; *National Colours:* Red, green and white shirts, red, green and black shorts and stockings.
Telephone: 002542 501825/35; *Cable:* KEFF NAIROBI; *Telex:* 24069 SPICERS KE; *Fax:* 002542 501120.

LESOTHO

Lesotho Football Association, P.O. Box 756, Maseru-100, Lesotho.
Founded: 1932; *Number of Clubs:* 88; *Number of Players:* 2,076; *National Colours:* Blue shirts, green shorts, white stockings.
Telephone: 00266 311879; *Cable:* LEFA MASERU; *Telex:* 4493, 4228; *Fax:* 00266 310586.

LIBERIA

Liberia Football Association, 110 Camp Johnson Road, P.O. Box 10-1066, 1000 Monrovia 10.
Founded: 1936; *National Colours:* Red shirts, white shorts, blue stockings.
Telephone: 00231 226284; *Cable:* LIBFOTASS MONROVIA; *Telex:* 44220 EXM IBR. *Fax:* 00231 225217.

LIBYA

Libyan Arab Football Federation, 7th October Stadium, P.O. Box 5137, Tripoli.
Founded: 1963; *Number of Clubs:* 89; *Number of Players:* 2,941; *National Colours:* Green shirts, white shorts, green stockings.
Telephone & fax: 0021821 4446610/3339150; *Telex:* 20896 LY.

MADAGASCAR

Federation Malagasy de Football, Immeuble Preservatrice Vie-Lot IBF-9B, Rue Rabearivelo-Antsahavola, Antananarivo 101.
Founded: 1961; *Number of Clubs:* 775; *Number of Players:* 23,536; *National Colours:* Red shirts, white shorts, green stockings.
Telephone: 0026120 2268374; *Telex:* 22265 AROSUR MG; *Fax:* 0026120 2268373.

MALAWI

Football Association of Malawi, P.O. Box 865, Blantyre.
Founded: 1966; *Number of Clubs:* 465; *Number of Players:* 12,500; *National Colours:* Red shirts, red and green shorts, green stockings.
Telephone & fax: 00265 674290; *Cable:* FOOTBALL BLANTYRE; *Telex:* 4526 SPORTS MI.

MALI

Federation Malienne De Football, Stade Mamdou Konate, B.P. 1020, Bamako.
Founded: 1960; *Number of Clubs:* 128; *Number of Players:* 5,480; *National Colours:* Green shirts, yellow shorts, red stockings.
Telephone: 00223 224254; *Cable:* MALIFOOT BAMAKO; *Telex:* 0985 1200 MJ; *Fax:* 00356 245136.

MAURITANIA

Federation De Foot-Ball De La Rep. Islamique. De Mauritanie, B.P. 566, Nouakchott.
Founded: 1961; *Number of Clubs:* 59; *Number of Players:* 1,930; *National Colours:* Green and yellow shirts, yellow shorts, green stockings.
Telephone: 00222 291032 (or) 50424; *Cable:* FOOTRIM NOUAKCHOTT; *Telex:* 577 MTN NKTT RIM; *Fax:* 00222 291031 (or) 250424 (or) 291077.

MAURITIUS

Mauritius Football Association, Chancery House, 2nd Floor Nos. 303-305, 14 Lislet Geoffroy Street, Port Louis.
Founded: 1952; *Number of Clubs:* 397; *Number of Players:* 29,375; *National Colours:* Red shirts, white shorts, red stockings with white tops.
Telephone: 00230 2121418; *Cable:* MFA PORT LOUIS; *Fax:* 00230 2084100.

MOROCCO

Federation Royale Marocaine De Football, Av. Ibn Sina, C.N.S. Bellevue, B.P. 51, Rabat.
Founded: 1955; *Number of Clubs:* 350; *Number of Players:* 19,768; *National Colours:* All red.
Telephone: 002127 672706/08; *Cable:* FERMAFOOT RABAT; *Telex:* 32940 FERMFOOT M. *Fax:* 002127 671070.

MOZAMBIQUE

Federacao Mocambicana De Futebol, Av. Samora Machel, 11-2, Caixa Postal 1467, Maputo.
Founded: 1978; *Number of Clubs:* 144; *National Colours:* Red shirts, black shorts, black and red stockings.
Telephone: 002581 300366; *Cable:* MOCAMBOLA MAPUTO; *Telex:* 6-747 MCID MO; *Fax:* 002581 300367.

NAMIBIA

Namibia Football Federation, Abraham Mashego Street 8521, Katurua Council of Churches in Namibia, P.O. Box 1345, Windhoek, Namibia.
Founded: 1990; *Number of Clubs:* 244; *Number of Players:* 7320; *National Colours:* All blue, red, green, yellow and white.
Telephone: 0026461 217621; *Fax:* 0026461 265693.

NIGER

Federation Nigerienne De Football (Fenifoot), Stade du 29 Juillet, B.P. 10299, Niamey.
Founded: 1967; *Number of Clubs:* 64; *Number of Players:* 1,525; *National Colours:* Orange shirts, white shorts, green stockings.
Telephone: 00227 725127/722147; *Cable:* FEDERFOOT NIGER NIAMEY; *Telex:* 5527; *Fax:* 00227 722147/734694.

NIGERIA

Nigeria Football Association, Plot 2033, Olusegun Obasanjo Way, Wuse Zone 7, Abuja, Nigeria.
Founded: 1945; *Number of Clubs:* 326; *Number of Players:* 80,190; *National Colours:* Green shirts, white shorts, green stockings.
Telephone: 002349 5237326; *Cable:* FOOTBALL ABUJA; *Telex:* 26570 NFA NG; *Fax:* 002349 5237327.

RWANDA

Federation Rwandaise De Football Amateur, B.P. 2000, Kigali.
Founded: 1972; *Number of Clubs:* 167; *National Colours:* Red, green and yellow shirts, green shorts, red stockings.
Telephone: 00250 84999; *Cable:* FERWAFA KIGALI; *Telex:* 22504 PUBLIC RW; *Fax:* 00250 76574.

SENEGAL

Federation Senegalaise De Football, Stade L.S. Senghor, Route De L'Aeroport De Yoff, B.P. 130 21, Dakar.
Founded: 1960; *Number of Clubs:* 75 (senior); *Number of Players:* 3,977; *National Colours:* Green shirts, yellow shorts, red stockings.
Telephone & fax: 00221 8273524; *Cable:* SENEFOOT DAKAR ; *Telex:* 13048 PUBLIDK SG.

SEYCHELLES

Seychelles Football Federation, P.O. Box 843, People's Stadium, Victoria-Mahe, Seychelles.
Founded: 1979; *National Colours:* Red and blue shirts, blue and red shorts, white stockings.
Telephone: 00248 323908 ext. 244; *Fax:* 00248 225468.

ST THOMAS AND PRINCIPE

Federation Santomense De Futebol, P.O. Box 42, Sao Tome.
Founded: 1975; *National Colours:* All green and yellow.
Telephone: 0023912 23431; *Telex:* 213 PUBLICO STP; *Fax:* 0023912 21365.

SIERRA LEONE

Sierra Leone Football Association, P.O. Box 672, National Stadium, Brookfields, Freetown.
Founded: 1967; *Number of Clubs:* 104; *Number of Players:* 8,120; *National Colours:* Green, white and blue shirts, white shorts, blue stockings with white tops.
Telephone: 00232 2224 1872; *Fax:* 00232 2222 7771.

SOMALIA

Somali Football Federation, c/o Conf. Afric. de Football, 5 Gabalaya Street, 11567, El Borg, Cairo, Egypt.
Founded: 1951; *Number of Clubs:* 46 (senior); *Number of Players:* 1,150; *National Colours:* All sky blue and white.
Telephone: 0020 2/3412497; *Cable:* SOMALIA FOOTBALL CAIRO; *Telex:* 93162 CAF UN; *Fax:* 0020 2/3420114 (CAF).

SOUTH AFRICA

South African Football Association, First National Bank Stadium, Nasrec/PO Box 910, Johannesburg 2000, South Africa.
Founded: 1991; *Number of Teams:* 51,944; *Number of Players:* 1,039,880; *National Colours:* Gold and black shirts, green shorts, white stockings.
Telephone: 002711 4943522; *Fax:* 002711 4943013.

SUDAN

Sudan Football Association, P.O. Box 437, Khartoum.
Founded: 1936; *Number of Clubs:* 750; *Number of Players:* 42,200; *National Colours:* Green shirts, white shorts, green stockings.
Telephone & fax: 0024911 776633; *Cable:* ALKOURA KHARTOUM; *Telex:* 23007 KORA SD.

SWAZILAND

National Football Association of Swaziland, P.O. Box 641, Mbabane.
Founded: 1968; *Number of Clubs:* 136; *National Colours:* Blue shirts, gold shorts, white stockings.
Telephone: 00268 46852; *Telex:* 2245 EXP WD; *Fax:* 00268 46206.

TANZANIA

Football Association of Tanzania, Uhuru/Shaurimoyo Road, Karume Memorial Stadium, P.O. Box 1574, Ilala/Dar Es Salaam.
Founded: 1930; *Number of Clubs:* 51; *National Colours:* Yellow shirts with black stripes, yellow shorts, yellow and black stockings with horizontal stripe.
Telephone: 0025551 117931; *Cable:* FAT DAR-ES-SALAAM; *Telex:* 41873 TZ; *Fax:* 0025551 117930.

TOGO

Federation Togolaise De Football, C.P. 5, Lome.
Founded: 1960; *Number of Clubs:* 144; *Number of Players:* 4,346; *National Colours:* White shirts, green shorts, red and yellow stockings with green stripes.
Telephone: 00228 221412; *Cable:* TOGOFOOT LOME; *Telex:* 5015 CNOT TG. *Fax:* 00228 221413.

TUNISIA

Federation Tunisienne De Football, 16 Rue de la Ligue Arabe, El-Menzah VI, Tunis 1004.
Founded: 1956; *Number of Clubs:* 215; *Number of Players:* 18,300; *National Colours:* Red shirts, white shorts, red stockings.
Telephone: 002161 233303; *Cable:* FOOTBALL TUNIS; *Telex:* 14783 FTFOOT TN; *Fax:* 002161 767929.

UGANDA

Federation of Uganda Football Associations, P.O. Box 22518, Kampala, Uganda.
Founded: 1924; *Number of Clubs:* 400; *Number of Players:* 1,518; *National Colours:* Yellow shirts with black stripes, black shorts with yellow stripes, yellow and red stockings.
Telephone: 0025641 342731; *Cable:* FUFA LUGOGO STADIUM, KAMPALA; *Telex:* 61605; *Fax:* 0025641 342731.

ZAMBIA

Football Association of Zambia, P.O. Box 34751, Lusaka.
Founded: 1929; *Number of Clubs:* 20 (senior); *Number of Players:* 4,100; *National Colours:* Copper shirts, black shorts, copper stockings.
Telephone: 002601 750254; *Cable:* FOOTBALL LUSAKA; *Fax:* 002601 225046.

ZIMBABWE

Zimbabwe Football Association, P.O. Box CY 114, Causeway, Harare.
Founded: 1965; *National Colours:* Green shirts, gold shorts, green and gold stockings.
Telephone: 002634 731262; *Cable:* SOCCER HARARE; *Telex:* 22299 SOCCER ZW; *Fax:* 002634 731265.

THE WORLD CUP 1930–2002

Year	Winners	Runners-up	Venue	Attendance	Referee
1930	Uruguay 4	Argentina 2	Montevideo	90,000	Langenus (B)
1934	Italy 2 *(after extra time)*	Czechoslovakia 1	Rome	50,000	Eklind (Se)
1938	Italy 4	Hungary 2	Paris	45,000	Capdeville (F)
1950	Uruguay 2	Brazil 1	Rio de Janeiro	199,854	Reader (E)
1954	West Germany 3	Hungary 2	Berne	60,000	Ling (E)
1958	Brazil 5	Sweden 2	Stockholm	49,737	Guigue (F)
1962	Brazil 3	Czechoslovakia 1	Santiago	68,679	Latychev (USSR)
1966	England 4 *(after extra time)*	West Germany 2	Wembley	93,802	Dienst (Sw)
1970	Brazil 4	Italy 1	Mexico City	107,412	Glockner (EG)
1974	West Germany 2	Holland 1	Munich	77,833	Taylor (E)
1978	Argentina 3 *(after extra time)*	Holland 1	Buenos Aires	77,000	Gonella (I)
1982	Italy 3	West Germany 1	Madrid	90,080	Coelho (Br)
1986	Argentina 3	West Germany 2	Mexico City	114,580	Filho (Br)
1990	West Germany 1	Argentina 0	Rome	73,603	Codesal (Mex)
1994	Brazil 0 *(Brazil won 3-2 on penalties aet)*	Italy 0	Los Angeles	94,194	Puhl (H)
1998	France 3	Brazil 0	St-Denis	75,000	Belqola (Mor)
2002	Brazil 2	Germany 0	Yokohama	69,029	Collina (I)

GOALSCORING AND ATTENDANCES IN WORLD CUP FINAL ROUNDS

Venue	*Matches*	*Goals (av)*	*Attendance (av)*
1930, Uruguay	18	70 (3.9)	434,500 (24,138)
1934, Italy	17	70 (4.1)	395,000 (23,235)
1938, France	18	84 (4.6)	483,000 (26,833)
1950, Brazil	22	88 (4.0)	1,337,000 (60,772)
1954, Switzerland	26	140 (5.4)	943,000 (36,270)
1958, Sweden	35	126 (3.6)	868,000 (24,800)
1962, Chile	32	89 (2.8)	776,000 (24,250)
1966, England	32	89 (2.8)	1,614,677 (50,458)
1970, Mexico	32	95 (2.9)	1,673,975 (52,311)
1974, West Germany	38	97 (2.5)	1,774,022 (46,684)
1978, Argentina	38	102 (2.7)	1,610,215 (42,374)
1982, Spain	52	146 (2.8)	2,064,364 (38,816)
1986, Mexico	52	132 (2.5)	2,441,731 (46,956)
1990, Italy	52	115 (2.2)	2,515,168 (48,368)
1994, USA	52	141 (2.7)	3,567,415 (68,604)
1998, France	64	171 (2.6)	2,775,400 (43,366)
2002, Japan/S. Korea	64	161 (2.5)	2,705,566 (42,274)

LEADING GOALSCORERS

Year	*Player*	*Goals*
1930	Guillermo Stabile (Argentina)	8
1934	Angelo Schiavio (Italy), Oldrich Nejedly (Czechoslovakia), Edmund Conen (Germany)	4
1938	Leonidas da Silva (Brazil)	8
1950	Ademir (Brazil)	9
1954	Sandor Kocsis (Hungary)	11
1958	Just Fontaine (France)	13
1962	Valentin Ivanov (USSR), Leonel Sanchez (Chile), Garrincha, Vava (both Brazil), Florian Albert (Hungary), Drazen Jerkovic (Yugoslavia)	4
1966	Eusebio (Portugal)	9
1970	Gerd Muller (West Germany)	10
1974	Grzegorz Lato (Poland)	7
1978	Mario Kempes (Argentina)	6
1982	Paolo Rossi (Italy)	6
1986	Gary Lineker (England)	6
1990	Salvatore Schillaci (Italy)	6
1994	Oleg Salenko (Russia) Hristo Stoichkov (Bulgaria)	6
1998	Davor Suker (Croatia)	6
2002	Ronaldo (Brazil)	8

CONFEDERATIONS CUP 2003

(in France)

PREVIOUS WINNERS

1992 Argentina; 1995 Denmark; 1997 Brazil; 1999 Mexico; 2001 France, 2003 France.

GROUP A

New Zealand 0, Japan 3
France 1, Colombia 0
Colombia 3, New Zealand 1
France 2, Japan 1
France 5, New Zealand 0
Japan 0, Colombia 1

	P	*W*	*D*	*L*	*F*	*A*	*Pts*
France	3	3	0	0	8	1	9
Colombia	3	2	0	1	4	2	6
Japan	3	1	0	2	4	3	3
New Zealand	3	0	0	3	1	11	0

GROUP B

Turkey 2, USA 1
Brazil 0, Cameroon 1
Cameroon 1, Turkey 0
Brazil 1, USA 0
Brazil 2, Turkey 2
USA 0, Cameroon 0

	P	*W*	*D*	*L*	*F*	*A*	*Pts*
Cameroon	3	2	1	0	2	0	7
Turkey	3	1	1	1	4	4	4
Brazil	3	1	1	1	3	3	4
USA	3	0	1	2	1	3	1

SEMI-FINALS

Cameroon 1, Colombia 0
France 3, Turkey 2

THIRD PLACE

Colombia 1, Turkey 2

CONFEDERATIONS CUP FINAL

France (0) 1 Cameroon (0) 0

Sunday, 29 June 2003

(at Stade de France, Paris, 51,985)

France: Barthez; Sagnol (Thuram 76), Lizarazu, Pedretti, Gallas, Desailly, Giuly, Cisse, Henry, Dacourt (Kapo 90), Wiltord (Pires 65).
Scorer: Henry (97).

Cameroon: Kameni; Perrier-Doumbe, Song, Mettomo, M'Bami, Djemba, Geremi, Mezague (Emana 91), N'Diefi (Eto'o 67), Idrissou, Atouba.

aet; France won on sudden death.

Referee: I. Valentin (Russia).

EURO 2004

■ *Denotes player sent off.*

GROUP 1

Nicosia, 7 September 2002, 11,898

Cyprus (1) 1 *(Okkas 14)*

France (1) 2 *(Cisse 39, Wiltord 52)*

Cyprus: Panayiotou N; Theodotou, Daskalakis (Michael 68), Ioakim, Konnafis, Spyrou, Kaiafas, Satsias, Nicolaou N (Agathocleous 74), Rauffmann (Yiasoumi 62), Okkas.
France: Coupet; Thuram, Christanval, Desailly, Silvestre, Wiltord (Kapo 79), Makelele, Zidane, Vieira, Marlet (Govou 70), Cisse.
Referee: Fandel (Germany).

Ljubljana, 7 September 2002, 15,000

Slovenia (1) 3 *(Debono 37 (og), Siljak 59, Cimerotic 90)*

Malta (0) 0

Slovenia: Simeunovic; Vugdalic, Bulajic, Knavs, Karic, Sukalo (Gajser 74), Acimovic (Radosavljevic 86), Zahovic, Pavlin, Siljak, Cimerotic.
Malta: Muscat; Said, Dimech, Carabott, Debono, Chetcuti, Agius, Giglio■, Mallia (Bogdanovic 71), Nwoko, Michael Mifsud (Mifsud A 88).
Referee: Borovilos (Greece).

Stade de France, 12 October 2002, 77,619

France (2) 5 *(Vieira 10, Marlet 35, 64, Wiltord 79, Govou 86)*

Slovenia (0) 0

France: Barthez; Thuram (Sagnol 84), Silvestre, Vieira, Gallas, Desailly, Wiltord (Cheyrou 87), Makelele, Marlet (Govou 80), Zidane, Henry.
Slovenia: Simeunovic; Gajser■, Karic (Filekovic 88), Sukalo, Vugdalic, Cipot, Zahovic, Radosavljevic (Zlogar 68), Siljak, Pavlin, Cimerotic (Ceh N 46).
Referee: Nielsen (Denmark).

Valletta, 12 October 2002, 4000

Malta (0) 0

Israel (0) 2 *(Balili 57, Revivo 77)*

Malta: Muscat; Said, Dimech, Chetcuti, Carabott, Debono, Agius (Mallia 84), Turner, Brincat (Mifsud A 76), Nwoko (Bogdanovic 64), Michael Mifsud.
Israel: Auat; Zano, Domb, Banin, Badir, Benado, Keissi, Balili (Benayoun 71), Revivo, Tal (Antebi 82), Berkovic.
Referee: Shebek (Ukraine).

Valletta, 16 October 2002, 12,000

Malta (0) 0

France (2) 4 *(Henry 25, 35, Wiltord 59, Carriere 84)*

Malta: Muscat; Carabott, Chetcuti, Debono (Miguel Mifsud 87), Said, Dimech, Agius, Michael Mifsud, Giglio, Nwoko (Bogdanovic 46), Brincat (Mallia 69).
France: Barthez; Thuram, Silvestre, Vieira (Dacourt 70), Gallas (Mexes 84), Desailly, Wiltord, Makelele, Marlet, Zidane, Henry (Carriere 78).
Referee: Tudor (Romania).

Nicosia, 20 November 2002, 5000

Cyprus (0) 2 *(Rauffmann 50, Okkas 74)*

Malta (0) 1 *(Michael Mifsud 90)*

Cyprus: Panayiotou N; Konnafis, Ioakim, Spyrou, Okkarides, Theodotou, Satsias (Michael), Kaiafas, Okkas, Rauffmann (Yiasoumi 71), Constantinou M (Nicolaou N 66).
Malta: Muscat; Said, Mamo (Miguel Mifsud 74), Giglio (Theuma 80), Chetcuti, Carabott, Agius, Dimech, Michael Mifsud, Bogdanovic, Mifsud A (Mallia 61).
Referee: Guenov (Bulgaria).

Limassol, 29 March 2003, 5000

Cyprus (0) 1 *(Rauffmann 61)*

Israel (1) 1 *(Afek 2)*

Cyprus: Panayiotou N; Okkarides, Ioakim (Nicolaou N 46) (Daskalakis 77), Konnafis, Spyrou, Theodotou, Engomitis (Rauffmann 60), Kaiafas, Tomic, Constantinou M, Okkas.
Israel: Auat; Benado, Ben-Haim, Keissi, Harazi A, Banin, Badir (Abuksis 85), Tal, Afek (Benayoun 73), Zandberg (Nimny 66), Revivo.
Referee: McCurry (Scotland).

Lens, 29 March 2003, 40,775

France (2) 6 *(Wiltord 36, Henry 38, 54, Zidane 57 (pen), 81, Trezeguet 70)*

Malta (0) 0

France: Barthez; Thuram (Sagnol 65), Lizarazu, Pedretti, Gallas, Silvestre, Wiltord (Govou 75), Makelele, Trezeguet, Zidane, Henry (Rothen 80).
Malta: Muscat; Carabott, Ciantar, Said, Vella, Mamo (Chetcuti 71), Bogdanovic (Turner 62), Dimech, Mallia, Michael Mifsud, Nwoko.
Referee: Bozinovski (Macedonia).

Palermo, 2 April 2003, 5000

Israel (1) 1 *(Afek 2)*

France (2) 2 *(Trezeguet 23, Zidane 45)*

Israel: Auat; Benado, Ben-Haim, Keissi, Harazi A, Abuksis, Banin (Benayoun 74), Tal (Badir 56), Afek, Turgeman (Zandberg 46), Revivo.
France: Barthez; Thuram, Lizarazu, Vieira, Gallas, Silvestre, Wiltord (Govou 66), Makelele, Trezeguet (Cisse 74), Zidane, Henry.
Referee: Barber (England).

Ljubljana, 2 April 2003, 5000

Slovenia (4) 4 *(Siljak 5, 14, Zahovic 39 (pen), Ceh A 43)*

Cyprus (1) 1 *(Constantinou M 10)*

Slovenia: Simeunovic; Cipot, Karic, Vugdalic, Bulajic, Zahovic, Ceh A, Pavlin, Sukalo, Koren (Zlogar 85), Siljak (Rakovic 90).
Cyprus: Panayiotou N; Konnafis (Ioakim 46), Daskalakis, Spyrou (Constantinou G 75), Theodotou, Kaiafas, Okkarides, Rauffmann (Charalambides 46), Tomic, Okkas, Constantinou M.
Referee: Gomes (Portugal).

Palermo, 30 April 2003, 1000

Israel (0) 2 *(Badir 88, Holtzman 90)*

Cyprus (0) 0

Israel: Elimelech; Zano, Afek, Benado, Ben-Haim, Banin (Badir 85), Keissi, Abuksis, Revivo, Turgeman (Benayoun 52), Zandberg (Holtzman 67).
Cyprus: Panayiotou N; Konnafis, Germanou, Nicolaou N, Tomic (Kaiafas 62), Engomitis (Chrisostomos 80), Theodotou, Nicolaou C (Yiasoumi 89), Okkarides, Okkas, Constantinou M.
Referee: Benes (Czech Republic).

Valletta, 30 April 2003, 2500

Malta (0) 1 *(Michael Mifsud 90)*

Slovenia (2) 3 *(Zahovic 15, Siljak 36, 57)*

Malta: Muscat; Ciantar, Vella, Carabott, Said, Turner, Dimech, Giglio (Camenzuli 69), Mallia, Michael Mifsud, Nwoko (Bogdanovic 63).
Slovenia: Simeunovic; Cipot, Vugdalic, Karic, Oslaj (Snofl 61), Sukalo, Ceh N, Zahovic, Pavlin, Siljak (Rakovic 90), Gajser (Koren 78).
Referee: Hanacsek (Hungary).

Antalya, 7 June 2003, 2500

Israel (0) 0

Slovenia (0) 0

Israel: Elimelech; Benado, Banin, Keissi, Afek (Zandberg 71), Nimny, Tal (Bachar 76), Abuksis (Holtzman 86), Revivo, Zano, Benayoun.
Slovenia: Simeunovic; Cipot, Vugdalic, Knavs, Gajser (Koren 71), Sukalo, Pavlin, Karic, Zahovic, Acimovic (Snofl 86), Siljak.
Referee: Busacca (Switzerland).

Ta'Qali, 7 June 2003, 3000

Malta (0) 1 *(Dimech 72)*

Cyprus (1) 2 *(Constantinou 23 (pen), 52)*

Malta: Darmanin■; Camenzuli, Said (Bogdanovic 86), Carabott, Vella, Giglio, Dimech, Mallia (Agius 66), Turner, Michael Mifsud, Nwoko (Muscat 23).
Cyprus: Panayiotou N; Konnafis, Charalambides (Garpozis 90), Daskalakis (Foukaris 65), Christodoulou, Satsias, Okkarides, Michael, Ilia, Okkas (Yiasoumi 78), Constantinou M.
Referee: Brugger (Austria).

Group 1 Table	P	W	D	L	F	A	Pts
France	5	5	0	0	19	2	15
Slovenia	5	3	1	1	10	7	10
Israel	5	2	2	1	6	3	8
Cyprus	6	2	1	3	7	11	7
Malta	7	0	0	7	3	22	0

GROUP 2

Sarajevo, 7 September 2002, 4500

Bosnia (0) 0

Romania (3) 3 *(Chivu 8, Munteanu D 10, Ganea 28)*

Bosnia: Piplica; Beslija (Brkic 41), Music, Hibic, Rizvic, Hota, Ikanovic (Huric 37), Bajramovic (Akrapovic 46), Salihamidzic, Muratovic, Mulina.
Romania: Stelea (Vintila 33); Contra, Radoi, Popescu, Chivu, Codrea (Ghioane 84), Munteanu D, Munteanu V, Mutu, Ganea, Niculae (Cernat 66).
Referee: Cardoso (Portugal).

Oslo, 7 September 2002, 25,114

Norway (0) 2 *(Riise 55, Carew 90)*

Denmark (1) 2 *(Tomasson 23, 72)*

Norway: Grodas; Basma, Berg, Johnsen R, Bergdolmo, Leonhardsen (Strand 77), Andersen T (Carew 77), Bakke (Larsen S 88), Riise, Iversen, Solskjaer.
Denmark: Sorensen; Helveg, Laursen, Lustu, Jensen N, Rommedahl (Michaelsen 59), Poulsen, Gravesen, Gronkjaer (Jensen C 70), Tomasson (Nielsen P 90), Sand.
Referee: Dallas (Scotland).

Copenhagen, 12 October 2002, 40,259

Denmark (0) 2 *(Tomasson 51 (pen), Sand 71)*

Luxembourg (0) 0

Denmark: Jensen S; Bogelund, Jensen N, Gravesen, Henriksen, Poulsen, Rommedahl (Gronkjaer 67), Jensen C (Lovenkrands 67), Tomasson, Sand, Jorgensen (Roll 75).
Luxembourg: Besic; Ferron, Deville F, Reiter, Hoffmann, Strasser, Remy, Holtz (Di Domenico 72), Leweck, Braun G (Huss 79), Cardoni.
Referee: Bede (Hungary).

Bucharest, 12 October 2002, 21,000

Romania (0) 0

Norway (0) 1 *(Iversen 84)*

Romania: Vintila; Contra, Rat, Radoi, Popescu, Chivu, Codrea, Munteanu D (Pancu 85), Ganea (Niculae 64), Moldovan (Ilie 64), Mutu.
Norway: Myhre; Bergdolmo, Basma, Bakke, Lundekvam, Berg, Iversen, Andersen T, Carew (Leonhardsen 80), Solskjaer (Rushfeldt 89), Riise.
Referee: Ivanov (Russia).

Luxembourg, 16 October 2002, 2056

Luxembourg (0) 0

Romania (4) 7 *(Moldovan 2, 5, Radoi 24, Contra 45, 47, 86, Ghioane 80)*

Luxembourg: Besic; Ferron, Deville F, Leweck, Hoffmann, Strasser, Holtz (Rohmann 76), Reiter, Remy, Braun G (Huss 71), Cardoni (Schneider 60).
Romania: Vintila; Contra, Rat, Munteanu D, Radoi, Popescu, Codrea (Ghioane 36), Moldovan (Cernat 69), Ilie, Ganea (Pancu 46), Miu.
Referee: Lajuks (Latvia).

Oslo, 16 October 2002, 24,169

Norway (2) 2 *(Lundekvam 7, Riise 27)*

Bosnia (0) 0

Norway: Olsen; Basma, Bergdolmo, Andersen T (Larsen S 90), Berg, Lundekvam, Leonhardsen (Carew 65), Bakke, Solskjaer (Rushfeldt 89), Iversen, Riise.
Bosnia: Tolja; Bosnjak (Mujcin 65), Papac, Bajramovic, Hibic, Konjic, Salihamidzic (Miskovic 85), Grujic, Baljic, Sabic (Huric 57), Music.
Referee: Benes (Czech Republic).

Zenica, 29 March 2003, 12,000

Bosnia (0) 2 *(Bolic 54, Barbarez 77)*

Luxembourg (0) 0

Bosnia: Hasagic; Biscevic (Berberovic 68), Konjic, Alihodzic, Bajramovic, Bolic (Turkovic 82), Beslija (Hrgovic 80), Baljic, Grujic, Music, Barbarez.
Luxembourg: Besic; Peters, Hoffmann, Strasser, Federspiel, Schauls, Remy, Molitor, Christophe (Huss 86), Braun G (Schneider 88), Leweck (Di Domenico 79).
Referee: Hyytia (Finland).

Bucharest, 29 March 2003, 50,000

Romania (1) 2 *(Mutu 5, Munteanu D 47)*

Denmark (1) 5 *(Rommedahl 9, 90, Gravesen 53, Tomasson 71, Contra 73 (og))*

Romania: Lobont; Radoi, Popescu, Filipescu, Chivu, Contra, Codrea (Reghecampf 60), Munteanu D, Pancu (Bratu 68), Ganea, Mutu.
Denmark: Sorensen; Rytter (Michaelsen 34), Henriksen, Laursen, Jensen N, Rommedahl, Poulsen (Weighorst 68), Gravesen, Lovenkrands (Jorgensen 56), Tomasson, Sand.
Referee: Gonzalez (Spain).

Copenhagen, 2 April 2003, 30,845

Denmark (0) 0

Bosnia (2) 2 *(Barbarez 23, Baljic 29)*

Denmark: Sorensen; Michaelsen, Henriksen, Albrechtsen, Jensen N (Frandsen 81), Rommedahl, Jensen C (Wieghorst 60), Gravesen, Jorgensen, Tomasson (Berg S 85), Sand.
Bosnia: Hasagic; Berberovic, Music, Konjic, Bajramovic, Hibic, Beslija (Mulina 84), Hrgovic (Grujic 67), Biscevic, Baljic (Blatnjak 77), Barbarez.
Referee: Stredak (Slovakia).

Luxembourg, 2 April 2003, 3000

Luxembourg (0) 0

Norway (0) 2 *(Rushfeldt 60, Solskjaer 74)*

Luxembourg: Besic; Peters, Federspiel, Hoffmann, Strasser, Remy, Schauls, Molitor, Braun G (Schneider 75), Leweck (Lassine 89), Christophe (Huss 83).
Norway: Olsen; Bergdolmo, Johnsen, Berg, Basma, Rudi (Tessem 46), Andersen T, Bakke (Larsen S 86), Riise, Flo T (Rushfeldt 46), Solskjaer.
Referee: Dobrinov (Bulgaria).

Copenhagen, 7 June 2003, 41,824

Denmark (1) 1 *(Gronkjaer 6)*

Norway (0) 0

Denmark: Sorensen; Helveg, Laursen, Henriksen, Jensen N, Wieghorst, Gravesen, Gronkjaer (Rommedahl 70), Jensen C (Larsen 62), Jorgensen (Nielsen P 83), Sand.
Norway: Olsen; Basma, Johnsen R, Lundekvam, Bakke, Iversen, Andersen T (Bergdolmo 46), Leonhardsen (Flo T 62), Riise, Carew, Solskjaer (Flo H 89).
Referee: Poll (England).

Craiova, 7 June 2003, 37,000

Romania (0) 2 *(Mutu 46, Ganea 88)*

Bosnia (0) 0

Romania: Lobont; Contra, Iencsi, Chivu, Rat, Radoi, Codrea (Bundea 66), Pancu, Ganea, Mutu (Miu 86), Ilie (Soava 73).
Bosnia: Hasagic; Berberovic (Blatnjak 73), Music, Konjic, Bajramovic, Hibic, Bolic, Beslija (Bartolovic 47), Grujic, Barbarez, Hrgovic.
Referee: Bossen (Holland).

Luxembourg, 11 June 2003, 6869

Luxembourg (0) 0

Denmark (1) 2 *(Jensen C 22, Gravesen 50)*

Luxembourg: Besic; Federspiel, Schauls, Strasser, Remy, Reiter, Molitor, Leweck, Braun G (Christophe 70), Posing, Braun M.
Denmark: Sorensen; Bogelund (Larsen 52), Laursen, Henriksen, Jensen N, Wieghorst, Gravesen, Gronkjaer (Rommedahl 63), Jensen C, Jorgensen, Sand (Skoubo 74).
Referee: Baskakov (Russia).

Oslo, 11 June 2003, 24,890

Norway (0) 1 *(Solskjaer 78 (pen))*

Romania (0) 1 *(Ganea 64)*

Norway: Olsen; Bergdolmo, Berg (Lundekvam 86), Johnsen R, Basma, Solskjaer, Bakke, Andersen T, Johnsen F (Flo T 70), Riise, Carew (Iversen 81).
Romania: Lobont; Contra, Iencsi, Chivu, Rat, Radoi, Soava, Pancu (Bratu 86), Ganea, Mutu, Ilie (Stoica 46).
Referee: Michel (Slovakia).

Group 2 Table	P	W	D	L	F	A	Pts
Denmark	6	4	1	1	12	6	13
Norway	6	3	2	1	8	4	11
Romania	6	3	1	2	15	7	10
Bosnia	5	2	0	3	4	7	6
Luxembourg	5	0	0	5	0	15	0

GROUP 3

Vienna, 7 September 2002, 18,300

Austria (2) 2 *(Herzog 4 (pen), 30 (pen))*

Moldova (0) 0

Austria: Manninger; Dospel, Baur, Martin Hiden, Panis, Schopp (Wimmer 58), Aufhauser, Herzog, Flogel, Vastic (Wagner 81), Wallner (Krankl 68).
Moldova: Hmaruc; Covalenco, Rebeja, Olexic, Sosnovschi, Priganiuc (Boret 68), Boicenco (Cebotari 46), Berco (Catinsus 46), Rogaciov, Ivanov, Clescenco.
Referee: Dougal (Scotland).

Eindhoven, 7 September 2002, 34,000

Holland (2) 3 *(Davids 35, Kluivert 37, Hasselbaink 73)*

Belarus (0) 0

Holland: Van der Sar; Ricksen, Stam, Frank de Boer, Zenden, Van der Meyde, Van Bommel, Cocu, Davids (Van der Vaart 70) (Reiziger 83), Kluivert, Van Nistelrooy (Hasselbaink 70).
Belarus: Shantalosov (Khomutovski 88); Kulchi, Lukhvich, Ostrovski, Shtanyuk, Gurenko, Khatskevich (Kovba 82), Hleb, Omelyunchuk (Shuneiko 76), Romashchenko■, Kutuzov.
Referee: Barber (England).

Minsk, 12 October 2002, 23,000

Belarus (0) 0

Austria (0) 2 *(Schopp 57, Akagunduz 89)*

Belarus: Tumilovich; Hleb, Gurenko, Lukhvich■, Ostrovski, Shtanyuk, Kulchi, Yaskovich (Omelyanchuk 51), Shuneiko (Vasilyuk 64), Khatskevich, Kutuzov (Ryndyuk 83).
Austria: Manninger; Schopp, Cerny, Martin Hiden, Baur, Dospel, Kovacevic (Aufhauser 90), Flogel, Kahraman (Herzog 82), Wallner (Akagunduz 75), Wagner.
Referee: Poulat (France).

Chisinau, 12 October 2002, 3000

Moldova (0) 0

Czech Republic (0) 2 *(Jankulovski 70 (pen), Rosicky 80)*

Moldova: Hmaruc; Catinsus, Cebotari, Sosnovschi■, Olexic, Covalenco, Rebeja, Pusca, Covalciuc (Budanov 70), Clescenco (Patula 46), Boret (Ivanov 65).
Czech Republic: Cech; Grygera, Jankulovski, Galasek (Jarosik 55), Bolf, Ujfalusi, Poborsky, Rosicky (Lokvenc 84), Vachousek (Dostalek 88), Koller, Stajner.
Referee: Irvine (Northern Ireland).

Vienna, 16 October 2002, 46,300

Austria (0) 0

Holland (3) 3 *(Seedorf 16, Cocu 20, Makaay 30)*

Austria: Manninger; Schopp, Weissenberger (Akagunduz 76), Martin Hiden■, Baur, Dospel, Flogel, Herzog (Aufhauser 46), Wallner (Scharner 80), Wagner, Cerny.
Holland: Van der Sar; Ricksen, Zenden (Bouma 69), Van Bommel (Ronald de Boer 77), Frank de Boer, Stam, Seedorf, Cocu, Makaay (Hasselbaink 80), Kluivert, Davids.
Referee: Collina (Italy).

Teplice, 16 October 2002, 12,850

Czech Republic (2) 2 *(Poborsky 7, Baros 23)*

Belarus (0) 0

Czech Republic: Cech; Jiranek (Grygera 86), Bolf, Ujfalusi, Poborsky, Galasek, Rosicky (Jarosik 90), Koller (Vachousek 56), Baros, Jankulovski, Nedved.
Belarus: Tumilovich; Yaskovich (Lavrik 26), Khrapkovski, Shuneiko (Omelyunchuk 46), Shtanyuk, Romashchenko, Gurenko, Kulchi, Hleb (Ryndyuk 69), Khatskevich, Kutuzov.
Referee: Fleischer (Germany).

Minsk, 29 March 2003, 8000

Belarus (1) 2 *(Kutuzov 43, Gurenko 58)*

Moldova (1) 1 *(Cebotari 14)*

Belarus: Tumilovich; Omelyunchuk, Kulchi, Ostrovski, Lavrik, Gurenko, Hleb (Romashchenko 80), Belkevich, Shuneiko, Khatskevich, Kutuzov (Kovba 87).
Moldova: Hmaruc; Olexic, Catinsus, Priganiuc, Covalenco, Testimitanu, Rebeja, Rogaciov (Popovich 25) (Berco 62), Covalciuc, Cebotari (Golban 79), Clescenco.
Referee: Verbist (Belgium).

Rotterdam, 29 March 2003, 45,000

Holland (1) 1 *(Van Nistelrooy 45)*

Czech Republic (0) 1 *(Koller 68)*

Holland: Waterreus; Ricksen, Stam, Frank de Boer, Van Bronckhorst (Van der Vaart 39), Seedorf, Van Bommel, Davids, Zenden, Kluivert, Van Nistelrooy (Makaay 81).
Czech Republic: Cech; Grygera, Bolf, Ujfalusi, Jankulovski, Poborsky, Galasek, Rosicky, Nedved, Smicer (Jiranek 79), Koller (Lokvenc 88).
Referee: Nielsen (Denmark).

Prague, 2 April 2003, 17,150

Czech Republic (2) 4 *(Nedved 19, Koller 32, 62, Jankulovski 57 (pen))*

Austria (0) 0

Czech Republic: Cech; Grygera, Bolf, Ujfalusi, Jankulovski, Poborsky, Galasek, Smicer (Rosicky 63), Nedved (Vachousek 74), Baros, Koller (Lokvenc 79).
Austria: Mandl; Schamer, Stranzl, Hieblinger, Pogatetz, Schopp, Aufhauser, Flogel (Wagner 46), Weissenberger, Herzog (Kovacevic■ 53), Haas (Dospel 64).
Referee: Lopez (Spain).

Tiraspol, 2 April 2003, 13,000

Moldova (1) 1 *(Boret 16)*

Holland (1) 2 *(Van Nistelrooy 37, Van Bommel 84)*

Moldova: Hmaruc; Covalenco, Olexic, Testimitanu, Catinsus, Priganiuc, Covalciuc (Berco 79), Ivanov, Boret, Cebotari (Pogreban 88), Clescenco (Golban 63).
Holland: Waterreus; Reiziger, Stam (Ricksen 63), Frank de Boer, Van Bommel, Davids, Seedorf (Ronald de Boer 65), Van der Vaart (Van Hooijdonk 74), Van Nistelrooy, Kluivert, Zenden.
Referee: Sars (France).

Minsk, 7 June 2003, 8000

Belarus (0) 0

Holland (0) 2 *(Overmars 62, Kluivert 68)*

Belarus: Tumilovich; Ostrovski, Lukhvich, Shtanyuk (Omelyunchuk 90), Shuneiko (Kovba 75), Belkevich, Romashchenko (Hleb 52), Gurenko, Kulchi, Kutuzov, Lavrik.
Holland: Van der Sar; Reiziger (Bosvelt 46), Frank de Boer, Stam, Van Bronckhorst (Overmars 60), Seedorf, Van Bommel, Cocu, Zenden, Kluivert, Van Nistelrooy (Van der Vaart 75).
Referee: Ovrevo (Norway).

Tiraspol, 7 June 2003, 10,000

Moldova (0) 1 *(Frunza 60)*

Austria (0) 0

Moldova: Hmaruc; Testimitanu, Priganiuc, Catinsus, Olexic, Ivanov, Frunza (Valuta 84), Covalciuc, Cebotari (Patula 77), Boret (Andriuta 67), Rogaciov.
Austria: Mandl; Schamer (Eder 79), Dospel (Cerny 56), Stranzl, Ehmann, Aufhauser, Schopp, Flogel, Wagner (Wallner 69), Haas, Kirchler.
Referee: Da Silva (Portugal).

Innsbruck, 11 June 2003, 8100

Austria (1) 5 *(Aufhauser 33, Haas 47, Kirchler 52, Wallner 62, Cerny 69)*

Belarus (0) 0

Austria: Mandl (Payer 85); Schamer, Dospel, Stranzl (Hieblinger 46), Ehmann, Aufhauser, Cerny, Flogel, Wagner, Haas (Wallner 60), Kirchler.
Belarus: Tumilovich; Kulchi, Ostrovski, Lukhvich, Shtanyuk (Khraphovsky 66), Gurenko, Omelyunchuk, Lavrik, Belkevich (Kovba 55), Romashchenko, Kutuzov (Vasilyuk 46).
Referee: Frojdfeldt (Sweden).

Olomouc, 11 June 2003, 12,097

Czech Republic (1) 5 *(Smicer 41, Koller 72 (pen), Stajner 81, Lokvenc 88, 90)*

Moldova (0) 0

Czech Republic: Cech; Grygera, Bolf, Ujfalusi, Jankulovski, Poborsky (Stajner 65), Galasek, Smicer (Baros 59), Rosicky, Nedved, Koller (Lokvenc 79).
Moldova: Hmaruc; Testimitanu, Priganiuc■, Catinsus, Olexic, Covalenco, Ivanov, Covalciuc (Pogreban 83), Cebotari (Frunza 76), Boret, Rogaciov (Patula 76).
Referee: Jakobsson (Iceland).

Group 3 Table	P	W	D	L	F	A	Pts
Czech Republic	5	4	1	0	14	1	13
Holland	5	4	1	0	11	2	13
Austria	6	3	0	3	9	8	9
Belarus	6	1	0	5	2	15	3
Moldova	6	1	0	5	3	13	3

GROUP 4

Riga, 7 September 2002, 9000

Latvia (0) 0

Sweden (0) 0

Latvia: Kolinko; Stepanovs IN, Astafjevs, Zemlinsky, Laizans, Blagonadezhdin, Isakov, Bleidelis, Rubins, Pahars (Stolcers 80), Verpakovsky.
Sweden: Hedman; Mellberg, Jakobsson, Michael Svensson, Antonelius, Linderoth, Alexandersson, Farnerud (Jonson 56), Magnus Svensson (Johansson 76), Ibrahimovic (Kallstrom 65), Allback.
Referee: De Bleeckere (Belgium).

Serravalle, 7 September 2002, 2000

San Marino (0) 0

Poland (0) 2 *(Kaczorowski 75, Kukielka 88)*

San Marino: Gasperoni F; Gennari, Vannucci (Selva R 83), Matteoni, Albani, Bacciocchi, Mauro Marani, Michele Marani, Moretti (Zonzini 70), Selva A, Ugolini (De Luigi 78).
Poland: Kowalewski; Glowacki, Klos, Bak J, Kaczorowski, Kukielka, Kaluzny (Marcin Zewlakow 60), Kosowski, Wichniarek (Dawidowski 46), Zurawski, Olisadebe (Lewandowski 80).
Referee: McKeon (Republic of Ireland).

Warsaw, 12 October 2002, 12,000

Poland (0) 0

Latvia (1) 1 *(Laizans 30)*

Poland: Dudek; Hajto, Michal Zewlakow (Surma 46), Kukielka, Zielinski, Ratajczak, Dawidowski, Lewandowski, Wichniarek (Marcin Zewlakow 46), Zurawski, Kosowski (Mieciel 63).
Latvia: Kolinko; Blagonadezhdin, Laizans, Rubins, Stepanovs IN, Zemlinsky, Isakov, Astafjevs, Verpakovsky (Stolcers 89), Pahars (Prohorenkovs 58), Bleidelis.
Referee: Busacca (Switzerland).

Stockholm, 12 October 2002, 35,084

Sweden (0) 1 *(Ibrahimovic 76)*

Hungary (1) 1 *(Kenesei 5)*

Sweden: Isaksson; Mellberg, Antonelius (Jonson 67), Linderoth, Jakobsson, Michael Svensson, Alexandersson (Kallstrom 59), Ljungberg, Andersson A, Ibrahimovic (Allback 76), Anders Svensson.
Hungary: Kiraly; Feher C, Low, Urban, Dragoner, Gyepes, Lipcsei, Lisztes, Tokoli (Feher M 59), Kenesei (Gera 70), Dardai.
Referee: Stark (Germany).

Budapest, 16 October 2002, 8000

Hungary (0) 3 *(Gera 49, 60, 85)*

San Marino (0) 0

Hungary: Kiraly; Feher C, Low, Urban, Dragoner, Gyepes, Lipcsei, Lisztes (Miriuta 84), Tokoli, Kenesei (Gera 46), Dardai (Feher M 78).
San Marino: Gasperoni F; Gennari, Gobbi, Bacciocchi, Valentini C (Zonzini 81), Albani, Moretti (Selva R 55), Michele Marani, Muccioli (Montagna 73), Selva A, Vannucci.
Referee: Orrason (Iceland).

Serravalle, 20 November 2002, 600

San Marino (0) 0

Latvia (0) 1 *(Valentini C 89 (og))*

San Marino: Gasperoni F; Valentini C, Matteoni, Gobbi, Gennari (Albani 86), Bacciocchi, Muccioli, Michele Marani (Zonzini 53), Selva A, Vannucci, Montagna (De Luigi 59).
Latvia: Kolinko; Stepanovs IN, Kolesnichenko (Prohorenkovs 57), Blagonadezhdin, Astafjevs, Zemlinsky, Isakov, Bleidelis (Stolcers 46), Rubins, Pahars, Verpakovsky (Mikholap 63).
Referee: Khudiev (Azerbaijan).

Chorzow, 29 March 2003, 48,000

Poland (0) 0

Hungary (0) 0

Poland: Dudek; Bak J, Hajto, Stolarczyk, Szymkowiak, Kaluzny, Swierczewski, Kosowski, Zajac (Dawidowski 71), Kuzba, Olisadebe.
Hungary: Kiraly; Feher C, Urban, Dragoner, Juhar, Lipcsei, Dardai, Lisztes, Low, Tokoli (Boor 85), Kenesei (Sebok 69).
Referee: De Santis (Italy).

Budapest, 2 April 2003, 30,000

Hungary (0) 1 *(Lisztes 65)*

Sweden (1) 2 *(Allback 34, 66)*

Hungary: Kiraly; Feher C, Juhar, Urban (Bodnar 61), Dragoner, Lipcsei (Boor 80), Dardai, Lisztes, Low, Tokoli (Sebok 68), Kenesei.
Sweden: Isaksson; Lucic, Michael Svensson, Edman, Mellberg, Andersson A, Anders Svensson (Kallstrom 61), Mjallby, Ljungberg, Larsson, Allback (Jonson 90).
Referee: Bastista (Portugal).

Ostrowiec, 2 April 2003, 8500

Poland (2) 5 *(Szymkowiak 4, Kosowski 27, Kuzba 55, 90, Karwan 82)*

San Marino (0) 0

Poland: Dudek; Bak J (Wasilewski 63), Zielinski, Sznaucner, Zajac (Karwan 46), Szymkowiak, Burkhardt, Kosowski, Zurawski, Kuzba, Olisadebe (Krzynowek 39).
San Marino: Gasperoni F; Albani, Bacciocchi, Matteoni, Michele Marani, Zonzini (Gasperoni B 67), Moretti, Muccioli, Selva A (Ugolini 89), Vannucci, Montagna (De Luigi 74).
Referee: Loizou (Cyprus).

Riga, 30 April 2003, 7500

Latvia (2) 3 *(Prohorenkovs 9, Bleidelis 20, 74)*

San Marino (0) 0

Latvia: Kolinko; Zirnis, Stepanovs IN, Zemlinsky, Laizans, Isakov, Prohorenkovs, Rubins, Bleidelis (Dobretsov 83), Verpakovsky (Rimkus 60), Mikholap (Stolcers 78).
San Marino: Gasperoni F; Valentini F, Gennari, Albani, Bacciocchi, Matteoni (Moretti 77), Muccioli (Gasperoni B 90), Michele Marani, Selva A, Vannucci, Montagna (De Luigi 64).
Referee: Byrne (Republic of Ireland).

Budapest, 7 June 2003, 3000

Hungary (0) 3 *(Szabics 51, 58, Gera 87)*

Latvia (1) 1 *(Verpakovsky 38)*

Hungary: Vegh; Urban, Dragoner (Gera 40), Juhar■, Feher C, Lisztes (Boor 77), Dardai, Lipcsei, Low, Kenesei (Lendvai 64), Szabics.
Latvia: Kolinko; Blagonadezhdin, Stepanovs IN, Zemlinsky, Isakov, Rubins, Astafjevs (Semyonov 85), Laizans, Bleidelis (Stolcers 79), Verpakovsky, Lobanov (Mikholap 71).
Referee: Merk (Germany).

Serravalle, 7 June 2003, 2184

San Marino (0) 0

Sweden (1) 6 *(Jonson 16, 59, 70, Allback 52, 85, Ljungberg 53)*

San Marino: Gasperoni F; Valentini C (Zonzini 66), Albani, Matteoni, Gennari, Moretti (Selva R 86), Bacciocchi, Selva A, Gasperoni B, Montagna, Vannucci (De Luigi 77).
Sweden: Isaksson; Lucic, Mellberg, Jakobsson, Edman, Mjallby (Nilsson 73), Andersson A, Kallstrom (Anders Svensson 57), Ljungberg (Johansson 73), Allback, Jonson.
Referee: Delevic (Serbia).

Serravalle, 11 June 2003, 1000

San Marino (0) 0

Hungary (2) 5 *(Boor 5, Lisztes 20, 82, Kenesei 62, Szabics 77)*

San Marino: Gasperoni F; Valentini C, Albani, Matteoni, Mauro Marani, Bacciocchi, Gasperoni B, Zonzini, De Luigi (Montagna 74), Selva R, Vannucci (Gennari 65).
Hungary: Vegh; Bodog, Dragoner, Szekeres (Fuzi 56), Boor, Lipcsei (Lendvai 74), Dardai (Zavadszky 80), Lisztes, Low, Kenesei, Szabics.
Referee: Clark (Scotland).

Stockholm, 11 June 2003, 35,220

Sweden (2) 3 *(Anders Svensson 16, 71, Allback 43)*

Poland (0) 0

Sweden: Isaksson; Lucic (Michael Svensson 87), Mellberg, Jakobsson, Edman, Ljungberg, Mjallby, Nilsson, Anders Svensson, Allback, Jonson (Magnus Svensson 72).
Poland: Dudek; Baszczynski (Klos 46), Bak J, Hajto, Stolarczyk, Szymkowiak (Burkhardt 76), Dawidowski, Zdebel, Kosowski (Zajac 64), Krzynowek, Wichniarek.
Referee: Veissiere (France).

Group 4 Table	*P*	*W*	*D*	*L*	*F*	*A*	*Pts*
Sweden	5	3	2	0	12	2	11
Hungary	6	3	2	1	13	4	11
Latvia	5	3	1	1	6	3	10
Poland	5	2	1	2	7	4	7
San Marino	7	0	0	7	0	25	0

GROUP 5

Toftir, 7 September 2002, 4000

Faeroes (2) 2 *(Petersen J 7, 13)*

Scotland (0) 2 *(Lambert 62, Ferguson B 83)*

Faeroes: Knudsen; Johannesen O, Hansen JK, Thorsteinsson, Jacobsen JR, Elltor (Lakjuni 89), Benjaminsen, Johnsson, Jacobsen C (Jacobsen R 76), Borg, Petersen J (Flotum 80).
Scotland: Douglas; Ross (Alexander 75), Crainey, Ferguson B, Weir, Dailly, Lambert, Dobie (Thompson S 83), Dickov (Crawford 46), Kyle, Johnston.
Referee: Granat (Poland).

Kaunas, 7 September 2002, 8500

Lithuania (0) 0

Germany (1) 2 *(Ballack 25, Stankevicius 58 (og))*

Lithuania: Stauce; Skarbalius, Stankevicius, Gleveckas, Dedura, Semberas, Zutautas, Razanauskas (Morinas 71), Mikalajunas, Poskus, Jankauskas (Fomenka 77).
Germany: Kahn; Linke, Ramelow, Metzelder, Frings, Schneider (Jeremies 85), Hamann, Ballack, Bohme, Jancker (Neuville 68), Klose.
Referee: Poll (England).

Reykjavik, 12 October 2002, 6611

Iceland (0) 0

Scotland (1) 2 *(Dailly 7, Naysmith 63)*

Iceland: Arason; Thorsteinsson, Vidarsson (Baldvinsson 66), Ingimarsson, Sigurdsson L, Hreidarsson, Gudnason (Gudjonsson B 77), Kristinsson R, Gudjohnsen E, Sigurdsson H (Helguson 46), Gunnarsson.
Scotland: Douglas; Ross, Naysmith (Anderson R 90), Dailly, Pressley, Wilkie, Lambert, Ferguson B, Crawford, Thompson S (Severin 89), McNamara (Davidson 34).
Referee: Sars (France).

Kaunas, 12 October 2002, 4000

Lithuania (2) 2 *(Razanauskas 23 (pen), Poskus 37)*

Faeroes (0) 0

Lithuania: Stauce; Zutautas (Barasa 75), Cesnauskis (Slavickas 77) (Stankevicius 84), Skarbalius, Poskus, Gleveckas, Razanauskas, Skerla, Fomenka, Dziaukstas, Mikalajunas.
Faeroes: Mikkelsen; Johannesen O, Jacobsen C (Flotum 60), Johnsson J (Jacobsen R 68), Petersen J, Thorsteinsson (Joensen J 73), Jacobsen JR, Hansen O, Benjaminsen, Hansen JK, Borg.
Referee: Delevic (Yugoslavia).

Hanover, 16 October 2002, 36,000

Germany (1) 2 *(Ballack 2 (pen), Klose 59)*

Faeroes (1) 1 *(Friedrich 45 (og))*

Germany: Kahn; Schneider (Kehl 87), Frings, Friedrich, Ramelow (Freier 46), Worns, Jeremies, Hamann, Jancker (Neuville 69), Klose, Ballack.
Faeroes: Mikkelsen; Thorsteinsson, Hansen JK, Benjaminsen, Johannesen O, Jacobsen JR, Borg (Elltor 71), Johnsson, Petersen J (Petersen H 87), Flotum (Jacobsen C 78), Hansen O.
Referee: Koren (Israel).

Reykjavik, 16 October 2002, 5000

Iceland (0) 3 *(Helguson 50, Gudjohnsen E 60, 73)*

Lithuania (0) 0

Iceland: Arason; Thorsteinsson (Gudjonsson B 37), Vidarsson, Ingimarsson, Gunnarsson, Hreidarsson, Gudnason, Stigsson (Einarsson 65), Helguson, Gudjohnsen E, Gudjonsson J (Sigurdsson H 75).
Lithuania: Stauce; Dziaukstas, Gleveckas, Skerla, Stankevicius, Cesnauskis■, Razanauskas, Mikalajunas, Barasa, Fomenka, Poskus.
Referee: Gilewski (Poland).

Nuremberg, 29 March 2003, 40,754

Germany (1) 1 *(Ramelow 8)*

Lithuania (0) 1 *(Razanauskas 73)*

Germany: Kahn; Friedrich, Worns, Rau (Freier 83), Frings, Ramelow, Hamann, Bohme (Rehmer 46), Schneider, Klose, Bobic (Kuranyi 72).
Lithuania: Stauce; Semberas, Zvirgdauskas, Dedura, Barasa, Morinas, Petrenko (Dziaukstas 87), Pukelevicius (Maciulevicius 46), Mikalajunas, Razanauskas, Jankauskas (Fomenka 90).
Referee: Torres (Spain).

Glasgow, 29 March 2003, 37,938

Scotland (1) 2 *(Miller 12, Wilkie 70)*

Iceland (0) 1 *(Gudjohnsen E 48)*

Scotland: Douglas; Wilkie, Alexander, Ferguson B, Pressley, Dailly, Lambert, Hutchison (Devlin 66), Crawford, Miller (McNamara 82), Naysmith.
Iceland: Arason; Thorsteinsson, Sigurdsson L, Bergsson, Gunnarsson (Gudjonsson T 74), Kristinsson R, Gudjonsson J, Ingimarsson, Vidarsson (Sigurdsson I 83), Gudjohnsen E (Gudmundsson T 89), Gretarsson.
Referee: Temmink (Holland).

Kaunas, 2 April 2003, 8000

Lithuania (0) 1 *(Razanauskas 74 (pen))*

Scotland (0) 0

Lithuania: Stauce; Semberas, Zvirgzdauskas, Dedura, Barasa, Morinas, Petrenko (Maciulevicius 71), Razanauskas, Gleveckas, Mikalajunas (Buitkus 89), Jankauskas (Fomenka 63).
Scotland: Gallacher; Alexander, Naysmith, Wilkie, Pressley, Dailly, McNamara (Gray 81), Lambert, Crawford (Devlin 57), Miller, Hutchison (Cameron 78).
Referee: Stuchlik (Austria).

Reykjavik, 7 June 2003, 6038

Iceland (0) 2 *(Sigurdsson H 49, Gudmundsson T 89)*

Faeroes (0) 1 *(Jacobsen JR 62)*

Iceland: Arason; Sigurdsson I (Gudmundsson T 75), Bergsson, Hreidarsson, Vidarsson, Kristinsson R, Sigurdsson L, Gudjonsson J, Sigurdsson H (Gretarsson 75), Gudjohnsen E, Gudjonsson T.
Faeroes: Mikkelsen; Jacobsen C, Joensen J, Jacobsen JR, Olsen, Borg, Jacobsen R, Petersen H (Johnsson 61), Benjaminsen, Petersen J, Flotum (Elltor 64).
Referee: Liba (Czech Republic).

Glasgow, 7 June 2003, 48,047

Scotland (0) 1 *(Miller 69)*

Germany (1) 1 *(Bobic 23)*

Scotland: Douglas; Ross (McNamara 75), Naysmith, Dailly, Pressley, Webster, Devlin (Rae 60), Cameron, Crawford, Miller (Thompson S 90), Lambert.
Germany: Kahn; Frings, Rau (Freier 57), Friedrich, Ramelow, Worns, Jeremies, Ballack, Bobic, Klose (Neuville 74), Schneider (Kehl 86).
Referee: Messina (Italy).

Torshavn, 11 June 2003, 6130

Faeroes (0) 0

Germany (0) 2 *(Klose 89, Bobic 90)*

Faeroes: Mikkelsen; Johannesen O, Joensen J, Thorsteinsson, Jacobsen JR, Jacobsen R, Benjaminsen, Johnsson, Borg (Elltor 61), Petersen J, Jacobsen C (Petersen JI 77).
Germany: Kahn (Rost 46); Friedrich, Freier, Rau (Hartmann 72), Ramelow, Worns, Jeremies (Klose 65), Kehl, Bobic, Neuville, Schneider.
Referee: Wegereef (Holland).

Kaunas, 11 June 2003, 8000

Lithuania (0) 0

Iceland (0) 3 *(Gudjonsson T 60, Gudjohnsen E 72, Hreidarsson 90)*

Lithuania: Stauce; Semberas■, Dedura, Barasa (Maciulevicius 72), Petrenko, Zvirgzdauskas, Zutautas (Karcemarskas 70), Morinas, Razanauskas, Jankauskas (Danilevicius 79), Skarbalius.
Iceland: Arason; Sigurdsson L, Bergsson, Hreidarsson, Vidarsson, Gunnarsson, Kristinsson R, Gudjonsson J (Gretarsson 89), Sigurdsson H (Gudmundsson T 82), Gudjohnsen E, Gudjonsson T.
Referee: Corpodea (Romania).

Group 5 Table	*P*	*W*	*D*	*L*	*F*	*A*	*Pts*
Germany	5	3	2	0	8	3	11
Iceland	5	3	0	2	9	5	9
Scotland	5	2	2	1	7	5	8
Lithuania	6	2	1	3	4	9	7
Faeroes	5	0	1	4	4	10	1

GROUP 6

Erevan, 7 September 2002, 9000

Armenia (0) 2 *(Art Petrossian 73, Sarkissian 90)*

Ukraine (2) 2 *(Serebrennikov 2, Zubov 33)*

Armenia: Berezovski; Artur Mkrtchian (Sarkissian 60), Hovsepian, Vardanian, Minasian (Voskanian 46), Khachatrian, Art Petrossian, Bilibio, Dokhoyan, Art Karamian, Arm Karamian (Movsisian 71).
Ukraine: Reva; Luzhny, Tymoshchuk, Yezersky■, Nesmachni, Kormiltsev, Serebrennikov, Gusin (Maksimioek 65) (Popov 90), Moroz, Zubov (Spivak 69), Vorobei.
Referee: Vuorela (Finland).

Athens, 7 September 2002, 17,000

Greece (0) 0

Spain (1) 2 *(Raul 8, Valeron 76)*

Greece: Nikopolidis; Patsatzoglou, Dabizas, Dellas, Fyssas (Vryzas 72), Konstantinidis (Karagounis 40), Zagorakis (Basinas 46), Tsartas, Giannakopoulos, Haristeas, Nikolaidis.
Spain: Casillas; Michel Salgado, Marchena, Garcia Calvo, Raul Bravo, Joaquin (Mendieta 59), Xavi (Baraja 59), Valeron (Cesar 87), Helguera, Vicente, Raul.
Referee: Merk (Germany).

Albacete, 12 October 2002, 16,000

Spain (1) 3 *(Baraja 19, 88, Guti 59)*

Northern Ireland (0) 0

Spain: Casillas; Michel Salgado, Raul Bravo, Xavi, Puyol, Helguera, Joaquin (Mendieta 79), Baraja, Raul (Morientes 63), Guti (Capi 83), Vicente.
Northern Ireland: Taylor; Hughes A, McCartney, Murdock, Taggart (McCann 70), Lomas, Johnson D, Mulryne, Gillespie, McVeigh (Healy 65), Horlock (Hughes M 65).
Referee: Dobrinov (Bulgaria).

Kiev, 12 October 2002, 55,000

Ukraine (0) 2 *(Vorobei 51, Voronin 90)*

Greece (0) 0

Ukraine: Reva; Tymoshchuk, Luzhny, Starostiak, Moroz (Radchenko 25), Gusin, Kormiltsev (Rebrov 71), Zubov, Kalinitchenko, Vorobei, Serebrennikov (Voronin 24).
Greece: Nikopolidis; Seitaridis, Lakis (Giannakopoulos 66), Dabizas, Dellas, Venetidis, Zagorakis (Basinas 69), Karagounis, Tsartas, Nikolaidis (Vryzas 66), Haristeas.
Referee: Temmink (Holland).

Athens, 16 October 2002, 5500

Greece (1) 2 *(Nikolaidis 2, 59)*

Armenia (0) 0

Greece: Nikopolidis; Seitaridis, Georgiadis (Giannakopoulos 46), Dellas, Dabizas, Venetidis (Vryzas 60), Basinas, Kafes, Haristeas, Nikolaidis, Tsartas (Zagorakis 46).
Armenia: Berezovski; Sarkissian (Melikian 82), Vardanian, Khachatrian (Minasian 46), Bilibio, Hovsepian, Art Petrossian, Art Karamian, Arm Karamian (Mkhitarian 66), Voskanian, Dokhoyan.
Referee: Ceferin (Slovenia).

Belfast, 16 October 2002, 9288

Northern Ireland (0) 0

Ukraine (0) 0

Northern Ireland: Taylor; Lomas, Horlock, Mulryne (McCann 80), Hughes A, McCartney, Gillespie, Johnson D (Murdock 84), McVeigh (Kirk 65), Healy, Hughes M.
Ukraine: Reva; Starostiak, Luzhny, Tymoshchuk, Kormiltsev (Lysytski 89), Gusin, Zubov, Kalynychenko (Rebrov 54), Voronin, Radchenko, Vorobei (Melashchenko 76).
Referee: Bolognino (Italy).

Erevan, 29 March 2003, 9000

Armenia (0) 1 *(Art Petrossian 87)*

Northern Ireland (0) 0

Armenia: Berezovski; Melikian, Dokhoyan, Hovsepian, Vardanian, Bilibio, Art Petrossian (Mkhitarian 89), Voskanian, Sarkissian (Artur Mkrtchian 89), Art Karamian (Agvan Mkrtchian 89), Arm Karamian.
Northern Ireland: Taylor; Hughes A, McCann, Lomas, Williams, Craigan, Gillespie, Johnson D, Healy, Quinn (Elliott 70), McVeigh.
Referee: Beck (Liechtenstein).

Kiev, 29 March 2003, 82,000

Ukraine (1) 2 *(Voronin 11, Gorchkov 90)*

Spain (0) 2 *(Raul 83, Etxeberria 87)*

Ukraine: Shovkovskyi; Nesmachni, Dmitrulin, Fedorov, Tymoshchuk, Kormiltsev (Kalynychenko 62), Gusin, Gorchkov, Voronin, Vorobei, Shevchenko (Serebrennikov 67).
Spain: Casillas; Michel Salgado, Aranzabal, Albelda (Xavi 65), Marchena, Cesar, Etxeberria, Baraja, Guti (Valeron 65), Raul, Vicente (Diego Tristan 77).
Referee: Riley (England).

Belfast, 2 April 2003, 7196

Northern Ireland (0) 0

Greece (1) 2 *(Haristeas 2, 55)*

Northern Ireland: Taylor; Hughes A, McCartney, Lomas, Williams, Craigan, Gillespie■, Johnson D, Healy (Kirk 68), Quinn■, McCann (McVeigh 68).
Greece: Nikopolidis; Giannakopoulos, Venetidis (Fyssas 70), Dabizas, Kyrgiakos, Konstantinidis, Zagorakis, Tsartas (Kafes 75), Haristeas, Nikolaidis (Vryzas 41), Karagounis.
Referee: Gilewski (Poland).

Amilivia, 2 April 2003, 13,500

Spain (0) 3 *(Diego Tristan 63, Helguera 69, Joaquin 90)*

Armenia (0) 0

Spain: Casillas; Michel Salgado, Bravo, Albelda, Helguera, Marchena, Etxeberria (Joaquin 46), Xavi (Vicente 54), Valeron (Baraja 63), Raul, Diego Tristan.
Armenia: Berezovski; Dokhoyan, Vardanian, Melikian, Hovsepian, Art Petrossian (Mkhitarian 81) (Minasian 84), Khachatrian, Voskanian, Sarkissian, Art Karamian (Bilibio 89), Arm Karamian.
Referee: Yefet (Israel).

Zaragoza, 7 June 2003, 32,000

Spain (0) 0

Greece (1) 1 *(Giannakopoulos 42)*

Spain: Casillas; Michel Salgado, Raul Bravo, Marchena (Sergio 76), Puyol, Helguera, Etxeberria (Joaquin 57), Valeron, Raul, Morientes, Vicente (De Pedro 57).
Greece: Nikopolidis; Seitaridis, Dellas, Dabizas, Kapsis, Venetidis■, Zagorakis, Tsartas (Karagounis 36), Giannakopoulos, Vryzas, Haristeas (Lakis 34).
Referee: Sars (France).

Lvov, 7 June 2003, 30,000

Ukraine (1) 4 *(Gorchkov 28, Shevchenko 65 (pen), 70, Fedorov 90)*

Armenia (1) 3 *(Sarkissian 13 (pen), 50, Art Petrossian 72 (pen))*

Ukraine: Shutkov; Luzhny, Fedorov, Nesmachni, Zakarlyuka (Radchenko 63), Popov (Kalynychenko 65), Gorchkov, Voronin, Rebrov (Venhlynsky 80), Shevchenko, Vorobei.
Armenia: Berezovski; Partsikian, Dokhoyan, Vardanian, Hovsepian, Art Petrossian (Bilibio 75), Khachatrian, Voskanian, Sarkissian, Art Karamian (Arutiunian 83), Arm Karamian.
Referee: Albrecht (Germany).

Athens, 11 June 2003, 15,000

Greece (0) 1 *(Haristeas 86)*

Ukraine (0) 0

Greece: Nikopolidis; Seitaridis, Dabizas, Dellas, Fyssas, Kapsis, Zagorakis (Tsartas 72), Lakis (Houtos 65), Karagounis, Vryzas (Haristeas 46), Giannakopoulos.
Ukraine: Shovkovskyi; Nesmachni, Fedorov, Golovko, Tymoshchuk, Gusin, Shevchuk, Zakarlyuka, Voronin, Shevchenko, Rebrov (Vorobei 61).
Referee: De Bleeckere (Belgium).

Belfast, 11 June 2003, 11,365

Northern Ireland (0) 0

Spain (0) 0

Northern Ireland: Taylor; Baird, Kennedy, Griffin, Hughes A, McCartney, Healy, Johnson, Smith (Williams 90), Jones (McVeigh 73), Doherty (Toner 80).
Spain: Casillas; Puyol, Juanfran, Sergio (Joaquin 66), Marchena, Helguera, Etxeberria (De Pedro 78), Baraja, Valeron, Raul, Vicente (Morientes 66).
Referee: Larsen (Denmark).

Group 6 Table	*P*	*W*	*D*	*L*	*F*	*A*	*Pts*
Greece	6	4	0	2	6	4	12
Spain	6	3	2	1	10	3	11
Ukraine	6	2	3	1	10	8	9
Armenia	5	1	1	3	6	11	4
Northern Ireland	5	0	2	3	0	6	2

GROUP 7

Vaduz, 7 September 2002, 1200

Liechtenstein (0) 1 *(Michael Stocklasa 90)*

Macedonia (1) 1 *(Hristov 7)*

Liechtenstein: Jehle; Ritter, Gigon (Burgmeier 83), Hasler D, Michael Stocklasa, Martin Stocklasa, Telser (D'Elia 83), Frick, Gerster, Beck T, Beck M (Buchel 46).
Macedonia: Milosevski; Braga (Grncarov 85), Sedloski, Nikolovski, Petrov, Mitreski I, Sumolikoski, Sakiri, Pandev (Stoikov 70), Hristov (Popov 58), Mitreski A.
Referee: Goduljan (Ukraine).

Istanbul, 7 September 2002, 20,000

Turkey (2) 3 *(Serhat 14, Arif 45, 65)*

Slovakia (0) 0

Turkey: Rustu; Fatih, Bulent K, Alpay, Hakan Unsal, Okan (Nihat 63), Tugay, Emre B (Cihan 78), Basturk, Serhat (Umit D 87), Arif.
Slovakia: Bucek; Karhan, Spilar, Dzurik, Labant (Michalik 61), Kisel, Cisovski, Kozlej (Reiter 55), Gresko (Hlinka 72), Janocko, Vittek.
Referee: Nieto (Spain).

Skopje, 12 October 2002, 12,000

Macedonia (1) 1 *(Grozdanovski 2)*

Turkey (1) 2 *(Okan 29, Nihat 54)*

Macedonia: Milosevski; Mitreski I, Vasovski, Sedloski, Stojanovski, Mitreski A, Trajanov (Nacevski 68), Sumolikoski (Petrov 46), Sakiri, Hristov (Popov 46), Grozdanovski.
Turkey: Rustu; Fatih, Okan (Umit D 79), Bulent K, Alpay, Tugay (Serhat 46), Emre B, Basturk, Arif (Hasan Sas 46), Nihat, Ergun.
Referee: Fisker (Denmark).

Bratislava, 12 October 2002, 30,000

Slovakia (1) 1 *(Nemeth S 24)*

England (0) 2 *(Beckham 65, Owen 82)*

Slovakia: Konig; Pinte (Kozlej 88), Leitner, Zeman, Dzurik, Hlinka, Karhan, Janocko (Mintal 88), Nemeth S, Petras, Vittek (Reiter 80).
England: Seaman; Neville G, Ashley Cole, Southgate, Woodgate, Butt, Beckham, Gerrard (Dyer 77), Heskey (Smith 90), Owen (Hargreaves 86), Scholes.
Referee: Messina (Italy).

Southampton, 16 October 2002, 32,095

England (2) 2 *(Beckham 14, Gerrard 36)*

Macedonia (2) 2 *(Sakiri 11, Trajanov 25)*

England: Seaman; Neville G, Ashley Cole, Gerrard (Butt 56), Campbell, Woodgate, Beckham, Scholes, Smith■, Owen, Bridge (Vassell 58).
Macedonia: Milosevski; Popov, Petrov, Sumolikoski, Sedloski, Vasovski, Grozdanovski, Mitreski A, Sakiri, Trajanov (Stojanovski 90), Toleski (Pandev 62).
Referee: Ibanez (Spain).

Istanbul, 16 October 2002, 15,000

Turkey (3) 5 *(Okan 7, Umit D 14, Ilhan 23, Serhat 81, 90)*

Liechtenstein (0) 0

Turkey: Rustu; Umit D, Ergun, Bulent K (Fatih 46), Alpay, Tugay, Okan (Hakan Unsal 60), Emre B, Ilhan (Serhat 79), Arif, Nihat.
Liechtenstein: Jehle; Telser, Michael Stocklasa, Nigg (Burgmeier 72), Hasler D, D'Elia, Martin Stocklasa (Beck M 79), Buchel (Ospelt 85), Beck T, Frick, Gerster.
Referee: Baskakov (Russia).

Vaduz, 29 March 2003, 3548

Liechtenstein (0) 0

England (1) 2 *(Owen 28, Beckham 53)*

Liechtenstein: Jehle; Telser, Hasler D, Michael Stocklasa, D'Elia, Beck T, Martin Stocklasa, Buchel (Beck M 86), Zech (Burgmeier 62), Frick (Nigg 82), Gerster.
England: James; Neville G, Bridge, Gerrard (Butt 66), Ferdinand, Southgate, Beckham (Murphy 70), Scholes, Heskey (Rooney 80), Owen, Dyer.
Referee: Kasnaferis (Greece).

Skopje, 29 March 2003, 8000

Macedonia (0) 0

Slovakia (1) 2 *(Petras 28, Reiter 90)*

Macedonia: Milosevski; Braga, Lazarevski (Stoikov 81), Sedloski, Mitreski I, Sumolikovski (Naumoski 52), Jancevski, Krstev M, Sakiri, Krstev S (Grozdanovski 61), Pandev.
Slovakia: Konig; Petras, Klimpl, Hlinka, Leitner, Karhan (Hanek 90), Demo (Labant 81), Michalik, Janocko, Nemeth S (Reiter 75), Vittek.
Referee: Duhamel (France).

Sunderland, 2 April 2003, 47,667

England (0) 2 *(Vassell 76, Beckham 90 (pen))*

Turkey (0) 0

England: James; Neville G, Bridge, Butt, Campbell, Ferdinand, Beckham, Scholes, Rooney (Dyer 89), Owen (Vassell 58), Gerrard.
Turkey: Rustu; Fatih (Hakan Sukur 79), Ergun, Alpay, Bulent K, Tugay, Okan (Umit D 59), Emre B, Basturk (Hasan Sas 70), Nihat, Ilhan.
Referee: Meier (Switzerland).

Trnava, 2 April 2003

Slovakia (1) 4 *(Reiter 18, Nemeth S 51, 64, Janocko 90)*

Liechtenstein (0) 0

Slovakia: Konig; Petras, Klimpl, Hlinka, Leitner, Karhan (Hanek 90), Demo (Labant 68), Michalik (Mintal 81), Janocko, Kozlej (Nemeth S 46), Reiter.
Liechtenstein: Jehle; Telser, Hasler D, Michael Stocklasa, D'Elia, Beck T, Martin Stocklasa, Buchel (Gigon 71), Burgmeier, Frick (Nigg 60), Gerster (Ospelt 85).
Match played behind closed doors.
Referee: Ceferen (Slovenia).

Skopje, 7 June 2003, 6000

Macedonia (1) 3 *(Sedloski 39 (pen), Krstev M 52, Stoikov 82)*

Liechtenstein (1) 1 *(Beck T 20)*

Macedonia: Milosevski; Sumolikoski, Sedloski, Vasovski, Lazarevski, Trajanov (Jancevski 60), Mitreski A, Sakiri (Bajevski 55), Stoikov, Naumoski (Dimitrovski 46), Krstev M.
Liechtenstein: Jehle; Ospelt, Hasler D, Gigon, Maierhofer (Wolfinger 89), D'Elia, Gerster, Frick, Telser, Beck M (Vogt 89), Beck T (Rohrer 79).
Referee: Jara (Czech Republic).

Bratislava, 7 June 2003, 15,000

Slovakia (0) 0

Turkey (1) 1 *(Nihat 12)*

Slovakia: Konig; Zeman, Hlinka (Vittek 46), Klimpl, Labant, Karhan (Mintal 71), Janocko, Petras, Demo, Michalik (Kisel 77), Nemeth S.
Turkey: Rustu; Fatih, Alpay, Bulent K, Ergun, Okan (Tayfun 58), Basturk (Volkan 80), Tugay, Emre B (Ibrahim 90), Nihat, Hakan Sukur.
Referee: Hauge (Norway).

Middlesbrough, 11 June 2003, 35,000

England (0) 2 *(Owen 62 (pen), 73)*

Slovakia (1) 1 *(Janocko 31)*

England: James; Mills (Hargreaves 43), Ashley Cole, Neville P, Southgate, Upson, Gerrard, Scholes, Rooney (Vassell 58), Owen, Lampard.
Slovakia: Konig; Hanek, Labant (Debnar 38), Zabavnik, Zeman, Petras, Demo (Mintal 55), Janocko, Nemeth S (Reiter 75), Vittek, Michalik.
Referee: Stark (Germany).

Istanbul, 11 June 2003, 22,000

Turkey (1) 3 *(Nihat 27, Gokdeniz 48, Hakan Sukur 59)*

Macedonia (2) 2 *(Grozdanovski 23, Sakiri 29)*

Turkey: Rustu; Fatih, Alpay (Yildirin 72), Bulent K, Ergun, Emre B (Gokdeniz 43), Tayfun (Okan 46), Tugay, Ibrahim, Hakan Sukur (Volkan 78), Nihat.
Macedonia: Milosevski; Sumolikoski, Sedloski, Vasovski, Lazarevski, Bozinovski (Poleski 76), Mitreski A, Sakiri, Stoikov, Grozdanovski (Nuhiji 56), Jancevski.
Referee: Rosetti (Italy).

Group 7 Table	*P*	*W*	*D*	*L*	*F*	*A*	*Pts*
Turkey	6	5	0	1	14	5	15
England	5	4	1	0	10	4	13
Slovakia	6	2	0	4	8	8	6
Macedonia	6	1	2	3	9	11	5
Liechtenstein	5	0	1	4	2	15	1

GROUP 8

Brussels, 7 September 2002, 20,000

Belgium (0) 0

Bulgaria (1) 2 *(Jankovic 17, Stilian Petrov 63)*

Belgium: De Vlieger; Vreven, Van Buyten, Simons, Van der Heyden (Peeters B 64), Englebert (Mpenza M 53), Vanderhaeghe, Baseggio, Goor, Mpenza E (Thijs 70), Sonck.
Bulgaria: Zdravkov; Kishishev, Kirilov, Petkov I, Petrov M, Peev (Petkov G 83), Stilian Petrov, Balakov, Petkov M (Zagorcic 90), Pazin, Jankovic (Chilikov 77).
Referee: Hauge (Norway).

Osijek, 7 September 2002, 12,000

Croatia (0) 0

Estonia (0) 0

Croatia: Pletikosa; Zivkovic, Babic, Simic, Tokic, Vugrinec, Tapalovic, Saric (Tomas 79), Maric T (Petric 60), Olic, Maric S (Rapajic 46).
Estonia: Poom; Allas, Stepanovs, Piroja, Saviauk, Rooba M, Reim, Kristal, Lindpere (Rooba U 59), Zelinski, Oper.
Referee: Marin (Spain).

Andorra, 12 October 2002, 700

Andorra (0) 0

Belgium (0) 1 *(Sonck 61)*

Andorra: Koldo; Ayala, Txema (Escura 66), Jonas, Lima A, Fernandez (Silva 6), Emiliano, Jimenez (Lucendo 75), Juli Sanchez, Ruiz, Sonejee.
Belgium: De Vlieger; De Cock, Dheedene, Buffel, Valgaeren, Simons, Vanderhaeghe, Baseggio (Thijs 81), Sonck (Soeters 90), Van Houdt, Goor.
Referee: Nalbandian (Armenia).

Sofia, 12 October 2002, 43,000

Bulgaria (2) 2 *(Stilian Petrov 22, Berbatov 37)*

Croatia (0) 0

Bulgaria: Zdravkov; Kishishev, Petov I, Stilian Petrov, Pazin, Kirilov, Peev (Ivanov G 90), Jankovic, Berbatov (Chilikov 39), Petrov M (Petrov G 66), Balakov.
Croatia: Pletikosa; Simic (Olic 18), Zivkovic, Tomas, Kovac R, Tudor, Vugrinec, Leko, Rapajic (Maric M 46), Boksic (Maric S 69), Stanic.
Referee: Frisk (Sweden).

Sofia, 16 October 2002, 38,000

Bulgaria (1) 2 *(Chilikov 37, Balakov 59)*

Andorra (0) 1 *(Lima A 81)*

Bulgaria: Zdravkov; Kishishev, Jankovic (Gonzo 77), Peev, Pazin, Kirilov, Stilian Petrov, Balakov (Svetoslav Petrov 62), Petrov M (Manchev 75), Chilikov, Petkov I.
Andorra: Koldo; Ayala, Jonas, Lima A■, Fernandez, Escura, Emiliano (Silva 64), Lima I, Jimenez (Marc 80), Sonejee, Ruiz.
Referee: Richards (Wales).

Tallinn, 16 October 2002, 4000

Estonia (0) 0

Belgium (1) 1 *(Sonck 2)*

Estonia: Poom; Allas, Rooba U, Anniste (Haavistu 46), Stepanovs, Piiroja, Reim, Kristal (Lindpere 83), Oper, Zelinski, Terehhov (Viikmae 60).
Belgium: De Vlieger; De Cock, Dheedene, Vanderhaeghe, Valgaeren, Simons, Buffel (Van Hout 89), Baseggio, Sonck, Van Houdt, Goor.
Referee: Riley (England).

Zagreb, 29 March 2003, 22,000

Croatia (1) 4 *(Srna 9, Prso 53, Maric T 68, Leko 76)*

Belgium (0) 0

Croatia: Pletikosa; Simic, Simunic, Kovac R, Zivkovic, Rapajic, Tudor (Kovac N 77), Srna, Rosso (Leko 46), Prso (Stanic 70), Maric T.
Belgium: Vandendriessche; De Cock (Deflandre 57), Valgaeren (Van Damme 67), Van Buyten, Van der Heyden, Buffel, Simons, Englebert (Baseggio 55), Goor, Sonck, Mpenza E.
Referee: Fandel (Germany).

Varazdin, 2 April 2003, 10,000

Croatia (2) 2 *(Rapajic 11 (pen), 44)*

Andorra (0) 0

Croatia: Pletikosa; Simic, Simunic (Kovac N 46), Kovac R, Zivkovic, Rapajic (Babic 65), Tudor, Srna, Leko, Prso, Maric T (Stanic 46).
Andorra: Koldo; Ayala, Txema, Jonas, Fernandez, Sonejee, Emiliano (Motwani 89), Marc, Pol Perez (Lucendo 79), Jimenez (Escura 55), Juli Sanchez.
Referee: Salomir (Romania).

Tallinn, 2 April 2003, 3200

Estonia (0) 0

Bulgaria (0) 0

Estonia: Poom; Allas, Lemsalu, Jaager, Rooba U, Leetma, Kristal, Oper, Haavistu (Reinumae 63), Terehov, Zelinski (Viikmae 63).
Bulgaria: Zdravkov; Kishishev, Pazin, Petkov I, Kirilov, Stilian Petrov, Peev, Balakov, Petrov M (Petkov M 70), Berbatov, Jankovic (Todorov 46).
Referee: Plautz (Austria).

La Vella, 30 April 2003, 500

Andorra (0) 0

Estonia (1) 2 *(Zelinski 26, 74)*

Andorra: Koldo; Ayala (Silva 90), Txema, Escura, Fernandez, Emiliano, Marc (Alvarez 80), Sonejee, Juli Sanchez, Ruiz, Jimenez (Lucendo 71).
Estonia: Poom; Allas, Stepanovs, Lemsalu, Rooba U, Reim, Haavistu (Reinumae 69), Kristal, Terehhov (Lindpere 55), Viikmae (Rooba M 89), Zelinski.
Referee: Aydin (Turkey).

Sofia, 7 June 2003, 42,000

Bulgaria (0) 2 *(Berbatov 53, Todorov 71 (pen))*

Belgium (1) 2 *(Stilian Petrov 31 (og), Clement 57)*

Bulgaria: Zdravkov; Stankov, Kirilov, Stoyanov, Petkov M, Borimirov, Stilian Petrov, Hristov (Manchev 72), Petrov M, Dimitrov (Alexandrov 81), Berbatov (Todorov 54).
Belgium: De Vlieger; Deflandre, Simons, Van Buyten, Dheedene, Mpenza M, Baseggio, Clement, Goor, Buffel, Sonck (Mpenza E 73).
Referee: Collina (Italy).

Tallinn, 7 June 2003, 2700

Estonia (2) 2 *(Allas 22, Viikmae 31)*

Andorra (0) 0

Estonia: Poom; Allas, Stepanovs, Piroja, Rooba U (Saviauk 49), Leetma, Kristal, Zahovalko, Haavistu (Rooba M 70), Viikmae, Lindpere (Reinumae 88).
Andorra: Koldo; Escura, Txema, Juli, Lima A, Lima I, Emiliano (Silva 83), Jimenez (Marc 53), Sonejee, Ruiz, Juli Sanchez.
Referee: Juhos (Hungary).

Ghent, 11 June 2003, 12,000

Belgium (2) 3 *(Goor 20, 65, Sonck 44)*

Andorra (0) 0

Belgium: De Vlieger; De Cock, Simons, Van Buyten, Dheedene (Van der Heyden 79), Clement, Baseggio, Goor (Soetars 83), Mpenza M, Sonck, Buffel (Martens 73).
Andorra: Koldo; Ayala, Txema, Jonas, Sonejee (Lucendo 81), Lima A, Lima I, Emiliano (Alvarez 70), Juli Sanchez (Escura 58), Fernandez, Marc.
Referee: Shmolik (Belarus).

Tallinn, 11 June 2003, 6000

Estonia (0) 0

Croatia (0) 1 *(Kovac N 77)*

Estonia: Poom; Allas (Zahovalko 82), Stepanovs, Piiroja, Rooba U, Leetma, Kristal, Oper, Rooba M (Reinumae 71), Lindpere (Lemsalu 83), Zelinski.
Croatia: Pletikosa; Simunic, Tomas, Zivkovic, Simic (Maric T 61), Babic (Leko 73), Rapajic (Rosso 79), Kovac N, Srna, Olic, Prso.
Referee: Hamer (Luxembourg).

Group 8 Table	*P*	*W*	*D*	*L*	*F*	*A*	*Pts*
Bulgaria	5	3	2	0	8	3	11
Croatia	5	3	1	1	7	2	10
Belgium	6	3	1	2	7	8	10
Estonia	6	2	2	2	4	2	8
Andorra	6	0	0	6	1	12	0

GROUP 9

Baku, 7 September 2002, 37,000

Azerbaijan (0) 0

Italy (1) 2 *(Akhmedov 32 (og), Del Piero 63)*

Azerbaijan: Kramarenko; Kuliyev K, Kerimov A, Akhmedov, Kuliyev E, Imamaliev, Kurbanov M (Musayev 68), Aliyev, Kurbanov K (Ismailov 90), Sadykhov, Agayev (Nabiev 88).
Italy: Buffon; Panucci, Nesta, Cannavaro, Coco, Gattuso, Di Biagio (Ambrosini 57), Del Piero, Tommasi, Inzaghi (Pirlo 78), Vieri (Montella 57).
Referee: Vassaras (Greece).

Helsinki, 7 September 2002, 35,833

Finland (0) 0

Wales (1) 2 *(Hartson 30, Davies 72)*

Finland: Niemi; Nylund (Johansson 69), Saarinen (Kopteff 78), Hyypia, Tihinen, Nurmela (Kottila 86), Riihilahti, Tainio, Kolkka, Litmanen, Kuqi.
Wales: Jones P; Delaney, Gabbidon, Savage, Melville, Pembridge, Speed, Johnson (Bellamy 76), Hartson, Davies, Giggs.
Referee: Plautz (Austria).

Helsinki, 12 October 2002, 11,853

Finland (1) 3 *(Akhmedov 14 (og), Tihinen 59, Hyypia 71)*

Azerbaijan (0) 0

Finland: Niemi; Pasanen, Saarinen, Riihilahti, Tihinen, Hyypia (Kuivasto 79), Nurmela, Tainio (Wiss 74), Sumiala (Kuqi 85), Litmanen, Kolkka.
Azerbaijan: Gasanzade; Kerimov A, Akhmedov, Agayev, Kuliyev K, Kuliyev E, Mamedov R (Mamedov F 90), Kurbanov M (Sadykhov 65), Kurbanov G, Aliyev, Imamaliev (Vasilyev 83).
Referee: Hamer (Luxembourg).

Naples, 12 October 2002, 42,661

Italy (1) 1 *(Del Piero 39)*

Yugoslavia (1) 1 *(Mijatovic 28)*

Italy: Buffon; Panucci, Zauri (Oddo 32), Pirlo (Ambrosini 34), Nesta, Cannavaro, Tommasi, Doni (Montella 46), Inzaghi, Del Piero, Gattuso.
Yugoslavia: Jevric; Lazetic, Dragutinovic, Vidic, Mihajlovic, Krstajic, Trobok, Mirkovic (Duljaj 8), Kovacevic D (Milosevic 69), Mijatovic (Kezman 66), Stankovic D.
Referee: Gonzalez (Spain).

Cardiff, 16 October 2002, 70,000

Wales (1) 2 *(Davies 12, Bellamy 71)*

Italy (1) 1 *(Del Piero 32)*

Wales: Jones P; Delaney, Speed, Pembridge, Melville, Gabbidon, Davies, Savage, Hartson, Bellamy (Blake 90), Giggs.
Italy: Buffon; Panucci, Zauri, Pirlo, Nesta, Cannavaro, Tommasi, Di Biagio (Gattuso 65) (Marazzina 85), Del Piero, Montella (Maccarone 70), Ambrosini.
Referee: Veissiere (France).

Belgrade, 16 October 2002, 35,000

Yugoslavia (0) 2 *(Kovacevic D 56, Mihajlovic 84 (pen))*

Finland (0) 0

Yugoslavia: Jevric; Njegus (Krstajic 46), Dragutinovic, Stankovic D, Vidic, Mihajlovic, Lazetic, Duljaj, Kovacevic D (Milosevic 71), Kezman (Brnovic N 62), Mijatovic.
Finland: Niemi; Saarinen, Kuivasto, Pasanen (Reini■ 63), Hyypia, Riihilahti, Nurmela, Tainio (Kuqi 82), Litmanen, Kolkka, Sumiala (Johansson 57).
Referee: Van Hulten (Holland).

Baku, 20 November 2002, 8000

Azerbaijan (0) 0

Wales (1) 2 *(Speed 9, Hartson 68)*

Azerbaijan: Gasanzade; Kerimov A (Mamedov F 46), Niftaliev, Sadykhov, Yadullayev, Akhmedov (Asadov 76), Kurbanov M (Ismailov 64), Imamaliev, Kurbanov A, Vasilyev, Aliyev.
Wales: Jones P; Delaney (Weston 71), Barnard, Robinson C (Trollope 90), Melville, Page, Davies, Speed, Earnshaw (Roberts N 89), Hartson, Giggs.
Referee: Huyghe (Belgium).

Podgorica, 13 February 2003, 8000

Yugoslavia (1) 2 *(Mijatovic 33 (pen), Lazetic 52)*

Azerbaijan (0) 2 *(Kurbanov G 58, 77)*

Yugoslavia: Jevric; Djordjevic, Dudic, Bunjevcevic, Vukic, Lazetic (Markovic 74), Boskovic, Stankovic D, Mijatovic (Ljuboja 70), Kezman (Duljaj 59), Milosevic.
Azerbaijan: Gasanzade; Kuliyev K, Sadykhov, Kuliyev E, Akhmedov, Kurbanov M (Mamedov F 90), Mamedov R, Imamaliev, Aliyev (Mamedov K 87), Kurbanov G, Ismailov (Musayev 55).
Referee: Granat (Poland).

Palermo, 29 March 2003, 34,074

Italy (2) 2 *(Vieri 6, 22)*

Finland (0) 0

Italy: Buffon; Panucci, Zambrotta, Zanetti C, Cannavaro, Nesta, Perrotta, Camoranesi, Totti (Miccoli 86), Delvecchio (Birindelli 69), Vieri (Corradi 82).
Finland: Niemi; Pasanen, Tihinen, Hyypia, Saarinen, Riihilahti (Johansson 36), Ilola, Nurmela (Kopteff 75), Tainio, Kolkka (Kuqi 89), Forssell.
Referee: Ivanov (Russia).

Cardiff, 29 March 2003, 72,500

Wales (3) 4 *(Bellamy 1, Speed 40, Hartson 44, Giggs 52)*

Azerbaijan (0) 0

Wales: Jones P; Davies, Speed (Trollope 46), Pembridge, Melville, Page, Oster, Savage (Robinson C 19), Hartson, Bellamy (Edwards 71), Giggs.
Azerbaijan: Gasanzade; Akhmedov, Kuliyev K, Aliyev (Tagizade 76), Kuliyev E (Yadullayev 46), Hajiyev (Mamedov F 46), Kurbanov M, Mamedov R, Kurbanov G, Imamaliev, Musayev.
Referee: Leuba (Switzerland).

Helsinki, 7 June 2003, 17,343

Finland (2) 3 *(Hyypia 20, Kolkka 45, Forssell 57)*

Serbia-Montenegro* (0) 0

Finland: Jaaskelainen; Pasanen, Hyypia, Tihinen, Saarinen, Valakari, Nurmela (Riihilahti 88), Vayrynen, Litmanen, Forssell (Kuqi 81), Kolkka (Kopteff 67).
Serbia-Montenegro: Jevric; Mirkovic (Kovacevic M 81), Vidic, Mihajlovic■, Dmitrovic, Duljaj, Markovic, Krstajic, Mijatovic (Vukic 46), Kovacevic D, Milosevic (Jestrovic 46).
Referee: Colombo (France).

Baku, 11 June 2003, 3500

Azerbaijan (0) 2 *(Kurbanov G 88 (pen), Aliyev 90)*

Serbia-Montenegro (1) 1 *(Boskovic 27)*

Azerbaijan: Kramarenko; Agayev (Tagizade 84), Akhmedov, Kuliyev E, Kerimov, Kuliyev K, Kurbanov M, Sadykhov, Aliyev, Kurbanov G (Yadullayev 90), Musayev (Ismailov 59).
Serbia-Montenegro: Jevric (Zilic 46); Mirkovic, Njegus, Djordjevic, Malbasa, Duljaj (Milosevic 88), Vukic, Krstajic, Boskovic, Kovacevic D, Mijatovic (Kovacevic N 68).
Referee: Fisker (Denmark).

Helsinki, 11 June 2003, 36,850

Finland (0) 0

Italy (1) 2 *(Totti 32, Del Piero 73)*

Finland: Jaaskelainen; Pasanen, Hyypia, Tihinen, Saarinen, Valakari (Riihilahti 82), Nurmela (Kopteff 69), Vayrynen, Litmanen, Forssell, Kolkka (Johansson 79).
Italy: Buffon; Panucci, Zambrotta, Perrotta, Nesta, Cannavaro (Legrottaglie 90), Zanetti C, Fiore (Oddo 83), Totti, Del Piero, Corradi (Delvecchio 85).
Referee: Siric (Croatia).

Group 9 Table	*P*	*W*	*D*	*L*	*F*	*A*	*Pts*
Wales	4	4	0	0	10	1	12
Italy	5	3	1	1	8	3	10
Finland	6	2	0	4	6	8	6
Serbia-Montenegro*	5	1	2	2	6	8	5
Azerbaijan	6	1	1	4	4	14	4

**Serbia-Montenegro: changed name from Yugoslavia in February 2003.*

GROUP 10

Moscow, 7 September 2002, 23,000

Russia (2) 4 *(Kariaka 20, Bestchastnykh 24, Kerzhakov 71, Babb 88 (og))*

Republic of Ireland (0) 2 *(Doherty 69, Morrison 76)*

Russia: Ovchinnikov; Loskov, Yanovsky, Ignachevitch, Onopko, Nizhegorodov, Kariaka, Aldonin, Bestchastnykh (Kerzhakov 46), Semak (Khokhlov 75), Gusev (Solomatin 28).
Republic of Ireland: Given; Finnan, Harte, Cunningham, Breen, Kinsella, McAteer (Doherty 65), Holland, Robbie Keane, Duff (Morrison 18), Kilbane (Babb 85).
Referee: Colombo (France).

Basle, 7 September 2002, 20,500

Switzerland (1) 4 *(Frei 37, Yakin H 63, Muller 74, Chapuisat 82)*

Georgia (0) 1 *(Arveladze A 62)*

Switzerland: Stiel; Haas, Henchoz, Yakin M, Magnin (Berner 83), Cabanas, Vogel (Celestini 68), Muller, Frei, Chapuisat, Yakin H (Wicky 74).
Georgia: Gvaramadze; Kobiashvili, Shekiladze, Kaladze, Sajaia (Rekhviashvili 46) (Kavelashvili 84), Nemsadze, Tskitishvili, Jamarauli, Demetradze, Arveladze A, Kinkladze (Burduli 46).
Referee: Krinak (Slovakia).

Tirana, 12 October 2002, 15,000

Albania (0) 1 *(Murati 79)*

Switzerland (1) 1 *(Yakin M 38)*

Albania: Strakosha; Fakaj, Duro (Sina 88), Murati, Cipi, Xhumba, Hasi, Lala, Vata F, Tare (Myrtaj 71), Haxhi (Bushi 60).
Switzerland: Stiel; Haas, Magnin, Cabanas (Cantaluppi 81), Yakin M, Muller, Vogel, Yakin H (Celestini 63), Frei (Thurre 84), Chapuisat, Wicky.
Referee: Erdemir (Turkey).

Dublin, 16 October 2002, 40,000

Republic of Ireland (0) 1 *(Magnin 78 (og))*

Switzerland (1) 2 *(Yakin H 45, Celestini 87)*

Republic of Ireland: Given; Kelly G, Harte (Doherty 86), Holland, Breen, Cunningham, Healy, Kinsella, Robbie Keane, Duff (Butler 82), Kilbane (Morrison 61).
Switzerland: Stiel; Haas, Magnin, Vogel, Yakin M, Muller, Cabanas, Yakin H (Celestini 84), Frei (Thurre 70), Chapuisat, Wicky (Cantaluppi 84).
Referee: Pedersen (Norway).

Moscow, 16 October 2002, 15,000

Russia (2) 4 *(Kerzhakov 3, Semak 42, 55, Onopko 52)*

Albania (1) 1 *(Duro 13)*

Russia: Ovchinnikov; Nizhegorodov, Ignachevitch, Smertin, Semak, Yanovsky, Onopko, Gusev (Yevseyev 81), Solomatin, Loskov (Aldonin 46), Kerzhakov (Popov 64).
Albania: Strakosha; Cipi, Xhumba, Fakaj, Murati, Hasi, Lala, Duro, Vata F (Sina 60), Tare (Myrtaj 69), Haxhi (Bushi 56).
Referee: Sundell (Sweden).

Tirana, 29 March 2003, 16,000

Albania (1) 3 *(Rraklli 20, Lala 80, Tare 83)*

Russia (0) 1 *(Kariaka 77)*

Albania: Strakosha; Beqiri, Cipi, Aliaj, Duro, Lala, Hasi, Murati (Bellai 68), Skela (Dede 84), Rraklli (Myrtaj 71), Tare.
Russia: Ovchinnikov; Nizhegorodov, Ignachevitch, Berezutski, Gusev (Bestchastnykh 56), Aldonin, Smertin (Yanovsky 73), Tochilin (Kariaka 46), Loskov, Semak, Kerzhakov.
Referee: Alaerts (Belgium).

Tbilisi, 29 March 2003, 15,000

Georgia (0) 1 *(Kobiashvili 61)*

Republic of Ireland (1) 2 *(Duff 18, Doherty 84)*

Georgia: Lomaia; Khizanishvili, Shashiashvili, Amisulashvili, Nemsadze, Tskitishvili, Jamarauli, Kinkladze (Didava 70), Kobiashvili, Ketsbaia (Demetradze 46), Iashvili.
Republic of Ireland: Given; Carr, O'Shea, Kinsella, Breen, Cunningham, Carsley, Holland, Doherty, Kilbane, Duff.
Referee: Vassaras (Greece).

Tirana, 2 April 2003, 17,000

Albania (0) 0

Republic of Ireland (0) 0

Albania: Strakosha; Duro, Murati (Bellai 67), Beqiri, Cipi, Aliaj, Lala, Hasi, Skela (Bushi 86), Rraklli (Myrtaj 69), Tare.
Republic of Ireland: Given; Carr, O'Shea, Holland, Breen, Cunningham, Carsley, Kinsella, Robbie Keane (Doherty 67), Duff, Kilbane.
Referee: Farina (Italy).

Tbilisi, 2 April 2003, 10,000

Georgia (0) 0

Switzerland (0) 0

Georgia: Lomaia; Khizanishvili, Kemoklidze, Khizaneishvili, Kvirkvelia, Tskitishvili, Nemsadze (Didava 46), Rekhviashvili, Kobiashvili, Demetradze (Ashvetia 72), Iashvili (Arveladze S 46).
Switzerland: Zuberbuhler; Haas, Berner, Vogel, Yakin M, Muller, Cabanas (Cantaluppi 68), Yakin H (Thurre 90), Frei (Celestini 59), Chapuisat, Wicky.
Referee: Trivkovic (Croatia).

Tbilisi, 30 April 2003, 11,000

Georgia (1) 1 *(Asatiani 11)*

Russia (0) 0

Georgia: Lomaia; Khizanishvili, Khizaneishvili, Kaladze, Tskitishvili, Nemsadze, Kvirkvelia, Burduli (Shashiashvili 80), Ashvetia (Alexidze 84), Asatiani (Didava 75), Demetradze.
Russia: Mandrykin; Nizhegorodov, Ignachevitch (Evsikov 14), Onopko, Aldonin (Sychev 79), Alenichev, Smertin, Titov, Kariaka, Semak, Izmailov (Kerzhakov 46).
Referee: Wack (Germany).

Dublin, 7 June 2003, 33,000

Republic of Ireland (1) 2 *(Robbie Keane 6, Aliaj (og) 90)*

Albania (1) 1 *(Skela 9)*

Republic of Ireland: Given; Carr, O'Shea, Kinsella (Carsley 55), Cunningham, Breen, Kilbane (Reid 76), Holland, Robbie Keane, Connolly (Doherty 65), Duff.
Albania: Strakosha (Beqaj 77); Beqiri, Cipi, Aliaj, Duro, Lala, Hasi, Skela, Murati (Bellai 57), Rraklli (Myrtaj 86), Tare.
Referee: Mikulski (Poland).

Basle, 7 June 2003, 30,500

Switzerland (2) 2 *(Frei 14, 16)*

Russia (1) 2 *(Ignachevitch 24, 68 (pen))*

Switzerland: Stiel; Haas, Yakin M, Muller (Henchoz 82), Magnin (Berner 61), Cabanas, Celestini, Wicky (Vogel 71), Yakin H, Frei, Chapuisat.
Russia: Ovchinnikov; Berezutski, Ignachevitch, Kovtun, Gusev, Smertin, Yanovski, Aldonin, Karaika (Bystrov 52), Popov (Sychev 46), Semak (Evsikov 82).
Referee: Ibanez (Spain).

Dublin, 11 June 2003, 36,000

Republic of Ireland (1) 2 *(Doherty 43, Robbie Keane 59)*

Georgia (0) 0

Republic of Ireland: Given; Carr, O'Shea, Carsley, Cunningham, Breen, Healy (Kinsella 86), Holland, Robbie Keane, Doherty (Lee 88), Kilbane.
Georgia: Lomaia; Khizanishvili, Khizaneishvili, Kaladze, Rekhviashvili, Burduli, Didava (Aleksidze 76), Asatiani, Amisulashvili, Demetradze (Daraselia 62), Arveladze S.
Referee: Gonzalez (Spain).

Geneva, 11 June 2003, 26,000

Switzerland (2) 3 *(Haas 10, Frei 32, Cabanas 72)*

Albania (1) 2 *(Lala 23, Skela 86 (pen))*

Switzerland: Stiel; Haas, Henchoz (Zwyssig 75), Yakin M, Berner, Cabanas, Vogel, Wicky (Spycher 64), Yakin H, Frei (Celestini 83), Chapuisat.
Albania: Strakosha; Beqiri, Cipi (Cana 46), Aliaj, Duro (Dragusha 74), Hasi, Lala, Skela, Bellai, Bushai (Rraklli 62), Tare.
Referee: Bennett (England).

Group 10 Table	P	W	D	L	F	A	Pts
Switzerland	6	3	3	0	12	7	12
Republic of Ireland	6	3	1	2	9	8	10
Russia	5	2	1	2	11	9	7
Albania	6	1	2	3	8	11	5
Georgia	5	1	1	3	3	8	4

EURO 2004 – REMAINING FIXTURES

GROUP 1
Cyprus, France, Israel, Malta, Slovenia.

06.09.03 France v Cyprus
06.09.03 Slovenia v Israel
10.09.03 Israel v Malta
10.09.03 Slovenia v France
11.10.03 Cyprus v Slovenia
11.10.03 France v Israel

GROUP 2
Denmark, Luxembourg, Norway, Romania, Bosnia.

06.09.03 Bosnia v Norway
06.09.03 Romania v Luxembourg
10.09.03 Luxembourg v Bosnia
10.09.03 Denmark v Romania
11.10.03 Norway v Luxembourg
11.10.03 Bosnia v Denmark

GROUP 3
Austria, Holland, Belarus, Moldova, Czech Republic.

06.09.03 Holland v Austria
06.09.03 Belarus v Czech Republic
10.09.03 Czech Republic v Holland
10.09.03 Moldova v Belarus
11.10.03 Austria v Czech Republic
11.10.03 Holland v Moldova

GROUP 4
Hungary, Poland, Sweden, San Marino, Latvia.

06.09.03 Latvia v Poland
06.09.03 Sweden v San Marino
10.09.03 Poland v Sweden
10.09.03 Latvia v Hungary
11.10.03 Sweden v Latvia
11.10.03 Hungary v Poland

GROUP 5
Germany, Iceland, Scotland, Faeroes, Lithuania.

20.08.03 Faeroes v Iceland
06.09.03 Scotland v Faeroes
06.09.03 Iceland v Germany
10.09.03 Germany v Scotland
10.09.03 Faeroes v Lithuania
11.10.03 Scotland v Lithuania
11.10.03 Germany v Iceland

GROUP 6
Greece, Northern Ireland, Spain, Ukraine, Armenia.

06.09.03 Armenia v Greece
06.09.03 Ukraine v Northern Ireland
10.09.03 Northern Ireland v Armenia
10.09.03 Spain v Ukraine
11.10.03 Greece v Northern Ireland
11.10.03 Armenia v Spain

GROUP 7
England, Liechtenstein, Turkey, Slovakia, Macedonia.

06.09.03 Liechtenstein v Turkey
06.09.03 Macedonia v England
10.09.03 England v Liechtenstein
10.09.03 Slovakia v Macedonia
11.10.03 Turkey v England
11.10.03 Liechtenstein v Slovakia

GROUP 8
Belgium, Bulgaria, Croatia, Estonia, Andorra.

06.09.03 Bulgaria v Estonia
06.09.03 Andorra v Croatia
10.09.03 Belgium v Croatia
10.09.03 Andorra v Bulgaria
11.10.03 Croatia v Bulgaria
11.10.03 Belgium v Estonia

GROUP 9
Finland, Italy, Wales, Serbia-Montenegro, Azerbaijan.

20.08.03 Serbia-Montenegro v Wales
06.09.03 Italy v Wales
06.09.03 Azerbaijan v Finland
10.09.03 Wales v Finland
10.09.03 Serbia-Montenegro v Italy
11.10.03 Italy v Azerbaijan
11.10.03 Wales v Serbia-Montenegro

GROUP 10
Albania, Republic of Ireland, Switzerland, Georgia, Russia.

06.09.03 Republic of Ireland v Russia
06.09.03 Georgia v Albania
10.09.03 Russia v Switzerland
10.09.03 Albania v Georgia
11.10.03 Russia v Georgia
11.10.03 Switzerland v Republic of Ireland

PLAY-OFFS
15/19.11.03

GROUP MATCHES
12/19.06.04

QUARTER-FINALS
30.06.04

SEMI-FINALS
01.07.04

FINAL
04.07.04

EUROPEAN FOOTBALL CHAMPIONSHIP

(formerly EUROPEAN NATIONS' CUP)

Year	*Winners*		*Runners-up*		*Venue*	*Attendance*
1960	USSR	2	Yugoslavia	1	Paris	17,966
1964	Spain	2	USSR	1	Madrid	120,000
1968	Italy After 1-1 draw	2	Yugoslavia	0	Rome	60,000 75,000
1972	West Germany	3	USSR	0	Brussels	43,437
1976	Czechoslovakia *(Czechoslovakia won on penalties)*	2	West Germany	2	Belgrade	45,000
1980	West Germany	2	Belgium	1	Rome	47,864
1984	France	2	Spain	0	Paris	48,000
1988	Holland	2	USSR	0	Munich	72,308
1992	Denmark	2	Germany	0	Gothenburg	37,800
1996	Germany *(Germany won on sudden death)*	2	Czech Republic	1	Wembley	73,611
2000	France *(France won on sudden death)*	2	Italy	1	Rotterdam	50,000

BRITISH AND IRISH INTERNATIONAL RESULTS 1872–2003

Note: In the results that follow, WC=World Cup, EC=European Championship, UI=Umbro International Trophy. TF = Tournoi de France. For Ireland, read Northern Ireland from 1921.

ENGLAND v SCOTLAND

Played: 110; England won 45, Scotland won 41, Drawn 24. Goals: England 192, Scotland 169.

			E	S
1872	30 Nov	Glasgow	0	0
1873	8 Mar	Kennington Oval	4	2
1874	7 Mar	Glasgow	1	2
1875	6 Mar	Kennington Oval	2	2
1876	4 Mar	Glasgow	0	3
1877	3 Mar	Kennington Oval	1	3
1878	2 Mar	Glasgow	2	7
1879	5 Apr	Kennington Oval	5	4
1880	13 Mar	Glasgow	4	5
1881	12 Mar	Kennington Oval	1	6
1882	11 Mar	Glasgow	1	5
1883	10 Mar	Sheffield	2	3
1884	15 Mar	Glasgow	0	1
1885	21 Mar	Kennington Oval	1	1
1886	31 Mar	Glasgow	1	1
1887	19 Mar	Blackburn	2	3
1888	17 Mar	Glasgow	5	0
1889	13 Apr	Kennington Oval	2	3
1890	5 Apr	Glasgow	1	1
1891	6 Apr	Blackburn	2	1
1892	2 Apr	Glasgow	4	1
1893	1 Apr	Richmond	5	2
1894	7 Apr	Glasgow	2	2
1895	6 Apr	Everton	3	0
1896	4 Apr	Glasgow	1	2
1897	3 Apr	Crystal Palace	1	2
1898	2 Apr	Glasgow	3	1
1899	8 Apr	Birmingham	2	1
1900	7 Apr	Glasgow	1	4
1901	30 Mar	Crystal Palace	2	2
1902	3 Mar	Birmingham	2	2
1903	4 Apr	Sheffield	1	2
1904	9 Apr	Glasgow	1	0
1905	1 Apr	Crystal Palace	1	0
1906	7 Apr	Glasgow	1	2
1907	6 Apr	Newcastle	1	1
1908	4 Apr	Glasgow	1	1
1909	3 Apr	Crystal Palace	2	0
1910	2 Apr	Glasgow	0	2
1911	1 Apr	Everton	1	1
1912	23 Mar	Glasgow	1	1
1913	5 Apr	Chelsea	1	0
1914	14 Apr	Glasgow	1	3
1920	10 Apr	Sheffield	5	4
1921	9 Apr	Glasgow	0	3
1922	8 Apr	Aston Villa	0	1
1923	14 Apr	Glasgow	2	2
1924	12 Apr	Wembley	1	1
1925	4 Apr	Glasgow	0	2
1926	17 Apr	Manchester	0	1
1927	2 Apr	Glasgow	2	1
1928	31 Mar	Wembley	1	5
1929	13 Apr	Glasgow	0	1
1930	5 Apr	Wembley	5	2
1931	28 Mar	Glasgow	0	2
1932	9 Apr	Wembley	3	0
1933	1 Apr	Glasgow	1	2
1934	14 Apr	Wembley	3	0
1935	6 Apr	Glasgow	0	2
1936	4 Apr	Wembley	1	1
1937	17 Apr	Glasgow	1	3
1938	9 Apr	Wembley	0	1
1939	15 Apr	Glasgow	2	1
1947	12 Apr	Wembley	1	1
1948	10 Apr	Glasgow	2	0
1949	9 Apr	Wembley	1	3
WC1950	15 Apr	Glasgow	1	0
1951	14 Apr	Wembley	2	3
1952	5 Apr	Glasgow	2	1
1953	18 Apr	Wembley	2	2
WC1954	3 Apr	Glasgow	4	2
1955	2 Apr	Wembley	7	2
1956	14 Apr	Glasgow	1	1
1957	6 Apr	Wembley	2	1
1958	19 Apr	Glasgow	4	0
1959	11 Apr	Wembley	1	0
1960	9 Apr	Glasgow	1	1
1961	15 Apr	Wembley	9	3
1962	14 Apr	Glasgow	0	2
1963	6 Apr	Wembley	1	2
1964	11 Apr	Glasgow	0	1
1965	10 Apr	Wembley	2	2
1966	2 Apr	Glasgow	4	3
EC1967	15 Apr	Wembley	2	3
EC1968	24 Jan	Glasgow	1	1
1969	10 May	Wembley	4	1
1970	25 Apr	Glasgow	0	0
1971	22 May	Wembley	3	1
1972	27 May	Glasgow	1	0
1973	14 Feb	Glasgow	5	0
1973	19 May	Wembley	1	0
1974	18 May	Glasgow	0	2
1975	24 May	Wembley	5	1
1976	15 May	Glasgow	1	2
1977	4 June	Wembley	1	2
1978	20 May	Glasgow	1	0
1979	26 May	Wembley	3	1
1980	24 May	Glasgow	2	0
1981	23 May	Wembley	0	1
1982	29 May	Glasgow	1	0
1983	1 June	Wembley	2	0
1984	26 May	Glasgow	1	1
1985	25 May	Glasgow	0	1
1986	23 Apr	Wembley	2	1
1987	23 May	Glasgow	0	0
1988	21 May	Wembley	1	0
1989	27 May	Glasgow	2	0
EC1996	15 June	Wembley	2	0
EC1999	13 Nov	Glasgow	2	0
EC1999	17 Nov	Wembley	0	1

ENGLAND v WALES

Played: 97; England won 62, Wales won 14, Drawn 21. Goals: England 239, Wales 90.

			E	W
1879	18 Jan	Kennington Oval	2	1
1880	15 Mar	Wrexham	3	2
1881	26 Feb	Blackburn	0	1
1882	13 Mar	Wrexham	3	5
1883	3 Feb	Kennington Oval	5	0
1884	17 Mar	Wrexham	4	0

			E	*W*
1885	14 Mar	Blackburn	1	1
1886	29 Mar	Wrexham	3	1
1887	26 Feb	Kennington Oval	4	0
1888	4 Feb	Crewe	5	1
1889	23 Feb	Stoke	4	1
1890	15 Mar	Wrexham	3	1
1891	7 May	Sunderland	4	1
1892	5 Mar	Wrexham	2	0
1893	13 Mar	Stoke	6	0
1894	12 Mar	Wrexham	5	1
1895	18 Mar	Queen's Club, Kensington	1	1
1896	16 Mar	Cardiff	9	1
1897	29 Mar	Sheffield	4	0
1898	28 Mar	Wrexham	3	0
1899	20 Mar	Bristol	4	0
1900	26 Mar	Cardiff	1	1
1901	18 Mar	Newcastle	6	0
1902	3 Mar	Wrexham	0	0
1903	2 Mar	Portsmouth	2	1
1904	29 Feb	Wrexham	2	2
1905	27 Mar	Liverpool	3	1
1906	19 Mar	Cardiff	1	0
1907	18 Mar	Fulham	1	1
1908	16 Mar	Wrexham	7	1
1909	15 Mar	Nottingham	2	0
1910	14 Mar	Cardiff	1	0
1911	13 Mar	Millwall	3	0
1912	11 Mar	Wrexham	2	0
1913	17 Mar	Bristol	4	3
1914	16 Mar	Cardiff	2	0
1920	15 Mar	Highbury	1	2
1921	14 Mar	Cardiff	0	0
1922	13 Mar	Liverpool	1	0
1923	5 Mar	Cardiff	2	2
1924	3 Mar	Blackburn	1	2
1925	28 Feb	Swansea	2	1
1926	1 Mar	Crystal Palace	1	3
1927	12 Feb	Wrexham	3	3
1927	28 Nov	Burnley	1	2
1928	17 Nov	Swansea	3	2
1929	20 Nov	Chelsea	6	0
1930	22 Nov	Wrexham	4	0
1931	18 Nov	Liverpool	3	1
1932	16 Nov	Wrexham	0	0
1933	15 Nov	Newcastle	1	2

			E	*W*
1934	29 Sept	Cardiff	4	0
1936	5 Feb	Wolverhampton	1	2
1936	17 Oct	Cardiff	1	2
1937	17 Nov	Middlesbrough	2	1
1938	22 Oct	Cardiff	2	4
1946	13 Nov	Manchester	3	0
1947	18 Oct	Cardiff	3	0
1948	10 Nov	Aston Villa	1	0
WC1949	15 Oct	Cardiff	4	1
1950	15 Nov	Sunderland	4	2
1951	20 Oct	Cardiff	1	1
1952	12 Nov	Wembley	5	2
WC1953	10 Oct	Cardiff	4	1
1954	10 Nov	Wembley	3	2
1955	27 Oct	Cardiff	1	2
1956	14 Nov	Wembley	3	1
1957	19 Oct	Cardiff	4	0
1958	26 Nov	Aston Villa	2	2
1959	17 Oct	Cardiff	1	1
1960	23 Nov	Wembley	5	1
1961	14 Oct	Cardiff	1	1
1962	21 Oct	Wembley	4	0
1963	12 Oct	Cardiff	4	0
1964	18 Nov	Wembley	2	1
1965	2 Oct	Cardiff	0	0
EC1966	16 Nov	Wembley	5	1
EC1967	21 Oct	Cardiff	3	0
1969	7 May	Wembley	2	1
1970	18 Apr	Cardiff	1	1
1971	19 May	Wembley	0	0
1972	20 May	Cardiff	3	0
WC1972	15 Nov	Cardiff	1	0
WC1973	24 Jan	Wembley	1	1
1973	15 May	Wembley	3	0
1974	11 May	Cardiff	2	0
1975	21 May	Wembley	2	2
1976	24 Mar	Wrexham	2	1
1976	8 May	Cardiff	1	0
1977	31 May	Wembley	0	1
1978	3 May	Cardiff	3	1
1979	23 May	Wembley	0	0
1980	17 May	Wrexham	1	4
1981	20 May	Wembley	0	0
1982	27 Apr	Cardiff	1	0
1983	23 Feb	Wembley	2	1
1984	2 May	Wrexham	0	1

ENGLAND v IRELAND

Played: 96; England won 74, Ireland won 6, Drawn 16. Goals: England 319, Ireland 80.

			E	*I*
1882	18 Feb	Belfast	13	0
1883	24 Feb	Liverpool	7	0
1884	23 Feb	Belfast	8	1
1885	28 Feb	Manchester	4	0
1886	13 Mar	Belfast	6	1
1887	5 Feb	Sheffield	7	0
1888	31 Mar	Belfast	5	1
1889	2 Mar	Everton	6	1
1890	15 Mar	Belfast	9	1
1891	7 Mar	Wolverhampton	6	1
1892	5 Mar	Belfast	2	0
1893	25 Feb	Birmingham	6	1
1894	3 Mar	Belfast	2	2
1895	9 Mar	Derby	9	0
1896	7 Mar	Belfast	2	0
1897	20 Feb	Nottingham	6	0
1898	5 Mar	Belfast	3	2
1899	18 Feb	Sunderland	13	2
1900	17 Mar	Dublin	2	0
1901	9 Mar	Southampton	3	0
1902	22 Mar	Belfast	1	0

			E	*I*
1903	14 Feb	Wolverhampton	4	0
1904	12 Mar	Belfast	3	1
1905	25 Feb	Middlesbrough	1	1
1906	17 Feb	Belfast	5	0
1907	16 Feb	Everton	1	0
1908	15 Feb	Belfast	3	1
1909	13 Feb	Bradford	4	0
1910	12 Feb	Belfast	1	1
1911	11 Feb	Derby	2	1
1912	10 Feb	Dublin	6	1
1913	15 Feb	Belfast	1	2
1914	14 Feb	Middlesbrough	0	3
1919	25 Oct	Belfast	1	1
1920	23 Oct	Sunderland	2	0
1921	22 Oct	Belfast	1	1
1922	21 Oct	West Bromwich	2	0
1923	20 Oct	Belfast	1	2
1924	22 Oct	Everton	3	1
1925	24 Oct	Belfast	0	0
1926	20 Oct	Liverpool	3	3
1927	22 Oct	Belfast	0	2

Year	Date	Venue	E	I
1928	22 Oct	Everton	2	1
1929	19 Oct	Belfast	3	0
1930	20 Oct	Sheffield	5	1
1931	17 Oct	Belfast	6	2
1932	17 Oct	Blackpool	1	0
1933	14 Oct	Belfast	3	0
1935	6 Feb	Everton	2	1
1935	19 Oct	Belfast	3	1
1936	18 Nov	Stoke	3	1
1937	23 Oct	Belfast	5	1
1938	16 Nov	Manchester	7	0
1946	28 Sept	Belfast	7	2
1947	5 Nov	Everton	2	2
1948	9 Oct	Belfast	6	2
wc1949	16 Nov	Manchester	9	2
1950	7 Oct	Belfast	4	1
1951	14 Nov	Aston Villa	2	0
1952	4 Oct	Belfast	2	2
wc1953	11 Nov	Everton	3	1
1954	2 Oct	Belfast	2	0
1955	2 Nov	Wembley	3	0
1956	10 Oct	Belfast	1	1
1957	6 Nov	Wembley	2	3
1958	4 Oct	Belfast	3	3
1959	18 Nov	Wembley	2	1
1960	8 Oct	Belfast	5	2
1961	22 Nov	Wembley	1	1
1962	20 Oct	Belfast	3	1
1963	20 Nov	Wembley	8	3
1964	3 Oct	Belfast	4	3
1965	10 Nov	Wembley	2	1
EC1966	20 Oct	Belfast	2	0
EC1967	22 Nov	Wembley	2	0
1969	3 May	Belfast	3	1
1970	21 Apr	Wembley	3	1
1971	15 May	Belfast	1	0
1972	23 May	Wembley	0	1
1973	12 May	Everton	2	1
1974	15 May	Wembley	1	0
1975	17 May	Belfast	0	0
1976	11 May	Wembley	4	0
1977	28 May	Belfast	2	1
1978	16 May	Wembley	1	0
EC1979	7 Feb	Wembley	4	0
1979	19 May	Belfast	2	0
EC1979	17 Oct	Belfast	5	1
1980	20 May	Wembley	1	1
1982	23 Feb	Wembley	4	0
1983	28 May	Belfast	0	0
1984	24 Apr	Wembley	1	0
wc1985	27 Feb	Belfast	1	0
wc1985	13 Nov	Wembley	0	0
EC1986	15 Oct	Wembley	3	0
EC1987	1 Apr	Belfast	2	0

SCOTLAND v WALES

Played: 102; Scotland won 60, Wales won 19, Drawn 23. Goals: Scotland 238, Wales 112.

Year	Date	Venue	S	W
1876	25 Mar	Glasgow	4	0
1877	5 Mar	Wrexham	2	0
1878	23 Mar	Glasgow	9	0
1879	7 Apr	Wrexham	3	0
1880	3 Apr	Glasgow	5	1
1881	14 Mar	Wrexham	5	1
1882	25 Mar	Glasgow	5	0
1883	12 Mar	Wrexham	3	0
1884	29 Mar	Glasgow	4	1
1885	23 Mar	Wrexham	8	1
1886	10 Apr	Glasgow	4	1
1887	21 Mar	Wrexham	2	0
1888	10 Mar	Edinburgh	5	1
1889	15 Apr	Wrexham	0	0
1890	22 Mar	Paisley	5	0
1891	21 Mar	Wrexham	4	3
1892	26 Mar	Edinburgh	6	1
1893	18 Mar	Wrexham	8	0
1894	24 Mar	Kilmarnock	5	2
1895	23 Mar	Wrexham	2	2
1896	21 Mar	Dundee	4	0
1897	20 Mar	Wrexham	2	2
1898	19 Mar	Motherwell	5	2
1899	18 Mar	Wrexham	6	0
1900	3 Feb	Aberdeen	5	2
1901	2 Mar	Wrexham	1	1
1902	15 Mar	Greenock	5	1
1903	9 Mar	Cardiff	1	0
1904	12 Mar	Dundee	1	1
1905	6 Mar	Wrexham	1	3
1906	3 Mar	Edinburgh	0	2
1907	4 Mar	Wrexham	0	1
1908	7 Mar	Dundee	2	1
1909	1 Mar	Wrexham	2	3
1910	5 Mar	Kilmarnock	1	0
1911	6 Mar	Cardiff	2	2
1912	2 Mar	Tynecastle	1	0
1913	3 Mar	Wrexham	0	0
1914	28 Feb	Glasgow	0	0
1920	26 Feb	Cardiff	1	1
1921	12 Feb	Aberdeen	2	1
1922	4 Feb	Wrexham	1	2
1923	17 Mar	Paisley	2	0
1924	16 Feb	Cardiff	0	2
1925	14 Feb	Tynecastle	3	1
1925	31 Oct	Cardiff	3	0
1926	30 Oct	Glasgow	3	0
1927	29 Oct	Wrexham	2	2
1928	27 Oct	Glasgow	4	2
1929	26 Oct	Cardiff	4	2
1930	25 Oct	Glasgow	1	1
1931	31 Oct	Wrexham	3	2
1932	26 Oct	Edinburgh	2	5
1933	4 Oct	Cardiff	2	3
1934	21 Nov	Aberdeen	3	2
1935	5 Oct	Cardiff	1	1
1936	2 Dec	Dundee	1	2
1937	30 Oct	Cardiff	1	2
1938	9 Nov	Edinburgh	3	2
1946	19 Oct	Wrexham	1	3
1947	12 Nov	Glasgow	1	2
wc1948	23 Oct	Cardiff	3	1
1949	9 Nov	Glasgow	2	0
1950	21 Oct	Cardiff	3	1
1951	14 Nov	Glasgow	0	1
wc1952	18 Oct	Cardiff	2	1
1953	4 Nov	Glasgow	3	3
1954	16 Oct	Cardiff	1	0
1955	9 Nov	Glasgow	2	0
1956	20 Oct	Cardiff	2	2
1957	13 Nov	Glasgow	1	1
1958	18 Oct	Cardiff	3	0
1959	4 Nov	Glasgow	1	1
1960	20 Oct	Cardiff	0	2
1961	8 Nov	Glasgow	2	0
1962	20 Oct	Cardiff	3	2
1963	20 Nov	Glasgow	2	1
1964	3 Oct	Cardiff	2	3
EC1965	24 Nov	Glasgow	4	1
EC1966	22 Oct	Cardiff	1	1

			S	*W*
1967	22 Nov	Glasgow	3	2
1969	3 May	Wrexham	5	3
1970	22 Apr	Glasgow	0	0
1971	15 May	Cardiff	0	0
1972	24 May	Glasgow	1	0
1973	12 May	Wrexham	2	0
1974	14 May	Glasgow	2	0
1975	17 May	Cardiff	2	2
1976	6 May	Glasgow	3	1
wc1976	17 Nov	Glasgow	1	0
1977	28 May	Wrexham	0	0
wc1977	12 Oct	Liverpool	2	0
1978	17 May	Glasgow	1	1
1979	19 May	Cardiff	0	3
1980	21 May	Glasgow	1	0
1981	16 May	Swansea	0	2
1982	24 May	Glasgow	1	0
1983	28 May	Cardiff	2	0
1984	28 Feb	Glasgow	2	1
wc1985	27 Mar	Glasgow	0	1
wc1985	10 Sept	Cardiff	1	1
1997	27 May	Kilmarnock	0	1

SCOTLAND v IRELAND

Played: 93; Scotland won 62, Ireland won 15, Drawn 16. Goals: Scotland 257, Ireland 81.

			S	*I*
1884	26 Jan	Belfast	5	0
1885	14 Mar	Glasgow	8	2
1886	20 Mar	Belfast	7	2
1887	19 Feb	Glasgow	4	1
1888	24 Mar	Belfast	10	2
1889	9 Mar	Glasgow	7	0
1890	29 Mar	Belfast	4	1
1891	28 Mar	Glasgow	2	1
1892	19 Mar	Belfast	3	2
1893	25 Mar	Glasgow	6	1
1894	31 Mar	Belfast	2	1
1895	30 Mar	Glasgow	3	1
1896	28 Mar	Belfast	3	3
1897	27 Mar	Glasgow	5	1
1898	26 Mar	Belfast	3	0
1899	25 Mar	Glasgow	9	1
1900	3 Mar	Belfast	3	0
1901	23 Feb	Glasgow	11	0
1902	1 Mar	Belfast	5	1
1902	9 Aug	Belfast	3	0
1903	21 Mar	Glasgow	0	2
1904	26 Mar	Dublin	1	1
1905	18 Mar	Glasgow	4	0
1906	17 Mar	Dublin	1	0
1907	16 Mar	Glasgow	3	0
1908	14 Mar	Dublin	5	0
1909	15 Mar	Glasgow	5	0
1910	19 Mar	Belfast	0	1
1911	18 Mar	Glasgow	2	0
1912	16 Mar	Belfast	4	1
1913	15 Mar	Dublin	2	1
1914	14 Mar	Belfast	1	1
1920	13 Mar	Glasgow	3	0
1921	26 Feb	Belfast	2	0
1922	4 Mar	Glasgow	2	1
1923	3 Mar	Belfast	1	0
1924	1 Mar	Glasgow	2	0
1925	28 Feb	Belfast	3	0
1926	27 Feb	Glasgow	4	0
1927	26 Feb	Belfast	2	0
1928	25 Feb	Glasgow	0	1
1929	23 Feb	Belfast	7	3
1930	22 Feb	Glasgow	3	1
1931	21 Feb	Belfast	0	0
1931	19 Sept	Glasgow	3	1
1932	12 Sept	Belfast	4	0
1933	16 Sept	Glasgow	1	2
1934	20 Oct	Belfast	1	2
1935	13 Nov	Edinburgh	2	1
1936	31 Oct	Belfast	3	1
1937	10 Nov	Aberdeen	1	1
1938	8 Oct	Belfast	2	0
1946	27 Nov	Glasgow	0	0
1947	4 Oct	Belfast	0	2
1948	17 Nov	Glasgow	3	2
1949	1 Oct	Belfast	8	2
1950	1 Nov	Glasgow	6	1
1951	6 Oct	Belfast	3	0
1952	5 Nov	Glasgow	1	1
1953	3 Oct	Belfast	3	1
1954	3 Nov	Glasgow	2	2
1955	8 Oct	Belfast	1	2
1956	7 Nov	Glasgow	1	0
1957	5 Oct	Belfast	1	1
1958	5 Nov	Glasgow	2	2
1959	3 Oct	Belfast	4	0
1960	9 Nov	Glasgow	5	2
1961	7 Oct	Belfast	6	1
1962	7 Nov	Glasgow	5	1
1963	12 Oct	Belfast	1	2
1964	25 Nov	Glasgow	3	2
1965	2 Oct	Belfast	2	3
1966	16 Nov	Glasgow	2	1
1967	21 Oct	Belfast	0	1
1969	6 May	Glasgow	1	1
1970	18 Apr	Belfast	1	0
1971	18 May	Glasgow	0	1
1972	20 May	Glasgow	2	0
1973	16 May	Glasgow	1	2
1974	11 May	Glasgow	0	1
1975	20 May	Glasgow	3	0
1976	8 May	Glasgow	3	0
1977	1 June	Glasgow	3	0
1978	13 May	Glasgow	1	1
1979	22 May	Glasgow	1	0
1980	17 May	Belfast	0	1
wc1981	25 Mar	Glasgow	1	1
1981	19 May	Glasgow	2	0
wc1981	14 Oct	Belfast	0	0
1982	28 Apr	Belfast	1	1
1983	24 May	Glasgow	0	0
1983	13 Dec	Belfast	0	2
1992	19 Feb	Glasgow	1	0

WALES v IRELAND

Played: 90; Wales won 42, Ireland won 27, Drawn 21. Goals: Wales 182, Ireland 127.

			W	*I*
1882	25 Feb	Wrexham	7	1
1883	17 Mar	Belfast	1	1
1884	9 Feb	Wrexham	6	0
1885	11 Apr	Belfast	8	2
1886	27 Feb	Wrexham	5	0
1887	12 Mar	Belfast	1	4
1888	3 Mar	Wrexham	11	0
1889	27 Apr	Belfast	3	1

			W	I
1890	8 Feb	Shrewsbury	5	2
1891	7 Feb	Belfast	2	7
1892	27 Feb	Bangor	1	1
1893	8 Apr	Belfast	3	4
1894	24 Feb	Swansea	4	1
1895	16 Mar	Belfast	2	2
1896	29 Feb	Wrexham	6	1
1897	6 Mar	Belfast	3	4
1898	19 Feb	Llandudno	0	1
1899	4 Mar	Belfast	0	1
1900	24 Feb	Llandudno	2	0
1901	23 Mar	Belfast	1	0
1902	22 Mar	Cardiff	0	3
1903	28 Mar	Belfast	0	2
1904	21 Mar	Bangor	0	1
1905	18 Apr	Belfast	2	2
1906	2 Apr	Wrexham	4	4
1907	23 Feb	Belfast	3	2
1908	11 Apr	Aberdare	0	1
1909	20 Mar	Belfast	3	2
1910	11 Apr	Wrexham	4	1
1911	28 Jan	Belfast	2	1
1912	13 Apr	Cardiff	2	3
1913	18 Jan	Belfast	1	0
1914	19 Jan	Wrexham	1	2
1920	14 Feb	Belfast	2	2
1921	9 Apr	Swansea	2	1
1922	4 Apr	Belfast	1	1
1923	14 Apr	Wrexham	0	3
1924	15 Mar	Belfast	1	0
1925	18 Apr	Wrexham	0	0
1926	13 Feb	Belfast	0	3
1927	9 Apr	Cardiff	2	2
1928	4 Feb	Belfast	2	1
1929	2 Feb	Wrexham	2	2
1930	1 Feb	Belfast	0	7
1931	22 Apr	Wrexham	3	2
1931	5 Dec	Belfast	0	4
1932	7 Dec	Wrexham	4	1
1933	4 Nov	Belfast	1	1
1935	27 Mar	Wrexham	3	1
1936	11 Mar	Belfast	2	3
1937	17 Mar	Wrexham	4	1
1938	16 Mar	Belfast	0	1
1939	15 Mar	Wrexham	3	1
1947	16 Apr	Belfast	1	2
1948	10 Mar	Wrexham	2	0
1949	9 Mar	Belfast	2	0
WC1950	8 Mar	Wrexham	0	0
1951	7 Mar	Belfast	2	1
1952	19 Mar	Swansea	3	0
1953	15 Apr	Belfast	3	2
WC1954	31 Mar	Wrexham	1	2
1955	20 Apr	Belfast	3	2
1956	11 Apr	Cardiff	1	1
1957	10 Apr	Belfast	0	0
1958	16 Apr	Cardiff	1	1
1959	22 Apr	Belfast	1	4
1960	6 Apr	Wrexham	3	2
1961	12 Apr	Belfast	5	1
1962	11 Apr	Cardiff	4	0
1963	3 Apr	Belfast	4	1
1964	15 Apr	Cardiff	2	3
1965	31 Mar	Belfast	5	0
1966	30 Mar	Cardiff	1	4
EC1967	12 Apr	Belfast	0	0
EC1968	28 Feb	Wrexham	2	0
1969	10 May	Belfast	0	0
1970	25 Apr	Swansea	1	0
1971	22 May	Belfast	0	1
1972	27 May	Wrexham	0	0
1973	19 May	Everton	0	1
1974	18 May	Wrexham	1	0
1975	23 May	Belfast	0	1
1976	14 May	Swansea	1	0
1977	3 June	Belfast	1	1
1978	19 May	Wrexham	1	0
1979	25 May	Belfast	1	1
1980	23 May	Cardiff	0	1
1982	27 May	Wrexham	3	0
1983	31 May	Belfast	1	0
1984	22 May	Swansea	1	1

OTHER BRITISH INTERNATIONAL RESULTS 1908–2002

ENGLAND

		v ALBANIA	E	A
WC1989	8 Mar	Tirana	2	0
WC1989	26 Apr	Wembley	5	0
WC2001	28 Mar	Tirana	3	1
WC2001	5 Sept	Newcastle	2	0

		v ARGENTINA	E	A
1951	9 May	Wembley	2	1
1953	17 May	Buenos Aires	0	0
(*abandoned after 21 mins*)				
WC1962	2 June	Rancagua	3	1
1964	6 June	Rio de Janeiro	0	1
WC1966	23 July	Wembley	1	0
1974	22 May	Wembley	2	2
1977	12 June	Buenos Aires	1	1
1980	13 May	Wembley	3	1
WC1986	22 June	Mexico City	1	2
1991	25 May	Wembley	2	2
WC1998	30 June	St Etienne	2	2
2000	23 Feb	Wembley	0	0
WC2002	7 June	Sapporo	1	0

		v AUSTRALIA	E	A
1980	31 May	Sydney	2	1
1983	11 June	Sydney	0	0
1983	15 June	Brisbane	1	0
1983	18 June	Melbourne	1	1
1991	1 June	Sydney	1	0
2003	12 Feb	West Ham	1	3

		v AUSTRIA	E	A
1908	6 June	Vienna	6	1
1908	8 June	Vienna	11	1
1909	1 June	Vienna	8	1
1930	14 May	Vienna	0	0
1932	7 Dec	Chelsea	4	3
1936	6 May	Vienna	1	2
1951	28 Nov	Wembley	2	2
1952	25 May	Vienna	3	2
WC1958	15 June	Boras	2	2
1961	27 May	Vienna	1	3
1962	4 Apr	Wembley	3	1
1965	20 Oct	Wembley	2	3
1967	27 May	Vienna	1	0
1973	26 Sept	Wembley	7	0
1979	13 June	Vienna	3	4

		v BELGIUM	E	B
1921	21 May	Brussels	2	0
1923	19 Mar	Highbury	6	1
1923	1 Nov	Antwerp	2	2
1924	8 Dec	West Bromwich	4	0
1926	24 May	Antwerp	5	3
1927	11 May	Brussels	9	1
1928	19 May	Antwerp	3	1
1929	11 May	Brussels	5	1
1931	16 May	Brussels	4	1
1936	9 May	Brussels	2	3
1947	21 Sept	Brussels	5	2

			E	*B*
1950	18 May	Brussels	4	1
1952	26 Nov	Wembley	5	0
WC1954	17 June	Basle	4	4*
1964	21 Oct	Wembley	2	2
1970	25 Feb	Brussels	3	1
EC1980	12 June	Turin	1	1
WC1990	27 June	Bologna	1	0*
1998	29 May	Casablanca	0	0
1999	10 Oct	Sunderland	2	1

*After extra time

		v BOHEMIA	*E*	*B*
1908	13 June	Prague	4	0

		v BRAZIL	*E*	*B*
1956	9 May	Wembley	4	2
WC1958	11 June	Gothenburg	0	0
1959	13 May	Rio de Janeiro	0	2
WC1962	10 June	Vina del Mar	1	3
1963	8 May	Wembley	1	1
1964	30 May	Rio de Janeiro	1	5
1969	12 June	Rio de Janeiro	1	2
WC1970	7 June	Guadalajara	0	1
1976	23 May	Los Angeles	0	1
1977	8 June	Rio de Janeiro	0	0
1978	19 Apr	Wembley	1	1
1981	12 May	Wembley	0	1
1984	10 June	Rio de Janeiro	2	0
1987	19 May	Wembley	1	1
1990	28 Mar	Wembley	1	0
1992	17 May	Wembley	1	1
1993	13 June	Washington	1	1
UI1995	11 June	Wembley	1	3
TF1997	10 June	Paris	0	1
2000	27 May	Wembley	1	1
WC2002	21 June	Shizuoka	1	2

		v BULGARIA	*E*	*B*
WC1962	7 June	Rancagua	0	0
1968	11 Dec	Wembley	1	1
1974	1 June	Sofia	1	0
EC1979	6 June	Sofia	3	0
EC1979	22 Nov	Wembley	2	0
1996	27 Mar	Wembley	1	0
EC1998	10 Oct	Wembley	0	0
EC1999	9 June	Sofia	1	1

		v CAMEROON	*E*	*C*
WC1990	1 July	Naples	3	2*
1991	6 Feb	Wembley	2	0
1997	15 Nov	Wembley	2	0
2002	26 May	Kobe	2	2

*After extra time

		v CANADA	*E*	*C*
1986	24 May	Burnaby	1	0

		v CHILE	*E*	*C*
WC1950	25 June	Rio de Janeiro	2	0
1953	24 May	Santiago	2	1
1984	17 June	Santiago	0	0
1989	23 May	Wembley	0	0
1998	11 Feb	Wembley	0	2

		v CHINA	*E*	*C*
1996	23 May	Beijing	3	0

		v CIS	*E*	*C*
1992	29 Apr	Moscow	2	2

		v COLOMBIA	*E*	*C*
1970	20 May	Bogota	4	0
1988	24 May	Wembley	1	1
1995	6 Sept	Wembley	0	0
WC1998	26 June	Lens	2	0

		v CROATIA	*E*	*C*
1996	24 Apr	Wembley	0	0

		v CYPRUS	*E*	*C*
EC1975	16 Apr	Wembley	5	0
EC1975	11 May	Limassol	1	0

		v CZECHOSLOVAKIA	*E*	*C*
1934	16 May	Prague	1	2
1937	1 Dec	Tottenham	5	4
1963	29 May	Bratislava	4	2
1966	2 Nov	Wembley	0	0
WC1970	11 June	Guadalajara	1	0
1973	27 May	Prague	1	1
EC1974	30 Oct	Wembley	3	0
EC1975	30 Oct	Bratislava	1	2
1978	29 Nov	Wembley	1	0
WC1982	20 June	Bilbao	2	0
1990	25 Apr	Wembley	4	2
1992	25 Mar	Prague	2	2

		v CZECH REPUBLIC	*E*	*C*
1998	18 Nov	Wembley	2	0

		v DENMARK	*E*	*D*
1948	26 Sept	Copenhagen	0	0
1955	2 Oct	Copenhagen	5	1
WC1956	5 Dec	Wolverhampton	5	2
WC1957	15 May	Copenhagen	4	1
1966	3 July	Copenhagen	2	0
EC1978	20 Sept	Copenhagen	4	3
EC1979	12 Sept	Wembley	1	0
EC1982	22 Sept	Copenhagen	2	2
EC1983	21 Sept	Wembley	0	1
1988	14 Sept	Wembley	1	0
1989	7 June	Copenhagen	1	1
1990	15 May	Wembley	1	0
EC1992	11 June	Malmo	0	0
1994	9 Mar	Wembley	1	0
WC2002	15 June	Niigata	3	0

		v ECUADOR	*E*	*Ec*
1970	24 May	Quito	2	0

		v EGYPT	*E*	*Eg*
1986	29 Jan	Cairo	4	0
WC1990	21 June	Cagliari	1	0

		v FIFA	*E*	*FIFA*
1938	26 Oct	Highbury	3	0
1953	21 Oct	Wembley	4	4
1963	23 Oct	Wembley	2	1

		v FINLAND	*E*	*F*
1937	20 May	Helsinki	8	0
1956	20 May	Helsinki	5	1
1966	26 June	Helsinki	3	0
WC1976	13 June	Helsinki	4	1
WC1976	13 Oct	Wembley	2	1
1982	3 June	Helsinki	4	1
WC1984	17 Oct	Wembley	5	0
WC1985	22 May	Helsinki	1	1
1992	3 June	Helsinki	2	1
WC2000	11 Oct	Helsinki	0	0
WC2001	24 Mar	Liverpool	2	1

		v FRANCE	*E*	*F*
1923	10 May	Paris	4	1
1924	17 May	Paris	3	1
1925	21 May	Paris	3	2
1927	26 May	Paris	6	0
1928	17 May	Paris	5	1
1929	9 May	Paris	4	1
1931	14 May	Paris	2	5
1933	6 Dec	Tottenham	4	1
1938	26 May	Paris	4	2
1947	3 May	Highbury	3	0
1949	22 May	Paris	3	1

			E	F
1951	3 Oct	Highbury	2	2
1955	15 May	Paris	0	1
1957	27 Nov	Wembley	4	0
EC1962	3 Oct	Sheffield	1	1
EC1963	27 Feb	Paris	2	5
WC1966	20 July	Wembley	2	0
1969	12 Mar	Wembley	5	0
WC1982	16 June	Bilbao	3	1
1984	29 Feb	Paris	0	2
1992	19 Feb	Wembley	2	0
EC1992	14 June	Malmo	0	0
TF1997	7 June	Montpellier	1	0
1999	10 Feb	Wembley	0	2
2000	2 Sept	Paris	1	1

		v GEORGIA	E	G
WC1996	9 Nov	Tbilisi	2	0
WC1997	30 Apr	Wembley	2	0

		v GERMANY	E	G
1930	10 May	Berlin	3	3
1935	4 Dec	Tottenham	3	0
1938	14 May	Berlin	6	3
1991	11 Sept	Wembley	0	1
1993	19 June	Detroit	1	2
EC1996	26 June	Wembley	1	1*
EC2000	17 June	Charleroi	1	0
WC2000	7 Oct	Wembley	0	1
WC2001	1 Sept	Munich	5	1

		v EAST GERMANY	E	EG
1963	2 June	Leipzig	2	1
1970	25 Nov	Wembley	3	1
1974	29 May	Leipzig	1	1
1984	12 Sept	Wembley	1	0

		v WEST GERMANY	E	WG
1954	1 Dec	Wembley	3	1
1956	26 May	Berlin	3	1
1965	12 May	Nuremberg	1	0
1966	23 Feb	Wembley	1	0
WC1966	30 July	Wembley	4	2*
1968	1 June	Hanover	0	1
WC1970	14 June	Leon	2	3*
EC1972	29 Apr	Wembley	1	3
EC1972	13 May	Berlin	0	0
1975	12 Mar	Wembley	2	0
1978	22 Feb	Munich	1	2
WC1982	29 June	Madrid	0	0
1982	13 Oct	Wembley	1	2
1985	12 June	Mexico City	3	0
1987	9 Sept	Dusseldorf	1	3
WC1990	4 July	Turin	1	1*

**After extra time*

		v GREECE	E	G
EC1971	21 Apr	Wembley	3	0
EC1971	1 Dec	Piraeus	2	0
EC1982	17 Nov	Salonika	3	0
EC1983	30 Mar	Wembley	0	0
1989	8 Feb	Athens	2	1
1994	17 May	Wembley	5	0
WC2001	6 June	Athens	2	0
WC2001	6 Oct	Old Trafford	2	2

		v HOLLAND	E	H
1935	18 May	Amsterdam	1	0
1946	27 Nov	Huddersfield	8	2
1964	9 Dec	Amsterdam	1	1
1969	5 Nov	Amsterdam	1	0
1970	14 Jun	Wembley	0	0
1977	9 Feb	Wembley	0	2
1982	25 May	Wembley	2	0
1988	23 Mar	Wembley	2	2
EC1988	15 June	Dusseldorf	1	3
WC1990	16 June	Cagliari	0	0
WC1993	28 Apr	Wembley	2	2
WC1993	13 Oct	Rotterdam	0	2
EC1996	18 June	Wembley	4	1
2001	15 Aug	Tottenham	0	2
2002	13 Feb	Amsterdam	1	1

		v HUNGARY	E	H
1908	10 June	Budapest	7	0
1909	29 May	Budapest	4	2
1909	31 May	Budapest	8	2
1934	10 May	Budapest	1	2
1936	2 Dec	Highbury	6	2
1953	25 Nov	Wembley	3	6
1954	23 May	Budapest	1	7
1960	22 May	Budapest	0	2
WC1962	31 May	Rancagua	1	2
1965	5 May	Wembley	1	0
1978	24 May	Wembley	4	1
WC1981	6 June	Budapest	3	1
WC1982	18 Nov	Wembley	1	0
EC1983	27 Apr	Wembley	2	0
EC1983	12 Oct	Budapest	3	0
1988	27 Apr	Budapest	0	0
1990	12 Sept	Wembley	1	0
1992	12 May	Budapest	1	0
1996	18 May	Wembley	3	0
1999	28 Apr	Budapest	1	1

		v ICELAND	E	I
1982	2 June	Reykjavik	1	1

		v REPUBLIC OF IRELAND	E	RI
1946	30 Sept	Dublin	1	0
1949	21 Sept	Everton	0	2
WC1957	8 May	Wembley	5	1
WC1957	19 May	Dublin	1	1
1964	24 May	Dublin	3	1
1976	8 Sept	Wembley	1	1
EC1978	25 Oct	Dublin	1	1
EC1980	6 Feb	Wembley	2	0
1985	26 Mar	Wembley	2	1
EC1988	12 June	Stuttgart	0	1
WC1990	11 June	Cagliari	1	1
EC1990	14 Nov	Dublin	1	1
EC1991	27 Mar	Wembley	1	1
1995	15 Feb	Dublin	0	1

(abandoned after 27 mins)

		v ISRAEL	E	I
1986	26 Feb	Ramat Gan	2	1
1988	17 Feb	Tel Aviv	0	0

		v ITALY	E	I
1933	13 May	Rome	1	1
1934	14 Nov	Highbury	3	2
1939	13 May	Milan	2	2
1948	16 May	Turin	4	0
1949	30 Nov	Tottenham	2	0
1952	18 May	Florence	1	1
1959	6 May	Wembley	2	2
1961	24 May	Rome	3	2
1973	14 June	Turin	0	2
1973	14 Nov	Wembley	0	1
1976	28 May	New York	3	2
WC1976	17 Nov	Rome	0	2
WC1977	16 Nov	Wembley	2	0
EC1980	15 June	Turin	0	1
1985	6 June	Mexico City	1	2
1989	15 Nov	Wembley	0	0
WC1990	7 July	Bari	1	2
WC1997	12 Feb	Wembley	0	1
TF1997	4 June	Nantes	2	0
WC1997	11 Oct	Rome	0	0
2000	15 Nov	Turin	0	1
2002	27 Mar	Leeds	1	2

		v JAPAN	E	J
UI1995	3 June	Wembley	2	1

		v KUWAIT	E	K
WC1982	25 June	Bilbao	1	0

		v LIECHTENSTEIN	E	L
EC2003	29 Mar	Vaduz	2	0

		v LUXEMBOURG	E	L
1927	21 May	Esch-sur-Alzette	5	2
WC1960	19 Oct	Luxembourg	9	0
WC1961	28 Sept	Highbury	4	1
WC1977	30 Mar	Wembley	5	0
WC1977	12 Oct	Luxembourg	2	0
EC1982	15 Dec	Wembley	9	0
EC1983	16 Nov	Luxembourg	4	0
EC1998	14 Oct	Luxembourg	3	0
EC1999	4 Sept	Wembley	6	0

		v MACEDONIA	E	M
EC2002	16 Oct	Southampton	2	2

		v MALAYSIA	E	M
1991	12 June	Kuala Lumpur	4	2

		v MALTA	E	M
EC1971	3 Feb	Valletta	1	0
EC1971	12 May	Wembley	5	0
2000	3 June	Valletta	2	1

		v MEXICO	E	M
1959	24 May	Mexico City	1	2
1961	10 May	Wembley	8	0
WC1966	16 July	Wembley	2	0
1969	1 June	Mexico City	0	0
1985	9 June	Mexico City	0	1
1986	17 May	Los Angeles	3	0
1997	29 Mar	Wembley	2	0
2001	25 May	Derby	4	0

		v MOLDOVA	E	M
WC1996	1 Sept	Chisinau	3	0
WC1997	10 Sept	Wembley	4	0

		v MOROCCO	E	M
WC1986	6 June	Monterrey	0	0
1998	27 May	Casablanca	1	0

		v NEW ZEALAND	E	NZ
1991	3 June	Auckland	1	0
1991	8 June	Wellington	2	0

		v NIGERIA	E	N
1994	16 Nov	Wembley	1	0
WC2002	12 June	Osaka	0	0

		v NORWAY	E	N
1937	14 May	Oslo	6	0
1938	9 Nov	Newcastle	4	0
1949	18 May	Oslo	4	1
1966	29 June	Oslo	6	1
WC1980	10 Sept	Wembley	4	0
WC1981	9 Sept	Oslo	1	2
WC1992	14 Oct	Wembley	1	1
WC1993	2 June	Oslo	0	2
1994	22 May	Wembley	0	0
1995	11 Oct	Oslo	0	0

		v PARAGUAY	E	P
WC1986	18 June	Mexico City	3	0
2002	17 Apr	Liverpool	4	0

		v PERU	E	P
1959	17 May	Lima	1	4
1962	20 May	Lima	4	0

		v POLAND	E	P
1966	5 Jan	Everton	1	1
1966	5 July	Chorzow	1	0
WC1973	6 June	Chorzow	0	2
WC1973	17 Oct	Wembley	1	1
WC1986	11 June	Monterrey	3	0
WC1989	3 June	Wembley	3	0
WC1989	11 Oct	Katowice	0	0
EC1990	17 Oct	Wembley	2	0
EC1991	13 Nov	Poznan	1	1
WC1993	29 May	Katowice	1	1
WC1993	8 Sept	Wembley	3	0

			E	P
WC1996	9 Oct	Wembley	2	1
WC1997	31 May	Katowice	2	0
EC1999	27 Mar	Wembley	3	1
EC1999	8 Sept	Warsaw	0	0

		v PORTUGAL	E	P
1947	25 May	Lisbon	10	0
1950	14 May	Lisbon	5	3
1951	19 May	Everton	5	2
1955	22 May	Oporto	1	3
1958	7 May	Wembley	2	1
WC1961	21 May	Lisbon	1	1
WC1961	25 Oct	Wembley	2	0
1964	17 May	Lisbon	4	3
1964	4 June	São Paulo	1	1
WC1966	26 July	Wembley	2	1
1969	10 Dec	Wembley	1	0
1974	3 Apr	Lisbon	0	0
EC1974	20 Nov	Wembley	0	0
EC1975	19 Nov	Lisbon	1	1
WC1986	3 June	Monterrey	0	1
1995	12 Dec	Wembley	1	1
1998	22 Apr	Wembley	3	0
EC2000	12 June	Eindhoven	2	3
2002	7 Sept	Villa Park	1	1

		v ROMANIA	E	R
1939	24 May	Bucharest	2	0
1968	6 Nov	Bucharest	0	0
1969	15 Jan	Wembley	1	1
WC1970	2 June	Guadalajara	1	0
WC1980	15 Oct	Bucharest	1	2
WC1981	29 April	Wembley	0	0
WC1985	1 May	Bucharest	0	0
WC1985	11 Sept	Wembley	1	1
1994	12 Oct	Wembley	1	1
WC1998	22 June	Toulouse	1	2
EC2000	20 June	Charleroi	2	3

		v SAN MARINO	E	SM
WC1992	17 Feb	Wembley	6	0
WC1993	17 Nov	Bologna	7	1

		v SAUDI ARABIA	E	SA
1988	16 Nov	Riyadh	1	1
1998	23 May	Wembley	0	0

		v SERBIA-MONTENEGRO	E	S-M
2003	3 June	Leicester	2	1

		v SLOVAKIA	E	S
EC2002	12 Oct	Bratislava	2	1
EC2003	11 June	Middlesbrough	2	1

		v SOUTH AFRICA	E	SA
1997	24 May	Old Trafford	2	1
2003	22 May	Durban	2	1

		v SOUTH KOREA	E	SK
2002	21 May	Seoguipo	1	1

		v SPAIN	E	S
1929	15 May	Madrid	3	4
1931	9 Dec	Highbury	7	1
WC1950	2 July	Rio de Janeiro	0	1
1955	18 May	Madrid	1	1
1955	30 Nov	Wembley	4	1
1960	15 May	Madrid	0	3
1960	26 Oct	Wembley	4	2
1965	8 Dec	Madrid	2	0
1967	24 May	Wembley	2	0
EC1968	3 Apr	Wembley	1	0
EC1968	8 May	Madrid	2	1
1980	26 Mar	Barcelona	2	0
EC1980	18 June	Naples	2	1
1981	25 Mar	Wembley	1	2
WC1982	5 July	Madrid	0	0
1987	18 Feb	Madrid	4	2
1992	9 Sept	Santander	0	1
EC 1996	22 June	Wembley	0	0
2001	28 Feb	Villa Park	3	0

		v SWEDEN	*E*	*S*
1923	21 May	Stockholm	4	2
1923	24 May	Stockholm	3	1
1937	17 May	Stockholm	4	0
1947	19 Nov	Highbury	4	2
1949	13 May	Stockholm	1	3
1956	16 May	Stockholm	0	0
1959	28 Oct	Wembley	2	3
1965	16 May	Gothenburg	2	1
1968	22 May	Wembley	3	1
1979	10 June	Stockholm	0	0
1986	10 Sept	Stockholm	0	1
WC1988	19 Oct	Wembley	0	0
WC1989	6 Sept	Stockholm	0	0
EC1992	17 June	Stockholm	1	2
UI1995	8 June	Leeds	3	3
EC1998	5 Sept	Stockholm	1	2
EC1999	5 June	Wembley	0	0
2001	10 Nov	Old Trafford	1	1
WC2002	2 June	Saitama	1	1

		v SWITZERLAND	*E*	*S*
1933	20 May	Berne	4	0
1938	21 May	Zurich	1	2
1947	18 May	Zurich	0	1
1948	2 Dec	Highbury	6	0
1952	28 May	Zurich	3	0
WC1954	20 June	Berne	2	0
1962	9 May	Wembley	3	1
1963	5 June	Basle	8	1
EC1971	13 Oct	Basle	3	2
EC1971	10 Nov	Wembley	1	1
1975	3 Sept	Basle	2	1
1977	7 Sept	Wembley	0	0
WC1980	19 Nov	Wembley	2	1
WC1981	30 May	Basle	1	2
1988	28 May	Lausanne	1	0
1995	15 Nov	Wembley	3	1
EC1996	8 June	Wembley	1	1
1998	25 Mar	Berne	1	1

		v TUNISIA	*E*	*T*
1990	2 June	Tunis	1	1
WC1998	15 June	Marseilles	2	0

		v TURKEY	*E*	*T*
WC1984	14 Nov	Istanbul	8	0
WC1985	16 Oct	Wembley	5	0
EC1987	29 Apr	Izmir	0	0
EC1987	14 Oct	Wembley	8	0
EC1991	1 May	Izmir	1	0
EC1991	16 Oct	Wembley	1	0
WC1992	18 Nov	Wembley	4	0
WC1993	31 Mar	Izmir	2	0
EC2003	2 Apr	Sunderland	2	0

		v UKRAINE	*E*	*U*
2000	31 May	Wembley	2	0

		v URUGUAY	*E*	*U*
1953	31 May	Montevideo	1	2
WC1954	26 June	Basle	2	4
1964	6 May	Wembley	2	1
WC1966	11 July	Wembley	0	0
1969	8 June	Montevideo	2	1
1977	15 June	Montevideo	0	0
1984	13 June	Montevideo	0	2
1990	22 May	Wembley	1	2
1995	29 Mar	Wembley	0	0

		v USA	*E*	*USA*
WC1950	29 June	Belo Horizonte	0	1
1953	8 June	New York	6	3
1959	28 May	Los Angeles	8	1
1964	27 May	New York	10	0
1985	16 June	Los Angeles	5	0
1993	9 June	Foxboro	0	2
1994	7 Sept	Wembley	2	0

		v USSR	*E*	*USSR*
1958	18 May	Moscow	1	1
WC1958	8 June	Gothenburg	2	2
WC1958	17 June	Gothenburg	0	1
1958	22 Oct	Wembley	5	0
1967	6 Dec	Wembley	2	2
EC1968	8 June	Rome	2	0
1973	10 June	Moscow	2	1
1984	2 June	Wembley	0	2
1986	26 Mar	Tbilisi	1	0
EC1988	18 June	Frankfurt	1	3
1991	21 May	Wembley	3	1

		v YUGOSLAVIA	*E*	*Y*
1939	18 May	Belgrade	1	2
1950	22 Nov	Highbury	2	2
1954	16 May	Belgrade	0	1
1956	28 Nov	Wembley	3	0
1958	11 May	Belgrade	0	5
1960	11 May	Wembley	3	3
1965	9 May	Belgrade	1	1
1966	4 May	Wembley	2	0
EC1968	5 June	Florence	0	1
1972	11 Oct	Wembley	1	1
1974	5 June	Belgrade	2	2
EC1986	12 Nov	Wembley	2	0
EC1987	11 Nov	Belgrade	4	1
1989	13 Dec	Wembley	2	1

SCOTLAND

		v ARGENTINA	*S*	*A*
1977	18 June	Buenos Aires	1	1
1979	2 June	Glasgow	1	3
1990	28 Mar	Glasgow	1	0

		v AUSTRALIA	*S*	*A*
WC1985	20 Nov	Glasgow	2	0
WC1985	4 Dec	Melbourne	0	0
1996	27 Mar	Glasgow	1	0
2000	15 Nov	Glasgow	0	2

		v AUSTRIA	*S*	*A*
1931	16 May	Vienna	0	5
1933	29 Nov	Glasgow	2	2
1937	9 May	Vienna	1	1
1950	13 Dec	Glasgow	0	1
1951	27 May	Vienna	0	4
WC1954	16 June	Zurich	0	1
1955	19 May	Vienna	4	1
1956	2 May	Glasgow	1	1
1960	29 May	Vienna	1	4
1963	8 May	Glasgow	4	1
	(*abandoned after 79 mins*)			
WC1968	6 Nov	Glasgow	2	1
WC1969	5 Nov	Vienna	0	2
EC1978	20 Sept	Vienna	2	3
EC1979	17 Oct	Glasgow	1	1
1994	20 Apr	Vienna	2	1
WC1996	31 Aug	Vienna	0	0
WC1997	2 Apr	Celtic Park	2	0
2003	30 Apr	Glasgow	0	2

		v BELARUS	*S*	*B*
WC1997	8 June	Minsk	1	0
WC1997	7 Sept	Aberdeen	4	1

		v BELGIUM	*S*	*B*
1947	18 May	Brussels	1	2
1948	28 Apr	Glasgow	2	0
1951	20 May	Brussels	5	0
EC1971	3 Feb	Liège	0	3

			S	*B*
EC1971	10 Nov	Aberdeen	1	0
1974	2 June	Brussels	1	2
EC1979	21 Nov	Brussels	0	2
EC1979	19 Dec	Glasgow	1	3
EC1982	15 Dec	Brussels	2	3
EC1983	12 Oct	Glasgow	1	1
EC1987	1 Apr	Brussels	1	4
EC1987	14 Oct	Glasgow	2	0
WC2001	24 Mar	Glasgow	2	2
WC2001	5 Sept	Brussels	0	2

		v BOSNIA	*S*	*B*
EC1999	4 Sept	Sarajevo	2	1
EC1999	5 Oct	Glasgow	1	0

		v BRAZIL	*S*	*B*
1966	25 June	Glasgow	1	1
1972	5 July	Rio de Janeiro	0	1
1973	30 June	Glasgow	0	1
WC1974	18 June	Frankfurt	0	0
1977	23 June	Rio de Janeiro	0	2
WC1982	18 June	Seville	1	4
1987	26 May	Glasgow	0	2
WC1990	20 June	Turin	0	1
WC1998	10 June	Sant-Denis	1	2

		v BULGARIA	*S*	*B*
1978	22 Feb	Glasgow	2	1
EC1986	10 Sept	Glasgow	0	0
EC1987	11 Nov	Sofia	1	0
EC1990	14 Nov	Sofia	1	1
EC1991	27 Mar	Glasgow	1	1

		v CANADA	*S*	*C*
1983	12 June	Vancouver	2	0
1983	16 June	Edmonton	3	0
1983	20 June	Toronto	2	0
1992	21 May	Toronto	3	1
2002	15 Oct	Easter Road	3	1

		v CHILE	*S*	*C*
1977	15 June	Santiago	4	2
1989	30 May	Glasgow	2	0

		v CIS	*S*	*C*
EC1992	18 June	Norrkoping	3	0

		v COLOMBIA	*S*	*C*
1988	17 May	Glasgow	0	0
1996	30 May	Miami	0	1
1998	23 May	New York	2	2

		v COSTA RICA	*S*	*CR*
WC1990	11 June	Genoa	0	1

		v CROATIA	*S*	*C*
WC2000	11 Oct	Zagreb	1	1
WC2001	1 Sept	Glasgow	0	0

		v CYPRUS	*S*	*C*
WC1968	17 Dec	Nicosia	5	0
WC1969	11 May	Glasgow	8	0
WC1989	8 Feb	Limassol	3	2
WC1989	26 Apr	Glasgow	2	1

		v CZECHOSLOVAKIA	*S*	*C*
1937	22 May	Prague	3	1
1937	8 Dec	Glasgow	5	0
WC1961	14 May	Bratislava	0	4
WC1961	26 Sept	Glasgow	3	2
WC1961	29 Nov	Brussels	2	4*
1972	2 July	Porto Alegre	0	0
WC1973	26 Sept	Glasgow	2	1
WC1973	17 Oct	Prague	0	1
WC1976	13 Oct	Prague	0	2
WC1977	21 Sept	Glasgow	3	1

**After extra time*

		v CZECH REPUBLIC	*S*	*C*
EC1999	31 Mar	Glasgow	1	2
EC1999	9 June	Prague	2	3

		v DENMARK	*S*	*D*
1951	12 May	Glasgow	3	1
1952	25 May	Copenhagen	2	1
1968	16 Oct	Copenhagen	1	0
EC1970	11 Nov	Glasgow	1	0
EC1971	9 June	Copenhagen	0	1
WC1972	18 Oct	Copenhagen	4	1
WC1972	15 Nov	Glasgow	2	0
EC1975	3 Sept	Copenhagen	1	0
EC1975	29 Oct	Glasgow	3	1
WC1986	4 June	Nezahualcayotl	0	1
1996	24 Apr	Copenhagen	0	2
1998	25 Mar	Glasgow	0	1
2002	21 Aug	Glasgow	0	1

		v ECUADOR	*S*	*E*
1995	24 May	Toyama	2	1

		v EGYPT	*S*	*E*
1990	16 May	Aberdeen	1	3

		v ESTONIA	*S*	*E*
WC1993	19 May	Tallinn	3	0
WC1993	2 June	Aberdeen	3	1
WC1997	11 Feb	Monaco	0	0
WC1997	29 Mar	Kilmarnock	2	0
EC1998	10 Oct	Edinburgh	3	2
EC1999	8 Sept	Tallinn	0	0

		v FAEROES	*S*	*F*
EC1994	12 Oct	Glasgow	5	1
EC1995	7 June	Toftir	2	0
EC1998	14 Oct	Aberdeen	2	1
EC1999	5 June	Toftir	1	1
EC2002	7 Sept	Toftir	2	2

		v FINLAND	*S*	*F*
1954	25 May	Helsinki	2	1
WC1964	21 Oct	Glasgow	3	1
WC1965	27 May	Helsinki	2	1
1976	8 Sept	Glasgow	6	0
1992	25 Mar	Glasgow	1	1
EC1994	7 Sept	Helsinki	2	0
EC1995	6 Sept	Glasgow	1	0
1998	22 Apr	Edinburgh	1	1

		v FRANCE	*S*	*F*
1930	18 May	Paris	2	0
1932	8 May	Paris	3	1
1948	23 May	Paris	0	3
1949	27 Apr	Glasgow	2	0
1950	27 May	Paris	1	0
1951	16 May	Glasgow	1	0
WC1958	15 June	Orebro	1	2
1984	1 June	Marseilles	0	2
WC1989	8 Mar	Glasgow	2	0
WC1989	11 Oct	Paris	0	3
1997	12 Nov	St Etienne	1	2
2000	29 Mar	Glasgow	0	2
2002	27 Mar	Paris	0	5

		v GERMANY	*S*	*G*
1929	1 June	Berlin	1	1
1936	14 Oct	Glasgow	2	0
EC1992	15 June	Norrkoping	0	2
1993	24 Mar	Glasgow	0	1
1998	28 Apr	Bremen	1	0
EC2003	7 June	Glasgow	1	1

		v EAST GERMANY	*S*	*EG*
1974	30 Oct	Glasgow	3	0
1977	7 Sept	East Berlin	0	1
EC1982	13 Oct	Glasgow	2	0
EC1983	16 Nov	Halle	1	2
1985	16 Oct	Glasgow	0	0
1990	25 Apr	Glasgow	0	1

		v WEST GERMANY	*S*	*WG*
1957	22 May	Stuttgart	3	1
1959	6 May	Glasgow	3	2
1964	12 May	Hanover	2	2
WC1969	16 Apr	Glasgow	1	1
WC1969	22 Oct	Hamburg	2	3
1973	14 Nov	Glasgow	1	1
1974	27 Mar	Frankfurt	1	2
WC1986	8 June	Queretaro	1	2

		v GREECE	*S*	*G*
EC1994	18 Dec	Athens	0	1
EC1995	16 Aug	Glasgow	1	0

		v HOLLAND	*S*	*H*
1929	4 June	Amsterdam	2	0
1938	21 May	Amsterdam	3	1
1959	27 May	Amsterdam	2	1
1966	11 May	Glasgow	0	3
1968	30 May	Amsterdam	0	0
1971	1 Dec	Rotterdam	1	2
WC1978	11 June	Mendoza	3	2
1982	23 Mar	Glasgow	2	1
1986	29 Apr	Eindhoven	0	0
EC1992	12 June	Gothenburg	0	1
1994	23 Mar	Glasgow	0	1
1994	27 May	Utrecht	1	3
EC1996	10 June	Birmingham	0	0
2000	26 Apr	Arnhem	0	0

		v HONG KONG XI	*S*	*HK*
†2002	23 May	Hong Kong	4	0

		v HUNGARY	*S*	*H*
1938	7 Dec	Glasgow	3	1
1954	8 Dec	Glasgow	2	4
1955	29 May	Budapest	1	3
1958	7 May	Glasgow	1	1
1960	5 June	Budapest	3	3
1980	31 May	Budapest	1	3
1987	9 Sept	Glasgow	2	0

		v ICELAND	*S*	*I*
WC1984	17 Oct	Glasgow	3	0
WC1985	28 May	Reykjavik	1	0
EC2002	12 Oct	Reykjavik	2	0
EC2003	29 Mar	Glasgow	2	1

		v IRAN	*S*	*I*
WC1978	7 June	Cordoba	1	1

		v REPUBLIC OF IRELAND	*S*	*RI*
WC1961	3 May	Glasgow	4	1
WC1961	7 May	Dublin	3	0
1963	9 June	Dublin	0	1
1969	21 Sept	Dublin	1	1
EC1986	15 Oct	Dublin	0	0
EC1987	18 Feb	Glasgow	0	1
2000	30 May	Dublin	2	1
2003	12 Feb	Glasgow	0	2

		v ISRAEL	*S*	*I*
WC1981	25 Feb	Tel Aviv	1	0
WC1981	28 Apr	Glasgow	3	1
1986	28 Jan	Tel Aviv	1	0

		v ITALY	*S*	*I*
1931	20 May	Rome	0	3
WC1965	9 Nov	Glasgow	1	0
WC1965	7 Dec	Naples	0	3
1988	22 Dec	Perugia	0	2
WC1992	18 Nov	Glasgow	0	0
WC1993	13 Oct	Rome	1	3

		v JAPAN	*S*	*J*
1995	21 May	Hiroshima	0	0

		v LATVIA	*S*	*L*
WC1996	5 Oct	Riga	2	0
WC1997	11 Oct	Glasgow	2	0
WC2000	2 Sept	Riga	1	0
WC2001	6 Oct	Glasgow	2	1

		v LITHUANIA	*S*	*L*
EC1998	5 Sept	Vilnius	0	0
EC1999	9 Oct	Glasgow	3	0
EC2003	2 Apr	Kaunas	0	1

		v LUXEMBOURG	*S*	*L*
1947	24 May	Luxembourg	6	0
EC1986	12 Nov	Glasgow	3	0
EC1987	2 Dec	Esch	0	0

		v MALTA	*S*	*M*
1988	22 Mar	Valletta	1	1
1990	28 May	Valletta	2	1
WC1993	17 Feb	Glasgow	3	0
WC1993	17 Nov	Valletta	2	0
1997	1 June	Valletta	3	2

		v MOROCCO	*S*	*M*
WC1998	23 June	St Etienne	0	3

		v NEW ZEALAND	*S*	*NZ*
WC1982	15 June	Malaga	5	2
2003	27 May	Tynecastle	1	1

		v NIGERIA	*S*	*N*
2002	17 Apr	Aberdeen	1	2

		v NORWAY	*S*	*N*
1929	28 May	Oslo	7	3
1954	5 May	Glasgow	1	0
1954	19 May	Oslo	1	1
1963	4 June	Bergen	3	4
1963	7 Nov	Glasgow	6	1
1974	6 June	Oslo	2	1
EC1978	25 Oct	Glasgow	3	2
EC1979	7 June	Oslo	4	0
WC1988	14 Sept	Oslo	2	1
WC1989	15 Nov	Glasgow	1	1
1992	3 June	Oslo	0	0
WC1998	16 June	Bordeaux	1	1

		v PARAGUAY	*S*	*P*
WC1958	11 June	Norrkoping	2	3

		v PERU	*S*	*P*
1972	26 Apr	Glasgow	2	0
WC1978	3 June	Cordoba	1	3
1979	12 Sept	Glasgow	1	1

		v POLAND	*S*	*P*
1958	1 June	Warsaw	2	1
1960	4 June	Glasgow	2	3
WC1965	23 May	Chorzow	1	1
WC1965	13 Oct	Glasgow	1	2
1980	28 May	Poznan	0	1
1990	19 May	Glasgow	1	1
2001	25 Apr	Bydgoszcz	1	1

		v PORTUGAL	*S*	*P*
1950	21 May	Lisbon	2	2
1955	4 May	Glasgow	3	0
1959	3 June	Lisbon	0	1
1966	18 June	Glasgow	0	1
EC1971	21 Apr	Lisbon	0	2
EC1971	13 Oct	Glasgow	2	1
1975	13 May	Glasgow	1	0
EC1978	29 Nov	Lisbon	0	1
EC1980	26 Mar	Glasgow	4	1
WC1980	15 Oct	Glasgow	0	0
WC1981	18 Nov	Lisbon	1	2
WC1992	14 Oct	Glasgow	0	0
WC1993	28 Apr	Lisbon	0	5
2002	20 Nov	Braga	0	2

		v ROMANIA	*S*	*R*
EC1975	1 June	Bucharest	1	1
EC1975	17 Dec	Glasgow	1	1
1986	26 Mar	Glasgow	3	0
EC1990	12 Sept	Glasgow	2	1
EC1991	16 Oct	Bucharest	0	1

		v RUSSIA	*S*	*R*
EC1994	16 Nov	Glasgow	1	1
EC1995	29 Mar	Moscow	0	0

		v SAN MARINO	*S*	*SM*
EC1991	1 May	Serravalle	2	0
EC1991	13 Nov	Glasgow	4	0
EC1995	26 Apr	Serravalle	2	0
EC1995	15 Nov	Glasgow	5	0
WC2000	7 Oct	Serravalle	2	0
WC2001	28 Mar	Glasgow	4	0

		v SAUDI ARABIA	S	SA
1988	17 Feb	Riyadh	2	2

		v SOUTH AFRICA	S	SA
2002	20 May	Hong Kong	0	2

		v SOUTH KOREA	S	SK
2002	16 May	Busan	1	4

		v SPAIN	S	Sp
WC1957	8 May	Glasgow	4	2
WC1957	26 May	Madrid	1	4
1963	13 June	Madrid	6	2
1965	8 May	Glasgow	0	0
EC1974	20 Nov	Glasgow	1	2
EC1975	5 Feb	Valencia	1	1
1982	24 Feb	Valencia	0	3
WC1984	14 Nov	Glasgow	3	1
WC1985	27 Feb	Seville	0	1
1988	27 Apr	Madrid	0	0

		v SWEDEN	S	Sw
1952	30 May	Stockholm	1	3
1953	6 May	Glasgow	1	2
1975	16 Apr	Gothenburg	1	1
1977	27 Apr	Glasgow	3	1
WC1980	10 Sept	Stockholm	1	0
WC1981	9 Sept	Glasgow	2	0
WC1990	16 June	Genoa	2	1
1995	11 Oct	Stockholm	0	2
WC1996	10 Nov	Glasgow	1	0
WC1997	30 Apr	Gothenburg	1	2

		v SWITZERLAND	S	Sw
1931	24 May	Geneva	3	2
1948	17 May	Berne	1	2
1950	26 Apr	Glasgow	3	1
WC1957	19 May	Basle	2	1
WC1957	6 Nov	Glasgow	3	2
1973	22 June	Berne	0	1
1976	7 Apr	Glasgow	1	0
EC1982	17 Nov	Berne	0	2
EC1983	30 May	Glasgow	2	2
EC1990	17 Oct	Glasgow	2	1
EC1991	11 Sept	Berne	2	2
WC1992	9 Sept	Berne	1	3
WC1993	8 Sept	Aberdeen	1	1
EC1996	18 June	Birmingham	1	0

		v TURKEY	S	T
1960	8 June	Ankara	2	4

		v URUGUAY	S	U
WC1954	19 June	Basle	0	7
1962	2 May	Glasgow	2	3
1983	21 Sept	Glasgow	2	0
WC1986	13 June	Nezahualcoyotl	0	0

		v USA	S	USA
1952	30 Apr	Glasgow	6	0
1992	17 May	Denver	1	0
1996	26 May	New Britain	1	2
1998	30 May	Washington	0	0

		v USSR	S	USSR
1967	10 May	Glasgow	0	2
1971	14 June	Moscow	0	1
WC1982	22 June	Malaga	2	2
1991	6 Feb	Glasgow	0	1

		v YUGOSLAVIA	S	Y
1955	15 May	Belgrade	2	2
1956	21 Nov	Glasgow	2	0
WC1958	8 June	Vasteras	1	1
1972	29 June	Belo Horizonte	2	2
WC1974	22 June	Frankfurt	1	1
1984	12 Sept	Glasgow	6	1
WC1988	19 Oct	Glasgow	1	1
WC1989	6 Sept	Zagreb	1	3

		v ZAIRE	S	Z
WC1974	14 June	Dortmund	2	0

†*match not recognised by FIFA*

WALES

		v ALBANIA	W	A
EC1994	7 Sept	Cardiff	2	0
EC1995	15 Nov	Tirana	1	1

		v ARGENTINA	W	A
1992	3 June	Tokyo	0	1
2002	13 Feb	Cardiff	1	1

		v ARMENIA	W	A
WC2001	24 Mar	Erevan	2	2
WC2001	1 Sept	Cardiff	0	0

		v AUSTRIA	W	A
1954	9 May	Vienna	0	2
EC1955	23 Nov	Wrexham	1	2
EC1974	4 Sept	Vienna	1	2
1975	19 Nov	Wrexham	1	0
1992	29 Apr	Vienna	1	1

		v AZERBAIJAN	W	A
EC2002	20 Nov	Baku	2	0
EC2003	29 Mar	Cardiff	4	0

		v BELARUS	W	B
EC1998	14 Oct	Cardiff	3	2
EC1999	4 Sept	Minsk	2	2
WC2000	2 Sept	Minsk	1	2
WC2001	6 Oct	Cardiff	1	0

		v BELGIUM	W	B
1949	22 May	Liège	1	3
1949	23 Nov	Cardiff	5	1
EC1990	17 Oct	Cardiff	3	1
EC1991	27 Mar	Brussels	1	1
WC1992	18 Nov	Brussels	0	2
WC1993	31 Mar	Cardiff	2	0
WC1997	29 Mar	Cardiff	1	2
WC1997	11 Oct	Brussels	2	3

		v BOSNIA	W	B
2003	12 Feb	Cardiff	2	2

		v BRAZIL	W	B
WC1958	19 June	Gothenburg	0	1
1962	12 May	Rio de Janeiro	1	3
1962	16 May	São Paulo	1	3
1966	14 May	Rio de Janeiro	1	3
1966	18 May	Belo Horizonte	0	1
1983	12 June	Cardiff	1	1
1991	11 Sept	Cardiff	1	0
1997	12 Nov	Brasilia	0	3
2000	23 May	Cardiff	0	3

		v BULGARIA	W	B
EC1983	27 Apr	Wrexham	1	0
EC1983	16 Nov	Sofia	0	1
EC1994	14 Dec	Cardiff	0	3
EC1995	29 Mar	Sofia	1	3

		v CANADA	W	C
1986	10 May	Toronto	0	2
1986	20 May	Vancouver	3	0

		v CHILE	W	C
1966	22 May	Santiago	0	2

		v COSTA RICA	W	CR
1990	20 May	Cardiff	1	0

		v CROATIA	W	C
2002	21 Aug	Varazdin	1	1

		v CYPRUS	W	C
WC1992	14 Oct	Limassol	1	0
WC1993	13 Oct	Cardiff	2	0

		v CZECHOSLOVAKIA	*W*	*C*
WC1957	1 May	Cardiff	1	0
WC1957	26 May	Prague	0	2
EC1971	21 Apr	Swansea	1	3
EC1971	27 Oct	Prague	0	1
WC1977	30 Mar	Wrexham	3	0
WC1977	16 Nov	Prague	0	1
WC1980	19 Nov	Cardiff	1	0
WC1981	9 Sept	Prague	0	2
EC1987	29 Apr	Wrexham	1	1
EC1987	11 Nov	Prague	0	2
WC1993	28 Apr	Ostrava†	1	1
WC1993	8 Sept	Cardiff†	2	2

†*Czechoslovakia played as RCS (Republic of Czechs and Slovaks).*

		v CZECH REPUBLIC	*W*	*CR*
2002	27 Mar	Cardiff	0	0

		v DENMARK	*W*	*D*
WC1964	21 Oct	Copenhagen	0	1
WC1965	1 Dec	Wrexham	4	2
EC1987	9 Sept	Cardiff	1	0
EC1987	14 Oct	Copenhagen	0	1
1990	11 Sept	Copenhagen	0	1
EC1998	10 Oct	Copenhagen	2	1
EC1999	9 June	Liverpool	0	2

		v ESTONIA	*W*	*E*
1994	23 May	Tallinn	2	1

		v FINLAND	*W*	*F*
EC1971	26 May	Helsinki	1	0
EC1971	13 Oct	Swansea	3	0
EC1987	10 Sept	Helsinki	1	1
EC1987	1 Apr	Wrexham	4	0
WC1988	19 Oct	Swansea	2	2
WC1989	6 Sept	Helsinki	0	1
2000	29 Mar	Cardiff	1	2
EC2002	7 Sept	Helsinki	2	0

		v FAEROES	*W*	*F*
WC1992	9 Sept	Cardiff	6	0
WC1993	6 June	Toftir	3	0

		v FRANCE	*W*	*F*
1933	25 May	Paris	1	1
1939	20 May	Paris	1	2
1953	14 May	Paris	1	6
1982	2 June	Toulouse	1	0

		v GEORGIA	*W*	*G*
EC1994	16 Nov	Tbilisi	0	5
EC1995	7 June	Cardiff	0	1

		v GERMANY	*W*	*G*
EC1995	26 Apr	Dusseldorf	1	1
EC1995	11 Oct	Cardiff	1	2
2002	14 May	Cardiff	1	0

		v EAST GERMANY	*W*	*EG*
WC1957	19 May	Leipzig	1	2
WC1957	25 Sept	Cardiff	4	1
WC1969	16 Apr	Dresden	1	2
WC1969	22 Oct	Cardiff	1	3

		v WEST GERMANY	*W*	*WG*
1968	8 May	Cardiff	1	1
1969	26 Mar	Frankfurt	1	1
1976	6 Oct	Cardiff	0	2
1977	14 Dec	Dortmund	1	1
EC1979	2 May	Wrexham	0	2
EC1979	17 Oct	Cologne	1	5
WC1989	31 May	Cardiff	0	0
WC1989	15 Nov	Cologne	1	2
EC1991	5 June	Cardiff	1	0
EC1991	16 Oct	Nuremberg	1	4

		v GREECE	*W*	*G*
WC1964	9 Dec	Athens	0	2
WC1965	17 Mar	Cardiff	4	1

		v HOLLAND	*W*	*H*
WC1988	14 Sept	Amsterdam	0	1
WC1989	11 Oct	Wrexham	1	2
1992	30 May	Utrecht	0	4
WC1996	5 Oct	Cardiff	1	3
WC1996	9 Nov	Eindhoven	1	7

		v HUNGARY	*W*	*H*
WC1958	8 June	Sanviken	1	1
WC1958	17 June	Stockholm	2	1
1961	28 May	Budapest	2	3
EC1962	7 Nov	Budapest	1	3
EC1963	20 Mar	Cardiff	1	1
EC1974	30 Oct	Cardiff	2	0
EC1975	16 Apr	Budapest	2	1
1985	16 Oct	Cardiff	0	3

		v ICELAND	*W*	*I*
WC1980	2 June	Reykjavik	4	0
WC1981	14 Oct	Swansea	2	2
WC1984	12 Sept	Reykjavik	0	1
WC1984	14 Nov	Cardiff	2	1
1991	1 May	Cardiff	1	0

		v IRAN	*W*	*I*
1978	18 Apr	Teheran	1	0

		v REPUBLIC OF IRELAND	*W*	*RI*
1960	28 Sept	Dublin	3	2
1979	11 Sept	Swansea	2	1
1981	24 Feb	Dublin	3	1
1986	26 Mar	Dublin	1	0
1990	28 Mar	Dublin	0	1
1991	6 Feb	Wrexham	0	3
1992	19 Feb	Dublin	1	0
1993	17 Feb	Dublin	1	2
1997	11 Feb	Cardiff	0	0

		v ISRAEL	*W*	*I*
WC1958	15 Jan	Tel Aviv	2	0
WC1958	5 Feb	Cardiff	2	0
1984	10 June	Tel Aviv	0	0
1989	8 Feb	Tel Aviv	3	3

		v ITALY	*W*	*I*
1965	1 May	Florence	1	4
WC1968	23 Oct	Cardiff	0	1
WC1969	4 Nov	Rome	1	4
1988	4 June	Brescia	1	0
1996	24 Jan	Terni	0	3
EC1998	5 Sept	Liverpool	0	2
EC1999	5 June	Bologna	0	4
EC2002	16 Oct	Cardiff	2	1

		v JAMAICA	*W*	*J*
1998	25 Mar	Cardiff	0	0

		v JAPAN	*W*	*J*
1992	7 June	Matsuyama	1	0

		v KUWAIT	*W*	*K*
1977	6 Sept	Wrexham	0	0
1977	20 Sept	Kuwait	0	0

		v LUXEMBOURG	*W*	*L*
EC1974	20 Nov	Swansea	5	0
EC1975	1 May	Luxembourg	3	1
EC1990	14 Nov	Luxembourg	1	0
EC1991	13 Nov	Cardiff	1	0

		v MALTA	*W*	*M*
EC1978	25 Oct	Wrexham	7	0
EC1979	2 June	Valletta	2	0
1988	1 June	Valletta	3	2
1998	3 June	Valletta	3	0

		v MEXICO	*W*	*M*
WC1958	11 June	Stockholm	1	1
1962	22 May	Mexico City	1	2

		v MOLDOVA	*W*	*M*
EC1994	12 Oct	Kishinev	2	3
EC1995	6 Sept	Cardiff	1	0

		v NORWAY	*W*	*N*
EC1982	22 Sept	Swansea	1	0
EC1983	21 Sept	Oslo	0	0
1984	6 June	Trondheim	0	1
1985	26 Feb	Wrexham	1	1
1985	5 June	Bergen	2	4
1994	9 Mar	Cardiff	1	3
WC2000	7 Oct	Cardiff	1	1
WC2001	5 Sept	Oslo	2	3

		v POLAND	*W*	*P*
WC1973	28 Mar	Cardiff	2	0
WC1973	26 Sept	Katowice	0	3
1991	29 May	Radom	0	0
WC2000	11 Oct	Warsaw	0	0
WC2001	2 June	Cardiff	1	2

		v PORTUGAL	*W*	*P*
1949	15 May	Lisbon	2	3
1951	12 May	Cardiff	2	1
2000	2 June	Chaves	0	3

		v QATAR	*W*	*Q*
2000	23 Feb	Doha	1	0

		v ROMANIA	*W*	*R*
EC1970	11 Nov	Cardiff	0	0
EC1971	24 Nov	Bucharest	0	2
1983	12 Oct	Wrexham	5	0
WC1992	20 May	Bucharest	1	5
WC1993	17 Nov	Cardiff	1	2

		v SAN MARINO	*W*	*SM*
WC1996	2 June	Serravalle	5	0
WC1996	31 Aug	Cardiff	6	0

		v SAUDI ARABIA	*W*	*SA*
1986	25 Feb	Dahran	2	1

		v SPAIN	*W*	*S*
WC1961	19 Apr	Cardiff	1	2
WC1961	18 May	Madrid	1	1
1982	24 Mar	Valencia	1	1
WC1984	17 Oct	Seville	0	3
WC1985	30 Apr	Wrexham	3	0

		v SWEDEN	*W*	*S*
WC1958	15 June	Stockholm	0	0
1988	27 Apr	Stockholm	1	4
1989	26 Apr	Wrexham	0	2
1990	25 Apr	Stockholm	2	4
1994	20 Apr	Wrexham	0	2

		v SWITZERLAND	*W*	*S*
1949	26 May	Berne	0	4
1951	16 May	Wrexham	3	2
1996	24 Apr	Lugano	0	2
EC1999	31 Mar	Zurich	0	2
EC1999	9 Oct	Wrexham	0	2

		v TUNISIA	*W*	*T*
1998	6 June	Tunis	0	4

		v TURKEY	*W*	*T*
EC1978	29 Nov	Wrexham	1	0
EC1979	21 Nov	Izmir	0	1
WC1980	15 Oct	Cardiff	4	0
WC1981	25 Mar	Ankara	1	0
WC1996	14 Dec	Cardiff	0	0
WC1997	20 Aug	Istanbul	4	6

		v REST OF UNITED KINGDOM	*W*	*UK*
1951	5 Dec	Cardiff	3	2
1969	28 July	Cardiff	0	1

		v UKRAINE	*W*	*U*
WC2001	28 Mar	Cardiff	1	1
WC2001	6 June	Kiev	1	1

		v USA	*W*	*USA*
2003	27 May	San Jose	0	2

		v URUGUAY	*W*	*U*
1986	21 Apr	Wrexham	0	0

		v USSR	*W*	*USSR*
WC1965	30 May	Moscow	1	2
WC1965	27 Oct	Cardiff	2	1
WC1981	30 May	Wrexham	0	0
WC1981	18 Nov	Tbilisi	0	3
1987	18 Feb	Swansea	0	0

		v YUGOSLAVIA	*W*	*Y*
1953	21 May	Belgrade	2	5
1954	22 Nov	Cardiff	1	3
EC1976	24 Apr	Zagreb	0	2
EC1976	22 May	Cardiff	1	1
EC1982	15 Dec	Titograd	4	4
EC1983	14 Dec	Cardiff	1	1
1988	23 Mar	Swansea	1	2

NORTHERN IRELAND

		v ALBANIA	*NI*	*A*
WC1965	7 May	Belfast	4	1
WC1965	24 Nov	Tirana	1	1
EC1982	15 Dec	Tirana	0	0
EC1983	27 Apr	Belfast	1	0
WC1992	9 Sept	Belfast	3	0
WC1993	17 Feb	Tirana	2	1
WC1996	14 Dec	Belfast	2	0
WC1997	10 Sept	Zurich	0	1

		v ALGERIA	*NI*	*A*
WC1986	3 June	Guadalajara	1	1

		v ARGENTINA	*NI*	*A*
WC1958	11 June	Halmstad	1	3

		v ARMENIA	*NI*	*A*
WC1996	5 Oct	Belfast	1	1
WC1997	30 Apr	Erevan	0	0
EC2003	29 Mar	Erevan	0	1

		v AUSTRALIA	*NI*	*A*
1980	11 June	Sydney	2	1
1980	15 June	Melbourne	1	1
1980	18 June	Adelaide	2	1

		v AUSTRIA	*NI*	*A*
WC1982	1 July	Madrid	2	2
EC1982	13 Oct	Vienna	0	2
EC1983	21 Sept	Belfast	3	1
EC1990	14 Nov	Vienna	0	0
EC1991	16 Oct	Belfast	2	1
EC1994	12 Oct	Vienna	2	1
EC1995	15 Nov	Belfast	5	3

		v BELGIUM	*NI*	*B*
WC1976	10 Nov	Liège	0	2
WC1977	16 Nov	Belfast	3	0
1997	11 Feb	Belfast	3	0

		v BRAZIL	*NI*	*B*
WC1986	12 June	Guadalajara	0	3

		v BULGARIA	*NI*	*B*
WC1972	18 Oct	Sofia	0	3
WC1973	26 Sept	Sheffield	0	0
EC1978	29 Nov	Sofia	2	0
EC1979	2 May	Belfast	2	0
WC2001	28 Mar	Sofia	3	4
WC2001	2 June	Belfast	0	1

		v CANADA	*NI*	*C*
1995	22 May	Edmonton	0	2
1999	27 Apr	Belfast	1	1

		v CHILE	*NI*	*C*
1989	26 May	Belfast	0	1
1995	25 May	Edmonton	1	2

		v COLOMBIA	*NI*	*C*
1994	4 June	Boston	0	2

		v CYPRUS	*NI*	*C*
EC1971	3 Feb	Nicosia	3	0
EC1971	21 Apr	Belfast	5	0
WC1973	14 Feb	Nicosia	0	1
WC1973	8 May	London	3	0
2002	21 Aug	Belfast	0	0

		v CZECHOSLOVAKIA	*NI*	*C*
WC1958	8 June	Halmstad	1	0
WC1958	17 June	Malmo	2	1*

**After extra time*

		v CZECH REPUBLIC	*NI*	*C*
WC2001	24 Mar	Belfast	0	1
WC2001	6 June	Teplice	1	3

		v DENMARK	*NI*	*D*
EC1978	25 Oct	Belfast	2	1
EC1979	6 June	Copenhagen	0	4
1986	26 Mar	Belfast	1	1
EC1990	17 Oct	Belfast	1	1
EC1991	13 Nov	Odense	1	2
WC1992	18 Nov	Belfast	0	1
WC1993	13 Oct	Copenhagen	0	1
WC2000	7 Oct	Belfast	1	1
WC2001	1 Sept	Copenhagen	1	1

		v FAEROES	*NI*	*F*
EC1991	1 May	Belfast	1	1
EC1991	11 Sept	Landskrona	5	0

		v FINLAND	*NI*	*F*
WC1984	27 May	Pori	0	1
WC1984	14 Nov	Belfast	2	1
EC1998	10 Oct	Belfast	1	0
EC1998	9 Oct	Helsinki	1	4
2003	12 Feb	Belfast	0	1

		v FRANCE	*NI*	*F*
1928	21 Feb	Paris	0	4
1951	12 May	Belfast	2	2
1952	11 Nov	Paris	1	3
WC1958	19 June	Norrkoping	0	4
1982	24 Mar	Paris	0	4
WC1982	4 July	Madrid	1	4
1986	26 Feb	Paris	0	0
1988	27 Apr	Belfast	0	0
1999	18 Aug	Belfast	0	1

		v GERMANY	*NI*	*G*
1992	2 June	Bremen	1	1
1996	29 May	Belfast	1	1
WC1996	9 Nov	Nuremberg	1	1
WC1997	20 Aug	Belfast	1	3
EC1999	27 Mar	Belfast	0	3
EC1999	8 Sept	Dortmund	0	4

		v WEST GERMANY	*NI*	*WG*
WC1958	15 June	Malmo	2	2
WC1960	26 Oct	Belfast	3	4
WC1961	10 May	Hamburg	1	2
1966	7 May	Belfast	0	2
1977	27 Apr	Cologne	0	5
EC1982	17 Nov	Belfast	1	0
EC1983	16 Nov	Hamburg	1	0

		v GREECE	*NI*	*G*
WC1961	3 May	Athens	1	2
WC1961	17 Oct	Belfast	2	0
1988	17 Feb	Athens	2	3
EC2003	2 April	Belfast	0	2

		v HOLLAND	*NI*	*H*
1962	9 May	Rotterdam	0	4
WC1965	17 Mar	Belfast	2	1
WC1965	7 Apr	Rotterdam	0	0
WC1976	13 Oct	Rotterdam	2	2
WC1977	12 Oct	Belfast	0	1

		v HONDURAS	*NI*	*H*
WC1982	21 June	Zaragoza	1	1

		v HUNGARY	*NI*	*H*
WC1988	19 Oct	Budapest	0	1
WC1989	6 Sept	Belfast	1	2
2000	26 Apr	Belfast	0	1

		v ICELAND	*NI*	*I*
WC1977	11 June	Reykjavik	0	1
WC1977	21 Sept	Belfast	2	0
WC2000	11 Oct	Reykjavik	0	1
WC2001	5 Sept	Belfast	3	0

		v REPUBLIC OF IRELAND	*NI*	*RI*
EC1978	20 Sept	Dublin	0	0
EC1979	21 Nov	Belfast	1	0
WC1988	14 Sept	Belfast	0	0
WC1989	11 Oct	Dublin	0	3
WC1993	31 Mar	Dublin	0	3
WC1993	17 Nov	Belfast	1	1
EC1994	16 Nov	Belfast	0	4
EC1995	29 Mar	Dublin	1	1
1999	29 May	Dublin	1	0

		v ISRAEL	*NI*	*I*
1968	10 Sept	Jaffa	3	2
1976	3 Mar	Tel Aviv	1	1
WC1980	26 Mar	Tel Aviv	0	0
WC1981	18 Nov	Belfast	1	0
1984	16 Oct	Belfast	3	0
1987	18 Feb	Tel Aviv	1	1

		v ITALY	*NI*	*I*
WC1957	25 Apr	Rome	0	1
1957	4 Dec	Belfast	2	2
WC1958	15 Jan	Belfast	2	1
1961	25 Apr	Bologna	2	3
1997	22 Jan	Palermo	0	2
2003	3 June	Campobasso	0	2

		v LATVIA	*NI*	*L*
WC1993	2 June	Riga	2	1
WC1993	8 Sept	Belfast	2	0
EC1995	26 Apr	Riga	1	0
EC1995	7 June	Belfast	1	2

		v LIECHTENSTEIN	*NI*	*L*
EC1994	20 Apr	Belfast	4	1
EC1995	11 Oct	Eschen	4	0
2002	27 Mar	Vaduz	0	0

		v LITHUANIA	*NI*	*L*
WC1992	28 Apr	Belfast	2	2
WC1993	25 May	Vilnius	1	0

		v LUXEMBOURG	*NI*	*L*
2000	23 Feb	Luxembourg	3	1

		v MALTA	*NI*	*M*
WC1988	21 May	Belfast	3	0
WC1989	26 Apr	Valletta	2	0
2000	28 Mar	Valletta	3	0
WC2000	2 Sept	Belfast	1	0
WC2001	6 Oct	Valletta	1	0

		v MEXICO	*NI*	*M*
1966	22 June	Belfast	4	1
1994	11 June	Miami	0	3

		v MOLDOVA	*NI*	*M*
EC1998	18 Nov	Belfast	2	2
EC1999	31 Mar	Chisinau	0	0

		v MOROCCO	*NI*	*M*
1986	23 Apr	Belfast	2	1

		v NORWAY	*NI*	*N*
1922	25 May	Bergen	1	2
EC1974	4 Sept	Oslo	1	2
EC1975	29 Oct	Belfast	3	0
1990	27 Mar	Belfast	2	3
1996	27 Mar	Belfast	0	2
2001	28 Feb	Belfast	0	4

		v POLAND	*NI*	*P*
EC1962	10 Oct	Katowice	2	0
EC1962	28 Nov	Belfast	2	0
1988	23 Mar	Belfast	1	1
1991	5 Feb	Belfast	3	1
2002	13 Feb	Limassol	1	4

		v PORTUGAL	*NI*	*P*
WC1957	16 Jan	Lisbon	1	1
WC1957	1 May	Belfast	3	0
WC1973	28 Mar	Coventry	1	1
WC1973	14 Nov	Lisbon	1	1
WC1980	19 Nov	Lisbon	0	1
WC1981	29 Apr	Belfast	1	0
EC1994	7 Sept	Belfast	1	2
EC1995	3 Sept	Lisbon	1	1
WC1997	29 Mar	Belfast	0	0
WC1997	11 Oct	Lisbon	0	1

		v ROMANIA	*NI*	*R*
WC1984	12 Sept	Belfast	3	2
WC1985	16 Oct	Bucharest	1	0
1994	23 Mar	Belfast	2	0

		v SLOVAKIA	*NI*	*S*
1998	25 Mar	Belfast	1	0

		v SOUTH AFRICA	*NI*	*SA*
1924	24 Sept	Belfast	1	2

		v SPAIN	*NI*	*S*
1958	15 Oct	Madrid	2	6
1963	30 May	Bilbao	1	1
1963	30 Oct	Belfast	0	1
EC1970	11 Nov	Seville	0	3
EC1972	16 Feb	Hull	1	1
WC1982	25 June	Valencia	1	0
1985	27 Mar	Palma	0	0
WC1986	7 June	Guadalajara	1	2
WC1988	21 Dec	Seville	0	4
WC1989	8 Feb	Belfast	0	2
WC1992	14 Oct	Belfast	0	0
WC1993	28 Apr	Seville	1	3
1998	2 June	Santander	1	4
2002	17 Apr	Belfast	0	5
EC2002	12 Oct	Albacete	0	3
EC2003	11 June	Belfast	0	0

		v SWEDEN	*NI*	*S*
EC1974	30 Oct	Solna	2	0
EC1975	3 Sept	Belfast	1	2
WC1980	15 Oct	Belfast	3	0
WC1981	3 June	Solna	0	1
1996	24 Apr	Belfast	1	2

		v SWITZERLAND	*NI*	*S*
WC1964	14 Oct	Belfast	1	0
WC1964	14 Nov	Lausanne	1	2
1998	22 Apr	Belfast	1	0

		v THAILAND	*NI*	*T*
1997	21 May	Bangkok	0	0

		v TURKEY	*NI*	*T*
WC1968	23 Oct	Belfast	4	1
WC1968	11 Dec	Istanbul	3	0
EC1983	30 Mar	Belfast	2	1
EC1983	12 Oct	Ankara	0	1
WC1985	1 May	Belfast	2	0
WC1985	11 Sept	Izmir	0	0
EC1986	12 Nov	Izmir	0	0
EC1987	11 Nov	Belfast	1	0
EC1998	5 Sept	Istanbul	0	3
EC1999	4 Sept	Belfast	0	3

		v UKRAINE	*NI*	*U*
WC1996	31 Aug	Belfast	0	1
WC1997	2 Apr	Kiev	1	2
EC2002	16 Oct	Belfast	0	0

		v URUGUAY	*NI*	*U*
1964	29 Apr	Belfast	3	0
1990	18 May	Belfast	1	0

		v USSR	*NI*	*USSR*
WC1969	19 Sept	Belfast	0	0
WC1969	22 Oct	Moscow	0	2
EC1971	22 Sept	Moscow	0	1
EC1971	13 Oct	Belfast	1	1

		v YUGOSLAVIA	*NI*	*Y*
EC1975	16 Mar	Belfast	1	0
EC1975	19 Nov	Belgrade	0	1
WC1982	17 June	Zaragoza	0	0
EC1987	29 Apr	Belfast	1	2
EC1987	14 Oct	Sarajevo	0	3
EC1990	12 Sept	Belfast	0	2
EC1991	27 Mar	Belgrade	1	4
2000	16 Aug	Belfast	1	2

REPUBLIC OF IRELAND

		v ALBANIA	*RI*	*A*
WC1992	26 May	Dublin	2	0
WC1993	26 May	Tirana	2	1
EC2003	2 Apr	Tirana	0	0
EC2003	7 June	Dublin	2	1

		v ALGERIA	*RI*	*A*
1982	28 Apr	Algiers	0	2

		v ANDORRA	*RI*	*A*
WC2001	28 Mar	Barcelona	3	0
WC2001	25 Apr	Dublin	3	1

		v ARGENTINA	*RI*	*A*
1951	13 May	Dublin	0	1
1979	29 May	Dublin	0	0*
1980	16 May	Dublin	0	1
1998	22 Apr	Dublin	0	2

**Not considered a full international*

		v AUSTRIA	*RI*	*A*
1952	7 May	Vienna	0	6
1953	25 Mar	Dublin	4	0
1958	14 Mar	Vienna	1	3
1962	8 Apr	Dublin	2	3
EC1963	25 Sept	Vienna	0	0
EC1963	13 Oct	Dublin	3	2
1966	22 May	Vienna	0	1
1968	10 Nov	Dublin	2	2
EC1971	30 May	Dublin	1	4
EC1971	10 Oct	Linz	0	6
EC1995	11 June	Dublin	1	3
EC1995	6 Sept	Vienna	1	3

		v BELGIUM	*RI*	*B*
1928	12 Feb	Liège	4	2
1929	30 Apr	Dublin	4	0
1930	11 May	Brussels	3	1
WC1934	25 Feb	Dublin	4	4
1949	24 Apr	Dublin	0	2
1950	10 May	Brussels	1	5
1965	24 Mar	Dublin	0	2
1966	25 May	Liège	3	2
WC1980	15 Oct	Dublin	1	1
WC1981	25 Mar	Brussels	0	1
EC1986	10 Sept	Brussels	2	2
EC1987	29 Apr	Dublin	0	0
WC1997	29 Oct	Dublin	1	1
WC1997	16 Nov	Brussels	1	2

		v BOLIVIA	*RI*	*B*
1994	24 May	Dublin	1	0
1996	15 June	New Jersey	3	0

		v BRAZIL	*RI*	*B*
1974	5 May	Rio de Janeiro	1	2
1982	27 May	Uberlandia	0	7
1987	23 May	Dublin	1	0

v BULGARIA			RI	B
WC1977	1 June	Sofia	1	2
WC1977	12 Oct	Dublin	0	0
EC1979	19 May	Sofia	0	1
EC1979	17 Oct	Dublin	3	0
WC1987	1 Apr	Sofia	1	2
WC1987	14 Oct	Dublin	2	0

v CAMEROON			RI	C
WC2002	1 June	Niigata	1	1

v CHILE			RI	C
1960	30 Mar	Dublin	2	0
1972	21 June	Recife	1	2
1974	12 May	Santiago	2	1
1982	22 May	Santiago	0	1
1991	22 May	Dublin	1	1

v CHINA			RI	C
1984	3 June	Sapporo	1	0

v CROATIA			RI	C
1996	2 June	Dublin	2	2
EC1998	5 Sept	Dublin	2	0
EC1999	4 Sept	Zagreb	0	1
2001	15 Aug	Dublin	2	2

v CYPRUS			RI	C
WC1980	26 Mar	Nicosia	3	2
WC1980	19 Nov	Dublin	6	0
WC2001	24 Mar	Nicosia	4	0
WC2001	6 Oct	Dublin	4	0

v CZECHOSLOVAKIA			RI	C
1938	18 May	Prague	2	2
EC1959	5 Apr	Dublin	2	0
EC1959	10 May	Bratislava	0	4
WC1961	8 Oct	Dublin	1	3
WC1961	29 Oct	Prague	1	7
EC1967	21 May	Dublin	0	2
EC1967	22 Nov	Prague	2	1
WC1969	4 May	Dublin	1	2
WC1969	7 Oct	Prague	0	3
1979	26 Sept	Prague	1	4
1981	29 Apr	Dublin	3	1
1986	27 May	Reykjavik	1	0

v CZECH REPUBLIC			RI	C
1994	5 June	Dublin	1	3
1996	24 Apr	Prague	0	2
1998	25 Mar	Olomouc	1	2
2000	23 Feb	Dublin	3	2

v DENMARK			RI	D
WC1956	3 Oct	Dublin	2	1
WC1957	2 Oct	Copenhagen	2	0
WC1968	4 Dec	Dublin	1	1
(abandoned after 51 mins)				
WC1969	27 May	Copenhagen	0	2
WC1969	15 Oct	Dublin	1	1
EC1978	24 May	Copenhagen	3	3
EC1979	2 May	Dublin	2	0
WC1984	14 Nov	Copenhagen	0	3
WC1985	13 Nov	Dublin	1	4
WC1992	14 Oct	Copenhagen	0	0
WC1993	28 Apr	Dublin	1	1
2002	27 Mar	Dublin	3	0

v ECUADOR			RI	E
1972	19 June	Natal	3	2

v EGYPT			RI	E
WC1990	17 June	Palermo	0	0

v ENGLAND			RI	E
1946	30 Sept	Dublin	0	1
1949	21 Sept	Everton	2	0
WC1957	8 May	Wembley	1	5
WC1957	19 May	Dublin	1	1
1964	24 May	Dublin	1	3
1976	8 Sept	Wembley	1	1
EC1978	25 Oct	Dublin	1	1
EC1980	6 Feb	Wembley	0	2
1985	26 Mar	Wembley	1	2
EC1988	12 June	Stuttgart	1	0
WC1990	11 June	Cagliari	1	1
EC1990	14 Nov	Dublin	1	1
EC1991	27 Mar	Wembley	1	1
1995	15 Feb	Dublin	1	0
(abandoned after 27 mins)				

v ESTONIA			RI	E
WC2000	11 Oct	Dublin	2	0
WC2001	6 June	Tallinn	2	0

v FINLAND			RI	F
WC1949	8 Sept	Dublin	3	0
WC1949	9 Oct	Helsinki	1	1
1990	16 May	Dublin	1	1
2000	15 Nov	Dublin	3	0
2002	21 Aug	Helsinki	3	0

v FRANCE			RI	F
1937	23 May	Paris	2	0
1952	16 Nov	Dublin	1	1
WC1953	4 Oct	Dublin	3	5
WC1953	25 Nov	Paris	0	1
WC1972	15 Nov	Dublin	2	1
WC1973	19 May	Paris	1	1
WC1976	17 Nov	Paris	0	2
WC1977	30 Mar	Dublin	1	0
WC1980	28 Oct	Paris	0	2
WC1981	14 Oct	Dublin	3	2
1989	7 Feb	Dublin	0	0

v GEORGIA			RI	G
EC2003	29 Mar	Tbilisi	2	1
EC2003	11 June	Dublin	2	0

v GERMANY			RI	G
1935	8 May	Dortmund	1	3
1936	17 Oct	Dublin	5	2
1939	23 May	Bremen	1	1
1994	29 May	Hanover	2	0
WC2002	5 June	Ibaraki	1	1

v WEST GERMANY			RI	WG
1951	17 Oct	Dublin	3	2
1952	4 May	Cologne	0	3
1955	28 May	Hamburg	1	2
1956	25 Nov	Dublin	3	0
1960	11 May	Dusseldorf	1	0
1966	4 May	Dublin	0	4
1970	9 May	Berlin	1	2
1975	1 Mar	Dublin	1	0†
1979	22 May	Dublin	1	3
1981	21 May	Bremen	0	3†
1989	6 Sept	Dublin	1	1

†v West Germany 'B'

v GREECE			RI	G
2000	26 Apr	Dublin	0	1
2002	20 Nov	Athens	0	0

v HOLLAND			RI	N
1932	8 May	Amsterdam	2	0
1934	8 Apr	Amsterdam	2	5
1935	8 Dec	Dublin	3	5
1955	1 May	Dublin	1	0
1956	10 May	Rotterdam	4	1
WC1980	10 Sept	Dublin	2	1
WC1981	9 Sept	Rotterdam	2	2
EC1982	22 Sept	Rotterdam	1	2
EC1983	12 Oct	Dublin	2	3
EC1988	18 June	Gelsenkirchen	0	1
WC1990	21 June	Palermo	1	1
1994	20 Apr	Tilburg	1	0
WC1994	4 July	Orlando	0	2
EC1995	13 Dec	Liverpool	0	2
1996	4 June	Rotterdam	1	3
WC2000	2 Sept	Amsterdam	2	2
WC2001	1 Sept	Dublin	1	0

v HUNGARY			RI	H
1934	15 Dec	Dublin	2	4
1936	3 May	Budapest	3	3

			RI	H
1936	6 Dec	Dublin	2	3
1939	19 Mar	Cork	2	2
1939	18 May	Budapest	2	2
WC1969	8 June	Dublin	1	2
WC1969	5 Nov	Budapest	0	4
WC1989	8 Mar	Budapest	0	0
WC1989	4 June	Dublin	2	0
1991	11 Sept	Gyor	2	1

		v ICELAND	RI	I
EC1962	12 Aug	Dublin	4	2
EC1962	2 Sept	Reykjavik	1	1
EC1982	13 Oct	Dublin	2	0
EC1983	21 Sept	Reykjavik	3	0
1986	25 May	Reykjavik	2	1
WC1996	10 Nov	Dublin	0	0
WC1997	6 Sept	Reykjavik	4	2

		v IRAN	RI	I
1972	18 June	Recife	2	1
WC2001	10 Nov	Dublin	2	0
WC2001	15 Nov	Tehran	0	1

		v N. IRELAND	RI	NI
EC1978	20 Sept	Dublin	0	0
EC1979	21 Nov	Belfast	0	1
WC1988	14 Sept	Belfast	0	0
WC1989	11 Oct	Dublin	3	0
WC1993	31 Mar	Dublin	3	0
WC1993	17 Nov	Belfast	1	1
EC1994	16 Nov	Belfast	4	0
EC1995	29 Mar	Dublin	1	1
1999	29 May	Dublin	0	1

		v ISRAEL	RI	I
1984	4 Apr	Tel Aviv	0	3
1985	27 May	Tel Aviv	0	0
1987	10 Nov	Dublin	5	0

		v ITALY	RI	I
1926	21 Mar	Turin	0	3
1927	23 Apr	Dublin	1	2
EC1970	8 Dec	Rome	0	3
EC1971	10 May	Dublin	1	2
1985	5 Feb	Dublin	1	2
WC1990	30 June	Rome	0	1
1992	4 June	Foxboro	0	2
WC1994	18 June	New York	1	0

		v LATVIA	RI	L
WC1992	9 Sept	Dublin	4	0
WC1993	2 June	Riga	2	1
EC1994	7 Sept	Riga	3	0
EC1995	11 Oct	Dublin	2	1

		v LIECHTENSTEIN	RI	L
EC1994	12 Oct	Dublin	4	0
EC1995	3 June	Eschen	0	0
WC1996	31 Aug	Eschen	5	0
WC1997	21 May	Dublin	5	0

		v LITHUANIA	RI	L
WC1993	16 June	Vilnius	1	0
WC1993	8 Sept	Dublin	2	0
WC1997	20 Aug	Dublin	0	0
WC1997	10 Sept	Vilnius	2	1

		v LUXEMBOURG	RI	I
1936	9 May	Luxembourg	5	1
WC1953	28 Oct	Dublin	4	0
WC1954	7 Mar	Luxembourg	1	0
EC1987	28 May	Luxembourg	2	0
EC1987	9 Sept	Dublin	2	1

		v MACEDONIA	RI	M
WC1996	9 Oct	Dublin	3	0
WC1997	2 Apr	Skopje	2	3
EC1999	9 June	Dublin	1	0
EC1999	9 Oct	Skopje	1	1

		v MALTA	RI	M
EC1983	30 Mar	Valletta	1	0
EC1983	16 Nov	Dublin	8	0
WC1989	28 May	Dublin	2	0
WC1989	15 Nov	Valletta	2	0
1990	2 June	Valletta	3	0
EC1998	14 Oct	Dublin	5	0
EC1999	8 Sept	Valletta	3	2

		v MEXICO	RI	M
1984	8 Aug	Dublin	0	0
WC1994	24 June	Orlando	1	2
1996	13 June	New Jersey	2	2
1998	23 May	Dublin	0	0
2000	4 June	Chicago	2	2

		v MOROCCO	RI	M
1990	12 Sept	Dublin	1	0

		v NIGERIA	RI	N
2002	16 May	Dublin	1	2

		v NORWAY	RI	N
WC1937	10 Oct	Oslo	2	3
WC1937	7 Nov	Dublin	3	3
1950	26 Nov	Dublin	2	2
1951	30 May	Oslo	3	2
1954	8 Nov	Dublin	2	1
1955	25 May	Oslo	3	1
1960	6 Nov	Dublin	3	1
1964	13 May	Oslo	4	1
1973	6 June	Oslo	1	1
1976	24 Mar	Dublin	3	0
1978	21 May	Oslo	0	0
WC1984	17 Oct	Oslo	0	1
WC1985	1 May	Dublin	0	0
1988	1 June	Oslo	0	0
WC1994	28 June	New York	0	0
2003	30 Apr	Dublin	1	0

		v PARAGUAY	RI	P
1999	10 Feb	Dublin	2	0

		v POLAND	RI	P
1938	22 May	Warsaw	0	6
1938	13 Nov	Dublin	3	2
1958	11 May	Katowice	2	2
1958	5 Oct	Dublin	2	2
1964	10 May	Kracow	1	3
1964	25 Oct	Dublin	3	2
1968	15 May	Dublin	2	2
1968	30 Oct	Katowice	0	1
1970	6 May	Dublin	1	2
1970	23 Sept	Dublin	0	2
1973	16 May	Wroclaw	0	2
1973	21 Oct	Dublin	1	0
1976	26 May	Poznan	2	0
1977	24 Apr	Dublin	0	0
1978	12 Apr	Lodz	0	3
1981	23 May	Bydgoszcz	0	3
1984	23 May	Dublin	0	0
1986	12 Nov	Warsaw	0	1
1988	22 May	Dublin	3	1
EC1991	1 May	Dublin	0	0
EC1991	16 Oct	Poznan	3	3

		v PORTUGAL	RI	P
1946	16 June	Lisbon	1	3
1947	4 May	Dublin	0	2
1948	23 May	Lisbon	0	2
1949	22 May	Dublin	1	0
1972	25 June	Recife	1	2
1992	7 June	Boston	2	0
EC1995	26 Apr	Dublin	1	0
EC1995	15 Nov	Lisbon	0	3
1996	29 May	Dublin	0	1
WC2000	7 Oct	Lisbon	1	1
WC2001	2 June	Dublin	1	1

		v ROMANIA	*RI*	*R*
1988	23 Mar	Dublin	2	0
WC1990	25 June	Genoa	0	0*
WC1997	30 Apr	Bucharest	0	1
WC1997	11 Oct	Dublin	1	1

*After extra time

		v RUSSIA	*RI*	*R*
1994	23 Mar	Dublin	0	0
1996	27 Mar	Dublin	0	2
2002	13 Feb	Dublin	2	0
EC2002	7 Sept	Moscow	2	4

		v SAUDI ARABIA	*RI*	*SA*
WC2002	11 June	Yokohama	3	0

		v SCOTLAND	*RI*	*S*
WC1961	3 May	Glasgow	1	4
WC1961	7 May	Dublin	0	3
1963	9 June	Dublin	1	0
1969	21 Sept	Dublin	1	1
EC1986	15 Oct	Dublin	0	0
EC1987	18 Feb	Glasgow	1	0
2000	30 May	Dublin	1	2
2003	12 Feb	Glasgow	2	0

		v SOUTH AFRICA	*RI*	*SA*
2000	11 June	New Jersey	2	1

		v SPAIN	*RI*	*S*
1931	26 Apr	Barcelona	1	1
1931	13 Dec	Dublin	0	5
1946	23 June	Madrid	1	0
1947	2 Mar	Dublin	3	2
1948	30 May	Barcelona	1	2
1949	12 June	Dublin	1	4
1952	1 June	Madrid	0	6
1955	27 Nov	Dublin	2	2
EC1964	11 Mar	Seville	1	5
EC1964	8 Apr	Dublin	0	2
WC1965	5 May	Dublin	1	0
WC1965	27 Oct	Seville	1	4
WC1965	10 Nov	Paris	0	1
EC1966	23 Oct	Dublin	0	0
EC1966	7 Dec	Valencia	0	2
1977	9 Feb	Dublin	0	1
EC1982	17 Nov	Dublin	3	3
EC1983	27 Apr	Zaragoza	0	2
1985	26 May	Cork	0	0
WC1988	16 Nov	Seville	0	2
WC1989	26 Apr	Dublin	1	0
WC1992	18 Nov	Seville	0	0
WC1993	13 Oct	Dublin	1	3
WC2002	16 June	Suwon	1	1

		v SWEDEN	*RI*	*S*
WC1949	2 June	Stockholm	1	3
WC1949	13 Nov	Dublin	1	3
1959	1 Nov	Dublin	3	2
1960	18 May	Malmo	1	4
EC1970	14 Oct	Dublin	1	1
EC1970	28 Oct	Malmo	0	1
1999	28 Apr	Dublin	2	0

		v SWITZERLAND	*RI*	*S*
1935	5 May	Basle	0	1
1936	17 Mar	Dublin	1	0
1937	17 May	Berne	1	0
1938	18 Sept	Dublin	4	0
1948	5 Dec	Dublin	0	1
EC1975	11 May	Dublin	2	1
EC1975	21 May	Berne	0	1
1980	30 Apr	Dublin	2	0
WC1985	2 June	Dublin	3	0
WC1985	11 Sept	Berne	0	0
1992	25 Mar	Dublin	2	1
EC2002	16 Oct	Dublin	1	2

		v TRINIDAD & TOBAGO	*RI*	*TT*
1982	30 May	Port of Spain	1	2

		v TUNISIA	*RI*	*T*
1988	19 Oct	Dublin	4	0

		v TURKEY	*RI*	*T*
EC1966	16 Nov	Dublin	2	1
EC1967	22 Feb	Ankara	1	2
EC1974	20 Nov	Izmir	1	1
EC1975	29 Oct	Dublin	4	0
1976	13 Oct	Ankara	3	3
1978	5 Apr	Dublin	4	2
1990	26 May	Izmir	0	0
EC1990	17 Oct	Dublin	5	0
EC1991	13 Nov	Istanbul	3	1
EC2000	13 Nov	Dublin	1	1
EC2000	17 Nov	Bursa	0	0

		v URUGUAY	*RI*	*U*
1974	8 May	Montevideo	0	2
1986	23 Apr	Dublin	1	1

		v USA	*RI*	*USA*
1979	29 Oct	Dublin	3	2
1991	1 June	Boston	1	1
1992	29 Apr	Dublin	4	1
1992	30 May	Washington	1	3
1996	9 June	Boston	1	2
2000	6 June	Boston	1	1
2002	17 Apr	Dublin	2	1

		v USSR	*RI*	*USSR*
WC1972	18 Oct	Dublin	1	2
WC1973	13 May	Moscow	0	1
EC1974	30 Oct	Dublin	3	0
EC1975	18 May	Kiev	1	2
WC1984	12 Sept	Dublin	1	0
WC1985	16 Oct	Moscow	0	2
EC1988	15 June	Hanover	1	1
1990	25 Apr	Dublin	1	0

		v WALES	*RI*	*W*
1960	28 Sept	Dublin	2	3
1979	11 Sept	Swansea	1	2
1981	24 Feb	Dublin	1	3
1986	26 Mar	Dublin	0	1
1990	28 Mar	Dublin	1	0
1991	6 Feb	Wrexham	3	0
1992	19 Feb	Dublin	0	1
1993	17 Feb	Dublin	2	1
1997	11 Feb	Cardiff	0	0

		v YUGOSLAVIA	*RI*	*Y*
1955	19 Sept	Dublin	1	4
1988	27 Apr	Dublin	2	0
EC1998	18 Nov	Belgrade	0	1
EC1999	1 Sept	Dublin	2	1

OTHER BRITISH AND IRISH INTERNATIONAL MATCHES 2002–03

FRIENDLIES

Villa Park, 7 September 2002, 40,058

England (1) 1 *(Smith 40)*

Portugal (0) 1 *(Costinha 79)*

England: James; Mills (Bridge 46); Ashley Cole (Hargreaves 46), Gerrard (Dunn 46), Ferdinand (Woodgate 46), Southgate, Bowyer (Sinclair 62), Butt (Murphy 63), Smith, Owen (Cole J 63), Heskey.
Portugal: Vitor Baia (Pereira 46); Beto (Nuno Gomes 46), Meara (Silva 78), Fernando Couto (Ferreira 46), Sergio Conceicao (Valente 46), Teixeira (Vidigal 65), Rui Costa (Boa Morte 46), Rui Jorge (Capucho 46), Figo (Viana 46), Pauleta (Santos 46), Sabrosa (Costinha 54).
Referee: T. Olembe.

West Ham, 12 February 2003, 34,590

England (0) 1 *(Jeffers 70)*

Australia (2) 3 *(Popovic 17, Kewell 42, Emerton 84)*

England (first half): James; Neville G, Ashley Cole, Lampard, Campbell, Ferdinand, Beckham, Scholes, Beattie, Owen, Dyer.
(second half): Robinson; Mills, Konchesky, Jenas, Brown, King, Murphy, Rooney, Jeffers, Vassell, Hargreaves.
Australia: Schwarzer; Neill, Lazaridis, Okon, Popovic, Moore, Emerton, Skoko (Bresciano 46), Chipperfield (Grella 76), Viduka (Sterjovski 84), Kewell (Aloisi 56).
Referee: M. Gonzalez (Spain).

Durban, 22 May 2003, 48,000

South Africa (1) 1 *(McCarthy 18 (pen))*

England (1) 2 *(Southgate 1, Heskey 64)*

South Africa: Baloyi; Mabizela, Radebe, Mokoena A, Molefe, Fredericks (Mazibuko 77), Sibaya, Mokoena T (Mendu 69), Buckley, Bartlett, McCarthy (Manyathele 68).
England: James (Robinson 46); Mills, Neville P, Gerrard (Barry 82), Ferdinand (Upson 46), Southgate, Beckham (Jenas 51), Scholes (Cole J 75), Heskey (Vassell 65), Owen, Sinclair (Lampard 58).
Referee: L. Chong (Mauritius).

Leicester, 3 June 2003, 30,900

England (1) 2 *(Gerrard 35, Cole J 82)*

Serbia-Montenegro (1) 1 *(Jestrovic 45)*

England: James; Mills (Carragher 61), Ashley Cole (Bridge 46), Neville P (Beattie 87), Southgate (Terry 46), Upson (Barry 84), Gerrard (Hargreaves 46), Lampard (Cole J 61), Heskey (Vassell 61), Owen (Rooney 46), Scholes (Jenas 46).
Serbia-Montenegro: Jevric (Zilic 67); Mirkovic (Brnovic 46), Stefanovic (Krstajic 50), Vidic (Kovacevic D 62), Markovic (Njegus 67), Duljaj (Boskovic 46), Kovacevic N (Malbasa 46), Dmitrovic (Trobok 46), Vukic (Djordjevic 46), Ilic (Mijatovic 67), Jestrovic (Milosevic 75).
Referee: P. Allaerts (Belgium).

Hampden Park, 21 August 2002, 28,766

Scotland (0) 0

Denmark (1) 1 *(Sand 8)*

Scotland: Douglas; Stockdale (Alexander 71), Naysmith (Johnston 71), Weir (Severin 77), Dailly, Ross, McNaughton (Crainey 46), Lambert (McInnes 81), Kyle, Thompson (Dobie 55), Ferguson B.
Denmark: Sorensen; Bogelund (Michaelson 46), Jensen N, Laursen (Wieghorst 66), Henriksen (Lustu 83), Rommedahl (Gronkjaer 46), Gravesen (Jensen C 46), Tomasson, Sand, Poulsen, Lovenkrands (Silberbauer 77).
Referee: L. Irvine (Northern Ireland).

Easter Road, 15 October 2002, 16,207

Scotland (1) 3 *(Crawford 11, 73, Thompson 50)*

Canada (1) 1 *(De Rosario 9 (pen))*

Scotland: Gallacher; Alexander, Ross (Davidson 46), Anderson, Pressley, Wilkie (Murray I 75), Devlin, Dailly, Thompson (McFadden 81), Crawford (Kyle 87), Gemmill (Severin 65).
Canada: Hirschfeld; Pozniak, De Guzman, Fenwick, McKenna, Hastings, Nsaliwa, Imhov (Xausa 82), Stalteri, Radzinski, De Rosario.
Referee: L. Huyghe (Belgium).

Braga, 20 November 2002, 8000

Portugal (2) 2 (Pauleta 8, 17)

Scotland (0) 0

Portugal: Quim (Nelson 85); Sergio Conceicao, Rui Jorge (Ferreiro 57), Fernando Couto, Neira, Rocha, Tiago, Pauleta, Simao (Neca 77), Figo (Ferreira 46).
Scotland: Douglas; Alexander, Ross (Devlin 46), Anderson (McInnes 22), Pressley, Wilkie (Severin 83), Dailly, Lambert (Williams 68), Dobie (Kyle 77), Crawford, Naysmith.
Referee: Anghelinei (Romania).

Hampden Park, 12 February 2003, 33,337

Scotland (0) 0

Republic of Ireland (2) 2 *(Kilbane 9, Morrison 17)*

Scotland: Sullivan (Gallacher 46); Alexander, Naysmith, Anderson, Caldwell S, Dailly, Ferguson B (Cameron 64), Lambert (Gemmill 46), Hutchison (Devlin 46), Crawford (Thompson 64), McCann (Smith 64).
Republic of Ireland: Kiely (Colgan 80); Carr, Harte, Breen (O'Brien 90), O'Shea (Dunne 80), Holland, Kinsella (Healy 77), Reid (Carsley 77), Morrison, Doherty (Connolly 73), Kilbane.
Referee: E. Braamhaar (Holland).

Hampden Park, 30 April 2003, 12,189

Scotland (0) 0

Austria (2) 2 *(Kirchler 27, Haas 33)*

Scotland: Gallacher; Devlin (Smith 84), Naysmith, Wilkie, Webster, Pressley, Burley (Cameron 63), Dailly (Gemmill 46), Thompson (Crawford 46), McFadden, Hutchison (Miller 61).
Austria: Mandl; Scharner, Ehmann, Stranzi, Dospel, Aufhauser, Schopp, Flogel, Wagner, Kirchler (Herzog 84), Haas (Brunmayr 63).
Referee: N. Vollquartz (Denmark).

Tynecastle, 27 May 2003, 10,016

Scotland (1) 1 *(Crawford 11)*

New Zealand (0) 1 *(Nelsen 47)*

Scotland: Douglas; Ross (Alexander 46), Naysmith, Dailly, Pressley, Webster, Devlin, McNamara (Kerr 82), Kyle (Gray 59), Crawford, McFadden.
New Zealand: Utting (Batty 46); Mulligan (Oughton 46), Davis, Zoricich (Smith 69), Nelsen, Jackson (De Gregorio 54), Elliott, Lines (Bouckenrooghe 80), Hickey, Burton, Coveny.
Referee: M. Ingvarsson (Sweden).

Varazdin, 21 August 2002, 6000

Croatia (0) 1 *(Petric 79)*

Wales (1) 1 *(Davies 11)*

Croatia: Pletikosa (Butina 60); Zivkovic, Tapalovic (Babic 75), Simunic, Kovac R (Vranjes 60), Kovac N (Leko 46), Saric, Vugrinec (Maric S 46), Rapaic (Bazina 60), Vlaovic (Petric 46), Maric T (Tomas 60).
Wales: Jones P; Delaney, Barnard (Weston 60), Robinson (Taylor 60), Gabbidon, Melville, Pembridge, Johnson, Hartson, Earnshaw (Trollope 80), Davies.
Referee: M. Frohlich (Germany).

Millennium Stadium, 12 February 2003, 25,000

Wales (1) 2 *(Earnshaw 8, Hartson 74)*

Bosnia (1) 2 *(Baljic 5, Barbarez 64)*

Wales: Ward (Crossley 46); Weston (Jones M 61), Speed, Melville, Page, Pembridge, Davies, Savage (Oster 88), Earnshaw (Koumas 76), Hartson (Taylor 82), Bellamy.
Bosnia: Hasagic; Berberovic, Konjic, Hibic, Music, Beslija, Biscevic (Valagic 90), Grujic (Mulina 77), Barbarez (Miakovic 78), Baljic (Hrgovic 78), Bolic (Halilovic 90).
Referee: D. Malcolm (Northern Ireland).

San Jose, 27 May 2003, 12,262

United States (1) 2 *(Donovan 41 (pen), Lewis 60)*

Wales (0) 0

United States: Rimando; Suarez (Petke 78), Brown, Agoos, Vanney, Stewart (Lagos 83), Convey (Ching 75), Mulrooney, Lewis, Donovan, Kirovski (Eskandarian 89).
Wales: Jones P (Ward 46); Jones M, Vaughan, Pembridge (Robinson 78), Melville, Williams, Davies, Oster (Pipe 70), Johnson, Koumas, Taylor (Roberts N 57).
Referee: B. Tellez (Mexico).

Windsor Park, 21 August 2002, 6922

Northern Ireland (0) 0

Cyprus (0) 0

Northern Ireland: Taylor; Griffin (Duff 46), McCartney, Horlock, Williams, Murdock, Gillespie (Feeney 87), Johnson, Healy, Quinn, Kennedy.
Cyprus: Panayiotu; Theodotou, Spyrou, Okkarides, Konnafis, Daskalakis (Nikaladu 46), Satsias, Eleftheriou, Okkas, Yiasoumi (Agathocleous 60), Nicolaou (Michali 43).
Referee: S. Jones (Wales).

Windsor Park, 12 February 2003, 6137

Northern Ireland (0) 0

Finland (0) 1 *(Hyypia 49)*

Northern Ireland: Taylor (Carroll 46); Hughes A, Kennedy, Williams, McCartney (Craigan 66), Lomas, Gillespie, Johnson, Healy, Quinn (Kirk 60), McVeigh (Elliott 76).
Finland: Jaaskelainen; Kuivasto, Hietanen, Hyypia (Heikkinen 69), Tihinen, Riihilahti, Nurmela, Vayrynan (Johansson 62), Valakari, Kolkka (Kopteff 76), Forssell (Kuqi 46).
Referee: D. McDonald (Scotland).

Campobasso, 3 June 2003, 18,270

Italy (1) 2 *(Corradi 31, Delvecchio 67)*

Northern Ireland (0) 0

Italy: Toldo; Oddo, Grosso (Birindelli 69), Legrotiaglio (Bonera 57), Cannavaro (Ferrari 46), Perrotta (Tommasi 57), Fiore, Ambrosini, Di Vaio (Nervo 69), Corradi (Delvecchio 46), Miccoli (Di Natale 57).
Northern Ireland: Taylor (Carroll 55); Baird, Kennedy (Williams 55), Griffin, Hughes A, McCartney, Johnson (Toner 69), Doherty (Elliott 87), Healy (Hamilton 76), Smith, McVeigh (Jones 55).
Referee: L. Baptista (Portugal).

Helsinki, 21 August 2002, 12,225

Finland (0) 0

Republic of Ireland (1) 3 *(Robbie Keane 12, Healy 74, Barrett 83)*

Finland: Jaaskelainen; Pasanen, Saarinen, Ilola (Riihilahti 59), Hyypia (Kuivasto 46), Tihinen, Nurmela (Kopteff 69), Tainio (Hietanen 80), Kolkka (Kottila 76), Litmanen, Johansson (Kuqi 59).
Republic of Ireland: Kiely (Given 75); Kelly G, Harte (Barrett 75), Breen, Cunningham (Doherty 46), Carsley (Holland 87), Butler (Kilbane 46), Kinsella (McPhail 46), McAteer (Healy 46), Robbie Keane (Goodwin 83), Duff (Delap 46).
Referee: R. Pedersen (Norway).

Athens, 20 November 2002, 5500

Greece (0) 0

Republic of Ireland (0) 0

Greece: Nikopolidis (Hiotis 46); Seitaridis (Patsatzoglou 46); Fyssas (Venetidis 46), Dabizas (Goumas 46), Kyrgiakos, Giannakopoulos (Georgiadis 46), Basinas (Zagorakis 60), Karagounis (Kafes 60), Tsartas (Amanatidis 46), Nikolaidis (Papadopoulos 46), Haristeas.
Republic of Ireland: Given; Finnan, Dunne, O'Shea, Cunningham, Holland, Healy, Carsley, McPhail, Crowe (Delap 85), Doherty.
Referee: A. Trentalange (Italy).

Dublin, 30 April 2003, 32,643

Republic of Ireland (1) 1 *(Duff 17)*

Norway (0) 0

Republic of Ireland: Given (Colgan 60); Carr, Harte (Finnan 60), Breen, Dunne, Holland, Kinsella (Carsley 65), Kilbane (Quinn 85), Robbie Keane (Crowe 90), Connolly (Healy 74), Duff (Lee 74).
Norway: Olsen (Holtan 46); Basma (Aas 56), Bergdolmo, Larsen S, Hangeland, Johnsen R (Hansen 46), Andersen (Johnsen F 90), Carew, Iversen (Rudi 65), Rushfeldt (Flo T 46), Leonhardsen.
Referee: M. McCurry (Scotland).

INTERNATIONAL APPEARANCES 1872–2003

This is a list of full international appearances by Englishmen, Irishmen, Scotsmen and Welshmen in matches against the Home Countries and against foreign nations. It does not include unofficial matches against Commonwealth and Empire countries. The year indicated refers to the season; ie 2002 is the 2001–02 season.

Explanatory code for matches played by all five countries: A represents Austria; Alb, Albania; Alg, Algeria; An, Angola; And, Andorra; Arg, Argentina; Arm, Armenia; Aus, Australia; B, Az, Azerbaijan; Bohemia; Bel, Belgium; Bl, Belarus; Bol, Bolivia; Bos, Bosnia; Br, Brazil; Bul, Bulgaria; C,CIS; Ca, Canada; Cam, Cameroon; Ch, Chile; Chn, China; Co, Colombia; Cr, Costa Rica; Cro, Croatia; Cy, Cyprus; Cz, Czechoslovakia; CzR, Czech Republic; D, Denmark; E, England; Ec, Ecuador; Ei, Republic of Ireland; EG, East Germany; Eg, Egypt; Es, Estonia; F, France; Fa, Faeroes; Fi, Finland; G, Germany; Ge, Georgia; Gr, Greece; H, Hungary; Hk, Hong Kong; Ho, Holland; Hon, Honduras; I, Italy; Ic, Iceland; Ir, Iran; Is, Israel; J, Japan; Jam, Jamaica; K, Kuwait; L, Luxembourg; La, Latvia; Li, Lithuania; Lie, Liechtenstein; M, Mexico; Ma, Malta; Mac, Macedonia; Mal, Malaysia; Mol, Moldova; Mor, Morocco; N, Norway; Ng, Nigeria; Ni, Northern Ireland; Nz, New Zealand; P, Portugal; Para, Paraguay; Pe, Peru; Pol, Poland; R, Romania; RCS, Republic of Czechs and Slovaks; R of E, Rest of Europe; R of UK, Rest of United Kingdom; R of W, Rest of World; Ru, Russia; S.Af, South Africa; S.Ar, Saudi Arabia; S, Scotland; Se, Sweden; Ser, Serbia-Montenegro; Sk, South Korea; Slo, Slovakia; Slv, Slovenia; Sm, San Marino; Sp, Spain; Sw, Switzerland; T, Turkey; Th, Thailand; Tr, Trinidad & Tobago; Tun, Tunisia; U, Uruguay; Uk, Ukraine; US, United States of America; USSR, Soviet Union; W, Wales; WG, West Germany; Y, Yugoslavia; Z, Zaire.
As at July 2003.

ENGLAND

Abbott, W. (Everton), 1902 v W (1)
A'Court, A. (Liverpool), 1958 v Ni, Br, A, USSR; 1959 v W (5)
Adams, T. A. (Arsenal), 1987 v Sp, T, Br; 1988 v WG, T, Y, Ho, H, S, Co, Sw, Ei, Ho, USSR; 1989 v D, Se, S.Ar.; 1991 v Ei (2); 1993 v N, T, Sm, T, Ho, Pol, N; 1994 v Pol, Ho, D, Gr, N; 1995 v US, R, Ei, U; 1996 v Co, N, Sw, P, Chn, Sw, S, Ho, Sp, G; 1997 v Ge (2); 1998 v I, Ch, P, S.Ar, Tun, R, Co, Arg; 1999 v Se, F; 2000 v L, Pol, Bel, S (2), Uk, P; 2001 v F, G (66)
Adcock, H. (Leicester C), 1929 v F, Bel, Sp; 1930 v Ni, W (5)
Alcock, C. W. (Wanderers), 1875 v S (1)
Alderson, J. T. (C Palace), 1923 v F (1)
Aldridge, A. (WBA), 1888 v Ni; (with Walsall Town Swifts), 1889 v Ni (2)
Allen, A. (Stoke C) 1960 v Se, W, Ni (3)
Allen, A. (Aston Villa), 1888 v Ni (1)
Allen, C. (QPR), 1984 v Br (sub), U, Ch; (with Tottenham H), 1987 v T; 1988 v Is (5)
Allen, H. (Wolverhampton W), 1888 v S, W, Ni; 1889 v S; 1890 v S (5)
Allen, J. P. (Portsmouth), 1934 v Ni, W (2)
Allen, R. (WBA), 1952 v Sw; 1954 v Y, S; 1955 v WG, W (5)
Alsford, W. J. (Tottenham H), 1935 v S (1)
Amos, A. (Old Carthusians), 1885 v S; 1886 v W (2)
Anderson, R. D. (Old Etonians), 1879 v W (1)
Anderson, S. (Sunderland), 1962 v A, S (2)
Anderson, V. (Nottingham F), 1979 v Cz, Se; 1980 v Bul, Sp; 1981 v N, R, W, S; 1982 v Ni, Ic; 1984 v Ni; (with Arsenal), 1985 v T, Ni, Ei, R, Fi, S, M, US; 1986 v USSR, M; 1987 v Se, Ni (2), Y, Sp, T; (with Manchester U), 1988 v WG, H, Co (30)
Anderton, D. R. (Tottenham H), 1994 v D, Gr, N; 1995 v US, Ei, U, J, Se, Br; 1996 v H, Chn, Sw, S, Ho, Sp, G; 1998 v S.Ar, Mor, Tun, R, Co, Arg; 1999 v Se, Bul, L, CzR, F; 2001 v F, I (sub); 2002 v Se (sub) (30)
Angus, J. (Burnley), 1961 v A (1)
Armfield, J. C. (Blackpool), 1959 v Br, Pe, M, US; 1960 v Y, Sp, H, S; 1961 v L, P, Sp, M, I, A, W, Ni, S; 1962 v A, Sw, Pe, W, Ni, S, L, P, H, Arg, Bul, Br; 1963 v F (2), Br, EG, Sw, Ni, W, S; 1964 v R of W, W, Ni, S; 1966 v Y, Fi (43)
Armitage, G. H. (Charlton Ath), 1926 v Ni (1)
Armstrong, D. (Middlesbrough), 1980 v Aus; (with Southampton), 1983 v WG; 1984 v W (3)
Armstrong, K. (Chelsea), 1955 v S (1)
Arnold, J. (Fulham), 1933 v S (1)
Arthur, J. W. H. (Blackburn R), 1885 v S, W, Ni; 1886 v S, W; 1887 v W, Ni (7)
Ashcroft, J. (Woolwich Arsenal), 1906 v Ni, W, S (3)
Ashmore, G. S. (WBA), 1926 v Bel (1)
Ashton, C. T. (Corinthians), 1926 v Ni (1)
Ashurst, W. (Notts Co), 1923 v Se (2); 1925 v S, W, Bel (5)
Astall, G. (Birmingham C), 1956 v Fi, WG (2)
Astle, J. (WBA), 1969 v W; 1970 v S, P, Br (sub), Cz (5)
Aston, J. (Manchester U), 1949 v S, W, D, Sw, Se, N, F; 1950 v S, W, Ni, Ei, I, P, Bel, Ch, US; 1951 v Ni (17)
Athersmith, W. C. (Aston Villa), 1892 v Ni, 1897 v S, W, Ni; 1898 v S, W, Ni; 1899 v S, W, Ni; 1900 v S, W (12)
Atyeo, P. J. W. (Bristol C), 1956 v Br, Se, Sp; 1957 v D, Ei (2) (6)
Austin, S. W. (Manchester C), 1926 v Ni (1)
Bach, P. (Sunderland), 1899 v Ni (1)
Bache, J. W. (Aston Villa), 1903 v W; 1904 v W, Ni; 1905 v S; 1907 v Ni; 1910 v Ni; 1911 v S (7)
Baddeley, T. (Wolverhampton W), 1903 v S, Ni; 1904 v S, W, Ni (5)
Bagshaw, J. J. (Derby Co), 1920 v Ni (1)
Bailey, G. R. (Manchester U), 1985 v Ei, M (2)
Bailey, H. P. (Leicester Fosse), 1908 v W, A (2), H, B (5)
Bailey, M. A. (Charlton Ath), 1964 v US; 1965 v W (2)
Bailey, N. C. (Clapham Rovers), 1878 v S; 1879 v S, W; 1880 v S; 1881 v S; 1882 v S, W; 1883 v S, W; 1884 v S, W, Ni; 1885 v S, W, Ni; 1886 v S, W; 1887 v S, W (19)
Baily, E. F. (Tottenham H), 1950 v Sp; 1951 v Y, Ni, W; 1952 v A (2), Sw, W; 1953 v Ni (9)
Bain, J. (Oxford University), 1887 v S (1)
Baker, A. (Arsenal), 1928 v W (1)
Baker, B. H. (Everton), 1921 v Bel; (with Chelsea), 1926 v Ni (2)
Baker, J. H. (Hibernian), 1960 v Y, Sp, H, Ni, S; (with Arsenal) 1966 v Sp, Pol, Ni (8)
Ball, A. J. (Blackpool), 1965 v Y, WG, Se; 1966 v S, Sp, Fi, D, U, Arg, P, WG (2), Pol (2); (with Everton), 1967 v W, S, Ni, A, Cz, Sp; 1968 v W, S, USSR, Sp (2), Y, WG; 1969 v Ni, W, S, R (2), M, Br, U; 1970 v P, Co, Ec, R, Br, Cz (sub), WG, W, S, Bel; 1971 v Ma, EG, Gr, Ma (sub), Ni, S; 1972 v Sw, Gr; (with Arsenal) WG (2), S; 1973 v W (3), Y, S (2), Cz, Ni, Pol; 1974 v P (sub); 1975 v WG, Cy (2), Ni, W, S (72)
Ball, J. (Bury), 1928 v Ni (1)
Ball, M. J. (Everton), 2001 v Sp (sub) (1)
Balmer, W. (Everton), 1905 v Ni (1)
Bamber, J. (Liverpool), 1921 v W (1)
Bambridge, A. L. (Swifts), 1881 v W; 1883 v W; 1884 v Ni (3)
Bambridge, E. C. (Swifts), 1879 v S; 1880 v S; 1881 v S; 1882 v S, W, Ni; 1883 v W; 1884 v S, W, Ni; 1885 v S, W, Ni; 1886 v S, W; 1887 v S, W, Ni (18)
Bambridge, E. H. (Swifts), 1876 v S (1)
Banks, G. (Leicester C), 1963 v S, Br, Cz, EG; 1964 v W, Ni, S, R of W, U, P (2), US, Arg; 1965 v Ni, S, H, Y, WG, Se; 1966 v Ni, S, Sp, Pol (2), WG (2), Y, Fi, U, M, F, Arg, P; 1967 v Ni, W, S, Cz; (with Stoke C), 1968 v W, Ni, S, USSR (2), Sp, WG, Y; 1969 v Ni, S, R (2), F, U, Br; 1970 v W, Ni, S, Ho, Bel, Co, Ec, R, Br, Cz; 1971 v Gr, Ma (2), Ni, S; 1972 v Sw, Gr, WG (2), W, S (73)
Banks, H. E. (Millwall), 1901 v Ni (1)
Banks, T. (Bolton W), 1958 v USSR (3), Br, A; 1959 v Ni (6)
Bannister, W. (Burnley), 1901 v W; (with Bolton W), 1902 v Ni (2)
Barclay, R. (Sheffield U), 1932 v S; 1933 v Ni; 1936 v S (3)
Bardsley, D. J. (QPR), 1993 v Sp (sub), Pol (2)
Barham, M. (Norwich C), 1983 v Aus (2) (2)
Barkas, S. (Manchester C), 1936 v Bel; 1937 v S; 1938 v W, Ni, Cz (5)
Barker, J. (Derby Co), 1935 v I, Ho, S, W, Ni; 1936 v G, A, S, W, Ni; 1937 v W (11)
Barker, R. (Herts Rangers), 1872 v S (1)
Barker, R. R. (Casuals), 1895 v W (1)
Barlow, R. J. (WBA), 1955 v Ni (1)
Barmby, N. J. (Tottenham H), 1995 v U (sub), Se (sub); (with Middlesbrough), 1996 v Co, N, P, Chn, Sw (sub), Ho (sub), Sp (sub); 1997 v Mol; (with Everton), 2000 v Br (sub), Uk (sub), Ma, G (sub), R (sub); (with Liverpool), 2001 v F, G, I, Sp; 2002 v Ho (sub), G, Alb, Gr (23)

Barnes, J. (Watford), 1983 v Ni (sub), Aus (sub), Aus (2); 1984 v D, L (sub), F (sub), S, USSR, Br, U, Ch; 1985 v EG, Fi, T, Ni, R, Fi, S, I (sub), M, WG (sub), US (sub); 1986 v R (sub), Is (sub), M (sub), Ca (sub), Arg (sub); 1987 v Se, T (sub), Br; (with Liverpool), 1988 v WG, T, Y, Is, Ho, S, Co, Sw, Ei, Ho, USSR; 1989 v Se, Gr, Alb, Pol, D; 1990 v Se, I, Br, D, U, Tun, Ei, Ho, Eg, Bel, Cam; 1991 v H, Pol, Cam, Ei, T, USSR, Arg; 1992 v Cz, Fi; 1993 v Sm, T, Ho, Pol, US, G; 1995 v US, R, Ng, U, Se; 1996 v Co (sub) (79)
Barnes, P. S. (Manchester C), 1978 v I, WG, Br, W, S, H; 1979 v D, Ei, Cz, Ni (2), S, Bul, A; (with WBA), 1980 v D, W; 1981 v Sp (sub), Br, W, Sw (sub); (with Leeds U), 1982 v N (sub), Ho (sub) (22)
Barnet, H. H. (Royal Engineers), 1882 v Ni (1)
Barrass, M. W. (Bolton W), 1952 v W, Ni; 1953 v S (3)
Barrett, A. F. (Fulham), 1930 v Ni (1)
Barrett, E. D. (Oldham Ath), 1991 v Nz; (with Aston Villa), 1993 v Br, G (3)
Barrett, J. W. (West Ham U), 1929 v Ni (1)
Barry, G. (Aston Villa), 2000 v Uk (sub), Ma (sub); 2001 v F, G (sub), Fi, I ; 2003 v S.Af (sub), Ser (sub) (8)
Barry, L. (Leicester C), 1928 v F, Bel; 1929 v F, Bel, Sp (5)
Barson, F. (Aston Villa), 1920 v W (1)
Barton, J. (Blackburn R), 1890 v Ni (1)
Barton, P. H. (Birmingham), 1921 v Bel; 1922 v Ni; 1923 v F; 1924 v Bel, S, W; 1925 v Ni (7)
Barton, W. D. (Wimbledon), 1995 v Ei; (with Newcastle U), Se, Br (sub) (3)
Bassett, W. I. (WBA), 1888 v Ni, 1889 v S, W; 1890 v S, W; 1891 v S, Ni; 1892 v S; 1893 v S, W; 1894 v S; 1895 v S, Ni; 1896 v S, W, Ni (16)
Bastard, S. R. (Upton Park), 1880 v S (1)
Bastin, C. S. (Arsenal), 1932 v W; 1933 v I, Sw; 1934 v S, Ni, W, H, Cz; 1935 v S, Ni, I; 1936 v S, W, G, A; 1937 v W, Ni; 1938 v S, G, Sw, F (21)
Batty, D. (Leeds U), 1991 v USSR (sub), Arg, Aus, Nz, Mal; 1992 v G, T, H (sub), F, Se; 1993 v N, Sm, US, Br; (with Blackburn R), 1994 v D (sub); 1995 v J, Br; (with Newcastle U), 1997 v Mol (sub), Ge, I, M, Ge, S.Af (sub), Pol (sub), F; 1998 v Mol, I, Ch, Sw (sub), P, S.Ar, Tun, R, Co (sub), Arg (sub); 1999 v Bul (sub), L; (with Leeds U), H, Se, Bul; 2000 v L, Pol (42)
Baugh, R. (Stafford Road), 1886 v Ni; (with Wolverhampton W) 1890 v Ni (2)
Bayliss, A. E. J. M. (WBA), 1891 v Ni (1)
Baynham, R. L. (Luton T), 1956 v Ni, D, Sp (3)
Beardsley, P. A. (Newcastle U), 1986 v Eg (sub), Is, USSR, M, Ca (sub), P (sub), Pol, Para, Arg; 1987 v Ni (2), Y, Sp, Br, S; (with Liverpool), 1988 v WG, T, Y, Is, Ho, H, S, Co, Sw, Ei, Ho; 1989 v D, Se, S.Ar, Gr (sub), Alb (sub+1), Pol, D; 1990 v Se, Pol, I, Br, U (sub), Tun (sub), Ei, Eg (sub), Cam (sub), WG, I; 1991 v Pol (sub), Ei (2), USSR (sub); (with Newcastle U), 1994 v D, Gr, N; 1995 v Ng, Ei, U, J, Se; 1996 v P (sub), Chn (sub) (59)
Beasant, D. J. (Chelsea), 1990 v I (sub), Y (sub) (2)
Beasley, A. (Huddersfield T), 1939 v S (1)
Beats, W. E. (Wolverhampton W), 1901 v W; 1902 v S (2)
Beattie, J. S. (Southampton), 2003 v Aus, Ser (sub) (2)
Beattie, T. K. (Ipswich T), 1975 v Cy (2), S; 1976 v Sw, P; 1977 v Fi, I (sub), Ho; 1978 v L (sub) (9)
Beckham, D. R. J. (Manchester U), 1997 v Mol, Pol, Ge, I, Ge, S.Af (sub), Pol, I, F; 1998 v Mol, I, Cam, P, S.Ar, Bel (sub), R (sub), Co, Arg; 1999 v L, CzR, F, Pol, Se; 2000 v L, Pol, S(2), Arg, Br, Uk, Ma, P, G, R; 2001 v F, G, I, Sp, Fi, Alb, M, Gr; 2002 v Ho, G, Alb, Gr, Se, Ho, I, Se, Arg, Ng, D, Br; 2003 v Slo, Mac, Aus, Lie, T, S.Af (60)
Becton, F. (Preston NE), 1895 v Ni; (with Liverpool), 1897 v W (2)
Bedford, H. (Blackpool), 1923 v Se; 1925 v Ni (2)
Bell, C. (Manchester C), 1968 v Se, WG; 1969 v W, Bul, F, U, Br; 1970 v Ni (sub), Ho (2), P, Br (sub), Cz, WG (sub); 1972 v Gr, WG (2), W, Ni, S; 1973 v W (3), Y, S (2), Ni, Cz, Pol; 1974 v A, Pol, I, W, Ni, S, Arg, EG, Bul, Y; 1975 v Cz, P, WG, Cy (2), Ni, S; 1976 v Sw, Cz (48)
Bennett, W. (Sheffield U), 1901 v S, W (2)
Benson, R. W. (Sheffield U), 1913 v Ni (1)
Bentley, R. T. F. (Chelsea), 1949 v Se; 1950 v S, P, Bel, Ch, USA; 1953 v W, Bel; 1955 v W, WG, Sp, P (12)
Beresford, J. (Aston Villa), 1934 v Cz (1)
Berry, A. (Oxford University), 1909 v Ni (1)
Berry, J. J. (Manchester U), 1953 v Arg, Ch, U; 1956 v Se (4)
Bestall, J. G. (Grimsby T), 1935 v Ni (1)
Betmead, H. A. (Grimsby T), 1937 v Fi (1)
Betts, M. P. (Old Harrovians), 1877 v S (1)
Betts, W. (Sheffield W), 1889 v W (1)
Beverley, J. (Blackburn R), 1884 v S, W, Ni (3)
Birkett, R. H. (Clapham Rovers), 1879 v S (1)
Birkett, R. J. E. (Middlesbrough), 1936 v Ni (1)
Birley, F. H. (Oxford University), 1874 v S; (with Wanderers), 1875 v S (2)
Birtles, G. (Nottingham F), 1980 v Arg (sub), I; 1981 v R (3)
Bishop, S. M. (Leicester C), 1927 v S, Bel, L, F (4)
Blackburn, F. (Blackburn R), 1901 v S; 1902 v Ni; 1904 v S (3)
Blackburn, G. F. (Aston Villa), 1924 v F (1)
Blenkinsop, E. (Sheffield W), 1928 v F, Bel; 1929 v S, W, Ni, F, Bel, Sp; 1930 v S, W, Ni, G, A; 1931 v S, W, Ni, F, Bel; 1932 v S, W, Ni, Sp; 1933 v S, W, Ni, A (26)
Bliss, H. (Tottenham H), 1921 v S (1)
Blissett, L. (Watford), 1983 v WG (sub), L, W, Gr (sub), H, Ni, S (sub), Aus (1+1 sub); (with AC Milan), 1984 v D (sub), H, W (sub), S, USSR (14)
Blockley, J. P. (Arsenal), 1973 v Y (1)
Bloomer, S. (Derby Co), 1895 v S, Ni; 1896 v W, Ni; 1897 v S, W, Ni; 1898 v S; 1899 v S, W, Ni; 1900 v S; 1901 v S, W; 1902 v S; W, Ni; 1904 v S; 1905 v S, W, Ni; (with Middlesbrough), 1907 v S, W (23)
Blunstone, F. (Chelsea), 1955 v W, S, F, P; 1957 v Y (5)
Bond, R. (Preston NE), 1905 v Ni, W; 1906 v S, W, Ni; (with Bradford C), 1910 v S, W, Ni (8)
Bonetti, P. P. (Chelsea), 1966 v D; 1967 v Sp, A; 1968 v Sp; 1970 v Ho, P, WG (7)
Bonsor, A. G. (Wanderers), 1873 v S; 1875 v S (2)
Booth, F. (Manchester C), 1905 v Ni (1)
Booth, T. (Blackburn R), 1898 v W; (with Everton), 1903 v S (2)
Bould, S. A. (Arsenal), 1994 v Gr, N (2)
Bowden, E. R. (Arsenal), 1935 v W, I; 1936 v W, Ni, A; 1937 v H (6)
Bower, A. G. (Corinthians), 1924 v Ni, Bel; 1925 v W, Bel; 1927 v W (5)
Bowers, J. W. (Derby Co), 1934 v S, Ni, W (3)
Bowles, S. (QPR), 1974 v P, W, Ni; 1977 v I, Ho (5)
Bowser, S. (WBA), 1920 v Ni (1)
Bowyer, L. D. (Leeds U), 2003 v P (1)
Boyer, P. J. (Norwich C), 1976 v W (1)
Boyes, W. (WBA), 1935 v Ho; (with Everton), 1939 v W, R of E (3)
Boyle, T. W. (Burnley), 1913 v Ni (1)
Brabrook, P. (Chelsea), 1958 v USSR; 1959 v Ni; 1960 v Sp (3)
Bracewell, P. W. (Everton), 1985 v WG (sub), US; 1986 v Ni (3)
Bradford, G. R. W. (Bristol R), 1956 v D (1)
Bradford, J. (Birmingham), 1924 v Ni; 1925 v Bel; 1928 v S; 1929 v Ni, W, F, Sp; 1930 v S, Ni, G, A; 1931 v W (12)
Bradley, W. (Manchester U), 1959 v I, US, M (sub) (3)
Bradshaw, F. (Sheffield W), 1908 v A (1)
Bradshaw, T. H. (Liverpool), 1897 v Ni (1)
Bradshaw, W. (Blackburn R), 1910 v W, Ni; 1912 v Ni; 1913 v W (4)
Brann, G. (Swifts), 1886 v S, W; 1891 v W (3)
Brawn, W. F. (Aston Villa), 1904 v W, Ni (2)
Bray, J. (Manchester C), 1935 v W; 1936 v S, W, Ni, G; 1937 v S (6)
Brayshaw, E. (Sheffield W), 1887 v Ni (1)
Bridge W. M. (Southampton), 2002 v Ho, I, Para, Sk (sub), Cam, Arg (sub), Ng (sub); 2003 v P (sub), Mac, Lie, T, Ser (sub) (12)
Bridges, B. J. (Chelsea), 1965 v S, H, Y; 1966 v A (4)
Bridgett, A. (Sunderland), 1905 v S; 1908 v S, A (2), H, B; 1909 v Ni, W, H (2), A (11)
Brindle, T. (Darwen), 1880 v S, W (2)
Brittleton, J. T. (Sheffield W), 1912 v S, W, Ni; 1913 v S; 1914 v W (5)
Britton, C. S. (Everton), 1935 v S, W, Ni, I; 1937 v S, Ni, H, N, Se (9)
Broadbent, P. F. (Wolverhampton W), 1958 v USSR; 1959 v S, W, Ni, I, Br; 1960 v S (7)
Broadis, I. A. (Manchester C), 1952 v S, A, I; 1953 v S, Arg, Ch, U, US; (with Newcastle U), 1954 v S, H, Y, Bel, Sw, U (14)
Brockbank, J. (Cambridge University), 1872 v S (1)
Brodie, J. B. (Wolverhampton W), 1889 v S, Ni; 1891 v Ni (3)
Bromilow, T. G. (Liverpool), 1921 v W; 1922 v S, W; 1923 v Bel; 1926 v Ni (5)
Bromley-Davenport, W. E. (Oxford University), 1884 v S, W (2)
Brook, E. F. (Manchester C), 1930 v Ni; 1933 v Sw: 1934 v S, W, Ni, F, H, Cz; 1935 v S, W, Ni, I; 1936 v S, W, Ni; 1937 v H; 1938 v W, Ni (18)
Brooking, T. D. (West Ham U), 1974 v P, Arg, EG, Bul, Y; 1975 v Cz (sub), P; 1976 v P, W, Br, I, Fi; 1977 v Ei, Fi, I, Ho, Ni, W; 1978 v I, WG, W, S (sub), H; 1979 v D, Ei, Ni, W

(sub), S, Bul, Se (sub), A; 1980 v D, Ni, Arg (sub), W, Ni, S, Bel, Sp; 1981 v Sw, Sp, R, H; 1982 v H, S, Fi, Sp (sub) (47)
Brooks, J. (Tottenham H), 1957 v W, Y, D (3)
Broome, F. H. (Aston Villa), 1938 v G, Sw, F; 1939 v N, I, R, Y (7)
Brown, A. (Aston Villa), 1882 v S, W, Ni (3)
Brown, A. S. (Sheffield U), 1904 v W; 1906 v Ni (2)
Brown, A. (WBA), 1971 v W (1)
Brown, G. (Huddersfield T), 1927 v S, W, Ni, Bel, L, F; 1928 v W; 1929 v S; (with Aston Villa), 1933 v W (9)
Brown, J. (Blackburn R), 1881 v W; 1882 v Ni; 1885 v S, W, Ni (5)
Brown, J. H. (Sheffield W), 1927 v S, W, Bel, L, F; 1930 v Ni (6)
Brown, K. (West Ham U), 1960 v Ni (1)
Brown, W. (West Ham U), 1924 v Bel (1)
Brown, W. M. (Manchester U), 1999 v H; 2001 v Fi (sub), Alb (sub); 2002 v Ho, Sk (sub), Cam; 2003 v Aus (sub) (7)
Bruton, J. (Burnley), 1928 v F, Bel; 1929 v S (3)
Bryant, W. I. (Clapton), 1925 v F (1)
Buchan, C. M. (Sunderland), 1913 v Ni; 1920 v W; 1921 v W, Bel; 1923 v F; 1924 v S (6)
Buchanan, W. S. (Clapham R), 1876 v S (1)
Buckley, F. C. (Derby Co), 1914 v Ni (1)
Bull, S. G. (Wolverhampton W), 1989 v S (sub), D (sub); 1990 v Y, Cz, D (sub), U (sub), Tun (sub), Ei (sub), Ho (sub), Eg, Bel (sub); 1991 v H, Pol (13)
Bullock, F. E. (Huddersfield T), 1921 v Ni (1)
Bullock, N. (Bury), 1923 v Bel; 1926 v W; 1927 v Ni (3)
Burgess, H. (Manchester C), 1904 v S, W, Ni; 1906 v S (4)
Burgess, H. (Sheffield W), 1931 v S, Ni, F, Bel (4)
Burnup, C. J. (Cambridge University), 1896 v S (1)
Burrows, H. (Sheffield W), 1934 v H, Cz; 1935 v Ho (3)
Burton, F. E. (Nottingham F), 1889 v Ni (1)
Bury, L. (Cambridge University), 1877 v S; (with Old Etonians), 1879 v W (2)
Butcher, T. (Ipswich T), 1980 v Aus; 1981 v Sp; 1982 v W, S, F, Cz, WG, Sp; 1983 v D, WG, L, W, Gr, H, Ni, S, Aus (3); 1984 v D, H, L, F, Ni; 1985 v EG, Fi, T, Ni, Ei, R, Fi, S, I, WG, US; 1986 v Is, USSR, S, M, Ca, P, Mor, Pol, Para, Arg; (with Rangers), 1987 v Se, Ni (2), Y, Sp, Br, S; 1988 v T, Y; 1989 v D, Se, Gr, Alb (2), Ch, S, Pol, D; 1990 v Se, Pol, I, Y, Br, Cz, D, U, Tun, Ei, Ho, Bel, Cam, WG (77)
Butler, J. D. (Arsenal), 1925 v Bel (1)
Butler, W. (Bolton W), 1924 v S (1)
Butt, N. (Manchester U), 1997 v M (sub), S.Af (sub); 1998 v Mol (sub), I (sub), Ch, Bel, CzR; 1999 v H; 2001 v I, Sp, Fi (sub), Alb, M (sub), Gr (sub); 2002 v Se, Ho (sub), I, Para, Arg, Ng, D, Br; 2003 v P, Slo, Mac (sub), Lie (sub), T (27)
Byrne, G. (Liverpool), 1963 v S; 1966 v N (2)
Byrne, J. J. (C Palace), 1962 v Ni; (with West Ham U), 1963 v Sw; 1964 v S, U, P (2), Ei, Br, Arg; 1965 v W, S (11)
Byrne, R. W. (Manchester U), 1954 v S, H, Y, Bel, Sw, U; 1955 v S, W, Ni, WG, F, Sp, P; 1956 v S, W, Ni, Br, Se, Fi, WG, D, Sp; 1957 v S, W, Ni, Y, D (2), Ei (2); 1958 v W, Ni, F (33)

Callaghan, I. R. (Liverpool), 1966 v Fi, F; 1978 v Sw, L (4)
Calvey, J. (Nottingham F), 1902 v Ni (1)
Campbell, A. F. (Blackburn R), 1929 v W, Ni; (with Huddersfield T), 1931 v W, S, Ni; 1932 v W, Ni, Sp (8)
Campbell, S. (Tottenham H), 1996 v H (sub), S (sub); 1997 v Ge, I, Ge, S.Af (sub), Pol, F, Br; 1998 v Mol, I, Cam, Ch, P, Mor, Bel, Tun, R, Co, Arg; 1999 v Se, Bul, L, CzR, Pol, Se, Bul; 2000 v S (2), Arg, Br, Uk, Ma, P, G, R; 2001 v F, Sp, Fi, Alb; (with Arsenal), 2002 v G, Alb, Ho, I, Sk, Cam, Se, Arg, Ng, D, Br; 2003 v Mac, Aus, T (54)
Camsell, G. H. (Middlesbrough), 1929 v F, Bel; 1930 v Ni, W; 1934 v F; 1936 v S, G, A, Bel (9)
Capes, A. J. (Stoke C), 1903 v S (1)
Carr, J. (Middlesbrough), 1920 v Ni; 1923 v W (2)
Carr, J. (Newcastle U), 1905 v Ni; 1907 v Ni (2)
Carr, W. H. (Owlerton, Sheffield), 1875 v S (1)
Carragher, J. L. (Liverpool), 1999 v H (sub); 2001 v I (sub), M (sub); 2002 v Ho, G (sub), Alb (sub), Se, Para (sub); 2003 v Ser (sub) (9)
Carrick, M. (West Ham U), 2001 v M (sub); 2002 v Ho (sub) (2)
Carter, H. S. (Sunderland), 1934 v S, H; 1936 v G; 1937 v S, Ni, H; (with Derby Co), 1947 v S, W, Ni, Ei, Ho, F, Sw (13)
Carter, J. H. (WBA), 1926 v Bel; 1929 v Bel, Sp (3)
Catlin, A. E. (Sheffield W), 1937 v W, Ni, H, N, Se (5)
Chadwick, A. (Southampton), 1900 v S, W (2)
Chadwick, E. (Everton), 1891 v S, W; 1892 v S; 1893 v S; 1894 v S; 1896 v Ni; 1897 v S (7)
Chamberlain, M (Stoke C), 1983 v L (sub); 1984 v D (sub), S, USSR, Br, U, Ch; 1985 v Fi (sub) (8)
Chambers, H. (Liverpool), 1921 v S, W, Bel; 1923 v S, W, Ni, Bel; 1924 v Ni (8)
Channon, M. R. (Southampton), 1973 v Y, S (2), Ni, W, Cz, USSR, I; 1974 v A, Pol, I, P, W, Ni, S, Arg, EG, Bul, Y; 1975 v Cz, P, WG, Cy (2), Ni (sub), W, S; 1976 v Sw, Cz, P, W, Ni, S, Br, I, Fi; 1977 v Fi, I, L, Ni, W, S, Br (sub), Arg, U; (with Manchester C), 1978 v Sw (46)
Charles, G. A. (Nottingham F), 1991 v Nz, Mal (2)
Charlton, J. (Leeds U), 1965 v S, H, Y, WG, Se; 1966 v W, Ni, S, A, Sp, Pol (2), WG (2), Y, Fi, D, U, M, F, Arg, P; 1967 v W, S, Ni, Cz; 1968 v W, Sp; 1969 v W, R, F; 1970 v Ho (2), P, Cz (35)
Charlton, R. (Manchester U), 1958 v S, P, Y; 1959 v S, W, Ni, USSR, I, Br, Pe, M, US; 1960 v W, S, Se, Y, Sp, H; 1961 v Ni, W, S, L, P, Sp, M, I, A; 1962 v W, Ni, S, A, Sw, Pe, L, P, H, Arg, Bul, Br; 1963 v S, F, Br, Cz, EG, Sw; 1964 v S, W, Ni, R of W, U, P, Ei, Br, Arg, US (sub); 1965 v Ni, S, Ho; 1966 v W, Ni, S, A, Sp, WG (2), Y, Fi, N, Pol, U, M, F, Arg, P; 1967 v Ni, W, S, Cz; 1968 v W, Ni, S, USSR (2), Sp (2), Se, Y; 1969 v S, W, Ni, R (2), Bul, M, Br; 1970 v W, Ni, Ho (2), P, Co, Ec, Cz, R, Br, WG (106)
Charnley, R. O. (Blackpool), 1963 v F (1)
Charsley, C. C. (Small Heath), 1893 v Ni (1)
Chedgzoy, S. (Everton), 1920 v W; 1921 v W, S, Ni; 1922 v Ni; 1923 v S; 1924 v W; 1925 v Ni (8)
Chenery, C. J. (C Palace), 1872 v S; 1873 v S; 1874 v S (3)
Cherry, T. J. (Leeds U), 1976 v W, S (sub), Br, Fi; 1977 v Ei, I, L, Ni, S (sub), Br, Arg, U; 1978 v Sw, L, I, Br, W; 1979 v Cz, W, Se; 1980 v Ei, Arg (sub), W, Ni, S, Aus, Sp (sub) (27)
Chilton, A. (Manchester U), 1951 v Ni; 1952 v F (2)
Chippendale, H. (Blackburn R), 1894 v Ni (1)
Chivers, M. (Tottenham H), 1971 v Ma (2), Gr, Ni, S; 1972 v Sw (1+1 sub), Gr, WG (2), Ni (sub), S; 1973 v W (3), S (2), Ni, Cz, Pol, USSR, I; 1974 v A, Pol (24)
Christian, E. (Old Etonians), 1879 v S (1)
Clamp, E. (Wolverhampton W), 1958 v USSR (2), Br, A (4)
Clapton, D. R. (Arsenal), 1959 v W (1)
Clare, T. (Stoke C), 1889 v Ni; 1892 v Ni; 1893 v W; 1894 v S (4)
Clarke, A. J. (Leeds U), 1970 v Cz; 1971 v EG, Ma, Ni, W (sub), S (sub); 1973 v S (2), W, Cz, Pol, USSR, I; 1974 v A, Pol, I; 1975 v P; 1976 v Cz, P (sub) (19)
Clarke, H. A. (Tottenham H), 1954 v S (1)
Clay, T. (Tottenham H), 1920 v W; 1922 v W, S, Ni (4)
Clayton, R. (Blackburn R), 1956 v Ni, Br, Se, Fi, WG, Sp; 1957 v S, W, Ni, Y, D (2), Ei (2); 1958 v S, W, Ni, F, P, Y, USSR; 1959 v S, W, Ni, USSR, I, Br, Pe, M, US; 1960 v W, Ni, S, Se, Y (35)
Clegg, J. C. (Sheffield W), 1872 v S (1)
Clegg, W. E. (Sheffield W), 1873 v S; (with Sheffield Albion), 1879 v W (2)
Clemence, R. N. (Liverpool), 1973 v W (2); 1974 v EG, Bul, Y; 1975 v Cz, P, WG, Cy, Ni, W, S; 1976 v Sw, Cz, P, W (2), Ni, S, Br, Fi; 1977 v Ei, Fi, I, Ho, L, S, Br, Arg, U; 1978 v Sw, L, I, WG, Ni, S; 1979 v D, Ei, Ni (2), S, Bul, A (sub); 1980 v D, Bul, Ei, Arg, W, S, Bel, Sp; 1981 v R, Sp, Br, Sw, H; (with Tottenham H), 1982 v N, Ni, Fi; 1983 v L; 1984 v L (61)
Clement, D. T. (QPR), 1976 v W (sub+1), I; 1977 v I, Ho (5)
Clough, B. H. (Middlesbrough), 1960 v W, Se (2)
Clough, N. H. (Nottingham F), 1989 v Ch; 1991 v Arg (sub), Aus, Mal; 1992 v F, Cz, C; 1993 v Sp, T (sub), Pol (sub), N (sub), US, Br, G (14)
Coates, R. (Burnley), 1970 v Ni; 1971 v Gr (sub); (with Tottenham H), Ma, W (4)
Cobbold, W. N. (Cambridge University), 1883 v S, Ni; 1885 v S, Ni; 1886 v S, W; (with Old Carthusians), 1887 v S, W, Ni (9)
Cock, J. G. (Huddersfield T), 1920 v Ni; (with Chelsea), v S (2)
Cockburn, H. (Manchester U), 1947 v W, Ni, Ei; 1948 v S, I; 1949 v S, Ni, D, Sw, Se; 1951 v Arg, P; 1952 v F (13)
Cohen, G. R. (Fulham), 1964 v U, P, Ei, US, Br; 1965 v W, S, Ni, Bel, H, Ho, Y, WG, Se; 1966 v W, S, Ni, A, Sp, Pol (2), WG (2), N, D, U, M, F, Arg, P; 1967 v W, S, Ni, Cz, Sp; 1968 v W, Ni (37)
Cole, A. (Manchester U), 1995 v U (sub); 1997 v I (sub); 1999 v F (sub), Pol, Se; 2000 v S (sub), Arg (sub); 2001 v F, G, Fi, Sp, Fi, Alb; 2002 v Ho, Gr (sub) (15)
Cole, A. (Arsenal), 2001 v Alb, M, Gr; 2002 v Ho, G, Alb, Gr, Sk, Se, Arg, Ng, D, Br; 2003 v P, Slo, Mac, Aus, Ser, Slo (19)
Cole, J. J. (West Ham U), 2001 v M (sub); 2002 v Ho (sub), I (sub), Para (sub), Sk (sub), Cam, Se (sub); 2003 v P, S.Af (sub), Ser (sub) (10)
Colclough, H. (C Palace), 1914 v W (1)

Coleman, E. H. (Dulwich Hamlet), 1921 v W (1)
Coleman, J. (Woolwich Arsenal), 1907 v Ni (1)
Collymore, S. V. (Nottingham F), 1995 v J, Br (sub); (with Aston Villa), 1998 v Mol (sub) (3)
Common, A. (Sheffield U), 1904 v W, Ni; (with Middlesbrough), 1906 v W (3)
Compton, L. H. (Arsenal), 1951 v W, Y (2)
Conlin, J. (Bradford C), 1906 v S (1)
Connelly, J. M. (Burnley), 1960 v W, N, S, Se; 1962 v W, A, Sw, P; 1963 v W, F; (with Manchester U), 1965 v H, Y, Se; 1966 v W, Ni, S, A, N, D, U (20)
Cook, T. E. R. (Brighton), 1925 v W (1)
Cooper, C. T. (Nottingham F), 1995 v Se, Br (2)
Cooper, N. C. (Cambridge University), 1893 v Ni (1)
Cooper, T. (Derby Co), 1928 v Ni; 1929 v W, Ni, S, F, Bel, Sp; 1931 v F; 1932 v W, Sp; 1933 v S; 1934 v S, H, Cz; 1935 v W (15)
Cooper, T. (Leeds U), 1969 v W, S, F, M; 1970 v Ho, Bel, Co, Ec, R, Cz, Br, WG; 1971 v EG, Ma, Ni, W, S; 1972 v Sw (2); 1975 v P (20)
Coppell, S. J. (Manchester U), 1978 v I, WG, Br, W, Ni, S, H; 1979 v D, Ei, Cz, Ni (2), W (sub), S, Bul, A; 1980 v D, Ni, Ei (sub), Sp, Arg, W, S, Bel, I; 1981 v R (sub), Sw, R, Br, W, S, Sw, H; 1982 v H, S, Fi, F, Cz, K, WG; 1983 v L, Gr (42)
Copping, W. (Leeds U), 1933 v I, Sw; 1934 v S, Ni, W, F; (with Arsenal), 1935 v Ni, I; 1936 v A, Bel; 1937 v N, Se, Fi; 1938 v S, W, Ni, Cz; 1939 v W, R of E; (with Leeds U), R (20)
Corbett, B. O. (Corinthians), 1901 v W (1)
Corbett, R. (Old Malvernians), 1903 v W (1)
Corbett, W. S. (Birmingham), 1908 v A, H, B (3)
Corrigan, J. T. (Manchester C), 1978 v I (sub), Br; 1979 v W; 1980 v Ni, Aus; 1981 v W, S; 1982 v W, Ic (9)
Cottee, A. R. (West Ham U), 1987 v Se (sub), Ni (sub); 1988 v H (sub); (with Everton) 1989 v D (sub), Se (sub), Ch (sub), S (7)
Cotterill, G. H. (Cambridge University), 1891 v Ni; (with Old Brightonians), 1892 v W; 1893 v S, Ni (4)
Cottle, J. R. (Bristol C), 1909 v Ni (1)
Cowan, S. (Manchester C), 1926 v Bel; 1930 v A; 1931 v Bel (3)
Cowans, G. (Aston Villa), 1983 v W, H, Ni, S, Aus (3); (with Bari), 1986 v Eg, USSR; (with Aston Villa), 1991 v Ei (10)
Cowell, A. (Blackburn R), 1910 v Ni (1)
Cox, J. (Liverpool), 1901 v Ni; 1902 v S; 1903 v S (3)
Cox, J. D. (Derby Co), 1892 v Ni (1)
Crabtree, J. W. (Burnley), 1894 v Ni; 1895 v Ni, S; (with Aston Villa), 1896 v W, S, Ni; 1899 v S, W, Ni; 1900 v S, W, Ni; 1901 v W; 1902 v W (14)
Crawford, J. F. (Chelsea), 1931 v S (1)
Crawford, R. (Ipswich T), 1962 v Ni, A (2)
Crawshaw, T. H. (Sheffield W), 1895 v Ni; 1896 v S, W, Ni; 1897 v S, W, Ni; 1901 v Ni; 1904 v W, Ni (10)
Crayston, W. J. (Arsenal), 1936 v S, W, G, A, Bel; 1938 v W, Ni, Cz (8)
Creek, F. N. S. (Corinthians), 1923 v F (1)
Cresswell, W. (South Shields), 1921 v W; (with Sunderland), 1923 v F; 1924 v Bel; 1925 v Ni; 1926 v W; 1927 v Ni; (with Everton), 1930 v Ni (7)
Crompton, R. (Blackburn R), 1902 v S, W, Ni; 1903 v S, W; 1904 v S, W, Ni; 1906 v S, W, Ni; 1907 v S, W, Ni; 1908 v S, W, Ni, A (2), H, B; 1909 v S, W, Ni, H (2), A; 1910 v S, W; 1911 v S, W, Ni; 1912 v S, W, Ni; 1913 v S, W, Ni; 1914 v S, W, Ni (41)
Crooks, S. D. (Derby Co), 1930 v S, G, A; 1931 v S, W, Ni, F, Bel; 1932 v S, W, Ni, Sp; 1933 v Ni, W, A; 1934 v S, Ni, W, F, H, Cz; 1935 v Ni; 1936 v S, W; 1937 v W, H (26)
Crowe, C. (Wolverhampton W), 1963 v F (1)
Cuggy, F. (Sunderland), 1913 v Ni; 1914 v Ni (2)
Cullis, S. (Wolverhampton W), 1938 v S, W, Ni, F, Cz; 1939 v S, Ni, R of E, N, I, R, Y (12)
Cunliffe, A. (Blackburn R), 1933 v Ni, W (2)
Cunliffe, D. (Portsmouth), 1900 v Ni (1)
Cunliffe, J. N. (Everton), 1936 v Bel (1)
Cunningham, L. (WBA), 1979 v W, Se, A (sub); (with Real Madrid), 1980 v Ei, Sp (sub); 1981 v R (sub) (6)
Curle, K. (Manchester C), 1992 v C (sub), H, D (3)
Currey, E. S. (Oxford University), 1890 v S, W (2)
Currie, A. W. (Sheffield U), 1972 v Ni; 1973 v USSR, I; 1974 v A, Pol, I; 1976 v Sw; (with Leeds U), 1978 v Br, W (sub), Ni, S, H (sub); 1979 v Cz, Ni (2), W, Se (17)
Cursham, A. W. (Notts Co), 1876 v S; 1877 v S; 1878 v S; 1879 v W; 1883 v S, W (6)
Cursham, H. A. (Notts Co), 1880 v W; 1882 v S, W, Ni; 1883 v S, W, Ni; 1884 v Ni (8)

Daft, H. B. (Notts Co), 1889 v Ni; 1890 v S, W; 1891 v Ni; 1892 v Ni (5)
Daley, A. M. (Aston Villa), 1992 v Pol (sub), C, H, Br, Fi (sub), D (sub), Se (7)
Danks, T. (Nottingham F), 1885 v S (1)
Davenport, P. (Nottingham F), 1985 v Ei (sub) (1)
Davenport, J. K. (Bolton W), 1885 v W; 1890 v Ni (2)
Davis, G. (Derby Co), 1904 v W, Ni (2)
Davis, H. (Sheffield W), 1903 v S, W, Ni (3)
Davison, J. E. (Sheffield W), 1922 v W (1)
Dawson, J. (Burnley), 1922 v S, Ni (2)
Day, S. H. (Old Malvernians), 1906 v Ni, W, S (3)
Dean, W. R. (Everton), 1927 v S, W, F, Bel, L; 1928 v S, W, Ni, F, Bel; 1929 v S, W, Ni; 1931 v S; 1932 v Sp; 1933 v Ni (16)
Deane, B. C. (Sheffield U), 1991 v Nz (sub + 1); 1993 v Sp (sub) (3)
Deeley, N. V. (Wolverhampton W), 1959 v Br, Pe (2)
Devey, J. H. G. (Aston Villa), 1892 v Ni; 1894 v Ni (2)
Devonshire, A. (West Ham U), 1980 v Aus (sub), Ni; 1982 v Ho, Ic; 1983 v WG, W, Gr; 1984 v L (8)
Dewhurst, F. (Preston NE), 1886 v W, Ni; 1887 v S, W, Ni; 1888 v S, W, Ni; 1889 v W (9)
Dewhurst, G. P. (Liverpool Ramblers), 1895 v W (1)
Dickinson, J. W. (Portsmouth), 1949 v N, F; 1950 v S, W, Ei, P, Bel, Ch, US, Sp; 1951 v Ni, W, Y; 1952 v W, Ni, S, A (2), I, Sw; 1953 v W, Ni, S, Bel, Arg, Ch, U, US; 1954 v W, Ni, S, R of E, H (2), Y, Bel, Sw, U; 1955 v Sp, P; 1956 v W, Ni, S, D, Sp; 1957 v W, Y, D (48)
Dimmock, J. H. (Tottenham H), 1921 v S; 1926 v W, Bel (3)
Ditchburn, E. G. (Tottenham H), 1949 v Sw, Se; 1953 v US; 1957 v W, Y, D (6)
Dix, R. W. (Derby Co), 1939 v N (1)
Dixon, J. A. (Notts Co), 1885 v W (1)
Dixon, K. M. (Chelsea), 1985 v M (sub), WG, US; 1986 v Ni, Is, M (sub), Pol (sub); 1987 v Se (8)
Dixon, L. M. (Arsenal), 1990 v Cz; 1991 v H, Pol, Ei (2), Cam, T, Arg; 1992 v G, T, Pol, Cz (sub); 1993 v Sp, N, T, Sm, T, Ho, N, US; 1994 v Sm; 1999 v F (22)
Dobson, A. T. C. (Notts Co), 1882 v Ni; 1884 v S, W, Ni (4)
Dobson, C. F. (Notts Co), 1886 v Ni (1)
Dobson, J. M. (Burnley), 1974 v P, EG, Bul, Y; (with Everton), 1975 v Cz (5)
Doggart, A. G. (Corinthians), 1924 v Bel (1)
Dorigo, A. R. (Chelsea), 1990 v Y (sub), Cz (sub), D (sub), I; 1991 v H (sub), USSR; (with Leeds U), 1992 v G, Cz (sub), H, Br; 1993 v Sm, Pol, US, Br; 1994 v H (15)
Dorrell, A. R. (Aston Villa), 1925 v W, Bel, F; 1926 v Ni (4)
Douglas, B. (Blackburn R), 1958 v S, W, Ni, F, P, Y, USSR (2), Br, A; 1959 v S, USSR; 1960 v Y, H; 1961 v Ni, W, S, L, P, Sp, M, I, A; 1962 v W, Ni, S, Pe, L, P, H, Arg, Bul, Br; 1963 v S, Br, Sw (36)
Downs, R. W. (Everton), 1921 v Ni (1)
Doyle, M. (Manchester C), 1976 v W, S (sub), Br, I; 1977 v Ho (5)
Drake, E. J. (Arsenal), 1935 v Ni, I; 1936 v W; 1937 v H; 1938 v F (5)
Dublin, D. (Coventry C), 1998 v Ch, Mor, Bel (sub); (with Aston Villa), 1999 v CzR (4)
Ducat, A. (Woolwich Arsenal), 1910 v S, W, Ni; (with Aston Villa), 1920 v S, W; 1921 v Ni (6)
Dunn, A. T. B. (Cambridge University), 1883 v Ni; 1884 v Ni; (with Old Etonians), 1892 v S, W (4)
Dunn, D. J. I. (Blackburn R), 2003 v P (sub) (1)
Duxbury, M. (Manchester U), 1984 v L, F, W, S, USSR, Br, U, Ch; 1985 v EG, Fi (10)
Dyer, K. C. (Newcastle U), 2000 v L, Pol (sub), Bel, Arg, Uk (sub); 2001 v F (sub), G (sub), I; 2002 v Para, Se (sub), D (sub), Br (sub); 2003 v Slo (sub), Aus, Lie, T (sub) (16)

Earle, S. G. J. (Clapton), 1924 v F; (with West Ham U), 1928 v Ni (2)
Eastham, G. (Arsenal), 1963 v Br, Cz, EG; 1964 v W, Ni, S, R of W, U, P, Ei, US, Br, Arg; 1965 v H, WG, Se; 1966 v Sp, Pol, D (19)
Eastham, G. R. (Bolton W), 1935 v Ho (1)
Eckersley, W. (Blackburn R), 1950 v Sp; 1951 v S, Y, Arg, P; 1952 v A (2), Sw; 1953 v Ni, Arg, Ch, U, US; 1954 v W, Ni, R of E, H (17)
Edwards, D. (Manchester U), 1955 v S, F, Sp, P; 1956 v S, Br, Se, Fi, WG; 1957 v S, Ni, Ei (2), D (2); 1958 v W, Ni, F (18)
Edwards, J. H. (Shropshire Wanderers), 1874 v S (1)
Edwards, W. (Leeds U), 1926 v S, W; 1927 v W, Ni, S, F, Bel, L; 1928 v S, F, Bel; 1929 v S, W, Ni; 1930 v W, Ni (16)

Ehiogu, U. (Aston Villa), 1996 v Chn (sub); (with Middlesbrough), 2001 v Sp (sub); 2002 v Ho (sub), I (sub) (4)
Ellerington, W. (Southampton), 1949 v N, F (2)
Elliott, G. W. (Middlesbrough), 1913 v Ni; 1914 v Ni; 1920 v W (3)
Elliott, W. H. (Burnley), 1952 v I, A; 1953 v Ni, W, Bel (5)
Evans, R. E. (Sheffield U), 1911 v S, W, Ni; 1912 v W (4)
Ewer, F. H. (Casuals), 1924 v F; 1925 v Bel (2)

Fairclough, P. (Old Foresters), 1878 v S (1)
Fairhurst, D. (Newcastle U), 1934 v F (1)
Fantham, J. (Sheffield W), 1962 v L (1)
Fashanu, J. (Wimbledon), 1989 v Ch, S (2)
Felton, W. (Sheffield W), 1925 v F (1)
Fenton, M. (Middlesbrough), 1938 v S (1)
Fenwick, T. (QPR), 1984 v W (sub), S, USSR, Br, U, Ch; 1985 v Fi, S, M, US; 1986 v R, T, Ni, Eg, M, P, Mor, Pol, Arg; (with Tottenham H), 1988 v Is (sub) (20)
Ferdinand, L. (QPR), 1993 v Sm, Ho, N, US; 1994 v Pol, Sm; 1995 v US (sub); (with Newcastle U), 1996 v P, Bul, H; 1997 v Pol, Ge, I (sub); (with Tottenham H), 1998 v Mol, S.Ar (sub), Mor (sub), Bel (17)
Ferdinand, R. G. (West Ham U), 1998 v Cam (sub), Sw, Bel (sub); 1999 v L, CzR, F (sub), H, Se (sub); 2000 v Arg (sub); 2001 v I; (with Leeds U), Sp, Fi, Alb, M, Gr; 2002 v G, Alb, Gr, Se, Ho, Sk, Cam, Se, Arg, Ng, D, Br; (with Manchester U), 2003 v P, Aus, Lie, T, S.Af (32)
Field, E. (Clapham Rovers), 1876 v S; 1881 v S (2)
Finney, T. (Preston NE), 1947 v W, Ni, Ei, Ho, F, P; 1948 v S, W, Ni, Bel, Se, I; 1949 v S, W, Ni, Se, N, F; 1950 v S, W, Ni, Ei, I, P, Bel, Ch, US, Sp; 1951 v W, S, Arg, P; 1952 v W, Ni, S, F, I, Sw, A; 1953 v W, Ni, S, Bel, Arg, Ch, U, US; 1954 v W, S, Bel, Sw, U, H, Y; 1955 v WG; 1956 v S, W, Ni, D, Sp; 1957 v S, W, Y, D (2), Ei (2); 1958 v W, S, F, P, Y, USSR (2); 1959 v Ni, USSR (76)
Fleming, H. J. (Swindon T), 1909 v S, H (2); 1910 v W, Ni; 1911 v W, Ni; 1912 v Ni; 1913 v S, W; 1914 v S (11)
Fletcher, A. (Wolverhampton W), 1889 v W; 1890 v W (2)
Flowers, R. (Wolverhampton W), 1955 v F; 1959 v S, W, I, Br, Pe, US, M (sub); 1960 v W, Ni, S, Se, Y, Sp, H; 1961 v Ni, W, S, L, P, Sp, M, I, A; 1962 v W, Ni, S, A, Sw, Pe, L, P, H, Arg, Bul, Br; 1963 v Ni, W, S, F (2), Sw; 1964 v Ei, US, P; 1965 v W, Ho, WG; 1966 v N (49)
Flowers, T. D. (Southampton), 1993 v Br; (with Blackburn R), 1994 v Gr; 1995 v Ng, U, J, Se, Br; 1996 v Chn; 1997 v I; 1998 v Sw, Mor (11)
Forman, Frank (Nottingham F), 1898 v S, Ni; 1899 v S, W, Ni; 1901 v S; 1902 v S, Ni; 1903 v W (9)
Forman, F. R. (Nottingham F), 1899 v S, W, Ni (3)
Forrest, J. H. (Blackburn R), 1884 v W; 1885 v S, W, Ni; 1886 v S, W; 1887 v S, W, Ni; 1889 v S; 1890 v Ni (11)
Fort, J. (Millwall), 1921 v Bel (1)
Foster, R. E. (Oxford University), 1900 v W; (with Corinthians), 1901 v W, Ni, S; 1902 v W (5)
Foster, S. (Brighton & HA), 1982 v Ni, Ho, K (3)
Foulke, W. J. (Sheffield U), 1897 v W (1)
Foulkes, W. A. (Manchester U), 1955 v Ni (1)
Fowler, R. B. (Liverpool), 1996 v Bul (sub), Cro, Chn (sub), Ho (sub), Sp (sub); 1997 v M; 1998 v Cam; 1999 v CzR (sub), Bul; 2000 v L, Pol, Br (sub), Uk, Ma (sub); 2001 v I (sub), Fi (sub), M, Gr; 2002 v Ho, Alb (sub), Gr, Se (sub); (with Leeds U), I (sub), Para (sub), Cam (sub), D (sub) (26)
Fox, F. S. (Millwall), 1925 v F (1)
Francis, G. C. J. (QPR), 1975 v Cz, P, W, S; 1976 v Sw, Cz, P, W, Ni, S, Br, Fi (12)
Francis, T. (Birmingham C), 1977 v Ho, L, S, Br; 1978 v Sw, L, I (sub), WG (sub), Br, W, S, H; (with Nottingham F), 1979 v Bul (sub), Se, A (sub); 1980 v Ni, Bul, Sp; 1981 v Sp, R, S (sub), Sw; (with Manchester C), 1982 v N, Ni, W, S (sub), Fi (sub), F, Cz, K, WG, Sp; (with Sampdoria), 1983 v D, Gr, H, Ni, S, Aus (3); 1984 v D, Ni, USSR; 1985 v EG (sub), T (sub), Ni (sub), R, Fi, S, I, M; 1986 v S (52)
Franklin, C. F. (Stoke C), 1947 v S, W, Ni, Ei, Ho, F, Sw, P; 1948 v S, W, Ni, Bel, Se, I; 1949 v S, W, Ni, D, Sw, N, F, Se; 1950 v W, S, Ni, Ei, I (27)
Freeman, B. C. (Everton), 1909 v S, W; (with Burnley), 1912 v S, W, Ni (5)
Froggatt, J. (Portsmouth), 1950 v Ni, I; 1951 v S; 1952 v S, A (2), I, Sw; 1953 v Ni, W, S, Bel, US (13)
Froggatt, R. (Sheffield W), 1953 v W, S, Bel, US (4)
Fry, C. B. (Corinthians), 1901 v Ni (1)
Furness, W. I. (Leeds U), 1933 v I (1)

Galley, T. (Wolverhampton W), 1937 v N, Se (2)
Gardner, T. (Aston Villa), 1934 v Cz; 1935 v Ho (2)
Garfield, B. (WBA), 1898 v Ni (1)
Garratty, W. (Aston Villa), 1903 v W (1)
Garrett, T. (Blackpool), 1952 v S, I; 1954 v W (3)
Gascoigne, P. J. (Tottenham H), 1989 v D (sub), S.Ar (sub), Alb (sub), Ch, S (sub); 1990 v Se (sub), Br (sub), Cz, D, U, Tun, Ei, Ho, Eg, Bel, Cam, WG; 1991 v H, Pol, Cam; (with Lazio), 1993 v N, T, Sm, T, Ho, Pol, N; 1994 v Pol, D; 1995 v J (sub), Se (sub), Br (sub); (with Rangers), 1996 v Co, Sw, P, Bul, Cro, Chn, Sw, S, Ho, Sp, G; 1997 v Mol, Pol, Ge, S.Af, Pol, I (sub), F, Br; 1998 v Mol, I, Cam; (with Middlesbrough), S.Ar (sub), Mor, Bel (57)
Gates, E. (Ipswich T), 1981 v N, R (2)
Gay, L. H. (Cambridge University), 1893 v S; (with Old Brightonians), 1894 v S, W (3)
Geary, F. (Everton), 1890 v Ni; 1891 v S (2)
Geaves, R. L. (Clapham Rovers), 1875 v S (1)
Gee, C. W. (Everton), 1932 v W, Sp; 1937 v Ni (3)
Geldard, A. (Everton), 1933 v I, Sw; 1935 v S; 1938 v Ni (4)
George, C. (Derby Co), 1977 v Ei (1)
George, W. (Aston Villa), 1902 v S, W, Ni (3)
Gerrard, S. G. (Liverpool), 2000 v Uk, G (sub); 2001 v Fi, M, Gr; 2002 v G, Alb, Gr, Ho, Para; 2003 v P, Slo, Mac, Lie, T, S.Af, Ser, Slo (18)
Gibbins, W. V. T. (Clapton), 1924 v F; 1925 v F (2)
Gidman, J. (Aston Villa), 1977 v L (1)
Gillard, I. T. (QPR), 1975 v WG, W; 1976 v Cz (3)
Gilliat, W. E. (Old Carthusians), 1893 v Ni (1)
Goddard, P. (West Ham U), 1982 v Ic (sub) (1)
Goodall, F. R. (Huddersfield T), 1926 v S; 1927 v S, F, Bel, L; 1928 v S, W, F, Bel; 1930 v S, G, A; 1931 v S, W, Ni, Bel; 1932 v Ni; 1933 v W, Ni, A, I, Sw; 1934 v W, Ni, F (25)
Goodall, J. (Preston NE), 1888 v S, W; 1889 v S, W; (with Derby Co), 1891 v S, W; 1892 v S; 1893 v W; 1894 v S; 1895 v S, Ni; 1896 v S, W; 1898 v W (14)
Goodhart, H. C. (Old Etonians), 1883 v S, W, Ni (3)
Goodwyn, A. G. (Royal Engineers), 1873 v S (1)
Goodyer, A. C. (Nottingham F), 1879 v S (1)
Gosling, R. C. (Old Etonians), 1892 v W; 1893 v S; 1894 v W; 1895 v W, S (5)
Gosnell, A. A. (Newcastle U), 1906 v Ni (1)
Gough, H. C. (Sheffield U), 1921 v S (1)
Goulden, L. A. (West Ham U), 1937 v Se, N; 1938 v W, Ni, Cz, G, Sw, F; 1939 v S, W, R of E, I, R, Y (14)
Graham, L. (Millwall), 1925 v S, W (2)
Graham, T. (Nottingham F), 1931 v F; 1932 v Ni (2)
Grainger, C. (Sheffield U), 1956 v Br, Se, Fi, WG; 1957 v W, Ni; (with Sunderland), 1957 v S (7)
Gray, A. A. (C Palace), 1992 v Pol (1)
Gray, M. (Sunderland), 1999 v H (sub), Se (sub), Bul (3)
Greaves, J. (Chelsea), 1959 v Pe, M, US; 1960 v W, Se, Y, Sp; 1961 v Ni, W, S, L, P, Sp, I, A; (with Tottenham H), 1962 v S, Sw, Pe, H, Arg, Bul, Br; 1963 v Ni, W, S, F (2), Br, Cz, Sw; 1964 v W, Ni, R of W, P (2), Ei, Br, U, Arg; 1965 v Ni, S, Bel, Ho, H, Y; 1966 v W, A, Y, N, D, Pol, U, M, F; 1967 v S, Sp, A (57)
Green, F. T. (Wanderers), 1876 v S (1)
Green, G. H. (Sheffield U), 1925 v F; 1926 v S, Bel, W; 1927 v W, Ni; 1928 v F, Bel (8)
Greenhalgh, E. H. (Notts Co), 1872 v S; 1873 v S (2)
Greenhoff, B. (Manchester U), 1976 v W, Ni; 1977 v Ei, Fi, I, Ho, Ni, W, S, Br, Arg, U; 1978 v Br, W, Ni, S (sub), H (sub); (with Leeds U), 1980 v Aus (sub) (18)
Greenwood, D. H. (Blackburn R), 1882 v S, Ni (2)
Gregory, J. (QPR), 1983 v Aus (3); 1984 v D, H, W (6)
Grimsdell, A. (Tottenham H), 1920 v S, W; 1921 v S, Ni; 1923 v W, Ni (6)
Grosvenor, A. T. (Birmingham), 1934 v Ni, W, F (3)
Gunn, W. (Notts Co), 1884 v S, W (2)
Guppy, S. (Leicester C), 2000 v Bel (1)
Gurney, R. (Sunderland), 1935 v S (1)

Hacking, J. (Oldham Ath), 1929 v S, W, Ni (3)
Hadley, N. (WBA), 1903 v Ni (1)
Hagan, J. (Sheffield U), 1949 v D (1)
Haines, J. T. W. (WBA), 1949 v Sw (1)
Hall, A. E. (Aston Villa), 1910 v Ni (1)
Hall, G. W. (Tottenham H), 1934 v F; 1938 v S, W, Ni, Cz; 1939 v S, Ni, R of E, I, Y (10)
Hall, J. (Birmingham C), 1956 v S, W, Ni, Br, Se, Fi, WG, D, Sp; 1957 v S, W, Ni, Y, D (2), Ei (2) (17)
Halse, H. J. (Manchester U), 1909 v A (1)
Hammond, H. E. D. (Oxford University), 1889 v S (1)
Hampson, J. (Blackpool), 1931 v Ni, W; 1933 v A (3)
Hampton, H. (Aston Villa), 1913 v S, W; 1914 v S, W (4)
Hancocks, J. (Wolverhampton W), 1949 v Sw; 1950 v W; 1951 v Y (3)

Hapgood, E. (Arsenal), 1933 v I, Sw; 1934 v S, Ni, W, H, Cz; 1935 v S, Ni, W, I, Ho; 1936 v S, Ni, W, G, A, Bel; 1937 v Fi; 1938 v S, G, Sw, F; 1939 v S, W, Ni, R of E, N, I, Y (30)
Hardinge, H. T. W. (Sheffield U), 1910 v S (1)
Hardman, H. P. (Everton), 1905 v W; 1907 v S, Ni; 1908 v W (4)
Hardwick, G. F. M. (Middlesbrough), 1947 v S, W, Ni, Ei, Ho, F, Sw, P; 1948 v S, W, Ni, Bel, Se (13)
Hardy, H. (Stockport Co), 1925 v Bel (1)
Hardy, S. (Liverpool), 1907 v S, W, Ni; 1908 v S; 1909 v S, W, Ni, H (2), A; 1910 v S, W, Ni; 1912 v Ni; (with Aston Villa), 1913 v S; 1914 v Ni, W, S; 1920 v S, W, Ni (21)
Harford, M. G. (Luton T), 1988 v Is (sub); 1989 v D (2)
Hargreaves, F. W. (Blackburn R), 1880 v W; 1881 v W; 1882 v Ni (3)
Hargreaves, J. (Blackburn R), 1881 v S, W (2)
Hargreaves, O. (Bayern Munich) 2002 v Ho, G (sub), I (sub), Para (sub), Sk, Cam, Se, Arg; 2003 v P (sub), Slo (sub), Aus (sub), Ser (sub), Slo (sub) (13)
Harper, E. C. (Blackburn R), 1926 v S (1)
Harris, G. (Burnley), 1966 v Pol (1)
Harris, P. P. (Portsmouth), 1950 v Ei; 1954 v H (2)
Harris, S. S. (Cambridge University), 1904 v S; (with Old Westminsters), 1905 v Ni, W; 1906 v S, W, Ni (6)
Harrison, A. H. (Old Westminsters), 1893 v S, Ni (2)
Harrison, G. (Everton), 1921 v Bel; 1922 v Ni (2)
Harrow, J. H. (Chelsea), 1923 v Ni, Se (2)
Hart, E. (Leeds U), 1929 v W; 1930 v W, Ni; 1933 v S, A; 1934 v S, H, Cz (8)
Hartley, F. (Oxford C), 1923 v F (1)
Harvey, A. (Wednesbury Strollers), 1881 v W (1)
Harvey, J. C. (Everton), 1971 v Ma (1)
Hassall, H. W. (Huddersfield T), 1951 v S, Arg, P; 1952 v F; (with Bolton W), 1954 v Ni (5)
Hateley, M. (Portsmouth), 1984 v USSR (sub), Br, U, Ch; (with AC Milan), 1985 v EG (sub), Fi, Ni, Ei, Fi, S, I, M; 1986 v R, T, Eg, S, M, Ca, P, Mor, Para (sub); 1987 v T (sub), Br (sub), S; (with Monaco), 1988 v WG (sub), Ho (sub), H (sub), Co (sub), Ei (sub), Ho (sub), USSR (sub); (with Rangers), 1992 v Cz (32)
Hawkes, R. M. (Luton T), 1907 v Ni; 1908 v A (2), H, B (5)
Haworth, G. (Accrington), 1887 v Ni, W, S; 1888 v S; 1890 v S (5)
Hawtrey, J. P. (Old Etonians), 1881 v S, W (2)
Haygarth, E. B. (Swifts), 1875 v S (1)
Haynes, J. N. (Fulham), 1955 v Ni; 1956 v S, Ni, Br, Se, Fi, WG, Sp; 1957 v W, Y, D, Ei (2); 1958 v W, Ni, S, F, P, Y, USSR (3), Br, A; 1959 v S, Ni, USSR, I, Br, Pe, M, US; 1960 v Ni, Y, Sp, H; 1961 v Ni, W, S, L, P, Sp, M, I, A; 1962 v W, Ni, S, A, Sw, Pe, P, H, Arg, Bul, Br (56)
Healless, H. (Blackburn R), 1925 v Ni; 1928 v S (2)
Hector, K. J. (Derby Co), 1974 v Pol (sub), I (sub) (2)
Hedley, G. A. (Sheffield U), 1901 v Ni (1)
Hegan, K. E. (Corinthians), 1923 v Bel, F; 1924 v Ni, Bel (4)
Hellawell, M. S. (Birmingham C), 1963 v Ni, F (2)
Hendrie, L. A. (Aston Villa), 1999 v CzR (sub) (1)
Henfrey, A. G. (Cambridge University), 1891 v Ni; (with Corinthians), 1892 v W; 1895 v W; 1896 v S, W (5)
Henry, R. P. (Tottenham H), 1963 v F (1)
Heron, F. (Wanderers), 1876 v S (1)
Heron, G. H. H. (Uxbridge), 1873 v S; 1874 v S; (with Wanderers), 1875 v S; 1876 v S; 1878 v S (5)
Heskey, E. W. (Leicester C), 1999 v H (sub), Bul (sub); 2000 v Bel (sub), S (sub), Arg; (with Liverpool), Uk (sub), Ma (sub), P (sub), R (sub); 2001 v Fi, I, Sp (sub), Fi (sub), Alb (sub), M, Gr; 2002 v G, Alb, Gr, Se, Ho, I, Sk, Cam, Se, Arg, Ng, D, Br; 2003 v P, Slo, Lie, S.Af, Ser (34)
Hibbert, W. (Bury), 1910 v S (1)
Hibbs, H. E. (Birmingham), 1930 v S, W, A, G; 1931 v S, W, Ni; 1932 v W, Ni, Sp; 1933 v S, W, Ni, A, I, Sw; 1934 v Ni, W, F; 1935 v S, W, Ni, Ho; 1936 v G, W (25)
Hill, F. (Bolton W), 1963 v Ni, W (2)
Hill, G. A. (Manchester U), 1976 v I; 1977 v Ei (sub), Fi (sub), L; 1978 v Sw (sub), L (6)
Hill, J. H. (Burnley), 1925 v W; 1926 v S; 1927 v S, Ni, Bel, F; 1928 v Ni, W; (with Newcastle U), 1929 v F, Bel, Sp (11)
Hill, R. (Luton T), 1983 v D (sub), WG; 1986 v Eg (sub) (3)
Hill, R. H. (Millwall), 1926 v Bel (1)
Hillman, J. (Burnley), 1899 v Ni (1)
Hills, A. F. (Old Harrovians), 1879 v S (1)
Hilsdon, G. R. (Chelsea), 1907 v Ni; 1908 v S, W, Ni, A, H, B; 1909 v Ni (8)
Hinchcliffe, A. G. (Everton), 1997 v Mol, Pol, Ge; 1998 v Cam; (with Sheffield W), Sw, S.Ar; 1999 v Bul (7)
Hine, E. W. (Leicester C), 1929 v W, Ni; 1930 v W, Ni; 1932 v W, Ni (6)
Hinton, A. T. (Wolverhampton W), 1963 v F; (with Nottingham F), 1965 v W, Bel (3)
Hirst, D. E. (Sheffield W), 1991 v Aus, Nz (sub); 1992 v F (3)
Hitchens, G. A. (Aston Villa), 1961 v M, I, A; (with Inter-Milan), 1962 v Sw, Pe, H, Br (7)
Hobbis, H. H. F. (Charlton Ath), 1936 v A, Bel (2)
Hoddle, G. (Tottenham H), 1980 v Bul, W, Aus, Sp; 1981 v Sp, W, S; 1982 v N, Ni, W, Ic, Cz (sub), K; 1983 v L (sub), Ni, S; 1984 v H, L, F; 1985 v Ei (sub), S, I (sub), M, WG, US; 1986 v R, T, Ni, Is, USSR, S, M, Ca, P, Mor, Pol, Para, Arg; 1987 v Se, Ni, Y, Sp, T, S; (with Monaco), 1988 v WG, T (sub), Y (sub), Ho (sub), H (sub), Co (sub), Ei (sub), Ho, USSR (53)
Hodge, S. B. (Aston Villa), 1986 v USSR (sub), S, Ca, P (sub), Mor (sub), Pol, Para, Arg; 1987 v Se, Ni, Y; (with Tottenham H), Sp, Ni, T, S; (with Nottingham F), 1989 v D; 1990 v I (sub), Y (sub), Cz, D, U, Tun; 1991 v Cam (sub), T (sub) (24)
Hodgetts, D. (Aston Villa), 1888 v S, W, Ni; 1892 v S, Ni; 1894 v Ni (6)
Hodgkinson, A. (Sheffield U), 1957 v S, Ei (2), D; 1961 v W (5)
Hodgson, G. (Liverpool), 1931 v S, Ni, W (3)
Hodkinson, J. (Blackburn R), 1913 v W, S; 1920 v Ni (3)
Hogg, W. (Sunderland), 1902 v S, W, Ni (3)
Holdcroft, G. H. (Preston NE), 1937 v W, Ni (2)
Holden, A. D. (Bolton W), 1959 v S, I, Br, Pe, M (5)
Holden, G. H. (Wednesbury OA), 1881 v S; 1884 v S, W, Ni (4)
Holden-White, C. (Corinthians), 1888 v W, S (2)
Holford, T. (Stoke), 1903 v Ni (1)
Holley, G. H. (Sunderland), 1909 v S, W, H (2), A; 1910 v W; 1912 v S, W, Ni; 1913 v S (10)
Holliday, E. (Middlesbrough), 1960 v W, Ni, Se (3)
Hollins, J. W. (Chelsea), 1967 v Sp (1)
Holmes, R. (Preston NE), 1888 v Ni; 1891 v S; 1892 v S; 1893 v S, W; 1894 v Ni; 1895 v Ni (7)
Holt, J. (Everton), 1890 v W; 1891 v S, W; 1892 v S, Ni; 1893 v S; 1894 v S, Ni; 1895 v S; (with Reading), 1900 v Ni (10)
Hopkinson, E. (Bolton W), 1958 v W, Ni, S, F, P, Y; 1959 v S, I, Br, Pe, M, US; 1960 v W, Se (14)
Hossack, A. H. (Corinthians), 1892 v W; 1894 v W (2)
Houghton, W. E. (Aston Villa), 1931 v Ni, W, F, Bel; 1932 v S, Ni; 1933 v A (7)
Houlker, A. E. (Blackburn R), 1902 v S; (with Portsmouth), 1903 v S, W; (with Southampton), 1906 v W, Ni (5)
Howarth, R. H. (Preston NE), 1887 v Ni; 1888 v S, W; 1891 v S; (with Everton), 1894 v Ni (5)
Howe, D. (WBA), 1958 v S, W, Ni, F, P, Y, USSR (3), Br, A; 1959 v S, W, Ni, USSR, I, Br, Pe, M, US; 1960 v W, Ni, Se (23)
Howe, J. R. (Derby Co), 1948 v I; 1949 v S, Ni (3)
Howell, L. S. (Wanderers), 1873 v S (1)
Howell, R. (Sheffield U), 1895 v Ni; (with Liverpool) 1899 v S (2)
Howey, S. N. (Newcastle U), 1995 v Ng; 1996 v Co, P, Bul (4)
Hudson, A. A. (Stoke C), 1975 v WG, Cy (2)
Hudson, J. (Sheffield), 1883 v Ni (1)
Hudspeth, F. C. (Newcastle U), 1926 v Ni (1)
Hufton, A. E. (West Ham U), 1924 v Bel; 1928 v S, Ni; 1929 v F, Bel, Sp (6)
Hughes, E. W. (Liverpool), 1970 v W, Ni, S, Ho, P, Bel; 1971 v EG, Ma (2), Gr, W; 1972 v Sw, Gr, WG (2), W, Ni, S; 1973 v W (3), S (2), Pol, USSR, I; 1974 v A, Pol, I, W, Ni, S, Arg, EG, Bul, Y; 1975 v Cz, P, Cy (sub), Ni; 1977 v I, L, W, S, Br, Arg, U; 1978 v Sw, L, I, WG, Ni, S, H; 1979 v D, Ei, Ni, W, Se; (with Wolverhampton W), 1980 v Sp (sub), Ni, S (sub) (62)
Hughes, L. (Liverpool), 1950 v Ch, US, Sp (3)
Hulme, J. H. A. (Arsenal), 1927 v S, Bel, F; 1928 v S, Ni, W; 1929 v Ni, W; 1933 v S (9)
Humphreys, P. (Notts Co), 1903 v S (1)
Hunt, G. S. (Tottenham H), 1933 v I, Sw, S (3)
Hunt, Rev K. R. G. (Leyton), 1911 v S, W (2)
Hunt, R. (Liverpool), 1962 v A; 1963 v EG; 1964 v S, US, P; 1965 v W; 1966 v S, Sp, Pol (2), WG (2), Fi, N, U, M, F, Arg, P; 1967 v Ni, W, Cz, Sp, A; 1968 v W, Ni, USSR (2), Sp (2), Se, Y; 1969 v R (2) (34)
Hunt, S. (WBA), 1984 v S (sub), USSR (sub) (2)
Hunter, J. (Sheffield Heeley), 1878 v S; 1880 v S, W; 1881 v S, W; 1882 v S, W (7)
Hunter, N. (Leeds U), 1966 v WG, Y, Fi, Sp (sub); 1967 v A; 1968 v Sp, Se, Y, WG, USSR; 1969 v R, W; 1970 v Ho, WG (sub); 1971 v Ma; 1972 v WG (2), W, Ni, S; 1973 v W (2) USSR (sub); 1974 v A, Pol, Ni (sub), S; 1975 v Cz (28)
Hurst, G. C. (West Ham U), 1966 v S, WG (2), Y, Fi, D, Arg, P; 1967 v Ni, W, S, Cz, Sp, A; 1968 v W, Ni, S, Se (sub),

WG, USSR (2); 1969 v Ni, S, R (2), Bul, F, M, U, Br; 1970 v W, Ni, S, Ho (1+1 sub), Bel, Co, Ec, R, Br, WG; 1971 v EG, Gr, W, S; 1972 v Sw (2), Gr, WG (49)

Ince, P. E. C. (Manchester U), 1993 v Sp, N, T (2), Ho, Pol, US, Br, G; 1994 v Pol, Ho, Sm, D, N; 1995 v R, Ei; (with Internazionale), 1996 v Bul, Cro, H, Sw, S, Ho, G; 1997 v Mol, Pol, Ge, I, M, Ge, Pol, I, F (sub), Br; (with Liverpool), 1998 v I, Cam, Ch (sub), Sw, P, Mor, Tun, R, Co, Arg; 1999 v Se, F; (with Middlesbrough), 2000 v Bel, S (2), Br, Ma (sub), P, G, R (53)
Iremonger, J. (Nottingham F), 1901 v S; 1902 v Ni (2)

Jack, D. N. B. (Bolton W), 1924 v S, W; 1928 v F, Bel; (with Arsenal), 1930 v S, G, A; 1933 v W, A (9)
Jackson, E. (Oxford University), 1891 v W (1)
James. D. B. (Liverpool), 1997 v M; (with Aston Villa), 2001 v I, Sp, M (sub); (with West Ham U), 2002 v Ho (sub + sub), I (sub), Sk (sub), Cam (sub); 2003 v P, Aus, Lie, T, S.Af, Ser, Slo (16)
Jarrett, B. G. (Cambridge University), 1876 v S; 1877 v S; 1878 v S (3)
Jefferis, F. (Everton), 1912 v S, W (2)
Jeffers, F. (Arsenal), 2003 v Aus (sub) (1)
Jenas, J. A. (Newcastle U), 2003 v Aus (sub), S.Af (sub), Ser (sub) (3)
Jezzard, B. A. G. (Fulham), 1954 v H; 1956 v Ni (2)
Johnson, D. E. (Ipswich T), 1975 v W, S; 1976 v Sw; (with Liverpool), 1980 v Ei, Arg, Ni, S, Bel (8)
Johnson, E. (Saltley College), 1880 v W; (with Stoke C), 1884 v Ni (2)
Johnson, J. A. (Stoke C), 1937 v N, Se, Fi, S, Ni (5)
Johnson, S. A. M. (Derby Co), 2001 v I (sub) (1)
Johnson, T. C. F. (Manchester C), 1926 v Bel; 1930 v W; (with Everton), 1932 v S, Sp; 1933 v Ni (5)
Johnson, W. H. (Sheffield U), 1900 v S, W, Ni; 1903 v S, W, Ni (6)
Johnston, H. (Blackpool), 1947 v S, Ho; 1951 v S; 1953 v Arg, Ch, U, US; 1954 v W, Ni, H (10)
Jones, A. (Walsall Swifts), 1882 v S, W; (with Great Lever), 1883 v S (3)
Jones, H. (Blackburn R), 1927 v S, Bel, L, F; 1928 v S, Ni (6)
Jones, H. (Nottingham F), 1923 v F (1)
Jones, M. D. (Sheffield U), 1965 v WG, Se; (with Leeds U), 1970 v Ho (3)
Jones, R. (Liverpool), 1992 v F; 1994 v Pol, Gr, N; 1995 v US, R, Ng, U (8)
Jones, W. (Bristol C), 1901 v Ni (1)
Jones, W. H. (Liverpool), 1950 v P, Bel (2)
Joy, B. (Casuals), 1936 v Bel (1)

Kail, E. I. L. (Dulwich Hamlet), 1929 v F, Bel, Sp (3)
Kay, A. H. (Everton), 1963 v Sw (1)
Kean, F. W. (Sheffield W), 1923 v S, Bel; 1924 v W; 1925 v Ni; 1926 v Ni, Bel; 1927 v L; (with Bolton W), 1929 v F, Sp (9)
Keegan, J. K. (Liverpool), 1973 v W (2); 1974 v W, Ni, Arg, EG, Bul, Y; 1975 v Cz, WG, Cy (2), Ni, S; 1976 v Sw, Cz, P, W (2), Ni, S, Br, Fi; 1977 v Ei, Fi, I, Ho, L; (with SV Hamburg), W, Br, Arg, U; 1978 v Sw, I, WG, Br, H; 1979 v D, Ei, Cz, Ni, W, S, Bul, Se, A; 1980 v D, Ni, Ei, Sp (2), Arg, Bel, I; (with Southampton), 1981 v Sp, Sw, H; 1982 v N, H, Ni, S, Fi, Sp (sub) (63)
Keen, E. R. L. (Derby Co), 1933 v A; 1937 v W, Ni, H (4)
Kelly, R. (Burnley), 1920 v S; 1921 v S, W, Ni; 1922 v S, W; 1923 v S; 1924 v Ni; 1925 v W, Ni, S; (with Sunderland), 1926 v W; (with Huddersfield T), 1927 v L; 1928 v S (14)
Kennedy, A. (Liverpool), 1984 v Ni, W (2)
Kennedy, R. (Liverpool), 1976 v W (2), Ni, S; 1977 v L, W, S, Br (sub), Arg (sub); 1978 v Sw, L; 1980 v Bul, Sp, Arg, W, Bel (sub), I (17)
Kenyon-Slaney, W. S. (Wanderers), 1873 v S (1)
Keown, M. R. (Everton), 1992 v F, Cz, C, H, Br, Fi, D, Fe, Se; (with Arsenal), 1993 v Ho, G (sub); 1997 v M, S.Af, I, Br; 1998 v Sw, Mor, Bel; 1999 v CzR, F, Pol, H, Se; 2000 v L, Pol, Bel, S, Arg, Br, Ma, P (sub), G, R; 2001 v F, G, Fi, M, Gr; 2002 v Ho, Gr, Para, Sk (sub), Cam (sub) (43)
Kevan, D. T. (WBA), 1957 v S; 1958 v W, Ni, S, P. Y, USSR (3), Br, A; 1959 v M, US; 1961 v M (14)
Kidd, B. (Manchester U), 1970 v Ni, Ec (sub) (2)
King, L. B. (Tottenham H), 2002 v I (sub); 2003 v Aus (sub) (2)
King, R. S. (Oxford University), 1882 v Ni (1)
Kingsford, R. K. (Wanderers), 1874 v S (1)
Kingsley, M. (Newcastle U), 1901 v W (1)
Kinsey, G. (Wolverhampton W), 1892 v W; 1893 v S; (with Derby Co), 1896 v W, Ni (4)
Kirchen, A. J. (Arsenal), 1937 v N, Se, Fi (3)
Kirton, W. J. (Aston Villa), 1922 v Ni (1)
Knight, A. E. (Portsmouth), 1920 v Ni (1)
Knowles, C. (Tottenham H), 1968 v USSR, Sp, Se, WG (4)
Konchesky, P. M. (Charlton Ath), 2003 v Aus (sub) (1)

Labone, B. L. (Everton), 1963 v Ni, W, F; 1967 v Sp, A; 1968 v S, Sp, Se, Y, USSR, WG; 1969 v Ni, S, R, Bul, M, U, Br; 1970 v S, W, Bel, Co, Ec, R, Br, WG (26)
Lampard, F. J. (West Ham U), 2000 v Bel; 2001 v Sp (sub); (with Chelsea), 2002 v Ho (sub), Se (sub), Ho (sub), I, Para (sub); 2003 v Aus, S.Af (sub), Ser, Slo (11)
Lampard, F. R. G. (West Ham U), 1973 v Y; 1980 v Aus (2)
Langley, E. J. (Fulham), 1958 v S, P, Y (3)
Langton, R. (Blackburn R), 1947 v W, Ni, Ei, Ho, F, Sw; 1948 v Se; (with Preston NE), 1949 v D, Se; (with Bolton W), 1950 v S; 1951 v Ni (11)
Latchford, R. D. (Everton), 1978 v I, Br, W; 1979 v D, Ei, Cz (sub), Ni (2), W, S, Bul, A (12)
Latheron, E. G. (Blackburn R), 1913 v W; 1914 v Ni (2)
Lawler, C. (Liverpool), 1971 v Ma, W, S; 1972 v Sw (4)
Lawton, T. (Everton), 1939 v S, W, Ni, R of E, N, I, R, Y; (with Chelsea), 1947 v S, W, Ni, Ei, Ho, F, Sw, P; 1948 v W, Ni, Bel; (with Notts Co), 1948 v S, Se, I; 1949 v D (23)
Leach, T. (Sheffield W), 1931 v W, Ni (2)
Leake, A. (Aston Villa), 1904 v S, Ni; 1905 v S, W, Ni (5)
Lee, E. A. (Southampton), 1904 v W (1)
Lee, F. H. (Manchester C), 1969 v Ni, W, S, Bul, F, M, U; 1970 v W, Ho (2), P, Bel, Co, Ec, R, Br, WG; 1971 v EG, Gr, Ma, Ni, W, S; 1972 v Sw (2), Gr, WG (27)
Lee, J. (Derby Co), 1951 v Ni (1)
Lee, R. M. (Newcastle U), 1995 v R, Ng; 1996 v Co (sub), N, Sw, Bul (sub), H; 1997 v M, Ge, S.Af, Pol, F (sub), Br (sub); 1998 v Cam (sub), Ch, Sw, Bel, Co (sub); 1999 v Se (sub), Bul, L (sub) (21)
Lee, S. (Liverpool), 1983 v Gr, L, W, Gr, H, S, Aus; 1984 v D, H, L, F, Ni, W, Ch (sub) (14)
Leighton, J. E. (Nottingham F), 1886 v Ni (1)
Le Saux, G. P. (Blackburn R), 1994 v D, Gr, N; 1995 v US, R, Ng, Ei, U, Se, Br; 1996 v Co, P (sub); 1997 v I, M, Ge, S.Af, Pol, I, F, Br; (with Chelsea), 1998 v I, Ch (sub), P, Mor, Bel, Tun, R, Co, Arg; 1999 v Se, Bul (sub), CzR, F, Pol, Se; 2001 v G (36)
Le Tissier, M. P. (Southampton), 1994 v D (sub), Gr (sub), N (sub); 1995 v R, Ng (sub), Ei; 1997 v Mol (sub), I (8)
Lilley, H. E. (Sheffield U), 1892 v W (1)
Linacre, H. J. (Nottingham F), 1905 v W, S (2)
Lindley, T. (Cambridge University), 1886 v S, W, Ni; 1887 v S, W, Ni; 1888 v S, W, Ni; (with Nottingham F), 1889 v S; 1890 v S, W; 1891 v Ni (13)
Lindsay, A. (Liverpool), 1974 v Arg, EG, Bul, Y (4)
Lindsay, W. (Wanderers), 1877 v S (1)
Lineker, G. (Leicester C), 1984 v S (sub); 1985 v Ei, R (sub), S (sub), I (sub), WG, US; (with Everton), 1986 v R, T, Ni, Eg, USSR, Ca, P, Mor, Pol, Para, Arg; (with Barcelona), 1987 v Ni (2), Y, Sp, T, Br; 1988 v WG, T, Y, Ho, H, S, Co, Sw, Ei, Ho, USSR; 1989 v Se, S.Ar, Gr, Alb (2), Pol, D; (with Tottenham H), 1990 v Se, Pol, I, Y, Br, Cz, D, U, Tun, Ei, Ho, Eg, Bel, Cam, WG, I; 1991 v H, Pol, Ei (2), Cam, T, Arg, Aus, Nz, Mal; 1992 v G, T, Pol, F (sub), Cz (sub), C, H, Br, Fi, D, F, Se (80)
Lintott, E. H. (QPR), 1908 v S, W, Ni; (with Bradford C), 1909 v S, Ni, H (2) (7)
Lipsham, H. B. (Sheffield U), 1902 v W (1)
Little, B. (Aston Villa), 1975 v W (sub) (1)
Lloyd, L. V. (Liverpool), 1971 v W; 1972 v Sw, Ni; (with Nottingham F), 1980 v W (4)
Lockett, A. (Stoke C), 1903 v Ni (1)
Lodge, L. V. (Cambridge University), 1894 v W; 1895 v S, W; (with Corinthians), 1896 v S, Ni (5)
Lofthouse, J. M. (Blackburn R), 1885 v S, W, Ni; 1887 v S, W; (with Accrington), 1889 v Ni; (with Blackburn R), 1890 v Ni (7)
Lofthouse, N. (Bolton W), 1951 v Y; 1952 v W, Ni, S, A (2), I, Sw; 1953 v W, Ni, S, Bel, Arg, Ch, U, US; 1954 v W, Ni, R of E, Bel, U; 1955 v Ni, S, F, Sp, P; 1956 v W, S, Sp, D, Fi (sub); 1959 v W, USSR (33)
Longworth, E. (Liverpool), 1920 v S; 1921 v Bel; 1923 v S, W, Bel (5)
Lowder, A. (Wolverhampton W), 1889 v W (1)
Lowe, E. (Aston Villa), 1947 v F, Sw, P (3)
Lucas, T. (Liverpool), 1922 v Ni; 1924 v F; 1926 v Bel (3)
Luntley, E. (Nottingham F), 1880 v S, W (2)
Lyttelton, Hon. A. (Cambridge University), 1877 v S (1)
Lyttelton, Hon. E. (Cambridge University), 1878 v S (1)

McCall, J. (Preston NE), 1913 v S, W; 1914 v S; 1920 v S; 1921 v Ni (5)
McCann, G. P. (Sunderland), 2001 v Sp (sub) (1)
McDermott, T. (Liverpool), 1978 v Sw, L; 1979 v Ni, W, Se; 1980 v D, Ni (sub), Ei, Ni, S, Bel (sub), Sp; 1981 v N, R, Sw, R (sub), Br, Sw (sub), H; 1982 v N, H, W (sub), Ho, S (sub), Ic (25)
McDonald, C. A. (Burnley), 1958 v USSR (3), Br, A; 1959 v W, Ni, USSR (8)
McFarland, R. L. (Derby Co), 1971 v Gr, Ma (2), Ni, S; 1972 v Sw, Gr, WG, W, S; 1973 v W (3), Ni, S, Cz, Pol, USSR, I; 1974 v A, Pol, I, W, Ni; 1976 v Cz, S; 1977 v Ei, I (28)
McGarry, W. H. (Huddersfield T), 1954 v Sw, U; 1956 v W, D (4)
McGuinness, W. (Manchester U), 1959 v Ni, M (2)
McInroy, A. (Sunderland), 1927 v Ni (1)
McMahon, S. (Liverpool), 1988 v Is, H, Co, USSR; 1989 v D (sub); 1990 v Se, Pol, I, Y (sub), Br, Cz (sub), D, Ei (sub), Eg, Bel, I; 1991 v Ei (17)
McManaman, S. (Liverpool), 1995 v Ng (sub), U (sub), J (sub); 1996 v Co, N, Sw, P (sub), Bul, Cro, Chn, Sw, S, Ho, Sp, G; 1997 v Pol, I, M; 1998 v Cam, Sw, Mor, Co (sub); 1999 v Pol, H; (with Real Madrid), 2000 v L, Pol, Uk, Ma (sub), P; 2001 v F (sub), Fi (sub+1), Alb, Gr (sub); 2002 v G (sub), Alb (sub), Gr (sub) (37)
McNab, R. (Arsenal), 1969 v Ni, Bul, R (1+1 sub) (4)
McNeal, R. (WBA), 1914 v S, W (2)
McNeil, M. (Middlesbrough), 1961 v W, Ni, S, L, P, Sp, M, I; 1962 v L (9)
Mabbutt, G. (Tottenham H), 1983 v WG, Gr, L, W, Gr, H, Ni, S (sub); 1984 v H; 1987 v Y, Ni, T; 1988 v WG; 1992 v T, Pol, Cz (16)
Macaulay, R. H. (Cambridge University), 1881 v S (1)
Macdonald, M. (Newcastle U), 1972 v W, Ni, S (sub); 1973 v USSR (sub); 1974 v P, S (sub), Y (sub); 1975 v WG, Cy (2), Ni; 1976 v Sw (sub), Cz, P (14)
Macrae, S. (Notts Co), 1883 v S, W, Ni; 1884 v S, Ni (5)
Maddison, F. B. (Oxford University), 1872 v S (1)
Madeley, P. E. (Leeds U), 1971 v Ni; 1972 v Sw (2), Gr, WG (2), W, S; 1973 v S, Cz, Pol, USSR, I; 1974 v A, Pol, I; 1975 v Cz, P, Cy; 1976 v Cz, P, Fi; 1977 v Ei, Ho (24)
Magee, T. P. (WBA), 1923 v W, Se; 1925 v S, Bel, F (5)
Makepeace, H. (Everton), 1906 v S; 1910 v S; 1912 v S, W (4)
Male, C. G. (Arsenal), 1935 v S, Ni, I, Ho; 1936 v S, W, Ni, G, A, Bel; 1937 v S, Ni, H, N, Se, Fi; 1939 v I, R, Y (19)
Mannion, W. J. (Middlesbrough), 1947 v S, W, Ni, Ei, Ho, F, Sw, P; 1948 v W, Ni, Bel, Se, I; 1949 v N, F; 1950 v S, Ei, P, Bel, Ch, US; 1951 v Ni, W, S, Y; 1952 v F (26)
Mariner, P. (Ipswich T), 1977 v L (sub), Ni; 1978 v L, W (sub), S; 1980 v W, Ni (sub), S, Aus, I (sub), Sp (sub); 1981 v N, Sw, Sp, Sw, H; 1982 v N, H, Ho, S, Fi, F, Cz, K, WG, Sp; 1983 v D, WG, Gr, W; 1984 v D, H, L; (with Arsenal), 1985 v EG, R (35)
Marsden, J. T. (Darwen), 1891 v Ni (1)
Marsden, W. (Sheffield W), 1930 v W, S, G (3)
Marsh, R. W. (QPR), 1972 v Sw (sub); (with Manchester C), WG (sub+1), W, Ni, S; 1973 v W (2), Y (9)
Marshall, T. (Darwen), 1880 v W; 1881 v W (2)
Martin, A. (West Ham U), 1981 v Br, S (sub); 1982 v H, Fi; 1983 v Gr, L, W, Gr, H; 1984 v H, L, W; 1985 v Ni; 1986 v Is, Ca, Para; 1987 v Se (17)
Martin, H. (Sunderland), 1914 v Ni (1)
Martyn, A. N. (C Palace), 1992 v C (sub), H; 1993 v G; (with Leeds U), 1997 v S.Af; 1998 v Cam, Ch, Bel; 1999 v CzR, F (sub); 2000 v L, Pol, Bel (sub), Uk, R; 2001 v Sp (sub), M; 2002 v Ho, Gr, Se, Ho, I, Sk, Cam (23)
Marwood, B. (Arsenal), 1989 v S.Ar (sub) (1)
Maskrey, H. M. (Derby Co), 1908 v Ni (1)
Mason, C. (Wolverhampton W), 1887 v Ni; 1888 v W; 1890 v Ni (3)
Matthews, R. D. (Coventry C), 1956 v S, Br, Se, WG; 1957 v Ni (5)
Matthews, S. (Stoke C), 1935 v W, I; 1936 v G; 1937 v S; 1938 v S, W, Cz, G, Sw, F; 1939 v S, W, Ni, R of E, N, I, Y; 1947 v S; (with Blackpool), 1947 v Sw, P; 1948 v S, W, Ni, Bel, I; 1949 v S, W, Ni, D, Sw; 1950 v Sp; 1951 v Ni, S; 1954 v Ni, R of E, H, Bel, U; 1955 v Ni, W, S, F, WG, Sp, P; 1956 v W, Br; 1957 v S, W, Ni, Y, D (2), Ei (54)
Matthews, V. (Sheffield U), 1928 v F, Bel (2)
Maynard, W. J. (1st Surrey Rifles), 1872 v S; 1876 v S (2)
Meadows, J. (Manchester C), 1955 v S (1)
Medley, L. D. (Tottenham H), 1951 v Y, W; 1952 v F, A, W, Ni (6)
Meehan, T. (Chelsea), 1924 v Ni (1)
Melia, J. (Liverpool), 1963 v S, Sw (2)
Mercer, D. W. (Sheffield U), 1923 v Ni, Bel (2)
Mercer, J. (Everton), 1939 v S, Ni, I, R, Y (5)
Merrick, G. H. (Birmingham C), 1952 v Ni, S, A (2), I, Sw; 1953 v Ni, W, S, Bel, Arg, Ch, U; 1954 v W, Ni, S, R of E, H (2), Y, Bel, Sw, U (23)
Merson, P. C. (Arsenal), 1992 v G (sub), Cz, H, Br (sub), Fi (sub), D, Se (sub); 1993 v Sp (sub), N (sub), Ho (sub), Br (sub), G; 1994 v Ho, Gr; 1997 v I (sub); (with Middlesbrough), 1998 v Sw, P (sub), Bel, Arg (sub); 1999 v Se (sub); (with Aston Villa), CzR (21)
Metcalfe, V. (Huddersfield T), 1951 v Arg, P (2)
Mew, J. W. (Manchester U), 1921 v Ni (1)
Middleditch, B. (Corinthians), 1897 v Ni (1)
Milburn, J. E. T. (Newcastle U), 1949 v S, W, Ni, Sw; 1950 v W, P, Bel, Sp; 1951 v W, Arg, P; 1952 v F; 1956 v D (13)
Miller, B. G. (Burnley), 1961 v A (1)
Miller, H. S. (Charlton Ath), 1923 v Se (1)
Mills, D. J. (Leeds U), 2001 v M (sub); 2002 v Ho (sub), Se (sub), I, Para (sub), Sk, Cam (sub), Se, Arg, Ng, D, Br; 2003 v P, Aus (sub), S.Af, Ser, Slo (17)
Mills, G. R. (Chelsea), 1938 v W, Ni, Cz (3)
Mills, M. D. (Ipswich T), 1973 v Y; 1976 v W (2), Ni, S, Br, I (sub), Fi; 1977 v Fi (sub), I, Ni, W, S; 1978 v WG, Br, W, Ni, S, H; 1979 v D, Ei, Ni (2), S, Bul, A; 1980 v D, Ni, Sp (2); 1981 v Sw (2), H; 1982 v N, H, S, Fi, F, Cz, K, WG, Sp (42)
Milne, G. (Liverpool), 1963 v Br, Cz, EG; 1964 v W, Ni, S, R of W, U, P, Ei, Br, Arg; 1965 v Ni, Bel (14)
Milton, C. A. (Arsenal), 1952 v A (1)
Milward, A. (Everton), 1891 v S, W; 1897 v S, W (4)
Mitchell, C. (Upton Park), 1880 v W; 1881 v S; 1883 v S, W; 1885 v W (5)
Mitchell, J. F. (Manchester C), 1925 v Ni (1)
Moffat, H. (Oldham Ath), 1913 v W (1)
Molyneux, G. (Southampton), 1902 v S; 1903 v S, W, Ni (4)
Moon, W. R. (Old Westminsters), 1888 v S, W; 1889 v S, W; 1890 v S, W; 1891 v S (7)
Moore, H. T. (Notts Co), 1883 v Ni; 1885 v W (2)
Moore, J. (Derby Co), 1923 v Se (1)
Moore, R. F. (West Ham U), 1962 v Pe, H, Arg, Bul, Br; 1963 v W, Ni, S, F (2), Br, Cz, EG, Sw; 1964 v W, Ni, S, R of W, U, P (2), Ei, Br, Arg; 1965 v Ni, S, Bel, H, Y, WG, Se; 1966 v W, Ni, S, A, Sp, Pol (2), WG (2), N, D, U, M, F, Arg, P; 1967 v W, Ni, S, Cz, Sp, A; 1968 v W, Ni, S, USSR (2), Sp (2), Se, Y, WG; 1969 v Ni, W, S, R, Bul, F, M, U, Br; 1970 v W, Ni, S, Ho, P, Bel, Co, Ec, R, Br, Cz, WG; 1971 v EG, Gr, Ma, Ni, S; 1972 v Sw (2), Gr, WG (2), W, S; 1973 v W (3), Y, S (2), Ni, Cz, Pol, USSR, I; 1974 v I (108)
Moore, W. G. B. (West Ham U), 1923 v Se (1)
Mordue, J. (Sunderland), 1912 v Ni; 1913 v Ni (2)
Morice, C. J. (Barnes), 1872 v S (1)
Morley, A. (Aston Villa), 1982 v H (sub), Ni, W, Ic; 1983 v D, Gr (6)
Morley, H. (Notts Co), 1910 v Ni (1)
Morren, T. (Sheffield U), 1898 v Ni (1)
Morris, F. (WBA), 1920 v S; 1921 v Ni (2)
Morris, J. (Derby Co), 1949 v N, F; 1950 v Ei (3)
Morris, W. W. (Wolverhampton W), 1939 v S, Ni, R (3)
Morse, H. (Notts Co), 1879 v S (1)
Mort, T. (Aston Villa), 1924 v W, F; 1926 v S (3)
Morten, A. (C Palace), 1873 v S (1)
Mortensen, S. H. (Blackpool), 1947 v P; 1948 v W, S, Ni, Bel, Se, I; 1949 v S, W, Ni, Se, N; 1950 v S, W, Ni, I, P, Bel, Ch, US, Sp; 1951 v S, Arg; 1954 v R of E, H (25)
Morton, J. R. (West Ham U), 1938 v Cz (1)
Mosforth, W. (Sheffield W), 1877 v S; (with Sheffield Albion), 1878 v S; 1879 v S, W; 1880 v S, W; (with Sheffield W), 1881 v W; 1882 v S, W (9)
Moss, F. (Arsenal), 1934 v S, H, Cz; 1935 v I (4)
Moss, F. (Aston Villa), 1922 v S, Ni; 1923 v Ni; 1924 v S, Bel (5)
Mosscrop, E. (Burnley), 1914 v S, W (2)
Mozley, B. (Derby Co), 1950 v W, Ni, Ei (3)
Mullen, J. (Wolverhampton W), 1947 v S; 1949 v N, F; 1950 v Bel (sub), Ch, US; 1954 v W, Ni, S, R of E, Y, Sw (12)
Mullery, A. P. (Tottenham H), 1965 v Ho; 1967 v Sp, A; 1968 v W, Ni, S, USSR, Sp (2), Se, Y; 1969 v Ni, S, R, Bul, F, M, U, Br; 1970 v W, Ni, S (sub), Ho (sub), Bel, P, Co, Ec, R, Cz, WG, Br; 1971 v Ma, EG, Gr; 1972 v Sw (35)
Murphy, D. B. (Liverpool), 2002 v Se (sub), I (sub), Para (sub), Sk; 2003 v P (sub), Aus (sub), Lie (sub) (7)

Neal, P. G. (Liverpool), 1976 v W, I; 1977 v W, S, Br, Arg, U; 1978 v Sw, I, WG, Ni, S, H; 1979 v D, Ei, Ni (2), S, Bul, A; 1980 v D, Ni, Sp, Arg, W, Bel, I; 1981 v R, Sw, Sp, Br, H; 1982 v N, H, W, Ho, Ic, F (sub), K; 1983 v D, Gr, L, W, Gr, H, Ni, S, Aus (2); 1984 v D (50)

Needham, E. (Sheffield U), 1894 v S; 1895 v S; 1897 v S, W, Ni; 1898 v S, W; 1899 v S, W, Ni; 1900 v S, Ni; 1901 v S, W, Ni; 1902 v W (16)
Neville, G. A. (Manchester U), 1995 v J, Br; 1996 v Co, N, Sw, P, Bul, Cro, H, Chn, Sw, S, Ho, Sp; 1997 v Mol, Pol, I, Ge, Pol, I (sub), F, Br (sub); 1998 v Mol, Ch, P, S.Ar, Bel, R, Co, Arg; 1999 v Bul, Pol; 2000 v L (sub), Pol, Br, Ma, P, G, R; 2001 v G, I, Sp (sub), Fi, Alb; 2002 v Ho, G, Alb, Gr, Se, Ho, I (sub), Para; 2003 v Slo, Mac, Aus, Lie, T (57)
Neville, P. J. (Manchester U), 1996 v Chn; 1997 v S.Af, Pol (sub), I, F, Br; 1998 v Mol, Cam, Ch, P (sub), S.Ar (sub), Bel; 1999 v L, Pol (sub), H, Se, Bul; 2000 v L (sub), Pol (sub), Bel (sub), S (2), Arg (sub), Br, Uk, Ma, P, G, R; 2001 v Fi, Sp, M, Gr; 2002 v Se (sub), Ho (sub), I (sub), Para (sub); 2003 v S.Af, Ser, Slo (40)
Newton, K. R. (Blackburn R), 1966 v S, WG; 1967 v Sp, A; 1968 v W, S, Sp, Se, Y, WG; 1969 v Ni, W, S, R, Bul, M, U, Br, F; (with Everton), 1970 v Ni, S, Ho, Co, Ec, R, Cz, WG (27)
Nicholls, J. (WBA), 1954 v S, Y (2)
Nicholson, W. E. (Tottenham H), 1951 v P (1)
Nish, D. J. (Derby Co), 1973 v Ni; 1974 v P, W, Ni, S (5)
Norman, M. (Tottenham H), 1962 v Pe, H, Arg, Bul, Br; 1963 v S, F, Br, Cz, EG; 1964 v W, Ni, S, R of W, U, P (2), US, Br, Arg; 1965 v Ni, Bel, Ho (23)
Nuttall, H. (Bolton W), 1928 v W, Ni; 1929 v S (3)

Oakley, W. J. (Oxford University), 1895 v W; 1896 v S, W, Ni; (with Corinthians), 1897 v S, W, Ni; 1898 v S, W, Ni; 1900 v S, W, Ni; 1901 v S, W, Ni (16)
O'Dowd, J. P. (Chelsea), 1932 v S; 1933 v Ni, Sw (3)
O'Grady, M. (Huddersfield T), 1963 v Ni; (with Leeds U), 1969 v F (2)
Ogilvie, R. A. M. M. (Clapham R), 1874 v S (1)
Oliver, L. F. (Fulham), 1929 v Bel (1)
Olney, B. A. (Aston Villa), 1928 v F, Bel (2)
Osborne, F. R. (Fulham), 1923 v Ni, F; (with Tottenham H), 1925 v Bel; 1926 v Bel (4)
Osborne, R. (Leicester C), 1928 v W (1)
Osgood, P. L. (Chelsea), 1970 v Bel, R (sub), Cz (sub); 1974 v I (4)
Osman, R. (Ipswich T), 1980 v Aus; 1981 v Sp, R, Sw; 1982 v N, Ic; 1983 v D, Aus (3); 1984 v D (11)
Ottaway, C. J. (Oxford University), 1872 v S; 1874 v S (2)
Owen, J. R. B. (Sheffield), 1874 v S (1)
Owen, M. J. (Liverpool), 1998 v Ch, Sw, P (sub), Mor (sub), Bel (sub), Tun (sub), R (sub), Co, Arg; 1999 v Se, Bul, L, F; 2000 v L (sub), Pol (sub), Bel (sub), S (2), Br, P, G, R; 2001 v F (sub), G, Sp, Fi, Alb, M, Gr; 2002 v Ho (sub), G, Alb, I, Para, Sk, Cam, Se, Arg, Ng, D, Br; 2003 v P, Slo, Mac, Aus, Lie, T, S.Af, Ser, Slo (50)
Owen, S. W. (Luton T), 1954 v H, Y, Bel (3)

Page, L. A. (Burnley), 1927 v S, W, Bel, L, F; 1928 v W, Ni (7)
Paine, T. L. (Southampton), 1963 v Cz, EG; 1964 v W, Ni, S, R of W, U, US, P; 1965 v Ni, H, Y, WG, Se; 1966 v W, A, Y, N, M (19)
Pallister, G. A. (Middlesbrough), 1988 v H; 1989 v S.Ar; (with Manchester U), 1991 v Cam (sub), T; 1992 v G; 1993 v N, US, Br, G; 1994 v Pol, Ho, Sm, D; 1995 v US, R, Ei, U, Se; 1996 v N, Sw; 1997 v Mol, Pol (sub) (22)
Palmer, C. L. (Sheffield W), 1992 v C, H, Br, Fi (sub), D, F, Se; 1993 v Sp (sub), N (sub), T, Sm, T, Ho, Pol, N, US, Br (sub); 1994 v Ho (18)
Pantling, H. H. (Sheffield U), 1924 v Ni (1)
Paravacini, P. J. de (Cambridge University), 1883 v S, W, Ni (3)
Parker, P. A. (QPR), 1989 v Alb (sub), Ch, D; 1990 v Y, U, Ho, Eg, Bel, Cam, WG, I; 1991 v H, Pol, USSR, Aus, Nz; (with Manchester U), 1992 v G; 1994 v Ho, D (19)
Parker, T. R. (Southampton), 1925 v F (1)
Parkes, P. B. (QPR), 1974 v P (1)
Parkinson, J. (Liverpool), 1910 v S, W (2)
Parlour, R. (Arsenal), 1999 v Pol (sub), Se (sub), Bul (sub); 2000 v L, S (sub), Arg (sub), Br (sub); 2001 v G (sub), Fi, I (10)
Parr, P. C. (Oxford University), 1882 v W (1)
Parry, E. H. (Old Carthusians), 1879 v W; 1882 v W, S (3)
Parry, R. A. (Bolton W), 1960 v Ni, S (2)
Patchitt, B. C. A. (Corinthians), 1923 v Se (2) (2)
Pawson, F. W. (Cambridge University), 1883 v Ni; (with Swifts), 1885 v Ni (2)
Payne, J. (Luton T), 1937 v Fi (1)
Peacock, A. (Middlesbrough), 1962 v Arg, Bul; 1963 v Ni, W; (with Leeds U), 1966 v W, Ni (6)
Peacock, J. (Middlesbrough), 1929 v F, Bel, Sp (3)
Pearce, S. (Nottingham F), 1987 v Br, S; 1988 v WG (sub), Is, H; 1989 v D, Se, S.Ar, Gr, Alb (2), Ch, S, Pol, D; 1990 v Se, Pol, I, Y, Br, Cz, D, U, Tun, Ei, Ho, Eg, Bel, Cam, WG; 1991 v H, Pol, Ei (2), Cam, T, Arg, Aus, Nz (2), Mal; 1992 v T, Pol, F, Cz, Br (sub), Fi, D, F, Se; 1993 v Sp, N, T; 1994 v Pol, Sm, Gr (sub); 1995 v R (sub), J, Br; 1996 v N, Sw, P, Bul, Cro, H, Sw, S, Ho, Sp, G; 1997 v Mol, Pol, I, M, S.Af, I; (with West Ham U), 2000 v L, Pol (78)
Pearson, H. F. (WBA), 1932 v S (1)
Pearson, J. H. (Crewe Alex), 1892 v Ni (1)
Pearson, J. S. (Manchester U), 1976 v W, Ni, S, Br, Fi; 1977 v Ei, Ho (sub), W, S, Br, Arg, U; 1978 v I (sub), WG, Ni (15)
Pearson, S. C. (Manchester U), 1948 v S; 1949 v S, Ni; 1950 v Ni, I; 1951 v P; 1952 v S, I (8)
Pease, W. H. (Middlesbrough), 1927 v W (1)
Pegg, D. (Manchester U), 1957 v Ei (1)
Pejic, M. (Stoke C), 1974 v P, W, Ni, S (4)
Pelly, F. R. (Old Foresters), 1893 v Ni; 1894 v S, W (3)
Pennington, J. (WBA), 1907 v S, W; 1908 v S, W, Ni, A; 1909 v S, W, H (2), A; 1910 v S, W; 1911 v S, W, Ni; 1912 v S, W, Ni; 1913 v S, W; 1914 v S, Ni; 1920 v S, W (25)
Pentland, F. B. (Middlesbrough), 1909 v S, W, H (2), A (5)
Perry, C. (WBA), 1890 v Ni; 1891 v Ni; 1893 v W (3)
Perry, T. (WBA), 1898 v W (1)
Perry, W. (Blackpool), 1956 v Ni, S, Sp (3)
Perryman, S. (Tottenham H), 1982 v Ic (sub) (1)
Peters, M. (West Ham U), 1966 v Y, Fi, Pol, M, F, Arg, P, WG; 1967 v Ni, W, S, Cz; 1968 v W, Ni, S, USSR (2), Sp (2), Se, Y; 1969 v Ni, S, R, Bul, F, M, U, Br; 1970 v Ho (2), P (sub), Bel; (with Tottenham H), W, Ni, S, Co, Ec, R, Br, Cz, WG; 1971 v EG, Gr, Ma (2), Ni, W, S; 1972 v Sw, Gr, WG (1+1 sub), Ni (sub); 1973 v S (2), Ni, W, Cz, Pol, USSR, I; 1974 v A, Pol, I, P, S (67)
Phelan, M. C. (Manchester U), 1990 v I (sub) (1)
Phillips, K. (Sunderland), 1999 v H; 2000 v Bel, Arg (sub), Br (sub), Ma; 2001 v I (sub); 2002 v Se, Ho (sub) (8)
Phillips, L. H. (Portsmouth), 1952 v Ni; 1955 v W, WG (3)
Pickering, F. (Everton), 1964 v US; 1965 v Ni, Bel (3)
Pickering, J. (Sheffield U), 1933 v S (1)
Pickering, N. (Sunderland), 1983 v Aus (1)
Pike, T. M. (Cambridge University), 1886 v Ni (1)
Pilkington, B. (Burnley), 1955 v Ni (1)
Plant, J. (Bury), 1900 v S (1)
Platt, D. (Aston Villa), 1990 v I (sub), Y (sub), Br, D (sub), Tun (sub), Ho (sub), Eg (sub), Bel (sub), Cam, WG, I; 1991 v H, Pol, Ei (2), T, USSR, Arg, Aus, Nz (2), Mal; (with Bari), 1992 v G, T, Pol, Cz, C, Br, Fi, D, F, Se; (with Juventus), 1993 v Sp, N, T, Sm, T, Ho, Pol, N, Br (sub), G; (with Sampdoria), 1994 v Pol, Ho, Sm, D, Gr, N; 1995 v US, Ng, Ei, U, J, Se, Br; (with Arsenal), 1996 v Bul (sub), Cro, H, Sw (sub), Ho (sub), Sp, G (62)
Plum, S. L. (Charlton Ath), 1923 v F (1)
Pointer, R. (Burnley), 1962 v W, L, P (3)
Porteous, T. S. (Sunderland), 1891 v W (1)
Powell, C. G. (Charlton Ath), 2001 v Sp, Fi, M (sub); 2002 v Ho (sub+sub) (5)
Priest, A. E. (Sheffield U), 1900 v Ni (1)
Prinsep, J. F. M. (Clapham Rovers), 1879 v S (1)
Puddefoot, S. C. (Blackburn R), 1926 v S, Ni (2)
Pye, J. (Wolverhampton W), 1950 v Ei (1)
Pym, R. H. (Bolton W), 1925 v S, W; 1926 v W (3)

Quantrill, A. (Derby Co), 1920 v S, W; 1921 v W, Ni (4)
Quixall, A. (Sheffield W), 1954 v W, Ni, R of E; 1955 v Sp, P (sub) (5)

Radford, J. (Arsenal), 1969 v R; 1972 v Sw (sub) (2)
Raikes, G. B. (Oxford University), 1895 v W; 1896 v W, Ni, S (4)
Ramsey, A. E. (Southampton), 1949 v Sw; (with Tottenham H), 1950 v S, I, P, Bel, Ch, US, Sp; 1951 v S, Ni, W, Y, Arg, P; 1952 v S, W, Ni, F, A (2), I, Sw; 1953 v Ni, W, S, Bel, Arg, Ch, U, US; 1954 v R of E, H (32)
Rawlings, A. (Preston NE), 1921 v Bel (1)
Rawlings, W. E. (Southampton), 1922 v S, W (2)
Rawlinson, J. F. P. (Cambridge University), 1882 v Ni (1)
Rawson, H. E. (Royal Engineers), 1875 v S (1)
Rawson, W. S. (Oxford University), 1875 v S; 1877 v S (2)
Read, A. (Tufnell Park), 1921 v Bel (1)
Reader, J. (WBA), 1894 v Ni (1)
Reaney, P. (Leeds U), 1969 v Bul (sub); 1970 v P; 1971 v Ma (3)
Redknapp, J. F. (Liverpool), 1996 v Co, N, Sw, Chn, S (sub); 1997 v M (sub), Ge (sub), S.Af; 1999 v Se, Bul, F, Pol (sub), H (sub), Bul; 2000 v Bel, S (2) (17)

Reeves, K. (Norwich C), 1980 v Bul; (with Manchester C), Ni (2)
Regis, C. (WBA), 1982 v Ni (sub), W (sub), Ic; 1983 v WG; (with Coventry C), 1988 v T (sub) (5)
Reid, P. (Everton), 1985 v M (sub), WG, US (sub); 1986 v R, S (sub), Ca (sub), Pol, Para, Arg; 1987 v Br; 1988 v WG, Y (sub), Sw (sub) (13)
Revie, D. G. (Manchester C), 1955 v Ni, S, F; 1956 v W, D; 1957 v Ni (6)
Reynolds, J. (WBA), 1892 v S; 1893 v S, W; (with Aston Villa), 1894 v S, Ni; 1895 v S; 1897 v S, W (8)
Richards, C. H. (Nottingham F), 1898 v Ni (1)
Richards, G. H. (Derby Co), 1909 v A (1)
Richards, J. P. (Wolverhampton W), 1973 v Ni (1)
Richardson, J. R. (Newcastle U), 1933 v I, Sw (2)
Richardson, K. (Aston Villa), 1994 v Gr (1)
Richardson, W. G. (WBA), 1935 v Ho (1)
Rickaby, S. (WBA), 1954 v Ni (1)
Ricketts, M. B. (Bolton W), 2002 v Ho (1)
Rigby, A. (Blackburn R), 1927 v S, Bel, L, F; 1928 v W (5)
Rimmer, E. J. (Sheffield W), 1930 v S, G, A; 1932 v Sp (4)
Rimmer, J. J. (Arsenal), 1976 v I (1)
Ripley, S. E. (Blackburn R), 1994 v Sm; 1998 v Mol (sub) (2)
Rix, G. (Arsenal), 1981 v N, R, Sw (sub), Br, W, S; 1982 v Ho (sub), Fi (sub), F, Cz, K, WG, Sp; 1983 v D, WG (sub), Gr (sub); 1984 v Ni (17)
Robb, G. (Tottenham H), 1954 v H (1)
Roberts, C. (Manchester U), 1905 v Ni, W, S (3)
Roberts, F. (Manchester C), 1925 v S, W, Bel, F (4)
Roberts, G. (Tottenham H), 1983 v Ni, S; 1984 v F, Ni, S, USSR (6)
Roberts, H. (Arsenal), 1931 v S (1)
Roberts, H. (Millwall), 1931 v Bel (1)
Roberts, R. (WBA), 1887 v S; 1888 v Ni; 1890 v Ni (3)
Roberts, W. T. (Preston NE), 1924 v W, Bel (2)
Robinson, J. (Sheffield W), 1937 v Fi; 1938 v G, Sw; 1939 v W (4)
Robinson, J. W. (Derby Co), 1897 v S, Ni; (with New Brighton Tower), 1898 v S, W, Ni; (with Southampton), 1899 v W, S; 1900 v S, W, Ni; 1901 v Ni (11)
Robinson, P. W. (Leeds U), 2003 v Aus (sub), S.Af (sub) (2)
Robson, B. (WBA), 1980 v Ei, Aus; 1981 v N, R, Sw, Sp, R, Br, W, S, Sw, H; 1982 v N; (with Manchester U), H, Ni, W, Ho, S, Fi, F, Cz, WG, Sp; 1983 v D, Gr, L, S; 1984 v H, L, F, Ni, S, USSR, Br, U, Ch; 1985 v EG, Fi, T, Ei, R, Fi, S, M, I, WG, US; 1986 v R, T, Is, M, P, Mor; 1987 v Ni (2), Sp, T, Br, S; 1988 v T, Y, Ho, H, S, Co, Sw, Ei, Ho, USSR; 1989 v S, Se, S.Ar, Gr, Alb (2), Ch, S, Pol, D; 1990 v Pol, I, Y, Cz, U, Tun, Ei, Ho; 1991 v Cam, Ei; 1992 v T (90)
Robson, R. (WBA), 1958 v F, USSR (2), Br, A; 1960 v Sp, H; 1961 v Ni, W, S, L, P, Sp, M, I; 1962 v W, Ni, Sw, L, P (20)
Rocastle, D. (Arsenal), 1989 v D, S.Ar, Gr, Alb (2), Pol (sub), D; 1990 v Se (sub), Pol, Y, D (sub); 1992 v Pol, Cz, Br (sub) (14)
Rooney, W. (Everton), 2003 v Aus (sub), Lie (sub), T, Ser (sub), Slo (5)
Rose, W. C. (Wolverhampton W), 1884 v S, W, Ni; (with Preston NE), 1886 v Ni; (with Wolverhampton W), 1891 v Ni (5)
Rostron, T. (Darwen), 1881 v S, W (2)
Rowe, A. (Tottenham H), 1934 v F (1)
Rowley, J. F. (Manchester U), 1949 v Sw, Se, F; 1950 v Ni, I; 1952 v S (6)
Rowley, W. (Stoke C), 1889 v Ni; 1892 v Ni (2)
Royle, J. (Everton), 1971 v Ma; 1973 v Y; (with Manchester C), 1976 v Ni (sub), I; 1977 v Fi, L (6)
Ruddlesdin, H. (Sheffield W), 1904 v W, Ni; 1905 v S (3)
Ruddock, N. (Liverpool), 1995 v Ng (1)
Ruffell, J. W. (West Ham U), 1926 v S; 1927 v Ni; 1929 v S, W, Ni; 1930 v W (6)
Russell, B. B. (Royal Engineers), 1883 v W (1)
Rutherford, J. (Newcastle U), 1904 v S; 1907 v S, Ni, W; 1908 v S, Ni, W, A (2), H, B (11)

Sadler, D. (Manchester U), 1968 v Ni, USSR; 1970 v Ec (sub); 1971 v EG (4)
Sagar, C. (Bury), 1900 v Ni; 1902 v W (2)
Sagar, E. (Everton), 1936 v S, Ni, A, Bel (4)
Salako, J. A. (C Palace), 1991 v Aus (sub), Nz (sub + 1), Mal; 1992 v G (5)
Sandford, E. A. (WBA), 1933 v W (1)
Sandilands, R. R. (Old Westminsters), 1892 v W; 1893 v Ni; 1894 v W; 1895 v W; 1896 v W (5)
Sands, J. (Nottingham F), 1880 v W (1)
Sansom, K. (C Palace), 1979 v W; 1980 v Bul, Ei, Arg, W (sub), Ni, S, Bel, I; (with Arsenal), 1981 v N, R, Sw, Sp, R, Br, W, S, Sw; 1982 v Ni, W, Ho, S, Fi, F, Cz, WG, Sp; 1983 v D, WG, Gr, L, Gr, H, Ni, S; 1984 v D, H, L, F, S, USSR, Br, U, Ch; 1985 v EG, Fi, T, Ni, Ei, R, Fi, S, I, M, WG, US; 1986 v R, T, Ni, Eg, Is, USSR, S, M, Ca, P, Mor, Pol, Para, Arg; 1987 v Se, Ni (2), Y, Sp, T; 1988 v WG, T, Y, Ho, S, Co, Sw, Ei, Ho, USSR (86)
Saunders, F. E. (Swifts), 1888 v W (1)
Savage, A. H. (C Palace), 1876 v S (1)
Sayer, J. (Stoke C), 1887 v Ni (1)
Scales, J. R. (Liverpool), 1995 v J, Se (sub), Br (3)
Scattergood, E. (Derby Co), 1913 v W (1)
Schofield, J. (Stoke C), 1892 v W; 1893 v W; 1895 v Ni (3)
Scholes, P. (Manchester U), 1997 v S.Af (sub), I, Br; 1998 v Mol, Cam, P, S.Ar, Tun, R, Co, Arg; 1999 v Se, Bul, L, F (sub), Pol, Se; 2000 v Pol, S (2), Arg, Br, Uk, Ma, P, G, R; 2001 v F, G, Fi, Sp, Fi, Alb, M, Gr; 2002 v Ho, G, Alb, Gr, Se, Ho, Para, Sk, Cam, Se, Arg, Ng, D, Br; 2003 v Slo, Mac, Aus, Lie, T, S.Af, Ser, Slo (57)
Scott, L. (Arsenal), 1947 v S, W, Ni, Ei, Ho, F, Sw, P; 1948 v S, W, Ni, Bel, Se, I; 1949 v W, Ni, D (17)
Scott, W. R. (Brentford), 1937 v W (1)
Seaman, D. A. (QPR), 1989 v S.Ar, D (sub); 1990 v Cz (sub); (with Arsenal), 1991 v Cam, Ei, T, Arg; 1992 v Cz, H (sub); 1994 v Pol, Ho, Sm, D, N; 1995 v US, R, Ei; 1996 v Co, N, Sw, P, Bul, Cro, H, Sw, S, Ho, Sp, G; 1997 v Mol, Pol, Ge (2), Pol, F, Br; 1998 v Mol, I, P, S.Ar, Tun, R, Co, Arg; 1999 v Se, Bul, L, F, Pol, H, Se, Bul; 2000 v Bel, S (2), Arg, Br, P, G; 2001 v F, G, Fi (2), Alb, Gr; 2002 v G, Alb, Para, Se, Arg, Ng, D, Br; 2003 v Slo, Mac (75)
Seddon, J. (Bolton W), 1923 v F, Se (2); 1924 v Bel; 1927 v W; 1929 v S (6)
Seed, J. M. (Tottenham H), 1921 v Bel: 1923 v W, Ni, Bel; 1925 v S (5)
Settle, J. (Bury), 1899 v S, W, Ni; (with Everton), 1902 v S, Ni; 1903 v Ni (6)
Sewell, J. (Sheffield W), 1952 v Ni, A, Sw; 1953 v Ni; 1954 v H (2) (6)
Sewell, W. R. (Blackburn R), 1924 v W (1)
Shackleton, L. F. (Sunderland), 1949 v W, D; 1950 v W; 1955 v W, WG (5)
Sharp, J. (Everton), 1903 v Ni; 1905 v S (2)
Sharpe, L. S. (Manchester U), 1991 v Ei (sub); 1993 v T (sub), N, US, Br, G; 1994 v Pol, Ho (8)
Shaw, G. E. (WBA), 1932 v S (1)
Shaw, G. L. (Sheffield U), 1959 v S, W, USSR, I; 1963 v W (5)
Shea, D. (Blackburn R), 1914 v W, Ni (2)
Shearer, A. (Southampton), 1992 v F, C, F; (with Blackburn R), 1993 v Sp, N, T; 1994 v Ho, D, Gr, N; 1995 v US, R, Ng, Ei, J, Se, Br; 1996 v Co, N, Sw, P, H (sub), Chn, Sw, S, Ho, Sp, G; (with Newcastle U), 1997 v Mol, Pol, I, Ge, Pol, F, Br; 1998 v Ch (sub), Sw, P, S.Ar, Tun, R, Co, Arg; 1999 v Se, Bul, L, F, Pol, H, Se, Bul; 2000 v L, Pol, Bel, S (2), Arg, Br, Uk, Ma, P, G, R (63)
Shellito, K. J. (Chelsea), 1963 v Cz (1)
Shelton A. (Notts Co), 1889 v Ni; 1890 v S, W; 1891 v S, W; 1892 v S (6)
Shelton, C. (Notts Rangers), 1888 v Ni (1)
Shepherd, A. (Bolton W), 1906 v S; (with Newcastle U), 1911 v Ni (2)
Sheringham, E. P. (Tottenham H), 1993 v Pol, N; 1995 v US, R (sub), Ng (sub), U, J (sub), Se, Br; 1996 v Co (sub), N (sub), Sw, Bul, Cro, H, Sw, S, Ho, Sp, G; 1997 v Ge, M, Ge, S.Af, Pol, I, F (sub), Br; (with Manchester U), 1998 v I, Ch, Sw (sub), P, S.Ar, Tun, R; 1999 v Se (sub), Bul (sub), Bul; 2001 v Fi, Alb (sub), M (sub); (with Tottenham H), 2002 v Gr (sub), Se (sub), I (sub), Para (sub), Sk (sub), Cam (sub), Arg (sub), Ng (sub), D (sub), Br (sub) (51)
Sherwood, T. A. (Tottenham H), 1999 v Pol, H, Se (3)
Shilton, P. L. (Leicester C), 1971 v EG, W; 1972 v Sw, Ni; 1973 v Y, S (2), Ni, W, Cz, Pol, USSR, I; 1974 v A, Pol, I, W, Ni, S, Arg; (with Stoke C), 1975 v Cy; 1977 v Ni, W; (with Nottingham F), 1978 v W, H; 1979 v Cz, Se, A; 1980 v Ni, Sp, I; 1981 v N, Sw, R; 1982 v H, Ho, S, F, Cz, K, WG, Sp; (with Southampton), 1983 v D, WG, Gr, W, Gr, H, Ni, S, Aus (3); 1984 v D, H, F, Ni, W, S, USSR, Br, U, Ch; 1985 v EG, Fi, T, Ni, R, Fi, S, I, WG; 1986 v R, T, Ni, Eg, Is, USSR, S, M, Ca, P, Mor, Pol, Para, Arg; 1987 v Se, Ni (2), Sp, Br; (with Derby Co), 1988 v WG, T, Y, Ho, S, Co, Sw, Ei, Ho; 1989 v D, Se, Gr, Alb (2), Ch, S, Pol, D; 1990 v Se, Pol, I, Y, Br, Cz, D, U, Tun, Ei, Ho, Eg, Bel, Cam, WG, I (125)
Shimwell, E. (Blackpool), 1949 v Se (1)
Shutt, G. (Stoke C), 1886 v Ni (1)
Silcock, J. (Manchester U), 1921 v S, W; 1923 v Se (3)
Sillett, R. P. (Chelsea), 1955 v F, Sp, P (3)
Simms, E. (Luton T), 1922 v Ni (1)

Simpson, J. (Blackburn R), 1911 v S, W, Ni; 1912 v S, W, Ni; 1913 v S; 1914 v W (8)
Sinclair, T. (West Ham U), 2002 v Se, I, Para (sub), Sk (sub), Cam (sub), Arg (sub), Ng, D, Br; 2003 v P (sub), S.Af (11)
Sinton, A. (QPR), 1992 v Pol, C, H (sub), Br, F, Se; 1993 v Sp, T, Br, G; (with Sheffield W), 1994 v Ho (sub), Sm (12)
Slater, W. J. (Wolverhampton W), 1955 v W, WG; 1958 v S, P, Y, USSR (3), Br, A; 1959 v USSR; 1960 v S (12)
Smalley, T. (Wolverhampton W), 1937 v W (1)
Smart, T. (Aston Villa), 1921 v S; 1924 v S, W; 1926 v Ni; 1930 v W (5)
Smith, A. (Nottingham F), 1891 v S, W; 1893 v Ni (3)
Smith, A. (Leeds U), 2001 v M (sub), Gr (sub); 2002 v Ho (sub); 2003 v P, Slo (sub), Mac (6)
Smith, A. K. (Oxford University), 1872 v S (1)
Smith, A. M. (Arsenal), 1989 v S.Ar (sub), Gr, Alb (sub), Pol (sub); 1991 v T, USSR, Arg; 1992 v G, T, Pol (sub), H (sub), D, Se (sub) (13)
Smith, B. (Tottenham H), 1921 v S; 1922 v W (2)
Smith, C. E. (C Palace), 1876 v S (1)
Smith, G. O. (Oxford University), 1893 v Ni; 1894 v W, S; 1895 v W; 1896 v Ni, W, S; (with Old Carthusians), 1897 v Ni, W, S; 1898 v Ni, W, S; (with Corinthians), 1899 v Ni, W, S; 1899 v Ni, W, S; 1901 v S (20)
Smith, H. (Reading), 1905 v W, S; 1906 v W, Ni (4)
Smith, J. (WBA), 1920 v Ni; 1923 v Ni (2)
Smith, Joe (Bolton W), 1913 v Ni; 1914 v S, W; 1920 v W, Ni (5)
Smith, J. C. R. (Millwall), 1939 v Ni, N (2)
Smith, J. W. (Portsmouth), 1932 v Ni, W, Sp (3)
Smith, Leslie (Brentford), 1939 v R (1)
Smith, Lionel (Arsenal), 1951 v W; 1952 v W, Ni; 1953 v W, S, Bel (6)
Smith, R. A. (Tottenham H), 1961 v Ni, W, S, L, P, Sp; 1962 v S; 1963 v S, F, Br, Cz, EG; 1964 v W, Ni, R of W (15)
Smith, S. (Aston Villa), 1895 v S (1)
Smith, S. C. (Leicester C), 1936 v Ni (1)
Smith, T. (Birmingham C), 1960 v W, Se (2)
Smith, T. (Liverpool), 1971 v W (1)
Smith, W. H. (Huddersfield T), 1922 v W, S; 1928 v S (3)
Sorby, T. H. (Thursday Wanderers, Sheffield), 1879 v W (1)
Southgate, G. (Aston Villa), 1996 v P (sub), Bul, H (sub), Chn, Sw, S, Ho, Sp, G; 1997 v Mol, Pol, Ge, M, Ge (sub), S.Af, Pol, I, F, Br; 1998 v Mol, I, Cam, Sw, S.Ar, Mor, Tun, Arg (sub); 1999 v Se, Bul, L, Bul; 2000 v Bel, S, Arg, Uk, Ma (sub), R (sub); 2001 v F (sub), G, Fi, I, M (sub); (with Middlesbrough), 2002 v Ho (sub), Se, Ho (sub), I, Para, Sk (sub), Cam (sub); 2003 v P, Slo, Lie, S.Af, Ser, Slo (55)
Southworth, J. (Blackburn R), 1889 v W; 1891 v W; 1892 v S (3)
Sparks, F. J. (Herts Rangers), 1879 v S; (with Clapham Rovers), 1880 v S, W (3)
Spence, J. W. (Manchester U), 1926 v Bel; 1927 v Ni (2)
Spence, R. (Chelsea), 1936 v A, Bel (2)
Spencer, C. W. (Newcastle U), 1924 v S; 1925 v W (2)
Spencer, H. (Aston Villa), 1897 v S, W; 1900 v W; 1903 v Ni; 1905 v W, S (6)
Spiksley, F. (Sheffield W), 1893 v S, W; 1894 v S, Ni; 1896 v Ni; 1898 v S, W (7)
Spilsbury, B. W. (Cambridge University), 1885 v Ni; 1886 v Ni, S (3)
Spink, N. (Aston Villa), 1983 v Aus (sub) (1)
Spouncer, W. A. (Nottingham F), 1900 v W (1)
Springett, R. D. G. (Sheffield W), 1960 v Ni, S, Y, Sp, H; 1961 v Ni, S, L, P, Sp, M, I, A; 1962 v W, Ni, S, A, Sw, Pe, L, P, H, Arg, Bul, Br; 1963 v Ni, W, F (2), Sw; 1966 v W, A, N (33)
Sproston, B. (Leeds U), 1937 v W; 1938 v S, W, Ni, Cz, G, Sw, F; (with Tottenham H), 1939 v W, R of E; (with Manchester C), N (11)
Squire, R. T. (Cambridge University), 1886 v S, W, Ni (3)
Stanbrough, M. H. (Old Carthusians), 1895 v W (1)
Staniforth, R. (Huddersfield T), 1954 v S, H, Y, Bel, Sw, U; 1955 v W, WG (8)
Starling, R. W. (Sheffield W), 1933 v S; (with Aston Villa), 1937 v S (2)
Statham, D. (WBA), 1983 v W, Aus (2) (3)
Steele, F. C. (Stoke C), 1937 v S, W, Ni, N, Se, Fi (6)
Stein, B. (Luton T), 1984 v F (1)
Stephenson, C. (Huddersfield T), 1924 v W (1)
Stephenson, G. T. (Derby Co), 1928 v F, Bel; (with Sheffield W), 1931 v F (3)
Stephenson, J. E. (Leeds U), 1938 v S; 1939 v Ni (2)
Stepney, A. C. (Manchester U), 1968 v Se (1)
Sterland, M. (Sheffield W), 1989 v S.Ar (1)
Steven, T. M. (Everton), 1985 v Ni, Ei, R, Fi, I, US (sub); 1986 v T (sub), Eg, USSR (sub), M (sub), Pol, Para, Arg; 1987 v Se, Y (sub), Sp (sub); 1988 v T, Y, Ho, H, S, Sw, Ho, USSR; 1989 v S; (with Rangers), 1990 v Cz, Cam (sub), WG (sub), I; 1991 v Cam; (with Marseille), 1992 v G, C, Br, Fi, D, F (36)
Stevens, G. A. (Tottenham H), 1985 v Fi (sub), T (sub), Ni; 1986 v S (sub), M (sub), Mor (sub), Para (sub) (7)
Stevens, M. G. (Everton), 1985 v I, WG; 1986 v R, T, Ni, Eg, Is, S, Ca, P, Mor, Pol, Para, Arg; 1987 v Br, S; 1988 v T, Y, Is, Ho, H (sub), S, Sw, Ei, Ho, USSR; (with Rangers), 1989 v D, Se, Gr, Alb (2), S, Pol; 1990 v Se, Pol, I, Br, D, Tun, Ei, I; 1991 v USSR; 1992 v C, H, Br, Fi (46)
Stewart, J. (Sheffield W), 1907 v S, W; (with Newcastle U), 1911 v S (3)
Stewart, P. A. (Tottenham H), 1992 v G (sub), Cz (sub), C (sub) (3)
Stiles, N. P. (Manchester U), 1965 v S, H, Y, Se; 1966 v W, Ni, S, A, Sp, Pol (2), WG (2), N, D, U, M, F, Arg, P; 1967 v Ni, W, S, Cz; 1968 v USSR; 1969 v R; 1970 v Ni, S (28)
Stoker, J. (Birmingham), 1933 v W; 1934 v S, H (3)
Stone, S. B. (Nottingham F), 1996 v N (sub), Sw (sub), P, Bul, Cro, Chn (sub), Sw (sub), S (sub), Sp (sub) (9)
Storer, H. (Derby Co), 1924 v F; 1928 v Ni (2)
Storey, P. E. (Arsenal), 1971 v Gr, Ni, S; 1972 v Sw, WG, W, Ni, S; 1973 v W (3), Y, S (2), Ni, Cz, Pol, USSR, I (19)
Storey-Moore, I. (Nottingham F), 1970 v Ho (1)
Strange, A. H. (Sheffield W), 1930 v S, A, G; 1931 v S, W, Ni, F, Bel; 1932 v S, W, Ni, Sp; 1933 v S, Ni, A, I, Sw; 1934 v Ni, W, F (20)
Stratford, A. H. (Wanderers), 1874 v S (1)
Streten, B. (Luton T), 1950 v Ni (1)
Sturgess, A. (Sheffield U), 1911 v Ni; 1914 v S (2)
Summerbee, M. G. (Manchester C), 1968 v S, Sp, WG; 1972 v Sw, WG (sub), W, Ni; 1973 v USSR (sub) (8)
Sunderland, A. (Arsenal), 1980 v Aus (1)
Sutcliffe, J. W. (Bolton W), 1893 v W; 1895 v S, Ni; 1901 v S; (with Millwall), 1903 v W (5)
Sutton, C. R. (Blackburn R), 1998 v Cam (sub) (1)
Swan, P. (Sheffield W), 1960 v Y, Sp, H; 1961 v Ni, W, S, L, P, Sp, M, I, A; 1962 v W, Ni, S, A, Sw, L, P (19)
Swepstone, H. A. (Pilgrims), 1880 v S; 1882 v S, W; 1883 v S, W, Ni (6)
Swift, F. V. (Manchester C), 1947 v S, W, Ni, Ei, Ho, F, Sw, P; 1948 v S, W, Ni, Bel, Se, I; 1949 v S, W, Ni, D, N (19)

Tait, G. (Birmingham Excelsior), 1881 v W (1)
Talbot, B. (Ipswich T), 1977 v Ni (sub), S, Br, Arg, U; (with Arsenal), 1980 v Aus (6)
Tambling, R. V. (Chelsea), 1963 v W, F; 1966 v Y (3)
Tate, J. T. (Aston Villa), 1931 v F, Bel; 1933 v W (3)
Taylor, E. (Blackpool), 1954 v H (1)
Taylor, E. H. (Huddersfield T), 1923 v S, W, Ni, Bel; 1924 v S, Ni, F; 1926 v S (8)
Taylor, J. G. (Fulham), 1951 v Arg, P (2)
Taylor, P. H. (Liverpool), 1948 v W, Ni, Se (3)
Taylor, P. J. (C Palace), 1976 v W (sub+1), Ni, S (4)
Taylor, T. (Manchester U), 1953 v Arg, Ch, U; 1954 v Bel, Sw; 1956 v S, Br, Se, Fi, WG; 1957 v Ni, Y (sub), D (2), Ei (2); 1958 v W, Ni, F (19)
Temple, D. W. (Everton), 1965 v WG (1)
Terry, J. G. (Chelsea), 2003 v Ser (sub) (1)
Thickett, H. (Sheffield U), 1899 v S, W (2)
Thomas, D. (Coventry C), 1983 v Aus (1+1 sub) (2)
Thomas, D. (QPR), 1975 v Cz (sub), P, Cy (sub+1), W, S (sub); 1976 v Cz (sub), P (sub) (8)
Thomas, G. R. (C Palace), 1991 v T, USSR, Arg, Aus, Nz (2), Mal; 1992 v Pol, F (9)
Thomas, M. L. (Arsenal), 1989 v S.Ar; 1990 v Y (2)
Thompson, P. (Liverpool), 1964 v P (2), Ei, US, Br, Arg; 1965 v Ni, W, S, Bel, Ho; 1966 v Ni; 1968 v Ni, WG; 1970 v S, Ho (sub) (16)
Thompson, P. B. (Liverpool), 1976 v W (2), Ni, S, Br, I, Fi; 1977 v Fi; 1979 v Ei (sub), Cz, Ni, S, Bul, Se (sub), A; 1980 v D, Ni, Bul, Ei, Sp (2), Arg, W, S, Bel, I; 1981 v N, R, H; 1982 v N, H, W, Ho, S, Fi, F, Cz, K, WG, Sp; 1983 v WG, Gr (42)
Thompson T. (Aston Villa), 1952 v W; (with Preston NE), 1957 v S (2)
Thomson, R. A. (Wolverhampton W), 1964 v Ni, US, P, Arg; 1965 v Bel, Ho, Ni, W (8)
Thornewell, G. (Derby Co), 1923 v Se (2); 1924 v F; 1925 v F (4)
Thornley, I. (Manchester C), 1907 v W (1)
Tilson, S. F. (Manchester C), 1934 v H, Cz; 1935 v W; 1936 v Ni (4)

Titmuss, F. (Southampton), 1922 v W; 1923 v W (2)
Todd, C. (Derby Co), 1972 v Ni; 1974 v P, W, Ni, S, Arg, EG, Bul, Y; 1975 v P (sub), WG, Cy (2), Ni, W, S; 1976 v Sw, Cz, P, Ni, S, Br, Fi; 1977 v Ei, Fi, Ho (sub), Ni (27)
Toone, G. (Notts Co), 1892 v S, W (2)
Topham, A. G. (Casuals), 1894 v W (1)
Topham, R. (Wolverhampton W), 1893 v Ni; (with Casuals) 1894 v W (2)
Towers, M. A. (Sunderland), 1976 v W, Ni (sub), I (3)
Townley, W. J. (Blackburn R), 1889 v W; 1890 v Ni (2)
Townrow, J. E. (Clapton Orient), 1925 v S; 1926 v W (2)
Tremelling, D. R. (Birmingham), 1928 v W (1)
Tresadern, J. (West Ham U), 1923 v S, Se (2)
Tueart, D. (Manchester C), 1975 v Cy (sub), Ni; 1977 v Fi, Ni, W (sub), S (sub) (6)
Tunstall, F. E. (Sheffield U), 1923 v S; 1924 v S, W, Ni, F; 1925 v Ni, S (7)
Turnbull, R. J. (Bradford), 1920 v Ni (1)
Turner, A. (Southampton), 1900 v Ni; 1901 v Ni (2)
Turner, H. (Huddersfield T), 1931 v F, Bel (2)
Turner, J. A. (Bolton W), 1893 v W; (with Stoke C) 1895 v Ni; (with Derby Co) 1898 v Ni (3)
Tweedy, G. J. (Grimsby T), 1937 v H (1)

Ufton, D. G. (Charlton Ath), 1954 v R of E (1)
Underwood A. (Stoke C), 1891 v Ni; 1892 v Ni (2)
Unsworth, D. G. (Everton), 1995 v J (1)
Upson, M. J. (Birmingham C), 2003 v S.Af (sub), Ser, Slo (3)
Urwin, T. (Middlesbrough), 1923 v Se (2); 1924 v Bel; (with Newcastle U), 1926 v W (4)
Utley, G. (Barnsley), 1913 v Ni (1)

Vassell, D. (Aston Villa), 2002 v Ho, I (sub), Para, Sk, Cam, Se, Ng (sub), Br (sub); 2003 v Mac (sub), Aus (sub), T (sub), S.Af (sub), Ser (sub), Slo (sub) (14)
Vaughton, O. H. (Aston Villa), 1882 v S, W, Ni; 1884 v S, W (5)
Veitch, C. C. M. (Newcastle U), 1906 v S, W, Ni; 1907 v S, W; 1909 v W (6)
Veitch, J. G. (Old Westminsters), 1894 v W (1)
Venables, T. F. (Chelsea), 1965 v Ho, Bel (2)
Venison, B. (Newcastle U), 1995 v US, U (2)
Vidal, R. W. S. (Oxford University), 1873 v S (1)
Viljoen, C. (Ipswich T), 1975 v Ni, W (2)
Viollet, D. S. (Manchester U), 1960 v H; 1962 v L (2)
Von Donop (Royal Engineers), 1873 v S; 1875 v S (2)

Wace, H. (Wanderers), 1878 v S; 1879 v S, W (3)
Waddle, C. R. (Newcastle U), 1985 v Ei, R (sub), Fi (sub), S (sub), I, M (sub), WG, US; (with Tottenham H), 1986 v R, T, Ni, Is, USSR, S, M, Ca, P, Mor, Pol (sub), Arg (sub); 1987 v Se (sub), Ni (2), Y, Sp, T, Br, S; 1988 v WG, Is, H, S (sub), Co, Sw (sub), Ei, Ho (sub); 1989 v Se, S.Ar, Alb (2), Ch, S, Pol, D (sub); (with Marseille), 1990 v Se, Pol, I, Y, Br, D, U, Tun, Ei, Ho, Eg, Bel, Cam, WG, I (sub); 1991 v H (sub), Pol (sub); 1992 v T (62)
Wadsworth, S. J. (Huddersfield T), 1922 v S; 1923 v S, Bel; 1924 v S, Ni; 1925 v S, Ni; 1926 v W; 1927 v Ni (9)
Wainscoat, W. R. (Leeds U), 1929 v S (1)
Waiters, A. K. (Blackpool), 1964 v Ei, Br; 1965 v W, Bel, Ho (5)
Walden, F. I. (Tottenham H), 1914 v S; 1922 v W (2)
Walker, D. S. (Nottingham F), 1989 v D (sub), Se (sub), Gr, Alb (2), Ch, S, Pol, D; 1990 v Se, Pol, I, Y, Br, Cz, D, U, Tun, Ei, Ho, Eg, Bel, Cam, WG, I; 1991 v H, Pol, Ei (2), Cam, T, Arg, Aus, Nz (2), Mal; 1992 v T, Pol, F, Cz, C, H, Br, Fi, D, F, Se; (with Sampdoria), 1993 v Sp, N, T, Sm, T, Ho, Pol, N, US (sub), Br, G; (with Sheffield W), 1994 v Sm (59)
Walker, I. M. (Tottenham H), 1996 v H (sub), Chn (sub); 1997 v I (3)
Walker, W. H. (Aston Villa), 1921 v Ni; 1922 v Ni, W, S; 1923 v Se (2); 1924 v S; 1925 v Ni, W, S, Bel, F; 1926 v Ni, W, S; 1927 v Ni, W; 1933 v A (18)
Wall, G. (Manchester U), 1907 v W; 1908 v Ni; 1909 v S; 1910 v W, S; 1912 v S; 1913 v Ni (7)
Wallace, C. W. (Aston Villa), 1913 v W; 1914 v Ni; 1920 v S (3)
Wallace, D. L. (Southampton), 1986 v Eg (1)
Walsh, P. (Luton T), 1983 v Aus (2 + 1 sub); 1984 v F, W (5)
Walters, A. M. (Cambridge University), 1885 v S, N; 1886 v S; 1887 v S, W; (with Old Carthusians), 1889 v S, W; 1890 v S, W (9)
Walters, K. M. (Rangers), 1991 v Nz (1)
Walters, P. M. (Oxford University), 1885 v S, Ni; (with Old Carthusians), 1886 v S, W, Ni; 1887 v S, W; 1888 v S, Ni; 1889 v S, W; 1890 v S, W (13)
Walton, N. (Blackburn R), 1890 v Ni (1)
Ward, J. T. (Blackburn Olympic), 1885 v W (1)
Ward, P. (Brighton & HA), 1980 v Aus (sub) (1)
Ward, T. V. (Derby Co), 1948 v Bel; 1949 v W (2)
Waring, T. (Aston Villa), 1931 v F, Bel; 1932 v S, W, Ni (5)
Warner, C. (Upton Park), 1878 v S (1)
Warren, B. (Derby Co), 1906 v S, W, Ni; 1907 v S, W, Ni; 1908 v S, W, Ni, A (2), H, B; (with Chelsea), 1909 v S, Ni, W, H (2), A; 1911 v S, Ni, W (22)
Waterfield, G. S. (Burnley), 1927 v W (1)
Watson, D. (Norwich C), 1984 v Br, U, Ch; 1985 v M, US (sub); 1986 v S; (with Everton), 1987 v Ni; 1988 v Is, Ho, S, Sw (sub), USSR (12)
Watson, D. V. (Sunderland), 1974 v P, S (sub), Arg, EG, Bul, Y; 1975 v Cz, P, WG, Cy (2), Ni, W, S; (with Manchester C), 1976 v Sw, Cz (sub), P; 1977 v Ho, L, Ni, W, S, Br, Arg, U; 1978 v Sw, L, I, WG, Br, W, Ni, S, H; 1979 v D, Ei, Cz, Ni (2), W, S, Bul, Se, A; (with Werder Bremen), 1980 v D; (with Southampton), Ni, Bul, Ei, Sp (2), Arg, Ni, S, Bel, I; 1981 v N, R, Sw, R, W, S, Sw, H; (with Stoke C), 1982 v Ni, Ic (65)
Watson, V. M. (West Ham U), 1923 v W, S; 1930 v S, G, A (5)
Watson, W. (Burnley), 1913 v S; 1914 v Ni; 1920 v Ni (3)
Watson, W. (Sunderland), 1950 v Ni, I; 1951 v W, Y (4)
Weaver, S. (Newcastle U), 1932 v S, 1933 v S, Ni (3)
Webb, G. W. (West Ham U), 1911 v S, W (2)
Webb, N. J. (Nottingham F), 1988 v WG (sub), T, Y, Is, Ho, S, Sw, Ei, USSR (sub); 1989 v D, Se, Gr, Alb (2), Ch, S, Pol, D; (with Manchester U), 1990 v Se, I (sub); 1992 v F, H, Br (sub), Fi, D (sub), Se (26)
Webster, M. (Middlesbrough), 1930 v S, A, G (3)
Wedlock, W. J. (Bristol C), 1907 v S, Ni, W; 1908 v S, Ni, W, A (2), H, B; 1909 v S, W, Ni, H (2), A; 1910 v S, W, Ni; 1911 v S, W, Ni; 1912 v S, W, Ni; 1914 v W (26)
Weir, D. (Bolton W), 1889 v S, Ni (2)
Welch, R. de C. (Wanderers), 1872 v S; (with Harrow Chequers), 1874 v S (2)
Weller, K. (Leicester C), 1974 v W, Ni, S, Arg (4)
Welsh, D. (Charlton Ath), 1938 v G, Sw; 1939 v R (3)
West, G. (Everton), 1969 v W, Bul, M (3)
Westwood, R. W. (Bolton W), 1935 v S, W, Ho; 1936 v Ni, G; 1937 v W (6)
Whateley, O. (Aston Villa), 1883 v S, Ni (2)
Wheeler, J. E. (Bolton W), 1955 v Ni (1)
Wheldon, G. F. (Aston Villa), 1897 v Ni; 1898 v S, W, Ni (4)
White, D. (Manchester C), 1993 v Sp (1)
White, T. A. (Everton), 1933 v I (1)
Whitehead, J. (Accrington), 1893 v W; (with Blackburn R), 1894 v Ni (2)
Whitfeld, H. (Old Etonians), 1879 v W (1)
Whitham, M. (Sheffield U), 1892 v Ni (1)
Whitworth, S. (Leicester C), 1975 v WG, Cy, Ni, W, S; 1976 v Sw, P (7)
Whymark, T. J. (Ipswich T), 1978 v L (sub) (1)
Widdowson, S. W. (Nottingham F), 1880 v S (1)
Wignall, F. (Nottingham F), 1965 v W, Ho (2)
Wilcox, J. M. (Blackburn R), 1996 v H; 1999 v F (sub); (with Leeds U), 2000 v Arg (3)
Wilkes, A. (Aston Villa), 1901 v S, W; 1902 v S, W, Ni (5)
Wilkins, R. G. (Chelsea), 1976 v I; 1977 v Ei, Fi, Ni, Br, Arg, U; 1978 v Sw (sub), L, I, WG, W, Ni, S, H; 1979 v D, Ei, Cz, Ni, W, S, Bul, Se (sub), A; (with Manchester U), 1980 v D, Ni, Bul, Sp (2), Arg, W (sub), Ni, S, Bel, I; 1981 v Sp (sub), R, Br, W, S, Sw, H (sub); 1982 v Ni, W, Ho, S, Fi, F, Cz, K, WG, Sp; 1983 v D, WG; 1984 v D, Ni, W, S, USSR, Br, U, Ch; (with AC Milan), 1985 v EG, Fi, T, Ni, Ei, R, Fi, S, I, M; 1986 v T, Ni, Is, Eg, USSR, S, M, Ca, P, Mor; 1987 v Se, Y (sub) (84)
Wilkinson, B. (Sheffield U), 1904 v S (1)
Wilkinson, L. R. (Oxford University), 1891 v W (1)
Williams, B. F. (Wolverhampton W), 1949 v F; 1950 v S, W, Ei, I, P, Bel, Ch, US, Sp; 1951 v Ni, W, S, Y, Arg, P; 1952 v W, F; 1955 v S, WG, F, Sp, P; 1956 v W (24)
Williams, O. (Clapton Orient), 1923 v W, Ni (2)
Williams, S. (Southampton), 1983 v Aus (1+1 sub); 1984 v F; 1985 v EG, Fi, T (6)
Williams, W. (WBA), 1897 v Ni; 1898 v W, Ni, S; 1899 v W, Ni (6)
Williamson, E. C. (Arsenal), 1923 v Se (2) (2)
Williamson, R. G. (Middlesbrough), 1905 v Ni; 1911 v Ni, S, W; 1912 v S, W; 1913 v Ni (7)
Willingham, C. K. (Huddersfield T), 1937 v Fi; 1938 v S, G, Sw, F; 1939 v S, W, Ni, R of E, N, I, Y (12)
Willis, A. (Tottenham H), 1952 v F (1)
Wilshaw, D. J. (Wolverhampton W), 1954 v W, Sw, U; 1955 v S, F, Sp, P; 1956 v W, Ni, Fi, WG; 1957 v Ni (12)

Wilson, C. P. (Hendon), 1884 v S, W (2)
Wilson, C. W. (Oxford University), 1879 v W; 1881 v S (2)
Wilson, G. (Sheffield W), 1921 v S, W, Bel; 1922 v S, Ni; 1923 v S, W, Ni, Bel; 1924 v W, Ni, F (12)
Wilson, G. P. (Corinthians), 1900 v S, W (2)
Wilson, R. (Huddersfield T), 1960 v S, Y, Sp, H; 1962 v W, Ni, S, A, Sw, Pe, P, H, Arg, Bul, Br; 1963 v Ni, F, Br, Cz, EG, Sw; 1964 v W, S, R of W, U, P (2), Ei, Br, Arg; (with Everton), 1965 v S, H, Y, WG, Se; 1966 v WG (sub), W, Ni, A, Sp, Pol (2), Y, Fi, D, U, M, F, Arg, P, WG; 1967 v Ni, W, S, Cz, A; 1968 v Ni, S, USSR (2), Sp (2), Y (63)
Wilson, T. (Huddersfield T), 1928 v S (1)
Winckworth, W. N. (Old Westminsters), 1892 v W; 1893 v Ni (2)
Windridge, J. E. (Chelsea), 1908 v S, W, Ni, A (2), H, B; 1909 v Ni (8)
Wingfield-Stratford, C. V. (Royal Engineers), 1877 v S (1)
Winterburn, N. (Arsenal), 1990 v I (sub); 1993 v G (sub) (2)
Wise, D. F. (Chelsea), 1991 v T, USSR, Aus (sub), Nz (2); 1994 v N; 1995 v R (sub), Ng; 1996 v Co, N, P, H (sub); 2000 v Bel (sub), Arg, Br, Ma, P (sub), G, R; 2001 v F, Fi (21)
Withe, P. (Aston Villa), 1981 v Br, W, S; 1982 v N (sub), W, Ic; 1983 v H, Ni, S; 1984 v H (sub); 1985 v T (11)
Wollaston, C. H. R. (Wanderers), 1874 v S; 1875 v S; 1877 v S; 1880 v S (4)
Wolstenholme, S. (Everton), 1904 v S; (with Blackburn R), 1905 v W, Ni (3)
Wood, H. (Wolverhampton W), 1890 v S, W; 1896 v S (3)
Wood, R. E. (Manchester U), 1955 v Ni, W; 1956 v Fi (3)
Woodcock, A. S. (Nottingham F), 1978 v Ni; 1979 v Ei (sub), Cz, Bul (sub), Se; 1980 v Ni; (with Cologne), Bul, Ei, Sp (2), Arg, Bel, I; 1981 v N, R, Sw, R, W (sub), S; 1982 v Ni (sub), Ho, Fi (sub), WG (sub), Sp; (with Arsenal), 1983 v WG (sub), Gr, L, Gr; 1984 v L, F (sub), Ni, W, S, Br, U (sub); 1985 v EG, Fi, T, Ni; 1986 v R (sub), T (sub), Is (sub) (42)
Woodgate, J. S. (Leeds U), 1999 v Bul; 2003 v P (sub), Slo, Mac (4)
Woodger, G. (Oldham Ath), 1911 v Ni (1)
Woodhall, G. (WBA), 1888 v S, W (2)
Woodley, V. R. (Chelsea), 1937 v S, N, Se, Fi; 1938 v S, W, Ni, Cz, G, Sw, F; 1939 v S, W, Ni, R of E, N, I, R, Y (19)
Woods, C. C. E. (Norwich C), 1985 v US; 1986 v Eg (sub), Is (sub), Ca (sub); (with Rangers), 1987 v Y, Sp (sub), Ni (sub), T, S; 1988 v Is, H, Sw (sub), USSR; 1989 v D (sub); 1990 v Br (sub), D (sub); 1991 v H, Pol, Ei, USSR, Aus, Nz (2), Mal; (with Sheffield W), 1992 v G, T, Pol, F, C, Br, Fi, D, F, Se; 1993 v Sp, N, T, Sm, T, Ho, Pol, N, US (43)
Woodward, V. J. (Tottenham H), 1903 v S, W, Ni; 1904 v S, Ni; 1905 v S, W, Ni; 1907 v S; 1908 v S, W, Ni, A (2), H, B; 1909 v W, Ni, H (2), A; (with Chelsea), 1910 v Ni; 1911 v W (23)
Woosnam, M. (Manchester C), 1922 v W (1)
Worrall, F. (Portsmouth), 1935 v Ho; 1937 v Ni (2)
Worthington, F. S. (Leicester C), 1974 v Ni (sub), S, Arg, EG, Bul, Y; 1975 v Cz, P (sub) (8)
Wreford-Brown, C. (Oxford University), 1889 v Ni; (with Old Carthusians), 1894 v W; 1895 v W; 1898 v S (4)
Wright, E. G. D. (Cambridge University), 1906 v W (1)
Wright, I. E. (C Palace), 1991 v Cam, Ei (sub), USSR, Nz; (with Arsenal), 1992 v H (sub); 1993 v N, T (2), Pol (sub), N (sub), US (sub), Br, G (sub); 1994 v Pol, Ho (sub), Sm, Gr (sub), N (sub); 1995 v US (sub), R; 1997 v Ge (sub), I (sub), M (sub), S.Af, I, F, Br (sub); 1998 v Mol, I, S.Ar (sub), Mor; (with West Ham U), 1999 v L (sub), CzR (33)
Wright, J. D. (Newcastle U), 1939 v N (1)
Wright, M. (Southampton), 1984 v W; 1985 v EG, Fi, T, Ei, R, I, WG; 1986 v R, T, Ni, Eg, USSR; 1987 v Y, Ni, S; (with Derby Co), 1988 v Is, Ho (sub), Co, Sw, Ei, Ho; 1990 v Cz (sub), Tun (sub), Ho, Eg, Bel, Cam, WG, I; 1991 v H, Pol, Ei (2), Cam, USSR, Arg, Aus, Nz, Mal; (with Liverpool), 1992 v F, Fi; 1993 v Sp; 1996 v Cro, H (45)
Wright, R. I. (Ipswich T), 2000 v Ma; (with Arsenal), 2002 v Ho (sub) (2)
Wright, T. J. (Everton), 1968 v USSR; 1969 v R (2), M (sub), U, Br; 1970 v W, Ho, Bel, R (sub), Br (11)
Wright, W. A. (Wolverhampton W), 1947 v S, W, Ni, Ei, Ho, F, Sw, P; 1948 v S, W, Ni, Bel, Se, I; 1949 v S, W, Ni, D, Sw, Se, N, F; 1950 v S, W, Ni, Ei, I, P, Bel, Ch, US, Sp; 1951 v Ni, S, Arg; 1952 v W, Ni, S, F, A (2), I, Sw; 1953 v Ni, W, S, Bel, Arg, Ch, U, US; 1954 v W, Ni, S, R of E, H (2), Y, Bel, Sw, U; 1955 v W, Ni, S, WG, F, Sp, P; 1956 v Ni, W, S, Br, Se, Fi, WG, D, Sp; 1957 v S, W, Ni, Y, D (2), Ei (2); 1958 v W, Ni, S, P, Y, USSR (3), Br, A, F; 1959 v W, Ni, S, USSR, I, Br, Pe, M, US (105)
Wylie, J. G. (Wanderers), 1878 v S (1)

Yates, J. (Burnley), 1889 v Ni (1)
York, R. E. (Aston Villa), 1922 v S; 1926 v S (2)
Young, A. (Huddersfield T), 1933 v W; 1937 v S, H, N, Se; 1938 v G, Sw, F; 1939 v W (9)
Young, G. M. (Sheffield W), 1965 v W (1)
R. E. Evans also played for Wales against E, Ni, S; J. Reynolds also played for Ireland against E, W, S.

NORTHERN IRELAND

Addis, D. J. (Cliftonville), 1922 v N (1)
Aherne, T. (Belfast C), 1947 v E; 1948 v S; 1949 v W; (with Luton T), 1950 v W (4)
Alexander, T. E. (Cliftonville), 1895 v S (1)
Allan, C. (Cliftonville), 1936 v E (1)
Allen, J. (Limavady), 1887 v E (1)
Anderson, J. (Distillery), 1925 v S.Af (1)
Anderson, T. (Manchester U), 1973 v Cy, E, S, W; 1974 v Bul, P; (with Swindon T), 1975 v S (sub); 1976 v Is; 1977 v Ho, Bel, WG, E, S, W, Ic; 1978 v Ic, Ho, Bel; (with Peterborough U), S, E, W; 1979 v D (sub) (22)
Anderson, W. (Linfield), 1898 v W, E, S; (with Cliftonville), 1899 v S (4)
Andrews, W. (Glentoran), 1908 v S; (with Grimsby T), 1913 v E, S (3)
Armstrong, G. J. (Tottenham H), 1977 v WG, E, W (sub), Ic (sub); 1978 v Bel, S, E, W; 1979 v Ei, D, Bul, E, Bul, E, S, W, D; 1980 v E, Ei, Is, S, E, W, Aus (3); 1981 v Se; (with Watford), P, S, P, S, Se; 1982 v S, Is, E, F, W, Y, Hon, Sp, A, F; 1983 v A, T, Alb, S, E, W; (with Real Mallorca), 1984 v A, WG, E, W, Fi; 1985 v R, Fi, E, Sp; (with WBA), 1986 v T, R (sub), E (sub), F (sub); (with Chesterfield), D (sub), Br (sub) (63)

Baird, C. P. (Southampton), 2003 v I, Sp (2)
Baird, G. (Distillery), 1896 v S, E, W (3)
Baird, H. C. (Huddersfield T), 1939 v E (1)
Balfe, J. (Shelbourne), 1909 v E; 1910 v W (2)
Bambrick, J. (Linfield), 1929 v W, S, E; 1930 v W, S, E; 1932 v W; (with Chelsea), 1935 v W; 1936 v E, S; 1938 v W (11)
Banks, S. J. (Cliftonville), 1937 v W (1)
Barr, H. H. (Linfield), 1962 v E; (with Coventry C), 1963 v E, Pol (3)
Barron, J. H. (Cliftonville), 1894 v E, W, S; 1895 v S; 1896 v S; 1897 v E, W (7)
Barry, J. (Cliftonville), 1888 v W, S; 1889 v E (3)
Barry, J. (Bohemians), 1900 v S (1)
Baxter, R. A. (Distillery), 1887 v S (1)
Baxter, S. N. (Cliftonville), 1887 v W (1)
Bennett, L. V. (Dublin University), 1889 v W (1)
Best, G. (Manchester U), 1964 v W, U; 1965 v E, Ho (2), S, Sw (2), Alb; 1966 v S, E, Alb; 1967 v E; 1968 v S; 1969 v E, S, W, T; 1970 v S, E, W, USSR; 1971 v Cy (2), Sp, E, S, W; 1972 v USSR, Sp; 1973 v Bul; 1974 v P; (with Fulham), 1977 v Ho, Bel, WG; 1978 v Ic, Ho (37)
Bingham, W. L. (Sunderland), 1951 v F; 1952 v E, S, W; 1953 v E, S, F, W; 1954 v E, S, W; 1955 v E, S, W; 1956 v E, S, W; 1957 v E, S, W, P (2), I; 1958 v S, E, W, I (2), Arg, Cz (2), WG, F; (with Luton T), 1959 v E, S, W, Sp; 1960 v S, E, W; (with Everton), 1961 v E, S, WG (2), Gr, I; 1962 v E, Gr; 1963 v E, S, Pol (2), Sp; (with Port Vale), 1964 v S, E, Sp (56)
Black, K. T. (Luton T), 1988 v Fr (sub), Ma (sub); 1989 v Ei, H, Sp (2), Ch (sub); 1990 v H, N, U; 1991 v Y (2), D, A, Pol, Fa; (with Nottingham F), 1992 v Fa, A, D, S, Li, G; 1993 v Sp, D (sub), Alb, Ei (sub), Sp; 1994 v D (sub), Ei (sub), R (sub) (30)
Black, T. (Glentoran), 1901 v E (1)
Blair, H. (Portadown), 1928 v F; 1931 v S; 1932 v S; (with Swansea), 1934 v S (4)
Blair, J. (Cliftonville), 1907 v W, E, S; 1908 v E, S (5)
Blair, R. V. (Oldham Ath), 1975 v Se (sub), S (sub), W; 1976 v Se, Is (5)
Blanchflower, J. (Manchester U), 1954 v W; 1955 v E, S; 1956 v S, W; 1957 v S, E, P; 1958 v S, E, I (2) (12)
Blanchflower, R. D. (Barnsley), 1950 v S, W; 1951 v E, S; (with Aston Villa), F; 1952 v W; 1953 v E, S, W, F; 1954 v E, S, W;

1955 v E, S (with Tottenham H), W; 1956 v E, S, W; 1957 v E, S, W, I, P (2); 1958 v E, S, W, I (2), Cz (2), Arg, F, WG; 1959 v E, S, W, Sp; 1960 v E, S, W; 1961 v E, S, W, WG (2); 1962 v E, S, W, Gr, Ho; 1963 v E, S, Pol (2) (56)
Bookman, L. J. O. (Bradford C), 1914 v W; (with Luton T), 1921 v S, W; 1922 v E (4)
Bothwell, A. W. (Ards), 1926 v S, E, W; 1927 v E, W (5)
Bowler, G. C. (Hull C), 1950 v E, S, W (3)
Boyle, P. (Sheffield U), 1901 v E; 1902 v E; 1903 v S, W; 1904 v E (5)
Braithwaite, R. M. (Linfield), 1962 v W; 1963 v P, Sp; (with Middlesbrough), 1964 v W, U; 1965 v E, S, Sw (2), Ho (10)
Breen, T. (Belfast C), 1935 v E, W; 1937 v E, S; (with Manchester U), 1937 v W; 1938 v E, S; 1939 v W, S (9)
Brennan, B. (Bohemians), 1912 v W (1)
Brennan, R. A. (Luton T), 1949 v W; (with Birmingham C), 1950 v E, S, W; (with Fulham), 1951 v E (5)
Briggs, W. R. (Manchester U), 1962 v W; (with Swansea T), 1965 v Ho (2)
Brisby, D. (Distillery), 1891 v S (1)
Brolly, T. H. (Millwall), 1937 v W; 1938 v W; 1939 v E, W (4)
Brookes, E. A. (Shelbourne), 1920 v S (1)
Brotherston, N. (Blackburn R), 1980 v S, E, W, Aus (3); 1981 v Se, P; 1982 v S, Is, E, F, S, W, Hon (sub), A (sub); 1983 v A (sub), WG, Alb, T, Alb, S (sub), E (sub), W; 1984 v T; 1985 v Is (sub), T (27)
Brown, J. (Glenavon), 1921 v W; (with Tranmere R), 1924 v E, W (3)
Brown, J. (Wolverhampton W), 1935 v E, W; 1936 v E; (with Coventry C), 1937 v E, W; 1938 v S, W; (with Birmingham C), 1939 v E, S, W (10)
Brown, N. M. (Limavady), 1887 v E (1)
Brown, W. G. (Glenavon), 1926 v W (1)
Browne, F. (Cliftonville), 1887 v E, S, W; 1888 v E, S (5)
Browne, R. J. (Leeds U), 1936 v E, W; 1938 v E, W; 1939 v E, S (6)
Bruce, A. (Belfast C), 1925 v S.Af (1)
Bruce, W. (Glentoran), 1961 v S; 1967 v W (2)
Buckle, H. R. (Cliftonville), 1903 v S; (with Sunderland), 1904 v E; (with Bristol R), 1908 v W (3)
Buckle, J. (Cliftonville), 1882 v E (1)
Burnett, J. (Distillery), 1894 v E, W, S; (with Glentoran), 1895 v E, W (5)
Burnison, J. (Distillery), 1901 v E, W (2)
Burnison, S. (Distillery), 1908 v E; 1910 v E, S; (with Bradford), 1911 v E, S, W; (with Distillery), 1912 v E; 1913 v W (8)
Burns, J. (Glenavon), 1923 v E (1)
Burns, W. (Glentoran), 1925 v S.Af (1)
Butler, M. P. (Blackpool), 1939 v W (1)

Campbell, A. C. (Crusaders), 1963 v W; 1965 v Sw (2)
Campbell, D. A. (Nottingham F), 1986 v Mor (sub), Br; 1987 v E (2), T, Y; (with Charlton Ath), 1988 v Y, T (sub), Gr (sub), Pol (sub) (10)
Campbell, James (Cliftonville), 1897 v E, S, W; 1898 v E, S, W; 1899 v E; 1900 v E, S; 1901 v S, W; 1902 v S; 1903 v E; 1904 v S (14)
Campbell, John (Cliftonville), 1896 v W (1)
Campbell, J. P. (Fulham), 1951 v E, S (2)
Campbell, R. M. (Bradford C), 1982 v S, W (sub) (2)
Campbell, W. G. (Dundee), 1968 v S, E; 1969 v T; 1970 v S, W, USSR (6)
Carey, J. J. (Manchester U), 1947 v E, S, W; 1948 v E; 1949 v E, S, W (7)
Carroll, E. (Glenavon), 1925 v S (1)
Carroll, R. E. (Wigan Ath), 1997 v Th (sub); 1999 v Ei (sub); 2000 v L, Ma; 2001 v Ma, D, Ic, CzR, Bul; (with Manchester U), 2002 v Lie (sub), Sp (sub); 2003 v Fi (sub), I (sub) (13)
Casey, T. (Newcastle U), 1955 v W; 1956 v W; 1957 v E, S, W, I, P (2); 1958 v WG, F; (with Portsmouth), 1959 v E, Sp (12)
Caskey, W. (Derby Co), 1979 v Bul, E, Bul, E, S (sub), D (sub); 1980 v E (sub); (with Tulsa R), 1982 v F (sub) (8)
Cassidy, T. (Newcastle U), 1971 v E (sub); 1972 v USSR (sub); 1974 v Bul (sub), S, E, W; 1975 v N; 1976 v S, E, W; 1977 v WG (sub); 1980 v E, Ei (sub), Is, S, E, W, Aus (3); (with Burnley), 1981 v Se, P; 1982 v Is, Sp (sub) (24)
Caughey, M. (Linfield), 1986 v F (sub), D (sub) (2)
Chambers, R. J. (Distillery), 1921 v W; (with Bury), 1928 v E, S, W; 1929 v E, S, W; 1930 v S, W; (with Nottingham F), 1932 v E, S, W (12)
Chatton, H. A. (Partick T), 1925 v E, S; 1926 v E (3)
Christian, J. (Linfield), 1889 v S (1)
Clarke, C. J. (Bournemouth), 1986 v F, D, Mor, Alg (sub), Sp, Br; (with Southampton), 1987 v E, T, Y; 1988 v Y, T, Gr, Pol, F, Ma; 1989 v Ei, H, Sp (1+1 sub); (with QPR), Ma, Ch; 1990 v H, Ei, N; (with Portsmouth), 1991 v Y (sub), D, A, Pol, Y (sub), Fa; 1992 v Fa, D, S, G; 1993 v Alb, Sp, D (38)
Clarke, R. (Belfast C), 1901 v E, S (2)
Cleary, J. (Glentoran), 1982 v S, W; 1983 v W (sub); 1984 v T (sub); 1985 v Is (5)
Clements, D. (Coventry C), 1965 v W, Ho; 1966 v M; 1967 v S, W; 1968 v S, E; 1969 v T (2), S, W; 1970 v S, E, W, USSR (2); 1971 v Sp, E, S, W, Cy; (with Sheffield W), 1972 v USSR (2), Sp, E, S, W; 1973 v Bul, Cy (2), P, E, S, W; (with Everton), 1974 v Bul, P, S, E, W; 1975 v N, Y, E, S, W; 1976 v Se, Y; (with New York Cosmos), E, W (48)
Clugston, J. (Cliftonville), 1888 v W; 1889 v W, S, E; 1890 v E, S; 1891 v E, W; 1892 v E, S, W; 1893 v E, S, W (14)
Cochrane, D. (Leeds U), 1939 v E, W; 1947 v E, S, W; 1948 v E, S, W; 1949 v S, W; 1950 v S, E (12)
Cockrane, G. (Cliftonville), 1903 v S (1)
Cochrane, G. T. (Coleraine), 1976 v N (sub); (with Burnley), 1978 v S (sub), E (sub), W (sub); 1979 v Ei (sub); (with Middlesbrough), D, Bul, E, Bul, E; 1980 v Is, E (sub), W (sub), Aus (1+2 sub); 1981 v Se (sub), P (sub), S, P, S, Se; 1982 v E (sub), F; (with Gillingham), 1984 v S, Fi (sub) (26)
Cochrane, M. (Distillery), 1898 v S, W, E; 1899 v E; 1900 v E, S, W; (with Leicester Fosse), 1901 v S (8)
Collins, F. (Celtic), 1922 v S (1)
Collins, R. (Cliftonville), 1922 v N (1)
Condy, J. (Distillery), 1882 v W; 1886 v E, S (3)
Connell, T. E. (Coleraine), 1978 v W (sub) (1)
Connor, J. (Glentoran), 1901 v S, E; (with Belfast C), 1905 v E, S, W; 1907 v E, S; 1908 v E, S; 1909 v W; 1911 v S, E, W (13)
Connor, M. J. (Brentford), 1903 v S, W; (with Fulham), 1904 v E (3)
Cook, W. (Celtic), 1933 v E, W, S; (with Everton), 1935 v E; 1936 v S, W; 1937 v E, S, W; 1938 v E, S, W; 1939 v E, S, W (15)
Cooke, S. (Belfast YMCA), 1889 v E; (with Cliftonville), 1890 v E, S (3)
Coote, A. (Norwich C), 1999 v Ca, Ei (sub); 2000 v Fi (sub), L (sub), Ma (sub), H (sub) (6)
Coulter, J. (Belfast C), 1934 v E, S, W; (with Everton), 1935 v E, S, W; 1937 v S, W; (with Grimsby T), 1938 v S, W; (with Chelmsford C), 1939 v S (11)
Cowan, J. (Newcastle U), 1970 v E (sub) (1)
Cowan, T. S. (Queen's Island), 1925 v W (1)
Coyle, F. (Coleraine), 1956 v E, S; 1957 v P; (with Nottingham F), 1958 v Arg (4)
Coyle, L. (Derry C), 1989 v Ch (sub) (1)
Coyle, R. I. (Sheffield W), 1973 v P, Cy (sub), W (sub); 1974 v Bul (sub), P (sub) (5)
Craig, A. B. (Rangers), 1908 v E, S, W; 1909 v S; (with Morton), 1912 v S, W; 1914 v E, S, W (9)
Craig, D. J. (Newcastle U), 1967 v W; 1968 v W; 1969 v T (2), E, S, W; 1970 v E, S, W, USSR; 1971 v Cy (2), Sp, S (sub); 1972 v USSR, S (sub); 1973 v Cy (2), E, S, W; 1974 v Bul, P; 1975 v N (25)
Craigan, S. (Partick T), 2003 v Fi (sub), Arm, Gr (3)
Crawford, A. (Distillery), 1889 v E, W; (with Cliftonville), 1891 v E, S, W; 1893 v E, W (7)
Croft, T. (Queen's Island), 1922 v N; 1924 v E; 1925 v S.Af (3)
Crone, R. (Distillery), 1889 v S; 1890 v E, S, W (4)
Crone, W. (Distillery), 1882 v W; 1884 v E, S, W; 1886 v E, S, W; 1887 v E; 1888 v E, W; 1889 v S; 1890 v W (12)
Crooks, W. J. (Manchester U), 1922 v W (1)
Crossan, E. (Blackburn R), 1950 v S; 1951 v E; 1955 v W (3)
Crossan, J. A. (Sparta-Rotterdam), 1960 v E; (with Sunderland), 1963 v W, P, Sp; 1964 v E, S, W, U, Sp; 1965 v E, S, Sw (2); (with Manchester C), W, Ho (2), Alb; 1966 v S, E, Alb, WG; 1967 v E, S; (with Middlesbrough), 1968 v S (24)
Crothers, C. (Distillery), 1907 v W (1)
Cumming, L. (Huddersfield T), 1929 v W, S; (with Oldham Ath), 1930 v E (3)
Cunningham, W. (Ulster), 1892 v S, E, W; 1893 v E (4)
Cunningham, W. E. (St Mirren), 1951 v W; 1953 v E; 1954 v S; 1955 v S; (with Leicester C), 1956 v E, S, W; 1957 v E, S, W, I, P (2); 1958 v S, W, I, Cz (2), Arg, WG, F; 1959 v E, S, W; 1960 v E, S, W; (with Dunfermline Ath), 1961 v W; 1962 v W, Ho (30)
Curran, S. (Belfast C), 1926 v S, W; 1928 v F, S (4)
Curran, J. J. (Glenavon), 1922 v W, N; (with Pontypridd), 1923 v E, S; (with Glenavon), 1924 v E (5)
Cush, W. W. (Glenavon), 1951 v E, S; 1954 v S, E; 1957 v W, I, P (2); (with Leeds U), 1958 v I (2), W, Cz (2), Arg, WG, F; 1959 v E, S, W, Sp; 1960 v E, S, W; (with Portadown), 1961 v WG, Gr; 1962 v Gr (26)

Dalrymple, J. (Distillery), 1922 v N (1)
Dalton, W. (YMCA), 1888 v S; (with Linfield), 1890 v S, W; 1891 v S, W; 1892 v E, S, W; 1894 v E, S, W (11)
D'Arcy, S. D. (Chelsea), 1952 v W; 1953 v E; (with Brentford), 1953 v S, W, F (5)
Darling, J. (Linfield), 1897 v E, S; 1900 v S; 1902 v E, S, W; 1903 v E, S (2), W; 1905 v E, S, W; 1906 v E, S, W; 1908 v W; 1909 v E; 1910 v E, S, W; 1912 v S (22)
Davey, H. H. (Reading), 1926 v E; 1927 v E, S; 1928 v E; (with Portsmouth), 1928 v W (5)
Davis, T. L. (Oldham Ath), 1937 v E (1)
Davison, A. J. (Bolton W), 1996 v Se; (with Bradford C), 1997 v Th; (with Grimsby T), 1998 v G (3)
Davison, J. R. (Cliftonville), 1882 v E, W; 1883 v E, W; 1884 v E, W, S; 1885 v E (8)
Dennison, R. (Wolverhampton W), 1988 v F, Ma; 1989 v H, Sp Ch (sub); 1990 v Ei, U; 1991 v Y (2), A. Pol, Fa (sub); 1992 v Fa, A, D (sub); 1993 v Sp (sub); 1994 v Co (sub); 1997 v I (sub) (18)
Devine, A. O. (Limavady), 1886 v E, W; 1887 v W; 1888 v W (4)
Devine, J. (Glentoran), 1990 v U (sub) (1)
Dickson, D. (Coleraine), 1970 v S (sub), W; 1973 v Cy, P (4)
Dickson, T. A. (Linfield), 1957 v S (1)
Dickson, W. (Chelsea), 1951 v W, F; 1952 v E, S, W; 1953 v E, S, W, F; (with Arsenal), 1954 v E, W; 1955 v E (12)
Diffin, W. J. (Belfast C), 1931 v W (1)
Dill, A. H. (Knock), 1882 v E, W; (with Down Ath), 1883 v W; (with Cliftonville), 1884 v E, S, W; 1885 v E, S, W (9)
Doherty, I. (Belfast C), 1901 v E (1)
Doherty, J. (Portadown), 1928 v F (1)
Doherty, J. (Cliftonville), 1933 v E, W (2)
Doherty, L. (Linfield), 1985 v Is; 1988 v T (sub) (2)
Doherty, M. (Derry C), 1938 v S (1)
Doherty, P. D. (Blackpool), 1935 v E, W; 1936 v E, S; (with Manchester C), 1937 v E, W; 1938 v E, S; 1939 v E, W; (with Derby Co), 1947 v E; (with Huddersfield T), 1947 v W; 1948 v E, W; 1949 v S; (with Doncaster R), 1951 v S (16)
Doherty, T. E. (Bristol C), 2003 v I, Sp (2)
Donaghey, B. (Belfast C), 1903 v S (1)
Donaghy, M. M. (Luton T), 1980 v S, E, W; 1981 v Se, P, S (sub); 1982 v S, Is, E, F, S, W, Y, Hon, Sp, F; 1983 v A, WG, Alb, T, Alb, S, E, W; 1984 v A, T, WG, S, E, W, Fi; 1985 v R, Fi, E, Sp, T; 1986 v T, R, E, F, D, Mor, Alg, Sp, Br; 1987 v E (2), T, Is, Y; 1988 v Y, T, Gr, Pol, F, Ma; 1989 v Ei, H; (with Manchester U), Sp (2), Ma, Ch; 1990 v Ei, N; 1991 v Y (2), D, A, Pol, Fa; 1992 v Fa, A, D, S, Li, G; (with Chelsea), 1993 v Alb, Sp, D, Alb, Ei, Sp, Li, La; 1994 v La, D, Ei, R, Lie, Co, M (91)
Donnelly, L. (Distillery), 1913 v W (1)
Doran, J. F. (Brighton), 1921 v E; 1922 v E, W (3)
Dougan, A. D. (Portsmouth), 1958 v Cz; (with Blackburn R), 1960 v S; 1961 v E, W, I, Gr; (with Aston Villa), 1963 v S, Pol (2); (with Leicester C), 1966 v S, E, Alb, W, WG, M; 1967 v E, S; (with Wolverhampton W), W; 1968 v S, W; 1969 v Is, T (2), E, S, W; 1970 v USSR (2), S, E; 1971 v Sp, Cy (2), E, S, W; 1972 v USSR (2), S, E, W; 1973 v Bul, Cy (43)
Douglas, J. P. (Belfast C), 1947 v E (1)
Dowd, H. O. (Glenavon), 1974 v W; (with Sheffield W), 1975 v N (sub), Se (3)
Dowie, I. (Luton T), 1990 v N (sub), U; 1991 v Y, D, A (sub), (with West Ham U), Y, Fa; (with Southampton) 1992 v Fa, A, D (sub), S (sub), Li; 1993 v Alb (2), Ei, Sp (sub), Li, La; 1994 v La, D, Ei (sub), R (sub), Lie, Co, M (sub); 1995 v A, Ei; (with C Palace) Ei, La, Ca, Ch, La; 1996 v P; (with West Ham U), A, N, G; 1997 v Uk, Arm, G, Alb, P, Uk, Arm, Th; 1998 v Alb, P; (with QPR), Slo, Sw, Sp; 1999 v T, Fi, Mol, G, Mol, Ca, Ei; 2000 v F, T, G (59)
Duff, M. J. (Cheltenham T), 2002 v Pol (sub); 2003 v Cy (sub) (2)
Duggan, H. A. (Leeds U), 1930 v E; 1931 v E, W; 1933 v E; 1934 v E; 1935 v S, W; 1936 v S (8)
Dunlop, G. (Linfield), 1985 v Is; 1987 v E, Y; 1990 v Ei (4)
Dunne, J. (Sheffield U), 1928 v W; 1931 v W, E; 1932 v E, S; 1933 v E, W (7)

Eames, W. L. E. (Dublin U), 1885 v E, S, W (3)
Eglington, T. J. (Everton), 1947 v S, W; 1948 v E, S, W; 1949 v E (6)
Elder, A. R. (Burnley), 1960 v W; 1961 v S, E, W, WG (2), Gr; 1962 v E, S, Gr; 1963 v E, S, W, Pol (2), Sp; 1964 v W, U; 1965 v E, S, W, Sw (2), Ho (2), Alb; 1966 v E, S, W, M, Alb; 1967 v E, S, W; (with Stoke C), 1968 v E, W; 1969 v E (sub), S, W; 1970 v USSR (40)
Elleman, A. R. (Cliftonville), 1889 v W; 1890 v E (2)
Elliott, S. (Motherwell), 2001 v Ma, D, Ic, N (sub), CzR, Bul (2), CzR; 2002 v D (sub), Ma, Pol (sub), Lie (sub), Sp; (with Hull C), 2003 v Fi (sub), Arm (sub), I (sub) (16)
Elwood, J. H. (Bradford), 1929 v W; 1930 v E (2)
Emerson, W. (Glentoran), 1920 v E, S, W; 1921 v E; 1922 v E, S; (with Burnley), 1922 v W; 1923 v E, S, W; 1924 v E (11)
English, S. (Rangers), 1933 v W, S (2)
Enright, J. (Leeds C), 1912 v S (1)

Falloon, E. (Aberdeen), 1931 v S; 1933 v S (2)
Farquharson, T. G. (Cardiff C), 1923 v S, W; 1924 v E, S, W; 1925 v E, S (7)
Farrell, P. (Distillery), 1901 v S, W (2)
Farrell, P. (Hibernian), 1938 v W (1)
Farrell, P. D. (Everton), 1947 v S, W; 1948 v E, S, W; 1949 v E, W (7)
Feeney, J. M. (Linfield), 1947 v S; (with Swansea T), 1950 v E (2)
Feeney, W. (Glentoran), 1976 v Is (1)
Feeney, W. J. (Bournemouth), 2002 v Lie, Sp; 2003 v Cy (sub) (3)
Ferguson, G. (Linfield), 1999 v Ca (sub); 2001 v N, CzR (sub), Bul (sub), CzR (sub) (5)
Ferguson, W. (Linfield), 1966 v M; 1967 v E (2)
Ferris, J. (Belfast C), 1920 v E, W; (with Chelsea), 1921 v S, E; (with Belfast C), 1928 v F, S (6)
Ferris, R. O. (Birmingham C), 1950 v S; 1951 v F; 1952 v S (3)
Fettis, A. W. (Hull C), 1992 v D, Li; 1993 v D; 1994 v M; 1995 v P, Ei, La, Ca, Ch, La; 1996 v P, Lie, A; (with Nottingham F), v N, G; 1997 v Uk, Arm (2); (with Blackburn R), 1998 v P, Slo, Sw, Sp; 1999 v T, Fi, Mol (25)
Finney, T. (Sunderland), 1975 v N, E (sub), S, W; 1976 v N, Y, S; (with Cambridge U), 1980 v E, Is, S, E, W, Aus (2) (14)
Fitzpatrick, J. C. (Bohemians), 1896 v E, S (2)
Flack, H. (Burnley), 1929 v S (1)
Fleming, J. G. (Nottingham F), 1987 v E (2), Is, Y; 1988 v T, Gr, Pol; 1989 v Ma, Ch; (with Manchester C), 1990 v H, Ei; (with Barnsley), 1991 v Y; 1992 v Li (sub), G; 1993 v Alb, Sp, D, Alb, Sp, Li, La; 1994 v La, D, Ei, R, Lie, Co, M; 1995 v P, A, Ei (31)
Forbes, G. (Limavady), 1888 v W; (with Distillery), 1891 v E, S (3)
Forde, J. T. (Ards), 1959 v Sp; 1961 v E, S, WG (4)
Foreman, T. A. (Cliftonville), 1899 v S (1)
Forsyth, J. (YMCA), 1888 v E, S (2)
Fox, W. T. (Ulster), 1887 v E, S (2)
Frame, T. (Linfield), 1925 v S.Af (1)
Fulton, R. P. (Larne), 1928 v F; (Belfast C), 1930 v W; 1931 v E, S, W; 1932 v W, E; 1933 v E, S; 1934 v E, W, S; 1935 v E, W, S; 1936 v S, W; 1937 v E, S, W; 1938 v W (21)

Gaffikin, G. (Linfield Ath), 1890 v S, W; 1891 v S, W; 1892 v E, S, W; 1893 v E, S, W; 1894 v E, S, W; 1895 v E, W (15)
Galbraith, W. (Distillery), 1890 v W (1)
Gallagher, P. (Celtic), 1920 v E, S; 1922 v S; 1923 v S, W; 1924 v S, W; 1925 v S, W, E; (with Falkirk), 1927 v S (11)
Gallogly, C. (Huddersfield T), 1951 v E, S (2)
Gara, A. (Preston NE), 1902 v E, S, W (3)
Gardiner, A. (Cliftonville), 1930 v S, W; 1931 v S; 1932 v E, S (5)
Garrett, J. (Distillery), 1925 v W (1)
Gaston, R. (Oxford U), 1969 v Is (sub) (1)
Gaukrodger, G. (Linfield), 1895 v W (1)
Gaussen, A. D. (Moyola Park), 1884 v E, S; (with Magherafelt), 1888 v E, W; 1889 v E, W (6)
Geary, J. (Glentoran), 1931 v S; 1932 v S (2)
Gibb, J. T. (Wellington Park) 1884 v S, W; 1885 v S, E, W; 1886 v S; 1887 v S, E, W; (with Cliftonville), 1889 v S (10)
Gibb, T. J. (Cliftonville), 1936 v W (1)
Gibson W. K. (Cliftonville), 1894 v S, W, E; 1895 v S; 1897 v W; 1898 v S, W, E; 1901 v S, W, E; 1902 v S, W; 1903 v S (14)
Gillespie, K. R. (Manchester U), 1995 v P, A, Ei; (with Newcastle U), Ei, La, Ca, Ch (sub), La (sub); 1996 v P, A, N, G; 1997 v Uk, Arm, Bel, P, Uk; 1998 v G, Alb, Slo, Sw; 1999 v T, Fi, Mol; (with Blackburn R), G, Mol; 2000 v F (sub), T (sub), G (sub), L, Ma, H; 2001 v Y (sub), CzR, Bul (2); 2002 v D, Ic, Pol, Lie, Sp; 2003 v Cy, Sp, Uk, Fi, Arm, Gr (47)
Gillespie, S. (Hertford), 1886 v E, S, W; 1887 v E, S, W (6)
Gillespie, W. (Sheffield U), 1913 v E, S; 1914 v E, W; 1920 v S, W; 1921 v E; 1922 v E, S, W; 1923 v E, S, W; 1924 v E, S, W; 1925 v E, S; 1926 v S, W; 1927 v E, W; 1928 v E; 1929 v E; 1931 v E (25)
Gillespie, W. (West Down), 1889 v W (1)
Goodall, A. L. (Derby Co), 1899 v S, W; 1900 v E, W; 1901 v E; 1902 v S; 1903 v E, W; (with Glossop), 1904 v E, W (10)

Goodbody, M. F. (Dublin University), 1889 v E; 1891 v W (2)
Gordon, H. (Linfield), 1895 v E; 1896 v E, S (3)
Gordon R. W. (Linfield), 1891 v S; 1892 v W, E, S; 1893 v E, S, W (7)
Gordon, T. (Linfield), 1894 v W; 1895 v E (2)
Gorman, W. C. (Brentford), 1947 v E, S, W; 1948 v W (4)
Gough, J. (Queen's Island), 1925 v S.Af (1)
Gowdy, J. (Glentoran), 1920 v E; (with Queen's Island), 1924 v W; (with Falkirk), 1926 v E, S; 1927 v E, S (6)
Gowdy, W. A. (Hull C), 1932 v S; (with Sheffield W), 1933 v S; (with Linfield), 1935 v E, S, W; (with Hibernian), 1936 v W (6)
Graham, W. G. L. (Doncaster R), 1951 v W, F; 1952 v E, S, W; 1953 v S, F; 1954 v E, W; 1955 v S, W; 1956 v E, S; 1959 v E (14)
Gray, P. (Luton T), 1993 v D (sub), Alb, Ei, Sp; (with Sunderland), 1994 v La, D, Ei, R, Lie (sub); 1995 v P, A, Ei, Ca, Ch (sub); 1996 v P (sub), Lie, A; (with Nancy), 1997 v Uk, Arm, G (sub); (with Luton T), 1999 v Mol (sub); (with Burnley), 2001 v Ma (sub), D (sub), Ic (sub); (with Oxford U), N (sub), CzR (sub) (26)
Greer, W. (QPR), 1909 v E, S, W (3)
Gregg, H. (Doncaster R), 1954 v W; 1957 v E, S, W, I, P (2); 1958 v E, I; (with Manchester U), 1958 v Cz, Arg, WG, F, W; 1959 v E, W; 1960 v S, E, W; 1961 v E, S; 1962 v S, Gr; 1964 v S, E (25)
Griffin, D. J. (St Johnstone), 1996 v G; 1997 v Uk, I, Bel (sub), Th; 1998 v G (sub), Alb; 1999 v Mol, Ei (sub); 2000 v L, Ma, H; (with Dundee U), 2001 v Y (sub), N (sub), CzR, Bul (2), CzR; 2002 v D, Ic, Ma, Pol; 2003 v Cy, I, Sp (25)

Hall, G. (Distillery), 1897 v E (1)
Halligan, W. (Derby Co), 1911 v W; (with Wolverhampton W), 1912 v E (2)
Hamill, M. (Manchester U), 1912 v E; 1914 v E, S; (with Belfast C), 1920 v E, S, W; (with Manchester C), 1921 v S (7)
Hamill, R. (Glentoran), 1999 v Ca (sub) (1)
Hamilton, B. (Linfield), 1969 v T; 1971 v Cy (2), E, S, W; (with Ipswich T), 1972 v USSR (1+1 sub), Sp; 1973 v Bul, Cy (2), P, E, S, W; 1974 v Bul, S, E, W; 1975 v N, Se, Y, E; 1976 v Se, N, Y; (with Everton), Is, S, E, W; 1977 v Ho, Bel, WG, E, S, W, Ic; (with Millwall), 1978 v S, E, W; 1979 v Ei (sub); (with Swindon T), Bul (2), E, S, W, D; 1980 v Aus (2 sub) (50)
Hamilton, G. (Portadown), 2003 v I (sub) (1)
Hamilton, J. (Knock), 1882 v E, W (2)
Hamilton, R. (Rangers), 1928 v S; 1929 v E; 1930 v S, E; 1932 v S (5)
Hamilton, W. D. (Dublin Association), 1885 v W (1)
Hamilton, W. J. (Distillery), 1908 v W (1)
Hamilton, W. J. (Dublin Association), 1885 v W (1)
Hamilton, W. R. (QPR), 1978 v S (sub); (with Burnley), 1980 v S, E, W, Aus (2); 1981 v Se, P, S, P, S, Se; 1982 v S, Is, E, W, Y, Hon, Sp, A, F; 1983 v A, WG, Alb (2), S, E, W; 1984 v A, T, WG, S, E, W, Fi; (with Oxford U), 1985 v R, Sp; 1986 v Mor (sub), Alg, Sp (sub), Br (sub) (41)
Hampton, H. (Bradford C), 1911 v E, S, W; 1912 v E, W; 1913 v E, S, W; 1914 v E (9)
Hanna, J. (Nottingham F), 1912 v S, W (2)
Hanna, J. D. (Royal Artillery, Portsmouth), 1899 v W (1)
Hannon, D. J. (Bohemians), 1908 v E, S; 1911 v E, S; 1912 v W; 1913 v E (6)
Harkin, J. T. (Southport), 1968 v W; 1969 v T; (with Shrewsbury T), W (sub); 1970 v USSR; 1971 v Sp (5)
Harland, A. I. (Linfield), 1922 v N; 1923 v E (2)
Harris, J. (Cliftonville), 1921 v W; (with Glenavon), 1925 v S.Af (2)
Harris, V. (Shelbourne), 1906 v E; 1907 v E, W; 1908 v E, W, S; (with Everton), 1909 v E, W, S; 1910 v E, S, W; 1911 v E, S, W; 1912 v E; 1913 v E, S; 1914 v S, W (20)
Harvey, M. (Sunderland), 1961 v I; 1962 v Ho; 1963 v W, Sp; 1964 v S, E, W, U, Sp; 1965 v E, S, W, Sw (2), Ho (2), Alb; 1966 v S, E, W, M, Alb, WG; 1967 v E, S; 1968 v E, W; 1969 v Is, T (2), E; 1970 v USSR; 1971 v Cy, W (sub) (34)
Hastings, J. (Knock), 1882 v E, W; (with Ulster), 1883 v W; 1884 v E, S; 1886 v E, S (7)
Hatton, S. (Linfield), 1963 v S, Pol (2)
Hayes, W. E. (Huddersfield T), 1938 v E, S; 1939 v E, S (4)
Healy, D. J. (Manchester U), 2000 v L, Ma, H; 2001 v Y, Ma, D, Ic; (with Preston NE), N, CzR, Bul (2), CzR; 2002 v D, Ic, Ma, Pol, Lie, Sp; 2003 v Cy, Sp (sub), Uk, Fi, Arm, Gr, I, Sp (26)
Healy, P. J. (Coleraine), 1982 v S, W, Hon (sub); (with Glentoran), 1983 v A (sub) (4)
Hegan, D. (WBA), 1970 v USSR; (with Wolverhampton W), 1972 v USSR, E, S, W; 1973 v Bul, Cy (7)
Henderson, J. (Ulster), 1885 v E, S, W (3)
Hewison, G. (Moyola Park), 1885 v E, S (2)
Hill, C. F. (Sheffield U), 1990 v N, U; 1991 v Pol, Y; 1992 v A, D; (with Leicester C), 1995 v Ei, La; 1996 v P, Lie, A, N, Se, G; 1997 v Uk, Arm, G, Alb, P, Uk, Arm, Th; (with Trelleborg), 1998 v G, Alb, P; (with Northampton T), Slo; 1999 v T (27)
Hill, M. J. (Norwich C), 1959 v W; 1960 v W; 1961 v WG; 1962 v S; (with Everton), 1964 v S, E, Sp (7)
Hinton, E. (Fulham), 1947 v S, W; 1948 v S, E, W; (with Millwall), 1951 v W, F (7)
Holmes, S. P. (Wrexham), 2002 v Lie (sub) (1)
Hopkins, J. (Brighton), 1926 v E (1)
Horlock, K. (Swindon T), 1995 v La, Ca; 1997 v G, Alb, I; (with Manchester C), v Bel, Uk, Arm, Th; 1998 v G, Alb, P; 1999 v T, Fi, G, Mol, Ca; 2000 v F, T, G, Ma (sub); 2001 v Y, Ma, D, Ic; 2002 v D, Ic, Ma, Sp; 2003 v Cy, Sp, Uk (32)
Houston, J. (Linfield), 1912 v S, W; 1913 v W; (with Everton), 1913 v E, S; 1914 v S (6)
Houston, W. (Linfield), 1933 v W (1)
Houston, W. J. (Moyola Park), 1885 v E, S (2)
Hughes, A. W. (Newcastle U), 1998 v Slo, Sw, Sp (sub); 1999 v T, Fi, Mol (sub), Ca, Ei; 2000 v F, T, L, H; 2001 v Y, Ma, D, Ic, N, CzR, Bul, CzR; 2002 v D, Ic, Pol, Sp; 2003 v Sp, Uk, Fi, Arm, Gr, I, Sp (31)
Hughes, M. E. (Manchester C), 1992 v D, S, Li, G; (with Strasbourg), 1993 v Alb, Sp, D, Ei, Sp, Li, La; 1994 v La, D, Ei, R, Lie, Co, M; 1995 v P, A, Ei (2) La, Ca, Ch, La; 1996 v P, Lie, A, N, G; (with West Ham U), 1997 v Uk, Arm, G, Alb, I, Uk; 1998 v G; (with Wimbledon), P, Slo, Sw, Sp; 1999 v T, Fi, Mol, G, Mol; 2000 v F, T, G, Fi, L (sub), Ma, H; 2001 v CzR, Bul (2), CzR; 2002 v D, Ic, Ma, Pol, Lie (sub); 2003 v Sp (sub), Uk (65)
Hughes, P. A. (Bury), 1987 v E, T, Is (3)
Hughes, W. (Bolton W), 1951 v W (1)
Humphries, W. M. (Ards), 1962 v W; (with Coventry C), 1962 v Ho; 1963 v E, S, W, Pol, Sp; 1964 v S, E, Sp; 1965 v S, Ho; (with Swansea T), 1965 v W, Alb (14)
Hunter, A. (Distillery), 1905 v W; 1906 v W, E, S; (with Belfast C), 1908 v W; 1909 v W, E, S (8)
Hunter, A. (Blackburn R), 1970 v USSR; 1971 v Cy (2), E, S, W; (with Ipswich T), 1972 v USSR (2), Sp, E, S, W; 1973 v Bul, Cy (2), P, E, S, W; 1974 v Bul, S, E, W; 1975 v N, Se, Y, E, S, W; 1976 v Se, N, Y, Is, S, E, W; 1977 v Ho, Bel, WG, E, S, W, Ic; 1978 v Ic, Ho, Bel; 1979 v Ei, D, S, W, D; 1980 v E, Ei (53)
Hunter, B. V. (Wrexham), 1995 v La; 1996 v P, Lie, A, Se, G; (with Reading), 1997 v Arm, G, Alb, I, Bel; 1999 v Ca, Ei; 2000 v F, T (15)
Hunter, R. J. (Cliftonville), 1884 v E, S, W (3)
Hunter, V. (Coleraine), 1962 v E; 1964 v Sp (2)

Irvine, R. J. (Linfield), 1962 v Ho; 1963 v E, S, W, Pol (2), Sp; (with Stoke C), 1965 v W (8)
Irvine, R. W. (Everton), 1922 v S; 1923 v E, W; 1924 v E, S; 1925 v E; 1926 v E; 1927 v E, W; 1928 v E, S; (with Portsmouth), 1929 v E; 1930 v S; (with Connah's Quay), 1931 v E; (with Derry C), 1932 v W (15)
Irvine, W. J. (Burnley), 1963 v W, Sp; 1965 v S, W, Sw, Ho (2), Alb; 1966 v S, E, W, M, Alb; 1967 v E, S; 1968 v E, W; (with Preston NE), 1969 v Is, T, E; (with Brighton & HA), 1972 v E, S, W (23)
Irving, S. J. (Dundee), 1923 v S, W; 1924 v S, E, W; 1925 v S, E, W; 1926 v S, W; (with Cardiff C), 1927 v S, E, W; 1928 v S, E, W; (with Chelsea), 1929 v E; 1931 v W (18)

Jackson, T. A. (Everton), 1969 v Is, E, S, W; 1970 v USSR (1+1 sub); (with Nottingham F), 1971 v Sp; 1972 v E, S, W; 1973 v Cy, E, S, W; 1974 v Bul, P, S (sub), E (sub), W (sub); 1975 v N (sub), Se, Y, E, S, W; (with Manchester U); 1976 v Se, N, Y; 1977 v Ho, Bel, WG, E, S, W, Ic (35)
Jamison, J. (Glentoran), 1976 v N (1)
Jenkins, I. (Chester C), 1997 v Arm, Th; 1998 v Slo; (with Dundee U), Sw, Sp; 2000 v Fi (6)
Jennings, P. A. (Watford), 1964 v W, U; (with Tottenham H), 1965 v E, S, Sw (2), Ho, Alb; 1966 v S, E, W, Alb, WG; 1967 v E, S; 1968 v S, E, W; 1969 v Is, T (2), E, S, W; 1970 v S, E, USSR (2); 1971 v Cy (2), E, S, W; 1972 v USSR, Sp, S, E, W; 1973 v Bul, Cy, P, E, S, W; 1974 v P, S, E, W; 1975 v N, Se, Y, E, S, W; 1976 v Se, N, Y, Is, S, E, W; 1977 v Ho, Bel, WG, E, S, W, Ic; (with Arsenal), 1978 v Ic, Ho, Bel; 1979 v Ei, D, Bul, E, Bul, E, S, W, D; 1980 v E, Ei, Is; 1981 v S, P, S, Se; 1982 v S, Is, E, W, Y, Hon, Sp, F; 1983 v Alb, S, E, W; 1984 v A, T, WG, S, W, Fi; 1985 v R, Fi, E, Sp, T; (with

Tottenham H), 1986 v T, R, E, F, D; (with Everton), Mor; (with Tottenham H), Alg, Sp, Br (119)
Johnson, D. M. (Blackburn R), 1999 v Ei (sub); 2000 v Fi (sub), L, Ma (sub), H (sub); 2001 v Y, Ma, Ic, N (sub), Bul (sub+1), CzR; 2002 v Ma, Pol; (with Birmingham C), Lie, Sp; 2003 v Cy, Sp, Uk, Fi, Arm, Gr, I, Sp (24)
Johnston, H. (Portadown), 1927 v W (1)
Johnston, R. S. (Distillery), 1882 v W; 1884 v E; 1886 v E, S (4)
Johnston, R. S. (Distillery), 1905 v W (1)
Johnston, S. (Linfield), 1890 v W; 1893 v S, W; 1894 v E (4)
Johnston, W. (Oldpark), 1885 v S, W (2)
Johnston, W. C. (Glenavon), 1962 v W; (with Oldham Ath), 1966 v M (sub) (2)
Jones, J. (Linfield), 1930 v S, W; 1931 v S, W, E; 1932 v S, E; 1933 v S, E, W; 1934 v S, E, W; 1935 v S, E, W; 1936 v E, S; (with Hibernian), 1936 v W; 1937 v E, W, S; (with Glenavon), 1938 v E (23)
Jones, J. (Glenavon), 1956 v W; 1957 v E, W (3)
Jones, S. (Distillery), 1934 v E; (with Blackpool), 1934 v W (2)
Jones, S. G. (Crewe Alex), 2003 v I (sub), Sp (2)
Jordan, T. (Linfield), 1895 v E, W (2)

Kavanagh, P. J. (Celtic), 1930 v E (1)
Keane, T. R. (Swansea T), 1949 v S (1)
Kearns, A. (Distillery), 1900 v E, S, W; 1902 v E, S, W (6)
Kee, P. V. (Oxford U), 1990 v N; 1991 v Y (2), D, A, Pol, Fa; (with Ards), 1995 v A, Ei (9)
Keith, R. M. (Newcastle U), 1958 v E, W, Cz (2), Arg, I, WG, F; 1959 v E, S, W, Sp; 1960 v S, E; 1961 v S, E, W, I, WG (2), Gr; 1962 v W, Ho (23)
Kelly, H. R. (Fulham), 1950 v E, W; (with Southampton), 1951 v E, S (4)
Kelly, J. (Glentoran), 1896 v E (1)
Kelly, J. (Derry C), 1932 v E, W; 1933 v E, W, S; 1934 v W; 1936 v E, S, W; 1937 v S, E (11)
Kelly, P. J. (Manchester C), 1921 v E (1)
Kelly, P. M. (Barnsley), 1950 v S (1)
Kennedy, A. L. (Arsenal), 1923 v W; 1925 v E (2)
Kennedy, P. H. (Watford), 1999 v Mol, G (sub); 2000 v F, T, G, Fi; 2001 v N, Bul (sub), CzR (sub); (with Wigan Ath), 2002 v D, Ic, Ma, Pol; 2003 v Cy, Fi, I, Sp (17)
Kernaghan, N. (Belfast C), 1936 v W; 1937 v S; 1938 v E (3)
Kirk, A. (Hearts), 2000 v H; 2001 v N (sub); 2003 v Uk (sub), Fi (sub), Gr (sub) (5)
Kirkwood, H. (Cliftonville), 1904 v W (1)
Kirwan, J. (Tottenham H), 1900 v W; 1902 v E, W; 1903 v E, S, W; 1904 v E, S, W; 1905 v E, S, W; (with Chelsea), 1906 v E, S, W; 1907 v W; (with Clyde), 1909 v S (17)

Lacey, W. (Everton), 1909 v E, S, W; 1910 v E, S, W; 1911 v E, S, W; 1912 v E; (with Liverpool), 1913 v W; 1914 v E, S, W; 1920 v E, S, W; 1921 v E, S, W; 1922 v E, S; (with New Brighton), 1925 v E (23)
Lawther, R. (Glentoran), 1888 v E, S (2)
Lawther, W. I. (Sunderland), 1960 v W; 1961 v I; (with Blackburn R), 1962 v S, Ho (4)
Leatham, J. (Belfast C), 1939 v W (1)
Ledwidge, J. J. (Shelbourne), 1906 v S, W (2)
Lemon, J. (Glentoran), 1886 v W; (with Belfast YMCA), 1888 v S; 1889 v W (3)
Lennon, N. F. (Crewe Alex), 1994 v M (sub); 1995 v Ch; 1996 v P, Lie, A; (with Leicester C), v N; 1997 v Uk, Arm, G, Alb, Bel, P, Uk, Arm, Th; 1998 v G, Alb, P, Slo, Sw, Sp; 1999 v T, Fi, Mol, G, Mol, Ei; 2000 v F, T, G, Fi, Ma, H; 2001 v D, Ic; (with Celtic), N, CzR, Bul (2); 2002 v Pol (sub) (40)
Leslie, W. (YMCA), 1887 v E (1)
Lewis, J. (Glentoran), 1899 v S, E, W; (with Distillery), 1900 v S (4)
Lockhart, H. (Russell School), 1884 v W (1)
Lockhart, N. H. (Linfield), 1947 v E; (with Coventry C), 1950 v W; 1951 v W; 1952 v W; (with Aston Villa), 1954 v S, E; 1955 v W; 1956 v W (8)
Lomas, S. M. (Manchester C), 1994 v R, Lie, Co (sub), M; 1995 v P, A; 1996 v P, Lie, A, N, Se, G; 1997 v Uk, Arm, G, Alb, I, Bel; (with West Ham U), P, Uk, Arm, Th; 1998 v Alb, P, Slo, Sw; 1999 v Mol, G, Mol, Ca; 2000 v F, T, G, L, Ma; 2001 v Ma, D, Ic; 2002 v Pol, Lie; 2003 v Sp, Uk, Fi, Arm, Gr (45)
Loyal, J. (Clarence), 1891 v S (1)
Lutton, R. J. (Wolverhampton W), 1970 v S, E; (with West Ham U), 1973 v Cy (sub), S (sub), W (sub); 1974 v P (6)
Lynas, R. (Cliftonville), 1925 v S.Af (1)
Lyner, D. R. (Glentoran), 1920 v E, W; 1922 v S, W; (with Manchester U), 1923 v E; (with Kilmarnock), 1923 v W (6)
Lytle, J. (Glentoran), 1898 W (1)

McAdams, W. J. (Manchester C), 1954 v W; 1955 v S; 1957 v E; 1958 v S, I; (with Bolton W), 1961 v E, S, W, I, WG (2), Gr; 1962 v E, Gr; (with Leeds U), Ho (15)
McAlery, J. M. (Cliftonville), 1882 v E, W (2)
McAlinden, J. (Belfast C), 1938 v S; 1939 v S; (with Portsmouth), 1947 v E; (with Southend U), 1949 v E (4)
McAllen, J. (Linfield), 1898 v E; 1899 v E, S, W; 1900 v E, S, W; 1901 v W; 1902 v S (9)
McAlpine, S. (Cliftonville), 1901 v S (1)
McArthur, A. (Distillery), 1886 v W (1)
McAuley, J. L. (Huddersfield T), 1911 v E, W; 1912 v E, S; 1913 v E, S (6)
McAuley, P. (Belfast C), 1900 v S (1)
McBride, S. D. (Glenavon), 1991 v D (sub), Pol (sub); 1992 v Fa (sub), D (4)
McCabe, J. J. (Leeds U), 1949 v S, W; 1950 v E; 1951 v W; 1953 v W; 1954 v S (6)
McCabe, W. (Ulster), 1891 v E (1)
McCambridge, J. (Ballymena), 1930 v S, W; (with Cardiff C), 1931 v W; 1932 v E (4)
McCandless, J. (Bradford), 1912 v W; 1913 v W; 1920 v W, S; 1921 v E (5)
McCandless, W. (Linfield), 1920 v E, W; 1921 v E; (with Rangers), 1921 v W; 1922 v S; 1924 v W, S; 1925 v S; 1929 v W (9)
McCann, G. S. (West Ham U), 2002 v Ma (sub), Pol (sub), Lie; 2003 v Sp (sub), Uk (sub); (with Cheltenham T), Arm, Gr (7)
McCann, P. (Belfast C), 1910 v E, S, W; 1911 v E; (with Glentoran), 1911 v S; 1912 v E; 1913 v W (7)
McCarthy, J. D. (Port Vale), 1996 v Se; 1997 v I, Arm, Th; (with Birmingham C), 1998 v P (sub), Slo (sub), Sp; 1999 v Fi (sub), Mol (sub), G (sub), Ca, Ei; 2000 v F, T, G, Fi; 2001 v N, Bul (sub) (18)
McCartney, A. (Ulster), 1903 v S, W; (with Linfield), 1904 v S, W; (with Everton), 1905 v E, S; (with Belfast C), 1907 v E, S, W; 1908 v E, S, W; (with Glentoran), 1909 v E, S, W (15)
McCartney, G. (Sunderland), 2002 v Ic, Ma, Pol (sub), Lie, Sp; 2003 v Cy, Sp, Uk, Fi, Gr, I, Sp (12)
McCashin, J. W. (Cliftonville), 1896 v W; 1898 v S, W; 1899 v S; 1903 v S (5)
McCavana, W. T. (Coleraine), 1955 v S; 1956 v E, S (3)
McCaw, D. (Malone), 1882 v E (1)
McCaw, J. H. (Linfield), 1927 v W; 1928 v F; 1930 v S; 1931 v E, S, W (6)
McClatchey, J. (Distillery), 1886 v E, S, W (3)
McClatchey, T. (Distillery), 1895 v S (1)
McCleary, J. W. (Cliftonville), 1955 v W (1)
McCleery, W. (Cliftonville), 1922 v N; (Linfield), 1930 v E, W; 1931 v E, S, W; 1932 v S, W; 1933 v E, W (10)
McClelland, J. (Mansfield T), 1980 v S (sub), Aus (3); 1981 v Se, S; (with Rangers), S, Se (sub); 1982 v S, W, Y, Hon, Sp, A, F; 1983 v A, WG, Alb, T, Alb, S, E, W; 1984 v A, T, WG, S, E, W, Fi; 1985 v R, Is; (with Watford), Fi, E, Sp, T; 1986 v T, F (sub); 1987 v E (2), T, Is, Y; 1988 v T, Gr, F, Ma; 1989 v Ei, H, Sp (2), Ma; (with Leeds U), 1990 v N (53)
McClelland, J. T. (Arsenal), 1961 v W, I, WG (2), Gr; (with Fulham), 1966 v M (6)
McCluggage, A. (Cliftonville), 1922 v N; (Bradford), 1924 v E; (with Burnley), 1927 v S, W; 1928 v S, E, W; 1929 v S, E, W; 1930 v W; 1931 v E, W (13)
McClure, G. (Cliftonville), 1907 v S, W; 1908 v E; (with Distillery), 1909 v E (4)
McConnell, E. (Cliftonville), 1904 v S, W; (with Glentoran), 1905 v S; (with Sunderland), 1906 v E; 1907 v E; 1908 v S, W; (with Sheffield W), 1909 v S, W; 1910 v S, W, E (12)
McConnell, P. (Doncaster R), 1928 v W; (with Southport), 1932 v E (2)
McConnell, W. G. (Bohemians), 1912 v W; 1913 v E, S; 1914 v E, S, W (6)
McConnell, W. H. (Reading), 1925 v W; 1926 v E, W; 1927 v E, S, W; 1928 v E, W (8)
McCourt, F. J. (Manchester C), 1952 v E, W; 1953 v E, S, W, F (6)
McCourt, P. J. (Rochdale), 2002 v Sp (sub) (1)
McCoy, R. K. (Coleraine), 1987 v Y (sub) (1)
McCoy, S. (Distillery), 1896 v W (1)
McCracken, E. (Barking), 1928 v F (1)
McCracken, R. (C Palace), 1921 v E; 1922 v E, S, W (4)
McCracken, R. (Linfield), 1922 v N (1)
McCracken, W. R. (Distillery), 1902 v E, W; 1903 v S, E; 1904 v E, S, W; (with Newcastle U), 1905 v E, S, W; 1907 v E; 1920 v E; 1922 v E, S, W; (with Hull C), 1923 v S (16)

McCreery, D. (Manchester U), 1976 v S (sub), E, W; 1977 v Ho, Bel, WG, E, S, W, Ic; 1978 v Ic, Ho, Bel, S, E, W; 1979 v Ei, D, Bul, E, Bul, W, D; (with QPR), 1980 v E, Ei, S (sub), E (sub), W (sub), Aus (1+1 sub); 1981 v Se (sub), P (sub); (with Tulsa R), S, P, Se; 1982 v S, Is, E (sub), F, Y, Hon, Sp, A, F; (with Newcastle U), 1983 v A; 1984 v T (sub); 1985 v R, Sp (sub); 1986 v T (sub), R, E, F, D, Alg, Sp, Br; 1987 v T, E, Y; 1988 v Y; 1989 v Sp, Ma, Ch; (with Hearts), 1990 v H, Ei, N, U (sub) (67)
McCrory, S. (Southend U), 1958 v E (1)
McCullough, K. (Belfast C), 1935 v W; 1936 v E; (with Manchester C), 1936 v S; 1937 v E, S (5)
McCullough, W. J. (Arsenal), 1961 v I; 1963 v Sp; 1964 v S, E, W, U, Sp; 1965 v E, Sw; (with Millwall), 1967 v E (10)
McCurdy, C. (Linfield), 1980 v Aus (sub) (1)
McDonald, A. (QPR), 1986 v R, E, F, D, Mor, Alg, Sp, Br; 1987 v E (2), T, Is, Y; 1988 v Y, T, Pol, F, Ma; 1989 v Ei, H, Sp, Ch; 1990 v H, Ei, U; 1991 v Y, D, A, Fa; 1992 v Fa, S, Li, G; 1993 v Alb, Sp, D, Alb, Ei, Sp, Li, La; 1994 v D, Ei; 1995 v P, A, Ei, La, Ca, Ch, La; 1996 v A (sub), N (52)
McDonald, R. (Rangers), 1930 v S; 1932 v E (2)
McDonnell, J. (Bohemians), 1911 v E, S; 1912 v W; 1913 v W (4)
McElhinney, G. M. A. (Bolton W), 1984 v WG, S, E, W, Fi; 1985 v R (6)
McEvilly, L. R. (Rochdale), 2002 v Sp (sub) (1)
McFaul, W. S. (Linfield), 1967 v E (sub); (with Newcastle U), 1970 v W; 1971 v Sp; 1972 v USSR; 1973 v Cy; 1974 v Bul (6)
McGarry, J. K. (Cliftonville), 1951 v W, F, S (3)
McGaughey, M. (Linfield), 1985 v Is (sub) (1)
McGibbon, P. C. G. (Manchester U), 1995 v Ca (sub), Ch, La; 1996 v Lie (sub); 1997 v Th; (with Wigan Ath), 1998 v Alb; 2000 v L (sub) (7)
McGrath, R. C. (Tottenham H), 1974 v S, E, W; 1975 v N; 1976 v Is (sub); 1977; (with Manchester U), Ho, Bel, WG, E, S, W, Ic; 1978 v Ic, Ho, Bel, S, E, W; 1979 v Bul (sub), E (2 sub) (21)
McGregor, S. (Glentoran), 1921 v S (1)
McGrillen, J. (Clyde), 1924 v S; (with Belfast C), 1927 v S (2)
McGuire, E. (Distillery), 1907 v S (1)
McGuire, J. (Linfield), 1928 v F (1)
McIlroy, H. (Cliftonville), 1906 v E (1)
McIlroy, J. (Burnley), 1952 v E, S, W; 1953 v E, S, W; 1954 v E, S, W; 1955 v E, S, W; 1956 v E, S, W; 1957 v E, S, W, I, P (2); 1958 v E, S, W, I (2), Cz (2), Arg, WG, F; 1959 v E, S, W, Sp; 1960 v E, S, W; 1961 v E, W, WG (2), Gr; 1962 v E, S, Gr, Ho; 1963 v E, S, Pol (2); (with Stoke C), 1963 v W; 1966 v S, E, Alb (55)
McIlroy, S. B. (Manchester U), 1972 v Sp, S (sub); 1974 v S, E, W; 1975 v N, Se, Y, E, S, W; 1976 v Se, N, Y, S, E, W; 1977 v Ho, Bel, E, S, W, Ic; 1978 v Ic, Ho, Bel, S, E, W; 1979 v Ei, D, Bul, E, Bul, E, S, W, D; 1980 v E, Ei, Is, S, E, W; 1981 v Se, P, S, P, S, Se; 1982 v S, Is; (with Stoke C), E, F, S, W, Y, Hon, Sp, A, F; 1983 v A, WG, Alb, T, Alb, S, E, W; 1984 v A, T, S, E, W, Fi; 1985 v Fi, E, T; (with Manchester C), 1986 v T, R, E, F, D, Mor, Alg, Sp, Br; 1987 v E (sub) (88)
McIlvenny, P. (Distillery), 1924 v W (1)
McIlvenny, R. (Distillery), 1890 v E; (with Ulster), 1891 v E (2)
McKeag, W. (Glentoran), 1968 v S, W (2)
McKeague, T. (Glentoran), 1925 v S.Af (1)
McKee, F. W. (Cliftonville), 1906 v S, W; (with Belfast C), 1914 v E, S, W (5)
McKelvey, H. (Glentoran), 1901 v W; 1903 v S (2)
McKenna, J. (Huddersfield), 1950 v E, S, W; 1951 v E, S, F; 1952 v E (7)
McKenzie, H. (Distillery), 1922 v N; 1923 v S (2)
McKenzie, R. (Airdrie), 1967 v W (1)
McKeown, N. (Linfield), 1892 v E, S, W; 1893 v S, W; 1894 v S, W (7)
McKie, H. (Cliftonville), 1895 v E, S, W (3)
McKinney, D. (Hull C), 1921 v S; (with Bradford C), 1924 v S (2)
McKinney, V. J. (Falkirk), 1966 v WG (1)
McKnight, A. D. (Celtic), 1988 v Y, T, Gr, Pol, F, Ma; (with West Ham U), 1989 v Ei, H, Sp (2) (10)
McKnight, J. (Preston NE), 1912 v S; (with Glentoran), 1913 v S (2)
McLaughlin, J. C. (Shrewsbury T), 1962 v E, S, W, Gr; 1963 v W; (with Swansea T), 1964 v W, U; 1965 v E, W, Sw (2); 1966 v W (12)
McLean, T. (Limavady), 1885 v S (1)
McMahon, G. J. (Tottenham H), 1995 v Ca (sub), Ch, La; 1996 v Lie, N (sub), Se, G; (with Stoke C), 1997 v Arm (sub), Alb (sub), Bel, P (sub), Uk (sub), Arm (sub), Th (sub); 1998 v G (sub), Alb (sub), P (sub) (17)
McMahon, J. (Bohemians), 1934 v S (1)
McMaster, G. (Glentoran), 1897 v E, S, W (3)
McMichael, A. (Newcastle U), 1950 v E, S; 1951 v E, S, F; 1952 v E, S, W; 1953 v E, S, W, F; 1954 v E, S, W; 1955 v E, W; 1956 v W; 1957 v E, S, W, I, P (2); 1958 v E, S, W, I (2), Cz (2), Arg, WG, F; 1959 v S, W, Sp; 1960 v E, S, W (40)
McMillan, G. (Distillery), 1903 v E; 1905 v W (2)
McMillan, S. T. (Manchester U), 1963 v E, S (2)
McMillen, W. S. (Manchester U), 1934 v E; 1935 v S; 1937 v S; (with Chesterfield), 1938 v S, W; 1939 v E, S (7)
McMordie, A. S. (Middlesbrough), 1969 v Is, T (2), E, S, W; 1970 v E, S, W, USSR; 1971 v Cy (2), E, S, W; 1972 v USSR, Sp, E, S, W; 1973 v Bul (21)
McMorran, E. J. (Belfast C), 1947 v E; (with Barnsley), 1951 v E, S, W; 1952 v E, S, W; 1953 v E, S, F; (with Doncaster R), 1953 v W; 1954 v E; 1956 v W; 1957 v I, P (15)
McMullan, D. (Liverpool), 1926 v E, W; 1927 v S (3)
McNally, B. A. (Shrewsbury T), 1986 v Mor; 1987 v T (sub); 1988 v Y, Gr, Ma (sub) (5)
McNinch, J. (Ballymena), 1931 v S; 1932 v S, W (3)
McParland, P. J. (Aston Villa), 1954 v W; 1955 v E, S; 1956 v E, S; 1957 v E, S, W, P; 1958 v E, S, W, I (2), Cz (2), Arg, WG, F; 1959 v E, S, W, Sp; 1960 v E, S, W; 1961 v E, S, W, I, WG (2), Gr; (with Wolverhampton W), 1962 v Ho (34)
McShane, J. (Cliftonville), 1899 v S; 1900 v E, S, W (4)
McVeigh, P. (Tottenham H), 1999 v Ca (sub); (with Norwich C), 2002 v Ic (sub), Pol (sub); 2003 v Sp, Uk, Fi, Arm, Gr (sub), I, Sp (sub) (10)
McVicker, J. (Linfield), 1888 v E; (with Glentoran), 1889 v S (2)
McWha, W. B. R. (Knock), 1882 v E, W; (with Cliftonville), 1883 v E, W; 1884 v E; 1885 v E, W (7)
Mackie, J. (Arsenal), 1923 v W; (with Portsmouth), 1935 v S, W (3)
Madden, O. (Norwich C), 1938 v E (1)
Magee, G. (Wellington Park), 1885 v E, S, W (3)
Magill, E. J. (Arsenal), 1962 v E, S, Gr; 1963 v E, S, W, Pol (2), Sp; 1964 v E, S, W, U, Sp; 1965 v E, S, Sw (2), Ho, Alb; 1966 v S; (with Brighton & HA), E, Alb, W, WG, M (26)
Magilton, J. (Oxford U), 1991 v Pol, Y, Fa; 1992 v Fa, A, D, S, Li, G; 1993 v Alb, D, Alb, Ei, Li, La; 1994 v La, D, Ei; (with Southampton), R, Lie, Co, M; 1995 v P, A, Ei (2), Ca, Ch, La; 1996 v P, N, G; 1997 v Uk (sub), Arm (sub), Bel, P; 1998 v G; (with Sheffield W), P, Sp; (with Ipswich T), 2000 v L; 2001 v Y, Ma, D, Ic, N, CzR, Bul; 2002 v D, Ic, Ma, Pol, Lie (52)
Maginnis, H. (Linfield), 1900 v E, S, W; 1903 v S, W; 1904 v E, S, W (8)
Mahood, J. (Belfast C), 1926 v S; 1928 v E, S, W; 1929 v E, S, W; 1930 v W; (with Ballymena), 1934 v S (9)
Manderson, R. (Rangers), 1920 v W, S; 1925 v S, E; 1926 v S (5)
Mansfield, J. (Dublin Freebooters), 1901 v E (1)
Martin, C. (Cliftonville), 1882 v E, W; 1883 v E (3)
Martin, C. (Bo'ness), 1925 v S (1)
Martin, C. J. (Glentoran), 1947 v S; (with Leeds U), 1948 v E, S, W; (with Aston Villa), 1949 v E; 1950 v W (6)
Martin, D. K. (Belfast C), 1934 v E, S, W; 1935 v S; (with Wolverhampton W), 1935 v E; 1936 v W; (with Nottingham F), 1937 v S; 1938 v E, S; 1939 v S (10)
Mathieson, A. (Luton T), 1921 v W; 1922 v E (2)
Maxwell, J. (Linfield), 1902 v W; 1903 v W, E; (with Glentoran), 1905 v W, S; (with Belfast C), 1906 v W; 1907 v S (7)
Meek, H. L. (Glentoran), 1925 v W (1)
Mehaffy, J. A. C. (Queen's Island), 1922 v W (1)
Meldon, P. A. (Dublin Freebooters), 1899 v S, W (2)
Mercer, H. V. A. (Linfield), 1908 v E (1)
Mercer, J. T. (Distillery), 1898 v E, S, W; 1899 v E; (with Linfield), 1902 v E, W; (with Distillery), 1903 v S (2), W; (with Derby Co), 1904 v E, W; 1905 v S (12)
Millar, W. (Barrow), 1932 v W; 1933 v S (2)
Miller, J. (Middlesbrough), 1929 v W, S; 1930 v E (3)
Milligan, D. (Chesterfield), 1939 v W (1)
Milne, R. G. (Linfield), 1894 v E, S, W; 1895 v E, W; 1896 v E, S, W; 1897 v E, S; 1898 v E, S, W; 1899 v E, W; 1901 v W; 1902 v E, S, W; 1903 v E, S (2); 1904 v E, S, W; 1906 v E, S, W (28)
Mitchell, E. J. (Cliftonville), 1933 v S; (with Glentoran), 1934 v W (2)
Mitchell, W. (Distillery), 1932 v E, W; 1933 v E, W; (with Chelsea), 1934 v W, S; 1935 v S, E; 1936 v S, E; 1937 v E, S, W; 1938 v E, S (15)
Molyneux, T. B. (Ligoniel), 1883 v E, W; (with Cliftonville), 1884 v E, W, S; 1885 v E, W; 1886 v E, W, S; 1888 v S (11)
Montgomery, F. J. (Coleraine), 1955 v E (1)

Moore, C. (Glentoran), 1949 v W (1)
Moore, P. (Aberdeen), 1933 v E (1)
Moore, R. (Linfield Ath), 1891 v E, S, W (3)
Moore, R. L. (Ulster), 1887 v S, W (2)
Moore, W. (Falkirk), 1923 v S (1)
Moorhead, F. W. (Dublin University), 1885 v E (1)
Moorhead, G. (Linfield), 1923 v S; 1928 v F, S; 1929 v S (4)
Moran, J. (Leeds C), 1912 v S (1)
Moreland, V. (Derby Co), 1979 v Bul (2 sub), E, S; 1980 v E, Ei (6)
Morgan, G. F. (Linfield), 1922 v N; 1923 v E; (with Nottingham F), 1924 v S; 1927 v E; 1928 v E, S, W; 1929 v E (8)
Morgan, S. (Port Vale), 1972 v Sp; 1973 v Bul (sub), P, Cy, E, S, W; (with Aston Villa), 1974 v Bul, P, S, E; 1975 v Se; 1976 v Se (sub), N, Y; (with Brighton & HA), S, W (sub); (with Sparta Rotterdam), 1979 v D (18)
Morrison, R. (Linfield Ath), 1891 v E, W (2)
Morrison, T. (Glentoran), 1895 v E, S, W; (with Burnley), 1899 v W; 1900 v W; 1902 v E, S (7)
Morrogh, D. (Bohemians), 1896 v S (1)
Morrow, S. J. (Arsenal), 1990 v U (sub); 1991 v A (sub), Pol, Y; 1992 v Fa, S (sub), G (sub); 1993 v Sp (sub), Alb, Ei; 1994 v R, Co, M (sub); 1995 v P, Ei (2), La; 1996 v P, Se; 1997 v Uk, G, Alb, I, Bel; (with QPR), P, Uk, Arm; 1998 v G, P, Slo, Sw, Sp; 1999 v T, Fi, Mol, G, Mol; 2000 v G, Fi (39)
Morrow, W. J. (Moyola Park), 1883 v E, W; 1884 v S (3)
Muir, R. (Oldpark), 1885 v S, W (2)
Mulholland, S. (Celtic), 1906 v S, E (2)
Mullan, G. (Glentoran), 1983 v S, E, W, Alb (sub) (4)
Mulligan, J. (Manchester C), 1921 v S (1)
Mulryne, P. P. (Manchester U), 1997 v Bel (sub), Arm (sub), Th; 1998 v Alb (sub), Sp (sub); 1999 v T, Fi; (with Norwich C), Ca; 2001 v Y, D (sub), Bul (sub), CzR; 2002 v D, Ic, Pol, Lie; 2003 v Sp, Uk (18)
Murdock, C. J, (Preston NE), 2000 v L (sub), Ma, H (sub); 2001 v Y, Ma, D, Ic, N, CzR, Bul (2), CzR; 2002 v D, Ma; 2003 v Cy, Sp, Uk (sub) (17)
Murphy, J. (Bradford C), 1910 v E, S, W (3)
Murphy, N. (QPR), 1905 v E, S, W (3)
Murray, J. M. (Motherwell), 1910 v E, S; (with Sheffield W), 1910 v W (3)

Napier, R. J. (Bolton W), 1966 v WG (1)
Neill, W. J. T. (Arsenal), 1961 v I, Gr, WG; 1962 v E, S, W, Gr; 1963 v E, W, Pol, Sp; 1964 v S, E, W, U, Sp; 1965 v E, S, W, Sw, Ho (2), Alb; 1966 v S, E, W, Alb, WG, M; 1967 v S, W; 1968 v S, E; 1969 v E, S, W, Is, T (2); 1970 v S, E, W, USSR (2); (with Hull C), 1971 v Cy, Sp; 1972 v USSR (2), Sp, S, E, W; 1973 v Bul, Cy (2), P, E, S, W (59)
Nelis, P. (Nottingham F), 1923 v E (1)
Nelson, S. (Arsenal), 1970 v W, E (sub); 1971 v Cy, Sp, E, S, W; 1972 v USSR (2), Sp, E, S, W; 1973 v Bul, Cy, P; 1974 v S, E; 1975 v Se, Y; 1976 v Se, N, Is, E; 1977 v Bel (sub), WG, W, Ic; 1978 v Ic, Ho, Bel; 1979 v Ei, D, Bul, E, Bul, E, S, W, D; 1980 v E, Ei, Is; 1981 v S, P, S, Se; (with Brighton & HA), 1982 v E, S, Sp (sub), A (51)
Nicholl, C. J. (Aston Villa), 1975 v Se, Y, E, S, W; 1976 v Se, N, Y, S, E, W; 1977 v W; (with Southampton), 1978 v Bel (sub), S, E, W; 1979 v Ei, Bul, E, Bul, E, W; 1980 v Ei, Is, S, E, W, Aus (3); 1981 v Se, P, S, P, S, Se; 1982 v S, Is, E, F, W, Y, Hon, Sp, A, F; 1983 v S (sub), E, W; (with Grimsby T), 1984 v A, T (51)
Nicholl, H. (Belfast C), 1902 v E, W; 1905 v E (3)
Nicholl, J. M. (Manchester U), 1976 v Is, W (sub); 1977 v Ho, Bel, E, S, W, Ic; 1978 v Ic, Ho, Bel, S, E, W; 1979 v Ei, D, Bul, E, Bul, E, S, W, D; 1980 v E, Ei, Is, S, E, W, Aus (3); 1981 v Se, P, S, P, S, Se; 1982 v S, Is, E; (with Toronto B), F, W, Y, Hon, Sp, A, F; (with Sunderland), 1983 v A, WG, Alb, T, Alb; (with Toronto B), S, E, W; 1984 v T; (with Rangers), WG, S, E; (with Toronto B), Fi; 1985 v R; (with WBA), Fi, E, Sp, T; 1986 v T, R, E, F, Alg, Sp, Br (73)
Nicholson, J. J. (Manchester U), 1961 v S, W; 1962 v E, W, Gr, Ho; 1963 v E, S, Pol (2); (with Huddersfield T), 1965 v W, Ho (2), Alb; 1966 v S, E, W, Alb, M; 1967 v S, W; 1968 v S, E, W; 1969 v S, E, W, T (2); 1970 v S, E, W, USSR (2); 1971 v Cy (2), E, S, W; 1972 v USSR (2) (41)
Nixon, R. (Linfield), 1914 v S (1)
Nolan, I. R. (Sheffield W), 1997 v Arm, G, Alb, P, Uk; 1998 v G, P; 2000 v G, Fi, L, Ma, H; (with Bradford C), 2001 v Y, Ma, Bul (2), CzR; (with Wigan Ath), 2002 v Sp (18)
Nolan-Whelan, J. V. (Dublin Freebooters), 1901 v E, W; 1902 v S, W; 1903 v S (5)

O'Boyle, G. (Dunfermline Ath), 1994 v Co (sub), M; (with St Johnstone), 1995 v P (sub), La (sub), Ca (sub), Ch (sub); 1996 v Se (sub), G (sub); 1997 v I (sub), Bel (sub); 1998 v Slo (sub), Sw (sub); 1999 v Fi (sub) (13)
O'Brien, M. T. (QPR), 1921 v S; (with Leicester C), 1922 v S, W; 1924 v S, W; (with Hull C), 1925 v S, E, W; 1926 v W; (with Derby Co), 1927 v W (10)
O'Connell, P. (Sheffield W), 1912 v E, S; (with Hull C), 1914 v E, S, W (5)
O'Doherty, A. (Coleraine), 1970 v E, W (sub) (2)
O'Driscoll, J. F. (Swansea T), 1949 v E, S, W (3)
O'Hagan, C. (Tottenham H), 1905 v S, W; 1906 v S, W, E; (with Aberdeen), 1907 v E, S, W; 1908 v S, W; 1909 v E (11)
O'Hagan, W. (St Mirren), 1920 v E, W (2)
O'Hehir, J. C. (Bohemians), 1910 v W (1)
O'Kane, W. J. (Nottingham F), 1970 v E, W, S (sub); 1971 v Sp, E, S, W; 1972 v USSR (2); 1973 v P, Cy; 1974 v Bul, P, S, E, W; 1975 v N, Se, E, S (20)
O'Mahoney, M. T. (Bristol R), 1939 v S (1)
O'Neill, C. (Motherwell), 1989 v Ch (sub); 1990 v Ei (sub); 1991 v D (3)
O'Neill, J. (Sunderland), 1962 v W (1)
O'Neill, J. P. (Leicester C), 1980 v Is, S, E, W, Aus (3); 1981 v P, S, P, S, Se; 1982 v S, Is, E, F, S, F (sub); 1983 v A, WG, Alb, T, Alb, S; 1984 v S (sub); 1985 v Is, Fi, E, Sp, T; 1986 v T, R, E, F, D, Mor, Alg, Sp, Br (39)
O'Neill, M. A. M. (Newcastle U), 1988 v Gr, Pol, F, Ma; 1989 v Ei, H, Sp (sub), Sp (sub), Ma (sub), Ch; (with Dundee U), 1990 v H (sub), Ei; 1991 v Pol; 1992 v Fa (sub), S (sub), G (sub); 1993 v Alb (sub + 1), Ei, Sp, Li, La; (with Hibernian), 1994 v Lie (sub); 1995 v A (sub), Ei; 1996 v Lie, A, N, Se; (with Coventry C), 1997 v Uk (sub), Arm (sub) (31)
O'Neill, M. H. M. (Distillery), 1972 v USSR (sub), (with Nottingham F), Sp (sub), W (sub); 1973 v P, Cy, E, S, W; 1974 v Bul, P, E (sub), W; 1975 v Se, Y, E, S; 1976 v Y (sub); 1977 v E (sub), S; 1978 v Ic, Ho, S, E, W; 1979 v Ei, D, Bul, E, Bul, D; 1980 v Ei, Is, Aus (3); 1981 v Se, P; (with Norwich C), P, S, Se; (with Manchester C), 1982 v S; (with Norwich C), E, F, S, Y, Hon, Sp, A, F; 1983 v A, WG, Alb, T, Alb, S, E; (with Notts Co), 1984 v A, T, WG, E, W, Fi; 1985 v R, Fi (64)
O'Reilly, H. (Dublin Freebooters), 1901 v S, W; 1904 v S (3)

Parke, J. (Linfield), 1964 v S; (with Hibernian), 1964 v E, Sp; (with Sunderland), 1965 v Sw, S, W, Ho (2), Alb; 1966 v WG; 1967 v E, S; 1968 v S, E (14)
Patterson, D. J. (C Palace), 1994 v Co (sub), M (sub); 1995 v Ei (sub+1), La, Ca, Ch (sub), La (sub); (with Luton T), 1996 v N (sub), Se; 1998 v Sw, Sp; (with Dundee U), 1999 v Fi, Mol, G, Mol, Ei (17)
Peacock, R. (Celtic), 1952 v S; 1953 v F; 1954 v W; 1955 v E, S; 1956 v E, S; 1957 v W, I, P; 1958 v S, E, W, I (2), Arg, Cz (2), WG; 1959 v E, S, W; 1960 v S, E; 1961 v E, S, I, WG (2), Gr; (with Coleraine), 1962 v S (31)
Peden, J. (Distillery), 1887 v S, W; 1888 v W, E; 1889 v S, E; 1890 v W, S; 1891 v W, E; 1892 v W, E; 1893 v E, S, W; 1896 v W, E, S; 1897 v W, S; 1898 v W, E, S; 1899 v W (24)
Penney, S. (Brighton & HA), 1985 v Is; 1986 v T, R, E, F, D, Mor, Alg, Sp; 1987 v E, T, Is; 1988 v Pol, F, Ma; 1989 v Ei, Sp (17)
Percy, J. C. (Belfast YMCA), 1889 v W (1)
Platt, J. A. (Middlesbrough), 1976 v Is (sub); 1978 v S, E, W; 1980 v S, E, W, Aus (3); 1981 v Se, P; 1982 v F, S, W (sub), A; 1983 v A, WG, Alb, T; (with Ballymena U), 1984 v E, W (sub); (with Coleraine), 1986 v Mor (sub) (23)
Pollock, W. (Belfast C), 1928 v F (1)
Ponsonby, J. (Distillery), 1895 v S, W; 1896 v E, S, W; 1897 v E, S, W; 1899 v E (9)
Potts, R. M. C. (Cliftonville), 1883 v E, W (2)
Priestley, T. J. M. (Coleraine), 1933 v S; (with Chelsea), 1934 v E (2)
Pyper, Jas. (Cliftonville), 1897 v S, W; 1898 v S, E, W; 1899 v S; 1900 v E (7)
Pyper, John (Cliftonville), 1897 v E, S, W; 1899 v E, W; 1900 v E, W, S; 1902 v S (9)
Pyper, M. (Linfield), 1932 v W (1)

Quinn, J. M. (Blackburn R), 1985 v Is, Fi, E, Sp, T; 1986 v T, R, E, F, D (sub), Mor (sub); 1987 v E (sub), T; (with Swindon T), 1988 v Y (sub), T, Gr, Pol, F (sub), Ma; (with Leicester C), 1989 v Ei, H (sub), Sp (sub+1); (with Bradford C), Ma, Ch; 1990 v H; (with West Ham U), N; 1991 v Y (sub); (with Bournemouth), 1992 v Li; (with Reading), 1993 v Sp, D, Alb (sub), Ei (sub), La (sub); 1994 v La, D (sub), Ei, R, Lie, Co, M; 1995 v P, A (sub), La (sub); 1996 v Lie, A (sub) (46)

Quinn, S. J. (Blackpool), 1996 v Se (sub); 1997 v Alb (sub), I, Bel, P, Uk (sub), Arm, Th (sub); 1998 v G, Alb; (with WBA), Slo, Sw; 1999 v T (sub), Fi (sub), Ei; 2000 v F (sub), T (sub), G (sub), Fi, L, Ma; 2001 v Y (sub), Bul (sub), CzR (sub); 2002 v Ma (sub); (with Willem II), 2003 v Cy, Fi, Arm, Gr (29)

Rafferty, P. (Linfield), 1980 v E (sub) (1)
Ramsey, P. C. (Leicester C), 1984 v A, WG, S; 1985 v Is, E, Sp, T; 1986 v T, Mor; 1987 v Is, E, Y (sub); 1988 v Y; 1989 v Sp (14)
Rankine, J. (Alexander), 1883 v E, W (2)
Rattray, D. (Avoniel), 1882 v E; 1883 v E, W (3)
Rea, R. (Glentoran), 1901 v E (1)
Redmond, R. (Cliftonville), 1884 v W (1)
Reid, G. H. (Cardiff C), 1923 v S (1)
Reid, J. (Ulster), 1883 v E; 1884 v W; 1887 v S; 1889 v W; 1890 v S, W (6)
Reid, S. E. (Derby Co), 1934 v E, W; 1936 v E (3)
Reid, W. (Hearts), 1931 v E (1)
Reilly, M. M. (Portsmouth), 1900 v E; 1902 v E (2)
Renneville, W. T. J. (Leyton), 1910 v S, E, W; (with Aston Villa), 1911 v W (4)
Reynolds, J. (Distillery), 1890 v E, W; (with Ulster), 1891 v E, S, W (5)
Reynolds, R. (Bohemians), 1905 v W (1)
Rice, P. J. (Arsenal), 1969 v Is; 1970 v USSR; 1971 v E, S, W; 1972 v USSR, Sp, E, S, W; 1973 v Bul, Cy, E, S, W; 1974 v Bul, P, S, E, W; 1975 v N, Y, E, S, W; 1976 v Se, N, Y, Is, S, E, W; 1977 v Ho, Bel, WG, E, S, Ic; 1978 v Ic, Ho, Bel; 1979 v Ei, D, E (2), S, W, D; 1980 v E (49)
Roberts, F. C. (Glentoran), 1931 v S (1)
Robinson, P. (Distillery), 1920 v S; (with Blackburn R), 1921 v W (2)
Robinson, S. (Bournemouth), 1997 v Th (sub); 1999 v Mol, Ei; 2000 v L (sub), H (sub) (5)
Rogan, A. (Celtic), 1988 v Y (sub), Gr, Pol (sub); 1989 v Ei (sub), H, Sp (2), Ma (sub), Ch; 1990 v H, N (sub), U; 1991 v Y (2), D, A; (with Sunderland), 1992 v Li (sub); (with Millwall), 1997 v G (sub) (18)
Rollo, D. (Linfield), 1912 v W; 1913 v W; 1914 v W, E; (with Blackburn R), 1920 v S, W; 1921 v E, S, W; 1922 v E; 1923 v E; 1924 v S, W; 1925 v W; 1926 v E; 1927 v E (16)
Roper, E. O. (Dublin University), 1886 v W (1)
Rosbotham, A. (Cliftonville), 1887 v E, S, W; 1888 v E, S, W; 1889 v E (7)
Ross, W. E. (Newcastle U), 1969 v Is (1)
Rowland, K. (West Ham U), 1994 v La (sub); 1995 v Ca, Ch, La; 1996 v P (sub), Lie (sub), N (sub), Se, G (sub); 1997 v Uk, Arm, I (sub); 1998 v Alb; (with QPR), 1999 v T, Fi, Mol, G, Ca, Ei (19)
Rowley, R. W. M. (Southampton), 1929 v S, W; 1930 v W, E; (with Tottenham H), 1931 v W; 1932 v S (6)
Rushe, F. (Distillery),1925 v S.Af (1)
Russell, A. (Linfield), 1947 v E (1)
Russell, S. R. (Bradford C), 1930 v E, S; (with Derry C), 1932 v E (3)
Ryan, R. A. (WBA), 1950 v W (1)

Sanchez, L. P. (Wimbledon), 1987 v T (sub); 1989 v Sp, Ma (3)
Scott, E. (Liverpool), 1920 v S; 1921 v E, S, W; 1922 v E; 1925 v W; 1926 v E, S, W; 1927 v E, S, W; 1928 v E, S, W; 1929 v E, S, W; 1930 v E; 1931 v E; 1932 v W; 1933 v E, S, W; 1934 v E, S, W; (with Belfast C), 1935 v S; 1936 v E, S, W (31)
Scott, J. (Grimsby), 1958 v Cz, F (2)
Scott, J. E. (Cliftonville), 1901 v S (1)
Scott, L. J. (Dublin University), 1895 v S, W (2)
Scott, P. W. (Everton), 1975 v W; 1976 v Y; (with York C), Is, S, E (sub), W; 1978 v S, E, W; (with Aldershot), 1979 v S (sub) (10)
Scott, T. (Cliftonville), 1894 v E, S; 1895 v S, W; 1896 v S, E, W; 1897 v E, W; 1898 v E, S, W; 1900 v W (13)
Scott, W. (Linfield), 1903 v E, S, W; 1904 v E, S, W; (with Everton), 1905 v E, S; 1907 v E, S; 1908 v E, S, W; 1909 v E, S, W; 1910 v E, S; 1911 v E, S, W; 1912 v E; (with Leeds City), 1913 v E, S, W (25)
Scraggs, M. J. (Glentoran), 1921 v W; 1922 v E (2)
Seymour, H. C. (Bohemians), 1914 v W (1)
Seymour, J. (Cliftonville), 1907 v W; 1909 v W (2)
Shanks, T. (Woolwich Arsenal), 1903 v S; 1904 v W; (with Brentford), 1905 v E (3)
Sharkey, P. G. (Ipswich T), 1976 v S (1)
Sheehan, Dr G. (Bohemians), 1899 v S; 1900 v E, W (3)
Sheridan, J. (Everton), 1903 v W, E, S; 1904 v E, S; (with Stoke C), 1905 v E (6)
Sherrard, J. (Limavady), 1885 v S; 1887 v W; 1888 v W (3)
Sherrard, W. C. (Cliftonville), 1895 v E, W, S (3)
Sherry, J. J. (Bohemians), 1906 v E; 1907 v W (2)
Shields, R. J. (Southampton), 1957 v S (1)
Silo, M. (Belfast YMCA), 1888 v E (1)
Simpson, W. J. (Rangers), 1951 v W, F; 1954 v E, S; 1955 v E; 1957 v I, P; 1958 v S, E, W, I; 1959 v S (12)
Sinclair, J. (Knock), 1882 v E, W (2)
Slemin, J. C. (Bohemians), 1909 v W (1)
Sloan, A. S. (London Caledonians), 1925 v W (1)
Sloan, D. (Oxford U), 1969 v Is; 1971 v Sp (2)
Sloan, H. A. de B. (Bohemians), 1903 v E; 1904 v S; 1905 v E; 1906 v W; 1907 v E, W; 1908 v W; 1909 v S (8)
Sloan, J. W. (Arsenal), 1947 v W (1)
Sloan, T. (Manchester U), 1979 v S, W (sub), D (sub) (3)
Sloan, T. (Cardiff C), 1926 v S, W, E; 1927 v W, S; 1928 v E, W; 1929 v E; (with Linfield), 1930 v W, S; 1931 v S (11)
Small, J. M. (Clarence), 1887 v E; (with Cliftonville), 1893 v E, S, W (4)
Smith, A. W. (Glentoran), 2003 v I, Sp (2)
Smith, E. E. (Cardiff C), 1921 v S; 1923 v W, E; 1924 v E (4)
Smith, J. E. (Distillery), 1901 v S, W (2)
Smyth, R. H. (Dublin University), 1886 v W (1)
Smyth, S. (Wolverhampton W), 1948 v E, S, W; 1949 v S, W; 1950 v E, S, W; (with Stoke C), 1952 v E (9)
Smyth, W. (Distillery), 1949 v E, S; 1954 v S, E (4)
Snape, A. (Airdrie), 1920 v E (1)
Sonner, D. J. (Ipswich T), 1998 v Alb (sub); (with Sheffield W), 1999 v G (sub), Ca (sub); 2000 v L (sub), Ma (sub), H; (with Birmingham C), 2001 v N (sub) (7)
Spence, D. W. (Bury), 1975 v Y, E, S, W; 1976 v Se, Is, E, W, S (sub); (with Blackpool), 1977 v Ho (sub), WG (sub), E (sub), S (sub), W (sub), Ic (sub); 1979 v Ei, D (sub), E (sub), Bul (sub), E (sub), S, W, D; 1980 v Ei; (with Southend U), Is (sub), Aus (sub); 1981 v S (sub), Se (sub); 1982 v F (sub) (29)
Spencer, S. (Distillery), 1890 v E, S; 1892 v E, S, W; 1893 v E (6)
Spiller, E. A. (Cliftonville), 1883 v E, W; 1884 v E, W, S (5)
Stanfield, O. M. (Distillery), 1887 v E, S, W; 1888 v E, S, W; 1889 v E, S, W; 1890 v E, S; 1891 v E, S, W; 1892 v E, S, W; 1893 v E, W; 1894 v E, S, W; 1895 v E, S; 1896 v E, S, W; 1897 v E, S, W (30)
Steele, A. (Charlton Ath), 1926 v W, S; (with Fulham), 1929 v W, S (4)
Stevenson, A. E. (Rangers), 1934 v E, S, W; (with Everton), 1935 v E, S; 1936 v S, W; 1937 v E, W; 1938 v E, W; 1939 v E, S, W; 1947 v S, W; 1948 v S (17)
Stewart, A. (Glentoran), 1967 v W; 1968 v S, E; (with Derby Co), 1968 v W; 1969 v Is, T (1+1 sub) (7)
Stewart, D. C. (Hull C), 1978 v Bel (1)
Stewart, I. (QPR), 1982 v F (sub); 1983 v A, WG, Alb, T, Alb, S, E, W; 1984 v A, T, WG, S, E, W, Fi; 1985 v R, Fi, Is, E, Sp, T; (with Newcastle U), 1986 v R, E, D, Mor, Alg (sub), Sp (sub), Br; 1987 v E, Is (sub) (31)
Stewart, R. K. (St Columb's Court), 1890 v E, S, W; (with Cliftonville), 1892 v E, S, W; 1893 v E, W; 1894 v E, S, W (11)
Stewart, T. C. (Linfield), 1961 v W (1)
Swan, S. (Linfield), 1899 v S (1)

Taggart, G. P. (Barnsley), 1990 v N, U; 1991 v Y, D, A, Pol, Fa; 1992 v Fa, A, D, S, Li, G; 1993 v Alb, Sp, D, Alb, Ei, Sp, Li, La; 1994 v La, D, Ei, R, Lie, Co, M; 1995 v P (sub), A, Ei (2), Ca, Ch, La; (with Bolton W), 1997 v G, Alb, I, Bel, P, Uk, Arm; 1998 v G, P, Sp; (with Leicester C), 2000 v H; 2001 v Ma, D, Ic, N; 2003 v Sp (51)
Taggart, J. (Walsall), 1899 v W (1)
Taylor, M. S. (Fulham), 1999 v G, Mol, Ca, Ei; 2000 v F, T, G, Fi, L (sub), Ma (sub), H; 2001 v Y, N, Bul, CzR; 2002 v D, Ic, Ma, Pol, Lie, Sp; 2003 v Cy, Sp, Uk, Fi, Arm, Gr, I, Sp (29)
Thompson, F. W. (Cliftonville), 1910 v E, S, W; (with Linfield), 1911 v W; (with Bradford C), 1911 v E; 1912 v E, W; 1913 v E, S, W; (with Clyde), 1914 v E, S (12)
Thompson, J. (Distillery), 1897 v S (1)
Thompson, R. (Queen's Island), 1928 v F (1)
Thompson, W. (Belfast Ath), 1889 v S (1)
Thunder, P. J. (Bohemians), 1911 v W (1)
Todd, S. J. (Burnley), 1966 v M (sub); 1967 v E; 1968 v W; 1969 v E, S, W; 1970 v S, USSR; (with Sheffield W), 1971 v Cy (2), Sp (sub) (11)
Toner, C. (Leyton Orient), 2003 v I (sub), Sp (sub) (2)
Toner, J. (Arsenal), 1922 v W; 1923 v W; 1924 v W, E; 1925 v E, S; (with St Johnstone), 1927 v E, S (8)
Torrans, R. (Linfield), 1893 v S (1)

Torrans, S. (Linfield), 1889 v S; 1890 v S, W; 1891 v S, W; 1892 v E, S, W; 1893 v E, S; 1894 v E, S, W; 1895 v E; 1896 v E, S, W; 1897 v E, S, W; 1898 v E, S; 1899 v E, W; 1901 v S, W (26)
Trainor, D. (Crusaders), 1967 v W (1)
Tully, C. P. (Celtic), 1949 v E; 1950 v E; 1952 v S; 1953 v E, S, W, F; 1954 v S; 1956 v E; 1959 v Sp (10)
Turner, A. (Cliftonville), 1896 v W (1)
Turner, E. (Cliftonville), 1896 v E (1)
Turner, W. (Cliftonville), 1886 v E, S; 1888 v S (3)
Twoomey, J. F. (Leeds U), 1938 v W; 1939 v E (2)
Uprichard, W. N. M. C. (Swindon T), 1952 v E, S, W; 1953 v E, S; (with Portsmouth), 1953 v W, F; 1955 v E, S, W; 1956 v E, S, W; 1958 v S, I, Cz; 1959 v S, Sp (18)

Vernon, J. (Belfast C), 1947 v E, S; (with WBA), 1947 v W; 1948 v E, S, W; 1949 v E, S, W; 1950 v E, S; 1951 v E, S, W, F; 1952 v S, E (17)

Waddell, T. M. R. (Cliftonville), 1906 v S (1)
Walker, J. (Doncaster R), 1955 v W (1)
Walker, T. (Bury), 1911 v S (1)
Walsh, D. J. (WBA), 1947 v S, W; 1948 v E, S, W; 1949 v E, S, W; 1950 v W (9)
Walsh, W. (Manchester C), 1948 v E, S, W; 1949 v E, S (5)
Waring, J. (Cliftonville), 1899 v E (1)
Warren, P. (Shelbourne), 1913 v E, S (2)
Watson, J. (Ulster), 1883 v E, W; 1886 v E, S, W; 1887 v S, W; 1889 v E, W (9)
Watson, P. (Distillery), 1971 v Cy (sub) (1)
Watson, T. (Cardiff C), 1926 v S (1)
Wattie, J. (Distillery), 1899 v E (1)
Webb, C. G. (Brighton), 1909 v S, W; 1911 v S (3)
Weir, E. (Clyde), 1939 v W (1)
Welsh, E. (Carlisle U), 1966 v W, WG, M; 1967 v W (4)
Whiteside, N. (Manchester U), 1982 v Y, Hon, Sp, A, F; 1983 v WG, Alb, T; 1984 v A, T, WG, S, E, W, Fi; 1985 v R, Fi, Is, E, Sp, T; 1986 v R, E, F, D, Mor, Alg, Sp, Br; 1987 v E (2), Is, Y; 1988 v T, Pol, F; (with Everton), 1990 v H, Ei (38)
Whiteside, T. (Distillery), 1891 v E (1)
Whitfield, E. R. (Dublin University), 1886 v W (1)
Whitley, Jeff (Manchester C), 1997 v Bel (sub), Th (sub); 1998 v Sp (sub); 2000 v Fi; 2001 v Y, D, N (7)
Whitley, Jim (Manchester C), 1998 v Sp; 1999 v T (sub); 2000 v Fi (sub) (3)
Williams, J. R. (Ulster), 1886 v E, S (2)
Williams, M. S. (Chesterfield), 1999 v G, Mol, Ca, Ei; (with Watford), 2000 v F, T, G, Fi, L, Ma, H (sub); (with Wimbledon), 2001 v Y, Ic (sub), N (sub), CzR, Bul, CzR; 2002 v Lie, Sp; 2003 v Cy, Fi; (with Stoke C), Arm, Gr, I (sub), Sp (sub) (25)
Williams, P. A. (WBA), 1991 v Fa (sub) (1)
Williamson, J. (Cliftonville), 1890 v E; 1892 v S; 1893 v S (3)
Willighan, T. (Burnley), 1933 v W; 1934 v S (2)
Willis, G. (Linfield), 1906 v S, W; 1907 v S; 1912 v S (4)
Wilson, D. J. (Brighton & HA), 1987 v T, Is, E (sub); (with Luton T), 1988 v Y, T, Gr, Pol, F, Ma; 1989 v Ei, H, Sp, Ma, Ch; 1990 v H, Ei, N, U; (with Sheffield W), 1991 v Y, D, A, Fa; 1992 v A (sub), S (24)
Wilson, H. (Linfield), 1925 v W, S.Af (2)
Wilson, K. J. (Ipswich T), 1987 v Is, E, Y; (with Chelsea), 1988 v Y, T, Gr (sub), Pol (sub), F (sub); 1989 v H (sub), Sp (2), Ma, Ch; 1990 v Ei (sub), N, U; 1991 v Y (2), A, Pol, Fa; 1992 v Fa, A, D, S; (with Notts Co), Li, G; 1993 v Alb, Sp, D, Sp, Li, La; 1994 v La, D, Ei, R, Lie, Co, M; (with Walsall), 1995 v Ei (sub), La (42)
Wilson, M. (Distillery), 1884 v E, S, W (3)
Wilson, R. (Cliftonville), 1888 v S (1)
Wilson, S. J. (Glenavon), 1962 v S; 1964 v S; (with Falkirk), 1964 v E, W, U, Sp; 1965 v E, Sw; (with Dundee), 1966 v W, WG; 1967 v S; 1968 v E (12)
Wilton, J. M. (St Columb's Court), 1888 v E, W; 1889 v S, E; (with Cliftonville), 1890 v E; (with St Columb's Court), 1893 v W, S (7)
Wood, T. J. (Walsall), 1996 v Lie (sub) (1)
Worthington, N. (Sheffield W), 1984 v W, Fi (sub); 1985 v Is, Sp (sub); 1986 v T, R (sub), E (sub), D, Alg, Sp; 1987 v E (2), T, Is, Y; 1988 v Y, T, Gr, Pol, F, Ma; 1989 v Ei, H, Sp, Ma; 1990 v H, Ei, U; 1991 v Y, D, A, Fa; 1992 v A, D, S, Li, G; 1993 v Alb, Sp, D, Ei, Sp, Li, La; 1994 v La, D, Ei, Lie, Co, M; (with Leeds U), 1995 v P, A, Ei (2), La, Ca (sub), Ch, La; 1996 v P, Lie, A, N, Se, G; (with Stoke C), 1997 v I, Bel (sub) (66)
Wright, J. (Cliftonville), 1906 v E, S, W; 1907 v E, S, W (6)
Wright, T. J. (Newcastle U), 1989 v Ma, Ch; 1990 v H, U; 1992 v Fa, A, S, G; 1993 v Alb, Sp, Alb, Ei, Sp, Li, La; 1994 v La; (with Nottingham F), D, Ei, R, Lie, Co, M (sub); 1997 v G, Alb, I, Bel; (with Manchester C), P, Uk; 1998 v Alb; 1999 v Ca (sub); 2000 v F (sub) (31)

Young, S. (Linfield), 1907 v E, S; 1908 v E, S; (with Airdrie), 1909 v E; 1912 v S; (with Linfield), 1914 v E, S, W (9)

SCOTLAND

Adams, J. (Hearts), 1889 v Ni; 1892 v W; 1893 v Ni (3)
Agnew, W. B. (Kilmarnock), 1907 v Ni; 1908 v W, Ni (3)
Aird, J. (Burnley), 1954 v N (2), A, U (4)
Aitken, A. (Newcastle U), 1901 v E; 1902 v E; 1903 v E, W; 1904 v E; 1905 v E, W; 1906 v E; (with Middlesbrough), 1907 v E, W; 1908 v E; (with Leicester Fosse), 1910 v E; 1911 v E, Ni (14)
Aitken, G. G. (East Fife), 1949 v E, F; 1950 v W, Ni, Sw; (with Sunderland), 1953 v W, Ni; 1954 v E (8)
Aitken, R. (Dumbarton), 1886 v E; 1888 v Ni (2)
Aitken, R. (Celtic), 1980 v Pe (sub), Bel, W (sub), E, Pol; 1983 v Bel, Ca (1+1 sub); 1984 v Bel (sub), Ni, W (sub); 1985 v E, Ic; 1986 v W, EG, Aus (2), Is, R, E, D, WG, U; 1987 v Bul, Ei (2), L, Bel, E, Br; 1988 v H, Bel, Bul, L, S.Ar, Ma, Sp, Co, E; 1989 v N, Y, I, Cy, F, Cy, E, Ch; 1990 v Y, F, N; (with Newcastle U), Arg (sub), Pol, Ma, Cr, Se, Br; (with St Mirren), 1992 v R (sub) (57)
Aitkenhead, W. A. C. (Blackburn R), 1912 v Ni (1)
Albiston, A. (Manchester U), 1982 v Ni; 1984 v U, Bel, EG, W, E; 1985 v Y, Ic, Sp (2), W; 1986 v EG, Ho, U (14)
Alexander, D. (East Stirlingshire), 1894 v W, Ni (2)
Alexander, G. (Preston NE), 2002 v Ng (sub), Sk, S.Af (sub), Hk (sub); 2003 v D (sub), Fa (sub), Ca, P, Ei, Ic, Li, Nz (sub) (12)
Allan, D. S. (Queen's Park), 1885 v E, W; 1886 v W (3)
Allan, G. (Liverpool), 1897 v E (1)
Allan, H. (Hearts), 1902 v W (1)
Allan, J. (Queen's Park), 1887 v E, W (2)
Allan, T. (Dundee), 1974 v WG, N (2)
Ancell, R. F. D. (Newcastle U), 1937 v W, Ni (2)
Anderson, A. (Hearts), 1933 v E; 1934 v A, E, W, Ni; 1935 v E, W, Ni; 1936 v E, W, Ni; 1937 v G, E, W, Ni, A; 1938 v E, W, Ni, Cz, Ho; 1939 v W, H (23)
Anderson, F. (Clydesdale), 1874 v E (1)
Anderson, G. (Kilmarnock), 1901 v Ni (1)
Anderson, H. A. (Raith R), 1914 v W (1)
Anderson, J. (Leicester C), 1954 v Fi (1)
Anderson, K. (Queen's Park), 1896 v Ni; 1898 v E, Ni (3)
Anderson, R. (Aberdeen), 2003 v Ic (sub), Ca, P, Ei (4)
Anderson, W. (Queen's Park), 1882 v E; 1883 v E, W; 1884 v E; 1885 v E, W (6)
Andrews, P. (Eastern), 1875 v E (1)
Archibald, A. (Rangers), 1921 v W; 1922 v W, E; 1923 v Ni; 1924 v E, W; 1931 v E; 1932 v E (8)
Archibald, S. (Aberdeen), 1980 v P (sub); (with Tottenham H), Ni, Pol, H; 1981 v Se (sub), Is, Ni, Is, Ni, E; 1982 v Ni, P, Sp (sub), Ho, Nz (sub), Br, USSR; 1983 v EG, Sw (sub), Bel; 1984 v EG, E, F; (with Barcelona), 1985 v Sp, E, Ic (sub); 1986 v WG (27)
Armstrong, M. W. (Aberdeen), 1936 v W, Ni; 1937 v G (3)
Arnott, W. (Queen's Park), 1883 v W; 1884 v E, Ni; 1885 v E, W; 1886 v E; 1887 v E, W; 1888 v E; 1889 v E; 1890 v E; 1891 v E; 1892 v E; 1893 v E (14)
Auld, J. R. (Third Lanark), 1887 v E, W; 1889 v W (3)
Auld, R. (Celtic), 1959 v H, P; 1960 v W (3)

Baird, A. (Queen's Park), 1892 v Ni; 1894 v W (2)
Baird, D. (Hearts), 1890 v Ni; 1891 v E; 1892 v W (3)
Baird, H. (Airdrieonians), 1956 v A (1)
Baird, J. C. (Vale of Leven), 1876 v E; 1878 v W; 1880 v E (3)
Baird, S. (Rangers), 1957 v Y, Sp (2), Sw, WG; 1958 v F, Ni (7)
Baird, W. U. (St Bernard), 1897 v Ni (1)
Bannon, E. (Dundee U), 1980 v Bel; 1983 v Ni, W, E, Ca; 1984 v EG; 1986 v Is, R, E, D (sub), WG (11)
Barbour, A. (Renton), 1885 v Ni (1)
Barker, J. B. (Rangers), 1893 v W; 1894 v W (2)
Barrett, F. (Dundee), 1894 v Ni; 1895 v W (2)
Battles, B. (Celtic), 1901 v E, W, Ni (3)
Battles, B. jun. (Hearts), 1931 v W (1)
Bauld, W. (Hearts), 1950 v E, Sw, P (3)

Baxter, J. C. (Rangers), 1961 v Ni, Ei (2), Cz; 1962 v Ni, W, E, Cz (2), U; 1963 v W, Ni, E, A, N, Ei, Sp; 1964 v W, E, N, WG; 1965 v W, Ni, Fi; (with Sunderland), 1966 v P, Br, Ni, W, E, I; 1967 v W, E, USSR; 1968 v W (34)
Baxter, R. D. (Middlesbrough), 1939 v E, W, H (3)
Beattie, A. (Preston NE), 1937 v E, A, Cz; 1938 v E; 1939 v W, Ni, H (7)
Beattie, R. (Preston NE), 1939 v W (1)
Begbie, I. (Hearts), 1890 v Ni; 1891 v E; 1892 v W; 1894 v E (4)
Bell, A. (Manchester U), 1912 v Ni (1)
Bell, J. (Dumbarton), 1890 v Ni; 1892 v E; (with Everton), 1896 v E; 1897 v E; 1898 v E; (with Celtic), 1899 v E, W, Ni; 1900 v E, W (10)
Bell, M. (Hearts), 1901 v W (1)
Bell, W. J. (Leeds U), 1966 v P, Br (2)
Bennett, A. (Celtic), 1904 v W; 1907 v Ni; 1908 v W; (with Rangers), 1909 v W, Ni, E; 1910 v E, W; 1911 v E, W; 1913 v Ni (11)
Bennie, R. (Airdrieonians), 1925 v W, Ni; 1926 v Ni (3)
Bernard, P. R. J. (Oldham Ath), 1995 v J (sub), Ec (2)
Berry, D. (Queen's Park), 1894 v W; 1899 v W, Ni (3)
Berry, W. H. (Queen's Park), 1888 v E; 1889 v E; 1890 v E; 1891 v E (4)
Bett, J. (Rangers), 1982 v Ho; 1983 v Bel; (with Lokeren), 1984 v Bel, W, E, F; 1985 v Y, Ic, Sp (2), W, E, Ic; (with Aberdeen), 1986 v W, Is, Ho; 1987 v Bel; 1988 v H (sub); 1989 v Y; 1990 v F (sub), N, Arg, Eg, Ma, Cr (25)
Beveridge, W. W. (Glasgow University), 1879 v E, W; 1880 v W (3)
Black, A. (Hearts), 1938 v Cz, Ho; 1939 v H (3)
Black, D. (Hurlford), 1889 v Ni (1)
Black, E. (Metz), 1988 v H (sub), L (sub) (2)
Black, I. H. (Southampton), 1948 v E (1)
Blackburn, J. E. (Royal Engineers), 1873 v E (1)
Blacklaw, A. S. (Burnley), 1963 v N, Sp; 1966 v I (3)
Blackley, J. (Hibernian), 1974 v Cz, E, Bel, Z; 1976 v Sw; 1977 v W, Se (7)
Blair, D. (Clyde), 1929 v W, Ni; 1931 v E, A, I; 1932 v W, Ni; (with Aston Villa), 1933 v W (8)
Blair, J. (Sheffield W), 1920 v E, Ni; (with Cardiff C), 1921 v E; 1922 v E; 1923 v E, W, Ni; 1924 v W (8)
Blair, J. (Motherwell), 1934 v W (1)
Blair, J. A. (Blackpool), 1947 v W (1)
Blair, W. (Third Lanark), 1896 v W (1)
Blessington, J. (Celtic), 1894 v E, Ni; 1896 v E, Ni (4)
Blyth, J. A. (Coventry C), 1978 v Bul, W (2)
Bone, J. (Norwich C), 1972 v Y (sub); 1973 v D (2)
Booth, S. (Aberdeen), 1993 v G (sub), Es (2 subs); 1994 v Sw, Ma (sub); 1995 v Fa, Ru; 1996 v Fi, Sm, Aus (sub), US, Ho, Sw (sub); (with Borussia Dortmund), 1998 v D, Fi, Co (sub), Mor (sub); (with Twente), 2001 v Pol; 2002 v Cro, Bel (sub), La (sub) (21)
Bowie, J. (Rangers), 1920 v E, Ni (2)
Bowie, W. (Linthouse), 1891 v Ni (1)
Bowman, D. (Dundee U), 1992 v Fi, US (sub); 1993 v G, Es; 1994 v Sw, I (6)
Bowman, G. A. (Montrose), 1892 v Ni (1)
Boyd, J. M. (Newcastle U), 1934 v Ni (1)
Boyd, R. (Mossend Swifts), 1889 v Ni; 1891 v W (2)
Boyd, T. (Motherwell), 1991 v R (sub), Sw, Bul, USSR; (with Chelsea), 1992 v Sw, R; (with Celtic), Fi, Ca, N, C; 1993 v Sw, P, I, Ma, G, Es (2); 1994 v I, Ma (sub), Ho (sub), A; 1995 v Fi, Fa, Ru, Gr, Ru, Sm; 1996 v Gr, Fi, Se, Sm, Aus, D, US, Co, Ho, E, Sw; 1997 v A, La, Se, Es (2), A, Se, W, Ma, Bl; 1998 v Bl, La, F, D, Fi (sub), Co, US, Br, N, Mor; 1999 v Li, Es, Fa, CzR, G, Fa, CzR; 2001 v La, Cro, Aus, Bel, Sm (sub), Pol; 2002 v Bel (72)
Boyd, W. G. (Clyde), 1931 v I, Sw (2)
Brackenbridge, T. (Hearts), 1888 v Ni (1)
Bradshaw, T. (Bury), 1928 v E (1)
Brand, R. (Rangers), 1961 v Ni, Cz, Ei (2); 1962 v Ni, W, Cz, U (8)
Branden, T. (Blackburn R), 1896 v E (1)
Brazil, A. (Ipswich T), 1980 v Pol (sub), H; 1982 v Sp, Ho (sub), Ni, W, E, Nz, USSR (sub); 1983 v EG, Sw; (with Tottenham H), W, E (sub) (13)
Bremner, D. (Hibernian), 1976 v Sw (sub) (1)
Bremner, W. J. (Leeds U), 1965 v Sp; 1966 v E, Pol, P, Br, I (2); 1967 v W, Ni, E; 1968 v W, E; 1969 v W, E, Ni, D, A, WG, Cy (2); 1970 v Ei, WG, A; 1971 v W, E; 1972 v P, Bel, Ho, Ni, W, E, Y, Cz, Br; 1973 v D (2), E (2), Ni (sub), Sw, Br; 1974 v Cz, WG, Ni, W, E, Bel, N, Z, Br, Y; 1975 v Sp (2); 1976 v D (54)
Brennan, F. (Newcastle U), 1947 v W, Ni; 1953 v W, Ni, E; 1954 v Ni, E (7)
Breslin, B. (Hibernian), 1897 v W (1)
Brewster, G. (Everton), 1921 v E (1)
Brogan, J. (Celtic), 1971 v W, Ni, P, E (4)
Brown, A. (St Mirren), 1890 v W; 1891 v W (2)
Brown, A. (Middlesbrough), 1904 v E (1)
Brown, A. D. (East Fife), 1950 v Sw, P, F; (with Blackpool), 1952 v USA, D, Se; 1953 v W; 1954 v W, E, N (2), Fi, A, U (14)
Brown, G. C. P. (Rangers), 1931 v W; 1932 v E, W, Ni; 1933 v E; 1934 v A; 1935 v E, W; 1936 v E, W; 1937 v G, E, W, Ni, Cz; 1938 v E, W, Cz, Ho (19)
Brown, H. (Partick T), 1947 v W, Bel, L (3)
Brown, J. (Cambuslang), 1890 v W (1)
Brown, J. B. (Clyde), 1939 v W (1)
Brown, J. G. (Sheffield U), 1975 v R (1)
Brown, R. (Dumbarton), 1884 v W, Ni (2)
Brown, R. (Rangers), 1947 v Ni; 1949 v Ni; 1952 v E (3)
Brown, R. jun. (Dumbarton), 1885 v W (1)
Brown, W. D. F. (Dundee), 1958 v F; 1959 v E, W, Ni; (with Tottenham H), 1960 v W, Ni, Pol, A, H, T; 1962 v Ni, W, E, Cz; 1963 v W, Ni, E, A; 1964 v Ni, W, N; 1965 v E, Fi, Pol, Sp; 1966 v Ni, Pol, I (28)
Browning, J. (Celtic), 1914 v W (1)
Brownlie, J. (Third Lanark), 1909 v E, Ni; 1910 v E, W, Ni; 1911 v W, Ni; 1912 v W, Ni, E; 1913 v W, Ni, E; 1914 v W, Ni, E (16)
Brownlie, J. (Hibernian), 1971 v USSR; 1972 v Pe, Ni, E; 1973 v D (2); 1976 v R (7)
Bruce, D. (Vale of Leven), 1890 v W (1)
Bruce, R. F. (Middlesbrough), 1934 v A (1)
Buchan, M. M. (Aberdeen), 1972 v P (sub), Bel; (with Manchester U), W, Y, Cz, Br; 1973 v D (2), E; 1974 v WG, Ni, W, N, Br, Y; 1975 v EG, Sp, P; 1976 v D, R; 1977 v Fi, Cz, Ch, Arg, Br; 1978 v EG, W (sub), Ni, Pe, Ir, Ho; 1979 v A, N, P (34)
Buchanan, J. (Cambuslang), 1889 v Ni (1)
Buchanan, J. (Rangers), 1929 v E; 1930 v E (2)
Buchanan, P. S. (Chelsea), 1938 v Cz (1)
Buchanan, R. (Abercorn), 1891 v W (1)
Buckley, P. (Aberdeen), 1954 v N; 1955 v W, Ni (3)
Buick, A. (Hearts), 1902 v W, Ni (2)
Burchill, M. J. (Celtic), 2000 v Bos (sub), Li, E (sub + sub), F (sub), Ho (sub) (6)
Burley, C. W. (Chelsea), 1995 v J, Ec, Fa; 1996 v Gr, Se, Aus, D, US, Co (sub), Ho (sub), E (sub), Sw; 1997 v A, La, Se, Es, A, Se, Ma, Bl; (with Celtic), 1998 v Bl, La, F, Co, US (sub), Br, N, Mor; 1999 v Fa, CzR; 2000 v Bos, Es, Bos, Li, E (2); (with Derby Co), Ho, Ei; 2001 v Cro, Aus, Bel, Sm; 2002 v Cro, Bel, La; 2003 v A (46)
Burley, G. (Ipswich T), 1979 v W, Ni, E, Arg, N; 1980 v P, Ni, E (sub), Pol; 1982 v W (sub), E (11)
Burns, F. (Manchester U), 1970 v A (1)
Burns, K. (Birmingham C), 1974 v WG; 1975 v EG (sub), Sp (2); 1977 v Cz (sub), W, Se, W (sub); (with Nottingham F), 1978 v Ni (sub), W, E, Pe, Ir; 1979 v N; 1980 v Pe, A, Bel; 1981 v Is, Ni, W (20)
Burns, T. (Celtic), 1981 v Ni; 1982 v Ho (sub), W; 1983 v Bel (sub), Ni, Ca (1 + 1 sub); 1988 v E (sub) (8)
Busby, M. W. (Manchester C), 1934 v W (1)

Cairns, T. (Rangers), 1920 v W; 1922 v E; 1923 v E, W; 1924 v Ni; 1925 v W, E, Ni (8)
Calderhead, D. (Q of S Wanderers), 1889 v Ni (1)
Calderwood, C. (Tottenham H), 1995 v Ru, Sm, J, Ec, Fa; 1996 v Gr, Fi, Se, Sm, US, Co, Ho, E, Sw; 1997 v A, La, Se, Es (2), A, Se; 1998 v Bl, La, F, D, Fi, Co, US, Br, N; 1999 v Li, Es; (with Aston Villa), Fa, CzR; 2000 v Bos (1 + sub) (36)
Calderwood, R. (Cartvale), 1885 v Ni, E, W (3)
Caldow, E. (Rangers), 1957 v Sp (2), Sw, WG, E; 1958 v Ni, W, Sw, Par, H, Pol, Y, F; 1959 v E, W, Ni, WG, Ho, P; 1960 v E, W, Ni, A, H, T; 1961 v E, W, Ni, Ei (2), Cz; 1962 v Ni, W, E, Cz (2), U; 1963 v W, Ni, E (40)
Caldwell, G. (Newcastle U), 2002 v F, Ng (sub), Sk, S.Af (4)
Caldwell, S. (Newcastle U), 2001 v Pol (sub); 2003 v Ei (2)
Callaghan, P. (Hibernian), 1900 v Ni (1)
Callaghan, W. (Dunfermline Ath), 1970 v Ei (sub), W (2)
Cameron, C. (Hearts), 1999 v G (sub), Fa (sub); 2000 v Li (sub), F, Ei (sub); 2001 v La (sub), Sm, Cro, Aus, Sm, Pol; (with Wolverhampton W), 2002 v Cro (sub), Bel (sub), La, F; 2003 v Ei (sub), Li (sub), A (sub), G (19)
Cameron, J. (Rangers), 1886 v Ni (1)
Cameron, J. (Queen's Park), 1896 v Ni (1)
Cameron, J. (St Mirren), 1904 v Ni; (with Chelsea), 1909 v E (2)

Campbell, C. (Queen's Park), 1874 v E; 1876 v W; 1877 v E, W; 1878 v E; 1879 v E; 1880 v E; 1881 v E; 1882 v E, W; 1884 v E; 1885 v E; 1886 v E (13)
Campbell, H. (Renton), 1889 v W (1)
Campbell, Jas (Sheffield W), 1913 v W (1)
Campbell, J. (South Western), 1880 v W (1)
Campbell, J. (Kilmarnock), 1891 v Ni; 1892 v W (2)
Campbell, John (Celtic), 1893 v E, Ni; 1898 v E, Ni; 1900 v E, Ni; 1901 v E, W, Ni; 1902 v W, Ni; 1903 v W (12)
Campbell, John (Rangers), 1899 v E, W, Ni; 1901 v Ni (4)
Campbell, K. (Liverpool), 1920 v E, W, Ni; (with Partick T), 1921 v W, Ni; 1922 v W, Ni, E (8)
Campbell, P. (Rangers), 1878 v W; 1879 v W (2)
Campbell, P. (Morton), 1898 v W (1)
Campbell, R. (Falkirk), 1947 v Bel, L; (with Chelsea), 1950 v Sw, P, F (5)
Campbell, W. (Morton), 1947 v Ni; 1948 v E, Bel, Sw, F (5)
Carabine, J. (Third Lanark), 1938 v Ho; 1939 v E, Ni (3)
Carr, W. M. (Coventry C), 1970 v Ni, W, E; 1971 v D; 1972 v Pe; 1973 v D (sub) (6)
Cassidy, J. (Celtic), 1921 v W, Ni; 1923 v Ni; 1924 v W (4)
Chalmers, S. (Celtic), 1965 v W, Fi; 1966 v P (sub), Br; 1967 v Ni (5)
Chalmers, W. (Rangers), 1885 v Ni (1)
Chalmers, W. S. (Queen's Park), 1929 v Ni (1)
Chambers, T. (Hearts), 1894 v W (1)
Chaplin, G. D. (Dundee), 1908 v W (1)
Cheyne, A. G. (Aberdeen), 1929 v E, N, G, Ho; 1930 v F (5)
Christie, A. J. (Queen's Park), 1898 v W; 1899 v E, Ni (3)
Christie, R. M. (Queen's Park), 1884 v E (1)
Clark, J. (Celtic), 1966 v Br; 1967 v W, Ni, USSR (4)
Clark, R. B. (Aberdeen), 1968 v W, Ho; 1970 v Ni; 1971 v W, Ni, E, D, P, USSR; 1972 v Bel, Ni, W, E, Cz, Br; 1973 v D, E (17)
Clarke, S. (Chelsea), 1988 v H, Bel, Bul, S.Ar, Ma; 1994 v Ho (6)
Cleland, J. (Royal Albert), 1891 v Ni (1)
Clements, R. (Leith Ath), 1891 v Ni (1)
Clunas, W. L. (Sunderland), 1924 v E; 1926 v W (2)
Collier, W. (Raith R), 1922 v W (1)
Collins, J. (Hibernian), 1988 v S.Ar; 1990 v EG, Pol (sub), Ma (sub); (with Celtic), 1991 v Sw (sub), Bul (sub); 1992 v Ni (sub), Fi; 1993 v P, Ma, G, P, Es (2); 1994 v Sw, Ho (sub), A, Ho; 1995 v Fi, Fa, Ru, Gr, Ru, Sm, Fa; 1996 v Gr, Fi, Se, Sm, Aus, D, US (sub), Co, Ho, E, Sw; (with Monaco), 1997 v A, La, Se, Es, A, Se, Ma; 1998 v Bl, La, F, Fi, Co, US, Br, N, Mor; (with Everton), 1999 v Li; 2000 v Bos, Es, Bos, E (2) (58)
Collins, R. Y. (Celtic), 1951 v W, Ni, A; 1955 v Y, A, H; 1956 v Ni, W; 1957 v E, W, Sp (2), Sw, WG; 1958 v Ni, W, Sw, H, Pol, Y, F, Par; (with Everton), 1959 v E, W, Ni, WG, Ho, P; (with Leeds U), 1965 v E, Pol, Sp (31)
Collins, T. (Hearts), 1909 v W (1)
Colman, D. (Aberdeen), 1911 v E, W, Ni; 1913 v Ni (4)
Colquhoun, E. P. (Sheffield U), 1972 v P, Ho, Pe, Y, Cz, Br; 1973 v D (2), E (9)
Colquhoun, J. (Hearts), 1988 v S.Ar (sub), Ma (sub) (2)
Combe, J. R. (Hibernian), 1948 v E, Bel, Sw (3)
Conn, A. (Hearts), 1956 v A (1)
Conn, A. (Tottenham H), 1975 v Ni (sub), E (2)
Connachan, E. D. (Dunfermline Ath), 1962 v Cz, U (2)
Connelly, G. (Celtic), 1974 v Cz, WG (2)
Connolly, J. (Everton), 1973 v Sw (1)
Connor, J. (Airdrieonians), 1886 v Ni (1)
Connor, J. (Sunderland), 1930 v F; 1932 v Ni; 1934 v E; 1935 v Ni (4)
Connor, R. (Dundee), 1986 v Ho; (with Aberdeen), 1988 v S.Ar (sub); 1989 v E; 1991 v R (4)
Cook, W. L. (Bolton W), 1934 v E; 1935 v W, Ni (3)
Cooke, C. (Dundee), 1966 v W, I; (with Chelsea), P, Br; 1968 v E, Ho; 1969 v W, Ni, A, WG (sub), Cy (2); 1970 v A; 1971 v Bel; 1975 v Sp, P (16)
Cooper, D. (Rangers), 1980 v Pe, A (sub); 1984 v W, E; 1985 v Y, Ic, Sp (2), W; 1986 v W (sub), EG, Aus (2), Ho, WG (sub), U (sub); 1987 v Bul, L, Ei, Br; (with Motherwell), 1990 v N, Eg (22)
Cormack, P. B. (Hibernian), 1966 v Br; 1969 v D (sub); 1970 v Ei, WG; (with Nottingham F), 1971 v D (sub), W, P, E; 1972 v Ho (sub) (9)
Cowan, J. (Aston Villa), 1896 v E; 1897 v E; 1898 v E (3)
Cowan, J. (Morton), 1948 v Bel, Sw; F; 1949 v E, W, F; 1950 v E, W, Ni, Sw, P, F; 1951 v E, W, Ni, A (2), D, F, Bel; 1952 v Ni, W, USA, D, Se (25)
Cowan, W. D. (Newcastle U), 1924 v E (1)
Cowie, D. (Dundee), 1953 v E, Se; 1954 v Ni, W, Fi, N, A, U; 1955 v W, Ni, A, H; 1956 v W, A; 1957 v Ni, W; 1958 v H, Pol, Y, Par (20)
Cox, C. J. (Hearts), 1948 v F (1)
Cox, S. (Rangers), 1949 v E, F; 1950 v E, F, W, Ni, Sw, P; 1951 v E, D, F, Bel, A; 1952 v Ni, W, USA, D, Se; 1953 v W, Ni, E; 1954 v W, Ni, E (24)
Craig, A. (Motherwell), 1929 v N, Ho; 1932 v E (3)
Craig, J. (Celtic), 1977 v Se (sub) (1)
Craig, J. P. (Celtic), 1968 v W (1)
Craig, T. (Rangers), 1927 v Ni; 1928 v Ni; 1929 v N, G, Ho; 1930 v Ni, E, W (8)
Craig, T. B. (Newcastle U), 1976 v Sw (1)
Crainey, S. (Celtic), 2002 v F, Ng; 2003 v D (sub), Fa (4)
Crapnell, J. (Airdrieonians), 1929 v E, N, G; 1930 v F; 1931 v Ni, Sw; 1932 v E, F; 1933 v Ni (9)
Crawford, D. (St Mirren), 1894 v W, Ni; 1900 v W (3)
Crawford, J. (Queen's Park), 1932 v F, Ni; 1933 v E, W, Ni (5)
Crawford, S. (Raith R), 1995 v Ec (sub); (with Dunfermline Ath), 2001 v Pol (sub); 2002 v F; 2003 v Fa (sub), Ic, Ca, P, Ei, Ic, Li, A (sub), Nz, G (13)
Crerand, P. T. (Celtic), 1961 v Ei (2), Cz; 1962 v Ni, W, E, Cz (2), U; 1963 v W, Ni; (with Manchester U), 1964 v Ni; 1965 v E, Pol, Fi; 1966 v Pol (16)
Cringan, W. (Celtic), 1920 v W; 1922 v E, Ni; 1923 v W, E (5)
Crosbie, J. A. (Ayr U), 1920 v W; (with Birmingham), 1922 v E (2)
Croal, J. A. (Falkirk), 1913 v Ni; 1914 v E, W (3)
Cropley, A. J. (Hibernian), 1972 v P, Bel (2)
Cross, J. H. (Third Lanark), 1903 v Ni (1)
Cruickshank, J. (Hearts), 1964 v WG; 1970 v W, E; 1971 v D, Bel; 1976 v R (6)
Crum, J. (Celtic), 1936 v E; 1939 v Ni (2)
Cullen, M. J. (Luton T), 1956 v A (1)
Cumming, D. S. (Middlesbrough), 1938 v E (1)
Cumming, J. (Hearts), 1955 v E, H, P, Y; 1960 v E, Pol, A, H, T (9)
Cummings, G. (Partick T), 1935 v E; 1936 v W, Ni; (with Aston Villa), E; 1937 v G; 1938 v W, Ni, Cz; 1939 v E (9)
Cummings, W. (Chelsea), 2002 v Hk (sub) (1)
Cunningham, A. N. (Rangers), 1920 v Ni; 1921 v W, E; 1922 v Ni; 1923 v E, W; 1924 v E, Ni; 1926 v E, Ni; 1927 v E, W (12)
Cunningham, W. C. (Preston NE), 1954 v N (2), U, Fi, A; 1955 v W, E, H (8)
Curran, H. P. (Wolverhampton W), 1970 v A; 1971 v Ni, E, D, USSR (sub) (5)

Dailly, C. (Derby Co), 1997 v W, Ma, Bl; 1998 v Bl, La, F, D, Fi, Co, US, Br, N, Mor; (with Blackburn R), 1999 v Li; 2000 v Bos (sub), Es, Bos, Li, E (2), F, Ho, Ei; 2001 v La, Sm, Aus; (with West Ham U), Pol; 2002 v Cro, Bel, La, F, Ng, Sk, S.Af, Hk; 2003 v D, Fa, Ic, Ca, P, Ei, Ic, Li, A, Nz, G (46)
Dalglish, K. (Celtic), 1972 v Bel (sub), Ho; 1973 v D (1+1 sub), E (2), W, Ni, Sw, Br; 1974 v Cz (2), WG (2), Ni, W, E, Bel, N (sub), Z, Br, Y; 1975 v EG, Sp (sub+1), Se, P, W, Ni, E, R; 1976 v D (2), R, Sw, Ni, E; 1977 v Fi, Cz, W (2), Se, Ni, E, Ch, Arg, Br; (with Liverpool), 1978 v EG, Cz, W, Bul, Ni (sub), W, E, Pe, Ir, Ho; 1979 v A, N, P, W, Ni, E, Arg, N; 1980 v Pe, A, Bel (2), P, Ni, W, E, Pol, H; 1981 v Se, P, Is; 1982 v Se, Ni, P (sub), Sp, Ho, Ni, W, E, Nz, Br (sub); 1983 v Bel, Sw; 1984 v U, Bel, EG; 1985 v Y, Ic, Sp, W; 1986 v EG, Aus, R; 1987 v Bul (sub), L (102)
Davidson, C. I. (Blackburn R), 1999 v Li (sub), Es, Fa, CzR, G, Fa, CzR; 2000 v Es, Bos, Li, E, F; (with Leicester C), 2001 v La, Pol; 2002 v La; 2003 v Ic (sub), Ca (sub) (17)
Davidson, D. (Queen's Park), 1878 v W; 1879 v W; 1880 v W; 1881 v E, W (5)
Davidson, J. A. (Partick T), 1954 v N (2), A, U; 1955 v W, Ni, E, H (8)
Davidson, S. (Middlesbrough), 1921 v E (1)
Dawson, A. (Rangers), 1980 v Pol (sub), H; 1983 v Ni, Ca (2) (5)
Dawson, J. (Rangers), 1935 v Ni; 1936 v E; 1937 v G, E, W, Ni, A, Cz; 1938 v W, Ho, Ni; 1939 v E, Ni, H (14)
Deans, J. (Celtic), 1975 v EG, Sp (2)
Delaney, J. (Celtic), 1936 v W, Ni; 1937 v G, E, A, Cz; 1938 v Ni; 1939 v W, Ni; (with Manchester U), 1947 v E; 1948 v E, W, Ni (13)
Devlin, P. J. (Birmingham C), 2003 v Ca, P (sub), Ei (sub), Ic (sub), Li (sub), A, Nz, G (8)
Dewar, G. (Dumbarton), 1888 v Ni; 1889 v E (2)
Dewar, N. (Third Lanark), 1932 v E, F; 1933 v W (3)
Dick, J. (West Ham U), 1959 v E (1)
Dickie, M. (Rangers), 1897 v Ni; 1899 v Ni; 1900 v W (3)

Dickov, P. (Manchester C), 2001 v Sm (sub), Cro (sub), Aus (sub); (with Leicester C), 2003 v Fa (4)
Dickson, W. (Dumbarton), 1888 v Ni (1)
Dickson, W. (Kilmarnock), 1970 v Ni, W, E; 1971 v D, USSR (5)
Divers, J. (Celtic), 1895 v W (1)
Divers, J. (Celtic), 1939 v Ni (1)
Divine, A. (Falkirk), 1910 v W (1)
Dobie, R. S. (WBA), 2002 v Sk, S.Af, Hk (sub); 2003 v D (sub), Fa, P (6)
Docherty, T. H, (Preston NE), 1952 v W; 1953 v E, Se; 1954 v N (2), A, U; 1955 v W, E, H (2), A; 1957 v E, Y, Sp (2), Sw, WG; 1958 v Ni, W, E, Sw; (with Arsenal), 1959 v W, E, Ni (25)
Dodds, D. (Dundee U), 1984 v U (sub), Ni (2)
Dodds, J. (Celtic), 1914 v E, W, Ni (3)
Dodds, W. (Aberdeen), 1997 v La (sub), W, Bl (sub); 1998 v Bl (sub); (with Dundee U), 1999 v Es (sub), Fa, G, Fa, CzR; 2000 v Bos, Es, Bos, Li (sub), E (2); (with Rangers), F, Ho, Ei; 2001 v La, Sm, Aus, Bel, Sm, Pol; 2002 v Cro (sub), Bel (26)
Doig, J. E. (Arbroath), 1887 v Ni; 1889 v Ni; (with Sunderland), 1896 v E; 1899 v E; 1903 v E (5)
Donachie, W. (Manchester C), 1972 v Pe, Ni, E, Y, Cz, Br; 1973 v D, E, W, Ni; 1974 v Ni; 1976 v R, Ni, W, E; 1977 v Fi, Cz, W (2), Se, Ni, E, Ch, Arg, Br; 1978 v EG, W, Bul, W, E, Ir, Ho; 1979 v A, N, P (sub) (35)
Donaldson, A. (Bolton W), 1914 v E, Ni, W; 1920 v E, Ni; 1922 v Ni (6)
Donnachie, J. (Oldham Ath), 1913 v E; 1914 v E, Ni (3)
Donnelly, S. (Celtic), 1997 v W (sub), Ma (sub); 1998 v La (sub), F (sub), D (sub), Fi (sub), Co (sub), US (sub); 1999 v Es (sub), Fa (10)
Dougall, C. (Birmingham C), 1947 v W (1)
Dougall, J. (Preston NE), 1939 v E (1)
Dougan, R. (Hearts), 1950 v Sw (1)
Douglas, A. (Chelsea), 1911 v Ni (1)
Douglas, J. (Renfrew), 1880 v W (1)
Douglas, R. (Celtic), 2002 v Ng, S.Af, Hk; 2003 v D, Fa, Ic, P, Ic, Nz, G (10)
Dowds, P. (Celtic), 1892 v Ni (1)
Downie, R. (Third Lanark), 1892 v W (1)
Doyle, D. (Celtic), 1892 v E; 1893 v W; 1894 v E; 1895 v E, Ni; 1897 v E; 1898 v E, Ni (8)
Doyle, J. (Ayr U), 1976 v R (1)
Drummond, J. (Falkirk), 1892 v Ni; (with Rangers), 1894 v Ni; 1895 v Ni, E; 1896 v E, Ni; 1897 v Ni; 1898 v E; 1900 v E; 1901 v E; 1902 v E, W, Ni; 1903 v Ni (14)
Dunbar, M. (Cartvale), 1886 v Ni (1)
Duncan, A. (Hibernian), 1975 v P (sub), W, Ni, E, R; 1976 v D (sub) (6)
Duncan, D. (Derby Co), 1933 v E, W; 1934 v A, W; 1935 v E, W; 1936 v E, W, Ni; 1937 v G, E, W, Ni; 1938 v W (14)
Duncan, D. M. (East Fife), 1948 v Bel, Sw, F (3)
Duncan, J. (Alexandra Ath), 1878 v W; 1882 v W (2)
Duncan, J. (Leicester C), 1926 v W (1)
Duncanson, J. (Rangers), 1947 v Ni (1)
Dunlop, J. (St Mirren), 1890 v W (1)
Dunlop, W. (Liverpool), 1906 v E (1)
Dunn, J. (Hibernian), 1925 v W, Ni; 1927 v Ni; 1928 v Ni, E; (with Everton), 1929 v W (6)
Durie, G. S. (Chelsea), 1988 v Bul (sub); 1989 v I (sub), Cy; 1990 v Y, EG, Eg, Se; 1991 v Sw (sub), Bul (2), USSR (sub), Sm; (with Tottenham H), 1992 v Sw, R, Sm, Ni (sub), Fi, Ca, N (sub), Ho, G; 1993 v Sw, I; 1994 v Sw, I; (with Rangers), Ho (2); 1996 v US, Ho, E, Sw; 1997 v A (sub), Se (sub), Ma (sub), Bl; 1998 v Bl, La, F, Fi (sub), Co, Br, N, Mor (43)
Durrant, I. (Rangers), 1988 v H, Bel, Ma, Sp; 1989 v N (sub); 1993 v Sw (sub), P (sub), I, P (sub); 1994 v I (sub), Ma; (with Kilmarnock), 1999 v Es, Fa (sub), G, Fa, CzR; 2000 v Bos (sub), Es, Ho (sub), Ei (sub) (20)
Dykes, J. (Hearts), 1938 v Ho; 1939 v Ni (2)

Easson, J. F. (Portsmouth), 1931 v A, Sw; 1934 v W (3)
Elliott, M. S. (Leicester C), 1998 v F (sub), D, Fi; 1999 v Li, Fa, CzR, Fa; 2000 v Ho, Ei; 2001 v La, Sm, Cro, Aus (sub), Bel, Sm; 2002 v Cro, Bel, La (18)
Ellis, J. (Mossend Swifts), 1892 v Ni (1)
Evans, A. (Aston Villa), 1982 v Ho, Ni, E, Nz (4)
Evans, R. (Celtic), 1949 v E, W, Ni, F; 1950 v W, Ni, Sw, P; 1951 v E, A; 1952 v Ni; 1953 v Se; 1954 v Ni, W, E, N, Fi; 1955 v Ni, P, Y, A, H; 1956 v E, Ni, W, A; 1957 v WG, Sp; 1958 v Ni, W, E, Sw, H, Pol, Y, Par, F; 1959 v E, WG, Ho, P; 1960 v E, Ni, W, Pol; (with Chelsea), 1960 v A, H, T (48)
Ewart, J. (Bradford C), 1921 v E (1)
Ewing, T. (Partick T), 1958 v W, E (2)

Farm, G. N. (Blackpool), 1953 v W, Ni, E, Se; 1954 v Ni, W, E; 1959 v WG, Ho, P (10)
Ferguson, B. (Rangers), 1999 v Li; 2000 v Bos, Es (sub), E (2), F, Ei; 2001 v La, Aus, Bel; 2003 v D, Fa, Ic, Ei, Ic (15)
Ferguson, D. (Rangers), 1988 v Ma, Co (sub) (2)
Ferguson, D. (Dundee U), 1992 v US (sub), Ca, Ho (sub); 1993 v G; (with Everton) 1995 v Gr; 1997 v A, Es (7)
Ferguson, I. (Rangers), 1989 v I, Cy (sub), F; 1993 v Ma (sub), Es; 1994 v Ma, A (sub), Ho (sub); 1997 v Es (sub) (9)
Ferguson, J. (Vale of Leven), 1874 v E; 1876 v E, W; 1877 v E, W; 1878 v W (6)
Ferguson, R. (Kilmarnock), 1966 v W, E, Ho, P, Br; 1967 v W, Ni (7)
Fernie, W. (Celtic), 1954 v Fi, A, U; 1955 v W, Ni; 1957 v E, Ni, W, Y; 1958 v W, Sw, Par (12)
Findlay, R. (Kilmarnock), 1898 v W (1)
Fitchie, T. T. (Woolwich Arsenal), 1905 v W; 1906 v W, Ni; (with Queen's Park), 1907 v W (4)
Flavell, R. (Airdrieonians), 1947 v Bel, L (2)
Fleck, R. (Norwich C), 1990 v Arg, Se, Br (sub); 1991 v USSR (4)
Fleming, C. (East Fife), 1954 v Ni (1)
Fleming, J. W. (Rangers), 1929 v G, Ho; 1930 v E (3)
Fleming, R. (Morton), 1886 v Ni (1)
Forbes, A. R. (Sheffield U), 1947 v Bel, L, E; 1948 v W, Ni; (with Arsenal), 1950 v E, P, F; 1951 v W, Ni, A; 1952 v W, D, Se (14)
Forbes, J. (Vale of Leven), 1884 v E, W, Ni; 1887 v W, E (5)
Ford, D. (Hearts), 1974 v Cz (sub), WG (sub), W (3)
Forrest, J. (Rangers), 1966 v W, I; (with Aberdeen), 1971 v Bel (sub), D, USSR (5)
Forrest, J. (Motherwell), 1958 v E (1)
Forsyth, A. (Partick T), 1972 v Y, Cz, Br; 1973 v D; (with Manchester U), E; 1975 v Sp, Ni (sub), R, EG; 1976 v D (10)
Forsyth, C. (Kilmarnock), 1964 v E; 1965 v W, Ni, Fi (4)
Forsyth, T. (Motherwell), 1971 v D; (with Rangers), 1974 v Cz; 1976 v Sw, Ni, W, E; 1977 v Fi, Se, W, Ni, E, Ch, Arg, Br; 1978 v Cz, W, Ni, W (sub), E, Pe, Ir (sub), Ho (22)
Foyers, R. (St Bernards), 1893 v W; 1894 v W (2)
Fraser, D. M. (WBA), 1968 v Ho; 1969 v Cy (2)
Fraser, J. (Moffat), 1891 v Ni (1)
Fraser, M. J. E. (Queen's Park), 1880 v W; 1882 v W, E; 1883 v W, E (5)
Fraser, J. (Dundee), 1907 v Ni (1)
Fraser, W. (Sunderland), 1955 v W, Ni (2)
Freedman, D. A. (C Palace), 2002 v La, F (2)
Fulton, W. (Abercorn), 1884 v Ni (1)
Fyfe, J. H. (Third Lanark), 1895 v W (1)

Gabriel, J. (Everton), 1961 v W; 1964 v N (sub) (2)
Gallacher, H. K. (Airdrieonians), 1924 v Ni; 1925 v E, W, Ni; 1926 v W; (with Newcastle U), 1926 v E, Ni; 1927 v E, W, Ni; 1928 v E, W; 1929 v E, W, Ni; 1930 v W, Ni, F; (with Chelsea), 1934 v E; (with Derby Co), 1935 v E (20)
Gallacher, K. W. (Dundee U), 1988 v Co, E (sub); 1989 v N, I; (with Coventry C), 1991 v Sm; 1992 v R (sub), Sm (sub), Ni (sub), N (sub), Ho (sub), G (sub), C; 1993 v Sw (sub), P; (with Blackburn R), P, Es (2); 1994 v I, Ma; 1996 v Aus (sub), D, Co (sub), Ho; 1997 v Se (sub), Es (2), A, Se, W, Ma, Bl; 1998 v Bl, La, F, Fi (sub), US, Br, N, Mor; 1999 v Li, Es, Fa, CzR; 2000 v Bos (sub); (with Newcastle U), Bos, Li (sub), E, F, Ei (sub); 2001 v Sm, Cro, Bel (sub), Sm (sub) (53)
Gallacher, P. (Sunderland), 1935 v Ni (1)
Gallacher, P. (Dundee U), 2002 v Hk (sub); 2003 v Ca, Ei (sub), Li, A (5)
Galloway, M. (Celtic), 1992 v R (1)
Galt, J. H. (Rangers), 1908 v W, Ni (2)
Gardiner, I. (Motherwell), 1958 v W (1)
Gardner, D. R. (Third Lanark), 1897 v W (1)
Gardner, R. (Queen's Park), 1872 v E; 1873 v E; (with Clydesdale), 1874 v E; 1875 v E; 1878 v E (5)
Gemmell, T. (St Mirren), 1955 v P, Y (2)
Gemmell, T. (Celtic), 1966 v E; 1967 v W, Ni, E, USSR; 1968 v Ni, E; 1969 v W, Ni, E, D, A, WG, Cy; 1970 v E, Ei, WG; 1971 v Bel (18)
Gemmill, A. (Derby Co), 1971 v Bel; 1972 v P, Ho, Pe, Ni, W, E; 1976 v D, R, Ni, W, E; 1977 v Fi, Cz, W (2), Ni (sub), E (sub), Ch (sub), Arg, Br; 1978 v EG (sub); (with Nottingham F), Bul, Ni, W, E (sub), Pe (sub), Ir, Ho; 1979 v A, N, P, N; (with Birmingham C), 1980 v A, P, Ni, W, E, H; 1981 v Se, P, Is, Ni (43)

Gemmill, S. (Nottingham F), 1995 v J, Ec, Fa (sub); 1996 v Sm, D (sub), US; 1997 v Es, Se (sub), W, Ma (sub), Bl (sub); 1998 v D, Fi; (with Everton), 1999 v G, Fa (sub); 2001 v Sm (sub), Pol (sub); 2002 v Cro (sub), F (sub), Ng, Sk, S.Af, Hk; 2003 v Ca, Ei (sub), A (sub) (26)
Gibb, W. (Clydesdale), 1873 v E (1)
Gibson, D. W. (Leicester C), 1963 v A, N, Ei, Sp; 1964 v Ni; 1965 v W, Fi (7)
Gibson, J. D. (Partick T), 1926 v E; 1927 v E, W, Ni; (with Aston Villa), 1928 v E, W; 1930 v W, Ni (8)
Gibson, N. (Rangers), 1895 v E, Ni; 1896 v E, Ni; 1897 v E, Ni; 1898 v E; 1899 v E, W, Ni; 1900 v E, Ni; 1901 v W; (with Partick T), 1905 v Ni (14)
Gilchrist, J. E. (Celtic), 1922 v E (1)
Gilhooley, M. (Hull C), 1922 v W (1)
Gillespie, G. (Rangers), 1880 v W; 1881 v E, W; 1882 v E; (with Queen's Park), 1886 v W; 1890 v W; 1891 v Ni (7)
Gillespie, G. T. (Liverpool), 1988 v Bel, Bul, Sp; 1989 v N, F, Ch; 1990 v Y, EG, Eg, Pol, Ma, Br (sub); 1991 v Bul (13)
Gillespie, Jas (Third Lanark), 1898 v W (1)
Gillespie, John (Queen's Park), 1896 v W (1)
Gillespie, R. (Queen's Park), 1927 v W; 1931 v W; 1932 v F; 1933 v E (4)
Gillick, T. (Everton), 1937 v A, Cz; 1939 v W, Ni, H (5)
Gilmour, J. (Dundee), 1931 v W (1)
Gilzean, A. J. (Dundee), 1964 v W, E, N, WG; 1965 v Ni, (with Tottenham H), Sp; 1966 v Ni, W, Pol, I; 1968 v W; 1969 v W, E, WG, Cy (2), A (sub); 1970 v Ni, E (sub), WG, A; 1971 v P (22)
Glass, S. (Newcastle U), 1999 v Fa (sub) (1)
Glavin, R. (Celtic), 1977 v Se (1)
Glen, A. (Aberdeen), 1956 v E, Ni (2)
Glen, R. (Renton), 1895 v W; 1896 v W; (with Hibernian), 1900 v Ni (3)
Goram, A. L. (Oldham Ath), 1986 v EG (sub), R, Ho; 1987 v Br; (with Hibernian), 1989 v Y, I; 1990 v EG, Pol, Ma; 1991 v R, Sw, Bul (2), USSR, Sm; (with Rangers), 1992 v Sw, R, Sm, Fi, N, Ho, G, C; 1993 v Sw, P, I, Ma, P; 1994 v Ho; 1995 v Fi, Fa, Ru, Gr; 1996 v Se (sub), D (sub), Co, Ho, E, Sw; 1997 v A, La, Es; 1998 v D (sub) (43)
Gordon, J. E. (Rangers), 1912 v E, Ni; 1913 v E, Ni, W; 1914 v E, Ni; 1920 v W, E, Ni (10)
Gossland, J. (Rangers), 1884 v Ni (1)
Goudie, J. (Abercorn), 1884 v Ni (1)
Gough, C. R. (Dundee U), 1983 v Sw, Ni, W, E, Ca (3); 1984 v U, Bel, EG, Ni, W, E, F; 1985 v Sp, E, Ic; 1986 v W, EG, Aus, Is, R, E, D, WG, U; (with Tottenham H), 1987 v Bul, L, Ei (2), Bel, E, Br; 1988 v H; (with Rangers), S.Ar, Sp, Co, E; 1989 v Y, I, Cy, F, Cy; 1990 v F, Arg, EG, Eg, Pol, Ma, Cr; 1991 v USSR, Bul; 1992 v Sm, Ni, Ca, N, Ho, G, C; 1993 v Sw, P (61)
Gould, J. (Celtic), 2000 v Li; 2001 v Aus (2)
Gourlay, J. (Cambuslang), 1886 v Ni; 1888 v W (2)
Govan, J. (Hibernian), 1948 v E, W, Bel, Sw, F; 1949 v Ni (6)
Gow, D. R. (Rangers), 1888 v E (1)
Gow, J. J. (Queen's Park), 1885 v E (1)
Gow, J. R. (Rangers), 1888 v Ni (1)
Graham, A. (Leeds U), 1978 v EG (sub); 1979 v A (sub), N, W, Ni, E, Arg, N; 1980 v A; 1981 v W (10)
Graham, G. (Arsenal), 1972 v P, Ho, Ni, Y, Cz, Br; 1973 v D (2); (with Manchester U), E, W, Ni, Br (sub) (12)
Graham, J. (Annbank), 1884 v Ni (1)
Graham, J. A. (Arsenal), 1921 v Ni (1)
Grant, J. (Hibernian), 1959 v W, Ni (2)
Grant, P. (Celtic), 1989 v E (sub), Ch (2)
Gray, A. (Hibernian), 1903 v Ni (1)
Gray, A. D. (Bradford C), 2003 v Li (sub), Nz (sub) (2)
Gray, A. M. (Aston Villa), 1976 v R, Sw; 1977 v Fi, Cz; 1979 v A, N; (with Wolverhampton W), 1980 v P, E (sub); 1981 v Se, P, Is (sub), Ni; 1982 v Se (sub), Ni (sub); 1983 v Ni, W, E, Ca (1+1 sub); (with Everton), 1985 v Ic (20)
Gray, D. (Rangers), 1929 v W, Ni, G, Ho; 1930 v W, E, Ni; 1931 v W; 1933 v W, Ni (10)
Gray, E. (Leeds U), 1969 v E, Cy; 1970 v WG, A; 1971 v W, Ni; 1972 v Bel, Ho; 1976 v W, E; 1977 v Fi, W (12)
Gray, F. T. (Leeds U), 1976 v Sw; 1979 v N, P, W, Ni, E, Arg (sub); (with Nottingham F), 1980 v Bel (sub); 1981 v Se, P, Is, Ni, Is, W; (with Leeds U), Ni, E; 1982 v Se, Ni, P, Sp, Ho, W, Nz, Br, USSR; 1983 v EG, Sw, Bel, Sw, W, E, Ca (32)
Gray, W. (Pollokshields Ath), 1886 v E (1)
Green, A. (Blackpool), 1971 v Bel (sub), P (sub), Ni, E; (with Newcastle U), 1972 v W, E (sub) (6)
Greig, J. (Rangers), 1964 v E, WG; 1965 v W, Ni, E, Fi (2), Sp, Pol; 1966 v Ni, W, E, Pol, I (2), P, Ho, Br; 1967 v W, Ni, E; 1968 v Ni, W, E, Ho; 1969 v W, Ni, E, D, A, WG, Cy (2); 1970 v W, E, Ei, WG, A; 1971 v D, Bel, W (sub), Ni, E; 1976 v D (44)
Groves, W. (Hibernian), 1888 v W; (with Celtic), 1889 v Ni; 1890 v E (3)
Guilliland, W. (Queen's Park), 1891 v W; 1892 v Ni; 1894 v E; 1895 v E (4)
Gunn, B. (Norwich C), 1990 v Eg; 1993 v Es (2); 1994 v Sw, I, Ho (sub) (6)

Haddock, H. (Clyde), 1955 v E, H (2), P, Y; 1958 v E (6)
Haddow, D. (Rangers), 1894 v E (1)
Haffey, F. (Celtic), 1960 v E; 1961 v E (2)
Hamilton, A. (Queen's Park), 1885 v E, W; 1886 v E; 1888 v E (4)
Hamilton, A. W. (Dundee), 1962 v Cz, U, W, E; 1963 v W, Ni, E, A, N, Ei; 1964 v Ni, W, E, N, WG; 1965 v Ni, W, E, Fi (2), Pol, Sp; 1966 v Pol, Ni (24)
Hamilton, G. (Aberdeen), 1947 v Ni; 1951 v Bel, A; 1954 v N (2) (5)
Hamilton, G. (Port Glasgow Ath), 1906 v Ni (1)
Hamilton, J. (Queen's Park), 1892 v W; 1893 v E, Ni (3)
Hamilton, J. (St Mirren), 1924 v Ni (1)
Hamilton, R. C. (Rangers), 1899 v E, W, Ni; 1900 v W; 1901 v E, Ni; 1902 v W, Ni; 1903 v E; 1904 v Ni; (with Dundee), 1911 v W (11)
Hamilton, T. (Hurlford), 1891 v Ni (1)
Hamilton, T. (Rangers), 1932 v E (1)
Hamilton, W. M. (Hibernian), 1965 v Fi (1)
Hannah, A. B. (Renton), 1888 v W (1)
Hannah, J. (Third Lanark), 1889 v W (1)
Hansen, A. D. (Liverpool), 1979 v W, Arg; 1980 v Bel, P; 1981 v Se, P, Is; 1982 v Se, Ni, P, Sp, Ni (sub), W, E, Nz, Br, USSR; 1983 v EG, Sw, Bel, Sw; 1985 v W (sub); 1986 v R (sub); 1987 v Ei (2), L (26)
Hansen, J. (Partick T), 1972 v Bel (sub), Y (sub) (2)
Harkness, J. D. (Queen's Park), 1927 v E, Ni; 1928 v E; (with Hearts), 1929 v W, E, Ni; 1930 v E, W; 1932 v W, F; 1934 v Ni, W (12)
Harper, J. M. (Aberdeen), 1973 v D (1+1 sub); (with Hibernian), 1976 v D; (with Aberdeen), 1978 v Ir (sub) (4)
Harper, W. (Hibernian), 1923 v E, Ni, W; 1924 v E, Ni, W; 1925 v E, Ni, W; (with Arsenal), 1926 v E, Ni (11)
Harris, J. (Partick T), 1921 v W, Ni (2)
Harris, N. (Newcastle U), 1924 v E (1)
Harrower, W. (Queen's Park), 1882 v E; 1884 v Ni; 1886 v W (3)
Hartford, R. A. (WBA), 1972 v Pe, W (sub), E, Y, Cz, Br; (with Manchester C), 1976 v D, R, Ni (sub); 1977 v Cz (sub), W (sub), Se, W, Ni, E, Ch, Arg, Br; 1978 v EG, Cz, W, Bul, W, E, Pe, Ir, Ho; 1979 v A, N, P, W, Ni, E, Arg, N; (with Everton), 1980 v Pe, Bel; 1981 v Ni (sub), Is, W, Ni, E; 1982 v Se; (with Manchester C), Ni, P, Sp, Ni, W, E, Br (50)
Harvey, D. (Leeds U), 1973 v D; 1974 v Cz, WG, Ni, W, E, Bel, Z, Br, Y; 1975 v EG, Sp (2); 1976 v D (2); 1977 v Fi (sub) (16)
Hastings, A. C. (Sunderland), 1936 v Ni; 1938 v Ni (2)
Haughney, M. (Celtic), 1954 v E (1)
Hay, D. (Celtic), 1970 v Ni, W, E; 1971 v D, Bel, W, P, Ni; 1972 v P, Bel, Ho; 1973 v W, Ni, E, Sw, Br; 1974 v Cz (2), WG, Ni, W, E, Bel, N, Z, Br, Y (27)
Hay, J. (Celtic), 1905 v Ni; 1909 v Ni; 1910 v W, Ni, E; 1911 v Ni, E; (with Newcastle U), 1912 v E, W; 1914 v E, Ni (11)
Hegarty, P. (Dundee U), 1979 v W, Ni, E, Arg, N (sub); 1980 v W, E; 1983 v Ni (8)
Heggie, C. (Rangers), 1886 v Ni (1)
Henderson, G. H. (Rangers), 1904 v Ni (1)
Henderson, J. G. (Portsmouth), 1953 v Se; 1954 v Ni, E, N; 1956 v W; (with Arsenal), 1959 v W, Ni (7)
Henderson, W. (Rangers), 1963 v W, Ni, E, A, N, Ei, Sp; 1964 v W, Ni, E, N, WG; 1965 v Fi, Pol, E, Sp; 1966 v Ni, W, Pol, I, Ho; 1967 v W, Ni; 1968 v Ho; 1969 v Ni, E, Cy; 1970 v Ei; 1971 v P (29)
Hendry, E. C. J. (Blackburn R), 1993 v Es (2); 1994 v Ma, Ho, A, Ho; 1995 v Fi, Fa, Gr, Ru, Sm; 1996 v Fi, Se, Sm, Aus, D, US, Co, Ho, E, Sw; 1997 v A, Se, Es (2), A, Se; 1998 v La, D, Fi, Co, US, Br, N, Mor; (with Rangers), 1999 v Li, Es, Fa, G; 2000 v Bos, Es, Bos, E (2); (with Coventry C), F; 2001 v La, Sm, Cro, Aus (sub); (with Bolton W), Bel, Sm (51)
Hepburn, J. (Alloa Ath), 1891 v W (1)
Hepburn, R. (Ayr U), 1932 v Ni (1)
Herd, A. C. (Hearts), 1935 v Ni (1)
Herd, D. G. (Arsenal), 1959 v E, W, Ni; 1961 v Ei, Cz (5)
Herd, G. (Clyde), 1958 v E; 1960 v H, T; 1961 v W, Ni (5)
Herriot, J. (Birmingham C), 1969 v Ni, E, D, Cy (2), W (sub); 1970 v Ei (sub), WG (8)

Hewie, J. D. (Charlton Ath), 1956 v E, A; 1957 v E, Ni, W, Y, Sp (2), Sw, WG; 1958 v H, Pol, Y, F; 1959 v Ho, P; 1960 v Ni, W, Pol (19)
Higgins, A. (Kilmarnock), 1885 v Ni (1)
Higgins, A. (Newcastle U), 1910 v E, Ni; 1911 v E, Ni (4)
Highet, T. C. (Queen's Park), 1875 v E; 1876 v E, W; 1878 v E (4)
Hill, D. (Rangers), 1881 v E, W; 1882 v W (3)
Hill, D. A. (Third Lanark), 1906 v Ni (1)
Hill, F. R. (Aberdeen), 1930 v F; 1931 v W, Ni (3)
Hill, J. (Hearts), 1891 v E; 1892 v W (2)
Hogg, G (Hearts), 1896 v E, Ni (2)
Hogg, J. (Ayr U), 1922 v Ni (1)
Hogg, R. M. (Celtic), 1937 v Cz (1)
Holm, A. H. (Queen's Park), 1882 v W; 1883 v E, W (3)
Holt, D. D. (Hearts), 1963 v A, N, Ei, Sp; 1964 v WG (sub) (5)
Holt, G. J. (Kilmarnock), 2001 v La (sub), Cro (sub); (with Norwich C), 2002 v F (sub) (3)
Holton, J. A. (Manchester U), 1973 v W, Ni, E, Sw, Br; 1974 v Cz, WG, Ni, W, E, N, Z, Br, Y; 1975 v EG (15)
Hope, R. (WBA), 1968 v Ho; 1969 v D (2)
Hopkin, D. (C Palace), 1997 v Ma, Bl; (with Leeds U), 1998 v Bl (sub), F (sub); 1999 v CzR; 2000 v Bos (2) (7)
Houliston, W. (Queen of the South), 1949 v E, Ni, F (3)
Houston, S. M. (Manchester U), 1976 v D (1)
Howden, W. (Partick T), 1905 v Ni (1)
Howe, R. (Hamilton A), 1929 v N, Ho (2)
Howie, H. (Hibernian), 1949 v W (1)
Howie, J. (Newcastle U), 1905 v E; 1906 v E; 1908 v E (3)
Howieson, J. (St Mirren), 1927 v Ni (1)
Hughes, J. (Celtic), 1965 v Pol, Sp; 1966 v Ni, I (2); 1968 v E; 1969 v A; 1970 v Ei (8)
Hughes, W. (Sunderland), 1975 v Se (sub) (1)
Humphries, W. (Motherwell), 1952 v Se (1)
Hunter, A. (Kilmarnock), 1972 v Pe, Y; (with Celtic), 1973 v E; 1974 v Cz (4)
Hunter, J. (Dundee), 1909 v W (1)
Hunter, J. (Third Lanark), 1874 v E; (with Eastern), 1875 v E; (with Third Lanark), 1876 v E; 1877 v W (4)
Hunter, R. (St Mirren), 1890 v Ni (1)
Hunter, W. (Motherwell), 1960 v H, T; 1961 v W (3)
Husband, J. (Partick T), 1947 v W (1)
Hutchison, D. (Everton), 1999 v CzR (sub), G; 2000 v Bos, Es, Li, E (2), F, Ho, Ei; (with Sunderland), 2001 v La, Sm, Cro, Aus, Bel, Sm; (with West Ham U), 2002 v Cro, Bel, La; 2003 v Ei, Ic, Li, A (23)
Hutchison, T. (Coventry C), 1974 v Cz (2), WG (2), Ni, W, Bel (sub), N, Z (sub), Y (sub); 1975 v EG, Sp (2), P, E (sub), R (sub); 1976 v D (17)
Hutton, J. (Aberdeen), 1923 v E, W, Ni; 1924 v Ni; 1926 v W, E, Ni; (with Blackburn R), 1927 v Ni; 1928 v W, Ni (10)
Hutton, J. (St Bernards), 1887 v Ni (1)
Hyslop, T. (Stoke C), 1896 v E; (with Rangers), 1897 v E (2)

Imlach, J. J. S. (Nottingham F), 1958 v H, Pol, Y, F (4)
Imrie, W. N. (St Johnstone), 1929 v N, G (2)
Inglis, J. (Rangers), 1883 v E, W (2)
Inglis, J. (Kilmarnock Ath), 1884 v Ni (1)
Irons, J. H. (Queen's Park), 1900 v W (1)
Irvine, B. (Aberdeen), 1991 v R; 1993 v G, Es (2); 1994 v Sw, I, Ma, A, Ho (9)

Jackson, A. (Cambuslang), 1886 v W; 1888 v Ni (2)
Jackson, A. (Aberdeen), 1925 v E, W, Ni; (with Huddersfield T), 1926 v E, W, Ni; 1927 v W, Ni; 1928 v E, W; 1929 v E, W, Ni; 1930 v E, W, Ni, F (17)
Jackson, C. (Rangers), 1975 v Se, P (sub), W; 1976 v D, R, Ni, W, E (8)
Jackson, D. (Hibernian), 1995 v Ru, Sm, J, Ec, Fa; 1996 v Gr, Fi (sub), Se (sub), Sm (sub), Aus (sub), D (sub), US; 1997 v La, Se, Es, A, Se, W, Ma, Bl; (with Celtic), 1998 v D, Fi, Co, US, Br, N; 1999 v Li, Es (sub) (28)
Jackson, J. (Partick T), 1931 v A, I, Sw; 1933 v E; (with Chelsea), 1934 v E; 1935 v E; 1936 v W, Ni (8)
Jackson, T. A. (St Mirren), 1904 v W, E, Ni; 1905 v W; 1907 v W, Ni (6)
James, A. W. (Preston NE), 1926 v W; 1928 v E; 1929 v E, Ni; (with Arsenal), 1930 v E, W, Ni; 1933 v W (8)
Jardine, A. (Rangers), 1971 v D (sub); 1972 v P, Bel, Ho; 1973 v E, Sw, Br; 1974 v Cz (2), WG (2), Ni, W, E, Bel, N, Z, Br, Y; 1975 v EG, Sp (2), Se, P, W, Ni, E; 1977 v Se (sub), Ch (sub), Br (sub); 1978 v Cz, W, Ni, Ir; 1980 v Pe, A, Bel (2) (38)
Jarvie, A. (Airdrieonians), 1971 v P (sub), Ni (sub), E (sub) (3)
Jenkinson, T. (Hearts), 1887 v Ni (1)
Jess, E. (Aberdeen), 1993 v I (sub), Ma; 1994 v Sw (sub), I, Ho (sub), A, Ho (sub); 1995 v Fi (sub); 1996 v Se (sub), Sm; (with Coventry C), US, Co (sub), E (sub); (with Aberdeen), 1998 v D (sub); 1999 v CzR, G (sub), Fa (sub), CzR (sub) (18)
Johnston, A. (Sunderland), 1999 v Es, Fa, CzR (sub), G, Fa, CzR; 2000 v Es, F (sub), Ei (sub); (with Rangers), 2001 v Sm (sub), Cro, Sm; (with Middlesbrough), 2002 v Ng (sub), Sk, S.Af, Hk; 2003 v D (sub), Fa (18)
Johnston, L. H. (Clyde), 1948 v Bel, Sw (2)
Johnston, M. (Watford), 1984 v W (sub), E (sub), F; 1985 v Y; (with Celtic), Ic, Sp (2), W; 1986 v EG; 1987 v Bul, Ei (2), L; (with Nantes), 1988 v H, Bel, L, S.Ar, Sp, Co, E; 1989 v N, Y, I, Cy, F, Cy, E, Ch (sub); (with Rangers), 1990 v F, N, EG, Pol, Ma, Cr, Se, Br; 1992 v Sw, Sm (sub) (38)
Johnston, R. (Sunderland), 1938 v Cz (1)
Johnston, W. (Rangers), 1966 v W, E, Pol, Ho; 1968 v W, E; 1969 v Ni (sub); 1970 v Ni; 1971 v D; (with WBA), 1977 v Se, W (sub), Ni, E, Ch, Arg, Br; 1978 v EG, Cz, W (2), E, Pe (22)
Johnstone, D. (Rangers), 1973 v W, Ni, E, Sw, Br; 1975 v EG (sub), Se (sub); 1976 v Sw, Ni (sub), E (sub); 1978 v Bul (sub), Ni, W; 1980 v Bel (14)
Johnstone, J. (Abercorn), 1888 v W (1)
Johnstone, J. (Celtic), 1965 v W, Fi; 1966 v E; 1967 v W, USSR; 1968 v W; 1969 v A, WG; 1970 v E, WG; 1971 v D, E; 1972 v P, Bel, Ho, Ni, E (sub); 1974 v W, E, Bel, N; 1975 v EG, Sp (23)
Johnstone, Jas (Kilmarnock), 1894 v W (1)
Johnstone, J. A. (Hearts), 1930 v W; 1933 v W, Ni (3)
Johnstone, R. (Hibernian), 1951 v E, D, F; 1952 v Ni, E; 1953 v E, Se; 1954 v W, E, N, Fi; 1955 v Ni, H; (with Manchester C), 1955 v E; 1956 v E, Ni, W (17)
Johnstone, W. (Third Lanark), 1887 v Ni; 1889 v W; 1890 v E (3)
Jordan, J. (Leeds U), 1973 v E (sub), Sw (sub), Br; 1974 v Cz (sub+1), WG (sub), Ni (sub), W, E, Bel, N, Z, Br, Y; 1975 v EG, Sp (2); 1976 v Ni, W, E; 1977 v Cz, W, Ni, E; 1978 v EG, Cz, W; (with Manchester U), Bul, Ni, E, Pe, Ir, Ho; 1979 v A, P, W (sub), Ni, E, N; 1980 v Bel, Ni (sub), W, E, Pol; 1981 v Is, W, E; (with AC Milan), 1982 v Se, Ho, W, E, USSR (52)

Kay, J. L. (Queen's Park), 1880 v E; 1882 v E, W; 1883 v E, W; 1884 v W (6)
Keillor, A. (Montrose), 1891 v W; 1892 v Ni; (with Dundee), 1894 v Ni; 1895 v W; 1896 v W; 1897 v W (6)
Keir, L. (Dumbarton), 1885 v W; 1886 v Ni; 1887 v E, W; 1888 v E (5)
Kelly, H. T. (Blackpool), 1952 v USA (1)
Kelly, J. (Renton), 1888 v E; (with Celtic), 1889 v E; 1890 v E; 1892 v E; 1893 v E, Ni; 1894 v W; 1896 v Ni (8)
Kelly, J. C. (Barnsley), 1949 v W, Ni (2)
Kelso, R. (Renton), 1885 v W, Ni; 1886 v W; 1887 v E, W; 1888 v E, Ni; (with Dundee), 1898 v Ni (8)
Kelso, T. (Dundee), 1914 v W (1)
Kennaway, J. (Celtic), 1934 v A (1)
Kennedy, A. (Eastern), 1875 v E; 1876 v E, W; (with Third Lanark), 1878 v E; 1882 v W; 1884 v W (6)
Kennedy, J. (Hibernian), 1897 v W (1)
Kennedy, J. (Celtic), 1964 v W, E, WG; 1965 v W, Ni, Fi (6)
Kennedy, S. (Aberdeen), 1978 v Bul, W, E, Pe, Ho; 1979 v A, P; 1982 v P (sub) (8)
Kennedy, S. (Partick T), 1905 v W (1)
Kennedy, S. (Rangers), 1975 v Se, P, W, Ni, E (5)
Ker, G. (Queen's Park), 1880 v E; 1881 v E, W; 1882 v W, E (5)
Ker, W. (Granville), 1872 v E; (with Queen's Park), 1873 v E (2)
Kerr, A. (Partick T), 1955 v A, H (2)
Kerr, B. (Newcastle U), 2003 v Nz (sub) (1)
Kerr, P. (Hibernian), 1924 v Ni (1)
Key, G. (Hearts), 1902 v Ni (1)
Key, W. (Queen's Park), 1907 v Ni (1)
King, A. (Hearts), 1896 v E, W; (with Celtic), 1897 v Ni; 1898 v Ni; 1899 v Ni, W (6)
King, J. (Hamilton A), 1933 v Ni; 1934 v Ni (2)
King, W. S. (Queen's Park), 1929 v W (1)
Kinloch, J. D. (Partick T), 1922 v Ni (1)
Kinnaird, A. F. (Wanderers), 1873 v E (1)
Kinnear, D. (Rangers), 1938 v Cz (1)
Kyle, K. (Sunderland), 2002 v Sk (sub), S.Af, Hk; 2003 v D, Fa, Ca (sub), P (sub), Nz (8)

Lambert, P. (Motherwell), 1995 v J, Ec (sub); (with Borussia Dortmund), 1997 v La (sub), Se (sub), A, Se, Bl; 1998 v Bl,

La; (with Celtic), Fi (sub), Co, US, Br, N, Mor; 1999 v Li, CzR, G, Fa, CzR; 2000 v Bos, Li, Ho, Ei; 2001 v Bel, Sm; 2002 v Cro, Bel, F, Ng; 2003 v D, Fa, Ic, P, Ei, Ic, Li, G (38)
Lambie, J. A. (Queen's Park), 1886 v Ni; 1887 v Ni; 1888 v E (3)
Lambie, W. A. (Queen's Park), 1892 v Ni; 1893 v W; 1894 v E; 1895 v E, Ni; 1896 v E, Ni; 1897 v E, Ni (9)
Lamont, D. (Pilgrims), 1885 v Ni (1)
Lang, A. (Dumbarton), 1880 v W (1)
Lang, J. J. (Clydesdale), 1876 v W; (with Third Lanark), 1878 v W (2)
Latta, A. (Dumbarton), 1888 v W; 1889 v E (2)
Law, D. (Huddersfield T), 1959 v W, Ni, Ho, P; 1960 v Ni, W; (with Manchester C), 1960 v E, Pol, A; 1961 v E, Ni; (with Torino), 1962 v Cz (2), E; (with Manchester U), 1963 v W, Ni, E, A, N, Ei, Sp; 1964 v W, E, N, WG; 1965 v W, Ni, E, Fi (2), Pol, Sp; 1966 v Ni, E, Pol; 1967 v W, E, USSR; 1968 v Ni; 1969 v Ni, A, WG; 1972 v Pe, Ni, W, E, Y, Cz, Br; (with Manchester C), 1974 v Cz (2), WG (2), Ni, Z (55)
Law, G. (Rangers), 1910 v E, Ni, W (3)
Law, T. (Chelsea), 1928 v E; 1930 v E (2)
Lawrence, J. (Newcastle U), 1911 v E (1)
Lawrence, T. (Liverpool), 1963 v Ei; 1969 v W, WG (3)
Lawson, D. (St Mirren), 1923 v E (1)
Leckie, R. (Queen's Park), 1872 v E (1)
Leggat, G. (Aberdeen), 1956 v E; 1957 v W; 1958 v Ni, H, Pol, Y, Par; (with Fulham), 1959 v E, W, Ni, WG, Ho; 1960 v E, Ni, W, Pol, A, H (18)
Leighton, J. (Aberdeen), 1983 v EG, Sw, Bel, Sw, W, E, Ca (2); 1984 v U, Bel, Ni, W, E, F; 1985 v Y, Ic, Sp (2), W, E, Ic; 1986 v W, EG, Aus (2), Is, D, WG, U; 1987 v Bul, Ei (2), L, Bel, E; 1988 v H, Bel, Bul, L, S.Ar, Ma, Sp; (with Manchester U), Co, E; 1989 v N, Cy, F, Cy, E, Ch; 1990 v Y, F, N, Arg, Ma (sub, Cr, Se, Br; (with Hibernian), 1994 v Ma, A, Ho; 1995 v Gr (sub), Ru, Sm, J, Ec, Fa; 1996 v Gr, Fi, Se, Sm, Aus, D, US; 1997 v Se, Es, A, Se, W (sub), Ma, Bl; (with Aberdeen), 1998 v Bl, La, D, Fi, US, Br, N, Mor; 1999 v Li, Es (91)
Lennie, W. (Aberdeen), 1908 v W, Ni (2)
Lennox, R. (Celtic), 1967 v Ni, E, USSR; 1968 v W, L; 1969 v D, A, WG, Cy (sub); 1970 v W (sub) (10)
Leslie, L. G. (Airdrieonians), 1961 v W, Ni, Ei (2), Cz (5)
Levein, C. (Hearts), 1990 v Arg, EG, Eg (sub), Pol, Ma (sub), Se; 1992 v R, Sm; 1993 v P, G, P; 1994 v Sw, Ho; 1995 v Fi, Fa, Ru (16)
Liddell, W. (Liverpool), 1947 v W, Ni; 1948 v E, W, Ni; 1950 v E, W, P, F; 1951 v W, Ni, E, A; 1952 v W, Ni, E, USA, D, Se; 1953 v W, Ni, E; 1954 v W; 1955 v P, Y, A, H; 1956 v Ni (28)
Liddle, D. (East Fife), 1931 v A, I, Sw (3)
Lindsay, D. (St Mirren), 1903 v Ni (1)
Lindsay, J. (Dumbarton), 1880 v W; 1881 v W, E; 1884 v W, E; 1885 v W, E; 1886 v E (8)
Lindsay, J. (Renton), 1888 v E; 1893 v E, Ni (3)
Linwood, A. B. (Clyde), 1950 v W (1)
Little, R. J. (Rangers), 1953 v Se (1)
Livingstone, G. T. (Manchester C), 1906 v E; (with Rangers), 1907 v W (2)
Lochhead, A. (Third Lanark), 1889 v W (1)
Logan, J. (Ayr U), 1891 v W (1)
Logan, T. (Falkirk), 1913 v Ni (1)
Logie, J. T. (Arsenal), 1953 v Ni (1)
Loney, W. (Celtic), 1910 v W, Ni (2)
Long, H. (Clyde), 1947 v Ni (1)
Longair, W. (Dundee), 1894 v Ni (1)
Lorimer, P. (Leeds U), 1970 v A (sub); 1971 v W, Ni; 1972 v Ni (sub), W, E; 1973 v D (2), E (2); 1974 v WG (sub), E, Bel, N, Z, Br, Y; 1975 v Sp (sub); 1976 v D (2), R (sub) (21)
Love, A. (Aberdeen), 1931 v A, I, Sw (3)
Low, A. (Falkirk), 1934 v Ni (1)
Low, T. P. (Rangers), 1897 v Ni (1)
Low, W. L. (Newcastle U), 1911 v E, W; 1912 v Ni; 1920 v E, Ni (5)
Lowe, J. (St Bernards), 1887 v Ni (1)
Lowe, J. (Cambuslang), 1891 v Ni (1)
Lundie, J. (Hibernian), 1886 v W (1)
Lyall, J. (Sheffield W), 1905 v E (1)

McAdam, J. (Third Lanark), 1880 v W (1)
McAllister, B. (Wimbledon), 1997 v W, Ma, Bl (sub) (3)
McAllister, G. (Leicester C), 1990 v EG, Pol, Ma (sub); (with Leeds U), 1991 v R, Sw, Bul, USSR (sub), Sm; 1992 v Sw (sub), Sm, Ni, Fi (sub), US, Ca, N, Ho, G, C; 1993 v Sw, P, I, Ma; 1994 v Sw, I, Ma, Ho, A, Ho; 1995 v Fi, Ru, Gr, Ru, Sm; 1996 v Gr, Fi, Se, Sm, Aus, D, US (sub), Co, Ho, E, Sw; (with Coventry C), 1997 v A, La, Es (2), A, Se, W, Ma, Bl; 1998 v Bl, La, F; 1999 v CzR (57)
McArthur, D. (Celtic), 1895 v E, Ni; 1899 v W (3)
McAtee, A. (Celtic), 1913 v W (1)
McAulay, J. (Arthurlie), 1884 v Ni (1)
McAulay, J. D. (Dumbarton), 1882 v W; 1883 v E, W; 1884 v E; 1885 v E, W; 1886 v E; 1887 v E, W (9)
McAuley, R. (Rangers), 1932 v Ni, W (2)
McAvennie, F. (West Ham U), 1986 v Aus (2), D (sub), WG (sub); (with Celtic), 1988 v S.Ar (5)
McBain, E. (St Mirren), 1894 v W (1)
McBain, N. (Manchester U), 1922 v E; (with Everton), 1923 v Ni; 1924 v W (3)
McBride, J. (Celtic), 1967 v W, Ni (2)
McBride, P. (Preston NE), 1904 v E; 1906 v E; 1907 v E, W; 1908 v E; 1909 v W (6)
McCall, J. (Renton), 1886 v W; 1887 v E, W; 1888 v E; 1890 v E (5)
McCall, S. M. (Everton), 1990 v Arg, EG, Eg (sub), Pol, Ma, Cr, Se, Br; 1991 v Sw, USSR, Sm; (with Rangers), 1992 v Sw, R, Sm, US, Ca, N, Ho, G, C; 1993 v Sw, P (2); 1994 v I, Ho, A (sub), Ho; 1995 v Fi (sub), Ru, Gr; 1996 v Gr, D, US (sub), Co, Ho, E, Sw; 1997 v A, La; 1998 v D (sub) (40)
McCalliog, J. (Sheffield W), 1967 v E, USSR; 1968 v Ni; 1969 v D; (with Wolverhampton W), 1971 v P (5)
McCallum, N. (Renton), 1888 v Ni (1)
McCann, N. (Hearts), 1999 v Li (sub); (with Rangers), CzR; 2000 v Bos, Es (sub), E, F (sub), Ho, Ei; 2001 v La, Sm, Aus (sub); 2002 v Cro, La, F, Ng; 2003 v Ei (16)
McCann, R. J. (Motherwell), 1959 v WG; 1960 v E, Ni, W; 1961 v E (5)
McCartney, W. (Hibernian), 1902 v Ni (1)
McClair, B. (Celtic), 1987 v L, Ei, E, Br (sub); (with Manchester U), 1988 v Bul, Ma (sub), Sp (sub); 1989 v N, Y, I (sub), Cy, F (sub); 1990 v N (sub), Arg (sub); 1991 v Bul (2), Sm; 1992 v Sw (sub), R, Ni, US, Ca (sub), N, Ho, G, C; 1993 v Sw, P (sub), Es (2) (30)
McClory, A. (Motherwell), 1927 v W; 1928 v Ni; 1935 v W (3)
McCloy, P. (Ayr U), 1924 v E; 1925 v E (2)
McCloy, P. (Rangers), 1973 v W, Ni, Sw, Br (4)
McCoist, A. (Rangers), 1986 v Ho; 1987 v L (sub), Ei (sub), Bel, E, Br; 1988 v H, Bel, Ma, Sp, Co, E; 1989 v Y (sub), F, Cy, E; 1990 v Y, F, N, EG (sub), Eg, Pol, Ma (sub), Cr (sub), Se (sub), Br; 1991 v R, Sw, Bul (2), USSR; 1992 v Sw, Sm, Ni, Fi (sub), US, Ca, N, Ho, G, C; 1993 v Sw, P, I, Ma, P; 1996 v Gr (sub), Fi (sub), Sm (sub), Aus, D (sub), Co, E (sub), Sw; 1997 v A, Se (sub), Es (sub), A (sub); 1998 v Bl (sub); (with Kilmarnock), 1999 v Li, Es (61)
McColl, A. (Renton), 1888 v Ni (1)
McColl, I. M. (Rangers), 1950 v E, F; 1951 v W, Ni, Bel; 1957 v E, Ni, W, Y, Sp, Sw, WG; 1958 v Ni, E (14)
McColl, R. S. (Queen's Park), 1896 v W, Ni; 1897 v Ni; 1898 v Ni; 1899 v Ni, E, W; 1900 v E, W; 1901 v E, W; (with Newcastle U), 1902 v E; (with Queen's Park), 1908 v Ni (13)
McColl, W. (Renton), 1895 v W (1)
McCombie, A. (Sunderland), 1903 v E, W; (with Newcastle U), 1905 v E, W (4)
McCorkindale, J. (Partick T), 1891 v W (1)
McCormick, R. (Abercorn), 1886 v W (1)
McCrae, D. (St Mirren), 1929 v N, G (2)
McCredie, A. (Rangers), 1893 v W; 1894 v E (2)
McCreadie, E. G. (Chelsea), 1965 v E, Sp, Fi, Pol; 1966 v P, Ni, W, Pol, I; 1967 v E, USSR; 1968 v Ni, W, E, Ho; 1969 v W, Ni, E, D, A, WG, Cy (2) (23)
McCulloch, D. (Hearts), 1935 v W; (with Brentford), 1936 v E; 1937 v W, Ni; 1938 v Cz; (with Derby Co), 1939 v H, W (7)
MacDonald, A. (Rangers), 1976 v Sw (1)
McDonald, J. (Edinburgh University), 1886 v E (1)
McDonald, J. (Sunderland), 1956 v W, Ni (2)
MacDougall, E. J. (Norwich C) 1975 v Se, P, W, Ni, E; 1976 v D, R (sub) (7)
McDougall, J. (Vale of Leven), 1877 v E, W; 1878 v E; 1879 v E, W (5)
McDougall, J. (Airdrieonians), 1926 v Ni (1)
McDougall, J. (Liverpool), 1931 v I, A (2)
McFadden, J. (Motherwell), 2002 v S.Af (sub); 2003 v Ca (sub), A, Nz (4)
McFadyen, W. (Motherwell), 1934 v A, W (2)
Macfarlane, A. (Dundee), 1904 v W; 1906 v W; 1908 v W; 1909 v Ni; 1911 v W (5)
Macfarlane, W. (Hearts), 1947 v L (1)
McFarlane, R. (Greenock Morton), 1896 v W (1)
McGarr, E. (Aberdeen), 1970 v Ei, A (2)
McGarvey, F. P. (Liverpool), 1979 v Ni (sub), Arg; (with Celtic), 1984 v U, Bel (sub), EG (sub), Ni, W (7)
McGeoch, A. (Dumbreck), 1876 v E, W; 1877 v E, W (4)

McGhee, J. (Hibernian), 1886 v W (1)
McGhee, M. (Aberdeen), 1983 v Ca (1+1 sub); 1984 v Ni (sub), E (4)
McGinlay, J. (Bolton W), 1994 v A, Ho; 1995 v Fa, Ru, Gr, Ru, Sm, Fa; 1996 v Se; 1997 v Se, Es (1 + sub), A (sub) (13)
McGonagle, W. (Celtic), 1933 v E; 1934 v A, E, Ni; 1935 v Ni, W (6)
McGrain, D. (Celtic), 1973 v W, Ni, E, Sw, Br; 1974 v Cz (2), WG, W (sub), E, Bel, N, Z, Br, Y; 1975 v Sp, Se, P, W, Ni, E, R; 1976 v D (2), Sw, Ni, W, E; 1977 v Fi, Cz, W (2), Se, Ni, E, Ch, Arg, Br; 1978 v EG, Cz; 1980 v Bel, P, Ni, W, E, Pol, H; 1981 v Se, P, Is, Ni, Is, W (sub), Ni, E; 1982 v Se, Sp, Ho, Ni, E, Nz, USSR (sub) (62)
McGregor, J. C. (Vale of Leven), 1877 v E, W; 1878 v E; 1880 v E (4)
McGrory, J. (Celtic), 1928 v Ni; 1931 v E; 1932 v Ni, W; 1933 v E, Ni; 1934 v Ni (7)
McGrory, J. E. (Kilmarnock), 1965 v Ni, Fi; 1966 v P (3)
McGuire, W. (Beith), 1881 v E, W (2)
McGurk, F. (Birmingham), 1934 v W (1)
McHardy, H. (Rangers), 1885 v Ni (1)
McInally, A. (Aston Villa), 1989 v Cy (sub), Ch; (with Bayern Munich), 1990 v Y (sub), F (sub), Arg, Pol (sub), Ma, Cr (8)
McInally, J. (Dundee U), 1987 v Bel, Br; 1988 v Ma (sub); 1991 v Bul (2); 1992 v US (sub), N (sub), C (sub); 1993 v G, P (10)
McInally, T. B. (Celtic), 1926 v Ni; 1927 v W (2)
McInnes, D. (WBA), 2003 v D (sub), P (sub) (2)
McInnes, T. (Cowlairs), 1889 v Ni (1)
McIntosh, W. (Third Lanark), 1905 v Ni (1)
McIntyre, A. (Vale of Leven), 1878 v E; 1882 v E (2)
McIntyre, H. (Rangers), 1880 v W (1)
McIntyre, J. (Rangers), 1884 v W (1)
MacKay, D. (Celtic), 1959 v E, WG, Ho, P; 1960 v E, Pol, A, H, T; 1961 v W, Ni; 1962 v Ni, Cz, U (sub) (14)
Mackay, D. C. (Hearts), 1957 v Sp; 1958 v F; 1959 v W, Ni; (with Tottenham H), 1959 v WG, E; 1960 v W, Ni, A, Pol, H, T; 1961 v W, Ni, E; 1963 v E, A, N; 1964 v Ni, W, N; 1966 v Ni (22)
Mackay, G. (Hearts), 1988 v Bul (sub), L (sub), S.Ar (sub), Ma (4)
McKay, J. (Blackburn R), 1924 v W (1)
McKay, R. (Newcastle U), 1928 v W (1)
McKean, R. (Rangers), 1976 v Sw (sub) (1)
McKenzie, D. (Brentford), 1938 v Ni (1)
Mackenzie, J. A. (Partick T), 1954 v W, E, N, Fi, A, U; 1955 v E, H; 1956 v A (9)
McKeown, M. (Celtic), 1889 v Ni; 1890 v E (2)
McKie, J. (East Stirling), 1898 v W (1)
McKillop, T. R. (Rangers), 1938 v Ho (1)
McKimmie, S. (Aberdeen), 1989 v E, Ch; 1990 v Arg, Eg, Cr (sub), Br; 1991 v R, Sw, Bul, Sm; 1992 v Sw, R, Ni, Fi, US, Ca (sub), N (sub), Ho, G, C; 1993 v P, Es (sub); 1994 v Sw, I, Ho, A, Ho; 1995 v Fi, Fa, Ru, Gr, Ru, Fa; 1996 v Gr, Fi, Se, D, Co, Ho, E (40)
McKinlay, D. (Liverpool), 1922 v W, Ni (2)
McKinlay, T. (Celtic), 1996 v Gr, Fi, D, Co, E, Sw; 1997 v A, La, Se, Es (sub + 1), A, Se, W, Ma, Bl; 1998 v Bl, La (sub), F (sub), US, Br (sub), Mor (sub) (22)
McKinlay, W. (Dundee U), 1994 v Ma, Ho (sub), A, Ho; 1995 v Fa (sub), Ru, Gr, Ru (sub), Sm (sub), J, Ec, Fa; 1996 v Fi (sub), Se (sub); (with Blackburn R), Sm (sub), Aus, D (sub), Ho (sub); 1997 v Se, Es (sub); 1998 v La (sub), F, D, Fi, Co (sub), US, Br (sub); 1999 v Es, Fa (29)
McKinnon, A. (Queen's Park), 1874 v E (1)
McKinnon, R. (Rangers), 1966 v W, E, I (2), Ho, Br; 1967 v W, Ni, E; 1968 v Ni, W, E, Ho; 1969 v D, A, WG, Cy; 1970 v Ni, W, E, Ei, WG, A; 1971 v D, Bel, P, USSR, D (28)
McKinnon, R. (Motherwell), 1994 v Ma; 1995 v J, Fa (3)
MacKinnon, W. (Dumbarton), 1883 v E, W; 1884 v E, W (4)
MacKinnon, W. W. (Queen's Park), 1872 v E; 1873 v E; 1874 v E; 1875 v E; 1876 v E, W; 1877 v E; 1878 v E; 1879 v E (9)
McLaren, A. (St Johnstone), 1929 v N, G, Ho; 1933 v W, Ni (5)
McLaren, A. (Preston NE), 1947 v E, Bel, L; 1948 v W (4)
McLaren, A. (Hearts), 1992 v US, Ca, N; 1993 v I, Ma, G, Es (sub + 1); 1994 v I, Ma, Ho, A; 1995 v Fi, Fa; (with Rangers), Ru, Gr, Ru, Sm, J, Ec, Fa; 1996 v Fi, Se, Sm (24)
McLaren, A. (Kilmarnock), 2001 v Pol (sub) (1)
McLaren, J. (Hibernian), 1888 v W; (with Celtic), 1889 v E; 1890 v E (3)
McLean, A. (Celtic), 1926 v W, Ni; 1927 v W, E (4)
McLean, D. (St Bernards), 1896 v W; 1897 v Ni (2)
McLean, D. (Sheffield W), 1912 v E (1)
McLean, G. (Dundee), 1968 v Ho (1)
McLean, T. (Kilmarnock), 1969 v D, Cy, W; 1970 v Ni, W; 1971 v D (6)
McLeish, A. (Aberdeen), 1980 v P, Ni, W, E, Pol, H; 1981 v Se, Is, Ni, Is, Ni, E; 1982 v Se, Sp, Ni, Br (sub); 1983 v Bel, Sw (sub), W, E, Ca (3); 1984 v U, Bel, EG, Ni, W, E, F; 1985 v Y, Ic, Sp (2), W, E, Ic; 1986 v W, EG, Aus (2), E, Ho, D; 1987 v Bel, E, Br; 1988 v Bel, Bul, L, S.Ar (sub), Ma, Sp, Co, E; 1989 v N, Y, I, Cy, F, Cy, E, Ch; 1990 v Y, F, N, Arg, EG, Eg, Cr, Se, Br; 1991 v R, Sw, USSR, Bul; 1993 v Ma (77)
McLeod, D. (Celtic), 1905 v Ni; 1906 v E, W, Ni (4)
McLeod, J. (Dumbarton), 1888 v Ni; 1889 v W; 1890 v Ni; 1892 v E; 1893 v W (5)
MacLeod, J. M. (Hibernian), 1961 v E, Ei (2), Cz (4)
MacLeod, M. (Celtic), 1985 v E (sub); 1987 v Ei, L, E, Br; (with Borussia Dortmund), 1988 v Co, E; 1989 v I, Ch; 1990 v Y, F, N (sub), Arg, EG, Pol, Se Br; (with Hibernian), 1991 v R, Sw, USSR (sub) (20)
McLeod, W. (Cowlairs), 1886 v Ni (1)
McLintock, A. (Vale of Leven), 1875 v E; 1876 v E; 1880 v E (3)
McLintock, F. (Leicester C), 1963 v N (sub), Ei, Sp; (with Arsenal), 1965 v Ni; 1967 v USSR; 1970 v Ni; 1971 v W, Ni, E (9)
McLuckie, J. S. (Manchester C), 1934 v W (1)
McMahon, A. (Celtic), 1892 v E; 1893 v E, Ni; 1894 v E; 1901 v Ni; 1902 v W (6)
McMenemy, J. (Celtic), 1905 v Ni; 1909 v Ni; 1910 v E, W; 1911 v Ni, W, E; 1912 v W; 1914 v W, Ni, E; 1920 v Ni (12)
McMenemy, J. (Motherwell), 1934 v W (1)
McMillan, I. L. (Airdrieonians), 1952 v E, USA, D; 1955 v E; 1956 v E; (with Rangers), 1961 v Cz (6)
McMillan, J. (St Bernards), 1897 v W (1)
McMillan, T. (Dumbarton), 1887 v Ni (1)
McMullan, J. (Partick T), 1920 v W; 1921 v W, Ni, E; 1924 v E, Ni; 1925 v E; 1926 v W; (with Manchester C), 1926 v E; 1927 v E, W; 1928 v E, W; 1929 v W, E, Ni (16)
McNab, A. (Morton), 1921 v E, Ni (2)
McNab, A. (Sunderland), 1937 v A; (with WBA), 1939 v E (2)
McNab, C. D. (Dundee), 1931 v E, W, A, I, Sw; 1932 v E (6)
McNab, J. S. (Liverpool), 1923 v W (1)
McNair, A. (Celtic), 1906 v W; 1907 v Ni; 1908 v E, W; 1909 v E; 1910 v W; 1912 v E, W, Ni; 1913 v E; 1914 v E, Ni; 1920 v E, W, Ni (15)
McNamara, J. (Celtic), 1997 v La (sub), Se, Es, W (sub); 1998 v D, Co, US (sub), N (sub), Mor; 2000 v Ho; 2001 v Sm; 2002 v Bel (sub), F (sub); 2003 v Ic (1+sub), Li, Nz, G (sub) (18)
McNaught, W. (Raith R), 1951 v A, W, Ni; 1952 v E; 1955 v Ni (5)
McNaughton, K. (Aberdeen), 2002 v Ng; 2003 v D (2)
McNiel, H. (Queen's Park), 1874 v E; 1875 v E; 1876 v E, W; 1877 v W; 1878 v E; 1879 v E, W; 1881 v E, W (10)
McNiel, M. (Rangers), 1876 v W; 1880 v E (2)
McNeill, W. (Celtic), 1961 v E, Ei (2), Cz; 1962 v Ni, E, Cz, U; 1963 v Ei, Sp; 1964 v W, E, WG; 1965 v E, Fi, Pol, Sp; 1966 v Ni, Pol; 1967 v USSR; 1968 v E; 1969 v Cy, W, E, Cy (sub); 1970 v WG; 1972 v Ni, W, E (29)
McPhail, J. (Celtic), 1950 v W; 1951 v W, Ni, A; 1954 v Ni (5)
McPhail, R. (Airdrieonians), 1927 v E; (with Rangers), 1929 v W; 1931 v E, Ni; 1932 v W, Ni, F; 1933 v E, Ni; 1934 v A, Ni; 1935 v E; 1937 v G, E, Cz; 1938 v W, Ni (17)
McPherson, D. (Kilmarnock), 1892 v Ni (1)
McPherson, D. (Hearts), 1989 v Cy, E; 1990 v N, Ma, Cr, Se, Br; 1991 v Sw, Bul (2), USSR (sub), Sm; 1992 v Sw, R, Sm, Ni, Fi, US, Ca, N, Ho, G, C; (with Rangers), 1993 v Sw, I, Ma, P (27)
McPherson, J. (Clydesdale), 1875 v E (1)
McPherson, J. (Vale of Leven), 1879 v E, W; 1880 v E; 1881 v W; 1883 v E, W; 1884 v E; 1885 v Ni (8)
McPherson, J. (Kilmarnock), 1888 v W; (with Cowlairs), 1889 v E; 1890 v Ni, E; (with Rangers), 1892 v W; 1894 v E; 1895 v E, Ni; 1897 v Ni (9)
McPherson, J. (Hearts), 1891 v E (1)
McPherson, R. (Arthurlie), 1882 v E (1)
McQueen, G. (Leeds U), 1974 v Bel; 1975 v Sp (2), P, W, Ni, E, R; 1976 v D; 1977 v Cz, W (2), Ni, E; 1978 v EG, Cz, W; (with Manchester U), Bul, Ni, W; 1979 v A, N, P, Ni, E, N; 1980 v Pe, A, Bel; 1981 v W (30)
McQueen, M. (Leith Ath), 1890 v W; 1891 v W (2)
McRorie, D. M. (Morton), 1931 v W (1)
McSpadyen, A. (Partick T), 1939 v E, H (2)
McStay, P. (Celtic), 1984 v U, Bel, EG, Ni, W, E (sub); 1985 v Y, Ic, Sp (2), W; 1986 v EG (sub), Aus, Is, U; 1987 v Bul, Ei (1+1 sub), L (sub), Bel, E, Br; 1988 v H, Bel, Bul, L, S.Ar, Sp, Co, E; 1989 v N, Y, I, Cy, F, Cy, E, Ch; 1990 v Y, F, N,

Arg, EG (sub), Eg, Pol (sub), Ma, Cr, Se (sub), Br; 1991 v R, USSR, Bul; 1992 v Sm, Fi, US, Ca, N, Ho, G, C; 1993 v Sw, P, I, Ma, P, Es (2); 1994 v I (sub), Ho; 1995 v Fi, Fa, Ru; 1996 v Aus; 1997 v Es (2), A (sub) (76)
McStay, W. (Celtic), 1921 v W, Ni; 1925 v E, Ni, W; 1926 v E, Ni, W; 1927 v E, Ni, W; 1928 v W, Ni (13)
McSwegan, G. (Hearts), 2000 v Bos (sub), Li (2)
McTavish, J. (Falkirk), 1910 v Ni (1)
McWattie, G. C. (Queen's Park), 1901 v W, Ni (2)
McWilliam, P. (Newcastle U), 1905 v E; 1906 v E; 1907 v E, W; 1909 v E, W; 1910 v E; 1911 v W (8)
Macari, L. (Celtic), 1972 v W (sub), E, Y, Cz, Br; 1973 v D; (with Manchester U), E (2), W (sub), Ni (sub); 1975 v Se, P (sub), W, E (sub), R; 1977 v Ni (sub), E (sub), Ch, Arg; 1978 v EG, W, Bul, Pe (sub), Ir (24)
Macauley, A. R. (Brentford), 1947 v E; (with Arsenal), 1948 v E, W, Ni, Bel, Sw, F (7)
Madden, J. (Celtic), 1893 v W; 1895 v W (2)
Main, F. R. (Rangers), 1938 v W (1)
Main, J. (Hibernian), 1909 v Ni (1)
Maley, W. (Celtic), 1893 v E, Ni (2)
Malpas, M. (Dundee U), 1984 v F; 1985 v E, Ic; 1986 v W, Aus (2), Is, R, E, Ho, D, WG; 1987 v Bul, Ei, Bel; 1988 v Bel, Bul, L, S.Ar, Ma; 1989 v N, Y, I, Cy, F, Cy, E, Ch; 1990 v Y, F, N, Eg, Pol, Ma, Cr, Se, Br; 1991 v R, Bul (2), USSR, Sm; 1992 v Sw, R, Sm, Ni, Fi, US, Ca (sub), N, Ho, G; 1993 v Sw, P, I (55)
Marshall, G. (Celtic), 1992 v US (1)
Marshall, H. (Celtic), 1899 v W; 1900 v Ni (2)
Marshall, J. (Third Lanark), 1885 v Ni; 1886 v W; 1887 v E, W (4)
Marshall, J. (Middlesbrough), 1921 v E, W, Ni; 1922 v E, W, Ni; (with Llanelly), 1924 v W (7)
Marshall, J. (Rangers), 1932 v E; 1933 v E; 1934 v E (3)
Marshall, R. W. (Rangers), 1892 v Ni; 1894 v Ni (2)
Martin, B. (Motherwell), 1995 v J, Ec (2)
Martin, F. (Aberdeen), 1954 v N (2), A, U; 1955 v E, H (6)
Martin, N. (Hibernian), 1965 v Fi, Pol; (with Sunderland), 1966 v I (3)
Martis, J. (Motherwell), 1961 v W (1)
Mason, J. (Third Lanark), 1949 v E, W, Ni; 1950 v Ni; 1951 v Ni, Bel, A (7)
Massie, A. (Hearts), 1932 v Ni, W, F; 1933 v Ni; 1934 v E, Ni; 1935 v E, Ni, W; 1936 v W, Ni; (with Aston Villa), 1936 v E; 1937 v G, E, W, Ni, A; 1938 v W (18)
Masson, D. S. (QPR), 1976 v Ni, W, E; 1977 v Fi, Cz, W, Ni, E, Ch, Arg, Br; 1978 v EG, Cz, W; (with Derby Co), Ni, E, Pe (17)
Mathers, D. (Partick T), 1954 v Fi (1)
Matteo, D. (Leeds U), 2001 v Aus, Bel, Sm; 2002 v Cro, Bel, F (6)
Maxwell, W. S. (Stoke C), 1898 v E (1)
May, J. (Rangers), 1906 v W, Ni; 1908 v E, Ni; 1909 v W (5)
Meechan, P. (Celtic), 1896 v Ni (1)
Meiklejohn, D. D. (Rangers), 1922 v W; 1924 v W; 1925 v W, Ni, E; 1928 v W, Ni; 1929 v E, Ni; 1930 v E, Ni; 1931 v E; 1932 v W, Ni; 1934 v A (15)
Menzies, A. (Hearts), 1906 v E (1)
Mercer, R. (Hearts), 1912 v W; 1913 v Ni (2)
Middleton, R. (Cowdenbeath), 1930 v Ni (1)
Millar, A. (Hearts), 1939 v W (1)
Millar, J. (Rangers), 1897 v E; 1898 v E, W (3)
Millar, J. (Rangers), 1963 v A, Ei (2)
Miller, C. (Dundee U), 2001 v Pol (1)
Miller, J. (St Mirren), 1931 v E, I, Sw; 1932 v F; 1934 v E (5)
Miller, K. (Rangers), 2001 v Pol (sub); (with Wolverhampton W), 2003 v Ic, Li, A (sub), G (5)
Miller, P. (Dumbarton), 1882 v E; 1883 v E, W (3)
Miller, T. (Liverpool), 1920 v E; (with Manchester U), 1921 v E, Ni (3)
Miller, W. (Third Lanark), 1876 v E (1)
Miller, W. (Celtic), 1947 v E, W, Bel, L; 1948 v W, Ni (6)
Miller, W. (Aberdeen), 1975 v R; 1978 v Bul; 1980 v Bel, W, E, Pol, H; 1981 v Se, P, Is (sub), Ni, W, Ni, E; 1982 v Ni, P, Ho, Br, USSR; 1983 v EG, Sw (2), W, E, Ca (3); 1984 v U, Bel, EG, W, E, F; 1985 v Y, Ic, Sp (2), W, E, Ic; 1986 v W, EG, Aus (2), Is, R, E, Ho, D, WG, U; 1987 v Bul, E, Br; 1988 v H, L, S.Ar, Ma, Sp, Co, E; 1989 v N, Y; 1990 v Y, N (65)
Mills, W. (Aberdeen), 1936 v W, Ni; 1937 v W (3)
Milne, J. V. (Middlesbrough), 1938 v E; 1939 v E (2)
Mitchell, D. (Rangers), 1890 v Ni; 1892 v E; 1893 v E, Ni; 1894 v E (5)
Mitchell, J. (Kilmarnock), 1908 v Ni; 1910 v Ni, W (3)
Mitchell, R. C. (Newcastle U), 1951 v D, F (2)
Mochan, N. (Celtic), 1954 v N, A, U (3)
Moir, W. (Bolton W), 1950 v E (1)
Moncur, R. (Newcastle U), 1968 v Ho; 1970 v Ni, W, E, Ei; 1971 v D, Bel, W, P, Ni, E, D; 1972 v Pe, Ni, W, E (16)
Morgan, H. (St Mirren), 1898 v W; (with Liverpool), 1899 v E (2)
Morgan, W. (Burnley), 1968 v Ni; (with Manchester U), 1972 v Pe, Y, Cz, Br; 1973 v D (2), E (2), W, Ni, Sw, Br; 1974 v Cz (2), WG (2), Ni, Bel (sub), Br, Y (21)
Morris, D. (Raith R), 1923 v Ni; 1924 v E, Ni; 1925 v E, W, Ni (6)
Morris, H. (East Fife), 1950 v Ni (1)
Morrison, T. (St Mirren), 1927 v E (1)
Morton, A. L. (Queen's Park), 1920 v W, Ni; (with Rangers), 1921 v E; 1922 v E, W; 1923 v E, W, Ni; 1924 v E, W, Ni; 1925 v E, W, Ni; 1927 v E, Ni; 1928 v E, W, Ni; 1929 v E, W, Ni; 1930 v E, W, Ni; 1931 v E, W, Ni; 1932 v E, W, F (31)
Morton, H. A. (Kilmarnock), 1929 v G, Ho (2)
Mudie, J. K. (Blackpool), 1957 v W, Ni, E, Y, Sw, Sp (2), WG; 1958 v Ni, E, W, Sw, H, Pol, Y, Par, F (17)
Muir, W. (Dundee), 1907 v Ni (1)
Muirhead, T. A. (Rangers), 1922 v Ni; 1923 v E; 1924 v W; 1927 v Ni; 1928 v Ni; 1929 v W, Ni; 1930 v W (8)
Mulhall, G. (Aberdeen), 1960 v Ni; (with Sunderland), 1963 v Ni; 1964 v Ni (3)
Munro, A. D. (Hearts), 1937 v W, Ni; (with Blackpool), 1938 v Ho (3)
Munro, F. M. (Wolverhampton W), 1971 v Ni (sub), E (sub), D, USSR; 1975 v Se, W (sub), Ni, E, R (9)
Munro, I. (St Mirren), 1979 v Arg, N; 1980 v Pe, A, Bel, W, E (7)
Munro, N. (Abercorn), 1888 v W; 1889 v E (2)
Murdoch, J. (Motherwell), 1931 v Ni (1)
Murdoch, R. (Celtic), 1966 v W, E, I (2); 1967 v Ni; 1968 v Ni; 1969 v W, Ni, E, WG, Cy; 1970 v A (12)
Murphy, F. (Celtic), 1938 v Ho (1)
Murray, I. (Hibernian), 2003 v Ca (sub) (1)
Murray, J. (Renton), 1895 v W (1)
Murray, J. (Hearts), 1958 v E, H, Pol, Y, F (5)
Murray, J. W. (Vale of Leven), 1890 v W (1)
Murray, P. (Hibernian), 1896 v Ni; 1897 v W (2)
Murray, S. (Aberdeen), 1972 v Bel (1)
Mutch, G. (Preston NE), 1938 v E (1)

Napier, C. E. (Celtic), 1932 v E; 1935 v E, W; (with Derby Co), 1937 v Ni, A (5)
Narey, D. (Dundee U), 1977 v Se (sub); 1979 v P, Ni (sub), Arg; 1980 v P, Ni, Pol, H; 1981 v W, E (sub); 1982 v Ho, W, E, Nz (sub), Br, USSR; 1983 v EG, Sw, Bel, Ni, W, E, Ca (3); 1986 v Is, R, Ho, WG, U; 1987 v Bul, E, Bel; 1989 v I, Cy (35)
Naysmith, G. A. (Hearts), 2000 v Ei; 2001 v La (sub), Sm, Cro; (with Everton), 2002 v Cro, Bel; 2003 v D, Ic, P, Ei, Ic, Li, A, Nz, G (15)
Neil, R. G. (Hibernian), 1896 v W; (with Rangers), 1900 v W (2)
Neill, R. W. (Queen's Park), 1876 v W; 1877 v E, W; 1878 v W; 1880 v E (5)
Nellies, P. (Hearts), 1913 v Ni; 1914 v W (2)
Nelson, J. (Cardiff C), 1925 v W, Ni; 1928 v E; 1930 v F (4)
Nevin, P. K. F. (Chelsea), 1986 v R (sub), E (sub); 1987 v L, Ei, Bel (sub); 1988 v L; (with Everton), 1989 v Cy, E; 1991 v R (sub), Bul (sub), Sm (sub); 1992 v US, G (sub), C (sub); (with Tranmere R), 1993 v Ma, P (sub), Es; 1994 v Sw, Ma, Ho, A (sub), Ho; 1995 v Fa, Ru (sub), Sm; 1996 v Se (sub), Sm, Aus (sub) (28)
Niblo, T. D. (Aston Villa), 1904 v E (1)
Nibloe, J. (Kilmarnock), 1929 v E, N, Ho; 1930 v W; 1931 v E, Ni, A, I, Sw; 1932 v E, F (11)
Nicholas, C. (Celtic), 1983 v Sw, Ni, E, Ca (3); (with Arsenal), 1984 v Bel, F (sub); 1985 v Y (sub), Ic (sub), Sp (sub), W (sub); 1986 v Is, R (sub), E, D, U (sub); 1987 v Bul, E (sub); (with Aberdeen), 1989 v Cy (sub) (20)
Nicholson, B. (Dunfermline Ath), 2001 v Pol; 2002 v La (2)
Nicol, S. (Liverpool), 1985 v Y, Ic, Sp, W; 1986 v W, EG, Aus, E, D, WG, U; 1988 v H, Bul, S.Ar, Sp, Co, E; 1989 v N, Y, Cy, F; 1990 v Y, F; 1991 v Sw, USSR, Sm; 1992 v Sw (27)
Nisbet, J. (Ayr U), 1929 v N, G, Ho (3)
Niven, J. B. (Moffatt), 1885 v Ni (1)

O'Connor, G. (Hibernian), 2002 v Ng (sub), Sk, Hk (sub) (3)
O'Donnell, F. (Preston NE), 1937 v E, A, Cz; 1938 v W; (with Blackpool), E, Ho (6)
O'Donnell, P. (Motherwell), 1994 v Sw (sub) (1)
Ogilvie, D. H. (Motherwell), 1934 v A (1)
O'Hare, J. (Derby Co), 1970 v W, Ni, E; 1971 v D, Bel, W, Ni; 1972 v P, Bel, Ho (sub), Pe, Ni, W (13)

O'Neil, B. (Celtic), 1996 v Aus; (with Wolfsburg), 1999 v G (sub); 2000 v Li, Ho (sub), Ei; (with Derby Co), 2001 v Aus (6)
O'Neil, J. (Hibernian), 2001 v Pol (1)
Ormond, W. E. (Hibernian), 1954 v E, N, Fi, A, U; 1959 v E (6)
O'Rourke, F. (Airdrieonians), 1907 v Ni (1)
Orr, J. (Kilmarnock), 1892 v W (1)
Orr, R. (Newcastle U), 1902 v E; 1904 v E (2)
Orr, T. (Morton), 1952 v Ni, W (2)
Orr, W. (Celtic), 1900 v Ni; 1903 v Ni; 1904 v W (3)
Orrock, R. (Falkirk), 1913 v W (1)
Oswald, J. (Third Lanark), 1889 v E; (with St Bernards), 1895 v E; (with Rangers), 1897 v W (3)

Parker, A. H. (Falkirk), 1955 v P, Y, A; 1956 v E, Ni, W, A; 1957 v Ni, W, Y; 1958 v Ni, W, E, Sw; (with Everton), Par (15)
Parlane, D. (Rangers), 1973 v W, Sw, Br; 1975 v Sp (sub), Se, P, W, Ni, E, R; 1976 v D (sub); 1977 v W (12)
Parlane, R. (Vale of Leven), 1878 v W; 1879 v E, W (3)
Paterson, G. D. (Celtic), 1939 v Ni (1)
Paterson, J. (Leicester C), 1920 v E (1)
Paterson, J. (Cowdenbeath), 1931 v A, I, Sw (3)
Paton, A. (Motherwell), 1952 v D, Se (2)
Paton, D. (St Bernards), 1896 v W (1)
Paton, M. (Dumbarton), 1883 v E; 1884 v W; 1885 v W, E; 1886 v E (5)
Paton, R. (Vale of Leven), 1879 v E, W (2)
Patrick, J. (St Mirren), 1897 v E, W (2)
Paul, H. McD. (Queen's Park), 1909 v E, W, Ni (3)
Paul, W. (Partick T), 1888 v W; 1889 v W; 1890 v W (3)
Paul, W. (Dykebar), 1891 v Ni (1)
Pearson, T. (Newcastle U), 1947 v E, Bel (2)
Penman, A. (Dundee), 1966 v Ho (1)
Pettigrew, W. (Motherwell), 1976 v Sw, Ni, W; 1977 v W (sub), Se (5)
Phillips, J. (Queen's Park), 1877 v E, W; 1878 v W (3)
Plenderleith, J. B. (Manchester C), 1961 v Ni (1)
Porteous, W. (Hearts), 1903 v Ni (1)
Pressley, S. J. (Hearts), 2000 v F (sub), Ei (sub); 2003 v Ic, Ca, P, Ic, Li, A, Nz, G (10)
Pringle, C. (St Mirren), 1921 v W (1)
Provan, D. (Rangers), 1964 v Ni, N; 1966 v I (2), Ho (5)
Provan, D. (Celtic), 1980 v Bel (2 sub), P (sub), Ni (sub); 1981 v Is, W, E; 1982 v Se, P, Ni (10)
Pursell, P. (Queen's Park), 1914 v W (1)

Quinn, J. (Celtic), 1905 v Ni; 1906 v Ni, W; 1908 v Ni, E; 1909 v E; 1910 v E, Ni, W; 1912 v E, W (11)
Quinn, P. (Motherwell), 1961 v E, Ei (2); 1962 v U (4)

Rae, G. (Dundee), 2001 v Pol; 2002 v La (sub); 2003 v G (sub) (3)
Rae, J. (Third Lanark), 1889 v W; 1890 v Ni (2)
Raeside, J. S. (Third Lanark), 1906 v W (1)
Raisbeck, A. G. (Liverpool), 1900 v E; 1901 v E; 1902 v E; 1903 v E, W; 1904 v E; 1906 v E; 1907 v E (8)
Rankin, G. (Vale of Leven), 1890 v Ni; 1891 v E (2)
Rankin, R. (St Mirren), 1929 v N, G, Ho (3)
Redpath, W. (Motherwell), 1949 v W, Ni; 1951 v E, D, F, Bel, A; 1952 v Ni, E (9)
Reid, J. G. (Airdrieonians), 1914 v W; 1920 v W; 1924 v Ni (3)
Reid, R. (Brentford), 1938 v E, Ni (2)
Reid, W. (Rangers), 1911 v E, W, Ni; 1912 v Ni; 1913 v E, W, Ni; 1914 v E, Ni (9)
Reilly, L. (Hibernian), 1949 v E, W, F; 1950 v W, Ni, Sw, F; 1951 v W, E, D, F, Bel, A; 1952 v Ni, W, E, USA, D, Se; 1953 v Ni, W, E, Se; 1954 v W; 1955 v H (2), P, Y, A, E; 1956 v E, W, Ni, A; 1957 v E, Ni, W, Y (38)
Rennie, H. G. (Hearts), 1900 v E, Ni; (with Hibernian), 1901 v E; 1902 v E, Ni, W; 1903 v Ni, W; 1904 v Ni; 1905 v W; 1906 v Ni; 1908 v Ni, W (13)
Renny-Tailyour, H. W. (Royal Engineers), 1873 v E (1)
Rhind, A. (Queen's Park), 1872 v E (1)
Richmond, A. (Queen's Park), 1906 v W (1)
Richmond, J. T. (Clydesdale), 1877 v E; (with Queen's Park), 1878 v E; 1882 v W (3)
Ring, T. (Clyde), 1953 v Se; 1955 v W, Ni, E, H; 1957 v E, Sp (2), Sw, WG; 1958 v Ni, Sw (12)
Rioch, B. D. (Derby Co), 1975 v P, W, Ni, E, R; 1976 v D (2), R, Ni, W, E; 1977 v Fi, Cz, W; (with Everton), W, Ni, E, Ch, Br; 1978 v Cz; (with Derby Co), Ni, E, Pe, Ho (24)
Ritchie, A. (East Stirlingshire), 1891 v W (1)
Ritchie, H. (Hibernian), 1923 v W; 1928 v Ni (2)
Ritchie, J. (Queen's Park), 1897 v W (1)
Ritchie, P. S. (Hearts), 1999 v G (sub), CzR; 2000 v Li, E; (with Bolton W), F, Ho (6)
Ritchie, W. (Rangers), 1962 v U (sub) (1)
Robb, D. T. (Aberdeen), 1971 v W, E, P, D (sub), USSR (5)
Robb, W. (Rangers), 1926 v W; (with Hibernian), 1928 v W (2)
Robertson, A. (Clyde), 1955 v P, A, H; 1958 v Sw, Par (5)
Robertson, D. (Rangers), 1992 v Ni; 1994 v Sw, Ho (3)
Robertson, G. (Motherwell), 1910 v W; (with Sheffield W), 1912 v W; 1913 v E, Ni (4)
Robertson, G. (Kilmarnock), 1938 v Cz (1)
Robertson, H. (Dundee), 1962 v Cz (1)
Robertson, J. (Dundee), 1931 v A, I (2)
Robertson, J. (Hearts), 1991 v R, Sw, Bul (sub), Sm (sub); 1992 v Sm, Ni (sub), Fi; 1993 v I (sub), Ma (sub), G, Es; 1995 v J (sub), Ec, Fa (sub); 1996 v Gr (sub), Se (16)
Robertson, J. N. (Nottingham F), 1978 v Ni, W (sub), Ir; 1979 v P, N; 1980 v Pe, A, Bel (2), P; 1981 v Se, P, Is, Ni, Is, Ni, E; 1982 v Se, Ni (2), E (sub), Nz, Br, USSR; 1983 v EG, Sw; (with Derby Co), 1984 v U, Bel (28)
Robertson, J. G. (Tottenham H), 1965 v W (1)
Robertson, J. T. (Everton), 1898 v E; (with Southampton), 1899 v E; (with Rangers), 1900 v E, W; 1901 v W, Ni, E; 1902 v W, Ni, E; 1903 v E, W; 1904 v E, W, Ni; 1905 v W (16)
Robertson, P. (Dundee), 1903 v Ni (1)
Robertson, T. (Queen's Park), 1889 v Ni; 1890 v E; 1891 v W; 1892 v Ni (4)
Robertson, T. (Hearts), 1898 v Ni (1)
Robertson, W. (Dumbarton), 1887 v E, W (2)
Robinson, R. (Dundee), 1974 v WG (sub); 1975 v Se, Ni, R (sub) (4)
Ross, M. (Rangers), 2002 v Sk, S.Af, Hk; 2003 v D, Fa, Ic, Ca, P, Nz, G (10)
Rough, A. (Partick T), 1976 v Sw, Ni, W, E; 1977 v Fi, Cz, W (2), Se, Ni, E, Ch, Arg, Br; 1978 v Cz, W, Ni, E, Pe, Ir, Ho; 1979 v A, P, W, Arg, N; 1980 v Pe, A, Bel (2), P, W, E, Pol, H; 1981 v Se, P, Is, Ni, Is, W, E; 1982 v Se, Ni, Sp, Ho, W, E, Nz, Br, USSR; (with Hibernian), 1986 v W (sub), E (53)
Rougvie, D. (Aberdeen), 1984 v Ni (1)
Rowan, A. (Caledonian), 1880 v E; (with Queen's Park), 1882 v W (2)
Russell, D. (Hearts), 1895 v E, Ni; (with Celtic), 1897 v W; 1898 v Ni; 1901 v W, Ni (6)
Russell, J. (Cambuslang), 1890 v Ni (1)
Russell, W. F. (Airdrieonians), 1924 v W; 1925 v E (2)
Rutherford, E. (Rangers), 1948 v F (1)

St John, I. (Motherwell), 1959 v WG; 1960 v E, Ni, W, Pol, A; 1961 v E; (with Liverpool), 1962 v Ni, W, E, Cz (2), U; 1963 v W, Ni, E, N, Ei (sub), Sp; 1964 v Ni; 1965 v E (21)
Sawers, W. (Dundee), 1895 v W (1)
Scarff, P. (Celtic), 1931 v Ni (1)
Schaedler, E. (Hibernian), 1974 v WG (1)
Scott, A. S. (Rangers), 1957 v Ni, Y, WG; 1958 v W, Sw; 1959 v P; 1962 v Ni, W, E, Cz, U; (with Everton), 1964 v W, N; 1965 v Fi; 1966 v P, Br (16)
Scott, J. (Hibernian), 1966 v Ho (1)
Scott, J. (Dundee), 1971 v D (sub), USSR (2)
Scott, M. (Airdrieonians), 1898 v W (1)
Scott, R. (Airdrieonians), 1894 v Ni (1)
Scoular, J. (Portsmouth), 1951 v D, F, A; 1952 v E, USA, D, Se; 1953 v W, Ni (9)
Sellar, W. (Battlefield), 1885 v E; 1886 v E; 1887 v E, W; 1888 v E; (with Queen's Park), 1891 v E; 1892 v E; 1893 v E, Ni (9)
Semple, W. (Cambuslang), 1886 v W (1)
Severin, S. (Hearts), 2002 v La (sub), Sk (sub), S.Af (sub), Hk; 2003 v D (sub), Ic (sub), Ca (sub), P (sub) (8)
Shankly, W. (Preston NE), 1938 v E; 1939 v E, W, Ni, H (5)
Sharp, G. M. (Everton), 1985 v Ic; 1986 v W, Aus (2 sub), Is, R, U; 1987 v Ei; 1988 v Bel (sub), Bul, L, Ma (12)
Sharp, J. (Dundee), 1904 v W; (with Woolwich Arsenal), 1907 v W, E; 1908 v E; (with Fulham), 1909 v W (5)
Shaw, D. (Hibernian), 1947 v W, Ni; 1948 v E, Bel, Sw, F; 1949 v W, Ni (8)
Shaw, F. W. (Pollokshields Ath), 1884 v E, W (2)
Shaw, J. (Rangers), 1947 v E, Bel, L; 1948 v Ni (4)
Shearer, D. (Aberdeen), 1994 v A (sub), Ho (sub); 1995 v Fi, Ru (sub), Sm, Fa; 1996 v Gr (7)
Shearer, R. (Rangers), 1961 v E, Ei (2), Cz (4)
Sillars, D. C. (Queen's Park), 1891 v Ni; 1892 v E; 1893 v W; 1894 v E; 1895 v W (5)
Simpson, J. (Third Lanark), 1895 v E, W, Ni (3)
Simpson, J. (Rangers), 1935 v E, W, Ni; 1936 v E, W, Ni; 1937 v G, E, W, Ni, A, Cz; 1938 v W, Ni (14)

Simpson, N. (Aberdeen), 1983 v Ni; 1984 v U (sub), F (sub); 1987 v E; 1988 v E (5)
Simpson, R. C. (Celtic), 1967 v E, USSR; 1968 v Ni, E; 1969 v A (5)
Sinclair, G. L. (Hearts), 1910 v Ni; 1912 v W, Ni (3)
Sinclair, J. W. E. (Leicester C), 1966 v P (1)
Skene, L. H. (Queen's Park), 1904 v W (1)
Sloan, T. (Third Lanark), 1904 v W (1)
Smellie, R. (Queen's Park), 1887 v Ni; 1888 v W; 1889 v E; 1891 v E; 1893 v E, Ni (6)
Smith, A. (Rangers), 1898 v E; 1900 v E, Ni, W; 1901 v E, Ni, W; 1902 v E, Ni, W; 1903 v E, Ni, W; 1904 v Ni; 1905 v W; 1906 v E, Ni; 1907 v W; 1911 v E, Ni (20)
Smith, D. (Aberdeen), 1966 v Ho; (with Rangers), 1968 v Ho (2)
Smith, G. (Hibernian), 1947 v E, Ni; 1948 v W, Bel, Sw, F; 1952 v E, USA; 1955 v P, Y, A, H; 1956 v E, Ni, W; 1957 v Sp (2), Sw (18)
Smith, H. G. (Hearts), 1988 v S.Ar (sub); 1992 v Ni, Ca (3)
Smith, J. (Ayr U), 1924 v E (1)
Smith, J. (Rangers), 1935 v Ni; 1938 v Ni (2)
Smith, J. (Aberdeen), 1968 v Ho (sub); (with Newcastle U), 1974 v WG, Ni (sub), W (sub) (4)
Smith, J. (Celtic), 2003 v Ei (sub), A (sub) (2)
Smith, J. E. (Celtic), 1959 v H, P (2)
Smith, Jas (Queen's Park), 1872 v E (1)
Smith, John (Mauchline), 1877 v E, W; 1879 v E, W; (with Edinburgh University), 1880 v E; (with Queen's Park), 1881 v W, E; 1883 v E, W; 1884 v E (10)
Smith, N. (Rangers), 1897 v E; 1898 v W; 1899 v E, W, Ni; 1900 v E, W, Ni; 1901 v Ni, W; 1902 v E, Ni (12)
Smith, R. (Queen's Park), 1872 v E; 1873 v E (2)
Smith, T. M. (Kilmarnock), 1934 v E; (with Preston NE), 1938 v E (2)
Somers, P. (Celtic), 1905 v E, Ni; 1907 v Ni; 1909 v W (4)
Somers, W. S. (Third Lanark), 1879 v E, W; (with Queen's Park), 1880 v W (3)
Somerville, G. (Queen's Park), 1886 v E (1)
Souness, G. J. (Middlesbrough), 1975 v EG, Sp, Se; (with Liverpool), 1978 v Bul, W, E (sub), Ho; 1979 v A, N, W, Ni, E; 1980 v Pe, A, Bel, P, Ni; 1981 v P, Is (2); 1982 v Ni, P, Sp, W, E, Nz, Br, USSR; 1983 v EG, Sw, Bel, Sw, W, E, Ca (2 + 1 sub); 1984 v U, Ni, W; (with Sampdoria), 1985 v Y, Ic, Sp (2), W, E, Ic; 1986 v EG, Aus (2), R, E, D, WG (54)
Speedie, D. R. (Chelsea), 1985 v E; 1986 v W, EG (sub), Aus, E; (with Coventry C), 1989 v Y (sub), I (sub), Cy (1+1 sub), Ch (10)
Speedie, F. (Rangers), 1903 v E, W, Ni (3)
Speirs, J. H. (Rangers), 1908 v W (1)
Spencer, J. (Chelsea), 1995 v Ru (sub), Gr (sub), Sm (sub), J; 1996 v Fi, Aus, D, US (sub), Co, Ho (sub), E, Sw (sub); 1997 v La; (with QPR), W (sub) (14)
Stanton, P. (Hibernian), 1966 v Ho; 1969 v Ni; 1970 v Ei, A; 1971 v D, Bel, P, USSR, D; 1972 v P, Bel, Ho, W; 1973 v W, Ni; 1974 v WG (16)
Stark, J. (Rangers), 1909 v E, Ni (2)
Steel, W. (Morton), 1947 v E, Bel, L; (with Derby Co), 1948 v F, E, W, Ni; 1949 v E, W, Ni, F; 1950 v E, W, Ni, Sw, P, F; (with Dundee), 1951 v W, Ni, E, A (2), D, F, Bel; 1952 v W; 1953 v W, E, Ni, Se (30)
Steele, D. M. (Huddersfield), 1923 v E, W, Ni (3)
Stein, C. (Rangers), 1969 v W, Ni, D, E, Cy (2); 1970 v A (sub), Ni (sub), W, E, Ei, WG; 1971 v D, USSR, Bel, D; 1972 v Cz (sub); (with Coventry C), 1973 v E (2 sub), W (sub), Ni (21)
Stephen, J. F. (Bradford), 1947 v W; 1948 v W (2)
Stevenson, G. (Motherwell), 1928 v W, Ni; 1930 v Ni, E, F; 1931 v E, W; 1932 v W, Ni; 1933 v Ni; 1934 v E; 1935 v Ni (12)
Stewart, A. (Queen's Park), 1888 v Ni; 1889 v W (2)
Stewart, A. (Third Lanark), 1894 v W (1)
Stewart, D. (Dumbarton), 1888 v Ni (1)
Stewart, D. (Queen's Park), 1893 v W; 1894 v Ni; 1897 v Ni (3)
Stewart, D. S. (Leeds U), 1978 v EG (1)
Stewart, G. (Hibernian), 1906 v W, E; (with Manchester C), 1907 v E, W (4)
Stewart, J. (Kilmarnock), 1977 v Ch (sub); (with Middlesbrough), 1979 v N (2)
Stewart, M. J. (Manchester U), 2002 v Ng (sub), Sk, S.Af (sub) (3)
Stewart, R. (West Ham U), 1981 v W, Ni, E; 1982 v Ni, P, W; 1984 v F; 1987 v Ei (2), L (10)
Stewart, W. E. (Queen's Park), 1898 v Ni; 1900 v Ni (2)
Stockdale, R. K. (Middlesbrough), 2002 v Ng, Sk (sub), S.Af, Hk; 2003 v D (5)
Storrier, D. (Celtic), 1899 v E, W, Ni (3)
Strachan, G. (Aberdeen), 1980 v Ni, W, E, Pol, H (sub); 1981 v Se, P; 1982 v Ni, P, Sp, Ho (sub), Nz, Br, USSR; 1983 v EG, Sw, Bel, Sw, Ni (sub), W, E, Ca (2 + 1 sub); 1984 v EG, Ni, E, F; (with Manchester U), 1985 v Sp (sub), E, Ic; 1986 v W, Aus, R, D, WG, U; 1987 v Bul, Ei (2); 1988 v H; 1989 v F (sub); (with Leeds U), 1990 v F; 1991 v USSR, Bul, Sm; 1992 v Sw, R, Ni, Fi (50)
Sturrock, P. (Dundee U), 1981 v W (sub), Ni, E (sub); 1982 v P, Ni (sub), W (sub), E (sub); 1983 v EG (sub), Sw, Bel (sub), Ca (3); 1984 v W; 1985 v Y (sub); 1986 v Is (sub), Ho, D, U; 1987 v Bel (20)
Sullivan, N. (Wimbledon), 1997 v W; 1998 v F, Co; 1999 v Fa, CzR, G, Fa, CzR; 2000 v Bos, Es, Bos, E (2), F, Ho, Ei; (with Tottenham H), 2001 v La, Sm, Cro, Bel, Sm, Pol; 2002 v Cro, Bel, La, F, Sk; 2003 v Ei (28)
Summers, W. (St Mirren), 1926 v E (1)
Symon, J. S. (Rangers), 1939 v H (1)

Tait, T. S. (Sunderland), 1911 v W (1)
Taylor, J. (Queen's Park), 1872 v E; 1873 v E; 1874 v E; 1875 v E; 1876 v E, W (6)
Taylor, J. D. (Dumbarton), 1892 v W; 1893 v W; 1894 v Ni; (with St Mirren), 1895 v Ni (4)
Taylor, W. (Hearts), 1892 v E (1)
Telfer, P. N. (Coventry C), 2000 v F (1)
Telfer, W. (Motherwell), 1933 v Ni; 1934 v Ni (2)
Telfer, W. D. (St Mirren), 1954 v W (1)
Templeton, R. (Aston Villa), 1902 v E; (with Newcastle U), 1903 v E, W; 1904 v E; (with Woolwich Arsenal), 1905 v W; (with Kilmarnock), 1908 v Ni; 1910 v E, Ni; 1912 v E, Ni; 1913 v W (11)
Thompson, S. (Dundee U), 2002 v F (sub), Ng, Hk; 2003 v D, Fa (sub), Ic, Ca; (with Rangers), Ei (sub), A, G (sub) (10)
Thomson, A. (Arthurlie), 1886 v Ni (1)
Thomson, A. (Third Lanark), 1889 v W (1)
Thomson, A. (Airdrieonians), 1909 v Ni (1)
Thomson, A. (Celtic), 1926 v E; 1932 v F; 1933 v W (3)
Thomson, C. (Hearts), 1904 v Ni; 1905 v E, Ni, W; 1906 v W, Ni; 1907 v E, W, Ni; 1908 v E, W, Ni; (with Sunderland), 1909 v W; 1910 v E; 1911 v Ni; 1912 v E, W; 1913 v E, W; 1914 v E, Ni (21)
Thomson, C. (Sunderland), 1937 v Cz (1)
Thomson, D. (Dundee), 1920 v W (1)
Thomson, J. (Celtic), 1930 v F; 1931 v E, W, Ni (4)
Thomson, J. J. (Queen's Park), 1872 v E; 1873 v E; 1874 v E (3)
Thomson, J. R. (Everton), 1933 v W (1)
Thomson, R. (Celtic), 1932 v W (1)
Thomson, R. W. (Falkirk), 1927 v E (1)
Thomson, S. (Rangers), 1884 v W, Ni (2)
Thomson, W. (Dumbarton), 1892 v W; 1893 v W; 1898 v Ni, W (4)
Thomson, W. (Dundee), 1896 v W (1)
Thomson, W. (St Mirren), 1980 v Ni; 1981 v Ni (sub+1) 1982 v P; 1983 v Ni, Ca; 1984 v EG (7)
Thornton, W. (Rangers), 1947 v W, Ni; 1948 v E, Ni; 1949 v F; 1952 v D, Se (7)
Toner, W. (Kilmarnock), 1959 v W, Ni (2)
Townsley, T. (Falkirk), 1926 v W (1)
Troup, A. (Dundee), 1920 v E; 1921 v W, Ni; 1922 v Ni; (with Everton), 1926 v E (5)
Turnbull, E. (Hibernian), 1948 v Bel, Sw; 1951 v A; 1958 v H, Pol, Y, Par, F (8)
Turner, T. (Arthurlie), 1884 v W (1)
Turner, W. (Pollokshields Ath), 1885 v Ni; 1886 v Ni (2)

Ure, J. F. (Dundee), 1962 v W, Cz; 1963 v W, Ni, E, A, N, Sp; (with Arsenal), 1964 v Ni, N; 1968 v Ni (11)
Urquhart, D. (Hibernian), 1934 v W (1)

Vallance, T. (Rangers), 1877 v E, W; 1878 v E; 1879 v E, W; 1881 v E, W (7)
Venters, A. (Cowdenbeath), 1934 v Ni; (with Rangers), 1936 v E; 1939 v E (3)

Waddell, T. S. (Queen's Park), 1891 v Ni; 1892 v E; 1893 v E, Ni; 1895 v E, Ni (6)
Waddell, W. (Rangers), 1947 v W; 1949 v E, W, Ni, F; 1950 v E, Ni; 1951 v E, D, F, Bel, A; 1952 v Ni, W; 1954 v Ni; 1955 v W, Ni (17)
Wales, H. M. (Motherwell), 1933 v W (1)
Walker, A. (Celtic), 1988 v Co (sub); 1995 v Fi, Fa (sub) (3)
Walker, F. (Third Lanark), 1922 v W (1)
Walker, G. (St Mirren), 1930 v F; 1931 v Ni, A, Sw (4)
Walker, J. (Hearts), 1895 v Ni; 1897 v W; 1898 v Ni; (with Rangers), 1904 v W, Ni (5)

Walker, J. (Swindon T), 1911 v E, W, Ni; 1912 v E, W, Ni; 1913 v E, W, Ni (9)
Walker, J. N. (Hearts), 1993 v G; (with Partick T), 1996 v US (sub) (2)
Walker, R. (Hearts), 1900 v E, Ni; 1901 v E, W; 1902 v E, W, Ni; 1903 v E, W, Ni; 1904 v E, W, Ni; 1905 v E, W, Ni; 1906 v Ni; 1907 v E, Ni; 1908 v E, W, Ni; 1909 v E, W; 1912 v E, W, Ni; 1913 v E, W (29)
Walker, T. (Hearts), 1935 v E, W; 1936 v E, W, Ni; 1937 v G, E, W, Ni, A, Cz; 1938 v E, W, Ni, Cz, Ho; 1939 v E, W, Ni, H (20)
Walker, W. (Clyde), 1909 v Ni; 1910 v Ni (2)
Wallace, I. A. (Coventry C), 1978 v Bul (sub); 1979 v P (sub), W (3)
Wallace, W. S. B. (Hearts), 1965 v Ni; 1966 v E, Ho; (with Celtic), 1967 v E, USSR (sub); 1968 v Ni; 1969 v E (sub) (7)
Wardhaugh, J. (Hearts), 1955 v H; 1957 v Ni (2)
Wark, J. (Ipswich T), 1979 v W, Ni, E, Arg, N (sub); 1980 v Pe, A, Bel (2); 1981 v Is, Ni; 1982 v Se, Sp, Ho, Ni, Nz, Br, USSR; 1983 v EG, Sw (2), Ni, E (sub); 1984 v U, Bel, EG; (with Liverpool), E, F; 1985 v Y (29)
Watson, A. (Queen's Park), 1881 v E, W; 1882 v E (3)
Watson, J. (Sunderland), 1903 v E, W; 1904 v E; 1905 v E; (with Middlesbrough), 1909 v E, Ni (6)
Watson, J. (Motherwell), 1948 v Ni; (with Huddersfield T), 1954 v Ni (2)
Watson, J. A. K. (Rangers), 1878 v W (1)
Watson, P. R. (Blackpool), 1934 v A (1)
Watson, R. (Motherwell), 1971 v USSR (1)
Watson, W. (Falkirk), 1898 v W (1)
Watt, F. (Kilbirnie), 1889 v W, Ni; 1890 v W; 1891 v E (4)
Watt, W. W. (Queen's Park), 1887 v Ni (1)
Waugh, W. (Hearts), 1938 v Cz (1)
Webster, A. (Hearts), 2003 v A, Nz, G (3)
Weir, A. (Motherwell), 1959 v WG; 1960 v E, P, A, H, T (6)
Weir, D. G. (Hearts), 1997 v W, Ma (sub); 1998 v F, D (sub), Fi (sub), N (sub), Mor; 1999 v Es, Fa; (with Everton), CzR, G, Fa, CzR; 2000 v Bos, Es, Bos, Li, E (2), Ho; 2001 v La, Sm (sub), Cro, Aus, Bel, Sm, Pol (sub); 2002 v Cro, Bel, La, F, Ng, Sk, S.Af, Hk; 2003 v D, Fa (37)
Weir, J. (Third Lanark), 1887 v Ni (1)
Weir, J. B. (Queen's Park), 1872 v E; 1874 v E; 1875 v E; 1878 v W (4)
Weir, P. (St Mirren), 1980 v Ni, W, Pol (sub), H; (with Aberdeen), 1983 v Sw; 1984 v Ni (6)
White, John (Albion R), 1922 v W; (with Hearts), 1923 v Ni (2)
White, J. A. (Falkirk), 1959 v WG, Ho, P; 1960 v Ni; (with Tottenham H), 1960 v W, Pol, A, T; 1961 v W; 1962 v Ni, W, E, Cz (2); 1963 v W, Ni, E; 1964 v Ni, W, E, N, WG (22)
White, W. (Bolton W), 1907 v E; 1908 v E (2)
Whitelaw, A. (Vale of Leven), 1887 v Ni; 1890 v W (2)
Whyte, D. (Celtic), 1988 v Bel (sub), L; 1989 v Ch (sub); 1992 v US (sub); (with Middlesbrough), 1993 v P, I; 1995 v J (sub), Ec; 1996 v US; 1997 v La; (with Aberdeen), 1998 v Fi; 1999 v G (sub) (12)
Wilkie, L. (Dundee), 2002 v S.Af (sub), Hk; 2003 v Ic, Ca, P, Ic, Li, A (8)
Williams, G. (Nottingham F), 2002 v Ng, Sk (sub), S.Af, Hk (sub); 2003 v P (sub) (5)
Wilson, A. (Sheffield W), 1907 v E; 1908 v E; 1912 v E; 1913 v E, W; 1914 v Ni (6)
Wilson, A. (Portsmouth), 1954 v Fi (1)
Wilson, A. N. (Dunfermline), 1920 v E, W, Ni; 1921 v E, W, Ni; (with Middlesbrough), 1922 v E, W, Ni; 1923 v E, W, Ni (12)
Wilson, D. (Queen's Park), 1900 v W (1)
Wilson, D. (Oldham Ath), 1913 v E (1)
Wilson, D. (Rangers), 1961 v E, W, Ni, Ei (2), Cz; 1962 v Ni, W, E, Cz, U; 1963 v W, E, A, N, Ei, Sp; 1964 v E, WG; 1965 v Ni, E, Fi (22)
Wilson, G. W. (Hearts), 1904 v W; 1905 v E, Ni; 1906 v W; (with Everton), 1907 v E; (with Newcastle U), 1909 v E (6)
Wilson, Hugh, (Newmilns), 1890 v W; (with Sunderland), 1897 v E; (with Third Lanark), 1902 v W; 1904 v Ni (4)
Wilson, I. A. (Leicester C), 1987 v E, Br; (with Everton), 1988 v Bel, Bul, L (5)
Wilson, J. (Vale of Leven), 1888 v W; 1889 v E; 1890 v E; 1891 v E (4)
Wilson, P. (Celtic), 1926 v Ni; 1930 v F; 1931 v Ni; 1933 v E (4)
Wilson, P. (Celtic), 1975 v Sp (sub) (1)
Wilson, R. P. (Arsenal), 1972 v P, Ho (2)
Winters, R. (Aberdeen), 1999 v G (sub) (1)
Wiseman, W. (Queen's Park), 1927 v W; 1930 v Ni (2)
Wood, G. (Everton), 1979 v Ni, E, Arg (sub); (with Arsenal), 1982 v Ni (4)
Woodburn, W. A. (Rangers), 1947 v E, Bel, L; 1948 v W, Ni; 1949 v E, F; 1950 v E, W, Ni, P, F; 1951 v E, W, Ni, A (2), D, F, Bel; 1952 v E, W, Ni, USA (24)
Wotherspoon, D. N. (Queen's Park), 1872 v E; 1873 v E (2)
Wright, K. (Hibernian), 1992 v Ni (1)
Wright, S. (Aberdeen), 1993 v G, Es (2)
Wright, T. (Sunderland), 1953 v W, Ni, E (3)
Wylie, T. G. (Rangers), 1890 v Ni (1)

Yeats, R. (Liverpool), 1965 v W; 1966 v I (2)
Yorston, B. C. (Aberdeen), 1931 v Ni (1)
Yorston, H. (Aberdeen), 1955 v W (1)
Young, A. (Everton), 1905 v E; 1907 v W (2)
Young, A. (Hearts), 1960 v E, A (sub), H, T; 1961 v W, Ni; (with Everton), Ei; 1966 v P (8)
Young, G. L. (Rangers), 1947 v E, Ni, Bel, L; 1948 v E, Ni, Bel, Sw, F; 1949 v E, W, Ni, F; 1950 v E, W, Ni, Sw, P, F; 1951 v E, W, Ni, A (2), D, F, Bel; 1952 v E, W, Ni, USA, D, Se; 1953 v W, E, Ni, Se; 1954 v Ni, W; 1955 v W, Ni, P, Y; 1956 v Ni, W, E, A; 1957 v E, Ni, W, Y, Sp, Sw (53)
Young, J. (Celtic), 1906 v Ni (1)
Younger, T. (Hibernian), 1955 v P, Y, A, H; 1956 v E, Ni, W, A; (with Liverpool), 1957 v E, Ni, W, Y, Sp (2), Sw, WG; 1958 v Ni, W, E, Sw, H, Pol, Y, Par (24)

WALES

Adams, H. (Berwyn R), 1882 v Ni, E; (with Druids), 1883 v Ni, E (4)
Aizlewood, M. (Charlton Ath), 1986 v S.Ar, Ca (2); 1987 v Fi; (with Leeds U), USSR, Fi (sub); 1988 v D (sub), Se, Ma, I; 1989 v Ho, Se (sub), WG; (with Bradford C), 1990 v Fi, WG, Ei, Cr; (with Bristol C), 1991 v D, Bel (2), L, Ei, Ic, Pol, WG; 1992 v Br, L, Ei, A, R, Ho, Arg, J; 1993 v Ei, Bel, Fa; 1994 v RCS, Cy; (with Cardiff C), 1995v Bul (39)
Allchurch, I. J. (Swansea T), 1951 v E, Ni, P, Sw; 1952 v E, S, Ni, R of UK; 1953 v S, E, Ni, F, Y; 1954 v S, E, Ni, A; 1955 v S, E, Ni, Y; 1956 v E, S, Ni, A; 1957 v E, S; 1958 v Ni, Is (2), H (2), M, Sw, Br; (with Newcastle U), 1959 v E, S, Ni; 1960 v E, S; 1961 v Ni, H, Sp (2); 1962 v E, S, Br (2), M; (with Cardiff C), 1963 v S, E, Ni, H (2); 1964 v E; 1965 v S, E, Ni, Gr, I, USSR; (with Swansea T), 1966 v USSR, E, S, D, Br (2), Ch (68)
Allchurch, L. (Swansea T), 1955 v Ni; 1956 v A; 1958 v S, Ni, EG, Is; 1959 v S; (with Sheffield U), 1962 v S, Ni, Br; 1964 v E (11)
Allen, B. W. (Coventry C), 1951 v S, E (2)
Allen, M. (Watford), 1986 v S.Ar (sub), Ca (1 + 1 sub); (with Norwich C), 1989 v Is (sub); 1990 v Ho, WG; (with Millwall), Ei, Se, Cr (sub); 1991 v L (sub), Ei (sub); 1992 v A; 1993 v Ei (sub); (with Newcastle U), 1994 v R (sub) (14)
Arridge, S. (Bootle), 1892 v S, Ni; (with Everton), 1894 v Ni; 1895 v Ni; 1896 v E; (with New Brighton Tower), 1898 v E, Ni; 1899 v E (8)
Astley, D. J. (Charlton Ath), 1931 v Ni; (with Aston Villa), 1932 v E; 1933 v E, S, Ni; 1934 v E, S; 1935 v S; 1936 v E, Ni; (with Derby Co), 1939 v E, S; (with Blackpool), F (13)
Atherton, R. W. (Hibernian), 1899 v E, Ni; 1903 v E, S, Ni; (with Middlesbrough), 1904 v E, S, Ni; 1905 v Ni (9)

Bailiff, W. E. (Llanelly), 1913 v E, S, Ni; 1920 v Ni (4)
Baker, C. W. (Cardiff C), 1958 v M; 1960 v S, Ni; 1961 v S, E, Ei; 1962 v S (7)
Baker, W. G. (Cardiff C), 1948 v Ni (1)
Bamford, T. (Wrexham), 1931 v E, S, Ni; 1932 v Ni; 1933 v F (5)
Barnard, D. S. (Barnsley), 1998 v Jam; 1999 v I, D, Bl, I, D; 2000 v Bl, Sw, Q, Fi, Br (sub), P; 2001 v Uk, Pol, Uk; 2002 v Arm (sub); (with Grimsby T), 2003 v Cro, Az (18)
Barnes, W. (Arsenal), 1948 v E, S, Ni; 1949 v E, S, Ni; 1950 v E, S, Ni, Bel; 1951 v E, S, Ni, P; 1952 v E, S, Ni, R of UK; 1954 v E, S; 1955 v S, Y (22)
Bartley, T. (Glossop NE), 1898 v E (1)
Bastock, A. M. (Shrewsbury), 1892 v Ni (1)
Beadles, G. H. (Cardiff C), 1925 v E, S (2)
Bell, W. S. (Shrewsbury Engineers), 1881 v E, S; (with Crewe Alex), 1886 v E, S, Ni (5)

Bellamy, C. D. (Norwich C), 1998 v Jam (sub), Ma, Tun; 1999 v D (sub), Sw (sub), I, D (sub); 2000 v Br (sub), P; (with Coventry C), 2001 v Bl, Arm, Uk; (with Newcastle U), 2002 v Arm, N, Bl, Arg; 2003 v Fi (sub), I, Bos, Az (20)
Bennion, S. R. (Manchester U), 1926 v S; 1927 v S; 1928 v S, E, Ni; 1929 v S, E, Ni; 1930 v S; 1932 v Ni (10)
Berry, G. F. (Wolverhampton W), 1979 v WG; 1980 v Ei, WG (sub), T; (with Stoke C), 1983 v E (sub) (5)
Blackmore, C. G. (Manchester U), 1985 v N (sub); 1986 v S (sub), H (sub), S.Ar, Ei, U; 1987 v Fi (2), USSR, Cz; 1988 v D (2), Cz, Y, Se, Ma, I; 1989 v Ho, Fi, Is, WG; 1990 v F; Ho, WG, Cr; 1991 v Bel, L; 1992 v Ei (sub), A, R (sub), Ho, Arg, J; 1993 v Fa, Cy, Bel, RCS; 1994 v Se (sub); (with Middlesbrough), 1997 v Bel (39)
Blake, N. A. (Sheffield U), 1994 v N, Se (sub); 1995 v Alb, Mol; 1996 v G (with Bolton W), I (sub); 1998 v T; 1999 v I, D, Bl; (with Blackburn R) Sw; 2000 v Bl, Sw, Q, Fi; 2001 v Bl (sub), N, Pol (2), Uk; 2002 v N (sub); (with Wolverhampton W), CzR; 2003 v I (sub) (23)
Blew, H. (Wrexham), 1899 v E, S, Ni; 1902 v S, Ni; 1903 v E, S; 1904 v E, S, Ni; 1905 v S, Ni; 1906 v E, S, Ni; 1907 v S; 1908 v E, S, Ni; 1909 v E, S; 1910 v E (22)
Boden, T. (Wrexham), 1880 v E (1)
Bodin, P. J. (Swindon T), 1990 v Cr; 1991 v D, Bel, L, Ei; (with C Palace), Bel, Ic, Pol, WG; 1992 v Br, G, L (sub); (with Swindon T), Ei (sub), Ho, Arg; 1993 v Ei, Bel, RCS, Fa; 1994 v R, Se, Es (sub); 1995 v Alb (23)
Boulter, L. M. (Brentford), 1939 v Ni (1)
Bowdler, H. E. (Shrewsbury), 1893 v S (1)
Bowdler, J. C. H. (Shrewsbury), 1890 v Ni; (with Wolverhampton W), 1891 v S; 1892 v Ni; (with Shrewsbury), 1894 v E (4)
Bowen, D. L. (Arsenal), 1955 v S, Y; 1957 v Ni, Cz, EG; 1958 v E, S, Ni, EG, Is (2), H (2), M, Se, Br; 1959 v E, S, Ni (19)
Bowen, E. (Druids), 1880 v S; 1883 v S (2)
Bowen, J. P. (Swansea C), 1994 v Es; (with Birmingham C), 1997 v Ho (2)
Bowen, M. R. (Tottenham H), 1986 v Ca (2 sub); (with Norwich C), 1988 v Y (sub); 1989 v Fi (sub), Is, Se, WG (sub); 1990 v Fi (sub), Ho, WG, Se; 1992 v Br (sub), G, L, Ei, A, R, Ho (sub), J; 1993 v Fa, Cy, Bel (1 + sub), RCS (sub); 1994 v RCS, Se; 1995 v Mol, Ge, Bul (2), G, Ge; 1996 v Mol, G, Alb, Sw, Sm; (with West Ham U), 1997 v Sm, Ho (2), Ei (sub) (41)
Bowsher, S. J. (Burnley), 1929 v Ni (1)
Boyle, T. (C Palace), 1981 v Ei, S (sub) (2)
Britten, T. J. (Parkgrove), 1878 v S; (with Presteigne), 1880 v S (2)
Brookes, S. J. (Llandudno), 1900 v E, Ni (2)
Brown, A. I. (Aberdare Ath), 1926 v Ni (1)
Browning, M. T. (Bristol R), 1996 v I (sub), Sm; 1997 v Sm, Ho (with Huddersfield T), S (sub) (5)
Bryan, T. (Oswestry), 1886 v E, Ni (2)
Buckland, T. (Bangor), 1899 v E (1)
Burgess, W. A. R. (Tottenham H), 1947 v E, S, Ni; 1948 v E, S; 1949 v E, S, Ni, P, Bel, Sw; 1950 v E, S, Ni, Bel; 1951 v S, Ni, P, Sw; 1952 v E, S, Ni, R of UK; 1953 v S, E, Ni, F, Y; 1954 v S, E, Ni, A (32)
Burke, T. (Wrexham), 1883 v E; 1884 v S; 1885 v E, S, Ni; (with Newton Heath), 1887 v E, S; 1888 v S (8)
Burnett, T. B. (Ruabon), 1877 v S (1)
Burton, A. D. (Norwich C), 1963 v Ni, H; (with Newcastle U), 1964 v E; 1969 v S, E, Ni, I, EG; 1972 v Cz (9)
Butler, J. (Chirk), 1893 v E, S, Ni (3)
Butler, W. T. (Druids), 1900 v S, Ni (2)

Cartwright, L. (Coventry C), 1974 v E (sub), S, Ni; 1976 v S (sub); 1977 v WG (sub); (with Wrexham), 1978 v Ir (sub); 1979 v Ma (7)
Carty, T. See McCarthy (Wrexham).
Challen, J. B. (Corinthians), 1887 v E, S; 1888 v E; (with Wellingborough GS), 1890 v E (4)
Chapman, T. (Newtown), 1894 v E, S, Ni; 1895 v S, Ni; (with Manchester C), 1896 v E; 1897 v E (7)
Charles, J. M. (Swansea C), 1981 v Cz, T (sub), S (sub), USSR (sub); 1982 v Ic; 1983 v N (sub), Y (sub), Bul (sub), S, Ni, Br; 1984 v Bul (sub); (with QPR), Y (sub), S; (with Oxford U), 1985 v Ic (sub), Sp, Ic; 1986 v Ei; 1987 v Fi (19)
Charles, M. (Swansea T), 1955 v Ni; 1956 v E, S, A; 1957 v E, Ni, Cz (2), EG; 1958 v E, S, EG, Is (2), H (2), M, Se, Br; 1959 v E, S; (with Arsenal), 1961 v Ni, H, Sp (2); 1962 v E, S; (with Cardiff C), 1962 v Br, Ni; 1963 v S, H (31)
Charles, W. J. (Leeds U), 1950 v Ni; 1951 v Sw; 1953 v Ni, F, Y; 1954 v E, S, Ni, A; 1955 v S, E, Ni, Y; 1956 v E, S, A, Ni; 1957 v E, S, Ni, Cz (2), EG; (with Juventus), 1958 v Is (2), H (2) M, Se; 1960 v S; 1962 v E, Br (2), M; (with Leeds U), 1963 v S; (with Cardiff C), 1964 v S; 1965 v S, USSR (38)
Clarke, R. J. (Manchester C), 1949 v E; 1950 v S, Ni, Bel; 1951 v E, S, Ni, P, Sw; 1952 v S, E, Ni, R of UK; 1953 v S, E; 1954 v E, S, Ni; 1955 v Y, S, E; 1956 v Ni (22)
Coleman, C. (C Palace), 1992 v A (sub); 1993 v Ei (sub); 1994 v N, Es; 1995 v Alb, Mol, Ge, Bul (2), G; 1996 v Mol; (with Blackburn R), I, Sw, Sm; 1997 v Sm; 1998 v Br; (with Fulham), Jam, Ma, Tun; 1999 v I, D, Bl, Sw, D; 2000 v Bl, Sw, Q, Fi; 2001 v Bl, N, Pol; 2002 v G (sub) (32)
Collier, D. J. (Grimsby T), 1921 v S (1)
Collins, W. S. (Llanelly), 1931 v S (1)
Conde, C. (Chirk), 1884 v E, S, Ni (3)
Cook, F. C. (Newport Co), 1925 v E, S; (with Portsmouth), 1928 v E, S; 1930 v E, S, Ni; 1932 v E (8)
Cornforth, J. M. (Swansea C), 1995 v Bul (sub), Ge (2)
Coyne, D. (Tranmere R), 1996 v Sw; (with Grimsby T), 2002 v CzR (sub) (2)
Crompton, W. (Wrexham), 1931 v E, S, Ni (3)
Cross, E. A. (Wrexham), 1876 v S; 1877 v S (2)
Crosse, K. (Druids), 1879 v S; 1881 v E, S (3)
Crossley, M. G. (Nottingham F), 1997 v Ei; 1999 v Sw (sub); 2000 v Fi; (with Middlesbrough), 2002 v Arg (sub), G; 2003 v Bos (sub) (6)
Crowe, V. H. (Aston Villa), 1959 v E, Ni; 1960 v E, Ni; 1961 v S, E, Ni, Ei, H, Sp (2); 1962 v E, S, Br, M; 1963 v H (16)
Cumner, R. H. (Arsenal), 1939 v E, S, Ni (3)
Curtis, A. (Swansea C), 1976 v E, Y (sub), S, Ni, Y (sub), E; 1977 v WG, S (sub), Ni (sub); 1978 v WG, E, S; 1979 v WG, S; (with Leeds U), E, Ni, Ma; 1980 v Ei, WG, T; (with Swansea C), 1982 v Cz, Ic, USSR, Sp, E, S, Ni; 1983 v N; 1984 v R (sub); (with Southampton), S; 1985 v Sp, N (1 + 1 sub); 1986 v H; (with Cardiff C), 1987 v USSR (35)
Curtis, E. R. (Cardiff C), 1928 v S; (with Birmingham), 1932 v S; 1934 v Ni (3)

Daniel, R. W. (Arsenal), 1951 v E, Ni, P; 1952 v E, S, Ni, R of UK; 1953 v S, E, Ni, F, Y; (with Sunderland), 1954 v E, S, Ni; 1955 v E, Ni; 1957 v S, E, Ni, Cz (21)
Darvell, S. (Oxford University), 1897 v S, Ni (2)
Davies, A. (Manchester U), 1983 v Ni, Br; 1984 v E, Ni; 1985 v Ic (2), N; (with Newcastle U), 1986 v H; (with Swansea C), 1988 v Ma, I; 1989 v Ho; (with Bradford C), 1990 v Fi, Ei (13)
Davies, A. (Wrexham), 1876 v S; 1877 v S (2)
Davies, A. (Druids), 1904 v S; (with Middlesbrough), 1905 v S (2)
Davies, A. O. (Barmouth), 1885 v Ni; 1886 v E, S; (with Swifts), 1887 v E, S; 1888 v E, Ni; (with Wrexham), 1889 v S; (with Crewe Alex), 1890 v E (9)
Davies, A. T. (Shrewsbury), 1891 v Ni (1)
Davies, C. (Charlton Ath), 1972 v R (sub) (1)
Davies, D. (Bolton W), 1904 v S, Ni; 1908 v E (sub) (3)
Davies, D. C. (Brecon), 1899 v Ni; (with Hereford); 1900 v Ni (2)
Davies, D. W. (Treharris), 1912 v Ni; (with Oldham Ath), 1913 v Ni (2)
Davies, E. Lloyd (Stoke C), 1904 v E; 1907 v E, S, Ni; (with Northampton T), 1908 v S; 1909 v Ni; 1910 v Ni; 1911 v E, S; 1912 v E, S; 1913 v E, S; 1914 v Ni, E, S (16)
Davies, E. R. (Newcastle U), 1953 v S, E; 1954 v E, S; 1958 v E, EG (6)
Davies, G. (Fulham), 1980 v T, Ic; 1982 v Sp (sub), F (sub); 1983 v E, Bul, S, Ni, Br; 1984 v R (sub), S (sub), E, Ni; 1985 v Ic; (with Manchester C), 1986 v S.Ar, Ei (16)
Davies, Rev. H. (Wrexham), 1928 v Ni (1)
Davies, Idwal (Liverpool Marine), 1923 v S (1)
Davies, J. E. (Oswestry), 1885 v E (1)
Davies, Jas (Wrexham), 1878 v S (1)
Davies, John (Wrexham), 1879 v S (1)
Davies, Jos (Newton Heath), 1888 v E, S, Ni; 1889 v S; 1890 v E; (with Wolverhampton W), 1892 v E; 1893 v E (7)
Davies, Jos (Everton), 1889 v S, Ni; (with Chirk), 1891 v Ni; (with Ardwick), v E, S; (with Sheffield U), 1895 v E, S, Ni; (with Manchester C), 1896 v E; (with Millwall), 1897 v E; (with Reading), 1900 v E (11)
Davies, J. P. (Druids), 1883 v E, Ni (2)
Davies, Ll. (Wrexham), 1907 v Ni; 1910 v Ni, S, E; (with Everton), 1911 v S, Ni; (with Wrexham), 1912 v Ni, S, E; 1913 v Ni, S, E; 1914 v Ni (13)
Davies, L. S. (Cardiff C), 1922 v E, S, Ni; 1923 v E, S, Ni; 1924 v E, S, Ni; 1925 v S, Ni; 1926 v E, Ni; 1927 v E, Ni; 1928 v S, Ni, E; 1929 v S, Ni, E; 1930 v E, S (23)
Davies, O. (Wrexham), 1890 v S (1)
Davies, R. (Wrexham), 1883 v Ni; 1884 v Ni; 1885 v Ni (3)
Davies, R. (Druids), 1885 v E (1)
Davies, R. O. (Wrexham), 1892 v Ni, E (2)

Davies, R. T. (Norwich C), 1964 v Ni; 1965 v E; 1966 v Br (2), Ch; (with Southampton), 1967 v S, E, Ni; 1968 v S, Ni, WG; 1969 v S, E, Ni, I, WG, R of UK; 1970 v E, S, Ni; 1971 v Cz, S, E, Ni; 1972 v R, E, S, N; (with Portsmouth), 1974 v E (29)
Davies, R. W. (Bolton W), 1964 v E; 1965 v E, S, Ni, D, Gr, USSR; 1966 v E, S, Ni, USSR, D, Br (2), Ch (sub); 1967 v S; (with Newcastle U), E; 1968 v S, Ni, WG; 1969 v S, E, Ni, I; 1970 v EG; 1971 v R, Cz; (with Manchester C), 1972 v E, S, Ni; (with Manchester U), 1973 v E, S (sub), Ni; (with Blackpool), 1974 v Pol (34)
Davies, S. (Tottenham H), 2001 v Uk (sub+1); 2002 v Arm, N, Bl, Arg, CzR, G; 2003 v Cro, Fi, I, Az, Bos, Az, US (15)
Davies, S. I. (Manchester U), 1996 v Sw (sub) (1)
Davies, Stanley (Preston NE), 1920 v E, S, Ni; (with Everton), 1921 v E, S, Ni; (with WBA), 1922 v E, S, Ni; 1923 v S; 1925 v S, Ni; 1926 v S, E, Ni; 1927 v S; 1928 v S; (with Rotherham U), 1930 v Ni (18)
Davies, T. (Oswestry), 1886 v E (1)
Davies, T. (Druids), 1903 v E, Ni, S; 1904 v S (4)
Davies, W. (Wrexham), 1884 v Ni (1)
Davies, W. (Swansea T), 1924 v E, S, Ni; (with Cardiff C), 1925 v E, S, Ni; 1926 v E, S, Ni; 1927 v S; 1928 v Ni; (with Notts Co), 1929 v E, S, Ni; 1930 v E, S, Ni (17)
Davies, William (Wrexham), 1903 v Ni; 1905 v Ni; (with Blackburn R), 1908 v E, S; 1909 v E, S, Ni; 1911 v E, S, Ni; 1912 v Ni (11)
Davies, W. C. (C Palace), 1908 v S; (with WBA), 1909 v E; 1910 v S; (with C Palace), 1914 v E (4)
Davies, W. D. (Everton), 1975 v H, L, S, E, Ni; 1976 v Y (2), E, Ni; 1977 v WG, S (2), Cz, E, Ni; 1978 v K; (with Wrexham), S, Cz, WG, Ir, E, S, Ni; 1979 v Ma, T, WG, S, E, Ni, Ma; 1980 v Ei, WG, T, E, S, Ni, Ic; 1981 v T, Cz, Ei, T, S, E, USSR; (with Swansea C), 1982 v Cz, Ic, USSR, Sp, E, S, F; 1983 v Y (52)
Davies, W. H. (Oswestry), 1876 v S; 1877 v S; 1879 v E; 1880 v E (4)
Davies, W. O. (Millwall Ath), 1913 v E, S, Ni; 1914 v S, Ni (5)
Davis, G. (Wrexham), 1978 v Ir, E (sub), Ni (3)
Day, A. (Tottenham H), 1934 v Ni (1)
Deacy, N. (PSV Eindhoven), 1977 v Cz, S, E, Ni; 1978 v K (sub), S (sub), Cz (sub), WG, Ir, S (sub), Ni; (with Beringen), 1979 v T (12)
Dearson, D. J. (Birmingham), 1939 v S, Ni, F (3)
Delaney, M. A. (Aston Villa), 2000 v Sw, Q, Br, P; 2001 v N, Pol, Arm, Uk (2); 2002 v Arm, N, Bl, Arg, CzR, G; 2003 v Cro, Fi, I, Az (19)
Derrett, S. C. (Cardiff C), 1969 v S, WG; 1970 v I; 1971 v Fi (4)
Dewey, F. T. (Cardiff Corinthians), 1931 v E, S (2)
Dibble, A. (Luton T), 1986 v Ca (1+1 sub); (with Manchester C), 1989 v Is (3)
Doughty, J. (Druids), 1886 v S; (with Newton Heath), 1887 v S, Ni; 1888 v E, S, Ni; 1889 v S; 1890 v E (8)
Doughty, R. (Newton Heath and Druids), 1888 v S, Ni (2)
Durban, A. (Derby Co), 1966 v Br (sub); 1967 v Ni; 1968 v E, S, Ni, WG; 1969 v EG, S, E, Ni, WG; 1970 v E, S, Ni, EG, I; 1971 v R, S, E, Ni, Cz, Fi; 1972 v Fi, Cz, E, S, Ni (27)
Dwyer, P. (Cardiff C), 1978 v Ir, E, S, Ni; 1979 v T, S, E, Ni, Ma (sub); 1980 v WG (10)

Earnshaw, R. (Cardiff C), 2002 v G; 2003 v Cro, Az, Bos (4)
Edwards, C. (Wrexham), 1878 v S (1)
Edwards, C. N. H. (Swansea C), 1996 v Sw (sub) (1)
Edwards, G. (Birmingham C), 1947 v E, S, Ni; 1948 v E, S, Ni; (with Cardiff C), 1949 v Ni, P, Bel, Sw; 1950 v E, S (12)
Edwards, H. (Wrexham Civil Service), 1878 v S; 1880 v E, S; 1882 v E, S; 1883 v S; 1884 v Ni; 1887 v Ni (8)
Edwards, J. H. (Wanderers), 1876 v S (1)
Edwards, J. H. (Oswestry), 1895 v Ni; 1897 v E, Ni (3)
Edwards, J. H. (Aberystwyth), 1898 v Ni (1)
Edwards, L. T. (Charlton Ath), 1957 v Ni, EG (2)
Edwards, R. I. (Chester), 1978 v K (sub); 1979 v Ma, WG; (with Wrexham), 1980 v T (sub) (4)
Edwards, R. O. (Aston Villa), 2003 v Az (sub) (1)
Edwards, R. W. (Bristol C), 1998 v T (sub), Bel, Ma (sub), Tun (sub) (4)
Edwards, T. (Linfield), 1932 v S (1)
Egan, W. (Chirk), 1892 v S (1)
Ellis, B. (Motherwell), 1932 v E; 1933 v E, S; 1934 v S; 1936 v E; 1937 v S (6)
Ellis, E. (Nunhead), 1931 v S; (with Oswestry), E; 1932 v Ni (3)
Emanuel, W. J. (Bristol C), 1973 v E (sub), Ni (sub) (2)
England, H. M. (Blackburn R), 1962 v Ni, Br, M; 1963 v Ni, H; 1964 v E, S, Ni; 1965 v E, D, Gr (2), USSR, Ni, I; 1966 v E, S, Ni, USSR, D; (with Tottenham H), 1967 v S, E; 1968 v E, Ni, WG; 1969 v EG; 1970 v R of UK, EG, E, S, Ni, I; 1971 v R; 1972 v Fi, E, S, Ni; 1973 v E (3), S; 1974 v Pol; 1975 v H, L (44)
Evans, B. C. (Swansea C), 1972 v Fi, Cz; 1973 v E (2), Pol, S; (with Hereford U), 1974 v Pol (7)
Evans, D. G. (Reading), 1926 v Ni; 1927 v Ni, E; (with Huddersfield T), 1929 v S (4)
Evans, H. P. (Cardiff C), 1922 v E, S, Ni; 1924 v E, S, Ni (6)
Evans, I. (C Palace), 1976 v A, E, Y (2), E, Ni; 1977 v WG, S (2), Cz, E, Ni; 1978 v K (13)
Evans, J. (Oswestry), 1893 v Ni; 1894 v E, Ni (3)
Evans, J. (Cardiff C), 1912 v Ni; 1913 v Ni; 1914 v S; 1920 v S, Ni; 1922 v Ni; 1923 v E, Ni (8)
Evans, J. H. (Southend U), 1922 v E, S, Ni; 1923 v S (4)
Evans, Len (Aberdare Ath), 1927 v Ni; (with Cardiff C), 1931 v E, S; (with Birmingham), 1934 v Ni (4)
Evans, M. (Oswestry), 1884 v E (1)
Evans, P. S. (Brentford), 2002 v CzR (sub) (1)
Evans, R. (Clapton), 1902 v Ni (1)
Evans, R. E. (Wrexham), 1906 v E, S; (with Aston Villa), Ni; 1907 v E; 1908 v E, S; (with Sheffield U), 1909 v S; 1910 v E, S, Ni (10)
Evans, R. O. (Wrexham), 1902 v Ni; 1903 v E, S, Ni; (with Blackburn R), 1908 v Ni; (with Coventry C), 1911 v E, Ni; 1912 v E, S, Ni (10)
Evans, R. S. (Swansea T), 1964 v Ni (1)
Evans, T. J. (Clapton Orient), 1927 v S; 1928 v E, S; (with Newcastle U), Ni (4)
Evans, W. (Tottenham H), 1933 v Ni; 1934 v E, S; 1935 v E; 1936 v E, Ni (6)
Evans, W. A. W. (Oxford University), 1876 v S; 1877 v S (2)
Evans, W. G. (Bootle), 1890 v E; 1891 v E; (with Aston Villa), 1892 v E (3)
Evelyn, E. C. (Crusaders), 1887 v E (1)
Eyton-Jones, J. A. (Wrexham), 1883 v Ni; 1884 v Ni, E, S (4)

Farmer, G. (Oswestry), 1885 v E, S (2)
Felgate, D. (Lincoln C), 1984 v R (sub) (1)
Finnigan, R. J. (Wrexham), 1930 v Ni (1)
Flynn, B. (Burnley), 1975 v L (2 sub), H (sub), S, E, Ni; 1976 v A, E, Y (2), E, Ni; 1977 v WG (sub), S (2), Cz, E, Ni; 1978 v K (2), S; (with Leeds U), Cz, WG, Ir (sub), E, S, Ni; 1979 v Ma, T, S, E, Ni, Ma; 1980 v Ei, WG, E, S, Ni, Ic; 1981 v T, Cz, Ei, T, S, E, USSR; 1982 v Cz, USSR, E, S, Ni, F; 1983 v N; (with Burnley), Y, E, Bul, S, Ni, Br; 1984 v N, R, Bul, Y, S, N, Is (66)
Ford, T. (Swansea T), 1947 v S; (with Aston Villa), 1947 v Ni; 1948 v S, Ni; 1949 v E, S, Ni, P, Bel, Sw; 1950 v E, S, Ni, Bel; 1951 v S; (with Sunderland), 1951 v E, Ni, P, Sw; 1952 v E, S, Ni, R of UK; 1953 v S, E, Ni, F, Y; (with Cardiff C), 1954 v A; 1955 v S, E, Ni, Y; 1956 v S, Ni, E, A; 1957 v S (38)
Foulkes, H. E. (WBA), 1932 v Ni (1)
Foulkes, W. I. (Newcastle U), 1952 v E, S, Ni, R of UK; 1953 v E, S, F, Y; 1954 v E, S, Ni (11)
Foulkes, W. T. (Oswestry), 1884 v Ni; 1885 v S (2)
Fowler, J. (Swansea T), 1925 v E; 1926 v E, Ni; 1927 v S; 1928 v S; 1929 v E (6)
Freestone, R. (Swansea C), 2000 v Br (1)

Gabbidon, D. L. (Cardiff C), 2002 v CzR; 2003 v Cro, Fi, I (4)
Garner, J. (Aberystwyth), 1896 v S (1)
Giggs, R. J. (Manchester U), 1992 v G (sub), L (sub), R (sub); 1993 v Fa (sub), Bel (sub + 1), RCS, Fa; 1994 v RCS, Cy, R; 1995 v Alb, Bul; 1996 v G, Alb, Sm; 1997 v Sm, T, Bel; 1998 v T, Bel; 1999 v I (2), D; 2000 v Bl, Fi; 2001 v Bl, N, Pol, Uk, Pol, Uk; 2002 v Arm, N, Arg, G; 2003 v Fi, I, Az (2) (40)
Giles, D. (Swansea C), 1980 v E, S, Ni, Ic; 1981 v T, Cz, T (sub), E (sub), USSR (sub); (with C Palace), 1982 v Sp (sub); 1983 v Ni (sub), Br (12)
Gillam, S. G. (Wrexham), 1889 v S (sub), Ni; (with Shrewsbury), 1890 v E, Ni; (with Clapton), 1894 v S (5)
Glascodine, G. (Wrexham), 1879 v E (1)
Glover, E. M. (Grimsby T), 1932 v S; 1934 v Ni; 1936 v S; 1937 v E, S, Ni; 1939 v Ni (7)
Godding, G. (Wrexham), 1923 v S, Ni (2)
Godfrey, B. C. (Preston NE), 1964 v Ni; 1965 v D, I (3)
Goodwin, U. (Ruthin), 1881 v E (1)
Goss, J. (Norwich C), 1991 v Ic, Pol (sub); 1992 v A; 1994 v Cy (sub), R (sub), Se; 1995 v Alb; 1996 v Sw (sub), Sm (sub) (9)
Gough, R. T. (Oswestry White Star), 1883 v S (1)
Gray, A. (Oldham Ath), 1924 v E, S, Ni; 1925 v E, S, Ni; 1926 v E, S; 1927 v S; (with Manchester C), 1928 v E, S; 1929 v E, S, Ni; (with Manchester Central), 1930 v S; (with Tranmere R), 1932 v E, S, Ni; (with Chester), 1937 v E, S, Ni; 1938 v E, S, Ni (24)

Green, A. W. (Aston Villa), 1901 v Ni; (with Notts Co), 1903 v E; 1904 v S, Ni; 1906 v Ni, E; (with Nottingham F), 1907 v E; 1908 v S (8)
Green, C. R. (Birmingham C), 1965 v USSR, I; 1966 v E, S, USSR, Br (2); 1967 v E; 1968 v E, S, Ni, WG; 1969 v S, I, Ni (sub) (15)
Green, G. H. (Charlton Ath), 1938 v Ni; 1939 v E, Ni, F (4)
Green, R. M. (Wolverhampton W), 1998 v Ma, Tun (2)
Grey, Dr W. (Druids), 1876 v S; 1878 v S (2)
Griffiths, A. T. (Wrexham), 1971 v Cz (sub); 1975 v A, H (2), L (2), E, Ni; 1976 v A, E, S, E (sub), Ni, Y (2); 1977 v WG, S (17)
Griffiths, F. J. (Blackpool), 1900 v E, S (2)
Griffiths, G. (Chirk), 1887 v Ni (1)
Griffiths, J. H. (Swansea T), 1953 v Ni (1)
Griffiths, L. (Wrexham), 1902 v S (1)
Griffiths, M. W. (Leicester C), 1947 v Ni; 1949 v P, Bel; 1950 v E, S, Bel; 1951 v E, Ni, P, Sw; 1954 v A (11)
Griffiths, P. (Chirk), 1884 v E, Ni; 1888 v E; 1890 v S, Ni; 1891 v Ni (6)
Griffiths, P. H. (Everton), 1932 v S (1)
Griffiths, T. P. (Everton), 1927 v E, Ni; 1929 v E; 1930 v E; 1931 v Ni; 1932 v Ni, S, E; (with Bolton W), 1933 v E, S, Ni; (with Middlesbrough), F; 1934 v E, S; 1935 v E, Ni; 1936 v S; (with Aston Villa), Ni; 1937 v E, S, Ni (21)

Hall, G. D. (Chelsea), 1988 v Y (sub), Ma, I; 1989 v Ho, Fi, Is; 1990 v Ei; 1991 v Ei; 1992 v A (sub) (9)
Hallam, J. (Oswestry), 1889 v E (1)
Hanford, H. (Swansea T), 1934 v Ni; 1935 v S; 1936 v E; (with Sheffield W), 1936 v Ni; 1938 v E, S; 1939 v F (7)
Harrington, A. C. (Cardiff C), 1956 v Ni; 1957 v E, S; 1958 v S, Ni, Is (2); 1961 v S, E; 1962 v E, S (11)
Harris, C. S. (Leeds U), 1976 v E, S; 1978 v WG, Ir, E, S, Ni; 1979 v Ma, T, WG, E (sub), Ma; 1980 v Ni (sub), Ic (sub); 1981 v T, Cz (sub), Ei, T, S, E, USSR; 1982 v Cz, Ic, E (sub) (24)
Harris, W. C. (Middlesbrough), 1954 v A; 1957 v EG, Cz; 1958 v E, S, EG (6)
Harrison, W. C. (Wrexham), 1899 v E; 1900 v E, S, Ni; 1901 v Ni (5)
Hartson, J. (Arsenal), 1995 v Bul, G (sub), Ge (sub); 1996 v Mol (sub), Sw; 1997 v Ho, T (sub), Ei; (with West Ham U), Bel (sub), S; 1998 v Bel, Jam, Ma, Tun; (with Wimbledon), 1999 v Sw (sub), I (sub), D; 2000 v Sw (sub); 2001 v N, Pol; (with Coventry C), Arm, Uk, Pol, Uk; (with Celtic), 2002 v N, Bl, Arg, CzR, G; 2003 v Cro, Fi, I, Az, Bos, Az (35)
Haworth, S. O. (Cardiff C), 1997 v S (sub); (with Coventry C), 1998 v Br, Jam (sub), Ma (sub), Tun (sub) (5)
Hayes, A. (Wrexham), 1890 v Ni; 1894 v Ni (2)
Hennessey, W. T. (Birmingham C), 1962 v Ni, Br (2); 1963 v S, E, H (2); 1964 v E, S; 1965 v S, E, D, Gr, USSR; 1966 v E, USSR; (with Nottingham F), 1966 v S, Ni, D, Br (2), Ch; 1967 v S, E; 1968 v E, S, Ni; 1969 v WG, EG, R of UK; 1970 v EG; (with Derby Co), E, S, Ni; 1972 v Fi, Cz, E, S; 1973 v E (39)
Hersee, A. M. (Bangor), 1886 v S, Ni (2)
Hersee, R. (Llandudno), 1886 v Ni (1)
Hewitt, R. (Cardiff C), 1958 v Ni, Is, Se, H, Br (5)
Hewitt, T. J. (Wrexham), 1911 v E, S, Ni; (with Chelsea), 1913 v E, S, Ni; (with South Liverpool), 1914 v E, S (8)
Heywood, D. (Druids), 1879 v E (1)
Hibbott, H. (Newtown Excelsior), 1880 v E, S; (with Newtown), 1885 v S (3)
Higham, G. G. (Oswestry), 1878 v S; 1879 v E (2)
Hill, M. R. (Ipswich T), 1972 v Cz, R (2)
Hockey, T. (Sheffield U), 1972 v Fi, R; 1973 v E (2); (with Norwich C), Pol, S, E, Ni; (with Aston Villa), 1974 v Pol (9)
Hoddinott, T. F. (Watford), 1921 v E, S (2)
Hodges, G. (Wimbledon), 1984 v N (sub), Is (sub); 1987 v USSR, Fi, Cz; (with Newcastle U), 1988 v D; (with Watford), D (sub), Cz (sub), Se, Ma (sub), I (sub); 1990 v Se, Cr; (with Sheffield U), 1992 v Br (sub), Ei (sub), A; 1996 v G (sub), I (18)
Hodgkinson, A. V. (Southampton), 1908 v Ni (1)
Holden, A. (Chester C), 1984 v Is (sub) (1)
Hole, B. G. (Cardiff C), 1963 v Ni; 1964 v Ni; 1965 v S, E, Ni, D, Gr (2), USSR, I; 1966 v E, S, Ni, USSR, D, Br (2), Ch; (with Blackburn R), 1967 v S, E, Ni; 1968 v E, S, Ni, WG; (with Aston Villa), 1969 v I, WG, EG; 1970 v I; (with Swansea C), 1971 v R (30)
Hole, W. J. (Swansea T), 1921 v Ni; 1922 v E; 1923 v E, Ni; 1928 v E, S, Ni; 1929 v E, S (9)
Hollins, D. M. (Newcastle U), 1962 v Br (sub), M; 1963 v Ni, H; 1964 v E; 1965 v Ni, Gr, I; 1966 v S, D, Br (11)

Hopkins, I. J. (Brentford), 1935 v S, Ni; 1936 v E, Ni; 1937 v E, S, Ni; 1938 v E, Ni; 1939 v E, S, Ni (12)
Hopkins, J. (Fulham), 1983 v Ni, Br; 1984 v N, R, Bul, Y, S, E, Ni, N, Is; 1985 v Ic (1 + 1 sub), N; (with C Palace), 1990 v Ho, Cr (16)
Hopkins, M. (Tottenham H), 1956 v Ni; 1957 v Ni, S, E, Cz (2), EG; 1958 v E, S, Ni, EG, Is (2), H (2), M, Se, Br; 1959 v E, S, Ni; 1960 v E, S; 1961 v Ni, H, Sp (2); 1962 v Ni, Br (2), M; 1963 v S, Ni, H (34)
Horne, B. (Portsmouth), 1988 v D (sub), Y, Se (sub), Ma, I; 1989 v Ho, Fi, Is; (with Southampton), Se, WG; 1990 v WG (sub), Ei, Se, Cr; 1991 v D, Bel (2), L, Ei, Ic, Pol, WG; 1992 v Br, G, L, Ei, A, R, Ho, Arg, J; (with Everton), 1993 v Fa, Cy, Bel, Ei, Bel, RCS, Fa; 1994 v RCS, Cy, R, N, Se, Es; 1995 v Mol, Ge, Bul, G, Ge; 1996 v Mol, G, I, Sw, Sm; (with Birmingham C), 1997 v Sm, Ho, T, Ei, Bel (59)
Howell, E. G. (Builth), 1888 v Ni; 1890 v E; 1891 v E (3)
Howells, R. G. (Cardiff C), 1954 v E, S (2)
Hugh, A. R. (Newport Co), 1930 v Ni (1)
Hughes, A. (Rhos), 1894 v E, S (2)
Hughes, A. (Chirk), 1907 v Ni (1)
Hughes, C. M. (Luton T), 1992 v Ho (sub); 1994 v N (sub), Se (sub), Es; 1996 v Alb; 1997 v Ei (sub); (with Wimbledon), 1998 v T, Bel (8)
Hughes, E. (Everton), 1899 v S, Ni; (with Tottenham H), 1901 v E, S; 1902 v Ni; 1904 v E, Ni, S; 1905 v E, Ni, S; 1906 v E, Ni; 1907 v E (14)
Hughes, E. (Wrexham), 1906 v S; (with Nottingham F), 1906 v Ni; 1908 v S, E; 1910 v Ni, E, S; 1911 v Ni, E, S; (with Wrexham), 1912 v Ni, E, S; (with Manchester C), 1913 v E, S; 1914 v N (16)
Hughes, F. W. (Northwich Victoria), 1882 v E, Ni; 1883 v E, Ni, S; 1884 v S (6)
Hughes, I. (Luton T), 1951 v E, Ni, P, Sw (4)
Hughes, J. (Cambridge University), 1877 v S; (with Aberystwyth), 1879 v S (2)
Hughes, J. (Liverpool), 1905 v E, S, Ni (3)
Hughes, J. I. (Blackburn R), 1935 v Ni (1)
Hughes, L. M. (Manchester U), 1984 v E, Ni; 1985 v Ic, Sp, Ic, N, S, Sp, N; 1986 v S, H, U; (with Barcelona), 1987 v USSR, Cz; 1988 v D (2), Cz, Se, Ma, I; (with Manchester U), 1989 v Ho, Fi, Is, Se, WG; 1990 v Fi, WG, Cr; 1991 v D, Bel (2), L, Ic, Pol, WG; 1992 v Br, G, L, Ei, R, Ho, Arg, J; 1993 v Fa, Cy, Bel, Ei, Bel, RCS, Fa; 1994 v RCS, Cy, N; 1995 v Ge, Bul, G, Ge; (with Chelsea), 1996 v Mol, I, Sm; 1997 v Sm, Ho, T, Ei, Bel; 1998 v T; (with Southampton), 1999 v I, D, Bl, Sw, I, D (72)
Hughes, P. W. (Bangor), 1887 v Ni; 1889 v Ni, E (3)
Hughes, W. (Bootle), 1891 v E; 1892 v S, Ni (3)
Hughes, W. A. (Blackburn R), 1949 v E, Ni, P, Bel, Sw (5)
Hughes, W. M. (Birmingham), 1938 v E, Ni, S; 1939 v E, Ni, S, F; 1947 v E, S, Ni (10)
Humphreys, J. V. (Everton), 1947 v Ni (1)
Humphreys, R. (Druids), 1888 v Ni (1)
Hunter, A. H. (FA of Wales Secretary), 1887 v Ni (1)

Jackett, K. (Watford), 1983 v N, Y, E, Bul, S; 1984 v N, R, Y, S, Ni, N, Is; 1985 v Ic, Sp, Ic, N, S, Sp, N; 1986 v S, H, S.Ar, Ei, Ca (2); 1987 v Fi (2); 1988 v D, Cz, Y, Se (31)
Jackson, W. (St Helens Rec), 1899 v Ni (1)
James, E. (Chirk), 1893 v E, Ni; 1894 v E, S, Ni; 1898 v S, E; 1899 v Ni (8)
James, E. G. (Blackpool), 1966 v Br (2), Ch; 1967 v Ni; 1968 v S; 1971 v Cz, S, E, Ni (9)
James, L. (Burnley), 1972 v Cz, R, S (sub); 1973 v E (3), Pol, S, Ni; 1974 v Pol, E, S, Ni; 1975 v A, H (2), L (2), S, E, Ni; 1976 v A; (with Derby Co), S, E, Y (2), Ni; 1977 v WG, S (2), Cz, E, Ni; 1978 v K (2); (with QPR), WG; (with Burnley), 1979 v T; (with Swansea C), 1980 v E, S, Ni, Ic; 1981 v T, Ei, T, S, E; 1982 v Cz, Ic, USSR, E (sub), S, Ni, F; (with Sunderland), 1983 v E (sub) (54)
James, R. M. (Swansea C), 1979 v Ma, WG (sub), S, E, Ni, Ma; 1980 v WG; 1982 v Cz (sub), Ic, Sp, E, S, Ni, F; 1983 v N, Y, E, Bul; (with Stoke C), 1984 v N, R, Bul, Y, S, E, Ni, N, Is; 1985 v Ic, Sp, Ic; (with QPR), N, S, Sp, N; 1986 v S, S.Ar, Ei, U, Ca (2); 1987 v Fi (2), USSR, Cz; (with Leicester C), 1988 v D (2); (with Swansea C), Y (47)
James, W. (West Ham U), 1931 v Ni; 1932 v Ni (2)
Jarrett, R. H. (Ruthin), 1889 v Ni; 1890 v S (2)
Jarvis, A. L. (Hull C), 1967 v S, E, Ni (3)
Jenkins, E. (Lovell's Ath), 1925 v E (1)
Jenkins, J. (Brighton), 1924 v Ni, E, S; 1925 v S, Ni; 1926 v E, S; 1927 v S (8)
Jenkins, R. W. (Rhyl), 1902 v Ni (1)

Jenkins, S. R. (Swansea C), 1996 v G; (with Huddersfield T), Alb, I; 1997 v Ho (sub), T, S; 1998 v T, Bel, Br, Jam; 1999 v I (sub), D; 2001 v Pol (sub), Uk (sub); 2002 v Arm, N (16)
Jenkyns, C. A. L. (Small Heath), 1892 v E, S, Ni; 1895 v E; (with Woolwich Arsenal), 1896 v S; (with Newton Heath), 1897 v Ni; (with Walsall), 1898 v S, E (8)
Jennings, W. (Bolton W), 1914 v E, S; 1920 v S; 1923 v Ni, E; 1924 v E, S, Ni; 1927 v S, Ni; 1929 v S (11)
John, R. F. (Arsenal), 1923 v S, Ni; 1925 v Ni; 1926 v E; 1927 v E; 1928 v E, Ni; 1930 v E, S; 1932 v E; 1933 v F, Ni; 1935 v Ni; 1936 v S; 1937 v E (15)
John, W. R. (Walsall), 1931 v Ni; (with Stoke C), 1933 v E, S, Ni, F; 1934 v E, S; (with Preston NE), 1935 v E, S; (with Sheffield U), 1936 v E, S, Ni; (with Swansea T), 1939 v E, S (14)
Johnson, A. J. (Nottingham F), 1999 v I, D, Bl, Sw; 2000 v Fi (sub), Br (sub), P (sub); (with WBA), 2003 v Cro, Fi, US (10)
Johnson, M. G. (Swansea T), 1964 v Ni (1)
Jones, A. (Port Vale), 1987 v Fi, Cz (sub); 1988 v D, (with Charlton Ath), D (sub), Cz (sub); 1990 v Hol (sub) (6)
Jones, A. F. (Oxford University), 1877 v S (1)
Jones, A. T. (Nottingham F), 1905 v E; (with Notts Co), 1906 v E (2)
Jones, Bryn (Wolverhampton W), 1935 v Ni; 1936 v E, S, Ni; 1937 v E, S, Ni; 1938 v E, S, Ni; (with Arsenal), 1939 v E, S, Ni; 1947 v S, Ni; 1948 v E; 1949 v S (17)
Jones, B. S. (Swansea T), 1963 v S, E, Ni, H (2); 1964 v S, Ni; (with Plymouth Arg), 1965 v D; (with Cardiff C), 1969 v S, E, Ni, I (sub), WG, EG, R of UK (15)
Jones, Charlie (Nottingham F), 1926 v E; 1927 v S, Ni; 1928 v E; (with Arsenal), 1930 v E, S; 1932 v E; 1933 v F (8)
Jones, Cliff (Swansea T), 1954 v A; 1956 v E, Ni, S, A; 1957 v E, S, Ni, Cz (2), EG; 1958 v EG, E, S, Is (2); (with Tottenham H), 1958 v Ni, H (2), M, Se, Br; 1959 v Ni; 1960 v E, S, Ni; 1961 v S, E, Ni, Sp, H, Ei; 1962 v E, Ni, S, Br (2), M; 1963 v S, Ni, H; 1964 v E, S, Ni; 1965 v E, S, Ni, D, Gr (2), USSR, I; 1967 v S, E; 1968 v E, S, WG; (with Fulham), 1969 v I, R of UK (59)
Jones, C. W. (Birmingham), 1935 v Ni; 1939 v F (2)
Jones, D. (Chirk), 1888 v S, Ni; (with Bolton W), 1889 v E, S, Ni; 1890 v E; 1891 v S; 1892 v Ni; 1893 v E; 1894 v E; 1895 v E; 1898 v S; (with Manchester C), 1900 v E, Ni (14)
Jones, D. E. (Norwich C), 1976 v S, E (sub); 1978 v S, Cz, WG, Ir, E; 1980 v E (8)
Jones, D. O. (Leicester C), 1934 v E, Ni; 1935 v E, S; 1936 v E, Ni; 1937 v Ni (7)
Jones, Evan (Chelsea), 1910 v S, Ni; (with Oldham Ath), 1911 v E, S; 1912 v E, S; (with Bolton W), 1914 v Ni (7)
Jones, F. R. (Bangor), 1885 v E, Ni; 1886 v S (3)
Jones, F. W. (Small Heath), 1893 v S (1)
Jones, G. P. (Wrexham), 1907 v S, Ni (2)
Jones, H. (Aberaman), 1902 v Ni (1)
Jones, Humphrey (Bangor), 1885 v E, Ni, S; 1886 v E, Ni, S; (with Queen's Park), 1887 v E; (with East Stirlingshire), 1889 v E, Ni; 1890 v E, S, Ni; (with Queen's Park), 1891 v E, S (14)
Jones, Ivor (Swansea T), 1920 v S, Ni; 1921 v Ni, E; 1922 v S, Ni; (with WBA), 1923 v E, Ni; 1924 v S; 1926 v Ni (10)
Jones, Jeffrey (Llandrindod Wells), 1908 v Ni; 1909 v Ni; 1910 v S (3)
Jones, J. (Druids), 1876 v S (1)
Jones, J. (Berwyn Rangers), 1883 v S, Ni; 1884 v S (3)
Jones, J. (Wrexham), 1925 v Ni (1)
Jones, J. L. (Sheffield U), 1895 v E, S, Ni; 1896 v Ni, S, E; 1897 v Ni, S, E; (with Tottenham H), 1898 v Ni, E, S; 1899 v S, Ni; 1900 v S; 1902 v E, S, Ni; 1904 v E, S, Ni (21)
Jones, J. Love (Stoke C), 1906 v S; (with Middlesbrough), 1910 v Ni (2)
Jones, J. O. (Bangor), 1901 v S, Ni (2)
Jones, J. P. (Liverpool), 1976 v A, E, S; 1977 v WG, S (2), Cz, E, Ni; 1978 v K (2), S, Cz, WG, Ir, E, S, Ni; (with Wrexham), 1979 v Ma, T, WG, S, E, Ni, Ma; 1980 v Ei, WG, T, E, S, Ni, Ic; 1981 v T, Ei, T, S, E, USSR; 1982 v Cz, Ic, USSR, Sp, E, S, Ni, F; 1983 v N; (with Chelsea), Y, E, Bul, S, Ni, Br; 1984 v N, R, Bul, Y, S, E, Ni, N, Is; 1985 v Ic, N, S, N; (with Huddersfield T), 1986 v S, H, Ei, U, Ca (2) (72)
Jones, J. T. (Stoke C), 1912 v E, S, Ni; 1913 v E, Ni; 1914 v S, Ni; 1920 v E, S, Ni; (with C Palace), 1921 v E, S; 1922 v E, S, Ni (15)
Jones, K. (Aston Villa), 1950 v S (1)
Jones, Leslie J. (Cardiff C), 1933 v F; (with Coventry C), 1935 v Ni; 1936 v S; 1937 v E, S, Ni; (with Arsenal), 1938 v E, S, Ni; 1939 v E, S (11)
Jones, M. G. (Leeds U), 2000 v Sw (sub), Q, Br, P; 2001 v Pol (sub); (with Leicester C), Arm (sub), Uk, Pol (sub); 2002 v Arm (sub), N (sub), Bl; 2003 v Bos (sub), US (13)
Jones, P. L. (Liverpool), 1997 v S (sub); (with Tranmere R), 1998 v T (sub) (2)
Jones, P. S. (Stockport Co), 1997 v S (sub); (with Southampton), 1998 v T (sub), Br, Jam, Ma; 1999 v I, D, Bl, Sw, I, D; 2000 v Bl, Sw, Q; 2001 v Bl, N, Pol, Arm, Uk, Pol, Uk; 2002 v Arm, N, Bl, Arg; 2003 v Cro, Fi, I, Az (2), US (31)
Jones, P. W. (Bristol R), 1971 v Fi (1)
Jones, R. (Bangor), 1887 v S; 1889 v E; (with Crewe Alex), 1890 v E (3)
Jones, R. (Leicester Fosse), 1898 v S (1)
Jones, R. (Druids), 1899 v S (1)
Jones, R. (Bangor), 1900 v S, Ni (2)
Jones, R. (Millwall), 1906 v S, Ni (2)
Jones, R. A. (Druids), 1884 v E, Ni, S; 1885 v S (4)
Jones, R. A. (Sheffield W), 1994 v Es (1)
Jones, R. S. (Everton), 1894 v Ni (1)
Jones, S. (Wrexham), 1887 v Ni; (with Chester), 1890 v S (2)
Jones, S. (Wrexham), 1893 v S, Ni; (with Burton Swifts), 1895 v S; 1896 v E, Ni; (with Druids), 1899 v E (6)
Jones, T. (Manchester U), 1926 v Ni; 1927 v E, Ni; 1930 v Ni (4)
Jones, T. D. (Aberdare), 1908 v Ni (1)
Jones, T. G. (Everton), 1938 v Ni; 1939 v E, S, Ni; 1947 v E, S; 1948 v E, S, Ni; 1949 v E, Ni, P, Bel, Sw; 1950 v E, S, Bel (17)
Jones, T. J. (Sheffield W), 1932 v Ni; 1933 v F (2)
Jones, V. P. (Wimbledon), 1995 v Bul (2), G, Ge; 1996 v Sw; 1997 v Ho, T, Ei, Bel (9)
Jones, W. E. A. (Swansea T), 1947 v E, S; (with Tottenham H), 1949 v E, S (4)
Jones, W. J. (Aberdare), 1901 v E, S; (with West Ham U), 1902 v E, S (4)
Jones, W. Lot (Manchester C), 1905 v E, Ni; 1906 v E, S, Ni; 1907 v E, S, Ni; 1908 v S; 1909 v E, S, Ni; 1910 v E; 1911 v E; 1913 v E, S; 1914 v S, Ni; (with Southend U), 1920 v E, Ni (20)
Jones, W. P. (Druids), 1889 v E, Ni; (with Wynstay), 1890 v S, Ni (4)
Jones, W. R. (Aberystwyth), 1897 v S (1)

Keenor, F. C. (Cardiff C), 1920 v E, Ni; 1921 v E, Ni, S; 1922 v Ni; 1923 v E, Ni, S; 1924 v E, Ni, S; 1925 v E, Ni, S; 1926 v S; 1927 v E, Ni, S; 1928 v E, Ni, S; 1929 v E, Ni, S; 1930 v E, Ni, S; 1931 v E, Ni, S; (with Crewe Alex), 1933 v S (32)
Kelly, F. C. (Wrexham), 1899 v S, Ni; (with Druids), 1902 v Ni (3)
Kelsey, A. J. (Arsenal), 1954 v Ni, A; 1955 v S, Ni, Y; 1956 v E, Ni, S, A; 1957 v E, Ni, S, Cz (2), EG; 1958 v E, S, Ni, Is (2), H (2), M, Se, Br; 1959 v E, S; 1960 v E, Ni, S; 1961 v E, Ni, S, H, Sp (2); 1962 v E, S, Ni, Br (2) (41)
Kenrick, S. L. (Druids), 1876 v S; 1877 v S; (with Oswestry), 1879 v E, S; (with Shropshire Wanderers), 1881 v E (5)
Ketley, C. F. (Druids), 1882 v Ni (1)
King, J. (Swansea T), 1955 v E (1)
Kinsey, N. (Norwich C), 1951 v Ni, P, Sw; 1952 v E; (with Birmingham C), 1954 v Ni; 1956 v E, S (7)
Knill, A. R. (Swansea C), 1989 v Ho (1)
Koumas, J. (Tranmere R), 2001 v Uk (sub); 2002 v CzR; (with WBA), 2003 v Bos (sub), US (4)
Krzywicki, R. L. (WBA), 1970 v EG, I; (with Huddersfield T), Ni, E, S; 1971 v R, Fi; 1972 v Cz (sub) (8)

Lambert, R. (Liverpool), 1947 v S; 1948 v E; 1949 v P, Bel, Sw (5)
Latham, G. (Liverpool), 1905 v E, S; 1906 v S; 1907 v E, S, Ni; 1908 v E; 1909 v Ni; (with Southport Central), 1910 v E; (with Cardiff C), 1913 v Ni (10)
Law, B. J. (QPR), 1990 v Se (1)
Lawrence, E. (Clapton Orient), 1930 v Ni; (with Notts Co), 1932 v S (2)
Lawrence, S. (Swansea T), 1932 v Ni; 1933 v F; 1934 v S, E, Ni; 1935 v E, S; 1936 v S (8)
Lea, A. (Wrexham), 1889 v E; 1891 v S, Ni; 1893 v Ni (4)
Lea, C. (Ipswich T), 1965 v Ni, I (2)
Leary, P. (Bangor), 1889 v Ni (1)
Leek, K. (Leicester C), 1961 v S, E, Ni, H, Sp (2); (with Newcastle U), 1962 v S; (with Birmingham C), v Br (sub), M; 1963 v E; 1965 v S, Gr; (with Northampton T), 1965 v Gr (13)
Legg, A. (Birmingham C), 1996 v Sw, Sm (sub); 1997 v Ho (sub), Ei; (with Cardiff C), 1999 v D (sub); 2001 v Arm (6)
Lever, A. R. (Leicester C), 1953 v S (1)

Lewis, B. (Chester), 1891 v Ni; (with Wrexham), 1892 v S, E, Ni; (with Middlesbrough), 1893 v S, E; (with Wrexham), 1894 v S, E, Ni; 1895 v S (10)
Lewis, D. (Arsenal), 1927 v E; 1928 v Ni; 1930 v E (3)
Lewis, D. (Swansea C), 1983 v Br (sub) (1)
Lewis, D. J. (Swansea T), 1933 v E, S (2)
Lewis, D. M. (Bangor), 1890 v Ni, S (2)
Lewis, J. (Bristol R), 1906 v E (1)
Lewis, J. (Cardiff C), 1926 v S (1)
Lewis, T. (Wrexham), 1881 v E, S (2)
Lewis, W. (Bangor), 1885 v E; 1886 v E, S; 1887 v E, S; 1888 v E; 1889 v E, Ni, S; (with Crewe Alex), 1890 v E; 1891 v E, S; 1892 v E, S, Ni; 1894 v E, S, Ni; (with Chester), 1895 v S, Ni, E; 1896 v E, S, Ni; (with Manchester C), 1897 v E, S; (with Chester), 1898 v Ni (27)
Lewis, W. L. (Swansea T), 1927 v E, Ni; 1928 v E, Ni; 1929 v S; (with Huddersfield T), 1930 v E (6)
Llewellyn, C. M. (Norwich C), 1998 v Ma (sub), Tun (sub) (2)
Lloyd, B. W. (Wrexham), 1976 v A, E, S (3)
Lloyd, J. W. (Wrexham), 1879 v S; (with Newtown), 1885 v S (2)
Lloyd, R. A. (Ruthin), 1891 v Ni; 1895 v S (2)
Lockley, A. (Chirk), 1898 v Ni (1)
Lovell, S. (C Palace), 1982 v USSR (sub); (with Millwall), 1985 v N; 1986 v S (sub), H (sub), Ca (1+1 sub) (6)
Lowrie, G. (Coventry C), 1948 v E, S, Ni; (with Newcastle U), 1949 v P (4)
Lowndes, S. (Newport Co), 1983 v S (sub), Br (sub); (with Millwall), 1985 v N (sub); 1986 v S.Ar (sub), Ei, U, Ca (2); (with Barnsley), 1987 v Fi (sub); 1988 v Se (sub) (10)
Lucas, P. M. (Leyton Orient), 1962 v Ni, M; 1963 v S, E (4)
Lucas, W. H. (Swansea T), 1949 v S, Ni, P, Bel, Sw; 1950 v E; 1951 v E (7)
Lumberg, A. (Wrexham), 1929 v Ni; 1930 v E, S; (with Wolverhampton W), 1932 v S (4)

McCarthy, T. P. (Wrexham), 1899 v Ni (1)
McMillan, R. (Shrewsbury Engineers), 1881 v E, S (2)
Maguire, G. T. (Portsmouth), 1990 v Fi (sub), Ho, WG, Ei, Se; 1992 v Br (sub), G (7)
Mahoney, J. F. (Stoke C), 1968 v E; 1969 v EG; 1971 v Cz; 1973 v E (3), Pol, S, Ni; 1974 v Pol, E, S, Ni; 1975 v A, H (2), L (2), S, E, Ni; 1976 v A, Y (2), E, Ni; 1977 v WG, Cz, S, E, Ni; (with Middlesbrough), 1978 v K (2), S, Cz, Ir, E (sub), S, Ni; 1979 v WG, S, E, Ni, Ma; (with Swansea C), 1980 v Ei, WG, T (sub); 1982 v Ic, USSR; 1983 v Y, E (51)
Mardon, P. J. (WBA), 1996 v G (sub) (1)
Marriott, A. (Wrexham), 1996 v Sw (sub); 1997 v S; 1998 v Bel, Br (sub), Tun (5)
Martin, T. J. (Newport Co), 1930 v Ni (1)
Marustik, C. (Swansea C), 1982 v Sp, E, S, Ni, F; 1983 v N (6)
Mates, J. (Chirk), 1891 v Ni; 1897 v E, S (3)
Mathews, R. W. (Liverpool), 1921 v Ni; (with Bristol C), 1923 v E; (with Bradford), 1926 v Ni (3)
Matthews, W. (Chester), 1905 v Ni; 1908 v E (2)
Matthias, J. S. (Brymbo), 1896 v S, Ni; (with Shrewsbury), 1897 v E, S; (with Wolverhampton W), 1899 v S (5)
Matthias, T. J. (Wrexham), 1914 v S, E; 1920 v Ni, S, E; 1921 v S, E, Ni; 1922 v S, E, Ni; 1923 v S (12)
Mays, A. W. (Wrexham), 1929 v Ni (1)
Medwin, T. C. (Swansea T), 1953 v Ni, F, Y; (with Tottenham H), 1957 v E, S, Ni, Cz (2), EG; 1958 v E, S, Ni, Is (2), H (2), M, Br; 1959 v E, S, Ni; 1960 v E, S, Ni; 1961 v S, Ei, E, Sp; 1963 v E, H (30)
Melville, A. K. (Swansea C), 1990 v WG, Ei, Se, Cr (sub); (with Oxford U), 1991 v Ic, Pol, WG; 1992 v Br, G, L, R, Ho, J (sub); 1993 v RCS, Fa (sub); (with Sunderland), 1994 v RCS (sub), R, N, Se, Es; 1995 v Alb, Mol (sub), Ge, Bul; 1996 v G, Alb, Sm; 1997 v Sm, Ho (2), T; 1998 v T; (with Fulham), 1999 v I, D; 2000 v Bl, Q, Fi, Br, P; 2001 v Bl, N, Pol, Arm, Uk, Pol, Uk; 2002 v Arm, Bl, Arg, CzR, G; 2003 v Cro, Fi, I, Az, Bos, Az, US (58)
Meredith, S. (Chirk), 1900 v S; 1901 v S, E, Ni; (with Stoke C), 1902 v E; 1903 v Ni; 1904 v E; (with Leyton), 1907 v E (8)
Meredith, W. H. (Manchester C), 1895 v E, Ni; 1896 v E, Ni; 1897 v E, Ni, S; 1898 v E, Ni; 1899 v E; 1900 v E, Ni; 1901 v E, Ni; 1902 v E, S; 1903 v E, S, Ni; 1904 v E; 1905 v E, S; (with Manchester U), 1907 v E, S, Ni; 1908 v E, Ni; 1909 v E, S, Ni; 1910 v E, S, Ni; 1911 v E, S, Ni; 1912 v E, S, Ni; 1913 v E, S, Ni; 1914 v E, S, Ni; 1920 v E, S, Ni (48)
Mielczarek, R. (Rotherham U), 1971 v Fi (1)
Millership, H. (Rotherham Co), 1920 v E, S, Ni; 1921 v E, S, Ni (6)
Millington, A. H. (WBA), 1963 v S, E, H; (with C Palace), 1965 v E, USSR; (with Peterborough U), 1966 v Ch, Br; 1967 v E, Ni; 1968 v Ni, WG; 1969 v I, EG; (with Swansea T), 1970 v E, S, Ni; 1971 v Cz, Fi; 1972 v Fi (sub), Cz, R (21)
Mills, T. J. (Clapton Orient), 1934 v E, Ni; (with Leicester C), 1935 v E, S (4)
Mills-Roberts, R. H. (St Thomas' Hospital), 1885 v E, S, Ni; 1886 v E; 1887 v E; (with Preston NE), 1888 v E, Ni; (with Llanberis), 1892 v E (8)
Moore, G. (Cardiff C), 1960 v E, S, Ni; 1961 v Ei, Sp; (with Chelsea), 1962 v Br; 1963 v Ni, H; (with Manchester U), 1964 v S, Ni; (with Northampton T), 1966 v Ni, Ch; (with Charlton Ath), 1969 v S, E, Ni, R of UK; 1970 v E, S, Ni, I; 1971 v R (21)
Morgan, J. R. (Cambridge University), 1877 v S; (with Swansea T), 1879 v S; (with Derby School Staff), 1880 v E, S; 1881 v E, S; 1882 v E, S, Ni; (with Swansea T), 1883 v E (10)
Morgan, J. T. (Wrexham), 1905 v Ni (1)
Morgan-Owen, H. (Oxford University), 1902 v S; 1906 v E, Ni; (with Welshpool), 1907 v S (5)
Morgan-Owen, M. M. (Oxford University), 1897 v S, Ni; 1898 v E, S; 1899 v S; 1900 v E; (with Corinthians), 1901 v S, E; 1903 v S; 1906 v S, E, Ni; 1907 v E (13)
Morley, E. J. (Swansea T), 1925 v E; (with Clapton Orient), 1929 v E, S, Ni (4)
Morris, A. G. (Aberystwyth), 1896 v E, Ni, S; (with Swindon T), 1897 v E; 1898 v S; (with Nottingham F), 1899 v E, S; 1903 v E, S; 1905 v E, S; 1907 v E, S; 1908 v E; 1910 v E, S, Ni; 1911 v E, S, Ni; 1912 v E (21)
Morris, C. (Chirk), 1900 v E, S, Ni; (with Derby Co), 1901 v E, S, Ni; 1902 v E; 1903 v E, S, Ni; 1904 v Ni; 1905 v E, S, Ni; 1906 v S; 1907 v S; 1908 v E, S; 1909 v E, S, Ni; 1910 v E, S, Ni; (with Huddersfield T), 1911 v E, S, Ni (27)
Morris, E. (Chirk), 1893 v E, S, Ni (3)
Morris, H. (Sheffield U), 1894 v S; (with Manchester C), 1896 v E; (with Grimsby T), 1897 v E (3)
Morris, J. (Oswestry), 1887 v S (1)
Morris, J. (Chirk), 1898 v Ni (1)
Morris, R. (Chirk), 1900 v E, Ni; 1901 v Ni; 1902 v S; (with Shrewsbury T), 1903 v E, Ni (6)
Morris, R. (Druids), 1902 v E, S; (with Newtown), Ni; (with Liverpool), 1903 v S, Ni; 1904 v E, S, Ni; (with Leeds C), 1906 v S; (with Grimsby T), 1907 v Ni; (with Plymouth Arg), 1908 v Ni (11)
Morris, S. (Birmingham), 1937 v E, S; 1938 v E, S; 1939 v F (5)
Morris, W. (Burnley), 1947 v Ni; 1949 v E; 1952 v S, Ni, R of UK (5)
Moulsdale, J. R. B. (Corinthians), 1925 v Ni (1)
Murphy, J. P. (WBA), 1933 v F, E, Ni; 1934 v E, S; 1935 v E, S, Ni; 1936 v E, S, Ni; 1937 v S, Ni; 1938 v E, S (15)

Nardiello, D. (Coventry C), 1978 v Cz, WG (sub) (2)
Neal, J. E. (Colwyn Bay), 1931 v E, S (2)
Neilson, A. B. (Newcastle U), 1992 v Ei; 1994 v Se, Es; 1995 v Ge; (with Southampton), 1997 v Ho (5)
Newnes, J. (Nelson), 1926 v Ni (1)
Newton, L. F. (Cardiff Corinthians), 1912 v Ni (1)
Nicholas, D. S. (Stoke C), 1923 v S; (with Swansea T), 1927 v E, Ni (3)
Nicholas, P. (C Palace), 1979 v S (sub), Ni (sub), Ma; 1980 v Ei, WG, T, E, S, Ni, Ic; 1981 v T, Cz, E; (with Arsenal), T, S, E, USSR; 1982 v Cz, Ic, USSR, Sp, E, S, Ni, F; 1983 v Y, Bul, S, Ni; 1984 v N, Bul, N, Is; (with C Palace), 1985 v Sp; (with Luton T), N, S, Sp, N; 1986 v S, H, S.Ar, Ei, U, Ca (2); 1987 v Fi (2) USSR, Cz; (with Aberdeen), 1988 v D (2), Cz, Y, Se; (with Chelsea), 1989 v Ho, Fi, Is, Se, WG; 1990 v Fi, Ho, WG, Ei, Se, Cr; 1991 v D (sub), Bel, L, Ei; (with Watford), Bel, Pol, WG; 1992 v L (73)
Nicholls, J. (Newport Co), 1924 v E, Ni; (with Cardiff C), 1925 v E, S (4)
Niedzwiecki, E. A. (Chelsea), 1985 v N (sub); 1988 v D (2)
Nock, W. (Newtown), 1897 v Ni (1)
Nogan, L. M. (Watford), 1992 v A (sub); (with Reading), 1996 v Mol (2)
Norman, A. J. (Hull C), 1986 v Ei (sub), U, Ca; 1988 v Ma, I (5)
Nurse, M. T. G. (Swansea T), 1960 v E, Ni; 1961 v S, E, H, Ni, Ei, Sp (2); (with Middlesbrough), 1963 v E, H; 1964 v S (12)

O'Callaghan, E. (Tottenham H), 1929 v Ni; 1930 v S; 1932 v S, E; 1933 v Ni, S, E; 1934 v Ni, S, E; 1935 v E (11)
Oliver, A. (Blackburn R), 1905 v E; (with Bangor), S (2)
Oster, J. M. (Everton), 1998 v Bel (sub), Br, Jam; (with Sunderland), 2000 v Sw; 2003 v Bos (sub), Az, US (7)
O'Sullivan, P. A. (Brighton), 1973 v S (sub); 1976 v S; 1979 v Ma (sub) (3)
Owen, D. (Oswestry), 1879 v E (1)

Owen, E. (Ruthin Grammar School), 1884 v E, Ni, S (3)
Owen, G. (Chirk), 1888 v S; (with Newton Heath), 1889 v S, Ni; 1893 v Ni (4)
Owen, J. (Newton Heath), 1892 v E (1)
Owen, Trevor (Crewe Alex), 1899 v E, S (2)
Owen, T. (Oswestry), 1879 v E (1)
Owen, W. (Chirk), 1884 v E; 1885 v Ni; 1887 v E; 1888 v E; 1889 v E, Ni, S; 1890 v S, Ni; 1891 v E, S, Ni; 1892 v E, S; 1893 v S, Ni (16)
Owen, W. P. (Ruthin), 1880 v E, S; 1881 v E, S; 1882 v E, S, Ni; 1883 v E, S; 1884 v E, S, Ni (12)
Owens, J. (Wrexham), 1902 v S (1)

Page, M. E. (Birmingham C), 1971 v Fi; 1972 v S, Ni; 1973 v E (1+1 sub), Ni; 1974 v S, Ni; 1975 v H, L, S, E, Ni; 1976 v E, Y (2), E, Ni; 1977 v WG, S; 1978 v K (sub+1), WG, Ir, E, S; 1979 v Ma, WG (28)
Page, R. J. (Watford), 1997 v T, Bel, S; 1998 v T, Bel (sub), Br, I; 2000 v Bl, Sw, Q, Fi, Br, P; 2001 v Bl, N, Pol, Arm, Uk, Pol, Uk; (with Sheffield U), 2002 v N, Bl (sub), Arg, CzR, G; 2003 v Az, Bos, Az (28)
Palmer, D. (Swansea T), 1957 v Cz; 1958 v E, EG (3)
Parris, J. E. (Bradford), 1932 v Ni (1)
Parry, B. J. (Swansea T), 1951 v S (1)
Parry, C. (Everton), 1891 v E, S; 1893 v E; 1894 v E; 1895 v E, S; (with Newtown), 1896 v E, S, Ni; 1897 v Ni; 1898 v E, S, Ni (13)
Parry, E. (Liverpool), 1922 v S; 1923 v E, Ni; 1925 v Ni; 1926 v Ni (5)
Parry, M. (Liverpool), 1901 v E, S, Ni; 1902 v E, S, Ni; 1903 v E, S; 1904 v E, Ni; 1906 v E; 1908 v E, S, Ni; 1909 v E, S (16)
Parry, T. D. (Oswestry), 1900 v E, S, Ni; 1901 v E, S, Ni; 1902 v E (7)
Parry, W. (Newtown), 1895 v Ni (1)
Pascoe, C. (Swansea C), 1984 v N, Is; (with Sunderland), 1989 v Fi, Is, WG (sub); 1990 v Ho (sub), WG (sub); 1991 v Ei, Ic (sub); 1992 v Br (10)
Paul, R. (Swansea T), 1949 v E, S, Ni, P, Sw; 1950 v E, S, Ni, Bel; (with Manchester C), 1951 v S, E, Ni, P, Sw; 1952 v E, S, Ni, R of UK; 1953 v S, E, Ni, F, Y; 1954 v E, S, Ni; 1955 v S, E, Y; 1956 v E, Ni, S, A (33)
Peake, E. (Aberystwyth), 1908 v Ni; (with Liverpool), 1909 v Ni, S, E; 1910 v S, Ni; 1911 v Ni; 1912 v E; 1913 v E, Ni; 1914 v Ni (11)
Peers, E. J. (Wolverhampton W), 1914 v Ni, S, E; 1920 v E, S; 1921 v S, Ni, E; (with Port Vale), 1922 v E, S, Ni; 1923 v E (12)
Pembridge, M. A. (Luton T), 1992 v Br, Ei, R; (with Derby Co), Ho, J (sub); 1993 v Bel (sub), Ei; 1994 v N (sub); 1995 v Alb (sub), Mol, Ge (sub); (with Sheffield W), 1996 v Mol, G, Alb, Sw, Sm; 1997 v Sm, Ho (2), T, Ei, Bel, S; 1998 v Bel, Br, Jam, Ma, Tun; (with Benfica), 1999 v D (sub), Bl, Sw, I (sub), D (sub); (with Everton), 2000 v Bl, Q, Fi; 2001 v Arm, Pol, Uk; 2002 v Bl, Arg, G; 2003 v Cro, Fi, I, Bos, Az, US (48)
Perry, E. (Doncaster R), 1938 v E, S, Ni (3)
Perry, J. (Cardiff C), 1994 v N (1)
Phennah, E. (Civil Service), 1878 v S (1)
Phillips, C. (Wolverhampton W), 1931 v Ni; 1932 v E; 1933 v S; 1934 v E, S, Ni; 1935 v E, S, Ni; 1936 v S; (with Aston Villa), 1936 v E, Ni; 1938 v S (13)
Phillips, D. (Plymouth Arg), 1984 v E, Ni, N; (with Manchester C), 1985 v Sp, Ic, S, Sp, N; 1986 v S, H, S.Ar, Ei, U; (with Coventry C), 1987 v Fi, Cz; 1988 v D (2), Cz, Y, Se; 1989 v Se, WG; (with Norwich C), 1990 v Fi, Ho, WG, Ei, Se; 1991 v D, Bel, Ic, Pol, WG; 1992 v L, Ei, A, R, Ho (sub), Arg, J; 1993 v Fa, Cy, Bel, Ei, Bel, RCS, Fa; (with Nottingham F), 1994 v RCS, Cy, R, N, Se, Es; 1995 v Alb, Mol, Ge, Bul (2), G, Ge; 1996 v Mol (sub), Alb, I (62)
Phillips, L. (Cardiff C), 1971 v Cz, S, E, Ni; 1972 v Cz, R, S, Ni; 1973 v E; 1974 v Pol (sub), Ni; 1975 v A; (with Aston Villa), H (2), L (2), S, E, Ni; 1976 v A, E, Y (2), E, Ni; 1977 v WG, S (2), Cz, E; 1978 v K (2), S, Cz, WG, E, S; 1979 v Ma; (with Swansea C), T, WG, S, E, Ni, Ma; 1980 v Ei, WG, T, S (sub), Ni, Ic; 1981 v T, Cz, T, S, E, USSR; (with Charlton Ath), 1982 v Cz, USSR (58)
Phillips, T. J. S. (Chelsea), 1973 v E; 1974 v E; 1975 v H (sub); 1978 v K (4)
Phoenix, H. (Wrexham), 1882 v S (1)
Pipe, D. R. (Coventry C), 2003 v US (sub) (1)
Poland, G. (Wrexham), 1939 v Ni, F (2)
Pontin, K. (Cardiff C), 1980 v E (sub), S (2)
Powell, A. (Leeds U), 1947 v E, S; 1948 v E, S, Ni; (with Everton), 1949 v E; 1950 v Bel; (with Birmingham C), 1951 v S (8)
Powell, D. (Wrexham), 1968 v WG; (with Sheffield U), 1969 v S, E, Ni, I, WG; 1970 v E, S, Ni, EG; 1971 v R (11)
Powell, I. V. (QPR), 1947 v E; 1948 v E, S, Ni; (with Aston Villa), 1949 v Bel; 1950 v S, Bel; 1951 v S (8)
Powell, J. (Druids), 1878 v S; 1880 v E, S; 1882 v E, S, Ni; 1883 v E, S, Ni; (with Bolton W), 1884 v E; (with Newton Heath), 1887 v E, S; 1888 v E, S, Ni (15)
Powell, Seth (WBA), 1885 v S; 1886 v E, Ni; 1891 v E, S; 1892 v E, S (7)
Price, H. (Aston Villa), 1907 v S; (with Burton U), 1908 v Ni; (with Wrexham), 1909 v S, E, Ni (5)
Price, J. (Wrexham), 1877 v S; 1878 v S; 1879 v E; 1880 v E, S; 1881 v E, S; (with Druids), 1882 v S, E, Ni; 1883 v S, Ni (12)
Price, P. (Luton T), 1980 v E, S, Ni, Ic; 1981 v T, Cz, Ei, T, S, E, USSR; (with Tottenham H), 1982 v USSR, Sp, F; 1983 v N, Y, E, Bul, S, Ni; 1984 v N, R, Bul, Y, S (sub) (25)
Pring, K. D. (Rotherham U), 1966 v Ch, D; 1967 v Ni (3)
Pritchard, H. K. (Bristol C), 1985 v N (sub) (1)
Pryce-Jones, A. W. (Newtown), 1895 v E (1)
Pryce-Jones, W. E. (Cambridge University), 1887 v S; 1888 v S, E, Ni; 1890 v Ni (5)
Pugh, A. (Rhostyllen), 1889 v S (sub) (1)
Pugh, D. H. (Wrexham), 1896 v S, Ni; 1897 v S, Ni; (with Lincoln C), 1900 v S; 1901 v S, E (7)
Pugsley, J. (Charlton Ath), 1930 v Ni (1)
Pullen, W. J. (Plymouth Arg), 1926 v E (1)

Rankmore, F. E. J. (Peterborough), 1966 v Ch (sub) (1)
Ratcliffe, K. (Everton), 1981 v Cz, Ei, T, S, E, USSR; 1982 v Cz, Ic, USSR, Sp, E; 1983 v Y, E, Bul, S, Ni, Br; 1984 v N, R, Bul, Y, S, E, Ni, N, Is; 1985 v Ic, Sp, Ic, N, S, Sp; 1986 v S, H, S.Ar, U; 1987 v Fi (2), USSR, Cz; 1988 v D (2), Cz; 1989 v Fi, Is, Se, WG; 1990 v Fi; 1991 v D, Bel (2), L, Ei, Ic, Pol, WG; 1992 v Br, G; (with Cardiff C), 1993 v Bel (59)
Rea, J. C. (Aberystwyth), 1894 v Ni, S, E; 1895 v S; 1896 v S, Ni; 1897 v S, Ni; 1898 v Ni (9)
Ready, K. (QPR), 1997 v Ei; 1998 v Bel, Br, Ma, Tun (5)
Reece, G. I. (Sheffield U), 1966 v E, S, Ni, USSR; 1967 v S; 1969 v R of UK (sub); 1970 v I (sub); 1971 v S, E, Ni, Fi; 1972 v Fi, R, E (sub), S, Ni; (with Cardiff C), 1973 v E (sub), Ni; 1974 v Pol (sub), E, S, Ni; 1975 v A, H (2), L (2), S, Ni (29)
Reed, W. G. (Ipswich T), 1955 v S, Y (2)
Rees, A. (Birmingham C), 1984 v N (sub) (1)
Rees, J. M. (Luton T), 1992 v A (sub) (1)
Rees, R. R. (Coventry C), 1965 v S, E, Ni, D, Gr (2), I, R; 1966 v E, S, Ni, R, D, Br (2), Ch; 1967 v E, Ni; 1968 v E, S, Ni; (with WBA), WG; 1969 v I; (with Nottingham F), 1969 v WG, EG, S (sub), R of UK; 1970 v E, S, Ni, EG, I; 1971 v Cz, R, E (sub), Ni (sub), Fi; 1972 v Cz (sub), R (39)
Rees, W. (Cardiff C), 1949 v Ni, Bel, Sw; (with Tottenham H), 1950 v Ni (4)
Richards, A. (Barnsley), 1932 v S (1)
Richards, D. (Wolverhampton W), 1931 v Ni; 1933 v E, S, Ni; 1934 v E, S, Ni; 1935 v E, S, Ni; 1936 v S; (with Brentford), 1936 v E, Ni; 1937 v S, E; (with Birmingham), Ni; 1938 v E, S, Ni; 1939 v E, S (21)
Richards, G. (Druids), 1899 v E, S, Ni; (with Oswestry), 1903 v Ni; (with Shrewsbury), 1904 v S; 1905 v Ni (6)
Richards, R. W. (Wolverhampton W), 1920 v E, S; 1921 v Ni; 1922 v E, S; (with West Ham U), 1924 v E, S, Ni; (with Mold), 1926 v S (9)
Richards, S. V. (Cardiff C), 1947 v E (1)
Richards, W. E. (Fulham), 1933 v Ni (1)
Roach, J. (Oswestry), 1885 v Ni (1)
Robbins, W. W. (Cardiff C), 1931 v E, S; 1932 v Ni, E, S; (with WBA), 1933 v F, E, S, Ni; 1934 v S; 1936 v S (11)
Roberts, A. M. (QPR), 1993 v Ei (sub); 1997 v Sm (sub) (2)
Roberts, D. F. (Oxford U), 1973 v Pol, E (sub), Ni; 1974 v E, S; 1975 v A; (with Hull C), L, Ni; 1976 v S, Ni, Y; 1977 v E (sub), Ni; 1978 v K (1+1 sub), S, Ni (17)
Roberts, G. W. (Tranmere R), 2000 v Fi (sub), Br, P; 2001 v Bl (4)
Roberts, I. W. (Watford), 1990 v Ho; (with Huddersfield T), 1992 v A, Arg, J; (with Leicester C), 1994 v Se; 1995 v Alb (sub), Mol; (with Norwich C), 2000 v Fi (sub), Br, P; 2001 v Bl, N (sub), Arm (sub); 2002 v Arm, Bl (sub) (15)
Roberts, Jas (Wrexham), 1913 v S, Ni (2)
Roberts, J. (Corwen), 1879 v S; 1880 v E, S; 1882 v E, S, Ni; (with Berwyn R), 1883 v E (7)
Roberts, J. (Ruthin), 1881 v S; 1882 v S (2)
Roberts, J. (Bradford C), 1906 v Ni; 1907 v Ni (2)
Roberts, J. G. (Arsenal), 1971 v S, E, Ni, Fi; 1972 v Fi, E, Ni; (with Birmingham C), 1973 v E (2), Pol, S, Ni; 1974 v Pol, E, S, Ni; 1975 v A, H, S, E; 1976 v E, S (22)
Roberts, J. H. (Bolton), 1949 v Bel (1)

Roberts, N. W. (Wrexham), 2000 v Sw (sub); (with Wigan Ath), 2003 v Az (sub), US (sub) (3)
Roberts, P. S. (Portsmouth), 1974 v E; 1975 v A, H, L (4)
Roberts, R. (Druids), 1884 v S; (with Bolton W), 1887 v S; 1888 v S, E; 1889 v S, E; 1890 v S; 1892 v Ni; (with Preston NE), S (9)
Roberts, R. (Wrexham), 1886 v Ni; 1887 v Ni; 1891 v Ni (3)
Roberts, R. (Rhos), 1891 v Ni; (with Crewe Alex), 1893 v E (2)
Roberts, R. L. (Chester), 1890 v Ni (1)
Roberts, W. (Llangollen), 1879 v E, S; 1880 v E, S; (with Berwyn R), 1881 v S; 1883 v S (6)
Roberts, W. (Wrexham), 1886 v E, S, Ni; 1887 v Ni (4)
Roberts, W. H. (Ruthin), 1882 v E, S; 1883 v E, S, Ni; (with Rhyl), 1884 v S (6)
Robinson, C. P. (Wolverhampton W), 2000 v Bl (sub), P (sub); 2001 v Arm (sub), Uk; 2002 v Arm, N, Bl (sub), Arg (sub); (with Portsmouth), 2003 v Cro, Az (1+sub), US (sub) (12)
Robinson, J. R. C. (Charlton Ath), 1996 v Alb (sub), Sw, Sm; 1997 v Sm, Ho (1 + sub), Ei, S; 1998 v Bel, Br; 1999 v I, D (sub), Bl, Sw, I, D; 2000 v Bl, Sw, Q, Fi, Br, P; 2001 v Bl, N, Pol, Arm; 2002 v N (sub), Bl, Arg (sub), CzR (30)
Rodrigues, P. J. (Cardiff C), 1965 v Ni, Gr (2); 1966 v USSR, E, S, D; (with Leicester C), Ni, Br (2), Ch; 1967 v S; 1968 v E, S, Ni; 1969 v E, Ni, EG, R of UK; 1970 v E, S, Ni, EG; (with Sheffield W), 1971 v R, E, S, Cz, Ni; 1972 v Fi, Cz, R, E, Ni (sub); 1973 v E (3), Pol, S, Ni; 1974 v Pol (40)
Rogers, J. P. (Wrexham), 1896 v E, S, Ni (3)
Rogers, W. (Wrexham), 1931 v E, S (2)
Roose, L. R. (Aberystwyth), 1900 v Ni; (with London Welsh), 1901 v E, S, Ni; (with Stoke C), 1902 v E, S; 1904 v E; (with Everton), 1905 v S, E; (with Stoke C), 1906 v E, S, Ni; 1907 v E, S, Ni; (with Sunderland), 1908 v E, S; 1909 v E, S, Ni; 1910 v E, S, Ni; 1911 v S (24)
Rouse, R. V. (C Palace), 1959 v Ni (1)
Rowlands, A. C. (Tranmere R), 1914 v E (1)
Rowley, T. (Tranmere R), 1959 v Ni (1)
Rush, I. (Liverpool), 1980 v S (sub), Ni; 1981 v E (sub); 1982 v Ic (sub), USSR, E, S, Ni, F; 1983 v N, Y, E, Bul; 1984 v N, R, Bul, Y, S, E, Ni; 1985 v Ic, N, S, Sp; 1986 v S, S.Ar, Ei, U; 1987 v Fi (2), USSR, Cz; (with Juventus), 1988 v D, Cz, Y, Se, Ma, I; (with Liverpool), 1989 v Ho, Fi, Se, WG; 1990 v Fi, Ei; 1991 v D, Bel (2), L, Ei, Pol, WG; 1992 v G, L, R; 1993 v Fa, Cy, Bel (2), RCS, Fa; 1994 v RCS, Cy, R, N, Se, Es; 1995 v Alb, Ge, Bul, G, Ge; 1996 v Mol, I (73)
Russell, M. R. (Merthyr T), 1912 v S, Ni; 1914 v E; (with Plymouth Arg), 1920 v E, S, Ni; 1921 v E, S, Ni; 1922 v E, Ni; 1923 v E, S, Ni; 1924 v E, S, Ni; 1925 v E, S; 1926 v E, S; 1928 v S; 1929 v E (23)

Sabine, H. W. (Oswestry), 1887 v Ni (1)
Saunders, D. (Brighton & HA), 1986 v Ei (sub), Ca (2); 1987 v Fi, USSR (sub); (with Oxford U), 1988 v Y, Se, Ma, I (sub); 1989 v Ho (sub), Fi; (with Derby Co), Is, Se, WG; 1990 v Fi, Ho, WG, Se, Cr; 1991 v D, Bel (2), L, Ei, Ic, Pol, WG; (with Liverpool), 1992 v Br, G, Ei, R, Ho, Arg, J; 1993 v Fa; (with Aston Villa), Cy, Bel (2), RCS, Fa; 1994 v RCS, Cy, R, N (sub); 1995 v Ge, Bul (2), G, Ge; (with Galatasaray), 1996 v G, Alb, Sm; (with Nottingham F), 1997 v Sm, Ho (2), T, Bel, S; 1998 v T, Bel, Br; (with Sheffield U), Ma, Tun; 1999 v I (sub), D, Bl; (with Benfica) Sw, I, D; (with Bradford C), 2000 v Bl, Sw, Fi (sub), Br; 2001 v Arm, Uk (sub) (75)
Savage, R. W. (Crewe Alex), 1996 v Alb (sub), Sw (sub), Sm (sub); 1997 v Ei (sub), S; (with Leicester C), 1998 v T, Bel, Jam, Tun; 1999 v I (sub), D, Bl, Sw; 2000 v Sw, Fi, Br; 2001 v Bl, N, Pol (2); 2002 v Arm, N, Arg, CzR, G; (with Birmingham C), 2003 v Fi, I, Bos, Az (29)
Savin, G. (Oswestry), 1878 v S (1)
Sayer, P. (Cardiff C), 1977 v Cz, S, E, Ni; 1978 v K (2), S (7)
Scrine, F. H. (Swansea T), 1950 v E, Ni (2)
Sear, C. R. (Manchester C), 1963 v E (1)
Shaw, E. G. (Oswestry), 1882 v Ni; 1884 v S, Ni (3)
Sherwood, A. T. (Cardiff C), 1947 v E, Ni; 1948 v S, Ni; 1949 v E, S, Ni, P, Sw; 1950 v E, S, Ni, Bel; 1951 v E, S, Ni, P, Sw; 1952 v E, S, Ni, R of UK; 1953 v S, E, Ni, F, Y; 1954 v E, S, Ni, A; 1955 v S, E, Y, Ni; 1956 v E, S, Ni, A; (with Newport Co), 1957 v E, S (41)
Shone, W. W. (Oswestry), 1879 v E (1)
Shortt, W. W. (Plymouth Arg), 1947 v Ni; 1950 v Ni, Bel; 1952 v E, S, Ni, R of UK; 1953 v S, E, Ni, F, Y (12)
Showers, D. (Cardiff C), 1975 v E (sub), Ni (2)
Sidlow, C. (Liverpool), 1947 v E, S; 1948 v E, S, Ni; 1949 v S; 1950 v E (7)
Sisson, H. (Wrexham Olympic), 1885 v Ni; 1886 v S, Ni (3)
Slatter, N. (Bristol R), 1983 v S; 1984 v N (sub), Is; 1985 v Ic, Sp, Ic, N, S, Sp, N; (with Oxford U), 1986 v H (sub), S.Ar, Ca (2); 1987 v Fi (sub), Cz; 1988 v D (2), Cz, Ma, I; 1989 v Is (sub) (22)
Smallman, D. P. (Wrexham), 1974 v E (sub), S (sub), Ni; (with Everton), 1975 v H (sub), E, Ni (sub); 1976 v A (7)
Southall, N. (Everton), 1982 v Ni; 1983 v N, E, Bul, S, Ni, Br; 1984 v N, R, Bul, Y, S, E, Ni, N, Is; 1985 v Ic, Sp, Ic, N, S, Sp, N; 1986 v S, H, S.Ar, Ei; 1987 v USSR, Fi, Cz; 1988 v D, Cz, Y, Se; 1989 v Ho, Fi, Se, WG; 1990 v Fi, Ho, WG, Ei, Se, Cr; 1991 v D, Bel (2), L, Ei, Ic, Pol, WG; 1992 v Br, G, L, Ei, A, R, Ho, Arg, J; 1993 v Fa, Cy, Bel, Ei, Bel, RCS, Fa; 1994 v RCS, Cy, R, N, Se, Es; 1995 v Alb, Mol, Ge, Bul (2), G, Ge; 1996 v Mol, G, Alb, I, Sm; 1997 v Sm, Ho (2), T, Bel; 1998 v T (92)
Speed, G. A. (Leeds U), 1990 v Cr (sub); 1991 v D, L (sub), Ei (sub), Ic, WG (sub); 1992 v Br, G (sub), L, Ei, R, Ho,Arg,J; 1993 v Fa, Cy, Bel, Ei, Bel, Fa (sub); 1994 v RCS (sub), Cy, R, N, Se; 1995 v Alb, Mol, Ge, Bul (2), G; 1996 v Mol, G, I, Sw (sub); (with Everton), 1997 v Sm (sub), Ho (2), T, Ei, Bel, S; 1998 v T, Br; (with Newcastle U), Jam, Ma, Tun; 1999 v I, D, Sw, I, D; 2000 v Bl, Sw, Q, Fi, Br, P; 2001 v Bl, N, Pol, Arm, Uk, Pol, Uk; 2002 v Bl, Arg, G; 2003 v Fi, I, Az, Bos, Az (73)
Sprake, G. (Leeds U), 1964 v S, Ni; 1965 v S, D, Gr; 1966 v E, Ni, USSR; 1967 v S; 1968 v E, S; 1969 v S, E, Ni, WG, R of UK; 1970 v EG, I; 1971 v R, S, E, Ni; 1972 v Fi, E, S, Ni; 1973 v E (2), Pol, S, Ni; 1974 v Pol; (with Birmingham C), S, Ni; 1975 v A, H, L (37)
Stansfield, F. (Cardiff C), 1949 v S (1)
Stevenson, B. (Leeds U), 1978 v Ni; 1979 v Ma, T, S, E, Ni, Ma; 1980 v WG, T, Ic (sub); 1982 v Cz; (with Birmingham C), Sp, S, Ni, F (15)
Stevenson, N. (Swansea C), 1982 v E, S, Ni; 1983 v N (4)
Stitfall, R. F. (Cardiff C), 1953 v E; 1957 v Cz (2)
Sullivan, D. (Cardiff C), 1953 v Ni, F, Y; 1954 v Ni; 1955 v E, Ni; 1957 v E, S; 1958 v Ni, H (2), Se, Br; 1959 v S, Ni; 1960 v E, S (17)
Symons, C. J. (Portsmouth), 1992 v Ei, Ho, Arg, J; 1993 v Fa, Cy, Bel, Ei, RCS, Fa; 1994 v RCS, Cy, R; 1995 v Mol, Ge (sub), Bul, G, Ge; (with Manchester C), 1996 v Mol, G, I, Sw; 1997 v Ho (2), Ei, Bel, S; (with Fulham), 1999 v I, D, Bl, Sw; 2000 v Q (sub); 2001 v Pol; 2002 v Arm, N, Bl (36)

Tapscott, D. R. (Arsenal), 1954 v A; 1955 v S, E, Ni, Y; 1956 v E, Ni, S, A; 1957 v Ni, Cz, EG; (with Cardiff C), 1959 v E, Ni (14)
Taylor, G. K. (C Palace), 1996 v Alb, I (sub); (with Sheffield U), Sw; 1997 v Sm (sub), Ho (sub), Ei (sub); 1998 v Bel (sub), Jam; (with Burnley), 2002 v CzR (sub); 2003 v Cro (sub), Bos (sub), US (12)
Taylor, J. (Wrexham), 1898 v E (1)
Taylor, O. D. S. (Newtown), 1893 v S, Ni; 1894 v S, Ni (4)
Thomas, C. (Druids), 1899 v Ni; 1900 v S (2)
Thomas, D. A. (Swansea T), 1957 v Cz; 1958 v EG (2)
Thomas, D. S. (Fulham), 1948 v E, S, Ni; 1949 v S (4)
Thomas, E. (Cardiff Corinthians), 1925 v E (1)
Thomas, G. (Wrexham), 1885 v E, S (2)
Thomas, H. (Manchester U), 1927 v E (1)
Thomas, M. (Wrexham), 1977 v WG, S (1+1 sub), Ni (sub); 1978 v K (sub), S, Cz, Ir, E, Ni (sub); 1979 v Ma; (with Manchester U), T, WG, Ma (sub); 1980 v Ei, WG (sub), T, E, S, Ni; 1981 v Cz, S, E, USSR; (with Everton), 1982 v Cz; (with Brighton & HA), USSR (sub), Sp, E, S (sub), Ni (sub); 1983 (with Stoke C), v N, Y, E, Bul, S, Ni, Br; 1984 v R, Bul, Y; (with Chelsea), S, E; 1985 v Ic, Sp, Ic, S, Sp, N; 1986 v S; (with WBA), H, S.Ar (sub) (51)
Thomas, M. R. (Newcastle U), 1987 v Fi (1)
Thomas, R. J. (Swindon T), 1967 v Ni; 1968 v WG; 1969 v E, Ni, I, WG, R of UK; 1970 v E, S, Ni, EG, I; 1971 v S, E, Ni, R, Cz; 1972 v Fi, Cz, R, E, S, Ni; 1973 v E (3), Pol, S, Ni; 1974 v Pol; (with Derby Co), E, S, Ni; 1975 v H (2), L (2), S, E, Ni; 1976 v A, Y, E; 1977 v Cz, S, E, Ni; 1978 v K, S; (with Cardiff C), Cz (50)
Thomas, T. (Bangor), 1898 v S, Ni (2)
Thomas, W. R. (Newport Co), 1931 v E, S (2)
Thomson, D. (Druids), 1876 v S (1)
Thomson, G. F. (Druids), 1876 v S; 1877 v S (2)
Toshack, J. B. (Cardiff C), 1969 v S, E, Ni, WG, EG, R of UK; 1970 v EG, I; (with Liverpool), 1971 v S, E, Ni, Fi; 1972 v Fi, E; 1973 v E (3), Pol, S; 1975 v A, H (2), L (2), S, E; 1976 v Y (2), E; 1977 v S; 1978 v K (2), S, Cz; (with Swansea C), 1979 v WG (sub), S, E, Ni, Ma; 1980 v WG (40)
Townsend, W. (Newtown), 1887 v Ni; 1893 v Ni (2)
Trainer, H. (Wrexham), 1895 v E, S, Ni (3)
Trainer, J. (Bolton W), 1887 v S; (with Preston NE), 1888 v S; 1889 v E; 1890 v S; 1891 v S; 1892 v Ni, S; 1893 v E; 1894 v

Ni, E; 1895 v Ni, E; 1896 v S; 1897 v Ni, S, E; 1898 v S, E; 1899 v Ni, S (20)

Trollope, P. J. (Derby Co), 1997 v S; 1998 v Br (sub); (with Fulham), Jam (sub), Ma, Tun; (with Coventry C), 2002 v CzR (sub); (with Northampton T), 2003 v Cro (sub), Az (sub+sub) (9)

Turner, H. G. (Charlton Ath), 1937 v E, S, Ni; 1938 v E, S, Ni; 1939 v Ni, F (8)

Turner, J. (Wrexham), 1892 v E (1)

Turner, R. E. (Wrexham), 1891 v E, Ni (2)

Turner, W. H. (Wrexham), 1887 v E, Ni; 1890 v S; 1891 v E, S (5)

Van Den Hauwe, P. W. R. (Everton), 1985 v Sp; 1986 v S, H; 1987 v USSR, Fi, Cz; 1988 v D (2), Cz, Y, I; 1989 v Fi, Se (13)

Vaughan, D. O. (Crewe Alex), 2003 v US (1)

Vaughan, Jas (Druids), 1893 v E, S, Ni; 1899 v E (4)

Vaughan, John (Oswestry), 1879 v S; 1880 v S; 1881 v E, S; 1882 v E, S, Ni; 1883 v E, S, Ni; (with Bolton W), 1884 v E (11)

Vaughan, J. O. (Rhyl), 1885 v Ni; 1886 v Ni, E, S (4)

Vaughan, N. (Newport Co), 1983 v Y (sub), Br; 1984 v N; (with Cardiff C), R, Bul, Y, Ni (sub), N, Is; 1985 v Sp (sub) (10)

Vaughan, T. (Rhyl), 1885 v E (1)

Vearncombe, G. (Cardiff C), 1958 v EG; 1961 v Ei (2)

Vernon, T. R. (Blackburn R), 1957 v Ni, Cz (2), EG; 1958 v E, S, EG, Se; 1959 v S; (with Everton), 1960 v Ni; 1961 v S, E, Ei; 1962 v Ni, Br (2), M; 1963 v S, E, H; 1964 v E, S; (with Stoke C), 1965 v Ni, Gr, I; 1966 v E, S, Ni, USSR, D; 1967 v Ni; 1968 v E (32)

Villars, A. K. (Cardiff C), 1974 v E, S, Ni (sub) (3)

Vizard, E. T. (Bolton W), 1911 v E, S, Ni; 1912 v E, S; 1913 v S; 1914 v E, Ni; 1920 v E; 1921 v E, S, Ni; 1922 v E, S; 1923 v E, Ni; 1924 v E, S, Ni; 1926 v E, S; 1927 v S (22)

Walley, J. T. (Watford), 1971 v Cz (1)

Walsh, I. (C Palace), 1980 v Ei, T, E, S, Ic; 1981 v T, Cz, Ei, T, S, E, USSR; 1982 v Cz (sub), Ic; (with Swansea C), Sp, S (sub), Ni (sub), F (18)

Ward, D. (Bristol R), 1959 v E; (with Cardiff C), 1962 v E (2)

Ward, D. (Notts Co), 2000 v P; (with Nottingham F), 2002 v CzR; 2003 v Bos, US (sub) (4)

Warner, J. (Swansea T), 1937 v E; (with Manchester U), 1939 v F (2)

Warren, F. W. (Cardiff C), 1929 v Ni; (with Middlesbrough), 1931 v Ni; 1933 v F, E; (with Hearts), 1937 v Ni; 1938 v Ni (6)

Watkins, A. E. (Leicester Fosse), 1898 v E, S; (with Aston Villa), 1900 v E, S; (with Millwall), 1904 v Ni (5)

Watkins, W. M. (Stoke C), 1902 v E; 1903 v E, S; (with Aston Villa); 1904 v E, S, Ni; (with Sunderland), 1905 v E, S, Ni; (with Stoke C), 1908 v Ni (10)

Webster, C. (Manchester U), 1957 v Cz; 1958 v H, M, Br (4)

Weston, R. D. (Arsenal), 2000 v P (sub); (with Cardiff C), 2003 v Cro (sub), Az (sub), Bos (4)

Whatley, W. J. (Tottenham H), 1939 v E, S (2)

White, P. F. (London Welsh), 1896 v Ni (1)

Wilcock, A. R. (Oswestry), 1890 v Ni (1)

Wilding, J. (Wrexham Olympians), 1885 v E, S, Ni; 1886 v E, Ni; (with Bootle), 1887 v E; 1888 v S, Ni; (with Wrexham), 1892 v S (9)

Williams, A. (Reading), 1994 v Es; 1995 v Alb, Mol, G (sub), Ge; 1996 v Mol, I; (with Wolverhampton W), 1998 v Br (sub), Jam; 1999 v I, D, I; (with Reading), 2003 v US (13)

Williams, A. L. (Wrexham), 1931 v E (1)

Williams, A. P. (Southampton), 1998 v Br (sub), Ma (2)

Williams, B. (Bristol C), 1930 v Ni (1)

Williams, B. D. (Swansea T), 1928 v Ni, E; 1930 v E, S; (with Everton), 1931 v Ni; 1932 v E; 1933 v E, S, Ni; 1935 v Ni (10)

Williams, D. G. (Derby Co), 1988 v Cz, Y, Se, Ma, I; 1989 v Ho, Is, Se, WG; 1990 v Fi, Ho; (with Ipswich T), 1993 v Ei; 1996 v G (sub) (13)

Williams, D. M. (Norwich C), 1986 v S.Ar (sub), U, Ca (2); 1987 v Fi (5)

Williams, D. R. (Merthyr T), 1921 v E, S; (with Sheffield W), 1923 v S; 1926 v S; 1927 v E, Ni; (with Manchester U), 1929 v E, S (8)

Williams, E. (Crewe Alex), 1893 v E, S (2)

Williams, E. (Druids), 1901 v E, Ni, S; 1902 v E, Ni (5)

Williams, G. (Chirk), 1893 v S; 1894 v S; 1895 v E, S, Ni; 1898 v Ni (6)

Williams, G. E. (WBA), 1960 v Ni; 1961 v S, E, Ei; 1963 v Ni, H; 1964 v E, S, Ni; 1965 v S, E, Ni, D, Gr (2), USSR, I; 1966 v Ni, Br (2), Ch; 1967 v S, E, Ni; 1968 v Ni; 1969 v I (26)

Williams, G. G. (Swansea T), 1961 v Ni, H, Sp (2); 1962 v E (5)

Williams, G. J. J. (Cardiff C), 1951 v Sw (1)

Williams, G. O. (Wrexham), 1907 v Ni (1)

Williams, H. J. (Swansea), 1965 v Gr (2); 1972 v R (3)

Williams, H. T. (Newport Co), 1949 v Ni, Sw; (with Leeds U), 1950 v Ni; 1951 v S (4)

Williams, J. H. (Oswestry), 1884 v E (1)

Williams, J. J. (Wrexham), 1939 v F (1)

Williams, J. T. (Middlesbrough), 1925 v Ni (1)

Williams, J. W. (C Palace), 1912 v S, Ni (2)

Williams, R. (Newcastle U), 1935 v S, E (2)

Williams, R. P. (Caernarvon), 1886 v S (1)

Williams, S. G. (WBA), 1954 v A; 1955 v E, Ni; 1956 v E, S, A; 1958 v E, S, Ni, Is (2), H (2), M, Se, Br; 1959 v E, S, Ni; 1960 v E, S, Ni; 1961 v Ni, Ei, H, Sp (2); 1962 v E, S, Ni, Br (2), M; (with Southampton), 1963 v S, E, H (2); 1964 v E, S; 1965 v S, E, D; 1966 v D (43)

Williams, W. (Druids), 1876 v S; 1878 v S; (with Oswestry), 1879 v E, S; (with Druids), 1880 v E; 1881 v E, S; 1882 v E, S, Ni; 1883 v Ni (11)

Williams, W. (Northampton T), 1925 v S (1)

Witcomb, D. F. (WBA), 1947 v E, S; (with Sheffield W), 1947 v Ni (3)

Woosnam, A. P. (Leyton Orient), 1959 v S; (with West Ham U), E; 1960 v E, S, Ni; 1961 v S, E, Ni, Ei, Sp, H; 1962 v E, S, Ni, Br; (with Aston Villa), 1963 v Ni, H (17)

Woosnam, G. (Newton White Star), 1879 v S (1)

Worthington, T. (Newtown), 1894 v S (1)

Wynn, G. A. (Wrexham), 1909 v E, S, Ni; (with Manchester C), 1910 v E; 1911 v Ni; 1912 v E, S; 1913 v E, S; 1914 v E, S (11)

Wynn, W. (Chirk), 1903 v Ni (1)

Yorath, T. C. (Leeds U), 1970 v I; 1971 v S, E, Ni; 1972 v Cz, E, S, Ni; 1973 v E, Pol, S; 1974 v Pol, E, S, Ni; 1975 v A, H (2), L (2), S; 1976 v A, E, S, Y (2), E, Ni; (with Coventry C), 1977 v WG, S (2), Cz, E, Ni; 1978 v K (2), S, Cz, WG, Ir, E, S, Ni; 1979 v T, WG, S, E, Ni; (with Tottenham H), 1980 v Ei, T, E, S, Ni, Ic; 1981 v T, Cz; (with Vancouver W), Ei, T, USSR (59)

Young, E. (Wimbledon), 1990 v Cr; (with C Palace), 1991 v D, Bel (2), L, Ei; 1992 v G, L, Ei, A; 1993 v Fa, Cy, Bel, Ei, Bel, Fa; 1994 v RCS, Cy, R, N; (with Wolverhampton W), 1996 v Alb (21)

REPUBLIC OF IRELAND

Aherne, T. (Belfast C), 1946 v P, Sp; (with Luton T), 1950 v Fi, E, Fi, Se, Bel; 1951 v N, Arg, N; 1952 v WG (2), A, Sp; 1953 v F; 1954 v F (16)

Aldridge, J. W. (Oxford U), 1986 v W, U, Ic, Cz; 1987 v Bel, S, Pol; (with Liverpool), S, Bul, Bel, Br, L; 1988 v Bul, Pol, N, E, USSR, Ho; 1989 v Ni, Tun, Sp, F (sub), H, Ma (sub), H; 1990 v WG; (with Real Sociedad), Ni, Ma, Fi (sub), T. E, Eg, Ho, R, I; 1991 v T, E (2), Pol; (with Tranmere R), 1992 v H (sub), T, W (sub), Sw (sub), US (sub), Alb, I, P (sub); 1993 v La, D, Sp, D, Alb, La, Li; 1994 v Li, Ni, CzR, I (sub), M (sub), N; 1995 v La, Ni, P, Lie; 1996 v La, P, Ho, Ru; 1997 v Mac (sub) (69)

Ambrose, P. (Shamrock R), 1955 v N, Ho; 1964 v Pol, N, E (5)

Anderson, J. (Preston NE), 1980 v Cz (sub), US (sub); 1982 v Ch, Br, Tr; (with Newcastle U), 1984 v Chn; 1986 v W, Ic, Cz; 1987 v Bul, Bel, Br, L; 1988 v R (sub), Y (sub); 1989 v Tun (16)

Andrews, P. (Bohemians), 1936 v Ho (1)

Arrigan, T. (Waterford), 1938 v N (1)

Babb, P. A. (Coventry C), 1994 v Ru, Ho, Bol, G, CzR (sub), I, M, N, Ho; (with Liverpool), 1995 v La, Lie, Ni (2), P, Lie, A; 1996 v La, P, Ho, CzR; 1997 v Ic; 1998 v Li (sub), R, Arg (sub), M; 1999 v Cro, Para (sub), Se (sub), Ni; 2000 v CzR (sub), S, M (sub), US, S.Af; (with Sunderland), 2003 v Ru (sub) (35)

Bailham, E. (Shamrock R), 1964 v E (1)

Barber, E. (Shelbourne), 1966 v Sp; (with Birmingham C), 1966 v Bel (2)

Barrett, G. (Arsenal), 2003 v Fi (sub) (1)

Barry, P. (Fordsons), 1928 v Bel; 1929 v Bel (2)

Beglin, J. (Liverpool), 1984 v Chn; 1985 v M, D, I, Is, E, N, Sw; 1986 v Sw, USSR, D, W; 1987 v Bel (sub), S, Pol (15)
Bermingham, J. (Bohemians), 1929 v Bel (1)
Bermingham, P. (St James' Gate), 1935 v H (1)
Braddish, S. (Dundalk), 1978 v T (sub), Pol (2)
Bonner, P. (Celtic), 1981 v Pol; 1982 v Alg; 1984 v Ma, Is, Chn; 1985 v I, Is, E, N; 1986 v U, Ic; 1987 v Bel (2), S (2), Pol, Bul, Br, L; 1988 v Bul, R, Y, N, E, USSR, Ho; 1989 v Sp, F, H, Sp, Ma, H; 1990 v WG, Ni, Ma, W, Fi, T, E, Eg, Ho, R, I; 1991 v Mor, T, E (2), W, Pol, US; 1992 v H, Pol, T, W, Sw, Alb, I; 1993 v La, D, Sp, W, Ni, D, Alb, La, Li; 1994 v Li, Sp, Ni, Ru, Ho, Bol, CzR, I, M, N, Ho; 1995 v Lie; 1996 v M, Bol (sub) (80)
Bradshaw, P. (St James' Gate), 1939 v Sw, Pol, H (2), G (5)
Brady, F. (Fordsons), 1926 v I; 1927 v I (2)
Brady, T. R. (QPR), 1964 v A (2), Sp (2), Pol, N (6)
Brady, W. L. (Arsenal), 1975 v USSR, T, Sw, USSR, Sw, WG; 1976 v T, N, Pol; 1977 v E, T, F (2), Sp, Bul; 1978 v Bul, N; 1979 v Ni, E, D, Bul, WG; 1980 v W, Bul, E, Cy; (with Juventus), 1981 v Ho, Bel, F, Cy, Bel; 1982 v Ho, F, Ch, Br, Tr; (with Sampdoria), 1983 v Ho, Sp, Ic, Ma; 1984 v Ic, Ho, Ma, Pol, Is; (with Internazionale), 1985 v USSR, N, D, I, E, N, Sp, Sw; 1986 v Sw, USSR, D, W; (with Ascoli), 1987 v Bel, S (2), Pol; (with West Ham U), Bul, Bel, Br, L; 1988 v L, Bul; 1989 v F, H (sub), H (sub); 1990 v WG, Fi (72)
Branagan, K. G. (Bolton W), 1997 v W (1)
Breen, G. (Birmingham C), 1996 v P (sub), Cro, Ho, US, M, Bol (sub); 1997 v Lie, Mac, Ic; (with Coventry C), v Mac; 1998 v Li (sub), R, CzR, Arg, M; 1999 v Ma, Y, Para, Se, Mac; 2000 v Y, Cro, Ma, Mac, T (2), Gr, S, M, US, S.Af; 2001 v Ho, P, Es, Fi, Cy, And (2); 2002 v Cy, Ir (2), Ru (sub), US, Cam, G, S.Ar, Sp; (with West Ham U), 2003 v Fi, Ru, Sw, S, Ge, Alb, N, Alb, Ge (56)
Breen, T. (Manchester U), 1937 v Sw, F; (with Shamrock R), 1947 v E, Sp, P (5)
Brennan, F. (Drumcondra), 1965 v Bel (1)
Brennan, S. A. (Manchester U), 1965 v Sp; 1966 v Sp, A, Bel; 1967 v Sp, T, Sp; 1969 v Cz, D, H; 1970 v S, Cz, D, H, Pol (sub), WG; (with Waterford), 1971 v Pol, Se, I (19)
Brown, J. (Coventry C), 1937 v Sw, F (2)
Browne, W. (Bohemians), 1964 v A, Sp, E (3)
Buckley, L. (Shamrock R), 1984 v Pol (sub); (with Waregem), 1985 v M (2)
Burke, F. (Cork Ath), 1952 v WG (1)
Burke, J. (Shamrock R), 1929 v Bel (1)
Burke, J. (Cork), 1934 v Bel (1)
Butler, P. J. (Sunderland), 2000 v CzR (1)
Butler, T. (Sunderland), 2003 v Fi, Sw (sub) (2)
Byrne, A. B. (Southampton), 1970 v D, Pol, WG; 1971 v Pol, Se (2), I (2), A; 1973 v F, USSR (sub), F, N; 1974 v Pol (14)
Byrne, D. (Shelbourne), 1929 v Bel; (with Shamrock R), 1932 v Sp; (with Coleraine), 1934 v Bel (3)
Byrne, J. (Bray Unknowns), 1928 v Bel (1)
Byrne, J. (QPR), 1985 v I, Is (sub), E (sub), Sp (sub); 1987 v S (sub), Bel (sub), Br, L (sub); 1988 v L, Bul (sub), Is, R, Y (sub), Pol (sub); (with Le Havre), 1990 v WG (sub), W, Fi, T (sub), Ma; (with Brighton & HA), 1991 v W; (with Sunderland), 1992 v T, W; (with Millwall), 1993 v W (23)
Byrne, P. (Dolphin), 1931 v Sp; 1932 v Ho; (with Drumcondra), 1934 v Ho (3)
Byrne, P. (Shamrock R), 1984 v Pol, Chn; 1985 v M; 1986 v D (sub), W (sub), U (sub), Ic (sub), Cz (8)
Byrne, S. (Bohemians), 1931 v Sp (1)

Campbell, A. (Santander), 1985 v I (sub), Is, Sp (3)
Campbell, N. (St Patrick's Ath), 1971 v A (sub); (with Fortuna Cologne), 1972 v Ir, Ec, Ch, P; 1973 v USSR, F (sub); 1975 v WG; 1976 v N; 1977 v Sp, Bul (sub) (11)
Cannon, H. (Bohemians), 1926 v I; 1928 v Bel (2)
Cantwell, N. (West Ham U), 1954 v L; 1956 v Sp, Ho; 1957 v D, WG, E (2); 1958 v D, Pol, A; 1959 v Pol, Cz (2); 1960 v Se, Ch, Se; 1961 v N; (with Manchester U), S (2); 1962 v Cz (2), A; 1963 v Ic (2), S; 1964 v A, Sp, E; 1965 v Pol, Sp; 1966 v Sp (2), A, Bel; 1967 v Sp, T (36)
Carey, B. P. (Manchester U), 1992 v US (sub); 1993 v W; (with Leicester C), 1994 v Ru (3)
Carey, J. J. (Manchester U), 1938 v N, Cz, Pol; 1939 v Sw, Pol, H (2), G; 1946 v P, Sp; 1947 v E, Sp, P; 1948 v P, Sp; 1949 v Sw, Bel, P, Se, Sp; 1950 v Fi, E, Fi, Se; 1951 v N, Arg, N; 1953 v F, A (29)
Carolan, J. (Manchester U), 1960 v Se, Ch (2)
Carr, S. (Tottenham H), 1999 v Se, Ni, Mac; 2000 v Y (sub), Cro, Ma, T (2), S, M, US, S.Af; 2001 v Ho, P, Es, And (sub), P, Es; 2003 v S, Ge, Alb, N, Alb, Ge (24)
Carroll, B. (Shelbourne), 1949 v Bel; 1950 v Fi (2)
Carroll, T. R. (Ipswich T), 1968 v Pol; 1969 v Pol, A, D; 1970 v Cz, Pol, WG; 1971 v Se; (with Birmingham C), 1972 v Ir, Ec, Ch, P; 1973 v USSR (2), Pol, F, N (17)
Carsley, L. K. (Derby Co), 1998 v R, Bel (1 + sub), CzR, Arg, M; 1999 v Cro (sub), Ma (sub), Para (sub); (with Blackburn R) Ni, Mac; 2000 v Y (sub), Cro, Ma, T; 2001 v Fi (sub); (with Coventry C), 2002 v Cro, Cy (sub), Ru (sub); (with Everton), S.Ar (sub); 2003 v Fi, Gr, S (sub), Ge, Alb, N (sub), Alb, Ge (28)
Cascarino, A. G. (Gillingham), 1986 v Sw, USSR, D; (with Millwall), 1988 v Pol, N (sub), USSR (sub), Ho (sub); 1989 v Ni, Tun, Sp, F, H, Sp, Ma, H; 1990 v WG (sub), Ni, Ma; (with Aston Villa), W, Fi, T, E, Eg, Ho (sub), R (sub), I (sub); 1991 v Mor (sub),T(sub), E (2 sub), Pol (sub), Ch (sub), US; (with Celtic), 1992 v Pol, T; (with Chelsea), W, Sw, US (sub); 1993 v W, Ni (sub), D (sub), Alb (sub), La (sub); 1994 v Li (sub), Sp (sub), Ni (sub), Ru, Bol (sub), G, CzR, Ho (sub); (with Marseille), 1995 v La (sub), Ni (sub), P (sub), Lie (sub), A (sub); 1996 v A (sub), P (sub), Ho, Ru (sub), P, Cro (sub), Ho; 1997 v Lie (sub), Mac, Ic; (with Nancy), v W, Mac, R (sub), Lie (sub); 1998 v Li (sub), Ic (sub), Li, R, Bel (2); 1999 v Cro (sub), Ma (sub), Y (sub), Para (sub), Se (sub), Ni (sub), Mac (sub); 2000 v Y (sub), Cro, Mac (sub), T (1 + sub) (88)
Chandler, J. (Leeds U), 1980 v Cz (sub), US (2)
Chatton, H. A. (Shelbourne), 1931 v Sp; (with Dumbarton), 1932 v Sp; (with Cork), 1934 v Ho (3)
Clarke, J. (Drogheda U), 1978 v Pol (sub) (1)
Clarke, K. (Drumcondra), 1948 v P, Sp (2)
Clarke, M. (Shamrock R), 1950 v Bel (1)
Clinton, T. J. (Everton), 1951 v N; 1954 v F, L (3)
Coad, P. (Shamrock R), 1947 v E, Sp, P; 1948 v P, Sp; 1949 v Sw, Bel, P, Se; 1951 v N (sub); 1952 v Sp (11)
Coffey, T. (Drumcondra), 1950 v Fi (1)
Colfer, M. D. (Shelbourne), 1950 v Bel; 1951 v N (2)
Colgan, N. (Hibernian), 2002 v D (sub); 2003 v S (sub), N (sub) (3)
Collins, F. (Jacobs), 1927 v I (1)
Conmy, O. M. (Peterborough U), 1965 v Bel; 1967 v Cz; 1968 v Cz, Pol; 1970 v Cz (5)
Connolly, D. J. (Watford), 1996 v P, Ho, US, M; 1997 v R, Lie; (with Feyenoord), 1998 v Li, Ic, Li, Bel (1 + sub), CzR, M; (with Wolverhampton W), 1999 v Y, Para (sub), Se, Ni (sub), Mac (sub); (with Excelsior), 2000 v T (1 + sub), CzR (sub), Gr; 2001 v Ho (sub), Fi (sub), Cy, And; (with Feyenoord), And; (with Wimbledon), 2002 v Cro (sub), Cy, Ir, D (sub), US (sub), Ng (sub), Sp (sub); 2003 v S (sub), N, Alb (37)
Connolly, H. (Cork), 1937 v G (1)
Connolly, J. (Fordsons), 1926 v I (1)
Conroy, G. A. (Stoke C), 1970 v Cz, D, H, Pol, WG; 1971 v Pol, Se (2), I; 1973 v USSR, F, USSR, N; 1974 v Pol, Br, U, Ch; 1975 v T, Sw, USSR, Sw, WG (sub); 1976 v T (sub), Pol; 1977 v E, T, Pol (27)
Conway, J. P. (Fulham), 1967 v Sp, T, Sp; 1968 v Cz; 1969 v A (sub), H; 1970 v S, Cz, D, H, Pol, WG; 1971 v I, A; 1974 v U, Ch; 1975 v WG (sub); 1976 v N, Pol; (with Manchester C), 1977 v Pol (20)
Corr, P. J. (Everton), 1949 v P, Sp; 1950 v E, Se (4)
Courtney, E. (Cork U), 1946 v P (1)
Coyle, O. C. (Bolton W), 1994 v Ho (sub) (1)
Coyne, T. (Celtic), 1992 v Sw, US, Alb (sub), US (sub), I (sub), P (sub); 1993 v W (sub), La (sub); (with Tranmere R), Ni; (with Motherwell), 1994 v Ru (sub), Ho, Bol, G (sub), CzR (sub), I, M, Ho; 1995 v Lie, Ni (sub), A; 1996 v Ru (sub); 1998 v Bel (sub) (22)
Crowe, G. (Bohemians), 2003 v Gr, N (sub) (2)
Cummins, G. P. (Luton T), 1954 v L (2); 1955 v N (2), WG; 1956 v Y, Sp; 1958 v D, Pol, A; 1959 v Pol, Cz (2); 1960 v Se, Ch, WG, Se; 1961 v S (2) (19)
Cuneen, T. (Limerick), 1951 v N (1)
Cunningham, K. (Wimbledon), 1996 v CzR, P, Cro, Ho (sub), US, Bol; 1997 v Ic (sub), W, R, Lie; 1998 v Li, Ic, Li, Bel (2), CzR; 1999 v Cro, Ma, Y, Para, Se, Ni, Mac; 2000 v Y, Cro, Ma, Mac, T (2), CzR, Gr; 2001 v Cy, And; 2002 v Ir (sub), Ru, D, US (sub), Ng, G (sub), Sp (sub); (with Birmingham C), 2003 v Fi, Ru, Sw, Gr, Ge, Alb (2), Ge (48)
Curtis, D. P. (Shelbourne), 1957 v D, WG; (with Bristol C), 1957 v E (2); 1958 v D, Pol, A; (with Ipswich T), 1959 v Pol; 1960 v Se, Ch, WG, Se; 1961 v N, S; 1962 v A; 1963 v Ic; (with Exeter C), 1964 v A (17)
Cusack, S. (Limerick), 1953 v F (1)

Daish, L. S. (Cambridge U), 1992 v W, Sw (sub); (with Coventry C), 1996 v CzR (sub), Cro, M (5)

Daly, G. A. (Manchester U), 1973 v Pol (sub), N; 1974 v Br (sub), U (sub); 1975 v Sw (sub), WG; 1977 v E, T, F; (with Derby Co), F, Bul; 1978 v Bul, T, D; 1979 v Ni, E, D, Bul; 1980 v Ni, E, Cy, Sw, Arg; (with Coventry C), 1981 v WG 'B', Ho, Bel, Cy, W, Bel, Cz, Pol (sub); 1982 v Alg, Ch, Br, Tr; 1983 v Ho, Sp (sub); 1984 v Is (sub), Ma; (with Birmingham C), 1985 v M (sub), N, Sp, Sw; 1986 v Sw; (with Shrewsbury T), U, Ic (sub), Cz (sub); 1987 v S (sub) (48)
Daly, J. (Shamrock R), 1932 v Ho; 1935 v Sw (2)
Daly, M. (Wolverhampton W), 1978 v T, Pol (2)
Daly, P. (Shamrock R), 1950 v Fi (sub) (1)
Davis, T. L. (Oldham Ath), 1937 v G, H; (with Tranmere R), 1938 v Cz, Pol (4)
Deacy, E. (Aston Villa), 1982 v Alg (sub), Ch, Br, Tr (4)
Delap, R. J. (Derby Co), 1998 v CzR (sub), Arg (sub), M (sub); 2000 v T (2), Gr (sub); (with Southampton), 2002 v US; 2003 v Fi (sub), Gr (sub) (9)
De Mange, K. J. P. P. (Liverpool), 1987 v Br (sub); (with Hull C), 1989 v Tun (sub) (2)
Dempsey, J. T. (Fulham), 1967 v Sp, Cz; 1968 v Cz, Pol; 1969 v Pol, A, D; (with Chelsea), 1969 v Cz, D; 1970 v H, WG; 1971 v Pol, Se (2), I; 1972 v Ir, Ec, Ch, P (19)
Dennehy, J. (Cork Hibernians), 1972 v Ec (sub), Ch; (with Nottingham F), 1973 v USSR (sub), Pol, F, N; 1974 v Pol (sub); 1975 v T (sub), WG (sub); (with Walsall), 1976 v Pol (sub); 1977 v Pol (sub) (11)
Desmond, P. (Middlesbrough), 1950 v Fi, E, Fi, Se (4)
Devine, J. (Arsenal), 1980 v Cz, Ni; 1981 v WG 'B', Cz; 1982 v Ho, Alg; 1983 v Sp, Ma; (with Norwich C), 1984 v Ic, Ho, Is; 1985 v USSR, N (13)
Doherty, G. M. T. (Luton T), 2000 v Gr (sub); (with Tottenham H), US, S.Af (sub); 2001 v Cy (sub), And (sub+1), P (sub), Es (sub); 2002 v US (sub); 2003 v Fi (sub), Ru (sub), Sw (sub), Gr, S, Ge, Alb (sub+sub), Ge (18)
Donnelly, J. (Dundalk), 1935 v H, Sw, G; 1936 v Ho, Sw, H, L; 1937 v G, H; 1938 v N (10)
Donnelly, T. (Drumcondra), 1938 v N; (Shamrock R), 1939 v Sw (2)
Donovan, D. C. (Everton), 1955 v N, Ho, N, WG; 1957 v E (5)
Donovan, T. (Aston Villa), 1980 v Cz; 1981 v WG 'B'(sub) (2)
Dowdall, C. (Fordsons), 1928 v Bel; (with Barnsley), 1929 v Bel; (with Cork), 1931 v Sp (3)
Doyle, C. (Shelbourne), 1959 v Cz (1)
Doyle, D. (Shamrock R), 1926 v I (1)
Doyle, L. (Dolphin), 1932 v Sp (1)
Duff, D. A. (Blackburn R), 1998 v CzR, M; 1999 v Cro, Ma, Y, Para, Se (sub), Ni, Mac; 2000 v Cro, Ma (sub), T (sub + sub), S (sub); 2001 v P (sub), Es (sub), Cy (sub), And, P (sub), Es; 2002 v Cro, Ho, Ru, D, US, Ng, Cam, G, S.Ar, Sp; 2003 v Fi, Ru, Sw, Ge, Alb, N, Alb (37)
Duffy, B. (Shamrock R), 1950 v Bel (1)
Duggan, H. A. (Leeds U), 1927 v I; 1930 v Bel; 1936 v H, L; (with Newport Co), 1938 v N (5)
Dunne, A. P. (Manchester U), 1962 v A; 1963 v Ic, S; 1964 v A, Sp, Pol, N, E; 1965 v Pol, Sp; 1966 v Sp (2), A, Bel; 1967 v Sp, T, Sp; 1969 v Pol, D, H; 1970 v H; 1971 v Se, I, A; (with Bolton W), 1974 v Br (sub), U, Ch; 1975 v T, Sw, USSR, Sw, WG; 1976 v T (33)
Dunne, J. (Sheffield U), 1930 v Bel; (with Arsenal), 1936 v Sw, H, L; (with Southampton), 1937 v Sw, F; (with Shamrock R), 1938 v N (2), Cz, Pol; 1939 v Sw, Pol, H (2), G (15)
Dunne, J. C. (Fulham), 1971 v A (1)
Dunne, L. (Manchester C), 1935 v Sw, G (2)
Dunne, P. A. J. (Manchester U), 1965 v Sp; 1966 v Sp (2), WG; 1967 v T (5)
Dunne, R. P. (Everton), 2000 v Gr, S (sub), M; 2001 v Ho, P, Es; (with Manchester C), Fi, And, P, Es; 2002 v Cro, Ho, Ru (sub), D (sub); 2003 v Gr, S (sub), N (17)
Dunne, S. (Luton T), 1953 v F, A; 1954 v F, L; 1956 v Sp, Ho; 1957 v D, WG, E; 1958 v D, Pol, A; 1959 v Pol; 1960 v WG, Se (15)
Dunne, T. (St Patrick's Ath), 1956 v Ho; 1957 v D, WG (3)
Dunning, P. (Shelbourne), 1971 v Se, I (2)
Dunphy, E. M. (York C), 1966 v Sp; (with Millwall), 1966 v WG; 1967 v T, Sp, T, Cz; 1968 v Cz, Pol; 1969 v Pol, A, D (2), H; 1970 v D, H, Pol, WG (sub); 1971 v Pol, Se (2), I (2), A (23)
Dwyer, N. M. (West Ham U), 1960 v Se, Ch, WG, Se; (with Swansea T), 1961 v W, N, S (2); 1962 v Cz (2); 1964 v Pol (sub), N, E; 1965 v Pol (14)

Eccles, P. (Shamrock R), 1986 v U (sub) (1)
Egan, R. (Dundalk), 1929 v Bel (1)
Eglington, T. J. (Shamrock R), 1946 v P, Sp; (with Everton), 1947 v E, Sp, P; 1948 v P; 1949 v Sw, P, Se; 1951 v N, Arg; 1952 v WG (2), A, Sp; 1953 v F, A; 1954 v F, L, F; 1955 v N, Ho, WG; 1956 v Sp (24)
Ellis, P. (Bohemians), 1935 v Sw, G; 1936 v Ho, Sw, L; 1937 v G, H (7)
Evans, M. J. (Southampton), 1998 v R (sub) (1)

Fagan, E. (Shamrock R), 1973 v N (sub) (1)
Fagan, F. (Manchester C), 1955 v N; 1960 v Se; (with Derby Co), 1960 v Ch, WG, Se; 1961 v W, N, S (8)
Fagan, J. (Shamrock R), 1926 v I (1)
Fairclough, M. (Dundalk), 1982 v Ch (sub), Tr (sub) (2)
Fallon, S. (Celtic), 1951 v N; 1952 v WG (2), A, Sp; 1953 v F; 1955 v N, WG (8)
Fallon, W. J. (Notts Co), 1935 v H; 1936 v H; 1937 v H, Sw, F; 1939 v Sw, Pol; (with Sheffield W), 1939 v H, G (9)
Farquharson, T. G. (Cardiff C), 1929 v Bel; 1930 v Bel; 1931 v Sp; 1932 v Sp (4)
Farrell, P. (Hibernian), 1937 v Sw, F (2)
Farrell, P. D. (Shamrock R), 1946 v P, Sp; (with Everton), 1947 v Sp, P; 1948 v P, Sp; 1949 v Sw, P (sub), Sp; 1950 v E, Fi, Se; 1951 v Arg, N; 1952 v WG (2), A, Sp; 1953 v F, A; 1954 v F (2); 1955 v N, Ho, WG; 1956 v Y, Sp; 1957 v E (28)
Farrelly, G. (Aston Villa), 1996 v P, US, Bol; (with Everton), 1998 v CzR, M; (with Bolton W), 2000 v US (6)
Feenan, J. J. (Sunderland), 1937 v Sw, F (2)
Finnan, S. (Fulham), 2000 v Gr, S; 2001 v P (sub), Es (sub), Fi, And (sub+sub); 2002 v Cro (sub), Ho (sub), Cy, Ir (2), Ru, US, Ng, Cam (sub), G, S.Ar, Sp; 2003 v Ru, Gr, N (sub) (22)
Finucane, A. (Limerick), 1967 v T, Cz; 1969 v Cz, D, H; 1970 v S, Cz; 1971 v Se, I (1+sub); 1972 v A (11)
Fitzgerald, F. J. (Waterford), 1955 v Ho; 1956 v Ho (2)
Fitzgerald, P. J. (Leeds U), 1961 v W, N, S; (with Chester), 1962 v Cz (2) (5)
Fitzpatrick, K. (Limerick), 1970 v Cz (1)
Fitzsimons, A. G. (Middlesbrough), 1950 v Fi, Bel; 1952 v WG (2), A, Sp; 1953 v F, A; 1954 v F, L, F; 1955 v Ho, N, WG; 1956 v Y, Sp, Ho; 1957 v D, WG, E (2); 1958 v D, Pol, A; 1959 v Pol; (with Lincoln C), 1959 v Cz (26)
Fleming, C. (Middlesbrough), 1996 v CzR (sub), P, Cro (sub), Ho (sub), US (sub), M, Bol; 1997 v Lie (sub); 1998 v R (sub), M (10)
Flood, J. J. (Shamrock R), 1926 v I; 1929 v Bel; 1930 v Bel; 1931 v Sp; 1932 v Sp (5)
Fogarty, A. (Sunderland), 1960 v WG, Se; 1961 v S; 1962 v Cz (2); 1963 v Ic (2), S (sub); 1964 v A (2); (with Hartlepools U), Sp (11)
Foley, D. J. (Watford), 2000 v S (sub), M (sub), US, S.Af; 2001 v Es (sub), Fi (6)
Foley, J. (Cork), 1934 v Bel, Ho; (with Celtic), 1935 v H, Sw, G; 1937 v G, H (7)
Foley, M. (Shelbourne), 1926 v I (1)
Foley, T. C. (Northampton T), 1964 v Sp, Pol, N; 1965 v Pol, Bel; 1966 v Sp (2), WG; 1967 v Cz (9)
Foy, T. (Shamrock R), 1938 v N; 1939 v H (2)
Fullam, J. (Preston NE), 1961 v N; (with Shamrock R), 1964 v Sp, Pol, N; 1966 v A, Bel; 1968 v Pol; 1969 v Pol, A, D; 1970 v Cz (sub) (11)
Fullam, R. (Shamrock R), 1926 v I; 1927 v I (2)

Gallagher, C. (Celtic), 1967 v T, Cz (2)
Gallagher, M. (Hibernian), 1954 v L (1)
Gallagher, P. (Falkirk), 1932 v Sp (1)
Galvin, A. (Tottenham H), 1983 v Ho, Ma; 1984 v Ho (sub), Is (sub); 1985 v M, USSR, N, D, I, N, Sp; 1986 v U, Ic, Cz; 1987 v Bel (2), S, Bul, L; (with Sheffield W), 1988 v L, Bul, R, Pol, N, E, USSR, Ho; 1989 v Sp; (with Swindon T), 1990 v WG (29)
Gannon, E. (Notts Co), 1949 v Sw; (with Sheffield W), 1949 v Bel, P, Se, Sp; 1950 v Fi; 1951 v N; 1952 v WG, A; 1954 v L, F; 1955 v N; (with Shelbourne), 1955 v N, WG (14)
Gannon, M. (Shelbourne), 1972 v A (1)
Gaskins, P. (Shamrock R), 1934 v Bel, Ho; 1935 v H, Sw, G; (with St James' Gate), 1938 v Cz, Pol (7)
Gavin, J. T. (Norwich C), 1950 v Fi (2); 1953 v F; 1954 v L; (with Tottenham H), 1955 v Ho, WG; (with Norwich C), 1957 v D (7)
Geoghegan, M. (St James' Gate), 1937 v G; 1938 v N (2)
Gibbons, A. (St Patrick's Ath), 1952 v WG; 1954 v L; 1956 v Y, Sp (4)
Gilbert, R. (Shamrock R), 1966 v WG (1)
Giles, C. (Doncaster R), 1951 v N (1)
Giles, M. J. (Manchester U), 1960 v Se, Ch; 1961 v W, N, S (2); 1962 v Cz (2), A; 1963 v Ic, S; (with Leeds U), 1964 v A (2),

Sp (2), Pol, N, E; 1965 v Sp; 1966 v Sp (2), A, Bel; 1967 v Sp, T (2); 1969 v A, D, Cz; 1970 v S, Pol, WG; 1971 v I; 1973 v F, USSR; 1974 v Br, U, Ch; 1975 v USSR, T, Sw, USSR, Sw; (with WBA), 1976 v T; 1977 v E, T, F (2), Pol, Bul; (with Shamrock R), 1978 v Bul, T, Pol, N, D; 1979 v Ni, D, Bul, WG (59)

Given, S. J. J. (Blackburn R), 1996 v Ru, CzR, P, Cro, Ho, US, Bol; 1997 v Lie (2); (with Newcastle U), 1998 v Li, Ic, Li, Bel (2), CzR, Arg, M; 1999 v Cro, Ma, Y, Para, Se, Ni; 2000 v Gr, S.Af; 2001 v Fi, Cy, And (2), P, Es; 2002 v Cro, Ho, Cy, Ir (2), Ru, US, Ng, Cam, G, S.Ar, Sp; 2003 v Fi (sub), Ru, Sw, Gr, Ge, Alb, N, Alb, Ge (52)

Givens, D. J. (Manchester U), 1969 v D, H; 1970 v S, Cz, D, H; (with Luton T), 1970 v Pol, WG; 1971 v Se, I (2), A; 1972 v Ir, Ec, P; (with QPR), 1973 v F, USSR, Pol, F, N; 1974 v Pol, Br, U, Ch; 1975 v USSR, T, Sw, USSR, Sw, WG; 1976 v T, N, Pol; 1977 v E, T, F (2), Sp, Bul; 1978 v Bul, N, D; (with Birmingham C), 1979 v Ni (sub), E, D, Bul, WG; 1980 v US (sub), Ni (sub), Sw, Arg; 1981 v Ho, Bel, Cy (sub), W; (with Neuchatel X), 1982 v F (sub) (56)

Glen, W. (Shamrock R), 1927 v I; 1929 v Bel; 1930 v Bel; 1932 v Sp; 1936 v Ho, Sw, H, L (8)

Glynn, D. (Drumcondra), 1952 v WG; 1955 v N (2)

Godwin, T. F. (Shamrock R), 1949 v P, Se, Sp; 1950 v Fi, E; (with Leicester C), 1950 v Fi, Se, Bel; 1951 v N; (with Bournemouth), 1956 v Ho; 1957 v E; 1958 v D, Pol (13)

Golding, J. (Shamrock R), 1928 v Bel; 1930 v Bel (2)

Goodman, J. (Wimbledon), 1997 v W, Mac, R (sub), Lie (sub) (4)

Goodwin, J. (Stockport Co), 2003 v Fi (sub) (1)

Gorman, W. C. (Bury), 1936 v Sw, H, L; 1937 v G, H; 1938 v N, Cz, Pol; 1939 v Sw, Pol; (with Brentford), H; 1947 v E, P (13)

Grace, J. (Drumcondra), 1926 v I (1)

Grealish, A. (Orient), 1976 v N, Pol; 1978 v N, D; 1979 v Ni, E, WG; (with Luton T), 1980 v W, Cz, Bul, US, Ni, E, Cy, Sw, Arg; 1981 v WG 'B', Ho, Bel, F, Cy, W, Bel, Pol; (with Brighton & HA), 1982 v Ho, Alg, Ch, Br, Tr; 1983 v Ho, Sp, Ic, Sp; 1984 v Ic, Ho; (with WBA), Pol, Chn; 1985 v M, USSR, N, D, Sp (sub), Sw; 1986 v USSR, D (45)

Gregg, E. (Bohemians), 1978 v Pol, D (sub); 1979 v E (sub), D, Bul, WG; 1980 v W, Cz (8)

Griffith, R. (Walsall), 1935 v H (1)

Grimes, A. A. (Manchester U), 1978 v T, Pol, N (sub); 1980 v Bul, US, Ni, E, Cy; 1981 v WG 'B' (sub), Cz, Pol; 1982 v Alg; 1983 v Sp (2); (with Coventry C), 1984 v Pol, Is; (with Luton T), 1988 v L, R (18)

Hale, A. (Aston Villa), 1962 v A; (with Doncaster R), 1963 v Ic; 1964 v Sp (2); (with Waterford), 1967 v Sp; 1968 v Pol (sub); 1969 v Pol, A, D; 1970 v S, Cz; 1971 v Pol (sub); 1972 v A (sub); 1974 v Pol (sub) (14)

Hamilton, T. (Shamrock R), 1959 v Cz (2) (2)

Hand, E. K. (Portsmouth), 1969 v Cz (sub); 1970 v Pol, WG; 1971 v Pol, A; 1973 v USSR, F, USSR, Pol, F; 1974 v Pol, Br, U, Ch; 1975 v T, Sw, USSR, Sw, WG; 1976 v T (20)

Harrington, W. (Cork), 1936 v Ho, Sw, H, L; 1938 v Pol (sub) (5)

Harte, I. P. (Leeds U), 1996 v Cro (sub), Ho, M, Bol; 1997 v Lie, Mac, Ic (sub), W, Mac (sub), R, Lie; 1998 v Li, Ic, Li, Bel (2), Arg, M; 1999 v Para; 2000 v Cro (sub), Ma (sub), CzR; 2001 v Ho, P, Es, Fi, Cy, And (2), P, Es; 2002 v Cro, Ho, Cy, Ir (2), Ru, D, US, Ng, Cam, G, S.Ar, Sp; 2003 v Fi, Ru, Sw, S, N (49)

Hartnett, J. B. (Middlesbrough), 1949 v Sp; 1954 v L (2)

Haverty, J. (Arsenal), 1956 v Ho; 1957 v D, WG, E (2); 1958 v D, Pol, A; 1959 v Pol; 1960 v Se, Ch; 1961 v W, N, S (2); (with Blackburn R), 1962 v Cz (2); (with Millwall), 1963 v S; 1964 v A, Sp, Pol, N, E; (with Celtic), 1965 v Pol; (with Bristol R), 1965 v Sp; (with Shelbourne), 1966 v Sp (2), WG, A, Bel; 1967 v T, Sp (32)

Hayes, A. W. P. (Southampton), 1979 v D (1)

Hayes, W. E. (Huddersfield T), 1947 v E, P (2)

Hayes, W. J. (Limerick), 1949 v Bel (1)

Healey, R. (Cardiff C), 1977 v Pol; 1980 v E (sub) (2)

Healy, C. (Celtic), 2002 v Ru, D (sub), US; 2003 v Fi (sub), Sw, Gr, S (sub), N (sub), Ge (9)

Heighway, S. D. (Liverpool), 1971 v Pol, Se (2), I, A; 1973 v USSR; 1975 v USSR, T, USSR, WG; 1976 v T, N; 1977 v E, F (2), Sp, Bul; 1978 v Bul, N, D; 1979 v Ni, Bul; 1980 v Bul, US, Ni, E, Cy, Arg; 1981 v Bel, F, Cy, W, Bel; (with Minnesota K), 1982 v Ho (34)

Henderson, B. (Drumcondra), 1948 v P, Sp (2)

Hennessy, J. (Shelbourne), 1965 v Pol, Bel, Sp; 1966 v WG; (with St Patrick's Ath), 1969 v A (5)

Herrick, J. (Cork Hibernians), 1972 v A, Ch (sub); (with Shamrock R), 1973 v F (sub) (3)

Higgins, J. (Birmingham C), 1951 v Arg (1)

Holland, M. R. (Ipswich T), 2000 v Mac (sub), M, US, S.Af; 2001 v P (sub), Fi, Cy (sub), And (2), P (sub), Es; 2002 v Ho, Cy, Ir (2), Ru (sub), D, US (sub), Ng, Cam, G, S.Ar, Sp; 2003 v Fi (sub), Ru, Sw, Gr, S, Ge, Alb, N, Alb, Ge (33)

Holmes, J. (Coventry C), 1971 v A (sub); 1973 v F, USSR, Pol, F, N; 1974 v Pol, Br; 1975 v USSR, Sw; 1976 v T, N, Pol; 1977 v E, T, F, Sp; (with Tottenham H), F, Pol, Bul; 1978 v Bul, T, Pol, N, D; 1979 v Ni, E, D, Bul; (with Vancouver W), 1981 v W (30)

Horlacher, A. F. (Bohemians), 1930 v Bel; 1932 v Sp, Ho; 1934 v Ho (sub); 1935 v H;1936 v Ho, Sw (7)

Houghton, R. J. (Oxford U), 1986 v W, U, Ic, Cz; 1987 v Bel (2), S (2), Pol, L; 1988 v L, Bul; (with Liverpool), Is, Y, N, E, USSR, Ho; 1989 v Ni, Tun, Sp, F, H, Sp, Ma, H; 1990 v Ni, Ma, Fi, E, Eg, Ho, R, I; 1991 v Mor, T, E (2), Pol, Ch, US; 1992 v H, Alb, US, I, P; (with Aston Villa), 1993 v D, Sp, Ni, D, Alb, La, Li; 1994 v Li, Sp, Ni, Bol, G (sub), I, M, N, Ho; (with C Palace), 1995 v P, A; 1996 v A, CzR; 1997 v Lie, R, Lie; (with Reading), 1998 v Li, R, Bel (1 + sub) (73)

Howlett, G. (Brighton & HA), 1984 v Chn (sub) (1)

Hoy, M. (Dundalk), 1938 v N; 1939 v Sw, Pol, H (2), G (6)

Hughton, C. (Tottenham H), 1980 v US, E, Sw, Arg; 1981 v Ho, Bel, F, Cy, W, Bel, Pol; 1982 v F; 1983 v Ho, Sp, Ma, Sp; 1984 v Ic, Ho, Ma; 1985 v M (sub), USSR, N, I, Is, E, Sp; 1986 v Sw, USSR, U, Ic; 1987 v Bel, Bul; 1988 v Is, Y, Pol, N, E, USSR, Ho; 1989 v Ni, F, H, Sp, Ma, H; 1990 v W (sub), USSR (sub), Fi, T (sub), Ma; 1991 v T; (with West Ham U), Ch; 1992 v T (53)

Hurley, C. J. (Millwall), 1957 v E; (with Sunderland), 1958 v D, Pol, A; 1959 v Cz (2); 1960 v Se, Ch, WG, Se; 1961 v W, N, S (2); 1962 v Cz (2), A; 1963 v Ic (2), S; 1964 v A (2), Sp (2), Pol, N; 1965 v Sp; 1966 v WG, A, Bel; 1967 v T, Sp, T, Cz; 1968 v Cz, Pol; 1969 v Pol, D, Cz, (with Bolton W), H (40)

Hutchinson, F. (Drumcondra), 1935 v Sw, G (2)

Irwin, D. J. (Manchester U), 1991 v Mor, T, W, E, Pol, US; 1992 v H, Pol, W, US, Alb, US (sub), I; 1993 v La, D, Sp, Ni, D, Alb, La, Li; 1994 v Li, Sp, Ni, Bol, G, I, M; 1995 v La, Lie, Ni, E, Ni, P, Lie, A; 1996 v A, P, Ho, CzR; 1997 v Lie, Mac, Ic, Mac, R; 1998 v Li, Bel, Arg (sub); 1999 v Cro, Y, Para, Mac; 2000 v Y, Mac, T (2) (56)

Jordan, D. (Wolverhampton W), 1937 v Sw, F (2)

Jordan, W. (Bohemians), 1934 v Ho; 1938 v N (2)

Kavanagh, G. A. (Stoke C), 1998 v CzR (sub); 1999 v Se (sub), Ni (sub) (3)

Kavanagh, P. J. (Celtic), 1931 v Sp; 1932 v Sp (2)

Keane, R. D. (Wolverhampton W), 1998 v CzR (sub), Arg, M; 1999 v Cro, Ma, Para, Se (sub), Ni, Mac; (with Coventry C), 2000 v Y, Ma, Mac, T, CzR, Gr, S, M, S.Af (sub); (with Internazionale), 2001 v Ho, P, Es, Fi, Cy, And, P; (with Leeds U), 2002 v Cro, Ho, Ir (2), Ru, D, US, Ng, Cam, G, S.Ar, Sp; 2003 v Fi; (with Tottenham H), Ru, Sw, Alb, N, Alb, Ge (44)

Keane, R. M. (Nottingham F), 1991 v Ch; 1992 v H, Pol, W, Sw, Alb, US; 1993 v La, D, Sp, W, Ni, D, Alb, La, Li; (with Manchester U), 1994 v Li, Sp, Ni, Bol, G, CzR (sub), I, M, N, Ho; 1995 v Ni (2); 1996 v A, Ru; 1997 v Ic, W, Mac, R, Lie; 1998 v Li, Ic, Li; 1999 v Cro, Ma, Y, Para; 2000 v Y, T (2), CzR; 2001 v Ho, P, Es, Cy, And, P; 2002 v Cro, Ho, Cy, Ir, Ru, Ng (58)

Keane, T. R. (Swansea T), 1949 v Sw, P, Se, Sp (4)

Kearin, M. (Shamrock R), 1972 v A (1)

Kearns, F. T. (West Ham U), 1954 v L (1)

Kearns, M. (Oxford U), 1971 v Pol (sub); (with Walsall), 1974 v Pol (sub), U, Ch; 1976 v N, Pol; 1977 v E, T, F (2), Sp, Bul; 1978 v N, D; 1979 v Ni, E; (with Wolverhampton W), 1980 v US, Ni (18)

Kelly, A. T. (Sheffield U), 1993 v W (sub); 1994 v Ru (sub), G; 1995 v La, Ni, E, Ni, P, Lie, A; 1996 v A, La, P, Ho; 1997 v Mac, Ic, Mac, R; 1998 v R, Arg (sub); 1999 v Para (sub), Mac; (with Blackburn R), 2000 v Y, Cro, Ma, Mac, T, CzR, S, US; 2001 v Ho, P, Es; 2002 v Cro (sub) (34)

Kelly, D. T. (Walsall), 1988 v Is, R, Y; (with West Ham U), 1989 v Tun (sub); (with Leicester C), 1990 v USSR, Ma; 1991 v Mor, W (sub), Ch, US; 1992 v H; (with Newcastle U), I (sub), P; 1993 v Sp (sub), Ni; (with Wolverhampton W), 1994 v Ru, N (sub); 1995 v E, Ni; (with Sunderland), 1996 v La (sub); 1997 v Ic, W (sub), Mac (sub); (with Tranmere R), 1998 v Li (sub), R (sub), Bel (sub) (26)

Kelly, G. (Leeds U), 1994 v Ru, Ho, Bol (sub), G (sub), CzR, N, Ho; 1995 v La, Lie, Ni (2), P, Lie, A; 1996 v A, La, P, Ho; 1997 v W (sub), R, Lie; 1998 v Ic, Li, Bel (2), CzR, Arg, M; 2000 v Cro, Mac, CzR; 2001 v Ho (sub), Fi, Cy, And (2), P, Es; 2002 v Cro, Ho, Ir (sub+sub), Ru (sub), D, US (sub), Ng (sub), Cam, G, S.Ar, Sp; 2003 v Fi, Sw (52)
Kelly, J. (Derry C), 1932 v Ho; 1934 v Bel; 1936 v Sw, L (4)
Kelly, J. A. (Drumcondra), 1957 v WG, E; (with Preston NE), 1962 v A; 1963 v Ic (2), S; 1964 v A (2), Sp (2), Pol; 1965 v Bel; 1966 v A, Bel; 1967 v Sp (2), T, Cz; 1968 v Pol, Cz; 1969 v Pol, A, D, Cz, D, H; 1970 v S, D, H, Pol, WG; 1971 v Pol, Se (2), I (2), A; 1972 v Ir, Ec, Ch, P; 1973 v USSR, F, USSR, Pol, F, N (47)
Kelly, J. P. V. (Wolverhampton W), 1961 v W, N, S; 1962 v Cz (2) (5)
Kelly, M. J. (Portsmouth), 1988 v Y, Pol (sub); 1989 v Tun; 1991 v Mor (4)
Kelly, N. (Nottingham F), 1954 v L (1)
Kendrick, J. (Everton), 1927 v I; (with Dolphin) 1934 v Bel, Ho; 1936 v Ho (4)
Kenna, J. J. (Blackburn R), 1995 v P (sub), Lie (sub), A (sub); 1996 v La, P, Ho, Ru (sub), CzR, P, Cro, Ho, US; 1997 v Lie, Mac, Ic, R (sub), Lie; 1998 v Li, Ic, R, Bel (1 + sub), CzR, Arg; 1999 v Cro (sub), Ma; 2000 v T (sub) (27)
Kennedy, M. F. (Portsmouth), 1986 v Ic, Cz (sub) (2)
Kennedy, M. J. (Liverpool), 1996 v A, La (sub), P, Ru, CzR, Cro, Ho (sub), US (sub), M, Bol (sub); 1997 v R, Lie; 1998 v Li, Ic (sub), R, Bel (2), (with Wimbledon), M (sub); 1999 v Ma (sub), Se, Ni, Mac; (with Manchester C), 2000 v Y, Ma, Mac, CzR, S, M, US (sub), S.Af (sub); 2001 v And; (with Wolverhampton W), 2002 v Cro, Cy, Ru (sub) (34)
Kennedy, W. (St James' Gate), 1932 v Ho; 1934 v Bel, Ho (3)
Keogh, J. (Shamrock R), 1966 v WG (sub) (1)
Keogh, S. (Shamrock R), 1959 v Pol (1)
Kernaghan, A. N. (Middlesbrough), 1993 v La, D (2), Alb, La, Li; 1994 v Li; (with Manchester C), Sp, Ni, Bol (sub), CzR; 1995 v Lie, E; 1996 v A, P (sub), Ho (sub), Ru, P, Cro (sub), Ho, US, Bol (22)
Kiely, D. L. (Charlton Ath), 2000 v T (sub + 1), Gr (sub), M; 2002 v Ru (sub), D; 2003 v Fi, S (8)
Kiernan, F. W. (Shamrock R), 1951 v Arg, N; (with Southampton), 1952 v WG (2), A (5)
Kilbane, K. D. (WBA), 1998 v Ic, CzR (sub), Arg; 1999 v Se (sub), Mac (sub); 2000 v Y, Cro (sub), Ma, T (2); (with Sunderland), CzR, Gr, S, M (sub), US, S.Af (sub); 2001 v Ho, P, Es, Fi, Cy, And (2), P, Es; 2002 v Cro (sub), Ho, Cy, Ir (2), Ru, US, Ng, Cam, G, S.Ar, Sp; 2003 v Fi (sub), Ru, Sw, S, Ge, Alb, N, Alb, Ge (46)
Kinnear, J. P. (Tottenham H), 1967 v T; 1968 v Cz, Pol; 1969 v A; 1970 v Cz, D, H, Pol; 1971 v Se (sub), I; 1972 v Ir, Ec, Ch, P; 1973 v USSR, F; 1974 v Pol, Br, U, Ch; 1975 v USSR, T, Sw, USSR, WG; (with Brighton & HA), 1976 v T (sub) (26)
Kinsella, J. (Shelbourne), 1928 v Bel (1)
Kinsella, M. A. (Charlton Ath), 1998 v CzR, Arg; 1999 v Cro, Ma, Y, Para, Se, Ni, Mac; 2000 v Y, Cro, Ma, Mac, T, CzR, Gr; 2001 v Ho, P, Es, Fi, Cy, And, P, Es; 2002 v Ir, D, US, Ng (sub), Cam, G, S.Ar, Sp; 2003 v Fi; (with Aston Villa), Ru, Sw, S, Ge, Alb, N, Alb, Ge (sub) (41)
Kinsella, O. (Shamrock R), 1932 v Ho; 1938 v N (2)
Kirkland, A. (Shamrock R), 1927 v I (1)

Lacey, W. (Shelbourne), 1927 v I; 1928 v Bel; 1930 v Bel (3)
Langan, D. (Derby Co), 1978 v T, N; 1980 v Sw, Arg; (with Birmingham C), 1981 v WG 'B', Ho, Bel, F, Cy, W, Bel, Cz, Pol; 1982 v Ho, F; (with Oxford U), 1985 v N, Sp, Sw; 1986 v W, U; 1987 v Bel, S, Pol, Br (sub), L (sub); 1988 v L (26)
Lawler, J. F. (Fulham), 1953 v A; 1954 v L, F; 1955 v N, H, N, WG; 1956 v Y (8)
Lawlor, J. C. (Drumcondra), 1949 v Bel; (with Doncaster R), 1951 v N, Arg (3)
Lawlor, M. (Shamrock R), 1971 v Pol, Se (2), I (sub); 1973 v Pol (5)
Lawrenson, M. (Preston NE), 1977 v Pol; (with Brighton), 1978 v Bul, Pol, N (sub); 1979 v Ni, E; 1980 v E, Cy, Sw; 1981 v Ho, Bel, F, Cy, Pol; (with Liverpool), 1982 v Ho, F; 1983 v Ho, Sp, Ic, Ma, Sp; 1984 v Ic, Ho, Ma, Is; 1985 v USSR, N, D, I, E, N; 1986 v Sw, USSR, D; 1987 v Bel, S; 1988 v Bul, Is (38)
Lee, A. D. (Rotherham U), 2003 v N (sub), Ge (sub) (2)
Leech, M. (Shamrock R), 1969 v Cz, D, H; 1972 v A, Ir, Ec, P; 1973 v USSR (sub) (8)
Lennon, C. (St James' Gate), 1935 v H, Sw, G (3)
Lennox, G. (Dolphin), 1931 v Sp; 1932 v Sp (2)
Lowry, D. (St Patrick's Ath), 1962 v A (sub) (1)
Lunn, R. (Dundalk), 1939 v Sw, Pol (2)
Lynch, J. (Cork Bohemians), 1934 v Bel (1)

McAlinden, J. (Portsmouth), 1946 v P, Sp (2)
McAteer, J. W. (Bolton W), 1994 v Ru, Ho (sub), Bol (sub), G, CzR (sub), I (sub), M (sub), N, Ho (sub); 1995 v La, Lie, Ni (2 sub), Lie; (with Liverpool), 1996 v La, P, Ho (sub), Ru; 1997 v Mac, Ic, W, Mac; 1998 v Ic (sub), Li, R; 1999 v Cro, Ma, Y; (with Blackburn R), Para, Se; 2000 v CzR (sub), S, M, US (sub), S.Af; 2001 v Ho, P, Es, Fi (sub), Cy; 2002 v Cro (sub), Ho; (with Sunderland), Ir (2), Ru (sub), D, Ng, Cam, S.Ar (sub); 2003 v Fi, Ru (51)
McCann, J. (Shamrock R), 1957 v WG (1)
McCarthy, J. (Bohemians), 1926 v I; 1928 v Bel; 1930 v Bel (3)
McCarthy, M. (Shamrock R), 1932 v Ho (1)
McCarthy, M. (Manchester C), 1984 v Pol, Chn; 1985 v M, D, I, Is, E, Sp, Sw; 1986 v Sw, USSR, W (sub), U, Ic, Cz; 1987 v S (2), Pol, Bul, Bel (with Celtic), Br, L; 1988 v Bul, Is, R, Y, N, E, USSR, Ho; 1989 v Ni, Tun, Sp, F, H, Sp; (with Lyon), 1990 v WG, Ni (with Millwall), W, USSR, Fi, T, E, Eg, Ho, R, I; 1991 v Mor, T, E, US; 1992 v H, T, Alb (sub), US, I, P (57)
McConville, T. (Dundalk), 1972 v A; (with Waterford), 1973 v USSR, F, USSR, Pol, F (6)
McDonagh, Jacko (Shamrock R), 1984 v Pol (sub), Ma (sub); 1985 v M (sub) (3)
McDonagh, J. (Everton), 1981 v WG 'B', W, Bel, Cz; (with Bolton W), 1982 v Ho, F, Ch, Br; 1983 v Ho, Sp, Ic, Ma, Sp; (with Notts Co), 1984 v Ic, Ho, Pol; 1985 v M, USSR, N, D, Sp, Sw; 1986 v Sw, USSR; (with Wichita Wings) D (25)
McEvoy, M. A. (Blackburn R), 1961 v S (2); 1963 v S; 1964 v A, Sp (2), Pol, N, E; 1965 v Pol, Bel, Sp; 1966 v Sp (2); 1967 v Sp, T, Cz (17)
McGee, P. (QPR), 1978 v T, N (sub), D (sub); 1979 v Ni, E, D (sub), Bul (sub); 1980 v Cz, Bul; (with Preston NE), US, Ni, Cy, Sw, Arg; 1981 v Bel (sub) (15)
McGoldrick, E. J. (C Palace), 1992 v Sw, US, I, P (sub); 1993 v D, W, Ni (sub), D; (with Arsenal), 1994 v Ni, Ru, Ho, CzR; 1995 v La (sub), Lie, E (15)
McGowan, D. (West Ham U), 1949 v P, Se, Sp (3)
McGowan, J. (Cork U), 1947 v Sp (1)
McGrath, M. (Blackburn R), 1958 v A; 1959 v Pol, Cz (2); 1960 v Se, WG, Se; 1961 v W; 1962 v Cz (2); 1963 v S; 1964 v A (2), E; 1965 v Pol, Bel, Sp; 1966 v Sp; (with Bradford), 1966 v WG, A, Bel; 1967 v T (22)
McGrath, P. (Manchester U), 1985 v I (sub), Is, E, N (sub), Sw (sub); 1986 v Sw (sub), D, W, Ic, Cz; 1987 v Bel (2), S (2), Pol, Bul, Br, L; 1988 v L, Bul, Y, Pol, N, E, Ho; 1989 v Ni, F, H, Sp, Ma, H; (with Aston Villa), 1990 v WG, Ma, USSR, Fi, T, E, Eg, Ho, R, I; 1991 v E (2), W, Pol, Ch (sub), US; 1992 v Pol, T, Sw, US, Alb, US, I, P; 1993 v La, Sp, Ni, D, La, Li; 1994 v Sp, Ni, G, CzR, I, M, N, Ho; 1995 v La, Ni, E, Ni, P, Lie, A; 1996 v A, La, P, Ho, Ru, CzR; (with Derby Co), 1997 v W (83)
McGuire, W. (Bohemians), 1936 v Ho (1)
McKenzie, G. (Southend U), 1938 v N (2), Cz, Pol; 1939 v Sw, Pol, H (2), G (9)
Mackey, G. (Shamrock R), 1957 v D, WG, E (3)
McLoughlin, A. F. (Swindon T), 1990 v Ma, E (sub), Eg (sub); 1991 v Mor (sub), E (sub); (with Southampton), W, Ch (sub); 1992 v H (sub), W (sub); (with Portsmouth), US (1 + sub), I (sub), P; 1993 v W; 1994 v Ni (sub), Ru, Ho (sub); 1995 v Lie (sub); 1996 v P, Cro, Ho, US, M, Bol (sub); 1997 v Lie, Mac, Ic, W, Mac; 1998 v Li (sub), Ic, Li, R, Bel, CzR (sub); 1999 v Y, Para (sub), Se, Ni (sub); 2000 v Cro, Ma (sub), Mac (42)
McLoughlin, F. (Fordsons), 1930 v Bel; (with Cork), 1932 v Sp (2)
McMillan, W. (Belfast Celtic), 1946 v P, Sp (2)
McNally, J. B. (Luton T), 1959 v Cz; 1961 v S; 1963 v Ic (3)
McPhail, S. (Leeds U), 2000 v S, US, S.Af; 2002 v Cro (sub), Cy (sub); 2003 v Fi (sub), Gr (7)
Macken, A. (Derby Co), 1977 v Sp (1)
Madden, O. (Cork), 1936 v H (1)
Maguire, J. (Shamrock R), 1929 v Bel (1)
Mahon, A. J. (Tranmere R), 2000 v Gr (sub), S.Af (2)
Malone, G. (Shelbourne), 1949 v Bel (1)
Mancini, T. J. (QPR), 1974 v Pol, Br, U, Ch; (with Arsenal), 1975 v USSR (5)
Martin, C. (Bo'ness), 1927 v I (1)
Martin, C. J. (Glentoran), 1946 v P (sub), Sp; 1947 v E; (with Leeds U), 1947 v Sp; 1948 v P, Sp; (with Aston Villa), 1949 v Sw, Bel, P, Se, Sp; 1950 v Fi, E, Fi, Se, Bel; 1951 v Arg; 1952 v WG, A, Sp; 1954 v F (2), L; 1955 v N, Ho, N, WG; 1956 v Y, Sp, Ho (30)
Martin, M. P. (Bohemians), 1972 v A, Ir, Ec, Ch, P; 1973 v USSR; (with Manchester U), 1973 v USSR, Pol, F, N; 1974 v Pol, Br, U, Ch; 1975 v USSR, T, Sw, USSR, Sw, WG;

(with WBA), 1976 v T, N, Pol; 1977 v E, T, F (2), Sp, Pol, Bul; (with Newcastle U), 1979 v D, Bul, WG; 1980 v W, Cz, Bul, US, Ni; 1981 v WG 'B', F, Bel, Cz; 1982 v Ho, F, Alg, Ch, Br, Tr; 1983 v Ho, Sp, Ma, Sp (52)
Maybury, A. (Leeds U), 1998 v CzR; 1999 v Ni (2)
Meagan, M. K. (Everton), 1961 v S; 1962 v A; 1963 v Ic; 1964 v Sp; (with Huddersfield T), 1965 v Bel; 1966 v Sp (2), A, Bel; 1967 v Sp, T, Sp, T, Cz; 1968 v Cz, Pol; (with Drogheda), 1970 v S (17)
Meehan, P. (Drumcondra), 1934 v Ho (1)
Milligan, M. J. (Oldham Ath), 1992 v US (sub) (1)
Monahan, P. (Sligo R), 1935 v Sw, G (2)
Mooney, J. (Shamrock R), 1965 v Pol, Bel (2)
Moore, A. (Middlesbrough), 1996 v CzR, Cro (sub), Ho, M, Bol; 1997 v Lie (sub), Mac (sub), Ic (sub) (8)
Moore, P. (Shamrock R), 1931 v Sp; 1932 v Ho; (with Aberdeen), 1934 v Bel, Ho; 1935 v H, G; (with Shamrock R), 1936 v Ho; 1937 v G, H (9)
Moran, K. (Manchester U), 1980 v Sw, Arg; 1981 v WG 'B', Bel, F, Cy, W (sub), Bel, Cz, Pol; 1982 v F, Alg; 1983 v Ic; 1984 v Ic, Ho, Ma, Is; 1985 v M; 1986 v D, Ic, Cz; 1987 v Bel (2), S (2), Pol, Bul, Br, L; 1988 v L, Bul, Is, R, Y, Pol, N, E, USSR, Ho; (with Sporting Gijon), 1989 v Ni, Sp, H, Sp, Ma, H; 1990 v Ni, Ma; (with Blackburn R), W, USSR (sub), Ma, E, Eg, Ho, R, I; 1991 v T (sub), W, E, Pol, Ch, US; 1992 v Pol, US; 1993 v D, Sp, Ni, Alb; 1994 v Li, Sp, Ho, Bol (71)
Moroney, T. (West Ham U), 1948 v Sp; 1949 v P, Se, Sp; 1950 v Fi, E, Fi, Bel; 1951 v N (2); 1952 v WG; (with Evergreen U), 1954 v F (12)
Morris, C. B. (Celtic), 1988 v Is, R, Y, Pol, N, E, USSR, Ho; 1989 v Ni, Tun, Sp, F, H (1+sub); 1990 v WG, Ni, Ma (sub), W, USSR, Fi (sub), T, E, Eg, Ho, R, I; 1991 v E; 1992 v H (sub), Pol, W, Sw, US (2), P; (with Middlesbrough), 1993 v W (35)
Morrison, C. H. (C Palace), 2002 v Cro (sub), Cy (sub), Ir (sub), Ru (sub), D, US (sub), Ng (sub); (with Birmingham C), 2003 v Ru (sub), Sw (sub), S (10)
Moulson, C. (Lincoln C), 1936 v H, L; (with Notts Co), 1937 v H, Sw, F (5)
Moulson, G. B. (Lincoln C), 1948 v P, Sp; 1949 v Sw (3)
Mucklan, C. (Drogheda U), 1978 v Pol (1)
Muldoon, T. (Aston Villa), 1927 v I (1)
Mulligan, P. M. (Shamrock R), 1969 v Cz, D, H; 1970 v S, Cz, D; (with Chelsea), 1970 v H, Pol, WG; 1971 v Pol, Se, I; 1972 v A, Ir, Ec, Ch, P; (with C Palace), 1973 v F, USSR, Pol, F, N; 1974 v Pol, Br, U, Ch; 1975 v USSR, T, Sw, USSR, Sw; (with WBA), 1976 v T, Pol; 1977 v E, T, F (2), Pol, Bul; 1978 v Bul, N, D; 1979 v E, D, Bul (sub), WG; (with Shamrock R), 1980 v W, Cz, Bul, US (sub) (50)
Munroe, L. (Shamrock R), 1954 v L (1)
Murphy, A. (Clyde), 1956 v Y (1)
Murphy, B. (Bohemians), 1986 v U (1)
Murphy, J. (C Palace), 1980 v W, US, Cy (3)
Murray, T. (Dundalk), 1950 v Bel (1)

Newman, W. (Shelbourne), 1969 v D (1)
Nolan, R. (Shamrock R), 1957 v D, WG, E; 1958 v Pol; 1960 v Ch, WG, Se; 1962 v Cz (2); 1963 v Ic (10)

O'Brien, A. J. (Newcastle U), 2001 v Es (sub); 2002 v Cro (sub), Ho (sub), Ru, US; 2003 v S (sub) (6)
O'Brien, F. (Philadelphia F), 1980 v Cz, E, Cy (sub) (3)
O'Brien, L. (Shamrock R), 1986 v U; (with Manchester U), 1987 v Br; 1988 v Is (sub), R (sub), Y (sub), Pol (sub); 1989 v Tun; (with Newcastle U), Sp (sub); 1992 v Sw (sub); 1993 v W; (with Tranmere R), 1994 v Ru; 1996 v Cro, Ho, US, Bol; 1997 v Mac (sub) (16)
O'Brien, M. T. (Derby Co), 1927 v I; (with Walsall), 1929 v Bel; (with Norwich C), 1930 v Bel; (with Watford), 1932 v Ho (4)
O'Brien, R. (Notts Co), 1976 v N, Pol; 1977 v Sp, Pol; 1980 v Arg (sub) (5)
O'Byrne, L. B. (Shamrock R), 1949 v Bel (1)
O'Callaghan, B. R. (Stoke C), 1979 v WG (sub); 1980 v W, US; 1981 v W; 1982 v Br, Tr (6)
O'Callaghan, K. (Ipswich T), 1981 v WG 'B', Cz, Pol; 1982 v Alg, Ch, Br, Tr (sub); 1983 v Sp, Ic (sub), Ma (sub), Sp (sub); 1984 v Ic, Ho, Ma; 1985 v M (sub), N (sub), D (sub), (with Portsmouth) E (sub); 1986 v Sw (sub), USSR (sub); 1987 v Br (21)
O'Connell, A. (Dundalk), 1967 v Sp; (with Bohemians), 1971 v Pol (sub) (2)
O'Connor, T. (Shamrock R), 1950 v Fi, E, Fi, Se (4)
O'Connor, T. (Fulham), 1968 v Cz; (with Dundalk), 1972 v A, Ir (sub), Ec (sub), Ch; (with Bohemians), 1973 v F (sub), Pol (sub) (7)
O'Driscoll, J. F. (Swansea T), 1949 v Sw, Bel, Se (3)
O'Driscoll, S. (Fulham), 1982 v Ch, Br, Tr (sub) (3)
O'Farrell, F. (West Ham U), 1952 v A; 1953 v A; 1954 v F; 1955 v Ho, N; 1956 v Y, Ho; (with Preston NE), 1958 v D; 1959 v Cz (9)
O'Flanagan, K. P. (Bohemians), 1938 v N, Cz, Pol; 1939 v Pol, H (2), G; (with Arsenal), 1947 v E, Sp, P (10)
O'Flanagan, M. (Bohemians), 1947 v E (1)
O'Hanlon, K. G. (Rotherham U), 1988 v Is (1)
O'Kane, P. (Bohemians), 1935 v H, Sw, G (3)
O'Keefe, E. (Everton), 1981 v W; (with Port Vale), 1984 v Chn; 1985 v M, USSR (sub), E (5)
O'Keefe, T. (Cork), 1934 v Bel; (with Waterford), 1938 v Cz, Pol (3)
O'Leary, D. (Arsenal), 1977 v E, F (2), Sp, Bul; 1978 v Bul, N, D; 1979 v E, Bul, WG; 1980 v W, Bul, Ni, E, Cy; 1981 v WG 'B',Ho, Cz, Pol; 1982 v Ho, F; 1983 v Ho, Ic, Sp; 1984 v Pol, Is, Chn; 1985 v USSR, N, D, Is, E (sub), N, Sp, Sw; 1986 v Sw, USSR, D, W; 1989 v Sp, Ma, H; 1990 v WG, Ni (sub), Ma, W (sub), USSR, Fi, T, Ma, R (sub); 1991 v Mor, T, E (2), Pol, Ch; 1992 v H, Pol, T, W, Sw, US, Alb, I, P; 1993 v W (68)
O'Leary, P. (Shamrock R), 1980 v Bul, US, Ni, E (sub), Cz, Arg; 1981 v Ho (7)
O'Mahoney, M. T. (Bristol R), 1938 v Cz, Pol; 1939 v Sw, Pol, H, G (6)
O'Neill, F. S. (Shamrock R), 1962 v Cz (2); 1965 v Pol, Bel, Sp; 1966 v Sp (2), WG, A; 1967 v Sp, T, Sp, T; 1969 v Pol, A, D, Cz, D (sub), H (sub); 1972 v A (20)
O'Neill, J. (Everton), 1952 v Sp; 1953 v F, A; 1954 v F, L, F; 1955 v N, Ho, N, WG; 1956 v Y, Sp; 1957 v D; 1958 v A; 1959 v Pol, Cz (2) (17)
O'Neill, J. (Preston NE), 1961 v W (1)
O'Neill, K. P. (Norwich C), 1996 v P (sub), Cro, Ho (sub), US (sub), M, Bol; 1997 v Lie, Mac (1 + sub); 1999 v Cro, Y (sub); (with Middlesbrough), Ni (sub); 2000 v Mac (sub) (13)
O'Neill, W. (Dundalk), 1936 v Ho, Sw, H, L; 1937 v G, H, Sw, F; 1938 v N; 1939 v H, G (11)
O'Regan, K. (Brighton & HA), 1984 v Ma, Pol; 1985 v M, Sp (sub) (4)
O'Reilly, J. (Brideville), 1932 v Ho; (with Aberdeen), 1934 v Bel, Ho; (with Brideville), 1936 v Ho; Sw, H, L; (with St James' Gate), 1937 v G, H, Sw, F; 1938 v N (2), Cz, Pol; 1939 v Sw, Pol, H (2), G (20)
O'Reilly, J. (Cork U), 1946 v P, Sp (2)
O'Shea, J. F. (Manchester U), 2002 v Cro (sub); 2003 v Gr, S, Ge, Alb (2), Ge (7)

Peyton, G. (Fulham), 1977 v Sp (sub); 1978 v Bul, T, Pol; 1979 v D, Bul, WG; 1980 v W, Cz, Bul, E, Cy, Sw, Arg; 1981 v Ho, Bel, F, Cy; 1982 v Tr; 1985 v M (sub); 1986 v W, Cz; (with Bournemouth), 1988 v L, Pol; 1989 v Ni, Tun; 1990 v USSR, Ma; 1991 v Ch; (with Everton) 1992 v US (2), I (sub), P (33)
Peyton, N. (Shamrock R), 1957 v WG; (with Leeds U), 1960 v WG, Se (sub); 1961 v W; 1963 v Ic, S (6)
Phelan, T. (Wimbledon), 1992 v H, Pol (sub), T, W, Sw, US, I (sub), P; (with Manchester C), 1993 v La (sub), D, Sp, Ni, Alb, La, Li; 1994 v Li, Sp, Ni, Ho, Bol, G, CzR, I, M, Ho; 1995 v E; 1996 v La; (with Chelsea), Ho, Ru, P, Cro, Ho, US, M (sub), Bol; (with Everton), 1997 v W, Mac; 1998 v R; (with Fulham), 2000 v S (sub), M, US, S.Af (42)

Quinn, A. (Sheffield W), 2003 v N (sub) (1)
Quinn, B. S. (Coventry C), 2000 v Gr, M, US (sub), S.Af (sub) (4)
Quinn, N. J. (Arsenal), 1986 v Ic (sub), Cz; 1987 v Bul (sub), Br (sub); 1988 v L (sub), Bul (sub), Is, R (sub), Pol (sub), E (sub); 1989 v Tun (sub), Sp (sub), H (sub); (with Manchester C), 1990 v USSR, Ma, Eg (sub), Ho, R, I; 1991 v Mor, T, E(2) W, Pol; 1992 v H, W (sub), US, Alb, US, I (sub), P; 1993 v La, D, Sp, Ni, D, Alb, La, Li; 1994 v Li, Sp, Ni; 1995 v La, Lie, Ni, E, Ni, P, Lie, A; 1996 v A, La, P, Ru, CzR, P (sub), Cro, Ho (sub), US; (with Sunderland), 1997 v Lie; 1998 v Li, Arg; 1999 v Ma, Y, Para, Se, Ni, Mac; 2000 v Y, Cro (sub), Ma, Mac, T, CzR, S, M, US (sub), S.Af; 2001 v Ho, P, Es, P, Es; 2002 v Ho (sub), Cy, Ir, Ru (sub), G (sub), S.Ar (sub), Sp (sub) (91)

Reid, C. (Brideville), 1931 v Sp (1)
Reid, S. J. (Millwall), 2002 v Cro, Ru, D (sub), US (sub), Ng (sub), Cam (sub), G (sub); 2003 v S, Alb (sub) (9)
Richardson, D. J. (Shamrock R), 1972 v A (sub); (with Gillingham), 1973 v N (sub); 1980 v Cz (3)
Rigby, A. (St James' Gate), 1935 v H, Sw, G (3)

Ringstead, A. (Sheffield U), 1951 v Arg, N; 1952 v WG (2), A, Sp; 1953 v A; 1954 v F; 1955 v N; 1956 v Y, Sp, Ho; 1957 v E (2); 1958 v D, Pol, A; 1959 v Pol, Cz (2) (20)
Robinson, J. (Bohemians), 1928 v Bel; (with Dolphin), 1931 v Sp (2)
Robinson, M. (Brighton & HA), 1981 v WG 'B', F, Cy, Bel, Pol; 1982 v Ho, F, Alg, Ch; 1983 v Ho, Sp, Ic, Ma; (with Liverpool), 1984 v Ic, Ho, Is; 1985 v USSR, N; (with QPR), N, Sp, Sw; 1986 v D (sub), W, Cz (24)
Roche, P. J. (Shelbourne), 1972 v A; (with Manchester U), 1975 v USSR, T, Sw, USSR, Sw, WG; 1976 v T (8)
Rogers, E. (Blackburn R), 1968 v Cz, Pol; 1969 v Pol, A, D, Cz, D, H; 1970 v S, D, H; 1971 v I (2), A; (with Charlton Ath), 1972 v Ir, Ec, Ch, P; 1973 v USSR (19)
Ryan, G. (Derby Co), 1978 v T; (with Brighton & HA), 1979 v E, WG; 1980 v W, Cy (sub), Sw, Arg (sub); 1981 v WG 'B' (sub), F (sub), Pol (sub); 1982 v Br (sub), Ho (sub), Alg (sub), Ch (sub), Tr; 1984 v Pol, Chn; 1985 v M (18)
Ryan, R. A. (WBA), 1950 v Se, Bel; 1951 v N, Arg, N; 1952 v WG (2), A, Sp; 1953 v F, A; 1954 v F, L, F; 1955 v N; (with Derby Co), 1956 v Sp (16)

Sadlier, R. T. (Millwall), 2002 v Ru (sub) (1)
Savage, D. P. T. (Millwall), 1996 v P (sub), Cro (sub), US (sub), M, Bol (5)
Saward, P. (Millwall), 1954 v L; (with Aston Villa), 1957 v E (2); 1958 v D, Pol, A; 1959 v Pol, Cz; 1960 v Se, Ch, WG, Se; 1961 v W, N; (with Huddersfield T), 1961 v S; 1962 v A; 1963 v Ic (2) (18)
Scannell, T. (Southend U), 1954 v L (1)
Scully, P. J. (Arsenal), 1989 v Tun (sub) (1)
Sheedy, K. (Everton), 1984 v Ho (sub), Ma; 1985 v D, I, Is, Sw; 1986 v Sw, D; 1987 v S, Pol; 1988 v Is, R, Pol, E (sub), USSR; 1989 v Ni, Tun, H, Sp, Ma, H; 1990 v Ni, Ma, W (sub), USSR, Fi (sub), T, E, Eg, Ho, R, I; 1991 v W, E, Pol, Ch, US; 1992 v H, Pol, T, W; (with Newcastle U), Sw (sub), Alb; 1993 v La, W (sub) (45)
Sheridan, J. J. (Leeds U), 1988 v R, Y, Pol, N (sub); 1989 v Sp; (with Sheffield W), 1990 v W, T (sub), Ma, I (sub); 1991 v Mor (sub), T, Ch, US (sub); 1992 v H; 1993 v La; 1994 v Sp (sub), Ho, Bol, G, CzR, I, M, N, Ho; 1995 v La, Lie, Ni, E, Ni, P, Lie, A; 1996 v A, Ho (34)
Slaven, B. (Middlesbrough), 1990 v W, Fi, T (sub), Ma; 1991 v W, Pol (sub); 1993 v W (7)
Sloan, J. W. (Arsenal), 1946 v P, Sp (2)
Smyth, M. (Shamrock R), 1969 v Pol (sub) (1)
Squires, J. (Shelbourne), 1934 v Ho (1)
Stapleton, F. (Arsenal), 1977 v T, F, Sp, Bul; 1978 v Bul, N, D; 1979 v Ni, E (sub), D, WG; 1980 v W, Bul, Ni, E, Cy; 1981 v WG 'B', Ho, Bel, F, Cy, Bel, Cz, Pol; (with Manchester U), 1982 v Ho, F, Alg; 1983 v Ho, Sp, Ic, Ma, Sp; 1984 v Ic, Ho, Ma, Pol, Is, Chn; 1985 v N, D, I, Is, E, N, Sw; 1986 v Sw, USSR, D, U, Ic, Cz (sub); 1987 v Bel (2), S (2), Pol, Bul, L; (with Ajax), 1988 v L, Bul, R, Y, N, E, USSR, Ho; (with Le Havre), 1989 v F, Sp, Ma; (with Blackburn R), 1990 v WG, Ma (sub) (71)
Staunton, S. (Liverpool), 1989 v Tun, Sp (2), Ma, H; 1990 v WG, Ni, Ma, W, USSR, Fi, T, Ma, E, Eg, Ho, R, I; 1991 v Mor, T, E (2), W, Pol, Ch, US; (with Aston Villa), 1992 v Pol, T, Sw, US, Alb, US, I, P; 1993 v La, Sp, Ni, D, Alb, La, Li; 1994 v Li, Sp, Ho, Bol, G, CzR, I, M, N, Ho; 1995 v La, Lie, Ni, E, Ni, P, Lie, A; 1996 v La, P, Ru; 1997 v Lie, Mac (2), W, R, Lie; 1998 v Li, Ic, Li, Bel (2), Arg; (with Liverpool), 1999 v Cro, Ma, Y, Se; 2000 v Y, Cro, Ma, Mac, CzR (sub), Gr; 2001 v Ho (sub), Fi (sub); (with Aston Villa), And (sub), P, Es; 2002 v Cro, Ho, Cy, Ir (2), Ru (sub), D, US (sub), Ng, Cam, G, S.Ar, Sp (102)
Stevenson, A. E. (Dolphin), 1932 v Ho; (with Everton), 1947 v E, Sp, P; 1948 v P, Sp; 1949 v Sw (7)
Strahan, F. (Shelbourne), 1964 v Pol, N, E; 1965 v Pol; 1966 v WG (5)
Sullivan, J. (Fordsons), 1928 v Bel (1)
Swan, M. M. G. (Drumcondra), 1960 v Se (sub) (1)
Synnott, N. (Shamrock R), 1978 v T, Pol; 1979 v Ni (3)

Taylor, T. (Waterford), 1959 v Pol (sub) (1)
Thomas, P. (Waterford), 1974 v Pol, Br (2)
Townsend, A. D. (Norwich C), 1989 v F, Sp (sub), Ma (sub), H; 1990 v WG (sub), Ni, Ma, W, USSR, Fi (sub), T, Ma (sub), E, Eg, Ho, R, I; (with Chelsea), 1991 v Mor, T, E (2), W, Pol, Ch, US; 1992 v Pol, W, US, Alb, US, I; 1993 v La, D, Sp, Ni, D, Alb, La, Li; (with Aston Villa), 1994 v Li, Ni, Ho, Bol, G, CzR, I, M, N, Ho; 1995 v La, Ni, E, Ni, P; 1996 v A, La, Ho, Ru, CzR, P; 1997 v Lie, Mac (2), Ic, R, Lie; 1998 v Li; (with Middlesbrough), Ic, Bel (2) (70)
Traynor, T. J. (Southampton), 1954 v L; 1962 v A; 1963 v Ic (2), S; 1964 v A (2), Sp (8)
Treacy, R. C. P. (WBA), 1966 v WG; 1967 v Sp, Cz; 1968 v Cz; (with Charlton Ath), 1968 v Pol; 1969 v Pol, Cz, D; 1970 v S, D, H (sub), Pol (sub), WG (sub); 1971 v Pol, Se (sub+1), I, A; (with Swindon T), 1972 v Ir, Ec, Ch, P; 1973 v USSR, F, USSR, Pol, F, N; 1974 v Pol; (with Preston NE), Br; 1975 v USSR, Sw (2), WG; 1976 v T, N (sub), Pol (sub); (with WBA), 1977 v F, Pol; (with Shamrock R), 1978 v T, Pol; 1980 v Cz (sub) (42)
Tuohy, L. (Shamrock R), 1956 v Y; 1959 v Cz (2); (with Newcastle U), 1962 v A; 1963 v Ic (2); (with Shamrock R), 1964 v A; 1965 v Bel (8)
Turner, C. J. (Southend U), 1936 v Sw; 1937 v G, H, Sw, F; 1938 v N (2); (with West Ham U), Cz, Pol; 1939 v H (10)
Turner, P. (Celtic), 1963 v S; 1964 v Sp (2)

Vernon, J. (Belfast C), 1946 v P, Sp (2)

Waddock, G. (QPR), 1980 v Sw, Arg; 1981 v W, Pol (sub); 1982 v Alg; 1983 v Ic, Ma, Sp, Ho (sub); 1984 v Ma (sub), Ic, Ho, Is; 1985 v I, Is, E, N, Sp; 1986 v USSR; (with Millwall), 1990 v USSR, T (21)
Walsh, D. J. (Linfield), 1946 v P, Sp; (with WBA), 1947 v Sp, P; 1948 v P, Sp; 1949 v Sw, P, Se, Sp; 1950 v E, Fi, Se; 1951 v N; (with Aston Villa), Arg, N; 1952 v Sp; 1953 v A; 1954 v F (2) (20)
Walsh, J. (Limerick), 1982 v Tr (1)
Walsh, M. (Blackpool), 1976 v N, Pol; 1977 v F (sub), Pol; (with Everton), 1979 v Ni (sub); (with QPR), D (sub), Bul, WG (sub); (with Porto), 1981 v Bel (sub), Cz; 1982 v Alg (sub); 1983 v Sp, Ho (sub), Sp (sub); 1984 v Ic (sub), Ma, Pol, Chn; 1985 v USSR, N (sub), D (21)
Walsh, M. (Everton), 1982 v Ch, Br, Tr; 1983 v Ic (4)
Walsh, W. (Manchester C), 1947 v E, Sp, P; 1948 v P, Sp; 1949 v Bel; 1950 v E, Se, Bel (9)
Waters, J. (Grimsby T), 1977 v T; 1980 v Ni (sub) (2)
Watters, F. (Shelbourne), 1926 v I (1)
Weir, E. (Clyde), 1939 v H (2), G (3)
Whelan, R. (St Patrick's Ath), 1964 v A, E (sub) (2)
Whelan, R. (Liverpool), 1981 v Cz (sub); 1982 v Ho (sub), F; 1983 v Ic, Ma, Sp; 1984 v Is; 1985 v USSR, N, I (sub), Is, E, N (sub), Sw (sub); 1986 v USSR (sub), W; 1987 v Bel (sub), S, Bul, Bel, Br, L; 1988 v L, Bul, Pol, N, E, USSR, Ho; 1989 v Ni, F, H, Sp, Ma; 1990 v WG, Ni, Ma, W, Ho (sub); 1991 v Mor, E; 1992 v Sw; 1993 v La, W (sub), Li (sub); 1994 v Li (sub), Sp, Ru, Ho, G (sub), N (sub); (with Southend U), 1995 v Lie, A (53)
Whelan, W. (Manchester U), 1956 v Ho; 1957 v D, E (2) (4)
White, J. J. (Bohemians), 1928 v Bel (1)
Whittaker, R. (Chelsea), 1959 v Cz (1)
Williams, J. (Shamrock R), 1938 v N (1)

BRITISH AND IRISH INTERNATIONAL GOALSCORERS SINCE 1872

Where two players with the same surname and initials have appeared for the same country, and one or both have scored, they have been distinguished by reference to the club which appears *first* against their name in the international appearances section.

ENGLAND

A'Court, A.	1
Adams, T. A.	5
Adcock, H.	1
Alcock, C. W.	1
Allen, A.	3
Allen, R.	2
Amos, A.	1
Anderson, V.	2
Anderton, D. R.	7
Astall, G.	1
Athersmith, W. C.	3
Atyeo, P. J. W.	5
Bache, J. W.	4
Bailey, N. C.	2
Baily, E. F.	5
Baker, J. H.	3
Ball, A. J.	8
Bambridge, A. L.	1
Bambridge, E. C.	11
Barclay, R.	2
Barmby, N. J.	4
Barnes, J.	11
Barnes, P. S.	4
Barton, J.	1
Bassett, W. I.	8
Bastin, C. S.	12
Beardsley, P. A.	9
Beasley, A.	1
Beattie, T. K.	1
Beckham, D. R. J.	11
Becton, F.	2
Bedford, H.	1
Bell, C.	9
Bentley, R. T. F.	9
Bishop, S. M.	1
Blackburn, F.	1
Blissett, L.	3
Bloomer, S.	28
Bond, R.	2
Bonsor, A. G.	1
Bowden, E. R.	1
Bowers, J. W.	2
Bowles, S.	1
Bradford, G. R. W.	1
Bradford, J.	7
Bradley, W.	2
Bradshaw, F.	3
Brann, G.	1
Bridges, B. J.	1
Bridgett, A.	3
Brindle, T.	1
Britton, C. S.	1
Broadbent, P. F.	2
Broadis, I. A.	8
Brodie, J. B.	1
Bromley-Davenport, W.	2
Brook, E. F.	10
Brooking, T. D.	5
Brooks, J.	2
Broome, F. H.	3
Brown, A.	4
Brown, A. S.	1
Brown, G.	5
Brown, J.	3
Brown, W.	1
Buchan, C. M.	4
Bull, S. G.	4
Bullock, N.	2
Burgess, H.	4
Butcher, T.	3
Byrne, J. J.	8
Campbell, S. J.	1
Camsell, G. H.	18
Carter, H. S.	7
Carter, J. H.	4
Chadwick, E.	3
Chamberlain, M.	1
Chambers, H.	5
Channon, M. R.	21
Charlton, J.	6
Charlton, R.	49
Chenery, C. J.	1
Chivers, M.	13
Clarke, A. J.	10
Cobbold, W. N.	6
Cock, J. G.	2
Cole, A.	1
Cole, J. J.	1
Common, A.	2
Connelly, J. M.	7
Coppell, S. J.	7
Cotterill, G. H.	2
Cowans, G.	2
Crawford, R.	1
Crawshaw, T. H.	1
Crayston, W. J.	1
Creek, F. N. S.	1
Crooks, S. D.	7
Currey, E. S.	2
Currie, A. W.	3
Cursham, A. W.	2
Cursham, H. A.	5
Daft, H. B.	3
Davenport, J. K.	2
Davis, G.	1
Davis, H.	1
Day, S. H.	2
Dean, W. R.	18
Devey, J. H. G.	1
Dewhurst, F.	11
Dix, W. R.	1
Dixon, K. M.	4
Dixon, L. M.	1
Dorrell, A. R.	1
Douglas, B.	11
Drake, E. J.	6
Ducat, A.	1
Dunn, A. T. B.	2
Eastham, G.	2
Edwards, D.	5
Ehiogu, U.	1
Elliott, W. H.	3
Evans, R. E.	1
Ferdinand, L.	5
Ferdinand, R. G.	1
Finney, T.	30
Fleming, H. J.	9
Flowers, R.	10
Forman, Frank	1
Forman, Fred	3
Foster, R. E.	3
Fowler, R. B.	7
Francis, G. C. J.	3
Francis, T.	12
Freeman, B. C.	3
Froggatt, J.	2
Froggatt, R.	2
Galley, T.	1
Gascoigne, P. J.	10
Geary, F.	3
Gerrard, S. G.	3
Gibbins, W. V. T.	3
Gilliatt, W. E.	3
Goddard, P.	1
Goodall, J.	12
Goodyer, A. C.	1
Gosling, R. C.	2
Goulden, L. A.	4
Grainger, C.	3
Greaves, J.	44
Grovesnor, A. T.	2
Gunn, W.	1
Haines, J. T. W.	2
Hall, G. W.	9
Halse, H. J.	2
Hampson, J.	5
Hampton, H.	2
Hancocks, J.	2
Hardman, H. P.	1
Harris, S. S.	2
Hassall, H. W.	4
Hateley, M.	9
Haynes, J. N.	18
Hegan, K. E.	4
Henfrey, A. G.	2
Heskey, E. W.	5
Hilsdon, G. R.	14
Hine, E. W.	4
Hinton, A. T.	1
Hirst, D. E.	1
Hitchens, G. A.	5
Hobbis, H. H. F.	1
Hoddle, G.	8
Hodgetts, D.	1
Hodgson, G.	1
Holley, G. H.	8
Houghton, W. E.	5
Howell, R.	1
Hughes, E. W.	1
Hulme, J. H. A.	4
Hunt, G. S.	1
Hunt, R.	18
Hunter, N.	2
Hurst, G. C.	24
Ince, P. E. C.	2
Jack, D. N. B.	3
Jeffers, F.	1
Johnson, D. E.	6
Johnson, E.	2
Johnson, J. A.	2
Johnson, T. C. F.	5
Johnson, W. H.	1
Kail, E. I. L.	2
Kay, A. H.	1
Keegan, J. K.	21
Kelly, R.	8
Kennedy, R.	3
Kenyon-Slaney, W. S.	2
Keown, M. R.	2
Kevan, D. T.	8
Kidd, B.	1
Kingsford, R. K.	1
Kirchen, A. J.	2
Kirton, W. J.	1
Langton, R.	1
Latchford, R. D.	5
Latherton, E. G.	1
Lawler, C.	1
Lawton, T.	22
Lee, F.	10
Lee, J.	1
Lee, R. M.	2
Lee, S.	2
Le Saux, G. P.	1
Lindley, T.	14
Lineker, G.	48
Lofthouse, J. M.	3
Lofthouse, N.	30
Hon. A. Lyttelton	1
Mabbutt, G.	1
Macdonald, M.	6
Mannion, W. J.	11
Mariner, P.	13
Marsh, R. W.	1
Matthews, S.	11
Matthews, V.	1
McCall, J.	1
McDermott, T.	3
McManaman, S.	3
Medley, L. D.	1
Melia, J.	1
Mercer, D. W.	1
Merson, P. C.	3
Milburn, J. E. T.	10
Miller, H. S.	1
Mills, G. R.	3
Milward, A.	3
Mitchell, C.	5
Moore, J.	1
Moore, R. F.	2
Moore, W. G. B.	2
Morren, T.	1
Morris, F.	1
Morris, J.	3
Mortensen, S. H.	23
Morton, J. R.	1
Mosforth, W.	3
Mullen, J.	6
Mullery, A. P.	1
Murphy, D. B	1
Neal, P. G.	5
Needham, E.	3
Nicholls, J.	1
Nicholson, W. E.	1
O'Grady, M.	3
Osborne, F. R.	3
Owen, M. J.	22
Own goals	24
Page, L. A.	1
Paine, T. L.	7
Palmer, C. L.	1
Parry, E. H.	1
Parry, R. A.	1
Pawson, F. W.	1

Payne, J.	2
Peacock, A.	3
Pearce, S.	5
Pearson, J. S.	5
Pearson, S. C.	5
Perry, W.	2
Peters, M.	20
Pickering, F.	5
Platt, D.	27
Pointer, R.	2
Quantrill, A.	1
Ramsay, A. E.	3
Revie, D. G.	4
Redknapp, J. F.	1
Reynolds, J.	3
Richardson, J. R.	2
Rigby, A.	3
Rimmer, E. J.	2
Roberts, F.	2
Roberts, H.	1
Roberts, W. T.	2
Robinson, J.	3
Robson, B.	26
Robson, R.	4
Rowley, J. F.	6
Royle, J.	2
Rutherford, J.	3
Sagar, C.	1
Sandilands, R. R.	3
Sansom, K.	1
Schofield, J.	1
Scholes, P.	13
Seed, J. M.	1
Settle, J.	6
Sewell, J.	3
Shackleton, L. F.	1
Sharp, J.	1
Shearer, A.	30
Shelton, A.	1
Shepherd, A.	2
Sheringham, E. P.	11
Simpson, J.	1
Smith, A.	1
Smith, A. M.	2
Smith, G. O.	11
Smith, Joe	1
Smith, J. R.	2
Smith, J. W.	4
Smith, R.	13
Smith, S.	1
Sorby, T. H.	1
Southgate, G.	2
Southworth, J.	3
Sparks, F. J.	3
Spence, J. W.	1
Spiksley, F.	5
Spilsbury, B. W.	5
Steele, F. C.	8
Stephenson, G. T.	2
Steven, T. M.	4
Stewart, J.	2
Stiles, N. P.	1
Storer, H.	1
Stone, S. B.	2
Summerbee, M. G.	1
Tambling, R. V.	1
Taylor, P. J.	2
Taylor, T.	16
Thompson, P. B.	1
Thornewell, G.	1
Tilson, S. F.	6
Townley, W. J.	2
Tueart, D.	2
Vassell, D.	4
Vaughton, O. H.	6
Veitch, J. G.	3
Violett, D. S.	1
Waddle, C. R.	6
Walker, W. H.	9
Wall, G.	2
Wallace, D.	1
Walsh, P.	1
Waring, T.	4
Warren, B.	2
Watson, D. V.	4
Watson, V. M.	4
Webb, G. W.	1
Webb, N.	4
Wedlock, W. J.	2
Weller, K.	1
Welsh, D.	1
Whateley, O.	2
Wheldon, G. F.	6
Whitfield, H.	1
Wignall, F.	2
Wilkes, A.	1
Wilkins, R. G.	3
Willingham, C. K.	1
Wilshaw, D. J.	10
Wilson, G. P.	1
Winckworth, W. N.	1
Windridge, J. E.	7
Wise, D. F.	1
Withe, P.	1
Wollaston, C. H. R.	1
Wood, H.	1
Woodcock, T.	16
Woodhall, G.	1
Woodward, V. J.	29
Worrall, F.	2
Worthington, F. S.	2
Wright, I. E.	9
Wright, M.	1
Wright, W. A.	3
Wylie, J. G.	1
Yates, J.	3

NORTHERN IRELAND

Anderson, T.	4
Armstrong, G.	12
Bambrick, J.	12
Barr, H. H.	1
Barron, H.	3
Best, G.	9
Bingham, W. L.	10
Black, K.	1
Blanchflower, D.	2
Blanchflower, J.	1
Brennan, B.	1
Brennan, R. A.	1
Brotherston, N.	3
Brown, J.	1
Browne, F.	2
Campbell, J.	1
Campbell, W. G.	1
Casey, T.	2
Caskey, W.	1
Cassidy, T.	1
Chambers, J.	3
Clarke, C. J.	13
Clements, D.	2
Cochrane, T.	1
Condy, J.	1
Connor, M. J.	1
Coulter, J.	1
Croft, T.	1
Crone, W.	1
Crossan, E.	1
Crossan, J. A.	10
Curran, S.	2
Cush, W. W.	5
Dalton, W.	4
D'Arcy, S. D.	1
Darling, J.	1
Davey, H. H.	1
Davis, T. L.	1
Dill, A. H.	1
Doherty, L.	1
Doherty, P. D.	3
Dougan, A. D.	8
Dowie, I.	12
Dunne, J.	4
Elder, A. R.	1
Elliott, S.	1
Emerson, W.	1
English, S.	1
Feeney, W	1
Ferguson, W.	1
Ferris, J.	1
Ferris, R. O.	1
Finney, T.	2
Gaffkin, J.	4
Gara, A.	3
Gaukrodger, G.	1
Gibb, J. T.	2
Gibb, T. J.	1
Gillespie, K. R.	1
Gillespie, W.	12
Goodall, A. L.	2
Griffin, D. J.	1
Gray, P.	6
Halligan, W.	1
Hamill, M.	1
Hamilton, B.	4
Hamilton, W. R.	5
Hannon, D. J.	1
Harkin, J. T.	2
Harvey, M.	3
Healy, D. J.	8
Hill, C. F.	1
Hughes, M. E.	5
Humphries, W.	1
Hunter, A. (*Distillery*)	1
Hunter, A. (*Blackburn R*)	1
Hunter, B. V.	1
Irvine, R. W.	3
Irvine, W. J.	8
Johnston, H.	2
Johnston, S.	2
Johnston, W. C.	1
Jones, S.	1
Jones, J.	1
Kelly, J.	4
Kernaghan, N.	2
Kirwan, J.	2
Lacey, W.	3
Lemon, J.	2
Lennon, N. F.	2
Lockhart, N.	3
Lomas, S. M.	3
Magilton, J.	5
Mahood, J.	2
Martin, D. K.	3
Maxwell, J.	2
McAdams, W. J.	7
McAllen, J.	1
Mcauley, J. L.	1
McCartney, G.	1
McCandless, J.	3
McCaw, J. H.	1
McClelland, J.	1
McCluggage, A.	2
McCracken, W.	1
McCrory, S.	1
McCurdy, C.	1
McDonald, A.	3
McGarry, J. K.	1
McGrath, R. C.	4
McIlroy, J.	10
McIlroy, S. B.	5
McKnight, J.	2
McLaughlin, J. C.	6
McMahon, G. J.	2
McMordie, A. S.	3
McMorran, E. J.	4
McParland, P. J.	10
McWha, W. B. R.	1
Meldon, J.	1
Mercer, J. T.	1
Millar, W.	1
Milligan, D.	1
Milne, R. G.	2
Molyneux, T. B.	1
Moreland, V.	1
Morgan, S.	3
Morrow, S. J.	1
Morrow, W. J.	1
Mulryne, P. P.	3
Murphy, N.	1
Neill, W. J. T.	2
Nelson, S.	1
Nicholl, C. J.	3
Nicholl, J. M.	1
Nicholson, J. J.	6
O'Boyle, G.	1
O'Hagan, C.	2
O'Kane, W. J.	1
O'Neill, J.	2
O'Neill, M. A.	4
O'Neill, M. H.	8
Own goals	6
Patterson, D. J.	1
Peacock, R.	2
Peden, J.	7
Penney, S.	2
Pyper, James	2
Pyper, John	1
Quinn, J. M.	12
Quinn, S. J.	3
Reynolds, J.	1
Rowland, K.	1
Rowley, R. W. M.	2
Sheridan, J.	2
Sherrard, J.	1
Sherrard, W. C.	2
Simpson, W. J.	5
Sloan, H. A. de B.	4
Smyth, S.	5
Spence, D. W.	3
Stanfield, O. M.	11
Stevenson, A. E.	5
Stewart, I.	2
Taggart, G. P.	7
Thompson, F. W.	2
Torrans, S.	1
Tully, C. P.	3
Turner, E.	1
Walker, J.	1
Walsh, D. J.	5
Welsh, E.	1
Whiteside, N.	9
Whiteside, T.	1
Whitley, Jeff	1
Williams, J. R.	1
Williams, M. S.	1
Williamson, J.	1
Wilson, D. J.	1
Wilson, K. J.	6
Wilson, S. J.	7
Wilton, J. M.	2
Young, S.	2

SCOTLAND

Aitken, R. (*Celtic*) 1
Aitken, R. (*Dumbarton*) 1
Aitkenhead, W. A. C. 2
Alexander, D. 1
Allan, D. S. 4
Allan, J. 2
Anderson, F. 1
Anderson, W. 4
Andrews, P. 1
Archibald, A. 1
Archibald, S. 4

Baird, D. 2
Baird, J. C. 2
Baird, S. 2
Bannon, E. 1
Barbour, A. 1
Barker, J. B. 4
Battles, B. Jr 1
Bauld, W. 2
Baxter, J. C. 3
Bell, J. 5
Bennett, A. 2
Berry, D. 1
Bett, J. 1
Beveridge, W. W. 1
Black, A. 3
Black, D. 1
Bone, J. 1
Booth, S. 6
Boyd, R. 2
Boyd, T. 1
Boyd, W. G. 1
Brackenridge, T. 1
Brand, R. 8
Brazil, A. 1
Bremner, W. J. 3
Brown, A. D. 6
Buchanan, P. S. 1
Buchanan, R. 1
Buckley, P. 1
Buick, A. 2
Burley, C. W. 3
Burns, K. 1

Cairns, T. 1
Calderwood, C. 1
Calderwood, R. 2
Caldow, E. 4
Cameron, C. 2
Campbell, C. 1
Campbell, John (*Celtic*) 5
Campbell, John (*Rangers*) 4
Campbell, P. 2
Campbell, R. 1
Cassidy, J. 1
Chalmers, S. 3
Chambers, T. 1
Cheyne, A. G. 4
Christie, A. J. 1
Clunas, W. L. 1
Collins, J. 12
Collins, R. Y. 10
Combe, J. R. 1
Conn, A. 1
Cooper, D. 6
Craig, J. 1
Craig, T. 1
Crawford, S. 4
Cunningham, A. N. 5
Curran, H. P. 1

Dailly, C. 4
Dalglish, K. 30
Davidson, D. 1
Davidson, J. A. 1
Delaney, J. 3
Devine, A. 1
Dewar, G. 1
Dewar, N. 4
Dickson, W. 4
Divers, J. 1
Dobie, R. S. 1
Docherty, T. H. 1
Dodds, D. 1
Dodds, W. 7
Donaldson, A. 1
Donnachie, J. 1
Dougall, J. 1
Drummond, J. 2
Dunbar, M. 1
Duncan, D. 7
Duncan, D. M. 1
Duncan, J. 1
Dunn, J. 2
Durie, G. S. 7

Easson, J. F. 1
Elliott, M. S. 1
Ellis, J. 1

Ferguson, B. 2
Ferguson, J. 6
Fernie, W. 1
Fitchie, T. T. 1
Flavell, R. 2
Fleming, C. 2
Fleming, J. W. 3
Fraser, M. J. E. 3
Freedman, D. A. 1

Gallacher, H. K. 23
Gallacher, K. W. 9
Gallacher, P. 1
Galt, J. H. 1
Gemmell, T. (*St Mirren*) 1
Gemmell, T. (*Celtic*) 1
Gemmill, A. 8
Gemmill, S. 1
Gibb, W. 1
Gibson, D. W. 3
Gibson, J. D. 1
Gibson, N. 1
Gillespie, Jas. 3
Gillick, T. 3
Gilzean, A. J. 12
Gossland, J. 2
Goudie, J. 1
Gough, C. R. 6
Gourlay, J. 1
Graham, A. 2
Graham, G. 3
Gray, A. 6
Gray, E. 3
Gray, F. 1
Greig, J. 3
Groves, W. 4

Hamilton, G. 4
Hamilton, J. (*Queen's Park*) 3
Hamilton, R. C. 14
Harper, J. M. 2
Harrower, W. 5
Hartford, R. A. 4
Heggie, C. 5
Henderson, J. G. 1
Henderson, W. 5
Hendry, E. C. J. 3
Herd, D. G. 3
Herd, G. 1
Hewie, J. D. 2
Higgins, A. (*Newcastle U*) 1
Higgins, A. (*Kilmarnock*) 4
Highet, T. C. 1
Holton, J. A. 2
Hopkin, D. 2
Houliston, W. 2
Howie, H. 1
Howie, J. 2
Hughes, J. 1
Hunter, W. 1
Hutchison, D. 6
Hutchison, T. 1
Hutton, J. 1
Hyslop, T. 1

Imrie, W. N. 1

Jackson, A. 8
Jackson, C. 1
Jackson, D. 4
James, A. W. 4
Jardine, A. 1
Jenkinson, T. 1
Jess, E. 2
Johnston, A. 2
Johnston, L. H. 1
Johnston, M. 14
Johnstone, D. 2
Johnstone, J. 4
Johnstone, Jas. 1
Johnstone, R. 9
Johnstone, W. 1
Jordan, J. 11

Kay, J. L. 5
Keillor, A. 3
Kelly, J. 1
Kelso, J. 1
Ker, G. 10
King, A. 1
King, J. 1
Kinnear, D. 1
Kyle, K. 1

Lambert, P. 1
Lambie, J. 1
Lambie, W. A. 5
Lang, J. J. 1
Law, D. 30
Leggat, G. 8
Lennie, W. 1
Lennox, R. 3
Liddell, W. 6
Lindsay, J. 6
Linwood, A. B. 1
Logan, J. 1
Lorimer, P. 4
Love, A. 1
Lowe, J. (*Cambuslang*) 1
Lowe, J. (*St Bernards*) 1

Macari, L. 5
MacDougall, E. J. 3
MacLeod, M. 1
Mackay, D. C. 4
Mackay, G. 1
MacKenzie, J. A. 1
MacKinnon, W. W. 6
Madden, J. 5
Marshall, H. 1
Marshall, J. 1
Mason, J. 4
Massie, A. 1
Masson, D. S. 5
McAdam, J. 1
McAllister, G. 5
McAulay, J. D. 1
McAvennie, F. 1
McCall, J. 1
McCall, S. M. 1
McCalliog, J. 1
McCallum, N. 1
McCann, N. 1
McClair, B. J. 2
McCoist, A. 19
McColl, R. S. 13
McCulloch, D. 3
McDougall, J. 4
McFarlane, A. 1
McFadyen, W. 2
McGhee, M. 2
McGinlay, J. 4
McGrory, J. 6
McGuire, W. 1
McInally, A. 3
McInnes, T. 2
McKie, J. 2
McKimmie, S. 1
McKinlay, W. 4
McKinnon, A. 1
McKinnon, R. 1
McLaren, A. 4
McLaren, J. 1
McLean, A. 1
McLean, T. 1
McLeish, A. 1
McLintock, F. 1
McMahon, A. 6
McMenemy, J. 5
McMillan, I. L. 2
McNeil, H. 5
McNeill, W. 3
McPhail, J. 3
McPhail, R. 7
McPherson, J. 8
McPherson, R. 1
McQueen, G. 5
McStay, P. 9
McSwegan, G. 1
Meiklejohn, D. D. 3
Millar, J. 2
Miller, K. 2
Miller, T. 2
Miller, W. 1
Mitchell, R. C. 1
Morgan, W. 1
Morris, D. 1
Morris, H. 3
Morton, A. L. 5
Mudie, J. K. 9
Mulhall, G. 1
Munro, A. D. 1
Munro, N. 1
Murdoch, R. 5
Murphy, F. 1
Murray, J. 1

Napier, C. E. 3
Narey, D. 1
Naysmith, G. A. 1
Neil, R. G. 2
Nevin, P. K. F. 5
Nicholas, C. 5
Nisbet, J. 2

O'Donnell, F. 2
O'Hare, J. 5
Ormond, W. E. 1
O'Rourke, F. 1
Orr, R. 1
Orr, T. 1
Oswald, J. 1
Own goals 15

Parlane, D. 1
Paul, H. McD. 2
Paul, W. 6
Pettigrew, W. 2
Provan, D. 1

Quinn, J. 7
Quinn, P. 1

Rankin, G. 2
Rankin, R. 2
Reid, W. 4
Reilly, L. 22
Renny-Tailyour, H. W. 1
Richmond, J. T. 1
Ring, T. 2
Rioch, B. D. 6
Ritchie, J. 1

Ritchie, P. S. 1
Robertson, A. 2
Robertson, J. 2
Robertson, J. N. 9
Robertson, J. T. 2
Robertson, T. 1
Robertson, W. 1
Russell, D. 1

Scott, A. S. 5
Sellar, W. 4
Sharp, G. 1
Shaw, F. W. 1
Shearer, D. 2
Simpson, J. 1
Smith, A. 5
Smith, G. 4
Smith, J. 1
Smith, John 13
Somerville, G. 1
Souness, G. J. 4
Speedie, F. 2
St John, I. 9
Steel, W. 12
Stein, C. 10
Stevenson, G. 4
Stewart, A. 1
Stewart, R. 1
Stewart, W. E. 1
Strachan, G. 5
Sturrock, P. 3

Taylor, J. D. 1
Templeton, R. 1
Thompson, S. 2
Thomson, A. 1
Thomson, C. 4
Thomson, R. 1
Thomson, W. 1
Thornton, W. 1

Waddell, T. S. 1
Waddell, W. 6
Walker, J. 2
Walker, R. 7
Walker, T. 9
Wallace, I. A. 1
Wark, J. 7
Watson, J. A. K. 1
Watt, F. 2
Watt, W. W. 1
Weir, A. 1
Weir, D. 1
Weir, J. B. 2
White, J. A. 3
Wilkie, L. 1
Wilson, A. 2
Wilson, A. N. 13
Wilson, D. (*Queen's Park*) 2
Wilson, D. (*Rangers*) 9
Wilson, H. 1
Wylie, T. G. 1

Young, A. 5

WALES

Allchurch, I. J. 23
Allen, M. 3
Astley, D. J. 12
Atherton, R. W. 2

Bamford, T. 1
Barnes, W. 1
Bellamy, C. D. 6
Blackmore, C. G. 1
Blake, N. A. 4
Bodin, P. J. 3
Boulter, L. M. 1
Bowdler, J. C. H. 3
Bowen, D. L. 1
Bowen, M. 3
Boyle, T. 1
Bryan, T. 1
Burgess, W. A. R. 1
Burke, T. 1
Butler, W. T. 1

Chapman, T. 2
Charles, J. 1
Charles, M. 6
Charles, W. J. 15
Clarke, R. J. 5
Coleman, C. 4
Collier, D. J. 1
Crosse, K. 1
Cumner, R. H. 1
Curtis, A. 6
Curtis, E. R. 3

Davies, D. W. 1
Davies, E. Lloyd 1
Davies, G. 2
Davies, L. S. 6
Davies, R. T. 9
Davies, R. W. 6
Davies, S. 5
Davies, Simon 3
Davies, W. 6
Davies, W. H. 1
Davies, William 5
Davis, W. O. 1
Deacy, N. 4
Doughty, J. 6
Doughty, R. 2
Durban, A. 2
Dwyer, P. 2

Earnshaw, R. 2
Edwards, G. 2
Edwards, R. I. 4
England, H. M. 4
Evans, I. 1
Evans, J. 1
Evans, R. E. 2
Evans, W. 1
Eyton-Jones, J. A. 1

Flynn, B. 7
Ford, T. 23
Foulkes, W. I. 1
Fowler, J. 3

Giles, D. 2
Giggs, R. J. 8
Glover, E. M. 7
Godfrey, B. C. 2
Green, A. W. 3
Griffiths, A. T. 6
Griffiths, M. W. 2
Griffiths, T. P. 3

Harris, C. S. 1
Hartson, J. 10
Hersee, R. 1
Hewitt, R. 1
Hockey, T. 1
Hodges, G. 2
Hole, W. J. 1
Hopkins, I. J. 2
Horne, B. 2
Howell, E. G. 3
Hughes, L. M. 16

James, E. 2
James, L. 10
James, R. 7
Jarrett, R. H. 3
Jenkyns, C. A. 1
Jones, A. 1
Jones, Bryn 6
Jones, B. S. 2
Jones, Cliff 16
Jones, C. W. 1
Jones, D. E. 1
Jones, Evan 1
Jones, H. 1
Jones, I. 1
Jones, J. L. 1
Jones, J. O. 1
Jones, J. P. 1
Jones, Leslie J. 1
Jones, R. A. 2
Jones, W. L. 6

Keenor, F. C. 2
Krzywicki, R. L. 1

Leek, K. 5
Lewis, B. 4
Lewis, D. M. 2
Lewis, W. 8
Lewis, W. L. 3
Lovell, S. 1
Lowrie, G. 2

Mahoney, J. F. 1
Mays, A. W. 1
Medwin, T. C. 6
Melville, A. K 3
Meredith, W. H. 11
Mills, T. J. 1
Moore, G. 1
Morgan, J. R. 2
Morgan-Owen, H. 1
Morgan-Owen, M. M. 2
Morris, A. G. 9
Morris, H. 2
Morris, R. 1
Morris, S. 2

Nicholas, P. 2

O'Callaghan, E. 3
O'Sullivan, P. A. 1
Owen, G. 2
Owen, W. 4
Owen, W. P. 6
Own goals 13

Palmer, D. 3
Parry, T. D. 3
Paul, R. 1
Peake, E. 1
Pembridge, M. 6
Perry, E. 1
Phillips, C. 5
Phillips, D. 2
Powell, A. 1
Powell, D. 1
Price, J. 4
Price, P. 1
Pryce-Jones, W. E. 3
Pugh, D. H. 2

Reece, G. I. 2
Rees, R. R. 3
Richards, R. W. 1
Roach, J. 2
Robbins, W. W. 4
Roberts, J. (*Corwen*) 1
Roberts, Jas. 1
Roberts, P. S. 1
Roberts, R. (*Druids*) 1
Roberts, W. (*Llangollen*) 2
Roberts, W. (*Wrexham*) 1
Roberts, W. H. 1
Robinson, J. R. C. 3
Rush, I. 28
Russell, M. R. 1

Sabine, H. W. 1
Saunders, D. 22
Savage, R. W. 2
Shaw, E. G. 2
Sisson, H. 4
Slatter, N. 2
Smallman, D. P. 1
Speed, G. A. 6
Symons, C. J. 2

Tapscott, D. R. 4
Thomas, M. 4
Thomas, T. 1
Toshack, J. B. 12
Trainer, H. 2

Vaughan, John 2
Vernon, T. R. 8
Vizard, E. T. 1

Walsh, I. 7
Warren, F. W. 3
Watkins, W. M. 4
Wilding, J. 4
Williams, A. 1
Williams, D. R. 2
Williams, G. E. 1
Williams, G. G. 1
Williams, W. 1
Woosnam, A. P. 3
Wynn, G. A. 1

Yorath, T. C. 2
Young, E. 1

REPUBLIC OF IRELAND

Aldridge, J. 19
Ambrose, P. 1
Anderson, J. 1

Barrett, G. 1
Bermingham, P. 1
Bradshaw, P. 4
Brady, L. 9
Breen, G. 6
Brown, D. 1
Byrne, J. (*Bray*) 1
Byrne, J. (*QPR*) 4

Cantwell, J. 14
Carey, J. 3
Carroll, T. 1
Cascarino, A. 19
Coad, P. 3
Connolly, D. J. 8
Conroy, T. 2
Conway, J. 3
Coyne, T. 6
Cummings, G. 5
Curtis, D. 8

Daly, G. 13
Davis, T. 4
Dempsey, J. 1
Dennehy, M. 2
Doherty, G. M. T. 4
Donnelly, J. 4
Donnelly, T. 1
Duff, D. A. 4
Duffy, B. 1
Duggan, H. 1
Dunne, J. 13
Dunne, L. 1
Dunne, R. P. 3

Eglington, T. 2
Ellis, P. 2

Fagan, F. 5
Fallon, S. 2
Fallon, W. 2
Farrell, P. 3
Finnan, S. 1
Fitzgerald, P. 2
Fitzgerald, J. 1
Fitzsimmons, A. 7
Flood, J. J. 4

Player	Goals
Fogarty, A.	3
Foley, D.	2
Fullam, J.	1
Fullam, R.	1
Galvin, A.	1
Gavin, J.	2
Geoghegan, M.	2
Giles, J.	5
Givens, D.	19
Glynn, D.	1
Grealish, T.	8
Grimes, A. A.	1
Hale, A.	2
Hand, E.	2
Harte, I. P.	8
Haverty, J.	3
Healy, C.	1
Holland, M. R.	4
Holmes, J.	1
Horlacher, A.	2
Houghton, R.	6
Hughton, C.	1
Hurley, C.	2
Irwin, D.	4
Jordan, D.	1
Kavanagh, G. A.	1
Keane, R. D.	16
Keane, R. M.	9
Kelly, D.	9
Kelly, G.	2
Kelly, J.	2
Kennedy, M.	3
Kernaghan, A. N.	1
Kilbane, K. D.	4
Kinsella, M. A.	3
Lacey, W.	1
Lawrenson, M.	5
Leech, M.	2
McAteer, J. W.	3
McCann, J.	1
McCarthy, M.	2
McEvoy, A.	6
McGee, P.	4
McGrath, P.	8
McLoughlin, A. F.	2
McPhail, S. J. P.	1
Mancini, T.	1
Martin, C.	6
Martin, M.	4
Mooney, J.	1
Moore, P.	7
Moran, K.	6
Morrison, C. H.	4
Moroney, T.	1
Mulligan, P.	1
O'Callaghan, K.	1
O'Connor, T.	2
O'Farrell, F.	2
O'Flanagan, K.	3
O'Keefe, E.	1
O'Leary, D. A.	1
O'Neill, F.	1
O'Neill, K. P.	4
O'Reilly, J. (*Brideville*)	2
O'Reilly, J. (*Cork*)	1
Own goals	10
Quinn, N.	21
Reid, S. J.	2
Ringstead, A.	7
Robinson, M.	4
Rogers, E.	5
Ryan, G.	1
Ryan, R.	3
Sheedy, K.	9
Sheridan, J.	5
Slaven, B.	1
Sloan, W.	1
Squires, J.	1
Stapleton, F.	20
Staunton, S.	7
Strahan, J.	1
Sullivan, J.	1
Townsend, A. D.	7
Treacy, R.	5
Touhy, L.	4
Waddock, G.	3
Walsh, D.	5
Walsh, M.	3
Waters, J.	1
White, J. J.	2
Whelan, R.	3

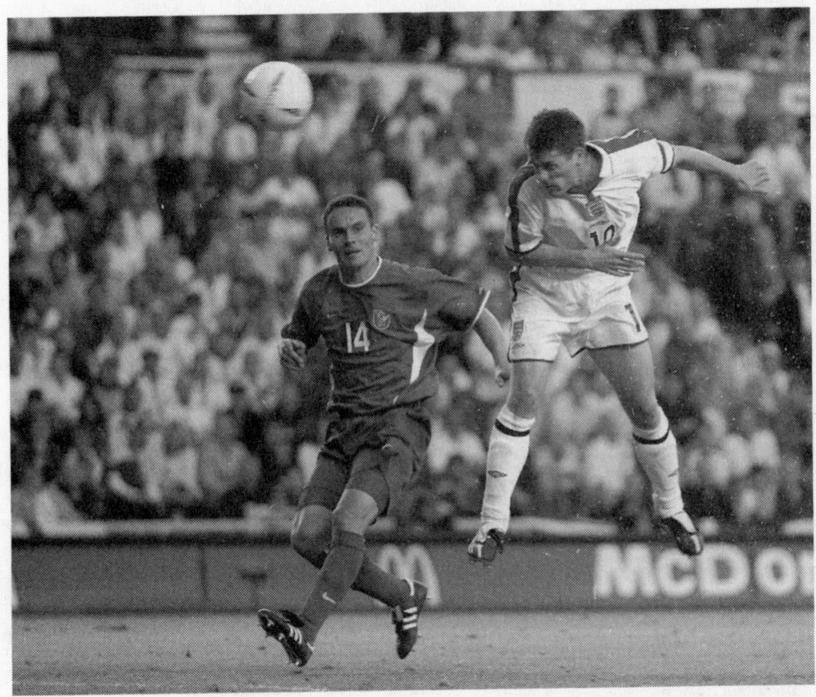

Michael Owen celebrated his 50th international appearance for England with two goals against Slovakia in a Euro 2004 tie. Here he heads home the second. (Actionimages)

SOUTH AMERICA

COPA LIBERTADORES 2002

SEMI-FINALS, FIRST LEG
Sao Caetano 2, America (Mex) 0
Olimpia 3, Gremio 2

SEMI-FINALS, SECOND LEG
America (Mex) 1, Sao Caetano 1
Gremio 1, Olimpia 0
Olimpia won 5-4 on penalties.

FINAL, FIRST LEG
Olimpia 0, Sao Caetano 1

FINAL, SECOND LEG
Sao Caetano 1, Olimpia 2
Olimpia won 4-2 on penalties.

COPA LIBERTADORES 2003

PRELIMINARY ROUND	P	W	D	L	F	A	Pts
Pumas	6	4	1	1	12	4	13
Cruz Azul	6	3	2	1	11	7	11
Estudiantes	6	2	1	3	7	9	7
Tachira	6	1	0	5	6	16	3

GROUP 1	P	W	D	L	F	A	Pts
Dep Cali	6	4	0	2	9	3	12
River Plate	6	4	0	2	10	7	12
Libertad	6	2	1	3	9	9	7
Emelec	6	1	1	4	6	15	4

GROUP 2	P	W	D	L	F	A	Pts
Paysandu	6	4	2	0	14	5	14
Cerro Porteno	6	2	2	2	8	11	8
Sporting Cristal	6	2	1	3	6	7	7
Univ Catolica	6	1	1	4	7	12	4

GROUP 3	P	W	D	L	F	A	Pts
Santos	6	4	2	0	16	4	14
America (Col)	6	3	1	2	11	11	10
El Nacional	6	1	3	2	4	6	6
12 de Octubre	6	1	0	5	7	17	3

GROUP 4	P	W	D	L	F	A	Pts
Cobreloa	6	2	3	1	9	5	9
Olimpia	6	2	3	1	9	6	9
Gimnasia	6	1	4	1	8	7	7
Alianza	6	1	2	3	6	14	5

GROUP 5	P	W	D	L	F	A	Pts
Gremio	6	3	1	2	10	7	10
Pumas	6	3	0	3	8	8	9
Bolivar	6	3	0	3	8	9	9
Penarol	6	2	1	3	12	14	7

GROUP 6	P	W	D	L	F	A	Pts
Racing Club	6	4	2	0	11	4	14
Nacional (Uru)	6	3	1	2	12	10	10
Universitario	6	1	4	1	8	8	7
Oriente	6	0	1	5	4	13	1

GROUP 7	P	W	D	L	F	A	Pts
Indep Medellin	6	4	0	2	9	6	12
Boca Juniors	6	3	2	1	10	7	11
Barcelona	6	1	2	3	8	10	5
Colo Colo	6	1	2	3	6	10	5

GROUP 8	P	W	D	L	F	A	Pts
Corinthians	6	5	0	1	15	6	15
Cruz Azul	6	3	0	3	12	11	9
Fenix	6	2	0	4	10	14	6
The Strongest	6	2	0	4	6	12	6

SECOND ROUND, FIRST LEG
Olimpia 2, Gremio 3
Cerro Porteno 0, Indep Medellin 1
Nacional (Uru) 4, Santos 4
Boca Juniors 0, Paysandu 1
Pumas 0, Cobreloa 1
America (Col) 1, Racing 1
River Plate 2, Corinthians 1
Cruz Azul 0, Dep Cali 0

SECOND ROUND, SECOND LEG
Indep Medellin 0, Cerro Porteno 1
Santos 2, Nacional (Uru) 2
Cobreloa 0, Pumas 0
Gremio 3, Olimpia 0
Dep Cali 0, Cruz Azul 0
Racing 0, America (Col) 0
Corinthians 1, River Plate 2
Paysandu 2, Boca Juniors 4

QUARTER-FINALS, FIRST LEG
River Plate 2, America (Col) 1
Cobreloa 1, Boca Juniors 2
Cruz Azul 2, Santos 2
Gremio 2, Indep Medellin 2

QUARTER-FINALS, SECOND LEG
America (Col) 4, River Plate 1
Boca Juniors 2, Cobreloa 1
Santos 1, Cruz Azul 0
Indep Medellin 2, Gremio 1

SEMI-FINALS, FIRST LEG
Santos 1, Indep Medellin 0
Boca Juniors 2, America (Col) 0

SEMI-FINALS, SECOND LEG
Indep Medellin 2, Santos 3
America (Col) 0, Boca Juniors 4

FINAL, FIRST LEG
Boca Juniors 2, Santos 0

FINAL, SECOND LEG
Santos 1, Boca Juniors 3

COPA SUDAMERICA 2002

VENEZUELA QUALIFYING GROUP
Dep Tachira 2, Monagas 0
Monagas 3, Dep Tachira 0

ARGENTINA GROUP 1
Racing 1, River Plate 0
River Plate 0, Racing 0

ARGENTINA GROUP 2
Gimnasia 3, Boca Juniors 1
Boca Juniors 0, Gimnasia 0

URUGUAY GROUP
Danubia 1, Nacional 1
Nacional 2, Danubia 0

VENEZUELA/MERCOSUR WINNERS GROUP
Monagas 0, San Lorenzo 3
San Lorenzo 5, Monagas 1

CHILE GROUP
Cobreloa 0, Santiago Wanderers 1
Santiago Wanderers 3, Cobreloa 2

PERU/ECUADOR GROUP
Aucas 1, Barcelona 2
Alianza 1, Universitario 0
Universitario 0, Alianza 1
Barcelona 1, Aucas 0
Barcelona 1, Alianza 0
Alianza 2, Barcelona 1
Alianza won 6-5 on penalties.

PARAGUAY/BOLIVIA GROUP
Bolivar 4, Oriente 2
Cerro Porteno 0, Libertad 2
Libertad 1, Cerro Porteno 0
Oriente 1, Bolivar 0
Bolivar 2, Libertad 0
Libertad 1, Bolivar 1

COLOMBIA GROUP
At Nacional 1, America 0
America 1, At Nacional 2

QUARTER-FINALS
Alianza 1, Nacional (Uru) 0
Nacional (Uru) 3, Alianza 1
San Lorenzo 3, Racing 1
Racing 2, San Lorenzo 0
San Lorenzo won 4-3 on penalties.

At Nacional 2, Santiago Wanderers 1
Santiago Wanderers 1, At Nacional 0
Santiago Wanderers won 6-5 on penalties.
Bolivar 4, Gimnasia 1
Gimnasia 2, Bolivar 0

SEMI-FINALS
Bolivar 2, San Lorenzo 1
San Lorenzo 4, Bolivar 2
At Nacional 2, Nacional (Uru) 1
Nacional (Uru) 2, At Nacional 1
At Nacional won 5-3 on penalties.

FINAL
At Nacional 0, San Lorenzo 4
San Lorenzo 0, At Nacional 0

AFRICA

CECAFA CUP 2002

(in Tanzania)

GROUP A	P	W	D	L	F	A	Pts
Tanzania	4	2	2	0	5	2	8
Kenya	4	2	1	1	6	3	7
Eritrea	4	1	2	1	5	7	5
Sudan	4	1	1	2	4	5	4
Burundi	4	0	2	2	3	6	2

GROUP B	P	W	D	L	F	A	Pts
Uganda	4	4	0	0	9	1	12
Rwanda	4	3	0	1	4	2	9
Zanzibar	4	1	1	2	1	3	4
Somalia	4	1	0	3	1	4	3
Ethiopia	4	0	1	3	0	5	1

SEMI-FINALS
Tanzania 3, Rwanda 0
Uganda 1, Kenya 3

THIRD PLACE
Uganda 1, Rwanda 2

FINAL
Tanzania 2, Kenya 3

AFRICAN NATIONS CUP 2004

GROUP 1
Djibouti withdrew.
Angola 0, Nigeria 0
Malawi 1, Angola 0
Malawi 0, Nigeria 1
Nigeria 4, Malawi 1
Nigeria 2, Angola 2
Angola 5, Malawi 1

GROUP 2
Niger 3, Ethiopia 1
Guinea 3, Liberia 0
Liberia 1, Niger 0
Ethiopia 1, Guinea 0
Ethiopia 1, Liberia 0
Guinea 2, Niger 0
Niger 1, Guinea 0
Liberia 1, Ethiopia 0
Liberia 1, Guinea 2
Ethiopia 2, Niger 0
Guinea 3, Ethiopia 0
Niger 1, Liberia 0

GROUP 3
Benin 4, Tanzania 0
Sudan 0, Zambia 1
Tanzania 1, Sudan 2
Zambia 1, Benin 1
Sudan 3, Benin 0
Tanzania 0, Zambia 1
Zambia 2, Tanzania 0
Benin 3, Sudan 0
Zambia 1, Sudan 1
Tanzania 0, Benin 1
Benin 3, Zambia 0
Sudan v Tanzania
Tanzania refused to play in Sudan, Sudan awarded the match.

GROUP 4
Congo 0, Burkina Faso 0
CAR 1, Mozambique 1
Burkina Faso 2, CAR 1
Mozambique 0, Congo 3
Mozambique 1, Burkina Faso 0
Congo 2, CAR 1
Burkina Faso 4, Mozambique 0
CAR 0, Congo 0
Burkina Faso 3, Congo 0
Mozambique 1, CAR 0
CAR 0, Burkina Faso 3
Congo 0, Mozambique 0

GROUP 5
Mauritania 0, Cape Verde 2
Kenya 3, Togo 0
Cape Verde 0, Kenya 1
Togo 1, Mauritania 0
Cape Verde 2, Togo 1
Kenya 4, Mauritania 0
Mauritania 0, Kenya 0
Togo 5, Cape Verde 2
Cape Verde 3, Mauritania 0
Togo 2, Kenya 0
Kenya 1, Cape Verde 0
Mauritania 0, Togo 0

GROUP 6
Seychelles 1, Eritrea 0
Zimbabwe 1, Mali 0
Eritrea 0, Zimbabwe 1
Mali 3, Seychelles 0
Eritrea 0, Mali 2
Zimbabwe 3, Seychelles 1
Mali 1, Eritrea 0
Seychelles 2, Zimbabwe 1
Eritrea 1, Seychelles 0
Mali 0, Zimbabwe 0
Seychelles 0, Mali 2
Zimbabwe 2, Eritrea 0

GROUP 7
Gabon 0, Morocco 1
Equatorial Guinea 1, Sierra Leone 3
Sierra Leone 2, Gabon 0
Morocco 5, Equatorial Guinea 0
Gabon 4, Equatorial Guinea 0
Sierra Leone 0, Morocco 0
Equatorial Guinea 2, Gabon 1
Morocco 1, Sierra Leone 0
Morocco 2, Gabon 0
Sierra Leone 2, Equatorial Guinea 0
Equatorial Guinea 0, Morocco 1
Gabon 2, Sierra Leone 0

GROUP 8
Sao Tome e Principe withdrew.
Lesotho 0, Senegal 1
Gambia 6, Lesotho 0
Gambia 0, Senegal 0
Senegal 3, Gambia 1
Senegal 3, Lesotho 0
Lesotho 1, Gambia 0

GROUP 9
Botswana 0, Swaziland 0
Libya 3, DR Congo 2
DR Congo 2, Botswana 0
Swaziland 2, Libya 1
Libya 0, Botswana 0
Swaziland 1, DR Congo 1
Botswana 0, Libya 1
DR Congo 2, Swaziland 0
DR Congo 2, Libya 1
Swaziland 3, Botswana 2
Botswana 0, DR Congo 0
Libya 6, Swaziland 2

GROUP 10
Guinea-Bissau withdrew.
Madagascar 1, Egypt 0
Mauritius 0, Madagascar 1
Mauritius 0, Egypt 1
Egypt 7, Mauritius 0
Egypt 6, Madagascar 0
Madagascar 0, Mauritius 2

GROUP 11
Ivory Coast 0, South Africa 0
South Africa 2, Burundi 0
Burundi 0, Ivory Coast 1
Ivory Coast 6, Burundi 1
South Africa 2, Ivory Coast 1
Burundi 0, South Africa 2

GROUP 12
Namibia 0, Algeria 1
Algeria 4, Chad 1
Chad 2, Namibia 0
Namibia 2, Chad 1
Algeria 1, Namibia 0
Chad 0, Algeria 0

GROUP 13
Uganda 1, Ghana 0
Ghana 4, Rwanda 2
Rwanda 0, Uganda 0
Uganda 0, Rwanda 1
Ghana 1, Uganda 1
Rwanda 1, Ghana 0
Competition still being played.

AFRICAN CHAMPIONS LEAGUE FINAL

FINAL, FIRST LEG
Raja (Morocco) 0, Zamalek (Egypt) 0

FINAL SECOND LEG
Zamalek 1, Raja 0

AFRICAN CUP-WINNERS' CUP

FINAL, FIRST LEG
WAC (Morocco) 1, Asante (Ghana) 0

FINAL, SECOND LEG
Asante 2, WAC 1

CAF CUP

FINAL, FIRST LEG
Kabylie (Algeria) 4, Tonnerre (Cameroon) 0

FINAL, SECOND LEG
Tonnerre 1, Kabylie 0

AFRICAN SUPER CUP

FINAL
Zamalek 3, WAC 1

ASIA

ARAB CUP 2002
(in Kuwait)

GROUP A	*P*	*W*	*D*	*L*	*F*	*A*	*Pts*
Saudi Arabia	4	3	1	0	8	3	10
Bahrain	4	2	1	1	6	3	7
Syria	4	2	0	2	8	6	6
Lebanon	4	1	1	2	5	7	4
Yemen	4	0	1	3	5	13	1

GROUP B	*P*	*W*	*D*	*L*	*F*	*A*	*Pts*
Jordan	4	2	2	0	6	3	8
Morocco U-23	4	1	2	1	5	4	5
Kuwait	4	1	2	1	6	6	5
Sudan	4	1	1	2	3	5	4
Palestine	4	0	3	1	7	9	3

SEMI-FINALS
Bahrain 2, Jordan 1
Saudi Arabia 2, Morocco U-23 0

FINAL
Saudi Arabia 1, Bahrain 0
Saudi Arabia won in sudden death.

TIGER CUP 2002
(in Indonesia and Singapore)

GROUP A	*P*	*W*	*D*	*L*	*F*	*A*	*Pts*
Vietnam	4	3	1	0	19	7	10
Indonesia	4	2	2	0	19	5	8
Myanmar	4	2	1	1	13	5	7
Cambodia	4	1	0	3	5	18	3
Philippines	4	0	0	4	3	24	0

GROUP B	*P*	*W*	*D*	*L*	*F*	*A*	*Pts*
Malaysia	3	2	1	0	8	2	7
Thailand	3	1	1	1	7	5	4
Singapore	3	1	1	1	3	6	4
Laos	3	0	1	2	3	8	1

SEMI-FINALS
Vietnam 0, Thailand 4
Malaysia 0, Indonesia 1

THIRD PLACE
Vietnam 2, Malaysia 1

FINAL
Indonesia 2, Thailand 2
Thailand won 4-2 on penalties.

ASIAN SUPER CUP

FINAL, FIRST LEG
Samsung Blue Wings (South Korea) 1, Al-Hilal (Saudi Arabia) 0

FINAL, SECOND LEG
Al-Hilal 1, Samsung Blue Wings 0
Samsung Blue Wings won 4-2 on penalties.

SAFF CHAMPIONSHIP 2003
(in Bangladesh)

GROUP A	*P*	*W*	*D*	*L*	*F*	*A*	*Pts*
Pakistan	3	3	0	0	4	1	9
India	3	1	1	1	5	2	4
Sri Lanka	3	1	1	1	3	3	4
Afganistan	3	0	0	3	0	6	0

GROUP B	*P*	*W*	*D*	*L*	*F*	*A*	*Pts*
Bangladesh	3	3	0	0	5	0	9
Maldives	3	2	0	1	9	3	6
Nepal	3	1	0	2	4	4	3
Bhutan	3	0	0	3	0	11	0

SEMI-FINALS
Pakistan 0, Maldives 1
Bangladesh 2, India 1

THIRD PLACE
Pakistan 1, India 2

FINAL
Maldives 1, Bangladesh 1
Bangladesh won 5-3 on penalties.

CONCACAF

CUP OF THE CHAMPIONS

FINAL
Morelia 0, Pachuca (Mexico) 1

OCEANIA

NATIONS CUP

FINAL
New Zealand 1, Australia 0

UEFA UNDER-21 CHAMPIONSHIP 2002–04

GROUP 1
Slovenia 1, Malta 0
Cyprus 0, France 1
Malta 0, Israel 1
France 1, Slovenia 0
Malta 0, France 3
Cyprus 2, Malta 0
Cyprus 2, Israel 0
France 2, Malta 0
Israel 0, France 3
Slovenia 2, Cyprus 0
Malta 0, Slovenia 0
Israel 0, Cyprus 3
Israel 0, Slovenia 0
Malta 0, Cyprus 1

GROUP 2
Norway 3, Denmark 0
Bosnia 2, Romania 1
Denmark 9, Luxembourg 0
Romania 0, Norway 1
Norway 0, Bosnia 0
Luxembourg 0, Romania 2
Bosnia 1, Luxembourg 0
Romania 0, Denmark 1
Denmark 3, Bosnia 0
Luxembourg 0, Norway 5
Romania 0, Bosnia 1
Denmark 2, Norway 0
Norway 2, Romania 1
Luxembourg 0, Denmark 6

GROUP 3
Holland 0, Belarus 1
Austria 1, Moldova 0
Belarus 0, Austria 1
Moldova 0, Czech Republic 2
Austria 1, Holland 1
Czech Republic 3, Belarus 0
Holland 0, Czech Republic 3
Belarus 3, Moldova 1
Czech Republic 3, Austria 1
Moldova 2, Holland 2
Belarus 2, Holland 1
Moldova 0, Austria 1
Czech Republic 3, Moldova 0
Austria 0, Belarus 2

GROUP 4
Latvia 0, Sweden 4
San Marino 1, Poland 5
Poland 3, Latvia 0
Sweden 1, Hungary 0
Hungary 4, San Marino 1
San Marino 0, Latvia 2
Poland 3, Hungary 2
Poland 7, San Marino 0
Hungary 5, Sweden 2
Latvia 4, San Marino 0
Hungary 3, Latvia 1
San Marino 1, Sweden 5
Sweden 1, Poland 1
San Marino 1, Hungary 2

GROUP 5
Lithuania 1, Germany 4
Iceland 0, Scotland 2
Iceland 1, Lithuania 2
Scotland 1, Iceland 0
Germany 1, Lithuania 0
Lithuania 2, Scotland 1
Scotland 2, Germany 2
Lithuania 3, Iceland 0

GROUP 6
Armenia 1, Ukraine 1
Greece 1, Spain 0
Ukraine 1, Greece 1
Spain 1, Northern Ireland 0
Northern Ireland 1, Ukraine 1
Greece 2, Armenia 1
Armenia 2, Northern Ireland 0
Ukraine 0, Spain 0
Northern Ireland 2, Greece 6
Spain 5, Armenia 0
Ukraine 4, Armenia 0
Spain 2, Greece 0
Northern Ireland 1, Spain 4
Greece 0, Ukraine 0

GROUP 7
Turkey 2, Slovakia 1
Portugal 1, Macedonia 0
Macedonia 0, Turkey 4
Slovakia 0, England 4
Turkey 4, Portugal 2
England 3, Macedonia 1
Portugal 4, England 2
Macedonia 0, Slovakia 2
Slovakia 0, Portugal 2
England 1, Turkey 1
Slovakia 0, Turkey 1
Macedonia 1, Portugal 4
Turkey 3, Macedonia 0
England 2, Slovakia 0

GROUP 8
Croatia 3, Estonia 1
Belgium 3, Bulgaria 1
Bulgaria 1, Croatia 3
Estonia 0, Belgium 1
Croatia 1, Belgium 1
Estonia 1, Bulgaria 1
Bulgaria 2, Belgium 1
Estonia 0, Croatia 0

GROUP 9
Finland 2, Wales 1
Azerbaijan 0, Italy 3
Finland 3, Azerbaijan 0
Italy 4, Serbia-Montenegro 1
Serbia-Montenegro 3, Finland 3
Wales 1, Italy 2
Azerbaijan 0, Wales 1
Serbia-Montenegro 3, Azerbaijan 0
Wales 1, Azerbaijan 0
Italy 1, Finland 0
Finland 1, Serbia-Montenegro 2
Finland 1, Italy 2
Azerbaijan 0, Serbia-Montenegro 2

GROUP 10
Russia 2, Republic of Ireland 0
Switzerland 2, Georgia 0
Albania 0, Switzerland 0
Georgia 0, Russia 3
Republic of Ireland 2, Switzerland 3
Russia 1, Albania 0
Georgia 1, Republic of Ireland 1
Albania 1, Russia 4
Albania 1, Republic of Ireland 0
Georgia 0, Switzerland 2
Switzerland 1, Russia 0
Republic of Ireland 0, Albania 3
Switzerland 2, Albania 1
Republic of Ireland 1, Georgia 1

Competition still being played.

UEFA UNDER-17 CHAMPIONSHIP

(Finals in Portugal)

GROUP A
Portugal 3, Denmark 2
Austria 1, Hungary 0
Portugal 1, Austria 0
Denmark 2, Hungary 0
Hungary 0, Portugal 2
Denmark 0, Austria 2

GROUP B
Spain 2, Italy 0
Israel 1, England 2
Israel 0, Spain 3
England 0, Italy 0
England 2, Spain 2
Italy 4, Israel 0

SEMI-FINALS
Portugal 2, England 2
Portugal won 3-2 on penalties.
Spain 5, Austria 2

MATCH FOR 3rd PLACE
Austria 1, England 0

FINAL
Portugal 2, Spain 1

UEFA UNDER-19 CHAMPIONSHIP

(Finals in Norway)

GROUP A
Norway 1, Slovakia 5
Spain 1, Czech Republic 1
Norway 0, Spain 3
Slovakia 5, Czech Republic 2
Czech Republic 1, Norway 0
Slovakia 1, Spain 3

Group A Table	P	W	D	L	F	A	Pts
Spain	3	2	1	0	7	2	7
Slovakia	3	2	0	1	11	6	6
Czech Republic	3	1	1	1	4	6	4
Norway	3	0	0	3	1	9	0

GROUP B
England 3, Germany 3
Belgium 1, Republic of Ireland 2
England 1, Belgium 1
Germany 3, Republic of Ireland 0
Republic of Ireland 3, England 2
Germany 2, Belgium 1

Group B Table	P	W	D	L	F	A	Pts
Germany	3	2	1	0	8	4	7
Republic of Ireland	3	2	0	1	5	6	6
England	3	0	2	1	6	7	2
Belgium	3	0	1	2	3	5	1

MATCH FOR 3rd PLACE
Slovakia 2, Republic of Ireland 1

FINAL
Spain 1, Germany 0

OLYMPIC FOOTBALL

Previous medallists

1896 Athens* — 1 Denmark, 2 Greece
1900 Paris* — 1 Great Britain, 2 France
1904 St Louis** — 1 Canada, 2 USA
1908 London — 1 Great Britain, 2 Denmark, 3 Holland
1912 Stockholm — 1 England, 2 Denmark, 3 Holland
1920 Antwerp — 1 Belgium, 2 Spain, 3 Holland
1924 Paris — 1 Uruguay, 2 Switzerland, 3 Sweden
1928 Amsterdam — 1 Uruguay, 2 Argentina, 3 Italy
1932 Los Angeles — no tournament
1936 Berlin — 1 Italy, 2 Austria, 3 Norway
1948 London — 1 Sweden, 2 Yugoslavia, 3 Denmark
1952 Helsinki — 1 Hungary, 2 Yugoslavia, 3 Sweden
1956 Melbourne — 1 USSR, 2 Yugoslavia, 3 Bulgaria
1960 Rome — 1 Yugoslavia, 2 Denmark, 3 Hungary
1964 Tokyo — 1 Hungary, 2 Czechoslovakia, 3 East Germany
1968 Mexico City — 1 Hungary, 2 Bulgaria, 3 Japan
1972 Munich — 1 Poland, 2 Hungary, 3 E Germany/USSR
1976 Montreal — 1 East Germany, 2 Poland, 3 USSR
1980 Moscow — 1 Czechoslovakia, 2 East Germany, 3 USSR
1984 Los Angeles — 1 France, 2 Brazil, 3 Yugoslavia
1988 Seoul — 1 USSR, 2 Brazil, 3 West Germany
1992 Barcelona — 1 Spain, 2 Poland, 3 Ghana
1996 Atlanta — 1 Nigeria, 2 Argentina, 3 Brazil
2000 Sydney — 1. Cameroon, 2. Spain, 3. Chile

* No official tournament
** No official tournament but gold medal later awarded by IOC

ENGLAND UNDER-21 RESULTS 1976–2003

EC UEFA Competition for Under-21 Teams

v ALBANIA

Year	Date		Venue	Eng	Alb
EC1989	Mar	7	Shkroda	2	1
EC1989	April	25	Ipswich	2	0
EC2001	Mar	27	Tirana	1	0
EC2001	Sept	4	Middlesbrough	5	0

v ANGOLA

Year	Date		Venue	Eng	Ang
1995	June	10	Toulon	1	0
1996	May	28	Toulon	0	2

v ARGENTINA

Year	Date		Venue	Eng	Arg
1998	May	18	Toulon	0	2
2000	Feb	22	Fulham	1	0

v AUSTRIA

Year	Date		Venue	Eng	Aus
1994	Oct	11	Kapfenberg	3	1
1995	Nov	14	Middlesbrough	2	1

v BELGIUM

Year	Date		Venue	Eng	Bel
1994	June	5	Marseille	2	1
1996	May	24	Toulon	1	0

v BRAZIL

Year	Date		Venue	Eng	B
1993	June	11	Toulon	0	0
1995	June	6	Toulon	0	2
1996	June	1	Toulon	1	2

v BULGARIA

Year	Date		Venue	Eng	Bul
EC1979	June	5	Pernik	3	1
EC1979	Nov	20	Leicester	5	0
1989	June	5	Toulon	2	3
EC1998	Oct	9	West Ham	1	0
EC1999	June	8	Vratsa	1	0

v CROATIA

Year	Date		Venue	Eng	Cro
1996	Apr	23	Sunderland	0	1

v CZECHOSLOVAKIA

Year	Date		Venue	Eng	Cz
1990	May	28	Toulon	2	1
1992	May	26	Toulon	1	2
1993	June	9	Toulon	1	1

v CZECH REPUBLIC

Year	Date		Venue	Eng	CzR
1998	Nov	17	Ipswich	0	1

v DENMARK

Year	Date		Venue	Eng	Den
EC1978	Sept	19	Hvidovre	2	1
EC1979	Sept	11	Watford	1	0
EC1982	Sept	21	Hvidovre	4	1
EC1983	Sept	20	Norwich	4	1
EC1986	Mar	12	Copenhagen	1	0
EC1986	Mar	26	Manchester	1	1
1988	Sept	13	Watford	0	0
1994	Mar	8	Brentford	1	0
1999	Oct	8	Bradford	4	1

v EAST GERMANY

Year	Date		Venue	Eng	EG
EC1980	April	16	Sheffield	1	2
EC1980	April	23	Jena	0	1

v FINLAND

Year	Date		Venue	Eng	Fin
EC1977	May	26	Helsinki	1	0
EC1977	Oct	12	Hull	8	1
EC1984	Oct	16	Southampton	2	0
EC1985	May	21	Mikkeli	1	3
EC2000	Oct	10	Valkeakoski	2	2
EC2001	Mar	23	Barnsley	4	0

v FRANCE

Year	Date		Venue	Eng	Fra
EC1984	Feb	28	Sheffield	6	1
EC1984	Mar	28	Rouen	1	0
1987	June	11	Toulon	0	2
EC1988	April	13	Besancon	2	4
EC1988	April	27	Highbury	2	2
1988	June	12	Toulon	2	4
1990	May	23	Toulon	7	3
1991	June	3	Toulon	1	0
1992	May	28	Toulon	0	0
1993	June	15	Toulon	1	0
1994	May	31	Aubagne	0	3
1995	June	10	Toulon	0	2
1998	May	14	Toulon	1	1
1999	Feb	9	Derby	2	1

v GEORGIA

Year	Date		Venue	Eng	Geo
EC1996	Nov	8	Batumi	1	0
EC1997	April	29	Charlton	0	0
2000	Aug	31	Middlesbrough	6	1

v GERMANY

Year	Date		Venue	Eng	Ger
1991	Sept	10	Scunthorpe	2	1
EC2000	Oct	6	Derby	1	1
EC2001	Aug	31	Frieburg	2	1

v GREECE

Year	Date		Venue	Eng	Gre
EC1982	Nov	16	Piraeus	0	1
EC1983	Mar	29	Portsmouth	2	1
1989	Feb	7	Patras	0	1
EC1997	Nov	13	Heraklion	0	2
EC1997	Dec	17	Norwich	4	2
EC2001	June	5	Athens	1	3
EC2001	Oct	5	Ewood Park	2	1

v HOLLAND

Year	Date		Venue	Eng	H
EC1993	April	27	Portsmouth	3	0
EC1993	Oct	12	Utrecht	1	1
2001	Aug	14	Reading	4	0
EC2001	Nov	9	Utrecht	2	2
EC2001	Nov	13	Derby	1	0

v HUNGARY

Year	Date		Venue	Eng	Hun
EC1981	June	5	Keszthely	2	1
EC1981	Nov	17	Nottingham	2	0
EC1983	April	26	Newcastle	1	0
EC1983	Oct	11	Nyiregyhaza	2	0
1990	Sept	11	Southampton	3	1
1992	May	12	Budapest	2	2
1999	April	27	Budapest	2	2

v ITALY

Year	Date		Venue	Eng	Italy
EC1978	Mar	8	Manchester	2	1
EC1978	April	5	Rome	0	0
EC1984	April	18	Manchester	3	1
EC1984	May	2	Florence	0	1
EC1986	April	9	Pisa	0	2
EC1986	April	23	Swindon	1	1
EC1997	Feb	12	Bristol	1	0
EC1997	Oct	10	Rieti	1	0
EC2000	May	27	Bratislava	0	2
2000	Nov	14	Monza*	0	0
2002	Mar	26	Valley Parade	1	1
EC2002	May	20	Basle	1	2
2003	Feb	11	Pisa	0	1

**Abandoned 11 mins; fog.*

v ISRAEL

Year	Date		Venue	Eng	Isr
1985	Feb	27	Tel Aviv	2	1

v LATVIA

Year	Date		Venue	Eng	Lat
1995	April	25	Riga	1	0
1995	June	7	Burnley	4	0

v LUXEMBOURG

Year	Date		Venue	Eng	Lux
EC1998	Oct	13	Greven Macher	5	0
EC1999	Sept	3	Reading	5	0

v MACEDONIA

Year	Date		Venue	Eng	M
EC2002	Oct	15	Reading	3	1

v MALAYSIA

Year	Date		Venue	Eng	Mal
1995	June	8	Toulon	2	0

v MEXICO

Year	Date		Venue	Eng	Mex
1988	June	5	Toulon	2	1
1991	May	29	Toulon	6	0
1992	May	25	Toulon	1	1
2001	May	24	Leicester	3	0

v MOLDOVA

Year	Date		Venue	Eng	Mol
EC1996	Aug	31	Chisinau	2	0
EC1997	Sept	9	Wycombe	1	0

v MOROCCO

Year	Date		Venue	Eng	Mor
1987	June	7	Toulon	2	0
1988	June	9	Toulon	1	0

v NORWAY

Year	Date		Venue	Eng	Nor
EC1977	June	1	Bergen	2	1
EC1977	Sept	6	Brighton	6	0
1980	Sept	9	Southampton	3	0
1981	Sept	8	Drammen	0	0
EC1992	Oct	13	Peterborough	0	2
EC1993	June	1	Stavanger	1	1
1995	Oct	10	Stavanger	2	2

			v POLAND	Eng	Pol
EC1982	Mar	17	Warsaw	2	1
EC1982	April	7	West Ham	2	2
EC1989	June	2	Plymouth	2	1
EC1989	Oct	10	Jastrzebie	3	1
EC1990	Oct	16	Tottenham	0	1
EC1991	Nov	12	Pila	1	2
EC1993	May	28	Zdroj	4	1
EC1993	Sept	7	Millwall	1	2
EC1996	Oct	8	Wolverhampton	0	0
EC1997	May	30	Katowice	1	1
EC1999	Mar	26	Southampton	5	0
EC1999	Sept	7	Plock	1	3

			v PORTUGAL	Eng	Por
1987	June	13	Toulon	0	0
1990	May	21	Toulon	0	1
1993	June	7	Toulon	2	0
1994	June	7	Toulon	2	0
EC1994	Sept	6	Leicester	0	0
1995	Sept	2	Lisbon	0	2
1996	May	30	Toulon	1	3
2000	Apr	16	Stoke	0	1
EC2002	May	22	Zurich	1	3
EC2003	Mar	28	Rio Major	2	4

			v REPUBLIC OF IRELAND	Eng	RoI
1981	Feb	25	Liverpool	1	0
1985	Mar	25	Portsmouth	3	2
1989	June	9	Toulon	0	0
EC1990	Nov	13	Cork	3	0
EC1991	Mar	26	Brentford	3	0
1994	Nov	15	Newcastle	1	0
1995	Mar	27	Dublin	2	0

			v ROMANIA	Eng	Rom
EC1980	Oct	14	Ploesti	0	4
EC1981	April	28	Swindon	3	0
EC1985	April	30	Brasov	0	0
EC1985	Sept	10	Ipswich	3	0

			v RUSSIA	Eng	Rus
1994	May	30	Bandol	2	0

			v SAN MARINO	Eng	SM
EC1993	Feb	16	Luton	6	0
EC1993	Nov	17	San Marino	4	0

			v SENEGAL	Eng	Sen
1989	June	7	Toulon	6	1
1991	May	27	Toulon	2	1

			v SERBIA-MONTENEGRO	Eng	S-M
2003	June	2	Hull	3	2

			v SCOTLAND	Eng	Sco
1977	April	27	Sheffield	1	0
EC1980	Feb	12	Coventry	2	1
EC1980	Mar	4	Aberdeen	0	0
EC1982	April	19	Glasgow	1	0
EC1982	April	28	Manchester	1	1
EC1988	Feb	16	Aberdeen	1	0
EC1988	Mar	22	Nottingham	1	0
1993	June	13	Toulon	1	0

			v SLOVAKIA	Eng	Slo
EC2002	June	1	Bratislava	0	2
EC2002	Oct	11	Trnava	4	0
EC2003	June	10	Sunderland	2	0

			v SLOVENIA	Eng	Slo
2000	Feb	12	Nova Gorica	1	0

			v SOUTH AFRICA	Eng	SA
1998	May	16	Toulon	3	1

			v SPAIN	Eng	Spa
EC1984	May	17	Seville	1	0
EC1984	May	24	Sheffield	2	0
1987	Feb	18	Burgos	2	1
1992	Sept	8	Burgos	1	0
2001	Feb	27	Birmingham	0	4

			v SWEDEN	Eng	Swe
1979	June	9	Vasteras	2	1
1986	Sept	9	Ostersund	1	1
EC1988	Oct	18	Coventry	1	1
EC1989	Sept	5	Uppsala	0	1
EC1998	Sept	4	Sundvall	2	0
EC1999	June	4	Huddersfield	3	0

			v SWITZERLAND	Eng	Swit
EC1980	Nov	18	Ipswich	5	0
EC1981	May	31	Neuenburg	0	0
1988	May	28	Lausanne	1	1
1996	April	1	Swindon	0	0
1998	Mar	24	Brugglifeld	0	2
EC2002	May	17	Zurich	2	1

			v USA	Eng	USA
1989	June	11	Toulon	0	2
1994	June	2	Toulon	3	0

			v TURKEY	Eng	Tur
EC1984	Nov	13	Bursa	0	0
EC1985	Oct	15	Bristol	3	0
EC1987	April	28	Izmir	0	0
EC1987	Oct	13	Sheffield	1	1
EC1991	April	30	Izmir	2	2
1991	Oct	15	Reading	2	0
EC1992	Nov	17	Orient	0	1
EC1993	Mar	30	Izmir	0	0
EC2000	May	29	Bratislava	6	0
EC2003	April	1	Newcastle	1	1

			v USSR	Eng	USSR
1987	June	9	Toulon	0	0
1988	June	7	Toulon	1	0
1990	May	25	Toulon	2	1
1991	May	31	Toulon	2	1

			v WALES	Eng	Wales
1976	Dec	15	Wolverhampton	0	0
1979	Feb	6	Swansea	1	0
1990	Dec	5	Tranmere	0	0

			v WEST GERMANY	Eng	WG
EC1982	Sept	21	Sheffield	3	1
EC1982	Oct	12	Bremen	2	3
1987	Sept	8	Ludenscheid	0	2

			v YUGOSLAVIA	Eng	Yugo
EC1978	April	19	Novi Sad	1	2
EC1978	May	2	Manchester	1	1
EC1986	Nov	11	Peterborough	1	1
EC1987	Nov	10	Zemun	5	1
EC2000	Mar	29	Barcelona	3	0
2002	Sept	6	Bolton	1	1

ENGLAND B RESULTS 1949–2003

Year	Date		Venue		
			v ALGERIA	Eng	Alg
1990	Dec	11	Algiers	0	0
			v AUSTRALIA	Eng	Aust
1980	Nov	17	Birmingham	1	0
			v AUSTRIA	Eng	Aus
1979†	June	12	Klagenfurt	1	0

†Abandoned 60 mins; waterlogged pitch.

Year	Date		Venue		
			v CHILE	Eng	Ch
1998	Feb	10	West Bromwich	1	2
			v CIS	Eng	CIS
1992	April	28	Moscow	1	1
			v CZECHOSLOVAKIA	Eng	Cz
1978	Nov	28	Prague	1	0
1990	April	24	Sunderland	2	0
1992	Mar	24	Budejovice	1	0
			v FINLAND	Eng	Fin
1949	May	15	Helsinki	4	0
			v FRANCE	Eng	Fra
1952	May	22	Le Havre	1	7
1992	Feb	18	Loftus Road	3	0
			v WEST GERMANY	Eng	WG
1954	Mar	24	Gelsenkirchen	4	0
1955	Mar	23	Sheffield	1	1
1978	Feb	21	Augsburg	2	1
			v HOLLAND	Eng	Hol
1949	May	18	Amsterdam	4	0
1950	Feb	22	Newcastle	1	0
1952	Mar	26	Amsterdam	1	0
			v ICELAND	Eng	Ice
1989	May	19	Reykjavik	2	0
1991	April	27	Watford	1	0
			v ITALY	Eng	Italy
1950	May	11	Milan	0	5
1989	Nov	14	Brighton	1	1
			v LUXEMBOURG	Eng	Lux
1950	May	21	Luxembourg	2	1
			v MALAYSIA	Eng	Mal
1978	May	30	Kuala Lumpur	1	1
			v MALTA	Eng	Mal
1987	Oct	14	Ta'Qali	2	0
			v NEW ZEALAND	Eng	NZ
1978	June	7	Christchurch	4	0
1978	June	11	Wellington	3	1
1978	June	14	Auckland	4	0
1979	Oct	15	Leyton	4	1
1984	Nov	13	Nottingham	2	0
			v NORTHERN IRELAND	Eng	NI
1994	May	10	Sheffield	4	2
			v NORWAY	Eng	Nor
1989	May	22	Stavanger	1	0
			v REPUBLIC OF IRELAND	Eng	RoI
1990	Mar	27	Cork	1	4
1994	Dec	13	Liverpool	2	0
			v RUSSIA	Eng	Rus
1998	Apr	21	Loftus Road	4	1
			v SCOTLAND	Eng	Sco
1953	Mar	11	Edinburgh	2	2
1954	Mar	3	Sunderland	1	1
1956	Feb	29	Dundee	2	2
1957	Feb	6	Birmingham	4	1
			v SINGAPORE	Eng	Sin
1978	June	18	Singapore	8	0
			v SPAIN	Eng	Sp
1980	Mar	26	Sunderland	1	0
1981	Mar	25	Granada	2	3
1991*	Dec	18	Castellon	1	0

**Spanish Olympic XI*

Year	Date		Venue		
			v SWITZERLAND	Eng	Swit
1950	Jan	18	Sheffield	5	0
1954	May	22	Basle	0	2
1956	Mar	21	Southampton	4	1
1989	May	16	Winterthur	2	0
1991	May	20	Walsall	2	1
			v USA	Eng	USA
1980	Oct	14	Manchester	1	0
			v WALES	Eng	Wales
1991	Feb	5	Swansea	1	0
			v YUGOSLAVIA	Eng	Yugo
1954	May	16	Ljubljana	1	2
1955	Oct	19	Manchester	5	1
1989	Dec	12	Millwall	2	1

BRITISH & IRISH INTERNATIONAL MANAGERS

England
Walter Winterbottom 1946–1962 (after period as coach); Alf Ramsey 1963–1974; Joe Mercer (caretaker) 1974; Don Revie 1974–1977; Ron Greenwood 1977–1982; Bobby Robson 1982–1990; Graham Taylor 1990–1993; Terry Venables (coach) 1994–1996; Glenn Hoddle 1996–1999; Kevin Keegan 1999–2000; Sven-Goran Eriksson from January 2001.

Northern Ireland
Peter Doherty 1951–1952; Bertie Peacock 1962–1967; Billy Bingham 1967–1971; Terry Neill 1971–1975; Dave Clements (player-manager) 1975–1976; Danny Blanchflower 1976–1979; Billy Bingham 1980–1994; Bryan Hamilton 1994–1998; Lawrie McMenemy 1998–1999; Sammy McIlroy from January 2000.

Scotland (since 1967)
Bobby Brown 1967–1971; Tommy Docherty 1971–1972; Willie Ormond 1973–1977; Ally MacLeod 1977–1978; Jock Stein 1978–1985; Alex Ferguson (caretaker) 1985–1986 Andy Roxburgh (coach) 1986–1993; Craig Brown 1993–2001; Berti Vogts from March 2002–

Wales (since 1974)
Mike Smith 1974–1979; Mike England 1980–1988; David Williams (caretaker) 1988; Terry Yorath 1988–1993; John Toshack 1994 for one match; Mike Smith 1994–1995; Bobby Gould 1995–1999; Mark Hughes from November 1999.

Republic of Ireland
Liam Tuohy 1971–1972; Johnny Giles 1973–1980 (after period as player-manager); Eoin Hand 1980–1985; Jack Charlton 1986–1996; Mick McCarthy 1996–2002; Brian Kerr from January 2003.

BRITISH AND IRISH UNDER-21 TEAMS 2002–03

▪ *Denotes player sent off.*

ENGLAND UNDER-21 INTERNATIONALS

Bolton, 6 September 2002, 10,511

England (0) 1 *(Wright-Phillips 80)*

Yugoslavia (1) 1 *(Lazovic 41)*

England: Kirkland; Samuel (Parnaby 78), Bramble, Barry, Konchesky (Lescott 89), Prutton (Etherington 73), Carrick, Jenas, Jeffers, Pennant (Wright-Phillips 60), Defoe (Ameobi 60).

Trnava, 11 October 2002, 3800

Slovakia (0) 0 *(Poncak▪)*

England (1) 4 *(Ameobi 34, Jeffers 63, 76, Cole J 87)*

England: Murray; Samuel, Konchesky (Clarke 81), Bramble (Dawson 69), Barry, Jenas, Prutton, Cole J, Jeffers, Ameobi (Taylor 81), Carrick.

Reading, 15 October 2002, 15,500

England (1) 3 *(Jeffers 32, 53, 73)*

Macedonia (0) 1 *(Baldovaliev 70)*

England: Kirkland (Murray 25); Samuel, Konchesky, Bramble, Barry, Jenas, Prutton, Cole J (Crouch 71), Jeffers, Ameobi (Wright-Phillips 55), Carrick.

Pisa, 11 February 2003, 3966

Italy (0) 1 *(Borrielio 75)*

England (0) 0

England: Murray (Grant 46); Samuel (Lescott 55), Taylor (McEveley 71), Barry, Dawson, Clarke, Prutton (Ambrose 79), Ameobi, Wright-Phillips (Nolan 61), Zamora (Bent D 71), Carrick.

Rio Major, 28 March 2003, 3000

Portugal (2) 4 *(Postiga 7, Barry 11 (og), Martins 61, Ronaldo 71)*

England (2) 2 *(Ameobi 9, 33)*

England: Bywater; Samuel, Konchesky, Bramble (Crouch 85), Dawson, Barry, Prutton (Pennant 69), Cole J, Ameobi▪, Defoe, Carrick (Stewart 46).

Newcastle, 1 April 2003, 21,085

England (1) 1 *(Jeffers 25)*

Turkey (1) 1 *(Sanil 13)*

England: Murray; Samuel (Johnson G 71), Konchesky, Jenas, Dawson, Clarke, Prutton, Cole J, Jeffers, Defoe (Cole C 64), Barry.

Hull, 2 June 2003, 24,004

England (1) 3 *(Ameobi 15, Defoe 68, Bent D 87)*

Serbia & Montenegro (0) 2 *(Petrovic 49, Stanic 85)*

England: Evans (Bywater 51); Parnaby (Johnson G 58), Konchesky, Pennant (Bent D 81), Jagielka, Clarke, Prutton, Sidwell, Ameobi (Cole C 51), Defoe, Zamora (Ambrose 58).

Sunderland, 10 June 2003, 11,223

England (1) 2 *(Dolezaj 40 (og), Jagielka 83)*

Slovakia (0) 0 *(Svrcek▪)*

England: Evans; Parnaby, Konchesky, Barry, Jagielka, Clarke, Prutton, Sidwell, Ameobi (Zamora 71), Defoe (Cole C 58), Pennant.

SCOTLAND UNDER-21 TEAMS 2002–03

Dunfermline, 20 August 2002, 2914

Scotland (1) 1 *(Canero 30)*

Denmark (1) 1 *(Bechmann 12)*

Scotland: Soutar (McGregor); McCunnie, Murray, Dowie, Doig, Kerr, Canero, Hughes (McLean), O'Connor, Stewart (McManus), Maloney (McFadden).

Hamilton, 4 September 2002, 3042

Scotland (1) 2 *(Maloney 3, Kennedy 84)*

Israel (1) 1 *(Barda 15)*

Scotland: McGregor (Gordon); McCunnie (Kennedy), Hammell, Dowie (Caldwell G), Doig, Kerr, Duff, Pearson (O'Brien), McFadden (Lynch), Stewart, Maloney.

St Mirren, 6 September 2002, 2351

Scotland (0) 1 *(Clyde 73 (og))*

Northern Ireland (1) 1 *(McEvilly 30)*

Scotland: Soutar (McEwan); McCunnie, Hammell, Kennedy, Doig, Kerr, Canero (Duff), Pearson (Lynch), McFadden (McLean), Stewart▪, Maloney (McManus).
Northern Ireland: Morris; Baird, Capaldi, Clyde, Simms, Melaugh, Close (McCann R), Toner, McEvilly (McFlynn), Browne (Braniff), Morrison (McCourt).

Hafnarfjordur, 11 October 2002, 700

Iceland (0) 0 *Skulason▪*

Scotland (1) 2 *(Kyle 17, Lynch 89)*

Scotland: Soutar; Caldwell G, Murray, Kennedy, Doig, Kerr, Duff, Williams, Kyle, Hughes (Fletcher), McManus (Lynch).

Dumfries, 14 October 2002, 3119

Scotland (2) 2 *(Caldwell G 9, Kerr 14)*

Ghana (0) 0

Scotland: Gordon (McEwan); Caldwell G, Hammell, Kennedy, Doig, Kerr, Duff (McParland), Murray (Simmons), McFadden (McLean), Hughes (O'Brien), McManus (Lynch).

Molenbeek, 19 November 2002, 276

Belgium (1) 2 *(Chatelle 25, Smolders 87)*

Scotland (0) 0

Scotland: Soutar (McGregor); Doig (Hammell), Caldwell G, Kennedy, Crainey, Hughes (Pearson), Murray, Kerr, Duff (Canero), Maloney (McLean), Lynch (Boyd).

Kilmarnock, 11 February 2003, 2987

Scotland (1) 2 *(Maloney 41, Lynch 68)*

Republic of Ireland (0) 0

Scotland: Soutar (McGregor); Caldwell G, Hammell, Kennedy, Doig (Crainey), Kerr, Canero (Duff), Pearson (Hughes), Kyle (Lynch), Williams (Stewart), Maloney (McFadden).
Republic of Ireland: Stack; Brennan, Tierney (Byrne R), Byrne C, Goodwin, Thompson (Hunt), Butler, Reid (Thornton), Barrett (Daly), Dempsey (Lester), Houlihan (Melligan).

Cumbernauld, 28 March 2003, 3192

Scotland (0) 1 *(Maloney 69)*

Iceland (0) 0

Scotland: Soutar; Caldwell G, Murray, Kennedy, Webster, Kerr, Canero, Williams, Kyle, Stewart (Hughes), McFadden (Maloney).

Vilnius, 1 April 2003, 950

Lithuania (1) 2 *(Kucys 34, Cesnauskis 82)*

Scotland (1) 1 *(Kyle 2)*

Scotland: Soutar; Caldwell G, Murray, Kennedy, Webster, Kerr, Canero (Lynch), Williams, Kyle, Stewart, McFadden (Maloney).

Dens Park, 29 April 2003, 2085

Scotland (0) 1 *(Lynch 65)*

Austria (0) 0

Scotland: Soutar (McGregor); Caldwell G, Pearson, Kennedy, Crainey, Kerr, Canero (Duff), Hughes (Noble), McManus (Lynch), Stewart (Montgomery), Maloney.

Kilmarnock, 6 June 2003, 5052

Scotland (2) 2 *(Lynch 15, Caldwell G 25)*

Germany (2) 2 *(Lauth 10, Balitsch 28)*

Scotland: Soutar; Caldwell G, Murray, Kennedy, Crainey, Kerr, Canero, Pearson, Kyle, Fletcher (Gallagher), Lynch (McManus).

NORTHERN IRELAND UNDER-21 TEAMS 2002–03

Almansa, **11 October 2002, 3000**

Spain (0) 1 *(Capaldi 90 (og))*

Northern Ireland (0) 0

Northern Ireland: Morris; Baird, Capaldi, Clyde, Simms, Melaugh, Close (Hughes), Toner, McEvilly (Braniff), Browne (McFlynn), McCourt.

Ballymena, 15 October 2002, 1000

Northern Ireland (1) 1 *(Baird 39)*

Ukraine (0) 1 *(Kabanov 83)*

Northern Ireland: Morris; Baird (Buchanan), Capaldi, Clyde, Simms, Melaugh, Close, Toner (Hughes), McEvilly, Browne (Black), McCourt.

Lurgan, 11 February 2003, 800

Northern Ireland (1) 3 *(Melaugh 45, McEvilly 88, McFlynn 89)*

Finland (0) 1 *(Oravainen 87)*

Northern Ireland: Morris (Blayney); Baird, Capaldi, Clyde, Simms, Melaugh (McFlynn), Hughes, Toner, Feeney (McEvilly), Braniff (Browne), Morrison (McCourt).

Abovyan, 28 March 2003, 600

Armenia (1) 2 *(Meloyan 25, Davytyan 65)*

Northern Ireland (0) 0

Northern Ireland: Morris; Close, Herron, McFlynn (Clingan), Simms, Capaldi, Hughes (McCourt), Melaugh, McEvilly, Feeney (Braniff), Morrison.

Belfast, 1 April 2003, 611

Northern Ireland (1) 2 *(Toner 35, McEvilly 58 (pen))*

Greece (3) 6 *(Lagos 4, Fotakis 38, Papadopoulos 41 (pen), 62, 82, Salpigidis 47)*

Northern Ireland: Morris; Baird (McCourt), Herron, Toner (McFlynn), Simms, Capaldi, Hughes, Melaugh, Braniff, Feeney (McEvilly), Morrison.

Lurgan, 10 June 2003, 1500

Northern Ireland (0) 1 *(Braniff 49)*

Spain (2) 4 *(Torres 1, 26, Lopes 60, Larena 68)*

Northern Ireland: Morris; Hughes, Capaldi, Duff S, Simms, Melaugh, McCann P (McFlynn), Close, Braniff, Browne (Clarke), Morrison (Campbell).

REPUBLIC OF IRELAND UNDER-21 TEAMS 2002–03

Helsinki, 20 August 2002

Finland (0) 0

Republic of Ireland (0) 1 *(Daly 90)*

Republic of Ireland: Murphy; Byrne S (Shelley), Byrne C, Goodwin (McGuinness), Tierney, Miller, Mattis (Doyle M), Keane (Gamble), Barrett (Doyle R), Burgess (Daly), Houlihan.

Moscow, 7 September 2002

Russia (2) 2 *(Pavlioutchenko 28, Kusov 29)*

Republic of Ireland (0) 0

Republic of Ireland: Murphy; Thompson, Goodwin, Byrne C, Tierney, Butler, Miller, Keane (Daly), Houlihan, Burgess (Reid), Barrett.

Kilkenny, 15 October 2002

Republic of Ireland (2) 2 *(Reid 1, Miller 8)*

Switzerland (1) 3 *(Cerrone 43, Rochat 74, Venlanthen 87)*

Republic of Ireland: Murphy; Thompson (Hunt), Goodwin, Byrne C, Tierney, Butler (Doyle M), Miller, Barrett, Houlihan, Reid (O'Flynn), Daly.

Tbilisi, 28 March 2003

Georgia (1) 1 *(Akhalaia 20)*

Republic of Ireland (0) 1 *(Hunt 84)*

Republic of Ireland: Stack; Brennan, Goodwin, Thompson (O'Connor), Paisley, Tierney (Byrne C), Miller, Thornton, Daly, Reid■, Houlihan (Hunt).

Tirana, 1 April 2003

Albania (0) 1 *(Rizvanolli 71)*

Republic of Ireland (0) 0

Republic of Ireland: Stack; Brennan, Goodwin, Byrne C, Thompson, Paisley (Rossiter (Ward)), Miller, Thornton, Daly, O'Connor (Hunt), Barrett.

Cork, 2 June 2003

Republic of Ireland (1) 2 *(O'Flynn 20, Miller 87)*

Germany (2) 2 *(Auer 30, Hitzlsperger 33)*

Republic of Ireland: Stack; Kelly, Cryan, Thompson, Capper, Butler (Elliott), Miller, Thornton (Houlihan), Reid (Ward), O'Flynn, Barrett.

Dublin, 6 June 2003

Republic of Ireland (2) 2 *(Barrett 43, O'Flynn 53)*

Albania (0) 1 *(Mansaku 85)*

Republic of Ireland: Stack; Kelly, Cryan, Thompson, Capper, Butler (Gilroy), Miller, Thornton, Reid, Barrett, O'Flynn (Elliott).
UEFA awarded Albania a 3-0 win; Miller was ineligible to play, having received two yellow cards.

Kilkenny, 10 June 2003

Republic of Ireland (0) 1 *(Cryan 53)*

Georgia (1) 1 *(Akhalaia 25)*

Republic of Ireland: Connor; Capper, Kelly, Cryan, Thompson, Gilroy■, Butler, Barrett, O'Flynn (Elliott), Thornton (O'Connor), Reid (Houlihan).

WALES UNDER-21 TEAMS 2002–03

Valkeakoski,6 September 2002, 1500

Finland (0) 2 *(Lagerblom 65, Sjolund 89)*

Wales (1) 1 *(Birchall 38)*

Wales: Brown; Moss, Price, Pejic, Day (Rees), Tolley, Valentine, Mumford (Gall), Birchall (Stock), Williams M, Vaughan.

Ninian Park, 15 October 2002, 2202

Wales (1) 1 *(Tolley 4)*

Italy (0) 2 *(Sculli 52, D'Agostino 81)*

Wales: Brown; Moss, Price (Collins), Pejic, Day, Tolley, Valentine, Mumford, Birchall (Williams G), Williams M, Fowler (Stock).

Baku, 19 November 2002, 2000

Azerbaijan (0) 0

Wales (0) 1 *(Gall 72)*

Wales: Brown; Moss, Price, Pejic, Day, Tolley, Pipe, Mumford, Birchall (Collins), Gall, Valentine (Byrne).

Barry, 28 March 2003, 1843

Wales (1) 1 *(Pipe 5)*

Azerbaijan (0) 0

Wales: Whitfield; Moss, Price, Rees, Day, Mumford, Pipe (Brough), Tolley, Collins, Williams G (Williams M), Vaughan.

BRITISH UNDER-21 APPEARANCES 1976–2003

ENGLAND

Ablett, G. (Liverpool), 1988 v F (1)
Adams, A. (Arsenal). 1985 v Ei, Fi; 1986 v D; 1987 v Se, Y (5)
Adams, N. (Everton), 1987 v Se (1)
Allen, B. (QPR), 1992 v H, M, Cz, F; 1993 v N (sub), T, P, Cz (sub) (8)
Allen, C. A. (Oxford U), 1995 v Br (sub), F (sub) (2)
Allen, C. (QPR), 1980 v EG (sub); (with C Palace), 1981 v N, R (3)
Allen, M. (QPR), 1987 v Se (sub); 1988 v Y (sub) (2)
Allen, P. (West Ham U), 1985 v Ei, R; (with Tottenham H), 1986 v R (3)
Allen, R. W. (Tottenham H), 1998 v F (sub), S.Af, Arg (sub) (3)
Ambrose, D. P. F. (Ipswich T), 2003 v I (sub); (with Newcastle U) Ser (sub) (2)
Ameobi, F. (Newcastle U), 2001 v Sp (sub), Fi (sub), Alb (sub), M, Gr (sub); 2002 v Ho (sub+1), Slv (sub), Sw (sub), I (sub), P (sub); 2003 v Y (sub), Slo, Mac, I, P, Ser, Slo (18)
Anderson, V. A. (Nottingham F), 1978 v I (1)
Anderton, D. R. (Tottenham H), 1993 v Sp, Sm, Ho, Pol, N, P, Cz, Br, S, F; 1994 v Pol, Sm (12)
Andrews, I. (Leicester C), 1987 v Se (1)
Ardley, N. C. (Wimbledon), 1993 v Pol, N, P, Cz, Br, S, F, 1994 v Pol (sub), Ho, Sm (10)
Ashcroft, L. (Preston NE), 1992 v H (sub) (1)
Atherton, P. (Coventry C), 1992 v T (1)
Atkinson, B. (Sunderland), 1991 v W (sub), Sen, M, USSR (sub), F; 1992 v Pol (sub) (6)
Awford, A. T. (Portsmouth), 1993 v Sp, N, T, P, Cz, Br, S, F; 1994 v Ho (9)

Bailey, G. R. (Manchester U), 1979 v W, Bul; 1980 v D, S (2), EG; 1982 v N; 1983 v D, Gr; 1984 v H, F (2), I, Sp (14)
Baker, G. E. (Southampton), 1981 v N, R (2)
Ball, M. J. (Everton), 1999 v Se, Bul, L, CzR, Pol; 2000 v L, D (sub) (7)
Barker, S. (Blackburn R), 1985 v Is (sub), Ei, R; 1986 v I (4)
Barmby, N. J. (Tottenham H), 1994 v D; 1995 v P, A (sub); (with Everton), 1998 v Sw (4)
Bannister, G. (Sheffield W), 1982 v Pol (1)
Barnes, J. (Watford), 1983 v D, Gr (2)
Barnes, P. S. (Manchester C), 1977 v W (sub), S, Fi, N; 1978 v N, Fi, I (2), Y (9)
Barrett, E. D. (Oldham Ath), 1990 v P, F, USSR, Cz (4)
Barry, G. (Aston Villa), 1999 v CzR, F, H; 2000 v Y; 2001 v Sp, Fi, Alb; 2002 v Ho, G, Alb, Gr, Ho (sub), Slv, I, P, Sw, I, P; 2003 v Y, Slo, Mac, I, P, T, Slo (25)
Bart-Williams, C. G. (Sheffield W), 1993 v Sp, N, T; 1994 v D, Ru, F, Bel, P; 1995 v P, A, Ei (2), La (2); (with Nottingham F), 1996 v P (sub), A (16)
Batty, D. (Leeds U), 1988 v Sw (sub); 1989 v Gr (sub), Bul, Sen, Ei, US; 1990 v Pol (7)
Bazeley, D. S. (Watford), 1992 v H (sub) (1)
Beagrie, P. (Sheffield U), 1988 v WG, T (2)
Beardsmore, R. (Manchester U), 1989 v Gr, Alb (sub), Pol, Bul, USA (5)
Beattie, J. S. (Southampton), 1999 v CzR (sub), F (sub), Pol, H; 2000 v Pol (5)
Beckham, D. R. J. (Manchester U), 1995 v Br, Mal, An, F; 1996 v P, A (sub), Bel, An, P (9)
Bent, D. A. (Ipswich T), 2003 v I (sub), Ser (sub) (2)
Bent, M. N. (Crystal Palace), 1998 v S.Af (sub), Arg (2)
Beeston, C (Stoke C), 1988 v USSR (1)
Benjamin, T. J. (Leicester C), 2001 v M (sub) (1)
Bertschin, K. E. (Birmingham C), 1977 v S; 1978 v Y (2) (3)
Birtles, G. (Nottingham F), 1980 v Bul, EG (sub) (2)
Blackwell, D. R. (Wimbledon), 1991 v W, T, Sen (sub), M, USSR, F (6)
Blake, M. A. (Aston Villa), 1990 v F (sub), Cz (sub); 1991 v H, Pol, Ei (2), W; 1992 v Pol (8)
Blissett, L. L. (Watford), 1979 v W, Bul (sub), Se; 1980 v D (4)
Booth, A. D. (Huddersfield T), 1995 v La (2 subs); 1996 v N (3)
Bothroyd, J. (Coventry C), 2001 v M (sub) (1)
Bowyer, L. D. (Charlton Ath), 1996 v N (sub), Bel, P, Br; (with Leeds U), 1997 v Mol, I, Sw, Ge; 1998 v Mol; 1999 v F, Pol; 2000 v D, Arg (13)
Bracewell, P. (Stoke C), 1983 v D, Gr (1 + 1 sub), H; 1984 v D, H, F (2), I (2), Sp (2); 1985 v T (13)
Bradbury, L. M. (Portsmouth), 1997 v Pol; (with Manchester C), 1998 v Mol (sub), I (sub) (3)
Bramble, T. M. (Ipswich T), 2001 v Ge, G, Fi, Alb (sub), M; 2002 v Ho (sub); (with Newcastle U), 2003 v Y, Slo, Mac, P (10)
Branch, P. M. (Everton), 1997 v Pol (sub) (1)
Bradshaw, P. W. (Wolverhampton W), 1977 v W, S; 1978 v Fi, Y (4)
Breacker, T. (Luton T), 1986 v I (2) (2)
Brennan, M. (Ipswich T), 1987 v Y, Sp, T, Mor, F (5)
Bridge, W. M. (Southampton), 1999 v H (sub); 2001 v Sp; 2002 v Ho, G, Alb, Gr, Ho (2) (8)
Bridges, M. (Sunderland), 1997 v Sw (sub); 1999 v F; (with Leeds U), 2000 v D (3)
Brightwell, I. (Manchester C), 1989 v D, Alb; 1990 v Se (sub), Pol (4)
Briscoe, L. S. (Sheffield W), 1996 v Cro, Bel (sub), An, Br; 1997 v Sw (sub) (5)
Brock, K. (Oxford U), 1984 v I, Sp (2); 1986 v I (4)
Broomes, M. C. (Blackburn R), 1997 v Sw, Ge (2)
Brown, M. R. (Manchester C), 1996 v Cro, Bel, An, P (4)
Brown, W. M. (Manchester U), 1999 v Se, Bul, L, CzR, Pol, Se, Bul; 2001 v G (8)
Bull, S. G. (Wolverhampton W), 1989 v Alb (2) Pol; 1990 v Se, Pol (5)
Bullock, M. J. (Barnsley), 1998 v Gr (sub) (1)
Burrows, D. (WBA), 1989 v Se (sub); (with Liverpool), Gr, Alb (2), Pol; 1990 v Se, Pol (7)
Butcher, T. I. (Ipswich T), 1979 v Se; 1980 v D, Bul, S (2), EG (2) (7)
Butt, N. (Manchester U), 1995 v Ei (2), La; 1996 v P, A; 1997 v Ge, Pol (7)
Butters, G. (Tottenham H), 1989 v Bul, Sen (sub), Ei (sub) (3)
Butterworth, I. (Coventry C), 1985 v T, R; (with Nottingham F), 1986 v R, T, D (2), I (2) (8)
Bywater, S. (West Ham U), 2001 v M (sub), Gr; 2002 v Ho (sub), I (sub); 2003 v P, Ser (sub) (6)

Cadamarteri, D. L. (Everton), 1999 v CzR (sub); 2000 v Y (sub); 2001 v M (sub) (3)
Caesar, G. (Arsenal), 1987 v Mor, USSR (sub), F (3)
Callaghan, N. (Watford), 1983 v D, Gr (sub), H (sub); 1984 v D, H, F (2), I, Sp (9)
Campbell, A. P. (Middlesbrough), 2000 v Y, T (sub), Slo (sub); 2001 v Ge (sub) (4)
Campbell, K. J. (Arsenal), 1991 v H, T (sub); 1992 v G, T (4)
Campbell, S. (Tottenham), 1994 v D, Ru, F, US, Bel, P; 1995 v P, A, Ei; 1996 v N, A (11)
Carbon, M. P. (Derby Co), 1996 v Cro (sub); 1997 v Ge, I, Sw (4)
Carr, C. (Fulham), 1985 v Ei (sub) (1)
Carr, F. (Nottingham F), 1987 v Se, Y, Sp (sub), Mor, USSR; 1988 v WG (sub), T, Y, F (9)
Carragher, J. L. (Liverpool), 1997 v I (sub), Sw, Ge, Pol; 1998 v Mol (sub), I, Gr, Sw (sub), F, S.Af, Arg; 1999 v Se, Bul, L, CzR, F, Pol, Se, Bul; 2000 v L, Pol, D, Arg, Y, I, T, Slo (27)
Carlisle, C. J. (QPR), 2001 v Ge (sub), G (sub), Fi (sub) (3)
Carrick, M. (West Ham U), 2001 v Ge, G, Fi, I, Gr; 2002 v Gr, Ho (2), P; 2003 v Y, Slo, Mac, I, P (14)
Casper, C. M. (Manchester U), 1995 v Mal (1)
Caton, T. (Manchester C), 1982 v N, H (sub), Pol (2), S; 1983 v WG (2), Gr; 1984 v D, H, F (2), I (2) (14)
Chadwick, L. H. (Manchester U), 2000 v L, D, Arg, I (sub), Slo (sub); 2001 v Ge (sub), I, Sp, Fi, Alb; 2002 v Ho, G, Alb (13)

Challis, T. M. (QPR), 1996 v An, P (2)
Chamberlain, M. (Stoke C), 1983 v Gr; 1984 v F (sub), I, Sp (4)
Chapman, L. (Stoke C), 1981 v Ei (1)
Charles, G. A. (Nottingham F), 1991 v H, W (sub), Ei; 1992 v T (4)
Chettle, S. (Nottingham F), 1988 v M, USSR, Mor, F; 1989 v D, Se, Gr, Alb (2), Bul; 1990 v Se, Pol (12)
Clark, L. R. (Newcastle U), 1992 v Cz, F; 1993 v Sp, N, T, Ho (sub), Pol (sub), Cz, Br, S; 1994 v Ho (11)
Clarke, P. M. (Everton), 2003 v Slo (sub), I, T, Ser, Slo (5)
Christie, M. N. (Derby Co), 2001 v Fi (sub), Sp, Fi, Alb, M, Gr; 2002 v Ho (sub), Gr (sub), Ho, Slv, P (11)
Clegg, M. J. (Manchester U), 1998 v Fr (sub), S.Af (sub) (2)
Clemence, S. N. (Tottenham H), 1999 v Se (sub) (1)
Clough, N. (Nottingham F), 1986 v D (sub); 1987 v Se, Y, T, USSR, F (sub), P; 1988 v WG, T, Y, S (2), M, Mor, F (15)
Cole, A. A. (Arsenal), 1992 v H, Cz (sub), F (sub); (with Bristol C), 1993 v Sm; (with Newcastle U), Pol, N; 1994 v Pol, Ho (8)
Cole, A. (Arsenal), 2001 v Ge, G, Fi, I (4)
Cole, C. (Chelsea), 2003 v T (sub), Ser (sub), Slo (sub) (3)
Cole, J. J. (West Ham U), 2000 v Arg (sub); 2001 v Ge, Gr; 2002 v G; 2003 v Slo, Mac, P, T (8)
Coney, D. (Fulham), 1985 v T (sub); 1986 v R; 1988 v T, WG (4)
Connor, T. (Brighton & HA), 1987 v Y (1)
Cooke, R. (Tottenham H), 1986 v D (sub) (1)
Cooke, T. J. (Manchester U), 1996 v Cro, Bel, An (sub), P (4)
Cooper, C. (Middlesbrough), 1988 v F (2), M, USSR, Mor; 1989 v D, Se, Gr (8)
Corrigan, J. T. (Manchester C), 1978 v I (2), Y (3)
Cort, C. E. R. (Wimbledon), 1999 v L (sub), CzR, H (sub), Se, Bul; 2000 v L (sub), Pol, D (sub), Arg, I, T, Slo (12)
Cottee, A. (West Ham U), 1985 v Fi (sub), Is (sub), Ei, R, Fi; 1987 v Sp, P; 1988 v WG (8)
Couzens, A. J. (Leeds U), 1995 v Mal (sub), An, F (sub) (3)
Cowans, G. S. (Aston Villa), 1979 v W, Se; 1980 v Bul, EG; 1981 v R (5)
Cox, N. J. (Aston Villa), 1993 v T, Ho, Pol, N; 1994 v Pol, Sm (6)
Cranson, I. (Ipswich T), 1985 v Fi, Is, R; 1986 v R, I (5)
Cresswell, R. P. W. (York C), 1999 v F (sub); (with Sheffield W) H (sub), Se, Bul (4)
Croft, G. (Grimsby T), 1995 v Br, Mal, An, F (4)
Crooks, G. (Stoke C), 1980 v Bul, S (2), EG (sub) (4)
Crossley, M. G. (Nottingham F), 1990 v P, USSR, Cz (3)
Crouch, P. J. (Portsmouth), 2002 v I (sub), P (sub), Sw; (with Aston Villa), 2003 v Mac (sub), P (sub) (5)
Cundy, J. V. (Chelsea), 1991 v Ei (2); 1992 v Pol (3)
Cunningham, L. (WBA), 1977 v S, Fi, N (sub); 1978 v N, Fi, I (6)
Curbishley, L. C. (Birmingham C), 1981 v Sw (1)
Curtis, J. C. K. (Manchester U), 1998 v I (sub), Gr, Sw, F, S.Af, Arg; 1999 v Se (sub), Bul, L, CzR, F, Pol (sub), H, Se (sub), Bul; 2000 v Pol (16)

Daniel, P. W. (Hull C), 1977 v S, Fi, N; 1978 v Fi, I, Y (2) (7)
Davies, K. C. (Southampton), 1998 v Gr (sub); (with Blackburn R), 1999 v CzR; (with Southampton), 2000 v Y (sub) (3)
Davis, K. G. (Luton T), 1995 v An; 1996 v Cro (sub), P (3)
Davis, P. (Arsenal), 1982 v Pol, S; 1983 v D, Gr (1 + 1 sub), H (sub); 1987 v T; 1988 v WG, T, Y, Fr (11)
Davis, S. (Fulham), 2001 v Fi, Alb, M, Gr; 2002 v Ho, G, Al, Ho (2), P, Sw (11)
Dawson, M. R. (Nottingham F), 2003 v Slo (sub), I, P, T (4)
Day, C. N. (Tottenham H), 1996 v Cro, Bel, Br; (with Crystal Palace), 1997 v Mol, Ge, Sw (6)
D'Avray, M. (Ipswich T), 1984 v I, Sp (sub) (2)
Deehan, J. M. (Aston Villa), 1977 v N; 1978 v N, Fi, I; 1979 v Bul, Se (sub); 1980 v D (7)
Defoe, J. C. (West Ham U), 2001 v M, Gr; 2002 v Ho (sub), G (sub), Alb, Gr, Ho (2), Slv, I, P (sub), Sw, I, P; 2003 v Y, P, T, Ser, Slo (19)
Dennis, M. E. (Birmingham C), 1980 v Bul; 1981 v N, R (3)
Dichio, D. S. E. (QPR), 1996 v N (sub) (1)
Dickens, A. (West Ham U), 1985 v Fi (sub) (1)
Dicks, J. (West Ham U), 1988 v Sw (sub), M, Mor, F (4)
Digby, F. (Swindon T), 1987 v Sp (sub), USSR, P; 1988 v T; 1990 v Pol (5)
Dillon, K. P. (Birmingham C), 1981 v R (1)
Dixon, K. (Chelsea), 1985 v Fi (1)
Dobson, A. (Coventry C), 1989 v Bul, Sen, Ei, US (4)
Dodd, J. R. (Southampton), 1991 v Pol, Ei, T, Sen, M, F; 1992 v G, Pol (8)
Donowa, L. (Norwich C), 1985 v Is, R (sub), Fi (sub) (3)
Dorigo, A. (Aston Villa), 1987 v Se, Sp, T, Mor, USSR, F, P; 1988 v WG, Y, S (2) (11)
Dozzell, J. (Ipswich T), 1987 v Se, Y (sub), Sp, USSR, F, P; 1989 v Se, Gr (sub); 1990 v Se (sub) (9)
Draper, M. A. (Notts Co), 1991 v Ei (sub); 1992 v G, Pol (3)
Duberry, M. W. (Chelsea), 1997 v Mol, Pol, Ge; 1998 v Mol, Gr (5)
Dunn, D. J. I. (Blackburn R), 1999 v CzR (sub); 2000 v I (sub), T, Slo; 2001 v Ge, G, Fi, I, Sp, M, Gr; 2002 v Ho, Gr, Ho (2), Slv, P, Sw, I, P (20)
Duxbury, M. (Manchester U), 1981 v Sw (sub), Ei (sub), R (sub), Sw; 1982 v N; 1983 v WG (2) (7)
Dyer, B. A. (Crystal Palace), 1994 v Ru, F, US, Bel, P; 1995 v P (sub); 1996 v Cro; 1997 v Mol, Ge; 1998 v Mol, Gr (10)
Dyer, K. C. (Ipswich T), 1998 v Mol, I, Gr, Sw, S.Af, Arg; 1999 v Se, Bul, CzR, Se; (with Newcastle U), 2000 v Y (11)
Dyson, P. I. (Coventry C), 1981 v N, R, Sw, Ei (4)

Eadie, D. M. (Norwich C), 1994 v F (sub), US; 1997 v Mol, Ge (2), I; 1998 v I (7)
Ebbrell, J. (Everton), 1989 v Sen, Ei, US (sub); 1990 v P, F, USSR, Cz; 1991 v H, Pol, Ei, W, T; 1992 v G, T (14)
Edghill, R. A. (Manchester C), 1994 v D, Ru; 1995 v A (3)
Ehiogu, U. (Aston Villa), 1992 v H, M, Cz, F; 1993 v Sp, N, T, Sm, T, Ho, Pol, N; 1994 v Pol, Ho, Sm (15)
Elliott, P. (Luton T), 1985 v Fi; 1986 v T, D (3)
Elliott, R. J. (Newcastle U), 1996 v P, A (2)
Elliott, S. W. (Derby Co), 1998 v F, Arg (sub) (2)
Etherington, N, (Tottenham H), 2002 v Slv (sub), I; 2003 v Y (sub) (3)
Euell, J. J. (Wimbledon), 1998 v F, Arg (sub); 1999 v Se (sub), Bul (se), Pol (sub), H (6)
Evans, R. (Chelsea), 2003 v Ser, Slo (2)

Fairclough, C. (Nottingham F), 1985 v T, Is, Ei; 1987 v Sp, T; (with Tottenham H), 1988 v Y, F (7)
Fairclough, D. (Liverpool), 1977 v W (1)
Fashanu, J. (Norwich C), 1980 v EG; 1981 v N (sub), R, Sw, Ei (sub), H; (with Nottingham F), 1982 v N, H, Pol, S; 1983 v WG (sub) (11)
Fear, P. (Wimbledon), 1994 v Ru, F, US (sub) (3)
Fenton, G. A. (Aston Villa), 1995 v Ei (1)
Fenwick, T. W. (C Palace), 1981 v N, R, Sw, Ei; (with QPR), R; 1982 v N, H, S (2); 1983 v WG (2) (11)
Ferdinand, R. G. (West Ham U), 1997 v Sw, Ge; 1998 v I, Gr; 2000 v Y (5)
Fereday, W. (QPR), 1985 v T, Ei (sub). Fi; 1986 v T (sub), I (5)
Flitcroft, G. W. (Manchester C), 1993 v Sm, Hol, N, P, Cz, Br, S, F; 1994 v Pol, Ho (10)
Flowers, T. (Southampton), 1987 v Mor, F; 1988 v WG (sub) (3)
Ford, M. (Leeds U), 1996 v Cro; 1997 v Mol (2)
Forster, N. M. (Brentford), 1995 v Br, Mal, An, F (4)
Forsyth, M. (Derby Co), 1988 v Sw (1)
Foster, S. (Brighton & HA), 1980 v EG (sub) (1)
Fowler, R. B. (Liverpool), 1994 v Sm, Ru (sub), F, US; 1995 v P, A; 1996 v P, A (8)
Froggatt, S. J. (Aston Villa), 1993 v Sp, Sm (sub) (2)
Futcher, P. (Luton T), 1977 v W, S, Fi, N; (with Manchester C), 1978 v N, Fi, I (2), Y (2); 1979 v D (11)

Gabbiadini, M. (Sunderland), 1989 v Bul, USA (2)
Gale, A. (Fulham), 1982 v Pol (1)
Gallen, K. A. (QPR), 1995 v Ei, La (2); 1996 v Cro (4)
Gardner, A. (Tottenham H), 2002 v I (sub) (1)
Gascoigne, P. (Newcastle U), 1987 v Mo, USSR, P; 1988 v WG, Y, S (2), F (2), Sw, M, USSR (sub), Mor (13)
Gayle, H. (Birmingham C), 1984 v I, Sp (2) (3)
Gernon, T. (Ipswich T), 1983 v Gr (1)
Gerrard, P. W. (Oldham Ath), 1993 v T, Ho, Pol, N, P, Cz, Br, S, F; 1994 v D, Ru; 1995 v P, A, Ei (2), La (2); 1996 v P (18)
Gerrard, S. G. (Liverpool), 2000 v L, Pol, D, Y (4)
Gibbs, N. (Watford), 1987 v Mor, USSR, F, P; 1988 v T (5)
Gibson, C. (Aston Villa), 1982 v N (1)
Gilbert, W. A. (C Palace), 1979 v W, Bul; 1980 v Bul; 1981 v N, R, Sw, R, Sw, H; 1982 v N (sub), H (11)
Goddard, P. (West Ham U), 1981 v N, Sw, Ei (sub); 1982 v N (sub), Pol, S; 1983 v WG (2) (8)
Gordon, D. (Norwich C), 1987 v T (sub), Mor (sub), F, P (4)
Gordon, D. D. (Crystal Palace), 1994 v Ru, F, US, Bel, P; 1995 v P, A, Ei (2), La (2); 1996 v P, N (13)
Grant, A. J. (Everton), 1996 v An (sub) (1)
Grant, L. A. (Derby Co), 2003 v I (sub) (1)
Granville, D. P. (Chelsea), 1997 v Ge (sub), Pol; 1998 v Mol (3)
Gray, A. (Aston Villa), 1988 v S, F (2)
Greening, J. (Manchester U), 1999 v H, Se (sub), Bul; 2000 v Pol; 2001 v Ge, G, Fi, I, Sp (sub), Fi, Alb; (with Middlesbrough), 2002 v Ho, G, Alb, Gr, Ho (sub), I, P (18)
Griffin, A. (Newcastle U), 1999 v H; 2001 v I, Sp (3)
Guppy, S. A. (Leicester C), 1998 v Sw (1)

Haigh, P. (Hull C), 1977 v N (sub) (1)
Hall, M. T. J. (Coventry C), 1997 v Pol (2), I, Sw, Ge; 1998 v Mol, Gr (2) (8)
Hall, R. A. (Southampton), 1992 v H (sub), F; 1993 v Sm, T, Ho, Pol, P, Cz, Br, S, F (11)
Hamilton, D. V. (Newcastle U), 1997 v Pol (1)
Hardyman, P. (Portsmouth), 1985 v Ei; 1986 v D (2)
Hargreaves, O. (Bayern Munich), 2001 v Ge (sub), I, Sp (3)
Harley, J. (Chelsea), 2000 v Arg (sub), T (sub), Slo (3)
Hateley, M. (Coventry C), 1982 v Pol, S; 1983 v Gr (2), H; (with Portsmouth), 1984 v F (2), I, Sp (2) (10)
Hayes, M. (Arsenal), 1987 v Sp, T; 1988 v F (sub) (3)
Hazell, R. J. (Wolverhampton W), 1979 v D (1)
Heaney, N. A. (Arsenal), 1992 v H, M, Cz, F; 1993 v N, T (6)
Heath, A. (Stoke C), 1981 v R, Sw, H; 1982 v N, H; (with Everton), Pol, S; 1983 v WG (8)
Hendon, I. M. (Tottenham H), 1992 v H, M, Cz, F; 1993 v Sp, N, T (7)
Hendrie, L. A. (Aston Villa), 1996 v Cro (sub); 1998 v Sw (sub); 1999 v Se, Bul, L, F, Pol; 2000 v L, D, Arg, Y, I, Slo (sub) (13)
Hesford, I. (Blackpool), 1981 v Ei (sub), Pol (2), S (2); 1983 v WG (2) (7)
Heskey, E. W. I. (Leicester C), 1997 v I, Ge, Pol (2); 1998 v I, Gr (2), Sw, F, S.Af, Arg; 1999 v Se, Bul, L; 2000 v L; (with Liverpool), Y (16)
Hilaire, V. (C Palace), 1980 v Bul, S (1+1 sub), EG (2); 1981 v N, R, Sw (sub); 1982 v Pol (sub) (9)
Hill, D. R. L. (Tottenham H), 1995 v Br, Mal, An, F (4)
Hillier, D. (Arsenal), 1991 v T (1)
Hinchcliffe, A. (Manchester C), 1989 v D (1)
Hinshelwood, P. A. (C Palace), 1978 v N; 1980 v EG (2)
Hirst, D. (Sheffield W), 1988 v USSR, F; 1989 v D, Bul (sub), Sen, Ei, US (7)
Hislop, N. S. (Newcastle U), 1998 v Sw (1)
Hoddle, G. (Tottenham H), 1977 v W (sub); 1978 v Fi (sub), I (2), Y; 1979 v D, W, Bul; 1980 v S (2), EG (2) (12)
Hodge, S. (Nottingham F), 1983 v Gr (sub); 1984 v D, F, I, Sp (2); (with Aston Villa), 1986 v R, T (8)
Hodgson, D. J. (Middlesbrough), 1981 v N, R (sub), Sw, Ei; 1982 v Pol; 1983 v WG (6)
Holdsworth, D. (Watford), 1989 v Gr (sub) (1)
Holland, C. J. (Newcastle U), 1995 v La; 1996 v N (sub), A (sub), Cro, Bel, An, Br; 1997 v Mol, Pol, Sw (10)
Holland, P. (Mansfield T), 1995 v Br, Mal, An, F (4)
Holloway, D. (Sunderland), 1998 v Sw (sub) (1)
Horne, B. (Millwall), 1989 v Gr (sub), Pol, Bul, Ei, US (5)
Howe, E. J. F. (Bournemouth), 1998 v S.Af (sub), Arg (2)
Hucker, P. (QPR), 1984 v I, Sp (2)
Huckerby, D. (Coventry C), 1997 v I (sub), Sw, Ge (sub), Pol (sub) (4)
Hughes, S. J. (Arsenal), 1997 v I, Sw, Ge, Pol; 1998 v Mol, I, Gr, Sw (sub) (8)
Humphreys, R. J. (Sheffield W), 1997 v Pol, Ge (sub), Sw (3)

Impey, A. R. (QPR), 1993 v T (1)
Ince, P. (West Ham U), 1989 v Alb; 1990 v Se (2)

Jackson, M. A. (Everton), 1992 v H, M, Cz, F; 1993 v Sm (sub), T, Ho, Pol, N; 1994 v Pol (10)
Jagielka, P. N. (Sheffield U), 2003 v Ser, Slo (2)
James, D. (Watford), 1991 v Ei (2), T, Sen, M, USSR, F; 1992 v G, T, Pol (10)
James, J. C. (Luton T), 1990 v F, USSR (2)
Jansen, M. B (Crystal Palace), 1999 v Se, Bul, L; (with Blackburn R) F (sub), Pol; 2000 v I (sub) (6)
Jeffers, F. (Everton), 2000 v L, Arg, I, T, Slo; 2001 v Ge; (with Arsenal), 2002 v Ho, G (sub), Alb; 2003 v Y, Slo, Mac, T (13)
Jemson, N. B. (Nottingham F), 1991 v W (1)
Jenas, J. A. (Newcastle U), 2002 v Slo, I, P (sub); 2003 v Y, Slo, Mac, T (7)
Joachim, J. K. (Leicester C), 1994 v D (sub); 1995 v P, A, Ei, Br, Mal, An, F; 1996 v N (9)
Johnson, G. M. C. (West Ham U), 2003 v T (sub), Ser (sub) (2)
Johnson, S. A. M. (Crewe Alex), 1999 v L (sub), CzR (sub), F (sub), Pol; (with Derby Co), Se, Bul; 2000 v D, Arg (sub), Y, I, T; 2001 v Fi; 2002 v Ho (sub), Alb (sub); (with Leeds U), P (15)
Johnson, T. (Notts Co), 1991 v H (sub), Ei (sub); 1992 v G, T, Pol; (with Derby Co), M, Cz (sub) (7)
Johnston, C. P. (Middlesbrough), 1981 v N, Ei (2)
Jones, D. R. (Everton), 1977 v W (1)
Jones, C. H. (Tottenham H), 1978 v Y (sub) (1)
Jones, R. (Liverpool), 1993 v Sm, Ho (2)

Keegan, G. A. (Manchester C), 1977 v W (1)
Kenny, W. (Everton), 1993 v T (1)
Keown, M. (Aston Villa), 1987 v Sp, Mor, USSR, P; 1988 v T, S, F (2) (8)
Kerslake, D. (QPR), 1986 v T (1)
Kilcline, B. (Notts C), 1983 v D, Gr (2)
King, A. E. (Everton), 1977 v W; 1978 v Y (2)
King, L. B. (Tottenham H), 2000 v L (sub), I, T, Slo; 2001 v I, Sp (sub), Fi; 2002 v G, Alb, Gr, Ho (2) (12)
Kirkland, C. E. (Coventry C), 2001 v M; (with Liverpool), 2002 v Gr, Ho (2), P (sub); 2003 v Y, Mac (7)
Kitson, P. (Leicester C), 1991 v Sen (sub), M, F; 1992 v Pol; (with Derby Co), M, Cz, F (7)
Knight, A. (Portsmouth), 1983 v Gr, H (2)
Knight, I. (Sheffield W), 1987 v Se (sub), Y (2)
Knight, Z. (Fulham), 2002 v Slo (sub), I (2), P (4)
Konchesky, P. M. (Charlton Ath), 2002 v Slo, P, Sw, I, P; 2003 v Y, Slo, Mac, P, T, Ser, Slo (12)
Kozluk, R. (Derby Co), 1998 v F, Arg (sub) (2)

Lake, P. (Manchester C), 1989 v D, Alb (2), Pol; 1990 v Pol (5)
Lampard, F. J. (West Ham U), 1998 v Gr (2), Sw, F, S.Af, Arg; 1999 v Se, Bul, L, CzR, F, Pol, Se; 2000 v L, Arg, Y, I, T, Slo (19)
Langley, T. W. (Chelsea), 1978 v I (sub) (1)
Lee, D. J. (Chelsea), 1990 v F; 1991 v H, Pol, Ei (2), T, Sen, USSR, F; 1992 v Pol (10)
Lee, R. (Charlton Ath), 1986 v I (sub); 1987 v Se (sub) (2)
Lee, S. (Liverpool), 1981 v R, Sw, H; 1982 v S; 1983 v WG (2) (6)
Le Saux, G. (Chelsea), 1990 v P, F, USSR, Cz (4)
Lescott, J. P. (Wolverhampton W), 2003 v Y (sub), I (sub) (2)

Lowe, D. (Ipswich T), 1988 v F, Sw (sub) (2)
Lukic, J. (Leeds U), 1981 v N, R, Ei, R, Sw, H; 1982 v H (7)
Lund, G. (Grimsby T), 1985 v T; 1986 v R, T (3)

McCall, S. H. (Ipswich T), 1981 v Sw, H; 1982 v H, S; 1983 v WG (2) (6)
McDonald, N. (Newcastle U), 1987 v Se (sub), Sp, T; 1988 v WG, Y (sub) (5)
McEveley, J. (Blackburn R), 2003 v I (sub) (1)
McGrath, L. (Coventry C), 1986 v D (1)
MacKenzie, S. (WBA), 1982 v N, S (2) (3)
McLeary, A. (Millwall), 1988 v Sw (1)
McMahon, S. (Everton), 1981 v Ei; 1982 v Pol; 1983 v D, Gr (2); (with Aston Villa), 1984 v H (6)
McManaman, S. (Liverpool), 1991 v W, M (sub); 1993 v N, T, Sm, T; 1994 v Pol (7)
Mabbutt, G. (Bristol R), 1982 v Pol (2), S; (with Tottenham H), 1983 v D; 1984 v F; 1986 v D, I (7)
Makin, C. (Oldham Ath), 1994 v Ru (sub), F, US, Bel, P (5)
Marriott, A. (Nottingham F), 1992 v M (1)
Marsh, S. T. (Oxford U), 1998 v F (1)
Marshall, A. J. (Norwich C), 1995 v Mal, An; 1997 v Pol, I (4)
Marshall, L. K. (Norwich C), 1999 v F (sub) (1)
Martin, L. (Manchester U), 1989 v Gr (sub), Alb (sub) (2)
Martyn, N. (Bristol R), 1988 v S (sub), M, USSR, Mor, F; 1989 v D, Se, Gr, Alb (2); 1990 v Se (11)
Matteo, D. (Liverpool), 1994 v F (sub), Bel, P; 1998 v Sw (4)
Matthew, D. (Chelsea), 1990 v P, USSR (sub), Cz; 1991 v Ei, M, USSR, F; 1992 v G (sub), T (9)
May, A. (Manchester C), 1986 v I (sub) (1)
Merson, P. (Arsenal), 1989 v D, Gr, Pol (sub); 1990 v Pol (4)
Middleton, J. (Nottingham F), 1977 v Fi, N; (with Derby Co), 1978 v N (3)
Miller, A. (Arsenal), 1988 v Mor (sub); 1989 v Sen; 1991 v H, Pol (4)
Mills, D. J. (Charlton Ath), 1999 v Se, Bul (sub), L, Pol, H, Se; (with Leeds U), 2000 v L, Pol, D, Arg, Y (sub), I, T, Slo (14)
Mills, G. R. (Nottingham F), 1981 v R; 1982 v N (2)
Mimms, R. (Rotherham U), 1985 v Is (sub), Ei (sub); (with Everton), 1986 v I (3)
Minto, S. C. (Charlton Ath), 1991 v W; 1992 v H, M, Cz; 1993 v T; 1994 v Ho (6)
Moore, I. (Tranmere R), 1996 v Cro (sub), Bel (sub), An, P, Br; 1997 v Mol (sub); (with Nottingham F), Sw (sub) (7)
Moran, S. (Southampton), 1982 v N (sub); 1984 v F (2)
Morgan, S. (Leicester C), 1987 v Se, Y (2)
Morris, J. (Chelsea), 1997 v Pol (sub), Sw (sub), Ge (sub); 1999 v Bul (sub), L (sub), CzR; 2000 v Pol (7)
Mortimer, P. (Charlton Ath), 1989 v Sen, Ei (2)
Moses, A. P. (Barnsley), 1997 v Pol; 1998 v Gr (sub) (2)
Moses, R. M. (WBA), 1981 v N (sub), Sw, Ei, R, Sw, H; 1982 v N (sub); (with Manchester U), H (8)
Mountfield, D. (Everton), 1984 v Sp (1)
Muggleton, C. D. (Leicester C), 1990 v F (1)
Mullins, H. I. (Crystal Palace), 1999 v Pol (sub), H, Bul (3)
Murphy, D. B. (Liverpool), 1998 v Mol, Gr (sub); 2000 v T, Slo (4)
Murray, P. (QPR), 1997 v I, Pol; 1998 v I, Gr (4)
Murray, M. W. (Wolverhampton W), 2003 v Slo, Mac (sub), I, T (4)
Mutch, A. (Wolverhampton W), 1989 v Pol (1)
Myers. A. (Chelsea), 1995 v Br, Mal, An (sub), F (4)

Naylor, L. M. (Wolverhampton W), 2000 v Arg; 2001 v M, Gr (3)
Nethercott, S. (Tottenham), 1994 v D, Ru, F, US, Bel, P; 1995 v La (2) (8)
Neville, P. J. (Manchester U), 1995 v Br, Mal, An, F; 1996 v P, N (sub); 1997 v Ge (7)
Newell, M. (Luton T), 1986 v D (1 + 1 sub), I (1 + 1 sub) (4)
Newton, A. L. (West Ham U), 2001 v Ge (1)
Newton, E. J. I. (Chelsea), 1993 v T (sub); 1994 v Sm (2)
Newton, S. O. (Charlton Ath), 1997 v Mol, Pol, Ge (3)
Nicholls, A. (Plymouth Arg), 1994 v F (1)
Nolan, K. A. J. (Bolton W), 2003 v I (sub) (1)

Oakes, M. C. (Aston Villa), 1994 v D (sub), F (sub), US, Bel, P; 1996 v A (6)
Oakes, S. J. (Luton T), 1993 v Br (sub) (1)
Oakley, M. (Southampton), 1997 v Ge; 1998 v F, S.Af, Arg (4)
O'Brien, A. J. (Bradford C), 1999 v F (1)
O'Connor, J. (Everton), 1996 v Cro, An, Br (3)
Oldfield, D. (Luton T), 1989 v Se (1)
Olney, I. A. (Aston Villa), 1990 v P, F, USSR, Cz; 1991 v H, Pol, Ei (2), T; 1992 v Pol (sub) (10)
Ord, R. J. (Sunderland), 1991 v W, M, USSR (3)
Osman, R. C. (Ipswich T), 1979 v W (sub), Se; 1980 v D, S (2), EG (2) (7)
Owen, G. A. (Manchester C), 1977 v S, Fi, N; 1978 v N, Fi, I (2), Y; 1979 v D, W; (with WBA), Bul, Se (sub); 1980 v D, S (2), EG; 1981 v Sw, R; 1982 v N (sub), H; 1983 v WG (2) (22)
Owen, M. J. (Liverpool), 1998 v Gr (1)

Painter, I. (Stoke C), 1986 v I (1)
Palmer, C. (Sheffield W), 1989 v Bul, Sen, Ei, US (4)
Parker, G. (Hull C), 1986 v I (2); (with Nottingham F), F; 1987 v Se, Y (sub), Sp (6)
Parker, P. (Fulham), 1985 v Fi, T, Is (sub), Ei, R, Fi; 1986 v T, D (8)
Parker, S. M. (Charlton Ath), 2001 v Ge (sub), G, Fi (sub), Alb (sub); 2002 v Ho (sub), G (sub), Alb, Slo, I (sub), Sw (sub), I (sub), P (sub) (12)
Parkes, P. B. F. (QPR), 1979 v D (1)
Parkin, S. (Stoke C), 1987 v Sp (sub); 1988 v WG (sub), T, S (sub), F (5)
Parlour, R. (Arsenal), 1992 v H, M, Cz, F; 1993 v Sp, N, T; 1994 v D, Ru, Bel, P; 1995 v A (12)
Parnaby, S. (Middlesbrough), 2003 v Y (sub), Ser, Slo (3)
Peach, D. S. (Southampton), 1977 v S, Fi, N; 1978 v N, I (2) (6)
Peake, A. (Leicester C), 1982 v Pol (1)
Pearce, I. A. (Blackburn R), 1995 v Ei, La; 1996 v N (3)
Pearce, S. (Nottingham F), 1987 v Y (1)
Pennant, J. (Arsenal), 2001 v M (sub), Gr (sub); 2002 v Ho (sub), Alb (sub), Gr, Ho (2), Slv, I (sub), P (sub), Sw, I, P; 2003 v Y, P (sub), Ser, Slo (17)
Pickering N. (Sunderland), 1983 v D (sub), Gr, H; 1984 v F (sub + 1), I (2), Sp; 1985 v Is, R, Fi; 1986 v R, T; (with Coventry C), D, I (15)
Platt, D. (Aston Villa), 1988 v M, Mor, F (3)
Plummer, C. S. (QPR), 1996 v Cro (sub), Bel, An, P (sub), Br (5)
Pollock, J. (Middlesbrough), 1995 v Ei (sub); 1996 v N, A (3)
Porter, G. (Watford), 1987 v Sp (sub), T, Mor, USSR, F, P (sub); 1988 v T (sub), Y, S (2), F, Sw (12)
Potter, G. S. (Southampton), 1997 v Mol (1)
Pressman, K. (Sheffield W), 1989 v D (sub) (1)
Proctor, M. (Middlesbrough), 1981 v Ei (sub), Sw; (with Nottingham F) 1982 v N, Pol (4)
Prutton, D. T. (Nottingham F), 2001 v Ge (sub), G (sub), Fi, Sp (sub), M, Gr (sub); 2002 v Ho (sub), G, Gr (sub), Slv (sub), I, Sw (sub), I, P; 2003 v Y, Slo, Mac; (with Southampton), I, P, T, Ser, Slo (22)
Purse, D. J. (Birmingham C), 1998 v F. S.Af (2)

Quashie, N. F. (QPR), 1997 v Pol; 1998 v Mol, Gr, Sw (4)
Quinn, W. R. (Sheffield U), 1998 v Mol (sub), I (2)

Ramage, C. D. (Derby Co), 1991 v Pol (sub), W; 1992 v Fr (sub) (3)
Ranson, R. (Manchester C), 1980 v Bul, EG; 1981 v R (sub), R, Sw (1 + 1 sub), H, Pol (2), S (10)
Redknapp, J. F. (Liverpool), 1993 v Sm, Pol, N, P, Cz, Br, S, F; 1994 v Pol, Ho (sub), D, Ru, F, US, Bel, P; 1995 v P, A; 1998 v Sw (19)
Redmond, S. (Manchester C), 1988 v F (2), M, USSR, Mor, F; 1989 v D, Se, Gr, Alb (2), Pol; 1990 v Se, Pol (14)
Reeves, K. P. (Norwich C), 1978 v I, Y (2); 1979 v N, W, Bul, Sw; 1980 v D, S; (with Manchester C), EG (10)

Regis, C. (WBA), 1979 v D, Bul, Se; 1980 v S, EG; 1983 v D (6)
Reid, N. S. (Manchester C), 1981 v H (sub); 1982 v H, Pol (2), S (2) (6)
Reid, P. (Bolton W), 1977 v S, Fi, N; 1978 v Fi, I, Y (6)
Richards, D. I. (Wolverhampton W), 1995 v Br, Mal, An, F (4)
Richards, J. P. (Wolverhampton W), 1977 v Fi, N (2)
Rideout, P. (Aston Villa), 1985 v Fi, Is, Ei (sub), R; (with Bari), 1986 v D (5)
Riggott, C. M. (Derby Co), 2001 v Sp (sub), Fi (sub), Alb, M (sub); 2002 v Ho (sub), Slv, P, Sw (8)
Ripley, S. (Middlesbrough), 1988 v USSR, F (sub); 1989 v D (sub), Se, Gr, Alb (2); 1990 v Se (8)
Ritchie, A. (Brighton & HA), 1982 v Pol (1)
Rix, G. (Arsenal), 1978 v Fi (sub), Y; 1979 v D, Se; 1980 v D (sub), Bul, S (7)
Roberts, A. J. (Millwall), 1995 v Ei, La (2); (with C Palace), 1996 v N, A (5)
Roberts, B. J. (Middlesbrough), 1997 v Sw (sub) (1)
Robins, M. G. (Manchester U), 1990 v P, F, USSR, Cz; 1991 v H (sub), Pol (6)
Robinson, P. P. (Watford), 1999 v Se, Bul; 2000 v Pol (3)
Robinson, P. W. (Leeds U), 2000 v D; 2001 v Ge, G, Fi, Sp; 2002 v Slv, I, P, Sw, I, P (11)
Robson, B. (WBA), 1979 v W, Bul (sub), Se; 1980 v D, Bul, S (2) (7)
Robson, S. (Arsenal), 1984 v I; 1985 v Fi, Is, Fi; 1986 v R, I (with West Ham U); 1988 v S, Sw (8)
Rocastle, D. (Arsenal), 1987 v Se, Y, Sp, T; 1988 v WG, T, Y, S (2), F (2 subs), M, USSR, Mor (14)
Roche, L. P. (Manchester U), 2001 v Fi (1)
Rodger, G. (Coventry C), 1987 v USSR, F, P; 1988 v WG (4)
Rogers, A. (Nottingham F), 1998 v F, S.Af, Arg (3)
Rosario, R. (Norwich C), 1987 v T (sub), Mor, F, P (sub) (4)
Rose, M. (Arsenal), 1997 v Ge (sub), I (2)
Rowell, G. (Sunderland), 1977 v Fi (1)
Ruddock, N. (Southampton), 1989 v Bul (sub), Sen, Ei, US (4)
Rufus, R. R. (Charlton Ath), 1996 v Cro, Bel, An, P, Br; 1997 v I (6)
Ryan, J. (Oldham Ath), 1983 v H (1)
Ryder, S.H. (Walsall), 1995 v Br, An, F (3)

Samuel, J. (Aston Villa), 2002 v I; 2003 v Y, Slo, Mac, I, P, T (7)
Samways, V. (Tottenham H), 1988 v Sw (sub), USSR, F; 1989 v D, Se (5)
Sansom, K. G. (C Palace), 1979 v D, W, Bul, Se; 1980 v S (2), EG (2) (8)
Scimeca, R. (Aston Villa), 1996 v P; 1997 v Mol, Pol, Ge, I; 1998 v Mol, I, Gr (2) (9)
Scowcroft, J. B. (Ipswich T), 1997 v Pol, Ge (2), I (sub); 1998 v Gr (sub) (5)
Seaman, D. (Birmingham C), 1985 v Fi, T, Is, Ei, R, Fi; 1986 v R, F, D, I (10)
Sedgley, S. (Coventry C), 1987 v USSR, F (sub), P; 1988 v F; 1989 v D (sub), Se, Gr, Alb (2), Pol; (with Tottenham H), 1990 v Se (11)
Sellars, S. (Blackburn R), 1988 v S (sub), F, Sw (3)
Selley, I. (Arsenal), 1994 v Ru (sub), F (sub), US (3)
Serrant, C. (Oldham Ath), 1998 v Gr (2) (2)
Sharpe, L. (Manchester U), 1989 v Gr; 1990 v P (sub), F, USSR, Cz; 1991 v H, Pol (sub), Ei (8)
Shaw, G. R. (Aston Villa), 1981 v Ei, Sw, H; 1982 v H, S; 1983 v WG (2) (7)
Shearer, A. (Southampton), 1991 v Ei (2), W, T, Sen, M, USSR, F; 1992 v G, T, Pol (11)
Shelton, G. (Sheffield W), 1985 v Fi (1)
Sheringham, T. (Millwall), 1988 v Sw (1)
Sheron, M. N. (Manchester C), 1992 v H, F; 1993 v N (sub), T (sub), Sm, Ho, Pol, N, P, Cz, Br, S, F; 1994 v Pol (sub), Ho, Sm (16)
Sherwood, T. A. (Norwich C), 1990 v P, F, USSR, Cz (4)
Shipperley, N. J. (Chelsea), 1994 v Sm (sub); (with Southampton), 1995 v Ei, La (2); 1996 v P, N, A (7)
Sidwell, S. J. (Reading), 2003 v Ser, Slo (2)
Simonsen, S. P. A. (Tranmere R), 1998 v F; (with Everton), 1999 v CzR, F, Bul (4)
Simpson, P. (Manchester C), 1986 v D (sub); 1987 v Y, Mor, F, P (5)
Sims, S. (Leicester C), 1977 v W, S, Fi, N; 1978 v N, Fi, I (2), Y (2) (10)
Sinclair, T. (QPR), 1994 v Ho, Sm, D, Ru, F, US, Bel, P; 1995 v P, Ei (2), La; 1996 v P; (with West Ham U), 1998 v Sw (5)
Sinnott, L. (Watford), 1985 v Is (sub) (1)
Slade, S. A. (Tottenham H), 1996 v Bel, An, P, Br (4)
Slater, S. I. (West Ham U), 1990 v P, USSR (sub), Cz (sub) (3)
Small, B. (Aston Villa), 1993 v Sm, T, Ho, Pol, N, P, Cz, Br, S, F; 1994 v Pol, Sm (12)
Smith, A. (Leeds U), 2000 v D, Arg (sub); 2001 v G, Fi, Sp; 2002 v I, P, Sw, I, P (10)
Smith, D. (Coventry C), 1988 v M, USSR (sub), Mor; 1989 v D, Se, Alb (2), Pol; 1990 v Se, Pol (10)
Smith, M. (Sheffield W), 1981 v Ei, R, Sw, H; 1982 v Pol (sub) (5)
Smith, M. (Sunderland), 1995 v Ei (sub) (1)
Smith, T. W. (Watford), 2001 v Ge (sub) (1)
Snodin, I. (Doncaster R), 1985 v T, Is, R, Fi (4)
Statham, B. (Tottenham H), 1988 v Sw; 1989 v D (sub), Se (3)
Statham, D. J. (WBA), 1978 v Fi, 1979 v W, Bul, Se; 1980 v D; 1983 v D (6)
Stein, B. (Luton T), 1984 v D, H, I (3)
Sterland, M. (Sheffield W), 1984 v D, H, F (2), I, Sp (2) (7)
Steven, T. (Everton), 1985 v Fi, T (2)
Stevens, G. (Brighton & HA), 1983 v H; (with Tottenham H), 1984 v H, F (1+1 sub), I (sub), Sp (1+1 sub); 1986 v I (8)
Stewart, J. (Leicester C), 2003 v P (sub) (1)
Stewart, P. (Manchester C), 1988 v F (1)
Stockdale, R. K. (Middlesbrough), 2001 v Ge (sub) (1)
Stuart, G. C. (Chelsea), 1990 v P (sub), F, USSR, Cz; 1991 v T (sub) (5)
Stuart, J. C. (Charlton Ath), 1996 v Bel, An, P, Br (4)
Suckling, P. (Coventry C), 1986 v D; (with Manchester C), 1987 v Se (sub), Y, Sp, T; (with C Palace), 1988 v S (2), F (2), Sw (10)
Summerbee, N.J. (Swindon T), 1993 v P (sub), S (sub), F (3)
Sunderland, A. (Wolverhampton W), 1977 v W (1)
Sutton, C. R. (Norwich), 1993 v Sp (sub), T (sub + 1),Ho, P (sub), Cz, Br, S, F; 1994 v Pol, Ho, Sm, D (13)
Swindlehurst, D. (C Palace), 1977 v W (1)
Sutch, D. (Norwich C), 1992 v H, M, Cz; 1993 v T (4)

Talbot, B. (Ipswich T), 1977 v W (1)
Taylor, M. (Blackburn R), 2001 v M (sub) (1)
Taylor, M. S. (Portsmouth), 2003 v Slo (sub), I (2)
Taylor, S. J. (Arsenal), 2002 v Ho, G, Alb (3)
Terry, J. G. (Chelsea), 2001 v Fi, Sp, Fi, Alb, M, Gr; 2002 v Ho (3) (9)
Thatcher, B. D. (Millwall), 1996 v Cro; (with Wimbledon), 1997 v Mol, Pol; 1998 v I (4)
Thelwell, A. A. (Tottenham H), 2001 v Sp (sub) (1)
Thirlwell, P. (Sunderland), 2001 v Ge (sub) (1)
Thomas, D. (Coventry C), 1981 v Ei; 1983 v WG (2), Gr, H; (with Tottenham H), I, Sp (7)
Thomas, M. (Luton T), 1986 v T, D, I (3)
Thomas, M. (Arsenal), 1988 v Y, S, F (2), M, USSR, Mor; 1989 v Gr, Alb (2), Pol; 1990 v Se (12)
Thomas, R. E. (Watford), 1990 v P (1)
Thompson, A. (Bolton W), 1995 v La; 1996 v P (2)
Thompson, D. A. (Liverpool), 1997 v Pol (sub), Ge; 2000 v L (sub), Pol (sub), D (sub), I, T (sub) (7)
Thompson, G. L. (Coventry C), 1981 v R, Sw, H; 1982 v N, H, S (6)
Thorn, A. (Wimbledon), 1988 v WG (sub). Y, S, F, Sw (5)
Thornley, B. L. (Manchester U), 1996 v Bel, P, Br (3)
Tiler, C. (Barnsley), 1990 v P, USSR, Cz; 1991 v H, Pol, Ei (2), T, Sen, USSR, F; (with Nottingham F), 1992 v G, T (13)

Unsworth, D. G. (Everton), 1995 v A, Ei (2), La; 1996 v N, A (6)
Upson, M. J. (Arsenal), 1999 v Se, Bul, L, F; 2000 v L, Pol, D; 2001 v I, Sp (sub), M (sub), Gr (11)

Vassell, D. (Aston Villa), 1999 v H (sub); 2000 v Pol (sub); 2001 v Ge, G, Fi, I, Fi, Alb; 2002 v Ho, G, Gr (11)
Venison, B. (Sunderland), 1983 v D, Gr; 1985 v Fi, T, Is, Fi; 1986 v R, T, D (2) (10)
Vernazza, P. A. P. (Arsenal), 2001 v G (sub); (with Watford), M (sub) (2)
Vinnicombe, C. (Rangers), 1991 v H (sub), Pol, Ei (2), T, Sen, M, USSR (sub), F; 1992 v G, T, Pol (12)

Waddle, C. (Newcastle U), 1985 v Fi (1)
Wallace, D. (Southampton), 1983 v Gr, H; 1984 v D, H, F (2), I, Sp (sub); 1985 v Fi, T, Is; 1986 v R, D, I (14)
Wallace, Ray (Southampton), 1989 v Bul, Sen (sub), Ei; 1990 v Se (4)
Wallace, Rod (Southampton), 1989 v Bul, Ei (sub), US; 1991 v H, Pol, Ei, T, Sen, M, USSR, F (11)
Walker, D. (Nottingham F), 1985 v Fi; 1987 v Se, T; 1988 v WG, T, S (2) (7)
Walker, I. M. (Tottenham H), 1991 v W; 1992 v H, Cz, F; 1993 v Sp, N, T, Sm; 1994 v Pol (9)
Walsh, G. (Manchester U), 1988 v WG, Y (2)
Walsh, P. M. (Luton T), 1983 v D (sub), Gr (2), H (4)
Walters, K. (Aston Villa), 1984 v D (sub), H (sub); 1985 v Is, Ei, R; 1986 v R, T, D, I (sub) (9)
Ward, P. D. (Brighton & HA), 1978 v N; 1980 v EG (2)
Warhurst, P. (Oldham Ath), 1991 v H, Pol, W, Sen, M (sub), USSR, F (sub); (with Sheffield W), 1992 v G (8)
Watson, D. (Norwich C), 1984 v D, F (2), I (2), Sp (2) (7)
Watson, D. N. (Barnsley), 1994 v Ho, Sm; 1995 v Br, F; 1996 v N (5)
Watson, G. (Sheffield W), 1991 v Sen, USSR (2)
Watson, S. C. (Newcastle U), 1993 v Sp (sub), N; 1994 v Sm (sub), D; 1995 v P, A, Ei (2), La (2); 1996 v N, A (12)
Weaver, N. J. (Manchester C), 2000 v L, Pol, Arg, I, T, Slo; 2001 v I, Fi, Alb; 2002 v Slv (sub) (10)
Webb, N. (Portsmouth), 1985 v Ei; (with Nottingham F), 1986 v D (2) (3)
Whelan, P. J. (Ipswich T), 1993 v Sp, T (sub), P (3)
Whelan, N. (Leeds U), 1995 v A (sub), Ei (2)
Wilson, M. A. (Manchester U), 2001 v Sp, Fi (sub), Alb, M (sub); (with Middlesbrough), 2002 v Ho (sub), Alb (sub) (6)
White, D. (Manchester C), 1988 v S (2), F, USSR; 1989 v Se; 1990 v Pol (6)
Whyte, C. (Arsenal), 1982 v S (1+1 sub); 1983 v D, Gr (4)
Wicks, S. (QPR), 1982 v S (1)
Wilkins, R. C. (Chelsea), 1977 v W (1)
Wilkinson, P. (Grimsby T), 1985 v Ei, R (sub); (with Everton), 1986 v R (sub), I (4)
Williams, D. (Sunderland), 1998 v Sw (sub); 1999 v F (2)
Williams, P. (Charlton Ath), 1989 v Bul, Sen, Ei, US (sub) (4)
Williams, P. D. (Derby Co), 1991 v Sen, M, USSR; 1992 v G, T, Pol (6)
Williams, S. C. (Southampton), 1977 v S, Fi, N; 1978 v N, I (1 + 1 sub), Y (2); 1979 v D, Bul, Se (sub); 1980 v D, EG (2) (14)
Winterburn, N. (Wimbledon), 1986 v I (1)
Wise, D. (Wimbledon), 1988 v Sw (1)
Woodcook, A. S. (Nottingham F), 1978 v Fi, I (2)
Woodgate, J. S. (Leeds U), 2000 v Arg (1)
Woodhouse, C. (Sheffield U), 1999 v H, Se, Bul; 2000 v Pol (sub) (4)
Woods, C. C. E. (Nottingham F), 1979 v W (sub), Se; (with QPR), 1980 v Bul, EG; 1981 v Sw; (with Norwich C), 1984 v D (6)
Wright, A. G. (Blackburn), 1993 v Sp, N (2)
Wright, M. (Southampton), 1983 v Gr, H; 1984 v D, H (4)
Wright, R. I. (Ipswich T), 1997 v Ge, Pol; 1998 v Mol, I, Gr (2), S.Af, Arg; 1999 v Se, Bul, L, Pol, H, Se; 2000 v Y (15)
Wright, S. J. (Liverpool), 2001 v Ge (sub), G, M (sub); 2002 v Ho (sub), G, Alb, Ho, Slv, I, P (10)
Wright, W. (Everton), 1979 v D, W, Bul; 1980 v D, S (2) (6)
Wright-Phillips, S. C. (Manchester C), 2002 v I; 2003 v Y (sub), Mac (sub), I (4)

Yates, D. (Notts Co), 1989 v D (sub), Bul, Sen, Ei, US (5)
Young, L. P. (Tottenham H), 1999 v H; 2000 v D (sub), Arg (sub), T, Slo; (with Charlton Ath), 2002 v Ho, Gr, Ho, P (sub), Sw, I, P (12)

Zamora, R. L. (Brighton & HA), 2002 v P (sub), I (sub), P (sub); 2003 v I, Ser, Slo (sub) (6)

SCOTLAND

Aitken, R. (Celtic), 1977 v Cz, W, Sw; 1978 v Cz, W; 1979 v P, N (2); 1980 v Bel, E; 1984 v EG, Y (2); 1985 v WG, Ic, Sp (16)
Albiston, A. (Manchester U), 1977 v Cz, W, Sw; 1978 v Sw, Cz (5)
Alexander, N. (Stenhousemuir), 1997 v P; 1998 v Bl, Ei, I; (with Livingston), 1999 v Li, Es, Bel (2), CzR, G (10)
Anderson, I. (Dundee), 1997 v Co (sub), US, CzR, P; 1998 v Bl, La, Fi, D (sub), Ei (sub), Ni; 1999 v G (sub), Ei, Ni, CzR; (with Toulouse), 2000 v Bos (15)
Anderson, R. (Aberdeen), 1997 v Es, A, Se; 1998 v La (sub), Fi, Ei, I; 1999 v Es, Bel, G, Ei, Ni, CzR; 2000 v Bos, Es (15)
Anthony, M. (Celtic), 1997 v La (sub), Es (sub), Col (3)
Archdeacon, O. (Celtic), 1987 v WG (sub) (1)
Archibald, A. (Partick T), 1998 v Fi, Ei, Ni, I; 1999 v Li (5)
Archibald, S. (Aberdeen), 1980 v B, E (2), WG; (with Tottenham H), 1981 v D (5)

Bagen, D. (Kilmarnock), 1997 v Es, A (sub), Se (sub), Bl (4)
Bain, K. (Dundee), 1993 v P, I, Ma, P (4)
Baker, M. (St. Mirren), 1993 v F, M, E; 1994 v Ma, A; 1995 v Gr, M, F (sub), Sk (sub); 1996 v H (sub) (10)
Baltacha, S. S. (St Mirren), 2000 v Bos, Li (sub), F (sub) (3)
Bannon, E. J. P. (Hearts), 1979 v US; (with Chelsea), P, N (2); (with Dundee U), 1980 v Bel, WG, E (7)
Beattie, J. (St Mirren), 1992 v D, US, P, Y (4)
Beaumont, D. (Dundee U), 1985 v Ic (1)
Bell, D. (Aberdeen), 1981 v D; 1984 v Y (2)
Bernard, P. R. J. (Oldham Ath), 1992 v R (sub), D, Se (sub), US; 1993 v Sw, P, I, Ma, P, F, Bul, M, E; 1994 v I, Ma (15)
Bett, J. (Rangers), 1981 v Se, D; 1982 v Se, D, I, E (2) (7)
Black, E. (Aberdeen), 1983 v EG, Sw (2), Bel; 1985 v Ic, Sp (2), Ic (8)
Blair, A. (Coventry C), 1980 v E; 1981 v Se; (with Aston Villa), 1982 v Se, D, I (5)
Bollan, G. (Dundee U), 1992 v D, G (sub), US, P, Y; 1993 v Sw, P, I, P, F, Bul, M, E; 1994 v Sw; 1995 v Gr; (with Rangers) v Ru, Sm (17)
Bonar, P. (Raith R), 1997 v A, La, Es (sub), Se (4)
Booth, S. (Aberdeen), 1991 v R (sub), Bul (sub + 1), Pol, F (sub); 1992 v Sw, R, D, Se, US, P, Y; 1993 v Ma, P (14)
Bowes, M. J. (Dunfermline Ath), 1992 v D (sub) (1)
Bowman, D. (Hearts), 1985 v WG (sub) (1)
Boyack, S. (Rangers), 1997 v Se (1)
Boyd, K. (Kilmarnock), 2003 v Bel (sub) (1)
Boyd, T. (Motherwell), 1987 v WG, Ei (2), Bel; 1988 v Bel (5)
Brazil, A. (Hibernian), 1978 v W (1)
Brazil, A. (Ipswich T), 1979 v N; 1980 v Bel (2), E (2), WG; 1981 v Se; 1982 v Se (8)
Brebner, G. I. (Manchester U), 1997 v Col, CzR (sub), US (sub), P; 1998 v Bl, La, Fi, D; (with Reading), 1999 v Li, Es, Bel (2), CzR, G, Ei, Ni, CzR; (with Hibernian), 2000 v Bos (18)
Brough, J. (Hearts), 1981 v D (1)
Browne, P. (Raith R), 1997 v A (1)
Buchan, J. (Aberdeen), 1997 v Se, Col, CzR, P; 1998 v Bl, La, Fi; 1999 v Li, Es, Bel, CzR, G, Ei (13)
Burchill, M. (Celtic), 1998 v Fi, D (sub); 1999 v Li, Es (sub), Bel (2), CzR, Ei, Ni, CzR; 2000 v Bos, Es; 2001 v La, Bel, Pol (15)
Burke, A. (Kilmarnock), 1997 v Es, A, Bl (sub); 1998 v Ei (sub) (4)

Burley, G. E. (Ipswich T), 1977 v Cz, W, Sw; 1978 v Sw, Cz (5)
Burley, C. (Chelsea), 1992 v D; 1993 v Sw, P, I, P; 1994 v Sw, I (sub) (7)
Burns, H. (Rangers), 1985 v Sp, Ic (sub) (2)
Burns, T. (Celtic), 1977 v Cz, W, E; 1978 v Sw; 1982 v E (5)

Caldwell, G. (Newcastle U), 2000 v F, Ni, W; 2002 v Cro, Bel, La; 2003 v Is (sub), Ic, Gh, Bel, Ei, Ic, Li, A, G (15)
Caldwell, S. (Newcastle U), 2001 v La, Cro, Bel; 2002 v Cro (4)
Campbell, S. (Dundee), 1989 v N (sub), Y, F (3)
Campbell, S. P. (Leicester C), 1998 v Fi (sub), D, Ei, Ni (sub), I; 1999 v Li, Es, Bel (2), CzR, G, Ei, Ni, CzR (sub); 2000 v Bos (sub) (15)
Canero, P. (Kilmarnock), 2000 v F; 2001 v La (sub), Cro (sub), Bel, Pol; 2002 v La (sub); 2003 v D, Ni, Bel (sub), Ei, ic, Li, A, G (14)
Carey, L. A. (Bristol C), 1998 v D (1)
Casey, J. (Celtic), 1978 v W (1)
Christie, M. (Dundee), 1992 v D, P (sub), Y (3)
Clark, R. (Aberdeen), 1977 v Cz, W, Sw (3)
Clarke, S. (St Mirren), 1984 v Bel, EG, Y; 1985 v WG, Ic, Sp (2), Ic (8)
Cleland, A. (Dundee U), 1990 v F, N (2); 1991 v R, Sw, Bul; 1992 v Sw, R, G, Se (2) (11)
Collins, J. (Hibernian), 1988 v Bel, E; 1989 v N, Y, F; 1990 v Y, F, N (8)
Connolly, P. (Dundee U), 1991 v R (sub), Sw, Bul (3)
Connor, R. (Ayr U), 1981 v Se; 1982 v Se (2)
Cooper, D. (Clydebank), 1977 v Cz, W, Sw, E; (with Rangers), 1978 v Sw, Cz (6)
Cooper, N. (Aberdeen), 1982 v D, E (2); 1983 v Bel, EG, Sw (2); 1984 v Bel, EG, Y; 1985 v Ic, Sp, Ic (13)
Crabbe, S. (Hearts), 1990 v Y (sub), F (2)
Craig, M. (Aberdeen), 1998 v Bl, La (2)
Craig, T. (Newcastle U), 1977 v E (1)
Crainey, S. D. (Celtic), 2000 v F (sub); 2003 v Bel, Ei (sub), A, G (5)
Crainie, D. (Celtic), 1983 v Sw (sub) (1)
Crawford, S. (Raith R), 1994 v A, Eg, P, Bel; 1995 v Fi, Ru,Gr, Ru, Sm, M, F (sub), Sk (sub), Br (sub); 1996 v Gr, Fi (sub), H (1 + sub), Sp (sub), F (sub) (19)
Creaney, G. (Celtic), 1991 v Sw, Bul (2), Pol, F; 1992 v Sw, R, G (2), Se (2) (11)
Cummings, W. (Chelsea), 2000 v F, Ni; 2001 v La, Cro, Bel, Pol; 2002 v Cro, Bel (8)

Dailly, C. (Dundee U), 1991 v R; 1992 v US, R; 1993 v Sw, P, I, Ic, P, F, Bul, M, E; 1994 v Sw, I, Ma, A, Eg, P, Bel; 1995 v Fi, Ru, Gr, Ru, Sm, M, F, Sk, Br; 1996 v Fi, Sm, H (2), Sp, F (34)
Dalglish, P. (Newcastle U), 1999 v Es, Bel, CzR; (with Norwich C), 2000 v Es (sub), Bos, Li (sub) (6)
Dargo, C. (Raith R), 1998 v Fi, Ei, Ni (sub), I; 1999 v Es, Bel (1+sub), CzR (sub), G, Ni (sub) (10)
Davidson, C. (St Johnstone), 1997 v Se, Bl (2)
Davidson, H. N. (Dundee U), 2000 v Es (sub), Li, F (3)
Dawson, A. (Rangers), 1979 v P, N (2); 1980 v B (2), E (2), WG (8)
Deas, P. A. (St Johnstone), 1992 v D (sub); 1993 v Ma (2)
Dennis, S. (Raith R), 1992 v Sw (1)
Dickov, P. (Arsenal), 1992 v Y; 1993 v F, M, E (4)
Dodds, D. (Dundee U), 1978 v W (1)
Dods, D. (Hibernian), 1997 v La, Es, Se (2), Bl (5)
Doig, C. R. (Nottingham F), 2000 v Ni, W; 2001 v La, Cro, Pol; 2003 v D, Is, Ni, Ic, Gh, Bel, Ei (12)
Donald, G. S. (Hibernian), 1992 v US (sub), P, Y (sub) (3)
Donnelly, S. (Celtic), 1994 v Eg, P, Bel; 1995 v Fi, Gr (sub); 1996 v Gr (sub), Sm, H (2), Sp, F (11)
Dow, A. (Dundee), 1993 v Ma (sub), Ic; (with Chelsea) 1994 v I (3)
Duffy, J. (Dundee), 1987 v Ei (1)
Dowie, A. (Rangers), 2003 v D, Is (2)
Duff, S. (Dundee U), 2003 v Is, Ni (sub), Ic, Gh, Bel, Ei (sub) (6)
Durie, G. S. (Chelsea), 1987 v WG, Ei, Bel; 1988 v Bel (4)
Durrant, I. (Rangers), 1987 v WG, Ei, Bel; 1988 v E (4)
Doyle, J. (Partick Th), 1981 v D, I (sub) (2)

Easton, C. (Dundee U), 1997 v Col, US, CzR, P; 1998 v Bl, Fi, D, Ei, Ni, I; 1999 v Li, Es, Bel (1+sub); 2000 v Li, F; 2001 v La (sub), Cro, Bel; 2002 v Cro, Bel (21)
Elliot, B. (Celtic), 1998 v Ni; 1999 v Li (sub) (2)
Esson, R. (Aberdeen), 2000 v Li, Ni; 2001 v La, Cro, Bel, Pol; 2002 v Bel (7)

Ferguson, B. (Rangers), 1997 v Col (sub), US, CzR, P; 1998 v Bl, La, Fi, D (sub), Ei, Ni, I; 1999 v Bel (12)
Ferguson, D. (Rangers), 1987 v WG, Ei, Bel; 1988 v E; 1990 v Y (5)
Ferguson, D. (Dundee U), 1992 v D, G, Se (2); 1993 v Sw, I, Ma (7)
Ferguson, D. (Manchester U), 1992 v US, P (sub), Y; 1993 v Sw, Ma (5)
Ferguson, I. (Dundee), 1983 v EG (sub), Sw (sub); 1984 v Bel (sub), EG (4)
Ferguson, I. (Clyde), 1987 v WG (sub), Ei; (with St Mirren), Ei, Bel; 1988 v Bel; (with Rangers), E (sub) (6)
Ferguson, R. (Hamilton A), 1977 v E (1)
Findlay, W. (Hibernian), 1991 v R, Pol, Bul (2), Pol (5)
Fitzpatrick, A. (St Mirren), 1977 v W (sub), Sw (sub), E; 1978 v Sw, Cz (5)
Flannigan, C. (Clydebank), 1993 v Ic (sub) (1)
Fleck, R. (Rangers), 1987 v WG (sub), Ei, Bel; (with Norwich C), 1988 v E (2); 1989 v Y (6)
Fletcher, D. B. (Manchester U), 2003 v Ic (sub) (1)
Fowler, J. (Kilmarnock), 2002 v Cro (sub), Bel, La (3)
Fraser, S. T. (Luton T), 2000 v Ni (sub), W; 2001 v La, Cro (4)
Freedman, D. A. (Barnet), 1995 v Ru (sub + 1), Sm, M, F, Sk, Br; (with C Palace), 1996 v Sm (sub) (8)
Fridge, L. (St Mirren), 1989 v F; 1990 v Y (2)
Fullarton, J. (St. Mirren), 1993 v F, Bul; 1994 v Ma, A, Eg, P, Bel; 1995 v M, F, Sk, Br; 1996 v Gr, Fi, H (sub + 1), Sp (sub), F (17)
Fulton, M. (St Mirren), 1980 v Bel, WG, E; 1981 v Se, D (sub) (5)
Fulton, S. (Celtic), 1991 v R, Sw, Bul, Pol, F; 1992 v G (2) (7)

Gallacher, K. (Dundee U), 1987 v WG, Ei (2), Bel (sub); 1988 v E (2); 1990 v Y (7)
Gallacher, P. (Dundee U), 1999 v Ei, Ni, CzR; 2000 v Bos, Es, Bos, F (7)
Gallagher, P. (Blackburn R), 2003 v G (sub) (1)
Galloway, M. (Hearts), 1989 v F; (with Celtic), 1990 v N (2)
Gardiner, J. (Hibernian), 1993 v F (1)
Geddes, R. (Dundee), 1982 v Se, D, E (2); 1988 v E (5)
Gemmill, S. (Nottingham F), 1992 v Sw, R (sub), G (sub), Se (sub) (4)
Germaine, G. (WBA), 1997 v Se (1)
Gilles, R. (St Mirren), 1997 v A (1 + sub), La, Es (2), Se, Bl (7)
Gillespie, G. (Coventry C), 1979 v US; 1980 v E; 1981 v D; 1982 v Se, D, I (2), E (8)
Glass, S. (Aberdeen), 1995 v M, F, Sk, Br; 1996 v Gr, Fi, H, Sp; 1997 v A (2), Es (11)
Glover, L. (Nottingham F), 1988 v Bel (sub); 1989 v N; 1990 v Y (3)
Goram, A. (Oldham Ath), 1987 v Ei (1)
Gordon, C. (Hearts), 2003 v Is (sub), Gh (2)
Gough, C. R. (Dundee U), 1983 v EG, Sw, Bel; 1984 v Y (2) (5)
Graham, D. (Rangers), 1998 v Bl (sub), La (sub), Fi (sub), D, Ei (sub), Ni, I; 1999 v Li (8)
Grant, P. (Celtic), 1985 v WG, Ic, Sp; 1987 v WG, Ei (2), Bel; 1988 v Bel, E (2) (10)
Gray S. (Celtic), 1995 v F, Sk, Br; 1996 v Gr, H, Sp, F (7)
Gray, S. (Aberdeen), 1987 v WG (1)
Gunn, B. (Aberdeen), 1984 v EG, Y (2); 1985 v WG, Ic, Sp (2), Ic; 1990 v F (9)

Hagen, D. (Rangers), 1992 v D (sub), US (sub), P, Y; 1993 v Sw (sub), P, Ic, P (8)
Hammell, S. (Motherwell), 2001 v Pol (sub); 2002 v La; 2003 v Is, Ni, Gh, Bel (sub), Ei (7)

Hamilton, B. (St Mirren), 1989 v Y, F (sub); 1990 v F, N (4)
Hamilton, J. (Dundee) 1995 v Sm (sub), Br; 1996 v Fi (sub), Sm, H (sub), Sp (sub), F; 1997 v A, La, Es, Se; (with Hearts), Es, A, Se (14)
Handyside, P. (Grimsby T), 1993 v Ic (sub), Bul, M, E; 1995 v Ru; 1996 v Fi, Sm (7)
Hannah, D. (Dundee U), 1993 v F (sub), Bul, M; 1994 v A, Eg, P, Bel; 1995 v Fi, Ru (sub), Gr, Ru, M, F, Sk, Br; 1996 v Gr (16)
Harper, K. (Hibernian), 1995 v Ru (sub); 1996 v Fi; 1997 v A (2), La, Es, Se (7)
Hartford, R. A. (Manchester C), 1977 v Sw (1)
Hartley, P. (Millwall), 1997 v A (sub) (1)
Hegarty, P. (Dundee U), 1987 v WG, Bel; 1988 v E (2); 1990 v F, N (6)
Hendry, J. (Tottenham H), 1992 v D (sub) (1)
Hetherston, B. (St Mirren), 1997 v Es (sub) (1)
Hewitt, J. (Aberdeen), 1982 v I; 1983 v EG, Sw (2); 1984 v Bel, Y (sub) (6)
Hogg, G. (Manchester U), 1984 v Y; 1985 v WG, Ic, Sp (4)
Hood, G. (Ayr U), 1993 v F, E (sub); 1994 v A (3)
Horn, R. (Hearts), 1997 v US, CzR, P; 1998 v Bl, La, D (sub) (6)
Howie, S. (Cowdenbeath), 1993 v Ma, Ic, P; 1994 v Sw, I (5)
Hughes, R. D. (Bournemouth), 1999 v CzR, Ei, Ni, CzR; 2000 v Bos, Es; 2001 v La, Cro, Bel (9)
Hughes, S. (Rangers), 2002 v La; 2003 v D, Ic, Gh, Be, Ei (sub), Ic (sub), A (8)
Hunter, G. (Hibernian), 1987 v Ei (sub); 1988 v Bel, E (3)
Hunter, P. (East Fife), 1989 v N (sub), F (sub); 1990 v F (sub) (3)

James, K. F. (Falkirk), 1997 v Bl (1)
Jardine, I. (Kilmarnock), 1979 v US (1)
Jess, E. (Aberdeen), 1990 v F (sub), N (sub); 1991 v R, Sw, Bul (2), Pol, F; 1992 v Sw, R, G (2), Se (1 + 1 sub) (14)
Johnson, G. I. (Dundee U), 1992 v US, P, Y; 1993 v Sw, P, Ma (6)
Johnston, A. (Hearts), 1994 v Bel; 1995 v Ru, 1996 v Sp (3)
Johnston, F. (Falkirk), 1993 v Ic (1)
Johnston, M. (Partick Th), 1984 v EG (sub); (with Watford), Y (2) (3)
Jordan, A. J. (Bristol C), 2000 v Bos (sub), Li, F (3)
Jupp, D. A. (Fulham), 1995 v Fi, Ru (2), Sm, M, F, Sk, Br; 1997 v Se (9)

Kirkwood, D. (Hearts), 1990 v Y (1)
Kennedy, J. (Celtic), 2003 v Is (sub), Ni, Ic, Gh, Bel, Ei, Ic, Li, A, G (10)
Kerr, B. (Newcastle U), 2003 v D, Is, Ni, Ic, Gh, Bel, Ei, Ic, Li, A, G (11)
Kerr, M. (Kilmarnock), 2001 v Pol (sub) (1)
Kerr, S. (Celtic), 1993 v Bul, M, E; 1994 v Ma, A, Eg, P, Bel; 1995 v Fi, Gr (10)
Kyle, K. (Sunderland), 2001 v La (sub), Cro (sub), Pol (sub); 2003 v Ic, Ei, Ic, Li, G (8)

Lambert, P. (St Mirren), 1991 v R, Sw, Bul (2), Pol, F; 1992 v Sw, R, G (2), Se (11)
Langfield, J. (Dundee), 2000 v W; 2002 v Cro (2)
Lauchlan, J. (Kilmarnock), 1998 v Ei, Ni, I; 1999 v CzR, G, Ni, CzR; 2000 v Bos, Es, Bos, Li (11)
Lavety, B. (St. Mirren), 1993 v Ic, Bul (sub), M (sub), E; 1994 v Ma, A (sub), Eg (sub), Bel (sub); 1995 v Fi (sub) (9)
Lavin, G. (Watford), 1993 v F, Bul, M; 1994 v Ma, Eg, P, Bel (7)
Leighton, J. (Aberdeen), 1982 v I (1)
Levein, C. (Hearts), 1985 v Sp, Ic (2)
Liddell, A. M. (Barnsley), 1994 v Ma (sub); 1995 v Sm (sub), M (sub), F, Sk; 1996 v Gr, Fi, Sm, H (2), Sp, F (sub) (12)
Lindsey, J. (Motherwell), 1979 v US (1)
Locke, G. (Hearts), 1994 v Ma, A, Eg, P; 1995 v Fi; 1996 v Fi, H; 1997 v Es, A, Bl (10)
Love, G. (Hibernian), 1995 v Ru (1)

Lynch, S. (Celtic), 2003 v Is (sub), Ni (sub), Ic (sub), Gh (sub), Bel; (with Preston NE) Ei (sub), Li (sub), A (sub), G (9)

McAllister, G. (Leicester C), 1990 v N (1)
McAlpine, H. (Dundee U), 1983 v EG, Sw (2), Bel; 1984 v Bel (5)
McAnespie, K. (St Johnstone), 1998 v Fi (sub); 1999 v G (sub); 2000 v Ni, W (4)
McAuley, S. (St. Johnstone), 1993 v P (sub) (1)
McAvennie, F. (St Mirren), 1982 v I, E; 1985 v Is, Ei, R (5)
McBride, J. (Everton), 1981 v D (1)
McBride, J. P. (Celtic), 1998 v Ni (sub), I (sub) (2)
McCall, S. (Bradford C), 1988 v E; (with Everton), 1990 v F (2)
McCann, N. (Dundee), 1994 v A, Eg, P, Bel; 1995 v Fi, Gr (sub), Sm; 1996 v Fi, Sm (9)
McClair, B. (Celtic), 1984 v Bel (sub), EG, Y (1 + 1 sub); 1985 v WG, Ic, Sp, Ic (8)
McCluskey, G. (Celtic), 1979 v US, P; 1980 v Bel (2); 1982 v D, I (6)
McCluskey, S. (St Johnstone), 1997 v Es (2), A, Se, Col, US, CzR; 1998 v Bl, La, D, Ei (sub), Ni, I; 1999 v Li (14)
McCoist, A. (Rangers), 1984 v Bel (1)
McConnell, I. (Clyde), 1997 v A (sub) (1)
McCracken, D. (Dundee U), 2002 v La (1)
McCulloch, A. (Kilmarnock); 1981 v Se (1)
McCulloch, I. (Notts Co), 1982 v E (2)
McCulloch, L. (Motherwell), 1997 v La (sub), Es (1 + sub), Se (sub + 1), A (sub), Col (sub); 1998 v Bl (sub), Fi (sub), D, Ei, Ni; 1999 v CzR, G (14)
McCunnie, J. (Dundee U), 2001 v Pol; 2002 v Cro; 2003 v D, Is, Ni (5)
MacDonald, J. (Rangers), 1980 v WG (sub); 1981 v Se; 1982 v Se (sub), L, I (2), E (2 sub) (8)
McDonald, C. (Falkirk), 1995 v Fi (sub), Ru, M (sub), F (sub), Br (sub) (5)
McEwan, C. (Clyde), 1997 v Col, US (sub), CzR (sub), P; (with Raith R), 1998 v Bl, La, Fi, D, Ei, Ni, I; 1999 v Li, Es (sub), Bel (2), CzR, G (sub) (17)
McEwan, D. (Livingston), 2003 v Ni (sub), Gh (sub) (2)
McFadden, J. (Motherwell), 2003 v D (sub), Is, Ni, Gh, Ei (sub), Ic, Li (7)
McFarlane, D. (Hamilton A), 1997 v Col, US (sub), P (sub) (3)
McGarry, S. (St Mirren), 1997 v US, CzR, P (sub) (3)
McGarvey, F. (St Mirren), 1977 v E; 1978 v Cz; (with Celtic), 1982 v D (3)
McGarvey, S. (Manchester U), 1982 v E (sub); 1983 v Bel, Sw; 1984 v Bel (4)
McGhee, M. (Aberdeen), 1981 v D (1)
McGinnis, G. (Dundee U), 1985 v Sp (1)
McGregor, A. (Rangers), 2003 v D (sub), Is, Bel (sub), Ei (sub), A (sub) (5)
McGrillen, P. (Motherwell), 1994 v Sw (sub), I (2)
McGuire, D. (Aberdeen), 2002 v Bel, La (2)
McInally, J. (Dundee U), 1989 v F (1)
McKenzie, R. (Hearts), 1997 v Es, Bl (2)
McKimmie, S. (Aberdeen), 1985 v WG, Ic (2) (3)
McKinlay, T. (Dundee), 1984 v EG (sub); 1985 v WG, Ic, Sp (2), Ic (6)
McKinlay, W. (Dundee U), 1989 v N, Y (sub), F; 1990 v Y, F, N (6)
McKinnon, R. (Dundee U), 1991 v R, Pol (sub); 1992 v G (2), Se (2) (6)
McLaren, A, (Hearts), 1989 v F; 1990 v Y, N; 1991 v Sw, Bul, Po1, F; 1992 v R, G, Se (2) (11)
McLaren, A. (Dundee U), 1993 v I, Ma (sub); 1994 v Sw, I (sub) (4)
McLaughlin, B. (Celtic), 1995 v Ru, Sm, M, Sk (sub), Br (sub); 1996 v Gr (sub), Sm (sub), H (8)
McLaughlin, J. (Morton), 1981 v D; 1982 v Se, D, I, E (2); 1983 v EG, Sw (2), Bel (10)
McLean, S. (Rangers), 2003 v D (sub), Ni (sub), Gh (sub), Bel (sub) (4)
McLeish, A. (Aberdeen), 1978 v W; 1979 v US; 1980 v Bel, E (2); 1987 v Ei (6)
MacLeod, A. (Hibernian), 1979 v P, N (2) (3)
McLeod, J. (Dundee U), 1989 v N; 1990 v F (2)

MacLeod, M. (Dumbarton), 1979 v US; (with Celtic), P (sub), N (2); 1980 v Bel (5)
McManus, T. (Hibernian), 2001 v Bel (sub), Pol (sub); 2002 v Cro, Bel, La; 2003 v D (sub), Ni (sub), Ic, Gh, A, G (sub) (11)
McMillan, S. (Motherwell), 1997 v A (sub + sub), Se, Bl (4)
McNab, N. (Tottenham H), 1978 v W (1)
McNally, M. (Celtic), 1991 v Bul; 1993 v Ic (2)
McNamara, J. (Dunfermline Ath), 1994 v A, Bel; 1995 v Gr, Ru, Sm; 1996 v Gr, Fi; (with Celtic), Sm, H (2), Sp, F (12)
McNaughton, K. (Aberdeen), 2002 v La (sub) (1)
McNichol, J. (Brentford), 1979 v P, N (2); 1980 v Bel (2), WG, E (7)
McNiven, D. (Leeds U), 1977 v Cz, W (sub), Sw (sub) (3)
McNiven, S. A. (Oldham Ath), 1996 v Sm (sub) (1)
McParland, A. (Celtic), 2003 v Gh (sub) (1)
McPhee, S. (Port Vale), 2002 v La (sub) (1)
McPherson, D. (Rangers), 1984 v Bel; 1985 v Sp; (with Hearts), 1989 v N, Y (4)
McQuilken, J. (Celtic), 1993 v Bul, E (2)
McStay, P. (Celtic), 1983 v EG, Sw (2); 1984 v Y (2) (5)
McWhirter, N. (St Mirren), 1991 v Bul (sub) (1)
Main, A. (Dundee U), 1988 v E; 1989 v Y; 1990 v N (3)
Malcolm, R. (Rangers), 2001 v Pol (1)
Maloney, S. (Celtic), 2002 v Cro (sub), Bel (sub), La; 2003 v D, Is, Ni, Bel, Ei, Ic (sub), Li (sub), A (11)
Malpas, M. (Dundee U), 1983 v Bel, Sw (1+1 sub); 1984 v Bel, EG, Y (2); 1985 v Sp (8)
Marshall, S. R. (Arsenal), 1995 v Ru, Gr; 1996 v H, Sp, F (5)
Mason, G. R. (Manchester C), 1999 v Li (sub); (with Dunfermline Ath), 2002 v Bel (2)
Mathieson, D. (Queen of the South), 1997 v Col; 1998 v La; 1999 v G (sub) (3)
May, E. (Hibernian), 1989 v Y (sub), F (2)
Meldrum, C. (Kilmarnock), 1996 v F (sub); 1997 v A (2), La, Es, Se (6)
Melrose, J. (Partick Th), 1977 v Sw; 1979 v US, P, N (2); 1980 v Bel (sub), WG, E (8)
Miller, C. (Rangers), 1995 v Gr, Ru; 1996 v Gr, Sp, F; 1997 v A, La, Es (8)
Miller, J. (Aberdeen), 1987 v Ei (sub); 1988 v Bel; (with Celtic), E; 1989 v N, Y; 1990 v F, N (7)
Miller, K. (Hibernian), 2000 v F, Ni, W; (with Rangers), 2001 v Cro, Bel; 2002 v Cro, Bel (7)
Miller, W. (Aberdeen), 1978 v Sw, Cz (2)
Miller, W. (Hibernian), 1991 v R, Sw, Bul, Pol, F; 1992 v R, G (sub) (7)
Milne, K. (Hearts), 2000 v F (1)
Milne, R. (Dundee U), 1982 v Se (sub); 1984 v Bel, EG (3)
Money, I. C. (St Mirren), 1987 v Ei; 1988 v Bel; 1989 v N (3)
Montgomery, N. A. (Sheffield U), 2003 v A (sub) (1)
Muir, L. (Hibernian), 1977 v Cz (sub) (1)
Murray, H. (St Mirren), 2000 v F (sub), Ni (sub), W (sub) (3)
Murray, I. (Hibernian), 2001 v Bel (sub), Pol; 2002 v Cro, Bel, La; 2003 v D, Ic, Gh, Bel, Ic, Li, G (12)
Murray, N. (Rangers), 1993 v P (sub), Ma, Ic, P; 1994 v Sw, I; 1995 v Fi, Ru, Gr, Sm; 1996 v Gr (sub), Fi, Sm, H (2), F (16)
Murray, R. (Bournemouth), 1993 v Ic (sub) (1)

Narey, D. (Dundee U), 1977 v Cz, Sw; 1978 v Sw, Cz (4)
Naysmith, G. (Hearts), 1997 v La, Es (1 + sub), Se, A, Col, US, CzR, P; 1998 v La, D; 1999 v Es, Bel (2), CzR, G, Ei, CzR; 2000 v Bos, Es, Bos, Li (22)
Neilson, R. (Hearts), 2000 v Ni (1)
Nevin, P. (Chelsea), 1985 v WG, Ic, Sp (2), Ic (5)
Nicholas, C. (Celtic), 1981 v Se; 1982 v Se; 1983 v EG, Sw, Bel; (with Arsenal), 1984 v Y (6)
Nicholson, B. (Rangers), 1999 v G, Ni, CzR (sub); 2000 v Bos (sub), Es, Bos, Li (7)
Nicol, S. (Ayr U), 1981 v Se; 1982 v Se, D; (with Liverpool), I (2), E (2); 1983 v EG, Sw (2), Bel; 1984 v Bel, EG, Y (14)
Nisbet, S. (Rangers), 1989 v N, Y, F; 1990 v Y, F (5)
Noble, D. J. (West Ham U), 2003 v A (sub) (1)

Notman, A. M. (Manchester U), 1999 v Li (sub), Es, Bel (sub+sub); 2000 v Li, F (sub), Ni, W; 2001 v La, Cro (10)

O'Brien, B. (Blackburn R), 1999 v Ei (sub), Ni (sub), CzR (sub); 2000 v Bos (sub); (with Livingston), 2003 v Is (sub), Gh (sub) (6)
O'Connor, G. (Hibernian), 2003 v D (1)
O'Donnell, P. (Motherwell), 1992 v Sw (sub), R, D, G (2), Se (1 + 1 sub); 1993 v P (8)
O'Neil, B. (Celtic), 1992 v D, G, Se (2); 1993 v Sw, P, I (7)
O'Neil, J. (Dundee U), 1991 v Bul (sub) (1)
O'Neill, M. (Clyde), 1995 v Ru (sub), F, Sk, Br; 1997 v Se (sub), Bl (sub) (6)
Orr, N. (Morton), 1978 v W (sub); 1979 v US, P, N (2); 1980 v Bel, E (7)

Parker, K. (St Johnstone), 2001 v Pol (sub) (1)
Parlane, D. (Rangers), 1977 v W (1)
Paterson, C. (Hibernian), 1981 v Se; 1982 v I (2)
Paterson, J. (Dundee U), 1997 v Col, US, CzR; 1999 v Bel (sub+sub); 2000 v Es, Bos, Li; 2002 v Cro (sub) (9)
Payne, G. (Dundee U), 1978 v Sw, Cz, W (3)
Peacock, L. A. (Carlisle U), 1997 v Bl (1)
Pearson, S. (Motherwell), 2003 v Is, Ni, Bel (sub), Ei, A, G (6)
Pressley, S. (Rangers), 1993 v Ic, F, Bul, M, E; 1994 v Sw, I, M, A, Eg, P, Bel; 1995 v Fi; (with Coventry C), Ru (2), Sm, M, F, Sk, Br; (with Dundee U), 1996 v Gr, Sm, H (2), Sp, F (26)
Provan, D. (Kilmarnock), 1977 v Cz (sub) (1)

Rae, A. (Millwall), 1991 v Bul (sub + 1), F (sub); 1992 v Sw, R, G (sub), Se (2) (8)
Rae, G. (Dundee), 1999 v Ei (sub), Ni, CzR; 2000 v Bos, Es, Bos (6)
Redford, I. (Rangers), 1981 v Se (sub); 1982 v Se, D, I (2), E (6)
Reid, B. (Rangers), 1991 v F; 1992 v D, US, P (4)
Reid, C. (Hibernian), 1993 v Sw, P, I (3)
Reid, M. (Celtic), 1982 v E; 1984 v Y (2)
Reid, R. (St Mirren), 1977 v W, Sw, E (3)
Renicks, S. (Hamilton A), 1997 v Bl (1)
Rice, B. (Hibernian), 1985 v WG (1)
Richardson, L. (St Mirren), 1980 v WG, E (sub) (2)
Ritchie, A. (Morton), 1980 v Bel (1)
Ritchie, P. R. (Hearts), 1996 v H; 1997 v A (2), La, Es (2), Se (7)
Robertson, A. (Rangers) 1991 v F (1)
Robertson, C. (Rangers), 1977 v E (sub) (1)
Robertson, D. (Aberdeen), 1987 v Ei (sub); 1988 v E (2); 1989 v N, Y; 1990 v Y, N (7)
Robertson, H. (Aberdeen), 1994 v Eg; 1995 v Fi (2)
Robertson, J. (Hearts), 1985 v WG, Ic (sub) (2)
Robertson, L. (Rangers), 1993 v F, M (sub), E (sub) (3)
Robertson, S. (St Johnstone), 1998 v Fi, Ni (2)
Roddie, A. (Aberdeen), 1992 v US, P; 1993 v Sw (sub), P, Ic (5)
Ross, T. W. (Arsenal), 1977 v W (1)
Rowson, D. (Aberdeen), 1997 v La, Es, Se (2), Bl (5)
Russell, R. (Rangers), 1978 v W; 1980 v Bel; 1984 v Y (3)

Salton, D. B. (Luton T), 1992 v D, US, P, Y; 1993 v Sw, I (6)
Scott, P. (St Johnstone), 1994 v A (sub), Eg (sub), P, Bel (4)
Scrimgour, D. (St Mirren), 1997 v US, CzR; 1998 v D (3)
Seaton, A. (Falkirk), 1998 v Bl (sub) (1)
Severin, S. D. (Hearts), 2000 v Es, Bos, Li (sub), F, Ni, W; 2001 v La, Bel; 2002 v Cro, Bel (10)
Shannon, R. (Dundee), 1987 v WG, Ei (2), Bel; 1988 v Bel, E (2) (7)
Sharp, G. (Everton), 1982 v E (1)
Sharp, R. (Dunfermline Ath), 1990 v N (sub); 1991 v R, Sw, Bul (4)
Sheerin, P. (Southampton), 1996 v Sm (1)
Shields, G. (Rangers), 1997 v A, La (2)
Simmons, S. (Hearts), 2003 v Gh (sub) (1)
Simpson, N. (Aberdeen), 1982 v I (2), E; 1983 v EG, Sw (2), Bel; 1984 v Bel, EG, Y; 1985 v Sp (11)
Sinclair, G. (Dumbarton), 1977 v E (1)

Skilling, M. (Kilmarnock), 1993 v Ic (sub); 1994 v I (2)
Smith, B. M. (Celtic), 1992 v G (2), US, P, Y (5)
Smith, G. (Rangers), 1978 v W (1)
Smith, H. G. (Hearts), 1987 v WG, Bel (2)
Sneddon, A. (Celtic), 1979 v US (1)
Soutar, D. (Dundee), 2003 v D, Ni, Ic, Bel, Ei, Ic, Li, A, G (9)
Speedie, D. (Chelsea), 1985 v Sp (1)
Spencer, J. (Rangers), 1991 v Sw (sub), F; 1992 v Sw (3)
Stanton, P. (Hibernian), 1977 v Cz (1)
Stark, W. (Aberdeen), 1985 v Ic (1)
Stephen, R. (Dundee), 1983 v Bel (sub) (1)
Stevens, G. (Motherwell), 1977 v E (1)
Stewart, C. (Kilmarnock), 2002 v La (1)
Stewart, J. (Kilmarnock), 1978 v Sw, Cz; (with Middlesbrough), 1979 v P (3)
Stewart, M. J. (Manchester U), 2000 v Ni; 2001 v La, Cro, Bel, Pol; 2002 v La; 2003 v D, Is, Ni, Ei (sub), Ic, Li, A (13)
Stewart, R. (Dundee U), 1979 v P, N (2); (with West Ham U), 1980 v Bel (2), E (2), WG; 1981 v D; 1982 v I (2), E (12)
Stillie, D. (Aberdeen), 1995 v Ru (2), Sm, M, F, Sk, Br; 1996 v Gr, Fi, Sm, H (2), Sp, F (14)
Strachan, G. D. (Aberdeen), 1980 v Bel (1)
Strachan, G. D. (Coventry C), 1998 v D, Ei; 1999 v Li, Es, Bel (2); 2000 v Li (7)
Sturrock, P. (Dundee U), 1977 v Cz, W, Sw, E; 1978 v Sw, Cz; 1982 v Se, I, E (9)
Sweeney, S. (Clydebank), 1991 v R, Sw (sub), Bul (2), Pol; 1992 v Sw, R (7)

Tarrant, N. K. (Aston Villa), 1999 v Ni (sub); 2000 v Es (sub), Bos (sub), Li, Ni (sub) (5)
Teale, G. (Clydebank), 1997 v La (sub), Es, Bl; (with Ayr U), 1999 v CzR (sub), G (sub), Ei (sub) (6)
Telfer, P. (Luton T), 1993 v Ma, P; 1994 v Sw (3)
Thomas, K. (Hearts), 1993 v F (sub), Bul, M, E; 1994 v Sw, Ma; 1995 v Gr; 1997 v A (8)
Thompson, S. (Dundee U), 1997 v US, CzR, P; 1998 v Bl, La; 1999 v G (sub), Ei, Ni, CzR; 2000 v Bos, Es, Bos (12)
Thomson, W. (Partick Th), 1977 v E (sub); 1978 v W; (with St Mirren), 1979 v US, N (2); 1980 v Bel (2), E (2), WG (10)
Tolmie, J. (Morton), 1980 v Bel (sub) (1)
Tortolano, J. (Hibernian), 1987 v WG, Ei (2)
Tweed, S. (Hibernian), 1993 v Ic; 1994 v Sw, I (3)

Wales, G. (Hearts), 2000 v F (1)
Walker, A. (Celtic), 1988 v Bel (1)
Wallace, I. (Coventry C), 1978 v Sw (1)
Walsh, C. (Nottingham F), 1984 v EG, Sw (2), Bel; 1984 v EG (5)
Wark, J. (Ipswich T), 1977 v Cz, W, Sw; 1978 v W; 1979 v P; 1980 v E (2), WG (8)
Watson, A. (Aberdeen), 1981 v Se, D; 1982 v D, I (sub) (4)
Watson, K. (Rangers), 1977 v E; 1978 v Sw (sub) (2)
Watt, M. (Aberdeen), 1991 v R, Sw, Bul (2), Pol, F; 1992 v Sw, R, G (2), Se (2) (12)
Webster, A. (Hearts), 2003 v Ic, Li (2)
Whiteford, A. (St Johnstone), 1997 v US (1)
Whyte, D. (Celtic), 1987 v Ei (2), Bel; 1988 v E (2); 1989 v N, Y; 1990 v Y, N (9)
Wilkie, L. (Dundee), 2000 v Bos, F, Ni, W; 2001 v La, Cro (6)
Will, J. A. (Arsenal), 1992 v D (sub), Y; 1993 v Ic (sub) (3)
Williams, G. (Nottingham F), 2002 v Bel (sub); 2003 v Ic, Ei, Ic, Li (5)
Wilson, S. (Rangers), 1999 v Es, Bel (2), G, Ei, CzR; 2000 v Bos (7)
Wilson, T. (St Mirren), 1983 v Sw (sub) (1)
Wilson, T. (Nottingham F), 1988 v E; 1989 v N, Y; 1990 v F (4)
Winnie, D. (St Mirren), 1988 v Bel (1)
Wright, P. (Aberdeen), 1989 v Y, F; (with QPR), 1990 v Y (sub) (3)
Wright, S. (Aberdeen), 1991 v Bul, Pol, F; 1992 v Sw, G (2), Se (2); 1993 v Sw, P, I, Ma; 1994 v I, Ma (14)
Wright, T. (Oldham Ath), 1987 v Bel (sub) (1)

Young, Darren. (Aberdeen), 1997 v Es (sub), Se, Col, CzR (sub), P; 1998 v La (sub); 1999 v CzR (sub), G (sub) (8)
Young, Derek. (Aberdeen), 2000 v W; 2001 v Cro (sub), Bel (sub), Pol; 2002 v Cro (5)

WALES

Aizlewood, M. (Luton T), 1979 v E; 1981 v Ho (2)

Baddeley, L. M. (Cardiff C), 1996 v Mol (sub), G (sub) (2)
Balcombe, S. (Leeds U), 1982 v F (sub) (1)
Barnhouse, D. J. (Swansea), 1995 v Mol; 1996 v Mol, Sm (3)
Bater, P. T. (Bristol R), 1977 v E, S (2)
Bellamy, C. D. (Norwich C), 1996 v Sm (sub); 1997 v Sm, T, Bel; 1998 v T, Bel, I; 1999 v I (8)
Birchall, A. S. (Arsenal), 2003 v Fi, I, Az (3)
Bird, A. (Cardiff C), 1993 v Cy (sub); 1994 v Cy (sub); 1995 v Mol, Ge (sub), Bul; 1996 v G (sub) (6)
Blackmore, C. (Manchester U), 1984 v N, Bul, Y (3)
Blake, N. (Cardiff C), 1991 v Pol (sub); 1993 v Cy, Bel, RCS; 1994 v RCS (5)
Blaney, S. D. (West Ham U), 1997 v Sm, Ho, T (3)
Bodin, P. (Cardiff C), 1983 v Y (1)
Bowen, J. P. (Swansea C), 1993 v Cy, Bel (2); 1994 v RCS, R (sub) (5)
Bowen, M. (Tottenham H), 1983 v N; 1984 v Bul, Y (3)
Boyle, T. (C Palace), 1982 v F (1)
Brace, D. P. (Wrexham), 1995 v Ge, Bul (2); 1997 v Sm Ho; 1998 v T (6)
Brough, M. (Notts Co), 2003 v Az (sub) (1)
Brown, J. R. (Gillingham), 2003 v Fi, I, Az (3)
Byrne, M. T. (Bolton W), 2003 v Az (sub) (1)

Cegielski, W. (Wrexham), 1977 v E (sub), S (2)
Chapple, S. R. (Swansea C), 1992 v R; 1993 v Cy, Bel (2), RCS; 1994 v RCS; Bul (2) (8)
Charles, J. M. (Swansea C), 1979 v E; 1981 v Ho (2)
Clark, J. (Manchester U), 1978 v S; (with Derby Co), 1979 v E (2)
Coates, J. S. (Swansea C), 1996 v Mol, G; 1997 v Ho, T (sub); 1998 v T (sub) (5)
Coleman, C. (Swansea C), 1990 v Pol; 1991 v E, Pol (3)
Collins, J. M. (Cardiff C), 2003 v I (sub), Az (sub+1) (3)
Coyne, D. (Tranmere R), 1992 v R; 1994 v Cy (sub), R; 1995 v Mol, Ge, Bul (2) (7)
Curtis, A. T. (Swansea C), 1977 v E (1)

Davies, A. (Manchester U), 1982 v F (2), Ho; 1983 v N, Y, Bul (6)
Davies, D. (Barry T), 1999 v D (sub) (1)
Davies, G. M. (Hereford U), 1993 v Bel, RCS; 1995 v Mol (sub), Ge, Bul (2); (with C Palace), 1996 v Mol (7)
Davies, I. C. (Norwich C), 1978 v S (sub) (1)
Davies, S. (Peterborough U), 1999 v D, Bl, Sw, I, D; (with Tottenham H), 2000 v S; 2001 v Bl, N, Pol, Arm (10)
Day, R. (Manchester C), 2000 v S (sub), Ni; 2001 v Uk, Pol, Uk; 2002 v Arm, N, Bl; 2003 v Fi, I, Az; (with Mansfield T), Az (10)
Deacy, N. (PSV Eindhoven), 1977 v S (1)
De-Vulgt, L. S. (Swansea C), 2002 v Arm (sub), Bl (2)
Dibble, A. (Cardiff C), 1983 v Bul; 1984 v N, Bul (3)
Doyle, S. C. (Preston NE), 1979 v E (sub); (with Huddersfield T), 1984 v N (2)
Dwyer, P. J. (Cardiff C), 1979 v E (1)

Earnshaw, R. (Cardiff C), 1999 v P (sub), I, D; 2000 v S, Ni; 2001 v Bl (sub), N, Pol (2), Uk (10)
Ebdon, M. (Everton), 1990 v Pol; 1991 v E (2)
Edwards, C. N. H. (Swansea C), 1996 v G; 1997 v Sm, Ho (2), T, Bel; 1998 v T (7)
Edwards, R. I. (Chester C), 1977 v S; 1978 v W (2)

Edwards, R. W. (Bristol C), 1991 v Pol; 1992 v R; 1993 v Cy, Bel (2), RCS; 1994 v RCS, Cy, R; 1995 v Ge, Bul; 1996 v Mol, G (13)
Evans, A. (Bristol R), 1977 v E (1)
Evans, K. (Leeds U), 1999 v I (sub), D; (with Cardiff C), 2001 v N (sub), Pol (sub) (4)
Evans, P. S. (Shrewsbury T), 1996 v G (1)
Evans, S. J. (Crystal Palace), 2001 v Bl, Arm (2)
Evans, T. (Cardiff C), 1995 v Bul (sub); 1996 v Mol, G (3)

Folland, R. W. (Oxford U), 2000 v Ni (sub) (1)
Foster, M. G. (Tranmere R), 1993 v RCS (1)
Fowler, L. A. (Coventry C), 2003 v I (1)
Freestone, R. (Chelsea), 1990 v Pol (1)

Gabbidon, D. L. (WBA), 1999 v D, P, Sw, I (sub), D; 2000 v Bl, Sw, S, Ni; (with Cardiff C), 2001 v N, Pol, Arm, Uk, Pol, Uk; 2002 v Arm, N (17)
Gale, D. (Swansea C), 1983 v Bul; 1984 v N (sub) (2)
Gall, K. A. (Bristol R), 2002 v N (sub), Bl (sub); 2003 v Fi (sub), Az (4)
Gibson, N. D. (Tranmere R), 1999 v D (sub), Bl (sub), P; 2000 v S (sub), Ni; (with Sheffield W), 2001 v Uk, Pol, Uk; 2002 v Arm, N, Bl (11)
Giggs, R. (Manchester U), 1991 v Pol (1)
Giles, D. C. (Cardiff C), 1977 v S; 1978 v S; (with Swansea C), 1981 v Ho; (with C Palace), 1983 v Y (4)
Giles, P. (Cardiff C), 1982 v F (2), Ho (3)
Graham, D. (Manchester U), 1991 v E (1)
Green, R. M. (Wolverhampton W), 1998 v I; 1999 v I, D, Bl, Sw, I, D; 2000 v Bl, S, Ni; 2001 v Bl, N, Pol, Arm, Uk, Pol (16)
Griffith, C. (Cardiff C), 1990 v Pol (1)
Griffiths, C. (Shrewsbury T), 1991 v Pol (sub) (1)

Hall, G. D. (Chelsea), 1990 v Pol (1)
Hartson, J. (Luton T), 1994 v Cy, R; 1995 v Mol, Ge, Bul; (with Arsenal), 1996 v G, Sm; 1997 v Sm, Ho (9)
Haworth, S. O. (Cardiff C), 1997 v Ho, T, Bel; (with Coventry C), 1998 v T, Bel; I; 1999 v I, D; (with Wigan Ath), Bl, Sw; 2000 v Bl, Sw (12)
Hillier, I. M. (Tottenham H), 2001 v Uk (sub), Pol (sub), Uk; (with Luton T), 2002 v Arm, N (5)
Hodges, G. (Wimbledon), 1983 v Y (sub), Bul (sub); 1984 v N, Bul, Y (5)
Holden, A. (Chester C), 1984 v Y (sub) (1)
Holloway, C. D. (Exeter C), 1999 v P, D (2)
Hopkins, J. (Fulham), 1982 v F (sub), Ho; 1983 v N, Y, Bul (5)
Hopkins, S. A. (Wrexham), 1999 v P (sub) (1)
Huggins, D. S. (Bristol C), 1996 v Sm (1)
Hughes, D. R. (Southampton), 1994 v R (1)
Hughes, R. D. (Aston Villa), 1996 v Sm; 1997 v Sm (sub), Ho (2), T, Bel; 1998 v T, Bel, I; 1999 v I, Sw, I; (with Shrewsbury T), 2000 v Sw (13)
Hughes, I. (Bury), 1992 v R; 1993 v Cy, Bel (sub), RCS; 1994 v Cy, R; 1995 v Mol, Ge, Bul; 1996 v Mol (sub), G (11)
Hughes, L. M. (Manchester U), 1983 v N, Y; 1984 v N, Bul, Y (5)
Hughes, W. (WBA), 1977 v E, S; 1978 v S (3)

Jackett, K. (Watford), 1981 v Ho; 1982 v F (2)
James, R. M. (Swansea C), 1977 v E, S; 1978 v S (3)
Jarman, L. (Cardiff C), 1996 v Sm; 1997 v Sm, Ho (2), Bel; 1998 v T, Bel; 1999 v I, P; 2000 v Bl (10)
Jeanne, L. C. (QPR), 1999 v P (sub), Sw, I: 2000 v Bl, Sw, S, Ni; 2001 v Bl (8)
Jelleyman, G. A. (Peterborough U), 1999 v D (sub) (1)
Jenkins, L. D. (Swansea C), 1998 v T (sub); 2000 v Bl, Sw, S, Ni; 2001 v N, Pol, Arm, Uk (9)
Jenkins, S. R. (Swansea C), 1993 v Cy (sub), Bel (2)
Jones, E. P. (Blackpool), 2000 v Ni (sub) (1)
Jones, F. (Wrexham), 1981 v Ho (1)
Jones, J. A. (Swansea C); 2001 v Pol, Uk; 2002 v N (sub) (3)
Jones, L. (Cardiff C), 1982 v F (2), Ho (3)
Jones, M. G. (Leeds U), 1998 v Bel; 1999 v I, D, Bl, Sw, I; 2000 v Sw (7)
Jones, P. L. (Liverpool), 1992 v R; 1993 v Cy, Bel (2), RCS; 1994 v RCS (sub), Cy, R; 1995 v Mol, Ge; 1996 v Mol, G (12)
Jones, R. (Sheffield W), 1994 v R; 1995 v Bul (2) (3)
Jones, V. (Bristol R), 1979 v E; 1981 v Ho (2)

Kendall, L. M. (Crystal Palace), 2001 v N, Pol (2)
Kendall, M. (Tottenham H), 1978 v S (1)
Kenworthy, J. R. (Tranmere R), 1994 v Cy; 1995 v Mol, Bul (3)
Knott, G. R. (Tottenham H), 1996 v Sm (1)

Law, B. J. (QPR), 1990 v Pol; 1991 v E (2)
Letheran, G. (Leeds U), 1977 v E, S (2)
Lewis, D. (Swansea C), 1982 v F (2), Ho; 1983 v N, Y, Bul; 1984 v N, Bu1, Y (9)
Lewis, J. (Cardiff C), 1983 v N (1)
Llewellyn, C. M. (Norwich C), 1998 v T (sub), Bel (sub), I; 1999 v I, D, Bl, I; 2000 v Bl, Sw, S; 2001 v N, Pol, Arm, Uk (14)
Loveridge, J. (Swansea C), 1982 v Ho; 1983 v N, Bul (3)
Low, J. D. (Bristol R), 1999 v P; (with Cardiff C), 2002 v Arm (sub), N (sub), Bl (1)
Lowndes, S. R. (Newport Co), 1979 v E; 1981 v Ho; (with Millwall), 1984 v Bul, Y (4)

McCarthy, A. J. (QPR), 1994 v RCS, Cy, R (3)
Maddy, P. (Cardiff C), 1982 v Ho; 1983 v N (sub) (2)
Margetson, M. W. (Manchester C), 1992 v R; 1993 v Cy, Bel (2), RCS; 1994 v RCS, Cy (7)
Martin, A. P. (Crystal Palace), 1999 v D (1)
Marustik, C. (Swansea C), 1982 v F (2); 1983 v Y, Bul; 1984 v N, Bul, Y (7)
Maxwell, L. J. (Liverpool), 1999 v Sw (sub), I; 2000 v Sw (sub), S, Ni; 2001 v Bl, Pol, Arm, Uk, Pol, Uk; (with Cardiff C), 2002 v Arm, N, Bl (sub) (14)
Meaker, M. J. (QPR), 1994 v RCS (sub), R (sub) (2)
Melville, A. K. (Swansea C), 1990 v Pol; (with Oxford U), 1991 v E (2)
Micallef, C. (Cardiff C), 1982 v F, Ho; 1983 v N (3)
Morgan, A. M. (Tranmere R), 1995 v Mol, Bul; 1996 v Mol, G (4)
Moss, D. M. (Shrewsbury T), 2003 v Fi, I, Az (2) (4)
Mountain, P. D. (Cardiff C), 1997 v Ho, T (2)
Mumford, A. O. (Swansea C), 2003 v Fi, I, Az (2) (4)

Nardiello, D. (Coventry C), 1978 v S (1)
Neilson, A. B. (Newcastle U), 1993 v Cy, Bel (2), RCS; 1994 v RCS, Cy, R (7)
Nicholas, P. (C Palace), 1978 v S; 1979 v E; (with Arsenal), 1982 v F (3)
Nogan, K. (Luton T), 1990 v Pol; 1991 v E (2)
Nogan, L. (Oxford U) 1991 v E (1)

Oster, J. M. (Grimsby T), 1997 v Sm (sub), Ho (sub), T, Bel; (with Everton), 1998 v T, Bel, I; 1999 v I, Sw (9)
Owen, G. (Wrexham), 1991 v E (sub), Pol; 1992 v R; 1993 v Cy, Bel (2); 1994 v Cy, R (8)

Page, R. J. (Watford), 1995 v Mol, Ge, Bul; 1996 v Mol (4)
Partridge, D. W. (West Ham U), 1997 v T (1)
Pascoe, C. (Swansea C), 1983 v Bul (sub); 1984 v N (sub), Bul, Y (4)
Pejic, S. M. (Wrexham), 2003 v Fi, I, Az (3)
Pembridge, M. (Luton T), 1991 v Pol (1)
Perry, J. (Cardiff C), 1990 v Pol; 1991 v E, Pol (3)
Peters, M. (Manchester C), 1992 v R; (with Norwich C), 1993 v Cy, RCS (3)
Phillips, D. (Plymouth Arg), 1984 v N, Bul, Y (3)
Phillips, G. R. (Swansea C), 2001 v Uk (sub); 2002 v Arm (sub), Bl (3)
Phillips, L. (Swansea C), 1979 v E; (with Charlton Ath), 1983 v N (2)
Pipe, D. R. (Coventry C), 2003 v As (2) (2)
Pontin, K. (Cardiff C), 1978 v S (1)
Powell, L. (Southampton), 1991 v Pol (sub); 1992 v R (sub); 1993 v Bel (sub); 1994 v RCS (4)
Price, J. J. (Swansea C), 1998 v I (sub); 1999 v I (sub), D, Bl, P; 2000 v Bl, Sw (7)
Price, M. D. (Everton), 2001 v Uk. Pol (sub), Uk; (with Hull C), 2002 v Arm, N, Bl; 2003 v Fi, I, Az (2) (10)
Price, P. (Luton T), 1981 v Ho (1)
Pugh, D. (Doncaster R), 1982 v F (2) (2)
Pugh, S. (Wrexham), 1993 v Bel (sub + sub) (2)

Ramasut, M. W. T. (Bristol R), 1997 v Ho, Bel; 1998 v T, I (4)
Ratcliffe, K. (Everton), 1981 v Ho; 1982 v F (2)
Ready, K. (QPR), 1992 v R; 1993 v Bel (2); 1994 v RCS, Cy (5)
Rees, A. (Birmingham C), 1984 v N (1)
Rees, J. (Luton T), 1990 v Pol; 1991 v E, Pol (3)
Rees, M. R. (Millwall), 2003 v Fi (sub), Az (2)
Roberts, A. (QPR), 1991 v E, Pol (2)
Roberts, C. J. (Cardiff C), 1999 v D (sub) (1)
Roberts, G. (Hull C), 1983 v Bul (1)
Roberts, G. W. (Liverpool), 1997 v Ho, T, Bel; 1998 v T, I; 1999 v I, D, Bl, P; (with Panionios) D; (with Tranmere R), 2000 v Sw (11)
Roberts, J. G. (Wrexham), 1977 v E (1)
Roberts, N. W. (Wrexham), 1999 v I (sub), P; 2000 v Sw (sub) (3)
Roberts, P. (Porthmadog), 1997 v Ho (sub) (1)
Roberts, S. I. (Swansea C), 1999 v Sw, I (sub), D; 2000 v Bl (sub), Ni; 2001 v Bl (sub), N, Pol, Arm, Uk; 2002 v Arm, N, Bl (13)
Roberts, S. W. (Wrexham), 2000 v S; 2001 v Bl, N (sub) (3)
Robinson, C. P. (Wolverhampton W), 1996 v Sm; 1997 v Sm, Ho (2), T, Bel (6)
Robinson, J. (Brighton & HA), 1992 v R; (with Charlton Ath), 1993 v Bel; 1994 v RCS, Cy, R (5)
Rowlands, A. J. R. (Manchester C), 1996 v Sm; 1997 v Sm, Ho (1 + sub), T (sub) (5)
Rush, I. (Liverpool), 1981 v Ho; 1982 v F (2)

Savage, R. W. (Crewe Alex), 1995 v Bul; 1996 v Mol, G (3)
Sayer, P. A. (Cardiff C), 1977 v E, S (2)
Searle, D. (Cardiff C), 1991 v Pol (sub); 1992 v R; 1993 v Cy, Bel (2), RCS; 1994 v RCS (6)
Slatter, D. (Chelsea), 2000 v Sw (sub), S; 2001 v Bl, N (sub), Pol (sub), Uk (sub) (6)
Slatter, N. (Bristol R), 1983 v N, Y, Bul; 1984 v N, Bul, Y (6)
Speed, G. A. (Leeds U), 1990 v Pol; 1991 v E, Pol (3)
Stevenson, N. (Swansea C), 1982 v F, Ho (2)
Stevenson, W. B. (Leeds U), 1977 v E, S; 1978 v S (3)
Stock, B. B. (Bournemouth), 2003 v Fi (sub), I (sub) (2)
Symons, K. (Portsmouth), 1991 v E, Pol (2)

Taylor, G. K. (Bristol R), 1995 v Ge, Bul (2); 1996 v Mol (4)
Thomas, D. J. (Watford), 1998 v T, Bel (2)
Thomas, J. A. (Blackburn R), 1996 v Sm; 1997 v Sm, Ho (2), T, Bel; 1998 v Bel; 1999 v D, Bl, P; 2000 v Bl (sub); 2001 v Bl, N, Pol, Arm, Uk, Pol, Uk; 2002 v Arm, N, Bl (21)
Thomas, Martin R. (Bristol R), 1979 v E; 1981 v Ho (2)
Thomas, Mickey R. (Wrexham), 1977 v E; 1978 v S (2)
Thomas, S. (Wrexham), 2001 v Pol, Uk; 2002 v Arm, N, Bl (5)
Thomas, D. G. (Leeds U), 1977 v E; 1979 v E; 1984 v N (3)
Tibbott, L. (Ipswich T), 1977 v E, S (2)
Tipton, M. J. (Oldham Ath), 1998 v I (sub); 1999 v P, Sw (sub); 2000 v Ni; 2001 v Arm (sub), Uk (sub) (6)
Tolley, J. C. (Shrewsbury T), 2001 v Pol, Uk (sub); 2003 v Fi, I, Az (2) (6)
Twiddy, C. (Plymouth Arg), 1995 v Mol, Ge; 1996 v G (sub) (3)

Vaughan, D. O. (Crewe Alex), 2003 v Fi, Az (2)
Vaughan, N. (Newport Co), 1982 v F, Ho (2)
Valentine, R. D. (Everton), 2001 v Pol, Uk; 2002 v Arm, N, Bl; (with Darlington), 2003 v Fi, I, Az (8)

Walsh, D. (Wrexham), 2000 v S, Ni; 2001 v Bl, Arm, Uk; 2002 v Arm, N, Bl (8)
Walsh, I. P. (C Palace), 1979 v E; (with Swansea C), 1983 v Bul (2)
Walton, M. (Norwich C.), 1991 v Pol (sub) (1)
Ward, D. (Notts Co), 1996 v Mol, G (2)
Weston, R. D. (Arsenal), 2001 v Bl, N, Pol; (with Cardiff C), Arm (4)
Whitfield, P. M. (Wrexham), 2003 v Az (1)
Williams, A. P. (Southampton), 1998 v Bel, I; 1999 v I, D (sub), Bl, Sw, I; 2000 v Bl, Sw (9)
Williams, A. S. (Blackburn R), 1996 v Sm; 1997 v Sm, Ho, Bel; 1998 v T, Bel, I; 1999 v I, D, Bl, P, Sw, I, D; 2000 v Bl, Sw (16)
Williams, D. (Bristol R), 1983 v Y (1)
Williams, D. I. L. (Liverpool), 1998 v I; 1999 v D, Bl; (with Wrexham) I, D; 2000 v Bl, S, Ni; 2001 v Bl (9)
Williams, E. (Caernarfon T), 1997 v Ho (sub), T (sub) (2)
Williams, G. (Bristol R), 1983 v Y, Bul (2)
Williams, G. A. (Crystal Palace), 2003 v I (sub), Az (2)
Williams, M. (Manchester U), 2001 v Pol (sub), Uk (sub); 2002 v Bl (sub); 2003 v Fi, I, Az (sub) (6)
Williams, S. J. (Wrexham), 1995 v Mol, Ge, Bul (2) (4)
Wilmot, R. (Arsenal), 1982 v F (2), Ho; 1983 v N, Y; 1984 v Y (6)
Wright, A. A. (Oxford U), 1998 v Bel, I (sub); 1999 v D (sub) (3)

Young, S. (Cardiff C), 1996 v Sm; 1997 v Sm, Ho (2), Bel (sub) (5)

NORTHERN IRELAND

Bailie, N. (Linfield), 1990 v Is; 1994 v R (sub) (2)
Baird, C. P. (Southampton), 2002 v G; 2003 v S, Sp, Uk, Fi, Gr (6)
Beatty, S. (Chelsea), 1990 v Is; (with Linfield), 1994 v R (2)
Black, J. (Tottenham H), 2003 v Uk (sub) (1)
Black, K. T. (Luton T), 1990 v Is (1)
Black, R. Z. (Morecambe), 2002 v G (1)
Blackledge, G. (Portadown), 1978 v Ei (1)
Blayney, A. (Southampton), 2003 v Fi (sub) (1)
Boyle, W. S. (Leeds U), 1998 v Sw (sub), S (sub); 2001 v CzR (sub), Bul (1+sub), CzR; 2002 v Ma (7)
Braniff, K. R. (Millwall), 2002 v G; 2003 v S (sub), Sp (sub), Fi, Arm (sub), Gr, Sp (7)
Brotherston, N. (Blackburn R), 1978 v Ei (sub) (1)
Browne, G. (Manchester C), 2003 v S, Sp, Uk, Fi (sub), Sp (5)
Buchanan, W. B. (Bolton W), 2002 v G (sub); 2003 v Uk (sub) (2)
Burns, L. (Port Vale), 1998 v Sw, S, Ei; 1999 v T, Fi, Mol, G, Mol, Ei; 2000 v F, T, G, Fi (13)

Campbell, S. (Ballymena U), 2003 v Sp (sub) (1)
Capaldi, A. C. (Birmingham C), 2002 v D (sub), Ic, Ma, G; 2003 v S, Sp, Uk, Fi, Arm, Gr; (with Plymouth Arg), Sp (11)
Carlisle, W. T. (Crystal Palace), 2000 v Fi (sub); 2001 v Ma, Ic, Bul (1+sub), CzR; 2002 v D, Ic, Ma (9)
Carroll, R. E. (Wigan Ath), 1998 v S, Ei; 1999 v T, Fi, Mol, G, Mol, Ei; 2000 v T, G, Fi (11)
Carson, S. (Rangers), 2000 v Ma; (wirh Dundee U), 2002 v D (sub) (2)
Clarke, L. (Peterborough U), 2003 v Sp (sub) (1)
Clarke, R. D. J. (Portadown), 1999 v Ei (sub), S; 2000 v F (sub), S, W (sub) (5)
Clingan, S. G. (Wolverhampton W), 2003 v Arm (sub) (1)
Close, B. (Middlesbrough), 2002 v Ic, Ma (sub), G; 2003 v S, Sp, Uk, Arm, Sp (8)
Clyde, M. G. (Wolverhampton W), 2002 v G; 2003 v S, Sp, Uk, Fi (5)
Connell, T. E. (Coleraine), 1978 v Ei (sub) (1)
Coote, A. (Norwich C), 1998 v Sw (sub), S, Ei; 1999 v T, Fi,Mol, G, Mol, Ei; 2000 v F, T, G (12)
Convery, J. (Celtic), 2000 v S, W; 2001 v D, Ic (4)

Devine, D. (Omagh T), 1994 v R (1)
Devine, J. (Glentoran), 1990 v Is (1)
Dickson, H. (Wigan Ath). 2002 v Ma (1)
Dolan, J. (Millwall), 2000 v Fi, Ma, S; 2001 v Ma, D, Ic (6)
Donaghy, M. M. (Larne), 1978 v Ei (1)
Dowie, I. (Luton T), 1990 v Is (1)

Duff, S. (Cheltenham T), 2003 v Sp (1)

Elliott, S. (Glentoran), 1999 v Fi (sub), Ei, S (sub) (3)

Feeney, L. (Linfield), 1998 v Ei (sub); 1999 v T, Fi, Mol; (with Rangers), G (sub), Ei, S; 2000 v Fi (8)
Feeney, W. (Bournemouth), 2002 v D, Ic (sub); 2003 v Fi, Arm, Gr (5)
Ferguson, M. (Glentoran), 2000 v T (sub), Ma (sub) (2)
Fitzgerald, D. (Rangers), 1998 v Sw, S; 1999 v T (sub), Fi (4)
Friars, S. M. (Liverpool), 1998 v Sw, S, Ei; (with Ipswich T), 1999 v T, Fi, Mol, G, Mol; 2000 v F, T, G, Ma, S, W; 2001 v Ma, D, Ic, CzR, Bul (2), CzR (21)

Gillespie, K. R. (Manchester U), 1994 v R (1)
Glendinning, M. (Bangor), 1994 v R (1)
Graham, G. L. (Crystal Palace), 1999 v S; 2000 v F, T, G, Fi (5)
Graham, R. S. (QPR), 1999 v Fi (sub), Mol, Ei (sub); 2000 v F (sub), T (sub), G (sub), Fi (sub), Ma, S, W; 2001 v Ma, D, CzR (sub), Bul (sub), CzR (sub) (15)
Gray, P. (Luton T), 1990 v Is (sub) (1)
Griffin, D. J. (St Johnstone), 1998 v S (sub), Ei; 1999 v T, Fi, G, Mol, Ei, S; 2000 v F, T (10)

Hamilton, G. (Blackburn R), 2000 v Ma (sub), S, W (sub); 2001 v Ma, D, Ic, CzR, Bul (2), CzR; (with Portadown), 2002 v Ic, Ma (12)
Hamilton, W. R. (Linfield), 1978 v Ei (1)
Harkin, M. P. (Wycombe W), Ma (sub), S (sub), W; 2001 v Ma (sub), D (sub), Ic, CzR, Bul (sub+1) (9)
Harvey, J. (Arsenal), 1978 v Ei (1)
Hawe, S. (Blackburn R), 2001 v Cz (1+sub) (2)
Hayes, T. (Luton T), 1978 v Ei (1)
Healy, D. J. (Manchester U), 1999 v Mol (sub), G (sub), Ei (sub), S; 2000 v F (sub), T, G, Fi (8)
Herron, C. J. (QPR), 2003 v Arm, Gr (2)
Holmes, S. (Manchester C), Ma, S, W; 2001 v Ma, D, Ic, CzR, Bul (2), CzR; (with Wrexham), 2002 v D, Ic, Ma (13)
Hughes, M. A. (Tottenham H), 2003 v Sp (sub), Uk (sub), Fi, Arm, Gr, Sp (6)
Hughes, M. E. (Manchester C), 1990 v Is (sub)
Hunter, M. (Glentoran), 2002 v G (sub) (1)

Ingham, M. (Sunderland), 2001 v CzR, Bul (2), CzR (4)

Johnson, D. M. (Blackburn R), 1998 v Sw, S, Ei; 1999 v T, Fi, G, Mol, Ei; 2000 v F, T, G (11)
Johnston, B. (Cliftonville), 1978 v Ei (1)

Kee, P. V. (Oxford U), 1990 v Is (1)
Kelly, D. (Derry C), 2000 v Ma, W; 2001 v Ma, Ic (sub), CzR, Bul (2), CzR; 2002 v D, Ic, Ma (11)
Kelly, N. (Oldham Ath), 1990 v Is (sub) (1)
Kirk, A. (Hearts), 1999 v S; 2000 v Ma, S, W; 2001 v Ma, D, Ic (sub); 2002 v D, Ic (9)

Lennon, N. F. (Manchester C), 1990 v Is; (with Crewe Alex), 1994 v R (2)
Lyttle, G. (Celtic), 1998 v Sw, S; (with Peterborough U), 1999 v T (sub), Mol (2), S; 2000 v G, Fi (8)

Magee, J. (Bangor), 1994 v R (sub) (1)
Magilton, J. (Liverpool), 1990 v Is (1)
Matthews, N. P. (Blackpool), 1990 v Is (1)
McAreavey, P. (Swindon T), 2000 v Ma, S; 2001 v Ma, D; 2002 v D, Ic (sub), Ma (sub) (7)
McBride, J. (Glentoran), 1994 v R (sub) (1)
McCallion, E. (Coleraine), 1998 v Sw (sub) (1)
McCann, G. S. (West Ham U), 2000 v S (sub), W; 2001 v D (sub), Ic, CzR, Bul (2), CzR; 2002 v D, Ic, Ma (11)
McCann, P. (Portadown), 2003 v Sp (1)
McCann, R. (Rangers), 2002 v G (sub); (with Linfield), 2003 v S (sub) (2)
McCartney, G. (Sunderland), 2001 v D, CzR, Bul (2); 2002 v D (5)
McCourt, P. J. (Rochdale), 2002 v G; 2003 v S (sub), Sp, Uk, Fi (sub), Arm (sub), Gr (sub) (6)
McCoy, R. K. (Coleraine), 1990 v Is (1)
McCreery, D. (Manchester U), 1978 v Ei (1)
McFlynn, T. M. (QPR), 2000 v Ma (sub), W (sub); 2001 v Ma (sub), CzR (sub), Bul (sub+sub), CzR; (with Woking), 2002 v D (sub), Ic (sub); (with Margate), G; 2003 v S (sub), Sp (sub), Fi (sub), Arm, Gr (sub), Sp (sub) (16)
McEvilly, L. (Rochdale), 2003 v S, Sp, Uk, Fi (sub), Arm, Gr (sub) (6)
McGibbon, P. C. G. (Manchester U), 1994 v R (1)
McGlinchey, B. (Manchester C), 1998 v Sw, S, Ei; (with Port Vale), 1999 v T, Fi, Mol, G, Mol, Ei, S; (with Gillingham), 2000 v F, G, T, Fi (14)
McIlroy, T. (Linfield), 1994 v R (sub) (1)
McKnight, P. (Rangers), 1998 v Sw; 1999 v T (sub), Mol (sub) (3)
McMahon, G. J. (Tottenham H),1994 v R (sub) (1)
McVeigh, A. (Ayr U), 2002 v G (sub) (1)
McVeigh, P. F. (Tottenham H), 1998 v S (sub), Ei; 1999 v T, Mol, G, Mol, Ei; 2000 v F, T (sub), G (sub), Fi (11)
Melaugh, G. M. (Aston Villa), 2002 v G; 2003 v S, Sp, Uk, Fi, Arm, Gr, Sp (8)
Millar, W. P. (Port Vale), 1990 v Is (1)
Miskelly, D. T. (Oldham Ath), 2000 v F, Ma, S, W; 2001 v Ma, D, Ic; 2002 v D, Ic, Ma (10)
Moreland, V. (Glentoran), 1978 v Ei (sub) (1)
Morgan, M, P. T. (Preston NE), 1999 v S (1)
Morris, E. J. (WBA), 2002 v G; (with Glentoran), 2003 v S, Sp, Uk, Fi, Arm, Gr, Sp (8)
Morrison, O. (Sheffield W), 2001 v Bul (sub); 2002 v Ma (sub); 2003, S, Fi; (with Sheffield U) v Arm, Gr, Sp (7)
Morrow, A. (Northampton T), 2001 v D (sub) (1)
Mulryne, P. P. (Manchester U), Sw, S, Ei; (with Norwich C), 1999 v G, Mol (5)
Murray, W. (Linfield), 1978 v Ei (sub) (1)

Nicholl, J. M. (Manchester U), 1978 v Ei (1)
Nixon, C. (Glentoran), 2000 v Fi (sub) (1)

O'Hara, G. (Leeds U), 1994 v R (1)
O'Neill, M. A. M. (Hibernian), 1994 v R (1)
O'Neill, J. P. (Leicester C), 1978 v Ei (1)

Patterson, D. J. (Crystal Palace), 1994 v R (1)

Quinn, S. J. (Blackpool), 1994 v R (1)

Robinson, S. (Tottenham H), 1994 v R (1)

Simms, G. (Hartlepool U), 2001 v Bul (2), CzR; 2002 v D, Ic, Ma, G; 2003 v S, Sp, Uk, Fi, Arm, Gr, Sp (14)
Skates, G. (Blackburn R), 2000 v Ma; 2001 v Ic (sub), CzR (2) (4)
Sloan, T. (Ballymena U), 1978 v Ei (1)

Taylor, M. S. (Fulham), 1998 v Sw (1)
Toner, C. (Tottenham H), 2000 v Ma (sub), S (sub), W; 2001 v D, Ic, CzR, Bul (2), CzR; 2002 v D, Ic, Ma; (with Leyton Orient), 2003 v S, Sp, Uk, Fi, Gr (17)

Waterman, D. G. (Portsmouth), 1998 v Sw, S, Ei; 1999 v T, Fi, Mol, G, Mol, Ei, S (sub); 2000 v F, T, G, Fi (14)
Wells, D. P. (Barry T), 1999 v S (1)
Whitley, Jeff (Manchester C), 1998 v Sw, S, Ei; 1999 v T, Fi, Mol, G, Ei, S; 2000 v F, G, T, Ma, S, W; 2001 v Ma, Ic (17)

FA SCHOOLS & YOUTH GAMES 2002–03

ENGLAND UNDER-20

Garry, Hoyte, Spicer, Small, Thomas (Arsenal); Myhill, Bewers, Hylton, Cooke S (Aston Villa); Carter (Birmingham C); Cole, Evans (Chelsea); O'Hanlon, Clarke (Everton); Leacock, Doherty (Fulham); Allaway, Simon Johnson (Leeds U); Otsemobor, Welsh (Liverpool); Fox, Mooniaruck (Manchester U); Davies, Dove (Middlesbrough); Chopra, Offiong (Newcastle U); Clark (Sunderland); Howard (Southampton); Bowditch, Ricketts, Burch (Tottenham H); Johnson G (West Ham U); Clare (Stockport Co); O'Neil (Portsmouth); Ashton (Crewe Alex); Austin (Barnsley); Lonergan (Preston NE), Davenport (Coventry C), Tonge (Sheffield U), Carruthers (Northampton T), Morgan (Wimbledon), Tyson (Reading), Bloomfield (Ipswich T), Duncan (QPR), Lee, McNamee (Watford).

23 Oct
Germany 1
England 2 *(Carter 1, O'Neil 48)*
(at Dessau).
England: Myhill; Bewers (Austin 46), Hylton, Carter (Howard 85), Clare (O'Hanlon 46), Garry, Chopra, O'Neil, Ashton, Cooke S (Fox 30), Thomas (Offiong 46).

27 Nov
England 3 *(Chopra 17, 62, Carter 44)*
Italy 5
(at Sunderland).
England: Lonergan (Allaway 46); Otsemobor, Hylton (Austin), Fox (Clark 75), Davenport, Garry, Chopra, O'Neil, Ashton (Offiong 52), Carter, Tonge (Thomas 68).

12 Dec
England 0
Switzerland 2
(at West Ham).
England: Lonergan (Lee 72); Hoyte (Hylton 74), Carruthers, Bowditch, Johnson G, Clarke, Thomas, O'Neil (Howard 66), Cole (Ricketts 46), Carter (Tonge 46), Morgan.

6 Feb
England 2 *(Tyson 9, 62)*
Germany 1
(at Reading).
England: Lonergan (Burch 72); Hoyte (O'Hanlon 73), Hylton, Bowditch (Fox 46), Leacock, Garry, Chopra, Welsh, Tyson (Mooniaruck 6), Carter, Howard (Cooke S 46).

19 Mar
Switzerland 1
England 1 *(Cole 25)*
(at Sion).
England: Burch (Evans 46); Bewers (Bowditch 41), Carruthers, Fox, Leacock, Davies, Dove (Bloomfield 1), Welsh, Cole, Chopra, Howard (Mooniaruck 61).

21 May
Italy 3
England 0
(at Lucca).
England: Burch (Lee 46); Otsemobor (Austin 46), Carruthers, Fox, Clare, O'Hanlon (Hylton 46), Dove (Spicer 55), Mooniaruck, Thomas, Howard, Doherty.

11 June
Portugal 3
England 0
(at Nimes).
England: Burch; Otsemobor, Carruthers, Fox, Hylton (Bowditch), Offiong, Thomas, Carter, Howard, Duncan (Small), Doherty (McNamee).

13 June
Argentina 8
England 0
(at Toulon).
England: Burch; Otsemobor, Carruthers, Fox, Hylton, Offiong (Spicer 63), Bowditch, Thomas (Simon Johnson 35), Howard (Dove 56), Duncan, McNamee.

15 June
Turkey 1
England 0
(at Toulon).
England: Burch; Otsemobor, Carruthers, Fox, Hylton, Offiong (Spicer), Bowditch, Thomas (Simon Johnson), Howard (Dove), Duncan, McNamee.

19 June
Japan 1
England 0
(at La Seyne).
England: Lonergan; Otsemobor, Carruthers, Carter, O'Hanlon (Fox), Dove (Mooniaruck), Howard, Doherty, Simon Johnson (Thomas), Spicer, Small.

ENGLAND UNDER-19

Hoyte, Garry, Pennant, Thomas, Bentley (Arsenal); Cooke S, Ridgewell, Whittingham (Aston Villa); Carter (Birmingham C); Watt, Donnelly (Blackburn R); Sam (Charlton Ath); Cole, Pidgeley (Chelsea); Schumacher, Rooney, Moogan A (Everton); Doherty, Leacock (Fulham); Kilgallon (Leeds U); Welsh, Otsemobor (Liverpool); Croft, Proffitt (Manchester C); Steele, Johnson E, Jones (Manchester U); Downing, Davies (Middlesbrough); Jenas, Chopra, Gardner (Newcastle U); Clark, Brown (Sunderland); Bowditch, McKie (Tottenham H); Johnson G (West Ham U); Grant, Camp, Mills (Derby Co); O'Neil (Portsmouth); Ashton (Crewe Alex); Bloomfield, Hogg (Ipswich T); Routledge (Crystal Palace); McNamee, Hand (Watford); Wright (Leicester C); Samba (Millwall); Young (Reading); Forrest (Bradford C); Taylor (Tranmere R); Reo-Coker (Wimbledon).

22 July+
Germany 3
England 3 *(Ashton 8, Thomas 28, Cole 74)*
(at Baerum).
England: Grant; Hoyte (Otsemobor 77), Garry, Jenas, Johnson G, Clark, Pennant, O'Neil, Ashton (Cole 70), Thomas (Chopra 72), Welsh.

24 July+
Belgium 1
England 1 *(Ashton 75)*
(at Kongsvinger).
England: Grant; Hoyte, Garry (Carter 80), Jenas, Johnson G, Clark, Pennant (Thomas 76), O'Neil, Cole (Ashton 67), Chopra, Bowditch.

26 July+
Republic of Ireland 3
England 2 *(Carter 11, Ashton 44)*
(at Honefoss).
England: Grant; Garry, Jenas, Johnson G, Clark (Otsemobor 75), Ashton, Cooke S, Thomas (Pennant 76), Chopra (Cole 77), Welsh, Carter.

18 Sept
Hungary 1
England 3 *(Doherty 43, Bentley 61, Watt 89)*
(at Budapest).
England: Steele (Camp 46); Hoyte, McKie (Whittingham 46), Bowditch, Johnson G (Mills 64), Ridgewell, Croft (Watt 64), Bloomfield (Jones 46), Johnson E, Bentley, Doherty (Brown 52).

10 Oct
England 2 *(Johnson E 53, Ridgewell 56)*
Yugoslavia 2
(at Kidderminster).
England: Steele (Camp 46); Welsh, Bentley, Johnson G (Kilgallon 67), Ridgewell, Hoyte, Downing (McNamee 46), Rooney (Johnson E 46), Bowditch (Schumacher 46), Routledge, Whittingham.

3 Nov+
England 3 *(Johnson E 1, own goal 16, Watt 83)*
Macedonia 0
(at Kidderminster).
England: Steele; Hoyte, McKie, Donnelly, Mills, Ridgewell, Croft (Whittingham 80), Welsh, Johnson E (Wright 80), Bentley, McNamee (Watt 70).

5 Nov+
England 9 *(Johnson E 1, Croft 18, 89, Bentley 20, 27, Ridgewell 29, Schumacher 52 (pen), Watt 54, Wright 88)*
Moldova 0
(at Rushden).
England: Steele; Hoyte, Donnelly, Mills, Ridgewell (Kilgallon 53), Croft, Welsh (Schumacher 46), Johnson E (Wright 85), Bentley, Watt, Whittingham.

7 Nov+
England 4 *(Donnelly 35, 36, 43, 53)*
Romania 0
(at Northampton).
England: Camp; Hoyte, McKie, Donnelly (Gardner 67), Mills (Wright 46), Ridgewell, Croft, Welsh, Johnson E (McNamee 80), Bentley, Watt.

24 Apr
Germany 3
England 2 *(Wright 40, 62)*
(at Saarbrucken).
England: Pidgeley (Young 46); Hoyte, McKie, Schumacher (Hand 46), Leacock (Forrest 76), Hogg, Samba (Taylor 46), Bowditch (Reo-Coker 57), Wright, Bentley (Moogan A 68), McNamee (Sam 84).

19 May+
Republic of Ireland 0
England 1 *(Donnelly 72)*
(at Dublin).
England: Steele; Hoyte, Whittingham, Welsh, Davies, Ridgewell, Routledge, Donnelly, Wright, Croft, Downing (McKie 90).

21 May+
Slovenia 0
England 3 *(Donnelly 18, 52, Wright 55)*
(at Dublin).
England: Steele; Hoyte (Taylor 72), Whittingham, Wright (Proffitt 62), Welsh, Davies, Ridgewell, Routledge, Donnelly, Downing, Schumacher.

23 May+
Switzerland 0
England 1 *(Wright 21)*
(at Drogheda).
England: Camp; Hoyte, Welsh, Ridgewell, Routledge (Watt 46), Donnelly, Wright, Downing, Mills, Schumacher, McKie.

ENGLAND UNDER-18

Small, Artry, Kilkenny (Arsenal); Grant (Aston Villa); Sadler, Luckett (Birmingham C); Sankofa, Long (Charlton Ath); Tillen (Chelsea); Brown (Everton); Doherty (Fulham); Carson (Leeds U); Raven, Smyth (Liverpool); Proffitt, Croft (Manchester C); Eagles, Eckersley (Manchester U); Turnbull, Peacock (Middlesbrough); Gardner, McDermott, Guy (Newcastle U); Dodds, Collins (Sunderland); Malcolm (Tottenham H); Cole M, Ferdinand A (West Ham U); Butcher, O'Grady (Leicester C); Young (Reading); Biggins, Groves (Nottingham F); Borrowdale (Crystal Palace); Hogg (Ipswich T); Samba (Millwall); Wilson (Crewe Alex); Henderson (Norwich C); Francis (Bradford C); Roma (Sheffield U).

13 Nov
France 3
England 0
(at Limoges).
England: Turnbull; Small, Dodds, Artry, Collins, Grant, Malcolm, Butcher, O'Grady, Eagles, Cole M.

14 Nov
Tunisia 0
England 4 *(Doherty 3, Proffitt 14, Samba 83, McDermott 85)*
(at Tunis).
England: Young (Carson 89); Biggins, Borrowdale, Gardner, Hogg, Sankofa, Samba, McDermott (Brown 46), Proffitt, Long (Groves 58), Doherty (Guy 43).

25 Jan#
Burkina Faso 2
England 3 *(Proffitt 21, Eckersley 25, Raven 90)*
(at Port Said).
England: Turnbull; Biggins, Eckersley (Sankofa 89), Gardner, Raven, Hogg, Brown, Croft, Proffitt (Smyth 63), Long, Doherty (Guy 86).

27 Jan#
Mali 1
England 1 *(Proffitt 47)*
(at Ismailia).
England: Young; Biggins, Eckersley, Gardner, Raven, Hogg, Croft (Sankofa 87), Proffitt (Doherty 80), Long, Groves, Smyth (Guy 65).

29 Jan#
Egypt 0
England 1 *(Guy 31)*
(at Ismailia).
England: Turnbull; Gardner, Raven, Hogg, Brown (McDermott 74), Croft (Smyth 82), Proffitt, Dodds, Groves, Guy, Sankofa.

1 Feb#
Nigeria 0
England 0
(at Ismailia).
England: Young; Biggins, Gardner, Raven, Doherty (Proffitt 46), McDermott (Long 46), Dodds, Groves, Guy (Croft 72), Sankofa, Smyth.

12 Mar
Switzerland 0
England 0
(at Lugano).
England: Carson (Young 46); Sankofa, Sadler, Gardner, Raven, Hogg (Collins 46), Samba (Wilson 46), Eagles, Guy, Long (Kilkenny 46), Smyth.

5 June
Sweden 1
England 2 *(Guy 4, Samba 48)*
(at Inatel).
England: Turnbull; Gardner, Henderson, Collins, Francis, Roma (Groves 46), Samba, Guy (Peacock 63), Proffitt (Kilkenny 46), Long (Ferdinand A 46), Tillen (Luckett 74).

6 June
Portugal 0
England 0
(at Inatel).
England: Carson; Gardner, Henderson, Collins, Ferdinand A, Kilkenny (Tillen 46), Francis, Luckett, Samba (Peacock 71), Guy, Long (Groves 66).

8 June
Spain 0
England 2 *(Henderson 8, Guy 63)*
(at Lisbon).
England: Turnbull (Carson 46); Tillen, Henderson (Wilson 80), Collins, Ferdinand A (Francis 46), Peacock (Samba 70), Kilkenny, Roma, Luckett, Groves, Guy.

ENGLAND UNDER-17

O'Hara, Jordan, Smith R (Arsenal); Bridges, Moore L, Nix (Aston Villa}; Anyon (Blackburn R); Gillan (Bolton W); Smith D, Pettigrew (Chelsea); Fontaine (Fulham); Lennon, Milner (Leeds U); Heaton, Jones (Manchester U); McMahon, Morrison, Taylor A (Middlesbrough); Taylor S, Webster (Newcastle U); Cranie (Southampton); Alnwick, Leadbitter, Smith D (Sunderland); Ifil (Tottenham H); Cohen, Noble (West Ham U); Ashikodi (Millwall); Bowditch (Ipswich T); Campbell, Rifat (Reading); Chapman, Fisher (Watford); Doyle, Holmes, Huddlestone (Derby Co); Forte, Ross (Sheffield U); Giddings (Coventry C); Jarvis (Norwich C); Martin (Wimbledon); O'Grady (Leicester C).

8 July
England 2 (Moore L 17, 38)
Italy 2
(at Oxford).
England: Jordan; Ifil, Gillen, Huddlestone, McMahon, Taylor S, Leadbitter (Doyle 69), Moore L (Bowditch 55), Forte (Smith R 66), O'Hara, Lennon.

11 July
England 2 *(Bowditch 49, 79)*
Czech Republic 0
(at Birmingham).
England: Martin; Ifil, Taylor S (McMahon 46), Milner, Leadbitter, Giddings, Taylor A, O'Hara (Huddlestone 68), Doyle, Bowditch, Smith R (Moore L 56).

14 July
England 1 *(Milner 8)*
Brazil 1
(at Oxford).
England: Martin; Ifil, Gillen (O'Hara 49), Huddlestone (Doyle 75), McMahon, Taylor S, Milner, Leadbitter, Moore L (Bowditch 70), Giddings, Lennon.

30 July**
Faeroes 0
England 4 *(Nix 41, Ross 53, Fisher 61, Smith D (Sunderland) 70)*
(at Alvakara).
England: Anyon; Smith D (Chelsea), Cohen, Campbell (Smith D (Sunderland) 69), Jones, Ashikodi, Chapman (Nix 41), Fisher (Jarvis 69), Pettigrew (Bridges 56), Ross, Webster (Noble 56).

31 July**
Sweden 3
England 5 *(Jarvis 20, 21, 37, 38, Fontaine 52)*
(at Kvarnvallen).
England: Alnwick; Bridges, Noble (Ross 41), Fontaine, Campbell (Cohen 56), Nix, Fisher (Chapman 66), Jarvis, Pettigrew (Smith D (Chelsea) 56), Smith D (Sunderland), Webster (Jones 61).

2 Aug**
Norway 1
England 2 *(Noble 19, Jones 78)*
(at Bjorknasvallen).
England: Anyon; Smith D (Chelsea), Noble, Cohen, Fontaine, Jones, Ashikodi, Nix, Jarvis (Campbell 59), Pettigrew, Ross (Webster 56).

3 Aug**
Iceland 0
England 1 *(own goal 89)*
(at Skogsvallen).
England: Alnwick; Bridges, Noble, Fontaine, Campbell (Jones 65), Chapman (Cohen 80), Fisher (Nix 60), Jarvis, Ross, Smith D (Sunderland), Webster.

12 Sept
USA 2
England 1
(at Gaeta).
England: Jordan; Ifil, Smith D (Sunderland), Taylor S, Lennon, Leadbitter (O'Hara 55), Moore L (Jarvis 41), Milner, Forte (Smith R 62), Fontaine, Ross (Huddlestone 50).

13 Sept
Yugoslavia 0
England 3
(at Gaeta)
England: Martin; Huddlestone, McMahon, Taylor S, Leadbitter (Smith D (Sunderland) 75), Milner (Lennon 47) (Ifil 68), O'Hara, Ross, Gillen, Jarvis (Forte 55), Smith R.

15 Sept
Russia 2
England 0
(at Formia).
England: Martin (Jordan 41); Smith D (Sunderland), Huddlestone (Leadbitter 41), McMahon, Lennon, Milner, Fontaine (Taylor S 57), O'Hara (Ifil 53), Ross, Jarvis, Smith R (Forte 40).

11 Dec
England 2 *(Huddlestone 29, Jarvis 66)*
France 0
(at Scunthorpe).
England: Heaton (Martin 41); Ifil, Taylor A (Giddings 41), Huddlestone (Lennon 49), Taylor S, Rifat (McMahon 46), Bowditch (Forte 55), Morrison, Jarvis (O'Grady 68), Leadbitter, Milner (Ross 54).

19 Feb
Greece 0
England 1
(at Drama).
England: Heaton (Anyon 60); Cranie, Giddings, Taylor S (Rifat 46), Lennon (Bowditch 16), Jarvis, O'Hara (Leadbitter 46), Holmes (Moore L 46), Taylor A (McMahon 46), Noble, Morrison (Doyle 46).

12 Mar+
England 2 *(Cranie 11, Jarvis 71 (pen))*
Czech Republic 0
(at Chester).
England: Heaton; Cranie, Moore L (Holmes 41), Taylor S, Leadbitter, Lennon (Morrison 57), Jarvis (Forte 75), Ifil, O'Hara, Doyle, Taylor A.

14 Mar+
England 5 *(Taylor S 8, 70, Leadbitter 14, Holmes 22, own goal 31)*
Slovakia 0
(at Bolton).
England: Heaton; Giddings, Moore L (Lennon 56), Taylor S, Leadbitter (O'Hara 58), Ifil, Doyle, Holmes (Forte 46), McMahon, Noble, Morrison.

16 Mar+
England 2 *(Noble 42, Lennon 75)*
Scotland 0
(at Tranmere).
England: Heaton; Cranie, Moore L, Taylor S, Leadbitter, Jarvis (Morrison 80), Ifil, Doyle, Holmes (Lennon 70), Taylor A, Noble.

7 May+
Israel 1
England 2 *(Bowditch 51, Milner 54)*
(at Penaguiao).
England: Heaton; Bowditch (Lennon 76), Cranie, Giddings, Moore L (Milner 20), Taylor S, Leadbitter, Jarvis, Huddlestone (Morrison 54), Ifil, Doyle.

9 May+
Italy 0
England 0
(at Chaves).
England: Heaton; Forte (Jarvis 48), Milner, Cranie, Taylor S, Leadbitter, Lennon, Doyle (Ifil 63), Taylor A, McMahon, Morrison (Bowditch 54).

11 May+
Spain 2
England 2 *(Taylor S 47, Milner 51)*
(at Villareal).
England: Martin; Bowditch, Milner, Cranie, Giddings, Taylor S, Jarvis (Taylor A 74), Huddlestone (Leadbitter 41), Ifil, Doyle, Morrison (Lennon 41).

14 May+
Portugal 2
England 2 *(Bowditch 8, Milner 21)*
Portugal won 3-2 on penalties.
(at Viseu).
England: Heaton; Bowditch, Milner, Cranie, Giddings, Taylor S, Leadbitter, Lennon, Jarvis (Moore L 52), Ifil, Doyle.

17 May+
Austria 1
England 0
(at Comba Dao).
England: Heaton; Bowditch, Forte (Milner 57), Taylor S, Jarvis, Huddlestone, Ifil, Doyle, Taylor A (Giddings 73), McMahon, Morrison (Lennon 54).

ENGLAND UNDER-16

Gilbert, Hislop, Lewis S, Moncur, Muamba, Murphy, Shimmin, Thomas (Arsenal); Bridges, Green, Osbourne, Paul (Aston Villa); Jones Z, Woods (Blackburn R); Ashton, Weston (Charlton Ath); Brand, Grant, Mancienne, Simmonds, Smith, Watkins (Chelsea); Lake, Wright (Everton); James, Ottley (Fulham); Parker, Walton S, Wilberforce (Leeds U); Guthrie, Holmes J (Liverpool); Baguley, Parillon (Manchester U); Knight, Wheater (Middlesbrough); Walton M (Newcastle U); Alnwick (Sunderland); Dawkins, Martin, Riley (Tottenham H); Henry, Welsh-Elliott, Noble (West Ham U); Ainsworth, Doyle, Holmes L (Derby Co); Ashikodi (Millwall); Berry (Crystal Palace); Castle (Reading); Davies (Wolverhampton W); Gilligan (Watford); Jones, Roberts (Crewe Alex); Lewis J (Norwich C); Mullarky, Rigby (Nottingham F); Porter (Leicester C).

18 Oct*
Northern Ireland 0
England 2 *(Moncur 5, A. N. Other)*
(at Ballymena).
England: Lewis J (Wilberforce 40); Grant (Henry 80), Wright, Guthrie (Gilligan 54), Moncur, Gilbert, Paul (Murphy 56), Lewis S, Walton M, Parillon (James 4), Holmes L.

1 Nov*
Wales 0
England 1 *(Ashikodi 21)*
(at Barry).
England: Lake (Thomas 40); Green, Parker, Muamba, Walton S, Brand, Berry (Dawkins 59), Rigby, Ashikodi (Osbourne 47), Smith (Baguley 46), Welsh-Elliott (Hislop 47).

12 Nov
England 0
Spain 1
(at Darlington).
England: Lewis J; Green, Ashton (Welsh-Elliott 46), Jones, Dawkins (Berry 50), Walton M (Ashikodi 65), Holmes L (Simmonds 50), Parker, Gilbert, Doyle (Walton S 70), Noble.

15 Nov
England 2 *(Ashikodi 43, Doyle 75)*
Holland 1
(at Gateshead).
England: Lake; Green, Ashton, Muamba (Doyle 80), Jones, Walton S (Gilbert 80), Simmonds, Holmes L, Noble, Ashikodi (Walton M 80), Berry (Dawkins 80).

18 Nov
England 2 *(Doyle 23 (pen), Berry 47)*
Germany 2
(at Sunderland).
England: Lake (Lewis J 47); Jones, Walton S, Simmonds (Green 77), Walton M (Ashikodi 68), Holmes L, Parker, Gilbert, Doyle, Noble, Berry (Dawkins 49).

29 Nov*
England 2 *(own goal 45, Paul 52)*
Scotland 1
(at Huddersfield).
England: Thomas (Knight 40); Ottley (Brand 40), Hislop, Roberts, Henry (Lewis S 67), Wheater, Mullarky (Paul 51), Gilligan (Guthrie 58), Osbourne, James, Murphy.

16 Apr
Russia 0
England 3 *(Paul 65, 80, Smith 34)*
(at Montaigu).
England: Alnwick; Walton M (Paul 56), Green (Gilbert 61), Jones, Cohen, Smith (James 55), Simmonds, Murphy (Porter 72), Castle, Roberts (Rigby 67), Ainsworth.

17 Apr
Gabon 0
England 2 *(Paul 64, Murphy 77)*
(at Bouffere).
England: Lewis J; Walton M (Murphy 53), Ashton, Green (Cohen 50), James, Gilbert (Jones 9), Paul (Simmonds 72), Smith (Roberts 40), Porter, Castle, Rigby.

19 Apr
France 3
England 1
(at Montaigu).
England: Alnwick; Ashton, Green, Jones, James (Porter 68), Cohen, Paul, Simmonds (Rigby 64), Murphy, Roberts, Ainsworth (Walton M 40).

21 Apr
Portugal 2
England 1
(at Montaigu).
England: Lewis J; Ashton, Green, Jones, Paul, Smith (James 50), Simmonds, Murphy (Ainsworth 64), Porter, Castle, Rigby (Roberts 44).

1 May
Israel 2
England 1 *(Weston 25)*
(at Ballymena).
England: Lake; Bridges (Riley 54), Moncur, Watkins, Davies, Weston (Welsh-Elliott 46), Holmes J, Muamba, Lewis S (Woods 62), Mancienne (Shimmin 58), Dawkins (Mullarky 54).

2 May
Czech Republic 2
England 1 *(Lewis S 1)*
(at Newforge).
England: Jones Z; Riley (Weston 54), Bridges, Woods (Davies 61), Shimmin, Martin (Muamba 70), Mullarky, Lewis S, Mancienne, Welsh-Elliott (Holmes J 26), Dawkins (Watkins 22).

3 May
Republic of Ireland 1
England 1 *(Weston 35)*
England won 6-5 on penalties.
(at Ballymena).
England: Jones Z; Woods (Martin 61), Moncur, Shimmin, Watkins, Mullarky (Welsh-Elliott 46), Davies, Weston, Holmes J (Bridges 67), Muamba (Lewis S 51), Mancienne.

5 May
Northern Ireland 0
England 1 *(Dawkins 1)*
(at Ballymena).
England: Lake; Riley (Moncur 52), Shimmin, Martin, Mullarky (Watkins 52), Davies, Holmes J, Muamba, Lewis S, Mancienne, Welsh-Elliott (Weston 59), Dawkins.

* Victory Shield; ** Nordic Tournament; # Meridian Cup; + UEFA Championship.

WOMEN'S FOOTBALL 2002–03

For the first time since the Women's National competition was formed, Arsenal Ladies failed to win any of the trophies on offer. Instead their mantle fell on the shoulders of Fulham Ladies, the only full time professional outfit, who swept the board. They defeated Arsenal 3–2 on penalty kicks in the Premier League Cup Final, the match being level 1–1 after extra time. Fulham also annexed the Women's FA Cup by beating Charlton Athletic 3–0 in front of an excellent 10,389 crowd at Selhurst Park. Finally they won the National League Division by 8 clear points from Doncaster Belles, even after having had a point deducted. They had an amazing goal difference of plus 50; and scored more (63) and conceded less (13) than any other team. Southampton Saints and Brighton were relegated. Aston Villa won the North Division with Ilkeston Town and Garswood Saints relegated; whilst Bristol Rovers won the Southern Division by 17 points with Barking relegated. The Premier League Reserve Cup was won by Birmingham City who beat Arsenal 2–1 but the Gunners did show some flair in the UEFA Women's Cup where they were England's representative. They reached the two-leg semi-final losing 8–2 on aggregate. However on the way they defeated teams from Spain, Belgium, Russia and Azerbaijan before going out to Fortuna Hjorring of Denmark.

The game in England is still going through a period of unprecedented growth and it is beginning to show at international level where there are more matches at all levels. England reached the fourth FIFA Women's World Cup play off whilst there are numerous games at Under 19 and Under 17 levels. The National Coach Hope Powell, who was recently awarded an OBE for services to the game, continues to produce fine teams despite the fact there are few professional players to call on. Even Fulham Ladies are set to go part-time next season. Nevertheless Brent Hills who is the Assistant National Coach told a large audience of London Football Coaches Association coaches who had seen him work with Arsenal's Under 14 year old girls, that most of the younger girls are set to become better than their older counterparts at all levels as time progresses and more funding is achieved. Women and girls football is still the fastest growing area of sport in the country and continues to attract ever more girls especially with the making of films such as 'Bend It Like Beckham'.

In April 2003 the FA relaunched the 'Get Involved' campaign to encourage more girls to play football. They set up a special hotline to give out details of local teams or taster courses. With its partner, Sport England, the FA is investing millions of pounds on five year schemes to encourage a progression from schools into club football to avoid the fall-out which has been noticed in boy's football. The aim is to appoint 46 full-time Women's Development Officers. More information on these aspects can be obtained from Kelly Simmons at the FA.

The Women's Football structure consists of Tessa Hayward – the Women's League Co-ordinator and Secretary for the Women's Premier League. Justine O'Donohoe – the League's Administrator. Helen Nicolaou – International Teams Development Co-ordinator. Sally Cunnington who deals with Youth teams. Mike Appelby – Leagues Manager for both women and men and Bev Ward – Media and Communication Officer.

KEN GOLDMAN

Fulham Ladies again showed their prowess in the FA Women's Cup final in which they defeated Charlton 3–0. (Actionimages)

NATIONAL DIVISION

		P	W	D	L	F	A	GD	Pts
1	Fulham*	18	16	2	0	63	13	50	49
2	Doncaster Belles	18	13	2	3	34	19	15	41
3	Arsenal	18	13	1	4	53	21	32	40
4	Charlton Athletic	18	10	4	4	44	20	24	34
5	Birmingham City	18	6	3	9	26	31	–5	21
6	Tranmere Rovers	18	6	3	9	25	48	–23	21
7	Leeds United	18	5	4	9	33	42	–9	19
8	Everton	18	5	1	12	18	38	–20	16
9	Southampton Saints	18	2	5	11	10	30	–20	11
10	Brighton & HA	18	1	1	16	18	62	–44	4

**Includes 1 point deducted*

NORTHERN DIVISION

		P	W	D	L	F	A	GD	Pts
1	Aston Villa	22	16	4	2	59	18	41	52
2	Sunderland	22	15	4	3	48	25	23	49
3	Oldham Curzon	22	14	2	6	48	29	19	44
4	Bangor City	22	11	4	7	46	37	9	37
5	Wolverhampton W	22	9	5	8	28	26	2	32
6	Liverpool	22	7	8	7	37	32	5	29
7	Lincoln City	22	6	7	9	38	46	–8	25
8	Manchester City	22	5	6	11	31	37	–6	21
9	Middlesbrough	22	6	2	14	25	44	–19	20
10	Sheffield W	22	5	5	12	15	36	–21	20
11	Ilkeston Town	22	5	4	13	24	44	–20	19
12	Garswood Saints	22	4	7	11	26	51	–25	19

SOUTHERN DIVISION

		P	W	D	L	F	A	GD	Pts
1	Bristol Rovers	20	17	1	2	76	19	57	52
2	Ipswich Town	20	11	2	7	49	36	13	35
3	Bristol City	20	10	5	5	47	34	13	35
4	Millwall Lionesses	20	10	4	6	41	33	8	34
5	Barnet	20	10	4	6	29	24	5	34
6	Chelsea	20	10	2	8	33	31	2	32
7	Merthyr Tydfil	20	9	3	8	30	34	–4	30
8	Langford	20	8	5	7	38	35	3	29
9	Wimbledon	20	5	1	14	27	48	–21	16
10	Enfield	20	3	2	15	32	59	–27	11
11	Barking	20	2	1	17	22	71	–49	7

NATIONAL DIVISION LEAGUE – PREVIOUS WINNERS

1992–93	Arsenal	1996–97	Arsenal	2000–01	Arsenal
1993–94	Doncaster Belles	1997–98	Everton	2001–02	Arsenal
1994–95	Arsenal	1998–99	Croydon	2002–03	Fulham
1995–96	Croydon	1999–00	Croydon		

THE FA WOMEN'S CUP 2002–03

FIRST QUALIFYING ROUND

Bury Girls & Ladies w.o. v Bolton Wanderers (Supporters) withdrew
Thameside Girls v Darlington RA 3-4
Stockport Celtic v Wigan 1-0
Doncaster Rovers w.o. v Morley Spurs withdrew
Kirklees v Thorpe United 0-4
Warldley Eagles v Mossley Hill 5-1
Tadcaster Albion v Chester-Le-Street Town 1-6
Penrith Sapphires v Gateshead Cleveland Hall 7-0
South Durham Royals v Newsham PH 1-12
Blyth Town v Southport 2-4
Bradford City v Preston North End 1-3
North Ferriby United v Bolton Wanderers 7-3
Droylsden v Greyhound Gunners 7-1
Durham City v Ossett Albion 4-3
Warrington Grange v Corwen 5-3
Windscale v Darwen 0-4
Killingworth YPC v Billingham 3-1
East Durham v Bolton Ambassadors 23-0
Leicester City v Buxton 13-0
Nettleham withdrew v Northampton Town w.o.
Pearl v Rushden & Diamonds 1-7
Loughborough v South Normanton Athletic 6-1
Kesteven & Grantham v Stone Dominoes 7-3
Southam United v Wollaston Victoria 2-7
Barwell v Kidderminster Harriers 2-3
Derby County v Great Wyrley 1-2
Oadby Town v Cambridge City 1-3
Leighfield Athletic v Belper Town 2-1
Abbey Rangers v Hitchin Town 0-7
London Colney v Slough 2-1
Tring Athletic v Mansfield Road 4-0
Berkshire Sports withdrew v Luton Town Belles w.o.
London Ladies v Crowborough Athletic 1-6

Hampton & Richmond Borough v Thatcham Town 1-10
Viking v MK Wanderers 5-5
MK Wanderers won 3-2 on penalties.
Hastings United v Royston Town 0-0
Hastings United won 4-3 on penalties.
Billericay Town v Barnet Copthall 2-1
Woodbridge Town v Caversham 2-1
Crystal Palace v Leighton Linslade 7-0
Tottenham Hotspur v Redhill 2-2
Tottenham Hotspur won 4-3 on penalties.
Wycombe Wanderers v Redbridge Raiders 1-3
Colney Heath v Basildon United 3-0
London Women v Sawbridgeworth Town 12-0
Dagenham & Redbridge v Brentwood Town 18-0
Harringey Borough v Woking 1-2
Brentford v Haywards Heath Town 5-3
Cogan Coronation v Southampton 1-0
Wadebridge Town withdrew v Corfe Hills United w.o.
Alphington v Okeford United 2-8
Torbay v Highridge United 15-0
Penzance v Newquay Ladies 2-6
Swindon Spitfires v Launceston 2-3
Rover Oxford w.o. v Marjons withdrew

SECOND QUALIFYING ROUND

Penrith Sapphires v Preston North End 1-2
Thorpe United w.o. v Kader withdrew
Stockport Celtic v Hopwood 0-4
Darlington RA v Killingworth YPC 4-2
Doncaster Rovers v Chester-Le-Street Town 0-1
Warrington Grange v Southport 2-3
Newsham PH v North Ferriby United 3-1
Durham City v Warldley Eagles 1-0
Bury Girls & Ladies v East Durham 0-10
Droylsden v Darwen 1-5
Kesteven & Grantham v Cambridge United 2-0
Leicester City v Kidderminster Harriers 7-1
Great Wyrley v Tamworth 1-0
Loughborough v Leighfield Athletic 1-0
Rushden & Diamonds v Cambridge City 4-2
Northampton Town v Wollaston Victoria 5-0
Billericay Town v Brentford 1-5
Clapton Orient v Chiswick United 2-0
Thame United v Hitchin Town 3-5
Crowborough Athletic v London Colney 6-2
MK Wanderers v Luton Town Belles 2-4
Woking v Colney Heath 4-2
Haywood United v Thatcham Town 3-1
Tring Athletic v Woodbridge Town 1-1
Tring Athletic won 6-5 on penalties.
Redbridge Raiders v Whitehawk 10-1
Dagenham & Redbridge v Tottenham Hotspur 5-3
Hastings United v Crystal Palace 1-5
Westbourne Girls & Ladies v London Women 2-1
Cogan Coronation v Torbay 0-5
Exeter Rangers v Keynsham Town 1-2
Newquay Ladies v Corfe Hills United 8-0
Rover Oxford v Plymouth Oak Villa 4-1
Launceston v Okeford United 4-7

FIRST ROUND

Chester-Le-Street Town v Darwen 4-2
Parkgate v Liverpool Feds 5-4
Darlington RA v Huddersfield Town 1-3
Stockport County v Blackpool Wren Rovers 4-0
Preston North End v Barnsley 2-3
Blackburn Rovers v Chesterfield 6-0
Southport v Chester City 0-2
Newsham PH v East Durham 2-4
Durham City v Newcastle 0-6
Gretna v Manchester United 3-6
Scunthorpe United v Leeds City Vixens 5-1
Thorpe United v Hopwood 5-1
Loughborough Students v Coventry City 1-0
Shrewsbury Town v Great Wyrley 10-1
Highfield Rangers v Lichfield Diamonds 5-6
Rushden & Diamonds v Loughborough 4-1
Ilkeston v Kesteven & Grantham 6-2
Peterborough United v Northampton Town 2-1
Cambridge University w.o. v Telford United failed to fulfil fixture.
Leicester City v Stafford Rangers 4-1
Hitchin Town v Reading 0-3
Chesham United v Brook House 0-2
Aylesbury United v Watford 1-13
Luton Town Belles v Denham United 1-2
West Ham United v Norwich City Racers 0-1
QPR Ladies v Crowborough Athletic 3-0
Dagenham & Redbridge v Tring Athletic 7-1
Woking v Reading Royals 2-2
Reading Royals won 3-2 on penalties.
Gillingham v Crystal Palace 2-1
Colchester United v Westbourne Girls & Ladies 4-0
Portsmouth v Bedford Town Belles 3-0
Brentford v Stowmarket Sophtlogic 1-2
Haywood United v Clapton Orient 4-0
Newquay Ladies v Keynsham Town 7-2
Newton Abbot v Exeter City 4-3
Cardiff City v Okeford United 10-2
Plymouth Argyle v Torbay 0-4
Rover Oxford v Swindon Town 2-1
Yeovil Town v Clevedon Town SBW 0-1
Bye: Redbridge Raiders

SECOND ROUND

Parkgate v Thorpe United 4-1
Newcastle v Chester-Le-Street Town 7-1
Chester City v Huddersfield Town 2-0
East Durham v Stockport County 2-1
Blackburn Rovers v Barnsley 4-0
Manchester United v Scunthorpe United 8-0
Peterborough United v Ilkeston 1-6
Cambridge University v Lichfield Diamonds 3-4
Leicester City v Loughborough Students 5-1
Rushden & Diamonds v Shrewsbury Town 5-2
Norwich City Racers v Stowmarket Sophtlogic 2-1
Reading Royals v Colchester United 8-1
Redbridge Raiders v Reading 1-0
Dagenham & Redbridge v Brook House 3-0
Denham United v Portsmouth 0-1
QPR Ladies v Watford 0-1
Haywood United v Gillingham 2-3
Newquay Ladies v Newton Abbot 4-2
Torbay v Rover Oxford 2-0
Cardiff City v Clevedon Town SBW 2-1

THIRD ROUND

Newcastle v Rushden & Diamonds 3-0
Manchester United v Ilkeston Town 3-0
Liverpool v Chester City 5-0
Wolverhampton Wanderers v Sheffield Wednesday 5-0
East Durham v Garswood Saints 7-0
Blackburn Rovers v Bangor City 4-0
Oldham Curzon v Sunderland 2-0
Leicester City v Manchester City 1-0
Lincoln City v Ilkeston 4-1
Parkgate v Aston Villa 2-7
Middlesbrough v Lichfield Diamonds 5-1
Portsmouth v Ipswich Town 3-4
Dagenham & Redbridge v Bristol Rovers 0-4
Gillingham v Torbay 1-3
Bristol City v Millwall Lionesses 2-0
Reading Royals v Wimbledon 2-1
Merthyr Tydfil v Norwich City Racers 2-1
Chelsea v Langford 3-1
Enfield v Cardiff City 0-1
Newquay Ladies v Watford 1-4
Barking v Redbridge Raiders 1-2
Bye: Barnet.

FOURTH ROUND

Bristol Rovers v Chelsea 4-3
Arsenal v Tranmere Rovers 2-0
Blackburn Rovers v Middlesbrough 3-2
Reading Royals v Aston Villa 2-3
Bristol City v Oldham Curzon 1-1
Oldham Curzon won 4-3 on penalties.
Lincoln City v Leicester City 2-1
Watford v Liverpool 1-1
Watford won 6-5 on penalties.
Newcastle v Birmingham City 0-5
Barnet v East Durham 1-6
Torbay v Manchester United 0-2
Redbridge Raiders v Ipswich Town 0-2
Charlton Athletic v Brighton & Hove Albion 4-0
Leeds United v Merthyr Tydfil 4-0

Cardiff City v Wolverhampton Wanderers	2-2
Wolverhampton Wanderers won 2-1 on penalties.	
Southampton Saints v Everton	2-1
Fulham v Doncaster Belles	2-0

FIFTH ROUND

Lincoln City v Watford	2-0
East Durham v Fulham	1-3
Birmingham City v Blackburn Rovers	7-2
Wolverhampton Wanderers v Arsenal	0-4
Manchester United v Charlton Athletic	0-8
Leeds United v Aston Villa	0-3
Ipswich Town v Oldham Curzon	2-3
Bristol Rovers v Southampton Saints	1-1
Bristol Rovers won 3-1 on penalties.	

SIXTH ROUND

Arsenal v Aston Villa	6-0
Fulham v Oldham Curzon	1-0
Bristol Rovers v Lincoln City	3-2
Birmingham City v Charlton Athletic	1-3

SEMI-FINALS

Bristol Rovers v Fulham	2-7
Charlton Athletic v Arsenal	1-0

THE FA WOMEN'S CUP FINAL

Monday, 5 May 2003
(at Selhurst Park)

Fulham (2) 3 *(Moore 18, Hills 36 (og), Williams 61 (og))*
Charlton Athletic (0) 0 10,389

Fulham: Johannessen; Jerray-Silver, Unitt, Haugenes, Pedersen, Phillip, McArthur, Duncan, Moore (Gibbons 85), Nwajei (Spacey 77), Yankey (Therkelsen 89).
Charlton Athletic: Cope; Stoney, Pond, Broadhurst (Smith 71), Loizou, Hills, Hunn (Williams 58), Lorton (Whitter 71), Barr, Walker, Rea.
Referee: G. Cain (Liverpool).

THE FA WOMEN'S CUP – PREVIOUS WINNERS

Year	*Winners*	*Runners-up*	*Score*
1971	Southampton	Stewarton & Thistle	4-1
1972	Southampton	Lee's Ladies	3-2
1973	Southampton	West Horn United	2-0
1974	Foxdens	Southampton	2-1
1975	Southampton	Warminster	4-2
1976	Southampton	QPR	2-1
1977	QPR	Southampton	1-0
1978	Southampton	QPR	8-2
1979	Southampton	Lowestoft	1-0
1980	St Helens	Preston North End	1-0
1981	Southampton	St Helens	4-2
1982	Lowestoft	Cleveland Spartans	2-0
1983	Doncaster Belles	St Helens	3-2
1984	Howbury Grange	Doncaster Belles	4-2
1985	Friends of Fulham	Doncaster Belles	2-0
1986	Norwich	Doncaster Belles	4-3
1987	Doncaster Belles	St Helens	2-0
1988	Doncaster Belles	Leasowe Pacific	3-1
1989	Leasowe Pacific	Friends of Fulham	3-2
1990	Doncaster Belles	Friends of Fulham	1-0
1991	Millwall Lionesses	Doncaster Belles	1-0
1992	Doncaster Belles	Red Star Southampton	4-0
1993	Arsenal	Doncaster Belles	3-0
1994	Doncaster Belles	Knowsley United	1-0
1995	Arsenal	Liverpool	3-2
1996	Croydon	Liverpool	1-1
	Croydon won 4-2 on penalties.		
1997	Millwall Lionesses	Wembley	1-0
1998	Arsenal	Croydon	3-2
1999	Arsenal	Southampton Saints	2-0
2000	Croydon	Doncaster Belles	2-1
2001	Arsenal	Fulham	1-0
2002	Fulham	Doncaster Belles	2-1
2003	Fulham	Charlton Atheltic	3-0

THE FA NATIONWIDE PREMIER LEAGUE CUP 2002–03

PRELIMINARY ROUND

Bristol City v Aston Villa	2-5
Langford v Merthyr Tydfil	2-1

FIRST ROUND

Arsenal v Sheffield Wednesday	11-0
Bangor City v Aston Villa	2-3
Barking v Garswood Saints	1-4
Brighton & Hove Albion v Barnet	2-0
Bristol Rovers v Southampton	3-0
Charlton Athletic v Enfield	7-1
Doncaster Belles v Everton	3-0
Fulham v Langford	6-2
Lincoln City v Leeds United	2-4
Manchester City v Ilkeston Town	5-2
Middlesbrough v Ipswich Town	0-1
Sunderland v Chelsea	4-0
Tranmere Rovers v Millwall Lionesses	4-0
Wolverhampton Wanderers v Liverpool	1-4
Wimbledon v Birmingham City	0-4

SECOND ROUND

Fulham v Liverpool	12-0
Doncaster Belles v Manchester City	2-1
Bristol Rovers v Oldham Curzon	2-0
Charlton Athletic v Garswood Saints	10-1
Tranmere Rovers v Ipswich Town	6-0
Sunderland v Aston Villa	2-3
Arsenal v Leeds United	3-0
Brighton & Hove Albion v Birmingham City	1-4

THIRD ROUND

Aston Villa v Charlton Athletic	1-0
Arsenal v Tranmere Rovers	1-0
Fulham v Birmingham City	5-0
Doncaster Belles v Bristol Rovers	7-0

SEMI-FINALS

Aston Villa v Fulham	1-2
Doncaster Belles v Arsenal	1-2

THE FA NATIONWIDE PREMIER LEAGUE CUP FINAL

Fulham v Arsenal	1-1
aet; Fulham won 3-2 on penalties.	

THE WOMEN'S PREMIER LEAGUE CUP – PREVIOUS WINNERS

Year	*Winners*	*Runners-up*	*Score*
1993	Arsenal	Knowsley	3-0
1994	Arsenal	Doncaster Belles	4-0
1995	Wimbledon	Villa Aztecs	2-0
1996	Wembley	Doncaster Belles	2-2
	Wembley won 5-3 on penalties.		
1997	Millwall Lionesses	Everton	2-1
1998	Arsenal	Croydon	3-2
1999	Arsenal	Everton	3-1
2000	Arsenal	Leeds United	5-1
2001	Arsenal	Tranmere Rovers	3-0
2002	Fulham	Birmingham City	7-1
2003	Fulham	Arsenal	1-1
	Fulham won 3-2 on penalties.		

THE FA WOMEN'S PREMIER LEAGUE RESERVE SECTION CUP 2002–03

PRELIMINARY ROUND

Oldham Curzon v Wolverhampton Wanderers	2-8
Wimbledon v Bristol Rovers	2-1

FIRST ROUND

Barking v Everton	0-9
Barnet v Doncaster Belles	2-5
Birmingham City w.o. v Ilkeston Town withdrawn	
Brighton & Hove Albion w.o. v Sheffield W withdrawn	
Chelsea v Arsenal	1-4
Enfield v Aston Villa	1-9
Fulham v Leeds United	4-1
Garswood Saints v Charlton Athletic	0-9
Lincoln City v Bangor City	6-3
Liverpool v Ipswich Town	3-1
Merthyr Tydfil v Manchester City	4-0
Middlesbrough v Langford	3-0
Millwall Lionesses v QPR	10-2
Southampton Saints v Wimbledon	3-0
Tranmere Rovers v Wolverhampton Wanderers	1-4

SECOND ROUND

Birmingham City v Merthyr Tydfil	5-0
Doncaster Belles v Brighton & Hove Albion	2-1
Fulham v Middlesbrough	5-0
Lincoln City v Millwall Lionesses	2-6
Liverpool v Aston Villa	4-3
Southampton Saints v Arsenal	2-5
Sunderland v Everton	0-3
Wolverhampton Wanderers v Charlton Athletic	0-4

THIRD ROUND

Arsenal v Liverpool	4-1
Birmingham City v Millwall Lionesses	4-2
Charlton Athletic v Doncaster Belles	5-0
Everton v Fulham	4-1

SEMI-FINALS

Charlton Athletic v Arsenal	0-4
Everton v Birmingham City	1-1

aet; Birmingham City won 5-3 on penalties.

THE FA WOMEN'S PREMIER LEAGUE RESERVE SECTION CUP FINAL

Sunday, 9 March 2003
(at Bishop Stortford FC)

Arsenal v Birmingham City	1-2

UEFA WOMEN'S CUP 2002–03

GROUP STAGE

Arsenal v Gomrukcu Baku *(Azerbaijan)*	6-0
Arsenal v Levante *(Spain)*	2-1
Arsenal v Eendracht Aalst *(Belgium)*	7-0

QUARTER-FINAL

CSK WS Samara *(Russia)* v Arsenal	0-2
Arsenal v CSK WS Samara *(Russia)*	1-1

SEMI-FINAL

Fortuna Hjorring *(Denmark)* v Arsenal	3-1
Arsenal v Fortuna Hjorring *(Denmark)*	1-6

FIFA WOMEN'S WORLD CUP

1991 USA 2, Norway 1 (in China)
1995 Norway 2, Germany 0 (in Sweden)
1999 USA 0, China 0 (in USA)
USA won 5-4 on penalties.

WOMEN'S OLYMPICS

1996 USA 2, China 1 (in Atlanta)
2000 Norway 3, USA 2 (in Sydney)

FIFA WOMEN'S UNDER-19'S CHAMPIONSHIP

2002 USA 1, Canada 0 (in Canada)

UEFA WOMEN'S CUP

2001–02 Frankfurt 2, Umea 0
2002–03 Umea 4, 3, Fortuna Hjorring 1, 0

UEFA WOMEN'S CHAMPIONSHIP

1984 Sweden 1, 0, England 0, 1
Sweden won 4-3 on penalties.
1987 Norway 2, Sweden 1
1989 Germany 4, Norway 1
1991 Germany 3, Norway 1
1993 Norway 1, Italy 0
1995 Germany 3, Sweden 2
1997 Germany 2, Italy 0
2001 Germany 1, Sweden 0
2002 France 1, 1, England 0, 0

UEFA WOMEN'S UNDER-19 CHAMPIONSHIP

1998 Denmark 2, 2, France 3, 0
1999 Sweden
2000 Germany 4, Spain 2
2001 Germany 3, Norway 2
2002 Germany 3, France 1
2003 Played 25/7/03 – 3/8/03, in Germany

WOMEN'S INTERNATIONAL RESULTS 2002–03

Date	*Match*	*Result*		*Venue*
SENIOR TEAM				
23/07/02	England v Nigeria	0-1	Lost	Norwich City FC
4th FIFA Women's World Cup Play Offs				
16/09/03	Iceland v England	2-2	Draw	Laugardalsvoliur Stadium
22/09/03	England v Iceland	1-0	Won	Birmingham City FC
17/10/02	England v France	0-1	Lost	Crystal Palace FC
16/11/02	France v England	1-0	Lost	Stade Geoffroy Gulchard
25/02/03	Italy v England	1-0	Lost	Stadio dei Pini T Bresciani, Viareggio
17/05/03	USA v England	6-0	Lost	Legion Field Stadium, Alabama
19/05/93	Canada v England	4-0	Lost	Catalogna Soccerplexe, Montreal
22/05/03	Canada v England	4-0	Lost	Frank Clair Stadium, Ottawa
UNDER-19 TEAM				
FIFA U19 Women's World Cup Finals 2002				
17/08/02	England v USA	1-5	Lost	Centennial Stadium, Canada
19/08/02	Chinese Taipei v England	0-4	Won	Centennial Stadium, Canada
21/08/02	Australia v England	0-0	Draw	Centennial Stadium, Canada
26/08/02	England v Canada	2-6	Lost	Edmonton Commonwealth Stadium, Canada
2nd UEFA Women's U19 Championship 2002–03, Round 1				
02/10/02	England v Lithuania	4-0	Won	Albena 1 Stadium, Bulgaria
04/10/02	England v Bulgaria	5-0	Won	Albena 1 Stadium, Bulgaria
06/10/02	England v Faroe Islands	5-1	Won	Albena 1 Stadium, Bulgaria
13/03/03	England v British Universities	2-0	Won	Lilleshall National Sports Centre
2nd UEFA Women's U19 Championship 2002–03, Round 2				
15/04/03	England v Republic of Ireland	3-0	Won	Bedford Town FC
17/04/03	Spain v England	1-1	Draw	Arlesey Town FC
19/04/03	Denmark v England	0-1	Won	Barton Rovers FC
15/05/03	Sweden v England	1-0	Lost	Vavarevallen, Sweden
UNDER-17 TEAM				
20/07/02	England v British Universities	2-2	Draw	Lilleshall National Sports Centre
Ballymena International Tournament				
02/05/03	England v Scotland	3-1	Won	Ballymena Showgrounds
03/05/03	England v Nothern Ireland	2-1	Won	Ballymena Showgrounds
05/05/03	England v USA	0-3	Lost	Ballymena Showgrounds
25/10/02	France v England	2-1	Lost	Clairefontaine

ENGLAND WOMEN'S INTERNATIONAL APPEARANCES 2002-03

Appearances include those as substitute.
Brown (University of Pittsburg) 5; Stoney (Charlton Athletic) 8; Unitt (Fulham) 8; Exley (Doncaster Belles) 8; Phillip (Fulham) 9; White (Arsenal) 4; Moore (Fulham) 7; Chapman (Fulham) 1; Walker, K. (Doncaster Belles) 7; Barr (Charlton Athletic) 7; Yankey (Fulham) 8; Hall (Leeds United) 1; McArthur (Fulham) 5; Fletcher (Arsenal) 1; Williams (Charlton Athletic) 5; Proctor (Brighton & HA) 1; Handley (Doncaster Belles) 6; Hunt (Doncaster Belles) 2; Burke (Leeds United) 4; Britton (Leeds United) 7; Nwajei (Fulham) 1; Cope (Charlton Athletic) 5; Smith (Leeds United) 5; Champ (Arsenal) 3; McDougall (Everton) 4; Bassett (Birmingham City) 3; Walker, C. (Charlton Athletic) 3; Pealling (Arsenal) 2; Maggs (Arsenal) 1; Hunn (Charlton Athletic) 1.

Goalscorers
Walker, K 2, Barr 1.

FOOTBALL AND THE LAW

In season 2002-03 Football and the Law carried on where it left off in the previous period. Arsenal's battle with its local trader in club merchandise symbols had a yo-yo existence after a London High Court judge's referral of its claim to the European Court. When it returned to England, the referring judge disputed its finding of facts. This in turn required the Court of Appeal to uphold Arsenal's claim to restrain the trader's breaches of Arsenal's trademark rights.

Dennis Wise also experienced more than one tribunal experience. His altercation with a Leicester City colleague led to termination of his contract. An initial claim by Wise for wrongful dismissal succeeded, but the club overruled the decision on an appeal hearing.

Similarly, Blackburn Rovers' Gary Flitcroft's High Court injunction against a newspaper's disclosure of his extra-marital affairs was reversed in the Court of Appeal.

Moving into higher levels in the game, the Premier League and its trading associate company Topps also obtained an injunction against Panini from infringing the Premier League's copyright in the badges and logos which appear on the shirts of players. This contrasted with the Football League's failure to uphold its television contract with Carlton and Granada, with the well-known knock-on financial consequences.

Closer to the field of play, Roy Keane was punished by the Football Association for claiming in his autobiography that he had deliberately injured Manchester City's Alf-Inge Haaland while Darren Pitcher of Crystal Palace failed to follow other successful claims for football tackle injuries against Huddersfield Town. Whatever the Laws of the Game decree, the law of the land becomes increasingly relevant to them.

EDWARD GRAYSON
Founder President, British Association for Sport and the Law.

UEFA REGIONS CUP

(Competition for European amateur teams)

1999 Veneto (Italy) 3, Madrid (Spain) 2
2001 Braga (Portugal) 2, Moravia (Czech Republic) 2
Moravia won 4-2 on penalties.
2003 Piemonte (Italy) 2, Maine (France) 1

MERIDIAN CUP

(competition for youth teams from Europe and Africa. Four teams from each continent.)

1997 Nigeria 3, Spain 2
1999 Portugal 0, Egypt 0
Portugal won 3-1 on penalties.

2001 Spain won 3 and drew 1.

Spain	10 points
Italy	9
Portugal	8
Czech Republic	8
Nigeria	4
Ghana	2
Cameroon	1
Mali	1

2003 Spain won all 4 matches.

Spain	12 points
Switzerland	8
France	8
England	8
Burkino Faso	2
Nigeria	2
Egypt	1
Mali	1

FUTURE CUP

(Competition for B International Teams)

17 Dec 2002, Mainz, 5200

Germany (1) 3 *(Kuranyi 16, Meier 58, Voigt 90)*
Scotland (1) 3 *(Kyle 43, Hughes 59, Malcolm 86)*

25 Feb 2003, Ataturk, 2000

Turkey (1) 1 *(Cayhun 37)*
Scotland (1) 1 *(Gray 18)*

20 May 2003, Partick, 1502

Scotland (2) 2 *(Hutchison 24, Kyle 26)*
Northern Ireland (0) 1 *(Jones 57)*

Scottish Players:
Alexander, G. (Preston NE); Alexander, N. (Cardiff C); Arthur (Partick T); Caldwell, G. (Newcastle U); Caldwell, S. (Newcastle U); Canero (Kilmarnock); Crainey (Celtic); Cummings (Chelsea); Dailly (West Ham U); Devlin (Birmingham C); Doig (Nottingham F); Fletcher (Manchester U); Gallacher (Dundee U); Glass (Watford); Gray (Bradford C); Harper (Portsmouth); Hughes (Rangers); Hutchison (West Ham U); Kennedy (Celtic); Kerr (Newcastle U); Kyle (Sunderland); Lynch (Preston NE); Malcolm (Rangers); McAllister (Aberdeen); McFadden (Motherwell); McGovern (Celtic); Miller (Wolverhampton W); Murray, I. (Hibernian); Murray, S. (Bristol C); Naysmith (Everton); Nicholson (Dunfermline Ath); Noble (West Ham U); Rae (Dundee); Ross (Rangers); Soutar (Dundee); Stillie (Dunfermline Ath); Stockdale (Middlesbrough); Webster (Hearts); Williams (Nottingham F); Wilson (Dunfermline Ath).

UNIBOND LEAGUE 2002–03

PREMIER DIVISION

			Home			*Goals*		*Away*			*Goals*			
		P	*W*	*D*	*L*	*F*	*A*	*W*	*D*	*L*	*F*	*A*	*GD*	*Pts*
1	Accrington Stanley	44	18	4	0	53	20	12	6	4	44	24	53	100
2	Barrow	44	14	5	3	41	21	10	7	5	43	31	32	84
3	Vauxhall Motors	44	14	3	5	46	19	8	7	7	35	27	35	76
4	Stalybridge Celtic	44	14	5	3	52	26	7	8	7	25	25	26	76
5	Worksop Town	44	9	6	7	42	35	12	3	7	40	32	15	72
6	Harrogate Town	44	10	4	8	38	31	11	4	7	37	32	12	71
7	Bradford (Park Avenue)	44	12	6	4	42	27	8	4	10	31	43	3	70
8	Hucknall Town	44	8	8	6	32	28	9	7	6	40	34	10	66
9	Droylsden	44	11	4	7	31	21	7	6	9	31	31	10	64
10	Whitby Town	44	8	4	10	38	38	9	8	5	42	31	11	63
11	Marine	44	10	5	7	39	31	7	5	10	24	29	3	61
12	Wakefield & Emley	44	8	12	2	22	16	6	6	10	24	32	–2	60
13	Runcorn FC Halton	44	9	6	7	33	37	6	9	7	36	37	–5	60
14	Altrincham	44	9	7	6	34	27	8	2	12	24	36	–5	60
15	Gainsborough Trinity	44	9	5	8	35	35	7	6	9	32	31	1	59
16	Ashton United	44	8	9	5	42	39	7	4	11	29	40	–8	58
17	Lancaster City	44	8	1	13	33	39	8	8	6	37	36	–5	57
18	Burscough	44	9	6	7	26	24	5	3	14	18	27	–7	51
19	Blyth Spartans	44	9	3	10	34	40	5	6	11	33	47	–20	51
20	Frickley Athletic	44	7	5	10	18	33	6	3	13	27	45	–33	47
21	Gateshead (R)	44	5	7	10	34	39	5	4	13	26	42	–21	41
22	Colwyn Bay	44	3	5	14	28	47	2	4	16	24	52	–47	24
23	Hyde United	44	3	4	15	22	47	2	4	16	18	51	–58	23

R = Relegated after playoff.

DIVISION ONE

			Home			*Goals*		*Away*			*Goals*			
		P	*W*	*D*	*L*	*F*	*A*	*W*	*D*	*L*	*F*	*A*	*GD*	*Pts*
1	Alfreton Town	42	11	5	5	51	29	15	4	2	55	30	47	87
2	Spennymoor United	42	15	2	4	44	15	12	4	5	37	27	39	87
3	Radcliffe Borough (P)	42	13	4	4	55	28	12	6	3	35	18	44	85
4	North Ferriby United	42	13	5	3	40	16	10	4	7	38	29	33	78
5	Chorley	42	13	4	4	47	21	8	6	7	33	30	29	73
6	Belper Town	42	11	5	5	28	24	9	8	4	25	18	11	73
7	Witton Albion	42	9	8	4	37	25	10	7	4	30	25	17	72
8	Matlock Town	42	11	4	6	34	28	9	6	6	33	20	19	70
9	Leek Town	42	11	4	6	33	24	9	5	7	30	22	17	69
10	Workington	42	11	4	6	42	31	8	6	7	31	29	13	67
11	Farsley Celtic	42	10	4	7	36	33	7	7	7	30	34	–1	62
12	Kendal Town	42	10	5	6	34	22	8	2	11	34	36	10	61
13	Bamber Bridge	42	9	3	9	28	24	6	6	9	27	35	–4	54
14	Guiseley	42	6	7	8	36	30	8	4	9	32	33	5	53
15	Bishop Auckland	42	9	8	4	36	30	4	2	15	22	53	–25	49
16	Lincoln United	42	6	4	11	35	32	6	5	10	32	45	–10	45
17	Stocksbridge PS	42	5	6	10	30	34	6	3	12	24	47	–27	42
18	Rossendale United	42	8	1	12	36	46	4	4	13	22	42	–30	41
19	Kidsgrove Athletic	42	7	4	10	27	33	2	7	12	22	38	–22	38
20	Ossett Town	42	4	8	9	20	34	4	1	16	19	46	–41	33
21	Eastwood Town	42	3	4	14	18	40	2	4	15	15	52	–59	23
22	Trafford	42	5	4	12	22	39	0	2	19	12	60	–65	21

P = Promoted after playoff.

LEADING GOALSCORERS (in order of League goals)

Premier Division

Lge	*Cup*	*Tot*	
33	3	36	Lutel James (Accrington Stanley)
31	2	33	Andy Whittaker (Lancaster City)
29	9	38	Terry Fearns (Vauxhall Motors)
24	6	30	Phil Eastwood (Stalybridge Celtic)
24	6	30	Paul Mullin (Accrington Stanley)
22	6	28	Lee Ellington (Gainsborough Trinity)
21	1	22	Aaron Wilford (Whitby Town)
19	8	27	Andy Todd (Worksop Town)
17	1	18	Andy Hayward (Bradford Park Avenue)

Division One

Lge	*Cup*	*Tot*	
34	9	43	Jodie Banin (Radcliffe Borough)
31	7	38	Gavin Knight (North Ferriby United)
24	9	33	Mike Moseley (Witton Albion)
24	7	31	Mick Godber (Alfreton Town)
21	1	22	Steve Preen (Spennymoor United) *Including 7 for Gateshead*
20	6	26	James Tevendale (Stocksbridge Park Steels)
20	5	25	Dave Whittaker (Leek Town)
17	8	25	Glenn Murray (Workington)
17	7	24	Danny Holland (Matlock Town)
17	7	24	Vill Powell (North Ferriby United)
16	2	18	Steve Taylor (Matlock Town)

ATTENDANCES

Premier Division

Highest Attendances: 2263 Accrington Stanley v Altrincham
1520 Barrow v Lancaster City
1501 Barrow v Blyth Spartans

Highest Average Attendance: 1133 Accrington Stanley

ATTENDANCES

Division One

Highest Attendances: 908 Matlock Town v Alfreton Town
742 Belper Town v Matlock Town
715 Alfreton Town v Belper Town

Highest Average Attendance: 388 Alfreton Town

UNIBOND LEAGUE – PREMIER DIVISION RESULTS 2002–03

	Accrington Stanley	Altrincham	Ashton United	Barrow	Blyth Spartans	Bradford (Park Avenue)	Burscough	Colwyn Bay	Droylsden	Frickley Athletic	Gainsborough Trinity	Gateshead	Harrogate Town	Hucknall Town	Hyde United	Lancaster City	Marine	Runcorn FC Halton	Stalybridge Celtic	Vauxhall Motors	Wakefield & Emley	Whitby Town	Worksop Town
Accrington Stanley	—	3-1	4-1	2-1	3-2	3-1	4-2	2-0	2-1	2-1	3-0	2-1	3-2	2-0	1-0	1-1	5-0	2-1	4-1	2-1	1-1	1-1	1-1
Altrincham	1-1	—	1-0	1-2	3-2	0-0	0-0	4-2	3-1	1-0	1-1	4-0	0-4	0-0	4-1	3-0	0-1	1-1	3-3	0-2	0-1	2-1	2-4
Ashton United	2-2	1-0	—	2-2	2-1	1-4	0-0	2-2	2-1	3-2	1-3	3-1	5-0	2-3	2-1	2-2	2-3	3-3	1-1	2-1	2-2	1-1	1-4
Barrow	1-0	4-0	0-3	—	2-1	3-2	3-0	2-1	0-0	2-1	3-2	2-0	1-2	1-1	3-0	2-2	1-0	3-0	1-0	1-2	1-1	2-2	3-1
Blyth Spartans	0-3	0-2	4-0	1-1	—	1-2	2-1	1-1	0-1	4-2	2-1	3-2	0-3	1-2	1-3	1-0	1-1	3-1	1-4	2-5	2-1	2-3	2-1
Bradford (Park Avenue)	1-1	1-1	1-1	2-2	5-1	—	3-2	4-2	3-1	2-2	1-0	2-0	1-0	0-3	5-1	0-1	2-1	3-2	2-1	1-0	1-1	2-3	0-1
Burscough	0-1	0-3	3-2	2-0	1-3	0-1	—	3-0	0-0	1-0	4-4	1-0	0-1	2-0	0-0	0-0	2-1	3-3	0-1	0-0	1-0	0-2	3-2
Colwyn Bay	1-2	2-3	1-1	3-4	1-2	2-0	1-3	—	0-3	2-3	0-3	2-3	0-1	3-6	2-0	1-1	0-2	1-3	1-1	1-1	3-2	1-1	0-2
Droylsden	2-2	1-0	0-1	0-2	7-0	2-0	1-0	2-1	—	3-1	3-0	0-2	2-1	0-0	0-1	1-5	0-1	2-0	1-1	1-1	1-0	2-1	0-1
Frickley Athletic	2-1	0-3	1-0	1-2	1-0	0-3	0-0	3-0	0-2	—	2-2	1-0	0-1	0-0	0-0	0-1	1-3	2-2	1-0	1-0	0-3	1-7	1-3
Gainsborough Trinity	1-5	2-1	1-2	0-2	3-2	2-2	0-1	2-1	1-4	2-0	—	0-1	1-2	2-2	4-2	2-1	0-0	1-1	1-1	2-1	4-1	0-1	4-2
Gateshead	5-1	0-0	0-1	2-2	3-0	1-1	1-0	2-2	0-2	2-2	1-1	—	2-3	1-5	2-1	3-3	1-2	2-3	0-1	3-2	0-1	1-3	2-3
Harrogate Town	0-2	3-0	0-1	3-2	3-1	5-2	2-1	4-1	0-0	1-2	0-2	1-3	—	2-0	3-1	1-3	1-1	3-1	1-0	2-2	1-2	0-2	2-2
Hucknall Town	2-1	4-1	2-3	0-3	0-2	1-2	3-1	2-1	2-0	1-0	0-0	1-1	1-1	—	2-0	1-1	2-1	3-3	2-2	1-2	1-1	1-2	0-0
Hyde United	3-3	0-2	1-1	1-3	1-1	3-1	1-0	0-2	1-3	2-3	1-5	0-1	1-5	0-1	—	2-3	0-2	0-2	0-1	1-0	0-1	3-3	1-4
Lancaster City	1-2	3-0	1-3	1-5	1-4	2-3	2-1	1-0	0-3	4-0	0-1	2-1	1-2	1-2	4-1	—	1-0	1-1	0-1	1-2	5-2	0-1	1-4
Marine	0-3	0-1	1-0	3-1	2-1	4-2	1-0	0-0	2-2	0-1	0-0	4-2	2-2	2-1	4-1	4-0	—	0-2	1-2	1-2	2-1	5-5	1-2
Runcorn FC Halton	0-2	3-2	3-2	1-1	2-2	2-0	0-2	6-2	0-0	0-1	0-5	1-1	2-1	0-3	1-1	1-4	2-1	—	1-0	0-5	4-1	1-1	3-0
Stalybridge Celtic	1-4	2-0	4-1	4-3	1-1	2-2	1-0	3-1	2-1	3-1	3-0	4-4	4-1	1-2	6-0	1-0	2-1	0-1	—	2-2	0-0	2-0	4-1
Vauxhall Motors	0-1	4-0	5-1	1-1	0-1	0-1	1-0	2-3	2-1	5-0	1-0	3-0	1-1	5-1	1-0	6-2	1-1	2-1	2-1	—	1-0	3-2	0-1
Wakefield & Emley	0-0	2-1	1-1	0-1	1-1	2-0	1-0	2-1	2-2	0-0	2-1	2-1	0-0	1-1	1-1	1-4	1-1	0-0	0-0	1-1	—	1-0	1-0
Whitby Town	0-3	0-1	3-2	1-1	4-4	0-1	0-2	1-0	5-2	3-1	3-0	2-2	4-2	3-3	3-2	2-3	2-0	0-3	1-2	1-2	0-1	—	0-1
Worksop Town	1-4	1-2	3-2	0-2	1-1	7-1	0-2	4-1	4-1	2-4	0-1	2-0	1-2	5-4	2-1	1-1	2-1	2-2	1-1	1-1	2-1	0-0	—

UNIBOND LEAGUE – DIVISION ONE RESULTS 2002–03

	Alfreton Town	Bamber Bridge	Belper Town	Bishop Auckland	Chorley	Eastwood Town	Farsley Celtic	Guiseley	Kendal Town	Kidsgrove Athletic	Leek Town	Lincoln United	Matlock Town	North Ferriby United	Ossett Town	Radcliffe Borough	Rossendale United	Spennymoor United	Stocksbridge Park Steels	Trafford	Witton Albion	Workington
Alfreton Town	—	1-1	1-2	4-1	1-3	4-1	2-0	1-3	4-3	2-0	1-2	2-2	2-0	3-4	5-1	3-2	3-0	1-1	1-1	6-1	1-1	3-0
Bamber Bridge	0-2	—	0-0	1-2	2-0	2-2	4-2	1-0	1-0	2-2	0-4	2-0	0-1	0-1	2-1	0-1	0-1	1-2	3-0	5-1	1-2	1-0
Belper Town	2-5	2-1	—	3-1	4-2	2-1	1-2	2-1	0-3	0-0	0-1	1-0	2-1	0-0	1-0	0-0	1-1	0-1	4-3	1-0	1-1	1-0
Bishop Auckland	0-0	2-2	2-2	—	2-1	3-0	1-1	1-1	2-0	1-0	1-1	1-1	1-5	1-3	3-1	1-3	5-3	3-2	2-1	2-0	0-0	2-3
Chorley	2-4	3-1	1-2	4-1	—	3-1	1-1	2-3	5-0	3-0	3-1	2-1	4-0	2-1	1-2	2-2	1-0	2-0	0-0	4-0	1-0	1-1
Eastwood Town	0-4	0-1	0-3	1-2	0-1	—	1-4	1-3	1-3	4-4	0-0	1-2	0-0	2-3	2-1	0-1	1-1	0-1	3-0	1-0	0-3	0-3
Farsley Celtic	0-3	2-1	0-1	3-0	3-3	2-1	—	2-2	0-1	5-4	4-3	4-1	1-5	0-1	1-0	1-1	1-0	1-1	2-0	4-3	0-1	0-1
Guiseley	2-2	3-3	0-0	7-0	2-1	4-0	0-1	—	1-2	0-0	2-2	4-0	0-3	1-2	2-6	0-0	3-1	0-2	1-2	2-0	0-1	2-2
Kendal Town	4-1	0-1	2-1	3-0	4-1	1-0	0-1	2-1	—	1-1	1-0	0-3	0-0	3-3	2-0	0-1	2-0	1-1	0-1	4-1	1-2	3-3
Kidsgrove Athletic	0-1	2-1	0-2	3-1	1-0	0-1	1-3	1-1	3-1	—	0-4	2-4	2-3	2-0	1-3	0-0	1-2	1-0	2-3	2-0	2-2	1-1
Leek Town	3-2	0-1	4-0	3-1	2-1	2-0	1-1	1-0	1-0	1-0	—	2-3	1-0	2-2	1-0	1-2	2-2	1-3	3-2	1-1	1-2	0-1
Lincoln United	1-3	1-1	0-1	3-3	1-2	6-0	4-1	2-3	3-1	0-2	0-0	—	1-5	4-2	0-0	0-1	1-2	0-2	2-0	5-0	0-1	1-2
Matlock Town	2-4	1-0	0-0	4-2	2-2	1-0	2-2	1-2	1-5	2-0	0-1	1-2	—	1-0	1-0	2-1	3-3	0-1	2-0	3-1	2-0	3-2
North Ferriby United	2-2	2-0	0-0	1-0	1-3	5-0	2-0	3-1	1-0	1-0	4-1	2-1	0-0	—	7-1	4-2	1-0	2-2	0-1	1-0	0-1	1-1
Ossett Town	1-2	4-0	1-2	2-1	1-2	1-0	1-1	0-0	2-2	2-2	0-5	1-1	0-0	0-4	—	0-4	2-1	0-1	1-3	0-0	1-1	0-2
Radcliffe Borough	2-4	2-1	1-1	1-0	1-1	1-1	3-0	2-1	2-4	5-1	0-1	4-1	0-1	2-0	7-1	—	2-1	7-4	4-0	4-2	4-2	1-1
Rossendale United	3-4	1-3	0-4	3-1	0-1	2-3	4-3	1-4	1-4	1-0	1-0	3-3	1-0	2-1	0-1	1-3	—	1-2	6-3	3-1	1-3	1-2
Spennymoor United	1-2	3-0	3-0	1-2	0-0	3-0	2-0	2-1	1-0	2-1	2-1	3-1	1-1	0-3	3-0	0-2	3-0	—	6-0	3-0	3-0	2-1
Stocksbridge Park Steels	2-3	1-1	0-0	3-1	1-4	2-1	1-3	2-3	1-1	3-4	0-1	1-1	1-1	1-2	2-0	0-1	5-1	0-3	—	2-0	1-1	1-2
Trafford	2-2	1-3	0-2	0-1	0-3	0-0	1-1	0-2	1-2	0-0	3-1	3-2	1-2	0-4	1-0	0-3	1-2	0-3	3-1	—	2-3	3-2
Witton Albion	1-2	1-2	1-1	1-0	1-1	1-1	2-2	5-0	3-1	1-0	0-0	1-2	0-4	1-1	2-0	2-2	2-0	5-3	1-1	4-1	—	2-1
Workington	0-3	3-3	2-1	2-2	1-1	7-2	0-1	1-0	2-1	2-1	0-1	5-1	2-1	2-1	2-1	1-3	2-1	1-2	1-2	3-0	3-3	—

UNIBOND LEAGUE CHALLENGE CUP 2002–03

FIRST ROUND
Belper Town 1, Matlock Town 4
Blyth Spartans 2, Bishop Auckland 3
Burscough 1, Colwyn Bay 3
Chorley 1, Bamber Bridge 0
Gateshead 6, Whitby Town 3 *aet*
Guiseley 3, Farsley Celtic 4
Hucknall Town 0, Gainsborough Trinity 3
Hyde United 2, Trafford 1
Lincoln United 1, North Ferriby United 2
Rossendale United 2, Droylsden 1
Stocksbridge Park Steels 2, Frickley Athletic 0
Witton Albion 3, Marine 5 *aet*
Workington 6, Kendal Town 0

SECOND ROUND
Altrincham 1, Hyde United 2
Ashton United 1, Vauxhall Motors 2
Barrow 3, Accrington Stanley 2
Bradford (Park Avenue) 2, Spennymoor United 2
aet; Bradford (Park Avenue) won 5-4 on penalties.
Eastwood Town 3, Kidsgrove Athletic 2
Harrogate Town 4, Bishop Auckland 0
Lancaster City 2, Leek Town 0
Marine 2, Stalybridge Celtic 0
Matlock Town 2, Worksop Town 3 *aet*
North Ferriby United 2, Gainsborough Trinity 3
Ossett Town 3, Farsley Celtic 0
Radcliffe Borough 3, Colwyn Bay 2
Runcorn FC Halton 1, Chorley 3
Stocksbridge Park Steels 1, Alfreton Town 4
Wakefield & Emley 1, Gateshead 3
Workington 2, Rossendale United 4

THIRD ROUND
Alfreton Town 4, Eastwood Town 1
Bradford Park Avenue 4, Ossett Town 5 *aet*
Gateshead 1, Harrogate Town 0
Marine 1, Hyde United 0
Radcliffe Borough 2, Barrow 1
Rossendale United 4, Lancaster City 1
Vauxhall Motors 2, Chorley 1
Worksop Town 3, Gainsborough Trinity 1

FOURTH ROUND
Gateshead 5, Alfreton Town 4 *aet*
Marine 1, Worksop Town 0
Radcliffe Borough 3, Ossett Town 4
Vauxhall Motors 0, Rossendale United 1

SEMI-FINALS
Gateshead 4, Rossendale United 0
Ossett Town 0, Marine 1

FINAL
Gatehead 0, 0, Marine 1, 2

PRESIDENT'S CUP

FIRST ROUND
Ashton United 4, Accrington Stanley 2
Colwyn Bay 2, Altrincham 1
North Ferriby United 2, Matlock Town 1
Runcorn FC Halton 2, Leek Town 1
Spennymoor United 5, Bishop Auckland 0
Stalybridge Celtic 4, Workington 1
Stocksbridge Park Steels 0, Kidsgrove Athletic 3
Wakefield & Emley 2, Farsley Celtic 1

SECOND ROUND
Ashton United 1, North Ferriby United 0
Runcorn FC Halton 3, Spennymoor United 1
Stalybridge Celtic 3, Colwyn Bay 0
Wakefield & Emley 5, Kidsgrove Athletic 1 *aet*

SEMI-FINALS
Ashton United 1, Wakefield & Emley 0
Runcorn FC Halton 2, Stalybridge Celtic 4

FINAL
Stalybridge Celtic 4, 2, Ashton United 2, 1

CHAIRMAN'S CUP

FIRST ROUND
Bamber Bridge 4, Burscough 2
Belper Town 0, Lincoln United 1 *aet*
Frickley Athletic 2, Whitby Town 1
Guiseley 1, Droylsden 3
Witton Albion 4, Trafford 2

SECOND ROUND
Bamber Bridge 8, Kendal Town 2
Blyth Spartans 3, Frickley Athletic 0
Droylsden 4, Witton Albion 2 *aet*
Lincoln United 0, Hucknall Town 2

SEMI-FINALS
Droylsden 1, Bamber Bridge 1
aet; Droylsden won 7-6 on penalties.
Hucknall Town 4, Blyth Spartans 1

FINAL
Droylsden 0, Hucknall Town 1 *aet*

LEAGUE CHALLENGE SHIELD

Accrington Stanley 2, Marine 0

UNIBOND LEAGUE PROMOTION PLAY-OFFS

SEMI-FINALS
Radcliffe Borough 1, North Ferriby United 0
Chorley 5, Gateshead 2

FINAL
Radcliffe Borough 2, Chorley 2
aet; Radcliffe Borough won 4-2 on penalties.

DR MARTENS LEAGUE 2002–03

PREMIER DIVISION

			Home			Goals		Away			Goals			
		P	W	D	L	F	A	W	D	L	F	A	GD	Pts
1	Tamworth	42	12	6	3	42	19	14	4	3	31	13	41	88
2	Stafford Rangers	42	11	7	3	43	18	10	5	6	33	22	36	75
3	Dover Athletic	42	11	4	6	21	20	8	10	3	21	15	7	71
4	Tiverton Town	42	11	4	6	34	22	8	8	5	36	21	27	69
5	Chippenham Town	42	9	9	3	30	14	8	8	5	29	23	22	68
6	Worcester City	42	12	6	3	39	27	6	7	8	21	22	11	67
7	Crawley Town	42	9	8	4	35	24	8	5	8	29	27	13	64
8	Havant & Waterlooville	42	10	6	5	35	30	5	9	7	32	34	3	60
9	Chelmsford City	42	8	5	8	31	28	7	7	7	34	35	2	57
10	Newport County	42	8	7	6	30	26	7	4	10	23	26	1	56
11	Hednesford Town	42	10	7	4	38	24	4	6	11	21	36	−1	55
12	Moor Green	42	8	7	6	29	19	5	7	9	20	39	−9	53
13	Hinckley United	42	9	6	6	35	29	3	10	8	26	35	−3	52
14	Bath City	42	8	7	6	27	22	5	6	10	23	39	−11	52
15	Welling United	42	8	7	6	27	25	5	5	11	28	33	−3	51
16	Grantham Town	42	10	5	6	39	28	4	4	13	20	37	−6	51
17	Weymouth	42	7	10	4	26	22	5	5	11	18	40	−18	51
18	Cambridge City	42	6	5	10	28	29	7	5	9	26	27	−2	49
19	Halesowen Town	42	7	8	6	20	17	5	5	11	32	46	−11	49
20	Hastings United	42	7	6	8	28	33	3	7	11	16	24	−13	43
21	Ilkeston Town	42	8	3	10	32	45	2	7	12	22	47	−38	40
22	Folkestone Invicta	42	5	4	12	35	42	2	3	16	22	63	−48	28

EASTERN DIVISION

			Home			Goals		Away			Goals			
		P	W	D	L	F	A	W	D	L	F	A	GD	Pts
1	Dorchester Town	42	17	1	3	70	21	11	8	2	44	19	74	93
2	Eastbourne Borough	42	16	3	2	59	17	13	3	5	33	16	59	93
3	Stamford	42	17	2	2	46	14	10	4	7	34	25	41	87
4	Salisbury City*	42	16	4	1	45	19	11	4	6	36	23	39	86
5	Bashley	42	13	6	2	56	19	10	6	5	34	25	46	81
6	King's Lynn	42	14	4	3	55	27	10	3	8	43	35	36	79
7	Rothwell Town	42	13	4	4	42	27	9	6	6	35	25	25	76
8	Banbury United	42	12	5	4	44	24	9	6	6	31	26	25	74
9	Tonbridge Angels	42	12	5	4	37	20	8	6	7	34	35	16	71
10	Histon	42	12	5	4	59	23	8	2	11	40	39	37	67
11	Ashford Town	42	12	4	5	35	22	6	5	10	28	35	6	63
12	Sittingbourne	42	8	6	7	30	28	7	2	12	27	41	−12	53
13	Burnham	42	9	4	8	35	35	6	3	12	27	44	−17	52
14	Fisher Athletic	42	5	2	14	22	43	10	3	8	35	37	−23	50
15	Chatham Town	42	9	2	10	29	33	5	3	13	25	51	−30	47
16	Newport (IoW)	42	7	3	11	26	39	5	3	13	27	48	−34	42
17	Dartford	42	7	4	10	35	35	4	4	13	13	43	−30	41
18	Erith & Belvedere	42	8	2	11	47	43	3	4	14	18	53	−31	39
19	Corby Town	42	5	6	10	26	42	4	5	12	23	42	−35	38
20	Fleet Town	42	3	6	12	11	31	5	2	14	23	49	−46	32
21	Spalding United	42	3	4	14	20	41	1	2	18	20	67	−68	18
22	St Leonards	42	2	3	16	19	46	2	1	18	19	70	−78	16

**3 points deducted for fielding an ineligible player.*

WESTERN DIVISION

			Home			Goals		Away			Goals			
		P	W	D	L	F	A	W	D	L	F	A	GD	Pts
1	Merthyr Tydfil	42	13	5	3	43	16	15	3	3	35	16	46	92
2	Weston-Super-Mare	42	11	5	5	38	27	15	2	4	39	15	35	85
3	Bromsgrove Rovers	42	14	3	4	47	20	9	4	8	26	21	32	76
4	Solihull Borough	42	12	6	3	43	17	9	7	5	34	31	29	76
5	Gloucester City	42	13	4	4	51	31	9	5	7	36	27	29	75
6	Mangotsfield United	42	13	5	3	60	21	8	5	8	46	32	53	73
7	Redditch United	42	15	1	5	48	17	7	5	9	28	25	34	72
8	Rugby United	42	15	3	3	39	16	5	6	10	19	27	15	69
9	Gresley Rovers	42	11	5	5	37	21	8	5	8	26	33	9	67
10	Taunton Town	42	9	5	7	36	36	11	2	8	40	42	−2	67
11	Sutton Coldfield Town	42	10	5	6	39	23	8	5	8	24	30	10	64
12	Evesham United	42	12	2	7	42	28	7	4	10	34	44	4	63
13	Clevedon Town	42	7	5	9	27	27	7	8	6	27	33	−6	55
14	Cirencester Town	42	9	3	9	34	39	6	4	11	28	43	−20	52
15	Cinderford Town	42	8	7	6	28	22	5	5	11	22	45	−17	50
16	Shepshed Dynamo	42	8	2	11	24	33	4	4	13	24	43	−28	42
17	Stourport Swifts	42	4	7	10	24	28	6	4	11	24	38	−18	41
18	Bedworth United	42	8	1	12	22	32	3	6	12	24	42	−28	40
19	Swindon Supermarine	42	5	3	13	26	39	6	2	13	26	46	−33	38
20	Atherstone United	42	5	7	9	26	34	4	3	14	19	44	−33	37
21	Rocester	42	5	5	11	16	30	4	5	12	18	44	−40	37
22	Racing Club Warwick	42	2	7	12	20	55	1	2	18	13	49	−71	18

DR MARTENS LEAGUE ATTENDANCES

Premier Average	628
Eastern Division Average	258
Western Division Average	232

DR MARTENS LEADING GOALSCORERS

(League and Cup)

PREMIER DIVISION

James Taylor (Havant & Waterlooville)	22
Gary Bull (Grantham Town)	17
Stephen Piearce (Hednesford Town)	17
David Sadler (Hinckley United)	17
Philip Everett (Tiverton Town)	16
Nathan Lamey (Moor Green)	16
Darren Middleton (Worcester City)	16
Martin Paul (Chippenham Town)	16
Dale Watkins (Chelmsford City)	16
Christopher Freestone (Ilkestone Town)	15
Lee Phillips (Weymouth)	15
Allan Tait (Folkestone Invicta)	15
Nicholas McDonnell (Crawley Town)	15
James Mudge (Tiverton Town)	14
Dennis Bailey (Stafford Rangers)	13
Paul Booth (Welling United)	13
Mark Cooper (Tamworth)	13
Charles Griffin (Chippenham Town)	13
Adam Webster (Worcester City)	13
Jason Ashby (Halesowen Town)	12
Daniel Davidson (Stafford Rangers)	12
Jai Martin (Moor Green)	12
James Millar (Folkestone Invicta)	12
Scott Rickards (Tamworth)	12
Daniel Simmonds (Hastings United)	12
Thomas Tyne (Dover Athletic)	12

EASTERN DIVISION

Norman Sylla (Banbury United)	32
Scott Ramsay (Eastbourne Borough)	30
Justin Keeler (Dorchester Town)	26
Martin Shepherd (Dorchester Town)	24
Kevin Byrne (Stamford)	23
Darren Adams (Erith & Belvedere)	22
Adrian Stone (Ashford Town)	21
Jason Turner (Rothwell Town)	21
Craig Davis (Bashley)	19
Matthew Groves (Dorchester Town)	19
David Staff (King's Lynn)	19
Adam Wallace (Salisbury City)	19
Christopher Bacon (Kings Lynn)	18
Michael Bartley (Burnham)	18
James Rowe (Histon)	18
Matthew Hann (Dorchester Town)	16
David Hassett (Ashford Town)	16
George Redknap (Banbury United)	16
Andrew Drury (Sittingbourne)	15
Daniel Gibbons (Bashley)	14
Richard Gillespie (Bashley)	14
Carl Holmes (King's Lynn)	14
Peter Munns (Histon)	14
Malcolm Ndekwe (Stamford)	14
Darren Pearce (Eastbourne Borough)	14

WESTERN DIVISION

David Seal (Mangotsfield United)	34
Andrew Corbett (Solihull Borough)	25
Simon Tucker (Sutton Coldfield)	25
Robert Beard (Rugby United)	21
Richard Ball (Stourport Swifts)	20
Cortez Belle (Merthyr Tydfil)	20
James Cox (Gloucester City)	19
Scott Griffin (Cinderford Town)	19
Adam Sims (Mangotsfield United)	19
Justin Pritchard (Merthyr Tydfil)	18
Andrew Hoskins (Gloucester City)	16
Kevin Charley (Atherstone United)	15
Gareth Hopkins (Cirencester Town)	15
Lee Ross (Bedworth United)	15
Gary Fisher (Taunton Town)	14
Simon Hollis (Redditch United)	14
Daniel O'Hagan (Weston-Super-Mare)	14
Jodie Bevan (Weston-Super-Mare)	13
Richard Burgess (Bromsgrove Rovers)	13
Matthew Lewis (Solihull Borough)	13
Morton Titterton (Solihull Borough)	13
Naveed Arshd (Redditch United)	12
James Dyson (Bromsgrove Rovers)	12
Wesley Joyce (Evesham United)	12

DR MARTENS LEAGUE CUP 2002–03

PRELIMINARY ROUND
Crawley Town 2, Sittingbourne 0
Mangotsfield United 3, Gloucester City 0

FIRST ROUND
Bedworth United 1, Atherstone United 0
Burnham 4, Erith & Belvedere 2
Chatham 0, Chelmsford City 3
Cirencester Town 3, Cinderford Town 1
Dartford 2, St Leonards 0
Grantham Town 3, Histon 1
Gresley Rovers 1, Hinckley United 2
Mangotsfield United 2, Weston-Super-Mare 0
Merthyr Tydfil 0, Chippenham Town 1
Moor Green 2, Stafford Rangers 1
Redditch United 4, Evesham United 5
Rocester 1, Hednesford Town 2
Rugby United 0, Cambridge City 3
Salisbury City 3, Dorchester Town 2
Shepshed Dynamo 3, Corby Town 2
Spalding United 1, Kings Lynn 3
Stamford 3, Rothwell Town 2
Solihull Borough 6, Racing Club Warwick 2
Stourport Swifts 1, Bromsgrove Rovers 4
Tonbridge Angels 1, Welling United 2
Fleet Town 0, Eastbourne Borough 1
Taunton Town 3, Swindon Supermarine 1
Bashley 3, Havant & Waterlooville 2
Crawley Town 1, Hastings United 0
Newport (IW) 3, Weymouth 1
Bath City 2, Tiverton Town 2
(Tiverton Town won 3-1 on penalties).
Dover Athletic 2, Folkestone Invicta 1
Fisher Athletic 1, Ashford Town 3
Newport County 2, Clevedon Town 0
Worcester City 0, Halesowen Town 1
Ilkeston Town 2, Banbury United 1
Tamworth 1, Sutton Coldfield 3

SECOND ROUND
Hinckley United 2, Moor Green 1
Solihull Borough 3, Bromsgrove Rovers 0
Chippenham Town 2, Bashley 1
Taunton Town 1, Mangotsfield United 7
Ashford Town 1, Crawley Town 2
Tiverton Town 4, Cirencester Town 2
Bedworth United 3, Hednesford Town 1
Dartford 1, Dover Athletic 6
Halesowen Town 4, Evesham United 3
Kings Lynn 2, Stamford 1
Newport (IW) 3, Salisbury City 2
Rugby United 2, Grantham Town 1
Shepshed Dynamo 3, Ilkeston Town 3
aet; Shepshed Dynamo won 4-2 on penalties.
Sutton Coldfield 2, Newport County 1
Welling United 2, Chelmsford City 3
Eastbourne Borough 2, Burnham 3

THIRD ROUND
Dover Athletic 0, Chelmsford City 1
Halesowen Town 4, Sutton Coldfield 1
Kings Lynn 3, Hinckley United 0
Mangotsfield United 0, Chippenham Town 1
Shepshed Dynamo 2, Grantham Town 5
Newport (IW) 1, Tiverton Town 7
Burnham 1, Crawley Town 4
Solihull Borough 2, Bedworth United 3

FOURTH ROUND
Bedworth United 0, Halesowen Town 2
Crawley Town 1, Chelmsford City 2
(tie awarded to Crawley Town; Chelmsford City fielded an ineligible player)
Kings Lynn 2, Grantham Town 0
Tiverton Town 2, Chippenham Town 3

SEMI-FINALS
Crawley Town 1, Kings Lynn 0
Halesowen Town 2, Chippenham Town 1

FINAL FIRST LEG
Halesowen Town 2, Crawley Town 1

FINAL SECOND LEG
Crawley Town 2, Halesowen Town 0

DR MARTENS LEAGUE – PREMIER DIVISION RESULTS 2002–03

	Bath City	Cambridge City	Chelmsford City	Chippenham Town	Crawley Town	Dover Athletic	Folkestone Invicta	Grantham Town	Halesowen Town	Hastings United	Havant & Waterlooville	Hednesford Town	Hinckley United	Ilkeston Town	Moor Green	Newport County	Stafford Rangers	Tamworth	Tiverton Town	Welling United	Weymouth	Worcester City
Bath City	—	1-1	0-1	1-1	0-1	1-0	2-0	3-2	3-0	1-0	1-1	4-1	2-2	1-1	1-1	4-3	0-1	0-2	0-1	0-2	1-1	1-0
Cambridge City	0-1	—	2-3	0-1	3-0	1-1	2-1	1-1	0-1	1-2	4-5	2-2	1-1	2-2	1-2	1-3	1-0	0-1	3-0	2-1	0-1	1-0
Chelmsford City	2-0	1-2	—	2-3	1-2	0-1	3-2	1-2	1-0	1-0	1-2	2-2	1-1	2-1	4-0	1-1	0-2	0-4	3-0	1-1	3-1	1-1
Chippenham Town	1-2	2-0	3-1	—	1-0	0-0	1-0	0-0	1-2	0-0	3-1	1-3	3-1	3-0	1-1	0-0	1-1	3-0	1-1	4-0	1-1	0-0
Crawley Town	1-2	4-2	0-0	1-1	—	0-3	2-2	2-0	4-0	1-1	2-1	2-2	0-2	2-1	2-2	2-0	2-4	1-0	1-1	1-0	5-0	0-0
Dover Athletic	2-0	2-1	1-0	0-1	2-1	—	2-1	2-1	0-3	1-0	0-0	1-0	2-0	1-1	1-2	0-0	0-2	0-3	0-0	2-1	0-2	2-1
Folkestone Invicta	2-4	0-3	3-2	1-2	1-3	1-2	—	0-2	2-2	1-0	3-3	4-1	4-0	0-3	0-1	2-3	1-2	2-3	1-1	2-2	4-1	1-2
Grantham Town	0-0	1-0	2-3	1-1	0-3	3-1	4-1	—	3-3	2-1	1-1	3-0	2-1	2-2	4-0	1-2	1-2	2-1	0-2	3-1	2-0	2-3
Halesowen Town	1-1	1-1	0-2	3-2	0-2	0-0	5-0	1-0	—	2-1	1-0	0-1	2-1	2-1	0-1	1-2	1-1	0-0	0-0	0-0	0-1	0-0
Hastings United	1-1	1-2	1-1	2-1	0-0	1-1	1-2	2-1	3-2	—	1-1	2-0	1-0	3-0	3-1	1-3	0-2	2-3	0-3	1-4	1-1	1-4
Havant & Waterlooville	3-1	0-2	1-0	1-0	2-4	1-1	6-2	3-3	3-1	0-0	—	2-1	2-2	1-3	3-3	1-0	1-1	0-3	2-1	1-0	0-1	2-1
Hednesford Town	2-2	3-2	2-2	1-3	0-0	2-2	3-1	1-0	3-2	1-0	3-0	—	0-0	6-2	0-0	1-0	2-2	0-1	2-3	4-1	0-1	2-0
Hinckley United	3-1	3-2	2-1	1-2	3-1	1-1	3-3	0-0	1-1	3-2	2-1	0-1	—	5-2	1-2	0-2	2-0	1-1	1-1	1-3	2-1	0-1
Ilkeston Town	1-1	0-2	2-2	2-6	2-1	0-1	2-1	1-2	1-3	3-1	1-5	3-1	1-1	—	2-0	1-0	2-5	0-1	1-3	1-6	3-1	3-2
Moor Green	1-0	1-1	1-1	1-0	0-2	0-2	3-0	3-0	4-0	0-0	0-1	0-1	2-2	5-0	—	1-2	1-1	0-2	2-1	1-0	2-2	1-1
Newport County	1-1	1-1	2-5	3-1	3-3	0-1	1-2	3-2	1-1	1-1	0-0	1-0	3-2	3-0	1-1	—	1-0	0-1	0-1	0-2	3-0	2-1
Stafford Rangers	5-0	0-1	1-1	0-0	2-1	3-1	6-0	4-0	4-2	1-1	1-3	1-1	2-2	2-0	4-0	1-0	—	1-2	2-1	1-1	0-0	2-1
Tamworth	6-1	3-1	3-1	0-1	1-1	1-2	2-0	3-1	3-1	2-0	3-3	1-0	2-0	1-1	2-2	0-0	2-1	—	1-1	2-0	3-0	1-2
Tiverton Town	2-1	0-2	3-3	1-1	0-1	0-0	4-0	0-2	4-2	0-1	3-1	2-1	0-2	3-1	1-0	3-1	2-1	0-1	—	3-1	3-0	0-0
Welling United	1-3	1-0	0-2	1-1	2-2	0-0	2-1	2-0	3-1	0-3	1-1	2-2	1-2	2-0	1-0	1-0	1-2	1-1	1-1	—	4-2	0-1
Weymouth	2-0	0-0	1-3	1-1	2-0	0-0	3-3	3-1	1-4	1-1	1-1	0-0	2-2	1-1	3-1	2-0	1-0	0-1	0-2	2-1	—	0-0
Worcester City	2-1	2-0	5-0	0-0	2-1	0-1	6-0	2-0	1-1	2-1	2-1	3-1	2-2	0-0	4-0	2-1	0-3	0-0	0-2	1-1	3-1	—

DR MARTENS LEAGUE – WESTERN DIVISION RESULTS 2002–03

	Atherstone United	Bedworth United	Bromsgrove Rovers	Cinderford Town	Cirencester Town	Clevedon Town	Evesham United	Gloucester City	Gresley Rovers	Mangotsfield United	Merthyr Tydfil	Racing Club Warwick	Redditch United	Rocester	Rugby United	Shepshed Dynamo	Solihull Borough	Stourport Swifts	Sutton Coldfield Town	Swindon Supermarine	Taunton Town	Weston-Super-Mare
Atherstone United	—	1-1	1-2	2-2	0-0	0-3	1-2	1-1	1-2	0-4	0-1	3-1	0-0	2-1	2-0	0-0	3-4	1-1	4-1	3-2	1-4	0-2
Bedworth United	2-1	—	2-1	2-1	0-1	0-2	2-1	2-2	1-2	0-1	2-1	2-1	1-0	1-2	1-3	1-4	0-1	3-2	0-2	0-1	0-1	0-2
Bromsgrove Rovers	3-0	1-0	—	5-2	5-1	5-1	0-1	2-4	4-1	2-1	1-2	1-0	0-0	4-1	3-2	1-0	1-1	3-0	2-0	1-3	3-0	0-0
Cinderford Town	2-2	1-1	1-0	—	2-1	1-1	1-3	4-0	2-2	2-1	1-1	0-0	1-0	0-0	1-2	2-3	1-2	1-0	0-1	1-0	4-0	0-2
Cirencester Town	3-1	3-1	2-0	1-1	—	0-1	1-2	0-3	1-3	2-5	2-0	1-0	2-0	1-0	2-0	2-4	0-1	0-4	3-1	3-3	5-5	0-4
Clevedon Town	1-2	1-2	1-1	2-3	2-4	—	3-1	1-1	0-0	0-2	0-1	2-1	1-0	1-2	1-0	2-1	1-1	1-1	1-2	2-1	4-0	0-1
Evesham United	3-0	4-3	1-0	3-1	4-1	2-4	—	0-1	1-0	1-0	0-2	4-0	1-2	3-0	0-0	5-1	2-1	1-3	0-0	3-2	1-2	3-5
Gloucester City	1-2	4-1	1-0	4-0	5-4	1-1	6-1	—	1-0	4-3	2-2	3-1	2-5	0-0	0-0	3-1	4-2	1-2	3-1	2-1	4-2	0-2
Gresley Rovers	4-1	1-0	2-0	3-0	3-1	2-3	3-0	1-1	—	2-1	0-1	2-0	0-0	2-0	1-1	3-3	1-1	1-2	0-1	2-1	2-3	2-1
Mangotsfield United	4-1	1-1	2-2	3-0	3-0	4-0	5-0	1-4	7-0	—	2-3	3-0	1-1	1-1	4-2	1-0	3-3	4-0	3-1	5-1	0-1	3-0
Merthyr Tydfil	5-0	1-0	2-0	0-0	2-0	1-0	2-0	3-2	1-1	0-0	—	3-0	2-2	4-1	3-0	3-0	2-3	1-3	2-2	4-0	1-0	1-2
Racing Club Warwick	0-4	2-3	1-1	0-2	1-2	2-2	0-6	1-6	1-5	2-2	1-2	—	0-3	1-1	1-4	2-0	1-1	1-0	0-0	2-2	1-7	0-2
Redditch United	2-0	2-1	2-1	3-0	4-0	0-1	2-1	1-0	1-2	3-3	0-1	4-1	—	0-1	3-1	4-0	2-0	5-0	4-1	2-1	1-2	3-0
Rocester	1-0	1-2	0-1	2-1	1-1	0-0	2-2	2-2	0-1	0-6	0-2	2-1	1-0	—	0-0	2-0	0-2	1-2	1-2	0-1	0-2	0-2
Rugby United	0-0	3-1	0-2	5-1	0-3	2-2	3-0	1-0	1-0	2-1	2-1	4-0	1-2	4-2	—	2-0	2-0	3-0	1-1	1-0	1-0	1-0
Shepshed Dynamo	1-2	4-1	0-5	4-0	1-2	2-1	0-1	1-0	0-0	2-1	0-2	4-3	0-4	2-0	1-0	—	1-3	1-1	0-2	0-2	0-2	0-1
Solihull Borough	1-0	1-1	2-2	0-1	2-0	2-0	2-2	2-1	4-0	4-2	0-0	4-0	2-1	5-0	0-1	1-1	—	2-0	0-0	2-0	7-2	0-3
Stourport Swifts	1-1	1-0	1-2	1-2	1-1	0-0	1-1	0-1	1-1	0-0	2-3	2-1	2-3	5-0	0-1	3-0	1-1	—	1-2	1-2	0-3	0-3
Sutton Coldfield Town	2-0	1-1	0-1	0-0	3-1	6-0	3-2	0-1	0-2	2-3	0-2	1-1	3-2	1-1	1-0	2-1	2-1	2-0	—	9-0	1-1	0-3
Swindon Supermarine	2-1	1-0	0-1	2-0	0-3	1-3	3-3	1-2	2-4	2-4	0-2	2-0	1-2	1-2	1-1	2-0	2-3	2-2	0-2	—	1-2	0-2
Taunton Town	2-0	5-1	0-3	0-2	1-1	1-1	3-2	0-2	3-0	1-5	1-4	2-1	3-1	3-1	1-1	1-4	1-1	3-1	2-1	1-2	—	2-2
Weston-Super-Mare	4-1	3-3	0-1	3-3	3-1	1-1	1-3	3-2	1-0	1-1	0-2	0-1	1-0	3-2	1-0	1-1	1-2	1-0	3-1	2-1	5-1	—

DR MARTENS LEAGUE – EASTERN DIVISION RESULTS 2002–03

	Ashford Town	Banbury United	Bashley	Burnham	Chatham Town	Corby Town	Dartford	Dorchester Town	Eastbourne Borough	Erith & Belvedere	Fisher Athletic	Fleet Town	Histon	King's Lynn	Newport (IoW)	Rothwell Town	Salisbury City	Sittingbourne	Spalding United	St Leonards	Stamford	Tonbridge Angels
Ashford Town	—	1-2	1-0	2-1	2-0	1-0	3-0	1-5	1-0	3-1	1-4	3-1	1-1	0-0	3-2	1-0	0-1	0-1	1-0	8-1	1-1	1-1
Banbury United	3-0	—	2-2	1-0	4-0	3-1	1-0	2-1	0-3	3-0	1-2	4-1	1-2	2-2	2-0	2-2	0-1	4-1	4-2	2-1	1-1	2-2
Bashley	4-1	0-0	—	4-2	4-0	2-0	4-0	0-0	1-6	0-0	4-1	4-0	5-1	1-2	5-1	1-1	3-1	4-0	1-1	6-0	2-1	1-1
Burnham	3-4	1-0	1-2	—	1-0	4-3	3-0	1-2	0-0	2-2	3-4	2-1	1-4	0-3	2-0	1-1	1-1	3-2	1-0	1-2	0-1	4-3
Chatham Town	1-1	3-4	1-0	2-0	—	3-2	0-1	0-4	0-3	1-2	0-1	3-1	1-1	1-3	2-1	2-1	0-2	2-0	3-1	2-1	1-2	1-2
Corby Town	2-5	2-1	2-2	0-1	2-2	—	1-1	2-5	2-2	1-4	0-2	1-1	1-0	1-1	2-0	1-3	0-4	1-3	2-0	2-0	0-1	1-4
Dartford	1-1	1-2	1-3	3-3	3-6	4-0	—	1-1	0-1	0-0	1-3	1-2	0-2	3-0	4-0	2-0	1-4	1-0	2-1	4-2	2-3	0-1
Dorchester Town	3-1	3-1	0-2	3-4	4-0	3-1	3-0	—	2-1	6-2	2-0	5-1	2-1	1-0	1-1	0-2	5-1	3-0	9-0	8-1	2-1	5-1
Eastbourne Borough	2-0	1-2	2-2	3-1	3-0	2-2	4-0	1-3	—	3-0	2-0	2-1	4-1	4-1	7-0	3-1	0-0	3-0	4-0	4-0	2-1	3-2
Erith & Belvedere	1-2	4-4	1-4	4-0	3-1	1-0	4-1	0-1	0-1	—	1-2	2-1	3-4	2-4	5-3	0-2	3-2	1-4	7-0	2-3	1-2	2-2
Fisher Athletic	0-2	0-1	1-2	2-0	3-0	0-1	1-1	1-5	2-4	1-1	—	0-1	3-2	0-5	1-3	0-3	0-1	2-5	2-1	3-1	0-3	0-1
Fleet Town	0-0	0-1	0-1	0-1	0-2	0-0	0-0	0-0	1-2	2-1	1-3	—	3-2	1-5	0-2	0-2	0-2	1-2	0-4	1-0	0-0	1-1
Histon	3-2	0-3	6-0	2-0	3-1	1-1	5-0	0-2	0-2	6-0	2-0	4-0	—	4-2	1-1	2-2	1-1	3-0	5-1	8-1	2-3	1-1
King's Lynn	1-0	2-1	2-1	5-1	7-2	4-1	2-0	2-2	2-0	3-0	1-1	5-0	2-8	—	1-3	3-4	3-1	1-1	4-0	1-1	1-0	3-0
Newport (IoW)	1-1	0-3	0-4	0-1	3-1	2-2	0-3	0-1	0-1	3-0	2-3	1-0	2-1	3-0	—	0-2	0-4	1-1	3-2	2-0	1-6	2-3
Rothwell Town	1-0	0-0	0-0	2-1	2-2	3-0	0-1	2-2	2-0	5-1	3-2	3-1	3-2	2-5	2-4	—	0-1	2-0	2-1	2-1	4-2	2-1
Salisbury City	3-1	0-0	2-2	5-2	2-0	3-1	3-0	0-0	1-2	2-1	3-1	2-1	3-2	2-1	3-2	0-0	—	3-0	1-0	3-2	2-1	2-0
Sittingbourne	2-1	0-0	1-0	2-2	0-1	2-2	1-2	0-3	0-2	4-1	1-1	3-0	0-1	1-2	0-0	0-0	3-2	—	5-2	2-1	1-4	2-1
Spalding United	0-2	4-1	0-2	1-5	0-2	1-2	1-1	2-2	0-1	1-0	2-2	0-1	1-2	1-2	0-3	2-4	1-4	1-2	—	1-0	0-0	1-3
St Leonards	2-3	0-3	1-2	0-0	0-4	1-3	3-1	0-2	1-1	0-1	2-3	3-5	0-2	0-4	3-1	0-2	0-2	1-3	1-1	—	0-1	1-2
Stamford	1-0	2-0	1-3	2-0	5-1	2-0	3-1	2-1	1-0	3-1	3-0	0-0	2-1	2-0	3-0	2-1	0-0	2-1	4-2	6-0	—	0-2
Tonbridge Angels	1-1	2-2	0-0	1-2	0-0	0-1	1-0	2-2	0-1	4-0	2-0	1-4	1-0	4-1	1-0	3-2	2-1	2-1	6-1	2-1	2-0	—

RYMAN FOOTBALL LEAGUE 2002–03

PREMIER LEAGUE

			Home			Goals		Away			Goals			
		P	W	D	L	F	A	W	D	L	F	A	GD	Pts
1	Aldershot Town	46	17	3	3	41	16	16	3	4	40	20	45	105
2	Canvey Island	46	14	7	2	63	27	14	1	8	49	29	56	92
3	Hendon	46	10	5	8	29	28	12	8	3	41	28	14	79
4	St Albans City	46	11	5	7	36	31	12	3	8	37	34	8	77
5	Basingstoke Town	46	14	3	6	44	27	9	4	10	36	33	20	76
6	Sutton United	46	13	6	4	44	29	9	3	11	33	33	15	75
7	Hayes	46	13	6	4	38	19	7	7	9	29	35	13	73
8	Purfleet	46	13	4	6	42	23	6	11	6	26	25	20	72
9	Bedford Town	46	14	3	6	42	27	7	6	10	24	31	8	72
10	Maidenhead United	46	8	7	8	40	37	8	10	5	35	26	12	65
11	Kingstonian	46	10	5	8	32	29	6	12	5	39	35	7	65
12	Billericay Town	46	10	5	8	27	21	7	6	10	19	23	2	62
13	Bishop's Stortford	46	9	6	8	39	35	7	5	11	35	37	2	59
14	Hitchin Town	46	7	8	8	36	32	8	5	10	33	35	2	58
15	Ford United	46	8	7	8	42	39	7	5	11	36	45	–6	57
16	Braintree Town	46	6	4	13	28	38	8	8	7	31	33	–12	54
17	Aylesbury United	46	9	8	6	34	33	4	7	12	28	42	–13	54
18	Harrow Borough	46	8	4	11	31	36	7	5	11	23	39	–21	54
19	Grays Athletic	46	9	6	8	26	24	5	5	13	27	35	–6	53
20	Heybridge Swifts	46	8	7	8	29	38	5	7	11	23	42	–28	53
21	Chesham United	46	8	7	8	35	39	6	3	14	21	42	–25	52
22	Boreham Wood	46	6	8	9	24	32	5	7	11	26	26	–8	48
23	Enfield	46	5	8	10	21	31	4	3	16	26	70	–54	38
24	Hampton & Richmond B	46	2	8	13	20	41	1	6	16	15	45	–51	23

DIVISION ONE NORTH

			Home			Goals		Away			Goals			
		P	W	D	L	F	A	W	D	L	F	A	GD	Pts
1	Northwood	46	17	2	4	66	26	11	5	7	43	30	53	91
2	Hornchurch	46	13	7	3	46	25	12	8	3	39	23	37	90
3	Hemel Hempstead Town	46	15	2	6	41	31	11	5	7	29	24	15	85
4	Slough Town	46	14	6	3	48	20	8	8	7	38	39	27	80
5	Uxbridge	46	13	6	4	35	18	10	4	9	27	23	21	79
6	Aveley	46	10	6	7	27	24	11	8	4	39	24	18	77
7	Berkhamsted Town	46	13	3	7	54	37	8	10	5	38	31	24	76
8	Thame United	46	13	5	5	50	17	7	7	9	34	34	33	72
9	Wealdstone	46	14	4	5	51	30	7	5	11	34	39	16	72
10	Harlow Town	46	11	6	6	28	21	9	6	8	38	32	13	72
11	Marlow	46	11	4	8	39	31	8	6	9	35	32	11	67
12	Barking & East Ham U	46	9	3	11	32	38	10	6	7	41	38	–3	66
13	Yeading	46	11	6	6	37	28	7	5	11	40	41	8	65
14	Great Wakering Rovers	46	9	8	6	36	31	8	6	9	28	39	–6	65
15	Oxford City	46	10	8	5	39	25	7	5	11	16	26	4	64
16	Arlesey Town	46	8	10	5	33	27	9	2	12	36	44	–2	63
17	East Thurrock United	46	11	6	6	48	35	6	4	13	27	44	–4	61
18	Wingate & Finchley	46	8	5	10	38	41	7	6	10	32	33	–4	56
19	Barton Rovers	46	9	4	10	23	27	6	3	14	30	38	–12	52
20	Tilbury	46	8	5	10	30	43	6	2	15	25	53	–41	49
21	Wivenhoe Town	46	5	5	13	30	43	4	6	13	26	51	–38	38
22	Leyton Pennant	46	4	4	15	18	35	5	3	15	20	46	–43	34
23	Wembley	46	4	7	12	33	53	3	4	16	24	58	–54	32
24	Hertford Town	46	3	4	16	25	54	3	2	18	21	65	–73	24

DIVISION ONE SOUTH

			Home			Goals		Away			Goals			
		P	W	D	L	F	A	W	D	L	F	A	GD	Pts
1	Carshalton Athletic	46	15	4	4	36	21	13	4	6	37	23	29	92
2	Bognor Regis Town	46	15	4	4	52	13	11	6	6	40	21	58	88
3	Lewes	46	13	6	4	48	23	11	10	2	58	27	56	88
4	Dulwich Hamlet	46	13	7	3	41	22	10	5	8	32	27	24	81
5	Whyteleafe	46	12	6	5	45	23	9	7	7	29	28	23	76
6	Bromley	46	11	5	7	36	29	10	8	5	34	24	17	76
7	Walton & Hersham	46	9	7	7	42	34	11	6	6	45	29	24	73
8	Horsham	46	10	5	8	45	31	11	4	8	35	27	22	72
9	Epsom & Ewell	46	12	5	6	37	34	7	7	9	30	32	1	69
10	Egham Town	46	9	8	6	30	34	10	2	11	32	37	–9	67
11	Tooting & Mitcham U	46	5	4	14	36	45	13	5	5	47	33	5	63
12	Worthing	46	10	5	8	44	38	7	7	9	34	37	3	63
13	Windsor & Eton	46	11	5	7	39	29	7	4	12	27	36	1	63
14	Leatherhead	46	9	8	6	39	28	7	5	11	32	38	5	61
15	Staines Town	46	8	9	6	32	30	6	7	10	25	33	–6	58
16	Banstead Athletic	46	8	5	10	35	34	6	10	7	23	25	–1	57
17	Ashford Town (Mx)	46	5	8	10	18	30	9	3	11	29	40	–23	53
18	Croydon	46	9	6	8	28	31	6	2	15	28	56	–31	53
19	Croydon Athletic	46	5	7	11	24	38	8	6	9	28	28	–14	52
20	Bracknell Town	46	6	5	12	29	44	6	11	6	28	30	–17	52
21	Corinthian Casuals	46	7	7	9	25	26	5	7	11	25	42	–18	50
22	Molesey	46	5	5	13	19	39	8	4	11	33	40	–27	48
23	Metropolitan Police	46	6	5	12	26	38	6	5	12	24	38	–26	46
24	Chertsey Town	46	2	3	18	20	64	1	4	18	23	75	–96	16

N.B. *Metropolitan Police beat Wembley 3-2 on aggregate in play-off to avoid relegation*

DIVISION TWO

			Home			Goals		Away			Goals			
		P	W	D	L	F	A	W	D	L	F	A	GD	Pts
1	Cheshunt	30	13	2	0	44	11	12	1	2	47	18	62	78
2	Leyton	30	13	1	1	46	8	8	4	3	31	14	55	68
3	Flackwell Heath	30	9	0	6	22	21	8	3	4	30	23	8	54
4	Abingdon Town	30	8	5	2	33	14	6	6	3	32	28	23	53
5	Hungerford Town	30	6	6	3	25	18	6	6	3	24	18	13	48
6	Leighton Town	30	7	2	6	34	24	7	1	7	27	19	18	45
7	Witham Town	30	8	4	3	26	19	4	4	7	14	24	–3	44
8	Ware	30	7	4	4	29	28	5	1	9	18	25	–6	41
9	Clapton	30	6	4	5	23	27	6	1	8	17	20	–7	41
10	Tring Town	30	7	2	6	29	29	4	3	8	20	29	–9	38
11	Kingsbury Town	30	5	7	3	17	13	4	4	7	21	35	–10	38
12	Edgware Town	30	6	0	9	28	32	4	3	8	21	33	–16	33
13	Wokingham Town	30	3	3	9	15	42	4	4	7	19	39	–47	28
14	Dorking	30	4	4	7	25	28	2	2	11	24	35	–14	24
15	Chalfont St Peter	30	4	2	9	18	31	2	3	10	16	32	–29	23
16	Camberley Town	30	2	2	11	11	28	2	2	11	12	33	–38	16

RYMAN FOOTBALL LEAGUE GOALSCORERS

PREMIER DIVISION	*Lge*	*BC*	*AMC*
45 Lee Boylan (Canvey Island)	38	7	
32 Craig McAllister (Basingstoke Town)	31	1	
25 Tim Sills (Kingstonian)	21	4	
22 Dean Roberts (Bedford Town)	21	1	
(includes 20 League and 1 Bryco goal for Barton Rovers)			
22 Neville Roach (Basingstoke Town)	20	2	
21 Darren Lynch (Bedford Town)	20	1	
22 Lawrence Yaku (Maidenhead United)	19	3	

DIVISION ONE NORTH	*Lge*	*BC*	*AMC*
25 Bryan Hammett (Hemel Hempstead Town)	25	–	
28 Matt Miller (Yeading)	24	4	
25 Chris Moore (Northwood)	24	–	
24 Sammy Winston (Slough Town)	24	–	
27 Scott Fitzgerald (Northwood)	23	2	
(includes 2 Charity Shield goals)			
24 Dell Davies (Wembley)	18	6	

DIVISION ONE SOUTH	*Lge*	*BC*	*AMC*
30 Gavin Geddes (Horsham)	30	–	
29 Matt Russell (Bognor Regis Town)	29	–	
28 Elliott Onochie (Tooting & Mitcham United)	28	–	
23 Lee Newman (Lewes)	20	3	
21 Matt Hynes (Dulwich Hamlet)	20	1	
(includes 14 League for Whyteleafe)			

DIVISION TWO	*Lge*	*BC*	*AMC*
23 Leon Archer (Cheshunt)	21	1	1
26 Jeff Wood (Leyton)	19	2	4
23 Daryl Cox (Cheshunt)	19	-	4
28 Emmannuel Williams (Leyton)	18	4	6

Lge, League; BC, Bryco Cup, AMC, Associate Members Cup

LEADING ATTENDANCES

PREMIER DIVISION
3553 Canvey Island v Aldershot Town
3419 Aldershot Town v Hendon

DIVISION ONE NORTH
583 Hornchurch v Berkhamsted Town
567 Northwood v Wealdstone

DIVISION ONE SOUTH
1147 Staines Town v Carshalton Athletic
1003 Bognor Regis Town v Worthing

DIVISION TWO
221 Cheshunt v Hungerford Town
197 Kingsbury Town v Edgware Town

TOTAL ATTENDANCES
435,340 (previous season 395,708)

RYMAN FOOTBALL LEAGUE – PREMIER DIVISION RESULTS 2002–03

	Aldershot Town	Aylesbury United	Basingstoke Town	Bedford Town	Billericay Town	Bishop's Stortford	Boreham Wood	Braintree Town	Canvey Island	Chesham United	Enfield	Ford United	Grays Athletic	Hampton & Richmond	Harrow Borough	Hayes	Hendon	Heybridge Swifts	Hitchin Town	Kingstonian	Maidenhead United	Purfleet	St Albans City	Sutton United
Aldershot Town	—	1-0	0-3	2-1	0-0	0-0	1-0	3-0	1-0	1-2	2-0	2-1	2-1	4-0	0-1	1-0	6-2	2-0	1-0	2-1	1-1	1-0	5-1	3-2
Aylesbury United	3-2	—	1-1	1-1	0-1	1-2	3-3	1-1	1-6	2-1	4-1	2-0	3-2	3-0	0-0	3-0	0-1	2-1	2-2	1-0	0-0	1-1	0-3	0-4
Basingstoke Town	0-1	2-2	—	2-1	2-0	3-1	1-1	2-1	2-1	1-2	2-3	3-0	3-1	3-1	1-2	3-1	0-2	2-2	3-0	0-1	3-2	2-1	3-1	1-0
Bedford Town	1-2	4-0	0-0	—	2-0	3-1	0-4	1-0	2-1	0-4	8-2	0-2	1-0	1-0	1-1	2-1	2-3	1-2	2-1	5-2	0-0	2-0	2-0	2-1
Billericay Town	0-1	1-1	1-0	4-0	—	1-1	0-0	1-2	2-1	1-0	0-1	1-3	4-1	0-2	1-0	1-1	0-0	2-0	1-2	0-2	2-0	1-3	1-0	2-0
Bishop's Stortford	1-1	2-2	3-1	1-1	1-0	—	1-4	1-1	1-2	2-1	1-0	0-1	1-3	2-1	4-0	2-3	4-1	2-0	2-3	2-2	3-4	2-2	0-2	1-0
Boreham Wood	0-1	1-2	1-5	0-1	1-3	1-1	—	1-2	1-3	0-0	2-1	3-2	0-2	0-0	2-2	2-0	1-1	0-0	2-2	2-1	0-3	0-0	1-0	3-0
Braintree Town	2-1	2-2	0-3	2-0	1-0	1-3	0-1	—	2-4	1-2	1-3	1-0	1-1	3-1	2-4	0-1	1-2	3-0	1-3	1-2	1-2	0-0	2-2	0-1
Canvey Island	0-1	2-1	4-0	1-1	3-0	0-4	1-0	1-1	—	4-1	10-1	3-1	2-0	4-0	2-1	2-2	4-4	4-1	3-1	1-1	3-2	2-2	6-1	1-1
Chesham United	1-3	1-3	3-2	1-3	0-2	3-1	3-1	1-1	2-4	—	2-2	2-2	2-1	1-0	1-1	2-3	1-1	3-0	2-1	0-4	0-0	1-1	1-3	2-0
Enfield	1-2	0-0	3-1	1-2	1-1	0-2	1-0	1-1	1-2	1-0	—	1-1	1-1	2-0	0-1	0-1	0-0	2-3	0-5	2-2	1-1	1-0	0-1	1-4
Ford United	2-3	1-2	2-3	2-0	0-2	3-2	1-1	3-0	1-3	2-0	3-1	—	1-0	3-0	2-0	3-3	1-3	3-3	2-2	2-2	0-3	1-1	1-1	3-4
Grays Athletic	0-0	3-1	1-2	0-0	1-0	1-0	2-1	1-2	1-2	1-0	3-0	1-2	—	1-1	4-1	1-0	0-2	0-2	1-1	1-1	1-4	2-1	0-1	0-0
Hampton & Richmond	1-3	3-1	0-2	0-2	1-1	1-0	0-4	0-1	0-2	1-3	0-1	2-3	1-1	—	0-2	1-1	1-1	1-1	0-2	2-2	1-1	1-1	2-3	1-3
Harrow Borough	0-2	2-2	1-2	0-2	1-2	2-2	2-0	2-2	1-2	3-0	2-0	4-0	0-4	1-0	—	1-3	1-3	2-1	2-0	2-1	1-1	1-2	0-4	0-1
Hayes	1-0	1-1	1-0	2-0	0-2	2-0	0-0	1-3	2-1	1-0	4-0	2-0	1-0	2-1	6-0	—	0-0	2-2	2-1	2-2	0-2	1-2	3-0	2-2
Hendon	1-3	3-1	2-1	0-2	2-1	0-3	0-2	2-0	1-0	0-1	3-0	3-1	1-0	3-3	1-1	2-0	—	0-0	2-1	1-1	1-1	1-2	0-2	0-2
Heybridge Swifts	0-4	1-0	2-4	1-0	1-1	3-3	1-0	2-0	0-2	0-0	2-1	4-4	1-1	1-0	0-1	1-0	0-4	—	3-1	2-4	0-0	0-2	3-3	1-3
Hitchin Town	1-3	2-3	1-0	2-1	1-0	0-1	2-1	0-0	2-3	1-1	7-1	2-2	3-3	1-1	1-0	2-3	2-2	0-1	—	0-0	2-3	1-1	1-2	2-0
Kingstonian	0-2	1-0	2-1	2-2	2-0	3-1	0-0	1-4	0-4	5-1	4-2	0-2	1-0	1-1	1-3	1-1	0-1	4-0	0-0	—	2-0	0-1	0-2	2-1
Maidenhead United	1-2	2-1	2-2	3-2	1-0	2-3	2-1	2-3	1-1	5-0	3-3	0-4	0-2	1-1	2-0	1-1	0-1	2-2	1-2	4-4	—	1-0	0-1	4-1
Purfleet	1-2	1-0	1-0	3-0	0-0	2-1	0-0	1-1	3-2	6-0	5-2	2-2	3-1	5-2	4-2	1-2	1-0	1-2	0-1	0-1	1-0	—	1-0	0-2
St Albans City	2-0	3-1	1-2	1-2	1-1	3-2	2-0	2-4	2-1	1-0	0-0	3-2	1-2	2-0	1-0	1-1	1-4	2-0	0-1	2-2	1-3	2-2	—	2-1
Sutton United	1-1	3-2	1-1	0-0	1-2	2-1	3-2	3-1	0-2	3-2	2-1	4-1	2-0	1-0	3-0	2-1	2-3	2-0	3-1	1-1	2-2	1-1	2-4	—

RYMAN FOOTBALL LEAGUE – DIVISION ONE NORTH RESULTS 2002–03

	Arlesey Town	Aveley	Barking & East Ham United	Barton Rovers	Berkhamsted Town	East Thurrock United	Great Wakering Rovers	Harlow Town	Hemel Hempstead Town	Hertford Town	Hornchurch	Leyton Pennant	Marlow	Northwood	Oxford City	Slough Town	Thame United	Tilbury	Uxbridge	Wealdstone	Wembley	Wingate & Finchley	Wivenhoe Town	Yeading
Arlesey Town	—	0-0	0-0	1-0	2-2	2-0	0-4	1-2	0-0	6-0	2-2	3-1	0-0	2-3	1-0	1-0	3-3	0-2	0-1	3-3	3-2	0-0	1-1	2-1
Aveley	3-3	—	1-2	2-1	0-3	1-0	1-1	1-0	1-1	1-0	0-2	0-1	1-0	1-2	0-0	1-1	1-2	2-0	2-1	1-2	2-0	1-0	3-1	1-1
Barking & East Ham United	3-1	1-3	—	0-3	3-5	4-0	0-4	3-1	0-1	1-0	1-1	2-0	1-2	0-0	0-0	2-1	2-1	1-0	0-1	2-0	1-5	0-2	3-4	2-3
Barton Rovers	1-0	1-1	1-2	—	0-0	0-4	0-0	1-0	2-0	2-1	0-1	0-1	1-2	3-2	1-2	2-2	1-0	2-3	1-0	0-1	1-2	0-3	1-0	2-0
Berkhamsted Town	1-2	1-2	2-2	3-1	—	3-0	4-2	2-2	1-0	4-0	1-1	2-0	1-4	3-4	4-2	3-1	2-3	3-0	0-1	1-5	3-1	1-0	6-2	3-2
East Thurrock United	2-1	0-1	0-4	2-5	1-1	—	5-0	0-0	2-0	5-1	4-3	0-1	3-3	2-3	2-1	0-2	1-1	3-1	1-0	2-2	5-0	2-0	3-3	3-2
Great Wakering Rovers	2-3	1-1	4-3	2-1	1-1	0-4	—	1-1	0-1	2-0	3-3	2-0	0-0	2-0	0-1	2-2	0-0	0-1	0-3	2-1	5-0	1-1	3-2	3-2
Harlow Town	3-1	2-1	3-2	0-0	1-1	1-0	2-0	—	0-2	0-2	0-0	0-0	2-1	1-3	0-0	2-2	2-0	2-0	0-1	0-1	2-1	0-2	3-1	2-0
Hemel Hempstead Town	1-1	0-1	2-1	2-1	2-3	4-1	2-3	0-2	—	3-1	1-3	2-1	1-0	3-2	1-0	2-2	3-1	3-2	1-3	2-1	2-1	1-0	1-0	2-1
Hertford Town	2-4	0-3	1-3	0-4	2-2	0-1	1-1	1-2	0-2	—	1-2	2-2	2-6	0-5	0-1	1-3	1-3	0-1	1-3	3-2	2-0	3-3	0-1	2-0
Hornchurch	4-3	0-1	5-1	1-1	5-3	1-1	2-1	1-2	2-2	2-1	—	2-1	0-3	1-0	3-1	3-2	1-1	2-0	0-0	3-0	6-0	1-0	0-0	1-1
Leyton Pennant	0-1	0-2	1-2	1-0	1-1	0-2	1-2	0-1	0-2	2-3	0-0	—	1-1	1-3	0-1	0-2	0-1	2-3	2-4	1-2	2-1	1-0	0-0	2-1
Marlow	1-0	4-3	1-2	3-1	0-0	1-4	0-0	4-1	0-2	4-1	2-3	4-0	—	1-0	1-2	2-3	2-1	2-0	0-0	2-0	0-1	2-2	2-1	1-4
Northwood	6-0	1-1	1-2	2-1	2-0	4-2	4-0	1-4	2-1	5-1	2-0	5-1	1-3	—	2-1	5-1	2-0	5-1	0-1	2-1	6-1	4-1	1-0	3-3
Oxford City	0-1	0-0	4-1	2-1	0-2	2-0	1-2	3-2	1-1	3-0	1-1	2-1	2-0	0-3	—	1-1	1-1	5-0	1-0	0-3	1-1	2-2	5-0	2-2
Slough Town	3-0	1-1	3-1	1-0	3-2	2-0	4-0	1-1	0-1	2-2	1-1	5-1	2-0	2-1	3-0	—	2-0	5-1	1-1	1-1	2-1	0-3	4-0	0-2
Thame United	2-1	1-1	2-1	1-0	1-1	1-3	2-0	0-0	8-2	0-0	0-1	3-1	4-0	0-1	1-0	1-1	—	3-0	4-0	4-2	5-0	0-1	7-0	0-1
Tilbury	1-4	1-1	0-1	3-1	2-1	1-1	1-1	3-2	1-0	2-1	1-2	1-1	0-2	0-3	0-0	3-0	1-6	—	1-4	2-0	2-1	1-3	0-3	3-5
Uxbridge	2-0	2-0	1-1	5-0	1-2	1-1	0-0	3-1	1-0	4-1	0-1	3-2	0-0	0-0	1-0	0-1	2-1	1-4	—	1-0	2-1	1-1	1-0	3-1
Wealdstone	1-3	0-2	2-2	2-3	3-0	3-0	4-2	1-1	0-2	4-0	1-0	1-0	2-0	4-4	4-0	3-2	1-2	4-1	2-1	—	1-1	3-2	3-2	2-0
Wembley	0-3	2-6	2-2	2-3	0-2	1-1	2-3	1-5	1-1	3-1	0-4	0-1	1-1	2-2	0-2	2-2	2-4	4-2	2-1	0-0	—	4-1	2-3	0-3
Wingate & Finchley	1-2	1-2	0-3	1-0	0-4	3-0	3-0	1-4	1-4	2-3	0-1	4-1	4-3	1-2	1-1	2-3	1-0	2-1	1-1	5-2	1-1	—	1-1	2-2
Wivenhoe Town	3-1	2-1	1-2	1-2	1-1	4-1	0-1	1-3	0-2	3-1	1-5	1-2	1-3	0-0	0-1	1-2	2-2	1-1	2-0	1-4	2-2	2-3	—	0-3
Yeading	2-1	3-5	1-1	1-1	0-1	5-1	0-1	2-1	1-2	5-1	1-2	2-1	2-1	1-0	1-0	0-2	1-1	1-1	1-0	1-1	2-1	3-2	1-1	—

RYMAN FOOTBALL LEAGUE – DIVISION ONE SOUTH RESULTS 2002–03

	Ashford Town (Mx)	Banstead Athletic	Bognor Regis Town	Bracknell Town	Bromley	Carshalton Athletic	Chertsey Town	Corinthian Casuals	Croydon	Croydon Athletic	Dulwich Hamlet	Egham Town	Epsom & Ewell	Horsham	Leatherhead	Lewes	Metropolitan Police	Molesey	Staines Town	Tooting & Mitcham United	Walton & Hersham	Whyteleafe	Windsor & Eton	Worthing
Ashford Town (Mx)	—	0-0	0-1	0-0	1-1	0-2	2-0	1-1	1-0	0-2	0-5	1-3	1-1	0-1	0-1	0-3	2-1	1-2	0-0	1-1	2-1	1-1	0-3	4-0
Banstead Athletic	2-3	—	0-1	0-1	3-3	0-2	3-1	4-0	2-3	0-1	4-1	3-2	4-0	1-1	1-1	1-1	1-0	2-5	0-1	2-1	0-4	1-0	1-2	0-0
Bognor Regis Town	8-0	1-0	—	0-1	1-1	1-0	6-0	1-1	3-1	2-0	0-1	3-1	3-0	1-3	0-0	0-2	4-0	1-1	3-0	3-0	3-0	3-0	2-1	3-0
Bracknell Town	1-1	1-1	3-1	—	2-1	1-4	4-2	3-2	2-2	0-3	0-4	0-1	0-3	1-2	5-2	1-2	1-2	0-3	0-0	2-2	0-1	0-1	1-0	1-4
Bromley	2-1	2-2	2-1	2-0	—	0-3	4-1	2-0	3-1	0-1	1-1	1-2	1-0	1-0	1-0	3-2	2-3	0-2	2-2	2-3	3-0	1-1	0-0	1-3
Carshalton Athletic	1-0	1-0	1-0	2-2	1-4	—	1-0	2-2	1-0	2-1	2-0	0-1	2-0	2-1	2-0	4-1	2-0	1-1	1-1	2-3	1-2	2-1	1-0	2-1
Chertsey Town	0-5	1-0	0-2	1-1	1-4	0-2	—	0-1	4-1	1-2	1-2	1-2	0-3	1-1	2-8	1-5	1-2	2-2	0-1	0-7	1-6	1-4	1-2	0-1
Corinthian Casuals	1-2	0-1	0-3	0-0	0-0	1-2	5-0	—	1-1	1-1	1-2	0-4	1-0	1-2	3-0	1-2	1-0	3-0	1-0	0-3	1-1	1-1	1-0	1-1
Croydon	2-1	0-0	0-6	1-1	1-1	1-2	3-1	0-3	—	1-1	1-0	3-1	0-0	0-2	1-2	1-3	1-0	1-0	3-1	0-1	2-2	2-0	0-2	4-1
Croydon Athletic	0-1	1-1	1-0	0-1	1-2	0-1	2-0	0-4	3-0	—	0-2	2-1	1-1	0-5	1-1	2-2	1-1	1-3	1-1	1-5	2-0	2-3	2-3	0-0
Dulwich Hamlet	2-0	0-0	0-0	2-2	0-2	1-0	3-1	4-2	0-1	2-1	—	2-0	3-1	3-1	3-2	2-2	1-1	1-0	1-0	4-0	1-1	2-3	2-0	2-2
Egham Town	0-3	0-0	1-6	0-3	1-0	1-1	3-3	3-1	1-0	1-1	3-0	—	0-3	1-0	1-1	1-5	0-0	2-1	2-1	2-0	3-3	0-1	1-1	3-0
Epsom & Ewell	3-0	1-3	1-1	3-2	1-2	1-4	3-0	0-0	4-0	1-0	3-3	1-0	—	1-1	2-1	0-7	1-0	1-0	1-0	2-2	1-0	1-3	4-0	1-5
Horsham	1-0	2-0	1-2	3-3	1-1	0-1	4-0	0-1	6-1	2-2	1-0	1-2	2-1	—	1-2	2-2	2-0	6-2	0-2	2-3	0-1	4-2	1-0	3-3
Leatherhead	2-0	2-2	0-0	1-1	1-1	0-3	3-3	2-2	5-2	4-2	3-1	0-2	1-1	0-2	—	0-1	6-2	0-1	0-1	1-1	4-0	1-0	2-0	1-0
Lewes	5-2	0-2	2-2	2-0	1-0	3-1	7-0	5-0	0-2	3-2	2-0	2-0	1-0	1-0	0-0	—	1-1	3-2	2-2	0-1	1-1	1-1	6-2	0-2
Metropolitan Police	1-1	1-3	0-2	2-2	2-2	1-2	2-1	2-1	3-2	3-0	1-1	2-3	0-1	0-1	2-1	0-3	—	0-2	2-2	0-2	0-2	0-1	0-2	2-1
Molesey	0-2	0-2	1-5	1-1	2-1	1-1	1-2	1-0	1-2	0-4	0-1	0-0	0-1	0-1	4-1	0-7	3-1	—	1-2	0-2	0-1	1-0	1-1	1-1
Staines Town	0-2	1-1	0-3	1-0	1-2	2-2	2-2	2-0	2-1	1-0	0-0	5-0	2-2	1-1	4-1	1-1	1-2	4-1	—	1-2	0-7	0-0	1-0	0-0
Tooting & Mitcham United	3-1	1-2	4-0	2-3	0-1	0-2	5-0	0-1	1-2	1-1	0-2	1-2	3-4	1-4	2-0	1-1	2-4	1-1	3-2	—	1-3	1-2	3-3	0-4
Walton & Hersham	0-2	1-1	0-0	3-1	2-1	3-0	5-2	1-1	2-0	3-1	1-3	4-2	0-0	2-3	1-3	2-2	2-0	3-0	1-2	2-2	—	2-2	0-2	2-4
Whyteleafe	0-1	1-0	3-1	0-1	1-2	3-1	3-3	5-0	4-1	0-0	0-0	2-1	2-2	4-1	1-0	2-2	1-0	1-2	3-0	1-2	2-2	—	2-0	4-1
Windsor & Eton	1-1	5-0	0-2	2-0	0-1	1-1	1-0	1-1	2-3	0-1	1-0	3-2	4-3	3-1	0-2	0-0	1-1	3-1	2-1	5-2	1-4	1-2	—	2-0
Worthing	5-0	3-2	1-1	2-2	0-1	2-0	3-1	3-1	5-2	0-1	2-3	0-0	1-3	2-1	1-3	2-2	1-3	3-1	4-3	0-2	0-3	0-0	4-3	—

RYMAN FOOTBALL LEAGUE – DIVISION TWO RESULTS 2002–03

	Abingdon Town	Camberley Town	Chalfont St Peter	Cheshunt	Clapton	Dorking	Edgware Town	Flackwell Heath	Hungerford Town	Kingsbury Town	Leighton Town	Leyton	Tring Town	Ware	Witham Town	Wokingham Town
Abingdon Town	—	4-0	3-1	1-2	2-2	2-1	1-1	2-3	0-0	1-1	3-1	5-1	6-1	1-0	0-0	2-0
Camberley Town	0-3	—	1-4	2-3	1-2	2-0	0-0	0-2	1-3	0-1	0-2	1-1	0-3	2-0	0-1	1-3
Chalfont St Peter	1-2	0-1	—	0-4	0-3	1-0	1-3	1-4	1-2	3-0	5-3	1-3	2-1	0-3	0-0	2-2
Cheshunt	4-1	2-1	3-0	—	3-0	1-0	6-1	3-1	0-0	7-0	2-1	1-1	3-2	2-1	3-1	4-1
Clapton	2-2	2-1	2-0	0-5	—	3-3	0-5	2-4	2-0	0-1	0-2	1-1	3-1	3-0	1-1	2-1
Dorking	2-2	2-0	2-2	3-6	0-1	—	1-2	1-2	1-1	1-1	2-1	0-7	0-1	1-2	4-0	5-0
Edgware Town	0-3	0-1	0-4	1-3	0-1	3-6	—	3-0	0-1	1-6	1-0	3-1	2-3	2-1	3-1	9-1
Flackwell Heath	0-4	3-2	1-0	0-2	2-1	3-0	3-1	—	1-3	2-0	1-0	0-2	3-2	2-1	1-2	0-1
Hungerford Town	1-1	1-0	5-1	1-3	3-0	2-0	3-2	1-2	—	2-2	1-0	0-2	1-1	1-1	1-1	2-2
Kingsbury Town	1-1	1-1	2-2	2-0	2-1	0-0	1-0	2-2	0-0	—	1-1	0-2	3-1	0-1	2-0	0-1
Leighton Town	3-3	2-1	2-0	0-5	0-1	3-0	8-0	3-3	2-3	5-2	—	0-1	0-1	2-1	2-0	2-3
Leyton	8-0	3-0	4-0	5-2	1-0	4-0	3-1	3-0	3-2	0-0	1-3	—	1-0	2-0	3-0	5-0
Tring Town	2-0	3-0	1-1	1-6	0-2	3-1	2-1	0-2	3-1	7-1	2-7	0-2	—	2-3	2-1	1-1
Ware	3-5	0-0	2-1	1-4	3-2	4-2	3-1	2-1	1-1	3-2	0-3	0-0	3-1	—	1-2	3-3
Witham Town	0-4	7-2	2-0	0-0	1-0	3-2	1-3	0-0	1-1	2-1	0-1	2-1	2-2	4-2	—	1-0
Wokingham Town	1-1	3-2	2-0	1-2	2-1	1-9	0-0	0-4	2-6	1-3	0-2	0-6	0-0	1-2	1-4	—

THE BRYCO CUP 2002–03

FIRST ROUND
Aveley 4, Bracknell Town 0
Barton Rovers 4, Croydon Athletic 1
Berkhamsted Town 4, Arlesey Town 4
Replay: Arlesey Town 3, Berkhamsted Town 2
Chertsey Town 3, Camberley Town 2
Cheshunt 6, Hertford Town 0
Clapton 2, Whyteleafe 2
Replay: Whyteleafe 1, Clapton 0
Corinthian Casuals 3, Edgware Town 1
East Thurrock United 3, Wokingham Town 1
Epsom & Ewell 1, Ashford Town (Middlesex) 4
Great Wakering Rovers 0, Bromley 1
Leighton Town 0, Chalfont St Peter 2
Lewes 3, Wivenhoe Town 0
Leyton Pennant 0, Flackwell Heath 1
Metropolitan Police 2, Hornchurch 6
Molesey 4, Barking & East Ham United 3
Tilbury 2, Hungerford Town 3
Ware 0, Marlow 1
Windsor & Eton 5, Egham Town 2
Witham Town 3, Leatherhead 0
Hemel Hempstead Town 1, Leyton 3
Wingate & Finchley 6, Dorking 5
Horsham 1, Abingdon Town 1
Replay: Abingdon Town 0, Horsham 3
Banstead Athletic 2, Tring Town 0
Kingsbury Town 0, Wembley 6

SECOND ROUND
Ashford Town (Middlesex) 3, Heybridge Swifts 1
Aveley 2, Marlow 0
Barton Rovers 1, Braintree Town 3
Billericay Town 5, Enfield 0
Cheshunt 1, Aldershot Town 0
Corinthian Casuals 2, Carshalton Athletic 1
Croydon 2, Banstead Athletic 0
Harlow Town 1, Grays Athletic 2
Windsor & Eton 0, Harrow Borough 4
Dulwich Hamlet 2, Chertsey Town 0
Flackwell Heath 0, Aylesbury United 3
Ford United 2, Tilbury 1
Hayes 0, Canvey Island 1
Hendon 4, Staines Town 2
Hungerford Town 0, Bishop's Stortford 0
Replay: Bishop's Stortford 7, Hungerford Town 1
Leyton 3, Wealdstone 0
Molesey 0, Hampton & Richmond Borough 1
Slough Town 1, Kingstonian 3
Uxbridge Town 1, Basingstoke Town 2
Witham Town 1, Wingate & Finchley 2
Lewes 3, Maidenhead United 3
Replay: Maidenhead United 0, Lewes 1
Northwood 4, Hornchurch 2
Thame United 2, East Thurrock United 3
Wembley 5, Oxford City 3
Whyteleafe 0, Yeading 3
Purfleet 0, Ford United 3
Bromley 0, Bedford Town 1
St Albans City 3, Bognor Regis Town 2
Horsham 1, Boreham Wood 3
Tooting & Mitcham United 1, Worthing 4
Walton & Hersham 0, Hitchin Town 1
Chalfont St Peter 1, Arlesey Town 2
Chesham United 2, Sutton United 3

THIRD ROUND
Hitchin Town 4, Boreham Wood 0
Bishop's Stortford 3, Basingstoke Town 1
East Thurrock United 0, Grays Athletic 1
Ford United 1, Billericay Town 3
Hendon 2, Arlesey Town 1
Kingstonian 3, Worthing 0
Wembley 0, Dulwich Hamlet 2
Yeading 4, Corinthian Casuals 0
Ashford Town (Middlesex) 1, St Albans City 2
Aveley 2, Northwood 1
Braintree Town 1, Harrow Borough 3
Lewes 6, Hampton & Richmond Borough 0
Leyton 3, Bedford Town 4
Aylesbury United 3, Sutton United 2
Cheshunt 1, Canvey Island 5
Croydon 1, Wingate & Finchley 3

FOURTH ROUND
Bedford Town 1, Yeading 2
Billericay Town 1, Bishop's Stortford 1
Replay: Bishop's Stortford 3, Billericay Town 0
Harrow Borough 2, Lewes 3
St Albans City 1, Dulwich Hamlet 2
Grays Athletic 1, Aylesbury United 0
Kingstonian 3, Aveley 1
Hendon 5, Wingate & Finchley 2
Hitchin Town 1, Canvey Island 3

FIFTH ROUND
Bishop's Stortford 1, Yeading 4
Dulwich Hamlet 4, Lewes 1
Canvey Island 6, Grays Athletic 0
Hendon 1, Kingstonian 0

SEMI-FINALS FIRST LEG
Canvey Island 4, Hendon 2
Dulwich Hamlet 1, Yeading 3

SEMI-FINALS SECOND LEG
Hendon 2, Canvey Island 2
Yeading 3, Dulwich Hamlet 3

FINAL
Yeading 2, Canvey Island 0

ASSOCIATE MEMBERS TROPHY

GROUP STAGE
Wokingham Town 1, Chalfont St Peter 8
Cheshunt 3, Edgware Town 0
Edgware Town 1, Tring Town 3
Flackwell Heath 1, Leighton Town 1
Ware 1, Witham Town 0
Wokingham Town 3, Leighton Town 2
Camberley Town 2, Hungerford Town 2
Chalfont St Peter 2, Leighton Town 1
Witham Town 1, Ware 2
Flackwell Heath 2, Chalfont St Peter 2
Cheshunt 3, Tring Town 0
Leighton Town 0, Flackwell Heath 2
Tring Town 0, Kingsbury Town 2
Abingdon Town 2, Camberley Town 2
Leyton 2, Witham Town 1
Ware 4, Clapton 1
Kingsbury Town 4, Edgware Town 1
Witham Town 1, Leyton 1
Wokingham Town 1, Flackwell Heath 2
Camberley Town 3, Dorking 1
Tring Town 1, Cheshunt 3
Leyton 4, Ware 0
Edgware Town 0, Kingsbury Town 1
Abingdon Town 3, Hungerford Town 0
Edgware Town 0, Cheshunt 1
Clapton 0, Leyton 2
Leyton 4, Clapton 0
Dorking 1, Hungerford Town 4
Ware 2, Leyton 8
Chalfont St Peter 0, Flackwell Heath 2
Hungerford Town 4, Abingdon Town 0
Kingsbury Town 0, Cheshunt 2
Clapton 0, Ware 2

QUARTER-FINALS
Cheshunt 1, Chalfont St Peter 0
Flackwell Heath 2, Ware 1
Hungerford Town 3, Kingsbury Town 3
Kingsbury Town won 6-5 on penalties.
Leyton 4, Camberley Town 0

SEMI-FINALS
Flackwell Heath 2, Leyton 2
Replay: Leyton 2, Flackwell Heath 0
Cheshunt 5, Kingsbury Town 0

FINAL
Leyton 2, Cheshunt 0

THE FA TROPHY 2002–03

PRELIMINARY ROUND

Chorley v Stocksbridge Park Steels 1-1, 0-1
Alfreton Town v Guiseley 5-0
Rocester v Workington 2-2, 2-2
Rocester won 4-3 on penalties.
Rossendale United v Witton Albion 2-2, 0-2
Farsley Celtic v Ossett Town 1-0
Trafford v Belper Town 2-0
Lincoln United v Bishop Auckland 4-3
Bamber Bridge v Leek Town 2-2, 1-3
North Ferriby United v Matlock Town 3-0
Radcliffe Borough v Eastwood Town 0-1
Shepshed Dynamo v Taunton Town 2-2, 0-3
Atherstone United v Gloucester City 0-1
Rothwell Town v Cinderford Town 4-0
Racing Club Warwick v Clevedon Town 0-1
Bromsgrove Rovers v Banbury United 0-1
Solihull Borough v Sutton Coldfield Town 2-0
Mangotsfield United v Stourport Swifts 4-2
Merthyr Tydfil v Evesham United 2-0
Bedworth United v Corby Town 0-1
Croydon Athletic v Tonbridge Angels 0-3
Histon v Wingate & Finchley 2-0
Leyton Pennant v Oxford City 0-2
East Thurrock United v Sittingbourne 2-0
Fleet Town v Epsom & Ewell 1-1, 0-2
Dorchester Town v Yeading 4-1
Aveley v Newport (IoW) 2-0
Spalding United v Barton Rovers 3-0
Harlow Town v Uxbridge 2-2, 2-1
Bracknell Town v Fisher Athletic 2-2, 7-4
Corinthian Casuals v Barking & East Ham United 4-3
Burnham v Arlesey Town 3-1
Wealdstone v Banstead Athletic 0-0, 1-0
Erith & Belvedere v St Leonards 2-0
Hornchurch v Walton & Hersham 2-6
Metropolitan Police v Dulwich Hamlet 1-1, 1-3
Hertford Town v Molesey 1-0
Northwood v Tooting & Mitcham United 0-2
Windsor & Eton v Ashford Town (Middlesex) 2-1
King's Lynn v Chertsey Town 4-0
Salisbury City v Dartford 2-0
Berkhamsted Town v Leatherhead 6-0
Slough Town v Wembley 2-0
Bashley v Marlow 1-2
Bognor Regis Town v Wivenhoe Town 5-2
Horsham v Tilbury 4-0

FIRST ROUND

Spennymoor United v Witton Albion 4-3
Blyth Spartans v North Ferriby United 5-3
Burscough v Marine 0-0, 3-1
Gresley Rovers v Harrogate Town 0-0, 0-3
Droylsden v Ashton United 2-1
Lincoln United v Alfreton Town 2-3
Stocksbridge Park Steels v Whitby Town 0-1
Gateshead v Hyde United 0-2
Leek Town v Eastwood Town 4-1
Farsley Celtic v Trafford 7-2
Rocester v Colwyn Bay 0-2
Kidsgrove Athletic v Frickley Athletic 1-1, 1-2
Gainsborough Trinity v Kendal Town 3-1
Mangotsfield United v Redditch United 3-1
Corby Town v Rothwell Town 0-5
Halesowen Town v Bath City 4-3
Grantham Town v Hinckley United 3-2
Banbury United v Gloucester City 1-1, 1-2
Weston-Super-Mare v Cirencester Town 1-1
Abandoned; waterlogged pitch 2-2, 2-3
Solihull Borough v Swindon Supermarine 7-1
Clevedon Town v Hednesford Town 2-4
Rugby United v Hucknall Town 2-1
Taunton Town v Merthyr Tydfil 1-2
Thame United v Bromley 3-2
Great Wakering Rovers v Ford United 2-2, 1-6
Burnham v Aylesbury United 0-2
Oxford City v Egham Town 4-2
Corinthian Casuals v Croydon 1-0
Hastings United v Chelmsford City 1-0
Hitchin Town v Chatham Town 3-1
Lewes v Slough Town 6-4
East Thurrock United v Kingstonian 1-3
Tooting & Mitcham United v Dulwich Hamlet 2-3
Aveley v Weymouth 1-4
Harlow Town v Wealdstone 2-0
Horsham v Ashford Town 2-0
Whyteleafe v Walton & Hersham 1-5
Worthing v Cambridge City 1-4
Staines Town v Epsom & Ewell 1-2
Carshalton Athletic v Folkestone Invicta 2-1
Bracknell Town v Heybridge Swifts 0-2
Windsor & Eton v Welling United 2-2, 5-3
Sutton United v Harrow Borough 2-1
Hemel Hempstead Town v Histon 2-3
Salisbury City v Erith & Belvedere 2-2, 0-2
Berkhamsted Town v Bishop's Stortford 2-2, 0-2
Eastbourne Borough v Hertford Town 4-1
Bognor Regis Town v Boreham Wood 2-0
Chippenham Town v Dorchester Town 4-1
Spalding United v Hampton & Richmond Borough 2-1
Marlow v Bedford Town 1-1, 2-1
Tonbridge Angels v Maidenhead United 3-2
King's Lynn v Stamford 1-2
Enfield v Basingstoke Town 1-2

SECOND ROUND

Droylsden v Colwyn Bay 1-2
Stafford Rangers v Alfreton Town 0-2
Moor Green v Blyth Spartans 2-3
Spennymoor United v Halesowen Town 1-1, 1-4
Tamworth v Accrington Stanley 4-1
Worksop Town v Solihull Borough 4-2
Runcorn FC Halton v Rugby United 0-3
Histon v Farsley Celtic 3-4
Harrogate Town v Burscough 2-2, 2-3
Vauxhall Motors v Frickley Athletic 4-2
Stalybridge Celtic v Rothwell Town 2-0
Wakefield & Emley v Spalding United 5-0
Leek Town v Hyde United 3-1
Ilkeston Town v Hednesford Town 3-1
Lancaster City v Stamford 6-1
Grantham Town v Gainsborough Trinity 0-1
Barrow v Whitby Town 4-2
Bradford Park Avenue v Altrincham 0-1
Chippenham Town v Aylesbury United 0-1
Hastings United v Eastbourne Borough 0-2
Heybridge Swifts v Weymouth 2-1
Dover Athletic v Ford United 2-0
Canvey Island v Carshalton Athletic 2-0
Windsor & Eton v Hitchin Town 3-1
Oxford City v Braintree Town 1-0
Gloucester City v Merthyr Tydfil 0-0, 1-0
St Albans City v Hayes 0-1
Havant & Waterlooville v Billericay Town 1-1, 2-1
Basingstoke Town v Sutton United 0-2
Horsham v Thame United 1-2
Kingstonian v Erith & Belvedere 5-1
Grays Athletic v Tiverton Town 3-1
Purfleet v Tonbridge Angels 3-2
Harlow Town v Lewes 0-3
Bishop's Stortford v Marlow 2-2, 2-3
Newport County v Epsom & Ewell 2-1
Chesham United v Walton & Hersham 0-0, 1-0
Bognor Regis Town v Hendon 1-4
Mangotsfield United v Dulwich Hamlet 0-1
Cambridge City v Crawley Town 0-1
Worcester City v Aldershot Town 1-0
Corinthian Casuals v Cirencester Town 0-4

THIRD ROUND

Farsley Celtic v Gainsborough Trinity 1-1, 1-2
Kettering Town v Altrincham 1-1, 3-3
Altrincham won 5-3 on penalties.
Chester City v Worksop Town 1-2
Leek Town v Southport 1-2
Alfreton Town v Halesowen Town 2-1
Leigh RMI v Vauxhall Motors 1-2
Rugby United v Telford United 0-2
Stalybridge Celtic v Scarborough 0-3
Northwich Victoria v Barrow 3-1
Wakefield & Emley v Burton Albion 1-0
Ilkeston Town v Burscough 0-3

Tamworth v Nuneaton Borough 3-0
Lancaster City v Morecambe 0-1
Colwyn Bay v Blyth Spartans 1-0
Halifax Town v Doncaster Rovers 4-1
Woking v Chesham United 3-0
Dover Athletic v Gravesend & Northfleet 1-0
Stevenage Borough v Oxford City 2-1
Forest Green Rovers v Barnet 4-2
Windsor & Eton v Thame United 3-2
Aylesbury United v Kingstonian 1-0
Eastbourne Borough v Farnborough Town 0-1
Gloucester City v Lewes 3-2
Dagenham & Redbridge v Marlow 5-2
Hayes v Crawley Town 2-1
Dulwich Hamlet v Margate 0-2
Canvey Island v Cirencester Town 5-1
Heybridge Swifts v Hendon 0-0, 1-2
Worcester City v Newport County 3-2
Purfleet v Grays Athletic 1-2
Hereford United v Yeovil Town 1-2
Sutton United v Havant & Waterlooville 1-3

FOURTH ROUND

Colwyn Bay v Havant & Waterlooville 0-2
Scarborough v Dover Athletic 1-1, 1-2
Halifax Town v Grays Athletic 3-2
Windsor & Eton v Vauxhall Motors 1-1, 3-0
Northwich Victoria v Canvey Island 2-1
Altrincham v Aylesbury United 0-1
Worksop Town v Hayes 2-3
Yeovil Town v Morecambe 2-1
Alfreton Town v Burscough 1-1, 0-2
Gainsborough Trinity v Forest Green Rovers 0-2
Worcester City v Margate 0-2
Dagenham & Redbridge v Southport 0-0, 2-2
Southport won 4-3 on penalties.
Gloucester City v Woking 0-0, 2-0
Wakefield & Emley v Hendon 0-0, 1-0
Tamworth v Stevenage Borough 3-0
Telford United v Farnborough Town 2-3

FIFTH ROUND

Dover Athletic v Forest Green Rovers 0-3
Margate v Tamworth 0-2
Farnborough Town v Halifax Town 2-0
Yeovil Town v Northwich Victoria 2-1
Burscough v Wakefield & Emley 5-0
Aylesbury United v Windsor & Eton 2-2, 1-1
Aylesbury United won 4-3 on penalties.
Gloucester City v Southport 1-1, 3-1
Havant & Waterlooville v Hayes 3-0

SIXTH ROUND

Farnborough Town v Tamworth 1-2
Aylesbury United v Gloucester City 2-1
Forest Green Rovers v Havant & Waterlooville 1-2
Yeovil Town v Burscough 0-2

SEMI-FINALS (two legs)

Aylesbury United v Burscough 1-1, 0-1
Tamworth v Havant & Waterlooville 1-0, 1-1

THE FA TROPHY FINAL

Sunday, 18 May 2003
(at Villa Park)

Burscough (1) 2 *(Martindale 26, 55)*
Tamworth (0) 1 *(Cooper 79)* 14,265

Burscough: Taylor M; Byrne (Black), Bowen, Macauley (White), Taylor J, Teale, Norman, Burns, Martindale (McHale), Wright, Lawless.
Tamworth: Acton; Warner, Follett, McGorry, Robinson, Walsh, Colley, Cooper, Rickards (Hatton), Sale (Hallam), Evans (Turner).
Referee: U. Rennie (Sheffield).

THE FA TROPHY – PREVIOUS WINNERS

Year	*Winners*	*Runners-up*	*Score*
1970	Macclesfield Town	Telford United	2-0
1971	Telford United	Hillingdon Borough	3-2
1972	Stafford Rangers	Barnet	3-0
1973	Scarborough	Wigan Athletic	2-1
1974	Morecambe	Dartford	2-1
1975	Matlock Town	Scarborough	4-0
1976	Scarborough	Stafford Rangers	3-2
1977	Scarborough	Dagenham	2-1
1978	Altrincham	Leatherhead	3-1
1979	Stafford Rangers	Kettering Town	2-0
1980	Dagenham	Mossley	2-1
1981	Bishop's Stortford	Sutton United	1-0
1982	Enfield	Altrincham	1-0
1983	Telford	Northwich Victoria	2-0
1984	Northwich Victoria	Bangor City	1-1
	Replay		2-1
1985	Wealdstone	Boston United	2-1
1986	Altrincham	Runcorn	1-0
1987	Kidderminster Harriers	Burton Albion	0-0
	Replay		2-1
1988	Enfield	Telford United	0-0
	Replay		3-2
1989	Telford United	Macclesfield Town	1-0
1990	Barrow	Leek Town	3-0
1991	Wycombe Wanderers	Kidderminster Harriers	2-1
1992	Colchester United	Witton Albion	3-1
1993	Wycombe Wanderers	Runcorn	4-1
1994	Woking	Runcorn	2-1
1995	Woking	Kidderminster Harriers	2-1
1996	Macclesfield Town	Northwich Victoria	3-1
1997	Woking	Dagenham & Redbridge	1-0
1998	Cheltenham Town	Southport	1-0
1999	Kingstonian	Forest Green Rovers	1-0
2000	Kingstonian	Kettering Town	3-2
2001	Canvey Island	Forest Green Rovers	1-0
2002	Yeovil Town	Stevenage Borough	2-0

THE FA VASE – PREVIOUS WINNERS

Year	*Winners*	*Runners-up*	*Score*
1975	Hoddesdon Town	Epsom & Ewell	2-1
1976	Billericay Town	Stamford	1-0
1977	Billericay Town	Sheffield	1-1
	Replay		2-1
1978	Blue Star	Barton Rovers	2-1
1979	Billericay Town	Almondsbury Greenway	4-1
1980	Stamford	Guisborough Town	2-0
1981	Wickham	Willenhall Town	3-2
1982	Forest Green Rovers	Rainworth MW	3-0
1983	VS Rugby	Halesowen Town	1-0
1984	Stansted	Stamford	3-2
1985	Halesowen Town	Fleetwood Town	3-1
1986	Halesowen Town	Southall	3-0
1987	St Helens Town	Warrington Town	3-2
1988	Colne Dynamoes	Emley	1-0
1989	Tamworth	Sudbury Town	1-1
	Replay		3-0
1990	Yeading	Bridlington Town	0-0
	Replay		1-0
1991	Guiseley	Gresley Rovers	4-4
	Replay		3-1
1992	Wimborne Town	Guiseley	5-3
1993	Bridlington Town	Tiverton Town	1-0
1994	Diss Town	Taunton Town	2-1
1995	Arlesey Town	Oxford City	2-1
1996	Brigg Town	Clitheroe	3-0
1997	Whitby Town	North Ferriby United	3-0
1998	Tiverton Town	Tow Law Town	1-0
1999	Tiverton Town	Bedlington Terriers	1-0
2000	Deal Town	Chippenham Town	1-0
2001	Taunton Town	Berkhamsted Town	2-1
2002	Whitley Bay	Tiptree United	1-0

THE FA VASE 2002–03

FIRST QUALIFYING ROUND

Blackpool Mechanics v Sheffield 0-0, 1-3
Chester-Le-Street Town v Eccleshill United 0-1
Nelson v Curzon Ashton 2-0
South Shields v Holker Old Boys 0-2
Thackley w.o. v Retford United removed from competition; no floodlights
West Allotment Celtic v Goole 2-1
Selby Town v Louth United 0-1
New Mills v Northallerton Town 1-5
Crook Town v Guisborough Town 1-3
Marske United v Prudhoe Town 1-2
Winsford United v Great Harwood Town 3-0
Brodsworth MW v Jarrow Roofing Boldon CA 3-2
Paulton Victoria v Hebburn Town 2-0
Easington Colliery v Warrington Town 0-1
Hatfield Main v Penrith 1-2
Chadderton v Glasshoughton Welfare 2-2, 0-6
Norton & Stockton Ancients v Washington 0-2
Oldham Town v Parkgate 0-6
Malvern Town v Rainworth MW 5-0
Causeway United v Bolehall Swifts 6-0
Willenhall Town v Marconi 6-0
Bourne Town v Bromyard Town 3-3
Bourne Town won 4-3 on penalties.
Kimberley Town v Carlton Town 3-4
Oldbury United v Dunkirk 5-2
Nettleham v Shawbury United 2-8
Handrahan Timbers v Congleton Town 0-3
Lye Town v Anstey Nomads 5-0
Heath Hayes v Tivedale 2-0
Glapwell v Westfields 3-1
Quorn v Blackstones 4-2
Biddulph Victoria v Kirby Muxloe 2-1
Blackwell MW v Lincoln Moorlands 1-0
Staveley MW v Cradley Town 0-1
Rolls Royce Leisure v Pegasus Juniors 3-1
Ledbury Town v Coventry Sphinx 3-2
Greenacres (Hemel Hempstead) w.o. v Downton Town withdrew
Ware v Hullbridge Sports 3-1
Whitton United v Enfield Town 1-3
Great Yarmouth Town v Clacton Town 1-3
Hoddesdon Town v Ruislip Manor 5-2
Fakenham Town v Ely City 1-3
Felixstowe & Walton United v Letchworth 2-0
Leyton v Brimsdown Rovers 1-0
Welwyn Garden City v Henley Town 2-1
Holmer Green v Bugbrooke St Michaels 3-1
Chalfont St Peter v Norwich United 0-2
Beaconsfield SYCOB v Harwich & Parkeston 3-2
Halstead Town v Thetford Town 2-0
Stowmarket Town v Harpenden Town 4-2
Brook House v Leighton Town 0-2
Brackley Town v Buckingham Town 1-4
Gorleston v Romford 4-1
Bury Town v Harringey Borough 2-1
Brightlingsea United withdrew v Clapton w.o.
Lowestoft Town v Edgware Town 4-3
Biggleswade Town v Cornard United 1-2
Long Buckby v Wootton Blue Cross 1-5
Westfield v Eastbourne Town 3-4
Horsham YMCA v Chipstead 1-1, 2-3
Wantage Town v Carterton Town 1-0
Merstham v Hartley Witney 6-0
Lordswood v Redhill 1-2
Whitstable Town v Raynes Park Vale 2-4
Godalming & Guildford v Three Bridges 1-0
Abingdon United v Chessington United 3-0
Ringmer v Eastbourne United 2-0
Farnham Town v Whitehawk 0-4
Ramsgate v Deal Town 1-2
Hungerford Town v Petersfield Town 4-0
East Preston v AFC Totton 0-3
Gosport Borough v Chichester City United 3-0
Eastleigh v Peacehaven & Telscombe 6-0
Pagham v Greenwich Borough 0-3
Frome Town v Downton 4-2
Poole Town v Christchurch 0-0, 0-2
Elmore v Harrow Hill 4-0
Paulton Rovers v Barnstaple Town 3-0
Wellington Town v Devizes Town 1-2
Clevedon United v Almondsbury Town 1-1, 4-2
Falmouth Town v Bristol Manor Farm 4-2
Portland United v Ilfracombe Town 0-1

SECOND QUALIFYING ROUND

Guisborough Town v Darwen 2-1
Woodleigh Sports v Horden CW 2-2, 1-2
Atherton Collieries v Cheadle Town 2-1
West Allotment Celtic v Warrington Town 1-1, 1-3
Bacup Borough v Cammell Laird 0-5
Squires Gate v Brandon United 2-4
Atherton LR v Sheffield 4-5
Thornaby v Willington 4-0
Kennek Ryehope CA v Northallerton Town 1-3
Esh Winning v Whickham 4-0
Penrith v Stand Athletic 3-0
Bridlington Town v North Shields 8-0
Newcastle Blue Star v Newcastle Benfield Saints 3-5
Louth United v Armthorpe Welfare 1-3
Fleetwood Town v Alsager Town 2-0
Harrogate Railway v Skelmersdale United 2-0
Alnwick Town v Ashington 0-7
Winsford United v Thackley 1-1, 2-3
Abbey Hey v Maltby Main 8-1
Nelson v Evenwood Town 2-1
Morpeth Town v Washington 3-1
Peterlee Newtown v Maine Road 3-1
Paulton Victoria v Seaham Red Star 2-1
Liversedge v Prudhoe Town 4-1
Washington Nissan v Flixton 0-1
Winterton Rangers v Parkgate 3-2
Tadcaster Albion v Eccleshill United 0-7
Shildon v Glasshoughton Welfare 6-3
Merton v Rossington Main 3-0
Brodsworth MW v Shotton Comrades 2-0
Pontefract Collieries v Holker Old Boys 5-1
Colne v Hall Road Rangers 1-3
Mossley v Ramsbottom United 3-1
Garforth Town v Formby 4-1
Worsborough Bridge MW v Yorkshire Amateur 0-1
Lye Town v Dudley Town 3-1
West Midlands Police v Holbeach United 1-4
Boston Town v Deeping Rangers 1-2
Oldbury United v Blackwell MW 6-1
Buxton v Daventry Town 1-0
St Andrews v Chasetown 0-1
Brierley & Hagley v Malvern Town 1-2
Stratford Town v Wednesfield 13-0
Holwell Sports v Congleton Town 1-2
Fernhill County Sports v Tipton Town 2-0
Cradley Town v Stafford Town 0-1
Coalville Town v Mickleover Sports 0-1
Meir KA v Ludlow Town 1-0
Shawbury United v Boldmere St Michaels 0-1
Gedling Town v Blaby & Whetstone Athletic 5-1
Highfield Rangers v South Normanton Athletic 2-5
Birstall United v Borrowash Victoria 1-2
Glapwell v Carlton Town 0-3
Barrow Town v Leamington 0-1
Willenhall Town v Friar Lane OB 1-0
Leek CSOB v Ledbury Town 1-5
Norton United v King's Heath 3-0
Biddulph Victoria v Rugby Town 0-1
Ibstock Welfare v Heath Hayes 8-0
Sutton Town v Glossop North End 5-6
Wellington v Alvechurch 2-4
Stone Dominoes v Causeway United 1-2
Shifnal Town v Rolls Royce Leisure 0-1
Long Eaton United v Pershore Town 2-1
Quorn v Shirebrook Town 1-2
Nuneaton Griff v Bourne Town 4-1
Downes Sports v Halesowen Harriers 0-5
Little Drayton Rangers v Pelsall Villa 1-4
Grosvenor Park v Gornal Athletic 4-0
Stansted v Bedford United & Valerio 2-1
Eton Manor v Buckingham Town 0-3
St Margaretsbury v Beaconsfield SYCOB 4-3
Ipswich Wanderers v Concord Rangers 1-1, 3-2
Harefield United v Northampton Spencer 3-1
Worboys Town v Needham Market 1-5
Burnham Ramblers v Somersham Town 2-1

Greenacres (Hemel Hempstead) v Stowmarket Town 3-1
Potters Bar Town v Bicester Town 6-1
Broxbourne Borough V&E v Tring Town 3-2
March Town United v Lowestoft Town 0-5
Eynesbury Rovers v Maldon Town 0-4
Basildon United v Enfield Town 0-2
Cheshunt v Leighton Town 2-0
Biggleswade United v London Colney 1-2
Leverstock Green v Cockfosters 1-0
Wootton Blue Cross v Holmer Green 2-0
Felixstowe & Walton United v Colney Heath 3-1
Welwyn Garden City v Rothwell Corinthians 1-2
Kempston Rovers v Norwich United 0-2
Woodbridge Town v Haverhill Rovers 0-5
Dunstable Town v Halstead Town 2-3
Stanway Rovers v Royston Town 5-1
Clacton Town v Potton United 3-1
Hanwell Town v Ely City 5-2
Leyton v Hoddesdon Town 5-1
Gorleston v Saffron Walden Town 1-1
(Match abandoned 113 minutes; Saffron Walden 2-1
Town had only six players on the pitch)
St Ives Town v Southall Town 3-4
Newmarket Town v Ilford 2-1
Bury Town v Brentwood 4-0
Witham Town v Yaxley 1-3
Southall v Flackwell Heath 0-1
Diss Town v Sawbridgeworth Town 2-0
Hadleigh United v Southend Manor 2-2, 0-4
Cornard United v Desborough Town 3-1
Woodford Town v Soham Town Rangers 1-4
Ware v Bowers United 4-3
Clapton v Langford 2-1
East Grinstead Town v Herne Bay 4-3
Bedfont v Hungerford Town 2-2, 5-2
Wantage Town v Saltdean United 1-0
Cray Wanderers v Godalming & Guildford 2-1
Alton Town v Erith Town 2-3
Hythe Town v Deal Town 1-1, 4-6
Sidlesham v Redhill 7-0
VCD Athletic v Littlehampton Town 2-1
Whitehawk v Reading Town 2-0
Oakwood v Lymington Town 1-3
Chessington & Hook United v Beckenham Town 4-3
Greenwich Borough v Wokingham Town 4-0
Cobham v Hillingdon Borough 3-1
Raynes Park Vale v BAT Sports 1-2
Camberley Town v Withdean 2000 0-2
Arundel v Hassocks 3-1
Gosport Borough v Ringmer 3-0
Slade Green v Viking Greenford 6-1
Sandhurst Town v Southwick 1-0
Lymington & New Milton v Wick 11-1
Blackfield & Langley v Eastleigh 1-7
Eastbourne Town v Winchester City 2-5
Fareham Town v Walton Casuals 0-1
Lancing v Hailsham Town 0-1
Chipstead v AFC Newbury 1-3
AFC Totton v Sidley United 2-1
Abingdon United v Milton United 2-0
Cove v Merstham 1-5
Tunbridge Wells v Didcot Town 0-2
Whitchurch United v Broadbridge Heath 0-7
Corsham Town v Brislington 2-0
Falmouth Town v Gloucester United 2-1
Westbury United v Elmore 2-1
Calne Town v Shepton Mallet 2-0
Bridport v Fareford Town 0-1
Ilfracombe Town v Torrington 1-2
Christchurch v Odd Down 2-0
Frome Town v Liskeard Athletic 0-1
Backwell United v Dawlish Town 6-1
Tuffley Rovers v Cullompton Rangers 3-1
Minehead Town v Chipping Norton Town 3-1
Hamworthy United v Bitton 2-3
Shortwood United v Wootton Bassett Town 5-1
Welton Rovers v Keynsham Town 3-2
Chard Town v Highworth Town 0-4
Paulton Rovers v Launceston 3-1
Cirencester Academy withdrew v Willand Rovers w.o.
Street v Yate Town 1-2
Exmouth Town v Bournemouth 0-1
Bridgwater Town v Pewsey Vale 9-1
Newton Abbot v Amesbury Town 3-3, 4-1
Devizes Town v Bishop Sutton 5-1
Clevedon United v Hook Norton 3-2

FIRST ROUND

Brandon United v Merton 3-0
Armthorpe Welfare v Bridlington Town 1-1, 3-3
Bridlington Town won 6-5 on penalties.
Eccleshill United v Paulton Victoria 1-3
Pontefract Collieries v Penrith 5-0
Abbey Hey v Liversedge 3-0
Esh Winning v Mossley 0-2
Salford City v Thackley 2-1
Warrington Town v Flixton 1-2
Nelson v Dunston FB 0-1
Garforth Town v Northallerton Town 0-1
Horden CW v Ashington 1-0
Peterlee Newtown v Ossett Albion 2-5
Hall Road Rangers v Hallam 4-3
Newcastle Benfield Saints v Morpeth Town 1-2
Nantwich Town v Fleetwood Town 0-3
Brodsworth MW v Billingham Synthonia 2-6
Cammell Laird v Shildon 4-1
Sheffield v Winterton Rangers 3-2
Yorkshire Amateur v Guisborough Town 1-2
Atherton Collieries v Harrogate Railway 4-6
Borrowash Victoria v Stafford Town 2-0
Rolls Royce Leisure v Long Eaton United 0-2
Stratford Town v Stourbridge 0-1
Malvern Town v Norton United 0-2
Congleton Town v Oldbury United 4-1
Pelsall Villa v Studley 1-3
Glossop North End v Ford Sports Daventry 1-2
Barwell v Ledbury Town 4-1
Nuneaton Griff v Grosvenor Park 0-1
Carlton Town v Lye Town 4-2
Boldmere St Michaels v Halesowen Harriers 2-1
Newcastle Town v Buxton 2-0
Stewarts & Lloyds v Deeping Rangers 3-0
Alvechurch v Rugby Town 0-3
Holbeach United v Fernhill County Sports 5-0
Meir KA v Causeway United 2-3
Gedling Town v Cogenhoe United 2-0
Wisbech Town v Chasetown 2-1
Willenhall Town v South Normanton Athletic 2-0
Bridgnorth Town v Shirebrook Town 0-2
Mickleover Sports v Leamington 2-0
Ibstock Welfare v Raunds Town 0-1
Burnham Ramblers v Bury Town 1-4
Hanwell Town v Greenacres (Hemel Hempstead) 8-3
Kingsbury Town v Cornard United 4-2
Southend Manor v Norwich United 2-3
Gorleston v Newmarket Town 3-2
Leverstock Green v Potters Bar Town 1-2
Buckingham Town v Clapton 4-1
Lowestoft Town v Ipswich Wanderers 5-1
London Colney v Broxbourne Borough V&E 2-0
Diss Town v Rothwell Corinthians 3-3, 5-0
St Margaretsbury v Stansted 8-0
Ware v Needham Market 3-0
Halstead Town v Stanway Rovers 2-3
Haverhill Rovers v Soham Town Rangers 0-3
Felixstowe & Walton United v Leyton 0-5
Enfield Town v North Leigh 3-1
Clacton Town v Southall Town 0-1
Wootton Blue Cross v Cheshunt 0-0, 2-0
Maldon Town v Harefield United 2-0
Yaxley v Flackwell Heath 5-1
Lymington & New Milton v Walton Casuals 5-2
Cowes Sports v Greenwich Borough 2-1
Whitehawk v Broadbridge Heath 3-0
Sandhurst Town v Gosport Borough 1-0
Lymington Town v Selsey 0-3
Chessington & Hook United v Abingdon United 2-1
Merstham v Withdean 2000 0-5
Maidstone United v Sidlesham 2-4
Winchester City v Cray Wanderers 5-2
Wantage Town v East Grinstead Town 5-2
Cobham v BAT Sports 5-3
Andover v AFC Newbury 3-1
AFC Wallingford v Arundel 0-1
Slade Green v Erith Town 0-2
Hailsham Town v Brockenhurst 1-2
Eastleigh v Deal Town 4-0
VCD Athletic v AFC Totton 1-5
Thatcham Town v Moneyfields 2-3
Bedfont v Didcot Town 1-3
St Blazey v Yate Town 3-2
Falmouth Town v Devizes Town 2-3
Newton Abbot v Willand Rovers 0-1

Clevedon United v Bournemouth 1-2
Bridgwater Town v Bitton 0-1
Shortwood United v Calne Town 1-0
Christchurch v Tuffley Rovers 4-2
Fareford Town v Team Bath 0-0, 2-5
Wimborne Town v Minehead Town 4-0
Welton Rovers v Highworth Town 5-0
Liskeard Athletic v Bideford 0-2
Corsham Town v Backwell United 1-0
Melksham Town v Paulton Rovers 1-4
Torrington v Westbury United 3-2
Bye: Thornaby

SECOND ROUND

Sheffield v Guisborough Town 1-2
Cammell Laird v Harrogate Railway 3-4
Pontefract Collieries v Northallerton Town 1-2
Billingham Synthonia v Whitley Bay 0-1
Consett v Billingham Town 1-4
Dunston FB v Tow Law Town 3-2
Ossett Albion v Durham City 0-4
Brigg Town v Horden CW 2-1
Abbey Hey v Hall Road Rangers 2-0
Morpeth Town v Brandon United 2-1
Thornaby v Fleetwood Town 1-1, 1-4
Bridlington Town v Paulton Victoria 2-1
Salford City v Mossley 1-2
Clitheroe v Bedlington Terriers 3-1
Prescot Cables v West Auckland Town 2-1
Flixton v St Helens Town 2-1
Mickleover Sports v Raunds Town 2-1
Borrowash Victoria v Rugby Town 0-3
Carlton Town v Oadby Town 1-2
Shirebrook Town v Congleton Town 5-4
St Neots Town v Newcastle Town 0-3
Boldmere St Michaels v Rushall Olympic 1-2
Stewarts & Lloyds v Ford Sports Daventry 2-3
Norton United v Gedling Town 1-2
Causeway United v Long Eaton United 2-1
Willenhall Town v Arnold Town 4-0
Wisbech Town v Holbeach United 2-2, 0-3
Barwell v Grosvenor Park 0-3
Heanor Town v Studley 0-2
Pickering Town v Stourbridge 3-2
Withdean 2000 v St Margaretsbury 2-2, 1-0
Cobham v Gorleston 0-1
Lowestoft Town v Sidlesham 5-0
Diss Town v Tiptree United 3-2
Sandhurst Town v Dorking 3-3, 1-4
Soham Town Rangers v Selsey 2-3
Potters Bar Town v Yaxley 0-1
Mildenhall Town v Maldon Town 2-4
Didcot Town v Wootton Blue Cross 1-2
Thamesmead Town v Leyton 3-1
Wroxham v Enfield Town 2-0
Chessington & Hook United v Ware 2-4
Norwich United v Stotfold 1-1, 2-1
London Colney v Milton Keynes City 2-2, 0-1
Arundel v Erith Town 1-0
Burgess Hill Town v Stanway Rovers 2-1
AFC Sudbury v Southall Town 1-0
Ash United v Kingsbury Town 4-1
Whitehawk v Abingdon Town 2-0
Buckingham Town v Bury Town 2-0
Hanwell Town v Dereham Town 2-1
Bitton v Wimborne Town 2-1
Devizes Town v Wantage Town 3-2
Christchurch v Torrington 3-2
Brockenhurst v Bemerton Heath Harlequins 1-0
Winchester City v Shortwood United 3-2
St Blazey v Hallen 1-0
Welton Rovers v Bournemouth 2-1
Moneyfields v Paulton Rovers 1-0
Eastleigh v Porthleven 1-3
Bideford v Cowes Sports 5-0
AFC Totton v Andover 2-0
Team Bath v Lymington & New Milton 2-3
Willand Rovers v Corsham Town 1-0

THIRD ROUND

Prescot Cables v Flixton 6-2
Rugby Town v Bridlington Town 1-2
Fleetwood Town v Abbey Hey 3-1
Grosvenor Park v Billingham Town 0-3
Pickering Town v Causeway United
Abandoned 31 minutes; injury to referee 2-2, 2-1
Dunston FB v Whitley Bay 0-2
Oadby Town v Mickleover Sports 2-2, 3-2
Clitheroe v Studley 4-1
Morpeth Town v Willenhall Town 3-2
Brigg Town v Rushall Olympic 2-1
Guisborough Town v Mossley 0-1
Northallerton Town v Shirebrook Town 6-3
Durham City v Gedling Town 7-3
Newcastle Town v Harrogate Railway 3-1
AFC Sudbury v Hanwell Town 6-0
Buckingham Town v Ash United 4-2
Moneyfields v Gorleston 0-4
Yaxley v Wroxham 0-1
Dorking v Ware 0-1
Holbeach United v Burgess Hill Town 1-4
Milton Keynes City v Diss Town 0-2
Wootton Blue Cross v Thamesmead Town 2-1
Ford Sports Daventry v Withdean 2000 0-2
Maldon Town v Selsey 3-0
Lowestoft Town v Norwich United 3-0
Whitehawk v Arundel 2-5
St Blazey v AFC Totton 5-1
Welton Rovers v Christchurch 0-5
Devizes Town v Bitton 2-2, 2-0
Willand Rovers v Lymington & New Milton 4-5
Bideford v Porthleven 3-2
Brockenhurst v Winchester City 0-7

FOURTH ROUND

Lymington & New Milton v Mossley 2-3
Newcastle Town v Winchester City 0-1
Northallerton Town v Burgess Hill Town 0-3
Wroxham v Prescot Cables 0-2
Ware v Clitheroe 0-1
Oadby Town v Bideford 4-2
Wootton Blue Cross v Whitley Bay 1-2
Maldon Town v Morpeth Town 3-0
Gorleston v Billingham Town 3-1
Durham City v AFC Sudbury 0-4
Devizes Town v Christchurch 3-1
Bridlington Town v Arundel 5-0
Withdean 2000 v Diss Town 2-2, 1-3
Lowestoft Town v Buckingham Town 2-0
Brigg Town v Fleetwood Town 3-1
Pickering Town v St Blazey 2-3

FIFTH ROUND

Brigg Town v Diss Town 4-1
Whitley Bay v Oadby Town 1-2
Gorleston v Bridlington Town 1-2
Lowestoft Town v Maldon Town 2-3
St Blazey v AFC Sudbury 1-1, 1-7
Mossley v Prescot Cables 2-1
Burgess Hill Town v Winchester City 1-2
Clitheroe v Devizes Town 1-3

SIXTH ROUND

Brigg Town v Bridlington Town 2-1
Devizes Town v Maldon Town 0-3
Oadby Town v Winchester City 1-0
Mossley v AFC Sudbury 0-2

SEMI-FINALS (two legs)

Oadby Town v Brigg Town 0-2, 1-1
Maldon Town v AFC Sudbury 0-1, 0-2

THE FA VASE FINAL

Saturday, 10 May 2003

(at Upton Park)

AFC Sudbury (1) 1 *(Rayner 28)*

Brigg Town (1) 2 *(Housham 2, Carter 70)* 6634

AFC Sudbury: Greygoose; Head (Norfolk 61), Spearing, Gardiner (Banya 78), Tracey, Bishop, Rayner, Anderson (Owen 71), Claydon, Bennett, Betson.
Brigg Town: Steer; Raspin, Carter, Rowland, Thompson G, Blanchard, Stones, Housham, Borman (Drayton 86), Roach, Stead (Thompson R 41).
Referee: M. Fletcher (Worcestershire).

THE FA YOUTH CUP 2002–03

FIRST QUALIFYING ROUND

Garforth Town v Curzon Ashton	0-1
Prudhoe Town v Yorkshire Amateur	4-1
Scarborough v Whitley Bay	6-2
Selby Town v Ossett Town	2-4
Leigh RMI v Wakefield & Emley	5-1
Consett v Witton Albion	2-3
Guiseley v Chadderton	1-5
Lancaster City v Morecambe	0-1
Altrincham v Frickley Athletic	5-0
Farsley Celtic v Pontefract Collieries	2-3
Chester City v Northwich Victoria	1-2
New Mills v Bradford (Park Avenue)	3-1
Barrow v Warrington Town	1-2
Workington v Doncaster Rovers	2-7
Chester-Le-Street Town v Southport	6-1
Halifax Town v Marine	1-1
Halifax Town won 5-4 on penalties.	
Harrogate Railway v Thackley	0-7
Burscough w.o. v Gretna withdrew	
Gornal Athletic v Congleton Town	5-0
Malvern Town w.o. v Holbeach United withdrew	
Rugby United v Belper Town	3-1
Lincoln United v Sutton Coldfield Town	1-3
Boldmere St Michaels v Kettering Town	1-2
Hucknall Town v Wisbech Town	1-0
Cradley Town v Arnold Town	3-2
Louth United v Mickleover Sports	1-2
Grantham Town v Lincoln Morlands	5-2
Quorn v Stone Dominoes	2-1
Hednesford Town v Oadby Town	1-3
Racing Club Warwick v Matlock Town	4-2
Coventry Sphinx v Gresley Rovers	3-3
Gresley Rovers won 5-4 on penalties.	
Nantwich Town v Lye Town	0-4
Chasetown v Bedworth United	1-5
Atherstone United v Long Buckby	2-0
Alfreton Town v Corby Town	3-0
Concord Rangers v Edgware Town	1-0
Histon v Uxbridge	3-1
Ruislip Manor v AFC Wallingford	4-2
Tie awarded to AFC Wallingford; Ruislip Manor fielded ineligible players.	
Clapton v Barton Rovers	2-9
Marlow v Hampton & Richmond Borough	0-3
Cogenhoe United v Southend Manor	0-4
Canvey Island v Royston Town	6-0
Hayes v Cambridge City	1-4
Heybridge Swifts v Sawbridgeworth Town	3-0
Leighton Town v Ilford	1-2
Hoddesdon Town v Henley Town	5-2
Cheshunt v Chesham United	0-2
Soham Town Rangers v Chelmsford City	2-3
Bedford Town v Bugbrooke St Michaels	2-4
Northampton Spencer v Haringey Borough	1-1
Haringey Borough won 3-1 on penalties.	
Stevenage Borough v Biggleswade United	7-0
Hullbridge Sports v Hornchurch	0-5
Tilbury v Welwyn Garden City	1-0
Wembley v Leyton	2-2
Leyton won 4-3 on penalties.	
St Ives Town v Diss Town	2-1
Beaconsfield SYCOB v Banbury United	1-0
Brentwood v Witham Town	2-0
Woodbridge Town v Dereham Town	4-1
Newmarket Town v Hemel Hempstead Town	0-4
Wingate & Finchley v Great Wakering Rovers	1-3
Purfleet v Bishop's Stortford	3-1
Great Yarmouth Town v Aylesbury United	0-5
Wealdstone v Ipswich Wanderers	0-3
Tie awarded to Wealdstone; Ipswich Wanderers fielded an ineligible player.	
Burnham Ramblers v Arlesey Town	0-1
Ware v Bowers United	8-1
Lowestoft Town v Bury Town	1-3
Northwood v Milton Keynes City	2-4
St Albans City v Berkhamsted Town	5-0
Hitchin Town v Potters Bar Town	0-2
Tie awarded to Hitchin Town; Potters Bar Town fielded an ineligible player.	
Halstead Town v Romford	1-4
Wokingham Town withdrew v Thame United w.o.	
Molesey v Fleet Town	7-1
Leatherhead v Horsham	5-1
Dartford v Gravesend & Northfleet	2-4
Farnborough Town v Aldershot Town	1-4
Walton & Hersham v Wick	1-3
Eastbourne Town v Moneyfields	3-1
Eastleigh v Banstead Athletic	4-2
Dover Athletic v Burgess Hill Town	6-2
North Leigh withdrew v Bracknell Town w.o.	
Chessington United v Chertsey Town	5-1
Sandhurst Town v Thatcham Town	3-4
Milton United v Tonbridge Angels	1-2
Littlehampton Town v Hillingdon Borough	0-3
Alton Town v Horndean	4-5
Gosport Borough v Croydon	1-2
Crowborough Athletic v Thamesmead Town	0-6
Merstham v Ashford Town (Middlesex)	1-3
Reading Town v Dulwich Hamlet	2-3
Abingdon United v Cobham	2-1
Hailsham Town v Three Bridges	0-6
Sittingbourne v Croydon Athletic	0-2
Saltdean United v Farnham Town	1-2
Eastbourne United v Havant & Waterlooville	2-10
Lewes v Pagham	2-0
Winchester City v Ramsgate	0-2
Chipstead v Tooting & Mitcham United	1-6
Carshalton Athletic v Basingstoke Town	4-2
Erith Town v AFC Newbury	2-1
Chatham Town v Kingstonian	0-3
Walton Casuals v Chichester City United	2-2
Chichester City United won 5-4 on penalties.	
Bashley withdrew v Westfield w.o.	
Swindon Supermarine v Cinderford Town	4-0
Worcester City v Newport County	4-0
Bitton v Cirencester Town	1-4
Yeovil Town v Chippenham Town	3-1
Gloucester City v Hereford United	6-2
Salisbury City v Evesham United	5-3
Forest Green Rovers v Bath City	1-5
Pershore Town v Mangotsfield United	0-4
Brislington v Clevedon Town	3-2
Paulton Rovers v Bournemouth	2-3
Frome Town v Corsham Town	1-0

SECOND QUALIFYING ROUND

Morecambe v Leigh RMI	3-1
Ossett Town v Pontefract Collieries	0-3
Scarborough v Chadderton	4-0
New Mills v Chester-Le-Street Town	0-2
Witton Albion v Halifax Town	1-9
Doncaster Rovers v Prudhoe Town	5-1
Curzon Ashton v Northwich Victoria	0-3
Burscough v Altrincham	2-1
Stocksbridge Park Steels v Warrington Town	2-0
Pickering Town v Thackley	1-3
Mickleover Sports v Racing Club Warwick	2-3
Worksop Town v Grantham Town	2-1
Tamworth v Sutton Coldfield Town	2-3
Hucknall Town v Kettering Town	0-2
Quorn v Malvern Town	1-2
Cradley Town v Gornal Athletic	2-1
Nuneaton Borough v Deeping Rangers	5-4
Bedworth United v Marconi	1-3
Tie awarded to Bedworth U; Marconi fielded an ineligible player.	
Oadby Town v Atherstone United	2-1
Burton Albion v Hinckley United	1-1
Burton Albion won 3-1 on penalties.	
Gresley Rovers v Alfreton Town	0-1
Lye Town v Rugby United	2-1
Ilford v Arlesey Town	4-1
Cambridge City v Hampton & Richmond Borough	5-0
Purfleet v St Albans City	0-4
Aylesbury United v Brentwood	0-1
Concord Rangers v Heybridge Swifts	1-2
Romford v Ware	0-3
Saffron Walden Town v Milton Keynes City	1-3
Tilbury v Hemel Hempstead Town	3-5
Harringey Borough v Leyton	1-0
Beaconsfield SYCOB v Canvey Island	0-5

Hitchin Town v Bugbrooke St Michaels 2-0
AFC Wallingford v Stevenage Borough 0-7
Woodbridge Town v Chelmsford City 1-4
Bury Town v St Ives Town 8-0
Hoddesdon Town v Wealdstone 6-3
Great Wakering Rovers v Histon 1-3
Southend Manor v Chesham United 0-2
Barton Rovers v Hornchurch 1-1
Barton Rovers won 4-2 on penalties.
Bracknell Town v Erith Town 1-1
Bracknell Town won 2-0 on penalties.
Eastleigh v Aldershot Town 2-2
Aldershot Town won 4-1 on penalties.
Ramsgate v Lordswood 4-0
Tooting & Mitcham United v Croydon Athletic 3-1
Thame United v Dover Athletic 0-4
Camberley Town v Kingstonian 1-4
Whyteleafe v Westfield 0-1
Ashford Town (Middlesex) v Havant & Waterlooville 0-5
Horndean v Dulwich Hamlet 1-3
Three Bridges v Eastbourne Town 5-3
Woking v Hillingdon Borough 3-2
Leatherhead v Croydon 2-4
Farnham Town v Tonbridge Angels 1-5
Chichester City United v Abingdon United 2-2
Abingdon United won 6-5 on penalties.
Chessington United v Carshalton Athletic 2-1
Lewes v Molesey 5-2
Wick v Thatcham Town 2-3
Gravesend & Northfleet v Thamesmead Town 2-1
Salisbury City v Gloucester City 2-1
Yeovil Town v Cirencester Town 1-1
Cirencester Town won 9-8 on penalties.
Worcester City v Devizes Town 9-2
Frome Town v Mangotsfield United 1-3
Bournemouth v Brislington 1-0
Swindon Supermarine v Bath City 0-5

THIRD QUALIFYING ROUND

Pontefract Collieries v Northwich Victoria 2-5
Halifax Town v Doncaster Rovers 0-2
Scarborough v Burscough 2-3
Stocksbridge Park Steels v Morecambe 0-3
Chester-Le-Street Town v Thackley 3-0
Cradley Town v Malvern Town 3-0
Kettering Town v Sutton Coldfield Town 2-3
Worksop Town v Lye Town 2-1
Alfreton Town v Bedworth United 5-5
Bedworth United won 7-6 on penalties.
Burton Albion v Oadby Town 1-2
Racing Club Warwick v Nuneaton Borough 0-5
Brentwood v Hoddesdon Town 0-1
Heybridge Swifts v Barton Rovers 0-3
Bury Town v St Albans City 0-2
Ilford v Canvey Island 3-0
Ware v Hitchin Town 2-3
Cambridge City v Histon 4-0
Haringey Borough v Milton Keynes City 2-1
Chelmsford City v Hemel Hempstead Town 1-0
Chesham United v Stevenage Borough 3-4
Tooting & Mitcham United v Chessington United 7-1
Dover Athletic v Gravesend & Northfleet 3-1
Abingdon United v Ramsgate 1-2
Bracknell Town v Three Bridges 1-4
Kingstonian v Woking 2-1
Aldershot Town v Lewes 4-0
Dulwich Hamlet v Westfield 9-0
Tonbridge Angels v Havant & Waterlooville 2-0
Thatcham Town v Croydon 1-5
Bath City v Salisbury City 3-3
Salisbury City won 3-2 on penalties.
Mangotsfield United v Bournemouth 4-4
Bournemouth won 5-4 on penalties.
Cirencester Town v Worcester City 4-3

FIRST ROUND

Port Vale v Chesterfield 5-2
Oldham Athletic v Hull City 2-3
Northwich Victoria v Tranmere Rovers 0-6
Huddersfield Town v Carlisle United 3-0
Chester-Le-Street Town v Hartlepool United 1-2
Crewe Alexandra v Barnsley 0-1
Darlington v Blackpool 2-3
Bury v Lincoln City 2-1
Stockport County v Doncaster Rovers 1-1
Doncaster Rovers won 3-1 on penalties.
Scunthorpe United v Morecambe 5-2
Burscough v Rochdale 2-1
Macclesfield Town v York City 0-1
Wigan Athletic v Wrexham 0-1
Nuneaton Borough v Cambridge United 1-5
Oadby Town v Kidderminster Harriers 3-1
Mansfield Town v Rushden & Diamonds 2-1
Shrewsbury Town v Northampton Town 0-2
Peterborough United v Cradley Town 8-1
Bedworth United v Notts County 0-1
Sutton Coldfield Town v Worksop Town 3-2
Dulwich Hamlet v Stevenage Borough 3-1
Tooting & Mitcham United v Tonbridge Angels 3-0
Dover Athletic v Chelmsford City 3-4
Brentford v Luton Town 0-3
Three Bridges v Hitchin Town 5-2
Croydon v Hoddesdon Town 1-3
Haringey Borough v St Albans City 1-6
Ilford v Wycombe Wanderers 1-4
Aldershot Town v Colchester United 1-4
Queens Park Rangers v Oxford United 1-0
Cambridge City v Sutton United 2-0
Ramsgate v Leyton Orient 3-4
AFC Bournemouth v Southend United 5-3
Kingstonian v Barton Rovers 2-3
Bournemouth v Cheltenham Town 0-4
Exeter City v Plymouth Argyle 2-1
Bristol City v Swansea City 5-3
Cirencester Town v Bristol Rovers 2-1
Torquay United v Cardiff City 0-3
Swindon Town v Salisbury City 4-0

SECOND ROUND

Port Vale v Hartlepool United 4-3
Wrexham v Sutton Coldfield Town 1-0
Tranmere Rovers v York City 2-0
Mansfield Town v Barnsley 1-2
Burscough v Blackpool 1-2
Hull City v Huddersfield Town 2-2
Huddersfield Town won 8-7 on penalties.
Oadby Town v Northampton Town 1-0
Notts County v Scunthorpe United 4-0
Bury v Doncaster Rovers 5-3
Exeter City v AFC Bournemouth 3-2
Dulwich Hamlet v Cambridge City 3-2
Cardiff City v Three Bridges 3-1
Barton Rovers v Cheltenham Town 1-3
Chelmsford City v Swindon Town 2-9
Wycombe Wanderers v Cirencester Town 2-0
Colchester United v St Albans City 4-2
Hoddesdon Town v Queens Park Rangers 1-0
Peterborough United v Leyton Orient 2-1
Cambridge United v Bristol City 1-0
Tooting & Mitcham United v Luton Town 1-3

THIRD ROUND

Walsall v Wolverhampton Wanderers 0-4
Fulham v Dulwich Hamlet 1-1
Fulham won 3-2 on penalties.
Portsmouth v Tottenham Hotspur 1-3
Grimsby Town v Chelsea 0-1
Bolton Wanderers v Cambridge United 0-1
Liverpool v Barnsley 1-2
Peterborough United v Nottingham Forest 1-0
Derby County v Southampton 0-2
Reading v Sheffield Wednesday 1-2
Ipswich Town v Notts County 1-2
Luton Town v Stoke City 1-0
Burnley v Crystal Palace 0-2
Sheffield United v Birmingham City 4-3
Manchester City v Wrexham 3-0
Hoddesdon Town v Swindon Town 1-4
Wycombe Wanderers v Tranmere Rovers 2-3
Brighton & Hove Albion v Wimbledon 1-2
Everton v Port Vale 0-1
West Ham United v Oadby Town 4-1
Blackburn Rovers v Blackpool 5-1
Coventry City v Leicester City 2-1
Arsenal v Colchester United 2-0
Cardiff City v Charlton Athletic 1-3
Leeds United v Gillingham 4-0
Watford v Exeter City 0-2

Middlesbrough v Bury	3-1
Rotherham United v Cheltenham Town	2-3
Millwall v West Bromwich Albion	2-0
Bradford City v Preston North End	2-0
Newcastle United v Manchester United	1-3
Norwich City v Aston Villa	2-1
Huddersfield Town v Sunderland	1-2

FOURTH ROUND

Tranmere Rovers v Cheltenham Town	3-0
Tottenham Hotspur v Swindon Town	1-0
Millwall v Arsenal	2-1
Cambridge United v Leeds United	2-4
West Ham United v Fulham	6-1
Luton Town v Bradford City	1-0
Charlton Athletic v Wolverhampton Wanderers	1-0
Southampton v Sunderland	0-1
Wimbledon v Norwich City	0-2
Crystal Palace v Notts County	3-1
Barnsley v Middlesbrough	0-1
Sheffield United v Coventry City	1-0
Port Vale v Chelsea	2-1
Blackburn Rovers v Exeter City	6-0
Manchester United v Sheffield Wednesday	2-0
Peterborough United v Manchester City	0-1

FIFTH ROUND

Crystal Palace v Tottenham Hotspur	0-1
Luton Town v Middlesbrough	1-1
Middlesbrough won 4-3 on penalties.	
West Ham United v Norwich City	2-1
Manchester United v Sheffield United	1-1
Manchester United won 4-3 on penalties.	
Leeds United v Blackburn Rovers	3-2
Tranmere Rovers v Port Vale	4-1
Sunderland v Charlton Athletic	2-2
Charlton Athletic won 4-3 on penalties.	
Millwall v Manchester City	0-1

SIXTH ROUND

Middlesbrough v Tottenham Hotspur	1-0
Manchester United v Tranmere Rovers	3-1
Leeds United v Charlton Athletic	0-1
Manchester City v West Ham United	2-0

SEMI-FINALS (two legs)

Middlesbrough v Manchester City	1-1, 2-1
Charlton Athletic v Manchester United	1-1, 0-2

THE FA YOUTH CUP FINAL (First Leg)

Tuesday, 15 April 2003

Middlesbrough (0) 0

Manchester United (1) 2 *(Richardson 4, Collett 89)* 8310

Middlesbrough: Turnbull; McMahon, Wheater, Davies, Bates, Harrison, Taylor, Liddle, Peacock (Kennedy 83), Brunt, Morrison.
Manchester United: Steele; Sims, Bardsley, McShane, Lawrence, Eagles, Jones, Richardson, Collett, Timm (Ebanks-Blake 59), Johnson.
Referee: R. Styles (Hampshire).

THE FA YOUTH CUP FINAL (Second Leg)

Friday, 25 April 2003

Manchester United (1) 1 *(Johnson 15)*

Middlesbrough (0) 1 *(Liddle 78)* 14,849

Manchester United: Steele; Sims, Bardsley, McShane (Howard 76), Lawrence, Eagles, Richardson (Poole 78), Jones, Collett, Johnson, Ebanks-Blake (Calliste 76).
Middlesbrough: Turnbull; McMahon, Bates, Wheater, Harrison (Reed 58), Morrison, Liddle, Taylor, Brunt (Masters 86), Peacock (Nordgren 46), Davies.
Referee: R. Styles (Hampshire).

THE FA YOUTH CUP – PREVIOUS WINNERS
(Aggregate Scores)

Year	*Winners*	*Runners-up*	*Score*
1953	Manchester United	Wolverhampton W	9-3
1954	Manchester United	Wolverhampton W	5-4
1955	Manchester United	West Bromwich Albion	7-1
1956	Manchester United	Chesterfield	4-3
1957	Manchester United	West Ham United	8-2
1958	Wolverhampton W	Chelsea	7-6
1959	Blackburn Rovers	West Ham United	2-1
1960	Chelsea	Preston North End	5-2
1961	Chelsea	Everton	5-3
1962	Newcastle United	Wolverhampton W	2-1
1963	West Ham United	Liverpool	6-5
1964	Manchester United	Swindon Town	5-2
1965	Everton	Arsenal	3-2
1966	Arsenal	Sunderland	5-3
1967	Sunderland	Birmingham City	2-0
1968	Burnley	Coventry City	3-2
1969	Sunderland	West Bromwich Albion	6-3
1970	Tottenham Hotspur	Coventry City	4-3
1971	Arsenal	Cardiff City	2-0
1972	Aston Villa	Liverpool	5-2
1973	Ipswich Town	Bristol City	4-1
1974	Tottenham Hotspur	Huddersfield Town	2-1
1975	Ipswich Town	West Ham United	5-1
1976	West Bromwich Albion	Wolverhampton W	5-0
1977	Crystal Palace	Everton	1-0*
1978	Crystal Palace	Aston Villa	1-0
1979	Millwall	Manchester City	2-0
1980	Aston Villa	Manchester City	3-2
1981	West Ham United	Tottenham Hotspur	2-1
1982	Watford	Manchester United	7-6
1983	Norwich City	Everton	6-5
1984	Everton	Stoke City	4-2
1985	Newcastle United	Watford	4-1
1986	Manchester City	Manchester United	3-1
1987	Coventry City	Charlton Athletic	2-1
1988	Arsenal	Doncaster Rovers	6-1
1989	Watford	Manchester City	2-1
1990	Tottenham Hotspur	Middlesbrough	3-2
1991	Millwall	Sheffield Wednesday	3-0
1992	Manchester United	Crystal Palace	6-3
1993	Leeds United	Manchester United	4-1
1994	Arsenal	Millwall	5-3
1995	Manchester United	Tottenham Hotspur	2-2
	Manchester United won 4-3 on penalties		
1996	Liverpool	West Ham United	4-1
1997	Leeds United	Crystal Palace	3-1
1998	Everton	Blackburn Rovers	5-3
1999	West Ham United	Coventry City	9-0
2000	Arsenal	Coventry City	5-1
2001	Arsenal	Blackburn Rovers	6-3
2002	Aston Villa	Everton	4-2

* One match only

THE FA SUNDAY CUP 2002–03

FIRST ROUND

Dickie Lewis v East Levenshulme	3-1
Clubmoor Nalgo v Fairweather Green WMC	1-2
East Bowling Unity v Ford Motors	3-2
Lobster v Bolton Woods	1-3
Taxi Club v Sandon	1-1
Taxi Club won 4-1 on penalties.	
Hetton Lyons Cricket Club v Oakenshaw	2-0
Norcoast v Prestige Brighams	2-1
Seymour v Redcar Workingmens	2-3
Hessle Rangers v Nicosia	0-3
Travellers v Three Horse Shoes	9-1
Linfield Yenton v Sporting Khalsa	5-0
St Gerards v St Joseph's (Luton)	0-2
Gossoms End v Hammer	1-4
Walsall Wood Royal Exchange v Slade Celtic	6-3
FC Houghton Centre v London Colney BCH	2-2
London Colney BCH won 4-2 on penalties.	
Schofields v Readflex Rangers	2-0
Brache Green Man withdrew v Capel Plough w.o.	
Standens Barn v Mackadown Lane S&S	1-2
Celtic SC (Luton) v Duke of York	0-3
St Margarets v St Joseph's (South Oxhey)	4-1
Theale (Sunday) v Quested	1-4
Ouzavich v Percival	2-3
Hexton v Lea Bridge Rangers	1-2
Lebeq Tavern Courage v Mayfair United	2-1
Southcote Video v Pioneer	3-8
General Panel Sports v Palmeston WMC	5-1

SECOND ROUND

Albion Sports v Dickie Lewis	3-2
Garston Woodcutter's v St Aloysius E	1-4
Clifton v Fairweather Green WMC	0-3
Hartlepool Lion Hillcarter v Smith & Nephew	3-0
A3 (Canada) v Britannia	3-2
East Bowling Unity v Shankhouse United	2-0
Bolton Woods v Canon	0-2
Orchard Park v Western Approaches	4-1
Burradon & New Fordley v Nicosia	4-3
Fantail Manfast v Hetton Lyons Cricket Club	4-3
Taxi Club v Redcar Workingmens	1-2
Allerton v Norcoast	5-1
Queens Park v Queensbury	4-0
Jolly Farmers v Linfield Yenton	1-0
Little Paxton v Travellers	2-4
Marden v St Joseph's (Luton)	0-3
Toll End v Trooper	7-2
Crawley Green v Hammer	0-1
Queensmen v Walsall Wood Royal Exchange	3-2
Casino Cars v London Colney BCH	1-0
Moat v Schofields	3-2
Belstone v Capel Plough	1-0
Lewsey Social v Mackadown Lane S&S	2-3
Biggleswade (Sunday) v Duke of York	1-5
Lodge Cottrell v St Margarets	3-4
Creekmoor Lions v Percival	5-5
Percival won 4-2 on penalties.	
General Panel Sports v Heybridge Social	4-2
Quested v Pioneer	5-4
Cavaliers (Reading) v Lea Bridge Rangers	0-2
Old Oak v Toby	1-1
Old Oak won 4-3 on penalties.	
Bournemouth Electric v Lebeq Tavern Courage	3-1
Rainham Sports v Reading Irish	0-4

THIRD ROUND

Burradon & New Fordley v Albion Sports	1-4
Hartlepool Lion Hillcarter v Fantail Manfast	1-0
Canon v Jolly Farmers	0-3
Fairweather Green WMC v Redcar Workingmens	1-0
St Aloysius E v Queens Park	5-1
Allerton v Orchard Park	3-1
A3 (Canada) v East Bowling Unity	3-2
Travellers v General Panel Sports	7-0
Duke of York v Lea Bridge Rangers	3-0
Reading Irish v Mackadown Lane S&S	5-0
Belstone v Hammer	2-3
St Joseph's (Luton) v Moat	7-0
Toll End v Casino Cars	0-1
Queensmen v Bournemouth Electric	3-1
St Margarets v Percival	5-1
Quested v Old Oak	7-0

FOURTH ROUND

Fairweather Green WMC v A3 (Canada)	1-3
Hartlepool Lion Hillcarter v St Aloysius E	4-2
Allerton v Jolly Farmers	4-0
Albion Sports v St Margarets	3-3
St Margarets won 4-2 on penalties.	
St Joseph's (Luton) v Queensmen	4-0
Reading Irish v Hammer	4-0
Casino Cars v Travellers	0-4
Duke of York v Quested	6-1

FIFTH ROUND

St Margarets v Hartlepool Lion Hillcarter	1-2
Allerton v A3 (Canada)	1-1
Allerton won 2-0 on penalties.	
Duke of York v Reading Irish	3-0
Travellers v St Joseph's (Luton)	1-3
Tie awarded to Travellers as St Joseph's (Luton) fielded an ineligible player.	

SEMI-FINALS

Hartlepool Lion Hillcarter v Allerton	1-3
Travellers v Duke of York	3-5

THE FA SUNDAY CUP FINAL

Duke of York v Travellers	3-1
(at Liverpool FC)	2203

THE FA SUNDAY CUP – PREVIOUS WINNERS

Year	*Winners*	*Runners-up*	*Score*
1965	London	Staffordshire	6-2
1966	Ubique United	Aldridge Fabrications	1-0
1967	Carlton United	Stoke Works	2-0
1968	Drovers	Brook United	2-0
1969	Leigh Park	Loke United	3-1
1970	Vention United	Ubique United	1-0
1971	Beacontree United	Saltley United	2-0
1972	Newtown Unity	Springfield Colts	4-0
1973	Carlton United	Wear Valley	2-1
1974	Newtown Unity	Brentford East	3-0
1975	Fareham Town Centipedes	Players Athletic Engineers	1-0
1976	Brandon United	Evergreen	2-1
1977	Langley Park Rams Head	Newtown Unity	2-0
1978	Arras	Lion Rangers	2-1
1979	Lobster	Carlton United	3-2
1980	Fantail	Twin Foxes	1-0
1981	Fantail	Mackintosh	1-0
1982	Dingle Rail	Twin Foxes	2-1
1983	Eagle	Lee Chapel North	1-1
	Replay		2-1
1984	Lee Chapel North	Eagle	4-3
1985	Hobbies United	Avenue	2-2
	Replay		1-1
	Second Replay		2-1
1986	Avenue	Glenn Sports	1-0
1987	Lodge Cottrell	Avenue	1-0
1988	Nexday	Humbledon Plains Farm	2-0
1989	Almithak	East Levenshulme	3-1
1990	Humbledon Plains Farm	Marston Sports	2-1
1991	Nicosia	Ouzavich	3-2
1992	Theale	Marston Sports	3-2
1993	Seymour	Bedfont Sunday	1-0
1994	Ranelagh Sports	Hartlepool Lion Hotel	2-0
1995	St Joseph's (Luton)	B&A Scaffolding	2-1
1996	St Joseph's (Luton)	Croxteth & Gilmoss RBL	2-1
1997	Marston United	Northwood	1-0
1998	Olympic Star	St Joseph's (Luton)	1-1
	Olympic Star won 5-3 on penalties.		
1999	Little Paxton	St Joseph's (Luton)	2-2
	Little Paxton won 4-3 on penalties.		
2000	Prestige Brighams	Albion Sports	1-0
2001	Hartlepool Lion Hillcarter	FC Houghton Centre	0-0
	Hartlepool Lion Hillcarter won 3-2 on penalties.		
2002	Britannia	Little Paxton	2-0

THE FA COUNTY YOUTH CUP 2002–03

FIRST ROUND

Isle of Man v Manchester	1-1
Isle of Man won 4-3 on penalties.	
Shropshire v Westmoreland	2-0
Cheshire v Leicestershire	1-0
North Riding v Derbyshire	7-0
Staffordshire v Northumberland	1-5
Sheffield & Hallamshire v Lincolnshire	2-1
Match awarded to Lincolnshire; Sheffield & Hallamshire fielded an over-age player.	
Herefordshire v Gloucestershire	2-0
Oxfordshire v Hampshire	6-4
Devon v Wiltshire	0-2
Surrey v Huntingdonshire	2-0
Worcestershire v Essex	3-1
London v Hertfordshire	3-2
Sussex v Dorset	3-6
Cambridgeshire v Army	2-2
Cambridgeshire won 4-3 on penalties.	
Northamptonshire v Berks & Bucks	1-0

SECOND ROUND

Cumberland v North Riding	0-3
East Riding v West Riding	4-1
Birmingham v Shropshire	3-0
Durham v Nottinghamshire	2-1
Cheshire v Lincolnshire	0-1
Lancashire v Northumberland	2-2
Northumberland won 3-2 on penalties.	
Liverpool v Isle of Man	3-2
Cornwall v Somerset	6-3
Dorset v Cambridgeshire	0-2
Suffolk v Bedfordshire	4-3
Norfolk v Surrey	2-0
London v Jersey	4-2
Kent v Northamptonshire	1-0
Guernsey v Oxfordshire	6-2
Herefordshire v Wiltshire	0-1
Worcestershire v Middlesex	1-2

THIRD ROUND

Birmingham v Durham	4-3
Suffolk v Northumberland	0-2
Lincolnshire v Middlesex	0-1
East Riding v Kent	1-5
Liverpool v Norfolk	1-0
Cambridgeshire v London	2-0
North Riding v Wiltshire	3-4
Guernsey v Cornwall	1-1
Guernsey won 4-2 on penalties.	

FOURTH ROUND

Wiltshire v Liverpool	1-2
Birmingham v Northumberland	0-1
Cambridgeshire v Middlesex	1-2
Kent v Guernsey	2-1

SEMI-FINALS

Northumberland v Middlesex	3-1
Liverpool v Kent	3-0

FA COUNTY YOUTH CUP FINAL

Liverpool v Northumberland	0-1
(at Southport FC)	315

THE FA COUNTY YOUTH CUP – PREVIOUS WINNERS
(Aggregate scores until 1970)

Year	*Winners*	*Runners-up*	*Score*
1945	Staffordshire	Wiltshire	3-2
1946	Berks & Bucks	Durham	4-3
1947	Durham	Essex	4-2
1948	Essex	Liverpool	5-3
1949	Liverpool	Middlesex	4-3
1950	Essex	Middlesex	4-3
1951	Middlesex	Leicestershire & Rutland	3-1
1952	Sussex	Liverpool	3-1
1953	Sheffield & Hallamshire	Hampshire	5-3
1954	Liverpool	Gloucestershire	4-1
1955	Bedfordshire	Sheffield & Hallamshire	2-0
1956	Middlesex	Staffordshire	3-2
1957	Hampshire	Cheshire	4-3
1958	Staffordshire	London	8-0
1959	Birmingham	London	7-5
1960	London	Birmingham	6-4
1961	Lancashire	Nottinghamshire	6-3
1962	Middlesex	Nottinghamshire	6-3
1963	Durham	Essex	3-2
1964	Sheffield & Hallamshire	Birmingham	1-0
1965	Northumberland	Middlesex	7-4
1966	Leicestershire & Rutland	London	6-5
1967	Northamptonshire	Hertfordshire	5-4
1968	North Riding	Devon	7-4
1969	Northumberland	Sussex	1-0
1970	Hertfordshire	Cheshire	2-1
1971	Lancashire	Gloucestershire	2-0
1972	Middlesex	Liverpool	2-0
1973	Hertfordshire	Northumberland	3-0
1974	Nottinghamshire	London	2-0
1975	Durham	Bedfordshire	2-1
1976	Northamptonshire	Surrey	7-1
1977	Liverpool	Surrey	3-0
1978	Liverpool	Kent.	3-1
1979	Hertfordshire	Liverpool	4-1
1980	Liverpool	Lancashire	2-0
1981	Lancashire	East Riding	3-2
1982	Devon	Kent	0-0
	Replay		3-2
1983	London	Gloucestershire	3-0
1984	Cheshire	Manchester	2-1
1985	East Riding	Middlesex	2-1
1986	Hertfordshire	Manchester	4-0
1987	North Riding	Gloucestershire	3-1
1988	East Riding	Middlesex	1-1
	Replay		5-3
1989	Liverpool	Hertfordshire	2-1
1990	Staffordshire	Hampshire	1-1
	Replay		2-1
1991	Lancashire	Surrey	6-0
1992	Nottinghamshire	Surrey	1-0
1993	Durham	Liverpool	4-0
1994	West Riding	Sussex	3-1
1995	Liverpool	Essex	3-2
1996	Durham	Gloucestershire	1-0
1997	Cambridgeshire	Lancashire	1-0
1998	Northumberland	West Riding	2-1
1999	Durham	Sussex	1-0
2000	Birmingham	Surrey	2-1
2001	Northamptonshire	Birmingham	3-0
2002	Birmingham	Durham	2-1

ENGLAND NATIONAL GAME XI

Italy 3
England 2 *(Kennedy, Boardman)* 1500
(at Cremona).
England: Baker; Lockwood, Rose, Johnson, Boardman, Peyton, Kennedy, Purser, Thompson, Sugden, Webster.
(Subs all used: Anderson, Weale, Lancaster, Blackburn, Way.)

Belgium 3
England 1 *(D'Sane)* 870
(at Ostend).
England: Key; Kennedy, Ward, Pullan, Duffy, Rivierre, Craney, Manuella, Wilde, McAllister, Rickards.
(Subs all used: Tomlinson, Bull, D'Sane, Keeling, Sims.)

Holland 0
England 0 950
(at Rotterdam).
England: Brown W; Kennedy, Guyett, Collins, Rose, Janney, Norris, Drummond, Elam, Blundell, Agogo.
(Subs all used: Johnson, Weale, Jackson, D'Sane, Rigoglioso.)

Lockwood, Johnson, Weale, Way, Skiverton, Jackson K (Yeovil Town); Baker, Rose (Hereford United); Boardman (Woking); Peyton (Nuneaton Borough); Kennedy, Ward, Duffy (Canvey Island); Purser, Agogo (Barnet); Thompson, Drummond, Elam, Rigoglioso (Morecambe); Sugden, Lancaster, Blackburn, Brown W, Collins, Guyett, Hatswell (Chester City); Webster, Anderson (Burton Albion); Key, Sims (Kingstonian); Pullan (Crawley Town); Rivierre (Welling United); Craney (Altrincham); Manuella (Aylesbury United); Wilde (Worcester City); McAllister (Basingstoke Town); Rickards (Tamworth); Tomlinson (Runcorn); Bull, D'Sane (Aldershot Town); Keeling (Purfleet); Janney, Terry (Dagenham & Redbridge); Norris, Blundell (Northwich Victoria); Jackson J (Gravesend & Northfleet); Whitman (Doncaster Rovers).

NB: Elam to Halifax Town in May.

FOUR NATIONS TOURNAMENT

England 4 *(Jackson 3, D'Sane)*
Republic of Ireland 0
(at Merthyr).
England: Weale; Kennedy (Hatswell), Guyett, Skiverton, Rose, Johnson (Terry), Way, Drummond, Elam, Jackson (Agogo), D'Sane.

Wales 0
England 2 *(Way, D'Sane)*
(at Merthyr).
England: Weale; Kennedy, Guyett, Skiverton (Hatswell), Rose, Johnson, Way (Terry), Drummond, Elam, Jackson, D'Sane (Whitman).

England 1 *(D'Sane)*
Scotland 1
(at Carmarthen).
England: Baker; Kennedy, Guyett, Boardman, Rose, Johnson, Whitman, Terry (Drummond), Norris (Elam), Agogo (Jackson), D'Sane.

	P	*W*	*D*	*L*	*F*	*A*	*Pts*
England	3	2	1	0	7	1	7
Scotland	3	1	1	1	6	6	4
Republic of Ireland	3	1	0	2	5	8	3
Wales	3	1	0	2	2	5	3

SCHOOLS FOOTBALL 2002–03

BOODLE & DUNTHORNE INDEPENDENT SCHOOLS FA CUP 2002–03

FIRST ROUND
Aldenham 0, Hampton 3
Birkdale 1, KES, Witley 2
Dover College 2, Bolton 14
Grange 1, Repton 5
Latymer Upper 1, City of London 0
St Bede's College (Manchester) 3, Highgate 2
St Bede's School (Hailsham) 3, Alleyn's 1
Wolverhampton GS 2, Lancing 2
(aet; Lancing won 3-0 on penalties).

SECOND ROUND
Ardingly 1, Hulme GS 4
Bolton 5, King's, Chester 1
Brentwood 4, Malvern 0
Forest 4, Wellingborough 0
Haileybury 0, Manchester GS 1
Hampton 0, Lancing 2 *(aet)*
Kimbolton 2, Winchester 4 *(aet)*
Latymer Upper 0, Eton 5
Millfield 6, Bury GS 1 *(aet)*
Oswestry 0, Bradfield 7
QEGS, Blackburn 2, Chigwell 4
Repton 6, KES, Witley 0
St Bede's College (Manchester) 5, Charterhouse 5
(aet; Charterhouse won 5-4 on penalties).
St Edmund's, Canterbury 0, John Lyon 2
St Mary's College 1, St Bede's School (Hailsham) 2
Westminster 4, Shrewsbury 0

THIRD ROUND
Bradfield 3, Hulme GS 0
Eton 1, Westminster 2
Forest 1, Millfield 2
John Lyon 2, Brentwood 6
Lancing 0, Winchester 0
(aet; Winchester won 4-2 on penalties).
Manchester GS 2, Chigwell 5
Repton 1, Bolton 4
St Bede's School (Hailsham) 3, Charterhouse 3
(aet; Charterhouse won 4-1 on penalties).

FOURTH ROUND
Bradfield 1, Westminster 0
Brentwood 1, Bolton 3
Charterhouse 2, Winchester 1
Chigwell 0, Millfield 1

SEMI-FINALS
Bradfield 3, Millfield 1
Charterhouse 0, Bolton 5

FINAL
(at Northampton Town FC)

Bolton 1 *(Parry)*
Bradfield 0
Bolton: D. Jones; J. Burrows, N. Price, P. Rainford, M. Pimblett, N. Pantelides (A. Marshall), P. Holowaty, S. McAllister, S. Pepper, D. Roberts, C. Parry.
Bradfield: A. Platt; M. Sydenham (E. Cheung), R. Knight, T. Storer, R. Stutley, N. Woodfroffe, J. Stutley (S. Parra), B. McGhee, M. Kember, J. Morris (M. Ellis), J. Price.
Referee: P. Jones (Loughborough).

UNIVERSITY FOOTBALL 2002–03

119th UNIVERSITY MATCH

(at QPR, 12th March 2003)

Oxford 1, Cambridge 0

Oxford: Alexander Hill; Mark Addley, Chris Woodcock, Mike Adamson, Andrew Durnford, Pete Hughes, Kevin Costello (Captain), Osman Akkaya, Thierry Richards, Brendan McGurk, Chris Bone. Subs: Neil Evans, Chris Paterson, Mathew Lowe, Patrick Walker (Goalkeeper).
Scorer: Thierry Richards.

Cambridge: Duncan Heath; Sion Lewis, Luke McNally, Ed Owles, Ben Allen, Paul Dimmock, Tim Hall, Dave Harding (Captain), Chris Fairbairn, Daniel Waistell, Andy Hall. Subs: Jonathan Hughes, Steve Jamison, Jim Wormington, Mike Phillips (Goalkeeper).

Referee: C R Wilkes.

UNIVERSITY OF LONDON UNION MEN'S COMPETITIONS

(Limited to one game against each member)

Premier Division One	*P*	*W*	*D*	*L*	*F*	*A*	*Pts*
King's College	12	10	2	0	41	7	32
Royal Holloway College	12	10	1	1	24	9	31
University College	12	10	0	2	35	9	30
Imperial College	12	8	2	2	41	13	26
London School of Economics	12	4	4	4	28	22	16
Imperial College School of Medicine	12	5	1	6	29	26	16
R Free, UC & Middx Hospitals M S	12	5	1	6	25	22	16
Sch. Oriental & African Studies	12	3	4	5	26	36	13
Guy's, King's & St. Thomas's M S	12	3	3	6	11	19	12
Queen Mary Westfield College	12	4	0	8	21	31	12
St Barts & R. London Hospitals M C	12	2	2	8	13	29	8
St George's Hospital M S	11	2	1	8	7	29	7
Goldsmiths' College	11	0	1	10	7	47	1

Premier Division Two	*P*	*W*	*D*	*L*	*F*	*A*	*Pts*
Imperial College Res	11	9	1	1	38	4	28
London School of Economics Res	11	9	0	2	40	13	27
University College Res	11	8	0	3	30	14	24
University College 3rd	11	6	1	4	30	26	19
Birkbeck College Students	11	5	2	4	34	31	17
Queen Mary Westfeld College Res	11	5	1	5	21	16	16
St George's Hospital M S Res	11	5	1	5	14	23	16
King's College 3rd	11	4	2	5	19	28	14
King' College Res	11	4	0	7	17	32	12
Imperial College Sch Med Res	11	3	1	7	25	40	10
Imperial College 3rd	11	3	0	8	16	27	9
St Barts & R. London Hosps M C Res	11	0	1	10	12	42	1

(Played as conventional Leagues)

Division 1	*P*	*W*	*D*	*L*	*F*	*A*	*Pts*
London School of Economics 3rd	22	19	2	1	72	28	59
Royal Holloway College Res	21	15	2	4	73	29	47
University College 4th	22	13	2	7	61	38	41
Royal Holloway College 3rd	22	12	5	5	48	25	41
Royal Holloway College 4th	22	11	6	5	34	25	39
London School of Economics 4th	22	11	2	9	39	35	35
Guy's, King's, St. Thomas's M S Res	22	9	2	11	41	49	29
Imperial College 4th	22	7	4	11	32	62	25
R Free, UC & Middx Hosps M S Res	21	7	5	9	31	32	26
Goldsmiths' College Res	20	7	3	10	35	45	24
King's College 4th	22	1	1	20	15	69	4
Imperial College Sch Med Res 3rd	22	1	0	21	16	60	3

Division 2	*P*	*W*	*D*	*L*	*F*	*A*	*Pts*
Guy's, King's, St. Thomas's MS 3rd	22	18	1	3	65	28	55
R Free, UC & Middx Hosp M S 3rd	22	16	4	2	81	17	52
Imperial College (R. School of Mines)	22	16	1	5	69	30	49
Royal Holloway College 5th	19	10	2	7	44	37	32
Imperial College Sch Med 4th	21	10	1	10	34	50	31
London School of Economics 5th	16	8	2	6	31	18	26
R Free, UC & Middx Hosps M S 4th	15	6	1	8	19	35	19
St Barts & R. London Hosps M C 3rd	20	6	0	14	27	54	18
Guy's, King's, St. Thomas's M S 4th	22	6	0	16	35	84	18
Wye College	17	4	2	11	13	23	14
Queen Mary Westfield College 3rd	15	4	0	11	28	48	12
Goldsmiths' College 3rd	15	2	0	13	13	35	6

Division 3	P	W	D	L	F	A	Pts
Royal Veterinary College	20	17	2	1	71	24	53
Imperial College 6th	22	13	6	3	72	52	45
University College 6th	21	12	4	5	66	27	40
Imperial College 5th	22	11	1	10	60	51	34
University College 7th	21	10	3	8	58	47	33
R College of Science (Imperial College)	22	9	3	10	48	49	30
Queen Mary Westfield College 4th	21	7	3	11	44	51	24
King's College 6th	20	7	2	11	44	57	23
Queen Mary Westfield College 5th	20	7	1	12	32	54	22
University College 5th	19	6	2	11	47	50	20
King's College 5th	19	5	3	11	26	60	18
London School of Economics 6th	21	5	0	16	30	76	15

Division 4	P	W	D	L	F	A	Pts
London School of Economics 7th	16	10	1	5	39	28	31
King's College 7th	15	10	1	4	45	36	31
Sch. of Oriental & African Studies Res	14	9	3	2	68	21	30
Royal Veterinary College Res	16	6	5	5	35	35	23
Guy's, King's, St. Thomas's M S 5th	16	5	4	7	31	46	19
School of Pharmacy	14	7	1	6	30	14	22
Imperial College 7th	15	5	3	7	29	36	18
St George's Hospital M S 3rd	16	5	2	9	31	44	17
R. School of Mines Res	16	2	0	14	19	67	6

CHALLENGE CUP
University College 4 R Free, UC & Mx Hosps MS 1

RESERVES' CHALLENGE CUP
Imperial College Res 0*:0 Imperial College 3rd 0*:1

RESERVES' PLATE
R Holloway 4th 2*:5p R Free, UC & Mx HMS 4th 2*:2p

VASE
King's College 5th 1*:2 Lon Sch Economis 5th 1*:1

UNIVERSITY OF LONDON UNION WOMEN'S LEAGUES

Premier Division	P	W	D	L	F	A	Pts
Guy's, King's & St. Thomas's M S	10	9	1	0	81	8	28
Queen Mary Westfield College	10	8	1	1	69	11	25
University College	9	4	0	5	35	35	12
London School of Economics	10	4	0	6	29	40	12
Imperial College	9	2	0	7	10	58	6
School of Oriental & African Studies	8	0	0	8	5	77	0

Division 1	P	W	D	L	F	A	Pts
Royal Holloway College	10	8	1	1	64	15	25
King's College	10	6	3	1	41	9	21
R Free, UC & Middx Hosps M S	10	3	1	6	8	19	10
Royal Veterinary College	9	2	3	4	10	17	9
Goldsmiths' College	9	3	0	6	2	65	9
St George's Hospital M S	10	2	2	6	19	19	8

Division 2	P	W	D	L	F	A	Pts
Guy's, King's, St. Thomas's MS Res	8	7	0	1	30	7	21
R Free, UC & Middx Hosps M S Res	8	5	0	3	18	15	15
University College Res	8	5	0	3	17	17	15
Wye College	8	3	0	5	10	26	9
Royal Holloway College Res	8	0	0	8	8	18	0

LONDON UNIVERSITY REPRESENTATIVE XI

v Royal Navy XI	Drawn	1–1
v Oxford University	Drawn	0–0
v Amateur Football Combination	Won	4–3
v Oxford University	Lost	0–3
v Amateur Football Alliance	Lost	0–1
v Deloitte Touche	Won	6–0
v United Hospitals	Lost	0–1
v Arthurian League	Lost	0–3
v Southern Amateur League	Lost	1–4
v Portobello College Dublin	Drawn	0–0
v University of Oslo	Drawn	0–0
v ASE Bucharest	Drawn	0–0

BRITISH UNIVERSITIES SPORTS ASSOCIATION CHAMPIONSHIP

MEN'S SEMI-FINALS
UW Swansea 1, Bath 1
UW Swansea won 4-3 on penalties.
Edge Hill 2, Northumbria 4

WOMEN'S SEMI-FINALS
Brighton 1, Bath 2
Loughborough 1, Liverpool (John Moores) 0

FINALS (AT TELFORD)

MEN'S
UW Swansea 1 (*Ryan*), Northumbria 0

WOMEN'S
Loughborough 4 (*Matthews 2, Naughter, Brackenbury*), Bath 0

FA PREMIER RESERVE LEAGUES 2002–03

FA PREMIER RESERVE LEAGUE – NORTH SECTION

	P	*W*	*D*	*L*	*F*	*A*	*GD*	*Pts*
Sunderland	28	17	4	7	51	26	+25	55
Middlesbrough	28	16	7	5	47	26	+21	55
Manchester C	28	17	3	8	55	27	+28	54
Aston Villa	28	16	4	8	59	44	+15	52
Liverpool	28	13	5	10	48	34	+14	44
Everton	28	12	7	9	44	36	+8	43
Leeds U	28	10	11	7	45	37	+8	41
Manchester U	28	12	5	11	45	37	+8	41
Bolton W	28	11	5	12	45	48	–3	38
Birmingham C	28	11	4	13	33	39	–6	37
WBA	28	8	11	9	27	31	–4	35
Newcastle U	28	8	9	11	44	43	+1	33
Blackburn R	28	10	3	15	34	51	–17	33
Sheffield W	28	3	5	20	21	55	–34	14
Bradford C	28	3	3	22	20	84	–64	12

Leading Appearances	
Vuoso (Manchester C)	27
Lynch (Manchester U)	27
Dyer (WBA)	27
Danns (Blackburn R)	26
Orr (Newcastle U)	26
Mkandawire (WBA)	26
Cooke (Aston Villa)	25
Kilgallon (Leeds U)	25
Pugh (Manchester U)	25
Chambers J (WBA)	25

Leading Goalscorers	
Mellor (Liverpool)	20
Chadwick (Everton)	16
Nardiello (Manchester U)	16
Osman (Everton)	12
Moore S (Aston Villa)	9
Fagan (Birmingham C)	9
Vuoso (Manchester C)	9
Proctor (Sunderland)	9
Baros (Liverpool)	8
Huckerby (Manchester C)	8
Macken (Manchester C)	8
Chopra (Newcastle U)	8

Sunderland League appearances
(includes playing substitutes): Arca 9; Atkinson 2; Babb 3; Bellion 11; Bjorklund 4; Black 15; Brown 2; Butler 11; Byrne 7; Capper 18; Clarke 17; Collins 4; Craddock 1; Davidson 5; Dickman 21; Emerson 9; Flo 2; Flynn 1; George 2; Gray 1; Graydon 8; Ingham 5; Kilbane 2; Kyle 12; Leadbitter 1; Macho 6; McAteer 2; McCann 1; McCartney 8; Medina 17; Myhre 1; Oster 11; Peeters 5; Phillips 1; Piper 4; Poom 7; Proctor 7; Reddy 2; Rossiter 15; Ryan 4; Schwarz 9; Scott 8; Shields 2; Stewart 12; Sullivan 2; Teggart 4; Thirlwell 7; Thornton 4; Toft 1; Turns 9; Varga 9; White 2; Whitley 8; Williams 13; Wright 1.
Goals: Proctor 9, Bellion 6, Graydon 6, Kyle 6, Oster 4, Stewart 3, Brown 2, Butler 2, Dickman 2, Varga 2, Collins 1, Flo 1, Kilbane 1, McCann 1, Medina 1, White 1, Williams 1, 2 own goals.

North Section Results 2002–2003

	Aston Villa	Birmingham C	Blackburn R	Bolton W	Bradford C	Everton	Leeds U	Liverpool	Manchester C	Manchester U	Middlesbrough	Newcastle U	Sheffield W	Sunderland	WBA
Aston Villa	—	2-1	2-5	5-0	4-0	4-0	3-2	3-0	2-4	2-2	1-2	4-2	1-0	1-4	2-2
Birmingham C	0-2	—	3-0	1-1	0-2	4-3	0-5	2-0	0-2	1-0	0-2	1-0	3-0	2-0	0-0
Blackburn R	1-2	2-1	—	1-2	3-0	0-2	2-1	0-2	0-3	0-5	0-2	0-4	2-1	1-2	0-0
Bolton W	1-2	3-2	0-2	—	2-0	1-1	1-3	1-2	2-1	1-1	1-2	3-2	1-1	1-3	1-2
Bradford C	0-3	0-4	1-3	1-3	—	0-3	1-3	1-7	0-5	1-3	1-2	1-1	4-3	1-2	0-0
Everton	1-2	2-2	2-2	2-1	2-1	—	1-2	5-1	1-0	1-0	0-2	1-2	3-0	0-0	1-1
Leeds U	1-1	0-2	3-0	2-3	3-0	1-1	—	1-2	0-5	2-1	0-0	0-0	2-1	2-2	1-1
Liverpool	3-0	2-0	2-1	1-2	5-0	1-3	1-2	—	1-1	1-1	0-1	1-2	1-1	1-3	3-1
Manchester C	1-2	2-1	3-0	2-1	1-0	0-1	3-3	0-1	—	5-0	0-1	3-2	3-0	2-1	1-1
Manchester U	6-2	3-0	1-3	1-2	2-0	1-4	2-0	0-2	1-0	—	0-0	2-3	3-0	1-3	1-0
Middlesbrough	0-0	2-0	3-1	1-3	9-0	3-1	1-1	2-1	0-1	1-1	—	4-2	2-1	1-3	0-0
Newcastle U	3-2	0-0	1-2	2-2	3-3	1-0	2-4	1-1	1-2	1-2	2-2	—	0-0	0-1	5-1
Sheffield W	0-2	0-1	2-2	1-5	0-1	0-1	0-0	0-4	1-3	0-2	1-2	0-2	—	2-1	0-2
Sunderland	1-2	1-2	1-0	3-1	4-1	2-0	1-1	0-0	3-0	1-0	4-0	1-0	2-3	—	2-0
WBA	2-1	3-0	0-1	1-0	4-0	2-2	0-0	0-2	1-2	1-3	1-0	0-0	0-3	1-0	—

FA PREMIER RESERVE LEAGUE – SOUTH SECTION

	P	*W*	*D*	*L*	*F*	*A*	*GD*	*Pts*
Watford	26	15	5	6	34	27	+7	50
Fulham	26	14	6	6	58	34	+24	48
Derby Co	26	13	7	6	46	30	+16	46
Arsenal	26	13	6	7	56	38	+18	45
West Ham U	26	10	11	5	29	26	+3	41
Tottenham H	26	10	5	11	32	33	–1	35
Charlton Ath	26	10	4	12	40	37	+3	34
Nottingham F	26	10	4	12	39	42	–3	34
Leicester C	26	10	3	13	31	43	–12	33
Chelsea	26	8	8	10	31	33	–2	32
Ipswich T	26	9	5	12	34	39	–5	32
Southampton	26	9	5	12	27	38	–11	32
Wimbledon	26	5	6	15	27	44	–17	21
Coventry C	26	4	9	13	18	38	–20	21

Leading Appearances	
Stevenson (Leicester C)	26
Nicolas (Chelsea)	25
Bloomfield (Ipswich T)	25
Ricketts (Tottenham H)	25
Smith J (Watford)	25
Westlake (Ipswich T)	24
Davies A (Southampton)	24
Cousins (Chelsea)	23
Hudson (Fulham)	23
Abidallah (Ipswich T)	23
Pullen (Ipswich T)	23
Westcarr (Nottingham F)	23
Lee (Watford)	23
Swonnell (Watford)	23
Herzig (Wimbledon)	23

Leading Goalscorers	
Hammond (Fulham)	13
Kneissl (Chelsea)	12
Cornwall (Fulham)	11
Pennant (Arsenal)	9
Murray (Derby Co)	9
Aliadiere (Arsenal)	8
Jeffers (Arsenal)	8
Willock (Fulham)	8
Stevenson (Leicester C)	8
Antoine-Courier (Nottingham F)	8
Bentley (Arsenal)	7
Norville (Watford)	7

Watford League appearances
(includes playing substitutes): Baardsen 1; Blackwell 1; Blizzard 5; Boothe 4; Bouazza 7; Brown 4; Buxton 1; Collins 5; Cook 8; Doyley 14; Dyche 5; E'Beyer 1; Fisken 12; Fitzgerald 6; Foley 7; Forde 4; Glass 4; Godfrey 16; Hand 7; Helguson 2; Herd 21; Hughes 3; Ifil 18; Johnson 14; Langston 3; Lee 23; Mahon 10; Matthews 3; McNamee 16; Mead 2; Noel-Williams 4; Norville 13; Patterson 2; Saunders 10; Smith J 25; Smith T 2; Swonnell 23; Vernazza 9; Watson 2; Williams G 1; Williams R 2; Wright 5; Young 10.
Goals: Norville 7, Foley 5, Godfrey 5, Fitzgerald 3, Noel-Williams 2, Smith J 2, Boothe 1, Bouazza 1, Collins 1, Forde 1, Glass 1, Langston 1, Wright 1, Young 1, 2 own goals.

South Section

Results

2002–2003

	Arsenal	Charlton Ath	Chelsea	Coventry C	Derby Co	Fulham	Ipswich T	Leicester C	Nottingham F	Southampton	Tottenham H	Watford	West Ham U	Wimbledon
Arsenal	—	6-1	0-2	4-1	1-2	1-5	2-0	3-3	7-2	3-1	2-0	1-1	1-2	2-1
Charlton Ath	4-1	—	2-1	4-0	1-1	0-1	1-1	1-2	0-2	1-0	1-0	1-2	0-1	1-1
Chelsea	1-1	4-1	—	1-0	0-1	3-4	3-2	2-1	3-0	0-1	0-2	1-5	0-0	2-2
Coventry C	1-1	1-3	0-0	—	2-0	1-2	0-3	0-2	0-3	0-0	1-1	0-1	0-0	1-1
Derby Co	0-0	1-0	0-2	2-0	—	1-0	4-1	2-2	2-3	1-1	4-0	3-1	3-0	4-1
Fulham	3-0	0-2	2-2	2-2	3-0	—	3-0	1-2	5-3	5-2	2-4	2-2	3-4	1-1
Ipswich T	3-0	2-1	3-2	1-3	1-3	0-2	—	1-1	2-1	0-1	2-1	0-1	1-1	3-1
Leicester C	0-2	2-1	0-2	0-1	1-3	0-4	0-3	—	2-1	3-0	0-1	1-0	2-1	1-4
Nottingham F	0-2	2-1	3-0	1-0	2-2	1-1	2-0	1-2	—	4-0	1-1	2-1	0-1	2-1
Southampton	1-3	1-3	0-0	1-1	2-2	0-2	2-1	0-1	1-0	—	3-1	0-1	3-0	4-2
Tottenham H	0-3	2-3	2-0	0-1	1-2	0-1	1-1	3-1	2-1	2-0	—	0-0	1-2	3-1
Watford	0-4	0-5	1-0	3-1	2-2	1-0	1-0	3-1	1-0	2-1	0-1	—	1-0	2-0
West Ham U	2-2	1-1	0-0	1-1	1-0	1-1	2-2	2-1	3-0	0-1	1-1	1-1	—	1-0
Wimbledon	2-4	2-1	0-0	1-0	2-1	1-3	0-1	1-0	2-2	0-1	0-2	0-1	0-1	—

AVON INSURANCE 2002–03

AVON INSURANCE LEAGUE PREMIER DIVISION

	P	*W*	*D*	*L*	*F*	*A*	*GD*	*Pts*
Sheffield U	20	11	4	5	36	19	17	37
Walsall	20	9	6	5	40	31	9	33
Huddersfield T	20	9	5	6	30	22	8	32
Barnsley	20	10	2	8	42	40	2	32
Preston NE	20	10	2	8	30	30	0	32
Wolverhamton W	20	9	3	8	31	28	3	30
Tranmere R	20	8	5	7	37	40	−3	29
Rotherham U	20	8	3	9	36	34	2	27
Burnley	20	8	1	11	35	37	−2	25
Oldham Ath	20	6	4	10	27	35	−8	22
Bury	20	3	3	14	24	52	−28	12

AVON INSURANCE LEAGUE DIVISION ONE (WEST)

	P	*W*	*D*	*L*	*F*	*A*	*GD*	*Pts*
Stoke C	18	12	2	4	42	22	20	38
Doncaster R	18	10	2	6	40	29	11	32
Shrewsbury T	18	9	3	6	32	23	9	30
Stockport Co	18	8	5	5	40	27	13	29
Macclesfield T	18	9	1	8	33	26	7	28
Rochdale	18	8	2	8	25	23	2	26
Wigan Ath	18	7	3	8	25	31	−6	24
Wrexham	18	6	1	11	27	40	−13	19
Blackpool	18	5	2	11	30	42	−12	17
Chesterfield	18	5	1	12	24	55	−31	16

AVON INSURANCE LEAGUE DIVISION ONE (EAST)

	P	*W*	*D*	*L*	*F*	*A*	*GD*	*Pts*
Hull C	20	13	4	3	31	13	18	43
Hartlepool U	20	11	4	5	42	21	21	37
Darlington	20	12	1	7	50	39	11	37
Grimsby T	20	10	3	7	27	33	−6	33
Boston U	20	10	1	9	33	30	3	31
Notts Co	20	8	3	9	29	17	12	27
Scunthorpe U	20	9	0	11	42	35	7	27
York C	20	8	2	10	26	37	−11	26
Mansfield T	20	7	3	10	30	53	−23	24
Lincoln C	20	7	2	11	32	42	−10	23
Scarborough	20	3	1	16	17	39	−22	10

AVON INSURANCE COMBINATION

	P	*W*	*D*	*L*	*F*	*A*	*GD*	*Pts*
Crystal Palace	25	16	5	4	60	23	37	53
Norwich C	25	14	8	3	44	18	26	50
Portsmouth	25	14	6	5	47	23	24	48
Plymouth Arg	25	15	3	7	48	36	12	48
Reading	25	14	4	7	53	32	21	46
Colchester U	25	13	5	7	37	24	13	44
Bristol C	25	13	5	7	47	40	7	44
Brighton & HA	25	11	8	6	41	24	17	41
Millwall	25	12	4	9	37	30	7	40
Cardiff C	25	11	7	7	31	24	7	40
Brentford	25	11	5	9	44	43	1	38
Southend U	25	11	5	9	37	38	−1	38
Oxford U	25	11	3	11	37	36	1	36
QPR	25	9	7	9	36	34	2	34
Swindon T	25	10	4	11	33	54	−21	34
Luton T	25	8	8	9	34	31	3	32
Leyton Orient	25	8	8	9	46	44	2	32
Cheltenham T	25	9	4	12	47	44	3	31
Cambridge U	25	8	5	12	40	45	−5	29
Peterborough U	25	8	4	13	44	48	−4	28
Wycombe W	25	7	4	14	27	48	−21	25
Bournemouth	25	5	6	14	40	57	−17	21
Bristol R	25	5	6	14	27	47	−20	21
Gillingham	25	4	9	12	24	45	−21	21
Northampton T	25	5	5	15	31	55	−24	20
Barnet	25	2	4	19	20	69	−49	10

FA ACADEMY UNDER-19 LEAGUE 2002–03

GROUP A	P	W	D	L	F	A	GD	Pts
Manchester C	28	18	5	5	50	27	+23	59
Nottingham F	28	15	9	4	37	25	+12	54
Manchester U	28	16	3	9	65	42	+23	51
Everton	28	14	3	11	52	32	+20	45
Liverpool	28	12	7	9	45	40	+5	43
Birmingham C	28	10	9	9	31	35	–4	39
Crewe Alex	28	11	4	13	37	49	–12	37
Wolverhampton W	28	8	9	11	38	35	+3	33
Sheffield U	28	7	4	17	37	57	–20	25
Stoke C	28	3	8	17	25	62	–37	17

GROUP B	P	W	D	L	F	A	GD	Pts
Blackburn R	28	18	5	5	69	31	+38	59
Barnsley	28	15	5	8	57	41	+16	50
Newcastle U	28	14	1	13	69	60	+9	43
Bolton W	28	13	3	12	39	43	–4	42
Sunderland	28	12	3	13	45	48	–3	39
Leeds U	28	11	5	12	32	38	–6	38
Derby Co	28	11	2	15	47	52	–5	35
Huddersfield T	28	10	4	14	39	52	–13	34
Middlesbrough	28	8	8	12	46	51	–5	32
Sheffield W	28	7	3	18	46	67	–21	24

GROUP C	P	W	D	L	F	A	GD	Pts
West Ham U	28	16	4	8	52	30	+22	52
Fulham	28	11	11	6	42	32	+10	44
Chelsea	28	9	7	12	42	39	+3	34
Southampton	28	9	7	12	43	51	–8	34
Reading	28	9	6	13	34	46	–12	33
Millwall	28	7	7	14	33	46	–13	28
Coventry C	28	8	4	16	33	48	–15	28
Crystal Palace	28	8	3	17	34	64	–30	27
Bristol C	28	3	7	18	27	65	–38	16

GROUP D	P	W	D	L	F	A	GD	Pts
Aston Villa	28	18	5	5	71	38	+33	59
Arsenal	28	17	4	7	53	31	+22	55
Ipswich T	28	15	2	11	36	29	+7	47
Leicester C	28	12	10	6	40	30	+10	46
Tottenham H	28	13	6	9	44	39	+5	45
Watford	28	11	7	10	43	43	0	40
Norwich C	28	11	7	10	35	36	–1	40
Charlton Ath	28	11	6	11	36	35	+1	39
Wimbledon	28	7	5	16	36	51	–15	26

UNDER-19 PLAY-OFFS

SEMI-FINALS
Aston Villa 2, West Ham U 0
Manchester C 0, Blackburn R 1

FINAL (two legs)
Blackburn R 5, Aston Villa 3
Aston Villa 0, Blackburn R 0

FA ACADEMY UNDER-17 LEAGUE 2002–03

GROUP A	P	W	D	L	F	A	GD	Pts
Manchester C	22	20	2	0	66	11	+55	62
Manchester U	22	15	2	5	44	29	+15	47
Sheffield U	22	10	5	7	34	24	+10	35
Wolverhampton W	22	10	5	7	21	19	+2	35
Everton	22	8	5	9	31	27	+4	29
Liverpool	22	8	4	10	22	35	–13	28
Crewe Alex	22	5	7	10	35	42	–7	22
Nottingham F	22	7	1	14	27	44	–17	22
Birmingham C	22	5	3	14	28	47	–19	18

GROUP B	P	W	D	L	F	A	GD	Pts
Leeds U	22	16	2	4	54	24	+30	50
Blackburn R	22	13	5	4	54	25	+29	44
Newcastle U	22	11	5	6	49	43	+6	38
Derby Co	22	11	3	8	33	30	+3	36
Middlesbrough	22	8	9	5	39	23	+16	33
Sunderland	22	7	4	11	22	41	–19	25
Sheffield W	22	5	3	14	28	53	–25	18
Bolton W	22	3	6	13	23	41	–18	15

GROUP C	P	W	D	L	F	A	GD	Pts
Southampton	22	12	6	4	51	32	+19	42
Fulham	22	8	7	7	36	32	+4	31
West Ham U	22	8	7	7	30	31	–1	31
Coventry C	22	7	5	10	33	37	–4	26
Millwall	22	7	2	13	32	53	–21	23
Bristol C	22	5	4	13	27	48	–21	19
Reading	22	3	6	13	26	54	–28	15
Crystal Palace	22	2	7	13	25	56	–31	13

GROUP D	P	W	D	L	F	A	GD	Pts
Aston Villa	22	13	8	1	55	30	+25	47
Arsenal	22	12	2	8	53	32	+21	38
Leicester C	22	11	3	8	53	37	+16	36
Tottenham H	22	9	4	9	35	36	–1	31
Wimbledon	22	9	3	10	41	44	–3	30
Ipswich T	22	8	4	10	40	43	–3	28
Charlton Ath	22	7	4	11	35	48	–13	25
Watford	22	7	3	12	41	52	–11	24

UNDER-17 PLAY-OFFS

GROUP 1	P	W	D	L	F	A	GD	Pts
Aston Villa	3	2	1	0	8	2	+6	7
Everton	3	2	0	1	4	4	0	6
West Ham U	3	1	1	1	6	4	+2	4
Middlesbrough	3	0	0	3	2	10	–8	0

GROUP 2	P	W	D	L	F	A	GD	Pts
Blackburn R	3	2	1	0	7	2	+5	7
Southampton	3	1	2	0	5	3	+2	5
Liverpool	3	0	2	1	1	5	–4	2
Tottenham H	3	0	1	2	4	7	–3	1

GROUP 3	P	W	D	L	F	A	GD	Pts
Manchester C	3	2	1	0	6	1	+5	7
Newcastle U	3	1	1	1	6	5	+1	4
Reading	3	0	2	1	3	5	–2	2
Watford	3	0	2	1	2	6	–4	2

GROUP 4	P	W	D	L	F	A	GD	Pts
Crystal Palace	3	3	0	0	4	1	+3	9
Ipswich T	3	1	1	1	4	4	0	4
Manchester U	3	1	0	2	3	4	–1	3
Derby Co	3	0	1	2	2	4	–2	1

GROUP 5	P	W	D	L	F	A	GD	Pts
Arsenal	3	2	0	1	10	3	+7	6
Wolverhampton W	3	2	0	1	7	9	–2	6
Sheffield W	3	1	1	1	2	3	–1	4
Bristol C	3	0	1	2	2	6	–4	1

GROUP 6	P	W	D	L	F	A	GD	Pts
Coventry C	3	3	0	0	11	2	+9	9
Leicester C	3	2	0	1	6	5	+1	6
Bolton W	3	1	0	2	2	6	–4	3
Birmingham C	3	0	0	3	1	7	–6	0

GROUP 7	P	W	D	L	F	A	GD	Pts
Sheffield U	3	3	0	0	11	2	+9	9
Sunderland	3	2	0	1	6	6	0	6
Charlton Ath	3	1	0	2	4	4	0	3
Fulham	3	0	0	3	1	10	–9	0

GROUP 8	P	W	D	L	F	A	GD	Pts
Leeds U	4	4	0	0	8	1	+7	12
Wimbledon	4	3	0	1	5	3	+2	9
Crewe Alex	4	2	0	2	3	5	–2	6
Nottingham F	4	1	0	3	4	6	–2	3
Millwall	4	0	0	4	0	5	–5	0

QUARTER-FINALS
Coventry C 1, Arsenal 2
Sheffield U 1, Leeds U 2
Aston Villa 0, Manchester C 2
Blackburn R 2, Crystal Palace 0

SEMI-FINALS
Manchester C 3, Blackburn R 2
Leeds U 1, Arsenal 0

FINAL
Manchester C 0, Leeds U 1 *aet*

FOOTBALL LEAGUE YOUTH TABLES 2002–03

UNDER 19s FINAL TABLES

DIVISION ONE NORTH

	P	W	D	L	F	A	GD	Pts
Tranmere R	9	7	1	1	17	4	13	22
Preston NE	9	7	0	2	34	9	25	21
Rotherham U	9	5	0	4	20	20	0	15
Scunthorpe U	9	4	1	4	12	19	–7	13
Wigan Ath	9	3	3	3	18	13	5	12
Shrewsbury T	9	4	0	5	10	19	–9	12
Port Vale	9	3	2	4	19	20	–1	11
Hartlepool U	9	3	1	5	15	15	0	10
Hull C	9	3	1	5	12	20	–8	10
Mansfield T	9	1	1	7	6	24	–18	4

DIVISION TWO NORTH

	P	W	D	L	F	A	GD	Pts
Oldham Ath	9	6	1	2	25	16	9	19
Notts Co	9	5	2	2	13	6	7	17
Doncaster R	9	4	4	1	17	9	8	16
Chester C	9	5	1	3	14	13	1	16
Stockport Co	9	3	4	2	10	9	1	13
Burnley	9	3	3	3	17	16	1	12
Bradford C	8	1	5	2	8	11	–3	8
Carlisle U	8	2	1	5	9	15	–6	7
Grimsby T	9	2	0	7	10	18	–8	6
Lincoln C	9	1	3	5	9	19	–10	6

DIVISION THREE NORTH

	P	W	D	L	F	A	GD	Pts
Wrexham	8	6	2	0	15	3	12	20
Chesterfield	8	4	3	1	9	8	1	15
York C	8	4	1	3	12	10	2	13
Halifax T	8	3	4	1	8	6	2	13
Macclesfield T	8	2	4	2	11	7	4	10
Bury	8	2	2	4	14	14	0	8
Darlington	8	1	3	4	11	14	–3	6
Rochdale	8	1	3	4	6	15	–9	6
Blackpool	8	1	2	5	5	14	–9	5

DIVISION ONE SOUTH

	P	W	D	L	F	A	GD	Pts
Brentford	9	5	4	0	18	12	6	19
Northampton T	9	3	6	0	14	11	3	15
Cardiff C	9	3	5	1	14	13	1	14
Plymouth Arg	9	3	4	2	14	9	5	13
WBA	9	3	4	2	13	12	1	13
Bristol R	9	3	1	5	12	18	–6	10
Peterborough U	9	1	6	2	13	14	–1	9
Swindon T	9	2	3	4	10	13	–3	9
Portsmouth	9	2	2	5	9	12	–3	8
Wycombe W	9	1	3	5	6	9	–3	6

DIVISION TWO SOUTH

	P	W	D	L	F	A	GD	Pts
Brighton & HA	8	7	1	0	19	4	15	22
Exeter C	8	5	2	1	19	8	11	17
Oxford U	8	5	1	2	16	13	3	16
Cambridge U	8	4	1	3	13	10	3	13
Luton T	8	1	6	1	11	7	4	9
Gillingham	8	2	2	4	8	13	–5	8
Cheltenham T	8	2	0	6	6	24	–18	6
AFC Bournemouth	8	1	2	5	10	14	–4	5
Leyton Orient	8	0	3	5	6	15	–9	3

DIVISION THREE SOUTH

	P	W	D	L	F	A	GD	Pts
Swansea C	8	6	1	1	17	9	8	19
Colchester U	8	5	0	3	19	12	7	15
Rushden & D	8	5	0	3	18	13	5	15
Southend U	8	4	1	3	14	15	–1	13
Torquay U	8	3	2	3	15	14	1	11
Walsall	8	3	1	4	10	10	0	10
QPR	8	3	1	4	10	11	–1	10
Kidderminster H	8	2	3	3	7	10	–3	9
Cirencester	8	0	1	7	5	21	–16	1

UNDER 17s FINAL TABLES

SOUTH WEST CONFERENCE

	P	W	D	L	F	A	GD	Pts
Cardiff C	20	15	1	4	54	21	33	46
Swindon T	20	14	1	5	67	23	44	43
AFC Bournemouth	18	11	4	3	46	25	21	37
Swansea C	20	8	7	5	46	35	11	31
Exeter C	20	9	4	7	37	36	1	31
Cheltenham T	19	5	8	6	33	43	–10	23
Oxford U	17	5	3	9	23	35	–12	18
Plymouth Arg	18	5	2	11	28	42	–14	17
Torquay U	19	5	2	12	24	49	–25	17
Cirencester	17	4	3	10	29	49	–20	15
Bristol R	18	3	3	12	29	58	–29	12

Clubs agreed to void remaining games as they are of no significance on title

SOUTH EAST CONFERENCE

	P	W	D	L	F	A	GD	Pts
Brighton & HA	22	15	3	4	49	23	26	48
Peterborough U	22	13	6	3	45	20	25	45
Leyton Orient	22	13	4	5	46	19	27	43
Luton Town	22	10	6	6	40	32	8	36
Wycombe W	22	9	6	7	38	45	–7	33
Cambridge U	22	8	5	9	41	37	4	29
Colchester U	22	7	5	10	37	50	–13	26
Portsmouth	22	5	7	10	44	41	3	22
QPR	22	3	11	8	28	41	–13	20
Gillingham	22	5	5	12	39	57	–18	20
Brentford	22	5	5	12	33	51	–18	20
Southend U	22	4	7	11	34	58	–24	19

NON-LEAGUE TABLES 2002–03

DORSET PREMIER

	P	W	D	L	F	A	GD	Pts
Hamworthy U	34	29	1	4	103	34	69	88
Gillingham T	34	27	6	1	89	25	64	87
Hamworthy Recreation	34	23	3	8	92	42	50	72
Westland Sports	34	20	5	9	73	49	24	65
Dorchester T Reserves	34	17	7	10	76	39	37	58
Sherborne T	34	15	9	10	59	42	17	54
Poole Borough	34	17	3	14	73	66	7	54
Holt U	34	12	13	9	68	56	12	49
Bridport Reserves	34	14	7	13	59	47	12	49
Wareham Rangers	34	13	7	14	64	71	−7	46
Bournemouth Sports	34	12	8	14	91	75	16	44
Stourpaine	34	13	3	18	62	72	−10	42
Shaftesbury	34	11	8	15	48	57	−9	41
Cobham Sports	34	9	4	21	39	78	−39	31
Sturminster Newton	34	7	8	19	40	70	−30	29
Blandford U	34	7	6	21	41	71	−30	27
Weymouth Sports	34	4	4	26	36	138	−102	16
Swanage T & Herston	34	3	4	27	29	110	−81	13

HAMPSHIRE PREMIER

	P	W	D	L	F	A	GD	Pts
Winchester City	38	36	1	1	181	18	163	109
Vosper Thorneycroft	38	29	5	4	116	40	76	92
East Cowes Vics	38	24	4	10	96	47	49	76
Poole T	38	21	6	11	79	55	24	69
Horndean	38	19	11	8	66	44	22	68
Locks Heath	38	19	5	14	84	70	14	62
Liss Athletic	38	18	8	12	95	86	9	62
Andover New Street	38	16	9	13	73	65	8	57
Stockbridge	38	17	4	17	86	75	11	55
Petersfield T	38	15	8	15	71	71	0	53
Amesbury T	38	15	5	18	76	88	−12	50
Ringwood T	38	13	10	15	75	79	−4	49
Portsmouth Royal Navy	38	14	7	17	62	84	−22	49
Bishops Waltham T	38	13	7	18	57	67	−10	46
Lymington T	38	11	11	16	75	91	−16	44
Pirelli General	38	10	7	21	45	92	−47	37
Brading T	38	10	7	21	58	110	−52	37
Fawley	38	6	5	27	43	130	−87	23
Hythe & Dibden	38	5	7	26	46	94	−48	22
AFC Aldermaston	38	3	5	30	37	115	−78	14

HAMPSHIRE DIVISION ONE

	P	W	D	L	F	A	GD	Pts
Hayling U	28	20	3	5	86	29	57	63
Verwood T	28	19	1	8	51	38	13	58
Colden Common	28	16	5	7	70	39	31	53
Paulsgrove	28	17	2	9	66	37	29	53
Fleet Spurs	28	15	6	7	57	36	21	51
Farnborough North End	28	14	5	9	69	47	22	47
Fleetlands	28	13	6	9	64	62	2	45
Micheldever	28	11	6	11	51	44	7	39
Tadley T	28	11	6	11	46	41	5	39
AFC Portchester	28	10	8	10	58	59	−1	38
Alresford T	28	11	5	12	39	50	−11	38
Clanfield	28	5	8	15	44	75	−31	23
Fareham Sacred Hearts	28	6	3	19	41	72	−31	21
Co-op Sports & Hilsea	28	3	5	20	34	81	−47	14
Yateley Green (−1)	28	3	3	22	26	92	−66	11

WEST MIDLANDS PREMIER

	P	W	D	L	F	A	GD	Pts
Westfields	42	32	6	4	119	30	89	102
Kington T	42	31	6	5	120	52	68	99
Tipton T	42	27	8	7	95	40	55	89
Little Drayton Rangers	42	26	5	11	113	66	47	83
Tividale	42	22	10	10	104	53	51	76
Malvern T	42	22	9	11	96	49	47	75
Shawbury U	42	21	9	12	86	68	18	72
Lye T	42	19	7	16	69	64	5	64
Ledbury T	42	18	9	15	90	75	15	63
Brierley & Hagley All	42	17	11	14	74	73	1	62
Heath Hayes	42	15	12	15	72	75	−3	57
Wolverhampton Cas	42	17	5	20	71	91	−20	56
Wellington	42	15	10	17	56	69	−13	55
Wolverhampton U	42	15	8	19	66	73	−7	53
Smethwick Sikh Temple	42	11	11	20	58	83	−25	44
Sedgley White Lions	42	11	9	22	48	74	−26	42
Ettingshall Holy Trinity	42	12	5	25	66	91	−25	41
Bustleholme	42	11	7	24	69	93	−24	40
Bromyard T	42	11	2	29	61	125	−64	35
Gornal Athletic	42	8	7	27	41	103	−62	31
Dudley T	42	7	9	26	46	112	−66	30
Walsall Wood	42	6	11	25	48	109	−61	29

MIDLAND COMBINATION

	P	W	D	L	F	A	GD	Pts
Alvechurch	42	30	7	5	126	48	78	97
Coventry Marconi	42	29	5	8	94	37	57	92
Leamington	42	27	9	6	92	48	44	90
Bolehall Swifts	42	27	5	10	82	53	29	86
Romulus	42	24	5	13	107	58	49	77
Rugby T	42	22	10	10	90	52	38	76
Coventry Sphinx	42	23	6	13	95	72	23	75
Fernhill County Sports	42	21	8	13	74	59	15	71
Highgate U (−3)	42	23	3	16	95	67	28	69
Meir KA	42	21	6	15	94	75	19	69
Castle Vale K H	42	19	6	17	86	66	20	63
Nuneaton Griff	42	17	3	22	66	80	−14	54
Continental Star	42	14	9	19	86	88	−2	51
Coleshill T	42	13	9	20	54	68	−14	48
Pershore T	42	13	7	22	74	86	−12	46
Massey Ferguson	42	13	7	22	85	112	−27	46
Feckenham	42	12	6	24	66	85	−19	42
West Midlands Police	42	11	9	22	56	87	−31	42
Handrahan Timbers	42	11	8	23	57	73	−16	41
Alveston	42	9	7	26	66	114	−48	34
Southam U	42	7	2	33	43	162	−119	23
Cheslyn Hay	42	4	7	31	47	145	−98	19

MIDLAND ALLIANCE

	P	W	D	L	F	A	GD	Pts
Stourbridge	42	31	8	3	96	27	69	101
Rushall Olympic (−3)	42	31	6	5	94	37	57	96
Stratford T	42	29	6	7	105	38	67	93
Oadby T	42	26	7	9	87	52	35	85
Quorn	42	25	9	8	115	55	60	84
Willenhall T	42	23	10	9	91	47	44	79
Studley	42	24	6	12	97	58	39	78
Oldbury U	42	22	7	13	88	58	30	73
Chasetown	42	20	8	14	79	64	15	68
Grosvenor Park	42	19	10	13	81	58	23	67
Causeway U	42	18	5	19	70	73	−3	59
Barwell	42	17	7	18	70	68	2	58
Biddulph Victoria	42	17	6	19	51	69	−18	57
Boldmere St Michaels	42	16	5	21	59	63	−4	53
Ludlow T	42	12	8	22	63	76	−13	44
Bridgnorth T	42	11	9	22	48	79	−31	42
Stafford T	42	11	8	23	61	93	−32	41
Pelsall Villa	42	10	11	21	64	97	−33	41
Cradley T	42	8	7	27	43	87	−44	31
Shifnal T	42	6	7	29	43	93	−50	25
Halesowen Harriers	42	4	6	32	44	107	−63	18
Wednesfield	42	4	0	38	19	169	−150	12

SEAGRAVE HAULAGE COMBINED COUNTIES

	P	W	D	L	F	A	GD	Pts
Withdean 2000	46	40	4	2	143	32	111	124
AFC Wallingford	46	37	4	5	129	33	96	115
AFC Wimbledon	46	36	3	7	125	46	79	111
Feltham	46	25	10	11	101	48	53	85
Bedfont	46	25	5	16	106	73	33	80
Sandhurst T	46	23	9	14	86	59	27	78
Godalming & Guildford	46	25	3	18	95	75	20	78
Raynes Park Vale	46	24	5	17	101	79	22	77
Ash U	46	23	5	18	110	83	27	74
North Greenford U	46	22	7	17	104	87	17	73
Hartley Wintney	46	23	4	19	88	84	4	73
Southall	46	19	11	16	91	77	14	68
Westfield	46	19	9	18	75	86	−11	66
Chessington & Hook	46	18	9	19	96	80	16	63
Reading T	46	18	6	22	67	79	−12	60
Chipstead	46	16	10	20	92	87	5	58
Merstham	46	16	10	20	61	80	−19	58
Walton Casuals	46	12	10	24	60	95	−35	46
Chessington U	46	13	6	27	56	84	−28	45
Frimley Green	46	13	5	28	65	98	−33	44
Cobham (−3)	46	11	10	25	61	108	−47	40
Farnham T	46	5	9	32	45	130	−85	24
Cove	46	5	6	35	46	160	−114	21
Viking Greenford (+3)	46	3	2	41	35	175	−140	14

SUSSEX DIVISION ONE

	P	W	D	L	F	A	GD	Pts
Burgess Hill T	38	29	4	5	97	27	70	91
Whitehawk	38	22	4	12	79	41	38	70
Horsham YMCA	38	21	6	11	101	51	50	69
Chichester City U	38	20	9	9	79	51	28	69
Sidlesham	38	20	6	12	65	62	3	66
Southwick	38	18	6	14	67	50	17	60
Ringmer	38	17	9	12	55	56	–1	60
Hassocks	38	16	8	14	67	65	2	56
Pagham	38	16	7	15	69	52	17	55
East Preston	38	16	6	16	63	66	–3	54
Selsey	38	14	11	13	59	44	15	53
Redhill	38	16	5	17	53	62	–9	53
Sidley U	38	15	6	17	55	51	4	51
Three Bridges	38	14	7	17	88	83	5	49
Hailsham T	38	13	8	17	54	60	–6	47
Shoreham	38	13	6	19	54	69	–15	45
Arundel	38	11	11	16	50	65	–15	44
Peacehaven & Telscombe	38	9	5	24	43	95	–52	32
Wick	38	7	5	26	51	123	–72	26
Littlehampton T	38	4	9	25	34	110	–76	21

SUSSEX DIVISION TWO

	P	W	D	L	F	A	GD	Pts
Rye & Iden U	34	27	4	3	77	35	42	85
Eastbourne T	34	25	7	2	97	28	69	82
East Grinstead T	34	17	12	5	67	39	28	63
Oakwood	34	17	5	12	70	55	15	56
Saltdean U	34	15	6	13	70	55	15	51
Westfield	34	13	10	11	54	53	1	49
Wealden	34	14	6	14	64	60	4	48
Eastbourne U	34	14	6	14	63	60	3	48
Lancing	34	12	11	11	47	49	–2	47
Steyning T	34	13	7	14	47	43	4	46
Shinewater Association	34	13	7	14	46	59	–13	46
Seaford T	34	11	7	16	51	51	0	40
Broadbridge Heath	34	11	5	18	54	74	–20	38
Worthing U	34	11	5	18	41	64	–23	38
Crawley Down Village	34	9	10	15	43	51	–8	37
Mile Oak	34	9	6	19	47	74	–27	33
Pease Pottage Village	34	9	4	21	38	79	–41	31
Oving SC	34	5	4	25	37	84	–47	19

DEVON

	P	W	D	L	F	A	GD	Pts
Dartmouth	38	29	5	4	96	32	64	92
Ivybridge T	38	26	8	4	135	55	80	86
Buckland Athletic	38	23	6	9	88	47	41	75
Vospers Oak Villa	38	21	4	13	72	57	15	67
Alphington	38	19	7	12	79	54	25	64
Newton Abbot Spurs	38	19	6	13	62	49	13	63
University of Exeter	38	19	3	16	85	76	9	60
Newton Abbot	38	16	11	11	67	57	10	59
Plymstock U	38	14	13	11	72	58	14	55
Cullompton Rangers	38	15	8	15	56	65	–9	53
Ottery St Mary	38	15	6	17	63	74	–11	51
Heavitree U	38	14	6	18	71	84	–13	48
Dartington SC	38	13	7	18	79	70	9	46
Appledore	38	12	9	17	51	69	–18	45
Elburton Villa	38	11	10	17	67	69	–2	43
Budleigh Salterton (–1)	38	12	8	18	58	77	–19	43
Exeter Civil Service	38	9	13	16	46	79	–33	40
Stoke Gabriel	38	7	6	25	58	92	–34	27
Crediton U	38	7	5	26	30	108	–78	26
Topsham T	38	7	3	28	29	92	–63	24

SPARTAN SOUTH MIDLANDS PREMIER

	P	W	D	L	F	A	GD	Pts
Dunstable T	36	26	6	4	104	32	72	84
Beaconsfield SYCOB	36	24	7	5	66	30	36	79
Potters Bar T	36	23	6	7	80	42	38	75
Harefield U	36	21	7	8	79	45	34	70
St Margaretsbury	36	18	6	12	79	60	19	60
London Colney	36	15	10	11	65	57	8	55
Ruislip Manor	36	15	8	13	47	56	–9	53
Hanwell T	36	16	4	16	94	82	12	52
Milton Keynes City	36	15	7	14	58	58	0	52
Hoddesdon T	36	14	9	13	54	48	6	51
Biggleswade T	36	13	6	17	60	67	–7	45
Hillingdon Borough	36	12	6	18	44	57	–13	42
Broxbourne B V&E (–3)	36	13	5	18	49	64	–15	41
Greenacres (Hemel)	36	11	6	19	66	77	–11	39
Haringey Borough	36	10	8	18	50	70	–20	38
Royston Town	36	10	7	19	46	63	–17	37
Brook House (–3)	36	10	9	17	36	67	–31	36
Bedford U & Valerio	36	7	8	21	40	74	–34	29
Holmer Green	36	5	3	28	40	108	–68	18

NORTH WEST COUNTIES DIVISION ONE

	P	W	D	L	F	A	GD	Pts
Prescot Cables	42	30	6	6	110	38	72	96
Clitheroe	42	28	8	6	97	38	59	92
Mossley	42	27	7	8	100	41	59	88
Newcastle T	42	23	12	7	83	52	31	81
Skelmersdale U	42	22	8	12	91	51	40	74
Nantwich T	42	19	11	12	90	74	16	68
St Helens T	42	17	14	11	77	60	17	65
Congleton T	42	19	8	15	72	62	10	65
Salford City	42	17	12	13	84	63	21	63
Fleetwood T	42	17	9	16	73	70	3	60
Alsager T	42	15	11	16	61	67	–6	56
Squires Gate	42	13	12	17	58	71	–13	51
Abbey Hey	42	12	13	17	56	73	–17	49
Atherton LR	42	11	12	19	65	86	–21	45
Ramsbottom U	42	11	11	20	73	83	–10	44
Warrington T	42	11	11	20	48	66	–18	44
Woodley Sports	42	11	9	22	62	85	–23	42
Curzon Ashton	42	11	9	22	60	87	–27	42
Atherton Collieries	42	11	7	24	52	85	–33	40
Glossop North End	42	10	9	23	55	104	–49	39
Flixton	42	10	8	24	44	112	–68	38
Winsford U	42	10	7	25	48	91	–43	37

NORTH WEST COUNTIES DIVISION TWO

	P	W	D	L	F	A	GD	Pts
Bacup Borough	34	25	2	7	91	32	59	77
Stone Dominoes	34	24	3	7	94	34	60	75
Maine Road	34	23	2	9	74	55	19	71
Padiham	34	19	6	9	69	44	25	63
Holker Old Boys	34	18	7	9	65	42	23	61
Great Harwood T	34	15	7	12	64	61	3	52
Nelson	34	13	12	9	50	40	10	51
Darwen	34	14	7	13	59	64	–5	49
Norton U	34	14	6	14	50	52	–2	48
Colne	34	14	5	15	65	53	12	47
Ashton T	34	12	9	13	50	53	–3	45
Castleton Gabriels	34	10	8	16	43	60	–17	38
Cheadle T	34	10	8	16	39	56	–17	38
Blackpool Mechanics	34	9	10	15	39	52	–13	37
Leek CSOB	34	8	9	17	46	57	–11	33
Daisy Hill	34	7	5	22	42	93	–51	26
Oldham T	34	4	12	18	40	86	–46	24
Chadderton	34	5	6	23	35	81	–46	21

NORTHERN COUNTIES EAST PREMIER

	P	W	D	L	F	A	GD	Pts
Bridlington T	38	29	5	4	92	32	60	92
Brigg T	38	22	6	10	75	42	33	72
Goole AFC	38	20	11	7	68	36	32	71
Buxton	38	21	7	10	84	56	28	70
Ossett Albion	38	21	7	10	70	52	18	70
Thackley	38	17	11	10	53	39	14	62
Sheffield	38	17	8	13	74	55	19	59
Eccleshill U	38	16	7	15	61	58	3	55
Liversedge	38	16	6	16	59	65	–6	54
Harrogate Railway	38	15	7	16	87	71	16	52
Glapwell	38	14	7	17	52	59	–7	49
Glasshoughton Welfare	38	13	9	16	66	74	–8	48
Pickering T	38	14	5	19	49	51	–2	47
Brodsworth Welfare	38	13	7	18	64	84	–20	46
Arnold T	38	12	8	18	58	53	5	44
Selby T	38	11	7	20	44	73	–29	40
Hallam	38	10	9	19	50	75	–25	39
Armthorpe Welfare	38	10	6	22	53	85	–32	36
Borrowash Victoria	38	9	5	24	41	97	–56	32
Garforth T	38	9	4	25	46	89	–43	31

NORTHERN COUNTIES EAST DIVISION ONE

	P	W	D	L	F	A	GD	Pts
Mickleover Sports	32	24	3	5	62	26	36	75
Shirebrook T	32	21	5	6	79	38	41	68
Long Eaton U	32	17	7	8	66	52	14	58
Pontefract Collieries	32	16	7	9	68	56	12	55
Hatfield Main	32	17	4	11	49	42	7	55
Gedling T	32	14	9	9	69	49	20	51
Lincoln Moorlands	32	14	6	12	56	42	14	48
Parkgate	32	12	10	10	66	52	14	46
Hall Road Rangers	32	12	8	12	55	67	–12	44
Winterton Rangers	32	10	8	14	48	54	–6	38
Yorkshire Amateur	32	10	8	14	39	45	–6	38
Rossington Main	32	9	10	13	45	59	–14	37
Louth U	32	10	6	16	48	62	–14	36
Worsborough Bridge	32	10	5	17	41	56	–15	35
Maltby Main	32	10	3	19	51	80	–29	33
Tadcaster Albion	32	6	5	21	31	58	–27	23
Staveley MW	32	5	6	21	34	69	–35	21

EASTERN COUNTIES PREMIER

	P	W	D	L	F	A	GD	Pts
AFC Sudbury	44	31	10	3	122	37	85	103
Wroxham	44	29	6	9	121	53	68	93
Soham T Rangers	44	25	11	8	91	62	29	86
Lowestoft T	44	25	7	12	108	65	43	82
Diss T	44	26	3	15	98	62	36	81
Wisbech T	44	23	9	12	101	73	28	78
Stowmarket T	44	22	9	13	65	56	9	75
Great Yarmouth T	44	19	11	14	67	57	10	68
Bury T	44	18	11	15	75	66	9	65
Mildenhall T (–1)	44	18	11	15	69	65	4	64
Clacton T	44	17	10	17	62	61	1	61
Tiptree U	44	17	7	20	73	90	–17	58
Histon Reserves	44	15	11	18	80	84	–4	56
Fakenham T	44	13	16	15	61	61	0	55
Gorleston	44	13	10	21	79	91	–12	49
Norwich U	44	13	10	21	44	63	–19	49
Maldon T	44	13	8	23	57	63	–6	47
Newmarket T	44	11	13	20	58	76	–18	46
Dereham T	44	12	9	23	55	86	–31	45
Woodbridge T	44	11	12	21	55	96	–41	45
Ipswich Wanderers	44	11	8	25	59	92	–33	41
Harwich & Parkeston	44	10	6	28	58	126	–68	36
Ely City (–4)	44	5	10	29	38	111	–73	21

EASTERN COUNTIES DIVISION ONE

	P	W	D	L	F	A	GD	Pts
Halstead T	36	24	7	5	76	37	39	79
King's Lynn Reserves	36	24	4	8	108	56	52	76
Whitton U	36	21	8	7	93	44	49	71
Hadleigh U	36	20	9	7	65	40	25	69
Stanway Rovers	36	19	10	7	78	39	39	67
Long Melford	36	18	10	8	69	38	31	64
Leiston	36	18	9	9	76	51	25	63
Swaffham T	36	18	3	15	62	62	0	57
Cambridge C Reserves	36	16	7	13	67	49	18	55
Haverhill Rovers	36	16	6	14	67	55	12	54
Needham Market	36	15	8	13	71	59	12	53
Godmanchester Rovers	36	10	13	13	53	53	0	43
Cornard U	36	11	5	20	44	70	–26	38
Somersham T	36	11	5	20	59	87	–28	38
March T U	36	9	10	17	54	86	–32	37
Felixstowe & Walton	36	10	6	20	51	71	–20	36
Thetford T	36	9	5	22	38	74	–36	32
Downham T	36	4	6	26	33	88	–55	18
Warboys T	36	2	3	31	18	123	–105	9

KENT

	P	W	D	L	F	A	GD	Pts	Av
Cray Wanderers	29	19	5	5	68	23	45	62	2.14
Maidstone U	30	18	9	3	76	31	45	63	2.10
Thamesmead T	30	19	6	5	76	39	37	63	2.10
Deal T	28	15	9	4	62	40	22	54	1.93
Ramsgate	30	16	7	7	59	35	24	55	1.83
Whitstable T	29	15	8	6	56	45	11	53	1.83
VCD Athletic	30	13	9	8	51	36	15	48	1.60
Hythe T	30	13	6	11	46	54	–8	45	1.50
Slade Green	29	10	5	14	57	54	3	35	1.21
Beckenham T	29	9	6	14	41	53	–12	33	1.14
Herne Bay	30	9	7	14	53	54	–1	34	1.13
Tunbridge Wells	29	7	8	14	51	66	–15	29	1.00
Lordswood	30	5	9	16	37	66	–29	24	0.80
Greenwich B	30	5	5	20	36	70	–34	20	0.67
Erith T	29	4	6	19	36	71	–35	18	0.62
Faversham T	22	2	1	19	18	86	–68	7	0.32

NB: Final positions based on average points per game as Faversham did not complete their fixtures.

KENT COUNTY PREMIER

	P	W	D	L	F	A	GD	Pts
Sevenoaks T	26	17	6	3	65	22	43	57
Stansfield O&BC	26	17	4	5	71	29	42	55
Old Roan	26	15	7	4	63	32	31	52
Lydd T	26	14	4	8	49	52	–3	46
Bearsted	26	11	10	5	45	28	17	43
Sheerness East	26	11	7	8	48	42	6	40
Greenways	26	10	7	9	50	47	3	37
Kennington	26	8	7	11	38	47	–9	31
Milton Athletic	26	9	3	14	47	46	1	30
New Romney	26	7	6	13	36	61	–25	27
Beauwater	26	7	4	15	29	56	–27	25
Wickham Park	26	6	4	16	27	54	–27	22
Crockenhill	26	5	6	15	40	54	–14	21
Snodland	26	5	5	16	33	71	–38	20

CENTRAL MIDLANDS SUPREME

	P	W	D	L	F	A	GD	Pts
Carlton T	38	22	9	7	80	46	34	75
Sutton T	38	23	5	10	75	47	28	74
South Normanton Ath	38	22	5	11	103	67	36	71
Retford U	38	19	11	8	69	40	29	68
Teversal	38	20	6	12	90	54	36	66
Dinnington T	38	19	9	10	78	50	28	66
Holbrook	38	17	12	9	67	49	18	63
Sandiacre T	38	17	10	11	67	60	7	61
Ripley T	38	17	9	12	81	57	24	60
Rolls Royce Leisure	38	19	3	16	72	64	8	60
Heanor T	38	17	6	15	78	50	28	57
Dunkirk	38	17	6	15	75	64	11	57
Barton T Old Boys	38	18	1	19	62	77	–15	55
Nettleham	38	11	9	18	52	72	–20	42
Greenwood Meadows	38	11	8	19	49	71	–22	41
Clipstone Welfare	38	11	7	20	50	73	–23	40
Askern Welfare	38	10	9	19	53	70	–17	39
Graham Street Prims	38	9	4	25	55	93	–38	31
Blackwell Miners Wel	38	8	4	26	65	106	–41	28
Bottesford T	38	4	5	29	40	151	–111	17

WESSEX

	P	W	D	L	F	A	GD	Pts
Eastleigh	42	32	7	3	115	32	83	103
Gosport Borough	42	27	7	8	94	43	51	88
AFC Totton	42	27	6	9	96	47	49	87
Wimborne T	42	26	7	9	113	44	69	85
Fareham T	42	22	10	10	78	47	31	76
Lymington & New Milton	42	22	8	12	89	56	33	74
Andover	42	22	7	13	95	63	32	73
Portland U	42	20	8	14	81	62	19	68
Thatcham T	42	18	13	11	68	58	10	67
Moneyfields	42	18	6	18	73	68	5	60
BAT Sports	42	18	6	18	57	65	–8	60
AFC Newbury	42	17	6	19	77	72	5	57
Christchurch	42	15	10	17	58	68	–10	55
Bournemouth	42	15	9	18	57	67	–10	54
Cowes Sports	42	13	13	16	57	55	2	52
Hamble ASSC	42	13	12	17	58	60	–2	51
Alton T	42	14	9	19	71	80	–9	51
Bemerton Heath H	42	13	5	24	59	83	–24	44
Downton	42	10	7	25	41	105	–64	37
Brockenhurst	42	7	5	30	50	118	–68	26
Blackfield & Langley	42	4	6	32	37	134	–97	18
Whitchurch U	42	4	3	35	27	124	–97	15

ESSEX SENIOR

	P	W	D	L	F	A	GD	Pts
Enfield T	32	23	6	3	77	28	49	75
Concord Rangers	32	23	2	7	83	46	37	71
Ilford	32	21	4	7	87	40	47	67
Southend Manor	32	20	7	5	73	43	30	67
Romford	32	21	4	7	63	34	29	67
Sawbridgeworth T	32	18	7	7	57	30	27	61
Bowers U	32	16	6	10	58	49	9	54
Burnham Ramblers	32	14	4	14	45	43	2	46
Barkingside	32	14	3	15	66	55	11	45
Waltham Abbey	32	12	6	14	45	41	4	42
Brentwood	32	12	5	15	44	62	–18	41
Saffron Walden T	32	10	4	18	49	57	–8	34
Basildon U	32	9	4	19	54	71	–17	31
Stansted	32	8	4	20	36	64	–28	28
Hullbridge Sports	32	5	3	24	35	89	–54	18
Eton Manor	32	3	8	21	43	98	–55	17
Woodford T	32	3	3	26	22	87	–65	12

ESSEX INTERMEDIATE

	P	W	D	L	F	A	GD	Pts
Bishop's Stortford S	22	15	2	5	52	16	36	47
Takeley	22	13	5	4	42	28	14	44
White Notley	22	14	0	8	57	34	23	42
Rayleigh T	22	12	4	6	46	33	13	40
Manford Way	22	12	4	6	32	28	4	40
Kelvedon Hatch	22	12	3	7	51	39	12	39
Epping	22	7	4	11	32	47	–15	25
Canning T	22	6	4	12	37	43	–6	22
Harold Wood Ath	22	5	5	12	35	51	–16	20
Frenford Senior	22	5	5	12	28	50	–22	20
Shell Club (Corringham)	22	5	3	14	26	46	–20	18
Wanstead T	22	4	5	13	25	48	–23	17

HELLENIC PREMIER

	P	W	D	L	F	A	GD	Pts
North Leigh	40	29	6	5	84	36	48	93
Yate T	40	25	8	7	87	42	45	83
Carterton T	40	22	17	1	61	29	32	83
Highworth T	40	23	10	7	79	41	38	79
Didcot T	40	22	6	12	77	39	38	72
Fairford T	40	21	8	11	65	30	35	71
Brackley T	40	18	12	10	84	43	41	66
Abingdon U	40	20	6	14	70	52	18	66
Bishops Cleeve	40	19	7	14	68	50	18	64
Henley T	40	17	10	13	69	48	21	61
Southall T	40	18	7	15	75	65	10	61
Hook Norton	40	15	13	12	67	55	12	58
Shortwood U	40	15	10	15	64	60	4	55
Tuffley Rovers	40	12	9	19	56	76	–20	45
Wootton Bassett T	40	10	10	20	36	70	–34	40
Gloucester U (–3)	40	9	8	23	48	89	–41	32
Almondsbury T	40	8	7	25	43	77	–34	31
Pegasus Juniors	40	8	7	25	45	108	–63	31
Pewsey Vale	40	7	8	25	45	93	–48	29
Bicester T	40	5	8	27	41	99	–58	23
Wantage T	40	5	7	28	36	98	–62	22

HELLENIC DIVISION ONE WEST

	P	W	D	L	F	A	GD	Pts
Slimbridge	38	29	6	3	114	26	88	93
Chipping Norton	38	24	10	4	76	33	43	82
Purton	38	25	1	12	99	49	50	76
Winterbourne U	38	22	6	10	80	41	39	72
Ardley U	38	21	6	11	93	47	46	69
Old Woodstock T	38	19	6	13	65	54	11	63
Kidlington	38	15	9	14	67	76	–9	54
Headington Amateurs	38	13	13	12	71	70	1	52
Cheltenham Saracens	38	13	12	13	61	54	7	51
Easington Sports	38	15	6	17	54	67	–13	51
Adderbury Park	38	14	8	16	70	85	–15	50
Shrivenham	38	13	10	15	55	65	–10	49
New College Academy	38	14	4	20	57	67	–10	46
Malmesbury Victoria	38	12	8	18	54	63	–9	44
Witney U	38	9	13	16	54	74	–20	40
Middle Barton	38	10	9	19	49	83	–34	39
Cirencester U	38	9	10	19	49	77	–28	37
Harrow Hill	38	10	5	23	45	78	–33	35
Clanfield	38	9	7	22	43	82	–39	34
Ross T	38	7	5	26	45	110	–65	26

HELLENIC DIVISION ONE EAST

	P	W	D	L	F	A	GD	Pts
Quarry Nomads	32	21	4	7	76	41	35	67
Penn & Tylers G (–3)	32	19	6	7	63	33	30	60
Finchampstead	32	17	9	6	61	32	29	60
Rayners Lane	32	18	5	9	66	40	26	59
Chalfont Wasps	32	18	4	10	67	44	23	58
Eton Wick	32	16	9	7	73	49	24	57
Milton U	32	14	9	9	53	40	13	51
Binfield	32	14	6	12	73	46	27	48
Letcombe	32	11	6	15	45	53	–8	39
Englefield Green	32	12	3	17	47	62	–15	39
RS Basingstoke	32	10	7	15	55	64	–9	37
Bisley Sports	32	10	7	15	43	64	–21	37
Hounslow Borough	32	9	8	15	61	73	–12	35
Prestwood	32	8	10	14	43	63	–20	34
Holyport	32	10	2	20	37	78	–41	32
Martin Baker Sports	32	4	11	17	41	74	–33	23
Drayton Wanderers	32	5	6	21	38	86	–48	21

LEICESTERSHIRE SENIOR

	P	W	D	L	F	A	GD	Pts
Coalville T	34	29	5	0	101	28	73	92
Barrow T	34	25	7	2	96	33	63	82
Thurnby Rangers	34	26	3	5	92	26	66	81
Loughborough Dynamo	34	19	3	12	75	55	20	60
Holwell Sports	34	19	2	13	61	39	22	59
St Andrews SC	34	18	4	12	68	56	12	58
Kirby Muxloe SC	34	17	6	11	63	44	19	57
Ibstock Welfare	34	17	4	13	68	47	21	55
Leicester YMCA	34	14	5	15	69	65	4	47
Ratby Sports	34	13	5	16	50	58	–8	44
Highfield Rangers	34	13	3	18	53	70	–17	42
Thurmaston T	34	12	5	17	46	63	–17	41
Birstall U	34	10	4	20	47	67	–20	34
Blaby & Whetstone Ath	34	8	6	20	36	68	–32	30
Downes Sports	34	8	5	21	44	69	–25	29
Ellistown	34	6	10	18	30	75	–45	28
Friar Lane OB (–3)	34	6	5	23	39	98	–59	20
Anstey Nomads	34	2	6	26	24	101	–77	12

NORTHERN DIVISION ONE

	P	W	D	L	F	A	GD	Pts
Brandon U	40	26	10	4	77	28	49	88
Bedlington Terriers	40	24	9	7	96	42	54	81
Billingham T (–3)	40	23	5	12	100	56	44	71
Billingham Synthonia	40	21	8	11	73	47	26	71
Durham City	40	21	5	14	77	54	23	68
Shildon	40	19	7	14	83	74	9	64
Guisborough T	40	19	6	15	58	43	15	63
Dunston Federation	40	17	11	12	52	43	9	62
Jarrow Roofing	40	17	7	16	64	67	–3	58
Whitley Bay (–3)	40	17	8	15	68	62	6	56
Morpeth T	40	15	11	14	67	67	0	56
Washington	40	16	8	16	52	60	–8	56
West Auckland T (–3)	40	16	9	15	87	74	13	54
Chester-Le-Street T	40	14	11	15	60	63	–3	53
Tow Law T	40	14	8	18	58	63	–5	50
Marske U	40	13	10	17	64	74	–10	49
Esh Winning (–3)	40	15	7	18	54	84	–30	49
Peterlee Newtown	40	8	9	23	44	89	–45	33
Prudhoe T	40	7	10	23	52	89	–37	31
Consett	40	7	8	25	44	83	–39	29
Newcastle Blue Star	40	3	9	28	37	105	–68	18

NORTHERN DIVISION TWO

	P	W	D	L	F	A	GD	Pts
Penrith	38	26	10	2	102	28	74	88
Horden CW	38	26	7	5	83	38	45	85
Thornaby	38	25	8	5	84	32	52	83
Seaham Red Star	38	26	4	8	91	45	46	82
Ashington	38	22	13	3	101	37	64	79
Washington Nissan	38	21	5	12	102	57	45	68
Easington Colliery	38	19	5	14	83	72	11	62
South Shields	38	16	11	11	86	70	16	59
Northallerton T	38	17	5	16	72	58	14	56
Whickham	38	14	9	15	68	72	–4	51
Kennek Ryhope CA	38	12	9	17	63	67	–4	45
Hebburn T	38	13	5	20	55	66	–11	44
Evenwood T	38	12	6	20	58	95	–37	42
Murton	38	10	8	20	55	95	–40	38
Alnwick T (–3)	38	10	8	20	50	69	–19	35
Crook T (–6)	38	11	8	19	64	92	–28	35
Shotton Comrades	38	8	5	25	46	103	–57	29
Norton & Stockton A	38	5	9	24	38	81	–43	24
Willington	38	6	5	27	50	132	–82	23
Eppleton CW (–15)	38	8	6	24	45	87	–42	15

UNITED COUNTIES PREMIER

	P	W	D	L	F	A	GD	Pts
Holbeach U	40	28	8	4	80	25	55	92
Newport Pagnell T	40	27	5	8	118	43	75	86
Wootton Blue Cross	40	22	10	8	72	33	39	76
Buckingham T	40	21	8	11	90	50	40	71
Deeping Rangers	40	20	9	11	68	58	10	69
S & L Corby	40	21	5	14	72	56	16	68
Yaxley	40	20	7	13	72	52	20	67
Boston T	40	20	5	15	62	57	5	65
Cogenhoe U	40	18	7	15	75	59	16	61
Daventry T	40	15	11	14	55	66	–11	56
Ford Sports Daventry	40	13	14	13	62	67	–5	53
Northampton Spencer	40	15	7	18	52	60	–8	52
St Neots T	40	16	4	20	59	69	–10	52
Woodford U	40	15	7	18	50	60	–10	52
Raunds T	40	15	6	19	52	58	–6	51
Blackstone	40	13	9	18	72	74	–2	48
Stotfold	40	11	13	16	69	69	0	46
Desborough T	40	10	13	17	48	75	–27	43
Bourne T	40	8	8	24	50	94	–44	32
Long Buckby	40	3	10	27	21	107	–86	19
Kempston Rovers	40	4	4	32	35	102	–67	16

UNITED COUNTIES DIVISION ONE

	P	W	D	L	F	A	GD	Pts
Sileby Rangers	30	23	3	4	96	26	70	72
Harrowby U	30	21	4	5	81	29	52	67
Irchester U	30	20	4	6	63	36	27	64
Eynesbury Rovers	30	19	3	8	77	36	41	60
Thrapston T	30	17	7	6	61	37	24	58
Potton U	30	16	6	8	63	40	23	54
Olney T	30	14	7	9	65	43	22	49
Rothwell Corinthians	30	12	6	12	49	44	5	42
St Ives T	30	11	9	10	47	50	–3	42
Cottingham	30	11	6	13	49	46	3	39
Northampton ON Ch	30	9	7	14	54	74	–20	34
Wellingborough W	30	8	2	20	39	72	–33	26
Bugbrooke St Michael	30	6	4	20	40	81	–41	22
Higham T	30	5	5	20	35	76	–41	20
Blisworth	30	4	6	20	30	94	–64	18
Burton Park Wanderers	30	2	5	23	27	92	–65	11

WESTERN PREMIER

	P	W	D	L	F	A	GD	Pts
Team Bath	34	27	3	4	109	28	81	84
Brislington	34	22	7	5	71	28	43	73
Bideford	34	21	7	6	105	35	70	70
Backwell U	34	21	4	9	70	33	37	67
Paulton Rovers	34	18	9	7	68	35	33	63
Bridgwater T	34	17	8	9	71	43	28	59
Bath City Reserves	34	14	5	15	66	57	9	47
Melksham T	34	12	7	15	65	68	–3	43
Odd Down	34	12	6	16	49	67	–18	42
Keynsham T	34	11	7	16	55	65	–10	40
Frome T	34	11	7	16	49	62	–13	40
Bishop Sutton	34	11	5	18	57	83	–26	38
Dawlish T	34	11	5	18	47	107	–60	38
Bridport	34	9	8	17	40	54	–14	35
Barnstaple T	34	8	8	18	41	68	–27	32
Welton Rovers	34	9	5	20	40	99	–59	32
Elmore	34	8	7	19	45	81	–36	31
Devizes T	34	6	8	20	40	75	–35	26

WESTERN DIVISION ONE

	P	W	D	L	F	A	GD	Pts
Torrington	36	27	5	4	113	47	66	86
Exmouth T	36	26	7	3	83	29	54	85
Westbury U	36	20	8	8	92	65	27	68
Hallen	36	19	6	11	70	56	14	63
Calne T	36	16	9	11	62	43	19	57
Clyst Rovers	36	17	5	14	67	55	12	56
Willand Rovers	36	16	6	14	63	53	10	54
Bitton	36	13	10	13	50	48	2	49
Shepton Mallet	36	13	10	13	53	55	–2	49
Chard T	36	12	10	14	59	60	–1	46
Bristol Manor Farm	36	14	4	18	56	71	–15	46
Wellington	36	12	8	16	49	57	–8	44
Larkhall Athletic	36	13	4	19	48	73	–25	43
Cadbury Heath	36	10	11	15	49	61	–12	41
Street (–6)	36	13	7	16	59	81	–22	40
Corsham T	36	8	12	16	44	51	–7	36
Weston St Johns	36	9	4	23	54	76	–22	31
Ilfracombe T	36	7	9	20	47	85	–38	30
Minehead	36	7	5	24	34	86	–52	26

SOUTH WESTERN

	P	W	D	L	F	A	GD	Pts
St Blazey	36	30	5	1	126	23	103	95
Tavistock	36	24	5	7	87	41	46	77
Porthleven	36	23	5	8	95	48	47	74
Plymouth Parkway	36	23	4	9	83	55	28	73
Liskeard Athletic	36	21	4	11	95	59	36	67
Wadebridge T	36	17	9	10	61	46	15	60
Launceston	36	18	6	12	79	78	1	60
Holsworthy	36	17	7	12	59	48	11	58
Saltash U	36	17	3	16	79	68	11	54
Falmouth T	36	16	5	15	60	61	–1	53
Newquay	36	13	4	19	64	77	–13	43
Penzance	36	12	5	19	53	55	–2	41
Torpoint Athletic	36	11	8	17	48	69	–21	41
Millbrook	36	12	4	20	56	80	–24	40
Callington T	36	11	6	19	64	80	–16	39
Truro City	36	9	6	21	44	74	–30	33
Penryn Athletic	36	7	7	22	51	84	–33	28
St Austell	36	7	6	23	45	108	–63	27
Bodmin T	36	3	3	30	30	125	–95	12

HIGHLAND LEAGUE

	P	W	D	L	F	A	GD	Pts
Deveronvale	28	21	6	1	90	24	66	69
Keith	28	17	1	10	66	35	31	52
Buckie Thistle	28	15	6	7	63	36	27	51
Cove Rangers	28	14	7	7	70	46	24	49
Nairn County	28	13	7	8	67	47	20	46
Fraserburgh	28	14	4	10	61	45	16	46
Clachnacuddin	28	13	4	11	46	50	–4	43
Huntly	28	12	5	11	53	42	11	41
Inverurie Locos	28	11	7	10	50	50	0	40
Lossiemouth	28	12	4	12	41	53	–12	40
Forres Mechanics	28	12	2	14	59	62	–3	38
Rothes	28	8	5	15	26	50	–24	29
Wick Academy	28	8	2	18	33	68	–35	26
Brora Rangers	28	3	6	19	30	77	–47	15
Fort William	28	2	4	22	20	90	–70	10

Non-League Cup winners

Albany Northern League – Shildon
Combined Counties – Withdean 2000
Devon – Plymstock United
Dorset – Dorchester Town
Foresters Essex – Ilford
Hellenic – Yate Town
Jewson Eastern Counties – Wroxham
Jewson Wessex – AFC Totton
Kent – Cray Wanderers
Leicestershire – Barrow Town
Midland Alliance – Stratford Town
Midland Combination – Alvechurch
Minerva – Harefield United
North West Counties – Mossley
Northern Counties East – Ossett Albion
Screwfix (Les Phillip Cup) – Bridgwater Town
South Western – Liskeard Athletic
Sussex County – Selsey
United Counties – Blackstone

County Cup winners

Bedfordshire – Dunstable Town
Berks & Bucks – Maidenhead United
Birmingham – Birmingham City
Cambridgeshire – Foxton
Cheshire – Crewe Alexandra
Derbyshire – Alfreton Town
Durham – Horden CW
East Anglian – East Thurrock United
East Riding – North Ferriby United
Essex Senior – Chelmsford City
Gloucester – Mangotsfield United
Hampshire – Aldershot Town
Hertfordshire – Berkhamsted Town
Huntingdonshire – St Neots Town
Isle of Wight – Newport (IoW)
Kent Senior – Margate
Lincolnshire – Gainsborough Trinity
London – Bromley
Manchester – Ashton United
Mid-Cheshire – Witton Albion
Middlesex – Hendon
Norfolk – Diss Town
Northants – Rothwell Town
Northern Alliance – West Allotment Celtic
Northumberland – Newcastle U Reserves
Notts – Hucknall Town
Oxfordshire – Oxford City
Sheffield & Hallamshire – Worksop Town
Shropshire – Shrewsbury Town
Somerset – Taunton Town
Staffordshire – Stafford Rangers
Suffolk – Long Melford
Surrey – Sutton United
Sussex Senior – Crawley Town
Wearside – Darlington Railway Athletic
West Cheshire – Ashville
West Riding – Harrogate Town
Wiltshire – Melksham Town
Wiltshire – Shrewton United
Worcestershire – Halesowen Town

AMATEUR FOOTBALL ALLIANCE 2002–03

AFA SENIOR CUP

Sponsored by Ladbrokes

1st ROUND PROPER
South Bank Cuaco 5 Old Cholmeleians 1
Old Finchleians 1* Old Salopians 0*
Polytechnic 0 Honourable Artillery Company 1
Brentham 1 Winchmore Hill 8
BB Eagles 3 The Rugby Clubs 1
Civil Service 4 Carshalton 3
Weirside Rangers 2 Glyn Old Boys 3
Mill Hill Village 3 Old Danes 4
Alleyn Old Boys 7 Old Minchendenians 1
Old Esthameians 5 University of Hertfordshire 0
Old Stationers 0 Old Latymerians 1
Crouch End Vampires 1*:4p Old Parmiterians 1*:5p
Latymer Old Boys 2 Old Wilsonians 0
Hale End Athletic 1 Parkfield 0
Cardinal Manning Old Boys 2 HSBC 7
Old Manorians 3 Old Sedcopians 1
Old Owens 7 Old Westminster Citizens 0
Old Salesians 3 Old Foresters 0
Old Challoners 0 Bromleians Sports 2
Nottsborough 11 William Fitt 1
Old Reptonians 2 Bank of England 4
UCL Academicals 4 Old Salvatorians 2
Old Hamptonians 7 Old Ignatians 1
Pegasus 0 Old Grammarians 3
Old Fairlopians 0 Old Meadonians 2
St Mary's College 0*:4p Old Aloysians 0*:3p
Hale End Athletic 3 Southgate County 2
Southgate Olympic 4 Ibis 1
Old Tenisonians 2*:2p E. Barnet O. Grammarians 2*:3p
Enfield Old Grammarians 2:2* Kew Association 2:5*
West Wickham 2 Albanian 0
Old Witleians 2 Old Actonians Association 4

2nd ROUND PROPER
South Bank Cuaco 2 Old Finchleians 0
Honourable Artillery Company 1 Winchmore Hill 4
Old Tiffinians 4 BB Eagles 2
Civil Service 5 Glyn Old Boys 0
Old Danes 1 Alleyn Old Boys 3
Old Esthameians 4* Old Latymerians 3*
Old Parmiterians 0* Latymer Old Boys 2*
HSBC 3 Old Manorians 2
Old Owens 2* Old Salesians 1*
Bromleians Sports 2 Nottsborough 0
Bank of England 4 UCL Academicals 0
Old Hamptonians 2 Old Grammarians 0
Old Meadonians 5 St Mary's College 0
Hale End Athletic 3 Southgate Olympic 0
E. Barnet O. Grammarians 4 Enfield O. Grammarians 0
West Wickham 0*:2p Old Actonians Association 0*:3p

3rd ROUND PROPER
South Bank Cuaco 2 Winchmore Hill 3
Old Tiffinians 0 Civil Service 6
Alleyn Old Boys 2*:4p Old Esthameians 2*:2p
Latymer Old Boys 6 HSBC 1
Old Owens 2* Bromleians Sports 3*
Bank of England 2 Old Hamptonians 0
Old Meadonians 1 Hale End Athletic 2
E. Barnet O.Grammarians 3 Old Actonians Association 5

4th ROUND PROPER
Winchmore Hill 1 Civil Service 0
Alleyn Old Boys 1 Latymer Old Boys 2
Bromleians Sports 1*:5p Bank of England 1*:4p
Hale End Athletic 1 Old Actonians Ass'n 3

SEMI-FINALS
Winchmore Hill 0*:4 Latymer Old Boys 0*:0
O. Bromleians Sports 1*:3p O. Actonians Ass'n 1*:2p

FINAL
Winchmore Hill 1 Bromleians Sports 0

**aet; p – penalties.*

OTHER CUP FINALS

ESSEX SENIOR
Hale End Athletic 2 Old Parkonians 0
MIDDLESEX SENIOR
Old Meadonians 2 Winchmore Hill 0
SURREY SENIOR
Old Wokingians 3:3* Nottsborough 3:5*
INTERMEDIATE
Old Camdenians 1st 3 UCL Academicals Res 2
JUNIOR
Old Aloysians 3rd 2* UCL Academicals 3rd 1*
MINOR
Old Magdalenians 1st 1 Nottsborough 4th 2
VETERANS
William Fitt 2 Old Parmiterians "A" 3
OPEN VETERANS
Awarded to Nalgo - opponents defaulted
GREENLAND
Old Owens 3 UCL Academicals 0
ESSEX INTERMEDIATE
Mount Pleasant P O 1st 1 Old Buckwellians Res 2
KENT INTERMEDIATE
Granby Sports 1st 0:1*:3p W. Wickham Res 0:1*:5p
MIDDLESEX INTERMEDIATE
Civil Service Res 1:3* E. Barnet O. Gramm'ns Res 1:3*
SURREY INTERMEDIATE
Old Tiffinians Res 1 Nottsborough Res 3
SENIOR NOVETS
Winchmore Hill 5th 2 Civil Service 5th 0
INTERMEDIATE NOVETS
Parkfield 6th 3 UCL Academicals 6th 0
JUNIOR NOVETS
Marsh 4th 1*:4p Old Kolsassians 1*:2p

SATURDAY YOUTH
U-18
Norsemen 6 Battersea Park Rangers 2
U-17
Devas 2 Shoreditch 5
U-16
Norsemen 4 Rockingham United 2
U-15
Bec United 2 Providence House 7
U-14
Pro Hawks 0 Santley United 2
U-13
Bethwin Boys "A" 2 Future Stars 5
U-12
Norseen 5 Accra 2000 2
U-11
Minchenden Youth "B" 1 Bec United 2

SUNDAY YOUTH
U-18
Alexandra Park 3 Young Parmiterians "A" 1
U-16
Sheen Tigers 3*:2p Percival Youth 3*:3p
U-15
Young Parmiterians "A" 3 Potters Bar United "A" 1
U-14
Alexandra Park "B" 4 Alexandra Park "A" 2
U-13
Alexandra Park "A" 2 Young Parmiterians 1
U-12 INVITATION
Alexandra Park 6 Young Parmiterans 4
U-12
Minchenden 3 Alexandra Park "A" 0
U-11
Norsemen 1*:4p Alexandra Park "B" 1*:3p

ARTHUR DUNN CUP

Old Salopians 2 Old Carthusians 1

ARTHURIAN LEAGUE

PREMIER DIVISION	P	W	D	L	F	A	Pts
Old Foresters	18	13	3	2	48	19	42
Old Brentwoods	18	9	2	7	44	36	29
Lancing Old Boys	18	9	2	7	32	35	29
Old Salopians	18	8	4	6	27	28	28
Old Carthusians	18	8	2	8	32	31	26
Old Harrovians	18	8	1	9	54	48	25
Old Westminsters	18	7	3	8	20	22	24
Old Etonians	18	7	3	8	32	43	24
Old Reptonians	18	3	8	7	30	34	17
Old Chigwellians	18	2	4	12	19	42	10

DIVISION 1	P	W	D	L	F	A	Pts
Old Cholmeleians	14	12	1	1	44	18	37
Old Bradfieldians	14	11	2	1	51	12	35
Old Witleians	14	7	3	4	26	23	24
Old Haberdashers	14	6	4	4	28	28	22
Old Aldenhamians	14	4	2	8	24	34	14
Old Malvernians	14	3	2	9	27	45	11
Old Wykehamists	14	2	2	10	19	37	8
Old Wellingburians*	14	2	2	10	22	44	5

DIVISION 2	P	W	D	L	F	A	Pts
Old Chigwellians Res	14	9	3	2	37	20	30
Old Salopians Res	14	7	2	5	38	30	23
Old Cholmeleians Res	14	7	2	5	36	28	23
Old Carthusians Res	14	6	4	4	31	24	22
Old Etonians Res	14	5	3	6	24	29	18
Old Carthusians 3rd	14	4	4	6	24	32	16
Old Etonians 3rd	14	3	4	7	21	28	13
Old Brentwoods Res	14	4	0	10	25	45	12

DIVISION 3	P	W	D	L	F	A	Pts
Lancing Old Boys Res	12	9	1	2	40	17	28
Old Foresters Res	12	8	1	3	27	22	25
Old Haileyburians	12	6	2	4	32	30	20
Old Bradfieldians Res	12	5	3	4	26	18	18
Old Cholmeleians 3rd	12	4	2	6	25	32	14
Old Foresters 3rd	12	3	1	8	25	31	10
Old Aldenhamians Res	12	2	0	10	15	40	6

**3 points deducted for breach of rule*

DIVISION 4 – 7 Teams
Won by Old Westminsters Res
DIVISION 5 – 6 Teams
Won by Old Bradfieldians 3rd
JUNIOR LEAGUE CUP
Old Chigwellians Res 4 Old Carthusians 3rd 1
DERRIK MOORE VETERANS' CUP
Old Carthusians 6 Old Aldenhamians 1
JIM DIXSON SIX-A-SIDE CUP
Won by Old Bradfieldians

LONDON FINANCIAL FOOTBALL ASSOCIATION

DIVISION ONE	P	W	D	L	F	A	Pts
Dresdner Kleinwort Wasserstein	16	13	2	1	54	21	41
Mount Pleasant Post Office	16	11	2	3	47	19	35
Zurich Eagle Star*	16	7	4	5	43	25	24
Granby Sports Club	16	5	5	6	27	25	20
Bank of America	16	5	5	6	31	38	20
National Westminster Bank	16	4	6	6	27	40	18
Royal Sun Alliance	16	4	5	7	31	44	17
Churchill Insurance	16	3	3	10	21	43	12
J P Morgan	16	3	2	11	24	50	11

Coutts & Co. *Record expunged – insufficient games*

DIVISION TWO	P	W	D	L	F	A	Pts
Marsh	16	11	2	3	55	27	35
Royal Sun Alliance Res	16	9	3	4	53	30	30
Citigroup	16	7	5	4	42	24	26
Citigroup Res	16	7	3	6	36	37	24
Granby Sports Club Res	16	6	4	6	34	33	22
National Westminster Bank Res	16	7	1	8	28	45	22
Marsh Res	16	6	2	8	36	38	20
Citigroup CIB	16	4	1	11	21	55	13
Royal Bank of Scotland	16	3	3	10	31	47	12

DIVISION THREE	P	W	D	L	F	A	Pts
Marsh 3rd	16	11	3	2	58	30	36
Coutts & Co. Res	16	10	0	6	40	31	30
Royal Sun Alliance 3rd	16	7	6	3	49	25	27
National Westminster Bank 3rd	16	8	3	5	41	34	27
Credit Suisse First Boston	16	8	3	5	36	34	27
National Westminster Bank 4th	16	6	4	6	34	25	22
Granby 3rd	16	4	3	9	28	40	15
Temple Bar	16	3	3	10	27	46	12
Foreign & Commonwealth Office*	16	2	1	13	20	68	6

DIVISION FOUR	P	W	D	L	F	A	Pts
National Westminster Bank 5th	14	10	2	2	55	29	32
Zurich Eagle Star Res	14	10	0	4	59	22	30
Marsh 4th	14	9	3	2	48	19	30
Granby 4th	14	6	3	5	36	34	21
South Bank Cuaco 6th	14	5	3	6	31	43	18
Bank of Ireland*	14	4	1	9	20	53	12
Royal Bank of Scotland Res	14	3	2	9	23	38	11
Temple Bar Res	14	1	2	11	22	56	5

GEFC *Record expunged – insufficient games*
**Point deducted for breach of rule*

CHALLENGE CUP
Zurich Eagle Star 3*:7p Weirside Rangers 3*:6p
SENIOR CUP
Coutts & Co. 5 Bank of America 0
JUNIOR CUP
Natwest Bank 5th 2 Natwest Bank 4th 1

LONDON LEGAL LEAGUE

DIVISION I	P	W	D	L	F	A	Pts
Slaughter & May	18	11	4	3	44	30	37
KPMG ICE	18	9	4	5	45	27	31
Denton Wilde Sapte (A)	18	8	6	4	38	34	30
Gray's Inn	18	8	5	5	37	32	29
Linklaters & Alliance	18	7	4	7	40	39	25
Watson Farley & Williams	18	7	3	8	28	31	24
Clifford Chance	18	7	3	8	35	39	24
Eversheds	18	5	6	7	28	34	21
CMS Cameron McKenna	18	6	1	11	26	30	19
Lovells	18	2	4	12	21	46	10

DIVISION II	P	W	D	L	F	A	Pts
Baker & McKenzie	18	12	2	4	58	37	38
Simmons & Simmons	18	10	6	2	39	27	36
Freshfields Bruckhaus Deringer	18	7	6	5	39	32	27
Titmuss Sainer Dechert	18	6	8	4	39	33	26
Norton Rose	18	7	3	8	41	42	24
Allen & Overy	18	7	1	10	39	43	22
Barlow Lyde & Gilbert	18	6	3	9	35	53	21
Nicholson Graham & Jones	18	5	4	9	41	42	19
Richards Butler	18	5	4	9	38	47	19
Herbert Smith	18	5	3	10	31	44	18

DIVISION III	P	W	D	L	F	A	Pts
Macfarlanes	18	13	3	2	63	26	42
Ashurst Morris Crisp	18	12	4	2	52	23	40
Financial Services A	18	12	3	3	44	29	39
Denton Wilde Sapte (B)	18	12	2	4	32	18	24
Stephenson Harwood	18	8	2	8	44	35	26
Pegasus (Inner Temple)	18	7	1	10	20	47	22
Mishcon de Reya*	18	5	2	11	34	33	16
Hammonds Suddards Edge	18	5	1	12	30	48	16
S J Berwin & Co	18	3	1	14	28	57	10
Taylor Joynson & Garrett	18	3	1	14	19	50	10

**Point deducted for breach of rule*

LEAGUE CHALLENGE CUP
Gray's Inn 4 Slaughter & May 1
WEAVERS ARMS CUP
Cameron McKenna 2 Simons & Simmons 3
INVITATION CUP
Lovells 2 Baker & McKenzie 3
REPRESENTATIVE MATCHES
v Amateur Football Combination Won 2-1

LONDON OLD BOYS CUPS

SENIOR
Old Ignatians 2* Old Meadonians 4*
INTERMEDIATE
Old Camdenians 1* Old Uxonians 0*

JUNIOR
Old Actonians Assn. 3rd 1 Mill Hill Village 3rd 0
MINOR
Old Actonians Assn. 5th 0*:4p Old Salvatorians 4th 0*:5p
DRUMMOND
Old Chigwellians 4th 3 Old Parmiterians 9th 2
NEMEAN
Old Danes 4th 4 Phoenix Old Boys 5th 1
OLYMPIAN
Old St Mary's 3rd 3 Mickleham O. Boxhillians Res 0
VETERANS
Old Vaughanians 0 Old Finchleians 2
**after extra time; p – kicks from the penalty mark*

OLD BOYS' INVITATION CUPS

SENIOR
Old Esthameians 4 Old Finchleians 0
JUNIOR
Old Owens Res 2 Old Parkonians Res 1
MINOR
Old Finchleians 0* Old Wilsonians 1*
4TH XIS
Old Finchleians 4th 1 Old Tenisonians 4th 0
5TH XIS
Old Tenisonians 5th 2 Alleyn Old Boys 5th 1
6TH XIS
Old Owens 6th 1 Old Stationers 6th 0
7TH XIS
Old Tenisonians 7th 3 Old Finchleians 7th 2
VETERANS'
E. Barnet O Grammarians 5 Old Lyonians 2

MIDLAND AMATEUR ALLIANCE

PREMIER DIVISION	P	W	D	L	F	A	Pts
Caribbean Cavaliers	22	18	3	1	107	32	57
Bracken Park	22	16	1	5	75	35	49
Ashland Rovers	22	15	3	4	67	34	48
Wollaton 3rd	22	13	3	6	57	41	42
Nottingham Trent University	22	12	3	7	67	62	39
Magdala Amateurs Res	22	10	3	9	77	73	33
Squareform Stealers	22	9	2	11	64	63	29
Nottinghamshire	22	7	4	11	42	41	25
Lady Bay	22	7	2	13	52	77	23
Old Elizabethans	22	6	2	14	76	76	20
Bassingfield	22	3	2	17	34	83	11
Woodborough United	22	1	2	19	27	128	5

DIVISION 1	P	W	D	L	F	A	Pts
Derbyshire Amateurs Res	24	20	1	3	86	31	61
Kirkby Autocentre	24	18	4	2	88	25	58
(fmly FLL Aerospace)							
Old Bemrosians	24	16	2	6	63	36	50
Sherwood Forest	24	13	2	9	63	47	41
Nottinghamshire Res	24	13	1	10	54	47	40
Beeston Old Boys Assn	24	11	6	7	57	35	39
County NALGO	24	11	4	9	78	65	37
Racing Athletic	24	10	6	8	48	49	36
Wollaton 4th	24	6	3	15	44	88	21
Southwell Arms	24	3	7	14	40	73	16
ASC Dayncourt Res	24	4	3	17	41	76	15
Bassingfield Res	24	3	6	15	33	69	15
Clinphone	24	4	3	17	28	82	15

DIVISION 2	P	W	D	L	F	A	Pts
Brunts Old Boys	28	20	3	5	99	41	63
Old Elizabethans Res	28	19	5	4	113	47	62
Kirkby Autocentre Res	28	18	3	7	81	46	57
Nottinghamshire 3rd	28	15	6	7	73	53	51
West Bridgford United	28	14	5	9	85	53	47
Caribbean Cavaliers Res	28	14	5	9	77	51	47
Keyworth United Res	28	14	4	10	58	43	46
Wollaton 5th	28	13	2	13	64	68	41
Jigsaw	28	11	7	10	98	65	40
Magdala Arms 3rd	28	11	5	12	90	113	38
Beeston O B Association Res	28	11	3	14	47	69	36
Dynamo	28	5	9	14	39	60	24
Old Bemrosians Res	28	4	8	16	51	89	20
Derbyshire Amateurs 3rd	28	4	1	23	37	125	13
Tibshelf Old Boys	28	3	2	23	42	131	11

LEAGUE SENIOR CUP
Nottinghamshire 3 Caribbean Cavaliers 2
LEAGUE INTERMEDIATE CUP
Derbyshire Amateurs Res 5 Beeston OB Association 1
LEAGUE MINOR CUP
Old Elizabethans Res 1 Caribbean Cavaliers 0

SOUTHERN AMATEUR LEAGUE

SENIOR SECTION

DIVISION 1	P	W	D	L	F	A	Pts
Old Salesians	22	14	6	2	45	15	48
Old Esthameians	22	10	7	5	38	22	37
Norsemen	22	8	7	7	36	26	31
Old Owens	22	9	4	9	35	34	31
Alleyn Old Boys***	22	9	5	8	28	32	29
Broomfield	22	8	5	9	26	42	29
Polytechnic	22	7	7	8	33	35	28
Old Actonians Association	22	8	4	10	25	31	28
HSBC	22	7	6	9	26	27	27
Civil Service	22	5	10	7	27	31	25
East Barnet Old Grammarians	22	6	5	11	29	34	23
BB Eagles *(fmly Barclays Bank)*	22	6	4	12	22	41	22

**3 points deducted for breach of rule*

DIVISION 2	P	W	D	L	F	A	Pts
Winchmore Hill	22	17	2	3	56	18	53
West Wickham	22	16	4	2	45	14	52
Nottsborough	22	12	8	2	56	22	44
Old Finchleians	22	9	7	6	46	37	34
Old Parkonians	22	10	1	11	25	39	31
South Bank Cuaco *(Merged)*	22	8	5	9	41	43	29
Old Stationers	22	7	5	10	34	40	26
Old Lyonians	22	7	3	12	45	44	24
Carshalton	22	7	3	12	36	47	24
Weirside Rangers *(fmly Lensbury)*	22	5	7	10	36	41	22
Lloyds TSB Bank	22	4	5	13	27	54	17
Crouch End Vampires	22	3	4	15	30	78	13

DIVISION 3	P	W	D	L	F	A	Pts
Bank of England	22	14	2	2	50	12	44
Old Parmiterians	22	12	3	3	60	22	39
Old Westminster Citizens	22	10	2	6	41	34	32
Kew Association	22	9	4	5	50	35	31
Alexandra Park	22	8	5	5	46	30	29
Old Latymerians	22	7	2	9	39	40	23
Merton	22	7	2	9	36	41	23
Ibis	22	4	2	12	22	47	14
Southgate Olympic	22	4	1	13	31	60	13
Brentham	22	3	1	14	23	77	10

RESERVE TEAM SECTION
Division 1–12 teams
Won by Polytechnic Res
Division 2–12 teams
Won by Nottsborough Res
Division 3–10 teams
Won by Ibis Res
THIRD TEAM SECTION
Division 1–12 teams
Won by Old Actonians Association 3rd
Division 2–12 teams
Won by Nottsborough 3rd
Division 3–10 teams
Won by Old Westminster Citizens 3rd
FOURTH TEAM SECTION
Division 1–12 teams
Won by Old Actonians Association 4th
Division 2–10 teams
Won by Old Owens 4th
Division 3–10 teams
Won by South Bank Cuaco 4th
FIFTH TEAM SECTION
Division 1–10 teams
Won by Winchmore Hill 5th
Division 2–10 teams
Won by Old Esthameians 5th
Division 3–8 teams
Won by Broomfield 5th
SIXTH TEAM SECTION
Division 1–11 teams
Won by Kew Association 6th
Division 2–10 teams
Won by East Barnet Old Grammarians 6th
MINOR SECTION:
Division 1–10 teams
Won by Old Parmiterians 7th
Division 2–10 teams
Won by Old Finchleians 8th
Division 3–10 teams
Won by Old Finchleians 9th

CHALLENGE CUPS
JUNIOR
Winchmore Hill 3rd 2 Ibis 3rd 1
MINOR
Carshalton 4th 4 Winchmore Hill 4th 1
SENIOR NOVETS
Norsemen 5th 1 Winchmore Hill 5th 0
INTERMEDIATE NOVETS
Carshalton 6th 2 Norsemen 6th 1
JUNIOR NOVETS
Old Finchleians 9th 5 Norsemen 7th 3

U-16 GIRLS CENTRE OF EXCELLENCE LEAGUE

	P	W	D	L	F	A	Pts
Arsenal	20	20	0	0	106	11	60
Southampton	20	15	2	3	117	23	47
Fulham	20	11	5	4	41	20	38
Reading	20	10	4	6	43	30	34
Charlton Athletic	19	9	3	7	38	30	30
Leyton Orient	20	9	3	8	34	47	30
Chelsea	20	6	3	11	21	43	21
Colchester United	19	6	2	11	30	43	20
Wimbledon	20	4	2	14	15	52	14
Brighton & Hove Albion	20	3	1	16	28	129	10
Millwall	20	2	3	15	15	61	9

AMATEUR FOOTBALL COMBINATION

(A merger of the former Old Boys' and Southern Olympian Leagues)

PREMIER DIVISION	P	W	D	L	F	A	Pts
Old Meadonians	19	15	3	1	51	19	48
Old Hamptonians	20	12	2	6	37	22	38
Hale End Athletic	20	8	6	6	45	36	30
Albanian	20	8	5	7	35	35	29
Old Aloysians	19	9	2	8	35	37	29
Old Wilsonians	20	8	4	8	39	39	28
UCL Academicals	20	7	6	7	40	36	27
Old Danes	20	5	5	10	33	49	20
Old Ignatians	20	6	2	12	27	46	20
Parkfield	20	4	7	9	34	45	19
Honourable Artillery Co.	20	4	4	12	30	42	16

SENIOR DIVISION 1	P	W	D	L	F	A	Pts
Old Salvatorians	20	16	1	3	58	24	49
Latymer Old Boys	20	15	2	3	50	19	47
Old Bealonians	20	13	1	6	61	24	40
Southgate County	20	10	3	7	49	38	33
Old Vaughanians	20	8	7	5	39	34	31
Old Tiffinians	20	8	3	9	44	41	27
Phoenix Old Boys	20	7	3	10	35	43	24
Cardinal Manning Old Boys	20	7	0	13	41	61	21
Mill Hill Village	20	5	2	13	41	55	17
Shene Old Grammarians	20	3	3	13	28	61	12
Ulysses*	20	3	3	13	32	78	9

SENIOR DIVISION 2	P	W	D	L	F	A	Pts
Old Tenisonians	22	15	2	5	47	20	47
Old Wokingians	22	13	7	2	55	32	46
Glyn Old Boys	22	12	3	7	39	37	39
Old Isleworthians	22	11	2	9	49	44	35
Enfield Old Gramms.	22	9	6	7	41	37	33
Old Dorkinians	22	8	8	6	34	33	32
Old Manorians	22	8	7	7	46	46	31
Old Grammarians	22	8	2	12	34	41	26
Old Suttonians	22	8	2	12	37	45	26
St Mary's College	22	5	4	13	35	50	19
Old Woodhouseians	22	4	6	12	35	49	18
King's Old Boys	22	4	5	13	38	56	17

SENIOR DIVISION 3	P	W	D	L	F	A	Pts
Economicals	20	15	1	4	75	29	46
Old Buckwellians	20	12	4	4	62	41	40
Queen Mary College Old Boys	20	10	5	5	50	30	35
University of Hertford	20	10	3	7	61	38	33
Wood Green Old Boys	20	9	4	6	51	43	31
Pegasus	20	9	4	7	42	40	31
Old Reigatians	20	7	4	9	31	38	25
Old Minchendenians	20	6	4	10	39	55	22
Brent	20	5	5	10	31	43	20
The Rugby Clubs	20	2	7	11	29	56	13
BBC	20	3	1	15	26	84	10

SENIOR DIVISION 4	P	W	D	L	F	A	Pts
Old Vaughanians Res	18	11	5	2	40	27	38
John Fisher Old Boys	18	11	3	4	56	33	36
Clapham Old Xaverians	18	10	4	4	53	33	34
City of London	18	10	2	6	51	45	32
Latymer Old Boys Res	18	6	6	6	40	34	24
Old Sedcopians	18	7	3	8	46	49	24
Centymca	18	6	2	10	41	46	20
Old Aloysians Res	18	3	7	8	38	37	16
Old Woodhouseians Res	18	4	3	11	32	61	15
Old Tenisonians Res*	18	3	3	12	24	56	9

SENIOR DIVISION 5 North	P	W	D	L	F	A	Pts
Parkfield Res	22	15	5	2	68	25	50
Old Challoners	22	12	8	2	58	21	44
UCL Academicals Res	22	13	3	6	65	26	42
Albanians Res	22	13	3	6	57	56	42
Old Tollingtonians	22	10	7	5	49	35	37
Hale End Athletic Res	22	9	2	11	54	53	29
Old Salvatorians Res	22	7	8	7	36	40	29
Pegasus Res	22	7	3	12	47	57	24
Egbertian	22	5	5	12	41	61	20
Mill Hill Village Res	22	4	6	12	33	60	18
Old Manorians Res*	22	5	3	14	28	78	15
Old Edmontonians	22	3	5	14	47	71	14

SENIOR DIVISION 5 South	P	W	D	L	F	A	Pts
Chertsey Old Salesians	21	16	3	2	69	33	51
Old Hamptonians Res	22	17	0	5	58	37	51
Old Wilsonians Res	20	14	1	5	45	17	43
Sinjuns	22	12	4	6	68	42	40
London Welsh	22	12	3	7	61	60	39
Witan	22	9	3	10	48	50	30
Honourable Artillery Co Res	22	8	3	11	48	54	27
Mickleham Old Boxhillians	22	7	5	10	54	54	26
St Mary's College Res	21	6	5	10	46	58	23
Old Meadonians Res	21	4	3	14	34	61	15
Old St Marys	21	3	3	15	24	54	12
Old Grammarians Res	22	2	5	15	45	80	11

**3 points deducted for breach of rule*

Intermediate Division North–11 teams
Won by Old Aloysians 3rd
Intermediate Division South–11 teams
Won by Old Thorntonians
Intermediate Division West–11 teams
Won by Hampstead Heathens

NORTHERN

Division 1–11 teams Won by Old Camdenians
Division 2–9 teams Won by Old Edmontonians 3rd
Division 3–10 teams Won by UCL Academicals 4th
Division 4–11 teams Won by Old Ignatians 4th
Division 5–9 teams Won by Ravenscroft Old Boys Res
Division 6–10 teams Won by Leyton County Old Boys Res
Division 7–10 teams Won by Southgate County 5th
Division 8–10 teams Won by Wood Green Old Boys 5th

SOUTHERN

Division 1–10 teams Won by Wandsworth Borough
Division 2–9 teams Won by Old Guildfordians
Division 3–10 teams Won by Centymca Res
Division 4–11 teams Won by Clapham Old Xaverians 3rd
Division 5–11 teams Won by Old Tiffinians 3rd
Division 6–11 teams Won by Sinjuns 3rd
Division 7–11 teams Won by Old Meadonians 8th
Division 8–11 teams Won by John Fisher Old Boys 5th
Division 9–10 teams Won by Old Guildfordians 3rd
Division 10–10 teams Won by Fulham Compton Old Boys 3rd

WESTERN

Division 1–10 teams Won by Old Salvatorins 3rd
Division 2–10 teams Won by Hampstead Heathens Res
Division 3–10 teams Won by Old Salvatorians 5th
Division 4–10 teams Won by Parkfield 5th
Division 5–9 teams Won by Old Kolsassians
Division 6–10 teams Won by Ealing Association Res

IMPORTANT ADDRESSES

The Football Association: A. Crozier, 25 Soho Square, London W1D 4FA. *020 7745 4545*

Scotland: David Taylor, Hampden Park, Glasgow G42 9AY. *0141 616 6000*

Northern Ireland (Irish FA): D. I. Bowen, 20 Windsor Avenue, Belfast BT9 6EG. *028 9066 9458*

Wales: D. Collins, 3 Westgate Street, Cardiff, South Glamorgan CF1 1DD. *029 2037 2325*

Republic of Ireland B. Menton (FA of Ireland): 80 Merrion Square South, Dublin 2. *00353 16766864*

International Federation (FIFA): P. O. Box 85 8030 Zurich, Switzerland. *00 411 384 9595. Fax: 00 411 384 9696*

Union of European Football Associations: Secretary, Route de Geneve 46, Case Postale CH-1260 Nyon, Switzerland. *0041 22 994 44 44. Fax: 0041 22 994 44 88*

THE LEAGUES

The Premier League: M. Foster, 11 Connaught Place, London W2 2ET. *020 7298 1600*

The Football League: Secretary, The Football League, Unit 5, Edward VII Quay, Navigation Way, Preston, Lancashire PR2 2YF. *01772 325800. Fax 01772 325801*

Scottish Premier League: R. Mitchell, Hampden Park, Somerville Drive, Glasgow G42 9BA. *0141 646 6962*

The Scottish League: P. Donald, Hampden Park, Glasgow G42 9AY. *0141 616 6000*

The Irish League: H. Wallace, 96 University Street, Belfast BT7 1HE. *028 9024 2888*

Football League of Ireland: D. Crowther, 80 Merrion Square, Dublin 2. *00353 16765120*

Nationwide Conference: J. A. Moules, Chief Executive, Riverside House, 14b High Street, Crayford, DA1 4HG. *01322 411021*

Central League: A. Williamson, The Football League, Unit 5, Edward VII Quay, Navigation Way, Preston, Lancashire PR2 2YF. *01772 325800. Fax 01772 325801*

Eastern Counties League: B. A. Badcock, 41 The Copse, Southwood, Farnborough, Hampshire GU14 0QD. *01252 387588*

Football Combination: D. A. Daughtery, 3 Eastergate, Little Common, Bexhill-on-Sea, East Sussex TN31 4NU. *01424 848061*

Hellenic League: B. King, 83 Queens Road, Carterton, Oxon OX18 3YF. *01993 212738*

Kent League: R. Vinter, Bakery House, The Street, Chilham, Canterbury, Kent CT4 8BX. *01227 730457*

Leicestershire Senior League: R. J. Holmes, 8 Huntsmans Close, Markfield, Leics LE67 9XE. *01530 243093*

Manchester League: P. Platt, 26A Stalybridge Road, Mottram Hyde, Cheshire SK14 6NE. *01457 763821*

Midland Combination: N. Harvey, 115 Millfield Road, Handsworth Wood, Birmingham B20 1ED. *0121 357 4172*

Northern Premier: R. D. Bayley, 22 Woburn Drive, Hale, Altrincham, Cheshire WA15 8LZ. *0161 980 7007*

Northern League: T. Golightly, 85 Park Road North, Chester-le-Street, Co Durham DH3 3SA. *0191 3882056*

Isthmian League: N. Robinson, 226 Rye Lane, Peckham SE15 4NL. *020 8409 1978. Fax: 020 7639 5726*

Southern League: D. J. Strudwick, P.O. Box 90, Worcester, WR3 8RX. *01905 757509*

Spartan South Midlands League: M. Mitchell, 26 Leighton Court, Dunstable, Beds LU6 1EW. *01582 667291*

United Counties League: R. Gamble, 8 Bostock Avenue, Northampton NN1 4LW. *01604 637766*

Western League: K. A. Clarke, 32 Westmead Lane, Chippenham, Wilts SN15 3HZ. *01249 464467*

West Midlands Regional League: N. R. Juggins, 14 Badger Way, Blackwell, Bromsgrove, Worcs B60 1EX. *0121 445 2953*

Northern Counties (East): B. Wood, 6 Restmore Avenue, Guiseley, Leeds LS20 9DG. *01943 874558*

Central Midlands Football League: Frank Harwood, 103 Vestry Road, Oakwood, Derby, Derbyshire DE21 2BN. *01332 832372*

Combined Counties League: Clive R. Tidey, 22 Silo Road, Farncombe, Godalming, Surrey GU7 3PA. *01483 428453*

Essex Senior League: David Walls, Bramley Cottage, 2 Birch Street, Colchester CO2 0NW. *0207 587 4139*

Lancashire Football League: Barbara Howarth, 86 Windsor Road, Great Harwood, Blackburn, Lancs BB6 7RR. *01254 886267*

Midland Football Alliance: Peter Dagger, 32 Drysdale Close, Wickhamford, Worcs WR11 6RZ. *01386 831763*

North West Counties Football League: G. J. Wilkinson, 46 Oaklands Drive, Penwortham, Preston, Lancs PR1 0XY. *01772 746312*

Wessex League: Tom Lindon, 63 Downs Road, South Wonston, Winchester, Hants SO21 3EW. *01962 884760*

South Western League: R. Rowe, 5 Alverton Gardens, Truro, Cornwall TR1 1JA. *01872 242190*

COUNTY FOOTBALL ASSOCIATIONS

Bedfordshire: P. D. Brown, Century House, Skimpot Road, Dunstable, Beds LU5 4JU. *01582 565111*

Berks and Bucks: B. G. Moore, 15a London Street, Faringdon, Oxon SN7 7HD. *01367 242099*

Birmingham County: D. Shelton, County FA Offices, Rayhall Lane, Great Barr, Birmingham B43 6JF. *0121 357 4278*

Cambridgeshire: R. K. Pawley, City Ground, Milton Road, Cambridge CB4 1FA. *01223 576770*

Cheshire: Mrs M. Dunford, The Cottage, Hartford Moss Rec Centre, Winnington, Northwich CW8 4BG. *01606 871166*

Cornwall: B. Cudmore, 1 High Cross Street, St. Austell, Cornwall PL25 4AB. *01726 74080*

Cumberland: G. Turrell, 17 Oxford Street, Workington, Cumbria CA14 2AL. *01900 872310*

Derbyshire: K. Compton, No 8–9 Stadium, Business Court, Millenium Way, Pride Park, Derby DE24 8HZ *01332 361422*

Devon County: C. Davidson, County HQ, Coach Road, Newton Abbot, Devon TQ12 1EJ. *01626 332077*

Dorset County: P. Hough, County Ground, Blandford Close, Hamworthy, Poole, Dorset BH15 4BF. *01202 682375*

Durham: J. Topping, 'Codeslaw', Ferens Park, Durham DH1 1JZ. *0191 3848653*

East Riding County: D. R. Johnson, 50 Boulevard, Hull HU3 2TB. *01482 221158*

Essex County: P. Sammons, 31 Mildmay Road, Chelmsford, Essex CM2 0DN. *01245 357727*

Gloucestershire: P. Britton, Oaklands Park, Almondsbury, Bristol BS32 4AG. *01454 615888*

Guernsey: D. Dorey, Haut Regard, St. Clair Hill, St. Sampson's, Guernsey, GY2 4DT, CI. *01481 246231*

Hampshire: L. Jones, William Pickford House, 8 Ashwood Gardens, off Winchester Road, Southampton SO16 7PW. *023 8079 1110*

Herefordshire: J. S. Lambert, County Ground Offices, Widemarsh Common, Hereford HR4 9NA. *01432 342179*

Hertfordshire: E. King, County Ground, Baldock Road, Letchworth, Herts SG6 2EN. *01462 677622*

Huntingdonshire: M. M. Armstrong, Cromwell Chambers, 8 St Johns Street, Huntingdon, Cambs PE29 6DD. *01480 414422*

Isle of Man: Mrs A. Garrett, P.O. Box 53, The Bowl, Douglas IOM IM99 1GY. *01624 615576*

Jersey: S. Monks, Rocqueberg View, Rue De Samares, St. Clement, Jersey JE2 6LS. *01534 852642*
Kent County: K. T. Masters, 69 Maidstone Road, Chatham, Kent ME4 6DT. *01634 843824*
Lancashire: J. Kenyon, The County Ground, Thurston Road, Leyland, Preston, Lancs PR5 1LF. *01772 624000*
Leicestershire and Rutland: P. Morrison, Holmes Park, Dog and Gun Lane, Whetstone, Leicester LE8 6FA. *0116 2867828*
Lincolnshire: J. Griffin, PO Box 26, 12 Dean Road, Lincoln LN2 4DP. *01522 524917*
Liverpool County: F. L. J. Hunter, Liverpool Soccer Centre, Walton Hall Park, Walton Hall Avenue, Liverpool L4 9XP. *0151 523 4488*
London: D. Fowkes, 6 Aldworth Grove, London SE13 6HY. *020 8690 9626*
Manchester County: John Dutton, Brantingham Road, Chorlton, Manchester M21 0TT. *0161 881 0299*
Middlesex County: P. J. Clayton, 39 Roxborough Road, Harrow, Middx HA1 1NS. *020 8424 8524*
Norfolk County: R. J. Howlett, Plantation Park, Blofield, Norwich, Norfolk, NR13 4PL. *01603 717177*
Northamptonshire: B. Walden, 2 Duncan Close, Moulton Park, Northampton NN3 6WL. *01604 670741*
North Riding County: M. Jarvis, Southlands Centre, Ormesby Road, Middlesbrough TS3 0HB. *01642 318603*
Northumberland: R. E. Maughan, Churchill Pavilion, Hartley Avenue, Whitley Bay NE26 3FA. *0191 2530656*
Nottinghamshire: M. Kilbee, 7 Clarendon Street, Nottingham NG1 5HS. *0115 9418954*
Oxfordshire: I. Mason, P.O. Box 62, Witney, Oxon OX28 1HA. *01993 778586*
Sheffield and Hallamshire: J. Hope-Gill, Clegg House, 69 Cornish Place, Cornish Street, Shalesmoor, Sheffield S6 3AF. *0114 241 4999*
Shropshire: D. Rowe, Gay Meadow, Abbey Foregate, Shrewsbury SY2 6AB. *01743 362769*
Somerset & Avon (South): Mrs H. Marchment, 30 North Road, Midsomer Norton, Radstock BA3 2QD. *01761 410280*
Staffordshire: B. J. Adshead, County Showground, Weston Road, Stafford ST18 0BD. *01785 256994*
Suffolk County: Felaw Maltings, 44 Felaw Street, Ipswich IP2 8SJ. *01473 407290*
Surrey County: R. Ward, 321 Kingston Road, Leatherhead, Surrey KT22 7TU. *01372 373543*
Sussex County: Ken Benham, County Office, Culver Road, Lancing, West Sussex BN15 9AX. *01903 753547*
Westmorland: P. G. Ducksbury, Unit 1, Angel Court, 21 Highgate, Kendal, Cumbria LA9 4DA. *01539 730946*
West Riding County: R. Carter, Fleet Lane, Woodlesford, Leeds LS26 8NX. *0113 2821222*
Wiltshire: M. G. Benson, Covingham Square, Covingham, Swindon SN3 5AA. *01793 525245*
Worcestershire: M. R. Leggett, Craftsman House, De Salis Drive, Hampton Lovett Industrial Estate, Droitwich WR9 0QE. *01905 827137*

OTHER USEFUL ADDRESSES

Amateur Football Alliance: M. L. Brown, 55 Islington Park Street, London N1 1QB. *020 7359 3493*
English Schools FA: Ms A. Pritchard, 1/2 Eastgate Street, Stafford ST16 2NN. *01785 51142*
Oxford University: M. Matthews, University College, Oxford OX1 4BH. *01865 276648*
Cambridge University: Dr J. A. Little, St Catherine's College, Cambridge CB2 1RL. *01223 334376*
Army: Major W. T. E. Thomson ASCB (MOD), Clayton Barracks, Thornhill Road, Aldershot, Hants GU11 2BG. *01252 348571/4*
Royal Air Force: Sqn Ldr R. Moorehouse, OC PACS, RAF Coltishall, Norwich. *01603 737361 ext 7306*
Royal Navy: Lt-Cdr S. Vasey, RN Sports Office, HMS Temeraire, Portsmouth, Hants PO1 2HB. *023 9272 2671*
British Universities Sports Association: G. Gregory-Jones, Chief Executive: BUSA, 8 Union Street, London SE1 1SZ. *020 7357 8555*
British Olympic Association: 6 John Prince's Street, London W1M 0DH. *020 7408 2029*
The Footbal Supporters Federation: Chairman: Ian D. Todd MBE, 8 Wyke Close, Wyke Gardens, Isleworth, Middlesex TW7 5PE. *020 8847 2905 (and fax). Mobile: 0961 558908.* National Secretary: Mike Williamson, 2 Repton Avenue, Torrishome, Morecambe, Lancs LA4 6RZ. *01524 425242, 07729 906329 (mobile).* National Administrator: Mark Agate, "The Stadium", 14 Coombe Close, Lordswood, Chatham, Kent ME5 8NU. *01634 319461 (and fax) 07931 635637 (mobile)*
National Playing Fields Association: Col. R. Satterthwaite, O.B.E., 578b Catherine Place, London, SW1.
Professional Footballers' Association: G. Taylor, 2 Oxford Court, Bishopsgate, Off Lower Mosley Street, Manchester M2 3WQ. *0161 236 0575*
Referees' Association: A. Smith, 1 Westhill Road, Coundon, Coventry CV6 2AD. *024 7660 1701*
Women's Football Alliance: Miss K. Doyle, The Football Association, 25 Soho Square, London W1D 4FA. *020 7745 4545*
Institute of Football Management and Administration: Camkin House, 8 Charles Court, Budbrooke Road, Warwick CV34 5LZ. *01926 411384. Fax: 01926 411041*
Football Administrators Association: as above.
Commercial and Marketing Managers Association: as above.
Management Stats Association: as above.
League Managers Association: as above.
The Association of Football Statisticians: R. J. Spiller, PO Box 5828, Basildon, Essex SS15 5GQ. *01268 416020 (and fax 01268-543559)*
The Football Programme Directory: David Stacey, 'The Beeches', 66 Southend Road, Wickford, Essex SS11 8EN. *01268 732041 (and fax)*
England Football Supporters Association: Publicity Officer, David Stacey, 'The Beeches', 66 Southend Road, Wickford, Essex SS11 8EN. *01268 732041 (and fax)*
World Cup (1966) Association: as above.
The Ninety-Two Club: 104 Gilda Crescent, Whitchurch, Bristol BS14 9LD.
Scottish 38 Club: Mark Byatt, 6 Greenfields Close, Loughton, Essex IG10 3HG. *0181 508 6088*
The Football Trust: Second Floor, Walkden House, 10 Melton Street, London NW1 2EJ. *020 7388 4504*
Association of Provincial Football Supporters Clubs in London: Stephen Moon, 32 Westminster Gardens, Barking, Essex IG11 0BJ. *020 8594 2367*
World Association of Friends of English Football: Carlisle Hill, Gluck, Habichthof 2, D24939 Flensburg, Germany. *0049 461 4700222*
Football Postcard Collectors Club: PRO: Bryan Horsnell, 275 Overdown Road, Tilehurst, Reading RG31 6NX. *0118 9424448 (and fax)*
UK Programme Collectors Club: Secretary, John Litster, 46 Milton Road, Kirkcaldy, Fife KY1 1TL. *01592 268718. Fax: 01592 595069*
Programme Monthly: as above.
Scottish Football Historians Association: as above.
Phil Gould (Licensed Football Agent), c/o Whoppit Management Ltd, P. O. Box 27204, London N11 2WS. *07071 732 468. Fax: 07070 732 469*
The Scandinavian Union of Supporters of British Football: Postboks, 15 Stovner, N-0913 Oslo, Norway.
Football Writers' Association: Executive Secretary, Ken Montgomery, 6 Chase Lane, Barkingside, Essex IG6 1BH. *0208 554 2455 (and fax)*
Programme Promotions: 47 The Beeches, Lampton Road, Hounslow, Middlesex TW3 4DF. Web: www.footballprogrammes.com

FOOTBALL CLUB CHAPLAINCY

Currently there are over sixty chaplains appointed to serve at Premier and Football League clubs and the number seems to increase overall by between two or three and five or six each year. The passing of the half century mark was regarded as significant by the chaplains themselves since it represented more than half the number of senior League clubs in England and Wales. Today, some two-thirds of those clubs enjoy the benefits that a chaplain can provide.

But chaplaincy in our sport is about much more than mere numbers – we would prefer there to be sixteen chaplains serving effectively than sixty simply being an anodyne presence at their clubs.

Actually though, there are sound reasons for believing that, at least, most of our number are delivering pastoral care and practical support where it is required, as well as demonstrating such genuine commitment and professionalism that it has earned them the respect of everyone connected with their clubs. That statement is confirmed by the way in which chaplaincy is now firmly accepted, approved and encouraged at the highest level of football in our country. The 2002 Chaplain's Conference at Lilleshall was addressed by – among others – the chief executives of the PFA and a leading Premier League club to demonstrate the fact that football's leading officials recognise that the chaplains offer a worthwhile, welcome, necessary and occasionally vital service to the clubs and the sport.

Delightfully too, there are instances where even the Church has accepted that sports ministry in general and football chaplaincy in particular are valid and appropriate ministries. It was not always so, and such progress is not universal, but some far-seeing denominations along with some of the structures within them, have appointed experienced football chaplains to advise upon and to seek to open up, Christian ministry in areas of sport and recreation.

There could be no better illustration of this dual acceptance of football chaplains within both sport and the Church than the Commonwealth Games held in Manchester last year, where some of our men were delighted to be invited to be involved, including several who had leading roles within the chaplaincy teams.

THE REV

OFFICIAL CHAPLAINS TO FA PREMIERSHIP AND FOOTBALL LEAGUE CLUBS

Rev Steven Hawkins—Bristol R; Rev Catherine Bell—Luton T; Rev Peter Bye—Carlisle U; Rev Ken Howles—Blackburn R; Rev David Langdon—QPR; Rev Andrew Taggart—Torquay U; Rev Gary Piper—Fulham; Rev David Jeans—Sheffield W; Rev Peter Amos—Barnsley; Rev Nigel Sands—Crystal Palace; Rev Barry Kirk—Reading; Rev Graham Spencer—Leicester C; Rev Martin Short and Very Rev John Richardson—Bradford C; Rev Kevan McCormack—Ipswich T; Rev John Boyers—Manchester U; Rev Allen Bagshawe—Hull C; Rev Martin Butt—Walsall; Rev David Tully—Newcastle U; Rev Derek Cleave—Bristol C; Rev Fr Alan Poulter and Fr Gerald Courell—Tranmere R; Rev Brian Rice—Hartlepool U; Rev Matt Baker and Rev Jeffrey Heskins—Charlton Ath; Mr John Graham—Watford; Rev Owen Beament—Millwall; Rev Michael Chantry—Oxford U; Rev Elwin Cockett—West Ham U; Rev Michael Futens—Derby Co; Rev Mick Woodhead—Sheffield U; Rev Ken Hawkins—Birmingham C; Rev Alan Comfort—Leyton Orient; Rev Simon Stevenette—Swindon T; Rev John Hall-Matthews—Wolverhampton W; Rev Steve Collis—Port Vale; Rev Chris Cullwick—York C; Rev Ken Baker—Northampton T; Rev Mark Hirst—Burnley; Rev Tony Porter—Manchester C; Rev Richard Hayton—Gillingham; Rev Clive Andrews—Notts Co; Fr Andrew McMahon—Southampton; Rev Chris Nelson—Preston North End; Rev Henry Corbett and Rev Harry Ross—Everton; Rev Paul Brown—Wrexham; Rev Jeff Howden—Plymouth Argyle; Rev Andy Rimmer and Mr Mick Mellows—Portsmouth; Rev Alan Hayday—Scunthorpe U; Rev James Booth—Southend U; Rev Philip Hearn—Kidderminster H; Rev David Ottley—Bury; Capt Nigel Tansley—Crewe Alex; Rev Billy Montgomery—Stockport Co; Rev Ken Hipkiss—WBA; Canon Roger Knight—Rushden & Diamonds; Rev Kevin Johns—Swansea C; Rev Anthony Wareham—Peterborough U; Revs David Male and Vaughan Pollard—Huddersfield T; Rev Jim Pearce—Yeovil T; Rev Brian Quow—Doncaster R.

The chaplains hope that those who read this page will see the value and benefit of chaplaincy work in football and will take appropriate steps to spread the word where this is possible. They would also like to thank the editors of the Football Yearbook *for their continued support for this specialist and growing area of work.*

The following addresses may be helpful: SCORE (Sports Chaplaincy Offering Resources and Encouragement), PO Box 123, Sale, Manchester M33 4ZA and Christians in Sport, Frampton House, Victoria Road, Bicester, OX26 6PB.

OBITUARIES

Gianni Agnelli (Born Turin, Italy, 12 March 1921. Died Turin, Italy, 24 January 2003.) Gianni Agnelli was perhaps more famous for his connections with the Fiat company, but he was also a key figure in the post-war history of Juventus, the club being owned by his family. Although only serving as club president for seven years (1947–54), he followed Juve's fortunes avidly and was an honorary president at the time of his death.

George Aitken (Born Lochgelly, Fife, 28 May 1925. Died Sunderland, 22 January 2003.) George Aitken was a big powerful left half who captained Sunderland for several seasons in the 1950s, making 267 senior appearances for the club. He had begun his professional career with East Fife, where he was a member of the team that won the Scottish League Cup in 1946–47 and 1948–49 and also played for Third Lanark prior to his move to Roker Park. George finished off with a season at Gateshead, the club's last in the Football League. He was capped eight times by Scotland.

Roger Albertsen (Born Tyssedal, Norway, 15 March 1957. Died Norway, 2 March 2003.) Roger Albertsen was perhaps best know as one of his country's goal-scorers in a famous 2–1 victory over England in September 1981. It was the first time Norway had beaten England and prompted one of the most colourful outbursts by a commentator in modern times. Roger won 25 caps and played at club level for ADO Den Haag, Feyenoord, Winterslag and Rosenborg.

Cecil Allan (Born circa 1915. Died May 2003.) Cecil Allen won his only cap for Northern Ireland against England in October 1935. A promising left back with Cliftonville, he later joined Chelsea but he had the misfortune to suffer a cartilage injury in his first match for the club's reserves and never made the first team at Stamford Bridge. Cecil later had a spell with Colchester United, then members of the Southern League before retiring from the senior game.

Frank Armstrong, CBE (Born Canonbie, Dumfriesshire, 27 July 1920. Died Saanichton, Vancouver Island, Canada, 24 August 2002.) Frank Armstrong was a reserve centre forward for Hibernian in the immediate post-war years before joining Cowdenbeath in February 1949. One of the highlights of his career was scoring a hat-trick against Rangers in a Scottish League Cup tie. He finished with a spell at Arbroath. Frank was awarded the CBE for his role in local government in the Highlands.

Jack Ash (Born Hebburn-on-Tyne, 31 December 1911. Died Huncoat, nr Accrington, 12 April 2003.) Jack Ash was a centre half for Accrington Stanley in the late 1930s and went on to join Southport for the 1938–39 season. He managed just four games for the Sandgrounders before returning to Accrington, where his career was effectively ended after he suffered a broken leg playing in an FA Cup tie against Chorley in November 1945.

Alan Ashman (Born Rotherham, 30 May 1928. Died Walsall, 30 November 2002.) Alan Ashman was best known as the manager of the West Bromwich Albion team that defeated Everton to win the 1968 FA Cup final. As a player he had been a prolific centre forward with Nottingham Forest and then Carlisle, for whom he scored a century of goals. He managed the Brunton Park club in two spells, taking them briefly to the top of the old First Division, Workington and Walsall, and also had a spell coaching in Greece with Olympiakos.

Bill Baxter (Born Leven, Fife, 21 September 1924. Died: East Wemyss, Fife, 9 November 2002.) Bill Baxter was a neat wing half who was mainly a reserve during his spell at Wolves, making 47 first-team appearances between 1945 and 1953. He did better at Aston Villa, for whom he played more than 100 games, later joining the coaching staff. He subsequently had spells as manager of East Fife and Raith Rovers.

Bobby Beattie (Born Stevenston, Ayrshire, 24 January 1916. Died Irvine, Ayrshire, 21 September 2002.) Bobby Beattie was a skilful inside forward who began his career with Kilmarnock before joining Preston in September 1937. He appeared for North End in the 1938 FA Cup final, when they beat Huddersfield Town 1-0 and went on to play 287 first-team games at Deepdale, scoring 55 goals. He later had a brief spell at Wigan before joining the coaching staff at Preston. Bobby won a single cap for Scotland, appearing against Wales in November 1938.

Len Beaumont (Born Huddersfield, 4 January 1915. Died Nottingham, 23 July 2002.) Len Beaumont was an outside right who served Huddersfield Town, Portsmouth and Nottingham Forest in the years leading up to the Second World War. However, he played most of his football in the emergency competitions that took place during the hostilities, making a total of 160 appearances for Forest, Mansfield and Lincoln City.

Stan Bentham (Born Leigh, 17 March 1915. Died Southport, 29 May 2002.) Stan Bentham was a hard-working inside right who was a regular in the Everton team that won the Football League title in 1938–39. Stan made over 200 appearances for the Toffees in the emergency wartime games and after retiring as a player in 1949 he was a member of the coaching staff at Goodison and later at Luton Town.

Ralph Birkett (Born Newton Abbott, 9 January 1913. Died Torquay, 8 July 2002.) Ralph Birkett was a pacy outside right who was capped once by England, appearing against Northern Ireland in October 1935. His professional career had begun at Torquay before he was snapped up by Arsenal in March 1933, however it was at Middlesbrough where he had his best years, scoring 36 goals in 101 games. He later had a spell at Newcastle before retiring from the full-time game.

Jack Bradley (Born Hemsworth, Yorkshire, 27 November 1916. Died Gorleston, Norfolk, 14 December 2002.) Like many of his generation, Jack Bradley lost his best playing years to the war. A powerful forward with a strong left foot, he appeared for Swindon and Chelsea before the hostilities began, resuming at Southampton in the 1946–47 season. He also played for Bolton and Norwich and his career total shows that he scored 55 goals in 190 senior games.

Tommy Cahill (Born Glasgow, 14 June 1931. Died Spain, 27 January 2003.) A product of Glasgow Junior football, Tommy Cahill joined Newcastle United in December 1951, but made only four first-team appearances for the Magpies. In the summer of 1955 he moved on to Barrow where he played over 300 games, mostly at left back, and won representative honours for Division Three North against their southern counterparts in April 1957.

Eddie Chapman (Born East Ham, London, 3 August 1923. Died October 2002.) As a player, Eddie Chapman was a speedy outside right or inside forward but he was mostly a reserve, playing on just seven occasions for West Ham shortly after the war. He also worked part-time in the office at Upton Park, and when his playing career came to an end he became club secretary in 1956, remaining in charge of administrative affairs until his retirement some 30 years later.

John Charles (Born Canning Town, London, 20 September 1944. Died Essex, 17 August 2002.) John Charles was one of the few black players in top-flight English football in the 1960s. He had captained the West Ham team that won the FA Youth Cup in 1963 and also won youth honours for England. A full back, he played 142 senior games for the Hammers between 1963 and 1971.

Jackie Chew (Born Blackburn, 13 May 1920. Died 19 October 2002.) Jackie Chew was outside right for Burnley when they were defeated by Charlton in the 1947 FA Cup final. He had previously been on Blackburn's books, playing a number of wartime games, but in May 1945 he signed for the Clarets for whom he made a total of 254 senior appearances. He also had a short spell with Bradford City before retiring from the full-time game in 1955.

Jim Clunie (Born Kirkcaldy, Fife, 4 September 1933. Died 12 May 2003.) Jim Clunie was coach for the Southampton team that won the FA Cup in 1976. He had followed manager Lawrie McMenemy from Grimsby and later had spells in charge of St Mirren and Kilmarnock. As a player he had been a talented centre half for Raith Rovers, Aberdeen (where he was a member of the team that won the Scottish League Cup in 1955–56), St Mirren and Bury. He also won one cap for the Scottish League representative team.

John Cord (Born circa 1957. Died October 2002.) John Cord was a determined defender who made nine first-team appearances for Brechin City in the early 1980s.

Fred Crack (Born Lincoln, 12 January 1919. Died Scarborough, 22 September 2002.) Fred Crack was a pacy outside left who featured regularly for Grimsby Town during the 1938–39 season, appearing for the Mariners in their FA Cup semi-final defeat by Wolves. He guested for a number of clubs during the war before a knee injury led to his retirement from the full-time game.

Chris Crowe (Born Newcastle, 17 June 1939. Died 2003.) Chris Crowe was a skilful inside forward who appeared for England against France in October 1962 and also won four caps at U-23 level. He played almost 400 Football League games for Leeds, Blackburn Rovers, Wolves, Nottingham Forest, Bristol City and Walsall.

George Dews (Born Ossett, 5 June 1921. Died 29 January 2003.) George Dews began his football career with Middlesbrough during the war years before joining Plymouth Argyle where he made over 250 senior appearances and helped the West Country club win the Division Three South title in 1951–52. Known as 'Gentleman Dews' for his courteous and sporting approach to the game, he finished his senior career at Walsall. George was also a professional cricketer with Worcestershire throughout the 1950s.

Dida (Born Maceio, Brazil, 16 March 1934. Died Brazil, 17 September 2002.) Dida was a member of the Brazilian squad that won the World Cup in 1958, although he did not appear in the final itself. A talented forward with the Flamengo club, for whom he scored 244 goals between 1954 and 1963, he won six caps for his country.

Frank Donovan (Born Pembroke Dock, 26 February 1919. Died 13 April 2003.) Frank Donovan was a Welsh amateur international winger in the early post-war years and a member of the Great Britain team for the 1948 Olympic Games tournament. A legendary figure in Pembrokeshire football, he played for almost 30 years in the Welsh League and also featured for Swansea Town during the 1950–51 season.

William Drennan (Born circa 1919. Died November 2002.) William Drennan was the secretary of the Irish FA from 1950 to 1983, and also served on various UEFA committees during this period. He was the holder of the UEFA Ruby Order of Merit.

Gordon Dreyer (Born Whitburn, Sunderland, 1 June 1914. Died Luton, 6 February 2003.) Gordon Dreyer was a product of Sunderland schools' football who went on to a professional career as a half back in the late 1930s. He made a total of 74 Football League appearances for Hartlepool, Hull City and Luton Town before retiring from the full-time game during the war.

Reg Drury (Born Hackney, London, 18 October 1928. Died Finchley, London, 12 June 2003.) Reg Drury was one of the best-known sports journalists of his day and from 1964 to 1992 he wrote for the *News of the World*, becoming the paper's chief football correspondent. He had begun his career in local papers, later moving to the weekly *Sport* magazine where he eventually became editor. A former chairman of the Football Writers' Association, he also had a spell with *Reynolds News* in the 1950s.

Len Duquemin (Born Cobo, Guernsey, 17 July 1924. Died 20 April 2003.) Len Duquemin was a hard-working centre forward who was a member of the Spurs' team that won the Second Division title in 1949–50 and the Football League championship the following season with their distinctive 'push and run' style. A product of Guernsey junior football, Len scored 114 goals in 274 league appearances during his time at White Hart Lane.

Cliff Durandt (Born Johannesburg, South Africa, 16 April 1940. Died South Africa, October 2002.) Cliff Durandt made his name playing as an inside forward for South Transvaal as a teenager but was quickly snapped up by Wolves. He never really established himself in the team at Molineux, despite making almost 50 appearances and later spent a couple of seasons at Charlton before returning to South Africa.

Brian Evans (Born Brynmawr, 2 December 1947. Died Swansea, 26 February 2003.) Brian Evans made over 400 appearances for Swansea Town between 1963 and 1973) and was a member of the team that won promotion from the Fourth Division in 1969–70. A tricky winger, he later played for Hereford United, and to date is the only player to win a full cap whilst on the club's books. Brian won a total of seven caps for Wales between 1972 and 1974.

Micky Fenton (Born Stockton-on-Tees, 30 October 1913. Died Stockton-on-Tees, 5 February 2003.) A slightly built centre forward with tremendous pace, Micky Fenton was one of the stars of the Middlesbrough team in the years either side of the war. He scored 162 goals from 269 games for Boro' and was capped by England against Scotland in April 1938. After retiring from playing, Micky joined the backroom staff at Ayresome Park and remained with the club through until the early 1960s.

Harry Ferrier (Born Ratho, Midlothian, 20 May 1920. Died Earles Colne, nr Colchester, Essex, 16 October 2002.) Harry Ferrier joined Barnsley as a teenager, but the war prevented him from making his debut and he managed just one senior appearance for the Yorkshire club, in an FA Cup tie in the 1945–46 season. He subsequently joined Portsmouth and was a regular at left back in the team that won successive Football League titles in 1948–49 and 1949–50. He remained a first choice until the end of the 1951–52 campaign and later managed Southern League clubs Gloucester City and Chelmsford.

Marc-Vivien Foé (Born Nkolo, Cameroon, 1 May 1975. Died Lyons, France, 26 June 2003.) Marc-Vivien Foé died in tragic circumstances after collapsing during the second half of the Confederations Cup semi-final between Cameroon and Colombia. A tall, powerful defensive midfield player, he made his debut for Cameroon at the age of 17 and came to the attention of the wider football world following his performances in the 1994 World Cup finals. He moved from Canon de Yaoundé to French club Racing Lens and over the next four seasons confirmed his reputation as a top-class player, helping his side to the French title in 1997–98. Marc-Vivien subsequently spent 18 months at West Ham then returned to France to play for Olympique Lyonnais, but spent the 2002–03 season on loan at Manchester City. A key member of the Cameroon national team, he had participated in three consecutive World Cup final tournaments and was a member of his country's teams that won the African Nations' Cup in 2000 and 2002.

Trevor Ford (Born Swansea, 1 October 1923. Died Swansea, 29 May 2003.) Trevor Ford was one of the biggest names in post-war British football. A tough, aggressive centre forward, he scored 23 goals in 38 appearances for Wales and when he moved from Aston Villa to Sunderland in October 1950 the transfer fee of £30,000 was a new British record. However, he also courted controversy and following comments over illegal payments (these were the days of the maximum wage) he received a lengthy suspension, during which time he played in the Netherlands for PSV Eindhoven. Trevor had begun his career with Swansea, netting 41 goals during the 1945–46 season, and scored regularly at club level throughout his career, which also included spells at Cardiff City and Newport County. His career tally amounted to 178 goals in 348 Football League games

Ron Garner (Born circa 1925. Died September 2002.) Ron Garner impressed as a goalkeeper in local football in the Coventry area during the war and went on to make 23 first-team appearances for Coventry City during the emergency competitions in 1943–44 and 1944–45.

Maurice Gerhard (Born Poland, 1920. Died Falkirk, 23 August 2002.) Maurice Gerhard settled in Scotland after serving in the Polish Free Army during the war and was the goalkeeper for the East Stirlingshire team that won the Scottish C Division title in 1947–48. He later had a spell in Division A with Stirling Albion before returning to play for East Stirlingshire.

Ron Gray (Born North Shields, 25 June 1920. Died Ipswich, October 2002.) A promising half back, Ron Gray lost out firstly to the war years and then an injury, which restricted him to just 29 first-team appearances for Watford. He subsequently spent lengthy spells on the backroom staff at both Vicarage Road and Millwall, managing both clubs, and was also in charge of Lincoln City in the late 1960s. He later acted as a scout for Ipswich and was credited with unearthing many of their stars of the 1970s and 1980s.

Mike Grice (Born Woking, Surrey, 3 November 1931. Died August 2002.) Mike Grice began his career at Colchester before being sold to West Ham in March 1956. A traditional-style outside right, he was a member of the Hammers' team that won promotion from Division Two in the 1957–58 season. Mike later played for Coventry before returning to Colchester, his career tally comprising 54 goals from 450 senior appearances.

Brian Hall (Born Derby, 9 March 1939. Died September 2002.) Brian Hall was an outside left with Mansfield Town during the early 1960s, but switched to playing at left back after he joined Colchester in March 1965. He went on to register more than 350 senior appearances for the U's and was a member of the team that sensationally knocked Leeds United out of the FA Cup in 1970–71.

Peter Harris (Born Portsmouth, 19 December 1925. Died Hayling Island, 2 January 2003.) An outstanding winger with tremendous pace and dribbling skills, Peter Harris was an important member of the Portsmouth team that won the Football League title in both 1948–49 and 1949–50. He remained loyal to Pompey throughout his career, scoring a club record total of 194 Football League goals, and amassing over 500 senior appearances. He once hit all five in a game against Aston Villa and was capped twice by England.

Geoff Hazledine (Born Arnold, Notts, 27 February 1932. Died 21 December 2002.) Geoff Hazledine made just one appearance for Derby County as a youngster before moving on to Midland League club Boston United. He went on to star for the York Street club in their remarkable 6–1 FA Cup second round victory at the Baseball Ground in 1955–56, when he netted a hat-trick. He subsequently returned to the full-time game, spending the 1957–58 season with Southport where he scored five times in 29 appearances.

Dave Helliwell (Born Blackburn, 28 March 1948. Died Blackburn, March 2003.) Dave Helliwell was a small, rather frail-looking winger who began his professional career as understudy to Bryan Douglas at Blackburn. He never really established himself in the team at Ewood Park and after a season at Lincoln he moved on to Workington in the summer of 1970. He became one of the stars of the Borough Park club, playing almost 200 games in a six-year spell before winding down with a season at Rochdale.

Wilson Hepplewhite (Born Washington, Co Durham, 11 June 1946. Died South Africa, 28 March 2003.) A former Arsenal apprentice, Wilson Hepplewhite joined Carlisle after a brief spell with Crook Town but made only a handful of appearances during his stay at Brunton Park. He later moved on to Hartlepool where he was a regular in the 1967–68 promotion team, mostly featuring at left half, although occasionally on the left wing. Wilson subsequently migrated to South Africa and played for the Port Elizabeth club.

Trevor Ford

George Hill (Born circa 1921. Died October 2002.) George 'Pud' Hill was a talented winger with Dundee in the immediate post-war years. He featured in the side that won the Scottish B Division title in 1946–47 and also played in the team that was defeated by Motherwell in the 1952 Scottish Cup final. He made almost 200 appearances for the Dens Park club before finishing his career with East Fife.

Frank Hindley (Born Worksop, 2 November 1914. Died Worksop, March 2003.) Frank Hindley was a dashing centre forward who made his bow in senior football for Nottingham Forest in the 1938–39 season. He joined Brighton & Hove Albion in the summer of 1939, featuring in the opening games of the new season before war brought an end to the proceedings. He guested for Forest and Mansfield Town during the hostilities and went on to make ten appearances for Brighton in the first post-war season before retiring.

Rob Hindmarch (Born Morpeth, Northumberland, 27 April 1961. Died Philadelphia, USA, 5 November 2002.) Rob Hindmarch was capped by England at youth level and went on to lead Sunderland back to Division One in 1979–80. An inspirational leader on the pitch he fell out of favour at Roker Park and after a brief loan spell at Portsmouth he moved on to Derby County. Here too he enjoyed success, assisting the Rams to successive promotions in 1985–86 and 1986–87. A solid central defender who was effective in the air, Rob concluded his career with a spell at Wolves. His untimely death was a result of motor neurone disease.

Bruce Howard (Born Sholing, 9 September 1921. Died Sholing, 15 January 2003.) Bruce Howard's experience of senior football amounted to two appearances for Southampton in the war years. One of these came on Christmas Day 1941 when visitors Bristol City turned up with just two men and had to make up their numbers with Saints' reserve players and members of the crowd. The home team won 5–2 and Bruce scored four times from the inside-left position.

Bobby Hunter (Born Shotts, Lanarkshire, 12 March 1931. Died Wilmslow, Cheshire, 8 July 2002.) Bobby Hunter was leading scorer for Hamilton Academicals in 1950–51, netting a total of 34 goals. He was subsequently sold to Motherwell, but rarely featured in the first team and eventually returned to Hamilton. He spent much of the 1954–55 season on loan at Swindon Town whilst carrying out National Service at a nearby RAF station.

Ian Hutchinson (Born Derby, 4 August 1948. Died London, 19 September 2002.) Ian Hutchinson was one of the stars of the Chelsea team of the early 1970s, and played a crucial role in the FA Cup victory over Leeds United in 1970, setting up David Webb's decisive goal during extra time in the replay. A big strong centre forward, he was powerful in the air and possessed an immense throw. Ian had begun his career in the Southern League with Burton Albion and then Cambridge United before his move to Stamford Bridge. He won two caps for England at U-23 level, featuring against Wales and Scotland in the 1970–71 season.

Joel (Born Catete, Rio de Janeiro, Brazil, 23 November 1931. Died 2002.) Joel was a member of the Brazil team that won the 1958 World Cup in Sweden. He featured in the group game against Austria, then lost his place to Garrincha and did not appear in the final. He won 15 caps between 1957 and 1961, while at club level with Flamengo he scored 115 goals in just over 400 appearances.

Ernie Johnson (Born Sheffield, 1917. Died March 2003.) Ernie Johnson was on the books of both Sheffield United and Nottingham Forest as a youngster without making a senior appearance. He subsequently joined New Brighton in October 1937, where he made nine first-team appearances, mostly at left half. After wartime service in the army he had a spell at Rotherham, again failing to make the first team, before stepping into non-league football with Worksop.

George Johnson (Born Esh, Co Durham, 6 October 1932. Died 11 August 2002.) George Johnson made just three appearances for Lincoln City, but one of these was in the club's record 11–1 victory over Crewe Alexandra in September 1951. He scored on that occasion, but eventually left Sincil Bank after five seasons of reserve-team football.

Sammy Kean (Born Dumbarton, circa 1917. Died Edinburgh, 17 April 2003.) Sammy Kean was one of the stars of the great Hibernian team of the late 1940s and played at left half in the team that won the Scottish League championship in 1947–48. He had begun playing for the Edinburgh club in the late 1930s and appeared alongside Matt Busby in the team that won the Scottish Summer Cup in 1941. Sammy won representative honours for Scotland against England in a wartime international (April 1943) and for the Scottish League. On retiring he was trainer at Hibernian and later with Dundee.

Mick Killourhy (Born New Springs, Wigan, February 1911. Died Southport, December 2002.) Mick Killourhy appeared in Wigan Borough's final Football League match in October 1931 before being sold by the club's liquidators to Sheffield United. A thoughtful inside forward, he was mostly a reserve at Bramall Lane, but saw more action at Doncaster for whom he scored 33 times in 68 appearances between 1936 and 1939.

Derek King (Born Hackney, London, 15 August 1929. Died Huntingdon, 16 June 2003.) Derek King made 19 appearances for Tottenham during a six-year spell at White Hart Lane during the 1950s. A dependable centre half, he was mostly a reserve for Spurs, and later spent a season at Swansea Town before retiring from the full-time game.

Frank King (Born Alnwick, Northumberland, 13 March 1917. Died 8 May 2003.) Frank King joined the Everton groundstaff at 16 but made little headway as a goalkeeper at Goodison, managing just 13 first-team appearances. He spent the 1937–38 season at Derby, but then war intervened and a broken ankle effectively ended his playing career. Frank subsequently qualified as a physiotherapist and was the trainer for the Luton Town team that reached the 1959 FA Cup final.

Andy Leigh (Born Rothesay, circa 1929. Died Dunfermline, 24 May 2003.) Andy Leigh made over 400 appearances for Raith Rovers between 1948 and 1963. A hard-working half back, he was a member of the team that lost out to Rangers in the 1948–49 Scottish League Cup final. He continued his association with the Starks Park club as coach and later groundsman, eventually retiring in 1994.

Willie Leishman (Born Motherwell, 17 April 1953. Died Carluke, 21 August 2002.) Willie Leishman was a defender who appeared as a youth international for Scotland, but failed to establish himself at club level for Motherwell. He subsequently made over 150 senior appearances for Albion Rovers and also featured for Dunfermline Athletic before retiring to join the Strathclyde Police in 1983.

Stan Leslie (Born Dumfries, 30 November 1971. Died Newcastle upon Tyne, 3 February 2003.) Stan Leslie was a defender who played 19 first-team games for Queen of the South in the early 1990s. He subsequently joined East of Scotland League club Annan Athletic, for whom he was still playing at the time of his death, which came as the result of a suspected brain haemorrhage.

Jack Lewis (Born Bloxwich, Walsall, 26 August 1919. Died Walsall, 25 December 2002.) Jack Lewis was a talented wing half who captained each of his three professional clubs. He joined Crystal Palace in July 1938 and later played for Bournemouth and Reading, scoring 23 goals in 240 senior appearances.

Keith Lindsey (Born Scunthorpe, 25 April 1946. Died 2003.) Keith Lindsey was a pacy, hard-tackling right back who made his debut as a teenager for Scunthorpe United at the start of the 1965–66 season. He went on to make over 200 Football League appearances in a career which saw him play for Doncaster, Cambridge United, Southend, Port Vale and Gillingham.

Ronnie Little (Born Carlisle, 24 January 1934. Died 28 November 2002.) Ronnie Little was an amateur outside right who made five appearances for Carlisle United in the 1955–56 season. A product of local football, he later played for Penrith and Gretna.

Tommy Lodge (Born Huddersfield, 16 April 1921. Died Skelmanthorpe, nr Huddersfield, 2002.) Tommy Lodge was a half back who played 34 times for Huddersfield during the war years, and a further two in peacetime. Although better known as a professional cricketer (he played on two occasions for Yorkshire in 1948), he also featured for St Johnstone during the 1950–51 season.

Billy McAdams (Born Belfast, 20 January 1934. Died Barrow in Furness, 13 October 2002.) Billy McAdams was a goal-scoring inside forward who won 15 caps for Northern Ireland between 1954 and 1962, registering a hat-trick in the World Cup qualifying match against West Germany in October 1960, although his team lost the match 4–3. He scored over 150 senior goals at club level, his career taking him to Manchester City, Bolton Wanderers, Leeds, Brentford, Queen's Park Rangers and Barrow.

Willie McCallum (Born circa 1942. Died 13 March 2003.) Willie McCallum was a towering centre half who made over 250 first-team appearances for Motherwell between 1959 and 1973. He later had brief spells with St Mirren, Dunfermline and Raith Rovers before retiring from the senior game.

Jim McConnon (Born Burnopfield, Co Durham, 21 June 1922. Died Altrincham, 26 January 2003.) Jim McConnon was a half back who joined Aston Villa shortly before the outbreak of war, but his senior experience was limited to just two games for Villa during the emergency competitions in 1944–45. He was also a talented cricketer for Glamorgan between 1950 and 1961, winning two caps for England against Pakistan in 1954.

Murray McDermott (Born Edinburgh, 2 February 1950. Died 7 March 2003.) Murray McDermott won schoolboy international honours for Scotland and joined Rangers as a teenager, but never made the first team at Ibrox. He later joined Raith Rovers where he was a highly regarded 'keeper and made over 500 senior appearances. Murray continued to play until his late 30s, featuring for Berwick Rangers, Morton, Arbroath, Meadowbank and Partick before bowing out with an appearance from the bench for Hearts in a UEFA Cup tie against St Patrick's.

Arthur McGachie (Born Lochore, Fife, circa 1904. Died Dunfermline, 20 December 2002.) Arthur McGachie was the last surviving member of the East Fife team that won promotion to the Scottish First Division in 1929–30. Principally a goal-scoring centre forward, he scored 115 times in 182 appearances for the Fife club, later also appearing for Dunfermline Athletic, Cowdenbeath, King's Park and Leith Athletic.

Doug McGibbon (Born Hamble, Southampton, 24 February 1919. Died Aylesbury, 25 October 2002.) Doug McGibbon was a centre forward with an excellent career record of 92 goals in 158 games. It would surely have been more had war not intervened, and his tally in the hostilities included six for Southampton in a 7–0 thrashing of Chelsea in December 1945. Doug began his career with the Saints in 1938 and later played for Fulham and Bournemouth

Bob McKinlay (Born Lochgelly, Fife, 10 October 1932. Died August 2002.) Bob McKinlay joined Nottingham Forest as a winger, but quickly switched to centre half and it was in this role that he established himself in the side, going on to make a club record of 614 Football League appearances between 1951 and 1970. He was a member of the team that defeated Luton Town to win the FA Cup in 1959 and skippered the side that came so close to a league and cup double in the 1966–67 season.

Bobby McLaughlin (Born Belfast, 6 December 1935. Died 2003.) Bobby McLaughlin began his career with Irish League club Distillery before joining Wrexham in January 1950. A combative wing half or inside forward, he then spent three seasons at Cardiff before moving on to Southampton. He made 177 first-team appearances for the Saints over the next six years before leaving the full-time game.

Billy McPhail (Born Glasgow, 2 February 1928. Died Glasgow, 4 April 2003.) Billy McPhail was something of a journeyman centre forward for Queen's Park and Clyde in the immediate post-war period, although he was a regular scorer, once netting five for the Shawfield club against Cowdenbeath. In May 1956 he surprisingly moved to Celtic and went on to gain legendary status for his role in scoring a hat-trick in the amazing 7–1 victory over Rangers in the 1957–58 Scottish League Cup final at Hampden Park. However, his stay at Parkhead was a brief one, for injury forced his retirement in the summer of 1958.

Mickey McWilliams (Died Bangor, Co Down, 10 September 2002.) Mickey McWilliams was a prominent left half in Irish football during the 1940s. He played for Belfast Celtic, Linfield and Ballymena, appearing for Linfield when they won the Irish Cup in 1945 and 1946.

Mostafa Kamel Mansour (Born Egypt, circa 1913. Died July 2002.) Mostafa Kamel Mansour played in goal for Egypt in both the 1934 World Cup finals and the 1936 Olympic Games and subsequently joined top Scottish amateur club Queen's Park where he featured regularly in the 1938–39 season. He later returned to Egypt and held the office of General Secretary of the CAF from 1958 to 1961.

Mauro (Born Poços de Caldas, Minas Gerais, Brazil, 30 August 1930. Died Poços de Caldas, Minas Gerais, Brazil, 18 September 2002.) Mauro captained the Brazil team that defeated Czechoslovakia to win the 1962 World Cup final. An elegant central defender, he won 28 caps for his country between 1949 and 1965. At club level he played for Sao Paulo, then Santos, and with the latter club he was a member of the team that won both the Copa Libertadores and the World Club Championship on two occasions.

Vic Metcalfe (Born Barrow, 3 February 1922. Died Huddersfield, 6 April 2003.) Vic Metcalfe joined Huddersfield Town as an amateur in 1939, but it was not until after the war that he made his senior debut for the club. He went on to make 434 appearances at Leeds Road, scoring 87 goals and won international honours for both England (two caps in May 1951) and the Football League. A talented outside left, he had great pace and skill and was considered one of the best crossers of the ball during the 1950s. Vic later had a spell at Hull City and also managed Halifax Town briefly in the mid-1960s.

Eddie Miller (Born Ulverston, 21 June 1920. Died 21 September 2002.) Eddie Miller was an inside forward for Barrow in the immediate post-war period. He played 16 times for the club during the war and added a further 132 senior appearances in peacetime, scoring 34 goals.

Sir Bert Millichip (Born Birmingham, 5 August 1914. Died Birmingham, 18 December 2002.) Bert Millichip was chairman of the Football Association from 1981 to 1996, a period of tremendous change within the game. The Premier League breakaway and the Taylor Report both occurred during his time at the helm. A West Bromwich solicitor, he had been chairman of his local club before his activities with the FA took over and he was knighted for his services to football in 1991.

Billy Morris (Born Colwyn Bay 31 July 1918. Died Bodelwyddan, near Rhyl, 31 December 2002.) Billy Morris was a skilful inside right who won five caps for Wales and appeared for Burnley in the 1947 FA Cup final. He played over 200 first-team games for the Clarets and after retiring as a player he joined the coaching staff at Turf Moor. Later he had two spells as manager of Wrexham (July 1960 to April 1961 and March to October 1963).

Trevor Morris, OBE, DFC (Born Gorlas, Carmarthenshire, 6 September 1920. Died Nottingham, 3 February 2003.) Trevor Morris played just one senior game for Ipswich Town and a handful of wartime outings for Cardiff before a broken leg ended his career. He subsequently joined the office staff at Ninian Park and served as manager of both Cardiff and Swansea City, taking the Swans to the semi-final of the FA Cup in 1963–64. He then served the FA of Wales as secretary from March 1971 until 1982 and in 1976 he was awarded an OBE for services to Welsh football.

Angus Morrison (Born Dingwall, 26 April 1924. Died Derby, 18 December 2002.) Angus Morrison was a versatile forward who missed out on a place in the Derby County line-up for the 1945–46 FA Cup final, despite having played a prominent part in ensuring the Rams reached Wembley. He went on to make over 250 appearances for Preston, for whom he played (and scored) in their 1954 FA Cup final defeat by West Bromwich Albion. He wound up his career with a season at Millwall.

Albert Mundy (Born Portsmouth, 12 May 1926. Died Portsmouth, 30 August 2002.) Albert Mundy created history by scoring one of the fastest goals on record when he netted after just six seconds for Aldershot against Hartlepool in October 1958. Initially a goal-scoring centre forward in the early days of his career with Portsmouth and Brighton, he spent much of his time at Aldershot playing as a right half. In all he scored 117 goals in 367 senior appearances.

Bobby Norris (Born circa 1938. Died March 2003.) Bobby Norris joined Dundee United from Junior outfit Rutherglen Glencairn and was a regular for the Tannadice Park club when they won promotion from the Scottish Second Division in 1959–60. An inside forward, he was soon on his way, however, and later played for a number of teams including St Mirren, South Shields, Stenhousemuir, Forfar and Stranraer before retiring from the game in his mid-20s.

Ray Parry (Born Derby, 19 January 1936. Died 23 May 2003.) An England schools international, Ray joined Bolton Wanderers and became the club's youngest-ever player when he lined-up against Wolves in October 1951, shortly before his 16th birthday. He went on to make nearly 300 appearances for the Trotters, and was a member of the team that defeated Manchester United in the 1958 FA Cup final. Ray won two England caps, featuring against Northern Ireland and Scotland in the 1959–60 season, and won representative honours for England U-23 and the Football League. He also played for Blackpool and Bury.

Bill Patrick (Born Lochgelly, Fife, 12 March 1932. Died 18 April 2003.) Bill Patrick made around 100 Football League appearances for Coventry City and Gillingham between 1955 and 1960. A versatile player he featured both at full back and centre forward during his career. He later had a lengthy spell with Southern League club Folkestone and was a member of the team that reached the FA Cup third round in 1965–66.

Johnny Pattillo (Born circa 1915. Died Craigie, Perth & Kinross, August 2002.) Johnny Pattillo made a fine start to his senior career with Aberdeen, scoring 15 goals in 14 appearances in his first season with the club, including four against Hibernian in January 1939. He continued to score regularly in wartime for the Dons, but in the summer of 1946 he was allowed to move on to Dundee where he was a member of the team that defeated Rangers to win the Scottish League Cup in 1951–52. He subsequently became player-manager, then manager of St Johnstone during the period 1953 to 1958.

Jeff Pears (Born York, 14 June 1920. Died York, 6 April 2003.) Jeff Pears was York City's reserve goalkeeper in the 1947–48 and 1948–49 seasons, and made three first-team appearances during his spell at the club. He later played in the Midland League for Scarborough.

Julio Perez (Born Montevideo, Uruguay, 19 June 1926 Died Montevideo, Uruguay, 21 September 2002.) Julio Perez was one of the stars of the Uruguay team that won the World Cup in 1950, setting up the winning goal in the decisive match against hosts Brazil at the Maracana Stadium. He won a total of 22 caps for his country and played at club level for Racing of Montevideo, River Plate (Buenos Aires) and Nacional.

Jack Ranshaw (Born Nettleham, nr. Lincoln, 19 December 1916. Died Nettleham, nr. Lincoln, 1 May 2003.) Jack Ranshaw enjoyed his best playing years during the war when he made over 100 appearances guesting for Grimsby Town, Chesterfield, Mansfield and Lincoln. He eventually signed for the Imps, for whom he made three appearances in the 1946–47 season. Jack returned to Sincil Bank as groundsman from 1953 to 1965.

Billy Reed (Born Ynyshir, Rhondda, 25 January 1928. Died January 2003.) Billy Reed was capped by Wales at schoolboy, amateur and full international levels, featuring for the senior team against Scotland and Yugoslavia in 1954. He began his professional career at Cardiff, but it was not until he joined Brighton & Hove Albion in August 1948 that he made his bow in senior football. He went on to make over 300 career appearances for the Seagulls, Ipswich and Swansea Town.

Dale Roberts (Born Newcastle, 8 October 1956. Died Ipswich, 5 February 2003.) Dale Roberts won England international youth honours and was also a member of the Ipswich Town team that won the FA Youth Cup in 1973 and 1975. However, injury prevented him from becoming a regular in the line-up at Portman Road and he moved on to Hull City where he played over 150 games before a pelvic injury brought his career to a close. He subsequently had spells on the coaching staff of Hull, Colchester and Ipswich, where he was still in post at the time of his death.

George Robertson (Born Bainsford, nr Falkirk, 20 April 1930. Died Plymouth, 23 March 2003.) George Robertson joined Plymouth Argyle at the start of 1950 and went on to make 382 first-team appearances over the next 14 years. A right back who was strong in the tackle and with good distribution, he was a member of the Argyle team that won the Third Division title in 1958–59. He remained loyal to the club, serving as groundsman and then manager of the club's youth hostel for many years.

Phil Rookes (Born Dulverton, Somerset, 23 April 1919. Died February 2003.) Phil Rookes began his senior career at Bradford City then moved on to Portsmouth in January 1938. He was a member of the Pompey team that won the London War Cup in 1942 and when peacetime football resumed he was a regular at right back in the line-up. He retained his place until January 1949, when an ankle injury sidelined him as the club went on to win the first of two successive Football League titles. Phil later spent two seasons at Colchester United before retiring from the full-time game.

Arthur Rowley (Born Wolverhampton, 21 April 1926. Died Shrewsbury, 18 December 2002.) Arthur Rowley was the most prolific goal-scorer in the Football League, scoring 434 goals in a career that spanned the period 1947 to 1965. He still holds the seasonal scoring records for both Leicester (44 goals in 1956–57) and Shrewsbury Town (38 in 1958–59) and has the highest overall total for the Gay Meadow club (152). Arthur had begun his career at West Bromwich Albion and later played for Fulham, but it was not until he arrived at Filbert Street that his talents began to emerge. Despite his success at scoring he won few representative honours, playing once for England B and once for the Football League team. He was player-manager and then manager for the Shrews for a decade to July 1968 and also had spells as manager of Sheffield United and Southend.

Denis Saunders (Born Scarborough, 19 December 1924. Died 16 February 2003.) Denis Saunders was a talented wing half who captained Pegasus to victory in the FA Amateur Cup in 1951 and 1953 and also won a single cap for England amateurs. Earlier in his career he had played a handful of games for Newport County. In later years he served as head of the FA School of Excellence at Lilleshall from 1984 to 1988.

Arthur Rowley

Pat Saward (Born Cobh, Co Cork, Ireland, 17 August 1928. Died Newmarket, Cambridgeshire, 20 September 2002.) Pat Saward was a talented wing half who won 18 caps for the Republic of Ireland between 1953 and 1962. He made his name in Division Three South for Millwall, joining Aston Villa in the summer of 1955. He was a member of the Villa team that defeated Manchester United in the 1957 FA Cup final and captained the side that won the Second Division title in 1959–60. He concluded his career with a spell at Huddersfield Town, later managing Brighton & Hove Albion from 1970 to 1973.

Juan Schiaffino (Born Montevideo, Uruguay, 25 July 1925. Died Montevideo, Uruguay, 13 November 2002.) Juan Schiaffino was one of the greatest talents in world football during the 1950s. He had been one of the stars of the Uruguay team that won the 1950 World Cup in Brazil, scoring the equaliser in the decisive game against the hosts and assisting his team to a 2–1 victory. A slightly built forward, he had superb control, exceptional positional sense and a great eye for goal. He helped Penarol to a string of domestic titles and after the 1954 World Cup finals he was sold to AC Milan for a then world record fee of £72,000. Juan won three Serie A titles with Milan and later played for Roma before returning to Uruguay. Whilst in Europe he won four caps for Italy between 1954 and 1958.

Harry Sharratt (Born Wigan, 16 December 1929. Died 19 August 2002.) Harry Sharratt was a top-class amateur goalkeeper in the 1950s, firstly for Yorkshire Amateurs and then Bishop Auckland, with whom he won three FA Amateur Cup winners' medals. He also made occasional appearances at senior level for Blackpool, Oldham and Nottingham Forest. Harry won four England amateur caps and toured the West Indies with an FA XI in the summer of 1955.

George Sherwood (Born Selby, 14 March 1917. Died 17 March 2003.) After failing to win a place in the line-up at Huddersfield, George Sherwood joined Stockport County in the summer of 1938 and went on to make 39 appearances at inside left in the 1938–39 season. He guested for York City, Hull and Doncaster during the war, joining his home town club Selby Town for the 1946–47 season.

Harold Spencer (Born Burnley, 30 April 1919. Died Burnley, 19 May 2003.) Harold Spencer was a half back who joined the Burnley groundstaff in 1935, turning professional two years later, but it was not until the 1946–47 season that he made his senior debut for the Clarets. Mostly a reserve at Turf Moor, he was a member of the team that won the Central League title in 1948–49. In the summer of 1950 he moved on to join Wrexham, making 11 appearances for the Division Three North club.

Garry Stewart (Born Inverness, 16 October 1981. Died Strathspey, 23 November 2002.) Garry Stewart was a young goalkeeper who made a single senior appearance for Ross County in 1998–99. His tragically early death was a result of a car crash.

Albert Stubbins (Born Wallsend, 13 July 1919. Died Cullercoats, 28 December 2002.) Albert Stubbins was a prolific goal-scorer for Newcastle United during the war years, netting 231 goals from just 188 appearances. In September 1946 he was sold to Liverpool and became a firm favourite at Anfield, scoring a further 83 goals. He was a member of the Reds side that won the Football League title in 1946–47 and also appeared in the team that lost to Arsenal in the 1950 FA Cup final. He went on to become a well-respected journalist for the *People* and in later life won further fame when he was included as one of the figures on the cover of the Beatles' album *Sgt Pepper's Lonely Hearts Club Band*.

Juan Schiaffino, the best of the 1954 World Cup inside forwards, dribbles for Uruguay v. Austria in the play-off for third place.

Frank Taylor, OBE (Born Barrow in Furness, 7 December 1920. Died 19 July 2002.) Frank Taylor was a football journalist who survived the Munich air crash in 1958 and went on to record the events in his book *The Day a Team Died* He made his way via local newspapers to the *Sheffield Telegraph* and then the *News Chronicle*, for whom he was working at the time of the crash. He later became senior sports columnist for the *Daily Mirror*. Frank was awarded the OBE for services to sport and journalism in 1978.

Eusebio Tejera (Born 6 January 1922. Died 10 November 2002.) Eusebio Tejera was a defender with the Uruguay team that won the World Cup in 1950. He won a total of 34 caps for his country and played at club level for Bella Vista, River Plate and Nacional.

Eddie Thomson (Born Rosewell, Edinburgh, 25 February 1947. Died Sydney, Australia, 20 February 2003.) Eddie Thomson was a solid defender who made over 250 appearances for Hearts and Aberdeen between 1967 and 1977. He eventually migrated to Australia, where he played for Sydney City and went on to coach the Australian national team between 1990 and 1996. He introduced many of the present day stars to international football and led the team to fourth place in the 1992 Olympic Games. Eddie also won three caps for Scotland at U-23 level.

Sam Thorpe (Born Sheffield, 2 December 1920. Died Sheffield, August 2002.) Sam Thorpe made two appearances as a wing half for Sheffield United in the late 1940s. Earlier he had featured in wartime for Liverpool, Tranmere Rovers and Southport while serving in the RAF.

Alan Wakeman (Born Walsall, 20 November 1920. Died Stafford, 15 December 2002.) Goalkeeper Alan Wakeman was capped six times by England schools in the 1930s but the best years of his career were lost to the war. He played over 200 games for Aston Villa during the hostilities but his peacetime tally of games amounted to just 31 for Villa, Doncaster Rovers and Shrewsbury Town.

Keith Walwyn (Born Nevis, West Indies, 17 February 1956. Died 15 April 2003.) Keith Walwyn was a big, old-fashioned style centre forward who was best known for his spell at York, where he scored 119 times in 245 appearances between 1981 and 1987. His goals helped the Minstermen win the Fourth Division title in 1983–84, when they became the first Football League club to register 100 points in a season. Keith also played for Chesterfield, Carlisle and Blackpool.

Jock Weir (Born Fauldhouse, 20 October 1923. Died 7 January 2003.) Jock Weir was a pacy player who could take either the outside-right or centre-forward berth. He made his name as a prolific scorer with Hibernian in the late 1940s and also played for Blackburn Rovers, Celtic, Falkirk, Llanelly and Dumbarton. He was a member of the Celtic team that defeated Motherwell to win the Scottish Cup in 1951.

Dick White (Born Scunthorpe, 18 August 1931. Died Nottingham, 15 June 2002.) Dick White came to prominence as a centre half with Scunthorpe United in their early years as a Football League club. He moved on to Liverpool in November 1955 and went on to make over 200 appearances during his time at Anfield, earning a reputation as a reliable, no-nonsense defender. Dick later had a couple of seasons with Doncaster before becoming player-manager of Kettering Town.

Ray Wilcox (Born Treharris, 12 April 1921. Died Newport, Gwent, 26 January 2003.) Ray Wilcox made more than 500 first-team appearances for Newport County in their Football League days, captaining the side that reached the FA Cup fifth round in 1948–49, the club's best-ever performance. His playing days spanned the period 1946 to 1960 and he then remained at Somerton Park as trainer for another decade.

Eric Wilkinson (Born Sheffield, 6 March 1931. Died Winkton, Dorset, 11 October 2002.) Eric Wilkinson was on the books of both Bradford City and Sheffield United without making a senior appearance. In the summer of 1955 he signed for Bournemouth and played four times as a wing half in the 1955–56 season before leaving the full-time game for a career in teaching.

Ken Wookey (Born Newport, Gwent, 23 February 1922. Died Newport, Gwent, 11 January 2003.) After wartime service in the RAF, Ken Wookey made his debut for Newport County in the 1946–47 season, but within a short space of time he had moved on to Bristol Rovers. He featured regularly at outside right for the Pirates over the next 18 months and also appeared for Swansea Town, Hereford and Ipswich Town.

Jasper Youell (Born Bilston, Staffs, 23 March 1925. Died Hastings, 1 July 2003.) As a youngster Jasper was on the books of West Bromwich Albion, but war then intervened and in August 1946 he signed for Portsmouth. Pompey were a First Division club at the time and Jasper was a reserve for the club's regular full backs, making 30 appearances in a six-year spell at Fratton Park. He later had a season at Barnsley, but an injury brought his full-time career to a close.

Ray Wilcox

THE FA BARCLAYCARD PREMIERSHIP AND NATIONWIDE FOOTBALL LEAGUE FIXTURES 2003–04

Reproduced under licence from Football Dataco Limited. All rights reserved. Licence No. PRINT/COU/THEFO070. Copyright © and Database Right The FA Premier League/The Football League Limited 2003. All rights reserved. No part of the Fixtures Lists may be reproduced stored or transmitted in any form without the prior written permission of Football DataCo Limited.

**Sky Sports; †Premiership Plus pay per view*

Saturday, 9 August 2003
Nationwide Football League Division 1
Bradford C v Norwich C
Burnley v Crystal Palace
Derby Co v Stoke C
Ipswich T v Reading
Millwall v Wigan Ath
Nottingham F v Sunderland* (5:35)
Preston NE v West Ham U* (12:30)
Rotherham U v Cardiff C
Sheffield U v Gillingham
Walsall v WBA
Watford v Coventry C
Wimbledon v Crewe Alex

Nationwide Football League Division 2
Barnsley v Colchester U
Bristol C v Notts Co
Luton T v Rushden & D'monds
Oldham Ath v Brighton & HA
Peterborough U v Hartlepool U
Plymouth Arg v Grimsby T
Port Vale v Bournemouth
QPR v Blackpool
Swindon T v Sheffield W
Tranmere R v Brentford
Wrexham v Chesterfield
Wycombe W v Stockport Co

Nationwide Football League Division 3
Carlisle U v York C
Huddersfield T v Cambridge U
Hull C v Darlington
Kidderminster H v Mansfield T
Leyton Orient v Doncaster R
Lincoln C v Oxford U
Macclesfield T v Boston U
Northampton T v Torquay U
Rochdale v Yeovil
Scunthorpe U v Bristol R
Southend U v Cheltenham T
Swansea C v Bury

Nationwide Conference
Barnet v Telford U
Exeter C v Halifax T
Forest Green R v Northwich Vic
Gravesend & N v Burton Alb
Leigh RMI v Dagenham & Red
Morecambe v Woking
Scarborough v Farnborough T T
Shrewsbury T v Margate
Stevenage B v Chester C
Tamworth v Hereford U

Sunday, 10 August 2003
Community Shield
Arsenal v Manchester U*

Nationwide Conference
Aldershot T v Accrington Stanley* (5:00)

Tuesday, 12 August 2003
Nationwide Conference
Accrington Stanley v Leigh RMI
Burton Alb v Shrewsbury T
Chester C v Tamworth
Dagenham & Red v Stevenage B
Farnborough T v Barnet
Halifax T v Morecambe
Hereford U v Forest Green R
Margate v Aldershot T
Northwich Vic v Scarborough
Telford U v Exeter C
Woking v Gravesend & N

Saturday, 16 August 2003
FA Barclaycard Premiership
Arsenal v Everton
Birmingham C v Tottenham H
Blackburn R v Wolverhampton W
Fulham v Middlesbrough
Leicester C v Southampton
Manchester U v Bolton W
Portsmouth v Aston Villa* (12:30)

Nationwide Football League Division 1
Cardiff C v Bradford C
Coventry C v Walsall
Crewe Alex v Ipswich T
Crystal Palace v Watford
Gillingham v Derby Co
Norwich C v Rotherham U
Reading v Nottingham F
Stoke C v Wimbledon
Sunderland v Millwall
WBA v Burnley* (5:35)
West Ham U v Sheffield U
Wigan Ath v Preston NE

Nationwide Football League Division 2
Blackpool v Wycombe W
Bournemouth v Barnsley
Brentford v Peterborough U
Chesterfield v Bristol C
Colchester U v Swindon T
Grimsby T v Port Vale
Hartlepool U v Tranmere R
Notts Co v Wrexham
Rushden & D'monds v Plymouth Arg
Sheffield W v Oldham Ath
Stockport Co v Luton T

Nationwide Football League Division 3
Boston U v Huddersfield T
Bristol R v Rochdale
Bury v Scunthorpe U
Cambridge U v Macclesfield T
Cheltenham T v Swansea C
Darlington v Kidderminster H
Doncaster R v Southend U
Mansfield T v Leyton Orient
Oxford U v Hull C
Torquay U v Lincoln C
Yeovil v Carlisle U
York C v Northampton T

Nationwide Conference
Accrington Stanley v Shrewsbury T
Burton Alb v Stevenage B
Chester C v Forest Green R
Dagenham & Red v Barnet
Farnborough T v Leigh RMI
Halifax T v Gravesend & N
Hereford U v Morecambe
Margate v Exeter C
Northwich Vic v Tamworth
Telford U v Aldershot T
Woking v Scarborough

Sunday, 17 August 2003
FA Barclaycard Premiership
Charlton Ath v Manchester C (3:00)
Leeds U v Newcastle U† (2:00)
Liverpool v Chelsea* (4:05)

Monday, 18 August 2003
Nationwide Football League Division 2
Brighton & HA v QPR* (8:00)

Saturday, 23 August 2003

FA Barclaycard Premiership
Bolton W v Blackburn R
Chelsea v Leicester C
Everton v Fulham
Manchester C v Portsmouth
Newcastle U v Manchester U* (12:00)
Southampton v Birmingham C
Tottenham H v Leeds U
Wolverhampton W v Charlton Ath

Nationwide Football League Division 1
Bradford C v Gillingham
Burnley v Wigan Ath
Derby Co v Reading
Ipswich T v Coventry C
Millwall v Crewe Alex
Nottingham F v Cardiff C
Preston NE v Sunderland* (5:35)
Rotherham U v West Ham U
Sheffield U v Norwich C
Walsall v Stoke C
Watford v WBA
Wimbledon v Crystal Palace

Nationwide Football League Division 2
Barnsley v Brighton & HA
Bristol C v Hartlepool U
Luton T v Grimsby T
Oldham Ath v Blackpool
Peterborough U v Sheffield W
Plymouth Arg v Stockport Co
Port Vale v Colchester U
QPR v Bournemouth
Swindon T v Notts Co
Tranmere R v Rushden & D'monds
Wrexham v Brentford
Wycombe W v Chesterfield

Nationwide Football League Division 3
Carlisle U v Bristol R
Huddersfield T v York C
Hull C v Cheltenham T
Kidderminster H v Bury
Leyton Orient v Yeovil
Lincoln C v Doncaster R
Macclesfield T v Torquay U
Northampton T v Darlington
Rochdale v Cambridge U
Scunthorpe U v Oxford U
Southend U v Mansfield T
Swansea C v Boston U

Nationwide Conference
Aldershot T v Woking
Barnet v Hereford U
Exeter C v Chester C
Forest Green R v Accrington Stanley
Gravesend & N v Telford U
Leigh RMI v Halifax T
Morecambe v Dagenham & Red
Scarborough v Burton Alb
Shrewsbury T v Farnborough T
Stevenage B v Northwich Vic
Tamworth v Margate

Sunday, 24 August 2003

FA Barclaycard Premiership
Aston Villa v Liverpool† (2:00)
Middlesbrough v Arsenal* (4:05)

Monday, 25 August 2003

FA Barclaycard Premiership
Blackburn R v Manchester C* (8:00)

Nationwide Football League Division 1
Cardiff C v Derby Co* (5:35)
Crewe Alex v Walsall
Crystal Palace v Sheffield U
Gillingham v Burnley
Norwich C v Wimbledon
Reading v Rotherham U* (12:30)
Stoke C v Millwall
Sunderland v Watford
WBA v Preston NE
West Ham U v Bradford C
Wigan Ath v Ipswich T

Nationwide Football League Division 2
Blackpool v Barnsley
Bournemouth v Swindon T
Brentford v Oldham Ath
Brighton & HA v Luton T
Chesterfield v Plymouth Arg
Colchester U v Bristol C
Grimsby T v Wycombe W
Hartlepool U v Port Vale
Notts Co v Peterborough U
Rushden & D'monds v QPR
Sheffield W v Wrexham
Stockport Co v Tranmere R

Nationwide Football League Division 3
Boston U v Carlisle U
Bristol R v Macclesfield T
Bury v Lincoln C
Cambridge U v Hull C
Cheltenham T v Kidderminster H
Darlington v Leyton Orient
Doncaster R v Huddersfield T
Mansfield T v Scunthorpe U
Oxford U v Swansea C
Torquay U v Rochdale
Yeovil v Northampton T
York C v Southend U

Nationwide Conference
Accrington Stanley v Scarborough
Burton Alb v Barnet
Chester C v Shrewsbury T
Dagenham & Red v Forest Green R
Farnborough T v Gravesend & N
Halifax T v Tamworth
Hereford U v Aldershot T
Margate v Stevenage B
Northwich Vic v Leigh RMI
Telford U v Morecambe
Woking v Exeter C

Tuesday, 26 August 2003

FA Barclaycard Premiership
Arsenal v Aston Villa
Charlton Ath v Everton
Leeds U v Southampton
Leicester C v Middlesbrough
Portsmouth v Bolton W

Wednesday, 27 August 2003

FA Barclaycard Premiership
Liverpool v Tottenham H
Manchester U v Wolverhampton W* (8:00)

Nationwide Football League Division 1
Coventry C v Nottingham F

Saturday, 30 August 2003

FA Barclaycard Premiership
Aston Villa v Leicester C
Bolton W v Charlton Ath
Chelsea v Blackburn R
Everton v Liverpool* (12:30)
Middlesbrough v Leeds U
Newcastle U v Birmingham C
Tottenham H v Fulham
Wolverhampton W v Portsmouth

Nationwide Football League Division 1
Bradford C v Sunderland
Burnley v Crewe Alex
Derby Co v WBA
Ipswich T v West Ham U
Millwall v Crystal Palace
Nottingham F v Norwich C
Preston NE v Stoke C
Rotherham U v Wigan Ath
Sheffield U v Coventry C
Walsall v Cardiff C
Watford v Gillingham
Wimbledon v Reading

Nationwide Football League Division 2
Barnsley v Notts Co
Bristol C v Grimsby T
Luton T v Hartlepool U
Oldham Ath v Rushden & D'monds
Peterborough U v Stockport Co
Plymouth Arg v Brighton & HA
Port Vale v Brentford
QPR v Chesterfield
Swindon T v Blackpool
Tranmere R v Colchester U
Wrexham v Bournemouth

Nationwide Football League Division 3
Carlisle U v Cambridge U
Huddersfield T v Bristol R
Hull C v Boston U
Kidderminster H v Oxford U
Leyton Orient v Cheltenham T
Lincoln C v York C
Macclesfield T v Yeovil
Northampton T v Doncaster R
Rochdale v Darlington
Scunthorpe U v Torquay U
Southend U v Bury
Swansea C v Mansfield T

Nationwide Conference
Aldershot T v Northwich Vic
Barnet v Halifax T
Exeter C v Farnborough T
Forest Green R v Margate
Gravesend & N v Chester C
Leigh RMI v Woking
Morecambe v Burton Alb
Scarborough v Telford U
Shrewsbury T v Dagenham & Red
Stevenage B v Hereford U
Tamworth v Accrington Stanley

Sunday, 31 August 2003

FA Barclaycard Premiership
Manchester C v Arsenal* (4:05)
Southampton v Manchester U† (2:00)

Monday, 1 September 2003

Nationwide Football League Division 2
Wycombe W v Sheffield W* (8:00)

Saturday, 6 September 2003

Nationwide Football League Division 1
Cardiff C v Watford
Coventry C v Bradford C
Crewe Alex v Preston NE
Crystal Palace v Ipswich T
Gillingham v Millwall
Norwich C v Derby Co
Reading v Walsall
Stoke C v Burnley
Sunderland v Rotherham U
WBA v Wimbledon
West Ham U v Nottingham F
Wigan Ath v Sheffield U

Nationwide Football League Division 2
Blackpool v Wrexham
Bournemouth v Bristol C* (12:05)
Brentford v Plymouth Arg
Brighton & HA v Swindon T
Chesterfield v Barnsley
Colchester U v QPR
Grimsby T v Peterborough U
Hartlepool U v Oldham Ath
Notts Co v Luton T
Rushden & D'monds v Wycombe W
Sheffield W v Tranmere R
Stockport Co v Port Vale

Nationwide Football League Division 3
Boston U v Scunthorpe U
Bristol R v Kidderminster H
Bury v Huddersfield T
Cambridge U v Lincoln C
Cheltenham T v Northampton T
Darlington v Carlisle U
Mansfield T v Macclesfield T
Oxford U v Southend U
Torquay U v Leyton Orient
Yeovil v Swansea C
York C v Rochdale

Nationwide Conference
Barnet v Accrington Stanley
Burton Alb v Woking
Dagenham & Red v Telford U
Exeter C v Stevenage B
Farnborough T v Hereford U
Halifax T v Northwich Vic
Leigh RMI v Forest Green R
Margate v Chester C
Morecambe v Aldershot T
Scarborough v Gravesend & N

Sunday, 7 September 2003
Nationwide Conference
Shrewsbury T v Tamworth* (12:30)

Monday, 8 September 2003
Nationwide Football League Division 3
Doncaster R v Hull C* (8:00)

Saturday, 13 September 2003
FA Barclaycard Premiership
Arsenal v Portsmouth
Blackburn R v Liverpool
Bolton W v Middlesbrough
Charlton Ath v Manchester U
Chelsea v Tottenham H
Everton v Newcastle U
Southampton v Wolverhampton W

Nationwide Football League Division 1
Bradford C v Preston NE
Cardiff C v Gillingham
Coventry C v Stoke C
Norwich C v Burnley
Nottingham F v Sheffield U
Rotherham U v Crewe Alex* (5:35)
Sunderland v Crystal Palace
Walsall v Derby Co
Watford v Millwall* (12:30)
WBA v Ipswich T
West Ham U v Reading
Wimbledon v Wigan Ath

Nationwide Football League Division 2
Blackpool v Bournemouth
Chesterfield v Notts Co
Colchester U v Brighton & HA
Hartlepool U v Grimsby T
Oldham Ath v Bristol C
Plymouth Arg v Luton T
Port Vale v Barnsley
QPR v Wycombe W
Rushden & D'monds v Brentford
Sheffield W v Stockport Co
Swindon T v Wrexham
Tranmere R v Peterborough U

Nationwide Football League Division 3
Bristol R v Boston U
Bury v Cheltenham T
Cambridge U v Torquay U
Carlisle U v Rochdale
Darlington v Doncaster R
Huddersfield T v Northampton T
Hull C v Southend U
Lincoln C v Leyton Orient
Macclesfield T v Kidderminster H
Oxford U v Mansfield T
Scunthorpe U v Swansea C
Yeovil v York C

Nationwide Conference
Accrington Stanley v Margate
Aldershot T v Shrewsbury T
Chester C v Halifax T
Forest Green R v Exeter C
Gravesend & N v Leigh RMI
Hereford U v Scarborough
Northwich Vic v Dagenham & Red
Stevenage B v Barnet
Tamworth v Morecambe
Telford U v Burton Alb
Woking v Farnborough T

Sunday, 14 September 2003
FA Barclaycard Premiership
Birmingham C v Fulham* (4:05)
Manchester C v Aston Villa† (2:00)

Monday, 15 September 2003
FA Barclaycard Premiership
Leicester C v Leeds U* (8:00)

Tuesday, 16 September 2003
Nationwide Football League Division 1
Burnley v Nottingham F
Crewe Alex v West Ham U
Crystal Palace v Bradford C
Gillingham v Norwich C
Ipswich T v Walsall
Millwall v Wimbledon
Preston NE v Coventry C
Reading v Cardiff C
Sheffield U v Rotherham U
Wigan Ath v WBA

Nationwide Football League Division 2
Barnsley v Oldham Ath
Bournemouth v Sheffield W
Brentford v Blackpool
Brighton & HA v Chesterfield
Bristol C v Tranmere R
Grimsby T v Swindon T
Luton T v Port Vale
Notts Co v Rushden & D'monds
Peterborough U v Plymouth Arg
Stockport Co v Hartlepool U
Wrexham v QPR
Wycombe W v Colchester U

Nationwide Football League Division 3
Cheltenham T v Oxford U
Doncaster R v Yeovil
Kidderminster H v Scunthorpe U
Leyton Orient v Hull C
Mansfield T v Bury
Northampton T v Carlisle U
Rochdale v Huddersfield T
Southend U v Lincoln C
Swansea C v Macclesfield T
Torquay U v Bristol R
York C v Darlington

Wednesday, 17 September 2003
Nationwide Football League Division 1
Derby Co v Watford
Stoke C v Sunderland

Nationwide Football League Division 3
Boston U v Cambridge U

Saturday, 20 September 2003
FA Barclaycard Premiership
Aston Villa v Charlton Ath
Fulham v Manchester C
Leeds U v Birmingham C
Liverpool v Leicester C
Newcastle U v Bolton W
Portsmouth v Blackburn R
Tottenham H v Southampton
Wolverhampton W v Chelsea* (12:30)

Nationwide Football League Division 1
Burnley v Bradford C
Crewe Alex v Nottingham F
Crystal Palace v WBA
Derby Co v Sunderland
Gillingham v West Ham U
Ipswich T v Wimbledon
Millwall v Walsall
Preston NE v Rotherham U
Reading v Coventry C
Sheffield U v Cardiff C
Stoke C v Norwich C* (5:35)
Wigan Ath v Watford

Nationwide Football League Division 2
Barnsley v Swindon T
Bournemouth v Rushden & D'monds
Brentford v Hartlepool U
Brighton & HA v Sheffield W
Bristol C v Port Vale
Grimsby T v Chesterfield
Luton T v QPR
Notts Co v Tranmere R
Peterborough U v Colchester U
Stockport Co v Blackpool
Wrexham v Plymouth Arg
Wycombe W v Oldham Ath

Nationwide Football League Division 3
Boston U v Bury
Cheltenham T v Cambridge U
Doncaster R v Oxford U
Kidderminster H v Lincoln C
Leyton Orient v Scunthorpe U
Mansfield T v Yeovil
Northampton T v Macclesfield T
Rochdale v Hull C
Southend U v Carlisle U
Swansea C v Huddersfield T
Torquay U v Darlington
York C v Bristol R

Nationwide Conference
Barnet v Aldershot T
Burton Alb v Hereford U
Dagenham & Red v Accrington Stanley
Farnborough T v Chester C
Gravesend & N v Exeter C
Halifax T v Margate
Leigh RMI v Tamworth

Northwich Vic v Morecambe
Scarborough v Forest Green R
Telford U v Stevenage B
Woking v Shrewsbury T

Sunday, 21 September 2003
FA Barclaycard Premiership
Manchester U v Arsenal* (4:05)
Middlesbrough v Everton† (2:00)

Monday, 22 September 2003
Nationwide Conference
Exeter C v Dagenham & Red* (8:00)

Tuesday, 23 September 2003
Nationwide Conference
Accrington Stanley v Burton Alb
Aldershot T v Farnborough T
Chester C v Northwich Vic
Forest Green R v Woking
Hereford U v Telford U
Margate v Barnet
Morecambe v Leigh RMI
Shrewsbury T v Halifax T
Stevenage B v Gravesend & N
Tamworth v Scarborough

Friday, 26 September 2003
FA Barclaycard Premiership
Arsenal v Newcastle U* (8:00)

Saturday, 27 September 2003
FA Barclaycard Premiership
Birmingham C v Portsmouth
Blackburn R v Fulham
Bolton W v Wolverhampton W
Chelsea v Aston Villa
Everton v Leeds U
Leicester C v Manchester U
Southampton v Middlesbrough

Nationwide Football League Division 1
Bradford C v Sheffield U* (12:30)
Cardiff C v Crewe Alex
Coventry C v Wigan Ath
Norwich C v Crystal Palace
Nottingham F v Derby Co
Rotherham U v Gillingham
Sunderland v Reading* (5:35)
Walsall v Preston NE
Watford v Ipswich T
WBA v Stoke C
West Ham U v Millwall
Wimbledon v Burnley

Nationwide Football League Division 2
Blackpool v Notts Co
Chesterfield v Brentford
Colchester U v Bournemouth
Hartlepool U v Brighton & HA
Oldham Ath v Luton T
Plymouth Arg v Barnsley
Port Vale v Wycombe W
QPR v Bristol C
Rushden & D'monds v Stockport Co
Sheffield W v Grimsby T
Swindon T v Peterborough U
Tranmere R v Wrexham

Nationwide Football League Division 3
Bristol R v Cheltenham T
Bury v Doncaster R
Cambridge U v Mansfield T
Carlisle U v Swansea C
Darlington v Boston U
Huddersfield T v Leyton Orient
Hull C v Kidderminster H
Lincoln C v Rochdale
Macclesfield T v York C
Oxford U v Northampton T
Scunthorpe U v Southend U
Yeovil v Torquay U

Nationwide Conference
Accrington Stanley v Woking
Aldershot T v Burton Alb
Chester C v Telford U
Exeter C v Scarborough
Forest Green R v Halifax T
Hereford U v Gravesend & N
Margate v Northwich Vic
Morecambe v Farnborough T
Shrewsbury T v Barnet
Stevenage B v Leigh RMI
Tamworth v Dagenham & Red

Sunday, 28 September 2003
FA Barclaycard Premiership
Charlton Ath v Liverpool† (2:00)
Manchester C v Tottenham H* (4:05)

Monday, 29 September 2003
Nationwide Football League Division 1
Walsall v Gillingham* (8:00)

Tuesday, 30 September 2003
Nationwide Football League Division 1
Bradford C v Derby Co* (12:30)
Cardiff C v Wigan Ath
Norwich C v Reading
Rotherham U v Stoke C
Sunderland v Ipswich T
Watford v Burnley
WBA v Millwall
Wimbledon v Sheffield U

Nationwide Football League Division 2
Blackpool v Grimsby T
Chesterfield v Bournemouth
Colchester U v Brentford
Hartlepool U v Wrexham
Oldham Ath v Stockport Co
Plymouth Arg v Bristol C
Port Vale v Peterborough U
QPR v Barnsley
Rushden & D'monds v Brighton & HA
Tranmere R v Wycombe W

Nationwide Football League Division 3
Bristol R v Mansfield T
Bury v York C
Cambridge U v Doncaster R
Carlisle U v Leyton Orient
Darlington v Southend U
Huddersfield T v Kidderminster H
Hull C v Swansea C
Lincoln C v Northampton T
Macclesfield T v Rochdale
Oxford U v Torquay U
Scunthorpe U v Cheltenham T
Yeovil v Boston U

Wednesday, 1 October 2003
Nationwide Football League Division 1
Coventry C v Crewe Alex
Nottingham F v Preston NE
West Ham U v Crystal Palace

Nationwide Football League Division 2
Sheffield W v Notts Co
Swindon T v Luton T

Saturday, 4 October 2003
FA Barclaycard Premiership
Fulham v Leicester C
Leeds U v Blackburn R
Liverpool v Arsenal* (12:30)
Manchester U v Birmingham C
Newcastle U v Southampton
Portsmouth v Charlton Ath
Tottenham H v Everton
Wolverhampton W v Manchester C

Nationwide Football League Division 1
Burnley v Walsall
Crewe Alex v Watford
Crystal Palace v Cardiff C
Derby Co v West Ham U* (5:35)
Gillingham v WBA
Ipswich T v Rotherham U
Millwall v Coventry C
Preston NE v Wimbledon
Reading v Bradford C
Sheffield U v Sunderland
Stoke C v Nottingham F
Wigan Ath v Norwich C

Nationwide Football League Division 2
Barnsley v Rushden & D'monds
Bournemouth v Hartlepool U
Brentford v Sheffield W
Brighton & HA v Blackpool
Bristol C v Swindon T
Grimsby T v QPR
Luton T v Tranmere R
Notts Co v Colchester U
Peterborough U v Oldham Ath
Stockport Co v Chesterfield
Wrexham v Port Vale
Wycombe W v Plymouth Arg

Nationwide Football League Division 3
Boston U v Oxford U
Cheltenham T v Yeovil
Doncaster R v Bristol R
Kidderminster H v Carlisle U
Leyton Orient v Macclesfield T
Mansfield T v Darlington
Northampton T v Hull C
Rochdale v Scunthorpe U
Southend U v Huddersfield T
Swansea C v Lincoln C
Torquay U v Bury
York C v Cambridge U

Nationwide Conference
Barnet v Morecambe
Burton Alb v Exeter C
Dagenham & Red v Chester C
Farnborough T v Tamworth
Gravesend & N v Forest Green R
Halifax T v Stevenage B
Leigh RMI v Aldershot T
Northwich Vic v Accrington Stanley
Scarborough v Shrewsbury T
Telford U v Margate
Woking v Hereford U

Sunday, 5 October 2003
FA Barclaycard Premiership
Aston Villa v Bolton W* (4:05)
Middlesbrough v Chelsea† (2:00)

Tuesday, 7 October 2003
Nationwide Conference
Barnet v Exeter C
Burton Alb v Chester C
Dagenham & Red v Margate
Farnborough T v Forest Green R

Gravesend & N v Aldershot T
Halifax T v Accrington Stanley
Leigh RMI v Shrewsbury T
Northwich Vic v Hereford U
Scarborough v Morecambe
Telford U v Tamworth
Woking v Stevenage B

Saturday, 11 October 2003

Nationwide Football League Division 1
Bradford C v Ipswich T
Burnley v Reading
Cardiff C v WBA
Derby Co v Wigan Ath
Gillingham v Sunderland
Norwich C v Coventry C
Preston NE v Watford
Rotherham U v Millwall
Sheffield U v Crewe Alex
Stoke C v Crystal Palace
Walsall v Nottingham F
Wimbledon v West Ham U

Nationwide Football League Division 2
Barnsley v Wrexham
Brighton & HA v Grimsby T
Bristol C v Peterborough U
Colchester U v Blackpool
Hartlepool U v Sheffield W
Luton T v Wycombe W
Notts Co v Bournemouth
Oldham Ath v Port Vale
Plymouth Arg v Tranmere R
QPR v Brentford
Rushden & D'monds v Chesterfield
Swindon T v Stockport Co

Nationwide Football League Division 3
Boston U v Cheltenham T
Cambridge U v Bury
Darlington v Bristol R
Huddersfield T v Torquay U
Hull C v Carlisle U
Kidderminster H v Southend U
Leyton Orient v Swansea C
Macclesfield T v Doncaster R
Mansfield T v York C
Oxford U v Yeovil
Rochdale v Northampton T
Scunthorpe U v Lincoln C

Nationwide Conference
Accrington Stanley v Farnborough T
Aldershot T v Halifax T
Chester C v Woking
Exeter C v Northwich Vic
Forest Green R v Burton Alb
Hereford U v Dagenham & Red
Margate v Leigh RMI
Morecambe v Gravesend & N
Shrewsbury T v Telford U
Stevenage B v Scarborough
Tamworth v Barnet

Tuesday, 14 October 2003

FA Barclaycard Premiership
Birmingham C v Chelsea

Nationwide Football League Division 1
Crewe Alex v Bradford C
Crystal Palace v Derby Co
Ipswich T v Burnley
Millwall v Preston NE
Reading v Gillingham
Sunderland v Cardiff C
Watford v Walsall
WBA v Sheffield U
Wigan Ath v Stoke C

Wednesday, 15 October 2003

FA Barclaycard Premiership
Fulham v Newcastle

Nationwide Football League Division 1
Coventry C v Wimbledon
Nottingham F v Rotherham U
West Ham U v Norwich C

Saturday, 18 October 2003

FA Barclaycard Premiership
Arsenal v Chelsea
Birmingham C v Aston Villa
Fulham v Wolverhampton W
Leeds U v Manchester U
Manchester C v Bolton W
Middlesbrough v Newcastle U
Portsmouth v Liverpool

Nationwide Football League Division 1
Coventry C v Cardiff C
Crewe Alex v Derby Co
Crystal Palace v Rotherham U
Ipswich T v Stoke C
Millwall v Sheffield U
Nottingham F v Wimbledon
Reading v Preston NE
Sunderland v Walsall
Watford v Bradford C
WBA v Norwich C
West Ham U v Burnley
Wigan Ath v Gillingham

Nationwide Football League Division 2
Blackpool v Hartlepool U
Bournemouth v Brighton & HA
Brentford v Luton T
Chesterfield v Swindon T
Grimsby T v Colchester U
Peterborough U v QPR
Port Vale v Plymouth Arg
Sheffield W v Rushden & D'monds
Stockport Co v Notts Co
Tranmere R v Oldham Ath
Wrexham v Bristol C
Wycombe W v Barnsley

Nationwide Football League Division 3
Bristol R v Cambridge U
Bury v Oxford U
Carlisle U v Macclesfield T
Cheltenham T v Rochdale
Doncaster R v Mansfield T
Lincoln C v Huddersfield T
Northampton T v Scunthorpe U
Southend U v Leyton Orient
Swansea C v Kidderminster H
Torquay U v Hull C
Yeovil v Darlington
York C v Boston U

Nationwide Conference
Accrington Stanley v Exeter C
Chester C v Hereford U
Dagenham & Red v Burton Alb
Farnborough T v Telford U
Forest Green R v Stevenage B
Leigh RMI v Barnet
Margate v Scarborough
Northwich Vic v Gravesend & N
Shrewsbury T v Morecambe
Tamworth v Aldershot T
Woking v Halifax T

Sunday, 19 October 2003

FA Barclaycard Premiership
Everton v Southampton* (4:05)
Leicester C v Tottenham H† (2:00)

Monday, 20 October 2003

FA Barclaycard Premiership
Blackburn R v Charlton Ath* (8:00)

Tuesday, 21 October 2003

Nationwide Football League Division 2
Blackpool v Rushden & D'monds
Bournemouth v Luton T
Brentford v Brighton & HA
Chesterfield v Hartlepool U
Grimsby T v Notts Co
Peterborough U v Barnsley
Port Vale v QPR
Stockport Co v Colchester U
Tranmere R v Swindon T
Wrexham v Oldham Ath
Wycombe W v Bristol C

Nationwide Football League Division 3
Bristol R v Leyton Orient
Bury v Hull C
Carlisle U v Scunthorpe U
Cheltenham T v Darlington
Doncaster R v Rochdale
Lincoln C v Macclesfield T
Northampton T v Kidderminster H
Southend U v Boston U
Swansea C v Cambridge U
Torquay U v Mansfield T
Yeovil v Huddersfield T
York C v Oxford U

Wednesday, 22 October 2003

Nationwide Football League Division 2
Sheffield W v Plymouth Arg

Saturday, 25 October 2003

FA Barclaycard Premiership
Aston Villa v Everton
Bolton W v Birmingham C* (12:30)
Chelsea v Manchester C
Liverpool v Leeds U
Manchester U v Fulham
Newcastle U v Portsmouth
Southampton v Blackburn R
Wolverhampton W v Leicester C

Nationwide Football League Division 1
Bradford C v Nottingham F
Burnley v Millwall
Cardiff C v West Ham U
Derby Co v Coventry C
Gillingham v Crystal Palace
Norwich C v Sunderland
Preston NE v Ipswich T
Rotherham U v WBA
Sheffield U v Reading
Stoke C v Crewe Alex
Walsall v Wigan Ath
Wimbledon v Watford

Nationwide Football League Division 2
Barnsley v Grimsby T
Brighton & HA v Stockport Co
Bristol C v Sheffield W
Colchester U v Chesterfield
Hartlepool U v Wycombe W
Luton T v Peterborough U
Notts Co v Brentford
Oldham Ath v Bournemouth
Plymouth Arg v Blackpool
QPR v Tranmere R

Rushden & D'monds v Wrexham
Swindon T v Port Vale

Nationwide Football League Division 3
Boston U v Torquay U
Cambridge U v Yeovil
Darlington v Bury
Huddersfield T v Carlisle U
Hull C v Lincoln C
Kidderminster H v Doncaster R
Leyton Orient v Northampton T
Macclesfield T v Southend U
Mansfield T v Cheltenham T
Oxford U v Bristol R
Rochdale v Swansea C
Scunthorpe U v York C

Sunday, 26 October 2003
FA Barclaycard Premiership
Charlton Ath v Arsenal† (2:00)
Tottenham H v Middlesbrough* (4:05)

Saturday, 1 November 2003
FA Barclaycard Premiership
Everton v Chelsea
Leeds U v Arsenal
Manchester U v Portsmouth
Middlesbrough v Wolverhampton W
Newcastle U v Aston Villa
Southampton v Manchester C
Tottenham H v Bolton W

Nationwide Football League Division 1
Burnley v Cardiff C
Coventry C v West Ham U
Crewe Alex v Reading
Ipswich T v Gillingham
Millwall v Nottingham F
Preston NE v Derby Co
Stoke C v Sheffield U
Walsall v Norwich C
Watford v Rotherham U
WBA v Sunderland
Wigan Ath v Crystal Palace
Wimbledon v Bradford C

Nationwide Football League Division 2
Brentford v Barnsley
Bristol C v Luton T
Chesterfield v Port Vale
Notts Co v Hartlepool U
Peterborough U v Brighton & HA
Plymouth Arg v Oldham Ath
Rushden & D'monds v Grimsby T
Sheffield W v Blackpool
Stockport Co v QPR
Swindon T v Wycombe W
Tranmere R v Bournemouth
Wrexham v Colchester U

Nationwide Football League Division 3
Bury v Yeovil
Cheltenham T v York C
Doncaster R v Torquay U
Hull C v Macclesfield T
Kidderminster H v Cambridge U
Leyton Orient v Rochdale
Lincoln C v Carlisle U
Mansfield T v Boston U
Oxford U v Darlington
Scunthorpe U v Huddersfield T
Southend U v Northampton T
Swansea C v Bristol R

Nationwide Conference
Aldershot T v Forest Green R
Barnet v Northwich Vic
Burton Alb v Farnborough T
Exeter C v Tamworth
Gravesend & N v Accrington Stanley
Halifax T v Dagenham & Red
Hereford U v Leigh RMI
Morecambe v Margate
Scarborough v Chester C
Stevenage B v Shrewsbury T
Telford U v Woking

Sunday, 2 November 2003
FA Barclaycard Premiership
Fulham v Liverpool† (2:00)
Leicester C v Blackburn R* (4:05)

Monday, 3 November 2003
FA Barclaycard Premiership
Birmingham C v Charlton Ath* (8:00)

Saturday, 8 November 2003
FA Barclaycard Premiership
Arsenal v Tottenham H
Aston Villa v Middlesbrough
Bolton W v Southampton
Charlton Ath v Fulham
Manchester C v Leicester C
Portsmouth v Leeds U
Wolverhampton W v Birmingham C† (12:30)

Nationwide Football League Division 1
Bradford C v Walsall
Cardiff C v Stoke C
Crystal Palace v Preston NE
Derby Co v Ipswich T
Gillingham v Crewe Alex
Norwich C v Millwall
Nottingham F v Watford
Reading v Wigan Ath
Rotherham U v Wimbledon
Sheffield U v Burnley
Sunderland v Coventry C
West Ham U v WBA

Sunday, 9 November 2003
FA Barclaycard Premiership
Chelsea v Newcastle U* (4:05)
Liverpool v Manchester U* (12:30)

Monday, 10 November 2003
FA Barclaycard Premiership
Blackburn R v Everton* (8:00)

Tuesday, 11 November 2003
Nationwide Conference
Accrington Stanley v Hereford U
Aldershot T v Exeter C
Barnet v Gravesend & N
Dagenham & Red v Farnborough T
Halifax T v Telford U
Leigh RMI v Scarborough
Margate v Woking
Morecambe v Chester C
Northwich Vic v Burton Alb
Shrewsbury T v Forest Green R
Tamworth v Stevenage B

Saturday, 15 November 2003
Nationwide Football League Division 1
Bradford C v WBA
Cardiff C v Preston NE
Crystal Palace v Crewe Alex
Derby Co v Burnley
Gillingham v Wimbledon
Norwich C v Watford
Nottingham F v Ipswich T
Reading v Millwall
Rotherham U v Coventry C
Sheffield U v Walsall
Sunderland v Wigan Ath
West Ham U v Stoke C

Nationwide Football League Division 2
Barnsley v Tranmere R
Blackpool v Chesterfield
Bournemouth v Peterborough U
Brighton & HA v Bristol C
Colchester U v Sheffield W
Grimsby T v Stockport Co
Hartlepool U v Rushden & D'monds
Luton T v Wrexham
Oldham Ath v Swindon T
Port Vale v Notts Co
QPR v Plymouth Arg
Wycombe W v Brentford

Nationwide Football League Division 3
Boston U v Leyton Orient
Bristol R v Bury
Cambridge U v Oxford U
Carlisle U v Mansfield T
Darlington v Lincoln C
Huddersfield T v Hull C
Macclesfield T v Scunthorpe U
Northampton T v Swansea C
Rochdale v Kidderminster H
Torquay U v Cheltenham T
Yeovil v Southend U
York C v Doncaster R

Nationwide Conference
Burton Alb v Halifax T
Chester C v Barnet
Exeter C v Morecambe
Farnborough T v Northwich Vic
Forest Green R v Tamworth
Gravesend & N v Shrewsbury T
Hereford U v Margate
Scarborough v Aldershot T
Stevenage B v Accrington Stanley
Telford U v Leigh RMI
Woking v Dagenham & Red

Saturday, 22 November 2003
FA Barclaycard Premiership
Birmingham C v Arsenal
Everton v Wolverhampton W
Leeds U v Bolton W
Leicester C v Charlton Ath
Manchester U v Blackburn R
Middlesbrough v Liverpool
Newcastle U v Manchester C
Southampton v Chelsea

Nationwide Football League Division 1
Burnley v Rotherham U
Coventry C v Gillingham
Crewe Alex v Sunderland
Ipswich T v Sheffield U
Millwall v Derby Co
Preston NE v Norwich C
Stoke C v Bradford C
Walsall v Crystal Palace
Watford v West Ham U
WBA v Reading
Wigan Ath v Nottingham F
Wimbledon v Cardiff C

Nationwide Football League Division 2
Brentford v Grimsby T
Bristol C v Barnsley
Chesterfield v Oldham Ath
Notts Co v Brighton & HA
Peterborough U v Blackpool

Plymouth Arg v Hartlepool U
Rushden & D'monds v Colchester U
Sheffield W v Luton T
Stockport Co v Bournemouth
Swindon T v QPR
Tranmere R v Port Vale
Wrexham v Wycombe W

Nationwide Football League Division 3
Bury v Northampton T
Cheltenham T v Carlisle U
Doncaster R v Boston U
Hull C v Yeovil
Kidderminster H v Torquay U
Leyton Orient v York C
Lincoln C v Bristol R
Mansfield T v Huddersfield T
Oxford U v Macclesfield T
Scunthorpe U v Cambridge U
Southend U v Rochdale
Swansea C v Darlington

Nationwide Conference
Accrington Stanley v Telford U
Aldershot T v Chester C
Barnet v Forest Green R
Dagenham & Red v Scarborough
Halifax T v Farnborough T
Leigh RMI v Exeter C
Margate v Burton Alb
Morecambe v Stevenage B
Northwich Vic v Woking
Shrewsbury T v Hereford U
Tamworth v Gravesend & N

Sunday, 23 November 2003
FA Barclaycard Premiership
Tottenham H v Aston Villa* (4:05)

Monday, 24 November 2003
FA Barclaycard Premiership
Fulham v Portsmouth* (8:00)

Tuesday, 25 November 2003
Nationwide Conference
Burton Alb v Leigh RMI
Chester C v Accrington Stanley
Exeter C v Shrewsbury T
Farnborough T v Margate
Forest Green R v Morecambe
Gravesend & N v Dagenham & Red
Hereford U v Halifax T
Scarborough v Barnet
Stevenage B v Aldershot T
Telford U v Northwich Vic
Woking v Tamworth

Saturday, 29 November 2003
FA Barclaycard Premiership
Arsenal v Fulham
Aston Villa v Southampton
Blackburn R v Tottenham H
Bolton W v Everton
Charlton Ath v Leeds U
Chelsea v Manchester U
Liverpool v Birmingham C
Manchester C v Middlesbrough
Portsmouth v Leicester C
Wolverhampton W v Newcastle U* (12:30)

Nationwide Football League Division 1
Bradford C v Millwall
Cardiff C v Ipswich T
Crystal Palace v Coventry C
Derby Co v Wimbledon
Gillingham v Stoke C
Norwich C v Crewe Alex
Nottingham F v WBA
Reading v Watford
Rotherham U v Walsall
Sheffield U v Preston NE
Sunderland v Burnley
West Ham U v Wigan Ath

Nationwide Football League Division 2
Barnsley v Stockport Co
Blackpool v Bristol C
Bournemouth v Brentford
Brighton & HA v Wrexham
Colchester U v Plymouth Arg
Grimsby T v Tranmere R
Hartlepool U v Swindon T
Luton T v Chesterfield
Oldham Ath v Notts Co
Port Vale v Rushden & D'monds
QPR v Sheffield W
Wycombe W v Peterborough U

Nationwide Football League Division 3
Boston U v Kidderminster H
Bristol R v Hull C
Cambridge U v Leyton Orient
Carlisle U v Doncaster R
Darlington v Scunthorpe U
Huddersfield T v Cheltenham T
Macclesfield T v Bury
Northampton T v Mansfield T
Rochdale v Oxford U
Torquay U v Southend U
Yeovil v Lincoln C
York C v Swansea C

Nationwide Conference
Accrington Stanley v Barnet
Aldershot T v Morecambe
Chester C v Margate
Forest Green R v Leigh RMI
Gravesend & N v Scarborough
Hereford U v Farnborough T
Northwich Vic v Halifax T
Stevenage B v Exeter C
Tamworth v Shrewsbury T
Telford U v Dagenham & Red
Woking v Burton Alb

Saturday, 6 December 2003
FA Barclaycard Premiership
Birmingham C v Blackburn R
Everton v Manchester C
Fulham v Bolton W
Leeds U v Chelsea
Leicester C v Arsenal
Manchester U v Aston Villa
Middlesbrough v Portsmouth
Newcastle U v Liverpool* (12:30)
Tottenham H v Wolverhampton W

Nationwide Football League Division 1
Burnley v Sheffield U
Coventry C v Sunderland
Crewe Alex v Gillingham
Ipswich T v Derby Co
Millwall v Norwich C
Preston NE v Crystal Palace
Stoke C v Cardiff C
Walsall v Bradford C
Watford v Nottingham F
WBA v West Ham U
Wigan Ath v Reading
Wimbledon v Rotherham U

Nationwide Conference
Barnet v Stevenage B
Burton Alb v Telford U
Dagenham & Red v Northwich Vic
Exeter C v Forest Green R
Farnborough T v Woking
Halifax T v Chester C
Leigh RMI v Gravesend & N
Margate v Accrington Stanley
Morecambe v Tamworth
Scarborough v Hereford U
Shrewsbury T v Aldershot T

Sunday, 7 December 2003
FA Barclaycard Premiership
Southampton v Charlton Ath* (4:05)

Saturday, 13 December 2003
FA Barclaycard Premiership
Arsenal v Blackburn R
Aston Villa v Wolverhampton W
Chelsea v Bolton W
Leicester C v Birmingham C
Liverpool v Southampton
Manchester U v Manchester C* (12:30)
Middlesbrough v Charlton Ath
Newcastle U v Tottenham H
Portsmouth v Everton

Nationwide Football League Division 1
Burnley v Coventry C
Crystal Palace v Nottingham F
Gillingham v Preston NE
Millwall v Ipswich T
Norwich C v Cardiff C
Rotherham U v Derby Co
Sheffield U v Watford
Stoke C v Reading
WBA v Crewe Alex
West Ham U v Sunderland
Wigan Ath v Bradford C
Wimbledon v Walsall

Nationwide Football League Division 2
Barnsley v Sheffield W
Blackpool v Luton T
Bournemouth v Grimsby T
Brighton & HA v Port Vale
Chesterfield v Tranmere R
Colchester U v Oldham Ath
Notts Co v Wycombe W
QPR v Hartlepool U
Rushden & D'monds v Bristol C
Stockport Co v Brentford
Swindon T v Plymouth Arg
Wrexham v Peterborough U

Nationwide Football League Division 3
Boston U v Northampton T
Bristol R v Yeovil
Bury v Rochdale
Cambridge U v Darlington
Cheltenham T v Doncaster R
Kidderminster H v Leyton Orient
Macclesfield T v Huddersfield T
Mansfield T v Lincoln C
Oxford U v Carlisle U
Scunthorpe U v Hull C
Swansea C v Southend U
Torquay U v York C

Nationwide Conference
Accrington Stanley v Aldershot T
Burton Alb v Gravesend & N
Chester C v Stevenage B
Dagenham & Red v Leigh RMI
Farnborough T v Scarborough
Halifax T v Exeter C
Hereford U v Tamworth
Margate v Shrewsbury T

Northwich Vic v Forest Green R
Telford U v Barnet
Woking v Morecambe

Sunday, 14 December 2003

FA Barclaycard Premiership
Leeds U v Fulham* (4:05)

Saturday, 20 December 2003

FA Barclaycard Premiership
Birmingham C v Middlesbrough
Blackburn R v Aston Villa
Bolton W v Arsenal
Charlton Ath v Newcastle U
Everton v Leicester C
Fulham v Chelsea
Manchester C v Leeds U
Southampton v Portsmouth
Tottenham H v Manchester U
Wolverhampton W v Liverpool

Nationwide Football League Division 1
Bradford C v Rotherham U
Cardiff C v Millwall
Coventry C v WBA
Crewe Alex v Wigan Ath
Derby Co v Sheffield U
Ipswich T v Norwich C
Nottingham F v Gillingham
Preston NE v Burnley
Reading v Crystal Palace
Sunderland v Wimbledon
Walsall v West Ham U
Watford v Stoke C

Nationwide Football League Division 2
Brentford v Swindon T
Bristol C v Stockport Co
Grimsby T v Wrexham
Hartlepool U v Colchester U
Luton T v Barnsley
Oldham Ath v QPR
Peterborough U v Rushden & D'monds
Plymouth Arg v Notts Co
Port Vale v Blackpool
Sheffield W v Chesterfield
Tranmere R v Brighton & HA
Wycombe W v Bournemouth

Nationwide Football League Division 3
Carlisle U v Torquay U
Darlington v Macclesfield T
Doncaster R v Swansea C
Huddersfield T v Oxford U
Hull C v Mansfield T
Leyton Orient v Bury
Lincoln C v Cheltenham T
Northampton T v Cambridge U
Rochdale v Boston U
Southend U v Bristol R
Yeovil v Scunthorpe U
York C v Kidderminster H

Nationwide Conference
Aldershot T v Margate
Barnet v Farnborough T
Exeter C v Telford U
Forest Green R v Hereford U
Gravesend & N v Woking
Leigh RMI v Accrington Stanley
Morecambe v Halifax T
Scarborough v Northwich Vic
Shrewsbury T v Burton Alb
Stevenage B v Dagenham & Red
Tamworth v Chester C

Friday, 26 December 2003

FA Barclaycard Premiership
Arsenal v Wolverhampton W
Birmingham C v Manchester C
Blackburn R v Middlesbrough
Charlton Ath v Chelsea
Fulham v Southampton
Leeds U v Aston Villa
Leicester C v Newcastle U
Liverpool v Bolton W
Manchester U v Everton
Portsmouth v Tottenham H

Nationwide Football League Division 1
Cardiff C v Walsall
Coventry C v Sheffield U
Crewe Alex v Burnley
Crystal Palace v Millwall
Gillingham v Watford
Norwich C v Nottingham F
Reading v Wimbledon
Stoke C v Preston NE
Sunderland v Bradford C
WBA v Derby Co
West Ham U v Ipswich T
Wigan Ath v Rotherham U

Nationwide Football League Division 2
Blackpool v Tranmere R
Bournemouth v Plymouth Arg
Brentford v Bristol C
Brighton & HA v Wycombe W
Chesterfield v Peterborough U
Colchester U v Luton T
Grimsby T v Oldham Ath
Hartlepool U v Barnsley
Notts Co v QPR
Rushden & D'monds v Swindon T
Sheffield W v Port Vale
Stockport Co v Wrexham

Nationwide Football League Division 3
Boston U v Lincoln C
Bristol R v Northampton T
Bury v Carlisle U
Cambridge U v Southend U
Cheltenham T v Macclesfield T
Darlington v Huddersfield T
Doncaster R v Scunthorpe U
Mansfield T v Rochdale
Oxford U v Leyton Orient
Torquay U v Swansea C
Yeovil v Kidderminster H
York C v Hull C

Nationwide Conference
Accrington Stanley v Morecambe
Burton Alb v Tamworth
Chester C v Leigh RMI
Dagenham & Red v Aldershot T
Farnborough T v Stevenage B
Halifax T v Scarborough
Hereford U v Exeter C
Margate v Gravesend & N
Northwich Vic v Shrewsbury T
Telford U v Forest Green R
Woking v Barnet

Sunday, 28 December 2003

FA Barclaycard Premiership
Aston Villa v Fulham
Bolton W v Leicester C
Chelsea v Portsmouth
Everton v Birmingham C
Manchester C v Liverpool
Middlesbrough v Manchester U
Newcastle U v Blackburn R
Southampton v Arsenal
Tottenham H v Charlton Ath
Wolverhampton W v Leeds U

Nationwide Football League Division 1
Bradford C v Coventry C
Burnley v Stoke C
Derby Co v Norwich C
Ipswich T v Crystal Palace
Millwall v Gillingham
Nottingham F v West Ham U
Preston NE v Crewe Alex
Rotherham U v Sunderland
Sheffield U v Wigan Ath
Walsall v Reading
Watford v Cardiff C
Wimbledon v WBA

Nationwide Football League Division 2
Barnsley v Chesterfield
Bristol C v Bournemouth
Luton T v Notts Co
Oldham Ath v Hartlepool U
Peterborough U v Grimsby T
Plymouth Arg v Brentford
Port Vale v Stockport Co
QPR v Colchester U
Swindon T v Brighton & HA
Tranmere R v Sheffield W
Wrexham v Blackpool
Wycombe W v Rushden & D'monds

Nationwide Football League Division 3
Carlisle U v Darlington
Huddersfield T v Bury
Hull C v Doncaster R
Kidderminster H v Bristol R
Leyton Orient v Torquay U
Lincoln C v Cambridge U
Macclesfield T v Mansfield T
Northampton T v Cheltenham T
Rochdale v York C
Scunthorpe U v Boston U
Southend U v Oxford U
Swansea C v Yeovil

Thursday, 1 January 2004

Nationwide Conference
Aldershot T v Dagenham & Red
Barnet v Woking
Exeter C v Hereford U
Forest Green R v Telford U
Gravesend & N v Margate
Leigh RMI v Chester C
Morecambe v Accrington Stanley
Scarborough v Halifax T
Shrewsbury T v Northwich Vic
Stevenage B v Farnborough T
Tamworth v Burton Alb

Saturday, 3 January 2004

Nationwide Football League Division 2
Barnsley v Blackpool
Bristol C v Colchester U
Luton T v Brighton & HA
Oldham Ath v Brentford
Peterborough U v Notts Co
Plymouth Arg v Chesterfield
Port Vale v Hartlepool U
QPR v Rushden & D'monds
Swindon T v Bournemouth
Tranmere R v Stockport Co
Wrexham v Sheffield W
Wycombe W v Grimsby T

Nationwide Football League Division 3
Carlisle U v Boston U

Huddersfield T v Doncaster R
Hull C v Cambridge U
Kidderminster H v Cheltenham T
Leyton Orient v Darlington
Lincoln C v Bury
Macclesfield T v Bristol R
Northampton T v Yeovil
Rochdale v Torquay U
Scunthorpe U v Mansfield T
Southend U v York C
Swansea C v Oxford U

Nationwide Conference
Accrington Stanley v Tamworth
Burton Alb v Morecambe
Chester C v Gravesend & N
Dagenham & Red v Shrewsbury T
Farnborough T v Exeter C
Halifax T v Barnet
Hereford U v Stevenage B
Margate v Forest Green R
Northwich Vic v Aldershot T
Telford U v Scarborough
Woking v Leigh RMI

Wednesday, 7 January 2004
FA Barclaycard Premiership
Aston Villa v Portsmouth
Bolton W v Manchester U
Chelsea v Liverpool
Everton v Arsenal
Manchester C v Charlton Ath
Middlesbrough v Fulham
Newcastle U v Leeds U
Southampton v Leicester C
Tottenham H v Birmingham C
Wolverhampton W v Blackburn R

Saturday, 10 January 2004
FA Barclaycard Premiership
Arsenal v Middlesbrough
Birmingham C v Southampton
Blackburn R v Bolton W
Charlton Ath v Wolverhampton W
Fulham v Everton
Leeds U v Tottenham H
Leicester C v Chelsea
Liverpool v Aston Villa
Manchester U v Newcastle U
Portsmouth v Manchester C

Nationwide Football League Division 1
Cardiff C v Rotherham U
Coventry C v Watford
Crewe Alex v Wimbledon
Crystal Palace v Burnley
Gillingham v Sheffield U
Norwich C v Bradford C
Reading v Ipswich T
Stoke C v Derby Co
Sunderland v Nottingham F
WBA v Walsall
West Ham U v Preston NE
Wigan Ath v Millwall

Nationwide Football League Division 2
Blackpool v QPR
Bournemouth v Port Vale
Brentford v Tranmere R
Brighton & HA v Oldham Ath
Chesterfield v Wrexham
Colchester U v Barnsley
Grimsby T v Plymouth Arg
Hartlepool U v Peterborough U
Notts Co v Bristol C
Rushden & D'monds v Luton T
Sheffield W v Swindon T
Stockport Co v Wycombe W

Nationwide Football League Division 3
Boston U v Macclesfield T
Bristol R v Scunthorpe U
Bury v Swansea C
Cambridge U v Huddersfield T
Cheltenham T v Southend U
Darlington v Hull C
Doncaster R v Leyton Orient
Mansfield T v Kidderminster H
Oxford U v Lincoln C
Torquay U v Northampton T
Yeovil v Rochdale
York C v Carlisle U

Saturday, 17 January 2004
FA Barclaycard Premiership
Aston Villa v Arsenal
Bolton W v Portsmouth
Chelsea v Birmingham C
Everton v Charlton Ath
Manchester C v Blackburn R
Middlesbrough v Leicester C
Newcastle U v Fulham
Southampton v Leeds U
Tottenham H v Liverpool
Wolverhampton W v Manchester U

Nationwide Football League Division 1
Bradford C v Cardiff C
Burnley v WBA
Derby Co v Gillingham
Ipswich T v Crewe Alex
Millwall v Sunderland
Nottingham F v Reading
Preston NE v Wigan Ath
Rotherham U v Norwich C
Sheffield U v West Ham U
Walsall v Coventry C
Watford v Crystal Palace
Wimbledon v Stoke C

Nationwide Football League Division 2
Barnsley v Bournemouth
Bristol C v Chesterfield
Luton T v Stockport Co
Oldham Ath v Sheffield W
Peterborough U v Brentford
Plymouth Arg v Rushden & D'monds
Port Vale v Grimsby T
QPR v Brighton & HA
Swindon T v Colchester U
Tranmere R v Hartlepool U
Wrexham v Notts Co
Wycombe W v Blackpool

Nationwide Football League Division 3
Carlisle U v Yeovil
Huddersfield T v Boston U
Hull C v Oxford U
Kidderminster H v Darlington
Leyton Orient v Mansfield T
Lincoln C v Torquay U
Macclesfield T v Cambridge U
Northampton T v York C
Rochdale v Bristol R
Scunthorpe U v Bury
Southend U v Doncaster R
Swansea C v Cheltenham T

Nationwide Conference
Aldershot T v Telford U
Barnet v Dagenham & Red
Exeter C v Margate
Forest Green R v Chester C
Gravesend & N v Halifax T
Leigh RMI v Farnborough T
Morecambe v Hereford U
Scarborough v Woking
Shrewsbury T v Accrington Stanley
Stevenage B v Burton Alb
Tamworth v Northwich Vic

Saturday, 24 January 2004
Nationwide Football League Division 2
Blackpool v Oldham Ath
Bournemouth v QPR
Brentford v Wrexham
Brighton & HA v Barnsley
Chesterfield v Wycombe W
Colchester U v Port Vale
Grimsby T v Luton T
Hartlepool U v Bristol C
Notts Co v Swindon T
Rushden & D'monds v Tranmere R
Sheffield W v Peterborough U
Stockport Co v Plymouth Arg

Nationwide Football League Division 3
Boston U v Swansea C
Bristol R v Carlisle U
Bury v Kidderminster H
Cambridge U v Rochdale
Cheltenham T v Hull C
Darlington v Northampton T
Doncaster R v Lincoln C
Mansfield T v Southend U
Oxford U v Scunthorpe U
Torquay U v Macclesfield T
Yeovil v Leyton Orient
York C v Huddersfield T

Nationwide Conference
Barnet v Margate
Burton Alb v Accrington Stanley
Dagenham & Red v Exeter C
Farnborough T v Aldershot T
Gravesend & N v Stevenage B
Halifax T v Shrewsbury T
Leigh RMI v Morecambe
Northwich Vic v Chester C
Scarborough v Tamworth
Telford U v Hereford U
Woking v Forest Green R

Saturday, 31 January 2004
FA Barclaycard Premiership
Arsenal v Manchester C
Birmingham C v Newcastle U
Blackburn R v Chelsea
Charlton Ath v Bolton W
Fulham v Tottenham H
Leeds U v Middlesbrough
Leicester C v Aston Villa
Liverpool v Everton
Manchester U v Southampton
Portsmouth v Wolverhampton W

Nationwide Football League Division 1
Cardiff C v Nottingham F
Coventry C v Ipswich T
Crewe Alex v Millwall
Crystal Palace v Wimbledon
Gillingham v Bradford C
Norwich C v Sheffield U
Reading v Derby Co
Stoke C v Walsall
Sunderland v Preston NE
WBA v Watford
West Ham U v Rotherham U
Wigan Ath v Burnley

Nationwide Football League Division 2
Blackpool v Swindon T

Bournemouth v Wrexham
Brentford v Port Vale
Brighton & HA v Plymouth Arg
Chesterfield v QPR
Colchester U v Tranmere R
Grimsby T v Bristol C
Hartlepool U v Luton T
Notts Co v Barnsley
Rushden & D'monds v Oldham Ath
Sheffield W v Wycombe W
Stockport Co v Peterborough U

Nationwide Football League Division 3
Boston U v Hull C
Bristol R v Huddersfield T
Bury v Southend U
Cambridge U v Carlisle U
Cheltenham T v Leyton Orient
Darlington v Rochdale
Doncaster R v Northampton T
Mansfield T v Swansea C
Oxford U v Kidderminster H
Torquay U v Scunthorpe U
Yeovil v Macclesfield T
York C v Lincoln C

Saturday, 7 February 2004
FA Barclaycard Premiership
Aston Villa v Leeds U
Bolton W v Liverpool
Chelsea v Charlton Ath
Everton v Manchester U
Manchester C v Birmingham C
Middlesbrough v Blackburn R
Newcastle U v Leicester C
Southampton v Fulham
Tottenham H v Portsmouth
Wolverhampton W v Arsenal

Nationwide Football League Division 1
Bradford C v West Ham U
Burnley v Gillingham
Derby Co v Cardiff C
Ipswich T v Wigan Ath
Millwall v Stoke C
Nottingham F v Coventry C
Preston NE v WBA
Rotherham U v Reading
Sheffield U v Crystal Palace
Walsall v Crewe Alex
Watford v Sunderland
Wimbledon v Norwich C

Nationwide Football League Division 2
Barnsley v Hartlepool U
Bristol C v Brentford
Luton T v Colchester U
Oldham Ath v Grimsby T
Peterborough U v Chesterfield
Plymouth Arg v Bournemouth
Port Vale v Sheffield W
QPR v Notts Co
Swindon T v Rushden & D'monds
Tranmere R v Blackpool
Wrexham v Stockport Co
Wycombe W v Brighton & HA

Nationwide Football League Division 3
Carlisle U v Bury
Huddersfield T v Darlington
Hull C v York C
Kidderminster H v Yeovil
Leyton Orient v Oxford U
Lincoln C v Boston U
Macclesfield T v Cheltenham T
Northampton T v Bristol R
Rochdale v Mansfield T
Scunthorpe U v Doncaster R
Southend U v Cambridge U
Swansea C v Torquay U

Nationwide Conference
Accrington Stanley v Dagenham & Red
Aldershot T v Barnet
Chester C v Farnborough T
Exeter C v Gravesend & N
Forest Green R v Scarborough
Hereford U v Burton Alb
Margate v Halifax T
Morecambe v Northwich Vic
Shrewsbury T v Woking
Stevenage B v Telford U
Tamworth v Leigh RMI

Tuesday, 10 February 2004
FA Barclaycard Premiership
Arsenal v Southampton
Birmingham C v Everton
Charlton Ath v Tottenham H
Leeds U v Wolverhampton W
Leicester C v Bolton W
Portsmouth v Chelsea

Wednesday, 11 February 2004
FA Barclaycard Premiership
Blackburn R v Newcastle U
Fulham v Aston Villa
Liverpool v Manchester C
Manchester U v Middlesbrough

Saturday, 14 February 2004
Nationwide Football League Division 1
Coventry C v Norwich C
Crewe Alex v Sheffield U
Crystal Palace v Stoke C
Ipswich T v Bradford C
Millwall v Rotherham U
Nottingham F v Walsall
Reading v Burnley
Sunderland v Gillingham
Watford v Preston NE
WBA v Cardiff C
West Ham U v Wimbledon
Wigan Ath v Derby Co

Nationwide Football League Division 2
Blackpool v Colchester U
Bournemouth v Notts Co
Brentford v QPR
Chesterfield v Rushden & D'monds
Grimsby T v Brighton & HA
Peterborough U v Bristol C
Port Vale v Oldham Ath
Sheffield W v Hartlepool U
Stockport Co v Swindon T
Tranmere R v Plymouth Arg
Wrexham v Barnsley
Wycombe W v Luton T

Nationwide Football League Division 3
Bristol R v Darlington
Bury v Cambridge U
Carlisle U v Hull C
Cheltenham T v Boston U
Doncaster R v Macclesfield T
Lincoln C v Scunthorpe U
Northampton T v Rochdale
Southend U v Kidderminster H
Swansea C v Leyton Orient
Torquay U v Huddersfield T
Yeovil v Oxford U
York C v Mansfield T

Nationwide Conference
Barnet v Shrewsbury T
Burton Alb v Aldershot T
Dagenham & Red v Tamworth
Farnborough T v Morecambe
Gravesend & N v Hereford U
Halifax T v Forest Green R
Leigh RMI v Stevenage B
Northwich Vic v Margate
Scarborough v Exeter C
Telford U v Chester C
Woking v Accrington Stanley

Saturday, 21 February 2004
FA Barclaycard Premiership
Aston Villa v Birmingham C
Bolton W v Manchester C
Charlton Ath v Blackburn R
Chelsea v Arsenal
Liverpool v Portsmouth
Manchester U v Leeds U
Newcastle U v Middlesbrough
Southampton v Everton
Tottenham H v Leicester C
Wolverhampton W v Fulham

Nationwide Football League Division 1
Bradford C v Crewe Alex
Burnley v Ipswich T
Cardiff C v Sunderland
Derby Co v Crystal Palace
Gillingham v Reading
Norwich C v West Ham U
Preston NE v Millwall
Rotherham U v Nottingham F
Sheffield U v WBA
Stoke C v Wigan Ath
Walsall v Watford
Wimbledon v Coventry C

Nationwide Football League Division 2
Barnsley v Wycombe W
Brighton & HA v Bournemouth
Bristol C v Wrexham
Colchester U v Grimsby T
Hartlepool U v Blackpool
Luton T v Brentford
Notts Co v Stockport Co
Oldham Ath v Tranmere R
Plymouth Arg v Port Vale
QPR v Peterborough U
Rushden & D'monds v Sheffield W
Swindon T v Chesterfield

Nationwide Football League Division 3
Boston U v York C
Cambridge U v Bristol R
Darlington v Yeovil
Huddersfield T v Lincoln C
Hull C v Torquay U
Kidderminster H v Swansea C
Leyton Orient v Southend U
Macclesfield T v Carlisle U
Mansfield T v Doncaster R
Oxford U v Bury
Rochdale v Cheltenham T
Scunthorpe U v Northampton T

Nationwide Conference
Accrington Stanley v Northwich Vic
Aldershot T v Leigh RMI
Chester C v Dagenham & Red
Exeter C v Burton Alb
Forest Green R v Gravesend & N
Hereford U v Woking
Margate v Telford U
Morecambe v Barnet

Shrewsbury T v Scarborough
Stevenage B v Halifax T
Tamworth v Farnborough T

Saturday, 28 February 2004

FA Barclaycard Premiership

Arsenal v Charlton Ath
Birmingham C v Bolton W
Blackburn R v Southampton
Everton v Aston Villa
Fulham v Manchester U
Leeds U v Liverpool
Leicester C v Wolverhampton W
Manchester C v Chelsea
Middlesbrough v Tottenham H
Portsmouth v Newcastle U

Nationwide Football League Division 1

Coventry C v Derby Co
Crewe Alex v Stoke C
Crystal Palace v Gillingham
Ipswich T v Preston NE
Millwall v Burnley
Nottingham F v Bradford C
Reading v Sheffield U
Sunderland v Norwich C
Watford v Wimbledon
WBA v Rotherham U
West Ham U v Cardiff C
Wigan Ath v Walsall

Nationwide Football League Division 2

Blackpool v Plymouth Arg
Bournemouth v Oldham Ath
Brentford v Notts Co
Chesterfield v Colchester U
Grimsby T v Barnsley
Peterborough U v Luton T
Port Vale v Swindon T
Sheffield W v Bristol C
Stockport Co v Brighton & HA
Tranmere R v QPR
Wrexham v Rushden & D'monds
Wycombe W v Hartlepool U

Nationwide Football League Division 3

Bristol R v Oxford U
Bury v Darlington
Carlisle U v Huddersfield T
Cheltenham T v Mansfield T
Doncaster R v Kidderminster H
Lincoln C v Hull C
Northampton T v Leyton Orient
Southend U v Macclesfield T
Swansea C v Rochdale
Torquay U v Boston U
Yeovil v Cambridge U
York C v Scunthorpe U

Nationwide Conference

Barnet v Tamworth
Burton Alb v Forest Green R
Dagenham & Red v Hereford U
Farnborough T v Accrington Stanley
Gravesend & N v Morecambe
Halifax T v Aldershot T
Leigh RMI v Margate
Northwich Vic v Exeter C
Scarborough v Stevenage B
Telford U v Shrewsbury T
Woking v Chester C

Tuesday, 2 March 2004

Nationwide Football League Division 1

Bradford C v Watford
Burnley v West Ham U
Cardiff C v Coventry C
Gillingham v Wigan Ath
Norwich C v WBA
Preston NE v Reading
Rotherham U v Crystal Palace
Sheffield U v Millwall
Walsall v Sunderland
Wimbledon v Nottingham F

Nationwide Football League Division 2

Barnsley v Peterborough U
Brighton & HA v Brentford
Bristol C v Wycombe W
Colchester U v Stockport Co
Hartlepool U v Chesterfield
Luton T v Bournemouth
Notts Co v Grimsby T
Oldham Ath v Wrexham
Plymouth Arg v Sheffield W
QPR v Port Vale
Rushden & D'monds v Blackpool

Nationwide Football League Division 3

Cambridge U v Swansea C
Darlington v Cheltenham T
Huddersfield T v Yeovil
Hull C v Bury
Kidderminster H v Northampton T
Leyton Orient v Bristol R
Macclesfield T v Lincoln C
Mansfield T v Torquay U
Oxford U v York C
Rochdale v Doncaster R
Scunthorpe U v Carlisle U

Wednesday, 3 March 2004

Nationwide Football League Division 1

Derby Co v Crewe Alex
Stoke C v Ipswich T

Nationwide Football League Division 2

Swindon T v Tranmere R

Nationwide Football League Division 3

Boston U v Southend U

Saturday, 6 March 2004

Nationwide Football League Division 1

Burnley v Preston NE
Crystal Palace v Reading
Gillingham v Nottingham F
Millwall v Cardiff C
Rotherham U v Bradford C
Sheffield U v Derby Co
Stoke C v Watford
WBA v Coventry C
West Ham U v Walsall
Wigan Ath v Crewe Alex
Wimbledon v Sunderland

Nationwide Football League Division 2

Barnsley v Luton T
Blackpool v Port Vale
Bournemouth v Wycombe W
Brighton & HA v Tranmere R
Chesterfield v Sheffield W
Colchester U v Hartlepool U
Notts Co v Plymouth Arg
QPR v Oldham Ath
Rushden & D'monds v Peterborough U
Stockport Co v Bristol C
Swindon T v Brentford
Wrexham v Grimsby T

Nationwide Football League Division 3

Boston U v Rochdale
Bristol R v Southend U
Bury v Leyton Orient
Cambridge U v Northampton T
Cheltenham T v Lincoln C
Kidderminster H v York C
Macclesfield T v Darlington
Mansfield T v Hull C
Oxford U v Huddersfield T
Scunthorpe U v Yeovil
Swansea C v Doncaster R
Torquay U v Carlisle U

Nationwide Conference

Accrington Stanley v Halifax T
Aldershot T v Gravesend & N
Chester C v Burton Alb
Exeter C v Barnet
Forest Green R v Farnborough T
Hereford U v Northwich Vic
Margate v Dagenham & Red
Morecambe v Scarborough
Shrewsbury T v Leigh RMI
Stevenage B v Woking
Tamworth v Telford U

Sunday, 7 March 2004

Nationwide Football League Division 1

Norwich C v Ipswich T

Saturday, 13 March 2004

FA Barclaycard Premiership

Birmingham C v Leicester C
Blackburn R v Arsenal
Bolton W v Chelsea
Charlton Ath v Middlesbrough
Everton v Portsmouth
Fulham v Leeds U
Manchester C v Manchester U
Southampton v Liverpool
Tottenham H v Newcastle U
Wolverhampton W v Aston Villa

Nationwide Football League Division 1

Bradford C v Wigan Ath
Cardiff C v Norwich C
Coventry C v Burnley
Crewe Alex v WBA
Derby Co v Rotherham U
Ipswich T v Millwall
Nottingham F v Crystal Palace
Preston NE v Gillingham
Reading v Stoke C
Sunderland v West Ham U
Walsall v Wimbledon
Watford v Sheffield U

Nationwide Football League Division 2

Brentford v Stockport Co
Bristol C v Rushden & D'monds
Grimsby T v Bournemouth
Hartlepool U v QPR
Luton T v Blackpool
Oldham Ath v Colchester U
Peterborough U v Wrexham
Plymouth Arg v Swindon T
Port Vale v Brighton & HA
Sheffield W v Barnsley
Tranmere R v Chesterfield
Wycombe W v Notts Co

Nationwide Football League Division 3

Carlisle U v Oxford U
Darlington v Cambridge U
Doncaster R v Cheltenham T
Huddersfield T v Macclesfield T
Hull C v Scunthorpe U
Leyton Orient v Kidderminster H
Lincoln C v Mansfield T
Northampton T v Boston U
Rochdale v Bury
Southend U v Swansea C

Yeovil v Bristol R
York C v Torquay U

Nationwide Conference
Burton Alb v Northwich Vic
Chester C v Morecambe
Exeter C v Aldershot T
Farnborough T v Dagenham & Red
Forest Green R v Shrewsbury T
Gravesend & N v Barnet
Hereford U v Accrington Stanley
Scarborough v Leigh RMI
Stevenage B v Tamworth
Telford U v Halifax T
Woking v Margate

Tuesday, 16 March 2004

Nationwide Football League Division 1
Bradford C v Crystal Palace
Cardiff C v Reading
Norwich C v Gillingham
Rotherham U v Sheffield U
Sunderland v Stoke C
Walsall v Ipswich T
Watford v Derby Co
WBA v Wigan Ath
Wimbledon v Millwall

Nationwide Football League Division 2
Blackpool v Brentford
Chesterfield v Brighton & HA
Colchester U v Wycombe W
Hartlepool U v Stockport Co
Oldham Ath v Barnsley
Plymouth Arg v Peterborough U
Port Vale v Luton T
QPR v Wrexham
Rushden & D'monds v Notts Co
Tranmere R v Bristol C

Nationwide Football League Division 3
Bristol R v Torquay U
Bury v Mansfield T
Cambridge U v Boston U
Carlisle U v Northampton T
Darlington v York C
Huddersfield T v Rochdale
Hull C v Leyton Orient
Lincoln C v Southend U
Macclesfield T v Swansea C
Oxford U v Cheltenham T
Scunthorpe U v Kidderminster H
Yeovil v Doncaster R

Wednesday, 17 March 2004

Nationwide Football League Division 1
Coventry C v Preston NE
Nottingham F v Burnley
West Ham U v Crewe Alex

Nationwide Football League Division 2
Sheffield W v Bournemouth
Swindon T v Grimsby T

Saturday, 20 March 2004

FA Barclaycard Premiership
Arsenal v Bolton W
Aston Villa v Blackburn R
Chelsea v Fulham
Leeds U v Manchester C
Leicester C v Everton
Liverpool v Wolverhampton W
Manchester U v Tottenham H
Middlesbrough v Birmingham C
Newcastle U v Charlton Ath
Portsmouth v Southampton

Nationwide Football League Division 1
Burnley v Wimbledon
Crewe Alex v Cardiff C
Crystal Palace v Norwich C
Derby Co v Nottingham F
Gillingham v Rotherham U
Ipswich T v Watford
Millwall v West Ham U
Preston NE v Walsall
Reading v Sunderland
Sheffield U v Bradford C
Stoke C v WBA
Wigan Ath v Coventry C

Nationwide Football League Division 2
Barnsley v Port Vale
Bournemouth v Blackpool
Brentford v Rushden & D'monds
Brighton & HA v Colchester U
Bristol C v Oldham Ath
Grimsby T v Hartlepool U
Luton T v Plymouth Arg
Notts Co v Chesterfield
Peterborough U v Tranmere R
Stockport Co v Sheffield W
Wrexham v Swindon T
Wycombe W v QPR

Nationwide Football League Division 3
Boston U v Bristol R
Cheltenham T v Bury
Doncaster R v Darlington
Kidderminster H v Macclesfield T
Leyton Orient v Lincoln C
Mansfield T v Oxford U
Northampton T v Huddersfield T
Rochdale v Carlisle U
Southend U v Hull C
Swansea C v Scunthorpe U
Torquay U v Cambridge U
York C v Yeovil

Nationwide Conference
Accrington Stanley v Stevenage B
Aldershot T v Scarborough
Barnet v Chester C
Dagenham & Red v Woking
Halifax T v Burton Alb
Leigh RMI v Telford U
Margate v Hereford U
Morecambe v Exeter C
Northwich Vic v Farnborough T
Shrewsbury T v Gravesend & N
Tamworth v Forest Green R

Saturday, 27 March 2004

FA Barclaycard Premiership
Arsenal v Manchester U
Birmingham C v Leeds U
Blackburn R v Portsmouth
Bolton W v Newcastle U
Charlton Ath v Aston Villa
Chelsea v Wolverhampton W
Everton v Middlesbrough
Leicester C v Liverpool
Manchester C v Fulham
Southampton v Tottenham H

Nationwide Football League Division 1
Bradford C v Burnley
Cardiff C v Sheffield U
Coventry C v Reading
Norwich C v Stoke C
Nottingham F v Crewe Alex
Rotherham U v Preston NE
Sunderland v Derby Co
Walsall v Millwall
Watford v Wigan Ath
WBA v Crystal Palace
West Ham U v Gillingham
Wimbledon v Ipswich T

Nationwide Football League Division 2
Blackpool v Stockport Co
Chesterfield v Grimsby T
Colchester U v Peterborough U
Hartlepool U v Brentford
Oldham Ath v Wycombe W
Plymouth Arg v Wrexham
Port Vale v Bristol C
QPR v Luton T
Rushden & D'monds v Bournemouth
Sheffield W v Brighton & HA
Swindon T v Barnsley
Tranmere R v Notts Co

Nationwide Football League Division 3
Bristol R v York C
Bury v Boston U
Cambridge U v Cheltenham T
Carlisle U v Southend U
Darlington v Torquay U
Huddersfield T v Swansea C
Hull C v Rochdale
Lincoln C v Kidderminster H
Macclesfield T v Northampton T
Oxford U v Doncaster R
Scunthorpe U v Leyton Orient
Yeovil v Mansfield T

Nationwide Conference
Burton Alb v Margate
Chester C v Aldershot T
Exeter C v Leigh RMI
Farnborough T v Halifax T
Forest Green R v Barnet
Gravesend & N v Tamworth
Hereford U v Shrewsbury T
Scarborough v Dagenham & Red
Stevenage B v Morecambe
Telford U v Accrington Stanley
Woking v Northwich Vic

Saturday, 3 April 2004

FA Barclaycard Premiership
Aston Villa v Manchester C
Fulham v Birmingham C
Leeds U v Leicester C
Liverpool v Blackburn R
Manchester U v Charlton Ath
Middlesbrough v Bolton W
Newcastle U v Everton
Portsmouth v Arsenal
Tottenham H v Chelsea
Wolverhampton W v Southampton

Nationwide Football League Division 1
Burnley v Norwich C
Crewe Alex v Rotherham U
Crystal Palace v Sunderland
Derby Co v Walsall
Gillingham v Cardiff C
Ipswich T v WBA
Millwall v Watford
Preston NE v Bradford C
Reading v West Ham U
Sheffield U v Nottingham F
Stoke C v Coventry C
Wigan Ath v Wimbledon

Nationwide Football League Division 2
Barnsley v Plymouth Arg
Bournemouth v Colchester U
Brentford v Chesterfield

Brighton & HA v Hartlepool U
Bristol C v QPR
Grimsby T v Sheffield W
Luton T v Oldham Ath
Notts Co v Blackpool
Peterborough U v Swindon T
Stockport Co v Rushden & D'monds
Wrexham v Tranmere R
Wycombe W v Port Vale

Nationwide Football League Division 3
Boston U v Darlington
Cheltenham T v Bristol R
Doncaster R v Bury
Kidderminster H v Hull C
Leyton Orient v Huddersfield T
Mansfield T v Cambridge U
Northampton T v Oxford U
Rochdale v Lincoln C
Southend U v Scunthorpe U
Swansea C v Carlisle U
Torquay U v Yeovil
York C v Macclesfield T

Nationwide Conference
Accrington Stanley v Chester C
Aldershot T v Stevenage B
Barnet v Scarborough
Dagenham & Red v Gravesend & N
Halifax T v Hereford U
Leigh RMI v Burton Alb
Margate v Farnborough T
Morecambe v Forest Green R
Northwich Vic v Telford U
Shrewsbury T v Exeter C
Tamworth v Woking

Saturday, 10 April 2004
FA Barclaycard Premiership
Arsenal v Liverpool
Birmingham C v Manchester U
Blackburn R v Leeds U
Bolton W v Aston Villa
Charlton Ath v Portsmouth
Chelsea v Middlesbrough
Everton v Tottenham H
Leicester C v Fulham
Manchester C v Wolverhampton W
Southampton v Newcastle U

Nationwide Football League Division 1
Bradford C v Reading
Cardiff C v Crystal Palace
Coventry C v Millwall
Norwich C v Wigan Ath
Nottingham F v Stoke C
Rotherham U v Ipswich T
Sunderland v Sheffield U
Walsall v Burnley
Watford v Crewe Alex
WBA v Gillingham
West Ham U v Derby Co
Wimbledon v Preston NE

Nationwide Football League Division 2
Blackpool v Brighton & HA
Chesterfield v Stockport Co
Colchester U v Notts Co
Hartlepool U v Bournemouth
Oldham Ath v Peterborough U
Plymouth Arg v Wycombe W
Port Vale v Wrexham
QPR v Grimsby T
Rushden & D'monds v Barnsley
Sheffield W v Brentford
Swindon T v Bristol C
Tranmere R v Luton T

Nationwide Football League Division 3
Bristol R v Doncaster R
Bury v Torquay U
Cambridge U v York C
Carlisle U v Kidderminster H
Darlington v Mansfield T
Huddersfield T v Southend U
Hull C v Northampton T
Lincoln C v Swansea C
Macclesfield T v Leyton Orient
Oxford U v Boston U
Scunthorpe U v Rochdale
Yeovil v Cheltenham T

Nationwide Conference
Accrington Stanley v Forest Green R
Burton Alb v Scarborough
Chester C v Exeter C
Dagenham & Red v Morecambe
Farnborough T v Shrewsbury T
Halifax T v Leigh RMI
Hereford U v Barnet
Margate v Tamworth
Northwich Vic v Stevenage B
Telford U v Gravesend & N
Woking v Aldershot T

Monday, 12 April 2004
FA Barclaycard Premiership
Aston Villa v Chelsea
Fulham v Blackburn R
Leeds U v Everton
Liverpool v Charlton Ath
Manchester U v Leicester C
Middlesbrough v Southampton
Newcastle U v Arsenal
Portsmouth v Birmingham C
Tottenham H v Manchester C
Wolverhampton W v Bolton W

Nationwide Football League Division 1
Burnley v Watford
Crewe Alex v Coventry C
Crystal Palace v West Ham U
Derby Co v Bradford C
Gillingham v Walsall
Ipswich T v Sunderland
Millwall v WBA
Preston NE v Nottingham F
Reading v Norwich C
Sheffield U v Wimbledon
Stoke C v Rotherham U
Wigan Ath v Cardiff C

Nationwide Football League Division 2
Barnsley v QPR
Bournemouth v Chesterfield
Brentford v Colchester U
Brighton & HA v Rushden & D'monds
Bristol C v Plymouth Arg
Grimsby T v Blackpool
Luton T v Swindon T
Notts Co v Sheffield W
Peterborough U v Port Vale
Stockport Co v Oldham Ath
Wrexham v Hartlepool U
Wycombe W v Tranmere R

Nationwide Football League Division 3
Boston U v Yeovil
Cheltenham T v Scunthorpe U
Doncaster R v Cambridge U
Kidderminster H v Huddersfield T
Leyton Orient v Carlisle U
Mansfield T v Bristol R
Northampton T v Lincoln C
Rochdale v Macclesfield T
Southend U v Darlington
Swansea C v Hull C
Torquay U v Oxford U
York C v Bury

Nationwide Conference
Aldershot T v Hereford U
Barnet v Burton Alb
Exeter C v Woking
Forest Green R v Dagenham & Red
Gravesend & N v Farnborough T
Leigh RMI v Northwich Vic
Morecambe v Telford U
Scarborough v Accrington Stanley
Shrewsbury T v Chester C
Stevenage B v Margate
Tamworth v Halifax T

Saturday, 17 April 2004
FA Barclaycard Premiership
Arsenal v Leeds U
Aston Villa v Newcastle U
Blackburn R v Leicester C
Bolton W v Tottenham H
Charlton Ath v Birmingham C
Chelsea v Everton
Liverpool v Fulham
Manchester C v Southampton
Portsmouth v Manchester U
Wolverhampton W v Middlesbrough

Nationwide Football League Division 1
Bradford C v Wimbledon
Cardiff C v Burnley
Crystal Palace v Wigan Ath
Derby Co v Preston NE
Gillingham v Ipswich T
Norwich C v Walsall
Nottingham F v Millwall
Reading v Crewe Alex
Rotherham U v Watford
Sheffield U v Stoke C
Sunderland v WBA
West Ham U v Coventry C

Nationwide Football League Division 2
Barnsley v Brentford
Blackpool v Sheffield W
Bournemouth v Tranmere R
Brighton & HA v Peterborough U
Colchester U v Wrexham
Grimsby T v Rushden & D'monds
Hartlepool U v Notts Co
Luton T v Bristol C
Oldham Ath v Plymouth Arg
Port Vale v Chesterfield
QPR v Stockport Co
Wycombe W v Swindon T

Nationwide Football League Division 3
Boston U v Mansfield T
Bristol R v Swansea C
Cambridge U v Kidderminster H
Carlisle U v Lincoln C
Darlington v Oxford U
Huddersfield T v Scunthorpe U
Macclesfield T v Hull C
Northampton T v Southend U
Rochdale v Leyton Orient
Torquay U v Doncaster R
Yeovil v Bury
York C v Cheltenham T

Nationwide Conference
Accrington Stanley v Gravesend & N
Chester C v Scarborough
Dagenham & Red v Halifax T
Farnborough T v Burton Alb
Forest Green R v Aldershot T
Leigh RMI v Hereford U
Margate v Morecambe
Northwich Vic v Barnet
Shrewsbury T v Stevenage B
Tamworth v Exeter C
Woking v Telford U

Saturday, 24 April 2004
FA Barclaycard Premiership
Birmingham C v Wolverhampton W
Everton v Blackburn R
Fulham v Charlton Ath
Leeds U v Portsmouth
Leicester C v Manchester C
Manchester U v Liverpool
Middlesbrough v Aston Villa
Newcastle U v Chelsea
Southampton v Bolton W
Tottenham H v Arsenal

Nationwide Football League Division 1
Burnley v Derby Co
Coventry C v Rotherham U
Crewe Alex v Crystal Palace
Ipswich T v Nottingham F
Millwall v Reading
Preston NE v Cardiff C
Stoke C v West Ham U
Walsall v Sheffield U
Watford v Norwich C
WBA v Bradford C
Wigan Ath v Sunderland
Wimbledon v Gillingham

Nationwide Football League Division 2
Brentford v Wycombe W
Bristol C v Brighton & HA
Chesterfield v Blackpool
Notts Co v Port Vale
Peterborough U v Bournemouth
Plymouth Arg v QPR
Rushden & D'monds v Hartlepool U
Sheffield W v Colchester U
Stockport Co v Grimsby T
Swindon T v Oldham Ath
Tranmere R v Barnsley
Wrexham v Luton T

Nationwide Football League Division 3
Bury v Bristol R
Cheltenham T v Torquay U
Doncaster R v York C
Hull C v Huddersfield T
Kidderminster H v Rochdale
Leyton Orient v Boston U
Lincoln C v Darlington
Mansfield T v Carlisle U
Oxford U v Cambridge U
Scunthorpe U v Macclesfield T
Southend U v Yeovil
Swansea C v Northampton T

Nationwide Conference
Aldershot T v Tamworth
Barnet v Leigh RMI
Burton Alb v Dagenham & Red
Exeter C v Accrington Stanley
Gravesend & N v Northwich Vic
Halifax T v Woking
Hereford U v Chester C
Morecambe v Shrewsbury T
Scarborough v Margate
Stevenage B v Forest Green R
Telford U v Farnborough T

Saturday, 1 May 2004
FA Barclaycard Premiership
Arsenal v Birmingham C
Blackburn R v Manchester U
Bolton W v Leeds U
Charlton Ath v Leicester C
Chelsea v Southampton
Liverpool v Middlesbrough
Manchester C v Newcastle U
Portsmouth v Fulham
Wolverhampton W v Everton

Nationwide Football League Division 1
Bradford C v Stoke C
Cardiff C v Wimbledon
Crystal Palace v Walsall
Derby Co v Millwall
Gillingham v Coventry C
Norwich C v Preston NE
Nottingham F v Wigan Ath
Reading v WBA
Rotherham U v Burnley
Sheffield U v Ipswich T
Sunderland v Crewe Alex
West Ham U v Watford

Nationwide Football League Division 2
Barnsley v Bristol C
Blackpool v Peterborough U
Bournemouth v Stockport Co
Brighton & HA v Notts Co
Colchester U v Rushden & D'monds
Grimsby T v Brentford
Hartlepool U v Plymouth Arg
Luton T v Sheffield W
Oldham Ath v Chesterfield
Port Vale v Tranmere R
QPR v Swindon T
Wycombe W v Wrexham

Nationwide Football League Division 3
Boston U v Doncaster R
Bristol R v Lincoln C
Cambridge U v Scunthorpe U
Carlisle U v Cheltenham T
Darlington v Swansea C
Huddersfield T v Mansfield T
Macclesfield T v Oxford U
Northampton T v Bury
Rochdale v Southend U
Torquay U v Kidderminster H
Yeovil v Hull C
York C v Leyton Orient

Sunday, 2 May 2004
FA Barclaycard Premiership
Aston Villa v Tottenham H

Saturday, 8 May 2004
FA Barclaycard Premiership
Birmingham C v Liverpool
Everton v Bolton W
Fulham v Arsenal
Leeds U v Charlton Ath
Leicester C v Portsmouth
Manchester U v Chelsea
Middlesbrough v Manchester C
Newcastle U v Wolverhampton W
Southampton v Aston Villa
Tottenham H v Blackburn R

Nationwide Football League Division 2
Brentford v Bournemouth
Bristol C v Blackpool
Chesterfield v Luton T
Notts Co v Oldham Ath
Peterborough U v Wycombe W
Plymouth Arg v Colchester U
Rushden & D'monds v Port Vale
Sheffield W v QPR
Stockport Co v Barnsley
Swindon T v Hartlepool U
Tranmere R v Grimsby T
Wrexham v Brighton & HA

Nationwide Football League Division 3
Bury v Macclesfield T
Cheltenham T v Huddersfield T
Doncaster R v Carlisle U
Hull C v Bristol R
Kidderminster H v Boston U
Leyton Orient v Cambridge U
Lincoln C v Yeovil
Mansfield T v Northampton T
Oxford U v Rochdale
Scunthorpe U v Darlington
Southend U v Torquay U
Swansea C v York C

Sunday, 9 May 2004
Nationwide Football League Division 1
Burnley v Sunderland
Coventry C v Crystal Palace
Crewe Alex v Norwich C
Ipswich T v Cardiff C
Millwall v Bradford C
Preston NE v Sheffield U
Stoke C v Gillingham
Walsall v Rotherham U
Watford v Reading
WBA v Nottingham F
Wigan Ath v West Ham U
Wimbledon v Derby Co

Saturday, 15 May 2004
FA Barclaycard Premiership
Arsenal v Leicester C
Aston Villa v Manchester U
Blackburn R v Birmingham C
Bolton W v Fulham
Charlton Ath v Southampton
Chelsea v Leeds U
Liverpool v Newcastle U
Manchester C v Everton
Portsmouth v Middlesbrough
Wolverhampton W v Tottenham H

FA BARCLAYCARD PREMIERSHIP FIXTURES 2003–04

Reproduced under licence from Football Dataco Limited. All rights reserved. Licence No. PRINT/COU/THEFO070.
Copyright © and Database Right The FA Premier League/The Football League Limited 2003. All rights reserved. No part of the Fixtures Lists may be reproduced stored or transmitted in any form without the prior written permission of Football DataCo Limited.

	Arsenal	Aston Villa	Birmingham C	Blackburn R	Bolton W	Charlton Ath	Chelsea	Everton	Fulham	Leeds U	Leicester C	Liverpool	Manchester C	Manchester U	Middlesbrough	Newcastle U	Portsmouth	Southampton	Tottenham H	Wolverhampton W
Arsenal	—	27.8	2.5	14.12	21.3	29.2	19.10	17.8	30.11	18.4	16.5	11.4	1.2	28.3	11.1	28.9	14.9	11.2	9.11	27.12
Aston Villa	18.1	—	22.2	21.3	5.10	21.9	13.4	26.10	29.12	8.2	31.8	24.8	4.4	16.5	9.11	18.4	8.1	30.11	2.5	14.12
Birmingham C	23.11	19.10	—	7.12	29.2	2.11	14.10	11.2	14.9	28.3	14.3	9.5	27.12	11.4	21.12	1.2	28.9	11.1	17.8	25.4
Blackburn R	14.3	21.12	16.5	—	11.1	19.10	1.2	9.11	28.9	11.4	18.4	14.9	28.8	2.5	27.12	12.2	28.3	29.2	30.11	17.8
Bolton W	21.12	11.4	26.10	24.8	—	31.8	14.3	30.11	16.5	2.5	29.12	8.2	22.2	8.1	14.9	28.3	18.1	9.11	18.4	28.9
Charlton Ath	26.10	28.3	18.4	22.2	1.2	—	27.12	27.8	9.11	30.11	2.5	28.9	17.8	14.9	14.3	21.12	11.4	16.5	11.2	11.1
Chelsea	22.2	28.9	18.1	31.8	14.12	8.2	—	18.4	21.3	16.5	24.8	8.1	26.10	30.11	11.4	9.11	29.12	2.5	14.9	28.3
Everton	8.1	29.2	29.12	25.4	9.5	18.1	2.11	—	24.8	28.9	21.12	31.8	7.12	8.2	28.3	14.9	14.3	19.10	11.4	23.11
Fulham	9.5	12.2	4.4	13.4	7.12	25.4	21.12	11.1	—	14.3	5.10	2.11	21.9	29.2	17.8	28.8	23.11	27.12	1.2	19.10
Leeds U	2.11	27.12	21.9	5.10	23.11	9.5	7.12	13.4	14.12	—	4.4	29.2	21.3	19.10	1.2	17.8	25.4	27.8	11.1	11.2
Leicester C	7.12	1.2	14.12	2.11	11.2	23.11	11.1	21.3	11.4	14.9	—	28.3	25.4	28.9	27.8	27.12	9.5	17.8	19.10	29.2
Liverpool	5.10	11.1	30.11	4.4	27.12	13.4	17.8	1.2	18.4	26.10	21.9	—	12.2	9.11	2.5	16.5	22.2	14.12	28.8	21.3
Manchester C	31.8	14.9	8.2	18.1	19.10	8.1	29.2	16.5	28.3	21.12	9.11	29.12	—	14.3	30.11	2.5	24.8	18.4	28.9	11.4
Manchester U	21.9	7.12	5.10	23.11	17.8	4.4	9.5	27.12	26.10	22.2	13.4	25.4	14.12	—	12.2	11.1	2.11	1.2	21.3	28.8
Middlesbrough	24.8	25.4	21.3	8.2	4.4	14.12	5.10	21.9	8.1	31.8	18.1	23.11	9.5	29.12	—	19.10	7.12	13.4	29.2	2.11
Newcastle U	13.4	2.11	31.8	29.12	21.9	21.3	25.4	4.4	18.1	8.1	8.2	7.12	23.11	24.8	22.2	—	26.10	5.10	14.12	9.5
Portsmouth	4.4	17.8	13.4	21.9	27.8	5.10	11.2	14.12	2.5	9.11	30.11	19.10	11.1	18.4	16.5	29.2	—	21.3	27.12	1.2
Southampton	29.12	9.5	24.8	26.10	25.4	7.12	23.11	22.2	8.2	18.1	8.1	14.3	2.11	31.8	28.9	11.4	21.12	—	28.3	14.9
Tottenham H	25.4	23.11	8.1	9.5	2.11	29.12	4.4	5.10	31.8	24.8	22.2	18.1	13.4	21.12	26.10	14.3	8.2	21.9	—	7.12
Wolverhampton W	8.2	14.3	9.11	8.1	13.4	24.8	21.9	2.5	22.2	29.12	26.10	21.12	5.10	18.1	18.4	30.11	31.8	4.4	16.5	—

NATIONWIDE FOOTBALL LEAGUE FIXTURES 2003–04

Reproduced under licence from Football Dataco Limited. All rights reserved. Licence No. PRINT/COU/THEFO070.
Copyright © and Database Right The FA Premier League/The Football League Limited 2003. All rights reserved. No part of the Fixtures Lists may be reproduced stored or transmitted in any form without the prior written permission of Football DataCo Limited.

DIVISION ONE	Bradford C	Burnley	Cardiff C	Coventry C	Crewe Alex	Crystal Palace	Derby C	Gillingham	Ipswich T	Millwall	Norwich C	Nottingham F	Preston NE	Reading	Rotherham U	Sheffield U	Stoke C	Sunderland	Walsall	Watford	WBA	West Ham U	Wigan Ath	Wimbledon
Bradford City	—	27.3	17.1	28.12	21.2	16.3	30.9	23.8	11.10	29.11	9.8	25.10	13.9	10.4	20.12	27.9	1.5	30.8	8.11	2.3	15.11	7.2	13.3	17.4
Burnley	20.9	—	1.11	13.12	30.8	9.8	24.4	7.2	21.2	25.10	3.4	16.9	6.3	11.10	22.11	6.12	28.12	9.5	4.10	12.4	17.1	2.3	23.8	20.3
Cardiff City	16.8	17.4	—	2.3	27.9	10.4	25.8	13.9	29.11	20.12	13.3	31.1	15.11	16.3	10.1	27.3	8.11	21.2	26.12	6.9	11.10	25.10	30.9	1.5
Coventry City	6.9	13.3	18.10	—	1.10	9.5	28.2	22.11	31.1	10.4	14.2	27.8	17.3	27.3	24.4	26.12	13.9	6.12	16.8	10.1	20.12	1.11	27.9	15.10
Crewe Alexandra	14.10	26.12	20.3	12.4	—	24.4	18.10	6.12	16.8	31.1	9.5	20.9	6.9	1.11	3.4	14.2	28.2	22.11	25.8	4.10	13.3	16.9	20.12	10.1
Crystal Palace	16.9	10.1	4.10	29.11	15.11	—	14.10	28.2	6.9	26.12	20.3	13.12	8.11	6.3	18.10	65.8	14.2	3.4	1.5	16.8	20.9	12.4	17.4	31.1
Derby County	12.4	15.11	7.2	25.10	3.3	21.2	—	17.1	8.11	1.5	28.12	20.3	17.4	23.8	13.3	20.12	9.8	20.9	3.4	17.9	30.8	4.10	11.10	29.11
Gillingham	31.1	25.8	3.4	1.5	8.11	25.10	16.8	—	17.4	6.9	16.9	6.3	13.12	21.2	20.3	10.1	29.11	11.10	12.4	26.12	4.10	20.9	2.3	15.11
Ipswich Town	14.2	14.10	9.5	23.8	17.1	28.12	6.12	1.11	—	13.3	21.12	24.4	28.2	9.8	4.10	22.11	18.10	12.4	16.9	20.3	3.4	30.8	7.2	20.9
Millwall	9.5	28.2	6.3	4.10	23.8	30.8	22.11	28.12	13.12	—	6.12	1.11	14.10	24.4	14.2	18.10	7.2	17.1	20.9	3.4	12.4	20.3	9.8	16.9
Norwich City	10.1	13.9	13.12	11.10	29.11	27.9	6.9	16.3	7.3	8.11	—	26.12	1.5	30.9	16.8	31.1	27.3	25.10	17.4	15.11	2.3	21.2	10.4	26.8
Nottingham Forest	28.2	17.3	23.8	7.2	27.3	13.3	27.9	20.12	15.11	17.4	30.8	—	1.10	17.1	15.10	13.9	10.4	9.8	14.2	8.11	29.11	28.12	1.5	18.10
Preston North End	3.4	20.12	24.4	16.9	28.12	6.12	1.11	13.3	25.10	21.2	22.11	12.4	—	2.3	20.9	9.5	30.8	23.8	20.3	11.10	7.2	9.8	17.1	4.10
Reading	4.10	14.2	16.9	20.9	17.4	20.12	31.1	14.10	10.1	15.11	12.4	16.8	18.10	—	25.8	28.2	13.3	20.3	6.9	29.11	1.5	3.4	8.11	26.12
Rotherham United	6.3	1.5	9.8	15.11	13.9	2.3	13.12	27.9	10.4	11.10	17.1	21.2	27.3	7.2	—	16.3	30.9	28.12	29.11	17.4	25.10	23.8	30.8	8.11
Sheffield United	20.3	8.11	20.9	30.8	11.10	7.2	6.3	9.8	1.5	2.3	23.8	3.4	29.11	25.10	16.9	—	17.4	4.10	15.11	13.12	21.2	17.1	28.12	12.4
Stoke City	22.11	6.9	6.12	3.4	25.10	11.10	10.1	9.5	2.3	25.8	20.9	4.10	26.12	13.12	12.4	1.11	—	17.9	31.1	6.3	20.3	24.4	21.2	16.8
Sunderland	26.12	29.11	14.10	8.11	1.5	13.9	27.3	14.2	30.9	16.8	28.2	10.1	31.1	27.9	6.9	10.4	16.3	—	18.10	25.8	17.4	13.3	15.11	20.12
Walsall	6.12	10.4	30.8	17.1	7.2	22.11	13.9	29.9	16.3	27.3	1.11	11.10	27.9	28.12	9.5	24.4	23.8	2.3	—	21.2	9.8	20.12	25.10	13.3
Watford	18.10	30.9	28.12	9.8	10.4	17.1	16.3	30.8	27.9	13.9	24.4	6.12	14.2	9.5	1.11	13.3	20.12	7.2	14.10	—	23.8	22.11	27.3	28.2
West Bromwich Albion	24.4	16.8	14.2	6.3	13.12	27.3	26.12	10.4	13.9	30.9	18.10	9.5	25.8	22.11	28.2	14.10	27.9	1.11	10.1	31.1	—	6.12	16.3	6.9
West Ham United	26.8	18.10	28.2	17.4	17.3	1.10	10.4	27.3	26.12	28.9	15.10	6.9	10.1	13.9	31.1	16.8	15.11	13.12	6.3	1.5	8.11	—	29.11	14.2
Wigan Athletic	13.12	31.1	13.4	20.3	6.3	1.11	14.2	18.10	26.8	10.1	4.10	22.11	16.8	6.12	26.12	6.9	14.10	24.4	28.2	20.9	16.9	9.5	—	3.4
Wimbledon	1..11	27.9	22.11	21.2	9.8	23.8	9.5	24.4	27.3	16.3	7.2	2.3	10.4	30.8	6.12	30.9	17.1	6.3	13.12	25.10	30.12	11.10	13.9	—

NATIONWIDE FOOTBALL LEAGUE FIXTURES 2003–04

Reproduced under licence from Football Dataco Limited. All rights reserved. Licence No. PRINT/COU/THEFO070.
Copyright © and Database Right The FA Premier League/The Football League Limited 2003. All rights reserved. No part of the Fixtures Lists may be reproduced stored or transmitted in any form without the prior written permission of Football DataCo Limited.

DIVISION TWO

	Barnsley	Blackpool	Bournemouth	Brentford	Brighton & HA	Bristol C	Chesterfield	Colchester U	Grimsby T	Hartlepool U	Luton T	Notts Co	Oldham Ath	Peterborough U	Plymouth Arg	Port Vale	QPR	Rushden & D	Sheffield W	Stockport Co	Swindon T	Tranmere R	Wrexham	Wycombe W
Barnsley	—	3.1	17.1	17.4	23.8	1.5	28.12	9.8	25.10	7.2	6.3	30.8	16.9	2.3	3.4	20.3	12.4	4.10	13.12	29.11	20.9	15.11	11.10	21.2
Blackpool	25.8	—	13.9	16.3	10.4	29.11	15.11	14.2	30.9	18.10	13.12	27.9	24.1	1.5	28.2	6.3	10.1	21.10	17.4	27.3	31.1	26.12	6.9	16.8
Bournemouth	16.8	20.3	—	29.11	18.10	6.9	12.4	3.4	13.12	4.10	21.10	14.2	28.2	15.11	26.12	10.1	24.1	20.9	16.9	1.5	25.8	17.4	31.1	6.3
Brentford	1.11	16.9	8.5	—	21.10	26.12	3.4	12.4	22.11	20.9	18.10	28.2	25.8	16.8	6.9	31.1	14.2	20.3	4.10	13.3	20.12	10.1	24.1	24.4
Brighton & Hove Albion	24.1	4.10	21.2	2.3	—	15.11	16.9	20.3	11.10	3.4	25.8	1.5	10.1	17.4	31.1	12.12	18.8	12.4	20.9	25.10	6.9	6.3	29.11	26.12
Bristol City	22.11	8.5	28.12	7.2	24.4	—	17.1	3.1	30.8	23.8	1.11	9.8	20.3	11.10	12.4	20.9	3.4	13.3	25.10	20.12	4.10	16.9	21.2	2.3
Chesterfield	6.9	24.4	30.9	27.9	16.3	16.8	—	28.2	27.3	21.10	8.5	13.9	22.11	26.12	25.8	1.11	31.1	14.2	6.3	10.4	18.10	13.12	10.1	24.1
Colchester United	10.1	11.10	27.9	30.9	13.9	26.8	25.10	—	20.2	6.3	26.12	10.4	13.12	27.3	29.11	24.1	6.9	1.5	15.11	2.3	15.8	31.1	17.4	16.3
Grimsby Town	28.2	12.4	13.3	1.5	14.2	31.1	20.9	18.10	—	20.3	24.1	21.10	26.12	6.9	10.1	16.8	4.10	17.4	3.4	15.11	16.9	29.11	20.12	25.8
Hartlepool United	26.12	20.2	10.4	27.3	27.9	24.1	2.3	20.12	12.9	—	31.1	17.4	6.9	10.1	1.5	25.8	13.3	15.11	10.10	16.3	29.11	16.8	30.9	25.10
Luton Town	20.12	13.3	2.3	21.2	3.1	17.4	29.11	7.2	23.8	30.8	—	28.12	3.4	25.10	20.3	16.9	20.9	9.8	1.5	17.1	12.4	4.10	15.11	11.10
Notts County	31.1	3.4	11.10	25.10	22.11	10.1	20.3	4.10	2.3	1.11	6.9	—	8.5	25.8	6.3	24.4	26.12	16.9	12.4	21.2	24.1	20.9	16.8	13.12
Oldham Athletic	16.3	23.8	25.10	3.1	9.8	13.9	1.5	13.3	7.2	28.12	27.9	29.11	—	10.4	17.4	11.10	20.12	30.8	17.1	30.9	15.11	21.2	2.3	27.3
Peterborough United	21.10	22.11	24.4	17.1	1.11	14.2	7.2	20.9	28.12	9.8	28.2	3.1	4.10	—	16.9	12.4	18.10	20.12	23.8	30.8	3.4	20.3	13.3	8.5
Plymouth Argyle	27.9	25.10	7.2	28.12	30.8	30.9	3.1	8.5	9.8	22.11	13.9	20.12	1.11	16.3	—	21.2	24.4	17.1	2.3	23.8	13.3	11.10	27.3	10.4
Port Vale	13.9	20.12	9.8	30.8	13.3	27.3	17.4	23.8	17.1	3.1	16.3	15.11	14.2	30.9	18.10	—	21.10	29.11	7.2	28.12	28.2	1.5	10.4	27.9
Queen's Park Rangers	30.9	9.8	23.8	11.10	17.1	27.9	30.8	28.12	10.4	13.12	27.3	7.2	6.3	21.2	15.11	2.3	—	3.1	29.11	17.4	1.5	25.10	16.3	13.9
Rushden & Diamonds	10.4	2.3	27.3	13.9	30.9	13.12	11.10	22.11	1.11	24.4	10.1	16.3	31.1	6.3	16.8	8.5	25.8	—	21.2	27.9	26.12	24.1	25.10	6.9
Sheffield Wednesday	13.3	1.11	17.3	10.4	27.3	28.2	20.12	24.4	27.9	14.2	22.11	1.10	16.8	24.1	22.10	26.12	8.5	18.10	—	13.9	10.1	6.9	25.8	31.1
Stockport County	8.5	20.9	22.11	13.12	28.2	6.3	4.10	21.10	24.4	16.9	16.8	18.10	12.4	31.1	24.1	6.9	1.11	3.4	20.3	—	14.2	25.8	26.12	10.1
Swindon Town	27.3	30.8	3.1	6.3	28.12	10.4	21.2	17.1	17.3	8.5	1.10	23.8	24.4	27.9	13.12	25.10	22.11	7.2	9.8	11.10	—	3.3	13.9	1.11
Tranmere Rovers	24.4	7.2	1.11	9.8	20.12	16.3	13.3	30.8	8.5	17.1	10.4	27.3	18.10	13.9	14.2	22.11	28.2	23.8	28.12	3.1	21.10	—	27.9	30.9
Wrexham	14.2	28.12	30.8	23.8	8.5	18.10	9.8	1.11	6.3	12.4	24.4	17.1	21.10	13.12	20.9	4.10	16.9	28.2	3.1	7.2	20.3	3.4	—	22.11
Wycombe Wanderers	18.10	17.1	20.12	15.11	7.2	21.10	23.8	16.9	3.1	28.2	14.2	13.3	20.9	29.11	4.10	3.4	20.3	28.12	1.9	9.8	17.4	12.4	1.5	—